GW00801711

© **PEÑÍN EDICIONES**

All rights reserved. No part of this publication may be reproduced, stored in a retrieval system or transmitted in any means, electronic, mechanical, photocopying, recording or otherwise, without the prior permission of the author.

Production team:
    Wine-tasting and management: José Peñin.
    Coordination: Antonio Mª Casado.
    Text editor: Ángeles Cosano.
    Assistant wine tasters: Antonio Mª Casado, Amaya Cervera,
        Maite Corsín, Bárbara Díaz.
    Data processing: Erika Laymus
    Designer: Mati Durán, Marta Gómez
    Front cover: Javier Herrán
    Database: Miguel Sáinz.

PUBLISHER: GRUPO PEÑÍN.
C/ Arga, 11
28002 Madrid.
Tel.: 00 34 91 411 94 64 Fax: 00 34 91 515 94 99
comunicacion@grupopenin.com
www.grupopenin.com

TRANSLATION: Cillero & de Motta / www.cillerodemotta.com

ISBN: 84-95203-27-8
Copyright:
Printer: RIVADENEYRA

DISTRIBUTOR: GRUPO COMERCIAL ANAYA
C/ Juan Ignacio Luca de Tena, 15
Tel: 00 34 91 393 88 00
28027 Madrid

CONTENTS

CONTENTS

INTRODUCTION

In this edition of the Peñín Guide there are more and better wines than ever before. Year after year we set out on the inexorable search for quality, clearly based on statistics and the huge database at our disposal, which without a doubt is the most extensive there is on Spanish wines.

Whilst the 2002 harvest did not go down in history because of the early autumn rains, 2003 suffered the same fate because of the unusual heat waves of the summer. At the time of finishing this book, it seems that the weather might be quite different for 2004. With a mild summer and therefore a slower ripening of the fruit, the quality could be much better. But we cannot be confident until the last bunch has entered the winepress.

Man finds himself in this ever changing crazy weather. There are more wines because to this age old profession of viticulture and winemaking, new travel companions are added; there are also better wines because of the wisdom of young oenologists committed to neutralizing the ravages of the weather. Before, bad harvests were not noticed thanks to the art of blending vintages. Nowadays, with more authentic harvests almost the same thing happens but this time as a result of an excellent knowledge of viticulture.

MORE THAN 6,000 WINES TASTED

The improvement in the quality of Spanish wine can be seen in the considerable increase of wines in the 80 to 90 points range (3,883 wines as opposed to the 3,090 in the 2004 edition) and the consequent reduction in the 70 to 80 points band (1,813 wines as opposed to the 2,172 in the 2004 edition). And all this, after tasting 400 more wines this year than for the 2004 edition. Finally, the podium of the 'Nineties' has increased, from the 225 wines in the 2004 Guide to the 288 in the present edition.

AN UNBELIEVABLE APATHY

In spite of being 15 years old and being the leading wine guide in Spain, when several wineries acknowledge that thanks to it their wines are sold on the international market, when practically 100% of foreign importers of Spanish wines consult the Peñín Guide and some even wait for the release of the new edition before placing their order, when it is published in German and the present edition may possibly be published in English and when the Guide is on the internet at **elvino.com**, the internet site on wines most consulted from abroad, it is unbelievable that there are still wineries that do not send us samples to be tasted. This is understandable in those wines that might get a low score, but the strangest thing is that in a lot of cases they are wines with more than 80 points.

The national bodegas, except for a few exceptions, suffer from apathy, which leads to disasters in the field of trade and, above all, exporting. They attend to those who come to the counter to buy a box even if it is the insignificant bar from around the corner, but they neglect the faxes, the emails, not to mention the letters, wherever they may come from. That is to say, they are more concerned about the tangible 25 from the cash sale because it is 'action', rather than the intangible communicational 'repercussion' of the guides. This insular attitude reaches its zenith in an institution such as the Rioja Designation Regulatory Council. A few years ago we decided to carry out the wine tasting at the regulatory councils, not only because it was logistically preferable but also to be closer to the source of information. But a person in charge at the Rioja headquarters informed us that they could not host the tastings for our guide as they would be obliged to do so for the other guides too. Our reply was categorical: "Naturally, there is nothing more profitable for the promotion of your wines than to welcome those who with their guides and publications, however small they might be, review and score the wines of the corresponding DO, and above all for free".

INNOVATIONS

On occasions, recently-bottled quality wines which will be released for the Christmas market are prematurely sent in for wine tasting – with hardly enough time for it to mature-on the closing dates so that they can enter the new edition of the Guide. As a result, the scores of these wines are lower than they would have been if they had been tasted some months later. This fact does not only affect the bodega by appearing for the whole year with a premature rating of a wine not precisely at its best, but the reader may also question our sensorial capability on seeing such an unfair rating. Therefore, we prefer to abstain from this compromise and repeat the wine tasting of previous vintages that may not be available from the bodega, but can still be found on the market. Only if the bodega insists will we agree to review wines under these unfavourable conditions but at their risk. In practice, some winemakers accept these conditions and others do not.

INDEPENDENT WINES

The dominance of the DO wines is losing ground to the progress of the *'Vinos de la Tierra'* VT (country wines). Only among the Castilla VT and the Castilla y León VT there are 300 wines of which 200 have been reviewed and 18 have a score of 90 points or more. In the 'hidden' region of Granada that encompasses the VT from the North of Granada, Southwest Granada and Contraviesa-Alpujarra, 60 different wines have been counted of which 40 have been reviewed and 25 received a score of 80 or more. In Zamora there are already 23 *Vinos de la Tierra* and 21 in Los Arribes. We could also include the 65 *Vinos de la Tierra* from Extremadura that have nothing to do with the Ribera de Guadiana DO and mention the more than 40 designations of *Vinos de la Tierra* from all over Spain.

The new Wine Law has sped up the legalising of these territories of which the majority are not so impatient as before to acquire a DO category, but at the same time the Autonomous Communities are not obsessed with speeding up this process.

BUYING GUIDE

The Peñin Guide is perhaps the only guide in the world that aspires to be a reference book rather than the traditional model of gathering together the wines of the elite, many of which pose a certain barrier because of their high cost.

In this edition we are going to be more explicit when it comes to pointing out the best quality/price ratio, as we are convinced it is more important to evaluate the best buys from 80 points and above. There are 27 wines for less than € 2 a bottle with this qualification. Likewise, there are 46 wines that cost less than one euro (!), some close to 80 points.

José Peñín

José Peñín

ACKNOWLEDGEMENTS

We would like to thank the following bodies: C.R. Ribera del Guadiana, Gran Canaria, Monte Lentiscal, Casa del Vino de Sauzal in Tenerife, C.R. de Valencia, Utiel-Requena, Vinos de Madrid, Bullas and Méntrida for their assistance in carrying out the wine tasting, as well as Pérez de Eulate from the Vinoteca de Palma de Mallorca.

USING THE BOOK

WINE PRODUCING REGIONS

At present there are 65 Designations of Origin in Spain. On going to press the Ribera de Uclés DO was on the point of being approved, and these wines appear in the present edition in the La Mancha or Castilla VT section and the wines from Gomera VT are now DO wines.

The only two *Vinos de Pago* (single vineyard wines) to date (Valdepusa and Finca Élez) which were already incorporated in the previous edition, no longer appear under a separate section and are integrated alphabetically among the rest of the DO wines.

The main incorporations this year are found among the *Vinos de la Tierra*, a mixed bag containing many great wines as well as curiosities, sometimes mediocre and very often experimental. As new entries we have Desierto de Almería, Ribera de Andarax, Serra de Tramuntana-Costa Nord and Valdejalón. Similarly, we have the recently approved Ribera del Queiles, from an old claim by the Guelbenzu company, that had left the Navarra DO some time ago –the first supra-regional designation of *Vinos de la Tierra*, as one section is found in Aragón and another in Navarra, and it is directly under the control of the Ministry of Agriculture- and El Terrerazo for the Mustiguillo bodega, which can, to all intents and purposes be considered *Vino de Pago*. Although the resolution has only been in force since the 2003 harvest, we have included all the wines from this bodega under this section.

All the DO wines appear in alphabetical order, while the rest of the labels reviewed and tasted appear under the section *Vinos de la Tierra*, if they are registered under this category (with the various names also sorted alphabetically), or under the section Other Regions-Other Wines. The latter is listed by Communities: Andalucía, Aragón, Baleares, Castilla-La Mancha, Castilla-León, Cataluña, Extremadura, La Rioja, Navarra and Valencia. Finally, the section Sparkling Wines - Traditional Method covers the sparkling wines produced in the same way as cavas – the system of second fermentation in bottle – but whose production areas do not fall under DO Cava nor under any other designation of origin.

In each chapter the following sections are found:
-Illustrative map of the DO and the main concentration of vineyards.
-General view of the area with a short commentary on its present situation and foreseeable future.
-General characteristics of its wines.
-Connection between bodegas and the wine tasting.

BODEGAS

These are listed alphabetically within the wine producing region in which they are found. In listing them, the more or less common terms in the sector have been removed such as bodega, cooperative, cava, etc., and the term that really 'names' the bodega is used; e.g. Bodegas Palacio is found under 'P', not 'B'.

The name, address and telephone number as well as the most relevant details of each bodega appear. This information was supplied by the producers on 15th July 2004. All the basic information (address, telephone numbers and wines on the market) has been updated practically 100% in this edition, although it is possible that other details (number of barrels, production, and percentage for exportation…) are from data gathered for the previous edition, as a result of not having received the requested information for the 2005 edition in time.

If the same company produce wines under different DO's or in different wine growing regions, the available data on them appears in all of them and in the index section by bodegas, as many entries as wine producing areas or regions appear in which they operate. The most frequent case is that of companies that produce cava and also other Catalonian DO wines.

WINES

The wines and the corresponding tastings make up the bulk of the text. The information on the bodega that produces them follows, according to the following specifications:

- Each wine appears with its name, maturation and vintage (if stated by the producer). The type of wine is also specified, the DO it belongs to, the approximate retail price the bodegas have provided and new to this edition, the countries they export to.
- The comments on the tasting highlight the main characteristics of the wines.
- The wines that do not have points and comments have not been tasted as the cellars did not send us samples and it is therefore due to circumstances beyond our control. In the case of wines within the 80 points range we attempted to acquire the sample by other means. Although, normally, the bodegas that think they can achieve a high score are quite determined when it comes to sending their wines to be reviewed.

The reproductions of the labels that appear in the guide are in no way linked to the quality of the wine. It is only a space contracted by the cellars to better locate their wines.

INDEX

Besides the usual alphabetical index by brands of wine and bodega, there is also an index with the best wines from each DO to easily distinguish the best from each area.

In addition, for 'The Podium' section, a list has been drawn up with comments by the author on the wines with the best points in this edition as well as all the wines with a score of 90 or more points.

Finally, as an innovation in this edition we have included a list of Designations of Origin and *Vinos de la Tierra* organized by Autonomous Communities, as well as another list of wine producers with all the associated companies.

HOW THE AUTOR DID THE WINE TASTING

The aim of the book is to quickly and efficiently inform the reader of the characteristics of the wines that can be found on the market during the last quarter of 2004 and the year 2005. The opinions expressed are the sole responsibility of the author and must only be evaluated in terms of the faith the reader has in his evaluation. These evaluations should, furthermore, be interpreted with a maximum margin of error of 6%.

Except in the case of wines with a marked character, the tasting has been simplified, highlighting only the most significant aspects easily detectable by any consumer. An overly detailed and technical description has been avoided, to our understanding clearly confusing for the average consumer. However, there is a list of terms that may seem technical for the unseasoned consumer.

WHEN ARE THE WINES TASTED?

The bulk of the tasting is carried out from 1st April to 20th July. Therefore, the samples that were received after these dates do not appear in the Guide. A tasting period for each area is established in such a way that the high number of tastings which have to be done in a relatively short period of time is systematised.

HOW WERE THE WINES RECEIVED?

We did not go looking for stragglers, except those we considered due to their quality and in view of past experience, would have a high score. The bodegas increasingly appreciate the prestige the Peñín Guide is gaining year after year and the amount of samples received is increasing. Almost all the best Spanish wines were sent in by the bodegas. The absentees on the other hand, were probably because the producers believed their wines would get very bad reviews, or because the cellar had sold their entire production due to demand or a low harvest. Occasionally, an obvious omission is the fault of Peñín editions. If it is attributable to the bodega we buy the wine on the market only – we repeat – only if the brand is relatively well-known.

SCORING SYSTEM

The American scoring system is used, in which 0 equals 50. This classification expresses the different qualities of the wine in a general way looking at the concepts detailed in each 10-point range. In view of the scoring the reader should look at this page for a general description related to this specific classification and then examine the description of the wine according to the following scale:

95-100 Exceptional wine.
Stands out among its type, year and the typical wines from the same region. Extraordinary impression on all the senses. Complex, full of registers on the nose as well as the palate due to a combination of factors, soil, variety, making and ageing; it is elegant and exceptional; i.e. it is not commercial and not well-known to the general public.

90-94 Excellent wine.
Wines with the same values as stated in the previous section but not as marked and with fewer nuances.

80-89 Very good wine.
The nuances gained during winemaking and/or ageing or those inherent of the grape variety stand out. A wine with specific characteristics but without the merits of the soil coming out in the wine.

70-79 Acceptable wine.
The wine has all the characteristics of the vine-variety and wine-growing region but somewhat diluted. It has no defects, but neither any virtues.

60-69 Below average wine.
An acceptable wine in which there are slight defects which do not excessively damage the whole.

50-59 Non-recommendable wine.
A wine acceptable from a health point of view but not a recreational one. It may be oxidized, have ageing defects, racked too late, or old wines in decline or young wines with a negative nose from fermentation.

HOW MANY WINES HAVE BEEN TASTED?

It is difficult to give a precise figure as the bulk of doubtful wines over 60 points were reviewed several times. More than 6,100 wines were tasted and reviewed with about 1,000 repeat tastings.

HOW ARE THE WINES CLASSIFIED AND THE POINTS AWARDED?

The author, like most specialized writers, is opposed to numerical reviews. However, a pure and simple description of the reviews without the aspect of points does not fully explain the differences between brands, when the non-expert consumer is faced with the dilemma of choosing between two or more similar descriptions. It is clear that the negative and positive reviews have their respective borders without the necessity of points. And we might think that it is sufficient to classify them as good, very good and excellent. But the author does not want to use these terms to classify them when a distinction needs to be made between a good wine with a score of 70 and another with a score of 75.

In this edition we have removed the '+' sign that was previously found in the different points ranges and we have only used numerical points. Therefore; a wine with 80+ will be scored 81, 82, 83 or 84, thus refining more and resolving the doubts of the readers and professionals, so that an 81 may be a far cry from an 84.

HOW ARE THE WINES TASTED?

Unlike comparative and competition tasting, José Peñín carried out the tastings with the labels uncovered and never scored a wine with only one sample, above all in wines with a score of 80 points or more.

This ensures that, unless the tasting of the same wines is carried out by various wine tasting groups or commissions in various sittings, the results obtained from a single blind tasting for an annual publication would never be fair except when the tasting is done with the label uncovered and the members have a general knowledge of the bodega. It is the taster's fair and objective opinion based on experience that makes him unbiased by the label. This is how the tastings were carried out.

We obtain a general impression of not only the results of the different tastings done at different places, situations and times, but also take into account the style or the segmentation of the quality of the bodega. It is strange that two bottles of the same brand, type and ageing method (Crianza, Reserva or Gran Reserva) have more than a three points difference (in the guide for example, 75 and 78) even though they are from different vintages. On the other hand it is more probable that a higher score is given due to profound changes in the winemaking style and the raw material obtained by the bodega.

The general knowledge of the winemaker (generally continuous) of each bodega throughout the last four years reduces the errors of blind tasting, where, at times, the defects inherent in certain bottles can be confused (not scored) with the defects in winemaking and ageing (scored) of the wine. With the new bodegas (or those that appear in the Guide for the first time and the style contrasts with the normal style of the producer being reviewed), José Peñín carries out a small survey among his colleagues and compares similarities with other collaborators.

In addition, the author is aware that in Spain, either because of the relatively uniform climatic reasons over a large part of the regions or – of course - the picaresque blending never abandoned by a large number of bodegas, the differences of the vintage are less than those of a change in style. This practice is normally stated and is also detected in the tasting.

TASTING OF PREMATURELY-BOTTLED WINES

In previous editions relatively lower scores appeared for good quality wines that were bottled in a period of less than three months. It is obvious that after six months this wine would deserve a higher score due to the improvement of its nose and palate and, with no opportunity for re-marking, they would have to wait for the following year's edition. The author, even though he is aware of the negative factors involved in reviewing a wine in this period (hermetic fruitiness, incomplete reaction of oak and wine, tannins very dry at times) and ignores this, cannot risk scoring higher than what his senses convey to him. Therefore, José Peñín recommends that the bodegas who are not completely sure of the development of the nose and palate of the wine do not send in samples under these conditions as it could incur a risk for them and it also discredits the author for erroneously scoring a wine too low. In these cases it is recommendable to review the previous vintage with its characteristics completely established, even if they are no longer available at the cellar, as it is possible that they could be on the market which is the most essential factor for publication in the Guide.

HOW TO INTERPRET THE TASTINGS

In each description of a wine two concepts appear:

OBJECTIVE. These are the 'evolutive' descriptions that are not conditioned by the state of the taster and his habits and be seen by any amateur wine taster.

Colour: The intensity and clarity; for example, if the wine is intense, open, pale, cloudy, crystalline, etc.

Aroma: The intensity, defects, an excess of aroma of an element in the wine (e.g.: wood and varietal type, fruity or otherwise, ageing, etc)

Taste: The intensity and structure; whether it is meaty, with body, full, the essential flavours (acidity, bitterness – tannins- sweet, acid, saline) and all those described in the aroma.

SUBJECTIVE. These are the 'non-evaluative' and personal descriptions referring to comparisons with other products that the author has come to know through experience and are there to orientate the reader. Examples: colour 'golden, cherry, old gold, mahogany, straw-coloured, etc.'; nose and palate 'roasted, jam, cherry, attic, etc.'

For another wine taster, for example, roasted could be the equivalent of toasted and attic described as dusty or old wood.

HOW TO INTERPRET THE INFORMATION ON THE BODEGAS

This is expressed schematically, which we believe allows one to see data such as the founding date, the size of the vineyard, sales etc of the majority of the bodegas reviewed at a glance.

We have therefore used an international system, simple and above all easy to interpret by using different icons:

⊞ Number of barrels.   ▮ Yearly sales.

▤ Capacity of tanks.   ◥ % of sales in the home market.

🍇 Number of hectares owned.   🌍 % exported.

⊞ Months aged in barrel.

We would like to point out the use of oak in many Spanish wines that are on the market that do not indicate the ageing such as oak, barrel, crianza etc. It is increasingly more common for the wines on the market to have been aged three or four months in the barrel with the aim of having a more finished and smoother wine. In this respect this new section that we have included and in which we state the amount of time the wine has been aged in oak is revealing as it gives the consumer a clearer idea of the contents of the bottle. However, it must also be stated that this data only appears if the producer has supplied it.

The abbreviations used to indicate the countries exported to and that are used internationally by ISO standards, are the following:

AD	Andorra	CM	Cameroon
AE	Arab Emirates	CN	China
AFR	Africa	CO	Colombia
AL	Albania	CR	Costa Rica
AN	Netherlands Antilles	CS	Serbia and Montenegro
AO	Angola	CU	Cuba
AR	Argentina	CV	Cabo Verde
ASIA	Asia	CY	Cyprus
AT	Austria	CZ	Czech Republic
AU	Australia	DE	Germany
BB	Barbados	DK	Denmark
BE	Belgium	DO	Dominican Republic
BJ	Republic of Benin	DZ	Algeria
BNL	Benelux	EC	Ecuador
BO	Bolivia	EE	Estonia
BR	Brazil	EL	Greece
BY	Byelorussia	ET	Ethiopia
CA	Canada	EUE	Eastern Europe
CAM	Central America and/or Caribbean	FI	Finland
CF	Central African Republic	FR	France
CG	Congo	GA	Gabon
CH	Switzerland	GM	Gambia
CI	Ivory Coast	GQ	Equatorial Guinea
CL	Chile	GT	Guatemala

HK ....Hong Kong	OCN ....Oceania
HN ....Honduras	PA...................................Panama
HU ....Hungary	PE ....Peru
ID...................................Indonesia	PF...Tahiti
IE ....Ireland	PH ....Philippines
IL ....Israel	PL ....Poland
IN ....India	PR ....Puerto Rico
IS..Iceland	PT ....Portugal
IT ....Italy	RU ....Russia
JO ....Jordan	SAM......................South America
JP ....Japan	SE......................................Sweden
KE ....Kenya	SDV ....Scandinavia
KR ....Korea	SG.................................Singapore
KY ....Cayman Islands	SI..Slovenia
KZ ....Kazakhstan	SK ....Slovakia
LB ....Lebanon	SN ....Senegal
LI ....Liechtenstein	SV ....El Salvador
LT ....Lithuania	TG ....Togo
LU ....Luxemburg	TH ....Thailand
LV ....Latvia	TR...................................Turkey
MA ....Morocco	TT ....Trinidad and Tobago
MK ....Macedonia	TW ....Taiwan
MT ....Malta	TZ ....Tanzania
MU ....Mauritius	UA....................................Ukraine
MX................................Mexico	UE ....Europe
MY ....Malaysia	UK ....United Kingdom
NAM......................North America	US ....United States
NC ....New Caledonia	UY ....Uruguay
NG ....Nigeria	VE ....Venezuela
NI ....Nicaragua	VN ....Vietnam
NL ....Netherlands	YG ....Yugoslavia
NO......................................Norway	ZA ....South Africa
NZ..............................New Zealand	

WINES NOT TASTED

There are two groups of wines not tasted:
a) Wines belonging to a bodega that sent in only some of their wines.
b) Wines belonging to a bodega that sent in none of their wines.

In the case of a) this might be because, either the wine had been sold out at the bodega (an absurd reason as the wine could be on the market), or because the producer believed that, as they were lower-quality brands, they would get a lower score. In the latter case we deduce that they are wines of an inferior quality to the others tasted and reviewed from these producers. As the wines we received allow us to recognize the style of the bodega we do not insist on tasting the missing ones.

In the case of b) we know with certainty that, except for very rare exceptions, the wines would not achieve a score of more than 79. However, we have gone to great lengths to update their basic information (address, telephone number and the wines sold) and of course we will keep on insisting that they send us samples for future editions.

VITICULTURE AND WINEMAKING

VITICULTURE AND WINEMAKING

THE VINE AND ITS ENVIRONMENT

THE MAKE-UP OF THE GRAPE AND ITS VEGETATIVE FUNCTION

Let us get to know the plant that produces the grape better: in which regions of the world it is planted, what conditions are necessary for it to survive and how the miracle of producing wine from the fruit is achieved.

The vines cultivated in the world are grouped into two well-defined regions in both hemispheres. Outside the two main zones defined below, vine-growing is merely coincidental.

The Northern hemisphere. They are found between 30º and 50º north, that is to say, from Morocco and Egypt up to Champagne, Burgundy and Moselle.

The Southern hemisphere. Vineyards are grown between 30º and 40º south, from Uruguay and the south of Brazil down to New Zealand.

The origin and the expansion of the vine. The Mediterranean area, from east to west, served as a cradle for its development and cultivation. From the 15th century it crossed the seas and was propagated along the colonization routes of the Empires of Spain, Portugal, England and Holland. The first vine stocks reached the Caribbean in 1493 and from there they spread all over America. The Dutch took it to South Africa two centuries later and the English immigrants introduced it to Australia in the second half of the 18th century.

Vineyards in the New World. They are without a doubt the heirs of Mediterranean viticulture, as most of them descend from grapes planted in the 15th century in the Canary Islands and Madeira. These grapes arrived on the islands representing the culmination of the historic voyage of the Greek Malvasia grape along the Mediterranean coastline.

WHAT IS THE VINE?

The vine is a shrub made up of roots, trunk, vine shoots, leaves, flowers and fruit. The plant is fed through the roots, by the absorption of moisture and the necessary mineral salts; the trunk and the shoots are mere transmission vehicles through which the water and the mineral components circulate.

The leaves. These are the most important organs of the vine: they convert the raw sap into the finished product, carrying out the vital functions of the plant (transpiration, respiration and photosynthesis). The molecules of acids, sugars, etc, which accumulate in the grape and condition its flavour, are formed from the oxygen and water in the leaves. This greenish substance called chlorophyll is responsible for capturing sufficient energy from the rays of sunlight to carry out all these processes.

HOW IS THE FRUIT OBTAINED AND HOW DOES IT DEVELOP?

THE CLUSTERS. The clusters appear, very green at first as they are saturated with chlorophyll, when the warm weather begins and the sap starts to rise. From this point on the whole plant dedicates its energy to developing the fruit as it gradually grows.

The **green grape**, not yet ripe, has a large concentration of tartaric, malic and to a lesser degree citric acids. The content of these substances depends to a large degree on the variety and on the geo-climatic conditions such as light, temperature and humidity which are decisive in the make-up of the organic acids.

THE 'VÉRAISON'. The point at which the fruit changes colour. It turns yellow if it is a white variety, and light red turning darker if it is a red variety.

RIPENING. During this process the acids give way to the sugars produced by the frenetic photosynthetic activity of the leaves. The trunks of the vines also contribute to the sweetness of the grape as they act as accumulators of sugar.

Due to the large amount of wood they have, **old vines** are capable of producing a more constant and better quality fruit. The larger quantity of roots (radial mass) also has an influence and increases the plants' ability to retain nutritive substances that protect them against water imbalances.

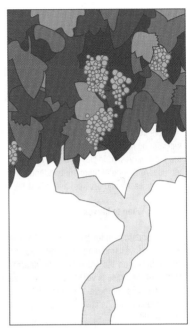

Foliage. The leaves are not only a simple 'adornment' of nature. They act as solar panels which store the energy that conditions the growth and ripening of the bunches. The right amount of leaves per vine (foliage mass) achieves an improved vegetative process.

THE COMPOSITION OF THE GRAPE

THE STALK. This is the woody part that forms the frame of the bunch. It supplies acids and phenolic substances – tannins – depending on whether it is used in the fermentation process or not. When used it adds acidity and astringency, but an uncontrolled use could produce certain unpleasant herbaceous traits.

THE GRAPE. This is divided into three parts:

The skin. The majority of the colorant and aromatic components in wines come from the skin: the phenolic or polyphenol compounds, mainly anthocyanins – red colorants – and tannins, which give the sensation of astringency and certain bitter tones which are noticeable in some wines. The aromatic substances are found in the inner layers of the skin, although there are varieties such as the *Moscatel* (Muscat) and the *Malvasia* whose pulp is also impregnated with these compounds.

Pulp. The main components of the must or squeezed pulp are water and sugars which by means of fermentation are transformed into wine. The pulp does not provide colour – except in some varieties known as 'Teinturier' grapes - and therefore it is possible to make white wines from red varieties, as long as the skins are not macerated with the must.

The pips. They are found in the pulp and differ according to the varieties. There are even varieties which do not have pips. They have a very hard outer shell and contribute tannins to the wine.

Other substances: Nitrogenous matter such as amino-acids, polypeptides and proteins that feed the yeasts activating the alcoholic fermentation; mineral substances that come from the water in the soil: potassium, phosphor, magnesium, calcium, sodium, iron, copper, zinc, fluoride, chlorine, iodine and bromide; vitamins that encourage the growth of the yeasts and bacteria; pectin, found in all fruit; mucilage and gums. The largest component however, is water, representing 80% of the total.

HARVESTING

This consists of the picking of the grapes to be transported to the bodegas where they will later be made into wine. This takes place from August (the earliest) to October and some are even harvested in November in the northern hemisphere depending on the latitude and altitude. At this point there are two fundamental aspects: the grape must be healthy (that is, free of diseases and bruises) and it is at the correct stage of ripening.

Deciding when to harvest.

This is fundamental for the quality of the wine. Rather than the balance between sugar and acidity that was traditionally sought. 'Polyphenol ripeness' is increasingly more important and is based on the analysis of the degree of tannins and anthocyanins in the fruit. The tasting of the grape is vital to check this 'ripeness' and above all, the tasting of the wooden part: the pips. If these are completely ripe there will be no risk of giving the wine a herbaceous and vegetative character during the long macerations that are currently used in good quality wines.

Which is best, mechanical harvesting or hand picking?

There is no end to this debate. Mechanical harvesting, which was revolutionary in reducing costs, facilitates picking at night and is very efficient, but it shakes the vine (which at times is quite aggressive for the plant) and the harvest is usually dirtier (more vegetative remains among the bunches). The vineyard of course, must be prepared for the machine with the appropriate distances between the rows of vines. On the positive side, besides the saving of salary bills, the grapes that fall into the baskets are more homogenous and on being ripe fall off easier thus making it possible to choose the ideal moment for harvesting. The great wines of the world, however, are still faithful to hand picking which involves expert grape pickers, the picking of selected bunches in the vineyard, harvesting the same vineyards several times to gather the grapes at the perfect point of ripeness, etc.

What is a late harvest?
A late harvest is carried out later than usual to pick the grapes that have been left on the vine to become overripe and which are normally used to produce sweet or raisin wines (due to the high concentration of sugar). In some cases, depending on the variety and climate, 'noble rot' occurs, when a fungus known as botrytis cinerea attacks the grape, increasing acidity and sugars and decreasing water content, also enriching the aromas in a special way. This is particularly prized in some of the world's best dessert wines, such as Sauternes.

THE TERROIR

This is the magical term the French use to speak about the intimate association that is established between the soil, the microclimate and one or more varieties adapted to this terrain, fundamental in producing a wine with its own personality and, therefore, having a different character to the rest.

The origin. Found in France. The *terroir* is the corner stone of the vine-growing philosophy in France and on which the system of designations of origin is based. It is used not only to mark out regions of a certain entity and size, but also to mark out small areas of only a few hectares: they are known as the *Crus* in Bordeaux and the even smaller *Clos* in Burgundy.

The concept in Spain. Although the system of designation of origin is similar, the geographical demarcations were carried out on a larger scale, either due to the influence of a group of vineyards, historical or even political reasons, and occasionally due to the soils and climate. *Vinos de Pago* have not been a serious option until recently, and only as the result of the increased concern for the vineyard.

The concept in the New World. Here the preference has been to give more importance to the variety than to the land, and the *terroir* has had the connotation of a poetic dream or a mere marketing ploy. But this posture contradicts the exquisite respect the Australians, Californians and even the Chileans have for their old vineyards, transmitting a greater complexity to the wine thanks to more numerous and deeper roots that absorb the minerals from the soil better. At present, they are also producing some exceptional quality *Vinos de Pago*.

What is the concept of *terroir*? Perhaps the most important philosophy associated with the *terroir* is the respect for all the components of nature (climate, soil, etc.) and that it therefore cannot undergo significant manipulation. In addition, the aim of achieving the greatest possible expression from the land demands recognized practices such as the limitation of the vineyard's production.

Are there better *terroirs* than others? When it comes to wines and *terroirs* there is no democracy. Therefore, there are *terroirs* that, given the nature of the soil and the climate, produce finer wines than others and even, for no apparent reason, wines with a greater complexity and the ability to age much better.

What are the main types of soil that produce quality wines? Neither the age or the geological composition, or the textures of the soil are the determining factors. We can find excellent wines born from clayey, slate, alluvium or calcareous soils etc. The only common factor seems to be the fact that these soils are not fertile (almost always incapable of being able to cultivate any other plant but the vine) and with excellent natural drainage (which may be improved by man if needs be) in such a way that the supply of water to the plant is strictly moderated and controlled; in other words, the soil has the necessary mechanisms to counteract a shortage or even an excess of water, depending on the latitude of the vineyards.

Is an ideal soil sufficient? We might think of a field with a top layer of stones (gravel, pebbles, slate), which increases heat and therefore ensures the ripening of the grape; followed by a second layer of sand that drains the water and below that a layer of clay to retain the humidity in the subsoil. This cross-section is found in many parts of Spain. Besides, the *terroir* must go hand in hand with an environmental and climatic factor which are in harmony with the soil. For example, a red wine from Priorat with the same soil but found at a higher altitude would be different. And the same would happen if the poorness of the telluric soil did not have fresh breezes coming off Montsant. In addition, it must not be forgotten that the better a variety is adapted to the soil and climate, the more character can be extracted from the soil.

THE BEST *TERROIRS* IN SPAIN

The Spanish *terroirs* in which these types of soils predominate are listed below (as far as possible in order of importance):

Slate soils. Priorat, some areas of Cebreros, Arribes del Duero, Ribeira Sacra, La Axarquia (Málaga), high areas of Valle de Guimar (Tenerife), small areas of Calatayud and the northeast of Empordà.

Stony soils, the best estates of Toro, certain estates of Tarragona (Falset, Conca de Barberà and Terra Alta), some areas of Ribera de Navarra, areas near the Duero in Rueda and certain areas of Rioja Baja.

Clayey calcareous soils, predominately limestone. Rioja Alavesa and surrounding regions, Sonsierra, Rioja Alta, the Valladolid area of the Ribera del Duero, Calatayud, Jumilla, Yecla, Jerez, Montilla-Moriles, Terra Alta, Alicante, Cigales, Costers del Segre and Somontano.

Sandy (siliceous) soils or with a granite base. Rías Baixas, Valdeorras, Ribeiro, Ribeira Sacra, Fermoselle, the area north of Méntrida, and the western area of Vinos de Madrid.

Volcanic soils. Lanzarote, Hierro, Valle de Güimar, Gran Canaria, Monte de Lentiscal, La Palma, Ycoden-Daute-Isora and Abona.

VARIETIES

THE MAIN SPANISH WHITE WINE VARIETIES

Airén

The main white grape variety from La Mancha, producing the largest single variety volume of wine in the world. When produced on a large scale without proper care, it provides very uninteresting wines. However, produced with greater care, it offers pale whites with a fruity nose that are smooth and pleasant on the palate but without any nuances of character.

ALBARIÑO

Mainly produced on the Atlantic coast of Galicia. Very good quality grape, probably originally from central Europe, typical of wet and less sunny regions. It is fruity and floral; the wine is characteristically oily and has a lingering taste.

CAYETANA BLANCA

Grown in Extremadura, mainly in Tierra de Barros. Adapts easily to clayey soils and warm climates; producing a light wine with pleasant and curious traces of scrubland herbs but without any traces of wildness; possessing a pleasant freshness, although losing it quickly after the second year in bottle.

GARNACHA BLANCA

This may be considered the Mediterranean white grape par excellence. Especially abundant in Cataluña (Empordà, Priorat and above all Terra Alta), it is characterised by pleasant hints of herbs, hay and scrubland, and a fleshiness and good level of alcohol on the palate tending to go rancid if barrel aged. There are excellent examples of barrel fermentation.

GODELLO

Another high quality Galician white cultivated in Valdeorras and Monterrei in the province of Galicia, as well as in Bierzo. Its high glycerol content, with resounding acidity, produces a pleasant bittersweet flavour together with a high alcohol content.

HONDARRABI ZURI

This variety is used to produce Txakoli in Vizcaya and Guipuzcoa. Perfectly adapted to a cool and humid environment, producing fresh and fruity wines, with pleasant hints of green apples, green grass, and a refreshing acidity.

LISTÁN BLANCA

Cultivated in the Canary Islands, providing a wine with curious nuances, somewhere between ripe grapes and mountain herbs. It is balsamic and even more so if it comes from vineyards found on dry and difficult soils (Valle de Güimar).

MACABEO (OR VIURA)

The basic variety of quality white Rioja wines and cavas. Its slow oxidation makes it ideal for barrel ageing. The wine is pale and light, with hints of green fruit. Recently an excellent side to *Macabeo* has been discovered being cultivated in poor, low yield fields, quite the contrary to current practices in Penedès and La Rioja.

MALVAR

This is the main stock of white wines produced in Madrid. It has a smooth texture, fruity with a certain sweetness. It combines well with *Airén* and is ideal for producing wines using the skin.

MALVASÍA

The most famous sweet wine of the Middle Ages, although it reigned throughout the Mediterranean region; it is now relegated to Italy, Portugal (it is the most important grape in Madeira) and Spain. Considered nobler than *Moscatel*, very aromatic whites are produced from it, with a highly original taste between musk and bitter. The best-known examples in Spain are the *Malvasias* from the Canary Islands, Sitges, and it is also produced in Navarra and La Rioja in smaller quantities.

MERSEGUERA

A variety that is cultivated in Valencia, basically in Alto Turia and on a lesser scale in Utiel-Requena. Produces whites with a grassy character with nuances of dry mountain herbs and a light almondy background; it has a little more body than the *Cayetana Blanca* and the *Airén*.

MOSCATEL (MUSCAT)

This is usually used to produce Mistela and produces aromatic, sharp wines that are very fragrant and fresh if recently made. It is grown in Levante, Cádiz, Málaga and the Ebro basin. In the latter area there is a type of *Moscatel de Grano Menudo* used in high quality sweet wines.

PALOMINO

This is the variety par excellence for Sherry. Its rapid evolution makes it ideal for producing 'Vinos Generosos' (fortified wines). It has little body and a fresh pungent flavour with nuances of bitter almonds. *Palomino* is also grown in the provinces of Galicia, León and Valladolid.

PARDINA

The most widely found white grape in Extremadura, especially abundant in the regions of Tierra de Barros and Ribera Baja. New wine-making methods are starting to discover a defined standard that is characterized by its mountain herbs and ripe fruit; a variety that can also unfold a great taste on the palate.

PARELLADA

Grown in the higher regions of Cataluña. It is a very fine grape and therefore difficult to produce. The low alcohol wines are pale, with delicate aromas and little body. It is also a complementary variety in the production of Cavas.

PEDRO XIMÉNEZ

Mainly grown in the provinces of Córdoba and Málaga. The wines from Montilla-Moriles are made from this grape and its rapid evolution makes it suitable for dry and sweet dessert wines, as well as for the sweet wines from Málaga combined with *Moscatel*. When used in dry wines it leaves a pleasant sensation of suppleness and sweetness.

PICAPOLL

A grape native to the Catalonian region of Pla del Bages, which is also grown in the Languedoc in France. According to some theories its name comes from the spots that appear on the skin and according to others from its sharp lemon acidity. Although it is traditionally used as a blend for other grapes (*Macabeo, Parellada...*), new wave producers such as Abadal have used it as a varietal due to its intense and fruity aromas (flowers and herbaceous).

TORRONTÉS

Used in blends for modern Ribeira wines – together with *Godello, Albariño, Treixadura* and *Loureiro* - producing high quality musts, a high production and a neutral taste, less intense and a better acidity than its companions. Outside Spain, it is the recipe for the best known whites from Chile.

TREIXADURA

This is a Galician grape from Ribeiro, similar to *Albariño* but not as refined and with less glycerol. Its taste is reminiscent of ripe apples and it combines perfectly with *Albariño*. Floral and fruity character, a good quality grape, however, it has a limited production.

VERDEJO

The white grape of Rueda, bordering the Duero and other regions of Castilla. It was the base for wines called 'Solera wines', 'rancios' and aged wines. Recently it has been added to the new tendency of fruity wines and it is used to make young whites, with greenish yellow tones and with a pleasant bitter touch on the palate. It has an excellent character if the vineyard is found on stony fields.

XAREL-LO

Very harmonious, but with more body than the classical Catalonian grapes, *Parellada* and *Macabeo*. When it ripens well and it is from a low yield, it has a good character.

GEOGRAPHICAL DISTRIBUTION OF THE MAIN SPANISH QUALITY WHITE VINES.

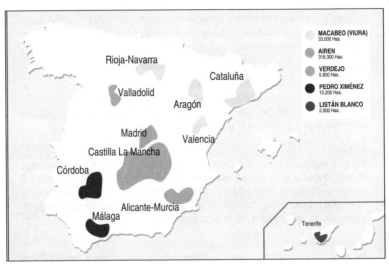

THE MAIN SPANISH RED WINE VARIETIES

BOBAL

Typical of the high areas of Levante and very abundant in Utiel-Requena. Intense colour, with brilliant reflections due to its high acidity, but low alcohol content. It has a fresh aroma, not too intense and makes good rosé wines. A more accentuated character of wild berries appears only when the grape is from old vines. An improved knowledge of low yield viticulture is producing some reds that are meatier and have more tannins with excellent possibilities for ageing.

CALLET

Native to Mallorca, for years it has been considered a second-rate grape, producing musts with very little colour and high yield production. However, young wine growers from around Felanitx have given it a new lease on life over the last few years thanks to selective work on old stock and low yield production, producing a wine with good colour and high alcohol content. It is usually mixed with *Cabernet*, *Manto Negro* or *Tempranillo* so that the wines age better and are more complex.

CARIÑENA

The dominant grape in Catalonian red wines which is also used in the production of wines in Rioja – where it is known as *Mazuelo* – and Aragón. It is a good complement to *Garnacha*, as it is more acidic and has a low oxidation level, making it ideal for ageing. Its taste only comes out when it is cultivated in very hot and open regions.

GARNACHA

The most extensively cultivated grape in Spain as it is easy to grow and gives good yields. Its body, fruitiness and meatiness make it an ideal complement for balanced blending. It tends to oxidise easily, and is used in some regions to make rancios and dessert wines. In recent years thanks to new technologies and faster harvesting an unforeseen quality for young reds and medium-aged reds is being discovered.

GARNACHA TINTORERA

The main characteristic of the grape is that the pulp is coloured, which makes it a very sought after grape to give colour to the bulk. Traditionally known as the Alicante Bouschet hybrid, some authors say it is an independent variety from the regions of Alicante, Toledo and Cuidad Real. In recent productions as a varietal wine in Almansa DO, it offers a grape with a great aromatic potency and very fruity character which also gives body and structure on the palate.

GRACIANO

This forms an important part of the blending in Riojan reds although it only occupies several hundred hectares in Rioja Alta and Navarra. Because of its fruity aroma, freshness and intense colour it is known as 'the grace of Rioja', even though it is difficult to grow and ripens very late with a brusque rise in sugar in the final stage. In recent years this vine has made a comeback and is used by quality wine producers in Rioja (Contino), and even in warmer areas such as Valencia, where surprising results are being obtained.

LISTÁN

This vine is cultivated in the Canary Islands and produces brilliant reds, with a marked balsamic nose and with hints of eucalyptus and very fresh and juicy red fruit. Very low in tannins, making it more suitable for producing young wines.

MANTO NEGRO

Native to the Balearic Islands, especially abundant in the DO Binissalem in Mallorca, but also found in Pla i Llevant. It gives characteristic ripe fruit aromas with hints of caramel. On the palate it is quite balanced, although it is normally blended with another local grape, *Callet*, or other international varieties.

MENCÍA

The cultivation of this grape is limited to the north eastern regions of the Iberian Peninsula, and it is found where the provinces of León and Zamora join Galicia. Very similar to *Cabernet Franc*, it produces fruity wines, rich in colour and acidity when it is cultivated in cool regions with sufficient water. Recently heavier and darker reds are being produced due to more careful winemaking and lower yields.

MONASTRELL

Typical variety from the Levante region, abounds in the Jumilla, Yecla, Alicante and Almansa DO´s. It is a very sweet and productive grape which traditionally has been used for rancios and dessert wines as it evolves quickly. It has a lovely colour, aromas of ripe grapes with hints of raisins and a powerful flavour, fruity, with few tannins, although on the whole, the wine is meaty. It needs to be combined with a slower evolving variety for the wines to be aged.

MORISTEL

This is cultivated in the Somontano DO and produces reds with a great fruity expression (brambles and red currants) and a slightly wild touch, which makes it better for young wines.

NEGRAMOLL

This is a grape cultivated in the Canary Islands, particularly on the island of La Palma. It has less character than the *Listán*, but a better tannin structure. If it is harvested late it sometimes has a tasty flavour of very ripe black fruit.

PRIETO PICUDO

This is cultivated between Benavente and Astorga and from this city to the border of the province of León with Palencia. It grows in extreme conditions; the wine has a dark cherry colour, developing aromas of red fruits similar to the *Mencía*, but with pleasant wild hints and it has a better structure. It is similar to the *Graciano*.

TEMPRANILLO

This is a noble Spanish grape par excellence and at the same time extremely widespread. Its name changes according to the region where it is found: *Tempranillo* in Rioja, T*into Fino* or *Tinto del País* in the Ribera del Duero, *Ull de Llebre* in Cataluña, *Cencibel* in La Mancha and *Tinto de Madrid* around the capital. Very fine and aromatic; producing excellent quality wines which can be aged for long periods due to their low oxidation level. It has a very fruity flavour and a characteristically ruby colour, especially in young wines.

GEOGRAPHICAL DISTRIBUTION OF THE MAIN SPANISH QUALITY RED VINES

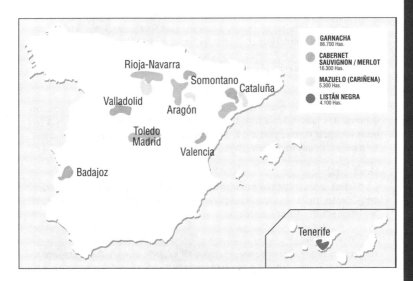

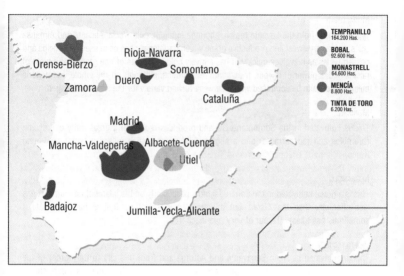

TEMPRANILLO 164.200 Has.
BOBAL 92.600 Has.
MONASTRELL 64.600 Has.
MENCÍA 8.800 Has.
TINTA DE TORO 6.200 Has.

THE MAIN FOREIGN VARIETIES CULTIVATED IN SPAIN

CABERNET FRANC (RED)

Like *Cabernet Sauvignon* it is from Bordeaux, but produces more supple and fruitier wines. It seems to be related to the *Mencía* which is extensively found in regions of Galicia and Castilla.

CABERNET SAUVIGNON (RED)

Originally from France and typical of the reds from Bordeaux. It is ideal for ageing, the colour is intense, it has strong tannins and a penetrating aroma of violets and berries. In Spain it has acclimatised perfectly to areas such as Penedès, Navarra and the Ribera del Duero, and it is difficult to find a red wine producing area in which this champion variety has not been planted in recent years.

CHARDONNAY (WHITE)

Comes from Burgundy in France and has become the most valued white grape in the world. The wines are characterised by a smoky aroma and good results are achieved when ageing in wood due to its high dry extract, glycerin and limited oxidation level. Perfectly adapted to different regions in Spain (Penedès, Costers del Segre, Navarra, Somontano, etc), it is being accepted by the Regulations of numerous Regulatory Councils.

GEWÜRZTRAMINER (WHITE)

Variety of the Traminer species, spicy flavour and traditionally from the Alsace region and Germany. It is cultivated on a limited scale in Somontano and Penedès, but the wines are not as famous as the ones produced in these European regions; in Spain the musky nuances are more prominent than the spicy ones.

MERLOT (RED)

From France, it has a dark blue colour and a very thick skin. Although it is an earlier grape than *Cabernet*, it does well in warm areas. It is widely grown in Somontano and Cataluña and to a lesser extent in Alicante and Murcia.

PETIT VERDOT (RED)

The grape is originally from Bordeaux, although it is hardly found in this region, and is relatively new to Spain, where it is associated more to the whims of the producers (Griñón,

Abadía Retuerta) than to specific geographical areas. Up to now the existing examples in Spain give aromatic sensations of ripe fruit, good intensity on the palate as well as the nose.

PINOT NOIR (RED)

A classic grape from Burgundy and Champagne. The fruit is small and has a dark violet skin which is a strong colorant. However, the wine loses colour faster than other types turning an orangey colour. In warm climates it loses its complexity and elegance. It is mainly grown in Cataluña.

RIESLING (WHITE)

The most famous white wines from Alsace, Moselle and the Rhine are produced from this grape. The grape is small and yellowish, and has a limited yield. In Spain it gives fresh, fruity and floral dry wine which is not as solemn and complex as in these European regions. It is mainly grown in Cataluña.

SAUVIGNON BLANC (WHITE)

A quality white grape with small fruit and a golden colour when ripe. It is mainly grown in Bordeaux (Graves) and the Loire area and it has acclimatised to other countries such as Argentina, Chile, Uruguay, California and above all New Zealand. In Spain it is mainly grown in Rueda DO and to a lesser extent in Cataluña. It has a taste of tropical fruits and a slight floral nuance.

SYRAH (RED)

This is the vine stock of the Rhone and Australia par excellence and is becoming very fashionable in Spain as it is ideally suited to warm areas. The grapes are ovoid and small with a very pleasant flavour. Its wine has a characteristic aroma of violets and very ripe black fruit. At present it is a very popular grape in Jumilla (the first place it was grown) where it is blended with *Monastrell*, as well as large parts of Spain with a Mediterranean–Continental climate.

VIOGNIER (WHITE)

The jewel of the Rhone valley is fast growing in popularity all over the world and is acclimatising well to Spain thanks to the similarity of the Mediterranean climate with its area of origin. A noble grape, which ages with grace. It has a floral and fruity character with hints of herbs and depth, and in good wines it has large doses of complexity.

VITICULTURE AND THE ALTITUDE TRIANGLE

It is true that the cooler climates are found in the north, but it is possible to reproduce similar climatic conditions in more southern areas: one only needs to increase the altitude.

In the northern hemisphere, between latitude 50 (the coldest viticulture area, at the level of Champagne) and 30 (the hottest, towards the centre of Morocco) vines are grown with a single annual crop picked around about the same dates and with an alcohol content of between 8% in the French region and 7% in the Maghrebi plains. The alcohol content of the grapes in the champagne area is not sufficient to produce still white wines, and therefore the must is used to produce sparkling wines.

The Bordeaux - Rioja - Ribeira - Tenerife equivalence.

In the north a more balanced alcohol content is found at Bordeaux where the vines are grown at a little over 10 metres above sea level. To find a wine with the same analytical characteristics to the south one would have to go as far as La Rioja. Here, at 450 metres above sea level (average level of the Riojan vineyards) the coolness of the higher altitude compensates for the warmer temperatures typical of the south. And if we continue our trip south we find that in the Ribera del Duero vines are grown at 800 metres to find the same climatic conditions and in Tenerife they are grown at a height of 1,300 metres above sea level.

The importance of the difference in day/night temperatures.

The importance is not so much in the daytime temperatures at these different altitudes above sea level being the same as in Bordeaux, as the strength of the sun in the south is greater, but in the drop in the nocturnal temperatures which compensates for the excessive sunlight during the day. The summer nights in Bordeaux are warmer than those in La Rioja and these in turn are warmer than the nights in Ribera, and the coolest of all are those of the very high vineyards of Vilaflor in Tenerife. Thus the loss of acidity generated by the heat is halted at night, above all in August and September, the main season for the ripening of the fruit. Therefore when the harvesting season arrives, the different parts of the grape are all in their prime; without having interrupted the ripening of the bunch during the day.

The graph below illustrates this strange relationship; however, specific microclimates of certain areas which could influence this graph, have not been taken into account.

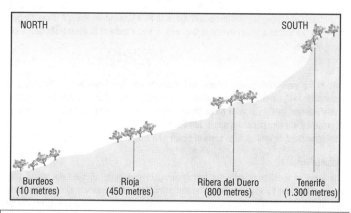

NORTH			SOUTH
Burdeos (10 metres)	Rioja (450 metres)	Ribera del Duero (800 metres)	Tenerife (1.300 metres)

VITICULTURE CLIMATES AND MICROCLIMATES

The role played by the climate on the development of the vine is decisive. Factors such as the temperature, the rainfall or the amount of sunshine will determine the making of different styles of wines. Spain moreover, influenced by the Atlantic and the Mediterranean, is subjected to a large number of climatic conditions over a very limited area.

The complex orography of Spain.

The high plateaux, the river valleys, terraces, plots and ravines represent the outline of the true back bone of what are the mountain ranges. These, curiously enough, run from northeast to southwest, and make up large catchment areas open from the west where 80% of the humid currents come in from; rains which appear precisely when the grape has not formed on the plant, but are necessary to feed the roots (which is what really matters). The low rainfall found in the Iberian Peninsula (due to the dominance of a permanent high pressure area over the Azores during the growing period of the vine) considerably reduces the percentage of moisture in comparison with a large part of Italy and the rest of Europe. This produces soils with a low organic level, poor production level but rich in minerals, which greatly favours the growing of vines.

Descriptions of all the climatic conditions that are found in Spain are listed below.

ATLANTIC CLIMATE

This is caused by the influence of the moisture from the ocean. It is characterised by mild temperatures and a certain degree of humidity, with rains all year round. There is a large mass of water situated to the west and the influence it has depends on the marine currents and the temperature differences of the water.

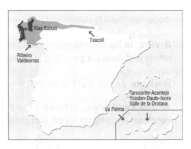

WINE PRODUCING REGIONS:

Northern Tenerife. The moisture does not come from the storms which occur more to the north, but from the humid trade winds from the north east, which, colliding with the warm air mass from the mountainous relief of Tenerife, create an accumulation of clouds known locally as 'panza de burro' (the donkey's paunch) which keep the level of humidity stable along the coastline from Tacoronte-Acentejo to the Valle de Orotava and to a certain degree up to the area of Ycoden - Daute - Isora.

Wines with high acidity, not very high alcohol content and a slight hint of malic acid.

Galicia. A region which is entirely influenced by the Atlantic, not only because of the level of humidity and the sea breezes, but also the frequency of the storms coming in from the west to the east, depositing great quantities of rain. In areas of the interior with less rainfall, micro-climates may form and therefore, the grape ripens more easily, such as Rosal and Condado de Tea.

Wines sometimes made from underripe rather than overripe grapes are high in malic acids, have a moderate alcohol content and high acidity.

Txakoli. Like Galicia, it has a 100% Atlantic climate with a high rainfall. This calls for the use of adapted varieties and does not allow for the use of alternative varieties with good acidity, except for grapes that do well in very cool and wet climates such as *Riesling*. The vines must face south, creating problems as the vineyards are found on the northern slopes.

Fresh whites, acidic, hints of green apples and floral. Very dry reds, slightly herbaceous and a red berry aroma.

ATLANTIC - CONTINENTAL CLIMATE

These are regions with a rainfall which comes from the Atlantic and at the same time have a certain proportion of a continental climate due to the lower nocturnal temperatures and in general, colder temperatures in winter.

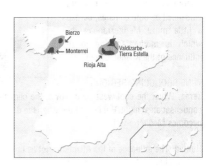

WINE PRODUCING REGIONS

Bierzo. This is a transitional region between Castilla and Galicia found at a lower altitude than the Castilian plateau. Because of the closeness of the Atlantic Ocean it has an Atlantic climate but with traces of a continental climate. It has less rainfall than Galicia and the nocturnal temperatures are lower and therefore the grape ripens more slowly and moderately, but it is also firmer.

Navarra. In the northern region (Valdizarbe and Tierra Estella) where the relief limits the influence of the sea, a good balance between Atlantic and a continental climate is found.

Rioja Alta. An area found to the west of northern Navarra.

Well-balanced wines, between 12 and 13 degrees, good ripening without a lot of sunshine; very elegant but not resounding.

CONTINENTAL – ATLANTIC CLIMATE

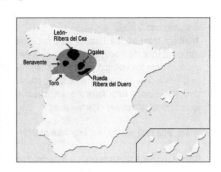

Characterised by the large contrast between day/night temperatures. The sunshine during the day allows for good ripening which the cold at night stops thus conserving the acidity. The Atlantic influence is due to the rains coming in from the ocean during spring and autumn.

WINE PRODUCING REGIONS

Castilla–León. Includes the Ribera del Duero DO and is situated in the river basin with the same name and is partly influenced by the altitude; Rueda to the southwest is at a lower altitude, more exposed and with a milder climate; Toro and Cigales.

Wines with a good colour and alcohol content, and very well conserved by the acidity.

ATLANTIC - MEDITERRANEAN CLIMATE

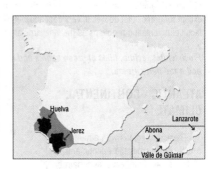

A strange combination in an area where both seas are very close. It is influenced by both climates, perhaps a little more Mediterranean, but which is moderated due to the influence of the Atlantic Ocean.

WINE PRODUCING REGIONS

Jerez. When the cool west wind blows, the climate is sufficiently Atlantic to form heavy condensation at night. But in summer when the drier easterly wind blows, the climate clearly becomes Mediterranean.

Huelva. The influence of the Atlantic is not as obvious as it is orientated towards the south and the climate is therefore more Mediterranean, in spite of being situated more to the west. **Wines with moderate alcohol and acidity** (in the case of Generoso wines, the most common wine in this area, this factor is not relevant as alcohol is added.)

CONTINENTAL – MEDITERRANEAN CLIMATE

The rainfall is similar to a Continental - Atlantic climate; it is at a lower altitude and therefore the vineyards can be closer to the sea in spite of being situated on a plateau.

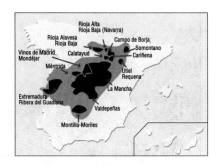

WINE PRODUCING REGIONS

Castilla-La Mancha, Montilla Moriles and Ribera del Guadiana; Campo de Borja, Cariñena and Calatayud in Aragón; Costers del Segre, south of Navarra, Rioja Baja and Rioja Alavesa.

Wines with a higher alcohol content and a lower acidity.

MEDITERRANEAN CLIMATE

This is characterised by its low rainfall and its low altitude.

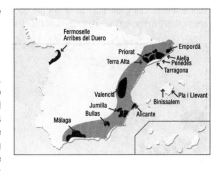

WINE PRODUCING REGIONS

Valencia, Clariano, Alto Turia, Alicante, Murcia with its two winegrowing regions Yecla and Jumilla; practically all the regions of Cataluña but especially the coastal region. The ripening period is longer and therefore the alcohol content is higher even when taking into consideration that vines with a long cycle are grown which are suited to warmer climates.

Full-bodied wines, alcoholic aroma, dry earth and very ripe or jammy black fruit.

VITICULTURAL MICROCLIMATES

These are climates that occur over small areas, such as a municipality, a vineyard or even a vine. In the section we will concentrate on those that affect a small territory and are more frequent in Spanish vineyards.

MOUNTAIN MICROCLIMATES. Affects the vineyards that are protected by forest areas and situated on uneven lands (slopes) and have different orientations (north, south, east, or west). The ripening of the grapes is different as the sun does not shine uniformly on the whole vineyard. We might even speak about small microclimates within the microclimate. However, the common factor is that they are 'protected areas'

Where are they found? At San Martin de Valdeiglesias (Madrid), La Axarquía (Málaga), Alto Turia, Sierra de Francia (Salamanca), Cebreros (Ávila) or the extraordinary Catalonian Priorat.

VALLEY MICROCLIMATES. These are very often found north of the 40º latitude. Normally, we find a river running through a valley acting as a hinge between the two slopes which are completely or partially protected by mountains. The vines grown on the slopes will have a shorter production cycle than those on the plain, but they also have different alcohol contents depending on the orientation and the slope of the ground.

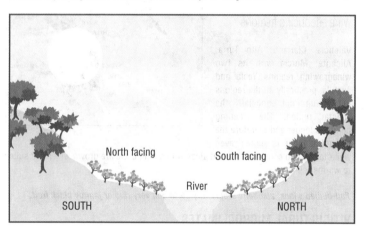

The valley slopes. The southern slope means more sun, as the rays of the sun are almost perpendicular, while on the northern slope the rays are oblique which cause a longer ripening and consequently more acidity and longevity. This is what happens at Ribera del Duero to the Vega Sicilia and Viña Mayor vineyards, found on the north-facing slopes which can produce grapes with the same alcohol content as those on the opposite slopes (Pesquera, Dehesa de los Canónigos, Hacienda Monasterio).

When the orientation of the valley is north–south and the slopes range from east to west, the ripening is also different. An east or southwest orientation in a northern latitude such as Côte de Nuits in Burgundy means they can take advantage of the sun from daybreak. But the same situation in Spain does not have any special advantages. The worst orientation is west, as the high temperatures during the day are capped with the excessive sun in the afternoon, the hottest time of the day.

The altitude factor. Ripening improves with an increase in altitude as it is away from the humidity and the greater coolness of the lower areas. Only when we go over 100 metres above the lowest level of the valley does the cold at night make ripening difficult. Equally, the vineyard on the plain will be more productive because of more water and will therefore be of inferior quality.

Where are they found? At vineyards found on the limit of growing conditions such as Ribera del Duero, the valley of Lerma (more exposed area with a harsher climate producing lighter wines), Rioja Alavesa (the effect of the foehn winds is added to the clouds that form along the mountain range and then scatter, the rainfall is lower and the wines are darker and have a higher alcohol content) and Rioja Alta (vineyards with less sunlight due to the higher rainfall and the slower ripening which gives less pigmented wines and more acidity).

FLUVIAL MICROCLIMATE Produced in areas found right against rivers and which also benefit from a valley climate. However, there is an element of risk in being so low and near a river. Due to the mass of water the ground temperature is lower, mists (greater risk of cryptogamic disease) and frost occur. Only when the soil is stony (typical of alluvial areas) is an excellent thermal affect created which helps ripening.

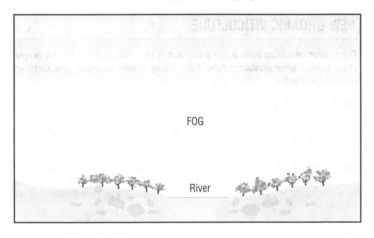

Where are they found? Certain Rueda vineyards near the Duero as well as the vineyards of Vega Sicilia and Abadia de Retuerta which extend along this river.

MARITIME MICROCLIMATE Determined by the positive influence that the sea has on very sunny areas which slows the growth process. It is very common in southern areas where varieties that need a lot of sunshine are grown, but which benefit from alternating temperatures thanks to the sea breezes.

Its influence on ageing. The influence of the sea also brings about a less oxidative and more placid ageing in wood, as occurs at El Puerto de Santa María and Sanlúcar de Barrameda. This used to be compulsory for the wines from Málaga (at the port of the city) and Oporto (near Vila Nova de Gaia, near the coast)

Where are they found? In the area of La Marina in Alicante, Banylus and Rivesaltes (Roussillin) on the French Mediterranean coast and Axarquía in Málaga, where the *Moscatel* grape needs a certain amount of moisture but also assured sunshine. In Jerez, the best vineyards are found on the highest hills facing the westerly sea breezes. In the north of

Tenerife, the trade winds from the northeast moderate the alcohol content of the grape and preserve the acidity.

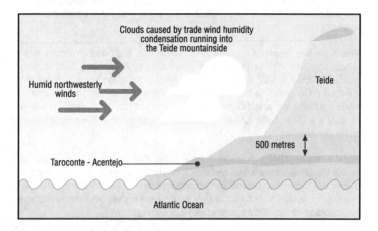

Clouds caused by trade wind humidity condensation running into the Teide mountainside

Teide

Humid northwesterly winds

500 metres

Taroconte - Acentejo

Atlantic Ocean

NEW ORGANIC VITICULTURE

The environmental movement has also reached the world of wines and for several years certain wine producers have been taking it very seriously. But there are several doctrines.

BIODYNAMICS FOR VITICULTURE

This is one of the most extreme practices and ideologies in viticulture, inspired by the theories of Rudolf Steiner, and borders on 'witchcraft'.

The Key: The emphasis is on the fertilisation of the soils and a new dimension which is added to wine through 'cosmic influences', defending the theory of the influence of the phases of the moon and the position of the planets when it comes to making the wine as well as vine growing.

They reject: Biodynamics, as an organic method, rejects all chemical products for fertilization, and they are replaced by organic extracts applied directly in small quantities and in very diluted concentrations, although the use of copper sulphate, the so called 'Bordeaux gravy', is not forbidden.

Who practices it: There are a good number of followers in France, above all in Burgundy and the system is especially used by vineyards such as Domaine Leflaive, Domaine Huet and Domaine Leroy. In Spain, this practice is used by a company in Mallorca and certain producers follow some of the theories, especially those related to the phases of the moon.

BIOLOGICAL VITICULTURE

Terminology used to refer to all types of viticultural methods in which organic farming is used in its different forms. It can be considered a philosophical tendency for the natural handling of the vine. It has a growing following amongst the Spanish wine growers who are committed to quality.

• **Objections.** They reject the use of chemical products such as herbicides, pesticides or fertilizers to avoid the residues being passed on to the wines.

- **Origin and achievements.** Very popular and widely accepted in the 1980s and a pioneering example of the current biological tendencies was the introduction of stock to create varieties that were resistant to phylloxera, certain eelworms and drought. The environment plays an important part in the viability of these practices as well as the make-up of the soils and the climatic conditions. Very efficient methods have been developed to prevent and eliminate fungal diseases with products which contain no chemical components.

- **Problems.** Low yields as the vines have to fight to find the necessary nutrients directly from a soil lacking additional nutrients. On the other hand, the use of organic material in the vineyard maintains the organic and chemical structure of the soil as well as improving water retention. Organic viticulture definitely defends a natural and biological way of maintaining and developing the vineyard.

ORGANIC WINE

Wine in whose production the use of sulphur dioxide and antioxidants are forbidden and whose grapes come from organic vineyards. In addition, the 'green' philosophy makes a very convincing commercial argument that is increasingly demanded by the consumer.

- **Origin and introduction.** In the 1990s organic farming became fashionable, with France as the cradle for this rediscovered traditional system. Although it is true that in areas with a Mediterranean climate this practice has fewer problems, as the cryptogamic diseases in vines hardly exist and it is naturally possible to avoid the use of chemical products. This is also true in Languedoc-Roussillon and in Provence, as well as in California and Australia. There is an increase in the number of companies that fall under the Regulation of Organic Agriculture (with their own label) in the different wine producing regions.

- **Criticism.** In the production of organic wines other practices and physical processes such as filtration are limited. Unfortunately, some of these prohibitions- according to the writer Jancis Robinson – do not have a scientific basis, particularly when the controlling bodies prohibit the use of tartaric acid for acidification, but authorise the addition of lemon juice on condition they come from organically produced fruit, even though tartaric acid is the main acid found naturally in wine and not citric acid. These very same bodies prohibit other physical processes without any apparent reason, such as centrifugation. This for example, could be good for the quality of the wine, and yet it has no influence on its organic character.

- **Are organic wines better?** Most definitely not. In some cases, they contain too many oxidants and we find bottles of the latest vintage, which have lost a lot of their fruity qualities due to the low doses of antioxidants that the wine itself generates but with the help of additional sulphur.

THE NEW CONCEPTS OF VITICULTURE

Working methods in vineyards have changed radically in recent times. The Californian and Australians have started a revolution with better quality in relatively high yields. European producers are also trying to maximize their vineyards. There is a whole series of new and old methods associated with new viticultural methods.

The main proponents of viticultural methods in the New World are the University of Davis (California), one of the most important researchers on the subject and the expert from New Zealand Richard Smart, who revolutionised viticulture with his work, *Sunlight into Wine*, and whose theories, thanks to his success as a travelling consultant, have been implanted by vineyards in large parts of the world (including some European and Spanish vineyards).

Canopy Management. This is a term used to describe a combination of practices in the vineyard. The concept is not exclusive to the New World and it is also being studied widely in Europe, although it is mainly applied in the New World producers as it works especially well in vineyards with vigorous growth. It is basically centred on the microclimate of the plant and the search for an optimum exposure of the leaves and the bunches to sunlight, an important quality factor that helps to improve the yield, obtain better quality grapes and combat diseases such as mildew and botrytis. To achieve optimum exposure different trellising methods are used (the most famous are the lyre system and the Scott-Henry and Smart-Dyson systems named after their inventors) and pruning techniques, green pruning and clearing away the leaves to achieve a better exposure to sunlight. Of course all modern trellising systems are also designed for mechanical harvesting.

Water Stress. This is the favourite term of modern viticulturists. This describes the 'psychological stress' a plant suffering from a water shortage goes through. This occurs naturally during the ripening phase in vineyards found in warm Mediterranean climates, and is considered a quality factor above all in reds (fruity concentration higher, control of yields) and currently this form of pressure is exerted on the plant in a controlled way and according to the wishes of the viticulturist. Present irrigation systems, associated with modern trellising systems, have even reached such levels of sophistication that a computer controls the determined quantity of water fed to the plant on one side and the other side of the roots alternatively. Underground irrigation also reduces evaporation.

Old Vines. Taking into account their heritage, old vines are one of the most sought after quality factors by European viticulturists. In Spain there are plenty of old vines, *Garnacha*, *Monastrell*, *Tempranillo*, *Tinta de Toro* and other varieties whose quality is now getting its just rewards. Old vines have lower yields (the yields decrease according to the age of the vines), but the quality of the grape is more stable and consistent and they may also have higher concentrations. Old stock is less vigorous, which means (according to the theory of canopy management) a better exposure of the leaves and bunches.

Root Mass. The root system of vines is another aspect which is increasingly important for viticulturist. A large portion of the work is orientated towards stimulating their growth towards the lower layers of the subsoil, to give the wine more mineral nuances and consequently a more defined character. Of course this must be on the basis of appropriate soils for the vine. Water stress also helps in this respect because if the plant is deprived of water on the top layers of the soil, it is forced to look for it in the depths of the subsoil.

THE MAKING OF WINE

HÓW IS WINE MADE?

Vinification is another crucial element for obtaining quality wines. Basically, the process of winemaking encompasses the following stages:

HARVESTING. This takes place between the first days of September and the middle of October although there are exceptions. Here the first selection is made, discarding the damaged bunches.

TRANSPORTING TO THE BODEGA. This must be done as carefully as possible so that the grapes are not damaged by too much pressure and to avoid premature fermentation. It is best is to use containers that do not exceed a capacity of 15 kg.

UNLOADING. This is carried out on the 'receiving hopper', a type of inverted cone, similar to a funnel, which deposits the grapes on a 'worm', which takes the grapes to the crusher. The fruit is analysed on the hopper to determine if it is disease-free and to check the levels of sugars and acids.

CRUSHING. The crusher squeezes the grape, but only sufficiently to stop the pips and the stalks or stems – the structural support of the bunch - breaking and contaminating the must. The resulting pulp is taken to the presses without coming into contact with the air to avoid fermentation starting.

WHITE WINES

PRESSING. The presses crush the grape using various pressures, producing different quality musts.

Free run musts: they are the finest, most aromatic, supplest and fruitiest (and therefore better quality) obtained statically (by gravity)

First, second and third or press musts: these are, in this order, the results of increasing pressures on the grape (greater pressure, lower quality). Each one is fermented separately and will produce different types of wine.

The marc: this is the excess pulp that remains in the press. It can be distilled to make Orujo (eau-de-vie) or be made into fertilisers or feed.

RACKING MUST. The method used to separate the herbaceous and aggressive parts of the grape from the must. The must is left to stand for several hours so that the suspended solid particles in it sink to the bottom, and the fermentation can take place in a clean and fruity must.

FERMENTATION. During this process the sugars in the must are turned into alcohol. This acohol fermentation is due to the action of the yeasts - micro fungi that are found in the soils of the vineyards - that without air, metabolize the sugars into alcohol and carbon dioxide.

During this process the temperature must be controlled as an excess could kill the yeasts and stop the fermentation. The density must also be checked to control the amount of sugar to be left in the must. This last point will determine the type of wine produced. One can distinguish between:

Dry white wine: the residual sugar content is not higher than 5 grams per litre.
Demi-sec white wine: the residual sugar content is not higher than 15 -30 grams per litre.

Sweet wine: more than 50 grams per litre of residual sugar.

To obtain the last two types of wine the fermentation must be stopped by chemical (adding sulphur dioxide) or physical means (cooling or overheating) at the moment the sugar content is appropriate for the type of wine desired.

BASIC PRODUCTION OF WHITE WINES

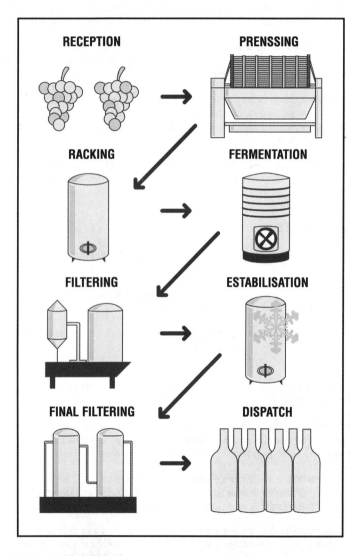

TYPES OF PRODUCTION.

'Virgin' fermentation. This is the most common practice and is only carried out with the must, that is to say, without any contact with the skins.

Skin maceration. This is a method of increasing the aromatic potential of the wine by extracting the many aromatic molecules from the skins. The must is macerated together with the skins impeding fermentation by means of cold treatment. This method, which is quite fashionable, gives the wine body, enriches the sensations on the palate, increases the strength of the aromas, improves evolution in the bottle and gives the wine a longer life.

Racking. This consists of transferring the wine from one container to another with the aim of leaving the solid particles behind. In the case of whites, the wine undergoes two or three rackings between November and January as during these dates the low temperatures prevent any contamination by micro-organisms. After this the qualities are selected and the corresponding mixtures take place to achieve the desired result.

Clarification. A clarifying agent is used to settle the particles in suspension that were left in the wine and which had not been removed by the racking.

Filtering. This has the same purpose as clarifying, but the method is different, and in this case the wine is passed through a porous material or membrane to remove the particles in suspension.

Bottling. The wine is finally bottled and is ready to be sold.

Rosés

They are produced in the same way as whites, except red grapes or a mixture of red and white grapes are used.

MACERATION. Before fermentation the wine undergoes a short cold maceration - to prevent fermentation – together with the skins (only for a few hours) to extract the colour.

RACKING AND FERMENTATION. The solid material is separated from the must, to carry out the primary fermentation (as though it were a white) with the resulting transformation of the sugars into alcohol due to the action of the yeasts.

What is claret? Rosé wine gets this name when the colouring process is carried out by fermenting the skins with the must. Clarets are therefore made in the same way as reds. In rural areas rosés are often called clarets.

RED WINES

These are made from the must of red grapes fermented with the solid parts of the grape (skin and pips).

DESTEMMING. Unlike whites, the resulting paste from the crusher goes through a 'stripping' process which consists of separating the grapes from the stalks to avoid the wine taking on herbaceous and bitter tastes from the woody part of the bunch during the maceration to get colour.

ALCOHOL FERMENTATION. Or 'tumultuous' due to the hectic activity of the yeasts in this stage. The sugars are converted into alcohol at the same time as the colorants from the skin dissolve in the must.

OVER-PUMPING. During alcohol fermentation carbon dioxide is formed. This forces the skins to the top forming a natural barrier called the 'cap'. Over-pumping consists in wetting this cap with the must to activate the extraction of the colour. The skins must also be stirred periodically, and this process is called 'punching'.

DRAWING OFF. Once the desired colour has been achieved, the liquid is decanted separating it from the solid matter which goes to the presses and then taken to another tank.

MALOLACTIC FERMENTATION. In red wines a second fermentation called malolactic fermentation, takes place, where malic acid, a sharp and vegetable acid, is converted into a smoother and creamier acid called lactic acid, which makes the wine finer and smoother.

BASIC PRODUCTION OF VINTAGE RED WINES

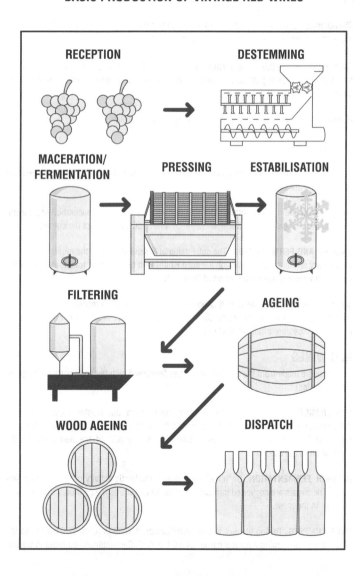

44

What is press wine? This is obtained as a result of the pressing of the solid remains from the first fermentation. It is very rich in colour and tannins, but must not be mixed with the rest unless it is of excellent quality and from ripe grapes.

Once the fermentations have been concluded, the wine is subjected to several rackings and clarification and stabilisation treatments to preserve the clarity of the bottled product. Finally, the wines are selected by qualities and bottled in the case of young wines or placed in barrels to be aged in wood.

GENEROSOS (FORTIFIED)

These are wines with a high alcohol content, normally between 15º and 23º. Although they are widely produced in different wine producing regions, they are closely linked to Andalucía.

• **The base wine.** This is a light wine from the *Palomino* grape about 11º, similar to a table wine.

• **Finos and Manzanillas.** They are made from the above-mentioned wine, as it permits biological ageing. Due to the addition of vinous alcohol of up to 15º and to the action of the yeast, the yeasts accumulate on the surface forming a cap called the 'flor' (fluer) or 'velo en flor' (veil), resulting in a pale colour; oxidation does not take place as the fluer cap prevents contact with the air and not because of less ageing in oak, as the ageing period is similar to that of medium-aged Amontillados and Olorosos.

• **Olorosos.** These are wines that due to their body are not used for Finos. Vinous alcohol of up to 19º is added to stop the formation of the 'velo en flor' and it therefore undergoes oxidative ageing in slightly warmer bodegas.

• **Amontillados**. These are Finos; as they oxidize and lose their attributes vinous alcohol is added to them to reach 17º. In this way the fluer is 'killed' and it develops into an oxidized wine in the same way as an Oloroso. The charm of these wines is the combination of the Fino and Oloroso characteristics.

• **Pedro Ximénez.** These are sweet wines made from grapes with the same name and which undergo a sun-drying phase; that is, the bunches are placed in the sun for 15 days to dehydrate the grape and to concentrate the sugars. They are aged, as the aforementioned wines, in oak casks.

• **Cream.** This is a mixture of Olorosos and sweet wines. They are mixed after they have been aged separately in their soleras or, less frequently, before.

AGEING. Generoso wines are aged in 550 litre American oak casks. A system of 'breeding' casks is used (casks which age wine, an oxidative or biological process depending on whether they are Olorosos or Finos respectively, or a mixture if they are Amontillados) and soleras (casks which are on the 'ground' row and whose wine is ready to be bottled. The casks of each type are placed, one on top of the other. When wine is drawn off (trickling) from the solera cask, this is replaced by wine which tickles down from the cask on top of it and so on successively from the rest of the 'breeders'.

FORTIFYING. This is the addition of alcohol to a wine of 11º to 15º thus initiating the Fino phase.

COUPAGE. To harmonize the qualities of the different types of wine before bottling.

What is 'Sobretabla' wine? This is the wine from the last harvest fortified with 15° alcohol and is 'bred' statically before being added to the Fino and Oloroso 'breeders'.

THE MAKING AND AGEING OF GENEROSOS

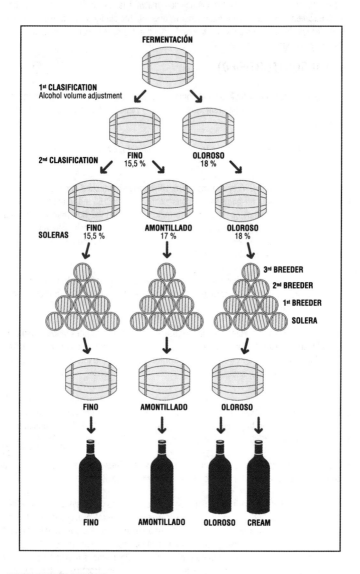

SPARKLING WINES

These are wines that contain carbon dioxide, because of the addition of yeasts and sucrose which produce a second fermentation.

Base wine. This is a pale, clean and fruity wine that does not exceed 11°.

SECOND FERMENTATION. (The first being the classical fermentation of transforming the must into wine). A mixture of sugar and yeasts is added to the base wine (tirage liqueur) which initiates a second fermentation in the bottle or a larger container during which carbon dioxide, so characteristic of sparkling wines, is generated.

BASIC PRODUCTION OF SPARKLING WINES
(Traditional method and charmat from left to right)

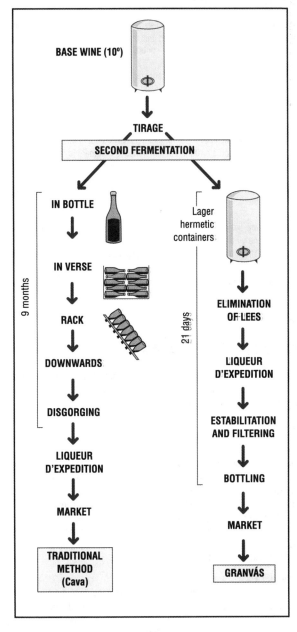

TRADITIONAL METHOD. Or the Champagne method, named after its origin. This refers to sparkling wines which undergo the second fermentation in the bottle and they are the best available on the market. They are made as follows:

AGEING. The bottles age in cellars for a minimum of nine months, usually in underground warehouses where the temperature and humidity are controlled. The bottles are placed flat (this is called 'in verse'), so that once the second fermentation has finished, the dead yeasts settle along the side of the bottle.

RIDDLING. Once the ageing has been completed, the bottles are placed upside down in a rack where they are gradually twisted and inclined until the yeasts fall into the neck of the bottle. Today, this process can also be done by computer controlled machines called gyropalettes.

DISGORGING. The necks of the bottles are frozen and uncapped, and a plug of all the yeasts flies out the bottles. The bottles are then filled up with liqueur d'expedition (the same type of wine or reserve wine which may have different amounts of sugar). They are then sealed, labelled and are ready to be sold.

TRANSFER METHOD. The second fermentation is carried out in the bottle and after that it is transferred to another bottle or tank. The difference is that there is no ageing in bottles with yeasts, as the wine lies for barely more than a few months.

CHARMAT (in large containers) In this case, the second fermentation is carried out in large stainless steel tanks for a period of 20 days.

Types of sparkling wines. The type depends on the amount of sugar used in the liqueur d'expedition or the vintage. One can distinguish between:
Brut nature: dry, no sugar added or up to 6gr/lt of residual sugar.
Brut: contains up to 15gr/lt
Dry: between 17 and 35gr/lt.
Demi-sec: between 33 and 50gr/lt.
Sweet: over 50gr/lt.
Gran Reserva: Aged for at least 30 months.

TRADITIONAL SPANISH WINES

These are the great historic wines, many of them almost forgotten and the vast majority not for daily consumption, but very important in the wine history of Spain and in the majority of cases, of first rate quality.

SWEET WINES

MISTELAS
Although they are called wines, they are really not as there is no fermentation. Mistelle is a mixture of grape juice with alcohol which is used as a sweet wine. The advantage of Mistelle is that it respects the fruity character of the variety incorporating ether to make a drink to be drunk on its own or to be aged. Moscatel is a famous Mistelle. It is produced from the variety with the same name, very apt for this system due to the large losses of aromas when fermented. Therefore, when people speak about a sweet Moscatel or a sweet wine from Moscatel, in the majority of cases it is a Mistelle. The regions where these wines are made extend from the Mediterranean basin up to Andalucía.

PARTIAL FERMENTATION.
The wines produced by this system are different to Mistelles in that the must is fermented up to a determined alcohol content (around 11o) and increased with the addition of vinous

alcohol. The fermentation process is stopped by freezing the water content in the wine or because the grape has a high sugar level and the wine does not finish fermenting, although it keeps it sweetness and a natural alcohol content by the conversion of the must into wine. This is common practice outside Spain and the most evident example is Port. Navarra is a pioneer of this system using the *Moscatel de Grano Menudo.*

LATE HARVEST.

The making of wines using this system is also relatively new in Spain. It is based on delaying the harvest for as long as possible to achieve a higher concentration of sugar in grapes that at times cannot ferment completely. It is similar to the partial fermentation system and used with grapes that have a few grams of residual sugar.

PASIFICADO WINE (RAISIN).

This group encompasses the well known Pedro Ximénez whose grapes, after harvesting, are dehydrated in the sun for 15 days. The loss in water means a concentration of sugar that makes fermentation difficult. In this way, in ninety percent of the cases this wine becomes a true Mistelle. The difficulty of achieving a natural fermentation is solved by the addition of alcohol. The same technique is used in some *Moscatel* raisin wines typical of Málaga and Jerez.

TOSTADILLO WINES

This system made the wines from Ribadavia, Pobla de Tribes, Liébana and the so called Rioja 'supurado' famous. They are all made in January from grapes cut and taken to drying barns where, due to the heat and the lack of humidity, they turn into raisins and become more concentrated. In fact, it is the same technique as dehydration, but, instead of using the sun, it is achieved by generating hot air in very dry spaces. This is quite widespread in Italy with 'pasito' and in France with 'vin de paile' and it is in its infancy in Galicia.

RANCIO WINES

STATIC AGEING.

These are the *Garnachas* from Empordà and Tarragona; wines which come from a variety prone to ageing through oxidation. The wine is aged in barrel or casks at a medium-high temperature. The alcohol content the wine reaches is natural (between 15o and 16o), as the grapes are rich in sugars. The same is true for the Rancios from Jumilla, made from Monastrell, slightly lighter than the *Garnachas* from Empordà and Tarragona. 'Fondillón' from Alicante is also a traditional Rancio wine. In this case the wine comes from a single harvest and, in theory, the losses produced by evaporation can only be replaced with wine from the same vintage, although this may not happen in practice.

WINES AGED IN GLASS CONTAINERS.

This is a relatively recent practice (barely 60 years old) in Cataluña and Rueda. It consists of storing the wine in glass demijohns exposed to the elements, with the aim of accelerating the ageing process by means of the sun and the heat, contrasted by the cold of the night. This somehow multiplies the days of ageing and the wine ages faster, and the absence of wood produces a certain burnt taste on the palate. In many cases a mixed ageing is carried out; first an oxidative ageing in wood and then in the glass demijohns.

YOUNG WINES

Submerged in floral and fruity aromas, turning its youth into a mass of floral and fruity aromas, turning its youth into a marvellous quality. And a young wine is where the quality of the varieties and the flavours of the grapes are best shown off.

Although Spain was a little slow in joining the international fashion of young wines, it is currently making quality whites, rosés and reds in this style. Winemakers from Penedès were pioneers in this, especially white wines. They replanted their vineyards with varieties more appropriate for this type of wine and have started to use new oenological techniques.

But young wines are not only found among the whites and rosés. Red wines also benefit from this fresher and fruitier style; the natural flavours are freed from the homogenizing effects of wood.

For the bodegas, the production and bottling of a quality young wine is more profitable as the wine does not have to be stored for long periods, there is less layout for stock and the losses in wine due to evaporation which are always present in barrel ageing are avoided.

Mention should also be made of common wine or 'litre' wine, which is like a mixture of remnant wines (vintages, origins or types of wine), and drunk mixed with soda. It is definitely a wine without pedigree, but which, when well made is not insignificant.

Of importance are:
The winemaking methods and a good selection of yeasts that can produce noteworthy wines even from common grapes.

Temperature control to preserve the aromas is possible and much easier due to the refrigerated stainless steel tanks.

A reminder: *young wines must be consumed within three or four years of the harvest date which is found on the label, as the qualities of freshness and fruitiness are quickly lost.*

WHAT IS 'NEW' WINE?

This is the most precocious of the young wines, almost ready to be drunk when just made and when it still has all the character of the grape. The French were pioneers with their 'Beaujolais', making it a resounding success, whose release is eagerly awaited each year.

How is it made? It is necessary to force fermentation, clarification and stabilisation by using centrifuge, filtering and cold treatments, unlike young wines, where these processes are slower. The fact that these wines have a shorter life is due to the low levels of tannin as the production is very fast and because of the rapid skin maceration.

What is carbonic maceration? This is a very common method in 'new' and young wines, that consists of working with whole bunches (without stripping) which are placed in a sealed tank that contains carbon dioxide. It may also happen that, due to the weight of the harvest, the berries that are at the bottom break and start the fermentation and thus give off carbon dioxide. The most important fact is that the fermentation must start inside the berry, and in this way, the specific character of each vine is respected. These wines are usually very fruity and aromatic, and because very few tannins are extracted they do not age well. It is better to drink them within the year.

What are the problems of young wines? Their limited life. Heat, their enemy, diffuses the aromas and flavours. They must be consumed during the winter and the spring following their harvesting and making.

Their history. Although they appear to be a recent invention, this is the first type of wine man consumed. It was what he drank immediately and hardly lasted to the next harvest. For centuries the arrival of the wine was a cause for celebration.

AGEING AND MATURATION

During ageing, in which maturation in barrel as well as in bottle is included, the wines can improve their qualities by acquiring some typical characteristics which are derived, above all, from the wood.

What should wines that have undergone ageing be like? They are normally wines that are robust, harsh and aggressive on the palate and intense and lively; aspects which slowly become more polished and refined during maturation.

THE BARREL. The oak container which houses the wine during its maturation. The most commonly used are 225-litre oak barrels, called the Bordeaux barrel.

What aspects of the barrel have an influence on the ageing of the wine?

* **The origin of the wood**. The most common is American oak, generally used because of its lower cost, but there is a growing use of French oak from the forests of Allier, Limousin or Nevers and recently oak from Eastern Europe is also being used.

* **The shape of the 'staves'** (each one of the planks that make up the barrel).

* **The age of the barrel.** New barrels or those that have not been used much transmit their character to the wine faster than old barrels, as old barrels slowly lose their character with use and it is necessary for the wine to remain in them for longer.

* **The length of time the wine stays in the barrel.** The longer the ageing, the greater the transfer of the character of the wood to the wine combined with an increase in oxidation, and the consequent loss of fruit.

How is the wine transferred to the barrel?

* Before the wine is transferred, the interior of the barrel is burnt with sulphur to sterilise it and eliminate the oxygen and the microbial remains inside .

* The wine is poured in slowly, by means of a tube which reaches the bottom to avoid a froth forming which would displace the sulphur dioxide formed by burning the sulphur.

* The barrel is sealed with a cork lid covered in hessian or the very latest are covered in silicone in such a way that they are as airtight as possible.

Conditions needed for proper ageing.

A stable low temperature (13°–15°C) in winter and summer, and a humidity of about 75%.

What is the racking? After the wine has been in the barrel for about six months, the wine is carefully transferred to another barrel ensuring that the accumulated deposits and impurities which have settled on the bottom during this period stay behind. Generally this operation is repeated with the same frequency until the wine has reached the desired point, but always at the winemaker's discretion and complying with the minimum requirements demanded by the competent authorities.

When it has been decided that the maturation in barrel is finished, complementary wines from the same vintage are blended to combine qualities and once the desired wine has been achieved it is bottled.

THE BOTTLE. After its stay in barrel, the wine needs bottle time for the fruit and wood characters to combine and harmonise. In the bottle, thanks to the lack of oxygen, the molecules of wine behave differently developing its bouquet and rounding off the harshness to reach its maximum expression.

It is important:
That the bottle is perfectly clean before the wine is added.

That the corks have a minimum length of 44mm and are free of smells and are not porous.

The placing of the bottles.
The bottles are laid horizontally side by side so that the wine is in contact with the cork, thus keeping it moist and sealed.

Where are the bottles kept? In 'wine cellars', completely isolated spots and generally found underground where there are no draughts and the temperature is constant with a relative humidity of 70%. In modern bodegas they are stored in the wooden or metal cages under the same conditions as underground cellars.

Does the evolution vary in the bottle? Definitely, but it is not the same for all wines. It depends on the quantity, the quality and the balance of the phenolic compounds they contain, especially tannins and total acidity.

Depending on the periods the wines undergo in their ageing phase - in barrel as well as in bottle- the words Crianza, Reserva or Gran Reserva can be placed on the back label, according to the following table which can depend on the regulations in force of each Designation of Origin:

MINIMUM PERIOD OF AGEING				
TYPES OF WINE		TOTAL	BARREL	BOTTLE
CRIANZA	White/Rosé	24 months	6 months	the rest
	Red	24 months	6 months	the rest
RESERVA	White/Rosé	24 months	6 months	the rest
	Red	36 months	12 months	the rest
GRAN RESERVA	White/Rosé	48 months	6 months	the rest
	Red	60 months	24 months	the rest

EVERYTHING ABOUT AGEING IN OAK

WHY IS WOOD FUNDAMENTAL FOR WINE?

A historic marriage. There was a time when wood and wine were inseparable. The wood was a multi-functional wrapping: it served as a recipient for the wine, assured the fermentation, helped with the maturation and made transportation easier.

The association between wine and wood started in the 17th century, coinciding with the development of maritime trade and the subsequent transportation of wine in large casks which gradually transferred part of their character to the wine. However, due to their large size and the disproportion between the volume of the wine and the wood in contact with the wine, this transfer was slow and small.

Nevertheless, this was the origin of the Oloroso, the first wine from Jerez, that captivated the senses of the English (the name comes from the contribution of the virtues the oak container imparted to the Oloroso wine from Quercus).

Something similar happened with Port, which gradually became immortal in the Vilanova de Gaia casks which gave it toasted flavours and aromas of exotic woods. The first oaks from Limonge in Bordeaux gave it an unmistakable bouquet of vanilla.

And so it was discovered that the wood invigorated the wine and at the same time gave the wine a certain maturity and solemnity. This fact was more evident when smaller barrels were made in which the proportion of oak to wine was greater.

The first wines aged in wood. The oak taste that the Jerez barrel transferred was to a large extent due to the southern heat and the rolling of the ships which produced heavy oxidation.

Influenced by the Jerez casks, Bordeaux got the idea of manufacturing their own barrels in which they stored a red wine high in tannins and acidity that was able to survive the action of the wood. With these they hoped to achieve the same aromatic intensity of the Jerez Quercus but in a more humid and cooler climate.

And years after the legendary 1855 classification that Bordeaux created for wines which offered hints of cedar and resins typical of prephylloxera oak barrels, the Gironde *Grands Crus* started to manufacture the 225-litre Bordeaux barrel which conferred characters to the wine which a larger recipient would keep to itself.

Meanwhile Rioja started to use, although on a smaller scale, the idea of the Bordeaux châteaux as cellars, importing the use and manufacture of the new 225-litre barrels which were called Bordeaux barrels.

Present-day barrels. These days the maturation in each bodega is mainly carried out in new barrels, carefully chosen from the best barrel-makers who guarantee the use of American, French or Russian oak; barrels which confer tannins and principal essential aromas to the wine.

WHAT IS HIDDEN BEHIND THE CHARACTERISTIC FLAVOUR OF OAK?

Between the oak and the wine there are innumerable reactions and exchanges which affect the evolution of the wine and can only be noticed when drinking it, such as the bitter tannins of the oak with the sweet tannins of the grapeskins or the fine hints of vanilla from the wood, enveloped in the fruity aroma of the variety.

The taste of yesteryear. The 'woody' and 'carpentry' flavours were normal in some old wines from Rioja, but this was more due to the weak constitution of the wine than to its long periods in barrel. Generally they were reds with a very open colour which usually matured prematurely, with evolved flavours, lacking nuances and over-oxidized. This was due to the excessive ventilation of the wine during racking, rather than the oxygen coming in through the pores and the staves of the wood.

Today's taste. These days, however, we have gone to the opposite extreme. The maturation periods in barrel have been decreased and the wine is bottled with fewer rackings. The profound flavours of the lees and the complex characters of the ripe skins are more pronounced, offering a pleasant freshness. And in this way the nuances acquired from the oak combine with the primary fruit flavours and with the characteristic features of the grape variety.

WHICH WOOD IS THE BEST?

Although the most commonly used wood in Spain is the American oak because of its price and availability, there is a growing tendency to use French oak or a combination of both.

French oak. The whites and reds matured in French oak barrels have a creamy or vanilla essence, and tend to sweeten slightly. It is more porous than American oak and it is therefore advisable to shorten the ageing.

American oak. The wine is more woody and aggressive due to the higher quantity of tannins in this wood. But this aggressiveness gives way to more supple toasty notes, with more aromas thanks to the heating of the wood when curving the staves.

Russian oak. It is used very little and it is characterised for imparting a perfume similar to cedar to the wine, but without losing the traces of European oak. It is creamier and not as harsh as American oak.

WHICH VARIETIES CAN BE AGED AND WHICH CANNOT?

To be able to support the wood, the variety has to have structure, personality and a slow oxidation as the barrel accelerates the oxidation process during the racking.

The most suitable.
Red wines which have a high tannin potential and the more noble whites which are not excessively aromatic.

* Reds: *Cabernet Sauvignon, Merlot, Syrah, Cabernet Franc, Nebbiolo, Sangiovese, Pinot Noir* and *Tempranillo.*

* Whites: *Chardonnay, Sémillon, Sauvignon Blanc, Viura, Verdejo* and *Viognier.*

The least suitable.
* The Galician *Treixadura* and *Albariño* do not combine well with the oak because of their heavy floral and fruity aromas which are reduced without being substituted by the complexity of the oak and the lees.

* The Andalusian grapes *Pedro Ximénez, Zalema* and *Palomino* – which oxidise very easily – go rancid very quickly and are therefore used for fortified wines (Generosos). The same goes for the *Airén* from *La Mancha,* the white *Cayetana* from Extremadura and the *Merseguera* from Valencia.

WHERE DO THE BEST WINES FOR MATURATION IN OAK COME FROM?

Taking into account that this is influenced by the climate and the geography of each winegrowing region, the best regions would be those with a slow ripening, and with a larger day/night temperature contrast: the cool nights impede the combustion of acids and the warm and sunny days provide more sugar.

The best regions.
* The **Ribera del Duero** produces wines high in acidity and alcohol and with more pigmentation; the necessary requirements for slow maturation in barrel.

* **Rioja Alta and Alavesa, Alto Penedès** and the regions of **Valdizarbe and Tierra Estella** in Navarra, as well as **Somontano and Bierzo** are also included in this list.

The least suitable.

The warmer regions such as **Aragón**, **Extremadura**, **La Mancha** and the south-eastern regions. Here the wines need less ageing in wood, not so much for the tendency of some varieties to oxidise but due to the faster ripening of the grape.

WHICH WINES AGE BEST?

Reds. Wines with a good make-up of tannins, pigmentation, high alcohol and acidity which, when consumed, in the same period as the maturation (three or four years after the harvesting) are harsh on the palate and whose aromas have not developed yet. They may have herbaceous touch from the skins and a hint of resin and pitch, typical of new oak. Normally the bodegas put them on the market three to five years after the harvest.

Whites. Normally, because they are low in tannins (except when they have been macerated with their skins) they have a transient life and in fact, the youthful, aromatic and penetrating character tends to disappear after two years.

However, a slow fermented white, aged in oak and bottled late, will prolong the life of the wine with the same expectancy as a red. This is due to the oak tannins imparted to the wine which compensate for the lack of tannins in white grapes (it must not be forgotten that the tannins are found in the grapeskin and that, normally, although things are starting to change, in white wines the must is not usually macerated with the skins).

Nowadays, in contrast to classical maturation which is heavy in wood and made the same way as reds, they are usually fermented in barrel on their lees and they undergo a well studied maturation where the molecules of the lees impede the characters of the oak being overbearing as can happen to whites aged in wood.

WHAT ARE WOOD SHAVINGS AND HOW ARE THEY USED?

The use of wood shavings is prohibited in Europe, but quite common in the New World for medium to low cost wines. It consists of replacing the traditional barrels for oak shavings which, when in contact with the wine, impart aromas and flavours typical of the wood. The big advantage is the saving in costs and the ability to offer the consumer wines with characters typical of 'aged' wines at very competitive prices. These shavings give a taste of wood which contrasts with the fruitiness and they do not harmonise in the first few months. This taste can be detected but not easily. The Australians usually add these shavings to the bunches when they are placed in the hopper.

EVERYTHING ABOUT THE CORK

Although the cork seems to be the least significant element in wine, it is highly valued, necessary and scarce, besides being of fundamental importance for the proper preservation of a wine.

DID YOU KNOW THAT...?

* Spain is the second largest producer of cork in the world, but our cork plantations are dwindling and are crying out for reforestation to halt the progressive disappearance of this irreplaceable raw material.

* For cork to be used as a seal, at least twenty years have to pass for the bark of the tree to achieve this flexibility and resistance.

The importance of cork.

* It is a light, impermeable and flexible natural product which compresses very well.

* It serves to stop the filtration of oxygen, micro-organisms and bacteria which could alter and contaminate the contents of the bottle.

THE PROPERTIES OF A GOOD CORK.

* It must be solid and compact.

* It must not have pores on either of its flat sides. The longitudinal dark streaks form spaces through which air as well as bacteria can enter, creating an ideal spot for infection that affects the quality and the life of the wine.

* Although the length is not always a guarantee of quality, corks of between 55mm and 65mm are normally used for Reserva and Gran Reserva wines. In Spain the standard length is usually 44mm for young and Crianza wines and 49mm for Reserva and Gran Reserva wines.

Things that must be changed... The mentality of some winemakers who do not pay enough attention to the corks. Although the better bodegas use quality corks, one can still find relatively high priced wines with measly corks which, without a doubt can accomplish their mission in the first few years but later on they prove defective.

HOW LONG DOES A CORK LAST?

Their average life expectancy is approximately 15 years. From this age on they start to 'age', and break up easily. And after ten years of use they progressively start to lose their elasticity and their natural moisture content.

On drying out, microscopic cavities form which become breeding grounds for mould. The mould ends up transferring the characteristic 'corked' aroma to the wine. However, it is important to point out that cork, on its own, does not transfer any taste or odour to the wine.

* *The cork of a bottle must be replaced after 15 years. This does not alter the characteristics of the wine.*

To ensure the correct functioning of the cork:

* Place the bottles in a horizontal position or upside down in such a way that the wine is in contact with the cork and it is kept at a constant temperature and humidity.

* Store wine at temperatures of no higher than 18ºC. The higher the temperature, the faster the ageing process and the greater the amount of evaporation through the cork. About 3ml/10 years is lost to evaporation at an average temperature of 20ºC.

HOW DO YOU KNOW IF THE CORK IS IN GOOD CONDITION?

The quality of the cork after opening the bottle is judged by its porosity, the colour it has and the area where the pigmentation is the greatest. A good cork will only be dark on the bottom side if the bottle contains an old wine, and purple in the case of a young wine.

The dark colour must never be along the side of the cork, as this indicates liquid escaping or the slightest contact with air.

The best cork... is totally natural, from cork plantations in dry regions where the growth of the tree, on being slower, guarantees a better make-up of the cork.

Some bodegas 'paraffin' their corks; i.e. they coat them with this substance, which, once treated, are odourless, insipid and impermeable, sealing and filling any possible cracks or natural holes. One can even find corks composed of two equal lengths that are stuck together with a fine layer of glue which also impedes the filtration of air into the wine.

STOPPERS FOR WINE: THE GREAT CONTROVERSY OF THE 21ST C

The unpleasant 'smell of cork' which destroys many wines is probably one of the most common defects and most recognisable even for amateurs. It is because of this that many producers and distributors, above all abroad, favour the new synthetic corks. We are mentioning these alternatives as you may soon find one of these when opening a bottle.

How many wines are spoilt because of the cork?

There are no reliable figures available on the quantity of wines which, to a lesser or greater extent, are ruined by this easily recognisable contamination caused by the cork, the *bouchoné* as the French say. A few years ago an Italian magazine spoke of about 15%, the Australian giant Southcorp say 5%, while a study carried out by the British WSA (Wine and Spirit Association) stated that after analysing 5,000 bottles, only 2.3% had significant anomalies and, of these, only 1.6% could be attributed to the cork. If we take into account the experience of tasting about 6,000 wines for our guide, our figures are similar to those of the latter survey.

What is TCA?

This is what causes the 'cork smell'. TCA is really an abbreviation for 2, 4, 6 trichloroanisole, a component associated with the use of substances which contain chlorophenols and whose use was widespread, until they were banned by the EU in the nineties for the treatment of wood. They are not harmful to one's health, but the main problem with TCA is that their presence, in even minute amounts (we are talking about a threshold of 20 nanograms/litre) is enough to contaminate the original characteristics of a wine. Its musty smell makes it easily recognizable, and it often coincides with the bad smell of cork.

'Brett' is something else.

'Brett' must not be confused with a cork problem. It is the name of a yeast (*brettanomyces*) found in the vine and the wine and it is characterised by its potential to destroy both. Normally it is noticed by a series of dirty aromas (stables, drains…) and to a lesser extent a smell of wet leather or even metallic smells. There are various types of 'brett' yeasts that can to a lesser or greater degree have negative effects on the wine. If the level is very low, its presence can even go unnoticed but, in any case, it is associated to a lack of hygiene in the wine cellar.

Not only the corks.

A French scientist Pascal Châtonnet, who headed a study on TCA, was the first person to discover this component in a wine from a tank (it has the same smell of humidity and mould) and therefore demonstrated that the problem is not only due to the corks. In fact, it has, on other occasions, been demonstrated to have come from the barrels, the wooden crates used to store the bottles and even the bottles themselves.

TCA, TeCA, PCA and TBA.

Recent research, headed by Châtonnet, has widened the spectrum of the 'guilty' to beyond just TCA. Within the chloroanisol family, to which TCA belongs, the mouldy character can also be produced by tetrachloroanisole (TeCA) or pentachloroanisole (PCA). But there is also a second source of infection by TBA (tribomoanisole), which belongs to the bromoanisole family. As in TCA, its perception threshold is quite low and its capacity to degrade wine is therefore quite high.

Strict control and prevention.

A lot of bodegas are replacing their wooden crates with metal crates and are demanding stricter quality control from the suppliers of the corks and barrels. The suppliers have implanted 'decontaminating' systems to ensure that their products are not contaminated. The cork industry has made advances which consist of applying microwaves to destroy micro-organisms, even in the centre of the cork. Other systems are based on heat to extract the chemical impurities or vapour under pressure, which destroys the spores of the mould and dilutes the substances that give rise to unpleasant aromas and tastes.

Synthetic corks.

These are a mixture of rubbers derived from petroleum (elastomers), although there are others that are a mixture of plastic and granulated cork. The prototypes were first made in France in the seventies, but they were not commercialised until the following decade. The British were the first to use them, thanks to the unconditional support of the large supermarket chains, which were fed up with having to face their customers' complaints about damaged corks.

Screw on caps.

However demystifying it seems, screw on caps appear to be the only system of proven efficiency, the only system which guarantees to keep the wine fresh and hardly ever result in losses or damage. The first examples were used in the Finos from Andalucía and at the same time in certain average quality Australian white wines. Why has good sense not triumphed in Europe? Plain and simply, because it is socially unacceptable. It would be like going to a gala dinner in trainers. Even the most illustrious wine experts expounding on their benefits has not helped. The wine industry, which needs to sell, has rejected them... although one is starting to hear lone voices from wine producers in the New World that are using them in some of their wines.

Other alternatives: glass and metal caps.

The increasing number of alternatives that are available shows, without a doubt, the importance the producers are giving to the fact that their wines might reach the consumer in a poor condition because of a faulty cork. There are bodegas that, after having used synthetic corks, have renounced them and have opted for other alternatives. Although in an experimental stage, we have heard news of a glass top designed by a German company. It is covered in a plastic membrane and then wrapped in aluminium. The only problem is that they require specific bottles to be able to fit. On the other hand, Chandon in Australia has just sealed one of its top quality sparkling wines with a metal cap (a designer cap, of course), the same as those used for beer bottles.

	ADVANTAGES	DISADVANTAGES
CORK	**Flexibility.** Fits like a glove in the neck of the bottle and moulds itself perfectly to it. **Easy to pull out.** This is due to its enormous flexibility. Any corkscrew can be used to open a bottle efficiently and easily. **Socially accepted.** Cork has been linked to wine for the last 300 years and forms part of the winegrowing culture of the planet. **Does the cork breathe?** Although it has not been proved, there are people who think that the cork lets minute quantities of air through which, in the case of wines that can be kept for long periods, has a positive influence on the reduction process that takes place in the bottle..	**Contamination.** A cork in bad condition can totally ruin a wine on its own and, in the majority of the cases makes it undrinkable. **Difficult to check.** It is impossible to guarantee that a batch is 100% problem-free, even in the case of the most expensive and the longest top quality corks. **The problem of 'returning' the bottle.** How does one complain about a bad wine when not in a restaurant.
SYNTHETIC CORKS	**Goodbye to the corked taste.** Wine with a synthetic cork will not have that horrible taste of mould which can be found in wines with a damaged cork. **Innocuous.** Synthetic corks used nowadays do not give strange aromas or tastes to the wine; they seal the bottles perfectly and completely isolate the wine. **Very effective in young wines.** They work very well in wines with a great turnover, which represent 80% of the world wine market. **They have the support of the wine industry.** Many of the great New World producers have been delighted to accept synthetic corks.	**Rigidity.** Despite the improvements to the prototypes, they are far from being as flexible as cork. **Difficult to pull out.** Even though any corkscrew can be used, their rigidity makes them much more difficult to pull out. **Not accepted socially.** The purists do not want wine (something enjoyable, traditional and socially acceptable) to be industrialised and made commonplace. **Reticence of some winemakers.** Some companies that have used them have had problems and others prefer to have more information regarding their effectiveness before using them.
SCREW TOP	**Restaurants and bodegas benefit.** Restaurants would avoid almost 5% of the wines being returned because of the wine being corked. The bodegas would also be grateful. **The wine would always be perfect.** The risk of the wine being corked or of it oxidising or turning sour because of contact with the air would be avoided. **Easy to open.** It is simple and fast to open without having to use a corkscrew. As the English wine expert Hugh Johnson said, 'if our forefathers had had them, they would have used them'. **They are better for white wines.** According to the Australian Wine Research Institute, these caps retain the sulphur dioxide better in white wines and therefore, they are protected against oxidation.	**Regulations, an obstacle.** The use of these caps is still not permitted in many European Designations. **Bad reputation.** For wine drinkers, these caps are cheap and tacky, relegated to poorer quality wines. This is thanks to the German producers who used them in cheap wines thirty years ago. **An artificial taste?** For some people, the screw top gives the wine an unpleasant taste of plastic or metal. **Not as ceremonious.** People in favour of 'uncorking' see it as a threat to this glamorous and tested ritual, endangering this protocol which forms part of the wine culture.

EVERYTHING ABOUT THE BOTTLE

From its rustic creation and use by the Greeks and Romans to 18th-century England, the bottle evolved continuously, although it was not until the 17th century when the concern for preserving the quality of the wine for as long as possible resulted in the adoption of the bottle.

THE ORIGIN

The Greeks and Romans. In the Classical Age, the Greeks and Romans stored their wine in amphorae made of wood, clay or animal skin. The biblical collection of bottles on display at the Ha'aretz Museum in Tel Aviv houses very fragile containers, only apt for serving wine but not at all appropriate for its conservation.

The Dutch. The traders from this country were concerned about the wine's short life and its deterioration when transported to the markets, and they started looking for systems to preserve wine; they were the first to add sulphur and alcohol to stop it going rancid during transportation.

THE BIRTH OF THE BOTTLE.

The inventor. The relationship between glass and wine was finally established in 1662 when Sir Kenelm Digby, a British courtier, manufactured the first tubular bottle with sloping shoulders and a long neck, with a cylindrical shape to be able to store it horizontally, and an external ring to adjust the string of the wooden stopper to seal the bottle.

This was the origin of the bottle as we know it, baptised by the Dutch as 'the English style bottle' and by the French, who adopted the bottle in 1707 to export their clarets, as the 'Bordeaux bottle'.

The first bottles. From the beginning they were olive green, almost translucent, but by mere chance (the smoke from the peat coal used in the ovens gave the glass the dark colour which would prove to be beneficial for the wine as it protected it from light).

The first tops. At first glass tops, which were made to fit the bottle with a paste made of grinding powder and oil, were used. The top was attached to the neck of the bottle by a string (this is the origin of the shape of the neck of present day bottles) and therefore every bottle had to have its own top, making the sealing process more expensive and complicated. Later wooden tops which were much more flexible than glass tops were used.

The advent of cork. Finally, when the wooden top was replaced by cork, a container which preserved the wine without it losing its main characteristics was achieved. However, wine, being alive, did not remain totally unalterable in the bottle.

THE EVOLUTIONARY PROCESSES WHICH TAKE PLACE WITHIN THE BOTTLE.

Reduction. This is the natural transformation which takes place in the wine within the bottle due to it having no contact with the air.

How does it take place? When wine is bottled it contains small quantities of dissolved carbon dioxide and oxygen. The stagnant air between the cork and the surface of the wine is absorbed by the wine creating a situation of 'asphyxia' in which the bacteria cannot reproduce. Moreover, if the cork is healthy and the bottle is kept in a cool place, the activity of the micro-organisms which change the taste and the smell of the wine is reduced.

DOES WINE IMPROVE IN THE BOTTLE?

Wine does not deteriorate because of the glass, however, its structure is modified.

Wine, when stored, can accentuate the characteristics it had before being bottled. And it is exactly these features acquired during its ageing in bottle which highlight some of the traits which will determine its quality.

What happens inside the bottle? The tannins from the grapes and the wood are rounded, reducing the primary characters (those from the original fruit) and increasing the notes which give the wine the hints of nuts, spices and wild herbs.

The influence of external factors. Light, heat and oxygen, depending on the amount of contact with the wine, produce a slower or faster evolution in the wine. The higher the temperature, the faster the wine evolves.

A wine bottled and stored at a constant temperature of between 10º and 14ºC has a better chance of keeping well than those that have been stored at higher temperatures.

The slower the evolution of the wine, the more harmonious the combination of the flavours of the grapes and those flavours acquired in the fermentation and maturation phases will be.

WHICH BOTTLE IS THE BEST?

The size of the bottle also plays an important role in the evolution of its contents. Although the image of wine is that of 750 ml bottles, widely used because they are easy to handle, wine is better protected in larger volumes.

Larger capacity glass containers retard the evolution of the wine, developing a wide variety of nuances which would have been lost in smaller containers.

The larger the container, the longer the life of the contents.

The magnum. With a capacity equivalent to two 750 ml bottles, it is the most suitable container for storing wine, as the same proportion of air exists in the chamber between the wine and the cork as in a standard bottle, but with a larger volume of wine, which slows its evolution. As the chamber of air between the top and the surface of the wine is the same as in a 750ml bottle, the same amount of oxygen is dissolved in double the amount of wine. In addition, the larger volume of liquid reduces the brusqueness of the changes in temperature, thus prolonging the ageing.

Cava. The larger bottle is also more appropriate for the ageing of this wine on its lees. Later, with the addition of the liqueur d'expedition there are fewer variations in the bottle. The only disadvantage is its weight, as the glass has to be thicker than normal to withstand the pressure generated by the carbon dioxide.

The 375 ml bottle is completely inappropriate for preserving wine.

HOW TO DESIGN A GREAT WINE

Listed below is a recipe in which the factors needed to achieve a good quality wine have been explained in order of importance. The work practices described are shared by the majority of the great labels, who set the standards for quality in the world of wine.

1. Cultivating and harvesting. These are fundamental for the grape to reach its greatest expression. The following practices are carried out:

* Organic treatment of the vineyard (organic fertilizers, green pruning to decrease yields).
* Limiting water to obtain a certain level of water stress in order to achieve smaller grapes and, therefore, a larger proportion of skin in the must.
* Controlling the foliage mass (the number of leaves needed to carry out a balanced photosynthesis).
* Determining the exact moment to harvest according to a phenolic ripeness (i.e. the skin of the grape is ripe and the seeds are dry) and not only 'sugar ripeness' (the balance between the level of alcohol and the acidity).
* Selecting the bunches on the vine.
* Controlling the ripeness of the skin.
* Selecting the bunches at the bodega (some exclusive bodegas even choose only the healthiest and ripest parts of the bunch).

2. Soil. The soil is responsible for the mineral nuances in the aroma and taste of the wine. It must:
* Be rich in minerals and poor in organic matter.

* Have a layer to permit good drainage (sand, stone, pebble, slate on a clayey calcareous substratum).

* Have water in the deeper layers so that the roots go through the different layers of soil in search of the water and in doing so, benefit from the different elements found in the different layers.

3. Varieties. The variety determines the style of wine. The ideal are old and noble vines (40 to 80 years old, these are the ones that have the most roots, some of which are very deep) such as *Tempranillo, Merlot, Cabernet Sauvignon, Syrah, Nebbiolo, Sangiovese, Garnacha, Pinot Noir, Cabernet Franc, Graciano*, etc.

4. Malolactic Fermentation and maturation. This determines a large proportion of the personality of the new quality wines. During the conversion of the malic acid bacteria into lactic acid, agents come into play which enrich the flavours (lees) but they decay easily.

* How is it carried out? Normally it must be done in new barrels together with the lees and the vegetal particles of the wine. These must be stirred periodically with a pole to better transmit their specific characters and stop them reducing and giving the wine a bad smell and taste (hints of stagnant water).

5. Selecting the barrels. The key to the fineness of the aroma and taste. Oak has gone from being a container to being the main ingredient in quality wines. What must be taken into account?

* The barrels must be new to take full advantage of the aromatic substances of the oak.

* The proportions of the different types of wood (American, French, or Russian oak), the drying and the period used for each wine.

* Choose the supplier carefully. Barrels are still handcrafted and the selection of the wood and the workmanship makes a barrel a work of art.

6. Micro-climate. The location of the vineyard is important, depending on if the field faces north or south, is on a flat or a slope.

* The best vineyards. They are found on the best ventilated hills and on higher ground. This situation produces more than sufficient acidity and thanks to direct sunlight, a considerable level of alcohol is achieved.

7. Alcohol fermentation. Fermentation with an exhaustive and precise temperature control of the must achieves a balance of the characters of the grape with those from the fermentation and maintains the character of the fruit intact during the extraction of the substances contained in the skin and the must.

* *To be kept in mind.* Over-pumping (wetting the solid mass of grapes that floats on top) or 'punching' (mechanical breaking of the mass or cap for the wine to penetrate through these gaps) dissolves the colour and the tannins better.

8. Skin maceration. (The skins with the must). Gives the wine a more fruity character. It is a process to extract, in the purest way and at low temperatures, the aromatic character of the grape before fermentation. In this way, the slight deterioration of its fruity potential produced by the temperature increase during fermentation is avoided.

9. Clarification by decanting and without filtration. The aim is to preserve the pigments and the compounds that enrich the aromas and the flavours of the wine.

* *Before.* The transparency of red wines was achieved by natural means, with prolonged resting in barrels and rackings.

* *Nowadays.* The reds are left in the barrel for just enough time for the wood to transmit the aromatic and tannic compounds of the ageing and this is not sufficient for all the sediments to disappear (pigments and bitartrate crystals). Therefore many labels warn the consumer of this fact.

SOME KEY POINTS OF NEW METHODS.

MICRO-OXYGENATION. Or *microbullage*, a French term which is used to refer to the injecting of oxygen into wine stored in tanks with very little aeration (steel vats) or in barrels for short periods of ageing to avoid bad aromas ('reduction off-odours' similar to stagnant water) which originate in the post-fermentation process or due to the lack of aeration.

This is carried out in young wines whose bottling has been advanced so much so that they did not receive the necessary dose of oxygen, as well as in wines aged in barrel, replacing the effects of the rackings and the long periods on the wine in wood. Therefore it is not necessary to lengthen the periods of ageing to give more aromas and flavours of oak, which would influence the characters of the wine. However, this practice of rapid micro-oxygenation does not achieve the attributes of oxygenation through the pores of the barrel that ageing in oak would give.

FINE LEES. These are the sediments that are left on the bottom of the containers after the fermentation of the wine: dead yeast, insoluble acids and the vegetal residues of the grape. When this wine is racked immediately after the alcohol fermentation, the 'larger' lees remain in the container, and the fine lees stay in the wine.

These compounds dissolve in the liquid, enrich the aromas of the wine, but for this to occur properly, the fine lees must have been oxygenated sufficiently not only through the pores of the wood but also by bâtonnage, a French word which describes the stirring of the liquid using a pole introduced into the mouth of the barrel.

This practice not only ensures that the lees remain in suspension, but it also ensures additional aeration, otherwise the settled lees would cause reduction or putrefaction due to the lack of oxygen with the resulting sulphuric (rotten eggs) or mercaptan (stagnant water) aromas.

FERMENTATION VESSELS

STAINLESS STEEL. These have been used in Spain since the end of the 70s.
Advantages: extremely aseptic and above all, excellent temperature control of the alcohol fermentation due to its sophisticated cooling system.
Disadvantages: its air-tightness impedes aeration and may cause the reduction of certain vegetal compounds; clarifying is more difficult, and in tanks larger than 15000 litres thermal currents occur due to the contrast of the external temperature with the totally controlled internal temperature, as well as strange electrostatic interferences caused by the steel.

WOOD. Traditionally wood has been the most used material in the making of quality wines.
Advantages: it allows the wine to 'breathe' better through its pores (a natural micro-oxygenation), the wines stabilize better after fermentation and they are more rounded.
Disadvantages: its high cost, the initial outlay as well as the maintenance; it needs to be cleaned thoroughly and receive continuous attention (repairs etc), besides the skilled staff needed.

CEMENT. This was the material used by the old wine presses and was found in almost all the cellars before the advent of stainless steel.
Advantages: lately it has been discovered that more uniform internal temperatures are obtained and therefore a better expression in the wine during the difficult phases of storing and ageing.
Disadvantages: one has to be extremely careful to avoid alterations in the wine caused by excessive temperatures, although refrigeration systems can be installed; absolute cleanliness is also required; it is not associated with quality wines (even though, the legendary Pétrus still uses cement to ferment its wines).

HOW TO SET UP A VINEYARD AND A WINE CELLAR

Owning a small vineyard and a small domestic cellar need not be an impossible task. I have listed some useful advice for those who wish to be 'on the other side of the bottle'.

There is always the possibility of buying good grapes and limiting oneself to making wine, but for the majority of people who have wine in their blood the crux of the matter is the vineyard and consequently, the great wines of the world come from exceptional vineyards, cultivated with great care and love. All modern oenologists state that the wine is made in the vineyard and not in the bodega.

THE VINEYARD.

WHERE?
Spain is basically a winegrowing country, and therefore there are many viticulture regions and zones (and not necessarily under a DO) in which to start. Needless to say the price of land in an acclaimed region is very high, but winemakers with a good nose have surprised the world by creating interesting wines, not only in isolated regions, but also regions with no tradition of winegrowing (see the pages in this guide).

Rights of use. These days one needs authorisation to plant a vineyard. If you want to start from zero and plant your own vineyard (this will complete the adventure) you will have to get the necessary permit. A lot more expensive in regions where the demand is high.

WHAT MUST BE TAKEN INTO ACCOUNT?
The soil. It must be poor; it is advisable to have it analysed for growing grapes, make sure it is healthy and check whether it lacks minerals such as iron and magnesium.

The orientation of the land. North, South, East or West. Depending on this the vineyard will receive more or less hours of sun (the slope and the altitude also influences this) or be exposed to more or less wind.

The microclimate. Apart from the general climatic conditions that affect the whole region, your plot will probably have special features that influence the development and the ripening of the grapes.

Root stock. One has to select the most suitable; one that is adapted to the soil, to the variety and the climate (be careful, there may be incompatible plants, and it is therefore best to ask for advice). Of course it must be an American rootstock resistant to phylloxera.

The grape variety. Are there native varieties that do well in the region? Are the conditions right for you to plant your favourite varieties with some guarantee of success? How many grapes and in what percentage? Look at the examples that work best in the region or, if you have decided to be a pioneer or you would like to experiment, ask for expert advice. If you fall within a DO and you would like to join it, you will have to adhere to their Regulations.

Planting and training the vine. Unless you have bought an old vine (in this case you will have to check the quality of the grapes; bear in mind that an old vine is a synonym of quality, but also low yields and viral diseases), these days all new vineyards are trellised; a more appropriate system that facilitates work in the vineyard. Normally the planting is linked to an irrigation system (at least drip irrigation, or a more sophisticated underground irrigation system). The majority of Spanish vineyards need watering at some point during their growing cycle.

The density of planting. This refers to the number of plants per hectare. In France and Italy it very high (up to 10,000 in some cases), but in Spain it is usually quite low (around 2,000 to 3,000). However, the latest theories advocate very high densities and very low yields per vine. However, in a DO one has to adhere to the regulations.

Crop management. A vineyard has its own work schedule: fertilising (it is better to avoid phytosanitary products, the ideal would be to follow organic viticulture), pruning, preventative treatments, cluster thinning (high yields generally mean low quality), harvesting…And do not forget, you will not get significant grapes until the fifth year. Vineyards are a long-term project.

THE COST.
Buying a plot of land, the right of use, the plants themselves and the cost of preparing a trellised vineyard with its irrigation system, will at best cost no less than 15,000 to 18,000 per hectare. Many famous wines in the world (e.g. Burgundy) do not come from large vineyards and, in any case, a hectare is more than enough to keep you busy making your 'own wine'. Of course if you are in a prestigious DO region the cost more than doubles.

THE BODEGA

If we agree with the philosophy that the vineyard is the most important, then the wine cellar is the second most important. An example to follow would be the 'garage' wines which, as the name indicates, can be made in a small space. For a modest production of 3,000 bottles no more is required. You might also consider the possibility of buying a lot of the equipment needed second hand, making sure they are in good condition.

WHAT MUST BE TAKEN INTO ACCOUNT?
Cleanliness. This is the most important factor in a cellar and it is not expensive. The aim is to have aseptic conditions. Cheap materials can be used to achieve this aim, without having to cover the floor with epoxy resin.

Receiving the grape. You will need a stainless steel hopper to receive the grapes and a stemmer to separate the stalk of the grape, unless you limit yourself to making carbonic macerated whites or reds, in which case it will not be necessary. And a grape pump to take the grapes to the fermentation tanks (if you design it yourself, you could also use gravity so that the destemmed grapes fall directly into the tanks; new techniques try to limit the pumping and handling of the grapes to a minimum).

Fermentation tanks. Stainless steel is completely aseptic but it is expensive. You will need it if you decide to make fruity whites. Wood is even more expensive, above all the maintenance and preservation. One could use everyday cement tanks with a cooling system to control the temperature. These days they are lined with glass tiles or epoxy resin to avoid problems, but they then lose their main advantage of keeping the temperature very stable. Mundane PVC tanks which serve perfectly well for fermentation are also available (seen more abroad than in Spain).

What is more important is to calculate the capacity needed for the size and layout of your vineyard; if you have different varieties, ideally, they should be worked separately. Small tanks for micro-fermentation are the order of the day at any self respecting cellar. They would be more suited to your work volume.

Besides the vinification, you will have to plan for the storage of the wine until you bottle.

Wine press. Taking into account your modest production, it will not be necessary to buy an expensive pneumatic press. Many innovative oenologists are returning to the old vertical presses which function very gently. This would probably be the ideal model for your bodega,.

Ageing. Do you want to stick to young wines or try your hand at wood? This makes the process a lot more expensive. How many barrels do you need to age your wine? French oak is a lot more expensive than American oak. And maturation means racking (although, why not try *microbullage*?). There is a thriving market for second hand barrels, but they must not be very old, and be careful with the dangers of TCA!

Externalise. You will have to have your wines analysed by a third party; it is not worth having your own laboratory for the moment, as it will make the project even more expensive. And the same with the bottling. You could go to one of the cooperatives or bodegas in the region. You will have to supply the bottles, labels (it could be fun to create a name and image for your own wines; or ask a friend who is good at designing) and a small space to store your wines.

THE COST.

The final cost will vary considerably according to the decisions taken on the equipment and material, and if you decide to buy new or second hand. The following prices will serve as a guide. A destemmer costs around 9000; a must pump 7,500; a racking pump 1,800; an American oak barrel 275; a French oak barrel 450.

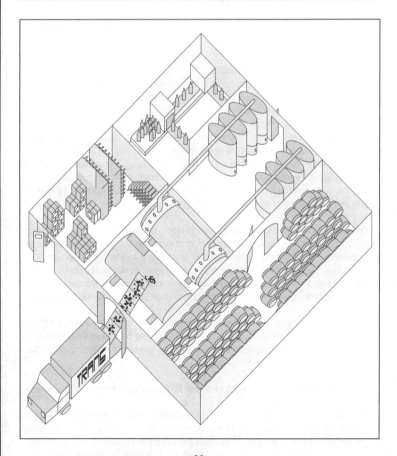

PRACTICAL MANUAL
FOR THE WINE TASTER

PRACTICAL MANUAL FOR THE WINE TASTER

BASIC NOTIONS

THE REASONS BEHIND THE BASIC WINE-TASTING RULES

This is the sequence that all good wine enthusiasts should follow, the recipe to discover a world of complex sensations, aromas and flavours. Below is a detailed liturgy that all wine lovers should follow.

1. - CHOOSING THE WINE.

Meat or fish, game or meat on the grill, fish done in the oven or in a casserole. Each dish demands a certain type of wine and vice versa.

Full bodied reds need a heavy meal; delicate meals on the other hand need lighter wines, no matter whether they are young or aged.

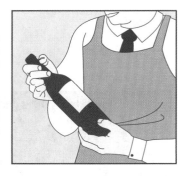

Why?
Because neither the meal nor the wine should dominate.

What you should know...
* Heavy whites or those aged or fermented in wood have a higher alcohol content.
* Light whites are generally from the latest vintage and are fruity and acid.
* Reds with body have a high alcohol and tannin content (Cabernets, wines from Toro, Ribera del Duero, Priorat, Jumilla, Alicante and the Gran Reservas from Rioja).
* The lighter reds are from Valdepeñas and La Mancha, some classic Crianzas from Rioja or those which –young or old- have undergone a short skin maceration.

2.- THE IDEAL TEMPERATURE.

A red wine should be drunk at between 16⁰ and 18⁰C; white wines are more expressive between 8⁰ and 10⁰C and rosés at about 12⁰C.

Why?
Because if we serve the wine colder, the quantity of aromas is less, as the aromatic molecules are not so volatile at low temperatures. And if it is too high, the alcohol evaporates very quickly and the emanation of the ethers attacks the palate and nose.

A red wine at 24⁰C placed in an ice bucket with water and ice requires 9 minutes to reach a serving temperature of 17°-18°C. A white wine must be served chilled and kept in an ice bucket with water and ice.

3. - OPENING THE BOTTLE BEFORE THE TIME

An aged wine (more than five years in the bottle) will reveal its aromas better if we open the bottle two hours before drinking it.

Why?
Because, on opening the bottle, the aromas are closed; false aromas produced by being enclosed in the bottle for so many years can appear, and in the case of young wines, due to early bottling, secondary aromas from the fermentation can appear.

What you should know...
* The aromas of leather or stagnated water that can appear in old wines disappear or are reduced after a while.
* By opening the bottle early, some of the acidity is eliminated by letting the acetic ether evaporate, a very volatile ester which produces a sensation of acidity. Sometimes, the light oxidation takes the sharpness off the tannins that are responsible for the bitter and astringent taste.

4. - HOW TO USE A DECANTER

A decanter enables us to have the best of the wine.

Why?
Because it accelerates the disappearance of the closed aromas that are caused by the bottle and, in the case of old wines, enables us to separate the colorants that have precipitated to the bottom of the bottle.

What you should know...
* Some red wines, likely to have very intense colours (Cabernet Sauvignon, reds from Priorat or Ribera del Duero, vintage Ports) must be decanted slowly into a glass decanter until just before the sediment appears.
* The aeration caused when decanting the wine at least half an hour before serving helps to dissipate the negative aromas but it can be dangerous for very old wines as the bouquet vanishes.

5. - THE GLASS.

The most appropriate are transparent, bowl shaped, with a tall stem and, if possible, of fine crystal.

Why?
Because in round glasses with a smaller top the wine can be swirled better, revealing more of the aromas of the wine.

What you should know...

* A narrower top makes it easier to drink and impedes the wine escaping from the corner of the mouth.
* The stem allows us to hold the glass without touching the bowl.
* A fine crystal glass shows the colour of the wine with more precision and has a pleasant feel on the mouth.

6. – OBSERVE.

By observing the wine we can pass judgement and know some of its attributes beforehand.

Why?

Because it is possible to see the age of the wine and consequently many of its traits.

What you should know...

* If the wine seems very fluid and a slight spritz appears on swirling it, it is a sign of its youth.
* If it is luminous and brilliant, closely related to its higher acidity, it is a confirmation that it is young.
* If it is heavy and 'thick', with tears on the sides of the glass, it is an indication that it has more glycerin and, therefore, more alcohol.
* If the red wine is dark with a garnet red or violet edge, this is due to its youth and richness in anthocyanins (deep red cherry colour).
* If it is slightly lighter with a brick red edge, it is a sign of ageing. The deep red colours (anthocyanins) are replaced by others, yellow brown (the tannins) which leave a smoother and not so bitter sensation on the palate.

7. – THE NOSE.

When we lift the glass to our nose, it reveals the majority of the wine's traits.

Why?

By swirling the glass, the aromas of the wine are stronger and we can distinguish the different types.

What you should know...

* The primary aromas (those from the grape) related to fruit or flowers; they are lighter aromas which are more volatile.
* If we swirl the glass, the secondary aromas also appear (wood, forest, fallen leaves, and yeasts); they are denser and are at the bottom of the glass, as well as the tertiary aromas (toast , vanilla, hazelnut, coffee and tobacco) in the case of old wines.

8. - ON THE PALATE.

The first sensation on the palate is quite a pronounced tangible effect which gives the wine a flavourful feel.

Why?

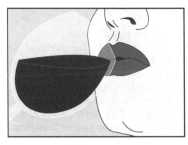

The sensation that is produced is a balanced combination of sweetness (alcohol), acidity (tartaric acid) and bitterness (tannins, either from the grape or the oak).

What you should know...

* Young wines enter the palate with a profusion of flavours. They are very rich in primary aromas; aromas which are more volatile and which disappear first (hints of fruit, flowers, blackberries, redcurrants, etc). The tangible sensation of harshness (astringency) that is usually produced on the palate is due to the high proportion of active tannins.

* Old wines have aromas which, although not as intense, have more subtle tones, and are denser and more intricate. The variety of tertiary tastes which are formed during the oxidative maturation (barrel) and reducing (bottle) leave a more persistent sensation on the palate

9. - FEEL.

Once on the palate, the wine does not reveal the flavours in such a spectacular way and it is necessary to breathe in a little to activate the aromatic properties.

Why?

Because, in this way a new batch of molecules which enter the nasal passages are evaporated in the opposite way (retronasal)

What you should know...

* A few moments after entering the mouth, the wines sets certain aromas free due to the temperature increase of the alcohol caused by the heat from the cavity of the mouth and consequently the tangible properties can be appreciated (tannins, acids, sweetness), but at the same time the aromatic potential is reduced.

* By breathing in a little air through the mouth and at the same time moving the wine about in the mouth, the oxidation caused by the air coming in creates the effect called 'retronasal' and gives a rounder sensation to the tannins. The fullness is due to the glycerin (oily, viscous sensation) which will be richer the higher the alcohol content.

10. - THE FINISH.

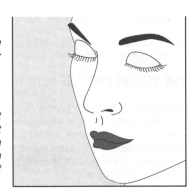

Once the wine has been swallowed, we can perceive new sensations, more or less intense.

Why?

Because there are nuances that do not appear in the nose or on the palate, but only come out when the wine has been swallowed due to the reaction of certain molecules of the wine with the enzymes of the saliva.

What you should know...

* Once the wine has been swallowed, the persistence of these sensations depend on the quality of the wine and the quantity of tertiary aromas and the variety.

* This persistence is due to the strength of the interaction of the aromatic molecules.

* Within the notes that did not appear before, neither in the nose or on the palate, should come out now, for example, very subtle hints such as the nuances of flint in some Sauvignons from alluvium regions or burnt and dark-roasted notes which are characteristic of some Californian Cabernet Sauvignons.

THE ESSENTIAL FLAVOURS OF WINE (PRACTICE AT HOME)

Divide and conquer, the old Spanish saying goes and it is very true. To know the different tastes in wine, there is nothing better than to forget about the wine for a few seconds and reproduce the sensations produced in a scientific and laboratory atmosphere. Let me explain how you can do it at home.

The sense of taste is found in the mouth, where the tongue and the taste buds are in charge of classifying the tastes and flavours. According to a study by David V. Smith and Robert Margolskee, the latter refers to the combined information from taste, smell and the tactile sensations in the mouth. Taste, on the other hand, is only related to sensations perceived by the mouth; bitter, salty, sour and sweet.

Let us concentrate on wine tasting; not only do we have to distinguish these four basic tastes (apparently easy), but also (this is the most important) their intensity or concentration in the wine, as this will determine its harmony or on the contrary, the lack of harmony. Because of this the following exercise not only takes into account the specific taste, but also its intensity. If you are able to detect the minimum quantities in the two exercises then you have the sensitivity to detect any defect in wine.

THE FIRST EXERCISE WITH WATER

Sweet. Dissolve 20 grams of sugar into a litre of water and you have a sweet taste in all its intensity. Then try for different solutions 5gr, 3gr, 2gr, and 1gr in a litre of water. Try to organize them in blind tasting by their intensity of sweetness.

Sour. To reproduce a sour taste, dissolve one gram of tartaric or citric acid in a litre of water. Then carry out the test with 'more or less acid' dissolving 0.7gr, 0.4gr and 0.1gr in a litre of water.

Salty. Dissolve 5gr of sodium chloride in a litre of water. Then prepare the other samples with different concentrations of 'salt': 2gr/lt, 1gr/lt and 0.5gr/lt.

Bitter. Dissolve 0.5gr of caffeine in a litre of water. To carry out the different concentrations of 'bitter' dissolve in a litre of water 0.25gr, 0.15gr, 0.10gr and 0.05gr per litre of water.

THE SECOND EXERCISE WITH WINE

Alcohol content. The alcohol modifies the balance of the rest of the flavours in the wine. To learn how to detect its level of influence on wine, try the following experiment. Take three bottles of white wine and three reds low in alcohol, about 11º (some Txakoli wines or red wines from Galicia will do). Leave one original sample of each wine and modify the other two by adding 9.5ml and 19ml of alcohol to increase the alcohol content to 12º and 13º respectively. Blind tasting.

Degree of sweetness. Take three bottles of a dry wine; keep an original sample and add 1gr and 2gr of sugar to the other two. Try to sort them in blind tasting by their intensity of sweetness.

Evaluating acidity. This is one of the most difficult aspects to taste. To learn how to detect it, take three bottles of red wine, reserve one and add 1gr and 2gr of citric or tartaric acid to the other two bottles. Once again, taste blind and sort them according to the degree of acidity.

Detecting the oily feeling. This is a quality which determines the weight of the wine on the palate and gives a pleasant sensation of roundness. To learn how to detect it, work with three samples of white wine and three of red wine; keep aside one of each and add 2 and 5grams of glycerin to each of the other whites; and 1 and 3 grams of glycerin to the reds.

Sulphur and acetic acid. These are the most common defects which are usually found in wines. The first, usually used in the making of the wine, especially in wines to be kept for a long time, can sometimes become evident in an exaggerated way. To learn how to recognize it, work with samples of red and dry white wine. Keep aside the original sample and add 10 and 20mg of sulphur dioxide to the others.

In the case of acetic acid (noticed by the vinegary hints), learn to identify it in different proportions working with four bottles of a young red wine in perfect condition (open on the nose). Keep aside an original sample and divide the rest into six samples. Add 0.2, 0.5, and 0.75 grams of acetic acid to the first three and to the other three add 50, 100 and 200mg of ethyl acetate.

The black glass. Obvious assessments such as a red smells like a red and a white smells like a white are not so obvious when one cannot see the colour of the wine. Try tasting in black glasses (or simply cover the glass in aluminium foil to the rim) a white wine that has lost its acidity (not a recent vintage, e.g. a 98 and from quite as warm climate: Valdepeñas, Terra Alta...), and a light red, not young, that has lost a large part of its fruity character and is not an intense varietal wine (*Garnacha*, *Mencía*, *Mazuelo*, *Monastrell* or *Tempranillo*). Are you able to tell the two wines apart?

EVERYTHING ABOUT THE COLOUR OF WINE

There is a whole series of nuances in wine which can only be appreciated through a comparative visualisation and provides valuable information about its characteristics.

* There is a basic principle for the colour of wines. Whites, with ageing, go darker; Reds become lighter.
* The more acidic wines have more of a glimmer, reds as well as whites.

WHITE WINES
* The darkening of white wines (ambers with reddish hues) in the bottle is due to oxidation from heat and light. The colouring session in wood after four months of ageing also gives it a more yellowish tone.

* The greenish glints indicate a higher acidity; apart from the fact that the characteristics of the variety could give it varying tones of yellow.

* *Chardonnay* always has a light yellow shade. On the other hand, a Sauvignon Blanc in similar circumstances has paler tones.

* A very brilliant pale white, with fast-moving beads is a young wine from cold regions rich in acids or made using modern methods of oenology with an early harvest low in sugars and, therefore rich in acids.

* A white which seems denser on pouring it into the glass will have come from warmer climates. A high alcohol content is usually directly proportional to the natural glycerin that makes the wine 'denser'.

RED WINES

* The time needed to extract the colorant during skin maceration with the must depends on the amount of sunlight the grape was exposed to during its vegetative phase.

* The wine, in its early stage, has a solid and intense colour. With the passing of the years it opens a little as the colour molecules tend to combine with one another becoming denser (going from a soluble state to colloidal and from this to insoluble, precipitating to the bottom of the bottle or barrel; these are the inoffensive sediments that many people confuse with the term 'chemical').

* Reds with brilliant glints and vermillion-blush rims come from northern regions and have high acid levels.

* Reds with violet tones with hints of brown are from warmer climates.

The colour of the wine definitely depends on the type of grape, the skin maceration, the ripeness of the grape, the time aged in wood and the ageing in bottle.

THE INFLUENCE OF THE WINEMAKING

THE FIRST PRACTICAL CASE: WHITES

Let us take two whites as examples: one made with new technology and the other made according to the most simple classic method used for table or common wines. And then we shall look at white wines made according to the increasingly more popular system of skin maceration.

Wine technology. It is a pale wine, the result of a controlled production and an early harvesting. The musts were filtered before fermentation, with the aim of preventing the herbaceous parts from giving excessive colour and flavours to the wine; later, the fermentation was controlled without exceeding 18º and finally, it was clarified.

It is very transparent with a high acid level which is reflected in its slightly greenish shine.
Traditional wine. Straw-yellow tones can be seen in it due to a more elementary vinification and a less rigorous racking than in the first. Perhaps there was not an exact control of the fermentation temperature and therefore the increased hints of oxidation are noticeable.
Wines with skin maceration. Whites that have been skin macerated (skin or peel of the grape) in their pre-fermentation stage (must) to obtain more structure, taste-smell complexity and density. It has certain amber hues produced by the yellow pigments (flavones) found in the skins.

THE SECOND PRACTICAL CASE: REDS

Here we have, as examples of the influence of the winemaking processes, two wines from the same vintage.
Wine with less colour. It has quite an open tone which indicates an early drawing off (separating the must, now wine, from the solid matter).

* They might have used more white grapes with the aim of smoothing it to cover a wider spectrum of consumers. This is the case of medium quality reds from Valdepeñas and La Mancha.

* It might have spent more time in barrel than the second and precipitated its colorants. However, this would be doubtful if the differences in the wood taste between the one and the other were not obvious.

Wine with more colour. It is more closed, either because it was macerated for longer or simply due to more sunshine in its region. The level of anthocyanins (red colour) and tannins (yellow) is a lot higher, which goes to show that a wine with these characteristics ages better. But perhaps, in the first phase of being on the market it comes up against customers who do not like the slightly harsher flavours.

ROSÉS
Supposedly the perfect rosé has a pale blush colour. If it was a very sunny season, the tone is redder as the skins of the red grapes have more colorants and it is difficult to separate the skin quickly enough to avoid the intensity of the colour. If it has been a rainy or cold year, the coloration is not as intense and it tends to have onion skin tones.

* The typical rosé oscillates between pink and onion skin tones. If the wine has been made under aseptic conditions, protected from the air, controlled fermentation and a moderate acidity, it has very lively blush tones and maybe slightly mauve reflections. With time the mauve reflections disappear, turning to yellowish and ochre tones.

CHAMPAGNE
The majority are made from red grapes with a rapid pressing. The must comes out quickly and is not left to 'run' among the broken skins to take on the red tones. Even so a certain blush nuance which is eliminated with carbon is unavoidable.

THE INFLUENCE OF AGEING

REDS
* **A red, the latest vintage.** It has the vermillion rims of a young wine, due to the large quantity of blue pigments that are found at this stage. In the same way, the rim is lively and brilliant with pronounced nuances of violet; characteristics which also betray the short life of this wine (see the glass at the bottom left of page 80).

* **A red aged for twenty years** in bottle (see the glass at the bottom right of page 80). Being in decline, it has more open tones, it has lost a lot of its anthocyanins and the brick coloured tones with glints of mahogany appearing and a predominance of yellow, the result of longer ageing.

ROSÉS
* **A rosé,** from the latest vintage (see the glass on the top left of page 80) has a raspberry pink colour due to a light reddish pigmentation with a bluish nuance which produces the raspberry tone.

* **A rosé that has been aged for twenty year**s in bottle has lost the brilliant bluish pink nuances (raspberry) to become more coppery-yellowish because of oxidation (see the glass on the top right of page 80).

WHITES
The inverse happens. If the wine is young (bottom left hand photo, page 79) it is characterised by a pale yellow tone, sharp and brilliant; the older one (see photo at the bottom right of page 79) has a more golden hue. Maybe this hue is due to the must having picked up the yellow pigments from the skins, flavones which, due to oxidation, modify the colour over time.

THE INFLUENCE OF AGEING IN WOOD

WHITES
The longer it stays in the barrel, the more intense the colour.

A wine aged in wood starts to present a golden shine after five months which continues to intensify with the ageing. However, if the wine has fermented with its lees in barrel, the influence of the oak is less and the colour somewhat paler than white wines that have only been aged in barrel due to the fermentative reaction of these compound solids.

Another illustrative example is Sherry, where the colour is not only due to the wood, but also to the defensive action of the yeasts in the Finos and the oxidative process in the case of Amontillados and Olorosos.

Finos. (Page 81, bottom left). There is degradation from the colourless tone at the rim to a pale yellow. This yellow tone is due to the two periods of the year in which the fluer disappears, and therefore the wine receives more oxygen.

Manzanilla. (Page 81, the same glass that is an example of Fino). With less ageing in wood than the Fino (although this is not always the case), the fluer, more permanent due to the humidity in the bodegas of Sanlúcar de Barrameda impedes oxidation. Therefore the wine stays pale and the greenish glints are more pronounced.

Amontillado. It is naturally inclined to oxidation, as it does not maintain its yeast completely and it is generally kept in barrel for longer than the previous ones. Therefore, it takes on its well defined orangey amber colour (page 81, the bottom centre glass).

Oloroso. The tones are more toasted; it has an orange and ochre background with yellow glims. On the one hand, there is more oxidation and on the other hand, concentration due to the evaporation of water and alcohol (see the glass at the bottom right of page 81).

THE INFLUENCE OF THE CLIMATE

The climate can have a definite influence on the colour of wines as may be seen in the following examples.

The wines from Sauternes and Central Europe. They are made from grapes left to ripen on the vine. The long ripening and the action of the noble rot cause the evaporation of the water content in the grapes, therefore the skin-must proportion favours pigmentation. The concentration of the sugars is greater and subsequently, they produce a greater intensity of colour due to the toasted colour of the belatedly ripened skins.

Pedro Ximénez wines. The grapes are dehydrated once they have been picked. The white grapes placed on mats and exposed to the sun, turn to raisins and take on a brown and ochre colour. The resultant wine is dark. This is due to a process similar to caramelising, as on the one hand the sun toasts the grapes and concentrates the sugar by reducing the volume of water and, on the other hand, oxidation is produced in the ageing in Solera which darkens it. Depending on the length of the ageing the colour will be lighter or darker (see photos on page 82).

Sunning in containers. This is only done in Rueda and Cataluña. It is the accelerated ageing of the wine stored in glass containers exposed to the elements; with the brusque day-night temperature differences it undergoes a similar process as an annual summer-winter ageing. The action of the sun can be seen in the yellow-reddish colour to which the white wine turns after a few months.

The colour of reds. It is clear that the pigmentation is produced by the sun on the grapes. However, a grape is not necessarily ripe for vinification when it is very black. The sugar level of the grape may not be sufficient (although unlikely in sunny climates). On the other hand, it is also quite common for the colour and the sugars to be optimum but the skin not to be ripe enough. This often happens in warm regions where, besides testing the sugar and acid levels with a refractometer, it is necessary to taste the peels and pips to check for ripeness. Occasionally, the pigmentation and the sugars form faster than the ripening of the skin. Therefore, paradoxically, there are reds from very sunny regions with herbaceous flavours although the colour is deep and the alcohol content is 12.5º or higher.

* A *Cabernet Sauvignon* from Lérida is exposed to more sunlight than a *Cabernet Sauvignon* from Bordeaux. The wines from the French region have a lively violet rim, while the ones from Lerida tend to have light ochre tones, but without losing the balance obtained from modern vinification.

* A Sauvignon from *Monastrell* in Cataluña or from Provence are not at all like ones from Jumilla or Alicante. In the latter two areas, the sun and the high alcohol content gives them a more bluish-brown tone, while in the north the tones are redder and more lively.

THE INFLUENCE OF THE VINE STOCK

RED WINES
* *Tempranillo.* When young it has a garnet red bigarreau cherry colour, with a vermillion-blush ribbon that gives it a sense of immaturity (see the glass on the top left of page 81).
* *Garnacha.* Violet rim and a slightly orangey cherry tone.
* *Cabernet Sauvignon.* Its nuances are more pronounced, with a brusque change from a solid ripe cherry base in the centre to very purple at the rim (see the glass on the top right of page 81).
* *The Garnacha Tintorera* (or *Alicante* in Galicia and León) not only has high levels of pigmentation in the skin but also in the must. And it is because of this that it is used in regions with little sunlight, such as Galicia, to compensate for the lack of colour typical of cooler climates.

ROSÉS WINES
* *Cariñena.* It has pomegranate tones at the rim.
* *Cabernet Sauvignon.* It has raspberry tones.
* *Garnacha.* Tones tending to shades of mauve.

WHITE WINES
* *Xarel-lo.* Produces a wine that tends to be straw yellow.
* *Parellada.* A paler wine due to the grapes not being completely ripe, as it is grown in higher regions. When blended with Xarel-lo, the wine has a higher alcohol content and moderate acidity, which makes a good blend for champagne.
* *Chardonnay.* A more yellow wine due to the colour of its skin.

GRAPHIC ILLUSTRATION OF THE COLOURS IN WINES

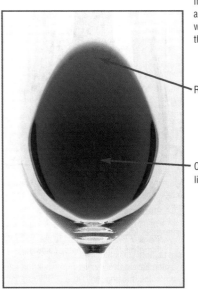

Interpretation of the colours in wines in a glass at an inclination of 45°, together with the most common terms used in the wine tastings in this guide:

Rim or border with a slightly violet hue

Cherry, medium-intensity and quite lively.

WHITE WINES

YOUNG WHITE WINE

Pale straw yellow. There are also green nuances, proof of its youth.

MATURE WHITE WINE, AGED FOR 20 YEARS IN BOTTLE

Golden yellow with hints of amber. (Due to oxidation the yellow becomes more intense and turns to shades of red).

ROSÉ WINES

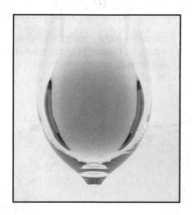

THE LATEST VINTAGE

Brilliant blush with a strawberry-raspberry hue. The blue tones that with the reddish tones, give a raspberry hue are associated with the youth of the wine.

20 YEARS OF AGEING IN BOTTLE

Blush salmon colour with coppery hints. (In rosés, time changes the colour to orangey hues, losing the lively blue tone that gives it the raspberry colour).

RED WINES

LATEST VINTAGE RIOJA

Medium-intensity cherry red with a violet rim (characteristic of its youth).

A RIOJA, AGED FOR 20 YEARS IN BOTTLE.

Ruby red with an orangey hue and a rim between ochre and brick. (This red wine is on the decline, the very brick coloured ochre is a sign of excessive oxidation).

TEMPRANILLO, CABERNET SAUVIGNON

The differences between these two varieties are quite clear: while the colour of the *Tempranillo* (the glass on the left) is dark cherry with a more orangey rim, the colour of the *Cabernet* (glass on the right) is more intense with a more violet rim, due to greater pigmentation from the skins as the grapes are smaller than the *Tempranillo's*.

VINOS GENEROSOS

MANZANILLA OR FINO

Pale yellow with greenish nuances. The paleness is due to the very little oxidation of the wine as it is protected by the cap that covers the surface.

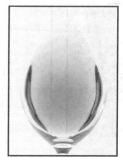

AMONTILLADO

A golden amber yellow. The more amber tones are caused by the oxidation phase of the Amontillado. Its golden nuance and brightness, more pronounced in an Oloroso, is due to the initial biological phase, the same as in the Fino.

OLOROSO

Iodised topaz colour. The browner and ochre colours with tones similar to those of iodine are the result of the heavy oxidative maturation it undergoes right from the start.

PEDRO XIMENEZ

Dark amber. This is an example of a younger and lighter PX and therefore, with less caramelisation of the sugar due to it being aged for less time in oak.

MATURE PEDRO XIMÉNEZ

Opaque cherry with a iodine coloured rim. The intensity of the colour is due to the caramelisation of the sugar in the oxidation phase of this wine during the long maturation period in casks.

EVERYTING ABOUT THE AROMA OF WINE

Although the nose is the organ we exercise least, it is vital. In fact, many of the pleasures of the mouth would be imperceptible if our sense of smell did not work. For the wine taster it is an irreplaceable tool and it is fair to consider it, as Max Leglise put it so beautifully, "the garden of the senses".

Our sense of smell is complex and mysterious and as such has its weaknesses.

Have you realized that…?
* You do not smell your everyday perfume but others do, or that a house has a smell that all but the owners notice.

* The nose is not reliable with usual smells; the nose gets tired.

It is important for the wine enthusiast to try and remember all the nuances detected with the first smell. Insistence is a sure way of increasing insensibility.

The importance of smell. Of the three gastronomic senses, smell is the most important. If we smell a rosé and we can see it, we will be convinced that it is a rosé. If we close our eyes, now we are not so sure; and even less so if we drink it.

Once we have smelt a wine at a wine tasting, we will have made approximately 80% of the evaluation.

Try it yourself… Bring an aged red wine without any defect to your nose and in it you will detect aromas of ripe red fruit harmonised with hints of new wood. Only with this information, added to its intense and brilliant colour, will we be able to say that it is a relatively young wine that has not been aged for very long in wood. The mouth will only confirm it, because of a certain astringency of the fruity tannins and the dry and bitter tannins of the wood, but all of these ingredients were announced beforehand by the notes perceived by the nose.

A reminder: The sense of smell is the most passive sense and, in general we do no really use it, unless aromas and smells reach us which due to their intensity and clarity catch our attention. If we concentrated on smelling all the time, we would be surprised at the multitude of aromas that surround us.

THE INFLUENCE OF THE SOIL

The type of soil modifies the aroma of wines very subtly.

Granite and sandy soils. They provide certain frankness to the wine and give it clean aromas that define its variety. They are the Galician wines or the *Garnachas* from San Martín de Valdeiglesias that are produced on soils that have low moisture retention.

Gravel or pebble fields (in some areas of Rueda and Toro). Produce wines with earthy aromas with flinty hints which blend with the nuances of the ripe grape produced by the thermal warming of the stones.

Slate soils and soils rich in minerals. In Priorat, Arribes del Duero, Cebreros and Axarquía the wines always have light hints of mineral, dark-roasted and toasted aromas, the same as those in the Portuguese Alto Duero, the cradle of Port.

Volcanic soils. The soils that are found in Lanzarote, Hierro, La Palma, and certain areas of Tenerife. Their wines have slightly burnt and iodised nuances.

Clayey soils (most of the Spanish soils). On retaining more moisture, the yield is higher but to the detriment of the quality. The wines are more neutral and, above all in the whites, one can taste certain herbaceous streaks if the vineyard is found on flat and damp areas. Clay is needed deep down in the subsoil to retain the moisture and to ensure the feeding of the roots.

Ferruginous soils. Difficult soils to grow quality wines on. In general, ferruginous clay soils give the grapes a high level of iron which should be eliminated. They are soils that give the wine a rustic and slightly burnt touch.

Calcareous fields (found in Burgundy - Côtes de Nuits– , Champagne, Jumilla, Jerez or Rioja Alavesa). These soils accentuate the quality of the wine with note of elegance; the wines are finer and more complex.

THE INFLUENCE OF THE CLIMATE

In cold and wet regions (such as **Txakolis** in the Basque Country, the **wines from Galicia and the north of Portugal**), the high rainfall impedes the complete ripening of the grape, thus producing wines low in alcohol and therefore with a high acidity level. The whites from these areas are noted for their high malic acid content, a slight hint of cider or apple, even when malolactic fermentation in forced to reduce the acidity.

However, the same variety can have a different character if there are marked changes in the climate. The Mediterranean varieties which dominate in Spain lose a lot of their aromatic potential in higher and wet regions.

This is what happens to a *Garnacha* grown in Rioja Alta and another in Rioja Baja. In the first case the wine is finer and more suitable for ageing but the higher acidity masks the aromas.

The opposite would be true for a *Parellada*, a white grape, fine and classy, which needs the cool temperatures of the higher regions of Penedès to be at its best and which loses part of its fineness in warmer climates.

THE INFLUENCE OF THE VINE STOCK

This is probably the most significant and constant element in the aroma of wines.
A global vision. The best varieties are cultivated in France, the result of post-phylloxera selection which forced them to identify the best grapes, due to their great aromatic and taste definition to which potency is added. These wines age more in barrel and evolve positively during their maturation. Some of the most highly valued grapes in the world are *Merlot, Cabernet Franc, Cabernet Sauvignon, Syrah, Sauvignon Blanc, Pinot Noir, Chardonnay*, etc.

But it is also true that the cooler French climate facilitates milder ripening and, proportionately, with less water retention (the fluvial location of the best French regions ensure good drainage), together with a more careful production, respects these primary characters.

What about Spain? Working with varieties is relatively new and we have only recently started to discover the potential and the personality of the *Tempranillo, Garnacha and Cariñena* grapes as a consequence of better control of the ripening of the grape. Other grapes that were forgotten because of their roughness in old production methods are reappearing today with a quality unimaginable ten years ago. This is the case of the *Pardina* from Extremadura, the *Moristel* from Huesca, the Catalonian *Trepat* and *Garro*, the Majorcan *Prensal*, the *Listán* from the Canary Islands or the *Dona Blanca* from Galicia.

Clones. The choosing of clones; that is, the selection of a particular botanical species of the same variety that is better adapted to the ecosystem of the region. Only clones whose wines have similar characteristics can be chosen from. A *Cabernet Sauvignon* from California would be more suited to the majority of the Spanish climates than a clone from Bordeaux because of the cooler climate it is used to.

THE INFLUENCE OF THE WINEMAKING

The aromas acquired during the winemaking process are called 'secondary'. These can be positive or negative.

Positive aromas. These are the aromas of yeast, the lactic nuances that produce a sweet and supple sensation on the palate, or the ethereal hints that have nuances of fine herbs from the lees.

Negative aromas.
* **Sulphide, sulphur, geranium, liquorice.** These can appear in young wines and indicate that the wine is not finished or has undergone microbiological breakdown of the sulphur dioxide due to the lack of aeration or late racking. The liquorice aromas are usually found in wines produced from Tempranillo because of semi-carbonic maceration. In general these negative smells and aromas are produced by alcohol and malolactic fermentation.

* **Banana**. Although it is not unpleasant, it appears in wines that have been bottled too early. It forms during vinification at low temperatures with selected yeasts. It is an aroma that is not as noticeable in late bottling.

* **Rustic and eau de vie aromas**. Typical of wines produced in unhygienic conditions, before the advent of stainless steel containers and the temperature control of fermentation. There was no racking (filtering or clarifying of the must) and the vegetable parts gave the wines undesirable flavours, although they were not always unwelcome. They did not control the alcohol content or the acidity, and the whites lacked the freshness that is so appreciated these days.

* **'Closed'**. This can be seen when opening a bottle of rosé or a prematurely bottled young wine or a wine that has been in the bottle for a long time but dissipate with aeration. Premature bottling never allows the wine to acquire the reducing aromas of ageing; and with time they even lose the primary aromas. Therefore, young wines as well as rosés must be consumed as soon as possible.

THE INFLUENCE OF AGEING

These are the aromas that the wine takes on while in the wooden barrels or casks. Peynaud said. "The knowledge of ageing is to conserve the virtues of youth for a long time". And this is what it is about, ageing wine without losing the fruity aromas. In Spain there are different maturation aromas depending on the wine preservation techniques.

Extended maturation. When the ageing is longer than two years, aldehyde aromas, very similar to acetones or nail varnish, start to appear due to the oxidation of the alcohol. At times one discovers very well defined aromas of wood which, in other cases, combine with hints of vanilla, mushroom, cinnamon, resin or nuts. When the wood is old it gives a rancid vanilla smell, and it is even more defined in old brandies. Musky aromas can also appear when bottle ageing is longer than 30 years.

Animal type aromas. This is typical of old wines that have been bottled for a long time and have asphyxiated or evaporated a lot in the bottle. Wines with very little pigmentation or tannins are susceptible to this, such as some reds, Chiantis or Burgundies.
* New leather, Moroccan leather.
* Wet dog.

Balsamic type aromas. Resin-like aromas produced by ageing in oak at medium to high conservation temperatures (Levante-Spain, Greek wines, wines from Tunisia, and some from Australia, California and South Africa). These 'medicine chest' aromas are also caused by the use of pine and chestnut. The caramelising of the wine that has evaporated between the staves of the barrel also contributes to this. Some smells with a hint of eucalyptus and bay could be due to phenolic immaturity (seeds and skin of the grape) which are produced in warm vineyards and contrast with the hints of sweetness or spirits from its high alcohol content. They must not be confused with the subtle aromas of the great wines from the Rhone which may have hints of eucalyptus.

* Pitch.
* Cedar wood.
* Incense.
* Eucalyptus (in some cases it is due to phenolic immaturity of the pips and peel of the grape).

Woody aromas. They are produced by recent ageing in wood, normally in 225-litre barrels. These aromas are usually found in regions with an Atlantic climate (Rioja, Castilla-León, Cataluña, France, northern Italy, etc).

* New oak barrel.
* Old wood.
* Cigar box.
* Green wood or kindling.

Toasty or smoky aroma. Aromas acquired during a long maturation in new toasted wood or from the peels of very ripe grapes (toasted).

* Black pepper.
* Roasted caramel.
* Roasted almonds.
* Coffee.
* Dark-roasted coffee.
* Cocoa.
* Chocolate.
* Toasted bread.
* Smoky flavours.
* Vanilla.
* Tobacco.

THE INFLUENCE OF THE BOTTLE

Normally, bottle conservation tempers the aromas of the wine and the aromas of maturation. This is called 'reduction' (changes of aroma and taste caused by the lack of oxygen in the bottle).

Negative aromas. Found in wines bottled with a lot of sulphur, and on being opened a few years later, one can notice unpleasant smells, such as to petrol and stagnant water.

Positive aromas. When the wine has a good balance of wood ageing, the quality of the prime material, is from an excellent vintage and an impeccable production, the reduction bouquets appear. They are similar to toasted honey, cinnamon, royal jelly and spicy aromas.

EVERYTHING ABOUT THE TASTE OF WINE

The sensations that a wine produces on the palate can be compared to a musical chord: the best combination occurs when the alcohol, acidity and tannins are in perfect harmony.

Taste, as pointed out in previous chapters, plays an easier role, as a good portion of the silhouette of the wine would have been revealed to the palate by the nose.

The taste components of a wine. Besides the tastes of acid, sweet or bitter, the wine holds back other flavours which a layman would not be able to describe.
These are taste sensations produced by:

* **The phenolic compounds** (found in the skins of the red grapes), where, according to the grape variety, the smoother or more mysterious complex tastes are born.

When all these tastes are combined it forms a conspiracy of tastes with a determined density, which is the body or extract of the wine, expressed in grams in the analyses.

* **The volatile substances which are created by fermentation** (alcohol, chemical and ethereal flavours).

* **The substances given off by the wood**.

The concept of balance. Without this, a wine would have a lack or have an excess of something. Let us have a look at some examples of this to explain this concept in a practical way.

* *Mature wines.* The youthful character has softened and, on maturing, the wine reaches its full splendour in roundness and harmony.

* *Wines with moderate alcohol.* The table type wine which dominates the world have about 11.5º - 12º - 12.5º alcohol. It is precisely in this range of alcohol that the other components (acidity, etc.) are neither aggressive nor weak provided that, of course, the harvest, the climate and the winemaking were optimum. They have a dry character.

* *Wines with a high alcohol content.* In wines with 13º or 14º, the alcohol must be enveloped by a higher participation of the other elements (body, acidity and tannins) for it not to be perceptible as a burning sensation caused by the high alcohol content. They have a slightly sweet taste.

A good wine must show itself to be a harmonious whole between the appearance, aroma and taste.

Appearance. Brightness and glimmer are common to whites, rosés and reds. Wines must always be transparent, sharp and brilliant.

Aroma and taste. In young wines as well as mature wines, the nose always defines the variety; and as far as flavours go, young wines are dominated by hints of fruit; and the mature wines by the nuances of ageing.

Tastes 'to order'. In France, and the whole of Europe in general, people are used to drier wines than the Spanish because their wines have less sugar than ours. This is the problem the Spanish producers have to confront when they export low-cost wines. On one hand, they must make modern wines with more acidity but, on the other hand, they have to keep their Spanish customers happy who are used to less dry wines.
Therefore the winemakers are faced with the arduous task of adapting their wines to the customers' taste, who ultimately have the last say. It is not so much a case of imitating the wine of the region in fashion, but adapting to the global tendencies that prevail at the moment.

THE MAIN SPANISH 'TASTES'.
Galician wines. Their acidity, above all in the whites, has been accepted and is even linked to specific foods such as seafood.
Rioja. The wine for special occasions. Their image has been copied by other regions through maturation in barrels and by means of advanced technology.

Ribera. This is a new taste, and smoother than Rioja. It is a red with body, rich colour and strong tannins that a lot of consumers have accepted.

Table wine. Due to its price it is one of the most popular wines. It is hypermarket wine or 'house wine' in a cheap restaurant, the result of the 'secret' blend of *Garnacha*, *Bobal*, *Airén* and *Monastrell*.

The taste of the different wineries. Each bodega has its own distinctive and specific traits regardless of the character or typology of the winemaking region where it is found, be it imposed by their regular customers or because of fidelity to a traditional identity.

This traditional aspect is mainly seen in wines which still have relatively long periods of maturation in oak and less to offer when it comes to more open colours.

TIPS FOR THE UNSEASONED ENTHUSIAST

We will analyze some of the most common terms used by laymen and their true meanings.

TASTES OF COGNAC!
For many consumers this is the expression used to define a good wine, an old wine or a noble wine.

The taste which slightly resembles brandy is due to the aldehydes caused by the oxidation of the alcohols during prolonged ageing in wood.

Wines are often likened to brandy because of the yellowish tones common to long maturation.

THIS WINE IS SOUR!
This expression is common among laymen who call the carbonic remains that can appear in a wine 'sour'.

The sour taste is produced by an elevated volatile acidity caused by bacteria which the experts call acetobacter (a sure way for the wine to turn into vinegar).
This defect is mainly found in bottles with damaged corks, as well as in wines which have been bottled with a very high volatile acidity. It is also found in unfinished bottles that have been left open.

IT'S A LITTLE ACID!
In Spain, where the wines from Mancha, Valdepeñas or Levante have always been drunk excessively, we are reluctant and sensitive to the acidity because we are used to it being masked by the alcohol. Nowadays this has been accentuated, above all in modern white wines, looking for the sensation of freshness it produces.

The acidity can also be confused with the bitterness produced by the personality of the grape. Or, in a wine made from non-virgin musts, where the solid particles or lees have left a certain bitterness in the must.

THIS WINE IS SUPPLE!
The suppleness is the roundness of the wine, the result of the period of ageing in bottle and good winemaking.

It is a velvety sensation, a normal term used in wine tasting which describes the slightly silky touch which is so pleasant on the palate.

The perception of smoothness is conditioned by the temperature of the wine. At 23º or 24ºC (too high to be consumed), reds become more supple, but the alcohol is more noticeable.

The 'most supple' wines:
* Reds from the southeast of Spain (Alicante, Jumilla and Yecla). Made from *Monastrell*, they have a slightly pasty, pleasant taste with a hint of glycerin, tears of viscosity which appear on the sides of the glass. Nowadays these wines are giving way to other more structured wines.

* Wines aged in wood and tempered in the bottle for a long time.
* Wines with little body, such as the wines low in acid from La Mancha, Extremadura, Valencia and Rueda, and even more glyceric wines made from *Chardonnay* and *Gewürztraminer* or from Tokay and Sauternes.
* Reds from La Mancha and Valdepeñas which have a high percentage of neutral white grapes that dilute the tannins of the red, producing a light smooth sensation. Nowadays this method is changing little by little in favour of darker and more full-bodied reds.

I LIKE THIS WINE!

If we could slow down the sensations produced by the wine, we would say that we like it as we notice the sensations of bitterness, acidity, and sweetness at the same time; a good aromatic sensation and on the palate it has a delicate and pleasant texture... Definitely, the balance.

Wine is a combination of simple flavours which cause a pleasant sensation on the palate. If the balance is not right or the acidity is low, we describe it as tender, as pseudo-sweet; if it has a low alcohol content, we say it is watery; if it lacks tannins, it is not elegant, it lacks virility and body; if it is too acid, we say it is angular.

SO-SO...

This is a derogatory term when applied to a young wine, with little body and an undetermined personality.

They are normally cheap wines, without a DO, litre or box wines whose main defect is a base of lees, a burning sensation and, sometimes an alcohol of unknown origin. They are wines transported in large tankers, above all to the local centres; there they are mixed and pasteurized before being bottled. Nowadays the best are the box wines of the large packaging companies. At least they do not have any flaws.

THIS WINE IS ROUGH!

Maybe one should do away with the term 'rough' because of its negative connotations. In sensorial vocabulary it is called astringent, which is a less aggressive sensation.

This roughness is found in young wines with a lot of body and above all with a lot of tannins; it is detected on the tongue as bitterness and roughness.

The more colour the wine has, the greater the sensation of roughness on the tongue, as generally more pigmentation is associated with a larger quantity of tannins. For experts, this astringency is an indication of the wines future and excellent maturity. And they are right.

THIS WINE IS WOODY!

This expression is used, almost always, to define wines with intense tones of wood, when this concept is absolutely false. This term makes reference to the wines from Madeira, wines historically oxidized by heat. The sensation is translated to a hint of this Portuguese wine in a bad sense of the word, like a rancid or off wine.

SMELLS OF CORK!

The cork is the only piece in wine manufacturing that cannot be individually controlled.

It seems that northern wines which have an appreciable acidity and low alcohol content degrade the cork more, or at least reveal the taste and smell of mould, that has developed in the microscopic cavities in the cork during the making and storage.

The smell of cork has often been confused with the smell of mould in some wines aged in old barrels which are stored in excessively damp cellars. Anyway the concept is the same: TCA

THE MOST COMMON TASTES AND AROMAS IN WINE

YOUNG WHITES:

* **Fruit:** green apples, lemon, banana and grapefruit.
* **Herbaceous:** fennel, mint, scrubland herbs, hay.

* **Flowers:** jasmine, petals.

WHITES AGED IN OAK.
* **Toasted:** dark-roasted, biscuit, cocoa.
* **Ripe fruit and nuts:** bitter almond, toasted almonds, golden apple, hazelnut.
* **Spices:** vanilla.

VERY OLD WHITES:
* Old wood, musky, rancid honey, toasted almonds, confectionery, walnuts.

YOUNG REDS:
* Black plums, blackberries, redcurrants, cherries, squashed black grapes, plum and blackberry jam.

REDS AGED IN OAK:
* The same features as young reds but less accentuated as well as vanilla, dark-roasted, cocoa, toasted bread, cedarwood.

OLD REDS:
* Leather, attics, vanilla, supple flavour, less body.

YOUNG ROSÉS:
* Raspberries, strawberries, violet sweets.

HOW TO DESCRIBE A WINE

It is not enough to say that 'I like this wine' or 'I do not like that one', or 'this one is better than the others'. Our taste memory should demand more, know why. And to do this we need to make notes and have a minimum vocabulary.

The amateur reader often criticises the metalanguage of the experts for not being understandable and a little elitist; however, we accept the difficult language of cars and computers as something natural.

It is not difficult to understand a description of a wine. In the descriptions we find different adjectives, nouns and comparisons with better known fruit and spices. When it says, for example, that a wine has hints of toast or coffee, two very different tastes and, of course, nothing to do with the taste or smell of wine, we are trying to arrive at the common note of these two products with the toasted hints in the inside of the oak barrel acquired during ageing.

On the following pages you will find the descriptions of the most common types of wine. In each case we start from a score card of a quality wine within each segment analysed, to then explain the reasons for using the different wine tasting terms. We also give clues on how to express the sensations of colour, aroma and taste a wine produces.

Whites, Rosés, Young Reds, and aged Reds, Finos, Olorosos, Amontillados, Cavas and Champagnes are all analysed by the expert.

A DESCRIPTION OF A QUALITY WHITE WINE FROM RUEDA AND FROM THE LATEST VINTAGE.

Greenish straw yellow. Fine and elegant on the nose, intense; aroma of exotic fruit

and citrus, fennel, flowers and fresh herbs. Flavourful and aromatic, enveloping, fresh, bitter, elegant in the retronasal passage.

Greenish straw yellow. Yellow in a young wine must be seen as pale which corresponds to the colour of straw; i.e. a mixture of pale yellow and green. Greenish is included as it is the predominant hue.

Fine and elegant on the nose. This is a way of expressing the harmony between the nuances that give hints of fruit, flowers and herbs which are cited afterwards as a comparison. Harmony is like a choir where no particular voice stands out but its absence would be noticed. The inclusion of a floral nuance and fine herbs always denotes a touch of elegance.

Intense. It is the first impression, clear and sharp, of the aroma of the wine without swirling the glass.

Aroma of exotic fruit and citrus. Exotic can be understood as a little known feature, remote and maybe close to tropical fruit, that could be from its maturity (tropical fruits are perceived as very sweet and therefore, very ripe). The critical word in this wine could be closer to grapefruit – not losing sight of the exoticism mentioned above- than to a lemon. In any case, by not specifically mentioning any citrus, we can leave it somewhere between a grapefruit and a lemon.

Fennel, flowers and fresh herbs. Express the hints of fine herbs with fennel predominating and the sensations of flower petals as a trait of youth. It is possible that they are the result of skin maceration (the herbaceous part of the grape) before fermentation. The adjective fresh is the way it penetrates the nose, the acidic and sweet tone of the wine.

Flavourful and aromatic. Flavourful is the 'cocktail' of the sweet sensation of the alcohol with the acidity perceived on the palate and that does not interfere with the combination of a good volume or density appropriate for the wine without being light or heavy. Aromatic as a taste sensation is what we perceive on the nose when the wine is on the palate and at the same time we breathe in through our mouth.

Enveloping, fresh, bitter. The first word describes the perception of density we feel on the palate due to good alcohol content; fresh is the counterpoint of the acidic balance; and bitter is a feature we gently perceive in wines made from the Verdejo grape.

Elegant in the retronasal passage. The aroma perceived on the nose from the palate breathing in through the mouth is called retronasal. In this case it is also delicate and elegant, the same as the direct aroma.

A DESCRIPTION OF A WHITE WINE FERMENTED IN BARREL AND AGED FOR SIX MONTHS IN BARREL

Straw-coloured with a brilliant golden glimmer. Fine aroma, with elegant smoky notes, fine herbs (a hint of fennel), lees. Oily on the palate, round, elegant, with an excellent point of acidity well-combined with the alcohol, hints of hay and ripe apples; very persistent .

Straw-coloured with a brilliant golden glimmer. The straw-coloured tones indicating a certain youthfulness combine with a golden hue which, in this case, the wine acquired from being in contact with wood and it gives us clues about the character that is behind the merely fruity and young side. Brilliant implies that the colour is lively.

Fine aroma. Implies a certain delicacy and a good aroma among the different aromatic nuances that are described below. It is a trait of good quality wines.

With elegant smoky notes. These are sensations imparted by the oak during fermentation and ageing and are almost more creamy (between butter, cream and vanilla) than toasted. This trait also transmits a sensation of fineness and elegance.

Fine herbs (a hint of fennel), lees. This refers to the hints of herbs with a delicate aroma (the fineness is specified in the perception), fennel, a herb with a fresh component which implies youth, dominates. But the lees, which are the sediments that remain in the barrel after fermentation, are also identified. It is an aroma between perfumed yeasts and dried grass or hay which makes this type of wine very complex.

Oily on the palate, round, elegant. It is oily because of the greasy or glycerin-enveloping sensation which gives volume on the palate. Very ripe grapes are used and therefore there is a high alcohol content which produces a slippery sensation. The roundness forms part of this perception of smoothness but without dissonant or aggressive elements. The elegance is now linked to the harmony and balance of all the components, producing a pleasant whole.

With an excellent point of acidity well-combined with the alcohol. This wine offers an intense sensation of sharpness and freshness and, at the same time, there is an enveloping feel, almost warm, due to the relatively high degree of alcohol. Again the wine is proof of having achieved a balance.

Hints of hay and ripe apples. The wine evokes tastes of fruit and dried grass. The ripe apple is identified, associated with a well-ripened grape base used in the making, and other similar sensations that had been detected earlier, on the nose.

Very persistent. This means that once you have swallowed the wine, the tastes and the aromatic sensations that were identified persist for a while, as an echo of its characteristics and personality.

A DESCRIPTION OF A QUALITY ROSÉ FROM NAVARRA AND FROM THE LATEST VINTAGE.

Blush with a strawberry hue, brilliant and lively; intense aroma, with hints of raspberries and rose petals; it is light, fresh, fruity and with good acidity on the palate, flavourful, easy drinking, and not very vinous.

Blush with a strawberry hue. The little pigmentation gives pink and strawberry colours in its most youthful stage and youth is one of its virtues.

Brilliant and lively. The brilliance is a quality, the result of good winemaking and acidity, lively is the sharpness or luminosity of a wine due to its youth.

Intense aroma. This is an indispensable condition of a good rosé.

With hints of raspberries and rose petals. In general it is a typical feature of rosés when they are fermented at low temperature and with selected yeasts. The floral hint is a quality of the free run musts (the first drops of the grape when pressing them) while a herbaceous taste is the result of a greater contact with the grapeskins, not appropriate in rosés.

Light, fresh, fruity. Light is a desired feature of rosés (they must not weigh on the mouth). Fresh is a sensation of acidity that is pleasant and which mixes with the sweet perception of alcohol; fruity in rosés is the combination of hints of red fruit, such as, barely ripe strawberry and raspberry.

With good acidity on the palate, flavourful. This is the touch of acidity that lingers in the mouth and leaves a hint of freshness; flavourful due to the natural residual sugars that some winemakers leave in the wine to be able to increase the acidity without being unpleasant and in this way provide a pleasanter palate.

Easy drinking, and not very vinous. A rosé is neither a very complex wine nor persistent in the mouth. Its main virtue is that it is light, fresh and that it is easy to drink and is not tiresome. A rosé should not be very vinous (heavy sensation transmitted by alcohol with low acidity).

A DESCRIPTION OF A QUALITY YOUNG RED FROM RIOJA AND FROM THE LATEST VINTAGE.

Dark garnet red cherry or bigarreau cherry with a lively violet edge. Fresh, intense, fruity and varietal aroma with hints of blackberries and redcurrants, and floral, lactic and aniseed notes. Well-formed, medium-bodied, fruity, flavourful and aromatic on the palate, with sweet tannins, a perfectly integrated acidity and persistent in the retronasal passage.

Dark garnet red cherry or bigarreau cherry. The colour is the result of a long ripe skin maceration (the skins of the grape) with the must.

With a lively violet edge. The violet colour that appears at the edge is a sign of its youth and freshness; the term lively refers to the luminosity which a good acidity gives.

Fresh, intense, fruity and varietal aroma. Fresh is the sensation of the fragrance of a young wine; intense is typical of a young wine; fruity the trace of grape that persists in the wine; and varietal is the type of grape, in this case Tempranillo.

With hints of blackberries and redcurrants. A comparison to known plants, such as black fruit from the bramble and the redcurrants that characterise wines that have not aged or matured.

And floral, lactic and aniseed notes. Floral because of the delicate notes from the fine musts, lactic because of the very faint lactic notes that still have not disappeared after the malolactic fermentation (transformation of malic acid – pungent - into lactic acid – smoother - usually carried out in red wines), aniseed is the fine herbaceous trait from good skins.

Well-formed, medium-bodied. A red that must be drunk young should have between a light and medium volume or body.

Fruity, flavourful and aromatic on the palate. Fruity from the sensations hinting of red fruit and ripe grape; flavourful from the nuances of sweetness and acidity integrated into its body or volume; aromatic because of the pleasant olfactory sensations from the palate.

With sweet tannins, a perfectly integrated acidity. The tannins (that slight roughness) are not dry or herbaceous as the skin was not completely macerated. They are therefore fruity (or sweet). Besides the wine has just the right amount of acidity; that is, the tannins and the acidity have combined to perfection with the rest of the substances that form the structure of the wine.

And persistent in the retronasal passage. When the wine has disappeared from the mouth and the aroma still persists internally.

A DESCRIPTION OF A RED CRIANZA FROM RIOJA

Very deep cherry with an orangey rim or border. Aroma of ripe black fruit (blackberries and jammy plums), fresh, with notes of new wood (toast, scrubland, dark-roasted) yet to be assembled. Fruity, medium-bodied with supple but marked tannins on the palate, somewhat dry from the wood but ripe from the fruit; fruity in the retronasal passage and flavourful and lively in the finish.

Very deep cherry with an orangey rim or border. Reminiscent of the bigarreau cherry (dark red) and in this case very intense. The rim is the side of the wine when we incline the glass and the liquid is about a centimetre from the lip. The orangey colour is the intermediate step between the violet or purple of a young wine and the tile or brick colour of an old wine.

Aroma of ripe black fruit (blackberries and jammy plums), reminiscent of wild fruit jam or crystallised fruit whose added sugar increases the density of their sweet aromas.

Fresh, with notes of new wood (toast, scrubland, dark-roasted) yet to be assembled. Fresh is the sensation of youth which the wine still expresses but with the addition of new toasted wood (the inside of the barrels are usually toasted). The hint of dark-roasted (caramelised coffee beans) is precisely this toasted aroma with a nuance of sweetness. The hint of scrubland is the combination of the notes of wet fallen leaves and wood from a cut tree. As this is a Crianza wine there is still trace of fruit from the wine itself and those of the wood are appreciated independently. Only subsequent ageing in the bottle would harmonise both nuances.

Fruity, medium-bodied. As it enters the mouth the first sensation is of ripe fruit; the ageing in wood is perceived afterwards in this type of wine. The medium-body is generally a characteristic of Crianzas from Rioja.

With supple but marked tannins on the palate. When the first fruity sensation fades the tactile molecules of the tannins come into play. In this case they are smooth as the Crianza wines have a limited life and, therefore they are to be consumed more or less immediately. The tannins are marked as the wine has still not been rounded in the bottle.

Somewhat dry from the wood but ripe from the fruit. The tannins from the oak are dry and slightly bitter, while the tannins from the grape are sweeter and riper. They can both be noticed separately as the wine has not been in the bottle long.

Fruity in the retronasal passage and a flavourful and lively in the finish. The retronasal is the olfactory sensation we experience when we take in air through the mouth with a little portion of wine in the mouth. Evidently it is fruity, as these olfactory molecules are the most volatile. The flavourful finish is the residue that still remains of alcohol and fruity sweetness with a persistent touch of acidity. All these features constitute a sign of youth and therefore, indicate that the wine has still got quite a lot of life.

A DESCRIPTION OF A QUALITY FINO OR MANZANILLA

Straw yellow with greenish glimmers. Sharp, saline (smell of low tide) aroma, with hints of flor (nuances of yeasts and mushrooms) and a slight nuance of wood, well-balanced. On the palate it has a broad spectrum of nuances, oily, bitter, dry, saline and flor in the retronasal passage and a persistent finish.

Straw yellow with greenish glimmers. The colour refers to the young aspect of the wine due to the lack of oxidation thanks to the protection (veil or whitish cap of the yeasts) which covers the surface of the wine and prevents the air from having an influence on the colour although the ageing is long.

Sharp, saline (smell of low tide) aroma. The term sharp refers to the intensity of a defined aroma, in this case the flor, which is noted by the trace of saline, similar to a port, or low tide.
With hints of flor (nuances of yeasts and mushrooms) and a slight nuance of wood, well-balanced. The flor, similar to a white mould covering the surface of the wine, impart hints of mushrooms and of course, bread yeast. The background of wood is the result of it being aged in oak casks for 5 years on average. All these nuances must be perfectly balanced.

On the palate it has a broad spectrum of nuances, oily, bitter, dry, saline. It is full because the nuances are felt throughout the mouth and very localised. Oily due to its alcohol (15.5º) and low acidity; bitter because this is the sensation of flor on the palate, while the tannins from the wood give their touch of dryness; the saline or slightly salty taste is a nuance which forms part of this dryness.

A DESCRIPTION OF A QUALITY MEDIUM-AGED AMONTILLADO

Colour between old gold and amber. Aroma reminiscent of flor, bitter almonds and hazelnuts, notes of aldehydes, slightly toasty nuances (pâtisserie, bakery). On the palate it is dry, quite sharp, bitter, but with a slight sensation of sweetness as it passes through and towards the back of the mouth, without the toasty and bitter character disappearing after swallowing.

Colour between old gold and amber. The amber is a yellow going dark because of the action of the oxygen as an Amontillado is born like a Fino (with a veil of flor which protects it from the air) and continues its evolution like an Oloroso; that is, the veil of flor is removed and therefore it is exposed to the action of the air.

Aroma reminiscent of flor, bitter almonds and hazelnuts. The hint of flor (see description of the Fino) is based on the biological beginning of the wine as a Fino. But once the veil is removed it goes into an oxidative phase (sherrifies) and acquires the typical features of bitter almond and hazelnut which characterise the wines that age exposed to air.

Notes of aldehydes, slightly toasty nuances (pâtisserie, bakery). These aldehyde notes are rancid touches from the oxidation of the alcohol by the action of the air in the ageing phase. The toasty nuances are from the interaction of the oxygen, the higher ageing temperature and the action of the wood. The resulting feature is normally a hint of baking of a cake or pastry.

On the palate it is dry, quite sharp, bitter, but with a slight sensation of sweetness as it passes through and towards the back of the mouth, without the toasty and bitter character disappearing after swallowing. It is dry and sharp due to its biological relationship (Fino), and bitter for the same reason and also because of the tannins from the oak. The sensation of sweetness is due to the alcohol (this wine has more alcohol than a Fino) and the oxidation. The toasty essence from the oxidation-wood and the bitter notes of the tannins from the oak are the last sensations that disappear in the mouth.

A DESCRIPTION OF A QUALITY MEDIUM-AGED OLOROSO

Light mahogany with a iodine-coloured glint. Sharp aroma with nuances of vanilla, cocoa, toast, hints of bakery and walnut and an essence of acetaldehydes. Slightly oily on the palate, soft nuances of sweetness and a bitter background of oak, certain structure on the palate and very persistent finish.

Light mahogany with a iodine-coloured glint. The oxidative ageing and at a higher temperature gives it a darker colour than an Amontillado and, of course, a Fino, although the length of ageing is the same for the three wines. The iodine-coloured glint with a hint of brown is due to the oxidation of the wine.

Sharp aroma with nuances of vanilla, cocoa, toast, hints of bakery and walnut and and an essence of acetaldehydes. These wines usually have an intense aroma. The touches of vanilla, cocoa, toast and the hints of baking and nuts are because of the oak-oxygen interaction which is perceived on the nose as a sensation of sweetness although on the palate it is dry. The nuance of acetaldehyde is due to the greater oxidation of the alcohol during maturation which can also be perceived in some wines (slight hints of acetones).

Slightly oily on the palate, soft nuances of sweetness. Without a doubt, the wines used for Olorosos are not as delicate as those used for Finos and Manzanillas; they appear to be 'fatter'. The larger quantity of glycerin (they are the Jerezs with the most alcohol) gives the sensation of more body, although at the same time they are smoother and, therefore, not as dry.

A bitter background of oak, certain structure on the palate and a very persistent finish. The oak tannins are bitter. The larger number of molecules produced by its high alcohol content, the transfer of more compounds from the oak due to the higher maturation temperature and the origin of the must produce a sensation of a more structured wine and consequently, it has a more persistent finish.

A DESCRIPTION OF A QUALITY YOUNG BRUT CAVA

Pale yellow with a greenish glint. Fresh, fruity aroma (green apples, peach), hints of bread yeast, notes of fennel and scrubland. Fresh on the palate, excellent balance of acidity and liqueur d'expédition; lively beads, light fruity notes and an elegant evolution (fennel, mint, dry mountain herbs).

Pale yellow with a greenish glint. The same colour as a well-made young wine without the least contact with the skins (pale) and whose greenish glints are typical of a complete absence of oxidation.

Fresh, fruity aroma (green apples, peach). Reminiscent of the wine and the grape which are still present in the Cava.

Hints of bread yeast, notes of fennel and scrubland. Without a doubt the aromas of yeast (placed in the bottle to carry out the second fermentation) are more noticeable during the first two years of the Cava's life (later they become less so and fuse with the lees). The hints of fennel and scrubland (wild notes) are reminiscent of its vegetal origin and the character transmitted by the lees. In the Brut, the aroma seems stickier than in the drier types (Brut Nature), but with an elegant reduction which changes the fruity aromas into more herbaceous and floral notes.

Fresh on the palate, excellent balance of acidity and liqueur d'expédition. The cava is young but the evolution in bottle has brought certain tranquillity to its components, in such a way that the acidity (a little higher than in still wines) is balanced with the sugar added during disgorging. This all gives a sensation of freshness and at the same time an elegant pleasantness.

Lively beads, light fruity notes and an elegant evolution (fennel, mint, dry mountain herbs). On the palate the bead is not very big. On the palate the sensation is of abundant beads, fresh and fruity (from the wine). The evocation of fine herbs is from the action of lees during the evolution in bottle, but without losing the primary attributes of the wine.

A DESCRIPTION OF A QUALITY CAVA BRUT RESERVA (BETWEEN THREE AND FIVE YEARS OLD).

Golden yellow. Aroma with notes of reduction (fennel, honey, bitter almonds, yeast, toast, withered petals) combined with very light fruity hints. On the palate, nuances of nuts, slightly generous, fine bead and embracing, quite supple through the mouth and slightly bitter in the finish.

Golden yellow. The Cava has acquired more tones and has turned to more golden tones due to its evolution in bottle.

Aroma with notes of reduction (fennel, honey, bitter almonds, yeast, toast, withered petals) combined with very light fruity hints. For so many years in bottle and in contact with the lees and the yeasts deposited over the length of the bottle, the cava loses its primary values and acquires spicier and aromas peculiar to it. They are pleasant herbaceous notes produced by the lees, honey (phenomenon caused by the reduction in bottle), and bitter almond (caused by slight oxidation). The nuances of yeasts and toast are due to the action of the dead yeasts found on the bottom of the bottle which give the wine spicier traits. The fruity hints remain despite the ageing.

On the palate, nuances of nuts, slightly generous, fine bead and embracing. In the same way as the aroma, the passing of time has transformed the green fruit and nuts (bitter almonds, walnuts or hazelnuts); on the palate the same happens, slightly more rancid tones but without being unpleasant. It has more body which is normal in more evolved wines. Logically the bubble will be finer and more embracing the longer it has remained in the bottle.

Quite supple through the mouth and slightly bitter in the finish. Time softens the acidity; however Cavas that have been on the lees in the bottle for longer produce more body on the palate, and sometimes this greater structure translates into a slightly more bitter tone.

LEARN TO TASTE AT HOME

EXTENDED AND CORRECTED WINE TASTING COURSE

By following the steps set out below, the reader can discover the main wine flavours in Spain, in reds as well as in whites. We have attempted to make a selection that covers the wine regions that are increasingly more active and offer better quality. This is an excellent way of becoming initiated into the art of wine tasting and can be done at home.

RED WINES

How to start. I have selected seven totally different types of wines as representative of the more specific flavours in Spanish wines.

Price. I have chosen the most easily available quality wines; the seven bottles should cost between 120 to 130, not very expensive if we bear in mind that besides using them for learning purposes, we have the pleasure of sharing them and when we divide the cost among 10 or 12 tasters it seems quite reasonable. The list also includes some more exclusive wines (for personality and scarcity) for those who wish to have a 'gourmet' tasting.

Wines chosen. The fundamental criterion of the selection made was to seek clear differences which would make the comparisons easier; all the wines are easily available on the market. May I suggest going to a specialist shop and explaining to them the purpose of the wines. They might find equivalent wines to those sought.

THE WINES
(Place seven glasses numbered 1 to 7 from left to right)

Glass nº 1
* **A young red wine made from** *Tempranillo,* **current style** (Canforrales, Tempranillo from La Mancha, Luberri from Rioja.).

Glass nº 2
* **A red Rioja, Gran Reserva, classic style**
 e.g.: a 904 Gran Reserva from Rioja Alta, Condes de los Andes, Castillo de Ygay.

Glass nº 3
* A modern red wine from Rioja. (Called 'highly expressive')
    e.g.: Barón de Chirel, Cirsion, Dalmau, Calvario, Torre Muga, Remírez de Ganuza, Viña el Pisón, etc.

Glass nº 4
* A very dark red Crianza or Reserva from Ribera del Duero
    e.g.: Pesquera, Alión, Viña Pedrosa, Pago de los Capellanes, Arzuaga, Malleolus, etc.

Glass nº 5
* A modern style red from Toro aged in wood (Crianza type).
    e.g.: Elías Mora, Estancia Piedra, Quinta la Quietud, Numanthia, etc

Glass nº 6
* A modern style red from Bierzo with a brief ageing in wood.
    e.g.: Dominio de Tares, Cepas Viejas, Tilenus, Luna Beberide, Corullón, etc.

Glass nº 7
* A Cabernet Sauvignon aged for three or four years in wood.
    e.g.: Raimat, Dehesa del Carrizal, Torres Mas La Plana, Enate, Viñas del Vero.

FIRST STEPS

Glasses. Obtain seven identical Bordeaux type glasses, similar to those used in a large number of restaurants.

Serving. The glasses must be filled with three fingers of wine and each bottle placed behind the corresponding glass.

Appearance. The wine must be visualised by inclining the glass forward until the wine almost reaches the rim of the glass. Hold it at about 15 centimetres from the chin to see the different nuances from the centre to the edge.

Nose. Place the nose gently at the mouth of the glass. If the aroma is not intense or not well defined, the wine should be gently swirled in a circular fashion by holding the glass at the bottom of the stem. It is advisable not to smell each one too long and to change glasses quickly to better appreciate the differences between them.

Taste. On taking the glass to the lips, sip a small amount (it is better to repeat than to take in large amounts which, due to the ethyl, could affect the taste.) The ideal is to spit into a spittoon (an ice bucket, a glass container with a large mouth or a cardboard box lined with plastic and some sawdust or sand on the bottom will do).
    It must be left in the mouth for a few seconds while at the same time chewing and half opening the mouth. Chewing is to enlarge and make the mouth cavity smaller. At the same time, taking in some air will strengthen the aromas of the wine (the temperature of the wine increases rapidly in the mouth) which, internally (retronasal), will then reach the sense of smell.

Posture. The taster should sit in front of the seven glasses placed on a white surface to see the colour contrasts, or even place a few blank sheets of paper in the manner of a table cloth. It is advisable to use natural or a halogen light.
    Each one of these steps should be followed with a glass in hand in the same sequence of wines as indicated below.
    Each wine must correspond to the glass to be able to compare better.

THE TASTING

First clue: the wines easiest to compare are glass 1 (young *Tempranillo*), glass 2 (classic Rioja), and glass 7 (*Cabernet Sauvignon*).

Second clue: the most difficult wines to compare are glass 3 (modern Rioja) and glass 4 (Ribera del Duero), and to a lesser extent glass 5 (Toro) and 6 (Bierzo). The reason for this is that all these wines are made using 'modern' methods, that is to say, concepts such as the selection of the grape, optimum ripeness of the grape, polyphenol extraction, the use of new woods with a greater use of French oak and, occasionally, techniques such as cold maceration prior to fermentation, the work with the tannins to obtain its maximum polymerisation or the work with the lees during ageing, Burgundy style. On occasions, and this is one of the great topical issues of modern wine, these techniques tend to homogenise the wines reducing the logical differences that should exist as a result of being made in different winegrowing regions (and therefore, with typical soils and climates).

Glass nº 1 – Young red, *Tempranillo*.
* Colour: This wine is a lively bigarreau cherry red with a clear violet hue towards the edges (seen clearly on inclining the glass).

* Nose. Quite intense (especially if carbonic maceration was used in its making) and possibly, it will be more open and expressive than the other wines (continue smelling the rest). It is the only wine with no wood, quite evident when compared to the rest, where to a greater or lesser extent one can appreciate the toasty nuances and the creamy and vanilla hints of oak. Therefore, its fruitiness and youth are its defining characteristics.

* Palate: Although it is quite intense and fruity, it has less structure or body than the others. The tannins can be slightly marked (stringent or harsh sensation on the palate) due to its youth, but the abundance of fruit balances the wine well and makes it very pleasant.

Glass nº 2.- Rioja Gran Reserva classic style.
* Colour: It is much less intense than the previous one, leaning towards orangey-brick red tones especially towards the edges and slightly darker and duller in the centre. All these features are characteristic of a more mature wine (it is the wine that has aged the longest by far in barrel).

* Nose. Vague reminder of wood in the drawers of antique furniture, a little like cedar (typical wood used to make craft items in Morocco). Compared to the rest it is more 'sherry-like'.

* Palate: It is slightly more bitter than the others because of the greater influence of oak. It is also lighter and rounder on the palate (the tannins from the fruit and the wood are completely rounded off and it is especially supple on the palate), spicier because of the wood during the long ageing process and more elegant; a typical and classic 'Gran Reserva' from Rioja. Also a slight acidic touch (compare with the others) characteristic of traditional winemaking, using this aspect to give a longer bottle life to their wines.

Glass nº 3.- A modern red Reserve wine from Rioja, called ' highly expressive'.
* Colour: Cherry (bigarreau), a lot darker than glass 2 and with violet edges (but less than glass 1) and orangey tones. Seems younger than its vintage. The reason: the bodega kept the wine in barrel for a shorter time and therefore there was less colour loss; at the same time skin maceration (skins and pips of the grape) was longer extracting more colour.

* Nose. It is very fruity although less than glass 1 (smell glass 1 again) and much more than glass 2, as less time in wood preserves the youthful characteristics although the vintage differences are less. The aroma of wood is hardly appreciable in the more toasty and creamy notes but they are more evident when compared to the young red wine (glass 1). The difference between these two, above all, is the oak of the Reserva and the fruitiness of the young wine (glass 1) that reminds us of blackberries or raspberry jelly.

*Palate: Seems harsher than the classic Rioja wine (glass 2) because of the tannins of the grape produced from the longer skin maceration. Certain bitterness in the finish (pleasant in this case) of new or almost new oak. If we compare it to the closest wine, the Ribera (glass 4) it is finer and more elegant, as the grapes were exposed to less sun. There is a big difference between this and the classic Gran Reserva (glass 2) even though they are from the same area.

Glass nº 4, - A red Crianza or very dark Reserva from Ribera del Duero.
* Colour: Except for some vintage exceptions it is darker than the 'highly expressive' Rioja although it has a more brilliant glimmer, almost as much as the *Cabernet Sauvignon* (glass 7). Except for the classic Rioja all the wines selected have quite a deep and intense colour, with orangey tones towards the rim in those from warmer regions such as Toro, and more violet or deep red in cooler areas such as Bierzo and La Rioja. The Ribera is halfway between the two.

* Nose: Although less intense, it seems 'sweeter' or less 'dry' than glass 3 (the most similar in style), due to the longer ageing of the grapes in the Castilian wine. The concentration of the colour and the ripeness of the grape with hints of preserve or black plum jam seem to 'conceal' the new or almost new wood that is not very pronounced in this wine.

* Palate: It is 'sweeter' than the Cabernet glass 7 (which is drier and harsher), but less than glass 5, the Toro, which has much riper sensations. It also has more body and the harshness (tannins) seems to 'submerge' into its volume and alcohol which characterises present-day reds from Ribera del Duero. It is slightly more acid than glass 3 (modern Rioja).

Glass nº 5, - A modern red from Toro, Crianza type.
* Colour: It is quite closed and intense but with tones more towards brown than violet. This is because the Toro region is very sunny.

* Nose: Sensations of ripeness more pronounced than in the previous two: jammy grapes and toasted grapeskins, which perfectly reflect the sunshine characteristic of the region. There are certain hints of earthiness in the background and thus it is not as elegant as the previous two. The level of ripeness is very evident when compared to glass 6, the Bierzo, where the fruit is fresher.

* Palate: It is very sweet and has a lot of ripe fruit, sometimes with viscous sensations even caramelised. The characteristic warmth of the wine can be felt; as the acid levels are lower than the Rioja, the Ribera or the Bierzo, the alcohol is evident. Thus it can seem rather heavy when compared to the previous ones, but it is also true that it is easier on the palate (no stringency), as the tannins are integrated with the alcohol. This fact is very evident when compared to the Ribera (glass nº 4) and, above all to the Cabernet (glass nº 7).

Glass nº 6, - A modern Bierzo aged in wood.
* Colour: It is also intense although maybe slightly less deep than the Ribera (glass nº 4) and the Toro (glass 5) but with especially brilliant tones with shades of violet and blue.

* Nose: A different variety to all the previous ones (made from *Tempranillo*), which brings out the personality of the *Mencía* grape. It is a slightly fresher fruit and has quite an intense

aroma of ripe red fruit. There are certain floral and spicy notes which do not come out in the others. It is especially different to glass n° 5 and compared to the warmth of the latter it is much more Atlantic.

* Palate: The *Mencía* is a variety with dry tannins, which might produce astringent tones if it were not so fruity. Modern methods achieve this and the wines are usually quite expressive and fruity. It has less body than the Ribera and the bitter sensation of the tannins is more evident than in the Toro and in the modern Rioja, but less than in the *Cabernet*.

Glass n° 7, - A three or four year-old *Cabernet Sauvignon*, aged in wood.
* Colour: Compared to the Ribera (glass 4) and the modern Rioja (glass 3), the closest wines, on the edges a narrower and lighter edge can be seen, typical of *Cabernet*.

* Nose: It is the most direct rival of the Castilian red due to the concentration of ripe fruit, although the aroma is quite different to the other reds with the same ageing. This is due to the defining character of the skin of the Cabernet (very ripe blackberries, a hint of paprika and green pepper). There are also nuances of wet forest or damp earth.

* Palate: the personality and the 'dry' astringency of the cabernet and the new oak is noticeable compared to the 'sweeter' Ribera and above all the Toro (glass 5) where the differences are more pronounced.

WHITE WINES

How to start. I have chosen the most different white wine flavours in Spain. A Penedès, an Albariño (Rias Baixas), a Rueda, a Chardonnay fermented in barrel, one or two years old and a wine with a high alcohol content, a white *Garnacha* from Priorat or Terra Alta, aged and fermented in barrel.

Price. The five bottles cost about 60, although once again the option of a 'gourmet' tasting presents itself.

Wines chosen. The wines chosen are easily available in shops and a perfect example of each winegrowing region.

THE WINES
(From left to right).

Glass n° 1
* A Penedès, the latest vintage.
  e.g. – Viña Sol, Heredad Segura Viudas, Bach, etc.

Glass n° 2
* A *Verdejo* de Rueda, the latest vintage.
  e.g.: Palacio de Bornos, José Pariente, Marqués de Riscal, Mantel Blanco, etc

Glass n° 3
* An *Albariño*, the latest vintage (Rias Baixa).
  e.g.: Terras Gauda, Fillaboa, Martín Códax, etc.

Glass n° 4
* A Mediterranean style white from Priorat or Terra Alta, the latest vintage.
  e.g.: Bárbara Forés, Vindemia, Mas Igneus, Morlanda…

Glass n° 5
* A *Chardonnay* fermented in barrel.

e.g.: Milmanda, Chivite Colección 125, Enate, etc.

Follow the same instructions set out for the red wines.

THE TASTING

Glass nº 1 Penedès.

* Colour: If compared to glass 2, and especially glass 3, it appears to be lighter in density (swirl both glasses) and paler.

* Nose: Fruity traces with hints of grass and green apples and a hint of lemon; it is the usual classic fruity white. Not as intense as glass 2, where there are nuances of fresh fruit and fennel, and glass 3, more exotic and floral (petals), whilst glass 4 has aromas of herbs and Mediterranean mountain. If we compare it to glass 5 we will notice the aromas of oak in it.

* Taste: The first thing we notice is that it is slightly more acid than the others and it is also lighter. It is fruity and fresh and easy drinking.

Glass nº 2 Rueda.

* Colour: It is slightly less pale than the previous one and has hints of straw.

* Nose: Fruity traces are more apparent and it is very fresh (also more than glasses 3 and 4), due to the fennel and green grass.

* Taste: Not as light as glass 1 and therefore, fuller on the palate, although not as dense as glass 3. The final is bitter and at times wild, a characteristic that does not appear in the other wines, leaving a final sensation on the palate.

Glass nº 3 Albariño (Rias Baixas).

* Colour: Very similar to glass 2, between straw and greenish tones, and an oily density.

* Nose: It appears more elegant and floral, with hints of ripe apples and herbs.

* Palate: Feels oilier and velvety, a deeper taste, such as tropical fruit, and not as dry as glasses 1 and 2.

Glass nº 4. A Mediterranean-style white from Priorat or Terra Alta.

* Colour: Similar to the previous one, but slightly more golden than green, because of the warmer climate it comes from. It is also a lot denser in the glass.

* Nose: Not as fruity as the previous ones but it has more spicy and Mediterranean mountain notes.

* Palate: It is the warmest of all, with a sensation of sweetness due to a higher alcohol content, somewhat dense, but supple and glyceric.

Glass 5. Chardonnay fermented in barrel.
* Colour: It is more yellow than any of the previous ones due to the pigmentation from the barrel.

* Nose: It is smoky with hints of butter, indicating the presence of the wood. But there are also fruity tones (ripe apples) and complex overtones of grass (hay) due to the action of the lees during fermentation. It is slightly less fruity than glasses 2 and 3 but more complex and subtle.

* Palate: It is more smoky and toasted on the palate than the rest, with a sensation of creamy vanilla.

RECOGNISING A WINE IN A BLIND TASTING

(An example of an experiment carried out in the summer of 2004)

This is the acid test for any connoisseur, the expert's dream and a tremendous feat when he gets it right. It is difficult, but not impossible to guess the wine without more clues than those offered to the senses.
The most impressive sight is to see a taster get the vintage right as it highlights his knowledge of the world of wine and shows the unbelievable relationship between the expert and the bottle.

During my many years as an oenologist, I have always had the wish to get the vintage right and to know who produced this unknown wine locked in a glass and hidden in a bottle. Some I have got right, but only because of having tasted them so often and this of course has no merit whatsoever. To get it right by deduction and a little intuition is praiseworthy. But one also needs experience and a sound knowledge gained by tasting so many different types of wines. It is the most difficult test one has to surpass to become a member of the exclusive Institute of Masters of Wine (IMW).

This is really a test of humility, serenity, analysis and the meditation of an expert wine taster when the moment of truth arrives. Generally, when doing blind wine tasting one is prone to mentally precipitate the identification of the wine, which then conditions the expert's expectations of the wine. When the taster sees he has made a mistake, he adjusts his score, increasing it if he thinks the wine was inferior or reducing it if the wine was better.

DEDUCTION BY ELIMINATION

This is the easiest way of identifying a wine: establishing 'what it isn't'. For example: if we try a red wine with a smooth and a slightly burning sensation on the palate, we can be sure that it is not a Galician wine. But this deduction must not exclusively be reached because of its high alcohol content as the wine could be from the slate and stony soils of Sil or Támega in a dry year. One would have to know beforehand that the number of reds in Galicia is much lower than whites, and therefore the probability of it being a Galician wine is less.

The 'could be factor' is the most disconcerting as there are many different options. The 'must be factor' is risking it. Let us look at a blind tasting based on a similar description to that found in the Guide to identify the wine by a process of elimination.

BLIND TASTING A RED WINE

Dark cherry with a brilliant garnet red edge. Finely toasted aroma (cocoa, coffee, peat), jammy, slightly mineral, warm. Powerful, very varietal, (overripe redcurrants, paprika) flavourful and very ripe tannins, very long.

Let us deduce its origin, make and vintage by taking into account that the wine must have some general characteristics associated with a region whose climate is present in the wine and with fewer alternatives than can be found in regions of many wines. The rest is up to the knowledge of the wine taster.

Colour. Dark cherry with a brilliant garnet red edge.

Deduction. We obviously have here a more or less recent vintage, as there is no indication of the colour having evolved. Is it a wine from the latest vintage? No, because there are no distinguishing violet nuances and it is quite deep , too much so for the concentrations which one expects to find in a young wine. Therefore it is obvious that the deep colour is due to a variety with a lot of colour and that a lot was extracted. The dullness could indicate a warm region. And so we are inclined to think that it could be a more or less modern wine, having been aged for between two to four years and from a very sunny region.

Nose. Finely toasted aroma (cocoa, coffee, peat), jammy, slightly mineral, warm.
Deduction. The nose reconfirms that we are not faced by a young wine because of the clear presence of wood. And, besides, it is the quality oak that leads us to think that it is from a quality winemaker. There are some very toasted notes, but also fine hints of cocoa, which leads us to think it is French oak. As a growing number of Spanish bodegas use this wood nowadays, the field is still wide.

What else does the nose reveal? Very ripe and jammy sensations, which automatically leads us to a vineyard in an especially sunny region. For the moment we can only eliminate Galicia, where the red wine, except from Ribeira Sacra and Valderras, does not have these characteristics at all; we can also eliminate wines from Bierzo and the higher regions of Spain which produce cooler wines than this one. We can also eliminate all wine-producing regions whose wines are not very high quality wines, as the fineness, the quality of the wood and the fruit show that this is a quality wine.

There is another very interesting point: the minerals we can appreciate in the wine. This limits the search to specific regions such as Priorat, where the soils give a distinct mineral nuance. Could it be the stony alluvium soils of Toro? It is not jammy or wild enough to be from this region. It could also be a single vineyard wine, found in an area not necessarily known for its soils, but where stony or shale soils are found.

What about the variety of the grape? Despite the signs of ripeness, we have here varietal characteristics of *Garnachas* or *Cariñenas* from warm regions with that jammy and slightly viscous hint, which identifies the wines from Tarragona (Priorat, Terra Alta or Montsant) although it could be a Priorat with larger quantities of foreign varieties. It could also be a *Tempranillo* grown in a warm region or a very mature *Merlot* or *Cabernet*. In this wine there is no clear varietal definition on the nose, the hints of oak and jam are heavier and do not enable us to identify the variety.

Taste. Powerful, very varietal (overripe redcurrants, paprika) flavourful and very ripe tannins, very long.

Deduction. At last, clear evidence that will put us on the right path. If the nose does not allow us to identify the variety clearly, the palate does. The notes of redcurrants and paprika lead us inexorably to foreign varieties and enable us to single out the *Tempranillo*. *Merlot* and *Cabernet Sauvignon* are typical of varieties from Bordeaux, but the hint of paprika is very characteristic of *Cabernets* found in hot climates, which allows us to tip the scales. It is, without a doubt, the main or the only variety of this wine.

The ripeness of the grape, on the other hand, indicates a Mediterranean style *Cabernet*. We have no alternative but to discard the Priorat as they do not produce wines with this grape as the main variety. What do we have now? A warm Cabernet from a quality producer, probably a single vineyard wine, and between two and four years old. In which Spanish regions do we find a wine of these characteristics? In Cataluña, Navarra, Castilla-La Mancha and moreover Somontano, but we should not forget that a wine was selected that agrees more with the temperature and soil and not the exceptions of regions identified with other features; therefore we have discarded the *Cabernet* from Ribera del Duero, and besides, they do not make varietal wines with this variety. In Alicante and Murcia the *Monastrell* reigns supreme, although in these regions they do not usually make such quality wines, except, perhaps, for Enrique Mendoza in Alicante; this is a candidate that may be considered. There are some in Castilla-La Mancha and in the region of Clariano in Valencia but they are relatively recent so they must be discarded.

Because of the ripeness of the fruit we might discard slightly warmer regions such as Navarra, Cataluña and Somontano but these are more varietal on the nose. The Costers del Segre, the single vineyard cabernets of Raimat are usually sold when they have aged more and with brick red edges. Avgvstvs (Penedès) is very warm but an 'Australian' touch is present; the Cabernet of Sot Lefriec is more spectacular than this one; Jean León is less mineral. Could it be one of the new experimental wines, Ex Ex from Castillo de Perelada? No, because they are usually more robust, concentrated and powerful. In Somontano the plainer wines of Enate and Viñas del Vero are lighter and the more 'luxurious' wines such as 2000 Enate Reserva Especial are very complex. Perhaps it is a Viñas del Vero Cabernet.

What are we left with?
Cataluña:
-Mas La Plana de Torres
-Mas Vilella (Jané Ventura)

Alicante:
-Enrique Mendoza

Castilla–La Mancha:
-Dominio de Valdepusa
-Dehesa del Carrizal
-Arrayán Cabernet

Somontano:
Viñas del Vero

CONCLUSIONS

Of all of these wines, the Mas Vilella from Jané Ventura has, in the latest vintages, had more cutting and fresher tannins than those found in our sample and it can therefore be discarded. The Torres Más La Plana has a 'fresher' line of Cabernet and lacks the touch of mineral hints. The Enrique Mendoza Cabernet from Alicante is darker and more concentrated, and although the red from Viñas del Vero from Somontano is made with ripe skins, there are not the stony hints found in this wine. In Toledo, Castilla-La Mancha, the best wines from this grape are produced. The latest vintages of Dominio de Valdepusa have a markedly Californian air about them, with heavy balsamic notes that are not found in this wine. The alluvium vineyards of Dehesa del Carrizal could be responsible for the hint of minerals. Arrayán has the same mineral nuances although they seem more complex and concentrated to me but I am not sure. It could be from between Dehesa del Carrizal and Arrayán, as the quality in both is close to 90 points.

Among the vintages of Dehesa del Carrizal over the last few years, 1999 was an exceptional year, although I do not think it can be because the colour is very intense and there would have to be orangey nuances towards the rim. I think 2000 was not quite as good. The 2002 vintage cannot be on the market yet, therefore it has to be the 2001 or the 2002 vintage of the Cabernet from Arrayán although I insist, it seems to be a bit concentrated; Could it be Dehesa del Carrizal 2001?

The red was a **DEHESA DEL CARRIZAL CABERNET SAUVIGNON 2001** from the bodega with the same name.

The date on which this tasting was written in this section was July 2004, and I would therefore like to remind readers if they have the opportunity of tasting this wine to take into account the variations associated with its evolution since then.

EXPAND YOUR KNOWLEDGE OF WINE TASTING

LOCAL SPAÑISH WINE FAIRS

An excellent way of getting to know Spanish wines is to go to the small fairs organised by town councils, Regulatory Councils and the associations of the different bodegas. There are more important national fairs - Fenavin (Ciudad Real), Bilbovinos (Bilbao), Food (Barcelona) and Gourmet (Madrid) - but we suggest the following fairs for the 'wine seeker', lover of different wines and enthusiast of the human touch and direct contact with the bodegas.

ANDALUCÍA			
WINE FAIR	**LOCATION**	**DATE**	**COMMENTS**
Wine day	Frailes	March	Wine Show, Vinos de la Tierra from Jaen
Ecological Agricultural Fair.	Cordoba	11 – 14th April	Organised by the National Competition of Ecological Wines. Tel.: 954 689 390
Vinicultural Fair of Alpujara	Laújar de Andarax	26 -28th April	Exhibition and wine tasting of Vinos de la Tierra from Laujar. Organised by the Town Council. Tel.: 950 514 161
Wine tasting of Wines from Montilla.	Cordoba	8 – 12th May	Competition of Wines from Montilla-Moriles. Organised by the CRDO of this region. Tel.: 957 475 484
Manzanilla Exhibition	Sanlúcar de Barrameda	28 May -2nd June	Exhibition of the Manzanilla winemaking bodegas of the region. Tel.: 956 385 229
Manzanilla Day.		23 – 29th June	
Exhibition of the wines from Chiclana.	Chiclana (Cádiz)	The end of June.	The bodegas from the Chiclana region take part. Organised by the Town Council. Tel.: 956 490 002
Moscatel Festival.	Chipiona (Cádiz)	14-17th August	Traditional Festival of Moscatels from the Chipiona region of Seville. Tel.: 956 377 150
Harvest Festival	La Palma del Condado	September	National tourist Festival with wines from the DO Condado de Huelva. Tel.: 954 924 526
Origin of Wine.	Cádiar (Granada)	5 - 9th October.	Traditional Festival based on the origin of wine (Vinos de la Tierra, Costa-Albondón). Tel: 958 768 031
Vinicultural Fair of Andalusia.	Montilla	25 - 27th October.	Organised by the Regulatory Council and the Town Council of Montilla. Tel: 957 475 484

ANDALUCÍA

Wine Exhibition of DO	Torremolinos (Málaga)	October-november	Exhibition of wines from Malaga. Organised by the Regulatory Council of Malaga at the Palcacio de Congresos in Torremolinos. Tel: 952 379 203

ARAGÓN

WINE FAIR	LOCATION	DATE	COMMENTS
Exhibition of the Wines from Aragon.	Zaragoza	4 – 5th March.	Exhibition of the Wines from Calatayud. Promoted by the Garnacha Cultural Association. Tel: 976 417 782
Piregourmet	Barbastro	12 - 15th April.	Exhibition of foods and DO Wines from Aragon. Barbastro Exhibition Centre. Tel: 974 311 919

CANARY ISLANDS

WINE FAIR	LOCATION	DATE	COMMENTS
Wine festival	No fixed venue.	April	Organised by the DO Valle de la Orotava. Tel.: 922 320 979
White Wine Competition.	Los Realejos (Tenerife)	Middle of May.	Exhibition of the wines from the region to celebrate the festival of San Isidro.
Vinicultural Fair of Alhóndiga	Tacoronte (Tenerife)	15 – 17th May.	A competition of regional wines, conferences and wine tasting. Organised by Cabildo de Tenerife. Tel.: 922 476 295

CASTILLA - LA MANCHA

WINE FAIR	LOCATION	DATE	COMMENTS
Exhibition of the Wines from Mondéjar.	Mondéjar (Guadalajara)	June	Exhibition of Wines from the region. Organised by the RC DO of Mondejar. Tel.: 949 385 284

CASTILLA Y LEÓN

WINE FAIR	LOCATION	DATE	COMMENTS
Week of Vineyards and Wine.	Ponferrada (León)	The end of February.	Organised by the Regulatory Council and the DO Bierzo. Tel.: 987 549 408
Vintoro	Toro (Zamora)	26 -28th April.	Organised by Fomentoro (Group of 27 bodegas). Tel.: 980 693 417
Wine Fair of Cacabelos	Cacabelos (León)	Beginning of May.	Exhibition of wine tasting of the wines from the region. Organised by the RC DO of Bierzo. Tel.: 987 549 408

CASTILLA Y LEÓN

Riberexpo	Peñafiel	18 – 20th May	Regional show of wines from the DO Ribera del Duero.
Harvest Festival and Wine Show.	Cigales (Valladolid)	End of September	Conferences, exhibitions and tasting wines from the region. Organised by the RC DO Cigales. Tel.: 983 580 074
Exhibition of regional products and Vino de la Tierra from Ávila.	Ávila	March	Exhibition and wine tasting of Vinos de la Tierra from Cebreros and other regions. Organised by the Sommelier Association of Avila.

CATALUÑA

WINE FAIR	LOCATION	DATE	COMMENTS
Divinum	Vilafranca del Penedès	April	Spring festival centred on wine. Organised by INCAVI. Tel.: 934 874 056
Exhibition of wines from Falset.	Falset	4 – 5th May.	Tasting and exhibition of the wines from DO Priorat and Montsant.. Organised by the Town Council of Falset. Tel.: 977 830 057
Festival of Vi de Reus	Reus	24th May.	Exhibition of the wines from the region. www.prioratdigital.com
Exhibition of the Wines from Empordá.	Figueras	11 – 15th September.	Traditional activities and tasting wines from the region. Organised by the RC DO Empordá-Costa Brava. Tel.: 972 507 513
Exhibition of the wines from Cataluña.	Barcelona	19 - 29th September	Traditional festivals centred around the festival of the Merced with an exhibition of bodegas with DO Catalonia. Tel.: 934 876 738
Cava Week.	San Sadurní D'Anoia (Barcelona)	5 - 13th October.	Open days of the cava-producing bodegas; exhibition of wines and the crowning of the Cava Queen. Organised by the RC DO of Cava and the Fraternity of Cava. Tel.: 938 912 803
Exhibition of Wines from Tarragona.	Tarragona	November (biannual).	Exhibition of wines with the DO of the province of Tarragona. Organised by the Chamber of Commerce of Tarragona. Tel.: 977 217 931

EXTREMADURA

WINE FAIR	LOCATION	DATE	COMMENTS
International Wine and Olive Exhibition.	Almendralejo (Badajoz)	April	The DO Ribera de Guadiana representing the wines of the region. Tel.: 924 671 302

GALICIA

WINE FAIR	LOCATION	DATE	COMMENTS
Exhibition of the Wines of Chantada.	Lugo	Middle of March.	Exhibition of regional wines with DO. Tel.: 982 182 376

GALICIA

Exhibition of the Wines of Amandi.	Sober (Lugo)	April	Traditional competition of wines from the region. Tel.: 982 456 005
Exhibition of the Wines of Ribeiro.	Ribadavia (Orense)	The end of April.	Exhibition and tasting of wines from Ribeiro. Organised by the CR DO of Ribeiro and the Town Council of Ribadavia. Tel.: 988 477 100
Exhibition of the Wines from Quiroga.	Quiroga (Lugo)	At Easter	Festival of Wines from the region. Organised by the Town Council of Quiroga. Tel.: 982 428 001
Exhibition of the Wines of Betanzos.	Betanzos (A Coruña)	Beginning of May	The wines from DO Ribeira Sacra with a sommelier competition. Tel.: 982 410 968
Exhibition of the Wines from Ribeira Sacra.	Monforte de Lemos (Lugo)	3rd week of May.	The wines from DO Ribeira Sacra with a sommelier competition. Tel.: 982 410 968
Exhibition of the Wines of Pantón.	Pantón (Lugo)	3rd week of May	Exhibition of the wines produced in this region. Tel.: 982 456 005
Exhibition of wines from Valdeorras.	A Rúa	May	Exhibition of wines with DO Valdeorras. Tel.: 988 300 295
Festival of red wines from Salnés.	Barrantes (Pontevedra)	June	Tasting of red wines from the Salnés region. Tel.: 986 718 499
Festival of wines from Rosal.	O Rosal (Pontevedra)	The end of July.	Exhibition of the wines from this sub-region of Rias Baixas.Tel: 986 625 000
Festival of wines from Albariño.	Cambados (Pontevedra)	The end of July.	Exhibition of Albariño wine. Organised by the Town Council of Cambados and DO Rias Baixas. Tel.: 986 854 850
Exhibition of wines from Condado.	Salvatierra de Miño	Last Sunday of August.	Exhibition of the wines from the sub-region of Rias Baixas, Condado de Tea. Tel.: 986 658 082
Exhibition of Albariño.	Barrantes (Lugo)	August.	Festival of the Albariño wines of the region. Organised by Town Council of Barrantes. Tel.: 986 718 499

MADRID

WINE FAIR	LOCATION	DATE	COMMENTS
Exhibition of the wines from Colmenar de Oreja.	Colmenar de Oreja	16 – 18th May.	Winemakers Association of Colmenar de Oreja
The week of wines from Arganda.	Arganda del Rey	Beginning of June.	Wine tasting and talks on the wines from the region. Tel.: 918 711 344

MURCIA

WINE FAIR	LOCATION	DATE	COMMENTS
Harvest Festival.	Bullas (Murcia)	Beginning of October.	Exhibition and wine tasting organised by the CR DO Bullas. Tel.: 968 652 601
The Festival of the Inmaculada.	Yecla (Murcia)	5th December.	Patron Saint festivals, attended by the bodegas Jumilla, Yecla, Bullas and Campo de Cartagena; wine tasting and competitions. Tel.: 968 366 742

NAVARRA

WINE FAIR	LOCATION	DATE	COMMENTS
Harvest Festival.	Olite	Beginning of September	Activities concerned with wine. Organised by the Olite Wine Fraternity. Tel.: 948 741 707

PAIS VASCO

WINE FAIR	LOCATION	DATE	COMMENTS
Txakoli Week	Lejona (Bizkaia)	The first fortnight of May.	Presentation of the Txakoli of Vizcaya harvest. Tel.: 944 555 063
Txakoli Eguna	Getaria (Guipúzcoa)	Beginning of September.	Exhibition of Txakoli products from the region.

VALENCIA

WINE FAIR	LOCATION	DATE	COMMENTS
Exhibition of food and Agriculture Quality.	Burriana	February.	Exhibition of the products from the region and the wines with DO Valencia. Organised by the Town Council of Burriana. Tel.: 964 510 062
Ferevin	Requena (Valencia)	End of August.	Exhibition of the wines from Utiel-Requena. Organised by the Town Council of Requena. Tel.: 962 170 504
Utiel Festival and Show.	Utiel (Valencia)	2nd week of September.	Promotional Pavilion of the wines from DO Utiel-Requena. Organised by the Town Council of Utiel. Tel.: 962 170 504

WINE AND SOCIETY

WINE AND SOCIETY

BASIC TIPS FOR BEGINNERS

WHAT SHOULD NOT BE DONE

* Buying wines: buy bargain aged reds older than ten years old, as they are in decline.
* Serving the wine: do not remove the capsule from the side of the bottle or pop a cava with the bottle in a vertical position.
* Storing wine: keep the bottles in the kitchen or in a pantry with smells of curing.
* At restaurants: ask for a cheap old wine unless they have an exemplary wine cellar.
* On drinking the wine: do not drink a bottle immediately after transporting it. Wait for at least 24 hours before consuming it.

GOOD MANNERS AT HOME

* The reds should be uncorked and placed on the table, and the whites and rosés in buckets with ice and water.
* The host should know the preferences of his guests.
* The host should taste the wine before serving it to check its state.
* The host should surprise one with an original wine.
* The host should start the series of reds beginning with the young and lighter wines to end off with the oldest and most expressive wines.

AT THE RESTAURANT

* Do not buy very old wines even if they are a bargain if the restaurant does not have a good system of storing them.
* Ask for the bottle to be brought to the table. The cold wines should be in a bucket at the side of the table.
* Do not trust a restaurant that only has well-known wines.
* Do not trust a restaurant that piles the wines up in the dining room.
* Do not be embarrassed to have a red wine chilled in an ice bucket (normally served at 23°C) for nine minutes in summer (the time it takes to go down to the serving temperature of 18°C).
* Trust a restaurant that has a wine cooling cabinet.
* Do not trust the restaurant that insists on serving you a particular wine without taking into account the food requested.
* Do not trust the free liqueur or drink offered at the end of a meal. It is preferable to pay for a known brand and return the drink if it is not up to standard.
* Beware of a 'house wine' without a label. If the house wine has the label of the restaurant, it is vital to know who the cellar is.
* Do not ask for a generic wine. Look at the restaurant and trust the unknown wines from lesser-known regions. It is an indication that the sommelier or the person in charge of the restaurant recognises their quality and is more capable of advising you.

HOW TO PASS AS AN EXPERT WITHOUT BEING ONE (OR MAYBE YOU ARE)

* Request new *Vinos de Pago* (single vineyard wines with the same soil and climate) and wines without a DO, a red from Priorat, Toro, Somontano and Ribera del Duero. Ask for a

white from Rias Baixas, Rueda and Chardonnays fermented in barrel.
* Drink cava as an aperitif.
* Have a wine-cooling cabinet with transparent doors at home.
* Buy wine directly from the bodega via mail.
* Go to any wine bar to taste wine by the glass.
* Be aware that the most interesting Galician reds are those from Ribeira Sacra.
* Request Pedro Ximénez with the desserts.
* Request a Rueda or a Rias Baixas which is not from the latest vintage (2-3 years maximum).
* Ask for a brandy at the temperature for reds (18°C) in a smaller glass.
* Participate in the internet forums.

PEOPLE WHO CLAIM TO BE WINE EXPERTS (BUT IN FACT AREN'T)

* Show off by quoting the same old French wines over and over (Petrus, Mouton Rothschild and Château Margaux)
* Repeat the hackneyed phrase 'the best wine in Spain is Rioja and perhaps, Ribera'.
* The barrel of wine from my village.
* Says he is a lover of wine but only remembers the Vega Sicilia and Viña Tondonia brands.
* Ask for a cognac in a very large warm glass.
* Cava with desserts.
* *The expression* 'traditional wine'
* The card with the vintages of Spanish wines.
* Say champagne with a glass of cava in their hand.
* Have a red at room temperature (always higher than 20°C in winter as well as in summer)
* Say 'this wine is natural and has no chemicals'
* Keep saying how 'sad' it is that the consumption of wine per person is on the decline (they drank worse wines before).
* Say that aged wine is better than young wine.
* Smooth light reds which taste of wood.
* Very large glasses for old wines and smaller glasses than those for water for other wines.
* A little basket to serve wines less than five years old.
* Cool down the glasses for white wines and rosés.
* Say that wines are more expensive now than twenty years ago.

SOME OF THE QUESTIONS THAT YOU WERE TOO SCARED TO ASK

Can one have reds with fish? If it is a blue fish there is no problem and neither is it a sacrilege to have a light bodied young red wine, up to three years old, with fish such as turbot, cod and other delicate fish if they are garnished or have a strong sauce.

Will this wine improve over time? The wine changes or worsens. A wine changes because it gains some attributes (becomes more supple, more spicy aromas appear), and it loses or harmonises others, such as the character of the grape and some sensorial elements of the terroir (soil and climate).

Does wine suffer when transported? Nowadays wines are sufficiently stabilised to undergo any onslaught. Only the flavours and the aromas get blocked (short aroma, without expression) in the days following the trip. After a fortnight they will have recovered.

Does white wine get worse over the years? Some wines aged intensively in wood are better after five years (the wood becomes smoother and the aromas of new oak wood combine with the slight hint of the grape and turn more honeyed and spicy). White wines such as *Albariño*, *Rueda* or *Chardonnay* fermented in wood are better after the second year.

Are rosés only for beginners? Not at all. What happens is that the measuring stick for reds and whites (type of ageing, variety and the terroir) is not applicable to rosés. Their freshness, their fruitiness and, above all their youth is of interest. Naturally, these factors are attractive to any consumer, experienced or not.

Why do the Finos and Manzanillas not last, even though they have a high alcohol content? All the wines from Jerez, sweet or dry, are made in the same way as Rancios (they oxidize with air and temperature) except for the Finos and Manzanillas which are made with no contact with oxygen under the veil or the cap that covers the surface of the wine in the cask and protects them from the air. From the moment the wine leaves the cask to be bottled, it is not protected by the 'fluer' or cap and it tends to go rancid. It is due to this that these wines are a lot paler and fresher, although they have the same period of maturation as an Amontillado or an Oloroso.

Is the must from red grapes red? The colour is the same as the must from white grapes. The pigmentation is only in the skin of the grapes. The must from the *Garnacha Tintorera*, an inferior quality grape, is the only exception.

Why do they usually use red grapes in champagne and the colour of the wine is white? Because they extract the must very quickly with very wide and shallow presses so that the must is not in contact with the skins long enough to be stained. Even so, the colour of sparkling wines sometimes has reddish reflections.

GOLDEN RULES FOR A GOOD WINE ENTHUSIAST

1.- Show some interest for the lesser-known wines.

2.-Wine is not only for meals, but to be enjoyed anytime.

3.-The sense of smell is the most important. The mouth only perceives sour, bitter, sweet and salty. The specific tastes of things is processed by our sense of smell, retronasal (internally from the mouth to the nose), but we only taste them on the palate.

4.-Do not obfuscate the beginner with a doctoral thesis on wine. The more you want to impress the beginner, the more difficult it will be for him to understand this culture.

5.-The acidity contrasts with the sugar and alcohol. A wine with only 12º alcohol, but with very low acidity seems to have more alcohol than a wine with 14º with a higher acidity level. A sweet wine would seem less so if we added tartaric acid (from grapes), citric acid (from oranges, lemons and grapefruit) or malic acid (from apples)

6.-Be tolerant. The more knowledge one has of wine, the more tolerant we are.

7.-Do not try to guess the name of the wine at a blind tasting if you don't want to be embarrassed. It would be better to say: this wine reminds me of X. If you got it wrong, nothing happens. But if you were fortunate enough to get it right, joy!

8.-With time red wine becomes lighter, and white wine goes darker and rosés go off.

9.-The violet edges in a red are a synonym of youth; an orangey edge means maturity, and an ochre edge on the decline. A straw yellow edge in whites means a young wine; a golden yellow, maturity; and reddish edges, decline.

HOW TO INTERPRET THE BOTTLE

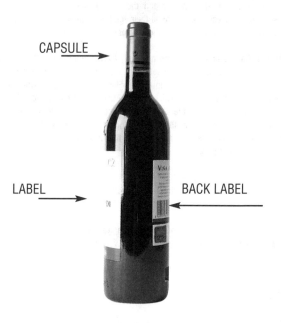

CAPSULE

LABEL

BACK LABEL

THE LABEL

The label is the identity card of the wine in which all the characteristics and the legal aspects of the wine appear.

The label reflects the distinctive name of the wine, the bottler, the alcohol content, volume of the contents, the name and address of the bodega, designation of origin and the export and health entry, and it is expressly forbidden to include any false or misleading information on the label.

The brands. Almost all self-respecting French wines include the word Château making reference to a recognized quality vineyard; the Spanish have traditionally preferred noble titles by naming their wines after mythical winemakers such as Marqués de Riscal or Marqués de Murrieta.

They also frequently use the name of the region where the grapes come from (Viña Pomal, Viña Tondonia); nowadays there is a very specific appreciation for the very fashionable *Vinos de Pago* or other wines which are trying to copy this concept: Finca (estate) Clos (term taken from Burgundy), Pago (vineyard), Dominio (dominion), Hacienda, Dehesa (meadow)...

D.O.
WINE
VINTAGE
REGISTERED BOTTLER
D.O. LOGOTYPE
ALCOHOL CONTENT
BODEGA
VOLUME

RIBERA DEL DUERO
DENOMINACIÓN DE ORIGEN

ENOA
1998

13% vol.
75 cl.

There are also those looking for grandeur: the castles (literal translation of the French word, but not the concept), palaces or 'the great' preceding the name. Although lately Latin names are fashionable: Aurus, Cirsion, Emeritus, Augustus, Summun, etc.

The design. The classic design seems to be working with no problem in the case of well-known wines. Any label seems to do for these wines (Pesquera for example). But when it comes to innovation in Europe, the Italians take the prize and, in general, the New World countries, up to the point that to be able to compete with these wines many European producers have copied their image.

In this field Spain is still behind the times, although there is no doubt that in the past five years it has taken a great stride forward. Nowadays it is not strange for a Spanish company to have their labels designed by American or London-based companies who produce works of art and go into the finest detail of all aspects of the image (the label, capsules, bottles, packaging, etc).

At any event, the most important thing is that the image of the label corresponds to the contents of the bottle. An excellent wine can be sold with a good label, but a great design is not sufficient to convert a mediocre wine into an excellent wine.

A blatant case: the Sherry labels. The people from the Jerez region have always been known as the wine Phoenicians, better salesmen than viticulturists or winemakers. After all Jerez wine was born from trade. The actual concept solera is nothing other than a trade concession that required a wine to be exactly like the one ordered previously in so far as maturation was concerned.

This philosophy is reflected on their labels. If the bodega is famous, its name is more important than the brand; if it is more commercial to highlight 'Manzanilla' or 'Pedro Ximénez' as a type of wine, the brand name (if it exists) appears in small letters. Expressions such as *'solera selecta'*, *'muy viejo'*, *'amoroso'*, etc, in different sizes produce a lot of confusion by the absence of legislation on the sizes of the words that identify the wine. They often use English words (dry, medium, old, rich...) with Jerez terms bordering on the curious and the anecdotal.

THE VINTAGE

This indicates the year in which the grapes were harvested. The fundamental reason is to indicate that this wine is different to others in terms of the climatic conditions the vineyard underwent.

Although it is normal to have the vintage on the label, and despite the fact that in many cases the veracity of the vintage is questionable, in Rioja and other trustworthy designations of origins they have been rigorously controlled since 1980. The practice of blending wines from different vintages and the fact that the climate in Spain is relatively similar in consecutive years, contributes to the fact that large differences between the different vintages cannot be appreciated.

THE SOLERA

The solera is obtained by legally blending different vintages. Generally on a bottle with the word solera a very old date appears. This is the date on which the wine was placed in the cask where it was aged for the first time, filling up the wine as it was extracted; therefore the wine is a mixture.

THE BACK LABEL

The back label is the official seal of the corresponding Designation of Origin and the guarantee of origin.

The back label also contains information on the ageing of the wine, Crianza, Reserva, Gran Reserva.

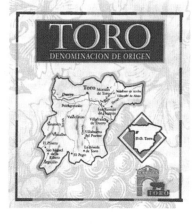

Since 1980 it has been obligatory to have the date of harvesting of a vintage wine, but if the wine is not an aged wine the words '*garantia de origen*' can figure to indicate the origin and make it clear that the wine was not aged in barrel.

The abbreviation CVC, making a comeback, means a 'combination of various vintages'; that is the wine is the result of blending different vintages. CVC wines are usually quite popular and are in no way related to Generoso wines aged in the solera system.

TYPES OF BOTTLE

BORGOÑA   BURDEOS   RIN

Nowadays in Spain we generally use the three types of bottles used by the French to differentiate between the different winegrowing regions. The most widely-used bottles are two variations of the tall cylindrical Bordeaux bottle. The authentic Bordeaux bottle is 3cm taller. The second bottle is the Burgundy bottle, which is also the oldest, and is wider and shorter. The third bottle is known as the Rhine bottle (Alsace-Germanic origin, from the regions of the Rhine). This bottle is thinner and taller and is generally used for whites and rosés. Recently, a cylindrical bottle with a long neck is becoming more popular for very expressive wines.

THE CAPSULE

The capsule is the covering on the top of the bottle and is fundamentally to guarantee that wine has not been opened. Lead is the most commonly used material (before they used sealing wax), although lately the lead is being replaced by less harmful materials such as plastic or tin to avoid any possible poisoning.

THE STOPPER

In 95% of the cases the wine stopper is cork, a naturally resistant and elastic material whose length can vary from about 44cm to 50cm, although nowadays synthetic stoppers are being used in Spanish wines (for more information on this and other alternatives see the section on 'Wine stoppers: the great controversy of the 21st century in the first section of this Guide, where the causes of 'the smell of cork' is also mentioned).

SERVING WINE

SERVING TEMPERATURE

This is a vitally important point, because serving the wine at its optimum temperature means nothing less than being able to fully appreciate the characteristics of the wine.

To achieve the sensation of freshness and vitality of a white wine or a Fino from Andalucía, these must be served between six and eight degrees. Rosés, because of their red wine traits combined with their white 'soul' are drunk at ten degrees, to be able to better appreciate their aromas and nuances.

Young reds, as well as Amontillados can be served at 14ºC, or perhaps 15ºC, because the fruity characters are hidden at lower temperatures, while older reds, aged for three years or more, and the Oloroso wines, are consumed at between 17º to 19ºC, depending on the age of the wine. This increase is because the aromas developed during its maturation phase are much more delicate. On the other hand they could be drowned out by the volatility of the alcohol if we serve the wine at a higher temperature.

Cavas can be consumed at an even lower temperature 4º to 6º due to the carbon dioxide which brings out the aromas.

To avoid the wine reaching the 24º that any house in Spain reaches during the summer, we can use a wine bucket filed with water and ice. If we place the red wine in the bucket for nine minutes its temperature will drop to 17º which will then go up to 18º in the glass. A young red should remain in the bucket for ten to twelve minutes, and the whites, rosés and cavas can be cooled at your discretion.

SERVING IN THE GLASS

The wine glass should be filled to about half or a little more. The bottle should be held at the bottom to reduce shaking, and when finishing, turn the bottle a quarter turn to avoid any drops falling.

LEFT OVER WINE

Bottles that have not been finished with a meal and are left for future consumption evolve differently; for example if it is a young red, it loses a lot of its fruitiness, going flat, without nuances. If it is an old wine, the aromas from ageing and its bouquet oxidize going rancid. The wine will eventually turn to vinegar.

A good method of maintaining the characteristics of the wine in half finished bottles is with the Vacu-Vin system. This consists of a pump, an air extractor and a rubber stopper which has an airtight seal, so the only aromas which remain in the bottle are from the wine as the air has been removed from the container. Bottles with this type of stopper must be stored upright.

It is not advisable to leave these wines in the fridge for more than one day, because the aromas of the fridge and dry ice flatten the aroma and the wine loses vitality and becomes oily on the palate.

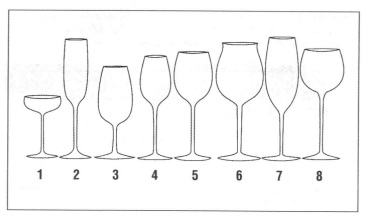

THE IDEAL GLASS

Champagne glass, Pompadour (nº 1). This glass and even flatter glasses can still be seen at toasts. It is not a very practical glass as it impedes smelling the wine and on having a very wide rim, the wine escapes from the side of the mouth with the slightest movement.

Flute glass (nº 2). Nowadays they are used for sparkling wines. Their main defect lies in the small surface of the liquid which impedes swirling to smell the wine. Very small bowl for the aromas.

Afnor wine glass (nº 3). This is valid for wine tasting although the volume is too small as there is not enough space to clearly see the wine's range of nuances along the rim of the glass. Not valid for the table as it is not very aesthetic.

Restaurant wine glass (nº 4). This glass, based on the Bordeaux glass and which has become well established over the last ten years, is widely used in restaurants, although it is not a very technical tasting glass.

A Bordeaux red wine glass (nº 5). This glass is ideal for tasting as well as for the table. Its larger volume and weight than the Anfor glass permits smoother movements for smelling. The glass is very thin (the thickness is very important to see the colour of the wine with more definition) and the mouth is wide enough to introduce the lips and the nose at the same time.

A Burgundy white wine glass (nº 6). A glass for easily-impressed people. The volume is too big; however, the quality of this glass is very good.

Champagne glass (nº 7). This is the best glass for champagne or cava. It is easy to see the ring of bubbles and as it has a slight bowl one can smell the wine.

A Burgundy red wine glass (nº 8). The bowl is too big. The advantage is the luminosity the wine has in these glasses due to the large surface of the liquid. The colour is not true as the large surface area tends to make the wine lighter. The mouth is very wide and any movement while drinking can lead to one spilling the wine.

THE INFLUENCE OF THE GLASS ON THE TASTE

The shape of the glass can change the taste of the wine, but to what extent can one appreciate the differences in the wine due to the different shapes and sizes glasses, all of them designed for drinking wine?

THE MOUTH. The mouth of the glass must close slightly to concentrate the aromas and to enable the glass to be swirled without spilling. The size of the mouth also determines which point of the mouth the wine goes to.

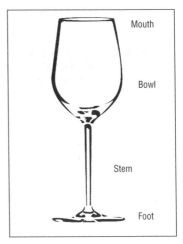

THE BOWL. The size of the bowl allows more or less space for the aromas to develop in the wine.

THE STEM. It is important for it to be compensated by the size of the bowl and long enough to hold the glass.

THE FOOT. As the support of the glass it must be big enough to provide stability to the glass. It can also be used to hold the glass.

KEY FACTORS

The differences can be so pronounced that even the most inexperienced person can see them. There is an almost scientific basis to wine glasses, thanks to the Reidel family, a Central European saga that has been dedicated to working with glass for the last ten generations. The fact that a glass is bigger or smaller, with a larger or smaller bowl, a wider or narrower mouth etc., will determine the perception of the wine. But, on which specific aspect of the wine does each one of these factors have an influence?

The size. The size influences the intensity and the quality of the aromas. The most important is the 'space' left to inhale, in which the aromas are set free.

Red wines, due to their greater alcohol content, demand bigger glasses, whilst for white wines small or medium sized glasses are more appropriate to appreciate the fruity notes.

The shape. The design is based on a study of the different varieties of grapes (aromatic intensity, tannins, alcohol, acidity, etc). We are not only trying to accentuate the good points of the wine, but to also hide the weak points.

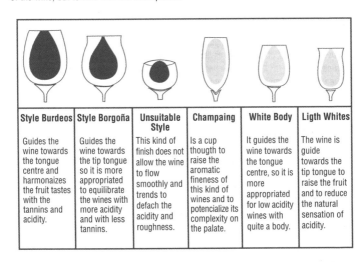

Style Burdeos	Style Borgoña	Unsuitable Style	Champaing	White Body	Ligth Whites
Guides the wine towards the tongue centre and harmonaizes the fruit tastes with the tannins and acidity.	Guides the wine towards the tip tongue so it is more appropriated to equilibrate the wines with more acidity and with less tannins.	This kind of finish does not allow the wine to flow smoothly and trends to defach the acidity and roughness.	Is a cup thougth to raise the aromatic fineness of this kind of wines and to potencialize its complexity on the palate.	It guides the wine towards the tongue centre, so it is more appropriated for low acidity wines with quite a body.	The wine is guide towards the tip tongue to raise the fruit and to reduce the natural sensation of acidity.

An inappropriate glass is capable of highlighting the least positive aspects of a wine.

The diameter of the rim. This determines the inclination of the head when drinking the wine. Glasses with a wide mouth force the head forward to sip the wine, while glasses with a narrow mouth force the head back. The posture when drinking the wine conducts the liquid to one or another zone of the mouth, where the principal tastes are registered (sweet, sour, salty, bitter).

The 'designer' decides which taste sensations of the wine he would like to enhance for each type of wine.

The thickness of the glass. Fine crystal is better for tasting. Besides giving a clearer and sharper view of the colour of the wine, there is a much narrower communication between the palate and the tactile sensation is much more pleasant.

THE PERCEPTION OF THE AROMAS AND TASTES

AROMAS. Reidel's theory makes a distinction between the three main types:

Floral and fruity. They are light and fragile, and ascend rapidly to the rim of the glass.

Green, mineral and earthy. Hints of the aromas of plants, and the minerals and soils, which are situated on an intermediate level.

Wood and alcohol, or related to these two elements. These are the most intense and remain at the bottom.

When the wine is swirled in the glass, the evaporation and the intensity increases, but this does not necessarily favour the mixing of these different layers of aromas. Thus the shape of the vessel can highlight or reveal some aromas more than others.

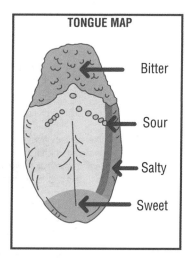

TONGUE MAP

Bitter

Sour

Salty

Sweet

TASTES. Once the wine has been taken into the mouth it comes into contact with the taste buds of the tongue and the palate. Because of the heat of the mouth cavity, volatile compounds are set free which rise to the nasal cavity where they reach the olfactory glands of the nose. These olfactory sensations have an important impact on our perception of the wine and, in this sense, taste is nothing else but a combination of tastes and aromas. In addition, the situation of the principal tastes on different parts of the tongue (tip, side, back…) enables one to describe one or the other.

A PRACTICAL DEMONSTRATION

What follows is a set of practical examples, taken from experience, to show what types of perceptions are altered by the use of one glass or another.

Different temperatures. The Chardonnay glass is designed to highlight the natural acidity of this type of wine and therefore the liquid is directed to the part of the tongue which registers this sensation. When tasting the same wine in a standard glass it does not give a sensation of freshness; it not only seems warmer, but also hotter.

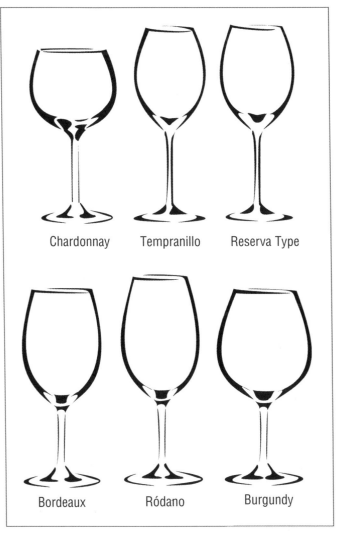

Chardonnay   Tempranillo   Reserva Type

Bordeaux   Ródano   Burgundy

Strengthens some aromas more than others. A *Cabernet* tasted in a Bordeaux glass is harmonious and complex; in a *Tempranillo* glass (smaller mouth) it seems closed and with more toasted and ageing aromas. On the other hand, the fruity concentration and the intensity a *Tempranillo* achieves in its glass is transformed into an apparently more alcoholic and less intense wine in a Cabernet glass.

In the case of a variety like *Verdejo*, changing the glass can turn a pleasantly fruity wine with green herbs nuances into another wine which only offers its more vegetative and herbaceous side without the slightest signs of finesse.

Burgundy red wines, with their complex and delicate bouquet, work better in a glass with a large bowl and a wide mouth, as the larger swirling surface brings out its great aromatic potential. Rhone-style wines, made from Mediterranean style varieties, *Syrah, Garnacha,*

Cariñena or *Monastrell* need a higher glass (the Rhone glass is a centimetre higher than a Bordeaux glass) which, thanks to the chimney effect, develops its typical spicy aromas.

The more complex a wine, the wider the mouth of the glass needs to be.

More or less tannins. The most surprising case is that of a Cabernet which, tasted in its glass (the Bordeaux glass directs the wine to the centre of the tongue) softens the tannins integrating them with the fruit and at the same time highlighting its complexity. But in a Tempranillo glass it seems to be full of tannins, harsh and extremely astringent.

A *Tempranillo* tasted in a Bordeaux glass seems a little diluted, rougher and the alcohol is more noticeable on the finish. A Rhone-style red in a Bordeaux glass seems to be much more acidic as the liquid is directed from the top of the tongue to the sides of the tongue. In a Rhone glass the liquid is directed to the tip of the tongue (where the sweet taste buds are found) to favour integration with the alcohol.

Does this mean that one should have as many glasses as wines? Of course not. Two models were made for Spanish red wines as demonstrated in the tasting and which are very appropriate for the majority of our wines. They are the Tempranillo glass and the Reserva glass, the latter being more appropriate for older wines and wines that have been aged longer. Its larger size and the wider mouth unfolds more complexities, while the first glass, with its more closed mouth, concentrates and strengthens the fruity aromas of the variety. Other glasses such as the Chianti, in which the wine tasting for this Guide was done, are very versatile. But if you are a true lover of Bordeaux reds or the Chardonnay whites, why not give yourself the luxury of owning the ideal glass for your favourite wine?

USEFUL ACCESSORIES

A basket for serving wine. They say that they stop the sediment of old wines falling into the glass. However, as we consume the wine, the level of the wine drops and it is necessary to tilt the basket more and this movement disturbs the sediment which makes it useless. It is ridiculous to use them for wines less than ten years old. The only baskets that are useful are the bolt style baskets.

Decanters. A bottle of old wine should be decanted very carefully to avoid the sediment on the bottom of the bottle from coming out (pigmentation and bitartrate crystals). Furthermore, it also serves to get rid of certain bad aromas (closed, reduction) produced by its long stay in the bottle. It also serves to decant young wines that have been prematurely bottled and have been kept in the bottle for more than two years.

THE ADVANTAGES AND DISADVANTAGES OF THE MOST COMMON CORKSCREWS

TWO-PRONG EXTRACTOR

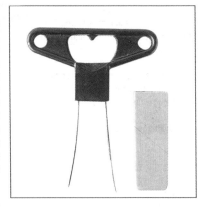

On extracting the opener from its sheath we can see two parallel prongs, one a little longer than the other. The longer one is introduced between the bottle and the cork and then the other on the other side. Slowly slip the prongs down the side of the cork, tilting the handle to avoid pushing it in completely vertically and pushing the cork all the way down too. When the two prongs have been completely inserted up to the handle, pull out the cork turning it at the same time.

Advantages: If you are skilled it is the fastest method. It is small and does not damage the cork (does not have a screw). It can also be used to insert the cork in the bottle again.

Disadvantages: One has to be quite skilled not to push the cork down into the bottle. It is not suitable for very old corks.

Availability: At some wine accessory shops. Approximate price: 6.

THE RABBIT

The fastest corkscrew available. It is a complex work of engineering, designed for those who have to do a lot of wine-tasting and have to open a lot of bottles quickly. The device is placed on the neck of the bottle, similar to pincers, moving the lever from left to right to introduce the screw and extract the cork.

Advantages: It is the fastest and the cork remains in perfect condition after being extracted. Only three turns of the screw!

Disadvantages: It is very expensive and the carbon screw has to be replaced after a certain number of uses. It sometimes fails to uncork a bottle if the lever is pushed in the opposite direction.

Availability: At some wine accessory shops or from the manufacturer: Screwpull. Ciencia,8. Pol. Industrial Massotes. 08850 Gavà (Barcelona).
Tel.: 934 224 040. screwpull@lecreuset.es. Approximate price: 159.

FROM THE 18th CENTURY

Reproduction of an eighteenth-century corkscrew. The first to use a screw. The screw is very short to make the least possible number of turns. Then the lever is put into position and the cork pulled out with ease.

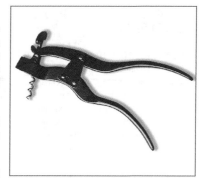

Advantages: Impeccable extraction and very little effort required, also making uncorking a ritual. Nice present.

Disadvantages: Not easy to use and slow.

Availability: At gift shops or wine accessory shops. Price: 12.

PUIGPULL

The inventor went to a lot of trouble to make sure the cork is extracted vertically. The instructions must be read very carefully to fully understand the complicated working of this jack-like device, with a moveable screw and ratchet. Once you have understood the instructions, the cork is extracted without effort with the jack system. The force required by the traditional waiter's opener compared to this opener, makes opening bottles with this device a mere ceremony.

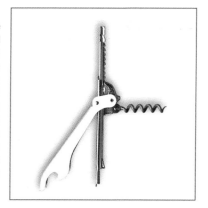

Advantages: The screw only has four turns, impeccable vertical extraction, robust and well made.

Disadvantages: Complicated to understand in the beginning, even after reading the instructions; slower than the classic waiter's lever corkscrew. The cork might crack at the sides depending on how the screw was inserted, as with all corkscrews without a guide.

Availability: At good gift shops and from the manufacturer: Oriente nº 5. 43700 El Vendrell (Tarragona). Tel. and fax: 00 34 977 587 220. Price: 12.40.

'LE CREUSET' SCREWPULL

Elegant looking corkscrew with a high quality screw, aided by a methacrylate guide to ensure that the screw enters the centre of the cork with a lever.

Advantages: The screw enters the centre of the cork without damaging the sides. The spiral is made from carbon with a very sharp point which goes through the cork without leaving bits of cork in the wine. The cork comes out impeccably and at times it is difficult to see that it has been pulled out by a corkscrew.

Disadvantages: The device has three independent parts (spiral, guide and lever) which are easy to lose. Once the cork has been extracted from the bottle it is difficult to extract it from the guide. Quite expensive.

Availability: At good gift shops and specialized shops. Price: 26.

WINGED CORKSCREW

The idea is perfect but the most important part has its shortcomings: the screw. The screw goes in easily due to the ring which acts as a guide and is placed on the top of the bottle. Once the spiral has been introduced into the cork, the wings open, and the cork is removed by pushing the levers down without force.

Advantages: Vertical introduction in the centre of the cork. Easy to use, no force needed.

Disadvantages: The spiral is die-cast and not made from forged steel. It is a very widely-used corkscrew. The major problem lies with the sharp spirals that rip the cork easily. It is not recommended for very old corks.

Availability: Can be bought at any hardware store. Price: 5.

WAITER'S CORKSCREW

This is the typical corkscrew seen in restaurants, which enables quick extraction with a lever.

Advantages: Effortless extraction as long as the screw is proportional in length to the anchor which is placed on the side of the top of the bottle and acts as a support for the lever.   Many manufactures do not bear this equilibrium in mind, and this means one has to use force to extract the last section of the cork. Easy to use and pocket-sized.

Disadvantages: During the final section of extraction, the cork might break or crack along the sides as the cork bends because the point of support of the anchor and the top of the spiral are quite separated.

Availability: At any hardware or wine accessory shop. Approximate price: 3.85 or more.

PULLTAPS

This is a sophisticated version of the waiter's corkscrew but without the cork being bent in the last phase, thanks to the dual anchor system, a longer and shorter one. The latter keeps the cork in a vertical position during the last phase of extraction.

Advantages: It is, without a doubt, the most recommendable corkscrew for size, speed, cleanness of extraction and price. It is of course a bit more expensive than the traditional waiter's corkscrew but this is possibly due to their limited availability.

Disadvantages: The only problem is the lack of a guide, which forces one to judge the verticality of the spiral during extraction.

Availability: At a very few wine accessory shops or from the manufacturer: Pulltex. Murcia, 33-A. Sant Boi de Llobregat (Barcelona). Tel.: 936 401 027, www.pulltex.com. Price: 27.

WHICH SHOULD I TURN, THE BOTTLE OR THE CORKSCREW?

Purists throw their hands up in horror when they see a waiter turn the bottle instead of the corkscrew.

This is not really serious, as the majority of wines do not have any sediment at the bottom of the bottle.

We must remember that when turning the bottle instead of the corkscrew, the chances of the spiral going in vertically are greater. When turning the bottle one only turns the bottle and not the wine, which remains practically still. However, it is a lot more aesthetic and ritualistic to see the waiter's wrist move.

BUYING WINE

WHERE AND HOW TO BUY

TASTE BEFORE BUYING

The easiest and cheapest way of getting to know the wines before buying the bottles is to try them in the wine bars that sell wine by the glass. We can compare the wines and decide which to buy without those last minute doubts.

WHICH WINES SHOULD I BUY?

Currently the most sold are the non-returnable bottles with a cork stopper and a capsule, but alongside these we find the returnable litre bottles and the modern tetra brick.

The tetra brick is hygienic and convenient, but it should only be used for everyday wines. Litre bottles are on the decline because of the bother of returning them and there are sometimes defects in the washing process despite the very strict controls.

Finally, in rural areas it is common to sell wine in demijohns, which means the wine has to be decanted into bottles or consumed very quickly to avoid it oxidizing.

BUYING AT THE BODEGA

In Spain there is not a tradition of buying directly from the bodegas, and besides, they are not very keen to have direct contact with the public. Generally the bodegas deal with the distributors but if they do deal with the public they tend to sell the wine at a price halfway between the wholesale price and the retail price to avoid problems with the distributors. However, recently, many bodegas have realised the importance of welcoming clients to their premises which are fitted out with shops and tasting rooms where the visitor can buy the wines at market prices.

BUYING FROM THE LOCAL DISTRIBUTOR

Distributors are not well known in Spain, and act as the link between the retail outlet and the bodega. They do not really sell to the general public but if they do, they charge the same price for the wine as the retail shop.

BUYING AT SUPERMARKETS AND HYPERMARKETS

Supermarkets and above all hypermarkets have the advantage of offering relatively young wines at tempting prices. The attraction of the hypermarkets lies in their 'offers of the month' or specific offers which means a large turnover and is based on heavy advertising campaigns. Recently there has been a major improvement in the range of wines offered by these establishments.

BUYING AT THE WINE CLUB

Wine clubs are interesting for two reasons: because they deliver the wine and because of their cultural function. Although one can expect wines of a certain quality at bargain prices, in the majority of the cases they offer unknown wines or wines which are already on the market but with different labels; however this is being controlled more by the bodegas.

BUYING AT THE GROCERY STORE

Barring exceptions, the grocer's is not the place to buy wines because the conditions the wines are stored in are frightening. In some cases, however one might find exceptional oenological treasures.

BUYING AT SPECIALIST SHOPS

These are the ideal places to buy wine and they are spreading all over Spain. The prices are higher but the service and personal attention is much better. Another advantage is the possibility of buying wines that have not been brought onto the market yet. There is also the disadvantage that some of them limit themselves to offering the wines supplied by the distributors.

BUYING OVER THE INTERNET

Since 1999 there has been an unusual interest in selling over the internet. With this method one can buy wine by following the instructions of the seller on the screen. The main advantage is not only the ease of shopping and paying using the computer, but also the access to a large amount of different wines in this virtual shop. The prices are similar or maybe even cheaper than those offered by the retail shops. However, there is no personal touch and it is impossible to taste the wines beforehand.

THE PRICES OF WINES

This is a determining factor when it comes to buying and a controversial issue in the light of the recent proliferation of wines costing over € 18 in Spain, something the Spanish consumer is not used to.

Is wine expensive? The price of Spanish wines has risen dramatically over the last decade, but it is also true that there has been a marked increase in quality over the same period. These days more wines are subject to a price/quality control, and can usually pass the test more or less successfully. And there are wines whose value goes beyond the commercial calculation of particular profit margins in terms of their manufacturing costs.

Why do some wines cost so much? Market demand sets the value of the product if it costs more than € 20. If the demand is greater than the supply, the middleman who has bought the vintage increases the price (and therefore its exclusivity) while the bodega stays out of this frenzy. But it is also true that the winemaker may want his share of the pie with the next vintage, however in practice they rarely participate in these crazy price hikes.

The most expensive wines. Buying a French Petrus or a Spanish Pingus satisfies the wish to have a wine that very few possess. In this case the price must be considered a social factor. The social value of a Rolex, even if it is not gold, is higher than a Seiko although both are equally accurate. While a luxury item is manufactured to demand, a *Grand Cru Classé* from Bordeaux, a L'Ermita from Priorat or the wines mentioned above depend on the size of their vineyards, without the possibility of increasing production due to the characteristics of the soil which transfers its personality to the wine.

Everyday wine. In reality, bottled wines are cheaper than 25 years ago. On the other hand, popular wines (local bulk wines and the common litre wines) from those times were proportionately cheaper than they are today. The wine lover has more money available than before, but he also wants more information on the product.

Be careful with bargains. While the offers of the Hypermarkets are interesting because of the space allocated to the product and the turnover of the product, bargains from shops and restaurants must be questioned. It is difficult to know if they want to get rid of a product that has been on their shelves for a long time under bad conditions or if, on the other hand, these wines are in the same condition as the wines sold at large supermarkets.

STORING AND PRESERVING

THE BODEGA AT HOME

THE BODEGA AT HOME

If you are thinking of building a house, think of the location of the bodega first. It would not be the first time that once the work has been finished, the storeroom almost always located next to the garage is converted into the wine cellar.

The following must therefore be kept in mind:

* The orientation.
* The thickness of the walls.
* The material used for the floor.
* Ventilation.
* The incompatibility of wine cellar/pantry.
* Noise.

Orientation. The orientations are listed below from best to worst.

1st North.
2nd Northeast.
3rd Northwest.
4th East.
5th West.
6th Southeast and Southwest.
7th South.

It is clear that the sun, the grape's great friend, is wine's enemy. Therefore the correct orientation will decrease temperature fluctuations and will help with insulation.

The thickness of the walls. The thickness of the walls is essential to maintain the ideal temperature for our wines.

They must be white, washable, and if possible cement with gravel, or Tyrolean plaster, as this system conserves moisture better if we wish to hose it down.

These walls of solid stone or brick found in buildings of yesteryear are more of a relic than a current option for storing our collection of wines, as their cost is high, and we would get the same results with good insulation using fibre glass, expanded polyurethane etc.

Nowadays, in numerous winemaking regions, we can find very modern cellars with maturation sheds on ground level with perfect sound and thermal insulation.

Therefore, it would not be a bad idea to cover the walls of your storeroom with the insulation material mentioned if it is found on the ground floor. It would also be a good idea to have the cellar face north, in the sense that the access to the cellar is in this direction.

Another factor is to have it semi-underground or underground as this offers the best conditions. But do not confuse the sensation of coolness found in a cellar where the temperature does not go below 20°C with the 15°C needed to preserve wine, as we would have to dig down 10 metres to achieve this, and this is definitely not cost-effective. It is easier to install an air conditioner capable of maintaining the temperature at a constant 14°C and the humidity at no less than 70% (Climacaves –Tel.: +34 938 432 575– at a cost of approximately 3,500).

As a matter of interest, with a humidity of 99% it is possible to store the bottles upright, as the cork will not shrink because of the moisture level. However, humidity levels of this sort would be too high and would lead to mould forming on the corks.

The material used for the floor. If you have taken into account the orientation and situation (subterranean or ground level) in your plans, remember that your floor also helps maintain moisture.

129

Do not use tiles or any material that is not porous. Old floor tiles are ideal, the ones that can be seen in typical old taverns, a floor of solid brick or any other material that absorbs moisture. However, the best in this case is also the cheapest: a floor of compacted or trodden earth and river sand.

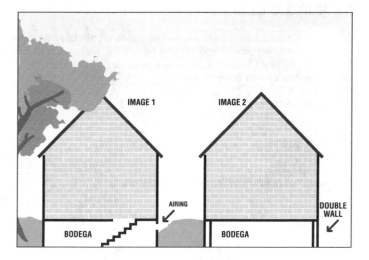

Ventilation. Subterranean rooms must be ventilated through a shunt or a ventilation conduct, or better still, build a conduit to the exterior. (Fig.1).

The same must be done in semi-underground cellars or, as a last resort, make holes in the door if the adjoining room has sufficient ventilation and is free of odours. (Fig. 2).

In rooms found on the ground floor, the windows should be bricked up, without taking out the frame as in the future the room could be used for other purposes by simply knocking the bricks out again.

The incompatibility of a wine cellar/pantry. Wine goes very well with the delights of the table but not in the cellar. Under no circumstances should we store perishable goods such as beans, fruit and vegetables in our wine cellar nor use it to cure meat. The smells generated by these articles disturb the peaceful rest of our reserve wines, as the smells come into contact with the precious liquid through the corks.

The custom of watering the floor with wine so that the 'cellar smells like a cellar' is not the most advisable thing to do. If the amount used is little there will be no problem. If on the other hand, it is a pool, the wine will turn into vinegar and the acetic microbes are not precisely wine's best friend.

Noise. The room adjoining the garage that the majority of wine lovers have to store their wines must be completely soundproofed and vibration free. We must not forget that the smoke and the smell of petrol from the car can be a real menace.

The soul of the vine is closer to a mystical monastic silence than to a rowdy party.

THE WINE RACKS

We have cool walls, an earthen or porous floor, subdued lighting, and the room is odour free. Now it is logically time to bring in the furniture: the wine racks.

Built-in shelves are appropriate because of their charm and rustic look.

To make them as cheap as possible, the niches should measure approximately 80cm x 80cm x 25cm deep (width of two bricks), if you want to place the tops of the bottles facing outwards.

If you would like to place them in the opposite position, the depth of the niche must be at least 30cm for the bottom of the bottle which is much heavier not to stick out.

If the size of the gap appears to be too big (fits 120 bottles) to store one make of wine, you can divide it into a maximum of 11 parts, by supporting a dividing board on each row, and the same in two or three parts.

To store Rhine bottles, which are longer, the depth of the niche must not be less than 35cm. However, given that

these types of bottle are generally used for whites and rosés, they can be placed in the lower niches or even on the floor, where it is cooler.

Be warned that placing these bottles one on top of the other in the same direction is unstable due to the shape of the bottles. Therefore it is better to place them alternately, in one direction and the other, to build a more solid block.

A wine rack can be built in the same way with boxes or wooden units by placing them one on top of the other and then dividing them with moveable boards. (Fig. 3).

Another way is to have wine racks made from wood, plastic or iron, with one bottle in each niche. This is probably a little more expensive but more practical as we have more mobility.

THE SELECTION AND THE AMOUNT OF BOTTLES

From 100 to 200 bottles are needed for the cellar to take shape. The ideal for a good wine enthusiast is to have six bottles of each wine and type except of course for the Gran Reservas.

Organize your wine cellar by regions. Do not forget that each region has its typical wine and that each dish has its soul mate.

It is best to place unique wines or wines that are no longer available in a separate place. If the space is limited, then place the Gran Reservas of each region on the bottom row separated from the everyday wines by a board.

If you have racks with independent niches, separate them into modules and know the limits of each space. Of course, each one must be clearly marked.

Each person must decide which wines they like best. If we have a normal diet then we should have about 50% red wines, 35% white wines and 15% rosés.

The reds should be made up of 70% light wines, bearing in mind that food nowadays is lighter. The rest can be full-bodied reds.

Aperitif or dessert wines do not need as much care as table wines, but they should be stored horizontally.

THE CELLAR BOOK

This is essential if we have a lot of wines stored, as the inexorable passage of time and humidity can destroy the labels. In addition, it is useful to keep information that could later be of interest.

The book must have spaces to write down the name of the wine, vintage, bottler, producer, date of purchase and its price, the quantity bought and the balance left as we consume it. It is also used to note down comments on the evolution of the wine and the situation of the bottle in the cellar.

If you are not so meticulous, buy some self-stick labels to stick on the top or bottom of the bottle with the following details:

a) Purchase date.

b) Purchase price.

c) A brief sensorial comment on the wine at the purchase date.

In this way you will know the genuine age of the wine and what is more important, its profitability. It must be remembered that the price increases are due to two factors: one because of the vintage and the other if it is not available on the market. The comments on the tasting done on the first day will be valuable to track the evolution of the wine.

THE MOST ELEMENTARY DOMESTIC CELLAR: FLATS AND APARTMENTS

A cool interior room must be used, and if possible cooled with an air conditioner of 1,500 BTU/hr (about € 700). The result is excellent: in winter with the heating switched off (16º) and in summer with the air conditioner (18º).

Wine-cooling cabinets are a good system for conserving wines. There are various sizes (between 50 and 120 bottles). It is advisable to buy one that has different temperatures according to the racks. The top racks are for the reds (18º). As we go lower rack by rack the temperature decreases. The rosés are kept in the central section (12º) and the whites and sparkling wines are stored on the bottom racks (5º-8º).

NUMBER OF BOTTLES AND TYPES OF WINE

The ideal would be 120 bottles (10 cases of 12) among which there should be a good representation of the majority of the Spanish wine-producing regions, and they can be distributed in the following way.

* 40 bottles of dark reds, full-bodied and with enough acid to store for up to 20 years: Ribera del Duero (Crianzas, Reservas and Gran Reservas), Rioja (some Crianzas, and almost all the Reservas and Gran Reservas), Priorat, Navarra (*Cabernet* and *Merlot*), Cataluña (*Cabernet* and *Merlot*).

* 20 bottles of not-so-dark reds to be kept for a maximum of eight years: (Crianzas from Rioja, Somontano, Toro).

* 10 bottles of lighter reds, or quick maturation to store for up to 20 years: Cariñena and the rest from Aragón, Jumilla, Alicante, Utiel-Requena, Bierzo.

* 10 bottles of very light reds, difficult to age (maximum 3 years): Extremadura, La Mancha, Valdepeñas, reds without ageing from all over Spain.

* 10 bottles of cava and young whites from the latest vintage from all regions in Spain.

* 10 bottles of whites to store for a maximum of five years from Rueda, Albariño, whites aged or fermented in wood from all regions, and whites made from the *Chardonnay* grape.

* 10 bottles of young rosés from the latest vintage from all regions in Spain.

* 10 bottles of aperitif and dessert wines, which can be stored for long periods: Olorosos, Pedro Ximénez, Ports, Amontillados, Tokay, Sauternes.

Note: the Finos and Manzanillas (dry Sherries) should be bought bottle by bottle and kept in the door of the fridge.

OTHER ASPECTS TO KEEP IN MIND

How to protect the label. The humidity needed to conserve the wine ends up damaging the labels. Therefore it is advisable, in the case of wines that we hope to store for a long time, to varnish the labels with transparent varnish (there is always the risk of the varnish cracking) or better still cover the body of the bottle with the plastic film that is used to cover foodstuffs.

Can a damaged label be replaced? For there not to be any problem with the authenticity of the bottle, the best thing would be to contact the producer. Some bodegas are often willing to replace the damaged label and even to undertake the 'restoration' of a venerable bottle (changing the bottle and cork).

Do the corks deteriorate in the cellar? The cork can give the wine bad odours. Although in the majority of cases the impregnation of this negative odour is prior to bottling, it could happen that a cork which was healthy becomes infected if it is near a product that gives off strong off-odours (for example, petrol). This is why one of the most important rules of the cellar is that it must be free of odours. One must also be careful of the cork leaking when it has lost elasticity due to drying out.

HOW LONG A WINE LASTS

A wine has youth, maturity and an old age. During the life of a wine there is a period of consumption and, within this an optimum stage. After this, its decline inevitably begins. We have listed some key factors concerning its preservation, as well as a graphical representation of its evolution to know when to drink the wine at its peak or when to throw out the bottle.

What does the optimum moment to drink the wine depend on? The different types of wine (white, rosé and red) depend on whether they have been aged in wood, their origin and even the grape variety used in their making. For example, a Jumilla reaches its peak before Rioja or Bordeaux wine. And the same is true of a *Garnacha* compared to a *Cabernet Sauvignon* or a *Tempranillo.*

How long does a wine last? It is difficult to know exactly. A red from Rioja improves over ten years, followed by a stationary period of no less than 5 years, and then begins to gradually go into decline. After this time the best thing that can happen to it is that it has the same characteristics as a wine that is 20 or 30 years older, providing it is kept in ideal conditions.

Does wine improve over time? It has not been fully proven. What is true is that the wine changes with time. However there is no doubt that the taste for the old – there is no doubt that it exists - can reach the sublime if it is an old and unrepeatable wine whose uncorking has deprived the rest of the world of the joy of a similar taste. Time is only positive to the extent in which it allows the components of the wine (wood, fruit, alcohol) to come together (hardly a few months) and the tannins to soften and be integrated, as long as the primary characters (grape and soil) disappear with the entry of the tertiary elements (those produced in the barrel and the bottle).

The importance of the temperature. Heat increases the speed of all the chemical reactions because the molecules have more energy and are more capable of reorganising and breaking up. In fact the speed of the chemical reactions doubles in the bottle for every 10º the temperature increases. Therefore the lower the temperature, the later the wine matures and

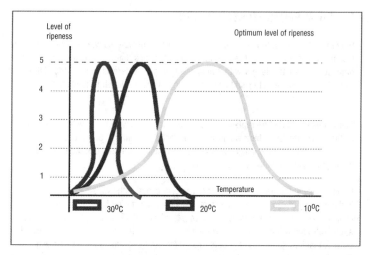

the longer it will last. But if we take the temperature down to 0ºC, the cold causes a large amount of tartaric deposits (in the shape of tiny crystals) which are not welcome either.

The importance of humidity. A wine preserved in a domestic wine cellar in La Coruña will last longer than one kept in similar conditions in Madrid. A humidity of 75% to 80% with sufficient ventilation is needed. Excessive humidity creates the danger of mould developing on the corks.

Which wines are not suitable for the basic rules of preservation? Those wines meant for immediate consumption, or if they were from a bad vintage, not balanced, have a low acidity or are low in tannins and the alcohol is not at least 12º. With these drawbacks their possibility of ageing is seriously reduced or even non-existent.

What has been taken into account in the graphs? The evolutionary periods are measured according to a standard method (not the ideal) of preserving wine; that is 10º in winter and 22º in summer and without the influence of the cork which should be in good condition. This is more or less the temperature of a domestic cellar at a weekend home or the backroom of a restaurant.

A reminder:

* Prematurely bottled red wines (Beaujolais nouveau, 'Cosechero' (Lit. grower wines) or *Novell* type wines) do not improve in bottle, losing their attributes of freshness and fruitiness after a few years.

* The variety also plays a part in the life of the wine. A wine made from *Tempranillo* ages more slowly than a wine from *Garnacha*. *Monastrell* wines go rancid more easily than others and tend to go rancid after six years.

* In the case of wines which age well it is advisable to change the corks every 15 years.

* When wood comes into play the wine has a longer life.

* The ideal preservation temperature varies between 10º and 16ºC.

WHITE WINES

Fruity whites that have not been in a barrel have a shorter life. The evolution which is expressed in the 'in decline' section of the graph means that, although the wine is fit for consumption, it has lost its fruitiness and freshness which are the characters which determine its personality. The possibility of prolonging the 'optimum moment' will depend on the nobility of the grape and its ability to retain these qualities for longer.

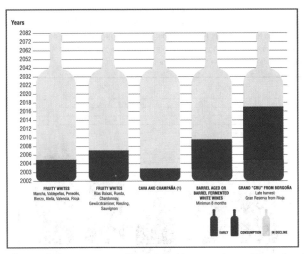

Cava and champagne are without a doubt more ephemeral once they have been disgorged and are put on sale. No sooner has the first year passed, their aroma and tastes evolve towards the almondy hints of oxidation. In the majority of cases there is no vintage year and the only reference we have is the purchase date.

The whites fermented and aged in barrel are protected by the tannins of the oak and have a longer life. There is even a period of just less than a year in which it is too early to drink them, as the wine and the oak are not harmonised. Their preservation of up to ten years is not because they maintain their fruitiness, but because of the transformation in bottle (reduction) and the harmonising with the qualities transferred by the wood.

ROSÉS AND YOUNG RED WINES

The difference between carbonic macerated reds and those bottled nor-mally lies in the

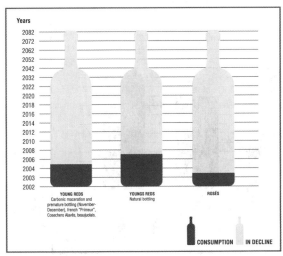

acquisition of fewer tannins by the former as their production is faster (less maceration of the skins) and their premature bottling.

Rosés have an even shorter life than whites as they immediately lose their raspberry traits (red fruit) which make up their main distinguishing identity.

RED WINES AGED IN BARREL

The wine's life is due to the grape variety and also to the influence of the climate. The Mediterranean reds (the first and second group) have a shorter life due to the type of wine grape used and the less vigorous tannins. Ribera del Duero wines (the last group), in spite of using the same varieties as those from Rioja (*Tempranillo* or *Tinto Fino*), enjoy a longer period of consumption due to the stronger tannins and acids.

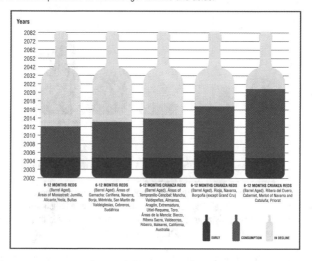

GREAT RESERVA AND GRAN RESERVA REDS

In these wines, except for the French wines, the early consumption stage takes place in the bodega within the regulations of a 'Reserva' and 'Gran Reserva' which lays down a minimum ageing period between barrel and bottle at three and five years respectively. The selection of the best vintages – the longest lived - and a greater extraction of tannins from the grape and wood, together with more acidity, results in a longer consumption period.

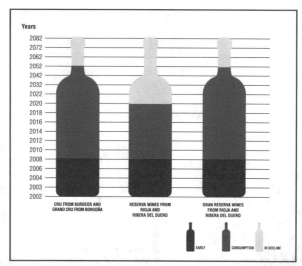

GENEROSO WINES

Generoso wines- an expression which alludes to their high alcohol content - have the longest life. Their oxidation during their prolonged ageing in wood and their high alcohol content – above all those in the first column - make them unalterable with age and even with an inappreciable evolution in the bottle over this period.

The wines in the second column, that is, those with a mixed barrel-bottle ageing (oxidoreduction) do evolve in the bottle (somewhat less in the Tokay due to its longer stay in cask).

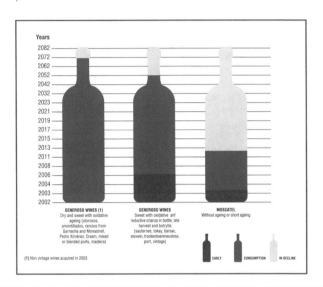

WINE AND FOOD

COMBINATIONS

It is important not to be influenced by tradition. The combination of wine and food should be flexible and a free choice. However, there are certain rules which must be kept in mind. Those we list as 'recommended' are the most orthodox associations, the 'tolerated' are the flexible list and the 'forbidden' are the ones not recommended.

YOUNG REDS AND REDS AGED FOR UP TO FOUR YEARS

● **Recommended with:** White and red meat, roast lamb, pork or beef, game, poultry, stews, rice dishes, pulses, mushrooms, cured cheese and blue cheese.

● **Tolerated with:** Fish and seafood in sauce, roast vegetables or stews, peppers, noodles, soups, sauces, smoked food, cold meats, omelettes, salads (substituting the vinegar for lemon), pickled meat, foie gras, cream cheese and spicy food.

● **Forbidden with:** Cooked fish or seafood, pickled fish, pickles, fish or seafood mousse, asparagus, leeks and artichokes.

RESERVA AND GRAN RESERVA REDS UP TO 10 YEARS OLD.

● **Recommended with:** White and red meat, roast lamb, pork or beef, game, poultry, stews, rice dishes, pulses, mushrooms, cured cheese and blue cheese.

● **Tolerated with:** Fish and seafood in sauce, roast vegetables or stews, peppers, noodles, soups, sauces, smoked food, cold meats, omelettes, salads (substituting the vinegar for lemon), pickled meat, foie gras.

● **Forbidden with:** Cooked and raw fish or seafood, pickled fish, pickles, fish or seafood mousse, asparagus, leeks and artichokes, cream cheese and spicy food.

RESERVA OR GRAN RESERVAS REDS FROM 10 YEARS OLD (7 YEARS MINIMUM IN BOTTLE)

● **Tolerated with:** Stewed meat, rice dishes, roast legumes, blue cheese, fish and seafood in sauce, roast or cooked vegetables, peppers, Italian noodles, smoked food, soups, sauces, cold meats, chorizo, omelettes, salads (substituting the vinegar for lemon), pickled meat, foie gras.

● **Forbidden with:** Cooked and raw fish or seafood, pickled fish, pickles, fish or seafood mousse, asparagus, leeks and artichokes, cream cheese and spicy food.

WHITES AGED IN WOOD, FINOS, CAVAS AND CHAMPAGNES

● **Recommended with:** Fish and seafood in sauce, fish or seafood mousse, foie gras, soups, sauces, smoked food, cold meats, omelettes, pickled meat, roast vegetables or vegetable stews.

● **Tolerated with:** Cooked and raw fish or seafood, pickled fish and meat, pickles, asparagus, leeks, rice dishes, bean stews, blue cheese, noodles, salads (substituting the vinegar for lemon), mushrooms, game, white and red meat, poultry, roast lamb, pork or beef, peppers and chorizo.

● **Forbidden with:** Artichokes.

YOUNG AND FRUITY WHITES

● **Recommended with:** Raw fish or seafood, cooked or in a sauce, fish or seafood mousse, smoked food, soup, sauces and cream cheese.

● **Tolerated with:** Foie gras, white meat, poultry, cooked or roasted vegetable, leeks, asparagus, rice dishes, pickled fish, salads dressed with lemon, mushrooms, omelettes.

● **Forbidden with:** Artichokes, peppers, chorizo, cold meats, cured cheese, game, blue cheese, red meat, roast lamb, pork or beef, pickles, pickled meat, beef stews, and bean stews.

ROSÉS AND CLARETS

● **Recommended with:** White meat, roast vegetables, noodles, rice dishes, mushrooms, soups, sauces, cold meats, poultry, omelettes, peppers.

● **Tolerated with:** Seafood and fish cooked and in sauce, fish or seafood mousse, red meat, game, roast lamb, pork or beef, meat stews, pickles, pickled fish and meat, chorizo, blue cheese, cooked vegetables, bean stews, salads dressed in lemon, foie gras, cream cheese, cured cheese, spicy and hot food, leeks and asparagus.

● **Forbidden with:** Artichokes.

SPECIAL COMBINATIONS

The most difficult products to combine due to spices, curing and smoking, vinaigrettes, hot food and metallic type tastes such as artichokes and asparagus go very well with heavily oxidized and aged wines (Generosos and Amontillados) due to their high alcohol content and the lingering tastes on the palate which neutralises any trace of these foods.

Blue cheeses such as those from Asturias and Cantabria (Cabrales) as well as Roquefort, with their strong, mouldy and spicy taste go very well with the smooth and slightly sweet Olorosos which soothe the palate.

AT THE RESTAURANT

This is probably the place where the ceremony of the serving of wine is best kept and represented, where the sommelier is the expert consultant and advisor.
At least in theory, because not all restaurants have the same level and their approach to wine can be quite inconsistent. However, in recent years many restaurants have improved their wine lists considerably and many wine bars and taverns have emerged.

Wine experts are increasingly necessary, somebody reliable to assist the client in choosing the wine which goes best with the food ordered, and without the price going through the roof, in addition to which the panorama of wines and origins is becoming increasingly more intricate.

WHAT THE CLIENT SHOULD DEMAND FROM THE SOMMELIER

* **A wide range of knowledge.** As a professional on wines, the sommelier should have a wide knowledge on his speciality and be prepared to answer the clients' questions about the characteristics of the different wines that make up the wine list and their appropriateness to accompany this or that dish.

* **Advice and a bit of psychology.** The sommelier will try to get to know the tastes of the diner and his knowledge of wines in a few seconds, and also take in the situation at the table: the confidence and trust of the customer, who the leader of the group is if there are several guests and what social pretences are hidden behind the ordering of a bottle (a business or social event, creating a pleasant atmosphere on a romantic date, etc.). You as the customer will help him in his task if you give the appropriate clues.

* **Impeccable service.** This process starts with the presentation of the bottle, intact, to the customer (always to the guest who selected the wine) for him to give his consent and check if the label corresponds to the wine and vintage ordered. The sommelier then removes the top of the capsule and uncorks the bottle, and has the guest taste the wine before serving it.

* **That the wine is in perfect condition**. The client should tell the sommelier about any problem with the wine: a defective cork which has contaminated the wine or any alteration that has modified its characteristics (vinegary, oxidised, etc), in which case the bottle must be changed, as well as any other factor which does not allow the wine to be enjoyed: e.g. the serving temperature is not correct, the glasses are not appropriate…

* **Any accessory needed for the wine.** For example, a decanter if it is an old wine or if it needs special breathing, a wine bucket in the case of cavas, whites, rosés and even reds in summer for the wine to remain at the ideal temperature, etc.

WINE AND HEALTH

Wine is not only a pleasure on our senses; it is also medicinal. Besides the traditional consumption of wine for its stimulant and calming properties, many studies in recent years speak about the beneficial effects of wine when drunk in moderation.

RESVERATROL AND THE 'FRENCH PARADOX'

It has been demonstrated that the beneficial effects of wine are due to compounds which are found in the seeds and the skin of the grapes, such as quercetin – a colorant in the fruit - flavones, tannins and polyphenols (mainly resveratrol).
Resveratrol, a substance produced by the grape to protect it against some common infections such as botrytis, has been shown to be an antioxidant and therefore it offers protection against certain diseases.

In recent years research has demonstrated that wine drunk in moderation (WHO recommends 300 to 400ml/day for men and 200ml to 300ml for women) has a preventative or moderating effect on certain illnesses. This has been demonstrated by the study called 'French Paradox', which shows a direct relationship between longevity and habitual wine consumption in one of the countries with the highest consumption of wine in the world and with a diet very rich in fats.

WHAT SHOULD BE KNOWN ABOUT ALCOHOL

* Its influence on the body depends on a multitude of factors, personal, social and psychological.

* Weight, physical constitution and even race determine the degree of tolerance and assimilation, especially in the case of women and native Africans who metabolize alcohol slower.

* A moderate consumption of wine is not fattening. A glass of red wine has the same calories as a sugar free yoghurt (between 70 to 100 calories).

* It helps with the digestion of certain foods and has a germicidal and antiseptic effect being used throughout history to disinfect wounds, a remedy against diphtheria, bronchitis and even as an anaesthetic.

* Regular consumption of more than the recommended half a bottle can cause gastrointestinal diseases, immunodeficiency, difficulties in assimilating vitamins, addiction (alcoholism), significant increase risk of cancer – especially liver cancer - and serious disorders of the central nervous system.

* A look at the statistical curve on the effects of alcohol yields surprising results in the shape of a 'U'. People who abstain and heavy drinkers have the same level of risk. The beneficial 400ml is found at the bottom of the 'U'. This demonstrates that moderate consumption of wine is the most beneficial.

THE VIRTUES OF TWO GLASSES A DAY (UP TO 40 CL)

Cardiovascular effects:
* Reduces the risk of heart attacks.
* Prevents clots forming.
* Reduces the risk of arteriosclerosis.

Anticancerogenic effects:
* The resveratrol content can prevent or reduce the probability of developing different cancers (skin, colon, prostate).

Metabolic effects:
* Dry and distilled wines improve glucose tolerance in diabetics.

Anti-infection effects:
* It is a germicide, disinfectant and antiseptic used for wounds.
* Reduces the risk of tooth decay.

Nutritional effects:
* Rich in iron, and sodium and potassium ions. Compatible with diets (a glass of white wine = 70kcal).

Neuropsychiatric effects:
* Improves general well being.
* Reduces inhibitions.
* Reduces stress.
* Reduces depression.
* Favours socialisation
* Improves cognitive functions.
* Reduces the probability of Alzheimer's disease and senile dementia.
* Analgesic effect.

YESTERYEAR AND TODAY

A THOUSAND YEARS OF SPANISH WINE

Let us review an eventful millennium in the history of Spanish wines to better understand present-day winemaking.

THE 11TH CENTURY. THE REBIRTH OF 'CHRISTIAN' VINEYARDS.

The reconstitution of Spanish vineyards in territories recaptured from the Arabs. Ordered by the feudal lords and the clergy, the tenant farmers started to occupy the lands of the Duero by means of the 'pressure' system, a Roman principle of repopulating conquered regions which were unclaimed. The lands were divided up among small land owners (mainly from Cantabria, the Basque Country and Galicia) who did not obtain ownership until the tilling of the soil and for this reason vineyards became one of the most important crops. The Catalonian clergy brought about amazing growth in remote regions such as Conca de Barberà (monastery of Poblet) and Priorat (monastery of Scala Dei), as did the Knights Templar in the areas under their control.

In 1002 the words Rioixia or Riojia appeared for the first time in the Charter of Miranda del Ebro to identify an area of present day Rioja and in 1099, Alfonso VI, established one of the first charters (privileges to promote certain crops and vineyards in general) in Miranda del Ebro, Laguardia and Navarrete.

12ᵀᴴ CENTURY. MONASTIC WINE

The monastic orders and in particular, the order of San Benito, consolidated the cultivation of vines in Spain especially along the Camino de Santiago. The first monastic vineyards were established in the remotest and highest regions of Castilla. In Pla de Bages and in the plains of Vic in the province of Barcelona the first significant terraced vineyards were established.

In 1158 the monk Raymond de Citeaux from Burgundy visited the Spanish Cistercian monasteries and promoted the cultivation of vines. He is credited with bringing a grape variety from Burgundy which with the passing of time was to become the *Tempranillo*.

13ᵀᴴ CENTURY. THE FIRST MENTION OF 'RIOJA'

The first mention of Rioja in reference to wines from the area between the rivers Oja and Najerilla. The increase in population and an improvement in cultivation methods encroached on the forests and uninhabited lands. Irrigation began to be used in the lands around the urban areas to cultivate grapes. The first local protectionist measures regarding local wine opposing grapes and wines from other municipalities were brought in and each Town council requested a royal grant for this privilege.

In 1264 the dividing up of the lands around Jerez which were recaptured from the Arabs was started. Each one of the Knights in charge of protecting the town of Jerez de la Frontera was awarded a little more than two hectares of the vineyards which were not pulled out by the Arabs.

14ᵀᴴ CENTURY. THE FIRST MEASURES OF PROTECTIONISM

Protectionist measures became widespread. In 1323, due to the great increase in the number of vineyards in Vallodolid, the city managed to get permission from King Alfonso XI to prohibit the entry of foreign wines. The same happened in Segovia and Peñafiel. King Sancho also restricted the entry of wines from Navarra into Castilla.

In 1532, and after having had several names, the Rioja region finally received the name of Rioxa.

Other important events of this century were the prohibition of Roman wines entering Castilla by King Sancho, the decline of viticulture due to epidemics, and trading in wine was established for the first time between Jerez and England. The Franciscan monk Eiximenis wrote the book '*Lo Terç del Crestià*' in which he described the art of moderation and the dangers of inebriation. Strangely enough he recommended drinking three or four glasses of wine at lunch and at dinner.

15ᵀᴴ CENTURY. JEREZ CROSSES BORDERS

Wine from Navarra reached its peak. The vineyards situated around Olite flourished thanks to the fact that the Prince of Viana resided in this area. Ribera de Tudela became the main wine-producing area in this region as it was an important producer of quality wines. *Verjus* (Agraz wine) became a highly prized speciality.

In 1483 the statutes of the *Gremio de las Pasas y la Vendimia de Jerez* guils were established, the first of its kind for a specific territory.

Jerez started to export. In the second half of the century a significant amount of wine from Jerez was exported to England and stored in Bristol. Fortified Jerez wine was aged for the first time in Jerez itself.

Wines that were enjoyed during this century were the above-mentioned Verjus, a white wine from Madrigal de las Altas Torres and a Generoso from Tierra de Medina. The growing of

'Vigrec' or *Malvasia* stock and *Moscatel* also became more widely spread along the whole Mediterranean coastline. The Catalonian entrepreneur Roger de Flor introduced the first *Malvasia* vines.

16TH CENTURY. THE SPLENDOUR OF GENEROSO WINES

Spanish wines were exported. The English discovered the first Spanish red wines on the Mediterranean coastline ('tent' or red from Alicante) as well as Sack (from the Spanish word 'sacar' which means to take out) from Jerez, the Canary Islands and Málaga.

Generoso wines were at their peak: the sweet toasted wine from Rivadavia, the white Generoso from Albillo de San Martín de Valdeiglesias and the Moscatels from Fuencarral and Hortaleza, these last two wines becoming very popular in 1561 when the Court moved to Madrid. The wines from Tierra de Medina (the present day Generoso) reached their zenith. The region of Alicante was mentioned for the first time and its wine was exported to Europe. The first prestigious red wine from Castilla was from Toro. In 1502 the Catholic Monarchs sanctioned by Royal Decree the setting up of the Fraternity of Winemakers of Málaga, with the aim of protecting the interests of winemakers and the cultivation of vines.

17TH CENTURY. THE PEAK OF 'CANARY SACK'

The prestige of Canary Sack outshone all other Spanish wines. In 1665 the English company called 'Compania de Canarias' was set up in Tenerife to control its monopoly. More highlights of this century: the trade of quality aged wines from Tierra de Medina (Añejos and Trasañejos); the wines from Cartuja de Porta Coeli became famous, an exquisite white sold by the traders from Valencia and the arrival of the first Dutch traders in Jerez to by buy wine to be distilled (called 'Holandas'); Charles I of England contributed to the trade of Jerez as it was his favourite wine. In this period, the largest part of the production was sold to England and Northern Europe through the first export offices situated temporarily in the port of Cádiz. Rivero, the first bodega in Jerez , was established in 1653 and is still functioning today.

18TH CENTURY. THE FIRST QUALITY WINES FROM JEREZ

The first English, Irish and French traders to set themselves up in Jerez were Osborne, Terry, Haurie, Gordon, Pemartín, Domecq, Lacoste and Harkon. The first permits were issued to allow the storing of wine at the place of origin and not only at the destination with the construction of the first high-roofed, cool, ventilated bodegas in Jerez. In 1733 the winemakers' guild of Jerez was established to control the production and trade of wine.

New wines emerged: mountain wine or sweet wine from the best vineyards from the mountains of Málaga. The first attempts at making 'Bordeaux-style' quality wines in Rioja by the priest Quintano. Catalonian wine flourished thanks to its naval fleet and to industry (cork, glass and barrel manufacturing). The first exports of wine from Rioja to America left from the port of Santander. The reds from Benicarlo ('Carlón') which were exported to Bordeaux to be mixed with the clarets from Gironde, thrived. These reds from Bajo Maestrazgo were sold by foreign traders such as Vagué, White, D´Elliseche and Trenor.

19TH CENTURY. THE MODERN ERA OF TABLE WINES

A serious crisis in Spanish wine during the first third of the century as a consequence of the Napoleonic war and the inactivity of the Royal Court. The winemakers guild is dissolved in 1834.

With the confiscation of Mendizábal (1850) new vineyards such as Finca de Lecanda in Valbuena de Duero were established. In 1852 the odium plague hit France, the same plague which would eventually destroy the *Malvasia* vineyards in Tenerife.

The first 'fine wines' were produced in Rioja according to the Bordeaux method at the *Bodega del Duque de la Victoria* owned by General Espartero.In 1860 the Marques de Riscal bodega was built. This was the first modern bodega built on the same lines as the Châteaux from Bordeaux. The first wines from Rioja were bottled here and the establishing of this bodega coincided with the settling of the first French traders in Rioja who were fleeing from odium. Howver, the first wine to be bottled in Spain was Tío Pepe (1850) of González Byass. In the second half of this century a large number of industrial-style bodegas were established: Cvne, López de Heredia, Faustino, Marqués de Murrieta, Franco Españolas, etc.

In 1876 the first outbreak of phylloxera was discovered on the Moclinejo estate in Málaga, although the disease did not spread through Spain until the eighteen-nineties .
1882 marked the first modern era of the splendour of Spanish wines, and by 1890 record quantities were being exported: 11 million hectolitres per year (90 % was exported to France as their vineyards had been destroyed by phylloxera). Vineyards extended over the largest area ever, covering 1,800,000 hectares. Vineyards in Rioja also reached their peak, covering the largest area ever: 62,000 hectares.

In 1872 the production of Cava was started and this changed the make-up of the 355, 000 hectares of vineyards in Cataluña, which until then had almost exclusively been under low quality red grape. The Catalonian market continued imitating: Cava was made in the Champagne style and the wholesalers at the port of Tarragona produced substitutes for Port, Jerez, and Málaga. Valdepeñas wine boomed in Madrid. In 1857 the consumption of this wine reached 115 litres per habitant per year .

20TH CENTURY. THE BIRTH OF THE DESIGNATIONS OF ORIGIN

In 1915 the red Vega Sicilia was born. During the first third of the century the decimated Spanish vineyards were reconstructed, the majority of the oenological areas were created and they extended to more profitable regions such as La Mancha and Extremadura. In 1932 the Wine Statutes were drawn up, the first oenological law in Spain. The first Regulatory Councils for the Designation of Origin such as Jerez and Rioja were constituted. The vineyards in Castilla-León and Cataluña as well as the number of individual and family winemakers decreased and resulted in the setting up of cooperatives. Others became suppliers to the industrial bodegas (growers and wholesalers).

There was a wine crisis from 1930 to 1949, and disastrous harvests from 1945 to 1949 resulting in the lowest yields in history: 10hl/hectare. The export of bulk wine made a comeback in the period from 1950 to 1979 giving an impetus to red wines (*Garnacha*, *Tintorera* and *Bobal*) as well as to quality wines (*Monastrell* and *Garnacha Tinta*) from Utiel-Requena, Manchuela, Almansa, Jumilla and Méntrida to be blended with white wines from La Mancha. Wine was exported to Africa and to the Soviet Union with the aid of huge subsidies from the Franco regime. In 1980 the technical and oenological renewal of the Spanish bodegas began as well as the up-rooting of 50% of the vineyards in La Mancha. The yields per hectare improved, there was more interest in quality wines, there was a reduction in bulk wine and an increase in bottled wine.

The nineties were the decade of quality. The vineyards, which had reached 1,670,000 hectares in 1979, were reduced to 1,179,000 hectares in 1997. There was a slow increase in the consumption of quality wines and the sales of common wine decreased considerably. In the second half of this decade Vinos de Pago made their appearance and there was a considerable improvement in the planting of low-yield vineyards. 'Highly Expressive' wines also came onto the scene. In these wines the influence of the terroir was more important than the winemaking techniques.

THE QUALITY PYRAMID OF SPANISH WINE

How are the different wine quality standards set out in Spain? Does this categorisation always correspond to true quality? Let us try to shed some light on the different qualitative levels that the consumer can find on the bottle and the innovations in the new Wine Law on this matter.

The new Wine Law has brought in a significant new qualitative classification of Spanish wine which the existing designations fall under and new categories have been created. However, what is really important is that it establishes the superimposition of levels; that is, the same plot of vineyards can produce grapes to make wines for only one or various levels of protection "provided that the grapes used and the wine produced comply with the established requisites for the level or the levels chosen, including the maximum yields assigned to the level per hectare".

Perhaps the most important aspect of the Law is that it considers wine as a foodstuff and not as an alcoholic drink subjected to the limitations of 'consumer warnings'. Another advantage is that it puts an end to the lobby of the DO's (the regions that in theory produce the best wines). From now on the quality of the harvest of each DO will not be determined by the interested parties who have always stated that all vintages were 'good', but by an external company who will be responsible for certification.

The name ***Vino de la Tierra de España*** will become a brand name which will take advantage of the heritage of the name of a country historically linked to wine and, therefore, with a certain responsibility for the image.

The law prohibits the blending of wines from different origins and bodegas. In addition, only grapes can be mixed but not musts or wines. In this respect, the Law is ahead of European regulation.

THE CATEGORIES OF THE NEW WINE LAW

TABLE WINES

This is the lowest rung of the ladder within the established categories. Wines, above all red wines, produced from the mixing (or not) of grapes from above all Mancha, Utiel-Requena or Extremadura have traditionally taken refuge under the umbrella of table wines. However, recently it has also been the banner for creative producers who have made wines in areas outside the DOs or any other recognized region (the pioneers of this were the Italians) but whose quality could be the same or better than many DO wines. The great innovation of the new Law in this category is the possibility of table wines mentioning a geographical location. In this way, two categories have been established in this section:

Table wine with a geographical indication. "For those who must specify the geographical location, a geographical area, the grape varieties and the types of wines used". Previously it was prohibited to mention the grape variety so as not to compete with other better quality wines.

Vino de la Tierra. Besides the previous requisites, a minimum alcohol content has been laid down and the physical-chemical and organoleptic characteristics of the wines used. This category remains more or less as it was: with a viticultural and oenological regulation not as strict as a DO. The equivalent of *Vinos de la Tierra* in France are *Vins du Pays* and in Italy IGT (*Indicazione Geografica Tipica*).

145

COMMENTS

The most important factor is the improved identification of wine, which must now indicate the vintage, the alcohol content and the details of ageing. This is definitely an improvement.

QUALITY WINE PRODUCED IN A SPECIFIC AREA

This is the second largest group laid out within the framework of the new Law and indicates superior level of quality over the previous ones. At the same time, it is divided into different levels of quality. They are reviewed in ascending order.

Table wine with a geographical location. This is a new category for Spanish wines. They are wines made in a specific region, using grapes from this region and whose quality, reputation or characteristics "are due to the geographical environment, human factor or both, regarding the production of the grape, the making of the wine or its ageing". They are identified on the label by 'Vino de calidad de...' (Quality wines from...) followed by the name of the place where they are produced.

Wines with *Denominación de Origen*. The concept is no different to the present *Denominaciones de Origen*. Wines from a delimited area of production and made within the parameters of quality and definition. Each DO is governed by a Regulatory Council, which is responsible for imposing the established rules in a Regulation which regulates aspects such as the authorised varieties, the yield per hectare, the winemaking methods, ageing, etc. If the status of *Vino de la Tierra* was the stage before achieving DO status, the new Law states that to accede to a DO, the production area must have been recognised previously (at least five years previously) to be able to produce quality wines with a geographical location.

COMMENTS

The innovation that the quality of the DOs could be certified by a specialist company without interests in the region is a great step forward, even though the mentioned certification company is appointed by the Councils themselves. It is understood that the morality of this company is in theory above the pressure that could be exerted on it by the Regulatory Council. Therefore, although the procedure can be improved, we have advanced.

Wines with *Denominacion de Origen Calificada*. (DOC) This is a superior level within the DO's of which there are already two examples in our country: Rioja and Priorat. The following is included among the requisites needed to achieve this status: that they have been recognized as a DO for ten years, that the products used be sold bottled at bodegas located within the area of production, or that there is an appropriate qualitative system by their control council.

COMMENTS

This category that seems to indicate a region of better quality wines is absurd. All the sections that figure in it are those that have always distinguished the DO's with the difference being that in the 'Qualified' all these sections are 'compulsory' (?). Other conditions needed for a DOC certification is having been a DO for at least 10 years and that DOC wines cannot be sold in bulk.

Vinos de Pago. This is one of the great innovations of the Law and also one of its most controversial points. It is a wine from a specific vineyard taking into account that the bodega and the bottling plant must be on the premises or on the boundary of the said premises. There are exceptional cases in which the competent Authority may grant permission for the winemaking, ageing and bottling installations to be located outside the vineyard but within the municipal boundaries or neighbouring area. If the entire vineyard is found within the area of a DOC, it will be called a *Vino de Pago Calificado*.

COMMENTS

The word *viña* (vineyard) of *Vino de Pago* has a long been used in a great number of Spanish brand names and was first used towards the end of the 19th century. But the categorising of *Vino de Pago*, although it is at the tip of the pyramid, does not guarantee a better quality than the rest of the categories, as the Law does not establish the denomination by means of a rigorous climatic and soil profile study of the property to establish the quality of the site, but simply by the fact of defining the wine as coming exclusively from this territory.

INDICATIONS RELATIVE TO THE CHARACTERISTICS OF THE WINES

• Article 3 sets out the following indications relative to the categories of ageing:

Noble. Wines aged for a minimum of 18 months in an oak container with a maximum capacity of 600 litres or in bottle.

Añejo. Wines aged for a minimum of 24 months in the same containers as mentioned above.

Viejo. Wines aged for a minimum of 36 months in oxidative maturation (thermal, light and oxygen).

This categorization is independent of the minimum periods already applied in the DO's (Crianza, Reserva, Gran Reserva), pointing out that the oak container has a maximum capacity of 330 litres.

In the section '**Gran Reserva**', the minimum period has been reduced to 18 months instead of 24.

COMMENTS

This typical Spanish idolizing of the ageing of wines still exists at a legislative level as if it were a factor of quality. All this terminology 'noble', 'añejo' or 'viejo' belong to a past that will not return as they follow the tradition of storing wines to 'reserve' them for a special occasion in the future. Age was considered something to boast about when in fact the wine in the wooden containers improved its qualitative life. In any case, it can only be seen in Generoso wines that have been aged by oxidation as the first element (the varietal and fruit value) is considerably reduced by the addition of alcohol prior to ageing. This can be understood in the evaluation of the age of a bottle with its specific vintage where the influence of external factors or oxidants is much less, or as a Spanish differentiation.

However, no other country has legislated the ageing of wines and only the Italian region of Brunello de Montalcino clings to this tradition and at the moment also uses minimum ageing. One must bear in mind that prolonged ageing introduces aromas and flavours produced by an external agent (the wood) and not by the internal and natural factors of the soil and variety.

QUALITY/PRICE RATIO AVAILABLE IN THE MARKET NOWADAYS

We have set up a pyramid of prices and quality which is related to what the consumer can find on the market and that is based on the wine tasting and the reviews in this Guide.

1. 90-100 points and more than € 18. Some prices could be as much as the € 300 a Pingus could cost, although the average is between € 30 and 120. The best wines from Spain are included. A mixed bag in which we can find: the best wines of the DOC's (Rioja, Priorat) and some DO's (mainly Ribera del Duero, Jerez, Rías Baixas, Toro, Jumilla, Penedès, Navarra, Somontano.) and some table wines (Leda, Mauro, Emeritus). In this last section there are quite a lot of labels that are future *Vinos de Pago* candidates.

2. 80-90 points and from € 6 to 30. The majority of the wines with DO, and some table wines and Vinos de la Tierra. The quality/price ratio is doubtful in those that cost more than € 18, unless they offer an original expression and characteristic of a specific soil (these could also be Vinos de Pago candidates). Excellent quality/price ratio for those around € 6 and are in the 80-85 points range and for those that cost € 12 between 85 and 90 points.

3. Between 75 and 80 points and from € 3 to € 12. Pleasant and serious wines. The most modest of the prestigious DO's, the average of certain denominations that have not got off the ground, a large part of the wines called *Vinos de la Tierra* and some table wines.

4. Below 75 points and less than € 5. The worst of the Spanish DO's, part of the *Vinos de la Tierra* and the bulk of the *Vinos de la Mesa* wines.

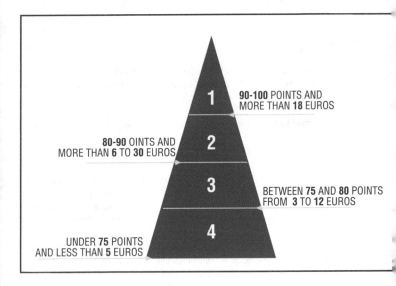

OTHER CATEGORIES OF WINE ONE SHOULD KNOW

They have no legal status on the label, but they are designations that are increasingly being and wine advocates:

A varietal wine.
In theory it is a wine that has been made from a single grape variety, although the law only demands a minimum of 80% to be able use it on the label. The varietal wines, promoted from the New World (although the pioneers were wines from Alsace), are still very fashionable and even Europe is committing itself to them. They have the advantage that, commercially, they are easily identifiable and the consumer has some idea of their style and characteristics. The most successful to date on the international market have been *Cabernet Sauvignon* and *Merlot* in reds and *Chardonnay* and *Sauvignon Blanc* in whites, but now there is a varied selection: *Pinot Noir, Syrah, Garnacha...*

Garage wine.
This term was first used in France to define a group of 'rebel' wines, made from very small productions and excellent quality and even the selection of the grape is taken to the extreme

and moreover they use any practice or technology to make them more expressive, potent or powerful. The French archetype of this is Valandraud from Bordeaux, where the term originated, as the cellar in which the wine was made was so small that it seemed to be the size of a garage. Without a doubt, Pingus (Ribera del Duero) in Spain, has taken full advantage of this concept. In California, these wines are well represented and are usually called *boutique* wines or culture wines.

'Alta Expresión' wine (highly expressive).

Although this term has created controversy, it is quite widely used. It came about to designate quality red wines from Rioja to set apart a new style from the traditional reserve wines. They are committed to the fruit and the expression of the terroir, more structure and potency, working with new wood (often French) and to shortening ageing, and therefore they are sold as reserves or with generic labels. Its use has extended to wines which share these characteristics in other winemaking regions in Spain.

2005 ANNEX

THE SPANISH BODEGA 100 YEARS AGO AND TODAY

The new millennium has left its mark on the majority of the Spanish bodegas. It is rare to find a bodega that has not been modernised, and they are now aseptic and use stainless steel as well as innovative designs. But what were these bodegas like a century ago? Let us see just how much Spanish bodegas have changed in a hundred years.

Quality wines have not changed much in the last hundred years. However, a hundred years ago there was a vast difference between fine wines and wines for general consumption.

Spanish cooperativism handled huge volumes of wine in not very hygienic conditions. The wine flowed in open channels, the rackings were done manually and cement and clay storage tanks were not very hygienic. The excess sulphur – used to stop the wine from rotting- eventually ended up in the wine. The classic 'coop smell' – a mixture of cement and mould - was produced by the combination of the dioxide with the wine.

The **fermentation** was carried out without control and at high temperatures, as the fruity character was not considered important and no effort was made to conserve it. In addition, they wanted premature oxidation to give the wines a certain maturity. The aim was to sell in bulk. The bodegas were businesses that transformed grapes into wine, and very little thought went into the quality of the end-product or the marketing the wine.

The **bottling** of table wine in Spain only started formally at the beginning of the seventies. The Government promoted the building of bottling plants on a regional level for hygienic reasons and to avoid fraud in the retail sector as until then wine had been sold in bulk. The result was a more hygienic wine which was flatter and with less character and taste.

The setting up of **cooperative plants** in Castilla-La Mancha in the fifties and seventies meant the construction of huge cement deposits and the use of continuous presses. Their priority was to give colour to the wine, either with Tintorera grapes that are very rich in anthocyanins or with double pulps – wines macerated with double the amount of pressed skins. And to top it all, this was done to produce red wines in a country where 85% of the grapes were whit.

THE BARREL MAKERS were employed to repair the barrels rather than to make them, resulting in the barrels being used for 20 or 30 years. During the last phases of the maturation there was a notable increase in the volatile acidity as they did not use sulphur as an antiseptic. It should be remembered that the practice of producing high alcohol content Generoso wines, so entrenched in Spain, was not consistent with the use of sulphur.

Oenologists as we understand the term did not arrive on the scene until practically the beginning of the eighties. Instead of oenologists, head winemakers who had basic notions of oenology acquired from the 'Escuela de Capataces de Requena' and the 'Escuela de la Vid in Madrid' were employed . Many of them were in charge of no less than ten bodegas whose only purpose was to prevent the wine from rotting. They were the 'wine doctors', and incidentally, were badly paid, as the wine producer believed that the wine made itself.

	IN THE PAST	NOW
HARVESTING	The grapes were transported in baskets or wooden crates to the mouths of the oak vats where they fermented in their skins. The harvesting was often associated with local festivals, to harvest festivals or to local folklore. And of course no batch was rejected unless it was obviously not suitable for the wine.	Harvesting is one of the most important moments for the wine, based on caring for the vine during the whole year, and taking into account the maximum amount of parameters to determine the ideal ripeness of the grape. Recently polyphenolic ripeness – of the components of the skin - is valued more than the acid/sugar ratio. The grape is selected in the vineyard itself and it is taken to the cellar as quickly as possible.
FERMENTATION	This took place in the oak vats or large earthenware jars where the wine fermented on its lees. The vats remained permanently open or closed; in the first case it was to facilitate the formation of the cap and thus avoid contact with the air. During fermentation the must was stirred once or twice a day. In regions where fine wines were produced, the wine fermented in a place away from the rest of the cellar's installations.	The stainless steel tanks and the temperature control are handled with meticulous care, besides attempts that are being made to devise a thousand and one ways to break the cap correctly and achieve more involvement of the skins and a better extraction of their components. Recently oak vats for fermentation are making a comeback, as it is felt that micro-oxygenation from the wood is beneficial and there are even those who praise the benefits of cement – we must not forget that the great Pétrus still ferment its wines in this material.
PRESERVING THE WINE	They used different capacity pine or oak casks from Jerez to Cataluña. In Castilla they used large underground oak vats to protect the wines from temperature changes and sunlight. In La Mancha they used baked earthenware jars as the region is very rich in clays – sometimes covered in a layer of pitch. In the 1920s they started using reinforced cement tanks, often lined out with glass tiles. They were placed against the walls and had a much larger capacity and conserved the wine much better.	Stainless steel is the most common material used for the conservation of wine because of its hygienic properties. However, many bodegas that still have their cement tanks find this material perfectly suitable for this purpose. Some companies use their wooden vats for this or use wood in general to harmonise the wines before they go to the barrel or once the maturation has been completed. The high cost of maintenance is the main problem with wood.
MATURATION	It must be made clear that maturation was an attribute of fine wines, as well as an indispensable part of Generosos and some Rancios. The wine was decanted into barrels after the first filtration and clarification and was left there for as long as possible until it was sold. It was not so much a period of maturation, as a period of preserving the wine until it was sold. In this sense, it is not strange that in days gone by bodegas had a certain affinity with dust and spiders' webs.	Maturation has become universal and democratic and all self respecting winemakers aspire to place a wine of this type on the market. These days the age of the barrels is closely monitored – old wood does not give off as many tannins and if it is not in perfect condition, it can give unpleasant touches of mould and dampness - and there is an absolute preference for new wood, and the amount of time in it – the exact time necessary for each type of wine. French oak is more popular than American or other exotic oaks from Hungary or Russia.

WINE ON THE INTERNET

We have selected the best web pages on Spanish and foreign wines for the 'web addicts' and for those who are comfortable on the web.

SPANISH WEBSITES

STAYING UP TO DATE

www.elvino.paginasamarillas.es
Get to know about wines: reports, the Peñin Guide, the Proensa Guide and the 300 best wines in the online magazine *Vino and Gastronomia*; online wine tasting courses, links and shopping.

www.elmundovino.elmundo.es
The web page of the newspaper *El Mundo*, designed for wine lovers who would like to know more: national and foreign news, wine tasting and lively chats, probably the best in Spain.

www.vinum.info/es
The online magazine of *Vinum* in Spanish and edited by Carlos Delgado´s wine critic team: reports, news, tastings and answers to wine amateurs' questions.

www.vinosnet.com
A little of everything: tasting, visits to bodegas and lots of news on the wine making world.

www.verema.com
A dynamic site calling themselves 'the virtual community on wines': new wines proposed by the amateur and thousands of opinions on their forum.

www.uec.es
The Spanish Union of Tasters offer course to beginners and advanced tasters, wine tasting and other products, and organised trips.

www.todovino.com
News, shopping (the wine club of the *ABC* newspaper), reviews of foreign news, articles and tasting by famous experts; also the Todovino Guide with the best wines of the year.

www.vinealis.com
Directed at wine professionals, full of news reports on new aspects in the sector, also in print form.

www.sobremesa.es
The *Sobremesa* publication of the Vinoseleccion group, specialising in wines and gastronomy, but an electronic version: new wines, trips, opinion column, interviews and reports… (subscriptions).

IN DEPTH.

www.infoagro.com/viticultura/viticultura.asp
Directed at professional viticulturists: research, shows and a simple search engine for bodegas and DOs.

www.enoforum.com
This is a portal on oenology and dedicated to the wine professional: interviews, news, events and a long list of sections.

www.enologo.com
The oenology web page of the Federación Española de Asociaciones de Enólogos (Spanish Federation of the Oenological Associations): for the professional looking for research carried out, the latest congresses or the Wine Law.

www.percepnet.com
A web page on the science of the senses: information on conferences, research or to download aroma wheels.

www.mapya.es/es/alimentación/alimentacion.htm
The Ministry of Agriculture where one can download statistical reports of grape varieties per region, lists of vintages or the Wine Law.

www.thewineacademy.com
International studies dedicated to the wine from the city of Marbella: courses, monographs, gourmet dinners and trips; in charge of the International Symposium on wine held in June.

www.culturadelvino.org
The foundation for Wine Culture's web page is still under construction, where they will soon have their legendary wine tasting and events dedicated to the promotion of wine as a cultural heritage.

www.fev.es
Statistics, figures, conferences and events organized by the Wine Federation, the official body of the sector. In short.

RESEARCH

http://biblioteca.unirioja.es/biblio/ser/sercdvino.html
A service of the Documentation of Wine of the University of Rioja: access to online magazines catalogues on vines and wines and other databases full of resources and links.

www.enologia.com
A search engine for oenology and viticulture sites, access to all the DO addresses, other wine pages, cellars, publications, associations, etc.; specialized chat and forums.

www.teledoc.urv.es/enovit/
To access and search for all types of magazines on oenology and viticiulture. The web site for the Oenology faculty of the University of Rovira i Virgil in Tarragona.

www.acenologia.com
A complete digital magazine on oenology: archive of articles, important search engine, downloading of technical books and the dates of the most interesting events.

SHOPPING ONLINE

www.reservaycata.com
Selection of wines by theme: the ten most sold wines, by grape variety, latest entries or according to food; also opinions and news on the viticultural regions.

www.vilaviniteca.es
The page of the enterprising Quim Vila from Barcelona with a complete selection of national wines (the latest and most original) and imported wines, dates for his wine tasting courses, profiles on bodegas and this month's favourites.

www.lavinia.es

Wines by season, seasonal offers and a club to receive offers for courses, Spanish and foreign wines; and a selection of wines and specialist gift articles.

www.pecadosoriginalesvinos.com

A specialist wine shop from Valladolid on wines from Ribera del Duero, specialising in internationally famous names.

www.santacecilia.es

The emblematic wine shop on wines from Madrid, now has an outlet on the web, with information on their wine list and tasting courses. Under construction.

www.vinoseleccion.com

The first Wine Club founded in Spain, with a selection of famous classic wines, inside and outside our borders; other delicacies available.

www.vivirelvino.com

The well known sommelier Jesus Flores has a magazine, guide, wine club, wine tasting school and now a web page where one can buy the wines he recommends in his tasting.

ESSENTIAL FAIRS

www.vinoble.com

The famous international exhibition held in spring dedicated to Noble wines, Fortified, Desert and Natural sweet wines organised in Jerez by the company Opus Wine.

www.gourmets.net

Page of the Gourmets Group, organised by the International Gourmets Club (Madrid in March), the Gourmet guide and the shopping club of wines and gourmet products (La Alacena).

www.salondelvino.com

National Wine exhibition held in November in Madrid, full of activities and prizes for the best wines.

www.alimentaria.com

The famous international food and drink show in Barcelona, with a large section on wines (Intervin), novelty forum and a must for professionals, held in March.

FOREIGN WEBSITES

TO BE UP TO DATE

www.winespectator.com

Digital version of the veteran American magazine, with wine and gastronomy, besides surveys, a manual on tasting, employment offers, etc.; a weekly online subscription is available with exclusive latest wine reviews.

www.foodandwine.com

Magazine on American gastronomy, wine and trips with a special section on wines, where to find articles, reports and an updated selection of wines.

www.decanter.com

The bible of English wines online, the contents of the magazine, news updates, wine tasting courses and a complete search engine on wines.

www.winereport.com
Page on Italian wines, with all the information on transalpine wines: maps, manual on how to taste them, list of wine producers, and the top wines according to the local guides.

www.wineint.com
The British magazine *Wine*, with interesting and straightforward reports on current issues and vineyards from anywhere in the world; contributions by the specialist on Spanish wines John Radford.

www.winepros.com
Page on Australian wines, with articles and reviews on wines, and information on the regions in Australia.

www.tizwine.com
Detailed information on wines in New Zealand: wine cellars, wines by price, links, trips and where to stay. A model page.

www.wineloverspage.com
Any doubts are solved on this page, aimed at wine lovers: multiple sections, reports and interactive forums. With Robin Carr's tasting notes.

www.wineanorak.com
Independent page, controversial and highly topical subjects; criticism of books and best buy guides on the English market.

www.argentinewines.com
Exclusive reports on Argentina, calendar of events and courses and wine reviews; organises wine tours to the most famous vineyards in the world.

www.chilevinos.com
Special offers on Chilean wines and the possibility of buying online; their magazine, international reports and news.

www.vitiviniccultura.cl
Aimed at wine professionals in Chile, with market figures and news from all over the world, events and services for winemakers.

www.ivp.pt
The Port and Duoro Wines Institute, their latest news, legislation and exhibitions. It also has an explanation on their wine types.

www.revistadevinhos.iol.pt
The best known publication on wines in Portugal, its contents and latest news items.

www.wineinstitute.org
The Californian voice on wine: figures, lists of cellars, the origin of each region, photos....

http://www.wosa.co.za/
The official South African web page on wines, where to find statistics, their history, regions, soils, recommended links and sites.

THE ONLINE GURUS

www.jancisrobinson.com
The famous English journalist gives her opinions and recommendations all over the world; with a special section for subscribers (purple pages) with access to The Oxford Companion dictionary. It also has the latest wine tastings and a questions and answer section.

www.erobertparker.com
The feared and admired American critic offers wines of the day, news on the sector, his books, food; on subscribing you receive The Wine Advocate, with a complete list of wine tasting per region.

www.ozclarke.com
The approachable and entertaining English taster sells his books on the internet and his recommendation for the month.

www.wineaccess.com/expert/tanzer
The author of the International Wine Cellar newsletter describes his latest tasting and gives his opinion on the changing market. A direct link to a selection of best buys (The Wine Analyst)

www.wine-pages.com
A best seller on the internet, directed by Tom Cannavan, reviews, reports, notes on the wine tasting of the rest of the British wine tasters, and even predictions about wines.

AUCTIONS

www.christies.com
The first wine auction house (1766), information on events, famous tastings and wine courses.

www.search.sothebys.com
In their wine section, a calendar of the latest bids for historical wines, in their London office as well as in New York.

www.winebid.com
From California; page on rarities and wines not found on the market. One can bid, buy or sell wines from any corner of the globe.

www.uvine.com
Wine market on the internet; aimed at investors looking for rare wines as well as consumers looking for specific vintages and competitive prices, no middlemen costs.

RESEARCH

www.bluewine.com
Wine and spirits portal, with an unending list of addresses ordered by subjects and the latest to join the web; also special reports on winegrowing regions.

www.vine2wine.com
More than 1,000 links to wines, classified by groups, with a brief explanation on each one and its origin.

IN DEPTH.

www.oiv.int
The International Office of the Vine and Wine: includes oenological standards, the latest reports of the commissions, geographical information and information on grapes. It is also a search engine for photographs of wine.

www.sommellerie-internationale.com/es/
The sommeliers site, with a notice board and advertisements for official competitions, database of professional associations and descriptions of wine growing regions.

www.wineserver.ucdavis.edu
The Oenology Faculty of the University of California, leader in viticulture research: one can consult the books in their library, scientific reports and download aroma wheels.

www.library.adelaide.edu.au/guide/agri/viti.html
The University of Adelaide's Faculty of Oenology: a powerful server with data bases and links on wine and viticulture.

www.history-of-wine.com
An interesting page in English on the history of wine, celebrations, why wine is popular, and wine geography by region, etc.

www.winebusiness.com
A business bulletin on wines and statistics for professionals of the wine industry, buying and selling of barrels, bulk prices; and also an employment section.

www.corkwatch.com
Everything about corks and their alternatives; newspaper reports, the problems of TCA (cork taint).

www.masters-of-wine.org
The prestigious diploma presented by the London Institute of Masters of Wine: information on education programme, group tasting and organized trips.

SHOPPING ONLINE

www.wineenthusiast.com
A shop window of accessories, cooling systems and other wine articles, with a direct link to the Enthusiast, an American wine magazine (www.winemag.com).

www.chateauonline.com
The large shop with wines from all over the world, especially French wines. *En primeur* sales, news and information on wine and special discounts.

www.wine-searcher.com
Look for any wine, who is selling it and at what price. This site guarantees to do it independently.

www.millesima.com
Catalogue of Grands Crus from Bordeaux and Burgundy; with the possibility of purchasing *en primeur* wine; good discounts and recommendations.

www.oddbins.com
The London wine and spirits chain, where one can buy any bottle in the world and at all prices.

www.bbr.com
British shop that specializes in fine wines and leading brands from all over the world, with recommendations and discounts on en primeur wines.

INTERNATIONAL FAIRS

www.vinexpo.com
The famous world exhibition of wines and spirits that is held in three cities: Chicago, Bordeaux and Tokyo.

www.vinitaly.com
The exhibition of Italian wines which is held on the first week of April in Verona.

www.messe-duesseldorf.de/prowein04/
The fair on European wines held in Düsseldorf during the first week in March.

www.mondialduvin.be/
Held in Brussels during the first week of May aimed at exploiting the potential of the Benelux market, third largest importer in the world.

www.oenologuesdefrance.fr/Vinalies_inter.htm
International competition of French wines alongside other countries, organized by the Union of French Oenologists since 1993. Held during the second week of February.

BODEGAS AND THE TASTING
OF THE WINES BY
DESIGNATION OF ORIGIN

DO ABONA

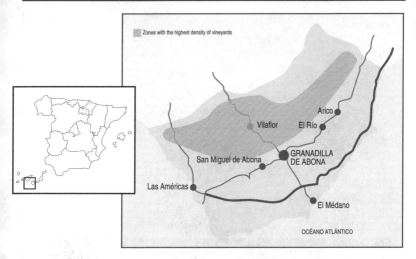

NEWS. Perhaps the most relevant aspect regarding the tasting of the wines of the 2003 vintage in this denomination is the large number of ecological wines which reached a score of 80 points. This kind of viticulture seems to be increasingly characterising a DO which has always prided itself on having a very low incidence of plagues and diseases, thanks mainly to the altitude factor. Hardly any fertilisers or herbicides are used in the majority of the vineyards, and the local winegrowers limit the use of sulphur dust to control powdery mildew.

In difficult years like 2003, the whites were saved, although not the reds, which, despite the obvious improvement in production, lack a certain degree of freshness and fruity expression, and in no case exceed 80 points. Once again, a sweet wine based on the outstanding Malvasía is the true winner, which should point out the route to be followed by the local winegrowers, perhaps ignoring the wishes of the administration which has during the past few years been leaning towards the reds and has in this regard been promoting the restructuring of the vineyards, especially in the higher regions, and the substitution of white varieties with red ones. The percentage of the latter has in almost 20 years risen from 5% to over 20% at present, with the hope of reaching 50% in the next 5 years.

Hectares of Vineyard	No. of Viticulturists	No. of Bodegas	2003 Harvest	2003 Production	Marketing
1,567	1,224	12	-	722,000 litres	100% Spain

LOCATION. In the southern area of the island of Tenerife, with vineyards which occupy the slopes of the Teide down to the coast. It covers the municipal districts of Adeje, Arona, Vilaflor, San Miguel de Abona, Granadilla de Abona, Arico and Fasnia.

CLIMATE. Mediterranean on the coastal belt, and gradually cools down inland as a result of the trade winds. Rainfall varies between 350 mm per year on the coast and

550 mm inland. In the highest region, Vilaflor, the vineyards do not benefit from these winds as they face slightly west. Nevertheless, the more than 200 Ha of this small plateau produce wines with an acidity of 8 g/l due to the altitude, but with an alcohol content of 13%, as this area of the island has the longest hours of sunshine.

SOIL. Distinction can be made between the sandy and calcareous soil inland and the more clayey, well drained soil of the higher regions, seeing as they are volcanic. The so-called 'Jable' soil is very typical, and is simply a very fine whitish volcanic sand, used by the local winegrower to cover the vineyards in order to retain humidity in the ground and to prevent weeds from growing. The vineyards are located at altitudes which range between 300 and 1,750 m (the better quality grapes are grown in the higher regions), which determines different grape harvesting dates in a period spanning the beginning of August up to October.

VARIETIES:
White: *Bastardo Blanco, Bermejuela, Forastera Blanca, Güal, Listán Blanca* (majority with 1,869 Ha), *Malvasía, Moscatel, Pedro Ximénez, Sabro, Torrontés, Verdello, Vijariego*. The white varieties make up the majority of the vineyards.
Red: *Bastardo Negro, Cabernet Sauvignon, Castellana Negra, Listán Negro, Listán Prieto, Malvasía Rosada, Moscatel Negro, Negramoll, Pinot Noir, Rubí Cabernet, Syrah, Tempranillo, Tintilla, Vijariego Negro*.

REGULATORY COUNCIL.
c/ Martín Rodríguez, 9. 38588 Porís de Abona - Arico. Tenerife.
Tel: 922 164 241. Fax: 922 164 135.
E-mail: crdoabona@terra.es

GENERAL CHARACTERISTICS OF THE WINES:

Whites	They have a pale yellow colour with a fruity and sometimes floral aroma and are dry, pleasant and well-balanced on the palate.
Rosés	They are characterised by their pink colour and are light and pleasant to drink, although less fragrant than those from Tacoronte.
Reds	Although less representative than the white wines, they have a deep cherry-red, with a red berries and bramble aroma and a somewhat light structure.

Sociedad Cooperativa CASMI

Carretera General del Sur, 5
38620 San Miguel de Abona (Tenerife)
☎: 922 700 300 - Fax: 922 700 301
bodega@casanmiguel.com
www.casmi.net

Established: 1985
▤ 269,200 litres ▼ 100%

VIÑA TAMAIDE 2003 SECO WHITE
VIÑA TAMAIDE 2003 SEMISECO WHITE
VIÑA TAMAIDE 2003 ROSÉ
VIÑA TAMAIDE 2003 RED

Cooperativa CUMBRES DE ABONA

Camino del Viso, s/n
38589 Arico (Santa Cruz de Tenerife)
☎: 922 768 604 - Fax: 922 768 234
cumbresabona@wanadoo.es

Established: 1989
▦ 30 ▤ 600,000 litres ❦ 4 has. ▼ 100%

ALMAZUL 2003 AFRUTADO WHITE

80 Pale. Aroma of ripe fruit (custard apples, mangoes) with mild toasty hints and herbs. Sweet, flavourful, fresh and fruity palate, pleasant.

ALMAVERDE 2003 JOVEN WHITE

80 Straw-coloured. Fresh, fruity aroma with notes of forest herbs and grapefruit. Light, fruity, fresh and flavourful palate, pleasant.

CUMBRES DE ABONA 2003 JOVEN WHITE
100% listán blanca

80 Straw-coloured. Fresh, fruity aroma with a mild suggestion of fragrant herbs. Fresh, flavourful palate with varietal character.

CUMBRES DE ABONA ECOLÓGICO 2003 JOVEN WHITE
100% listán blanca

83 Straw-coloured. Fresh aroma with character, mild notes of Mediterranean hillside herbs and a ripe fruit hint. Fresh, flavourful palate, original and with character, flavourful.

FLOR DE CHASNA 2003 JOVEN WHITE
100% listán blanca

79 Straw-coloured. Aroma with herbaceous hints, foresty essence and reduction notes. Slightly better on the palate with varietal character, flavourful, fresh and supple with a subtle sweetness.

FLOR DE CHASNA AFRUTADO 2003 JOVEN WHITE
100% listán blanca

68 Pale. Aroma with light reduction notes (late racking), somewhat fruity. Slightly more expressive, flavourful palate, nearly a demi-sec.

TESTAMENTO MALVASÍA DULCE 2003 JOVEN WHITE
100% malvasía

87 Greenish yellow. Aroma with notes of sweet fruit (pineapples, melons), fresh and quite intense. Sweet palate with a good fruit expression evoking fragrant herbs (lavender, fennel), flavourful and persistent with pleasant reminiscences.

FLOR DE CHASNA 2003 SEMISECO WHITE
100% listán blanca

66 Straw-coloured. Aroma with unusual toasty flavours and herbs. Sweet palate with a carbonic suggestion, flavourful and better than in the nose.

FLOR DE CHASNA 2003 SEMISECO WHITE
CUMBRES DE ABONA 2003 JOVEN ROSÉ
CUMBRES DE ABONA 2003 RED

EL TOPO

Finca Frontos.Lomo Grande, 3
Los Blanquitos Ctra. TF28, K.m.70, 2
38600 Granadilla de Abona
(Santa Cruz de Tenerife)
☎: 922 777 253 - Fax: 922 777 253
bodega@tierrasdefrontos.com

Established: 2002
▦ 20 ▤ 100,000 litres ❦ 25 has. ▼ 100%

TIERRA DE FRONTOS CLÁSICO 2003 BARRICA WHITE
albillo, malvasia, marmajuelo, güal

80 Straw-coloured. Aroma with light notes of smokiness and ripe fruit (mangoes and custard apples). Fresh palate with light smoky notes and fragrant herbs in the retronasal passage.

TIERRA DE FRONTOS CLÁSICO 2003 WHITE
albillo, malvasia, güal, marmajuelo

83 Straw-coloured. Slightly short but clear aroma with slight nuances of quite complex fruit. A good expression on the palate, flavourful, warm and with character, persistent.

TIERRA DE FRONTOS JABLE 2003 WHITE
90% listán blanca, 10% albillo

80 Straw-coloured. Fresh, quite fruity aroma with notes of forest herbs. Fresh, fruity palate, better than in the nose, with a certain sweetness and with a retronasal effect of fragrant herbs (lavender, rosemary), flavourful.

TIERRA DE FRONTOS 2003 ROSÉ
listán negro

83 Lively raspberry. Powerful aroma with notes of forest red fruit (brambles), fresh. Powerful palate with copious fruit (raspberries, cassis) and a suggestion of sweetness, flavourful.

TIERRA DE FRONTOS 2003 RED
50% listán prieto, 40% listán negro, 10% cabernet sauvignon

79 Garnet red cherry. Fruity, clear aroma, varietal. Fruity and slightly flabby palate, flavourful.

TIERRA DE FRONTOS TIERRA 2003 RED
listán negro

80 Garnet red cherry. Aroma of fresh red fruit (cassis, redcurrants and brambles) with notes of fallen leaves and with character. Dry, light, flavourful and slightly flabby palate.

HIMACOPASA

Avenida Reyes Católicos, 23
38005 Santa Cruz de Tenerife (Tenerife)
☎: 922 218 155 - Fax: 922 215 666
sofusa@gruposocas.com

Established: 1996
🛢 150 🛢 300,000 litres 🍇 76 has.
🍷 100%

LOMO BERMEJO 2003 SECO WHITE

80 Straw-coloured. Aroma with notes of scrubland herbs with ripe fruit. Fruity, fresh, flavourful palate, slightly oily.

LOMO BERMEJO 2003 SEMISECO WHITE

JOSÉ JEREMÍAS AMARAL DELGADO

Carretera General del Sur, 23
38580 Villa de Arico, Arico (Tenerife)
☎: 922 768 386

AUCHÓN ECOLÓGICO 2003 JOVEN WHITE
100% listán blanca

77 Straw-coloured. Quite short, closed-in aroma with a mild fruity nuance. Fresh palate with ripe fruit and fragrant herbs in the retronasal passage.

AUCHÓN 2003 AFRUTADO WHITE

LA ORTIGOSA

Subida a Vista el Valo, 1
38592 Icor-Arico (Tenerife)
☎: 608 248 992
lblanca@canaryart.com
www.bodegaslaortigosa.com

Established: 1994
🛢 50 🛢 51,000 litres 🍇 2.8 has.
🍷 100%

LEÑA BLANCA 2003 F. BARRICA WHITE
100% listán blanca

78 Straw-coloured with a golden glimmer. Aroma with fine smoky, creamy notes and mountain

herbs. Dry, light, quite flavourful palate with a somewhat weak expression.

MALVANERA 2003 WHITE

73 Straw-coloured. Slightly fruity, fresh aroma. Low acidity, quite sweet and forest herbs.

MALVANERA 2003 RED

63 Garnet red. Aroma with viscous notes (raisins). Slightly flat palate without nuances.

Sociedad Cooperativa LAS ERAS DE ARICO

Chajana, s/n
38592 Icor- Arico (Tenerife)
☎: 922 277 141 - Fax: 922 271 311

VIÑA CHAJAÑA WHITE
VIÑA CHAJAÑA ECOLÓGICO RED

MARISOL DÍAZ QUINTERO

Avenida Mencey de Abona, 5
38600 Granadilla (Santa Cruz de Tenerife)
☎: 922 770 190 - Fax: 922 770 190

Established: 19987
🛢 17,600 litres 🍇 1.68 has. 🍷 100%

PEDREGAL 2003 JOVEN WHITE
PEDREGAL 2003 JOVEN RED

PEDRO HERNÁNDEZ TEJERA

Carretera Archifira, s/n
38570 Fasnia (Tenerife)
☎: 616 920 832

VIÑA ARESE 2003 JOVEN WHITE

79 Straw-coloured. Fresh aroma of fine herbs, fruity. Light, fresh, flavourful palate with something of a varietal character.

VIÑA ARESE 2003 JOVEN RED

73 Garnet red cherry with a carbonic hue. Fresh, fruity aroma of medium ripeness with traces of fermentation. Dry, slightly fruity palate, slightly lacking in ripeness.

RAFAEL YUSEF DELGADO

Carretera General, 21
38595 Charco del Pino
Granadilla de Abona (Tenerife)
☎: 922 633 084

Established: 1973
🛢 15,000 litres 🍇 1.5 has. 🍷 100%

DO ABONA

CHIÑAMA 2003 JOVEN RED

80 Quite dark cherry. Aroma with notes of skins and ripe fruit, fruity with hints of minerals and mountain herbs. Warm, ripe, flavourful palate slightly low in acidity but well-balanced overall.

CHIÑAMA ECOLÓGICO 2003 JOVEN RED

80 Intense cherry. Aroma with notes of overripe grapes and earthiness (clayey notes). Fleshy, quite flavourful palate with barely any tannins (quite limited quality of the harvest).

TOMÁS FRÍAS GONZÁLEZ

Carretera Los Cazadores, s/n
38500 Fasnia (Santa Cruz de Tenerife)
☎: 922 164 301

VERA DE LA FUENTE 2003 JOVEN WHITE

77 Straw-coloured. Fresh, quite fruity aroma with mild notes of forest herbs. Fresh, light, flavourful palate with a ripe retronasal effect (custard apples).

VERA DE LA FUENTE 2003 JOVEN RED

65 Garnet red with a glacé cherry hue. Aroma with a slight off-odour (late racking) and slightly muted fruit. Slightly sweet yet vegetative on the palate, discreet.

VIÑA VIEJA

Carretera General de Sur, 6
38620 San Miguel de Abona (Tenerife)
☎: 922 700 565 - Fax: 922 700 565

ALBA SUR ECOLÓGICO 2003 WHITE

82 Straw-coloured. Aroma with unusual nuances of tropical fruit and forest herbs, fresh and with aromatic intensity. Mild notes of sweetness on the palate, warm, flavourful and with original overtones.

LAS GALGAS 2003 WHITE

75 Straw-coloured. Aroma with a slight off-odour from reduction in the tank, slightly fruity. Fresh, light palate with a foresty hint, herbs.

ALBASUR ECOLÓGICO 2003 JOVEN RED

80 Garnet red. Powerful, fruity aroma with light mineral notes, fresh (brambles), Flavourful, fruity palate, warm but with fresh fruit in the retronasal passage.

LAS GALGAS 2003 RED

70 Garnet red. Short, slightly fruity aroma, quite hard. Slightly flabby palate, discreet.

VIÑAFLOR TENERIFE

Carretera Arona a Vilaflor, km. 14
38613 Vilaflor (Tenerife)
☎: 606 218 693
bodegaviniaflor@yahoo.de
Established: 1999
🌐 50 🛢 40,000 litres 🍇 3 has. 🇪🇸 100%

VIÑAFLOR ECOLÓGICO 2003 WHITE
listán blanca, moscatel, albillo

70 Straw-coloured with a slight greenish hue. Aroma with notes of forest herbs, a fruity hint and a mild evolution. Fresh, quite flavourful, fruity palate.

VIÑAFLOR 2003 JOVEN WHITE
listán blanca, moscatel

68 Straw-coloured. Aroma with a mild off-odour (quite late racking). Fresh, light palate, potential for originality if it had received bodega airing.

VIÑAFLOR ECOLÓGICO 2003 JOVEN ROSÉ
listán negro, rubí cabernet, cabernet sauvignon

68 Dark strawberry. Flat aroma without fruity nuances. Without fruit expression and freshness on the palate, discreet.

ABOLENGO 2003 JOVEN RED
listán negro, rubí cabernet, cabernet sauvignon, castellana, tintilla

79 Garnet red cherry. Slightly short, fresh, fruity aroma. Slightly flabby, fruity palate, clear and clean.

ABOLENGO ECOLÓGICO 2003 JOVEN RED
listán negro, rubí cabernet, cabernet sauvignon, castellana, tintilla

79 Garnet red cherry. Fruity aroma despite the mild hint of reduction (late racking). Slightly better palate, light bodied and slightly flabby.

DO ALELLA

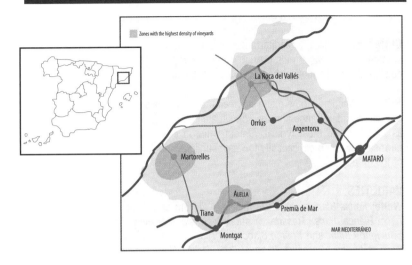

Zones with the highest density of vineyards

La Roca del Vallés

Orrius

Argentona

Martorelles

MATARÓ

ALELLA

Tiana

Premià de Mar

Montgat

MAR MEDITERRÁNEO

NEWS. The hot and dry summer of 2003 caused the foreign grape varieties, used to colder climates, to suffer, especially the white Chardonnay.

The decrease in the number of DO winegrowers already considered to be small is rather significant, as well as the reduced amount of wine destined for export, in marked contrast to the general trend of seeking out foreign markets as a solution to the progressive downturn in the national market.

Hectares of Vineyard	No. of Viticulturists	No. of Bodegas	2003 Harvest	2003 Production	Marketing
560	36	6	VG whites/ Excellent reds	800,000 litres	98% Spain 2% Foreign

On a more positive note, we were able to assess the quality of two bodegas whose wines were not present in the previous edition, Roura and Alella Vinícola, although we regret not being able to obtain samples from the most outstanding bodega in the region in our Guide 2004, Alta Alella, which reached a score of 90 points with its Orbes. Together with the notable performance of Parxet, with two barrel-fermented whites in which the oak compensated for the relative deficiencies of the grapes in the last two vintages (2002 and 2003), we would like to stress the good results of Roura with the foreign white varieties, which, also with the subtle intervention of the wood, achieves a high varietal expression whose complexity is enhanced by the great work with the lees.

LOCATION. It extends over the regions of El Maresme and el Vallès in Barcelona. It covers the municipal districts of Alella, Argentona, Cabrils, El Masnou, La Roca del Vallès, Martorelles, Montornès del Vallès, Montgat, Orrius, Premià de Dalt, Premià de Mar, Santa Mª de Martorelles, Sant Fost de Campsentelles, Teià, Tiana,

Vallromanes, Vilanova del Vallès and Vilasar de Salt. The main feature of this region is the urban environment which surrounds this small stretch of vineyards; in fact, one of the smallest DOs in Spain.

CLIMATE. A typically Mediterranean microclimate with mild winters and hot dry summers. The coastal hills play an important role, as they protect the vines from cold winds and condense the humidity from the sea.

SOIL. Distinction can be made between the clayey soils of the interior slope of the coastal mountain range and the soil situated along the coastline. The latter, known as *Sauló*, is the most typical. Almost white in colour, it is renowned for it high permeability and great capacity to retain sunlight, which makes for a better ripening of the grapes.

VARIETIES:

White: *Pansa Blanca* (similar to the *Xarel·lo* from other regions in Catalonia), *Garnatxa Blanca, Pansa Rosada, Picapoll, Malvasía, Macabeo, Parellada, Chardonnay, Sauvignon Blanc* and *Chenin Blanc.*
Red (minority): *Garnatxa Negra, Ull de Llebre (Tempranillo), Merlot, Pinot Noir, Syrah* and *Cabernet Sauvignon.*

REGULATORY COUNCIL.

Masía Can Magarda, s/n. 08328 Alella (Barcelona).
Tel: 935 559 153. Fax: 935 405 249.
E-mail: doalella@doalella.org
Website: www.doalella.org

GENERAL CHARACTERISTICS OF THE WINES:

Whites	These are the most characteristic of the region. One can distinguish between the traditional Alella, light, fruity and quite supple (although not sweet), and the other dry wines with a pale straw colour which are fresh, fruity, well-balanced, slightly supple with a persistent aroma. There are also examples of white wines fermented in barrels.
Rosés	These are not the most abundant, although very good rosé wines are produced which are very flavourful on the palate.
Reds	The most interesting examples in the region are those that include foreign varieties in the blend, especially *Merlot* and *Cabernet Sauvignon*, which stand out for their unique fruity character.

ALELLA VINÍCOLA CAN JONC

Rambla Angel Guimerá, 62
08328 Alella (Barcelona)
☎: 935 403 842 - Fax: 935 401 648
comercial@alellavinicola.com
www.alellavinicola.com

Established: 1906

🍷 450 📊 932,000 litres 🍇 115 has.

🍾 93% 🌐7%: -US -CH

MARFIL 2003 JOVEN SECO WHITE
100% pansa blanca

78 Brilliant gold. Powerful, varietal aroma with fruit, white flowers and slight exotic hints (grape-fruit, pineapple). Flavourful, somewhat fruity pala-te with spicy and nutty notes, slightly warm.

IVORI 2003 F. BARRICA WHITE
pansa blanca, pansa roja, garnacha blanca

85 Straw-coloured with a golden hue. Not very intense yet elegant aroma (lees, smoky scents, a citrus fruit nuance). Oily palate, notes of well-inte-grated toasty oak and fruit, good acidity and a citrus finish.

MARFIL 2003 SEMISECO WHITE
100% pansa blanca

81 Pale with coppery nuances. Intense aroma of ripe white fruit (slightly reduced), hints of petals and sweet spices. Flavourful palate with quality bittersweet notes, and hints of jammy fruit; slightly warm but with good fruit weight.

MARFIL CHARDONNAY 2002 WHITE
100% chardonnay

83 Pale gold. Intense aroma of ripe white fruit, flo-ral hints, lees, perfumed soap and nuts. Flavourful palate with fine bitter notes, slightly warm and oily with zesty hints and excellent acidity.

ONA 2004 ROSÉ

83 Deep raspberry with a coppery glint. Intense aroma, ripe red fruit, floral nuances (petals) and herbs, fine toasty skins. Flavourful palate, fruity, herbaceous and citrus fruit pulp notes, marked acidity.

MARFIL 2003 RED

84 Red with a violet rim. Aroma of ripe red fruit with jammy forest fruit, spicy. Fresh, flavourful, medium-bodied palate.

MARFIL NEGRE 2002 CRIANZA RED
garnacha tinta, cabernet sauvignon, merlot

76 Not very deep cherry. Spicy aroma of wood with a notion of red fruit. Light palate without many nuances and not very persistent

MARFIL 2003 ROSÉ
60% garnacha, 30% merlot, 10% cabernet sauvignon

81 Deep raspberry with an orangey hue. Not very intense aroma with red stone fruit, spicy hints and herbs. Flavourful, fruity palate with fine bitter notes, citrus fruit and good acidity.

ALTA ALELLA

Cau D' En Genis, s/n
08391 Tiana (Barcelona)
☎: 934 644 949 - Fax: 934 642 401
carmenet@carmenet.es

Established: 2000

🍷 80 📊 150,000 litres 🍇 8 has.

🍾 90% 🌐10%: -DE -FR -UK -AD

ALTA ALELLA PARVUS 2003 SECO WHITE
ALTA ALELLA LANIUS 2003 SECO WHITE
ALTA ALELLA PARVUS 2003 ROSÉ
ALTA ALELLA ORBUS 2001 CRIANZA RED
ALTA ALELLA MATARÓ 2003 DULCE RED

Celler ALTRABANDA

Bienni, 2
08107 Martorelles (Barcelona)
☎: 935 704 534 - Fax: 935 704 534
serralademarina@pc-serveis.com

Established: 2000

SERRALADA DE MARINA JOVEN WHITE
SERRALADA DE MARINA F. BARRICA
WHITE

DO ALELLA

Celler J. MESTRE

Camí Baix d'Alella, s/n
08391 Tiana (Barcelona)
☎: 934 691 220 - Fax: 934 693 742
Established: 1989
🍷 20 📊 50,000 litres 🌿 4.5 has. 🍇 100%

JUAN MESTRE

PARXET

Mas Parxet s/n
08391 Tiana (Barcelona)
☎: 933 950 811 - Fax: 933 955 500
parxet@parxet.es - www.parxet.es
Established: 1920
🍷 40 📊 1,500,000 litres 🌿 200 has.
🍇 85% 🌐15%: -US -UK -JP -DE -BE -DK

MARQUÉS DE ALELLA CLÁSICO 2003 JOVEN WHITE
100% pansa blanca

84 Pale yellow with a greenish hue. Not very intense aroma with a certain finesse, notes of white fruit and notions of freshness (mint, fennel, ripe limes). Fresh on the palate with fine bitter notes, green apples and excellent acidity.

MARQUÉS DE ALELLA ALLIER 2002 F. BARRICA WHITE
100% chardonnay

86 Golden yellow. Intense aroma of ripe white fruit with fine smoky and creamy oak notes, hints of lees and fine herbs. Flavourful and ripe on the palate with smoky notes, well-integrated spices and fruit and a slightly acidic edge.

MARQUÉS DE ALELLA ALLIER ACOT 2003 F. BARRICA WHITE
100% chardonnay

88 Pale yellow with a golden hue. Not very intense aroma of great finesse with an excellent suggestion of Chardonnay (apples, fine herbs) and a smoky and creamy oak (vanilla) nuance. Ripe on the palate with well-integrated oak and fruit, well-balanced and long.

ROURA

Vall de Rials, s/n
08328 Alella (Barcelona)
☎: 933 527 456 - Fax: 933 524 339
roura.mari@terra.es - www.roura.es
Established: 1987
🍷 270 📊 373,000 litres 🌿 45 has.
🍇 70% 🌐30%: -SE -DE -US -BE -UK -JP -CH -FR

ROURA SAUVIGNON BLANC 2003 JOVEN WHITE
100% sauvignon blanc

85 Golden yellow. Intense, very fine aroma with fruit, white flowers, mild exotic hints (melon, mango) and fresh overtones of grapeskins. Flavourful palate with fine bitter and bittersweet notes, slightly warm with a mineral suggestion.

ROURA XAREL.LO 2003 JOVEN WHITE
100% xarel.lo

81 Pale with greenish nuances. Intense aroma of fruit and white flowers, fresh citrus and mineral overtones. Fresh, fruity palate with a slightly oily texture and excellent acidity.

ROURA CHARDONNAY NEVERS 2002 F. BARRICA WHITE
100% chardonnay

85 Intense gold. Powerful aroma of ripe white fruit, lees, creamy, spicy oak and a suggestion of reduction. Flavourful palate with predominant toasty oak notes, oily and warm, quite persistent.

ROURA MERLOT 2003 JOVEN ROSÉ
100% merlot

78 Pale cherry. Not very intense, fresh aroma with fine notes of red fruit. Flavourful, spicy palate (skins), slightly warm and oily.

ROURA TEMPRANILLO CABERNET 2000 SEMICRIANZA RED
50% tempranillo, 50% cabernet sauvignon

75 Cherry with an orangey hue. Toasty aroma of wood, vanilla and very sweet notes. Acidic, warm palate with not very noticeable fruit and wood tannins.

ROURA TEMPRANILLO CABERNET 2000 CRIANZA RED
50% tempranillo, 50% cabernet sauvignon

76 Ruby red cherry. Aroma of skins, not a very ripe Tempranillo typification and mild toasty scents. Drying on the palate with noticeable tannins and slight hints of roasted coffee in the retronasal passage.

ROURA MERLOT 1999 RESERVA RED
100% merlot

77 Cherry with an orangey edge. Aroma of ripe red forest fruit, varietal typification, vanilla and well-integrated wood. Light palate with supple wood and fruit tannins and toasty hints and chocolate in the retronasal passage.

ROURA MERLOT RESERVA ESPECIAL 1998 RED
100% merlot

77 Cherry with a brick red rim. Toasty aroma of wood, eucalyptus, red fruit and spices. Drying on the palate with bitter notes, not very long.

ROURA MERLOT 1997 RESERVA ESPECIAL RED

DO ALICANTE

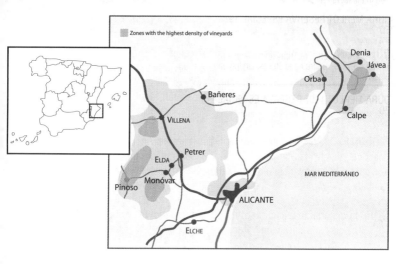

Zones with the highest density of vineyards

Denia
Jávea
Orba
Bañeres
Calpe
VILLENA
Petrer
ELDA
Monóvar
MAR MEDITERRÁNEO
Pinoso
ALICANTE
ELCHE

NEWS. The dry-farmed crops yielded high alcohol contents, which emphasised the most traditional expression of the wines from the region, where the average in 2003 was over 14° (14.1° to be precise). The increase in production over the previous vintage (around 21%) was a consequence of the rainfall during the winter. In general, the grapes were quite healthy (thanks to the high temperatures of the summer, and especially to the contrast in day-night temperatures), which promised a much better harvest than that of 2002, although perhaps the excessive youth of the stock planted over the past few years which has recently entered production can be noted when tasting the young wines of 2003.

Hectares of Vineyard	No. of Viticulturists	No. of Bodegas	2003 Harvest	2003 Production	Marketing
14,254	3,134	48 producers, (26 bottlers)	Good	16,922,000 litres	63% Spain 37% foreign

The whites, which seem oily, warm and with hardly any fruity expression, are definitely not the most outstanding. The oenologists seem to remain committed to sacrificing the fruity expression of the aged and medium aged red wines for marked wooden notes and, on occasions, somewhat mature notes. Therefore, once again, the Fondillones and sweet wines obtain the best scores, a terrain in which Gutiérrez de la Vega plays a major role.

With regard to dry wines, Enrique Mendoza is still the brightest star (followed somewhat behind by Salvador Poveda), with his extraordinary work with foreign varieties, without forgetting his desire to take full advantage of the local Monastrell, trying to do away with the warmth and the toasty notes of the skin, typical of the variety, to obtain fresher wines.

The efforts made to boost foreign markets, especially the USA and Nordic countries (Sweden and Denmark) is quite significant. There has also been a sharp decrease in the number of bottling bodegas, dropping from 34 to only 26. In general, the good quality of the harvest is notable, with bulk wine (which in the Valencian Community still remains the most convenient solution for unhealthy balance sheets) at extremely low prices. The winegrowers received 0.23 € / kg for *Bobal* and 0.19 € /kg for *Tempranillo*.

LOCATION. In the province of Alicante (covering 51 municipal districts), and a small part of the province of Murcia. The vineyards extend over areas close to the coast (in the surroundings of the capital city of Alicante, and especially in the area of La Marina, a traditional producer of Moscatel), as well as in the interior of the province.

CLIMATE. Distinction must be made between the vineyards situated closer to the coastline, where the climate is clearly Mediterranean and somewhat more humid, and those inland, which receive continental influences and have a lower level of rainfall.

SOIL. In general, the majority of the soils in the region are of a dun limestone type, with little clay and hardly any organic matter.

VARIETIES:
White: *Merseguera, Moscatel de Alejandría, Macabeo, Planta Fina, Verdil, Airén, Chardonnay* and *Sauvignon Blanc*.
Red: *Monastrell, Garnacha Tinta (Alicante or Giró), Garnacha Tintorera, Bobal, Tempranillo, Cabernet Sauvignon, Merlot, Pinot Noir* and *Syrah*.

REGULATORY COUNCIL.
Orense, 3, Entlo. Dcha. 03003 Alicante.
Tel: 965 984 478. Fax: 965 229 295.
E-mail: crdo.alicante@crdo-alicante.org

GENERAL CHARACTERISTICS OF THE WINES:

Whites	The young white wines produced from local varieties are usually pale yellow, with an honest, fruity aroma, although maybe not too intense, and are pleasant to drink. There are also some *Chardonnays* which reflect the character of the variety, but full of hints of ripe fruit due to the Mediterranean climate. More significant still are the sweet Muscatels of the region of Marina, which are reminiscent of honey, with grapey hints and a musky character characteristic of the variety.
Rosés	These are pink with a fresh fruity aroma and are easy and pleasant to drink.
Reds	The red wines are characteristic of the Mediterranean climate. They are warm, meaty with a fine structure; on the nose they may develop balsamic aromas (fallen leaves, eucalyptus). There is also a range of more classic reds without too much extraction of colour, which unfortunately may appear a bit rusty.
Fondillón	This is the historic wine of the region (old wine with a high alcohol content and a rusty character). Sometimes, it is produced as a Rancio wine and other times it is mixed with Mistelas.

DO ALICANTE

A. & M. NAVARRO

Pintor Juan Gris, 26
03400 Villena (Alicante)
☎: 965 801 486 - Fax: 965 800 978
direccion@aymnavarro.com
www.aymnavarro.com

Established: 1956

🌐 400 ▯ 1,500,000 litres 🍇 60 has.
🚩 30% 🍷70%

TERRA NATURA MOSCATEL WHITE

80 Intense golden. Musky aroma of honey, medium-intensity. Sweet, flavourful, light palate with a herby hint, very well-mannered.

TERRA NATURA SELECCIÓN 2003 WHITE
100% macabeo

79 Pale with golden nuances. Slightly intense aroma of ripe white fruit with floral hints. Flavourful palate with fine notes of bitterness and citrus fruit and with good acidity.

TERRA NATURA 2003 ROSÉ
100% tempranillo

80 Brilliant raspberry. Intense aroma of red fruit with hints of sweetness and macerated skins. Flavourful palate with fine bitter notes and good acidity.

TERRA NATURA 2003 RED
100% tempranillo

78 Medium-hue ruby red with a garnet red hue. Aroma of well-ripened foresty strawberries and sun-drenched skins, highly perfumed. Drying palate with very pungent tannins and considerable persistence.

MIGUEL NAVARRO 1999 CRIANZA RED
100% tempranillo

71 Cherry with a brick red hue. Aroma of stewed fruit with very sweet notes and overripe fruit. Drying, light palate evoking bitter almonds in the retronsal passage.

MIGUEL NAVARRO 1998 RESERVA RED
100% cabernet sauvignon

70 Very dark and quite deep garnet red. Highly viscous aroma almost of Mistelle, without varietal character, unusual. Drying, pungent, earthy palate.

MIGUEL NAVARRO 2002 OAK AGED RED
ALEBUS 2002 OAK AGED RED
GRAN FONDILLÓN 1964 RESERVA

Cooperativa de ALGUEÑA

Carretera Rodriguillo, s/n
03668 Algueña (Alicante)
☎: 965 476 113 - Fax: 965 478 113

TORREVIÑAS LÁGRIMA 2003 ROSÉ
100% monastrell

76 Intense raspberry. Powerful aroma of ripe red fruit with hints of sun-drenched skins and oily hints. Flavourful and fruity palate with fine bitter notes of citrus fruit (blood oranges). Somewhat oily, with an acidic edge.

TORREVIÑAS DOBLE PASTA 2003 RED
100% monastrell

80 Deep cherry with a violet edge. Powerful, concentrated aroma of jammy fruit with hints of sun-drenched skins. Fleshy and concentrated on the palate with well-integrated ripe fruit and grape tannins and a bitter nuance (liquorice).

TORREVIÑAS TEMPRANILLO 2003 RED
85% tempranillo, 15% otras

79 Cherry with a violet rim. Powerful aroma of very ripe fruit (macerated black fruit) and toasty hints of grapeskins. Flavourful, fleshy and round on the palate with a good expression of ripe fruit and a slightly oily texture.

BERNABÉ NAVARRO

Ctra Villena-Cañada, km. 3 Finca Casa Balaguer
03400 Villena (Alicante)
☎: 966 770 353 - Fax: 966 770 353
info@bodegasbernabenarro.com
www.bodegasbernabenavarro.gestionaweb.com

Established: 2000

🌐 200 ▯ 150,000 litres 🍇 40 has. 🚩 100%

BERYNA 2002 RED
50% monastrell, 25% cabernet sauvignon , 25% syrah

86 Intense cherry with a violet edge. Intense, fruity aroma with fine toasty oak over a nuance of slightly underripe skins (Monastrell) and mineral notes. Fleshy, warm and flavourful on the palate, toasty flavours (chocolate and coffee), ripe Cabernet in the retronasal passage, noticeable oak tannins.

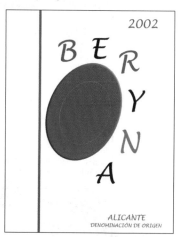

2002

BERYNA

ALICANTE
DENOMINACIÓN DE ORIGEN

BERYNA 2000 CRIANZA RED

79 Intense cherry with a saffron edge. Powerful aroma of fine toasty oak notes and ripe black fruit (quite viscous nuance). Flavourful and fleshy on the palate, oak tannins with an element of greeness, bitter with a slightly oily texture.

BOCOPA

Autovía Alicante-Madrid, km. 39
Paraje Les Pedreres,
03610 Petrer (Alicante)
☎: 966 950 489 - Fax: 966 950 406
info@bocopa.com
www.bocopa.com

Established: 1987

🌐 1,000 📊 15,500,000 litres 🍇 8,000 has.

🍷 70% 🌐30%: -DE -FR -BE -NL -CH -IT -FI -DK -JP -US -PT -MT -MX -DK.

MARINA ALTA GRAN SELECCIÓN 2003 JOVEN WHITE
100% moscatel de Alejandría

81 Pale. Powerful, fresh aroma of great finesse with excellent varietal expression (musk, anise). Fresh and flavourful on the palate with fine bittersweet notes, hints of crystallised fruit and excellent acidity.

TERRETA ROSÉ 2003 JOVEN ROSÉ
100% monastrell

79 Brilliant raspberry. Intense, slightly fruity aroma with a spicy nuance of skins. Fresh flavourful palate of red fruit (red grapefruit pulp) with a slightly acidic edge.

MARQUÉS DE ALICANTE 1999 CRIANZA RED
40% monastrell, 30% tempranillo, 15% cabernet sauvignon, 15% merlot

76 Garnet red cherry with a saffron edge. Intense aroma with predominant toasty and creamy oak notes. Flavourful on the palate with hints of aged wood, a fruity nuance and an acidic edge.

LAUDUM 2000 CRIANZA RED
85% monastrell, 10% merlot, 5% cabernet sauvignon

76 Garnet red cherry with a coppery edge. Intense aroma with well-integrated fruit and oak and spicy hints of skins. Flavourful on the palate with a certain oaky and fruity freshness and an acidic edge.

LAUDUM 2001 CRIANZA RED
85% monastrell, 10% merlot, 5% cabernet sauvignon

80 Brilliant garnet red cherry. Not very intense aroma with predominant spicy oak notes. Flavourful on the palate with overtones of freshness and varietal character, well-integrated oak and fruit.

SOL DE ALICANTE VINO DE LICOR
monastrell

88 Intense garnet red cherry. Powerful aroma of ripe black fruit with hints of sun-drenched skins and a spicy hint of terroir. Flavourful, concentrated, unctuous and sweet on the palate with refreshing acidity.

DULCENEGRA VINO DE LICOR
LAUDUM ECOLÓGICO NATURE 2003 JOVEN RED
LAUDUM BARRICA ESPECIAL 2000 SEMICRIANZA RED
MARQUÉS DE ALICANTE 1999 CRIANZA RED
FONDILLON ALONE 1970

BODEGA Y VIÑEDOS DEL ARZOBISPO

Carretera de Hurchillo, km. 1, 500
03300 Orihuela (Alicante)
☎: 965 302 340 - Fax: 966 741 176
bvarzobispo@ctv.es
www.bvarzobispo.com

Established: 2000

🌐 130 📊 500,000 litres 🍇 35 has.

🍷 90% 🌐10%: -SE -BE -PT -FR -DE

ARZOBISPO LOAZES LÁGRIMA 2002 ROSÉ
100% monastrell

78 Pale cherry with an orangey glint. Powerful aroma of sour cherries in liqueur with hints of petals and fine reduction. Flavourful palate of jammy red fruit with spicy hints (cinnamon), slightly warm, oily and distinctive.

ARZOBISPO LOAZES MONASTRELL ROBLE RED
100% monastrell

74 Not very deep cherry. Aroma with sweet notes and very ripe red fruit, somewhat viscous with mild toasty scents. Light palate with polished tannins and good acidity.

ARZOBISPO LOAZES DOBLE PASTA RED
100% monastrell

79 Red cherry with a coppery edge. Intense, fruity aroma with hints of macerated skins. Flavourful, fleshy palate with rough tannins and bitter hints, somewhat warm and spicy.

ARZOBISPO LOAZES 1998 CRIANZA RED
monastrell, tempranillo, cabernet sauvignon

80 Dark cherry with a brick red edge. Somewhat intense aroma with predominant spicy oak notes and a black fruit nuance. Flavourful, spicy and warm on the palate with hints of liquorice, dark-roasted flavours and jammy fruit.

MISTELA DE TEULADA SANT JUST MOSCATEL DULCE
100% moscatel

78 Old gold. Not a very intense aroma yet characteristic and musky. Sweet, flavourful palate, very well-mannered.

ARZOBISPO LOAZES COSECHA RED
ARZOBISPO LOAZES TEMPRANILLO RED

BODEGAS ESTEBAN

Paraje Hondo de Carboneras, 14
Finca Atalaya
03400 Villena (Alicante)
☎: 965 806 021 - Fax: 965 814 437
lentiscares@terra.es

Established: 1997

🛢 50 ▤ 60,000 litres 🍇 50 has.
🍷 80% 🍇20%

VIÑA ELENA MACABEO 2003 WHITE
LENTISCARES 2002 CRIANZA RED

BROTONS

Partida Culebrón, 59
03658 Pinoso (Alicante)
☎: 965 477 267 - Fax: 965 477 602
asolei.3057@cajarural.com

Established: 1955

▤ 500,000 litres 🍇 40 has. 🍷 100%

CASERÍO CULEBRÓN RED
monastrell

72 Orangey red. Aroma with sweet notes, ripe red fruit and faint hints of black olives. Light on the palate with not very marked tannins, fresh.

CULEBRÓN SYRAH-MONASTRELL RED
syrah, monastrell

83 Intense cherry with a violet edge. Powerful aroma with ripe black fruit, notes of sun-drenched skins and a spicy and earthy nuance. Concentrated on the palate with grape tannins well-integrated with the fruit notes, a toasty nuance, liquorice and hints of terroir.

CULEBRÓN 2003 RED
100% syrah

85 Cherry with a violet hue. Powerful aroma of very ripe black fruit with hints of petals and a spicy nuance of skins. Flavourful and fleshy on the palate quite concentrated with very fine grape tannins and a spicy nuance (liquorice).

CULEBRÓN MERLOT 2002 RED
100% merlot

82 Garnet red cherry with a coppery edge. Powerful aroma of jammy black fruit (blackberries) with spicy hints of skins and a creamy oak nuance. Flavourful, fleshy and very ripe on the palate with a slight varietal expression (a herbaceous and paprika nuance) and hints of liquorice.

CULEBRÓN 2000 RED
100% syrah

76 Garnet red with an orangey rim. Aroma with sweet, viscous notes. Warm and light on the palate with tart tannins.

GRAN FONDILLON 1964 RESERVA

81 Amber. Toasty aroma of aged wood and acetaldehydes. Toasty on the palate, pastries, aged wood with a rancid character, long.

Bodega CAMPO DE SAN BLAS

Barrio de la Estación, 12
03630 Sax (Alicante)
☎: 965 474 137 - Fax: 965 474 137

🛢 25 🍷 95% 🍇5%

ERMITA SAN BLAS WHITE SEMI-SECO

70 Pale yellow with a golden hue. Not very intense aroma of ripe fruit with hints of reduction. Flavourful on the palate with bitter notes (herbs, almonds), without fruit expression and high in acidity.

CASTILLO DE SAX WHITE

70 Pale with coppery hues. Not very intense aroma with hardly any fruit expression. Quite fresh and bitter on the palate with a slightly oily texture.

CASTILLO DE SAX JOVEN ROSÉ

69 Fairly pale raspberry with a coppery glint. Short aroma, slightly fresh without fruit nuances. Quite flavourful palate with stone fruit and a warm hint.

TROPEZÓN ROSÉ

71 Blush with an orangey hue. Not very expressive, viscous aroma. Sweet and light on the palate, not outstanding.

CASTILLO DE SAX JOVEN RED

70 Intense cherry. Not very intense aroma with a fruity nuance. Flavourful on the palate with bitter notes and without great nuances, good acidity.

RINCÓN DEL MORO MERLOT RED

71 Intense cherry with a brick red edge. Fairly intense aroma of ripe red fruit with spicy hints of wood. Dry, bitter and pleasant on the palate, flawless.

CASTILLO DE SAX 2000 CRIANZA RED

72 Almost opaque cherry. Powerful aroma of jammy black fruit with warm and overripe notes. Flavourful and fleshy on the palate with marked and rough grape and oak tannins; oily, very ripe fruit.

CÁNTARA 4

Camino Alcalali, 5
03727 Jalón (Alicante)
☎: 966 480 758 - Fax: 966 480 758
viñamelada@tarraco.seric.es

Established: 1985

🛢 40 ▤ 37,000 litres 🍇 3.6 has. 🍷 100%

VIÑAMELADA 1998 CRIANZA RED

E. MENDOZA

Partida El Romeral, s/n
03580 Alfás del Pi (Alicante)
☎: 965 888 639 - Fax: 965 889 232
bodegas-mendoza@bodegasmendoza.com
www.bodegasmendoza.com

Established: 1989

🍷 850 ▤ 500,000 litres 🌿 100 has.

📦 50% 🌐50%: -DE -DK -NL -AT -UK -BE -FR -SE -LU -DK -CH -JP -PR -MX -RU -US -KR -BR

ENRIQUE MENDOZA CHARDONNAY 2003 JOVEN WHITE
100% chardonnay

84 Brilliant gold. Intense aroma of white stone fruit with notes of flowers, fine lees, light tropical hints and curry. Flavourful and bitter on the palate, slightly warm and oily with spicy notes of skins and excellent acidity.

ENRIQUE MENDOZA CHARDONNAY 2003 FERMENTADO EN BARRICA WHITE
100% chardonnay

85 Golden. Powerful aroma of ripe apples (somewhat reduced), lees, petals, with a suggestion of honey and creamy oak (vanilla) notes. Flavourful, slightly warm and oily on the palate with fine bitter notes, fragrant herbs and a spicy finish, lacking acidity.

ENRIQUE MENDOZA MOSCATEL DE LA MARINA 2003 WHITE
100% moscatel

89 Pale gold. Intense aroma with fine, quite varietal notes of overripeness (musk) and fresh, zesty overtones. Flavourful, unctuous palate with quality bittersweet notes, somewhat spicy, rich in nuances and long.

ENRIQUE MENDOZA SHIRAZ 2002 RED
100% shiraz

88 Cherry with a purple hue. Expressive aroma with grape variety character (flowers, spices) and toasty skins (elegant earthiness). Fleshy, very fruity palate with well-integrated fine smoky flavours, very fruity tannins and a varietal finish.

ENRIQUE MENDOZA MERLOT 2000 RED
100% merlot

85 Opaque garnet red. Deep aroma of well-ripened black fruit with balsamic notes (fallen leaves) and hints of minerals. Fleshy palate with very fresh fruit tannins, fruit/wood harmony and a pleasant, slightly bitter finish.

ENRIQUE MENDOZA PINOT NOIR 2000 RED
100% pinot noir

86 Cherry with a garnet red edge. Fine aroma with earthy notes (hints of stones) and a nuance of well-ripened black fruit. Flavourful palate with fruity and fresh tannins, regional balsamic character and a long finish.

ENRIQUE MENDOZA CABERNET SAUVIGNON 2000 CRIANZA RED
100% cabernet sauvignon

84 Garnet red. Aroma with notes of animals and leathers (a certain reduction) with a balsamic and oaky hint (cocoa). Fleshy palate with round fruit and slightly pungent wood tannins, very fresh.

ENRIQUE MENDOZA CABERNET SAUVIGNON - SHIRAZ 1999 RESERVA RED
65% cabernet sauvignon, 35% shiraz

87 Almost opaque cherry. Aroma of black fruit with notes of cedar and spicy grapes. Fleshy, flavourful palate with fresh and fruity tannins, spicy with a pleasant earthy finish.

ENRIQUE MENDOZA SELECCIÓN PEÑÓN DE IFACH 1999 RESERVA RED
60% cabernet sauvignon, 20% merlot, 20% shiraz

85 Garnet red. Expressive aroma of Cabernet with balsamic and bush notes and a nuance of black fruit. Fleshy, flavourful palate with good freshness, notes of sun-drenched skins and a certain crianza reduction aftertaste.

ENRIQUE MENDOZA SANTA ROSA 1999 RESERVA RED
70% cabernet sauvignon, 15% merlot, 15% shiraz

92 Very deep cherry. Concentrated aroma of fine smoky wood and fresh black fruit (skins, ink), with an elegant suggestion of reduction (earthiness) and an expression of flowers and broom. Fleshy palate with powerful but oily fruit tannins and a certain oaky astringence yet to be integrated; an expression of grapes in the aftertaste.

DOLÇ DE MENDOZA 2001 RED DULCE
60% merlot, 10% cabernet sauvignon, 10% shiraz, 10% pinot, 10% monastrell

91 Very deep brilliant cherry. Original aroma of raisins, overripening (black olives, dates), fine reduction and complex smoky, toasty notes. Sweet, powerful, fleshy palate with excellent freshness, expression of the fruit and a very pleasant bitter finish.

ENRIQUE MENDOZA MOSCATEL DE MENDOZA 2003

FRANCISCO YAGO PUCHE

Finca El Mojón. Paraje La Boquera
30510 Villena (Alicante)
☎: 968 790 765 - Fax: 968 790 765
boyago@terra.es

Established: 2001

🍷 50 ▤ 530,000 litres 🌿 90 has. 📦 100%

BOYAGO 2003 JOVEN RED
40% monastrell, 40% tempranillo, 20% garnacha

82 Cherry with a violet hue. Intense aroma of ripe black fruit (blackberries) with hints of terroir and sun-drenched skins. Flavourful, concentrated, fruity and ripe on the palate with a suggestion of liquorice.

BOYAGO 2001 JOVEN RED
BOYAGO 2002 JOVEN RED
BOYAGO 2001 CRIANZA RED

Bodegas GUTIÉRREZ DE LA VEGA

Canalejas, 4
03792 Parcent (Alicante)
☎: 966 405 266 - Fax: 966 405 257
gutivega@arrakis.es
www.arrakis.es/gutivega

Established: 1978

200 ▯ 70,000 litres 🍇 10 has.
🍷 75% 🥃25%

CASTA DIVA COSECHA DORADA 2003 WHITE
100% moscatel

82 Pale yellow with greenish nuances. Intense aroma with a fine varietal expression (musk, exotic fruit, pollen). Dry, bitter palate with fine herbs and pronounced citrus acidity.

CASTA DIVA LA DIVA 2003 OAK AGED WHITE DULCE
100% moscatel

89 Golden yellow. Expressive aroma of citrus fruit (oranges) with quince, a nuance of exotic herbs and light toasty wood. Sweet, bitter palate with an expression of green fruit pulp; reminiscent of mountain herbs (thyme) and loquats, very fresh.

CASTA DIVA COSECHA MIEL 2002 WHITE DULCE
100% moscatel

90 Brilliant gold. Generous, expressive palate with sun-drenched grapes and a nuance of quince and citrus fruit (grapefruit), spicy. Sweet palate with a Muscatel character and hints of light smoky crianza with a very pleasant bitter finish, very fresh.

CASTA DIVA RESERVA REAL 2002 WHITE DULCE
100% moscatel

90 Brilliant gold. Generous, expressive palate with sun-drenched grapes and a nuance of quince and citrus fruit (grapefruit), spicy. Sweet palate with a Muscatel character and hints of light smoky crianza, with a very pleasant bitter finish, very fresh.

CASTA DIVA ROJO Y NEGRO 2002 RED
40% monastrell, 10% cariñena, 40% merlot, 10% cabernet sauvignon

82 Dark garnet red. Toasty aroma of black berries with mineral hints and a floral hint. Concentrated palate with powerful wood tannins over the abundant fruit; fresh with a slightly astringent finish.

VIÑA ULISES 2001 CRIANZA RED

78 Medium-hue cherry. Aroma with light reduction notes, not very new wood and leather. Drying, vinous palate with slightly marked wood tannins and a suggestion of wood in the retronasal passage.

CASTA DIVA TAMBOURINE 2001 RED
garnacha, monastrell, cabernet sauvignon

77 Nearly opaque garnet red. Aroma with reduction notes (animals, leather), fine cocoa and ripe fruit. Fleshy, concentrated, very pungent palate (oak tannins), with a woody finish.

CASTA DIVA FONDILLÓN 1995 OAK AGED FONDILLÓN DULCE
100% monastrell

88 Brilliant deep cherry. Complex aroma of jammy plums, fine smoky notes and an expression of terroir. Sweet palate with red wine character, good fruit-wood balance and round, powerful tannins, very original with a fresh finish.

CASTA DIVA FONDILLÓN 15 AÑOS OAK AGED DULCE

92 Cherry with an orangey hue. Elegant, spicy and very subtle aroma with mild smokiness (cocoa), hints of earth and well-integrated varnish. Powerful, sweet palate with a long crianza expression (cedar, spices tobacco), excellent acidity, long with toasty grapes.

CASTA DIVA MONTE DIVA 2003 FERMENTADO EN BARRICA WHITE SECO
CASTA DIVA CAVATINA TENDER DULCE
CASTA DIVA FURTIVA LÁGRIMA 2003 WHITE DULCE
ROJO Y NEGRO COSECHA ROJA 2001 RED

JAUME & FULLANA

La Senia, 2
03728 Alcalali (Alicante)
☎: 658 846 467 - Fax: 963 441 570
sebastiandejaime@ono.com

Established: 1999

97 ▯ 40,000 litres 🍇 6 has. 🍷 100%

LES MARINES 2003 CRIANZA WHITE
100% moscatel

82 Pale straw. Fresh, grapey aroma and a herby suggestion. Slightly oily, flavourful palate with complex overtones of mountain and Mediterranean herb flavours and spicy tones.

TOSSALS DEL POP 2000 CRIANZA RED
cabernet sauvignon, merlot, garnacha

79 Cherry with an orangey edge. Very dark-roasted aroma (very toasty coffee), with a suggestion of skins and sun-drenched fruit. Quite powerful palate of ripe fruit with oak tannins in the finish.

DO ALICANTE

LADERA DE PINOSO

Paraje El Sequé, 59
03650 Pinoso (Alicante)
☎: 945 600 119 - Fax: 945 600 850
elseque@artadi.com

Established: 1999

🍷 200 📊 150,000 litres 🍇 40 has.

🍷 40% 🌐60%

EL SEQUÉ 2002 OAK AGED RED
monastrell, syrah, cabernet sauvignon

88 Intense cherry. Very fruity, varietal aroma (dry earth, brambles) with a jammy hint. Oily, warm palate with ripe fruit (jam) and earthy hints, flavourful, very varietal Monastrell.

LADERAS DE EL SEQUÉ 2003 RED

Cooperativa Nuestra Señora de LAS VIRTUDES

Carretera de Yecla, 9
03400 Villena (Alicante)
☎: 965 802 187 - Fax: 965 813 387
coopvillena@coopvillena.com
www.coopvillena.com

Established: 1961

🍷 212 📊 9,000,000 litres

VINALOPÓ 2003 WHITE
macabeo

80 Pale yellow. Intense, fruity aroma with hints of white stone fruit and hay and traces of citrus fruit. Flavourful, quite fresh on the palate, fruity with fine bitter notes and good acidity.

VINALOPÓ 2003 ROSÉ
monastrell, tempranillo

79 Fairly pale raspberry. Intense, fruity aroma with fresh citrus overtones. Flavourful and very fresh on the palate with red fruit notes, hints of ripe citrus fruit and good acidity.

VINALOPÓ 2003 RED
monastrell, tempranillo, cabernet sauvignon

80 Brilliant cherry with a violet glint. Intense, fruity aroma with spicy hints of skins and herbaceous and varietal freshnes (Cabernet). Fresh and fruity on the palate with a slightly oily texture, pleasant.

VINALOPÓ SELECCIÓN BARRICA 2002 RED
monastrell

81 Garnet red cherry with a coppery edge. Intense aroma with predominant toasty and spicy oak notes and hints of petals. Flavourful on the palate with well-integrated oak and fruit and a bitter nuance (chocolate, liquorice).

VINALOPÓ 2001 CRIANZA RED
monastrell, cabernet sauvignon

79 Garnet red cherry with a brick red edge. Intense aroma with predominant toasty oak notes and hints of reduction. Flavourful on the palate with slightly marked tannins, a spicy oak nuance and high quality hints of herbs.

VINALOPÓ 2000 RESERVA RED
monastrell, cabernet sauvignon

78 Garnet red cherry with a coppery edge. Powerful aroma with predominant toasty oak notes and a suggestion of fine reduction. Flavourful on the palate with promising although quite marked tannins and hints of liquorice and bitter chocolate.

Bodegas MURVIEDRO

Ampliación Polígono El Romeral, s/n
46340 Requena (Valencia)
☎: 962 329 003 - Fax: 962 329 002
murviedro@murviedro.es
www.murviedro.es

Established: 1927

🍷 1,500 📊 7,100,000 litres

🍷 5% 🌐95%

TRAVITANA 2002 OAK AGED RED
monastrell

84 Garnet red cherry with a slightly coppery edge. Powerful aroma with predominant toasty oak notes over the very ripe fruit. Flavourful and fleshy on the palate with good concentration, well-integrated oak and fruit, somewhat rough tannins, a liquorice nuance and hints of terroir.

Cooperativa de PINOSO

Paseo de la Constitución, 82
03650 Pinoso (Alicante)
☎: 965 477 040 - Fax: 965 477 040
labodegadepinoso@yahoo.es

Established: 1932

🍷 50 📊 10,000,000 litres 🍇 3,000 has.

🍷 90% 🌐10%

LA TORRE DEL RELOJ 2003 RED
100% tempranillo

82 Deep cherry with a violet edge. Powerful, fruity aroma with hints of sun-drenched skins and a suggestion of underbrush. Flavourful and fleshy on the palate with very fine grape tannins, very pleasant.

LA TORRE DEL RELOJ 2003 RED
100% monastrell

83 Cherry with a violet edge. Intense, fruity aroma (blackberries) with hints of ripe skins. Flavourful on the palate with grape tannins well-integrated with the ripe fruit, notions of liquorice and good varietal expression.

DO ALICANTE

VERMADOR 2003 RED
100% monastrell

80 Garnet red cherry. Intense aroma with a certain finesse, fruity notes and high quality herbaceous hints. Flavourful and slightly fleshy on the palate with very fine grape tannins, a suggestion of ripe red fruit and excellent acidity.

Bodegas PRIMITIVO QUILES

Mayor, 4
03640 Monóvar (Alicante)
☎: 965 470 099 - Fax: 966 960 235
primitivoquiles@terra.es
www.primitivoquiles.com

PRIMITIVO QUILES MONASTRELL 2001 CRIANZA RED
monastrell

87 Dark cherry with a coppery edge. Intense, ripe aroma with fine toasty oak notes and a balsamic nuance. Flavourful, fleshy palate with ripe oak tannins well-integrated with grape tannins, an oily texture and excellent varietal, crianza expression.

RASPAY 1999 RESERVA RED

86 Garnet red cherry with a brick red edge. Powerful aroma with predominant reduction notes (aged wood, varnishes, prunes) and a balsamic nuance. Powerful and oily on the palate with bitter crianza notes, ripe and fairly rough tannins; varietal expression, bitter chocolate and high quality rancid hints.

GRAN IMPERIAL 1892 RESERVA ESPECIAL RED

87 Dark mahogany. Intense aroma of sultanas with notes of vanilla, old Solera, crystallised fruit and coffee. Sweet on the palate with a syrupy expression, notes of nuts and coffee; complex and very fresh.

PRIMITIVO QUILES MOSCATEL VINO DE LICOR DULCE

82 Golden with an amber glint. Fresh grapey aroma with toasty notes of skins, honey and oranges. Sweet and warm on the palate, fresh with notes of peaches and vanilla and a pleasant bitter finish.

PRIMITIVO QUILES MOSCATEL EXTRA WHITE LICOR NOBLE

84 Mahogany with an orangey rim. Fresh aroma of orange peel with notes of varnish and toffee. Sweet and fresh on the palate with bitter traces (hazelnuts), pleasant and well-balanced with the acidity.

PRIMITIVO QUILES FONDILLÓN 1948 GRAN RESERVA RED

85 Mahogany with an orange edge. Aroma of crystallised fruit (oranges) with varnish and notes of sweet almonds, complex. Dry, fresh palate,

hints of Solera and vanilla from the oak; a slightly sweet nutty finish.

PRIMITIVO QUILES CONO-4 RED

SALVADOR POVEDA

Benjamín Palencia, 19
03640 Monóvar (Alicante)
☎: 965 471 139 - Fax: 965 473 389
salvadorpoveda@salvadorpoveda.com
www.salvadorpoveda.com

Established: 1919
🏛 1,210 ▯ 2,000,000 litres 🍇 150 has.
🍷 30% 🍷70%

TOSCAR MONASTRELL 2003 RED
100% monastrell

85 Dark cherry with a garnet red and orange glint. Powerful, very fruity and varietal aroma (brambles), fresh. Fruity, fresh, light palate, an excellent young Monastrell, clean and flavourful.

POVEDA TEMPRANILLO 2001 CRIANZA RED
tempranillo

85 Brilliant garnet red cherry. Powerful aroma, very fruity and well-ripened, conserving its fresh fruit, varietal and with a fine smoky hint. Fresh, fruity aroma, rich in varietal expression and with an elegant and subtle oak presence, flavourful.

POVEDA CABERNET-MERLOT 2001 CRIANZA RED
60% cabernet sauvignon, 40% merlot

87 Quite intense cherry. Fine, toasty aroma of ripe fruit with a slight varietal expression. Round, full and flavourful palate with excellent fruit expression well-balanced with the toasty oak, good acidity.

BORRASCA 2001 CRIANZA RED
100% monastrell

82 Intense cherry. Aroma with mild nuances of overripening (jammy fruit) and toasty oak. Fleshy palate with oak tannins and stewed fruit, flavourful and slightly less relevant than the previous vintage.

BORRASCA CLASSIC 2000 CRIANZA RED
100% monastrell

88 Quite intense cherry with an orange edge. Powerful aroma with mineral notes, ripe fruit and fine toasty oak notes. Full, fleshy palate with flavourful and ripe tannins, warm and very varietal with peat in the retronasal passage.

FONDILLÓN GRAN RESERVA GENEROSO

88 Mahogany. Powerful aroma with hints of pâtisserie, nuts and rancid oxidative notes. Sweet palate with pâtisserie, caramel and toasty flavours with rancid hints and hazelnuts in the retronasal passage.

CANTALUZ 2002 WHITE
ROSELLA 2002 ROSÉ

VIÑA VERMETA 1999 CRIANZA RED
VIÑA VERMETA 1998 RESERVA RED

Bodegas SANBERT

Partida Alfaquinet
03650 Pinoso (Alicante)
☎: 965 978 603 - Fax: 965 978 603

Established: 1999

🍷 400 🌿 160 has. 🇪🇸 100%

CAMPS DE GLÒRIA RODRIGUILLO COSECHA ESPECIAL WHITE
moscatel, merseguera

79 Brilliant gold. Intense aroma of ripe stone fruit with spicy and exotic hints and fine musky notes of Muscatel. Flavourful, bitter, oily palate with a creamy and spicy suggestion.

RODRIGUILLO RED
monastrell

81 Intense cherry with a dark red hue. Intense aroma of very varietal ripe fruit with herbaceous and underbrush notions. Powerful, fleshy palate with slightly marked tannins and a slightly viscous and sweet fruit hint, warm and oily.

RODRIGUILLO CRIANZA RED
monastrell

77 Dark garnet red cherry. Intense, fruity aroma with toasty oak notes and a suggestion of petals and damp earth. Flavourful, bitter palate with unintegrated oak/fruit and marked acidity.

CAMPS DE GLÒRIA RODRIGUILLO 1999 RESERVA RED
monastrell

80 Garnet red cherry with a saffron rim. Quite intense aroma with a suggestion of finesse, toasty oak notes and a suggestion of ripe fruit. Flavourful palate with slightly rough and oily tannins and predominant bitter notes (dark-roasted flavours, liquorice).

Cooperativa Agrícola
SANT VICENTE FERRER

Avenida Las Palmas, 32
03725 Teulada (Alicante)
☎: 965 740 051 - Fax: 965 740 489
bodega@coop-santvicent.com

Established: 1940

🛢 1,000,000 litres 🇪🇸 100%

VIÑA TEULADA VENDIMIA SELECCIONADA BLANC DE LA MARINA ALTA 2003 WHITE
moscatel

79 Straw-coloured. Intense aroma of jammy grapes evoking talcum powder and white flor with a herby nuance. Light and dry on the palate with mountain herbs and a bitter finish, somewhat lacking in acidity.

MISTELA SELECTA DE TEULADA MOSCATEL
moscatel

81 Coppery. Aroma of crystallised fruit, orange peel and musky notes with fresh overtones. Sweet palate with pleasant toasty notes, slightly pasty, orange peel in the finish.

TEULADA MOSCATEL

Compañía de Vinos de
TELMO RODRÍGUEZ

Siete Infantes de Lara, 5 Oficina 1
26006 Logroño (La Rioja)
☎: 941 511 128 - Fax: 941 511 131
cia@fer.es

AL MUVEDRE 2003 JOVEN RED
100% monastrell

83 Quite intense cherry with an orange edge. Spirituous aroma of jammy fruit with hints of earthiness. Warm, supple palate with ripe fruit, slightly spirituous with supple tannins.

VALLE DEL CARCHE

Polígono CC-13 Casas del Señor
03640 Monovar (Alicante)
☎: 965 978 050 - Fax: 965 980 060

Established: 1865

🍷 325 🛢 1,200,000 litres 🌿 165 has.
🇪🇸 75% 🍇25%

PORTICHUELO 2003 WHITE
100% sauvignon blanc

79 Very pale with a greenish hue. Fairly intense, fruity aroma (mild exotic hints) and fresh overtones. Dry on the palate with fine bitter notes and a slightly oily texture, pleasant.

PORTA REGIA TEMPRANILLO 2003 RED
100% tempranillo

80 Cherry with a violet hue. Intense aroma of ripe red fruit with good varietal expression (underbrush, spicy hints of skins). Flavourful and fruity on the palate with quite firm grape tannins although well-integrated with the sweet notes of the fruit, good acidity.

LISANDRO 2002 RED
tempranillo, cabernet sauvignon

78 Garnet red cherry with a coppery edge. Not very intense, slightly fruity aroma with toasty hints of wood. Flavourful and slightly fleshy on the palate with marked tannins, a ripe fruit nuance and an acidic edge.

PORTA REGIA MONASTRELL RED
100% monastrell

74 Ruby red. Slightly alcoholic aroma with varietal expression. Without great nuances on the palate, powerful and fleshy tannins.

PORTA REGIA SYRAH RED
100% syrah

72 Garnet red with a ruby hue. Aroma of ripe red fruit with light notes of salted meat. Fresh, not very expressive and ripe on the palate.

PORTA REGIA MERLOT RED
100% merlot

79 Cherry with a violet edge. Intense aroma of ripe bilberries and blackberries, expressive. Flavourful and pleasant on the palate, with a vegetative note and a slightly astringent finish.

DOMUS ROMANS CRIANZA RED
tempranillo, cabernet sauvignon, merlot

79 Garnet red cherry with a brick red edge. Intense aroma with predominant spicy oak notes and a ripe red fruit nuance with hints of fine reduction. Flavourful on the palate with slightly drying oak tannins and bitter crianza notes.

DOMUS ROMANS 1998 RESERVA RED
tempranillo, cabernet sauvignon, merlot

79 Brilliant garnet red cherry. Powerful aroma with predominant toasty oak notes, a jammy fruit nuance and a slight reduction. Flavourful on the palate with dark-roasted notes, lacks balance.

VAGUADA 2002 WHITE
PORTA REGIA 2002 ROSÉ
VAGUADA 2002 ROSÉ
VAGUADA 2002 RED

VIÑA PRADO

Camino del Prado, 15
03650 Pinoso (Alicante)
☎: 965 478 762

VIÑA PRADO BRONCE 2003 JOVEN RED
tempranillo

80 Garnet red cherry with a violet edge. Intense aroma of ripe fruit with hints of petals and a spicy nuance of skins. Flavourful and fruity on the palate with quite fresh grape tannins, fine herbaceous notes and a slightly acidic edge.

ROMÁNTICO VICTORIA 2003 OAK AGED RED
tempranillo

85 Garnet red cherry. Powerful aroma of jammy black fruit with smoky and creamy hints of oak. Flavourful on the palate with well-integrated fruit and oak with bitter hints (chocolate) and balsamic flavours, excellent acidity.

VIÑA PRADO PLATA 2002 CRIANZA RED
tempranillo

85 Garnet red cherry with a violet edge. Powerful aroma with excellent varietal expression (red fruit, underbrush) and hints of sun-drenched skins. Powerful, flavourful and fleshy on the palate with well-integrated grape tannins and fruit, spicy (liquorice).

VIÑA PRADO ORO 2002 RESERVA RED

80 Garnet red cherry. Intense aroma of macerated red fruit with hints of creamy oak and fresh overtones. Flavourful and fleshy on the palate with promising although quite rough tannins and a spicy aroma in the retronasal passage (pepper) with herbaceous and slightly mineral hints.

DO ALMANSA

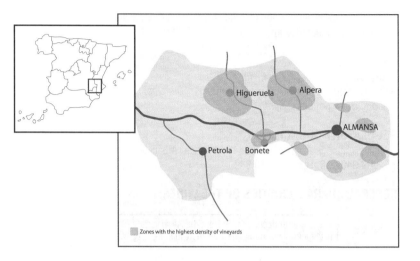

Zones with the highest density of vineyards

NEWS. A consequence of the atypical climatology of 2003 in Almansa was a rather high alcohol content, good polyphenolic ripening and precise acidity. The excellent quality of the *Garnacha Tintorera* can once be praised. It is no surprise that after the great success of the single-variety vinification of this DO, its neighbours from La Mancha are starting to recover this variety for their wines. It is worth pointing out the recent incorporation of the *Verdejo* and *Sauvignon Blanc* varieties, called upon to improve the generally poor quality of the whites in the region, although as yet we have no examples.

Hectares of Vineyard	No. of Viticulturists	No. of Bodegas	2003 Harvest	2003 Production	Marketing
7,100	3,150	6	Good	2,500,000 litres	25% Spain 75% foreign

There has also been a significant increase in exports, rising from 50% to 75% of the production, which is based on the appreciation of the English, German and Nordic consumer for the easy and full-bodied fruit of the *Garnacha Tintorera*, always accompanied by a fresh background. Thanks to the carbonic maceration, it is pleasant and complex on the palate.

LOCATION. In the eastern region of the province of Albacete. It covers the municipal areas of Almansa, Alpera, Bonete, Corral Rubio, Higueruela, Hoya Gonzalo, Pétrola and the municipal district of El Villar de Chinchilla.

CLIMATE. Of a continental type, somewhat less extreme than the climate of La Mancha, although the summers are very hot, with temperatures which easily reach 40 °C. Rainfall, on the other hand, is scant, an average of about 350 mm a year. The majority of the vineyards are situated on the plains, although there are a few situated on the slopes.

SOIL. The soil is limy, poor in organic matter and with some clayey areas. The vineyards are situated at an altitude of about 700 m.

VARIETIES:
White: *Airén, Verdejo* and *Sauvignon Blanc.*
Red: *Garnacha Tintorera* (most popular), *Cencibel (Tempranillo), Monastrell* (second most popular), *Syrah.*

REGULATORY COUNCIL.
Méndez Núñez, 5. Aptdo. 158. 02640 Almansa (Albacete).
Tel: 967 340 258. Fax: 967 310 842.

GENERAL CHARACTERISTICS OF THE WINES:

Whites	These are produced mainly from the *Airén* variety. They are pale yellow, light, fruity and pleasant, in line with the wines from La Mancha.
Rosés	These are pink or salmon pink; fresh and fruity with an honest aroma and are usually full-bodied and easy drinking.
Reds	The *Garnacha Tintorera* has over the past few years recovered the prominence of the DO, producing strong, fruity, fresh and meaty wines, especially since it is now bottled more selectively instead of being sold in bulk. Up to then, the most characteristic reds were the young wines of *Cencibel*, with an intense cherry colour and a fruity character. All of them stand out for a certain acidity on the palate due to the altitude of the vineyards.

DO ALMANSA

AGRO-ALMANSA

Carretera N-330, Km 96, 5
02640 Almansa (Albacete)
☎: 967 345 315 - Fax: 967 345 315

Established: 2003
🍾 100 📖 150,000 litres 🍇 85 has.

VIÑA ATALAYA 2003 RED

PIQUERAS

Zapateros, 11
02640 Almansa (Albacete)
☎: 967 341 482 - Fax: 967 345 480
bodpiqueras@almansa.org
www.bodegaspiqueras.es

Established: 1915
🍾 3000 📖 1,700,000 litres 🍇 80 has.
🚢 18% 🌐82%: -DE -CH -FI -DK -US -CA
-JP -PR -FR -AT -BE

CASTILLO DE ALMANSA COLECCIÓN 2003
WHITE
CASTILLO DE ALMANSA COLECCIÓN 2003
ROSÉ
CASTILLO DE ALMANSA COLECCIÓN 2003
RED
CASTILLO DE ALMANSA 2001 CRIANZA RED
CASTILLO DE ALMANSA 2000 RESERVA RED

SANTA ROSA

Valle Inclán, 2 - 4ºG
02640 Almansa (Albacete)
☎: 967 342 296 - Fax: 967 310 481
crisgramage@terra.es

Established: 2002
🍾 41 📖 110,000 litres 🍇 39 has. 🚢 100%

MATAMANGOS COLECCIÓN OAK AGE 2002
RED
monastrell, garnacha tintorera

85 Garnet red cherry. Spicy aroma (pepper) with
notes of ripe skins and toasty wood integrated with
the fruit. Fleshy, expressive and very fresh palate;
slightly marked toasty oak in the finish with nuances of the vine varieties.

MATAMANGOS 2003 OAK AGE RED

TINTORALBA

Cooperativa, s/n
02690 Alpera (Albacete)
☎: 967 330 108 - Fax: 967 330 903
tintoralba@tintoralba.com
www.tintoralba.com

Established: 2001
🍾 400 📖 20,000,000 litres 🍇 5000 has.
🚢 50% 🌐50%

TINTORALBA 2003 MACERACIÓN
CARBÓNICA RED
100% garnacha tintorera

86 Deep ruby red. Aroma of ripe red fruit, jammy
black fruit and underbrush, intense with varietal
character. Warm, fleshy palate with obvious tannins and black fruit.

TINTORALBA 2000 CRIANZA RED
garnacha tintorera, syrah

85 Cherry with an orangey edge. Very clean
toasty aromas of vanilla with balsamic notes (mint,
liquorice) and ripe red fruit. Powerful palate with a
good assemblage of wood and grape tannins and
toasty notes (coffee).

HIGUERUELA 2003 RED
garnacha tintorera

80 Very deep cherry. Intense, floral (violets)
aroma of ripe black fruit. Balanced, fleshy and persistent on the palate with a slightly vegetative
nuance.

SANTA CRUZ DE ALPERA 2003 RED

83 Intense garnet red cherry. Powerful aroma of
ripe black fruit, fresh overtones of macerated skins
and floral hints. Flavourful, fleshy palate of red
fruit, spicy hints of skins and damp earth.

TINTORALBA SELECCIÓN 2000 CRIANZARED

DO ARABAKO TXAKOLINA

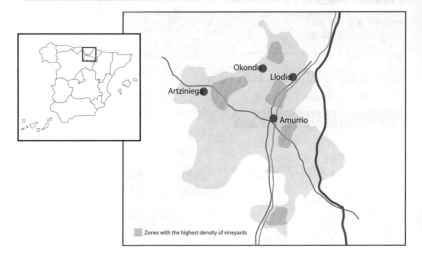

Zones with the highest density of vineyards

NEWS. As pointed out in the previous edition, the surface of the vineyards which fall under the DO Arabako Txakolina, which in 1989 did not exceed 20 Ha, is now in its third campaign approaching 70 Ha in production of a total of 76 Ha (including the newly allocated surface). Good news for the recovery of a historical vineyard for which there are documentary records dating back to the year 760 and which covered 550 Ha in 1877. The production figures for 2003 are an exact replica of the previous

Hectares of Vineyard	No. of Viticulturists	No. of Bodegas	2002 Harvest	2002 Production	Marketing
76	35	2	Very Good	150,165 litres	90% Basque Country and the rest of Spain 10% foreign

year and the quality also remains within similar parameters, although the need to incorporate more bodegas is evident if it wants to reach the same level of recognition and importance currently held by the other two DOs of Basque Txakoli.

LOCATION. It covers the region of Aiara (Ayala), situated in the north west of the province of Alava on the banks of the Nervion river basin. Specifically, it is made up of the municipalities of Amurrio, Artziniega, Aiara (Ayala), Laudio (Llodio) and Okondo.

CLIMATE. Similar to that of the DO Bizkaiko Txakolina, determined by the influence of the Bay of Biscay, although somewhat less humid and slightly drier and fresher. In fact, the greatest risk in the region stems from frost in the spring. However, it should not be forgotten that part of its vineyards borders on the innermost plantations of the DO Bizkaiko Txakolina.

SOIL. A great variety of formations are found, ranging from clayey to fundamentally stony, precisely those which to date are producing the best results and where fairly stable grape ripening is achieved.

VARIETIES:
Main: *Hondarrabi Zuri* (80%).
Authorized: *Petit Manseng, Petit Corbu* and *Gross Manseng.*

REGULATORY COUNCIL.
Plaza Dionisio Aldama (Galería Comercial). Apto. 36. 01470 Amurrio (Álava).
Tel: 945 892 308. Fax: 945 891 211.
E-mail: dotxakolialava@mundofree.com
Website: www.arabakotxakolina.com

GENERAL CHARACTERISTICS OF THE WINES:

Whites	Produced mainly from the autochthonous variety *Hondarrabi Zuri*, the Txakoli from Álava is very similar to those from the other two provinces of the Basque Country, especially those from Bizkaia. They are pale steely or greenish, with hints of fresh herbs and a fruity character slightly more aged than their neighbours. On the palate, they are slightly more round and full-bodied thanks to a slightly higher alcohol content and, although fresh, they are less acidic on the palate.

ARABAKO TXAKOLINA

Maskuribai s/n
Edf. El Salvador
01470 Amurrio (Álava)
☎: 945 891 211 - Fax: 945 891 211

Established: 1992
26 has. 89% 11%: -FR -MX -CU

XARMANT 2003 WHITE
70% hondarrabi zuri, 20% gross manseng, 5% petit manseng, 5% petit courbu

79 Pale yellow. Intense aroma of ripe white fruit and hints of petals. Fresh, flavourful palate with excellent fruit-acidity balance.

CASA DEL TXAKOLI

Alday, 40
01470 Amurrio (Álava)
☎: 947 890 703

Established: 1973
1,500 litres 0.25 has. 100%

MAHATXURI WHITE

DO BIERZO

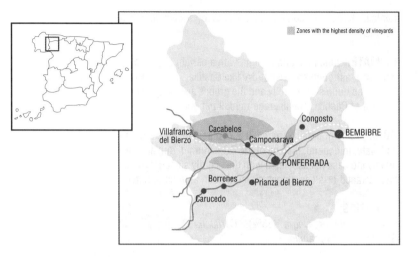

Zones with the highest density of vineyards

Congosto
Villafranca del Bierzo
Cacabelos
Camponaraya
BEMBIBRE
PONFERRADA
Borrenes
Prianza del Bierzo
Carucedo

NEWS. One important fact to start off with: the percentage of grapes grown for wine with DO rose from 56.8% in the 2002 harvest to 86.2% in the 2003 harvest, which makes the excellent quality of this vintage and the good potential for ageing the reds clearly evident. Both the alcohol content and the polyphenolic compounds (colour) are very high, although the poor acidity called for corrections which no one is willing to reveal.

Hectares of Vineyard	No. of Viticulturists	No. of Bodegas	2003 Harvest	2003 Production	Marketing
4,096	5,067	45	Very Good	5,109,911 litres	94% Spain 6% foreign

In this DO, there are two very different wine cultures which share little more than a common variety, the traditional *Mencía*, which occupies two thirds of the vineyards and whose great challenge is still its behaviour during ageing: on the one hand, the Berciana league, with bodegas such as Guerra and Cepas del Bierzo, whose wines have more in common with the Spanish cooperative of yesteryear than with modern oenological techniques; on the other hand, the new wave of young winegrowers who have arrived in the region drawn by the particular nature of its of slaty soils similar to those of the Priorat and a climatology which promises matchless *terroir* wines.
The Cepas Viejas of Dominio de Tares is quite excellent, having risen from 91 points in the 2001 vintage to 94 in the 2002 vintage, as are the 2002 Corullón of J. Palacios, and the novel Mencía of Paixar, which has deservedly risen to 90 points. Amongst the young wines, the Pétalos del Bierzo of J. Palacios stands out, closely followed by Castro Ventosa. Particularly significant is the fact that the once expressive rosés of the region hardly reach 80 points, which may hint at a slow withdrawal.

LOCATION. In the north west of the province of León. It covers 23 municipal areas and occupies several valleys in mountainous terrain and a flat plain at a lower altitude than the plateau of León, with higher temperatures accompanied by more rainfall. It may be considered an area of transition between Galicia, León and Asturias.

CLIMATE. Quite mild and benign, with a certain degree of humidity due to Galician influence, although somewhat dry like Castilla. Thanks to the low altitude, late frost is avoided quite successfully and the grapes are usually harvested one month before the rest of Castilla. The average rainfall per year is 721 mm.

SOIL. In the mountain regions, it is made up of a mixture of fine elements, quartzite and slate. In general, the soil of the DO is humid, dun and slightly acidic. The greater quality indices are associated with the slightly sloped terraces close to the rivers, the half-terraced or steep slopes situated at an altitude of between 450 and 1,000 m.

VARIETIES:
Red: *Mencía* or *Negra* (65%), *Garnacha Tintorera* (5.5%), *Merlot, Cabernet Sauvignon, Tempranillo.*
White: *Doña Blanca* (10%), *Palomino* (15%), *Malvasía* (3%), *Godello* (1.5%).

REGULATORY COUNCIL.
Los Morales, 1. Apto. Correos 41. 24540 Cacabelos (León).
Tel: 987 549 408. Fax: 987 547 077.
E-mail: info@crdobierzo.es
Website: www.crdobierzo.es

GENERAL CHARACTERISTICS OF THE WINES:

Whites	These are pale yellow, light, fresh and fruity, although not too defined. The ones with most character are those that contain the *Godello* variety.
Rosés	The colour can range from onion skin to pink tones; on the nose, strawberry and raspberry aromas dominate, typical of the *Mencía* variety, which must make up at least 50% of the blend. In general, they are light and supple.
Reds	These are the most characteristic wines of the denomination. Those that most stand out are the young wines of normal vinification or produced using the carbonic maceration procedure. Sometimes there is a risk of a slightly low acidity due to the fast ripening of the *Mencia* in such a mild climate. They have an intense cherry colour with a brilliant violet edge and are fruity with a very robust aroma (strawberries, blackberries) typical of the variety; on the palate they are dry, light and fruity with a great varietal character. Barrel-aged red wines are also produced.

Bodega del ABAD 2000

Carretera N-VI, km 396
24549 Carracedelo (León)
☎: 987 562 417 - Fax: 987 562 428
vinos@bodegadelabad
www.bodegadelabad.com

Established: 2000
🍾 900 📊 400,000 litres 🌿 21 has. 🍷 100%

ABAD DOM BUENO 2004 FERMENTADO EN BARRICA WHITE
100% godello

77 Yellow straw with a greenish nuance. Aroma of butter, yeast, white fruit and toasty wood. Bittersweet notes on the palate with dry wood tannins.

ABAD DOM BUENO 2003 JOVEN RED
100% mencía

80 Intense cherry with a violet edge. Powerful, fruity aroma with fine herbaceous varietal notes and hints of sun-drenched skins. Fresh palate with a mild carbonic hint, flavourful tannicity, an acidic edge and hints of terroir.

CARRACEDO 2003 OAK AGED RED
mencía   🍷 4

87 Almost opaque cherry with a violet edge. Intense aroma of jammy red fruit with toasty hints of fine wood (cocoa, coffee). Flavourful and fleshy on the palate with well-integrated oak/fruit, fresh tannins and varietal notes in the retronasal passage.

ABAD DOM BUENO 2001 ROBLE RED
100% mencía   🍷 3

80 Very deep cherry. Powerful, very ripe aroma with mild animal reduction off-odours, a hint of ripe fruit and toasty oak. Better in the mouth; flavourful and fleshy with well-assembled oak and fruit, a slightly oily texture, with fine herbaceous notes and hints of underbrush.

ABAD DOM BUENO 2000 CRIANZA RED
100% mencía

79 Dark garnet red cherry. Intense, ripe aroma with mild reduction off-odours (late racking) and a nuance of toasty oak. Fleshy on the palate, well-integrated tannins and fruit and a spicy nuance (liquorice, pepper).

ABAD DOM BUENO 2001 CRIANZA RED
100% mencía

80 Intense cherry with a coppery edge. Intense, very ripe aroma of creamy and spicy oak notes with a reduction nuance (lees). Flavourful on the palate with slightly marked tannins, a dark-roasted and balsamic nuance and an acidic edge.

ADRIÁ

Ctra. Antigua Madrid - La Coruña, km. 408
24500 Villafranca del Bierzo (León)

☎: 987 540 347 - Fax: 987 540 347
mteijon@telefonica.net
www.bodegasdria.com

Established: 2002
🌿 25 has. 🍷 100%

VEGA MONTÁN 2003 JOVEN WHITE
85% doña blanca, 15% godello

79 Pale with a greenish hue. Fairly intense aroma with notes of green fruit and hints of fine herbs. Fresh and quite flavourful on the palate with fine bitter and citrus fruit notes.

VEGA MONTÁN GODELLO 2003 FERMENTADO EN BARRICA WHITE
100% godello

82 Pale yellow with a golden hue. Intense aroma with predominant smoky oak notes and ripe white fruit. Fresh palate with a mild carbonic hint, fine bitter notes, creamy wood and good acidity.

VEGA MONTÁN GODELLO 2003 WHITE
100% godello

78 Pale yellow with a golden hue. Powerful aroma of white stone fruit with quality hints of herbs and citrus fruit. Fresh on the palate with fine bitter notes, flavour and good varietal character; slightly oily and warm.

VEGA MONTÁN 2003 JOVEN RED
100% mencía

80 Dark garnet red cherry. Intense aroma of jammy red fruit, mild herbaceous hints (bramble) and toasty hints of skins. Fleshy, supple palate with flavourful, slightly oily tannins and hints of terroir.

VEGA MONTÁN MENCÍA 2003 ROBLE RED
100% mencía

83 Deep cherry. Fruity aroma (strawberries, liquorice) and fine smoky oak tones. Fleshy palate with fruity tannins, notes of liquorice and spices, long and pleasant.

VEGA MONTÁN 2001 CRIANZA RED
100% mencía

77 Deep cherry. Smoky aroma with notes of oak over the fruit and some reduction. Dry palate with slightly dry wood tannins, ripe fruit, slightly warm.

VEGA MONTÁN 2003 ROSÉ

AGRIBERGIDUM

Antigua Carretera N-VI, km. 403, 5
24547 Pieros (León)
☎: 987 546 279 - Fax: 987 548 026
info@agribergidum.com
www. agribergidum.com

Established: 1999
🍾 225 📊 520,000 litres 🌿 50 has.

🍷 95% 🍇5%: -US -NL -DE -BE

ODORUS 2003 WHITE
100% godello

83 Straw-coloured with a steely hue. Aroma of ripe white fruit, pears, peaches and butter. Fresh on the palate with good acidity and hay in the retronasal passage.

CASTRO BERGIDUM 2003 JOVEN RED
100% mencía

83 Intense cherry with a violet edge. Powerful, fruity aroma with an excellent varietal expression (red fruit, herbaceous hints, toasty skins). Flavourful on the palate with slightly marked tannins, a strong presence of fruit and good acidity.

FRUCTUS 2003 RED
100% mencía

83 Cherry. Aroma of ripe red fruit jam and lactics (strawberry yoghurt). Flavourful, quite fleshy palate with flavourful tannins.

CASTRO BERGIDUM 2002 ROBLE RED
100% mencía

85 Orangey red. Aroma of superripe fruit and withered flowers. Flavourful on the palate with good wood, well-balanced.

TERRAS CÚA 2002 OAK AGED RED
100% mencía 🍷12

87 Cherry with a garnet red-violet edge. Medium-intensity aroma of toasty wood with a mineral nuance. Good assemblage of concentrated fruit and wood on the palate, expressive and flavourful with ripe grape and wood tannins in the finish.

ENCOMIENDA TEMPLARIA 2001 CRIANZA RED
100% mencía

82 Garnet red cherry with a violet glint. Intense aroma with predominant toasty oak notes and hints of brambles and underbrush. Flavourful and fleshy on the palate, with quite marked although promising tannins and slightly mineral hints.

CASTRO BERGIDUM 2001 WHITE
VIÑA VON CADABAL 2003 WHITE
CASTRO BERGIDUM 2003 ROSÉ
VIÑA VON CADABAL 2003 RED

Viñedos y Bodegas ARTURO GARCÍA

La Escuela, 3
24516 Perandones-Villadecanes (León)
☎: 987 418 157 - Fax: 987 425 727
info@bodegarturo.com
www.bodegarturo.com
Established: 2000
🍷 150 🍷 200,000 litres 🍇 20 has.
🍷 80% 🍇20%: -CH -US -UK -DK -FI -PR

HACIENDA ELSA 2003 WHITE
godello

80 Golden yellow. Powerful aroma of ripe white fruit with hints of exotic fruit and a nuance of flowers (acacia). Flavourful and fruity on the palate with fine bitter notes, well structured.

HACIENDA ELSA 2003 ROSÉ
mencía

76 Quite pale raspberry with an orangey hue. Fairly intense aroma of red fruit with spicy hints of skins. Dry and bitter on the palate with not very fine herbaceous hints.

VALDERICA RED
mencía

63 Garnet red with a ruby red hue. Aroma with off-odours that mask the rest. Light and vinous on the palate, greenness.

HACIENDA ELSA 2003 RED
mencía

83 Brilliant purplish cherry. Aroma of concentrated black berries, notes of liquorice and slate, very varietal. Dry, flavourful palate with good freshness, oily fruit tannins and a bitter finish.

SOLAR DE SAEL 2003 ROBLE RED
mencía 🍷4

83 Almost opaque cherry with a violet edge. Powerful palate of very ripe black fruit, with hints of sun-drenched skins and toasty oak. Flavourful, concentrated palate with slightly marked yet promising tannins, and a bitter nuance. Quite viscous with warm hints.

SOLAR DE SAEL 2002 CRIANZA RED

Bodegas y Viñedos BERGIDENSES

Antigua N-VI km. 400.
Apartado de Correos, 62
24540 Cacabelos (León)
☎: 987 546 725 - Fax: 987 546 725
carlos.fdez@psfd.ictnet.es
Established: 1995
🍷 9 🍷 220,000 litres 🍇 9 has.
🍷 95% 🍇5%

VIÑA GARNELO 2003 JOVEN WHITE
100% godello

80 Pale yellow with carbonic and lemony hints. Intense, fresh aroma of green apples with hints of fresh herbs. Flavourful on the palate with fine bitter notes and fresh citrus fruit.

VEGA DEL CÚA 2003 JOVEN RED
100% mencía

80 Garnet red cherry. Slightly short, smoky aroma of sour cherries and sun-drenched skins. Flavourful, expressive palate with fruity tannins, good acidity and very pleasant.

TÉGULA 2001 CRIANZA RED
100% mencía

82 Cherry with a garnet red edge. Aroma of ripe black fruit with slightly sweet, oak vanillas. Dry palate with slightly marked wood over the fruit, slightly oily, pleasant tannins, good freshness but a woody finish.

VEGA DEL CÚA 2001 JOVEN RED

BERNARDO ÁLVAREZ

San Pedro, 71
24430 Villadecanes (León)
☎: 987 562 129 - Fax: 987 562 129

Established: 1940

60 📖 1,000,000 litres 🍇 43 has.🍷 100%

VIÑA MIGARRON 2003 WHITE
doña blanca, godello, jerez

72 Yellow straw with a greenish rim. Aroma with light reduction notes and a little varietal expression. Slightly drying and light on the palate with medium acidity.

CAMPO REDONDO GODELLO 2003 WHITE
godello

70 Yellow straw. Aroma without great fruit expression with a slight hint of citrus fruit. Light and only well-mannered on the palate.

VIÑA MIGARRÓN 2003 ROSÉ
mencía

77 Brilliant raspberry. Fairly intense aroma of red fruit and fresh overtones. Fresh and flavourful on the palate with a mild carbonic hint and fine bitter notes.

VIÑA MIGARRÓN 2002 RED
mencía

77 Cherry with a violet hue. Intense, fruity aroma with hints of herbs and slightly balsamic. Flavourful palate with fresh overtones, hints of greeness and a slightly acidic edge.

CAMPO REDONDO 2002 ROBLE RED
mencía

82 Intense cherry. Aroma of red fruit with well-balanced floral and toasty oak notes. Flavourful, fresh palate with a good expression of ripe fruit and agreeable, oily tannins.

VIÑA MIGARRÓN 2000 CRIANZA RED
mencía

75 Garnet red cherry. Intense aroma with predominant creamy oak notes, a reduction nuance (leather) and ripe fruit. Flavourful palate with fleshy overtones and hints of aged wood, lacking symmetry.

BROCO MARTÍNEZ

Carretera N-VI, km. 402
24516 Parandones (León)
☎: 987 689 015

SEÑORÍO DEL PINAR GODELLO 2002 WHITE
VIÑA DEL CONDE MENCÍA 2002 RED

Bodegas del BURBIA

Traversía la Constitución s/n
24549 Carracedelo (León)
☎: 987 403 712 - Fax: 987 403 712
isidro@casardeburbia.com
www.casardeburbia.com

Established: 1972

152 🍇 27 has. 🍷 65%

🌍35%: -DE -US

CASAR DE BURBIA 2002 ROBLE RED
100% mencía

81 Quite dark garnet red cherry. Aroma with a hint of oak, not integrated with the fruit but clean and powerful. Flavourful, fresh palate, with a hint of sawn oak.

CASAR DE BURBIA HOMBROS 2002 RED
95% mencía, 5% garnacha tintorera

84 Dark garnet red cherry. Aroma with notes of fresh black fruit and ripe nuances of sawn oak. Fruity, flavourful palate, with drying notes of oak; ripe with good acidity.

CASTRO VENTOSA

Finca El Barredo, s/n
24530 Valtuille de Abajo (León)
☎: 987 562 148 - Fax: 987 562 191
bodegascastrov@terra.es

Established: 1987

250 📖 litres 🍇 60 has.

🍷 90% 🌍10%: -PR -DE -UK

CASTRO VENTOSA 2003 RED
100% mencía

86 Deep cherry. Spicy aroma of sun-drenched skins with a fine expression of the vine variety. Fleshy, fruity palate of liquorice and pitch (complex fruit), long.

VALTUILLE CEPAS CENTENARIAS 2001 OAK AGED RED
100% mencía   16

88 Deep cherry with a violet edge. Not very intense aroma of great finesse, with predominant notes of macerated red fruit. Flavourful, fleshy and concentrated on the palate with fine ripe tannins, excellent symmetry and hints of skins and spices in the retronasal passage.

CASTRO VENTOSA VINTAGE 2002 OAK AGED RED
100% mencía   14

88 Very deep cherry. Intense aroma of black fruit, fine toasty oak, a balsamic nuance and slightly mineral. Fleshy palate quite rough, sweet tannins, spicy notes and excellent acidity and potential.

CEPAS DEL BIERZO

Carretera de Sanabria, 111
24400 Ponferrada (León)
☎: 987 412 333 - Fax: 987 412 912
coocebie@coocebier.e.telefonica.net

Established: 1966

⊕ 24 🗑 8,300,000 litres
🍇 1,000 has. 🍷 100%

ESCARIL 2002 JOVEN WHITE
palomino, godello

63 Pale yellow with a greenish hue. Intense sherry aroma, without fruit expression. Better palate, quite fresh.

FANEIRO 2002 JOVEN WHITE
palomino, doña blanca

67 Pale yellow. Quite fresh aroma, without fruit expression. Quite fresh and bitter on the palate.

FANEIRO 2002 JOVEN ROSÉ
mencía , palomino

70 Pale cherry with an orangey glint. Powerful aroma of very ripe red fruit (crystallised fruit notes). Flavourful palate of toasty notes and a nuance of sweetness.

ESCARIL 2002 JOVEN ROSÉ
mencía , doña blanca

72 Brilliant raspberry with coppery nuances. Flat aroma without fruit expression. Slightly better in the mouth with bitter and fruity notes and good acidity.

FANEIRO 2002 JOVEN RED
100% mencía

74 Garnet red cherry. Intense, slightly fruity aroma with hints of damp earth, not very expressive. Flavourful palate with bitter notes, a fruity nuance and a slightly oily texture.

DON OSMUNDO 2000 RED
100% mencía

70 Garnet red cherry. Intense aroma with not very fine reduction notes, a very ripe fruit nuance and toasty hints of skins. Quite flavourful palate with fleshy overtones and an acidic edge, lacking symmetry.

DON OSMUNDO 2003 FERMENTADO EN BARRICA RED
GODELLO VIZBAYO 2002 WHITE

COBERTIZO DE VIÑA RAMIRO

San Pelayo, 2
24530 Valtuille de Abajo (León)
☎: 987 562 157

Established: 1994

🍇 7 has.

COBERTIZO 2003 RED

Cooperativa COMARCAL VINÍCOLA DEL BIERZO

Carretera Columbrianos a Ocero s/n
24412 Cabañas Raras (León)
☎: 987 421 755 - Fax: 987 421 755
lopezbsu@terra.es

Established: 1965

⊕ 137 🗑 3,000,000 litres
🍇 450 has. 🍷 100%

CABAÑAS ORO GODELLO 2003 WHITE
CABAÑAS ORO 2003 WHITE
CABAÑAS ORO DOÑA BLANCA 2003 WHITE
CABAÑAS ORO 2003 ROSÉ
CABAÑAS ORO 2003 RED
CABAÑAS ORO 2000 OAK AGED RED
CABAÑAS ORO 2000 CRIANZA RED

Viñedos y Bodegas COMENDADOR

Carretera Toral-Sorribas
24550 Sorribas (Leon)
☎: 606 598 846

LAGAR DE AMADOR MENCÍA 2003 RED
100% mencía

84 Intense cherry. Very expressive aroma of black berries (liquorice, violets) with spicy grape hints and a character of skins. Flavourful, fresh, very fruity palate with a Mencía character.

VISANU 2003 RED
100% mencía

83 Intense cherry with a strawberry edge. Aroma of spiced fruit, liquorice, flowers, with character. Fleshy, flavourful palate, very fresh acidity and a very lively red fruit sensation in the finish.

VILLARROMANA DEL MIRADOR 2003 RED
100% mencía

83 Brilliant cherry. Very fresh aroma of red fruit, spices and Mencía varietal notes. Flavourful, fruity palate of macerated strawberries and liquorice, very fresh acidity.

DESCENDIENTES DE J. PALACIOS

Calvo Sotelo, 6
24500 Villafranca del Bierzo (León)
☎: 987 540 821 - Fax: 987 540 851

Established: 1999

⊕ 180 🗑 120,000 litres 🍇 26 has.

☛ 35% ⏺65%: -US U.K. -IE -FR -FI -DE - DK -DK -RU -CH -IT -JP -DO -BR

CORULLÓN 2002 RED

90 Deep cherry with a violet edge. Elegant aroma of expressive black fruit with a fine woody contribution and a marked suggestion of earth (hints of stones). Fleshy, powerful palate with very elegant wood tannins well-assembled with the fruit, fruity with a generous floral finish, mineral and very fresh.

PÉTALOS DEL BIERZO 2003 RED

88 Intense cherry. Fresh, very fruity aroma with varietal notes (brambles), very expressive fresh fruit and a mild toasty suggestion. Dry, very fruity, fresh and flavourful palate.

VILLA DE CORULLÓN 2002 RED

Viñedos y Bodegas
DOMINIO DE TARES

Los Barredos, 4. Polígono Bierzo Alto
24318 San Román de Bembibre (León)
☎: 987 514 550 - Fax: 987 514 570
info@dominiodetares.com
www.dominiodetares.com

Established: 2000

🌐 850 ▤ 350,000 litres ⚘ 20 has.

☛ 50% ⏺50%

DOMINIO DE TARES GODELLO 2003 FERMENTADO EN BARRICA WHITE
godello

84 Pale yellow with a golden glint. Intense aroma of white fruit with fine hints of exotic fruit and hay, smoky oak and a slightly mineral nuance. Flavourful on the palate with very fine oak tannins, rich, bitter and herby notes, somewhat oily and warm.

DOMINIO DE TARES CEPAS VIEJAS 2002 OAK AGED RED
mencía   🌐9

94 Intense cherry. Powerful, very fruity aroma of great expression, nuances and fine integrated toasty oak. Full, oily, round palate with polished tannins and a complex retronasal passage of cocoa and aromatic coffee.

BEMBIBRE 2002 CRIANZA RED
100% mencía

88 Very deep cherry with a violet edge. Powerful aroma with predominant toasty oak notes and a nuance of black macerated fruit, skins and balsamic flavours. Concentrated on the palate with well-integrated fruit/oak, fleshy overtones and mineral hints.

TARES P. 3 2001 CRIANZA RED
mencía

88 Almost opaque cherry. Powerful aroma of fine creamy and toasty oak notes with a ripe fruit and fine reduction nuance (lees). Fleshy on the palate with slightly marked although promising tannins, a good fruit weight despite the alcohol (13,8%), and fine bitter notes (liquorice, dark-roasted flavours).

ESTEFANÍA

Carretera dehesas - Posada del Birezo, s/n
24390 Ponferrada (León)
☎: 987 420 015 - Fax: 987 420 015
cascudo@tilenus.com
www.tilenus.com

Established: 1999

🌐 1,000 ▤ 220,000 litres ⚘ 36 has.

☛ 75% ⏺25%: -US -CH -SE -JP -DE -UK -MX

TILENUS MENCÍA 2000 RED
100% mencía

88 Deep intense cherry. Aroma of fine notes of oak (spices and smoky scents), ripe skins and very ripe black fruit. Concentrated, powerful palate of rounded black fruit, polished wood tannins and an astringent, persistent fruit finish (slightly mineral, liquorice).

TILENUS ENVEJECIDO EN ROBLE 2002 ROBLE RED
100% mencía   🌐4

85 Deep cherry. Fruity aroma (slightly spicy red fruit) with character of the skins and very fine toasty notes. Dry, concentrated palate with good fruit-wood balance; Mencía expression, long.

TILENUS PAGOS DE POSADA 2000 RESERVA RED
mencía

84 Ruby red cherry. Balsamic aromas (liquorice, toffee) with a light reduction nuance. Fleshy, round palate with good fruit/wood symmetry; mineral.

TILENUS 2003 JOVEN RED
TILENUS 2001 CRIANZA RED

Bodegas y Viñedos GANCEDO

El Parque, 9
24548 Quilós (León)
☎: 987 563 278 - Fax: 987 563 278

Established: 1998

🌐 23 ▤ 58,000 litres ⚘ 10.5 has.

☛ 90% ⏺10%

VAL DE PAXARIÑAS "CAPRICHO" 2003 SEMI-DULCE
godello, doña blanca

82 Yellow straw with a greenish rim. Aroma of ripe white fruit (pears, apples). Semi-sweet, pungent (carbon dioxide) and intense on the palate.

VAL DE PAXARIÑAS "OTOÑO" 2002 OAK AGED RED
mencía   🍷 12

85 Intense cherry with a violet edge. Intense aroma with superripe red stone fruit, creamy hints of oak and a nuance of lees. Better, fresh and fleshy on the palate with well-combined oak and fruit, fine spicy balsamic notes and an element of terroir.

VAL DE PAXARIÑAS "PRIMAVERA" 2003 RED

HEREDEROS DE MARTÍNEZ FUENTE

Las Flores s/n
24530 Valtuille de Abajo (León)
☎: 987 561 256 - Fax: 987 562 217
mencía 1970@hotmail.com

Established: 2001

🛢 20 ▪ 150,000 litres 🍇 35 has.

🍷 35% 🌐65%: -US -IE

PUCHO MENCÍA 2003 OAK AGED RED
100% mencía

80 Light garnet red. Aroma of slightly ripe red fruit with spices and tobacco of the skins. Fresh, flavourful palate with fruity, fairly ripe tannins.

Bodegas y Viñedos
HIJOS DE LISARDO GARCÍA

Carretera Parandones - Horta, 32
24516 Parandones-Toral de los Vados (León)
☎: 987 544 009 - Fax: 987 544 034
comercial@vinosmiranda.com

Established: 1920

▪ 450,000 litres 🍇 40 has. 🍷 100%

VIÑA MIRANDA 2003 WHITE
godello

81 Pale yellow with coppery nuances. Fairly intense aroma with white fruit notes and hints of exotic fruit. Flavourful on the palate with fine bitter notes, hints of herbs and a certain citrus fruit and mineral freshness.

VIÑA MIRANDA 2002 RED
mencía

83 Deep intense cherry. Floral aroma of red fruit with violet sweets nuances and fine hints of skins. Fleshy, fruity palate, nuances of the vine variety, very fresh and pleasant.

LA SERRANA

Los Pinares, 69
24530 Villadecanes (León)

☎: 689 005 595 - Fax: 987 463 167
bodegaslaserrana@yahoo.es

UTTARIS 2003

LOBATO FOLGUERAL

Carretera Cacabelos , 11 Bajo
24550 Sorribas (Leon)
☎: 619 709 426 - Fax: 987 547 019
lfolgueral@terra.es
www.lfolgueral.com

FOLGUERAL RED

Bodega y Viñedos LUNA BEBERIDE

Carretera Madrid-Coruña, km. 402
24540 Cacabelos (León)
☎: 987 549 002 - Fax: 987 549 214
info@lunabeberide.com
www.lunabeberide.com

Established: 1987

🛢 400 ▪ 400,000 litres 🍇 80 has.

MENCÍA LUNA BEBERIDE 2003 RED
100% mencía

84 Dark cherry with a violet rim. Powerful, fruity aroma with an excellent varietal young wine expression, a nuance of terroir and macerated skins. Flavourful, fleshy palate with ripe, oily tannins, liquorice and excellent structure.

LUZDIVINA AMIGO

Carretera Villafranca 10
24516 Parandones (León)
☎: 987 544 826
bodegaluz@iespana.es

Established: 2002

🛢 30 ▪ 50,000 litres 🍇 5 has. 🍷 100%

VIÑADEMOYA 2003 JOVEN RED
100% mencía

84 Very deep cherry with a violet edge. Intense, ripe aroma with red stone fruit, fine, toasty skins and a terroir nuance. Fleshy palate with fine, flavourful, spicy tannins, fine herbaceous notes, liquorice and minerals.

BALOIRO 2002 RED
100% mencía

86 Almost opaque cherry. Fine aroma of very ripe black fruit, toasty hints of skins and oak spices. Fruity, fleshy palate of powerful black fruit with well-integrated oily wood tannins and a long finish.

BALOIRO 2003 JOVEN RED
VIÑADEMOYA 2002 RED

DO BIERZO

Viñedos y Bodegas MARTÍNEZ YEBRA

San Pedro, 96
24530 Villadecanes (León)
☎: 987 562 082 - Fax: 987 562 082

Established: 1977
🍷 60 📊 234,000 litres
🍇 12 has. 💪 100%

TRES RACIMOS 2003 GODELLO WHITE
Godello

84 Straw-coloured with a coppery hue. Powerful aroma, fine smoky notes, white stone fruit, hints of exotic fruit and apricot skin, a slightly vinous nuance. Flavourful, fresh palate, with predominant notes of oak, fresh mineral and white fruit overtones, excellent acidity, slightly warm and oily finish.

TRES RACIMOS 2003 MENCÍA RED
Mencía

85 Garnet red cherry, very lively. Intense aroma, fine notes of varietal ripe fruit with a creamy oak nuance. Powerful, flavourful, fresh palate, well-integrated fruit/oak, with bitter varietal nuances. Hints of liquorice and bitter chocolate in the retronasal passage, slightly oily, long.

VIÑADECANES 2003RED

82 Garnet red cherry with a violet edge. Intense aroma, ripe red fruit, quality varietal nuances, spicy hints of skins. Flavourful, fresh palate, fresh fruit, notes of strawberry jelly, excellent acidity.

VIÑADECANES 2000 CRIANZA RED

83 Intense garnet cherry. Powerful aroma, with predominant toasty oak notes and a nuance of macerated black fruit. Flavourful palate, ripe and oily tannins, fresh overtones of brambles, spicy and chocolate hints in the retronasal passage.

Bodegas OTERO SANTÍN

Ortega y Gasset, 10
24400 Ponferrada (León)
☎: 987 410 101 - Fax: 987 418 544

Established: 1940
🍷 40 📊 500,000 litres 🍇 20 has.
💪 90% 🍷10%

OTERO SANTÍN JOVEN WHITE

73 Pale with greenish nuances. Slightly intense aroma with a hint of fruity and herby freshness. Flavourful palate with bitter notes, without great expression.

OTERO SANTÍN JOVEN ROSÉ

79 Brilliant raspberry with coppery nuances. Slightly intense, fruity aroma with hints of petals. Flavourful, somewhat fruity palate with the spicy freshness of skins, hints of citrus fruit and good acidity.

OTERO SANTÍN MENCÍA JOVEN RED
mencía

80 Garnet red cherry with a violet edge. Balsamic aroma of red fruit and ink. Flavourful, fresh, light and varietal on the palate.

VALDECAMPO MENCÍA JOVEN RED
mencía

81 Garnet red cherry. Medium-intensity aroma, red berries, fresh. Flavourful palate with ripe red fruit and a good structure, alcohol well-integrated in the wine, quite persistent.

OTERO SANTÍN 1997 CRIANZA RED
mencía

78 Cherry with a brick red edge. Not very intense aroma of toasty notes (coffee) with a slight reduction. Round, slightly flavourful palate with dry, polished wood tannins.

Bodegas y Viñedos PAIXAR

Ribadeo, 56
24500 Villafranca del Bierzo (León)
☎: 987 549 002 - Fax: 987 549 214

PAIXAR MENCÍA 2001 RED
100% mencía

90 Intense cherry. Aroma with an excellent fruit expression of fresh ripe fruit in harmony with the oak and mineral nuances. Powerful, fresh, flavourful and varietal palate; precise and ripe tannins.

PAIXAR 2002 CRIANZA RED

Bodegas PEIQUE

Calle del Bierzo s/n
24530 Valtuille de Abajo (León)
☎: 987 562 044 - Fax: 987 562 044
bopei@navegalia.com

Established: 1999

⊕ 45 ▤ 122,000 litres ⊌ 7 has.

☛ 85% 🍇15%: -US -NL -CH -JP

PEIQUE 2003 RED
100% mencía

84 Almost opaque cherry with a violet edge. Powerful aroma with an excellent varietal expression (red fruit, hints of brambles) and spicy hints of skins. Flavourful, fleshy and concentrated on the palate with slightly marked tannins which give an excellent structure to the fruit, hints of minerals.

PEIQUE SELECCIÓN DE VIÑEDOS VIEJOS 2001 OAK AGED RED
100% mencía   ⊕ 12

83 Deep cherry with a violet edge. Fairly intense, very fine aroma of jammy black fruit with a fine toasty oak nuance and hints of underbrush. Powerful and fleshy on the palate, with some concentration, slightly marked tannins and with a mild note of greeness, very flavourful.

PÉREZ CARAMÉS

Peña Picón, s/n
24500 Villafranca del Bierzo (León)
☎: 987 540 197 - Fax: 987 540 314
1018fp@teleline.es

Established: 1986

⊕ 156 ⊌ 32 has. ☛ 30%

🍇70%: -CH -FI -DE -BE -JP -MX

EL VINO DE LOS CÓNSULES DE ROMA 2002 JOVEN RED
100% mencía

78 Deep cherry. Aroma of black bramble berries with balsamic notes and a plummy hint. Fleshy palate with fresh but slightly green fruit tannins (herbs).

CASAR DE VALDAIGA 2001 RED
100% mencía

79 Dark cherry with a garnet red edge. Intense aroma with fresh overtones of red fruit, not very ripe skins and spicy hints. Flavourful, quite fresh palate without great crianza expression.

CASAR DE VALDAIGA 2000 CRIANZA RED
100% mencía

80 Garnet red cherry with a brick red edge. Powerful, toasty aroma with hints of reduction (varnish). Flavourful palate with fine bitter crianza notes (dark-roasted flavours, jam) and good acidity.

EL VINO DE LOS CÓNSULES DE ROMA 2000 CRIANZA RED
100% mencía

80 Garnet red cherry. Quite intense aroma with the freshness of oak and skins and rich varietal notes. Flavourful, quite fleshy palate with a nuance of sweet fruit.

PITTACUM

De la Iglesia, 11
24546 Arganza (León)
☎: 987 548 054 - Fax: 987 548 054
pittacum@ pittacum.com
www.pittacum.com

Established: 1999

⊕ 250 ▤ 200,000 litres ⊌ 4 has.

PITTACUM 2002 OAK AGED RED
100% mencía   ⊕ 6

86 Very deep cherry with a violet edge. Intense aroma with predominant notes of macerated red fruit. Fleshy palate with slightly marked although promising oak tannins, a ripe, toasty fruit nuance, good acidity and well-balanced.

PRADA A TOPE

La Iglesia, s/n
24546 Canedo (León)
☎: 902 400 101 - Fax: 987 567 000
info@pradaatope.es
www.pradaatope.es

Established: 1984

⊕ 300 ▤ 400,000 litres ⊌ 30 has.

☛ 85% 🍇15%: -CH -DE -AU -US

PALACIO DE CANEDO 2003 WHITE
100% godello

73 Golden yellow. Powerful, fruity aroma with smoky and creamy oak notes. Dry and warm on the palate with an oily texture, toasty oak and barely any fruit expression.

PALACIO DE CANEDO 2003 ROSÉ
85% mencía , 15% godello

80 Lively raspberry. Intense aroma of ripe red fruit (syrupy hints) and toasty hints of skins. Flavourful palate with fine bitter notes and good acidity.

PRADA A TOPE 2003 MACERACIÓN CARBÓNICA RED
mencía

84 Cherry with a violet hue. Intense, fruity aroma (strawberry syrup) and toasty notes of skins. Fresh, flavourful palate, with fleshy overtones, fine bitter notes of liquorice, warm, with good acidity.

PALACIO DE CANEDO 2003 RED
100% mencía

83 Almost opaque cherry with a violet hue. Powerful, fruity, very concentrated aroma with toasty notes and spicy skins and a terroir nuance. Fleshy, flavourful palate with ripe, oily tannins, a certain elegance and expression of young wine.

PRADA A TOPE 1996 GRAN RESERVA RED
100% mencía

82 Garnet red cherry with a brick red edge. Intense aroma with predominant spicy notes of reduction (leathers, rotting waste). Flavourful, fleshy palate with a ripe fruit nuance (prunes) and good crianza expression.

SEÑORÍO DE PEÑALBA

Polígono Industrial del Bierzo, parc. 31-32
24560 Toral de los Vados (León)
☎: 987 545 271 - Fax: 987 544 828

Established: 1989

⊞ 10,000 🗑 13,000,000 litres 🍇 100 has.

🇪🇸 75% 🌐25%: -US -MX -CU -DO -DE -DK -NL -SE -DK -CH -UK -BE

SEÑORÍO DE PEÑALBA 2003 WHITE
SEÑORÍO DE PEÑALBA 1998 CRIANZA RED
SEÑORÍO DE PEÑALBA 1997 RESERVA RED

VALSANZO SELECCIÓN

Manuel Azaña, 9 Edif. Ambassador, Local 15
47014 (Valladolid)
☎: 677 448 608 - Fax: 983 784 096
valsanzo@telefonica.net

⊞ 250 🗑 150,000 litres 🍇 80 has.

🇪🇸 30% 🌐70%

TERRAS CÚA 2002 CRIANZA RED
100% mencía

87 Cherry with a garnet red-violet edge. Medium intensity aroma with toasty wood and a suggestion of minerals. Expressive, flavourful palate with good concentrated fruit/wood integration, and ripe grape and wood tannins in the finish.

Vinos VALTUILLE

La Fragua, s/n
24530 Valtuille de Abajo (León)
☎: 987 562 112 - Fax: 987 549 425

Established: 2000

🗑 90,000 litres 🍇 12 has.

PAGO DE VALDONESE 2003 JOVEN RED

Comercial Vinícola VILLAFRANQUINA

El Cotelo, s/n
24500 Villafranca del Bierzo (León)
☎: 987 540 237 - Fax: 987 542 364

Established: 1966

⊞ 300 🗑 10,000,000 litres
🍇 2,000 has. 🇪🇸 100%

DON MARIANO 2003 RED
PADORNIÑA 2003 RED

VINIMUSA

Avenida José Antonio, 2
24546 Arganza (León)
☎: 987 546 705 - Fax: 987 546 705

CASAR DE SAMPIRO MENCÍA 2002 RED

VINOS DEL BIERZO

Avenida de la Constitución, 106
24540 Cacabelos (León)
☎: 987 546 150 - Fax: 987 549 236
info@vinosdelbierzo.com
www.vinosdelbierzo.com

Established: 1963

⊞ 1,000 🗑 14,000,000 litres 🍇 1,100 has.
🇪🇸 90% 🌐10%

GUERRA 2002 WHITE
palomino, doña blanca

69 Pale with greenish nuances. Fairly intense aroma with mild notes of fermentation. Quite flavourful palate with herby hints and fresh overtones.

SEÑORÍO DEL BIERZO 2003 WHITE
100% godello

75 Pale yellow. Intense, slightly fruity aroma with fine spicy notes of skins and hints of fine herbs. Flavourful on the palate without great fruit expression and slightly oily.

VIÑA ORO 2003 WHITE
doña blanca, godello

DO BIERZO

70 Pale yellow with golden nuances. Intense, ripe aroma without great fruit expression. Flavourful and bitter on the palate with an acidic edge.

GUERRA 2002 ROSÉ
100% mencía

64 Intense salmon pink with an orangey hue. Aroma with oxidation notes, somewhat oily. Bitter palate with an oily texture, without expression.

VIÑA ORO 2003 ROSÉ
100% mencía

71 Raspberry with an orangey hue. Not very intense aroma without great nuances and with a slightly spicy and sweet nuance. Quite flavourful and bitter on the palate, lacking symmetry.

VIÑA ORO 2003 RED
mencía

80 Intense cherry-raspberry. Fresh, fruity aroma (macerating strawberries). Dry, fruity palate with character of the vine variety, fresh.

VINOS GUERRA 2002 RED
100% mencía

72 Garnet red with an orangey hue. Slightly alcoholic aroma with reduction notes (leather, wet hide). Marked, drying tannins on the palate.

GUERRA 2002 OAK AGED RED
100% mencía

76 Brick red. Discreet aroma of slightly reduced fruit, tobacco notes of the crianza. Flavourful, fresh palate with notes of reduction in the bottle.

GUERRA 1998 CRIANZA RED
100% mencía

72 Brick red. Slightly reduced fruit aroma, spicy notes, muted. Flavourful palate, fresh but without fruit expression.

SEÑORÍO DEL BIERZO 1997 RESERVA RED
100% mencía

79 Brick red. Toasty aroma with reduction notes (tobacco, orange peel) of the crianza. Flavourful, fresh palate with complex crianza notes and a pleasant finish (creamy).

FONTOUSAL 2002 WHITE
FONTOUSAL 2002 ROSÉ
GUERRA 2003 MACERACIÓN CARBÓNICA RED
FONTOUSAL 2002 RED

VIÑAS BIERZO

Carretera Ponferrada a Cacabelos s/n
24410 Camponaraya (León)
☎: 987 463 009 - Fax: 987 450 323
vdelbierzo@granbierzo.com
www.granbierzo.com

Established: 1963

⊕ 300 ▯ 14,000,000 litres ⚜ 800 has.

🍷 98% 🌐2%: -US -UK -FR -CH -BE -DE

NARAYA WHITE
VALMAGAZ WHITE
NARAYA ROSÉ
MARQUÉS DE CORNATEL 2003 WHITE
VALMAGAZ 2002 ROSÉ
VALDERRETILLAS 2003 RED
NARAYA 2003 RED
VALMAGAZ MENCIA 2002 RED
MARQUÉS DE CORNATEL 2002 RED
GRAN BIERZO 2000 CRIANZA RED
GRAN BIERZO 1997 RESERVA RED
FUNDACION 1963 2000 RESERVA RED

VITICULTORES BERCIANOS

República Argentina, 1-E
24400 Ponferrada (León)
☎: 987 412 083 - Fax: 987 412 088
galiciano@galiciano.com
www.galiciano.com

Established: 2000

⊕ 40 ▯ 200,000 litres 🍷 90% 🌐10%

GRAN RIOCUA JOVEN RED
RIOCUA ROBLE RED
GRAN RIOCUA ROBLE RED

DO BINISSALEM MALLORCA

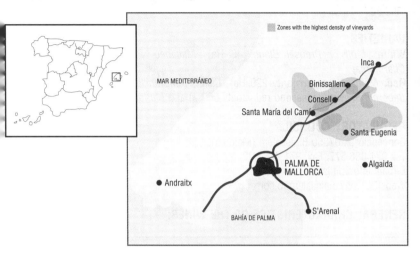

Zones with the highest density of vineyards

MAR MEDITERRÁNEO

Inca
Binissallem
Consell
Santa María del Camí
Santa Eugenia
PALMA DE MALLORCA
Algaida
Andraitx
S'Arenal
BAHÍA DE PALMA

NEWS. The year in which the DO exceeded 500 Ha (in 1990, the year of its creation, only 300 Ha were registered) was ironically a year of low production, mainly caused by the low yield due to one of the driest and hottest summers in living memory on the island (besides the heavy hail which affected the village of Binissalem). Despite this, the alcohol content was not excessively high due to the rainfall in september which corrected the sugar content of the fruit.

Hectares of Vineyard	No. of Viticulturists	No. of Bodegas	2003 Harvest	2003 Production	Marketing
508	145	12	Very Good	1,008,145 litres	98% Spain 2% foreign

Regarding quality, it is not easy to find young wines amongst the highest rated, among which the most outstanding is the Manto Negro González Súñer; nonetheless, its toasty notes acquired from its ageing in wood are more evident than its fruity notes. Perhaps the time has come to reconsider the possibility of incorporating a greater percentage of foreign varieties in blends in which the local *Manto Negro* is still prominent. It is no secret that the wines of Binissalem are losing ground in favour of their neighbours from Pla i Llevant, whose finest examples are produced with *Cabernet Sauvignon, Syrah* and *Merlot*.

LOCATION. In the central region on the island of Majorca. It covers the municipal areas of Santa María del Camí, Binissalem, Sencelles, Consell and Santa Eugenia.

CLIMATE. Mild Mediterranean, with dry, hot summers and short winters. The average rainfall per year is around 450 mm. The production region is protected from the northerly winds by the Sierra de Tramuntana and the Sierra de Alfabia mountain ranges.

SOIL. The soil is of a brownish-grey or dun limey type, with limestone crusts on occasions. The slopes are quite gentle, and the vineyards are situated at an altitude ranging from 75 to 200 m.

VARIETIES:
White: *Moll or Prensal Blanc* (46 Ha), *Macabeo, Parellada, Moscatel and Chardonnay.*
Red: *Manto Negro* (majority 229 Ha), *Callet, Tempranillo, Syrah, Monastrell* and *Cabernet Sauvignon* (second red variety 56 Ha) and *Merlot.*

REGULATORY COUNCIL.
Concepció, 7. 07350 Binissalem (Majorca).
Tel: 971 886 577. Fax: 971 886 522.
E-mail: info@binissalemdo.com
Website: www.binissalemdo.com

GENERAL CHARACTERISTICS OF THE WINES:

Whites	These are straw yellow in colour. They are characterised by their wild, fruity traits, with hints of mountain herbs and a very Mediterranean character; the best, in which the personality of the local *Prensal* grapes stands out, provide a great complexity of nuances and excellent balance on the palate.
Rosés	These are pink and are characterised by their hints of aged wood, typical of the vineyards that receive a lot of sunshine.
Reds	These are the most characteristic of the region and represent almost three quarters of the production of the denomination. There are young and, especially, aged wines. Their character is determined by the peculiarities of the *Manto Negro* autochthonous variety, which provides an essence of ripe fruits and hints of caramel; on the palate, the wines are well-balanced and persistent.

DO BINISSALEM MALLORCA

ANTONIO NADAL

Finca Son Roig. Camino Son Roig, s/n
07350 Binissalem (Baleares)
☎: 971 451 146 - Fax: 971 771 502
bodegasantonionadal@hotmail.com
www.binissalemdo.com

Established: 1960

🍶 180 🗄 300,000 litres
🍇 29 has. 💯 100%

BLANC DE MOLL 2003 WHITE
ROS 2003 ROSÉ
TRES UVAS 2001 RED
TRES UVAS 2002 RED
TINTO DE AÑAROS 2001 OAK AGED RED
TRES UVAS 2000 CRIANZA RED
TRES UVAS 1999 CRIANZA RED
TRES UVAS 1999 RESERVA RED
TRES UVAS 1998 RESERVA RED
TRES UVAS 1997 RESERVA RED

Vinyes i Vins CA SA PADRINA

Camí dels Horts, s/n
07140 Sencelles (Balears)
☎: 686 933 991 - Fax: 971 616 336
casapadrina@hotmail.com

Established: 1999

🍶 40 🗄 25,000 litres 🍇 10 has.
💯 98% 🌍2%: -DE -FR

MANTONEGRO GONZÁLEZ SUÒER 2003
ROBLE RED
manto negro, syrah, cabernet sauvignon, merlot

85 Cherry with an orangey hue. Fine, toasty aroma (cocoa toffee) with an expression of ripe fruit. Light, round palate with foresty scrubland herbs in the retronasal passage and persistent but restrained tannins.

JAUME DE PUNTIRÓ

Plaza Nova, 23
07320 Santa María del Cami (Baleares)
☎: 971 620 023 - Fax: 971 620 023

Established: 1981

🍶 107 🗄 120,000 litres 🍇 11 has.
💯 90% 🌍10%: -DE -CH -LU

JAUME DE PUNTIRÓ 2003 JOVEN WHITE
100% prensal blanc

83 Pale. Fresh aroma with fruit, white flowers, fine exotic hints and herbs. Flavourful palate with spicy notes, minerals and good acidity.

JAUME DE PUNTIRÓ DAURAT 2002
F. BARRICA WHITE
100% prensal blanc

78 Pale gold. Intense aroma with predominant wood notes and hints of fennel. Flavourful, bitter palate with hardly any fruit expression and good acidity.

BUC 2001 CRIANZA RED

85 Garnet red cherry with a brick red glint. Intense, ripe aroma with fine reduction notes (tobacco, leather, cedar, smoky oak). Flavourful, fleshy palate with an excellent crianza expression and a suggestion of terroir.

J.P. 2001 CRIANZA RED

89 Fairly intense cherry. Aroma with mineral notes (dry earth), forest herbs, fine toasty scents and good fruit expression. Slightly fleshy, warm palate with mineral notes and ripe fruit, warm and slightly spirituous.

JAUME DE PUNTIRÓ CARMESÍ 2001
CRIANZA RED
manto negro, callet

85 Dark garnet red cherry. Powerful aroma of very ripe fruit with fine toasty oak, a suggestion of Mediterranean herbs and notions of terroir. Fleshy, concentrated palate with ripe and oily tannins, liquorice and toasty oak.

JAUME DE PUNTIRÓ VERMELL 2002
JOVEN RED

JOSÉ L. FERRER (FRANJA ROJA)

Conquistador, 103
07350 Binissalem (Balears)
☎: 971 511 050 - Fax: 971 870 084
bfroja.encata@bitel.es
www.vinosferrer.com

Established: 1931

🍶 1,800 🗄 2,000,000 litres 🍇 80 has.
💯 92% 🌍8%: -DE -NL -AT -DK -JP

JOSÉ L. FERRER BLANC DE BLANCS 2003
WHITE
71% moll, 14% parellada, 10% moscatel, 5% macabeo

80 Pale with a greenish hue. Intense, very fine aroma of fruit and white flowers with fine notes of herbs and anise and hints of citrus fruit. Flavourful, bitter palate with an acidic edge.

VERITAS 2003 F. BARRICA WHITE
97% moll, 3% parellada

79 Pale golden yellow. Slightly intense aroma with smoky oak notes and without great nuances. Flavourful, bitter palate with a slightly acidic edge.

JOSÉ L. FERRER 2003 ROSÉ
53% manto negro, 25% tempranillo, 15% callet, 3% cabernet sauvignon, 4% otras

201

80 Deep raspberry with a coppery hue. Quite intense aroma of red stone fruit with jammy hints. Fresh palate with fine bitter notes, slightly oily with a hint of spices and a suggestion of minerals.

BINISSALEM AUTÉNTICO 2003 JOVEN RED
60% manto negro, 30% cabernet sauvignon, 7% tempranillo, 2% callet, 1% syrah

79 Not very deep cherry with a brick red glint. Slightly intense, fruity aroma with toasty hints of skins. Flavourful palate with fresh, spicy and balsamic overtones, pleasant with good acidity.

AÑADA JOSÉ L. FERRER 2002 OAK AGED RED
60% manto negro, 21% cabernet sauvignon, 16% tempranillo, 3% callet, other
🍷 6

79 Not very deep cherry with an orange glint. Quite intense aroma of ripe fruit with a spicy hint of oak. Flavourful palate, more expressive than in the nose, bitter, slightly warm and oily.

JOSÉ L. FERRER 2001 CRIANZA RED
58% manto negro, 21% cabernet sauvignon, 15% tempranillo, 3% callet, 4% other

78 Garnet red cherry with a brick red glint. Intense aroma with predominant notes of spices and fine reduction. Flavourful palate with a certain crianza expression and without great nuances.

VERITAS 2001 CRIANZA RED
56% manto negro, 26% cabernet sauvignon, 17% tempranillo, 1% callet

79 Fairly deep cherry with a brick red edge. Quite intense, ripe aroma with spicy oak notes and fine reduction. Flavourful, very bitter palate and a slightly acidic edge.

JOSÈ L. FERRER RESERVA ESPECIAL 2000 RED
56% manto negro, 20% tempranillo, 17% cabernet sauvignon, 4% callet, 3% other

88 Quite intense cherry. Fine, toasty aroma with good fruit expression with toasty, elegant notes well-integrated in the wine. Round, oily, elegant palate, the vigneron's best wine.

VERITAS 1999 RESERVA RED
65% manto negro, 28% cabernet sauvignon, 7% tempranillo

86 Cherry with an orangey edge. Fine, toasty aroma (cocoa, toffee) with slightly jammy fruit due to the evolution in bottle, overall harmony in the nose. Round, oily, elegant, fresh palate with sweet and fine tannins and quite persistent.

JOSÉ L. FERRER 1998 GRAN RESERVA RED
66% manto negro, 18% cabernet sauvignon, 15% tempranillo, 1% callet

84 Garnet red cherry with a brick red glint. Powerful, ripe aroma with fine reduction notes (tobacco, cedar, old furniture). Flavourful, expressive palate, slightly warm and bitter with good acidity.

BRUT VERITAS 2001 BRUT NATURE
76% moll, 11% moscatel, 7% macabeo, 6% parellada

83 Brilliant gold with a slightly robust and persistent bead. Intense aroma of ripe white fruit (exotic hints) with good crianza expression (fine lees) and a floral essence. Dry, creamy palate with fine bitter notes (cumin, nuts) and excellent acidity.

VERITAS DOLÇ 2003 MOSCATEL
100% moscatel de grano menudo

78 Straw-coloured with a greenish edge. Herbaceous aroma with scrubland herbs and a suggestion of ripeness. Sweet, flavourful palate with good bitterness that balances the sweetness and a herby finish.

JOAN MIR 1997 RESERVA ESPECIAL RED

MACIÀ BATLE

Camí Coanegra, s/n
07320 Santa María del Camí (Balears)
☎: 971 140 014 - Fax: 971 140 086
correo@maciabatle.com
www.maciabatle.com

Established: 1998
🛢 550 📦 500,000 litres 🌿 50 has.
🍷 80% 🌐20%: -DE -SE -DK -UK

MACIÀ BATLE BLANC DE BLANCS 2003 JOVEN WHITE
80% prensal blanc, 20% chardonnay

81 Pale gold with a greenish hue. Intense, fresh aroma with white fruit, hints of flowers and fennel. Flavourful, very bitter palate (with slight notes of greeness), pleasant.

MACIÀ BATLE BLANC DE BLANCS ÚNIC 2003 F. BARRICA WHITE
70% prensal blanc, 30% chardonnay

83 Brilliant gold. Powerful aroma with predominant oak notes (smoky, vanilla) and varietal hints of Chardonnay. Dry, flavourful, slightly warm, oily, bitter palate with mountain herbs and toffee in the retronasal passage.

MACIÀ BATLE 2003 JOVEN ROSÉ
80% manto negro, 10% callet, 5% cabernet sauvignon, 5% syrah

82 Intense raspberry with a coppery hue. Slightly intense and fruity aroma with hints of sun-drenched skins and fresh herby and terroir overtones. Flavourful palate with fine bitter and toasty notes.

PAGOS DE MARÌA 2001 RED
59% manto negro, 21% cabernet sauvignon, 16% syrah, 4% merlot

88 Garnet red cherry. Aroma with mild balsamic notes, red fruit, varietal expression and fine toasty scents, elegant. Round palate with expression and spicy notes, supple but precise tannins and an excellent retronasal effect.

MACIÀ BATLE 2001 CRIANZA RED
80% manto negro, 10% callet, 10% cabernet sauvignon

83 Brilliant cherry with a saffron glint. Intense, ripe aroma with predominant notes of fine reduction. Flavourful, fleshy palate with slightly drying tannins and a balsamic suggestion, liquorice.

MACIÀ BATLE RESERVA PRIVADA 2000 RED
80% manto negro, 10% callet, 10% cabernet sauvignon

86 Cherry with an orange edge. Fine, delicate aroma with toasty hints of pastries and cocoa and ripe fruit but with expression. Round palate with oily tannins well-integrated in the wine, a good evolution in the bottle.

MACIÀ BATLE 2003 RED

Vins NADAL

Ramón Llull, 2
07350 Binissalem (Balears)
☎: 971 511 058 - Fax: 971 870 150
albaflor@vinsnadal.com - info@vinsnadal.net
www.vinsnadal.com

Established: 1995

⊕ 100 ▤ 175,000 litres ❦ 8 has.
🏆 90% (🌐10%: -DE

ALBAFLOR 2003 ROSÉ
85% manto negro , 15% cabernet sauvignon

75 Deep raspberry with a coppery nuance. Intense aroma with toasty, slightly sweet notes. Flavourful, warm palate without great fruit expression.

ALBAFLOR 2003 JOVEN RED
cabernet sauvignon, manto negro

79 Lively garnet red cherry. Intense aroma of red fruit with nuances of sweetness and macerated skins. Flavourful palate with slightly rough and quite elegant tannins and a suggestion of sweetness and spices.

ALBAFLOR 2001 CRIANZA RED
70% manto negro , 30% cabernet sauvignon

75 Garnet red cherry with a brick red edge. Intense, toasty aroma with fine spicy and reduction notes. Flavourful, bitter palate without great nuances.

ALBAFLOR 2000 RESERVA RED
manto negro , cabernet sauvignon

77 Not very intense garnet red cherry with a coppery hue. Slightly intense aroma of red fruit with fine notes of spices and reduction.. Flavourful, supple palate without great nuances and with a hint of spices and reduction.

ALBAFLOR 2003 WHITE
SYRAH 110 VINS NADAL 2003 RED
MERLOT 110 VINS NADAL 2002 RED

PERE ANTONI LLABRÉS

C. de Sor Francinaina Cirer, 14
07040 Sencelles (Balears)

☎: 971 872 418 - Fax: 971 872 418

SERRAL DE CAN RAMIS

RAMANYÀ

Quarter VIII, 16
07320 Santa Maria del Carmí (Baleares)
☎: 971 620 040 - Fax: 971 140 045
ramanya@terra.es

Established: 2003
⊕ 24 ▤ 33,000 litres ❦ 14 has. 🏆 100%

RAMANYÀ 2003 OAK AGED RED
70% manto negro, 30% callet, syrah, cabernet sauvignon

83 Garnet red cherry with a coppery glint. Intense, ripe aroma with fine smoky oak notes, balsamic and terroir hints. Fleshy, flavourful palate with rough, oily tannins and smoky notes and liquorice in the retronasal passage.

RAMANYÀ 2003 WHITE
100% prensal blanc

80 Brilliant pale with a greenish hue. Intense, fresh aroma with white fruit and hints of flowers (orange blossom) and fine herbs. Flavourful palate with bitter and slightly mineral notes, good acidity.

RAMANYÀ VI DOLÇ RED
manto negro

83 Cherry with a redcurrant edge. Aroma of macerated red fruit with notes of flowers and ripe skins. Sweet, fruity palate with acidity-sweetness symmetry, hints of sloes in liqueur and a bitter finish.

Bodegas RIBAS

Montanya, 2
07330 Consell (Balears)
☎: 971 622 673 - Fax: 971 622 746
hhribas@hotmail.com

Established: 1986
⊕ 220 ▤ 170,000 litres ❦ 40 has.
🏆 70% (🌐30%

SIÓ CONTRAST 2000 F. BARRICA WHITE

86 Golden yellow. Powerful aroma, rich in crianza nuances, hints of ripe fruit, spices, flowers (acacia) and Mediterranean herbs. Powerful, warm palate with fine bitter notes and smoky oak, very long.

SIO CONTRAST 2001 RED
gorgollasa

84 Garnet red cherry. Medium-intensity, fruity, fresh aroma of fine toasty oak notes (cocoa). Fresh, fruity, very well-balanced, somewhat elegant palate with supple and light tannins.

SIÓ DE RIBAS 2000 RED

DO BINISSALEM MALLORCA

Celler SANTA EUGÈNIA

Balanguera 40
07142 Santa Eugenia (Mallorca)
☎: 971 144 494 - Fax: 971 144 494

Established: 2001
⊕ 24 ▤ 95,000 litres 🍇 6,5 has. 🍷 100%

VINYA TAUJANA 2002 OAK AGED RED
70% manto negro, 30% cabernet sauvignon

78 Ruby red cherry with an orange glint. Intense aroma with predominant reduction notes and a creamy essence of oak. Flavourful palate with bitter notes (liquorice, dark-roasted flavours, dry earth).

VINYA TAUJANA 2003 WHITE
moll

81 Pale yellow. Intense aroma of fruit and white flowers with an essence of lees. Flavourful palate with fine bitter notes, fragrant herbs and spicy hints of skins, a suggestion of minerals and noticeable acidity.

DO BIZKAIKO TXAKOLINA

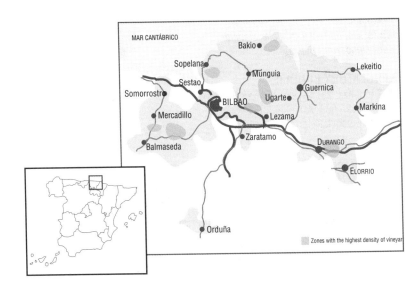

NEWS. The 2003 harvest was excellent, not only in the main Txakoli DO, but also in the whole Basque wine region. The drought and the high temperatures brought forward the harvesting by an average of 10 to 14 days, with an optimum ripening of the grapes. But, apart from the optimistic statements by the Regulatory Council, what is indeed evident in the Txakolis of the last few vintages is that they are more characterised and interesting wines (especially the whites), where the producers have taken full advantage of the varietal potential of the *Hondarrabi Zuri*. In a sunny year like 2003, the fruity expression proves to be very fresh, with hints of ripe apple and an oily mouthfeel quite characteristic of the stock. There was also a notable increase in volume, brought about by the entering into production of a new vineyard. We are delighted that, after calling on the producers to send us samples of their wines, we have more than doubled the number of tasting samples in relation to the previous edition, although there are still many to be assessed.

Hectares of Vineyard	No. of Viticulturists	No. of Bodegas	2003 Harvest	2003 Production	Marketing
195	275	74	Very Good	710,000 litres	100% Spain

LOCATION. In the province of Vizcaya. The production region covers both coastal areas and other areas inland.

CLIMATE. Quite humid and mild due to the influence of the Bay of Biscay which tempers the temperatures. Fairly abundant rainfall, with an average of 1,000 to 1,300 mm per year.

SOIL. Mainly clayey, although slightly acidic on occasions, with a fairly high organic matter content.

VARIETIES:
White: *Hondarrabi Zuri, Folle Blanche.*
Red: *Hondarrabi Beltza.*

REGULATORY COUNCIL.
Bº Garaioltza, 23. 48196 Lezama (Vizcaya).
Tel: 944 555 063. Fax: 944 556 245.
E-mail: prvegetal@lorra-cg.net
Website: www.bizkaikotxakolina.org

GENERAL CHARACTERISTICS OF THE WINES:

Whites	These are the most characteristic of the denomination. They are characterised by their dull, straw yellow with, on occasions, green glimmer; their aroma combines floral and fruity notes, although they have a more herbaceous character than those of Getaria due to the *Folle Blanche* variety, together with the *Hondarrabi Zuri* variety. on the palate they are light, easy drinking and have a freshness that gives them their high acidity.
Rosés	In the region, this type of wine is known as 'Ojo de Gallo', rooster's eye. They represent a very small proportion of the production; they are fresh and light, although on the palate they tend to be quite acidic.
Reds	As with the rosé wines they are also a minority product; in fact, they are only produced in regions with a certain tradition. In general, they are excessively acidic.

AGIRRE LLONA

Barrio Olagoien, 178
48178 Lezama (Vizcaya)
☎: 944 556 272
Established: 1992

AGIRRE LLONA WHITE
AGIRRE LLONA ROSÉ
AGIRRE LLONA RED

AITABITXI

Bº Goitioltza, 45
48196 Lezama (Vizcaya)
☎: 944 556 554 - Fax: 944 571 817
bodegaitabitxi@hotmail.com

AITABITXI 2003 WHITE
60% hondarrabi zuri, 40% folle blanche

78 Pale with a greenish hue. Intense aroma of white fruit with hints of petals and an essence of lees. Flavourful, bitter palate with hints of aniseed and citrus fruit and an acidic edge.

AITABITXI 2003 ROSÉ
50% hondarrabi zuri, 30% folle blanch, 20% hondarrabi beltza

76 Brilliant salmon. Intense aroma of slightly reduced ripe fruit (lees, withered petals). Fresh, flavourful, spicy palate with not very fine bitter hints, good acidity.

Txakoli ARITXOLA

Eguskiza, s/n
48200 Durango (Vizcaya)
☎: 946 811 285 - Fax: 946 811 285
arritxola1@txakoliarritxola.com
www.txakoliarritxola.com
Established: 1992
🍷 6 📊 13,000 litres 🍇 3 has. 🍷 100%

TXAKOLI ARITXOLA

Txakoli ARTEBAKARRA

Bº San Isidro, 24
48160 Derio (Vizcaya)
☎: 944 541 292 - Fax: 944 540 196
Established: 1950
📊 6,000 litres 🍇 1 has. 🍷 100%

ARTEBAKARRA WHITE

AXPE (JOSE A. BILBAO)

Bº Atxondoa, Cº Axpe, 13

48300 Markina - Xemein (Vizcaya)
☎: 946 168 285 - Fax: 946 168 285

AXPE

AYARZA

Bº Aretxalde, 44
48196 Lezama (Vizcaya)
📊 2,500 litres 🍷 100%

TXAKOLI AYARZA

DONIENE-GORRONDONA

Bº Benta -Alde, 10
48130 Bakio (Vizcaya)
☎: 946 194 795 - Fax: 946 195 831
gorrondona@euskalnet.net
www.bakio.com
🍷 10 📊 80,000 litres 🍇 12 has.
🍷 95% 🍇 5%: -US -AD

DONIENE 2003 JOVEN WHITE
100% hondarrabi zuri

81 Brilliant pale. Intense aroma of white fruit with fine floral and herby notes. Fresh, flavourful palate with spicy hints of skins and pronounced citrus acidity.

GORRONDONA 2003 JOVEN RED
100% hondarribi beltza

81 Dark cherry with a dark red edge. Powerful aroma with fine smoky, very varietal skins and hints of nettles. Flavourful, fleshy palate, with good fruit expression and a quality herbaceous essence, excellent acidity.

GORRONDONA 2003 JOVEN WHITE
DONIENE 2003 F. BARRICA WHITE
GORRONDONA 2003 RED

EGUZKITZA-URIARTE

Barrio Acillcona-Cº Eguskiza
48113 Fika (Vizcaya)
☎: 946 153 140 - Fax: 946 153 535
Established: 1867
📊 200,000 litres 🍇 10 has.
🍷 75% 🍇 25%

CASERÍO EGUZKITZA - URIARTE WHITE
CASERÍO EGUZKITZA - URIARTE ROSÉ

ERDIKOETXE LANDETXEA

Goitioltza, 38
48196 Lezama (Vizcaya)

DO BIZKAIKO TXAKOLINA

☎: 944 573 285 - Fax: 944 573 285
erdikoetxelandetxea@hotmail.com

Established: 2000
📦 8,000 litres 🍇 2 has.

ERDIKOETXE 2003 WHITE

80 Brilliant pale yellow. Intense aroma of white fruit with hints of petals and an essence of fine lees. Flavourful, fresh palate with green apples and grapey hints, slightly oily with excellent acidity.

ERDIKOETXE 2003 RED

76 Brilliant cherry with an orangey hue. Powerful, toasty aroma with a light hint of reduction (dried peaches) and a smoky essence. Flavourful palate with slightly marked tannins and notes of liquorice and fallen leaves.

GUEREDIAGA

Zubitalde Auzoa, 22
48195 Larrabetzu (Vizcaya)
☎: 944 558 095

🌐 8 📦 600 litres 🍷 100%

TXAKOLI LARRABETZUCO TORRE WHITE
TXAKOLI LARRABETZUCO TORRE RED

GURE AHALEGINAK

Bº Ibazurra, 1
48460 Orduña (Vizcaya)
☎: 945 384 126 - Fax: 945 384 126
maitedurana@euskalnet.net

Established: 1990
🍇 2 has. 🍷 100%

GURE AHALEGINAK 2003 WHITE

74 Very pale. Slightly intense aroma with fruit, white flowers and hints of citrus fruit. Fresh, quite flavourful palate without great fruit expression.

OSTEBI 2003 WHITE

77 Pale with greenish nuances. Not very intense aroma of white fruit and fine floral hints. Fresh, flavourful palate with spicy hints and good citrus acidity.

ITSASMENDI

Barrio Arane, s/n - Aptdo. Correos 241
48300 Gernika (Vizcaya)
☎: 677 580 362 - Fax: 946 270 316
bitsasmendi@euskalnet.net

Established: 1994
📦 190,000 litres 🍇 27 has.
🍷 90% 🌐10%: -US -DE

AHIEN 2003 WHITE
hondarrabi zuri

84 Pale with greenish nuances. Powerful aroma with predominant notes of herbs, smoky skins and white fruit. Flavourful palate with bitter notes, fine herbs and hints of citrus fruit in the finish.

ITSAS MENDI VENDIMIA TARDÍA 2002 DULCE WHITE
hondarrabi zuri

84 Brilliant golden yellow. Intense aroma with smoky and spicy notes, hints of citrus fruit and overripening. Bittersweet on the palate with fresh overtones (skins, phosphorous), notes of botrytis and a pronounced citrus acidity.

TXAKOLI ITSASMENDI BEREZIA 2003 WHITE
100% hondarrabi zuri

84 Yellow straw with a greenish rim. Floral and quite dense aroma of green fruit. Flavourful palate, well-balanced with flowers in the retronasal passage.

TXAKOLI ARANE 2003 WHITE

ITURRIALDE

Mantzorri-Bidea, 9
Apartado de Correos nº 6
48100 Mungia (Vizcaya)
☎: 946 742 706 - Fax: 946 741 221
aretxondo@euskalnet.net

Established: 1995
📦 62,000 litres 🍇 5,5 has.
🍷 95% 🌐5%

AMUNATEGI 2003 SECO WHITE

80 Brilliant pale with a greenish hue. Intense aroma of flor and white fruit with hints of fine lees and exotic notes (pineapples, grapefruit). Fresh, flavourful palate with fine bitter notes and excellent acidity.

ARETXONDO 2003 WHITE
hondarrabi zuri

82 Pale straw. Fresh aroma of apples and hay, expressive and varietal. Very fresh palate with excellent acidity, slightly oily and very Hondarrabi.

BION-ETXEA 2003 WHITE
100% munhe mahatsa

82 Pale with a greenish nuance. Not very intense yet clean aroma of ripe fruit (an exotic element), dried grass and lees. Oily, fresh palate of good fruit and herbs and notes of sweetness well-balanced with the bitter finish.

EGIA ENEA 2003 SECO WHITE

75 Yellow straw. Ripe aroma, unusual for a 2003 wine (orange peel, honey and pollen). Light palate with orange peel and good acidity, bitter.

DO BIZKAIKO TXAKOLINA

LARRONDO 2003 SECO WHITE

78 Yellow straw. Fresh, fruity aroma of aniseed. Fruity, slightly oily palate, easy drinking.

MARKO 2003 SECO WHITE

81 Pale with a greenish glint. Slightly intense aroma with a certain finesse of white fruit (apricot skins). Fresh, flavourful palate with fine bitter notes and rich hints of citrus fruit.

NEKESOLO 2003 SECO WHITE

79 Pale yellow with a greenish hue. Fresh aroma of green apples with hints of herbs and citrus fruit (sweet limes). Fresh, spicy, flavourful palate with excellent acidity.

JOSÉ ETXEBARRÍA URRUTIA

Txonebarri-C. Igartua, s/n
48110 Gatika (Vizcaya)
☎: 946 742 010

TXAKOLI ETXEBARRÍA

Txakoli LLARENA

Eras de Polankos, 13
48460 Orduña (Vizcaya)
☎: 945 384 300

Established: 1965
🍷 100%

TXAKOLI LLARENA WHITE

NUESTRA SEÑORA DE LA ANTIGUA

Burgos, 20
48460 Orduña (Vizcaya)
☎: 696 198 194 - Fax: 945 383 509

Established: 1996
🛢 10 🗄 25,000 litres 🌿 5 has.
🍷 99% 🍇1%

TXAKOLI VINO DEL AÑO WHITE

RUFINO ISASI

Bº Orobio, Cº Arazola
48200 Iurreta (Vizcaya)
☎: 946 251 069

TXAKOLI ISASI WHITE

SASIA BASERRIA

Sasia, 7
48810 Alonsotegi (Vizcaya)
☎: 944 980 179
jaldama@eresmas.net
Established: 1948

SASIA BASERRIA

TXORIERRI

Caserío Torre, 132, Bº Aretxalde
48196 Lezama (Vizcaya)
☎: 944 556 239

Established: 1883
🗄 25,000 litres 🌿 4 has. 🍷 100%

TXORIERRI TXAKOLINA WHITE

VIRGEN DE LOREA

Barrio de Lorea
48860 Otxaran-Zalla (Vizcaya)
☎: 946 390 296 - Fax: 946 670 521

Established: 1990
🗄 40,000 litres 🌿 10 has.

ARETXAGA JOVEN WHITE
SEÑORÍO DE OTXARAN JOVEN WHITE
SEÑORÍO DE OTXARAN RED

XABIER ARETXABALETA

Arteaga Auzoa, 107
48170 Zamudio (Vizcaya)
☎: 944 521 431 - Fax: 944 521 431

MAGALARTE 2003 WHITE

83 Pale yellow with a greenish hue. Powerful aroma of fruit and white flowers (exotic hints) with hints of herbs and fine lees. Flavourful, fruity aroma with excellent balance.

DO BULLAS

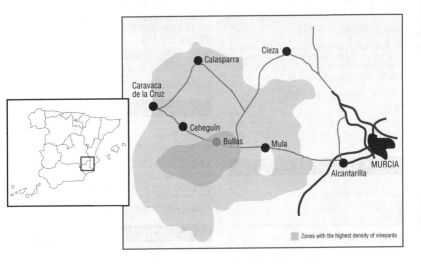

Zones with the highest density of vineyards

NEWS. There has been a considerable increase in production: from just over 5 million kilograms in 2002 up to 8 million in 2003, with perfectly healthy grapes. Nevertheless, there are too many fruity notes or rather hints on the brink of over-ripeness which reduce the typification of the *Monastrell*. Moreover, the best wines of the DO, the Partal of Bodegas Balcona, are all aged (the best of which is a Reserva of 99).

Amongst the young wines, the best rated wine is the Siscar of Bodegas Madroñal which, together with the Carrascalejo, is the only young single-variety wine made of Monastrell with a score of more than 80 points. This variety, which must form part of the wines of the DO with a percentage of at least 60%, still remains the 'little darling' of the region, although some positive reports on the behaviour of foreign varieties in certain blends are starting to appear, as well as on the *Tempranillo* and the *Garnacha*.

Hectares of Vineyard	No. of Viticulturists	No. of Bodegas	2003 Harvest	2003 Production	Marketing
3,000	800	10	Good	1,509,288 litres	76% Spain 24% foreign

Quite notable the increase of 500 Ha in the total area of the vineyards which fall under the DO, as well as the fact that the good export figures have been maintained, especially to countries in the European Union, such as Germany and the Netherlands.

LOCATION. In the province of Murcia. It covers the municipal areas of Bullas, Cehegín, Mula and Ricote, and several vineyards in the vicinity of Calasparra, Moratalla and Lorca.

CLIMATE. Mediterranean, with an average annual temperature of 15.6 °C and low rainfall (average of 300 mm per year). The heavy showers and storms which occur in the region are another defining element.

SOIL. Brownish-grey limey soil, with limestone crusts, and alluvial. The terrain is rugged and determined by the layout of the little valleys, each with their own microclimate. Distinction can be made between 3 areas: one to the north north-east with an altitude of 400 – 500 m; another in the central region, situated at an altitude of 500 – 600 m; and the third in the western and north-western region, with the highest altitude (500 – 810 m), the highest concentration of vineyards and the best potential for quality.

VARIETIES:
White: *Macabeo* (main) and *Airén*.
Red: *Monastrell* (main), *Tempranillo, Cabernet Sauvignon, Syrah, Merlot* and *Garnacha*.

REGULATORY COUNCIL.
Avda. de Murcia, 4. 30180 Bullas (Murcia).
Tel: 968 652 601. Fax: 968 652 601.
E-mail: crdob@iespaña.es

GENERAL CHARACTERISTICS OF THE WINES:

Whites	Produced with *Macabeo* and *Airén*, they are pale yellow and have pleasant fruity notes.
Rosés	The varietal character of those produced with *Monastrell* stands out. They are light, pleasant and easy drinking. Those produced from *Garnacha* are full-bodied on the palate.
Reds	Those produced from *Monastrell* and *Tempranillo* stand out for their Mediterranean character, sun-drenched fruit and fruity character, although they are less rounded than those of Jumilla and Alicante. On the other hand, their inclusion in the blend of the new varieties recently approved by the Council should afford greater structure and longevity to the red wines.

DO BULLAS

A. GARCÍA NOGUEROL

Carretera de Murcia, 102
30430 Cehegín (Murcia)
☎: 968 740 027 - Fax: 968 742 788

ALPARGATERO 2003 JOVEN RED

75 Garnet red cherry. Fruity and warm aroma. Fresh, flavourful, fruity palate, discreet.

Cooperativa Vinícola
AGRARIA SAN ISIDRO

Polígono Industrial Marimingo, Parcela 19.
C/ Altiplano, s/n
30180 Bullas (Murcia)
☎: 968 652 160 - Fax: 968 652 160
bodegasanisidro@terra.es

Established: 1957

🍶 50 📊 1,935,000 litres 🍇 370 has.
🍷 90% 🍏10%: -FI -DE -SE

CEPAS DEL ZORRO 2003 JOVEN WHITE
100% macabeo

79 Pale. Fresh, fruity, clean aroma with notes of green apples and herbs. Fresh, fruity, pleasant and flavourful palate.

CEPAS DEL ZORRO 2003 JOVEN ROSÉ
90% monastrell, 10% garnacha

75 Raspberry. Fresh, fruity aroma, despite mild hints of reduction. Fresh, fruity palate, not very prominent.

CEPAS DEL ZORRO 2003 JOVEN RED
60% monastrell, 25% tempranillo, 15% syrah

80 Garnet red cherry with a purple hue. Fresh, fruity aroma with slightly reduced notes (late racking). Better palate, flavourful and fruity (ripe black fruit).

CEPAS DEL ZORRO 2º AÑO 2003 RED
100% monastrell

66 Garnet red cherry. Fresh aroma, varietal, with a suggestion of very typified Monastrell, a hint of reduction. Highly developed palate, late racking. Not very clear.

CEPAS DEL ZORRO 2001 CRIANZA RED
70% monastrell, 20% tempranillo, 10% syrah

75 Garnet red cherry. Short aroma, without nuances. Slightly reduced. Light, slightly flavourful, warm palate with flabby tannins. Without expression.

BALCONA

Carretera de Avilés, Paraje "El Aceniche"
30180 Bullas (Murcia)
☎: 968 652 891 - Fax: 968 652 666

bodegabalcona@larural.es
www.paralelo40.org/partal

Established: 1998

🍶 125 📊 40,000 litres 🍇 12 has.
🍷 60% 🍏40%: -US -CH -DE -UK

PARTAL 37 BARRICAS SELECCIÓN 2002 RED
65% monastrell, 15% syrah, 10% tempranillo, 10% cabernet sauvignon

87 Very deep cherry. Aroma of concentrated jammy blackberries. A mild suggestion of well-integrated, toasty flavours (dark-roasted flavours with a hint of chocolate). Fleshy, flavourful palate, rich in expression of fruit and earth; persistent and ripe tannins with a long fruity nuance.

PARTAL 2001 CRIANZA RED
60% monastrell, 10% tempranillo, 15% cabernet sauvignon, 15% syrah

86 Intense cherry. Aroma of very ripe black fruit with mineral hints. Well-integrated wood, creamy. Fleshy palate of ripe black fruit and well-integrated wood; powerful, ripe tannins, highly flavourful.

PARTAL 1999 RESERVA RED
60% monastrell, 20% tempranillo, 15% cabernet sauvignon, 5% syrah

88 Intense cherry with a lively violet rim. Powerful aroma, rich in varietal expression and fruity with fine notes of crianza (cocoa, vanilla, tobacco), ripe fruit and nuances of minerals. Generous, with fleshy overtones and flavourful palate, ripe black fruit and creamy wood tannins; full, good persistence.

PARTAL 2000 CRIANZA RED

CARRASCALEJO

Finca El Carrascalejo, s/n
30180 Bullas (Murcia)
☎: 968 652 003 - Fax: 968 652 003
carrascalejo@carrascalejo.com
www.carrascalejo.com

Established: 1850

🍶 65 📊 500,000 litres 🍇 100 has. 🍷 100%

CARRASCALEJO 2003 ROSÉ
100% monastrell

77 Raspberry. Aroma with herbaceous notes, a fruity suggestion, a hint of freshness. Fresh, fruity palate, better than in the nose.

CARRASCALEJO 2003 RED
100% monastrell

81 Intense cherry with a violet hue. Aroma with fruit notes and pressed skins (bunches). Rustic hints. Fleshy, fresh palate, with dry tannins, fruity, young in style, flavourful, with body.

DO BULLAS

CARRASCALEJO 2000 CRIANZA RED
60% monastrell, 40% cabernet sauvignon

60 Garnet red cherry. Slightly reduced aroma, slightly overripe fruit, without nuances, viscous, warm. Mild carbonic notes on the palate, without finish and with a hint of refermentation.

FERNANDO CARREÑO PEÑALVER

Andalucía, 40
30430 Cehegín (Murcia)
☎: 968 740 004 - Fax: 968 740 004
bodegascarreño@mixmail.com

Established: 1930
48 500,000 litres 100%

MARMALLEJO MONASTRELL 2002 CRIANZA RED
50% monastrell, 40% tempranillo, 10% cabernet sauvignon

85 Garnet red cherry with a coppery edge. Intense, ripe aroma with fine smoky oak notes, a spicy suggestion and notions of terroir. Flavourful palate with quite marked but promising tannins, slightly warm and bitter with a suggestion of fresh fruit and liquorice.

MARMALLEJO MONASTRELL 2001 RED
50% monastrell, 40% tempranillo, 10% cabernet sauvignon

80 Intense cherry with coppery glints. Aroma with light reduction notes, less fruity than in our previous edition. Round, fruity palate, quite flavourful.

Bodegas LOS CEPEROS

Pago Los Ceperos
30430 Cehegín (Murcia)
☎: 968 271 370 - Fax: 968 271 326
info@losceperos.com

Established: 1997
60 80,000 litres 25 has.
20% 80%: -DK -DE -SE -PL

CEPEROS 2003 RED
70% monastrell, 15% cabernet sauvignon, 15% merlot

81 Intense cherry. Fruity aroma, very ripe black fruit, hints of ink and concentrated skins. Fleshy, full, flavourful palate, powerful, ripe tannins.

CEPEROS 2000 RED
70% monastrell, 15% cabernet sauvignon, 15% merlot

78 Intense cherry with a lively violet edge. Aroma with very jammy notes, almost overly ripe fruit. Fleshy palate with a muted fruit expression, sweet tannins, quite flavourful.

CEPEROS 1999

Bodegas MADROÑAL

Partal, 6
30180 Bullas (Murcia)
☎: 968 655 183 - Fax: 968 652 423
siscar@terra.com

Established: 2001
40,000 litres 8 has. 100%

SISCAR 2003 JOVEN RED
monastrell

82 Very intense cherry. Powerful aroma, rich in black fruit expression, dates, very expressive and varietal; very unlike the Jumilla and Alicante wines. Powerful, very fleshy palate, abundant sweet tannins, a rustic but typified hint.

MADROÑAL 2001 CRIANZA RED
monastrell, merlot

70 Quite intense cherry. Discreet aroma, notes of oak and slightly overripe fruit, notes of late racking. Fruity, lightly flabby and warm on the palate, quite flavourful.

MUNDO ENOLÓGICO Q & M

Herrera, 22
30180 Bullas (Murcia)
☎: 968 654 205 - Fax: 968 654 205
pilarquesadagil@yahoo.es

Established: 1998
12 30,000 litres 4 has.
90% 10%: -DE -NL

MERCADER QUESADA MONASTRELL 2003 JOVEN RED
100% monastrell

79 Garnet red cherry. Not very intense aroma, slightly lacking in fruit expression, with mineral notes. Medium-bodied, fruity, earthy, flavourful palate.

MERCADER QUESADA MONASTRELL 2002 OAK AGED RED
100% monastrell

78 Intense cherry. Aroma with notes of slightly woody oak, ripe fruit, hints of maceration. Fleshy, flavourful ripe palate, well-mannered.

MERCADER QUESADA 2003 OAK AGED RED
MERCADER QUESADA 2002 OAK AGED RED

Cooperativa Agrovinícola NUESTRA SEÑORA DEL ROSARIO

Avenida de la Libertad s/n
30180 Bullas (Murcia)
☎: 968 652 075 - Fax: 968 653 765
cnsrosario@bullas.net

www.bullas.net

Established: 1950

415 ▦ 4,000,000 litres ❦ 1,200 has.
66% 34%

LAS REÑAS MACABEO 2003 WHITE
macabeo

80 Pale with greenish glints. Fruity, fresh, pleasant aroma. Fresh, fruity palate, reminiscent of apples, flavourful.

LAS REÑAS MONASTRELL 2003 ROSÉ
monastrell

82 Fairly light raspberry. Fruity aroma (red stone fruit), very fresh. Generous, slightly dense palate, fruit well-enveloped by the alcohol, flavourful, persistent.

LAS REÑAS 2002 RED
monastrell

79 Intense garnet red cherry. Aroma of ripe fruit with a hint of overripening, hints of sweetness. Fleshy palate with body and ripe, dry and firm tannins.

LAS REÑAS MONASTRELL 2001 OAK AGED RED
monastrell, tempranillo

78 Deep cherry with a brick red edge. Aroma of jammy fruit, notes of well-mannered evolution. Flavourful, slightly round, warm palate with slightly muted tannins, quite flavourful.

LAS REÑAS MONASTRELL 2001 DULCE RED
monastrell

77 Garnet red cherry. Short aroma, without viscous or ripe fruit expression, with light, fine reduction notes. Sweet palate, without body, with few nuances yet quite flavourful.

LAS REÑAS MONASTRELL-SHIRAZ 2000 CRIANZA RED
80% monastrell, 20% syrah

78 Quite intense cherry. Fruity aroma, with reduction overtones, quite viscous, without great nuances. Flavourful, warm, balsamic palate; slightly flabby tannins, well-mannered.

LAS REÑAS SELECCIÓN 2000 RED
80% monastrell, 20% syrah

85 Cherry with a violet hue and vivacious overtones. Fine aroma, with well-integrated hints of wood and excellent reduction in the bottle. Round, flavourful palate with rich and ripe tannins, persistent.

SEÑORÍO DE BULLAS 1998 RESERVA RED
monastrell

81 Garnet red cherry. Aroma with fine notes of reduction (tobacco, cocoa), integrated fruit/wood. Flavourful, round palate, good evolution in the bottle; with fine overtones and supple tannins.

DO CALATAYUD

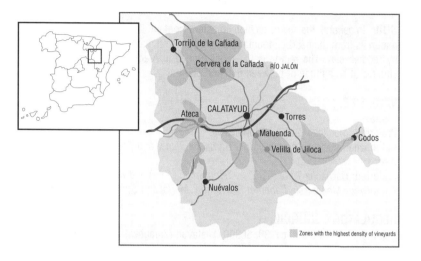

Zones with the highest density of vineyards

NEWS. The 2003 harvest was characterized by a sharp increase in production (41% in relation to 2002), boosted by the plentiful rainfall during the first part of the vegetative cycle and the absence of frost in the spring. In September, after a dry and very hot summer (with temperatures of up to 40 °C), there were rains, torrential in some cases, which caused certain outbreaks of botrytis, although the quality was not affected as the grapes were harvested very selectively in these areas.

Hectares of Vineyard	No. of Viticulturists	No. of Bodegas	2003 Harvest	2003 Production	Marketing
5,940	2,702	9 bottlers	Very Good	6,268,500 litres	30% Spain 70% foreign

Moreover, this increase in the volume of harvested grapes forced an inspection at the beginning of the summer of 2004 of the vineyards in the region to contain the production and to prevent an excess of grapes resulting in poorer quality.
The *Garnacha* of the Cooperativa San Alejandro with its Baltasar Gracián is exceptional (both the Viñas Viejas 2002, with 92 points, and the Reserva 2000 with 89), which last year hardly reached 80 points, although Castillo de Maluenda exceeds it in the production of young wines using the same variety.

LOCATION. It is situated in the western region of the province of Zaragoza, along the foothills of the Sistema Ibérico, outlined by the network of rivers woven by the different tributaries of the Ebro: Jalón, Jiloca, Manubles, Mesa, Piedra and Ribota, and covers 46 municipal areas of the Ebro Valley.

CLIMATE. Semi-arid and dry, although somewhat cooler than Cariñena and Borja, with cold winters, an average annual temperature which ranges between 12 and 14

°C, and a period of frost of between 5 and 7 months which greatly affects the production. The average rainfall ranges between 300 – 550 mm per year, with great day/night temperature contrasts during the ripening season.

SOIL. In general, the soil has a high limestone content. It is formed by rugged stony materials from the nearby mountain ranges and is on many occasions accompanied by reddish clay. The region is the most rugged in Aragón, and the vineyards are situated at an altitude of between 550 and 880 m.

VARIETIES:
White:
Preferred: *Macabeo* (25%) and *Malvasía*.
Authorized: *Moscatel de Alejandría, Garnacha Blanca* and *Chardonnay*.
Red:
Preferred: *Garnacha Tinta* (61.9%), *Tempranillo* (10%) and *Mazuela*.
Authorized: *Monastrell, Cabernet Sauvignon, Merlot* and *Syrah*.

REGULATORY COUNCIL.
Pol. Industrial La Charluca, 39. 50300 Calatayud (Zaragoza). Apdo. Correos 40.
Tel: 976 884 260. Fax: 976 885 912.
E-mail: comercial.crdoc@efor.es

GENERAL CHARACTERISTICS OF THE WINES:

Whites	These are pale yellow and are characterised by their fresh, fruity style. There is some experience with fermentation in barrels.
Rosés	These constitute the most characteristic product of the region and are excellent value for money. Produced mainly from *Garnacha*, they stand out for their fine varietal expression, their brilliant raspberry colour, their freshness, their strong aroma and their full-bodiedness, typical of the variety.
Reds	The *Garnacha* grapes give these wines a lively dark colour. The finest examples have quite a strong aroma, with notes of ripe black fruit; on the palate they are full-bodied and sometimes somewhat warm.

AGUSTÍN CUBERO

Polígono La Charluca, Nave 1
50300 Calatayud (Zaragoza)
☎: 976 882 332 - Fax: 976 887 512
bodegascuberocalatayud@efor.es

Established: 1996

🛢 320 📊 500,000 litres 🍇 64 has.

🍷 70% 🍾30%: -CH -DE -NL -US

ATALAYA 1999 JOVEN RED
ATALAYA REAL RED
MARQUÉS DE LAS NAVAS RED

Bodegas ALBADA

Avenida de la Cooperativa, s/n
50310 Villarroya de la Sierra (Zaragoza)
☎: 976 780 136 - Fax: 976 303 035
info@albada.com
www.bodegas-albada.com

Established: 2001

🛢 100 📊 120,000 litres 🍷 40% 🍾60%

ALBADA 2001 RED
100% garnacha

83 Cherry with a violet hue. Fairly intense aroma of toasty oak notes and a nuance of well-integrated jammy fruit. Flavourful, fleshy palate with good concentration and rough tannins, a good crianza expression, well-balanced.

Bodegas y Vinos
ANGEL LUIS PABLO URIOL

Camino de Calatayud s/n
50293 Terrer (Zaragoza)
☎: 976 898 400 - Fax: 976 898 401
valdepablo@valdepablo.com
www.valdepablo.com

Established: 1928

🛢 500 🍷 40% 🍾60%: -DE -NL -BE -FR -UK -US -JP -NG

DOM YAGO 2003 ROSÉ
garnacha

80 Salmon pink. Good intensity, harmonious aroma of ripe red fruit. Flavourful palate, sweet red fruit and agreeable bitter counterpoint.

SEÑORÍO DE SAN VICÉN 2003 JOVEN RED
tempranillo, garnacha

77 Brilliant garnet red cherry. Intense aroma with notes of red fruit and hints of sun-drenched skins. Flavourful palate with firm grape tannins, a mild hint of greeness and fine bitter notes.

DOM YAGO 2003 RED
tempranillo

76 Garnet red cherry with a violet hue. Intense, ripe aroma with ripe fruit, sun-drenched skins and a balsamic nuance. Flavourful palate, slightly marked tannins, with predominant bitter notes and an acidic edge.

DOM YAGO 1999 CRIANZA RED
garnacha, tempranillo

77 Garnet red cherry with a brick red glint. Intense aroma with predominat wood and reduction notes (tobacco, leather). Flavourful palate with warm notes and a good expression of traditional crianza.

SEÑORÍO DE SAN VICÉN 2003 JOVEN WHITE
DOM YAGO 2003 WHITE
SEÑORÍO DE SAN VICÉN 2003 JOVEN ROSÉ

CASTILLO DE MALUENDA

Pº Cortés de Aragón, 4. Local, 2
50300 Calatayud (Zaragoza)
☎: 976 889 251 - Fax: 976 889 252
informacion@castillodemaluenda.com
www.castillodemaluenda.com

Established: 1999

🛢 2,500 📊 12,000,000 litres 🍇 1,800 has.

🍷 30% 🍾70%: -UK -US -DE -NL -BE -DK -CH -JP -FR

CASTILLO DE MALUENDA GARNACHA-SYRAH 2003 JOVEN RED
60% garnacha, 20% tempranillo, 20% syrah

84 Cherry with a violet edge. Powerful aroma of red fruit, notes of sun-drenched skins, hints of petals, underbrush and a high quality herbaceous nuance. Flavourful and fleshy on the palate with grape tannins that give good structure, hints of minerals.

CASTILLO DE MALUENDA VIÑAS VIEJAS 2003 JOVEN RED
100% garnacha

86 Deep cherry with a violet edge. Powerful aroma with predominant notes of toasty skins, ripe fruit and hints of bramble and minerals. Fresh, very flavourful palate with excellent structure (fine tannicity) and hints of terroir.

CASTILLO DE MALUENDA TEMPRANILLO-CABERNET SAUVIGNON 2003 JOVEN RED
65% tempranillo, 30% cabernet sauvignon, 5% garnacha

86 Deep cherry with a violet edge. Powerful aroma with an excellent varietal fruit expression, ripe redcurrants, herbaceous and underbrush hints. Flavourful, fleshy, well-structured palate (strong tannicity), liquorice, good acidity and very long.

CASTILLO DE MALUENDA TEMPRANILLO 2003 OAK AGED RED
100% tempranillo

81 Deep cherry with a violet edge. Intense aroma of ripe fruit, toasty oak hints and a fine reduction. Flavourful palate of somewhat rough tannins that envelop the ripe fruit and fine bitter notes.

NAVITUM 2002 RED
50% merlot, 50% cabernet sauvignon

81 Garnet red cherry with a violet-coppery edge. Intense aroma of jammy black fruit, spicy notes and minerals. Flavourful palate with slightly marked tannins, well-structured and slightly warm with a spicy finish of liquorice and terracotta.

CLARAVAL 2001 RED
60% garnacha, 30% syrah, 10% cabernet sauvignon

83 Deep garnet red cherry. Fairly intense aroma with spicy wood notes and a ripe fruit nuance. Flavourful, fleshy palate with ripe, slightly rough tannins, fine spicy notes of liquorice, earth and balsamic flavours.

CASTILLO DE MALUENDA 2000 CRIANZA RED
60% tempranillo, 30% garnacha, 10% cabernet sauvignon

80 Brilliant cherry with a coppery edge. Quite intense aroma, with spicy oak notes, a ripe fruit nuance and hints of a fine reduction. Flavourful palate with a certain finesse, warm notes and minor fruit expression.

CASTILLO DE MALUENDA 2003 WHITE
CASTILLO DE MALUENDA 2003 JOVEN ROSÉ
CASTILLO DE MALUENDA 2003 JOVEN RED
LA OLMEDILLA 2003 JOVEN ROSÉ
VIÑA AGÜERO 1998 CRIANZA RED
CASTILLO DE MALUENDA 1997 RESERVA RED

LANGA HERMANOS

Carretera Nacional II, km. 241, 700
Apartado 49
50300 Calatayud (Zaragoza)
☎: 976 881 818 - Fax: 976 884 463
info@bodegas-langa.com
www.bodegas-langa.com

Established: 1982

⊕ 150 ▤ 8,250 litres ⚘ 50 has.

▶ 75% ◉25%: -UK -DE -BE -NL -LU -PL

REYES DE ARAGÓN ECOLÓGICO 2003 FERMENTADO EN BARRICA RED
merlot, syrah

83 Cherry with a violet hue. Intense aroma, with spicy oak notes, a ripe fruit nuance and light reduction. Flavourful, fleshy palate with fruit well enveloped by the oak, bitter notes (dark-roasted flavours) and balsamic hints.

REYES DE ARAGÓN CEPAS VIEJAS 2003 RED
100% garnacha

80 Intense cherry with a violet edge. Powerful aroma of jammy fruit and fine reduction notes. Flavourful, fleshy palate with toasty and spicy notes of the vine variety and hints of smoky earth.

CASTILLO DE AYUD 2001 CRIANZA RED
tempranillo, garnacha

82 Garnet red cherry with a coppery edge. Powerful, very ripe aroma with toasty hints and some reduction (late racking). Better palate, flavourful and fleshy with well-integrated oak/fruit; a ripe fruit nuance and with bitter and balsamic hints.

CASTILLO DE AYUD 1996 RESERVA RED
tempranillo, garnacha

84 Garnet red cherry with a coppery edge. Powerful aroma of fine toasty oak notes, a ripe fruit nuance and hints of terroir. Flavourful palate, with excellent crianza expression (well-integrated oak/fruit), fine bitter notes; long.

NIÑO JESÚS

Las Tablas, s/n
50313 Aniñón (Zaragoza)
☎: 976 899 150 - Fax: 976 896 160
njesusani@zaz.servicom.es

Established: 1978

▤ 2,300,000 litres ⚘ 318 has.

▶ 80% ◉20%: -UK -US

ESTECILLO 2003 WHITE
100% macabeo

80 Brilliant pale yellow with golden nuances. Not very intense, quite fruity aroma with spicy hints of skins (long maceration) and hints of herbs. Flavourful palate with fine bitter notes and good acidity.

ESTECILLO 2003 ROSÉ
100% garnacha

80 Brilliant raspberry. Fairly intense aroma, with fruity notes and spicy, warm hints. Flavourful palate with fresh overtones, bitter notes of quality and hints of citrus fruit.

ESTECILLO 2003 RED
garnacha, tempranillo

79 Intense cherry with a violet edge. Intense, fruity aroma with fine spicy notes of skins and hints of terroir. Flavourful and fruity on the palate tannins with a mild hint of greeness, slightly warm and pleasant.

ESTECILLO 2000 CRIANZA RED
85% garnacha, 15% tempranillo

78 Intense garnet red cherry. Powerful aroma with hints of toast, creamy oak, jammy fruit and a mild hint of reduction. Flavourful, fleshy on the palate with slightly dry tannins, lacking balance.

SAN ALEJANDRO

Carretera Calatayud - Cariñena, km. 16
50330 Miedes de Aragón (Zaragoza)
☎: 976 892 205 - Fax: 976 890 540
bodegas@san-alejandro.com
www.san-alejandro.com

Established: 1962

🌐 1,000 📊 6,000,000 litres 🍇 1,200 has.

🍷 20% (🌍80%: -DE -BE -UK -US -FR -JP
-NL -SE -NO

BALTASAR GRACIÁN VENDIMIA SELECCIONADA 2003 ROSÉ
100% garnacha

79 Brilliant raspberry. Fairly intense aroma with notes of red fruit and warm hints. Fresh, flavourful on the palate with hints of citrus fruit and good acidity.

VIÑAS DE MIEDES 2003 RED
100% garnacha

80 Garnet red cherry with a violet edge. Fairly intense aroma of red fruit, fine spiced and mineral notes. Fresh, flavourful on the palate with slightly fresh tannins, well-structured.

VIÑAS DE MIEDES VIÑAS VIEJAS 2003 RED
100% garnacha

81 Brilliant cherry with a violet glint. Intense aroma of red fruit, fine, spicy hints of skins, bramble and terroir. Fresh, flavourful, fleshy palate, with a slightly oily texture, ripe and very pleasant.

BALTASAR GRACIÁN EXPRESIÓN 2001 OAK AGED RED
53% garnacha, 19% tempranillo, 28% syrah

85 Garnet red cherry with a coppery glint. Intense aroma, well-integrated fruit/oak, with a suggestion of good Garnacha, varietal expression and hints of flowers. Fleshy, flavourful palate with excellent structure and balance.

BALTASAR GRACIÁN GARNACHA VIÑAS VIEJAS 2002 OAK AGED RED
100% garnacha

92 Intense cherry. Deep, spirituous aroma of ripe black fruit and fine notes of toasty oak (coffee), quite a strong expression of an unusual Garnacha. Full, fleshy palate with flavourful, almost sweet tannins with an excellent oak association, generous and warm.

BALTASAR GRACIÁN VARIETALES 2002 OAK AGED RED
10% syrah, 33% tempranillo, 13% merlot, 4% cabernet sauvignon

83 Cherry with a violet hue. Powerful aroma of toasty wood notes, a nuance of ripe black fruit and hints of sun-drenched skins. Flavourful, fleshy palate with slightly marked tannins, a dark-roasted hint, liquorice, spices and hints of fine herbs.

BALTASAR GRACIÁN VENDIMIA SELECCIONADA 2002 RED
garnacha

81 Intense cherry. Fresh, fruity aroma with notes of Garnacha and a mild evolutive nuance. Flavourful with vine variety sweetness on the palate, fresh; better than in the nose.

BALTASAR GRACIÁN 2001 CRIANZA RED
60% garnacha, 30% tempranillo, 10% Syrah

85 Garnet red cherry with a saffron edge. Powerful aroma with fine toasty oak notes and a ripe fruit and underbrush nuance. Fleshy, concentrated palate, well-integrated oak/fruit, excellent structure with a balsamic nuance.

BALTASAR GRACIÁN 2000 RESERVA RED
70% garnacha, 20% tempranillo, 10% cabernet sauvignon

89 Garnet red cherry with a coppery edge. Powerful aroma of black fruits in maceration, a nuance of toasty oak, a fine reduction and hints of sour cherries in liqueur. Fleshy palate, well-integrated oak/fruit, rich in nuances, with excellent crianza expression and a mineral suggestion.

BALTASAR GRACIÁN VENDIMIA SELECCIÓN 2003 WHITE
VIÑAS DE MIEDES 2003 WHITE
VIÑAS DE MIEDES WHITE SEMISECO
VIÑAS DE MIEDES 2003 ROSÉ

SAN GREGORIO

Carretera Villalengua s/n
50312 Cervera de la Cañada (Zaragoza)
☎: 976 899 206 - Fax: 976 896 240
montearmantes@bodegasangregorio.com
www.bodegasangregorio.com

Established: 1965

🌐 120 📊 3,750,000 litres 🍇 950 has.

🍷 20% (🌍80%: -UK -NL -DE -US -DK -DK

MONTE ARMANTES 2003 ROSÉ
garnacha, tempranillo

82 Raspberry blush. Fine, fresh aroma of red fruit. Flavourful, fresh palate of red fruit, well-crafted.

MARQUÉS DE CASTILLO GARNACHA 2003 RED
100% garnacha

83 Cherry with a violet hue. Intense, fruity aroma with spicy notes of the skins and hints of terroir. Flavourful, very fresh palate with excellent presence of tannins in the fruit, well-structured and long.

MONTE ARMANTES CARMESÍ GARNACHA-TEMPRANILLO 2003 RED
50% tempranillo, 50% garnacha

85 Very deep cherry with a violet edge. Powerful aroma of macerated black fruit and hints of smoky earth. Powerful, concentrated, well-structured

DO CALATAYUD

palate (strong tannicity), with fine bitter notes (liquorice) in the finish.

MONTE ARMANTES GARNACHA 2003 RED
garnacha

82 Intense cherry with a violet edge. Fairly intense aroma of black fruit with balsamic notes and spicy skins. Flavourful palate with slightly marked tannins, warm notes and good fruit weight.

MONTE ARMANTES GARNACHA-TEMPRANILLO 2003 RED
50% garnacha, 50% tempranillo

83 Cherry with a violet hue. Intense aroma with predominant ripe, red fruit, hints of figs and sun-drenched skins. Fleshy palate with fresh overtones (flavourful tannins), spices and terroir.

TRES OJOS GARNACHA 2003 RED
100% garnacha

84 Garnet red cherry with a violet hue. Intense aroma with black fruit notes, spicy hints of skins and a terroir nuance. Flavourful palate with fine, well-integrated bitter notes and fruit and balsamic hints, very rich.

MONTE ARMANTES SYRAH-GARNACHA 2003 RED
70% syrah, 30% garnacha

79 Cherry with a violet hue. Powerful aroma of very ripe black fruit and a terroir nuance. Concentrated on the palate with jammy fruit notes, fine tannicity and a slightly mineral nuance, ripe though lacks complexity.

TRES OJOS TEMPRANILLO 2003 RED
100% tempranillo

80 Garnet red cherry. Not very intense aroma with fresh overtones of red fruit and balsamic hints. Flavourful palate with quite marked grape tannins, warm notes and good fruit weight

MONTE ARMANTES TEMPRANILLO 2000 CRIANZA RED
tempranillo

82 Garnet red cherry with a violet edge. Powerful aroma with predominant toasty oak notes and a fine touch of sour cherries in liqueur. Flavourful palate with slightly marked oak tannins, ripe fruit and hints of liquorice and terroir.

MONTE ARMANTES TEMPRANILLO 2001 CRIANZA RED
tempranillo

82 Deep cherry with a coppery edge. Intense aroma of fine spicy notes of oak, a ripe fruit nuance and fine reduction notes. Flavourful palate with slightly marked yet promising tannins, a ripe fruit nuance and bitter notes (liquorice, dark-roasted flavours).

MONTE ARMANTES SELECCIÓN 20 BARRICAS 2000 RESERVA RED
100% tempranillo

80 Garnet red cherry with a brick red edge. Intense aroma with predominant toasty and spicy

oak notes. Flavourful, fleshy palate with creamy overtones, slightly marked tannins, a fruity nuance, dark-roasted and liquorice hints.

MONTE ARMANTES 2001 FERMENTADO EN BARRICA WHITE
MONTE ARMANTES 2003 WHITE
VIEJO ARMANTES WHITE
HUGE JUICY RED GARNACHA 2003 RED
VIÑA FUERTE GARNACHA 2003 RED
VIÑA SARDANA TEMPRANILLO 2003 RED

Sociedad Cooperativa
VIRGEN DE LA PEANA

Carretera N II km 221
50200 Ateca (Zaragoza)
☎: 976 842 164 - Fax: 976 842 164

Established: 1945

66 🗄 2,500,000 litres
366 has. 🍷 100%

CASTILLO DE ALCOCER WHITE

76 Yellow straw with a coppery glint. Intense, slightly fruity aroma with a suggestion of herbs and nuts. Without great fruit expression on the palate, slightly warm.

CASTILLO DE ALCOCER ROSÉ

73 Pale raspberry with an orangey glint. Slightly intense, fruity aroma with warm hints of spicy skins. Warm palate without great fruit expression.

CASTILLO DE ALCOCER 2003 JOVEN RED
70% tempranillo, 30% garnacha

79 Cherry with a violet edge. Fairly intense aroma of ripe red fruit and spicy hints of skins. Fleshy, somewhat fresh palate with flavourful grape tannins and good acidity.

CASTILLO DE ALCOCER 1999 CRIANZA RED
80% tempranillo, 20% garnacha

77 Garnet red cherry with a brick red edge. Powerful aroma with predominant toasty and creamy oak notes. Flavourful, slightly fleshy palate with damp wood notes and balsamic hints.

CASTILLO DE ALCOCER 2003 CRIANZA RED

VIRGEN DE LA SIERRA

Avenida de la Cooperativa, 21-23
50310 Villarroya de la Sierra (Zaragoza)
☎: 976 899 015 - Fax: 976 899 132
coovillarroya@cepymenet.es

Established: 1954

200 🗄 5,000,000 litres 🍷 5% 🌐95%:
-UK -IE -DE -NL -BE -FR -AT -CH -DK -IT -US -CA

CRUZ DE PIEDRA 2003 WHITE
100% macabeo

81 Pale yellow. Intense aroma of white fruit, hints of exotic fruit, a nuance of herbs and citrus fruit. Intense on the palate with fresh overtones, flavourful, fine bitter notes and good acidity.

CRUZ DE PIEDRA 2003 ROSÉ
100% garnacha

81 Intense raspberry with coppery nuances. Fairly intense aroma of red fruit with spicy hints of skins and fresh overtones of citrus fruit. Flavourful palate with fine bitter notes and excellent acidity.

CRUZ DE PIEDRA 2003 RED
100% garnacha

84 Intense cherry with a violet edge. Powerful, ripe aroma of red fruit, with a spicy nuance of skins and terracotta. Fruity on the palate with ripe, slightly rough tannins, a certain mineral freshness and good acidity.

CRUZ DE PIEDRA LAS NAVAS VENDIMIA SELECCIONADA 2001 OAK AGED RED
100% garnacha

83 Deep cherry with a violet edge. Fairly intense aroma with jammy fruit and a nuance of toasty oak. Powerful, fleshy palate with a certain concentration, slightly marked tannins, balsamic flavours, liquorice and hints of earth.

ALBADA 2001 SEMICRIANZA RED
MONTEMAGUILLO 2001 CRIANZA RED

DO CAMPO DE BORJA

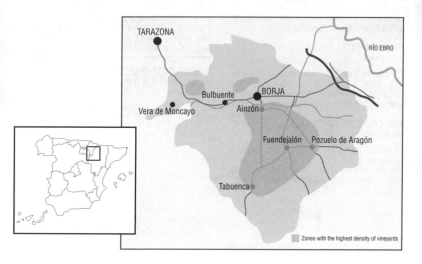

Zones with the highest density of vineyards

NEWS. The 2003 harvest was quite unusual, with plentiful rainfall in the spring and a severe summer drought: temperatures remained above 38 °C for a period of almost 3 months. The result: a poor expression for the white varieties, but a *Garnacha* in good form, perhaps not only regarding its nature and character, but also its age, seeing as most is from old vineyards of a quality that has caused the neighbours from Rioja to start eyeing them. The queen of the varieties of the DO,

Hectares of Vineyard	No. of Viticulturists	No. of Bodegas	2003 Harvest	2003 Production	Marketing
7,414	2,010	16	Good	18,000,000 litres	42% Spain 58% foreign

which occupies 75% of the vineyards, lives up to expectations in the single-variety wines (the Fagus and the Coto de Hayas of Bodegas Aragonesas are exceptional), but at present loses full points in blends with the *Tempranillo* and *Cabernet Sauvignon*, grape varieties whose best single-variety examples, the Aliana and Ruberte of Bodegas Ruberte, only just manage to exceed 80 points.

LOCATION. The DO Campo de Borja is made up of 16 municipal areas, situated in the north west of the province of Zaragoza and 60 km from the capital city, in an area of transition between the mountains of the Sistema Ibérico (at the foot of the Moncayo) and the Ebro Valley: Agón, Ainzón, Alberite, Albeta, Ambel, Bisimbre, Borja, Bulbuente, Burueta, El Buste, Fuendejalón, Magallón, Malejan, Pozuelo de Aragón, Tabuenca and Vera del Moncayo.

CLIMATE. A rather extreme continental climate, with cold winters and dry, hot summers. One of its main characteristics is the influence of the 'Cierzo', a cold and dry north-westerly wind. Rainfall is rather scarce, with an average of between 350 and 450 mm per year.

SOIL. The most abundant are brownish-grey limey soils, terrace soils and clayey ferrous soils. The vineyards are situated at an altitude of between 350 and 700 m on small slightly rolling hillsides, on terraces of the Huecha river and the Llanos de Plasencia, making up the Somontano del Moncayo.

VARIETIES:
White: *Macabeo, Moscatel, Chardonnay.*
Red: *Garnacha* (majority with 75%), *Tempranillo, Mazuela, Cabernet Sauvignon, Merlot, Syrah.*

REGULATORY COUNCIL.
Subida de San Andrés, 6. 50570 Ainzón (Zaragoza).
Tel: 976 852 122. Fax: 976 868 806.
E-mail: vinos@campodeborja.com
Website: www.campodeborja.com

GENERAL CHARACTERISTICS OF THE WINES:

Whites	Mainly produced from *Macabeo*, they are light, fresh and pleasant. There is also experience with white wines fermented in barrels.
Rosés	With notably fine quality, they are produced mainly from *Garnacha*; they are somewhat fresher than those of *Cariñena* and stand out for the full-bodied character that the variety provides.
Reds	Also based on the *Garnacha*, they are the most important type of wine in the region. In their youth, dark cherry coloured, they have a fine intense aroma and offer notes of ripe black fruit; they are flavourful, fruity and meaty. The Crianza reds are somewhat lighter and more round; the Reservas and Gran Reservas produced in the traditional manner, however, may have animal nuances and hints of reduced fruit with the rusty character of the *Garnacha*.

AGROFRAGO

Carretera Soria, km. 55'400
50520 Magallón (Zaragoza)
☎: 976 863 006 - Fax: 976 863 006

Established: 1994

🍷 30 🛢 227,000 litres 🍇 25 has. 🌿 100%

GREGORIANO 2003 JOVEN RED
60% tempranillo, 30% garnacha, 10% cabernet sauvignon

72 Garnet red cherry. Intense, ripe, not very fine aroma of reduced red fruit. Slightly better on the palate, flavourful and fruity with sweet and toasty hints of skins.

GRAN GREGORIANO 2001 CRIANZA RED
60% tempranillo, 30% garnacha, 10% cabernet sauvignon

78 Garnet red with an orange edge. Aroma of black pepper and spices with grape character but dominated by wood. Fleshy palate with powerful and astringent oak tannins; finish generous in nuances.

GRAN GREGORIANO 1999 RESERVA RED
60% tempranillo, 30% garnacha, 10% cabernet sauvignon

81 Ruby red with a brick red hue. Aroma with reduction notes (leathers, spices, tobacco) and a suggestion of Cabernet. Fleshy palate with round and oily tannins, a complex crianza with a powerful finish.

GREGORIANO 2003 JOVEN WHITE
GREGORIANO 2003 JOVEN ROSÉ
GRAN GREGORIANO JOVEN RED

ANTONIO TOLOSA

Constitución s/n
50529 Fuendejalón (Zaragoza)
☎: 976 862 418

Established: 1970

🍷 50 🛢 150,000 litres 🍇 40 has. 🌿 100%

CHURRO 2003 JOVEN RED
CHURRO 1998 RESERVA RED

Bodegas ARAGONESAS

Carretera Magallón, s/n
50529 Fuendejalón (Zaragoza)
☎: 976 862 153 - Fax: 976 862 363
barag@bodegasaragonesas.com
www.bodegasaragonesas.com

Established: 1984

🍷 3,500 🛢 1,300,000 litres 🍇 3,500 has.
🌿 50%% 🌐50%: -FR -UK -IE -DE -NL -BE -US -CA -VE -CH -SE -DK -FI -RU -LT -PL.

COTO DE HAYAS 2002 FERMENTADO EN BARRICA WHITE
chardonnay, moscatel , macabeo

77 Pale golden yellow. Intense, fruity aroma of ripe apples, with creamy hints of wood and light musky tones. Somewhat fruity and warm on the palate with harsh bitter notes and a lack of fruit-oak-acidity balance.

COTO DE HAYAS 2003 WHITE
chardonnay

81 Pale golden yellow. Intense, fruity aroma with hints of flowers and citrus fruit. Flavourful, fruity palate with fine bitter notes and good acidity.

COTO DE HAYAS 2003 ROSÉ
garnacha, tempranillo

81 Lively raspberry blush. Intense aroma of ripe red fruit with an essence of aniseed. Flavourful, very fruity palate with mountain herbs, very pleasant.

COTO DE HAYAS TEMPRANILLO CABERNET 2003 JOVEN RED
85% tempranillo, 15% cabernet sauvignon

83 Medium-hue garnet red. Aroma of ripe and sweet red fruit (raspberries, blackberries) with light lactic notes. Fleshy, flavourful palate with good acidity and weighty fruit.

CRUCILLON 2003 JOVEN RED
100% garnacha

77 Lively garnet red cherry. Intense, fruity aroma with an essence of withered petals and slightly reduced red stone fruit. Flavourful palate with slightly marked tannins and a slightly acidic edge.

MOLILLA 2003 JOVEN RED
100% garnacha

80 Intense cherry. Clear aroma of bitter red fruit with an essence of sweetness. Flavourful palate with fruity tannins, quite ripe but with good character, a fresh finish.

DON RAMÓN 2002 OAK AGED RED
75% garnacha, 25% tempranillo

80 Garnet red cherry. Intense aroma of red stone fruit with sweet hints of macerated skins and spicy oak. Flavourful palate with a good oak/fruit integration, spicy with good fruit weight.

COTO DE HAYAS GARNACHA CENTENARIA 2003 OAK AGED RED
100% garnacha

89 Dark cherry with a purplish edge. Powerful aroma with excellent expression of ripe red fruit, hints of macerated skins and fine smoky oak. Fleshy, powerful, varietal palate with slightly marked tannins, oily with jammy fruit and liquorice and terroir in the finish.

FAGUS DE COTO DE HAYAS 2002 OAK AGED RED
100% garnacha

92 Dark cherry. Powerful, very fine aroma, rich in stone fruit nuances, graphite and sun-drenched skins, with spicy hints of wood (pepper, creamy vanilla). Flavourful palate with fleshy overtones and jammy red fruit, slightly sweet and warm with tremendous potential.

COTO DE HAYAS 2003 RED
100% garnacha

84 Garnet red cherry with a violet hue. Intense aroma of red stone fruit and fine spicy notes of skins. Flavourful, fruity palate with slightly drying tannins and warm hints.

CASTILLO DE FUENDEJALON
2000 CRIANZA RED
75% garnacha, 25% tempranillo

84 Not very intense cherry. Aroma of thyme, spicy with lactic notes. Warm palate with well-integrated tannins and a suggestion of wood and balsamic notes in the retronasal passage, good crianza.

MOSÉN CLETO 2001 CRIANZA RED
75% garnacha, 25% tempranillo

79 Garnet red cherry. Slightly intense aroma with spicy oak notes and an essence of slightly reduced ripe fruit. Flavourful, quite fleshy palate without great nuances and with an essence of slightly aged wood.

COTO DE HAYAS 2000 RESERVA RED
100% garnacha

83 Deep intense cherry. Aroma of black fruit with expression and well-integrated hints of smokiness and spices. Fleshy, spicy palate with oily but ripe tannins and freshness; finish generous in nuances.

VIÑA TITO 2003 JOVEN RED
80% garnacha, 20% tempranillo

81 Garnet red with a strawberry edge. Perfumed aroma of strawberry syrup. Flavourful, well-balanced, persistent palate with a suggestion of ripe red fruit in the retronasal passage.

DUQUE DE SEVILLA 1998 RESERVA RED
70% garnacha, 30% tempranillo

77 Cherry. Toasty aroma of spices over red fruit. Flavourful, slightly woody palate with fleshy tannins, quite expressive.

COTO DE HAYAS MOSCATEL 2003 VINO DE LICOR
100% moscatel

84 Straw-coloured. Intense, fresh, fruity aroma (grapes) of fresh herbs, subtle. Very flavourful palate with a great expression of fresh grapes, syrupy and very well-balanced.

COTO DE HAYAS 2003 ROSÉ
MAGALLÓN 2003 JOVEN RED
DON RAMÓN 2001 CRIANZA RED
CASTILLO DE FUENDEJALON
COTO DE HAYAS MISTELA 2002 VINO DE LICOR

BORDEJÉ

Carretera Borja - Rueda, km. 3
50570 Ainzón (Zaragoza)
☎: 976 868 080 - Fax: 976 868 989
ainzon@bodegasbordeje.com
www.bodegasbordeje.com

Established: 1770
⊞ 200 ▤ 500,000 litres ❦ 60 has.
🍷 100%

BORDEJÉ 2003 JOVEN ROSÉ
ABUELO NICOLÁS 2003
PAGO DE HUECHASECA 2003 JOVEN RED
BORDEJÉ 1996 RESERVA RED
DON PABLO 1998 RESERVA RED
PAGO DE ROMEROSO 1999 RESERVA RED
GREGORIO 2003 JOVEN RED

Bodegas BORSAO

Carretera Nac. 122, km. 63
50540 Borja (Zaragoza)
☎: 976 867 116 - Fax: 976 867 752
info@bodegasborsao.com
www.bodegasborsao.com

Established: 2001
⊞ 1,100 ▤ 10,000,000 litres 🍷 35%
🌐65%: -DE -NL -BE -CH -UK -JP -US -AU -AT -CA -CR -BR -IL -RU

BORSAO SELECCIÓN 2003 JOVEN RED
cabernet sauvignon, tempranillo, garnacha

85 Garnet red cherry a violet hue. Powerful aroma of red stone fruit with notes of macerated skins and hints of sweetness. Fruity palate with flavourful tannins, good varietal expression and fine notes of spices and terroir.

BORSAO TRES PICOS GARNACHA 2002 RED
garnacha

83 Very deep garnet red. Spicy, balsamic aroma with a suggestion of ripe fruit. Flavourful, fleshy palate with a good fruit /wood tannin integration and an intense suggestion of cask crianza in the retronasal passage.

BORSAO SELECCIÓN 2001 CRIANZA RED
garnacha, cabernet sauvignon

87 Dark cherry with a deep red edge. Intense, ripe aroma of black fruit, macerated skins, highly perfumed (petals, balsamic flavours) and spicy hints of wood. Flavourful palate with a degree of fruit expression slightly subdued by the alcohol.

BORSAO SELECCIÓN 2000 RESERVA RED
garnacha, cabernet sauvignon, tempranillo

86 Dark very lively cherry. Intense aroma with the freshness of red fruit, skins and oak. Flavourful palate with fleshy overtones, varietal expression and rough tannins (a mild hint of greeness), warm.

BORSAO PRIMIZIA 2003 RED

CAYTUSA

Bodegas Bajas, s/n
50570 Ainzón (Zaragoza)
☎: 976 867 552 - Fax: 976 867 552
bodegascaytusa@hotmail.com

Established: 1986

200,000 litres 🍷 80% 🌐20%: -FR -VE -CR -US

MONASTERIO DE VERUELA RED
MONASTERIO DE VERUELA 2001 CRIANZA RED
MONASTERIO DE VERUELA 2000 RESERVA RED

CRIANZAS Y VIÑEDOS SANTO CRISTO

Carretera de Tabuenca, s/n
50570 Ainzón (Zaragoza)
☎: 976 869 696 - Fax: 976 868 097
info@bodegas-santo-cristo.com
www.odegas-santo-cristo.com

Established: 1956

900 8,400,000 litres 1,185 has.
🍷 34% 🌐66%: -NL -DE -UK -DK -SE -DK -IE -FR -US -BE

VIÑA COLLADO 2003 JOVEN ROSÉ
100% garnacha

76 Raspberry blush. Medium-intensity, mildly fruity aroma. Fruity, bitter palate, well-mannered overall.

VIÑA COLLADO 2003 JOVEN RED
garnacha, tempranillo

82 Ruby red with a strawberry glimmer. Somewhat alcoholic aroma of strawberry jelly, not very intense. Slightly marked tannins on the palate, light, with a suggestion of strawberries in the retronasal passage, persistent.

PEÑAZUELA DE AINZÓN SELECCIÓN 2001 ROBLE RED
80% garnacha, 10% tempranillo, 10% cabernet sauvignon

85 Intense cherry. Aroma of black fruit, notes of spices and white flowers with expression of the vine varieties and a smoky essence. Fleshy palate with red fruit pulp, tobacco notes and fruity, well-balanced tannins, fine oak in the finish.

VIÑA AINZON 2001 CRIANZA RED
70% garnacha, 30% tempranillo

80 Not very intense cherry. Aroma of strawberry syrup with notes of vanilla, slightly short. Bitter notes on the palate, persistent with a suggestion of wood in the retronasal passage.

VIÑA AINZÓN 1999 RESERVA RED
60% garnacha, 40% tempranillo

83 Garnet red cherry. Intense aroma with predominant burnt notes. Flavourful, bitter palate (dark-roasted flavours, liquorice) with slightly rough tannins, fairly potential.

MOSCATEL AINZÓN VINO DE LICOR
moscatel, moscatel de grano menudo

78 Lemon yellow. Discreet, not very clear aroma of sun-drenched grapes and notes of ripe bananas. Sweet, unctuous palate without great freshness with a tropical fruit finish.

VIÑA COLLADO 2003 JOVEN WHITE
VIÑA AINZÓN RESERVA PREMIUM 1998 RESERVA RED

DELFÍN PARDOS BONA

Subida San Andrés, 5
50540 Ainzón (Zaragoza)
☎: 670 776 860 - Fax: 976 567 410
delfinp@able.es
www.valdetalon.com

VALDETALÓN CABERNET SAUVIGNON 2003 RED
100% cabernet sauvignon

82 Deep cherry. Aroma of black fruit with hints of liquorice and a toasty suggestion of skins. Round, very fresh palate, fruity and pleasant.

MARECA

Carraborja, s/n
50547 Tabuenca (Zaragoza)
☎: 976 865 795 - Fax: 976 785 869

Established: 1998

40 110,000 litres 12 has. 🍷 100%

MARECA 2001 CRIANZA RED
MARECA TEMPRANILLO 2000 CRIANZA RED
MARECA 2000 RESERVA RED

Bodegas MURVIEDRO

Ampliación Polígono El Romeral, s/n
46340 Requena (Valencia)
☎: 962 329 003 - Fax: 962 329 002
murviedro@murviedro.es
www.murviedro.es

Established: 1927

1,500 7,100,000 litres 🍷 5% 🌐95%

SANTERRA GARNACHA 2003 RED
garnacha

82 Deep cherry. Clear, varietal aroma with notes of strawberries and flowers. Fruity palate, slightly bitter yet pleasant, slightly alcoholic with a fresh retronasal effect and a floral finish.

ROMÁN

Carretera Gallur - Agreda, 1
50546 Balbuente (Zaragoza)
☎: 976 852 936

PORTAL DE MONCAYO 2003 JOVEN RED
SENDA DE HOYAS 2003 JOVEN RED

RUBERTE

Tenor Fleta, 7
50520 Magallón (Zaragoza)
☎: 976 858 063 - Fax: 976 858 475
bodegasruberte@telefonica.net

Established: 1982

🌐 305 🍶 700,000 litres 🍇 22,75 has.

🍷 40% 🍇60%: -US -DE -UK -CH -DK -SE -NL -JP

MUZA ALCORAZ 2003 WHITE
100% macabeo

78 Brilliant pale. Fresh, fruity aroma with hints of flowers and fine herbs. Fresh palate of white fruit with spicy hints and a slightly acidic edge.

MUZA ALCORAZ 2003 ROSÉ
100% garnacha

74 Raspberry blush. Clean, fresh aroma of red fruit but with a vegetative essence (vine shoots). Very vegetative palate (green asparagus) and a suggestion of red fruit.

MUZA ALCORAZ 2003 JOVEN RED
60% tempranillo, 40% garnacha

77 Garnet red cherry with a violet hue. Intense, fresh, fruity aroma with notes of macerated skins and hints of damp earth. Flavourful, fruity palate with fairly lively grape tannins.

RUBERTE 2003 JOVEN RED
100% tempranillo

82 Deep intense cherry. Aroma of clear red fruit with a certain fruit expression (spices). Fleshy, very fresh palate with strawberry pulp, somewhat herbaceous yet pleasant with sweet tannins.

ALIANA 2001 ROBLE RED
100% cabernet sauvignon

83 Dark cherry. Perfumed aroma of toasty wood and elegant leathers with light notes of green pepper. Drying, flavourful palate with well-integrated wood and fruit tannins.

MORAVIÑA 1999 OAK AGED RED
45% merlot, 25% cabernet sauvignon, 20% tempranillo, 10% garnacha

77 Garnet red cherry with a brick red glint. Slightly intense aroma with predominant smoky oak notes and a nuance of mild reduction (tobacco). Flavourful palate with overripe fruit and a nuance of bitterness and slightly aged wood.

RUBERTE GARNACHA 2000 RED
RUBERTE 1996 OAK AGED RED
RUBERTE 1999 CRIANZA RED
RUBERTE 1995 GRAN RESERVA RED

DO CARIÑENA

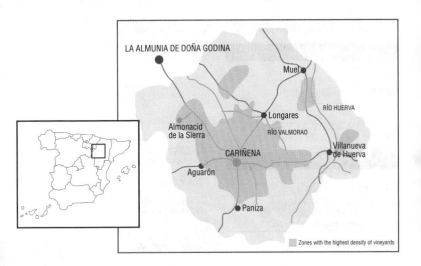

Zones with the highest density of vineyards

NEWS. The 2003 harvest in Cariñena was characterised by a spring with plentiful rainfall and higher than usual temperatures, as well as an absence of frost. However, the early harvesting period expected for that year, given the hot and dry summer, did not materialise because of the rains at the end of August, which eventually delayed it. All this resulted in a good phytosanitary state of the grapes, with a increase in production of 10% in relation to 2002, and a volume of 75% of red grapes as against 25% of white, 95% of which were from cooperatives.

A somewhat rhetorical, but necessary, question: seeing as the percentage of *Garnacha* in the vineyards of Cariñena exceeds 55%, why is it that the single-variety model, which is proving to be so successful for its neighbours from Campo de Borja and Calatayud, is not applied? Care, the best wine of the DO and the top wine of Bodegas Añadas (the result of a 9 million € investment), which has leapt onto the podium of the great wines with a score of 91 points, has a third of *Cabernet Sauvignon*. However, this is an exception to the rule. Even with blending Cariñena does not seem able to produce wines scoring around 85 points. There is a long road ahead for the third 'C' in Aragon's stable.

Hectares of Vineyard	No. of Viticulturists	No. of Bodegas	2003 Harvest	2003 Production	Marketing
16,676	3,500	33	Good	32,000,000 litres	38% Spain 62% foreign

LOCATION. In the province of Zaragoza, and occupies the Ebro valley covering 14 municipal areas: Aguarón, Aladrén, Alfamén, Almonacid de la Sierra, Alpartir, Cariñena, Cosuenda, Encinacorba, Longares, Mezalocha, Muel, Paniza, Tosos and Villanueva de Huerva.

CLIMATE. A continental climate, with cold winters, hot summers and low rainfall. The viticulture is also influenced by the effect of the 'Cierzo'.

SOIL. Mainly poor; either brownish-grey limey soil, or reddish dun soil settled on rocky deposits, or brownish-grey soil settled on alluvial deposits. The vineyards are situated at an altitude of between 400 and 800 m.

VARIETIES:
White:
Preferred: *Macabeo* (majority 20%).
Authorized white: *Garnacha Blanca, Moscatel Romano, Parellada* and *Chardonnay*.
Red:
Preferred red: *Garnacha Tinta* (majority 55%), *Tempranillo, Mazuela* (or *Cariñena*).
Authorized red: *Juan Ibáñez, Cabernet Sauvignon, Syrah* and *Merlot*.

REGULATORY COUNCIL.
Cno. de la Platera, 7. 50400 Cariñena (Zaragoza).
Tel: 902 190 713.
Tel: 976 793 031. Fax: 976 621 107.
E-mail: consejoregulador@docarinena.com

GENERAL CHARACTERISTICS OF THE WINES:

Whites	These are not the most important of the region. They are characterised by their straw yellow colour, notes of ripe fruit and fruity character.
Rosés	Most are the result of new technology: they are pink, with fine fruit intensity and flavourful on the palate, thanks to the intervention of the *Garnacha*.
Reds	These are the wines par excellence of the region, quite robust with a warm character. The young wines have a dark cherry colour with hints of violet and aromas of ripe fruit reminiscent of blackberries and plums; thanks to the *Garnacha*, they are also very flavourful on the palate. The Crianza wines maintain these characteristics, although they are more supple due to being aged in barrels; these may display balsamic notes and dark-roasted flavours; on the palate they are supple and warm. These long-aged wines, if only produced from *Garnacha*, may have rough notes due to the fact that this grape variety does not age very well.

DO CARIÑENA

Bodegas AÑADAS

Carretera Aguarón, Km 47, 100
50400 Cariñena (Zaragoza)
☎: 976 302 271 - Fax: 976 213 946
bodega@carewines.com
www.carewines.com

Established: 2000

⊕ 700 ▤ 740,000 litres ⚘ 100 has.
🍷 60% 🌐40%: -IT -CH -DE -US -PR

CARE 2002 OAK AGED RED
65% garnacha, 35% cabernet sauvignon

89 Dark cherry. Intense aroma with predominant fruity notes (cherries, bilberries), fresh skins and a spicy essence of oak. Powerful, flavourful, quite fleshy palate with marked but quite promising tannins, a warm and oily texture and cocoa in the retronasal passage.

CARE 2001 OAK AGED RED
60% garnacha, 40% cabernet sauvignon

91 Dark cherry with a lively violet edge. Intense aroma of great finesse with excellent red stone fruit, toasty notes of oak, spicy skins and a balsamic, quite viscous suggestion. Powerful, warm palate with a good oak/fruit integration and spicy, bitter hints (cocoa liquorice) in the finish.

BODEGAS DEL SEÑORÍO

Afueras, s/n
50108 Almonacid de la Sierra (Zaragoza)
☎: 976 627 225 - Fax: 976 627 225
Jmartinez@bodegasdelaobra.com
www.bodegasdelaobra.com

Established: 1947

⊕ 400 ▤ 300,000 litres ⚘ 50 has.
🍷 40% 🌐60%: -DE -CH -DK -MX -FR -FI

VIÑA VELERMA 2003 JOVEN RED
DOBL EXCELENT 1999 CRIANZA RED
SENDA LASARDA 1999 CRIANZA RED
SEÑORÍO DE LA OBRA 1999 RESERVA RED

CAMINO DEL BOSQUE

Camino del Bosque, s/n
50108 Almomacid de la Sierra (Zaragoza)
☎: 976 627 311 - Fax: 976 352 735

CAMINO DEL BOSQUE RED

CONDALES DEL NORTE, P.T.

García Ximénez, 101
50450 Muel (Zaragoza)
☎: 976 140 003 - Fax: 976 141 107

bodegascondales@able.es
www.bodegascondales.com

Established: 1958

⊕ 350 ▤ 560,000 litres 🍷 55% 🌐45%

CORONA CONDAL CRIANZA RED
DUQUE DE VALÓN CRIANZA RED
DUQUE DE VALÓN RESERVA RED

COVINCA

Carretera Valencia, s/n
50460 Longares (Zaragoza)
☎: 976 142 653 - Fax: 976 142 402
covinca@rsc.es

Established: 1987

⊕ 3,000 ▤ 20,000,000 litres ⚘ 3,000 has.
🍷 35% 🌐65%: -DE -UK -BE -NL -DK -FI -AT -DK -CA -US -BR -CR -SG

MARQUES DE BALLESTER 2003 WHITE
MARQUES DE BALLESTER 2003 ROSÉ
MARQUES DE BALLESTER 2003 RED
TORRELONGARES 2003 JOVEN WHITE
TORRELONGARES 2003 JOVEN ROSÉ
TORRELONGARES 2003 JOVEN RED
VIÑA ORIA 2003 JOVEN RED
MARQUÉS DE BALLESTER 2001 CRIANZA RED
TORRELONGARES 2001 CRIANZA RED
VIÑA ORIA 2001 CRIANZA RED
MARQUÉS DE BALLESTER 1998 RESERVA RED
TORRELONGARES 1998 RESERVA RED
MARQUÉS DE BALLESTER 1996 GRAN RESERVA RED
TORRELONGARES 1996 GRAN RESERVA RED

GENARO TEJERO

Ronda del Muro, s/n
50400 Cariñena (Zaragoza)
☎: 976 620 183 - Fax: 976 620 183
info@bodegasgenarotejero.com

Established: 1875

⊕ 300 ▤ 1,100,000 litres ⚘ 25 has.
🍷 80% 🌐20%

VIÑA POMONIA JOVEN RED
VIÑA POMONIA CRIANZA RED
SYRIUS RED

Bodegas GRAN DUCAY

Carretera Nacional 330, km. 450
50400 Cariñena (Zaragoza)
☎: 976 620 400 - Fax: 976 620 398
bsv@sanvalero.com

DO CARIÑENA

www.bodegasanvalero.com

Established: 1944

🏭 9,000 📦 20,000,000 litres 🍇 3,500 has.
🍷 50% 🌐50%: -UK -DE -CH -CA -US -
DO -FI -JP -FR

MONTE DUCAY 2003 JOVEN WHITE
MONTE DUCAY 2003 JOVEN ROSÉ
MONTE DUCAY 2003 JOVEN RED
CARINVS 2001 FERMENTADO EN BARRICA
JOVEN RED
MONTE DUCAY 2001 CRIANZA RED
IMPERIAL CARINVS 1998 RESERVA RED
MARQUÉS DE TOSOS 2000 RESERVA RED
MONTE DUCAY 1998 GRAN RESERVA RED
DON MENDO 2002 VINO DE LICOR

GRANDES VINOS Y VIÑEDOS

Carretera Valencia , km. 46, 300
50400 Cariñena (Zaragoza)
☎: 976 621 261 - Fax: 976 621 253
marketing@grandesvinos.com
www.grandesvinos.com

Established: 1997

🏭 7,500 📦 36,500,000 litres 🍇 5.800 has.
🍷 60% 🌐40%

CORONA DE ARAGÓN 2003 JOVEN WHITE
100% macabeo

80 Yellow straw. Medium-intensity, fresh, clean aroma with good fruit expression. Flavourful palate with white fruit, slightly warm in the finish.

MONASTERIO DE LAS VIÑAS 2003 WHITE
100% macabeo

73 Straw-coloured. Slightly short aroma of yeast with weak fruit. Quite dense on the palate, well-mannered but without great expression.

CORONA DE ARAGÓN 2003 JOVEN ROSÉ
100% cabernet sauvignon

72 Salmon-pink. Medium-intensity aroma with considerable vegetative notes and a suggestion of red fruit. A tannic palate with a carbonic edge and an element of greeness.

MONASTERIO DE LAS VIÑAS 2003 JOVEN ROSÉ
100% garnacha

73 Salmon blush. Medium-intensity aroma with a suggestion of red fruit and not very expressive. Bitter on the palate with sweetish notes and well-mannered overall.

CORONA DE ARAGÓN CABERNET SAUVIGNON 2003 JOVEN RED
100% cabernet sauvignon

80 Garnet red cherry with a violet edge. Medium-intensity, spicy aroma with balsamic notes. Generous, flavourful and concentrated on the palate with ripe fruit and a ripe Cabernet character.

CORONA DE ARAGÓN CARIÑENA 2003 JOVEN RED
85% cariñena, tempranillo, syrah

82 Lively violet garnet red. Medium-intensity aroma with balsamic notes (mint, bay leaf). Flavourful, intense palate with a good expression of ripe fruit, balsamic notes and spices; very pleasant.

CORONA DE ARAGÓN TEMPRANILLO 2003 JOVEN RED
100% tempranillo

80 Cherry with a lively violet rim. Intense, spicy aroma (pepper) with a vegetative suggestion. Flavourful palate with well-integrated alcohol and balsamic notes; long.

MONASTERIO DE LAS VIÑAS 2003 JOVEN RED
garnacha, tempranillo, cariñena

82 Lively garnet red cherry. Medium-intensity aroma of red fruit, fresh, with a balsamic and floral nuance (violets). Flavourful, intense palate with good fruit expression and toasty skins, long.

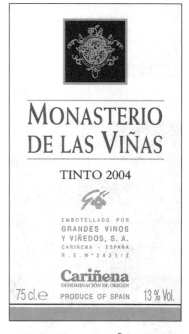

MONASTERIO DE LAS VIÑAS CABERNET SAUVIGNON 2003 JOVEN RED
100% cabernet sauvignon

75 Cherry with a violet edge. Perfumed aroma of flowers (violets) and underripe red fruit. A slightly astringent, light palate, well-mannered overall.

MONASTERIO DE LAS VIÑAS TEMPRANILLO 2003 JOVEN RED
100% tempranillo

75 Cherry. Not very intense aroma of sun-drenched skins and underripe red fruit. Vinous, light palate with good acidity.

ANAYÓN 2001 SEMICRIANZA RED
cabernet sauvignon, merlot, tempranillo

88 Deep intense cherry. Aroma with warm notes, slightly spirituous, with a mineral nuance (dry earth). Slightly jammy fruit with notes of fine oak. Powerful, fleshy palate, ripe tannins with a hint of sweetness and jammy fruit, slightly spirituous.

CORONA DE ARAGÓN 2000 CRIANZA RED
tempranillo, cariñena, cabernet sauvignon, garnacha

83 Garnet red cherry. Intense aroma with predominant spicy oak notes, skins and red stone fruit. Flavourful palate with good fruit/oak integration, fresh herbaceous overtones and bitter notes (liquorice, dark-roasted flavours), somewhat warm.

MONASTERIO DE LAS VIÑAS 2001 CRIANZA RED
garnacha, tempranillo, cariñena, cabernet sauvignon

80 Cherry. Perfumed aroma with sweet notes, ripe red fruit and light, toasty wood. Supple palate with well-integrated tannins and toasty wood.

VALDEMADERA 2000 CRIANZA RED
garnacha, mazuelo, tempranillo

77 Intense cherry. Spicy aroma with notes of tobacco and an essence of ripe plums. Flavourful palate with fruity tannins, balanced wood and an expressive finish.

CORONA DE ARAGÓN 1999 RESERVA RED
tempranillo, cabernet sauvignon, cariñena, garnacha

78 Not very deep cherry. Spicy aroma with balsamic notes, tobacco, and toasty hints. Good acidity and slightly warm on the palate.

MONASTERIO DE LAS VIÑAS 2000 RESERVA RED
garnacha, tempranillo, cariñena, cabernet sauvignon

80 Cherry with a brick red nuance. Slightly viscous, not very intense aroma of toasty wood and slightly balsamic notes. Flavourful with good balance between the fruit and wood.

CORONA DE ARAGÓN 1996 GRAN RESERVA RED
tempranillo, cabernet sauvignon, cariñena, garnacha

83 Deep cherry with an orangey edge. Not very intense, spicy aroma (cinnamon, vanilla cloves), with crianza character. Flavourful palate with noticeable fruit, well-assembled with the wood; younger than what could be expected of a '96.

MONASTERIO DE LAS VIÑAS 1996 GRAN RESERVA RED
garnacha, tempranillo, cariñena, cabernet sauvignon

79 Cherry with an orangey hue. Aroma with a hint of reduction, jammy tomatoes and spices. Well-balanced on the palate with polished tannins and toasty notes.

Bodegas IGNACIO MARÍN

San Valero, 1
50400 Cariñena (Zaragoza)
☎: 976 621 129 - Fax: 976 621 031
comercial@ignaciomarin.com
www.ignaciomarin.com

Established: 1903

🛢 1,400 🗄 1,800,000 litres 🍇 117 has.
🍷 40% 🌐60%

BARÓN DE LAJOYOSA CENTENARIO PLATA 2003 OAK AGED RED
50% garnacha, 50% cabernet sauvignon

84 Very lively garnet red. Aroma of jammy plums and integrated toasty tones (pepper, fine smoky notes). Fleshy, very fresh, flavourful palate with well-structured wood.

CAMPO MARÍN 1999 RESERVA RED
50% tempranillo, 30% garnacha, 20% cariñena

82 Garnet red cherry with a brick red glint. Powerful, ripe aroma with fine reduction notes (leather, old furniture). Flavourful, bitter palate with slightly drying tannins.

DUQUE DE MEDINA 1998 RESERVA RED
DUQUE DE MEDINA 2002 RED
DUQUE DE MEDINA 2000 CRIANZA RED
DUQUE DE MEDINA 2000 GRAN RESERVA RED
CASTILLO DE VIÑARAL 1999 CRIANZA RED
BARÓN DE LAJOYOSA 1996 GRAN RESERVA RED

BARÓN DE LAJOYOSA MOSCATEL VINO DE LICOR

JOSE ANTONIO VALERO TORRES

La Iglesia, 44
50461 Alfamen (Zaragoza)
☎: 976 626 130

Established: 1950

⊞ 25 ▤ 500,000 litres ☙ 10 has. ▼ 100%

CAMPO HERVATO
HERVATO
VIÑA HERVATO

MANUEL MONEVA E HIJOS

Avenida Zaragoza, 10
50108 Almonacid de la Sierra (Zaragoza)
☎: 976 627 020 - Fax: 976 627 334

Established: 1900

⊞ 100 ▤ 800,000 litres ☙ 40 has.
▼ 60% ⊕40%

VIÑA VADINA 2003 RED

Bodegas y Viñedos MONFIL

Avenida del Ejército 20,
50400 Cariñena (Zaragoza)
☎: 976 470 849 - Fax: 976 472 328
monfil@public.ibercaja.es
www.monfil.com

Established: 1998

MONFIL 2003 JOVEN RED
70% garnacha, 30% tempranillo

75 Garnet red cherry. Intense, fruity aroma with predominant herbaceous notes (vine shoots) and skins. Flavourful palate with fine tannins and lacking fruit expression.

MONFIL 2001 CRIANZA RED
70% garnacha, 30% tempranillo

76 Lively garnet red cherry. Not very intense aroma with an essence of spicy oak and the freshness of red fruit. Flavourful palate with a good oak/fruit integration, hints of sweetness.

MONFIL 1998 RESERVA RED

78 Garnet red with a brick red rim. Aroma of jammy red fruit, honey and thyme. Slightly drying and light on the palate with hints of honey in the retronasal passage.

Viñedos y Bodegas PABLO

Avenida Zaragoza, 16

50108 Almonacid de la Sierra (Zaragoza)
☎: 976 627 037 - Fax: 976 627 102
vinedosybodegaspablo@wanadoo.es

Established: S XVIII

⊞ 136 ▤ 348,000 litres ☙ 50 has.
▼ 70% ⊕30%: -US

GRAN VÍU 2001 CRIANZA RED
garnacha, cabernet sauvignon, tempranillo, syrah

85 Intense cherry. Aroma of ripe black fruit with an essence of toasty skins and a mineral expression. Fleshy palate with concentrated black fruit and good symmetry between the round fruit tannins and wood, traces of terroir in the finish.

GRAN VÍU 2000 RESERVA RED
garnacha, cabernet sauvignon, tempranillo

84 Deep cherry. Aroma predominated by toasty oak with an essence of jammy fruit and hints of soil and minerals. Fleshy, ripe palate, slightly flavourful with toasty oak and obvious yet integrated oak tannins.

GRAN VÍU 2000 CRIANZA RED
GRAN VÍU 2003 CRIANZA RED

SEÑORÍO DE AYLES

Finca Ayles. Carretera A-1101 km. 24
50152 Mezalocha (Zaragoza)
☎: 976 140 473 - Fax: 976 140 268
info@bodegasayles.com
www.bodegasayles.com

Established: 1998

⊞ 300 ▤ 800,000 litres ☙ 54 has.
▼ 40% ⊕60%: -US -DE -DK -CH -AT -UK

AYLÉS MERLOT-TEMPRANILLO 2002 OAK AGED RED
50% merlot, 50% tempranillo

84 Garnet red cherry. Fresh aroma of jammy red fruit with an essence of spicy oak and damp earth. Flavourful palate with a good fruit/oak integration and excellent varietal fruit expression, good acidity.

AYLÉS 2001 CRIANZA RED
cabernet sauvignon, tempranillo, merlot

86 Dark cherry with a garnet red edge. Intense, very fine, fruity aroma (redcurrants, cherries) with fine toasty oak, hints of graphite and balsamic notes. Flavourful palate with slightly drying yet promising tannins and rough hints of skins, slightly warm.

AYLÉS 2003 JOVEN RED
cabernet sauvignon, merlot, tempranillo, garnacha

85 Almost opaque cherry with a violet edge. Quite complex aroma of black fruit with notions of terroir and fallen leaves. Fleshy, round palate with weighty fruit tannins and an aftertaste of cocoa and bramble notes; slightly warm but fresh.

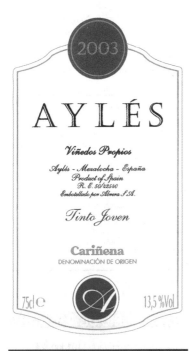

SOLAR DE URBEZO

San Valero, 14
50400 Cariñena (Zaragoza)
☎: 976 621 968 - Fax: 976 620 549
info@solardeurbezo.es
www.solardeurbezo.es

Established: 1995

🏭 300 ᠍ 980,000 litres 🍇 100 has.

🇪🇸 45% 🌐 55%

URBEZO CHARDONNAY 2003 JOVEN WHITE
100% chardonnay

83 Straw-coloured. Quite intense, varietal aroma with hints of ripe fruit and creamy toasty flavours. Powerful, oily, warm, varietal and slightly spirituous palate.

URBEZO CHARDONNAY 2002 WHITE

84 Brilliant pale yellow. Intense aroma, fresh overtones of varietal fruit, a suggestion of fine lees. Flavourful palate, white fruit, quality citrus hints, a slightly smoky nuance of the cask, excellent acidity.

VIÑA URBEZO 2004 RED

84 Very deep violet cherry. Intense aroma, forest fruit, notes of macerated skins, a bramble suggestion. Flavourful palate, fruity, fine herbaceous hints, excellent acidity.

DANCE DEL MAR 2003 RED

79 Deep garnet red cherry. Intense aroma, ripe, slightly sweet fruit, fresh overtones of the terroir. Flavourful, fresh palate, with fleshy overtones, slightly marked grape tannins, bitter.

URBEZO CARIÑENA-SYRAH 2002 RED

84 Garnet red cherry. Intense aroma, ripe red fruit, creamy hints of the crianza, a slightly organic suggestion. Better on the palate, flavourful, good fruit/oak integration, well-balanced, fresh overtones of skins and mineral in the finish.

URBEZO SELECCIÓN ROBLE 2000 RED

83 Garnet red cherry with a coppery glint. Quite intense aroma, with fine overtones, good fruit/oak integration. Flavourful palate, slightly marked tannins, an oily texture, a bitter hint (liquorice, cocoa), marked acidity.

SOLAR DE URBEZO 2001 CRIANZA RED

84 Garnet red cherry with a saffron edge. Intense aroma, with predominant toasty notes of the crianza, hints of fruit and new leather. Flavourful palate, slightly marked tannins, a bitter hint(dark-roasted flavours), slightly warm and oily.

URBEZO 10º ANIVERSARIO 2000 RESERVA RED

86 Garnet red cherry with a coppery edge. Quite intense aroma, with predominant spicy notes of the crianza, a jammy red fruit suggestion. Powerful palate, creamy, slightly marked but promising tannins, slightly oily and long, good acidity.

VIÑA URBEZO 2002 JOVEN RED

SUCESORES DE MANUEL PIQUER

Polígono Las Norias
50450 Muel (Zaragoza)
☎: 976 141 156 - Fax: 976 141 156
bodegaspiquer@bodegaspiquer.com
www.bodegaspiquer.com

Established: 1963

⊞ 100 🗄 130,000 litres 🇪🇸 85% 🌐15%: -
DK -US -NL -MX

VALTUERTA 2003 JOVEN WHITE
VALTUERTA 2003 JOVEN ROSÉ
VALTUERTA 2003 JOVEN RED
VALDETOME 2000 CRIANZA RED
VALDETOME 1997 RESERVA RED

TOSOS ECOLÓGICA

Cuevas, 2
50154 Tosos (Zaragoza)
☎: 976 147 040 - Fax: 976 147 040
btososecol@terra.es
www.bodegastososecológica.com

Established: 1994

⊞ 42 🗄 80.000 litres 🌾 20 has.
🍷 60%% 🌐40%: -UK -DE -IT -BE

CORDIS NATURA 2003 WHITE
100% macabeo

75 Pale gold. Intense aroma of white fruit and a certain varietal character (flowers, exotic fruit). Flavourful, very warm palate with oily hints.

CORDIS NATURA 2003 ROSÉ
100% garnacha

76 Pale blush with a coppery hue. Intense aroma with smoky hints of skins and a suggestion of red fruit. Flavourful, somewhat varietal palate (spices) with fruit expression muted by the alcohol.

CORDIS NATURA 2003 JOVEN RED
70% garnacha, 10% mazuelo, 20% tempranillo

75 Dark garnet red cherry. Powerful, fruity aroma with raisiny hints. Fleshy palate with slightly marked tannins and a jammy suggestion (overripening).

LÁGRIMA VIRGEN 1999 RESERVA RED
60% garnacha, 20% tempranillo, 20% mazuelo

79 Garnet red cherry with a brick red edge. Powerful aroma with predominant reduction notes (prunes, leather, old furniture). Flavourful, bitter, warm palate with a dark-roasted finish.

LÁGRIMA VIRGEN 2002 OAK AGED RED

LÁGRIMA VIRGEN 2000 CRIANZA RED

Sociedad Cooperativa
VIRGEN DEL AGUILA

Carretera Valencia, km. 53
50480 Paniza (Zaragoza)
☎: 976 622 515 - Fax: 976 622 958
info@bodegasvirgenaguila.com
www.bodegasvirgenaguila.com

Established: 1953

⊞ 15,000 🗄 13,000,000 litres 🌾 2,200 has.
🍷 50% 🌐50%: -DE-DK-CH-SE-NL-BE-US

VAL DE PANIZA 2003 JOVEN RED
30% garnacha, 30% tempranillo, 20% cabernet sauvignon, 20% syrah

80 Dark cherry with a garnet red rim. Intense aroma of ripe fruit (redcurrants, cherries, plums) with hints of skins. Flavourful, fleshy palate with ripe tannins and hints of sweet fruit.

CASTILLO DE PANIZA 2003 RED
50% tempranillo, 30% cariñena, 20% garnacha

77 Dark garnet red cherry. Quite intense and fruity aroma with notions of terroir. Flavourful, fleshy palate with somewhat drying but elegant tannins, liquorice and terracotta, pleasant.

SEÑORÍO DEL ÁGUILA 2000 CRIANZA RED
50% tempranillo, 30% garnacha, 20% cabernet sauvignon

73 Dark cherry. Intense, fruity aroma with spicy hints of oak (somewhat aged). Flavourful, bitter palate with a suggestion of sweet fruit and lacking crianza symmetry.

SEÑORÍO DEL ÁGUILA 1998 RESERVA RED
50% tempranillo, 20% garnacha, 20% cabernet sauvignon, 10% cariñena

73 Dark cherry with a garnet red edge. Powerful, spicy aroma with hints of reduction (prunes, old furniture). Flavourful, bitter palate (hints of aged wood).

VAL DE PANIZA 2003 JOVEN WHITE
VAL DE PANIZA 2003 JOVEN ROSÉ
CASTILLO DE PANIZA 2000 CRIANZA RED
CASTILLO DE PANIZA 1999 RESERVA RED

WINNER WINES

Adelfas, 18 3ºB
28007 Madrid (Madrid)
☎: 915 019 042 - Fax: 915 017 794
winnerwines@ibernoble.com
www.winnerwines.es

Established: 1986

⊞ 500 🗄 1,000,000 litres 🌾 400 has.
🍷 8% 🌐92%: -US -CA -MX -DO -PR -SG -
JP -CH -IT -FR -DE -SE -FI -DK -BE -AT -DK.

NAIF 1999 RESERVA RED
GLAMOUR 1999 RESERVA RED

DO CATALUNYA

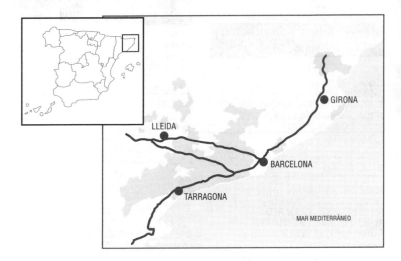

NEWS. The proposal of an 'umbrella' DO for wines from Catalonia is starting to take shape after 5 years in operation, with an increase of 23% in bottled wine, now exceeding 38 million bottles, half of which were exported to international markets where they were received with sharp increases in percentage terms in some cases (87% in the Netherlands, 64% in the United Kingdom, 35% in Germany). The 2003 harvest was considered to be very good. The summer temperatures brought about an average increase of over one degree in the alcohol content, although they also led to a decrease in acidity. The wines of Mas Gil (Clos D'Agon, Clos Valmaña) and the red wine Ca N'Estruc, which once again is among the finest, are extraordinary. As is the white Clos D'Agon, which, with the trilogy of white varieties of the Rhone (*Viognier, Roussanne* and *Marsanne*) and the 95 points awarded to it, has become the best white wine in Spain.

Hectares of Vineyard	No. of Viticulturists	No. of Bodegas	2003 Harvest	2003 Production	Marketing
8,894	3,218	103	Very Good	38,341,209 litres	49% Spain 51% foreign

LOCATION. The production area covers the traditional vine-growing Catalonian regions, and practically coincides with the current DOs present in Catalonia plus a few municipal areas with vine-growing vocation.

CLIMATE AND SOIL. Depending on the location of the vineyard, the same as those of the Catalonian DOs, whose characteristics are defined in this guide. See Alella, Empordà-Costa Brava, Conca de Barberà, Costers del Segre, Montsant, Penedès, Pla de Bages, Priorat, Tarragona and Terra Alta.

VARIETIES:
White:
Recommended: *Chardonnay, Garnacha Blanca, Macabeo, Muscat, Parellada, Riesling, Sauvignon Blanc, Xarel·lo.*
Authorized: *Gewürztraminer, Subirat Parent (Malvasía), Malvasía de Sitges, Picapoll, Pedro Ximénez.*
Red:
Recommended: *Cabernet Franc, Cabernet Sauvignon, Garnacha, Garnacha Peluda, Merlot, Monastrell, Pinot Noir, Samsó (Cariñena), Trepat, Ull de Llebre (Tempranillo).*
Authorized: *Garnacha Tintorera, Syrah.*

REGULATORY COUNCIL.
Passeig Sunyer, 4-6. 43202 Reus (Tarragona).
Tel: 977 328 103. Fax: 977 321 357.
E-mail: info@do-catalunya.com
Website: www.do-catalunya.com

GENERAL CHARACTERISTICS OF THE WINES:

Whites	In general, the autochthonous varieties from Catalonia predominate, *Macabeo, Xarel·lo* and *Parellada*. They are straw yellow and have a fresh and fruity aroma; on the palate they are light and easy drinking. One can also find some *Chardonnay*, which are somewhat fruitier, typical of the variety, although not excessively, as they come from high-yield vineyards.
Rosés	These are quite modern; most are pink or raspberry pink in colour and the aroma is fresh and fruity with hints of red berries; on the palate they are light and correct.
Reds	These may be produced from autochthonous grapes, especially *Ull de Llebre (Tempranillo) and Garnacha*. Cherry-coloured, they tend to be fruity on the nose with notes of wild berries; on the palate they are fruity, without too much body, although easy drinking. There are also examples of foreign varieties, especially *Cabernet*, which can have balsamic and, on occasions, vegetative notes and which have a greater structure on the palate.

ALBET I NOYA

Can Vendrell, s/n
08739 Sant Pau D'Ordal (Barcelona)
☎: 938 994 812 - Fax: 938 994 930
albetinoya@albetinoya.com
www.albetinoya.com
Established: 1977
🏛 875 🗄 1,000,000 litres 🍇 42 has.
🍷 25% 🌐75%: -CH -DE -FR -UK -NL -BE -JP -US

ALBET I NOYA VINYA LAIA 2002 CRIANZA RED

83 Cherry with a brick red rim. Spicy, balsamic aroma of green pepper. Quite aggressive tannins on the palate, greeness, good acidity, persistence and balsamic hints in the retronasal passage.

ALTA ALELLA

Cau D' En Genis s/n
08391 Tiana (Barcelona)
☎: 934 644 949 - Fax: 934 642 401
carmenet@carmenet.es
Established: 2000
🏛 80 🗄 150,000 litres 🍇 8 has.
🍷 90% 🌐10%: -DE -FR -UK -AD

ALTA ALELLA SYRAH 2001 RED
ALTA ALELLA CABERNET SAUVIGNON 2001 RED

ANOIA

Del Mas, 29
08787 Carme (Barcelona)
☎: 938 080 111 - Fax: 938 080 125
info@banoia.com
www.banoia.com
Established: 1976
🗄 300,000 litres 🍷 75% 🌐25%

PRINCIPAT VI DE L'ANY 2003 JOVEN WHITE
80% xarel.lo, 10% macabeo, 10% parellada

78 Pale golden yellow. Not very intense aroma with notes of white fruit. Flavourful palate with bitter notes, fragrant herbs and fresh overtones.

PRINCIPAT VI DE L'ANY 2003 JOVEN RED
75% garnacha, 25% cariñena

78 Not very deep cherry. Intense, spicy aroma with red fruit and underripe skins. Flavourful palate with warm hints which subdue the fruit expression.

CEP D'ART 2001 CRIANZA RED
30% cabernet sauvignon, 25% garnacha, 25% cariñena, 20% merlot

79 Not very deep cherry. Toasty aroma of wood, dark-roasted flavours and balsamic nuances. Drying, slightly warm palate with very marked tannins, persistent.

PRINCIPAT VI DE L'ANY 2003 JOVEN ROSÉ

BACH

Carretera Martorell - Capellades, km. 20, 5
08635 Sant Esteve de Sesrovires (Barcelona)
☎: 937 714 052 - Fax: 937 713 177
codinfo@codorniu.es
www.grupocodorniu.com
Established: 1915
🏛 7,500 🗄 10,000,000 litres 🍇 150 has.
🍷 88% 🌐12%

VIÑA EXTRÍSIMA CRIANZA RED

BOHIGAS

Finca Can Maciá s/n
08711 Ódena (Barcelona)
☎: 938 048 100 - Fax: 938 032 366
comercial@bohigas.es
www.bohigas.es
🗄 400,000 litres 🍇 60 has.
🍷 60% 🌐40%: -UE -US

BOHIGAS BLANC DE BLANCS 2003 JOVEN WHITE
xarel.lo, parellada

82 Brilliant gold. Powerful, fruity aroma with exotic hints (melons, ripe pineapples) and fine floral notes. Fresh, flavourful palate with white fruit, fine bitter notes and excellent acidity.

BOHIGAS CHARDONNAY 2003 FERMENTADO EN BARRICA WHITE
100% chardonnay

85 Brilliant gold. Intense aroma with a good expression of varietal fruit (ripe apples), fine hints of lees and smoky oak and fragrant herbs. Flavourful palate with a good fruit/oak balance and excellent acidity.

BOHIGAS 2003 JOVEN ROSÉ
trepat

78 Pale raspberry with a coppery hue. Intense aroma of foresty red fruit with slightly sweet and toasty hints of skins. Flavourful, slightly meaty and fruity palate with a slightly acidic edge.

BOHIGAS 2003 ROBLE RED
tempranillo, merlot, cabernet sauvignon

84 Dark cherry with a violet edge. Intense, fruity aroma with hints of macerated skins a suggestion of underbrush and fine toasty oak notes. Flavourful, meaty palate with ripe, oily tannins, good acidity and hints of liquorice in the finish.

BOHIGAS CABERNET SAUVIGNON 2001 OAK AGED RED
100% cabernet sauvignon

85 Dark cherry with a deep red-violet edge. Intense aroma of fine smoky oak with very varietal fruit notes (redcurrants, red stone fruit). Powerful, concentrated palate with slightly marked but fine tannins, excellent varietal expression (pepper) and spices and hints of cedar in the retronasal passage.

BOHIGAS 2001 CRIANZA RED
tempranillo, merlot, cabernet sauvignon

85 Dark cherry with a dark red edge. Powerful aroma of toasty oak, an essence of jammy fruit, fine balsamic and reduction hints. Meaty palate with good fruit/oak integration, bitter notes, good acidity and crianza expression.

BOHIGAS 1999 RESERVA RED
tempranillo, merlot, cabernet sauvignon

85 Dark cherry with a dark red edge. Powerful aroma with predominant burnt notes, spices and fine reduction (petals). Meaty palate with good fruit/oak integration and bitter hints (liquorice, dark-roasted flavours), slightly warm and oily.

CA N'ESTRUC

Carretera C-1414, km. 1, 05
08292 Esparreguera (Barcelona)
☎: 937 777 017 - Fax: 937 771 108
canestruc@vilaviniteca.es

Established: 1981

🍷 80 📊 120,000 litres 🍇 26 has.

🍷 95% 🌐5%

IDOIA BLANC 2003 FERMENTADO EN BARRICA WHITE
40% xarel.lo, 30% macabeo, 30% chardonnay

87 Straw-coloured. Smoky aroma of cut grass (hay) with ripe apples and fine lees. Fresh, fruity palate with a smoky retronasal effect, flavourful.

CA N'ESTRUC BLANC 2003 WHITE
83% xarel.lo, 12% macabeo, 5% chardonnay

87 Straw-coloured. Powerful aroma rich in fragrant herbs notes, fresh green fruit and varietal notes. Fresh, light, fragrant and flavourful palate, with character and varietal overtones.

IDOIA NEGRE 2003 FERMENTADO EN BARRICA RED
50% syrah, 40% cabernet, 10% petit verdot, tanat, merlot

90 Intense cherry. Aroma with good fruit expression (fresh fruit, varietal character) and fine toasty notes. Medium-bodied, fresh palate with fine toasty flavours and excellent acidity, easy drinking, elegant and very fruity but with fine toasty oak.

CA N'ESTRUC 2003 ROSÉ

CA N'ESTRUC 2003 RED

Cellers CAMP TARRAGONA

Sant Cristòfol, 29
43765 La Secuita (Tarragona)
☎: 977 611 382 - Fax: 977 611 356
camptarragona@terra.es

Established: 2002

🍷 300 📊 150,000 litres 🍇 45 has.

🍷 30% 🌐70%: -US -PR -DE -BE -AT

GAMEZ ALBA CHARDONNAY 2002 FERMENTADO EN BARRICA WHITE
100% chardonnay

80 Brilliant gold. Intense aroma with predominant smoky oak notes, with an essence of ripe fruit and nutty notes. Flavourful palate with bitter hints of wood, without great fruit expression.

GAMEZ ALBA 150 BARRICAS 2002 OAK AGED RED
80% merlot, 20% tempranillo

84 Dark cherry with a deep red edge. Intense aroma of red fruit and fine spicy oak notes. Flavourful palate with somewhat fresh oak tannins, slightly warm and slightly potential.

GAMEZ ALBA 2002 RED
80% cabernet sauvignon, 10% merlot, 10% tempranillo

84 Dark garnet red cherry. Powerful, fruity aroma of fine toasty oak. Flavourful palate with promising yet slightly drying tannins, spicy with notions of terroir.

CAVAS DEL AMPURDÁN

Plaza del Carme, 1
17491 Perelada (Girona)
☎: 972 538 011 - Fax: 972 538 277
perelada@castilloperelada.com
www.perelada.com

Established: 1923

📊 1,800,000 litres 🍷 99% 🌐1%

MASIA PERELADA 2003 JOVEN WHITE
80% macabeo, 20% garnacha blanca

80 Pale with coppery nuances. Aroma of ripe fruit, white flowers and citrus fresh overtones. Flavourful, bitter palate with hints of herbs, spices and ripe citrus pulp.

MASIA PERELADA 2003 ROSÉ
60% garnacha, 40% tempranillo

77 Fairly deep raspberry with coppery nuances. Somewhat fruity and warm aroma. Flavourful palate with fruity notes and spicy hints of skins, slightly warm.

MASIA PERELADA 2002 RED
80% garnacha, 20% tempranillo

83 Garnet red cherry. Intense aroma of jammy red fruit (fine hints of reduction), petals and fine toasty oak. Flavourful, bitter palate with a good fruit/oak integration and a spicy and sweet retronasal effect.

CLOS VITIS

Vilafranca, 27
08770 Sant Sadurni D'anoia (Barcelona)
☎: 696 -29 818

CLOS VITIS CABERNET MERLOT 1999 CRIANZA RED
CLOS VITIS CABERNET MERLOT 2000 RED
CLOS VITIS TEMPRANILLO SYRAH 2001 RED

Caves CONDE DE CARALT

Ctra Sant Sadurní-Sant Pere de Riudebitlles, km. 5
08770 Sant Sadurní D'Anoia (Barcelona)
☎: 938 917 070 - Fax: 938 996 006
www.condecaralt.es

Established: 1954
🗃 2,000,000 litres 🌿 200 has.
🍷 90% 🍇10%

CONDE DE CARALT BLANC DE BLANCS 2003 JOVEN WHITE
macabeo, xarel.lo, parellada

80 Golden straw with a carbonic hue. Intense aroma of ripe white stone fruit with hints of flowers and a spicy suggestion of skins. Fresh, flavourful, slightly fruity palate with fine bitter notes and good acidity.

CONDE DE CARALT CHARDONNAY 2002 OAK AGED WHITE
100% chardonnay

82 Pale yellow with a golden hue. Intense aroma of green apples with smoky hints of oak and a suggestion of citrus fruit. Fresh, flavourful, bitter palate with marked citrus acidity.

CONDE DE CARALT 2003 ROSÉ
tempranillo, garnacha, cariñena

80 Deep raspberry. Intense aroma of foresty red fruit with spicy hints of skins. Fresh, flavourful palate with fine bitter notes and excellent acidity.

CONDE DE CARALT 1999 RESERVA RED
tempranillo, cabernet sauvignon

80 Dark cherry with a deep red edge. Powerful aroma with toasty and creamy oak notes, a suggestion of ripe fruit and hints of macerated skins. Generous palate with a good fruit/oak integration and fine notes of reduction and notions of fresh fruit in the finish.

Cardenal Vidal y Barraguer, 2
08870 Sitges (Barcelona)
☎: 938 940 003 - Fax: 938 146 090

Established: 1935
🍾 30 🗃 15,000 litres 🌿 2,5 has. 🍇 100%

MALVASÍA DE SITGES LLOPIS I BOFILL VINO DE LICOR DULCE
malvasía

82 Amber with a coppery rim. Aroma of pâtisserie with toasty and honeyed notes. Sweet palate with hints of crystallised fruit, sun-drenched grapes and a fresh finish.

MALVASÍA SECA DE SITGES LLOPIS I BOFILL
malvasía

80 Old gold. Toasty aroma with rancid notes of Mistelle (varnish, viscosity). Dry palate, high in acidity with almond and iodine notes and a slightly astringent finish.

MOSCATELL LLOPIS I BOFILL 2000 MISTELA
moscatel

85 Old gold. Powerful, fresh aroma of Muscatel grapes with notes of jammy fruit and complex overtones. Flavourful palate with sweetness well-integrated with the bitterness of the wine (fruit pulp), and a notion of Mistelle.

JAUME SERRA

Finca El Padruell, s/n
08800 Vilanova i la Geltru (Barcelona)
☎: 938 936 404 - Fax: 938 142 262
jaumeserra@jgc.es
www.vinosdefamilia.com

Established: 1985
🍾 3,500 🗃 3,500,000 litres 🌿 76 has.
🍷 95% 🍇5%: -US-UK -DE -IT -LT -JP -FR -AT -NL

VIÑA DEL MAR AZUL 2003 WHITE SEMI DULCE
60% xarel.lo, 40% macabeo

72 Brilliant pale yellow. Intense, fruity aroma with hints of withered petals. Flavourful, fruity, syrupy palate, lacking in acidity.

VIÑA DEL MAR AZUL 2003 WHITE SECO
50% macabeo, 25% xarel.lo, 25% parellada

70 Brilliant pale. Not very intense aroma with quite fruity notes. Slightly fresh palate without great nuances.

VIÑA DEL MAR AZUL 2003 ROSÉ
tempranillo, cariñena
72 Blush. Intense aroma of ripe red fruit and strawberry jelly. Light, bitter palate, lacking fruit.

VIÑA DEL MAR AZUL 2003 OAK AGED RED

60% tempranillo, 40% cariñena

72 Garnet red cherry with a coppery edge. Somewhat intense fruity aroma with hints of reduction. Quite flavourful fruity palate with drying notes of oak.

VIÑA DEL MAR AZUL 2002 RED
60% tempranillo, 40% cariñena

76 Intense cherry. Spicy aroma (cloves, pepper); red fruit pulp. Somewhat bitter and fresh on the palate with nuances of tobacco and grapes and with slightly green tannins.

ALBATROS WHITE DE AGUJA
ALBATROS ROSÉ DE AGUJA

JEAN LEON

Finca Chateau León - Afueras, s/n
08775 Torrelavit (Barcelona)
☎: 938 995 512 - Fax: 938 995 517
jeanleon@jeanleon.com - www.jeanleon.com
Established: 1963
🗄 1,300 🗄 292,500 litres 🍇 67 has.
🍷 60% 🌐40%: -CH -DE -US -JP -UK

JEAN LEON TERRASOLA SAUVIGNON
BLANC 2003 JOVEN WHITE
75% sauvignon blanc, 25% garnacha

83 Yellow straw. Powerful aroma of ripe fruit and grapey notes with a musky hay essence. Flavourful, full palate with an oily note, easy drinking; ripe Sauvignon.

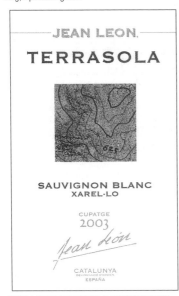

JEAN LEON TERRASOLA MUSCAT 2003
JOVEN WHITE
87% muscat, 13% parellada

82 Greenish straw. Medium-intensity, fresh

aroma of jammy grapes with a green grass nuance. Slightly unctuous and flavourful on the palate with jammy grapes and notions of the vine variety.

JEAN LEON TERRASOLA SYRAH-
CARIÑENA 2002 JOVEN RED
83% syrah, 17% cariñena

84 Bigarreau cherry with a garnet red-violet edge. Medium-intensity aroma with hints of red plums and a balsamic nuance. Flavourful, powerful palate with good Syrah fruit expression, with slightly evident tannins and a balsamic finish.

JOAN SARDÁ

Carretera Vilafranca- St. Jaume dels
Domenys, km. 8, 100
08732 Castellvi de la Marca (Barcelona)
☎: 937 720 900 - Fax: 937 721 495
joansarda@joansarda
www.joansarda.com
Established: 1927
🗄 450 🗄 2,900,000 litres 🍇 20 has.
🍷 50% 🌐50%: -CU -JP -CR -DE -US -KE

MASIA RIBOT 2003 WHITE
50% macabeo, 50% xarel.lo
73 Pale steel. Grapey aroma with white fruit, fresh overtones and a rustic suggestion. Light, with marked acidity and a bitter finish.

MASIA RIBOT 2003 ROSÉ

74 Blush with a salmon hue. Not very intense yet clear aroma of slightly overripe fruit. Light, fresh palate with an element of acidity, well-mannered.

FEIXES DEL PORT 2001 RED
100% lledoner

78 Dark cherry. Toasty aroma with smoky notes over a fruity essence (flowers). Round, flavourful palate with freshness and smoky herbaceous notes in the retronasal passage.

MASIA RIBOT 2002 RED
tempranillo

78 Intense cherry. Clean aroma of strawberries and smoky notes. Fresh, flavourful and round on the palate with Tempranillo character.

MOSCATELL SARDÁ VINO DE LICOR
moscatel

80 Golden amber. Aroma of Muscatel and orange peel with a creamy nuance (vanilla). Sweet and unctuous on the palate, fresh with notes of peaches (Muscatel), a fresh finish.

LEONARDO CANO PEÑA
(Vins i caves Artesanals Vallbona d'Anoia)

Nou 79
08785 Vallbona d'Anoia (Barcelona)
☎: 937 760 223 - Fax: 937 760 223
canop@eresmas.com

Established: 2000
⊕ 50 🗄 10,000 litres 🇪🇸 100%

CASTELL DE LEONARD 2001 FERMENTADO EN BARRICA WHITE
CASTELL DE LEONARD 2000 OAK AGED RED

MAS GIL

Afueras de Calonge - Apdo. 117
17251 Calonge (Girona)
☎: 972 661 486 - Fax: 972 661 462
info@closdagon.com
www.closdagon.com

Established: 1987
⊕ 120 🗄 70,000 litres 🍇 14 has.
🍷40% 🌐60%: -CH -US -UK -DE -FR

CLOS D'AGON 2003 JOVEN WHITE
36% roussanne, 46% viognier, 18% marsanne

95 Lively golden. Powerful aroma with a rich expression of scrubland herbs, sweet fruit and fine smoky hints. Oily, elegant and smoky palate.

CLOS D'AGON 2001 OAK AGED RED
60% cabernet sauvignon, 20% merlot, 20% syrah

93 Intense cherry. Powerful aroma of ripe black fruit with very expressive mineral suggestions.

Full, oily, powerful and ripe palate with fine toasty oak and with minerals in the retronasal passage (dry earth), flavourful and well-displayed tannins.

CLOS VALMAÑA 2001 CRIANZA RED
cabernet sauvignon, syrah

91 Intense cherry with an orange edge. Aroma with mineral notes, ripe black fruit, a suggestion of dried mountain herbs and damp hints of oak (tobacco). Oily, round and elegant palate with minerals, flavourful and full, with character.

CLOS D'AGON 2001 JOVEN WHITE
CLOS D'AGON 2002 JOVEN WHITE
CLOS D'AGON 1999 RED
CLOS D'AGON 2000 RED
CLOS D'AGON 2001 RED
CLOS D'AGON 2002 RED
CLOS VALMAÑA 2000 CRIANZA RED
CLOS VALMAÑA 2002 CRIANZA RED

MIGUEL TORRES

Miguel Torres Carbó, 6
08720 Vilafranca del Penedés (Barcelona)
☎: 938 177 400 - Fax: 938 177 444
webmaster@torres.es
www.torres.es

Established: 1870
⊕ 20,000 🗄 28,000,000 litres 🍇 2122
has.🍷 50% 🌐50%: 120 países

NEROLA 2003 WHITE
50% xarel.lo, 50% garnacha blanca

88 Straw-coloured. Aroma with fresh notes and herbs, fruity and varietal (grapefruit). Fresh, light, flavourful, fruity palate with character.

SAN VALENTÍN MEDIUM 2003 WHITE SEMIDULCE
parellada

80 Pale. Fine orange blossom aroma with hints of peach. Flavourful palate with well-balanced alcohol-acidity; a floral finish.

DE CASTA 2003 ROSÉ
garnacha, mazuelo

83 Fairly deep raspberry with a coppery hue. Intense aroma of ripe red fruit with toasty hints of skins. Fresh, flavourful palate with fine bitter notes and notes of slightly sweet fruit, excellent acidity.

NEROLA 2002 RED
80% syrah, 20% monastrell

87 Intense cherry. Powerful aroma of ripe black fruit with fine toasty oak and mild spicy and animal hints (leather, tobacco). Ripe fruit on the palate with toasty oak and grapes, flavourful with ripe and persistent tannins.

MONT MARÇAL VINÍCOLA

DO CATALUNYA

Finca Manlleu, s/n
08732 Castellví de la Marca (Barcelona)
☎: 938 918 281 - Fax: 938 919 045
direccion@mont-marcal.com
www.mont-marcal.com

Established: 1975
⊕ 500 ▤ 500,000 litres ⚘ 40 has.
🍷 20% 🌰80%

MAS MARÇAL 2001 CRIANZA RED
tempranillo, garnacha, merlot, mazuelo

84 Dark garnet red cherry with a brick red edge. Intense aroma with fine spicy and creamy wood notes and a suggestion of ripe black fruit. Flavourful, meaty palate with well-integrated, bitter fruit and oak, long with a suggestion of fine reduction.

MAS MARÇAL 2003 RED
garnacha, merlot, samsó, syrah

82 Cherry with a lively violet hue. Fresh, fruity aroma with hints of macerated skins, violets and damp earth. Powerful, meaty palate with very flavourful grape tannins, fine bitter notes (liquorice) and good acidity.

OLIVEDA

La Roca, 3
17750 Capmany (Girona)
☎: 972 549 012 - Fax: 972 549 106
comercial10@grupoliveda.com
www.grupoliveda.com

Established: 1948
⊕ 600 ▤ 1,300,000 litres ⚘ 50 has.
🍷 75% 🌰25%: -DE -CH -BE -NL -DK -LU -FR -AD -US

MASÍA OLIVEDA PRIMERA FLOR 2003 WHITE
50% macabeo, 25% garnacha blanca, 25% parellada

80 Pale with greenish nuances. Intense, fresh aroma with a certain finesse, fruit, white flowers, jammy hints and fine herbs. Fresh, flavourful palate with fine bittersweet notes and rich hints of citrus fruit.

MASIA OLIVEDA 2000 CRIANZA RED
tempranillo, garnacha, syrah

82 Garnet red. Aroma of ripe red fruit, toasty wood and viscous notes. Meaty palate with well-integrated tannins, persistent.

MASIA OLIVEDA 2001 RED
tempranillo, garnacha, syrah

80 Cherry with a brick red edge. Somewhat viscous aroma of little intensity. Drying on the palate with slightly marked tannins and medium persistence.

MASÍA OLIVEDA PRIMERA FLOR 2003 ROSÉ DULCE
MASIA OLIVEDA 2000 OAK AGED RED

DULCE

PERE GUARDIOLA

Carretera GI-602, km. 2, 9
17750 Capmany (Gerona)
☎: 972 549 096 - Fax: 972 549 097
vins@pereguardiola.com
www.pereguardiola.com

Established: 1989
⊕ 252 ▤ 275,000 litres ⚘ 38 has.
🍷 87% 🌰13%: -BE -DE

ROCABERDI 2003 JOVEN WHITE
60% macabeo, 40% xarel.lo

79 Pale yellow. Intense aroma with fruit, white flowers, exotic hints (melon, pineapple) and citrus fruit. Flavourful palate with bitter notes and quality citrus fruit.

ROCABERDI 2003 JOVEN ROSÉ
100% cariñena

79 Salmon pink. Clean, fresh, fruity aroma. Light, fresh, pleasant palate, easy drinking.

ROCABERDI 2002 RED
50% cariñena, 50% garnacha

80 Intense cherry. Aroma of spicy strawberries with balsamic hints. Flavourful, fresh palate with a sensation of strawberries and fruity tannins.

ROCABERDI 1999 CRIANZA RED

Bodegas PINORD

Doctor Pasteur, 6
08720 Vilafranca del Penedés (Barcelona)
☎: 938 903 066 - Fax: 938 170 979
pinord@pinord.es
www.pinord.com

Established: 1942
⊕ 2,000 ▤ 4,000,000 litres ⚘ 100 has.
🍷 78% 🌰22%: -US -DE -UK -JP -FR -AT -BE -DK -FI -EL -IT -MT -NL -DK -MX -BR -DO -IE -IS

MASIA GAUDIANA 2003 RED

81 Garnet red cherry. Intense aroma of red fruit with the spicy freshness of skins, sweet and balsamic hints. Flavourful palate with herbaceous hints, quite varietal spicy hints and good acidity.

RAMÓN ROQUETA

Carretera de Vic, 83
08241 Manresa (Barcelona)
☎: 938 743 511 - Fax: 938 737 204
marketing@roqueta.com
www.roqueta.com

Established: 1898

🏭 600 🍷 50% 🌐50%

RAMÓN ROQUETA CHARDONNAY 2003 WHITE
100% chardonnay

83 Brilliant pale yellow. Intense, ripe aroma with a certain varietal character of ripe apples and a suggestion of fine lees. Flavourful palate rich in spicy nuances and lees. Slightly fruity, warm and oily.

SYNERA 2003 WHITE SEMI-DULCE
70% macabeo, 30% moscatel

74 Golden. Intense, fruity aroma with predominant notes of musky Muscatel and floral hints. Fresh, flavourful and bitter on the palate with an unrefined sugary essence and an acidic edge.

SYNERA 2003 WHITE
70% macabeo, 30% moscatel

79 Pale yellow with golden nuances. Intense aroma of white fruit, apricot skin, floral and citrus fruit nuances. Flavourful, fruity palate with fine bitter notes and reminiscent of herb soap.

RAMÓN ROQUETA CABERNET SAUVIGNON 2003 ROSÉ
100% cabernet sauvignon

80 Blush. Intense, fresh, clean aroma. Flavourful palate with weighty fruit, well-balanced and fresh.

SYNERA 2003 ROSÉ
50% garnacha, 50% tempranillo

78 Pale blush. Intense aroma of red fruit with a certain finesse. Light, quite flavourful palate with a suggestion of bitterness, yet fresh; a strawberry beads gum finish.

RAMÓN ROQUETA CABERNET SAUVIGNON 2002 OAK AGED RED
100% cabernet sauvignon

85 Dark cherry with a coppery edge. Powerful aroma with a good varietal expression (redcurrants, cedar, paprika) and toasty notes of wood (pitch, coffee). Powerful palate with marked yet fine tannins, flavourful, spicy and bitter (liquorice, dark-roasted flavours).

RAMÓN ROQUETA TEMPRANILLO 2002 OAK AGED RED
100% tempranillo

81 Dark cherry with a lively violet edge. Intense, varietal aroma (black fruit, underbrush) with hints of macerated skins and toasty oak. Flavourful, bitter palate with a good fruit/oak integration.

SYNERA 2002 OAK AGED RED
cabernet sauvignon, tempranillo

77 Cherry with an orangey hue. Spicy aroma of ripe red fruit and sun-drenched skins. Flavourful, ripe palate with good oak/fruit harmony, easy.

RAMÓN ROQUETA MERLOT 2002 CRIANZA RED
100% merlot

84 Dark cherry with a purplish edge. Intense aroma with excellent varietal expression (paprika, redcurrants, underbrush) and a balsamic essence. Flavourful palate with fruity notes and fine smoky oak. Slightly drying and warm.

RENÉ BARBIER

Afueras, s/n
08770 Sant Sadurní D'Anoia (Barcelona)
☎: 938 917 000 - Fax: 938 911 254
renebarbier@renebarbier.es

MEDITERRANEAM WHITE
MEDITERRANEAM ROSÉ
MEDITERRANEAM RED

Vinos ROSTEI

Cami Mas Rostei, s/n
17255 Begur (Girona)
☎: 972 622 638 - Fax: 972 304 400
dambois@teleline.es

Established: 1986

🏭 20 📊 10,100 litres 🌿 2 has. 🇪🇸 100%

ROSTEI 2000 CRIANZA RED
60% cabernet sauvignon, 40% merlot

81 Garnet red cherry with a saffron edge. Powerful, spicy, very varietal aroma (cedar, paprika) with fine toasty crianza notes. Flavourful palate with slightly drying tannins, spicy notes, tobacco and good acidity.

ROSTEI 1999 OAK AGED RED

Celler Cooperatiu de SALELLES

Carretera D'Igualada, s/n
08240 Manresa (Barcelona)
☎: 938 720 572 - Fax: 938 720 572
coopsalelles@coopsalelles.com
www.coopsalelles.com

Established: 1926

🏭 25 📊 500,000 litres 🍷 100%

DEGÀ DE SALELLES OAK AGED RED
90% tempranillo, 10% cabernet sauvignon

83 Lively garnet red cherry. Intense aroma of ripe red stone fruit with spicy hints of wood. Flavourful palate with meaty overtones, slightly sweet fruit and slightly lively but fine tannins with hints of skins and fresh fruit in the finish.

SOL DE BRUGAS

Carretera 244, km. 18
08736 Mediona (Barcelona)
☎: 938 988 183 - Fax: 938 988 300

Established: 1995

260,000 litres 🍇 11 has.

20% 🌐80%: -BE -DE -IE -US -JP -DK

SOL DE BRUGAS MERLOT 2000 RED
SOL DE BRUGAS CABERNET SAUVIGNON
2000 RED
SOL DE BRUGAS SYRAH 2000 RED

VINS GRAU

Ctra. C-37 de Igualada a Manresa, km. 75, 5
08255 Maians-(Castellfollit de Boix)
(Barcelona)
☎: 938 356 002 - Fax: 938 356 002
vinsgrau@troc.es
www.vinsgrau.com

Established: 1966

125 300,000 litres 🍇 15 has.

90% 🌐10%: -DK -AT -CH -DE

CLOS ESTRADA 2003 WHITE
CLOS ESTRADA 2002 OAK AGED RED
CLOS JORMÀ 2003 RED

DO CAVA

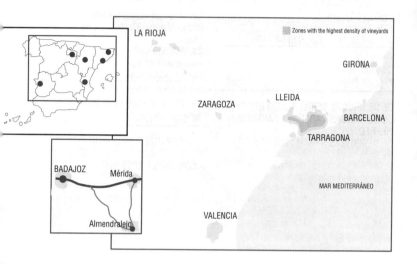

LA RIOJA

Zones with the highest density of vineyards

GIRONA

ZARAGOZA

LLEIDA

BARCELONA

TARRAGONA

MAR MEDITERRÁNEO

BADAJOZ   Mérida

Almendralejo

VALENCIA

NEWS. The high temperatures of 2003 reduced the aromatic complexity of the wines, although, due to their nature, Cavas gain a large amount of their character during the ageing process. Therefore, the wines tasted for this edition, which are all mainly from the 2002 harvest, consolidate their quality on the better expression and fineness of the yeast notes (lees, withered petals) together with a delicate fruit and, in the best of examples, strong hints of ripe citrus pulp. We will have to wait for another year to discover what the grapes of the 2003 harvest were like.

Hectares of Vineyard	No. of Viticulturists	No. of Bodegas	2003 Harvest	2003 Production	Marketing
32,009	6,848	272	Good	160,986,000 litres	46% Spain 54% foreign

Secondly, the consumption figures of Cava in the national market seem to have recovered slightly, perhaps as a result of the efforts that the Instituto del Cava is making with its promotion.

Of the 419 wines tasted, 151 exceed 85 points and more than 200 received between 80 and 84 points, which results in a more than acceptable quality standard. Regarding the style, the producers remain committed to the pattern of fresh wine, in which the ageing attributes are more in line with the delicacy, the fineness and the dry character of the Brut Nature. With respect to the varieties, the producers no longer seem to resort to the *Chardonnay*, as expected 2 or 3 years ago, although it is indeed the dominant variety in the better rated Cavas, as is the case with the Gramona Colección de Arte, or the classic, as far as we are concerned, Jaume Codorníu 450 Aniversario.

Another aspect of interest arises from the assessment of the rosé Cavas, where the *Pinot Noir*, the *Monastrell* and the *Garnacha* seem to perform better than the indigenous *Trepat*. The latter, without reaching exceptional scores, displays good varietal notes and quality in notable single-variety exceptions such as Freixenet

Trepat 1998, Carles Andreu, Martín Soler (Soler i Degollada), Agustí Torrelló, or blended, in the Lavit of Segura Viudas or the 999 of Loxarel.

LOCATION. The defined Cava region covers the sparkling wines produced according to the traditional method of a second fermentation in the bottle of 63 municipalities in the province of Barcelona, 52 in Tarragona, 12 in Lleida and 5 in Girona, as well as those of the municipal areas of Laguardia, Moreda de Álava and Oyón in Álava, Almendralejo in Badajoz, Mendavia and Viana in Navarra, Requena in Valencia, Ainzón and Cariñena in Zaragoza, and a further 18 municipalities of La Rioja.

CLIMATE. That of each producing region stated in the previous epigraph. Nevertheless, the region in which the largest part of the production is concentrated (Penedès) has a Mediterranean climate, with some production areas being cooler and situated at a higher altitude.

SOIL. This also depends on each producing region.

VARIETIES:
White: *Macabeo (Viura), Xarel·lo, Parellada, Subirat (Malvasía Riojana)* and *Chardonnay.*
Red: *Garnacha Tinta, Monastrell, Trepat* and *Pinot Noir.*

REGULATORY COUNCIL.
Avinguda Tarragona, 24. 08720 Vilafranca del Penedés (Barcelona).
Tel: 938 903 104. Fax: 938 901 567.
E-mail: consejo@cava.es
Website: www.crcava.es

GENERAL CHARACTERISTICS OF THE WINES:

Young Cavas	Their youth is due to a shorter ageing period in the bottle (the minimum stipulated by the Council is nine months). They are somewhat lighter, fresher and easier to drink; they have notes of fruit and vegetables.
With longer ageing periods	(For the Gran Reserva, the wines have to be aged for a minimum of 30 months in the bottle). They have more complex notes due to the longer time that the yeasts remain in the bottles. There is a distinction between the more traditional styles, normally with aromas of dried fruit and bitter almonds, sometimes also due to the inclusion of old wine in the expedition liqueur, although this custom is gradually dying out. The more modern styles combine slightly fruity and floral notes, even herbs, with hints of toast and nuts; they are also characterised by their refinement and elegance, typical of champagne.
Chardonnay-based	These are characterised by their greater body on the palate and a light oily mouthfeel; on the nose they may sometimes develop aromas of tropical fruit.

A. CANALS NADAL

Ponent, 2
08733 El Pla del Penedés (Barcelona)
☎: 938 988 081 - Fax: 938 989 050
cava@canalsnadal.com
www.canalsnadal.com

Established: 1915

190,000 litres ❦ 20 has.🚩 75% 🍇25%

ANTONI CANALS NADAL RESERVA BRUT
40% macabeo, 40% xarel.lo, 20% parellada

84 Brilliant straw with fine and persistent beads. Somewhat intense, ripe aroma, with a good expression of the crianza over a ripe fruit nuance. Dry, creamy palate with notes of ripe lemons and excellent acidity, hints of nuts.

ANTONI CANALS NADAL 2000 BRUT NATURE
40% macabeo, 40% xarel.lo, 20% parellada

85 Straw-coloured with a golden hue. Fresh aroma with fine notes of reduction (withered petals), citrus fruit and white fruit. Dry, creamy palate with excellent fruit-crianza-acidity balance.

ANTONI CANALS NADAL BRUT CUPADA SELECCIÓ BRUT NATURE
45% xarel.lo, 35% macabeo, 20% parellada

84 Pale yellow with a greenish glint. Powerful, very fresh aroma with notes of green apples and fine notes of reduction (lees, withered petals). Dry palate with fine bitter notes, hints of sweet limes, without great nuances, pleasant.

Cooperativa AGR. I CAIXA AGR. ESPLUGA

Lluís Carulla, 15
43440 L'Esplugá de Francolí (Tarragona)
☎: 977 870 105 - Fax: 977 870 026
coespluga@retemail.es

Established: 1902

200 4,000,000 litres
❦ 582 has. 🚩 100%

FRANCOLI BRUT
FRANCOLI BRUT NATURE
FRANCOLI SEMI-SECO

AGUSTÍ TORELLÓ

La Serra, s/n
08770 Sant Sadurní d'Anoia (Barcelona)
☎: 938 911 173 - Fax: 938 912 616
agistitorello@agustitorello.com
www.agustitorello.com

Established: 1954

32 ❦ 28 has. 🚩 80% 🍇20%

AGUSTÍ TORELLÓ MATA TREPAT 2002 RESERVA BRUT ROSÉ
100% trepat

83 Brilliant blush. Intense, ripe aroma with spicy hints of skins and mild reduction (petals, lees). Creamy, fresh and dry on the palate without great crianza expression, pleasant.

AGUSTÍ TORELLÓ MATA 2001 RESERVA BRUT
46% macabeo, 28% xarel.lo, 26% parellada

87 Brilliant pale. Intense aroma of great finesse, with lees, fennel, a suggestion of petals and white fruit. Fresh, dry and creamy on the palate with fine bitter notes (almonds, anise, herbs) and excellent acidity.

AGUSTÍ TORELLÓ MATA BARRICA 2000 RESERVA BRUT NATURE
100% macabeo

85 Brilliant pale. Intense aroma with ripe fruit, fine smoky wood, lees, flowers and honey. Dry, flavourful palate with well-integrated beads, slightly marked tannins and fine bitter crianza notes (herbs and nuts).

AGUSTÍ TORELLÓ MATA 2000 GRAN RESERVA BRUT NATURE
45% macabeo, 30% xarel.lo, 25% parellada

89 Straw-coloured with golden nuances. Powerful, ripe aroma with hints of withered petals and flowers (acacia) and fresh overtones of new almonds. Very dry, fine palate with quality bitter notes (almonds, anise, fine herbs) and good acidity.

AGUSTÍ TORELLÓ MATA MAGNUM 1998 GRAN RESERVA BRUT NATURE
macabeo, xarel.lo, parellada

91 Brilliant straw. Intense, very fine aroma with predominant reduction notes (withered petals, bakery, bitter almonds) over a suggestion of white fruit and ripe grapefruit. Generous palate with well-integrated beads and fine bitter notes, well-balanced with a powerful finish of herbs and nuts.

KRIPTA 1999 GRAN RESERVA BRUT NATURE
44% macabeo, 30% xarel.lo, 26% parellada

88 Pale yellow with golden nuances. Intense aroma with mild reduction notes (lees, anise, fine herbs, bitter almonds). Flavourful and creamy palate (well-integrated beads) with fine bitter and citrus notes, excellent acidity.

ALBET I NOYA

Can Vendrell, s/n
08739 Sant Pau D'Ordal (Barcelona)
☎: 938 994 812 - Fax: 938 994 930
albetinoya@albetinoya.com
www.albetinoya.com

DO CAVA

Established: 1977

875 1,000,000 litres 42 has.

25% 75%: -CH -DE -FR -UK -NL -BE -JP -US

ALBET I NOYA BRUT 21 2000
70% chardonnay, 30% parellada

87 Straw-coloured with a golden glint. Intense aroma, fruity, (ripe apples, green fruit) with a fine reduction nuance. Dry, creamy palate, excellent expression of crianza (nuts) and hints of honey and citrus fruit, good acidity.

ALBET I NOYA RESERVA BRUT
25% chardonnay, 25% xarel.lo, 25% parellada, 25% macabeo

82 Brilliant straw. Intense aroma, ripe with an excellent crianza-acidity balance and a ripe citrus fruit nuance. Creamy palate with fine bitter and bittersweet notes, good acidity, without great nuances of crianza, pleasant.

ALBET I NOYA RESERVA BRUT ROSÉ
100% pinot noir

89 Brilliant raspberry with a coppery glint. Powerful aroma with excellent varietal expression, a spicy nuance, and fine crianza notes (lees, nuts). Dry, fresh palate with well-integrated beads and fine bitter notes, good acidity, very long, with hints of underbrush and liquorice in the retronasal passage.

ALBET I NOYA RESERVA DULCE
25% chardonnay, 25% xarel.lo, 25% parellada, 25% macabeo

83 Very pale yellow with a greenish hue. Intense aroma, of green apples with a crystallised nuance and fine lees. Sweet palate with fine bitter notes, well-balanced, very pleasant.

CAN VENDRELL DE LA CODINA RESERVA BRUT
33% xarel.lo, 33% macabeo, 33% parellada

85 Very pale yellow with a greenish hue. Intense, fruity aroma (green apples) with a fine reduction notes (lees). Generous palate, rich in nuances with bitter notes (almonds) and a nuance of crystallised fruit, good acidity.

ALBET I NOYA RESERVA BRUT NATURE
25% chardonnay, 25% xarel.lo, 25% parellada, 25% macabeo

86 Brilliant straw. Intense, very fine aroma with fine notes of white fruit, a nuance of lees and hints of high quality citrus fruit. Dry palate with excellent fruit-crianza-acidity balance and predominant bitter notes (almonds) in the retronasal passage.

ALELLA VINÍCOLA CAN JONC

Rambla Ángel Guimerá, 62
08328 Alella (Barcelona)
☎: 935 403 842 - Fax: 935 401 648
comercial@alellavinicola.com
www.alellavinicola.com

Established: 1906

450 932,000 litres 115 has.

93% 7%: -US -CH

MARFIL GRAN SELECCIÓN BRUT NATURE

Cava ALMIRALL

Diputació, 29
08770 Sant Sadurní D'Anoia (Barcelona)
☎: 938 912 939 - Fax: 938 912 939

Established: 1950

3 has. 100%

ALMIRALL 2000 BRUT
ALMIRALL 1998 GRAN RESERVA BRUT NATURE
ALMIRALL 2002 SEMI-SECO

ALSINA & SARDÁ

Barrio Les Tarumbes, s/n
08733 Pla del Penedés (Barcelona)
☎: 938 988 132 - Fax: 938 988 671
alsina@ialsinasarda.com
www.readysoft.es/alsina

Established: 1986

135 1.150.000 litres 40 has.

70% 30%

ALSINA & SARDÁ 2000 RESERVA BRUT
macabeo, xarel.lo, parellada

84 Brilliant gold. Powerful aroma with a good expression of traditional crianza (nuts, mountain herbs) and a hint of spices (cumin). Dry palate with a well-integrated bead and toasted nuts, lacking acidity.

ALSINA & SARDÁ BRUT
macabeo, xarel.lo, parellada

83 Golden straw. Intense aroma with notes of herbs and nuts and a toasty suggestion of fine lees. Dry, creamy palate (well-integrated bead) with a hint of ripe fruit, bitter and pleasant, lacking an element of acidity.

ALSINA & SARDÁ BRUT ROSÉ

80 Intense raspberry with a coppery hue. Intense, fruity aroma with fine notes of sweet fruit, a suggestion of lees and withered petals and spicy hints. Flavourful palate with fine bitter notes, hints of citrus fruit and a slightly acidic edge.

ALSINA & SARDÁ 1999 GRAN RESERVA BRUT NATURE
40% macabeo, 40% xarel.lo, 20% parellada

86 Straw-coloured. with a golden hue. Powerful aroma with fine notes of citrus fruit pulp, an expression of lees and a suggestion of nuts and mountain herbs. Powerful, creamy, bitter aroma with a fine crianza expression and excellent acidity.

ALTA ALELLA

Cau D' En Genis s/n
08391 Tiana (Barcelona)
☎: 934 644 949 - Fax: 934 642 401
carmenet@carmenet.es
Established: 2000
⊕ 80 📊 150,000 litres 🌿 8 has.
🍷 90% 🌐10%-DE -FR -UK -AD

MIRGIN 2001 BRUT NATURE
chardonnay

80 Straw-coloured with golden nuances. Subtle aroma of flowers and white fruit with a hint of fine lees. Dry, bitter palate (almonds) with dried herbs and elevated acidity.

ALTA ALELLA PRIVAT MIRGIN ROSÉ 2002 BRUT NATURE

AMETLLER CIVILL

Rovira Roja, 10
08731 Sant Martí Sarroca (Barcelona)
☎: 933 208 439 - Fax: 933 208 437
ametller@ametller.com
www.ametller.com
Established: 1999
🌿 38 has. 🍷 50%
🌐50%:-NL -SE -DK -JP -UK -CH

MANUEL DE CABANYES BRUT
parellada, xarel.lo, macabeo

82 Straw-coloured with a greenish glint. Quite intense aroma with a nuance of ripe white fruit and light notes of citrus fruit and bakery. Fresh, dry, creamy palate with fine bitter notes and good acidity, pleasant yet without great crianza expression.

MANUEL DE CABANYES RESERVA BRUT NATURE
parellada, xarel.lo, macabeo

84 Pale yellow. Quite intense aroma of ripe white fruit with fine reduction notes and hints of grape-fruit. Very dry palate with well-integrated beads, fine bitter notes, well-crafted crianza and a suggestion of freshness (citrus fruits).

MANUEL DE CABANYES GRAN RESERVA BRUT NATURE
parellada, xarel.lo, macabeo

85 Brilliant straw. Quite intense, ripe aroma with fine reduction notes (withered petals, acacia, bakery). Dry, creamy palate with fine bitter notes (almonds, herbs, cumin), good acidity (hints of citrus fruit).

ANTONI VILAMAJÓ SAUMELL

Pol. Can Ferrer I -Parcela 5
08770 Sant Sadurní D'Anoia (Barcelona)
☎: 938 183 313 - Fax: 933 493 009

A. VILAMAJÓ BRUT
A. VILAMAJÓ GRAN RESERVA BRUT NATURE
A. VILAMAJÓ GRAN RESERVA ESPECIAL BRUT NATURE

ANTONIO MASCARÓ

Casal, 9
08720 Vilafranca del Penedés (Barcelona)
☎: 938 901 628 - Fax: 938 901 358
mascaro@mascaro.es
www.mascaro.es
Established: 1946
⊕ 1,000 🌿 40 has. 🍷 85% 🌐15%

MASCARÓ NIGRUM BRUT

83 Straw-coloured. Fine aroma of mountain herbs with well-assembled notes of lees and mild aniseed notes. Dry, fresh, herbaceous palate with good beads and expression of anise.

CUVÉE ANTONIO MASCARÓ GRAN RESERVA EXTRA BRUT
50% parellada, 35% macabeo, 15% chardonnay

80 Pale yellow. Not very intense aroma with finesse and notes of aniseed and fine lees. Dry, fresh palate, with fine bitter notes (almonds), pleasant although without great crianza expression.

MASCARÓ "MONARCH" GRAN RESERVA BRUT
90% parellada, 10% chardonnay

80 Lemon. Aroma of green fruit with a suggestion of citrus fruit (fruit pulp), and a nutty crianza nuance. Flavourful palate with a good sweet-bitter symmetry and herbs in the finish.

MASCARÓ BRUT NATURE
80% parellada, 20% macabeo

83 Straw-coloured with a greenish edge. Aroma of fine herbs with a nuance of pleasant lees and hints of aniseed. Flavourful, very fresh palate with an expression of herbs and spices (varietal), fine beads.

MASCARÓ ROSADO "RUBOR AURORAE" BRUT
MASCARÓ NIGRUM SEMI-SECO

ARTESANOS VINÍCOLAS

L'Avella, 13 "Can Gabatx" - Bustia, 24
08739 Font-Rubi (Barcelona)
☎: 938 979 422 - Fax: 938 979 422
Established: 1985
🛢 25 📊 15,000 litres 🌿 25 has.
🍷 60% 🌐40%

EMILIA FREIXEDAS RESERVA BRUT
FAMILIA FREIXEDAS CRIANZA BRUT NATURE

ARVIC ARETEY

Pº Colón, 4
08002 Barcelona (Barcelona)
☎: 933 102 262 - Fax: 933 100 671
info@aretey.com
www.aretey.com

ARETEY BRUT ROSÉ
ARETEY BRUT VINTAGE GRAN RESERVA
ARETEY RESERVA BRUT

Cavas AVINYÓ

Masia Can Fontanals, s/n
08793 Avinyonet del Penedés (Barcelona)
☎: 938 970 055 - Fax: 938 970 691
www.avinyo.com
Established: 1982
🛢 50 📊 450,000 litres 🌿 33 has.
🍷 80% 🌐20%-US -CH

AVINYÓ BRUT NATURE
macabeo, xarel.lo, parellada

81 Pale yellow. Intense aroma with excellent crianza expression (lees, withered petals). Dry, flavourful palate with high quality bitter notes and an excellent suggestion of dried herbs and citrus fruit.

AVINYÓ SELECCIÓ LA TICOTA GRAN RESERVA BRUT NATURE
macabeo, xarel.lo

85 Straw-coloured. Intense aroma of well-characterised crianza (fine lees, bakery, nuts) over a delicate suggestion of citrus fruit (límes pulp) and aniseed. Dry, flavourful palate with fine bitter notes and excellent crianza-acidity balance.

AVINYÓ RESERVA BRUT

BACH

Carretera Martorell - Capellades, km. 20, 5
08635 Sant Esteve de Sesrovires (Barcelona)
☎: 937 714 052 - Fax: 937 713 177
codinfo@codorniu.es
www.grupocodorniu.com
Established: 1915
🛢 7,500 📊 10,000,000 litres 🌿 150 has.
🍷 88% 🌐12%

BACH RESERVA DE LA MASÍA BRUT
50% chardonnay, 25% xarel.lo, 25% macabeo

82 Pale yellow. Powerful, ripe aroma (green apples, white fruit) with predominant reduction notes (withered petals, pâtisserie). Generous palate with fine bitter notes, bittersweet notes, a fruity nuance and good acidity.

Cavas BERTHA

Avernó, 14
08770 Sant Sadurní de Noya (Barcelona)
☎: 938 910 903 - Fax: 938 911 091
cavabertha@hotmail.com
Established: 1989
🌿 4 has. 🍷 100%

BERTHA 2000 GRAN RESERVA ROSÉ
BERTHA COSECHA 2001 GRAN RESERVA
BERTHA RESERVA BRUT NATURE
BERTHA SIGLO XXI 1999 GRAN RESERVA

BLANCHER ESPUMOSOS DE CAVA

Plaça Pont Romà, 5
08770 Sant Sadurní D'Anoia (Barcelona)
☎: 938 183 286 - Fax: 938 911 961
blancher@blancher.es
www.blancher.es
Established: 1955
📊 500,000 litres 🌿 10 has. 🍷 80% 🌐20%

BLANCHER RESERVA BRUT NATURE ROSÉ
100% garnacha

81 Not very deep brilliant raspberry. Fruity, varietal aroma (spices, red fruit) with a nuance of sweet fruit. Dry, fresh, slightly creamy palate with fine bitter notes of skins and crianza, good acidity.

BLANCHER RESERVA BRUT NATURE
macabeo, xarel.lo, parellada

79 Straw-coloured. Not very intense aroma with overtones of white fruit freshness and a fine reduction nuance. Dry, bitter palate, high in acidity, lacks balance, better crianza expression.

CAPDEVILA PUJOL RESERVA ESPECIAL BRUT NATURE
xarel.lo, parellada, macabeo

85 Straw-coloured. Not very intense aroma of ripe white fruit with fine notes of crianza in the bottle (lees, hints of fennel). Dry palate with excellent acidity-fruit-reduction balance, very fine.

BLANCHER DE LA TIETA GRAN RESERVA BRUT NATURE
xarel.lo, parellada, macabeo

84 Straw-coloured with a golden hue. Intense aroma of ripe white fruit with hints of fine reduction (withered petals, lees). Dry, creamy palate (well-integrated beads) with fine bitter notes of crianza and hints of citrus fruit in the retronasal passage, good acidity.

BLANCHER ESPECIAL BRUT
BLANCHER OBRAC RESERVA BRUT
MAGNUM CAPDEVILA PUJOL BRUT NATURE
BLANCHER EXTRA SEMI-SECO
BLANCHER EXTRA ROSÉ SEMI-SECO
BLANCHER DOLÇ CLASSIC DULCE

BODEGA Y VIÑEDOS DEL ARZOBISPO

Carretera de Hurchillo, km. 1, 500
03300 Orihuela (Alicante)
☎: 965 302 340 - Fax: 966 741 176
bvarzobispo@ctv.es
www.bvarzobispo.com

Established: 2000

130 🍷 500,000 litres 🍇 35 has.

90% 🍷10%-SE -BE -PT -FR -DE

SANT JUST BRUT
macabeo, xarel.lo, parellada

78 Pale yellow with a golden hue. Intense aroma of ripe white fruit with floral notes and a certain finesse, without great crianza expression. Dry, creamy palate with a nuance of sweetness, lacking balance.

SANT JUST BRUT NATURE
macabeo, xarel.lo, parellada

80 Pale with a greenish glint. Not very intense aroma, with fresh overtones, white stone fruit, exotic hints and withered petals. Dry palate, fresh with fine bitter notes and a toasty nuance of the crianza.

BOHIGAS

Finca Can Maciá s/n
08711 Ódena (Barcelona)
☎: 938 048 100 - Fax: 938 032 366
comercial@bohigas.es
www.bohigas.es

🍷 400,000 litres 🍇 60 has.

🇪🇸 60% 🍷40%-UE -US

BOHIGAS 2000 BRUT
40% macabeo, 25% xarel.lo, 35% parellada

86 Golden yellow with fine and persistent beads. Quite intense aroma of ripe white fruit with hints of lees and a honeyed nuance. Generous palate, rich in crianza nuances (toasted nuts), well-balanced and long.

MAS MACIÀ BRUT
macabeo, xarel.lo, parellada

83 Intense golden yellow. Powerful, very ripe aroma with reduction notes and a slightly vinous nuance. Dry, creamy palate (well-integrated beads) with fine notes of nuts and Mediterranean herbs, an expression of old wine and good acidity.

BOHIGAS 2000 GRAN RESERVA BRUT
30% macabeo, 10% xarel.lo, 45% parellada, 15% chardonnay

84 Brilliant straw with a golden glint. Intense aroma, ripe, with a fine reduction nuance (nuts) and vinous hints. Dry, flavourful palate, well-integrated beads, excellent crianza expression, good acidity.

BOHIGAS 2000 BRUT NATURE
30% macabeo, 10% xarel.lo, 45% parellada, 15% chardonnay

87 Golden yellow with fine beads. Powerful, ripe aroma, rich in reduction notes (withered petals, nuts). Dry, creamy palate with excellent crianza expression, very long.

BOHIGAS BRUT NATURE

83 Pale yellow with a greenish hue. Powerful aroma of green apples with ripe white fruit and reduction notes (withered petals, fine lees). Dry, fresh palate, rich in bitter crianza nuances, citrus fruits.

BOLET VINOS Y CAVAS

Finca Mas Lluet
08732 Castellvi de la Marca (Barcelona)
☎: 938 918 153 - Fax: 938 918 153
sat.maslluet@sefes.es
www.cavasbolet.com

Established: 1983

24 🍷 400,000 litres 🍇 65 has.

95% 🍷5%-DE -BE

BOLET 1999 GRAN RESERVA EXTRA BRUT
macabeo, xarel.lo, parellada

85 Straw-coloured with a golden hue. Powerful, ripe aroma with good crianza expression (withered petals, lees, nuts) and a vinous nuance. Dry, creamy, balanced palate with fine bitter and toasty crianza notes, good acidity.

BOLET 2001 BRUT
macabeo, xarel.lo, parellada

84 Straw-coloured with a golden glint, slightly robust beads. Not very intense aroma with fine notes of ripeness and reduction (withered petals, nuts, herbs). Generous, creamy palate with fine bitter notes, very pleasant.

BOLET 2000 BRUT NATURE
macabeo, xarel.lo, parellada

85 Straw-coloured with a golden hue. Intense, ripe aroma with fine notes of crianza (nuts, lees) and hints of honey. Generous palate with bitter notes fine toasty crianza notes, long.

BONET CABESTANY

Tarragona, 19
08770 Sant Sadurní D'Anoia (Barcelona)
☎: 938 911 624 - Fax: 938 911 624
cavasbonet@hotmail.com

Established: 1989
🏴 100%

BONET CABESTANY BRUT NATURE
BONET CABESTANY RESERVA BRUT NATURE
BONET CABESTANY CHARDONNAY RESERVA
ESPECIAL BRUT NATURE

BORDEJÉ

Carretera Borja - Rueda, km. 3
50570 Ainzón (Zaragoza)
☎: 976 868 080 - Fax: 976 868 989
ainzon@bodegasbordeje.com
www.bodegasbordeje.com

Established: 1770
🌐 200 📦 500,000 litres
🍇 60 has. 🏴 100%

BORDEJÉ CHARDONNAY BRUT NATURE
BORDEJÉ MILENIO BRUT NATURE

CA N'ESTELLA

Masia Can Estella
08791 Sant Esteve Sesrovires (Barcelona)
☎: 934 161 387 - Fax: 934 161 620
canestella@canestella.ce.telefonica.net

Established: 1998
🌐 140 📦 200,000 litres 🍇 40 has.
🏴 40% 🌍60%-DE -UK -NL -DK -SE

RABETLLAT I VIDAL BRUT CA N'ESTELLA
50% macabeo, 50% xarel.lo

80 Brilliant straw with a greenish hue. Powerful aroma of green apples with fine notes of crianza (lees) and a nuance of sweet limes. Dry palate with well-integrated beads, fresh (without great crianza expression), high in acidity.

RABETLLAT I VIDAL BRUT NATURE
85% chardonnay, 15% macabeo

83 Brilliant straw with fine beads. Not very intense, fresh aroma of white fruit with a nuance of flowers, hints of lees and ripe lemon. Dry, creamy palate with fine bitter notes (almonds, herbs), good acidity.

Cellers CAL FERU

Arquitecte César Martinell, 3
08770 Sant Sadurní D'Anoia (Barcelona)
☎: 938 910 163 - Fax: 938 913 343
calferu@telefonica.net

Established: 1934
🏴 100%

HENRI NOVEL BRUT NATURE
MIQUEL ROIG RESERVA BRUT NATURE
VIMONT BRUT NATURE

Cellers CAMP TARRAGONA

Sant Cristòfol, 29
43765 La Secuita (Tarragona)
☎: 977 611 382 - Fax: 977 611 356
camptarragona@terra.es

Established: 2002
🌐 300 📦 150,000 litres 🍇 45 has.
🏴 30% 🌍70%-US -PR -DE -BE -AT

GRAN D'ABBATIS 2001 BRUT NATURE
100% parellada

82 Yellow with a golden rim. Perfumed aroma (flowers) with overtones of crianza notes (fine lees). Well-balanced, fruity palate (white fruit), fresh with fizzy beads.

CAN FEIXES (HUGUET)

Finca Can Feixes
08785 Cabrera D'Anoia (Barcelona)
☎: 937 718 227 - Fax: 937 718 031
canfeixes@canfeixes.com

Established: 1768
🌐 250 📦 310.000 litres 🍇 80 has.
🏴 60% 🌍40%-US -DE -NL -BE -UK -AT -
CH -FI -MX

HUGUET 2001 RESERVA BRUT
64% parellada, 25% chardonnay, 11% macabeo

83 Pale with a greenish glint. Fresh aroma of green apples with a nuance of fine lees. Dry, fresh palate with fine bitter notes and excellent citrus fruit nuance (sweet limes), lacks crianza expression.

HUGUET 2001 RESERVA BRUT NATURE
64% parellada, 25% chardonnay, 11% macabeo

84 Straw-coloured with a greenish glint. Intense, very fresh aroma of green apples, without great crianza expression with mild hints of lees and balsamic flavours. Dry, fresh palate with good acidity and fine citrus notes, very flavourful.

Celler CAN PUJOL

Duc de la Victoria, 9
08800 Vilanova i la Geltrú (Barcelona)
☎: 938 931 535 - Fax: 938 143 063
cellercanpujol@cellercanpujol.com
www.cellercanpujol.com

Established: 1989
⊞ 60 ▤ 125,000 litres

TORRENTS & CARBÓ BRUT
xarel.lo, macabeo, parellada

82 Golden straw. Aroma of tropical fruit, perfumed (acacia), with hints of fresh lees. Flavourful palate, slightly oily palate with fine beads; good freshness, with almondy notes in the finish.

TORRENTS & CARBÓ BRUT NATURE
xarel.lo, macabeo, parellada

82 Straw-coloured. Aroma of fresh fruit with fine lees and notes of herbs and flowers. Dry palate with a slightly rustic expression, good fruit-wood balance and robust beads.

TORRENTS & CARBÓ GRAN RESERVA BRUT NATURE
xarel.lo, macabeo, parellada

84 Straw-coloured with a greenish hue. Intense aroma of ripe white fruit, with notes of fine reduction (withered petals, lees), and a honeyed nuance. Dry, fresh palate with excellent fruit-crianza-acidity balance.

L'AVI TAPET BRUT
CAVA BLAU TORRENTS & CARBÓ GRAN RESERVA BRUT NATURE

CAN QUETU

Tarragona, 33
08770 Barcelona (Sant Sadurní D'Anoia)
☎: 938 911 214 - Fax: 938 914 104
canquetu@tiscali.es

Established: 1954
⊞ 100 ▤ 50,000 litres 🍷 90% 🌍10%

CAN QUETU BRUT
CAN QUETU BRUT ROSÉ
CAN QUETU BRUT NATURE
CAN QUETU BRUT NATURE ROSÉ
CAN QUETU 1996 RESERVA BRUT NATURE
CAN QUETU 1998 RESERVA BRUT NATURE
CAN QUETU BOTELLA ESPECIAL RESERVA
CAN QUETU SEMI-SECO
ROIG VIRGILI NATURE SELECCIÓ 1998
ROIG VIRGILI RESERVA NATURE 1998

CAN RÀFOLS DELS CAUS

Can Rafols del Caus s/n
08739 Avinyonet del Penedés (Barcelona)
☎: 938 970 013 - Fax: 938 970 370
canrafols@seker.es

Established: 1980
⊞ 150 ▤ 300,000 litres 🍷 50 has.
🍷 67% 🌍33%

PARISAD GRAN RESERVA 1998 EXTRA BRUT

89 Golden yellow. Powerful aroma, rich in crianza nuances (spices, nuts, fine lees). Fresh palate, creamy (well-integrated bead), robust overtones, excellent balance, spicy nuances in the finish, long.

GRAN CAUS BRUT ROSÉ
GRAN CAUS RESERVA EXTRA BRUT
GRAN CAUS BRUT NATURE

Cellers de
CAN SURIOL DEL CASTELL

Castell de Grabuac
08736 Font-Rubí (Barcelona)
☎: 938 978 426 - Fax: 938 978 364
cansuriol@suriol.com
www.suriol.com

Established: 1987
⊞ 50 ▤ 280,000 litres 🍷 25 has.
🍷 60% 🌍40%-BE

AZIMUT 2000 BRUT NATURE
33% macabeo, 33% xarel.lo, 33% parellada

82 Pale yellow with a golden glint. Powerful aroma with predominant reduction notes (lees, nuts). Very dry palate, bitter (almonds, balsamic flavours), good crianza expression.

SURIOL COLLITA PROPIA 1994 BRUT NATURE
30% macabeo, 30% xarel.lo, 35% parellada

83 Golden yellow. Powerful aroma with predominant reduction notes (lees, nuts, hints of varnish). Dry palate with well-integrated beads, fine bitter crianza notes, and an old wine character, very long.

SURIOL COLLITA PROPIA 1996 RESERVA BRUT NATURE
macabeo, xarel.lo, parellada

83 Golden yellow. Powerful aroma with predominant reduction notes (lees, nuts, varnishes). Dry palate, well-integrated beads, fine notes of crianza (nuts), good old wine character.

DO CAVA

CANALS & MUNNÉ

Ctra. Sant Sadurní - Vilafranca, km. 0, 5
08770 Sant Sadurní d'Anoia (Barcelona)
☎: 938 910 318 - Fax: 938 911 945
canalsmunne@troc.es
www.troc.es/canals&munne
Established: 1915
🌐 350 🛢 600,000 litres 🍇 20 has.
🍷 75% 🌐25%-CH -UK -IT -PT -DE -BE -DK

CANALS & MUNNÉ GRAN DUC XXI 1998
RESERVA ESPECIAL BRUT NATURE
50% chardonnay, 30% xarel.lo, 20% parellada

86 Pale with a golden hue. Intense aroma of ripe apples with, good crianza expression (withered petals, bakery). Dry palate with good balance between acidity and crianza and fine bitter notes (nuts, cumin, mountain herbs).

CANALS & MUNNÉ INSUPERABLE 2002 BRUT
CANALS & MUNNÉ 2001 GRAN RESERVA BRUT
CANALS & MUNNÉ 2000 RESERVA
CANALS & MUNNÉ EL SERRAT DEL GUINEU 1999 GRAN RESERVA BRUT NATURE

CANALS Y DOMINGO

Carretera Sant Sadurní-Vilafranca, km. 1
08770 Sant Sadurní d' Anoia (Barcelona)
☎: 938 910 391 - Fax: 938 910 391
Established: 1963
🛢 700.000 litres 🍇 3 has. 🍷 100%

CANALS Y DOMINGO BRUT
CANALS Y DOMINGO BRUT NATURE

CANALS Y NUBIOLA

Plaza Santiago Rusinyol, s/n
08770 Sant Sadurní D'Anoia (Barcelona)
☎: 938 917 025 - Fax: 938 910 126
Established: 1915
🛢 2.000.000 litres 🍇 3 has.
🍷 90% 🌐10%

CANALS & NUBIOLA 2002 BRUT
40% xarel.lo, 30% parellada, 30% macabeo

78 Pale with greenish nuances. Intense, fruity aroma with hints of withered petals and lees. Flavourful, creamy palate with notes of jammy fruit and good acidity, pleasant.

CANALS & NUBIOLA 2002 BRUT NATURE
33% xarel.lo, 33% parellada, 33% macabeo

78 Pale with greenish nuances. Intense aroma of fruit, white flowers and hints of herbs and fennel. Very fresh palate with a well-integrated bead and fine bitter notes (almonds).

Bodegas CAPITÀ VIDAL

Carretera Villafranca-Igualada, km. 30
08733 Pla del Penedés (Barcelona)
☎: 938 988 630 - Fax: 938 988 625
capitavidal@capitavidal.com
capitavidal.com
Established: 1985
🍇 50 has. 🍷 90% 🌐10%

FUCHS DE VIDAL BRUT CINCO BRUT
30% macabeo, 40% xarel.lo, 30% parellada

85 Straw-coloured with fine beads. Intense aroma with fine notes of white fruit over a nuance of lees. Dry, fresh, creamy palate with fine bitter notes and good acidity.

FUCHS DE VIDAL CUVÉE ESPECIAL BRUT NATURE
35% macabeo, 40% xarel.lo, 25% parellada

83 Brilliant yellow. Not very intense aroma with notes of ripe apples and fine reduction (lees, withered petals). Ripe, creamy palate with well-integrated beads, good acidity.

PALAU SOLÁ BLANC DE BLANCS BRUT NATURE
35% macabeo, 40% xarel.lo, 25% parellada

87 Pale. Not very intense aroma but of great finesse with fruit and white flowers, hints of lees and sweet limes. Dry, very fresh palate with excellent acidity and balance.

FUCHS DE VIDAL 1999 GRAN RESERVA BRUT NATURE
macabeo, xarel.lo, parellada

84 Straw-coloured with a golden hue. Intense aroma with fine reduction notes (withered petals, nuts) over a nuance of ripe apples. Creamy, ripe palate with a hint of cumin and toasty crianza notes, lacks acidity.

GRAN FUCHS BRUT NATURE
CAPITÀ VIDAL BANDA BRUT NATURE

Cavas CARDONER

Vilarnau, 41
08770 Sant Sadurní D'Anoia (Barcelona)
☎: 938 912 955 - Fax: 938 911 313
cavas@cardoner.com
Established: 1983
🍷 80% 🌐20%

CARDONER BRUT
CARDONER BRUT NATURE
CARDONER SEMI-SECO

DO CAVA

Cava CARLES ANDREU

Sant Sebastià, 19
43423 Pira (Tarragona)
☎: 977 887 404 - Fax: 977 887 404
info@cavandreu.com
www.cavandreu.com

Established: 1991

🍾 4 📦 24,000 litres 🍇 60 has. 🍷 100%

CARLES ANDREU BRUT
parellada, macabeo

83 Pale yellow with a greenish glint. Intense, fruity aroma (apples), with good reduction notes (withered petals, yeasts). Dry palate with fine bitter notes and a fruity nuance (ripe citrus fruit), good acidity.

CARLES ANDREU EXTRA BRUT ROSÉ
trepat

84 Very deep raspberry. Fruity, not very intense aroma with hints of lees. Dry palate with well-integrated beads, fine bitter notes and a toasty, quite spicy crianza nuance, good acidity.

CARLES ANDREU RESERVA BRUT NATURE
parellada, macabeo

85 Brilliant straw. Not very intense aroma with fine reduction notes (lees, withered petals) over a nuance of ripe white fruit with hints of honey. Dry palate with fine bitter crianza notes, excellent balance.

CARLES ANDREU BRUT NATURE
parellada, macabeo

83 Pale with a greenish glint. Not very intense aroma of white fruit with hints of fine reduction (petals). Dry, fresh, creamy palate with fine bitter notes, well-balanced, a sweet nuance in the retronasal passage.

CARMENET

Pelegrí Torelló, 14
08770 Sant Sadurní D'Anoia (Barcelona)
☎: 934 644 949 - Fax: 934 642 401
carmenet@carmenet.es

Established: 1953

🍾 60 📦 150,000 litres 🍇 9 has.
🍶 200,000 litres. 🍷 80%
🌐20%-US -DE -FR -UK -AD

PRIVAT RESERVA BRUT
macabeo, xarel.lo, parellada

84 Yellow straw with a golden rim. Unusual aroma of fresh herbs with white fruit, intense with a fine crianza expression. Vinous palate with bitter notes of fruit pulp, good acidity, slightly short.

PRIVAT EVOLUCIÓ RESERVA BRUT NATURE
chardonnay

87 Brilliant golden yellow with fine beads. Powerful, very aromatic and ripe aroma with floral notes (acacia) and lees, honeyed hints. Flavourful, creamy palate with fine bitter notes and the character of a still wine, excellent, original crianza expression.

PRIVAT LAIETÀ RESERVA BRUT NATURE
chardonnay

85 Golden with fine and persistent beads. Very fine aroma with notes of ripe white fruit, hints of fine reduction (cumin) and a floral nuance. Fresh, bitter, creamy palate, excellent acidity.

PRIVAT RESERVA BRUT NATURE
chardonnay

83 Golden yellow. Aroma of ripe white fruit and yeasts with reduction notes. Ripe palate with overtones of bitterness and good varietal and crianza expression.

PRIVAT OPUS EVOLUTIUM GRAN RESERVA BRUT NATURE
chardonnay

88 Yellow with a golden hue. Intense aroma of great finesse with floral notes, ripe apples (varietal expression) and a nuance of fine lees. Fresh, dry palate, rich in nuances with notes of white fruit, crianza spices, herbs and citrus fruit, excellent acidity.

Cellers CAROL VALLÈS

Can Parellada s/n - Corral del Mestre
08739 Subirats (Barcelona)
☎: 938 989 078 - Fax: 938 988 413
info@cellerscarol.com
www.cellerscarol.com

Established: 1996

🍇 10 has. 🍷 80% 🌐20%-AD -CH

GUILLEM CAROL MILLENIUM 1997 GRAN RESERVA BRUT
35% parellada, 30% xarel.lo, 20% macabeo, 15% chardonnay

85 Pale yellow with a golden glint. Not very intense aroma of ripe white fruit with hints of lees and honey. Dry, fresh palate with fine bitter crianza notes, excellent acidity.

PARELLADA I FAURA 2002 BRUT NATURE
60% parellada, 30% macabeo, 10% xarel.lo

85 Pale yellow with a golden glint. Not very intense aroma of great finesse with notes of white fruit and fine notes of crianza (toasted nuts, fennel, withered petals). Dry, creamy palate with fine bitter notes (almonds) and hints of citrus fruit in the retronasal passage, very long.

PARELLADA I FAURA MILLENIUM 2001 RESERVA BRUT NATURE
40% parellada, 40% macabeo, 20% xarel.lo

84 Golden yellow. Quite intense aroma with predominant ripe apple notes over a nuance of fine reduction (withered petals). Dry palate, fine bitter crianza notes, hints of herbs, good acidity.

GUILLEM CAROL 1997 GRAN RESERVA BRUT NATURE
40% xarel.lo, 40% parellada, 20% chardonnay

84 Yellow straw with a golden glint. Quite intense, very fine aroma of green fruit with a nuance of fine lees. Dry, fresh palate with good crianza expression (bitter almonds, dried herbs), excellent acidity.

GUILLEM CAROL 1999 GRAN RESERVA BRUT

CASTELL D'AGE

Carretera, 6-8
08782 La Beguda Baixa (Barcelona)
☎: 937 725 181 - Fax: 937 727 061
info@castelldage.com
www.castelldage.com

Established: 1989

🌐 400 📊 110,000 litres 🍇 60 has.
📛 20% 🌐80%: UE

CASTELL D'AGE GRAN RESERVA BRUT
macabeo, parellada, chardonnay

77 Straw-coloured with a greenish edge. Discreet aroma of ripe fruit with notes of lees reduction. Dry, fresh, somewhat rustic palate with herbaceous expression, long.

ANNE MARIE COMTESSE BRUT NATURE
xarel.lo, parellada, macabeo

82 Straw-coloured with a greenish edge. Fine toasty aroma with hints of almonds and a nuance of herbs. Dry, fresh palate with an expression of herbs and fine beads, slightly short.

ANNE MARIE COMTESSE BRUT NATURE ROSÉ
xarel.lo, parellada, macabeo

81 Strawberry blush. Fresh aroma of rose petals with a nuance of red fruit. Dry, fresh palate with fine beads, jammy red fruit and hints of bitterness.

CASTELL D'AGE CHARDONNAY GRAN RESERVA BRUT NATURE
chardonnay

78 Straw-coloured with a green glint. Toasty aroma with a very pleasant light buttery and herbaceous nuance; tropical fruit. Flavourful palate, a little vinous with herbs in the finish, long.

CASTELL D'AGE GRAN RESERVA BRUT NATURE
macabeo, parellada, chardonnay

83 Straw-coloured with a greenish hue. Slightly intense, ripe aroma, with predominant crianza notes (withered petals, fine lees) and a nuance of ripe grapefruit. Fresh, dry palate with fine bitter notes (almonds, fine herbs), long.

POCULUM BONI GENI GRAN RESERVA ANNE MARIE COMTESSE SEMI-SECO

CASTELL DE VILARNAU

Vilarnau, 34-36
08770 Sant Sadurní D'Anoia (Barcelona)
☎: 938 912 361 - Fax: 938 912 913
castelldevilarnau@gonzalezbyass,.es
www.gonzalezbyass.es

Established: 1982

📊 85.000 litres 🍇 16 has. 📛 30%
🌐70%-UK -DE -CH -DK -IS -NL -BE -SE -EC -IT -VE

ALBERT DE VILARNAU 2000 FERMENTADO EN BARRICA BRUT
70% macabeo, 20% parellada, 10% chardonnay

87 Straw-coloured with a golden glint and fine beads. Intense, ripe aroma with fine hints of reduction (withered petals) and a sweet suggestion of wood. Generous palate, rich in nuances with fine bitter notes of oak; almonds and dried herbs, good acidity and structure, very fine.

CASTELL DE VILARNAU 2000 BRUT NATURE
100% chardonnay

87 Straw-coloured with a coppery glint and fine and persistent beads. Fine aroma with notes of ripe white fruit and a nuance of mild reduction (honey, withered petals, fine lees). Dry, creamy palate with fine bitter notes and nuts, excellent acidity.

CASTELL DE VILARNAU BRUT
CASTELL DE VILARNAU BRUT ROSÉ
CASTELL DE VILARNAU VINTAGE 1998 GRAN RESERVA BRUT
CASTELL DE VILARNAU BRUT NATURE
CASTELL DE VILARNAU SEMI-SECO

Celler CASTELL DEL MIRALL

Masia Can Gustems, s/n
08792 La Granada (Barcelona)
☎: 938 974 558 - Fax: 938 974 708
enologia@castelldelmirall.com
www.castelldelmirall.com

Established: 2000

🌐 200 📊 800,000 litres 🍇 50 has.
📛 85% 🌐15%-DE -BE -UK -US -FR

FERRÉ I CATASÚS RESERVA BRUT NATURE
macabeo, xarel.lo, parellada

83 Straw-coloured. Quite intense aroma of ripe white fruit with fine reduction notes (withered petals, fine lees). Dry, creamy palate with fine bitter notes (almonds, cumin) and notes of citrus fruit, high in acidity.

CASTELL SANT ANTONI

Passeig del Parc, 13
08770 Sant Sadurní de D'Anoia (Barcelona)
☎: 938 183 099 - Fax: 938 183 099
cava@castellsantantoni.com
www.castellsantantoni.com

Established: 1963

🗄 15,000 litres 🍇 20 has. 🍷 100%

CASTELL SANT ANTONI RESERVA ESPECIAL BRUT ROSÉ
100% garnacha

84 Brilliant raspberry. Not very intense, fruity aroma with very varietal spicy notes and fine lees. Flavourful, creamy palate, rich in nuances with fine bitter notes, good acidity.

CASTELL SANT ANTONI RESERVA ESPECIAL BRUT
macabeo, xarel.lo, parellada

85 Pale yellow. Intense aroma with fine reduction notes (lees, withered petals) over a nuance of superripe white fruit. Dry, creamy palate with fine bitter notes (almonds) and a nuance of citrus fruit and crystallised white fruit, very pleasant.

CASTELL SANT ANTONI GRAN RESERVA BRUT NATURE
macabeo, xarel.lo, parellada

87 Straw-coloured with a greenish glint. Somewhat intense aroma with good crianza expression (fine lees) over a grapefruit and ripe white fruit nuance. Dry, fresh palate with fine bitter notes, excellent acidity and balance, very fine.

CASTELL SANT ANTONI "CUVÉE MILLENNIUM" GRAN RESERVA BRUT NATURE
macabeo, xarel.lo, parellada

88 Straw-coloured with a golden glint. Powerful aroma of ripe fruit over a toasty crianza nuance (fine lees, cumin). Dry palate with well-integrated beads and an excellent balance between bitter crianza notes (nuts, herbs) and acidity.

CASTELL SANT ANTONI "GRAN BRUT" BRUT NATURE
macabeo, xarel.lo, parellada

86 Slightly pale straw with a greenish glint. Intense, ripe aroma of fine lees with a delicate nuance of grapefruit. Very dry palate with well-integrated beads and fine crianza notes (dried herbs, cumin, toasty flavours); good acidity, very fine.

CASTELL SANT ANTONI GRAN RESERVA BRUT NATURE ROSÉ
garnacha

88 Very deep raspberry with a coppery glint. Powerful aroma, with excellent varietal (spices, underbrush) and crianza (lees) expression. Dry, flavourful, creamy palate with fine bitter notes (nuts, orange peel), very long.

CASTELL SANT ANTONI MAGNUM GRAN RESERVA BRUT NATURE
macabeo, xarel.lo, parellada

88 Pale yellow. Intense aroma with predominant reduction notes (withered petals, lees), hints of honey and a nuance of ripe fruit. Dry, fresh palate with excellent fruit-crianza-acidity balance and a hint of citrus fruit, long.

CASTELLBLANCH

Avenida Casetes Mir, s/n
08770 Sant Sadurní D'Anoia (Barcelona)
☎: 938 917 025 - Fax: 938 910 126
castellblanch@castellblanch.es
www.castellblanch.es

Established: 1908

🗄 2,000,000 litres 🍇 250 has.

🍷 75% 🌐 25%-DE -UK -JP -US -CH -IT

GRAN CASTELL 1999 GRAN RESERVA BRUT
40% parellada, 25% macabeo, 20% xarel.lo, 15% chardonnay

80 Straw-coloured. Intense aroma with predominant notes of ripe white fruit and a hint of fine lees. Fresh, flavourful palate with fine bitter notes, very pleasant but lacking crianza expression.

CASTELLROIG

Ctra Sant Sadurní d'Anoia - Vilafranca del Penedés, km. 1
08739 Subirats (Barcelona)
☎: 938 911 927 - Fax: 938 996 092
info@castellroig.com
www.castellroig.com

Established: 1988

🌐 100 🗄 170,000 litres 🍇 25 has.

🍷 65% 🌐 35%-DK -NL -CH -BE -AD -US

CASTELLROIG 1998 GRAN RESERVA BRUT NATURE
82% xarel.lo, 18% macabeo

84 Pale with a greenish glint. Quite intense aroma with notes of ripe white fruit, and a nuance of reduction (withered petals, almonds, honey). Dry, creamy palate with fine bitter notes, well-balanced.

CASTELLROIG 2000 RESERVA BRUT NATURE
68% xarel.lo, 22% macabeo, 10% parellada

85 Pale yellow with a greenish glint. Intense aroma of well-balanced notes of fruit and crianza. Dry, creamy palate with fine bitter notes (toasted nuts, herbs), excellent acidity.

CASTELLROIG 2001 RESERVA BRUT NATURE
40% xarel.lo, 48% macabeo, 12% parellada

83 Brilliant straw with a greenish glint. Intense aroma, fresh, fruity (green apples), with a light nuance of reduction (fine lees) and hints of citrus fruit. Dry palate with fine bitter notes (almonds) and notes of sweet limes in the retronasal passage.

CASTELLROIG 2001 RESERVA BRUT
CASTELLROIG 2000 RESERVA BRUT
CASTELLROIG MAGNUM 1998 GRAN RESERVA BRUT NATURE
CASTELLROIG RESERVA FAMILIAR 1999 GRAN RESERVA BRUT NATURE

Cavas del
CASTILLO DE PERELADA

Avenida Barcelona, 78
08720 Vilafranca del Penedés (Barcelona)
☎: 938 180 676 - Fax: 938 180 926
bodegas@castilloperelada.com
www.castilloperelada.com

Established: 1923

▤ 3,500,000 litres ⬛ 85% 🌐15%-NL -DE -DK -FI -SE -UK -BE -PE -TT -JP

CASTILLO PERELADA BRUT ROSÉ
garnacha, monastrell

80 Blush. Fresh aroma of red fruit with floral hints (petals), fine lees and herbs. Dry, flavourful palate with a well-integrated bead and rich bitter and citrus notes.

CASTILLO PERELADA RESERVA BRUT
40% macabeo, 30% xarel.lo, 30% parellada

79 Pale with greenish nuances. Intense aroma with a certain finesse of fruit and white flowers with fine notes of citrus fruit and herbs, fresh, lacking crianza expression. Flavourful, creamy palate with a citrus and bitter freshness (sweet almonds).

TORRE GALATEA BRUT ROSÉ
50% monastrell, 25% garnacha, 25% trepat

85 Brilliant raspberry. Intense aroma of fine smoky skins, spices and red fruit with hints of fine lees. Flavourful and creamy on the palate with fine bitter crianza notes, a spicy essence and hints of high quality citrus fruit; well-balanced.

CASTILLO PERELADA 2002 BRUT NATURE
macabeo, xarel.lo, parellada

83 Straw-coloured with a greenish hue. Fairly intense aroma of ripe fruit with hints of reduction (fine lees, withered petals). Dry and creamy on the palate with fine bitter and citrus notes and good acidity.

CASTILLO PERELADA CHARDONNAY 2000 BRUT NATURE
100% chardonnay

88 Pale yellow with a golden hue. Powerful aroma of ripe apples with fine reduction notes (lees, nuts, cumin) and a nuance of withered petals. Dry and creamy on the palate with bitter almonds, fine herbs, and a slightly oily texture, rich in nuances, well-balanced.

CASTILLO PERELADA CUVÉE ESPECIAL 2002 BRUT NATURE
macabeo, xarel.lo, parellada, chardonnay

86 Brilliant straw. Intense aroma of ripe white fruit with fine reduction notes and hints of citrus fruit. Fresh and dry on the palate with a well-integrated bead, bitter almonds, hints of citrus fruit and herbs in the finish, good acidity.

GRAN CLAUSTRO CASTILLO PERELADA 2002 BRUT NATURE
45% chardonnay, 20% macabeo, 20% parellada, 15% xarel.lo

85 Brilliant pale yellow. Fairly intense aroma with a certain finesse, ripe white fruit, a nuance of lees and hints of fennel. Flavourful and creamy on the palate with fine bitter notes (almonds, cumin), good acidity and crianza expression.

CASTILLO PERALADA SEMI-SECO
macabeo, xarel.lo, parellada

80 Pale golden yellow. Intense aroma with fine notes of fruit and flowers and hints of aniseed. Fresh, flavourful palate with hints of jammy black fruit, good acidity.

CASTILLO PERALADA SECO
50% macabeo, 25% xarel.lo, 25% parellada

80 Pale lemony yellow. Intense aroma of ripe white stone fruit with hints of withered petals. Flavourful, creamy palate with a light bittersweet nuance, very fresh.

CATASÚS I CASANOVAS

Sant Isidre, 36
08770 Sant Sadurní D'Anoia (Barcelona)
☎: 938 183 716 - Fax: 934 590 710
info@masxarot.com
www.masxarot.com

Established: 1993

▤ 11,000 litres ⬛ 40% 🌐60%

PLA DE PLANILS BRUT
MAS XAROT RESERVA BRUT
MAS XAROT BRUT NATURE
MAS XAROT GRAN RESERVA BRUT NATURE
PLA DE PLANILS BRUT NATURE

CAYTUSA

Bodegas Bajas, s/n
50570 Ainzón (Zaragoza)

☎: 976 867 552 - Fax: 976 867 552
bodegascaytusa@hotmail.com
Established: 1986
▨ 200,000 litres 🍷 80%
🌍20%-FR -VE -CR -US

1986 GRAN RESERVA 1999
macabeo, parellada, chardonnay

77 Brilliant pale with fine beads. Intense, slightly fresh aroma (green apples), hints of herbs, nuts (raw almonds) and fine lees. Flavourful, bitter palate with toasted nuts. and withered petals in the retronasal passage.

CODORNÍU

Avenida Jaume Codorníu, s/n
08770 Sant Sadurní D'Anoia (Barcelona)
☎: 938 183 232 - Fax: 938 910 822
smartin@codorniu.es
www.grupocodorniu.com
Established: 1551
▨ 36,000,000 litres 🌿 3,245 has.
🍷 80% 🌍20%

ANNA DE CODORNÍU RESERVA BRUT
chardonnay, xarel.lo, parellada

88 Golden yellow with fine beads. Powerful aroma with notes of ripe apples and fine notes of reduction (lees, nuts, Mediterranean herbs). Creamy palate, rich in nuances with excellent balance and a slightly oily texture, very long.

CODORNÍU NON PLUS ULTRA CUVÉE REINA Mª CRISTINA BRUT
chardonnay, xarel.lo, macabeo

88 Straw-coloured with a golden glint. Intense aroma with notes of petals and fine lees and hints of ripe apples and toasty bakeries. Dry, very flavourful palate, rich in nuances, with fine bitter notes (nuts, mountain herbs), very long; powerful retronasal effect (walnuts, oriental spices), excellent acidity.

CODORNÍU PINOT NOIR BRUT ROSÉ
100% pinot noir

84 Brilliant salmon with a coppery glint and barely perceptible beads. Subtle aroma with fine notes of red stone fruit over a suggestion of lees. Dry palate with fine bitter notes and hints of nuts and fragrant herbs in the retronasal passage.

GRAN CODORNÍU BRUT
macabeo, xarel.lo, parellada

86 Pale yellow with a golden glint. Not very intense aroma, very fine with notes of lees and white fruit and a suggestion of ripe grapefruit. Dry palate with well-integrated beads, fine bitter notes and good acidity.

JAUME CODORNÍU BRUT
chardonnay, parellada

89 Straw-coloured with a golden glint. Intense aroma with fine notes of reduction (withered petals) over a nuance of ripe white fruit. Dry, flavourful palate with excellent acidity, fine toasty (nuts) crianza notes and overtones of freshness.

JAUME CODORNÍU MAGNUM 450 ANIVERSARI BRUT
chardonnay, parellada

91 Yellow straw with a golden hue. Powerful aroma, rich in crianza nuances (herbs, cumin, bakery) over a hint of ripe white fruit. Powerful, dry palate with excellent balance between acidity and crianza, creamy (well-integrated beads)and oily, complex, long.

VINYA CODORNIU BRUT NATURE

87 Straw-coloured with a yellow hue. Aroma with toasty notes (phosphorous, Pedernal) with a fine nuance of lees and jammy fruit. Fresh palate with excellent bead, flavourful with a bitter hint, dry, elegant.

CUVÉE RAVENTÓS BRUT NATURE

COLET VINOS Y CAVAS

Camí del Salinar, s/n
08739 Pacs del Penedés (Barcelona)
☎: 938 170 809 - Fax: 938 170 809
colet_cava@jet.es
www.coletcava.com
Established: 1994
▨ 60 ▨ 80,000 litres 🌿 22 has.
🍷 75% 🌍25%

COLET ASSEMBLAGE EXTRA BRUT

83 Very pale salmon. Intense, fruity aroma with fine notes of reduction (withered petals, lees). Dry, creamy palate (well-integrated beads) with fine bitter notes, a spicy nuance and good acidity.

COLET GRAND CUVÉE BLANC DE BLANCS EXTRA BRUT

86 Pale yellow. Powerful, ripe aroma, with predominant reduction notes (withered petals, toasty and honey hints). Dry, creamy palate with fine bitter notes (almonds); a nuance of dried herbs, good acidity.

COLET TRADITIONNELLE BLANC DE BLANCS EXTRA BRUT

81 Very pale straw. Not very intense aroma of ripe white fruit with a nuance of fine reduction (lees, floral hints). Generous, creamy palate, without great crianza expression yet very pleasant, a mild nuance of sweetness.

COMERCIAL VINÍCOLA DEL NORDEST

Espolla, 9
17752 Mollet de Peralada (Girona)

☎: 972 563 150 - Fax: 972 545 134
vinicola@vinicoladelnordest.com
www.vinicoladelnordest.com

Established: 1977

⊕ 80 🍶 1,000,000 litres 🍇 200 has.
🍷 95% 🌍5%

ANUBIS RESERVA BRUT
ANUBIS RESERVA BRUT NATURE
ANUBIS RESERVA SEMI-SECO

Caves CONDE DE CARALT

Ctra Sant Sadurní-Sant Pere de
Riudebitlles, km. 5
08770 Sant Sadurní D'Anoia (Barcelona)
☎: 938 917 070 - Fax: 938 996 006
www.condecaralt.es

Established: 1954

🍶 2,000,000 litres 🍇 200 has.
🍷 90% 🌍10%

CONDE DE CARALT BRUT
macabeo, xarel.lo, parellada

77 Pale yellow. Not very intense aroma, with fresh overtones, notes of green apples and a nuance of citrus fruit. Dry, fresh palate, creamy, lacks balance and crianza expression.

CONDE DE CARALT BLANC DE BLANCS BRUT

82 Straw-coloured. Intense aroma of ripe white fruit with hints of Mediterranean herbs, hints of citrus fruit and fine lees. Dry, fresh palate with fine bitter notes, good acidity, very pleasant.

CONDE DE VALICOURT

Sant Antoni, 33-35-39
08770 Sant Sadurní D'Anoia (Barcelona)
☎: 938 910 036 - Fax: 938 910 696
valicourt@wanadoo.es

Established: 1940

CONDE DE VALICOURT RESERVA BRUT
CONDE DE VALICOURT RESERVA BRUT
NATURE
CONDE DE VALICOURT PAS DE SUCRE
RESERVA

COVIDES

Finca Prunamala s/n
08770 Sant Sadurní d'Anoia (Barcelona)
☎: 938 172 552 - Fax: 938 171 798
covides@covides.com
comercial@covides.com
www.covides.com

Established: 1964

⊕ 550 🍶 30,000,000 litres 🍇 3,000 has.
🍷 71% 🌍29%

CAVA DUC DE FOIX RESERVA ESPECIAL

79 Brilliant straw with a golden hue. Quite intense aroma with notes of green apples, a suggestion of freshness and mild hints of reduction (bitter almonds). Dry, bitter palate with toasty notes of crianza, dried grass and limes in the retronasal passage.

DUC DE FOIX BRUT
macabeo, xarel.lo, parellada

80 Straw-coloured with a greenish hue. Intense aroma with overtones of freshness, ripe white fruit and hints of herbs and fine reduction. Fresh, dry palate with bitter and citrus notes, refreshing acidity.

XÈNIUS BRUT
macabeo, xarel.lo, parellada

79 Brilliant straw with a golden glint. Intense, fruity, fresh aroma with a great crianza expression (mild nuance of lees). Creamy palate with fine bittersweet notes, fresh, very pleasant.

XÈNIUS RESERVA BRUT
macabeo, xarel.lo, parellada

84 Straw-coloured with a greenish hue. Intense aroma with notes of white fruit and citrus fruit and fine hints of reduction (withered petals, ees, almonds). Dry palate with fine bitter notes and hints of dried herbs, good acidity, very fine.

DUC DE FOIX BRUT NATURE
macabeo, xarel.lo, parellada

79 Straw-coloured with a greenish glint. Fresh, quite intense aroma of green apples with poor crianza expression. Dry, fresh palate with good acidity and without great nuances.

DUC DE FOIX BRUT

COVIVES

Major, 39
43812 Montferri (Tarragona)
☎: 977 606 579 - Fax: 977 606 579
vives-ambros@tinet.org
www.tinet.org/vives-ambros

Established: 1996

⊕ 2 🍶 40.000 litres 🍇 24 has. 🍷 100%

VIVES-AMBROS RESERVA BRUT
VIVES-AMBROS GRAN RESERVA BRUT
NATURE

CRIANZAS Y VIÑEDOS SANTO CRISTO

Carretera de Tabuenca, s/n
50570 Ainzón (Zaragoza)

☎: 976 869 696 - Fax: 976 868 097
info@bodegas-santo-cristo.com
www.bodegas-santo-cristo.com

Established: 1956

🛢 900 🛢 8,400,000 litres 🍇 1,185 has.

🍷 34% 🌐66%-NL -DE -UK -DK -SE -DK -
IE -FR -US -BE

REINANTE EXTRA BRUT

CRISTINA COLOMER BERNAT

Diputació, 58 Apdo. 16
08770 Sant Sadurní D'Anoia (Barcelona)
☎: 938 910 804 - Fax: 938 913 034
ccolomer@cavescolomer.com
www.cavescolomer.com

Established: 1943

1907 CUPATGE JOAN COLOMER COSTA BRUT NATURE
xarel.lo, macabeo, parellada

86 Straw-coloured. Intense, ripe aroma with fine toasty and bakery notes, hints of withered petals and aniseed. Dry, fresh, very flavourful palate with great symmetry between acidity and crianza and a powerful retronasal effect (herbs, nuts, citrus fruit).

COLOMER 1907 BRUT NATURE
xarel.lo, macabeo, montonèc

81 Pale yellow. Intense, fresh aroma with fine notes of lees over a suggestion of citrus fruit. Dry palate, without great crianza expression, with citrus fruit notes and a hint of mountain herbs.

COLOMER HOMENATGE SALVADOR DALÍ BRUT NATURE

85 Pale yellow. Intense aroma with a fine crianza expression (lees, toasted nuts) and high quality citrus hints. Dry palate with well-integrated beads, hints of dried herbs and good acidity, long; light mineral notes in the retronasal passage.

CRISTINA COLOMER BRUT NATURE
xarel.lo, macabeo, parellada, chardonnay

85 Pale yellow. Quite intense aroma with fine notes of crianza over a suggestion of ripe limes. Dry palate with notes of herbs and nuts and good acidity; light notes of minerals in the retronasal passage, very long.

CRISTINA COLOMER BRUT D'AUTOR HOMENATGE GAUDÍ BRUT NATURE
xarel.lo, macabeo, parellada, chardonnay

83 Straw-coloured with fine and constant beads. Intense aroma of well-characterised crianza (fine lees, nuts, hints of fennel). Dry, flavourful palate with fine bitter notes (nuts), good acidity and citrus hints in the retronasal passage.

1907 BRUT NATURE

CUSCÓ BERGA

Esplugues, 7
08793 Les Gunyoles D'Avinyonet (Barcelona)
☎: 938 970 164 - Fax: 938 970 563
cuscoberga@cuscoberga.com
www.cuscoberga.com

Established: 1985

🛢 16 🛢 25,000 litres 🍇 3 has.🍷 100%

CUSCÓ BERGA 2001 BRUT
40% parellada, 35% macabeo, 25% xarel.lo

83 Straw-coloured with a golden glint. Not very intense aroma of white fruit with hints of a fine reduction (withered petals). Dry, bitter palate with hints of cumin in the retronasal passage, good acidity.

CUSCÓ BERGA 2001 BRUT NATURE
40% xarel.lo, 40% parellada, 20% macabeo

83 Pale yellow with a golden hue. Intense aroma of ripe white fruit with a fine reduction nuance. Dry and fresh palate with well-integrated beads; hints of bitter almonds, excellent acidity.

CUSCÓ BERGA 2002 BRUT ROSÉ
CUSCÓ BERGA 1999 GRAN RESERVA BRUT
CUSCÓ BERGA 2003 SEMI-SECO

Celler Cooperatiu D'ARTÉS

Cr. Rocafort, 44
08271 Artés (Barcelona)
☎: 938 305 325 - Fax: 938 306 289

Established: 1908

🛢 110 🛢 360,000 litres 🇪🇸 92%

🌐8%-DK -DE

LLUIS GUITART 2003 EXTRA BRUT
ARTIUM ROSÉ 2003 EXTRA BRUT
ARTIUM 2002 EXTRA BRUT
ARTIUM 2001 BRUT NATURE
ARTIUM 2000 GRAN RESERVA BRUT NATURE
ARTIUM 2003 SEMI-SECO
LLUIS GUITART 2003 SEMI-SECO

DOMINIO DE LA VEGA

Carretera Madrid - Valencia, km. 270, 650
46390 San Antonio. Requena (Valencia)
☎: 962 320 570 - Fax: 962 320 330
info@dominiodelavega.com
www.dominiodelavega.com

Established: 2001

DOMINIO DE LA VEGA BRUT

DO CAVA

Vins EL CEP

Can Llopart de Les Alzines, s/n
08770 Sant Sadurní D'Anoia (Barcelona)
☎: 938 912 353 - Fax: 938 183 956
info@elcep.com
www.elcep.com
Established: 1980
⊞ 45 ▤ 500,000 litres ⚜ 200 has.
▼ 65% 🌢35%

L'ALZINAR GRAN RESERVA BRUT NATURE
MARQUÉS DE GELIDA GRAN SELECCIÓ BRUT NATURE
MARQUÉS DE GELIDA RESERVA BRUT NATURE

Bodegas ESCUDERO

Carretera de Arnedo, s/n
26587 Gravalos (La Rioja)
☎: 941 398 008 - Fax: 941 398 070
www.bodegasescudero.com
Established: 1952
⊞ 1,300 ▤ 800,000 litres ⚜ 120 has.
▼ 80% 🌢20%-CH -DE -UK -DK -FR

BENITO ESCUDERO ABAD BRUT
100% viura

78 Straw-coloured. Aroma with notes of yeasts (crianza) over the fruit (ripe apples, tropical fruit), slightly rustic. Dry palate with high acidity, flavourful with persistent beads; aftertaste without obvious nuances, quite short.

BENITO ESCUDERO ABAD BRUT NATURE
100% viura

80 Straw-coloured. Ripe aroma with toasty notes over the fruit (apples, bananas). Dry palate with fine beads; fruity, without great crianza expression, quite short.

BENITO ESCUDERO ABAD SEMI-SECO
100% viura

75 Straw-coloured. Medium-intensity aroma, fruity, slightly short in lees character. Demi-sec palate, lacking slightly in freshness, long, somewhat aggressive beads.

DIORO BACO EXTRA BRUT
DIORO BACO VENDIMIA SELECCIONADA EXTRA BRUT

EUDALD MASSANA NOYA

Finca El Maset s/n
08739 Sant Pau D'Ordal (Barcelona)
☎: 938 994 124 - Fax: 938 994 139
bodega@massananoya.com

www.massananoya.com
Established: 1994
⊞ 50 ▤ 190,000 litres ⚜ 25 has.
▼ 95% 🌢5%-DE -CH -BE -JP

EUDALD MASSANA NOYA MIL.LENNI BRUT NATURE
40% xarel.lo, 30% macabeo, 25% chardonnay, 5% parellada

78 Yellow straw with a golden glint. Intense, ripe aroma with traditional crianza expression (withered petals, honey, toasted nuts). Dry, flavourful palate with bitter notes, good acidity.

EUDALD MASSANA NOYA BRUT
EUDALD MASSANA NOYA BRUT NATURE
EUDALD MASSANA NOYA RESERVA BRUT NATURE
EUDALD MASSANA NOYA SEMI-SECO

EXPLOTACIÓN VITIVINÍCOLA DEL PENEDÉS MONTSARRA

Finca Heredad Montsarra
08739 Torrelles de Foix (Barcelona)
☎: 938 991 359 - Fax: 938 991 376
jmarti@bardinet.es

MONTSARRA BRUT NATURE

EXPLOTACIONES SADURNÍ BEGUES

Masía Can Sadurní
08859 Begues (Barcelona)
☎: 936 390 161 - Fax: 936 390 161
sadurnibeguas@troc.es
www.troc.es/sadurni-begas
Established: 1966
⚜ 250 has.

ARRELS MONTAU DE SADURNÍ BRUT
MONTAU DE SADURNÍ BRUT
MONTAU DE SADURNÍ CHARDONNAY BRUT
MONTAU DE SADURNÍ GRAN RESERVA BRUT
SENYOR DEL MONTNEGRE BRUT
MONTAU DE SADURNÍ BRUT NATURE

Bodegas FAUSTINO

Carretera de Logroño, s/n
01320 Oyón (Alava)
☎: 945 622 500 - Fax: 945 622 106
⊞ 25,000 ⚜ 650 has.

CAVA FAUSTINO RESERVA BRUT
macabeo, chardonnay

85 Brilliant pale. Intense, ripe aroma of white fruit with mild reduction notes (withered petals, lees) and a suggestion of honey and crystallised citrus fruit peel. Flavourful, creamy palate with fresh fruit, hints of herbs and excellent acidity.

FÉLIX TORNÉ CALDÚ

Espiells, 8
08770 Sant Sadurní D'Anoia (Barcelona)
☎: 938 183 045 - Fax: 938 912 132
tornebel@jazzfree.com

Established: 1989

🍾 73,000 litres 🍇 12 has. 🍷 100%

TORNÉ & BEL BRUT NATURE
macabeo, xarel.lo, parellada

81 Straw-coloured with a greenish hue. Intense, ripe aroma with fine notes of reduction (lees) and hints of citrus fruit (ripe lemons). Dry palate with bitter notes of crianza (almonds, cumin), good acidity.

TORNÉ & BEL CHARDONNAY-MACABEU BRUT NATURE
50% macabeo, 50% chardonnay

82 Pale yellow with fine beads. Quite intense, ripe aroma with a nuance of fine lees. Dry, creamy, bitter palate with a nuance of green apples, refreshing acidity.

TORNÉ & BEL CRIANÇA EN BÓTA DE ROURE OAK AGED BRUT NATURE
chardonnay, macabeo

85 Straw-coloured with a greenish glint. Intense aroma of ripe white fruit with fine notes of reduction (lees) and sweet hints of wood. Dry, fresh palate with flavourful notes of bitter crianza (almonds, cumin) and hints of citrus fruit, very long, high in acidity.

TORNÉ & BEL RESERVA BRUT NATURE
40% macabeo, 40% xarel.lo, 20% parellada

80 Pale yellow with a greenish hue. Intense, ripe aroma with a nuance of lees and grapefruit. Dry, fresh palate with notes of bitter almonds and hints of citrus fruit, lacking crianza-acidity balance.

TORNÉ & BEL RESERVA BRUT

Cavas FERRET

Avenida de Catalunya, 36
08736 Guardiola de Font-Rubí (Barcelona)
☎: 938 979 148 - Fax: 938 979 285
ferret@cavasferret.com
www.cavasferret.com

Established: 1941

🌐 120 🍾 600,000 litres 🍇 12 has.
🍷 80% 🌍20%-DE -UK -NL -DK -BE -SE -CH

FERRET 2000 GRAN RESERVA BRUT
parellada, xarel.lo, macabeo

85 Brilliant golden yellow. Powerful, ripe aroma of white fruit pulp with hints of fine reduction (withered petals, cumin, dried grass). Dry, creamy palate with fine toasty crianza notes, a hint of herbs and nuts.

FERRET BRUT
parellada, xarel.lo, macabeo

86 Straw-coloured with a golden hue. Intense aroma with notes of white fruit over a nuance of well-characterised crianza (withered petals, dried herbs). Creamy palate (well-integrated beads), rich in nuances, with fruit complementing the crianza toasty flavours, excellent acidity.

FERRET BRUT NATURE
parellada, xarel.lo, macabeo

86 Straw-coloured. Expressive aroma of good fruit with fine notes of lees and a nuance of ripeness (lees reduction). Flavourful, balanced palate; fresh acidity, fruit notes and well-assembled crianza.

FERRET RESERVA BRUT NATURE ROSÉ

85 Blush with a coppery edge. Fine aroma of red berries and bakery with a nuance of lees. Flavourful palate with good alcohol-acidity balance; fine beads, long.

ALTRE NOS FERRET RESERVA BRUT NATURE
parellada, xarel.lo, macabeo, chardonnay

89 Pale yellow. Intense aroma of great finesse with a fine crianza nuance (lees, cumin) and overtones of white fruit and mountain herbs. Generous, creamy palate (well-integrated beads), rich in nuances with excellent crianza-acidity balance.

EZEQUIEL FERRET 1997 GRAN RESERVA BRUT NATURE

89 Pale with a golden hue. Powerful aroma of well-characterised crianza (withered petals, fine lees, nuts), with a hint of ripe white fruit. Dry, ripe, creamy palate with fine bitter notes, well-balanced, excellent acidity, very long.

Cava FONPINET

Joan Maragall, 14
08770 Sant Sadurní D'Anoia (Barcelona)
☎: 938 910 228 - Fax: 938 910 211

Established: 1943

FONPINET BRUT
FONPINET RESERVA BRUT
FONPINET BRUT NATURE

FONPINET RESERVA BRUT NATURE
FONPINET CHARDONNAY RESERVA
ESPECIAL BRUT NATURE
FONPINET SEMI-SECO
FONPINET ROSÉ

FRANCISCO DOMÍNGUEZ CRUCES

Lavernó, 22-27
08770 Sant Sadurní D'Anoia (Barcelona)
☎: 938 910 182 - Fax: 938 910 411
vinosycavas@elxamfra.com
www.ruralcat.com

Established: 1988

🍷 55 📊 20,000 litres 🌿 80% 🍇20%

XAMFRÀ BRUT ROSÉ
XAMFRÀ RESERVA BRUT
XAMFRÀ CASA GRAN RESERVA BRUT
XAMFRÀ RESERVA BRUT NATURE
XAMFRÀ RESERVA SEMI-SECO

FREIXA RIGAU

Santa Lucía, 15
17750 Capmany (Girona)
☎: 972 549 012 - Fax: 972 549 106
comercial@grupoliveda.com
www.grupoliveda.com

Established: 1948

📊 1,000,000 litres 🌿 50 has.
🌿 85% 🍇15%-DE -CH -UK -DK -NL -BE

FREIXA RIGAU BRUT DE BRUT
35% macabeo, 35% parellada, 25% xarel.lo5%

80 Golden yellow with fine beads. Powerful aroma, ripe, with predominant reduction notes (nuts, varnishes, balsamic flavours). Very dry, creamy palate, fine bitter notes, good acidity.

FREIXA RIGAU NATURE CHARDONNAY BRUT NATURE
100% chardonnay

84 Golden yellow. Intense aroma with good varietal expression, fine hints of petals and lees, hints of crystallised fruit. Dry, bitter palate, toasted nuts, good acidity.

NATURE MIL.LESSIMA RESERVA DE FAMILIA BRUT NATURE
40% macabeo, 30% parellada, 30% xarel.lo

85 Pale yellow. Intense aroma of white fruit and well-integrated crianza notes (lees). Dry palate, fine bitter notes, hints of herbs and ripe citrus fruit.

BRUT D'OLIVEDA BRUT
FREIXA RIGAU BRUT ROSÉ
EXTRA D'OLIVEDA SEMI-SECO
ROSAT D'OLIVEDA ROSÉ SEMI-SECO

FREIXENET

Joan Sala, 2
08770 Sant Sadurní D'Anoia (Barcelona)
☎: 938 917 000 - Fax: 938 913 095
freixenet@freixenet.es
www.freixenet.es

Established: fin. s. XIX

🍷 2,000 📊 32,000,000 litres 🌿 1,000 has.
🌿 40% 🍇60%-DE -UK -US -SE -JP -CH - CA -DK -DK -NL -AR -FI -BE -RU -AT -TW - VE -FR -AU -MX -IT

BRUT BARROCO RESERVA BRUT
40% parellada, 30% macabeo, 30% xarel.lo

85 Straw-coloured with a golden hue. Intense aroma, with predominant notes of ripe apples, a fine crianza nuance (withered petals). Dry, creamy palate (well-integrated beads), fine bitter notes; well-balanced, good acidity.

FREIXENET CARTA NEVADA BRUT
33% parellada, 33% macabeo, 33% xarel.lo

75 Straw-coloured. Fresh aroma with notes of green apples and hints of citrus fruit without great crianza expression. Fresh, fruity palate with fine bitter notes and a nuance of light sweetness, good acidity.

FREIXENET ROSÉ BRUT ROSÉ
30% garnacha, 70% trepat

80 Not very deep raspberry with a coppery glint. Quite intense, fruity aroma with notes of fine reduction (petals, nuts) and ripe cherry. Fresh, dry, bitter palate, high in acidity, lacking balance.

FREIXENET TREPAT 1998 BRUT
100% trepat

86 Brilliant golden yellow with a coppery glint. Powerful aroma of superripe white fruit with hints of spices and honey and fine reduction notes (yeasts, petals). Generous, creamy palate with fine bitter notes (nuts, cumin, herbs), very long, flavourful and original.

RESERVA REAL RESERVA BRUT
macabeo, xarel.lo, parellada, otras

85 Pale yellow. Intense, ripe aroma with predominant reduction notes (yeasts, withered petals). Dry, creamy palate with well-characterised crianza and fine notes of citrus fruit and bitter almonds in the retronasal passage.

CUVÉE D.S. 1999 RESERVA BRUT
40% macabeo, 40% xarel.lo, 20% parellada

86 Brilliant straw with a greenish hue. Intense aroma of ripe white fruit with a nuance of lees and withered petals and hints of crystallised fruit. Dry, creamy palate with fruity notes over a bitter (almonds) crianza nuance (hints of hay), good acidity.

FREIXENET MONASTRELL-XAREL.LO 1999 GRAN RESERVA BRUT
50% monastrell, 50% xarel.lo

82 Amber with a coppery glint. Intense, ripe aroma with notes of fine lees and an excellent vinous nuance. Dry palate with fine bitter notes (nuts, herbs, cumin, fine toasty flavours), good acidity.

FREIXENET VINTAGE 2000 BRUT NATURE
40% macabeo, 30% parellada, 30% xarel.lo

84 Pale yellow with fine and persistent beads. Not very intense aroma with a certain finesse, rich in nuances (green apples, hints of lees). Fresh, dry palate with fine bitter notes, hints of herbs and notes of sweet lime in the retronasal passage.

FREIXENET MALVASÍA 2001 GRAN RESERVA DULCE
100% malvasía

83 Pale yellow with a golden glint. Not very intense aroma with notes of flowers and fine reduction (withered petals) over a nuance of ripe apples. Flavourful palate with bittersweet notes, a fine suggestion of bitterness (nuts) and of crystallised fruit.

GRAN CARTA NEVADA BRUT
CORDÓN NEGRO BRUT
CUVÉE CASA BATLLÓ 1999 GRAN RESERVA BRUT
CORDÓN NEGRO SECO

FRIGULS

Diputació, 44
08770 Sant Sadurní D'Anoia (Barcelona)
☎: 938 910 166
friguls@cavafriguls.com
www.cavafriguls.com
Established: 1930

FRIGULS EXTRA BRUT
FRIGULS GRAN RESERVA BRUT
FRIGULS BLANC DE BLANCS BRUT

GASTÓN COTY

Avernó, 30
08770 Sant Sadurní D'Anoia (Barcelona)
☎: 902 176 197 - Fax: 938 913 461
lorigan@lorigancava.com
www.lorigancava.com
Established: 1906
🍷 50 🌿 3 has. 🇪🇸 100%

L'O DE L'ORIGAN BRUT NATURE
macabeo, xarel.lo, parellada, chardonnay

90 Golden. Powerful aroma rich in toasty, oxidative notes and mountain herbs, complex, unusual and individual. Generous, ripe palate with toasty lees, an oxidative hint, withered petals and nuts, excellent acidity and pleasantly sweet.

Cava GIBERT

Doctor Ferrer, 10
08271 Artes (Barcelona)
☎: 938 305 008 - Fax: 938 306 004
cavagibert@cavagibert.com
www.cavagibert.com
Established: 1920
🇪🇸 98% 🌐2%

GIBERT GRAN RESERVA BRUT NATURE

81 Pale with greenish nuances. Intense aroma with a certain finesse, of ripe white fruit, a suggestion of withered petals and hints of fennel. Dry, flavourful palate with well-integrated beads, bitter notes and a slightly acidic edge.

GIRÓ DEL GORNER

Masia Giró del Gorner, s/n
08797 Puigdálber (Barcelona)
☎: 938 988 032 - Fax: 938 988 032
gorner@girodelgorner.com
www.girodelgorner.com
Established: 1976
🍷 40 🛢 400,000 litres 🌿 45 has.
🍷 80% 🌐20%-JP -BE -DE -AD -CH

GORNER 2001 BRUT
50% macabeo, 30% parellada, 20% xarel.lo

83 Straw-coloured. Fresh aroma of white fruit (pears), very pleasant withered petals and hints of almonds. Flavourful palate with good acidity; fine beads with green fruit character rather than crianza, persistent.

GORNER 1999 GRAN RESERVA BRUT NATURE
50% macabeo, 30% xarel.lo, 20% parellada

83 Straw-coloured with a greenish edge. Perfumed aroma (violets, acacias) with fruity notes (pears) and a fresh herby nuance. Dry, herbaceous palate with expression of the vine variety, good bead and long.

GORNER 2000 GRAN RESERVA BRUT NATURE
50% macabeo, 30% xarel.lo, 20% parellada

80 Pale yellow with a greenish glint. Not very intense, fresh aroma with a certain finesse, varietal expression and fine reduction notes. Dry, very fresh palate with excellent bitter notes, high in acidity.

GIRÓ RIBOT

Finca El Pont, s/n
08792 Santa Fe del Penedés (Barcelona)
☎: 938 974 050 - Fax: 938 974 311
giroribot@giroribot.es
www.giroribot.es

Established: 1977

🌐 25 📖 1,500,000 litres 🍇 50 has.

🍷 25% 🌐75%-US -CR -CU -IE -DK -DK -
FI -DE -CH -NL -BE -FR -IT -IL -JP

GIRÓ RIBOT BRUT
50% macabeo, 30% xarel.lo, 20% parellada

83 Pale yellow. Quite intense aroma with predominant notes of white fruit, a nuance of fine lees and honeyed hints. Dry, creamy palate with fine bitter notes, bittersweet notes and good acidity.

PAUL CHENEAU BLANC DE BLANCS BRUT
45% macabeo, 40% xarel.lo, 15% parellada

84 Pale yellow with a greenish glint. Intense aroma with notes of green fruit, a fine nuance of reduction (lees, flowers) and citrus fruit. Dry, creamy palate, rich in nuances with excellent fruit-crianza-acidity balance.

GIRÓ RIBOT "MARE" 1999 GRAN RESERVA BRUT NATURE
50% xarel.lo, 30% macabeo, 20% parellada

88 Yellow straw with a golden glint. Intense aroma, ripe, very fine, with fine notes of crianza (lees, bitter almonds) well-integrated with the fruit. Dry palate with fine bitter notes, well-balanced and very long.

GIRÓ RIBOT GRAN RESERVA BRUT NATURE
50% macabeo, 30% xarel.lo, 20% parellada

84 Straw-coloured with a golden glint. Intense aroma with notes of well-integrated ripe white fruit and crianza (petals, lees). Dry, bitter palate, fine reduction notes (nuts, balsamic flavours), excellent acidity.

MASIA PARERA BRUT

GRAMONA

Industria, 36
08770 Sant Sadurní D'Anoia (Barcelona)
☎: 938 910 113 - Fax: 938 183 284
cava@gramona.com
alonsorafael@gramona.com
www.gramona.com

Established: 1921

🌐 150 📖 500,000 litres 🍇 29 has.

🍷 85% 🌐15%-US -DE -DK -BE -RU -CZ -
LU -NL -CA -AD -CH

GRAMONA PINOT NOIR 2001 GRAN RESERVA BRUT ROSÉ
100% pinot noir

87 Brilliant salmon with fine beads. Not very intense aroma with fine varietal hints (red stone fruit, spicy hints) over a suggestion of lees, slightly mineral. Dry palate with fine bitter notes, fruity and mineral hints, long.

GRAMONA IMPERIAL 2000 GRAN RESERVA BRUT
40% macabeo, 40% xarel.lo, 20% chardonnay

86 Straw-coloured with a golden glint and fine beads. Not very intense, fresh aroma with a nuance of fine reduction (lees) and rich citrus hints. Dry palate with well-integrated beads and fine bitter notes; elegant, well-structured although lacking crianza expression.

GRAMONA ALLEGRO RESERVA BRUT
40% macabeo, 20% chardonnay, 20% xarel.lo, 20% parellada

83 Brilliant straw with fine and persistent beads. Intense aroma of green apples, lacks crianza expression. Dry palate with bitter and rich citrus fruit notes, excellent acidity.

GRAMONA ARGENT 1999 GRAN RESERVA BRUT
chardonnay

88 Pale yellow with a greenish hue. Intense aroma with excellent crianza expression (lees, withered petals, bitter almonds) over a nuance of green apples. Dry palate with fine bitter notes, toasty crianza notes and hints of dried grass, excellent acidity.

GRAMONA III LUSTROS 1998 GRAN RESERVA BRUT NATURE
70% xarel.lo, 30% macabeo

87 Straw-coloured with a greenish glint. Intense, ripe aroma with a good crianza expression (nuts, Mediterranean herbs) and a nuance of ripe fruit (apples, limes) with fine bitter notes, good acidity. Dry, creamy palate (well-integrated beads) with fine bitter notes, good acidity.

GRAMONA COLECCIÓN DE ARTE MILENIO GRAN RESERVA BRUT NATURE
100% chardonnay

90 Golden yellow. Powerful aroma of ripe apples with toasty crianza notes (nuts, withered petals) and a nuance of honey and rosemary. Dry, creamy palate (well-integrated beads) with well-balanced bitter crianza and sweet fruit notes, excellent acidity, long.

GRAMONA GRAN CUVÉE DE POSTRE GRAN RESERVA SEMI-DULCE
33% xarel.lo, 33% macabeo, 33% parellada

82 Pale yellow. Not very intense aroma of ripe fruit with a nuance of sweetness. Fresh, creamy palate with fine bittersweet notes; a bitter nuance of crianza, good acidity, very pleasant.

DO CAVA

GRAMONA LA SUITE GRAN RESERVA SECO
33% xarel.lo, 33% macabeo, 33% parellada

83 Brilliant straw. Intense aroma with overtones of freshness and a mild nuance of grapefruit and cough medicine. Dry palate with fine bitter notes (almonds, cumin, dried herbs) and hints of citrus fruit, better than in the nose.

GRAMONA CELLER BATLLE 1996 BRUT

Bodegas GRAN DUCAY

Carretera Nacional 330, km. 450
50400 Cariñena (Zaragoza)
☎: 976 620 400 - Fax: 976 620 398
bsv@sanvalero.com
www.bodegasanvalero.com

Established: 1944

🍮 9,000 🗒 20,000,000 litres 🌿 3,500 has.
🍷 50% 🌐50%-UK -DE -CH -CA -US -DO -FI -JP -FR

GRAN DUCAY 2003

Cellers GRAU DORIA

Eliseo Oliver, s/n
08811 Canyelles (Barcelona)
☎: 938 973 263

Established: 1989

🌿 7 has.🍷 100%

GRAU DORIA BRUT
GRAU DORIA BRUT NATURE
GRAU DORIA SEMI-SECO

GRIMAU DE PUJADES

Castell de Les Pujades s/n
08732 Castellví de la Marca (Barcelona)
☎: 938 918 031 - Fax: 938 918 426
grimau@grimau.com
www.grimau.com

Established: 1988

🍮 200 🗒 250,000 litres 🌿 23 has.
🍷 80% 🌐20%

GRIMAU DE PUJADES BRUT NATURE
macabeo, xarel.lo, parellada

83 Straw-coloured. Intense aroma with excellent crianza expression (lees, withered petals, bakery) over notes of white fruit and citrus fruit pulp. Dry palate, rich in nuances (aniseed notes, herbs, citrus fruit) with good acidity.

GRIMAU RESERVA FAMILIAR BRUT NATURE

85 Pale yellow. Intense aroma of fine lees with hints of petals and a suggestion of white fruit and citrus fruit. Dry, flavourful palate, rich in nuances with fine bitter notes (herbs and nuts) and excellent crianza expression.

TRENCADÍS DE GRIMAU BRUT NATURE

83 Pale with a golden glint. Intense aroma with good crianza expression (lees, flowers) and a hint of ripe white fruit. Dry, flavourful palate with well-integrated beads, hints of bitter almonds and fragrant herbs, very rich.

Cellers GRIMAU GOL

Nord, 8
08720 Vilafranca del Penedés (Barcelona)
☎: 938 181 372 - Fax: 938 920 812
emarti@duartdesio.com
www.duartdesio.com

Established: 1987

🍮 285 🗒 800,000 litres 🌿 40 has.
🍷 55% 🌐45%

DUART DE SIÓ BRUT
DUART DE SIÓ BRUT NATURE
CAN MILA DE LA ROCA GRAN RESERVA BRUT NATURE
DUART DE SIÓ VINET TRANSPARENT BLAU BRUT NATURE

Cava GUILERA

Masia Artigas, s/n
08734 Lavern-Subirats (Barcelona)
☎: 938 993 085 - Fax: 938 993 491
guilera@cavaguilera.com
www.cavaguilera.com
www.artesansdelavid.com

GUILERA BRUT
GUILERA EXTRA BRUT
GUILERA GRAN NATURE BRUT NATURE

HERETAT MAS JORNET

Avenida Penedes, 62
08730 La Rapita - Monjos (Barcelona)
☎: 938 980 484 - Fax: 938 983 005
vinesicavesmasjornet@catanet.com
www.vinesicavesmasjornet.com

Established: 1987

🍮 125 🗒 50,000 litres 🌿 10 has.
🍷 80% 🌐20%-CH -DE

MAS JORNET BRUT DE BRUTS BRUT
macabeo, xarel.lo, parellada

78 Golden yellow. Powerful, ripe aroma with fine reduction notes. Better on the palate, dry, with a well-characterised crianza (toasted nuts, herbs, bitter notes), good acidity.

MAS JORNET BRUT NATURE ROSÉ

76 Onion-skin. Toasty aroma of nuts, flower petals and mountain herbs. Dry, flavourful palate, slightly bitter yet fresh, fruity finish.

HERETAT MONT-RUBÍ

Abellà, 1
08736 Font Rubí (Barcelona)
☎: 938 979 066 - Fax: 934 732 292
mont.rubi@salvat-lab.es

Established: 1985

🍷 30 📗 30,000 litres 🍇 340 has.

🍷 75% 🌐25%-US -CH

MONT-RUBÍ BRUT
MONT-RUBÍ BRUT NATURE
MONT-RUBÍ GRAN RESERVA BRUT NATURE
MONT-RUBÍ (SPECIAL BOTTLE) 1999 GRAN
RESERVA BRUT NATURE

Cavas HILL

Bonavista, 2
08734 Moja (Olérdola) (Barcelona)
☎: 938 900 588 - Fax: 938 170 246
cavashill@cavashill.com
www.cavashill.com

Established: 1887

🍷 980 📗 214,000 litres 🍇 50 has.

🍷 80% 🌐20%

CAVAS HILL BLANC DE BLANCS ORO RESERVA BRUT
macabeo, xarel.lo, parellada

79 Straw-coloured. Quite intense aroma of ripe white fruit with fresh overtones over a nuance of light reduction. Dry palate with fine bitter notes, good acidity, pleasant.

CAVAS HILL BLANC DE BLANCS ORO RESERVA BRUT NATURE
macabeo, xarel.lo, parellada

80 Straw-coloured with a greenish glint. Aroma of ripe white fruit with a fine nuance of reduction (lees). Dry, creamy palate with fine bitter notes.

CAVAS HILL BRUT DE BRUT ARTESANÍA 2001 RESERVA BRUT NATURE
45% macabeo, 35% xarel.lo, 20% parellada

80 Pale. Slightly intense aroma with fine reduction notes (withered petals) over a nuance of ripe white fruit. Dry, bitter palate with notes of dried grass, good acidity, lacking crianza expression.

CAVAS HILL BRUTÍSIMO 2001 GRAN RESERVA BRUT NATURE
parellada, xarel.lo, chardonnay, macabeo

79 Straw-coloured with a greenish glint and fine and constant beads. Not very intense, fresh aroma,

of ripe white fruit with hints of herbs. Dry, creamy palate with bitter notes, lacking crianza-acidity symmetry.

RESERVA DE ORO BRUT
RESERVA DE ORO BRUT NATURE
RESERVA DE ORO SEMI-SECO
RESERVA DE ORO SECO

Bodegas J. TRIAS

Comerç, 6
08720 Vilafranca del Penedés (Barcelona)
☎: 938 902 627 - Fax: 938 901 724
bodegas@jtrias.com
www.jtrias.com

Established: 1932

🍷 55 📗 135,000 litres 🍇 15 has.

🍷 90% 🌐10%: -DK-DE-TR-CU-CH-CY-PL

TRIAS BRUT
TRIAS BATLLE RESERVA BRUT
TRIAS BATLLE BRUT NATURE
TRIAS BATLLE RESERVA BRUT NATURE
TRIAS BATLLE ROSADO BRUT NATURE
TRIAS SEMI-SECO

JANÉ VENTURA

Carretera Calafell, 2
43700 El Vendrell (Tarragona)
☎: 977 660 118 - Fax: 977 661 239
janeventura@janeventura.com
www.janeventura.com

Established: 1914

🍷 200 📗 400,000 litres 🍇 15 has.

🍷 80% 🌐20%-SE -NL -CH -BE -DK -AT -US -PR

JANÉ VENTURA BRUT ROSÉ
100% garnacha

85 Very deep raspberry. Powerful aroma of ripe red fruit with a hint of lees and spicy notes, Dry palate, rich in nuances, creamy (well-integrated beads), good acidity and excellent balance between fruit and crianza.

JANÉ VENTURA RESERVA BRUT

85 Straw-coloured with a greenish glint. Intense aroma, very fresh, rich in nuances (white fruit, fine lees, herbs, citrus fruit). Dry palate, creamy (well-integrated beads), excellent acidity.

JANÉ VENTURA 2000 GRAN RESERVA BRUT NATURE
xarel.lo, macabeo, parellada

85 Yellow straw with a golden glint. Intense aroma with excellent crianza profile (fine lees, withered petals) over a suggestion of ripe white fruit. Dry, flavourful palate with well-integrated beads, fine notes of nuts and Mediterranean herbs and citrus hints, good acidity.

JANÉ VENTURA RESERVA BRUT NATURE

86 Straw-coloured with a greenish glint. Intense aroma with notes of green apples and fine reduction notes (nuts, Mediterranean herbs, fine lees). Dry, creamy palate with rich bitter notes and citrus hints in the retronasal passage.

JAUME GIRÓ I GIRÓ

Montaner i Oller, s/n
08770 Sant Sadurní d'Anoia (Barcelona)
☎: 938 910 165 - Fax: 938 911 271
cavagiro@interbook.net
www.cavagiro.com

Established: 1926
🍇 85% 🍇15%

JAUME GIRÓ I GIRÓ BOMBONETTA BRUT

81 Very pale with a greenish glint. Aromatic with overtones of finnesse, white fruit and a fine nuance of reduction (fennel, lees). Dry, creamy palate with light bitter notes, floral hints and sweet almonds, good acidity.

JAUME GIRÓ I GIRÓ DE CAL REI GRAN RESERVA BRUT

84 Raspberry with a coppery hue. Powerful, fruity aroma with a toasty crianza nuance and hints of fine lees. Dry, bitter, creamy palate (well-integrated beads) with hints of nuts and balsamic nuances, good acidity, very long.

JAUME GIRÓ I GIRÓ GRAN RESERVA BRUT NATURE

84 Yellow straw with a greenish hue. Not very intense aroma, fine, with excellent crianza expression (bitter almonds, balsamic flavours). Dry palate with fine bitter notes, refreshing acidity.

JAUME GIRÓ I GIRÓ RESERVA BRUT NATURE

80 Very pale straw with quite robust beads. Not very intense, fresh aroma with a nuance of fine reduction. Dry palate with mild bitter notes (almonds) and hints of herbs and citrus fruit, very pleasant.

JAUME GIRÓ I GIRÓ SELECTE RESERVA BRUT NATURE

82 Straw-coloured with a greenish glint. Intense aroma with fine reduction notes (lees, withered petals) and hints of citrus fruit. Generous, fresh palate with a certain finesse, pleasant although without strong crianza expression; good acidity.

GRANDALLA BRUT
JAUME GIRÓ I GIRÓ BRUT ROSÉ
JAUME GIRÓ I GIRÓ ELABORACIÓN
ARTESANA BRUT NATURE

JAUME LLOPART ALEMANY

Calle Font Rubí, 9
08736 Font-Rubí (Barcelona)
☎: 938 979 133 - Fax: 938 979 133
info@jaumellopartalemany.com
www.jaumellopartalemany.com
Established: 1985
🍇 50 has. 🍇 85% 🍇15%-AD -NL

SEROLG BRUT
JAUME LLOPART ALEMANY 2001 BRUT
SEROLG BRUT NATURE
JAUME LLOPART ALEMANY 2001 BRUT NATURE
JAUME LLOPART ALEMANY 2001 BRUT NATURE ROSÉ
SEROLG GRAN CUVÉE RESERVA
JAUME LLOPART ALEMANY 2000 GRAN RESERVA

JAUME SERRA

Finca El Padruell, s/n
08800 Vilanova i la Geltru (Barcelona)
☎: 938 936 404 - Fax: 938 142 262
jaumeserra@jgc.es
www.vinosdefamilia.com
Established: 1985
🍇 30 has. 🍇 55% 🍇45%-US -UK -DE -IT -LT -JP -FR -AT -NL -BR -MX

CRISTALINO BRUT
50% macabeo, 35% parellada, 15% xarel.lo

74 Straw-coloured with a golden glint. Intense aroma, fine reduction notes (varnishes, nuts). Better on the palate, with bitter and balsamic notes, good acidity.

JAUME SERRA RESERVA BRUT ROSÉ
40% pinot noir, 60% trepat

81 Brilliant raspberry. Quite intense aroma of ripe red fruit with a nuance of lees and withered petals. Fresh, creamy palate, hints of nuts, very pleasant.

JAUME SERRA BRUT NATURE
50% macabeo, 25% parellada, 25% xarel.lo

82 Straw-coloured with a golden edge. Intense aroma of ripe fruit and flowers with hints of toasted nuts and fresh herbs. Flavourful palate with good acidity; slightly oily although not too heavy.

JAUME SERRA RESERVA BRUT NATURE
45% macabeo, 25% parellada, 15% xarel.lo, 15% chardonnay

77 Straw-coloured. Honeyed aroma with sweet notes of honey and flowers over the fruit. Flavourful, slightly sweet palate with dominant crianza nuances; herby notes in the finish.

JAUME SERRA VINTAGE 2000 BRUT NATURE
30% macabeo, 30% chardonnay, 25% parellada, 15% xarel.lo

78 Golden. Ripe aroma with crianza reduction notes and a tropical fruit nuance. Fresh, slightly oily palate with an expression of honey and nuts over the fruit.

CRISTALINO SEMI-SECO
50% macabeo, 35% parellada, 15% xarel.lo

80 Brilliant yellow with a golden hue. Not very intense aroma with hints of nuts and crystallised fruit. Flavourful, creamy palate, fine bitter notes, excellent balance.

JOAN BLANCH

Avenida Catalunya, 8
43812 Puigpelat (Tarragona)
☎: 933 074 504 - Fax: 933 076 219
blanch@cellersblanch.com
cellersblanch.com

Established: 1980

⊞ 25 ▤ 90.000 litres ※ 25 has.🍷 100%

CELLER BLANCH BRUT
CELLER BLANCH BRUT ROSÉ
CELLER BLANCH BRUT NATURE
CELLER BLANCH SEMI-SECO

Caves JOAN BUNDÓ

Camí de la Font del Lleó s/n
08796 Pacs del Penedés (Barcelona)
☎: 938 902 157 - Fax: 938 902 157

Established: 1997

🍷 100%

JOAN BUNDÓ PONS BRUT
JOAN BUNDÓ PONS BRUT NATURE

JOAN PUJOL VILALLONGA

Eduard Gibert, 44
08940 Cornella de Llobregat (Barcelona)
☎: 933 770 761

Established: 1928

TRIANON 1999 BRUT NATURE

JOAN RAVENTÓS ROSELL

Heretat Vall-Ventós, s/n
Ctra. Sant Sadurní - Masquefa, km. 6, 5
08783 Masquefa (Barcelona)
☎: 937 725 251 - Fax: 937 727 191
correu@raventosrosell.com
www.raventosrosell.com

Established: 1985

⊞ 300 ▤ 350,000 litres ※ 100 has.

🍷 50% 🍇50%-DE -CH -NL -BE -DK -FI -RU -US -CA -CO

JOAN RAVENTÓS ROSELL GRAN HERETAT RESERVA BRUT
50% macabeo, 40% chardonnay, 10% parellada

78 Golden. Ripe aroma with reduced lees and dominant crianza notes over the fruit, toasty flavours. Dry, flavourful, slightly oily palate with a bitter character (almonds), short.

JOAN RAVENTÓS ROSELL DONE'S ROSÉ BRUT NATURE ROSÉ
85% pinot noir, 15% chardonnay

75 Onion-skins. Discreet aroma with notes of reduced lees and overripe fruit. Dry, somewhat bitter, well-balanced, reduced fruit notes.

JOAN RAVENTÓS ROSELL BRUT RESERVA GRADIVA RESERVA BRUT NATURE
JOAN RAVENTÓS ROSELL BRUT NATURE HERETAT BRUT NATURE

JOAN SARDÁ

Ctra. Vilafranca- St. Jaume dels Domenys, km. 8, 100
08732 Castellvi de la Marca (Barcelona)
☎: 937 720 900 - Fax: 937 721 495
joansarda@joansarda.com
www.joansarda.com

Established: 1927

⊞ 450 ▤ 2,900,000 litres ※ 20 has.

🍷 50% 🍇50%-CU -JP -CR -DE -US -KE

CAVA SARDÁ BRUT
macabeo, xarel.lo, parellada

83 Pale yellow. Not very intense aroma with notes of green apples and a reduction nuance (withered petals, honeyed hints). Dry, bitter palate, a nuance of light sweetness, well-balanced.

SARDÁ GRAN RESERVA BRUT NATURE
xarel.lo, parellada, macabeo

78 Pale yellow. Intense aroma, ripe, with predominant crianza notes (withered petals, nuts, balsamic flavours). Dry, creamy palate, bitter notes, lacking balance.

JOAN SARDÁ MILLENIUM
macabeo, parellada, xarel.lo

85 Brilliant straw with a golden hue. Intense aroma, very fine with well-integrated notes of ripe white fruit and crianza (lees). Fresh, creamy palate with quality bittersweet notes, fine bitter balsamic nuance, good acidity.

DO CAVA

JOSÉ MARÍA ROSELL MIR

Masel de Can Ros.
08739 Subirats (Barcelona)
☎: 938 911 354 - Fax: 938 911 311
jmrosell@hotmail.com

Established: 1982
🌐 200 🍾 350,000 litres 🍇 30 has.
🍷 90% 🌐10%-DK -CA -NL

CAN GUINEU BRUT
CAN GUINEU BRUT NATURE
ROSELL MIR BRUT NATURE

JOSEP FERRET I MATEU

Avenida Penedés, 27
08730 Sta. Margarida i Els Monjos (Barcelona)
☎: 938 980 583 - Fax: 938 980 584
ferretmateu@ferretmateu.com

Established: 1942

CAL VERMELL BRUT
macabeo, xarel.lo, chardonnay

83 Very pale straw with a greenish hue. Not very intense, fresh aroma with finesse, notes of white fruit and a nuance of fine lees. Dry, creamy palate with fine bitter notes; rich in nuances with refreshing acidity.

MON PRIVÉ BRUT
macabeo, xarel.lo, chardonnay

85 Straw-coloured with a golden glint. Intense aroma with a good balance of white fruit and crianza notes (withered petals, lees) and a nuance of ripe citrus fruit. Generous palate, rich in nuances with good structure, fine bitter notes and excellent acidity.

CAL VERMELL BRUT NATURE
macabeo, xarel.lo, chardonnay

81 Pale yellow. Ripe, intense aroma with notes of white fruit, somewhat musky hints of truffles. Dry, slightly fruity palate with fine bitter notes, good acidity (ripe grapefruit).

FERRET I MATEU BRUT NATURE
macabeo, xarel.lo, parellada

84 Brilliant pale yellow. Intense, fresh, fruity aroma (green apples) with fine notes of reduction. Dry, fresh palate with fine bitter notes, well-balanced, very pleasant.

MARIA MATEU RESERVA BRUT NATURE
macabeo, xarel.lo, chardonnay

82 Straw-coloured with a greenish glint. Powerful aroma of ripe fruit with fine reduction notes (lees) and a nuance of citrus fruit and bitter almonds. Very dry palate with fine bitter notes and sweet limes, high in acidity.

MON PRIVÉ BRUT NATURE
macabeo, xarel.lo, chardonnay

77 Brilliant straw with a golden hue. Intense aroma of superripe white fruit with a not very fine hint of reduction. Dry, slightly creamy palate, lacking balance.

MON PRIVÉ SEMI-SECO
macabeo, xarel.lo, chardonnay

79 Golden yellow. Powerful aroma of superripe white fruit with reduction notes (withered petals, yeasts). Flavourful palate with notes of crystallised fruit, lacks acidity.

JOSEP FONT VERDIELL

Vilafranca, 7
08770 Sant Sadurní D'Anoia (Barcelona)
☎: 938 911 913 - Fax: 938 911 913

Established: 1982
🍾 3,670 litres 🍷 95% 🌐5%

JOSEP FONT VERDIELL EXTRA BRUT
ISACH BALCELLS BRUT NATURE
ISACH BALCELLS GRAN RESERVA

Celler JOSEP M. FERRET

B. L'Alzinar, 68
08736 Font-Rubí (Barcelona)
☎: 938 979 037 - Fax: 938 979 414
celler.ferret@sefes.es

Established: 1997
🍾 35,000 litres 🍇 1 has.
🍷 85% 🌐15%-DE -AD -US -CR

J.M. FERRET GUASCH 1998 RESERVA BRUT NATURE ROSÉ
60% garnacha, 40% pinot noir

82 Quite intense onion skin. Fresh aroma of red stone fruit with a hint of fine lees. Dry palate with well-integrated beads, fine bitter notes and a suggestion of Meiterranean herbs and nuts.

JOSEP M. FERRET GUASCH 1999 RESERVA BRUT NATURE
50% parellada, 30% xarel.lo, 20% macabeo

79 Pale yellow. Intense aroma, rich in crianza nuances (fine lees, mountain herbs) with high quality citrus fruit notes. Dry palate with a hint of dried herbs, not as expressive as in the nose.

JOSEP M. FERRET GUASCH 2001 BRUT NATURE
70% parellada, 20% xarel.lo, 10% macabeo

82 Straw-coloured. Powerful aroma of ripe white fruit and a fine hint of reduction in bottle (lees, withered petals). Dry, flavourful palate with well-integrated beads, fine bitter notes and an excellent hint of anise and citrus fruit.

JOSEP M. FERRET GUASCH 2001 BRUT
JOSEP M. FERRET GUASCH 1999 RESERVA
 BRUT
FERRET GUASCH COUPAGE SARA
 RESERVA BRUT NATURE

JOSEP MASACHS

Carretera Sant Martí Sarroca, km. 7
08737 Torrellles de Foix (Barcelona)
☎: 938 990 017 - Fax: 938 991 561
infocm@cavasmasachs.com
www.cavasmasachs.com

Established: 1940

🍶 1,200,000 litres 🌿 40 has. 🍷 79%
🌐21%-DE -CH -NL -DK -UK -US -MX

GRAN VERNIER BRUT
LOUIS DE VERNIER BRUT
JOSEP MASACHS BRUT ROSÉ
LOUIS DE VERNIER BRUT ROSÉ
JOSEP MASACHS RESERVA BRUT
CAROLINA DE MASACHS RESERVA BRUT
JOSEP MASACHS BRUT DE BRUTS BRUT
NATURE
JOSEP MASACHS BRUT NATURE
JOSEP MASACHS GRAN RESERVA BRUT
NATURE
LOUIS DE VERNIER MILLENNIUM CUVÉE
 BRUT NATURE
LOUIS DE VERNIER RESERVA BRUT
 NATURE
MASACHS MILLENNIUM CUVÉE BRUT
 NATURE
LOUIS DE VERNIER SEMI-SECO
LOUIS DE VERNIER EXTRA SECO

JOSEP TORRES SIBILL

Industria 4
08770 Sant Sadurní d'Anoia (Barcelona)
☎: 938 910 903 - Fax: 938 910 903
www.cavabertha.com

Established: 1989

🍷 100%

BERTHA RESERVA BRUT
BERTHA GRAN RESERVA BRUT
BERTHA 1999 GRAN RESERVA BRUT
NATURE
BERTHA RESERVA BRUT NATURE
BERTHA S.XXI 1999 GRAN RESERVA BRUT
NATURE
BERTHA RESERVA SECO

JUVÉ & CAMPS

Sant Venat, 1
08770 Sant Sadurní D'Anoia (Barcelona)
☎: 938 911 000 - Fax: 938 912 100

juveycamps@juveycamps.com
www. juveycamps.com

Established: 1921

🍶 1,000 🍶 5,000,000 litres 🌿 430 has.
🍷 90% 🌐10%

GRAN JUVÉ & CAMPS 2000 RESERVA BRUT
35% macabeo, 35% parellada, 30% xarel.lo

85 Golden yellow with fine and persistent beads. Quite intense aroma, with predominant reduction notes (lees) over a nuance of ripe fruit. Dry palate with bitter crianza notes (almonds, dried herbs) with hints of citrus fruit in the retronasal passage.

JUVÉ & CAMPS CINTA PÚRPURA RESERVA
BRUT
35% macabeo, 35% parellada, 30% xarel.lo

82 Pale yellow with a golden glint. Intense aroma with predominant crianza notes (lees, withered flowers) over a nuance of white fruit with hints of honey. Generous palate, rich in bitter nuances with good acidity and hints of citrus fruit in the finish.

JUVÉ & CAMPS RESERVA DE LA FAMILIA
2000 GRAN RESERVA BRUT NATURE
35% macabeo, 35% parellada, 30% xarel.lo

84 Pale yellow. Intense, ripe aroma, with predominant crianza notes (withered petals, fine lees). Dry, fresh palate with fine bitter notes (herbs, almonds) and hints of high quality citrus fruit.

MILESIMÉ CHARDONNAY GRAN RESERVA
BRUT
100% chardonnay

84 Golden yellow with fine and persistent beads. Intense aroma with excellent varietal expression, a ripe and spicy nuance, of fine lees and jammy fruit. Dry, fresh, creamy palate with fine bitter notes, good acidity.

R. CINCTA PÚRPURA BRUT
GRAN JUVÉ GRAN RESERVA BRUT

LA XARMADA

Hisenda Casa Llivi, s/n
08796 Pacs del Penedés (Barcelona)
☎: 938 171 237 - Fax: 938 171 546
laxarmada@laxarmada.com
www. laxarmada.com

Established: 1977

🍶 120 🍶 600,.000 litres 🌿 100 has.
🍷 70% 🌐30%

LA XARMADA HERETAT DE SANGENÍS
BRUT NATURE

82 Brilliant pale, yellow. Intense aroma of white fruit (exotic hints) with fine lees, petals and a suggestion of syrup. Fresh, dry palate with notes of ripe lemon, creamy (well-integrated beads), with a slightly oily texture and good acidity.

DO CAVA

LA XARMADA HERETAT DE SANGENÍS ROSADO BRUT NATURE

79 Pale raspberry with hardly any beads. Intense aroma of ripe red fruit with fine reduction notes (withered petals, lees) and a crystallised hint. Dry palate with fine bitter notes (nuts), an oily texture, original.

LANGA HERMANOS

Carretera Nacional II, km. 241, 700
Apartado 49
50300 Calatayud (Zaragoza)
☎: 976 881 818 - Fax: 976 884 463
info@bodegas-langa.com
www.bodegas-langa.com

Established: 1982

150 🛢 8.250 litres 🍇 50 has.

🍷 75% 🍇25%-UK -DE -BE -NL -LU -PL

J. LANGA RESERVA FAMILIAR 2002 RESERVA BRUT NATURE
60% macabeo, 40% chardonnay

85 Pale yellow with a golden glint. Intense aroma with notions of the freshness of green fruit, fine reduction notes (nuts, cumin). Dry, creamy palate with fine bitter notes, excellent symmetry.

REYES DE ARAGÓN GRAN RESERVA BRUT NATURE
70% chardonnay, 30% macabeo

81 Pale yellow. Intense aroma with a certain finesse, white fruit with a nuance of lees and withered petals. Fresh, fruity palate with a good crianza expression (cumin, nuts), pleasant.

J. LANGA 2002 BRUT

LAR DE BARROS-INVIOSA

La Fuente, 8
06200 Almendralejo (Badajoz)
☎: 924 671 235 - Fax: 924 665 932
info@lardebarros.com
www.lardebarros.com

Established: 1931

2,500 🛢 2,000,000 litres 🍇 400 has.

🍷 60% 🍇40%-US -MX -CA -JP -PR -TW
-PL -CH -SE -DK -DE -DK -UK -NL -BE -FR

BONAVAL BRUT
macabeo, chardonnay

76 Pale gold. Slightly intense, fruity aroma with a nuance of fine lees. Fresh, flavourful, dry palate without great crianza nuances.

BONAVAL SECO
macabeo

76 Pale gold with fine beads. Slightly intense aroma of ripe white fruit with hints of flowers and lees. Fresh, flavourful palate with hints of citrus fruit.

BONAVAL NUEVO MILENIO 2000 BRUT NATURE
macabeo

80 Brilliant gold. Powerful, ripe aroma with a fine toasty crianza (nuts, cumin, mountain herbs). Fresh, flavourful, slightly creamy palate with fine bitter notes.

Cavas LAVERNOYA

Sant Pere, 17
08770 Sant Sadurní D'Anoia (Barcelona)
☎: 938 912 202 - Fax: 938 911 159
lavernoya@troc.es
www.troc.es/lavernoya

Established: 1890

🍷 75% 🍇25%

LACRIMA BACCUS RESERVA BRUT

85 Brilliant yellow straw. Not very intense aroma with a certain finesse, of green apples and hints of bitter almonds. Dry, creamy palate with good crianza expression, bitter and well-balanced.

LAVERNOYA GRAN CUVÉE BRUT

79 Pale yellow with a golden glint. Not very intense aroma, fruity (mildly crystallised nuance), hints of reduction (withered petals). Creamy palate with fine bitter notes, overtones of fruit-crianza-acidity balance, without great crianza expression.

LACRIMA BACCUS GRAN RESERVA BRUT NATURE

78 Golden straw. Aroma of ripe fruit (apples) with musky notes (honey and flowers). Ripe, fresh palate with notes of golden delicious apples, an oily texture and fizzy beads, short.

LACRIMA BACCUS PRIMERÍSIMO GRAN CUVÉE RESERVA BRUT NATURE

85 Brilliant golden yellow. Not very intense aroma of ripe white fruit with fresh overtones, a nuance of nuts and hints of minerals and herbs. Dry palate with well-integrated beads, good acidity.

LACRIMA BACCUS SUMMUM GRAN RESERVA BRUT NATURE

85 Golden yellow. Powerful, very fine, ripe aroma with fine reduction notes, a nuance of honey and toasted nuts. Dry palate, with fresh overtones, well-characterised crianza, hints of herbs and bitterness in the retronasal passage, good acidity.

LEONARDO CANO PEÑA
(Vins i caves Artesanals Vallbona d'Anoia)

Nou 79
08785 Vallbona d'Anoia (Barcelona)
☎: 937 760 223 - Fax: 937 760 223
canop@eresmas.com

Established: 2000

DO CAVA

🛢 50 ▐ 10,000 litres 🍷 100%

CASTELL DE LEONARD 2002 BRUT
NATURE
CASTELL DE LEONARD 2003 BARREL
AGED BRUT NATURE

Cava LINCON
(SALVADOR MATA OLIVA)

Passatge Terol, 11
08770 Sant Sadurní D'Anoia (Barcelona)
☎: 938 911 178 - Fax: 938 911 779

Established: 1923

🍷 100%

LINCON RESERVA EXTRA BRUT
MATA GABARRÓ RESERVA BRUT NATURE

LLOPART

Ctr.a de Sant Sadurni al Ordal, km. 4
08739 Subirats (Barcelona)
☎: 938 993 125 - Fax: 938 993 038
llopart@llopart.es - llopart.es

Established: 1887

🛢 90 ▐ 350.000 litres 🍇 70 has.

🍷 90% 🌐10%-JP -DE -DK -US

EX-VITE LLOPART BRUT
40% macabeo, 60% xarel.lo

84 Pale yellow. Not very intense aroma of great finesse with white fruit and a nuance of lees. Generous palate with subtle and well-integrated beads, somewhat oily with fine notes of crianza (almonds, cumin, nuts) and good old wine character, lacking acidity.

LLOPART ROSÉ RESERVA BRUT
60% monastrell, 40% garnacha

84 Raspberry with a coppery glint. Quite intense aroma of red stone fruit with quite varietal spicy hints and a nuance of fine lees. Dry, fresh, fruity palate with well-integrated beads and fine bitter notes, good acidity.

IMPERIAL LLOPART GRAN RESERVA BRUT
40% xarel.lo, 30% macabeo, 15% parellada, 15% chardonnay

87 Straw-coloured with greenish nuances. Intense aroma with predominant reduction notes (lees, withered petals, hints of honey) and a nuance of ripe white fruit. Dry, creamy palate with fine bitter notes and an excellent crianza-acidity balance.

INTEGRAL LLOPART BRUT NATURE
25% macabeo, 45% parellada, 30% chardonnay

82 Straw-coloured with a greenish hue. Intense aroma of green fruit with fine reduction notes (lees). Dry, fresh palate with hints of high quality citrus fruit, good acidity, a hint of finesse yet without crianza expression.

LLOPART RESERVA BRUT NATURE
macabeo, xarel.lo, parellada, chardonnay

83 Brilliant straw with a greenish glint. Intense aroma of ripe white fruit with hints of fine reduction (withered petals, almonds). Dry, fresh palate with less crianza expression and hints of high quality citrus fruit.

LEOPARDI VINTAGE 1999 GRAN RESERVA BRUT NATURE
40% macabeo, 30% xarel.lo, 15% parellada, 15% chardonnay

83 Pale with a golden glint. Powerful aroma of well-integrated white fruit and crianza notes with a hint of citrus fruit (lemon peel). Dry, fresh, bitter palate with slightly mineral nuance, high in acidity.

LLOPART NÉCTAR TERRENAL 2001 SEMI-DULCE
xarel.lo, parellada

84 Brilliant pale yellow with fine and persistent beads. Intense aroma with predominant reduction notes (lees, withered petals) and a nuance of white fruit. Flavourful, creamy palate with fine bittersweet notes and hints of crystallised fruit, bitter, long.

LOXAREL

Masia Can Mayol, s/n
08735 Vilobí del Penedés (Barcelona)
☎: 938 978 001 - Fax: 938 978 111
canmayol@interceller.com
www.wloxarel.com

999 DE LOXAREL BRUT ROSÉ
trepat, pinot noir

83 Very deep raspberry. Intense aroma with predominant reduction notes and slightly vinous hints. Dry palate with fine bitter notes, well-integrated beads and an old wine character, spicy and original.

LOXAREL VINTAGE 1999 RESERVA BRUT NATURE
macabeo, xarel.lo, parellada

85 Pale yellow with a golden glint. Intense aroma with fine reduction notes, a nuance of ripe fruit and hints of wax and lemon peel. Dry, flavourful palate with fine bitter crianza notes and a nuance of toasted nuts, good acidity.

MM DE LOXAREL 2000 RESERVA ROSÉ
pinot noir, chardonnay

87 Golden yellow with coppery hues. Powerful aroma, rich in crianza nuances (toasted nuts, fine lees), over a hint of ripe apples and honey. Dry palate with subtle and well-integrated beads with a good expression of old wine, spicy, slightly oily with refreshing acidity.

RESERVA FAMILIAR DE LOXAREL
macabeo, xarel.lo, parellada, chardonnay

87 Yellow straw with a golden glint. Powerful, ripe aroma with notes of lees and toasted crianza nuts with hints of fragrant herbs. Dry, generous, creamy palate with oily hints and rich bitter notes.

DO CAVA

LUDEN

Masía Grabuac
08736 Font Rubí (Barcelona)
☎: 938 978 129 - Fax: 932 325 128

Established: 1986

🗟 52,500 litres 🍇 35 has.
🍷 20% 🍇80%-BE -DE -UK

LUDEN BRUT
LUDEN BRUT NATURE
LUDEN EXTRA BRUT

M. RIGOL ORDI

Fullerachs, 9
08770 Sant Sadurní D'Anoia (Barcelona)
☎: 938 910 194 - Fax: 938 910 226
cavamro@mariarigolordi.com
www.mariarigolordi.com

Established: 1986

🍷 100%

MARÍA RIGOL ORDI BRUT NATURE
MARÍA RIGOL ORDI RESERVA BRUT
  NATURE
MARIOR CAVA GRAN RESERVA BRUT
  NATURE

Cava MAGUST

Carretera BP-2151, 142
08776 Sant Pere de Riudebitlles (Barcelona)
☎: 938 997 054 - Fax: 938 997 054
cavamagust@terra.es

Established: 1996

🌐 5 🗟 20,000 litres 🍇 3 has.🍷 100%

MAGUST BRUT NATURE
MAGUST COLE.LECCIÓ RESERVA BRUT
  NATURE

MARÍA CASANOVAS

Montserrat, 117
08770 Sant Sadurní d'Anoia (Barcelona)
☎: 938 910 812 - Fax: 938 911 572
mariacasanovas@brutnature.com
www.brutnature.com

Established: 1982

🍷 95% 🍇5%

MARÍA CASANOVAS 2001 GRAN RESERVA
BRUT NATURE
MARÍA CASANOVAS 2002 RESERVA BRUT
NATURE ROSÉ

Celler MARIOL

Les Forques, s/n
43786 Batea (Tarragona)
☎: 934 367 628 - Fax: 934 500 281
celler@cellermariol.es
www.cellermariol.es

Established: 1945

🌐 600 🗟 3,100,000 litres 🍇 50 has.
🍷 50% 🍇50%

CELLER MARIOL 36 MESES BRUT
CELLER MARIOL BRUT NATURE
CELLER MARIOL ARTESANAL 48 MESES
BRUT NATURE
CELLER MARIOL BRUT NATURE

MARQUÉS DE MONISTROL

Monistrol D'Anoia, s/n
08770 Sant Sadurní D'Anoia (Barcelona)
☎: 938 910 276 - Fax: 938 183 328
adelgado@haciendas-espana.com
www.marquesdemonistrol.com

Established: 1882

🌐 8,000 🗟 6,000,000 litres
🍷 60% 🍇40%

MARQUÉS DE MONISTROL MILLÉSIMÉ
1997 GRAN RESERVA BRUT ROSÉ
pinot noir, monastrell

85 Fairly pale brilliant raspberry. Intense aroma
of ripe red fruit with spicy hints and fine reduction
notes (withered petals, lees). Dry and creamy on
the palate with red stone fruit, fine bitter notes and
hints of minerals.

CLOS MONISTROL 1998 RESERVA EXTRA
BRUT
macabeo, xarel.lo, parellada

84 Pale yellow with golden nuances. Not very
intense, ripe aroma with fine reduction notes.
Fresh, dry and creamy on the palate (well-integrated bead) with good crianza expression and hints
of wax and citrus fruit.

MARQUÉS DE MONISTROL BRUT NATURE
macabeo, xarel.lo, parellada

83 Straw-coloured with golden nuances. Intense
aroma of ripe white fruit, hints of fine lees and withered petals with a nuance of honey. Dry and creamy on the palate with very flavourful bitter notes
evoking the freshness of citrus fruits.

MARQUÉS DE MONISTROL MILLÉSIMÉ
1997 GRAN RESERVA BRUT NATURE
chardonnay

84 Pale with greenish nuances. Powerful aroma of green apples and fine reduction notes (withered petals, lees, waxy hints). Flavourful and creamy on the palate with a slightly oily texture and fine bitter notes.

MARRUGAT

Doctor Pasteur, 6
08720 Vilafranca del Penedés (Barcelona)
☎: 938 903 066 - Fax: 938 170 979
pinord@pinord.es
www.pinord.com
Established: 1942
▥ 2,000 ▤ 4,000,000 litres ⚘ 100 has.
🍷 78% 🍇22%

MARRUGAT CHARDONNAY RESERVA BRUT
chardonnay

75 Golden yellow. Intense aroma, with predominant not very fine reduction notes (varnishes, lees), and a nuance of ripe fruit. Dry, bitter palate, lacking balance.

MARRUGAT GRAN BRUT RESERVA BRUT
macabeo, xarel.lo, parellada

79 Brilliant yellow straw. Intense aroma, very ripe with traditional crianza expression (withered petals, lees). Bitter, creamy palate, lacking balance.

MARRUGAT SEMI-SECO
macabeo, xarel.lo, parellada

81 Pale yellow, with a golden hue. Intense aroma, with predominant reduction notes (withered petals, lees, nuts) over a nuance of ripe fruit. Generous, creamy palate, notes of crystallised fruit, good acidity.

MARRUGAT RESERVA FAMILIAR
macabeo, xarel.lo, parellada

80 Golden yellow. Intense aroma with predominant reduction notes (nuts, balsamic flavours). Dry, bitter palate with fresh overtones and good acidity.

MARRUGAT RESERVA SELECCIONADA 2002 BRUT
MARRUGAT 2000 GRAN RESERVA BRUT NATURE

MAS CODINA

El Gorner, Mas Codina s/n
08797 Puigdalber (Barcelona)
☎: 938 988 166 - Fax: 938 988 166
cavesmascodina@hotmail.com
Established: 1970
▥ 44 ▤ 300,000 litres ⚘ 40 has. 🍷 75%
🍇25%-FR -DE -NL -DK -CH -UK -US -BE

MAS CODINA 2001 BRUT
48% macabeo, 20% parellada, 18% xarel.lo, 14% chardonnay

84 Straw-coloured with a golden hue. Not very intense aroma of ripe white fruit with a toasty (cumin, nuts) crianza nuance. Dry, creamy palate with fine bitter notes and hints of herbs and citrus fruit in the retronasal passage, excellent acidity.

MAS CODINA 2001 BRUT NATURE
MAS CODINA 2000 RESERVA ESPECIAL BRUT NATURE

MAS COMTAL

Mas Comtal, 1
08739 Avinyonet del Penedés (Barcelona)
☎: 938 970 052 - Fax: 938 970 591
mascomtal@arrakis.es
www.mascomtal.com
Established: 1993
▥ 200 ▤ 220,000 litres ⚘ 40 has.
🍷 50% 🍇50%

MAS COMTAL 2002 BRUT NATURE
chardonnay, xarel.lo

85 Straw-coloured with a greenish edge. Herbaceous aroma with notes of fine lees, flowers and green fruit pulp. Fresh palate with expression of herbs; slightly tropical, fine beads, long.

Cavas MAS FERRER

S. Sebastia, 25 C'al Avi
08739 Subirats (Barcelona)
☎: 938 988 292 - Fax: 938 988 545
info@elmasferrer.com
www.elmasferrer.com
Established: 1987
🍷 95% 🍇5%

EL MAS FERRER BRUT ROSÉ
60% pinot noir, 40% garnacha

79 Brilliant raspberry. Fruity aroma, with a hint of lees and withered petals. Dry, very bitter palate with elevated acidity and a suggestion of red stone fruit.

EL MAS FERRER RESERVA BRUT
40% xarel.lo, 30% macabeo, 30% parellada

82 Straw-coloured. Aroma of fine crianza (toasty, a suggestion of lees) with well-balanced white fruit and hints of flor. Dry palate with well-balanced bittersweetness, fruitier than in the nose; light crianza, long.

EL MAS FERRER SEGLE XXI GRAN RESERVA EXTRA BRUT
40% xarel.lo, 35% macabeo, 25% parellada

DO CAVA

86 Straw-coloured. Fine aroma with crianza expression (withered flowers, bakery) and white fruit notes. Dry, flavourful palate with fine and integrated beads and notes of flowers and herbs, persistent.

EL MAS FERRER BRUT NATURE
40% xarel.lo, 35% parellada, 25% macabeo

84 Straw-coloured. Floral aroma of white fruit (pears) with notes of fennel and herbs over fine lees. Dry, flavourful palate with good acidity; fruity and generous (herbaceous).

MAS OLIVÉ

Plaza Pont Roma, 17
08770 Sant Sadurní D'Anoia (Barcelona)
☎: 938 910 310 - Fax: 938 910 409
cavamasolive@yahoo.es

Established: 1929

🛢 50 ⬛ 40,000 litres 🍇 15 has.

🍷 85% 🌐15%-NL -US

J. RAVENTÓS ROIG RESERVA BRUT NATURE
40% macabeo, 35% parellada, 25% xarel.lo

84 Straw-coloured with a golden hue. Powerful, ripe aroma with fine reduction notes (lees, fragrant herbs). Dry, creamy palate with fine bitter notes, crianza fine toasty flavours and excellent acidity.

MAS OLIVER TRADICIÓ FAMILIAR RESERVA BRUT NATURE
45% macabeo, 30% parellada, 25% xarel.lo

80 Pale yellow. Intense, slightly fresh aroma of ripe apples with notes of citrus fruit and fine reduction. Dry palate with predominant bitter and citrus notes, not very well-balanced but pleasant.

Caves MAS TINELL

Ctra de Vilafranca-St. Martí Sarroca, km. 0,5
08720 Vilafranca del Penedés (Barcelona)
☎: 938 170 586 - Fax: 938 170 500
manuel@mastinell.com
www.mastinell.com

Established: 1989

⬛ 370,000 litres 🍇 4 has. 🍷 95% 🌐5%

CRISTINA 1998 GRAN RESERVA EXTRA BRUT
macabeo, parellada, chardonnay

86 Pale yellow with a greenish hue. Powerful aroma with excellent crianza expression (withered petals, fine lees, honey). Generous, flavourful, balanced palate with well-integrated beads, good acidity.

HERETAT MAS TINELL GRAN RESERVA EXTRA BRUT
macabeo, xarel.lo, parellada

87 Pale yellow with a greenish glint. Intense, fresh aroma with notes of green apples and a fine nuance of reduction. Very dry palate with fine notes of bitter almonds and fennel; hints of citrus fruit and herbs, excellent acidity, very long.

HERETAT MAS TINELL RESERVA BRUT ROSÉ

84 Blush with a coppery edge. Lively aroma of strawberries with notes of almonds and a nuance of fine petals. Dry, flavourful palate with good fruit-crianza balance; fruity, slightly bitter.

HERETAT MAS TINELL BRUT REAL RESERVA BRUT
macabeo, xarel.lo, parellada

82 Pale yellow with a golden glint. Light, slightly fruity aroma (green apples) with fine lees. Generous palate with fine bitter notes and a nuance of white fruit with hints of crystallisation, pleasant.

HERETAT MAS TINELL GRAN RESERVA BRUT NATURE
macabeo, xarel.lo, parellada

83 Straw-coloured. Fresh, herbaceous aroma of fine bakery, elegant. Flavourful palate, high in acidity; toasty lees notes, fruity, long (green fruit pulp).

HERETAT MAS TINELL RESERVA ESPECIAL RESERVA BRUT NATURE

86 Brilliant pale yellow. Not very intense aroma with overtones of freshness, green fruit and a nuance of fine lees. Dry, creamy palate with fine bitter crianza notes (almonds, herbs), very fine with excellent acidity and hints of minerals in the retronasal passage.

BRUT REAL RESERVA
MAS TINELL RESERVA ESPECIAL BRUT NATURE

MASET DEL LLEÓ

Av. Barcelona, 31
08734 Sant Pere Molanta (Barcelona)
☎: 902 200 250 - Fax: 938 921 333
info@maset.com
www.maset.com

Established: 1777

🛢 150 ⬛ 400,000 litres 🍇 50 has.

🍷 90% 🌐10%-DE -US

MASET DEL LLEÓ BRUT
xarel.lo, macabeo, parellada

84 Pale yellow. Intense aroma of fine lees with a suggestion of ripe fruit (apples, limes) and hints of herbs. Rich in nuances on the palate with good crianza-acidity-sweetness balance.

L'AVI PAU MASET DEL LLEÓ CUVÉE BRUT NATURE
chardonnay, macabeo, parellada

82 Straw-coloured. Powerful aroma with a good crianza expression and a predominant suggestion of citrus notes. Generous, dry palate with well-integrated beads, slightly subtle notes of lees, nuts and herbs with predominant citrus notes (sweet limes).

MASET DEL LLEÓ RESERVA BRUT NATURE
xarel.lo, macabeo, parellada

83 Straw-coloured with a golden glint. Not very intense aroma with a certain finnesse and a good crianza expression (lees, withered petals) over a nuance of white fruit. Dry palate with well-integrated beads, well-balanced and very pleasant; fine hints of almonds and aniseed in the retronasal passage.

MASET DEL LLEÓ RESERVA BRUT NATURE
xarel.lo, macabeo, parellada

83 Straw-coloured. Fruity aroma (ripe apples), with toasty flavours and a hint of fine herbs, fine. Dry, flavourful palate with good acidity and an aftertaste of crianza nuances, long.

MASET DEL LLEÓ EXTRA BRUT

MASÍA PAPIOL

Masovería Papiol s/n
43720 L'Arboç del Penedés (Tarragona)
☎: 977 670 056 - Fax: 977 671 313
masiapapiol@masiapapiol.e.telefonica.net
Established: 1991
⊞ 10 🗄 160,000 litres
🌱 118 has.🥾 100%

SANT PONÇ GRAN RESERVA EXTRA BRUT
SANT PONÇ BRUT NATURE

MASÍA PUIGMOLTÓ

Barrio de Sant Marçal, s/n
08732 Castellet i La Gornal (Barcelona)
☎: 938 918 076 - Fax: 932 115 730
puigmolt@mento.net
Established: 1975
⊞ 20 🗄 100,000 litres 🌱 25 has.
🥾 95% 🌐5%

PUIGMOLTÓ GRAN RESERVA BRUT
60% xarel.lo, 20% macabeo, 20% parellada

86 Pale golden yellow. Intense, very fine aroma with notes of white stone fruit well-integrated with the crianza (lees, withered petals). Dry, creamy palate with fine bitter notes (almonds, mountain herbs) and hints of high quality citrus fruit.

PUIGMOLTÓ BRUT NATURE
50% xarel.lo, 30% macabeo, 20% parellada

82 Pale with golden nuances. Powerful, fresh aroma of green fruit, hints of flowers and fine lees. Very dry palate with bitter notes, citrus fruits, fresh herbs, wax and minerals.

PUIGMOLTÓ RESERVA BRUT

MASÍA SAGUÉ

Avinguda U, 43-45
08794 Les Cabanyes (Barcelona)
☎: 938 920 850 - Fax: 938 921 760
bodega@masiasague.com
www.masiasague.com
Established: 1919
⊞ 20 🗄 4,000,000 litres 🌱 80 has.
🥾 80% 🌐20%-DE -JP -NL -DK -IE -CH

MASÍA SAGUÉ RESERVA BRUT
40% macabeo, 40% xarel.lo, 20% parellada

83 Straw-coloured. Intense aroma of white fruit over a fine nuance of reduction (flowers, lees). Dry, creamy palate (well-integrated beads) with fine bitter notes (almonds, dried herbs), excellent acidity.

MASÍA SAGUÉ RESERVA BRUT NATURE
macabeo, xarel.lo, parellada

83 Brilliant straw with quite robust beads. Not very intense aroma of ripe white fruit with a nuance of fragrant herbs, fennel and a hint of bakeries. Dry, creamy palate with fine bitter notes and hints of grapefruit in the retronasal passage, good acidity.

MASÍA SAGUÉ GRAN RESERVA BRUT NATURE
macabeo, xarel.lo, parellada

86 Straw-coloured with fine and persistent beads. Fine aroma with balance between notes of ripe white fruit and crianza (lees, herbs). Dry, creamy palate with fine bitter notes, fine toasty flavours and a nuance of rich citrus fruit, long.

MASÍA SAGUÉ RESERVA SEMI-SECO

Cavas MESTRES

Plaça Ajuntament, 8
08770 Sant Sadurní D'Anoia (Barcelona)
☎: 938 910 043 - Fax: 938 911 611
mestrescava@bsab.com
Established: 1928
⊞ 35 🗄 150,000 litres 🌱 80 has.
🥾 95% 🌐5%-DK -UK

MESTRES MAS VIA 1990 GRAN RESERVA BRUT
60% xarel.lo, 20% macabeo, 20% parellada

77 Golden. Honeyed aroma with notes of reduction in the bottle (toasty flavours). Dry, fresh palate with ripe notes (orange peel), not very generous.

MESTRES 1312 2002 BRUT NATURE
60% xarel.lo, 30% macabeo, 10% parellada

78 Straw-coloured. Slightly short aroma with notes of fine petals and a suggestion of yeasts. Dry, fresh palate, without strong cava character, slightly vinous.

MESTRES 1996 GRAN RESERVA BRUT NATURE ROSÉ
60% xarel.lo, 20% macabeo, 10% parellada, 10% monastrell

68 Coppery with a golden edge. Aroma with crianza notes (varnishes, toasty flavours) and reduced fruit. Viscous, vinous palate without nuances nor beads.

MESTRES CLOS NOSTRE SENYOR MILLÉSIMÉ 1997 GRAN RESERVA BRUT NATURE
60% xarel.lo, 20% macabeo, 20% parellada

80 Straw-coloured. Ripe aroma of long ageing (bakery) with a suggestion of withered flowers. Flavourful, fruity palate; without strong notes of lees, better in the nose, somewhat short.

MESTRES COQUET 2001 BRUT NATURE
60% xarel.lo, 30% macabeo, 10% parellada

85 Pale yellow. Intense aroma with predominant reduction notes (withered petals, bakery) over notes of ripe apples. Fresh, creamy palate (well-integrated beads), bitter hints, good acidity.

MESTRES VISOL RESERVA PARTICULAR RESERVA BRUT NATURE
60% xarel.lo, 25% macabeo, 15% parellada

86 Brilliant golden with a coppery glint. Intense aroma of fine lees with a fine tannic note and fresh citrus overtones. Dry palate with well-integrated beads, notes of herbs, a nuance of aniseed and nuts, excellent acidity.

MESTRES CUPATGES BRUT
MESTRES CUPATGES BRUT NATURE
MESTRES CLOS DAMIANA GRAN RESERVA BRUT NATURE

Caves MIQUEL PONS

Del Mig, 17
08792 La Granada del Penedes (Barcelona)
☎: 938 974 064 - Fax: 938 974 064
cavamiquelpons@redestb.es

Established: 1992

🌐 80 🗄 20,000 litres 🌿 20 has.
🍷 98% 🍇2%

MIQUEL PONS BRUT
MIQUEL PONS BRUT NATURE
MIQUEL PONS SEMI-SECO

MONASTELL

Girona, 30
08770 Sant Sadurní D'Anoia (Barcelona)
☎: 938 910 396 - Fax: 938 183 716

Established: 1954

🌐 10 🗄 25,000 litres 🍷 70% 🍇30%

MONASTELL BRUT
MONTSANT BRUT
MONASTELL BRUT NATURE
MONTSANT BRUT NATURE
ROCA GIBERT BRUT NATURE

MONT MARÇAL VINÍCOLA

Finca Manlleu, s/n
08732 Castellví de la Marca (Barcelona)
☎: 938 918 281 - Fax: 938 919 045
direccion@mont-marcal.com
www.mont-marcal.com

Established: 1975

🌐 500 🗄 500,000 litres 🌿 40 has.
🍷 20% 🍇80%

EXTREMARIUM DE MONT MARÇAL RESERVA BRUT

82 Greenish straw. Aroma of lemons with notes of fresh herbs and flowers; a nuance of toasty bread. Flavourful palate with green fruit pulp, high in acidity; persistent.

MONT MARÇAL M.M. RESERVA BRUT ROSÉ

80 Raspberry with a coppery hue. Quite intense aroma of red stone fruit with good varietal expression (spices, underbrush), with a nuance of fine lees. Dry, fruity palate with fine bitter crianza notes, pleasant.

MONT MARÇAL RESERVA BRUT

84 Straw-coloured. Toasty aroma (bakery) with hints of honey and fresh flowers. Fresh, flavourful palate with good balance between the sugar and the bitterness; fruity.

MONT MARÇAL GRAN RESERVA

68 Lemon with a golden glint. Musky, quite dirty aroma; rancid notes. Vinous, fresh palate, without beads, oily but without cava expression.

MONT MARÇAL RESERVA BRUT NATURE

Caves MONT-FERRANT

Abat Escarré, 1
17300 Blanes (Girona)
☎: 934 191 000 - Fax: 934 193 170
montferrant@montferrant.com
www.montferrant.com

Established: 1865

🍷 95% 🍇5%

AGUSTÍ-VILARET 1999 EXTRA BRUT
65% chardonnay, 15% parellada, 10% xarel.lo, 10% macabeo

88 Pale yellow with a golden glint, fine and persistent beads. Intense aroma of ripe white fruit with a nuance of grapefruits and fine reduction (withered petals, nuts). Elegant, well-balanced palate with fine bitter and toasty crianza notes, good acidity.

BERTA BOUZY EXTRA BRUT
50% parellada, 20% xarel.lo, 20% macabeo, 10% chardonnay

86 Straw-coloured with a golden glint. Not very intense aroma but of great finesse with fine crianza notes (lees, herbs, nuts). Well-balanced palate with rich bitter notes and a nuance of spicy and toasty crianza, flavourful with well-integrated beads, long.

GRAN CUVÉE BRUT
parellada, xarel.lo, chardonnay

86 Brilliant straw with a greenish hue. Intense, fresh aroma with notes of dried herbs and a nuance of toasted nuts. Dry, creamy palate with fine bitter notes, good acidity, very long.

MONT-FERRANT RODOLPHE BOURLON EXTRA BRUT
21% macabeo, 21% xarel.lo, 55% parellada, 3% chardonnay

88 Brilliant straw with a golden glint. Not very intense, very fine aroma of white fruit with notes of citrus fruit and fine lees. Dry, creamy palate with bitter crianza notes (almonds, cumin, dried herbs), excellent acidity.

MONT-FERRANT BRUT ROSÉ
60% monastrell, 40% garnacha

87 Brilliant raspberry. Intense aroma of red stone fruit with a slightly varietal spicy nuance and hints of sweetness (strawberry jelly). Dry, fresh, creamy, flavourful palate; fine bitter notes, excellent acidity, long.

MONT-FERRANT BLANES NATURE BRUT EXTRA
33% macabeo, 33% parellada, 29% xarel.lo, 5% chardonnay

86 Straw-coloured with a golden hue. Intense aroma of ripe white fruit and fine reduction notes with a crystallised fruit nuance. Dry, creamy palate with fine bitter notes, high quality hints of citrus fruit (sweet limes) and nuts, excellent acidity.

MONT-FERRANT R.D. 2000 RESERVA EXTRA BRUT
29% xarel.lo, 33% parellada, 33% macabeo, 5% chardonnay

85 Straw-coloured with a golden glint. Somewhat intense aroma with notes of ripe fruit and a fine reduction nuance (fine lees, fine herbs). Dry, creamy palate with fine bitter notes, well-crafted crianza and excellent acidity.

LUIS JUSTO VILLANUEVA BRUT NATURE
38% parellada, 33% macabeo, 29% xarel.lo

87 Straw-coloured with a golden hue. Not very intense, fresh aroma with fine notes of reduction (lees) over a nuance of green apples. Dry, creamy, balanced palate with fine bitter nuance, excellent acidity.

MONT-FERRANT BLANES & BLANES BRUT NATURE
55% parellada, 21% xarel.lo, 21% macabeo, 3% chardonnay

87 Straw-coloured with a golden hue, quite robust and persistent beads. Intense aroma with predominant crianza notes and a nuance of ripe apples. Dry, creamy palate (well-integrated beads), bitter, with a nuance of grapefruit and toasty (herbs, cumin, nuts) crianza hints, very fine.

MONT-FERRANT VINTAGE 2000 BRUT NATURE
55% parellada, 21% xarel.lo, 21% macabeo, 3% chardonnay

85 Straw-coloured with a golden glint. Not very intense aroma with overtones of finesse, an excellent crianza note and ripe fruit complement. Dry, creamy palate, fine bitter (nuts, cumin, herbs) crianza notes, very fine and long.

SANT LLAMI EXTRA BRUT
TRADICIÓ BRUT
MEDALLA D'OR BRUT
L´ AMERICANO RESERVA BRUT

MONTESQUIUS

Rambla de la Generalitat s/n
08770 Sant Sadurni D'Anoia (Barcelona)
☎: 938 910 800 - Fax: 938 911 747
montesquius@montesquiuscom
www.montesquius.com

Established: 1918

🍷 90% 🍇10%

DAMA DE COLL DE JUNY GRAN RESERVA BRUT

87 Straw-coloured with a golden glint. Intense aroma with overtones of freshness, a nuance of crianza (lees, withered petals) and fine beads. Dry, creamy palate with fine bitter notes (nuts, dried grass), excellent acidity.

MONTESQUIUS GRAN RESERVA BRUT NATURE

88 Brilliant gold. Powerful aroma with fine notes of reduction (lees, withered petals, bakery) and a nuance of dried herbs, Dry palate with fine creamy and nutty hints, well-integrated beads, excellent acidity.

NADAL

Finca Can Nadal s/n
08775 El Pla del Penedés (Barcelona)
☎: 938 988 036 - Fax: 938 988 443
nadal@Tnadal.com - visita@nadal.com

DO CAVA

www.nadal.com

Established: 1943

🌐 16 🍷 1,600,000 litres 🍇 100 has.

🍷 90% 🌐10%-NL -DK -CH -AD -CR -BE -JP -SG -AT -BO

NADAL ESPECIAL 1999 EXTRA BRUT
parellada, macabeo, xarel.lo

86 Very pale with a greenish glint. Intense aroma with predominant notes of ripe white fruit, a nuance of fine reduction (lees, herb-honey, nuts). Dry, bitter palate with a quality citrus fruit nuance, well-balanced and very fine.

NADAL SALVATGE 1998 EXTRA BRUT
macabeo, xarel.lo, parellada

85 Straw-coloured with a greenish edge. Fresh, clean aroma of fine lees and pâtisserie with a bitter nuance of fruit pulp. Dry, fresh palate with an oily but lively texture; almonds and herbs in the finish.

NADAL BRUT
NADAL BRUT ROSÉ
RAMON NADAL GIRÓ 1997 BRUT

Caves NAVERÁN (SADEVE)

Can Parellada Sant Martí Sadevesa
08775 Torrelavit (Barcelona)
☎: 938 988 274 - Fax: 938 989 027
sadeve@naveran.com
www.naveran.com

Established: 1986

🌐 400 🍷 900,000 litres 🍇 110 has.

🍷 60% 🌐40%-FR -US -PR -JP -BE -NL -UK -IE -SE -CH -DE

DAMA DE NAVERÁN 2001 EXTRA BRUT
85% chardonnay, 15% parellada

83 Pale yellow with a golden glint. Ripe, not very intense aroma with hints of fine reduction and hints of ripe grapefruit and honey. Dry, fresh, fruity palate with fine bitter notes and hints of citrus fruit, good acidity.

NAVERÁN BLANC DE BLANCS 2001 RESERVA BRUT
parellada, xarel.lo, macabeo

78 Straw-coloured with a greenish glint. Not very intense aroma with a certain finesse (green fruit, withered petal nuance). Dry palate with bitter notes and a nuance of sweet limes, pleasant.

NAVERÁN "N DE N" 2000 BRUT NATURE
20% parellada, 40% xarel.lo, 20% macabeo, 20% chardonnay

84 Brilliant straw with a greenish glint. Powerful, ripe aroma with reduction notes (withered petals, yeasts). Dry, creamy palate (well-integrated beads), fine bitter crianza notes, good acidity, a nuance of grapefruit.

NAVERÁN ODISEA 2000 RESERVA BRUT NATURE
60% chardonnay, 40% parellada

80 Golden yellow. Powerful, ripe aroma with predominant reduction notes (yeasts), crystallised fruit nuance. Better, dry, creamy palate with fine bitter notes, a nuance of cumin, herbs and bitter almonds.

NAVERÁN PERLES ROSES 2001 BRUT NATURE ROSÉ
100% pinot noir

78 Brilliant salmon. Intense, ripe aroma with predominant reduction notes, hints of honey, not very clear. Dry, fruity, spicy palate with fine bitter notes, good acidity.

Bodegas OLARRA

Poligono de Cantabria 1, s/n
26006 Logroño (La Rioja)
☎: 941 235 299 - Fax: 941 253 703
bodegasolarra@bodegasolarra.es
www.bodegasolarra.es

Established: 1973

🌐 25,000 🍷 50% 🌐50%

AÑARES BRUT NATURE
100% viura

78 Very pale straw. Quite intense aroma with fine notes of yeast and withered petals and a hint of ripe white fruit. Dry, fresh, flavourful palate with fine bitter crianza notes.

AÑARES BRUT NATURE

OLIVE BATLLORI

Barrio Els Casots, s/n
08739 Subirats (Barcelona)
☎: 938 993 103 - Fax: 938 995 700

Established: 1941

🍷 75,000 litres 🍇 15 has. 🍷 100%

ANTONIETA BATLLORI BRUT
OLIVE BATLLORI BRUT
GRAN BRUT OLIVE BATLLORI BRUT
ANTONIETA BATLLORI BRUT NATURE
GRAN D'ART BRUT NATURE
OLIVE BATLLORI BRUT NATURE
ANTONIETA BATLLORI SEMI-SECO
OLIVE BATLLORI SEMI-SECO

OLIVELLA I BONET

Casetes Puigmoltó, 26
43720 L'Arboç (Tarragona)
☎: 977 670 433 - Fax: 977 670 433

Established: 1988

MONT CARANAC CHARDONNAY BRUT
OLIVELLA I BONET BRUT
OLIVELLA I BONET BRUT NATURE

Bodegas ONDARRE

Carretera de Aras, s/n
31230 Viana (Navarra)
☎: 948 645 300 - Fax: 948 646 002
bodegasondarre@bodegasondarre.es
www.bodegasondarre.es
Established: 1984
⊕ 12,000 ⚘ 55% ⚘45%

ONDARRE SELECCIÓN MILLENNIUM BRUT
100% viura

83 Pale with a straw-coloured glint. Aroma of fine crianza (fine yeasts, toasty flavours) over ripe fruit. Dry, flavourful, slightly sweet, fruity palate with less character than crianza, persistent.

ONDARRE RESERVA BRUT

Caves ORIOL ROSSELL

Can Cassanyes
43729 St. Marçal-Castellet i Gornal (Barcelona)
☎: 977 671 061 - Fax: 977 671 050
or@ofitecnica.net
Established: 1979
⚘ 80 has. ⚘ 88% ⚘12%-JP -DE -NL -BE -UK -FR -US -AD

ORIOL ROSSELL 2003 BRUT ROSÉ
trepat

79 Raspberry with a coppery hue and slightly robust beads. Not very intense aroma, fruity with spicy hints of skins and a suggestion of sweetness. Flavourful, fresh palate, pleasant.

ORIOL ROSSELL 2002 RESERVA BRUT NATURE
macabeo, xarel.lo, parellada

82 Straw-coloured with a greenish glint. Not very intense aroma, with fine notes of white fruit and hints of lees and fragrant herbs. Dry palate with excellent acidity and fine bitter notes, fresh, without great crianza expression.

ORIOL ROSSELL 1999 GRAN RESERVA BRUT NATURE
macabeo, xarel.lo, parellada

86 Straw-coloured with a golden hue. Not very intense, fine aroma with well-integrated notes of white fruit and petals (crianza). Dry, fresh, creamy palate with elegant bitter notes, ripe grapefruit, good acidity.

ORIOL ROSSELL RESERVA DE LA PROPIETAT 2000 GRAN RESERVA BRUT NATURE
macabeo, xarel.lo, parellada

87 Brilliant straw. Somewhat intense, very fine aroma with a nuance of lees, herbs and ripe citrus fruit. Dry palate with fine bitter notes, excellent acidity.

PAGÉS ENTRENA

Ctra de Piera-Sant Sadurní D'Anoia, km. 10,1
08784 Sant Jaume Sesoliveres (Barcelona)
☎: 938 183 827 - Fax: 938 913 147
cava@pagesentrena.com
www.pagesentrena.com
Established: 1987
⬛ 187,700 litres ⚘ 100%

JOAN PAGÉS 2000 BRUT
PAGÉS ENTRENA 1999 BRUT
JOAN PAGÉS 2000 BRUT NATURE
PAGÉS ENTRENA 1999 BRUT NATURE
JOAN PAGÉS 2000 SEMI-SECO
PAGÉS ENTRENA 1999 SEMI-SECO

Bodegas PARATÓ

Can Respall de Renardes
08733 Pla del Penedés (Barcelona)
☎: 938 988 182 - Fax: 938 988 510
info@parato.es
www.parato.es
Established: 1975
⊕ 150 ⬛ 800,000 litres ⚘ 94 has.
⚘ 70% ⚘30%-DE -BE -CH

PARATÓ BRUT
macabeo, xarel.lo, parellada

84 Pale yellow with a greenish glint. Intense aroma of white fruit with hints of a fine reduction (withered petals). Flavourful, creamy palate with fine bitter notes, green fruit and good acidity.

ELIAS-TERNS GRAN RESERVA BRUT NATURE
macabeo, xarel.lo, parellada

86 Pale yellow. Not very intense aroma with finesse, hints of lees over a nuance of white fruit and ripe limes. Dry palate with fine bitter notes (almonds), well-integrated beads and good acidity.

PARATÓ BRUT NATURE
macabeo, xarel.lo, parellada

83 Pale yellow with a coppery glint. Powerful, ripe aroma with a nuance of withered petals and hints of honey. Dry, creamy palate with notes of ripe apples and well-integrated, bitter hints of crianza.

RENARDES CUVÉE ESPECIAL BRUT NATURE
macabeo, xarel.lo, parellada

85 Pale yellow. Intense, ripe aroma with predominant reduction notes (withered petals). Dry on the palate with fine bitter notes (herbs, anise) and hints of high quality citrus fruit.

PARÉS BALTÁ

Masía Can Baltá, s/n
08796 Pacs del Penedés (Barcelona)
☎: 938 901 399 - Fax: 938 901 143
paresbalta@paresbalta.com
www.paresbalta.com

Established: 1790

🍾 500 📇 1,300,000 litres 🍇 175 has.

🍷 80% 🌐20%

PARÉS BALTÀ CUVÉE DE CAROL BRUT
PARÉS BALTÀ BRUT NATURE

PARXET

Mas Parxet s/n
08391 Tiana (Barcelona)
☎: 933 950 811 - Fax: 933 955 500
parxet@parxet.es
wwwparxet.es

Established: 1920

🍾 40 📇 1,500,000 litres 🍇 200 has.

🍷 85% 🌐15%-US -UK -JP -DE -BE -DK

PARXET MAXIMUN 2000 GRAN RESERVA BRUT
macabeo, parellada, pansa blanca

85 Straw-coloured. Generous aroma of fine tropical fruit with notes of sun-drenched skins and a nuance of well-integrated lees (herbs). Dry, fresh, fruity palate with notes of spices and yeast.

PARXET RESERVA BRUT

83 Straw-coloured. Elegant aroma of fine lees, mountain herbs and anise. Dry palate with good freshness and a spicy, herby character; without great crianza notes.

PARXET PINOT NOIR BRUT
100% pinot noir

84 Intense salmon with a coppery glint. Powerful aroma with fresh overtones, spicy hints of skins, a nuance of balsamic flavours and fine reduction notes. Dry, creamy palate, fine bitter notes, good acidity.

PARXET BRUT
macabeo, parellada, pansa blanca

84 Straw-coloured. Complex aroma (honey, green grass, a suggestion of terroir) with reduction notes. Flavourful palate with good ripeness and freshness, a generous finish.

PARXET ANIVERSARIO PA83 BRUT NATURE
chardonnay

88 Golden yellow with fine and persistent beads. Powerful aroma, ripe, excellent varietal and crianza expression (lees, nuts, balsamic flavours). Dry palate, well-integrated beads, rich in nuances, good crianza expression.

PARXET BRUT NATURE
macabeo, parellada, pansa blanca

80 Pale yellow. Intense aroma of white fruit with fine hints of spices and toasty crianza notes. Dry, slightly creamy palate with notes of bitter almonds and balsamic flavours, a little lacking in balance.

PARXET TITIANA BRUT NATURE
chardonnay

86 Brilliant yellow with a golden glint. Intense aroma with excellent varietal expression (ripe apples), a fine reduction nuance (petals, balsamic flavours, honey). Dry, creamy palate with fine bitter notes (nuts) and good acidity.

PARXET CUVÉE DESSERT BRUT NATURE
pinot noir, chardonnay

84 Intense salmon with coppery hues. Intense aroma, fruity, with a nuance of crystallised fruit and fine reduction. Generous, sweet, creamy palate, well-balanced (a bitter nuance) with hints of citrus fruit in the retronasal passage.

PARXET RESERVA SEMI-SECO
macabeo, parellada, pansa blanca

84 Straw-coloured with a golden hue. Intense aroma with notes of fine reduction (lees, fennel, balsamic flavours). Generous, creamy palate, fine bitter notes, hints of crystallised fruit, well-balanced.

PARXET GRAPA BRUT

PERE MUNNÉ DURÁN

San Josep, 10-11-12
08784 Sant Jaume Sesrovires (Barcelona)
☎: 937 860 148 - Fax: 937 854 247

Established: 1989

🍾 8 📇 800 litres 🍇 3 has. 🍷 100%

MUNGUST 2001
PERE MUNNÉ DURÁN 2002 BRUT

PERE RIUS

Masia Pere Rius
08732 Castellvi de la Marca (Barcelona)
☎: 938 918 274 - Fax: 938 918 223
cavapererius@eresmas.com

Established: 1990
🍇 20 has. 🍷 100%

MASÍA PERE RIUS 2000 GRAN RESERVA
RIUS PLANAS 2001 RESERVA

PERE VENTURA

Carretera de Vilafranca, km. 0, 4
08770 Sant Sadurní D'Anoia (Barcelona)
☎: 938 183 371 - Fax: 938 912 679
pventura@interceller.com
www.pereventura.com

Established: 1992
🛢 500 📦 150,000 litres 🍇 14 has.
🍷 65% 🌐35% -UE

PERE VENTURA TRESOR BRUT NATURE
xarel.lo, macabeo, parellada, chardonnay

85 Straw-coloured with a golden hue. Powerful aroma with a fine expression of lees and well-integrated very ripe white fruit with spicy hints of crianza and a suggestion of withered petals. Dry, creamy palate with fine bitter notes (nuts, mountain herbs) and excellent acidity.

PERE VENTURA RESERVA SEMI-SECO
xarel.lo, macabeo

85 Pale gold. Powerful, floral aroma (acacia) with crystallised white fruit and a nuance of lees and withered petals. Flavourful palate with fine bittersweet notes and a bitter hint (almonds, mountain herbs) with excellent acidity.

PERE VENTURA RESERVA BRUT
PERE VENTURA RESERVA BRUT ROSÉ
TRESOR RESERVA BRUT NATURE
CUPATGE D'HONOR RESERVA BRUT NATURE
LA PUBILLA RESERVA BRUT NATURE
PERE VENTURA RESERVA ROSÉ SEMI-SECO

Cavas PUIG MUNTS

Revall, 38
08760 Martorell (Barcelona)
☎: 937 755 216 - Fax: 937 740 213
puigmunts@terra.es
www.puigmnts.com

Established: 1940
🍇 254 has. 🍷 95%
🌐5%-DE -LV -PL -AD -US -TR

PUIG MUNTS RESERVA BRUT
PUIG MUNTS RESERVA BRUT NATURE
PUIG MUNTS GRAN RESERVA BRUT NATURE
PUIG MUNTS RESERVA SEMI-SECO
PUIG MUNTS RESERVA SECO

PUPITRE

Avinguda Jacint Verdaguer, 8
43720 L'Arboc del Penedés (Tarragona)
☎: 977 670 055 - Fax: 977 670 353
caycra@caycra.com
www.caycra.com

Established: 1919
🛢 500 📦 15,000,000 litres 🍇 1,100 has.
🍷 70% 🌐30%

CASTELL GORNAL BRUT
CASTELL GORNAL BRUT NATURE
PUPITRE BRUT NATURE
PUPITRE CHARDONNAY BRUT NATURE
PUPITRE CHARDONNAY GRAN RESERVA BRUT NATURE

RAMÓN CANALS CANALS

Av. Mare de Deu Montserrat, 9
08769 Castellví de Rosanes (Barcelona)
☎: 937 755 446 - Fax: 937 741 719
cava@rcanalscanals.com
www.rcanalscanals.com

Established: 1974
🛢 150 📦 50,000 litres 🍇 20 has.
🍷 80% 🌐20%-US -JP -DE -AD -UK

R. CANALS CANALS RESERVA BRUT
DURAN GRAN RESERVA BRUT NATURE
R. CANALS CANALS BRUT NATURE ROSÉ
R. CANALS CANALS SEMI-SECO
R. CANALS CANALS GRAN RESERVA BRUT NATURE

RAMÓN VIDAL MORGADES

Nou, 6
43815 Les Pobles (Tarragona)

DO CAVA

☎: 977 638 554 - Fax: 977 638 554
vidaliferre@teleline.es

Established: 1991
🍇 14 has. 🍷 100%

VIDAL I FERRE RESERVA BRUT NATURE
VIDAL I FERRE RESERVA BRUT
VIDAL I FERRE SEMI-SECO

RAVENTOS GUASCH

Industria, 29-31
08770 Sant Sadurni D'Anoia (Barcelona)
☎: 938 910 400 - Fax: 938 910 425
cava@raventossoler.com
www.raventossoler.com

Established: 1925
🍷 100%

RAVENTÓS SOLER BRUT
MAGNUM RAVENTÓS SOLER RESERVA
BRUT NATURE
RAVENTÓS SOLER RESERVA BRUT NATURE
RAVENTÓS SOLER SEMI-SECO
RAVENTÓS SOLER SECO

RAVENTÓS I BLANC

Plaça del Roure
08770 Sant Sadurní D'Anoia (Barcelona)
☎: 938 183 262 - Fax: 938 312 500
raventos@raventos.com
www.raventos.com

Established: 1986
🍾 172 🛢 683,000 litres 🍇 90 has.
🍷 80% 🌐20%-DE -UK -CH -AT -BE -NL -
US -JP

L'HEREU DE RAVENTÓS I BLANC BRUT
60% macabeo, 20% xarel.lo, 20% parellada

85 Brilliant yellow. Intense, fresh aroma with fine citrus notes (tangerines, orange blossom) and a nuance of lees. Dry, fresh, creamy palate with fine bitter notes and hints of herbs, very pleasant.

RAVENTÓS I BLANC 2000 RESERVA BRUT
50% macabeo, 30% xarel.lo, 15% parellada, 5% chardonnay

83 Very pale straw with fine beads. Not very intense aroma with a hint of freshness and a nuance of ripe fruit and reduction (fine lees). Dry, creamy, fresh palate with good acidity-crianza balance, long.

RAVENTÓS I BLANC 1999 GRAN RESERVA
BRUT NATURE
40% xarel.lo, 30% macabeo, 25% parellada, 5% chardonnay

84 Straw-coloured. Intense aroma with fine notes of crianza (withered petals, bakery) well-integrated

with the white fruit and citrus fruit. Dry, very fresh palate with good acidity, without obvious crianza expression, grapefruit in the retronasal passage.

RAVENTÓS I BLANC GRAN RESERVA
PERSONAL MANUEL RAVENTÓS 1998 BRUT
NATURE
40% parellada, 25% macabeo, 25% xarel.lo, 10% chardonnay

85 Pale yellow with a golden glint. Fresh aroma of ripe white fruit with hints of fine lees. Dry, creamy palate (well-integrated beads) with fine bitter notes, good acidity.

L'HEREU DE RAVENTÓS I BLANC 2002
BRUT NATURE

RECAREDO

Tamarit, 10
08770 Sant Sadurní D'Anoia (Barcelona)
☎: 938 910 214 - Fax: 938 911 697
cava@recaredo.es
www.recaredo.com

Established: 1924
🍾 145 🛢 400,000 litres 🍇 45 has.
🍷 98% 🌐2%-AD -DE -JP

RECAREDO 2001 BRUT NATURE
45% xarel.lo, 40% macabeo, 15% parellada

83 Straw-coloured with a greenish glint and fine beads. Fresh aroma of white fruit with a fine nuance of reduction. Dry, creamy palate (well-integrated beads) with a bitter nuance of crianza (dried herbs, almonds), good acidity.

RECAREDO BRUT DE BRUTS 1999 BRUT
NATURE
60% macabeo, 40% xarel.lo

88 Pale yellow with fine beads. Intense aroma with excellent crianza expression (lees) and varietal typification (Macabeo) with a ripe citrus fruit nuance. Very dry, fresh, fine aroma, rich in nuances (herbs, sweet almonds, lime, fennel), excellent acidity.

RENÉ BARBIER

Afueras, s/n
08770 Sant Sadurní D'Anoia (Barcelona)
☎: 938 917 000 - Fax: 938 911 254
renebarbier@renebarbier.es

RENÉ BARBIER MEDITERRANEAM RESERVA
BRUT

REXACH BAQUES

Santa María, 12
08736 Guardiola de Font-Rubí (Barcelona)
☎: 938 979 170 - Fax: 938 979 335

Established: 1929

DO CAVA

🗄 70,000 litres 🍇 19 has. 🍾 100%

REXACH BAQUES 1999 GRAN RESERVA BRUT NATURE

RIMARTS

Avenida Cal Mir, 42
08770 Sant Sadurní D'Anoia (Barcelona)
☎: 938 912 775 - Fax: 938 912 775
rimarts@rimarts.net
www.rimarts.net

Established: 1987
🍾 90% 🌐10%

UVAE 2002 BRUT NATURE

89 Brilliant gold. Intense aroma, very fine and rich in nuances (lees, flowers, citrus fruit, spicy and honeyed notes, with a suggestion of broom). Powerful, fresh, complex, creamy palate, excellent citrus acidity and Crianza expression (nuts), very long.

RIMARTS GRAN RESERVA BRUT NATURE
30% xarel.lo, 30% macabeo, 30% parellada, 10% chardonnay

86 Straw-coloured with a greenish hue. Intense, very fine aroma with excellent expression of white fruit and reduction notes (lees, bitter almonds) and hints of honey. Dry, creamy, fresh, somewhat oily palate with well-crafted crianza, refreshing acidity.

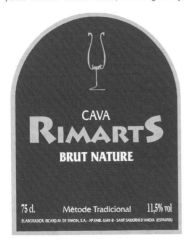

RIMARTS CHARDONNAY RESERVA ESPECIAL BRUT NATURE
macabeo, xarel.lo, parellada, chardonnay

86 Straw-coloured with a golden glint. Intense aroma, ripe with white fruit, fine hints of lees and the toasty notes of crianza (nuts, cumin). Dry palate, rich in bitter nuances with excellent acidity.

RIMARTS BRUT NATURE
70% chardonnay, 30% xarel.lo

81 Straw-coloured. Intense aroma of withered petals with crianza expression and a nuance of ripe apple. Flavourful, fresh palate with notes of green fruit pulp, without obvious crianza nuances, long.

RIMARTS BRUT
RIMARTS SEMI-SECO

ROBERT J. MUR

Rambla de la Generalitat s/n
08770 Sant Sadurni D'Anoia (Barcelona)
☎: 938 910 800 - Fax: 938 911 747
roberjmur@robertjmur.com
www.robertjmur.com

Established: 1897
🍇 20 has. 🍾 85% 🌐15%-DE -UK -FR -JP -MX -US -CA

ROBERT J. MUR TRADICIÓ 2001 RESERVA BRUT
40% parellada, 30% xarel.lo, 30% macabeo

80 Straw-coloured with a golden glint. Fine aroma with a good crianza expression over a nuance of slightly fresh white fruit. Dry palate with fine bitter notes (Mediterranean herbs), creamy, good acidity.

ROBERT J. MUR 2000 GRAN RESERVA BRUT NATURE
40% macabeo, 40% xarel.lo, 20% parellada

89 Yellow straw with a golden glint. Slightly subtle aroma with fine nuances of fennel and fine lees. Dry, very elegant palate with creamy hints, excellent crianza-acidity balance, rich in nuances, very long.

ROBERT J. MUR TRADICIÓ 2001 RESERVA BRUT NATURE
40% parellada, 30% xarel.lo, 30% macabeo

83 Brilliant yellow with a golden glint. Intense aroma with fine notes of crianza (lees, withered petals, hint of cumin). Fresh palate with bitter notes (nuts, mountain herbs) and hints of ripe limes.

ROBERT J. MUR MILLESIMÉE 1997 BRUT NATURE
50% xarel.lo, 50% chardonnay

79 Brilliant gold. Intense aroma with fine notes of crianza and fresh overtones (citrus fruit). Creamy palate with fine bitter notes, a nuance of white fruit and overtones of acidic freshness.

Caves ROGER GOULART

Major, 6
08635 Sant Esteve Sesrovires (Barcelona)
☎: 934 191 000 - Fax: 934 193 170
rogergoulart@rogergoulart.com

Established: 1882

🍷 80% 🌐20%

ROGER GOULART 2000 RESERVA BRUT
NATURE
macabeo, xarel.lo, parellada

86 Brilliant straw. Intense aroma, of great finesse, very fresh with a hint of citrus notes and fresh herbs. Dry palate with excellent acidity balance and a toasty suggestion of crianza.

ROGER GOULART BRUT ROSÉ
garnacha, monastrell

81 Pale pink. Aroma of fresh strawberries and withered petals, quite ripe. Flavourful palate with red fruit, slightly vinous with a slightly toasty finish; good bittersweet balance.

ROGER GOULART GRAN CUVÉE 1999
EXTRA BRUT
macabeo, xarel.lo, parellada

85 Pale yellow with a golden hue. Intense, very fine aroma with excellent balance between ripe fruit and crianza (withered petals, nuts). Dry, creamy palate with fine bitter notes and good acidity.

ROGER GOULART RESERVA BRUT
macabeo, xarel.lo, parellada

85 Straw-coloured. Intense, very fresh aroma with hints of citrus fruit and herbs, without great crianza expression but with fine nuances. Dry, fresh, elegant palate with excellent acidity.

ROGER GOULART GRAN RESERVA EXTRA
BRUT
macabeo, xarel.lo, parellada, chardonnay

87 Straw-coloured with a golden glint and. fine beads. Fine aroma, without great crianza expression with notes of white fruit and a suggestion of fresh herbs, fennel and citrus fruit. Fresh palate with excellent acidity, creamy hints and a suggestion of grapefruit in the retronasal passage.

ROGER GOULART GRAN RESERVA

Cava ROMAGOSA TORNÉ

Finca - Rodamilans - La Serra
08731 Sant Martí Sarroca (Barcelona)
☎: 938 991 353 - Fax: 938 991 558
montse@romagosatorné.com

Established: 1864

🍷 75% 🌐25%-BE -DE

ROMAGOSA TORNÉ BRUT

ROMAGOSA TORNÉ RESERVA BRUT
ROMAGOSA TORNÉ GRAN RESERVA BRUT
ROMAGOSA TORNÉ BRUT DE BRUTS
RESERVA BRUT
ROMAGOSA TORNÉ BRUT NATURE
ROMAGOSA TORNÉ SEMI-SECO

ROSELL GALLART

Cl. Montserrat, 56
08770 Sant Sadurní d'Anoia (Barcelona)
☎: 938 912 073 - Fax: 938 183 539
rosellgallart@terra.es

Established: 1845

🍇 5 has. 🍷 100%

ROSELL GALLART BRUT NATURE
50% xarel.lo, 30% macabeo, 20% parellada

87 Golden yellow with fine and persistent beads. Intense aroma of ripe apples and fine reduction notes (nuts, pâtisserie). Dry, bitter palate with excellent crianza expression, well-balanced and long.

TERESA MATA I GARRIGA BRUT NATURE
50% xarel.lo, 30% macabeo, 20% parellada

84 Straw-coloured with a golden hue. Intense, ripe, very elegant aroma with a fine reduction nuance (withered petals, honey, fennel). Dry, creamy, bitter palate (almonds, fine herbs) with a fresh lime in the finish.

ROSELL RAVENTOS CRISTAL BRUT
NATURE

ROSELL I FORMOSA

Rambla de la Generalitat, 14
08770 Sant Sadurní D'Anoia (Barcelona)
☎: 938 911 013 - Fax: 938 911 967
rformosa@roselliformosa.com
www.roselliformosa.com

Established: 1948

🍷 99% 🌐1%-DE -NL -DK

ROSELL I FORMOSA BRUT
45% macabeo, 30% xarel.lo, 25% parellada

78 Pale yellow. Intense, ripe aroma with a hint of flowers and fine lees. Flavourful, generous palate with fresh overtones, fine notes of white fruit and citrus fruit, pleasant.

ROSELL I FORMOSA BRUT ROSÉ
50% garnacha, 50% monastrell

82 Brilliant cherry. Intense aroma with notes of ripe red fruit, hints of petals and fine lees. Dry, flavourful, very fresh palate with well-integrated beads, fine bitter notes and a hint of sweet fruit.

DAURAT "BRUT DE BRUTS" BRUT NATURE
macabeo, xarel.lo, parellada

82 Pale yellow. Intense aroma of ripe fruit with a fine suggestion of crianza (lees, flowers). Fresh, dry palate, rich in fruit nuances (apples, ripe limes pulp) with hints of aniseed and mountain herbs.

ROSELL I FORMOSA GRAN RESERVA SEMI-SECO
45% macabeo, 30% xarel.lo, 25% parellada

80 Pale yellow. Quite intense aroma with fine lees over a floral nuance of ripe white fruit. Generous, ripe palate with fine bitter notes and hints of citrus fruit in the retronasal passage, well-balanced.

ROSELL I FORMOSA GRAN RESERVA BRUT NATURE

ROSMAS

Provença, 10
08770 Sant Sadurní D'Anoia (Barcelona)
☎: 938 911 041 - Fax: 938 183 021
rosmas@rosmas.com
www.rosmas.com

Established: 1950
🗄 17,000 litres 🚩 100%

ROSMAS 2001 GRAN RESERVA BRUT NATURE
ROSMAS 2002 BRUT NATURE
ROSMAS BRUT DEL RACO 2002 BRUT NATURE

ROURA

Vall de Rials, s/n
08328 Alella (Barcelona)
☎: 933 527 456 - Fax: 933 524 339
roura.mari@terra.es
www.roura.es

Established: 1987
🌐 270 🗄 373,000 litres 🌿 45 has.
🚩 70% 🍇30%-SE -DE -US -BE -UK -JP - CH -FR

ROURA BRUT
50% chardonnay, 50% xarel.lo

81 Golden with a fine and persistent bead. Intense, ripe aroma with mild reduction notes (withered petals, pâtisserie, nuts). Dry, and creamy on the palate with spicy, bitter notes, a classic expression of the crianza.

ROURA 5 * BRUT NATURE
50% chardonnay, 50% xarel.lo

85 Brilliant gold. Intense aroma of ripe apples with a good expression of traditional crianza and predominant fine reduction notes (spices, nuts, bakery). Fresh, dry and creamy on the palate with quality bitter notes and good acidity.

ROURA BRUT NATURE
50% chardonnay, 50% xarel.lo

82 Pale gold. Intense, ripe aroma with predominant reduction notes (lees, withered petals, nuts). Dry palate with a well-integrated bead, fine bitter crianza notes (almonds, cumin), hints of wax and good acidity.

ROVELLATS

Finca Rovellats
08731 Sant Marti Sarroca (Barcelona)
☎: 934 880 575 - Fax: 934 880 819
rovellats@cavasrovellats.com
ww.cavasrovellats.com

Established: 1940
🌿 210 has. 🚩 75% 🍇25%

ROVELLATS 2000 GRAN RESERVA BRUT NATURE
60% xarel.lo, 26% macabeo, 14% parellada

85 Straw-coloured with a golden glint. Not very intense aroma with finesse, ripe white fruit, notes of fine reduction (lees) and hints of citrus fruit. Flavourful palate with well-integrated beads, notes of fennel and herbs, bitter almonds and good acidity.

ROVELLATS 2002 RESERVA ESPECIAL BRUT ROSÉ
monastrell, tempranillo

87 Brilliant raspberry. Intense, ripe aroma with a mild reduction nuance (lees, petals, crystallised fruit). Dry, fruity palate with well-integrated beads and fine bitter crianza notes, excellent symmetry.

ROVELLATS IMPERIAL 2001 BRUT
ROVELLATS 2002 RESERVA ESPECIAL BRUT
ROVELLATS CHARDONNAY 2000 GRAN RESERVA BRUT NATURE
ROVELLATS EXTRA 2002 RESERVA SEMI-SECO
ROVELLATS MASIA S. XV MILLESIMÉE 1998 GRAN RESERVA BRUT NATURE

Cavas SANSTRAVÉ

General Mola, 10
43412 Solivella (Tarragona)
☎: 977 892 165 - Fax: 977 892 073
bodega@sanstrave.com
www.sanstrave.com

Established: 1985
🛢 60 🍶 80,000 litres 🍇 22 has.
🍷 85% 🌐15%

SANSTRAVÉ GRAN RESERVA BRUT NATURE
macabeo, parellada, chardonnay

85 Pale yellow with a fine and persistent bead.
Not very intense, fine aroma with notes of crianza
(lees, withered petals) and well-integrated white
fruit. Dry palate, rich in crianza nuances (bitter
almonds, herbs), good acidity.

Cooperativa Vinícola SARRAL

Avenida de la Conca, 33
43424 Sarral (Tarragona)
☎: 977 890 031 - Fax: 977 890 136
cavaportell@covisal.es
www.cava-portell.com

Established: 1907
🛢 125 🍶 7,000,000 litres 🍇 1,115 has.
🍷 85% 🌐15%-DE -DK -MX -FR

PORTELL 2003 BRUT ROSÉ
100% trepat

81 Brilliant raspberry with a coppery glint.
Intense aroma of red stone fruit, fine spicy notes
and lees, with a slightly sweet nuance. Dry palate
with fine bitter notes, fresh, good acidity.

PORTELL 2002 BRUT NATURE
80% macabeo, 20% parellada

75 Pale yellow with a greenish glint. Not very
intense aroma of white fruit with hints of citrus fruit
and lees. Dry, fresh palate with bitter notes (lemon
pips), lacking balance.

PETRIGNANO 1999 GRAN RESERVA BRUT
NATURE
85% macabeo, 15% parellada

83 Pale yellow with a greenish glint. Intense
aroma of green fruit with fine lees, citrus fruit and
herby hints. Dry palate with fine bitter crianza
notes (almonds, fennel) and good acidity.

PORTELL VINTAGE 2000 GRAN RESERVA
BRUT NATURE
65% macabeo, 35% parellada

78 Pale yellow with a greenish hue. Not very
intense aroma of ripe white fruit with fresh overtones and hints of lees. Dry, slightly creamy palate
without great nuances, pleasant.

PORTELL 2003 ROSÉ SEMI-SECO
100% trepat

78 Not very deep raspberry with coppery hues.
Quite intense aroma with predominant reduction
notes and a nuance of crystallised fruit. Fresh,
very sweet palate, without great nuances.

PORTELL 2003 BRUT
PORTELL MAGNUM BRUT NATURE
PORTELL 2003 WHITE SEMI-SECO

SEGURA VIUDAS

Apdo. Correos, 30
08775 Torrelavit (Barcelona)
☎: 938 917 070 - Fax: 938 996 006
seguraviudas@seguraviudas.com
www.seguraviudas.com

Established: 1954
🛢 2,100 🍶 25,000,000 litres 🍇 50 has.
🍷 40% 🌐60%

HEREDAD RESERVA BRUT

84 Straw-coloured with a greenish edge. Fine
aroma of tropical fruit (papaya, a suggestion of
citrus fruit) with hints of herbs and well-balanced,
elegant lees. Flavourful, slightly sweetish palate,
fresh but with more fruit character than crianza,
distinctive.

SEGURA VIUDAS BRUT VINTAGE 1999
67% macabeo, 33% parellada

86 Yellow straw with a golden glint. Intense
aroma with a nuance of ripe white fruit, hints of
fine reduction (withered petals, cumin). Dry palate
with fine bitter crianza notes, excellent acidity.

SEGURA VIUDAS CAVA LAVIT BRUT ROSÉ
trepat, garnacha, monastrell

85 Blush with a coppery edge. Intense aroma of
fresh rose petals and harmonised red fruit and
nuts. Flavourful palate, very fresh, expression of
red berry pulp and well-balanced crianza; a pleasant bitter finish.

CONDE DE CARALT CHARDONNAY BRUT
NATURE
85% chardonnay, 15% otras

80 Brilliant straw with a greenish hue. Fresh
aroma with a good varietal profile (ripe apples),
fine reduction notes (withered petals) and a honeyed nuance. Dry, fresh palate, very bitter (almonds,
dried grass), fine suggestion of citrus fruit.

SEGURA VIUDAS ARIA BRUT NATURE

82 Straw-coloured with a greenish glint. Fresh
intense aroma with hints of green fruit and bitter
almonds and a nuance of sweet limes. Fresh, dry
palate with fine bitter notes, pleasant although without great crianza expression.

DO CAVA

SEGURA VIUDAS LAVIT BRUT NATURE
macabeo, parellada

86 Brilliant straw with a golden hue. Not very intense aroma but of great finesse with white fruit and fine reduction notes (lees, dried herbs). Dry palate, with fresh overtones, fine bitter notes and an excellent crianza-acidity balance, very long.

TORRE GALIMANY 2000 BRUT NATURE
xarel.lo, macabeo, parellada

88 Brilliant golden yellow. Intense aroma, with fresh overtones, ripe apples, fine reduction notes (honey, withered petals, nuts). Dry, creamy palate, rich in nuances with fine bitter notes, well-balanced, long.

SEGURA VIUDAS RESERVA BRUT

SIGNAT

Escultor Llimona, s/n
08328 Alella (Barcelona)
☎: 935 403 400 - Fax: 935 401 471
signat@eresmas.com
Established: 1987
▤ 70,000 litres ▥ 7 has. ▼ 95% ☁5%

CAVA SIGNAT BRUT NATURE
40% xarel.lo, 30% parellada, 20% macabeo, 10% chardonnay

88 Pale yellow with a golden glint. Intense, ripe aroma (white stone fruit) with fine crianza notes (lees, petals, nuts). Dry on the palate with a slightly oily texture, rich in nuances, with excellent fruit-crianza-acidity symmetry.

SIGNAT RESERVA IMPERIAL BRUT
20% macabeo, 35% xarel.lo, 30% parellada, 10% chardonnay

91 Straw-coloured with a golden hue. Intense, fresh, very elegant aroma with excellent crianza expression (lees, anise) and a green fruit nuance. Fresh on the palate with fine bitter notes (almonds, herbs, cumin), a powerful aroma in the retronasal passage and hints of minerals.

SIMÓ DE PALAU

Carretera N-240, km. 39
43440 L'Esplugá de Francoli (Tarragona)
☎: 977 862 599 - Fax: 977 875 039
caves@simodepalau.com
www.simodepalau.com
Established: 1991
▼ 75% ☁25%

SIMÓ DE PALAU BRUT
SIMÓ DE PALAU BRUT NATURE
SIMÓ DE PALAU GRAN RESERVA BRUT NATURE

SOLA RAVENTÓS

Industria, 38-40
08770 Sant Sadurní D'Anoia (Barcelona)
☎: 938 910 837 - Fax: 938 911 144
cava@solaraventos.com
www.solaraventos.com
Established: 1898
▤ 10,000 litres ▼ 100%

RESERVADA CRIANZA BRUT
BRUT DE LA GAFA RESERVA BRUT NATURE
MARÍA ROIG RESERVA ESPECIAL BRUT NATURE
SOLA II GRAN RESERVA BRUT NATURE

SOLER Y DEGOLLADA

Barri La Serra d Sabanell, s/n
08736 Font-Rubí (Barcelona)
☎: 938 988 220 - Fax: 938 988 681
info@cavamartinsoler.com
www.cavamartinsoler.com
Established: 1965
▤ 325,000 litres ▥ 20 has.
▼ 98% ☁2%-DE -FR -BE

MARTIN SOLER MASIA 1616 EXTRA BRUT
30% macabeo, 30% xarel.lo, 20% chardonnay, 20% parellada

84 Straw-coloured. Toasty aroma of fine pâtisserie over flowers and fine lees. Flavourful palate with elegant beads, generous with fruit and crianza symmetry and perfumed soap in the retronasal passage.

MARTIN SOLER BRUT NATURE
35% macabeo, 30% xarel.lo, 25% parellada

83 Straw-coloured with a golden glint. Intense aroma of ripe fruit with hints of bakery and petals. Dry, creamy palate with fine bitter notes (nuts, herbs, cumin), good acidity.

MARTIN SOLER ROSADO BRUT NATURE
100% trepat

84 Fairly deep salmon. Powerful aroma of red stone fruit with spicy and a mildely sweet nuance and hints of fine lees. Dry palate with fine bitter notes, a rich bittersweet nuance and hints of ripe fruit and nuts and crystallised fruits in the retronasal passage.

MARTIN SOLER BRUT
MARTIN SOLER ROSADO BRUT
MARTIN SOLER SEMI-SECO
MARTIN SOLER ROSÉ SEMI-SECO
MARTIN SOLER EXTRA SECO

DO CAVA

SOLER-JOVÉ

Finca Prunamala, Parc. 2
08770 Sant Sadurní D'Anoia (Barcelona)
☎: 938 910 503 - Fax: 938 911 153
solerjove@sct.ictnet.es
www.solerjove.com

Established: 1985

🌐 200 🗄 275,000 litres 🍷 60%

🌍40%-DE -UK -DK -DK -SE

SOLER JOVÉ 1999 GRAN RESERVA BRUT
SOLER JOVÉ 2000 GRAN RESERVA BRUT
NATURE

Bodegues SUMARROCA

El Rebato, s/n
08739 Subirats (Barcelona)
☎: 938 911 092 - Fax: 938 911 778
sumarroca@sumarroca.es
www.sumarroca.es

Established: 1983

🌐 727 🗄 3,500,000 litres 🌱 460 has.

🍷 80% 🌍20%-US -CH -DE -GT -JP -NL -
UK -SE -BR -BE -SV

CAVA SUMARROCA RESERVA BRUT
42% parellada, 27% macabeo, 24% xarel.lo, 7% chardonnay

83 Pale yellow, with a greenish hue. Intense very fresh aroma with notes of green apples, fine lees and a nuance of ripe lemons. Fresh, dry palate, bitter (almonds) with well-integrated beads, without great crianza expression but very pleasant.

CAVA SUMARROCA GRAN BRUT ALLIER
40% chardonnay, 40% xarel.lo, 20% parellada

87 Pale yellow with coppery hues. Intense aroma of fine toasty notes of oak, hints of lees, balsamic flavours and nuts. Dry, creamy palate with fresh overtones, fine bitter crianza notes, well-balanced.

CAVA SUMARROCA PINOT NOIR BRUT ROSÉ
100% pinot noir

84 Brilliant raspberry. Not very intense aroma with a certain finesse of red stone fruit with a balsamic nuance and lees. Dry, creamy palate with fine bitter notes, rich in varietal expression, slightly high acidity.

SUMARROCA GRAN BRUT BRUT
60% chardonnay, 30% parellada, 10% macabeo

85 Pale yellow with a golden glint. Powerful aroma, ripe, fine reduction notes (nuts, lees), on a honeyed nuance. Dry, creamy palate, fine bitter notes, good acidity and crianza expression.

CAVA SUMARROCA GRAN RESERVA BRUT NATURE
42% parellada, 27% macabeo, 24% xarel.lo, 7% chardonnay

83 Brilliant golden yellow. Intense aroma with predominant reduction notes (nuts, hints of varnish). Dry palate with fine bitter notes, high in acidity.

CAVA SUMARROCA CUVÉE 1999 GRAN RESERVA BRUT NATURE
60% chardonnay, 40% parellada

83 Pale yellow with a golden glint. Intense aroma, fine reduction notes (almonds, balsamic flavours). Dry palate with a certain freshness, bitter (herbs, nuts), good acidity.

TORELLÓ

Can Martí de Baix Apdo. 8,
08770 Sant Sadurní D'Anoia (Barcelona)
☎: 938 910 793 - Fax: 938 910 877
torello@torello.es
www.torello.es

Established: 1951

🌐 60 🗄 700,000 litres 🌱 110 has.

🍷 85% 🌍15%-JP -MX -IT -AD

TORELLÓ 2001 GRAN RESERVA BRUT
39% xarel.lo, 36% macabeo, 25% parellada

86 Straw-coloured with a greenish hue and fine and persistent beads. Fresh aroma of great finesse and green apples with fine reduction notes. Dry palate with excellent acidity-fruit-crianza balance, notes of citrus fruits, bitterness and dried grass.

GRAN TORELLÓ 2000 GRAN RESERVA BRUT NATURE
38% xarel.lo, 36% macabeo, 26% parellada

85 Very pale with a greenish glint. Intense aroma of great finesse with an excellent crianza expression (lees, withered petals, dried herbs) and a nuance of grapefruit. Very dry, creamy palate with bitter notes, refreshing acidity.

TORELLÓ 2000 GRAN RESERVA BRUT NATURE
41% xarel.lo, 38% macabeo, 21% parellada

86 Very pale with a greenish glint. Intense aroma with predominant reduction notes (withered petals, fine lees) over a nuance of ripe white fruit. Dry, creamy palate with fine bitter notes and a hint of grapefruit, good acidity.

TORELLÓ 2001 BRUT ROSÉ
TORELLÓ MAGNUM 2000 GRAN RESERVA BRUT NATURE

Cavas y Vinos TORRE ORIA

Carretera Pontón - Utiel, km. 3
46390 Derramador - Requena (Valencia)
☎: 962 320 289 - Fax: 962 320 311

info.torreoria@natra.es
www.torreoria.com

Established: 1897

🏭 4,500 📊 4,500,000 litres 🍇 20 has.

🍷 35% 🌐65%-DK -DK -SE -FI -DE -UK -
NL -BE -CH -RU -LT -JP -PH MK -US -MX

TORRE ORIA BRUT
100% macabeo

77 Pale yellow with a greenish glint. Intense aroma of ripe apples with a reduction nuance (withered petals, honey). Dry and flavourful on the palate with bitter hints (dried herbs, almonds) and good acidity.

TORRE ORIA RESERVA BRUT
90% macabeo, 10% parellada

79 Pale yellow with greenish nuances. Intense aroma of ripe fruit with a reduction nuance (honey, withered petals, herbs). Fresh and dry on the palate with bitter crianza notes (almonds, cumin), pleasant.

MARQUÉS DE REQUENA BRUT NATURE
90% macabeo, 10% parellada

74 Straw-coloured with a greenish glint. Powerful, ripe aroma with a not very fine crianza nuance. Dry, fresh and creamy on the palate with bitter notes and a slightly acidic edge.

TORRE ORIA BRUT NATURE
90% macabeo, 10% parellada

73 Pale yellow with a greenish glint. Not very intense aroma of white fruit without great crianza expression. Dry, fresh and creamy on the palate with bitter notes and high acidity.

TORRE ORIA CENTENARIO BRUT NATURE
90% macabeo, 10% parellada

80 Golden yellow. Intense aroma of ripe apples with a nuance of withered petals, honey and crème pâtissière. Dry, fresh and creamy on the palate (well-integrated beads) with fine bitter notes (nuts) and good acidity.

TORRE ORIA EXTRA SEMI-SECO
100% macabeo

75 Pale yellow with a golden hue. Intense aroma of ripe white fruit with a fine reduction (honey, withered petals). Flavourful and creamy on the palate with bittersweet notes and a crystallised fruit nuance; pleasant.

TORRE ORIA ROSÉ SEMI-SECO
100% garnacha

77 Intense raspberry. Not very intense aroma of ripe red fruit with hints of freshness. Fresh and fruity on the palate with spicy hints of skins and a crystallised fruit nuance, very pleasant.

TORRENS & MOLINER

Avenida Casetes del Mir, 28
08770 Sant Sadurní D'Anoia (Barcelona)

☎: 938 911 033 - Fax: 938 911 761
tormol@torrensmoliner.com
www.torrensmoliner.com

Established: 1986

📊 25,000 litres 🍇 5 has.

🍷 85% 🌐15%-MX -NL

TORRENS & MOLINER GRAN RESERVA BRUT NATURE

TROBAT

Castelló, 5
17780 Garriguella (Gerona)
☎: 972 530 092 - Fax: 972 552 530
albertsabido@b.mark.es
www. bodegastrobat.com

Established: 1965

🏭 60 📊 300,000 litres 🍷 100%

CELLER TROBAT BRUT

79 Pale yellow with a golden glint. Intense, ripe, fruity aroma with crianza expression (withered petals). Dry, bitter palate, lacking balance.

GRAN AMAT BRUT

84 Pale yellow with a greenish glint. Intense, fruity aroma with a nuance of crystallised fruit, fine lees and hints of honey. Dry, creamy, fresh palate with fine bitter notes, good acidity and hints of nuts in the retronasal passage, very long.

CELLER TROBAT BRUT NATURE

82 Brilliant yellow with a golden glint and fine beads. Intense aroma with predominant notes of ripe white fruit (a crystallised nuance) and hints of fine lees. Dry palate with fine bitter notes and a fruity nuance (apples, grapefruit), good acidity.

Vins-Caves TUTUSAUS

Can Tutusaus, s/n
08795 Olesa de Bonesvalls (Barcelona)
☎: 938 984 155
cavestutusaus@hotmail.com

Established: 1987

🏭 10 📊 20,000 litres 🍇 8 has.

🍷 85% 🌐15%-BE -NL

CAVA TUTUSAUS 2001 BRUT NATURE
xarel.lo, macabeo, parellada, chardonnay

85 Straw-coloured with a golden glint. Intense aroma with excellent crianza expression (fine lees, spices, nuts) over a suggestion of white fruit. Dry palate with fine bitter notes, dried herbs, well-integrated beads and an excellent crianza character.

CAVA TUTUSAUS 2002 BRUT

U MES U FAN TRES

Masia Navinés (Els Pujols)
08736 Font-Rubí (Barcelona)
☎: 938 974 069 - Fax: 938 974 724
navines@interceller.com

Established: 2000
🌐 350 🍾 30 has. 🍇 15% 🌍85%

1 + 1 = 3 2000 BRUT NATURE

87 Straw-coloured with a greenish hue. Clean aroma with predominant notes of herbs, hints of aniseed and toast. Fresh palate evoking a good crianza (toast), green fruit, with a fine bitter finish and good balance.

DOGA 2000

VALLFORMOSA

La Sala, 45
08735 Vilobi del Penedés (Barcelona)
☎: 938 978 286 - Fax: 938 978 355
vallformosa@vallformosa.es
www.vallformosa.es

Established: 1865
🌐 2,500 🛢 5,200,000 litres 🍾 397 has.
🍇 73% 🌍27%-UE -SAM

CARLA DE VALLFORMOSA RESERVA BRUT
30% macabeo, 30% parellada, 40% xarel.lo

83 Pale yellow. Quite intense aroma, with predominant notes of ripe white fruit and a fine reduction nuance. Dry, fresh palate, fine bitter notes, balsamic hints in the retronasal passage.

CHANTAL DE VALLFORMOSA BRUT ROSÉ
80% garnacha, 20% monastrell

79 Fairly deep intense salmon. Powerful aroma of very ripe red fruit, hints of petals and pâtisserie. Flavourful palate, a nuance of sweetness, without great crianza expression.

GALA DE VALLFORMOSA 1999 RESERVA BRUT
25% macabeo, 25% xarel.lo, 25% parellada, 25% chardonnay

86 Yellow straw with a golden glint. Quite intense ripe aroma with fine reduction notes (lees, withered petals) and a honeyed nuance. Generous palate with rich bitter crianza notes, well-integrated beads, well-balanced and long.

ORIOL BRUT
60% parellada, 40% chardonnay

70 Straw-coloured with a greenish edge. Aroma with notes of yeasts without great fruit nuances. Flavourful palate, with acidity-bitterness balance and herbs in the finish.

VALLFORMOSA BRUT
35% macabeo, 30% xarel.lo, 35% parellada

84 Pale yellow with a greenish glint. Intense aroma of green fruit with a nuance of fine lees, hints of wax and lemon peel. Dry, very fresh palate with fine bitter notes (herbs, almonds) and ripe limes in the retronasal passage.

ERIC DE VALLFORMOSA BRUT NATURE
40% chardonnay, 60% parellada

83 Straw-coloured. Intense aroma of fine lees with notes of hazelnuts and honey and a nuance of flowers. Herbaceous, fresh palate with good acidity; very pleasant bitter notes.

VALLFORMOSA BRUT NATURE
40% macabeo, 30% xarel.lo, 30% parellada

82 Pale yellow. Quite intense aroma, very fine, fruity with hints of balsamic flavours and lees. Dry, creamy palate, fine bitter notes, good acidity.

VALLFORMOSA SEMI-SECO
35% macabeo, 30% xarel.lo, 35% parellada

85 Straw-coloured with a greenish glint. Intense very fresh aroma of green apples with fine reduction notes and hints of citrus fruit. Generous palate, rich in nuances with notes of crystallised fruit and a flavourful bitter nuance of crianza, excellent acidity.

VALLFORMOSA EXTRA SECO
40% macabeo, 30% xarel.lo, 30% parellada

84 Yellow straw with a greenish hue. Not very intense aroma, a certain finesse, a ripe fruit nuance and fine notes of petals. Creamy palate, fine bitter notes with a nuance of crystallised fruit, well-balanced.

VALLORT VINYATERS

Ca la Marta
08737 Torrelles de Foix (Barcelona)
☎: 677 503 267 - Fax: 938 180 612
vallort@airtel.net

Established: 2000
🛢 250,000 litres 🍇 100%

VALLORT VINYATERS 1999

Celler VELL

Partida Mas Solanes, s/n
08770 Sant Sadurní D'Anoia (Barcelona)
☎: 938 910 290 - Fax: 938 183 246
info@cellervell.com
www.cellervell.com

Established: 1954
🛢 20,000 litres 🍾 2 has. 🍇 98% 🌍2%

CELLER VELL EXTRA BRUT
xarel.lo, macabeo, parellada, chardonnay

83 Straw-coloured with a golden hue. Intense aroma with notes of white fruit, fine reduction notes (lees, withered petals). Dry and creamy on the palate (well-integrated beads) with fresh overtones, bitter and quality citrus hints.

CELLER VELL ROSÉ EXTRA BRUT
70% garnacha, 30% pinot noir

80 Brilliant raspberry. Not very intense aroma with fresh overtones of red stone fruit and hints of lees. Dry, fresh and slightly creamy on the palate with fine bitter and citrus notes.

ESTRUCH CLASSIC BRUT NATURE
xarel.lo, parellada, macabeo, chardonnay

84 Brilliant pale yellow. Fairly intense aroma with fresh overtones of green fruit and a nuance of fine lees. Fresh, flavourful and slightly creamy palate, good acidity.

EL CELLER VELL BRUT
CELLER VELL ESTRUCH RESERVA EXTRA BRUT
EL CELLER VELL BRUT NATURE
EL CELLER VELL SEMI-SECO
EL CELLER VELL ROSÉ SEMI-SECO

Caves VIDAL I FERRÉ

Nou, 6
43815 Les Pobles (Tarragona)
☎: 977 638 554 - Fax: 977 638 554
vidaliferre@teleline.es
Established: 1991
🍇 24 has. 🍷 100%

VIDAL I FERRÉ RESERVA BRUT
macabeo, xarel.lo, parellada

81 Brilliant straw with a greenish glint. Not very intense aroma of white fruit with fine reduction notes (withered petals, fennel). Fresh on the palate with hints of ripe apple and fine bitter notes; well-balanced.

VIDAL I FERRÉ RESERVA BRUT NATURE
macabeo, xarel.lo, parellada

85 Pale yellow with a golden hue. Intense, very elegant aroma with notes of ripe apples, fine toasty crianza and hints of lees, cumin and fennel. Fresh and dry on the palate, slightly creamy with fine bitter crianza notes and good acidity.

VIDAL I FERRÉ SEMI-SECO
macabeo, xarel.lo, parellada

83 Pale yellow with a greenish glint. Powerful aroma of white fruit with hints of a fine reduction (lees, anise). Fresh and creamy on the palate with notes of crystallised fruit, excellent acidity and hints of ripe lemon.

Celler Cooperatiu
VILAFRANCA DEL PENEDÉS

Camí de Sant Pau Paratge les Clotes s/n
08720 Vilafranca del Penedés (Barcelona)
☎: 938 171 035 - Fax: 938 900 418
cellervila@cellervila.com - cellervila.com
Established: 1933
🍾 300 🍶 10,000,000 litres 🍇 1,055 has.
🍷 90% 🌐10%-IE -JP -DE -BE -NL

CASTELLER BRUT
xarel.lo, macabeo, parellada

80 Straw-coloured with golden nuances and quite robust beads. Intense aroma with a hint of lees and ripe white fruit. Dry, flavourful palate with fine bitter notes, without great complexity but with good crianza character.

CHENINE BRUT
macabeo, parellada, xarel.lo

76 Pale, very subdued. Fresh aroma without great nuances with a hint of lees. Slightly better on the palate, dry, quite flavourful with bitter notes and well-integrated fruit but without an obvious crianza character.

CASTELLER BRUT NATURE
macabeo, parellada, xarel.lo

77 Pale yellow. Subtle aroma with a suggestion of ripe white fruit and hints of herbs. Dry, fresh palate with fine bitter notes, without great crianza expression.

CASTELLER GRAN RESERVA BRUT NATURE
40% macabeo, 40% parellada, 20% xarel.lo

80 Yellow straw. Intense aroma of white fruit with a hint of lees and citrus fruit. Dry, flavourful palate with Mediterranean herbs, fine bitter notes and ripe limes; lacks crianza expression.

CHENINE BRUT NATURE
macabeo, parellada, xarel.lo

75 Pale. Not very intense aroma with a hint of white fruit. Dry palate without great crianza expression with hints of citrus fruit and mountain herbs.

CHENINE SEMI-SECO
macabeo, parellada, xarel.lo

79 Brilliant straw with fine bead. Intense aroma with a hint of freshness and a suggestion of withered petals and pâtisserie. Dry, fresh, flavourful, supple palate without great nuances and with scarcely any sweet notes.

VINÍCOLA DE NULLES

Raval Sant Joan, 7
43887 Nulles (Tarragona)
☎: 977 602 622 - Fax: 977 602 622
casinulles@casinulles.com

www.casinulles.com
Established: 1917
⊕ 26 ▤ 3,500,000 litres ▧ 440 has.
🍷 80% 🌐20%-JP -DE -CH

1917 2002 BRUT
ADERNATS 2003 BRUT
CAMPASSOS 2003 BRUT
ADERNATS ELABORACIÓ ARTESANAL
2003 BRUT
ADERNATS BRUT DE BRUTS 2001 BRUT
1917 2002 BRUT NATURE
ADERNATS 2003 BRUT NATURE
CAMPASSOS 2003 BRUT NATURE
ADERNATS ESPECIAL 2001 BRUT NATURE
ADERNATS 2003 SEMI-SECO
CAMPASSOS 2003 SEMI-SECO

VIÑA TORREBLANCA

Finca Masia Torreblanca, s/n
08734 Miquel D'Olérdola (Barcelona)
☎: 938 915 066 - Fax: 938 900 102
torreblanca@retemail.es
Established: 1995
▧ 22 has. 🍷 17% 🌐83%

TORREBLANCA 2001 RESERVA EXTRA BRUT
73% chardonnay, 11% parellada, 9% macabeo, 7% xarel.lo

82 Pale yellow with a golden glint. Intense aroma of ripe white fruit with fine lees. Fresh palate with fine bitter notes, slightly high acidity and citrus hints in the retronasal passage.

TORREBLANCA BRUT
40% parellada, 35% macabeo, 25% xarel.lo

84 Pale yellow with a golden glint. Intense aroma with good crianza expression and a nuance of white fruit. Flavourful palate with well-integrated beads, fine notes of herbs and citrus fruit and excellent acidity and balance.

TORREBLANCA BRUT ROSÉ

82 Very intense blush. Fruity aroma of fresh red stone fruit with fine balanced yeasts. Flavourful, slightly sweet palate with good full-throttle fruit and fine beads; persistent.

MASBLANC EXTRA BRUT
TORREBLANCA EXTRA SECO

Cooperativa de
VITICULTORS DE MONTBLANC

Muralla de Santa Tecla, 54 - 56
43400 Montblanc (Tarragona)
☎: 977 860 016 - Fax: 977 860 929
info@cavapontvell.com
www.cavapontvell.com
Established: 1918

▤ 4,000,000 litres 🍷 95% 🌐5%-DE -UK

PONT VELL 2002 BRUT
60% macabeo, 40% parellada

78 Brilliant straw with a greenish glint. Intense, ripe aroma, not very fine, with predominant reduction notes. Fresh, slightly fruity palate with a suggestion of bitter crianza and lacking great nuances.

PONT VELL 2002 BRUT NATURE
60% macabeo, 40% parellada

77 Straw-coloured with a golden glint. Powerful aroma of ripe apples with reduction notes (withered petals, nuts) and hints of honey. Flavourful, fruity palate with fine bitter notes, without noticeable nuances.

PONT VELL 2002 SEMI-SECO
60% macabeo, 40% parellada

84 Golden straw. Aroma with reduction overtones, fine herb notes and a ripe fruit nuance. Flavourful, quite sweet palate with pleasant bitter notes, well-balanced and fresh.

PONT VELL MIL.LENIUM 2001 RESERVA BRUT NATURE

Cava VIVES AMBRÒS

Mayor, 39
43812 Montferri (Tarragona)
☎: 639 521 652 - Fax: 977 606 579
vives-ambros@tinet.org
wwwtinet.org/vives-ambros
Established: 1996
⊕ 2 ▤ 40,000 litres ▧ 24 has.
🍷 90% 🌐10%-DE -BE -PT

VIVES AMBRÒS 2001 RESERVA BRUT
40% macabeo, 30% xarel.lo, 30% parellada

85 Very pale with a greenish hue. Not very intense aroma with a certain finesse, notes of white fruit and hints of petals and herb-honey. Dry palate with fine bitter notes (almonds), excellent acidity.

VIVES AMBRÒS 2000 GRAN RESERVA BRUT NATURE
40% macabeo, 30% xarel.lo, 20% chardonnay, 10% parellada

84 Pale yellow with a greenish glint and fine beads. Intense aroma of great finesse with white fruit and a nuance of minerals and fine lees with fine balsamic notes. Dry palate with bitter crianza notes and notes of sweet lime in the retronasal passage.

VIVES AMBRÒS TRADICIÓ 1999 GRAN RESERVA BRUT NATURE
60% xarel.lo, 40% macabeo

85 Straw-coloured with a golden glint. Intense aroma of ripe apples, and fine reduction notes (lees, withered petals, honey, nuts). Dry, creamy palate with fine bitter notes (almonds, fine herbs), good acidity.

DO CAVA

Cellers VIVES GAU

Mas de la Basserola
43714 El Pla de Manlleu (Barcelona)
☎: 977 638 619 - Fax: 977 639 196

MAS DE LA BASSEROLA BRUT NATURE
parellada, macabeo

84 Straw-coloured with a greenish hue. Intense, very fresh aroma with notes of green apples, fine yet without great crianza expression. Dry, very fresh palate; fine notes of citrus fruit (sweet limes), hints of bitter almonds, good acidity.

MAS DE LA BASSEROLA SELECCIÓ BRUT NATURE
parellada, macabeo

79 Straw-coloured with a golden glint. Not very intense aroma of white fruit, lacking noticeable nuances. Dry palate with fine bitter notes (sweet almonds, dried herbs), pleasant.

WINNER WINES

Adelfas, 18 3ºB
28007 Madrid (Madrid)
☎: 915 019 042 - Fax: 915 017 794
rsaseta@winnerwines.es
www.winnerwines.es

Established: 1986

🌐 550 📊 1,200,000 litres 🍇 400 has.

🍷 8% 🍇92% -US -CA -MX -DO -PR -SG -JP -CH -IT -FR -DE -SE -FI -DK -BE -AT -DK

JUVENALS RESERVA BRUT
50% macabeo, 30% parellada, 20% xarel.lo

78 Straw-coloured with few beads. Not very intense, clean aroma, fresh overtones and a fine suggestion of lees. Generous palate with white fruit and a suggestion of mild sweetness; hints of herbs, slightly lacking in acidity.

Cava XAMÓS

Virgen de Montserrat, 5
08130 Santa Perpetua de la Mogoda (Barcelona)
☎: 932 462 287 - Fax: 935 604 560
xamos@xamos.net
www.xamos.net

Established: 1987

🌐 15

DOGMA BRUT NATURE

XEPITUS

La Vinya, 19
08770 Sant Sadurní D'Anoia (Barcelona)
☎: 938 912 271

Established: 1975

🍷 100%

XEPITUS BRUT
XEPITUS BRUT NATURE
LA GRAMALLA RESERVA BRUT NATURE
XEPITUS SEMI-SECO
XEPITUS SAECO

DO CIGALES

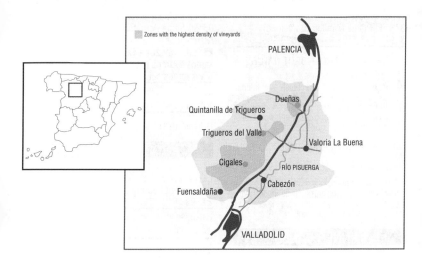

Zones with the highest density of vineyards

PALENCIA
Dueñas
Quintanilla de Trigueros
Trigueros del Valle
Valoria La Buena
Cigales
RÍO PISUERGA
Fuensaldaña
Cabezón
VALLADOLID

NEWS. The year 2003 saw a grape harvest of almost 11 million kilograms, almost doubling the six and a half million of 2002, setting a new record for the DO. 122 Ha of new vineyard entered production, with *Tempranillo* present in 70% of the vineyard, followed by *Garnacha* (16%) and smaller percentages of white grapes used to blend with rosé wines. A year with almost two vintages: an earlier harvest for grapes destined for rosés (in search of greater acidity, freshness and a strong aroma) and a later one, about fifteen days afterwards, for the red varieties.

Cigales was also affected by the hot temperatures of the summer, which reduced the acidity, thereby calling for corrections. More than half of the wines tasted reached a score of 80 points. It is clear that the red wines are in infinitely better shape than the rosés which brought so much fame to the DO. The latter slowly seem to be forming part of the past.

Hectares of Vineyard	No. of Viticulturists	No. of Bodegas	2003 Harvest	2003 Production	Marketing
2,860	660	34 bottlers. 1 producer	Excellent red wines. Very good rosés.	7,700,000 litres	95% Spain 5% foreign

LOCATION. The region stretches to the north of the Duero depression and on both sides of the Pisuerga, bordered by the Cérvalos and the Torozos hills. The vineyards are situated at an altitude of 750 m; the DO extends from part of the municipal area of Valladolid (the wine estate known as 'El Berrocal') to the municipality of Dueñas in Palencia, also including Cabezón de Pisuerga, Cigales, Corcos del Valle, Cubillas de Santa Marte, Fuensaldaña, Mucientes, Quintanilla de Trigueros, San Martín de Valvení, Santovenia de Pisuerga, Trigueros del Valle and Valoria la Buena.

CLIMATE. The climate is continental with Atlantic influences, and is marked by great contrasts in temperature, both yearly and day/night. The summers are extremely dry; the winters are harsh and prolonged, with frequent frost and fog; rainfall is irregular.

SOIL. The soil is sandy and limy with clay loam which is settled on clay and marl. It has an extremely variable limestone content which, depending on the different regions, ranges between 1% and 35%.

TYPES OF WINE.
Rosés:
Cigales Nuevo. Produced with at least 60% of the *Tinto del País* variety and at least 20% of white varieties. The vintage must be displayed on the label.
Cigales. Produced with at least 60% of the *Tinto del País* variety and at least 20% of white varieties. Marketed from 31st December of the following year.
Reds. Produced with at least 85% of the *Tinto del País* and the *Garnacha Tinta* varieties.

VARIETIES:
White: *Verdejo, Albillo.*
Red: *Tinto del País* (*Tempranillo*), *Garnacha Tinta, Garnacha Gris.*

REGULATORY COUNCIL.
Corro Vaca, 5. 47270 Cigales (Valladolid).
Tel: 983 580 074. Fax: 983 586 590.
E-mail: consejo@do-cigales.es
Website: www.do-cigales.es

GENERAL CHARACTERISTICS OF THE WINES:

Rosés	There is a distinction between the more traditional rosé wines, with the classic onion skin colour, fresh, fruity, with medium-intensity, aromatic and light and supple on the palate; and the more modern rosé wines: raspberry-coloured with more powerful aromas and greater fruitiness on the palate. There are also Crianza rosé wines aged for a minimum of six months in barrel and one year in the bottle.
Reds	Young and Crianza wines are produced. The first are typical fresh, fruity red wines that are pleasant and easy drinking. Those that are aged in barrels are quite correct and well-balanced. The best stand out for having obtained more colour and greater concentration, thanks to the use of finer wood and a greater fruity expression and to the *Terroir*.

DO CIGALES

ANDRÉS HERRERO VALLEJO

San Antón s/n
47194 Mucientes (Valladolid)
☎: 983 587 765
rulherrero@terra.es
Established: 1979
🍇 12 has. 🍷 100%

SURCOS 2003 ROSÉ

70 Brilliant raspberry. Intense aroma of slightly reduced ripe fruit. Quite flavourful, warm palate with fruit expression muted by the alcohol.

BURPAGARARRI

Malpique, s/n
47270 Cigales (Valladolid)
☎: 983 474 085 - Fax: 983 474 085
info@ovidiogarcia.com
www.ovidiogarcia.com
Established: 2000
🛢 60 📊 120,000 litres 🍇 7 has.🍷 100%

OVIDIO GARCÍA "COLECCIÓN PRIVADA" 2001 CRIANZA RED
100% tempranillo

84 Dark cherry. Powerful aroma of black fruit with fine toasty oak and creamy and balsamic hints. Flavourful palate with a good oak/fruit integration, bitter (liquorice, dark-roasted flavours) good acidity.

OVIDIO GARCÍA 2003 ROSÉ

CÉSAR PRÍNCIPE

Ronda
47194 Fuensaldaña (Valladolid)
☎: 629 779 282 - Fax: 983 583 242
Established: 1980
🛢 100 📊 120,000 litres 🍇 40 has.
🇪🇸 85% 🌐15%

CÉSAR PRÍNCIPE 2001 ROBLE RED
tempranillo ⊕ 15

90 Ruby red cherry. Aroma of ripe red stone fruit, jammy forest fruits, toasty flavours, coffee, leathers and certain notes of overripening. Powerful, warm, spirituous palate and slightly evident wood tannins, flavourful.

CÉSAR PRÍNCIPE 2000 ROBLE RED
tempranillo ⊕ 15

87 Cherry. Aroma with fine reduction notes, spices and very ripe red fruit. Warm palate with flavourful, slightly marked tannins and pleasant bitter notes.

Cooperativa de CIGALES

Las Bodegas s/n
47270 Cigales (Valladolid)
☎: 983 580 135 - Fax: 983 580 682
bcc@bodegacooperativacigales.com
www.bodegacooperativacigales.com
Established: 1957
🛢 200 📊 3,200,000 litres 🍇 700 has.
🍷 80% 🌐20%: -IT -DE -CH

VIÑATORONDOS 2003 JOVEN ROSÉ
65% tempranillo, 20% albillo, 10% garnacha, 10% verdejo

73 Brilliant raspberry. Fresh aroma of red fruit without great nuances. Flavourful, slightly fruity aroma with a slightly acidic edge.

VILLULLAS 2003 JOVEN ROSÉ
65% tempranillo, 20% albillo, 10% garnacha, 10% verdejo

73 Pale raspberry with a coppery hue. Not very intense aroma with hardly any fruit nuances. Quite flavourful, spicy and warm on the palate.

TORONDOS 2002 ROBLE ROSÉ
tempranillo, albillo, garnacha, verdejo

71 Orangey blush. Powerful, evolved aroma (nuts, clay, spices). Flavourful warm palate without fruit expression.

TORONDOS 2003 RED
100% tempranillo

86 Deep cherry with a violet edge. Concentrated aroma of jammy plums with notes of liquorice and cocoa and a floral suggestion, complex. Fleshy, powerful palate with ripe black fruit and a good fruit expression, freshness and pleasantly bitter overtones in the finish.

VIÑATORONDOS JOVEN RED
100% tempranillo

82 Dark cherry. Powerful, ripe aroma with hints of sun-drenched skins and damp earth. Flavourful palate with slightly drying tannins, ripe fruit, spices and chocolate, quite long.

TORONDOS 2000 CRIANZA RED
100% tempranillo

84 Cherry with a garnet red edge. Good intensity aroma with reduction notes (tobacco, cigar box, leather). Ripe fruit on the palate, flavourful with terroir notes, toasty wood and a long, spicy finish.

TORONDOS 2001 CRIANZA RED
100% tempranillo

83 Cherry with a slightly orangey edge. Medium-intensity, ripe fruit (with a viscous hint) and ink. Ripe palate of integrated fruit, integrated alcohol with drying tannins in the finish.

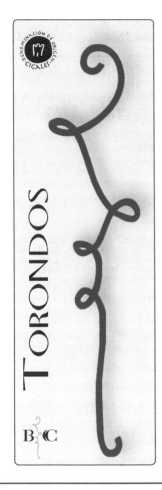

TORONDOS CIGALES NUEVO 2003 ROSÉ

Hijos de CRECENCIA MERINO

Corrales s/n
47280 Corcos del Valle (Valladolid)
☎: 983 580 118 - Fax: 983 580 118
Established: 2001
🍷 150,000 litres 🌿 17 has. 🚩 100%

VIÑA CATAJARROS 2003 ROSÉ

EMETERIO FERNÁNDEZ

Carretera Cigales km 1
47194 Fuensaldaña (Valladolid)
☎: 983 583 244 - Fax: 983 583 172
lalegua@lalegua.com
www.lalegua.com

Established: 1997
🏭 400 🍷 400,000 litres 🌿 80 has.
🚩 50% 🌐50%

LA LEGUA CAPRICHO 2001 FERMENTADO EN BARRICA RED
100% tempranillo

77 Intense cherry. Balsamic aroma (fallen leaves) of fresh red fruit with a nuance of liquorice. Flavourful, fruity palate with notes of green seeds and a slightly astringent finish.

VALDETAN 2002 ROBLE RED
100% tempranillo

77 Cherry. Spicy aroma with smoky notes and toasty skins. Flavourful, slightly bitter palate with a certain ripeness and a pleasant finish.

LA LEGUA 2001 CRIANZA RED
95% tempranillo, 5% cabernet sauvignon

81 Garnet red cherry. Not very intense yet harmonious aroma with ripe red fruit, hints of aniseed and oak spices. Flavourful, and round on the palate with red fruit and toasty wood.

LA LEGUA 1999 CRIANZA RED
tempranillo

77 Garnet red with an orangey edge. Aroma of ripe fruit with spices and marked wood. Flavourful, spicy palate with fruity tannins (a suggestion of ripeness).

LA LEGUA 1999 RESERVA RED
92% tempranillo, 8% cabernet sauvignon

82 Cherry with an orangey hue. Aroma with fine reduction notes (leather, tobacco, cedar), balsamic and fresh. Fresh, fleshy and slightly light palate with good persistence and a balsamic suggestion.

VALDETAN 2003 JOVEN RED

Hijos de FÉLIX SALAS

Corrales, s/n
47280 Corcos del Valle (Valladolid)
☎: 983 580 378 - Fax: 983 580 262
Established: 1890
🏭 344 🍷 734,600 litres 🌿 80 has.
🚩 85% 🌐15%: -BE -NL -DK

VIÑA PICOTA 2003 ROSÉ
80% tempranillo, 20% albillo, verdejo, garnacha

80 Pale raspberry. Intense, fruity aroma with fine spicy notes of skins. Flavourful palate with red stone fruit, notes of bitterness and, herbs and good acidity.

FÉLIX SALAS 2003 ROSÉ
80% tempranillo, 20% verdejo, albillo, garnacha

76 Brilliant raspberry with a coppery hue. Quite intense and fresh aroma of red fruit, without great nuances. Flavourful, bitter palate with marked citrus acidity.

DO CIGALES

VIÑA PERROTE 2003 ROSÉ
70% tempranillo, albillo, garnacha, verdejo

78 Brilliant raspberry. Fresh aroma of red stone fruit with hints of flowers and herbs. Flavourful, bitter palate with a slightly acidic edge.

FÉLIX SALAS 2002 JOVEN RED

73 Cherry with a violet hue. Not very intense yet clean aroma of red fruit and notes of caramel. Very astringent palate.

FÉLIX SALAS 2000 CRIANZA RED
95% tempranillo, 5% cabernet sauvignon

76 Garnet red with an orange edge. Spicy, toasty aroma with a hint of red fruit. Flavourful, light palate with sweet crianza notes and muted fruit.

FÉLIX SALAS 2000 RESERVA RED
90% tempranillo, 10% cabernet sauvignon

79 Cherry with an orangey edge. Not very intense aroma of red berries and notes of oak. Red fruit on the palate with a very toasty wood finish, a well-mannered ensemble.

FÉLIX SALAS 2003 JOVEN RED
PRELADO DE ARMEDILLA 2000 CRIANZA RED

FINCA MUSEUM

Carretera Cigales -Corcos, km. 3
47270 Cigales (Valladolid)
☎: 983 581 029 - Fax: 983 581 030
fincamuseum@telefonica.net

Established: 2000
4,800 2,000,000 litres 105 has.
40% 60%

MUSEUM REAL 2001 RESERVA RED

86 Intense cherry with a coppery edge. Intense aroma of jammy black fruit with fine toasty oak and a freshness evoking macerated skins. Flavourful palate with rough and slightly oily tannins, a good oak/fruit integration and spicy and bitter notes, good acidity.

MUSEUM REAL 2000 RESERVA RED

85 Garnet red cherry. Medium-intensity but fine aroma of spicy notes (tobacco) and well-integrated red fruit and wood. Flavourful palate, good red fruit and toasty wood, with oily tannins and quite persistent.

FRUTOS VILLAR

Carretera Burgos, km. 113, 7
47270 Cigales (Valladolid)
☎: 983 586 868 - Fax: 983 580 180
frutosvillar@cic.es
www.frutosvillar.com
Established: 1960

2,100 3,000,000 litres 110 has.
80% 20%: -DE -FR -UK -US -RU -MX -PT

CALDERONA NUEVO 2003 JOVEN ROSÉ
100% tempranillo

80 Salmon pink. Not very intense, yet clean, fresh and fruity aroma. Sweet overtones on the palate, with red fruit, slightly oily and pleasant.

CALDERONA ÉLITE 2003 JOVEN ROSÉ
100% tempranillo

81 Salmon pink. Medium intensity, fine aroma of ripe red fruit with a nuance of aniseed. Flavourful, fruity and light on the palate, very pleasant.

CALDERONA TEMPRANILLO 2003 JOVEN RED
100% tempranillo

83 Cherry with a raspberry edge. Intense aroma of red bramble fruit with complex liquorice and mountain herbs. Fleshy, fruity palate with fresh and flavourful fruit tannins and a slightly bitter, drying finish (minerals).

CALDERONA TEMPRANILLO 2002 JOVEN RED
100% tempranillo

82 Deep cherry. Toasty aroma with smoky hints and a suggestion of ripe black fruit. Fleshy, fresh palate with marked oak tannins in a flavourful finish with vanilla and spices.

CALDERONA ÉLITE 2001 RED

86 Deep cherry. Aroma of fine crianza (smoky wood, anise) with jammy black fruit and a nuance of earthiness. Fleshy palate with fresh and round tannins and wood well-integrated with the fruit; a fruity (skins), elegant finish.

CALDERONA 1998 RESERVA RED
100% tempranillo

85 Very dark cherry. Aroma of toasty skins with jammy dates and plums and elegant wood notes. Flavourful palate with a good assemblage of fine wood and fruit, supple tannins and a fruity finish.

VIÑA CANSINA MACERACIÓN 2003 ROSÉ
CONDE ANSÚREZ 2003 ROSÉ
VIÑA CALDERONA 2003 ROSÉ
CONDE ANSÚREZ TEMPRANILLO 2003 RED
CONDE ANSÚREZ 2002 JOVEN RED
VIÑA CANSINA 2002 RED
CALDERONA 2000 CRIANZA RED
CONDE ANSÚREZ 2000 CRIANZA RED
CALDERONA 1998 RESERVA RED

GONZÁLEZ LARA

Carretera Fuensaldaña s/n
47194 Mucientes (Valladolid)
☎: 983 587 881 - Fax: 983 587 881

gonzalezlara@bodegasgonzalezlara.com
bodegasgonzalezlara.com

Established: 1990

🌐 100 📊 750,000 litres 🍇 35 has.
🍷 90% 🔵10%

FUENTE DEL CONDE 2003 ROSÉ
tinta del país, garnacha

76 Raspberry blush. Short, quite fruity aroma with lactic notes. Better on the palate; fruity, quite well-structured, slightly warm but well-balanced.

VIÑA ZAPATA 2003 ROSÉ

69 Raspberry blush. Quite short aroma, lack of racking and a fruity hint. Bitter palate with a carbonic edge lacking fruit.

FUENTE DEL CONDE 1999 CRIANZA RED

HERMÓGENES

La Horca, s/n
47194 Fuensaldaña (Valladolid)
☎: 983 233 638

Established: 1933

🌐 12 📊 2,752 litres 🍷 100%

SEÑORÍO DE FUENSALDAÑA 2003 ROSÉ
PAGO SOMBRÍO 2001 CRIANZA ROSÉ

LEZCANO-LACALLE

Carretera de Valoria, s/n
47282 Trigueros (Valladolid)
☎: 983 586 940 - Fax: 983 586 697
oficina@bodegaslezcano.com
www.bodegaslezcano.com

Established: 1991

🌐 110 📊 130,000 litres 🍇 16 has.
🍷 85% 🔵15%: -NL -BE -DE -ASIA

DOCETAÑIDOS 2003 ROSÉ
80% tempranillo, 20% albillo, verdejo, sauvignon blanc

79 Brilliant raspberry. Intense aroma of very ripe red fruit. Intense, flavourful palate with red fruit, nuts, well-balanced.

LEZCANO-LACALLE 2000 RESERVA RED
80% tempranillo, 20% merlot

81 Cherry with a garnet red edge. Somewhat closed aroma of jammy fruit and a balsamic nuance. Red berries on the palate with earthy notes, considerable wood presence and dry oak tannins in the finish.

LEZCANO-LACALLE DÚ 2000 RESERVA RED
60% tempranillo, 40% cabernet sauvignon

87 Garnet red cherry. Intense aroma of black fruit with hints of macerated skins, spicy oak and a fine balsamic hint. Flavourful, fleshy and concentrated

palate with a good oak/fruit integration and a nuance of liquorice and sweet fruit, excellent acidity.

M. LUISA CENTENO VÁSQUEZ

Valentín Madruga, 23
47270 Cigales (Valladolid)
☎: 983 580 202
barri.001@teleline.es

Established: 1970

📊 48,000 litres 🍇 7 has. 🍷 100%

EMILIANUS 2003 ROSÉ

75 Salmon pink with an orangey hue. Quite intense aroma of smoky skins. with hardly any fruit expression. Flavourful, spicy and slightly warm on the palate with good acidity.

Bodegas y Viñedos PILCAR

Carretera Trigueros - Valoria km. 10, 6
47200 Valoria la Buena (Valladolid)
☎: 983 502 265 - Fax: 983 502 253
info@pilcar.com
www.pilcar.com

Established: 1998

🌐 200 📊 225,000 litres 🍇 15 has.
🍷 50% 🔵50%: -CH -NL -BE -UK -JP -US -DE -AT

CARREDUEÑAS 2003 JOVEN RED
100% tempranillo

79 Dark cherry with a garnet red-violet edge. Powerful, fruity aroma with slightly green hints of skins and notions of terroir. Flavourful, fleshy palate with slightly marked tannins and marked acidity.

CARREDUEÑAS 2003 ROBLE RED
100% tempranillo   🛢4

82 Garnet red cherry. Intense, fruity aroma with fine spicy oak notes and hints of fresh skins. Flavourful palate with fleshy overtones and quite fresh tannins, good acidity, easy drinking.

VIÑA CONCEJO 2001 CRIANZA RED
100% tempranillo

80 Garnet red cherry. Medium-intensity aroma of jammy fruit and toasty wood. Flavourful, concentrated palate with considerable weight of the wood and very dry oak in the finish.

VIÑA CONCEJO 1999 RESERVA RED
100% tempranillo

84 Dark cherry with a garnet red edge. Intense aroma with fine toasty and jammy fruit notes, a slightly balsamic suggestion and a hint of damp earth. Flavourful, fleshy palate with a good oak/fruit integration, ripe fruit and hints of liquorice.

CARREDUEÑAS 2003 ROSÉ
CARREDUEÑAS 1999 CRIANZA RED
CARREDUEÑAS 1998 RESERVA RED

PINEDO MENESES

Picón del Rollo
47280 Corcor del Valle (Valladolid)
☎: 983 586 877 - Fax: 983 586 877

Established: 1992
🏭 10 🛢 98,000 litres 🍇 10 has. 🍷 100%

PINEDO MENESES 2003 ROSÉ
CORQUEÑO 2003 ROSÉ
PINEDO MENESES 2003 RED

RODRÍGUEZ SANZ

Santa María, 6
47270 Cigales (Valladolid)
☎: 983 580 006 - Fax: 983 580 006
rodriguezsanz@telefonica.net

Established: 1931
🛢 200,000 litres 🍇 20 has.
🍷 90% 🍇10%: -CH

ROSAN 2003 JOVEN ROSÉ
80% tinto fino, 10% garnacha, 10% albillo

73 Brilliant raspberry. Quite intense, fruity aroma without great nuances. Fresh, flavourful palate with marked citrus acidity.

Hijos de RUFINO IGLESIAS

Trascastillo s/n
47194 Mucientes (Valladolid)
☎: 983 587 778 - Fax: 983 587 778
carramill@teleline.es

Established: 1948
🛢 500,000 litres 🍇 6 has.
🍷 95% 🍇5%: -UE

CARRATRAVIESA 2003 JOVEN ROSÉ
70% tempranillo, 20% garnancha, 10% albillo, verdejo

78 Blush. Fresh, clean and fruity aroma with strawberries. Fruity, pleasant with an element of acidity and slightly warm.

RUFINO IGLESIAS 2º AÑO ROSÉ
60% tempranillo, 30% garnancha, 10% albillo, verdejo

70 Onion skins. Aroma of somewhat overripe fruit (with signs of evolution). suggestions of red fruit on the palate, light and slightly rustic.

MILLATOS 2002 JOVEN RED
100% tempranillo

78 Deep cherry with a violet edge. Aroma of black bramble fruit, slightly balsamic and maceration. Fleshy palate of fresh red fruit and pungent tannins, fresh.

Bodegas SAN ANTÓN

Zona de las bodegas
47194 Mucientes (Valladolid)
☎: 983 587 862
bodegasananton@usuarios.retecal.es

PANEDAS 2000 CRIANZA RED
tempranillo

81 Garnet red cherry. Not very intense aroma but with well-integrated fruit and wood. Flavourful on the palate with expression, pleasant and easy drinking.

SANTA RUFINA

Pago Fuente La Teja Polígono 3
Parcela 102
47290 Cubillas de Santa Marta (Valladolid)
☎: 983 585 202 - Fax: 983 585 202
santarufina@terra.es

Established: 1997
🏭 1,800 🛢 850,000 litres 🍇 84 has.
🍷 50% 🍇50%: -DE -US -FI -DK -CH -FR

VIÑA RUFINA "PAGO DE SALLANA" 2003 ROSÉ
50% tempranillo, 30% verdejo, 10% albillo, 10% viura

71 Pale blush. Not very fine aroma with hints of sulphur. Slightly better on the palate; flavourful and spicy with a slightly acidic edge.

VIÑA RUFINA "PAGO DE SALLANA" 2001 ROBLE JOVEN RED
85% tinta del pais, 15% cabernet sauvignon

82 Deep cherry. Toasty aroma of dark-roasted notes over black fruit. Fleshy, toasty palate with fruit tannins slightly muted by the fruit yet round.

VIÑA RUFINA "PAGO DE SALLANA" 2000 CRIANZA RED
85% tinta del pais, 15% cabernet sauvignon

78 Dark garnet red. Aroma of ripe black fruit with notes of reduction in wood (leather, animal skins). Fleshy palate with rough oak tannins, traces of earthiness and slightly warm.

VIÑA RUFINA ALTA GAMA VENDIMIA SELECCIONADA 1999 RESERVA RED
100% tempranillo

84 Cherry with a garnet red edge. Fine aroma with an expression of terroir, well-ripened black fruit, complex notes (pitch, dry earth, animals) and a toasty hint. Flavourful, light palate with round, oily yet fresh tannins and toasty wood notes.

VIÑA RUFINA ALTA GAMA VENDIMIA SELECCIONADA 1998 GRAN RESERVA RED
100% tempranillo

81 Garnet red with a brick red edge. Aroma with crianza notes (reduction, varnish, animal skins) and a nuance of jammy fruit. Fleshy, earthy palate with toasty oak notes, flavourful, noticeable wood tannins and a fresh finish.

VIÑA RUFINA "PAGO DE SALLANA" 2000 CRIANZA RED
VIÑA RUFINA "PAGO DE SALLANA" 2000 RESERVA RED
VIÑA RUFINA PAGOS DE SALLANA 1999 RESERVA RED
VIÑA RUFINA "PAGO DE SALLANA" 1999 GRAN RESERVA RED
VIÑA RUFINA "PAGO DE SALLANA" 1998 GRAN RESERVA RED

SINFORIANO VAQUERO CENTENO

Carretera Mucientes - Villalba
Mucientes (Valladolid)
☎: 983 587 789 - Fax: 983 587 789

Established: 1956
⊞ 25 ▥ 250,000 litres ⚘ 40 has. ☛ 100%

SINFORIANO TEMPRANILLO 2001 CRIANZA RED
100% tempranillo

87 Very deep cherry. Intense aroma of perfectly ripe fruit, very elegant crianza (smoky flavours, cocoa) and balsamic hints. Fleshy on the palate with slightly dry wood tannins, slightly warm fruit tannins but with good acidity, flavourful.

SOLAR DE LAGUNA

Calle de La Fuente, s/n
47282 Trigueros del Valle (Valladolid)
☎: 983 586 771 - Fax: 983 586 850

Established: 1991
⊞ 50 ▥ 600,000 litres

SOLAR DE LAGUNA 2003 JOVEN ROSÉ
tempranillo, albillo, verdejo

60 Salmon pink. Off-odours from the tank without fruit.

CASTILLO DE ROBLES 2003 JOVEN ROSÉ
tempranillo, albillo, verdejo

74 Raspberry with an orangey glint. Intense aroma of ripe red fruit and hints of reduction (withered petals). Flavourful, bitter palate with marked citrus acidity.

ALARDE 2003 JOVEN ROSÉ
tinto fino, verdejo, albillo, garnacha

73 Pale blush. Intense, ripe aroma without great fruit expression but with hints of reduction. Flavourful, fresh, quite fruity aroma with marked acidity.

GRAN SOLAR DE LAGUNA 2003 FERMENTADO EN BARRICA ROSÉ
tempranillo

80 Deep raspberry. Powerful aroma of red fruit, fine smoky oak and a creamy hint. Flavourful, bitter palate with fine spicy notes and good acidity.

GRANDÓN 2002 JOVEN RED
tempranillo

78 Garnet red. Aroma of ripe black fruit with toasty notes and a hint of mild reduction. Flavourful, fresh palate with supple wood tannins that predominate the fruit.

GRANDÓN 2000 CRIANZA RED
tempranillo

80 Deep cherry. Toasty aroma with dark-roasted oak notes over jammy black fruit. Fleshy, fresh, toasty palate with a slightly earthy finish.

CARROSANTOS 2003 JOVEN ROSÉ
CASTILLO DE ROBLES 2002 JOVEN RED
GRANDÓN 2003 JOVEN RED
CASTILLO DE ROBLES 2003 JOVEN RED

Compañía de Vinos de
TELMO RODRÍGUEZ

Siete Infantes de Lara, 5. Oficina 1
26006 Logroño (La Rioja)
☎: 941 511 128 - Fax: 941 511 131
cia@fer.es

VIÑA 105 2003 JOVEN RED

TRASLANZAS

Barrio de las Bodegas, s/n
47194 Mucientes (Valladolid)
☎: 639 641 123 - Fax: 946 020 263
traslanzas@euskalnet.com

Established: 1998
⊞ 65 ▥ 20,000 litres ⚘ 20 has.
☛ 60% ✈40%: -AT -DE -US -CH

TRASLANZAS 2001 OAK AGED RED
100% tinta del país

90 Very deep cherry. Aroma of ripe black fruit with notes of terroir and hints of minerals (animals), complex and concentrated. Fleshy on the palate with powerful fruit tannins integrated with wood tannins; slightly oily with traces of minerals and cocoa from the oak.

VALDELOSFRAILES

Carretera Cubillas, s/n
47359 Cubillas de Santa María (Valladolid)
☎: 983 485 024 - Fax: 983 107 104
aclareco@matarromera.es
www. matarromera.es

Established: 1998
⊞ 500 ▥ 350,000 litres ⚘ 60 has.

🐗 70% 🐦30%: -DE -AD AT -BE -BR -CA - CU CL -DK -EC -FR -UK -NL -IT -JP -MX - DK -PA -PE -PR -SE -CH -US -CZ -DO

VALDELOSFRAILES 2003 ROSÉ
100% tinto fino

78 Onion skins. Not very intense yet clean aroma and a suggestion of red fruit. Flavourful, fruity palate with good acidity and a pleasant bitterness in the finish.

VALDELOSFRAILES 2003 RED
100% tinto fino

77 Garnet red with a violet hue. Aroma of tank that disappears with airing, ripe red fruit. Light and not very persistent on the palate.

VALDELOSFRAILES PRESTIGIO 2001 OAK AGED RED
100% tinto fino

83 Cherry with a garnet red edge. Somewhat closed aroma of ripe fruit with light reduction notes that fade. Flavourful, expressive palate of ripe red fruit, creamy wood notes and evident yet ripe and slightly drying oak tannins.

VALDELOSFRAILES VENDIMIA SELECCIONADA 2001 OAK AGED RED
100% tinto fino   🛢 12

86 Dark cherry with a dark red hue. Powerful aroma with a good expression of ripe forest fruit, fine spicy oak notes and notions of terroir. Flavourful, fleshy palate, with good fruit/oak integration, fresh overtones of skins and liquorice, damp earth and spices in the finish.

Camino de las Bodegas, s/n
47290 Cubillas de Santa Marta (Valladolid)
☎: 983 585 085 - Fax: 983 585 186
bodegasvaleriano@wanadoo.es
Established: 1993
🛢 50 🛢 250,000 litres 🌿 20 has. 🐗 100%

VIÑA SESMERO 2003 JOVEN ROSÉ
70% tempranillo, 15% garnacha, 15% verdejo

74 Pale raspberry. Quite intense, fruity aroma without great nuances. Flavourful palate with freshness and good citrus acidity.

VALERIANO 2003 FERMENTADO EN BARRICA ROSÉ
100% tempranillo

77 Brilliant raspberry. Intense, slightly fruity aroma of fine smoky wood with a spicy hint. Flavourful, slightly bitter palate, lacking fruit expression with a slightly acidic edge.

VALERIANO 2003 JOVEN RED
100% tempranillo

76 Cherry with a violet edge. Not very clean aroma of skins, that improves with airing. Light, slightly warm palate with not very persistent tannins.

VALERIANO 2002 CRIANZA RED
100% tempranillo

82 Cherry with a garnet red edge. Good intensity aroma of red berries and an expressive floral edge. Flavourful palate with abundant red fruit and toasty wood notes, very pleasant.

VALERIANO 2000 CRIANZA RED
100% tempranillo

81 Deep cherry. Floral, fruity aroma with very sweet notes and toasty wood. Warm, flavourful palate with marked tannins and smoky notes.

EL BERRROJO 2003 JOVEN ROSÉ
VIÑA SESMERO 2003 JOVEN ROSÉ
EL BERRROJO 2003 JOVEN RED

Carretera Trigueros, km. 10, 6
47200 Valoria la Buena (Valladolid)
☎: 983 400 114 - Fax: 983 400 114
vegapisuerga@vegapisuerga.com
www.vegapisuerga.com
Established: 1997
🛢 140 🛢 535,000 litres 🌿 80 has.
🐗 98% 🐦2%

MALVANEGRA
CARRAMONTEA

DO CONCA DE BARBERÀ

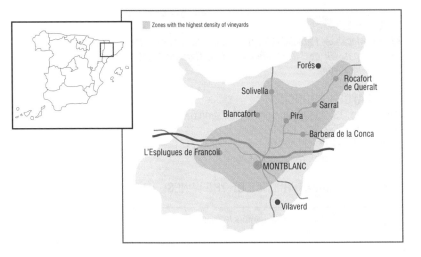

Zones with the highest density of vineyards

Forés
Rocafort de Queralt
Solivella
Sarral
Blancafort
Pira
Barbera de la Conca
L'Esplugues de Francolí
MONTBLANC
Vilaverd

NEWS. Under the threat, as in the rest of Spain, of the extreme relentless heat wave suffered by the vineyards, the refreshing rains of 17th August came to the rescue, boosting a correct ripening of the grapes and preserving their health, especially the red varieties. The Council, probably urged in the same way as the rest of the denominations in Catalonia by the initiative displayed by the DO Catalunya, has authorized the white varieties *Chardonnay* and *Sauvignon Blanc*, together with the red varieties *Cabernet Sauvignon, Merlot, Syrah* and *Pinot Noir*. The reason: to boost the quality of wines in a more contemporary context, which the market seems to demand.

There has also been a significant increase in export figures, which have risen from 10% of the total production to 36% in the last campaign.

Hectares of Vineyard	No. of Viticulturists	No. of Bodegas	2003 Harvest	2003 Production	Marketing
5,871	2,235	17	Very Good	30,438 hectolitres	64% Spain 36% export

The best results of this denomination were achieved by the large groups (Torres, Codorníu), together with La Xarmada, with wines in the region of 90 points. Particularly noteworthy is Concavins, whose wines produced with foreign varieties are being awarded scores of over 85 points with increasing frequency.

LOCATION. In the north of the province of Tarragona with a production area covering 14 municipalities, to which two new ones have recently been added: Savallà del Comtat and Vilanova de Prades.

CLIMATE. Mediterranean and continental influences, as the vineyards occupy a river valley surrounded by mountain ranges without direct contact with the sea.

SOIL. The soil is mainly brownish-grey and limy. The vines are cultivated on slopes protected by woodland. An important aspect is the altitude which gives the wines a fresh, light character.

VARIETIES:

White: *Macabeo, Parellada* (majority 3300 Ha) *Chardonnay, Sauvignon Blanc.*
Red: *Trepat, Ull de Llebre (Tempranillo), Garnatxa, Cabernet Sauvignon, Merlot, Syrah, Pinot Noir.*

REGULATORY COUNCIL.

Sant Josep, 18. 43400 Montblanc (Tarragona).
Tel: 977 861 232. Fax: 977 862 424.
E-mail: cellers@do-conca.org
Website: www.doconcadebarbera.com

GENERAL CHARACTERISTICS OF THE WINES:

Whites	Pale and brilliant, they are fruity, pleasant to drink and very light, although not excessively aromatic.
Rosés	Raspberry-pink coloured, quite modern in their production style, with red fruit aromas, slightly fresh, flavourful and well-balanced.
Reds	These are quite light and easy drinking, for the moment, with characteristics more adapted to producing young wines than for Crianza wines, except in the case of the most experienced producers who produce powerful, meaty and concentrated red wines.

DO CONCA DE BARBERÁ

ABADÍA DE POBLET

Paasseig de l'Abat Conill, 6
43448 Poblet (Tarragona)
☎: 977 870 358 - Fax: 977 870 191
codinfo@codorniu.es/smartin@codorniu.es
www.grupocodorniu.com

Established: 1989
97 9 has. 100%

ABADÍA DE POBLET 2002 ROBLE RED
100% pinot noir

87 Garnet red cherry with a brick red edge.
Intense aroma of ripe fruit with excellent varietal
expression (spices, wet horsehair), toasty hints of
oak and cola. Flavourful, fleshy palate with a good
fruit/oak integration, leather and spices (pepper) in
the retronasal passage and excellent acidity.

LES MASIES DE POBLET 2001 RED
ABADÍA DEPOBLET 2001 RED

Cooperativa AGR. I CAIXA AGR. ESPLUGA

Lluis Carulla, 15
43440 L'Esplugá de Francoli (Tarragona)
☎: 977 870 105 - Fax: 977 870 026
coespluga@retemail.es

Established: 1902
200 4,000,000 litres 582 has.
100%

FRANCOLI WHITE SEMISECO
FRANCOLI ROSÉ
FRANCOLI NEGRE RED
SPLUGEN ROSAT ROSÉ
SPLUGEN NEGRE RED

Cooperativa AGRÍCOLA DE PIRA

Avenida Arnau de Ponç, 16
43423 Pira (Tarragona)
☎: 977 887 007 - Fax: 977 887 007
copira@do-conca.org

MIRALPEIX WHITE
macabeo, parellada

75 Pale yellow with a greenish hue. Intense
aroma of green fruit with notes of spices and
herbs. Flavourful, bitter palate with an acidic edge.

MIRALPEIX JOVEN ROSÉ
trepat

76 Pale raspberry with a coppery hue. Intense,
slightly fruity aroma with fine smoky skins.
Flavourful palate with pronounced citrus acidity.

MIRALPEIX RED
ull de llebre

74 Cherry. Aroma of ripe red fruit with spices and
a suggestion of viscosity. Round, fresh and very
flavourful palate, ripe.

Cooperativa Agrícola de BARBERÀ

Comercio, 40
43422 Barberà de la Conca (Tarragona)
☎: 977 887 035 - Fax: 977 887 035

Established: 1894
4,000,000 litres 100%

CABANAL 2003 WHITE
CABANAL 2003 ROSÉ
CABANAL 2003 RED

Cooperativa Agrícola i CAIXA AGRÍCOLA DE BLANCAFORT

Plaza de Arbres, 11
43411 Blancafort (Tarragona)
☎: 977 892 115 - Fax: 977 892 002
blancafort@retemail.es

Established: 1896
20 3,500,000 litres 100%

BLANCA FLOR NEGRE DE FLOR 2003
JOVEN WHITE
BLANCA FLOR BLANC DE FLOR 2003 FER-
MENTADO EN BARRICA WHITE
BLANCA FLOR ROSA TREPAT 2003 JOVEN
ROSÉ
BLANCA FLOR ULL DE LLEBRE Y
CABERNET 2003 JOVEN RED

CONCAVINS

Carretera Montblanc-Barbera, s/n
43422 Barberá de la Conca (Tarragona)
☎: 977 887 030 - Fax: 977 887 032
comercial@bodegasconcavins.com
www.bodegasconcavins.com

Established: 1988
1,100 3,000,000 litres 40 has.
20%% 80%: -US -CA -UK -DE -JP -
NL -BE -DK -AT -SE -CH

CLOS MONTBLANC CHARDONNAY PREMIUM
2003 FERMENTADO EN BARRICA WHITE
100% chardonnay

81 Pale gold. Powerful aroma with good varietal
expression (ripe apples, hay) and smoky hints of
skins. Flavourful palate with fresh mineral overtones, fruit partially subdued by the alcohol.

DO CONCA DE BARBERÁ

CASTILLO DE MONTBLANC VIURA CHARDONNAY 2003 WHITE
70% viura, 30% chardonnay

80 Straw-coloured with golden nuances. Intense aroma of ripe white fruit with exotic hints (bananas) and flowers. Flavourful palate with fine notes of bitterness, citrus fruit and fresh mineral overtones.

CLOS MONTBLANC SAUVIGNON BLANC PREMIUM 2003 WHITE
100% sauvignon blanc

79 Pale yellow with a golden hue. Not very intense aroma with a certain finesse and varietal expression (notes of exotic fruit, heather). Fresh, flavourful and warm on the palate.

CLOS MONTBLANC PREMIUM 2003 ROSÉ
cabernet sauvignon, merlot, tempranillo

76 Salmon blush. Not very intense but fine, somewhat ripe (petals, nuts). A touch of flavour on the palate. Fruity but with quite marked tannins.

CASTILLO DE MONTBLANC TEMPRANILLO 2003 RED
85% tempranillo, 15% cabernet sauvignon

83 Garnet red cherry with a coppery glint. Powerful, ripe, varietal aroma with smoky hints of skins and fallen leaves. Flavourful palate with ripe tannins, spicy and balsamic with liquorice and terracotta in the retronasal passage.

CLOS MONTBLANC CABERNET SAUVIGNON PREMIUM 2000 CRIANZA RED
100% cabernet sauvignon

86 Dark cherry with a saffron edge. Powerful aroma, rich in varietal nuances with fine notes of toasty, sweet oak. Flavourful palate with a good oak/fruit integration, bitter, vigorous and long.

CLOS MONTBLANC CABERNET-MERLOT PREMIUM 2000 CRIANZA RED
70% cabernet sauvignon, 30% merlot

86 Cherry. Aroma with light notes of fine reduction (leather, tobacco) and wood. Flavourful palate with well-integrated tannins and a mild suggestion of green peppers in the retronasal passage.

CLOS MONTBLANC MERLOT PREMIUM 2002 CRIANZA RED
100% merlot

84 Medium-hue garnet red. Spicy aroma of not very intense jammy tomatoes. Drying and warm on the palate with quite aggressive wood tannins and lactic suggestions in the retronasal passage.

CLOS MONTBLANC PINOT NOIR PREMIUM 2002 CRIANZA RED
100% pinot noir

82 Cherry with an orangey hue. Aroma of black olives, toasty wood and smoky tones. Well-balanced on the palate with good wood/fruit integration and good acidity.

CLOS MONTBLANC SYRAH PREMIUM 2002 CRIANZA RED
100% syrah

86 Dark cherry. Powerful aroma of jammy black fruit and petals (violets) with spicy notes of skins and toasty oak. Flavourful palate with a good oak/fruit integration, rich in bitter nuances (chocolate, liquorice), with excellent acidity.

CLOS MONTBLANC MASÍA LES COMES 2000 RESERVA RED
70% cabernet sauvignon, 30% merlot

84 Dark cherry. Powerful aroma with excellent varietal expression (redcurrants, paprika, fallen leaves) and spicy oak notes. Flavourful palate with a good oak/fruit integration, hints of coffee and jammy fruit with a herbaceous and terracotta suggestion.

LA XARMADA

Hisenda Casa Llivi, s/n
08796 Pacs del Penedés (Barcelona)
☎: 938 171 237 - Fax: 938 171 546
laxarmada@laxarmada.com
www.laxarmada.com

Established: 1977

120 🛢 600,000 litres 🍇 100 has.

🍷 70% 🌐30%

LA XARMADA FERMENTADO EN BARRICA WHITE
50% chardonnay, 50% chenin blanc

81 Brilliant pale yellow. Intense aroma of ripe white fruit with fine smoky oak notes, hints of fine herbs, spices and ripe citrus fruit. Flavourful palate without obvious fruit expression with a slightly oily texture, fine bitter notes, good acidity.

LA XARMADA MOSCAT WHITE DULCE
100% moscatel

80 Very pale yellow. Intense aroma with a hint of freshness, notes of crystallised citrus fruit, fine musky, floral hints and fine herbs. Bitterswet notes of quality on the palate, fresh with fine bitter notes, original.

LA XARMADA MERLOT-CABERNET SAUVIGNON 2003 JOVEN ROSÉ
90% merlot, 10% cabernet sauvignon

83 Very deep raspberry. Powerful, fruity aroma (strawberry jelly), with spicy notes of skins and hints of underbrush. Powerful, flavourful palate with red fruit, fine bitter and citrus hints and good acidity.

LA XARMADA TEMPRANILLO-SYRAH 2003 JOVEN RED
40% tempranillo, 40% syrah, 10% cabernet sauvignon, 10% merlot

82 Very deep cherry with a violet hue. Intense aroma of great finesse, notes of red fruit, hints of violets and a notion of terroir. Flavourful palate with quite marked grape tannins, good fruit weight, bitterness and good acidity.

DO CONCA DE BARBERÁ

LA XARMADA TURDUS SELECCIÓ 2002 OAK AGED RED
60% tempranillo, 40% syrah

84 Intense cherry with a violet edge. Intense aroma with predominant toasty oak notes, jammy red fruit and a spicy notion of terroir. Flavourful palate with promising yet quite marked tannins, slightly bitter notes and a balsamic and mineral nuance.

LA XARMADA TURDUS SELECCIÓ 2001 OAK AGED RED
60% tempranillo, 40% syrah

86 Brilliant cherry with a saffron edge. Intense aroma with spicy oak notes, red fruit and a hint of mineral freshness. Flavourful, supple palate with well-integrated oak and fruit, fine bitter notes and excellent acidity.

LA XARMADA 2001 CRIANZA RED
50% syrah, 20% merlot, 30% cabernet sauvignon

83 Deep cherry with a coppery-violet edge. Fairly intense aroma with notes of red fruit, violets, spicy hints of skins and toasty oak. Flavourful palate with promising yet slightly marked tannins, a slight varietal expression, a herbaceous balsamic undertone and a slightly acidic edge.

LA XARMADA MISTELA SWEET

81 Intense raspberry with a coppery hue. Powerful, fruity aroma (jammy red fruit), quite fleshy with figs and spicy hints. Flavourful palate with fine bittersweet notes predominant over the jammy fruit, pleasant.

LICOROSO LA XARMADA VINO DE LICOR

83 Golden amber. Aroma of sun-drenched white fruit with quince and honey, viscous and slightly toasty notes. Sweet palate with notes of quite sweet almonds, not very fresh, quite heavy with a fruity finish (sweetish pears)

LA XARMADA 2003 JOVEN WHITE
LA XARMADA KOSHER WHITE
LA XARMADA KOSHER RED
LA XARMADA SELECCIÓ 2002 RED
LA XARMADA 2002 OAK AGED RED
LA XARMADA SEMICRIANZA RED

Celler MAS FORASTER

Camino Ermita de Sant Josep, s/n
43400 Montblanc (Tarragona)
☎: 977 860 229 - Fax: 977 875 037
foraster@teleline.es
www.josepforaster.com

Established: 1998
🌐 92 🍷 70,000 litres 🌿 22 has.
🍷 60% 🌍40%: -DE -UK -BE
-NL -FR -AT -AD -LU -CH -MX

JOSEP FORASTER 2003 JOVEN RED
85% tempranillo, 15% cabernet sauvignon

85 Bigarreau cherry with a violet edge. Intense, expressive, harmonious aroma of red fruit and balsamic flavour. Flavourful, and fruity on the palate, fresh and lively with noticeable but ripe tannins; an excellent young wine.

JOSEP FORASTER SELECCIÓ 2001 OAK AGED RED
90% cabernet sauvignon, 10% tempranillo

86 Quite intense cherry with a garnet red-orangey edge. Not very intense yet fine spicy aroma (pepper) with toasty oak and balsamic flavour, harmonious. Generous, flavourful palate with ripe redcurrants well-blended with the oak and ripe tannins.

JOSEP FORASTER 2002 CRIANZA RED
80% cabernet sauvignon, 20% tempranillo

86 Dark cherry. Powerful aroma of fine wood notes, a ripe, varietal and fruity essence, balsamic hints, fallen leaves and minerals. Flavourful palate with an excellent crianza expression and Mediterranean character.

MIGUEL TORRES

Miguel Torres Carbó, 6
08720 Vilafranca del Penedés (Barcelona)

☎: 938 177 400 - Fax: 938 177 444
webmaster@torres.es
www.torres.es

Established: 1870

⊞ 20,000 ▯ 28,000,000 litres ⚘ 2,122 has.
🍖 50% 🌐50%: 120 países

MILMANDA 2002 FERMENTADO EN BARRICA WHITE
100% chardonnay

89 Pale golden yellow. Intense aroma with a fine integration of the varietal fruit notes and smoky oak and a suggestion of fine herbs (mint, fennel). Flavourful palate with slightly fresh oak tannins, fine bitter notes, a slightly oily texture and hints of herbs with anise and minerals in the finish.

GRANS MURALLES 2000 OAK AGED RED
garnacha tinta, mazuelo, monastrell, garró, samsó

88 Deep cherry with a purplish edge. Intense, very elegant aroma of jammy black fruit with toasty oak notes (slightly fresh) and balsamic notes. Flavourful and quite promising on the palate, with somewhat drying tannins and fine bitter notes, lacking fruit expression.

RENDE MASDEU

Avenida Catalunya, 44
43440 L'Espluga de Francolí (Tarragona)
☎: 977 871 361 - Fax: 977 871 361
rendemasdeu@worldonline.es

Established: 1987

⊞ 115 ▯ 60,000 litres ⚘ 23 has.
🍖 90% 🌐10%: -CH -BE

ARNAU 2001 RED
RENDÉ MASDEU 2000 RED
RENDÉ MASDEU 2000 CRIANZA RED
RENDÉ MASDEU 1998 RESERVA RED

ROSA MARÍA TORRES

Avenida Anguera, 2
43424 Sarral (Tarragona)
☎: 977 890 013 - Fax: 977 890 173
info@rosamariatorres.com
www.rosamariatorres.com

Established: 1993

⊞ 150 ▯ 350,000 litres ⚘ 110 has.

VIOGNIER 2002 FERMENTADO EN BARRICA WHITE
100% viognier

79 Golden. Intense aroma with predominant smoky and creamy oak notes with an essence of ripe fruit (apricots). Flavourful, spicy palate with caramelised hints and fine herbs.

CASTRELL D'ARFÉS WHITE

72 Straw-coloured. Aroma of slightly overripe fruit yet well-mannered. Light palate and a rustic edge.

CASTRELL D'ARFÉS 2000 OAK AGED RED
100% cabernet sauvignon

78 Cherry with a brick red edge. Spicy aroma of smoke and red fruit. Marked wood tannins on the palate, short with a suggestion of green peppers in the retronasal passage.

VINYA PLANS 2002 RED
cabernet sauvignon

78 Cherry with an orangey edge. Aroma with varietal typification of green peppers and notes of greeness. Warm, short palate with a persistent suggestion of the green peppers in the retronasal passage.

SUSEL 2003 RED
65% cabernet franc, 35% syrah

78 Deep garnet red with a violet edge. Aroma of red fruit, light mineral notes and skins. Fleshy palate with supple tannins though with a note of greeness, light bitter notes and medium persistence.

SUSELA 2002 ROSÉ
CASTRELL D'ARFÉS 2002 OAK AGED RED
CASTRELL D'ARFÉS 2003 RED

Cavas SANSTRAVÉ

General Mola, 10
43412 Solivella (Tarragona)
☎: 977 892 165 - Fax: 977 892 073
bodega@sanstrave.com
www.sanstrave.com

Established: 1985

⊞ 60 ▯ 80,000 litres ⚘ 22 has.
🍖 85% 🌐15%

GASSET BLANC SANSTRAVÉ 2001 FERMENTADO EN BARRICA WHITE
100% chardonnay

84 Brilliant gold. Powerful aroma of smoky oak, a slightly varietal ripe fruit essence, and hints of perfumed soap. Flavourful, creamy palate (caramel) with spicy oak notes and hints of ripe fruit in the finish.

PARTIDA DELS JUEUS SANSTRAVÉ 2003 RED
40% merlot, 20% garnacha, 20% tempranillo, 20% cabernet sauvignon

83 Dark cherry with a garnet red edge. Powerful, fruity aroma with hints of macerated skins and an essence of terroir. Flavourful, fruity palate with fine bitter notes, an excellent expression of young wine.

SANSTRAVÉ SYRAH 2003 RED
100% syrah

84 Bigareau cherry with a lively violet edge. Intense, viscous aroma of very ripe black fruit. Powerful, fleshy and warm on the palate with a good expression of very ripe fruit (cherries in liqueur), quite persistent.

GASSET NEGRE SANSTRAVÉ 2000 RESERVA RED
60% cabernet sauvignon, 30% tempranillo, 10% merlot

86 Dark red cherry. Powerful aroma with fine varietal notes, oak, balsamic and fallen leaves nuance. Flavourful, fleshy palate with good oak/fruit integration, a bitter hint (jammy fruit, liquorice, dark-roasted flavours) and excellent acidity.

Cooperativa Vinícola SARRAL

Avenida de la Conca, 33
43424 Sarral (Tarragona)
☎: 977 890 031 - Fax: 977 890 136
cavaportell@covisal.es
www.cava-portell.com

Established: 1907

125 | 7,000,000 litres | 1,115 has.

85% | 15%: -DE -DK -MX -FR

PORTELL WHITE SEMI-SWEET
macabeo, parellada

72 Straw-coloured. Not very intense aroma, with weak fruit and yeast. Quite well-balanced sweetness-acidity on the palate but without great nuances.

PORTELL BLANC DE BLANCS 2003 WHITE
75% macabeo, 25% parellada

76 Straw-coloured. Not very intense yet clean aroma of hay and yeast. Fresh, light palate, slightly bitter but well-balanced with the acidity.

PORTELL MARINADA 2003 WHITE DE AGUJA
70% macabeo, 30% parellada

80 Pale gold. Intense aroma of ripe fruit, exotic hints and withered petals. Fresh palate, with fine carbonic hints and jammy fruit, bitter, herby and very rich.

PORTELL 2003 FERMENTADO EN BARRICA ROSÉ
100% trepat

79 Pale raspberry. Intense, slightly fruity aroma with fine smoky oak. Flavourful, bitter palate with hints of herbs and marked acidity.

PORTELL MESTRAL 2003 ROSÉ DE AGUJA
100% trepat

79 Pale raspberry. Intense aroma of red stone fruit, spices and herbs. Fresh, bitter palate without great fruit expression with a quality citrus fruit hint.

PORTELL TREPAT 2003 ROSÉ
100% trepat

73 Blush. Not very intense aroma but fresh, fruity (strawberry jelly) and herby hint. Bitter, tannic palate, lacking fruit.

PORTELL MERLOT 2002 RED
100% merlot

78 Cherry with a garnet red-violet edge. Medium-intensity, ripe aroma with vanilla, spicy oak and jammy fruit. Lively, acidic palate with a hint of greeness, a medium structure and a toasty oak finish.

PORTELL ULL DE LLEBRE 2001 RED
cabernet sauvignon, tempranillo

75 Garnet red cherry. Slightly short aroma with bramble berries and sun-drenched grapes. Round, light and fruity on the palate, easy drinking.

PORTELL MACABEO 2003 OAK FERMENTED WHITE
FLOR DE RAIM 2003 WHITE
PORTELL 2001 CRIANZA RED
PORTELL 2000 RESERVA RED
VINYA D'EN GREC 2003 RED

DO CONDADO DE HUELVA

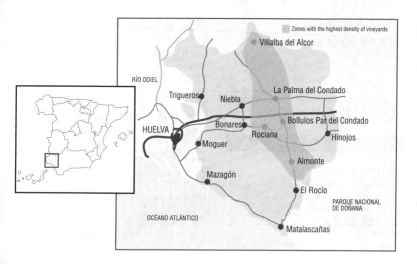

NEWS. This region is almost at a standstill. Its classic wines more or less seem to be holding ground, although the whites of a young and fruity style are of a somewhat dubious quality. It seems strange that a denomination which is striving to modernise itself and adapt to modern times with wines of a more modern type, besides having all the required technological means at their disposal, produces white wines which are clearly trailing behind the rest in Spain and is one of the regions with the highest count of defective wines, an obstacle which the remaining DOs in Spain have gradually been doing away with.

Hectares of Vineyard	No. of Viticulturists	No. of Bodegas	2003 Harvest	2003 Production	Marketing
5,311	2,876	19 bottlers	Good	11,328,660 litres	90% Spain 10% foreign

Nevertheless, the relatively good performance during tasting of the wines of Vinícola del Condado is worthy of mention, which is in fact the largest wine cooperative in Andalusia, both in terms of production (representing 45% of the total of the DO) and in number of members (over a thousand). More interesting news from Huelva is the research project on the evolution of colour according to the pre-fermentation maceration conditions at controlled temperatures for red wines. Although the only red tasted was Don Frede, obtaining a score of 80 points, we may have some surprises in store, seeing as Andalusia in general is revealing itself, against all predictions, as a region of great interest for red varieties.

LOCATION. In the south east of Huelva. It occupies the plain of Bajo Guadalquivir. The production area covers the municipal areas of Almonte, Beas, Bollullos Par del Condado, Bonares, Chucena, Gibraleón, Hinojos, La Palma del Condado, Lucena del

Puerto, Manzanilla, Moguer, Niebla, Palos de la Frontera, Rociana del Condado, San Juan del Puerto, Villalba del Alcor, Villarrasa and Trigueros.

CLIMATE. Mediterranean in nature, with certain Atlantic influences. The winters and springs are fairly mild, with long hot summers. The average annual temperature is 18 °C, and the average rainfall per year is around 550 mm, with a relative humidity of between 60% and 80%.

SOIL. In general, flat and slightly rolling terrain, with fairly neutral sound soils of medium fertility. The soil is mainly reddish, brownish-grey with alluvium areas in the proximity of the Guadalquivir.

VARIETIES:
White: *Zalema* (majority with 86% of vineyards), *Palomino, Listán de Huelva, Garrido Fino, Moscatel de Alejandría* and *Pedro Ximénez.*

REGULATORY COUNCIL.
Avda. 28 de Febrero, s/n. 21710 Bollullos Par del Condado (Huelva).
Tel: 959 410 322. Fax: 959 413 859.
E-mail: consejoregulador@vinosconcadohuelva.com
Website: www.condadohuelva.org

GENERAL CHARACTERISTICS OF THE WINES:

Young Whites	Produced from the autochthonous *Zalema* variety, they are characterised by their slightly vegetative notes with hints of scrubland; they are pleasant and easy drinking.
Condado Pálido	These are quite similar to the other Finos of Andalusia (Jerezanos and Montillanos). *Palomino* grapes are used in their production, the same as those used for Jerez, although they have somewhat less biological character.
Condado Viejo	These are the most traditional wines of the region, although now only produced in a few cellars, and come from the oldest Soleras.

A. VILLARÁN

San Vicente, 25
21710 Bollullos del Condado (Huelva)
☎: 959 410 377 - Fax: 959 408 133

PEDRO XIMÉNEZ PEDRO XIMÉNEZ DULCE SOLERA 1934 GENEROSO

Bodegas ANDRADE

Avenida Coronación, 35
21710 Bollullos del Condado (Huelva)
☎: 959 410 106 - Fax: 959 411 305
1,800 ⬧ 100 has. 🍷 100%

CASTILLO DE ANDRADE 2003 JOVEN WHITE

80 Pale straw. Fresh aroma with green fruit and apples. Fresh, flavourful palate, pleasant bitter note, expressive.

PUENTE DEL REY 2003 JOVEN WHITE

80 Straw-coloured. Aroma of ripe fruit (bananas, pears, apples), good intensity. Flavourful, pleasant palate with bitter expression, well-mannered.

ANDRADE VINO DE PASAS DULCE

70 Dark mahogany. Aroma with weak character, evoking vine gratings (dried grass) with a nuance of raisins. Sweet palate of old wood, a little coarse.

DOCEAÑERO CREAM SEMI-DULCE

75 Old gold. Aroma of acetone and nuts with crianza character. Sweet palate with a hint of syrup and toasty notes.

DOCEAÑERO OLOROSO

79 Old gold. Aroma with notes of varnish, wood nuts. Old wood on the palate and a iodised finish.

MURALLAS DE NIEBLA WHITE

77 Very pale. Medium-intensity aroma of ripe fruit (bananas, apples). Sweet, fruity, well-mannered palate.

Bodegas CONTRERAS RUIZ

Almonte, 5
21720 Rociana del Condado (Huelva)
☎: 959 416 426 - Fax: 959 416 744
Established: 1982
120 🗄 1,000,000 litres ⬧ 40 has.
🍷 97% 🌐3%

VIÑA BARREDERO 2003 JOVEN WHITE

77 Pale straw. Not very intense but fruity aroma (ripe apples) with notes of white flor. Fairly flavourful, fruity and fresh on the palate.

VIÑA CONTRERAS 2003 JOVEN WHITE

75 Very pale. Slightly fruity aroma of hay. Light palate with notes of sweetness and a bitter counterpoint; well-mannered.

LAS BOTAS CONDADO VIEJO

75 Amber. Medium-intensity aroma of nail varnish, varnishes, and slightly overripe fruit. Dry palate of toasty wood and varnishes.

DÍAZ

Avenida de la Paz, 43
21710 Bollullos del Condado (Huelva)
☎: 959 410 340 - Fax: 959 408 095
Established: 1955
550 🗄 292,500 litres 🍷 100%

DON BACO MOSCATEL DULCE

82 Dark mahogany with a iodised rim. Powerful aroma of raisins with caramelised notes and aged wood. Sweet and raisiny palate with an element of orange peel in the finish, sweet.

LA CONCHA CONDADO PÁLIDO WHITE

74 Straw-coloured with a greenish hue. Slightly short, vinous aroma of aged cask. Dry and bitter palate, well-mannered but without great expression.

SOLERA 1955 CONDADO VIEJO

79 Old gold. Medium-intensity aroma with rancid notes of nuts and aged Solera. Dry, pungent and bitter on the palate with carpentry in the finish.

DOÑANA

Labradores, 2 Pol. El Lirio
21710 Bollullos del Condado (Huelva)
☎: 959 411 513 - Fax: 959 411 513

VIÑA DOÑANA 2003 JOVEN WHITE

Bodegas IGLESIAS

Teniente Merchante, 2
21710 Bollullos del Condado (Huelva)
☎: 959 410 439 - Fax: 959 410 463
biglesias@arrakis.es
www.bodegasiglesias.com
Established: 1937
1,300 🗄 2,000,000 litres ⬧ 15 has.

%UZ JOVEN WHITE
100% zalema

76 Pale straw. Aroma of good intensity with a fruit expression (ripe apples) of the vine variety. Pleasant, well-mannered palate with an element of acidity.

UZT JOVEN WHITE
100% zalema

74 Straw-coloured with a coppery glimmer. Medium-intensity aroma with marked notes of banana. Slightly overripe fruit on the palate, notes of sweetness, well-mannered.

LETRADO ZALEMA SOLERA GENEROSO
zalema

82 Amber-topaz. Good intensity aroma, nuts (almonds) and toasty hints. Dry palate with notes of pâtisserie, nuts, hazelnuts and toasty walnut in the finish.

EXQUISITA CRIANZA BIOLÓGICA GENEROSO
zalema, listán

80 Yellow straw. Aroma with notes of flor, saline hints and almond, clean. Round, supple palate with almondy notes, very saline with a very toasty wood finish.

PAR VINO NARANJA DULCE

73 Mahogany. Intense aroma of caramelised orange peel and sweet tangerines. Very sweet, slightly pasty palate, evoking tangerines, a little cloying.

RICAHEMBRA GENEROSO DULCE
zalema, pedro ximénez

80 Dark mahogany. Aroma of varnish with a raisiny expression and a suggestion of spices and dark-roasted flavours. Sweet, dense palate with notes of sweet almonds and white cocoa; a slightly heavy finish.

MARQUÉS DE VILLALÚA

Maestro Beño, 20
21860 Villalba del Alcor (Huelva)
☎: 959 420 905
www.marquesdevillalua.es

Established: 2000
200000 litres 🌳 8 has. 🍷 100%

AGUADULCE DE VILLALÚA 2003 JOVEN WHITE SEMI-DULCE
100% zalema

65 Pale straw. Short aroma of yeasts with off-odour overtones. Quite sweet on the palate, weak fruit.

MARQUÉS DE VILLALÚA 2003 JOVEN WHITE

75 Yellow straw. Fresh aroma of jammy grapes with mild musky notes. Light and flavourful on the palate with an element of sweetness to counterpoint the bitter notes.

MARQUÉS DE VILLALÚA 2003 JOVEN WHITE SEMI-DULCE

NUESTRA SEÑORA DE LA GUÍA

Avenida de la Constitución 1-3
21700 La Palma del Condado (Huelva)
☎: 959 400 795
coopeguia@wanadoo.es

Established: 1957
1,000,000 litres 🍷 100%

PALMERINO JOVEN WHITE
100% zalema

75 Straw-coloured with a greenish hue. Medium-intensity, fruity and fresh aroma. Fresh and fruity on the palate with bitter-sweet symmetry.

PALMERINO 2003 WHITE

NUESTRA SEÑORA DEL SOCORRO

Carril de los Moriscos
21720 Rociana del Condado (Huelva)
☎: 959 416 108 - Fax: 959 416 108
vitivinicolasocorro@interalimentaria.net

EL GAMO JOVEN WHITE

73 Pale straw. Medium-intensity, mildly fruity aroma. Fresh palate despite slightly weak fruit.

VIÑAGAMO JOVEN WHITE

72 Pale straw. Short but clean, fruity aroma. Elements of acidity on the palate but well-mannered as a whole.

DON FREDE 2003 RED
cabernet sauvignon, syrah, tempranillo

77 Intense cherry. Aroma of red fruit with hints of maceration (eucalyptus and liquorice). Dry, fruity, slightly green palate, a dry finish.

OLIVEROS

Rábida, 12
21710 Bollullos Par del Condado (Huelva)
☎: 959 410 057 - Fax: 959 410 057
oliveros@bodegasoliveros.com
www.bodegasoliveros.com

Established: 1940
🍾 4500 🗄 22000000 litres 🌳 380 has.
🇪🇸 90% 🌐10%: -UE -US Asia

BELROSE MOSCATEL DULCE
moscatel

DO CONDADO DE HUELVA

82 Light mahogany. Viscous aroma with a Muscatel character and notes of lemon peel, original. Sweet, very fresh, perfumed palate (notes of perfumed soap) with hints of fresh grapes and flowers; slightly warm finish.

VINO NARANJA RED
zalema, pedro ximénez

83 Mahogany. Aroma of orange jelly and vanilla with a hint of sun-drenched fruit. Sweet palate with a good bitter character, bittersweet balance and an expression of orange and fine toasty oak.

JUAN JAIME 2003 JOVEN WHITE
OLIVEROS 1996 OLOROSO

Bodegas
PRIVILEGIO DEL CONDADO

San José, 2
21710 Bollullos del Condado (Huelva)
☎: 959 410 261 - Fax: 959 410 171
comercial@vinicoladelcondado.com
www.vinicoladelcondado.com

Established: 1955

1,000 ᵇ 40,000,000 litres 2,000 has. 95% 5%

DON CONDADO 2003 JOVEN WHITE SEMIDULCE
zalema

60 Pale straw. Aroma with mild fruity notes and fermentation off-odours. Sweet palate with muted fruit.

MIORO GRAN PRIVILEGIO DEL CONDADO 2003 JOVEN WHITE SECO
zalema, moscatel

81 Pale straw. Fresh, fruity, herbaceous, perfumed aroma. Flavourful, fruity palate, easy drinking, with pleasant bitter notes in the finish.

MIORO PRIVILEGIO DEL CONDADO 2003 JOVEN WHITE
100% zalema

71 Straw-coloured. Medium-intensity aroma of yeasts, weak fruit. Well-mannered and bitter on the palate, lacking in fruit.

MISTERIO DULCE
zalema

80 Mahogany. Aroma of stewed fruit (plums and raisins) and a pâtisserie nuance. Sweet flavourful on the palate with crystallised fruit and toasty notes.

MISTERIO FINO
listán blanca

73 Straw-coloured. Aroma of ripe fruit with a nutty hint. Dry and bitter palate, more expressive than in the nose.

MISTERIO OLOROSO SECO
listán negro

86 Amber. Intense, nutty aroma of pastries and toasty notes with complex overtones. Slightly glyceric, flavourful and dry palate with toasted nuts and good crianza.

MISTERIO CREAM DULCE
listán

81 Mahogany. Medium-intensity, raisiny, toasty aroma with hints of acetaldehydes. Flavourful, sweet palate of crystallised fruit, good crianza, long.

VDM MOSCATEL DULCE
moscatel

74 Intense gold. Aroma with acetone notes, old wood and a nuance of Muscatel, lacking character. Slightly better in the mouth, sweet, flavourful palate with toasty notes.

Bodegas
SÁENZ-DEL DIEZMO NUEVO

Sor Ángela de la Cruz, 56
21800 Moguer (Huelva)
☎: 959 370 004 - Fax: 959 371 840

Established: 1787

200 ᵇ 100,000 litres 100%

VIÑA EL PATRIARCA JOVEN WHITE

68 Very pale. Aroma with a mild off-odour in the nose and a citrus fruit nuance. A lack of fruitiness on the palate.

EL PATRIARCA 1972
PATRIARCA CONDADO PÁLIDO 2000 FINO

SAUCI

Doctor Fleming, 1
21710 Bollullos del Condado (Huelva)
☎: 959 410 524 - Fax: 959 410 331
bodegassauci@terra.es
www.bodegasauci.es

Established: 1925
600 ᵇ 400,000 litres 7 has. 100%

ESPINAPURA FINO
100% palomino

83 Straw-coloured. Pungent aroma with nuts (almonds) and flor. Bitter, powerful and dry palate with a toasted almond and saline finish.

RIODIEL OLOROSO

78 Light mahogany. Aroma of varnish, orange peel and dark-roasted flavours, slightly warm. Powerful, bitter palate (nuts) with good acidity, long with generous nuances.

SAUCI CREAM
75% palomino, 25% pedro ximénez

79 Mahogany. Aroma of old wood, toasty flavours, nuts. Sweet palate of stewed fruit and carpentry; well-integrated alcohol, quite persistent.

VINO DULCE SAUCI FINO
100% pedro ximénez

82 Dark copper. Aroma of sweet raisins with spicy and coffee notes, orange peel. Sweet, generous palate (toasty flavours, coffee, bakery); very fresh.

RIODIEL FINO

VINÍCOLA MANZANILLERA

Santa María, 23
21890 Manzanilla (Huelva)
☎: 959 415 055 - Fax: 959 415 055

RETAMARES JOVEN WHITE

VINÍCOLA VALVERDEJO

Carretera Gibraleón - Trigueros km 2
21500 Gibraleón (Huelva)
☎: 959 240 215 - Fax: 959 240 900
mateobarba@vinicolavalverdejo.com
www.vinicolavalverdejo.com

MATEO BARBA
PANTORRANO

Agroalimentaria VIRGEN DEL ROCÍO

Avenida de Cabezudos, s/n
21730 Almonte (Huelva)
☎: 959 406 146 - Fax: 959 450 689
www. raigal.com

RAIGAL 2003 JOVEN WHITE

72 Pale with a coppery glimmer. Fairly short aroma of slightly overripe fruit (bananas). Slightly mild palate without fruit expression; well-mannered but lacking harmony.

TEJARES WHITE

55 Pale straw. Obvious flaws in the nose and on the palate.

TEJARES CONDADO DULCE VINO DE LICOR
zalema

78 Mahogany. Medium-intensity aroma of varnishes and Solera with a nuance of raisins. Sweet, flavourful palate with stewed fruit, pleasant.

TEJARES CONDADO PÁLIDO WHITE

74 Straw-coloured. Aroma of aged cask, flowers and nuts. Dry and very bitter palate of aged wood.

TEJARES CONDADO VIEJO VINO DE LICOR
zalema

77 Pale copper. Toasty aroma with notes of cask, varnish and spices. Dry, fresh, slightly alcoholic palate with an aftertaste of nuts.

RAIGAL BRUT

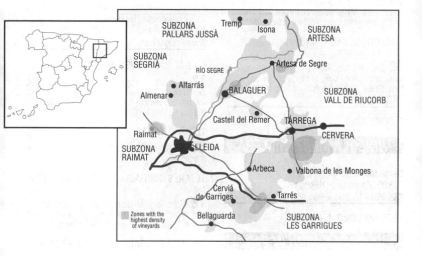

NEWS. Together with the surprising newcomer of the DO, the Geol of Tomás Cusiné, the stars of the region are the Cérvoles Selecció en Vinya, which returns to the giddy heights of the 90s, together with 1780 of Castell del Remei (apparently determined to present its credentials in the national market following years of success in foreign markets, with export figures of up to 70% of its production). Do not be fooled however; these three bodegas are simply three slices of the same pie: Cérvoles is owned by Castell del Remei, and Geol is a personal project of one of the two brothers who own this bodega.

Hectares of Vineyard	No. of Viticulturists	No. of Bodegas	2003 Harvest	2003 Production	Marketing
4,144	701	16 bottlers. 9 producers	Very Good	87,019 hectolitres	77% Spain 22% foreign

Also worthy of mention are the qualitative notes of Comalats (whose wines lack some of the expression of a couple of years ago) and Vinya L'Hereu, as well as L'Olivera, especially its Blanc de Marges, for defending the local varieties (*Macabeo, Parellada*). Of the 20 red wines of the DO which exceeded a score of 85 points, only nine include some percentage (and usually very modest) of *Garnacha* or *Tempranillo*, as opposed to the *Cabernet Sauvignon, Merlot, Syrah,* or *Pinot Noir* which give rise to an excellent varietal expression; in the white wines, only the Macabeo and the Parellada appear together with the preeminent *Chardonnay* (and to a lesser extent the *Riesling* and the *Müller-Thurgau*), and there seems to be no trace of the *Garnacha Blanca*, which in previous years used to liven up the character of the wines of Catalonia.

LOCATION. In the southern regions of Lleida, and a few municipal areas of Tarragona. It covers the sub-regions of: Artesa de Segre, Garrigues, Pallars Jussà, Raimat, Segrià and Valls del Riu Corb.

CLIMATE. Rather dry continental climate in all the sub-regions, with minimum temperatures often dropping below zero in winter, summers with maximum temperatures in excess of 35° on occasions, and fairly low rainfall figures: 385 mm/year in Lleida and 450 mm/year in the remaining regions.

SOIL. The soil is mainly calcareous and granitic in nature. Most of the vineyards are situated on soils with a poor organic matter content, brownish-grey limestone, with a high percentage of limestone and very little clay.

VARIETIES:
Preferred white: *Macabeo, Xarel·lo, Parellada, Chardonnay, Garnacha Blanca.*
Authorized white: *Albariño, Riesling, Sauvignon Blanc.*
Preferred red: *Garnacha Negra, Ull de Llebre (Tempranillo), Cabernet Sauvignon, Merlot, Monastrell, Trepat, Samsó, Pinot Noir.*
Authorized red: *Syrah.*

REGULATORY COUNCIL.
Complex de la Capallera, 97. 25192 Lleida.
Tel: 973 270 494 / 973 264 583.
E-mail: secretari@costersdelsegre.es
Website: www.costersdelsegre.es

GENERAL CHARACTERISTICS OF THE WINES:

Whites	There is a distinction between those produced from traditional grapes (*Macabeo, Parellada* and *Xarel·lo*), which follow the parameters of the white wines from other Catalonian regions. They are light, fruity and fresh with good acidity indexes. In addition, there are the *Chardonnays*, both young and barrel-aged wines, with fine varietal character and following the Mediterranean interpretation of this variety.
Rosés	Produced from *Ull de Llebre (Tempranillo), Merlot* or *Cabernet Sauvignon*, the wines are pink, with a fine fruit character, fresh and characterised by the personality of the variety used.
Reds	The wines have a Mediterranean character, single varietal or a mixture of autochthonous and foreign varieties. In general they are warm, with a powerful aroma and character of ripe fruit. Some may develop balsamic aromas and, on the palate, they are characterised by their warmth and flavourfulness.

Celler de CANTONELLA

Avenida Les Garrigues, 26
25471 La Pobla de Cèrvoles (Lleida)
☎: 973 580 200 - Fax: 973 718 312
info@castelldelremei.com
www.cervoles.com

Established: 1997

🌐 300 📊 250,000 litres 🍇 40 has.

🍷 30% 🍇70%: -US -DE -CA -FI -AT -PR -BE -FR -UK -MX -CH -SG -DK -NL -SE -PE

CÉRVOLES 2003 FERMENTADO EN BARRICA WHITE
sauvignon blanc, macabeo

84 Pale straw. Intense aroma of fine smoky oak, a fresh fruit hint and fragrant herbs. Generous, flavourful palate with fresh, ripe fruit, a herby finish and oak yet to be integrated.

CÉRVOLES 2000 RESERVA RED
cabernet sauvignon, tempranillo, merlot

89 Dark cherry with a garnet red edge. Powerful aroma with predominant toasty oak notes (coffee, pitch), somewhat varietal ripe fruit (redcurrants) and hints of graphite. Powerful, flavourful palate with a good fruit/oak integration, dark-roasted hints and excellent acidity.

CÉRVOLES 2001 RESERVA RED
cabernet sauvignon, tempranillo, merlot

89 Dark garnet red cherry. Powerful, warm aroma of ripe fruit with a hint of minerals (stone and dry earth) and fine toasty flavours. Round palate with flavourful and ripe tannins and creamy oak in the retronasal passage.

CÉRVOLES SELECCIÓ EN VINYA 2001 RESERVA RED
cabernet sauvignon, tempranillo, garnacha

91 Dark cherry with a deep red edge. Powerful aroma of black fruit with fine hints of overripening, graphite and pitch. Powerful, concentrated aroma with slightly rough tannins, fine bitter notes (liquorice dark-roasted flavours) and excellent potential.

CAR VINÍCOLAS REUNIDAS

Carretera, 19
25340 Verdu (Lleida)
☎: 973 310 732 - Fax: 973 310 616

Established: 1974
📊 800,000 litres 🍷 100%

SOT NERAL SEMICRIANZA RED

CASA PARDET

Bonaire, 19
25340 Verdú (Lleida)

☎: 973 347 023 - Fax: 973 348 079
info@casapardet.com
www.casapardet.com

Established: 1992

🌐 90 📊 200,000 litres 🍇 8 has.

🍷 40% 🍇60%: -CH -DE -UK -BE

CASA PARDET 2000 CRIANZA RED
100% cabernet sauvignon

78 Nearly opaque cherry. Concentrated aroma of black fruit and nuts (dried peaches, dates) with obvious toasty scents and hints of dust. Fleshy palate with rough wood tannins (cocoa) and a varietal and woody aftertaste.

CASA PARDET TEMPRANILLO 1995 RESERVA RED
100% tempranillo

73 Ruby red with a brick red rim. Discreet aroma of fruit with dominant oak (reduction). Light, spicy and flavourful on the palate with toasty notes over the fruit.

CASA PARDET 2003 ORGANIC WHITE
CASA PARDET 1999 CRIANZA RED

CASA PATAU

Costa del Senyor, s/n
25139 Menarguens (Lleida)
☎: 973 180 367 - Fax: 973 180 367
patau2@eresmas.com
www.casapatau.com

Established: 2001

🌐 24 📊 90,000 litres 🍇 4,6 has. 🍷 100%

CASA PATAU MACABEU 2003 WHITE
100% macabeo

60 Straw-coloured with a golden hue. Aroma with evident off-odours that do not disappear with airing. Absence of nuances or hints of fruit on the palate.

CASA PATAU ULL DE LLEBRE 2003 RED
tempranillo, merlot

75 Garnet red cherry with coppery nuances. Powerful, ripe aroma of black fruit with hints of reduction (petals). Flavourful palate with sweetish notes (overextraction) and an acidic edge.

CASA PATAU 2002 CRIANZA RED
cabernet sauvignon

67 Garnet red with an orangey edge. Discreet aroma with notes of stables and obvious greeness. Flavourful palate, without fruit expression and with predominant off-odours.

CASTELL DEL REMEI

Finca Castell del Remei
25333 Castell del Remei (Lleida)

☎: 973 580 200 - Fax: 973 718 312
info@castelldelremei.com
www.castelldelremei.com

Established: 1780

⊕ 1,700 ▤ 800,000 litres ⚜ 80 has.
🍷 30% ☝70%: -US -NL -DE -CA -UK -BE
-JP -FR -CH -AT -DK -AD -DK -FI -SE -SG -
PE -MX -IS -EL

CASTELL DEL REMEI BLANC PLANELL 2003 JOVEN WHITE
sauvignon blanc, macabeo

86 Straw-coloured. Aroma of mountain herbs (lavender) and fruit (green apples), fresh. Fresh, fruity, slightly oily palate with very ripe sweet fruit in the retronasal passage.

ODA BLANC 2003 FERMENTADO EN BARRICA WHITE
chardonnay, macabeo

88 Straw-coloured. Fresh, fruity aroma with cut grass (hay) and creamy notes. Fresh, fruity, oily, smoky and flavourful palate, very varietal and of medium expression

GOTIM BRU 2002 CRIANZA RED
cabernet sauvignon, tempranillo, merlot

85 Dark cherry. Powerful aroma with fine notes of toast and fresh fruit and varietal traces. Flavourful, fresh palate with very harmonious wood and fruit.

ODA 2001 CRIANZA RED
cabernet sauvignon, tempranillo, merlot

87 Intense cherry. Aroma with creamy and fine toasty wood and jammy fruit (blackberries and plums). Fleshy palate with very ripe fruit, toasty, spirituous and warm

1780 2000 RESERVA RED
cabernet sauvignon, garnacha, merlot

91 Intense cherry. Toasty, powerful, fine, smoky aroma (cocoa, coffee), with ripe black fruit. Powerful, fleshy palate rich in expression of jammy black fruit and hints of minerals, spirituous and full-bodied.

Celler COMALATS

Jaume Bonet Celler Comalats
43427 Vallfogona de Riucorb (Tarragona)
☎: 977 880 111 - Fax: 977 880 111

Established: 1993

⊕ 25 ▤ 100,000 litres ⚜ 12,5 has.
🍷 50% ☝50%: -DE -NL -BE

COMALATS 2001 RED
100% cabernet sauvignon

85 Dark cherry. Powerful aroma of very ripe black fruit with hints of macerated skins and spices (paprika, cocoa). Flavourful, slightly fleshy palate with marked yet very elegant tannins and fine bitter notes (liquorice, pitch), warm but with good fruit weight.

COMALATS 2002 RED
100% cabernet sauvignon

84 Dark cherry. Powerful aroma with an excellent expression of overripe black fruit, fine smoky oak and hints of terroir. Flavourful, warm palate with rough, slightly drying tannins, quality herbaceous hints (somewhat varietal) and hot paprika and dark-roasted flavours in the finish.

COMALATS 2000 RESERVA RED
100% cabernet sauvignon

88 Dark cherry with a coppery rim. Intense, very fine aroma of jammy black fruit, toasty oak notes and a balsamic, spicy nuance. Powerful, flavourful palate with supple overtones, good fruit/oak integration, very varietal ripe fruit and hints of graphite and terroir in the retronasal passage.

Cooperativa D'ARTESA DE SEGRE

Carretera Artesa - Montblanc, km. 1
25730 Artesa de Segre (Lleida)
☎: 973 402 037 - Fax: 973 402 204
pere@coopartesa.com
www.coopartesa.com

Established: 1958

⊕ 292 ▤ 690,000 litres ⚜ 140 has.
🍷 80% ☝20%

DEL IRIS SAUVIGNON BLANC 2002 WHITE

78 Straw-coloured. Not very intense, fruity aroma (tropical fruits), with a nuance of mountain herbs. Fresh, slightly bitter palate with a green fruit pulp, without great nuances but pleasant.

ARTESIÀ CABERNET SAUVIGNON 1999 CRIANZA RED

82 Deep cherry with an orange edge. Quite ripe aroma of jammy black fruit with notes of vanilla. Fleshy, fresh palate with good fruit but obvious oak; strong yet fine tannins.

L'OLIVERA

La Plana s/n
25268 Vallbona de les Monges (Lleida)
☎: 973 330 276 - Fax: 973 330 276
olivera@olivera.org - olivera.org

Established: 1989

⊕ 88 ▤ 86600 litres ⚜ 12 has.
🍷 85% ☝15%: -FR -DE -BE -DK -AD -UK
-AT -IT

BLANC DE SERÈ 2003 WHITE
60% macabeo, 30% parellada, 10% chardonnay

75 Yellow straw. Quite intense, fresh aroma of ripe green fruit. Light, fruity palate, pleasant.

BLANC DE MARGES 2002 FERMENTADO EN BARRICA WHITE
50% parellada, 25% chardonnay, 25% macabeo

DO COSTERS DEL SEGRE

85 Brilliant gold. Powerful aroma with predominant smoky notes of fine lees and a suggestion of wax. Flavourful palate with fine bitter notes, an oily texture and good acidity.

AGALIU 2003 FERMENTADO EN BARRICA WHITE
EIXADERS 2003 FERMENTADO EN BARRICA WHITE
MISSENYORA 2003 FERMENTADO EN BARRICA WHITE
BLANC DE ROURE 2002 OAK AGED WHITE

MONESTIR DEL TALLAT

Adminstracion. Carretera Reus-El Morell, Km. 738
43760 El Morrell (Tarragona)
☎: 977 840 655 - Fax: 977 842 146
vermut@vermutyzaguirre.com
www.vermutyzaguirre.com

Established: 1995

🌐 130 🍷 88,000 litres 🌿 45 has.

🍷 75% 🌐25%: -BE -NL -IT -AD -CH -DE -LV -RU -IE

ERMITA DELS DIUMENGES 2001 FERMENTADO EN BARRICA WHITE
80% chardonnay, 20% riesling

73 Golden. Powerful aroma with toasty oak notes and a nuance of wax and mountain herbs. Flavourful palate with predominant toasty wood notes, toffee and herbs, lacking fruit expression.

MONESTIR DEL TALLAT CABERNET SAUVIGNON 2000 RESERVA RED
100% cabernet sauvignon

79 Deep garnet red cherry. Powerful aroma of very varietal fruit (green pepper) with toasty oak notes, hints of cedar and a balsamic suggestion. Flavourful, spicy palate (spicy paprika) with somewhat fresh oak, good acidity.

MONESTIR DEL TALLAT MERLOT 2000 RESERVA RED
merlot

83 Deep garnet red. Intense aroma of red fruits of the forest (blackberries raspberries), light hints of violets and a suggestion of minerals. Fleshy, well-balanced palate, with toasty wood in the retronasal passage.

ERMITA DELS DIUMENGES 2002 FERMENTADO EN BARRICA WHITE

MONESTIR DEL TALLAT CABERNET SAUVIGNON 1999 RESERVA RED
MONESTIR DEL TALLAT MERLOT 1999 RESERVA RED

PAGOS ÚNICOS

Constancia, 41
41010 (Sevilla)
☎: 954 276 488 - Fax: 954 276 477
tierranuestra@reservaycata.com

Established: 1997

🌐 65 🍷 15,000 litres 🍷 70% 🌐30%: -UK -US -DE -DK -BE -AT

A. PAÍS 2000 BARREL AGED RED
40% tempranillo, 20% garnacha, 25% merlot, 15% cabernet sauvignon

85 Garnet red cherry with a brick red edge. Powerful aroma of ripe fruit and fine toasty reduction notes (tobacco, leather). Flavourful palate with a good oak/fruit integration. Slightly drying and warm with fine bitter notes.

SIGNOS 2000 BARREL AGED RED
garnacha, tempranillo, cabernet sauvignon

85 Garnet red cherry. Intense aroma with predominant toasty oak notes and a nuance of jammy black fruit. Flavourful palate with a good oak/fruit integration, hints of prunes, bitter notes (liquorice, dark-roasted flavours) and lactic hints in the finish.

"SIGNOS PAGO LAS PIEDRAS" 2002 CRIANZA RED

RAIMAT

Afueras, s/n
25111 Raimat (Lleida)
☎: 973 724 000 - Fax: 973 724 061
smartin@codorniu.es
www.raimat.com

Established: 1918

🌐 15,000 🍷 8,000,000 litres 🌿 2.300 has.
🇪🇸 71% 🌐29%

RAIMAT CHARDONNAY 2003 JOVEN WHITE
chardonnay

85 Yellow straw. Intense, fine aroma of ripe apples with notes of lemons, hay, and lavender and excellent expression. Fresh and flavourful on the palate, with lively acidity which gives the wine nerve.

RAIMAT CHARDONNAY SELECCIÓN ESPECIAL 2002 CRIANZA WHITE
100% chardonnay

85 Yellow straw. Powerful aroma of toasty oak, with smoky, buttery and varietal notes. Creamy and flavourful with glycerin on the palate, a long, smoky finish.

RAIMAT TEMPRANILLO 2001 CRIANZA RED
100% tempranillo

77 Garnet red cherry with a saffron edge. Intense aroma with predominant, animal reduction notes, with a suggestion of tobacco and jammy fruit. Flavourful palate with not very fine bitter notes and hints of overripening.

RAIMAT CABERNET SAUVIGNON 1999 CRIANZA RED
85% cabernet sauvignon, 15% merlot

88 Dark garnet red cherry with a brick red edge. Powerful aroma of toasty oak and skins with mild reduction notes (cedar, prunes) and balsamic notes. Flavourful, fleshy, ripe palate with excellent varietal expression, slightly oily with liquorice and dark-roasted flavours.

RAIMAT MERLOT 1999 CRIANZA RED
95% merlot, 5% cabernet sauvignon

84 Dark cherry with a brick red hue. Intense, ripe aroma and a varietal character of quality (redcurrants, spices, damp earth). Flavourful palate with a good oak/fruit integration, fine bitter notes (liquorice, dark-roasted flavours) and good acidity.

RAIMAT CABERNET SAUVIGNON MAS CASTELL 1995 RESERVA RED
100% cabernet sauvignon

87 Cherry with a brick red edge. Powerful aroma of pitch, tobacco and a balsamic suggestion (eucalyptus, fallen leaves). Intense, generous palate with peppery notes, spices and a ripe Cabernet character.

RAIMAT CABERNET SAUVIGNON VALLCORBA 1995 RESERVA RED
100% cabernet sauvignon

89 Quite dark cherry with a brick red edge. Intense aroma with fine balsamic notes (fallen leaves), spices (pepper, pepper) and jammy fruit. Powerful, fleshy and full on the palate with well-assembled fine toasty wood and balsamic notes, spices in the retronasal passage; long.

RAIMAT EL MOLÍ 1995 RESERVA RED
100% cabernet sauvignon

84 Intense cherry with a brick red edge. Powerful, ripe aroma with predominant reduction notes (cedar, clay, old furniture, prunes). Flavourful, supple palate slightly varietal and balsamic, with a good expression of a classic Reserva.

RAIMAT CABERNET SAUVIGNON 1995 RESERVA RED
85% cabernet sauvignon, 15% merlot

89 Intense cherry with a brick red edge. Intense aroma with predominant reduction notes (leather, dates, old furniture). Flavourful, supple palate, rich in nuances, dark-roasted flavours, spices, an excellent expression of Reserva.

RAIMAT 4 VARIETALES 1994 GRAN RESERVA RED
51% cabernet sauvignon, 26% merlot, 15% tempranillo, 8% pinot noir

85 Ruby red with a brick red rim. Aroma of fine crianza (pepper, smokiness, leather) with balsamic notes, quite complex. Powerful, fleshy palate with wood tannins predominating the good fruit weight; a long cocoa finish, with cedar and consistent tannins.

RAIMAT GRAN BRUT BRUT
70% chardonnay, 30% pinot noir

87 Brilliant pale gold. Intense, ripe aroma with an excellent crianza expression (lees, withered petals), a hint of white stone fruit and honey. Flavourful and creamy on the palate with fine notes of herbs and ripe citrus fruit, excellent acidity.

RAIMAT CHARDONNAY 2003 JOVEN WHITE
RAIMAT CABERNET SAUVIGNON 1999 CRIANZA RED
RAIMAT MERLOT 1999 CRIANZA RED
RAIMAT TEMPRANILLO 2001 CRIANZA RED
RAIMAT GRAN BRUT BRUT
RAIMAT CABERNET SAUVIGNON 1995 RESERVA RED

Celler TEIXIDÓ

Carretera Balaguer, 26
25130 Algerri (LLeida)
☎: 973 426 209 - Fax: 973 426 209

Established: 1989
🍷 40 📇 100,000 litres 🍇 6 has.

TEIXIDÓ

TOMÁS CUSINÉ

Plaza Sant Sebastià, 13
25547 El Vilosell (Lleida)
☎: 609 717 196 - Fax: 973 176 029
info@tomascusine.com
Established: 2003

GEOL 2003 BARREL AGED RED
60% merlot, 40% cabernet sauvignon

91 Dark cherry with unintegrated toasty hints of oak and fruit, elegant with character and hints of minerals. Mineral, complex palate with silky tannins, oily with a great ripe fruit expression, excellent and medium-bodied.

VALL DE BALDOMAR

De lo Font, s/n
25737 Baldomar (Lleida)
☎: 973 402 205 - Fax: 932 104 040
baldomar@smc.es
Established: 1989
🍷 100 📇 160,000 litres 🍇 20 has.
🍖 50% 🍏 50%

BALDOMÀ 2003 WHITE
müller thurgau, macabeo

83 Yellow straw. Intense, grapey aroma with excellent ripe, fresh fruit over a suggestion of herbs. Abundant fresh fruit on the palate, a little bitter.

CRISTIARI 2003 WHITE
müller thurgau, pinot bianco

85 Golden. Not very intense yet fine aroma, notes of lees and fragrant herbs with a nutty hint. Somewhat bitter palate with notes of herbs but lacking the fruit and the body of the previous vintage.

CRISTIARI D'ALÒS MERLOT 2003 ROBLE RED
merlot

89 Medium-hue garnet red. Spicy, slightly alcoholic though not very intense aroma. Well-balanced and round on the palate with good persistence and hints of coffee in the retronasal passage.

BALDOMÀ 2003 RED
merlot, tempranillo, cabernet sauvignon

78 Intense cherry. Spicy aroma with smoky notes over a nuance of sun-drenched skins and balsamic hints. Flavourful palate with quite pungent fruit tannins (green seeds) and a slightly warm finish evoking creamy wood.

BALDOMÀ SELECCIÓ 2002 RED
merlot, bobal, cabernet sauvignon

77 Ruby red with a brick red rim. Toasty aroma with crianza reduction notes and a nuance of ripe fruit. Flavourful, light palate without grape expression and with mild smokiness, short.

CRISTIARI 2000 CRIANZA RED
merlot, cabernet sauvignon

85 Cherry with a brick red hue. Aroma with toasty notes, elegant reduction (coffee, tobacco) and notes of bell pepper. Somewhat green palate with integrated tannins, a good fruit weight, the bell pepper notes reappear in the retronasal passage.

VILA CORONA

Camí els Nerets, s/n
25654 Vilamitjana (Lleida)
☎: 973 652 638 - Fax: 973 652 638
vila-corona@teleline.es

Established: 1993

🍷 30 📦 320,000 litres 🍇 7,35 has.
🍷 80% 🌍20%: -BE -DK

VILA CORONA CHARDONNAY 2003 WHITE
100% chardonnay

85 Greenish straw. Fresh aroma of ripe apples, white fruit, hay and green grass. Fresh, varietal and prominent on the palate with a certain complexity of herbs in the finish, persistent.

VILA CORONA RIESLING 2003 WHITE
100% riesling

82 Straw-coloured. Intense, grapey aroma of ripe white fruit and herbs. Fresh, flavourful palate of aromatic herbs, well-balanced and easy drinking.

VILA CORONA CABERNET SAUVIGNON 2001 CRIANZA RED
85% cabernet sauvignon, 15% tempranillo

78 Intense cherry. Toasty aroma of ripe black fruit with slightly sweet spices. Flavourful palate with fresh overtones and a nuance of the vine variety (pepper), well-balanced.

VILA CORONA MERLOT 2002 RED
100% merlot

76 Ruby red. Aroma with spices and smoky notes over ripe red fruit. Flavourful, light palate with balsamic notes, easy drinking.

NERET JOVEN RED

VINYA L'HEREU

Molí s/n
25739 Sero (Artesa de Segre) (Lleida)
☎: 639 311 175 - Fax: 973 400 472
apijuan@telefonica.net

Established: 2002

🍷 28 📦 90,000 litres 🍇 14 has.
🍷 60% 🌍40%: -AD -US

EL PETIT GREALÓ SERÓ 2003 JOVEN RED
50% syrah, 25% cabernet sauvignon, 25% merlot

87 Very dark deep cherry. Toasty aroma with exotic spices (incense), abundant black fruit (dates, plums), and dry stones, original. Fleshy, powerful palate with woody tannins over abundant fruit and a slightly bitter finish (bitter cocoa and minerals).

FLOR DE GREALÓ 2002 BARREL AGED RED
50% merlot, 25% cabernet sauvignon, 25% syrah

86 Dark cherry. Aroma with notes of dry stone with spices and a nuance of jammy fruit and fine smoky wood. Fleshy, bitter palate with marked oak tannins, powerful with an intense notion of terroir.

DO DOMINIO DE VALDEPUSA

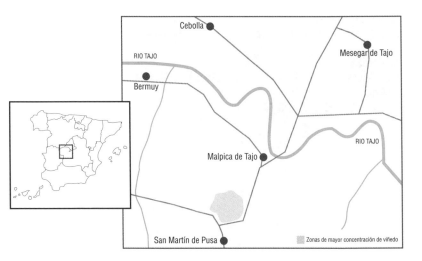

NEWS. Carlos Falcó, the Marquis of Griñón, is a visionary in the Spanish vineyard. Not only did he secretly introduce the foreign stocks *Cabernet Sauvignon* and *Chardonnay* into his estate in La Mancha near Toledo back in the 70s, but he also put into practice a wine-growing style considered revolutionary at the time in Spain which he gradually assimilated from his trips learning about oenology around the world. He also brought to Spain, after passing through the prestigious Davis University, and at the hands of the wine-growing guru from New Zealand, Richard Smart, the new formulas for the layout of vines; rather a whole new philosophy on maximizing the amount of sun absorbed by the grapes. This is what is known today as 'Canopy Management'.

He also dared to evade the issue of the DOs and make do without the official black label, without renouncing high quality. Finally, his efforts have paid off, and two years ago he managed to position his wines at the top of the pyramid after eventually being awarded the recognition of Vinos de Pago with the approval of the Autonomous Government of Castilla La Mancha.

His pet grape varieties have been, besides the *Cabernet Sauvignon*, which brought him his first successes, the likewise French varieties *Syrah* –he made the first fine Syrah in Spain, being the pioneer of a variety which is proving to be very successful in Spain– and *Petit Verdot* –a very rare stock not frequently used round the world, to which he also managed to give a special dimension–.

LOCATION. The bodega is situated on the estate, which has been owned by the family since 1262, in the vicinity of Malpica de Tajo (Toledo), in the valley of the river Pusa.

CLIMATE. This region has a continental climate, harsh and extreme, which requires the use of irrigation. The summers are hot and dry, with extremely little rainfall each year, usually coinciding with the harvesting season.

SOIL. The soil is mainly clayey calcareous in nature.

VARIETIES:
White: *Chardonnay.*
Red: *Cabernet Sauvignon, Syrah, Petit Verdot, Merlot* and *Graciano.*

ADDRESS.
Ctra. San Martín de Pusa, Km. 6.500. Finca Casadevacas. 45692 Malpica de Tajo (Toledo).
Tel: 952 597 222. Fax: 925 789 416.

DOMINIO DE VALDEPUSA

Carretera San Marín de Pusa, km. 6, 500
Finca Casadevacas
45692 Malpica de Tajo (Toledo)
☎: 925 597 222 - Fax: 925 789 416
egener@arcobu.com
www.marquesdegrinon.com

Established: 1989

🛢 700 📊 370,000 litres 🍇 42 has.

🚩 35% 🌐65%

MARQUÉS DE GRIÑÓN EMERITVS 2000 RESERVA RED

92 Intense cherry. Powerful aroma, with a suggestion of mineral expression, earthy hints, jammy black fruit, carob. Powerful, meaty, balsamic, and spirituous palate, sweet tannins, slightly warm.

DOMINIO DE VALDEPUSA SYRAH 2001 RED
100% syrah

89 Intense cherry with a slightly orangey edge. Aroma of ripe fruit, balsamic hints with fallen leaves, with an essence of minerals, slightly short fruit expression. Meaty palate, sweet and firm tannins. Jammy black fruit, flavourful, not very long.

DOMINIO DE VALDEPUSA CABERNET SAUVIGNON 2001 RED
100% cabernet sauvignon

90 Quite intense cherry with an orange edge. Fine and toasty aroma, ripe varietal, evoking earthiness (dry clay) Meaty palate, ripe, flavourful and well-balanced on the palate.

DOMINIO DE VALDEPUSA PETIT VERDOT 2001 RED
100% petit verdot

88 Very intense cherry. Toasty aroma, fairly impenetrable with balsamic notes, hints of pitch, and dry forest. Powerful and meaty palate, jammy black fruit, sweet tannins, a toasty and balsamic retronasal effect.

SUMMA VARIETALIS 2002 BARREL AGED RED

DO EL HIERRO

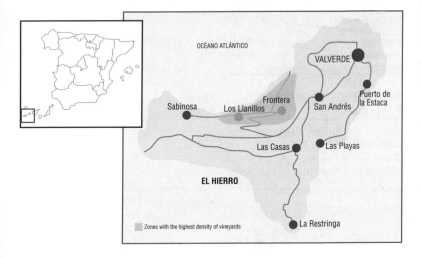

NEWS. The Gran Salmor, a sweet wine which in fact seems to be heading in what is considered the most reliable direction for the future of quality wines on the island, this time seems slightly less expressive than the previous vintage. Meanwhile, another of the wines of the same bodega (and the only one whose samples we had access to within the DO) is the wine which managed to pull it off as far as scoring is concerned, obtaining 80 points. The Viña Frontera wines, despite the difficulty of identifying such a variety of different wines under the same brand, due to their greater or lesser residual sugar content and to the variable percentages of the

Hectares of Vineyard	No. of Viticulturists	No. of Bodegas	2003 Harvest	2003 Production	Marketing
192	298	5 bottlers	Good	312,000 kilos	Mainly in the Canary Islands.

dominant varieties, are perhaps the only ones which are worthwhile in El Hierro. The remaining wines have in recent years been subjected to continuous disqualification by the Regulatory Council.

With regard to the varieties, the *Verijadiego*, blended with the *Listán Blanca*, is at present the top scorer, followed by the *Bremajuelo* which does not seem to be producing wines of great interest.

LOCATION. On the island of El Hierro, part of the Canary Islands. The production area covers the whole island, although the main growing regions are Valle del Golfo, Sabinosa, El Pinar and Echedo.

CLIMATE. Fairly mild in general, although higher levels of humidity are recorded in high mountainous regions. Rainfall is relatively low.

SOIL. Volcanic in origin, with a good water retention and storage capacity. Although the vineyards were traditionally cultivated in the higher regions, at present most of them are found at low altitudes, resulting in an early ripening of the grapes.

VARIETIES:

White: *Verijadiego* (majority with 50% of all white varieties), *Listán Blanca, Bremajuelo, Uval (Gual), Pedro Ximénez, Baboso, Gual* and *Moscatel*.
Red: *Listán Negro, Negramoll, Baboso Negro* and *Verijadiego Negro*.

REGULATORY COUNCIL.

Oficina de Agricultura. El Matorral, s/n. 38911 Frontera (El Hierro).
Tel: 922 556 064 / 922 559 744. Fax: 922 55 96 91.
E-mail: doelhierro@hotmail.com

GENERAL CHARACTERISTICS OF THE WINES:

Whites	These are the most characteristic wines of the island. They are produced mainly from the *Vijariego* and *Listán Blanco* varieties. They are straw yellow, quite fresh and fruity and, on occasions, they have notes of tropical fruit.
Rosés	These are characterised by their orangey raspberry colour and are quite fresh and fruity.
Reds	These are characterised by their good quality. Likewise, they are quite full-bodied and fruity.

DIEGO S. ACOSTA PADRÓN

Los Mocanes, 40
38911 Frontera (Tenerife)
☎: 922 559 543

Established: 1999
🗍 3,000 litres 🍷 2% 🍇98%

VIÑA DIEGOS 2002 WHITE

EL TESORO

Licenciado Bueno, 7
38900 Valverde (El Hierro)
☎: 922 550 780 - Fax: 922 550 780

BODEGAS EL TESORO WHITE
BODEGAS EL TESORO RED

UWE URBACH

El Matorral, 60
38911 Frontera (El Hierro)
☎: 922 559 581 - Fax: 922 559 581

Established: 1996
🌐 21 🗍 15,000 litres 🍇 5 has. 🍷 100%

TEGAMÓN WHITE
GOTA DE VINO RED

VIÑA FRONTERA

El Matorral, s/n
38911 Frontera (Tenerife)
☎: 922 556 016 - Fax: 922 556 042
coopfrontera@cooperativafrontera.com
www.cooperativafrontera.com

Established: 1986
🌐 60 🗍 600,000 litres 🍷 100%

VIÑA FRONTERA 2003 JOVEN WHITE
100% verijadiego blanco

70 Straw-coloured. Aroma with notes of evolution, very ripe raisiny grapes. Fresh, fruity, flavourful and sweet palate, foresty notes.

VIÑA FRONTERA 2001 F. BARRICA SECO WHITE
50% verijadiego, 40% listán blanco, 5% pedro ximénez, 5% uval

70 Reddish gold. Aroma of wood with muted fruit and overtones of oxidative evolution. Concealed fruit and evident oak on the palate.

VIÑA FRONTERA 2003 SECO WHITE
40% verijadiego, 40% listán blanco, 10% pedro ximénez, 5% baboso blanco, 5% uval

78 Straw-coloured. Powerful aroma, rich in notes of foresty herbs and sweet fruit. Fresh, flavourful palate with quite wild herbs.

VIÑA FRONTERA 2003 SECO WHITE
95% bremajuelo, 5% pedro ximénez

70 Straw-coloured. Sweet and foresty aroma with notes of herbs, fruity. A foresty suggestion on the palate, quite low on fruit.

VIÑA FRONTERA 2003 SEMISECO WHITE
60% verijadiego, 40% listán blanco

79 Straw-coloured. Fresh, fruity aroma of foresty herbs. Sweet, flavourful and fruity palate.

GRAN SALMOR OAK AGED DULCE WHITE

Reddish gold. Aroma with woody oak notes and ripe fruit (jam and crystallised fruit). Sweet palate with bitter oak and something of a varietal character, flavourful.

VIÑA FRONTERA 2003 SEMIDULCE WHITE
60% verijadiego, 40% listán blanco

80 Straw-coloured. Fresh, somewhat short, fruity aroma with notes of sweet fruit and fragrant herbs. Sweet, flavourful and fruity palate, fresh.

VIÑA FRONTERA 2003 ROSÉ
GRAN SALMOR 2001 DULCE RED
VIÑA FRONTERA 2003 RED
VIÑA FRONTERA 2000 DULCE RED
VIÑA FRONTERA 2000 CRIANZA RED

DO EMPORDÀ-COSTA BRAVA

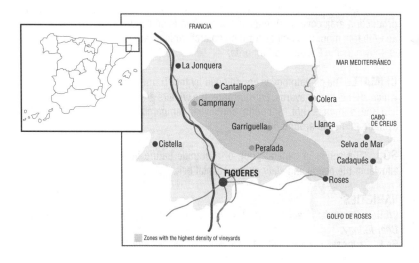

Zones with the highest density of vineyards

NEWS. An unusual year in climatological terms, with extreme meteorological conditions. With less rainfall than usual during the winter and an exceptionally hot summer, there was a lot of nail-biting before the rains eventually arrived days before the grape harvest. The reason for this is that a lack of humidity dehydrates the plant and stunts its growth (the grapes receive no sugars or acids), consequently affecting the yield and the quality of the grapes. The late rains, together with the north wind during the harvest, saved the quality but required some extra dedication from the oenologists.

Hectares of Vineyard	No. of Viticulturists	No. of Bodegas	2003 Harvest	2003 Production	Marketing
2,033	549	31	Very Good	65,000 hectolitres	95% Spain 5% foreign

Excellent work by Castillo de Perelada with all their top quality wines, with four of them scoring 90 points, and the Gran Claustro wines which, thanks to their modernity and concentration, are gradually catching up with the Ex Ex series. In a league of their own: Garbet (95 points) and Ex Ex 4 (93 points) with a superb *Syrah*. Castillo de Perelada, with an exemplary philosophy for technological renovation and research, and with Josep Lluís Pérez (Clos Martinet) and Simó Serra at the head of its oenological department, currently has 150 Ha of vineyard spread over 4 different estates in the DO Empordà: El Garrigal, Malaveïna, Garbet and Espolla.

The singular and idiosyncratic Oliver Contí is once again on the podium and, beating a path to the door of the 90s, we find the Ctònia and Gneis of Masia Serra, as well as the sweet wines (one of the region's most prized jewels) of Martí Fabra.

It is strange that the young wine awarded the most points, the Floresta 2003 of Pere Guardiola, is also one of the very few (together with the Sauló of Celler Espelt) that defends the national varieties against the increasingly omnipresent foreign grape varieties, which seem to be called upon to determine the future character of the region's wines.

LOCATION. In the far north west of Catalonia, in the province of Girona. The production area covers 40 municipal areas and is situated the slopes of the Rodes and Alberes mountain ranges forming an arch which leads from Cape Creus to what is known as the Garrotxa d'Empordà.

CLIMATE. The climatology is conditioned by the 'Tramontana', a strong north wind which affects the vineyards. Furthermore, the winters are mild, with hardly any frost, and the summers hot, although somewhat tempered by the sea breezes. The average rainfall is around 600 mm.

SOIL. The soil is in general poor, of a granitic nature in the mountainous areas, alluvial in the plains and slaty on the coastal belt.

VARIETIES:
White: *Garnacha Blanca* (200 Ha), *Macabeo* (100 Ha), *Moscatel, Xarel·lo* and *Chardonnay.*
Red: *Cariñena* (majority with 1,815 Ha), *Garnacha Tinta* (150 Ha), *Ull de Llebre (Tempranillo), Cabernet Sauvignon* and *Merlot.*

REGULATORY COUNCIL.
Avda. Marignane, 2. Apto. Correos 186. 17600 Figueres (Gerona).
Tel: 972 507 513. Fax: 972 510 058.
E-mail: doempcb@teleline.es

GENERAL CHARACTERISTICS OF THE WINES:

Whites	Those produced from autochthonous varieties are fresh and flavourful on the palate and persistent; their aroma is reminiscent of hay and apples. Single variety wines from *Chardonnay* are also produced.
Rosés	These are pink-raspberry coloured with a fruity aroma and are relatively intense, fresh and light.
Reds	*Novell* red wines are produced (they are marketed immediately after the harvest to be consumed within the year) with a deep cherry-red colour, easy drinking with good indices of acidity and a red berry aroma. The Crianza wines are aromatic with notes of spices; on the palate they are flavourful and pleasant to drink.
Licorosos	Traditional wines of the region produced from *Garnacha*. Red amber in colour, the aroma has notes of Mistela and Rancio; on the palate they stand out for their sweetness and stickiness.

DO EMPORDÁ-COSTA BRAVA

Cooperativa Vinícola ALT EMPORDÀ

Carretera de Roses, 3
17493 Vilajuica ()
☎: 972 530 043 - Fax: 972 552 019

CASTELL DE QUERMANÇÓ 2003 WHITE
macabeo

75 Brilliant gold. Intense aroma of white fruit with toasty skins and hints of petals. Quite flavourful on the palate with notes of nuts, herbs and a mild evolution.

CASTELL DE QUERMANÇÓ 2002 ROSÉ
garnacha, cariñena, merlot

76 Pale cherry with an orangey hue. Not very intense aroma of red stone fruit with a fine viscous element. Flavourful palate with notes of evolution and a sweet essence, warm with nuts and mountain herbs.

VINYA DELS DOLMENS 2002 CRIANZA RED
80% garnacha, 20% cariñena

81 Garnet red cherry with a saffron edge. Intense aroma with toasty oak notes, an essence of ripe fruit and a fine reduction (tobacco, leather, prunes). Flavourful palate with rough and oily tannins, bitter notes (coffee, liquorice) and viscous hints.

CASTELL DE QUERMANÇÓ 2002 RED
garnacha, cariñena, merlot

73 Ruby red cherry with a coppery glint. Slightly intense, fruity aroma with hints of evolution (nuts, spices, an essence of acetaldehydes). Flavourful, light, slightly fruity palate.

MERLOT CASTELL DE QUERMANÇÓ 2000 RED
merlot

73 Garnet red with an orangey rim. Aroma of cheese with reduction notes and not very noble woods. Acidic, short, light palate, without varietal expression with a persistent suggestion of cheese in the retronasal passage.

GARNATXA D'EMPORDÁ CDQ 1999 SWEET
garnacha

83 Mahogany. Medium-intensity aroma with rancid notes, caramel and pastries. Sweet, generous palate with very toasty notes and nuts, quite old but very well-mannered wood.

MOSCATELL D'EMPORDÁ CDQ 2003 DULCE
moscatel

85 Lively golden. Musky aroma of honey and crystallised fruit, fresh. Flavourful, sweet palate with notes of herbs and toasty skins, fresh and well-balanced.

CASTELL DE BIART

Carretera de Vilarnadal - Perelada, s/n
17763 Masarac (Alt Empordá)

☎: 972 510 008 - Fax: 972 555 165

CASTELL DE BIART 2003 JOVEN WHITE
macabeo, xarel.lo

65 Pale steel. Not very intense, unclear aroma of yeast. Without expression on the palate and with an edge of acidity.

CASTELL DE BIART XAREL.LO 2003 WHITE
100% xarel.lo

70 Pale greenish. Aroma of yeast and hay, slightly flat and without expression of the vine variety. Sweet-acidic notes on the palate yet to be assembled.

CASTELL DE BIART SAUVIGNON BLANC 2002 WHITE

79 Pale steel. Aroma of aromatic herbs and grapefruit, not very varietal. Notes of hay, smokiness and citrus fruit on the palate, bitter.

CASTELL DE BIART 2003 ROSÉ
garnacha , syrah

77 Lively raspberry. Medium-intensity, balsamic aroma (fallen leaves) of red fruit. Menthol and balsamic notes on the palate, slightly spicy, curious.

CASTELL DE BIART 2003 RED
100% tempranillo

80 Garnet red cherry. Balsamic, fresh aroma of red fruit. Flavourful and pleasant on the palate with fresh fruit, slightly warm in the finish.

CASTELL DE BIART 2001 CRIANZA RED
merlot, garnacha tinta, cariñena

84 Cherry with an orange edge. Aroma with very sweet notes, jammy tomatoes and very ripe red fruit. Warm palate with ripe fruit; well-balanced.

CASTILLO DE CAPMANY

Plaza del Fort, 5
17750 Capmany (Girona)
☎: 972 549 043 - Fax: 972 549 043
castillodecapmany@terra.es

Established: 1994

🍷 55 📊 60,000 litres 🌿 11 has.

🍇 60% 🌍40%: -DE -FR

MOLL DE ALBA 2001 CRIANZA RED
cabernet sauvignon, merlot, garnacha

80 Quite deep garnet red. Aroma of wood with tobacco, spices and mild notes of sweetness. Drying palate with slightly marked wood tannins, not very persistent.

CASTILLO OLIVARES 2002 RED
cabernet sauvignon, merlot, garnacha

80 Cherry with light orange notes. Aroma of sun-drenched skins, perfumed and quite floral. Drying palate with greeness, light bitter notes and a suggestion of cocoa in the retronasal passage.

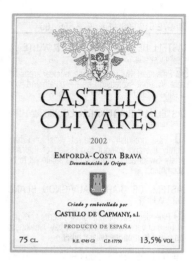

MOLL DE ALBA 2000 CRIANZA RED
cabernet sauvignon, merlot, garnacha

86 Deep cherry with a brick red edge. Powerful aroma of fine toasty oak notes with a varietal accent and fine reduction notes (tobacco, cedar, prunes). Flavourful, supple palate with fine bitter notes (liquorice), slightly oily with hints of Cabernet paprika.

Cavas del
CASTILLO DE PERELADA

Pl. del Carmen, 1
17491 Perelada (Girona)
☎: 972 538 011 - Fax: 972 538 277
bodegas@castilloperelada.com
www.castilloperelada.com

Established: 1923
🍷 4,600 🛢 2,100,000 litres 🍇 132 has.
🍷 85% 🍏15%

CASTILLO DE PERELADA CHARDONNAY 2003 JOVEN WHITE
100% chardonnay

87 Brilliant pale. Intense aroma of white fruit with notes of anise and fennel and fine citrus notes. Flavourful palate with fine spicy notes, a mineral freshness and excellent acidity.

CASTILLO DE PERELADA SAUVIGNON BLANC 2003 JOVEN WHITE
100% sauvignon blanc

80 Straw-coloured with a greenish hue. Medium-intensity, clean, fresh aroma with notes of herbs and grapefruit. Flavourful palate with a bitter counterpoint and white fruit, pleasant.

CASTILLO DE PERELADA BLANC DE BLANCS 2003 WHITE
macabeo, xarel.lo, chardonnay

81 Brilliant pale yellow. Intense aroma of ripe white fruit with floral hints (acacia) and a fresh grapeskins freshness. Flavourful, bitter palate with less fruit expression than in the nose, good acidity.

CASTILLO DE PERELADA 2003 JOVEN ROSÉ
70% garnacha, 20% cariñena, 10% tempranillo

80 Intense raspberry with a coppery glint. Quite intense aroma of red stone fruit with spicy hints of skins. Flavourful, fruity palate with a grapeskins and fine herb freshness, good acidity.

CASTILLO DE PERELADA CABERNET SAUVIGNON 2003 JOVEN ROSÉ
100% cabernet sauvignon

82 Brilliant blush cherry. Powerful aroma of ripe red fruit with sweet and spicy hints of skins (suggestion of varietal paprika). Flavourful, fruity palate with meaty overtones and a spicy essence, slightly warm and oily.

GRAN CLAUSTRO 2000 OAK AGED RED
45% cabernet sauvignon, 25% merlot, 17% cariñena, 13% garnacha

90 Dark cherry with an orangey edge. Powerful aroma of concentrated fruit and spices (pepper), very balsamic, fine woods. Powerful, flavourful and concentrated on the palate with well-assembled ripe black fruit and wood and ripe tannins with a long viscous finish.

CASTILLO DE PERELADA 2001 CRIANZA RED
tempranillo, garnacha, cabernet sauvignon

84 Cherry with an orangey rim. Toasty wood aroma of good reduction, balsamic flavours and coffee. Warm on the palate with good tannins and toffee notes in the retronasal passage.

CASTILLO DE PERELADA CABERNET SAUVIGNON 2000 CRIANZA RED
100% cabernet sauvignon

DO EMPORDÁ-COSTA BRAVA

87 Garnet red cherry with a saffron edge. Intense, very fine aroma of jammy black fruit with quite varietal spicy hints (paprika) and nuances of oak. Flavourful palate with rough and oily tannins, a fruity essence, liquorice, pitch, balsamic notions and good varietal and crianza character.

CASTILLO DE PERELADA 2001 RESERVA RED
cabernet sauvignon, merlot, garnacha, cariñena

87 Cherry with a garnet red-orangey edge. Fine aroma with balsamic notes, ripe fruit, toasty wood and a perfumed nuance. Powerful, very flavourful and somewhat concentrated on the palate with pleasant toasty notes, jammy fruit, ripe tannins and chocolate in the finish.

CASTILLO DE PERELADA 2000 RESERVA RED
cabernet sauvignon, merlot, garnacha, cariñena

86 Fairly dark cherry with a garnet red edge. Intense, spicy aroma (pepper, tobacco) with fine toasty oak and ripe redcurrants. Powerful, flavourful, balsamic palate with well-integrated creamy oak, long.

CASTILLO DE PERELADA TORRE GALATEA CABERNET SAUVIGNON 2000 RESERVA RED
100% cabernet sauvignon

88 Almost opaque cherry. Powerful aroma with copious nuances, jammy fruit, toastiness, varietal paprika and fine reduction (cedar, prunes). Flavourful palate with a good fruit/oak integration, fine bitter notes (pitch, liquorice) and excellent acidity.

FINCA GARBET DE CASTILLO DE PERELADA 2001 RESERVA RED
75% syrah, 25% cabernet sauvignon

95 Lively Bigarreau cherry with a garnet red edge. Intense aroma of ripe macerated fruit with a viscous edge and spices (pepper), and a herby nuance; complex. Powerful on the palate with a silky texture, red fruit syrup, well-integrated fine woods, herby notes in the retronasal passage and ripe polymerised tannins; long.

GRAN CLAUSTRO DE CASTILLO DE PERELADA 2001 RESERVA RED
54% cabernet sauvignon, 27% merlot, 12% cariñena, 7% garnacha

90 Cherry with a garnet red edge. Intense aroma of concentrated ripe fruit (redcurrants), ink and fine woods. Generous, flavourful and powerful on the palate with well-assembled superripe fruit and wood, ripe and oily tannins and a long toasty finish.

CASTILLO DE PERELADA EX EX 4 2001 RED
100% syrah

93 Very deep cherry with a garnet red edge. Powerful yet fine balsamic aroma (eucalyptus), with character of skins, ink and exotic wood (sandalwood). Powerful palate of concentrated, ripe, black fruit, with balsamic notes, finely integrated wood and sweet but ripe tannins, long, with a viscous hint in the finish.

CASTILLO DE PERELADA FINCA MALAVEÏNA 2001 RED
40% cabernet sauvignon, 30% merlot, 30% garnacha

91 Intense cherry. Powerful, toasty, mineral aroma (peat, chocolate) with very ripe black fruit. Warm, powerful, meaty palate with abundant and ripe tannins, flavourful and slightly spirituous with a mineral retronasal effect.

CASTILLO DE PERELADA DON MIGUEL MATEU 1999 RESERVA RED

COMERCIAL VINÍCOLA DEL NORDEST

Espolla, 9
17752 Mollet de Peralada (Girona)
☎: 972 563 150 - Fax: 972 545 134
vinicola@vinicoladelnordest.com
www.vinicoladelnordest.com

Established: 1977

🍶 80 🗒 1,000,000 litres 🍇 200 has.
🇪🇸 95% 🌐5%

COVEST CHARDONNAY 2003 JOVEN WHITE
100% chardonnay

80 Pale. Intense, clean and fruity aroma of mountain herbs and ripe fruit. Flavourful palate with notes of hay, pleasant and easy drinking.

COVEST 2003 WHITE
85% macabeo, 15% garnacha blanca

70 Pale with a greenish hue. Not very intense aroma with mild herby notes and weak fruit. Well-mannered on the palate but with an edge of acidity.

VINYA FARRIOL SECO WHITE
macabeo, garnacha blanca

72 Straw-coloured. Medium-intensity aroma with notes of cough medicine and a balsamic nuance. Slightly flabby on the palate with notes of herbal tea, without great expression.

VINYA FARRIOL WHITE SEMIDULCE
macabeo, garnacha blanca

71 Straw-coloured. Medium-intensity aroma with herby notes. A slightly sweet, fruity palate, well-mannered but lacking acidity.

COVEST 2003 ROSÉ
70% cariñena, 30% garnacha

80 Blush. Intense, fresh aroma of ripe red fruit with a herby suggestion. Flavourful, lively, fruity and fresh on the palate, easy drinking.

VINYA FARRIOL 2003 SECO ROSÉ
cariñena, garnacha

60 Salmon with an ochre nuance. Evolved aroma and palate, without fruit expression.

VINYA FARRIOL SEMIDULCE ROSÉ
cariñena, garnacha

69 Onion-skins. Faint aroma of fried foods with off-odours from the tank. Better in the mouth, with a good sweet and fruity integration.

COVEST 2003 RED
60% cariñena, 40% garnacha

75 Garnet red cherry with a violet edge. Powerful, fruity palate with spicy hints of skins and notes of damp earth. Flavourful palate of very ripe fruit (hints of raisins).

COVEST CABERNET SAUVIGNON 2003 RED
100% cabernet sauvignon

83 Dark cherry with a purplish edge. Intense aroma of black fruit with a spicy and very varietal essence (paprika) and damp foliage. Flavourful, meaty palate with a good fruit weight, slightly marked yet fine grape tannins, liquorice and spicy skins, slightly oily.

COVEST MERLOT 2003 RED
100% merlot

77 Intense cherry with a purplish rim. Powerful aroma with a varietal expression (redcurrants, nettle, underbrush) and a toasty suggestion of skins. Flavourful palate with slightly herbaceous tannins (elements of greeness) and an acidic edge.

VINYA FARRIOL SECO RED
cariñena

73 Pale cherry with a brick red glint. Intense, not very fine aroma of slightly reduced ripe red fruit and balsamic notes (reminiscent of vermouth). Better on the palate, flavourful with fresh overtones (red stone fruit, terracotta).

GARRIGAL 2002 CRIANZA RED
80% garnacha , 20% cariñena

78 Ruby red cherry with an orange hue. Somewhat intense aroma of jammy black fruit and spicy reduction notes (tanned hide, aged wood). Flavourful and slightly warm on the palate, with bitter notes and nuts in the finish

VINYA FARRIOL SEMIDULCE RED
100% cariñena

71 Garnet red cherry with a brick red glint. Powerful aroma with predominant balsamic notes, thyme and Mediterranean herbs. Flavourful, slightly fruity and sweet on the palate with bitter notes, lacks balance.

ANUBIS NEGRE DE LES COSTES 2001 CRIANZA RED
58% merlot, 30% cabernet sauvignon, 12% garnacha

79 Cherry with a brick red edge. Not very intense, balsamic aroma with a slight varietal expression. Slightly warm and spicy on the palate with balsamic notes in the retronasal passage.

ANUBIS GRAN RESERVA GARNATXA DE L'EMPORDÀ DULCE NATURAL
garnacha blanca, garnacha tinta

83 Mahogany with coppery nuances. Powerful aroma with mild reduction notes (aged wood, cigar box) and currents. Sweet, unctuous palate with spicy and bitter notes (chocolate, herbs) and fresh acidity.

COVEST MOSCATELL DE L'EMPORDÀ DULCE NATURAL
100% moscatel

85 Golden with amber nuances. Powerful, overripe aroma with notes of honey and musk, a certain grapeskins freshness and currents. Flavourful, unctuous palate with fine, raisiny notes and good acidity.

VINYA FARRIOL 2003 RED SEMIDULCE
COVEST GARNATXA DE L'EMPORDÁ RESERVA DULCE
COVEST ULL DE LLEBRE 2003 DULCE

Celler Cooperatiu D'ESPOLLA

Carretera Roses, s/n
17753 Espolla (Gerona)
☎: 972 563 049 - Fax: 972 563 178
espolla@clae.es

Established: 1931

3,000,000 litres 308 has. 95% 5%

MACABEU D'ESPOLLA WHITE
100% macabeo

68 Yellow straw. Slightly artificial cough medicine aroma. Weak fruit on the palate, vegetative, bitter.

MACABEU D'ESPOLLA SUAU WHITE

73 Greenish straw-coloured. Fruity aroma with aromatic herbs. Balsamic and sweet on the palate, well-mannered.

ESPOLLA 1999 CRIANZA RED

73 Garnet red cherry with a brick red rim. Powerful aroma with not very fine reduction off-odours notes (pitch). Better on the palate; flavourful, with an oily texture, reduced fruit notes, spices and balsamic hints.

DO EMPORDÁ-COSTA BRAVA

ESPOLLA GARNATXA DE L'EMPORDÀ DULCE NATURAL
65% garnacha blanca, 35% garnacha tinta

82 Amber with greenish nuances. Intense aroma with predominant spicy and smoky notes of wood and mild reduction hints (old furniture). Flavourful, somewhat unctuous and sweet palate with good acidity.

ESPOLLA MUSCAT D'EMPORDÀ DULCE NATURAL
100% moscatel

84 Pale golden yellow. Intense aroma with a slight varietal expression and notes of flowers, spices and zest. Flavourful, sweetish and somewhat unctuous palate with the freshness of herbs and nuts, good acidity.

Celler ESPELT

Paratge Mas Satlle s/n
17493 Vilajuiga (Girona)
☎: 972 531 727 - Fax: 972 531 741
info@cellerespelt.com
www.cellerespelt.com

Established: 1999

600 ▯ 1,200,000 litres ▯ 130 has.
▯ 95% ▯5%

ESPELT CHARDONNAY 2003 JOVEN WHITE
100% chardonnay

83 Pale gold. Powerful aroma with ripe apples, floral hints (acacia) and a honeyed nuance. Quite fresh on the palate with fine bitter hints, spicy skins, minerals, fine herbs and wax.

VAILET 2003 JOVEN WHITE
50% macabeo, 50% garnacha blanca

74 Straw-coloured. Aroma of slightly reduced fruit. Quite flavourful on the palate with sweet-sour notes, weak fruit.

QUINZE ROURES 2003 FERMENTADO EN BARRICA WHITE
55% chardonnay, 22% macabeo, 23% garnacha blanca

79 Brilliant gold. Intense aroma with predominant caramelised oak notes and an essence of Mediterranean herbs. Flavourful palate with fine bitter wood notes and nuts, somewhat warm and oily.

MARENY 2003 WHITE
50% sauvignon blanc, 50% muscat

77 Pale straw. Musky, intense and very Muscatel aroma. Fresh, fruity palate with a slight edge of acidity, yet well-mannered.

ESPELT GARNATXA DE L'EMPORDÀ JOVEN ROSÉ
garnacha

80 Orangey. Intense aroma with spices, toasty skins, nuts, honey and dried peaches. Sweet on the palate with fine toasty, bittersweet notes, and a spicy, slightly balsamic suggestion.

CORALÍ 2003 ROSÉ
70% merlot, 25% cabernet sauvignon, 5% garnacha

75 Raspberry blush. Intense aroma of slightly overripe red fruit with balsamic notes. Flavourful, balsamic palate, fresher than in the nose, pleasant.

ESPELT LLEDONER 2003 ROSÉ
100% lledoner

70 Lively raspberry. Aroma of slightly reduced and evolved fruit. An element of acidity on the palate with nuts and weak fruit.

SAULÓ 2003 JOVEN RED
80% garnacha, 20% cariñena

83 Garnet red cherry with a violet edge. Powerful, very fresh and fruity aroma with an excellent expression of young wine, a certain herbaceous Cariñena, freshness and spicy hints of skins. Fresh, flavourful palate with foresty red fruit, slightly warm with good acidity.

TERRES NEGRES 2001 RED
80% cabernet sauvignon, 20% cariñena

76 Dark cherry with an orangey edge. Medium-intensity, spicy aroma of slightly reduced fruit. Dark-roasted flavours and pitch on the palate with very noticeable extraction.

ESPELT VIDIVÍ 2001 CRIANZA RED
30% cariñena, 20% cabernet sauvignon, 18% merlot, 17% tempranillo, 15% garnacha

82 Cherry with a brick red edge. Intense spicy aroma with balsamic notes and green peppers. Flavourful palate with concentrated fruit, strong toasty oak, and a hint of pitch; slightly warm but quite long.

AIRAM GARNATXA DE L'EMPORDÀ DULCE NATURAL
garnacha, garnacha blanca

86 Dark amber with an orange glint. Powerful, spicy aroma (cinnamon, oriental spices), with hints of overripe skins, a certain woody freshness and cocoa powder. Flavourful, spicy palate with fine bittersweet notes of jammy fruit, somewhat unctuous and long.

ESPELT MOSCATELL DE L'EMPORDÁ 15/5 MOSCATEL
100% moscatel

80 Old gold. Musky aroma of crystallised fruit and honey. Flavourful, varietal, sweet and pleasant on the palate.

SOLIVENT MOSCATELL DE L'EMPORDÁ GARNATXA DE L'EMPORDÀ SWEET
100% moscatel

80 Golden amber. Spicy aroma of toasty grapes with nuances of incense and quince. Sweet, unctuous palate of raisins, and crystallised fruit, slightly pasty, lacking freshness with a very sweet finish.

Cooperativa Agrícola de GARRIGUELLA

Carretera de Roses, s/n
17780 Garriguella (Girona)

☎: 972 530 002 - Fax: 972 531 747
coopgarriguella@cdgir.com
www.crae.com/coopetivagarriguella.com
Established: 1963
🛢 80 ▯ 1,980,000 litres 🍷 100%

DINARELLS 2004 WHITE
100% macabeo

73 Pale with golden nuances. Ripe aroma with hints of withered petals and slightly reduced white fruit. Flavourful palate with fine bitter notes and an acidic edge.

DINARELLS 2004 ROSÉ
garnacha, cariñena

79 Brilliant raspberry. Not very intense aroma of red fruit. Better on the palate, flavourful with ripe fruit, a slightly oily texture, very sweet, with good acidity.

DINARELLS 2003 RED
garnacha, cariñena

75 Lively garnet red cherry. Slightly flat, delicate fruity aroma. Better in the mouth, flavourful, fruity and easy drinking.

GARIGUELLA 2002 CRIANZA RED
garnacha, cariñena, cabernet sauvignon, merlot

79 Garnet red cherry with a brick red edge. Powerful aroma with not very fine reduction notes (evoking stables) and black fruit. Flavourful, meaty palate with slightly marked tannins, a slightly oily texture, sweet fruit and dark-roasted flavours.

GARNATXA D'EMPORDÁ DULCE ROSÉ PUNTILS 2003 RED
VINYA GARRIGUELLA NOVELL 2003 RED

Celler GENERI

Plaza Teresa Palleja, 3
17707 Agullana (Girona)
☎: 972 535 505 - Fax: 972 535 505
Established: 1997
🛢 12 ▯ 8,000 litres 🍇 2.5 has. 🍷 100%

PRAT D'EGNA 2000 RED
merlot, cabernet sauvignon

85 Dark cherry. Powerful aroma with excellent varietal expression (paprika, redcurrants, damp earth) and fine toasty oak. Flavourful palate with a good fruit/oak integration, predominant notes of spicy skins and wood; slightly oily with excellent acidity.

PRAT D'EGNA 2002 ROBLE WHITE

Celler MARÍA PAGÈS

Pujada, 6
17750 Capmany (Girona)

☎: 972 549 160 - Fax: 972 549 160
cellermpages@terra.es
Established: 1993
🛢 60 ▯ 80,000 litres 🍇 10 has. 🍷 100%

SERRASAGUÉ 2003 WHITE
chardonnay, garnacha blanca

75 Gold with a coppery hue. Clean, original aroma with notes of herbs and aniseed. Light palate also with abundant aniseed notes, quite unusual.

SERRASAGUÉ 2003 ROSÉ
tempranillo, garnacha tinta

77 Brilliant salmon. Not very intense aroma with an essence of aniseed and hardly any fruit nuances. Flavourful palate with fine bitter notes, slightly warm with an essence of crystallised fruit and a mild sweetness.

VI NOVELL 2003 JOVEN RED
tempranillo, cariñena, garnacha

78 Not very deep cherry. Perfumed aroma with sweet notes and a suggestion of raisins. Light, not very persistent palate with a suggestion of raisins in the retronasal passage.

SERRASAGUÉ 2000 CRIANZA RED
tempranillo, garnacha, cariñena

78 Deep cherry. Earthy aroma of jammy black fruit with marked toasty notes. Meaty palate with marked oak tannins, earthy nuances and bitter cocoa in the finish.

Celler MARTÍ FABRA

Barrio Vic, 26
17751 Sant Climent Sescebes (Girona)
☎: 972 563 011 - Fax: 972 563 011
celermartifabra@cdgir.com
Established: 1946
🛢 120 ▯ 300,000 litres 🍇 20 has.
🍷 70% 🍇30%

VERD ALBERA 2003 WHITE
100% moscatel

82 Pale with greenish nuances. Intense, fresh aroma of green fruit, fennel, anise, and balsamic herbs. Flavourful, very fresh palate with the same notes as in the nose, excellent acidity, original.

LLADONER 2003 ROSÉ
90% garnacha, 10% tempranillo

79 Quite pale cherry with a coppery hue. Intense, fruity aroma with notes of withered petals and macerated red fruit. Flavourful, slightly meaty palate with spicy and fruity hints.

MARTÍ FABRA SELECCIÓ VINYES VELLES 2001 RED
70% garnacha, 10% cariñena, 10% tempranillo, 5% syrah, 5% cabernet sauvignon

DO EMPORDÁ-COSTA BRAVA

85 Garnet red cherry with a saffron edge. Not very intense aroma of ripe fruit, fine hints of reduction (leather, dates) and toasty hints of oak. Flavourful palate with a good oak/fruit integration, fine bitter notes (liquorice, dark-roasted flavours) and excellent acidity.

MASÍA CARRERAS 2000 RED
60% garnacha, 20% cariñena, 10% tempranillo, 5% syrah, 5% cabernet sauvignon

85 Garnet red cherry with a brick red edge. Intense, very fine aroma with predominant reduction notes (tobacco, leather), and a balsamic and spicy oak suggestion. Flavourful palate with a good oak/fruit integration, well-balanced with hints of dates, leather and spices in the retronasal passage.

MASÍA CARRERAS 1998 RED
60% garnacha, 20% cariñena, 10% tempranillo, 5% syrah, 5% cabernet sauvignon

85 Dark cherry with a coppery-brick red edge. Powerful aroma of jammy black fruit, spicy hints of oak, a balsamic suggestion and fine reduction. Flavourful, powerful palate with a good fruit/oak integration, dark-roasted hints and balsamic notes and liquorice in the finish.

MASIA CARRERAS GRAN RESERVA DE LA FAMILIA 1945 GRAN RESERVA DULCE NATURAL

88 Mahogany with an orangey rim. Powerful aroma with fine raisiny and crianza notes (carpentry, nuts). Flavourful and somewhat unctuous on the palate with toasty and bitter crianza notes, a certain raisin skins freshness, mountain herbs and notions of ageing.

MASÍA PAIRAL CAN CARRERAS 2000 DULCE
100% moscatel

89 Brilliant gold. Intense, fruity aroma with excellent varietal expression (flowers, musk) and a suggestion of freshness. Flavourful and slightly unctuous on the palate with fine varietal notes (fresh grapes), hints of marzipan and syrup and good acidity.

MASÍA PAIRAL CAN CARRERAS 1986 DULCE NATURAL
garnacha blanca, garnacha tinta, garnacha rosada

84 Mahogany with an ochre rim. Intense aroma with notes of caramel and raisiny fruit, with fig bread and an aged wood nuance. Sweet, spicy palate (cinnamon, cocoa), with hints of bitter orange marmelade.

FLOR D'ALBERA 2003 FERMENTADO EN BARRICA WHITE
VINYA COMAMILLANA 2003 WHITE
VINYA COMAMILLANA 2003 RED
VI NOVELL 2003 RED

MAS ESTELA

Mas Estela
17489 Selva de Mar (Girona)

☎: 972 126 176 - Fax: 972 388 011
masestela@hotmail.com

Established: 1989

🍷 82 🛢 72,000 litres 🌿 15 has.

🍷 40% 🌐60%: -FR -CH -IT -AT -LU -DE -UK -NL

VINYA SELVA DE MAR 2002 FERMENTADO EN BARRICA WHITE
60% chardonnay, 40% muscat d'Alexandria

82 Golden. Aroma with musky notes, green grass, white flowers and honey. Flavourful palate with herbal tea, white fruit and jammy grapes; very aromatic retronasal effect.

ESTELA SOLERA RED DULCE NATURAL
100% garnacha tinta

83 Ruby red cherry with amber nuances. Somewhat intense aroma of fine toasty notes and dates, with spicy hints (vanilla). Flavourful palate with a certain raisiny freshness and cocoa powder.

VINYA SELVA DE MAR 2000 OAK AGED RED
75% garnacha, 25% syrah

86 Deep cherry. Deep aroma of ripe black fruit (plums), slightly warm with earthy notes (flowers) and toastiness. Meaty palate with weighty fruit, marked yet oily oak tannins and an aftertaste of bitter cocoa.

VINYA SELVA DE MAR 2002 OAK AGED RED
55% garnacha, 30% syrah, 15% carñena

81 Deep cherry. Aroma of very ripe red fruit with a fine smoky essence, slightli warm. Flavourful, expressive, slightly alcoholic palate without great freshness with a balsamic finish.

VINYA SELVA DE MAR MAS ESTELA 2001 OAK AGED RED
75% garnacha, 25% syrah

83 Dark cherry. Intense, not very fine aroma (a suggestion of off-odours, late racking), toasty with an expression of overripe fruit, a balsamic essence and notions of terroir. Flavourful, meaty palate with concentrated overtones, rough tannins, viscous hints (liquorice, sour cherries) and an essence of skins.

VINYA SELVA DE MAR 2001 OAK AGED RED
QUINDALIS MAS ESTELA 2002 OAK AGED RED

Vinyes i Cellers MAS LLUNES

Carretera de Roses, s/n
17780 Garriguela (Girona)
☎: 972 530 089 - Fax: 972 530 112

Established: 2000

🍷 40 🛢 239,000 litres 🌿 40 has.

EMPÓRION 2001 CRIANZA RED
45% cabernet sauvignon, 35% merlot, 20% garnacha tinta

86 Dark cherry. Intense aroma with fine varietal notes (bilberries, paprika) and spicy oak with a balsamic suggestion. Flavourful palate with ripe and fine tannins, an excellent varietal fruit expression, balsamic and spicy hints.

Bodegas MAS VIDA

Afuera s/n
17741 Cistella (Girona)
☎: 972 546 384

MASVIDA CHARDONNAY 2002 WHITE
100% chardonnay

83 Pale with greenish nuances. Intense aroma of white fruit, fine herbaceous notes of lees and smoky hints of oak. Powerful, flavourful palate with a good fruit/oak integration, hints of smokiness and vanilla in the retronasal passage and good acidity.

MAS VIDA CABERNET SAUVIGNON 2000 RED
100% cabernet sauvignon

84 Very deep cherry with a garnet red edge. Intense aroma of dark-roasted flavours, pitch and jammy fruit. Warm, flavourful and varietal on the palate with a good expression of Mediterranean Cabernet.

MASIA SERRA

Dels Solés, 20
17750 Cantallops (Girona)
☎: 629 335 022 - Fax: 972 514 006
gestec@tiservinet.es
Established: 1995
🍷 65 📊 24,000 litres 🍇 10 has.
🍷 55% 🌐 45%

CTÒNIA 2002 OAK AGED WHITE
100% garnacha blanca

89 Pale golden yellow. Powerful aroma with predominant smoky oak notes, a suggestion of white fruit and hints of fine herbs. Flavourful palate with a good fruit/oak integration, a slightly warm, oily texture, waxy hints and powerful hints of toffee, minerals and Mediterranean herbs in the retronasal passage.

GNEIS 2001 OAK AGED RED
cabernet sauvignon, merlot, garnacha tinta

89 Very deep cherry with a purplish edge. Powerful aroma with predominant toasty notes, of jammy black fruit, balsamic notes, glacé cherry liqueur and terracotta. Flavourful, meaty palate with slightly ripe, oily tannins, fine varietal notes (spicy paprika) and good fruit weight.

INO GARNATXA DE L'EMPORDÀ DULCE NATURAL
100% garnacha blanca

86 Amber with greenish nuances. Intense aroma with a certain finesse, predominant vanilla notes and Solera (pâtisserie, nuts). Flavourful palate with fine bittersweet notes, quite sweet, dense, with a spicy nuance (cocoa, cinnamon, nutmeg) and excellent acidity.

OLIVEDA

La Roca, 3
17750 Capmany (Girona)
☎: 972 549 012 - Fax: 972 549 106
comercial10@grupoliveda.com
www.grupoliveda.com
Established: 1948
🍷 600 📊 1,300,000 litres 🍇 50 has.
🍷 75% 🌐 25%: -DE -CH -BE -NL -DK -LU -FR -AD -US

RIGAU ROS 2003 JOVEN WHITE
60% xarel.lo, 30% chardonnay, 10% macabeo

80 Pale straw. Powerful, fresh aroma with a fruity character (apples), fennel and mint. Flavourful and well-mannered palate, less expressive than in the nose.

RIGAU ROS CHARDONNAY 2003 FERMENTADO EN BARRICA WHITE
chardonnay

76 Straw-coloured. Intense aroma of smoky oak with an essence of citrus fruit and ripe white fruit. Fresh, pleasant palate but with considerably weighty and unintegrated wood.

RIGAU ROS 2003 ROSÉ
70% merlot, 20% garnacha, 10% cariñena

71 Raspberry. Slightly short aroma of red fruit and citrus fruit with light vegetative notes. Slightly carbonic on the palate with weak fruit.

DON JOSÉ 2000 CRIANZA RED
80% tempranillo, 10% cariñena, 10% cabernet sauvignon

82 Cherry with an orangey hue. Aroma of dried herbs and toasty skins with a saline edge. Flavourful, expressive palate with wood-fruit symmetry, a hint of muted fruit and balsamic notes.

RIGAU ROS 1999 CRIANZA RED
50% cabernet sauvignon, 25% cariñena, 25% garnacha

77 Ruby red with an orangey hue. Aroma of ripe black fruit with reduction notes, spices and balsamic flavours. Light, fresh, spicy palate with toasty wood notes, very flavourful.

RIGAU ROS CABERNET SAUVIGNON 1998 GRAN RESERVA RED
90% cabernet sauvignon, 10% tempranillo

77 Cherry with an orangey hue. Aroma with notes of reduction and sweet hints. Drying palate with not very marked fruit tannins.

RIGAU ROS GRAN RESEVA 1998 GRAN RESERVA RED
cabernet sauvignon, garnacha, cariñena

77 Cherry with an orangey rim. Aroma with viscous, slightly sweet notes and ripe red fruit. Light, not very persistent palate with reduction notes in the retronasal passage.

CLOS PRIMAT 2003 JOVEN WHITE
CLOS PRIMAT 2003 JOVEN ROSÉ
CLOS PRIMAT 2003 JOVEN RED
VI NOVELL EMPORDÁ 2003 JOVEN RED
RIGAU ROS 1998 RESERVA RED
GARNACHA DEL EMPORDÁ RED SWEET

Celler OLIVER CONTI

Puignau, s/n
17600 Capmany (Girona)
☎: 972 193 161 - Fax: 972 193 040
oliverconti@oliverconti.com
www.oliverconti.com
Established: 1991
🛢 60 🛢 130,000 litres 🍇 15 has.
🍷 63% 🍇37%: -BE -NL -US -UK -FR -CH

OLIVER CONTI 1999 WHITE
50% gewürztraminer, 50% sauvignon blanc

87 Golden straw. Medium-intensity, spicy aroma with mild reduction notes and nuts. White fruit, saline notes, raw almonds and dry on the palate, slightly warm in the finish.

OLIVER CONTI 2000 RED
70% cabernet sauvignon, 20% merlot, 10% cabernet franc

90 Intense cherry. Complex aroma, rich in expression of minerals and fine lees with a smoky essence (cocoa), very elegant. Round and flavourful with good acidity on the palate, notes of ripe fruit and a mineral retronasal effect, flavourful and ripe yet perceptible tannins.

OLIVER CONTI 2000 WHITE
OLIVER CONTI 1999 RED

Cooperativa Agrícola PAU I ROSES

Carretera Roses, s/n
17494 Pau (Girona)
☎: 972 530 140 - Fax: 972 530 528
pauroses@paurosescooperativa.com
www.viemporda.com - www.oliemporda.com
Established: 1961

🛢 300 🛢 1,200,000 litres 🍇 150 has.
🍷 95% 🍇5%: -US -DE -UK -BE

SINOLS 2002 FERMENTADO EN BARRICA WHITE
garnacha blanca, macabeo

83 Pale yellow with golden nuances. Intense aroma of ripe white fruit with predominant creamy oak notes. Flavourful palate with notes of very ripe white stone fruit, a slightly oily texture, hints of wax and herbs.

VINYA VERDERA BLANC DE BLANCS 2003 WHITE
garnacha blanca, macabeo

80 Pale with greenish nuances. Intense, quite fruity aroma with good varietal expression of the Garnacha (wax, flowers). Fresh, flavourful palate of green fruit, balsamic herbs, fine bitter notes and citrus fruit.

SINOLS 2003 ROSÉ
garnacha, cariñena, cabernet sauvignon

83 Brilliant light cherry. Powerful aroma with ripe red fruit, toasty notes of skins and slightly sweet hints. Flavourful, meaty palate with fine toasty notes and a certain tannic freshness, citrus fruit and good acidity.

VINYA VERDERA ROSAT FLOR 2003 ROSÉ
garnacha blanca, cariñena

81 Very deep, brilliant raspberry. Intense aroma of red fruit, hints of flowers and lees. Fresh, flavourful palate with slightly sweet red fruit, fine bitter notes and excellent acidity.

VINYA VERDERA NEGRE 2003 RED

80 Garnet red cherry with a violet hue. Slightly intense aroma of black fruit with fresh notes of maceration and spicy skins. Flavourful, fruity palate with somewhat ripe and firm tannins and excellent acidity.

SINOLS ANTIMA 2001 RED
cariñena

85 Dark garnet red cherry. Powerful aroma with predominant burnt notes and viscous, balsamic notions. Flavourful, meaty palate with a good oak/fruit integration and very ripe fruit, slightly oily with a dark-roasted suggestion.

SINOLS VI DE GUARDA 2000 OAK AGED RED
70% cabernet sauvignon, 20% garnacha, 10% tempranillo

82 Dark cherry with a deep red edge. Intense, ripe aroma of jammy black fruit, balsamic notes and toasty oak. Flavourful, bitter palate with a good fruit/oak association and a spicy, slightly varietal finish (paprika) with liquorice.

SINOLS VI DE GUARDA 2001 OAK AGED RED
cabernet sauvignon, garnacha, tempranillo

83 Dark cherry with a coppery-violet edge. Intense aroma with predominant toasty oak notes and hints of slightly reduced ripe fruit. Flavourful palate with a certain concentration, ripe, oily tannins, fine bitter hints and balsamic notes.

SINOLS 2001 CRIANZA RED
garnacha, cariñena, cabernet sauvignon

82 Garnet red cherry with a saffron hue. Powerful aroma with predominant mild reduction notes (leather, tobacco) and a balsamic nuance. Flavourful, supple palate of jammy fruit, fine bitter notes and refreshing acidity.

SINOLS COROMINA 2001 RED

85 Dark garnet red cherry. Powerful aroma of jammy black fruit with fine toasty hints of oak and a balsamic hint of sour cherries in liqueur. Flavourful, meaty palate with a certain concentration, slightly marked but fine tannins and a spicy essence.

SINOLS GARNATXA DE L'EMPORDÀ DULCE NATURAL
garnacha

86 Amber with a coppery hue. Intense aroma of toasty skins with the freshness of overripe red fruit and spicy and delicately sweet notes. Flavourful, somewhat sweet and unctuous palate with macerated skins, cocoa powder, a fig nuance and good acidity.

SINOLS MOSCATELL DE L'EMPORDÀ 2003 DULCE NATURAL
moscatel

87 Brilliant pale. Intense, very fine aroma with very varietal musky notes and the freshness of ripe pineapples, flowers and citrus fruit. Flavourful, bitter palate with fine bittersweet notes and crystallised lemon peel, spicy and somewhat unctuous with refreshing acidity.

PERE GUARDIOLA

Carretera GI-602, km. 2, 9
17750 Capmany (Gerona)
☎: 972 549 096 - Fax: 972 549 097
vins@pereguardiola.com
www.pereguardiola.com

Established: 1989

🍷 252 🛢 275,000 litres 🍇 38 has.
🍷 87% 🌐13%: -BE -DE

JONCARIA 2002 FERMENTADO EN BARRICA WHITE
100% moscatel

85 Straw-coloured. Intense, musky, fresh aroma of jammy grapes and herbs, barely perceptible oak. Flavourful, and varietal on the palate with mild smoky notes well-integrated in the wine, a curious experience.

JONCARIA 2003 FERMENTADO EN BARRICA WHITE
100% moscatel

83 Straw-coloured with a greenish nuance. Intense, fine aroma with musky notes of Mediterranean hills. Spicy and slightly hot on the palate with character of the vine variety and greater consistency on the palate due to the oak contribution.

FLORESTA 2003 WHITE
60% macabeo, 40% chardonnay

78 Straw-coloured with a greenish nuance. Medium-intensity aroma of ripe white fruit. with a certain complexity of mountain herbs. Less expressive on the palate; light and easy drinking.

FLORESTA 2003 ROSÉ
garnacha, cariñena

80 Lively raspberry blush. Intense aroma of jammy raspberries and caramelised notes. Fresh and light with red fruit on the palate, bitter.

FLORESTA 2003 RED
55% tempranillo, 45% garnacha

85 Brilliant garnet red cherry. Intense, fruity aroma with hints of macerated skins, a suggestion of herbaceous freshness and minerals. Flavourful, fresh palate of red stone fruit, spicy notes of skins and good acidity.

CLOS FLORESTA 2000 OAK AGED RED
40% cabernet sauvignon, 45% merlot, 10% garnacha, 5% cariñena

86 Dark cherry with a saffron edge. Powerful aroma of jammy black fruit with fine toasty oak and spicy hints of skins and black olives. Flavourful, meaty palate with a good oak/fruit integration, with fine notes of spices and brand new leather in the retronasal passage, good acidity.

TORRE DE CAPMANY GRAN RESERVA GARNATXA DE L'EMPORDÀ DULCE NATURAL
100% garnacha blanca

82 Brilliant mahogany. Somewhat intense aroma with fine crianza notes, toasty and pâtisserie hints, currents. Sweet on the palate with quality bittersweet notes, spices, nuts and Catalonian cream custard.

TORRE DE CAPMANY CRIANZA SWEET FLORESTA 1999 CRIANZA RED

Cooperativa Agrícola de RICARDELL

Carretera Madrid - Francia, km. 762
17706 Pont de Molins (Girona)
☎: 972 529 219 - Fax: 972 529 219

Established: 1935

🛢 2,800,000 litres 🍇 97 has.
🍷 97% 🌐3%: -DK -DE -FR

VINYA ORLINA 2003 JOVEN WHITE
macabeo

65 Straw-coloured. Aroma of reduced fruit and lack of racking.

VINYA ORLINA 2003 JOVEN ROSÉ
60% cariñena, 40% garnacha

73 Raspberry pink. Not very intense, yet clean and fruity aroma. Sweetish on the palate, well-mannered.

TRABUCAIRE 2002 RED
50% garnacha, 50% cariñena

75 Garnet red cherry. Slightly intense, ripe aroma with reduction notes (tobacco, aged wood) and a balsamic nuance. Flavourful palate with fine bitter notes and a suggestion of macerating herbs.

VINYA ORLINA 2002 RED
60% cariñena, 40% garnacha

79 Dark garnet red cherry. Slightly intense, ripe aroma of jammy black fruit, with spicy notes of oak and a balsamic nuance. Flavourful palate with round, oily tannins and good acidity.

GARNATXA D'EMPORDÁ RICARDELL 2001 DULCE

Cellers SANTAMARÍA

Plaza Mayor, 6
17750 Capmany (Girona)
☎: 972 549 033 - Fax: 972 549 022
ridi@ctv.es

Established: 1955

🛢 200 🗄 240,000 litres 🌿 12 has.

🍷 80% 🍾20%: -UK -DE -CH

GRAN RECOSIND 1994 GRAN RESERVA RED
garnacha, cariñena, tempranillo, cabernet sauvignon, macabeo

88 Intense garnet red cherry with a brick red edge. Intense aroma of great finesse, with a traditional Reserva expression (old furniture, nuts, cedar, balsamic notes and dark-roasted flavours). Flavourful, supple palate with a good fruit/oak integration, liquorice, spices and dark-roasted flavours in the finish.

GRAN RECOSIND 2000 CRIANZA RED

TROBAT

Castelló, 5
17780 Garriguella (Gerona)
☎: 972 530 092 - Fax: 972 552 530
albertsabido@b.mark.es
www.bodegastrobat.com

Año de fundación: 1965

🛢 60 🗄 300,000 litres 🍷 100%

AMAT CABERNET SAUVIGNON RED
AMAT MERLOT RED

VINYES DELS ASPRES

Requesens, s/n
17708 Cantallops (Girona)
☎: 972 463 146 - Fax: 972 420 662
laselva@jalberti.com

Established: 2001

🛢 65 🗄 60,000 litres 🌿 38 has.

🍷 78% 🍾22%

BLANC DELS ASPRES 2002 FERMENTADO EN BARRICA WHITE
100% garnacha blanca

81 Brilliant gold. Intense aroma of fine smoky notes of oak with white fruit suggestion and spicy hints. Flavourful palate with slightly drying oak tannins, fine notes of vanilla, smoky wood and mountain herbs with mineral notes in the retronasal passage.

NEGRE DELS ASPRES 2001 CRIANZA RED
cabernet sauvignon, garnacha tinta, cariñena, syrah

85 Garnet red cherry. Intense, very fine aroma of black fruit with spicy hints of oak and notes of black olives. Flavourful palate with ripe tannins, fine, very varietal herbaceous notes and waxy hints, spices and terroir.

VI DE PANSES 2001 DULCE RED
100% garnacha

82 Amber with an orange glint. Aroma with stewed fruit notes, an element of reduction and hints of varnish. Sweet palate with a very ripe grape expression and orange peel, unctuous, without freshness and persistent.

BAC DE LES GINESTERES 1997 GARNATXA DE L'EMPORDÀ DULCE NATURAL
100% garnacha

83 Light mahogany. Woody aroma (smoky hints, cedar), spices, a suggestion of stewed white fruit and varnish. Flavourful, fresh palate with rancid notes (almonds), a certain bitterness and hints of pears in liqueur.

DO FINCA ÉLEZ

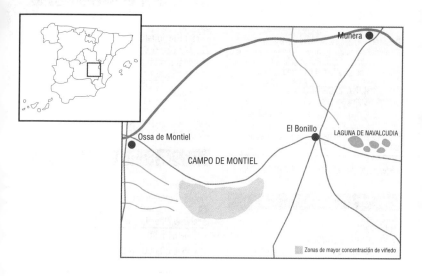

NEWS. The first to be awarded the denomination for 'Vinos de Pago' (estate wines) by the Autonomous Government of Castilla-La Mancha. It belongs to the multifaceted Manuel Manzaneque who, besides being a 'bodeguero' (wine-maker), is an author and theatre producer. The privileged enclave, due to its ideal altitude and cool nights which contrast with the prolonged sunshine in the region, together with the poor soil, allows for wines of a very high quality to be produced. The bodega already made this quite clear with its white *Chardonnay*, which was an instant success in the 90s and was rated one of the best white wines in the country under the supervision of the prestigious oenologist Michel Poudou, who opted for a markedly Burgundy style. Over the years, Finca Élez has increasingly been cultivating red stock, up to 40 Ha of vineyard, which today surrounds the bodega. More prone to blending, the recipe used to produce the Finca Élez brands and its expressive red Escena, the bodega also labels a 100% Syrah.

LOCATION. The estate, at an altitude of over 1,000 m, is situated in the heart of the Sierra de Alcaraz, in the south of the province of Albacete, in the vicinity of the town of El Bonillo.

CLIMATE. The climatology is conditioned by the day-night temperature contrast and the cooling effect that the high altitude has on the vineyards.

SOIL. In general, franc-sandy, limy, with run-off water and a high mineral content.

VARIETIES:
White: *Chardonnay.*
Red: *Cabernet Sauvignon, Merlot, Tempranillo* and *Syrah.*

REGULATORY COUNCIL.
Finca Elez. Ctra. Ossa de Montiel a El Bonillo. 02610 El Bonillo (Albacete).
Tel: 967 585 003. Fax: 967 585 003.
E-mail: manuelmanzaneque@wanadoo.es

MANUEL MANZANEQUE

Finca Elez
Ctra. Ossa de Montiel - El Bonillo
02610 El Bonillo (Albacete)
☎: 967 585 003 - Fax: 967 585003
manuelmanzaneque@wanadoo.es

Established: 1993

🍷 550 ▌ 40 has. 🍷 70%

🌍 30%: UK-BR-MX-DE-CH-SE-AT-JP

MANUEL MANZANEQUE CHARDONNAY 2003 WHITE
100% chardonnay

85 Lemon with a greenish edge. Intense aroma of tropical fruit with a fine smoky nuance and floral notes. Flavourful palate with expression of fresh fruit over the toasty oak; green fruit pulp (bitter) and and oily texture in the finish.

MANUEL MANZANEQUE ESCENA 2002 RED
100% tempranillo

84 Cherry. Aroma of stewed red fruit, floral with slightly green pips. New wood on the palate, somewhat drying, good acidity.

MANUEL MANZANEQUE NUESTRO SYRAH 2002 RED
100% syrah

83 Brilliant deep cherry. Aroma of red berries and well-balanced mild smoky flavours and spicy notes. Fleshy, fresh palate with slightly bitter fruit tannins; well-integrated smoky wood, a dry finish.

MANUEL MANZANEQUE FINCA ELEZ 2001 CRIANZA RED
65% cabernet sauvignon, 20% merlot, 15% tempranillo

85 Garnet red. Medium-intensity aroma of black fruits with spices and smoky (crianza) hints. Dry palate with freshness, fleshy, somewhat woody but flavourful.

MANUEL MANZANEQUE NUESTRA SELEC-CIÓN 2001 RED

DO GETARIAKO TXAKOLINA

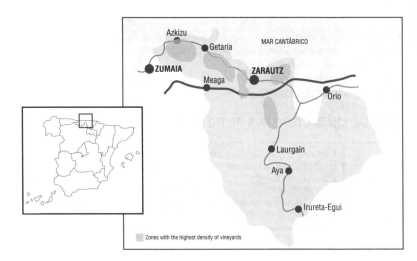

Zones with the highest density of vineyards

NEWS. The 2003 harvest was of a high quality. After a very cold winter, the mild temperatures of the spring helped the settling of the flower and the hot summer brought the harvest some 15 days forward. One of the consequences of the heat, the low acidity, was not a complete disaster in an area whose wines are generally considered to be 'too acidic'.

Despite the fact that some trials have been carried out with red wines (hardly reaching 1500 bottles), the only one we had access to displayed notes verging on this defect. 95% of the vineyards are occupied by the white variety *Hondarrabi Zuri* and only the remaining 5% by the red variety. These two varieties have traditionally been harvested at the same time, as the old vineyards of these two varieties are intermingled and they are used together to produce the white Txakoli.

Hectares of Vineyard	No. of Viticulturists	No. of Bodegas	2003 Harvest	2003 Production	Marketing
177	59	17	Good	1,000,000 litres	98% Spain 2% foreign

LOCATION. On the coastal belt of the province of Guipuzcoa, covering the vineyards situated in the municipal areas of Aia, Getaria and Zarauz, at a distance of about 25 km from San Sebastián.

CLIMATE. Fairly mild, thanks to the influence of the Bay of Biscay. The average annual temperature is 13°C, and the rainfall is plentiful with an average of 1,600 mm per year.

SOIL. The vineyards are situated in small valleys and gradual hillsides at altitudes of up to 200 m. They are found on humid brownish-grey limy soil, which are rich in organic matter.

VARIETIES:
White: *Hondarrabi Zuri* (majority with 90% of all vineyards).
Red: *Hondarrabi Beltza.*

REGULATORY COUNCIL.
Parque Aldamar, 4 bajo. 20808 Getaria (Gipuzkoa).
Tel / Fax: 943 140 383.
E-mail: info@getariakotxakolina.com.
Website: www.getariakotxakolina.com

GENERAL CHARACTERISTICS OF THE WINES:

Whites	Produced from the autochthonous variety *Hondarrabi Zuri*; nevertheless, they may include a small percentage of red grapes (*Hondarrabi Beltza*) in the blend. The Txakoli from Getaria is characterised by its pale steely colour; the clean and frank aroma of the wine, with pleasant herby notes and, in the best case, with floral traits; on the palate it is very fresh due to its high acidity, and light; it may also seem a bit carbonic.

AGERRE TXAKOLINA

Agerre Baserria - Bº Askizu
20808 Getaria (Guipúzcoa)
☎: 943 140 446 - Fax: 943 140 446
txakaguerre@terra.es

Established: 1957
🛢 9 📊 9,000 litres 🍇 100%

AGERRE 2002 WHITE
90% hondarrabi zuri, 10% hondarribi beltza

78 Pale. Not very intense aroma with green apple notes and fresh citrus overtones. Fresh palate of ripe fruit with a slightly oily texture, well-balanced.

SAN MARTIN 2002 WHITE

AIZPURUA

San Prudentzio Auzoa, 36
20808 Getaria (Guipúzcoa)
☎: 943 140 696

Established: 1930
📊 50,000 litres 🍇 6.5 has. 🍇 100%

AIALLE 2002 WHITE
hondarrabi zuri

83 Pale yellow. Intense aroma of ripe fruit, fine hints of lees and ripe citrus fruits. Flavourful palate with a slightly oily texture, spicy, slightly exotic hints and fine bitter notes.

AIZPURUA 2003 WHITE

77 Very pale with a greenish hue. Intense, fairly ripe aroma with green fruit, fine citrus hints and a waxy nuance. Fresh palate with bitter and citrus fruit notes and refreshing acidity.

AKARREGI TXIKI

Akarregi Txiki Baserria
20808 Guetaria (Guipúzcoa)
☎: 943 140 726 - Fax: 943 140 726

AKARREGI TXIKI 2003 WHITE

81 Pale with greenish nuances. Powerful, fresh aroma with green apple notes and quality glyceric hints. Fresh palate of green fruit, fine hints of bitterness and citrus fruit.

AMEZTOI

Barrio Eitzaga, 10
20808 Getaria (Guipúzcoa)
☎: 943 140 918 - Fax: 943 140 918
amestoycb@euskalnet.net
Established: 1995

🌐 20 📊 202,000 litres 🍇 18 has.
🇪🇸 85% 🍇15%

AMEZTOI 2003 WHITE
hondarrabi zuri

82 Pale yellow with a golden glint. Intense, fruity aroma with fine spicy and citrus fruit notes. Fresh, flavourful palate, rich in nuances, hints of fine herbs and excellent acidity.

ANDER REZABAL

Casas Itsas- Begi, 628
20800 Zarautz (Guipúzcoa)
☎: 943 580 899 - Fax: 943 580 899

Established: 1996
🌐 12 📊 55,000 litres 🍇 9 has. 🍇 100%

ARRI 2003 WHITE
hondarrabi zuri

80 Brilliant pale yellow. Intense, very fresh aroma of green fruit, fine aniseed notes (fennel) and hints of citrus fruit peel. Flavourful palate with complex overtones (herbs, anise, citrus fruit).

REZABAL 2003 WHITE
hondarrabi zuri

77 Straw-coloured with a greenish hue. Intense, very fresh aroma of green fruit, waxy hints and a nuance of citrus fruit (sweet limes). Fresh palate, fine carbonic notes and good acidity.

ARREGI

Bº San Martín de Ibaieta
20800 Zarautz (Guipúzcoa)
☎: 943 580 835 - Fax: 943 580 835

Established: 1996
📊 40,000 litres 🍇 3 has. 🍇 100%

ARREGI 2003 WHITE

81 Pale yellow. Intense aroma of white fruit, fine citrus hints and fresh overtones. Fresh, flavourful, slightly creamy palate (fine carbonics), with rich herbaceous and citrus notes.

BASA LORE

Basa-Lore Baserria
20800 Zarautz (Guipúzcoa)
☎: 943 132 231 - Fax: 943 132 231
🍇 16 has. 🍇 100%

BASA-LORE 2003 WHITE

79 Pale yellow with carbonic hints. Not very intense aroma of ripe white fruit with hints of citrus fruit. Fresh palate of green apples with fine hints of ripe lemon.

DO GETARIAKO TXAKOLINA

EIZAGUIRRE

Azpeiti Bidea, 18
20800 Zarautz (Guipúzcoa)
☎: 943 130 303 - Fax: 943 130 303

Established: 1930
🍇 10.5 has. 🍷 90% 🌐10%: -US -UE

EIZAGUIRRE 2003 WHITE

ETXETXO

Etxetxo Baserria
20808 Getaria (Guipúzcoa)
☎: 943 140 085 - Fax: 943 140 146

ETXETXO 2003 WHITE

79 Pale with a coppery glint. Intense, fruity aroma with floral hints. Flavourful palate with white fruit, fine bitter notes, a slightly oily texture and refreshing acidity.

Txakoli GAINTZA

Caserío Gaintza
20808 Getaria (Guipúzcoa)
☎: 943 140 032 - Fax: 943 896 038

Established: 1923
🛢 150,000 litres 🍇 10 has.
🍷 90% 🌐10%: -FR

GAINTZA 2003 WHITE
80% hondarrabi zuri, 20% hondarribi beltza

81 Very pale with a greenish hue. Intense, very fresh aroma with fine notes of green apples and hints of fairly ripe citrus fruit. Flavourful, fresh palate with good fruit-acidity balance.

GAÑETA

Agerre Goikoa Baserria
20808 Getaria (Guipúzcoa)
☎: 943 140 174 - Fax: 943 140 174

GAÑETA 2003 WHITE
hondarrabi zuri

78 Very pale. Intense, fresh, fruity aroma with hints of herbs and a citrus fruit nuance (sweet limes). Fresh, flavourful palate with some fruit-acidity balance.

Bodegas SANTARBA

Santa Bárbara, 7 buzon Nº 8
20800 Zarautz (Guipúzcoa)
☎: 943 140 452 - Fax: 943 140 452

Established: 1950

🍷 9 🛢 45000 litres 🍇 8.5 has.
🍷 100%

SANTARBA 2003 WHITE
hondarrabi zuri, hondarribi beltza

78 Pale with a greenish hue. Intense aroma of green apples and fine citrus hints. Flavourful palate, with quality bitter notes, slightly fruity with good acidity.

TALAI-BERRI

Talaimendi 728
20800 Zarautz (Gipuzkoa)
☎: 943 132 750 - Fax: 943 132 750
talaiberri@euskalnet.net

Established: 1992
🛢 100,000 litres 🍇 12 has.
🍷 90% 🌐10%: -US -DE -FR -JP

TALAI-BERRI 2003 WHITE
95% hondarrabi zuri, 5% hondarribi beltza

79 Pale yellow. Intense, slightly fruity aroma with hints of flowers. Flavourful palate, fine hints of bitterness and citrus fruit with good fruit-acidity balance.

TALAI-BERRI TXAKOLINA 2003 RED
100% hondarribi beltza

71 Cherry with a violet hue. Powerful aroma with mild reduction off-odours (ash, sackcloth) and a nuance of underripe, red fruit. Slightly better in the mouth, quite flavourful on the palate with slightly marked tannins, hints of greeness and terroir.

TXOMIN ETXANIZ

Finca Ametzmendi
20808 Getaria (Guipúzcoa)
☎: 943 140 702 - Fax: 943 140 702

🍷 33 🛢 300,000 litres 🍇 30 has.
🍷 80% 🌐20%: -US -FR G.B. -BE -NL -DE

TXOMIN ETXANIZ 2004 WHITE
85% hondarrabi zuri, 15% hondarribi beltza

84 Pale with a golden hue. Intense aroma of white fruit, with fine spicy notes and ripe citrus fruit. Generous on the palate, rich in nuances, with notes of fine herbs and a fruity hint, a slightly oily texture and excellent acidity.

352

25# DO GETARIAKO TXAKOLINA

Txakoli ULACIA

Cristóbal Balenciaga, 9
20808 Getaria (Guipúzcoa)
☎: 943 140 893

45,000 litres ⚘ 3 has. 🍷 100%

ULACIA 2003 WHITE

80 Brilliant pale. Fairly intense aroma with a certain finesse, white fruit notes and spicy hints. Fresh, flavourful palate with complex overtones (herbs, cumin) and good acidity.

Txakoli ZUDUGARAI

Carretera Zarautz - Aia
B. Laurgain
20809 Aia (Guipúzcoa)
☎: 943 830 386 - Fax: 943 835 952
txakolizudugarai@euskalnet.net

ZUDUGARAI 2003 WHITE

DO GRAN CANARIA

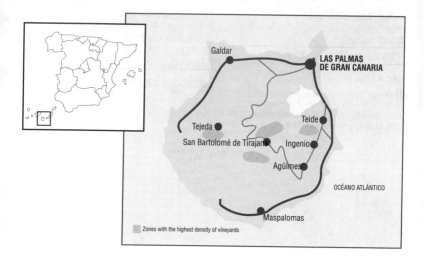

Galdar

LAS PALMAS DE GRAN CANARIA

Teide

Tejeda

San Bartolomé de Tirajana

Ingenio

Agüimes

OCÉANO ATLÁNTICO

Maspalomas

Zones with the highest density of vineyards

NEWS. The Regulatory Council, which was recognized by the Ministerial Order of 10th December 2003, regards the harvest of this year as being merely 'fair'. Not many bodegas dared to let their brands see the light, proof that this was not an exceptional harvest. Only 7 samples were sent to the Guide, opposed to the 15 received the previous year. Curiously enough, although the number of wines tasted is not very representative, after a sweet wine, the highest rated wines were two reds, displaying balsamic notes of significant interest.

LOCATION. The production region covers 99% of the island of Gran Canaria, as the climate and the conditions of the terrain allow for the cultivation of grapes at altitudes close to sea level up to the highest mountain tops. The DO incorporates all the municipal areas of the island, except for the Tafira Protected Landscape which falls under an independent DO, Monte de Lentiscal, also fully covered in this Guide.

Hectares of Vineyard	No. of Viticulturists	No. of Bodegas	2003 Harvest	2003 Production	Marketing
150	242	26	Fair	150,000 litres	100% local market

CLIMATE. As with the other islands of the archipelago, the differences in altitude give rise to several microclimates which create specific characteristics for the cultivation of the vine. Nevertheless, the climate is conditioned by the influence of the trade winds which blow from the east and whose effect is more evident in the higher-lying areas.

SOIL. The vineyards are found both in coastal areas and on higher grounds at altitudes of up to 1500 m, resulting in a varied range of soils.

VARIETIES:

White:
Preferred: *Malvasía, Güal, Marmajuelo (Bermejuela), Vijariego, Albillo* and *Moscatel.*
Authorized: *Listán Blanco, Burrablanca, Torrontés, Pedro Ximénez, Brebal.*

Red:
Preferred: *Listán Negro, Negramoll, Tintilla, Malvasía Rosada.*
Authorized: *Moscatel Negra.*

REGULATORY COUNCIL.

Antonio Perera, s/n. 35320 Vega de San Mateo (Gran Canaria).
Tel: 928 66 09 70.

GENERAL CHARACTERISTICS OF THE WINES:

Whites	Yellow straw, the aroma tends to be of herbs with fruity notes. Sweet wines from *Moscatel* are also produced with the characteristic musky nuance of the variety, with honey and herb notes.
Rosés	These have an onion skin colour; they are fruity, but with a character still to be defined.
Reds	With a deep cherry-red colour, they offer some fruity notes and characteristic balsamic hints, without too much body on the palate.

D.O. GRAN CANARIA

ANSITE

Martínez de Escobar 16
35110 Santa Lucía (Las Palmas de Gran Canaria)
☎: 608 359 154

GRAN ANSITE

Vino EL CASERÍO

Bajada La Socorra, 6
35108 Fataga (Gran Canaria)
☎: 928 798 271

EL CASERÍO 2003 WHITE
EL CASERÍO 2003 ROSÉ
EL CASERÍO 2003 RED

EL EUCALIPTO

Camino General del Palmital, 16
35200 Telde (Gran Canaria)
☎: 928 696 718

EL EUCALIPTO

EL RINCÓN

Bajada La Socorra, 7
35108 Fataga (Gran Canaria)
☎: 928 798 362

EL RINCÓN

EL SOLAPÓN

El Caidero, 8
35350 Artenara (Gran Canaria)
☎: 928 672 670

ARTENATUR LICOR NOBLE 2003 GENEROSO

80 Golden. Aroma of Muscatel, musky. Fiery, with Mistelle on the palate, sweet and very flavourful.

FRONTÓN DE ORO

Camaretas, 13
35320 San Mateo (Gran Canaria)
☎: 928 660 661 - Fax: 928 711 405

FRONTÓN DE ORO

HOYA CHIQUITA

Carretera Hoya Chiquita, 44
35309 Santa Brígida (Gran Canaria)

☎: 928 640 555

HOYA CHIQUITA

LA MONTAÑA

La Solana, 89 (Utiaca)
35328 Vega de San Mateo (Las Palmas)
☎: 928 642 897 - Fax: 928 642 897
Established: 1984
🛢 10,000 litres 🍇 1 has. 🚩 100%

LA MONTAÑA 2003 JOVEN WHITE

75 Yellow straw. Fresh, fruity, somewhat musky, warm aroma with dried mountain herbs. Warm, foresty and slightly fruity.

LA MONTAÑA 2003 JOVEN RED
listán negro, negramoll

60 Intense cherry. Aroma with a mild raisiny and vegetative hint. Flat palate without nuances, with a suggestion of viscosity.

LA ORILLA

La Orilla de El Palmital, 15
35218 Telde (Las Palmas de Gran Canaria)
☎: 928 572 629

LA ORILLA 2003 JOVEN DULCE WHITE
100% malvasía

60 Lively golden. Aroma with a slight off-odour (late racking). Sweet, not very clear, unexpressive palate, mediocre.

LA ORILLA 2003 JOVEN RED

50 Muted garnet red. Off-odour aroma and on the palate, lacking structure, flat, without nuances.

Bodegas LAS TIRAJANAS

Oficial Mayor José Rubio, s/n
35290 San Bartolomé de Tirajana
(Gran Canaria)
☎: 649 487 804

LAS TIRAJANAS

MOGARÉN

Las Moranas, 2. Las Vegas
35217 Valsequillo
(Las Palmas de Gran Canaria)
☎: 607 381 093

MOGARÉN 2003 JOVEN RED

77 Slightly subdued garnet red cherry. Vegetative, balsamic aroma (eucalyptus). Fresh, slightly fruity palate with vegetative hints.

D.O. GRAN CANARIA

GRAN MOGARÉN 2003 ROBLE RED
🛢2

79 Quite intense cherry. Fresh aroma, slightly vegetative but with a suggestion of mild creamy wood. Balsamic palate with a fruity hint and noticeable tannins.

RAMOSAT

Paraje Las Carboneras, s/n
35110 Santa Lucía de Tirajana
(Gran Canaria)
☎: 617 135 848

VIÑA EL CARDÓN JOVEN WHITE

VINOS DE JUAN INGLÉS

Montaña Las Palmas
35200 Telde (Las Palmas de Gran Canaria)
☎: 928 693 443

JUAN INGLÉS RED

VIÑA ANGOA

Camino Los Pérez, 67
35017 Las Palmas de Gran Canaria
(Gran Canaria)
☎: 928 352 871

VIÑA ANGOA RED

VIÑA CENTRO

Lomo Espino, 330
35309 Santa Brígida
(Las Palmas de Gran Canaria)
☎: 928 641 204

VIÑA CENTRO 2003 JOVEN RED

DO JEREZ - XÉRÈS- SHERRY
MANZANILLA DE SANLÚCAR DE BARRAMEDA

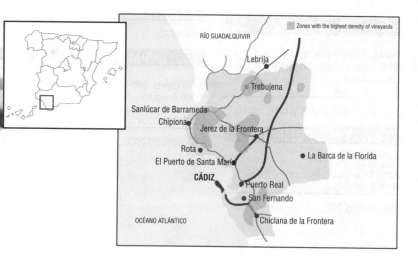

NEWS. Midway through its Strategic Plan 2002-2006, it is now time for reflection in Jerez, whose Regulatory Council remains firm on one of its key issues: that of bringing production in line with sales. The grape harvest from the 10,500 Ha of registered vineyard was just over 109 million kilograms, a slight decrease (4.4%) from the previous year.

But to achieve the level of adjustment promised by the Plan, stocks have to be reduced; i.e. more needs to be sold, seeing as most of the bodegas have an excess stock of aged wine. And Jerez has still not managed to assimilate the drop in sales,

Hectares of Vineyard	No. of Viticulturists	No. of Bodegas	2003 Harvest	2003 Production	Marketing
10,500	2,836	64	Good	546,096 wineskins	20% Spain 80% foreign

for the 2002-2003 period, of about 2% in the foreign market and 3% in the national market, and about 6% in 2003. In this year, the bodegas registered with the Council sold 68 million bottles, of which 80% were destined for export. Nevertheless, it is worth remembering that the classified Jerez wines (VORS and VOS), according to the new categories created in 2001, saw an increase of 37% in sales during the period 2002-2003, reaching a volume of 142,364 bottles.

The best of all is that these ups and downs in the figures have still had no effect on the exceptional quality of the wines of the Marco de Jerez. Of the 184 wines tasted (all receiving scores of over 70 points, and therefore without any defects whatsoever), 173 scored 80 points or more, and 122 above 85 points. At the top of the podium, although with a diametrically opposite nature, and with a score of 97 points, we find the extremely dense Santa Ana 1861 of Emilio Hidalgo, an exceptionally aged Pedro Ximénez, and the Manzanilla San León of Herederos de Argüeso, a flagship wine below € 6.

LOCATION. In the province of Cádiz. The production area covers the municipal districts of Jerez de la Frontera, El Puerto de Santa María, Chipiona, Trebujena, Rota, Puerto Real, Chiclana de la Frontera and some estates in Lebrija.

CLIMATE. Warm with Atlantic influences. The west winds play an important role, as they provide humidity and help to temper the conditions. The average annual temperature is 17.5°C, with an average rainfall of 600 mm per year.

SOIL. The so-called 'Albariza' soil is a key factor regarding quality. This type of soil is practically white and is rich in calcium carbonate, clay and silica. It is excellent for retaining humidity and storing winter rainfall for the dry summer months. Moreover, this soil determines the so-called 'Jerez superior'. It is found in Jerez de la Frontera, Puerto de Santa María, Sanlúcar de Barrameda and certain areas of Trebujena. The remaining soil, known as 'Zona', is muddy and sandy.

VARIETIES:
White: *Palomino* (90%), *Pedro Ximénez, Moscatel, Palomino Fino, Palomino de Jerez.*

REGULATORY COUNCIL.
Avda. Álvaro Domecq, 2. 11405 Jerez de la Frontera (Cádiz).
Tel: 956 332 050. Fax: 956 338 908.
E-mail: vinjerez@sherry.org
Website: www.sherry.org

GENERAL CHARACTERISTICS OF THE WINES:

Manzanilla and Fino	These are straw yellow in colour. They are characterised by their salty notes, typical of the biological ageing under the Velo en Flor (more pronounced in the case of the Manzanilla), and by the bitter notes conferred by ageing.
Oloroso	With completely oxidative ageing, the range can be varied depending on the higher or lower scale level (i.e. the number of sacas of Solera wine to be bottled) and, consequently, the greater or lesser refreshing with unaged wine for the first criadera. In the very old wines, it is customary to tone them down with Mistela of Pedro Ximénez which provide notes of sweetness to mitigate the bitter tannins of the oak.
Pedro Ximénez	These are characterised by their marked taste of raisin, although some have a small percentage of Oloroso to reduce the sweetness. On the palate they are flavourful and sweet.
Cream	These combine the bitter notes of the Olorosos with hints of toast and the sweetness of the Pedro Ximénez.

Bodegas 501 DEL PUERTO

Valdés, 9
11500 El Puerto de Sta. María (Cádiz)
☎: 956 855 511 - Fax: 956 873 053
brandy501@infonegocio.com
www.bodegas501.com
Established: 1783
⊕ 3,800 ◫ 4,000,000 litres 🍷 58% 🌐42%:
-NG -SK -MT -GQ -AD -DE -BE -UK -ZA

501 MARINERO FINO
palomino

77 Brilliant straw. Slightly warm aroma with mild notes of flor. Dry, oily and slightly alcoholic on the palate, without great character.

GADES 501 AMONTILLADO
palomino

89 Old gold. Fine aroma with light notes of pâtisserie and pungent dry nuances of Amontillado. Slightly sweet, flavourful palate with hints of carpentry and acetones, persistent.

501 TERCIOS OLOROSO
palomino, pedro ximénez

80 Old gold. Very sweet aroma with notes of pâtisserie, a rancid nuance (saline). Flavourful palate with traces of bitterness, suggestions of bitter almond and an unctuous finish.

501 ZURBARÁN CREAM
palomino, pedro ximénez

85 Mahogany with an iodised rim. Aroma of toasted nuts, jammy figs, vanilla and coffee. Concentrated, flavourful, toasty palate (coffee, sweet almonds).

501 RIBERA DEL PUERTO JOVEN WHITE

ALMOCADÉN

Jardinillo, 16
11404 Jerez de la Frontera (Cádiz)
☎: 956 185 324 - Fax: 956 187 526
almocaden@bodegsalmocaden.com
www.bodegsalmocaden.com
Established: 1988
⊕ 1,800 ◫ 800,000 litres 🌐 50 has.
🍷 90% 🌐10%: -DE -DK -US

ALMOCADEN CREAM
ALMOCADEN AMONTILLADO
ALMOCADEN OLOROSO
ALMOCADEN PEDRO XIMÉNEZ

BARBADILLO

Luis de Eguilaz, 11
11540 Sanlúcar de Barrameda (Cádiz)
☎: 956 385 500 - Fax: 956 385 501
barbadillo@barbadillo.com
www.barbadillo.com
Established: 1821
⊕ 50,000 ◫ 5,000,000 litres 🌐 500 has.
🍷 60% 🌐40%: -UK -DE -US -NL -BE

SOLEAR MANZANILLA

88 Straw-coloured. Medium-intensity aroma, fresh, young, with hints of flor, well-balanced. Supple, slightly bitter and flavourful palate, easy drinking.

PRÍNCIPE AMONTILLADO

88 Golden with a reddish hue. Powerful aroma with notes of nuts and oak and pungent organic hints. Powerful, bitter palate with notes of Solera and carpentry, very dry with oak tannins.

CUCO OLOROSO SECO
100% palomino

83 Old gold. Creamy aroma (vanilla) with a saline and pâtisserie expression, slightly sweet. Dry, fresh, slightly pungent palate (crianza) with oak and bitter almonds in the finish.

SAN RAFAEL OLOROSO DULCE
pedro ximénez, palomino

87 Brilliant amber with a coppery hue. Intense aroma with spicy crianza notes and a fine suggestion of acetaldehyde, broom and nuts. Flavourful, sweet palate, slightly warm and unctuous with fine bitter notes of aged wood.

OBISPO GASCÓN PALO CORTADO
100% palomino

85 Old gold. Aroma with pungent notes of oxidised flor and oak. Bittersweet notes on the palate with old Solera, varnish and aldehyde.

LA CILLA PEDRO XIMÉNEZ
100% pedro ximénez

82 Mahogany. Aroma of sun-drenched raisins with oxidative crianza notes (fine reduction). Sweet palate with dried fruit, very unctuous on the palate, without great freshness and with a creamy finish.

EVA CREAM
pedro ximénez, palomino

88 Old gold with an amber hue. Intense aroma of toasty and creamy crianza notes with a good Oloroso expression and a fine suggestion of cocoa and raisins. Powerful, flavourful palate with an excellent sweetness-aging symmetry, spicy (cocoa), very long.

LAURA MOSCATEL
100% moscatel

86 Mahogany with a coppery hue. Powerful aroma with creamy and toasty crianza notes (vanilla, cocoa) and a slightly varietal and dried fruit suggestion. Powerful, unctuous palate with fine notes of aged Solera, persistent.

MUYEINA MANZANILLA
AMONTILLADO VORS AMONTILLADO
LA CILLA PALO CORTADO
BARBADILLO VORS OLOROSO SECO
BARBADILLO VORS OLOROSO DULCE
PALO CORTADO VORS PALO CORTADO

BARÓN

Carretera Sanlúcar - Chipiona, km. 1
11540 Sanlúcar de Barrameda (Cádiz)
☎: 956 360 796 - Fax: 956 365 256
hiescay@teleline.es

Established: 1871

⬜ 5,000 🍇 70 has. 🍷 90% 🍷10%

ATALAYA MANZANILLA
BARÓN MANZANILLA
MICAELA MANZANILLA
ATALAYA AMONTILLADO
ATALAYA MOSCATEL
ATALAYA CREAM SEMI-DULCE

CARBAJO RUIZ

Carretera Trebujena, km. 1
11540 Sanlúcar de Barrameda (Cádiz)
☎: 956 381 060 - Fax: 956 381 060
carbajoruiz@terra.es

Established: 1875

⬜ 900 🍶 250,000 litres
🍇 12 has. 🍷 100%

PREDILECTA MANZANILLA

CÉSAR FLORIDO ROMERO

Padre Lerchundi, 35-37
11550 Chipiona (Cádiz)
☎: 956 371 285 - Fax: 956 370 222
florido@bodegasflorido.com
www.bodegasflorido.com

Established: 1887

⬜ 1,500 🍶 1,000,000 litres🍷 95% 🍷5%

CÉSAR FINO
CRUZ DEL MAR CREAM DULCE
CÉSAR FLORIDO DORADO MOSCATEL
CÉSAR FLORIDO ESPECIAL MOSCATEL
CÉSAR FLORIDO PASAS MOSCATEL

DELGADO ZULETA

Carretera Sanlucar-Chipiona, km. 1, 5
11540 Sanlúcar de Barrameda (Cádiz)
☎: 956 360 133 - Fax: 956 360 780
bodegas@delgadozuleta.com

Established: 1744

⬜ 7,000 🍷 84% 🍷16%: -UK -NL -BE -
DE -FR -AT -JP -CA -AU -DK -DK

LA GOYA MANZANILLA
100% palomino

88 Crystalline straw. Slightly short but fine, fresh and delicate aroma with a hint of flor. Saline, fresh and pleasant palate, slightly bitter and persistent.

QUO VADIS SOLERA AMONTILLADO

86 Golden with an olive green hue. Pungent aroma of carpentry with hints of varnish and aldehyde. Powerful and bitter on the palate with more evident oak tannins than in our previous edition, very dry with a subtle notion of flor.

MONTEAGUDO PEDRO XIMÉNEZ
100% pedro ximénez

81 Dark mahogany with an iodised rim. Intense aroma of raisins with hints of vanilla and a suggestion of Solera. Very sweet palate with jammy raisins and dates, without enough acidity.

DIOS BACO

Manuel María González
Edificio Alameda, Portal 1-1ºB
11403 Jerez de la Frontera (Cádiz)
☎: 956 333 337 - Fax: 956 333 825
diosbaco@ozu.es
www.bacosherry.com

Established: 1848

⬜ 1,500 🍶 500,000 litres🍇 38 has.
🍷 40% 🍷60%: -US -DK -DE -BE

BULERÍA FINO
100% palomino

78 Straw-coloured. Clear but simple aroma with well-defined saline and mask notes and mild and very fine nutty nuances. Flavourful, slightly oily palate with bitter notes, somewhat vinous.

DIOS BACO OLOROSO

83 Mahogany with a yellowish edge. Creamy aroma of pâtisserie, almonds and toast. Dry, slightly pungent palate, round with a glyceric sensation and a hazelnut finish.

OXFORD 1970 PEDRO XIMÉNEZ
100% pedro ximénez

90 Very dark mahogany. Fine aroma with notes of Solera, spicy dried fruit, toasty flavours and chocolate, complex. Sweet, considerably fresh palate, flavourful with saline jammy dates notes, syrupy.

BULERÍA AMONTILLADO
BACO IMPERIAL VORS 20 AÑOS
 AMONTILLADO
BACO IMPERIAL VORS 30 AÑOS OLOROSO
BULERÍA CREAM DULCE
ESNOBISTA MOSCATEL

DIPLOMÁTICO

Polígono Bertola. Avenida Sanlúcar
11408 Jerez de la Frontera (Cádiz)
☎: 956 140 290 - Fax: 956 141 922

LOS 48 MANZANILLA

EL MAESTRO SIERRA

Plaza de Silos, 5
11403 Jerez de la Frontera (Cádiz)
☎: 956 342 433 - Fax: 956 326 191
info@maestrosierra.com
www.maestrosierra.com

Established: 1830

1,500 🗐 500,000 litres 🍷 70% 🍇30%

EL MAESTRO SIERRA FINO
100% palomino

87 Straw-coloured. Aroma with light notes of old flor and humid yet fresh and saline notes. Dry, slightly pungent, saline, bitter and flavourful palate.

EL MAESTRO SIERRA AMONTILLADO
100% palomino

84 Amber. Expressive aroma with notes of Fino and nuts and a suggestion of well-integrated varnish. Dry palate with a saline character, slightly pungent with bitter and flavourful notes.

EL MAESTRO SIERRA VIEJO 1830 AMONTILLADO
100% palomino

88 Golden with a reddish hue. Pungent aroma of carpentry, wood. Dry palate with oak in the retronasal passage and bitter oak notes; warm, long and flavourful.

OLOROSO 1/14
100% palomino

85 Amber with a mahogany rim. Creamy aroma slightly marked by Solera with pâtisserie hints and toffee. Pungent, quite warm palate with a sweet sensation and a nutty, iodised, bitter and harmonised finish.

OLOROSO EXTRA VIEJO 1/7 OLOROSO
100% palomino

88 Old gold. Aroma of fine varnish with notes of pâtisserie, toasted nuts and slight reduction. Round, fresh palate of nuts (bitter almonds), orange peel and a saline nuance in the aftertaste; long.

EL MAESTRO SIERRA 15 AÑOS OLOROSO
100% pedro ximénez

86 Dark amber with a coppery hue. Fine aroma with good crianza expression (cocoa, pâtisserie, varnish) and a slightly varietal and raisiny suggestion. Powerful, dry, flavourful palate with a slightly sweet and toasty suggestion, pastries, nuts, hints of cereal and excellent Solera.

EL MAESTRO SIERRA PEDRO XIMÉNEZ
100% pedro ximénez

82 Old amber. Spicy aroma with hints of cedar and Solera and notes of Mistelle. Flavourful, sweet palate evoking old Solera with an aftertaste of sweet almonds.

EL MAESTRO SIERRA PEDRO XIMÉNEZ VIEJÍSIMO
100% pedro ximénez

90 Almost opaque mahogany. Aroma of sultanas with complex toasty flavours (cocoa, cinnamon) and a suggestion of old Solera, spicy. Syrupy on the palate with quite heavy sweetness and without freshness with jammy figs, powerful and round.

EL MAESTRO SIERRA CREAM DULCE
palomino, pedro ximénez

87 Mahogany with an amber hue. Powerful aroma of aged wood and bakery with a good expression of Oloroso hint (walnuts). Good turns between sweet and bitter notes on the palate with toasty crianza, persistent.

EL MAESTRO SIERRA AMOROSO
palomino, pedro ximénez

83 Old amber. Aroma with notions of Amontillado (flor, almonds) and notes of pâtisserie. Sweet, saline aroma with slightly pungent but pleasant bitterness; a very pleasant almondy finish.

EMILIO HIDALGO

Clavel, 29
11402 Jerez de la Frontera (Cádiz)
☎: 956 341 078 - Fax: 956 320 922
emidalgo@teleline.es

Established: 1874

4500 🗐 3,600,000 litres 🍷 30%
🍇70%: -DE -NL -DK -UK -IT -JP -US

GOBERNADOR OLOROSO SECO
100% palomino

83 Amber with an orangey hue. Sweet aroma of sweet almonds, pastries and cream. Dry, pleasant and round palate; simple and without great nuances.

MARQUÉS DE RODIL PALO CORTADO
100% palomino

85 Brilliant amber. Complex aroma with saline hints, a suggestion of varnish and well-integrated Solera. Generous, fresh palate with glyceric notes (bitter almonds), slightly pungent with integrated crianza nuances.

PRIVILEGIO 1860 PALO CORTADO
100% palomino

89 Brilliant old gold. Complex aroma of aged Solera, varnish and reduction notes with a saline suggestion and oven-roasted nuts. Fresh, flavourful palate with character, well-blended crianza notes and iodine and almond hint.

EMILIO HIDALGO PEDRO XIMÉNEZ
100% pedro ximénez

83 Mahogany with a yellowish edge. Sweet palate with slightly sweet sultanas and a suggestion of aged Solera. Fleshy, very sweet palate with jammy raisins and figs, without great freshness.

SANTA ANA 1861 PEDRO XIMÉNEZ
100% pedro ximénez

97 Opaque chocolatey mahogany (stains the glass). Toasty aroma, concentrated, raisins and dates, with carob and chocolate. Dense, unctuous palate with good weight, raisins and dates; toasty, intense and persistent notes in the retronasal passage; extraordinary.

MORENITA CREAM
70% palomino, 30% pedro ximénez

83 Light mahogany with a yellow edge. Toasty aroma of jammy raisins with hints of Solera. Sweet palate with a hint of Mistelle, toasty and very flavourful, easy drinking.

PANESA FINO
CHARITO MANZANILLA

EMILIO LUSTAU

Calle Arcos, 53
11402 Jerez de la Frontera (Cádiz)
☎: 956 341 597 - Fax: 956 347 789
lustau2@a2000.es
www.emilio-lustau.com

Established: 1986

15,000 500 litres 170 has. 10%
90%: -UK -NL -DE -BE -DK -SE -JP -US -CA -IE -PT -IT

JARANA FINO

90 Brilliant straw with a greenish edge. Intense aroma of yeast with a floral character, notes of harbours and iodine. Generous, flavourful palate with a Fino character and an almondy and saline nuance, very long.

LUSTAU PAPIRUSA MANZANILLA
100% palomino

89 Straw-coloured with a yellow glimmer. Powerful aroma with mild notes of flor but stronger in notes of dried mountain herbs. Dry palate with dried herbs in the retronasal passage, slightly pungent, bitter and flavourful.

LUSTAU RESERVA EMPERATRIZ EUGENIA SOLERA OLOROSO

87 Slightly light mahogany. Toasty aroma, slightly viscous and with a suggestion of pâtisserie. Supple, flavourful palate, sweet and bitter in the finish.

LUSTAU ESCUADRILLA AMONTILLADO

83 Old gold. Toasty aroma of pastries with a suggestion of Solera and vinous hints closer to the cut stalks. Supple palate with bitter hints, Solera and a suggestion of pâtisserie.

LUSTAU EMILÍN MOSCATEL
100% moscatel

86 Mahogany with an amber hue. Powerful aroma with fine toasty oak, hints of spices (vanilla, cocoa) and dried fruit. Flavourful palate with very marked notes of raisins, unctuous with a suggestion of spices and hints of fine Solera.

SAN EMILIO PEDRO XIMÉNEZ
pedro ximénez

84 Mahogany with an orange edge. Aroma with a hint of crianza complexity, sun-drenched raisins and Mistelle notes with a suggestion of nuts. Flavourful and sweet but fairly fresh on the palate with notes of spicy raisins and a syrupy sensation.

FAUSTINO GONZÁLEZ

Beato Juan Grande, 7
11403 Jerez de la Frontera (Cádiz)
☎: 956 342 599 - Fax: 956 344 417

CRUZ VIEJA OLOROSO

FEDERICO PATERNINA

Carretera Morabita, km. 2
11407 Jerez de la Frontera (Cádiz)
☎: 956 186 112 - Fax: 956 303 500
marketing@paternina.com
www.paternina.com

Established: 1810

11,000 200,000 litres 80% 20%

FINO IMPERIAL AMONTILLADO
100% palomino

88 Old gold with a coppery hue. Powerful aroma with a fine Solera expression and with saline and iodised notes over a spicy hint of oak and nuts. Very dry, powerful palate with a marked oak character, bitter, very long.

VICTORIA REGINA OLOROSO
100% palomino

88 Light mahogany. Aroma with notes of acetaldehyde and pâtisserie with a nutty nuance. A suggestion of sweetness blended with bitter oak notes on the palate, warm and spirituous

VIEJA SOLERA PEDRO XIMÉNEZ
100% pedro ximénez

88 Dark mahogany. Aroma of dates with notes of carpentry and vanilla with fine Solera. Concentrated, unctuous, syrupy palate, evoking toasty and dark-roasted flavours with a flavourful finish.

PEMARTIN FINO
BERTOLA FINO
BERTOLA MANZANILLA
VICTORIA MANZANILLA
PEMARTIN AMONTILLADO
BERTOLA MEDIUM OLOROSO
PEMARTÍN CREAM DULCE
BERTOLA CREAM DULCE

GARVEY

Ronda de Circunvalación, s/n
11407 Jerez de la Frontera (Cádiz)
☎: 956 319 650 - Fax: 956 319 824
atencionalcliente@grupogarvey.com
www.grupogarvey.com

Established: 1780

🍇 36,000 📊 80,000 litres🍇 100 has.

SAN PATRICIO FINO

87 Straw-coloured. Medium-intensity aroma with mild hints of flor. Supple, slightly dry, flavourful palate with hints of flor, saline.

TÍO GUILLERMO AMONTILLADO
palomino

78 Old gold. Intense aroma of varnish and carpentry with a suggestion of reduction. Unctuous palate of bitter almonds with saline notes; better in the mouth.

OÑANA AMONTILLADO
palomino

91 Old gold. Aroma with notes of varnish, old flor and pâtisserie. Sweet notes on the palate with a pungent and bitter aftertaste, very intense, long and persistent.

PUERTA REAL OLOROSO
100% palomino

83 Old gold. Toasty aroma of old Solera and nuts. Dry, bitter palate with varnish tostado and toasty hints in the retronasal passage.

ASALTO AMOROSO OLOROSO
palomino, pedro ximénez

85 Old gold. Pungent aroma of Solera and nuts. Dry palate with sweetness in the mouth, toasty and persistent.

FLOR DE JEREZ CREAM OLOROSO DULCE
palomino, pedro ximénez

87 Mahogany with an orange rim. Toasty aroma (oven-baked bread), with chocolate and a nuance of fine Solera. Sweet on the palate with pleasant hints of bitter almonds and pâtisserie, almost syrupy with a saline hint in the retronasal, expressive.

OCHAVICO OLOROSO
100% palomino

88 Mahogany. Powerful aroma, rich in toasty nuances of pastries with a suggestion of old Solera and nuts. Round, sweet, toasty and slightly bitter palate, flavourful and persistent.

JAUNA PALO CORTADO
palomino

86 Old gold. Aroma with notes of old Solera (nuts, varnish) and a toasty hint. Very dry, pungent palate with varnish and wood.

GARVEY PEDRO XIMÉNEZ

85 Mahogany with a yellow edge. Fine aroma of varnish and toasty crianza with a spicy nuance. Flavourful, fresh palate with saline notes and the bitter pleasant suggestion of nuts, long (syrup).

GRAN ORDEN PEDRO XIMÉNEZ
pedro ximénez

91 Chocolatey mahogany. Powerful, toasty aroma with notes of jammy raisins, dates and carob. Sweet palate with a hint of Oloroso in the retronasal passage, flavourful and long with hints of dates.

GARVEY CREAM DULCE
palomino, pedro ximénez

83 Old gold. Toasty aroma with fine notes of varnish and a nuance of bakery. Sweet, almost syrupy on the palate with bitter hints that balance the sugar and sun-drenched raisins in the finish.

TÍO GUILLERMO AMONTILLADO
FLOR DEL MUSEO OLOROSO DULCE
GARVEY 1780 VOS OLOROSO
GARVEY 1780 VORS OLOROSO
GARVEY 1780 VOS PEDRO XIMÉNEZ
GARVEY 1780 VORS PEDRO XIMÉNEZ

Grupo GARVEY-JOSÉ DE SOTO

R. Circunvalación - Bellavista
11403 Jerez de la Frontera (Cádiz)
☎: 956 319 650 - Fax: 956 319 824

Established: 1780

🍇 8,000 📊 3,000,000 litres🍇 100 has.

🐂 15% 🌍85%: -US -DE -PH -NG -UK -MX

DON JOSÉ MARÍA FINO

86 Straw-coloured. Fine, dry aroma of flor, clean and fresh. Slightly supple, not very pungent or bitter and flavourful on the palate, with weak flor.

DON JOSÉ MARÍA MANZANILLA

88 Dark straw. Aroma with notes of crianza (almonds) and flor (saline), fresh. Slightly buttery, flavourful, supple and bitter on the palate; a hint of slightly overripe Manzanilla flor, pleasant.

JUNCAL MANZANILLA
palomino

83 Yellow straw. Slightly ripe aroma with mask notes almonds. Unctuous, enveloping, fresh palate with saline hints and a fresh finish.

SOTO FINO
DON JOSÉ MARÍA AMONTILLADO
DON JOSÉ MARÍA OLOROSO
DON JOSÉ MARÍA OLOROSO DULCE
SOTO PEDRO XIMÉNEZ
SOTO CREAM

Bodega GASPAR FLORIDO

Avenida de Trebujena, 15
11540 Sanlúcar de Barrameda (Cádiz)
☎: 956 360 124 - Fax: 956 360 124
bodega@manzanillasanlucar.com
www.manzanillasanlucar.com

Established: 1942

⊞ 6,000 🗄 1,500,000 litres

🍷 95% 🌐5%: -DE -JP

25 G.F. JEREZ VIEJÍSIMO AMONTILLADO
listán blanca, palomino

80 Dark old gold. Aroma with notes of old furniture and acetone, slightly volatile but very complex, aged Solera. Powerful, very bitter and woody palate with oak tannins; persistent and a little excessive.

PLEAMAR MANZANILLA
listán, palomino

89 Straw-coloured. Fresh, slightly pungent, dry and saline aroma of seasoned cask. Dry, clean, flavourful and bitter palate, persistent.

OLOROSO MUY VIEJO GF
listán, palomino

78 Mahogany. Aroma with notes of Mistelle, Solera, without great nuances. Palate with a certain sweetness, without great nuances.

GRAN SOLERA GF OLOROSO
listán, palomino

86 Old gold. Aroma with complex notes of Solera, varnish, salts and a suggestion of coffee. Sweet palate with balanced, flavourful, bitter notes and a finish reminiscent of Fino and almonds.

AB CREAM GF CREAM
listán, palomino

86 Mahogany with an orangey edge. Toasty aroma of oven-roasted nuts with a suggestion of raisins and hints of Solera. Sweet, fresh, flavourful and reminiscent palate, with notes of chocolate liqueurs and hazelnuts and a pleasant bitter hint in the finish.

GONZÁLEZ BYASS

Manuel María González, 12
11403 Jerez de la Frontera (Cádiz)
☎: 956 357 000 - Fax: 956 357 043
atencion@gonzalezbyass.es
www.gonzalezbyass.es

Established: 1835

⊞ 100,000 🗄 60,000,000 litres🍇 601 has.

🍷 41% 🌐59%: -UK -DE -NL -JP -CH -BE -MX -US -RU

TÍO PEPE FINO

93 Straw-coloured. Fresh, saline aroma of clean flor, slightly pungent, harmonious. Dry, well-balanced and persistent on the palate with a good saline retronasal effect.

GADITANO FINO
palomino

82 Straw-coloured with a greenish edge. Clean aroma of green grass with saline notes and reduction overtones(mushrooms, withered flowers). Oily, dry and slightly pungent palate with light notes of flor; a slightly short finish.

EL ROCÍO MANZANILLA

88 Straw-coloured. Fine, fresh, saline aroma with hints of clean and powerful flor. Dry, supple, fresh, slightly saline and flavourful on the palate with a slightly bitter finish.

DEL DUQUE AMONTILLADO

92 Old gold. Powerful, fine aroma, with toasty notes of pâtisserie and a pungent suggestion of almonds. Dry palate, with fatness and with volume, complex, toasty, baked and flavourful.

VIÑA AB AMONTILLADO SECO
palomino

85 Brilliant gold. Expressive aroma with crianza notes (varnish, vanilla, toffee), and ripe fruit (orange peel, reduction). Oily, warm and enveloping on the palate with nutty notes (almonds), bitter hints and a saline finish with character.

ALFONSO OLOROSO SECO

86 Old gold with a nuance of mahogany. Aroma with oak and vinous notes with a suggestion of pâtisserie. Dry, flavourful palate with supple overtones, toasty.

MATUSALEM OLOROSO DULCE

89 Dark mahogany. Toasty aroma of pastries with hazelnuts and walnuts, old Solera and a hint of popcorn. Sweet, powerful palate with a bitter aftertaste of Oloroso, flavourful, full and persistent.

GONZÁLEZ BYASS DE AÑADA 1978 OLOROSO

90 Old gold. Powerful aroma of carpentry and pâtisserie, pungent with notes of clean and fine oak. Generous, full, bitter, acetonic palate with hints of varnish and slightly incisive wood; less complex than previous years.

APÓSTOLES PALO CORTADO

88 Toasted mahogany. Powerful aroma, with toasty notes of pâtisserie, nuts, Solera and Havana cigars. Sweet, toasty and powerful on the palate with a warm bitter suggestion of Oloroso, old Solera, long.

NOÉ SOLERA PEDRO XIMÉNEZ

92 Very intense with a mahogany edge. Powerful aroma of harmonious toasty notes, dates and aldehydes. Sweet palate with a dry suggestion of Oloroso, flavourful and well-balanced with toasty notes in the retronasal passage (coffee), persistent.

NÉCTAR CREAM

89 Dark caramelised mahogany. Aroma of raisin liqueur, toasty, fruity. Very sweet, flavourful palate, raisins, a hint of dates, long.

SOLERA 1847 SWEET CREAM

82 Dark mahogany. Toasty aroma, quite viscous, with a suggestion of nuts and pâtisserie. Sweet, flavourful, toasty palate, with unharmonised swe-etness.

GUTIÉRREZ COLOSÍA

Avenida Bajamar, 40
11500 El Puerto de Sta. María (Cádiz)
☎: 956 852 852 - Fax: 956 542 936
export@gutierrez-colosia.com
www.gutierrez-colosia.com

Established: 1838

⊜ 1,200

GUTIÉRREZ COLOSÍA FINO
100% palomino

82 Straw-coloured. Clear aroma with notes of flor and nuts. Flavourful palate with good fresh-ness and well-integrated bitter overtones, slightly vinous, well-mannered finish.

CAMPO DE GUÍA FINO

78 Straw-coloured. Intense flor aroma with floral and nutry notes. Slightly sweet and watery on the palate with a discreet finish.

GUTIÉRREZ COLOSÍA MANZANILLA
100% palomino

88 Brilliant gold. Powerful aroma with fine notes of flor and bitter almonds. Dry, powerful, flavour-ful palate with a fine saline suggestion, long.

GUTIÉRREZ COLOSÍA AMONTILLADO SECO
100% palomino

88 Old gold. Intense aroma with a certain fines-se, fine notes of Solera, notions of flor and quality saline hints. Flavourful palate with an excellent expression of Amontillado, nuts, aged wood, and a saline suggestion, slightly oily.

SANGRE Y TRABAJADERO OLOROSO

80 Mahogany. Aroma with notes of Solera and a vinous suggestion of Mistelle. Dry and vinous palate, lacks solera, flavourful.

GUTIERREZ COLOSÍA OLOROSO

82 Old gold. Expressive aroma of Solera with nuts, carpentry and salty hints. Dry, bitter palate with saline notes and a pungent finish.

GUTIÉRREZ COLOSÍA 1/2 PALO CORTADO
100% palomino

88 Amber with an iodised edge. Complex and intense aroma of fine varnish with hints of Solera and toasted nuts. Dry, slightly bitter and pungent palate with notes of acetaldehyde and bitter almonds in the finish.

GUTIÉRREZ COLOSÍA PEDRO XIMÉNEZ
pedro ximénez

84 Dark mahogany. Clear aroma of raisins with spicy hints and a suggestion of Solera. Sweet palate with crystallised fruit, almost syrupy with pâtisserie notes and an almondy retronasal effect.

GUTIÉRREZ COLOSÍA SOLEADO MOSCATEL

85 Mahogany. Powerful aroma of raisins and caramel with honeyed notes and orange peel. Unctuous and sweet palate but with an element of freshness, crystallised fruit, sweet.

GUTIÉRREZ COLOSÍA CREAM

86 Old amber. Complex aroma with hints of pâtisserie, toffee, Fino (saline) and cream. Sweet, flavourful palate of considerable freshness with rancid nuances and nuts; orange peel.

MARI PEPA CREAM SEMI-DULCE
palomino, pedro ximénez

85 Amber with a coppery hue. Slightly intense aroma with notes of caramel and a toasty sugges-tion of quite fine Oloroso. Sweet, flavourful and unctuous palate with hints of dates, fresh spicy overtones and nuts, long.

HARVEYS

Calle Pintor Muñoz Cebrián, s/n
11403 Jerez de la Frontera (Cádiz)
☎: 956 346 000 - Fax: 956 349 427
jerez@domecq.es
www.domecq.es

Established: 1796

⊜ 48,000 🗌 10,000,000 litres 🌿 600 has.

🥃 1% 🍷99%

GRAN SOLERA OLOROSO
85% palomino, 15% pedro ximénez

80 Old gold. Aroma with light toasty notes of pâtisserie, viscous nuances, nuts. Sweet palate with hints of Oloroso, nuts, flavourful.

HARVEYS MEDIUM AMONTILLADO
93% palomino, 7% pedro ximénez

83 Amber. Aroma with notes of toffee and pâtis-serie with a rancid hint (flor). Semi-sweet palate with notes of Solera (vanilla) and almonds in the finish, original.

HARVEYS BRISTOL CREAM
80% palomino, 20% pedro ximénez

85 Mahogany with a reddish hue. Toasty and vis-cous aroma, nuts. Flavourful palate of a sweet whilst dry very well-integrated Oloroso.

HARVEYS PALE CREAM SEMI-SECO CREAM

85 Straw-coloured. Clear, saline aroma with a flor expression; quite warm with nuts and mountain herbs. Demi-sec, slightly pungent palate with light notes of flor, well-integrated bitterness and a long finish with almonds and herbs, original.

HEREDEROS DE ARGÜESO

Mar, 8
11540 Sanlúcar de Barrameda (Cádiz)
☎: 956 385 116 - Fax: 956 368 169
argueso@argueso.es
www.argueso.es

Established: 1822

⊕ 12,000 ▤ 6,000,000 litres ▧ 50 has.
▼ 85% ◐15%: -DE -UK -NL -BE -US -CA

SAN LEÓN MANZANILLA
100% palomino

97 Straw-coloured. Powerful aroma, fresh with saline and iodised notes of clean flor and a suggestion of mountain herbs. Dry, fresh, bitter, saline palate, rich in organic expression in the retronasal passage.

ARGÜESO AMONTILLADO VIEJO
100% palomino

88 Mahogany. Powerful, pungent aroma with mild toasty notes of Solera and nuts (hazelnuts and walnuts). Powerful, pungent, bitter palate, old with very persistent oak tannins.

HEREDEROS DE NICOLÁS MARTÍN

Polígono Industrial El Portal C/2 - P. 78
11408 Jerez de la Frontera (Cádiz)
☎: 956 237 476 - Fax: 956 143 849
info@bodegashmartin.com
www.bodegashmartin.com

Established: 1969

⊕ 1,500 ▤ 750,000 litres ▧ 25 has.
▼ 80% ◐20%

CERRO DE SANTIAGO FINO
CERRO DE SANTIAGO AMONTILLADO
CERRO DE SANTIAGO OLOROSO SECO
CERRO DE SANTIAGO PEDRO XIMÉNEZ
CERRO DE SANTIAGO CRIANZA MOSCATEL
CERRO DE SANTIAGO CREAM

Bodegas HIDALGO-LA GITANA

Banda de Playa, 42
11540 Sanlúcar de Barrameda (Cádiz)
☎: 956 385 304 - Fax: 956 363 844
bodegashidalgo@lagitana.es
www.lagitana.es

Established: 1792

⊕ 10,000 ▤ 3,200,000 litres ▧ 75 has.
▼ 75% ◐25%: -UE -CA -US -SAM- ASIA

LA GITANA MANZANILLA
100% palomino fino

87 Pale straw. Short, clean aroma with a hint of flor, very fine. Dry, fresh and flavourful palate, slightly saline, well-balanced and finer than last year's vintage.

PASTRANA MANZANILLA
100% palomino fino

90 Golden with a greenish hue. Powerful aroma with notes of old flor, a nuance of Solera and mountain herbs. Bitter, flavourful palate with structure but with a pungent hint, better balanced than last year's vintage.

PASTRANA AMONTILLADO
100% palomino fino

90 Old gold. Powerful aroma, aldehydic, of old Solera and oak. Dry, slightly organic and flavourful palate, with good wood, elegant.

VIEJO HIDALGO OLOROSO
100% palomino fino

84 Old gold. Aroma with pungent, dry notes, toasty flavours and aldehyde. Dry, woody, pungent, warm and flavourful on the palate.

JEREZ CORTADO HIDALGO 20 AÑOS VOS PALO CORTADO
100% palomino fino

82 Brilliant amber. Aroma of pâtisserie and sweet toasty flavours. Dry, fresh and flavourful palate with slightly flat traces of Solera.

PALO CORTADO VIEJO HIDALGO V.O.R.S. 30 YEARS

90 Old gold. Fine, toasty aroma of nuts and fine pâtisserie. Dry bitter palate with toasty notes in the retronasal passage (pastries, nuts), flavourful.

VIEJO NAPOLEÓN PEDRO XIMÉNEZ
100% pedro ximénez

89 Mahogany with a coppery edge. Elegant aroma of fine toasty flavours and vanilla with a suggestion of raisins and spices, slightly saline. Round, sweet palate with a pleasant bitter hint, quite fresh with a very long creamy retronasal effect.

JEREZ CORTADO HIDALGO AMONTILLADO VIEJO "HIDALGO"

HIJOS DE RAINERA PÉREZ MARÍN

Misericordia, 1
11540 Sanlúcar de Barrameda (Cádiz)
☎: 956 319 564 - Fax: 956 319 869
laguita@laguita.com
www.laguita.com

Established: 1852

🌐 22,000 📊 5,204,000 litres 🍇 275 has.

🍷 30% 🌐70%: AN -DE -AR -AU -AT -CO -BE -DK -US -PH -FI -FR -UK -IL -NL -UK - IE -JP -LV -MX -DK -NZ -PA -PL -PR -DO - RU -SE -CH

LA GUITA MANZANILLA

89 Straw-coloured. Not very intense aroma, mild saline notes, fresh. Bitter on the palate, fresh, clean, delicate, light, notes of flor.

J. FERRIS M.

Carretera CA-602, km. 16
11500 Sanlucar de Barrameda (Cádiz)
☎: 956 235 100 - Fax: 956 235 011
bodega@bodegasferris.com

Established: 1975

🌐 10,000 📊 2,000,000 litres 🍇 35 has.

🍷 5% 🌐95%

LAS 3 CÁNDIDAS FINO
palomino

80 Straw-coloured. Slightly rustic aroma of yeast with iodised notes of aged cask and a suggestion of flor. Fresh, slightly bitter, vinous palate, without great character.

PICONERA MANZANILLA

74 Pale. Somewhat vinous aroma, not a great deal of flor but clean. Light palate of aged wood, lacking character.

LAS 3 CÁNDIDAS AMONTILLADO
palomino

87 Old gold with an amber hue. Intense aroma with fine notes of cocoa and nuts and a mild suggestion of sweetness. Dry, powerful aroma with fine bitter notes (nuts, herbs, aged wood) and a slightly oily texture, very long.

LAS 3 CÁNDIDAS OLOROSO

84 Toasted amber. Deep aroma of Solera with walnuts and toasty pastries. Fresh palate with flavourful overtones, reminiscent of almonds and with a saline suggestion, long.

J. FERRIS PEDRO XIMÉNEZ
pedro ximénez

85 Dark mahogany. Intense aroma with crianza notes (toast, vanilla, cedar) and spices of sundrenched fruit. Fleshy and almost syrupy on the palate with good alcoholic freshness, long.

J. FERRIS MOSCATEL
moscatel

76 Amber with an orange glint. Marked aroma of oranges with a hint of viscosity and a creamy suggestion of pâtisserie, creamy. Sweet palate with almondy notes and crystallised fruit, slightly artificial.

LAS 3 CÁNDIDAS CREAM
palomino, pedro ximénez

85 Mahogany with an amber hue. Intense aroma, rich in crianza nuances with predominant toasty and slightly sweet (vanilla, cocoa) oak notes. Generous palate with fine bitter notes and a good expression of Oloroso hint, spicy.

JUAN C. GRANT

Bolos, 1 y 3
11500 El Puerto de Sta. María (Cádiz)
☎: 956 870 406 - Fax: 956 870 406
info@bodegasgrant.com
www.bodegasgrant.com
Established: 1841

VALEROSO FINO
LA GARROCHA MANZANILLA
LA GARROCHA AMONTILLADO
LA GARROCHA OLOROSO
LA GARROCHA PEDRO XIMÉNEZ
LA GARROCHA CREAM DULCE
LA GARROCHA MOSCATEL

LA CIGARRERA

Plaza Madre de Dios, s/n
11540 Sanlúcar de Barrameda (Cádiz)
☎: 956 381 285 - Fax: 956 383 824
lacigarrera@lacigarrera.com
ww.lacigarrera.com

Established: 1758
⊞ 600 ▦ 40,000 litres 📏 90%
🍇10%: -US -JP -DK -DE

LA CIGARRERA MANZANILLA
100% palomino

86 Straw-coloured. Aroma with mild hints of wood and flor. Dry, bitter palate, powerful but not very complex.

LA CIGARRERA AMONTILLADO
100% palomino

86 Golden. Aroma with notes somewhere between flor, and nuts, old Solera. Pungent palate with oak and oxidative notes, bitter.

LA CIGARRERA PEDRO XIMÉNEZ
100% pedro ximénez

84 Mahogany with an orange rim. Aroma of toasty grapes, fresh, with a suggestion of cedar and vanilla. Sweet and toasty on the palate with good freshness and notes of dates and raisins in the mouth, long.

LA CIGARRERA MOSCATEL
100% moscatel

85 Mahogany. Intense toasty aroma of dates and dark-roasted flavours with a Muscatel nuance (orange peel). Flavourful palate with a syrupy expression and toasty hints standing out over the grapes, persistent.

LUIS CABALLERO

San Francisco, 24
11500 El Puerto de Sta. María (Cádiz)
☎: 956 851 810 - Fax: 956 859 204

MACARENA MANZANILLA
palomino

87 Brilliant golden yellow. Powerful aroma with notes of flor, an iodised suggestion of aged cask. Bitter, flavourful palate with pungent and saline hints, quite persistent.

DON LUIS AMONTILLADO

84 Old gold. Aroma of toasted nuts with notes of orange peel (reduction), resins and hints of well-integrated Solera. Round, flavourful, slightly glyceric palate with saline notes and a sweet almonds aftertaste.

CABALLERO OLOROSO REAL

88 Mahogany. Powerful aroma with creamy oak notes and a hint of fine Solera notes (varnish, nuts, pâtisserie). Powerful, bitter and creamy palate with iodised notes, quite complex.

LERCHUNDI MOSCATEL DE CHIPIONA

86 Mahogany. Toasty aroma of caramelised dates with a nuance of vanilla (Crianza) and a suggestion of spices and coffee. Flavourful palate with freshness and reminiscent oranges and Muscatel in reduction, long and almondy.

MANOLA CREAM

84 Old gold with an iodised rim. Toasty aroma with a hint of jammy figs and a suggestion of old Solera. Concentrated, flavourful palate with notions of nougat and good acidity.

M. GIL LUQUE

Ctra. de Lebrija, km. 3 "Viña El Telégrafo"
11407 Jerez de la Frontera (Cádiz)
☎: 956 319 564 - Fax: 956 319 869
gilluque@laguita.com
www.mgilluque.com

Established: 1912
⊞ 2,100 ▦ 6,000,000 litres 🌿 55 has.
📏 30% 🍇70%: -AN -DE -AR -AU -AT -CO
-BE -DK -US -PH -FI -FR -IL -NL -UK -IE -
JP -LV -MX -DK -NZ -PA -PL -PR -DO -RU -
SE -CH

LEYENDA AMONTILLADO
100% palomino

72 Old gold. Aroma of Solera and aldehyde. Semi-sweet palate with toasty hints and carpentry, without Oloroso character.

DE BANDERA VORS AMONTILLADO
100% palomino

86 Old gold. Pungent aroma with oak notes, carpentry with hints of oxidised flor. Powerful dry, varnishy and pungent palate.

LUQUE CLASSIC AMONTILLADO SEMI-SECO
100% palomino

86 Old gold with a coppery hue. Powerful, clean aroma of Solera and aged oak with a fine suggestion of nuts, herbs and varnish. Powerful, dry palate with notes of fine sweetness and vanillas and toasty oak (a mild suggestion of toffee), bitter and long.

DE BANDERA VORS OLOROSO
100% palomino

83 Not very clear old gold with reddish hues. Pungent aroma with oak notes, nuts and Solera. Very dry, pungent and bitter on the palate, very old with varnish.

LUQUE CLASSIC OLOROSO
100% palomino

85 Mahogany. Aroma with notes of old Solera, pastries and nuts. Dry palate with notes of sweetness, toasty with hints of pastries and bitter oak in the finish, flavourful.

LEYENDA OLOROSO
palomino

83 Amber. Intense aroma of Solera and varnish with nutty notes and saline overtones. Dry, expressive and fresh palate with a saline and almondy character, long.

DE BANDERA VORS PALO CORTADO
100% palomino

83 Slightly cloudy old gold. Toasty pâtisserie aroma with pungent hints and aldehyde. Dry palate of bitter almonds with a suggestion of sweetness.

LEYENDA SOLERA PEDRO XIMÉNEZ

83 Mahogany with a saffron edge. Aroma with toffee notes, toasty, caramel. Sweet palate, fresh, notes of orange rind, a slightly viscous finish.

LEYENDA ORO PEDRO XIMÉNEZ
100% pedro ximénez

86 Mahogany. Sweet, toasty aroma, caramel, aged Solera, raisins. Sweet, flavourful, toasty palate, reminiscent of dates and raisins.

LEYENDA CREAM DULCE
80% palomino, 20% pedro ximénez

83 Old gold. Aroma of Mistelle with hints of varnish and a nuance of Solera. Sweet, chocolatey, almost syrupy on the palate with a suggestion of orange, slightly sweet.

LUQUE CLASSIC CREAM DULCE
80% palomino, 20% pedro ximénez

80 Old gold. Hazelnut aroma with hints of acetaldehyde and a suggestion of pâtisserie. Sweet, flavourful palate with toasted nuts, round with a sweet almond aftertaste.

LUQUE CLASSIC MOSCATEL
100% moscatel

78 Amber with a brick red rim. Fresh aroma of orange peel with crianza hints of toasty flavours and varnish, without notes of Muscatel. Very fresh, somewhat bitter, dense and slightly pasty on the palate.

DE BANDERA GRAN RESERVA MOSCATEL
100% moscatel

84 Mahogany with a yellow edge. Aroma of complex aged Solera with a dark-roasted suggestion of pâtisserie, without Muscatel expression. Fleshy, almost syrupy palate, reminiscent of Muscatel, good freshness with toasty flavours and toasted nuts and a very long finish.

LUQUE CLASSIC FINO
LUQUE CLASSIC PEDRO XIMÉNEZ
DE BANDERA VORS PEDRO XIMÉNEZ
LUQUE CLASSIC CREAM PALE CREAM

MANUEL ARAGÓN BAIZÁN

Calle Olivo, 1
11130 Chiclana de la Frontera (Cádiz)
☎: 956 400 756 - Fax: 956 532 907
granero@teleline.es

Established: 1795

🍾 800 📊 250,000 litres 🌱 60 has.

🍷 85% 🌍 15%: -FR -IT -UK

EL NETO AMONTILLADO SECO
TÍO ALEJANDRO OLOROSO SECO
GRANERO SECO
GLORIA MOSCATEL DULCE
CREAM VIEJO A. SEMI- DULCE
LOS CUATRO MOSCATEL DULCE
NARANJA MOSCATEL DULCE

MARQUÉS DEL REAL TESORO (JOSÉ ESTEVEZ)

Carretera Nacional IV, km. 640
11408 Jerez de la Frontera (Cádiz)
☎: 956 321 004 - Fax: 956 340 829
visitas@grupoestevez.com
www.realtesoro.com

Established: 1760

⊕ 15,000 🗄 7,000,000 litres 🍇 225 has.

🍷 45% 🍇55%

TÍO MATEO FINO
100% palomino

92 Straw-coloured with a greenish edge. Clear, clean aroma of flor with subtle saline and herbaceous hints. Oily, long, slightly warm palate with character and bitter notes well-assembled yet fresh.

DEL PRÍNCIPE AMONTILLADO
100% palomino

86 Amber with a yellowish edge. Generous aroma of pâtisserie with hints of varnish, orange peel and nuts. Dry palate, slightly dry Solera with notes of almonds and carpentry (bitter), long.

COVADONGA OLOROSO
100% palomino

90 Very old gold. Complex aroma of carpentry with notes of varnish and reduction and a suggestion of hazelnuts. Dry and flavourful palate, slightly pungent due to the alcohol with traces of well-combined Solera overall, fresh with a very interesting almond finish.

PX VIEJO REAL TESORO PEDRO XIMÉNEZ
100% pedro ximénez

82 Mahogany with an iodised edge. Aroma of sultanas, figs and well-integrated toasty flavours (coffee and sweet vanilla). Very sweet, slightly pasty palate, with notes of fig bread and a sweet, syrupy finish.

MIGUEL M. GÓMEZ

Avenida de la Libertad
11500 El Puerto de Sta. María (Cádiz)
☎: 956 850 150 - Fax: 956 850 264

Established: 1816

⊕ 8.000 🍇 70 has. 🍷 10% 🍇90%

ALAMEDA FINO
GÓMEZ 1855 AMONTILLADO
MENTIDERO OLOROSO
TRIPLE DULCE PEDRO XIMÉNEZ
PIE DE REY CREAM DULCE

OSBORNE Y CÍA

Fernán Caballero, 3
11500 El Puerto de Sta. María (Cádiz)
☎: 956 869 000 - Fax: 956 869 078
comunicacion@osborne.es
www.osborne.es

Established: 1772

⊕ 17,500 🗄 10,000,000 litres 🍇 210 has.

🍷 50% 🍇50%: -NL -DE -UK -US

FINO QUINTA
100% palomino

94 Straw-coloured. Powerful, slightly pungent aroma with notes of very clean flor (salted meat, low tide). Full, generous palate, slightly oily, bitter and clean.

COQUINERO FINO AMONTILLADO
100% palomino

91 Straw-coloured with a golden glimmer. Powerful, pungent aroma of flor with light oxidative notes (almonds and hazelnuts). Full, oily, flavourful palate, slightly bitter with great persistence.

CARA DE GALLO MANZANILLA
100% palomino

79 Straw-coloured. Dry aroma with light notes of flor, slightly vinous. Fresh, light palate with a moderate flor expression.

OSBORNE RARE SHERRY SOLERA AOS AMONTILLADO SECO

90 Old gold with a light mahogany hue. Fine, toasty aroma with nutty notes (hazelnuts and almonds). Dry palate with aldehyde and old Solera, clean, bitter, slightly pungent, persistent.

BAILEN OLOROSO SECO
100% palomino

85 Old gold. Clear, toasty aroma of pastries with excellent balance between wine and oak. Flavourful, toasty palate with notes of vanilla and pastries, well-balanced, persistent.

10RF MEDIUM OLOROSO SEMI-DULCE
palomino, pedro ximénez

79 Old gold. Aroma with toasty notes, a hint of Mistelle and nuts. Quite fruity toasty palate with viscous notes.

OSBORNE RARE SHERRY SOLERA INDIA OLOROSO

95 Old gold with a dark mahogany hue. Powerful aroma with notes of acetaldehyde and old Solera with pungent hints of wood and nuts, toasty flavours. Dry, bitter, full, warm, old on the palate with aldehyde in the retronasal passage, very persistent, with fatness.

OSBORNE RARE SHERRY SOLERA BC 200 OLOROSO

94 Old gold with a light mahogany hue. Fine, powerful aroma, rich in toasty nuances with a suggestion of creamy wood, old Solera and toasted nuts. Full, generous, warm palate, sweet and flavourful, persistent, rich in toasty and spicy nuances.

OSBORNE RARE SHERRY PALO CORTADO SEMI-DULCE

92 Old gold with a mahogany hue. Powerful aroma, rich in fine pâtisserie notes and a mild floral and creamy nuance. Full, unctuous, elegant, oily palate with toasty pastries in the retronasal passage, flavourful.

1827 PEDRO XIMÉNEZ
100% pedro ximénez

83 Dark mahogany. Toasty aroma with Oloroso notes (nuts) and pâtisserie. Sweet, flavourful palate with a suggestion of Oloroso, toasty.

OSBORNE RARE SHERRY PX VORS 30 AÑOS PEDRO XIMÉNEZ SWEET

95 Chocolatey with a dark mahogany edge. Powerful, toasty aroma (dates, carob, dark-roasted flavour, caramelised pastries). Sweet, unctuous, warm, powerful and toasty palate with a bitter suggestion of Oloroso, old Solera, persistent with aldehyde in the retronasal passage.

SANTA MARÍA CREAM
palomino, pedro ximénez

83 Old gold with a coppery glint. Toasty aroma with Mistelle and hints of toasty caramel. Sweet, flavourful palate with perfect in wood and wine, light overtones.

PEDRO DOMECQ

San Ildefonso, 3
11403 Jerez de la Frontera (Cádiz)
☎: 956 151 500 - Fax: 956 338 674
jerez@domecq.es - domecq.es

Established: 1730

⊞ 100,000 ▤ 15,000,000 litres
🌱 1,100 has. 🍇 10% 🍷90%

LA INA FINO

93 Straw-coloured. Fresh aroma, slightly shorter than previous vintages with very fresh and clear pungent and saline hints. Dry, bitter, slightly pungent and flavourful on the palate with good persistence, medium-intensity retronasal effect.

BOTAINA SOLERA AMONTILLADO
100% palomino

91 Golden with a greenish hue. Powerful aroma, rich in organic and oxidative expression, very harmonious. Dry, bitter palate with pungent hints of well-integrated wood and flor, flavourful; long and persistent.

CAPUCHINO VORS AMONTILLADO
100% palomino

93 Old gold. Powerful aroma, rich in nuances of toasty pâtisserie and nuts, old Solera. Full, dry, warm, oily and bitter palate with good wood/wine harmony and a good oxidative balance.

AMONTILLADO 51-1ª VORS AMONTILLADO
100% palomino

91 Old gold. Powerful aroma with good oak/wine balance and excellent oxidation with a nuance of old Amontillado. Dry, harmonious palate with a pungent hint; dry and flavourful.

LA RAZA OLOROSO
85% palomino, 15% pedro ximénez

85 Mahogany. Toasty aroma of coffee, caramel, pâtisserie. Sweet, toasty, supple palate, with fatness, flavourful.

SIBARITA VORS OLOROSO VIEJO
98% palomino, 2% pedro ximénez

90 Mahogany. Fine, toasty aroma (fine pastries cocoa) and a nutty nuance. Oak tannins on the palate with very sweet hints and fine toasty hints on the retronasal passage, persistent and long.

VENERABLE 30 AÑOS PEDRO XIMÉNEZ
100% pedro ximénez

95 Opaque. Concentrated aroma of dates, jam, carob, very toasty, coffee. Dense, unctuous, sweet and toasty palate (coffee, chocolate), very complex and persistent.

RÍO VIEJO OLOROSO
LA RAZA OLOROSO VIEJO SWEET
LA INA PEDRO XIMÉNEZ
VIÑA 25 PEDRO XIMÉNEZ

PEDRO ROMERO

Trasbolsa, 84
11540 Sanlúcar de Barrameda (Cádiz)
☎: 956 360 736 - Fax: 956 361 027
pedroromero@pedroromero.es
www.pedroromero.es

Established: 1860

⊞ 12,000 ▤ 3,610,000 litres 🍇 70%
🍷30%: -US -CA -FR -UK -NL -BE -DK -AU -JP -SAM

PEDRO ROMERO MANZANILLA
100% palomino

90 Straw-coloured. Fresh, saline and iodised aroma with hints of clean flor. Dry, bitter, complex overtones, flavourful and fresh palate.

AURORA MANZANILLA
100% palomino

86 Pale with a greenish edge. Clear aroma with obvious mask notes (yeast, nuts) and a certain finnesse. Flavourful, intense palate with a saline and almond expression, long.

DON PEDRO ROMERO VORS GAMA PRESTIGE MUY VIEJO AMONTILLADO
100% palomino

85 Old gold. Complex aroma with Solera notes (cream, vanilla), hints of reduction and a suggestion of well-assembled flor. Flavourful, saline, slightly pungent and warm palate with marked nutty notes and an iodised finish.

DON PEDRO ROMERO VORS GAMA PRESTIGE MUY VIEJO OLOROSO
100% palomino

81 Light mahogany. Aroma with notes of acetaldehyde (varnish), old Solera (carob) and nuts. Bitter palate with slightly pungent wood.

HIJO DE PEDRO ROMERO VILLAREAL GAMA PRESTIGE VORS PALO CORTADO
100% palomino

88 Old gold with a mahogany hue. Powerful, toasty aroma of pâtisserie. Dry, pungent, bitter, flavourful palate, well-balanced.

VIÑA EL ALAMO PEDRO XIMÉNEZ
100% pedro ximénez

78 Dark amber. Toasty aroma of fresh grapes with notes of Mistelle (peaches) Sweet, very warm palate with a sensation of orange peel, without freshness.

VIÑA EL ALAMO AMONTILLADO
VIÑA EL ALAMO DRY OLOROSO
VIÑA EL ALAMO MEDIUM OLOROSO
VIÑA EL ALAMO CREAM OLOROSO
VIÑA EL ALAMO MOSCATEL

PILAR ARANDA

Álamos, 23
11401 Jerez de la Frontera (Cádiz)
☎: 956 339 634 - Fax: 917 258 630
mariasen@wanadoo.es
alvarodomecq.com

Established: 1800
🍷 1,200 🍇 60% 🌐40%

LA JANDA FINO

85 Straw-coloured with a golden edge. Intense aroma of flor with a flor character, notes of sweet almonds and a hint of fine crianza. Flavourful, slightly oily and fresh on the palate with saline suggestions and a slightly alcoholic finish.

LA JACA MANZANILLA

82 Straw-coloured. Somewhat ripe aroma with nutty notes without floral elegance and a suggestion of dried herbs. Flavourful, with almonds on the palate, clean and with bitter overtones but without intensity.

1730 AMONTILLADO

82 Old gold. Creamy, vanilla aroma with light notes of iodine and fine freshness. Fresh, flavourful palate with slightly flat nuances and mild cask notes; short.

1730 OLOROSO

80 Old gold. Toasty aroma of old Solera with toasty hints, nuts and a pâtisserie nuance. Dry, slightly pungent palate with hints of wood and iodine in the retronasal passage.

ALBUREJO OLOROSO

83 Old gold with an amber hue. Intense aroma with creamy and toasty Solera notes and hints of varnish. Dry, slightly unctuous and oily palate with a fine suggestion of sweetness alternating between bitter and nutty notes.

1730 PALO CORTADO

83 Old gold. Aroma with notes of old Solera with hints of oven-baked pastries and varnish. Dry, pungent palate with toasty notes in the retronasal passage, bitter, flavourful and more harmonious than on other occasions.

1730 PEDRO XIMÉNEZ

88 Very dark mahogany. Aroma of chocolate and coffee with notes of Solera, vanilla and dates. Sweet, intense palate, evoking coffee and toasty wood; not very fresh, long.

ARANDA CREAM

85 Old gold. Saline aroma (flor, nuts) with toasty crianza and orange peel. Expressive and very sweet palate with notes of bitter almonds, very long.

REY FERNANDO DE CASTILLA

Jardinillo, 7 - 11
11404 Jerez de la Frontera (Cádiz)
☎: 956 182 454 - Fax: 956 182 222

Established: 1837
🍷 1,000 🛢 200,000 litres 🌿 10 has.

🍷 40% 🌐60%: -UK -FR -CH -JP -IT -BE - US -SE -DK -DK -FI -MX -CA -RU -PH -PL - CZ -LV

FERNANDO DE CASTILLA FINO
100% palomino

87 Golden with an amber hue. Intense, full aroma, rich in crianza nuances (nuts, mountain herbs, hints of varnish) with a mild suggestion of flor. Flavourful, full palate with a ripe and original Fino expression, herbs and nuts.

FERNANDO DE CASTILLA AMONTILLADO

90 Golden. Powerful aroma with notes of wood and nuts with pungent notes of flor. Dry, powerful palate, with wood, bitter, very long.

FERNANDO DE CASTILLA OLOROSO
100% palomino

83 Old gold. Slightly pungent aroma of broom and Solera. Dry, pungent palate with old Solera, bitter.

FERNANDO DE CASTILLA PALO CORTADO

86 Old gold. Aroma with vinous notes, a nuance of wood and Solera and slightly wet hints. Dry palate, with pâtisserie and nuts in the retronasal passage, slightly bitter.

FERNANDO DE CASTILLA PEDRO XIMÉNEZ
100% pedro ximénez

93 Very dark mahogany. Aroma of Solera (vanilla, cocoa, cedar) with saline and spicy hints and a suggestion of dates and chocolates. Spicy, sweet and very complex palate with fresh overtones, syrupy with a dark-roasted and long in the retronasal passage.

SAINZ DE BARANDA

Bolsa, 169
11540 Sanlúcar de Barrameda (Cádiz)
☎: 956 369 882 - Fax: 956 362 125
msdbr@hotmail.com - elbuenvino.com

Established: 1915

600 🗒 100,000 litres 🍇 7,5 has.

🍷 95% 🍇5%

TÍA CARI MANZANILLA
SAINZ DE BARANDA MANZANILLA

SÁNCHEZ ROMATE HERMANOS

Lealas 26-28
11403 Jerez de la Frontera (Cádiz)
☎: 956 182 212 - Fax: 956 185 276
comercial@romate.com
www.romate.com

Established: 1781

6,500 🗒 500,000 litres 🍇 110 has.

🍷 40% 🍇60%

NPU AMONTILLADO
100% palomino

90 Gold with a greenish glimmer. Powerful aroma with harmonised organic and oxidative notes. Dry, pungent, bitter palate with symmetry between evolution, flor and wood.

LA SACRISTÍA DE ROMATE AMONTILLADO
100% palomino

86 Old gold. Aroma with notes of pâtisserie, more Oloroso than Amontillado. Dry, flavourful, bitter palate with a hint of carpentry.

LA SACRISTÍA DE ROMATE OLOROSO
100% palomino

90 Mahogany. Aroma with fine notes of toasty pastries, old Solera and hazelnuts. Full palate with sweet overtones, warm flavourful and toasty.

DON JOSÉ OLOROSO
100% palomino

89 Mahogany. Toasty aroma of fine pâtisserie with notes of old Solera. Dry, warm palate with aldehyde and iodine in the retronasal passage, flavourful, with fatness.

DUQUESA PEDRO XIMÉNEZ
100% pedro ximénez

90 Very intense with a mahogany rim. Raisiny, toasty, fruity aroma. Sweet pasty, toasty, powerful, spirituous, full, unctuous and flavourful palate.

LA SACRISTÍA DE ROMATE PEDRO XIMÉNEZ
100% pedro ximénez

87 Very intense. Toasty aroma with rancid flavours and hints of varnish. Sweet palate with hints of volatile acidity that without undermining the flavour makes it slightly less complex.

IBERIA CREAM DULCE
palomino, pedro ximénez

87 Mahogany with an amber hue. Powerful aroma of toasty crianza, rich in aged nuances and hints of fine oxidation (varnish, pâtisserie, nuts). Powerful, toasty and unctuous palate with raisiny notes and a suggestion of bitterness, warm with hints of broom and nuts in the retronasal passage.

LA SACRISTÍA DE ROMATE CREAM
palomino, pedro ximénez

88 Mahogany with an iodised edge. Complex aroma of old Solera with notes of raisins and cedar and hints of good reduction. Long, complex palate with excellent flavour, toasty hazelnuts and orange peel and a well-blended bitter finish.

MARISMEÑO FINO
LA PEPA MANZANILLA
REGENTE PALO CORTADO
CARDENAL CISNEROS PEDRO XIMÉNEZ

SANDEMAN

Pizarro, 10
11403 Jerez de la Frontera (Cádiz)
☎: 956 151 700 - Fax: 956 303 534

the.don@sandeman.com
www.sandeman.com

Established: 1790

 27,000 ☷ 19,000,000 litres 360 has.

🍷 5% 🍇95%

DON FINO
100% palomino

85 Straw-coloured with a greenish edge. Intense flor aroma, herbaceous notes and a suggestion of original salted meat nuances. Fresh, slightly oily palate with a sensation of fresh herbs, mild notes of nuts and clay, long.

DON AMONTILLADO SEMI-SECO
98% palomino, 2% pedro ximénez

80 Old gold. Aroma with notes of forest herbs and a suggestion of flor, pungent. Notes of wood on the palate, sweet with a bitter unharmonised finish.

CHARACTER AMONTILLADO SEMI-SECO
95% palomino, 5% pedro ximénez

84 Old gold. Elegant aroma of fine lees, oven-baked pâtisserie and a nuance of Solera. Demi-sec palate with a Fino expression, almondy notes and a nutty retronasal effect.

ROYAL ESMERALDA VOS 20 AÑOS AMONTILLADO SECO
100% palomino

88 Very old gold. Aroma of resin with notes of Solera, a hint of iodine and well-assembled pâtisserie and toffees. Flavourful palate with hints of well-assembled crianza, fresh, notes of pastries and combined notes of Fino and Oloroso, persistent.

ARMADA RICH CREAM OLOROSO
80% palomino, 20% pedro ximénez

85 Orangey gold. Spicy aroma (curry) with fine vanilla, nutty Solera and a saline hint. Sweet and creamy palate with integrated bitter notes, long in nutty nuances.

ROYAL CORREGIDOR VOS OLOROSO 20 AÑOS
85% palomino, 15% pedro ximénez

88 Mahogany with an amber hue. Powerful aroma with an excellent Solera expression, fine spicy oak notes (cocoa, vanilla), nuts and orange peel. Powerful, unctuous, spicy palate with notes of chocolate in the finish.

ROYAL AMBROSANTE VOS 20 AÑOS PEDRO XIMÉNEZ
100% pedro ximénez

95 Almost opaque mahogany. Quite quite closed, very concentrated aroma of freshly baked cakes with notes of coffee and well-integrated old Solera. Powerful palate with good Pedro Ximénez expression, fine toasty hints and chocolate, generous retronasal effect (fig bread, spices), long and fresh.

RARE FINO BARREL SELECTED

TRADICIÓN

Plaza Cordobeses, 3
11407 Jerez de la Frontera (Cádiz)
☎: 956 168 628 - Fax: 956 333 029
recarpet@arrakuis.es

Established: 1998

🍾 950 🍷 90% 🍇10%: -US -CA -AT -DE

TRADICIÓN MUY VIEJO VORS AMONTILLADO
100% palomino

88 Old gold. Aroma with notes of new wood and oxidative hints of Solera, hazelnuts and pâtisserie. Dry, bitter palate with nuts in the retronasal passage, persistent with a very bitter finish.

TRADICIÓN MUY VIEJO VORS 30 AÑOS OLOROSO
100% palomino

81 Brilliant old gold. Aroma of varnish and acetaldehyde with a suggestion of Solera (nuts). Fresh palate with marked Solera, flavourful and almondy hints.

TRADICIÓN MUY VIEJO VORS PALO CORTADO

89 Fairly dark gold. Aroma with notes of clean Solera, nuts and furniture. Dry, bitter palate with notes of oak, notes of carpentry not harmonised with the wine.

TRADICIÓN MUY VIEJO VOS PEDRO XIMÉNEZ

VALDESPINO

Carretera Nacional IV, km. 640
11408 Jerez de la Frontera (Cádiz)
☎: 956 321 004 - Fax: 956 340 829
visitas@grupoestevez.com
www.realtesoro.com

Established: 1875

🍾 14,000 ☷ 4,000,000 litres 155 has.

🍷 50% 🍇50%

INOCENTE FINO
100% palomino

90 Straw-coloured with a greenish edge. Clean flor aroma with a saline character (iodine) and a hint of well-assembled sweet almonds. Dry palate heavy on glycerin, well-integrated bitter taste overall with saline notes in the finish, round.

TÍO DIEGO AMONTILLADO
100% palomino

84 Old gold with an iodised edge. Very toasty aroma with notes of orange peel and pâtisserie. Round, dry, slightly warm palate with almondy notes, long and with a saline hint in the finish.

EL CANDADO PEDRO XIMÉNEZ
100% pedro ximénez

88 Mahogany with an amber edge. Generous aroma of spices with toasty Solera, dates and a suggestion of cedar and dark-roasted flavours. Sweet palate with notes of honey and figs, quite fresh with a toffee and Solera finish.

VIÑA LA CALLEJUELA

Camino Reventón Chico, s/n
11540 Sanlucar de Barrameda (Cádiz)
☎: 956 361 553
callejuela@vodafone.es
Established: 1998
🌐 400 🛢 500,000 litres🍇 35 has. 🍷 100%

VIÑA LA CALLEJUELA MANZANILLA

WILLIAMS & HUMBERT

Carretera N-IV, km. 641, 75
11408 Jerez de la Frontera (Cádiz)
☎: 956 353 400 - Fax: 956 353 411
williams@williams-humbert.com - williams-humbert.com
Established: 1877
🌐 70,000 🛢 35,000,000 litres
🍇 500 has. 🍷 35% 🍇65%

DRYSACK FINO
palomino

85 Straw-coloured. Intense aroma of flor with notes of nuts, toast and with a saline character. Unctuous, fresh and bitter on the palate (herbaceous), well-integrated with a complex almond finish; long.

ALEGRÍA MANZANILLA

83 Straw-coloured. Powerful aroma, with notes of flor in old casks, fresh. Bitter notes on the palate, flavourful, dry and slightly pungent.

JALIFA VORS "30 YEARS" AMONTILLADO

89 Old gold. Aroma with mild notes of pâtisserie, nuts, toasty flavours, caramel. Dry, powerful, old palate with oak tannins, bitter and persistent.

DRY SACK MEDIUM DRY OLOROSO

89 Old gold. Fine aroma of pâtisserie, cocoa and vanilla. Harmonious palate, well-crafted and conceived, flavourful and sweet, with a hint of dryness at the same time.

DRY SACK "SOLERA ESPECIAL" 15 AÑOS OLOROSO

89 Dark brownish mahogany. Toasty aroma (hazelnuts, pâtisserie), concentrated and harmonious. Sweet and toasty with caramel on the palate, flavourful with nuts and pâtisserie.

DON GUIDO SOLERA ESPECIAL PEDRO XIMÉNEZ

93 Very intense nearly opaque. Aroma of jam, coffee and chocolate, very toasty and complex. Dense, corporeal, full and unctuous, oily palate; very sweet and flavourful, excellent.

DO JUMILLA

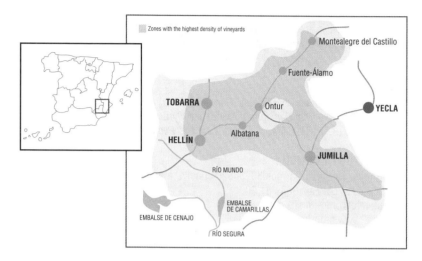

Zones with the highest density of vineyards

Montealegre del Castillo
Fuente-Álamo
TOBARRA
Ontur
YECLA
Albatana
HELLÍN
JUMILLA
RÍO MUNDO
EMBALSE DE CENAJO
EMBALSE DE CAMARILLAS
RÍO SEGURA

NEWS. Although there has been a significant decrease in the number of hectares and winegrowers in Jumilla, the number of bodegas in this region, which is maintaining an excellent level of quality and whose 2003 harvest was considered to be very good, is still growing.

In 2003, the plateau in Murcia dramatically suffered from the tremendous heat wave, along with the rest of Spain, with the difference that extreme weather conditions are commonplace in areas with this latitude, and the local *Monastrell* displays its finest values, in both sweet and dry red wines. The grapes were not harvested earlier, as expected, because the high temperatures meant that the grapes could not ripen properly, and time had to be given for this process to conclude.

Worthy of mention are the four aces of Casa Castillo (Julia Roch e Hijos), which has managed to place 4 of its wines on the podium, two of which are different vintages (2002 and 2003) of the formidable Valtosca, which with 94 points has become the best single-variety *Syrah* in Spain. The same can be said of the *Viognier*, also a white Rhone variety which obtained 85 points and has a notable varietal expression in the Casa de la Ermita (at only € 5).

Hectares of Vineyard	No. of Viticulturists	No. of Bodegas	2003 Harvest	2003 Production	Marketing
33,000	2,900	37	Very Good	23,503,027 litres	51% Spain 49% foreign

LOCATION. Midway between the provinces of Murcia and Albacete, this DO spreads over a large region in the southeast of Spain and covers the municipal areas of Jumilla (Murcia) and Fuente Álamo, Albatana, Ontur, Hellín, Tobarra and Montealegre del Castillo (Albacete).

CLIMATE. Continental in nature with Mediterranean influences. It is characterized by its aridity and low rainfall (270 mm) which is mainly concentrated in spring and autumn. The winters are cold and the summers dry and quite hot.

SOIL. The soil is mainly brownish-grey, brownish-grey limestone and limy. In general, it is poor in organic matter, with great water retention capacity and medium permeability.

VARIETIES:
Red: *Monastrell* (main 35,373 Ha), *Garnacha Tinta, Garnacha Tintorera, Cencibel (Tempranillo), Cabernet Sauvignon, Merlot* and *Syrah*.
White: *Airén* (3,751 Ha), *Macabeo, Malvasía* and *Pedro Ximénez*.

REGULATORY COUNCIL.
San Roque, 15. Apdo Correos 66. 30520 Jumilla (Murcia).
Tel: 968 781 761. Fax: 968 781 900.
E-mail: info@crdo-jumilla.com
Website: www.crdo-jumilla.com

GENERAL CHARACTERISTICS OF THE WINES:

Whites	Although they are not the most characteristic of the region, those produced from *Macabeo* are superior to those produced from *Airen*. In general, the white wines of Jumilla are straw yellow in colour; they have a moderate fruity character and a certain body on the palate; moreover, they are balanced and flavourful.
Rosés	These tend have a salmon pink colour; the aroma is quite fruity and has a good aromatic intensity; on the palate they are flavourful, some with slightly more body and a bit warmer.
Reds	These are the region's wines par excellence, based on a variety, the *Monastrell* that, subject to the production techniques, provides wines with a lot of intense colour, with characteristic aromas of ripe black fruit and occasionally dried fruit; on the palate the best are very powerful with excellent tannin structure, flavourful and meaty. The Crianzas combine this fruity character with the contributions of the wood, and in the case of the older wines, although oxidation notes may still appear, the evolutionary trend of the variety is controlled more and more.

DO JUMILLA

Bodegas 1890

Carretera Venta del Olivo, km. 2, 5
30520 Jumilla (Murcia)
☎: 968 757 099 - Fax: 968 757 099
elisam@jgc.es
www.vinosdefamilia.com

Established: 1890

4,525 🛢 10,000,000 litres 🌿 70 has.

🍷 80% 🍇20%

MAYORAL COSECHA 2003 JOVEN RED
60% monastrell, 40% tempranillo

82 Intense cherry. Fresh aroma with smoky notes, spices, toasty skins and blackberries. Fresh, flavoured earthy palate with black fruit in the finish.

MAYORAL CABERNET SAUVIGNON 2002 OAK AGED RED
100% cabernet sauvignon

85 Deep cherry. Varietal aroma of ripe black fruit, with spicy notes (paprika) and a well-structured toasty hint. Flavourful palate, good fruit/wood balance; good freshness and suple, integrated tannins.

MAYORAL SELECCIÓN 2002 OAK AGED RED
40% cabernet sauvignon, 30% tempranillo, 30% monastrell

82 Deep cherry with a garnet red edge. Spicy aroma with fine notes of oak reduction overtones and a suggestion of ripe black fruit. Fleshy palate with marked oak tannins, a suggestion of terroir and a fresh finish.

MAYORAL SYRAH 2002 OAK AGED RED
100% syrah

83 Deep cherry. Aroma of jammy black fruit, fine spices, hints of earth and a ripe hint. Fresh, flavourful palate with polished fruit tannins and assembled with the oak, a spicy finish.

MAYORAL 2001 CRIANZA RED
70% tempranillo, 30% monastrell

85 Very deep cherry Toasty aroma with light smoky hints, notes of terroir and a nuance of ripe black fruit. Flavourful palate with good alcohol-acidity balance, toasty notes and persistence (red fruit).

MAYORAL 2000 RESERVA RED
70% monastrell, 30% tempranillo

84 Deep cherry with a garnet red edge. Fine smoky aroma of toasty skins with hints of cumin and a certain crianza complexity. Fleshy palate with rough yet round wood tannins; a nuance of earth and a vanilla finish.

AGAPITO RICO

Casas de la Hoya, s/n - El Carche
30520 Jumilla (Murcia)
☎: 968 435 137 - Fax: 968 435 509

carchelo@interbook.net
Established: 1989

850 🛢 700,000 litres 🌿 100 has.

🍷 25% 🍇75%

CARCHELO 2003 JOVEN RED
50% monastrell, 30% syrah, 20% merlot

87 Intense violet cherry. Expressive aroma of red fruit with hints of maceration. Fleshy palate, round, fresh, fruity tannins with acidity well-integrated in the alcohol and a fruity finish.

CARCHELO "TARDO" 2003 JOVEN RED
100% merlot

81 Brilliant cherry with a violet hue. Powerful aroma of black fruit and sun-drenched skins with hints of terroir, figs and slightly crystallised notes. Fleshy and sweetish palate with ripe black fruit, good acidity and fresh overtones.

ALTICO MERLOT 2002 JOVEN RED
100% merlot

82 Garnet red. Aroma of red fruit, intense, toasty flavours, balsamic. Well-balanced on the palate with predominat wood, flavourful.

CARCHELO SYRAH 2002 JOVEN RED
100% syrah

88 Deep intense cherry. Varietal, spicy aroma with notes of fresh grapes. Dry, round palate with fruity tannins and some tannicity.

CANALIZO SYRAH 2000 CRIANZA RED
100% syrah

88 Deep cherry. Fruity aroma with a fine expression of the skins, integrated toasty notes and a floral nuance. Flavourful palate with fruity, powerful tannins, smoky nuances and very fresh acidity.

CARCHELO 2000 CRIANZA RED
50% monastrell, 30% syrah, 20% merlot

85 Deep cherry. Aroma of well-ripened black berries, spices (cocoa, black pepper), and elegant, well-integrated oak. Fruity palate with fleshy and flavourful fruit tannins, good acidity and a generous toasty crianza finish.

CARCHELO MERLOT 1997 CRIANZA RED
CARCHELO 1996 RESERVA RED

ASENCIO CARCELEN

Barón del Solar, 3
30520 Jumilla (Murcia)
☎: 968 780 418 - Fax: 968 780 145
vb-a.carcelen@terra.es

Established: 1876

300 🛢 3,000,000 litres 🌿 300 has.

🍷 85% 🍇15%

PURA SANGRE 1997 RESERVA RED

CON SELLO 1996 GRAN RESERVA RED
SOL Y LUNA MONASTRELL RED DULCE

BLEDA

Avenida de Yecla, 26
30520 Jumilla (Murcia)
☎: 968 780 012 - Fax: 968 782 699
wines@bodegasbleda.com

Established: 1935

845 ⬛ 2,000,000 litres ❦ 220 has.

🍷 20% 🍇80%

CASTILLO DE JUMILLA MACABEO 2003 JOVEN WHITE
100% macabeo

81 Brilliant pale with greenish nuances. Intense aroma of fruit and white flowers with hints of fine herbs. Flavourful, bitter palate with rich hints of citrus fruit, somewhat warm and oily.

CASTILLO DE JUMILLA 2003 JOVEN ROSÉ
100% monastrell

80 Cherry with coppery nuances. Powerful aroma of red stone fruit, slightly sweet with toasty notes of skins. Flavourful, bitter, spicy palate, somewhat warm and oily with hints of herbs.

CASTILLO DE JUMILLA MONASTRELL 2003 JOVEN RED
100% monastrell

77 Cherry with a violet edge. Aroma of skins, slightly alcoholic, with ripe red fruit and underbrush. Warm palate with fleshy tannins and noticeable acidity, bitter.

CASTILLO DE JUMILLA MONASTRELL - TEMPRANILLO 2003 JOVEN RED
60% monastrell, 40% tempranillo

84 Dark cherry with a purplish edge. Powerful aroma of jammy cherries, black fruit, with hints of macerated skins and a nuance of damp earth. Flavourful palate with slightly marked, sweet tannins, spicy and long with hints of liquorice.

MONTESINOS 2002 RED
cabernet sauvignon

76 Medium-hue garnet red. Aroma with sweet notes and very ripe red fruit. Warm and drying on the palate, not very well-balanced.

MONTESINOS MERLOT 2002 RED
100% merlot

78 Garnet red. Somewhat alcoholic aroma of jammy red fruit. Warm palate with polished though slightly drying tannins, not very persistent.

MONTESINOS SYRAH 2002 RED
100% syrah

78 Medium-hue cherry red. Medium-intensity, fresh aroma of ripe red fruit. Drying and short on the palate with slightly agressive tannins.

CASTILLO DE JUMILLA 2000 CRIANZA RED
55% monastrell, 45% tempranillo

82 Red cherry with a saffron edge. Intense aroma of ripe red stone fruit, spicy oak notes and hints of reduction (leather). Flavourful palate with a good fruit/oak integration, dark-roasted flavours and cocoa, somewhat warm.

DIVUS 2001 CRIANZA RED
90% monastrell, 10% cabernet sauvignon

84 Deep garnet red. Aroma of vanilla, new wood, hints of varnish and superripe fruit. Drying on the palate with slightly marked wood tannins, fleshy and slightly short.

DIVUS 2002 CRIANZA RED
95% monastrell, 5% merlot

82 Quite deep garnet red. Toasty aroma of very clean wood, jammy ripe fruit and spices. Fleshy, well-balanced and round on the palate with toasty hints in the retronasal passage.

CASTILLO DE JUMILLA 1999 RESERVA RED

79 Medium-hue cherry. Perfumed, not very intense aroma with light, toasty wood, balsamic hints and spices. Drying on the palate with not very marked wood or fruit tannins, light with toasty hints.

ORO VIEJO SOLERA RED
100% monastrell

83 Amber. Aroma with notes of rancid wine, sweet with toasty wood and bitter almonds. Drying palate with bitter notes and a suggestion of nuts (bitter almonds) and honey in the retronasal passage.

CARCHE 2002 JOVEN RED
MONTESINOS TEMPRANILLO 2002 RED
CARCHE 2000 CRIANZA RED
CASTILLO DE JUMILLA 1998 RESERVA RED

Bodegas y Viñedos
CASA DE LA ERMITA

Avenida de la Asunción, 42 bajo
30520 Jumilla (Murcia)
☎: 968 783 035 - Fax: 968 716 063
bodega@casadelaermita.com
www.casadelaermita.com

Established: 1999

2,200 ⬛ 1,134,000 litres ❦ 120 has.

🍷 20% 🍇80%: -US -JP U K -DE -FR -DK
-NL -BE -DK -SE -FI -AT-CH -MX -PE -CA -
IT -SG -LU -PL -SK -SY -PA

CASA DE LA ERMITA 2003 WHITE
100% viognier

85 Pale gold. Intense aroma of apricot skin with fine herbs, tropical nuances and petals. Flavourful, fruity, slightly warm and oily on the palate with good acidity, spices and a suggestion of minerals.

CASA DE LA ERMITA 2003 RED
monastrell, tempranillo, cabernet sauvignon, merlot, syrah

75 Red with a violet hue. Balsamic aroma of ripe red fruit and sun-drenched skins. Skin greeness on the palate with an element of acidity.

MONASTERIO DE SANTA ANA CABERNET 2003 JOVEN RED
100% cabernet sauvignon

82 Cherry with an orangey edge. Medium-intensity, balsamic aroma with spicy hints. Flavourful palate with notes of redcurrants and toasty skins and woods, well-balanced.

MONASTERIO DE SANTA ANA MONASTRELL 2003 JOVEN RED
100% monastrell

80 Quite dark cherry with a garnet red-orangey edge. Intense, balsamic aroma, ripe black fruit. Warm palate with sun-drenched skins and slightly drying tannins.

MONASTERIO DE SANTA ANA SYRAH 2003 JOVEN RED
100% syrah

82 Cherry with a garnet red edge. Powerful aroma of red plums with a floral edge, clean and expressive. Flavourful palate with good, prominent fruity character and fresh overtones, well-balanced.

CASA DE LA ERMITA MONASTRELL 2002 RED
100% monastrell

82 Garnet red cherry with a saffron edge. Powerful aroma with predominant reduction notes (damp horsehair) and a slightly fruity nuance. Flavourful palate with well-integrated fruit/oak, fine bitter notes and notes of terroir, with good acidity.

CASA DE LA ERMITA PETIT VERDOT 2001 OAK AGED RED
100% petit verdot

88 Almost opaque cherry. Fine varietal concentrated aroma of black fruit (flowers, balsamic flavours) and toasty notes. Fleshy, powerful palate with quite aggressive wood tannins, good freshness and with minerals and abundant fruit in the finish.

CASA DE LA ERMITA 2001 CRIANZA RED
monastrell, tempranillo, cabernet sauvignon

81 Deep garnet red. Spicy aroma with notes of toasty skins and a hint of flowers. Flavourful, fleshy palate with fruity, round but somewhat ripe tannins.

CASA DE LA ERMITA DULCE 2001 RED
100% monastrell

87 Garnet red cherry with a saffron hue. Powerful aroma of jammy black fruit with notes of sun-drenched skins and hints of figs and damp earth. Powerful, concentrated palate with rich, bittersweet notes, a slightly oily palate, fine bitter notes and hints of liquorice and terroir in the retronasal passage.

MONASTERIO DE SANTA ANA MERLOT 2003 JOVEN RED

DELAMPA

Carretera Jumilla - Yecla, km. 79, 3
30520 Jumilla (Murcia)
☎: 968 435 035 - Fax: 968 435 035

DELAMPA WHITE
DELAMPA ROSÉ
DELAMPA MONASTRELL RED
DELAMPA CRIANZA RED

FINCA LUZÓN

Carretera de Cieza, km. 3, 1
30520 Jumilla (Murcia)
☎: 968 784 135 - Fax: 968 784 135
info@fincaluzon.com
www.fincaluzon.com

Established: 1978

🍇 2,000 📦 10,500,000 litres 🍷 500 has.

🇪🇸 15% 🌐85%: -US -UK -DE -DK -CH -SE -FR -JP

FINCA LUZÓN 2003 JOVEN RED
40% monastrell, 20% merlot, 20% cabernet sauvignon, 10% tempranillo, 10% syrah

87 Very dark garnet red. Aroma with lactic fermentation notes and ripe red fruit. Flavourful and fleshy on the palate with good acidity and a spicy aroma in the retronasal passage.

ALTOS DE LUZÓN 2002 CRIANZA RED
50% monastrell, 25% cabernet sauvignon, 25% tempranillo

90 Intense cherry with an orangey rim. Toasty aroma of fine wood, quinces and balsamic flavours. Flavourful and full-bodied on the palate with symmetry between the fruit and wood and persistent tannins.

CASTILLO DE LUZÓN 2001 CRIANZA RED
50% monastrell, 20% merlot, 30% cabernet sauvignon

82 Garnet red with a brick red rim. Aroma with light hints of viscosity. Slightly marked tannins, spicy notes and an element of overripening on the palate.

FINCA LUZÓN 2003 WHITE
FINCA LUZÓN 2003 ROSÉ
MARÍA JESÚS 2002 CRIANZA RED SWEET

FINCA OMBLANCA

Ctra. Jumilla - Aontur, s/n
30520 Jumilla (murcia)
☎: 968 780 850
comercial@fincaomblanca.com
www.fincaomblanca.com

DO JUMILLA

DELAÍN MONASTRELL 2003 OAK AGED RED
🍾 3

82 Deep cherry. Aroma of well-ripened red fruit, pleasant spicy hints, a varietal nuance (flowers). Fresh, elegant, flavourful palate, with the character of the grape variety; not evident wood.

HUERTAS

Carretera de Murcia
30520 Jumilla (Murcia)
☎: 968 783 061 - Fax: 968 781 180
vinos@bodegashuertas.es
www.bodegashuertas.es

Established: 1996

🌐 600 📊 10,500,000 litres 🍇 300 has.

🎩 60% 🍇40%

RODREJO 2003 WHITE
50% airén, 50% macabeo

75 Pale. Intense, fruity aroma with hints of exotic fruit. Flavourful palate with white fruit and without great nuances.

RODREJO 2003 ROSÉ
100% monastrell

80 Very deep raspberry. Powerful aroma of very ripe red fruit with hints of withered petals. Flavourful, fleshy palate with the spicy freshness of skins, pleasant.

RODREJO 2003 RED
70% monastrell, 30% tempranillo

84 Garnet red cherry. Intense, varietal, expressive aroma with an important fruity presence and a floral edge. Very flavourful, full palate of fresh ripe fruit and well-integrated alcohol.

RODREJO MONASTRELL - TEMPRANILLO 2002 RED
80% monastrell, 20% tempranillo

82 Dark garnet red cherry. Intense aroma of black fruit, fine spicy notes, hints of flowers and underbrush. Flavourful, fleshy palate with predominant ripe fruit notes, round, slightly oily tannins and good acidity.

RODREJO SELECCIÓN 2000 RED
100% monastrell

75 Cherry with an orangey hue. Not very intense aroma, of slightly overripe red fruit and a suggestion of lees. Warm and light on the palate, well-mannered.

ARANZO 2000 CRIANZA RED

77 Dark cherry. Not very intense, spicy aroma (pepper) with light reduction notes. Fleshy and fruity on the palate, slightly warm with polished tannins.

ARANZO 1999 CRIANZA RED
100% monastrell

81 Cherry with an orangey hue. Aroma with smoky notes, lactics, spices and red stone fruit.

Fleshy, well-balanced palate with well-integrated wood tannins.

ARANZO 1998 CRIANZA RED
100% monastrell

82 Cherry with a brick red rim. Clean, not very intense aroma of ripe red fruit and light reduction. Wood tannins and well-integrated fruit on the palate, well-balanced.

ARANZO 1999 RESERVA RED
100% monastrell

80 Cherry with a brick red hue. Perfumed aroma with ripe red stone fruit, flowers and varietal notes. Fleshy, well-balanced palate with well-integrated tannins.

ARANZO 1998 RESERVA RED
100% monastrell

77 Cherry with a brick red hue. Aroma of toasty wood and light notes of jammy red fruit. Slightly drying on the palate with light, bitter notes.

RODREJO 2001 RESERVA RED
100% monastrell

72 Cherry with an orangey hue. Perfumed aroma with a suggestion of lees without great varietal typification. Round, polished on the palate.

ARANZO 1996 RESERVA RED

Bodegas JUAN GIL

Paraje de la Aragona, Pol. 214 Parcela 2-D
30520 Jumilla (Murcia)
☎: 968 716 045 - Fax: 968 716 051
info@bodegasjuangil.com

Established: 2003

🌐 250 📊 3,500,000 litres 🍇 90 has.

JUAN GIL 2003 OAK AGED RED
100% monastrell
🍾 4

86 Very deep cherry with a violet edge. Powerful aroma of black fruit with an excellent expression of young wine and a hint of oaky freshness (spices). Fresh, fleshy palate with well-integrated grape and oak tannins and good acidity.

JULIA ROCH E HIJOS

Finca Casa Castillo
Carretera Jumilla - Hellín, km. 15, 7
30520 Jumilla (Murcia)
☎: 968 781 691 - Fax: 968 716 238
juliaroch@interbook.net

Established: 1991

🌐 350 📊 565,000 litres 🍇 192 has.

🎩 25% 🍇75%: -US -JP -NZ -MX

CASA CASTILLO VENDIMIA 2003 JOVEN RED
85% monastrell, 15% tempranillo

85 Cherry with a raspberry hue. Fresh aroma of intense red berries, flowers (violets) and pleasant maceration notes, slightly mineral. Flavourful, bitter palate with ripe tannins and a good mineral component; lively red fruit.

CASA CASTILLO MONASTRELL 2003 RED
100% monastrell

85 Bigarreau cherry. Aroma of red fruit (bigarreau cherries, raspberries) with lactic tones and balsamic nuances. Flavourful, powerful palate with good slightly drying tannins and a bitter nuance.

VALTOSCA 2003 OAK AGED RED
100% syrah

94 Very intense cherry. Deep aroma with a rich fruit expression, very ripe with hints of bunches and a note of dried fruit, mineral. Powerful, warm, spirituous, very fleshy palate with sweet tannins and a toasty retronasal effect (pitch, peat, chocolate), very complex.

VALTOSCA 2002 RED
100% syrah

93 Intense cherry with a lively violet edge. Toasty aroma of minerals, with jammy fruit notes (jam, chocolate, dark-roasted flavours), rich in fruit expression and wood. Powerful, fleshy palate with very ripe tannins, jammy black fruit, earthy hints and minerals, complex.

LAS GRAVAS 2001 CRIANZA RED
monastrell, cabernet sauvignon, syrah

93 Very intense cherry. Medium-intensity aroma, jammy and toasty hints (coffee, dates). Powerful, fleshy, and full palate with very ripe and persistent tannins, good fruit/wood assemblage, more elegant than Pie Franco.

CASA CASTILLO PIE FRANCO 2000 OAK AGED RED
100% monastrell

93 Intense cherry. Mineral aroma of new wood (carpentry), pipe tobacco and jammy fruit. Very spiritous, warm palate with powerful and very concentrated tannins, hints of alcoholic sweetness and a very mineral retronasal effect.

CASA CASTILLO 1999 CRIANZA RED

Cooperativa Nuestra Señora de
LA ENCARNACIÓN

Avenida Guardia Civil, 106
02500 Tobarra (Albacete)
☎: 967 325 033 - Fax: 967 325 033

SEÑORÍO DE TOBARRA

Bodegas **MURVIEDRO**

Ampliación Polígono El Romeral, s/n
46340 Requena (Valencia)

☎: 962 329 003 - Fax: 962 329 002
murviedro@murviedro.es
www.murviedro.es
Established: 1927
🛢 1,500 🛢 7,100,000 litres 🏴 5% 🌐95%

SANTERRA MONASTRELL 2003 RED
monastrell

84 Deep raspberry. Aroma of black fruit, hints of bramble berries, slightly spicy. Fleshy, powerful palate with highly polished tannins and clear varietal flavour; harmonious.

OLIVARES

Vereda Real, s/n
30520 Jumilla (Murcia)
☎: 968 780 180 - Fax: 968 756 474
bodolivares@eresmas.com
Established: 1930
🛢 400 🛢 5,000,000 litres 🍇 275 has.
🏴 60% 🌐40%

ALTOS DE LA HOYA 2002 RED
90% monastrell, 10% garnacha

80 Dark cherry with a deep red edge. Somewhat intense aroma of jammy black fruit with hints of macerated skins and a nuance of toasty oak. Flavourful palate with fine bitter notes and notions of wax, slightly oily and spicy with liquorice and pitch in the finish.

OLIVARES 2000 RED DULCE
100% monastrell

94 Dark cherry. Powerful, concentrated aroma of jammy black fruit, macerated skins, dried fruit tones and terroir. Concentrated palate with a dried fruit character, unctuous, sweet with vigorous tannins, cocoa powder and excellent acidity.

PEDRO LUIS MARTÍNEZ

Barrio Iglesias, 55
30520 Jumilla (Murcia)
☎: 968 780 142 - Fax: 968 716 256
export@alceno.com
www.alceno.com
Established: 1870
🛢 80 🛢 3,400,000 litres 🏴 40%
🌐60%: -US -JP -UE

ALCEÑO 2003 JOVEN WHITE
95% macabeo, 5% airén

80 Straw-coloured with golden nuances. Intense aroma of ripe white fruit with spicy hints of skins. Flavourful, fruity palate with a slightly oily texture and fine notes of herbs.

ALCEÑO 2003 ROSÉ
70% monastrell, 25% tempranillo, 5% syrah

80 Pale cherry. Quite intense aroma of red stone fruit with sweet hints (strawberry jelly). Fresh, quite fruity palate with rich spicy and bitter notes.

ROMEO 2003 JOVEN RED
100% monastrell

82 Garnet red cherry with a coppery edge. Intense aroma of forest fruit with notes of macerated skins and balsamic hints. Flavourful, light palate with hints of jammy fruit and the freshness of skins and damp earth, slightly warm.

ALCEÑO 2003 RED
50% monastrell, 30% tempranillo, 20% syrah

84 Cherry with a lively violet hue. Clear aroma of strawberry pulp with maceration notes and a nuance of the vine varieties (flowers, spices). Fleshy, fruity palate with pleasant mineral tones and good fruit-wood balance.

ALCEÑO SELECCIÓN 2002 ROBLE RED
60% monastrell, 20% tempranillo, 20% syrah

85 Dark garnet red cherry. Powerful, concentrated aroma of jammy black fruit with fine toasty oak and hints of tobacco. Flavourful palate with rough and oily tannins, well-integrated fruit and bitter notes (pitch, liquorice, dark-roasted flavours), slightly warm.

ALCEÑO SELECCIÓN 2001 CRIANZA RED
34% monastrell, 33% tempranillo, 34% syrah

84 Deep cherry. Aroma of very ripe red fruit, blackberries and forest fruit, spicy. Well-balanced, fleshy, spicy palate with a good fruit /wood tannin integration, long.

ALCEÑO SELECCIÓN 2000 CRIANZA RED
60% monastrell, 20% tempranillo, 20% syrah

86 Deep garnet red. Expressive aroma of toasty skins with mineral notes and a nuance of ripeness and fine spices. Fleshy, flavourful palate with an excellent fruit-wood balance; considerable freshness and an earthy finish.

ROMEO 2001 CRIANZA RED
100% monastrell

83 Garnet red cherry with a brick red rim. Intense aroma with predominant spicy and fine reduction notes (tobacco, leather). Flavourful, supple palate with a good fruit/oak integration, round and oily tannins, spicy.

Bodegas SAN DIONISIO

Carretera Higuera, s/n
02651 Fuenteálamo (Albacete)
☎: 967 543 032 - Fax: 967 543 136
sandionisio@bodegassandionisio.es
www.bodegassandinisio.es

Established: 1957
⊕ 125 ▤ 15,000,000 litres ⬝ 5,400 has.
🍷 70% 🌐30%: -IT -DE -PT -DK

SEÑORÍO DE FUENTEÁLAMO SELECCIÓN 2003 MACERACIÓN CARBÓNICA RED
70% monastrell, 30% tempranillo

81 Intense cherry with a raspberry edge. Intense balsamic aroma of red fruit and maceration (flowers). Fleshy, fresh palate with black fruit and liquorice; firm tannins, long.

SEÑORIO DE FUENTEÁLAMO 2000 CRIANZA RED
60% monastrell, 40% tempranillo

78 Cherry with a brownish edge. Toasty aroma with dark-roasted flavours over the fruit, earthy and animal hints. Flavourful, fresh, supple palate with well-balanced fruit-wood.

SEÑORIO DE FUENTEÁLAMO (150 CL.) 1999 CRIANZA RED
70% monastrell, 30% cencibel

84 Intense cherry. Powerful aroma of very ripe fruit with earthy notes and an oaky nuance. Fleshy, warm and flavourful on the palate with stewed fruit and toasty oak in the retronasal passage.

SEÑORÍO DE FUENTEÁLAMO 1998 RESERVA RED
60% monastrell, 40% cencibel

75 Garnet red with a brick red edge. Aroma of old wood (dust, animals) with a suggestion of very ripe fruit. Flavourful palate with good acidity and marked toasty flavours; without great crianza expression.

SEÑORÍO DE FUENTEÁLAMO MACABEO SELECCIÓN 2003 WHITE
SEÑORIO DE FUENTEÁLAMO MONASTRELL 2003 JOVEN ROSÉ
SEÑORIO DE FUENTEÁLAMO CENCIBEL SELECCIÓN RED
SEÑORÍO DE FUENTEÁLAMO MONASTRELL 2003 RED
SEÑORÍO DE FUENTEÁLAMO 1998 RESERVA RED

Bodegas SAN ISIDRO

Carretera Murcia, s/n
30520 Jumilla (Murcia)
☎: 968 780 700 - Fax: 968 782 351
bsi@bsi.es
www.corpbsi.com - www.bsi.es

Established: 1935
⊕ 2,000 ▤ 52,000,000 litres ⬝ 4,000 has.
🍷 55% 🌐45%

SABATACHA 2003 FERMENTADO EN BARRICA WHITE

77 Pale with a golden hue. Intense aroma with predominant smoky oak notes. Flavourful palate with hints of quite fresh oak and a nuance of ripe fruit, lacking balance.

SABATACHA AIRÉN 2003 WHITE
100% airén

76 Brilliant pale. Quite intense, fruity aroma with hints of petals. Flavourful palate with the freshness of spices and citrus fruit.

SABATACHA MONASTRELL 2003 ROSÉ
monastrell

74 Intense raspberry with a coppery glint. Intense aroma of slightly reduced red fruit (withered petals). Flavourful palate with a somewhat oily and warm texture, spicy notes of skins and hints of herbs.

SABATACHA GRAN NOVAL 2003 MACERACIÓN CARBÓNICA RED
monastrell

82 Garnet red with a violet hue. Spicy, earthy aroma with overripe fruit. Good expression on the palate, fleshy, with chewy tannins, powerful.

SABATACHA MONASTRELL 2003 RED
monastrell

72 Cherry. Discreet aroma with off-odours of elaboration. Fleshy, fresh palate, without fruit expression.

BSI MONASTRELL 2003 RED
monastrell

82 Ruby red. Viscous aromas of ripe fruit, fruity and floral. Palate with very fleshy and powerful tannins, not very persistent.

SABATACHA SYRAH 2002 OAK AGED RED
100% syrah

78 Garnet red. Aroma with fine reduction notes, vinous and alcoholic. Very ripe fruit on the palate and very warm, lacks great nuances.

GÉMINA CUVÉE SELECCIÓN 2001 RED
monastrell

87 Deep garnet red cherry. Powerful aroma of jammy black fruit with fine toasty oak notes and a notion of terroir. Flavourful, fleshy palate with promising but slightly marked tannins, a good fruit/oak integration, spicy and long.

GENUS MONASTRELL SYRAH 2001 RED
80% monastrell, 20% syrah

78 Garnet red. Aroma of very ripe fruit with spicy notes of sun-drenched skins and hints of vanilla-flavoured wood. Flavourful palate with fruity but sweet tannins; fresh but without great character.

BSI MONASTRELL ECOLÓGICO 2000 OAK AGED RED
monastrell   🍷 6

81 Dark garnet red cherry. Intense aroma with predominant notes of toasty oak and skins, spicy. Flavourful palate with fine bitter notes, slightly warm and spicy with hints of fresh skins in the retronasal passage.

SABATACHA MONASTRELL 2000 CRIANZA RED
monastrell

78 Dark garnet red. Spicy aroma of ripe toasty skins and a suggestion of minerals. Fleshy, fla-vourful palate with ripe fruit well-integrated with the oak and complex hints of the vine variety.

SABATACHA MONASTRELL 1995 RESERVA RED
monastrell

74 Brick red garnet. Ripe aroma of caramel and sun-drenched skins. Fleshy palate without fruit nuances but with sweet notes.

GÉMINA PREMIUN RESERVA 1996 RED

77 Very deep cherry. Very toasty aroma of overripe fruit, alcoholic and rustic. Warm, drying palate without great expression.

LACRIMA VIÑA CRISTINA DULCE
100% monastrell

77 Quite intense mahogany. Aroma with notes of aged wood, raisins and pastries. Slightly drying and aged wood on the palate, a rancid character.

Cooperativa del Campo **SAN JOSÉ**

Camino de Hellín, s/n
02652 Ontur (Albacete)
☎: 967 324 212 - Fax: 967 324 186
export@villadeontur.com
www.villadeontur.com

Established: 1947

🛢 100 📟 220 litres 🌿 2,500 has.

🍇 70% 🌐30%

CASTILLO DE ONTUR RED
DOMINIO DE ONTUR OAK AGED RED
DOMINIO DE ONTUR 2002 CRIANZA RED
DOMINIO DE ONTUR 1999 CRIANZA RED

SEÑORÍO DEL CONDESTABLE

Avenida Reyes Católicos, 47
30520 Jumilla (Murcia)
☎: 968 781 011 - Fax: 968 781 100
www.byb.es

Established: 1963

🛢 1,500 📟 16,220,000 litres

🍇 63,9% 🌐36,1%

SEÑORÍO DE ROBLES MONASTRELL 2003 ROSE
100% monastrell

80 Raspberry with a coppery glint. Intense, fruity aroma with spicy hints of skins. Flavourful, fleshy and slightly oily on the palate with fine spicy notes, hints of herbs and good acidity.

SEÑORÍO DE ROBLES MONASTRELL 2003 ROSE
100% monastrell

82 Intense raspberry with coppery nuances. Intense aroma of slightly reduced red fruit with hints of petals. Flavourful palate with fine bitter and citrus notes and the freshness of grapeskins.

DO JUMILLA

SEÑORÍO DE ROBLES MONASTRELL 2003 RED
100% monastrell

82 Cherry. Clear aroma with a nuance of clean strawberries and fine pepper. Flavourful, fruity palate, very fresh and with a very pleasant strawberry flavour.

SEÑORÍO DEL CONDESTABLE 2000 CRIANZA RED
100% monastrell

82 Brilliant cherry with a brick red edge. Intense aroma of smoky oak notes with a reduction nuance (leathers). Flavourful on the palate with fine bitter notes and a good crianza expression, very pleasant.

SEÑORÍO DEL CONDESTABLE 1999 RESERVA RED
100% monastrell

82 Not very deep cherry. Spicy aroma of vanilla, toasty and balsamic flavour. A good fruit/wood integration and well-balanced on the palate with light bitter notes.

SILVANO GARCÍA

Avenida de Murcia, 29
30520 Jumilla (Murcia)
☎: 968 780 767 - Fax: 968 916 125
bodegas@silvanogarcia.com
www.silvanogarcia.com

Established: 1925

150 2,500,000 litres 40 has.

80% 20%: -US

VIÑA HONDA 2003 WHITE
100% macabeo

76 Straw-coloured with coppery nuances. Quite intense aroma with predominant notes of lees and toasty hints of skins. Flavourful, somewhat fruity, warm and oily palate with bitter hints.

VIÑA HONDA 2003 ROSÉ
100% monastrell

78 Cherry with coppery nuances. Somewhat intense and fruity aroma with hints of petals and fine lees. Flavourful palate with fine bitter and citrus notes and a spicy hint.

SILVANO GARCÍA MONASTRELL 2003 RED DULCE
100% monastrell

86 Opaque cherry. Aroma with notes of jammy black fruit, toasty with a notion of skins and terroir and a raisiny hint. Sweet, powerful, concentrated palate with fine bitter hints (cocoa), lacking freshness.

VIÑA HONDA 2003 RED
70% monastrell, 20% tempranillo, 10% syrah

80 Dark cherry with a purplish edge. Intense aroma of jammy black fruit with hints of sun-drenched skins and fresh overtones of damp earth. Flavourful palate with marked, slightly sweet tannins (hints of overextraction), fine bitter notes and good acidity.

VIÑA HONDA 2001 CRIANZA RED
70% monastrell, 20% tempranillo, 10% cabernet sauvignon

81 Garnet red cherry. Powerful aroma with predominant toasty oak notes and a fine reduction nuance (tobacco). Powerful, concentrated and flavourful on the palate with well-integrated fruit/oak, spices, dark-roasted flavours and liquorice in the retronasal passage.

SILVANO GARCÍA MOSCATEL 2003 DULCE WHITE

SIMÓN

Carretera Madrid, 15
02653 Albatana (Albacete)
☎: 967 323 340 - Fax: 967 323 340
bodsimon@hotmail.com
joaquin444@hotmail.com

Established: 1942

150 900,000 litres 150 has.

70% 30%: -DE -UK -US -NL -BE -DK

GALÁN DEL SIGLO 2003 JOVEN RED
GALÁN DEL SIGLO 2001 CRIANZA RED
GALÁN DEL SIGLO 2003 CRIANZA RED
GALÁN DEL SIGLO 1996 RESERVA RED
GALÁN DEL SIGLO 1989 GRAN RESERVA RED

Bodegas TORRECASTILLO

Carretera de Bonete, km. 0,4
02650 Montealegre del Castillo (Albacete)
☎: 967 582 188 - Fax: 967 582 188
bodega@torrecastillo.com
www.torrecastillo.com

Established: 1997

75 450,000 litres 105 has. 100%

TORRE CASTILLO 2003 ROSÉ
monastrell

80 Brilliant raspberry. Intense, fruity aroma with hints of fine herbs and peach skins. Flavourful, fresh palate with fine notes of spices and citrus fruit.

TORRE CASTILLO 2003 OAK AGED RED
monastrell

79 Cherry with a purple hue. Clear aroma of fresh red berries with balsamic notions. Fresh, flavourful palate with red fruit in the finish, very pleasant.

TORRE CASTILLO 2001 CRIANZA RED
monastrell

84 Garnet red. Concentrated aroma of ripe black fruit with notes of dates and hints of earthiness.

Fleshy, powerful palate with earthy wood tannins, well-balanced and slightly warm.

VALLE DEL CARCHE

Polígono CC-13 Casas del Señor
03640 Monovar (Alicante)
☎: 965 978 050 - Fax: 965 980 060

Established: 1865

🛢 325 ▯ 1,200,000 litres 🍇 165 has.

🇪🇸 75% ⊕25%

VEGA CARCHE MERLOT 2002 ROSÉ
VEGA CARCHE MERLOT 2002 RED
VEGA CARCHE MONASTRELL 2002 RED
VEGA CARCHE SYRAH 2002 RED
VEGA CARCHE TEMPRANILLO 2002 RED
CASTILLO MAESTRAL 1998 CRIANZA RED

Vitivinícola de Albacete Sociedad Cooperativa Limitada VITIALBA

Carretera de la Higuera s/n
02651 Fuenteálamo (Albacete)
☎: 669 876 376 - Fax: 967 543 136
mesparcia@vitialba.es - vitialba@vitialba.es
www.vitialba.es

Established: 1999

🛢 400 ▯ 30,000,000 litres 🍇 12,000 has.

🇪🇸 80% ⊕20%

VITIALBA DOMUS

DO LA GOMERA

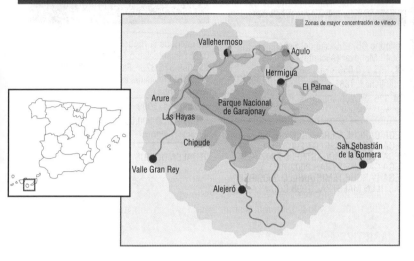

Zonas de mayor concentración de viñedo

Vallehermoso
Agulo
Hermigua
El Palmar
Arure
Parque Nacional
de Garajonay
Las Hayas
Chipude
San Sebastián
de la Gomera
Valle Gran Rey
Alejeró

NEWS. A new addition to this Guide, which is growing day by day in the number of DOs –the next will be Uclés– as the interest shown by the autonomous communities in recognising their wine-growing heritage increases. The DO Gomera was approved together with Gran Canaria, although it had difficulties in adjusting to the requirements demanded by the regulations, and therefore there have been no wines with the new official label until this year. In principle, of the six bodegas present on the island, only three of them have been integrated into the Regulatory Council, whilst the remaining three are still marketing their wines under the umbrella of Vinos de la Tierra of La Gomera and, on occasions, not even this. The Inter-Island Council appears to be much more interested in promoting the island than the wine producers themselves to market its wines. Perhaps the DO may serve as an impulse to set up a common project within the very fragmented viticultural reality made up of multiple plots which barely reach a hectare in size.

Hectares of Vineyard	No. of Viticulturists	No. of Bodegas	2002 Harvest	2002 Production	Marketing
100	146	3	Good	56,500 litres	100% local

With regard to quality, the only worthy wines are those of the Sociedad Vinícola La Gomera, headed by the Inter-Island Council, which has learnt the lesson that in order to obtain good results from the predominant stock, the white *Forastera*, it must be planted in the higher regions of the Garajonay where it is protected from the humidity and heat, and production must be reduced as much as possible.

A peculiar fact of these wines is that they do not display the same ash aromas of the other neighbouring islands. The constant erosion that La Gomera is subjected to has resulted in a complicated geography full of ravines, with no signs of volcanic eruptions and, therefore, without this character in its soil.

LOCATION. The majority of the vineyards are found in the north of the island, in the vicinity of the towns of Vallehermoso (some 385 Ha) and Hermigua. The remaining vineyards are spread out over Agulo, Valle Gran Rey –near the capital city of La Gomera, San Sebastián– and Alajeró, on the slopes of the Garajonay peak.

CLIMATE. The island benefits from a subtropical climate together with, as one approaches the higher altitudes of the Garajonay peak, a phenomenon of permanent humidity known as 'mar de nubes' (sea of clouds) caused by the trade winds. This humid air from the north collides with the mountain range, thereby creating a kind of horizontal rain resulting in a specific ecosystem made up of luxuriant valleys. The average temperature is 20°C all year round.

SOIL. The most common soil in the higher mountain regions is deep and clayey, while, as one approaches lower altitudes towards the scrubland, the soil is more Mediterranean with a good many stones and terraces similar to those of the Priorat.

VARIETIES:
White: *Forastera* (90%), *Gomera Blanca, Listán Blanca* and *Marmajuelo*.
Red: *Listán Negra* (5%), *Negramoll* (2%); experimental: *Tintilla Castellana, Cabernet Sauvignon* and *Rubí Cabernet*.

REGULATORY COUNCIL.
Avda. Guillermo Ascanio, 16, 1°. Vallehermoso 38840 La Gomera.
Tel: 922 800 801. Fax: 922 801 146.

GENERAL CHARACTERISTICS OF THE WINES:

Whites	Almost all the wines are based on the *Forastera*, and are produced according to traditional methods: they are usually a little overripe and have rustic and warm notes. The best examples are from the higher and less humid areas, with wild and scrubland notes.
Reds	The warm climate leaves its mark on most of the young red wines of the island, with a somewhat sweet taste with balsamic notes. The greenness that can be seen in many of them is the result of the high production that on occasions the varietal pattern of the *Listán Negra* and the *Negramoll* have, from which they are produced.

Sociedad Vinícola GOMERA

Avenida Pedro Garcia Cabrera, 3
38840 Vallehermoso (La Gomera)
☎: 922 801 203 - Fax: 922 800 545

Established: 1995

130,000 litres 5 has.

ASOCADO 2003 WHITE
forastera blanca

78 Straw-coloured. Fresh, fruity aroma, with notes of foresty herbs and with character. Fruity, fresh, flavourful palate, good acidity with ripe foresty hints.

ASOCADO VENDIMIA SELECCIONADA 2003 WHITE
forastera blanca

80 Straw-coloured. Fruity, fresh aroma with foresty notes (scrubland herbs) and considerable varietal expression. Fresh, fruity aroma, with character, flavourful with very interesting foresty notes.

ASOCADO RED

Comunidad de Bienes MONTORO

La Castellana, s/n
38820 Hermigua (La Gomera)
☎: 922 880 307

Established: 1950

12,450 litres 30 has. 100%

MONTORO AFRUTADO WHITE

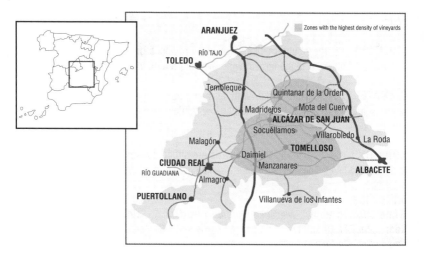

NEWS. The 2003 harvest represented an increase in production of almost 15% in relation to 2002, mostly thanks to the regions of Cuenca and Toledo. Very healthy grapes, although lacking some acidity, with a significant increase (35%) in the amount of red grapes harvested, the result of new vineyards entering into production with *Cabernet Sauvignon, Merlot, Syrah* and *Tempranillo* planted at the end of last century to replace the then omnipresent *Airén*.

The DO La Mancha is still a large umbrella for many different things. More and more interesting companies are being born with quality wines (Pagos del Vicario, Wilmot,

Hectares of Vineyard	No. of Viticulturists	No. of Bodegas	2003 Harvest	2003 Production	Marketing
191,699	21,604	195 bottlers	Very Good	48,888,505 litres	62% Spain 38% foreign

etc.), although many opt to use the official label of VT Castilla (the case with Dueto of Bodegas Fontana, with 93 points, or the Ercavio of Más Que Vinos).

As novelties, we have seen some wines produced with blends of *Garnacha Tintorera* or with this grape as a single-variety wine, so broadening the spectrum of tastes, together with an increase of 46% in export figures…; all in all, things are moving in La Mancha.

With respect to quality, of the 281 wines tasted, only 25 reached or exceeded 85 points. Undeniably the best was El Vínculo of Alejandro Fernández, whose rise in La Mancha runs parallel with a slight loss in quality in its original region of the Duero; the novel Mano a Mano, behind which is our colleague, the journalist Víctor Rodríguez; followed closely by the excellent Chardonnay of Blas Muñoz, the Canforrales, and several of the Fontal of Bodegas Fontana. Brilliant performance by the Finca Antigua wines, also from Cuenca (we will need to go into greater detail about geographic specifications from now on), with a really high average quality (all

its wines are rated above 85 points), and to a lesser extent, Casa Gualda.
The white wines have not yet managed to achieve high scores (with the exception of the aforementioned Blas Muñoz), and the best single-variety wines made of *Macabeo, Airén* or even the once promising *Sauvignon Blanc* hardly exceed 80 points.

LOCATION. On the southern plateau in the provinces of Albacete, Ciudad Real, Cuenca and Toledo. It is the largest wine-growing region in Spain and in the world.

CLIMATE. Extreme continental, with temperatures ranging between 40/45°C in summer and −10/12°C in winter. Rather low rainfall, with an average of about 375 mm per year.

SOIL. The terrain is flat and the vineyards are situated at an altitude of about 700 m above sea level. The soil is generally sandy, limy and clayey.

VARIETIES:
White: *Airén* (majority), *Macabeo, Pardilla, Chardonnay, Sauvignon Blanc.*
Red: *Cencibel* (majority amongst red varieties), *Garnacha, Moravia, Cabernet Sauvignon, Merlot* and *Syrah.*

REGULATORY COUNCIL.
Avda. de Criptana, 73. 13600 Alcázar de San Juan (Ciudad Real).
Tel: 926 541 523 / 926 541 592. Fax: 926 58 80 40.
E-mail: consejo@lamanchado.es
Webiste: www.lamanchado.es and www.lamanchawines.com

GENERAL CHARACTERISTICS OF THE WINES:

Whites	Most of them are produced from *Airén*; they are fresh and fruity, sometimes with notes of tropical fruit (melon, banana, pineapple) and somewhat limited on the palate. Those produced from *Macabeo* are a bit more balanced and intense, and are fruity, fresh and very pleasant to drink.
Rosés	The colour can range from onion skin to pink; on the nose they are fresh and fruity; on the palate they are supple and very light.
Reds	At present, this is the type of the highest quality in the region. Based on the *Cencibel (Tempranillo)*, one can especially find young red wines with a good colour, which are fresh, fruity and with a varietal character on the nose; on the palate they are meaty and quite flavourful. Those aged in wood generally maintain these characteristics, although they are more supple due to the contribution of the barrel. The Reservas and Gran Reservas follow the line of the traditional wines from Rioja, as far as the conception of their ageing. There are also single variety *Cabernet Sauvignon* wines that add to the characteristics of this variety, quite warm notes, typical of the sunshine of the region.

AGROCINEGÉTICA JOMA

Ct. Villarrobledo-Barrax, km. 14'
02600 Villarrobledo (Albacete)
☎: 967 440 200 - Fax: 967 440 204
martinez@lapina.es

VIÑA ORCE MACABEO 2003 JOVEN WHITE

ALCASOR

Isaac Peral, 15
45350 Noblejas (Toledo)
☎: 925 140 220 - Fax: 925 140 651

JÁNTIPE WHITE
GRAN CONDADO RED
JÁNTIPE RED

Bodega y Viña ALDOBA

Carretera Alcázar
13700 Tomelloso (Ciudad Real)
☎: 926 505 654 - Fax: 926 505 652
aldoba@allozo.com

Established: 1998
🍇 20 has. 🍷 90% 🌐10%

ALDOBA SELECCIÓN 2003 WHITE
100% macabeo

78 Brilliant pale. Slightly intense aroma of white stone fruit and fresh overtones. Flavourful palate with bitter notes, quality citrus fruit and hints of herbs.

ALDOBA SELECCIÓN 2003 RED
100% tempranillo

80 Garnet red cherry with a violet hue. Intense, fruity aroma with quality varietal hints (skins, damp earth). Flavourful palate with quite noticeable, fine tannins, liquorice and excellent acidity.

ALDOBA TEMPRANILLO 1999 RESERVA RED
100% tempranillo

80 Garnet red cherry with an orange glint. Powerful aroma with predominant reduction notes (leather, varnish). Flavourful palate with ripe, oily tannins and bitter, spicy notes, slightly warm.

ALDOBA 2001 CRIANZA RED

AMANCIO MENCHERO MÁRQUEZ

Legión Extranjera, 27
13260 Bolaños de Calatrava (Ciudad Real)
☎: 926 870 076 - Fax: 926 871 558

Established: 1930
🍷 24 🛢 1,000,000 litres 🍷 100%

FINCA MORIANA 2001 RED

Sociedad Cooperativa
ÁNGEL DEL ALCÁZAR

Carretera de Lillo, s/n
45860 Villacañas (Toledo)
☎: 925 160 548 - Fax: 925 160 548
angeldelalcazar@hotmail.com
Established: 1965
🍷 10 🛢 14,000,000 litres 🍷 90% 🌐10%

HACEDOR AIRÉN WHITE
HACEDOR MACABEO WHITE
HACEDOR CRIANZA RED
HACEDOR CENCIBEL RED

ANTONIO BALLESTEROS

Camino Villatobas, 1
45350 Noblejas (Toledo)
☎: 925 140 153 - Fax: 925 140 153
joseballesteros@wanadoo.es
www.ballesteros.es

Established: 1909
🍷 88 🛢 500,000 litres 🍇 20 has. 🍷 100%

VALLE REAL 2003 WHITE
airén

77 Brilliant pale. Slightly intense aroma of ripe white fruit with mountain herbs and hints of citrus fruit. Flavourful, bitter palate, with fresh acidity.

VALLE REAL 2003 ROSÉ
100% tempranillo

78 Brilliant salmon. Somewhat intense and fruity aroma with hints of dried flowers. Fresh, flavourful palate with citrus fruit freshness.

VALLE REAL 2003 RED
tempranillo

79 Deep cherry. Aroma of quite ripe black fruit, clear. Fresh, fruity palate with supple tannins and mineral nuances, pleasant.

VALLE REAL TEMPRANILLO 2000 OAK AGED RED
cencibel 🍷7

77 Cherry with an orange edge. Aroma with notes of animal fur, somewhat rustic with a nuance of ripe plums. Fleshy, earthy palate with good quality notes; good freshness.

Bodegas ASOCIADAS

Plaza Santa Quiteria, 24, 1 Pt

13600 Alcázar de San Juan (Ciudad Real)
☎: 926 547 404 - Fax: 926 547 702
baco@dominiodebaco.com
www.ofimanchega.com/b.a.co

DOMINIO DE BACO MACABEO WHITE

70 Yellow straw. Aroma with red fruit notes and skins. Without fruit on the palate, slightly oily and low in acidity.

DOMINIO DE BACO 2001 RED
cencibel

78 Cherry with an orangey hue. Aroma of toasted wood, liquorice and fruit. Greeness on the palate, with high acidity and not very persistent.

DOMINIO DE BACO AIRÉN WHITE
ABADIA DE BACO MACERACIÓN CARBÓNICA RED

AURELIO PURIFICACIÓN

Menéndez Pidal. 4
45460 Manzaneque (Toledo)
☎: 925 320 062 - Fax: 925 320 062

Established: 1972

🍷 2,500,000 litres 🌿 50 has. 🍷 100%

CASTILLO DE MANZANEQUE WHITE
CASTILLO DE MANZANEQUE RED

AYUSO

Miguel Caro, 6
02600 Villarrobledo (Albacete)
☎: 967 140 458 - Fax: 967 144 925
comercialayuso@telefonica.net
www.bodegasayuso.es

Established: 1947

🌐 12,000 🍷 40,000,000 litres 🌿 310 has.
🍷 75% 🌍25%: -DE -BE -CA -DK -US -EE -FI -FR -NL -IE -JP -MX -DK -NZ -PR -CZ - DO -SE -CH

ESTOLA 2003 ROBLE WHITE
airén

73 Pale with golden nuances. Quite intense aroma of smoky oak notes with scarcely any fruit expression. Quite flavourful palate with fresh overtones, hints of herbs and slightly drying oak.

ARMIÑO 2003 WHITE SEMIDULCE
100% airén

77 Pale yellow. Somewhat intense aroma of green apple peel and spicy hints. Fresh palate with carbonic hints, green fruit and fine bittersweet notes.

CASTILLO DE BENIZAR MACABEO 2003 WHITE
100% macabeo

71 Straw-coloured with coppery nuances. Quite intense aroma with fresh overtones, scarcely any fruit expression. Quite flavourful, bitter palate.

VIÑA Q 2003 WHITE
100% airén

79 Pale gold. Quite intense aroma with a certain finesse and varietal expression, white fruit, smoky skins and fine herbs. Fresh, flavourful palate, rich in citrus acidity.

CASTILLO DE BENIZAR CABERNET SAUVIGNON 2003 ROSÉ
100% cabernet sauvignon

81 Brilliant cherry. Somewhat intense aroma of blackberries and hints of herbs. Flavourful, fruity palate with bitter notes and quite varietal spices, excellent acidity.

VIÑA Q 2003 ROSÉ
100% cencibel

81 Pale cherry. Intense, fruity aroma, ripe and sweet with hints of petals. Flavourful palate of red fruit and a spicy nuance; slightly warm and oily.

CASTILLO DE BENIZAR TEMPRANILLO 2003 RED
100% tempranillo

67 Not very deep cherry. Vinous aroma of the tank without much expression of the vine variety. No great nuances on the palate.

ESTOLA 1999 RESERVA RED
100% cencibel

80 Ruby red cherry with a brick red glint. Intense aroma with predominant reduction notes (leather, aged wood, a nuance of black olives). Flavourful, supple palate with a peppery hint of oak, slightly warm with hints of tobacco and leather in the retro-nasal passage.

ESTOLA 2000 RESERVA RED
100% cencibel

80 Garnet red cherry with a brick red edge. Intense aroma with predominant spicy and reduction notes (leather, old furniture, prunes). Flavourful, supple palate with somewhat rough tannins, hints of liquorice, slightly warm.

ESTOLA 1994 GRAN RESERVA RED
65% cencibel, 35% cabernet sauvignon

85 Cherry. Aroma of very ripe, jammy red fruit and woody notes; quite viscous. Supple palate with good wood/fruit integration, a classic.

VIÑA Q 2003 RED

BALLESTEROS

Virtudes, 13
13340 Albaladejo (Ciudad Real)
☎: 926 387 458 - Fax: 926 387 034
bdgasballesteros@eresmas.com

Established: 1989

🍷 50 📋 195,000,litres 🍇 7 has. 🍷 100%

ARCADUZ JOVEN WHITE
ARCADUZ JOVEN RED

BIBIANO

Buñuelo, 8
16670 El Provencio (Cuenca)
☎: 967 165 056 - Fax: 967 166 264
alfredo.martinez@ictnet.es

Established: 1929

🍷 50 📋 1,000,000 litres 🍇 50 has.

🍷 90% 🌐10%

BIBIANO WHITE
CINCO ESTRELLAS WHITE
VEREDA DEL ZÁNCARA RED
CINCO ESTRELLAS CRIANZA RED

Sociedad Agraria de Transformación
BODEGAS VERDÚGUEZ

Los Hinojosos, 1
45810 Villanueva de Alcardete (Toledo)
☎: 925 167 493 - Fax: 925 166 148
verduguez@bodegasverduguez.com
www.bodegasverduguez.com

Established: 1950

🍷 280 📋 1,500,000 litres 🍇 128 has.

🍷 28% 🌐72%: -UK -FR -NL -FI -DK -CZ -DE -AT -BE -IE -US -MX -CR -CO -BR Chile -JP -RU -CU

PALACIOS REALES SAUVIGNON BLANC 2003 JOVEN WHITE
100% sauvignon blanc

80 Pale gold. Fresh, fruity aroma with a slight varietal expression (pineapple, bananas). Flavourful palate with bitter, fruity notes, hints of citrus fruit and good acidity.

PALACIOS REALES CABERNET SAUVIGNON 2003 JOVEN RED
cabernet sauvignon

82 Very deep cherry. Peppery aroma of black fruit, varietal. Fleshy and flavourful with ripe fruit on the palate with freshness and earthy traces in the finish.

PALACIOS REALES TEMPRANILLO 2003 JOVEN RED
100% tempranillo

82 Intense cherry. Very clear aroma of red berries, fresh with balsamic notes. Flavourful, very fresh palate with mineral and fruity notes.

PALACIOS REALES TEMPRANILLO 2000 CRIANZA RED
100% tempranillo

80 Deep cherry. Spicy aroma with smoky oak notes and a nuance of quite ripe red fruit. Flavourful, very fresh palate with traces of strawberry pulp.

PALACIOS REALES CHARDONNAY 2003 JOVEN WHITE
PALACIOS REALES MACABEO 2003 JOVEN WHITE
PALACIOS REALES AIRÉN 2002 WHITE
PALACIOS REALES MERLOT 2003 JOVEN RED
PALACIOS REALES SYRAH 2003 JOVEN RED
PALACIOS REALES TEMPRANILLO 1999 RESERVA RED
PALACIOS REALES TEMPRANILLO 2002 RED
PALACIOS REALES TEMPRANILLO 1997 GRAN RESERVA RED

Sociedad Cooperativa del
CAMPO SAN ISIDRO

Tarazona, 58
02636 Villagordo del Júcar (Albacete)
☎: 967 455 282 - Fax: 967 455 282
isivillal@ucaman.es

VILLA DEL JÚCAR FERMENTADO EN BARRICA WHITE
VILLA DEL JÚCAR MACABEO WHITE
VILLA DEL JÚCAR ROSÉ
VILLA DEL JÚCAR CENCIBEL RED

CAMPOS REALES BODEGAS L
(Cooperativa Nuestra Señora del Rosario)

Castilla-La Mancha, 4
16670 El Provencio (Cuenca)
☎: 967 166 066 - Fax: 967 165 032
info@bodegascamposreales.com
www.bodegascamposreales.com

Established: 1950

🍷 400 📋 25,000,000 litres 🍇 3,500 has.

🍷 50% 🌐50%: -US -UK -DE -SE -AT -NL -BR -CR -NZ

CANFORRALES LUCÍA 100 AÑOS AIRÉN 2002 WHITE
100% airen

80 Pale steel. Not very intense yet clean aroma of lavender and hay, fruity. Light, flavourful palate with a herby complexity, easy drinking.

CANFORRALES SOFÍA MACABEO 2003 WHITE

80 Pale steel. Medium-intensity aroma of ripe apples with a nuance of fragrant herbs. Light, quite flavourful palate, very well-mannered.

CANFORRALES ALMA CHARDONNAY SAUVIGNON 2003 RED
chardonnay, sauvignon blanc

72 Pale steel. Not very intense aroma with a mild off-odour and a nuance of ripe fruit. Light, slightly rustic palate, bitter.

CANFORRALES 2003 ROSÉ
100% garnacha

80 Pale raspberry. Not very intense yet fine aroma (petals, raspberries, strawberry jelly). Flavourful, fruity palate, easy drinking.

CANFORRALES CLÁSICO TEMPRANILLO 2003 RED

86 Bigarreau cherry with a lively violet edge. Powerful, fresh, harmonious aroma of ripe fruit (blackberries, raspberries) and an excellent varietal expression. Powerful, generous and fresh on the palate, with an important fruit presence, liquorice and very well-balanced.

CANFORRALES SYRAH 2003 RED
syrah

84 Bigarreau cherry with a lively violet edge. Medium-intensity, fine aroma with spicy skins and ripe red fruit. Flavourful, fresh palate with red fruit and a nuance of liquorice, expressive.

CANFORRALES SYRAH 2003 ROBLE RED
syrah

85 Cherry with a lively violet edge. Intense aroma of very ripe but fresh red fruit with a nuance of liquorice, spicy (vanilla), with a floral edge. Generous, flavourful palate with abundant red fruit and very toasty oak yet to be assembled.

CANFORRALES TEMPRANILLO 2003 ROBLE RED
tempranillo

85 Almost deep cherry with a violet edge. Clear aroma of black bramble fruit with mineral and balsamic notes, concentrated. Fleshy, powerful palate with abundant jammy fruit, long (black berries, minerals, ink).

CAMPOS REALES 1999 CRIANZA RED
tempranillo, cabernet sauvignon, merlot

84 Cherry with a coppery glint. Intense, ripe aroma with fine smoky wood hints. Fleshy palate with flavourful tannicity, a somewhat oily texture and good acidity.

CANFORRALES 1999 CRIANZA RED
tempranillo, cabernet sauvignon

86 Very deep cherry with a purplish hue. Aroma of black bramble fruit with balsamic and graphite notes and a toasty hint, intense. Fleshy palate with fruity and fresh tannins and very well-assembled wood; a complex finish (cocoa, pitch, liquorice).

CAMPOS REALES 1998 RESERVA RED
tempranillo, cabernet sauvignon

85 Deep cherry. Intense aroma of ripe black fruit; mineral and expressive with integrated wood.

Fleshy, very flavourful palate; polished wood tannins, supple and with good fruit.

CANFORRALES 1998 RESERVA RED
tempranillo, cabernet sauvignon

86 Intense cherry with a garnet red edge. Spicy aroma (vanilla, pepper) with ink, black fruit and a good crianza. Powerful, very flavourful palate with toasty oak, round tannins and black fruit in the finish.

CANFORRALES MACABEO 2002 WHITE
CANFORRALES 2002 RED
CAMPOS REALES TEMPRANILLO 2002 RED

Hermanos CAÑADAS ZARRAUTE

Cardenal Cisneros, 21
45350 Noblejas (Toledo)
☎: 925 140 209 - Fax: 925 140 964

Established: 1989

🌐 100 📦 1,000,000 litres 🍇 20 has.

🍷 100%

CAÑAZATE WHITE
SEÑORÍO DE CAÑADAS WHITE
CAÑAZATE RED
SEÑORÍO DE CAÑADAS RED

CASAGRANDE

Matadero, 1
45749 Villamuelas (Toledo)
☎: 925 346 524 - Fax: 925 346 524
gmdiego@mixmail.com

Established: 1975

🌐 420 📦 3,500,000 litres 🍷 70%

🌍 30%: -SE -JP -AD -UK

CASTILLO DE MORA RED
CASTILLO DE MORA 1999 OAK AGED RED

CENTRO ESPAÑOLAS

Carretera Alcázar, km. 1
13700 Tomelloso (Ciudad Real)
☎: 926 505 653 - Fax: 926 505 652
allozo@allozo.com
www.allozo.com

Established: 1991

🌐 3,500 📦 3,500,000 litres 🍇 243 has.

🍷 30% 🌍 70%

ALLOZO AIRÉN 2003 JOVEN WHITE
100% airén

75 Brilliant pale yellow. Not very intense aroma with a suggestion of spices and hay. Flavourful, quite fruity palate with a slightly acidic edge.

ALLOZO MACABEO 2003 JOVEN WHITE
100% macabeo

79 Pale yellow. Slightly intense aroma of fruit and white flowers without great nuances. Fresh, quite fruity palate with excellent citrus acidity.

ALLOZO TEMPRANILLO 2003 JOVEN ROSÉ
100% tempranillo

78 Pale raspberry. Fresh, slightly fruity aroma (red stone fruit) with spicy hints. Flavourful, very fresh palate with hints of citrus fruit and herbs on a slightly weak fruit nuance.

ALLOZO TEMPRANILLO 2003 JOVEN RED
100% tempranillo

81 Dark garnet red cherry. Quite intense aroma of very ripe and slightly reduced fruit with a spicy suggestion of skins. Flavourful, bitter palate with ripe and slightly oily tannins, liquorice and balsamic notes in the retronasal passage.

ALLOZO TEMPRANILLO MERLOT PAGO LOMA LOS FRAILES 2003 JOVEN RED
50% tempranillo, 50% merlot

76 Cherry with an orange edge. Medium-intensity aroma of not very ripe black fruit and black olives. Warm, somewhat green palate with noticeable tannins.

ALLOZO TEMPRANILLO-CABERNET SAUVIGNON PAGO LOMA LOS FRAILES 2003 JOVEN RED
50% tempranillo, 50% cabernet sauvignon

77 Deep cherry. Aroma of red fruit pulp with hints of pepper and a smoky hint. Flavourful palate with a bitter greeness and a rustic hint.

ALLOZO FINCA LOS CANTOS 2000 RED
100% tempranillo

71 Cherry with an orangey edge. Medium-intensity aroma with reduction off-odours and boiled fruit, without great expression. Supple palate with an adequate wood weight.

ALLOZO TEMPRANILLO 2000 CRIANZA RED
100% tempranillo

76 Cherry with an orangey edge. Aromas of reduction, spicy, balsamic notes. Bitter notes on the palate with quite noticeable tannins.

ALLOZO TEMPRANILLO 1998 RESERVA RED
100% tempranillo

78 Cherry with a brick red edge. Toasty, balsamic aroma, with spicy reduction notes. Warm palate with somewhat noticeable tannins and a toasty retronasal effect.

ALLOZO TEMPRANILLO 1997 GRAN RESERVA RED
100% tempranillo

80 Brick red. Toasty aromas of wood, chocolate and black fruit. Spicy, flavourful palate with very ripe fruit in the retronasal passage.

VERDIAL 2003 JOVEN RED

CERVANTINO

Grande, 66
13670 Villarubia de los Ojos (Ciudad Real)
☎: 926 898 018 - Fax: 926 266 514
cervantino@b-lozano.com

Established: 2000

150,000 litres 75% 25%

CERVANTINO 2003 WHITE
airén

79 Pale with greenish nuances. Somewhat intense aroma of fruit, white flowers and hints of herbs. Fresh palate with bitter notes and good citrus acidity.

CERVANTINO 2003 RED
100% tempranillo

77 Garnet red. Aroma of red fruit pulp with notes of sun-drenched skins. Fresh and round on the palate with somewhat muted fruit.

SOCIEDAD AGRARIA DE TRANSFORMACIÓN
COLOMAN

Goya, 17
13620 Pedro Muñoz (Ciudad Real)
☎: 926 586 410 - Fax: 926 586 656
coloman@satcoloman.com
www.satcoloman.com

Established: 1965

⊕ 50 🛢 27,800,000 litres 🍇 4,210 has.
🍷 99% 🌐1%: -FR

COLOMÁN 2003 WHITE
100% airén

77 Pale yellow. Quite intense aroma of slightly reduced ripe fruit. Better on the palate, flavourful and fruity with fine bitter notes, slightly oily with good acidity.

COLOMÁN 2003 ROSÉ
100% cencibel

72 Pale raspberry. Not very fine aroma with a fruity nuance, tank off-odours. Somewhat fruity and spicy on the palate with sweet notes.

COLOMÁN 2001 CRIANZA RED
100% cencibel

82 Deep cherry. Fruity aroma (blackberries, wild redcurrants), an earthy and toasty hint. Fleshy palate with traces of earthiness, fruity tannins, fresh and well-balanced.

COLOMÁN 2003 RED
100% cencibel

82 Garnet red with a violet edge. Aroma of vanilla and toasty wood. Drying on the palate with slightly marked and fresh oak tannins and a good fruit weight.

SEÑORÍO CAÑADAS JOVEN WHITE
COLOMÁN 2003 CRIANZA RED
SEÑORÍO CAÑADAS RED
VOGLIAMO 2000 RED

Sociedad Cooperativa Agraria
CORZA DE LA SIERRA

Maestro Lara, 65
13345 Cózar (Ciudad Real)
☎: 926 365 125 - Fax: 926 365 287
corza@ucaman.es

Established: 1964

⊕ 100 🛢 14,000,000 litres 🍇 2.100 has.
🍷 100%

CORZAVIN
REFLEJOS

COSECHEROS EMBOTELLADORES

Camino de Villatobas, 4
45350 Noblejas (Toledo)
☎: 925 140 292 - Fax: 925 140 962
cosecheros@embotelladores.e.telefonica.net

Established: 1967

⊕ 1,000 🛢 3,500,000 litres
🍶 3,000,000 litres. 🍷 75% 🌐25%: -UE

CUEVAS REALES 1999 CRIANZA RED
tempranillo, cabernet sauvignon

76 Cherry with a brick red edge. Aroma with crianza character (quite dry wood, varnish). Light, supple, somewhat spicy palate with considerable oak weight but well-mannered.

CUEVAS REALES 1998 RESERVA RED
tempranillo, cabernet sauvignon

74 Cherry with a brick red edge. Short aroma with notes of oak and a viscous hint. Light palate with slightly marked wood tannins but well-mannered overall.

Sociedad Cooperativa
CRISTO DE LA VEGA (CRISVE)

General Goded, 6
13630 Socuéllamos (Ciudad Real)
☎: 926 530 388 - Fax: 926 530 024
cristo.vega@interbook.net

Established: 1955

⊕ 400 🛢 90,000,000 litres 🍇 14,000 has.
🍷 25% 🌐75%

YUGO 2003 JOVEN WHITE
airén

82 Pale with greenish nuances. Somewhat intense aroma with a good varietal fruit expression (quite exotic white fruit, fine herbs). Flavourful palate with slight bitter notes and excellent acidity.

YUGO 2003 JOVEN ROSÉ
garnacha, tempranillo

80 Brilliant cherry with a violet hue. Somewhat intense, fruity aroma without great nuances. Flavourful, quite fruity palate with predominant bitter notes, spices and fine herbs.

YUGO SYRAH-TEMPRANILLO 2003 JOVEN RED
syrah, tempranillo

79 Garnet red cherry with a violet hue. Powerful aroma of black fruit (reduction notes), notes of petals and damp earth. Flavourful palate with sweetish fruit (hints of overextraction), bitter notes in the finish.

MARQUÉS DE CASTILLA 1999 CRIANZA RED
cencibel, cabernet sauvignon

80 Garnet red cherry with a coppery edge. Slightly intense aroma with spicy hints and reduction notes (tobacco). Flavourful palate with good oak/fruit integration; bitter with noticeable acidity.

SIGLO XVI 1999 CRIANZA RED

80 Garnet red cherry. Quite intense aroma of somewhat reduced ripe fruit, petals and spicy oak notes. Flavourful palate with a good fruit/oak integration, quite rough and oily tannins and quality bitter notes.

MARQUÉS DE CASTILLA 1998 RESERVA RED

80 Not very deep cherry. Aroma with viscous notes, sweet, with ripe red fruit. Flavourful palate with an earthy feel.

Bodegas DEL CARMEN

Carmen, 22
13179 Pozuelo de Calatrava (Ciudad Real)
☎: 926 840 340 - Fax: 926 840 340
bodegavcarmen@teleline.net

Established: 1928
2,300,000 litres 20 has. 100%

15 DE MAYO WHITE
15 DE MAYO RED

DEL SAZ (VIDAL DEL SAZ RODRÍGUEZ)

Maestro Manzanares, 57
13610 Campo de Criptana (Ciudad Real)
☎: 926 562 424 - Fax: 926 562 659
bodegasdelsaz@infonegocio.com

Established: 1974
60 6,000,000 litres 70 has.
100%

VIDAL DEL SAZ 2004 JOVEN WHITE

79 Pale yellow. Intense aroma, varietal (white flowers), a suggestion of sweet limes. Flavourful, bitter palate, marked citrus acidity, partially concealed fruit.

VIDAL DEL SAZ 2003 JOVEN ROSÉ

80 Intense raspberry. Intense aroma, forest fruit, fresh citrus overtones. Very fresh, flavourful palate, marked citrus acidity which subdues the fruit expression.

VIDAL DEL SAZ TEMPRANILLO 2002 ROBLE RED

78 Garnet red cherry with a violet edge. Powerful aroma, a spicy hint (tumeric) over a suggestion of forest fruit. Flavourful palate, very bitter, lacking balance and fruit expression, marked acidity.

VIDAL DEL SAZ 2000 CRIANZA RED

81 Dark garnet red cherry. Powerful aroma, ripe, fine reduction notes, a suggestion of skins and toasty oak. Powerful, flavourful palate, ripe and oily tannins, bitter hints (liquorice).

Cooperativa Agrícola EL PROGRESO

Avenida de la Virgen, 89
13670 Villarubia de los Ojos (Ciudad Real)
☎: 926 896 088 - Fax: 926 896 135
cooprogres@isid.es

Established: 1917
200 45,000 litres 9,700 has.

OJOS DEL GUADIANA AIRÉN 2003 JOVEN WHITE
airén

79 Brilliant pale. Intense aroma of white fruit, with hints of flowers and hay. Flavourful palate, less expressive than in the nose, with quality bitter and fruit notes.

OJOS DEL GUADIANA 2003 ROSÉ
tempranillo

77 Deep raspberry. Intense aroma of very ripe red fruit and hints of petals; slightly sweet and warm. Flavourful, fruity aroma with warm notes and bitter hints.

OJOS DEL GUADIANA TEMPRANILLO 2003 JOVEN RED
100% tempranillo

77 Garnet red cherry with a violet hue. Intense, fruity aroma with sweet notions (strawberry jelly). Flavourful, fruity palate with fleshy overtones and a hint of greeness to the tannins.

OJOS DEL GUADIANA 2001 CRIANZA RED

80 Not very deep cherry. Aroma of jammy tomatoes, not very intense and somewhat lactic. Warm, toasty palate, medium persistence.

OJOS DEL GUADIANA 2000 RESERVA RED
cencibel

82 Very deep cherry. Lactic aroma with sweet notes, vanilla and well-integrated wood. Fleshy, warm palate with bitter notes, well-balanced.

Alejandro Fernández Tinto Pesquera
"EL VINCULO"

Avenida Juan Carlos I s/n
13610 Campo de Criptana (Ciudad Real)
☎: 926 563 709 - Fax: 926 563 709

Established: 1999

🌐 1.300 🗒 10 litres 🍷 60%% 🍇40%:

EL VÍNCULO 2002 ROBLE RED

92 Very intense cherry. Complex toasty aroma (dark-roasted flavour, chocolate) and ripe jammy fruit. Powerful, fleshy, full, flavourful and toasty on the palate with good fruit/oak integration and complex overtones, warm.

Bodegas ENOMAR

Carretera Córdoba - Tarragona, km. 322
16630 Mota del Cuervo (Cuenca)
☎: 967 182 570 - Fax: 967 180 628
bodegasenomar@eresmas.com

Established: 1995

🌐 127 🗒 450,000 litres 🍷 90% 🍇10%: -
FR -DK -DE -CH -PR

BENENGELI MACABEO 2003 WHITE
100% macabeo

78 Pale with greenish nuances. Not very intense aroma with a certain finesse, herbs and hints of citrus fruit. Flavourful palate with bitter notes and good acidity.

CASCO ANTIGUO MACABEO WHITE
100% macabeo

72 Pale with greenish nuances. Slightly intense, fruity aroma. Quite flavourful palate without great expression, an acidic edge.

BENENGELI TEMPRANILLO 2003 ROSÉ
100% cencibel

76 Lively raspberry with coppery nuances. Somewhat intense, fruity aroma with hints of herbs and peach skins. Flavourful, bitter palate with fine spicy notes of skins and an acidic edge.

CASCO ANTIGUO TEMPRANILLO ROSÉ
100% cencibel

74 Brilliant raspberry. Not very intense aroma of ripe red fruit (somewhat reduced). Flavourful palate with spicy hints of skins and fresh overtones.

BENENGELI TEMPRANILLO 2003 RED
100% cencibel

79 Intense cherry with a coppery edge. Intense, fruity aroma with spicy notes of skins and a terracotta nuance. Flavourful, bitter palate with rough and fine tannins and rich bitter notes.

CASCO ANTIGUO CABERNET SAUVIGNON RED
100% cabernet sauvignon

76 Garnet red. Spicy aroma (pepper) with marked greeness. Fleshy with flavourful fruit tannins and notes of herbs on the palate, supple and varietal.

CASCO ANTIGUO SYRAH RED
100% syrah

72 Deep cherry. Aroma of ripe fruit with notes of off-odours and a rustic suggestion. Fleshy, powerful and ripe palate with flavourful tannins yet weak in character.

CASCO ANTIGUO TEMPRANILLO RED
100% cencibel

82 Garnet red. Aroma of black fruit (blackberries, redcurrants) with notes of liquorice, clear. Fleshy palate with a bitter but pleasant finish; notes of black berries and good freshness.

BENENGELI 2000 CRIANZA RED
100% cencibel

82 Dark garnet red cherry. Somewhat intense aroma of ripe fruit with toasty oak notes and hints of terracotta. Flavourful palate with somewhat fresh and rough oak tannins and fine spicy and reduction notes (leather, tobacco).

BENENGELI 1999 RESERVA RED
50% cencibel, 50% cabernet sauvignon

82 Garnet red cherry with a brick red rim. Intense aroma with predominant oak notes (spices, dark-roasted flavours) and runny liquorice. Flavourful

DO LA MANCHA

palate with a good oak/fruit integration, bitter notes and good acidity.

CASCO ANTIGUO MERLOT RED

ENTREMONTES (NUESTRA SEÑORA DE LA PIEDAD)

Circunvalación, s/n
45800 Quintanar de la Orden (Toledo)
☎: 925 180 930 - Fax: 925 180 480
comercial@bodegasentremontes.com
Established: 1954
📕 33,000,000 litres 🍇 5,800 has.
🍷 50% 🍏50%

CLAVELITO AIRÉN 2003 WHITE
airén

77 Brilliant pale yellow. Not very intense aroma with the finesse of herbs and spicy skins. Flavourful palate with bitter notes and noticeable citrus acidity.

CLAVELITO 2003 ROSÉ
cencibel

78 Intense salmon-pink. Somewhat intense aroma of red fruit with hints of petals. Flavourful palate with fine spicy and bitter notes, good acidity.

ENTREMONTES GARNACHA 2003 RED
garnacha

76 Dark cherry with a purplish rim. Powerful aroma of black fruit with somewhat varietal notes of spices and flowers. Flavourful palate with fleshy overtones, obvious tannins and an acidic edge.

ENTREMONTES SYRAH 2003 RED
syrah

77 Very dark cherry with a purplish edge. Powerful aroma of black fruit with hints of petals and toasty notes of skins. Flavourful, bitter palate with fleshy overtones and a slightly acidic edge.

ENTREMONTES TEMPRANILLO 2003 RED
cencibel

79 Dark cherry with a purplish edge. Powerful, fruity aroma with excellent varietal expression (flowers, damp earth). Flavourful palate with somewhat noticeable tannins, hints of overripening and a liquorice nuance.

ENTREMONTES ROBLE 2002 OAK AGED RED
tempranillo

80 Dark cherry with a purplish rim. Aroma of black fruit, fine toasty oak and quality spices. Flavourful palate with somewhat noticeable tannins, ripe fruit and bitter notes (liquorice).

ENTREMONTES ROBLE 1999 CRIANZA RED
tempranillo

80 Garnet red cherry with a saffron edge. Intense aroma with predominant toasty oak notes and a nuance of slightly reduced stone fruit. Flavourful, bitter palate (dark-roasted flavours, liquorice), with a balsamic and jammy fruit hint.

ENTREMONTES 1999 RESERVA RED
tempranillo

81 Garnet red cherry with a saffron edge. Somewhat intense aroma of jammy black fruit, with toasty hints and quite sweet oak notes. Flavourful palate with slightly marked yet rich tannins and hints of spices and reduction notes in the finish (tobacco, leather).

EVARISTO MATEOS

Mayor, 62
45350 Noblejas (Toledo)
☎: 925 140 082 - Fax: 925 140 573
evaristomateos@telefonica.net
www.evaristomateos.com
Established: 1964
🛢 500 🍇 5 has. 🍷 80% 🍏20%: -DE -CH

EVARISTO I 2003 WHITE
100% airén

79 Pale yellow. Slightly intense, fruity aroma with hints of flowers and spicy skins. Fresh, quite flavourful on the palate with fine herbs and good acidity.

EVARISTO I 2003 JOVEN RED
100% tempranillo

75 Cherry. Aroma of sweetish strawberries, clear. Flavourful, fruity palate with strawberry pulp notes, simple.

EVARISTO I 1999 CRIANZA RED
100% tempranillo

77 Cherry with an orangey hue. Aroma of resin, wood and ripe red fruit with balsamic notes. Well-mannered on the palate with a slight edge of acidity.

SEMBRADOR 1998 RESERVA RED
100% tempranillo

78 Garnet red. Ripe aroma with notes of sun-drenched skins and sweet vanilla. Fleshy palate with wood tannins perceptible over ripe black fruit, quite warm.

EXPLOTACIONES HERMANOS DELGADO

Villarrobledo, 37
13630 Socuéllamos (Ciudad Real)
☎: 625 339 887 - Fax: 926 532 645
info@bodegaehd.com
www.bodegaehd.com
Established: 1995
🛢 100 📕 3,000,000 litres 🍇 200 has.

🚩 25% 🍷75%: -DE -BE -DK -FR -NL -IE -
LV -UK -ZA -RU -CH

SEÑORÍO DE LOS SANTOS 2003 WHITE
100% airén

80 Pale with golden nuances. Fresh, quite fruity
aroma with exotic notes (pineapple, bananas) and
fine herbs. Flavourful palate with a certain finesse,
of white fruit, spices, citrus fruit.

SEÑORÍO DE LOS SANTOS 2003 ROSÉ
100% tempranillo

75 Brilliant blush. Somewhat intense, fruity
aroma with not very fine notes (stewed meat).
Better on the palate; quite flavourful, with hints of
spices and quality citrus fruit notes.

SEÑORÍO DE LOS SANTOS 2003 RED
100% tempranillo

77 Cherry with a garnet red edge. Vinous, not
very intense tank off-odours. Obvious tannins and
good acidity on the palate, pleasant, with medium
persistence.

SEÑORÍO DE LOS SANTOS 2002 OAK AGED RED
80% tempranillo, 20% garnacha

76 Cherry. Aroma of jammy tomatoes and toasty
wood with notions of earthiness. Quite incisive
tannins on the palate with bitter notes and good
acidity, slightly short.

FINCA ANTIGUA

Ctra Quintanar - Los Hinojosos, km. 11, 5
16417 Los Hinojosos (Cuenca)
☎: 969 129 700 - Fax: 969 129 496
info@fincaantigua.com
www.bujanda.com

Established: 2003
🍷 5,000 📦 6,000,000 litres 🌿 100 has.
🚩 40% 🍷60%: -UK -DE -US

FINCA ANTIGUA CABERNET 2002 OAK AGED RED
100% cabernet sauvignon

87 Dark garnet red cherry. Intense aroma of very
varietal black fruit with peppery hints, balsamic
hints and a spicy, oaky freshness. Flavourful vigorous palate with varietal characterisation, supple
with a good oak/fruit integration, slightly warm.

FINCA ANTIGUA TEMPRANILLO 2002 OAK AGED RED
100% tempranillo

86 Deep cherry. Intense aroma with predominant
ripe fruit notes, hints of macerated skins and a
nuance of damp earth. Flavourful palate with quite
rough and oily tannins, good varietal expression,
bitter, long.

FINCA ANTIGUA 2001 CRIANZA RED
60% tempranillo, 20% cabernet sauvignon, 20% merlot

85 Dark cherry with a garnet red edge. Intense
aroma with spicy oak notes, a very varietal ripe
fruit nuance (redcurrants). Flavourful palate with
promising but quite noticeable tannins, spicy and
balsamic hints and a notion of fresh skins in the
retronasal passage.

FINCA ANTIGUA 2000 RESERVA RED
75% merlot, 20% cabernet sauvignon, 5% syrah

86 Almost opaque cherry. Powerful, concentrated
palate with fine smoky notes of oak and a very
varietal fruity freshness (skins, damp earth).
Flavourful, supple palate with a good oak/fruit
integration, rich in bitter nuances (liquorice, dark-
roasted flavours, jam).

FINCA LA BLANCA

Princesa, 84
45840 Puebla de Almoradiel (Toledo)
☎: 925 178 440 - Fax: 925 178 432
fincalablanca@ole.es
www.capel-vinos.es

Established: 1996
🍷 750 📦 800,000 litres 🌿 840 has.
🚩 80% 🍷20%

RIBERA DE LOS MOLINOS 2003 WHITE

73 Brilliant pale. Somewhat intense aroma of
slightly reduced very ripe white fruit. Quite flavourful and fresh on the palate with an acidic edge.

MONTE DON LUCIO MACABEO 2003 WHITE
100% macabeo

80 Brilliant pale yellow. Intense, very perfumed and
varietal aroma (white stone fruit, exotic and floral
hints). Flavourful palate with fine bitter and somewhat tropical fruit notes and a slightly acidic edge.

RIBERA DE LOS MOLINOS 2003 ROSÉ

75 Brilliant blush. Somewhat intense, fruity
aroma. Fresh palate with bitter notes, slightly oily
with an acidic edge.

MONTE DON LUCIO CABERNET SAUVIG-NON 2003 RED
100% cabernet sauvignon

82 Garnet red cherry with a violet edge. Intense
aroma of red stone fruit with a very varietal spicy
hint (paprika) and hints of macerated skins.
Flavourful palate with somewhat obvious and fine
tannins, spicy notes and good acidity.

MONTE DON LUCIO TEMPRANILLO 2003 RED
100% tempranillo

79 Cherry with a violet hue. Clean, lactic aroma,
red stone fruit. Well-balanced, flavourful palate with
polished tannins and a balsamic retronasal effect.

RIBERA DE LOS MOLINOS 2003 RED

79 Garnet red cherry with a violet edge. Quite
intense aroma of stone fruit with hints of nettles and

the freshness of damp earth. Flavourful, bitter palate with slightly marked tannins and an acidic edge.

MONTE DON LUCIO 1999 RESERVA RED

78 Cherry with a brick red edge. Toasty aromas of wood, dark-roasted flavours, with slightly balsamic notes. Well-mannered palate but with slight notes of greeness.

FONTANA

Extramuros, s/n
16411 Fuente de Pedro Naharro (Cuenca)
☎: 969 125 433 - Fax: 969 125 387
bf@bodegasfontana.com
www.bodegasfontana.com

Established: 1997

2,150 ▦ 5,000,000 litres ▽ 500 has.

60% 40%: -US -CH -DK -DE -NL -UK -PR -JP

FONTAL TEMPRANILLO 2003 ROBLE RED
90% tempranillo, 5% cabernet sauvignon, 5% merlot

85 Cherry with a purplish hue. Concentrated aroma of black fruit with notes of skins and mineral nuances. Fleshy with good fruit on the palate and integrated acidity, fine smoky, barely perceptible wood, very fresh.

FONTAL 2001 CRIANZA RED
85% tempranillo, 15% cabernet sauvignon

84 Deep cherry. Aroma of well-ripened black fruit with sun-drenched hints and a nuance of earthy notes. Fleshy palate with well-assembled wood tannins, round with a bitter finish (cocoa, liquorice).

GRAN FONTAL SELECCIÓN 2000 RESERVA RED
100% tempranillo

87 Cherry. Smoky aroma with fine notes of oak (earthiness, a mineral suggestion) and a nuance of black berries. Fleshy palate with excellent freshness, grape variety character, fresh with a bitter and overall harmonised finish.

FREEWINE

Castilla La Mancha, 4
16670 El Provencio (Cuenca)
☎: 609 119 248 - Fax: 916 160 246
victorre@telefonica.net

Established: 2003

500 ▦ 250,000 litres ▽ 10 has.

25% 75%: -US -CA -JP -DE -NL -CH

MANO A MANO 2003 ROBLE JOVEN RED
tempranillo

90 Intense cherry with a lively violet edge. Aroma with fine smoky oak notes (cocoa) and ripe but fresh fruit, elegant. Fresh fruit on the palate, powerful, with a wealth of fruit expression and evoking forest herbs.

GARRÓN

Fernández de los Ríos, s/n
45470 Los Yébenes (Toledo)
☎: 925 320 140 - Fax: 925 320 140
vinosgarronsa@terra.es

Established: 1942

28 ▦ 3,600,000 litres 100%

EL MADROÑAL WHITE
GARRONCETE WHITE
GARRONCETE RED
EL MADROÑAL 2001 CRIANZA RED

HERMANOS RUBIO

Carretera de Villamuelas, s/n
45740 Villasequilla (Toledo)
☎: 925 310 284 - Fax: 925 325 133
bodegasrubio@terra.es

Established: 1934

450 ▦ 2,700,000 litres 80%

20%: -HU -RU -DE -MX -CH -DK -NL

SEÑORÍO DE ZOCODOVER 2003 WHITE
airén

76 Pale gold. Intense aroma of ripe white stone fruit with exotic hints. Fresh, fruity palate with a somewhat oily texture and a slight dilution in the finish.

VIÑA ALAMBRADA 2003 WHITE
100% airén

DO LA MANCHA

77 Pale with greenish nuances. Intense, spicy aroma, without great fruit expression. Better on the palate, fresh and flavourful with notes of herbs and pronounced citrus acidity.

SEÑORÍO DE ZOCODOVER 2003 ROSÉ
garnacha, cencibel

70 Brilliant blush. Fresh aroma without great fruit expression. Quite flavourful and fresh on the palate with some dilution.

VIÑA ALAMBRADA 2003 ROSÉ
75% tempranillo, 25% garnacha

73 Brilliant blush. Not very intense aroma with a certain spicy freshness of the fruit. Quite flavourful and oily on the palate, lacking expression.

SEÑORÍO DE ZOCODOVER CENCIBEL 2003 RED
100% tempranillo

77 Deep cherry. Vinous aroma of sun-drenched skins, alcohol and post-fermentation. Sweetish notes on the palate and red fruit in the retronasal passage

SEÑORÍO DE ZOCODOVER 1999 CRIANZA RED
100% tempranillo

78 Dark garnet red cherry with a purplish edge. Intense aroma with mild off-odours (late racking) and a nuance of slightly reduced fruit. Flavourful, fruity palate with quite rough and oily tannins and a nuance of spices and liquorice.

VIÑA ALAMBRADA 1999 CRIANZA RED
100% tempranillo

78 Intense cherry. Aroma of foresty red fruit with balsamic hints and a nuance of liquorice. Flavourful, very fresh palate with fruity tannins, better in the mouth.

SEÑORÍO DE ZOCODOVER 1997 RESERVA RED
100% tempranillo

82 Dark cherry with a saffron rim. Intense aroma of toasty oak and jammy red fruit. Flavourful palate with quite noticeable and sweet tannins and quality bitter (pitch, dark-roasted flavours, liquorice) notes.

VEGA CEDRON 1999 RESERVA RED
100% tempranillo

79 Garnet red with a purple edge. Aroma with light reduction notes of old wood. Supple, spicy palate with considerable wood weight.

BARÓN DE SABAS RED

Vinos ISIDORO DÍAZ-REGAÑÓN

Mayor, 24-b
45350 Noblejas (Toledo)
☎: 925 140 174 - Fax: 925 141 106

PUERTA BISAGRA RED

ISIDRO CICUÉNDEZ MADERO

Virgen de las Angustias, 1
45840 La Puebla de Almoradiel (Toledo)
☎: 925 178 063 - Fax: 925 178 042

Established: 1920

🛢 53 500,000 litres 140 has.
100%

CHOZO DE LA MOLINERA 1998 CRIANZA RED

ISLA

Nuestra Señora de la Paz, 9
13210 Villarta San Juan (Ciudad Real)
☎: 926 640 004 - Fax: 926 640 004
bisla@terra.es
www.bodegasisla.com

Established: 1993

🛢 40 5,000,000 litres 200 has.
80% 20%: -DE -FI -SE -DK -CZ

ISLA ORO WHITE
airén

72 Straw-coloured. Not very fine aroma with off-odours in the tank. Better on the palate, somewhat fresh and spicy.

ISLA ORO RED
cencibel

70 Deep garnet red. Vinous aroma of very ripe red fruit and withered blossom. Drying on the palate with rough tannins, without great expression.

ISLA ORO 2001 CRIANZA RED
tempranillo

73 Deep cherry. Very ripe aroma of sun-drenched skins with mineral notes. Flavourful, light palate, without fruit, slightly short.

J. GARCÍA CARRIÓN LA MANCHA

Guarnicionero, s/n
30520 Daimiel (Ciudad Real)
☎: 926 260 094 - Fax: 926 260 091
flozano@jgarciacarrion.es
www.vinosdefamilia.com

Established: 2000

🛢 492 110,700 litres 60% 40%: -US -DE -UK -FR -IT -CZ -DK -NL

DON LUCIANO TEMPRANILLO 2003 RED
100% tempranillo

78 Cherry with a violet rim. Aroma of red fruit and rustic overtones. Medium-bodied palate, slightly astringent but very well-mannered.

DON LUCIANO CABERNET 2002 RED
100% cabernet sauvignon

77 Cherry. Aroma with mild notes of the tank and slightly vegetative. Medium-bodied palate with quite marked Cabernet tannins, a well-mannered ensemble.

DON LUCIANO 2001 CRIANZA RED
100% tempranillo

80 Garnet red cherry. Aromas of toasty wood (toffee), vanilla and slight reduction notes. Flavourful palate with dry oak tannins and toasty notes in the retronasal passage.

DON LUCIANO MERLOT 2002 RED
100% merlot

80 Cherry. Aroma of jammy tomatoes and red fruit. Medium-bodied palate with vegetative overtones but pleasant and easy drinking.

DON LUCIANO 2003 WHITE
DON LUCIANO 2003 ROSÉ
DON LUCIANO SYRAH 2002 RED
DON LUCIANO 1999 RESERVA RED

Bodegas J. SANTOS

Sagunto, 6
45850 La Villa de Don Fadrique (Toledo)
☎: 925 195 120 - Fax: 925 195 650
exportjsantos@telefonica.net

Established: 1900

🍷 400 📊 9,000,000 litres 🍇 600 has.

🚢 40% 🌐60%: -DE -NL -AT

JULIÁN SANTOS 2003 WHITE
100% airén

75 Brilliant pale yellow. Not very intense aroma with a white fruit nuance. Better on the palate, flavourful and bitter with hints of herbs and noticeable citrus acidity.

MONTE DEL ALCALDE 2003 ROSÉ
100% garnacha

77 Very lively deep raspberry. Intense aroma with a certain finesse, red fruit and fresh skins overtones. Flavoured palate with bitter notes and citrus fruit.

MONTE DEL ALCALDE CENCIBEL 2002 RED
cencibel

75 Not very deep cherry. Aroma of very ripe red fruit, withered petals, intense. Vinous palate, raisins and medium persistence.

JULIÁN SANTOS 1999 CRIANZA RED
100% cencibel

73 Garnet red cherry with a purplish rim. Quite intense aroma of red fruit with hints of quite fresh oak. Flavourful, fruity palate with a mild suggestion of greeness (wood) and an acidic edge.

DON FADRIQUE 1998 RESERVA RED
100% cencibel

82 Glacé cherry. Varietal aroma with sweetish notes, toasty wood and jammy red fruit. Good fruit weight on the palate with bitter notes and well-integrated wood tannins.

DON FADRIQUE 1996 GRAN RESERVA RED
100% cencibel

74 Garnet red cherry with an orangey hue. Intense aroma with reduction notes (varnish, slightly aged wood). Flavourful palate with slightly drying tannins and warm hints.

JACINTO JARAMILLO E HIJOS

Calvario, 31
13160 Torralba de Calatrava (Ciudad Real)
☎: 926 811 332 - Fax: 926 811 340
bodegasjaramillo@vegazacatena.com
www.vegazacatena.com

Established: 1927

🍷 150 📊 3,000,000 litres 🍇 25 has.

🚢 100%

VEGA ZACATENA JOVEN RED
VEGA ZACATENA CRIANZA RED
VEGA ZACATENA RESERVA RED

Cooperativa JESÚS DEL PERDÓN

Polígono Industrial, s/n
13200 Manzanares (Ciudad Real)
☎: 926 610 309 - Fax: 926 610 516
yuntero@yuntero.com
www.yuntero.com

Established: 1954

🍷 2,000 📊 25,000,000 litres 🍇 3,605 has.

🚢 60% 🌐40%: -UE -CH -JP -AU -US -CO -PH

YUNTERO CHARDONNAY 2003 FERMENTADO EN BARRICA WHITE
100% chardonnay

78 Pale yellow with greenish nuances. Powerful aroma with predominant smoky oak notes and hints of wax. Flavourful palate with bitter notes, hints of herbs and a noticeable oak presence.

CASA LA TEJA AIRÉN 2003 WHITE
100% airén

77 Pale. Not very intense aroma, quite fruity with hints of herbs. Flavourful palate, with bitter notes and citrus fruit.

MUNDO DE YUNTERO AIRÉN ECOLÓGICO 2003 WHITE
100% airén

79 Pale with greenish nuances. Slightly intense aroma of white fruit, with hints of flowers and fennel. Flavourful palate with bitter notes and herbs.

YUNTERO MACABEO 2003 WHITE
100% macabeo

80 Pale with a lemony hue. Somewhat intense, varietal aroma of ripe white stone fruit (exotic hints) and herbs. Flavourful palate with slight bitter notes and good acidity.

YUNTERO TEMPRANILLO 2003 ROSÉ
100% tempranillo

78 Lively raspberry. Intense aroma of red stone fruit, with hints of herbs and citrus fruit. Flavourful palate with spicy notes and noticeable citrus acidity.

CASA LA TEJA TEMPRANILLO 2003 RED
100% tempranillo

76 Garnet red cherry with a violet hue. Intense, fruity aroma with hints of macerated skins. Flavourful, bitter palate with quite noticeable tannins (overextraction).

MUNDO DE YUNTERO TEMPRANILLO ECOLÓGICO 2003 RED
100% tempranillo

76 Cherry with a violet hue. Somewhat intense aroma of black fruit and spicy hints of skins. Flavourful palate with somewhat noticeable tannins, fine bitter notes and a slightly acidic edge.

YUNTERO 2001 CRIANZA RED
80% tempranillo, 20% cabernet sauvignon

76 Cherry with an orangey hue. Toasty aromas of new wood, vanilla and pepper. Oily palate with quite noticeable wood tannins.

YUNTERO CABERNET SAUVIGNON 1999 CRIANZA RED
100% cabernet sauvignon

81 Dark cherry with a saffron edge. Intense aroma of jammy black fruit, hints of spices and mild reduction (leather). Flavourful, fleshy palate with quite rough, fine tannins and liquorice and balsamic notes in the retronasal passage.

YUNTERO 50 ANIVERSARIO 2000 RESERVA ESPECIAL RED
80% tempranillo, 20% cabernet sauvignon

84 Cherry. Aroma of ripe red fruit, very sweet wood, jammy fruit and balsamic notes. Warm palate with a good oak/fruit integration; fleshy and persistent.

YUNTERO 1999 RESERVA RED
70% tempranillo, 20% cabernet sauvignon

75 Brick red. Short aroma with certain notes of ripe fruit and toasty wood. Metallic notes on the palate; without great expression.

YUNTERO 1997 GRAN RESERVA RED
80% tempranillo, 20% cabernet sauvignon

80 Intense cherry with a brick red edge. Intense aroma with predominant toasty oak notes and a sweet slightly reduced fruit nuance. Flavourful, supple palate of jammy fruit, liquorice and dark-roasted flavours.

CASA LA TEJA 2001 CRIANZA RED
CASA LA TEJA 1999 RESERVA RED
CASA LA TEJA 1997 GRAN RESERVA RED

JESÚS FERNÁNDEZ VERDÚGUEZ

Carretera Madrid-Alicante, s/n
45810 Villanueva de Alcardete (Toledo)
☎: 925 598 009 - Fax: 925 167 487
celiafer@airtel.net
www.galeon.com/picurnio

EL PICURNIO WHITE
EL PICURNIO ROSÉ
EL PICURNIO RED

JOSÉ LUIS GUILLERMO MENDIETA

Avenida de La Mancha, 42
45860 Villacañas (Toledo)
☎: 925 160 439 - Fax: 925 160 912
bodegasguillermo@wanadoo.es

Established: 1900

🛢 280 | 13,250,000 litres 🚩 100%

VIÑA CIBELINA WHITE
CIBELINO CRIANZA RED
VIÑA CIBELINA RED

Cooperativa Nuestra Señora de LA ASUNCIÓN

Santa Misión, 19
45310 Villatobas (Toledo)
☎: 925 152 102 - Fax: 925 152 152
vinotobas@ucaman.es

Established: 1958

🛢 13,000,000 litres 🍇 1,900 has.

🚩 60% 🍇40%

MORAYO AIRÉN WHITE
DON ANDRÉS RED

Sociedad Cooperativa LA CANDELARIA

c/San Clemente, 13
16612 Casas de Los Pinos (Cuenca)
☎: 969 383 291 - Fax: 969 383 291
la.candelaria@wanadoo.es

Established: 1959

DO LA MANCHA

🛢 54 🛢 10,000,000 litres 🍷 100%

LOS PINOS 2003 WHITE
LOS PINOS 2001 CRIANZA RED
LOS PINOS 2001 RED

Cooperativa LA DEFENSA

Avenida de Castilla - La Mancha, 38
45379 Santa Cruz de la Zarza (Toledo)
☎: 925 143 234 - Fax: 925 143 234
ladefensa@inicia.es

LA DEFENSA WHITE
LA DEFENSA RED

Cooperativa Agrícola LA HUMANIDAD

Avenida Castilla - La Mancha, 6 y 13
45820 El Toboso (Toledo)
☎: 925 197 043 - Fax: 925 197 043
lahumildad@ucaman.es

Established: 1917
🛢 60 🍇 3,500 has.

QUIÑÓN DE ROSALES CENCIBEL RED
QUIÑÓN DE ROSALES TEMPRANILLO RED

Sociedad Cooperativa LA MAGDALENA

Carretera de la Roda, s/n
16611 Casas de Haro (Cuenca)
☎: 967 380 722 - Fax: 967 380 722
vmoragona@ucaman.es

Established: 1958
🛢 250 🛢 6,400,000 litres 🍇 1,400 has.
🍷 85% 🍷15%

VEGA MORAGONA 2003 ROSÉ
VEGA MORAGONA 1999 RESERVA RED

Cooperativa Nuestra Señora de LA MUELA

Real, 16
45880 Corral de Almaguer (Toledo)
☎: 925 190 161 - Fax: 925 207 434
cooplamuela@bzn.es
www.cooperativalamuela.com

Established: 1953
🛢 24,000,000 litres 🍷 80% 🍷20%

CASTILLO DE LA MUELA RED

Cooperativa Agrícola LA REMEDIADORA

Alfredo Atienza, 149

02630 La Roda (Albacete)
☎: 967 440 600 - Fax: 967 441 465
remediador@ucaman.es
www.laremediadora.com

Established: 1946
🛢 150 🛢 33,750 litres 🍇 1,500 has.
🍷 95% 🍷5%: -BE -DE

LA VILLA REAL MACABEO 2002 JOVEN
WHITE
100% macabeo

78 Pale with a coppery glint. Slightly intense aroma of ripe fruit (reduction notes), floral hints. Flavourful palate with toasty and spicy hints and with a suggestion of nuts.

LA VILLA REAL 2003 JOVEN ROSÉ
100% cencibel

80 Very deep raspberry. Powerful aroma with very ripe red stone fruit, spicy hints of skins; slightly sweet and warm. Flavourful palate with slight bitter notes, long with hints of overextraction.

LA VILLA REAL 2003 JOVEN RED
50% cencibel, 50% cabernet sauvignon

77 Garnet red cherry with a violet hue. Somewhat intense, fruity aroma with hints of macerated skins. Flavourful, slightly oily and bitter on the palate with gentle hints of overextraction.

LA VILLA REAL 2000 CRIANZA RED
100% cencibel

83 Garnet red cherry. Intense, ripe aroma with spicy oak notes, a certain balsamic and slightly varietal fruit freshness. Flavourful palate with bitter notes (dark-roasted flavours, pitch), warm hints, spices and fresh skins in the retronasal passage.

LA VILLA REAL 2001 CRIANZA RED
cencibel, cabernet sauvignon

81 Lively garnet red cherry. Slightly intense aroma with predominant notes of black fruit and fine toasty oak. Flavourful palate with good oak/fruit integration; very bitter with quite varietal spicy hints (paprika).

LA VILLA REAL 1999 RESERVA RED

Cooperativa Nuestra Señora de LA SOLEDAD

Carretera Tarancón, s/n
16411 Fuente de Pedro Naharro (Cuenca)
☎: 969 125 085 - Fax: 969 125 085
info@bodegasoledad.com
www.bodegasoledad.com

Established: 1958
🛢 42 🛢 20,433,360 litres 🍇 2,798 has.
🍷 99,5% 🍷 5%: -FR

RIBERA DEL RIANSARES 2003 WHITE
RIBERA DEL RIANSARES 2003 ROSÉ
RIBERA DEL RIANSARES 2003 RED
RIBERA DEL RIANSARES 2001 CRIANZA RED

LA TERCIA-VINOS ECOLÓGICOS

Almagro, 6
13600 Alcázar de San Juan (Ciudad Real)
☎: 926 541 512 - Fax: 926 550 104
bodegalatercia@terra.es
www.bodegalatercia.com
Established: 1940
🌐 25 📋 125,000 litres 🍇 47 has.
🍷 85% 🍇15%: -DE -CH

YEMANUEVA AIRÉN 2003 WHITE
100% airén

72 Brilliant pale. Intense aroma with somewhat reduced ripe fruit and petals. Flavourful palate with fruity fresh overtones and bitter notes.

YEMANUEVA TEMPRANILLO 2003 JOVEN RED
100% tempranillo

79 Garnet red cherry with a violet hue. Powerful, ripe aroma with hints of somewhat reduced fruit and a suggestion of damp earth. Flavourful palate with slightly marked but fine tannins and fine bitter notes.

YEMASERENA TEMPRANILLO SELECCIÓN LIMITADA 2001 OAK AGED RED
100% tempranillo

81 Dark garnet red cherry. Powerful aroma of jammy black fruit with fine toasty oak. Flavourful, fleshy palate with quite rough and oily tannins, liquorice and dark-roasted notes.

YEMASERENA 2002 CRIANZA RED

Cooperativa del Campo LA UNIÓN

Barrio San José, s/n
02100 Tarazona de la Mancha (Albacete)
☎: 967 480 074 - Fax: 967 480 294
cclaunion@terra.es
www.cop-launion.com
Established: 1956
🌐 400 📋 30,000,000 litres 🍷 60%
🍇40%

CASA ANTONETE MACABEO 2003 JOVEN WHITE
100% macabeo

80 Yellow straw. Clean aroma of ripe fruit (bananas, apples) and hay. Flavourful palate with ripe fruit, expressive and slightly low in acidity yet very pleasant.

CASA ANTONETE 2000 FERMENTADO EN BARRICA WHITE

79 Straw-coloured with golden nuances. Medium-intensity aroma with toasty oak notes, burnt hints and slightly subdued fruit. Flavourful palate with considerable woody presence and a nuance of ripe fruit.

CASA ANTONETE CENCIBEL 2003 JOVEN ROSÉ
100% cencibel

77 Lively raspberry blush. Intense aroma of ripe red fruit (strawberry syrup). Flavourful palate with ripe red fruit and slightly weak acidity yet expressive.

CASA ANTONETE 2000 OAK AGED ROSÉ

73 Salmon with an ochre hue. Aroma with predominant and slightly dry wood, clean but with weak fruit. Marked wood tannins on the palate without a trace of fruit.

CASA ANTONETE CENCIBEL 2003 JOVEN RED
100% cencibel

80 Dark cherry with a coppery edge. Intense aroma of red stone fruit with sweet hints and toasty skins. Flavourful, fruity and bitter on the palate with ripe, firm tannins and good acidity.

CASA ANTONETE CENCIBEL 2001 CRIANZA RED
100% cencibel

83 Dark cherry with a garnet red edge. Powerful aroma of toasty oak and a jammy fruit hint. Flavourful, fleshy palate with a good oak/fruit integration and fine bitter notes (liquorice, dark-roasted flavours).

CASA ANTONETE CENCIBEL 2000 RESERVA RED
100% cencibel

82 Dark cherry with a saffron edge. Intense aroma of jammy black fruit, toasty oak and hints of sour cherries in liqueur. Flavourful palate with a good fruit/oak integration, supple with bitter notes of the crianza.

Cooperativa LA VID Y LA ESPIGA

San Anton, 30
16415 Villamayor de Santiago (Cuenca)
☎: 969 139 069 - Fax: 969 139 069
vidyespiga@ucaman.es
Established: 1944
🌐 83 📋 9,969,693 litres 🍇 1388 has.
🍷 100%

AÑADOR 2003 JOVEN WHITE
airén

77 Pale with golden nuances. Somewhat intense, fruity aroma with hints of herbs. Fresh palate with quality bitter notes and hints of citrus fruit.

DO LA MANCHA

AÑADOR TEMPRANILLO 2003 RED
tempranillo

80 Garnet red cherry with a violet hue. Powerful, fruity aroma with spicy notes of skins, sweet notes and damp earth. Fleshy palate with slightly marked but flavourful tannins and fine, bitter, slightly varietal notes.

Bodegas y Viñedos LADERO

Carretera Alcázar, km. 1
13700 Tomelloso (Ciudad Real)
☎: 926 505 653 - Fax: 926 505 652
miguelangel@allozo.com

Established: 1992

⬡ 500 🛢 500,000 litres 🍇 30 has.

🍷 10% 🌐 90%

LADERO SELECCIÓN MACABEO 2003 JOVEN WHITE
100% macabeo

79 Brilliant pale. Not very intense aroma with hints of fruit and white flowers. Better on the palate, flavourful, fresh and quite fruity, with hints of spices and herbs, slightly oily.

LADERO TEMPRANILLO 2003 JOVEN RED
100% tempranillo

78 Not very deep cherry. Somewhat alcoholic aroma of red fruit and sun-drenched skins. Drying on the palate with notes of greeness.

LADERO TEMPRANILLO 2001 CRIANZA RED
100% tempranillo

79 Garnet red cherry. Intense aroma with smoky wood notes, a suggestion of black fruit and hints of dry earth. Flavourful, fleshy palate with unassembled oak/fruit and hints of slightly fresh oak (greeness).

LADERO TEMPRANILLO 1999 RESERVA RED
100% tempranillo

80 Garnet red cherry with a brick red glint. Intense aroma with reduction notes (leathers, raisins) and spicy hints of oak. Flavourful palate with a good fruit/oak integration and bitter hints (dark-roasted flavours, liquorice).

LADERO TEMPRANILLO 2000 CRIANZA RED
100% tempranillo

80 Garnet red cherry with a brick red edge. Not very intense aroma with predominant toasty oak notes. Flavourful palate with fine bitter notes, quite rough and fine tannins, spicy and pleasant.

LEGANZA

Carretera Madrid-Alicante, km. 121, 700
45800 Quintanar de la Orden (Toledo)
☎: 925 564 452 - Fax: 925 564 021

⬡ 6,000

CONDESA DE LEGANZA 2003 WHITE
CONDESA DE LEGANZA 2003 ROSÉ
CONDESA DE LEGANZA CRIANZA RED
CONDESA DE LEGANZA 1995 RESERVA RED

LORETO

San Antón, 4
13630 Socuéllamos (Ciudad Real)
☎: 926 539 013 - Fax: 926 539 132
info@bodegasloreto.com
www.bodegasloreto.com

Established: 1980

⬡ 20 🛢 10,500,000 litres 🍇 2,000 has.

🍷 90% 🌐10%

CASA LEANDRO 2000 CRIANZA RED
MONTENO CENCIBEL 2003 RED

Industria Vinícola LOS CANDEALES

Paseo del Carmen, s/n
13250 Daimiel (Ciudad Real)
☎: 926 850 765 - Fax: 926 850 765
cereales@meyca.es

VEGA DE AZUER WHITE
VEGA DE AZUER CRIANZA RED
VEGA DE AZUER RESERVA RED

Cooperativa Nuestra Señora de LOS REMEDIOS

Cooperativa, 2
45100 Sonseca (Toledo)
☎: 925 380 322 - Fax: 925 381 617

Established: 1967
🌐 60 📊 7,000,000 litres 🍇 3,000 has.
🍷 100%

VIÑA SANDERUELO 2003 JOVEN WHITE
GOROPA WHITE
VIÑA SANDERUELO 2002 ROSÉ
GOROPA 2003 ROSÉ
GOROPA 2003 JOVEN RED
VIÑA SANDERUELO 2002 RED
EL BROSQUIL 2000 CRIANZA RED
DE NEIVA 2001 CRIANZA RED
DE NEIVA 1999 RESERVA RED

Bodegas LOZANO

Grande, 67
13670 Villarrubia de los Ojos (Ciudad Real)
☎: 926 898 018 - Fax: 926 266 514
bodegaslozano@bodegas-lozano.com
www.bodegas-lozano.com

Established: 1947
📊 7,500,000 litres 🍇 140 has. 🍷 90%
🌐10%

LOBAR WHITE
LOBAR RED

LOZANO

Avenida Reyes Católicos, 156
02600 Villarrobledo (Albacete)
☎: 967 141 907 - Fax: 967 138 087
c.nacional@bodegas-lozano.com
www.bodegas-lozano.com

Established: 1920
🌐 6,500 📊 25,000,000 litres 🍇 200 has.
🍷 15% 🌐85%: -DE -UK -DK -JP -CA -US
-FR -PL -RU

ABANICO SHIRAZ 2004 TINTO

82 Intense cherry with a strawberry edge. Intense aroma of forest red fruits with hints of eucalyptus and maceration notes. Fleshy, fruity palate, fruit tannins, hints of liquorice and aromatic herbs.

ABANICO

S P A I N

ABANICO DE SABORES - SPECTRUM OF FLAVOURS

SHIRAZ

2004

LA MANCHA DENOMINACION DE ORIGEN

ALC 13% vol. 750 ml ℮

ORISTÁN 2002 TINTO CRIANZA

83 Deep cherry. Aroma of black fruit, aromatic herbs, paprika notes, well-integrated smoky flavours. Fleshy palate, fresh tannins, fruity, herbaceous notes (Cabernet).

ORISTÁN 1998 GRAN RESERVA TINTO

80 Garnet red with a ruby red edge. Toasty aroma, ripe red fruit, notes of Cabernet (paprika). Supple palate, well-balanced, fine oak notes and sensations of sweet red fruit, round.

DELMIO MACABEO 2002 WHITE

DO LA MANCHA

AÑORANZA AIRÉN 2003 WHITE
AÑORANZA 2003 ROSÉ
DELMIO TEMPRANILLO 2003 RED
AÑORANZA 2003 RED
DELMIO GARNACHA 2003 RED
ORISTAN 2000 CRIANZA RED
AÑORANZA 2001 CRIANZA RED
ORISTAN 2002 CRIANZA RED
ORISTAN 1998 RESERVA RED
ORISTAN 1997 GRAN RESERVA RED

LUIS FERNÁNDEZ FERNÁNDEZ

Campo, 47
13620 Pedro Muñoz (Ciudad Real)
☎: 926 586 642

Established: 1999

100,000 litres 🍇 15 has. 🛢 100%

DON MAMBRINO BRUT NATURE
DON MAMBRINO SPARKLING SEMI-SECO
ANDANTE CULTIVO ECOLÓGICO EXTRA
BRUT SEMI-SECO

Cooperativa Nuestra Señora de
MANJAVACAS

Camino Real, 7
16630 Mota del Cuervo (Cuenca)
☎: 967 180 025 - Fax: 967 181 120
scam@eacsl.com
www.zagarron.com

Established: 1948

🍾 350 🛢 25,000,000 litres 🛢 60% 🌐 40%

ZAGARRÓN WHITE
ZAGARRÓN ROSÉ
ZAGARRÓN RED

MARTÍN PUIG

Feria, 8 (Finca La Gallega)
16600 San Clemente (Cuenca)
☎: 969 300 071 - Fax: 969 302 154

Established: 1920

🛢 1,200,000 litres 🍇 120 has. 🛢 100%

CASA DE OMA 2001 JOVEN RED

MAZORRAL

Polígono Industrial El Salvador,
Avenida 2º P. 69
02630 La Roda (Albacete)
☎: 968 302 250 - Fax: 968 302 138
mazorral@mazorral.com
www.mazorral.com

Established: 2000

🍾 2,000 🛢 1,500,000 litres 🛢 80%
🌐 20%: -DE -UK -SE -RU -PL -US -CA -DO
-JP -IL.

CASTILLO GUIJOSA SELECCIÓN LIMITADA
2003 JOVEN WHITE
100% sauvignon blanc

78 Brilliant pale gold. Intense aroma of slightly
reduced ripe white fruit and hints of herbs. Better
on the palate, flavourful and fruity with exotic
hints; somewhat oily.

CASTILLO GUIJOSA SELECCIÓN LIMITADA
2003 JOVEN RED
100% tempranillo

78 Cherry. Smoky aroma of ripe black fruit with
rustic hints (animals). Flavourful palate with fresh
fruit tannins and ripeness compensated by acidity.

CASTILLO GUIJOSA SELECCIÓN LIMITADA
2003 ROBLE RED
100% tempranillo

73 Deep cherry with a brick red edge. Aroma of
ripe plums with notes of varnish. Fleshy, slightly
rustic palate with obvious oak tannins, ripe.

CASTILLO GUIJOSA SELECCIÓN LIMITADA
2000 OAK AGED RED
cabernet sauvignon

82 Deep cherry. Balsamic aromas with sweetish
notes, liquorice and red fruit. Warm palate with
good fruit/wood integration and dark-roasted flavours in the retronasal passage.

CASTILLO ESTABLÉS 1999 CRIANZA RED
70% tempranillo, 30% cabernet sauvignon

82 Cherry with a brick red edge. Aroma of toasty
wood, balsamic flavours, liquorice and ripe red
fruit. Fleshy and persistent on the palate, well-
integrated, with a long finish.

CAMPO MAZORRAL 1999 RESERVA RED
70% tempranillo, 30% cabernet sauvignon

82 Garnet red with a brick red edge.
Concentrated aroma of ripe black fruit with earthy
and mineral notes. Fleshy palate with a pleasant
bitterness (liquorice), flavourful, round fruit tannins, powerful.

CASTILLO ESTABLÉS 1999 RESERVA RED
tempranillo, cabernet sauvignon

77 Garnet red with a brick red edge. Ripe aroma
of sun-drenched skins with a nuance of mineral
notes. Ripe, flavourful, fresh palate without great
fruit nuances and an earthy finish.

CAMPO FRÍO SELECCIÓN LIMITADA 2003
JOVEN WHITE
CAMPO SECO SELECCIÓN LIMITADA 2000
OAK AGED RED
CAMPO SECO SELECCIÓN LIMITADA 1999
OAK AGED RED
CAMPO MAZORRAL 1999 CRIANZA RED
RONCERO VINO DE LICOR

MONTALVO WILMOT

Finca Los Cerrillos
Carretera Ruidera km. 10, 200
13170 Argamasilla de Alba (Ciudad Real)
☎: 926 699 069 - Fax: 926 699 069
alejandromontalvo@ya.com -

Established: 2001

⊞ 218 ▤ 694,000 litres ⚜ 34 has.

🍷 70% 🌐30%: -IE -CH -DE -UK

WILMOT 2003 JOVEN RED
100% cabernet sauvignon

83 Fairly deep cherry with a violet hue. Powerful, ripe aroma an excellent varietal expression (redcurrants, fine herbacity) and hints of minerals. Flavourful, fleshy palate with excellent fruit-tannins-acidity symmetry.

WILMOT 2003 JOVEN RED
tempranillo, cabernet sauvignon

84 Intense cherry with a violet edge. Intense aroma of ripe fruit with hints of figs and a suggestion of terroir. Flavourful palate with excellent tannins, fine hints of minerals and balsamics, long.

Viñedos y Bodegas MUÑOZ

Carretera Villarrubia, 11
45350 Noblejas (Toledo)
☎: 925 140 070 - Fax: 925 141 334
vibomu@teleline.es

Established: 1940

⊞ 600 ▤ 7,500,000 litres ⚜ 70 has.

🍷 25% 🌐75%

BLAS MUÑOZ CHARDONNAY 2003 FERMENTADO EN BARRICA WHITE
100% chardonnay

87 Golden yellow. Aroma of toasty wood, butter, light smoky notes and flowers. Warm, oily palate with quite noticeable wood tannins and toasty wood and lees in the finish.

ARTERO MACABEO 2003 WHITE
100% macabeo

80 Straw-coloured. Clean, medium-intensity aroma of ripe white stone fruit. Fresh on the palate, well-balanced with medium persistence.

ARTERO TEMPRANILLO 2003 ROSÉ
100% tempranillo

82 Intense raspberry. Intense, fruity aroma with fine spicy notes of skins and hints of herbs. Flavourful, fresh palate with bitter notes, hints of citrus fruit and excellent acidity.

ARTERO 2000 CRIANZA RED
50% merlot, 50% tempranillo

86 Dark cherry with a saffron edge. Powerful, ripe aroma with fine toasty oak notes, and a certain varietal character (red fruit, damp earth). Powerful, flavourful palate with good fruit/oak integration, slightly oily and with good fruit-alcohol balance despite its 14-15 %.

ARTERO TEMPRANILLO 2003 RED
100% tempranillo

80 Dark cherry with a purplish rim. Powerful aroma with spicy notes of skins; very varietal (red fruit, damp earth, dried flowers). Flavourful, fleshy palate with an excellent fruit expression, fine, firm tannins and good acidity.

ARTERO MERLOT 1998 RESERVA RED
100% merlot

85 Garnet red cherry. Powerful aroma of ripe black fruit, fine toasty oak, notes of wax and damp earth. Flavourful palate with ripe, oily tannins, and fine spicy, bitter notes (chocolate, After Eights).

MUÑOZ MONTOYA E HIJOS

Duque de Alba, 60
13620 Pedro Muñoz (Ciudad Real)
☎: 926 569 033 - Fax: 926 569 045

Established: 1999

⊞ 100 ▤ 50,000 litres ⚜ 35 has. 🇪🇸 100%

CUNA DEL MAYO 2002 WHITE
CUNA DEL MAYO 2002 RED
CUNA DEL MAYO 2002 MACERACIÓN
CARBÓNICA RED
CUNA DEL MAYO 2002 CRIANZA RED

NARANJO

Felipe II, 5
13150 Carrión de Calatrava (Ciudad Real)
☎: 926 814 155 - Fax: 926 815 335
info@bodegasnaranjo.com
www.bodegasnaranjo.com

Established: 1898

⊞ 800 ▤ 8,500,000 litres ⚜ 10 has.

🍷 95% 🌐5%

VIÑA CUERVA 2003 JOVEN WHITE
VIÑA CUERVA 2003 JOVEN ROSÉ
VIÑA CUERVA 2000 CRIANZA RED
VIÑA CUERVA 1998 RESERVA RED
VIÑA CUERVA MERLOT TEMPRANILLO
2001 CRIANZA RED

NUESTRA SEÑORA DE LA CABEZA

Tapias, 8
16708 Pozoamargo (Cuenca)

DO LA MANCHA

☎: 969 387 173 - Fax: 969 387 202
info@casagualda.com
www.casagualda.com

Established: 1958

🍶 535 ▪ 5,000,000 litres 🌿 900 has.

🍷 80% ⊕20%: -US -NL -DE -CH -UK

CASA GUALDA ALLIER 2002 FERMENTADO EN BARRICA WHITE
90% macabeo, 10% chardonnay

77 Pale with golden nuances. Intense aroma with predominant notes of quite fresh oak and slightly reduced white fruit. Fresh, flavourful and quite fruity on the palate; lacking balance.

CASA GUALDA CENCIBEL 2003 JOVEN RED
85% cencibel, 8% merlot, 7% cabernet sauvignon

82 Dark cherry with a purplish edge. Powerful aroma with a fine varietal expression (red fruit, petals, damp earth). Flavourful palate with quite noticeable, rich tannins, spicy notes and liquorice.

CASA GUALDA SINGULAR 2003 RED
bobal, syrah, cencibel

86 Very deep cherry. Powerful aroma of jammy black fruit, fine toasty oak and a balsamic nuance. Flavourful palate with good oak/fruit integration, bitter notes (dark-roasted flavours, liquorice), excellent acidity and promising.

CASA GUALDA SELECCIÓN C & J 2001 ROBLE RED
100% cencibel

84 Deep cherry. Spicy, smoky aroma of ripe red fruit. Fleshy palate with noticeable wood tannins and toasty notes in the retronasal passage.

CASA GUALDA CENCIBEL-CABERNET SAUVIGNON 2000 CRIANZA RED
50% cencibel, 50% cabernet sauvignon

82 Cherry with an orangey hue. Aroma with lactic hints, very sweet wood and jammy tomatoes. Warm, vinous palate with well-structured wood and fruit tannins and paprika in the retronasal passage.

CASA GUALDA SELECCIÓN C & J 2000 ROBLE RED

Sociedad Cooperativa del Campo
NUESTRA SEÑORA DE LA PAZ

Cervantes, 96
13210 Villarta de San Juan (Ciudad Real)
☎: 926 640 111 - Fax: 926 640 630
bodega@tintobel.com
www.tintobel.com

Established: 1954

🍶 69 ▪ 14,800,000 litres 🍷 100%

MATICES MACABEO 2003 JOVEN WHITE
80% macabeo, 20% airén

75 Pale gold with coppery nuances. Ripe, quite fruity aroma with toasty hints of skins and fine herbs. Flavourful palate of nuts, lacking fresh fruit expression.

MATICES 2003 JOVEN RED
100% tempranillo

78 Dark cherry with a violet edge. Powerful, fruity aroma with hints of petals and damp earth. Flavourful palate with quite rough but rich tannins and with fine bitter notes (liquorice).

ALTOVELA 2003 JOVEN WHITE
100% airén

80 Pale yellow. Slightly intense, fruity aroma with spicy hints and citrus fruit pulp. Flavourful, bitter palate with fragrant herbs and good acidity.

ALTOVELA 2003 JOVEN WHITE
100% macabeo

76 Pale with golden nuances. Slightly intense aroma with hints of varietal fruit and fragrant herbs. Flavourful, bitter palate with fine citrus acidity.

ALTOVELA 2003 JOVEN ROSÉ

78 Pale raspberry. Slightly intense aroma of red fruit with hints of petals and fine lees. Flavourful, fruity palate with spicy hints

ALTOVELA SYRAH 2003 JOVEN RED
syrah

80 Dark cherry. Intense aroma of black fruit with hints of petals and a sweet hint. Flavourful palate with fine bitter notes, weighty ripe fruit despite the alcohol and hints of spices and liquorice.

ALTOVELA TEMPRANILLO 2003 JOVEN RED
tempranillo

77 Cherry with a violet rim. Aroma of strawberries and red fruit with varietal typification. Slightly warm, light, short palate with good varietal expression.

TINTOBEL 2000 CRIANZA RED
100% tempranillo

78 Dark cherry with a garnet red edge. Somewhat intense aroma of jammy black fruit and toasty oak. Flavourful palate with somewhat ripe, oily tannins, bitter notes, warm and overextraction hints.

Cooperativa
NUESTRA SRA. DE LA PAZ

Ctra. Madrid-Alicante km 99,800
45880 Corral de Almaguer (Toledo)
☎: 925190269 - Fax: 925190268
cooplapaz@hotmail.com

Established: 1965

🍶 200 ▪ 40,000,000 litres 🌿 5,000 has.

🇪🇸 75% ⊕25%

CAMPO AMABLE CENCIBEL 1998 CRIANZA RED
cencibel

74 Medium-hue cherry. Toasty aroma of wood with balsamic hints, a lactic suggestion and notes of greeness. Drying palate, green, light and short, without great varietal expression.

Sociedad Cooperativa Andaluza NUESTRA SEÑORA DE LA VEGA

Carretera Castellar de Santiago, s/n
13344 Torre de Juan Abad (Ciudad Real)
☎: 926 383 026 - Fax: 926 383 026

Established: 1964
🏺 100%

SEÑORÍO DE QUEVEDO WHITE
SEÑORÍO DE QUEVEDO RED

Cooperativa Agraria NUESTRA SEÑORA DE LAS NIEVES

Santo Domingo, 11
13270 Almagro (Ciudad Real)
☎: 926 860 344 - Fax: 926 860 344

Established: 1950
🗟 3,500,000 litres 🍇 780 has. 🏺 100%

GRAN FUCARES WHITE
GRAN FUCARES ROSÉ
GRAN FUCARES RED

Sociedad Cooperativa Agraria NUESTRA SEÑORA DE ROSARIO

Carretera de la Solana, 34
13230 Membrilla (Ciudad Real)
☎: 926 636 660 - Fax: 926 637 309

Established: 1965
🗟 20,000,000 litres 🍇 2,500 has. 🏺 100%

GALAN DE MEMBRILLA AIRÉN 2003 WHITE
GALAN DE MEMBRILLA TEMPRANILLO 2002 RED

Sociedad Cooperativa Agraria NUESTRA SEÑORA DE RUS

Carretera Almarcha, 50
16600 San Clemente (Cuenca)
☎: 969 300 155 - Fax: 969 300 281
cooprus@puentederus.com
www.puentederus.com

Established: 1945
🍾 200 🗟 30,000,000 litres 🍇 3,500 has.
🏺 80% 🌍20%: -PT -FR -DE

PUENTE DE RUS 2003 WHITE
PUENTE DE RUS 2003 ROSÉ
PUENTE DE RUS 2003 JOVEN RED
PUENTE DE RUS 2001 CRIANZA RED

Cooperativa NUESTRA SEÑORA DEL EGIDO

Sendilla, 1
45840 Puebla de Almoradiel (Toledo)
☎: 925 178 052 - Fax: 925 178 052
coopegido.3081@cajarural.com

Established: 1954
🍾 50 🗟 33,200,000 litres 🍇 6.000 has.
🏺 60% 🌍40%

PIRUBÍ WHITE
PIRUBÍ RED

Sociedad Cooperativa NUESTRA SEÑORA DEL ESPINO

San Miguel, 34
13230 Membrilla (Ciudad Real)
☎: 926 637 475 - Fax: 926 636 616
coopvirgenespino@eresmas.com

Established: 1957
🍾 60 🗟 21,000,000 litres 🍇 2,300 has.
🏺 100%

REZUELO AIRÉN 2003 WHITE
REZUELO CENCIBEL 2003 RED
REZUELO CENCIBEL 2001 CRIANZA RED
GRAN REZUELO 2000 RESERVA RED

Sociedad Cooperativa NUESTRA SEÑORA DEL PILAR

Extramuros, s/n
45810 Villanueva de Alcardete (Toledo)
☎: 925 166 375 - Fax: 925 166 611
coopnspilar.3081@cajarural.com

Established: 1973
🍾 35 🗟 24,500,000 litres
🍇 3,800 has.

DO GRUMIER 2003 JOVEN WHITE
ALCARDET 2002 WHITE
SIERRA JABALERAS 2003 RED
SIERRA JABALERAS 2003 RED

Sociedad Cooperativa Agraria
PEÑARROYA

Carretera de Villarta de San Juan, s/n
13710 Argamasilla de Alba (Ciudad Real)
☎: 926 523 456 - Fax: 926 522 175
penarroya@ucaman.es

Established: 1958

12,000,000 litres

CASA DEL BACHILLER SANSÓN
CARRASCO 2003 WHITE
100% airén

78 Brilliant pale. Intense aroma with a good somewhat varietal fruit expression. Fresh, quite flavourful on the palate with bitter notes and quality citrus fruit, slightly oily.

CASA DEL BACHILLER SANSÓN
CARRASCO 2003 WHITE
100% macabeo

79 Brilliant pale. Intense, perfumed aroma with a good varietal fruit expression (exotic hints). Fresh, fruity palate with hints of herbs, spicy skins and good acidity.

CASA DEL BACHILLER SANSÓN
CARRASCO 2003 RED
100% cencibel

77 Very deep garnet red. Lactic and perfumed aroma of very ripe red fruit. Relatively obvious tannins on the palate, slightly hard.

Sociedad Cooperativa
PURÍSIMA CONCEPCIÓN

Carretera Minaya-San Clemente, s/n
16610 Casas de Fernando Alonso (Cuenca)
☎: 969 383 043 - Fax: 969 383 153
purisima@ucaman.es

Established: 1958

300 15,000,000 litres 2,300 has.
70% 30%: -UK -US -PT -NL

TEATINOS SIGNVM 2001 CRIANZA RED

ROMERO DE ÁVILA SALCEDO

Avenida Constitución, 4
13240 La Solana (Ciudad Real)
☎: 926 631 426 - Fax: 926 634 189
info@bodegasromerodeavila.com
www.bodegasromerodeavila.com

Established: 1961

50 1,500,000 litres 50 has.
80% 20%: -DE -UK -US

FRODO ECOLÓGICO 2002 WHITE
FRODO ECOLÓGICO 2002 RED
PORTENTO TEMPRANILLO 2002 RED
PORTENTO MERLOT 2002 RED
PORTENTO SYRAH 2002 RED
PORTENTO 2000 CRIANZA RED

SALCEDO BALMASEDA

Fray Luis León, 1
13420 Malagón (Ciudad Real)
☎: 926 800 043 - Fax: 926 800 409

Established: 1975

50 2,000,000 litres 130 has.
100%

GUADARBAIRE WHITE
GUADARBAIRE RED
SALCEDO CRIANZA RED

SAN FERNANDO

Paseo de la Constitución, 2
13320 Villanueva de los Infantes (Ciudad Real)
☎: 926 360 209 - Fax: 926 360 209

Established: 1987

1,000,000 litres 100%

SAN FERNANDO 2000 RED
SAN FERNANDO 2001 CRIANZA RED

Sociedad Cooperativa AgroVitivinícola
SAN ISIDRO

Dos de Mayo, 21
13620 Pedro Muñoz (Ciudad Real)
☎: 926 586 057 - Fax: 926 568 380
mail@viacotos.com
www.viacotos.com

Established: 1954

50 4,500 has 80% 20%

AMIGO SANCHO MACABEO WHITE
LA HIJUELA AIRÉN WHITE
AMIGO SANCHO TEMPRANILLO RED
LA HIJUELA TEMPRANILLO RED
GRAN AMIGO SANCHO EDICIÓN LIMITADA
CRIANZA RED

Cooperativa SAN ISIDRO

Camino Esperilla, s/n
45810 Villanueva de Alcardete (Toledo)
☎: 925 167 429 - Fax: 925 166 673
calidadsanisidro@telefonica.net

Established: 1954

🍷 300 📊 32,000,000 litres 🍇 4600 has.
🍷 45% 🍇55%

MAJASVERDES 2003 JOVEN WHITE
macabeo

76 Pale yellow with golden nuances. Intense aroma of ripe white fruit (slightly reduced) with hints of withered petals. Flavourful, fruity palate, slightly warm and oily.

AZÁN ORGANIC WINE 2003 JOVEN RED
100% tempranillo

69 Medium-hue cherry. A slightly unusual aroma (overripe fruit, thyme) with a rustic hint. Marked acidity on the palate, without fruit.

GRANDUC SELECCIÓN TEMPRANILLO 2003 JOVEN RED
90% tempranillo, 10% cabernet sauvignon

75 Bigarreau cherry with a violet edge. Intense, juvenile aroma (blackberries, plums) with a nuance of liquorice, fresh. Fruity palate but with highly marked vegetative tannins.

GRANDUC SELECCIÓN TEMPRANILLO GARNACHA 2002 JOVEN RED
50% tempranillo, 50% garnacha

76 Cherry with a violet edge. Not very intense but fruity aroma, clean. Light and quite flavourful palate, well-mannered overall.

MAJASVERDES 2003 JOVEN RED
cencibel

75 Bigarreau cherry with a violet edge. Medium-intensity, fruity aroma (red cherries, strawberries). Light, slightly tannic and vegetative palate with a red fruit finish. Good value.

PINGOROTE 1999 CRIANZA RED
80% tempranillo, 20% cabernet sauvignon

75 Cherry with an orange edge. Slightly short yet clean aroma with crianza notes. Light palate with dry wood tannins and a flavourful edge.

MAJASVERDES 2003 JOVEN WHITE

Cooperativa
SAN ISIDRO LABRADOR

Ramón y Cajal, 42
16640 Belmonte (Cuenca)
☎: 967 170 289 - Fax: 967 170 289
isbelmonte@ucaman.es

Established: 1945

📊 5,981,200 litres 🍷 100%

VISIBEL 2003 WHITE
VISIBEL 2003 RED

Sociedad Cooperativa Limitada
SANTA CATALINA

Cooperativa, 2
13240 La Solana (Ciudad Real)
☎: 926 632 194 - Fax: 926 631 085
losgalanes@ucaman.es

Established: 1959

🍷 102 📊 18,000,000 litres 🍇 14,000 has.
🍷 70% 🍇30%: -DK -DE -FR

LOS GALANES 2003 JOVEN WHITE
airén

79 Pale gold. Intense aroma of white fruit and exotic hints; somewhat floral and varietal. Fresh, fruity palate with noticeable citrus acidity.

LOS GALANES 2003 JOVEN RED
tempranillo

80 Cherry with a violet rim. Aroma of red fruit with varietal typification, somewhat vinous. Slightly marked tannins with light bitter notes but a good fruit weight.

LOS GALANES 1999 CRIANZA RED
tempranillo

82 Garnet red. Aromas of toasty wood, lactic notes and jammy tomatoes with good intensity. Fleshy, well-balanced palate with well-integrated wood and fruit tannins.

LOS GALANES 1997 RESERVA RED

Cooperativa **SANTA QUITERIA**

Avenida Provincia, s/n
13680 Fuente El Fresno (Ciudad Real)
☎: 926 806 110 - Fax: 926 806 110

Established: 1970

🍷 10 📊 8,000,000 litres 🍷 100%

FRONTILES WHITE
FRONTILES RED

Sociedad Agraria de Transformación
SANTA RITA

San Agustín, 14
16630 Mota del Cuervo (Cuenca)
☎: 967 180 071 - Fax: 967 182 277

Established: 1972

🍷 300 📊 4,000,000 litres 🍇 700 has.
🍷 80% 🍇20%: -SE -DE -FR -BE -CH -NL

VARONES 2003 JOVEN WHITE
100% macabeo

81 Pale with a golden hue. Intense aroma of ripe white fruit with floral and jammy notions. Flavourful, fruity palate with fine bitter notes and excellent acidity.

VERONÉS 2003 JOVEN WHITE
100% airén

78 Pale with a golden hue. Slightly fruity, floral aroma. Flavourful, bitter palate with fresh overtones and good acidity.

VERONÉS 2003 JOVEN RED
100% tempranillo

83 Very intense cherry with a violet edge. Fruity aroma with the pulp of jammy red bramble fruit, a nuance of liquorice and a suggestion of minerals. Very fresh, fruity palate and a complex hint (skins).

VARONES 1998 CRIANZA RED
100% tempranillo

79 Cherry with a brick red edge. Not very intense aroma with crianza notes and a nuance of slightly overripe fruit, spicy. Round, supple, flavourful palate with a slightly woody presence.

VARONES 1997 RESERVA RED
100% tempranillo

84 Garnet red cherry. Powerful aroma with predominant crianza notes (tobacco, smoky notes, spices) and a ripe fruit hint. Flavourful, fleshy palate with good oak/fruit integration, slightly warm buena acidez. with good acidity.

SANTÍSIMO CRISTO DEL ESPÍRITU SANTO

Avenida Fundadores Coop., 69
13420 Malagón (Ciudad Real)
☎: 926 802 640 - Fax: 926 801 040
scespiritu@ucaman.es

Established: 1908
🍷 100%

TRADICIONAL QUINTANARES CENCIBEL RED
QUINTANARES CABERNET SAUVIGNON RED

Cooperativa SANTO NIÑO DE LA BOLA

Angel Moya, 24
16650 Las Mesas (Cuenca)
☎: 967 155 074 - Fax: 967 167 317
lasmesas@arrakis.es

PICORZO AIRÉN WHITE
PICORZO RED
TARAY TEMPRANILLO RED

SEÑORÍO DEL JÚCAR

Avenida Albacete, 23
02230 Madrigueras (Albacete)
☎: 967 484 334 - Fax: 967 485 065
bodegas@bsjucar.e.telefonica.net

Established: 1982

🍾 300 🛢 2,000,000 litres 🌿 60 has.
🍷 90% 🌍10%: -DE -UK -US -CI

COVASYERMAS 2003 JOVEN RED
100% tempranillo

76 Cherry with a violet edge. Aroma of foresty red fruit with hints of spices and slightly green. Flavourful with bitter (liquorice) fruit on the palate, good freshness.

COVASYERMAS 2000 OAK AGED RED
80% tempranillo, 20% cabernet sauvignon

78 Cherry with a brick red hue. Aroma of wood with little intensity. Warm palate with very noticeable tannins, very well-mannered but without great nuances.

COVASYERMAS 1999 RESERVA RED
80% tempranillo, 20% cabernet sauvignon

81 Garnet red cherry with a brick red edge. Intense aroma with predominant spicy, reduction notes (tobacco, leather). Flavourful palate with quite rough, rich tannins, liquorice and dark-roasted flavours.

Grupo SOLIS VINTNERS

Carretera Santa Cruz km. 4, 5
16400 Tarancón (Cuenca)
☎: 969 320 200 - Fax: 969 321 274
gruposolis@gruposolis.net
www.gruposolis.net

Established: 2000
🍾 900 🛢 25,000,000 litres 🍷 80% 🌍20%

PLAZA MAYOR AIRÉN-MACABEO 2004 JOVEN WHITE
airen, macabeo

77 Pale with coppery nuances. Somewhat intense aroma of white stone fruit with floral hints. Flavourful, fruity palate with quality bitter hints.

PLAZA MAYOR GARNACHA 2004 JOVEN ROSÉ
100% garnacha

75 Intense raspberry. Fresh aroma with red stone fruit and foresty strawberries. Quite flavourful, fruity palate with spicy hints of skins, lacking acidity.

MONASTERIO DE UCLÉS 2003 JOVEN RED
tempranillo

74 Lively garnet red cherry. Not very intense, fruity aroma. Fresh, fruity palate with the freshness of macerated skins.

PLAZA MAYOR 2003 JOVEN RED
tempranillo

78 Ruby red with a strawberry edge. Aroma of strawberries and raspberries, with sweet notes, sun-drenched skins and lactics. Fresh, well-balanced palate with good varietal character and strawberries in the retronasal passage.

TORRES FILOSO

Carretera San Clemente, km. 1
02600 Villarrobledo (Albacete)
☎: 967 144 426 - Fax: 967 146 419
torresfiloso@arrakis.es
www.torresfiloso.com

Established: 1921

⊞ 220 📦 150,000 litres 🍇 20 has.

🍷 70% 🌐30%: -DE -US

ARBOLES DE CASTILLEJO 2003 JOVEN WHITE
JUAN JOSÉ 2001 RED
AD PATER 2001 RED
ARBOLES DE CASTILLEJO 2003 RED

TRINIDAD FUENTES GARCÍA

La Torre, 53
13750 Castellar de Santiago (Ciudad Real)
☎: 926 340 360 - Fax: 926 340 360
bodegfuentes@vodafone.es

⊞ 50 📦 1,450,000 litres 🍇 10 has.

🍷 95% 🌐5%: -DK -DE

VEGAGIL 2003 JOVEN WHITE
100% airén

72 Brilliant straw with greenish nuances. Intense aroma of white fruit with mild off-odours from the tank. Better on the palate, flavourful and fruity, with a slight dilution in the finish.

VEGAGIL 2002 JOVEN RED
100% tempranillo

73 Not very deep cherry. Aroma with very sweet notes of red fruit jelly, perfumed, with a suggestion of cough medicine. Medium-bodied palate with obvious tannins.

MATA DE MENCALIZ 2001 ROBLE RED
100% cencibel

80 Cherry. Fruity aroma of strawberries with mineral notes. Flavourful, very fresh palate with hints of stones, very pleasant.

MATA DE MENCÁLIZ 2001 CRIANZA RED
100% tempranillo

70 Brick red. Very toasty wood aroma of very ripe red fruit and jam. Light, drying palate with very noticeable wood tannins.

VEGAGIL 2003 RED

VIHUCAS DISTRIBUCIONES Y SERVICIOS

Mayor, 3
45860 Villacañas (Toledo)
☎: 925 160 309 - Fax: 925 160 309
vihucas@vihucas.com
www.vihucas.com

Established: 1982

VIHUCAS 2000 FERMENTADO EN BARRICA WHITE
VIHUCAS 2001 OAK AGED RED
VIHUCAS 1999 CRIANZA RED
VIHUCAS 2000 CRIANZA RED

Cooperativa Vinícola de VILLARROBLEDO

Carretera de Munera, km. 0, 5
02600 Villarrobledo (Albacete)
☎: 967 140 276 - Fax: 967 146 657
info@vinicolavillarrobledo.com
www.vinicolavillarrobledo.com

Established: 1998

⊞ 675 📦 19,700,000 litres 🍇 3,500 has.

🍷 50% 🌐50%: -FR -DK -SE -DK -DE

R. ELIPA 2003 WHITE
ROCHALES 2003 WHITE
DON OCTAVIO 2003 RED
R. ELIPA 2000 CRIANZA RED
DON OCTAVIO 1999 RESERVA RED
DON OCTAVIO 1996 GRAN RESERVA RED

VINÍCOLA DE CASTILLA

Polígono Industrial Calle I
13200 Manzanares (Ciudad Real)
☎: 926 647 800 - Fax: 926 610 466
nacional@vinicoladecastilla.com
www.vinicoladecastilla.com

Established: 1976

⊞ 8,000 📦 19,000,000 litres 🍇 250 has.

🍷 50% 🌐50%: -UK -DE -JP -US -PR -PH -BE -CH -EE -RU -BR -TW

SEÑORÍO DE GUADIANEJA CHARDONNAY 2003 FERMENTADO EN BARRICA WHITE
100% chardonnay

80 Pale gold hue. Somewhat intense aroma with fruity and floral notes and a spicy nuance of skins and smoky oak. Flavourful palate with ripe white fruit and fine bitter notes.

SELECCIÓN VINÍCOLA DE CASTILLA 1996 CRIANZA WHITE
50% viura, 30% airén, 20% chardonnay

77 Pale gold. Powerful aroma with predominant vanilla oak notes. Flavourful palate with fine bitter notes, hints of herbs and creamy oak.

CASTILLO DE ALHAMBRA AIRÉN 2003 WHITE
100% airén

76 Brilliant straw. Somewhat intense aroma evoking the freshness of fruit and white flowers with hints of herbs. Flavourful palate with spicy notes of skins and notes of exotic fruit.

GRAN VERDAD 2003 WHITE
100% airén

73 Pale with golden nuances. Not very intense aroma evoking freshness. Flavourful, fresh palate with fine bitter notes, pleasant.

SEÑORÍO DE GUADIANEJA MACABEO 2003 WHITE
macabeo

79 Brilliant pale. Intense aroma with fresh and fruity overtones (white fruit with exotic hints). Flavourful palate with fine spicy and bitter notes, mountain herbs and varietal expression.

CASTILLO DE ALHAMBRA 2003 ROSÉ
100% garnacha

79 Deep raspberry. Intense aroma of red stone fruit with spicy hints of skins, slightly warm. Flavourful palate with a spicy freshness (varietal), pleasant.

FINCA VIEJA 2003 ROSÉ
100% garnacha

78 Raspberry with a coppery hue. Not very intense aroma evoking the freshness of red stone fruit. Flavourful palate with spicy hints of skins, a sweet hint, good acidity.

SEÑORÍO DE GUADIANEJA GARNACHA 2003 ROSÉ
90% garnacha, 10% tempranillo

80 Brilliant raspberry. Intense aroma of red stone fruit with toasty hints of skins. Flavourful, fruity palate with fine bitter and herby notes, peach skins.

CASTILLO DE ALHAMBRA TEMPRANILLO 2003 JOVEN RED
100% tempranillo

80 Deep cherry. Aroma with lactic notes, ripe red stone fruit and skins. Drying on the palate, slightly warm with good acidity, fleshy and varietal.

SEÑORÍO DE GUADIANEJA TEMPRANILLO 2003 JOVEN RED
100% cencibel

78 Cherry. Intense aroma of red fruit and sun-drenched skins. Very noticeable tannins with good acidity on the palate.

SEÑORÍO DE GUADIANEJA MERLOT 2003 OAK AGED RED
100% merlot

78 Cherry with a strawberry edge. Aroma of red fruit and blackberries with a suggestion of flowers. Warm palate with a good fruit weight and supple tannins.

BALADA CENCIBEL ECOLÓGICO 2003 RED
100% cencibel

75 Very deep garnet red. Aroma of sun-drenched skins, slightly alcoholic, vinous. Warm palate with slightly marked tannins despite the good fruit weight.

FINCA VIEJA TEMPRANILLO 2003 RED
tempranillo

79 Dark cherry. Intense, fruity aroma with hints of sun-drenched skins. Flavourful palate with red stone fruit, a certain spicy freshness and good acidity.

SEÑORÍO DE GUADIANEJA SYRAH 2003 RED
100% syrah

73 Garnet red with a violet hue. Alcoholic aroma of ripe red fruit and earth. Warm palate with bitter notes.

FINCA VIEJA 2001 CRIANZA RED
100% tempranillo

74 Garnet red cherry with a saffron edge. Intense, ripe aroma with not very fine reduction notes. Flavourful, somewhat fleshy palate with the character of reduced fruit.

LA LLANURA 2001 CRIANZA RED
100% tempranillo

80 Not very deep cherry. Aroma of toasty wood and underripe fruit. Light, warm palate with quite noticeable wood tannins.

GRAN VERDAD 2000 CRIANZA RED
100% tempranillo

75 Cherry with an orangey hue. Aroma with very sweet notes, reduction, and jammy red fruit; overall well-mannered on the palate.

SELECCIÓN VINÍCOLA DE CASTILLA 1995 CRIANZA RED
50% cencibel, 30% cabernet sauvignon, 20% merlot

78 Garnet red cherry with coppery nuances. Somewhat intense aroma of jammy fruit, with spicy oak notes and hints of reduction (tobacco). Flavourful palate with a good fruit/oak integration, bitter notes, hints of aged wood and noticeable acidity.

SEÑORÍO DE GUADIANEJA 2001 CRIANZA RED
91% tempranillo, 9% merlot

80 Not very deep cherry with an orangey hue. Toasty aroma of wood, earthy with ripe red fruit. Fresh palate with a good wood/fruit integration and a smoky retronasal effect.

FINCA VIEJA 1997 RESERVA RED
100% tempranillo

77 Garnet red cherry with a brick red glint. Not very intense aroma with spicy hints of oak and a notion of the freshness of red fruit. Flavourful, supple palate with drying notes of oak.

GUADIANEJA VIÑAS 50 AÑOS 1998 RESERVA ESPECIAL RED
100% cencibel

83 Garnet red cherry. Toasty aromas with an expression of reduction, earthy and somewhat varietal. Spicy, warm palate with good wood tannins well-integrated with the fruit, nice, somewhat pungent finish.

FINCA VIEJA 1996 GRAN RESERVA RED
100% tempranillo

78 Not very deep cherry with an orange glint. Not very intense aroma of slightly reduced fruit with spicy hints. Flavourful palate with fine bitter crianza notes, slightly warm.

SEÑORÍO DE GUADIANEJA CABERNET SAUVIGNON 1992 GRAN RESERVA RED
100% cabernet sauvignon

84 Cherry with an orangey hue. Powerful aroma with predominant slightly varietal reduction notes (tobacco, cedar, old furniture, jammy bilberries). Flavourful, supple palate with slightly marked but fine tannins, good acidity.

SEÑORÍO DE GUADIANEJA TEMPRANILLO 1991 GRAN RESERVA RED
100% tempranillo

85 Garnet red cherry with a brick red edge. Slightly intense aroma with mild reduction notes (tobacco, old furniture, jammy prunes). Flavourful, supple palate with hints of aged wood and spices, with a good expression of Gran Reserva.

S&G BLANCO 2002 OAK AGED DULCE NATURAL
moscatel, macabeo

74 Brilliant gold. Intense, spicy aroma of slightly reduced white fruit, dried peaches, hay and spices (curry). Sweet and bitter on the palate, without great expression.

S&G TINTO 2002 OAK AGED RED DULCE NATURAL
syrah, tempranillo

76 Lively garnet red cherry. Intense aroma of black fruit with spicy notes of skins and hints of sackcloth. Flavourful, slightly sweet palate with bitter oak notes and hints of cocoa powder.

CANTARES SPARKLING EXTRA BRUT
90% viura, 10% airén

74 Pale with a greenish hue and a persistent not very fine bead. Fresh, quite intense aroma of fruit and white flowers without great crianza expression. Dry and bitter on the palate with quality citrus fruit notes.

BALADA ECOLÓGICO 2003 WHITE
CASTILLO DE MANZANARES 2000 WHITE
FINCA VIEJA 2003 WHITE
LA LLANURA 2003 JOVEN WHITE
VIÑA DEL CASTILLO 2003 WHITE
SEÑORÍO DE GUADIANEJA SEMIDULCE WHITE
GRAN VERDAD 2003 ROSÉ
VIÑA DEL CASTILLO 2003 ROSÉ
CANTARES SPARKLING SEMI SECO
CASTILLO DE MANZANARES 2000 OAK AGED RED
VIÑA DEL CASTILLO 2000 CRIANZA RED
SEÑORÍO DE GUADIANEJA 1999 RESERVA RED

VINÍCOLA DE TOMELLOSO

Carretera Toledo - Albacete, km. 130, 8
13700 Tomelloso (Ciudad Real)
☎: 926 513 004 - Fax: 926 538 001
javier@vinicolatomelloso.com
www.vinicolatomelloso.com

Established: 1986

🍪 1,100 🗄 6,000,000 litres 🍇 2,500 has.
🐾 60% 🌍40%

TORRE DE GAZATE AIRÉN 2003 JOVEN WHITE
100% airén

80 Pale with golden nuances. Somewhat intense aroma of fruit, white flowers and spicy hints. Flavourful, fruity palate with good fruit-alcohol-acidity balance.

AÑIL 2003 JOVEN WHITE
90% macabeo, 10% chardonnay

80 Brilliant pale with greenish nuances. Intense aroma of fruit and ripe white flowers (hints of fine reduction). Fresh, fruity palate with spicy notes of skins, a certain citrus freshness and herbs.

TORRE DE GAZATE SAUVIGNON BLANC 2003 JOVEN WHITE
100% sauvignon blanc

81 Pale with golden nuances. Somewhat intense aroma of ripe white fruit and hints of fine herbs. Flavourful palate with quite varietal fruit (exotic hints), with spicy notes of skins and good acidity.

TORRE DE GAZATE 2003 JOVEN ROSÉ
100% cabernet sauvignon

82 Pale cherry with coppery nuances. Powerful aroma of very ripe fruit (toasty, sweet hints). Generous, flavourful and fruity on the palate, with bitter notes and good acidity.

TORRE DE GAZATE CENCIBEL 2003 JOVEN RED
100% cencibel

80 Garnet red cherry. Intense aroma of ripe strawberries, blackberries and balsamic notes. Warm, varietal, flavourful palate with fruit in the retronasal passsage.

ALSUR 2000 CRIANZA RED
cencibel, cabernet sauvignon, syrah

81 Lively garnet red cherry. Fruity aroma with notes of sun-drenched skins, slightly varietal Tempranillo hints (damp earth, red fruit). Flavourful palate with a good oak/fruit integration and rich bitter notes (liquorice).

FINCA CERRADA 2000 CRIANZA RED
cencibel, cabernet sauvignon, syrah

84 Garnet red cherry. Intense aroma of black fruit with hints of macerated skins and spicy notes of oak. Flavourful palate with ripe red stone fruit, a good oak/fruit integration, a good varietal fruit expression, liquorice and terroir.

TORRE DE GAZATE 2000 CRIANZA RED
70% cencibel, 30% cabernet sauvignon

80 Cherry. Aroma of wood with balsamic notes, vinous. Bitter on the palate with well-integrated tannins, medium persistence and toasty notes in the retronasal passage.

TORRE DE GAZATE 1998 RESERVA RED
50% cencibel, 50% cabernet sauvignon

83 Glacé cherry. Varietal aroma of Cabernet (paprika) with black fruit, balsamic hints and toasty wood. Dry palate with well-structured tannins, long, with vanilla in the retronasal passage.

TORRE DE GAZATE CABERNET SAUVIGNON 1996 GRAN RESERVA RED
100% cabernet sauvignon

80 Brick red. Aroma with reduction notes, green pepper, toasty wood and black olives. Spicy, fleshy palate with polished tannins.

MANTOLÁN BRUT NATURE
100% macabeo

79 Brilliant gold with a very light bead. Powerful aroma of ripe fruit (exotic hints), with hints of flowers and a toasty suggestion of skins and fine herbs. Fresh, dry and creamy palate with bitter notes (nuts, mountain herbs) and good acidity.

TORRE DE GAZATE 1999 CRIANZA RED

VINOS Y BODEGAS

Carretera de las Mesas, km. 1
13630 Socuéllamos (Ciudad Real)
☎: 926 531 067 - Fax: 926 532 249
export@vinosybodegas.com
www.vinosybodegas.com

Established: 1996
📖 300 ⚖ 4,500,000 litres 🍷 10%
🌐90%: -UE Africa Asia América

REAL BODEGA MACABEO 2003 WHITE
100% macabeo

81 Pale with a golden hue. Powerful aroma of white fruit with hints of apricot skins and perfumed soap. Flavourful palate with fine bitter and, varietal notes with a suggestion of aniseed and good citrus acidity.

REAL BODEGA CABERNET SAUVIGNON 2003 RED
cabernet sauvignon

78 Intense cherry with a violet edge. Not very intense, somewhat fruity and vegetative aroma. Medium bodied palate with vegetative notes, red fruit and bitter tannins.

REAL BODEGA SYRAH 2003 RED
100% syrah

79 Dark cherry with a violet edge. Powerful aroma of black fruit, fine toasty notes and petals. Flavourful palate with slightly drying tannins and a fruit expression slightly muted by the alcohol.

REAL BODEGA TEMPRANILLO 2003 RED
100% tempranillo

79 Cherry with a violet edge. Clean, fruity aroma of brambles. Fruity, flavourful, slightly astringent on the palate with bitter tannins.

REAL BODEGA TEMPRANILLO 2001 CRIANZA RED
tempranillo

75 Intense cherry with an orangey edge. Aroma with viscous notes (overripe fruit) and toasty notes. Somewhat flabby palate with drying oak tannins and ripe black fruit.

AÑADAS DE ORO 2003 RED
LA VIEJA ESTACIÓN 2003 RED
REAL BODEGA TEMPRANILLO 1997 RESERVA RED

VIÑASORO

Carretera Alcázar - Manzanares, km. 7
13600 Alcázar de San Juan (Ciudad Real)
☎: 918 596 910 - Fax: 918 596 088
alejandro@bodegas-vinasoro.com
www.bodegas-vinasoro.com

⊞ 300 ▦ 350.000 litres ⚘ 80 has.

VIÑASORO VARIETAL MERLOT 2002 RED
merlot

80 Garnet red cherry. Intense aroma with a certain varietal profile (black fruit, underbrush) and a toasty suggestion of skins. Flavourful palate with quite rough, oily tannins, and a spicy, bitter hint (liquorice, dark-roasted flavours).

VIÑASORO 1996 RESERVA RED

77 Cherry with a coppery glint. Not very intense aroma with quite fruity notes and a spicy suggestion of oak. Flavourful palate with fleshy overtones, without great nuances.

VIÑEDOS MEJORANTES

Carretera de Villafranca, km. 2
45860 Villacañas (Toledo)
☎: 925 201 036 - Fax: 925 200 023
portillejo@portillejo.com
www.portillejo.com
Established: 1994

⊞ 600 ▦ 2,000,000 litres ⚘ 250 has.

🍷 80% ⚘20%: -UK -DE -CH -NL -BE

PORTILLEJO 2003 WHITE
macabeo

79 Pale. Slightly intense aroma with a certain spicy finnesse, fruity, with hints of flowers and bananas. Flavourful palate with fine bitter notes and good acidity.

PORTILLEJO 2003 JOVEN RED
tempranillo

78 Dark cherry. Somewhat intense aroma of black fruit and fresh overtones of macerated skins. Flavourful, bitter palate with hints of liquorice, damp earth and an acidic edge.

PORTILLEJO 2003 JOVEN RED
merlot

80 Cherry with a violet hue. Not very intense aroma of sun-drenched skins and ripe red fruit. Generous tannins on the palate and fruit in the retronasal passsage.

PORTILLEJO 2003 OAK AGED RED
cabernet sauvignon

83 Garnet red cherry. Lactic aromas of ripe red fruit and earth. Balanced palate with good persistence and red fruit in the retronasal passage.

PORTILLEJO 2002 OAK AGED RED
merlot

78 Cherry with a garnet red edge. Aroma with light reduction notes (leather), spices and vanilla. Somewhat warm on the palate with red fruit in the retronasal passage.

PORTILLEJO 2002 OAK AGED RED
cabernet sauvignon

81 Cherry with an orangey hue. Spicy aroma of hot paprika and ripe black fruit. Flavourful palate, well-balanced with well-structured tannins and medium persistence.

PORTILLEJO 2000 CRIANZA RED
cabernet sauvignon

83 Cherry with an orangey hue. Somewhat alcoholic, vinous aroma of green pepper and light, toasty wood. Persistent palate of green pepper.

PORTILLEJO 1999 CRIANZA RED
cabernet sauvignon

79 Cherry with an orangey rim. Peppery aroma with underripe red fruit and sweet notes. Fleshy palate of medium persistence.

PORTILLEJO 1998 RESERVA RED
cabernet sauvignon

80 Cherry with an orangey hue. Aroma of toasty wood, pepper and alcohol. Bitter on the palate with polished tannins and medium persistence.

PORTILLEJO 1999 RESERVA RED
cabernet sauvignon

80 Cherry with a brick red nuance. Aroma with reduction notes and roasted green peppers. Warm, dry palate with noticeable wood tannins, well mannered but somewhat lacking in fruit.

PORTILLEJO 2003 SEMICRIANZA RED

VIÑEDOS Y CRIANZAS

Avenida Juan Carlos I, 28
16400 Tarancón (Cuenca)
☎: 969 327 099 - Fax: 969 327 199
viñedosycrianzas@telefonica.net
Established: 2000
🛢 1,000 🛢 800,000 litres 🍇 300 has.
🍷 95% 🍇5%

LAMÁN

VIÑEDOS Y RESERVAS

Carretera Quintanar, km. 2
45810 Villanueva de Alcardete (Toledo)
☎: 925 167 536 - Fax: 925 167 558
vr@fedeto.es
www.cuevassantoyo.com
Established: 1987
🍇 100 has. 🍷 90% 🍇10%: -DE -US

CUEVAS SANTOYO 201 BRUT
CAROLUS RESERVA IMPERIAL 2000 BRUT
NATURE
CUEVAS SANTOYO 2002 SEMISECO

VIRGEN DE LAS VIÑAS

Carretera Argamasilla de Alba s/n
13700 Tomelloso (Ciudad Real)
☎: 926 510 865 - Fax: 926 512 130
atencion.cliente@vinostomillar.com
www.vinostomillar.com
Established: 1961
🛢 2,500 🛢 125,000,000 litres
🍇 22,500 has.🍷 85% 🍇15%: -DE -UK -NL

LORENZETE AIRÉN 2003 JOVEN WHITE
100% airén

79 Brilliant pale. Intense, quite fruity aroma with a slight varietal expression (fine herbs, fruit, white flowers). Flavourful palate with bitter notes; slightly oily with good acidity.

ROCÍO LÓPEZ LÓPEZ 2003 JOVEN SEMI SECO WHITE
100% airén

78 Pale with greenish nuances. Somewhat intense, fruity aroma with hints of fine herbs. Sweet, slightly dense palate with quality bittersweet notes and a bitter, citrus fruit nuance.

TOMILLAR 2003 FERMENTADO EN BARRICA WHITE
airén

75 Brilliant pale with golden nuances. Intense aroma of ripe white fruit with a smoky oaky freshness and fine herbs. Flavourful palate with slightly drying tannins (some greeness) and bitter notes.

TOMILLAR TEMPRANILLO 2003 JOVEN ROSÉ
100% cencibel

77 Very deep raspberry. Slightly intense aroma with hardly any fruit expression and hints of dried flowers. Flavourful, bitter on the palate, slightly warm and oily.

TOMILLAR TEMPRANILLO 2003 JOVEN RED
100% cencibel

81 Cherry with a violet hue. Intense, fruity aroma with very sweet notes (caramel) and hints of sun-drenched skins. Flavourful palate with ripe, sweet tannins, toasty notes of skins good acidity.

TOMILLAR 2001 RED
100% tempranillo

80 Garnet red cherry. Somewhat intense, ripe aroma with spicy notes of quite varietal fruit (petals, underbrush). Flavourful palate with ripe, oily tannins, toasty notes of crianza and good acidity.

TOMILLAR 1999 CRIANZA RED
100% cencibel

80 Garnet red cherry with a brick red edge. Slightly intense aroma of jammy black fruit, with spicy hints of oak and reduction notes. Flavourful palate with somewhat rough tannins, quite promising and bitter notes.

TOMILLAR 1997 RESERVA RED
cabernet sauvignon, tempranillo

76 Garnet red cherry with a coppery edge. Not very intense aroma with predominant toasty oak and skins. Flavourful palate with quite bitter tannins (aged wood) and a spicy nuance (varietal paprika).

DON EUGENIO 1996 GRAN RESERVA RED
100% tempranillo

81 Garnet red cherry with a coppery edge. Intense aroma with predominant spicy oak notes. Flavourful palate with a good fruit/oak integration, mild reduction notes (nuts, prunes), balsamic and toasty nuances.

TOMILLAR FERMENTADO EN BARRICA WHITE
TOMILLAR NUEVO WHITE

DO LA PALMA

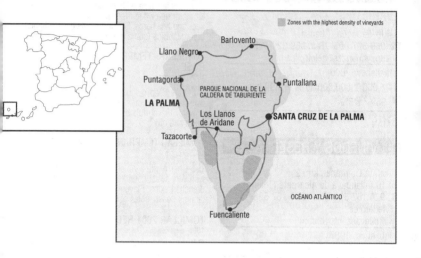

Zones with the highest density of vineyards

Barlovento
Llano Negro
Puntagorda
Puntallana
PARQUE NACIONAL DE LA CALDERA DE TABURIENTE
LA PALMA
Los Llanos de Aridane
SANTA CRUZ DE LA PALMA
Tazacorte
OCÉANO ATLÁNTICO
Fuencaliente

NEWS. As with the rest of the wines from the islands, there is not much to comment on, as very few wines have 'come forward' for tasting. We have only received three samples, all from the same bodega (Carballo), and only one wine of the current vintage, 2003. It is worth highlighting, with the scant information we have, the recovery of two red varieties, the *Castellana* and the *Listán Prieto*, as well as the return to a 'normal' production level after the climatological loss of 2002: the one and a half million kilograms harvested in 2003 almost doubles the 800,000 of the previous year.

Hectares of Vineyard	No. of Viticulturists	No. of Bodegas	2003 Harvest	2003 Production	Marketing
869	1,265	16	-	1,500,000 kilos	Mainly in La Palma, Tenerife and Gran Canaria.

LOCATION. The production area covers the whole island of San Miguel de La Palma, and is divided into three distinct sub-regions: Hoyo de Mazo, Fuencaliente and Northern La Palma.

CLIMATE. Variable according to the altitude and the direction that the vineyards face. The relief is a fundamental aspect in La Palma, seeing as it gives rise to different climates and microclimates; one must not forget that it has the highest altitudes in relation to surface area of all the Canary Islands. Nevertheless, as it is situated in the Atlantic, it benefits from the effects of the trade winds (humid and from the northwest), which temper the temperatures and tone down the climatic contrasts.

SOIL. The vineyards are situated at altitudes of between 200 m and 1,400 m above sea level in a coastal belt ranging in width which surrounds the whole island. Due to the ragged topography, the vineyards occupy the steep hillsides in the form of small terraces. The soil is mainly of volcanic origin.

VARIETIES:

White: *Malvasía, Güal* and *Verdello* (main)*; Albillo, Bastardo Blanco, Bermejuela, Bujariego, Burra Blanca, Forastera Blanca, Listán Blanco, Moscatel, Pedro Ximénez, Sabro* and *Torrontés.*

Red: *Negramol* (main), *Listán Negro (Almuñeco), Bastardo Negro, Malvasía Rosada, Moscatel Negro, Tintilla, Castellana* and *Listan Prieto.*

SUB REGIONS:

Hoyo de Mazo: incorporates the municipal districts of Villa de Mazo, Breña Baja, Breña Alta and Santa Cruz de La Palma, at altitudes of between 200 m and 700 m. The vines grow over the terrain on hillsides covered with volcanic stone ('Empedrados') or with volcanic gravel ('Picón Granado'). White and mainly red varieties are grown.

Fuencaliente: incorporates the municipal districts of Fuencaliente, El Paso, Los Llanos de Aridane and Tazacorte. The vines grow over terrains of volcanic ash at altitudes of between 200 m and 1900 m. The white varieties and the sweet Malvasia stand out.

Northern La Palma: situated at an altitude of between 100 m and 200 m, covering the municipal areas of Puntallana, San Andrés and Sauces, Barlovento, Garafía, Puntagorda and Tijarafe. The region is richer in vegetation and the vines grow on trellises and using the goblet system. The traditional 'Tea Wines' are produced here.

REGULATORY COUNCIL.

Dr. Acosta Gómez, 7. 38740 Fuencaliente (La Palma).
Tel / Fax: 922 444 404.
E-mail: cr.vinoslapalma@terra.es
Website: www.malvasiadelapalma.com

GENERAL CHARACTERISTICS OF THE WINES:

Whites	Produced mainly from *Bujariego* or combined with *Listán Blanco*. They are dry, fruity with certain rustic notes; on occasion they also display mineral and volcanic nuances. They are the most classic wines of the island; nevertheless, they are sweet wines from *Malvasia*, complex and original with notes that are reminiscent of fine herbs.
Rosés	The colour ranges from salmon to pink. The wines are light, fruity and delicate.
Reds	Produced mainly from *Negramol*, they usually have a deep cherry-red colour. As with the rosés, these wines are also fresh and light.
Tea Wine	A characteristic wine from La Palma, normally produced from *Negramol, Listán Prieto* and *Albillo*, and aged in tea (Canary oak), which gives it intense aromas and tastes of resin that combine with the fruity and herbaceous touches of the grape.

CARBALLO

Carretera Las Indias, 74
38740 Fuencaliente - La Palma (Tenerife)
☎: 922 444 140 - Fax: 922 444 140
sipaorga@mail.ddnet.es

Established: 1990
⊕ 10 ⊟ 100,000 litres ⚘ 8 has. 🐄 100%

BRISAS DEL SUR 1999 WHITE
listán blanca

78 Golden. Toasty aroma of jammy and crystallised fruit with notes of almonds and woody oak. Dry palate with bitter oak, somewhat aged but flavourful.

CARBALLO 2003 WHITE
100% listán blanca

70 Straw-coloured. Fresh, fruity and slightly evolved aroma. Dry, quite fruity palate, discreet.

MALVASÍA DULCE CARBALLO 2000 WHITE

88 Golden. Toasty aroma of foresty honey with crystallised fruit. Unctuous, sweet palate evoking the bitterness of the vine variety with a toasty oak retronasal effect, flavourful and original, this bodega's best wine.

CARLOS FERNÁNDEZ FELIPE

Las Ledas, 40
38710 Breña Baja (Canarias)
☎: 922 434 439 - Fax: 922 434 439

VIÑA ETNA NEGRAMOLL RED
VIÑA ETNA VERDELLO DULCE WHITE

Bodegas EL HOYO

Carretera Hoyo de Mazo, 60 Callejones
38738 Villa de Mazo (Santa Cruz de Tenerife)
☎: 922440616 - Fax: 922428569
info@bodegaselhoyo.com
www.bodegaselhoyo.com

Established: 1994
⊕ 36 ⊟ 530,000 litres ⚘ 110 has.
🐄 95% ⚘5%: -DE -VE

HOYO DE MAZO 2003 WHITE
HOYO DE MAZO 2002 DULCE WHITE
MAZEGAS 2003 WHITE

EUFROSINA PÉREZ RODRÍGUEZ

Briesta, 3 El Castillo
38788 Villa de Garafia (La Palma)
☎: 922 400 447 - Fax: 922 400 447

Established: 1998

⊕ 4 ⊟ 26,000 litres ⚘ 2 has. 🐄 100%

EL NÍSPERO WHITE
EL NÍSPERO RED

JORGE L. RODRÍGUEZ

Llano El Molino, La Galga
38710 Puntallana (La Palma)
☎: 922 430 165 - Fax: 922 430 712

TABOCO RED

JUAN MATÍAS TORRES PÉREZ

Ciudad Real 10 Canarios
38740 Fuentecaliente de la Palma
(Santa Cruz de Tenerife)
☎: 922 444 219 - Fax: 922 444 219

Established: 1895
⊕ 42 ⊟ 32,000 litres ⚘ 2 has. 🐄 100%

VID SUR 2003 OAK AGED WHITE
VID SUR 2003 OAK AGED RED

LAS TOSCAS

Nogales, 1 El Granel
38700 Puntallana (La Palma)
☎: 922 430 020 - Fax: 922 416 642
lastoscas@infopalma.com
infopalma.com/latoscas

Established: 1994
⊕ 14 ⊟ 60,000 litres ⚘ 3.8 has.
🐄 90% ⚘10%

VIÑA LAS TOSCAS WHITE
VIÑA LAS TOSCAS RED

LLANOVID

Los Canarios, s/n
38740 Fuencaliente - La Palma (Tenerife)
☎: 922 444 078 - Fax: 922 444 394
vinosteneguia@ctv.es
www.vinosteneguia.com

Established: 1985
⊕ 62 ⊟ 1,060,000 litres ⚘ 240 has.

TENEGUÍA MALVASÍA 2003 F. BARRICA
 AFRUTADO SECO WHITE
TENEGUÍA MALVASÍA 2003 JOVEN WHITE
TENEGUÍA ALBILLO 2003 WHITE
TENEGUÍA CALETAS 2003 F. BARRICA
WHITE
TENEGUÍA 2003 ROSÉ
TENEGUÍA 2001 2003 JOVEN RED
TENEGUÍA NEGRAMOLL RED

DO LA PALMA

TENEGUÍA 2000 CRIANZA RED
TENEGUÍA MALVASÍA 1997 BRUT DULCE

MELQUIADES CAMACHO HERNÁNDEZ

San Nicolás, 450- Las Manchas
38760 Los Llanos de Aridane (La Palma)
☎: 922 494 208

NAMBROQUE LISTÁN WHITE
NAMBROQUE NEGRAMOLL RED

ONÉSIMA PÉREZ RODRÍGUEZ

Las Tricias
38738 Garafía (La Palma)
☎: 922 463 481 - Fax: 922 463 481

VITEGA 2003 WHITE
VITEGA 2003 F. BARRICA WHITE
VITEGA ALBILLO 2003 WHITE
VITEGA 2003 ROSÉ
VITEGA 2003 RED
VITEGA ALMUÑECO 2003 RED
VITEGA NEGRAMOLL 2003 RED
VITEGA TEA 2003 RED

Bodega PERDOMO

Joaquina, 12 (Las Tricias)
38738 Garafía (La Palma)
☎: 922 400 089 - Fax: 922 400 183

PIEDRA JURADA WHITE
PIEDRA JURADA RED

TAMANCA

Las Manchas (San Nicolás), s/n
38750 El Paso (La Palma)
☎: 922 494 155 - Fax: 922 494 296

TAMANCA WHITE
TAMANCA RED

Agrícola VELHOCO

Juan Mayor, 32
38700 Velhoco (La Palma)
☎: 922 414 340 - Fax: 922 413 531
lastoscas@infolapalma.com

ORO DE RISCO AFRUTADO WHITE
ORO DE RISCO AFRUTADO RED

Cooperativa Agrícola VIRGEN DEL PINO

Camino de la Cooperativa, 6 El Pinar
38738 Puntagorda (La Palma)
☎: 922 493 211 - Fax: 922 493 211

VIÑA TRAVIESA AFRUTADO WHITE
VIÑA TRAVIESA AFRUTADO RED

DO LANZAROTE

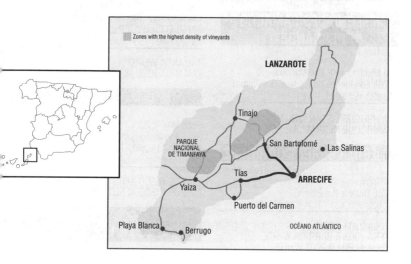

NEWS. Another poor harvest, perhaps more in terms of quantity than quality, which, as the Regulatory Council admits, amounts to 'a step backwards in the marketplace'. Either way, expectations for 2004 are around two million kilograms, whereas in 2003 just over one and a half million kilograms were harvested. The lack of grapes is paralyzing the work of the island's bodegas, which experienced exceptional prosperity at the turn of the century, with an average production of three million kilograms per year. Despite a few outbreaks of powdery mildew, the grapes have generally been healthy.

Hectares of Vineyard	No. of Viticulturists	No. of Bodegas	2003 Harvest	2003 Production	Marketing
2,209	1,677	14 bottlers,	Very Good	1,023,987 litres	98% Spain 2%foreign

Nevertheless, we find it rather difficult to assess the quality of the wines with a mere three samples. As with La Palma, only one bodega supplied us with samples for tasting, and once again a sweet wine (although in this case based on *Moscatel* instead of *Malvasía*) took the honours with a score close to 90 points.

LOCATION. On the island of Lanzarote. The production area covers the municipal areas of Tinajo, Yaiza, San Bartolomé, Haría and Teguise.

CLIMATE. Dry subtropical in nature, with low rainfall (about 200 mm per year) which is spread out irregularly throughout the year. On occasions, the Levante wind (easterly), characterised by its low humidity and which carries sand particles from the African continent, causes a considerable increase in the temperatures.

SOIL. Volcanic in nature (locally known as 'Picón'). In fact, the cultivation of vines

428

is made possible thanks to the ability of the volcanic sand to perfectly retain the water from dew and the scant rainfall. The island is relatively flat (the maximum altitude is 670 m) and the most characteristic form of cultivation is in 'hollows' surrounded by semicircular walls which protect the plants from the wind. This singular layout of the vineyards causes an extremely low density of stock per hectare.

VARIETIES:

White: *Malvasía* (majority 75%), *Pedro Ximénez, Diego, Listán Blanco, Moscatel, Burrablanca, Breval.*
Red: *Listán Negra* (15%) and *Negramoll.*

REGULATORY COUNCIL.

c/ Arrecife, 9. 35550 San Bartolomé (Lanzarote).
Tel: 928 521 048. Fax: 928 521 049.
E-mail: consejo@crdolanzarote.e.telefonica.net

GENERAL CHARACTERISTICS OF THE WINES:

Whites	The most characteristic wines of the island are the white *Malvasia* wines. They have vegetative aromas with volcanic and mineral nuances. There are more classical and traditional wines, which have a yellow amber colour, with almond and mellow aromas; the young white wines, which have a golden yellow colour, great varietal aromas, sometimes with aromas of fennel or mint, and are flavourful on the palate; and the semi-sec, with similar characteristics, but sweeter on the palate.
Rosés	In general, they have a pink or raspberry pink colour and are quite fresh and fruity.
Reds	These are usually mid-tone, with a deep cherry-red colour; they are somewhat warm and have a good structure on the palate.

BARRETO

Guardafría, 2
35550 San Bartolomé (Lanzarote)
☎: 928 520 717 - Fax: 928 520 866
barreto@infolanz.es
Established: 1980
⊞ 200 ▤ 800,000 l. ※ 40has.
▼ 97% ◑3%

EL CAMPESINO WHITE
EL CAMPESINO RED

CASTILLO DE GUANAPAY

Teruel, 5
35500 Arrecife (Lanzarote)
☎: 928 807 148

CASTILLO DE GUANAPAY WHITE
CASTILLO DE GUANAPAY ROSÉ
CASTILLO DE GUANAPAY RED

EL GRIFO

El Islote, 121
35550 San Bartolomé de Lanzarote
(Las Palmas de Gran Canaria)
☎: 928 524 036 - Fax: 928 832 634
bodegas@elgrifo.com
www.elgrifo.com
Established: 1775
⊞ 300 ▤ 1,000,000 litres ※ 40 has.
▼ 90% ◑10%: -DE -US

EL GRIFO MALVASÍA 2003 SEMIDULCE
WHITE
EL GRIFO MALVASÍA 2003 SECO
EL GRIFO MALVASÍA 2003 SECO WHITE
EL GRIFO 2003 ROSÉ
EL GRIFO 2003 OAK AGED RED
EL GRIFO 2003 RED
EL GRIFO MALVASÍA 2003 DULCE WHITE

Bodega LA GERIA

Carretera de la Geria, km. 19
35570 Yaiza-Lanzarote
(Las Palmas de Gran Canaria)
☎: 928 510 743 - Fax: 928 511 370
www.lageria.com
Established: 1990
⊞ 70 ▤ 450,000 litres ※ 10 has.
▼ 98% ◑2%

LA GERIA 2003 SEMI-DULCE WHITE
LA GERIA 2003 SECO WHITE

LA GERIA 2003 DULCE WHITE
LA GERIA 2003 ROSÉ
LA GERIA 2003 RED
LA GERIA VINO DE LICOR

Bodegas LA VEGUETA

C. Camino Las Huertitas, 3
35560 La Vegueta - Tinajo (Lanzarote)
☎: 928 511 434 - Fax: 928 823 598
Established: 2000
⊞ 25 ▤ 55,000 litres ※ 4 has. ▼ 100%

BODEGAS LA VEGUETA 2003 SECO
WHITE
100% malvasía

77 Straw-coloured. Fruity, fresh, varietal aroma with hints of minerals. Fresh, slightly fruity palate with herbs.

BODEGAS LA VEGUETA 2002 RED
75% negra moll, 25% listán negro

80 Quite dark cherry. Fresh, fruity aroma with a suggestion of Granadina and brambles. Supple, slightly flabby yet clean palate, fruity and varietal.

BODEGAS LA VEGUETA 2000 OAK AGED
VINO DE LICOR
100% moscatel

88 Golden. Toasty aroma of pâtisserie, honey, and crystallised fruit. Sweet, unctuous palate with a suggestion of Muscatel and very ripe grapes, flavourful, toasty and persistent.

MOZAGA

Carretera Arrecife a Tinajo, km. 8
35562 Mozaga (Lanzarote)
☎: 928 520 485 - Fax: 928 521 409
bodegasmozaga@hotmail.com
Established: 1973
⊞ 500 ▤ 1,200,000 litres ▼ 100%

BODEGA MOZAGA WHITE
BODEGA MOZAGA ROSÉ
BODEGA MOZAGA RED

REYMAR

Los Dolores, 13
35560 Tinajo (Lanzarote)
☎: 928 840 737 - Fax: 928 840 737

REYMAR MISTELA WHITE
REYMAR MALVASÍA SECO WHITE
REYMAR MOSCATEL DULCE WHITE
REYMAR ROSÉ
REYMAR OAK AGED RED

DO LANZAROTE

TIMANFAYA

Camino Volcán I, 16
35550 Macher-Tías
(Las Palmas de Gran Canaria)
☎: 606 323 811 - Fax: 928 510 061
bodegas_timanfaya@hotmail.com

Established: 1999
⊕ 14 ▤ 18,000 litres ☙ 1.3 has. ☛ 100 %

TIMANFAYA MALVASIA 2003 WHITE
TIMANFAYA 2000 RED
TIMANFAYA 1999 CRIANZA RED
CENIZAS DE TIMANFAYA DULCE NATURAL
2000 MOSCATEL
CENIZAS DE TIMANFAYA MOSCATEL VINO
DE LICOR
CENIZAS DE TIMANFAYA NATURAL MOSCATEL

TINACHE

La Vegueta, 73
35560 Tinajo (Lanzarote)
☎: 928 840 849 - Fax: 928 840 849
bodegas@tinache.net - tinache.net

Established: 1975
⊕ 200 ▤ 230000 litres ☙ 20 has.
☛ 90% ☘10%

TINACHE MALVASÍA SECO WHITE
TINACHE MOSCATEL SECO WHITE
TINACHE MOSCATEL DULCE WHITE
TINACHE F. BARRICA ROSE
TINACHE ROSÉ

VEGA DE YUCO

La Vegueta, 127
35560 Tinajo (Lanzarote)
☎: 928 812 925 - Fax: 928 812 925

Established: 1997
▤ 100,000 litres ☛ 100%

PRINCESA ICO SEMIDULCE WHITE
VEGA DE YUCO WHITE
VEGA DE YUCO ROSÉ
VEGA DE YUCO RED

DO MÁLAGA and DO SIERRAS DE MÁLAGA

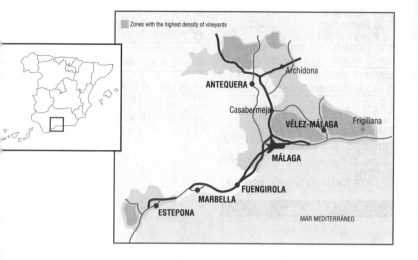

Zones with the highest density of vineyards

Archidona
ANTEQUERA
Casabermeja
VÉLEZ-MÁLAGA   Frigiliana
MÁLAGA
FUENGIROLA
MARBELLA
ESTEPONA   MAR MEDITERRÁNEO

NEWS. The Regulatory Council of the DOs of Málaga and Sierras de Málaga, a common body governing both, has carried out exemplary work over the past few years, managing to strike the difficult balance between protecting the traditional production methods and including new high quality products (whites, reds and dry rosés) by promoting new regions with extraordinary potential, such as the Zona Norte and the vineyards of Ronda. As a result of this policy, somewhere between visionary and real, it hopes to double the number of registered bodegas by 2006. With respect to the 2003 harvest, the heatwave at the beginning of August resulted in significant losses, to a greater degree in Axarquía and the Zona Norte and less significant on the Costa Occidental.

Hectares of Vineyard	No. of Viticulturists	No. of Bodegas	2003 Harvest	2003 Production	Marketing
1,172,6	427	14	Very Good	5,000,000 litres	63% Spain 37% foreign

Amongst the new generation of dry wines, the barrel-fermented Chardonnay produced by Federico Schatz in Ronda with organic crops stands out, along with the excellent profile that Juan Manuel Vetas, also from the mountainous vineyards, is drawing from the two Cabernets (the *Sauvignon* and the *Franc*). And on the topic of top quality foreign varieties: the red Gadea of Tierras de Mollina, a single-variety *Syrah*, has soon after its release reached a score of 84 points, with outstanding fruity notes and quite remarkable Terruño notes, hitherto unthinkable at such southerly latitudes. Regarding the sweet wines, the *Moscatel* has by far outscored the *Pedro Ximénez*, which with the Don Juan of López Hermanos alone stands amongst the very best with 90 points.

LOCATION. In the province of Málaga. It covers 54 municipal areas along the coast (in the vicinity of Málaga and Estepona) and inland (along the banks of the river

Genil), together with the new sub-region of Serranía de Ronda, a region to which the two new municipal districts of Cuevas del Becerro and Cortes de la Frontera have been added. It incorporates the *Colombard* (white) and the *Petit Verdot* (red), (...).

CLIMATE. Varies depending on the production area. In the northern region, the summers are short with high temperatures, and the average rainfall is in the range of 500 mm; in the region of Axarquía, protected from the northerly winds by the mountain ranges and facing south, the climate is somewhat milder due to the influence of the Mediterranean; whilst in the west, the climate can be defined as dry subhumid.

SOIL. It varies from red Mediterranean soil with limestone components in the northern region to decomposing slate on steep slopes of the Axarquía.

VARIETIES:
White: DO Málaga: *Pedro Ximénez* and *Moscatel*; DO Sierras de Málaga: *Chardonnay, Moscatel, Pedro Ximénez, Macabeo* and *Sauvignon Blanc, Colombard.*
Red (only DO Sierras de Málaga)**:** *Romé, Cabernet Sauvignon, Merlot, Syrah, Tempranillo, Petit Verdot.*

REGULATORY COUNCIL.
Fernando Camino, 2, 3° 3. 29016 Málaga.
Tel: 952 228 493. Fax: 952 227 990.
E-mail: info@vinomalaga.com   Website: www.vinomalaga.com

GENERAL CHARACTERISTICS OF THE WINES:

Traditional Wines	Their personality is marked by the grape syrup, the must that is concentrated or dehydrated by the heat that caramelises the wine and gives it its characteristic colour, sweetness and mellowness. There is a distinction between the 'Málaga', a sweet wine produced from the first must of the grape, the Pedro Ximénez and the Moscatel, which are produced from the grapes of the same name.
Modern Wines	Produced from autochthonous and foreign varieties, they are marked by the heat of the climate, especially in the case of the red wines, which are very sunny with 'scorched' notes. The new natural sweet whites offer pleasant soft, mellow aromas and are very fresh on the palate, and sweet at the same time.

TYPOLOGY OF CLASSIC WINES:
Liqueur wines: from 15 to 22% vol.
Natural sweet wines: from 15 to 22 % vol. obtained from the *Moscatel* or *Pedro Ximénez* varieties, from musts with a minimum sugar content of 244 grams/litre.
Naturally sweet wines (with the same varieties, over 13% vol. and from musts with 300 grams of sugar/litre) and still wines (from 10 to 15% vol.).
Depending on their ageing:
Málaga Joven: Unaged still wines.
Málaga Pálido: Unaged non-still wines.
Málaga: Wines aged for between 6 and 24 months.
Málaga Noble: Wines aged for between 2 and 3 years.
Málaga Añejo: Wines aged for between 3 and 5 years.
Málaga Trasañejo: Wines aged for over 5 years.

A. MUÑOZ CABRERA

San Bartolomé, 5
29738 Moclinejo (Málaga)
☎: 952 400 594 - Fax: 952 400 743
dimobe@terra.es

Established: 1927

⊞ 70 ▤ 146.000 litres

🌿 2 has. 🍷 100%

VALMOCLIN DULCE
moscatel

75 Slightly peaty amber. Aroma of raisins in syrup, viscous. Light and with not much glycerin on the palate; easy drinking with raisiny aroma in the retronasal passage.

SEÑORÍO DE BROCHES MOSCATEL DULCE NATURAL
moscatel

80 Straw-coloured with a golden hue. Musky aroma with honeyed notes and orange peel. Unctuous, sweet (almost pasty) palate, musky, apricots.

ZUMBRAL MOSCATEL
EL LAGAR DE CABRERA 2003 MOSCATEL SECO

ANTIGUA CASA DE GUARDIA

Carretera Olias-Comares, s/n.
Finca El Romerillo
29197 Bda. de Olías (Málaga)
☎: 952 030 714 - Fax: 952 252 150
antiguacasadeguardia@wanadoo.es

Established: 1840

⊞ 230 ▤ 10,000 litres

🌿 15 has. 🍷 100%

GUARDIA MOSCATEL DULCE

78 Mahogany. Viscous aroma with toasted raisins, without fruit expression and slightly dominated by the oak. Sweet, fresh palate with flavourful fruit and good balance, better in the mouth.

GUINDA MOSCATEL DULCE

75 Light mahogany. Pungent aroma of varnish with notes of oak over the fruit liqueur. Sweet, flavourful palate without freshness with notes of sour cherry in the finish.

PAJARETE 1908 PEDRO XIMÉNEZ DULCE

80 Mahogany. Aroma of Muscatel, toasty crianza and a nuance of raisins. Sweet, and flavourful on the palate with notes of oak over the fruit and a fresh, spicy finish.

VERDIALES CREAM PEDRO XIMÉNEZ SEMI-DULCE

82 Dark amber. Aroma with notes of cedar, spices and varnish. Fresh, and flavourful on the palate with notes of crianza over the fruit, hints of pâtisserie and nuts.

PEDRO XIMEN 1908 PEDRO XIMÉNEZ

78 Old gold. Toasty aroma with notes of toasty almonds and white chocolate. Unctuous, very sweet palate, evoking crianza (vanilla) with a suggestion of toasty raisins.

VERDIALES SECO PEDRO XIMÉNEZ

78 Old gold with a mahogany glint. Fine pâtisserie aroma with a suggestion of orange and carpentry. Sweet, fresh palate with toasty notes, without great nuances.

VERDIALES CREAM PEDRO XIMÉNEZ SEMI-DULCE

F. SCHATZ

Finca Sanguijuela s/n.
Apdo. Correos 131
29400 Ronda (Málaga)
☎: 952 871 313 - Fax: 952 161 825
bodega@f-schatz.com
www.f-schatz.com

Established: 1982

⊞ 50 ▤ 20,000 litres 🌿 3 has.

🍷 70% 🍇30%

SCHATZ CHARDONNAY 2002 FERMENTADO EN BARRICA WHITE
100% chardonnay

86 Golden yellow. Intense aroma with excellent varietal expression (ripe apples, fragrant herbs), creamy oak notes and hints of wax. Flavourful on the palate with ripe fruit, fine smoky flavours and a slightly oily texture, well-balanced.

FINCA SANGUIJUELA PINOT-NOIR 2001 CRIANZA RED
100% pinot noir   ⊞ 12

76 Cherry with a brick red edge. Medium-intensity aroma of light raisiny fruit and a balsamic nuance. Light on the palate with the weight of the wood concealing the fruit; a well-mannered ensemble.

FINCA SANGUIJUELA PETIT-VERDOT 2001 CRIANZA RED
100% petit verdot   ⊞ 12

80 Garnet red cherry. Intense aroma marked menthol (eucalyptus); curious. Fresh, flavourful on the palate with ripe fruit and balsamic notes well-integrated with the wood.

GOMARA

Lima, 6 Polígono Industrial El Viso
29006 Málaga (Málaga)

☎: 952 342 075 - Fax: 952 360 011
bodegas@gomara.com
www.gomara.com

Established: 1994

🍷 85% ♦15%: -US -FR -IT -CZ -JP -BE -CH -FI -KR -DE -PH -CA -AT -NL

GOMARA TRASAÑEJO MÁLAGA
100% pedro ximénez

80 Mahogany. Spicy aroma with notes of Solera and a hint of crianza reduction. Flavourful, fresh palate with nutty notes and citrus fruit overtones.

GOMARA AÑEJO SECO
100% pedro ximénez

78 Old gold. Intense aroma of carpentry, nuts and Solera. Dry, flavourful palate with a sweet almond nuance and a crianza finish, long.

MALAGA CREAM GOMARA SEMI-DULCE
95% pedro ximénez, 5% moscatel

80 Old gold. Creamy aroma with notes of vanilla and orange peel (Muscatel). Sweet fresh palate (citrus fruit) and a suggestion of almonds, simple.

PAJARETE SEMI-DULCE
100% pedro ximénez

86 Intense amber with a greenish hue. Intense aroma with good crianza expression (aged wood, varnish) and a slightly smoky hint, spicy and varietal. Dry palate with mildly sweet hints, slightly unctuous with hints of pastries, nuts and balsamic herbs.

MÁLAGA DULCE GOMARA
90% pedro ximénez, 10% moscatel

85 Intense mahogany. Powerful aroma with predominant toasty and creamy oak notes, and a suggestion of dried fruit. Flavourful, unctuous palate with dried notes and a suggestion of the spicy freshness of skins and dates, very pleasant.

GRAN GOMARA DULCE
70% pedro ximénez, 30% moscatel

85 Old gold with a mahogany hue. Powerful aroma with acetaldehyde notes over a creamy suggestion of oak and dried fruit. Flavourful, sweet palate, with a fine bitter suggestion and fig bread, quite unctuous and pleasant.

LACRIMAE CHRISTI GOMARA DULCE
GOMARA FINO
MÁLAGA MOSCATEL
MÁLAGA PEDRO XIMÉNEZ

JUAN MANUEL VETAS MARTÍN

Camino Nador. Finca El Baco
29350 Arriate (Málaga)
☎: 952 870 539 - Fax: 952 870 539
elbacoarriate@hotmail.com

Established: 2000

🍶 12 📦 9,000 litres 🌿 1 has.

VETAS PETIT VERDOT CRIANZARED
100% petit verdot

83 Very deep cherry with a garnet red edge. Powerful aroma with predominant notes of ripeness and fine reduction and very varietal herbaceous hints. Fleshy, flavourful palate slightly marked yet promising tannins, powerful retronasal effect (liquorice, toasty flavours, prunes).

VETAS SELECCIÓN RED
40% cabernet sauvignon, 40% cabernet franc, 20% otras

85 Very deep cherry. Powerful aroma with toasty notes of oak, a nuance of black fruit, balsamic flavours and fine terroir. Flavourful, fleshy, concentrated palate with well-integrated oak and fruit. Notes of liquorice and minerals in the retronasal passage.

LARIOS PERNOD RICARD

César Vallejos, 24 Polígono Industrial Gaudalhorce
29004 Málaga (Málaga)
☎: 952 247 056 - Fax: 952 240 382
asantana@prlarios.es

Established: 1875

🍶 2,000 📦 3,000,000 litres 🍷 20% ♦80%

MÁLAGA LARIOS ROBLE DULCE
90% pedro ximénez, 10% moscatel

80 Mahogany with an amber edge. Slightly short, toasty aroma of vanilla with a hint of carpentry. Flavourful palate with good freshness and sweet almondy notes, slightly viscous.

LÓPEZ GARCÍA

Cisne, 14 - 18
29009 Málaga (Málaga)
☎: 952 306 593 - Fax: 952 306 593
bodlopga@teleline.es

MÁLAGA CREAM OLOROSO DULCE
MÁLAGA EMBRUJO ESPECIAL DULCE

LÓPEZ HERMANOS

Canadá 10 - Pol. Ind. . El Viso
29006 Málaga (Málaga)
☎: 952 319 454 - Fax: 952 359 819
bodegas@lopezhermanos.com
www.lopezhermanos.com

Established: 1885

🍶 6,000 📦 3,000,000 litres 🌿 250 has.

🍷 75% ♦25%: -UE AMÉRICA

BARÓN DE RIVERO 2003 WHITE
70% moscatel, 30% chardonnay

80 Straw-coloured with a greenish hue. Aroma of fruity grapes, ripe character, and a herby suggestion. Flavourful, fresh, lively palate of green fruit.

MOSCATEL NARANJA WHITE
100% moscatel

82 Golden straw. Intense, fresh aroma of orange peel, sweet tangerines and a herbaceous suggestion. Sweet, light palate, easy drinking with agreeable herby notes and a tangerine finish; very pleasant.

PICO PLATA MOSCATEL DULCE
100% moscatel

80 Mahogany. Toasty aroma with notes of cocoa, cedar and a suggestion of varnish. Sweet and quite heavy on the palate, without great freshness; with notes of cocoa and raisins in the retronasal passage.

SOL DE MÁLAGA DULCE DE LICOR
50% moscatel, 50% pedro ximénez

83 Mahogany. Aroma of toasty grapes with notes of Solera (orange peel), and Muscatel. Sweet, flavourful palate with fruity fresh overtones, spicy and pleasant.

DON SALVADOR MOSCATEL DULCE DE LICOR
100% moscatel

90 Pitch black. Toasty aroma of raisins and dates. Sweet palate with jammy raisins and dates and a suggestion of Muscatel, toasty, concentrated, full and powerful palate, a typical classic.

IBERIA MOSCATEL DULCE DE LICOR
100% moscatel de Alejandría

85 Old amber. Fresh aroma of peaches, clean grapes and well-integrated toasty notes (toffee, vanilla). Flavourful palate, sweet yet fresh with fruity notes and suggestions of orange and cream in the finish.

DON JUAN PEDRO XIMÉNEZ DULCE DE LICOR
100% pedro ximénez

90 Very dark mahogany. Toasty aroma with notes of Solera, chocolate and jammy dates with hints of varnish. Sweet, toasty palate with an almondy sensation (slightly saline) and citrus fruit notes (orange peel), very fresh.

CHORRERA CREAM AÑEJO 1998 OLOROSO DULCE
100% pedro ximenez

86 Mahogany with an orange rim. Toasty aroma of oven-roasted nuts and a suggestion of varnish. Sweet palate with pleasantly bitter hints, raisiny undertones and an almondy finish.

TRAJINERO 1998 OLOROSO SECO
100% pedro ximénez

83 Brilliant amber. Saline aroma of vanilla and orange peel with a suggestion of sweet Solera. Flavourful, fresh palate with bitter almond nuances and a citrus edge.

SECO TRASAÑEJO 1998 VINO DE LICOR
100% pedro ximénez

88 Reddish Mahogany. Pungent, dry aroma of hazelnuts, toasty. Dry, bitter and old with aldehyde on the palate.

MÁLAGA VIRGEN 2000 DULCE DE LICOR
100% pedro ximénez

80 Mahogany. Vanilla aroma with notes of cedar, liquorice and marked toasty hints. Flavourful, very sweet palate lacking freshness, with notes of raisins and coffee in the finish.

RESERVA DE FAMILIA 2000 PEDRO XIMÉNEZ DULCE DE LICOR
100% pedro ximenez

81 Mahogany with an orange edge. Toasty aroma slightly saline with notes of old Solera and a suggestion of spices. Sweet palate with quite heavy dried fruit weight, notions of chocolate and a generous finish.

RESERVA DE FAMILIA 2000 MOSCATEL DULCE DE LICOR
100% muscat de Alejandria

89 Reddish amber. Fine Muscatel aroma of ripe berries, toasty with creamy vanilla. Sweet, unctuous, very sweet, full, and flavourful palate, persistent, excellent and fine Muscatel.

TRES LEONES 2002 MOSCATEL DULCE
100% moscatel

89 Brilliant gold with a coppery hue. Intense, very varietal aroma (musk, quince, flowers, fine herbs, a grapey freshness of skins). Powerful, flavourful palate with fine bittersweet notes, a hint of the freshness of citrus fruits. and good acidity.

CARTOJAL 2003 PALE CREAM
100% moscatel

82 Straw-coloured. Herbaceous aroma of acidic fruit pulp (papaya) and a suggestion of damp earth. Sweet, and flavourful on the palate with good freshness, fruity, a pleasantly bitter finish.

KINA SAN CLEMENTE

LÓPEZ-MADRID

Avenida José Ortega y Gasset, km. 7, 5
29196 El Tajaral (Málaga)
☎: 952 433 189 - Fax: 952 437 647
lopezmadrid@eresmas.com
www.lopezmadrid.com
Established: 1946

🍾 130 🛢 100,000 litres 🍇 2 has.
🍷 90% 🌍10%: -NL -DE

DEL ABUELO DULCE
70% pedro ximénez, 30% moscatel

83 Mahogany with a yellow edge. Toasty aroma with dark-roasted flavours, an expression of raisins and some suggestion of Solera reduction. Flavourful palate of Muscatel with good harmony of between sweetness-acidity, chocolate notions and slightly sweet finish.

ZAR 1997 TRASAÑEJO MÁLAGA DULCE
70% pedro ximénez, 30% moscatel

85 Dark mahogany. Aroma with vanilla notes, figs and casks (coffee). Sweet, long palate with long-lasting freshness, pleasantly bitter notes in the finish, generous.

MAESTRO 2003 MOSCATEL DULCE
100% moscatel

78 Straw-coloured with a golden edge. Floral aroma with notes of exotic fruit and a suggestion of honey. Sweet palate without Muscatel nuances, a fresh sensation.

SOLIVIÑA 2003 WHITE
PEDRO XIMEN 2001 MÁLAGA

Bodegas QUITAPENAS

Avenida Juan Sebastian Elcano, 149
29017 Málaga ()
☎: 952 290 129 - Fax: 952 290 016
ventas@bodegas-quitapenas.com
www.bodegasquitapenas.com
Established: 1880

🍾 360 🛢 435,000 litres 🍷 60%
🌍40%: -FR -US -PL -PA

MONTES DE MÁLAGA PAJARETE CREAM
100% pedro ximénez

82 Clear mahogany with an iodised edge. Aroma of Mistelle with notes of peaches in syrup, toasted nuts and Catalonian cream custard. Flavourful palate with bitter almond overtones, round and fresh.

VEGASOL 2003 WHITE SECO
moscatel

78 Pale. Intense, slightly fruity and varietal aroma (musk) with overtones of spicy freshness and minerals. Dry, flavourful palate with bitter notes, herbs and marked citrus acidity.

MÁLAGA VIÑA 2003 OAK AGED DULCE
70% Pedro Ximénez, 30% Moscatel

78 Mahogany. Viscous aroma, toasty grapes and hints of oven-baked pâtisserie. Flavourful, fresh palate with notes of toast and ripe dates in the finish.

MÁLAGA VIEJO ABUELO 10 AÑOS 1990 TRASAÑEJO DULCE
90% pedro ximénez, 10% Moscatel

85 Mahogany with an iodised rim. Concentrated aroma of dark-roasted flavours, raisins and spices with a spicy and toasty suggestion. Sweet on the palate with vanilla, almost syrupy with sensations of toasty grapes and chocolate.

MÁLAGA PX OLD SWEET 2000
100% pedro ximénez

80 Old amber Viscous, marmelade aroma with notes of Solera and dried wheat. Sweet and light but without great freshness on the palate, with crystallised fruit, long.

QUITAPENAS MÁLAGA 2001 DULCE
30% moscatel, 70% pedro ximénez

78 Dark mahogany. Dark-roasted flavour, very toasty aroma with marked oak notes (varnish). Sweet palate with coffee, smoky hints, and freshness without great grape nuances.

QUITAPENAS DORADO 2003 MOSCATEL DULCE
100% moscatel

77 Old gold. Aroma of very ripe toasty grapes with notes of orange peel and spices. Unctuous, very sweet palate, quite heavy with lemony finish.

DOMARE 2002 CRIANZA RED
JUNKITO 2003 JOVEN PALE CREAM DULCE
MÁLAGA ORO VIEJO TRASAÑEJO 1997
OAK AGED DULCE TRASAÑEJO

R. Y F. ANGULO VARONA

Poeta Rilque, 21
29400 Ronda (Málaga)
☎: 609 642 555 - Fax: 952 870 086

SIERRA HIDALGA JOVEN RED

80 Dark garnet red cherry. Intense, fruity aroma with fine spicy and toasty skin notes, suggestion of dry earth. Fleshy palate with slightly marked flavourful tannins, slightly warm and oily with good fruit weight and excellent acidity.

Compañía de Vinos de
TELMO RODRIGUEZ

Siete Infantes de Lara, 5 Oficina 1
26006 Logroño (La Rioja)
☎: 941 511 128 - Fax: 941 511 131
cia@fer.es

MR 2003 JOVEN WHITE DULCE
100% moscatel

89 Straw-coloured with a greenish glimmer. Powerful, grapey, musky aroma with hints of herbs and flowers. Sweet, unctuous, very sweet palate with a rich hint of minerals, elegant, flavourful, persistent and very fruity.

MOLINO REAL 2002 WHITE DULCE
100% moscatel

90 Straw-coloured with a golden glimmer. Elegant aroma with hints of honey, fresh and slightly less complex than previous years. Sweet, flavourful, fresh and grapey palate.

TIERRAS DE MOLLINA

Avenida de las Américas, s/n Cortijo Colarte
29532 Mollina (Málaga)
☎: 952 741 052 - Fax: 952 741 053
tierrademollina@tierrasdemollina.net
www.tierrasdemollina.net

Established: 1993

🛢 504 ☘ 97 has.

MONTESPEJO 2003 JOVEN WHITE
doradilla, moscatel

79 Pale yellow. Intense aroma of ripe white fruit with hints of apricot skin, crystallised fruit and flowers. Fresh, flavourful and fruity on the palate with fine spicy notes of skins and excellent acidity.

GADEA 2003 JOVEN RED
100% syrah

84 Dark cherry with a violet edge. Powerful aroma with a good varietal expression (black fruit, petals, skins) and a suggestion of dry earth. Fleshy palate with rough, sweet tannins, an excellent structure, hints of liquorice and good acidity.

CARPE DIEM DULCE NATURAL WHITE
100% pedro ximenez

80 Straw-coloured with a golden edge. Floral aroma with notes of stewed white fruit (pears) and a suggestion of ripeness. Flavourful, sweet palate with well-balanced acidity and a mild suggestion of Muscatel.

CARPE DIEM TRASAÑEJO MÁLAGA DULCE
100% pedro ximénez

80 Mahogany with an iodised edge. Intense dark-roasted aroma with toasty hints and chocolate. Fleshy, sweet palate with a harmonious bitterness and a caramel finish.

MONTELOBO JOVEN WHITE
CARPE DIEM AÑEJO MÁLAGA DULCE

DO MANCHUELA

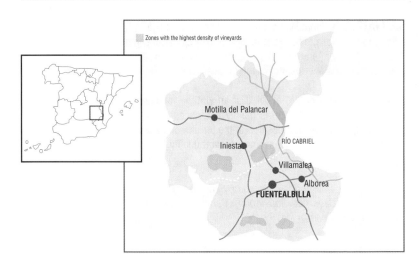

Zones with the highest density of vineyards

Motilla del Palancar

Iniesta

RÍO CABRIEL

Villamalea

Alborea

FUENTEALBILLA

NEWS. As with the rest of the DOs of Castilla-La Mancha, Manchuela has, since its creation in 2000, been committed to the restructuring of its vineyards and grape varieties (Castilla-La Mancha is beneficiary of approximately half of the funds awarded to Spain by the European Union for this kind of plan). This explains the significant increase in the number of hectares of vineyards (over 400 Ha in the past year) and winegrowers (over 100).

Hectares of Vineyard	No. of Viticulturists	No. of Bodegas	2003 Harvest	2003 Production	Marketing
4,105	1,108	34	-	-	95% Spain 5% foreign

As far as quality is concerned, and together with the exceptional performance over the past two years of the wines of Finca Sandoval (with its brands Finca Sandoval and Salia), practically all the wines tasted are comfortably situated around 80 points, with a good defence of the varietal values of the *Cencibel* or *Tempranillo* (the Realce of the Unión Campesina Iniestense is quite impressive at € 1.5), the *Bobal* (the Azúa at € 1.70 and the Azúa Selección from old vines at € 3.20, both of which scored close to 85 points, are extraordinary) and, to a lesser extent, the *Cabernet Sauvignon*. The whites of the region have not yet managed to cause much impression, although of the 7 wines tasted, single-variety wines based on the *Macabeo* or blended with the less expressive *Albillo*, reached scores ranging between 75 and 80 points, with no trace of defects, of course, and even at times displaying some complexity. And all this always below the symbolic price of € 2.00.

LOCATION. The production area covers the territory situated in the southeast of the province of Cuenca and the northeast of Albacete, between the rivers Júcar and

Cabriel. It comprises 70 municipal districts, 26 of which are in Albacete and the rest in Cuenca.

CLIMATE. The climate is continental in nature, with cold winters and hot summers, although the cool and humid winds from the Mediterranean during the summer help to lower the temperatures at night, so creating favourable day-night temperature contrasts for a slow ripening of the grapes.

SOIL. The vineyards are situated at an altitude ranging between 600 and 700 m above sea level. The terrain is mainly flat, except for the ravines outlined by the rivers. Regarding the composition of the terrain, below a clayey surface of gravel or sand, the soil is limy, which is an important quality factor for the region.

VARIETIES:
White: *Albillo, Chardonnay, Macabeo, Sauvignon Blanc, Verdejo.*
Red: *Bobal, Cabernet Sauvignon, Cencibel (Tempranillo), Garnacha, Merlot, Monastrell, Moravia Dulce, Syrah.*

REGULATORY COUNCIL.
Matadero, 5. 02260 Fuentealbilla (Albacete).
Tel: 967 477 535. Fax: 967 477 505.
E-mail: domanchuela@wanadoo.es.

GENERAL CHARACTERISTICS OF THE WINES:

Whites	Normally produced from *Macabeo*, they have a straw yellow colour, apple fruity aromas, and are pleasant and easy drinking.
Rosés	These have a raspberry colour; the *Bobal* variety gives intense fruity aromas to raspberry, and on occasion hints of herbs; on the palate they are flavourful, fresh and balanced.
Reds	Cherry-coloured, they are very similar to the wines from La Mancha, with notes of blackberries and, on occasions, with an earthy background; they are supple, flavourful and warm on the palate. Those produced from *Bobal* have a better defined fruity expression (blackberry) and are very flavourful.

DO MANCHUELA

ADEGAS VINSA

Infesta, 96
15319 Betanzos (A Coruña)
☎: 981 776 453 - Fax: 981 771 211
export@adegasvinsa.com
www. adegasvinsa.com

Established: 1958
100 ▤ 10,500,000 litres 🌿 5 has.
🍷 32% 🍇68%

CASTILLO COLINA RED

Vinos CAMBRONERO

Extramuros, s/n
02260 Fuentealbilla (Albacete)
☎: 967 472 503 - Fax: 967 472 516
info@franchete.com
ww.wfranchete.com

Established: 1983
▤ 1,200,000 litres 🌿 65 has.
🍷 70% 🍇30%: -PT -US

FRANCHETE 2002 RED
tempranillo

74 Cherry with a brick red hue. Short aroma of slightly overripe fruit. Warm, round palate fruitier than in the nose.

FRANCHETE 2000 OAK AGED RED
cabernet sauvignon

72 Garnet red cherry with a saffron edge. Intense aroma with a not very fine suggestion of reduction. Quite flavourful palate with poor crianza expression and an acidic edge.

FRANCHETE 2003 WHITE
FRANCHETE 2003 OAK AGED RED
FRANCHETE ROSÉ

Cooperativa CEREAL-VINÍCOLA NTRA. SEÑORA DE LA CABEZA

Carretera Villamalea, 32
02200 Casas Ibáñez (Albacete)
☎: 967 460 105 - Fax: 967 460 266
info@coop-cabeza.com
www.coop-cabeza.com

Established: 1946
240 ▤ 15,000,000 litres 🌿 2,140 has.
🍷 70% 🍇30%: -PT -IT -FR

VIARIL 2003 WHITE
100% macabeo

79 Straw-coloured. Intense aroma with fruit, white flowers and exotic nuances. Flavourful, slightly warm palate with fine bitter notes and hints of herbs.

VIARIL 2003 RED
100% cencibel

77 Dark cherry with a violet hue. Intense, fruity aroma with hints of skins and notions of terroir. Flavourful palate with slightly marked tannins (overextraction).

VIARIL 2001 CRIANZA RED
70% cabernet sauvignon, 30% bobal

80 Cherry with a strawberry rim. Aroma of cocoa, toasty wood, ripe red fruit and strawberry syrup. Slightly drying tannins on the palate, well-balanced with a suggestion of sweet and toasty flavours in the retronasal passage.

VIARIL 2000 RESERVA RED
70% cencibel, 20% cabernet sauvignon, 10% bobal

79 Not very deep Bigarreau cherry. Aroma with reduction notes, leathers, toasty wood and a hint of nuts. Light yet fresh palate with a suggestion of wood in the retronasal passage.

VIARIL 2003 ROSÉ
CHOZO BLANCO 2003 JOVEN RED

Cooperativa del Campo DULCE NOMBRE DE JESÚS

Niño Jesús, 25
16280 Villarta (Cuenca)
☎: 962 189 006 - Fax: 962 189 125
info@villavid.com
www.villavid.com

Established: 1952
▤ 13,000,000 litres 🌿 2,500 has.
🍷 95% 🍇5%

VILLAVID MACABEO JOVEN WHITE
100% macabeo

80 Pale gold. Powerful aroma of ripe white fruit with hints of flowers, dried grass and a suggestion of perfumed soap. Flavourful, bitter palate with good acidity.

VILLAVID 2003 JOVEN ROSÉ
100% boba

80 Lively blush. Intense, fresh, quite fruity aroma with spicy, sweetish hints. Flavourful palate with very varietal fine bitter notes, pleasant.

VILLAVID TEMPRANILLO 2002 JOVEN RED
100% tempranillo

82 Intense brilliant cherry. Intense aroma of jammy red fruit, with hints of flowers and sweet liquorice. Fleshy, bitter palate (earthiness) with round, fresh tannins and good freshness.

FINCA SANDOVAL

CM-3222, km. 26, 800
Ledaña (Cuenca)
☎: 616 444 805 - Fax: 915 864 848
consulto@terra.es

Established: 2001

⊕ 170 🔟 80,000 litres 🍇 11 has.
🍷 30% 🌐70%

FINCA SANDOVAL 2002 RED
91% syrah, 9% monastrell

94 Very intense cherry. Aroma of ripe berry skins but with fresh hints of controlled ripening, very well-enveloped by the fine toasty oak and a light mineral nuance. Fleshy palate, dry and marked but ripe tannins, excellent wood combination with the wood; a good expression of a non-fruit concentrate Mediterranean red.

SALIA 2002 RED
55% syrah , 45% monastrell

89 Quite intense cherry. Aroma with notes of ripe forest fruit with a light, earthy nuance of Monastrell, and toasty, creamy oak. Fruity palate, brambles in the retronasal passage. Good Monastrell acidity, fine hints of creamy wood.

Sociedad Cooperativa Agraria
INMACULADA CONCEPCIÓN

Carretera Campillo, s/n
16200 Motilla del Palancar (Cuenca)
☎: 969 331 071 - Fax: 969 331 680
coopmotilla.3064@cajarural.com

Established: 1952

🔟 6,000,000 litres 🍇 1,100 has.
🍷 70% 🌐30%

ROBLE ALTO RED
100% cencibel

75 Dark cherry with a garnet red edge. Slightly intense, fruity aroma with toasty notes of skins. Flavourful palate with hints of overripening.

Cooperativa del Campo
SAN ANTONIO ABAD

Valencia, 41
02270 Villamalea (Albacete)
☎: 967 483 023 - Fax: 967 483 536
antoniabad@ucaman.es
lamanchuela.net/sanantoni

Established: 1947

⊕ 500 🔟 25,000,000 litres 🍇 4,500 has.
🍷 80% 🌐20%: -UK -DE -BE -NL

ALTOS DEL CABRIEL 2002 WHITE
100% macabeo

79 Pale with greenish nuances. Fresh, fruity aroma (green apples) with hints of citrus fruit and herbs. Fresh, fruity palate with good citrus acidity.

MARICUBAS WHITE
100% macabeo

77 Pale gold. Intense, fruity aroma with smoky notes and a spicy slightly varietal hint. Flavourful palate with smoky notes, dried grass and fruit slightly subdued by the alcohol.

ALTOS DEL CABRIEL 2003 ROSÉ
100% bobal

78 Lively raspberry. Intense aroma of red fruit with smoky hints of skins and a suggestion of sweetness. Flavourful, fresh palate with sweetish fruit and good acidity.

ALTOS DEL CABRIEL 2002 RED
100% cencibel

78 Garnet red cherry with a violet hue. Intense aroma with predominant reduction notes (not very fine animal hints). Better on the palate, flavourful, fruity with good acidity.

MARICUBAS CENCIBEL CRIANZA RED
tempranillo

75 Cherry with an orangey hue. Ripe aroma (dried peaches, cherry liqueur) with a toasty hint. Round, supple palate with drying wood tannins.

VIÑAMALEA 2001 CRIANZA RED
100% cencibel

78 Dark garnet red cherry. Intense aroma with predominant toasty oak notes and a nuance of somewhat varietal ripe fruit. Flavourful palate with slightly marked tannins, drying notes and a suggestion of jammy fruit, spices and liquorice.

Sociedad Cooperativa
SAN GREGORIO MAGNO

Carretera de Ledaña, s/n
02246 Navas de Jorquera (Albacete)
☎: 967 482 134 - Fax: 967 482 134
sangregorio@amialbacete.com

Established: 1958

⊕ 30 🔟 5,000,000 litres

MONTE MIRÓN CENCIBEL 2001 RED
tempranillo

74 Garnet red cherry. Medium-intensity aroma of ripe fruit, slightly rustic. A touch of flavour on the palate with ripe fruit and old wood.

MONTE MIRÓN CENCIBEL 2000 CRIANZA RED
cencibel

74 Not very intense cherry. Not very clear, slightly rustic aroma with an earthy hint. Slightly marked tannins on the palate, drying, not a very clean retronasal effect.

Cooperativa del Campo SAN ISIDRO

Extramuros, s/n
02215 Alborea (Albacete)
☎: 967 477 067 - Fax: 967 477 096
Established: 1959
▦ 120 ▤ 4,500,000 litres ※ 920 has.
☗ 99% ◔1%: -UK -BE

ALTERÓN 2003 F. BARRICA WHITE
100% macabeo

75 Pale with a golden hue. Powerful aroma with predominant smoky oak notes and hints of aniseed. Flavourful, bitter palate with slightly fresh oak and fruit slightly subdued by the alcohol.

ALTERÓN ROSÉ
100% bobal

79 Deep raspberry. Slightly intense, fruity aroma with hints of petals. Flavourful palate of red fruit with a very varietal hint and good acidity.

ALTERÓN 2000 RESERVA RED
100% bobal

82 Deep cherry. Aroma of black fruit with light smoky hints and fine spices. Round, fresh palate with slightly drying wood tannins; an earthy finish.

ALTERÓN 2001 RED

Cooperativa Agraria SAN ISIDRO

Virgen, 15
16220 Quintanar del Rey (Cuenca)
☎: 967 496 313 - Fax: 967 495 048

ZAÍNO 2003 RED
cencibel

80 Dark cherry. Powerful aroma of black fruit with sweet hints, toasty skins and a nuance of damp earth. Powerful, fruity, varietal and slightly warm on the palate.

Sociedad Cooperativa Agraria SANTA MARÍA MAGDALENA

Real, 5
16250 Castillejo de Iniesta (Cuenca)
☎: 962 187 508 - Fax: 962 187 508

PERCHEL JOVEN ROSÉ

Cooperativa UNIÓN CAMPESINA INIESTENSE

San Idefonso, 1
16235 Iniesta (Cuenca)
☎: 967 490 120 - Fax: 967 490 777
comercial@cooperativauci.com
Established: 1944
▦ 800 ▤ 54,000,000 litres
※ 7,000 has. ☗ 70%
◔30%: -FR -IT -PT -DE -BE -US -NL -AT

REALCE 2003 JOVEN WHITE
100% viura

79 Greenish straw. Not very intense yet clear quite fruity aroma with a nuance of herbs. Light, slightly flavourful palate with hay and slightly warm; well-crafted.

REALCE 2003 JOVEN ROSÉ
100% bobal

79 Brilliant raspberry. Intense, fruity aroma with fine spicy and citrus fruit hints. Flavourful palate with a good fruit weight despite the alcohol (13.5%).

REALCE 2003 JOVEN RED
100% tempranillo

84 Intense cherry with a violet edge. Aroma of fresh black fruit with maceration notes, toasty skins and a certain complexity. Fleshy, very varietal palate (spicy skins) with fresh fruit tannins; long.

REALCE 2001 CRIANZA RED
100% tempranillo

80 Dark cherry with a brick red rim. Quite intense, ripe aroma with notes of slightly reduced fruit (petals, prunes) and toasty oak. Flavourful palate with slightly rough tannins, a suggestion of sweet fruit and the toasty notes of the crianza.

REALCE 2000 RESERVA RED
100% bobal

82 Garnet red cherry. Aroma of an elegant crianza (smoky, creamy flavours) over a nuance of

DO MANCHUELA

jammy plums with complex hints and ink. Fleshy palate with round and flavourful tannins and good fruit; wood integrated overall with a fresh finish.

Bodegas y Viñedos VEGA TOLOSA

Benjamín Palencia, 15
02200 Casas Ibáñez (Albacete)
☎: 967 460 804
info@vegatolosa.com
www.vegatolosa.com

Established: 1992

🏭 25 ▤ 1,120,000 litres ✿ 112 has.
🍷 20% ✪80%: -NL -DE -CH -US

VEGA TOLOSA 2003 JOVEN RED
cabernet sauvignon, syrah

80 Brilliant purplish cherry. Clear aroma of intense red fruit and liquorice hints. Fleshy, fresh and flavourful on the palate with red fruit (pulp) and a persistent finish.

MAGYAR ALLIER 2003 ROBLE RED
40% cabernet sauvignon, 40% syrah, 20% tempranillo

79 Not very deep cherry. Aroma with viscous notes and black fruit. Well-integrated tannins on the palate, flavourful with a suggestion of skins in the retronasal passage.

VINÍCOLA MANCHUELA

Beaterio, 36
02270 Villamalea (Albacete)
☎: 963 951 325 - Fax: 963 951 325
vinos@gualberto.com - gualberto.com

🏭 150 ▤ 4,000,000 litres ✿ 80 has.
🍷 95% ✪5%

GUALBERTO CRIANZA RED

Cooperativa del Campo
VIRGEN DE LAS NIEVES

Santa Ana, 8
02247 Cenizate (Albacete)
☎: 967 482 006 - Fax: 967 482 805
cooperativa@virgendelasnieves.com
www.virgendelasnieves.com

Established: 1956

🏭 125 ▤ 13,492,602 litres
🍷 70% ✪30%: -PT -FR

ARTESONES DE CENIZATE 2001 CRIANZA RED
100% cencibel

77 Deep cherry. Aroma of very ripe black fruit, warm with a fine smoky hint. Fleshy palate with round tannins and well-integrated wood and a fruity and generous bitter cocoa finish.

ARTESONES DE CENIZATE 2003 JOVEN WHITE
ARTESONES DE CENIZATE 2003 JOVEN RED

VITIVINOS ANUNCIACIÓN

Camino de Cabezuelas, s/n
02270 Villamalea (Albacete)
☎: 967 483 114 - Fax: 967 483 964
vitivinos@wanadoo.es

Established: 1969

🏭 1,000 ▤ 8,200,000 litres ✿ 1,500 has.
🍷 75% ✪25%: -DK -NL -US

AZUA 2003 JOVEN WHITE
80% albillo, 20% macabeo

77 Straw-coloured. Aroma of slightly ripe white fruit with hints of fine skins. Flavourful palate, without great nuances; good acidity, without character.

AZUA 2003 JOVEN ROSÉ
100% bobal

80 Very intense blush. Fresh, fruity aroma (strawberries), slightly sweet. Flavourful palate with good acidity and red fruit in the finish.

AZUA 2003 F. BARRICA RED
100% bobal

83 Dark cherry with raspberry on the edge. Intense aroma of blackberries and raspberries with fine balsamic and smoky notes. Fruity palate with high acidity, abundant fruit with round, oily tannins and a fruity finish (blackberries).

AZUA SELECCIÓN BOBAL VIEJO 2001 CRIANZA RED
100% bobal

82 Intense cherry. Aroma of red bramble fruit with hints of fermentation and eucalyptus. Fleshy palate with dry and slightly woody tannins and good but slightly drying fruit; fresh.

AZUA SELECCIÓN BOBAL VIEJO 2000 RED
AZUA SELECCIÓN BOBAL VIEJO 2000 CRIANZA RED
AZUA 1998 RESERVA RED

DO MÉNTRIDA

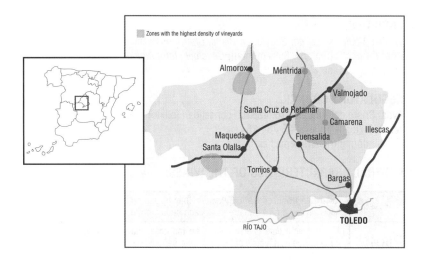

Zones with the highest density of vineyards

NEWS. Everything points to a profound change in the wine-growing attitude of the region. Together with a notable decrease in the number of hectares under cultivation (around 2,000 Ha last year), of vine growers (around 400) and bodegas (almost half), some wines have achieved exceptional scores of 90 points. What does this mean? Fundamentally, the slow but steady abandoning of the old values of cooperative farming and buying and selling in bulk, with bodegas producing high quality wines on a small scale on the verge of being incorporated into the denomination.

Nevertheless, the bulk of the points reveal that there is still a long way to go. There is a huge difference between the highflying Arrayán and the rest, and only the Vega Gitania wines accompany the notable wine of the La Verdosa estate with scores higher than 80 points. The common bodegas at least offer wines with fewer defects than in previous years, in spite of the fact that the 2003 harvest was not exceptional.

Hectares of Vineyard	No. of Viticulturists	No. of Bodegas	2003 Harvest	2003 Production	Marketing
10,385	1.800	23	-	2,452,000 litres	50% domestic 50% export

LOCATION. In the north of the province of Toledo. It borders with the provinces of Ávila and Madrid to the north, with the Tajo to the south, and with the Sierra de San Vicente to the west. It is made up of 51 municipal areas of the province of Toledo.

CLIMATE. Continental, dry and extreme, with long, cold winters and hot summers. Late frosts in spring are quite common. The average rainfall is between 300 mm and 500 mm, and is irregularly distributed throughout the year.

SOIL. The vineyards are at an altitude of between 400 m and 600 m, although some municipal districts of the Sierra de San Vicente reach an altitude of 800 m. The soil is mainly sandy-clayey, with a medium to loose texture.

VARIETIES:

White: *Albillo, Macabeo, Sauvignon Blanc, Chardonnay* and *Verdejo.*
Red: *Garnacha* (majority 85% of total), *Cencibel (Tempranillo), Cabernet Sauvignon, Merlot, Syrah* and *Petit Verdot.*

REGULATORY COUNCIL.

Avda. Cristo del Amparo, 16. 45510 Fuensalida (Toledo).
Tel: 925 785 185. Fax: 925 784 154.
E-mail: domentrida@retemail.es

GENERAL CHARACTERISTICS OF THE WINES:

Rosés	Normally produced from *Garnacha,* they have a raspberry pink colour; they have a fruity aroma and are meaty and supple on the palate.
Reds	These have a dark cherry colour; on the nose, they are noticeable for their hints of ripe fruit typical of long ripening periods; on the palate they are meaty, warm and supple.

DO MÉNTRIDA

ACEITES Y VINOS NATURALES

Paseo de la Estación, s/n
45685 Montearagón (Toledo)
☎: 925 865 041 - Fax: 925 865 167
aceites@aceitesyvinosnaturales.com

Established: 1900

🏭 450 📊 300,000 litres 🍇 60 has.

🍷 80% 🍇20%: -CH -TW

RIBERA DEL TAJO 2003 JOVEN RED
RIBERA DEL TAJO 2002 RED
VIÑA EBORA OAK AGED RED
VIÑAREN OAK AGED RED

ANGEL COLADO PAVÓN

Paseo de la Estación, s/n
45555 Montearagón (Toledo)
☎: 925 865 278 - Fax: 925 865 278

Established: 1934

🍷 100%%

ALARICHE 2003 RED

ANTONIO POVEDA MERINO

Avenida de Madrid, 22
45940 Valmojado (Toledo)
☎: 918 170 030 - Fax: 918 170 793

Established: 1947

POVEDA

Cooperativa
CONDES DE FUENSALIDA

Avenida San Crispín, 129
45510 Fuensalida (Toledo)
☎: 925 784 823 - Fax: 925 784 823
condes-fuensalida@hotmail.com
www.condesdefuensalida.iespana.es

Established: 1974

🏭 50 📊 4,000,000 litres 🍇 1.200 has.

🍷 90% 🍇10%

CONDES DE FUENSALIDA JOVEN ROSÉ

65 Strawberry. Very evolved, flat aroma, without fruit. Flat palate, without expression or fruitiness.

CONDES DE FUENSALIDA JOVEN RED

67 Dark cherry. Evolved aroma without nuances. Flat, flabby palate without nuances.

CONDES DE FUENSALIDA 2001 CRIANZA RED
60% cabernet sauvignon, 25% garnacha, 15% tempranillo

73 Garnet red cherry with a ruby red glint. Aroma with notes of woody oak that masks the fruit. Notes of ripe fruit on the palate and persistent oak in the retronasal passage.

COSECHEROS ABASTECEDORES

Avenida San Crispín, 129
45510 Fuensalida (Toledo)
☎: 913 043 240 - Fax: 913 040 713
casa@coabsa.es
www.cosecherosabastecedores.es

PALACIO DE FUENSALIDA

DELISPAIN

Fray Pedro Payo Piñeño, 17 bajo
15009 A Coruña (A Coruña)
☎: 670 522 577 - Fax: 881 924 492
delispain@delispain.com
www.delispain.com

VEGA GITANIA 2003 ROSÉ
90% garnacha, 10% tempranillo

79 Lively raspberry. Intense, fruity aroma with slightly sweet and spicy hints. Flavourful palate with fine bitter notes and marked citrus acidity.

VEGA GITANIA PREMIUM 2003 RED
60% tempranillo, 40% garnacha

83 Dark cherry with a lively violet edge. Intense, fruity aroma with herbaceous hints (nettles) and spicy skins. Fresh palate with carbonic hints, fruity with a slightly oily texture and marked and flavourful tannins, bitter.

VEGA GITANIA 2003 RED
100% garnacha

82 Lively garnet red cherry. Intense aroma of red stone fruit, with a hint of varietal freshness (spices, fallen leaves) and macerated skins. Flavourful palate with slightly marked grape tannins, bitter with a good varietal and young wine expression.

Viñedos y Bodegas EL BARRO

Camino El Lomo, s/n
45180 Camarena (Toledo)
☎: 918 174 160 - Fax: 918 174 301
elbarro@ccae.es - grandvulture.com

🏭 478 📊 375.000 litres 🍇 75 has.

🍷 65% 🍇35%

MAJAZUL TEMPRANILLO CRIANZA RED
PORTALIE SYRAH-CABERNET SAUVIGNON CRIANZA RED
PORTALIE MERLOT-TEMPRANILLO CRIANZA RED

GARVA

Topete, 72
45930 Méntrida (Toledo)
☎: 918 177 304 - Fax: 918 177 304

DANZANTE

Viñedos y Bodegas GONZÁLEZ

Real, 86
45180 Camarena (Toledo)
☎: 918 174 063 - Fax: 918 174 136
bodegasgonzalez@yahoo.es

Established: 1898

🌐 66 ▨ 1,500,000 litres

🍇 75 has. 🚩 100%

VIÑA BISPO 2002 JOVEN WHITE
VIÑA BISPO 2002 JOVEN ROSÉ
VIÑA BISPO JOVEN RED
VIÑA BISPO TEMPRANILLO 2002 JOVEN RED
VIÑA BISPO 2002 CRIANZA RED

LA CASA DE LAS CUATRO RAYAS

Finca La Verdosa
45513 Santa Cruz del Retamar (Toledo)
☎: 647 342 097 - Fax: 916 632 796
comercial@arrayan-laverdosa.com
www.arrayan-laverdosa.com

Established: 1999

🌐 206 ▨ 150,000 litres 🍇 26 has.

🚩 50% 🌐50%: -NL -DE -CH

ARRAYÁN CABERNET SAUVIGNON 2003 RED
100% cabernet sauvignon

89 Very intense cherry. Toasty aroma, ripe black fruit, jammy notes, fairly impenetrable, meaty, powerful and flavourful palate, very ripe and firm tannins, dark-roasted retronasal effect.

ARRAYÁN SYRAH 2003 RED
100% syrah

92 Very intense cherry. Quite impenetrable aroma but rich in very ripe black fruit sensations, earthy hints, minerals and toasty oak nuances. Robust and meaty palate, well-displayed tannins, very ripe fruit, dark-roasted retronasal effect.

ARRAYÁN PREMIUM 2003 RED
55% syrah, 20% merlot, 10% petit verdot, 15% cabernet sauvignon

89 Intense cherry. Intense aroma, mild notes with an earthy and very toasty essence. Powerful, meaty and flavourful palate, good expression.

ARRAYÁN MERLOT 2003 OAK AGED RED
100% merlot

87 Intense cherry. Fruity and toasty aroma, slightly reduced and vegetative, ripe fruit. Meaty palate, with vigorous, powerful and flavourful tannins.

ARRAYÁN PETIT VERDOT 2003 OAK AGED RED
100% petit verdot

93 Intense cherry. Fine and toasty aroma (cocoa, coffee, creamy vanilla), slightly mineral. Generous and full palate with a pleasant contrast between the dry but ripe tannins and the sweetness of the alcohol, persistent.

ARRAYÁN SYRAH 2002 RED
100% syrah

93 Intense cherry. Spirituous, mineral aroma (dry earth) of jammy plums with toasty hints of dark-roasted flavours and chocolate. Generous, very ripe, toasty, spirituous and warm palate with sweet tannins and very toasty and ripe flavours.

ARRAYÁN PREMIUM 2002 RED
55% syrah, 20% merlot, 10% petit verdot, 15% cabernet sauvignon

89 Intense cherry. Aroma with notes of ripe skins (ink), an earthy nuance (minerals) and toasty oak (dark-roasted flavours and pitch). Round, warm, very expressive palate with good acidity despite the alcohol, flavourful.

ARRAYÁN CABERNET SAUVIGNON 2002 RED
100% cabernet sauvignon

90 Intense cherry. Aroma with good varietal expression of Cabernet from warm regions (paprika) and well-integrated, toasty, creamy oak. Meaty, full and flavourful palate with blackcurrants and very fine toasty oak in the retronasal passage.

ARRAYÁN PETIT VERDOT 2002 OAK AGED RED
100% petit verdot

89 Intense cherry. Aroma with predominant oak notes over the fruit, with jammy black fruit, good fruit expression and toasty oak. Meaty palate with new wood, very ripe almost jammy fruit and sweet and very flavourful tannins.

LA CERCA

Lepanto, s/n
45950 Casarrubios del Monte (Toledo)
☎: 918 172 456 - Fax: 918 172 456
bodegaslacerca@hotmail.com

Established: 1957

🌐 110 ▨ 2,000,000 litres 🍇 10 has.

🚩 90% 🌐10%: -US -FI -NL -PT

D. CECILIO 2003 JOVEN ROSÉ

68 Raspberry. Lightly evolved and reduced aroma, without nuances. Fresh palate, slightly better than in the nose, mildly fruity.

DON CECILIO 2003 JOVEN RED

67 Dark cherry. Slightly raisiny aroma without freshness or fruitiness. Flat palate, without nuances or fruit.

D. CECILIO 2003 RED

75 Straw-coloured. Fresh, very fruity aroma, foresty yet pleasant hints. Very dry on the palate with a slightly acidic edge, fresh.

MOLINO VIEJO 1999 CRIANZA RED
tempranillo, garnacha

75 Intense cherry. Toasty aroma of ripe fruit (stewed plums) with a nuance of oak well-integrated with the wine. Slightly meaty palate with hints of toasty and burnt flavours (notes of burnt wood), flavourful.

MOLINO VIEJO 2000 CRIANZA RED
tempranillo, garnacha

79 Garnet red cherry. Fresh aroma, fruity but with fine oak nuances. Fresh, fruity palate with character, flavourful.

MOLINO VIEJO 2001 CRIANZA RED
tempranillo, cabernet sauvignon

76 Garnet red cherry with a light ruby red edge. Aroma with light notes of slightly woody oak with ripe fruit. Flavourful, round palate with oak in the retronasal passage and slightly flabby tannins.

MOLINO VIEJO 1999 RESERVA RED
100% tempranillo

79 Slightly intense cherry with a ruby red glint. Aroma with toasty oak notes, partially concealed fruit (mild jammy fruit nuances). Round, flavourful palate with a toasty oak retronasal effect, flabby wine tannins and a bitter oak aftertaste.

MOLINO VIEJO 2000 RESERVA RED
100% tempranillo

77 Intense cherry. Toasty aroma of fruit and oak with complex overtones. Round, flavourful palate with light varietal nuances and oak in the retronasal passage.

DON CECILIO 2003 WHITE
DON CECILIO 2003 ROSÉ
MOLINO VIEJO 1999 CRIANZA RED

Cooperativa Nuestra Señora de
LA NATIVIDAD

San Roque, 1
45930 Méntrida (Toledo)
☎: 918 177 004 - Fax: 918 177 004
natividad.3081@cajarural.com
Established: 1945
⊕ 50 ▤ 2,000,000 litres 🍷 100%%

VEGA BERCIANA JOVEN ROSÉ
100% garnacha

69 Raspberry. Aroma with notes of evolution and notions of overripe fruit (a suggestion of overripeness). Aroma with reduced notes, without fruit, vinous.

VEGA BERCIANA JOVEN RED
100% garnacha

74 Fairly dark cherry. Aroma with a slight varietal expression of quite jammy ripe fruit. Warm, slightly flabby palate with hardly any tannins or acidity.

VEGA BERCIANA 2001 CRIANZA RED
100% tempranillo

70 Ruby red cherry. Aroma with light woody oak notes without fine toasty wood with mild jammy notes. Round, warm palate with woody oak and burnt flavours in the retronasal passage, slightly flavourful.

Cooperativa Nuestra Señora de **LINARES**

Inmaculada, 95
45920 Torre de Esteban Hambrán (Toledo)
☎: 925 795 452 - Fax: 925 795 452
Established: 1965
▤ 4,200,000 litres

FORTITUDO

Cooperativa **NUESTRA SEÑORA
DE GRACIA**

Extramuros s/n
Casarrubios del Monte (Toledo)
☎: 918 172 531

VIÑA TORMANTOS WHITE

70 Slightly golden yellow. Aroma with ripe notes, a hint of evolution, slightly overripe fruit. Warm on the palate with a suggestion of sweetness, without nuances.

VIÑA TORMANTOS JOVEN ROSÉ

70 Light garnet red. Aroma with slight notes of overripe fruit and an element of overripening. Fresh, and fruity palate with tannic notes of skins and with a mild sweetness.

Sociedad Cooperativa **NUESTRA
SEÑORA DE LA CARIDAD**

Carretera Toledo - Valmojado, s/n
45180 Camarena (Toledo)
☎: 918 174 850 - Fax: 918 174 235
Established: 1963
⊕ 80 ▤ 3,000,000 litres

🌿 980 has. 🍷 100%

EL GARBOSO JOVEN RED

70 Garnet red cherry. Aroma with light notes of evolution-overripening, slightly sweet. Quite low in acidity on the palate with raisiny hints in the retronasal passage, overripe.

EL GARBOSO RED
tempranillo, garnacha

65 Garnet red cherry. Lightly fruity and vegetative aroma, quite sweet. Slightly sweet and vegetative palate.

EL GARBOSO TEMPRANILLO JOVEN RED

Sociead Cooperativa Comarcal Vitivinícola
SAN ISIDRO

Carretera Toledo-Valmojado, km. 24
45180 Camarena (Toledo)
☎: 918 174 347 - Fax: 918 174 632
cosanisidro@hotmail.com

Established: 1972

🗄 4,500,000 litres 🌿 780 has.
🍷 85% 🌍15%: -US -TW -DO

BASTIÓN DE CAMARENA ROSÉ
90% tempranillo, 10% garnacha

70 Raspberry. Fruity aroma with varietal character, fresh. Slightly fruity palate, without great nuances.

CAMPO DE CAMARENA 2003 ROSÉ
100% garnacha

73 Lively raspberry. Fresh aroma, fruity yet slightly vinous. Fresh, mildly fruity palate, well-mannered.

CAMPO DE CAMARENA 2003 RED

65 Quite lively garnet red cherry. Aroma with vegetative notes of unripe skins, without fruit nuances. Flat palate without fruit and flabby.

BASTIÓN DE CAMARENA 2003 RED

63 Dark cherry. Aroma with overtones of raisiny notes and a vegetative nuance. Flat palate, without fruitiness, slightly cooked.

CAMPO DE CAMARENA WHITE

Cooperativa SANTA MARÍA MAGDALENA

Santa M. Magdalena, 2
45960 Chozas de Canales (Toledo)
☎: 918 176 142 - Fax: 918 176 191

ROCANALES

Cooperativa Agrícola SANTO CRISTO DE LA SALUD

Carretera Méntrida, s/n
45920 Torre de Esteban Hambrán (Toledo)
☎: 925 795 114 - Fax: 925 795 114
coopcrist@telefonica.net

Established: 1975

🍶 25 🗄 3,576,000 litres 🌿 1,200 has.

SEÑORIO DE ESTEBAN HAMBRÁN 2003 JOVEN ROSÉ
garnacha, tempranillo

69 Raspberry pink. Aroma of slight reduction in the tank, without fruit. Slightly flat palate without nuances or fruitiness.

SEÑORIO DE ESTEBAN HAMBRÁN TEMPRANILLO-GARNACHA 2003 RED
tempranillo, garnacha

60 Garnet red cherry. Vegetative aroma, without fruit, quite sweet. Flat palate without expression or fruitiness.

TORRESTEBAN 2002 CRIANZA RED

Cooperativa SANTO DOMINGO GUZMÁN

Aldea del Fresno, s/n
45940 Valmojado (Toledo)
☎: 918 170 904 - Fax: 918 170 633

EL INDIANO DE VALMOJADO JOVEN ROSÉ

67 Raspberry pink. Slightly reduced aroma without fruit, flat. No nuances or fruitiness on the palate.

LOS COTOS DE VALMOJADO JOVEN RED

64 Garnet red cherry. Aroma with light notes of stewed meat, without fruit. Flat palate without nuances or acidity.

COTO DE VALMOJADO

TAVASA

Carretera N-V, km. 40, 700
45950 Casarrubios del Monte (Toledo)
☎: 918 170 810 - Fax: 918 170 905
tavasa@tavasa.es
www.tavasa.es

HEREDAD DE CASARRUBIOS

DO MONDÉJAR

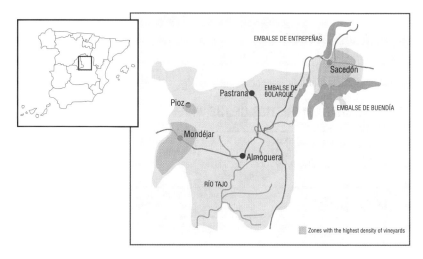

NEWS. We must mention the scant response to our request for samples, with only one wine tasted (by the way, an exceptional Syrah called Tierra Rubia) and, in general, the profound disregard shown by the bodegas of this DO towards a guide such as ours, which is starting to make headway on the international scene. This is a pity because, except for a couple of wines, the samples tasted in the previous edition easily achieved scores of between 75 and 80 points. Moreover, we believe that Guadalajara, in a certain sense, has the same potential for quality as the neighbouring Cuenca, whose wines are among the best of the DO La Mancha.

Hectares of Vineyard	No. of Viticulturists	No. of Bodegas	2003 Harvest	2003 Production	Marketing
3,000	900	5	Good	200,000 litres	90% Spain 10% foreign

LOCATION. In the southwest of the province of Guadalajara. It is made up of the municipal districts of Albalate de Zorita, Albares, Almoguera, Almonacid de Zorita, Driebes, Escariche, Escopete, Fuenteovilla, Illana, Loranca de Tajuña, Mazuecos, Mondéjar, Pastrana, Pioz, Pozo de Almoguera, Sacedón, Sayatón, Valdeconcha, Yebra and Zorita de los Canes.

CLIMATE. Temperate Mediterranean. The average annual temperature is around 18°C and the average rainfall is 500 mm per year.

SOIL. The south of the Denomination is characterized by red soil on lime-clayey sediments, and the north (the municipal districts of Anguix, Mondéjar, Sacedón, etc.) which has brown limestone soil on lean sandstone and conglomerates.

VARIETIES:

White (40%): *Malvar* (majority 80% of white varieties), *Macabeo* and *Torrontés*.
Red (60%): *Cencibel* (*Tempranillo* – represents 95% of red varieties) and *Cabernet Sauvignon* (5%) and *Syrah*.

REGULATORY COUNCIL.

Pza. Mayor, 10. 19110 Mondéjar (Guadalajara).
Tel / Fax: 949 385 284.
E-mail: crdom@crdomondejar.com

GENERAL CHARACTERISTICS OF THE WINES:

Whites	Those produced according to the more modern style tend to have a pale straw yellow colour; they have a fruity, fresh aroma and on the palate they are light and fruity; in the more traditional wines, however, there may appear notes of over-ripening.
Rosés	In general, they are light, supple and quite pleasant, although without excessive aromatic intensity.
Reds	These are probably the most interesting of the region. Produced mainly from *Cencibel*, their style resembles those from La Mancha: good aromatic intensity, with a presence of ripe fruit, supple and flavourful on the palate.

DO MONDEJAR

MARISCAL

Carretera de Perales, km. 71
19110 Mondejar (Guadalajara)
☎: 949 385 138 - Fax: 949 387 740

Established: 1913

850 ▤ 7,000,000 litres 🍇 1600 has.

🍷 60% 🍇40%: -DE -DK -SE -DK -BE -CO -UY -GT

TIERRA RUBIA 2003 RED
syrah

84 Bigarreau cherry with a violet edge. Intense, clean and expressive aroma (cherries and very ripe red plums). Very flavourful and intense on the palate with high quality fresh fruit and quite persistent.

VEGA TAJUÑA 2003 WHITE
PAGO DE ARIS TORRONTÉS 2002 WHITE
VEGA TAJUÑA 2003 RED
SEÑORÍO DE MARISCAL 1998 CRIANZA RED
CUEVA DE LOS JUDÍOS 1998 RESERVA RED

Sociedad Cooperativa SAN DONATO

Estudio, 1
19162 Pioz (Guadalajara)
☎: 949 272 058 - Fax: 949 222 354

CASTILLO DE PIOZ

Sociedad Cooperativa
SANTA MARÍA MAGDALENA

Carretera Perales - Albares, km. 71, 200
19110 Mondejar (Guadalajara)
☎: 949 385 139 - Fax: 949 387 727

Established: 1965

50 ▤ 7,000,000 litres 🍇 900 has.

🍷 100%

VALMORES WHITE
JARDINILLO 2003 WHITE
JARDINILLO 2003 ROSÉ
JARDINILLO TEMPRANILLO 2002 RED
JARDINILLO TEMPRANILLO 2001 OAK AGED RED

Sociedad Cooperativa VIÑA SACEDÓN

Carretera Sacedón - Buendía, s/n
19120 Sacedón (Guadalajara)
☎: 949 351 156 - Fax: 949 351 048

Established: 1994

55 ▤ 500,000 litres 🍇 170 has.

🍷 100%

VIÑA SACEDÓN JOVEN RED
VIÑA SACEDÓN CRIANZA RED
VIÑA SACEDÓN RESERVA RED

DO MONTE LENTISCAL

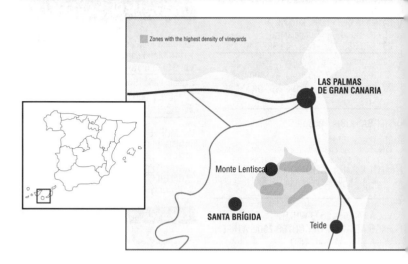

Zones with the highest density of vineyards

LAS PALMAS DE GRAN CANARIA

Monte Lentiscal

SANTA BRÍGIDA

Teide

NEWS. Possibly due to the future unification of the denominations of Gran Canaria, the Regulatory Council of Monte de Lentiscal has practically refused to communicate with us. Mondalón Picachos is the only wine cellar whose wines (all) achieved scores of 80 points. The 2003 harvest, which was promising in terms of quality, was frustrated by the rains at the end of the season, with the result that the wines were empty, without any fruitiness, although with an alcohol content resulting from an ever-present sun.

LOCATION. On the island of Gran Canaria. The production region comprises part of the municipal districts of Las Palmas of Gran Canaria, Santa Brígida and Teide, and consists of a protected natural area which is dominated by the Pico de Bandama crater. Historically, the region was 50% larger, but the DO could not be given its old extension due to the pressure from residential development.

Hectares of Vineyard	No. of Viticulturists	No. of Bodegas	2003 Harvest	2003 Production	Marketing
200	60	10	-	-	Entirely in the Canary Islands.

CLIMATE. The climate is Atlantic in nature, dry with little rainfall (around 300 mm per year). The average temperature is between 16° and 25°C. As with the rest of the islands of the archipelago, it is exposed to the trade winds that blow from the east affecting mainly the high altitude vineyards. The region is also exposed to the Sirocco from the Sahara, which is usually accompanied by large clouds of sand dust, which can last for weeks and negatively affect grapevine cultivation.

SOIL. The fundamental element is the volcanic character of the terrain, the so-called 'Picón', which tends to give the wines a marked personality. The vineyards are at an altitude of between 150 m and 550 m in the interior of the island, relatively far from the sea.

VARIETIES:
White:
Preferred: *Albillo, Breval, Güal, Malvasía, Marmajuelo* or *Bremejuela, Pedro Ximénez, Vijariego.*
Authorized: *Burrablanca, Listán Blanco, Torrontés.*

Red:
Preferred: *Listán Negra, Negra Común, Negramoll, Malvasía, Tintilla.*
Authorized: *Moscatel Negra.*

REGULATORY COUNCIL.
La Cultura, s/n. 35017 Las Palmas de Gran Canaria.
Tel: 928 35 22 35. Fax: 928 35 70 34.

GENERAL CHARACTERISTICS OF THE WINES:

Whites	Mainly produced from *Listán Blanca*, they have a straw yellow colour with notes of mountain herbs; on the palate there may appear notes of vegetables, but also a pleasant oily mouthfeel.
Rosés	Pink in colour, they should present a pattern of red berries and some notes of herbs; on the palate, they are light and easy drinking.
Reds	Produced mainly from *Listán Negra*, they have a deep cherry-red colour. On the nose, they have a fruity character together with balsamic notes; they are fruity on the palate and quite light.

DO MONTE LENTISCAL

DIEGO CAMBRELENG ROCA

Carretera Bandama, 4
35310 Santa Brígida (Gran Canaria)
☎: 928 350 975 - Fax: 928 311 120

VANDAMA 2003 JOVEN RED

58 Slightly muted cherry. Aroma with reduction off-odours (hydrogen sulphide). Flat palate, without nuances, mediocre.

FAMILIA FLICK FINCA EL GARITÓN

Las Arenillas, 65
35319 T.M. Santa Brígida (Gran Canaria)
☎: 928 289 055 - Fax: 928 206 512
juergenflick@grupoflick.com
www.grupoflick.com

Established: 1873

🍷 25 📊 25,000 litres 🍇 7.44 has.
🍾 100%

VIÑA MONTEALTO 2003 OAK AGED RED
listan negro, negramoll

60 Dark cherry. Very vegetative aroma without fruit. Flat palate, without fruitiness or nuances.

FRANCISCO PEÑATE RIVERO

El Palmital, 14
35218 Telde (Las Palmas de Gran Canaria)
☎: 928 572 318 - Fax: 928 572 318

VIÑA ROCONATELDE 2003 JOVEN RED

71 Garnet red. Short aroma, muted fruit without nuances. Light palate, not very fruity and unexpressive.

HEREDEROS CARMEN RODRÍGUEZ MILLÁN

Carretera Bandama, 68. Monte Lentiscal
35300 Santa Brígida
(Las Palmas de Gran Canaria)
☎: 928 350 937
juancmillan@hotmail.com

Established: 1912

🍇 11 has.

VIÑA MOCANAL 2003 JOVEN RED
80% listán negro, 20% negramoll

65 Quite dark cherry. Fruity aroma (fresh fruit, raspberries, slight vegetative hint). Fruity palate but with nuances ranging from herbaceous to vegetative.

VIÑA MOCANAL 2003 JOVEN SECO WHITE
VIÑA MOCANAL 2002 MOSCATEL

LAUREANO ROCA DE ARMAS

35300 Santa Brígida
(Las Palmas de Gran Canaria)

MONTE ROCA 2003 JOVEN RED

70 Garnet red cherry. Slightly fruity and vegetative aroma, balsamic. Fresh, quite fruity palate, good acidity and simple.

MANUEL QUINTANA NARANJO

Cuesta del Reventón, 62
35300 Santa Brígida
(Las Palmas de Gran Canaria)
☎: 928 351 838

MONTEGO RED

MONDALÓN PICACHOS

Cuesta del Mondalón, 6
35017 Palmas de Gran Canaria (Palmas de Gran Canaria)
☎: 928 356 066

Established: 1994

MONDALÓN 2003 WHITE

80 Pale yellow. Clear, fresh aroma with mild varietal notes, fruity. Fresh, fruity palate, pleasant and well-balanced.

MONDALÓN 2003 SEMI-DULCE WHITE

81 Yellow. Fruity, slightly musky aroma with fragrant herbs. Fresh, light, clear and very fruity palate, pleasant and with good acidity.

MONDALÓN 2003 DULCE WHITE

86 Yellow straw. Fresh, fruity, musky aroma of jammy fruit. Sweet, fragrant, fresh, flavourful palate, very fruity.

MONDALÓN 2003 OAK AGED RED
tintilla

80 Garnet red cherry. Powerful aroma rich in fresh fruit (raspberries) and a slight suggestion of wood. Light, fresh, fruity palate, pleasant and very varietal can be drunk young despite the mild vegetative nuance.

SANTIAGO ROBAINA LEÓN

Carretera Los Hoyos, 271 Plaza Perdida
35017 Palmas de G. Canaria (Gran Canaria)
☎: 928 355 871

DO MONTE LENTISCAL

PLAZA PERDIDA 2003 JOVEN RED

68 Garnet red cherry. Slightly viscous and raisiny aroma. Muted fruit on the palate, without nuances, discreet.

SARAMEMA

Tomás Quevedo Ramírez, 8
35300 Santa Brígida (Gran Canaria)
☎: 928 356 670 - Fax: 928 354 939

LOS LIRIOS 2003 JOVEN RED

72 Garnet red. Not very clear aroma with a slightly varietal suggestion. Light, fresh, slightly vegetative and fruity palate.

TABLERO DE LA DATA

Carretera de los Hoyos 185
35017 Las Palmas (Gran Canaria)
☎: 928 430 708

MARQUÉS DE LA DATA 2003 JOVEN RED

59 Garnet red cherry. Slightly fruity with a mild corked aroma. Fruity, warm, not very clear palate, mediocre.

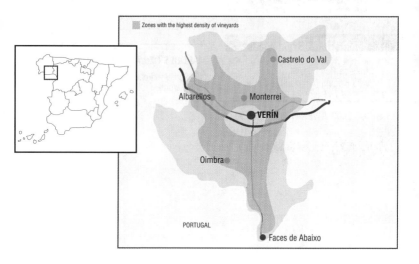

NEWS. Expectations were met, both in quality and quantity, thanks to a year with exceptional sunshine. After the dreadful 2002 harvest, Monterrei achieved a million kilograms of exceptionally healthy grapes with good alcohol content. The white varieties dominate (mainly *Godello* – also called *Verdello* in the region – and *Treixadura*), which make up 60% of the total. Many labels, both white and red wines, achieved scores of more than 80 points, some of which even surpassed 85, as in the case of Vendimia Seleccionada of Bernabé Jiménez and the white wine from Terra do Gargalo (86 points) of Roberto Verino.

The issue of the Crianza wines still has to be settled, for which the Regulatory Council is still debating the possibility of the authorising foreign varieties, which age better in barrels than the local Mencía or Bastardo varieties.

Hectares of Vineyard	No. of Viticulturists	No. of Bodegas	2003 Harvest	2003 Production	Marketing
660	545	14	Excellent	800,000 litres	90% Spain 10% Foreign

LOCATION. In the east of the province of Orense, on the border with Portugal. The vineyards occupy the valley of Monterrei, and it is made up of the municipal districts of Verín, Monterrei, Oimbra and Castrelo do Vall.

CLIMATE. Midway between the Atlantic and Continental influences. Drier than in the rest of Galicia, with maximum temperatures of 35°C in summer and minimum of –5°C in winter.

SOIL. The vineyards cover the slopes of the mountains and valleys irrigated by the Támega river and its tributaries. The soil is quite clayey, deep, rather heavy and, in some places, somewhat sandy.

VARIETIES:

White: *Doña Blanca, Verdello (Godello)* and *Treixadura (Verdello Louro).*
Red: *Mencía, Bastardo (*or *María Ardoña).*

SUB-REGIONS:

Val de Monterrei. Comprising the vineyards situated in the valley region (therefore, more level terrains) and covering the parishes and municipal districts belonging to the following city councils: Castrelo do Val (Castrelo do Val, Pepín and Nocedo); Monterrei (Albarellos, Infesta, Monterrei and Vilaza); Oimbra (Oimbra, Rabal, O Rosal and San Cibrao); Verín (Abedes, Cabreiroa, Feces da Baixo, Feces de Cima, Mandín, Mourazos, Pazos, Queizás, A Rasela, Tamagos, Tamaguelos, Tintores, Verín, Vilela and Vilamaior do Val).
Ladeira de Monterrei. These vineyards occupy the hills. The parishes and municipal districts that make up this sub-region are: Castrelo do Val (Gondulfes and Servoi), Oimbra (As Chas and A Granxa), Monterrey (Flariz, Medeiros, Mixós, Estevesiños and Vences) and Verín (Queirugas).

REGULATORY COUNCIL.

Galerías Maga. Avda. Luis Espada, 89. 32600 Verín (Ourense).
Tel: 988 590 007. Fax: 988 410 634.
E-mail: info@domonterrei.com
Website: www.crdomonterrei.com

GENERAL CHARACTERISTICS OF THE WINES:

Whites	These have a straw yellow colour and are fresh and pleasant. Those produced from autochthonous grapes, as opposed to the flatter of the *Palomino* variety, are more intense and fruity, flavourful on the palate, with a good alcohol-acidity balance.
Reds	With a deep cherry-red colour, these are mainly young red wines which have a good fruity character, although, on occasions, there are herbaceous notes; on the palate they are light and fruity.

Bodegas BERNABÉ JIMÉNEZ

Rua Laureano Peláez, 25
32600 Verín (Orense)
☎: 988 410 314 - Fax: 988 410 350

GRAN BERNABÉ VENDIMIA SELECCIONADA 2003 WHITE
godello, treixadura

80 Pale yellow with a greenish hue. Intense, ripe aroma with white fruit notes and slightly exotic hints. Flavourful palate with fine bitter notes, hints of herbs and citrus fruit, good acidity.

GRAN BERNABÉ VENDIMIA SELECCIONADA 2003 RED
mencía

85 Very deep cherry with a violet hue. Powerful aroma of red fruit with a very varietal character (spicy skins, a herbaceous essence, brambles, underbrush). Flavourful, meaty palate with elegant tannins and excellent symmetry.

CASTRO DE LOBARZÁN

Carretera de Requeixo, 51
32618 Villaza - Monterrei (Ourense)
☎: 988 418 163 - Fax: 988 418 163
lobarzan@wanadoo.es
www.lobarzan.com

Established: 2000
▦ 16,000 litres ❦ 4 has. 🍷 100%

CASTRO DE LOBARZÁN GODELLO 2003 WHITE
godello

83 Straw-coloured with a greenish hue. Intense aroma with predominant herby notes over a nuance of very varietal fruit. Fresh, flavourful palate with green fruit and excellent acidity.

CASTRO DE LOBARZÁN MENCÍA 2003 RED
mencía

82 Cherry with a violet hue. Powerful, fruity aroma with hints of sun-drenched skins and spicy notes of the vine variety. Meaty, flavourful, slightly warm palate with better tannic expression than the previous vintage.

GARGALO

Rua Do Castelo, 59
32600 Verín (Ourense)
☎: 988 590 203 - Fax: 988 590 295
gargalo@verino.es
www.verino.es

Established: 1997
⊕ 20 ▦ 220,000 litres ❦ 18 has.
🍷 90% 🍇10%

TERRA DO GARGALO 2003 WHITE
arauxa, mencía, bastardo

83 Deep cherry with a violet edge. Intense, fruity aroma with fine, spicy hints of skins and a rich herbaceous nuance (brambles). Fresh, flavourful palate with fine grape tannins, good fruit expression and excellent acidity.

TERRA DO GARGALO CARBALLO 2001 ROBLE RED
arauxa, mencía, bastardo

84 Garnet red cherry. Not very intense aroma of red fruit with fine toasty and mildly creamy oak notes and rich herbaceous hints. Flavourful palate with predominant fruit notes, spicy hints and a good oak/fruit integration, well-structured with hints of liquorice.

TERRA DO GARGALO 2003 RED
godello, dona blanca, treixadura

86 Pale yellow with a greenish hue. Powerful, fruity aroma (of green apples) with fine notes of lees and flowers. Fresh, flavourful palate with fine bitter notes and hints of citrus fruit and herbs.

Adegas LADAIRO

Lg. O'Rosal, s/n
32613 Oimbra (Orense)
☎: 988 422 757

LADAIRO 2003 F. BARRICA WHITE
godello, treixadura

78 Pale yellow with a golden hue. Fairly intense aroma of ripe white fruit with creamy hints (vanilla) of oak. Fruity palate with an oily texture, lacking expression and acidity.

LADAIRO 2003 WHITE
godello

81 Pale yellow. Intense, slightly fruity aroma with fresh overtones and varietal expression. Generous, flavourful palate with ripe white fruit (hints of exotic fruit) and a slightly oily texture.

LADAIRO 2003 RED
mencía

80 Garnet red cherry with a violet edge. Fairly intense aroma of red fruit with toasty hints of skins. Fresh, flavourful, fruity palate with slightly marked tannins (notes of greeness) and good acidity.

Adegas MADREVELLA

Carretera Portugal, s/n - Tamagos
32697 Verín (Ourense)
☎: 988 414 097

MADREVELLA 2003 WHITE
treixadura

83 Pale yellow with a coppery hue. Intense, fruity aroma with a good varietal expression (aromatic herbs, white fruit). Flavourful palate with fine bitter and slightly mineral notes, good acidity.

Bodegas del NUEVO MILENIO

Carrero Blanco, 33 (Albarellos)
32618 Monterrei (Ourense)
☎: 988 425 959 - Fax: 988 425 949
gdiez@pazodemonterrey.es
www.pazodemonterrey.es

Established: 2003

🛢 63 📦 200,000 litres 🍇 4 has.
🍷 70% 🌿30%: -US -TW -UE

PAZO DE MONTERREY 2003 WHITE
65% treixadura, 35% godello

82 Pale. Not very intense aroma with fresh white fruit overtones and herby hints. Flavourful, fruity and slightly oily palate with smoky skins and quality citrus hints.

PAZO DE MONTERREY 2003 OAK AGED WHITE
TIERRAS DE VERÍN 2003 RED

Adegas O CABILDO

Cabildo, 10
32613 Oimbra (Orense)
☎: 670 601 625

Established: 2004
📦 60,000 litres 🍇 6 has.

CASAL DO CABILDO WHITE
godello, treixadura, dona blanca

77 Pale with a greenish hue. Fairly intense aroma of ripe white fruit, with floral hints. Flavourful palate with fine bitter notes, a slightly oily texture and lacking acidity.

Bodegas y Viñedos
QUINTA DA MURADELLA

Avenida Luis Espada, 99. Entresuelo, dcha.
32600 Verín (Ourense)
☎: 988 411 724 /4000 - Fax: 988 590 427
muradella@wanadoo.es

Established: 1999
🛢 10 📦 30,000 litres 🍇 12,5 has. 🍷 100%

ALANDA 2003 JOVEN WHITE
75% doña blanca, 20% treixadura, 5% monstruosa

83 Straw-coloured with coppery hues. Intense aroma of green fruit with fresh overtones and fine notes of lees. Dry palate with fine bitter notes and hints of herbs, slightly warm.

GORVIA VERDELLO 2003 WHITE
100% verdejo

84 Brilliant straw. Intense aroma, fruity with good varietal expression, hints of greengage plums, a herby nuance. Fresh, fruity palate with fine mineral notes and good acidity.

GORVIA F. BARRICA 2003 WHITE
100% doña blanca

82 Straw-coloured with a coppery glint. Quite intense aroma with fresh overtones, fine hints of ripe fruit and a herbaceous nuance of lees. Fresh, flavourful, somewhat oily and warm palate; well-crafted with barely perceivable oak.

GORVIA TINTO 2003 RED
100% mencía

84 Deep cherry with a violet edge. Powerful, ripe aroma with excellent varietal expression (ripe red fruit, hints of herbs) and a nuance of toasty wood. Flavourful, meaty palate with predominant notes of oak, slightly warm, promising.

ALANDA TINTO 2003 OAK AGED RED
60% bastardo, 35% tempranillo, 5% mencía

79 Cherry with a violet hue. Intense aroma with fresh overtones, black fruit notes and hints of sun-drenched skins. Meaty, slighty warm palate with very flavourful grape tannins, good acidity.

GORVIA TINTO 2002 OAK AGED RED
100% mencía

80 Intense cherry with a coppery edge. Powerful aroma with good varietal expression and well-integrated fruit and wood. Fresh, flavourful palate with slightly drying oak tannins, a spicy nuance and fine bitter notes, pleasant.

Adegas QUINTA DO BUBLE

Casas dos Montes
32613 Oimbra (Orense)
☎: 988 411 698

QUINTA DO BUBLE 2003 WHITE
verdejo

74 Pale yellow. Fairly intense, fruity aroma with fresh ripe citrus overtones. Fresh palate with fine bitter notes and good acidity.

Adega VALDERELLO

Rua Máximo 1 Albarellos de Monterrey
32618 Monterrei (Ourense)
☎: 606 767 005
Established: 2001

VALDERELLO JOVEN WHITE
VALDERELLO JOVEN RED

DO MONTILLA - MORILES

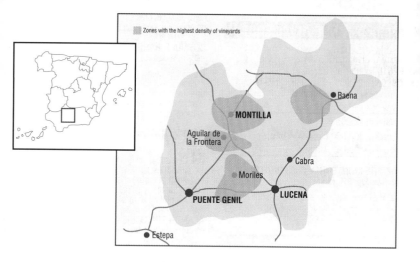

NEWS. Just like Jerez, Montilla-Moriles is seeking out both markets and an identity. As for its promotion abroad, its main clients in terms of volume are European: the Netherlands, the United Kingdom and Belgium. As for identity, and taking into account that traditional production has declined over the last few years, there is still interest in young dry white wines. In this edition, they all achieved scores of 70 points or more (thanks to the absence of defects), and the best examples display a certain taste and pleasant notes of citrus fruits.

As part of this 'modernisation', it should be remembered that almost 400 vine growers from Montilla-Moriles have adopted the restructuring and conversion of vineyards to cultivate red varieties (*Syrah, Cabernet Sauvignon* and *Tempranillo*) in trellised vineyards, a conduction system that enables the mechanisation of the vineyards and the lowering of production costs. Casa Villa Cevallos, a red wine of Pérez Barquero produced from *Tempranillo, Merlot, Cabernet Sauvignon* and *Syrah*, achieved a score of 83 points, and so jumps on the bandwagon of the new and undreamed-of generation of Andalusian red wines that are transforming the viticultural landscape of this region.

Hectares of Vineyard	No. of Viticulturists	No. of Bodegas	2003 Harvest	2003 Production	Marketing
9,215	4,052	70 Producers	Very Good	19,336,503 litres	83% Spain 17% foreign

LOCATION. To the south of Córdoba. It covers all the vineyards of the municipal districts of Montilla, Moriles, Montalbán, Puente Genil, Montruque, Nueva Carteya and Doña Mencía, and part of the municipal districts of Montemayor, Fernán-Núñez, La Rambla, Santaella, Aguilar de la Frontera, Lucena, Cabra, Baena, Castro del Río and Espejo.

CLIMATE. Semi-continental Mediterranean, with long, hot, dry summers and short winters. The average annual temperature is 16.8°C and the average rainfall is between 500 mm and 1,000 mm per year.

SOIL. The vineyards are situated at an altitude of between 125 m and 640 m. The soils are franc, franc-sandy and, in the higher regions, calcareous ('Albarizas'), which are precisely those of best quality, and which predominate in what is known as the Upper Sub-Region, which includes the municipal districts of Montilla, Moriles, Castro del Río, Cabra and Aguilar de la Frontera.

VARIETIES:
White: *Pedro Ximénez* (main variety), *Layrén, Baladí, Moscatel* and *Torrontés*.
Red: *Tempranillo, Syrah* and *Cabernet Sauvignon*.

SUB-REGIONS: There is a difference between the vineyards in the flatter regions and in the higher regions (Sierra de Montilla and Moriles Alto). The latter, situated on calcareous soil, are the best quality of the DO and comprise just over 2,000 Ha.

REGULATORY COUNCIL.
Rita Pérez, s/n. 14550 Montilla (Córdoba).
Tel: 957 650 800. Fax: 957 652 866.
E-mail: crdo@montilla-moriles.org
Website: www.montilla-motiles.org

GENERAL CHARACTERISTICS OF THE WINES:

Young Whites	Created relatively recently, they are light and fruity wines for rapid consumption.
Finos	Produced following the classical biological procedure of 'velo en flor'. With saline aromas of yeast and bitter almonds, they differ from the Jerezanos in being less dry on the palate.
Olorosos	These are mahogany coloured, with aromas of confectionery; they are sweet and flavourful on the palate.
Amontillados	Amber or old gold in colour. Nutty aroma (almonds and hazelnut); on the palate they have sweet notes with certain notes of biological ageing due to their origin as Finos.
Pedro Ximénez	This is the Montilla-Moriles wine par excellence. Produced from sun-dried grapes, the colour may range from mahogany to very dark browns, thoroughly dense and concentrated. Unmistakable due to its aroma of raisins and dates, with a hint of toast; on the palate it is sweet, mellow and flavourful.

DO MONTILLA-MORILES

A. DOBLAS MARTOS

Avenida 28 de Febrero, 25
14510 Moriles (Córdoba)
☎: 957 537 942 - Fax: 957 537 942
bodegas@adoblasmartos.com

Established: 1984
⊕ 400 🖺 40,000 litres 🌿 6 has. 🍷 100%

DOBLAS FINO
DOBLAS AMONTILLADO
DOBLAS PEDRO XIMÉNEZ

A. MIGUEL OJEDA CHACÓN

Calle 28 de Febrero, 12
14510 Moriles (Córdoba)
☎: 957 537 445 - Fax: 957 537 445
moriles@bodegassanpablo.com

Established: 1903
🍷 100%

SAN PABLO FINO
SAN PABLO AMONTILLADO
LAGAR DE SAN PABLO PEDRO XIMÉNEZ
SAN PABLO PALE CREAM

AGUERA

Carreteros, 4
14540 La Rambla (Córdoba)
☎: 957 684 262

Established: 1958
⊕ 250 🖺 320,000 litres 🍷 100%

FINO CA

ALVEAR

María Auxiliadora, 1
14550 Montilla (Córdoba)
☎: 957 650 100 - Fax: 957 650 135
info@alvear.es
www.alvear.es

Established: 1729
⊕ 16,000 🖺 11,000,000 litres 🌿 300 has.
🍷 60% 🥂40%

MARQUÉS DE LA SIERRA 2003 WHITE
pedro ximénez, riesling, chardonnay, sauvignon blanc

76 Brilliant pale yellow. Intense, grapey aroma with notes of flowers, spices and an essence of slightly reduced fruit. Flavourful, fresh and quite fruity on the palate with an acidic edge.

FINO CB FINO
100% pedro ximénez

89 Pale straw. Dry, slightly pungent and saline aroma. Dry and bitter palate with hints of flor and nuances of flavourful foresty herbs.

CAPATAZ FINO
100% pedro ximénez

90 Straw-coloured with a yellow glimmer. Deep aroma with notes of old flor and bitter almonds and nuances of foresty herbs. Slightly lardy, dry and full palate, persistent.

ALVEAR FINO EN RAMA 2000
100% pedro ximénez

90 Light gold. Powerful aroma, rich in notes of flor with scrubland herbs, almonds and saline. Full, generous, bitter palate with a supple and glyceric edge, very persistent and flor typification.

ALVEAR SOLERA FUNDACIÓN AMONTILLADO DULCE

87 Old gold with a coppery hue. Powerful aroma with fine notes of acetaldehyde, clean evoking Fino with nuts and mountain herbs. Flavourful, dry palate, rich in crianza nuances with a saline essence, aged, quite vital and persistent.

CARLOS VII MUY VIEJO AMONTILLADO
100% pedro ximénez

87 Golden amber. Powerful aroma, with pungent notes of oak and flor, nuts and mild hints of pâtisserie. Dry warm, flavourful and pungent on the palate with aldehyde in the retronasal passage, persistent and flavourful.

ASUNCIÓN OLOROSO
100% pedro ximénez

88 Mahogany with an amber hue. Aroma with nutty notes (hazelnuts, almonds) and a slightly viscous edge. Quite a sweet palate with toasty notes in the retronasal passage, flavourful.

ALVEAR PX SOLERA 1830 RESERVA PEDRO XIMÉNEZ
100% pedro ximénez

98 Chocolate black with a mahogany edge. Generous aroma, rich in nuances of dark chocolate, dates, raisins with Solera oxidative notes and jammy raisins. Dense, unctuous, full palate rich in nuances of raisins and jams, notions of honey, carob, chocolate and Turkish coffee.

PX SOLERA 1830 PEDRO XIMÉNEZ
100% pedro ximénez

96 Chocolatey with a mahogany hue. Powerful aroma rich in expression, toasty and raisiny, evoking dates and coffee. Round palate, slightly less dense but with a clearer flavour than the first 1830, typical of P.X.

ALVEAR PX 1927 SOLERA PEDRO XIMÉNEZ DULCE
100% pedro ximénez

87 Toasted mahogany. Toasty, viscous aroma with a suggestion of raisins and pastries. Sweet, flavourful, toasty palate with a suggestion of jammy raisins.

PEDRO XIMÉNEZ DE AÑADA 2002 PEDRO XIMÉNEZ
100% pedro ximénez

89 Brilliant deep amber. Powerful aroma, rich in dried fruit nuances and toasty hints of skins, with fresh overtones, a nuance of aged cask, clean, rosemary-honey. Unctuous palate, fine toasty oak hints, a nuance of dried fruit with alcoholic, spicy hints (ginger).

PEDRO XIMÉNEZ COSECHA 2002 OAK AGED PEDRO XIMÉNEZ
100% pedro ximénez

88 Brilliant amber with coppery hues. Intense aroma, notes of raisins, hints of new wood, a nuance of dates and toasty hints of skins. Powerful palate, unctuous with fresh oak overtones and hints of fig bread and oriental spices in the retro-nasal passage, original.

ALVEAR PX RESERVA 1998 RESERVA PEDRO XIMÉNEZ
100% pedro ximénez

91 Opaque with a mahogany rim. Powerful aroma of chocolate and spices with fresh varietal and raisiny hints and a suggestion of orange peel and fine pâtisserie. Unctuous palate rich in nuances of raisins and reduction and pâtisserie, succulent and very long.

FESTIVAL PALE CREAM
100% pedro ximénez

82 Brilliant lemon. Aroma with discreet notes of flor, salinity, warm and floral petals. Sweet palate with suggestions of sweet almonds and hints of Fino, enveloping and long.

ALVEAR SOLERA CREAM

100% pedro ximénez

88 Mahogany with a coppery-greenish hue. Powerful, clean aroma with fine oxidative notes, toasty with aged wood, varnish and a slightly sweet and raisiny suggestion. Flavourful palate with fine sweet notes, slightly aged and bitter (broom, wood, nuts), quite vital.

ARAGÓN Y COMPAÑÍA

Camino de la Estación, s/n
14900 Lucena (Córdoba)
☎: 957 500 046 - Fax: 957 502 935
gerencia@aragonycia.com
Established: 1946
🍷 2,500 🛢 1,500,000 litres 🏆 98% 🌐2%

LAGAR DE CAMPOARAS JOVEN WHITE DE AGUJA
100% pedro ximénez

78 Pale steel. Aroma of white fruit, evoking flowers with a hint of honeycombs and citrus fruit (limes). Fruity palate with very subtle beads, hints of sweetness.

BOABDIL VIEJÍSIMO GRAN RESERVA AMONTILLADO
100% pedro ximénez

78 Old gold. Aroma of vanilla, varnish and nuts; slightly marked by the crianza. Dry palate with bitter notes and almondy notes; better in the mouth.

MORILES 47 FINO
100% pedro ximénez

77 Straw-coloured. Mild aroma of flor with notes of reduced lees, without great character. Dry palate with notes of flor and almonds in the finish.

MORILES P.G. FINO
100% pedro ximénez

80 Straw-coloured with a golden glint. Fruity aroma with rancid notes (butters) and a vegetative nuance. Dry, bitter, slightly pungent palate; oily structure but quite characterless structure.

PILYCRIM PALE CREAM
100% pedro ximénez

76 Pale. Quite intense aroma with light notes of flor and a herby nuance. Fresh, slightly dense and sweet palate with fine bitter notes, quite flavourful.

PACORRITO AMONTILLADO
100% pedro ximénez

84 Old gold. Expressive aroma of nuts, varnish and hints of flor and pâtisserie. Dry palate with sweet notes of almonds and orange peel; persistent.

ARACELI PEDRO XIMÉNEZ
100% pedro ximénez

80 Mahogany. Intense aroma of raisins with notes of cocoa and dark-roasted flavours, quite sweet. Sweet, flavourful palate with undertones of freshness compensating the sweetness, pleasant.

PATRICIA CREAM SWEET

CONCEPCIÓN SÁNCHEZ RODRÍGUEZ

M. López Aguilera, 3
14510 Moriles (Córdoba)
☎: 957 537 095

J. M. FINO EN RAMA

CONDE DE LA CORTINA

María Auxiliadora, 1
14550 Montilla (Córdoba)
☎: 957 650 100 - Fax: 957 650 135
Established: 1973
🌐 4,000 📊 1,200,000 litres 🍷 100%

CONDE DE LA CORTINA FINO
CONDE DE LA CORTINA DULCE
CONDE DE LA CORTINA MOSCATEL

CRISMONA

Baena, 25
14860 Doña Mencía (Córdoba)
☎: 957 695 514 - Fax: 957 676 342
Established: 1904
🌐 2,000 📊 2,000,000 litres
🍇 90 has. 🍷 100%

LOS CABALES FINO
PERICO FINO
CRISMONA OLOROSO
CRISMONA RESERVA ESPECIAL PEDRO XIMÉNEZ
CRISMONA PEDRO XIMÉNEZ

CRUZ CONDE

Ronda Canillo, 4
14550 Montilla (Córdoba)
☎: 957 652 000 - Fax: 957 653 619
avilchez@bodegascruzconde.es
www.bodegascruzconde.es
Established: 1902
🌐 5,725 📊 5,200,000 litres 🍇 26 has.
🍷 70%🌐30%: -MX -NL -UK -BE -US -EC -FR -DE

VIÑA TERCIA WHITE
C.C. FINO
DONERRE FINO
C.C. AMONTILLADO
MERCEDES OLOROSO
PALE CREAM C.C. SEMI-DULCE

CRUZ CONDE MOSCATEL

DELGADO

Cosano, 2
14500 Puente Genil (Córdoba)
☎: 957 600 085 - Fax: 957 604 571
fino@bodegasdelgado.com
www.bodegasdelgado.com
Established: 1874
🌐 6,000 📊 2,000,000 litres 🍷 96%🌐4%

SEGUNDA BOTA FINO
pedro ximénez

82 Golden. Clear, clean and iodised aroma, nuts (Solera). Oily palate, a pleasantly bitter hint in the finish, very oily with a saline essence, almonds in the finish, long; slightly lacking in freshness.

DELGADO 1874 AMONTILLADO NATURAL MUY VIEJO

90 Golden amber. Fine aroma of well-integrated Solera, pâtisserie (marzipan) and saline essence. Generous palate with a good Fino expression, almondy notes, pleasantly bitter, very long in the finish.

DELGADO 1874 OLOROSO VIEJO

90 Light mahogany with a yellowish edge. Complex aroma of elegant varnish (carpentry, sweet almonds), with a white chocolate suggestion. Flavourful, fresh palate with a hint of nuts, pâtisserie and Solera, rather pungent in the finish but with character.

DELGADO 1874 PEDRO XIMÉNEZ
pedro ximénez

88 Very dark mahogany with an iodised edge. Intense aroma of toasty raisins (baked bread), hints of complex Solera (hazelnuts and cocoa) . Sweet palate with bitter raisins which balance the sweetness, fig and caramel notes in the retronasal passage.

LAGAR DE BENAZOLA WHITE SEMI-SECO
LAGAR DE SAN ANTONIO WHITE SECO

ESPEJO

Avenida Marqués de la Vega Armijo, 57
14550 Montilla (Córdoba)
☎: 957 650 412 - Fax: 957 654 037
bodegasespejo@arrakis.es
Established: 1976
🌐 3.200 📊 2.400.000 litres 🍇 150 has.
🍷 95%🌐5%

BRAVADO FINO
95% pedro ximénez, 5% montúa de pila

80 Golden. Expressive aroma of flor; hints of nuts and fresh grapes. Flavourful palate, pleasant yet slightly ripe.

AMABLE AMONTILLADO
95% pedro ximénez, 5% airén

79 Golden. Aroma marked by the flor with notes of salinity and of reduction nuances. Dry, slightly pungent palate; without the characteristic notes of Amontillado ageing.

ESPEJO PEDRO XIMÉNEZ DULCE
100% pedro ximénez

83 Mahogany with an amber rim. Aroma of cocoa, dates, pâtisserie and figs, generous. Sweet, flavourful palate, better in the nose; fresh with fig bread in the finish.

GRACIA HERMANOS

Avenida Marqués de la Vega de Armijo, 103
14550 Montilla (Córdoba)
☎: 957 650 162 - Fax: 957 652 335
comercial@bodegasgracia.com
www.bodegasgracia.com

Established: 1952
🛢 6,000 🛢 8,500,000 litres 🍇 110 has.
🍷 80% 🍷 20%

VIÑA VERDE 2003 JOVEN WHITE

78 Pale with a greenish glint. Fruity aroma (papayas, ripe limes). Flavourful palate, with marked green fruit pulp acidity, quite sweet fruity and long.

TAUROMAQUIA FINO

85 Straw-coloured. Expressive, clear flor aroma with bitter almond and pâtisserie notes. Flavourful, fresh palate with a Fino character (almonds, salines) and a slightly short finish.

TAUROMAQUIA AMONTILLADO

86 Old gold. Complex aroma of varnish, well-blended Solera, essence of pâtisserie and reduction (orange). Generous, flavourful and expressive on the palate with more Oloroso character, and a slightly almondy and saline finish.

TAUROMAQUIA OLOROSO

85 Gold with a coppery edge. Creamy aroma of pâtisserie, toffee and a suggestion of Solera. Very fresh and flavourful palate, with a degree of persistence. Sweet notes in the finish.

TAUROMAQUIA PEDRO XIMÉNEZ

83 Mahogany with an iodised rim. Intense raisiny aroma with an essence of spice and toasty caramel. Sweet palate with sweet sensations, lacking freshness,Chocolate in the finish.

JESÚS NAZARENO

Avenida Cañete de las Torres, 33

14850 Baena (Córdoba)
☎: 957 670 225 - Fax: 957 690 873
bodejenaza@arrakis.es

Established: 1963
🛢 2,200 🛢 2,000,000 litres
🍇 275 has. 🇪🇸 100%

DON BUENO AFRUTADO WHITE
PEÑAS DE OMAR CRIANZA RED
BAENA FINO
CANCIONERO DE BAENA FINO
MORANA PALE CREAM DULCE
MINGUILLAR PEDRO XIMÉNEZ DULCE

Cooperativa Agrícola LA AURORA

Carretera Córboba - Málaga, km. 44
14550 Montilla (Córdoba)
☎: 957 650 362 - Fax: 957 654 642

FINO AMANECER

76 Straw-coloured with a golden edge. Ripe aroma with light notes of flor and nuts. Dry, slightly vinous palate with pungent and oily hints, evolved.

Cooperativa Vitivinícola LA PURÍSIMA

Carretera de Aguilar, km. 92
14500 Puente Genil (Córdoba)
☎: 957 600 147 - Fax: 957 600 350
administracion@vinoleapurisima.com
www.vinoleapurisima.com

Established: 1970
🛢 1,700 🛢 4,500,000 litres 🍷 100%

CASTILLO DE ALJONOZ JOVEN WHITE
SEMI-SECO

71 Pale with a greenish hue. Intense aroma with hints of varnish and dried herbs. Better on the palate, flavourful with light carbonic hints, quite fruity and bitter.

MONTE CAÑERO FINO

80 Straw-coloured with a golden edge. Not very intense aroma of flor, hints of herbs and yeast. Dry, oily palate with a herby expression and slight bitterness.

PEDRO XIMÉNEZ SWEET

74 Amber aroma of ripe grapes, toasty notes of skins and hints of pâtisserie. Very sweet, cloying and unctuous on the palate without great expression.

Cooperativa Agrícola LA UNIÓN

Avenida de Italia, 1
14550 Montilla (Córdoba)
☎: 957 651 855 - Fax: 957 651 855

coop_launion@terra.es

Established: 1979

🌐 2,700 🛢 15,000,000 litres 🍇 1,500 has.
🍷 14.500.000,litros. 🍷 80%
🌍20%: -IT -FR -PT

ALGARABÍA WHITE AFRUTADO

72 Pale greenish yellow. Powerful aroma with fruit, white flowers and jammy hints. Dry, flavourful palate without great fruit expression but with an acidic edge.

TRES PALACIOS FINO
100% pedro ximénez

80 Straw-coloured with a greenish edge. Expressive aroma with notes of mountain herbs, with a nuance of flor, fresh. Flavourful, quite bitter and pleasant on the palate with warm overtones and a herbaceous finish.

FINO 79

LAMA

Ronda Povedano, 9
14860 Doña Mencía (Córdoba)
☎: 957 676 016 - Fax: 957 676 023
bodegaslama@terra.es -
geocities.com/bodegaslama

Established: 1885

🌐 25 🛢 300,000 litres 🍷 100%

PX MENCÍA PEDRO XIMÉNEZ DULCE
MENCÍA FINO

LOS GABRIELES

Monturque, 72
14510 Moriles (Córdoba)
☎: 957 537 078 - Fax: 957 537 928
rmclygm@hotmail.com

Established: 1950

🌐 250 🛢 12,000 litres 🍷 100%

LOS GABRIELES FINO
LOS GABRIELES AMONTILLADO
LOS GABRIELES PEDRO XIMÉNEZ

LUQUE

La Molinera, 3
14860 Doña Mencía (Córdoba)
☎: 957 676 029 - Fax: 957 676 029

Established: 1920

🌐 3.500 🛢 750,000 litres 🍇 8 has.
🍷 100%

SOLERA ANDALUZA FINO
100% pedro ximénez

73 Straw-coloured. Aroma with notes of varnish, toasted hints and a suggestion of very ripe fruit. Warm, ripe palate with pungent notes of a dominant crianza.

LOS LUQUES (IMPERIAL) FINO
100% pedro ximénez

72 Golden yellow. Aroma of varnish with toasty hints over the hints of flor. Unctuous palate without freshness; almondy notes and a discreet, warm finish.

FINO EL PATO
100% pedro ximénez

72 Brilliant gold. Aroma with noticeable crianza notes (varnish, orange peel) and an essence of light saline notes. Flavourful, warm palate with unctuous notes slightly dominated by the wood.

EL ABUELO SOLERA 1888 AMONTILLADO
100% pedro ximénez

82 Mahogany with an orange rim. Creamy aroma with toffee and hints of varnish. Intense bitter palate, dry, slightly pungent with a flor expression and an intense finish.

VIEJO OLOROSO
100% pedro ximénez

75 Old gold. Aroma of crystallised fruit with hints of pâtisserie. Slightly flat, uncomplex palate with mild Solera notes.

LUQUE PEDRO XIMÉNEZ
100% pedro ximénez

80 Mahogany. Aroma of Mistelle with notes of vanilla and a suggestion of raisins and sweet fruit. Sweet palate with a syrupy sensation, without great freshness.

BODEGA LUQUE MOSCATEL DULCE
PALE CREAM CHIPI SEMI- DULCE

MAILLO E HIJOS

Ancha, 4
14550 Montilla (Córdoba)
☎: 957 650 651

SAAVEDRA FINO
CREAM VIEJO
SIERRA DE MONTILLA

MARÍN

Pérez Galdós, 2
14520 Fernán Núñez (Córdoba)
☎: 957 380 110 - Fax: 957 380 110

Established: 1895

🌐 1,200 🛢 370,000 litres 🍷 100%

EL CAPRICHO FINO
MARÍN FINO
PERIQUITO FINO
VIEJO MARÍN AMONTILLADO
MARÍN PEDRO XIMÉNEZ
MARÍN PALE CREAM DULCE
LOS MARINES

MÁRQUEZ PANADERO

Ronda de Canillo, 4
14550 Montilla (Córdoba)
☎: 957 651 250 - Fax: 957 653 619
avilchez@bodegascruzconde.es
www.cellerepelt.com

Established: 1886

🌐 6,000 🇪🇸 100%

CALERITO FINO
EL PIREO FINO
LA NIÑA FINO
AMARGOSO FINO
FRAGANTE OLOROSO
P.X. SOÑADOR PEDRO XIMÉNEZ

MORA CHACÓN DE LUCENA

Carretera Córdoba - Málaga, km. 74
14900 Lucena (Córdoba)
☎: 957 502 211 - Fax: 957 502 211
www.morachacon.com

Established: 1891

🌐 600 📦 64,500 litres 🇪🇸 100%

DON SANTOGO FINO
SANTOGO FINO
DON SANTOGO AMONTILLADO
SANTOGO OLOROSO
SANTOGO PALE CREAM

MORENO

Fuente de la Salud, 2
14006 Córdoba ()
☎: 957 767 605 - Fax: 957 279 907
moreno@morenosa.com

Established: 1957

🌐 8,000

BENAVIDES FINO

82 Brilliant straw. Aroma with iodised notes, slight ripeness, nuts and a mask suggestion. Expressive, slightly pungent palate with an oily texture and a round almondy finish.

MUSA FINO

85 Straw-coloured with a greenish hue. Intense mask aroma with hints of sweet almonds and sea salt. Round, slightly oily and flavourful palate with pleasant nutty and flor sensations and a fresh

finish.

MUSA AMONTILLADO

72 Amber. Slightly flat aroma of very ripe grapes and vanilla. Dry, slightly bitter palate with saline notes and a pungent finish.

SIETE SABIOS AMONTILLADO

76 Old gold. Aroma of vanilla with oak notes (varnish). Flavourful palate with warm notes, a slightly flat expression; almondy finish.

CABRIOLA AMONTILLADO

80 Old gold. Slightly warm aroma with predominant crianza notes (varnish). A wood dominated palate with bitter traces (nuts) and a slightly saline finish.

MUSA OLOROSO

76 Old gold. Aroma with slightly marked Solera (vanilla, varnish). Dry, and slightly bitter palate with nutty notes and an oak and almondy finish.

SOLERA OLOROSA PLATINO

84 Old gold. Creamy aroma with pâtisserie, hints of Solera and complex overtones. Dry, unctuous, almondy and slightly vinous on the palate with a fresh finish.

FUNDACIÓN 1819 OLOROSO

87 Amber. Expressive aroma of nuts (sweet almonds) with a Fino character and with rancid, well-integrated wood notes. Dry palate with bitter notes of a good Fino (flor, almonds), unctuous and long.

ALBOROQUE PALO CORTADO

78 Old gold. Intense aroma of varnish with very sweet notes of pâtisserie. Dry, pungent palate with nutty hints and a discreet finish.

MUSA PEDRO XIMÉNEZ

78 Amber. Intense, quite sweet aroma of fresh grapes with notes of orange peel. Sweet, and pasty on the palate, without great freshness, with a pâtisserie finish.

UNA VIDA PEDRO XIMÉNEZ

80 Mahogany. Fine aroma of toasty crianza, dates, fresh grapes with hints of spices. Sweet and very unctuous on the palate without sufficient acidity, with grapey notes and good length.

VIRGILIO PEDRO XIMÉNEZ

88 Nearly opaque mahogany. Concentrated aroma of raisins and fine toasty flavours (cocoa, spices), dates and nuts. Sweet, almost syrupy on the palate, unctuous with suggestions of toasty grapes and fresh overtones, very long.

Bodegas NAVARRO

Avenida Antonio y Miguel Navarro, 1

14550 Montilla (Córdoba)
☎: 957 650 644 - Fax: 957 650 122
bodegasnavarro@bodegasnavarro.com
bodegasnavarro.com

Established: 1830

▥ 2,500 ▤ 3,200,000 litres

☕ 90% 🍷10%-DE -FR

FINO SOLERA FUNDACIÓN 1830 NAVARRO
pedro ximénez

78 Golden. Aroma of mild flor with toasty Solera and yeast. Dry, oily palate, slightly warm and without great saline expression herby notes.

SOLERA FUNDACIÓN 1830 PEDRO XIMÉNEZ
pedro ximénez

85 Mahogany with an orange edge. Aroma of toasted nuts with notes of raisins and fresh dates and a suggestion of well-integrated Solera. Sweet, long palate with fresh character and notes of raisins and sweet pastries, a complex finish.

ANDALUCÍA FINO
NAVARRO FINO
NUESTRA SRA. DE LA AURORA FINO
SOLERA 1830 VIEJO AMONTILLADO
NAVARRO OLOROSO
NAVARRO VIEJO OLOROSO
SOLERA FUNDACIÓN 1830 AMONTILLADO
NAVARRO PEDRO XIMÉNEZ

NAVISA INDUSTRIAL VINÍCOLA ESPAÑOLA

Carretera Montalbán, s/n
14550 Montilla (Córdoba)
☎: 957 650 450 - Fax: 957 651 747
navisa@globalnet.es
www.navisa.es

POMPEYO FINO
pedro ximénez

74 Greenish straw. Ripe aroma (bananas) with notes of yeast. Dry, vinous palate without Fino expression, herbaceous notes.

VEGA MARÍA JOVEN WHITE
VIÑA RAMA JOVEN WHITE
COBOS FINO
MONTEBELLO FINO
MONTULIA FINO
CERINOLA AMONTILLADO
DOS PASAS PEDRO XIMÉNEZ
MONTEBELLO MOSCATEL DULCE
TRES PASAS PEDRO XIMÉNEZ
SOLDORAO PALE CREAM DULCE

PÉREZ BARQUERO

Avenida Andalucía, 27
14550 Montilla (Córdoba)

☎: 957 650 500 - Fax: 957 650 208
comercial@perezbarquero.com
www.perezbarquero.com

Established: 1905

▥ 9,000 ▤ 13,000,000 litres

🍇 110 has. ☕ 51% 🍷49%

VIÑA AMALIA 2003 JOVEN WHITE

75 Straw-coloured. Slightly flat aroma, ripe fruit. Flavourful palate, pleasantly bitter (citrus fruit), without great grape nuances.

CASA VILLA ZEVALLOS BARREL AGED RED
tempranillo, merlot, cabernet sauvignon, syrah   ▨ 6

83 Deep garnet red. Concentrated aroma of black fruit, well-integrated toasty notes (cocoa), and a spicy suggestion. Meaty and powerful on the palate, with ripe tannins, well-balanced oak; a slightly drying but elgant finish.

GRAN BARQUERO FINO
100% pedro ximénez

82 Greenish straw. Clean aroma of fresh flor (iodine) with a suggestion of yeast and fennel notes. Dry, slightly vinous palate with saline notes, without much flavour and slightly glyceric in the finish.

GRAN BARQUERO AMONTILLADO

84 Brownish amber. Toasty aroma of oven-roasted nuts and varnish. Flavourful, quite bitter and pleasant on the palate with sweet almondy notes, a slightly saline finish.

GRAN BARQUERO OLOROSO

86 Old gold with a coppery edge. Fine aroma of pâtisserie, cream, and toasty flavours. Very flavourful and expressive on the palate with fresh notes of citrus fruit, nuts and well-integrated Solera.

GRAN BARQUERO PEDRO XIMÉNEZ
100% pedro ximénez

84 Mahogany with a yellowish edge. Aroma of sweet grapes with sweet chocolate and a suggestion of Solera. Sweet palate without great freshness, with intense notes of fig bread, syrupy, slightly heavy sugar.

PEDRO XIMÉNEZ DE COSECHA

83 Old gold. Sweet and intense raisiny aroma with creamy vanilla and Solera notes. Sweet palate with notes of sweet almonds and pâtisserie, lacking freshness.

CORAZÓN LATINO PALE CREAM DULCE
LA CAÑADA PEDRO XIMÉNEZ

ROBLES

Carretera Córdoba-Málaga, km. 447, 5
14550 Montilla (Córdoba)

DO MONTILLA-MORILES

☎: 957 650 063 - Fax: 957 653 140
info@bodegasrobles.com
www.ctv.es/USERS/brobles

Established: 1927
🏺 3,000 🗄 2,100,000 litres
🍷 90% 🍇10%

PIEDRA LUENGA BIO PALE DRY FINO
100% pedro ximénez

75 Greenish straw. Not very intense, saline, nutty aroma. Dry, saline palate, well-mannered but without great nuances.

PIEDRA LUENGA BIO PEDRO XIMÉNEZ
100% pedro ximénez

78 Amber with an orangey hue. Aroma of sun-drenched grapes, orange peel and tropical fruit pulp. Very sweet, unctuous palate, without freshness, with quince and marzipan, very persistent.

VINO DE PASAS ROBLES PEDRO XIMÉNEZ
100% pedro ximénez

84 Old amber. Spicy aroma with crianza notes over raisins and hints of Mistelle. Round, unctuous palate with notes of citrus fruit (orange peel) and a creamy and generous finish.

CASTILLO DE MONTILLA 2001 WHITE
CASTILLO DE MONTILLA WHITE
ROBLES FINO
PATACHULA FINO
COPEO FINO
FINITO 12 AÑADA FINO
SELECCIÓN ROBLES NATURAL FINO
PATACHULA PALE CREAM FINO DULCE
ABUELO PEPE OLOROSO
SELECCIÓN ROBLES OLOROSO
PATACHULA CREAM OLOROSO
SELECCIÓN 1927 PEDRO XIMÉNEZ
BESO DE ANGEL MOSCATEL
ROBLES CREAM

SAN RAFAEL

Barroso, 10
14003 Córdoba (Córdoba)
☎: 957 479 324 - Fax: 957 479 324

Established: 1980
🏺 500 🗄 50,000 litres 🍷 100%

MORILES FINO FILIGRANA

75 Straw-coloured. Floral, slightly fruity aroma with light mask notes. Vinous palate with little flor character and a sweet sensation.

MONTILLA OLOROSO

73 Mahogany. Aroma dominated by varnish, varnished wood notes. Slightly pungent, warm palate with light nutty hints.

P.X. VIEJO PEDRO XIMÉNEZ

70 Amber. Aroma of Muscatel, very sweet

(freshly pressed grapes). Excessively sweet, slightly aggressive palate without fresh nuances.

SILLERO

Fernán Gómez, 11
14540 La Rambla (Córdoba)
☎: 957 684 069 - Fax: 957 684 464

🏺 2,000 🗄 157,000 litres 🍷 100%

ANACLETO FINO
LAS CÁRMENES FINO
SILLERO FINO
RONDALLA OLOROSO
SILLERO DULCE

SOC. DE PLATEROS

Cruz Conde, 3
14008 Córdoba
☎: 957 481 639

PLATINO FINO

Compañía Vinícola del SUR

Burgueños, 9
14550 Montilla (Córdoba)
☎: 957 650 200 - Fax: 957 652 335
vinsur@fiab.es

Established: 1962
🏺 2,000 🗄 3,500,000 litres 🍇 110 has.
🍷 75% 🍇25%

MONTECRISTO FINO
MONTECRISTO AMONTILLADO
MONTECRISTO OLOROSO
MONTECRISTO PEDRO XIMÉNEZ

TORO ALBALÁ

Carretera General de Málaga, s/n
14920 Aguilar de la Frontera (Córdoba)
☎: 957 660 046 - Fax: 957 661 494
info@talbala.com
www.talbala.com

Established: 1844
🏺 6,800 🗄 1,000,000 litres 🍇 39 has.
🍷 58% 🍇42%

ELÉCTRICO FINO DEL LAGAR

84 Yellow with a greenish edge. Saline aroma with hints of mountain herbs, quite ripe yet clean. Oily palate with good freshness, slightly pungent with well-balanced notes of flor and crianza and fennel in the finish.

VIEJÍSIMO SOLERA 1922

80 Old gold. Intense aroma with predominant notes of varnish and a suggestion of nuts. Powerful, bitter and quite unctuous palate with fine notes of herbs and nuts, lacking complexity.

DON P.X. 2002 PEDRO XIMÉNEZ
100% pedro ximenez

89 Toasted old gold. Aroma of fine pastries and toasted nuts with hints of raisins and jam. Very sweet, spirituous, dense and sweet palate with raisins.

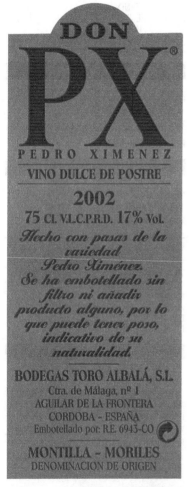

DON P.X. 1975 RESERVA PEDRO XIMÉNEZ
100% pedro ximénez

92 Opaque with a mahogany edge. Toasty aroma of old Solera (ripe dates, carob) and caramel. Sweet, toasty palate with old Solera and a suggestion of Oloroso and jammy dates, flavourful.

DON P.X. ECOLÓGICO 2002 PEDRO XIMÉNEZ
100% pedro ximénez

88 Reddish amber. Aroma with viscous notes and toasty hazelnuts and a suggestion of old Oloroso Solera. Sweet, pasty, flavourful, sweet, unctuous, concentrated palate, flavourful with aldehyde in the retronasal passage.

TORRES BURGOS

Ronda San Francisco, 1
14900 Lucena (Córdoba)
☎: 957 501 062 - Fax: 957 503 692
Established: 1890
⊕ 1,850 🌶 100%

CASTILLO DEL MORAL 2002 WHITE
100% pedro ximénez

74 Pale with a greenish edge. Discreet aroma of muted fruit and dominant ripeness. Dry, fresh palate with well-mannered fruit.

TB ETIQUETA NEGRA FINO
100% pedro ximénez

80 Straw-coloured with a greenish glint. Expressive aroma with hints of flor and notes of fennel. Round palate with poor saline nuances, slightly flat in nuances, an oily finish.

MORILES 1890 TORRES BURGOS AMONTILLADO
100% pedro ximénez

83 Amber. Aroma slightly dominated by Solera, with saline hints and toasted nuts. Dry palate with an expression of bitter almonds and notes of flor

TB PEDRO XIMÉNEZ
100% pedro ximénez

80 Old gold. Aroma of Mistelle with hints of Solera and vanilla and a raisiny essence. Fruity palate with crystallised fruit and quite heavy sugar weight; a vanilla finish.

WHY CRYM PALE CREAM SEMI-DULCE
100% pedro ximénez

77 Very pale with a greenish hue. Intense aroma with a hint of the freshness of crystallised citrus fruit peel. Fresh, flavourful, quite sweet palate with rich bittersweet notes.

VÍBORA

Ronda de Canillo, 4
14900 Montilla (Córdoba)
☎: 957 651 250 - Fax: 957 653 619
avilchez@bodegascruzconde.es
www.bodegascruzconde.es
Established: 1886
⊕ 3,820 🍶 2,100,000 litres 🌶 100%

ANA MARÍA FINO
DONCELES FINO
VÍBORA FINO

DO MONTSANT

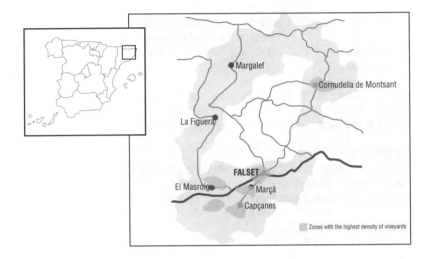

Zones with the highest density of vineyards

NEWS. Of the 63 wines from Montsant tasted for this edition, 34 surpassed 85 points, most of which were wines that were sold for less than € 12, which makes the region an excellent alternative to the ever pricier Priorats. Above this high average quality, Joan D'Anguera and Venus La Universal stand out with wines that constitute the most powerful and characteristic expression of Montsant. Also, an extraordinary achievement by Celler de Capçanes, based on the excellent harvest of 2001, with all its wines achieving scores above 85 points; as was the case with El Masroig, where, together with an excellent 2001 harvest, the good showing of the young white wines is equally patent, particularly those of carbonic maceration, and also the very elegant Ètim, and the Laurona de Europvin, which constantly achieved scores of nearly 90 points.

The 2002 harvest also promises generous maturity without losing the attributes of freshness and *terroir* commendably linked to this DO, with all the wines of this harvest achieving scores above 86 points.

Hectares of Vineyard	No. of Viticulturists	No. of Bodegas	2003 Harvest	2003 Production	Marketing
2,058	785	27	Very Good	6,500,000 kilos	51% Spain 49% foreign

LOCATION. In the region of Priorat (Tarragona). It is made up of Baix Priorat, part of Alt Priorat and various municipal districts of Ribera d'Ebre that were already integrated into the Falset sub-region. In total, 16 municipal districts: La Bisbal de Falset, Cabaces, Capçanes, Cornudella de Montsant, La Figuera, Els Guiamets, Marçá, Margalef, El Masroig, Pradell, La Torre de Fontaubella, Ulldemolins, Falset, El Molar, Darmós and La Serra d'Almos. The vineyards are located at widely variable altitudes, ranging between 200 m to 700 m above sea level.

CLIMATE. Although the vineyards are located in a Mediterranean region, the mountains that surround the region isolate it from the sea to a certain extent, resulting in a somewhat more Continental climate. Due to this, it benefits from the contrasts in day/night temperatures, which is an important factor in the ripening of the grapes. However, it also receives the sea winds, laden with humidity, which help to compensate for the lack of rainfall in the summer. The average rainfall is between 500 and 600 mm per year.

SOIL. There are mainly three types of soil: compact calcareous soils with pebbles on the borders of the DO; granite sands in Falset; and siliceous slate (the same stony slaty soil as Priorat) in certain areas of Falset and Cornudella.

VARIETIES:
White: *Chardonnay, Garnacha Blanca, Macabeo, Moscatel, Pansal, Parellada.*
Red: *Cabernet Sauvignon, Cariñena, Garnacha Tinta, Garnacha Peluda, Merlot, Monastrell, Picapoll, Syrah, Tempranillo* and *Mazuela.*

REGULATORY COUNCIL.
Plaça de la Quartera, 6. 43730 Falset (Tarragona).
Tel: 977 831 742. Fax: 977 830 676.
E-mail: info@domontsant.com
Website: www.domontsant.com

GENERAL CHARACTERISTICS OF THE WINES:

Whites	The most characteristic are the white wines based on *Garnacha Blanca*, which gives wines with body and a certain structure and the characteristic notes of herbs and hints of Mediterranean woodland, typical of the variety. The white wines from *Macabeo* are a little lighter and refined, fresh and fruity.
Rosés	There are not many examples, but in general they are produced from *Garnacha*. They are flavourful and fruity, maybe a little corporeal, but very pleasant with good red berry definition.
Reds	These are, without doubt, the most characteristic wines of the DO. They are produced almost exclusively from *Garnacha* or from a blend of this variety and *Mazuelo* with foreign varieties, especially *Cabernet Sauvignon* or *Syrah*. The young wines are fruity, meaty and flavourful. The best examples amongst those aged in barrels have high levels of fruitiness: they are powerful, meaty, with a high alcohol content. Mineral notes may also appear. They are reminiscent of Priorat wines, perhaps with less extraction and weight.
Traditional Wines	Liqueurs (sweet) are produced mainly from *Garnacha*. They are usually sticky and mellow on the palate, with aromas and a taste of raisins and preserved fruit.

AGRÍCOLA FALSET-MARÇA

Miquel Barceló, 31
43730 Falset (Tarragona)
☎: 977 830 105 - Fax: 977 830 363
sira@falsetmarca.com
www.falsetmarca.com

Established: 1913

🌐 1,000 📊 1,632,250 litres 🍇 210 has.

🍷 60% (🍷40%: -FR -BE -JP -AU -NZ -MX
AE-SAM -DE -DK -NL

ÈTIM VEREMA TARDANA 2002 CRIANZA DULCE WHITE
100% garnacha blanca

90 Golden yellow. Original aroma of stewed white fruit, quince, rosemary honey and light smoky scents. Sweet palate with a syrupy expression, crystallised fruit, good alcoholic acidity and a complex, citrus finish (grapefruit and apples).

MARTIUS 2003 WHITE
100% garnacha

84 Yellow straw. Intense aroma of great finesse with notes of ripe white fruit, smoky hints of oak and a nuance of herbs and minerals. Flavourful on the palate with the freshness of minerals and citrus fruit and a white fruit hint, well-balanced.

MARTIUS 2003 ROSÉ
66% garnacha, 34% syrah

86 Very deep raspberry. Intense aroma with an excellent expression of ripe red fruit, spicy hints of skins, minerals and fine lees. Flavourful palate with red stone fruit, hints of citrus fruit and minerals and excellent acidity.

ÈTIM SELECTION SYRAH 2001 OAK AGED RED
100% syrah

91 Very deep cherry with a coppery-violet edge. Powerful aroma with predominant notes of macerated red fruit, fine toasty oak and a mineral nuance. Fleshy, very flavourful palate with promising although quite evident tannins, fruit very well-integrated with the oak, a slight varietal expression, liquorice and underbrush.

ÈTIM VEREMA TARDANA
2002 OAK AGED DULCE RED
100% garnacha

89 Lively garnet red cherry. Intense aroma of black fruit with spicy notes and macerated overripe skins. Flavourful, powerful and concentrated on the palate, with fine tannins and a very oily texture, excellent expression of raisiny skins with cocoa and hints of minerals.

MARTIUS 2002 OAK AGED RED
garnacha, samsó, syrah

83 Very deep cherry with a violet edge. Not very intense aroma with predominant ripe fruit notes and a nuance of toasty oak. Fleshy, flavourful palate with slightly astringent tannins, bitter, slightly warm.

CASTELL DE FALSET 2000 RED
50% garnacha, 35% cabernet sauvignon, 15% tempranillo

87 Deep cherry with a garnet red edge. Complex aroma of crianza over fruit (tobacco, animals); with hints of sun-drenched skins and a slate nuance. Fleshy, powerful palate with long, drying wood tannins yet to be assembled, a good fruit nuance, long.

ÈTIM SELECTION VEREMA
SOBREMADURADA 2001DULCE RED
60% garnacha, 40% cariñena

88 Cherry. Aromas of toasty wood, smoky scents and very ripe red fruit. Sweet palate, marked but ripe tannins with good acidity; fleshy.

IMUS 2003 RED
SYRAH 2001 CRIANZA RED
ÈTIM SELECCIÓ GARNATXA 2001 RED

Cooperativa Agrícola
AUBACS I SOLANS

Carretera, 1
43736 La Figuera (Tarragona)
☎: 977 825 228
aubacsisolans@wanadoo.es

Established: 1931

🌐 6 📊 200,000 litres 🍇 55 has. 🍷 100%

AUBACS I SOLANS ROSÉ
AUBACS I SOLANS RED
AUBACS I SOLANS CRIANZA RED

Cooperativa Agrícola
BAIX PRIORAT, ELS GUIAMETS

Esgésia, 1
43777 Els Guiamets (Tarragona)
☎: 977 413 018 - Fax: 977 413 014
coop_guiamets@yahoo.es.es

Established: 1913

🌐 120 📊 1,000,000 litres 🍇 275 has.

🍷 50% (🍷50%

LO METS 2004 RED

85 Dark cherry with a violet hue. Powerful, fruity aroma, ripe black fruit, fine spicy and skins notes, a nuance of damp earth. Powerful, flavourful palate, slightly marked tannins, fine bitter notes (liquorice, bitter chocolate) very long.

LO METS 2003 JOVEN RED

84 Straw-coloured with a golden hue. Intense, varietal aroma, white fruit and flowers, a nuance of quality citrus fruit, spicy and mineral hints. Powerful, flavourful palate, concentrated, fine bitter notes, fragrant herbs, excellent citrus acidity.

GRAN METS 2003 OAK AGED RED

86 Garnet red cherry. Intense aroma, ripe fruit, with toasty, quite organic crianza nuances. Powerful, flavourful palate, slightly marked but promising tannins, fine bitter notes, quite long.

ISIS 2003 OAK AGED RED

85 Very dark garnet red cherry. Intense aroma, with predominant notes of ripe red fruit and fine spicy and terroir notes. Powerful, flavourful palate, oak tannins yet to be assembled with the fruit, excellent acidity, promising.

ISIS 2002 OAK AGED RED

87 Dark garnet red cherry. Powerful, ripe aroma, jammy red fruit, toasty oak notes, a suggestion of terroir. Flavourful palate, excellent crianza expression, well-balanced, fresh mineral overtones, with bitter nuances (chocolate, liquorice) in the finish.

VALL SELLADA 2003 JOVEN WHITE
VALL SELLADA 2003 FERMENTADO EN BARRICA WHITE

Cellers BARONÍA DEL MONTSANT

Comte Rius, 1
43360 Cornudella de Montsant (Tarragona)
☎: 977 821 483 - Fax: 938 924 402
englora@baronia-m.com
www.baronia-m.com

Established: 1997

🍷 40 🛢 10,000 litres 🍇 3 has.

🍾 20% 🌐80%

CLOS D'ENGLORA FERMENTAT EN BARRICA 2003 WHITE
ENGLORA 2002 SEMICRIANZA RED
CLOS D'ENGLORA AV 14 2000 CRIANZA RED
CLOS D'ENGLORA AV 21 1999 RESERVA RED
CLOS D'ENGLORA NEGRE DOLÇ 1998 RESERVA DULCE RED

BUIL & GINÉ

Apdo. de Correo 63
43730 Falset (Tarragona)
☎: 977 830 483 - Fax: 977 830 373
esther@builgine.com
www.builgine.com

Established: 1996

17-XI 2001 OAK AGED RED
garnacha, cariñena, tempranillo

84 Dark garnet red cherry. Intense aroma with predominant balsamic and dark-roasted flavours notes. Flavourful, fleshy palate with good oak/fruit integration and jammy fruit and liquorice in the finish.

Cellers CAPAFONS-OSSÓ

Del Bosquet, 6
43730 Falset (Tarragona)
☎: 977 831 204 - Fax: 977 831 367
cellers@capafons-osso.com
www.capafons-osso.com

Established: 1992

🍷 100 🛢 40,000 litres 🍇 17,5 has.

🍾 50% 🌐50%: -US -AD -BE -FR -NL -IT -CH -MX -DE

ROIGENC 2003 JOVEN ROSÉ
100% syrah

84 Very deep raspberry. Powerful, fruity aroma (strawberries, raspberries, red stone fruit) with a spicy nuance of skins. Flavourful and fruity on the palate with fine bitter notes and hints of citrus fruit, somewhat oily and warm, with good acidity.

MASIA ESPLANES 2001 CRIANZA RED
35% cabernet sauvignon, 40% merlot, 10% garnancha, 15% syrah

89 Very intense cherry with a saffron edge. Powerful aroma with predominant notes of red stone fruit (an element of prunes) and fine toasty oak. Flavourful on the palate with fine bitter notes (chocolate, liquorice), hints of minerals and a spicy ripe fruit nuance.

VESSANTS 2001 CRIANZA RED
35% cabernet sauvignon, 25% merlot, 25% garnancha, 15% cariñena

83 Intense cherry. Powerful aroma of red fruit with toasty hints of oak, slightly warm. Flavourful on the palate with fruit and oak yet to be integrated, rich in nuances, bitter and with good acidity.

Celler de CAPÇANES

Llebaria, s/n
43776 Capçanes (Tarragona)
☎: 977 178 319 - Fax: 977 178 319
cellercapcanes@cellercapcanes.com

Established: 1933

🍷 2,000 🛢 2,000,000 litres 🍇 300 has.

🍾 20% 🌐80%

MAS DONÍS 2003 JOVEN RED
80% garnacha, 20% Syrah

84 Intense cherry with a violet edge. Powerful, fruity aroma with hints of sun-drenched skins and fine spicy hints of the vine variety with a mineral nuance. Generous on the palate and rich in nuances (fruit, balsamic flavours) with slightly marked tannins, hints of earth and good acidity.

FLOR DE PRIMAVERA 2001 ROBLE RED
40% garnacha, 45% cabernet sauvignon, 15% tempranillo, 5% cariñena

91 Very deep garnet red cherry with a coppery edge. Powerful aroma of fine toasty oak well-integrated with macerated black fruit notes, with balsamic and mineral hints. Powerful on the palate with slightly marked although promising tannins, an oily and slightly warm texture and a good fruit weight, well-balanced and very long.

CABRIDA 2001 OAK AGED RED
100% garnacha

90 Garnet red. Fine aroma of dry earth, minerals and very elegant crianza reduction. Powerful, expressive and fleshy palate with well-balanced fruit-wood and a generous retronasal effect of red fruit, soil, spices.

COSTERS DEL GRAVET 2001 OAK AGED RED
30% garnacha, 50% cabernet sauvignon, 15% cariñena, 5% tempranillo

86 Intense cherry with a coppery edge. Powerful aroma of well-integrated spicy oak and black fruit notes with a fine mineral hint. Powerful and concentrated on the palate with well-integrated oak/fruit and bitter notes (chocolate, pitch), excellent symmetry, long.

LASENDAL 2002 OAK AGED RED
85% garnacha, 15% syrah

87 Very deep cherry with a coppery edge. Intense aroma of fine toasty oak notes with a very ripe red stone fruit nuance. Flavourful on the palate with slightly marked tannins, fine bitter notes (chocolate, dark-roasted flavours) and a spicy fruit nuance.

MAS COLLET 2001 CRIANZA RED
30% garnacha, 20% cabernet sauvignon, 20% tempranillo, 30% cariñena

85 Very deep garnet red cherry. Powerful aroma rich in spicy nuances and very varietal herbs (paprika, underbrush) with fine toasty wood. Flavourful on the palate with ripe and oily tannins and fine bitter notes, excellent acidity.

MAS COLLET 2002 CRIANZA RED
30% garnacha, 20% cabernet sauvignon, 20% tempranillo, 30% cariñena

87 Garnet red cherry with a coppery edge. Powerful aroma of toasty oak, jammy fruit, balsamic hints and terroir. Fleshy, concentrated palate with a good fruit/oak integration, liquorice and dark-roasted flavours, slightly warm and oily.

MAS TORTÓ 2001 CRIANZA RED
70% garnacha, 10% syrah, 10% merlot, 10% cabernet sauvignon

89 Very deep cherry with a coppery edge. Powerful aroma with well-integrated fruit/oak and fine balsamic hints. Powerful on the palate with rough tannins and well-characterised crianza with a nuance of pitch and minerals and an excellent Mediterranean expression.

VALL DEL CALÀS 2001 CRIANZA RED
50% merlot, 30% garnacha, 20% tempranillo

86 Garnet red cherry with a coppery edge. Powerful aroma with predominant toasty oak notes, hints of fruit and sun-drenched skins and a terroir nuance. Powerful on the palate with promising although slightly marked tannins, paprika-flavoured varietal nuances (Merlot), herbaceous hints and good acidity.

PANSAL DEL CALÀS VINO DE LUGAR 2001 JOVEN VINO DE LICOR
60% garnacha, 40% cariñena

85 Very deep cherry with a saffron edge. Not very intense aroma with predominant notes of toasty skins and raisins. Powerful, and unctuous on the palate with quality bittersweet notes, oily, with fine hints of spices and slightly mineral.

MAS COLLET 2003 JOVEN WHITE
CAPÇANES 2003 JOVEN ROSÉ

Unió Agraria Cooperativa
CELLERS UNIÓ

Joan Oliver, 16-24
Mas de les Animes
43206 Reus (Tarragona)
☎: 977 330 055 - Fax: 977 330 070
f.gimenez@cellersunio.com
www.cellersunio.com

Established: 1942

🌐 6,500 📦 6,000,000 litres 🍇 2110 has.

🍷 25% 🌍75%: -DE -DK -US -NL -JP

PERLAT SELECCIÓ ESPECIAL 2001 RESERVA RED

88 Dark garnet red cherry. Intense aroma, a certain finesse and richness of nuances (violets, jammy red fruit, mineral flavours). Powerful, flavourful palate, ripe, excellent crianza expression, well-balanced, mineral, long.

PERLAT 2003 CRIANZA RED

84 Intense garnet red cherry. Intense aroma, very fresh red fruit, fine mineral notes, hints of Mediterranean herbs. Flavourful, fresh palate, fine herbaceous, very varietal hints, excellent acidity and balance.

DO MONTSANT

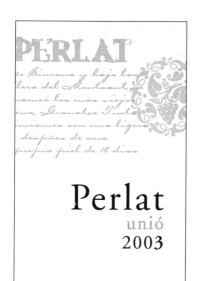

PERLAT 2° ANY 2002 CRIANZA RED

COLL DEL MONTSANT

Llull, 184 4° 3ª
08005 (Barcelona)
☎: 699 985 447 - Fax: 933 051 097
colldelmontsant@hotmail.com

Established: 2000
📖 20,000 litres 🍇 6 has. 🇪🇸 100%

COLL DEL TARTACÓ 2002 RED
80% cariñena, 20% garnacha

86 Cherry with an orangey edge. Floral aroma with slight viscous notes and jammy tomatoes. Flavourful, well-balanced and long on the palate with lively acidity.

Cooperativa de CORNUDELLA

Comte de Rius, s/n
43360 Cornudella (Tarragona)
☎: 977 821 031 - Fax: 977 821 031
info@cornudella.net

www.cornudella.net
Established: 1922
📖 1,500,000 litres 🍇 97 has.

EL CODOLAR 2003 JOVEN WHITE
macabeo

75 Pale with a greenish hue. Not very intense, slightly fruity aroma with hints of green apples and herbs. Fresh and flavourful on the palate with hints of citrus fruit.

EL CODOLAR 2003 JOVEN ROSÉ
garnacha, cariñena

74 Brilliant raspberry. Fairly intense aroma with fresh overtones, notes of sun-drenched skins but scarce fruit expression. Flavourful, fresh and pleasant on the palate.

LES TROIES 2003 JOVEN RED
garnacha tinta

75 Cherry-raspberry. Fresh aroma of red berries, flowers, liquorice and fine smoky notes. Fruity on the palate with hints of slightly bitter fruit pulp and high acidity.

CASTELL DE SIURANA 2001 OAK AGED RED
garnacha, tempranillo, cariñena

76 Brilliant cherry with an orangey glint. Fairly intense aroma with hints of ash, sackcloth and red stone fruit. Supple, quite flavourful palate with pronounced fruity freshness but scarcely any crianza expression.

Celler EL MASROIG

Passeig de L'Arbre, s/n
43736 El Masroig (Tarragona)
☎: 977 825 050 - Fax: 977 825 315
cellermasroig@retemail.es
Established: 1917
🍷 350 📖 2,700,000 litres 🍇 500 has.
🍾 50% 🔴 50%

LES SORTS 2003 WHITE

86 Pale with a greenish hue. Intense aroma of green fruit, fine notes of herbs, aniseed (fennel) and floral hints. Flavourful on the palate with fine bitter notes and quality hints of minerals and citrus fruit.

LES SORTS 2003 MACERACIÓN CARBÓNICA RED

85 Intense cherry with a violet edge. Powerful, fruity, ripe aroma with fine hints of herbs and brambles and sun-drenched skins. Powerful on the palate with an excellent expression of ripe fruit, spicy hints of skins and fine mineral notes in the finish.

SOLÀ FRED 2003 RED

82 Garnet red cherry with a violet hue. Powerful aroma of black fruit with spicy notes of skins and a suggestion of underbrush and minerals.

Flavourful on the palate with firm tannins well-integrated with the sweet fruit notes.

CASTELL DE LES PINYERES 2002 CRIANZA RED
garnacha, cariñena, tempranillo, cabernet sauvignon

82 Garnet red cherry with a coppery edge. Intense aroma of ripe red fruit with toasty oak notes and balsamic hints. Flavourful on the palate with slightly marked tannins, a ripe fruit nuance and bitter hints of liquorice.

LES SORTS VINYES VELLES 2001 CRIANZA RED
40% garnacha, 30% cariñena, 30% cabernet sauvignon

89 Very deep cherry with a coppery edge. Powerful aroma with predominant toasty oak notes, ripe fruit and hints of minerals. Powerful and concentrated on the palate with quite marked although promising tannins, ripe fruit and hints of pitch, very expressive and long.

MAS.ROIG 2001 CRIANZA RED
15% garnacha, 75% cariñena, 10% cabernet sauvignon

91 Deep cherry with a violet edge. Powerful aroma of fine toasty oak with a nuance of black fruit and balsamic flavours and light mineral notes. Flavourful on the palate with slightly marked but fine and promising tannins, notes of pitch, fine dark-roasted flavours, ripe fruit and spices, excellent.

ENRIC ANGUERA CEDÓ

Sant Pere, 2
43792 Darmós - Tivissa (Tarragona)
☎: 977 405 857 - Fax: 977 404 106
Established: 1960
90,000 litres 12 has. 100%

RECLOT ANGUERA DOMÈNECH 2003 RED
60% tempranillo, 20% garnacha, 20% monastrell

77 Light cherry. Fruity (sour cherries), fresh, spicy aroma (slight notes of reduction). Flavourful palate with very pleasant bitter notes (clay) and woody fruit in the finish (orange).

ESCOLA D'ENOLOGIA JAUME CIURANA IES PRIORAT

Carretera Porrera, s/n
43730 Falset (Tarragona)
☎: 977 830 338 - Fax: 977 830 338

ESCOLA D'ENOLOGIA JAUME CIURANA 2000 CRIANZA RED

83 Intense cherry. Fruity aroma (strawberries, flowers) and agreeable, spicy notes. Dry, very fresh palate with fruity tannins, without nuances of crianza and very well-balanced.

EUROPVIN FALSET

Carretera Bellmunt s/n
43730 Falset (Tarragona)
☎: 977 831 712 - Fax: 977 831 712
europvin@infonegocio.com
Established: 1999
100 100,000 litres 5 has.
30% 70%: -US -DE -CH -UK Países Escandinavios -NL -BE -BR -JP

6 VINYES DE LAURONA 2002 OAK AGED RED
60% garnacha, 40% cariñena   14

88 Deep cherry. Spicy, complex aroma with smoky notes of toasty skins, hints of pitch and minerals. Fleshy, fresh palate with powerful oak tannins well-balanced with the fruit and a liquorice and black fruit finish (plum).

6 VINYES DE LAURONA 2001 OAK AGED RED
60% garnacha, 40% cariñena   14

89 Intense cherry with a coppery-violet edge. Powerful, ripe aroma of creamy oak notes, a suggestion of fine lees and toast. Fleshy palate with rough, ripe, fine tannins well-integrated with the ripe fruit notes, bitter hints of terroir, very long.

LAURONA 2001 OAK AGED RED
30% garnacha, 30% cariñena, 15% syrah, 15% merlot, 10% cabernet sauvignon   12

88 Garnet red cherry with a coppery edge. Intense aroma with a certain finesse, predominant spicy oak, balsamic and fine reduction notes and a nuance of macerated red fruit. Flavourful palate with well-integrated oak/fruit, excellent crianza expression, balsamic and mineral.

LAURONA 2002 OAK AGED RED
40% garnacha, 20% cariñena, 15% syrah, 15% merlot, 10% cabernet sauvignon   12

88 Deep cherry. Intense, very fine aroma with well-integrated toasty oak and red stone fruit notes and a fine mineral element. Fleshy on the palate with ripe and slightly sweet tannins, fine hints of bitterness (chocolate, liquorice) and quality herbs; very long.

Cellers FOLCH

Avenida 11 de Setembre, s/n
43736 El Masroig (Tarragona)
☎: 977 825 009 - Fax: 977 825 009
cellersfolch@tinet.org
Established: 1952
20 960,000 litres 2 has.
90% 10%: -NL -DE -DK -SE

FRUCTUS 2003 WHITE
80% garnacha, 20% macabeo

79 Pale gold. Powerful aroma with spicy notes, mountain herbs and a poor fruit expression. Fresh, flavourful, slightly warm and oily on the palate with a suggestion of minerals.

MAS DE DALT 2003 JOVEN RED
35% tempranillo, 35% garnacha, 30% cariñena

75 Dark cherry with a violet rim. Intense aroma with light hints of evolution (dried peaches). Better on the palate, flavourful, slightly fruity and warm.

MAS DE DALT SELECCIÓN 2003 JOVEN RED
35% cariñena, 30% garnacha, 20% tempranillo, 15% cabernet sauvignon

77 Medium-hue cherry. Medium-intensity, ripe aroma of liquorice. Slightly concentrated fruit on the palate, well-mannered.

MAS DE DALT 2001 OAK AGED RED
35% cariñena, 30% garnacha, 20% tempranillo, 15% cabernet sauvignon

77 Not very deep orange. Aroma with very sweet notes of almost overripe red fruit. Very sweet, evolved palate with hints of honey in the retronasal passage.

Celler FRANCESC MASDEU

Major, 99
43736 El Masroig (Tarragona)
☎: 977 825 017 - Fax: 977 825 017
francescmasdeu@terra.es
Established: 1956
🍷 5 📦 70,000 litres 🌿 9 has.
🍇 60% 🍂40%

MASDEU 2003 JOVEN RED
garnacha, cariñena

80 Intense violet cherry. Aroma of red bramble berries with notes of vine shoots and a nuance of earth. Round palate with very fresh tannins, notes of liquorice and black berries, very polished.

MASDEU 2002 CRIANZA RED
garnacha, cariñena

75 Lively garnet red cherry. Lightly evolved aroma with very toasty wood. Ripe, warm palate with considerable wood weight.

Cellers GRIPOLL DECLARA

La Font, 8
53736 El Molar (Tarragona)
☎: 977 825 339 - Fax: 977 825 158
cgripolldeclara@terra.es
www.cgripolldeclara.com
Established: 2001
🍷 70 📦 23,000 litres 🌿 7 has.
🍇 60% 🍂40%: -US -PT -BE -CH

TOSSALS 2001 CRIANZA RED
garnacha, cariñena, cabernet sauvignon

88 Dark cherry with a violet edge. Powerful aroma of jammy black fruit, fine, toasty, creamy oak notes and balsamic hints. Powerful and concentrated on the palate with ripe, slightly oily tannins that envelop the fruit notes, fine hints of bitterness and minerals in the retronasal passage.

JOAN D'ANGUERA

Mayor s/n
43746 Darmós (Tarragona)
☎: 977 418 006 - Fax: 977 418 302
anguerabeyme@teleline.es
www.cellerjoandanguera.com
Established: 1820
🍷 200 📦 200,000 litres 🌿 39 has.
🍇 30% 🍂70%: -US -JP -CH -UK -DK -CA -FR -BE -DE -MX -NL -SE

JOAN D'ANGUERA 2003 JOVEN RED
45% syrah, 35% garnacha, 20% cabernet sauvignon

80 Brilliant cherry with a violet edge. Intense aroma with red stone fruit and herbaceous hints. Fresh, flavourful palate with slightly marked yet fine grape tannins, good fruit weight and good acidity.

EL BUGADER 2001 CRIANZA RED
70% syrah, 15% cabernet sauvignon, 15% garnacha

94 Very deep cherry. Intense aroma of jammy black fruit with a toasty oak nuance (very fine) and mineral hints. Powerful, very concentrated palate with well-integrated wood/fruit, ripe and oily tannins and fine spicy mineral notes.

FINCA L'ARGATA 2002 CRIANZA RED
40% syrah, 35% cabernet sauvignon, 15% garnacha, 10% cariñena

92 Very deep cherry. Concentrated but fresh aroma with well-integrated black fruit and wood (peat, slate, flowers), and character of the vine varieties. Powerful, fresh palate with fruity, slightly oily tannins, well-integrated smoky wood and a generous finish with notes of bitter cocoa and spices.

LA COVA DELS VINS

Bosquet, 5 (4 - 4)
43730 Falset (Tarragona)
☎: 600 807 325@filete
fax:covavins@wanadoo.es
Established: 2002
🍷 12 📦 12,000 litres

TERRÒS 2002 CRIANZA RED
50% garnacha, 25% Syrah, 25% cariñena

86 Very deep cherry with a violet edge. Powerful aroma of jammy black fruit with toasty oak notes and sour cherries in liqueur. Powerful and concentrated on the palate with slightly marked although promising tannins, rich in expression of bitter notes (chocolate, liquorice, pitch) with a mineral nuance.

Celler MAGÍ BAIGET

Nou, 26
43360 Cornudella de Montsant (Tarragona)
☎: 657 969 185 - Fax: 977 312 005
magi@btlink.net
www.pymesnetwork.com/celler
Established: 2002
🛢 35 🛢 15,000 litres 🍇 5 has.
🍷 60% 🌐40%: -DK -SE -US

CINGLES BLAUS SELECCIÓ 2002 CRIANZA RED
65% garnacha, 35% Syrah

87 Intense cherry with a violet edge. Powerful aroma with fine toasty oak, very ripe red fruit, a balsamic nuance and a fine reduction (lees). Fleshy, concentrated on the palate with flavourful tannins well-integrated with the fruit and spicy, bitter hints in the retronasal passage.

MAS DE L'ABUNDÀNCIA

Camí de Gratallops, s/n
43736 El Masroig (Tarragona)
☎: 637 415 263

MAS DE L'ABUNDÀNCIA 2002 OAK AGED RED
50% cabernet sauvignon, 25% garnacha, 25% cariñena
🛢 12

86 Deep cherry. Concentrated aroma of black fruits, toasty flavours, cocoa in the oak with hints of minerals and tobacco. Concentrated on the palate, abundant, polished, oily fruit and wood tannins with an aftertaste of slate notes and quite a dry finish.

FLVMINIS 2003 RED
60% cabernet sauvignon, 20% garnacha, 20% cariñena

81 Garnet red cherry with a coppery edge. Fairly intense aroma with notes of red stone fruit, minerals and fresh overtones. Fresh, fruity palate with slightly marked grape tannins, flavourful, well-structured and with good acidity.

NOGUERALS

Tou, 5
43360 Cornudella de Montsant (Tarragona)
☎: 977 821 020
wwwnoguerals@hotmail.com
Established: 2000
🛢 30 🛢 15,800 litres 🍇 4,5 has. 🍷 100%

CORBATERA 2002 RED
75% garnacha, 25% cabernet sauvignon

83 Deep intense cherry. Expressive aroma of wood spices, ripe black fruit and a terroir hint. Flavourful, very fresh palate with fruity tannins and slightly marked wood, long.

CORBATERA 2001 CRIANZA RED

Cooperativa Agricola SANT JAUME APOSTOL S.C.C.L.

Saltadora, 17
43363 Ulldemolins (Tarragona)
☎: 977 561 613 - Fax: 977 561 613

LES PEDRENYERES 2003 OAK AGED WHITE
garnacha blanca, macabeo
🛢 5

80 Pale yellow with a coppery hue. Intense aroma of ripe white fruit with a smoky and creamy oak hint. Flavourful on the palate with a slightly oily and warm texture, hints of fruit and herbs and a slightly mineral nuance.

ULLDEMOLINS GARNATXA RED
garnacha

72 Cherry red. Aroma with viscous notes and very ripe red fruit, slightly alcoholic. Warm on the palate, without great nuances.

SARMIENTO I DI GALANTE

Finca El Maset
43775 Marçà (Tarragona)
☎: 977 262 143 - Fax: 977 262 143
Established: 2001
🛢 15 🛢 500 litres 🍇 6 has.

ORCELLA ORSUS 2002 OAK AGED RED
90% garnacha, 10% syrah
🛢 12

83 Garnet red cherry. Concentrated aroma, of elegant toasty notes, ripe black fruit and a vanilla nuance. Flavourful palate of tobacco and animal skins, round tannins, slightly warm.

ORCELLA ARDEA 2002 CRIANZA RED
60% garnacha, 30% cabernet sauvignon, 10% merlot

83 Cherry. Aroma of ripe red fruit with jammy forest fruit. Warm, well-balanced and pleasant on the palate.

COOPERATIVA AGRÍCOLA DE LA SERRA D'ALMOS

Major, 23
43746 Serra D'Almos (Tarragona)
☎: 977 418 125 - Fax: 977 418 399
serracoop@retemail.es

DO MONTSANT

MUSSEFRES RED

TERRES DE CODOLS I LLICORERA

Comte de Rius, 2
43360 Cornudella (Tarragona)
☎: 977 821 074 - Fax: 977 821 074
adegalegas@nexo.es

Established: 1998

⊕ 400 ▤ 1,000,000 litres ※ 50 has.

🚩 80% 🌐20%

CLOS DELS CODOLS 2001 RED

86 Very deep cherry. Powerful, very fine aroma with toasty oak notes, ripe fruit and fine mineral hints. Flavourful, fleshy palate with slightly marked although promising tannins and hints of jammy fruit, well-balanced and very long.

VENDRELL RIVED

Carretera Marçà-La Torre, s/n
43775 Marçà (Tarragona)
☎: 977 178 150
jmvendrell@terra.es

Established: 2000

⊕ 30 ▤ 25,000 litres ※ 18 has.

🚩 20% 🌐80%: -US -CH

SERÉ 2003 OAK AGED RED
80% garnacha, 20% tempranillo

76 Cherry with a violet hue. Slightly alcoholic aroma without obvious fruit expression. Warm on the palate with vegetative notes and slightly marked tannins.

L'ALLEU 2002 CRIANZA RED
70% garnacha, 10% cariñena, 10% cabernet sauvignon, 10% tempranillo

84 Fairly deep brilliant cherry. Intense aroma of black fruit with spicy hints of oak, slightly warm. Flavourful and fleshy on the palate with slightly marked, rough and quite promising tannins, a nuance of spices and very ripe fruit, chocolate, long.

L'ALLEU 2001 CRIANZA RED

VENUS LA UNIVERSAL

Carretera Porrera, s/n
43730 Falset (Tarragona)
☎: 977 830 545 - Fax: 639 121 244

Established: 1999

⊕ 105 ▤ 50,000 litres ※ 4 has.

🚩 40% 🌐60%

VENUS 2001 RED
50% syrah, 50% cariñena

93 Intense cherry. Aroma with crianza notes (spices, pipe tobacco, pepper and new oak) and a jammy note with a subtle, complex suggestion of the wine press. Powerful, fleshy, flavourful and ripe palate with wood and fruit tannins.

DIDO 2003 RED

92 Intense deep cherry. Powerful, mineral aroma, very ripe fruit and toasty oak. Fleshy, powerful, full palate, obvious tannins, creamy oak in the retronasal passage (cocoa, chocolate), ripe fruit, mineral, warm.

VENUS 2002 RED
50% syrah, 50% cariñena

89 Intense cherry. Aroma with good fresh fruit expression (brambles, plums), earthy hints (clay, stones). Fresh, flavourful palate, fruity, slightly elegant, creamy oak in the retronasal passage.

VIÑAS DEL MONTSANT

Partida Coll de Mora , s/n
43775 Marçà (Tarragona)
☎: 977 831 309 - Fax: 977 831 356
fraguerau@tiscali.es

Established: 2001

⊕ 300 ▤ 110,000 litres ※ 42 has.

🚩 70%% 🌐30%: -US

FRA GUERAU 2002 OAK AGED RED
15% garnacha, 15% cariñena, 20% cabernet sauvignon, 20% merlot, 20% syrah, 5% tempranillo, 5% monastrell

87 Garnet red cherry with a saffron edge. Powerful aroma of macerated black fruit with fine spicy oak notes. Flavourful, fleshy and supple on the palate with well-integrated oak/fruit, well-balanced with balsamic and bitter notes and hints of sweet fruit in the retronasal passage.

FRA GUERAU 2001 JOVEN RED

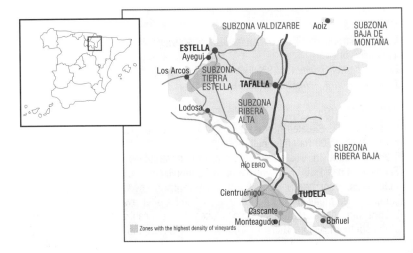

Zones with the highest density of vineyards

NEWS. Navarra is in vogue and its name is starting to be heard even in the foreign markets beyond the traditional rosé wines (less interesting, by the way, in the past few years). The main reason is quality and competitive prices, which makes the region an alternative to Rioja or Ribera del Duero. Of the 300 wines tasted, 85 surpassed 85 points and the rest maintained a good level.

Hectares of Vineyard	No. of Viticulturists	No. of Bodegas	2003 Harvest	2003 Production	Marketing
17,335	6,122	88 bottlers	Good	72,285,225	66% Spain 34% foreign

The 2003 harvest was 15 days early (it started on 16th August) due to the high temperatures in July and August. In general terms, the harvest was good, maybe a little affected by the rain and the sharp fall in temperatures in September.
The *Garnacha* grape, used to produce single variety wines, is going from strength to strength with four wines surpassing 85 points: Santa Cruz de Artazu of Artadi (89), the Palacio de Sada (2002 and 2003) and El Chaparral of Vega Sindoa. And the excellent average quality of Palacio de Otazu, with six wines above 87 marks, or the extraordinary wines of Javier Asensio.

LOCATION. In the province of Navarra. It draws together areas of different climates and soils, which produce wines with diverse characteristics.

CLIMATE. Typical of dry, sub-humid regions in the northern fringe, with average rainfall of between 593 mm and 683 mm per year. The climate in the central region is transitional and changes to drier conditions in southern regions, where the average annual rainfall is a mere 448 mm.

SOIL. The diversity of the different regions is also reflected in the soil. Reddish or yellowish and stony in the Baja Montaña, brownish-grey limestone and limestone in

Valdizarbe and Tierra Estella, limestone and alluvium marl in the Ribera Alta, and brown and grey semi-desert soil, brownish-grey limestone and alluvium in the Ribera Baja.

VARIETIES:

White: *Chardonnay* (2%), *Garnacha Blanca, Malvasía, Moscatel de Grano Menudo, Viura* (6% of total).
Red: *Cabernet Sauvignon* (9%), *Garnacha Tinta* (majority 42% of total), *Graciano, Mazuela, Merlot, Tempranillo* (29%).

SUB-REGIONS:

Baja Montaña. Situated northeast of Navarra, it comprises 22 municipal districts with around 2,500 Ha under cultivation.
Tierra Estella. In western central Navarra, it stretches along the Camino de Santiago. It has 1,800 Ha of vineyards in 38 municipal districts.
Valdizarbe. In central Navarra. It is the key centre of the Camino de Santiago. It comprises 25 municipal districts and has 1,100 Ha of vineyards.
Ribera Alta. In the area around Olite, it takes in part of central Navarra and the start of the southern region. There are 26 municipal districts and 3,300 Ha of vineyards.
Ribera Baja. In the south of the province, it is the most important in terms of size (4,600 Ha). It comprises 14 municipal districts.

REGULATORY COUNCIL.

Rúa Romana s/n. 31390 Olite (Navarra).
Tel: 948 741 812. Fax: 948 741 776.
E-mail: consejoregulador@vinonavarra.com
Website: www.vinonavarra.com

GENERAL CHARACTERISTICS OF THE WINES:

Whites	Although a minority product with respect to the red and rosé wines, young wines and wines fermented in barrels are also produced from the *Chardonnay* variety: golden yellow in colour, the best are characterised by their creamy and toasted aromas, which are well combined with fruit, and by their varietal character. Amongst the sweet wines, the whites from the *Moscatel de Grano Menudo*, a traditional variety which is slowly being recovered, stand out. There are few examples, although of high quality: grapey and honey aromas on the nose; flavourful, complex and fresh on the palate.
Rosés	Most are produced from *Garnacha*, although there are also examples from *Tempranillo* and *Cabernet Sauvignon*. Raspberry pink coloured, they are very fresh and fruity with a great character of red berries; on the palate they are balanced, flavourful and fruity.
Reds	These vary according to the varieties and the regions they are produced in. In the northern regions, where the *Tempranillo* predominates, the wines have a more Atlantic character; the aroma is more reminiscent of red berries; they are fresher with higher levels of acidity. In the south, the varietal character of the *Garnacha* stands out: the wines are warmer, with notes of ripe black fruit, round and supple on the palate. As well as these, there are the single variety wines from foreign varieties (mainly *Cabernet Sauvignon* and *Merlot*, with a marked varietal character), together with the red wines that combine autochthonous and foreign grape varieties.

Bodegas y Viñedos ALZANIA

Cardiel, 1
31210 Los Arcos (Navarra)
☎: 607 214 279 - Fax: 619 222 537
alzania@knet.es

Established: 1999

🌐 136 📊 275,000 litres 🍇 8,5 has.

🍷 40% 🌍60%: -DE -NL -AT -DK -CH -UK -RU -MX -US

ALZANIA 2002 CRIANZA RED
58% tempranillo, 34% garnacha, 8% merlot

88 Almost opaque cherry. Fine, concentrated aroma of toasty skins, foresty black fruit (blackberries), toasty notes and a suggestion of minerals. Fleshy, slightly tannic palate, very fruity and powerful with well-balanced smoky notes, for keeping.

ALZANÍA SELECCIÓN PRIVADA 2002 CRIANZA RED
68% cabernet sauvignon, 32% tempranillo

87 Dark cherry. Powerful aroma with predominant toasty notes (coffee, pitch) of oak and a nuance of jammy fruit. Flavourful, fleshy palate with promising yet slightly drying tannins and a nuance of spices and terroir.

Señorío de ANDIÓN

Carretera Pamplona-Zaragoza, km. 38
31390 Olite (Navarra)
☎: 948 712 193 - Fax: 948 712 343
info@lanavarra.com - lanavarra.com

Established: 2003

🌐 550 🍇 60 has. 🍷 80%

🌍20%: -UE -ASIA -US -CA -CAM

SEÑORÍO DE ANDIÓN 2001 CRIANZA RED
cabernet sauvignon, merlot, tempranillo, graciano

87 Black cherry. Powerful, concentrated aroma with jammy black fruit notes, toasty hints of oak and a balsamic suggestion of sour cherries in liqueur. Flavourful, fleshy palate with a good oak/fruit integration, slightly warm with liquorice and spices in the retronasal passage.

Cooperativa ÁNGEL DE LA GUARDA

Carretera De Larraga, s/n
31252 Berbinzana (Navarra)
☎: 948 722 056 - Fax: 948 711 489

Established: 1946

📊 1,000,000 litres 🍷 80% 🌍20%

ERETAS RED

ARDOA

Las Mercedes, 31, 4º
48930 Getxo (Vizcaya)
☎: 944 315 872 - Fax: 944 315 873
info@ardoa.com

Established: 2002

🍷 5% 🌍95%: -UE -US

AZCÚNAGA CABERNET SAUVIGNON-MERLOT 2000 CRIANZA RED
50% tempranillo, 30% cabernet sauvignon, 20% merlot

85 Dark cherry with an orangey edge. Intense aroma of jammy fruit with dark-roasted and caramelised notes. Full, fleshy and flavourful on the palate with good assemblage of fruit and wood, concentrated.

AZCÚNAGA 1999 RESERVA RED
50% tempranillo, 30% cabernet sauvignon, 20% merlot

86 Cherry with an orangey edge. Medium-intensity yet fine, balsamic and toasty aroma of damp earth. Flavourful and full on the palate with balsamic notes that add freshness, ripe fruit well-integrated with the oak, ripe tannins, persistent.

AZCÚNAGA SELECCIÓN PRIVADA 1999 RESERVA RED
30% tempranillo, 40% cabernet sauvignon, 30% merlot

87 Cherry with an orangey edge. Medium-intensity, balsamic (fallen leaves) and fine aroma of ripe red fruit. Powerful, concentrated and flavourful on the palate with a good fruit expression, toasty oak and spicy crianza in the finish.

ReSerVa 1999
SeLecCióN PrIvadA
NaVaRrА
DEnOmInAtion dE oRIgEN

AZcúNAgA

ARISTU

Carretera N-240 Pamplona-Saca, km. 35
31440 Lumbier (Navarra)
☎: 948 398 098 - Fax: 948 880 290
baristu@teleline.es
www.aristu.com

Established: 1994

⊕ 150 📦 400,000 litres 🍇 40 has.

🍷 75% 🌐25%: -US -DE -CH -FR -SE -IE

MAZTEGUI GARNACHA 2003 RED
ARISTU GARNACHA 2002 RED
SEÑORÍO DE ARISTU 2000 CRIANZA RED
ARISTU 1999 RESERVA RED

ARMENDARIZ

Avenida El Salvador, 11-Bajo
31370 Falces (Navarra)
☎: 948 734 135 - Fax: 948 714 902
josepueyo@teleline.es

Established: 1888

⊕ 241 📦 1,400,000 litres 🍇 25 has.

🍷 95% 🌐5%: -FR -DE -BE

ARMENDARIZ 2003 WHITE
ARMENDARIZ 2003 ROSÉ
JUANRON 2003 ROSÉ
VALDESANJUAN 2003 ROSÉ
DON JUAN 2003 ROSÉ
ARMENDARIZ 2003 RED
ARMENDARIZ 2001 CRIANZA RED
ARMENDARIZ 2000 RESERVA RED

Vinos y Viñedos AROA

Berokia, 7
31292 Zurukoain (Navarra)
☎: 948 555 394 - Fax: 948 555 395
info@aroawines.com - aroawines.com

Established: 1998

⊕ 150 📦 120,000 litres 🍇 16 has.

🍷 45% 🌐55%: -DE -FR -BE -UK -IE -CH -US

AROA DEIERRI 2002 OAK AGED RED
43% cabernet sauvignon, 42% merlot, 15% tempranillo

88 Garnet red cherry. Aroma with light notes between vegetative (geranium leaves) and mineral nuances and fine lees. Round, oily and flavourful on the palate with harmonious oak and fruit and complex overtones.

AROA JAUNA 2001 CRIANZA RED
36% merlot, 35% cabernet sauvignon, 29% tempranillo

73 Not very deep cherry. Aroma with marked vegetative notes (green peppers) that sully the fruitiness. Slightly more fruit on the palate, well-mannered but lacking expression.

AROA 2001 RESERVA RED
43% merlot, 42% cabernet sauvignon, 15% tempranillo

83 Deep cherry with a coppery-violet edge. Not very intense aroma, jammy red fruit notes with a toasty oak hint and elements of minerals and

cedar. Flavourful palate with fine bitter notes (well-integrated oak/fruit) and a spicy and balsamic nuance.

AROA JAUNA 2002 CRIANZA RED
AROA TEMPRANILLO 2003 RED

Bodegas y Viñedos ARTAZU

Mayor, 3
31195 Artazu (Navarra)
☎: 945 600 119 - Fax: 945 600 850
artazu@artadi.com

Established: 2000

⊕ 200 🍷 40% 🌐60%

SANTA CRUZ DE ARTAZU 2002 OAK AGED RED
garnacha

89 Dark garnet red cherry. Fresh, very fruity aroma with very fine toasty nuances (cocoa). A rich fruit expression blended with fine toasty oak nuances on the palate, flavourful and persistent, more elegant and less expressive than the previous vintage.

ARTAZURI 2003 ROSÉ SECO
ARTAZURI 2003 RED SECO

ASENSIO VIÑEDOS Y BODEGAS

Mayor, 84
31293 Sesma (Navarra)
☎: 948 698 040 - Fax: 948 698 097
info@bodegasasensio.com
www.bodegasasensio.com

Established: 1994

⊕ 614 📦 428,000 litres 🍇 70 has.

🍷 20% 🌐80%

JAVIER ASENSIO 2000 CRIANZA RED
50% cabernet sauvignon, 30% merlot, 20% tempranillo

90 Deep cherry with a saffron edge. Powerful aroma of black fruit with fresh, spicy Cabernet overtones and balsamic notes with fine toasty oak. Flavourful palate with well-integrated oak/fruit, and hints of liquorice and underbrush.

JAVIER ASENSIO CABERNET SAUVIGNON 2000 RESERVA RED
cabernet sauvignon

89 Very deep cherry. Powerful, ripe,very concentrated and varietal aroma of toasty oak and a slightly mineral suggestion. Powerful, flavourful palate with ripe, oily tannins and fine herbaceous, spicy (paprika, liquorice) and very varietal notes in the reteronasal passage.

DO NAVARRA

JAVIER ASENSIO 2000 RESERVA RED
50% cabernet sauvignon, 30% merlot, 20% tempranillo

91 Very dark, garnet red cherry. Powerful aroma though somewhat quite closed with toasty oak notes, well-integrated jammy black fruit and hints of graphite. Powerful, flavourful palate with quite rough and very promising tannins, hints of liquorice and balsamic notes in the retronasal passage.

JAVIER ASENSIO MERLOT 2000 RESERVA RED
merlot

89 Intense cherry with a coppery edge. Powerful aroma with toasty oak and skins with good varietal expression (jammy black fruit, paprika, fallen leaves). Flavourful, fleshy palate with quite firm tannins, fine notes of dark-roasted flavours and liquorice, and acidic, spicy in the retronasal passage.

BROJAL 2000 RESERVA RED

91 Garnet red cherry with a coppery edge. Powerful aroma with toasty notes of oak and skins, very varietal fruit (paprika), underbrush and wet earth. Powerful and very concentrated on the palate with rough tannins, good fruit/oak integration and fine bitter notes; liquorice, balsamic notes and hot paprika in the retronasal passage.

Bodegas AZPEA

Itúrbero, s/n
31440 Lumbier (Navarra)
☎: 948 880 433 - Fax: 948 880 433
bodegasazpea@wanadoo.es
Established: 2000
🍷 34 📊 120,000 litres 🍇 20 has.
🇪🇸 95% 🌐5%: -DE -BE -FR

AZPEA VIURA 2003 WHITE
100% viura

75 Yellow straw. Not very varietal aroma with subtle hints of flowers. Fruity palate, high in acidity and quite bitter.

AZPEA MOSCATEL 2003 WHITE DULCE
moscatel de grano menudo

81 Pale yellow. Aroma of white flowers and quince, not very intense yet clean. Slightly carbonic on the palate, sweet, with good acidity.

AZPEA 2003 ROSÉ
garnacha

80 Intense raspberry. Powerful aroma of red fruit, hints of sweetness and toasty skins. Flavourful, with fresh fruity overtones and hints of citrus fruit, good acidity.

AZPEA 2001 JOVEN RED
33% garnacha, 33% tempranillo, 33% cabernet sauvignon

83 Deep cherry with a violet edge. Powerful aroma of black fruit, fresh spicy overtones and skins with dark-roasted oak. Flavourful, slightly fleshy palate with slightly marked tannins and fine bitter notes (good fruit/oak combination), slightly warm.

AZPEA SELECCIÓN 2001 RED
80% cabernet sauvignon, 20% garnacha

84 Very deep cherry. Intense aroma of ripe black fruit, with toasty hints of oak without great varietal character. Flavourful, fleshy palate with ripe and slightly oily tannins, fine herbaceous hints of Cabernet and good acidity.

AZUL Y GARANZA BODEGAS

c/San Juan, s/n
31310 Carcastillo (Navarra)
☎: 948 725 677 - Fax: 948 725 677
info@azulygaranza.com
www.azulygaranza.com
Established: 2000
🍷 120 📊 300,000 litres 🍇 35 has.
🇪🇸 30% 🌐70%: -US -DE -CH -FI -UK

ROSA DE AZUL Y GARANZA 2003 ROSÉ
tempranillo, garnacha

82 Brilliant raspberry with a coppery hue. Intense, very fine aroma of red fruit with floral hints (rose petals) and spicy skins. Fresh, fruity palate with fine bitter notes and good acidity.

AZUL Y GARANZA 2003 OAK AGED RED
tempranillo, cabernet sauvignon

84 Garnet red cherry with a violet hue. Slightly intense aroma of red fruit with a spicy nuance of skins and toasty hints of oak. Flavourful palate with slightly marked although promising tannins, spicy with balsamic and mineral hints.

SEIS DE AZUL Y GARANZA 2002 OAK AGED RED
merlot, cabernet sauvignon

85 Garnet red cherry with a coppery edge. Powerful aroma with macerated red fruit and fine smoky and spicy oak notes. Flavourful palate with fine wood tannins, ripe fruit and balsamic hints, liquorice and minerals in the retronasal passage.

SEIS DE AZUL Y GARANZA 2003 CRIANZA ROSÉ
SEIS DE AZUL Y GARANZA 2003 RED

BEAMONTE

Vía Romana, s/n
31520 Cascante (Navarra)
☎: 948 811 000 - Fax: 948 811 407

Established: 1938

🗄 1,200,000 litres

BEAMONTE WHITE
BEAMONTE ROSÉ
BEAMONTE RED
LEÓN MARZOT RED
BEAMONTE CRIANZA RED
BEAMONTE RESERVA RED

CAMILO CASTILLA

Santa Bárbara, 40
31591 Corella (Navarra)
☎: 948 781 021 - Fax: 948 780 515
comercial@bodegascamilocastilla.com

Established: 1856

🌐 600 🗄 833,000 litres 🍇 53.27 has.

🚢 75% 🍷25%: -DE -CH -BE -NL -DK -MX -UK

CAPRICHO DE GOYA VINO DE LICOR DULCE
100% moscatel

91 Very deep mahogany. Powerful, concentrated aroma with predominant dried fruit notes (dates, molasses) on a long crianza hint (cocoa, dark-roasted flavours, pâtisserie, old furniture). Powerful, unctuous palate with dark-roasted notes, spices (cinnamon), a creamy, refreshing acidity and powerful hints of toffee in the retronasal passage, very long.

MONTECRISTO 2003 OAK AGED WHITE SECO
100% moscatel de grano menudo

79 Pale yellow with a golden hue. Intense aroma with good varietal expression (flowers, musk, smoky hints of oak). Fresh, dry, slightly bitter palate with creamy hints of wood and an acidic edge.

MONTECRISTO 2003 JOVEN ROSÉ
100% garnacha

80 Very deep raspberry. Powerful aroma of ripe red fruit, toasty hints of skins and floral notes with a terroir nuance. Flavourful, slightly fruity and

spicy palate with a slightly oily and warm texture that conceals the fruit.

MONTECRISTO 2000 CRIANZA RED
70% tempranillo, 15% cabernet sauvignon, 10% mazuelo, 5% graciano

79 Garnet red cherry. Powerful aroma with ripe fruit, fine reduction notes and underbrush. Flavourful palate with quite fresh oak tannins and a slightly acidic edge.

MONTECRISTO SELECCIÓN FINCA MARINA 1999 RESERVA RED
50% tempranillo, 30% cabernet sauvignon, 20% mazuelo

79 Garnet red cherry with a coppery edge. Intense, ripe aroma with fine herbaceous hints and spicy hints of oak. Flavourful palate with jammy fruit, very marked tannins and mild hints of greeness, bitter with good acidity.

MONTECRISTO 2003 MOSCATEL
moscatel

83 Yellow with a golden glint. Aroma of ripe quince, slightly alcoholic, with hints of citrus fruit (grapefruit). Warm, sweet and unctuous on the palate.

VINO PARA CONSAGRAR WHITE
GOYA OAK AGED MOSCATEL
RAYO DE SOL OAK AGED MOSCATEL

CAMINO DEL VILLAR

Camino del Villar. N-161, km. 3
31591 Corella (Navarra)
☎: 948 401 321 - Fax: 948 781 414
sales@vinaaliaga.com
www.vinaaliaga.com

Established: 1998

🌐 449 🗄 800,000 litres 🍇 55 has.

🚢 40% 🍷60%: -DE -NL -BE -AT -CH -FR -BR -RU -DK -IE -UK -CA -US -TR

VIÑA ALIAGA ROSADO DE LÁGRIMA 2003 ROSÉ
100% garnacha

79 Brilliant raspberry. Fairly intense aroma with fruity notes, spicy hints of skins and fresh overtones. Flavourful, very fresh palate, slightly oily and warm with high quality citrus fruit hints.

VIÑA ALIAGA TEMPRANILLO 2002 RED
100% tempranillo

82 Garnet red cherry with a coppery-violet edge. Intense aroma of black fruit with toasty hints of grapes and a slightly creamy hint. Flavourful palate with quite marked tannins, well-structured with fresh mineral overtones.

VIÑA ALIAGA GARNACHA VIEJA 2002 RED
100% garnacha

81 Intense cherry with a violet edge. Powerful aroma of ripe red fruit with spicy notes of skins and a suggestion of terroir. Flavourful palate with slightly green tannins, quite concentrated.

VIÑA ALIAGA ANTONIO CORPUS 2002 OAK AGED RED
90% garnacha, 10% cabernet sauvignon

88 Very deep cherry with a violet edge. Powerful, very fine aroma of perfectly ripe red fruit with fine spicy notes of skins and notions of terroir. Powerful and very concentrated on the palate with well-integrated oak and fruit, good turns between bitter and sweet notes and excellent varietal expression, very long.

VIÑA ALIAGA CUVÉE 2001 OAK AGED RED
85% tempranillo, 15% cabernet sauvignon   6

82 Garnet red cherry. Intense aroma of macerated black fruit, hints of toasty oak and spicy skins with notes of minerals. Flavourful palate with promising but quite marked tannins, herbaceous hints of Cabernet, with fine bitter notes and good acidity.

VIÑA ALIAGA 2000 CRIANZA RED
80% tempranillo, 20% cabernet sauvignon

83 Garnet red cherry with a brick red edge. Intense aroma with predominant toasty oak notes and hints of jammy fruit. Powerful and flavourful palate with slightly fresh oak tannins and a good expression of ripe fruit, balsamic flavours and liquorice.

VIÑA ALIAGA 1999 RESERVA RED
100% tempranillo

85 Garnet red cherry with an orangey glint. Not very intense aroma with a certain finesse, spicy wood notes, tobacco and notions of terroir. Flavourful palate with complementary fruit and oak, predominant dark-roasted flavours and bitter chocolate notes, well-balanced.

VIÑA ALIAGA GRAN SELECCIÓN 2000 RESERVA RED
70% cabernet sauvignon, 30% tempranillo

88 Garnet red cherry with a coppery edge. Powerful aroma with predominant smoky oak and fine reduction notes (tobacco) with a suggestion of jammy fruit. Flavourful and with fleshy overtones on the palate, with a good fruit/oak integration, excellent acidity.

CARLOS MAGAÑA

Avenida Rio Aragón, 1
31490 Caseda (Navarra)
☎: 948 434 332 - Fax: 948 434 115
bodegas@carlosmagana.com
www.carlosmagana.com

Established: 1999

 550 1,000,000 litres 10 has.

 50% 50%

VEGA DE CÁSEDA 2000 CRIANZA RED
merlot, cabernet sauvignon

82 Garnet red cherry with a coppery edge. Powerful aroma of jammy black fruit, with fine herbaceous, spicy (paprika); and very varietal notes with a suggestion of creamy oak. Flavourful palate with slightly marked tannins and a predominant bitter and toasty notes (liquorice, dark-roasted flavours).

MELIUS 2000 CRIANZA RED
merlot, cabernet sauvignon

80 Garnet red cherry. Not very intense aroma with a certain finesse, with macerated red fruit and spicy oak notes. Flavourful palate with quite rough tannins, a mild note of greeness and predominant bitter notes in the retronasal passage, lacks balance.

MELIUS 1998 RESERVA RED
merlot, cabernet sauvignon

84 Garnet red cherry. Intense aroma with a good oak/fruit integration, fine toasty notes, spicy and balsamic hints. Flavourful palate with a slight varietal expression (redcurrants, paprika), good fruit-tanicity-acidity balance and fine bitter notes in the retronasal passage.

CARRICAS

Rua Romana, 11
31390 Olite (Navarra)
☎: 948 740 106 - Fax: 948 740 106
Established: 1910
 3,000,000 litres 60 has.

MONT-PLANÉ WHITE
MONT-PLANÉ ROSÉ
MONT-PLANÉ RED

CASTILLO DE MONJARDÍN

Viña Rellanada, s/n
31242 Villamayor de Monjardín (Navarra)
☎: 948 537 412 - Fax: 948 537 436
monjardín@interbook.net
www.monjardin.es

Established: 1988

 1,800 1,500,000 litres 135 has.

 60% 40%: -DE -UK -FR -NL -DK -SE -JP -CA -US -PT -CH

CASTILLO DE MONJARDÍN 2003 JOVEN WHITE
100% chardonnay

83 Pale yellow with a golden hue. Intense aroma of ripe white fruit with exotic hints of flowers and honeyed notes. Fresh, flavourful palate with green apples, fine bitter notes and hints of high quality citrus fruit.

DO NAVARRA

CASTILLO DE MONJARDÍN 2001 FERMENTADO EN BARRICA WHITE
100% chardonnay

85 Brilliant golden yellow. Intense aroma of ripe white fruit with fine spicy and creamy oak notes, floral hints and lees. Fresh, flavourful palate with green apples, fine oak tannins, hints of quality citrus fruit and good acidity.

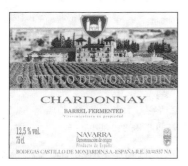

CASTILLO DE MONJARDÍN 2000 RESERVA WHITE
100% chardonnay

89 Golden yellow. Powerful aroma with a good oak/fruit integration, an excellent varietal expression (apples, hay), a suggestion of creamy wood, lees and honeyed notes. Flavourful palate, rich in nuances with a slightly oily, warm texture and excellent symmetry and acidity.

CASTILLO DE MONJARDÍN 2003 FERMENTADO EN BARRICA ROSÉ
100% merlot

81 Deep raspberry with a coppery hue. Powerful, ripe aroma of red fruit with spicy and toasty hints of skins. Generous, fleshy palate with ripe and slightly oily tannins, a good weight of very varietal fruit and refreshing acidity.

TINTO MONJARDÍN 2003 JOVEN RED
tempranillo, merlot

83 Fairly deep cherry with a violet hue. Powerful, fruity aroma with spicy notes (paprika) and fine notes of herbs and underbrush. Flavourful, fruity palate with fleshy overtones, fine grape tannins and excellent structure and acidity.

CASTILLO DE MONJARDÍN MERLOT 2001 OAK AGED RED
100% merlot

83 Garnet red cherry. Not very intense aroma of black fruit with toasty and creamy oak notes. Flavourful palate with well-integrated oak/fruit, fine bitter and toasty notes and refreshing acidity.

CASTILLO DE MONJARDÍN 2001 CRIANZA RED
85% merlot, 15% cabernet sauvignon

85 Intense cherry. with a saffron edge. Powerful aroma with excellent varietal expression (paprika, underbrush) and spicy hints of wood. Flavourful, slightly supple palate with fine tannins and good varietal and crianza expression.

CASTILLO DE MONJARDÍN 1999 RESERVA RED
cabernet sauvignon, tempranillo

84 Deep cherry with a saffron edge. Powerful aroma of black fruit with an excellent varietal profile (fine herbaceous notes) and smoky hints of oak. Flavourful, fleshy palate with well-integrated oak/fruit, notes of liquorice and an element of minerals in the retronasal passage.

DEYO MONJARDÍN 2002 RED
100% merlot

82 Deep cherry with a violet edge. Powerful, fruity aroma with hints of sun-drenched skins and an excellent varietal expression (paprika, red fruit). Flavourful, fleshy palate with very fine tannins and good acidity.

CASTILLO DE MONJARDÍN 2002 FERMENTADO EN BARRICA WHITE
CASTILLO DE MONJARDÍN 2001 CRIANZA RED
CASTILLO DE MONJARDÍN 1994 GRAN RESERVA RED
ESENCIA MONJARDÍN 2000 GRAN RESERVA RED

CIRBONERA

Ribera, s/n
31592 Cintruénigo (Navarra)
☎: 948 811 033 - Fax: 948 815 160
info@bodegacirbonera.com
www.bodegacirbonera.com

Established: 1920

DO NAVARRA

🍇 725 📊 13,000,000 litres 🍷 1.400 has.
🍷 80% 🍇20%

CAMPO LASIERPE 2003 WHITE
viura

78 Pale yellow with a golden hue. Intense aroma of ripe white fruit with fine floral notes (petals) and an element of lees. Flavourful palate with white fruit, bitter hints (hay, almonds) and a slightly oily texture.

CAMPO LASIERPE 2003 ROSÉ
100% garnacha

80 Brilliant raspberry. Intense aroma of red fruit, optimum ripeness and spicy hints of skins with a citrus fruit nuance. Fresh, flavourful palate with fine spicy notes (white pepper) and good acidity.

CAMPO LASIERPE 2002 OAK AGED RED
tempranillo, garnacha

82 Garnet red cherry with a coppery edge. Intense aroma of red fruit with spicy hints of skins, fine toasty notes and notes of underbrush. Flavourful, fruity palate with ripe and fine tannins, spicy hints (liquorice, pepper) and slightly mineral in the retronasal passage.

DOMINIO LASIERPE 1999 CRIANZA RED
tempranillo, cabernet sauvignon, merlot

82 Garnet red cherry. Fairly intense aroma of spicy oak notes with a nuance of black fruit and a herbaceous freshness. Flavourful, supple palate with well-associated oak/fruit, well-balanced, with excellent crianza expression.

DOMINIO LASIERPE 1999 RESERVA RED
tempranillo, cabernet sauvignon, merlot

81 Garnet red cherry with a brick red rim. Intense aroma with predominant notes of oak and a fine reduction, hints of prune stones. Flavourful, supple palate, spicy notes, very pleasant.

CORELLANAS

Santa Bárbara, 29
31591 Corellana (Navarra)
☎: 948 780 029 - Fax: 948 781 542
bcorellanas@line-pro.es

Established: 1900

🛢 120 📊 750,000 litres 🍷 45 has.
🍷 80% 🍇20%

VIÑA RUBICÁN 2003 WHITE
60% viura, 40% moscatel

79 Pale yellow. Intense aroma of fine floral and mildly musky Muscatel notes. Fresh, flavourful palate with rich bittersweet notes, bitter hints and citrus fruit.

VIÑA RUBICÁN 2003 ROSÉ
100% garnacha

79 Brilliant raspberry. Intense aroma of ripe red fruit with toasty notes of skins and a suggestion of crystallised fruit. Flavourful, fruity palate with a slightly oily and warm texture.

VIÑA RUBICÁN 2003 RED
100% tempranillo

80 Fairly deep cherry with a violet edge. Intense aroma of ripe red fruit with floral hints (petals) and toasty skins. Flavourful palate with firm tannins, a hint of sweet fruit, bitterness and a slightly oily texture.

VIÑA RUBICÁN 2000 CRIANZA RED
85% tempranillo, 15% garnacha

83 Garnet red cherry with a coppery edge. Fairly intense aroma of jammy black fruit with toasty oak notes. Flavourful palate, with a good oak/fruit integration, fine bitter notes and a slightly oily, warm texture, well-crafted crianza, pleasant.

VIÑA RUBICÁN 1997 RESERVA RED
33% cabernet sauvignon, 33% tempranillo, 33% merlot

80 Garnet red cherry with a coppery edge. Intense aroma with toasty oak notes, fine notes of spices and jammy fruit. Flavourful and fleshy with quite marked oak tannins and toasty wood notes, pleasant.

SARASATE 2003 MOSCATEL DULCE NATURAL
100% moscatel

86 Pale with a golden glint. Intense aroma with good varietal expression (musk, white flowers), honeyed hints and spices. Flavourful palate with rich bittersweet notes, unctuous with notes of aniseed and fine herbs, refreshing acidity.

MARQUÉS DE SARASATE WHITE
MARQUÉS DE SARASATE ROSÉ
MARQUÉS DE SARASATE RED
CASTILLO DE BLENDO RED

COSECHEROS REUNIDOS

Carretera Beire, nº 1
31390 Olite (Navarra)
☎: 948 740 067 - Fax: 948 740 067
cosecheros@ucan.es
www.vinosdeolite.com

Established: 1913

📊 3,000,000 litres 🍷 300 has.
🍷 95% 🍇5%

VIÑA JUGUERA ROSÉ
VIÑA JUGUERA RED
VIÑA JUGUERA TEMPRANILLO RED

DÁMASO GARBAYO ALDUAN

Rubio, 4
31592 Cintruénigo (Navarra)

☎: 948 811 869 - Fax: 948 811 154

Established: 1734

⊞ 25 ▤ 1,370,000 litres

🍇 20 has. 🍷 100%

VIÑA JAVIER GARBAYO 1999 CRIANZA RED
VIÑA JAVIER GARBAYO 1995 CRIANZA RED

Bodegas ESCALERA

Merindad de estella, 14
31390 Olite (Navarra)
☎: 661 265 235
bodegasescalera@hotmail.com

Established: 2002

⊞ 100 ▤ 230,000 litres 🍇 25 has.

SEÑORÍO DE LANDIBAR 2002 ROSÉ
SEÑORÍO DE LANDIBAR 2002 OAK AGED RED
SEÑORÍO DE LANDIBAR 2002 RED

FERNÁNDEZ DE ARCAYA

La Serna, 31
31210 Los Arcos (Navarra)
☎: 948 640 072 - Fax: 948 441 060
noelia@fernandezdearcaya.com
www.fernandezdearcaya.com

Established: 1990

⊞ 850 ▤ 600,000 litres 🍇 94 has.

🍷 80% 🌐20%: -DE -NL -BE -DK -UK -FR -SE -US -JP

VIÑA PERGUITA 2003 WHITE
viura, chardonnay

81 Brilliant pale yellow. Intense aroma of ripe white fruit with hints of exotic fruit and fine herbs. Flavourful palate with fine bitter notes, a slightly oily texture and good acidity.

VIÑA PERGUITA 2003 ROSÉ
tempranillo, garnacha, cabernet sauvignon

79 Pale raspberry with an orangey hue. Intense aroma of red stone fruit with spicy hints of skins and a hint of citrus fruit freshness. Flavourful, slightly fruity and fresh palate with refreshing acidity.

VIÑA PERGUITA RED
100% tempranillo

78 Deep cherry. Aroma of caramel with hints of sun-drenched skins and spices. Flavourful palate with high acidity and ripe but not heavy fruit; a spicy finish.

VIÑA PERGUITA 1998 CRIANZA RED
85% tempranillo, 10% cabernet sauvignon, 5% merlot

78 Garnet red cherry. Aroma of ripe fruit with notes of orange peel (reduction). Flavourful, light palate with polished wood tannins, well-mannered.

VIÑA PERGUITA 1999 CRIANZA RED
85% tempranillo, 10% cabernet sauvignon, 5% merlot

78 Pale garnet red. Aroma with reduction notes and nuts, smoky. Flavourful palate with high acidity and bitter notes (wood tannins), ripe.

FERNÁNDEZ DE ARCAYA 1999 RESERVA RED
cabernet sauvignon

80 Garnet red cherry. Aroma of caramel with notes of vanilla and toasty oak and a suggestion of Cabernet. Fleshy, slightly oily palate, with a good wood/fruit integration and notes of green peppers.

FERNÁNDEZ DE ARCAYA 1998 RESERVA RED
cabernet sauvignon

77 Brick red. Aroma with reduction notes, spices (attics). Flavourful, slightly bitter palate of black pepper with good acidity and supple tannins.

FERNÁNDEZ DE ARCAYA 1997 RESERVA RED
cabernet sauvignon

81 Deep garnet red with a brick red edge. Spicy aroma (white pepper) with notes of toasty skins and cocoa. Fleshy palate with incisive ripe fruit tannins, vanilla and spices, well-balanced.

VIÑA PERGUITA 1996 RESERVA RED
70% tempranillo, 20% cabernet sauvignon, 10% merlot

82 Garnet red cherry with a brick red edge. Intense aroma with predominant reduction notes (leather, tobacco). Flavourful, fleshy and supple palate with a good oak/fruit integration and a good expression of traditional crianza.

FERNÁNDEZ DE ARCAYA 1996 RESERVA RED
cabernet sauvignon

76 Garnet red with a brick red edge. Aroma with notes of dust, old wood and a suggestion of ripe fruit. Flavourful, fresh palate, spicy with wood reduction nuances.

DO NAVARRA

FERNÁNDEZ DE ARCAYA 1995 RESERVA RED
100% cabernet sauvignon

82 Very deep cherry with a mahogany edge. Aroma of full-throttle fruit, concentrated with notes of toasty skins, spices and fine cocoa. Fleshy palate with flavourful tannins of slightly ripe fruit with well-integrated wood and chocolate in the finish.

FERNÁNDEZ DE ARCAYA 1994 RESERVA RED
100% cabernet sauvignon

80 Deep cherry with a garnet red edge. Earthy, slightly varietal aroma with hints of jammy black fruit and well-assembled wood. Powerful palate with round fruit tannins, slightly oily with integrated smoky crianza and green peppers in the finish.

Finca FINCA ZUBASTÍA

Extramuros, s/n
31494 Lerga (Navarra)
☎: 948 199 733 - Fax: 948 199 732
roberto@basanda.es

Established: 2003
⊕ 80 ▯ 800,000 litres ⚘ 40 has.
🍷 40% 🍇60%: -DE

ADA FINCA ZUBASTÍA 2003 JOVEN RED
garnacha, merlot, tempranillo, cabernet sauvignon

85 Dark cherry with a violet rim. Intense aroma with an excellent fruit expression (redcurrants, red stone fruit) and hints of terroir. Flavourful palate with slightly drying vigorous tannins, warm, with a good fruit weight, spicy and long.

GARCÍA BURGOS

Hernán Cortés 2
31521 Murchante (Navarra)
☎: 948 850 147 - Fax: 948 850 147
info@bodegasgarciaburgos.com

www.bodegasgarciaburgos.com

Established: 2002
⊕ 55 ▯ 52,000 litres ⚘ 40 has.
🍷 30% 🍇70%: -US

GARCÍA BURGOS VENDIMIA SELECCIO-NADA 2002 CRIANZA RED
70% cabernet sauvignon, 30% tempranillo

83 Intense cherry with a garnet red rim. Fruity aroma (red fruit, redcurrants) with earthy and mineral nuances, deep. Fruity and earthy palate with a presence of red fruit, well-balanced and long (liquorice).

GARCÍA BURGOS VENDIMIA SELECCIO-NADA 2003 CRIANZA RED
70% cabernet sauvignon, 30% tempranillo

85 Garnet red cherry with a violet edge. Intense, fresh aroma, ripe red fruit, mineral nuances. Flavourful palate, red fruit, optimum ripeness, with slightly lively tannins, a spicy hint, complex (plums, mineral flavours), excellent structure and acidity.

GARCÍA BURGOS LA CANTERA DE SANTA ANA 2002 CRIANZA

87 Garnet red cherry. Intense, fresh aroma of ripe black fruit with a spicy and terroir suggestion. Flavourful palate, excellent fruit weight and varietal expression, with slightly marked but promising oak tannins, nuances of soil, complex, quite long.

HEREDERO DEL CONDE DE NAVASQÜÉS

Rua de San Francisco, 25
31390 Olite (Navarra)
☎: 948 703 590 - Fax: 948 703 261
bodega-navasques@ole.com

Established: 1999
🌐 600 🍷 10% 🌍90%

BODEGAS NAVASQÜES RED
BODEGAS NAVASQÜES CRIANZA RED

Bodegas HEREDEROS DE LUIS GARCÍA MARTÍNEZ

Mayor, 58
31521 Murchante (Navarra)
☎: 948 838 192 - Fax: 948 838 192
lgmoooo6@teleline.es

Established: 1958
🌐 200 🥃 620,000 litres 🌿 38 has.
🍷 90% 🌍10%: -DE

COLMARES MERLOT 2002 OAK AGED RED
COLMARES 2000 CRIANZA RED
COLMARES 2001 RED

Bodega INURRIETA

Carretera Falces-Miranda de Arga, km.30
31370 Falces (Navarra)
☎: 948 737 309 - Fax: 948 737 310
info@bodegainurrieta.com
www.bodegainurrieta.com

INURRIETA ORCHÍDEA 2003 JOVEN WHITE
65% viura, 35% chardonnay

85 Straw-coloured. Expressive aroma of white fruit (pears, green apples) with notes of citrus fruit and tropical fruit and a floral nuance. Dry, flavourful, powerful palate with a good acidity-bitterness balance; slightly oily with fruit expression, persistent.

INURRIETA MEDIODÍA 2003 JOVEN ROSÉ
100% garnacha

83 Intense pink. Fresh aroma of strawberry pulp, slightly sweet (hints of caramel), with herbaceous overtones. Dry, fresh palate with well-balanced acidity and bitterness; fruit expression.

INURRIETA RECUERDOS Y TEXTURAS DEL NORTE 2002 OAK AGED RED
cabernet sauvignon, merlot

85 Cherry. Aroma of red fruit, spices (thyme), leathers and minerals. Good acidity on the palate, well-balanced, slightly bitter.

INURRIETA "SUR" 2002 RED
65% garnacha, 20% tempranillo, 15% graciano

86 Deep cherry with a strawberry edge. Intense aroma of bramble red berries, spicy (pepper, cumin); with notes of aromatic herbs and sun-drenched skins. Fresh palate with slightly dry wood tannins cloaked by the round fruit and an aftertaste of Mediterranean herbs; original and long.

INURRIETA ORCHÍDEA 2003 JOVEN WHITE
INURRIETA MEDIODIA 2003 JOVEN ROSÉ
INURRIETA CUATROCIENTOS 2001 CRIANZA RED

IRACHE

Monasterio de Irache, 1
31240 Ayegui (Navarra)
☎: 948 551 932 - Fax: 948 554 954
irache@irache.com
www.irache.com

Established: 1891
🌐 8,000 🥃 10,000,000 litres 🌿 120 has.
🍷 70% 🌍30%

CASTILLO IRACHE 2003 WHITE
100% chardonnay

81 Brilliant, golden yellow. Intense aroma with fresh fruit overtones (ripe apples), varietal expression and hints of fine herbs. Fresh, flavourful palate with fine bitter notes, well-balanced.

CASTILLO IRACHE 2003 JOVEN RED
tempranillo

79 Cherry with a violet hue. Perfumed aroma of quite ripe red stone fruit. Light, fresh palate but not very varietal.

GRAN IRACHE 2000 CRIANZA RED
tempranillo, cabernet sauvignon, merlot, mazuelo, graciano

76 Very deep cherry. Peppery aroma with notes of very toasty skins and very ripe fruit. Fleshy palate with ripe fruit, abundant fruit tannins, well-integrated wood and a Cabernet aftertaste.

DO NAVARRA

CASTILLO IRACHE 1999 RESERVA RED
tempranillo, cabernet sauvignon, merlot, mazuelo

78 Deep cherry. Aroma of quite ripe black fruit, spices and woody sweetish vanilla. Concentrated palate with slightly oily fruit tannins, smoky and spicy crianza and a pleasant bitter finish.

IRACHE WHITE
ROSADO IRACHE JOVEN ROSÉ
CASTILLO IRACHE 2003 ROSÉ
FUENTE CERRADA ECOLÓGICO JOVEN RED
IRACHE TEMPRANILLO RED
REAL IRACHE RED
TINTO VIÑA IRACHE 2003 RED
IRACHE MERLOT CRIANZA RED
IRACHE CABERNET CRIANZA RED
PRADO DE IRACHE RESERVA RED
REAL IRACHE 1994 GRAN RESERVA RED
REAL IRACHE 1996 GRAN RESERVA RED
FUENTE DE IRACHE 1976 GRAN RESERVA RED
REAL IRACHE 1970 GRAN RESERVA RED
REAL IRACHE 1973 GRAN RESERVA RED
REAL IRACHE 1964 GRAN RESERVA RED

J. ANDRÉS PÉREZ FONSECA

Camino de Itúrbero, s/n
31440 Lumbier (Navarra)
☎: 948 880 425 - Fax: 948 880 433

AZPEA 2002 RED
garnacha, cabernet sauvignon, tempranillo

84 Very deep cherry with a purple edge. Aroma of very well-ripened black fruit (jammy plums, blackberries) with notes of cocoa and skins. Dry, fresh palate with marked but round fruit tannins; slightly alcoholic with overall freshness.

AZPEA SELECCIÓN 2002 RED
100% cabernet sauvignon

85 Almost opaque very deep cherry. Aroma of concentrated fruit with nuances of bitter cocoa and green but pleasant grapes. Fresh palate with drying and well-assembled oak tannins that partially conceal the fruit; warm but round with herbs in the finish.

JULIÁN CHIVITE

Ribera, 34
31592 Cintruénigo (Navarra)
☎: 948 811 000 - Fax: 948 811 407
info@bodegaschivite.com
www.bodegaschivite.com
Established: 1647
▥ 18,000 ✣ 550 has. ⚑ 32% ⚐68%

CHIVITE COLECCIÓN 125 2002 FERMENTADO EN BARRICA WHITE
100% chardonnay

93 Brilliant gold. Powerful, smoky, very varietal, fine aroma with cut grass (hay) and ripe apples. Powerful, oily and elegant palate with smoky hints in the retronasal passage, complex, very persistent and long.

CHIVITE COLECCIÓN 125 VENDIMIA TARDÍA 2002 WHITE DULCE
100% moscatel

93 Brilliant gold. Smoky, powerful aroma with notes of honey and ripe fruit, fresh and pleasantly volatile. Generous, flavourful, full and unctuous palate, long with ripe Muscatel grapes and excellent acidity.

GRAN FEUDO 2003 WHITE
100% chardonnay

82 Golden straw. Not very intense yet fine aroma of white fruit with a nuance of fennel. Flavourful, fresh and varietal on the palate with good fruit expression and fresh acidity.

GRAN FEUDO 2003 WHITE DULCE
100% moscatel

90 Straw-coloured with a yellow glint. Powerful, musky, grapey, fresh and fruity aroma. Sweet, fresh palate with excellent acidity, complex, unctuous and more fragrant than ever.

GRAN FEUDO 2003 ROSÉ
100% garnacha

82 Brilliant raspberry. Intense aroma of red stone fruit with fresh overtones of citrus fruit. Fresh, flavourful palate with spicy notes of skins, bitter and quite varietal.

GRAN FEUDO 2000 CRIANZA RED
tempranillo, garnacha, cabernet sauvignon

86 Dark cherry with a brick red rim. Intense aroma of toasty oak with a suggestion of jammy black fruit and balsamic hints. Flavourful palate with a good oak/fruit integration, fine bitter notes and excellent acidity.

GRAN FEUDO 1998 RESERVA RED
tempranillo, cabernet sauvignon, merlot

85 Garnet red cherry with a brick red edge. Intense aroma with a good fruit/toasty oak integration and a balsamic and spicy suggestion. Flavourful palate with good crianza expression and bitter notes (liquorice graphite, dark-roasted flavours), hints of wax and minerals.

GRAN FEUDO VIÑAS VIEJAS 1998 RESERVA RED
tempranillo, garnacha, merlot

86 Dark cherry with a garnet red glint. Powerful aroma of fine smoky oak, a nuance of jammy black fruit, balsamic and terroir notions. Flavourful, concentrated palate with a good fruit/oak integration, bitter notes (chocolate, dark-roasted flavours) and good acidity.

CHIVITE COLECCIÓN 125 2000 RESERVA RED
66% tempranillo, 20% merlot, 14% cabernet sauvignon

90 Intense cherry. Fine, fairly quite closed, elegant, toasty aroma (cocoa) with notes of tanned leather and fresh fruit. Round, oily, elegant palate with fresh fruit and very fine, flavourful tannins, very persistent.

CHIVITE COLECCIÓN 125 1996 GRAN RESERVA RED
100% tempranillo

88 Cherry with a brick red hue. Spicy aroma of jammy fruit with notes of a fine evolution in the bottle (leather, tobacco). Round, spicy, fine, complex palate, very lively.

Cooperativa LA CRUZ

Autovía del Camino, s/n
31130 Mañeru (Navarra)
☎: 948 341 002 - Fax: 948 348 036
cooparga.3008@cajarural.com
Established: 1960
🍇 50 ▤ 1,750,000 litres
🍷 110 has. 🐂 100%

BELARDI 2003 WHITE
BELARDI 2003 ROSÉ
BELARDI 2002 RED
BELARDI 2001 CRIANZA RED

LEZAUN

Egiarte s/n
31292 Lakar-Yerri (Navarra)
☎: 948 541 339 - Fax: 948 536 055
info@lezaun.com
www.lezaun.com
Established: 1993
🍇 350 ▤ 400,000 litres 🍷 35 has.
🐂 65% 🐦35%

EGIARTE 2003 JOVEN ROSÉ
100% garnacha

79 Brilliant raspberry with coppery nuances. Slightly intense aroma of red fruit and toasty skins. Flavourful palate, slightly oily and warm with fine spicy notes.

EGIARTE GRACIANO-GARNATXA VIÑAS VIEJAS 2001 JOVEN RED
50% graciano, 50% garnacha

80 Dark cherry with a purplish edge. Powerful, fruity aroma with a slight varietal expression (spices, petals) and fine toasty oak. Flavourful, fleshy palate, with rough and oily tannins and fruit with notions of overripening.

LEZAUN TEMPRANILLO 2003 JOVEN RED
100% tempranillo

77 Cherry with a violet hue. Intense, fruity aroma with spicy notes of skins. Flavourful, fleshy, slightly oily and bitter palate with a slightly acidic edge.

EGIARTE 2003 JOVEN RED
70% tempranillo, 30% merlot

84 Quite dark cherry with a purplish edge. Powerful aroma of macerated black fruit with toasty hints of skins and underbrush. Flavourful, fleshy palate with a spicy freshness (maceration) and slightly varietal with liquorice.

LEZAUN GAZAGA 2002 OAK AGED RED
60% tempranillo, 30% cabernet sauvignon, 10% merlot

84 Dark cherry. Intense aroma of jammy black fruit with hints of sun-drenched skins and a suggestion of underbrush and varietal paprika. Flavourful, fleshy palate with a good oak/fruit integration, slightly warm and spicy.

EGIARTE MERLOT SELECCIÓN 2002 RED
100% merlot

81 Brilliant garnet red cherry. Powerful aroma with a good varietal expression (redcurrants, paprika, fallen leaves) and toasty hints of skins. Flavourful, fleshy palate with a good fruit weight despite the 15 degrees.

EGIARTE 2001 CRIANZA RED
60% tempranillo, 30% merlot, 10% cabernet sauvignon

84 Dark cherry. Powerful aroma of jammy red fruit with a herbaceous freshness (varietal hints of Merlot) and smoky oak notes. Powerful palate with notes of sweet fruit, slightly warm, with hints of liquorice and terroir in the retronasal passage.

LEZAUN 2001 CRIANZA RED
45% cabernet sauvignon, 35% merlot, 20% tempranillo

81 Dark cherry. Intense aroma with predominant toasty oak notes and a suggestion of jammy black fruit. Flavourful palate with slightly marked tannins, slightly warm and oily with good expression of fruit and crianza, liquorice in the finish.

DO NAVARRA

LUIS GURPEGUI MUGA

Carretera Pamplona, s/n
31330 Villafranca (Navarra)
☎: 948 670 050 - Fax: 948 670 259
bodegas@gurpegui.es
www.gurpegui.es

🌐 2,500 🛢 2,400,000 litres 🛢 80% 🌐20%

MONTE ORY 2003 ROSÉ
garnacha

76 Brilliant strawberry. Aroma of light strawberry flavours, fresh herbs. Warm, oily, unexpressive palate.

MONTE ORY TEMPRANILLO-MERLOT 2003 JOVEN RED
tempranillo, merlot

76 Garnet red cherry. Not very intense aroma yet clean and fruity, red berries. Flavourful, fruity palate with an expressive note, slightly green but pleasant and easy drinking.

SAN ACISCLO 2003 ROSÉ
MENDIANI 2003 ROSÉ
SESTERO 2003 ROSÉ
MONTE ORY TEMPRANILLO-CABERNET SAUVIGNON 2003 JOVEN RED
SAN ACISCLO 2003 JOVEN RED
MENDIANI 2003 JOVEN RED
SESTERO 2003 JOVEN RED
MONTE ORY 1998 CRIANZA RED
MONTE ORY 1997 RESERVA RED

MACAYA

Carretera Estella, 28
31251 Larraga (Navarra)
☎: 948 711 549 - Fax: 948 711 788
info@bodegasmacaya.com
www.bodegasmacaya.com
Established: 1999

🌐 300 🍇 17 has. 🛢 40% 🌐60%: -AD -DE -CH -NL -LU -DK -UK -SE -JP -PR

CONDADO DE ALMARA 2000 RED
100% cabernet sauvignon

82 Garnet red with an orangey hue. Aroma with light reduction notes and leathers, spicy with ripe fruit. Fleshy on the palate with obvious wood tannins and coffee in the retronasal passage.

CONDADO DE ALMARA 2002 RED
100% tempranillo

82 Garnet red. Aroma of ripe red fruit, varietal typification, lactic notes and spices. Slightly aggressive wood tannins on the palate but flavourful; well-mannered.

CONDADO DE ALMARA SELECCIÓN 2002 RED
100% tempranillo

82 Brilliant deep cherry. Fine smoky aroma of ripe skins with a spicy nuance. Round, fresh palate with good oak/fruit balance, pleasant.

ALMARA TEMPRANILLO 2000 CRIANZA RED
100% tempranillo

78 Garnet red with an orange rim. Aroma of toasty wood, smoky meat, cedar and balsamic flavours. Good balance between the wood tannins and the fruit on the palate, good acidity.

ALMARA 2000 CRIANZA RED
50% tempranillo, 50% cabernet sauvignon

80 Deep garnet red. Aroma of paprika with ripe red fruit and varietal expression. Body on the palate with dry oak tannins and toasty notes in the retronasal passage.

ALMARA CABERNET SAUVIGNON 2000 CRIANZA RED
100% cabernet sauvignon

76 Brilliant garnet red. Aroma of ripe black fruit with honeyed notes, dark-roasted flavours and a smoky hint. Fleshy palate of plums, with very sweet toffee and good fruit-wood symmetry.

CONDADO DE ALMARA 2001 CRIANZA RED
50% cabernet sauvignon, 50% tempranillo

78 Deep garnet red. Toasty, dark-roasted flavours aroma of ripe fruit (plums). Fleshy palate with marked oak tannins well-integrated with the fruit and notes of chocolate in the finish.

CONDADO DE ALMARA 2000 RESERVA RED
70% tempranillo, 30% cabernet sauvignon

80 Garnet red cherry with an orange edge. Very spicy, balsamic and fine reduction aroma. Fresh palate with ripe fruit and oak well-integrated with the fruit, slightly ripe.

MARCO REAL

Carretera Pamplona/Zaragoza, km. 38
31390 Olite (Navarra)
☎: 948 712 193 - Fax: 948 712 343
info@lanavarra.com
www.bodegasmarcoreal.com
Established: 1988

🌐 4,300 🛢 4,200,000 litres 🍇 200 has.
🛢 65% 🌐35%: -UE -ASIA -US -CA -CAM

HOMENAJE 2003 JOVEN WHITE
90% viura, 10% chardonnay, moscatel

74 Straw-coloured. Medium-intensity aroma of white fruit with lemony notes and a mild off-odour suggestion. Better in the mouth, fruity and light palate, easy drinking.

HOMENAJE 2003 JOVEN ROSÉ
90% garnacha, tempranillo, cabernet sauvignon, merlot

78 Blush. Intense aroma with notes of strawberry jelly and very ripe red fruit sensation. Fresher and flavourful on the palate, easy drinking, with a bitter, cleansing finish.

HOMENAJE 2002 MACERACIÓN CARBÓNICA RED
100% tempranillo

83 Bigarreau cherry with a violet rim. Intense aroma with a floral edge (violets) and notes of strawberry jelly, expressive. Powerful, flavourful and varietal on the palate with good fruit expression and dry tannins, very pleasant.

HOMENAJE 2002 JOVEN RED
50% tempranillo, 40% merlot, 5% cabernet sauvignon, 5% garnacha

75 Cherry. Not very intense aroma of slightly overripe red fruit. Warm palate with noticeable tannins, well-mannered overall.

HOMENAJE 2000 CRIANZA RED
25% cabernet sauvignon, 50% tempranillo, 5% garnacha, 20% merlot

79 Dark cherry with a brick red edge. Intense aroma with predominant toasty and fine reduction notes (leather). Flavourful palate with fleshy overtones and spicy varietal notions (paprika) with liquorice, slightly warm.

MARCO REAL COLECCIÓN PRIVADA 2001 CRIANZA RED
25% cabernet sauvignon, 45% tempranillo, 25% merlot, 5% graciano

86 Dark cherry with a saffron edge. Powerful aroma with spicy oak notes and a fine suggestion of reduction. Flavourful, supple palate with a good fruit/oak integration and ripe tannins, slightly warm and oily, spicy, long.

HOMENAJE 1999 RESERVA RED
30% cabernet sauvignon, 40% tempranillo, 5% garnacha, 25% merlot

82 Dark garnet red cherry. Intense aroma with fine reduction notes (leather, tobacco) with a slightly varietal ripe fruit nuance (redcurrants). Flavourful, supple palate with a good fruit/oak integration and notions of liquorice and sweet fruit in the finish.

MARCO REAL RESERVA DE FAMILIA 2000 RESERVA RED
50% tempranillo, 20% cabernet sauvignon, 25% merlot, 5% graciano

84 Dark garnet red cherry. Intense, very fine aroma of spicy oak notes with a balsamic suggestion of jammy fruit. Flavourful, supple palate with ripe and slightly oily tannins and warm notes.

MÁXIMO ABETE BODEGAS Y VINOS

P. Sales Muruzábal, 30
31495 San Martín de Unx (Navarra)
☎: 948 738 120 - Fax: 948 738 120
maximoab@teleline.es

GUERINDA 2003 JOVEN ROSÉ
GUERINDA 2003 JOVEN RED
GUERINDA 2001 CRIANZA RED

MONASTERIO DE LA OLIVA

Carretera Caparroso-Carcastillo, km. 17, 5
31310 Carcastillo (Navarra)
☎: 948 725 626 - Fax: 948 715 855
bodegasoliva@infonegocio.com
Established: 1927

🍷 244 📊 300,000 litres 🌿 20 has. 🍾 75%
🌍 25%: -FR -BE -IT -DE -NL -CH -HN -PR

MONASTERIO DE LA OLIVA 2003 ROSÉ
100% garnacha

67 Coppery. Flat aroma, without fruit. Evolved on the palate, fresh, flat.

MONASTERIO DE LA OLIVA 2003 RED
80% tempranillo, 20% merlot

77 Cherry. Aroma of black fruit, clean, a suggestion of maceration. Fleshy, earthy, and slightly alcoholic on the palate, a slightly pungent finish.

MONASTERIO DE LA OLIVA 2000 CRIANZA RED
30% tempranillo, 40% merlot, 30% cabernet sauvignon

76 Garnet red with a brick red edge. Aroma of black fruit, sun-drenched skins and toasty flavour. Toasty palate dominated by oak, with ripe and slightly drying tannins.

MONASTERIO DE LA OLIVA 1998 RESERVA RED
40% merlot, 30% cabernet sauvignon, 30% tempranillo

75 Brick red. Toasty aroma with notes of aged cask (traces of animal skins), and a viscous hint. Flavourful palate with bitter tannins, warm, with hints of evolution.

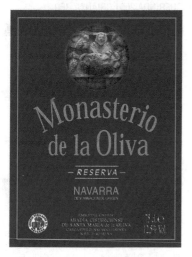

MONASTERIO DE LA OLIVA 2003 VINO DE LICOR DULCE DE LICOR
50% garnacha, 50% tempranillo

66 Onion skin. Slightly evolved aroma, sun-drenched notes (toasty caramel), liquorice. Sweet, flavourful, warm palate with fresh overtones, without fruity notes.

MONASTERIO DE LA OLIVA 2001 CRIANZA RED

Cooperativa Vinícola MURCHANTINA

Carretera de Tudela, s/n
31521 Murchante (Navarra)
☎: 948 838 030 - Fax: 948 838 677
murchantina@meganet.es
Established: 1958
🏭 4,350 📊 12,000,000 litres 🍇 900 has.
🍷 90% 🌐10%

REMONTE CHARDONNAY 2003 FERMENTADO EN BARRICA WHITE
chardonnay

79 Pale gold. Intense aroma of fine smoky wood and ripe white fruit. Flavourful palate with somewhat fresh oak tannins and bitter hints, pleasant.

REMONTE 2003 ROSÉ
garnacha

81 Pale raspberry with a coppery hue. Intense, fresh aroma of forest red fruit and hints of herbs. Flavourful, bitter palate with marked citrus acidity.

REMONTE 2001 RED

80 Cherry with a brick red edge. Aroma with balsamic notes, spicy oak and a ripe red fruit hint. Flavourful, fresh and balsamic on the palate with dry oak tannins.

KARRIKIRI 2001 RED
60% tempranillo, 20% cabernet sauvignon, 20% merlot

78 Cherry with an orangey hue. Smoky aroma of green peppers, varietal and with a hint of reduction. Ripe on the palate with flavourful, fresh tannins and light toasty hints.

REMONTE CABERNET SAUVIGNON 2000 CRIANZA RED
cabernet sauvignon

82 Cherry with a brick red rim. Fine, spicy aroma of a good crianza and a fresh balsamic hint. Flavourful, expressive palate with good fruit-wood harmony and a toasty finish.

REMONTE 1998 RESERVA RED

78 Garnet red with a brick red edge. Ripe aroma with marked crianza notes and reduction. Flavourful palate with very ripe fruit tannins, marked wood notes in the finish and bitter overtones of earth.

Bodegas y Viñedos NEKEAS

Las Huertas s/n
31154 Añorbe (Navarra)
☎: 948 350 296 - Fax: 948 350 300
nekeas@ibernet.com
Established: 1993
🏭 3.000 📊 2,200,000 litres 🍇 225 has.
🍷 25% 🌐75%: -DE -NL -SE -CH -UK -IE -FR -US -CA -BE -DK -IL -DK

NEKEAS VIURA-CHARDONNAY 2003 JOVEN WHITE
70% viura, 30% chardonnay

80 Pale yellow with golden nuances. Intense, fruity aroma with hints of fine herbs. Generous palate with white fruit and a slightly warm and oily texture, hay and fine spicy notes (cumin) in the retronasal passage.

DO NAVARRA

ODAIZA DE VEGA SINDOA 2002 FERMENTADO EN BARRICA WHITE
100% chardonnay

84 Brilliant golden yellow. Powerful aroma of fine smoky wood with a suggestion of very varietal ripe fruit (apples, hay). Flavourful palate with fairly fresh oak tannins, well-balanced, slightly warm and oily with refreshing acidity and a fine mineral note in the retronasal passage.

MAIETAS DE VEGA SINDOA 2001 OAK AGED RED
garnacha, merlot

83 Very deep garnet red cherry. Powerful aroma with a good expression of red fruit, a suggestion of spicy oak, balsamic hints (Mediterranean herbs) and fallen leaves. Flavourful palate with slightly marked tannins, an excellent expression of ripe fruit and fresh overtones of the oak and the acidity.

NEKEAS 2001 CRIANZA RED
50% cabernet sauvignon, 30% tempranillo, 20% merlot

88 Fairly deep cherry with a coppery edge. Intense, very fine aroma with excellent Cabernet varietal expression and a notion of spicy oak. Flavourful palate with a good oak/fruit integration, with a certain herbaceous freshness, fine bitter notes and excellent acidity.

NEKEAS MERLOT 2001 CRIANZA RED
100% merlot

87 Deep cherry with a coppery edge. Intense aroma of jammy redcurrants with spicy hints of skins and oak and a suggestion of fallen leaves. Flavourful palate with promising yet quite marked tannins, slightly bitter toasty notes (pitch, chocolate, liquorice) and notions of terroir.

IZAR DE NEKEAS 1998 RESERVA RED
45% cabernet sauvignon, 30% tempranillo, 25% merlot

88 Garnet red cherry with a saffron edge. Powerful aroma of ripe black fruit with hints of cedar and an excellent Bordeaux expression. Flavourful and fleshy palate, quite supple, with ripe and oily tannins, fine spicy notes (paprika) and an excellent crianza expression.

EL CHAPARRAL DE VEGA SINDOA 2001 RED
100% garnacha

85 Intense cherry. Aroma with a marked woody accent, although fine and creamy. Faint varietal notes yet fruity. Fresh palate, light yet flavourful vegetative hints; medium ripening, pleasant, with some varietal expression.

MARAIN DE VEGA SINDOA 2001 RED
merlot

87 Intense cherry. Deep aroma, varietal (ripe bunch grape vines, blackcurrants), with toasty notes of creamy oak, harmonious. Fleshy overtones on the palate, good ripeness yet with freshness. Dry but flavourful tannins.

NEKEAS CHARDONNAY "CUVÉE ALLIER" 2003 FERMENTADO EN BARRICA WHITE
NEKEAS 2003 JOVEN ROSÉ
NEKEAS 1999 RESERVA RED
NEKEAS 2003 JOVEN RED

NUESTRA SEÑORA DEL CAMINO

Avenida de los Fueros, 18
31522 Monteagudo (Navarra)
☎: 948 843 102 - Fax: 948 843 161
bodegadelcamino@bodegadelcamino.com
www.bodegadelcamino.com

Established: 1954

322 ▯ 2,000,000 litres ▮ 210 has.
▮70% ▮30%:-DK -DE -FR -NL -AT -PE -GT

CONDE DE ARTOIZ 2003 WHITE
100% viura

74 Pale with a greenish hue. Fresh, fruity aroma of yeast. Fresh, well-mannered palate, with a sweetness in the finish.

CONDE DE ARTOIZ 2003 ROSÉ
100% garnacha

72 Raspberry blush. Aroma of slightly reduced red fruit (withered petals). A flavourful note with sweetness on the palate.

CONDE DE ARTOIZ 2002 RED
50% tempranillo, 50% garnacha

73 Dark red cherry with a brick red edge. Intense, fruity aroma with a not very fine herbaceous hint. Flavourful, bitter palate with slightly marked tannins, lacking balance.

MONTITURA VENDIMIA SELECIONADA 2000 OAK AGED RED
60% tempranillo, 30% garnacha, 10% mazuelo ▮6

78 Garnet red cherry with a saffron edge. Intense, ripe aroma with spicy hints of oak and a suggestion of slightly reduced fruit. Flavourful, fruity palate with fleshy overtones, a slightly oily texture and a spicy finish.

PEDRO DE IVAR 2001 CRIANZA RED
70% tempranillo, 20% garnacha, 10% mazuelo

80 Cherry with a garnet red edge. Medium-intensity aroma of toasty oak with notes of leather and a hint of animals over ripe fruit. Fresh palate with well-balanced fruit-oak; good acidity with polished and slightly drying tannins in the finish.

PEDRO DE IVAR PRESTIGIO 2001 CRIANZA RED
60% tempranillo, 40% garnacha

501

87 Very deep cherry. Aroma of concentrated black fruit with cocoa notes and spices, very complex with mild traces of minerals. Fleshy palate, very fresh with round wood tannins integrated with the ripe fruit; long, very fruity and round.

VIÑA RIÑANCO 2003 WHITE
VIÑA RIÑANCO 2003 ROSÉ
VIÑA RIÑANCO 2002 RED
MONTITURA MACERACIÓN CARBÓNICA RED

Bodega NUESTRA SEÑORA DEL ROMERO

Ctra de Tarazona, 33 Apdo. de Correos, 24
31520 Cascante (Navarra)
☎: 948 851 411 - Fax: 948 844 504
info@bodegasdelromero.com
www.bodegasdelromero.com
Established: 1951

🍷 3,200 📊 13,000,000 litres 🍇 1,250 has.
🇪🇸 40% 🌐60%: -DE -DK -UK -FR -NL

MALÓN DE ECHAIDE 2003 WHITE
100% viura

79 Golden yellow. Slightly intense, fruity aroma with hints of hay and slightly spicy notions. Flavourful, slightly fruity palate with rich bitter hints and good acidity.

TORRECILLA 2003 ROSÉ
100% garnacha

80 Pale raspberry with an orangey hue. Intense aroma of ripe red fruit with spicy notes of skins. Flavourful, fruity aroma with spices and quality citrus fruit notes.

MALÓN DE ECHAIDE 2003 ROSÉ
100% garnacha

79 Brilliant raspberry. Powerful, ripe aroma of red fruit and hints of withered petals. Flavourful, fleshy palate with fresh overtones, spicy fruity notes, a slightly oily texture and good acidity.

MALÓN DE ECHAIDE TEMPRANILLO 2002 RED
100% tempranillo

73 Cherry with an orangey hue. Aroma with reduction notes. Poorly balanced palate with a light greeness and without great nuances.

TORRECILLA 2002 RED
70% tempranillo, 30% garnacha

79 Garnet red cherry with an orangey glint. Intense aroma with spicy oak notes and a slight note of greeness. Flavourful palate with fine bitter notes (liquorice, dark-roasted flavours) and a good expression of traditional crianza.

MALÓN DE ECHAIDE GARNACHA VIEJA 2003 RED
100% garnacha

84 Garnet red cherry with violet shades. Powerful, ripe aroma of red fruit, notes of sun-drenched skins, a spicy suggestion of terroir. Flavourful, fleshy palate with a certain concentration, quite marked grape tannins, fine bitter notes and excellent acidity.

SEÑORÍO DE YÁNIZ TEMPRANILLO 2003 RED
100% tempranillo

77 Intense cherry with a purplish edge. Intense aroma of red fruit with the freshness of maceration. Fresh palate with a varietal fruit expression, light carbonic hints and an acidic edge.

TORRECILLA 1999 CRIANZA RED
85% tempranillo, 10% garnacha, 5% cabernet sauvignon

77 Not very deep brick red cherry. Toasty, spicy aroma with light lactic notes. Light, slightly green palate and a toasty finish.

PLANDENAS 1996 RESERVA RED
80% tempranillo, 10% garnacha, 10% cabernet sauvignon

76 Garnet red cherry with a brick red edge. Intense aroma with predominant reduction notes. Flavourful palate with a good oak/fruit integration, bitter (dark-roasted flavours), and reduction (prunes, aged wood) notes.

MALÓN DE ECHAIDE 1996 RESERVA RED
100% cabernet sauvignon

85 Cherry with a brick red edge. Intense aroma with predominant toasty oak notes of jammy black fruit and an excellent varietal expression (paprika). Flavourful and supple palate with a good fruit/oak integration, notions of liquorice with ripe fruit and dark-roasted flavours in the retronasal passage.

VIÑA PAROT 1995 RESERVA RED
85% cabernet sauvignon, 15% tempranillo

83 Ruby red cherry with an orangey edge. Powerful aroma with predominant reduction notes (cedar, dates, old furniture). Flavourful, supple palate with a good expression of a classic Reserva, spices and tobacco.

SEÑOR DE CASCANTE 1995 GRAN RESERVA RED
85% tempranillo, 15% cabernet sauvignon

84 Garnet red cherry with a brick red glint. Fairly intense aroma with predominant spicy oak notes and hints of fine reduction. Flavourful palate with a good oak/fruit integration, fine bitter notes and good crianza expression.

MALÓN DE ECHAIDE 1999 CRIANZA RED
MALÓN DE ECHAIDE CABERNET 1996 RESERVA RED

OCHOA

Alcalde Maillata, 2
31390 Olite (Navarra)
☎: 948 740 006 - Fax: 948 740 048
info@bodegasochoa.com
www.bodegasochoa.com

Established: 1845

🍷 2,700 ⬛ 1,800,000 litres 🍇 143 has.

🍷 30% 🍷70%

OCHOA VIURA-CHARDONNAY 2003 WHITE
70% viura, 30% chardonnay

79 Pale yellow. Powerful aroma of ripe white fruit, with hints of exotic fruit, and floral hints (withered petals). Flavourful, quite fruity palate with fine bitter notes, a slightly oily texture, fine herbs and an acidic edge.

OCHOA DULCE MOSCATEL 2003 WHITE
100% moscatel

87 Golden yellow. Raisiny, dense, fresh aroma of white flowers and quince. Sweet palate with body and good acidity, unctuous, persistent.

OCHOA ROSADO DE LÁGRIMA 2002 ROSÉ
50% garnacha, 50% cabernet sauvignon

84 Intense raspberry. Powerful aroma with fresh overtones and varietal expression (red stone fruit, herbaceous and spicy hints of skins). Flavourful and fleshy on the palate with fruity fresh overtones (raspberries, citrus fruit) and excellent acidity.

OCHOA GARNACHA 2003 ROSÉ
100% garnacha

82 Brilliant raspberry with coppery nuances. Not very intense aroma of ripe red fruit and toasty notes of skins. Flavourful palate with fleshy overtones, fine spicy varietal notes, a slightly oily texture and excellent acidity.

OCHOA GARNACHA-TEMPRANILLO 2002 RED
60% tempranillo, 40% garnacha

75 Cherry with an orangey rim. Aroma of reduction notes (leathers, ink). Medium-bodied palate, a well-mannered ensemble.

OCHOA GRACIANO-GARNACHA 2002 RED
graciano, garnacha

80 Cherry. Aroma with light reduction notes, liquorice and jammy tomatoes. Spicy, medium-bodied palate and a toasty finish.

OCHOA VENDIMIA SELECCIONADA 2000 RED
cabernet sauvignon, merlot

88 Garnet red cherry. Powerful aroma with an excellent varietal and crianza expression. Expressive and vigorous palate with a good oak/fruit integration, ripe and oily tannins and excellent fruit weight, well-balanced.

OCHOA CABERNET SAUVIGNON 2001 CRIANZA RED
100% cabernet sauvignon

82 Garnet red with an orangey rim. Varietal aroma with light reduction notes and hints of leather. Balsamic and medium-bodied palate with a toasty finish.

OCHOA MERLOT 2001 CRIANZA RED
100% merlot

75 Cherry with a brick red edge. Quite alcoholic and slight reduction aroma. An edge of acidity on the palate with slightly noticeable tannins and a toasty finish.

OCHOA TEMPRANILLO 2001 CRIANZA RED
100% tempranillo

86 Deep cherry with a brick red edge. Intense, ripe aroma with fine toasty oak. Flavourful and fleshy on the palate with ripe and oily tannins and excellent crianza expression, well-balanced with toasty and spicy notes in the retronasal passage.

OCHOA 1999 RESERVA RED
55% tempranillo, 30% cabernet sauvignon, 15% merlot

85 Garnet red cherry with a brick red edge. Intense, ripe aroma with fine reduction notes (leather), with a suggestion of toasty oak, spicy quite varietal notes (paprika), balsamic flavours and underbrush. Fleshy, flavourful and supple palate with a good fruit/oak integration, well-balanced.

OCHOA 1998 GRAN RESERVA RED
55% tempranillo, 30% cabernet sauvignon, 15% merlot

88 Garnet red cherry with a coppery edge. Powerful aroma with good crianza expression (leather, spices). Flavourful palate with a good oak/fruit integration, rich in herbaceous Cabernet nuances, balsamic flavours, liquorice, fine toasty notes and excellent acidity.

Sociedad Cooperativa Agraria ORVALAIZ

Carretera Pamplona-Estella, s/n
31151 Obanos (Navarra)
☎: 948 344 437 - Fax: 948 344 401
bodega@orvalaiz.es

Established: 1993

🌐 830 🍷 3,000,000 litres 🍇 400 has.

🍷 66% 🌐34%

VIÑA ORVALAIZ 2003 ROSÉ
tempranillo, garnacha

81 Intense raspberry. Powerful aroma with predominant notes of toasty skins and red stone fruit. Flavourful palate with a hint of freshness, a suggestion of spices and citrus fruit and fine bitter notes.

ORVALAIZ CABERNET SAUVIGNON 2003 ROSÉ
cabernet sauvignon

81 Brilliant raspberry. Fairly intense aroma of red stone fruit and a slight varietal suggestion (herbaceous notes, fallen leaves). Fresh palate with firm ripe grape tannins, hints of citrus fruit and excellent acidity.

ORVALAIZ MERLOT 2001 RED
100% merlot

82 Cherry with an orangey edge. Toasty, spicy aromas of black olives and the varietal. Fleshy palate with balance between the fruit and the wood.

ORVALAIZ CABERNET SAUVIGNON 2001 RED
100% cabernet sauvignon

83 Garnet red cherry with a coppery edge. Powerful aroma with an excellent varietal expression (paprika, herbaceous hints) and fine toasty notes. Flavourful palate with quite marked tannins, a very ripe stone fruit suggestion and spicy and bitter notes (liquorice, chocolate) in the retronasal passage.

VIÑA ORVALAIZ GARNACHA 2001 RED
garnacha

79 Garnet red cherry with a coppery rim. Intense aroma of fine spicy and creamy oak notes with a ripe fruit hint. Flavourful palate with marked tannins (a slight note of greenness) and good acidity.

VIÑA ORVALAIZ 2002 RED
tempranillo, cabernet sauvignon

74 Cherry. Aroma of green pepper, floral, with some green notes. Warm palate with well-integrated tannins but some greeness.

VIÑA ORVALAIZ TEMPRANILLO 2002 RED
tempranillo

79 Intense cherry with a violet edge. Intense aroma of jammy red fruit and fine toasty notes with a balsamic suggestion and terroir. Flavourful palate with quite marked tannins, a slight note of greeness, fine bitter notes and good acidity.

SEPTENTRIÓN 2000 ROBLE RED
85% tempranillo, 15% cabernet sauvignon   🌐 12

84 Deep garnet red cherry. Powerful aroma of black fruit with fine smoky oak and mineral fresh overtones. Flavourful and fleshy on the palate with ripe tannins, fine herbaceous hints of Cabernet and good acidity.

SEPTENTRIÓN 2001 ROBLE RED
85% tempranillo, 15% cabernet sauvignon   🌐 12

86 Ruby red cherry. Slightly alcoholic aroma of toasty flavours, lactics, vanilla and balsamic flavours. Creamy palate, slightly polished wood tannins with toasty flavours and coffee in the retronasal passage.

ORVALAIZ 2000 CRIANZA RED
85% tempranillo, 15% cabernet sauvignon

85 Garnet red cherry with a brick red edge. Powerful aroma with predominant toasty oak notes and a suggestion of jammy fruit. Flavourful palate with well-blended fruit/oak and an excellent varietal and crianza expression.

Señorío de OTAZU (GABARBIDE)

Señorío de Otazu, s/n
31174 Echauri (Navarra)
☎: 948 329 200 - Fax: 948 329 353
comercial@otazu.com - otazu.es

Established: 1989

🌐 2,000 🍷 800,000 litres 🍇 110 has.

🍷 60% 🌐40%: -DE -AT -US -IE -JP -BE - UK -DK -VE -FR

PALACIO DE OTAZU CHARDONNAY 2000 FERMENTADO EN BARRICA WHITE
100% chardonnay

88 Straw-coloured with a golden glimmer. Fresh, fruity aroma with fine smoky notes, elegant. Light, oily palate with a very fine toasty retronasal effect (creamy vanilla), flavourful and persistent with an excellent oak association.

PALACIO DE OTAZU CHARDONNAY 2002 WHITE
100% chardonnay

87 Straw-coloured. Aroma with smoky notes of the vine variety, hints of ripe fruit and hay. Fresh, oily, ripe varietal and flavourful palate with mineral nuances.

PALACIO DE OTAZU 2000 CRIANZA RED
70% merlot, 20% cabernet sauvignon, 10% tempranillo

87 Garnet red cherry. Aroma with good expression of fresh fruit and floral hint (violets, petals) and fine and imperceptible toasty oak notes. Light palate with good varietal expression and a well-proportioned oak-wine assemblage, flavourful.

PALACIO DE OTAZU 1999 RESERVA RED
70% merlot, 20% cabernet sauvignon, 10% tempranillo

89 Dark cherry. Powerful aroma, with copious fine toasty notes (cocoa, vanilla, toffee) and an expression of fresh fruit, well-integrated and elegant. Fresh, flavourful palate with fine toasty notes of oak and a varietal hint (redcurrants, damp earth), fruity with dry but ripe tannins.

RESERVA
1999

PALACIO DE
OTAZU
NAVARRA
DENOMINACION DE ORIGEN
GABARBIDE, S. A.
ECHAURI-NAVARRA-ESPAÑA

EMBOTELLADO EN ORIGEN
ESTATE BOTTLED
RED WINE
PRODUCT OF SPAIN

Alc.13 % vol.
750 ml.℮
N.R.E. 31/4/805-NA

PALACIO DE OTAZU RESERVA ESPECIAL 1999 RED

92 Intense cherry. Complex aroma, rich in toasty creamy notes (aromatic coffee, cocoa), mineral notes and fresh fruit, varietal. Round, elegant, fine and complex palate with an excellent fruit expression

with a delicate ageing process and a varietal retro-nasal effect (Bordeaux, redcurrants, damp earth).

ALTAR 1999 RESERVA ESPECIAL RED

91 Intense cherry with an orange edge. Powerful aroma of fresh fruit, with toasty hints, caramel and creamy oak nuances. Fleshy palate, dry but ripe, with a good varietal expression of fresh fruit.

PALACIO DE AZCONA (NAVAYERRI)

Carretera Ugar, s/n
31177 Azcona (Navarra)
☎: 948 542 294 - Fax: 948 542 294
info@palaciodeazcona.com
www.palaciodeazcona.com

Established: 1996

536 | 600,000 litres | 37 has.

40% | 60%

PALACIO DE AZCONA TEMPRANILLO 2003 RED
PALACIO DE AZCONA MERLOT 2003 RED
PALACIO DE AZCONA 2000 CRIANZA RED
PALACIO DE AZCONA 1999 RESERVA RED

PALACIO DE LA VEGA

Condesa de la Vega, s/n
31263 Dicastillo (Navarra)
☎: 948 527 009 - Fax: 948 527 333
www.palaciodelavega.com

Established: 1991

4,600 | 3,000,000 litres | 35 has.

20% | 80%: -DE -UK -DK -DK -SE -CH

PALACIO DE LA VEGA CHARDONNAY 2003 FERMENTADO EN BARRICA WHITE
100% chardonnay

87 Brilliant golden yellow. Intense aroma with predominant creamy, smoky oak notes and a slightly varietal, ripe fruit suggestion. Flavourful, slightly warm and oily on the palate; a good oak/fruit integration and hints of fine herbs.

PALACIO DE LA VEGA 2003 ROSÉ
90% garnacha, 10% cabernet sauvignon

80 Brilliant slightly pale raspberry. Intense aroma of foresty strawberries, hints of petals and slightly reduced fruit. Flavourful palate with fine spicy notes of skins; slightly oily with hints of citrus fruit.

PALACIO DE LA VEGA TEMPRANILLO 2003 RED
100% tempranillo

83 Quite dark cherry with a garnet red edge. Slightly intense aroma with a good varietal expression (black fruit, underbrush) and hints of macerated skins. Fruity palate with flavourful and firm grape tannins, fine spicy notes and fresh acidity.

PALACIO DE LA VEGA MERLOT 2000 CRIANZA RED
100% merlot

86 Dark cherry with a brick red edge. Powerful aroma of tobacco and slightly reduced fruit with fine toasty oak and a nuance of damp earth. Flavourful palate with slightly marked tannins, a slightly sweet fruity hint and bitter notes (liquorice, dark-roasted flavours).

PALACIO DE LA VEGA 2000 CRIANZA RED
70% cabernet sauvignon, 30% tempranillo

84 Dark red cherry with a brick red edge. Intense aroma with spicy oak notes, a hint of Cabernet, herbaceous freshness and notions of macerated red fruit and fallen leaves. Flavourful palate with round and oily tannins, fine bitter notes (liquorice) and good acidity.

PALACIO DE LA VEGA TEMPRANILLO 1999 RESERVA RED
100% tempranillo

85 Dark cherry with a saffron edge. Not very intense aroma, jammy black fruit with toasty hints of oak. Flavourful palate with a good fruit/oak integration and fine bitter notes, with a suppleness and spicy and mineral freshness.

CONDE DE LA VEGA 2000 RESERVA RED
cabernet sauvignon, tempranillo, merlot

88 Dark cherry. Powerful, ripe aroma of jammy black fruit with fine spicy and toasty wood notes. Flavourful palate with a mineral and herbaceous freshness (Cabernet), a good fruit/oak integration, supple with excellent acidity.

PALACIO DE LA VEGA CABERNET SAUVIGNON 2000 RESERVA RED
100% cabernet sauvignon

87 Dark cherry with a coppery edge. Powerful, very varietal aroma (paprika, redcurrants) with fine spicy wood notes. Flavourful palate with round and slightly oily tannins, a good oak/fruit integration, bitter notes and fine dark-roasted flavours.

PALACIO DE LA VEGA CHARDONNAY 2003 WHITE

PALACIO DE MURUZÁBAL

Calle La Cruz, s/n
31152 Muruzábal (Navarra)
☎: 948 344 279 - Fax: 948 344 325
a.marino@eresmas.net

Established: 1991
🍷 255 ▯ 50,000 litres 🍇 34 has.
🍷 20% 🌐80%: -IE -DE -UK -CH -PR

PALACIO DE MURUZÁBAL 2000 FERMENTADO EN BARRICA WHITE
100% chardonnay

89 Golden straw. Slightly closed aroma with fine bitter notes and sweet ripe fruit. Generous palate, much better than in the nose (fragrant herbs) with sweet fruit and smoky and creamy flavours in the retronasal passage, flavourful, persistent.

PALACIO DE MURUZÁBAL COSECHA PARTICULAR 1998 RESERVA RED
PALACIO DE MURUZÁBAL 1998 GRAN RESERVA RED

PARRALDEA

Jardín, 10
31152 Muruzábal (Navarra)
☎: 948 344 146 - Fax: 948 344 146
bodegaparraldea@terra.es

Established: 1995
🍷 95 ▯ 50,000 litres 🍇 11 has.
🍷 50% 🌐50%: -DE -BE -CH -NL

FIDELIUM FINCA PARRALDEA 2001 CRIANZA RED
FIDELIUM COLECCIÓN ESPECIAL 2001 CRIANZA RED

Bodegas PÉREZ LAHERA

Vaquero Jacoste, 4
31500 Tudela (Navarra)
☎: 948 821 263 - Fax: 948 821 263
info@servimatic.net
www.servimatic.net/bpi

Established: 1925
🍷 350 ▯ 500,000 litres 🍷 100%

VALDETELLAS ROSÉ
VALDETELLAS JOVEN RED
VIÑA UGUETA CRIANZA RED
VALDETELLAS CRIANZA RED

PIEDEMONTE

Rua Romana, s/n
31390 Olite (Navarra)
☎: 948 712 406 - Fax: 948 740 090
laboratorio@piedemonte.com
www.piedemonte.com

Established: 1992
🍷 2170 ▯ 4,000,000 litres 🍇 350 has.
🍷 40% 🌐60%

PIEDEMONTE CHARDONNAY 2003 WHITE
chardonnay

79 Pale yellow with golden nuances. Not very intense aroma with a certain finesse and varietal expression (ripe apples). Flavourful, fruity palate (exotic hints) with fresh overtones and good acidity.

PIEDEMONTE 2003 WHITE
100% viura

78 Yellow straw. Intense aroma of ripe white fruit with hints of exotic fruit and petals. Flavourful, fleshy palate with a slightly oily texture.

PIEDEMONTE MOSCATEL 2003 WHITE
moscatel de grano menudo

84 Yellow straw with a greenish nuance. Dense aroma with faint notes of honey and white fruit. Sweet palate with good acidity, well-balanced.

PIEDEMONTE 2003 ROSÉ
100% garnacha

79 Lively raspberry. Intense aroma with a slight varietal expression (spices, fallen leaves, stone fruit) and a citrus fruit nuance. Flavourful palate with fresh overtones and fine bitter notes.

PIEDEMONTE TEMPRANILLO 2003 RED
100% tempranillo

82 Garnet red cherry. Intense aroma with a good varietal expression (black fruit, underbrush) and toasty hints of skins. Flavourful palate with fleshy overtones, toasty notes of grapes, with liquorice and terroir in the retronasal passage.

PIEDEMONTE MERLOT 2003 RED
100% merlot

84 Dark cherry with a purplish edge. Powerful aroma with a good varietal expression (black fruit, petals, damp earth) and toasty hints of skins. Flavourful and fleshy palate with ripe fruit, slightly ripe and oily grape tannins and fine bitter notes.

PIEDEMONTE SELECCIÓN 2002 RED
tempranillo, cabernet sauvignon , merlot

85 Garnet red cherry. Powerful aroma with spicy oak notes and a suggestion of very varietal ripe fruit (redcurrants, fallen leaves, damp earth). Flavourful, fleshy palate with a good oak/fruit integration and fine bitter notes (cocoa, liquorice) with spices (pepper) in the retronasal passage.

PIEDEMONTE 2000 CRIANZA RED
cabernet sauvignon, tempranillo, merlot

79 Very deep cherry. Powerful aroma of very varietal fruit (herbaceous hints) with a spicy oak nuance. Flavourful palate with marked tannins (a note of oaky greeness) and scarcely any fruit weight.

PIEDEMONTE CABERNET SAUVIGNON 2000 CRIANZA RED
100% cabernet sauvignon

85 Dark cherry with a coppery edge. Powerful aroma of ripe black fruit with hints of reduction (prunes), toasty oak and damp earth. Flavourful,

fleshy palate with fine bitter notes (a good oak/fruit integration) and dark-roasted flavours and liquorice in the retronasal passage, with a mild note of spices (paprika) in the finish.

PIEDEMONTE 1999 RESERVA RED

84 Cherry with an orangey edge. Aroma with fine reduction notes (leather, tobacco) and a balsamic bouquet. Flavourful palate with black fruit, damp earth and well-integrated wood, well-balanced.

PRÍNCIPE DE VIANA

Mayor, 191
31521 Murchante (Navarra)
☎: 948 838 640 - Fax: 948 818 574
info@principedeviana.com - principedevia-na.com

Established: 1983

🌐 11,000 🛢 5,500,000 litres 🍇 400 has.

🍷 55% 🍇45%: -UK -DE -SE -DK -NL -EE -CH -PL -RU -US -MX -PE CHILE -CA -KR - JP -PH -MY

PRÍNCIPE DE VIANA CHARDONNAY 2003 FERMENTADO EN BARRICA WHITE
100% chardonnay

78 Straw-coloured with a golden edge. Aroma of ripe fruit (tropical), with a nuance of smoky notes. Flavourful palate with predominant fruit over wood, good freshness and peaches and citrus fruit in the finish.

PRÍNCIPE DE VIANA GARNACHA 2003 ROSÉ
100% garnacha

77 Brilliant blush. Aroma of red fruit with cara-melised hints. Somewhat warm, flavourful palate, fruity; sweet strawberries in the finish.

PRÍNCIPE DE VIANA CABERNET SAUVIG-NON 2003 ROSÉ
100% cabernet sauvignon

82 Brilliant raspberry. Intense aroma of ripe red fruit with a light note of crystallised fruit. Flavourful and fleshy on the palate with a slightly oily texture and a spicy grape nuance; excellent acidity.

PRÍNCIPE DE VIANA TEMPRANILLO 2003 OAK AGED RED
100% tempranillo

84 Very deep cherry with a violet edge. Powerful aroma with an excellent varietal fruit expression (red fruit, underbrush), spices and toasty hints of skins. Fleshy, flavourful palate with fine grape tannicity (hints of oak) and fresh overtones in the retronasal passage.

PRÍNCIPE DE VIANA 2000 CRIANZA RED
40% tempranillo, 60% cabernet sauvignon

82 Cherry with an orangey edge. Not very intense, slightly spicy aroma with a balsamic nuance.

DO NAVARRA

Flavourful and well-balanced on the palate with well-integrated wood, pleasant.

PRÍNCIPE DE VIANA GARNACHA VIÑAS VIEJAS 2003 CRIANZA RED
100% garnacha

83 Very deep brilliant cherry. Aroma of macerated red fruit with floral notes, aromatic herbs and integrated cocoa notes. Fruity and fleshy on the palate with assembled fruit and wood, very fresh acidity and redcurrants and herbs in the finish.

PRÍNCIPE DE VIANA 1423 1999 RESERVA RED
50% tempranillo, 30% cabernet sauvignon, 20% merlot

85 Cherry with an orangey edge. Intense aroma of well-assembled wood and fruit with a balsamic nuance; fine. Flavourful, varietal and powerful on the palate with well-integrated wood and present but round tannins.

PRÍNCIPE DE VIANA 1999 RESERVA RED
33% tempranillo, 33% cabernet sauvignon, 33% merlot

87 Cherry with a brick red edge. Medium-intensity aroma with good crianza notes (cocoa, toasty flavours) that are well-assembled with the fruit. Powerful and flavourful on the palate with ripe but fresh black fruit, a good concentration and a toasty, persistent finish.

AGRAMONT 2003 WHITE
AGRAMONT 2003 ROSÉ
AGRAMONT 2002 RED

Bodegas y Viñedos QUADERNA VIA

Paraje Yumberri, par 203
31241 Iguzquiza (Navarra)
☎: 948 554 083 - Fax: 948 558 540
vinaebro@ctv.es
Established: 1998
🌐 500 3,500,000 litres 70 has.
25% 75%: -DE -UK -NL -SE -BE -CA

QUADERNA VIA ESPECIAL 2003 RED
QUADERNA VIA 2003 MACERACIÓN CARBÓNICA RED
QUADERNA VIA TEMPRANILLO 2001 CRIANZA RED
QUADERNA VIA CABERNET 2001 CRIANZA RED
QUADERNA VIA 2001 RESERVA RED

Cooperativa SAN FRANCISCO JAVIER

Arrabal, 2
31491 Sada (Navarra)
☎: 948 877 013

PALACIO DE SADA 2003 ROSÉ
100% garnacha

82 Brilliant raspberry. Intense, ripe aroma of red stone fruit with a spicy, slightly varietal nuance. Flavourful, very fresh, quite fruity palate with a slightly acidic edge.

PALACIO DE SADA 2003 JOVEN RED
garnacha

88 Cherry with a violet rim. Aroma of very ripe red stone fruit (plums, Bigarreau cherry) and notes of skins. Fleshy, varietal palate with good acidity, long.

PALACIO DE SADA 2001 CRIANZA RED

85 Deep cherry with a violet edge. Intense aroma of jammy black fruit with fine toasty oak notes and notions of terroir. Flavourful, concentrated palate with a good oak/fruit integration, fine bitter notes (chocolate, liquorice, dark-roasted flavours) and excellent acidity.

PALACIO DE SADA 2002 RED
garnacha

85 Ruby garnet red. Perfumed aroma of ripe red fruit, quince and slightly viscous. Flavourful, fleshy palate with noticeable tannins.

Sociedad Cooperativa SAN JOSÉ

Avenida Navarra, s/n
31591 Corella (Navarra)
☎: 948 780 058 - Fax: 948 780 058
coopsanjose@telefonica.net
Established: 1952
🌐 200 4,500,000 litres 100%

SEÑORÍO DE CORELLA ROSÉ
CONDE ALPERCHE RED
SEÑORÍO DE CORELLA RED

Bodegas SAN MARTÍN

Carretera de Sanguesa, s/n
31495 San Martín de Unx (Navarra)
☎: 948 738 294 - Fax: 948 738 293
admbodegasm@hotmail.com
Established: 1914
🌐 226 8,000,000 litres 845 has.
88% 12%: -US -CU -DK -DE -NL -AT -DO -FR

ILAGARES 2003 WHITE
100% viura

77 Pale gold. Quite intense aroma with spicy notes of skins and a nuance of perfumed soap. Flavourful, bitter, somewhat fruity and warm palate with a slightly acidic edge.

ILAGARES 2003 ROSÉ
100% garnacha

74 Intense raspberry. Ripe, somewhat fruity aroma with hints of petals. Flavourful, somewhat unctuous and warm on the palate without great nuances.

SEÑORÍO DE UNX 2000 CRIANZA RED
100% tempranillo

72 Cherry. Not very intense aroma of not very ripe red fruit with sharp green notes. Light, not very persistent palate reminiscent of toast and light hints of varnish in the retronasal passage.

ILAGARES 2002 RED
70% tempranillo, 30% garnacha

78 Dark cherry with a garnet red edge. Intense aroma with predominant spicy notes of skins, a suggestion of ripe black fruit and underbrush. Flavourful, spicy palate with slightly marked tannins and a certain warmth.

ILAGARES 2003 RED
70% tempranillo, 30% garnacha

78 Garnet red cherry with a violet hue. Intense aroma with good varietal, young wine expression, with toasty hints of skins and underbrush. Fresh, flavourful palate with slightly marked tannins (a mild hint of greeness) and marked acidity.

Cooperativa SAN MIGUEL

Chirria, s/n
31494 Eslava (Navarra)
☎: 948 733 185 - Fax: 948 733 288
torreslava@wanadoo.es

Established: 1939

🍷 110 ⬛ 3,000,000 litres
🍇 225 has. 🍷 100%

SIRGÚN 2003 ROSÉ
garnacha, tempranillo

81 Intense raspberry. Not very intense, fruity aroma with a hint of citrus fruit freshness. Flavourful, very fresh palate with fine bitter notes, spicy skins, red stone fruit and good acidity.

SIRGÚN CEPAS VIEJAS 2002 RED
100% garnacha

84 Garnet red cherry with a coppery edge. Fairly intense aroma with good varietal expression (red fruit, spicy notes) and spicy hints of oak. Flavourful palate with some concentration, fine bitter notes (with a good oak/fruit integration) and excellent acidity.

SIRGÚN 2001 CRIANZA RED
garnacha, tempranillo

84 Intense garnet red cherry. Intense aroma with fine toasty oak notes, red stone fruit, quite varietal spicy hints and a balsamic suggestion. Flavourful palate with promising although quite marked tannins, well-balanced and long.

VEGA SIRGÚN 2003 ROSÉ
VEGA SIRGÚN 2003 RED

Cooperativa SAN RAIMUNDO ABAD

Lejalde, 25
31593 Fitero (Navarra)
☎: 948 776 056 - Fax: 948 844 963
raimundo@ucan.es

Established: 1940

🍷 80 ⬛ 3.800.000 litres
🍇 415 has. 🍷 100%

VIRREY PALAFOX 2003 ROSÉ
VIRREY PALAFOX 2003 RED
SOLOSOTO 2001 OAK AGED RED
MONASTERIO DE FITERO 2000 CRIANZA RED

Bodega SAN RAMÓN

San Ramón, 1
31580 Lodosa (Navarra)
☎: 948 693 675 - Fax: 948 662 399

Established: 1967

⬛ 700,000 litres 🍇 54 has. 🍷 100%

CALDERÍN 2003 JOVEN ROSÉ
GRANEL 2003 JOVEN ROSÉ
VINO CALDERÍN 2003 JOVEN RED
GRANEL 2003 JOVEN RED

Bodegas SAN SALVADOR

Carretera de Alto, 102
31243 Arróniz (Navarra)
☎: 948 537 128 - Fax: 948 537 662

Established: 1947

GALCÍBAR 2003 WHITE
viura

77 Brilliant pale yellow. Not very intense, slightly fruity, ripe aroma with floral hints (petals). Flavourful palate with bitter notes and a ripe white fruit nuance.

GALCÍBAR 2003 ROSÉ
garnacha

78 Intense raspberry. Ripe aroma of red fruit with a spicy nuance of skins and hints of terroir. Flavourful palate with fresh overtones, a varietal character (spices) and hints of ripe red grapefruit with a slightly acidic edge.

VIÑA ARNATA 2003 ROSÉ
garnacha

75 Very deep raspberry. Intense aroma of somewhat reduced ripe red fruit with mild off-odours from the tank. Flavourful palate with fresh spicy overtones, fruity and somewhat warm.

CASTILUZAR 2003 RED
tempranillo

77 Cherry. Simple aroma of red fruit (pulp) and hints of maceration. Fresh and fruity on the palate, without great nuances.

GALCÍBAR 2002 RED
tempranillo

77 Garnet red. Aroma with crianza notes (animal skins) and spices. Flavourful palate with good acidity, ripe fruit; slightly toasty but pleasant flavours quite rustic.

VIÑA ARNATA 2002 JOVEN RED
tempranillo

77 Garnet red cherry with a violet hue. Intense aroma of slightly reduced ripe fruit, petals, spices and underbrush. Flavourful, fruity palate with slightly marked tannins (a mild note of greeness) and good acidity.

GALCÍBAR 1999 CRIANZA RED
tempranillo

80 Garnet red cherry with a saffron edge. Powerful aroma of ripe red fruit with spicy, creamy (vanilla) wood notes. Flavourful palate with well-integrated oak/fruit, fruity, spicy and pleasant.

VIÑA ARNATA 1999 CRIANZA RED
tempranillo

78 Dark cherry with a brick red rim. Powerful aroma of ripe black fruit (reduction) and spicy oak notes. Flavourful palate with quite fresh tannins, spicy hints and liquorice.

CASTILUZAR 2000 CRIANZA RED
tempranillo

71 Garnet red with an orangey edge. Aroma with crianza reduction notes and flat fruit. Fresh and subdued on the palate, without fruit.

GALCÍBAR 1997 RESERVA RED
tempranillo

80 Garnet red cherry with a brick red edge. Intense, ripe aroma with mild reduction off-odours (late racking). Better in the mouth; flavourful, supple palate with well-integrated fruit/oak and good acidity.

GALCÍBAR 1999 CRIANZA RED

Cooperativa SANTO CRISTO DEL AMPARO

Carretera Lumbier, s/n
31460 Aibar (Navarra)
☎: 948 877 009 - Fax: 948 877 004
Established: 1938
📦 5,000,000 litres 🇪🇸 100%

VAL DE SORETA 2003 JOVEN ROSÉ
VAL DE SORETA 2002 RED

Bodega de SARRÍA

Finca Señorío de Sarría
31100 Puente La Reina (Navarra)
☎: 948 202 202 - Fax: 948 340 140
info@bodesa.net - bodegadesarria.com
Established: 1953
⊕ 6,000 📦 3,000,000 litres 🌿 210 has.
🍷 80% 🌍20%: -FR -DE -UK -US -IE -JP -MX -CA -PL -DK -FI

SEÑORÍO DE SARRÍA CHARDONNAY 2003 JOVEN WHITE
chardonnay

85 Pale golden yellow. Intense aroma of ripe apples, fine notes of spices and fragrant herbs. Flavourful, quite fruity palate, with a warm, slightly oily texture and excellent acidity.

SEÑORÍO DE SARRÍA VIÑEDO Nº 3 2003 FERMENTADO EN BARRICA WHITE
100% chardonnay

87 Pale gold. Intense aroma of fine toasty oak notes, well-integrated with ripe white fruit and fragrant herbs. Flavourful, slightly warm and creamy on the palate with spicy, bitter oak and excellent acidity.

SEÑORÍO DE SARRÍA 2003 JOVEN ROSÉ
100% garnacha

79 Brilliant raspberry. Fresh, somewhat fruity aroma with predominant spicy and very varietal notes. Fresh, flavourful palate with red stone fruit, spicy, slightly warm and oily with good citrus acidity.

SEÑORÍO DE SARRÍA VIÑEDO Nº 5 2003 ROSÉ
100% garnacha

78 Raspberry blush. Good intensity, fresh aroma of red fruit and a slightly vegetative suggestion (vine shoots). Flavourful palate with fleshy overtones, red stone fruit, slightly warm and oily, well-mannered.

SEÑORÍO DE SARRÍA VIÑEDO Nº 8 2002 OAK AGED RED
100% mazuelo ⊕ 12

86 Dark cherry with a purplish edge. Powerful, very fine aroma with a slight varietal expression (black fruit, hints of petals and spices) and toasty oak. Flavourful, fleshy palate with slightly marked but fine tannins, bitter (liquorice).

SEÑORÍO DE SARRÍA VIÑEDO Nº 9 2002 OAK AGED RED
100% cabernet sauvignon ⊕ 6

84 Nearly opaque cherry. Concentrated aroma of black fruit with earthy hints (a mineral suggestion). Fleshy, fresh, well-balanced palate with notes of the vine variety; somewhat tannic fruit, for keeping.

SEÑORÍO DE SARRÍA VIÑEDO Nº 4 2002 OAK AGED RED
100% merlot   6

82 Fairly dark cherry with a garnet red edge. Medium-intensity, fresh, balsamic aroma with a touch of Bordeaux. Flavourful palate with fresh, ripe fruit, very balsamic (pepper), spicy and warm with a light herbaceous hint.

SEÑORÍO DE SARRÍA VIÑEDO Nº 7 2002 OAK AGED RED
100% graciano   6

78 Brilliant garnet red cherry. Very balsamic aroma (pine, resins). Medium-bodied palate with bitter tannins and a toasty wood finish with red fruit but not very varietal.

SEÑORÍO DE SARRÍA VIÑEDO SOTÉS 2002 OAK AGED RED
merlot, tempranillo, cabernet sauvignon, mazuelo, garnacha, graciano   6

82 Very deep cherry with a garnet red edge. Somewhat closed aroma of concentrated black fruit, sun-drenched skins, dark-roasted flavours and minerals. Flavourful palate with very bitter wood tannins without fruit tannin integration, warm and balsamic.

SEÑORÍO DE SARRÍA 1999 CRIANZA RED
50% tempranillo, 40% cabernet sauvignon, 10% garnacha

77 Garnet red. Aroma with reduction notes and fine spices. Fleshy, fresh palate, without great fruit, slightly rustic.

SEÑORÍO DE SARRÍA 1997 RESERVA RED
merlot, cabernet sauvignon, graciano

82 Brilliant deep garnet red. Elegant crianza aroma (terroir, smoky hints) and notes of ripe skins. Fleshy, flavourful palate with dominant oak tannins but rounded with the fruit and a spicy finish.

SEÑORÍO DE SARRÍA 1996 GRAN RESERVA RED
merlot, cabernet sauvignon, graciano

83 Lively garnet red. Concentrated toasty aroma of cocoa, fine reduction and a suggestion of ripe fruit. Fleshy palate with good freshness, round, flavourful oak tannins and a spicy finish.

SEÑORÍO DE SARRÍA MOSCATEL 2002 DULCE
100% moscatel

85 Intense golden. Aroma of quince, orange peel and sun-drenched grapes. Sweet, unctuous palate, evoking citrus fruit, slightly pasty with a bakery finish (marzipan), long.

SEÑORÍO DE URDAIZ

Carretera Madrid s/n
31591 Corella (Navarra)
☎: 916 398 228 - Fax: 916 343 830
carmeng@swd.es

Established: 1940

223 ⚗ 658,000 litres 🍷 80%

🍇20%: -UK -DE -SDV -CH -AT -DK -BE

ARX ROJO 2003 JOVEN RED
60% tempranillo, 40% cabernet sauvignon

84 Garnet red cherry. Intense aroma of ripe red stone fruit with hints of terroir and sun-drenched skins, optimum ripeness. Fresh, flavourful on the palate, excellent fruit-crianza-acidity symmetry.

ARX NEGRO 2003 JOVEN RED
60% tempranillo, 40% merlot

87 Very deep cherry. Intense aroma of black fruit, with an excellent varietal expression, spicy notes of skins and a nuance of petals and underbrush. Powerful, concentrated palate with flavourful tannins and refreshing acidity.

Cooperativa Vinícola de TAFALLA

Carretera Estella, s/n
31300 Tafalla (Navarra)
☎: 948 700 088 - Fax: 948 755 433
vinicolatafalla@eresmas

TORRE BERATXA 2003 ROSÉ
garnacha

79 Brilliant pale raspberry. Intense, fruity aroma (strawberries, white fruit) with spicy hints of skins. Flavourful, quite fruity palate with a slightly warm and oily texture and good acidity.

VIÑA NAVA 2003 ROSÉ
garnacha, tempranillo

83 Brilliant raspberry with an orangey hue. Intense aroma of red stone fruit, fine spicy notes of skins and hints of high quality citrus fruit. Flavourful, fleshy palate of red fruit; slightly warm with refreshing acidity.

VIÑA NAVA 2003 RED
tempranillo

84 Very deep cherry with a violet hue. Powerful, fruity aroma with an excellent varietal expression (black fruit, underbrush) and hints of terroir.

Flavourful on the palate with quite marked grape tannins though well-complemented by the sweet fruit, hints of liquorice, excellent acidity.

Bodegas VALCARLOS

Carretera Circunvalación, s/n
31210 Los Arcos (Navarra)
☎: 948 640 866 - Fax: 948 640 866
ignacio_vela@bodegasvalcarlossl.es
www.bodegasvalcarlos.com

Established: 2000

🍷 5,000 📦 3,000,000 litres 🍇 55 has.

🍾 60% 🌐40%: -DE -UK -DK -CH -US -AU -MX -TH -FR -PR -SE -NO

MARQUÉS DE VALCARLOS 2003 JOVEN WHITE
85% viura, 15% chardonnay

79 Yellow straw. Aroma of ripe tropical fruit and white flowers. Supple palate with good acidity and a somewhat short finish.

MARQUÉS DE VALCARLOS 2003 JOVEN ROSÉ
75% tempranillo, 25% merlot

78 Intense raspberry. Not very intense aroma of red stone fruit with a hint of freshness. Flavourful palate with fine spicy notes of the vine variety and citrus fruit hints.

FORTIUS CABERNET 1999 CRIANZA RED
100% cabernet sauvignon

85 Garnet red cherry with a brick red edge. Powerful aroma with predominant toasty oak notes and fine notes of fruit and reduction. Flavourful, fleshy and supple palate with spicy notes (paprika), ripe and firm tannins, liquorice, balsamic flavours and fine toasty notes in the retronasal passage.

FORTIUS MERLOT 2000 CRIANZA RED
100% merlot

84 Garnet red cherry with a brick red edge. Powerful aroma, toasty oak notes, a ripe red fruit suggestion (slightly viscous) and fine reduction (leather). Flavourful, supple palate, excellent crianza expression and quite varietal (paprika).

MARQUÉS DE VALCARLOS 2000 CRIANZA RED
80% tempranillo, 20% cabernet sauvignon

81 Garnet red cherry with a brick red edge. Powerful aroma with good Cabernet expression (paprika) and fine spicy oak notes. Flavourful palate with quite marked tannins, slightly fresh oak and good acidity.

MARQUÉS DE VALCARLOS 1998 RESERVA RED
60% cabernet sauvignon, 40% tempranillo

78 Intense cherry with a brick red edge. Intense aroma with predominant reduction notes (varnish, leather). Flavourful palate with slightly astringent tannins and good acidity.

ÉLITE DE FORTIUS 2000 RESERVA RED
merlot, cabernet sauvignon

89 Quite intense cherry. Fine, elegant aroma with creamy toast (cocoa) and varietal notes (redcurrants, paprika). Round, oily palate with varietal expression and fine toasty hints, flavourful.

MARQUÉS DE VALCARLOS 1997 GRAN RESERVA RED
tempranillo, cabernet sauvignon

85 Garnet red cherry with a brick red edge. Intense aroma with spicy oak notes, a jammy hint and reduction notes (aged wood). Flavourful palate with predominant bitter notes and balanced overtones, notes of dark-roasted flavours and liquorice in the retronasal passage.

FORTIUS 1999 RESERVA RED
FORTIUS 1998 GRAN RESERVA RED

Bodegas y Viñas VALDELARES

Carretera Eje del Ebro, Km.58
31579 Carcar (Navarra)
☎: 656 849 602

VALDELARES 2003 JOVEN ROSÉ
33% tempranillo, 33% cabernet sauvignon, 33% merlot

82 Very brilliant rosé with a coppery hue. Fresh aroma of sweetish strawberries with a red fruit pulp and a very pleasant hint of greeness (varietal). Fresh, fruity palate with the expression of the vine varieties and fruit weight, a little warm but compensated by a fresh acidity.

VALDELARES 2003 JOVEN RED
50% tempranillo, 50% merlot

81 Very deep cherry. Aroma of ripe black fruit (a hint of sun-toasted plums) with earthy notes and a suggestion of cocoa. Dry palate with round fruit tannins, slightly lacking in flavour; good freshness with quite green grape notes.

VALDELARES 2002 JOVEN RED
40% tempranillo, 40% cabernet sauvignon, 20% merlot

78 Deep cherry. Aroma of vanilla with sweetish notes of unassembled wood, ripe plums and a hint of spicy fruit. Dry palate with drying cask tannins, a good fruit weight concealed by the wood and a slightly bitter finish.

Bodegas VEGA DEL CASTILLO

Rua Romana, 7
31390 Olite (Navarra)
☎: 948 740 012 - Fax: 948 741 074
www.vegadelcastillo.com

VEGA DEL CASTILLO LÁGRIMA 2003 ROSÉ
MERAK 2001 RED
VEGA DEL CASTILLO TEMPRANILLO 2003 RED
VEGA DEL CASTILLO 2001 CRIANZA RED
VEGA DEL CASTILLO CABERNET SAUVIGNON 2003 RED

VICENTE MALUMBRES

Santa Bárbara, 15
31591 Corella (Navarra)
☎: 948 401 920 - Fax: 948 401 653
info@malumbres.com
www.malumbres.com

Established: 1930

⊕ 400 ▤ 550,000 litres ❧ 60 has.

🍷 20% 🍇80%: -DE -UK -NL -CH -FR -DK -BE IT

VICENTE MALUMBRES 2000 FERMENTADO EN BARRICA WHITE
100% chardonnay

77 Golden. Intense aroma of ripe white stone fruit and spicy notes of oak. Flavourful palate, lacking fruit-oak-alcohol symmetry with a slightly ripe oily texture.

MALUMBRES 2003 WHITE
100% viura

79 Pale yellow with golden nuances. Slightly intense aroma of ripe white stone fruit and creamy oak notes. Flavourful palate with ripe fruit, and a spicy suggestion, slightly warm with hints of wax and hay.

MALUMBRES 2003 ROSÉ
100% garnacha

78 Slightly dark raspberry. Intense aroma of red stone fruit and hints of petals. Flavourful palate with fresh overtones of spice and citrus fruit.

MALUMBRES GRACIANO 2000 CRIANZA RED
graciano

87 Dark garnet red with a coppery edge. Powerful aroma of black fruit, flowers, spicy skins, damp earth and toasty hints of oak. Flavourful, fleshy palate with good varietal crianza expression; spicy, vigorous and long.

MALUMBRES 2003 RED
85% garnacha, 15% tempranillo

82 Brilliant cherry with shades of violet. Intense, fresh aroma with varietal Garnacha notes (spices, violets) and hints of damp earth. Flavourful palate of black fruit with fine, ripe tannins and excellent acidity.

MALUMBRES PRIMEROS VIÑEDOS 2000 RED
100% garnacha

82 Quite dark cherry. Intense, quite concentrated aroma (black fruit, toasty hints of skins) and a spicy oak suggestion. Flavourful, fleshy and supple on the palate with fine, spicy, very varietal notes and good acidity.

MALUMBRES 2000 CRIANZA RED

80 Dark red cherry with a saffron edge. Intense aroma with varietal presence (spices, violets) and spicy hints of oak. Flavourful palate with mild reduction notes (tobacco) and ripe tannins; slightly warm.

MALUMBRES GARNACHA 2000 CRIANZA RED
100% garnacha

84 Dark cherry with a saffron edge. Intense, ripe aroma with a good varietal profile (spices, flowers), spicy freshness overtones of the oak, underbrush. Flavourful, fleshy palate with a good fruit/oak integration, hints of liquorice and fine bitter notes (chocolate).

MALUMBRES 2001 CRIANZA RED
60% tempranillo, 30% garnacha, 10% merlot

84 Dark cherry. Slightly intense aroma of black fruit, fine hints of skins, toasty oak and damp earth. Flavourful, slightly warm palate with round, oily tannins, a good fruit weight and fresh overtones.

MALUMBRES 2000 RESERVA RED
40% tempranillo, 40% garnacha, 20% cabernet sauvignon

84 Deep garnet red cherry. Intense, very fine aroma of macerated black fruit fine spicy oak notes and fresh terracota overtones. Flavourful, supple palate, a good oak/fruit integration and dark-roasted flavours in the retronasal passage.

VIÑA ONTINAR 2003 WHITE
VIÑA ONTINAR 2003 ROSÉ

DO NAVARRA

VIÑA ONTINAR 2003 RED
MALUMBRES PRIMEROS VIÑEDOS 1998 RED

VINÍCOLA CORELLANA

Carretera del Villar, s/n
31591 Corella (Navarra)
☎: 948 780 617 - Fax: 948 401 894
vcorellana@eresmas.com

Established: 1989

⊞ 1,092 ⊠ 2,000,000 litres ⚇ 110 has.

⬛ 20% ⊕80%: -FR -DE -NL -CH -US

REYNOBLE GRACIANO 2002 JOVEN RED
100% graciano

81 Garnet red cherry. Intense aroma of red fruit with fine herbaceous notes (brambles), a spicy nuance and hints of underbrush. Flavourful, fruity palate with fleshy overtones and firm tannins, slightly warm, with refreshing acidity.

REYNOBLE CABERNET SAUVIGNON 2002 JOVEN RED
100% cabernet sauvignon

81 Very deep cherry with a purplish hue. Fruity aroma (strawberries) with notes of eucalyptus and a hint of green. Fleshy palate with flavourful slightly ripe fruit tannins, floral notes and well-integrated smoky oak (cocoa) .

REYNOBLE 2001 CRIANZA RED
70% tempranillo, 20% cabernet sauvignon, 10% garnacha

78 Garnet red cherry with a coppery edge. Intense aroma with fresh red fruit overtones, a spicy nuance (paprika) and a mild suggestion of reduction (leathers). Flavourful palate with slightly marked tannins, lacks symmetry.

REYNOBLE 1995 GRAN RESERVA RED
80% tempranillo, 10% cabernet sauvignon, 10% garnacha

83 Garnet red cherry with a coppery edge. Powerful, ripe aroma with spicy oak notes, black fruit and a fine reduction nuance. Flavourful, fleshy palate with well-integrated oak/fruit, well-balanced with a good expression of traditional crianza.

VIÑA ZORZAL 2003 JOVEN WHITE
REYNOBLE 2003 JOVEN WHITE
VIÑA ZORZAL 2003 JOVEN ROSÉ
REYNOBLE 2003 JOVEN ROSÉ
VIÑA ZORZAL 2003 JOVEN RED
REYNOBLE GARNACHA DE VIÑAS VIEJAS 2003 JOVEN RED
REYNOBLE TEMPRANILLO 2003 JOVEN RED
CÁMARA ALTA 2001 CRIANZA RED
REYNOBLE 1995 RESERVA RED
CÁMARA ALTA 1998 RESERVA RED
CÁMARA ALTA 1995 GRAN RESERVA RED

VINÍCOLA NAVARRA

Avenida Pamplona, 25
31398 Tiebas-Muruarte de Reta (Navarra)
☎: 948 360 131 - Fax: 948 360 544
vinicola@byb.es
www.byb.es

Established: 1864

⊞ 4,500 ⊠ 3,500,000 litres ⚇ 11 has.

⬛ 75.5% ⊕24.5%

CASTILLO DE JAVIER 2003 ROSÉ
100% garnacha

83 Very deep raspberry. Powerful, fruity aroma (red stone fruit) with warm and somewhat spicy hints of skins. Flavourful palate with foresty strawberries, fine bitter notes and hints of citrus fruit.

LAS CAMPANAS 2003 ROSÉ
100% garnacha

78 Brilliant raspberry. Not very intense aroma, somewhat fruity and fresh. Flavourful palate with fleshy overtones, a slightly oily texture and fine spicy notes of skins.

LAS CAMPANAS TEMPRANILLO 2003 JOVEN RED
tempranillo, cabernet, graciano, merlot

80 Cherry with a garnet red edge. Intense, clean aroma of red berries (raspberries), and brambles. Flavourful, fresh and very fruity palate; an easy drinking young wine.

CASTILLO DE JAVIER 2000 CRIANZA RED
tempranillo, cabernet sauvignon, merlot

84 Garnet red cherry with a saffron glint. Slightly intense aroma with a certain finesse, jammy black fruit and spicy hints of wood. Flavourful, supple palate with a good oak/fruit integration and hints of bitterness and fallen leaves in the retronasal passage.

DO NAVARRA

LAS CAMPANAS 2000 CRIANZA RED
80% tempranillo, 20% cabernet sauvignon

80 Garnet red cherry with a brick red edge. Somewhat intense aroma with spicy oak notes a fruity nuance and reduction hints. Flavourful and fleshy on the palate with jammy black fruit and somewhat ripe and oily tannins.

LAS CAMPANAS 1997 RESERVA RED
70% tempranillo, 30% cabernet sauvignon

83 Garnet red cherry with a brick red edge. Intense aroma with predominant reduction notes and slightly varietal, spicy and herbaceous hints (Cabernet). Flavourful, fleshy and supple palate with good crianza expression.

CASTILLO DE JAVIER 1999 RESERVA RED
tempranillo, cabernet sauvignon, merlot

85 Fairly deep cherry with a saffron edge. Not very intense aroma of fine toasty oak, black fruit notes and a certain spicy, herbaceous freshness (fallen leaves, paprika). Flavourful palate with a good fruit/oak integration; supple, with spicy notions and refreshing acidity.

VIÑA MAGAÑA

San Miguel , 9
31523 Barillas (Navarra)
☎: 948 850 034 - Fax: 948 851 536
bodegas@vinamagana.com
www.vinamagana.com

Established: 1968
🍾 1,100 ▤ 950,000 litres 🍇 110 has.
🍷 20% 🌐80%

CALCHETAS 2001 OAK AGED RED
merlot, cabernet sauvignon, syrah, malbec

95 Quite intense cherry. Powerful aroma, rich in toasty nuances (cocoa, coffee, fruit), complex with warm notes, ripe fruit and minerals. Full, oily, powerful palate with abundant and silky tannins; long and exceptional with a rich expression of ripe but fresh black fruit; flavourful.

TORCAS 2002 RED
37% merlot, 32% cabernet sauvignon, 21% syrah, 10% malbec

92 Fairly intense cherry. Fine aroma with creamy toasty oak notes and fresh fruit. Round, oily palate with excellent tannins and ripe fruit, sweet, very flavourful and persistent tannins, glyceric.

VIÑA MAGAÑA MERLOT 2001 RESERVA RED
100% merlot

88 Dark garnet red. Aroma of ripe black fruit with overtones of the vine variety and crianza complexity (pitch, spices, smoky flavours) and a hint of sun-drenched skins. Powerful palate with black fruit character (liquorice), will keep well, a long finish.

DIGNUS 2000 CRIANZA RED
BARÓN DE MAGAÑA FINCA LA SARDA 2000 CRIANZA RED
BARÓN DE MAGAÑA FINCA LA SARDA MERLOT 2000 CRIANZA RED
VIÑA MAGAÑA 1996 RESERVA RED
VIÑA MAGAÑA MERLOT 1982 GRAN RESERVA RED
VIÑA MAGAÑA 1985 GRAN RESERVA RED

VIÑA VALDORBA

Carretera de la Estación, s/n
31395 Garinoain (Navarra)
☎: 659 098 794 - Fax: 948 720 505

Established: 2000
🍾 400 ▤ 200,000 litres 🍷 50%
🌐50%: -NL -DE -UK -IS -FI -DK -DK -AT

EOLO 2000 CRIANZA RED
25% merlot, 25% tempranillo, 25% graciano, 25% cabernet sauvignon

86 Garnet red cherry with a brick red edge. Powerful aroma of fine smoky oak notes with undertones of fresh fruit, spicy hints of skins and a fine reduction (leathers). Flavourful palate with a good fruit/oak integration, fine bitter notes and balsamic and mineral hints in the retronasal passage.

EOLO GARNACHA 2001 CRIANZA RED
100% garnacha

84 Garnet red cherry with a coppery edge. Powerful aroma with predominant spicy notes of the vine variety, a balsamic notion and toasty oak. Flavourful palate with a good oak/fruit integration, fine bitter notes and hints of terroir.

EOLO GRACIANO 2001 CRIANZA RED
100% graciano

85 Deep cherry with a coppery edge. Intense aroma of black fruit with toasty oak notes and balsamic notes. Flavourful palate, fleshy overtones, with an excellent varietal and crianza expression, with bitter and mineral notes in the retronasal passage.

GRAN EOLO 2000 RESERVA RED
40% cabernet sauvignon, 30% tempranillo, 30% merlot

87 Deep cherry, with a coppery edge. Intense aroma of black fruit with a spicy oak nuance and fine notes of cedar and dried leaves. Flavourful palate with well-integrated oak and fruit, fine bitter notes (chocolate, coffee), a good fruit weight and an excellent crianza expression.

EOLO 2001 RED

VIÑEDOS DE CALIDAD

Carretera Tudela, s/n
31591 Corella (Navarra)
☎: 948 782 014 - Fax: 948 782 164

javierc@arrakis.es

Established: 1954

750 | 2,000,000 litres | 60 has.

40% 60%: -DE -SE -DK -FI -CH -FR -NL -BE -UK

ALEX GARNACHA 2003 ROSÉ
100% garnacha

79 Salmony-pink. Medium-intensity, warm aroma of red fruit. Flavourful palate with pleasant, sweet notes.

ALEX 2000 CRIANZA RED
70% tempranillo, 20% merlot, 10% graciano

79 Cherry with an orangey edge. Medium-intensity, ripe aroma with mild spicy notes. Flavourful palate with an element of overextraction and very noticeable tannins in the finish.

ALEX TEMPRANILLO 2003 RED
100% tempranillo

80 Cherry with a garnet red edge. Medium-intensity aroma of balsamic notes and red fruit. Flavourful palate of concentrated red fruit, toasty skins and light overextraction.

ALEX SELECCIÓN DE BODEGA 2000 RESERVA RED
50% tempranillo, 50% merlot

84 Cherry with a garnet red edge. Intense aroma of well-assembled fruit (blackberries) and wood with mild balsamic notes. Flavourful, intense palate with ripe fruit and somewhat incisive tannins, long.

ALEX VIURA 2003 WHITE
ALEX GRACIANO 2000 CRIANZA RED
ALEX MERLOT 2000 CRIANZA RED

VIRGEN BLANCA Sociedad Cooperativa

Carretera de Calahorra s/n
31260 Lerín (Navarra)
☎: 948 530 058 - Fax: 948 530 589
info@bodegavirgenblanca.com
www.virgenblanca.com

Established: 1956

2,300 | 4,500,000 litres | 480 has.

70% 30%

VIÑA SARDASOL ROSADO DE LÁGRIMA 2003 ROSÉ
garnacha

78 Brilliant raspberry. Fresh aroma of ripe red fruit and hints of petals with a slightly varietal, spicy nuance. Flavourful, bitter palate with red stone fruit and an acidic edge.

VIÑA SARDASOL MERLOT 2003 RED
merlot

85 Intense cherry. Aroma of red fruit with spices, toasty skins and a light smoky suggestion. Fleshy, fruity palate with flavourful fruit tannins (macerating red fruit) and a spicy, pleasant, varietal finish.

VIÑA SARDASOL TEMPRANILLO 2002 RED
tempranillo

80 Deep cherry with a coppery edge. Powerful aroma of ripe red fruit with spicy hints of oak and an underbrush nuance. Flavourful palate with slightly marked tannins, fresh red fruit overtones and a slightly acidic edge.

VIÑA SARDASOL TEMPRANILLO - MERLOT 2002 RED
tempranillo, merlot

82 Deep cherry. Smoky aroma with spicy hints and well-integrated ripe skins. Fleshy palate with round and oily tannins, vanilla and notes of the vine variety (animals, strawberries), long.

VIÑA SARDASOL 2000 CRIANZA RED

81 Garnet with a brick red rim. Balsamic, toasty aroma of red fruit in liqueur. Fleshy palate with good acidity, well-balanced.

VIÑA SARDASOL 1999 RESERVA RED
tempranillo, cabernet sauvignon, merlot

83 Garnet red cherry with a brick red edge. Intense aroma evoking spicy hints of wood and red stone fruit with a prune hint. Flavourful, supple palate with well-associated oak and fruit, bitter hints (chocolate) and pepper and new leather in the retronasal passage.

DO PENEDÈS

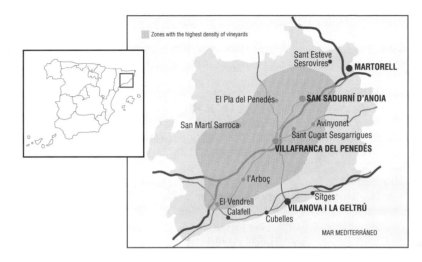

Zones with the highest density of vineyards

Sant Esteve Sesrovires • MARTORELL

El Pla del Penedés — SAN SADURNÍ D'ANOIA

San Martí Sarroca

Avinyonet
Sant Cugat Sesgarrigues
VILLAFRANCA DEL PENEDÉS

l'Arboç

El Vendrell
Calafell
Cubelles

Sitges
VILANOVA I LA GELTRÚ

MAR MEDITERRÁNEO

NEWS. The vineyards of Penedès did not escape the rigours of the 2003 summer in Spain, although the rains at the end of August and the subsequent normalisation of the temperatures in part mitigated the problems caused by the excessive heat on the ripening of the grapes.

In general, of the 409 wines tasted, 291 surpassed 80 points, with their fruitiness standing out, even in those wines that had only been aged in oak for a short period of time. We were glad to see again the red wines of Cavas Avinyó, with excellent single-variety work with *Merlot* and *Cabernet Sauvignon*. Also, Mas Comtal with one of the best Rosé wines, not only of Catalonia but in the whole of Spain. Of enormous interest is the tasting of the always hard-to-find Parés Baltà, which is in perfect shape and among the wines with the highest scores, behind the leading bunch (wines produced exclusively from foreign grapes), the best 'national' is the Finca Els Camps of Jané Ventura, a single-variety wine of *Tempranillo* that reached a score of 88 points and which is only in thirteenth position within the DO.

Hectares of Vineyard	No. of Viticulturists	No. of Bodegas	2003 Harvest	2003 Production	Marketing
27,547	5,678	157 bottlers	Very Good	51,810,194 litres	65% Spain 35% foreign

LOCATION. In the province of Barcelona, between the pre-coastal Catalonian mountain range and the plains that lead to the Mediterranean coast. There are three different areas: Penedès Superior, Penedès Central or Medio and Bajo Penedès.

CLIMATE. Mediterranean, in general warm and mild; warmer in the Bajo Penedès region due to the influence of the Mediterranean Sea, with slightly lower temperatures in Medio Penedés and Penedés Superior, where the climate is typically pre-coastal (greater contrasts between maximum and minimum temperatures, more frequent frosts and annual rainfall which at some places can reach 990 litres per square metre).

SOIL. There is deep soil, not too sandy or too clayey, permeable, which retains the rainwater well. The soil is poor in organic matter and not very fertile.

VARIETIES:
White: *Macabeo* (6,622 Ha), *Xarel·lo* (7,833 Ha), *Parellada* (6,045 Ha), *Chardonnay* (1,038 Ha), *Riesling, Gewürztraminer, Chenin Blanc, Moscatel de Alejandría.*
Red: *Garnacha, Merlot* (1,554 Ha), *Cariñena, Ull de Llebre (Tempranillo – 1,507 Ha), Pinot Noir, Monastrell, Cabernet Sauvignon* (11,487 Ha) and *Syrah.*

SUB-REGIONS:
Penedés Superior. The vineyards reach an altitude of 800 m; the traditional, characteristic variety is the Parellada, which is better suited to the cooler regions.
Penedés Central or Medio. Cava makes up a large part of the production in this region; the most abundant traditional varieties are Macabeo and Xarel·lo.
Bajo Penedés. This is the closest region to the sea, with a lower altitude and wines with a markedly Mediterranean character.

REGULATORY COUNCIL.
Pol. Industrial Domenys II. Plaça Àgora. 08720 Vilafranca del Penedés.
Apdo. Correos 226.
Tel: 938 904 811. Fax: 938 904 754.
E-mail: dopenedes@dopenedes.es.

GENERAL CHARACTERISTICS OF THE WINES:

Whites	The classical wines of the region, produced with the *Macabeo, Xarel·lo, Parellada* varieties, which stand out for their fruity character and extreme lightness. They are fresh wines, and are pleasant to drink within the year. Barrel-fermented wines are also starting to appear, mainly single variety wines of *Xarel·lo* and *Macabeo*, with a greater capacity to age due to the contribution of the tannins of the wood. Another important group is the *Chardonnay* white wines, whether young (fruity, with lemony notes and fine varietal character) or fermented in barrels, which combine the fruity personality of *Chardonnay* with the creamy notes of the oak.
Rosés	Modern in style, raspberry pink coloured, powerful, aromatic and fresh. They are produced from varieties as diverse as *Tempranillo, Cabernet, Merlot* or *Pinot Noir.*
Reds	Those produced from autochthonous grapes, generally *Garnacha* and *Tempranillo,* are young red wines, and are pleasant and easy drinking, although, on occasions, they may be a bit light and have certain herbal notes due to overproduction in the vineyard. Regarding those aged in wood, they may come from foreign varieties (mainly *Cabernet* and *Merlot*) or combined with local grape varieties. They integrate the notes of fine wood with fruity aromas with a good intensity; on the palate they are concentrated and meaty.

A. CANALS NADAL

Ponent, 2
08733 El Pla del Penedés (Barcelona)
☎: 938 988 081 - Fax: 938 989 050
cava@canalsnadal.com
www.canalsnadal.com

Established: 1915
190,000 litres 20 has.
75% 25%

ANTONI CANALS NADAL XAREL.LO 2002 FERMENTADO EN BARRICA WHITE
100% xarel.lo

82 Pale with a greenish edge. Aroma with a tropical fruit finish, light creamy wood and notes of fennel. Flavourful palate of white and tropical fruit well-integrated with the wood, good freshness.

A. CANALS NADAL BLANC D´ANYADA 2003 WHITE
macabeo, xarel.lo

77 Pale with a straw-coloured glint. Tropical aroma (papaya, a nuance of citrus fruit pulp), fairly ripe. Flavourful, warm, slightly sweet palate (evokes peaches) with light beads.

ANTONI CANALS NADAL D'ANYADA 2002 RED
tempranillo

84 Brilliant cherry. Fairly intense, fruity aroma (red fruit) with fresh overtones and hints of terroir. Flavourful, fruity palate, with ripe grape tannins, a slightly oily texture, sun-drenched skins and good acidity.

ANTONI CANALS NADAL CABERNET SAUVIGNON - MERLOT 2001 CRIANZA RED
60% cabernet sauvignon, 40% merlot

84 Very deep cherry with a saffron edge. Intense aroma of black fruit with hints of sun-drenched skins and a nuance of toasty oak. Flavourful, fleshy palate with quite rough tannins well-assembled with the fruit; powerful aroma in the retronasal passage (bitter chocolate).

ALBET I NOYA

Can Vendrell, s/n
08739 Sant Pau D'Ordal (Barcelona)
☎: 938 994 812 - Fax: 938 994 930
albetinoya@albetinoya.com
www.albetinoya.com

Established: 1977
875 1,000,000 litres 42 has.
25% 75%: -CH -DE -FR -UK -NL -BE -JP -US

CAN VENDRELL 2003 JOVEN WHITE
50% xarel.lo, 27% chardonnay, 14% macabeo, 9% sauvignon blanc

84 Pale yellow. Powerful, fruity aroma (ripe apples, hints of tropical fruit) with fresh citrus overtones. Fresh, flavourful and supple palate with excellent acidity.

ALBET I NOYA COL.LECCIÓ CHARDONNAY 2003 FERMENTADO EN BARRICA WHITE
100% chardonnay

84 Yellow straw with a greenish rim. Aroma of ripe white stone fruit, butters and yeasts. Well-balanced, round, oily palate with medium persistence; varietal notions in the retronasal passage.

ALBET I NOYA COL.LECCIÓ XAREL.LO 1999 FERMENTADO EN BARRICA WHITE
100% xarel.lo   4

83 Golden yellow. Aroma of new casks, pastries and ripe quinces. Palate with marked notes of wood over fruit and bitter notes, quite light.

ALBET I NOYA LIGNUM 2002 FERMENTADO EN BARRICA WHITE
52% sauvignon blanc, 48% chardonnay   3

88 Yellow-straw with a greenish hue. Aroma with notes of fine wood, white fruit (pears) and quinces. Well-balanced palate with good freshness, round tannins and a good fruit-wood balance; long.

ALBET I NOYA EL BLANC XXV 2002 WHITE
25% chardonnay, 25% xarel.lo, 25% parellada, 25% macabeo

87 Straw-coloured. Good, intense, aroma with notes of aniseed and herbs (fennel, mint). Fresh, oily palate, expressive, very good alcohol-acidity balance.

ALBET I NOYA XAREL-LO CLÀSSIC 2000 WHITE
100% xarel.lo

85 Straw-coloured with a greenish hue. Not very intense yet fine aroma of ripe fruit (apples) with fine notes of herbs (fennel) and flowers (lavender). Flavourful, fresh palate with lively acidity, well-balanced.

ALBET I NOYA PINOT NOIR MERLOT CLÀSSIC 2003 ROSÉ
pinot noir, merlot

82 Raspberry blush. Good intensity, fresh aroma of red fruit, fine. Flavourful, fresh palate with good bitter-acidic balance and quite persistent.

CAN VENDRELL 2003 JOVEN RED
66% tempranillo, 34% cabernet sauvignon

84 Garnet red cherry with a violet rim. Intense aroma of black fruit with spicy hints of skins and a very fine herbaceous and varietal nuance. Fresh palate with flavourful, somewhat rough grape tannins, excellent acidity and young wine expression.

ALBET I NOYA TEMPRANILLO CLASIC 2003 RED
tempranillo

80 Cherry with a violet hue. Aroma with mild notes of the tank, lees and green fruit. Drying tannins on the palate, warm, with body.

ALBET I NOYA COL.LECCIÓ CABERNET SAUVIGNON 2000 OAK AGED RED
100% cabernet sauvignon   14

89 Garnet red cherry. Fairly intense aroma with predominant toasty notes of oak and a nuance of macerated black fruit. Powerful and concentrated on the palate with fairly rough though promising oak tannins; excellent aroma in the retronasal passage (ripe fruit, liquorice, pitch).

ALBET I NOYA COL.LECCIÓ SYRAH 2000 OAK AGED RED
100% syrah   14

86 Cherry with a ruby red hue. Aroma of ink with elegant notions of reduction, red fruit and jammy tomatoes. Round, quite bitter, well-balanced and fleshy palate.

ALBET I NOYA LIGNUM 2001 OAK AGED RED
garnacha, cariñena, cabernet sauvignon   6

83 Cherry with an orangey hue. Perfumed aroma of light toasty and balsamic flavours, spicy. Palate with body, good acidity and well-integrated wood-fruit tannins, fairly warm.

ALBET I NOYA NURIA 2001 OAK AGED RED
95% merlot, 3% caladoc, 2% petit syrah

80 Bigarreau cherry. Fruity aroma of ink. Palate with an edge of marked acidity, fruity and well-mannered.

ALBET I NOYA COL.LECCIÓ TEMPRANILLO 1999 RED
100% tempranillo

83 Red with an orangey hue. Aroma with sweet, jammy, balsamic notes. Drying, fleshy palate with overtones of varietal expression.

ALBET I NOYA EL NEGRE 25 ANYS 1999 RED

89 Garnet red cherry. Intense aroma of toasty oak notes with a ripe fruit (jamminess), and balsamic nuance. Powerful, concentrated palate with quite marked, rough, promising oak tannins and an oily texture; excellent aroma in the retronasal passage (chocolate, spices).

ALBET I NOYA DOLÇ ADRIÀ 2000 RED SWEET
syrah, tempranillo

89 Nearly opaque cherry. Powerful aroma of jammy black fruit with spicy hints of oak, notes of sun-drenched skins and raisiny notes. Powerful, concentrated, unctuous palate with fine notes of sweet fruit (prunes) and a powerful aroma in the retronasal passage (cocoa, spices, balsamic flavours).

ALBET I NOYA RESERVA MARTÍ 1998 RED

90 Very deep cherry with a coppery edge. Powerful, concentrated aroma of fine smoky and toasty oak notes and perfectly ripe black fruit. Powerful palate with well-integrated grape and fruit tannins and fine varietal notes (paprika), very complex (liquorice, spices, balsamic flavours) and long.

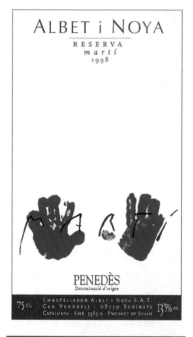

ALEMANY I CORRIO

Melió, 78
08720 Vilafranca del Penedés (Barcelona)
☎: 938 172 587 - Fax: 938 172 587
sotlefriec@totpenedes.com

Established: 1999
🍷 18 🛢 228 litres 🍇 8 has.
🏳 20% 🌍80%

SOT LEFRIEC 2001 OAK AGED RED

95 Very intense cherry. Medium-intensity aroma with ripe black fruit, mineral notes and toasty flavours (chocolate, coffee). Full palate, rich in fruit expression (ripe redcurrants) and toasty oak (peat, pitch, hints of carpentry), flavourful.

PAS CURTEI 2003 RED

88 Intense garnet red cherry. Powerful aroma rich in fine toasty notes (cocoa, toffee, vanilla) and ripe fruit with fresh overtones. Fresh, slightly light, fine palate with good acidity, easy drinking, with fine toasty oak and fresh tannins.

ALSINA & SARDÁ

Barrio Les Tarumbes, s/n
08733 Pla del Penedés (Barcelona)
☎: 938 988 132 - Fax: 938 988 671
alsina@ialsinasarda.com -
www.readysoft.es/alsina

Established: 1986
135 ▤ 1,150,000 litres 🍇 40 has.
🍷 70% 🍷30%

ALSINA & SARDÁ CHARDONNAY 2003 FERMENTADO EN BARRICA WHITE
chardonnay

81 Pale yellow with a greenish hue. Intense aroma with smoky oak notes, hints of slightly ripe fruit, creamy (vanilla). Fresh, flavourful palate, with bittersweet notes and a bitter suggestion of oak, smoky, slightly varietal and long.

ALSINA & SARDÁ CHARDONNAY XAREL.LO 2003 WHITE
chardonnay, xarel.lo

83 Pale with a greenish hue. Intense, fruity aroma with hints of exotic fruit and white flowers. Flavourful, fruity palate with fine bitter and citrus notes.

ALSINA & SARDÁ MERLOT 2003 ROSÉ
merlot

79 Very lively raspberry. Intense, fresh, fruity aroma with hints of sweetness and petals. Flavourful palate with notes of slightly sweet red fruit, slightly bitter and oily with hints of citrus fruit.

ARNAU D'ALSINA SARDÁ 2003 JOVEN RED
merlot

85 Dark deep red cherry. Powerful, fruity aroma with a good varietal expression of young wine (redcurrants, damp earth, sweet hints). Flavourful, fleshy palate with slightly sweet fruit, toasted skins, a slightly oily texture and good acidity.

ALSINA & SARDÁ MERLOT 2001 OAK AGED RED
merlot   ▤ 3

77 Dark cherry with a dark red edge. Powerful, ripe aroma with a slight varietal expression (redcurrants, underbrush) and toasty oak notes. Flavourful, bitter palate, lacking balance, fruit-oak fusion, acidic edges.

ALSINA & SARDÁ CRIANZA 1999 CRIANZA RED
cabernet sauvignon, tempranillo

80 Cherry with a brick red edge. Toasty aroma with prominent wood overripe red fruit and hints of reduction. Flavourful, with pungent oak tannins and good freshness.

AMETLLER CIVILL

Rovira Roja, 10
08731 Sant Martí Sarroca (Barcelona)
☎: 933 208 439 - Fax: 933 208 437
ametller@ametller.com
www.ametller.com

Established: 1999
🍇 38 has. 🍷 50%
🌍50%: -NL -SE -DK -JP -UK -CH

AMETLLER XARE.LO - CHARDONNAY 2003 FERMENTADO EN BARRICA WHITE
70% xarel.lo, 30% chardonnay

80 Pale with golden nuances. Quite intense aroma of white stone fruit with hints of flowers and smoky oak. Flavourful, somewhat fruity palate with fine bitter notes (herbs, toasty flavours) and good acidity.

AMETLLER SELECCIÓ 2003 WHITE
65% xarel.lo, 25% parellada, 10% macabeo

83 Pale yellow with a golden glint. Fairly intense, fresh aroma with notes of green apples and hints of exotic fruit. Fresh palate with fine bitter notes and excellent acidity.

AMETLLER 2000 CRIANZA RED
tempranillo, cabernet sauvignon, merlot

82 Deep cherry with a saffron edge. Intense aroma of red fruit and toasty oak with a slightly herbaceous nuance. Flavourful palate with ripe tannins, hints of liquorice and overripe fruit in the finish.

AMETLLER CABERNET SAUVIGNON MERLOT 1999 RESERVA RED

ANTONIO MASCARÓ

Casal, 9
08720 Vilafranca del Penedés (Barcelona)
☎: 938 901 628 - Fax: 938 901 358
mascaro@mascaro.es
www.mascaro.es

Established: 1946
1.000 🍇 40 has.🍷 85% 🍷15%

MASCARÓ CABERNET SAUVIGNON 1996 RESERVA RED
100% cabernet sauvignon

78 Cherry with an orangey edge. Medium-intensity aroma with vegetative notes (green peppers, vine shoots) and a fruity nuance. Flavourful palate which also has a vegetative touch yet, on the whole, well-mannered.

ANIMA MASCARÓ 1996 GRAN RESERVA RED
90% cabernet sauvignon, 10% merlot

80 Cherry with an orangey edge. Medium-intensity aroma with nuances of reduction (tobacco), red fruit and green peppers. Flavourful, quite fruity palate with a vegetative nuance and with acidic overtones that do not sully the whole.

ARVIC ARETEY

Pº Colón, 4
08002 Barcelona (Barcelona)
☎: 933 102 262 - Fax: 933 100 671
info@aretey.com
www.aretey.com

ARETEY CABERNET SAUVIGNON 2000 RED
ARETEY CS EDICIÓN EXCLUSIVA 1999 RED
ARETEY TEMPRANILLO-MERLOT 2002 RED
GRAN ARETEY COUPAGE SELECCIÓN 2000 RED

AVGVSTVS-FORUM

Carretera Sant Vicenç s/n
43700 El Vendrell (Tarragona)
☎: 977 666 910 - Fax: 977 666 590
avgvstvs@wanadoo.es

Established: 1989

🍷 200 📊 200,000 litres 🌿 10 has.

🍇 50% 🌐50%: -US -JP -MX -CA -AU -NZ -UK -FR -DE -DK -DK -SE -FI -PL -NL -BE - LU -CH -AT -AD -PT -IE

AVGVSTVS CHARDONNAY 2003
FERMENTADO EN BARRICA WHITE
100% chardonnay

86 Straw-coloured with a golden hue. Good, intense aroma with notes of hay and dried grass, smoky oak notes and a nuance of fresh fruit. Flavourful, oily palate, varietal with fine smoky notes and citrus fruit in the finish, persistent.

AVGVSTVS 2003 JOVEN ROSÉ
100% cabernet sauvignon

84 Brilliant raspberry. Powerful, ripe and fruity aroma with a spicy nuance of skins. Dry, generous palate, rich in nuances with a slightly oily texture, very varietal notes and excellent structure and acidity.

AVGVSTVS CABERNET FRANC 2002 OAK AGED RED
100% cabernet franc   🍷3

87 Garnet red cherry with a saffron edge. Intense aroma of great finesse with predominant toasty notes of oak and varietal expression (red fruit, hints of nettles). Flavourful palate with well-integrated fruit and oak and spicy hints in the retronasal passage, very long.

AVGVSTVS CABERNET SAUVIGNON-MERLOT 2000 OAK AGED RED
50% cabernet sauvignon, 50% merlot   🍷12

85 Very deep garnet red cherry. Not very intense aroma of toasty oak notes (dark-roasted flavours, pitch). Flavourful palate with slightly rough tannins and an oily texture with well-integrated oak and fruit, good acidity.

AVGVSTVS EVTYCHES 1999 OAK AGED RED
70% cabernet sauvignon, 30% merlot   🍷12

86 Garnet red cherry with a brick red edge. Powerful aroma with spicy wood notes, a ripe fruit nuance and a good varietal expression (truffles, underbrush). Flavourful palate with ripe tannins, a slightly oily texture and liquorice and dark-roasted flavours in the retronasal passage.

AVGVSTVS MERLOT 2002 OAK AGED RED
100% merlot   🍷6

86 Garnet red cherry with a violet edge. Not very intense, very fine aroma of spicy oak notes, red stone fruit and hints of terroir. Flavourful palate with an excellent varietal expression, ripe tannins, herbaceous and rich bitter hints and good acidity.

AVGVSTVS TRAJANUS 1998 CRIANZA RED
70% cabernet sauvignon, 25% merlot, 5% cabernet franc

89 Intense cherry with a brick red edge. Intense aroma of ripe black fruit (hints of prunes) and fine toasty wood. Flavourful palate with ripe, oily tannins and excellent crianza expression and good acidity.

AVGVSTVS TRAJANUS 1997 CRIANZA RED

Cavas AVINYÓ

Masia Can Fontanals, s/n
08793 Avinyonet del Penedés (Barcelona)
☎: 938 970 055 - Fax: 938 970 691
www.avinyo.com

Established: 1982

🍷 50 📊 450,000 litres 🌿 33 has.

🍇 80% 🌐20%: -US -CH

ESTEVE I VIA JOVEN WHITE DE AGUJA
macabeo, xarel.lo, parellada

72 Pale. Aroma of slightly overripe fruit (mild evolution). Better in the mouth, a fruity, mildly sweet yet well-mannered.

AVINYÓ MERLOT 2001 CRIANZA RED
100% merlot

88 Garnet red cherry with a coppery edge. Intense aroma of smoky oak notes with a ripe fruit nuance and fine varietal notions (underbrush). Flavourful on the palate with well-integrated fruit and oak, smoky notes and notes of a fine reduction; hints of minerals, excellent symmetry and acidity.

AVINYÓ CABERNET SAUVIGNON 2001 RESERVA RED
100% cabernet sauvignon

89 Very deep cherry with a violet edge. Powerful aroma of jammy black fruit with fine toasty oak notes, good varietal expression and a balsamic hint. Flavourful and concentrated on the palate with quite rough but promising tannins; well-integrated fruit and wood, excellent.

BACH

Carretera Martorell - Capellades, km. 20, 5
08635 Sant Esteve de Sesrovires (Barcelona)
☎: 937 714 052 - Fax: 937 713 177
codinfo@codorniu.es
www.grupocodorniu.com

Established: 1915

🏢 7,500 🛢 10,000,000 litres
🍇 150 has. 🍷 88% 🍇12%

BACH CABERNET SAUVIGNON 1999 CRIANZA RED
100% cabernet sauvignon

80 Quite intense cherry with an orange edge. Aroma with nuances of early reduction (leather, balsamic flavours) with oak notes. Round, slightly varietal, animal (leather) on the palate, without great nuances.

BACH CABERNET SAUVIGNON 2000 CRIANZA RED
100% cabernet sauvignon

80 Cherry with orangey hues. Toasty, smoky, balsamic aroma. Good acidity on the palate, well-balanced and pleasant.

BACH MERLOT 2001 CRIANZA RED
100% merlot

80 Cherry with an orangey edge. Toasty aroma of sun-drenched skins and spices. Light palate with ripe, fresh tannins and a spicy finish.

BACH TEMPRANILLO 1999 CRIANZA RED
100% tempranillo

85 Deep cherry. Aroma of ripe black fruit; complex notes of skins with a suggestion of earth and vanilla. Flavourful palate with fruity tannins and sensations of red fruit, well-integrated fine smoky flavours and an earthy, bitter cocoa finish.

BACH TEMPRANILLO 1999 CRIANZA RED
100% tempranillo

84 Fairly deep cherry with a brick red edge. Intense aroma with a good varietal expression (ripe red fruit), fine toasty oak and a balsamic suggestion. Flavourful palate, with well-integrated oak/fruit, fine bitter notes, with fresh spicy overtones and fruit in the finish.

BACH MERLOT 2002 CRIANZA RED
100% merlot

84 Cherry with an orangey hue. Aroma with good red fruit varietal character, underbrush and dark-roasted notes. Fleshy palate with good balance between the fruit and wood tannins.

BACH CABERNET SAUVIGNON 2000 CRIANZA RED

BLANCHER ESPUMOSOS DE CAVA

Plaça Pont Romà, 5
08770 Sant Sadurní D'Anoia (Barcelona)
☎: 938 183 286 - Fax: 938 911 961
blancher@blancher.es
www.blancher.es

Established: 1955

🛢 500,000 litres 🍇 10 has.

🍷 80% 🍇20%

BLANCHER SELECCIÓ 2002 WHITE
BLANCHER XAREL.LO MONOVARIETAL 2003 WHITE
BLANCHER 2001 CRIANZA RED
BLANCHER MERCÉ 2002 CRIANZA RED

BOLET VINOS Y CAVAS

Finca Mas Lluet
08732 Castellvi de la Marca (Barcelona)
☎: 938 918 153 - Fax: 938 918 153
sat.maslluet@sefes.es
www.cavasbolet.com

Established: 1983

🏢 24 🛢 400,000 litres 🍇 65 has.

🍷 95% 🍇5%: -DE -BE

BOLET 2003 SECO WHITE
macabeo, xarel.lo, parellada

69 Straw-coloured. Fairly short, fruity aroma with mild off-odours. Weak fruit and bitterness on the palate.

BOLET XAREL.LO 2003 WHITE
100% xarel.lo

80 Straw-coloured. Very intense aroma of ripe apples with a herby nuance, elegant. Flavourful palate with ripe fruit, well-balanced and pleasant.

BOLET 2003 ROSÉ
merlot, cabernet sauvignon, tempranillo

78 Raspberry with a coppery glint. Fairly intense aroma of red stone fruit and toasty hints of skins. Flavourful palate with red fruit, predominant bitter notes and an acidic edge.

DO PENEDÈS

BOLET MERLOT 2003 ROSÉ
100% merlot

78 Intense raspberry. Not very intense, slightly fruity aroma with a spicy nuance of skins and hints of terroir. Flavourful and fresh on the palate with notes of ripe red fruit and high acidity.

BOLET COUPAGE 2003 RED
merlot, cabernet sauvignon, tempranillo

74 Garnet red cherry. Intense aroma with a mild reduction off-odour from the tank and a sweet fruit nuance. Flavourful on the palate with predominant bitter notes and an acidic edge.

BOLET MERLOT 2000 OAK AGED RED
100% merlot

75 Ruby red with a brick red hue. Perfumed aroma of green fruit. Astringent palate with slightly drying wood and underripe fruit tannins.

CA N'ESTELLA

Masia Can Estella
08791 Sant Esteve Sesrovires (Barcelona)
☎: 934 161 387 - Fax: 934 161 620
canestella@canestella.ce.telefonica.net

Established: 1998

⊕ 140 🛢 200,000 litres 🍇 40 has.

🍷 40% 🌐60%: -DE -UK -NL -DK -SE

CLOT DELS OMS CHARDONNAY 2003 FERMENTADO EN BARRICA WHITE
100% chardonnay

84 Straw-coloured. Fine aroma of smoky wood well-integrated with the herby notes and fruity tones. Very oily and flavourful palate; excellent balance, fine wood to be integrated.

CLOT DELS OMS FINCA CA N'ESTELLA CHARDONNAY 2003 WHITE
100% chardonnay

83 Straw-coloured. Not very intense yet fine aroma of ripe apples, expressive. Flavourful, fruity palate with an element of acidity but well-balanced.

CLOT DELS OMS FINCA CA N'ESTELLA SELECCIÓN 2003 WHITE
40% chardonnay, 30% macabeo, 30% xarel.lo

81 Straw-coloured. Not very intense yet fine aroma (apples, herbs) with good ripeness. Flavourful palate with ripe apples and an element of acidity which adds freshness.

CLOT DELS OMS FINCA CA N'ESTELLA SELECCIÓN 2003 ROSÉ
90% merlot, 10% cabernet sauvignon

82 Raspberry blush. Fresh, medium-intensity aroma of cherries, green grass and petals. Flavourful, fresh, fruity and expressive on the palate; good elaboration.

CLOT DELS OMS VS 2001 OAK AGED RED
60% merlot, 40% cabernet sauvignon ⊕ 14

84 Garnet red cherry with a saffron edge. Not very intense aroma with predominant spicy oak notes. Flavourful palate with well-integrated fruit and oak, a spicy, ripe nuance and hints of liquorice and balsamic flavours.

CLOT DELS OMS MERLOT 2001 OAK AGED RED
100% merlot ⊕ 10

79 Cherry with a brick red edge. Not very intense aroma of toasty oak notes. Flavourful palate with ripe tannins, a slightly oily texture and a ripe fruit nuance and notions of liquorice.

CLOT DELS OMS CABERNET SAUVIGNON 2001 OAK AGED RED
cabernet sauvignon ⊕ 12

84 Intense cherry with a coppery edge. Intense aroma with good varietal expression, a herbaceous nuance and toasty hints of wood. Flavourful on the palate with quite marked, rough and sweet tannins, fine bitter notes.

CAM CAMPS

Can Camps, s/n
08810 Olivella (Barcelona)
☎: 938 970 013

PEDRADURA 2000 RED

89 Very deep garnet red cherry. Powerful aroma, ripe red fruit, fine creamy (cocoa) and spicy oak notes, mineral nuances and a hint of chocolate. Powerful, oily palate, slightly marked but promising tannins, flint nuances, aromatic herbs and sweet fruit, expressive, long.

CAN FEIXES (HUGUET)

Finca Can Feixes
08785 Cabrera D'Anoia (Barcelona)
☎: 937 718 227 - Fax: 937 718 031
canfeixes@canfeixes.com

Established: 1768

⊕ 250 🛢 310,000 litres 🍇 80 has.

🍷 60% 🌐40%: -US -DE -NL -BE -UK -AT -CH -FI -MX

CAN FEIXES CHARDONNAY 2001 FERMENTADO EN BARRICA WHITE
100% chardonnay ⊕ 8

89 Pale yellow with a golden glint. Intense, very fine aroma with good balance between the ripe fruit notes and the creamy wood notes. Generous palate with an opulence of nuances and excellent balance with hints of herbs, toasty and fine bitter and mineral notes in the retronasal passage.

DO PENEDÈS

CAN FEIXES SELECCIÓ 2003 JOVEN WHITE
40% parellada, 35% macabeo, 20% chardonnay, 5% pinot noir

84 Pale yellow. Not very intense aroma of white fruit with hints of fennel. Flavourful, fresh palate with excellent fruit-acidity balance.

CAN FEIXES 1999 RESERVA ESPECIAL RED
65% cabernet sauvignon, 35% merlot

87 Fairly deep cherry with a brick red edge. Powerful aroma, fine spicy notes of oak with a mild reduction nuance and very ripe fruit (prunes). Flavourful palate with well-integrated fruit and oak; powerful aroma of chocolate, liquorice and spices in the retronasal passage.

CAN FEIXES SELECCIÓ 2001 CRIANZA RED
40% merlot, 40% cabernet sauvignon, 20% tempranillo

84 Garnet red cherry with a saffron edge. Powerful, very varietal aroma of fine toasty oak with balsamic hints. Flavourful palate with fresh overtones of wood, expressive, vigorous and with good acidity.

CAN MIRET D'OLIVELLA

Can Miret d'Olivella
08010 Olivella (Barcelona)
☎: 639 351 174 - Fax: 938 960 024
canmiret@jazzfree.com
Established: 2000
30 | 30,000 litres | 13,4 has.
80% | 20%

CLAR DE CASTANYER XAREL.LO 2003 FERMENTADO EN BARRICA WHITE
100% xarel.lo

79 Pale yellow. Intense aroma with predominant smoky wood notes (chestnuts) and dried herbs. Dry, flavourful on the palate with fresh overtones and slightly drying wood tannins without great fruit expression and a nuance of dead leaves.

Celler CAN PUJOL

Duc de la Victoria, 9
08800 Vilanova i la Geltrú (Barcelona)
☎: 938 931 535 - Fax: 938 143 063
cellercanpujol@cellercanpujol.com
www.cellercanpujol.com
Established: 1989
60 | 125,000 litres

TORRENTS & CARBÓ XAREL.LO 2002 FERMENTADO EN BARRICA WHITE
xarel.lo

77 Straw-coloured with a greenish edge. Aroma of wood lees with notes of herbs and a ripe fruit nuance. Bitter palate with freshness and good fruit and fine wood character; harmonious, better in the mouth.

TORRENTS & CARBÓ XAREL.LO 2002 WHITE
xarel.lo

71 Pale with a greenish edge. Aroma of ripe fruit with discreet nuances and overtones of off-odours. High acidity on the palate, without great fruit presence, light.

TORRENTS & CARBÓ MEDITERRANI 2003 WHITE
xarel.lo, macabeo

77 Straw-coloured. Fruity, fresh aroma with citrus fruit pulp, tropical (pineapples, passion fruit). Flavourful, fresh, fruity palate, pleasant as a whole but without great expression.

TORRENTS & CARBÓ MEDITERRANI 2003 ROSÉ
tempranillo

78 Brilliant pale blush. Aroma of red berries with a hint of herbs, pleasant. Fresh, flavourful palate with a good fruit expression, slightly fizzy (alcohol).

TORRENTS & CARBÓ MERLOT 2003 ROSÉ
merlot

81 Raspberry blush. Medium-intensity, fine aroma of red fruit with a nuance of green grass. Flavourful palate with pleasant bitter-acidic notes, quite persistent.

TORRENTS & CARBÓ MEDITERRANI 2003 RED
100% tempranillo

79 Brilliant cherry with a violet edge. Not very intense aroma with a fruity nuance and a good varietal expression. Flavourful palate with an edge of greeness to the grape tannins and good acidity.

TORRENTS & CARBÓ CABERNET-MERLOT 2000 CRIANZA RED
50% cabernet sauvignon, 50% merlot

82 Garnet red cherry with a coppery edge. Intense aroma with predominant spicy oak notes and a fine reduction nuance. Flavourful palate with quite rough and oily tannins; complementary fruit and oak.

CAN QUETU

Tarragona, 33
08770 Barcelona (Sant Sadurní D'Anoia)
☎: 938 911 214 - Fax: 938 914 104
canquetu@tiscali.es
Established: 1954
100 | 50,000 litres | 90% | 10%

CAN QUETU 2003 WHITE
CAN QUETU CHARDONNAY 2003 FERMENTADO EN BARRICA WHITE
CAN QUETU ROSÉ
CAN QUETU CABERNET SAUVIGNON ROBLE RED
CAN QUETU 2001 ROBLE RED

CAN RÀFOLS DELS CAUS

Can Rafols del Caus s/n
08739 Avinyonet del Penedés (Barcelona)
☎: 938 970 013 - Fax: 938 970 370
canrafols@seker.es

Established: 1980

🍷 150 📚 300,000 litres 🍇 50 has.

🍷 67% 🍇33%

LA CALMA 2001 WHITE

91 Brilliant yellow. Intense, fresh aroma, slightly floral, citrus fruit notes, a spicy and balsamic suggestion. Intense, fresh palate, rich in mineral nuances over a fine toasty hint of the crianza, crystallised citrus fruit nuances (tangerine segments), excellent acidity, very long.

EL ROCALLÍS 2000 WHITE

88 Golden yellow. Intense, very fresh aroma, fine herbs, a toasty suggestion, balsamic and crystallised fruit notes. Intense, toasty palate, fine bitter notes, excellent acidity, mineral and citrus hints in the finish.

GRAN CAUS 2001 RED

92 Garnet red cherry with a saffron hue. Powerful, ripe aroma, black fruit, nuances of smoky skins, opulent, creamy, a spicy suggestion of the crianza. Powerful palate, fresh overtones, fine toasty notes, red stone fruit, slightly oily, balsamic nuances and a slightly sweet finish, very long.

CAUS LUBIS 1999 RED

91 Dark cherry with a saffron hue. Powerful aroma, quite viscous and sweet fruit, fine toasty notes, a balsamic suggestion. Powerful palate, sweet, fine bitter notes, spicy fruit nuances, sweet in the finish, very long.

RESERVA ESPECIAL 20 ANIVERSARI 1998 RED

90 Dark cherry with a saffron edge. Powerful, spicy (curry), very fine aroma, jammy red fruit. Powerful palate, well-structured, rich in balsamic nuances, a suggestion of chocolate and sweet fruit, very long.

CELLERS DE CAN SURIOL DEL CASTELL

Castell de Grabuac
08736 Font-Rubí (Barcelona)
☎: 938 978 426 - Fax: 938 978 364
cansuriol@suriol.com
www.suriol.com

Established: 1987

🍷 50 📚 280,000 litres 🍇 25 has.
🍷 60% 🍇40%: -BE

SURIOL VINYA CELLER MASIA 2003 FERMENTADO EN BARRICA WHITE
chenin blanc, xarel.lo

81 Straw-coloured. Medium-intensity aroma of ripe fruit and smoky oak. Flavourful palate, slightly oily with good fruit, pleasant.

AZIMUT PINOT NOIR 2003 ROSÉ
100% pinot noir

65 Raspberry. Aroma with notes of nuts, quite evolved. Weak fruit on the palate, well evolved.

SURIOL MERLOT 2003 ROSÉ
100% merlot

77 Salmon pink. Medium-intensity aroma with balsamic notes and red fruit. Flavourful palate with bitter notes, slightly tannic.

SURIOL VINYA CELLER MASIA 2001 CRIANZA RED
pinot noir

85 Deep cherry with a coppery edge. Powerful aroma with fine toasty oak, a nuance of ripe black fruit and hints of sour cherries in liqueur. Flavourful palate with well-integrated oak and fruit, fine bitter notes and good acidity.

AZIMUT SANG DE DRAC 2002 RED
100% merlot

85 Garnet red cherry with a violet edge. Powerful aroma of black fruit and a good varietal expression (underbrush). Flavourful, fruity and ripe on the palate with spicy hints of skins, fine toasty notes and excellent acidity.

FLOR AZIMUT 2001 WHITE
VI ROSAT PINOT RESERVA DE SURIOL 2003 ROSÉ
CUPATGE SURIOL 2003 RED

CANALS & MUNNÉ

Carretera Sant Sadurní a Vilafranca, km. 0,5
08770 Sant Sadurní d'Anoia (Barcelona)
☎: 938 910 318 - Fax: 938 911 945
canalsmunne@troc.es
www.troc.es/canals&munne

Established: 1915

🍷 350 📚 600,000 litres 🍇 20 has. 🍷 75%
🍇25%: -CH -UK -IT -PT -DE -BE -DK

CANALS & MUNÉE PRÍNCEPS 2003 JOVEN WHITE
40% xarel.lo, 30% parellada, 30% chardonnay

81 Straw-coloured. Good intensity aroma of apples and ripe pears, expressive. Flavourful, fresh and fruity on the palate; pleasant.

CANALS & MUNÉE PINCEPS 2003 WHITE
CANALS & MUNÉE NOIR PRÍNCEPS 2000
RESERVA RED

Bodegas CAPITÀ VIDAL

Carretera Villafranca-Igualada, km. 30
08733 Pla del Penedés (Barcelona)
☎: 938 988 630 - Fax: 938 988 625
capitavidal@capitavidal.com
www.capitavidal.com

Established: 1985

🍇 50 has. 🍷 90% 🌐10%

CLOS VIDAL BLANC DE BLANCS 2004 WHITE
50% macabeo, 30% xarel.lo, 20% parellada

80 Pale straw. Fruity aroma, typical Penedès. Flavourful, slightly oily palate with notes of hay and herbs integrated with the fruit, very pleasant.

CLOS VIDAL CUVÉE 2004 JOVEN ROSÉ
45% garnacha, 35% tempranillo, 20% cariñena

80 Salmon pink. Good intensity aroma of ripe red fruit, harmonious. Flavourful, fresh and very fruity on the palate; easy drinking.

CLOS VIDAL MERLOT 2002 CRIANZA RED
85% merlot, 15% tempranillo

85 Garnet red cherry with a coppery edge. Intense aroma of jammy black fruit with a spicy oak nuance. Flavourful, fleshy palate with ripe and fairly rough tannins, well-integrated oak and fruit, very pleasant.

CLOS VIDAL 2000 RESERVA RED

CARMENET

Pelegrí Torelló, 14
08770 Sant Sadurní D'Anoia (Barcelona)
☎: 934 644 949 - Fax: 934 642 401
carmenet@carmenet.es

Established: 1953

🍷 60 📊 150,000 litres 🍇 9 has.
🍶 200,000 litres.

🍷 80% 🌐20%: -US -DE -FR -UK -AD

PRIVAT CABERNET SAUVIGNON 2002 ROSÉ
cabernet sauvignon

65 Raspberry with a salmon hue. Aroma with clear notes of evolution (a 2002). Slightly better on the palate, with fresh overtones, yet well evolved.

PRIVAT MERLOT 2000 RED
100% merlot

84 Garnet red cherry. Intense aroma with fine notes of smoky oak, perfectly ripe red fruit and an underbrush nuance. Flavourful, fleshy palate with well-integrated fruit and oak and fine bitter notes (chocolate, liquorice) in the retronasal passage.

PRIVAT CABERNET SAUVIGNON 2000 RED
100% cabernet sauvignon

80 Garnet red cherry with a coppery edge. Intense, ripe aroma with fine toasty oak notes and a mild reduction nuance. Flavourful palate, lacking fruit-crianza-acidity symmetry.

CASTELL D'AGE

Carretera, 6-8
08782 La Beguda Baixa (Barcelona)
☎: 937 725 181 - Fax: 937 727 061
info@castelldage.com
www.castelldage.com

Established: 1989

🍷 400 📊 110,000 litres 🍇 60 has.
🍷 20% 🌐80%: UE

CASTELL D'AGE CHARDONNAY ECOLÓGICO
2003 FERMENTADO EN BARRICA WHITE
100% chardonnay

75 Pale yellow. Not very intense aroma with smoky oak notes over a nuance of mildly varietal ripe fruit (apples). Fresh, flavourful palate, lacking fruit-oak-acidity symmetry.

CASTELL D'AGE BLANC DE BLANCS
ECOLÓGICO 2003 WHITE
100% macabeo

78 Very pale yellow. Not very intense aroma of white fruit with a nuance of exotic fruit notes, not very clean. Flavourful palate, high in acidity and lacking balance.

CASTELL D'AGE ECOLÓGICO 2003 ROSÉ
100% cabernet sauvignon

83 Raspberry blush. Intense aroma of red fruit and strawberry jelly. Very flavourful palate with a hint of glycerin and ripe red fruit, excellent acidity and a bitter finish.

CASTELL D'AGE CABERNET SAUVIGNON
2001 CRIANZA RED
100% cabernet sauvignon

79 Garnet red cherry with a coppery edge. Intense aroma of jammy black fruit and paprika with a toasty oak nuance. Flavourful palate with good oak/fruit integration and bitter notes; pleasant although without great nuances.

CASTELL D'AGE MERLOT ECOLÓGICO 2002
CRIANZA RED
85% merlot, 15% cabernet sauvignon

80 Very deep garnet red cherry. Not very intense aroma of black fruit with jammy notions, a toasty and mildly creamy oak nuance. Flavourful, fleshy palate with well-integrated oak and fruit, a liquorice nuance, spicy, long and without great varietal overtones.

CASTELL D'AGE TEMPRANILLO ECOLÓGICO
2001 CRIANZA RED

CASTELL DE VILARNAU

Vilarnau, 34-36
08770 Sant Sadurní D'Anoia (Barcelona)
☎: 938 912 361 - Fax: 938 912 913
castelldevilarnau@gonzalezbyass.es
www.gonzalezbyass.es

Established: 1982

85,000 litres ❦ 16 has.

30% ❦70%: -UK -DE -CH -DK -IS -NL -BE -SE -EC -IT -VE

LES PLANES DE VILARNAU CHARDONNAY 2003 WHITE
100% chardonnay

85 Straw-coloured with a greenish hue. Fine aroma of ripe apples and pears, good intensity. Flavourful, oily palate with excellent balance between alcohol and acidity, expressive and persistent.

LES PLANES DE VILARNAU PINOT NOIR 2003 ROSÉ
85% pinot noir, 15% merlot

70 Raspberry with a violet hue. Intense aroma of very ripe fruit with a light evolution. Fairly flavourful but also with notes of evolution.

LES PLANES DE VILARNAU CABERNET SAUVIGNON 2001 CRIANZA RED
85% cabernet sauvignon, 15% merlot

84 Garnet red cherry with a violet edge. Intense aroma with predominant toasty oak notes. Flavourful palate with a good varietal expression (black fruit, paprika) and promising although slightly marked tannins; slightly oily with hints of chocolate and liquorice in the retronasal passage.

Celler CASTELL DEL MIRALL

Masia Can Gustems, s/n
08792 La Granada (Barcelona)
☎: 938 974 558 - Fax: 938 974 708
enologia@castelldelmirall.com
www.castelldelmirall.com

Established: 2000

200 800,000 litres ❦ 50 has.

85% ❦15%: -DE -BE -UK -US -FR

FERRÉ I CATASÚS BLANC D'EXPRESSIÓ 2003 JOVEN WHITE
chardonnay, parellada, sauvignon blanc, xarel.lo

83 Straw-coloured. Clean, intense aroma of tropical fruit (pineapples, passion fruit) with hints of ripe fruit. Dry, fruity palate with tropical and quite herbaceous notes, bitter nuances, persistent.

FERRÉ I CATASÚS XAREL.LO 2003 JOVEN WHITE
100% xarel.lo

85 Yellow straw with a greenish rim. Aroma of ripe white fruit, ripe pears, quinces. Oily, round, well-balanced palate, medium persistence.

FERRÉ I CATASÚS CHARDONNAY 2003 FERMENTADO EN BARRICA WHITE
100% chardonnay

85 Pale gold. Intense, very fine aroma with a good oak/fruit integration, hints of fine lees, nuts and wax. Powerful palate with smoky oak notes that envelop the fruit; slightly warm and oily with fine bitter notes (herbs, nuts).

FERRÉ I CATASÚS MERLOT 2003 ROSÉ
merlot

76 Brilliant raspberry. Fresh, clear aroma of red stone fruit, lively, slightly ripe. Flavourful palate, quite warm but with freshness; hints of slightly green fruit (astringence).

CAMERLOT 2000 CRIANZA RED
merlot, cabernet sauvignon, tempranillo

77 Deep cherry. Toasty aroma with slightly green and spicy notes over the fruit. Fleshy, fresh palate with dry wood tannins.

FERRÉ I CATASÚS MERLOT 2001 CRIANZA RED

77 Deep cherry. Aroma of ripe black fruit with notes of aged wood and fine spicy Merlot. Fleshy palate, slightly dominated by the wood; slightly drying tannins, good freshness and well-integrated alcohol.

CASTELLROIG

Carretera Sant Sadurní d'Anoia a Vilafranca del Penedès, km. 1
08739 Subirats (Barcelona)
☎: 938 911 927 - Fax: 938 996 092
info@castellroig.com
www.castellroig.com

Established: 1988

100 170,000 litres ❦ 25 has.

65% ❦35%: -DK -NL -CH -BE -AD -US

CASTELLROIG XAREL.LO 2003 JOVEN WHITE
10% xarel.lo

79 Straw-coloured with a greenish hue. Short, yet clean and fruity aroma. Palate with an element of carbonic and sweet and bitter notes in symmetry; pleasant.

CASTELLROIG SELECCIÓ 2003 FERMENTADO EN BARRICA WHITE
62% chardonnay, 35% xarel.lo

85 Straw-coloured with a greenish hue. Somewhat closed yet fine aroma (ripe fruit and smoky flavours). Flavourful, oily palate with a good fruit expression (citrus fruit, apples), long, with oak that does not weigh on the flavours but boosts them.

CASTELLROIG 2003 ROSÉ
54% ull de llebre, 46% merlot

74 Lively raspberry. Medium-intensity aroma, slighty flawed in the nose with very ripe red fruit and nuts. Fresh, quite bitter palate with an element of acidity.

CASTELLROIG SELECCIÓ 2001 OAK AGED RED
65% cabernet sauvignon, 35% merlot   🍷 12

86 Very deep cherry. Not very intense aroma with overtones of varietal fruit expression (bilberries, paprika), ripe fruit and a nuance of toasty oak. Flavourful palate with ripe oily tannins and fine bitter notes (liquorice, chocolate) in the retronasal passage, excellent acidity.

CASTELLROIG ULL DE LLEBRE-MERLOT 2001 OAK AGED RED
70% ull de llebre, 30% merlot   🍷 12

84 Garnet red cherry. Not very intense aroma with toasty oak notes and a nuance of ripe black fruit (hints of sun-drenched skins). Flavourful palate with well-integrated fruit and oak, ripe and oily tannins, excellent crianza expression, well-balanced.

CATASÚS I CASANOVAS

Sant Isidre, 36
08770 Sant Sadurní D'Anoia (Barcelona)
☎: 938 183 716 - Fax: 934 590 710
info@masxarot.com
www.masxarot.com

Established: 1993
🛢 11,000 litres 🍷 40% 🍇60%

MAS XAROT PANER DE BLANCS WHITE
MAS XAROT ROSAT FOGO'S WHITE
MAS XAROT CABERNET SAUVIGNON RED
MAS XAROT GRAN GRESOL RED

COLET VINOS Y CAVAS

Camí del Salinar, s/n
08739 Pacs del Penedés (Barcelona)
☎: 938 170 809 - Fax: 938 170 809
colet_cava@jet.es
www.coletcava.com

Established: 1994
🍷 60 🛢 80,000 litres 🍇 22 has.
🍷 75% 🍇25%

XAREL.LO ORIGEN 1/5 2001 WHITE
xarel.lo

82 Pale yellow. Intense aroma of ripe fruit and fine creamy oak notes. Flavourful, slightly warm palate with good crianza expression and hints of minerals.

GEWÜRZTRAMINER ORIGEN 1/5 2002 WHITE
gewürztraminer

83 Golden yellow. Powerful, very varietal aroma of fruit and white flowers (acacia) with musky and mineral hints. Generous palate, rich in nuances with fine bitter notes (cumin, dried grass) and refreshing acidity.

COVIDES

Finca Prunamala s/n
08770 Sant Sadurní d'Anoia (Barcelona)
☎: 938 172 552 - Fax: 938 171 798
covides@covides.com
comercial@covides.com
www.covides.com

Established: 1964
🍷 550 🛢 30,000,000 litres 🍇 3,000 has.
🍷 71% 🍇29%

DUC DE FOIX CHARDONNAY 2003 FERMENTADO EN BARRICA WHITE
100% chardonnay

83 Straw-coloured. Medium-intensity, fine aroma with lemony notes, smoky flavours and butters. Flavourful, fresh palate with an oily element and well-integrated oak.

DUC DE FOIX 2003 SECO WHITE

80 Straw-coloured with a greenish hue. Good, intense aroma of ripe fruit with a nuance of green grass and lavender. Fresh and fruity on the palate, easy drinking.

DUC DE FOIX CABERNET 2003 ROSÉ
cabernet sauvignon, merlot

80 Lively raspberry. Not very intense aroma although fresh and clean with red fruit. Flavourful and very fruity on the palate with citric acidity that gives much freshness and a bitter finish that refreshes the mouth.

DUC DE FOIX CABERNET SAUVIGNON 1998 RESERVA RED
cabernet sauvignon

80 Garnet red cherry with a coppery edge. Intense aroma with predominant spicy oak notes, a ripe fruit nuance and hints of fine reduction. Flavourful palate with quite marked oak tannins and a bitter nuance (liquorice), lacking balance.

DUC DE FOIX CABERNET SAUVIGNON 2003 RED
cabernet sauvignon, merlot, syrah

83 Cherry with a violet edge. Intense, fruity aroma with fine smoky notes of skins and an excellent varietal expression (paprika). Flavourful palate with ripe grape tannins, a fine herbaceous nuance and good acidity.

DUC DE FOIX MERLOT 2003 RED
100% merlot

82 Brilliant cherry with a violet edge. Fruity aroma with some varietal notes (black fruit, herbaceous hints) and a spicy nuance of skins. Flavourful palate with ripe tannins and fine bitter notes, good acidity.

CUSCÓ BERGA

Esplugues, 7
08793 Les Gunyoles D'Avinyonet (Barcelona)
☎: 938 970 164 - Fax: 938 970 563
cuscoberga@cuscoberga.com
www.cuscoberga.com

Established: 1985

🍶 16 🗄 25,000 litres 🍇 3 has. 🛢 100%

CUSCÓ BERGA CABERNET SAUVIGNON - MERLOT 2003 ROSÉ
80% cabernet sauvignon, 20% merlot

79 Raspberry with a coppery hue. Intense aroma with spicy hints of skins and hints of fine reduction. Flavourful, fruity palate with a slightly oily texture, pleasant.

CUSCÓ BERGA CABERNET SAUVIGNON 2002 OAK AGED RED
80% cabernet sauvignon, 20% merlot   🍶 12

84 Intense cherry with a coppery edge. Powerful aroma with smoky oak notes, a suggestion of ripe fruit, hints of cedar and a herbaceous nuance. Flavourful, fleshy palate with ripe, rough tannins, a nuance of black fruit, chocolate and hints of terroir.

CUSCÓ BERGA CABERNET SAUVIGNON - MERLOT 2001 CRIANZA RED
80% cabernet sauvignon, 20% merlot

87 Intense cherry. Toasty, fruity, complex aroma with mineral notes. Fleshy, powerful palate, rich in fruit expression with enough nuances of well-integrated wood, flavourful.

CUSCÓ BERGA NOVELL 2002 WHITE
CUSCÓ BERGA XARDONNAY 2002 WHITE
CUSCÓ BERGA NOVELL 2003 RED

CUSCOMAS

Cups, s/n Apartat 78
08784 La Foresta (Piera)
☎: 938 912 349 - Fax: 938 912 349
cuscomas@terra.es
www.cuscoicomas.com

Established: 1989

🛢 95% 🌐5%

CUSCO I COMAS WHITE
CUSCO I COMAS ROSÉ

CUSCO I COMAS MERLOT RED
CUSCO I COMAS RED
CUSCOMAS RED

Vins EL CEP

Can Llopart de Les Alzines, s/n
08770 Sant Sadurní D'Anoia (Barcelona)
☎: 938 912 353 - Fax: 938 183 956
info@elcep.com
www.elcep.com

Established: 1980

🍶 45 🗄 500,000 litres 🍇 200 has.

🛢 65% 🌐35%

L'ALZINAR CHARDONNAY FERMENTADO EN BARRICA WHITE
L'ALZINAR XAREL.LO FERMENTADO EN BARRICA WHITE
MARQUÉS DE GÉLIDA BLANC DE BLANCS WHITE
L'ALZINAR GRAN CUBÍ RED
L'ALZINAR MERLOT CRIANZA RED
L'ALZINAR ULL DE LLEBRE CRIANZA RED

EUDALD MASSANA NOYA

Finca El Maset s/n
08739 Sant Pau D'Ordal (Barcelona)
☎: 938 994 124 - Fax: 938 994 139
bodega@massananoya.com
www.massananoya.com

Established: 1994

🍶 50 🗄 190,000 litres 🍇 25 has.

🛢 95% 🌐5%: -DE -CH -BE -JP

EUDALD MASSANA NOYA "AVI TON" XAREL.LO 2003 OAK AGED WHITE
100% xarel.lo

83 Straw-coloured with a greenish hue. Intense, fruity aroma with fine creamy and spicy oak notes. Flavourful, fruity palate with complementary fruit and oak tannins; hints of bitter almonds and herbs in the retronasal passage.

EUDALD MASSANA NOYA "LA CREUETA" 2001 CRIANZA RED
70% cabernet sauvignon, 30% merlot

82 Garnet red cherry. Intense aroma of black fruit with good varietal expression (paprika) and toasty hints of oak. Flavourful palate with a good fruit/oak integration, predominant fruit notes, spicy.

EUDALD MASSANA NOYA "COUPAGE" 2003 JOVEN WHITE
EUDALD MASSANA NOYA "L'ALZINARET" WHITE
EUDALD MASSANA NOYA "COUPAGE" 2003 JOVEN ROSÉ

DO PENEDÈS

EUDALD MASSANA NOYA "COUPAGE" 2002 RED

EXPLOTACIONES SADURNÍ BEGUES

Masía Can Sadurní
08859 Begues (Barcelona)
☎: 936 390 161 - Fax: 936 390 161
sadurnibeguas@troc.es
www.troc.es/sadurni-begas

Established: 1966
🌳 250 has.

ARRELS MONTAU DE SADURNÍ WHITE
MONTAU DE SADURNÍ WHITE
SENYOR DEL MONTNEGRE BLANC DE
BLANCS WHITE
ARRELS MONTAU DE SADURNÍ ROSÉ
SENYOR DEL MONTNEGRE ROSÉ
ARRELS MONTAU DE SADURNÍ RED
SENYOR DEL MONTNEGRE RED

Cavas FERRET

Avenida de Catalunya, 36
08736 Guardiola de Font-Rubí (Barcelona)
☎: 938 979 148 - Fax: 938 979 285
ferret@cavasferret.com
www.cavasferret.com

Established: 1941
📦 120 🛢 600,000 litres 🌳 12 has.
🍷 80% 🌐20%: -DE -UK -NL -DK -BE -SE -CH

FERRET BLANC DE BARRICA 2001
FERMENTADO EN BARRICA WHITE
50% xarel.lo, 50% chardonnay

81 Straw-coloured with a golden hue. Aroma of good reduction (vanilla, nutmeg, toasty oak). Flavourful, oily palate with smoky notes, fresh; good evolution.

FERRET AGUJA 2003 WHITE
parellada, xarel.lo, macabeo

72 Straw-coloured with a greenish hue. Short but clean aroma of green fruit. Robust beads on the palate, fresh, slightly weak in fruit but with a well-mannered ensemble.

FERRET CELLER DEL MINGO 2003 WHITE
parellada, xarel.lo, macabeo

80 Straw-coloured. Good, intense, very fruity aroma (ripe fruit), expressive. Fresh and flavourful palate, well elaborated, a good example of a classic Penedès.

FERRET XAREL.LO 2003 WHITE
100% xarel.lo

80 Straw-coloured. Medium-intensity aroma of ripe fruit (apples) and mountain herbs. Flavourful palate with an element of acidity which adds nerve, very fresh.

FERRET AGUJA 2003 ROSÉ
tempranillo, garnacha

79 Raspberry blush. Not very intense yet clean aroma of red berries. Fresh, fruity palate with somewhat robust beads, a pleasant sweet-acidic-bitter combination; well-elaborated.

FERRET CABERNET SAUVIGNON 2003 ROSÉ
100% cabernet sauvignon

75 Lively raspberry. Medium-intensity aroma of red fruit, slightly flawed in the nose. Better on the palate, flavourful, fresh with red fruit and with an element of acidity.

FERRET CELLER DEL MINGO 2003 ROSÉ
tempranillo, cariñena

76 Blush with a raspberry hue. Medium-intensity, clean aroma of red fruit and nuts. A touch of flavour and fruit on the palate, slightly lacking in acidity though a well-mannered ensemble.

FERRET MERLOT 2003 OAK AGED RED
100% merlot

86 Garnet red cherry with a violet edge. Powerful, ripe aroma with good varietal expression, hints of sun-drenched skins, notes of fine reduction (leathers) and toasty oak. Flavourful palate with well-integrated fruit and oak, fine bitter notes (chocolate, liquorice, Mediterranean herbs).

FERRET CELLER DEL MINGO 2001 RED
tempranillo, merlot

83 Garnet red cherry. Intense aroma with fine smoky oak notes, a nuance of ripe black fruit and hints of terroir. Flavourful palate, well-integrated oak and fruit, a light acidic edge.

FERRET 1999 CRIANZA RED
50% tempranillo, 26% cabernet sauvignon, 24% merlot

86 Intense cherry with a coppery edge. Powerful aroma with fine notes of smoky oak, an excellent fruit expression (varietal hints), a mineral nuance. Flavourful palate with ripe rannins well-integrated with the fruit; spicy with good acidity.

FERRET 1998 RESERVA RED
50% tempranillo, 30% cabernet sauvignon, 20% merlot

82 Cherry with a brick red edge. Intense aroma, with predominant toasty notes of oak and a fine reduction nuance. Flavourful palate with well-integrated fruit and oak, fine bitter notes and an acidic edge.

FERRET RESERVA ESPECIAL 2001 RED

85 Dark cherry with a purplish edge. Intense aroma with predominant and very varietal peppery and balsamic notes and fine smoky oak. Flavourful palate with a good fruit/oak integration, spicy, vigorous and with excellent acidity.

FINCA ELS CUCONS

Finca Els Cucons, s/n
08810 Sant Pere de Ribes (Barcelona)
☎: 938 961 370

VINYA ARNERA XAREL.LO 2003 WHITE

78 Brilliant pale yellow. Intense aroma with fresh varietal overtones, floral and citrus nuances. Flavourful palate, lacking fruit expression (a slight hint of greeness), drying hints, good citrus acidity.

FINCA VALLDOSERA

Masia Les Garrigues, s/n (Urb. Can Trebal)
08734 Olérdola (Barcelona)
☎: 938 143 047 - Fax: 938 935 590
general@fincavalldosera.com
www.fincavalldosera.com

Established: 1980

🌐 75 📊 200,000 litres 🍇 32 has.

FINCA VALLDOSERA SUBIRAT PARENT 2003 DULCE
CLOS DEL CALAU 2001 CRIANZA RED
GRAVALS D'EN CAYO 2001 CRIANZA RED

Cava FONPINET

Joan Maragall, 14
08770 Sant Sadurní D'Anoia (Barcelona)
☎: 938 910 228 - Fax: 938 910 211

Established: 1943

CHATEAU DE BELCASTEL WHITE
CHATEAU DE BELCASTEL ROSÉ
FONPINET CABERNET SAUVIGNON RED
FONPINET MERLOT RED

FRANCISCO DOMÍNGUEZ CRUCES

Lavernó, 22-27
08770 Sant Sadurní D'Anoia (Barcelona)
☎: 938 910 182 - Fax: 938 910 411
vinosycavas@elxamfra.com
www.ruralcat.com

Established: 1988

🌐 55 📊 20,000 litres 🍷 80% 🌐20%

XAMFRÀ CUVÉE 2003 JOVEN WHITE
xarel.lo, macabeo, chardonnay

80 Very pale. Not very intense yet fine aroma of ripe apples with a herby nuance. Palate with an element of acidity but pleasant and easy drinking.

XAMFRÀ CHARDONNAY 2003 FERMENTADO EN BARRICA WHITE
100% chardonnay

60 Straw-coloured. Aroma with obvious off-odours in the nose and on the palate.

XAMFRÀ CUVÉE 2003 JOVEN ROSÉ
100% merlot

81 Brilliant raspberry. Intense aroma of ripe red fruit with a spicy nuance of skins. Flavourful and spicy on the palate, slightly fruity with good acidity.

XAMFRÁ CABERNET SAUVIGNON CRIANZA RED
100% cabernet sauvignon

78 Garnet red cherry. Aroma of varietal typification, green fruit and alcohol. Astringent, warm, slightly vinous on the palate, medium-bodied.

XAMFRÀ CUVÉE 2003 JOVEN RED
XAMFRÀ SELECCIÓN 2003 OAK AGED RED

GIRÓ DEL GORNER

Masia Giró del Gorner, s/n
08797 Puigdálber (Barcelona)
☎: 938 988 032 - Fax: 938 988 032
gorner@girodelgorner.com
www.girodelgorner.com

Established: 1976

🌐 40 📊 400,000 litres 🍇 45 has.
🍷 80% 🌐20%: -JP -BE -DE -AD -CH

GORNER 2003 WHITE
40% macabeo, 45% xarel.lo, 15% parellada

79 Pale yellow with a greenish hue. Intense aroma of green fruit with a fine nuance of fennel. Fresh, flavourful palate, pleasant and high in acidity.

MERLOT ROSADO GORNER 2003 ROSÉ
100% merlot

79 Fairly pale raspberry. Intense, fresh aroma with notes of red stone fruit and hints of petals. Fresh palate with fine bitter notes and hints of spicy paprika.

GOMER 2000 RESERVA RED
MERLOT ROSADO GORNER 2003 ROSÉ

GIRÓ RIBOT

Finca El Pont, s/n
08792 Santa Fe del Penedés (Barcelona)
☎: 938 974 050 - Fax: 938 974 311
giroribot@giroribot.es
www.giroribot.es

Established: 1977

🌐 25 📊 1,500,000 litres 🍇 50 has.

☛ 25% 👁75%: -US -CR -CU -IE -DK -DK -FI -DE -CH -NL -BE -FR -IT -IL -JP

GIRÓ RIBOT CHARDONNAY 2003 FERMENTADO EN BARRICA WHITE
50% chardonnay, 30% xarel.lo, 20% parellada

80 Pale yellow with a golden hue. Powerful aroma with predominant spicy and creamy oak notes. Flavourful palate with well-integrated wood and fruit, a nuance of nuts and fragrant herbs, excellent acidity.

GIRÓ RIBOT BLANC DE BLANCS 2003 WHITE
xarel.lo, parellada

76 Pale yellow with a greenish glint. Fairly intense aroma with notes of green fruit and fine notes of citrus fruit. Fresh, bitter palate with lemon peel and high acidity.

GIRÓ RIBOT CHARDONNAY 2003 WHITE
50% chardonnay, 30% xarel.lo, 20% parellada

79 Pale yellow. Intense, fresh aroma with notes of green apples and Mediterranean herbs. Dry palate with fine bitter notes and good acidity.

GIRÓ RIBOT MUSCAT 2003 WHITE
50% moscatel, 30% xarel.lo, 20% parellada

77 Pale yellow. Intense, very varietal aroma (musk) with a nuance of ripe white fruit. Fresh palate with fine bitter notes of sweet limes, high acidity.

GRAMONA

Industria, 36
08770 Sant Sadurní D'Anoia (Barcelona)
☎: 938 910 113 - Fax: 938 183 284
cava@gramona.com/
alonsorafael@gramona.com
www.gramona.com

Established: 1881

🛢 150 📦 500,000 litres 🍇 29 has.

☛ 80% 👁20%: -US -DE -DK -BE -RU -CZ -LU -NL -CA -AD -CH

GRAMONA GESSAMÍ 2003 JOVEN WHITE
60% moscatel de Alejandría, 30% sauvignon blanc, 10% moscatel de frontignan

82 Pale yellow. Intense aroma with good varietal expression and quality floral hints. Flavourful palate, fine bitter notes, and quite sweet fruit, herbs, aniseed, excellent acidity.

GRAMONA MAS ESCORPÍ CHARDONNAY 2003 JOVEN WHITE
100% chardonnay

88 Brilliant gold. Powerful aroma of ripe fruit with excellent varietal expression, floral notes (acacia), fine lees and a suggestion of spices. Powerful, oily palate with excellent fruit-alcohol-acidity symmetry and a suggestion of light mineral notes.

GRAMONA SAUVIGNON BLANC 2003 FERMENTADO EN BARRICA WHITE
100% sauvignon blanc

89 Pale golden yellow. Intense, very fine aroma of ripe white fruit with exotic hints (papaya) and fine herbs. Powerful, flavourful palate with ripe fruit, smoky oak (hints of caramel) and fine bitter and mineral notes in the finish.

GRAMONA GRA A GRA 2001 WHITE DULCE NATURAL
chardonnay, sauvignon blanc

90 Pale gold. Intense aroma with an excellent expression of botrytised grapes, a suggestion of spices and flowers, fine herbs and hints of crystallised citrus fruit peel. Powerful, unctuous palate with a fine sweetness, a bitter essence and excellent acidity.

VI DE GEL RIESLING 2003 WHITE DULCE
100% riesling

86 Brilliant gold. Intense aroma evoking the freshness of white stone (hints of apricot skins) and citrus fruit. Flavourful, sweet, slightly dense palate with good sugar-acidity-alcohol symmetry and fine bitter notes in the finish.

VI DE GEL GEWÜRZTRAMINER 2003 WHITE DULCE
100% gewürztraminer

86 Brilliant gold. Intense, fresh aroma of fruit and white flowers, slightly varietal with a suggestion of cyrystallised citrus fruit. Flavourful palate with fine bitter notes, fine sweet notes and excellent citrus acidity.

PRIMEUR GRAMONA 2003 ROSÉ
40% syrah, 30% merlot, 30% pinot noir

80 Lively raspberry. Intense aroma with notes of red stone fruit, toasty notes of skins with a slightly sweet essence. Flavourful palate with slightly marked tannins, a suggestion of alternation between bitter and sweet notes.

MERLOT & CO. 2001 RED
70% merlot, 30% syrah

88 Very intense cherry. Deep aroma of fresh varietal and ripe fruit with fine toasty and creamy hints well-integrated with the wine. Fleshy, ripe palate with fresh fruit and fruity tannins, subtle creamy flavours in the retronasal passage, flavourful and well-structured.

BRU DE GRAMONA 2000 RESERVA RED

GRIMAU DE PUJADES

Castell de Les Pujades s/n
08732 Castellví de la Marca (Barcelona)
☎: 938 918 031 - Fax: 938 918 426
grimau@grimau.com
www.grimau.com

DO PENEDÈS

Established: 1988

🛢 200 📋 250,000 litres 🍇 23 has.

🍷 80% 🌐20%

GRIMAU CHARDONNAY 2002 FERMENTADO EN BARRICA WHITE
100% chardonnay

81 Golden. Medium-intensity aroma with smoky notes, butters and a note of reduction. Glycerin on the palate, pleasant with considerable wood weight and good acidity.

GRIMAU BLANC DE BLANCS 2003 WHITE
35% macabeo, 30% xarel.lo, 25% parellada, 10% chardonnay

83 Straw-coloured with a greenish hue. Good, intense aroma of ripe apples, expressive with a fine herby nuance. Flavourful, fresh palate with good fruit expression and pleasant bitter notes.

GRIMAU MERLOT 2003 ROSÉ
100% merlot

80 Brilliant raspberry with a coppery glint. Intense aroma of ripe red fruit with a spicy nuance and fine hints of reduction. Generous, flavourful palate with red fruit, a nuance of sweetness and good acidity.

GRIMAU RUBICUNDUS 2000 CRIANZA RED
100% tempranillo

84 Deep cherry with a coppery edge. Fairly intense aroma with predominant toasty oak notes over the ripe fruit (slightly jammy). Flavourful palate with well-integrated oak and fruit and bitter hints of fine crianza (chocolate, liquorice, balsamic flavours).

GRIMAU CABERNET SAUVIGNON 1999 RESERVA RED

82 Intense cherry with a coppery edge. Intense aroma of macerated black fruit with fine toasty wood notes. Flavourful palate with promising although quite marked tannins and a balsamic nuance; bitter with hints of sour cherries in liqueur.

GRIMAU NEGRAL 2002 RED

Cellers GRIMAU GOL

Nord, 8
08720 Vilafranca del Penedés (Barcelona)
☎: 938 181 372 - Fax: 938 920 812
emarti@duartdesio.com
www.duartdesio.com

Established: 1987

🛢 285 📋 800,000 litres 🍇 40 has.

🍷 55% 🌐45%

CAN MILA DE LA ROCA CLASSIC PENEDÉS WHITE

DUART DE SIÓ BRISA SOL WHITE
DUART DE SIÓ PRIMAVERA WHITE
DUART DE SIÓ BRISA SOL ROSÉ
DUART DE SIÓ FLORAL ROSÉ
HERETAT CAN MILA DE LA ROCA ROSÉ
DUART DE SIÓ LA GITANETA RED
DUART DE SIÓ NEGRE GRANA RESERVA RED
CAN MILA DE LA ROCA GRAN RESERVA RED

HERETAT MAS JORNET

Avenida Penedes, 62
08730 La Rapita - Monjos (Barcelona)
☎: 938 980 484 - Fax: 938 983 005
vinesicavesmasjornet@catanet.com
www.vinesicavesmasjornet.com

Established: 1987

🛢 125 📋 50,000 litres 🍇 10 has.

🍷 80% 🌐20%: -CH -DE

MAS JORNET WHITE
30% macabeo, 30% xarel.lo, 40% parellada

73 Pale. Slightly fruity aroma with slightly ripe tropical notes. Fresh, flavourful palate with fairly sweet notes.

MAS JORNET JOVEN RED
50% cabernet sauvignon, 50% tempranillo

76 Fairly deep cherry with a violet edge. Intense fruity aroma with mild off-odours from the tank. Flavourful palate with quite marked but high quality grape tannins and good acidity.

MAS JORNET 1998 CRIANZA RED
100% cabernet sauvignon

80 Nearly opaque cherry with a violet edge. Powerful aroma of jammy black fruit with a nuance of toasty oak. Flavourful palate with fine bitter crianza notes and good acidity.

MAS JORNET 2000 RED

Cavas HILL

Bonavista, 2
08734 Moja (Olérdola) (Barcelona)
☎: 938 900 588 - Fax: 938 170 246
cavashill@cavashill.com
www.cavashill.com

Established: 1887

🛢 980 📋 214,000 litres 🍇 50 has.

🍷 80% 🌐20%

MASIA HILL 2003 JOVEN WHITE
90% xarel.lo, 10% macabeo

78 Straw-coloured with a golden hue. Fairly intense, fruity aroma without great nuances. Flavourful on the palate with fine bitter notes, hints of citrus fruit and a slightly acidic edge.

DO PENEDÈS

ORO PENEDÈS HILL 2003 JOVEN WHITE
muscat, xarel.lo

80 Pale yellow. Powerful, fruity aroma (exotic fruit notes) with a fine musky nuance. Generous on the palate with a slightly oily texture, fruity with fresh overtones and lacking acidity.

BLANC BRUC HILL 2002 FERMENTADO EN BARRICA WHITE
xarel.lo, sauvignon blanc, chardonnay

83 Yellow straw. Not very intense yet fine aroma with smoky oak and a citrus fruit nuance (grapefruit). Fresh on the palate with good fruit framed by the wood, well-crafted.

CHARDONNAY HILL 2002 FERMENTADO EN BARRICA WHITE
100% chardonnay

80 Golden yellow. Powerful aroma with predominant smoky and creamy oak notes (vanilla) and a ripe fruit essence. Flavourful on the palate with slightly marked oak tannins; lacking balance.

SAUVIGNON BLANC HILL 2003 WHITE
100% sauvignon blanc

81 Yellow straw. Not very intense aroma with a citrus fruit essence (grapefruit). Slightly oily and flavourful on the palate and more varietal than in the nose; good acidity and well-balanced.

MASÍA HILL 2003 ROSÉ
60% tempranillo, 40% garnacha

79 Intense raspberry. Powerful aroma of ripe red fruit with spicy hints of skins. Flavourful and fruity on the palate with bitter and quality citrus fruit notes and a slightly acidic edge.

MASÍA HILL 2003 JOVEN RED
100% tempranillo

83 Intense cherry with a violet edge. Powerful, fruity, very fresh aroma with excellent varietal expression (red fruit, underbrush). Powerful and fruity on the palate with very flavourful grape tannins, well-balanced.

MERLOT HILL 2000 CRIANZA RED
100% merlot

84 Garnet red cherry with a saffron edge. Powerful aroma with an excellent varietal expression (bilberries, underbrush, paprika) and fine toasty oak. Flavourful on the palate with promising although slightly marked oak tannins and good acidity.

GRAN CIVET HILL 2001 CRIANZA RED
50% tempranillo, 35% cabernet sauvignon, 15% merlot

84 Garnet red cherry with a coppery edge. Intense aroma with predominant smoky oak notes, a ripe fruit nuance and spicy, quite varietal notes (paprika). Flavourful on the palate with well-integrated oak/fruit and a balsamic nuance (herbs, liquorice).

CABERNET SAUVIGNON HILL 1999 RESERVA RED
100% cabernet sauvignon

83 Garnet red cherry with a coppery edge. Intense aroma of fine toasty oak with a good suggestion of the vine variety (paprika, black fruit). Flavourful on the palate with well-integrated oak/fruit, spices (paprika) and fine reduction notes (tobacco).

GRAN TOC HILL 1999 RESERVA RED
60% tempranillo, 25% cabernet sauvignon, 15% merlot

87 Garnet red cherry with a saffron edge. Intense aroma of toasty oak notes and a ripe fruit nuance with hints of a fine reduction. Flavourful on the palate with well-integrated oak/fruit, excellent balance and powerful in the retronasal passage (balsamic flavours and minerals).

GRAN RESERVA HILL 1998 GRAN RESERVA RED
60% cabernet sauvignon, 30% tempranillo, 10% syrah

80 Garnet red cherry with a coppery edge. Intense aroma with predominant wood notes and a suggestion of reduction. Flavourful on the palate with slightly marked oak tannins, hints of aged wood and a herbaceous nuance, lacking balance.

BLANC BRUC 2002 FERMENTADO EN BARRICA WHITE

Bodegas J. TRIAS

Comerç, 6
08720 Vilafranca del Penedés (Barcelona)
☎: 938 902 627 - Fax: 938 901 724
bodegas@jtrias.com
www.jtrias.com

Established: 1932

55 🛢 135,000 litres 🍇 15 has.

🍷 90% 🌐10%: -DK -DE -TR -CU -CH -CY -PL

TRIAS BATLLE BLANC DE BLANCS 2003 WHITE
TRIAS BATLLE 2003 ROSÉ
SAIRT CABERNET SAUVIGNON 2001 CRIANZA RED
SAIRT 2001 CRIANZA RED
TRIAS BATLLE 2003 RED

JANÉ VENTURA

Carretera Calafell, 2
43700 El Vendrell (Tarragona)
☎: 977 660 118 - Fax: 977 661 239
janeventura@janeventura.com
www.janeventura.com

Established: 1914

200 🛢 400,000 litres 🍇 15 has.

🍷 80% 🌐20%: -SE -NL -CH -BE -DK -AT -US -PR

DO PENEDÈS

JANÉ VENTURA 2003 JOVEN WHITE
90% xarel.lo, 8% parellada, 2% subirat parent

83 Straw-coloured. Fresh, fruity aroma with varietal notes. Fruity fresh palate with excellent alcohol-acidity balance, flavourful.

JANÉ VENTURA "FINCA ELS CAMPS" MACABEU 2003 FERMENTADO EN BARRICA WHITE
95% macabeo, 5% xarel.lo

86 Straw-coloured with a yellow glimmer. Fresh aroma with fine smoky notes, fresh fruit and bitter hints of the vine variety. Acidity is greater than the 2001 vintage, this mutes the fruit expression associated with the ageing oak lees.

JANÉ VENTURA 2003 ROSÉ
90% tempranillo, 10% cariñena

84 Raspberry. Fresh, fragrant aroma with hints of redcurrants and strawberries. Fruity, clean, flavourful and very dry on the palate.

JANÉ VENTURA VINYA PALFURIANA 2003 ROBLE RED
50% tempranillo, 50% merlot

85 Quite intense cherry. Powerful aroma of ripe fruit with a suggestion of freshness and the varietal with fine toasty notes. Powerful, fruity palate with excellent varietal ripeness supporting the fresh fruit, with fine, creamy oak tannins and good flavour though lacking wood/fruit assemblage.

JANÉ VENTURA "FINCA ELS CAMPS" ULL DE LLEBRE 2001 OAK AGED RED
100% tempranillo

88 Intense cherry. Fine, toasty aroma (cocoa, tobacco, coffee) with macerated black fruit. Fruity palate, rich in varietal expression, toasty and spirituous with wood tannins dominating the ripe fruit, very flavourful.

JANÉ VENTURA "FINCA ELS CAMPS" ULL DE LLEBRE 2002 OAK AGED RED
95% tempranillo, 5% cabernet sauvignon

87 Intense cherry. Powerful, creamy, toasty aroma (coffee, cocoa) with ripe fruit. Fleshy, fruity palate with slighty pronounced tannins, good acidity and creamy toasty oak in the retronasal passage.

JANÉ VENTURA MARGALLÓ 2002 CRIANZA RED
60% tempranillo, 20% merlot, 20% cabernet sauvignon

87 Quite intense cherry with an orange edge. Powerful, creamy aroma (cocoa, aromatic coffee) and fresh, varietal Merlot notes. Fresh, fruity, varietal palate with marked acidity and excellent oak expression.

JANE VENTURA "MAS VILELLA" 2000 CRIANZA RED
100% cabernet sauvignon

91 Intense cherry. Fine, toasty aroma with nuances of fine oak and well-integrated ripe fruit. Round, flavourful palate with oily tannins; harmonious with good freshness, light mineral notes and jammy black fruit.

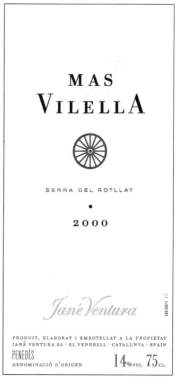

JANÉ VENTURA "MAS VILELLA" 2001 CRIANZA RED
100% cabernet sauvignon

93 Intense cherry. Toasty aroma (pitch peat, chocolate) with ripe fruit but fresh overtones without running to jam. Fleshy palate with powerful tannins, full, toasty and flavourful, less Mediterranean than the 2000 harvest.

JANÉ VENTURA CARINYENA+GARNATXA VINYES VELLES 2001 OAK AGED RED
JANÉ VENTURA "FINCA ELS CAMPS" ULL DE LLEBRE 2002 OAK AGED RED
JANÉ VENTURA SUMOLL VINYES VELLES 2001 OAK AGED RED
JANÉ VENTURA "MAS VILELLA" 2002 CRIANZA RED

JAUME GIRÓ I GIRÓ

Montaner i Oller, s/n
08770 Sant Sadurní d'Anoia (Barcelona)
☎: 938 910 165 - Fax: 938 911 271
cavagiro@interbook.net
www.cavagiro.com

Established: 1926
🍷 85% 🍇15%

JAUME GIRÓ I GIRÓ CABERNET-MERLOT 2001 RED
cabernet sauvignon, merlot

79 Deep cherry. Powerful, fruity aroma with excellent varietal expression (paprika) and a nuance of toasty oak. Flavourful, fleshy palate with slightly marked tannins, rich in fruit nuances although with an excess of herbaceous and acidic notes.

JAUME LLOPART ALEMANY

Calle Font Rubí, 9
08736 Font-Rubí (Barcelona)
☎: 938 979 133 - Fax: 938 979 133
info@jaumellopartalemany.com
www.jaumellopartalemany.com

Established: 1985
🍇 50 has. 🍷 85% 🍇15%: -AD -NL

JAUME LLOPART ALEMANY 2003 JOVEN WHITE
JAUME LLOPART ALEMANY 2003 ROSÉ
JAUME LLOPART ALEMANY 2003 RED

JAUME SERRA

Finca El Padruell, s/n
08800 Vilanova i la Geltru (Barcelona)
☎: 938 936 404 - Fax: 938 142 262
jaumeserra@jgc.es
www.vinosdefamilia.com

Established: 1985
🍷 3,000 🛢 2,400,000 litres 🍇 76 has.

🍷 75% 🍇25%: -US -UK -DE -IT -LT -JP - FR -AT -NL

JAUME SERRA OPERA PRIMA 2003 WHITE SECO
35% macabeo, 50% chardonnay, 15% muscat

80 Pale with golden nuances. Quite intense aroma of fruit and white flowers with fine notes of perfumed soap. Flavourful, fresh palate with rich bitter notes and with good acidity.

JAUME SERRA XAREL.LO 2003 WHITE SEMIDULCE
100% xarel.lo

72 Straw-coloured with a greenish hue. Medium-intensity, mildly fruity aroma. Aroma with notes of herbs (rosemary) and good balance between sweetness and bitterness.

JAUME SERRA CHARDONNAY 2003 FERMENTADO EN BARRICA WHITE SECO
100% chardonnay

78 Yellow straw. Aroma with creamy wood notes dominating the fruit. Flavourful, slightly oily palate, with slightly more fruit and a toasty oak finish.

JAUME SERRA MACABEO 2003 WHITE SECO
100% macabeo

78 Straw-coloured. Medium-intensity aroma of ripe fruit (bananas, pears) Fruity palate with an element of acidity; well-mannered.

JAUME SERRA TEMPRANILLO 2003 ROSÉ
100% tempranillo

77 Brilliant raspberry. Slightly intense aroma with the varietal and spicy freshness of skins. Fresh, slightly fruity palate with fine bitter hints of citrus fruit and good acidity.

JAUME SERRA CABERNET SAUVIGNON 2002 ROBLE RED
100% cabernet sauvignon   🛢 4

83 Garnet red cherry with a coppery edge. Powerful aroma of toasty oak notes with a ripe fruit nuance and elements of a fine reduction. Flavourful palate with quite ripe and oily tannins, hints of spices and leathers and good acidity.

JAUME SERRA MERLOT SELECCIÓN 2002 ROBLE RED
100% merlot   🛢 4

80 Garnet red cherry. Intense, ripe aroma with black fruit and a not very clean oak nuance. Flavourful palate with fine bitter notes, toasty hints of oak and good acidity.

JAUME SERRA TEMPRANILLO 2002 ROBLE RED
100% tempranillo   🛢 4

80 Garnet red cherry with a coppery edge. Intense aroma of macerated black fruit with a spicy oak nuance and hints of fine reduction. Flavourful palate with bitter notes (dark-roasted flavours, Mediterranean herbs), an acidic edge.

JAUME SERRA TEMPRANILLO 2002 OAK AGED RED
100% tempranillo   🛢 3

75 Garnet red cherry. Not very intense aroma of red fruit with spicy hints of oak. Flavourful and fruity on the palate with a slightly oily texture, without great nuances.

JAUME SERRA 2000 CRIANZA RED
75% cabernet sauvignon, 25% tempranillo

80 Garnet red with a saffron edge. Not very intense aroma with spicy hints of oak. Flavourful palate with well-integrated fruit and oak, a nuance of ripe black fruit and bitter hints.

JAUME SERRA 1998 RESERVA RED
50% cabernet sauvignon, 20% tempranillo, 30% merlot

80 Very deep cherry with a brick red edge. Intense aroma of fine toasty oak with a balsamic nuance of ripe black fruit (hints of prunes).

Flavourful palate with a good expression of traditional crianza; fruity nuance, liquorice, dark-roasted flavours.

JAUME SERRA SELECCIÓN 2003 FERMENTADO EN BARRICA RED

JEAN LEÓN

Finca Chateau León - Afueras, s/n
08775 Torrelavit (Barcelona)
☎: 938 995 512 - Fax: 938 995 517
jeanleon@jeanleon.com
www.jeanleon.com

Established: 1963

🌐 1,300 📦 292,500 litres 🍷 67 has.

🍷 60%/🌐40%: -CH -DE -US -JP -UK

JEAN LEÓN PETIT CHARDONNAY 2003 JOVEN WHITE
100% chardonnay

87 Straw-coloured with a greenish hue. Good intensity, fine, elegant aroma of ripe white fruit, a citrus fruit nuance and fine smoky notes. Flavourful, oily palate with good balance between the ripe fruit and the smoky wood notes; good acidity.

JEAN LEÓN CHARDONNAY 2002 FERMENTADO EN BARRICA WHITE
100% chardonnay

89 Straw-coloured. Powerful, elegant aroma with smoky oak notes (butter, walnuts), fine lees and with a nuance of aromatic herbs. Flavourful, very oily, powerful palate with ripe fruit and a long, smoky finish.

JEAN LEÓN VINYA PALAU 2001 CRIANZA RED
merlot

85 Cherry with an orangey hue. Aroma with terroir character (earth, dust), jam and ripe fruit. Fleshy, flavourful, mineral on the palate and very pleasant.

ZEMIS PAGO JEAN LEON 2000 CRIANZA RED
60% cabernet sauvignon, 30% merlot, 10% cabernet franc

89 Intense cherry with an orange edge. Powerful, spicy, peppery aroma with a ripe fruit suggestion and nuances of oak. Full, oily, powerful, fleshy palate, rich in spicy expression with very ripe fruit.

JEAN LEÓN CABERNET SAUVIGNON 1999 RESERVA RED
85% cabernet sauvignon, 15% cabernet franc

85 Cherry with a garnet red edge. Powerful aroma with peppery notes, tobacco, toasty wood and crianza character. Ripe fruit on the palate with balsamic notes, creamy wood. Good alcohol/wine integration and ripe tannins.

JEAN LEÓN CABERNET SAUVIGNON 1996 GRAN RESERVA RED
85% cabernet sauvignon, 15% cabernet franc

85 Cherry with a brick red edge. Aroma with good reduction notes (tobacco, spices) and a nuance of jammy fruit. Round, spicy, flavourful palate with polished tannins and bitter notes of oak.

JEAN LEÓN MERLOT 2002 CRIANZA RED

JOAN FERRAN ROSES VILA

Can Roig
08732 Castellvi de la Marca (Barcelona)
☎: 938 919 130 - Fax: 938 904 351
rosesvila@yahoo.es
www.rosesvila.com

Established: 2000

🌐 30 📦 100,000 litres 🍷 30 has.

🍷 50% 🌐50%: -UK -IE -CH -CU -US

ROSÉS VILA 2003 JOVEN RED

JOAN LLOPART PONS

Finca Llopart
08736 Font Rubí (Barcelona)
☎: 938 989 059 - Fax: 938 989 059
raurell@cal.magmet.com

Established: 1982

📦 400,000 litres 🍷 100 has. 🍷 100%

RAURELL WHITE
RAURELL ROSÉ
RAURELL RED

JOAN RAVENTÓS ROSELL

Heretat Vall-Ventós, s/n
Carretera Sant Sadurní a Masquefa, km. 6,5
08783 Masquefa (Barcelona)
☎: 937 725 251 - Fax: 937 727 191
correu@raventosrosell.com
www.raventosrosell.com

Established: 1985

🌐 300 📦 350,000 litres 🍷 100 has.

🍷 50% 🌐50%: -DE -CH -NL -BE -DK -FI -RU -US -CA -CO

HERETAT VALL-VENTÓS BLANC PRIMER 2003 JOVEN WHITE

82 Pale yellow with a coppery hue. Fresh, fruity aroma of green apples with, fine hints of petals (acacia) and honeyed scents. Fresh, flavourful palate with white stone fruit, excellent acidity.

HERETAT VALL-VENTÓS CHARDONNAY 2003 JOVEN WHITE
100% chardonnay

80 Golden yellow. Powerful aroma with a slight varietal expression (ripe apples), a honeyed nuance and hints of lees. Flavourful, fruity palate with a slightly oily texture and hints of Mediterranean herbs, high in acidity.

HERETAT VALL-VENTÓS CHENIN 2003 JOVEN WHITE
100% chenin blanc

79 Golden with a coppery glint. Powerful, ripe aroma with predominant reduction notes (lees, withered petals, nuts). Improved, fresh palate with hints of white stone fruit, spices, good acidity.

HERETAT VALL-VENTÓS SAUVIGNON BLANC 2003 JOVEN WHITE
100% sauvignon blanc

81 Golden yellow. Powerful aroma of white stone fruit (apricots) and fine hints of exotic fruit. Flavourful, fresh palate, good acidity.

HERETAT VALL-VENTÓS BLANC DE NOIR 2003 JOVEN ROSÉ
100% pinot noir

80 Salmon. Intense aroma of red fruit with a spicy nuance of skins. Flavourful, fruity palate with a slightly warm and oily texture.

HERETAT VALL-VENTÓS MERLOT 2003 JOVEN ROSÉ
100% merlot

77 Pale raspberry with a coppery glint. Fairly intense aroma of ripe red fruit with warm hints. Flavourful palate with predominant warm notes, slightly oily with a nuance of sweet fruit.

HERETAT VALL-VENTÓS ROSAT PRIMER 2003 JOVEN ROSÉ
75% pinot noir, 25% merlot

78 Pale raspberry with a coppery glint. Intense aroma of red fruit with a spicy nuance of skins; slightly warm. Flavourful palate with fine bitter notes and quite oily and warm texture, good acidity.

HERETAT VALL-VENTÓS VIÑA BORDOY 2001 JOVEN RED
75% tempranillo, 25% merlot

80 Garnet red cherry. Intense aroma of ripe red fruit and fine toasty oak. Flavourful palate with notes of macerated fruit, fresh overtones (good acidity) and hints of spices and terroir, pleasant.

HERETAT VALL-VENTÓS TEMPRANILLO 2001 OAK AGED RED
100% tempranillo   ⊕ 6

76 Fairly deep cherry with a saffron glint. Intense, ripe aroma with toasty hints of oak and mild reduction off-odours. Fairly flavourful, bitter palate, lacking balance (excess acidity, poor integration of oak and fruit).

HERETAT VALL-VENTÓS MERLOT 2001 OAK AGED RED
100% merlot   ⊕ 6

81 Garnet red cherry with a saffron edge. Powerful aroma of ripe red fruit and underbrush with a toasty, spicy (pepper) oak nuance. Flavourful palate with slightly fresh tannins (note of greeness), good acidity.

HERETAT VALL-VENTÓS CABERNET SAUVIGNON 2000 CRIANZA RED
100% cabernet sauvignon

79 Garnet red cherry. Powerful, ripe aroma with varietal character overtones (paprika) and a not very clean nuance of wood. Flavourful, fleshy palate with fresh fruit overtones, lacking balance.

HERETAT VALL-VENTÓS BLANC PRIMER 2003 JOVEN WHITE
HERETAT VALL-VENTÓS PINOT NOIR 2003 JOVEN RED
HERETAT VALL-VENTÓS 2000 RESERVA RED

JOAN SARDÁ

Ctra Vilafranca- St. Jaume dels Domenys, km. 8, 100
08732 Castellvi de la Marca (Barcelona)
☎: 937 720 900 - Fax: 937 721 495
joansarda@joansarda
www.joansarda.com

Established: 1927

⊕ 450 ▤ 2,900,000 litres ※ 20 has.

🞂 50% 🕐50%: -CU -JP -CR -DE -US -KE

JOAN SARDÁ CHARDONNAY 2003 WHITE
100% chardonnay

82 Straw-coloured with a greenish edge. Aroma of green fruit with notes of lees and mountain herbs. Fresh and fruity on the palate with herbaceous expression of the vine variety, persistent.

MARINER BLANC DE BLANCS 2003 WHITE
50% chardonnay, 50% xarel.lo

75 Straw-coloured with a greenish glint. Medium-intensity aroma of discreet white fruit with hints of flor. Light and well-balanced on the palate, fresh although without obvious fruit expression.

VIÑA SARDÀ 2003 WHITE
70% macabeo, 30% chardonnay

73 Straw-coloured with a greenish edge. Discreet aroma of fruit ripe overtones. Dry on the palate with high acidity, slightly carbonic, lacking marked fruit character.

VIÑA SARDÀ 2003 ROSÉ
100% garnacha

72 Pale pink. Aroma of slightly muted red fruit, discreet. Fresh on the palate with mountain herbs, well-mannered.

JOAN SARDÁ CABERNET SAUVIGNON 2003 ROSÉ
100% cabernet sauvignon

74 Brilliant pink. Fresh aroma of red fruit with discreet flower petals. Flavourful and quite ripe on the palate with marked carbonic smells and slightly muted fruit.

VIÑA SARDÀ 2002 RED
100% tempranillo

78 Garnet red cherry. Not very intense aroma with notes of red fruit and spicy hints. Flavourful, fruity palate with quite marked tannins (vegetative notes) and good acidity.

JOAN SARDÁ CABERNET SAUVIGNON 2000 CRIANZA RED
100% cabernet sauvignon

83 Deep cherry. Spicy aroma with notes of toasty skins and tobacco, complex crianza overtones. Fleshy, dry and fresh on the palate with well-balanced superripe fruit and wood; a toasty finish.

JOAN SARDÁ MERLOT 2000 CRIANZA RED
100% merlot

77 Cherry with a garnet red rim. Aroma of ripe black fruit with a nuance of smoky notes. Fleshy on the palate with obvious wood tannins; spices in the finish.

JOAN SARDÁ TEMPRANILLO 2000 CRIANZA RED
100% tempranillo

77 Garnet red cherry. Aroma of red fruit with hints of jam, tobacco and pitch (crianza). Flavourful and fresh on the palate with quite aggressive wood tannins; spicy notes in the finish.

GRAN VINYA SARDÁ 1999 RESERVA RED
100% tempranillo

80 Intense cherry. Spicy aroma with notes of tobacco and attics (aged wood). Flavourful on the palate, better crianza expression, round tannins and pleasant freshness.

Celler JORDI LLUCH

Barrio Les Casetes
08777 Sant Quinti de Mediona (Barcelona)
☎: 938 988 138 - Fax: 938 988 138
vinyaescude@vinyaescude.com
www.vinyaescude.com

Established: 1984

🌐 20 📊 500,000 litres 🍇 20 has.

🍷 90% 🌐10%: -NL

VINYA ESCUDÉ 2003 JOVEN WHITE
50% macabeo, 30% xarel.lo, 20% parellada

72 Straw-coloured with a greenish edge. Slightly discreet aroma of white fruit with hints of citrus fruit. Fruity palate, without great fruit nuances, fresh.

VINYA ESCUDÉ MERLOT 2003 JOVEN ROSÉ
100% merlot

80 Raspberry. Good intensity aroma of ripe red fruit. Flavourful, fresh, very fruity palate, very pleasant and easy drinking.

VINYA ESCUDE ROSAT NOVELL 2003 JOVEN ROSÉ
70% tempranillo, 30% merlot

73 Brilliant blush. Aroma of slightly ripe red fruit with a nuance of nutty notes. Flavourful, slightly warm palate, without great freshness.

VINYA ESCUDÉ 2003 JOVEN RED
80% tempranillo, 20% merlot

79 Intense cherry with a violet edge. Intense, fruity aroma with spicy hints of skins and a high quality herbaceous nuance. Flavourful palate with an edge of greeness to the grape tannins and refreshing acidity.

VINYA ESCUDÉ CABERNET SAUVIGNON 2000 CRIANZA RED
100% cabernet sauvignon

80 Garnet red cherry with a coppery edge. Intense aroma of spicy oak notes with a ripe fruit nuance and a fine reduction. Flavourful palate with well-integrated fruit and oak, fine bitter notes and good crianza expression.

VINYA ESCUDÉ MERLOT 2000 CRIANZA RED

JOSÉ MARÍA ROSELL MIR

Masel de Can Ros.
08739 Subirats (Barcelona)
☎: 938 911 354 - Fax: 938 911 311
jmrosell@hotmail.com

Established: 1982

🌐 200 📊 350,000 litres 🍇 30 has.

🍷 90% 🌐10%: -DK -CA -NL

PLA DE LA CREU 2003 JOVEN WHITE
100% xarel.lo

78 Straw-coloured. Aroma of exotic fruit (ripe pineapples) and fine herbs. Light, fruity and fresh on the palate with fairly ripe notes.

ROSELL MIR 2003 WHITE SECO
xarel.lo, macabeo

82 Pale yellow with carbonic hints. Intense aroma of white fruit with hints of ripe citrus fruit and a herbaceous nuance. Fresh, flavourful and ripe on the palate with a slightly oily texture, fine bitter notes and good acidity.

ROSELL MIR CAN GUINEU 2003 RED
cabernet franc, merlot

82 Garnet red cherry. Fairly intense fruity aroma with hints of sun-drenched skins and a slightly herbaceous nuance. Ripe palate with a good varietal expression (black fruit, underbrush), pleasant.

ROSELL MIR PLA DE LA CREU 2002 RED

81 Garnet red cherry with a saffron edge. Fairly intense aroma of black fruit with spicy hints of skins and a fairly toasty nuance. Flavourful palate with a good varietal expression (paprika), ripe and somewhat oily tannins, good acidity.

PLA DE LA CREU 2003 ROSÉ
CAN GUINEU 2003 FERMENTADO EN BARRICA RED
ROSELL MIR CABERNET SAUVIGNON CRIANZA RED
ROSELL MIR MERLOT CRIANZA RED
PLA DE LA CREU 2002 CRIANZA RED

JOSEP FERRET I MATEU

Avenida Penedés, 27
08730 Sta. Margarida i Els Monjos (Barcelona)
☎: 938 980 583 - Fax: 938 980 584
ferretmateu@ferretmateu.com
Established: 1942

FERRET I MATEU CHARDONNAY 2003 WHITE

80 Straw-coloured with a greenish glint. Not very intense aroma with a certain finesse, of white stone fruit and exotic hints. Flavourful, fruity palate with a slightly oily texture, very pleasant.

FERRET I MATEU NOVELL VINYA SANT GALDERIC 2003 WHITE

81 Straw-coloured. Intense aroma of ripe white fruit with exotic hints (melons). Fresh, fruity palate with notes of herbs and good acidity.

FERRET I MATEU SAUVIGNON BLANC 2003 WHITE
sauvignon blanc

82 Straw-coloured. Intense aroma with good varietal expression (green fruit and hints of citrus fruit). Generous palate, rich in white fruit nuances with a suggestion of balsamic herbs and good acidity.

MON MARITIM BLANCO DE AGUJA SEMI SECO WHITE
macabeo, xarel.lo, parellada

78 Straw-coloured. Not very intense aroma of white fruit with fresh overtones. Dry palate with carbonic hints and bitter notes, high in acidity.

MON MARITIM ROSADO DE AGUJA SEMI SECO ROSÉ
tempranillo, garnacha

70 Brilliant raspberry. Very fruity aroma of strawberry syrup. Fresh palate with carbonic hints, not very fine bittersweet notes and a bitter nuance.

FERRET I MATEU NOVELL VINYA SANT GALDERIC 2003 ROSÉ

79 Brilliant raspberry. Fairly intense aroma of red fruit with spicy hints of skins. Flavourful, fresh, slightly warm palate, good acidity.

ÁGATA CABERNET SAUVIGNON RED
cabernet sauvignon

77 Cherry with an orangy edge. Intense aroma with predominant reduction notes (varnish, prune stones). Better on the palate, flavourful with ripe and sweet tannins and hints of spices and minerals.

MARIA MATEU CABERNET SAUVIGNON 1997 RED

79 Cherry with an orangey edge. Intense aroma with predominant reduction notes (varnishes). Flavourful palate with ripe tannins, a good expression of traditional crianza.

FERRET I MATEU NOVELL VINYA SANT GALDERIC 2003 RED

77 Brilliant cherry with a violet edge. Intense aroma of red fruit with balsamic notes and notes of petals (mild tank off-odours). Fresh, flavourful palate, good acidity.

VIÑA LARANDA FERRET I MATEU 2001 RED
tempranillo

81 Cherry with a coppery edge. Intense, fruity aroma with good varietal expression and balsamic hints. Flavourful, slightly fleshy palate with a good expression of ripe fruit and herbaceous hints in the retronasal passage.

FERRET I MATEU MERLOT 2003 RED
merlot

79 Garnet red cherry. Intense aroma of very ripe black fruit with balsamic hints and macerated fruit. Better, flavourful, fleshy palate with black fruit, fine toasty notes and herbaceous hints.

Celler JOSEP M. FERRET

B. L'Alzinar, 68
08736 Font-Rubí (Barcelona)
☎: 938 979 037 - Fax: 938 979 414
celler.ferret@sefes.es
Established: 1997
🗌 35,000 litres 🍇 1 has.
🍷 85% 🌐15%: -DE -AD -US -CR

FERRET GUASCH GEBRE 2003 WHITE SECO
80% xarel.lo, 20% macabeo

77 Straw-coloured. Medium-intensity aroma of ripe fruit. Acidic and bitter notes on the palate, pleasant.

FERRET GUASCH GEBRE 2003 ROSÉ
100% cabernet sauvignon

83 Brilliant raspberry. Not very intense, fruity aroma with good varietal expression. Flavourful palate with a spicy nuance of skins, hints of high quality citrus fruit, excellent acidity.

AMYSTIS 1997 CRIANZA RED
30% cabernet sauvignon, 30% merlot, 30% tempranillo, 10% syrah

74 Strawberry with a brick red rim. Aroma with hints of the tank, reduction overtones, aged wood. Drying palate, light with not very much persistence.

JOSEP MASACHS

Carretera Sant Martí Sarroca, km. 7
08737 Torrellles de Foix (Barcelona)
☎: 938 990 017 - Fax: 938 991 561
infocm@cavasmasachs.com
www.cavasmasachs.com

Established: 1940
📦 1,200,000 l. litres 🍇 40 has. 🇪🇸 79%
🌐21%: -DE -CH -NL -DK -UK -US -MX

PAINOUS WHITE SECO
PICANT D'OR AGUJA WHITE
JOSEP MASACHS 2002 WHITE SECO
JOSEP MASACHS CHARDONNAY 2002 JOVEN WHITE
PAINOUS WHITE SEMISECO
DALINA DE MASACHS WHITE
PAINOUS ROSÉ
PICANT D'OR AGUJA ROSÉ
JOSEP MASACHS 2002 JOVEN ROSÉ
PAINOUS TEMPRANILLO JOVEN RED
JOSEP MASACHS TEMPRANILLO 2002 JOVEN RED
JOSEP MASACHS MERLOT 2002 JOVEN RED
JOSEP MASACHS CABERNET SAUVIGNON RED
JOSEP MASACHS TEMPRANILLO CRIANZA RED

JUVÉ & CAMPS

Sant Venat, 1
08770 Sant Sadurní D'Anoia (Barcelona)
☎: 938 911 000 - Fax: 938 912 100
juveycamps@juveycarnps.com
www.juveycamps.com

Established: 1921
🍶 1,000 📦 5,000,000 litres 🍇 430 has.
🚩 90% 🌐10%

ERMITA D'ESPIELLS "BLANC FLOR" 2003 JOVEN WHITE
40% macabeo, 20% xarel.lo, 40% parellada

82 Pale yellow. Fresh aroma with hints of green fruit, hints of bitter almonds and mountain herbs. Dry palate, with fine bitter notes and good acidity.

LA MIRANDA D'ESPIELLS 2002 FERMENTADO EN BARRICA WHITE
chardonnay

85 Golden yellow. Powerful aroma with predominant toasty notes of oak, an excellent varietal expression (apples) and hints of citrus fruit peel. Generous palate with well-integrated wood and fruit and fine hints of reduction (nuts).

LA MIRANDA D'ESPIELLS CHARDONNAY FLOR 2001 WHITE
100% chardonnay

84 Pale yellow with golden nuances. Not very intense aroma with fine notes of ripe apple, and hints of herbs. Dry palate with fine bitter notes and slightly marked tannins; nuts and mountain herbs; excellent acidity, very long.

CASA VELLA D'ESPIELLS CABERNET SAUVIGNON 1998 RED
100% cabernet sauvignon

74 Cherry with a brick red edge. Intense varietal aroma (black fruit, paprika) with light not very fine crianza off-odours (aged wood, lack of racking). Bitter palate with high acidity, lacking balance.

LA MIRANDA D'ESPIELLS 2003 JOVEN WHITE

Cavas LAVERNOYA

Sant Pere, 17
08770 Sant Sadurní D'Anoia (Barcelona)
☎: 938 912 202 - Fax: 938 911 159
lavernoya@troc.es
www.troc.es/lavernoya

Established: 1890
🚩 75% 🌐25%

LACRIMA BACCHUS BLANC DE BLANCS 2003 JOVEN WHITE
macabeo, xarel.lo, chardonnay

78 Straw-coloured. Medium-intensity aroma of very ripe fruit (bananas, pineapple). Fruity palate with an element of acidity; well-mannered ensemble.

LAVERNOYA MERLOT 2002 ROSÉ
merlot

80 Pale cherry with an orange hue. Intense aroma with fine spicy notes of skins and a reduction nuance. Flavourful, generous and dry on the palate with fine bitter notes and hints of nuts and Mediterranean herbs.

LAVERNOYA MERLOT 2001 CRIANZA RED
100% merlot

85 Very deep cherry with a coppery edge. Intense aroma of jammy black fruit with spicy hints of oak. Flavourful, fleshy palate with well-integrated oak and grape tannins, and a powerful aroma in the retronasal passage (liquorice, chocolate, prune stones).

LAVERNOYA CABERNET 1999 RED
cabernet sauvignon

86 Garnet red cherry with a coppery edge. Powerful aroma with an excellent varietal fruit expression (bilberries, paprika) and a spicy oak nuance. Flavourful, fleshy palate with ripe fruit and fine bitter crianza notes (bitter chocolate, liquorice).

NU DE LAVERNOYA 1999 RED
cabernet sauvignon, merlot

85 Garnet red cherry. Intense aroma with predominant smoky notes of oak and a fine reduction nuance (tobacco). Flavourful palate with well-integrated fruit and oak, excellent acidity with bitter and spicy notes (liquorice, chocolate) in the retronasal passage.

LLOPART

Carretera de Sant Sadurni al Ordal, km. 4
08739 Subirats (Barcelona)
☎: 938 993 125 - Fax: 938 993 038
llopart@llopart.es - llopart.es

Established: 1887

🌐 90 🗄 350,000 litres 🍇 70 has.
🚩 90% 🌐10%: -JP -DE -DK -US

LLOPART CHARDONNAY 2003 FERMENTADO EN BARRICA WHITE
100% chardonnay

83 Straw-coloured with a greenish hue. Not very intense aroma with a certain finesse, complementary white fruit and creamy, smoky oak notes. Dry, bitter palate, without great fruit expression, with a nuance of minerals and balsamic flavours.

CASTELL DE SUBIRATS 2000 RESERVA RED
merlot, cabernet sauvignon, tempranillo

85 Deep cherry with a saffron edge. Powerful aroma with an excellent varietal expression (black fruit, paprika, underbrush) and toasty hints of oak. Flavourful palate with well-integrated oak and fruit tannins; spicy, liquorice, very long.

LOXAREL

Masia Can Mayol, s/n
08735 Vilobí del Penedés (Barcelona)
☎: 938 978 001 - Fax: 938 978 111
canmayol@interceller.com
www.loxarel.com

CORA DE LOXAREL 2003 WHITE
moscatel, chardonnay, xarel.lo

82 Pale straw. Fine aroma with musky notes, ripe fruit (bananas, pineapples) and perfume. Fruity palate with notes of herbs, a mild sweetness and a bitter and mineral finish.

PETIT ARNAU DE LOXAREL 2003 ROSÉ
merlot, pinot noir

82 Raspberry. Intense aroma of jammy strawberries and redcurrants, expressive. Flavourful palate with copious fruit, good symmetry between fruit and bitter notes.

OPS DE LOXAREL 2003 OAK AGED RED
merlot, cabernet sauvignon, tempranillo

81 Garnet red cherry. Intense, fresh aroma with good expression of red fruit. Flavourful, fresh and expressive palate, well prepared.

LOXAREL 2001 RESERVA RED
100% cabernet sauvignon

85 Intense cherry. Aroma of ripe black fruit with smoky nuances of reduction and spices (cloves). Powerful, fleshy palate with spicy black fruit; well-assembled toasty crianza; long.

LOXAREL 1999 RESERVA RED
100% cabernet sauvignon

84 Dark cherry with a coppery edge. Intense aroma with fresh overtones of red fruit, a spicy oak nuance and balsamic hints. Flavourful palate with an excellent varietal expression, quite fresh oak tannins and good acidity.

GAIA DE LOXAREL 2003 OAK AGED WHITE
EOS DE LOXAREL 2003 OAK AGED RED
MAS CARGOLS DE LOXAREL 2002 RED

Cava MAGUST

Carretera BP-2151, 142
08776 Sant Pere de Riudebitlles (Barcelona)
☎: 938 997 054 - Fax: 938 997 054
cavamagust@terra.es

Established: 1996

🌐 5 🗄 20,000 litres 🍇 3 has 🚩 100%

MAGUST ROSÉ
MAGUST RED
MAGUST CRIANZA RED

MARÍA CASANOVAS

Montserrat, 117
08770 Sant Sadurní d'Anoia (Barcelona)
☎: 938 910 812 - Fax: 938 911 572
mariacasanovas@brutnature.com
www.brutnature.com

Established: 1982

🚩 95% 🌐5

ROIG OLLÉ XAREL.LO MACERAT WHITE
ROIG OLLÉ CABERNET SAUVIGNON ROSÉ
ROIG OLLÉ CABERNET SAUVIGNON RED

MARQUÉS DE MONISTROL

Monistrol D'Anoia, s/n
08770 Sant Sadurní D'Anoia (Barcelona)
☎: 938 910 276 - Fax: 938 183 328
adelgado@haciendas-espana.com
www.marquesdemonistrol.com

Established: 1882

🏭 8,000 📊 6,000,000 litres 🍷 60% 🌍40%

MARQUÉS DE MONISTROL BLANC DE BLANCS WHITE

77 Pale with greenish nuances. Intense, fruity, slightly oily aroma. Flavourful on the palate with fine bitter notes, hints of fine citrus fruit and a waxy nuance.

MARTÍ SERDÁ

Ctra. D'Igualada a Vilafranca, km. 31.300
08792 Santa Fe del Penedés (Barcelona)
☎: 938 974 411 - Fax: 938 974 405
martiserda@troc.es
www.martiserda.com

Established: 1986

🏭 100 📊 500,000 litres 🍇 30 has.
🍷 95% 🌍5%

MARTÍ SERDÁ FERMENTADO EN BARRICA
 WHITE
MARE NOSTRUM DE AGUJA WHITE
MARE NOSTRUM DE AGUJA ROSÉ
MARTÍ SERDÁ MERLOT RED

MAS CODINA

El Gorner, Mas Codina s/n
08797 Puigdalber (Barcelona)
☎: 938 988 166 - Fax: 938 988 166
cavesmascodina@hotmail.com

Established: 1970

🏭 44 📊 300,000 litres 🍇 40 has. 🍷 75%
🌍25%: -FR -DE -NL -DK -CH -UK -US -BE

MAS CODINA CUPATGE 2003 JOVEN WHITE
50% macabeo, 25% chardonnay, 20% xarel.lo, 5% moscatel

78 Pale with a greenish edge. Clear, varietal aroma with a suggestion of flowers and a nuance of lychees. Flavourful, fresh, slightly sweet palate, pleasant.

MAS CODINA COUPATGE 2003 JOVEN ROSÉ
60% merlot, 40% cabernet sauvignon

70 Raspberry with a salmon hue. Not very intense aroma, somewhat flawed, weak fruit. Better on the palate, fruity though with overtones of greeness.

MAS CODINA "VINYA FERRER" 1999 CRIANZA RED
100% cabernet sauvignon

87 Garnet red cherry with a coppery edge. Powerful aroma of macerated black fruit with hints of sour cherries in liqueur and fine spicy notes of oak. Flavourful on the palate with well-integrated

wood and fruit; fine bitter and balsamic notes and excellent acidity.

MAS COMTAL

Mas Comtal, 1
08739 Avinyonet del Penedés (Barcelona)
☎: 938 970 052 - Fax: 938 970 591
mascomtal@arrakis.es
www.mascomtal.com

Established: 1993

🏭 200 📊 220,000 litres 🍇 40 has.
🍷 50% 🌍50%

PETREA 2002 OAK AGED WHITE
chardonnay, xarel.lo

88 Golden yellow. Powerful aroma with predominant toasty oak notes, white stone fruit and spicy hints of lees, herbs and citrus fruit peel. Flavourful palate with well-integrated oak/fruit; complex, slightly warm and with good acidity.

MAS COMTAL POMELL DE BLANC 2003 WHITE
xarel.lo, chardonnay

84 Yellow straw with a greenish rim. Aroma of fresh herbs with a hint of tropical fruit and a not very intense aroma of fine lees. Very fresh palate with fruity notions.

MAS COMTAL ROSADO DE LÁGRIMA 2003 ROSÉ
merlot

86 Raspberry blush. Intense, sweet aroma (of strawberry and raspberry jelly) with a suggestion of herbs and aniseed. Intense palate with abundant sweet fruit well-complemented by bitter notes, excellent balance, long.

MAS COMTAL ANTISTIANA 2000 RED

89 Brilliant garnet red. Complex aroma of very ripe black fruit with hints of fine varnish and earth (orange peel). Fresh, flavourful palate, firm fruit tannins well-integrated with the oak; a fruity, very fresh finish with an earthy component.

PÉTREA 2000 RED
merlot

85 Cherry with an orangey rim. Mineral aroma of red fruit and new wood. Fleshy, round and persistent on the palate with marked tannins.

Sociedad Agraria de Transformación
MAS LLUET

Cal Tessu-Sant Marçal
08732 Castellví de la Marca (Barcelona)
☎: 938 918 153 - Fax: 938 918 153
sat.maslluet@sefes.es

MAS LLUET MERLOT RED

MAS OLIVÉ

Plaza Pont Roma, 17
08770 Sant Sadurní D'Anoia (Barcelona)
☎: 938 910 310 - Fax: 938 910 409
cavamasolive@yahoo.es

Established: 1929

🏭 50 🛢 40,000 litres 🍇 15 has.

🍷 85% 🍷15%: -NL -US

MAS OLIVER 2001 CRIANZA RED
85% cabernet sauvignon, 15% merlot

84 Deep cherry with a coppery edge. Intense aroma of ripe black fruit with a fine reduction nuance. Flavourful and fruity on the palate with well-integrated oak and a rich bitter nuance (liquorice, balsamic flavours), well-crafted crianza.

MAS OLIVÉ CABERNET RED

Caves MAS TINELL

Ctra. de Vilafranca-St. Martí Sarroca, km. 0,5
08720 Vilafranca del Penedés (Barcelona)
☎: 938 170 586 - Fax: 938 170 500
manuel@mastinell.com
www.mastinell.com

Established: 1989

🛢 370,000 litres 🍇 4 has. 🍷 95% 🍷5%

L'ALBA MAS TINELL BLANC DE LLUNA 2003 WHITE

83 Pale. Intense, fine aroma of ripe apples and white flor, overall harmony. Fresh, very fruity and expressive palate with good acidity-bitterness balance.

HERETAT MAS TINELL CHARDONNAY 2003 WHITE

84 Straw-coloured with a greenish hue. Fresh aroma of green apples and herbs, not very intense yet fine. Slightly oily palate with notes of green herbs and good fruit; very fresh and pleasant.

ARTE MAS TINELL 1998 RESERVA RED
50% cabernet sauvignon, 50% merlot

87 Garnet red cherry with a coppery edge. Intense aroma with an excellent varietal expression (black fruit, a herbaceous nuance, hints of paprika) and a toasty oak nuance. Flavourful, fleshy palate with ripe fruit and fairly ripe and rough oak tannins and a powerful effect in the retronasal passage (chocolate, liquorice, terroir).

MASET DEL LLEÓ

Av. Barcelona, 31
08734 Sant Pere Molanta (Barcelona)

☎: 902 200 250 - Fax: 938 921 333
info@maset.com
www.maset.com

Established: 1777

🏭 150 🛢 400,000 litres 🍇 50 has.

🍷 90% 🍷10%: -DE -US

MASET DEL LLEÓ BLANC DE BLANCS 2003 JOVEN WHITE
xarel.lo

82 Straw-coloured. Medium-intensity aroma of ripe apples; fine. Flavourful palate with a good sweetness-acidity balance; very pleasant drinking.

FLOR DEL MAR MASET DEL LLEÓ CHARDONNAY 2003 WHITE
chardonnay

72 Straw-coloured with a golden hue. Not very intense aroma of evolved fruit. Ripe fruit on the palate, lacking great expression but well-mannered.

MASET DEL LLEÓ MERLOT 2003 ROSÉ
merlot

79 Raspberry blush. Fairly short, yet clean aroma of nuts and red fruit. Flavourful and fruity on the palate, easy drinking.

MASET DEL LLEÓ CABERNET SAUVIGNON 2000 RESERVA RED
100% cabernet sauvignon

80 Intense cherry with a brick red edge. Intense aroma with predominant toasty wood notes and a nuance of jammy fruit. Slightly better in the mouth, flavourful palate with well-integrated fruit and oak.

MASET DEL LLEÓ GRAN ROBLE 2000 RESERVA RED
100% tempranillo

81 Intense cherry with a brick red edge. Intense aroma of jammy black fruit, toasty oak notes and a reduction nuance. Flavourful palate with ripe, oily tannins and a good expression of traditional crianza with a spicy nuance.

MASET DEL LLEÓ MERLOT 2000 RESERVA RED
merlot

75 Intense cherry with a coppery edge. Intense aroma with predominant reduction notes (leather, varnishes). Flavourful palate with astringent overtones, lacking balance.

MASÍA L'HEREU

Monistrol D'Anoia, s/n
08770 Sant Sadurni D'Anoia (Barcelona)
☎: 938 910 276 - Fax: 938 183 328
adelgado@haciendas-espana.com
www.haciendas-espana.com

Established: 1882

DO PENEDÈS

⊕ 8,000

MASÍA L'HEREU CABERNET SAUVIGNON 2000 ROBLE RED
cabernet sauvignon　　　　　　　　　　⊕ 17

85 Red with a brick red hue. Aroma of toasty wood, varietal typification and spices. Medium-bodied palate with lively acidity and good balance between the fruit tannins and wood.

MASÍA L'HEREU 2000 OAK AGED RED
cabernet sauvignon, merlot　　　　　　　⊕ 18

86 Very deep cherry. Powerful aroma with an excellent varietal expression (redcurrants, paprika), fine toasty oak and a balsamic essence. Flavourful, fleshy palate with ripe and oily tannins, a good oak/fruit integration, balsamic hints and spices and terroir in the retronasal passage.

MASÍA L'HEREU RESERVA PRIVADA 1999 RESERVA RED
cabernet sauvignon, merlot, tempranillo

84 Cherry with a brick red rim. Toasty, earthy aroma with light reduction notes. Flavourful, well-balanced palate with toasty notes in the retronasal passage.

MASÍA L'HEREU CHARDONNAY 2003 WHITE
MASÍA L'HEREU MERLOT 2001 CRIANZA RED

MASÍA PAPIOL

Masovería Papiol s/n
43720 L'Arboç del Penedés (Tarragona)
☎: 977 670 056 - Fax: 977 671 313
masiapapiol@masiapapiol.e.telefonica.net
Established: 1991
⊕ 10 🗄 160,000 litres
🌿 118 has. 🏴 100%

SANT PONÇ WHITE

MASÍA PUIGMOLTÓ

Barrio de Sant Marçal, s/n
08732 Castellet i La Gornal (Barcelona)
☎: 938 918 076 - Fax: 932 115 730
puigmolt@mento.net
Established: 1975
⊕ 20 🗄 100,000 litres 🌿 25 has.
🏴 95% 🌐5%

MASÍA PUIGMOLTÓ WHITE
MASÍA PUIGMOLTÓ ROSÉ
MASÍA PUIGMOLTÓ RED
MASÍA PUIGMOLTÓ 2001 CRIANZA RED

MASÍA SAGUÉ

Avinguda U, 43-45
08794 Les Cabanyes (Barcelona)
☎: 938 920 850 - Fax: 938 921 760
bodega@masiasague.com
www.masiasague.com
Established: 1919
⊕ 20 🗄 4,000,000 litres 🌿 80 has.
🏴 80% 🌐20%: -DE -JP -NL -DK -IE -CH

MASÍA SAGUÉ BLANC DE BLANCS 2003 WHITE
70% xarel.lo, 30% macabeo, parellada

83 Pale yellow. Intense aroma of white fruit with fine hints of minerals and green grass. Flavourful palate of ripe apples, fine vegetative notes and excellent balance.

MASÍA SAGUÉ ROSÉ 2003 ROSÉ
50% cabernet sauvignon, 25% merlot, 25% tempranillo

81 Very lively raspberry. Intense aroma of red fruit with hints of spices, slightly mineral. Dry, flavourful palate with red fruit, spicy notes of skins and excellent acidity.

MANUEL DE CABANYES 2000 CRIANZA RED
33% cabernet sauvignon, 33% tempranillo, 33% merlot

84 Garnet red cherry with a coppery edge. Powerful aroma, with predominant smoky notes and spicy oak notes. Flavourful, fruity palate with quite rough tannins and an oily texture; excellent expression of the crianza and quite long.

MASÍA SAGUÉ MERLOT 2002 RED
100% merlot

86 Intense cherry with a coppery edge. Intense aroma with an excellent varietal expression (black fruit, paprika, underbrush) and fine reduction notes. Flavourful palate with ripe, oily tannins, a powerful finish with bitter notes (chocolate, liquorice) and excellent acidity.

MASÍA SAGUÉ TEMPRANILLO 2001 RED
100% tempranillo

81 Garnet red cherry with a saffron edge. Not very intense aroma with fine notes of ripe fruit and toasty oak. Flavourful palate with well-integrated wood and fruit, a spicy nuance and a light acidic edge.

MASÍA SAGUÉ CABERNET SAUVIGNON 2000 RED
MANUEL DE CABANYES 1997 RESERVA RED

Cavas MESTRES

Plaça Ajuntament, 8
08770 Sant Sadurní D'Anoia (Barcelona)
☎: 938 910 043 - Fax: 938 911 611

mestrescava@bsab.com

Established: 1928

🛢 35 📊 150,000 litres 🌿 80 has.

🍷 95% 🍇5%: -DK -UK

MESTRES 2003 WHITE
macabeo, xarel.lo, chardonnay

75 Pale. Fruity aroma (pears) without great nuances of grapes, hints of flor. Simple, fruity and fresh on the palate.

MESTRES 2003 RED
tempranillo

84 Intense cherry with a violet edge. Intense, fresh, fruity aroma (excellent varietal character) with hints of petals and terroir. Flavourful palate with somewhat rough, ripe grape tannins and excellent acidity.

MESTRES MERLOT 2001 OAK AGED RED
merlot   🛢 8

86 Garnet red cherry with a coppery edge. Intense aroma of well-integrated fruit and oak with hints of prune stones and terroir. Flavourful, fruity palate with ripe, round tannins, fine bitter notes (liquorice, chocolate) and excellent symmetry.

MIGUEL TORRES

Miguel Torres Carbó, 6
08720 Vilafranca del Penedés (Barcelona)
☎: 938 177 400 - Fax: 938 177 444
webmaster@torres.es
www.torres.es

Established: 1870

🛢 20,000 📊 28,000,000 litres 🌿 2,122 has.

🍷 50% 🍇50%

FRANSOLA 2003 JOVEN WHITE
90% sauvignon blanc, 10% parellada

84 Straw-coloured with a yellow glimmer. Aroma with notes of very ripe Sauvignon (bananas, passion fruit), warm with mountain herbs. Notes of sweetness and hints of ripe fruit on the palate, less expressive than other years, flavourful.

VIÑA ESMERALDA 2003 JOVEN WHITE
85% moscatel, 15% gewürztraminer

85 Pale with golden nuances. Intense, fruity aroma with an excellent varietal expression (musky Muscatel, apricots) and hints of aniseed. Fresh, flavourful palate with fine bittersweet notes (sweet almonds), good acidity.

GRAN VIÑA SOL 2003 OAK AGED WHITE
85% chardonnay, 15% parellada

88 Brilliant pale yellow. Fresh aroma with an excellent varietal expression (green apples, hay, fennel) and fine hints of smoky oak. Fresh on the palate with white fruit, fine bitter notes and creamy (vanilla) hints of oak, excellent acidity.

WALTRAUD 2003 WHITE
100% riesling

87 Pale with golden nuances. Intense aroma of great finesse and varietal expression (honeyed, aniseed) over a suggestion of white stone fruit. Flavourful palate with fine bittersweet notes, jammy fruit and pollen, excellent acidity.

ATRIUM 2003 RED
100% merlot

87 Dark cherry with a purplish edge. Powerful aroma with good varietal expression (redcurrants, underbrush), fine toasty oak and a balsamic nuance. Flavourful and fleshy on the palate with slightly marked but fine and sweet tannins and fine bitter notes, the best Atrium in the last few years.

MAS LA PLANA 2000 OAK AGED RED
100% cabernet sauvignon

91 Intense cherry. Aroma with copious spicy and fruity nuances (redcurrants, coffee, dry underbrush) with toasty, creamy notes of oak and black fruit. Round, oily, elegant palate with flavourful and sweet yet persistent tannins, flavourful and long. One of the best Mas la Plana.

MAS BORRÁS 2002 OAK AGED RED
100% pinot noir

88 Cherry with an orange edge. Aroma with toasty notes, hints of brambles, ripe cassis and fine toasty oak. Round, oily palate with small and polished tannins, light, but persistent. Excellent sun-drenched Pinot Noir.

GRAN CORONAS 2001 RED
85% cabernet sauvignon, 15% tempranillo

83 Deep cherry. Powerful aroma of jammy black fruit with fine toasty oak notes and a suggestion of very varietal herbaceous freshness. Flavourful palate with slightly drying tannins and predominant toasty notes of oak and fruit.

GRAN SANGRE DE TORO 2001 RESERVA RED
60% garnacha tinta, 25% mazuelo, 15% syrah

81 Not very deep garnet red. Slightly alcoholic aroma with light notes of red fruit. Drying, warm palate with marked tannins and viscous notes in the retronasal passage.

RESERVA REAL 2000 RED
cabernet sauvignon, merlot, cabernet franc

94 Very intense cherry. Fine, delicate, toasty aroma of very ripe fruit and toasty notes (coffee, chocolate and pastries). Full, generous, fleshy and elegant palate with notes of southern Cabernet in the retronasal passage and lively but flavourful tannins, well-integrated in the wine. Outstanding improvement in a year.

MONASTELL

Girona, 30
08770 Sant Sadurní D'Anoia (Barcelona)

☎: 938 910 396 - Fax: 938 183 716

Established: 1954

🏭 10 🗄 25,000 litres 🏴 70% 🌐30%

ROCA GIBERT XAREL.LO FERMENTADO EN
BARRICA WHITE
ROCA GIBERT CABERNET SAUVIGNON RED

MONT MARÇAL VINÍCOLA

Finca Manlleu, s/n
08732 Castellví de la Marca (Barcelona)
☎: 938 918 281 - Fax: 938 919 045
direccion@mont-marcal.com
www.mont-marcal.com

Established: 1975

🏭 500 🗄 500,000 litres 🍇 40 has.
🏴 20% 🌐80%

MONT MARÇAL JOVEN WHITE
macabeo, xarel.lo, parellada

80 Straw-coloured with a greenish hue. Intense
aroma, fruity (green apples, hints of tropical fruit)
with a nuance of petals. Fresh, flavourful palate
with green fruit, good acidity.

MONT MARÇAL CHARDONNAY
FERMENTADO EN BARRICA WHITE
chardonnay

79 Pale yellow with a golden glint. Fairly intense
aroma with notes of ripe white fruit, creamy hints
of oak and a suggestion of honey. Flavourful palate, without great varietal character, lacks fruit-acidity-alcohol symmetry.

MONT MARÇAL JOVEN ROSÉ
tempranillo, merlot

82 Brilliant raspberry. Intense, very fresh aroma
of red stone fruit and a spicy nuance of skins.
Fresh, fruity palate with flavourful tannicity and
good acidity.

MONT MARÇAL JOVEN RED
tempranillo, merlot

84 Very deep cherry with a violet edge. Powerful,
fruity aroma with macerated black fruit and hints of
underbrush. Flavourful palate with very ripe fruit
and sun-drenched skins, good fruit-tanicity- acidity balance.

MONT MARÇAL CABERNET SAUVIGNON
1999 RESERVA RED
90% cabernet sauvignon, 10% merlot

84 Very deep cherry. Powerful aroma of ripe
black fruit with a toasty oak nuance, balsamic hints
and lees. Flavourful, concentrated palate with
complementary fruit-wood association and refreshing acidity.

MONT MARÇAL CABERNET-MERLOT 2000
RESERVA RED
cabernet sauvignon, merlot

83 Deep cherry with a saffron edge. Powerful,
very ripe aroma with excellent varietal expression
(paprika) and a toasty oak nuance. Flavourful,
fruity palate with well-integrated oak and hints of
spices and liquorice.

MONT MARÇAL MERLOT 2001 RED
merlot

83 Deep cherry with a saffron edge. Powerful
aroma with good varietal expression (black fruit,
underbrush). Flavourful, fruity palate with fine
herbaceous hints, well-integrated oak and fruit,
high acidity.

Caves MONT-FERRANT

Abat Escarré, 1
17300 Blanes (Girona)
☎: 934 191 000 - Fax: 934 193 170
montferrant@montferrant.com
www.montferrant.com

Established: 1865

🏴 95% 🌐5%

MAS FERRANT SONATINA WHITE
MAS FERRANT PINYA DE ROSA RED

MONTCAU

Can Castany, s/n
08790 Gelida (Barcelona)
☎: 937 790 066 - Fax: 937 914 850
montcau@interceller.com
www.interceller.com/montcau

Established: 1995

🏭 100 🗄 32,000 litres 🍇 40 has.
🏴 50% 🌐50%

BLANC D'ARQUER CHARDONNAY FERMEN-
TADO EN BARRICA WHITE
ALGENDARET WHITE
ALGENDARET RED

MONTESQUIUS

Rambla de la Generalitat s/n
08770 Sant Sadurni D'Anoia (Barcelona)
☎: 938 910 800 - Fax: 938 911 747
montesquius@montesquiuscom
www.montesquius.com

Established: 1918

🏴 90% 🌐10%

MONTESQUIUS WHITE
MONTESQUIUS ROSÉ
MONTESQUIUS CHARDONNAY ROSÉ
MONTESQUIUS RED

NADAL

Finca Can Nadal s/n
08775 El Pla del Penedés (Barcelona)
☎: 938 988 036 - Fax: 938 988 443
nadal@tnadal.com - visita@nadal.com
www.nadal.com

Established: 1943

🍇 16 🛢 1,600,000 litres 🍃 100 has.

🍷 90% 🌐10%: -NL -DK -CH -AD -CR -BE -JP -SG -AT -BO

DOLÇ D'OCTUBRE VENDIMIA TARDÍA 1998 WHITE DULCE
NADAL 1510 2000 WHITE
FINCA BOADELLA TRADICIONAL 2001 WHITE

Caves NAVERÁN (SADEVE)

Can Parellada Sant Martí Sadevesa
08775 Torrelavit (Barcelona)
☎: 938 988 274 - Fax: 938 989 027
sadeve@naveran.com
www.naveran.com

Established: 1986

🍇 400 🛢 900,000 litres 🍃 110 has.

🍷 60% 🌐40%: -FR -US -PR -JP -BE -NL -UK -IE -SE -CH -DE

MANUELA DE NAVERÁN 2002 CRIANZA WHITE
100% chardonnay

80 Golden yellow. Powerful aroma with predominant reduction notes. Generous palate with a slightly oily and warm texture with notes of nuts and spicy hints in the retronasal passage.

NAVERÁN BLANC DE BLANCS DE LA FINCA 2003 WHITE
20% macabeo, 50% xarel.lo, 30% chardonnay

82 Straw-coloured. Fairly intense aroma of white fruit with hints of green grass. Flavourful palate, with a slightly oily texture and fine bitter notes, good acidity.

NAVERÁN ROSADO DE LA FINCA 2003 RED
60% ull de llebre, 15% merlot, 15% pinot noir, 10% cabernet sauvignon

78 Brilliant raspberry. Intense, fruity aroma with fresh overtones. Fruity palate with an oily and warm texture, pleasant.

NAVERÁN CABERNET DE LA FINCA 2002 RED
60% tempranillo, 20% cabernet sauvignon, 20% merlot

79 Cherry with a saffron edge. Slightly intense aroma of black fruit with a paprika nuance and spicy hints of oak. Flavourful palate with ripe tan-

nins and an overpronounced herbaceous character in the retronasal passage.

NAVERÁN MERLOT 2001 RED
100% merlot

84 Very deep garnet red cherry. Powerful aroma of toasty oak with a nuance of superripe black fruit and hints of fine reduction. Fruity, fleshy palate with well-integrated oak and fruit; fine spicy notes, liquorice, good acidity.

NAVERÁN PINOT NOIR 2003 RED

70 Dark cherry. Aroma with notes of warm, rapid ripening and greenish skins with hints of sweetness. Flat palate, unusual and overripe aroma expressive and uninteresting green skins.

NAVERÁN 2000 CRIANZA RED
merlot, cabernet sauvignon

85 Garnet red cherry with a coppery edge. Intense aroma of jammy black fruit with fine reduction notes and toasty oak. Flavourful palate, rich in nuances with a good fruit/oak integration and balsamic and dark-roasted hints.

NAVERÁN DON PABLO 2000 RESERVA RED
100% cabernet sauvignon

86 Very deep garnet red cherry. Intense aroma with great finesse, jammy black fruit and toasty oak. Flavourful, fleshy palate with oak tannins complementing the fruit and a powerful effect in the retronasal passage (chocolate, balsamic flavours).

NAVERÁN CLOS DEL PI 1998 RESERVA RED
80% cabernet sauvignon, 10% merlot, 10% syrah

85 Very deep cherry with a coppery edge. Powerful aroma of very ripe black fruit with fine balsamic notes, toasty oak and reduction hints. Flavourful, fleshy palate with somewhat rough, ripe tannins; rich in nuances (liquorice, dark-roasted flavours), long.

CLOS ANTONIA 2002 CRIANZA WHITE

OLIVE BATLLORI

Barrio Els Casots, s/n
08739 Subirats (Barcelona)
☎: 938 993 103 - Fax: 938 995 700

Established: 1941

🛢 75,000 litres 🍃 15 has. 🍷 100%

OLIVE BATLLORI CABERNET SAUVIGNON 2000 RED

OLIVELLA I BONET

Casetes Puigmoltó, 26
43720 L'Arboç (Tarragona)
☎: 977 670 433 - Fax: 977 670 433

Established: 1988

OLIVELLA I BONET CABERNET SAUVIGNON RED
OLIVELLA I BONET MERLOT RED

PAGÉS ENTRENA

Ctra de Piera-Sant Sadurní D'Anoia, km. 10.1
08784 Sant Jaume Sesoliveres (Barcelona)
☎: 938 183 827 - Fax: 938 913 147
cava@pagesentrena.com
www.pagesentrena.com

Established: 1987
⊟ 187,700 litres ⚐ 100%

BARÓ DE VALLS 2002 WHITE
BARÓ DE VALLS 1999 CRIANZA RED

Bodegas PARATÓ

Can Respall de Renardes
08733 Pla del Penedès (Barcelona)
☎: 938 988 182 - Fax: 938 988 510
info@parato.es
www.parato.es

Established: 1975
⊕ 150 ⊟ 800,000 litres ⚘ 94 has.
⚐ 70% ⊕30%: -DE -BE -CH

PARATÓ COUPAGE 2003 JOVEN WHITE
50% macabeo, 30% parellada, 20% xarel.lo

74 Straw-coloured. Short aroma of nearly overripe yet clean fruit. Light, fresh palate with an element of acidity.

PARATÓ XAREL.LO 2003 JOVEN WHITE
100% xarel.lo

78 Pale straw. Medium-intensity aroma of green apples with a citrus fruit nuance (grapefruit). Fresh on the palate with an element of acidity, fruity and well-mannered.

PARATÓ XAREL.LO 2003 FERMENTADO EN BARRICA WHITE
100% xarel.lo

77 Straw-coloured with a coppery hue. Aroma with creamy wood notes that slightly conceal the fruit. Palate with heavy oak, dominated by dry tannins; well-mannered.

PARATÓ XAREL.LO XXV 2002 WHITE DULCE
100% xarel.lo

80 Golden yellow. Medium-intensity aroma with lemony notes and crystallised fruit. Sweet, flavourful and glyceric on the palate with notes of lemon sorbet, pleasant.

PARATÓ PINOT NOIR 2003 JOVEN ROSÉ
100% pinot noir

75 Lively raspberry. Not very intense aroma of very ripe fruit and a note of evolution. Better on the palate, fresh, flavourful and slightly bitter.

RENARDES 2001 OAK AGED RED
tempranillo, cabernet sauvignon ⬤ 6

82 Very deep cherry with a garnet red hue. Not very intense aroma with a nuance of black, macerated fruit and fine smoky wood hints. Flavourful palate with rough but promising tannins.

PARATÓ CLASSIC 2000 CRIANZA RED
75% tempranillo, 25% cabernet sauvignon

84 Very deep cherry with a coppery edge. Not very intense aroma with a certain finesse and well-integrated fruit and oak. Flavourful palate with quite rough tannins though ripe and oily; a ripe fruit nuance, spicy with bitter hints and liquorice.

PARÉS BALTÁ

Masía Can Baltá, s/n
08796 Pacs del Penedès (Barcelona)
☎: 938 901 399 - Fax: 938 901 143
paresbalta@paresbalta.com
wwwparesbalta.com

Established: 1790
⊕ 500 ⊟ 1,300,000 litres ⚘ 175 has.
⚐ 80% ⊕20%

PARÉS BALTÀ MAS DE CAROL 2003 FERMENTADO EN BARRICA WHITE
100% chardonnay

87 Golden yellow. Powerful aroma with predominant smoky, creamy wood notes, ripe apples and fine herbs. Flavourful palate with good varietal expression, and spicy notes (vanilla) of oak; generous and oily with excellent acidity.

ABSIS 2000 RESERVA RED
tempranillo, merlot, cabernet sauvignon, shiraz

91 Deep cherry. Aroma of black fruit with a fine character of skins, well-assembled wood (smoky flavours, spices). Fleshy, powerful palate with oily but marked tannins; persistent (liquorice, balsamic flavours), with varietal expression, long.

PARÉS BALTA MAS PONS 2003 WHITE
ELECTIO 2003 WHITE
RADIX SHIRAZ 2003 ROSÉ
MAS IRENE 1999 RESERVA RED

PERE MUNNÉ DURÁN

San Josep, 10-11-12
08784 Sant Jaume Sesrovires (Barcelona)
☎: 937 860 148 - Fax: 937 854 247

Established: 1989
⊕ 8 ⊟ 800 litres ⚘ 3 has. ⚐ 100%

PERE MUNNÉ DURÁN 2000 OAK AGED RED

PERE RIUS

Masia Pere Rius
08732 Castellvi de la Marca (Barcelona)
☎: 938 918 274 - Fax: 938 918 223
cavapererius@eresmas.com

Established: 1990
🌱 20 has. 🏴 100%

MASÍA PERE RIUS 2003 ROSÉ
MASÍA PERE RIUS 2002 RED

PERE VENTURA

Carretera de Vilafranca, km. 0.4
08770 Sant Sadurní D'Anoia (Barcelona)
☎: 938 183 371 - Fax: 938 912 679
pventura@interceller.com
www.pereventura.com

Established: 1992
🌐 500 📊 150,000 litres 🌱 14 has.
🏴 65% 🌍35%: -UE -NAM

PERE VENTURA CHARDONNAY 2003
JOVEN WHITE
100% chardonnay

82 Pale gold. Intense aroma with a good expression of varietal fruit (apples) and slightly exotic and floral hints. Flavourful, fruity palate with fine bitter notes and good acidity.

PERE VENTURA CHARDONNAY-XAREL.LO
2003 OAK AGED WHITE
50% chardonnay, 50% xarel.lo

80 Brilliant straw. Intense aroma of fine smoky oak with a spicy and slightly floral essence. Flavourful palate with fruit expression slightly muted by the alcohol and bitter oak notes.

INÈDIT 2003 ROSÉ
merlot

84 Very deep raspberry. Intense aroma with fine notes of ripe red stone fruit, hints of sun-drenched skins and spicy and slightly mineral hints. Flavourful, fruity palate with quality notes of bitterness and citrus fruit, a slightly oily texture.

PERE VENTURA CUPATGE 1999 RESERVA
ESPECIAL RED
cabernet sauvignon, merlot

82 Cherry with a ruby red edge. Smoky aroma with rustic hints and sun-drenched skins. Spicy palate with ripe tannins, dominant oak, fresh overtones and some reduction.

PERE VENTURA TEMPRANILLO 2001
CRIANZA RED
tempranillo, cabernet sauvignon

77 Cherry with a garnet red edge. Aroma of ripe black fruit, some evolution and an earthy essence. Flavourful, slightly rustic palate with marked oak tannins over the fruit, fresh.

PERE VENTURA CABERNET SAUVIGNON
2000 RESERVA RED
cabernet sauvignon, tempranillo

82 Cherry with a ruby red edge. Peppery, varietal, slightly rustic aroma. Fleshy, powerful palate, with ripe, finished tannins, notes of Cabernet and a bitter, very well-balanced wood finish.

PERE VENTURA 2003 WHITE SECO

Sociedad Agraria de Transformación
PIJOAN ESCOFET

Finca Mas Les Planes. Apdo. nº5
43717 La Bisbal del Penedés (Tarragona)
☎: 977 169 906 - Fax: 977 169 907
pijoanescofet@terra.es

Established: 1999
🌐 40 📊 55,000 litres 🌱 40 has.
🏴 50% 🌍50%

MIL.LIARI ROSA DE LES CLOTES
 FERMENTADO EN BARRICA WHITE
MIL.LIARI CHARDONNAY WHITE
MIL.LIARI XAREL.LO WHITE
MIL.LIARI CABERNET SAUVIGNON ROSÉ
MIL.LIARI MERLOT-CABERNET SAUVIGNON
RED

Bodegas PINORD

Doctor Pasteur, 6
08720 Vilafranca del Penedés (Barcelona)
☎: 938 903 066 - Fax: 938 170 979
pinord@pinord.es
www.pinord.com

Established: 1942
🌐 2,000 📊 4,000,000 litres 🌱 100 has.
🏴 78% 🌍22%: -US -DE -UK -JP -FR -AT
-BE -DK -FI -EL -IT -MT -NL -DK -MX -BR -
DO -IE -IS

PINORD CHARDONNAY 2003 JOVEN WHITE
100% chardonnay

80 Pale golden yellow. Fairly intense aroma with overtones of fresh varietal fruit and hints of dried grass. Flavourful and bitter on the palate with fine spicy and herby notes, a slightly oily texture and good acidity.

PINORD VIÑA CHATEL BLANC DE BLANCS
2003 JOVEN WHITE
macabeo, xarel.lo, parellada

82 Pale with a greenish hue. Intense aroma with green apple notes, green grass and rich hints of citrus fruit. Fresh, flavourful and bitter on the palate with a slightly acidic edge.

PINORD VIÑA MIREIA 2003 JOVEN WHITE
moscatel, gewürztraminer

75 Steely straw. Aroma of very ripe white stone fruit, perfumed with sweet notes. Warm and light on the palate with an element of sweetness.

PINORD CHARDONNAY 2000 FERMENTADO EN BARRICA WHITE
100% chardonnay

75 Brilliant yellow. Aroma of wax and vanilla with very ripe peaches. Very obvious wood tannins on the palate.

PINORD LA NANSA 2003 WHITE DE AGUJA
100% macabeo

76 Pale with a greenish hue. Fairly intense, fresh and fruity aroma. Fresh on the palate with a fine carbonic hint, excellent bitter notes and good acidity.

PINORD REYNAL 2003 WHITE DE AGUJA
macabeo, xarel.lo, parellada

79 Pale yellow. Not very intense aroma of ripe white fruit with hints of petals. Flavourful on the palate with pleasant bittersweet notes, fresh and creamy overtones.

PINORD VIÑA CHATEL TEMPRANILLO 2003 JOVEN ROSÉ
tempranillo, cariñena

78 Brilliant raspberry. Fairly intense aroma of ripe red fruit with oily hints. Dry and flavourful on the palate with fine bitter notes, hints of citrus fruit and a slightly acidic edge.

PINORD COLL DE BOU MERLOT 2003 OAK AGED ROSÉ
100% merlot

81 Brilliant raspberry. Intense, ripe aroma of red fruit with a toasty and slightly creamy suggestion. Generous and fruity on the palate with fine bitter notes and an oily and warm texture.

PINORD 2003 ROSÉ DE AGUJA
tempranillo, garnacha

72 Raspberry with coppery nuances. Powerful aroma of very ripe red fruit with hints of lees. Fruity, slightly creamy and pleasant on the palate.

PINORD PI DEL NORD CABERNET SAUVIGNON 1998 OAK AGED RED
100% cabernet sauvignon

88 Garnet red cherry with an orangey edge. Intense aroma with fine toasty and creamy oak notes and an excellent varietal expression (redcurrants, paprika). Flavourful and fleshy on the palate with oak tannins well-integrated with fruit tannins and a fine bitter nuance (chocolate, liquorice).

PINORD CLOS 15 MERLOT 2001 CRIANZA RED
100% merlot

83 Cherry with an orangey hue. Aroma with toasty and mildly vegetative notes (pepper) and fruity hints. Powerful, fruity, varietal, pleasant palate with dry Merlot tannins and a suggestion of fresh fruit.

PINORD VIÑA CHATEL TEMPRANILLO 2001 CRIANZA RED
tempranillo, merlot

82 Cherry with an orangey edge. Intense, spicy (pepper), slightly balsamic aroma with oak notes well-integrated with the fruit. Flavourful, balsamic and balanced on the palate with a spicy finish and an adequate woody contribution.

PINORD CHATELDON CABERNET SAUVIGNON 2000 RESERVA RED
cabernet sauvignon, merlot

86 Garnet red cherry with a saffron edge. Intense aroma of ripe black fruit with fine herbaceous notes and a spicy wood nuance. Flavourful on the palate with well-integrated oak/fruit, an excellent varietal and crianza expression;. well-balanced and long.

PINORD CHATELDON CABERNET SAUVIGNON 1997 GRAN RESERVA RED
cabernet sauvignon, merlot

81 Cherry with a brick red edge. Aroma with reduction notes (tobacco, vanilla) and toasty wood (coffee). Round and flavourful on the palate with jammy fruit, well-mannered despite the rather pronounced oak notes.

PINORD REYNAL 2003 RED DE AGUJA

Cavas PUIG MUNTS

Revall, 38
08760 Martorell (Barcelona)
☎: 937 755 216 - Fax: 937 740 213
puigmunts@terra.es
www.puigmnts.com

Established: 1940

🌱 254 has. 🍷 95% 🌐5%: -DE -LV -PL -AD -US -TR

PUIG MUNTS WHITE
PUIG MUNTS ROSÉ
PUIG MUNTS RED

PUPITRE

Avinguda Jacint Verdaguer, 8
43720 L'Arboc del Penedés (Tarragona)
☎: 977 670 055 - Fax: 977 670 353
caycra@caycra.com
www.caycra.com

DO PENEDÈS

Established: 1919

🌐 500 📊 15,000,000 litres 🍇 1,100 has.

🍷 70% 🍇30%

PUPITRE CHARDONNAY 2002 OAK AGED
 WHITE
CASTELL GORNAL CHARDONNAY 2003
 WHITE
CASTELL GORNAL BLANC DE BLANCS 2003
 WHITE
CASTELL GORNAL 2003 JOVEN ROSÉ
CASTELL GORNAL 2003 JOVEN RED
PUPITRE CABERNET SAUVIGNON 2000
 CRIANZA RED
PUPITRE TEMPRANILLO 2000 CRIANZA RED
CASTELL GORNAL MERLOT 2003 CRIANZA
 RED

RAMÓN CANALS CANALS

Av. Mare de Deu Montserrat, 9
08769 Castellví de Rosanes (Barcelona)
☎: 937 755 446 - Fax: 937 741 719
cava@rcanalscanals.com
www.rcanalscanals.com

Established: 1974

🌐 150 📊 50,000 litres 🍇 20 has.

🍷 80% 🍇20%: -US -JP -DE -AD -UK

CHARDONNAY R. CANALS CANALS 2002
 WHITE
MASIA SUBIRANA XAREL.LO 2003 WHITE
VINYA DELS ANGELS 2003 WHITE
VINYA DELS ANGELS ROSÉ
RAMON CANALS CANALS CABERNET
 SAUVIGNON 2003 ROSÉ
MASIA SUBIRANA CABERNET SAUVIGNON
 2001 OAK AGED RED
MERLOT R. CANALS CANALS 2001 OAK
 AGED RED

RAVENTOS GUASCH

Industria, 29-31
08770 Sant Sadurni D'Anoia (Barcelona)
☎: 938 910 400 - Fax: 938 910 425
cava@raventossoler.com
www.raventossoler.com

Established: 1925

🍷 100%

RAVENTÓS SOLER WHITE
RAVENTÓS SOLER RED

RAVENTÓS I BLANC

Plaça del Roure
08770 Sant Sadurní D'Anoia (Barcelona)

☎: 938 183 262 - Fax: 938 312 500
raventos@raventos.com
www.raventos.com

Established: 1986

🌐 172 📊 683,000 litres 🍇 90 has.

🍷 80% 🍇20%: -DE -UK -CH -AT -BE -NL
SDV -US -JP

PERFUM DE VI BLANC 2003 JOVEN WHITE
60% macabeo, 40% moscatel

84 Straw-coloured. Intense, fresh aroma; grapey and musky. Flavourful, full palate with an expressive touch of glycerin, fruity, well-balanced and very well elaborated.

PRELUDI CLOS DEL SERRAL 2003 WHITE
50% xarel.lo, 35% macabeo, 15% chardonnay

84 Straw-coloured with a greenish hue. Good, intense, expressive aroma of apples and fine, ripe pears. Flavourful palate with abundant fresh, ripe fruit and good acidity.

RAVENTÓS I BLANC CHARDONNAY 2003
WHITE
100% chardonnay

86 Brilliant pale yellow. Intense aroma with fresh overtones, notes of green apples and hints of high quality citrus fruit. Fresh and very flavourful on the palate, with excellent varietal expression, well-balanced and with a mineral nuance.

LA ROSA DE RAVENTÓS I BLANC 2003 ROSÉ
100% merlot

85 Lively raspberry. Intense, expressive aroma with red fruit (cherries) and strawberry jelly. Very flavourful, fresh and fruity on the palate with a pleasant bitter counterpoint, long, excellent elaboration.

L'HEREU DE RAVENTÓS I BLANC 2003
JOVEN RED
70% tempranillo, 20% merlot, 10% cabernet sauvignon

83 Cherry with a violet hue. Lactic aroma (strawberry cream) with blackberries and red stone fruit. Robust and ripe tannins on the palate, well-balanced and medium to low-bodied.

ISABEL NEGRA 2001 OAK AGED RED
50% merlot, 50% cabernet sauvignon

88 Intense cherry with a saffron edge. Powerful aroma of ripe fruit with excellent varietal character, a spicy oak nuance and balsamic hints. Flavourful palate with well-integrated fruit and oak, fine bitter notes, excellent structure and balance.

ISABEL NEGRA 2002 OAK AGED RED
50% merlot, 50% cabernet sauvignon

86 Intense cherry. Aroma with peppery Cabernet Sauvignon and fine toasty oak notes. Fleshy, flavourful, varietal palate, fruity.

MONTSERRAT BLANC 2003 WHITE

RECAREDO

Tamarit, 10
08770 Sant Sadurní D'Anoia (Barcelona)
☎: 938 910 214 - Fax: 938 911 697
cava@recaredo.es
www.recaredo.com

Established: 1924

⊞ 145 ▤ 400,000 litres ❧ 45 has.

🍷 98% 🌐 2%: -AD -DE -JP

RECAREDO CHARDONNAY CRIANZA
WHITE

Vins REFILAT

Agustí Manaut, 15
17539 Bolvir de Cerdanya (Girona)
☎: 972 895 03 - Fax: 972 883 156
refilat@mailpersonal.com

Established: 1863

⊞ 120 ▤ 180,000 litres 🍷 100%

REFILAT WHITE
70% xarel.lo, 15% macabeo, 15% parellada

82 Straw-coloured with a coppery glint. Intense, somewhat fresh aroma of ripe white fruit with fine hints of exotic fruit. Fresh, fruity, dry palate with a slightly oily texture, and excellent acidity.

REFILAT ROSÉ
50% tempranillo, 50% cabernet sauvignon

81 Brilliant raspberry. Intense aroma of ripe red fruit and fresh overtones. Fresh, flavourful palate with fine spicy notes of skins and excellent acidity.

REFILAT 1999 CRIANZA RED
20% tempranillo, 40% cabernet sauvignon, 40% merlot

86 Very deep cherry with a coppery edge. Powerful aroma with an excellent varietal expression, fine smoky oak notes and hints of terroir. Flavourful, fleshy palate with well-integrated oak and grape tannins, spicy notes (paprika, pepper), a fine herbaceous nuance and bitter chocolate.

REFILAT RED

RENÉ BARBIER

Afueras, s/n
08770 Sant Sadurní D'Anoia (Barcelona)
☎: 938 917 000 - Fax: 938 911 254
renebarbier@renebarbier.es

RENÉ BARBIER CHARDONNAY SELECCIÓN
2002 FERMENTADO EN BARRICA WHITE
chardonnay

85 Golden yellow. Intense aroma with predominant smoky and creamy oak notes. Flavourful on the palate with excellent varietal expression (ripe apples) and well-integrated oak and fruit with fine toasty notes of dried herbs in the retronasal passage, very long.

RENÉ BARBIER CHARDONNAY VARIETAL 2003 WHITE
chardonnay

77 Very pale yellow. Fresh, slightly fruity aroma with good varietal expression (apples, fine herbs). Flavourful and quite fruity on the palate with a slightly acidic edge.

RENÉ BARBIER KRALINER 2003 WHITE
xarel.lo, macabeo, parellada

83 Pale yellow with a greenish glint. Intense, fruity aroma with fresh overtones of citrus fruit and herbs. Fresh on the palate with notes of green apples, hints of citrus fruit and a slightly acidic edge.

RENÉ BARBIER TRADICIÓN 2003 ROSÉ
garnacha, tempranillo, monastrell

83 Very lively raspberry. Intense, fresh aroma of ripe red fruit (crystallised nuance) with spicy hints of skins. Fresh and fruity on the palate with fine bitter notes, a slightly oily texture and a rich nuance of citrus fruit.

RENÉ BARBIER CABERNET SAUVIGNON 1999 RED

80 Very deep garnet red. Toasty aroma, with fine fruit reduction notes, a varietal essence (paprika). Fleshy palate, marked and drying oak tannins, black fruit, spices, slightly warm and ripe finish.

RENÉ BARBIER CABERNET SAUVIGNON VARIETAL 2002 RED
cabernet sauvignon

81 Cherry with an orangy hue. Aroma with hints of reduction and varietal typification. Good acidity with quite marked tannins, medium-bodied.

RENÉ BARBIER CLASSIC RED SEMISECO
tempranillo, garnacha, monastrell

74 Cherry with a garnet red-orangey edge. Slightly short, closed aroma and a ripe fruit nuance. Round, supple palate without great fruit expression yet well-mannered.

RENÉ BARBIER XAREL.LO VARIETAL 2002
WHITE
RENÉ BARBIER 2002 RED

RIMARTS

Avenida Cal Mir, 42
08770 Sant Sadurní D'Anoia (Barcelona)
☎: 938 912 775 - Fax: 938 912 775

rimarts@rimarts.net
www.rimarts.net

Established: 1987

🍇 90% 🍷10%

RIMARTS CHARDONNAY 2001 WHITE
65% chardonnay, 25% otras

86 Brilliant yellow with a golden hue. Powerful aroma with an excellent varietal expression (ripe apples, white petals) and smoky and creamy hints of wood. Flavourful, slightly oily and warm on the palate with excellent toasty oak, herby notes and wax, long.

RIMARTS MERLOT 2003 ROSÉ
100% merlot

85 Brilliant raspberry. Intense, fruity aroma (cassis syrup) with hints of spices and orange peel. Flavourful on the palate with fine bitter notes, fine toasty skins and excellent acidity.

RIMARTS CABERNET SAUVIGNON - MERLOT 2001 OAK AGED RED
66% cabernet sauvignon, 34% merlot

85 Garnet red cherry with a coppery edge. Intense aroma with very varietal fruit notes (redcurrants, paprika) and fine spicy oak notes. Flavourful on the palate with well-integrated oak/fruit, fine bitter (chocolate, pitch) and balsamic notes.

ROBERT J. MUR

Rambla de la Generalitat s/n
08770 Sant Sadurni D'Anoia (Barcelona)
☎: 938 910 800 - Fax: 938 911 747
roberjmur@robertjmur.com
www.robertjmur.com

Established: 1897

🍇 20 has. 🍷 85% 🍷15%: -DE -UK -FR -JP Benelux -MX -US -CA

ROBERT J. MUR JOVEN WHITE SECO
ROBERT J. MUR JOVEN ROSÉ
ROBERT J. MUR JOVEN RED
ROBERT J. MUR CABERNET SAUVIGNON CRIANZA RED

Cava ROMAGOSA TORNÉ

Finca - Rodamilans - La Serra
08731 Sant Martí Sarroca (Barcelona)
☎: 938 991 353 - Fax: 938 991 558
montse@romagosatorné.com

Established: 1864

🍷 75% 🍷25%: -BE -DE

ROMAGOSA TORNÉ JOVEN WHITE
ROMAGOSA TORNÉ JOVEN ROSÉ
ROMAGOSA TORNÉ RESERVA RED

ROSELL GALLART

Cl. Montserrat, 56
08770 Sant Sadurní d'Anoia (Barcelona)
☎: 938 912 073 - Fax: 938 183 539
rosellgallart@terra.es

Established: 1845

🍇 5 has. 🍷 100%

VINUET XAREL.LO JOVEN WHITE
VINUET CRIANZA RED

ROVELLATS

Finca Rovellats
08731 Sant Marti Sarroca (Barcelona)
☎: 934 880 575 - Fax: 934 880 819
rovellats@cavasrovellats.com
www.cavasrovellats.com

Established: 1940

🍇 210 has. 🍷 75% 🍷25%

ROVELLATS BLANC DE PRIMAVERA 2003 JOVEN WHITE
ROVELLATS CHARDONNAY 2003 JOVEN WHITE
ROVELLATS BLANC DE MACERACIÓ 2001 CRIANZA WHITE
ROVELLATS BRU DE TARDOR 2001 RED

SEGURA VIUDAS

Apdo. Correos , 30
08775 Torrelavit (Barcelona)
☎: 938 917 070 - Fax: 938 996 006
seguraviudas@seguraviudas.com
www.seguraviudas.com

Established: 1954

🍷 2,100 🍷 25,000,000 litres 🍇 50 has. 🍷 40% 🍷60%

CREU DE LAVIT 2003 WHITE
xarel.lo

85 Straw-coloured with a greenish glint. Fine aroma of slightly ripe white fruit with expression of fine lees (lavender) and notes of nuts. Flavourful and slightly oily on the palate with good freshness and predominant fruit with hints of herbs of the vine variety, lacking woody presence.

VIÑA HEREDAD BLANC DE BLANCS 2003 WHITE
macabeo, xarel.lo, parellada

83 Pale yellow with a greenish glint. Fairly intense aroma of green fruit with hints of petals and ripe citrus fruit. Fresh and dry on the palate with excellent acidity.

VIÑA HEREDAD 2003 ROSÉ
tempranillo, garnacha, cariñena

75 Raspberry with an orangey hue. Intense aroma with fruity notes and spicy hints of skins. Quite fresh on the palate with fine bitter notes and an acidic edge.

MAS D'ARANYÓ 2000 RESERVA RED

83 Cherry with a garnet red edge. Medium-intensity aroma with a note of reduction and ripe fruit. Very flavourful, powerful palate with ripe fruit and toasty wood, quite persistent.

SEGURA VIUDAS CABERNET SAUVIGNON 2002 RED
100% cabernet sauvignon

78 Deep cherry with a saffron edge. Intense, slightly fruity aroma, very varietal (paprika) with herbaceous hints. Dry, bitter palate with very marked grape tannins and a lack of fruit-acidity-alcohol symmetry.

SOLA RAVENTÓS

Industria, 38-40
08770 Sant Sadurní D'Anoia (Barcelona)
☎: 938 910 837 - Fax: 938 911 144
cava@solaraventos.com
www.solaraventos.com

Established: 1898

🔲 10,000 litres 🍷 100%

SOLA RAVENTÓS JOVEN WHITE
SOLA RAVENTÓS ROSÉ
SOLA RAVENTÓS RED
SOLA RAVENTÓS CABERNET SAUVIGNON RED

SOLER Y DEGOLLADA

Barri La Serra d Sabanell, s/n
08736 Font-Rubí (Barcelona)
☎: 938 988 220 - Fax: 938 988 681
info@cavamartinsoler.com
www.cavamartinsoler.com

Established: 1965

🔲 325,000 litres 🌿 20 has.

🍷 98% 🌐2%: -DE -FR -BE

MARTIN SOLER WHITE SECO
macabeo, xarel.lo, parellada

79 Very pale yellow. Intense, fruity aroma of green fruit with fine exotic notes and green grass. Dry, bitter palate with fresh overtones and high acidity.

MARTIN SOLER ROSÉ

80 Raspberry with a coppery glint. Intense aroma of very ripe red fruit with mild hints of reduction.

Flavourful, fruity palate with spicy notes of skins and good acidity.

MARTIN SOLER 2000 CRIANZA RED

74 Garnet red cherry. Intense aroma of black fruit with not very fine hints of crianza in the oak. Flavourful palate without great fruit expression, with bitter notes, lacks balance.

SOLER-JOVÉ

Finca Prunamala, Parc. 2
08770 Sant Sadurní D'Anoia (Barcelona)
☎: 938 910 503 - Fax: 938 911 153
solerjove@sct.ictnet.es
www.solerjove.com

Established: 1985

⊕ 200 🔲 275,000 litres 🍷 60%

🌐40%: -DE -UK -DK -DK -SE

SOLER JOVÉ 2003 WHITE
SOLER JOVÉ 2003 ROSÉ
SOLER JOVÉ 2000 CRIANZA RED

Bodegues SUMARROCA

El Rebato, s/n
08739 Subirats (Barcelona)
☎: 938 911 092 - Fax: 938 911 778
sumarroca@sumarroca.es
www.sumarroca.es

Established: 1983

⊕ 727 🔲 3,500,000 litres 🌿 460 has.

🍷 80% 🌐20%: -US -CH -DE -GT -JP -NL -UK -SE -BR -BE -SV

SUMARROCA BLANC DE BLANCS 2003 WHITE
41% xarel.lo, 20% macabeo, 22% parellada, 10% moscatel, 7% sauvignon blanc

78 Straw-coloured. Fairly short aroma with a nuance of fruit and hay. Fruity palate with an element of acidity, pleasant.

SUMARROCA CHARDONNAY 2003 WHITE
100% chardonnay

84 Straw-coloured. Very intense, fine aroma of ripe fruit (apples) with a nuance of hay, harmonious. Flavourful, varietal, ripe Chardonnay on the palate, excellent symmetry.

SUMARROCA GEWÜRZTRAMINER 2003 WHITE
100% gewürztraminer

82 Yellow straw. Intense aroma of green herbs and musky notes. Fruity, flavourful, well-balanced palate.

SUMARROCA GRAN BLANC DE BLANCS 2003 WHITE
50% chardonnay, 27% moscatel, 16% sauvignon blanc, 7% riesling

84 Straw-coloured. Intense aroma of ripe fruit (apples, pears), grapey, harmonious. Flavourful on the palate with an oily element and fine smoky oak well-integrated with ripe fruit; well-elaborated.

SUMARROCA MUSCAT 2003 WHITE
100% moscatel

82 Straw-coloured. Medium-intensity aroma, grapey and musky with a herby nuance. Flavourful, herby palate with good acidity, well-balanced.

SUMARROCA RIESLING 2003 WHITE
100% riesling

80 Straw-coloured. Not very intense aroma although fresh and fruity (grapey). Flavourful, fruity palate but without vine variety character.

SIRIUS 2003 RED
65% tempranillo, 30% garnacha, 5% merlot

83 Brilliant cherry with a coppery edge. Intense, ripe aroma with fine smoky notes of oak and balsamic hints. Flavourful on the palate with ripe tannins, fine bitter notes and excellent acidity.

BORIÁ SUMARROCA 2001 RED
77% syrah, 12% cabernet sauvignon, 11% merlot

91 Very deep garnet red cherry. Intense, very fine aroma of well-integrated toasty oak and black fruit notes with a slightly mineral and balsamic nuance. Powerful, concentrated and ripe on the palate with slightly marked yet promising oak tannins; fine bitter notes (chocolate, liquorice, pitch), well-structured and long.

SUMARROCA SANTA CREU DE CREIXÀ 2001 RED
36% tempranillo, 18% syrah, 17% garnacha, 12% cabernet franc

80 Garnet red with a ruby red hue. Aroma of dark-roasted flavours and chocolate with a nuance of red fruit. A somewhat astringent, drying palate with wood that conceals the fruit, little persistent.

SUMARROCA CABERNET SAUVIGNON 2000 OAK AGED RED
100% cabernet sauvignon
🍷 15

86 Garnet red cherry with a coppery edge. Intense aroma with predominant toasty notes of oak, and a balsamic nuance and jammy black fruit. Flavourful on the palate with well-integrated fruit and oak; fine bitter crianza notes (chocolate, pitch).

SUMARROCA MERLOT 1999 CRIANZA RED
100% merlot

83 Brick garnet red. Aroma with varietal typification (pepper, earth) and mountain herbs. Slightly herbaceous, drying palate with well-integrated wood and fine toasty notes in the retronasal passage.

SUMARROCA SAUVIGNON BLANC 2003 WHITE
SUMARROCA 2003 ROSÉ
SUMARROCA PINOT NOIR 2003 ROSÉ

TORELLÓ

Can Martí de Baix Apdo. 8,
08770 Sant Sadurni D'Anoia (Barcelona)
☎: 938 910 793 - Fax: 938 910 877
torrello@torello.es
www.torello.es

Established: 1951

🌐 60 📊 700,000 litres 🍇 110 has.

🍷 85% 🌐15%: -JP -MX -IT -AD

CRISALYS 2003 WHITE
100% xarel.lo

84 Pale with a greenish edge. Intense aroma of tropical fruit (papaya, pineapple) with herbaceous notes and toasty hints of skins. Bitter, fresh palate with good acidity, green fruit pulp character; long.

RAIMONDA 2001 CRIANZA RED
40% cabernet sauvignon, 30% merlot, 30% tempranillo

79 Garnet red with an orangey rim. Aroma of not very ripe red fruit, toasty, pepper. Drying palate, light, slightly astringent.

BLANC TRANQUILLE 2003 WHITE

Bodegas TORRE DEL VEGUER

Urb. Torre de Veguer, s/n
08810 Sant Pere de Ribes (Barcelona)
☎: 938 963 190 - Fax: 932 374 931
torredelveguer@torredelveguer.com
www.torredelveguer.com

Established: 1995

🌐 100 📊 92,000 litres 🍇 70 has.

🍷 90% 🌐10%

TORRE DEL VEGUER MUSCAT 2003 WHITE
100% muscat de Frotignan

82 Pale straw. Intense aroma, grapey, fresh, varietal. Flavourful, full, fresh, fruity and very pleasant palate with a herby finish.

TORRE DEL VEGUER SAUVIGNON BLANC 2003 WHITE
100% sauvignon blanc

84 Straw-coloured with a greenish hue. Very intense aroma of exotic fruit (grapefruit, passion fruit). Flavourful, oily and overwhelming palate with ripe fruit; well-balanced, quite persistent.

TORRE DEL VEGUER MERLOT 2003 ROSÉ
100% merlot

81 Raspberry with a violet hue. Intense, fresh and fruity aroma. Flavourful palate of sweet fruit, expressive, well-balanced and well-elaborated.

MARQUES DE FERRER-VIDAL 2001 OAK AGED RED
60% merlot, 12,5% cariñena, 12,5% tempranillo, 15% cabernet sauvignon

77 Garnet red cherry with a saffron edge. Intense aroma with mild reduction off-odours (tobacco, varnishes). Flavourful palate with a ripe fruit nuance and spicy hints of oak, lacks balance (high acidity).

TORRE DEL VEGUER CABERNET SAUVIGNON 2001 OAK AGED RED
85% cabernet sauvignon, 7% cariñena, 4% tempranillo, 4% merlot

83 Intense cherry with a saffron edge. Intense aroma, fresh overtones of varietal fruit, spicy notes of the crianza. Intense palate, with predominant crianza notes, a suggestion of ripe fruit (herbaceous hints), spicy and white chocolate nuances, a waxy suggestion, marked acidity.

RAÏMS DE LA IMMORTALITAT 1999 RESERVA RED
95% cabernet sauvignon, 5% pinot noir

88 Intense cherry with a brick red edge. Intense aroma of jammy black fruit with a toasty wood nuance. Powerful, concentrated palate with fairly rough oak tannins well-integrated with the grape tannins and a slightly oily texture, excellent aroma in the retronasal passage of chocolate and spices.

RAÏMS DE LA IMMORTALITAT 2001 WHITE
TORRE DEL VEGUER 2000 OAK AGED RED

TORRENS & MOLINER

Avenida Casetes del Mir, 28
08770 Sant Sadurní D'Anoia (Barcelona)
☎: 938 911 033 - Fax: 938 911 761
tormol@torrensmoliner.com
www.torrensmoliner.com

Established: 1986

▦ 25,000 litres ❦ 5 has.

🍷 85% 🌐15%: -MX -NL

TORRENS & MOLINER D'ANYADA 2003 WHITE
TORRENS & MOLINER 2002 CRIANZA RED
TORRENS & MOLINER 2001 RESERVA RED

Vins-Caves TUTUSAUS

Can Tutusaus, s/n
08795 Olesa de Bonesvalls (Barcelona)
☎: 938 984 155
cavestutusaus@hotmail.com
Established: 1987

▦ 10 ▤ 20,000 litres ❦ 8 has.
🍷 85% 🌐15%: -BE -NL

TUTUSAUS - VACC DOCINA 2003 RED

U MES U FAN TRES

Masia Navinés (Els Pujols)
08736 Font-Rubí (Barcelona)
☎: 938 974 069 - Fax: 938 974 724
navines@interceller.com

Established: 2000

▦ 350 ❦ 30 has.
🍷 15% 🌐85%

XAREL.LO 1+1=3 2001 FERMENTADO EN BARRICA WHITE
100% xarel.lo

82 Yellow straw. Good intensity aroma with lactic wood notes and a nuance of white fruit. Flavourful, slightly oily and warm on the palate with wood yet to be integrated and a bitter finish.

CABERNET SAUVIGNON 1+1= 3 2003 ROSÉ
100% cabernet sauvignon

83 Lively raspberry. Intense, expressive aroma with forest fruits (raspberries, berries, redcurrants) with a nuance of herbs. Flavourful, fresh palate with red fruit, good acidity and nerve.

DOGA 1998 OAK AGED RED
tempranillo, cabernet sauvignon, merlot

85 Garnet red cherry with a coppery hue. Powerful, very fine aroma with an excellent expression of slightly varietal ripe fruit (redcurrants, paprika) and a fine reduction (cedar, tobacco). Flavourful palate with a good fruit/oak integration, spicy and slightly warm.

DÉFORA 1998 RED
77% garnacha, 23% cabernet sauvignon

86 Deep cherry with a garnet red edge. Slightly warm aroma of jammy black fruit, fine crianza (smoky hints, truffles, cedar), with an earthy hint. Fleshy palatewith toasty oak slightly rough but fresh wood tannins and a round supple finish.

CALIU 2001 SEMICRIANZA RED
51% tempranillo, 49% cabernet sauvignon

85 Deep cherry. A deep aroma of black fruit, toasty hints, fine varnish and minerals. Fresh palate with sensations of fruit, bitter overtones in the finish (pulp) and flavourful tannins.

VALLFORMOSA

La Sala, 45
08735 Vilobi del Penedés (Barcelona)
☎: 938 978 286 - Fax: 938 978 355
vallformosa@vallformosa.es -

www.vallformosa.es

Established: 1865

🍷 2,500 📊 5,200,000 litres 🍇 397 has.

🇪🇸 73% 🌐27%: -UE América Latina

CLOS MASET SELECCIÓN ESPECIAL 2000 CRIANZA RED
100% cabernet sauvignon

91 Intense cherry. Powerful aroma with notes of jammy redcurrants and toasty flavours (dark-roasted flavours, carob, pitch) with a hint of mineral notes. Powerful, warm, very ripe, quite spirituous and fleshy palate with flavourful and abundant tannins.

MAS CABALLÉ DE VALLFORMOSA 2001 FERMENTADO EN BARRICA WHITE
VALLFORMOSA CHARDONNAY 2003 WHITE
CLAUDIA DE VALLFORMOSA 2003 WHITE
VALLFORMOSA MARINA AGUJA WHITE
VIÑA BLANCA VALLFORMOSA 2003 WHITE
VALLFORMOSA MARINA AGUJA ROSÉ
VIÑA ROSADA VALLFORMOSA 2003 ROSÉ
VALLFORMOSA CABERNET SAUVIGNON 2000 RED
MASIA FREYÉ MERLOT DE VALLFORMOSA 2000 RED
MAS LA ROCA SYRAH DE VALLFORMOS 2000 RED
VIÑA BRUNA VALLFORMOSA 2002 RED
VALLFORMOSA TEMPRANILLO 2001 CRIANZA RED
VALLFORMOSA 2000 RESERVA RED
VALLFORMOSA 1998 GRAN RESERVA RED

VALLORT VINYATERS

Ca la Marta
08737 Torrelles de Foix (Barcelona)
☎: 677 503 267 - Fax: 938 180 612
vallort@airtel.net

Established: 2000

📊 250,000 litres 🍷 100%

VALLORT VINYATERS 1998 RED

VEGA DE RIBES

Masía La Serra
08810 Sant Pere de Ribes (Barcelona)
☎: 938 960 024 - Fax: 938 960 024
vegaribes@troc.es
www.troc.es/vegaribes

VEGA DE RIBES 2004 WHITE

77 Straw-coloured with a golden hue. Intense aroma, fruit and white flowers, some varietal expression, exotic nuances. Fresh palate, marked acidity, citrus notes that conceal the fruit expression.

SASSERRA MALVASÍA DE SITGES 2001 WHITE

84 Intense gold. Intense aroma, ripe white fruit, apricot skin, nuances of flower honey and Mediterranean herbs. Fresh palate, dry, with hints of sweet almonds, dried grass and citrus fruit zest in the retronasal passage, good acidity.

VEGA DE RIBES 2003 WHITE
VEGA DE RIBES 2003 RED

VILADELLOPS VINÍCOLA

Finca Viladellops
08734 Olérdola (Barcelona)
☎: 938 188 371 - Fax: 934 141 245
www.viladellops.com

FINCA VILADELLOPS 2002 FERMENTADO EN BARRICA WHITE

80 Golden. Aroma with notes of nuts, toasty hints, quite evolved. Palate without nuances, without fruit, ripe, bitter notes, lacking varietal complexity.

FINCA VILADELLOPS 2003 RED

84 Garnet red cherry with a violet edge. Powerful, fruity, ripe aroma, fine spicy notes with jam and mineral nuances. Fresh, flavourful palate, slightly marked but promising tannins, with a suggestion of terracotta, marked acidity, long.

FINCA VILADELLOPS 2003 FERMENTADO EN BARRICA WHITE

84 Brilliant gold. Intense aroma, ripe white fruit, fine toasty oak notes, a suggestion of lees, broom and dried fallen leaves. Flavourful, dry, slightly warm and oily palate, spicy and slightly mineral hints in the finish, good acidity.

Celler Cooperatiu
VILAFRANCA DEL PENEDÉS

Camí de Sant Pau Paratge les Clotes s/n
08720 Vilafranca del Penedés (Barcelona)
☎: 938 171 035 - Fax: 938 900 418
cellervila@cellervila.com
www.cellervila.com

Established: 1933

🍷 300 📊 10,000,000 litres 🍇 1055 has.

🇪🇸 90% 🌐10%: -IE -JP -DE -BE -NL

CASTELLER GRAN CHARDONNAY 2003 WHITE SECO
100% chardonnay

73 Pale yellow with a golden hue. Fairly intense aroma with notes of green fruit and a nuance of Mediterranean herbs. Flavourful palate with fine bitter notes and good acidity.

DO PENEDÈS

CASTELLER BLANC DE BLANCS WHITE SEMIDULCE

79 Pale straw. Fresh, fruity aroma (ripe apples) with good intensity. Flavourful, fresh palate with an element of acidity, pleasant.

CASTELLER GRAN XAREL.LO 2003 WHITE
100% xarel.lo

84 Straw-coloured with a greenish hue. Fine aroma with ripe fruit (apples, pears, melon), overall harmony. Flavourful, fruity, fresh and well-balanced palate.

CASTELLER ROSÉ

72 Brilliant raspberry with a coppery glint. Not very intense aroma with red fruit notes and a spicy nuance. Dry, bitter palate with hardly any fruit expression and high acidity.

CASTELLER GRAN ROSAT 2003 ROSÉ
merlot, cabernet sauvignon

77 Raspberry with a coppery glint. Intense, fruity aroma with hints of fine reduction (withered petals). Fruity palate with a slightly oily texture and fine bitter notes.

CASTELLER GRAN CABERNET 2002 RED
100% cabernet sauvignon

77 Cherry with a brick red rim. Light aroma of reduction and varietal typification. Bitter green fruit tannins on the palate.

CASTELLER 2003 FERMENTADO EN BARRICA RED

81 Intense cherry with a violet edge. Intense, fruity aroma with a good varietal expression (paprika, black fruit). Flavourful palate with slightly marked oak tannins yet well-associated with the fruit tannins, very pleasant.

CASTELLER BARRICA 2001 OAK AGED RED
merlot, cabernet sauvignon

79 Garnet red cherry with a saffron edge. Intense aroma of ripe black fruit, spicy varietal hints (paprika) and toasty oak. Flavourful on the palate with well-integrated oak and fruit, very bitter elements and traces of overripe fruit.

CASTELLER BARRICA 2002 JOVEN WHITE
CASTELLER WHITE
CASTELLER GRAN MERLOT 2002 RED
CASTELLER 2000 OAK AGED RED

VINUET

Cl. Montserrat, 56
08770 Sant Sadurní d'Anoia (Barcelona)
☎: 938 912 073 - Fax: 938 183 539
rosellgallart@terra.es

Established: 1845

🍷 20 🛢 5,000 litres 🍇 5 has. 🍷 100%

VINUET XAREL.LO 2003 JOVEN WHITE
90% xarel.lo, 10% chardonnay

74 Straw-coloured with a greenish hue. Medium-intensity aroma of lightly evolved fruit. Fairly fruity palate although without vine variety expression.

VINUET 2001 CRIANZA RED
50% cabernet sauvignon, 50% merlot

81 Brilliant cherry with a coppery edge. Not very intense aroma, slightly fruity with spicy notes of oak. Flavourful palate with well-integrated fruit and oak, a nuance of jammy fruit, toasty oak notes and good acidity.

VIÑA TORREBLANCA

Finca Masia Torreblanca, s/n
08734 Miquel D'Olérdola (Barcelona)
☎: 938 915 066 - Fax: 938 900 102
torreblanca@retemail.es

Established: 1995

🍇 22 has. 🍷 17% 🍇83%

TORREBLANCA LES ATZAVARES 2003 WHITE SECO
parellada, macabeo, xarel.lo, chardonnay

80 Pale yellow. Intense aroma of ripe white fruit with exotic hints. Generous, fruity palate, slightly oily with refreshing acidity.

TORREBLANCA MERLOT 2003 ROSÉ
merlot

82 Fairly deep raspberry. Intense aroma of red stone fruit with fresh overtones. Flavourful palate with a slightly oily texture, spicy hints of skins and a mineral nuance.

TORREBLANCA CABERNET SAUVIGNON 1999 RESERVA RED

84 Deep cherry with a saffron edge. Fairly intense aroma of redcurrants with spicy hints of oak. Flavourful, fleshy palate with slightly marked yet promising tannins; fine herbaceous and fruit notes with a slightly oily texture and excellent acidity.

Cellers VS 96-CAN BONASTRE

Can Bonastre Santa Magdalena
08783 Masquefa (Barcelona)
☎: 937 726 167 - Fax: 937 727 929
canbonastre@canbonastre.com
www.canbonastre.com

Established: 1996

🍷 150 🛢 500,000 litres 🍇 100 has.
🍷 90% 🍇10%

CAN BONASTRE MERLOT 2000 OAK AGED RED
100% merlot

🍷 3

DO PENEDÈS

76 Cherry with a coppery edge. Intense aroma of black fruit with an underbrush nuance, fine toasty oak notes and a mild reduction nuance. Flavourful palate with not very fine bitter notes (notes of greeness) and an acidic edge.

CAN BONASTRE CHARDONNAY 2002 WHITE
CAN BONASTRE PINOT NOIR 2000 RED
CAN BONASTRE MERLOT 1999 CRIANZA RED
CAN BONASTRE CABERNET SAUVIGNON 2000 CRIANZA RED

WINNER WINES

Adelfas, 18 3°B
28007 Madrid
☎: 915 019 042 - Fax: 915 017 794
rsaseta@winnerwines.es
www.winnerwines.es

Established: 1986

550 📦 1,200,000 litres 🍇 400 has.

🍷 8% 🌐92%: -US -CA -MX -DO -PR -SG -JP -CH -IT -FR -DE -SE -FI -DK -BE -AT -DK

JUVENALS CHARDONNAY 2003 FERMENTADO EN BARRICA WHITE
100% chardonnay

80 Straw-coloured with a greenish hue. Medium-intensity aroma with smoky oak notes over fruit notes. Flavourful palate with ripe fruit but with enough oak.

JUVENALS 2003 RED
100% cabernet sauvignon

82 Cherry with a violet edge. Intense aroma with a good expression of young, varietal wine (ripe black fruit). Fresh, fruity palate with quite marked grape tannins and hints of freshness.

JUVENALS 1998 RESERVA RED
100% cabernet sauvignon

83 Intense cherry with a brick red edge. Not very intense aroma with mild reduction notes (new leather, tobacco), and a nuance of ripe black fruit. Flavourful palate with complementary fruit and wood tannins, good acidity.

Cava XAMÓS

Virgen de Montserrat, 5
08130 Sta Perpetua de la Mogoda (Barcelona)
☎: 932 462 287 - Fax: 935 604 560
xamos@xamos.net
www.xamos.net

Established: 1987

15

XAMOS 1997 RED
XAMÓS 1998 RED
XAMÓS MERLOT 1998 RED

DO PLA DE BAGES

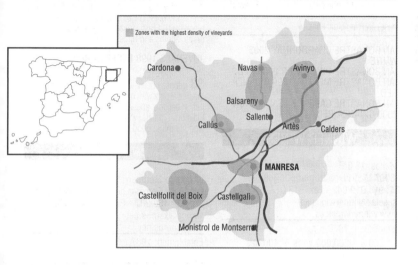

Zones with the highest density of vineyards

Cardona● Navas Avinyo

Balsareny
Sallent●
Callús Artés Calders

MANRESA

Castellfollit del Boix Castellgalí

Monistrol de Montserrat

NEWS. With the excellent performance of the red wines and the original Abadal *picapoll* white and another of the great names of the DO, Solergibert, Pla de Bages can be considered a region with interesting varietal expressions, not only for the autochthonous varieties, which are in the process of being 'recovered', but also for the two foreign *Cabernets* (*Sauvignon* and *Franc*) and the *Merlot*. In general, the Adadal is rightly regarded as being one of the best wines of Catalonia – even their rosés are impeccable – and, in the tasting of its Selecció 2001, this impressive red wine, which had a score of 90 points in the previous edition, reached 93 points, with excellent prospects for ageing well in the bottle.

Hectares of Vineyard	No. of Viticulturists	No. of Bodegas	2003 Harvest	2003 Production	Marketing
550	100	7	Very Good	1,750,000 litres	78% Spain 22% abroad

LOCATION. Covering one of the eastern extremes of the Central Catalonian Depression; it covers the natural region of Bages, of which the city of Manresa is the urban centre. To the south the region is bordered by the Montserrat mountain range, the dividing line which separates it from Penedés. It comprises the municipal areas of Fonollosa, Monistrol de Caldres, Sant Joan de Vilatorrada, Artés, Avinyó, Balsareny, Calders, Callús, Cardona, Castellgalí, Castellfollit del Boix, Castellnou de Bages, Manresa, Mura, Navarcles, Navàs, El Pont de Vilomara, Rajadell, Sallent, Sant Fruitós de Bages, Sant Mateu de Bages, Sant Salvador de Guardiola, Santpedor, Santa María d'Oló, Súria and Talamanca.

CLIMATE. Mid-mountain Mediterranean, with little rainfall (500 mm to 600 mm average annual rainfall) and greater temperature contrasts than in the Penedés.

SOIL. The vineyards are situated at an altitude of about 400 m. The soil is franc-clayey, franc-sandy and franc-clayey-sandy.

VARIETIES:

White: *Chardonnay, Gewürztraminer, Macabeo, Picapoll, Parellada, Sauvignon Blanc.*
Red: *Sumoll, Ull de Llebre (Tempranillo), Merlot, Cabernet Franc, Cabernet Sauvignon, Syrah* and *Garnacha.*

REGULATORY COUNCIL.

Casa de La Culla. La Culla, s/n. 08240 Manresa (Barcelona).
Tel: 938 748 236. Fax: 938 748 094.
E-mail: info@dopladebages.com
Website: www.dopladebages.com

GENERAL CHARACTERISTICS OF THE WINES:

Whites	These are of similar character to the Penedés white wines; they are young and fruity, and are the result of modern technology, both those that use autochthonous varieties and those based on *Chardonnay*.
Rosés	Produced mainly from *Merlot* and *Cabernet Sauvignon*, they have a raspberry pink colour and are clean and fruity on the nose with a good fruit expression of the grapes they are produced from.
Reds	Deep cherry-red coloured, fresh, with a pronounced character of the Viníferas that they are based on. The fine varietal character of those produced from *Cabernet Sauvignon* stands out.

ABADAL MASIES D'AVINYÓ

08279 Sta María D'Horta D'Avinyó (Barcelona)
☎: 938 757 525 - Fax: 938 748 326
info@abadal.net
www.abadal.net

Established: 1983
🍷 2,140 🛢 480,000 litres 🍇 70 has.
🍾 80% 🌍 20%

ABADAL CHARDONNAY 2002 FERMENTADO EN BARRICA WHITE
100% chardonnay

85 Golden yellow, with a coppery glint. Powerful palate of white fruit well-integrated with the smoky, creamy oak notes and hints of herbs and fine lees. Flavourful palate, well-integrated fruit/oak, spicy citrus fruit hints (lemongrass) and fresh mineral overtones.

ABADAL CHARDONNAY 2002 WHITE
100% chardonnay

85 Straw-coloured. Powerful, fine aroma of ripe fruit, lemon notes and lees. Sweet fruit on the palate contrasting with a fresh acidity and a bitter finish. Oily texture and a long citrus finish.

ABADAL PICAPOLL 2003 WHITE
100% picapoll

87 Straw-coloured. Powerful, fresh, expressive aroma of exotic fruit (maracuya, pasion fruit) and a nuance of citrus fruit and fennel. Oily, full, flavourful palate with good fruit expression, hints of hay and agreeable bitter notes in the finish.

ABADAL CABERNET SAUVIGNON 2003 ROSÉ
100% cabernet sauvignon

85 Raspberry blush. Powerful, fresh palate of red fruit, very fine and expressive. Flavourful palate with excellent texture and fruit notions; a superb Rosé.

ABADAL CABERNET FRANC-TEMPRANILLO 2002 OAK AGED RED
60% cabernet franc, 40% tempranillo

88 Very dark cherry. Powerful aroma with excellent toasty oak notes and skins, varietal character (paprika, damp earth), balsamic hints and fresh mineral overtones. Flavourful palate with slightly marked yet promising tannins, fine bitter notes and an excellent structure.

ABADAL SELECCIÓ 2001 OAK AGED RED
40% cabernet sauvignon, 40% cabernet franc, 20% syrah

93 Dark cherry. Powerful aroma with an excellent varietal expression of the crianza (cedar, macerated fruit, toasty flavours, balsamic hints). Flavourful, fleshy palate with ripe, promising tannins, slightly fresh in the retronasal passage, very rich in fruit nuances and excellent acidity.

ABADAL SELECCIÓ 2000 RED
40% cabernet sauvignon, 40% cabernet franc, 20% syrah

89 Intense cherry. Aroma of well-crafted fine toasty oak notes and fruit with a nuance of black fruit (redcurrants, truffles). Generous palate with a fresh varietal character (Bordeaux-style); flavourful and generous with fine tannins.

ABADAL 2000 CRIANZA RED
50% cabernet sauvignon, 50% merlot

87 Dark cherry. Powerful aroma with toasty notes of oak, well-integrated black fruit, varietal presence (paprika, underbrush) and waxy hints. Flavourful, fleshy palate, excellent fruit weight with liquorice and balsamic notes in the retronasal passage.

ABADAL MERLOT 2001 CRIANZA RED
100% merlot

86 Cherry with a garnet red edge. Powerful, balsamic aroma of pepper and redcurrants. Flavourful and intense on the palate with concentrated black fruit, ripe, well-crafted round tannins, a good wood assemblage and a spicy finish.

ABADAL 3.9 2000 RESERVA RED
85% cabernet sauvignon, 15% syrah

88 Almost opaque cherry. Powerful aroma with predominant ripe fruit varietal notes (redcurrants, paprika, cedar), fine toasty oak and a balsamic suggestion. Flavourful palate with a good oak/fruit integration and a certain spicy, mineral freshness.

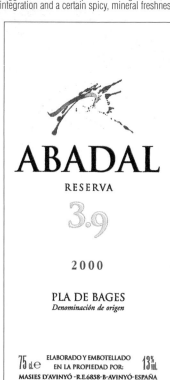

ABADAL
RESERVA
3.9
2000
PLA DE BAGES
Denominación de origen

75 cl.e ELABORADO Y EMBOTELLADO EN LA PROPIEDAD POR: 13% vol.
MASIES D'AVINYÓ -R.E.6858-B-AVINYÓ-ESPAÑA

DO PLA DE BAGES

ABADAL 2000 RESERVA RED
60% merlot, 30% cabernet sauvignon, 10% Syrah

89 Very deep cherry. Spicy aroma, with minerals and pepper. Round, very well-balanced, persistent palate with balsamic flavours in the retronasal passage.

Celler Cooperatiu D'ARTÉS

Cr. Rocafort, 44
08271 Artés (Barcelona)
☎: 938 305 325 - Fax: 938 306 289

Established: 1908

🛢 110 📦 360,000 litres

🍷 92% 🌐8%: -DK -DE

ARTIUM PICAPOLL 2003 FERMENTADO EN BARRICA WHITE
100% picapoll

75 Golden. Powerful aroma with predominant smoky and creamy (vanilla, luke-warm butter) wood notes. Flavourful, fine toasty palate, lacking great varietal fruit expression.

ARTIUM PICAPOLL 2003 WHITE
100% picapoll

79 Pale gold. Quite intense aroma of white stone fruit with hints of flowers and lees. Flavourful, somewhat fruity palate with fine bitter notes and good acidity.

ARTIUM 2000 RED
ARTIUM 2001 RED
ARTIUM 2002 RED
ARTIUM ROCAS ALBAS 2002 RED

FARGAS-FARGAS

Casa Quico
08240 Salelles - Manresa (Barcelona)
☎: 938 358 547

FARGAS-FARGAS CABERNET SAUVIGNON 2000 RED
cabernet sauvignon

86 Dark cherry with a brick red rim. Powerful aroma with mild varietal notes (redcurrants, paprika) and fine toasty oak. Flavourful palate with quite rough, oily tannins, an excellent crianza expression and hints of reduction (tobacco) in the retronasal passage.

MAS DE SANT ISCLE

Casa Vilanova
08272 Sant Fruitós de Bages (Barcelona)
☎: 938 743 806

Established: 1996

🛢 35 🌱 3 has.

MAS DE SANT ISCLE PICAPOLL 2003 WHITE
100% picapoll

79 Straw-coloured. Medium-intensity aroma of ripe fruit (apricots) and white flower. Flavourful palate with ripe fruit, slightly lacking in acidity.

MAS DE SANT ISCLE SAUVIGNON BLANC 2003 WHITE
100% sauvignon blanc

80 Straw-coloured. Medium-intensity aroma with herb notes and fresh ripe fruit. Flavourful and grapey on the palate, oily, not very varietal but pleasant.

MAS DE SANT ISCLE ULL DE LLEBRE 2003 RED
100% tempranillo

80 Brilliant cherry with a coppery hue. Not very intense aroma with fine varietal hints and warm notes. Flavourful palate with firm yet very elegant tannins, red fruit and excellent acidity.

Celler Cooperatiu de SALELLES

Carretera D'Igualada, s/n
08240 Manresa (Barcelona)
☎: 938 720 572 - Fax: 938 720 572
coopsalelles@coopsalelles.com
www.coopsalelles.com

Established: 1926

🛢 25 📦 500,000 litres 🍷 100%

AS DE COPES 2003 WHITE
AS DE COPES 2002 RED

Celler SOLERGIBERT

Calle Barquera 40
08271 Artés (Barcelona)
☎: 938 305 084 - Fax: 938 305 763
josep@cellersolergibert.com
www.cellersolergibert.com

Established: 1868

🛢 170 📦 150,000 litres 🌱 11 has.

🍷 100%

SOLERGIBERT PICAPOLL 2003 OAK AGED RED
100% picapoll

84 Brilliant pale yellow. Intense aroma with a certain finesse, white fruit, hints of herbs, zest and fine smoky oak. Flavourful palate with the freshness of white fruit, aniseed, lees and fine citrus acidity.

SOLERGIBERT CABERNET SAUVIGNON 1999 RESERVA RED
85% cabernet sauvignon, 15% cabernet franc

85 Dark garnet red cherry. Powerful aroma with a good Mediterranean varietal expression (paprika, herbaceous and balsamic freshness) and spicy oak notes. Flavourful, bitter palate with hints of aniseed and jammy fruit.

ENRIC SOLERGIBERT GRAN SELECCIÓ 2000 RESERVA RED
85% cabernet sauvignon, 15% cabernet franc

85 Garnet red cherry with a brick red edge. Powerful aroma with predominant varietal fruit notes (redcurrants, paprika) and a spicy hint of oak. Flavourful, supple palate with a good fruit/oak integration, spicy and slightly oily.

CONXITA SERRA GRAN SELECCIÓ 2000 RESERVA RED
SOLERGIBERT CABERNET SAUVIGNON 2000 RESERVA RED
SOLERGIBERT MERLOT 2000 RESERVA RED

VINS GRAU

Ctra C-37 de Igualada a Manresa, km. 75,5
08255 Maians-Castellfollit de Boix (Barcelona)
☎: 938 356 002 - Fax: 938 356 002
vinsgrau@troc.es
www.vinsgrau.com

Established: 1966

⊜ 125 ⧯ 300,000 litres ❦ 15 has.
🏴 90% ⊕10%: -DK -AT -CH -DE

JAUME GRAU I GRAU MERLOT 2003 ROSÉ
100% merlot

80 Brilliant raspberry. Powerful, fruity aroma with fine spicy notes of skins. Flavourful, fruity palate, somewhat oily and warm, very pleasant.

JAUME GRAU I GRAU TEMPRANILLO 2001 OAK AGED RED
70% tempranillo, 10% merlot, 20% cabernet sauvignon

78 Garnet red cherry. Intense, fruity aroma with spicy hints of oak. Flavourful palate with very ripe fruit and predominant, not very fine, bitter oak notes.

JAUME GRAU I GRAU CABERNET SAUVIGNON 1999 CRIANZA RED
100% cabernet sauvignon

74 Garnet red cherry. Intense aroma with predominant smoky notes of oak and a nuance of ash. Fairly flavourful palate, lacks fruit-acidity-tannicity balance.

JAUME GRAU I GRAU MACABEO 2003 JOVEN WHITE
JAUME GRAU I GRAU PICAPOLL 2003 FERMENTADO EN BARRICA WHITE
VINYA MAIANS VELL 2003 JOVEN WHITE
VINYA MAIANS VELL 2003 JOVEN ROSÉ
CLOS ESTRADA 2003 ROSÉ
VINYA MAIANS VELL TEMPRANILLO 2002 JOVEN RED
VINYA MAIANS VELL 2003 JOVEN RED
JAUME GRAU I GRAU 1998 RESERVA RED

DO PLA I LLEVANT

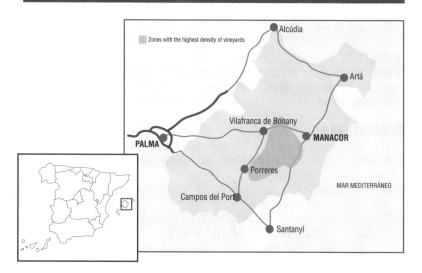

NEWS. A dead heat between the 'Miquels' at 90 points: the Ses Ferritges of Miquel Oliver, a magnificent blend of *Cabernet Sauvignon, Merlot, Syrah* and *Callet* for less than € 10, and Miquel Gelabert's impeccable Torrent Negre Selecció Privada. The white wines, especially the *Chardonnay*, of the 2003 harvest, are splendid in the entire Balearic region. Awaiting approval is the inclusion of *Pinot Noir* and *Riesling* among the authorised varieties of the DO, almost certainly with a view to reinforcing the already extraordinary average quality of the region in which the 37 wines tasted had scores above 77 points. A curious observation is that of these 37 wines, 18 were of the 2003 harvest; although the Crianza red wines are the most outstanding, the white wines are very good (generally fermented in barrels), and even the rosés, which extends the range and the market potential of this small insular DO.

Hectares of Vineyard	No. of Viticulturists	No. of Bodegas	2003 Harvest	2003 Production	Marketing
283	102	9	Very Good	972,995 litres	95% Spain 5% foreign

LOCATION. The production region covers the eastern part of Majorca and consists of 18 municipal districts: Algaida, Ariany, Artá, Campos, Capdepera, Felanitx, Lluchamajor, Manacor, Mª de la Salud, Montuiri, Muro, Petra, Porreres, Sant Joan, Sant Llorens des Cardasar, Santa Margarita, Sineu and Vilafranca de Bonany.

CLIMATE. Mediterranean, with an average temperature of 16°C and with slightly cool winters and dry, hot summers. The constant sea breeze during the summer has a notable effect on these terrains close to the coast. The wet season is in autumn and the average annual rainfall is between 450 mm and 500 mm.

SOIL. The soil is made up of limestone rocks, which give limy-clayey soils. The reddish colour of the terrain is due to the presence of iron oxide. The clays and calcium and magnesium carbonates, in turn, provide the whitish colour which can also be seen in the vineyards.

VARIETIES:
White: *Prensal Blanc, Macabeo, Parellada, Moscatel* and *Chardonnay.*
Red: *Callet* (majority), *Manto Negro, Fogoneu, Tempranillo, Monastrell, Cabernet Sauvignon, Merlot* and *Syrah.*

REGULATORY COUNCIL.
Molí de N'Amengual. Duzay, 3. 07260 Porreres (Islas Baleares).
Provisional address: Edifici de l'Antic Escorxador, s/n. Carretera de Porreres Montuïri. 07260. Porreres.
Tel / Fax: 971 168 569.
E-mail: plaillevant@wanadoo.es

GENERAL CHARACTERISTICS OF THE WINES:

Whites	The characteristics of the white wines are conditioned by the peculiarities of the foreign varieties. The *Premsal* grape gives wines that singularly express the 'terruño' character of the region.
Rosés	These follow in the line of the rosés of Binissalem, although the distinction comes from those produced from French grape varieties. The sensorial definition of these varieties does not prevent them, in certain cases, from being a little heavy on the nose.
Reds	These share the style that characterises the Mediterranean adaptation of the French varieties they are produced from. Thus, they give off balsamic hints in the nose; on the palate they offer supple and ripe tannins; they are flavourful and full bodied.

ARMERO I ADROVER

Camada Real s/n
07200 Felanitx (Balears)
☎: 971 827 103 - Fax: 971 827 103
luisarmero@armeroiadrover.com
www.armeroiadrover.com

Established: 1992

🛢 10 🗄 87,800 litres 🍇 21 has.

🍷 99% 🍷1%

ARMERO I ADROVER COLLITA DE FRUITS 2003 FERMENTADO EN BARRICA WHITE
100% chardonnay

85 Pale yellow with a golden hue. Intense aroma with excellent varietal expression and fine smoky oak notes. Flavourful palate with fine bitter notes and hints of new wood, slightly oily.

ARMERO ADROVER 2003 WHITE
chardonnay, prensal

81 Pale yellow with a greenish hue. Fresh aroma of white fruit with notes of fennel. Fresh, flavourful palate with fine bitter and herby notes and marked citrus acidity.

ARMERO ADROVER 2003 ROSÉ
syrah, callet

80 Deep raspberry with a coppery hue. Powerful aroma of ripe red fruit with sweet and slightly toasty hints. Flavourful, slightly fleshy, warm palate with ripe fruit and a hint of spices.

ARMERO ADROVER 2003 RED
syrah, callet

85 Dark cherry, quite luminous. Powerul aroma of red forest fruits, complex. Fresh and fruity palate, light and flavourful, very fresh and varietal expression of fruit.

ARMERO I ADROVER COLLITA DE FRUITS 2003 OAK AGED RED
callet, cabernet sauvignon, merlot

84 Dark cherry with a dark red-violet edge. Powerful aroma of ripe black fruit with toasty oak. Meaty palate with ripe and oily tannins, slightly warm with notes of spices and liquorice, an oily texture and a good fruit weight.

CAN MAJORAL

Carrer Campanar, s/n
07210 Algaida (Balears)
☎: 971 665 867 - Fax: 971 665 867
bodega@canmajoral.com
www.canmajoral.com

Established: 1994

🛢 96 🗄 50,000 litres 🍇 12 has.

🍷 90% 🍷10%: -DE

CAN MAJORAL SON BLANC 2003 FERMENTADO EN BARRICA WHITE
100% chardonnay

82 Brilliant pale gold. Powerful aroma with predominant creamy and smoky oak notes and ripe white fruit. Flavourful, creamy palate with good fruit-wood symmetry, slightly warm and oily.

BUTIBALAUSÍ 2003 WHITE
prensal blanc, parellada, chardonnay

79 Pale yellow with a greenish hue. Intense, fruity aroma with hints of fine herbs. Flavourful palate with fine bitter notes and marked acidity.

BUTIBALAUSÍ 2003 ROSÉ
tempranillo, callet, manto negro

82 Lively blush. Intense aroma of foresty red fruit with sweet hints and a herby and citrus fruit hint. Fresh (carbonic hints), quite fruity and bitter on the palate with marked citrus acidity.

CAN MAJORAL SON ROIG 2001 CRIANZA RED
cabernet sauvignon, syrah, merlot

84 Very dark cherry. Powerful aroma of jammy black fruit with toasty oak notes, a balsamic hint and notions of terroir. Meaty, concentrated and bitter palate (hints of overripening), slightly warm and oily.

BUTIBALAUSÌ 2002 RED

81 Quite dark cherry. Aroma with light reduction notes (late racking), toasty oak and ripe fruit. Round palate with ripe fruit, spicy and toasty.

CAN MAJORAL S'HERETAT 2001 CRIANZA RED

GALNÉS I FERRER

Barracar Alt, 56
07250 Petra (Balears)
☎: 971 561 088 - Fax: 971 561 088

GALNÉS I FERRER RED

JAUME MESQUIDA

Vileta, 7
07260 Porreres - Mallorca (Balears)
☎: 971 647 106 - Fax: 971 168 205
info@jaumemesquida.com
www.jaumemesquida.com

Established: 1945

🛢 450 🗄 200,000 litres 🍇 25 has.

🍷 95% 🍷5%: -DE

JAUME MESQUIDA CHARDONNAY 2003 WHITE
100% chardonnay

79 Pale gold. Intense aroma, of ripe white fruit with good varietal expression and a suggestion of spices. Flavourful, quite fruity palate with fragrant herbs.

JAUME MESQUIDA CABERNET SAUVIGNON 2000 ROBLE RED
cabernet sauvignon

84 Intense cherry with an orange edge. Spicy aroma with a nuance of ripe fruit, varietal expression, elegant with hints of damp earth. Round, oily palate with sweet and flavourful tannins, fine toasty oak and fruit, has improved over the last year.

CABERNET SAUVIGNON

2 0 0 0

Pla i Llevant - Mallorca
· DENOMINACIÓ D'ORIGEN ·

DES DE 1945
Jaume Mesquida

JAUME MESQUIDA MERLOT 2000 RED
100% merlot

82 Dark ruby red with a brick red hue. Aroma with tanned oak notes (wax), and animal notes (leather). Oily, round palate with a hint of aldehyde and somewhat weak tannins for a year 2000 wine.

JAUME MESQUIDA SELECCIÓ FAMILIAR SHIRAZ 2000 RED
syrah

86 Cherry with a brick red hue. Somewhat short aroma with oak/fruit balance and a spicy hint. Round, balsamic palate with scrubland herbs and oily tannins, more expressive in the mouth than in the nose.

MARÍA ESTHER 2000 ROBLE RED

Vins MIQUEL GELABERT

Salas, 50
07500 Manacor (Balears)
☎: 971 821 444 - Fax: 971 821 444
vinsmq@vinsmiquelgelabert.com
www.vinsmiquelgelabert.com

Established: 1985

🍷 104 📊 40,000 litres 🌿 8 has.

📦 70% 🌍30%: -DE

MUSCAT 2003 JOVEN WHITE
50% moscatel de grano menudo, 50% moscatel de Málaga

85 Pale yellow with a greenish hue. Intense, very fine aroma with an excellent varietal expression, musky notes, slightly exotic hints and a suggestion of flowers and aniseed. Flavourful, bitter palate with good acidity.

CHARDONNAY 2003 FERMENTADO EN BARRICA WHITE
100% chardonnay

87 Golden with a lemony hue. Powerful aroma, with smoky, creamy (vanilla) oak notes and ripe varietal hints (apples). Powerful palate with a good oak/fruit integration and a warm, oily texture, spicy and long.

VINYA SON CAULES 2002 OAK AGED WHITE
40% macabeo, 30% parellada, 20% prensal blanc, 10% moscatel

82 Brilliant pale yellow. Intense aroma with white fruit, exotic hints, smoky oak, floral touches (acacia) and herbs. Flavourful palate, rich in nuances with fine bitter notes and good acidity.

VINYA SON CAULES 2002 ROSÉ
callet, mantonegro, tempranillo

82 Brilliant intense salmon pink. Powerful, ripe aroma of slightly reduced red fruit (lees petals). Flavourful palate with fine bitter notes, herbs and marked citrus acidity.

GRAN VINYA SON CAULES 2001 OAK AGED RED
75% callet, 5% mantonegro, 5% cabernet sauvignon, 5% merlot, 5% syrah, 5% fogoneu

88 Intense cherry. Fine, toasty aroma with certain fruit expression well-integrated with the creamy oak. Round, full palate with body and precise but ripe and flavourful tannins, long.

MIQUEL GELABERT CABERNET SAUVIGNON 2001 OAK AGED RED
85% cabernet sauvignon, 15% merlot

84 Dark cherry. Aroma with a good integration between toasty notes and fruit expression. Round palate with supple tannins, mild animal notes in the retronasal passage (leather), flavourful.

TORRENT NEGRE 2001 OAK AGED RED
40% cabernet sauvignon, 25% merlot, 35% syrah

93 Intense cherry. Fine, elegant, spicy aroma with hints of black fruit with fine toasty oak and great varietal expression. Powerful palate, rich in fruity and mineral expression with perceptible tannins although integrated in the wine and an elegant retronasal effect.

TORRENT NEGRE SELECCIÓ PRIVADA 2001 OAK AGED RED
100% syrah

90 Intense cherry. Powerful, mineral, spicy aroma with good fruit expression combined with fine toasty flavours (chocolate, toffee) of creamy oak. Meaty, full, warm, powerful, flavourful palate with obvious yet ripe tannins. Has improved over the last year.

VINYA SON CAULES 2002 OAK AGED RED
ull de llebre, callet, manto negro, syrah

86 Deep cherry with coppery nuances. Powerful aroma with predominant oak notes (toasty flavours, cocoa) and a mineral and balsamic suggestion. Powerful palate with a good oak/fruit integration and fine bitter notes (liquorice dark roasted flavours, terracotta), slightly oily.

Vinyes i Bodegues MIQUEL OLIVER

Font, 26
07520 Petra (Baleares)
☎: 971 561 117 - Fax: 971 561 117
bodega@miqueloliver.com
www.miqueloliver.com

Established: 1912

🍷 500 📖 200,000 litres 🌿 10 has.

🍷 90% 🌍10%: -DE -CH -AT -MX

SON CALÓ BLANC DE BLANCS 2003 JOVEN WHITE
100% prensal blanc

84 Pale yellow with a greenish hue. Intense aroma of white fruit with hints of apricot skins and fresh aniseed and mineral overtones. Fresh palate with fine bittersweet notes, varietal with good acidity.

MUSCAT ORIGINAL MIQUEL OLIVER 2003 WHITE
60% moscatel, 40% moscatel

82 Very pale yellow with a golden hue. Intense, fresh aroma with a good varietal expression (white fruit, musk, fennel). Fresh palate with a fine expression of fruit and herbs, slightly mineral, good citrus acidity.

AIA 2002 SEMICRIANZA RED
100% merlot

87 Quite dark cherry. Aroma with light notes of ripe fruit and fine toasty scents with good and elegant fruit expression. Fresh, varietal palate with fruity and flavourful tannins and a well-balanced retronasal effect.

SES FERRITGES 2001 RESERVA RED
30% cabernet sauvignon, 30% merlot, 30% callet, 10% syrah

90 Intense cherry. Powerful aroma, rich in expression of minerals and fine toasty scents (chocolate, dark-roasted flavours) with ripe fruit and some fruity nuances. Meaty, warm, powerful palate with minerals; flavourful and very ripe tannins, complex.

GRAN CHARDONNAY MIQUEL OLIVER 1999 CRIANZA WHITE
SON CALÓ 2003 JOVEN ROSÉ
SON CALÓ 2003 JOVEN RED
MONT FERRUTX 2000 CRIANZA RED
SES FERRITGES 1996 GRAN RESERVA RED

PERE SEDA

Cid Campeador, 22
07500 Manacor (Mallorca)
☎: 971 605 087 - Fax: 971 604 856
pereseda@pereseda.com
www.pereseda.com

Established: Final s. XIX

🍷 300 📖 1,200.000,litres 🌿 35 has.

🍷 98% 🌍2%: -DE

PERE SEDA CHARDONNAY 2003 JOVEN WHITE
100% chardonnay

83 Brilliant pale yellow. Powerful aroma of somewhat varietal ripe fruit (ripe apples) and fragrant herbs. Flavourful palate with spicy hints of skins and a hint of minerals, with a warm, oily texture.

L'ARXIDUC PERE SEDA 2003 WHITE
82% parellada, 18% otras

80 Pale with a golden hue. Intense aroma with fruit and white flowers, fine hints of exotic fruit and notes of aniseed and herbs. Flavourful, fresh palate with marked citrus acidity.

L'ARXIDUC PERE SEDA 2003 ROSÉ
merlot, tempranillo

82 Lively blush. Intense aroma of ripe red fruit slightly sweet. Flavourful palate with fine bitter notes and marked citrus acidity.

PERE SEDA NOVELL 2003 JOVEN RED
manto negro, callet, tempranillo

77 Dark garnet red cherry. Powerful aroma of slightly reduced ripe fruit with hints of damp earth. Flavourful palate with fleshy overtones, slightly rough tannins and bitter and sweet notions, oily.

DO PLA I LLEVANT

L'ARXIDUC PERE SEDA 2000 OAK AGED RED
manto negro, callet, tempranillo   🌐6

78 Garnet red cherry. Intense aroma with toasty oak notes and a suggestion of jammy fruit. Meaty palate, with a hint of slightly aged and sweet wood, bitter, without great nuances.

PERE SEDA 2000 CRIANZA RED
cabernet sauvignon, tempranillo, merlot, syrah

83 Dark cherry with a coppery-dark red edge. Intense, spicy aroma with fine reduction notes (animals). Meaty, flavourful palate with slightly rough, oily tannins, hints of liquorice and terroir, slightly warm.

MOSSÈN ALCOVER 2001 RESERVA RED
50% cabernet sauvignon, 50% callet

86 Cherry with an orangey hue. Aroma with excellent fruit expression combined with fine toasty oak (cocoa, vanilla). Round, oily palate with fruit expression and fine spices, long and persistent with a good evolution in the bottle and supple tannins.

PERE SEDA 1999 RESERVA RED
tempranillo, cabernet sauvignon, merlot, callet, manto negro

85 Garnet red cherry with a brick red edge. Powerful aroma with predominant toasty oak and reduction notes (tobacco, leather, cedar, old furniture). Flavourful, supple palate with a good oak/fruit integration, good acidity and a slightly warm, oily texture.

GVIVM MERLOT-CALLET 2001 RED
50% merlot, 50% callet

85 Dark garnet red cherry. Aroma with balsamic and toasty notes (pitch, coffee, and iodine). Round, elegant, balsamic palate with supple tannins, flavourful.

CHARDONNAY PERE SEDA 2003 OAK AGED WHITE

Vins TONI GELABERT

Camí dels Horts de Llodrá km. 1,3
Son Fangos
07500 Manacor (Balears)
☎: 971 552 409 - Fax: 971 552 409
info@vinstonigelabert.com
www.vinstonigelabert.com

Established: 1980

🛢 65 ⬛ 24,000 litres 🍇 5 has.

🍷 90% 🍏10%: -DE

VINYA SON FANGOS 2003 WHITE
85% prensal blanc, 15% moscatel de grano menudo

85 Pale yellow. Powerful, complex aroma with fruit, white flowers, exotic hints, herbs and a nuance of aniseed. Flavourful palate with fine notes of bitterness, herbs and excellent acidity.

TONI GELABERT CHARDONNAY 2003 OAK AGED WHITE
100% chardonnay

86 Pale yellow with a greenish hue. Quite intense aroma with fine notes of white fruit well-integrated with the smoky oak. Flavourful, slightly warm and oily on the palate with excellent varietal expression, fine bitter notes and good acidity.

SES HEREVES 2001 OAK AGED RED
40% merlot, 30% cabernet sauvignon, 30% syrah

87 Quite dark cherry. Fruity aroma with ripe varietal hints (paprika), dry earth and fine toasty creamy oak. Round, oily palate with a good integration between varietal expression and fine toasty wood, complex.

MERLOT TONI GELABERT 2002 RED
100% merlot

83 Garnet red cherry. Aroma with varietal notes and a suggestion of early reduction, fruity with toasty hints. Round, fruity, varietal, pleasant palate.

NEGRE DE SA COLONIA 2001 CRIANZA RED

DO Ca. PRIORAT

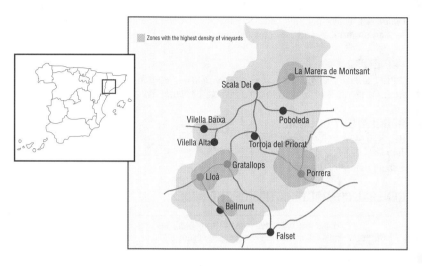

Zones with the highest density of vineyards

La Marera de Montsant
Scala Dei
Vilella Baixa
Poboleda
Vilella Alta
Torroja del Priorat
Gratallops
Lloà
Porrera
Bellmunt
Falset

NEWS. Priorat, a word on everybody's lips, and not only due to the international impact of its finest wines, sought everywhere for their unique character, the heritage of the exceptional *terroir* it is blessed with. Now – and the market was screaming out for this – a significant number of bodegas have proposed launching second brands at more reasonable prices. And, very sensibly so, some producers were of the opinion that one could not sell wines from young vineyards at the same price. 40% of the stock of Priorat is more than 20 years old, 35% between 8 and 20 years old, and the remaining 25% less than 7 years old. For this reason the Regulatory Council is trying to ensure that there are no imbalances between the supply of a grape, generally young, and its price.

Hectares of Vineyard	No. of Viticulturists	No. of Bodegas	2003 Harvest	2003 Production	Marketing
1,600	600	52	Very Good	2,100,000 kilos	51% Spain 49% foreign

Regardless of the 'price' question, of the 89 wines tasted, 42 achieved scores of 88 points and 14 equalled or surpassed 90 points, up to 98 for the exceptional and very elegant L'Ermita of Álvaro Palacios.

LOCATION. In the province of Tarragona. It is made up of the municipal districts of La Morera de Montsant, Scala Dei, La Vilella, Gratallops, Bellmunt, Porrera, Poboleda, Torroja, Lloá, Falset and Mola.

CLIMATE. Although with Mediterranean influences, it is temperate and dry. One of the most important characteristics is the practical absence of rain during the summer, which ensures very healthy grapes. The average rainfall is between 500 and 600 mm per year.

SOIL. This is probably the most distinctive characteristic of the region and precisely what has catapulted it to the top positions in terms of quality, not only in Spain, but around the world. The soil, thin and volcanic, is composed of small pieces of slate (*llicorella*), which give the wines a markedly mineral character. The vineyards are located on terraces and very steep slopes.

VARIETIES:
White: *Chenin Blanc, Macabeo, Garnacha Blanca, Pedro Ximénez.*
Red: *Cariñena, Garnacha, Garnacha Peluda, Cabernet Sauvignon, Merlot, Syrah.*

REGULATORY COUNCIL.
Bassa, 9. 43737 Torroja del Priorat.
Tel / Fax: 977 839 495.
E-mail: crdopriorat@inicia.es

GENERAL CHARACTERISTICS OF THE WINES:

Whites	These are produced mainly from *Macabeo* and *Garnacha Blanca*. Straw yellow coloured, they have fruity aromas and are reminiscent of mountain herbs; on the palate, they also show their Mediterranean character: they are somewhat warm with wild notes.
Rosés	These are maybe the least characteristic of the region. Due to the rather warm climate in which the grapes ripen, they are known for their ripe fruit notes; on the palate they are warm and flavourful.
Reds	The star product of the region. Produced from *Garnacha* and *Cariñena* combined in the high ranges with lesser percentages of foreign varieties; they are characterised by their very cloudy intense cherry colour. The best offer a nose with great complexity, with notes of very ripe fruit and the marked character of terruño (due to the effect of the slaty soil) that provide abundant mineral notes. On the palate, they have great character and structure; they are powerful, meaty, warm, and at the same time emphatically acidic, markedly tannic and very persistent.
Rancios and Sweet Wines	The traditional Rancios of the region have aromas of almonds and notes of mountain herbs; on the palate they are warm, flavourful with fine oxidative evolution. There is also a range of sweet wines produced according to more traditional criteria. They have a cloudy cherry colour; the aroma is of black fruit, almost raisin-like and notes of toast due to their ageing in oak; on the palate they are sweet, sticky, very fruity and well-balanced due to their good acidity.

ALVARO PALACIOS

Afores s/n
43737 Gratallops (Tarragona)
☎: 977 839 195 - Fax: 977 839 197
alvaropalacios@ctv.es

Established: 1989

🍷 700 🗄 200,000 litres❦ 24 has.

🚩 35% 🌐65%

L'ERMITA 2002 CRIANZA RED
80% garnacha, 20% cabernet sauvignon

97 Garnet red cherry with an orangey hue. Fine, elegant aroma of minerals with fine toast, cocoa and ripe fruit with mild floral notes, complex and very expressive. Medium-bodied, oily, round palate with minerals and fine toasty flavours in the retronasal passage and silky tannins within a persistent and elegant yet light structure.

FINCA DOFÍ 2002 CRIANZA RED
55% garnacha, 45% cabernet sauvignon, syrah, merlot

94 Intense cherry with an orange edge. Deep and complex aroma of minerals, ripe fruit, fine toasty oak, barely perceptible yet slightly creamy tannins. Generous, fleshy and elegant palate, polished tannins with toasty notes in the retronasal passage, very fine.

LES TERRASSES 2002 CRIANZA RED
60% cariñena, 30% garnacha, 10% cabernet sauvignon, syrah

88 Dark cherry with an orange edge. Fruity aroma with fresh overtones, mineral and creamy notes of oak well-blended with the wine. Generous, flavourful palate, very well-balanced, warm, with flavourful and sweet tannins; minerals and fine toasty flavours in the retronasal passage.

Celler ARDÈVOL I ASSOCIATS

Barceloneta, 14
43739 Porrera (Tarragona)
☎: 977 828 057 - Fax: 977 828 057
cellerardevol@terra.es

Established: 1999

🍷 60 🗄 20,000 litres❦ 10 has.

🚩 10% 🌐90%: -US -BE -IT -CH -SAM

TERRA D'HOM 2001 CRIANZA RED
COMA D'EN ROMEU 2002 CRIANZA RED

BUIL & GINÉ

Apdo. de Correo 63
43730 Falset (Tarragona)
☎: 977 830 483 - Fax: 977 830 373
esther@builgine.com
www.builgine.com

Established: 1996

GINÉ GINÉ 2001 RED
garnacha, cariñena

82 Garnet red cherry. Ripe aroma with viscous notes and toasty oak. Flavourful, powerful, fleshy and warm on the palate with very ripe fruit.

JOAN GINÉ GINÉ 2000 OAK AGED RED
garnacha, cariñena, cabernet sauvignon   🍷12

86 Dark cherry with a brick red rim. Intense, very fine aroma with black berries, fine toasty oak, balsamic and terracotta nuance. Flavourful palate with ripe, oily tannins, bitter (liquorice, dark-roasted flavours) with a jammy fruit hint.

PLERET 2000 OAK AGED RED
garnacha, cariñena, cabernet sauvignon, syrah, merlot

88 Dark cherry. Powerful aroma of fine toasty oak and ripe fruit with balsamic and slightly viscous notes. Flavourful palate with round and oily tannins, bitter (liquorice, dark-roasted flavours, graphite) with excellent acidity.

Bodegas y Viñedos del CAL GRAU

Ctra. El Molar - El Lloar, km. 2,5
43736 El Molar (Priorat)
☎: 661 861 971
miguelps@bodegascalgrau.com

Established: 2001

❦ 40 has.

LES ONES 2002 CRIANZA RED
55% cariñena, 35% garnacha, 10% syrah

92 Intense cherry. Powerful, very mineral aroma (slate, dry stones), with ripe fruit (jammy plums) and toasty hints of fine oak. Powerful, fleshy, warm and flavourful palate, very mineral.

Celler CAL PLA

Prat de la Riba, 1
43739 Porrera (Tarragona)
☎: 977 828 125 - Fax: 977 828 125
joan.sangenis@terra.es

Established: 1996

🍷 140 🗄 50,000 litres❦ 20 has. 🚩 70%

🌐30%: -US -DK -CH -UK -DE -IT -NL

CELLER CAL PLA 2001 OAK AGED RED
60% garnacha, 40% cariñena

77 Orangey cherry. Aroma with reduction notes, with smoky and spicy hint. Ripe, somewhat evolved palate with bitter, expressive tannins.

PLANOTS 2001 CRIANZA RED
60% garnacha, 40% cariñena

88 Intense cherry. Smoky, spices aroma (pepper) with mineral notes. Fleshy, powerful palate, with flavourful, fruity tannins, good fruit/oak integration and a generous finish in crianza nuances.

MAS D'EN COMPTE 2001 CRIANZA RED
60% garnacha, 40% cariñena

84 Cherry with a garnet red edge. Spicy aroma with notes of ripe skins and expressive, toasty crianza hints. Fleshy palate with quite pungent yet pleasant oak tannins (leather, animal skins).

MAS D'EN COMPTE 2003 WHITE

Cellers CAPAFONS-OSSÓ

del Bosquet, 6
43730 Falset (Tarragona)
☎: 977 831 204 - Fax: 977 831 367
cellers@capafons-osso.com
www.capafons-osso.com
Established: 1992
🌐 100 📊 40,000 litres 🍇 17.5 has.
🍷 50% 🌍50%: -US -AD -BE -FR -NL -IT -CH -MX -DE

MAS DE MASOS 2001 RED
35% garnacha peluda, 30% cabernet sauvignon, 20% garnacha, 10% cariñena, 5% syrah

89 Very dark cherry. Powerful aroma of toasty oak with spicy hints, skins, a balsamic and jammy fruit suggestion. Powerful, concentrated palate with good oak/fruit integration, a viscous edge, balsamic hints, and fine notes of exotic spices and minerals in the finish, promising.

MASOS D'EN CUBELLS 2001 OAK AGED RED
30% cabernet sauvignon, 30% garnacha, 20% cariñena, 10% merlot, 10% syrah

88 Dark cherry. Intense, very fine aroma rich in ripe fruit nuances (jammy hints) and oak crianza. Powerful, fleshy palate with good fruit/oak integration, fine bitter notes, spices and good acidity, promising.

MAS DE MASOS 2000 CRIANZA RED
35% garnacha peluda, 30% cabernet sauvignon, 20% garnacha, 10% cariñena, 5% syrah

87 Deep cherry. Spicy aroma (pepper), with notes of furniture, meat and jammy plums. Fleshy, powerful palate with mineral and fruit expression, a round finish.

ENLLAC 2002 JOVEN WHITE

Cellers CARTOIXA DE MONTSAVAT

Ereta, 10
43375 La Vilella Alta (Tarragona)
☎: 977 839 299 - Fax: 977 839 136
correu@cellerscartoixa.com
www.cellerscartoixa.com
Established: 1996
🌐 90 📊 25,000 litres 🍇 5 has.

🍷 20% 🌍80%

BLANC DE MONTSALVAT 2002 WHITE

89 Slightly cloudy golden yellow. Powerful aroma with smoky and creamy (vanilla, jelly) oak notes, a suggestion of ripe white fruit and hints of citrus fruit and herbs. Flavourful palate with a good fruit/oak integration, lactic flavours and a suggestion of exotic fruit and spices, slightly mineral, original.

MONTGARNATX 2002 RED
garnacha, cariñena

86 Dark garnet red cherry. Fruity, slightly mineral aroma with fine toasty notes. Warm, fleshy, flavourful and spirituous on the palate with ripe fruit, better than the '99.

MONTSALVAT 2001 RED

91 Intense cherry. Powerful aroma rich in ripe fruit expression (jammy plums), fine toasty flavours (cocoa, coffee), creamy oak and minerals. Powerful, warm, fleshy, full and spirituous on the palate with mineral hints (dry earth, stones), flavourful and persistent.

Celler CECILIO

Piró, 28
43737 Gratallops (Tarragona)
☎: 977 839 181 - Fax: 977 839 507
cellercecilio@hotmail.com
Established: 1942
🌐 80 📊 42,000 litres 🍇 8.5 has.
🍷 40% 🌍60%: -NL -DK -CH -US -DE

CELLER CECILIO 2003 WHITE
100% garnacha blanca

83 Coppery gold. Powerful aroma of white fruit with fine exotic and spicy hints of skins. Fresh, flavourful palate with slightly drying tannins, bittersweet (slightly crystallised fruit) with fine bitter notes and a citrus pulp, good acidity.

CELLER CECILIO 2002 RED
40% garnacha, 40% cariñena, 20% cabernet sauvignon

85 Deep cherry. Toasty, smoky aroma with hints of minerals and ripe black fruit. Fleshy, powerful palate, with round, expressive tannins and an earthy finish.

L'ESPILL 2001 RED
cabernet sauvignon, cariñena, garnacha

85 Dark cherry with a dark red-coppery edge. Intense aroma of slightly reduced ripe fruit, hints of leather and spicy oak. Fleshy palate with good fruit/oak integration, exotic spices, prunes, fine bitter notes, terroir and a warm, slightly oily texture, very long.

L'ESPILL 2000 OAK AGED RED
30% cabernet sauvignon, 60% garnacha, 20% cariñena

82 Cherry. Aroma of red fruit, green notes of skins and mineral hints. Flavourful palate with pleasant, fruity bitter tannins and herbaceous hints.

CELLER CECILIO 2003 RED

Unió Agraria Cooperativa CELLERS UNIÓ

Joan Oliver, 16-24 Mas de les Animes
43206 Reus (Tarragona)
☎: 977 330 055 - Fax: 977 330 070
f.gimenez@cellersunio.com
www.cellersunio.com
Established: 1942
🍷 6,500 📦 6,000,000 litres🍇 2,110 has.
🇪🇸 25% 🌐75%: -DE -DK -US -NL -JP

ROUREDA LLICORELLA 2002 CRIANZA RED
45% garnacha tinta, 35% cariñena, 20% syrah

86 Garnet red cherry with brick red nuances. Intense aroma of spicy notes of oak on a ripe fruit hint (blackberries). Flavourful, supple palate with a fresh spicy overtones, skins and minerals, slightly warm and very long.

CIMS DE PORRERA

Carretera de Torroja, s/n
43739 Porrera (Tarragona)
☎: 977 828 233 - Fax: 977 828 187
cims@arrakis.es
Established: 1996
🍷 300 📦 125,000 litres 🍷 25% 🌐75%

SOLANES 2001 CRIANZA RED
50% cariñena, 20% garnacha, 15% cabernet sauvignon, 10% merlot, 5% syrah

85 Dark cherry with a purplish edge. Powerful aroma of ripe fruit with spicy notes of skins, fine toasty oak and a balsamic and quite viscous hint. Flavourful palate with a good fruit/oak integration, bitter with a spicy finish (black pepper) and a suggestion of minerals.

CIMS DE PORRERA 2001 CRIANZA RED
90% cariñena, 10% garnacha

89 Dark cherry with a garnet red edge. Intense aroma with a certain finesse, with black berries, spicy hints of skins, balsamic hints, pitch and prunes. Flavourful palate with a good oak/fruit integration, sour cherries in liqueur and a good fruit weight despite the alcohol, balsamic and long.

CLOS BERENGUER

Carretera T-734 del Masroig, PK 8, 3
43736 El Molar (Tarragona)
☎: 606 453 536 - Fax: 977 361 390
closberenguer@terra.es

CLOS BERENGUER 2001 RED

83 Cherry with a garnet red edge. Aroma ripe red bramble fruit with well-integrated smoky notes. Fresh palate with notes of fresh cherries, fruity tannins and a bitter cocoa finish.

CLOS BERENGUER 2002 WHITE

CLOS ERASMUS

La Font, 1
43737 Gratallops (Tarragona)
☎: 977 839 022 - Fax: 977 839 179
closerasmus@terra.es
Established: 1994
🍷 20 🍇 7 has. 🍷 10% 🌐90%

CLOS ERASMUS PRIORAT RED

CLOS FIGUERAS

Carrer La Font, 38
43737 Gratallops (Tarragona)
☎: 977 831 712 - Fax: 977 831 712
europvin@infonegocio.com
Established: 1996
🍷 60 📦 20,000 litres🍇 25 has.
🍷 40% 🌐60%: -US -CH -DE -PR -JP -UK

FONT DE LA FIGUERA 2003 WHITE

85 Golden with a coppery hue. Fruity aroma (papaya, ripe grapefruit), expressive, musky hints and well-integrated, fine smoky nuances. Flavourful, fruity, fresh palate, with quite volume, evoking tropical fruit, slight bitterness contrasting with the weight of the alcohol, smoky.

FONT DE LA FIGUERA 2002 RED
50% garnacha, 30% cariñena, 15% syrah, 5% nonastrell

85 Deep cherry with a redcurrant edge. Aroma of well-ripened black fruit, spicy, with a slatey character, elegant toasty flavours. Fleshy, supple palate, with black fruit weight, toasty flavours (cocoa), elegant, mineral traces in the retronasal passage.

CLOS FIGUERAS 2001 RED
40% garnacha, 30% cariñena, 20% syrah, 10% mouvedre

89 Nearly opaque cherry with a garnet red edge. Aroma of black fruit, hints of cassis, chocolates (elegant wood), complex (mineral flavours, ripe plums). Fleshy, powerful palate with fresh overtones, bitter cocoa in the finish (yet to be assembled; lacks last year's complexity).

CLOS MOGADOR

Camí Manyetes s/n

43737 Gratallops (Tarragona)
☎: 977 839 171 - Fax: 977 839 426
closmogador@terra.es

Established: 1979

🌐 60 📖 17,250 litres 🍇 20 has.

🍷 20% 🌐80%: -UE E.U. -TW -JP -AU

CLOS MOGADOR 2002 CRIANZA RED
37% garnacha, 30% cabernet sauvignon, 20% syrah, 13% cariñena

91 Intense cherry. Aroma with mineral nuances, jammy black fruit and creamy toast (chocolate, coffee). Fleshy, warm, powerful and mineral on the palate with abundant, sweet tannins, spirituous.

CLOS MANYETES 2001 RESERVA RED
70% cariñena, 30% garnacha

88 Intense cherry. Toasty aroma of stewed black fruit and spirituous hints. Warm, spirituous palate and sweet tannins, powerful and fleshy, with an earthy retronasal effect.

COSTERS DEL SIURANA

Manyetes, s/n
43737 Gratallops (Tarragona)
☎: 977 839 276 - Fax: 977 839 371
info@costersdelsiurana.com
www.costersdelsiurana.com

Established: 1987

🌐 200 📖 120,000 litres 🍇 50 has.

🍷 50% 🌐50%: -US -JP -CA -UE

CLOS DE L'OBAC 2002 ROBLE RED
garnacha, cabernet sauvignon, merlot, cariñena

89 Dark cherry with a violet rim. Powerful aroma of spicy oak with fine hints of ripe fruit and minerals. Intense, concentrated and elegant on the palate, rich in balsamic nuances with good fruit/oak integration, spicy and long.

MISERERE 2002 CRIANZA RED
tempranillo, cabernet sauvignon, merlot, garnacha

88 Dark garnet red cherry. Powerful aroma with well-integrated spicy oak notes and fruit, cocoa, balsamic hints and minerals. Powerful, fleshy palate with slightly rough, oily tannins, spices, an oily texture, balsamic and terroir hints.

DOLÇ DE L'OBAC 2002 RED DULCE

88 Intense brilliant cherry. Elegant aroma of jammy black fruit, with smoky notes, pitch and a fine smoky hint. Sweet, flavourful and very expressive on the palate with minerals, sun-drenched skins and a highly integrated tannicity.

KYRIE 2001 CRIANZA WHITE
CLOS DE L'OBAC 2001 CRIANZA RED DULCE

DE MULLER

Camí Pedra Estela, 34
43205 Reus (Tarragona)
☎: 977 757 473 - Fax: 977 771 129
demuller1@infonegocio.com

Established: 1851

🌐 1,200 📖 3,850,000 litres 🍇 132 has.

🍷 35% 🌐65%: -US; -CA -MX -CO -PE -SE -UK -FR -FI -DK -DE -RU -LT -JP -BJ -ET -CH -DE -SE

LEGITIM DE MULLER 2000 ROBLE RED
60% garnacha tinta, 20% merlot, 10% syrah, 10% cariñena

85 Dark cherry with a brick red edge. Powerful aroma with predominant toasty oak notes and hints of reduction (tobacco, cedar, cigar box). Flavourful palate with ripe, oily tannins, spicy with rich reduction hints and liquorice.

LES PUSSES DE MULLER 2001 OAK AGED RED
50% merlot, 50% syrah   🌐12

87 Dark garnet red cherry. Powerful, ripe aroma with toasty, spicy notes of oak and a slight varietal hint (jammy redcurrants, spices, petals, underbrush). Powerful, fleshy palate with a good fruit/oak integration, warm and oily with a suggestion of sweet fruit, liquorice and dark-roasted flavours.

LO CABALÓ 1998 RESERVA RED
70% garnacha tinta, 10% merlot, 10% syrah, 10% cariñena

88 Dark deep red cherry. Powerful, fruity aroma (redcurrants, cherries, skins), with smoky oak notes and a hint of Bordeaux (cedar). Fleshy palate with good fruit/oak integration and a warm, oily texture, spicy and very long.

PRIORAT DOM JOAN FORT 1865 VINO DE LICOR
DOM BERENGUER 1918 RANCIO DULCE

ELS CUPS

Major, 4
43376 Poboleda (Tarragona)
☎: 977 827 010 - Fax: 977 827 302
populetus@terra.es

Established: 2000

🌐 14 📖 17,000 litres 🍇 6 has. 🍷 100%

POPULETUS 2002 WHITE
ELS CUPS 2003 ROBLE RED
ELS CUPS 2000 ROBLE RED
ELS CUPS 2001 ROBLE RED

Celler FUENTES

Montsent, 2

43738 Bellmunt del Priorat (Tarragona)
☎: 977 830 675 - Fax: 977 830 675
cellersfuentes@granclos.com
www.cellersfuentes.com

Established: 1995

⊞ 140 ▤ 50,000 litres 30 has.

🍷 80% 🍇20%

VINYA LLISARDA FERMENTADO EN BARRICA
 WHITE
FINCA EL PUIG CRIANZA RED
GRAN CLOS 2000 CRIANZA RED

JOAN AMETLLER

Ctra La Morera de Monsant-Cornudella, km.3,2
43360 La Morera de Monsant (Tarragona)
☎: 933 208 439 - Fax: 933 208 437
ametller@ametller.com
www.ametller.com

Established: 2003

⊞ 115 ▤ 42,000 litres 23 has.

🍷 18% 🍇82%: -NL -SE -JP -UK -DE -MX

ELS IGOLS 2001 RED

JOAN BLANCH

Avenida Catalunya, 8
43812 Puigpelat (Tarragona)
☎: 933 074 504 - Fax: 933 076 219
blanch@cellersblanch.com
www.cellersblanch.com

Established: 1980

⊞ 25 ▤ 90,000 litres 25 has. 🍷 100%

VI DEL RACÓ CRIANZA RED
VI DEL RACÓ RESERVA RED
VI DEL RACÓ DOLÇ CRIANZA DULCE

Celler JOAN SIMÓ

Onze de Setembre, 7
43739 Porrera (Tarragona)
☎: 977 830 325 - Fax: 977 830 325
cellerjoansimo@airtel.net

Established: 1999

⊞ 60 ▤ 25,000 litres 11 has.

🍷 20% 🍇80%: -US -BE -CH -DE -CA

LES SENTIUS 2002 ROBLE RED
60% garnacha, 20% cariñena, 10% cabernet sauvignon,
10% syrah

83 Intense cherry with a violet edge. Slightly ripe
aroma of spices (pepper) and a mineral suggestion. Flavourful, fresh palate with expressive red
fruit tannins, slightly mineral.

LES ERES "VINYES VELLES" 2002 OAK AGED
RED
50% garnacha peluda, 35% cariñena, 15% cabernet sauvignon

80 Dark cherry with a purplish edge. Powerful
aroma with notes of burnt oak, a suggestion of
petrol, graphite and Chinese ink. Fleshy, concentrated palate with bitter notes (liquorice, dark-
roasted flavours), lacks fruit nuances.

LES ERES "VINYES VELLES" 2001 OAK AGED
RED

Celler de L'ENCASTELL

Castell, 13
43739 Porrera (Tarragona)
☎: 977 828 146 - Fax: 977 828 146
roquers@roquers.com
www.roquers.com

Established: 1999

⊞ 80 ▤ 25,000 litres 7.5 has. 🍷 30%

🍇70%: -UK -US -IT -DK. -SE -BE -CH -AD

MARGE 2002 OAK AGED RED
50% garnacha, 20% cabernet sauvignon, 15% merlot, 15%
syrah   ⊞ 8

86 Dark deep red cherry. Intense aroma with
good oak/fruit integration, fine balsamic notes and
minerals. Fleshy, slightly warm and oily on the
palate, rich in bitter nuances with jammy fruit,
liquorice, balsamic flavours, terroir and spices in
the retronasal passage.

ROQUERS DE PORRERA 2002 CRIANZA RED
40% garnacha, 40% cariñena, 20% cabernet sauvignon,
merlot, syrah

87 Very deep cherry. Fine aroma with concentrated
black plums, smoky flavours and well-assembled
cocoa with an earthy hint. Fleshy, powerful palate,
with expressive fruit tannins integrated with the
wood (cocoa), a round and slightly pungent finish.

LA CONRERIA DE SCALA DEI

Mitja Galta, 32
43379 Scala Dei (Tarragona)
☎: 977 -82 -55 - Fax: 977 -82 -55
laconreria@scaladei.org
www.scaladei.org

Established: 1997

⊞ 90 ▤ 60,000 litres 24 has. 🍷 85%

🍇15%: -US -DE -JP -DK -CH -PR -IT -AT

NONA 2002 FERMENTADO EN BARRICA
WHITE
100% garnacha

92 Gold with a reddish glimmer. Deep, original
aroma with notes of fragrant herbs (lavender, mint
and fennel) and apples. Full, complex, flavourful,

mineral palate with ripe fruit and bitter hints very well neutralised by the alcohol. It has improved since last year's tasting.

LES BRUGUERES 2003 WHITE
100% garnacha

89 Coppery. Intense, very fine aroma of ripe white fruit with hints of flowers and fine lees. Generous palate with a slightly warm, oily texture and spicy, smoky hints, fruity with a mineral finish and notes of fresh fruit, original.

IUGITER 2001 OAK AGED RED
10% cabernet sauvignon, 5% cariñena, 85% garnacha

85 Dark cherry with a brick red rim. Powerful, ripe aroma with fine reduction notes, a toasty and spicy oak hint. Fleshy, concentrated palate with good oak/fruit integration, rough, slightly warm and oily sweet tannins with a mineral suggestion.

IUGITER SELECCIÓ DE VINYES VELLES 2000 CRIANZA RED
60% garnacha, 30% cabernet sauvignon, 10% cariñena

89 Very deep garnet red cherry. Intense, very fine, concentrated aroma of ripe black fruit, with fine smoky, creamy oak notes, spicy hints and terracotta. Flavourful, fleshy palate with good fruit/oak integration, balsamic hints and a viscous edge (liquorice); very long.

LA CONRERIA 2002 RED
garnacha, merlot, cabernet

82 Deep cherry. Clear aroma of red fruit with notes of fallen leaves. Fresh, flavourful palate with fruit tannins, a Mediterranean nuance (broom) and a fresh finish.

LA PERLA DEL PRIORAT

Mas dels Frares, s/n
43736 El Molar (Tarragona)
☎: 977 825 202 - Fax: 977 825 202
laperladelpriorat@telefonica.net

Established: 1997

🍷 144 🛢 85,000 litres🌿 17 has.

🍷 30% 🌐70%: -UK -US -BE -DK -DE -CH

CLOS LES FITES 2002 CRIANZA RED
55% garnacha, 25% cariñena, 20% cabernet sauvignon

85 Not very deep cherry. Aroma of ripe fruit with minerals and balsamic flavour. Fresh, flavourful palate with good wood/fruit integration and a suggestion of toasty wood in the retronasal passage.

COMTE PIRENNE 2002 CRIANZA RED
50% garnacha, 30% cariñena, 20% cabernet sauvignon

88 Intense cherry. Powerful aroma rich in varietal expression, spirituous, with minerals and very ripe black fruit. Fleshy, powerful, spirituous palate with sweet and flavourful tannins, smoky and persistent.

CLOS LES FITES 2002 WHITE
CLOS LES FITES 2003 CRIANZA RED

LLICORELLA VINS

Carrer de l'Era, 11
43737 Torroja del Priorat (Tarragona)
☎: 639 893 498
administracio@llicorellavins.com
www.llicorellavins.com

Established: 2001

🍷 12 🛢 11,000 litres 🍷 80%

🌐20%: -US -FR

MAS SAURA 2001 RED
50% garnacha, 25% syrah, 15% cabernet sauvignon, 10% cariñena

88 Very deep cherry. Intense aroma of well-ripened black fruit, with harmonised smoky flavours and subitle cocoa. Fleshy, with chewy, ripe tannins, an excellent fruit-wood balance, round finish.

MAS SAURA 2002 OAK AGED RED
MAS SAURA 2003 OAK AGED RED

MAS D'EN COSME VITICULTORS

Carretera de Porrera, s/n
43730 Falset (Tarragona)
☎: 977 830 483 - Fax: 977 830 373
www.masdencosme.com

Established: 1999

🌿 12 has.

BABOIX 2000 OAK AGED RED
garnacha, cariñena, tempranillo, cabernet sauvignon, merlot
🍷 12

85 Dark cherry with a saffron rim. Powerful aroma with predominant toasty wood notes, balsamic and jammy fruit suggestion. Flavourful, bitter palate (good oak/fruit integration) with hints of liquorice, terroir and sweet fruit.

Viticultors MAS D'EN GIL

Finca Mas D'En Gil, s/n
43738 Bellmunt del Priorat (Tarragona)
☎: 977 830 192 - Fax: 977 830 152
mail@masdengil.com
www.masdengil.com

Established: 1998

🍷 270 🛢 245,000 litres🌿 45 has.

🍷 80% 🌐20%: -UE -US -JP

COMA VELLA 2002 RED

89 Very deep garnet red cherry. Powerful aroma, ripe, notes of red stone fruit, fresh varietal overtones with very fine wood, smoky and spicy hints of the crianza. Powerful palate, fresh, very flavourful, excellent varietal expression, complex, well-balanced, slightly marked but promising wood tannins, excellent acidity, very long.

CLOS FONTÀ 2002 RED

92 Intense garnet red cherry. Intense aroma, rich in ripe fruit nuances (jammy red fruit) with a fine creamy hint (cocoa) of the oak, a slightly mineral and balsamic suggestion. Powerful, supple, ripe palate, excellent fruit weight (in spite of the 14.5%), polished and oily tannins, fresh mineral overtones, liquorice and balsamic hints in the finish.

GRAN BUIG 1998 RED

91 Dark cherry. Aroma with notes of carpentry and earthy mineral hints, stewed fruit. Fleshy palate, full and warm, oak in the retronasal passage, carpentry, long, very ripe sweet tannins.

Celler MAS DE LES PERERES

Mas de Les Pereres, s/n
43376 Poboleda (Tarragona)
☎: 977 827 257 - Fax: 977 827 257
Dirk.Hoet@village.uunet.be

NUNCI ABOCAT 2003 FERMENTADO EN BARRICA WHITE

90 Brilliant golden yellow. Powerful aroma, rich in nuances of ripe white fruit and highly fragrant scrubland herbs with notes of fine and creamy oak. Warm palate with body, full, sweet and spiritous; Mediterranean and persistent.

NUNCI BLANC 2002 FERMENTADO EN ÇBARRICA WHITE

88 Gold with a coppery glimmer. Aroma with creamy notes and ripe fruit with hints of mountain herbs. Dense, warm, very sweet (more so than advocat) palate, flavourful, and long.

NUNCI COSTERO 2002 CRIANZA RED

90 Intense cherry. Aroma with nuances of ripe skins and toasty flavours, with a suggestion of minerals and toasty oak notes well-integrated with the wine. Full, generous palate with character, flavourful with silky grape tannins although with slightly marked wood tannins.

NUNCI NEGRE 2002 RED

91 Intense cherry. Intense aroma of fine toasty oak with excellent black fruit character, varietal and mineral. Fleshy, powerful, warm and expressive palate with minerals in the retronasal passage, excellent balance between oak and wine, slightly spirituous.

NUNCI 2003 FERMENTADO EN BARRICA WHITE

Celler MAS DOIX

Carme, 115
43376 Poboleda (Tarragona)
☎: 639 356 172 - Fax: 933 216 790
masdoix@bsab.com
Established: 1998
🛢 90 🛢 40,000 litres 🍇 20 has.
🍷 25% 🌐75%

SALANQUES 2001 CRIANZA RED
60% garnacha, 20% cariñena, 7% merlot, 7% cabernet sauvignon, 6% syrah

88 Deep intense cherry. Toasty aroma of spices (black pepper, cocoa) over jammy fruit. Woody, fresh palate with noticeable oak tannins; heavy fruit, yet to be assembled.

DOIX 2001 CRIANZA RED
50% garnacha, 47% cariñena, 3% merlot

90 Very intense cherry. Powerful aroma of minerals, chocolate and carob with a nuance of fine carpentry. Powerful, spirituous, warm, slightly viscous and full palate with flavourful and very ripe tannins and a suggestion of minerals.

Celler MAS GARRIAN

Camí Rieres, s/n
43736 El Molar (Tarragona)
☎: 977 262 118 - Fax: 977 825 120
masgarriansl@wanadoo.es
Established: 2000
🛢 50 🛢 35,000 litres 🍇 45 has.
🍷 50% 🌐50%: -FI -US -BE -CH -CA

CLOS SEVERI 2001 CRIANZA RED
40% garnacha, 25% cariñena, 25% cabernet sauvignon, 10% syrah

85 Deep cherry. Clear and clean aroma of red fruit with a mountain herb edge. Flavourful, fresh palate with red fruit tannins and barely perceptible fine wood.

MAS DEL CAMPEROL 2001 CRIANZA RED
40% cariñena, 25% garnacha, 25% cabernet sauvignon, 10% syrah

85 Intense cherry. Intense, mineral aroma with fine smoky notes (cocoa) and expressive fruit skins. Fleshy palate, quite powerful, well-integrated toasty notes and an astringent finish (bramble fruit).

MAS DEL CAMPEROL 2000 CRIANZA RED
CLOS SEVERI 2002 CRIANZA RED

MAS IGNEUS

Diputación, 39
08770 Sant Sadurni d'Anoia (Barcelona)

DO Ca. PRIORAT

☎: 938 183 445 - Fax: 938 914 094
info@anpiwines.com

Established: 1919

🌐 250 📊 240,000 litres 🍇 125 has. 🇪🇸 20%

🌍80%: -DE -CH -NL -PDV -US -SAM

BARRANC DELS CLOSOS 2003 JOVEN WHITE
50% macabeo, 30% garnacha blanca, 20% pedro ximénez

89 Pale yellow with a greenish hue. Intense, very fine aroma with notes of flowers and slightly exotic fresh fruit (melon), notes of fennel. Flavourful, slightly fruity and warm palate with fresh mineral overtones, long.

MAS IGNEUS FA 104 2003 JOVEN WHITE
100% garnacha blanca

89 Pale with a greenish hue. Intense, very fine aroma with excellent varietal notes (green fruit, hints of exotic fruit and fine herbs) and smoky oak suggestions. Powerful, slightly fruity palate with rich herb nuances, warm and oily.

BARRANC DELS CLOSOS 2002 OAK AGED RED
70% garnacha tinta, 30% cariñena

86 Dark deep red cherry. Slightly intense aroma with smoky, spicy notes of oak, a nuance of ripe fruit and macerated skins. Powerful palate with marked but promising tannins and a spicy fresh soil overtones, slightly warm but with good fruit weight and liquorice.

MAS IGNEUS FA 206 2001 RED

MAS IGNEUS FA 112 2000 OAK AGED RED

COSTERS DE MAS IGNEUS 2001 OAK AGED RED

MAS MARTINET

Carretera Falset - Gratallops, km. 6
43730 Falset (Tarragona)
☎: 629 238 236 - Fax: 639 121 244
masmartinet@masmartinet.com
www.masmartinet.com

Established: 1989

🌐 300 📊 60,000 litres 🍇 15 has.

🍷 40% 🌍60%: -DE -CH -US -PR -OTHERS

MARTINET BRU 2002 CRIANZA RED
garnacha, cabernet sauvignon, merlot

87 Deep cherry. Mineral aroma of jammy red fruit with a sun-drenched nuance. Fleshy palate with marked but oily oak tannins, overtones of reduction notes (dry earth, animal skins), quite light.

CLOS MARTINET 2001 CRIANZA RED
40% garnacha, 25% syrah, 20% cabernet sauvignon, 15% cariñena

95 Intense cherry. Deep, toasty aroma of ripe fruit (jammy prunes, dark-roasted flavours) with a nuance of finesse; wood and fruit to be assembled, with complex notes of evolution in bottle. Powerful, spirituous and flavourful palate (chocolate); sweet grape tannins well-integrated with the creamy oak tannins.

CLOS MARTINET 2002 CRIANZA RED

MAS PERINET

Finca Mas Perinet, s/n T-702 km. 1, 6
43360 La Morera de Montsant (Tarragona)
☎: 977 827 113 - Fax: 977 827 480

Established: 1998

🌐 230 📊 166,000 litres 🍇 18 has.

PERINET 2002 OAK AGED RED

MASÍA DUCH

Carretera de las Vilellas, km. 13
Finca el Tancat
43379 Scala Dei (Tarragona)
☎: 977 773 513 - Fax: 977 341 215

Established: 1985

🌐 300 📊 300,000 litres 🍇 20 has.

🍷 80% 🌍20%

BRESSOL 2000 RED
80% garnacha, 20% cabernet sauvignon

72 Dark cherry with an orange edge. Very reduced aroma (wet leather) without fruit or minerals. Supple, slightly sweet expressionless palate.

EL TANCAT 1999 RED
80% cabernet sauvignon, 20% garnacha

79 Quite intense cherry with an orange edge. Aroma with reduction notes (tobacco, leather), dried mountain herbs and toasty hints. Supple, round and slightly reduced on the palate with muted fruit.

NOGUERALS

Tou, 5
43360 Cornudella de Montsant (Tarragona)
☎: 977 821 020
noguerals@hotmail.com

Established: 2000
🌐 30 🛢 15,800 litres 🍇 4.5 has. 🍷 100%

ABELLARS 2002 CRIANZA RED
50% garnacha, 25% cariñena, 15% cabernet sauvignon, 10% syrah

90 Deep cherry. Powerful aroma of subtle, ripe black fruit, and a suggestion of earth and liquorice, complex. Fleshy palate with promising fresh, fruity tannins, well-assembled smoky wood and a round, toasty aftertaste.

Celler PASANAU

La Bassa, s/n
43361 La Morera de Montsant (Tarragona)
☎: 974 827 049 - Fax: 974 827 049
pasanaugerm@retemail.es
www.bodegapasanau.com

Established: 1995
🌐 120 🛢 82,500 litres 🍇 14 has.
🍷 50% 🌍50%: -UE -US -CA -CH -JP -MX

PASANAU CEPS NOUS 2002 RED
44% garnacha, 30% merlot, 20% mazuelo, 6% syrah

83 Intense cherry. Marked peppery aroma with balsamic hints and a suggestion of ripe red fruit. Fresh, flavourful palate with fruity tannins, spicy, round.

PASANAU FINCA LA PLANETA 2001 RED
60% cabernet sauvignon, 40% garnacha

90 Very deep cherry. Powerful aroma of fine toasty wood, liquorice and earth with a suggestion of jammy plums. Fleshy, powerful palate with earthy and ripe tannins, chocolate and a mild expression of soil in the finish.

PASANAU LA MORERA DE MONTSANT 2001 RED
62% garnacha, 24% cabernet sauvignon, 14% merlot

89 Dark cherry with a dark red-coppery edge. Powerful aroma of ripe black fruit (reduction hints), spicy oak notes, balsamic and terroir suggestion. Fleshy, flavourful palate with good fruit/oak integration, and ripe, oily tannins, slightly warm but with excellent fruit weight; very long.

PASANAU LA MORERA DE MONTSANT 2000 RED

Celler del PONT

Del Riu, 1 Baixos
43374 La Vilella Baixa (Tarragona)
☎: 977 828 231 - Fax: 977 828 231
cellerdelpont@mixmail.com

Established: 1998
🌐 24 🛢 8,000 litres 🍷 40%
🌍60%: -US -DE -CH -UK -DK -AD -JP -CA

LO GIVOT 2002 CRIANZA RED
33% cariñena, 32% garnacha negra, 25% cabernet sauvignon, 10% syrah

88 Garnet red with a violet edge. Aroma of elegant black fruit with a hint of soil (minerals), earthy, and well-integrated toasty flavoured notes. Fruity palate, with flavourful tannins, toasty aroma, slightly warm; a fresh finish and marked earthy flavour.

LO GIVOT 2001 RED
33% cariñena, 32% garnacha negra, 25% cabernet sauvignon, 10% syrah

87 Dark garnet red. Earthy aroma, expressive black fruit, fine reduction, floral. Fleshy palate, mineral, reminiscent of liquorice and fruit with ripe and oily tannins. Slightly warm but made up for the acidity.

Bodegas BG RAFAEL BORDALAS GARCÍA

Carretera T-210, km. 9, 5
43737 Gratallops (Tarragona)
☎: 977 839 513 - Fax: 977 839 434
bodegasbg@yahoo.es

Established: 1998
🌐 30 🛢 15,000 litres 🍇 25 has. 🍷 20%

DO Ca. PRIORAT

🍇80%: -EA -BE-UK-SE -DK -MX -DE -CH -PR

EL SI DEL MOLÍ 2003 OAK AGED WHITE
70% garnacha blanca, 30% viura

83 Brilliant gold. Powerful aroma with a hint of sherry, toasty wood notes and a suggestion of ripe white fruit. Powerful, flavourful, warm and oily palate with predominant notes of lees and smoky wood, lacking balance.

GUETA LUPIA 2001 CRIANZA RED
55% garnacha, 35% cariñena, 5% merlot, 5% cabernet sauvignon

88 Brilliant deep cherry. Mineral aroma with an expression of toasty skins and a suggestion of liquorice. Fleshy palate with both powerful and fruity tannins and a well-integrated soily character.

GUETA LUPIA 2002 RED

Celler RIPOLL SANS

Baixada Consolació, 4
43737 Gratallops (Tarragona)
☎: 977 -83 -61 - Fax: 977 -83 -61
mripoll@closabatllet.com
www.closabatllet.com

Established: 2000

🍷 36 📊 20,000 litres🌿 9 has. 🇪🇸 10%
🍇90%: -US -DE -CH -UK -AT -JP -NO

CLOSA BATLLET 2003 OAK AGED WHITE
escanyavells

78 Golden. Aroma with a predominant suphorous odour, hints of almonds and partially concealed fruit. Warm, flavourful palate with bitter hints.

CLOSA BATLLET 2002 OAK AGED RED
65% cariñena, 21% garnacha, 6% cabernet sauvignon, 6% syrah

87 Dark cherry with a purplish rim. Intense, ripe aroma of black fruit (hints of reduction) and fine smoky oak. Fleshy palate with good fruit/oak integration, excellent fruit-alcohol balance, a slightly viscous edge, liquorice and terroir.

ROSA M. BARTOLOMÉ VERNET

Nou, 3
43738 Bellmunt del Priorat (Tarragona)
☎: 977 320 449 - Fax: 977 320 448
cellerbartolome@hotmail.com

Established: 1997

🍷 28 📊 13,000 litres🌿 6 has.
🇪🇸 50% 🍇50%: -US -CH -BE

PRIMITIU DE BELLMUNT 2002 OAK AGED RED
60% garnacha, 40% cariñena

88 Deep cherry with a violet edge. Aroma of well-ripened red fruit, mountain herbs and well-integrated cocoa. Fleshy, with ripe, fresh tannins, complex toasty notes, expressive fruit and round in the finish.

ROTLLAN TORRÁ

Balandra, 6
43737 Torroja del Priorat (Tarragona)
☎: 902 177 000 - Fax: 933 050 112
priorat@teleline.es
www.rotllantorra.com

Established: 1982

🍷 350 📊 250,000 litres🌿 24 has.
🇪🇸 50% 🍇50%

TIRANT 2001 OAK AGED RED
25% garnacha, 25% cabernet sauvignon, 25% cariñena, 10% merlot, 15% syrah

82 Very intense cherry. Aroma with notes of overripening (port), toasty hints (chimneys) and earthy hints. Fleshy, mineral, viscous and warm on the palate, spirituous and slightly fiery.

AMADIS 2001 OAK AGED RED
40% garnacha, 25% cabernet sauvignon, 20% cariñena, 10% syrah, 5% merlot

81 Intense cherry. Toasty, spirituous and somewhat evolved aroma (hints of sweetness, port). Fleshy, and jammy on the palate with carob beans, overripe or evolved.

ARIANE 1998 OAK AGED RED
25% cariñena, 25% cabernet sauvignon, 25% syrah, 15% garnacha, 10% merlot

83 Intense cherry with a slightly brick red edge. Very reduced aroma (wet leather, saddles) with jammy fruit. Round, flavourful palate with sweet, very obvious but not very expressive tannins.

BALANDRA 2001 OAK AGED RED

Celler SABATÉ

Nou, 6
43374 La Vilella Baixa (Tarragona)
☎: 977 839 209 - Fax: 977 839 209
cellersabate@hotmail.com

Established: 1910

🍷 60 📊 50,000 litres🌿 29 has.
🇪🇸 70% 🍇30%: -BE -DK -CH A-DE

MAS PLANTADETA GARNATXA 2003 FERMENTADO EN BARRICA WHITE
100% garnacha blanca

84 Pale gold. Powerful aroma with fine smoky and spicy notes of oak and a suggestion of slightly varietal and ripe fruit. Flavourful, spicy palate, slightly warm and oily with a smoky and herby finish.

MAS PLANTADETA GARNATXA 2003 ROBLE RED
100% garnacha

80 Dark cherry with a dark red edge. Powerful, fruity aroma with hints of macerated skins, a toasty hint and mild reduction in the tank. Fleshy, quite viscous palate of very ripe fruit (slight hints of overextraction); flavourful.

MAS PLANTADETA 2001 CRIANZA RED
70% garnacha, 20% cariñena, 10% cabernet sauvignon

85 Garnet red cherry with a brick red glint. Powerful aroma with fine smoky, spicy (oriental spices), oak notes, a toasty and jammy fruit hint. Powerful, concentrated palate with good fruit/oak integration, bitter hints of fine sweetness and good acidity.

MAS PLANTADETA SOLERA 35 AÑOS RANCIO

SANGENÍS I VAQUÉ

Pl. Catalunya, 3
43739 Porrera (Tarragona)
☎: 977 828 238 - Fax: 977 828 068
celler@sangenisvaque.com
Established: 1985
⊞ 125 ❦ 13 has. ❦ 20% ❦80%

GARBINADA 2001 RED
VALL POR 2001 RED
PORRERA 2001 RED
CLOS MONLLEO 2000 RED
CORANYA 2000 RED

Cellers de SCALA DEI

Rambla de la Cartoixa, s/n
43379 Scala Dei (Tarragona)
☎: 977 827 027 - Fax: 977 827 044
codinfo@codorniu.es
www.grupocodorniu.com
Established: 1973
⊞ 288 ❦ 90 has. ❦ 80% ❦20%

SCALA DEI PRIOR 2001 CRIANZA RED
garnacha, syrah, cabernet sauvignon

87 Cherry with a garnet red edge. Aroma of plums with balsamic notes, slightly varietal and a fine toasty hint. Fruity, flavourful palate with round, fresh tannins and a generous pleasant finish.

SCALA DEI CARTOIXA 2000 RESERVA RED
48% cabernet sauvignon, 47% garnacha, 5% Syrah

84 Deep cherry. Toasty, vanilla aroma with ripe red fruit, a suggestion of soil and spices. Round, flavourful palate with ripe fruit tannins, and marked oak, yet to be assembled.

Celler VALL-LLACH

Del Pont, 9
43739 Porrera (Tarragona)
☎: 977 828 244 - Fax: 977 828 325
celler@vallllach.com
www.vallllach.com
Established: 1997
⊞ 360 ▤ 120,000 litres ❦ 38 has.
♦ 90,000 litros. ❦ 30% ❦70%: -US -DE -CH -FR -IT -DK -BE -BR -PE -MX -IL -AT -RU -CA

VALL-LLACH 2002 OAK AGED RED
60% cariñena, 25% merlot, 10% cabernet sauvignon

90 Intense cherry. Fine toasty aroma with mineral notes and jammy fruit, less complex than previous years. Warm, spirituous, flavourful and mineral on the palate with pronounced yet slightly sweet tannins.

IDUS DE VALL-LLACH 2002 OAK AGED RED
40% cariñena, 20% merlot, 25% cabernet sauvignon, 10% garnacha, 5% syrah

89 Intense cherry. Aroma with fine toasty oak, minerals and ripe fruit. Fleshy, warm, flavourful palate with stewed black fruit, minerals and sweet, persistent tannins.

EMBRUIX DE VALL-LLACH 2002 OAK AGED RED
30% cariñena, 30% garnacha, 30% cabernet sauvignon, 10% syrah

90 Intense cherry. Fine toasty, very complex aroma (coffee, chocolate), hints of minerals and black fruit. Round, complex, mineral and warm on the palate, spirituous, very elegant and long.

VINÍCOLA DEL PRIORAT

Calle Piró, s/n
43737 Gratallops (Tarragona)
☎: 977 839 167 - Fax: 977 839 201
info@vinicoladelpriorat.com
www.vinicoladelpriorat.com
Established: 1991
⊞ 125 ▤ 750,000 litres ❦ 200 has.
❦ 20% ❦80%: -DE -CH -NL -BE -DK -UK -CA -US -JP -IL -NZ -PT -NO

ONIX CLÁSSIC 2003 JOVEN RED
50% garnacha tinta, 50% samsó

81 Cherry with a glacé cherry hue. Slightly closed aroma, spirituous, quite mineral with very ripe fruit. Warm palate with supple tannins and slightly fiery.

ONIX SELECCIÓ 2000 CRIANZA RED
100% samsó

81 Quite intense cherry. Aroma with light notes of overripening and a slightly viscous edge. Toasty aroma with viscous overtones and supple, sweet tannins, spirituous.

ONIX EVOLUCIÓ 2001 CRIANZA RED
50% samsó, 30% cabernet sauvignon, 20% garnacha tinta

82 Intense cherry. Slightly raisiny aroma with a viscous edge and toasty hints. Fleshy, and warm on the palate, spirituous and slightly viscous.

VIÑEDOS DE ITHACA

Roquer del Ros
43737 Gratallops (Tarragona)
☎: 977 660 080 - Fax: 977 668 666
mail@vinedosdeithaca.com
www.vinedosdeithaca.com

Established: 1999

⊞ 60 ▤ 40,000 litres 20 has. 🍷 60%
🌐40%: -UK -US -DE -BE -NL -IT -CH -DK -DK -FR -PT

ODYSSEUS PX 2003 WHITE
100% pedro ximénez

89 Fairly reddish gold. Aroma with sweet notes (custard apples) and a mild mineral suggestion, complex, curious. Powerful, mineral, unusual and flavourful palate, persistent and sweet.

ODYSSEUS GB 2003 WHITE
100% garnacha blanca

88 Straw-coloured with a golden hue. Intense aroma of ripe fruit (sweet and exotic notes) with hints of flowers and fine lees. Powerful palate with slightly sweet fruit, nuances of citrus pulp, a suggestion of minerals and excellent acidity.

ODYSSEUS R 2003 ROSÉ
60% cariñena, 20% garnacha, 10% petit verdot, 10% touriga

90 Raspberry. Powerful, fresh and fruity aroma (raspberries and strawberries). Powerful palate rich in fruity nuances, sweet and warm with a suggestion of minerals, a curious Rosé, exotic and out of context.

ODYSSEUS 2001 OAK AGED RED
38% garnacha, 30% cabernet sauvignon, 25% cariñena, 7% touriga

90 Intense cherry. Powerful, toasty, warm and mineral aroma of jammy black fruit. Warm, mineral palate with flavourful, sweet tannins and very elegant toasty ripe fruit.

VITICULTORS DEL PRIORAT

Partida Palells, Mas Subirat
43738 Bellmunt del Priorat (Tarragona)
☎: 977 262 268 - Fax: 977 262 268
morlanda@inicia.es - morlanda.com

Established: 1997

⊞ 260 ▤ 80,000 litres 22 has.
🍷 50% 🌐50%: -US -DE -MX -PE

MORLANDA 2003 JOVEN WHITE
garnacha

81 Light gold. Aroma with light notes of oxidative evolution and notions of scrubland herbs, ripe fruit and nuts. Powerful, warm palate with nuances of oak not yet integrated with the wine, flavourful and with a hint of evolution.

MORLANDA VI DE GUARDA 2001 OAK AGED (12) RED
60% garnacha, 30% cariñena, 10% cabernet sauvignon
⊞ 12

84 Quite dark cherry with an orange edge. Aroma with precocious reduction notes, hints of minerals and stewed fruit. Round, warm and flavourful on the palate with weak tannins.

PRIOR TERRAE 1998 RESERVA RED

DO RÍAS BAIXAS

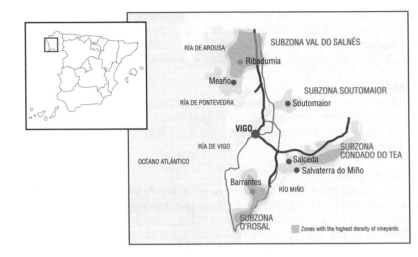

NEWS. Regardless of the praise of the wine producers and Regulatory Council with respect to the 2003 Harvest (it was said to be excellent 'in quality and quantity'), it is true that the heat had an effect, especially in the loss of acidity and freshness in most of the wines.

Hectares of Vineyard	No. of Viticulturists	No. of Bodegas	2003 Harvest	2003 Production	Marketing
2,643	5,690	179	-	10,785,600 litres	85% Spain 15% Abroad

Production increased by 20% and exports are continuing to rise (13%), close to a million litres now, mainly to the USA.

Mention should be made of cold maceration when evaluating the quality of the wine – a highly controversial topic, in view of the fact that, although it provides more heat and even aroma (rather in the line of skin yeasts), in general, it takes away freshness and the expression of varietal fruit displayed by those first Albariños that started to gain ground in international markets in the nineties.

In our opinion, despite the expectations generated by the 2003 harvest, qualitatively there has not been a huge leap forward with respect to 2002. Although the large brands and well-established firms (Señorans, Adegas Galegas, Fillaboa, Barrantes, Do Ferreiro, Lusco, etc.) all produce excellent wines, there are quite a few wines that do not achieve scores of 80 points, which makes it evident that export is seen as an easy way to bottle more wine without paying attention to the quality.

LOCATION. In the southwest of the province of Pontevedra, covering five distinct sub-regions: Val do Salnés, O Rosal, Condado do Tea, Soutomaior and Ribeira do Ulla.

CLIMATE. Atlantic, with moderate, mild temperatures due to the influence of the sea, high relative humidity and abundant rainfall (the annual average is around 1600 mm). There is less rainfall further downstream of the Miño (Condado de Tea), and as a consequence the grapes ripen earlier.

SOIL. Sandy, shallow and slightly acidic, which makes fine soil for producing quality wines. The predominant type of rock is granite, and only in the *Concellos* of Sanxenxo, Rosal and Tomillo is it possible to find a narrow band of metamorphous rock. Quaternary deposits are very common in all the sub-regions.

VARIETIES:
White: *Albariño* (majority), *Loureira Blanca* or *Marqués, Treixadura* and *Caíño Blanco* (preferred); *Torrontés* and *Godello* (authorized).
Red: *Caíño Tinto, Espadeiro, Loureira Tinta* and *Sousón* (preferred); *Mencía* and *Brancellao* (authorized).

SUB-REGIONS:
Val do Salnés. This is the historic sub-region of the *Albariño* (in fact, here, almost all the white wines are produced as single-variety wines from this variety) and is centred around the municipal district of Cambados. It has the flattest relief of the four sub-regions.
Condado do Tea. The furthest inland, it is situated in the south of the province on the northern bank of the Miño. It is characterized by its mountainous terrain. The wines must contain a minimum of 70% of *Albariño* and *Treixadura*.
O Rosal. In the extreme southwest of the province, on the right bank of the Miño river mouth. The warmest sub-region, where river terraces abound. The wines must contain a minimum of 70% of *Albariño* and *Loureira*.
Soutomaior. Situated on the banks of the Verdugo River, about 10 km from Pontevedra, it consists only of the municipal district of Soutomaior. It produces only single-varietals of *Albariño*.
Ribeira do Ulla. A new sub-region along the Ulla River, which forms the landscape of elevated valleys further inland. It comprises the municipal districts of Vedra and part of Padrón, Deo, Boquixon, Touro, Estrada, Silleda and Vila de Cruce. Red wines predominate.

REGULATORY COUNCIL.
Centro de Apoyo de Cabanas. 36143 Salcedo (Pontevedra).
Tel: 986 854 850 / 864 530. Fax: 986 86 45 46.
E-mail: consejo@igatel.net - Website: www.doriasbaixas.com

GENERAL CHARACTERISTICS OF THE WINES:

Whites	Marked by the personality of the *Albariño*. They have a colour that ranges from pale yellow to greenish yellow. The aroma is of herbs and flowers with excellent intensity that may be reminiscent of rather ripe apples, apricot, fennel or mint. On the palate they stand out for their oily and glycerine-like mouthfeel, their fruity character and persistence (the best examples have good doses of complexity and elegance).
Reds	At present there is very limited production. The first examples reveal a markedly Atlantic character; the wines are a very brilliant violet cherry colour; they stand out for their notes of red berries and herbs reminiscent of eucalyptus and, on the palate, for their high acidity.

DO RÍAS BAIXAS

Bodegas A CAPELA

AIOS, 129 - NOALLA
36990 Sanxenxo (Pontevedra)
☎: 986 723 021 - Fax: 986 723 021
nati_d_t@hotmail.com

Established: 1980

📦 20,000 litres 🍷 100%

A CAPELA 2003 WHITE

ADONIS NÚÑEZ CORES

Cabanelas
36636 Ribadumia (Pontevedra)
☎: 986 710 068

ADONIS AFRUTADO WHITE

Bodegas AGNUSDEI

Bouza, 19- Besoaño
36968 Axix-Simes -Meaño (Pontevedra)
☎: 609 149 716 - Fax: 986 710 827

Established: 2002

📦 650,000 litres 🍇 30 has.

🍷 85% 🌐15%: -DE -US -UK

AGNUSDEI ALBARIÑO 2003 WHITE
100% albariño

82 Yellow straw. Medium-intensity aroma of ripe
fruit (bananas, pears) Flavourful palate with ripe
fruit and slightly low acidity but pleasant.

AGRO DE BAZÁN

Tremoedo, 46
36628 Vilanova de Arousa (Pontevedra)
☎: 986 555 562 - Fax: 986 555 799
agrodebazan@agrodebazansa.es

Established: 1982

🛢 42 📦 600,000 litres 🍇 15 has.

🍷 90% 🌐10%: -CH -NL -DE -US -PR -UK
-AD -BE

GRANBAZÁN LIMOUSIN 2001 WHITE
GRANBAZÁN AMBAR 2003 WHITE
GRANBAZÁN VERDE 2003 WHITE
CONTRAPUNTO 2003 WHITE

ALBARIÑO ZÁRATE

Bouza, 23
36668 Padrenda - Meaño (Pontevedra)
☎: 986 718 503 - Fax: 986 718 503

info@albarino-zarate.com
www.albarino-zarate.com

Established: 1925

📦 60,000 litres 🍇 7 has. 🍷 100%

ZÁRATE 2003 WHITE
ZÁRATE EL PALOMAR 2003 WHITE

ALDEA DE ABAIXO

Novas s/n
36770 O'Rosal (Pontevedra)
☎: 986 626 121 - Fax: 986 626 121

Established: 1991

📦 60,000 litres 🍇 10 has. 🍷 100%

SEÑORÍO DA TORRE 2003 WHITE
80% albariño, 15% loureira, 5% caíño

83 Pale straw. Intense aroma, fresh and fine, with
an important fruity presence (green apples) and a
nuance of fennel. Fresh and flavourful palate with
an oily touch, flavourful, nervy and expressive.

GRAN NOVAS ALBARIÑO 2003 WHITE
100% albariño

84 Yellow straw. Not very intense aroma but of
great finesse (grapefruit, fennel, lavender).
Flavourful palate with good fruit expression,
slightly weak acidity yet very pleasant.

ARAGUNDE

Carretera Iglesia, 3. Barrantes
36636 Ribadumia (Pontevedra)
☎: 986 710 135

CASAL DA TORRE ALBARIÑO WHITE

Adega ARRAIANA

Sela - Estación, s/n
36494 Arbo (Pontevedra)
☎: 986 853 366 - Fax: 986 661 522

Established: 1990

📦 30,000 litres 🍇 3 has. 🍷 100%

TEOTONIO 2003 WHITE
DON RAMÓN 2003 WHITE
DON RAMÓN 2003 RED

Pazo AS BARREIRAS

El Casal, 2
36458 Salvaterra do Miño (Pontevedra)
☎: 986 252 411 - Fax: 986 252 788
bvs2000@teleline.es

Established: 1999

75,000 litres 6 has.

SEÑORÍO DE LAZOIRO WHITE

AS LAXAS

As Laxas, 16
36430 Arbo (Pontevedra)
☎: 986 665 444 - Fax: 986 665 554
aslaxas@comunired.com

Established: 1989

450,000 litres 18 has. 90%

10%: -DE -CH -PR -US -BE -SE -JP -NL

LAXAS ALBARIÑO 2003 WHITE
albariño

81 Brilliant straw. Not very intense, varietal and hay aroma. Flavourful palate with a carbonic element and pleasantly bitter notes.

BÁGOA DO MIÑO LÁGRIMA 2003 WHITE
albariño

79 Straw-coloured with a coppery hue. Not very intense aroma with the character of slightly overripe fruit. Bitter on the palate without great fruit expression, a well-mannered ensemble.

BARREIRO AMADO

O Santo, 13 - Nantes
36969 Sanxenxo (Pontevedra)
☎: 986 723 751 - Fax: 986 723 751

Established: 1989

35,000 litres 1 has. 100%

DA OCA JOVEN WHITE

Adegas BEIRAMAR

Bruñeiras, 7
36440 As Neves (Pontevedra)
☎: 986 667 210 - Fax: 986 667 210
adegas-beiramar@terra.es

Established: 1986

225,000 litres 14 has.

35% 65%: -US -NL -IE

CARQUEIXAL ALBARIÑO 2003 WHITE
100% albariño

75 Yellow straw. Somewhat flat aroma of yeast. Better in the mouth, somewhat flavourful and with sweet fruit on the palate although without great varietal expression.

MONTE DO CEO CONDADO DO TEA 2003 WHITE
75% albariño, 12% treixadura, 13% foureiro

76 Yellow straw. Not very intense aroma, clean but with slightly weak fruit and yeast. Quite sweet on the palate, an uncommon although well-mannered ensemble.

BELISARDO RODRÍGUEZ ROMERO

Entienza, 29
36471 Salc. de Caselas (Pontevedra)
☎: 986 349 227

FINCA PORTELIÑA WHITE

BENITO AMIL PADÍN

Cobas de Lobos, 104 Vilariño
36633 Cambados (Pontevedra)
☎: 986 542 570 - Fax: 986 524 451

Established: 1988

20,000 litres 3 has. 100%

CASA DA BARCA WHITE
QUINTELA DA BARCA WHITE

BENJAMÍN MIGUEZ NOVAL

Porto de Abaixo, 10 Porto
36458 Salvaterra de Miño (Pontevedra)
☎: 986 122 705
benjaminmiguez@mundo-r.com
www.bodegasdegalicia.com/mariabargiela

Established: 1995

4 8,000 litres 2 has. 100%

MARÍA BARGIELA 2003 WHITE
90% albariño, 8% treixadura, 2% loureira

69 Straw-coloured with a coppery nuance. Evolved fruit aroma, lacking expression. Also evolved on the palate.

BOUZA DE CARRIL

Avenida Caponiñas, 14 - Barrantes
36636 Ribadumia (Pontevedra)
☎: 986 710 471 - Fax: 986 710 471

Established: 1997

6 21,000 litres 3 has.

99% 1%: -DE -CH -BE

ALBARIÑO BOUZA DE CARRIL 2003 WHITE
100% albariño

78 Pale straw. Medium-intensity, fruity and fresh aroma. Flavourful palate with sweet notes, pleasant and well-mannered overall.

BOUZA DO REI

Lugar de Puxafeita, s/n
36636 Ribadumia (Pontevedra)
☎: 986 710 257 - Fax: 986 718 393
bouzadorei@terra.es

Established: 1983

📦 800,000 litres 🌿 80 has.

🍷 90% ⊕10%: -US -DE -CH -AT -AR

CASTEL DE BOUZA 2003 WHITE
100% albariño

79 Yellow straw. Intense, fresh, fruity aroma although lacking varietal expression. Slightly carbonic on the palate, pleasant and well-mannered.

BOUZA DO REI 2003 WHITE
100% albariño

79 Yellow straw. Medium-intensity, slightly varietal aroma of ripe fruit. Fresh, somewhat bitter palate without great varietal expression.

CARLOS CASTRO SERANTES

Travesía do Freixo, 3
36636 Ribadumia (Pontevedra)
☎: 986 710 550
www.tomadadecastro@terra.es

Established: 1998

📦 24,000 litres 🌿 2 has. 🍷 100%

TOMADA DE CASTRO 2002 WHITE
100% albariño

74 Golden straw with a greenish nuance. Slightly short aroma of nuts, a baked apple hint. Light palate, slightly weak in fruit but well-mannered overall.

RÍA DE AROSA 2003 WHITE
100% albariño

79 Straw-coloured with a greenish nuance. Fresh, fruity and grapey aroma. Flavourful and somewhat unctuous on the palate, not very varietal but fresh and well-balanced.

Bodegas CASTRO MARTÍN

Puxafeita, 3.
36636 Ribadumia (Pontevedra)
☎: 986 710 202 - Fax: 986 710 607
info@bodegascastromartin.com
www.bodegascastromartin.com

Established: 1981

🛢 2 📦 300,000 litres 🌿 10 has.

🍷 70% ⊕30%

CASAL CAEIRO ALBARIÑO 2003 WHITE
100% albariño

85 Pale yellow with golden nuances. Slightly intense aroma with predominant ripe stone fruit notes and hints of flowers and lees. Fresh and flavourful on the palate with spicy hints of skins and herbs, good acidity, lacking fruit expression.

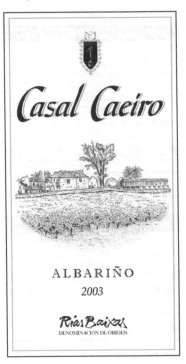

BODEGA CASTRO MARTÍN ALBARIÑO 2003 WHITE
100% albariño

84 Brilliant golden yellow. Slightly intense aroma of ripe white fruit with toasty hints of skins. Fresh and flavourful on the pa late with ripe fruit, rich in bitter and spicy nuances, a herby hint and an oily texture, very rich.

AVIAN ALBARIÑO 2003 JOVEN WHITE
100% albariño

84 Pale with golden nuances. Intense aroma of ripe white fruit with exotic hints and fine toasty skins. Flavourful and fruity palate with an oily texture, well-structured.

CASAL CAEIRO VENDIMIA SELECCIONADA 2002 FERMENTADO EN BARRICA WHITE

Adegas CASTROBREY

Camanzo
3643 Vila de Cruces (Pontevedra)
☎: 986 411 612 - Fax: 986 411 612
bodegas@castrobrey.com
www.castrobrey.com

Established: 1985

🗄 250,000 litres 🍇 10 has.

🍷 87% 🌐13%: -US -CH -FR

SEÑORÍO DE REGAS 2003 WHITE
SEÑORÍO DE CRUCES 2003 WHITE
CASTRO VALDES ALBARIÑO 2003 WHITE

CHAVES

Condesa, 3
36636 Barrantes-Ribadumia (Pontevedra)
☎: 986 710 015 - Fax: 986 718 240
bodegaschaves@terra.es

Established: 1955

🗄 165,000 litres 🍇 9 has.

🍷 80% 🌐20%: -US -UK

FLOR DE CASTEL WHITE
VIÑA BARRANTIÑOS WHITE
PONTE DA BARCA WHITE
CASTEL DE FORNOS 2002 JOVEN WHITE
CASTEL DE FORNOS SELECCIÓN 2003 JOVEN WHITE

COMERCIAL OULA

Lg. Abelleira, s/n - Baión
36614 Vilanova de Arousa (Pontevedra)
☎: 986 508 180 - Fax: 986 511 523

Established: 1988

🗄 155,000 litres 🍇 25 has. 🍷 85% 🌐15%

PAZO DE BAIÓN WHITE
VIONTA WHITE

Adega CONDES DE ALBAREI

Lg. A Bouza, 1
36639 Castrelo Cambados (Pontevedra)
☎: 986 543 535 - Fax: 986 524 251
inf@salnesur.es

www.condesdealbarei.com

Established: 1988

🍶 50 🗄 2,000,000 litres 🍇 165 has.

🍷 80% 🌐20%

CONDES DE ALBAREI CARBALLO GALEGO 2002 FERMENTADO EN BARRICA WHITE
albariño

83 Brilliant pale yellow. Intense aroma with ripe white fruit (hints of crystallised fruit) and a suggestion of spicy oak and floral nuance (orange blossom). Flavourful palate of ripe white fruit, a slightly oily texture with fine herbs, spices (vanilla) and citrus fruit in the retronasal passage.

CONDES DE ALBAREI 2003 WHITE
100% albariño

81 Yellow straw. Intense aroma of ripe fruit (bananas, pears). Fresh and flavourful with notes of hay on the palate and a slight varietal expression.

ENXEBRE VENDIMIA SELECCIONADA 2003 WHITE
albariño

83 Straw-coloured with a coppery hue. Medium-intensity aroma of ripe fruit with a herby nuance. Flavourful, with hay on the palate and pleasant bitter notes.

CONSTANTINA SOTELO ARES

Castriño, 9-Castelo
36630 Cambados (Pontevedra)
☎: 986 524 704

ADEGA SOTELO AFRUTADO WHITE

COSECHEROS REUNIDOS DE SOUTOMAIOR

Alexandre Boveda, 3 A
36691 Soutomaior (Pontevedra)
☎: 986 705 292
bodega@cosecherosdesoutomaior.com
www.cosecherosdesoutomaior.com

Established: 1992

🗄 26,000 litres 🍇 2,5 has. 🍷 100%

MARIA VINYALS ALBARIÑO WHITE

COTO DE XIABRE

Rúa Xiabre, 58
36610 Villagarcía de Arousa (Pontevedra)
☎: 986 504 985 - Fax: 986 507 924
maiordemendoza@terra.es
www.maiordemendoza.com

Established: 1995

DO RÍAS BAIXAS

🗄 100,000 litres 🍇 10 has.
🍷 90% 🌐10%: -US -NL -UK -DK -IT

MAIOR DE MENDOZA ALBARIÑO 2003 WHITE
100% albariño

85 Golden yellow. Powerful, fruity aroma with hints of tropical fruit and a toasty suggestion of skins. Flavourful palate with fresh overtones, ripe white fruit, toasty notes and good acidity.

A Portela, s/n San Juan de Tabagón
36760 O'Rosal (Pontevedra)
☎: 986 609 060 - Fax: 986 609 313
couto@bodegascouto.com

Established: 2000
🗄 70,000 litres

SERRA DA ESTRELA 2003 WHITE
100% albariño

80 Yellow straw. Medium-intensity aroma of fruit (grapefruit) and hay. Quite flavourful and bitter on the palate, pleasant.

Adega DA SERRA

Montesiña, s/n
36691 Soutomaior (Pontevedra)
☎: 986 705 161 - Fax: 986 705 637

Established: 1993

VAL DO CASTELO WHITE

DAVID MARTÍNEZ SOBRAL

Figueiro
36992 Tomiño (Pontevedra)
☎: 986 620 127 - Fax: 986 620 127
bodegaspedrega@arrakis.es

Established: 1991
🗄 40,000 litres 🍇 6 has.
🍷 98% 🌐2%: -PR

LAGAR PEDREGALES WHITE

DIVINA FERNÁNDEZ GIL

Pazo Casa Grande Almuiña
36439 Arbo (Pontevedra)
☎: 986 413 611 - Fax: 986 412 366

Established: 1875
🗄 100,000 litres 🍇 6 has. 🇪🇸 100%

GRAN ALMUIÑA WHITE
TORRE ALMUIÑA WHITE
ALMUIÑA WHITE
CASA GRANDE ALMUIÑA RED

Adega DO MOLLON

Avenida Buenos Aires 19- local 35
32004 Ourense (Ourense)
☎: 988 222 272 - Fax: 988 226 641
axeourense@line-pro.es

Established: 2000
🗄 25,000 litres 🍇 21 has. 🍷 95% 🌐5%

POMBARES JOVEN WHITE
POMBARES JOVEN RED
ADEGA DO MOLLON JOVEN RED

Adega DOS EIDOS

Padriñán, 65
36960 Sanxenxo (Pontevedra)
☎: 986 690 009 - Fax: 986 690 009
info@adegaeidos.com
www.adegaeidos.com

EIDOS ALBARIÑO 2003 WHITE
100% albariño

87 Fairly pale gold. Powerful aroma of ripe white fruit with fine spicy notes and a fine hint of perfumed soap. Powerful palate with smoky notes of skins, fine bitter hints (nuts) and a suggestion of zest, excellent acidity.

VEIGAS ALBARIÑO 2003 WHITE

Adega DURÁN

Rua Pardo Bazán, 1
36630 Cambados (Pontevedra)
☎: 986 542 354 - Fax: 986 716 312
adegaduran@ventomareiro.com

Established: 1989

🪵 50,000 litres

VENTO MAREIRO ALBARIÑO RIAS BAIXAS WHITE

ESCUDEIRO

Avenida Rosalia de Castro-Barrantes
36636 Ribadumia (Pontevedra)
☎: 986 710 777 - Fax: 986 710 777

Established: 1906
🌐 3 🪵 75,000 litres 🍇 12 has. 🍷 100%

VERDÍA 2002 ROBLE WHITE
ALBARIÑO VIÑA ROEL 2003 WHITE
RIBERA DEL UMIA ALBARIÑO 2003 WHITE
VIÑA ROEL 2003 WHITE

Palacio de FEFIÑANES

Pza. de Fefiñanes, s/n
36630 Cambados (Pontevedra)
☎: 986 542 204 - Fax: 986 524 512
feninan@arrakis.es

🍷 80% 🌐20%: -US -UK -JP -DK -SE -AD -DE

ALBARIÑO DE FEFIÑANES III AÑO 2001 WHITE
100% albariño

88 Brilliant pale. Intense aroma of great finesse, with good varietal and Crianza expression, ripe white fruit, fine herbs, nuts and hints of flowers (acacia). Flavourful palate with fine bitter notes (herbs), hints of chocolate, ripe citrus fruit and good acidity.

1583 ALBARIÑO DE FEFIÑANES 2002 OAK AGED WHITE
ALBARIÑO DE FEFIÑANES 2003 WHITE

FELICIANO DOPAZO PADÍN

Bichona, 21 - Villalonga
36990 Sanxenxo (Pontevedra)
☎: 986 720 518

Established: 1946
🌐 10 🪵 15,000 litres 🍇 5 has.
🍷 75% 🌐25%

DOPAZO MARTÍNEZ WHITE

FERNANDO DIEGUEZ OTERO

J. Fuentes Echevarría, s/n
36650 Caldas de Rei (Pontevedra)
☎: 986 530 658 - Fax: 986 540 905

info@aquiscelenis.com
www.aquiscelenis.com

Established: 1995
🪵 15,000 litres 🍇 5 has.
🍷 80% 🌐20%: -US

ALBARIÑO AQUIS CEPAS VIEJAS 2003 WHITE

FILLABOA

Lugar de Fillaboa, s/n
36459 Salvaterra do Miño (Pontevedra)
☎: 986 658 132 - Fax: 986 664 212
info@bodegasfillaboa.com
www.bodegasfillaboa.com

Established: 1988
🌐 4 🪵 300,000 litres 🍇 50 has.
🍷 90% 🌐10%

ALBARIÑO FILLABOA 2003 JOVEN WHITE
100% albariño

88 Pale yellow. Intense aroma of green apples, with mild exotic hints, fennel and fresh citrus and saline overtones. Fresh and flavourful on the palate with excellent varietal expression, fine bitter notes, fine herbs and excellent acidity.

ALBARIÑO FILLABOA 2002 FERMENTADO EN BARRICA WHITE
100% albariño

90 Yellow straw. Very elegant aroma of ripe and at the same time fresh fruit perfectly harmonised with the smoky oak, very varietal. Powerful, oily palate with pleasant bitter notes well-integrated with the oak, good acidity.

ALBARIÑO FILLABOA 2003 FERMENTADO EN BARRICA WHITE
100% albariño

90 Pale yellow with golden nuances. Intense aroma with fine smoky and creamy oak notes well-integrated with the ripe fruit, hints of fine herbs. Powerful palate with fine spicy (cumin) and bitter notes and an oily, slightly warm texture.

ALBARIÑO FILLABOA SELECCIÓN FINCA MONTE ALTO 2002 WHITE
100% albariño

92 Pale yellow with golden nuances. Intense aroma of white stone fruit notes with hints of exotic fruit, flowers (jasmine) and lees. Flavourful palate, rich in toasty nuances of skins with a slightly oily texture and a powerful effect of spices and ripe fruit in the retronasal passage.

FRANCISCO ALFONSO REBOREDA (PEDRALONGA)

Santiaguiño de Godos, 17

DO RÍAS BAIXAS

36615 Caldas de Reis (Pontevedra)
☎: 986 535 201
www.bodegasdegalicia.com/pedralonga
Established: 1997
🗋 21,000 litres 🍇 7,7 has. 🚩 100%

ALBARIÑO PEDRALONGA JOVEN WHITE
PEDRALONGA JOVEN RED

FRANCISCO LAMEIRO FERREIRA

Baldranes - Cerqueiro, 17
36460 Tuy (Pontevedra)
☎: 986 629 137 - Fax: 986 629 137
f.lameiro@terra.es
www.adegaslameiro.com
Established: 1950
🗋 35,000 litres 🍇 3 has. 🚩 100%

ALBARIÑO 3º MILENIO WHITE
CONDADO DE TEA 3º MILENIO WHITE

Adegas GALEGAS

Meder, s/n
36457 Salvaterra do Miño (Pontevedra)
☎: 986 657 400 - Fax: 986 657 371
galiciano@galiciano.com
www.galiciano.com
Established: 1995
🍾 120 🗋 600,000 litres 🍇 47 has.
🚩 70% 🌐30%: -UE -US -CA América del
Sur Paises del Este -JP

DON PEDRO SOUTOMAIOR TEMPO 1999
FERMENTADO EN BARRICA WHITE
100% albariño

86 Lively golden. Intense aroma of honeyed, smoky oak and fine reduction notes. Oily, slightly dense palate with toasty oak. Well-balanced with good acidity.

GRAN VEIGADARES 2002 FERMENTADO EN
BARRICA WHITE
100% albariño

85 Pale straw with a coppery glimmer. Intense aroma with reduction notes (honey, petals) and quite noticeable oak. Oily, round and smoky on the palate with butter and vanilla in the finish.

VEIGADARES 2003 FERMENTADO EN
BARRICA WHITE
85% albariño, 10% treixadura, 5% loureiro

90 Lively yellow straw. Powerful, fine and varietal aroma of ripe fruit (apples, pears) very well-integrated with the smoky oak. Powerful, oily pala-

te with smoky and abundant notes of ripe fruit, complex and harmonious.

BOUZA GRANDE CONDADO 2001 WHITE
75% albariño, 20% treixadura, 5% loureiro

85 Lively straw-coloured. Medium-intensity aroma of fine reduction notes (petals, honeyed notes, herbs). Oily palate with notes of herbs (fennel, aniseed) and wax.

O DEUS DIONISOS 2003 WHITE
100% albariño

82 Brilliant pale yellow. Not very intense aroma with a certain finesse and varietal expression (white fruit and flowers). Flavourful palate with fine spicy notes, hints of sweet limes and refreshing acidity.

DON PEDRO SOUTOMAIOR MACERADO EN
NEVE CARBÓNICA 2003 WHITE
100% albariño

88 Straw-coloured with a coppery glint. Powerful aroma of ripe fruit (apples, pears, peaches), with a fine suggestion of fennel, harmonious. Powerful, oily palate with body, good acidity and a pleasant complexity of herbs, very long.

DON PEDRO SOUTOMAIOR 2003 WHITE
100% albariño

81 Yellow straw. Not very intense yet clean aroma of green fruit and hay. Fresh and flavourful on the palate, good acidity and very well-mannered.

RUBINES 2003 WHITE
100% albariño

85 Yellow straw. Not very intense yet clean aroma of ripe fruit, fine. Fresh on the palate with lively acidity, an oily note and pleasant bitter notes, well-balanced.

SEÑORÍO DE RUBIOS 2000 RED

GALLAECIA PREMIUM

Fray Pedro Payo Piñeño, 17 bajo
15009 A Coruña (A Coruña)
☎: 670 522 577 - Fax: 881 924 492
delispain@delispain.com
www.gallaeciapremium.com
Established: 2003

CARTA OUTONO 2002 OAK AGED WHITE
CARTA OUTONO 2003 WHITE

Adegas GÁNDARA

Porto Mirón, 25
36459 Salvatierra de Miño (Pontevedra)
☎: 986 639 110
adegasgandara@hotmail.com
adegasgandara.com
Established: 2000

🛢 17,100 litres 🍇 3 has. 🍷 100%

ADEGAS GÁNDARA ALBARIÑO 2003 WHITE
100% albariño

81 Yellow straw. Fresh, ripe fruit aroma but not very intense. Flavourful palate with lightly spicy, bitter notes.

SOBRESEIXAL 2003 WHITE

GERARDO MÉNDEZ

Galiñanes - Lores, 10
36968 Meaño (Pontevedra)
☎: 986 747 046 - Fax: 986 747 046
adoferreiro@terra.es
www.bodegasgerardomendez.com

Established: 1973
🛢 50,000 litres 🍇 5 has.
🍷 70% 🌐30%: -US -PR

DO FERREIRO CEPAS VELLAS 2002 WHITE
100% albariño

89 Pale golden yellow. Intense aroma, rich in nuances of white stone fruit with floral and toasty hints of skins and a suggestion of lees and fine herbs. Flavourful palate with an element of ripe fruit, spicy hints (cumin) and a slightly oily texture.

ALBARIÑO DO FERREIRO 2003 WHITE
100% albariño

89 Brilliant pale yellow. Intense, very fine aroma with fresh overtones (green apples, citrus fruit, fennel, fresh herbs). Flavourful, fresh and fruity palate with a slightly oily texture although the fleshy traces of skins maceration are noticeable, good acidity.

Adegas GRAN VINUM

Fermín Bouza Brey, 9 5ºB
36600 Vilagarcía de Arousa (Pontevedra)
☎: 986 555 742 - Fax: 986 555 742
info@adegasgranvinum.com
www.adegasgranvinum.com

🛢 60,000 litres

GRAN VINUM 2002 WHITE
albariño

82 Pale yellow. Intense, ripe aroma of white fruit with notes of exotic fruit and toasty hints of skins. Flavourful palate with ripe fruit and a slightly oily texture, fine toasty notes in the retronasal passage.

ESENCIA DIVIÑA 2003 WHITE
albariño

79 Pale yellow with golden nuances. Slightly intense aroma with a good varietal expression (white stone fruit, fennel, hints of citrus fruit). Very fresh and flavourful on the palate with notes of citrus fruit (high in acidity), lacking fruit expression.

MAR DE VIÑAS 2003 WHITE
albariño

77 Pale yellow with golden nuances. Slightly intense, fruity aroma (apples, apricots) with the spicy freshness of skins. Flavourful palate with fruity and citrus notes and a slightly acidic edge.

Adega HEREDEROS JOAQUÍN GIL ARMADA

Plaza de Fefiñans, s/n
36630 Cambados (Pontevedra)
☎: 986 524 877 - Fax: 986 542 628
bodegajgilarmada@pazodefefinans.com
www.pazodefefinans.com

Established: 1974
🍇 7 has.

JOAQUÍN GIL ARMADA 2002 JOVEN WHITE

JORGE TABOAS CARRERA

Adega Canedo
36860 Ponteareas (Pontevedra)
☎: 986 641 736
adegaruben@eresmas.com

Established: 1997
🍷 20 🛢 30,000 litres 🍇 3 has. 🍷 100%

VILLA DEL CORPUS 2003 WHITE
BAIXABEN 2003 WHITE

JOSÉ ANGEL BOADO CHAVES

O Casal, 10. San Félix de Lois
36636 Ribadumia (Pontevedra)
☎: 986 712 183

Established: 1974
🛢 60,000 litres 🍇 9 has. 🍷 100%

O CASAL WHITE

JOSÉ CASTRO REY

Leiro
36636 Ribadumia (Pontevedra)
☎: 986 211 033

SEÑORÍO DA REGAS WHITE

JOSÉ DOMÍNGUEZ POMBO

Aios, 83
36990 Sanxenxo (Pontevedra)

DO RÍAS BAIXAS

☎: 986 727 024 - Fax: 986 724 379
inelsa@inelsa.com

Established: 1992

📦 15,000 litres 🍇 1.5 has. 🍷 100%

VIÑA TORRIÑAS WHITE

JULIÁN GONZÁLEZ AREAL

Finca Lavandeira - Rebordans
36712 Tui (Pontevedra)
☎: 986 601 414 - Fax: 986 601 414

Established: 1991

📦 18,000 litres 🍇 2,5 has 🍷 100%

CANÓNIGO AREAL WHITE

LA VAL

San Miguel de Tabagón, 19
36760 O'Rosal (Pontevedra)
☎: 986 610 728 - Fax: 986 611 635
laval@bodegaslaval.com
www.bodegaslaval.com

Established: 1985

🛢 30 📦 650,000 litres 🍇 65 has.

🍷 90% 🌐10%: -CH -DE -UK -NL -BE -DK
-JP -US -PR-CO -DO -VE

LA VAL ALBARIÑO 2001 FERMENTADO EN BARRICA WHITE
100% albariño

88 Golden yellow. Intense aroma with predominant very varietal ripe fruit notes (hints of exotic fruit and fine herbs) over the smoky and creamy oak notes. Powerful, flavourful palate with a good oak/fruit integration, smoky and vanilla hints in the retronasal passage, fine waxy notes.

ALBARIÑO ORBALLO 2003 WHITE
100% albariño

82 Lively straw-coloured. Quite complex aroma of mountain herbs and hay, delicate. Fresh and flavourful on the palate with lively acidity, easy drinking.

TORRES DE ARANTEI 2003 WHITE
100% albariño

83 Brilliant pale yellow. Intense aroma of green fruit with hints of flowers and herbs. Flavourful palate with fine bitter notes and the freshness of citrus fruits.

VIÑA LUDY 2003 WHITE
70% albariño, 15% treixadura, 10% loureira, 5% caíno

80 Brilliant pale yellow. Somewhat intense aroma of white stone fruit with fresh overtones. Fresh, flavourful palate with fine bitter and citrus notes, good acidity.

LA VAL ALBARIÑO 2003 WHITE
100% albariño

81 Pale with golden nuances. Slightly intense aroma of ripe white fruit with hints of flowers and lees. Fresh palate with green apples and fine bitter notes of citrus fruit, pleasant although lacking great varietal expression.

LAGAR DE BESADA

Pazo, 11
36968 Xil-Meaño (Pontevedra)
☎: 986 747 473 - Fax: 986 747 473
maria.sineiro@psfd.ictnet.es

Established: 1988

🛢 5 📦 92,000 litres 🍇 2.4 has. 🍷 100%

VIÑA BALADIÑA 2002 WHITE
100% albariño

85 Lively golden. Powerful aroma of fine reduction notes (nuts herbs, hints of wax and petals) with a slight varietal expression. Intense and flavourful on the palate, rich in crianza nuances, original.

VIÑA BALADIÑA SELECCIÓN DE FAMILIA 2003 WHITE
100% albariño

84 Yellow straw. Medium-intensity aroma of ripe fruit with a fennel nuance. Oily, flavourful and expressive on the palate, somewhat spicy and very well-balanced.

EX-LIBRIS 2003 WHITE
100% albariño

81 Pale straw. Not very intense yet clean aroma of ripe fruit. Flavourful palate with bitter notes, pleasant and easy drinking.

LAGAR DE CANDES

Pereira, 6
36968 Meaño (Pontevedra)
☎: 986 747 241 - Fax: 986 747 742

Established: 2002

📦 15,000 litres 🍇 2 has. 🍷 100%

LAGAR DE CANDES ALBARIÑO 2003 WHITE
100% albariño

68 Golden. Not very clear aroma of windfall fruit. Flat palate without fruit.

LAGAR DE COSTA

Sartaxes, 8 - Castrelo
36639 Cambados (Pontevedra)
☎: 986 299 731 - Fax: 986 299 731
carmencarrete@auna.com

Established: 1950

📦 45,000 litres 🍇 6 has. 🍷 100%

DO RÍAS BAIXAS

LAGAR DE COSTA 2003 WHITE
100% albariño

85 Pale with lime green nuances. Intense, fresh aroma of green fruit with hints of flowers and fine lees. Flavourful palate rich in nuances of white fruit, spicy hints of skins and the freshness of herbs and citrus fruit, good acidity.

LAGAR DE FORNELOS

Barrio de Cruces Fornelos
36778 La Guardia - O'Rosal (Pontevedra)
☎: 986 625 875 - Fax: 986 625 011
lagar@riojalta.com
www.riojalta.com
Established: 1988
🍇 76 has. 🍷 70% 🌐30%: -UK-DE-MX-US

LAGAR DE CERVERA 2003 WHITE
100% albariño

89 Brilliant straw. Quite fresh and fragrant aroma of a certain complexity. Complex palate with a suggestion of bitter notes and sweet fruit; with good expression.

ALBARIÑO 2003
LAGAR DE CERVERA
RÍAS BAIXAS

LAGAR DE PINTOS

Cabanelas, 6.
36636 Ribadumia (Pontevedra)
☎: 986 710 001 - Fax: 986 710 203
lagar.de.pintos@corevia.com
Established: 1887
🍾 22 🛢 200,000 litres 🍇 7 has.
🍷 80% 🌐20%

LAGAR DE PINTOS 2003 WHITE
100% albariño

79 Straw-coloured. Medium-intensity aroma of slightly overripe fruit (bananas). Very ripe fruit also on the palate, flavourful and well-mannered overall.

LAGAR DE PINTOS 2002 FERMENTADO EN BARRICA WHITE

CASTIÑERA 2003 WHITE

LAGAR DE REY

Carballoso - Xil
36968 Meaño (Pontevedra)
☎: 986 743 189 - Fax: 986 743 189
marisaconf@yahoo.es
Established: 1997
🛢 10,000 litres 🍇 2 has. 🍷 100%

LAGAR DE REI 2003 WHITE
100% albariño

78 Straw-coloured with a greenish hue. Good intensity aroma of green fruit and herbs. Light and fruity on the palate; well-mannered.

LAGAR DO FREIXO

Freixo, 4
36636 Ribadumia (Pontevedra)
☎: 986 718 216 - Fax: 986 718 216
Established: 1992
🛢 22,000 litres 🍇 2 has. 🍷 100%

LAGAR DO FREIXO WHITE

LUIS PADÍN REY

Piñeiros, 16
36990 Villalonga-Xanxenxo (Pontevedra)
☎: 986 745 829
Established: 1995
🍾 10 🛢 20,000 litres 🍇 2 has.
🍷 80% 🌐20%

D'ARVELOS WHITE
D'ARVELOS RED

LUSCO DO MIÑO

Alxen
36459 Salvaterra do Miño (Pontevedra)
☎: 986 658 519 - Fax: 986 244 113
luscodominho@yahoo.es
Established: 1997
🛢 50,000 litres 🍇 5 has.
🍷 50% 🌐50%: -US -JP -BE -DE -UK -AU

LUSCO 2003 WHITE
100% albariño

91 Straw-coloured. Fresh, fruity aroma with notions of cut grass (hay). Fruity, fresh palate with flowers in the retronasal passage, very flavourful, complex and slightly elegant.

DIVERSUS 2003 WHITE

DO RÍAS BAIXAS

M. DEL CARMEN VARELA TORRES

Cabeza de Boi, 5. Armenteira
36192 Meis (Pontevedra)
☎: 986 710 591

ALBARIÑO SAN ERO 2003 JOVEN WHITE
100% albariño

76 Yellow straw. Weak fruit aroma with a light varietal suggestion but a little flat. Better in the mouth, with a flavourful hint, pleasant.

MAR DE FRADES

Ande-Rubians, 39
36619 Vilagarcía de Arousa (Pontevedra)
☎: 986 508 071 - Fax: 986 565 538
mardefrades@mardefrades.com
www.mardefrades.com

Established: 1987

🛢 20 ▮ 350,000 litres 🍇 6 has.
🍷 90% 🌐10%: -US -PR -AD -CH -CZ

MAR DE FRADES 2003 JOVEN WHITE
100% albariño

85 Yellow straw. Powerful, fine aroma of ripe fruit (bananas, apples, pears) with a herby nuance. Flavourful, expressive palate with ripe fruit and good acidity.

MAR DE FRADES ARAUTIAM 2003 FERMENTADO EN BARRICA WHITE
100% albariño

87 Straw-coloured with a coppery nuance. Powerful, expressive aroma of ripe fruit (apples, apricots) and smoky oak. Oily, powerful, flavourful and varietal on the palate, well-balanced with good oak integration.

ALGAREIRO 2003 JOVEN WHITE

Bodegas MARQUÉS DE VIZHOJA

Finca La Moreira
36430 Arbo (Pontevedra)
☎: 986 665 825 - Fax: 986 665 960
marquesdevizhoja.@marquesdevizhoja.com
www.marquesdevizhoja.com

Established: 1966

▮ 1,125,000 litres 🍇 35 has.
🍷 80% 🌐20%: -DE -IT -CH -UK -BE -JP - PR -US -AD

TORRE LA MOREIRA 2003 WHITE

84 Brilliant straw. Intense aroma, fine, excellent varietal expression (fruit and white flowers, citrus and spicy hints). Fresh, fruity, flavourful palate, with predominant citrus notes in the finish, excellent acidity.

SEÑOR DA FOLLA VERDE 2003 WHITE

81 Brilliant yellow. Intense aroma, smoky, ripe fruit (apples, apricots), spicy nuances of skins. Fresh, flavourful palate, white fruit, fine herbaceous hints, slightly acidic edge.

MARTÍN CÓDAX

Burgans, 91
36663 Vilariño-Cambados (Pontevedra)
☎: 986 526 040 - Fax: 986 526 901
comercial@martincodax.com
www.martincodax.com

Established: 1986

🛢 110 ▮ 2,200,000 litres 🍇 215 has.
🍷 70% 🌐30%: -US -UK -DE -CH

BURGANS ALBARIÑO 2003 JOVEN WHITE
100% albariño

85 Yellow straw. Intense, fine, harmonious aroma of ripe fruit (apples, pears) and herbs. Flavourful, varietal, oily and round on the palate with sweet fruit and pleasant bitter notes.

MARTÍN CÓDAX 2003 JOVEN WHITE
100% albariño

83 Pale with golden nuances. Intense, fruity aroma with fennel and fine herbs. Fresh, flavourful palate with notes of green apple, hints of citrus fruit and a slightly acidic edge.

ORGANISTRUM 2002 FERMENTADO EN BARRICA WHITE
albariño

84 Lively yellow straw. Not very intense yet fine aroma of fresh fruit with herby and smoky nuances. Flavourful palate with creamy hints of oak and an element of acidity.

GALLAECIA 2002 WHITE

Bodega MARTINEZ SERANTES

Cruceiro Vello, calle Raul Alfonsin, 3
36636 Ribadumia (Pontevedra)
☎: 986 718 074 - Fax: 986 718 087
franxamar@franxamar.com
www.franxamar.com

Established: 1996
▨ 115,000 litres ▼ 4 has.
▟ 90% ♠10%: -US

FRANXAMAR 2003 WHITE
100% albariño

83 Straw-coloured with a greenish nuance. Medium-intensity aroma of ripe fruit (bananas, pears) with a herby nuance. Flavourful palate with an oily hint, and lively acidity with ripe fruit.

DONA ROSA 2003 WHITE
100% albariño

78 Yellow straw. Medium-intensity aroma of ripe fruit (bananas) with a herby nuance. An edge of acidity and ripe fruit on the palate, well-mannered.

MONTE SACRO

Carrasqueira - Cabarcos, s/n
36638 Sisán - Ribadumia (Pontevedra)
☎: 986 718 402 - Fax: 986 718 402

Established: 1989
▤ 20 ▨ 60,000 litres ▼ 2 has.
▟ 70% ♠30%: -FR

MONTE SACRO CEPAS VELLAS 2002 FERMENTADO EN BARRICA WHITE
ALBARIÑO NOR 2003 WHITE
MONTE SACRO VENDIMIA SELECCIONADA 2003 WHITE

MORGADÍO

Albeos
36429 Creciente (Pontevedra)
☎: 988 261 212 - Fax: 988 261 213

info@morgadio.com
www.morgadio.com

Established: 1982
▨ 500,000 litres ▼ 40 has.
▟ 80% ♠20%: -US -DE -NL -BE -VE

TORRE FORNELOS 2003 WHITE
100% albariño

83 Straw-coloured. Good intensity aroma of white fruit and a herby hint. Flavourful palate with an oily touch; fresh, with a pleasant bitterness in the finish.

MORGADÍO ALBARIÑO 2003 WHITE
100% albariño

87 Brilliant golden yellow. Intense aroma of white fruit (hints of exotic fruit) with notes of flowers and herbs. Flavourful and slightly fruity on the palate with fine bitter notes, spicy hints of skins, a slightly oily texture and an excellent structure.

COTO DE ALBEOS 2003 WHITE

NANCLARES

Castriño, 13 - Castrelo
36639 Cambados (Pontevedra)
☎: 986 520 763 - Fax: 986 524 958
bodega@bodegasnanclares.com
www.bodegasnanclares.com

Established: 1997
▤ 8 ▨ 7,000 litres ▼ 1,2 has. ▟ 100%

ALBERTO NANCLARES ALBARIÑO 2003 WHITE
100% albariño

79 Pale straw. Not very intense aroma of green fruit. Flavourful palate with an oily touch and hints of hay; a well-mannered ensemble.

SOVERRIBAS DE NANCLARES 2001 FERMENTADO EN BARRICA WHITE

O AFORADO

Eiras
36760 O'Rosal (Pontevedra)
☎: 986 620 292 - Fax: 986 620 121
labodega@aforado.com
www.aforado.com

Established: 1982
▨ 96,100 litres ▼ 8 has. ▟ 100%

AFORADO 2003 JOVEN WHITE
80% albariño, 15% caíño, 5% marqués

87 Pale with a golden hue. Intense, very fine aroma of ripe white fruit with floral notes and fine herbs. Flavourful, slightly fruity palate with fine bitter notes and hints of spices and minerals in the retronasal passage.

PABLO LÓPEZ FRANCO

Rúa de Corgo, 67
36980 O Grove (Pontevedra)
☎: 986 730 180

AGRO VELLO WHITE

PABLO PADÍN

Ameiro, 24 - Dena
36967 Meaño (Pontevedra)
☎: 986 743 231 - Fax: 986 745 791
segrel@teleline.es

Established: 1987

250,000 litres 3 has.

80% 20%: -DE -NL -BE -CH -FR -AD -UK -IE -US

ALBARIÑO SEGREL ÁMBAR 2003 WHITE
100% albariño

86 Pale yellow with golden nuances. Powerful, fruity aroma with hints of flowers and herbs and a suggestion of varietal typification. Fresh and fruity palate with a slightly oily texture, fine bitter notes, toasty skins and excellent acidity.

ALBARIÑO SEGREL 2003 WHITE
100% albariño

85 Brilliant pale with greenish nuances. Intense, ripe aroma of white stone fruit with fine toasty hints of skins. Flavourful and fruity palate with notes of herbs, spicy hints and fine bitter notes of ripe citrus fruit, good acidity.

ALBARIÑO EIRAL 2002 WHITE
ALBARIÑO SEGREL 2003 WHITE

PAZO DE BARRANTES

Finca Pazo de Barrantes, Barrantes
36636 Ribadumia (Pontevedra)
☎: 986 718 211 - Fax: 986 710 424
barrantes@marquesdemurrieta.com

Established: 1991

223,220 litres 12 has. 65% 35%

PAZO DE BARRANTES ALBARIÑO 2003 WHITE
100% albariño

90 Greenish straw. Powerful aroma rich in herby expression of fennel, mint, fresh fruit and a mineral edge. Fresh, fragrant palate with excellent acidity, the best Barrantes of all time.

PAZO DE SEÑORANS

Vilanoviña
36616 Meis (Pontevedra)
☎: 986 715 373 - Fax: 986 715 569
pazosenorans@pazodesenorans.com
www.pazodesenorans.com

PAZO DE SEÑORANS 2003 JOVEN WHITE
100% albariño

87 Straw-coloured with a greenish nuance. Intense, fine aroma of fennel, green herbs and white fruit. Fresh and flavourful on the palate, with well-balanced fresh fruit and acidic, bitter notes.

PAZO DE SEÑORANS SELECCIÓN DE AÑADA 2000 WHITE
100% albariño

89 Lively straw-coloured with a greenish nuance. Delicate, complex aroma of petals, lavender and white flowers. Very oily and flavourful on the palate, with body, ripe fruit and well-integrated alcohol, complex.

Pazo de PONDAL

Cabeiras Merelle, 10
36436 Arbo (Pontevedra)
☎: 935 677 088 - Fax: 935 677 078
info@pazopondal.com
www.pazopondal.com

Established: 1988

6 43,000 litres 10 has.

60% 40%: -US -UK -NL -AD -CU -PA

PAZO PONDAL ALBARIÑO 2003 WHITE
100% albariño

83 Straw-coloured. Fresh, fruity aroma of hay and ripe white fruit. Flavourful, oily palate with pleasant bitter notes, well-balanced.

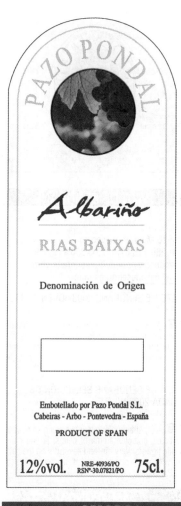

Pazo de la PEDREIRA

Souto, 5
36638 Sisán - Ribadumia (Pontevedra)
☎: 986 718 494

🍷 6 📦 15,000 litres 🍇 2,5 has. 🏴 100%

PAZO DE LA PEDREIRA WHITE

Comunidad de Bienes PINTOS

Lugo, 13
36630 Cambados (Pontevedra)
☎: 986 542 188

Established: 1940

🍷 24 🍇 2 has. 🏴 100%

OUSO DA TORRE ALBARIÑO WHITE

PORTA DO RIO MIÑO

A Lomba, 49
36770 O' Rosal (Pontevedra)
☎: 986 625 242 - Fax: 986 625 258

Established: 1980

📦 250,000 litres 🏴 100%

OSTIUM MINII ALBARIÑO WHITE
ROSAL CINCO ROSAS WHITE

Pazo QUINTEIRO DA CRUZ

Lois
36636 Ribadumia (Pontevedra)
☎: 986 501 011 - Fax: 986 501 011

Established: 1979

🍷 6 📦 18,000 litres 🍇 3.5 has.
🏴 95% 🍇5%

QUINTEIRO DA CRUZ ALLIER 2002 ROBLE
WHITE
QUINTEIRO DA CRUZ 2003 WHITE

ROBALIÑO

Pazo de Almuíña, 10
36430 Arbo (Pontevedra)
☎: 986 665 082 - Fax: 986 665 012
bodegasrobalino@bodegasrobalino.com
www.geocities.com/bodegasrobalino

Established: 1991

🍷 15 📦 200,000 litres 🍇 25 has.
🏴 90% 🍇10%: -US -DE -VE -CH -IT -BR
-FR -UK

LIÑAR DE VIDES 2003 WHITE
100% albariño

81 Greenish straw. Medium-intensity aroma of ripe fruit, lavender and white flowers. Flavourful and slightly unctuous on the palate with a considerable fruity presence.

ROSA GONZÁLEZ GONZÁLEZ

Piñeiros, 7 - Vilalonga
36990 Sanxenxo (Pontevedra)
☎: 986 744 796

Established: 1982

📦 15,000 litres 🍇 2 has. 🏴 75% 🍇25%

FONTE DO OURO JOVEN WHITE

ROSA TORRES VARELA

Aios, 129 - Noalla

DO RÍAS BAIXAS

36990 Sanxenxo (Pontevedra)
☎: 986 542 571

A CAPELA AFRUTADO WHITE

Pazo de SAN MAURO

Porto s/n
36458 Salvaterra de Miño (Pontevedra)
☎: 986 658 285 - Fax: 986 664 208
info@pazosanmauro.com
www.pazosanmauro.com

Established: 1988
▤ 105,000 litres ⚘ 30 has. ▰ 92% ⊕8%

SANAMARO 2002 WHITE
95% albariño, 5% loureira

80 Brilliant pale. Slightly intense aroma with the freshness of white fruit and hints of herbs and fine lees. Flavourful, slightly spicy and warm on the palate with bitter notes, lacking fruit expression.

PAZO SAN MAURO CONDADO 2003 WHITE
albariño, treixadura, loureira, torrontes

83 Yellow straw. Intense aroma of ripe fruit (bananas, pears). Ripe fruit and good acidity on the palate, flavourful and well-balanced.

PAZO SAN MAURO ALBARIÑO 2003 WHITE
albariño

85 Straw-coloured with a greenish nuance. Fresh, intense and fine aroma of fennel. Flavourful palate with fresh acidity and ripe fruit, very well-balanced.

Bodega SANTIAGO ROMA

Catariño, 5 Besomaño
36636 Ribadumia (Pontevedra)
☎: 986 718 477 - Fax: 986 718 477
bodega@santiagoroma.com
www.santiagoroma.com

Established: 1997
▤ 30,000 litres ⚘ 3 has. ▰ 90% ⊕10%

ALBARIÑO SANTIAGO ROMA SELECCIÓN 2003 WHITE
100% albariño

82 Pale yellow. Slightly intense aroma of fine fruity notes and herbs. Flavourful and fruity on the palate with toasty hints of skins and an oily texture, pleasant, lacking freshness.

ALBARIÑO SANTIAGO ROMA 2003 WHITE
100% albariño

85 Brilliant pale yellow. Intense, fruity aroma with a good varietal expression (herbs, citrus fruit, hints of exotic fruit) and hints of fine lees. Fresh palate with notes of green apple and the freshness of citrus fruit and herbs, with fine spicy notes and good acidity.

SANTIAGO RUIZ

Rua do Vinicultor Santiago Ruiz
36760 San Miguel de Tabagón-O Rosal (Pontevedra)
☎: 986 614 083 - Fax: 986 614 142
info@bodegaslan.com
www.bodegaslan.com

Established: 1892
▤ 130,000 litres ⚘ 40 has.
▰ 50% ⊕50%: -DE -EE -US -PR -JP -CR

SANTIAGO RUIZ 2003 WHITE
70% albariño, 20% loureira, 10% treixadura

83 Yellow straw with a greenish rim. Floral aroma of fresh herbs and fine yeasts. Good acidity on the palate, green notes long with bay leaves in the retronasal passage.

Adegas SANTOS LÓPEZ

Carretera de Currás, 46 Caleiro
36629 Vilanova de Arosa (Pontevedra)
☎: 986 554 433 - Fax: 986 554 435

Established: 1999
▤ 60,000 litres ⚘ 0,5 has. ▰ 100%

TORRE DE CÁLAGO 2003 WHITE
100% albariño

75 Straw-coloured with a greenish nuance. Medium-intensity aroma of slightly overripe fruit with a herby nuance. Fresh palate with bitter notes and an element of acidity.

Señorío de SOBRAL

Porto - Sobral
36459 Salvaterra do Miño (Pontevedra)
☎: 986 415 144 - Fax: 986 421 744
comercial@ssobral.com
www.ssobral.com

Established: 1978
⊕ 45 ▤ 325,000 litres ⚘ 5 has.
▰ 80% ⊕20%: -NL -DE -UK -CH

SEÑORÍO DE SOBRAL 2003 WHITE
100% albariño

83 Greenish straw. Slightly intense, fruity and quite expressive aroma. Flavourful palate of ripe fruit, oily and well-balanced.

Adegas TERRA SANTA

Avenida de Villagarcía, 100
36630 Cambados (Pontevedra)
☎: 986 542 947 - Fax: 986 542 947

DO RÍAS BAIXAS

Established: 1999
🛢 41.500 litres 🚩 100%

TERRA SANTA ALBARIÑO 2003 WHITE
VIÑA DOZO 2003 WHITE

TERRAS GAUDA

Carretera Tui - A Guarda
36760 O'Rosal (Pontevedra)
☎: 986 621 001 - Fax: 986 621 084
terrasgauda@terrasgauda.com
www.terrasgauda.com

Established: 1990

🛢 800,000 litres 🍇 82 has.

🚩 80% 🌰20%: -DE -UK -CH -DK -BE -IE
-NL -JP -RU -US -PR -VE -MX

TERRAS GAUDA ETIQUETA NEGRA 2002
70% albariño, 20% loureira, 10% caíno

84 Straw-coloured with a coppery glimmer. Powerful aroma of smoky wood and ripe apricots. Fresh on the palate with considerable wood weight and good acidity.

ABADÍA DE SAN CAMPO 2003 WHITE
100% albariño

85 Yellow straw. Intense, fresh, varietal aroma of ripe apples with a herby nuance. Flavourful, fresh palate, with an oily element, very pleasant.

TERRAS GAUDA 2003 WHITE
70% albariño, 20% loureira, 10% caíno

86 Straw-coloured. Slightly closed yet fine aroma of fresh and ripe fruit (apples, apricots). Fresh, flavourful and varietal on the palate with lively acidity that emphasises the flavours.

TERRAS GAUDA ETIQUETA NEGRA 2003
AGED ON THE LEES WHITE
TERRAS GAUDA 2002 WHITE
ABADÍA DE SAN CAMPO 2003 WHITE

Adegas TOLLODOURO

Estrada Tui-A Guarda, km. 45
36760 Eiras O Rosal (Pontevedra)
☎: 986 609 810 - Fax: 986 609 811
tollodouro@retemail.es

Established: 2000

🛢 250 litres 🍇 52 has.🚩 90% 🌰10%: -US

TOLLODOURO ROSAL 2003 JOVEN WHITE
albariño, loureira, treixadura, caíno

81 Pale. Not very intense yet clean aroma of lavender and white flowers. Flavourful palate with notes of aromatic herbs, pleasant.

PONTELLÓN ALBARIÑO 2003 JOVEN WHITE
100% albariño

82 Yellow straw. Not very intense yet fine aroma of lavender and herbal tea. Flavourful and bitter palate of grapefruit and herbs; quite persistent.

VALDAMOR

Valdamor, 8
36968 Xil - Meaño (Pontevedra)
☎: 986 747 111 - Fax: 986 747 743
clientes@valdamor.es
www.valdamor.es

Established: 1990

🍾 50 🛢 700,000 litres 🚩 75% 🌰25%: -
UK -US -CH -DE -AD -JP -SE -DK -DO -PR

VALDAMOR 2003 JOVEN WHITE
100% albariño

85 Pale straw. Intense aroma of ripe fruit (apples, bananas), harmonious. Flavourful and expressive with hay on the palate, well-balanced and very pleasant.

VALDAMOR 2001 BARREL AGED WHITE
100% albariño

83 Straw-coloured with a coppery nuance. Aroma of reduction notes (honey and petals) with a certain finesse. Flavourful and smoky with cocoa on the palate, a bitter finish.

NAMORIO 2002 JOVEN WHITE
VALDAMOR 2003 JOVEN WHITE
NAMORIO 2003 JOVEN WHITE
VALDAMOR 2003 OAK AGED WHITE

Adega VALDÉS

Santa Cruz de Rivadulla
15885 vedra (A Coruña)
☎: 981 212 439 - Fax: 981 509 226
comercial@adegavaldes.com
www.adegavaldes.com

ALBARIÑO GUNDIAN 2003 WHITE
100% albariño

83 Straw-coloured. Aroma of tropical fruit (loquats, ripe pineapples) with notes of citrus fruit and wet straw. Flavourful and full-bodied on the palate with good alcohol-acidity balance, slightly oily with pleasant fruit and an aftertaste of herbs.

PAZO VILADOMAR 2003 WHITE
treixadura, albariño

85 Pale yellow. Intense, very fruity aroma with a good varietal expression (Treixadura), white fruit, hints of exotic fruit and a nuance of hay and citrus fruit. Flavourful and fleshy on the palate with ripe apples, notes of fennel and excellent acidity.

VALDUMIA

Camino novo s/n - Zamar
36619 Rubianes - Vilagarcía de Arousa
(Pontevedra)
☎: 986 507 922 - Fax: 986 565 142
comercial@valdumia.net

Established: 1985

220,000 litres 🍇 2 has. 🍷 96% 🌐4%

VALDUMIA SELECCIÓN DE AÑADA 2001
WHITE
100% albariño

84 Golden yellow. Slightly intense aroma of ripe
fruit with toasty and spicy notes of skins.
Flavourful palate with ripe fruit, an oily texture, a
fine crianza expression and spices, slightly creamy
and long.

VALDUMIA 2002 WHITE
albariño

80 Pale gold. Slightly short, fruity aroma with hints
of exotic fruit. Better in the mouth, flavourful
palate with white fruit, fine toasty notes of skins and the
freshness of herbs and citrus fruit, good acidity.

Adegas VALMIÑOR

A Portela, s/n San Juan de Tabagón
36760 O'Rosal (Pontevedra)
☎: 986 609 060 - Fax: 986 609 313
valminor@adegasvalminor.com
www.adegasvalminor.com

Established: 1997

450,000 litres 🍷 80% 🌐20%: -US -MX
-PR -AU -JP -UK -DE -IE -IT -DK -NL -BE -
PT -CH -FI -DK -AD

VALMIÑOR 2003 JOVEN WHITE
100% albariño

84 Brilliant straw. Powerful aroma of ripe fruit
(pears, bananas, pineapple) with a suggestion of
hay. Slightly bitter on the palate with less fruit than
in the nose, but well-mannered and pleasant.

DÁVILA 2003 JOVEN WHITE
65% albariño, 25% treixadura, 10% loureira

91 Lively straw-coloured. Powerful aroma
with a good fruit expression (ripe apples, apricots, lychees) and a suggestion of white flowers
and fennel. Oily, powerful and expressive on the
palate with a carbonic element and slightly
marked acidity that will allow it to last a long
time, persistent.

Hermanos VÁZQUEZ ABAL

Carballal, 3. Barrantes
36636 Ribadumia (Pontevedra)
☎: 986 710 981 - Fax: 986 520 007
carballal@carballal.net

Established: 1985

75,000 litres 🍇 6 has.

CARBALLAL WHITE

VEIGA SERANTES

Escusa, 10
36600 Ribadumia (Pontevedra)
☎: 986 710 092 - Fax: 986 710 092
veigaserantes@terra.es

Established: 1988

100,000 litres 🍇 25 has. 🍷 100%

VEIGA SERANTES 2003 WHITE
100% albariño

69 Straw-coloured with a greenish nuance.
Aroma with notes of somewhat overripe fruit and
nuts. Bitter on the palate with weak fruit.

DO RÍAS BAIXAS

VICENTE DOMÍNGUEZ SANSILVESTRE

O Santo, 16
36969 Sanxenxo (Pontevedra)
☎: 986 857 146 - Fax: 986 863 084
adegadosan@yahoo.es
www.adegasdosan.com

Established: 1992
▤ 16,800 litres ⚘ 1 has. 🍷 100%

ADEGA DOSAN ALBARIÑO 2002 WHITE
100% albariño

73 Straw-coloured with a greenish nuance. Aroma with notes of yeast, weak fruit and spicy nuances. Somewhat oily palate with an edge of acidity, lacks harmony.

ADEGA DOSAN ALBARIÑO 2003 WHITE
100% albariño

70 Straw-coloured with a copper glimmer. Somewhat short aroma of overripe fruit. An edge of acidity on the palate, lacks harmony.

Adega VIEITES

Laxe - Cambados
36634 Cambados (Pontevedra)
☎: 986 542 481 - Fax: 986 542 481

Established: 1988
▤ 30,000 litres ⚘ 5 has. 🍷 100%

FORMIGAL 2003 WHITE

Pazo de VILLAREI

Vía Rápida del Salnés, km. 5
36637 San Martiño de Meis (Pontevedra)
☎: 986 710 827 - Fax: 986 710 827
villarei@byb.es
www.byb.es

Established: 1993
🌐 13 ▤ 300,000 litres ⚘ 81 has.

VILLAREI ALBARIÑO 2003 WHITE
100% albariño

87 Brilliant pale with greenish nuances. Intense, fresh aroma with a good varietal expression (fine herbs, green fruit). Fresh palate with fine bitter and citrus notes and excellent acidity.

PAZO DE VILLAREI 2003 WHITE

VIÑA BLANCA DO SALNES

Lugar de Baltar, 15. Castrelo
36639 Cambados (Pontevedra)
☎: 986 542 910 - Fax: 986 542 910

Established: 1986
▤ 36,000 litres ⚘ 10 has.

ALBARIÑO VIÑA BLANCA DEL SALNES WHITE

VIÑA NORA

Bruñeiras, 7
36440 As Neves (Pontevedra)
☎: 986 667 210 - Fax: 916 160 246
victorre@telefonica.net

Established: 2002
▤ 250,000 litres ⚘ 15 has.
🍷 30% 🌐70%: -US -JP -DE -NL

NORA 2003 JOVEN WHITE
100% albariño

92 Straw-coloured. Floral aroma with fragrant herbs, fine, elegant and fruity. Generous, full, persistent palate with excellent alcohol-acidity balance.

PEITÁN 2003 JOVEN WHITE
albariño

88 Straw-coloured with a yellow hue. Powerful aroma with mineral notes, fresh cut grass (hay) and white fruit. Oily, powerful palate with body but with freshness and acidity.

VIÑA REMESAL

Abelleira, 21 Randufe
36713 Tui (Pontevedra)
☎: 986 600 006 - Fax: 986 600 006

Established: 1990
⚘ 3 has. 🍷 100%

VIÑA REMESAL

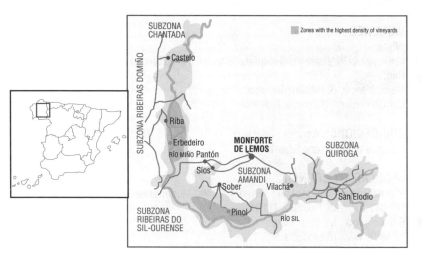

NEWS. Extraordinary growth in grape production (33%) in the Ribeira Sacra in 2003. The *Mencía* harvest alone surpassed the entire 2002 harvest by more than 100,000 kg.

As for quality, the bulk of the scores range from 70 to 80 points. Wines with defects are disappearing; nonetheless, the *Mencía* of this region, although basically correct, does not seem to acquire a style or an expression which permits it to escape its local borders. And it has a tough job, with fierce competition among Spanish wines, as far as red wines are concerned.

Hectares of Vineyard	No. of Viticulturists	No. of Bodegas	2003 Harvest	2003 Production	Marketing
1,200	2,807	89 bottles	-	3,311,617 kilos	92,3%Spain 1.26% foreign

As for the white wines, it seems that the *Godello* is more frequently being mentioned on the label, and has become a selling point, although the Peza do Rei is the only single-variety wine produced from this grape that has surpassed 80 points.

LOCATION. The region extends along the banks of the rivers Miño and Sil in the south of the province of Lugo and the northern region of the province of Orense; it is made up of 17 municipal districts in this region.

CLIMATE. Quite variable depending on the specific area. Less rain and slightly cooler climate and greater Continental influence in the Sil valley, and greater Atlantic character in the Miño valley. Altitude, on the other hand, also has an effect, with the vineyards closer to the rivers and with a more favourable orientation (south-southeast) being slightly warmer.

SOIL. In general, the soil is highly acidic, although the composition varies greatly from one area to another. The vineyards are located on steep terraces and are no higher than 400 m to 500 m above sea level.

VARIETIES:
White:
Main: *Albariño, Loureira, Treixadura, Godello, Doña Blanca* and *Torrontés.*
Red:
Main: *Mencía, Brancellao Merenzao.*
Complimentary: *Garnacha Tintorera.*

SUB-REGIONS: Amandi, Chantada, Quiroga-Bibei, Ribeiras do Miño (in the province of Lugo) and Ribeiras do Sil.

REGULATORY COUNCIL.
Rua Pescadeira, s/n (Antiguo Torreón). 27400 Monforte de Lemos (Lugo).
Tel: 982 410 968. Fax: 982 411 265.
E-mail: info@ribeirasacra.org
Website: www.ribeirasacra.org

GENERAL CHARACTERISTICS OF THE WINES:

Whites	Single variety wines are produced from *Albariño* and *Godello*. The former have a greenish yellow colour with a fruity character and potency typical of *Albariño*; the latter are somewhat fresher than those of Valdeorras and less glycerine-like on the palate. There are also other white wines, the result of the blending of different varieties; these have a straw yellow colour and a fruity aroma.
Reds	The single variety wines of *Mencía*, the most characteristic of the region, have a deep-red mid-tone colour; on the nose they are very fresh and aromatic; on the palate, they are dry, fruity and without a pronounced structure.

ALFONSO FERNÁNDEZ RODRÍGUEZ

Barantes e Abaixo
27421 Sober (Lugo)
☎: 982 152 519

OS CANARES RED

79 Brilliant garnet red cherry. Not very intense aroma of brambles, red fruit and earth. Quite flavourful on the palate, with red fruit and a certain characteristic terroir presence.

Adega ALGUEIRA

Francos - Doade
27460 Sober (Lugo)
☎: 629 208 917 - Fax: 982 402 714
Algueira@navegalia.com
Established: 1998
⊞ 5 ▤ 55,000 litres ▧ 5 has. ⛴ 100%

BRANDÁN GODELLO 2003 WHITE
100% godello

79 Pale golden yellow with greenish nuances. Intense aroma with a certain finesse and varietal nuances (white and exotic fruit, fennel). Flavourful, bitter palate with a slightly acidic edge.

ALGUEIRA 2003 ROBLE RED
100% mencía   ⊞ 10

84 Deep intense cherry. Fine smoky aroma (balsamic flavours) of toasty skins with a nuance of black fruit, complex. Fleshy palate with very fresh yet weighty tannins; character of the vine variety, elegant.

ALVAREZ PIÑEIRO

Vilachá de Salvadur
27413 Puebla de Brollón (Lugo)
☎: 982 401 888 - Fax: 982 410 833
Established: 1997
▤ 25,000 litres ▧ 1 has. ⛴ 100%

CONDE OMAR

AMEDO

Tarrio, San Fiz
27500 Chantada (Lugo)
☎: 982 184 488 - Fax: 982 184 488
Established: 1997
▤ 140,000 litres ▧ 8 has. ⛴ 85% ⚑15%

DONANDREA GODELLO 2003 WHITE
100% godello

77 Pale. Intense aroma of white fruit, hints of flowers, fine notes of herbs and citrus fruit. Fresh, flavourful palate that lacks fruit expression.

DONDARÍO MENCÍA 2003 RED
100% mencía

73 Garnet red with a lively violet edge. Not very intense aroma of red fruit with a suggestion of light off-odours. Fruity, fresh and light on the palate with fairly evident tannins.

AMELIA ALVAREZ REGUDÍN

Carretera de Orense, 58 - Ferreira
27430 Pantón (Lugo)
☎: 982 456 206

ALBARDE 2003 JOVEN RED
100% mencía

76 Lively garnet red cherry. Not very intense yet fresh aroma of red berries and varietal character. Fruity but astringent palate with a rustic hint; well-mannered overall.

AMELIA LEDO VENCE

Sobrado - San Pedro de Líncora
27514 Chantada (Lugo)
☎: 982 440 989 - Fax: 982 440 989
terrasbendaña@europuntoahorro.com
Established: 2000
▤ 30,000 litres ▧ 4 has. ⛴ 100 %

TERRAS BENDAÑA 2002 RED
100% mencía

70 Lively garnet red cherry. Mild evolved aroma yet with a nuance of red fruit. Light, somewhat rustic palate without great fruit expression but well-mannered.

ANTONIO RODRÍGUEZ ALVAREZ

Cruz - Lumeares
32764 A Teixeira (Ourense)
☎: 988 207 432

VIÑA ORIAL RED

Adega BARALLAS

Campo 1, Bulso
27422 Sober (Lugo)
☎: 982 152 582

BARALLAS RED

BOURIZA

Campo da Festa, 21

27466 Rosende - Sober (Lugo)
☎: 982 460 507
bouriza@latinmail.com

Established: 1996

🍷 9 🍶 20,500 litres 🍇 3 has. 🍷 100%

BOURIZA MENCÍA 2003 RED
100% mencía

72 Garnet red cherry. Not very intense aroma, slightly fruity but with mild off-odours. Slightly carbonic on the palate, with ink, well-mannered overall.

CARLOS DÍAZ DIAZ

Calvo Sotelo 65 -2º B
27600 Sarria (Lugo)
☎: 982 152 425 - Fax: 982 533 864

ESTRELA 2003 RED
100% mencía

75 Medium-hue cherry. Slightly short aroma, without great fruit expression yet well-mannered. Light, slightly fruity and pleasant on the palate.

CARMEN PÉREZ PÉREZ

Sanmil, 41 Santa Cruz de Brosmos
27425 Sober (Lugo)
☎: 982 152 508

🍶 22,000 litres 🍇 2 has. 🍷 100%

GUIMARO MENCÍA 2003 RED
100% mencía

78 Cherry with a violet edge. Not very intense aroma with blackberries (ripe berries). Flavourful, fresh and fruity palate, easy drinking.

CARMEN RODRÍGUEZ RODRÍGUEZ

Vilacha - Doade
27424 Sober (Lugo)
☎: 982 153 702

VIÑA A FRIEIRA 2003 RED

78 Garnet red cherry. Medium-intensity aroma of ripe red fruit and lactic notes, harmonious. Quite flavourful on the palate, fresh and balsamic with bitter tannins.

CASA MOREIRAS

Celso Emilio Ferreiro 7- 4º B
36003 Vigo (Lugo)
☎: 982 456 174 - Fax: 986 480 209
Established: 1692

🍷 75.000 🍇 10 has. 🍷 100%

CASA MOREIRAS MENCÍA 2002 RED
mencia

78 Bigarreau cherry with a lively violet edge. Medium-intensity aroma of ripe fruit (strawberries, redcurrants) and a spicy hint. A somewhat astringent but fruity palate, pleasant; very well-mannered.

CASA MOREIRAS GODELLO 2002 WHITE

CÉSAR ENRÍQUEZ "CACHÍN"

Abeleda
32765 A Texeira (Ourense)
☎: 988 203 450

Established: 1993

🍶 25.000 litres 🍇 4 has. 🍷 100%

PEZA DO REI 2003 JOVEN WHITE
100% godello

82 Pale gold. Intense, fruity aroma with a certain varietal character (white fruit, exotic hints, fennel). Flavourful, fruity palate with fine notes of bitterness and citrus fruit.

PEZA DO REI 2003 JOVEN RED
100% mencía

81 Bigarreau cherry with a lively violet edge. Expressive aroma of good intensity with lactic notes and ripe red berries. A touch of flavour on the palate with ripe red fruit and ripe polished tannins, very pleasant.

Adegas COSTOYA

Boga - A Abeleda
32764 A Teixeira (Ourense)
☎: 981 578 222 - Fax: 981 578 222

ALODIO 2003 JOVEN RED
mencía, merenzao, brancellao

76 Cherry with a garnet red edge. Medium-intensity aroma of ink, brambles, a slightly vegetative suggestion. Quite flavourful palate of toasty skins, well-mannered overall.

DARÍA FERREIRO LÓPEZ

Soto, 14 Nogueira
27515 Chantada (Lugo)
☎: 982 441 259 - Fax: 982 982

CABO DO MUNDO 2003 RED
100% mencía

81 Garnet red with a lively violet edge. Short but clean aroma with good expression of red fruit and a floral hint. Flavourful, varietal and intense on the palate with macerated red fruit and a degree of persistence.

DOMINGO LÓPEZ FERNÁNDEZ

Doade, 54
27424 Sober (Lugo)
☎: 982 152 458

VIÑA CICHÓN 2003 JOVEN RED
mencía

72 Bigarreau cherry with a violet edge. Medium-intensity aroma with notes of evolution (overripe fruit). Livelier on the palate; ripe fruit and overtones of vine variety expression.

DON BERNARDINO (EMILIO RODRÍGUEZ DÍAZ)

Santa Cruz de Brosmos, 9
27425 Sober (Lugo)
☎: 982 182 397 - Fax: 982 403 600
info@donbernardino.com
www.donbernardino.com

Established: 1990
🌐 40 ▯ 70,000 litres 🍇 4,5 has. 🍷 100%

DON BERNARDINO 2003 RED
100% mencia

79 Garnet red cherry. Not very intense yet clean aroma of blackberries with a balsamic hint. Notes of skins and red fruit on the palate with a certain expression and persistence.

DON BERNARDINO 2003 ROBLE RED
DON BERNARDINO 2003 RED
ANTERGO 2003 RED

Adega DON RAMÓN

Rubín - Rozabales
27413 Monforte de Lemos (Lugo)
☎: 982 155 770

Established: 1993
🌐 89 ▯ 30,000 litres 🍇 2 has. 🍷 100%

DON RAMÓN MENCÍA 2003 JOVEN RED
mencía

72 Lively garnet red cherry. Not very intense aroma, slightly herbaceous (vine shoots), with a nuance of red fruit. Astringent palate with red fruit, lacks harmony.

DON RAMÓN JOVEN WHITE

EDELMIRO DOMÍNGUEZ GLEZ

O Bao de Oleiros- Os Peares
27528 Carballedo (Lugo)

☎: 988 200 000

CALEXOTES GODELLO 2003 WHITE
godello

72 Pale yellow with golden nuances. Intense, not very fine aroma of somewhat reduced ripe fruit. Flavourful, vinous palate, without great nuances.

CALEXOTE MENCÍA 2003 RED
mencía

74 Garnet red with a slightly violet edge. Not very intense aroma of brambles and balsamic flavours. Light, fruity palate, well-mannered overall.

ELADIO MARTÍNEZ FERNÁNDEZ

Doade
27424 Sober (Lugo)
☎: 982 152 304

Established: 1970
▯ 15,000 litres 🍇 3 has. 🍷 100%

ANZIO MENCÍA 2003 RED
mencía

80 Bigarreau cherry with a violet edge. Aroma of toasty skins, fallen leaves, brambles and ripe red fruit. Flavourful, fresh palate with good fruit expresión, very pleasant.

ENOLÓGICA TÉMERA

Boga, 24
32267 Abeleda - A Teixeira (Ourense)
☎: 606 595 494
jorge@ternera.com
www.ternera.com

Established: 2001
🌐 12 ▯ 10,000 litres

THÉMERA 2002 OAK AGED RED
mencía

80 Dark cherry with an orangey edge. Aroma with spicy oak notes, ink, skins and balsamic flavour. Slightly drying tannins on the palate, spices, lacking in fruit weight but very original.

THÉMERA 2001 CRIANZA RED

ERMITAS RODRÍGUEZ PÉREZ

Lobios - Cima de Lama
27423 Sober (Lugo)
☎: 982 152 500

VIÑA SANCOSMEDE MENCÍA 2003 RED
mencía

76 Cherry with a lively violet edge. Medium-intensity aroma with a good expression of red fruit although a little overripe. Light, fruity and round on the palate, easy drinking.

ERNESTO RODRÍGUEZ PÉREZ

Adega Can Celiño
27460 Sober (Lugo)
☎: 982 152 410

Established: 2002
🍷 100%

VIÑA PEÓN 2003 RED

76 Lively garnet red cherry. Not very intense, slightly vegetative aroma with a nuance of red fruit. Light, fresh, fruity palate; very well-mannered.

ISABEL LÓPEZ LÓPEZ

San Román de Acedre - Budian
27430 Pantón (Lugo)
☎: 982 182 350 - Fax: 982 456 606
a.nogueiras.@wanadoo.es

Established: 1994
20,000 litres 🍇 2 has. 🍷 100%

CAPILLA 2003 RED
100% mencía

76 Cherry with a lively violet edge. Not very intense, yet clean fresh aroma of red fruit and Atlantic woodland. Quite flavourful palate of toasty skins with a hint of overextraction but well-mannered overall.

JESÚS CONDE RODRÍGUEZ

Piantes - Santa Cruz de Brosmos
27425 Sober (Lugo)
☎: 982 152 948

CONDE DE PIANTES MENCÍA 2003 RED
100% mencía

76 Bigarreau cherry with a lively violet edge. Intense aroma of very sweet red fruit. Balsamic, spicy palate with an exotic touch, slightly lacking in freshness.

JESÚS EXPÓSITO HUETE

Cibrisqueiros, 25 Piuca- Pombeiro
27470 Pantón (Lugo)
☎: 982 200 208

Established: 1994

12.000 litres 🍇 3,5 has. 🍷 100%

PEDRA POMBEIRA RED

80 Garnet red cherry. Fresh, fine aroma with pleasant notes of red berries and a balsamic hint. Flavourful, fruity and balsamic on the palate with evident but pleasant tannins.

JESÚS MARIÑO SÁNCHEZ

Guxeba - Santiago de Arriba
27514 Chantada (Lugo)
☎: 982 440 077

Established: 2001
6,000 litres 🍇 1,7 has. 🍷 100%

GUXEBA 2003 RED
100% mencía

76 Bigarreau cherry with a garnet red edge. Short, not very expressive aroma, quite rustic. Better on the palate, fresh, fruity and varietal with a fleshy edge.

GUXEBA 2003 WHITE

JOSÉ ANTONIO FORTES LÓPEZ

Saviñao s/n
27514 Chantada (Lugo)
☎: 982 440 883

Established: 2002
40,000 litres 🍇 3 has. 🍷 100%

VIÑA DO FORTES 2003 RED
100% mencía

74 Brilliant garnet red cherry. Not very intense, slightly rustic aroma of brambles. Light palate with red fruit, balsamic and bitter.

JOSÉ BLANCO LÓPEZ

Hermida, 8
27514 Chantada (Lugo)
☎: 657 805 731 - Fax: 982 440 281

ADEGA DO VEIGA MENCÍA 2003 RED
100% mencía

60 Dark cherry with a lively violet edge. Not very clear, strange aroma of cologne and herbaceous hints. Very astringent palate, with greenness, without fruit.

JOSÉ M. CASTRO SESSE

Puente - Canabal
27440 Sober (Lugo)
☎: 982 460 071

CASTRO SESSE

JOSÉ M. RODRÍGUEZ GONZÁLEZ

Vilachá - Doade
27424 Sober (Lugo)
☎: 982 460 613

PRISCILLVS 2003 RED
mencía, brancellao, merenzao

79 Cherry with a lively violet edge. Intense, expressive aroma of jammy strawberries, varietal. Fresh, light, fruity palate, better in the nose.

DÉCIMA 2003 RED
100% mencía

79 Garnet red cherry. Not very intense aroma with balsamic notes and a nuance of red fruit. Quite flavourful palate with a good expression of red fruit, very pleasant.

JOSÉ MANUEL OTERO CASTRO

O Puzo - San Fiz
27516 Chantada (Lugo)
☎: 982 255 354

CONDE DE VIDÁS

JOSÉ MANUEL VIDAL LÓPEZ

Carballeda - Lobios
27423 Sober (Lugo)
☎: 982 152 627

VIÑA MEZQUITA 2003 JOVEN RED
mencía

80 Bigarreau cherry with a violet edge. Not very intense but fresh aroma of blackberries and toasty skins. Fresh palate with ripe red fruit, not very long but expressive.

JOSÉ MOSQUERA CAMPOS

Regueira - Barantes
27421 Sober (Lugo)
☎: 982 460 591

VIÑA DOS ROMANOS

JOSÉ PÉREZ LÓPEZ

Tellada 11- Santa Cruz de Brosmos,
27425 Sober (Lugo)
☎: 982 152 962

ADEGA DO VAL 2003 JOVEN RED

81 Cherry with a garnet red edge. Intense, fresh, balsamic aroma (fallen leaves) with ink and ripe red fruit. Flavourful, fresh and well-balanced on the palate with a good expression of sweet red fruit.

OS SANTOS RED

JOSÉ RODRÍGUEZ GÓMEZ

Cantón - Amandi
27423 Sober (Lugo)
☎: 982 460 504

VAL DA LENDA 2003 RED
100% mencía

80 Garnet red cherry. Medium-intensity aroma of blackberries, fresh, balsamic and clean. Flavourful, expressive and varietal on the palate, well-characterised with a degree of persistence.

JOSÉ RODRÍGUEZ PRIETO

Barantes
27421 Sober (Lugo)
☎: 982 152 570

VIÑA DO REGUEIRAL JOVEN RED
SEÑORÍO DO CAÑÓN

JOSÉ VÁZQUEZ ÁLVAREZ

Cristosende, s/n
32765 A Texeira (Orense)
☎: 988 266 159

VIÑA PEDERNEIRA 2003 RED

72 Garnet red cherry. Not very intense, somewhat rustic aroma with a suggestion of red fruit. Light on the palate, well-mannered but without great expression.

LEIRABELLA

Leira Vella - Sacardebois
32747 Parada do Sil (Ourense)
☎: 988 290 003 - Fax: 988 290 003

LEIRABELLA 2003 RED

80 Brilliant garnet red cherry. Intense, fruity aroma (strawberry beadsgum), varietal. Light, quite flavourful, fresh palate, easy drinking with red fruit in the finish.

M. BERTA PÉREZ PIÑEIRO (CASA NOGUEDO)

Noguedo - Santiorxo
27422 Sober (Lugo)

☎: 982 152 610 - Fax: 982 411 014
Established: 1980
⊞ 12 🗄 15,000 litres 🍇 1,5 has.🍷 100%

CASA NOGUEDO MENCÍA 2003 JOVEN RED
100% mencía

80 Garnet red cherry. Medium-intensity aroma with red fruit and balsamic flavours. Flavourful palate of concentrated expressive red fruit, with good acidity and varietal character.

M. DEL CARMEN PRADO FERREIRO

Lobios, 30
27423 Sober (Lugo)
☎: 982 152 575

GULLUFRE

M. ISOLINA MOREIRAS MÉNDEZ

A Sariña
27517 Chantada (Lugo)
☎: 982 440 856
Established: 2002
⊞ 5 🗄 25,000 litres 🍇 1 has. 🍷 100%

RIBAZO 2003 WHITE
100% godello

78 Pale yellow. Intense, fresh, slightly fruity aroma. Flavourful palate with white fruit notes, a spicy hint and good acidity.

RIBAZO 2003 RED
100% mencía

78 Lively garnet red cherry. Fresh aroma, a classic northern wine, balsamic with red fruit. Light, quite flavourful palate with the character of the skins and with a light but pleasant greeness.

MANUEL FERNÁNDEZ RODRÍGUEZ

Lobios 54
27423 Sober (Lugo)
☎: 982 401 872 - Fax: 982 456 150

VÉRITAS MENCÍA 2003 RED
100% mencía

74 Bigarreau cherry with a violet edge. Not very intense aroma of ripe fruit with mild off-odours (needs airing). Warm palate with a fleshy edge and ripe fruit, slightly lacking in freshness.

MANUEL LÓPEZ LÓPEZ

Piñeiro, 26 A - Diomondi
27548 O Saviñao (Lugo)
☎: 982 452 253

PALACIO DE DIOMONDI MENCÍA 2003 RED
100% mencía

78 Garnet red with an orangey edge. Clean aroma with notes of almost overripe red fruit. Flavourful, round palate with oily tannins and ripe fruit, slightly lacking in acidity but very well-mannered.

MANUEL PÉREZ PIÑA

Pista de Santa Mariña, s/n
27770 Portomarín (Lugo)
☎: 982 545 024 - Fax: 982 545 071

TERRA PORTUS 2003 WHITE

69 Golden yellow. Powerful aroma of cider with rustic overtones. Flavourful, vinous palate without great nuances.

TERRA PORTUS MENCÍA 2003 RED
100% mencía

73 Brilliant garnet red cherry. Medium-intensity aroma with lactic notes, red fruit (strawberries) and a balsamic hint. Fairly light on the palate, bitter and with weak fruit.

MANUEL PRIMITIVO LAREU LÓPEZ

Fondo de Vila - Sabadelle
27517 Chantada (Lugo)
☎: 982 162 320

SABATELIUS MENCÍA 2003 JOVEN RED
100% mencía

69 Lively garnet red cherry. Aroma with red fruit notes and quite strong off-odours. Better on the palate: quite flavourful and fruity.

MANUELA VALDÉS PÉREZ

Suiglesia - Figueiroá 22
27460 Sober (Lugo)
☎: 982 460 545

TEAR 2003 RED

81 Bigarreau cherry with a violet edge. Slightly intense aroma of macerated red fruit and sun-drenched skins. Flavourful, slightly fleshy palate, expressive and varietal with ripe red fruit.

MARCELINO ALVAREZ GONZÁLEZ

A Carqueixa - Proendos
27460 Sober (Lugo)
☎: 982 460 043

MARCELINO I 2003 JOVEN RED
mencía

78 Bigarreau cherry with a garnet red edge. Aroma of toasty skins, brambles and a somewhat rustic hint. Quite flavourful on the palate with concentrated ripe fruit and a sunny character.

Adegas MARCOS

Vilachá - Doade
27424 Sober (Lugo)
☎: 982 152 285 - Fax: 982 152 285
Established: 1989
🍶 1 🗄 30,000 litres 🍇 3 has.
🍷 95% 🍇5%: -IE

CRUCEIRO 2003 RED
100% mencia

78 Cherry with a violet edge. Not very intense yet clean aroma with an expression of red fruit. Quite flavourful, fresh, fruity palate, easy drinking.

MARIBEL RODRÍGUEZ GONZÁLEZ

A Cal - Amandi
27423 Sober (Lugo)
☎: 982 152 633

O BARREIRO 2003 RED

71 Garnet red cherry. Medium-intensity aroma of slightly burnt skins and dark-roasted notes. Light, well-mannered palate but without great expression.

MAXIMINO LÓPEZ VÁZQUEZ

Espasantes
27450 Pantón (Lugo)
☎: 982 456 595

TERRAS MOURAS RED
mencia

78 Lively cherry. Aroma of black fruit with notes of fallen leaves and a suggestion of scrubland. Flavourful, fresh palate with expressive red fruit.

MONDELO

Bendollo, 29
27329 Quiroga (Lugo)
☎: 982 185 353 - Fax: 928 140 600
Established: 1996
🍶 10 🗄 70,000 litres 🍇 1,5 has.
🍷 95% 🍇5%

PORVIDE 2003 WHITE
godello

70 Pale gold. Aroma with predominant notes of evolution (reduced fruit). Quite flavourful palate with an acidic edge, without nuances.

PORVIDE RED

80 Garnet red cherry. Not very intense yet clean aroma with blackberries and a floral and balsamic hint. Light, balsamic palate with an expression of sun-drenched red fruit and a degree of persistence.

Adegas MOURE

Buenos Aires, 12 - Escairón
27540 O Saviñao (Lugo)
☎: 982 452 031 - Fax: 982 452 700
abadiadacova@adegasmoure.com
www.abadiadacova.com
Established: 1956
🍶 44 🗄 170,000 litres 🍇 10 has.
🍷 90% 🍇10%

ABADÍA DA COVA GODELLO 2003 WHITE
85% godello, 10% albariño, 5% treixadura

83 Brilliant gold. Powerful, fruity aroma (fine exotic touches) with a floral hint. Flavourful palate with white fruit, spicy notes of skins and fine hints of bitterness and citrus fruit.

ABADÍA DA COVA ALBARIÑO 2003 WHITE
85% albariño, 10% godello, 5% treixadura

80 Pale gold. Intense aroma of ripe fruit with hints of jammy grapes and herbs. Flavourful palate with fruit expression slightly muted by the alcohol, bitter with good acidity.

ABADIA DA COVA MENCÍA 2002 OAK AGED RED
100% mencia   🍶 9

77 Garnet red with a violet edge. Not very intense aroma of skins, slightly alcoholic. Drying palate with very marked wood tannins and a suggestion of raisins in the retronasal passage.

ABADIA DA COVA 2003 RED
100% mencía

79 Very deep garnet red with a ruby red hue. Aroma of red fruit and skins. Notes of greeness on the palate, light, without great presence.

DO RIBEIRA SACRA

GODELLO ABADIADA COVA WHITE
CIMBRO RED

OSCAR FIGUEIRAS SÁNCHEZ

Reguengo de Arriba
27517 Chantada (Lugo)
☎: 982 440 823

VIÑA AS COVAS RED

78 Lively cherry. Aroma of strawberries with smoky notes and hints of fruit pulp. Fresh, flavourful palate with pleasantly sweet fruit.

PABLO DOMINGO GONZÁLEZ GÓMEZ

Margaride - Quintá do Lor
27321 Quiroga (Lugo)
☎: 982 155 534

DON COSME

PEDRO PÉREZ FERNÁNDEZ

Camilo, 30 - Bolmente
27421 Sober (Lugo)
☎: 982 152 518

VIÑA FERREIRO RED

Adegas PINCELO

Lg. Pincelo - La Sariña
27515 Chantada (Lugo)
☎: 982 441 660 - Fax: 982 441 281
Established: 1985
🍶 80,000 litres 🍇 5 has 🍷 100%

PINCELO RED

75 Medium-hue ruby red with a garnet red nuance. Lactic aroma of strawberries with sweet notes, pleasant. Slightly drying on the palate, watery, with a suggestion of strawberry jelly in the retronasal passage.

EL ORIGEN 2002 RED

74 Not very deep cherry. Aroma of skins, not very intense and fresh. Pungent, green and light on the palate, without much persistence.

VIÑA PORTOTIDE RED

Adegas PÍO

O Cobo - Piñeiro
32789 Puebla de Trives (Ourense)

☎: 988 330 162 - Fax: 988 331 010
Established: 1998
🍶 30,000 litres 🍇 5 has 🍷 95% 🍇5%

DON PÍO GODELLO 2002 WHITE
100% godello

73 Pale with a greenish nuance. Ripe aroma of slightly reduced white fruit (withered petals) and fine herbs. Fresh palate with a note of greeness to the tannins and scarcely any fruit expression.

DON PÍO 2002 RED
100% mencia

76 Almost opaque cherry. Concentrated aroma of black fruit with hints of greeness. Fleshy, slightly astringent palate (green seeds) with hints of cocoa in the finish.

DOÑA LUISA WHITE
FUENTE GUA RED

Adega PONTE DA BOGA

Lugar do Couto, Sampaio
32764 Castro Caldelas (Ourense)
☎: 988 203 306 - Fax: 988 203 299
ponteboga@yahoo.es
Established: 1999
🍶 355,000 litres 🍇 6 has 🍷 90% 🍇10%:

PONTE DA BOGA 2003 WHITE
100% godello

79 Pale yellow with golden nuances. Intense, quite fruity aroma with hints of grapes and soap perfumed with fine herbs. Flavourful palate with fine bitter notes and a slightly acidic edge.

PONTE DA BOGA 2003 RED
mencia

76 Lively garnet red cherry. Not very intense aroma of brambles and ripe red fruit. Fruity, quite flavourful and varietal on the palate, easy drinking.

PONTE LOMA RED

Adegas PONTE MOURULLE

Sans Xulian de Insua
27550 Toboada (Lugo)
☎: 982 465 318
Established: 2001
🍶 80,000 litres 🍷 100%

VALDOMENDE MENCÍA 2003 RED
100% mencía

82 Dark cherry with a purplish edge. Intense, fruity, ripe aroma with notes of macerated skins. Flavourful palate with red stone fruit, very varietal fine, herbaceous notes and good acidity.

PROMOTORA LOSADA FERNÁNDEZ

Joaquín González, s/n
27430 Ferreira de Pantón (Lugo)
☎: 982 456 213 - Fax: 982 456 213

Established: 1999

🛢 12 🛢 30,000 litres ⚜ 3 has. 🍷 100%

DON VENTURA 2003 RED
100% mencía

83 Biggareau cherry with a lively violet edge. Fresh, balsamic aroma (fallen leaves) with earthy notes and redcurrants. Intense, generous palate with a good Atlantic wine expression (balsamic) and a fleshy edge.

RABELAS

San Fiz
27516 Chantada (Lugo)
☎: 982 440 809 - Fax: 982 440 880

OS CIPRESES 2003 RED
100% mencía

75 Bigarreau cherry with a lively violet edge. Slightly intense aroma of ripe red fruit (strawberry jelly), varietal. Somewhat flavourful and a little rustic on the palate, lacking freshness.

OS CIPRESES 2003 WHITE

RECTORAL DE AMANDI

Amandi
27423 Sober (Lugo)
☎: 988 384 200

RECTORAL DE AMANDI 2003 RED
100% mencía

75 Brilliant garnet red cherry. Slightly short aroma, with notes of brambles and liquorice hints. Fruity, bitter palate, well-mannered overall.

REGINA VIARUM

Doade s/n
27424 Sober (Lugo)
☎: 986 401 699 - Fax: 986 409 945
clientes@reginaviarum.es -
www.reginaviarum.es

Established: 2002

🛢 22 🛢 220,000 litres ⚜ 20 has.
🍷 95% 🍇5%

VÍA IMPERIAL 2003 RED
100% mencía

83 Dark cherry with a dark red edge. Powerful, ripe aroma with fine notes of red fruit and the spicy freshness of skins. Flavourful, fresh palate with rough tannins, fleshy overtones and excellent acidity.

REGINA VIARUM 2003 RED
100% mencía

85 Dark garnet red cherry. Powerful aroma of ripe black fruit a suggestion of petals and notions of terroir. Flavourful, fleshy palate, rich in fruit nuances with firm tannins well-blended with the sweet fruit notes, spicy hints, toast and liquorice.

SAIÑAS (JAVIER FERNÁNDEZ GONZÁLEZ)

Espasantes
27450 Pantón (Lugo)
☎: 982 456 228 - Fax: 982 456 150
saleta16@hotmail.com

Established: 1993

🛢 16 🛢 69,000 litres ⚜ 5'8 has.
🍷 99,5% 🍇0,5%

SAIÑAS 2003 JOVEN RED
100% mencía

78 Garnet red. Fresh aroma, with notes of brambles and a balsamic hint. Fresh, light palate of red fruit, well-mannered overall.

JAVIER FERNÁNDEZ 2003 RED

78 Bigarreau cherry with a lively violet edge. Fresh, balsamic aroma of ripe red fruit with a mild evolution. Better on the palate: fresh, flavourful, varietal and expressive.

JAVIER FERNÁNDEZ 2002 RED

71 Brilliant garnet red cherry. Aroma with burnt notes, ink and balsamic flavours. Astringent, bitter palate with weak fruit.

Adegas SAN JOSÉ

Santa Mariña de Eiré
27439 Pantón (Lugo)
☎: 982 456 545 - Fax: 982 456 545
adegas@infonegocio.com

Established: 1992

🛢 400,000 litres ⚜ 1 has 🍷 95% 🍇5%

RIBEIRA DE VALBOA GODELLO 2003 WHITE
100% godello

78 Straw-coloured. Intense, fresh, slightly fruity aroma (green apples) with fine herbs. Fresh palate with fine bitter notes and without great fruit expression.

RIBEIRA DE PANTÓN 2003 RED
80% mencía, 20% garnacha

79 Cherry with a lively violet edge. Medium-intensity aroma of red fruit, brambles and a good varietal expression. Light, fresh palate with a balsamic nuance, well-mannered overall.

RIBEIRA DE VALBOA 2003 RED
100% mencía

78 Cherry with a garnet red edge. Medium-intensity aroma of ripe blackberries and fallen leaves. Light and pleasant on the palate with red fruit, easy drinking.

Adega SAN MAMED

Salgueiros - Rozabales 8
27413 Monforte de Lemos (Lugo)
☎: 982 155 235

Established: 1999

📦 30,000 litres 🍇 3 has. 🍷 100%

SAN MAMED 2003 RED
mencia

76 Garnet red cherry. Good intensity aroma with ink and slightly overripe red fruit. A touch of flavour on the palate, fruity and bitter with liquorice in the finish.

SANTA MARÍA DE NOGUEIRA

Eirexe-Nogueira
27515 Chantada (Lugo)
☎: 982 128 900 - Fax: 982 128 641
discosta@hotmail.com

Established: 1992

📦 185,000 litres 🍇 1,5 has. 🍷 100%

MONTEQUINTELA MENCÍA 2003 RED
100% mencía

78 Bigarreau cherry with a lively violet edge. Medium-intensity aroma of sun-drenched skins with a balsamic hint (fallen leaves) and certain expression. Light palate with red fruit, pleasant and easy drinking.

SOUTELO

Roberto Baamonde 2 -1º
27400 Monforte de Lemos (Lugo)
☎: 982 410 778 - Fax: 982 411 534
bodegasoutelo@hotmail.com
www.bodegasoutelo.com

Established: 2000

📦 23,000 litres 🍇 0.4 has.

CARDENAL RODRIGO DE CASTRO 2003 JOVEN RED
100% mencia

72 Garnet red. Not very intense aroma with notes of brambles, and a nuance of red fruit. Light palate without great nuances but well-mannered overall.

Adegas TEIXEIRO LEMOS

Pincelo - A Sariña
27515 Chantada (Lugo)
☎: 982 171 666 - Fax: 982 441 281

Established: 1999

📦 15,000 litres 🍇 3.5 has. 🍷 100%

DIEGO DE LEMOS RED

72 Cherry with a violet edge. Aroma of underripe fruit with a suggestion of the tank, not very clean. Light palate with good acidity, bitter.

TOMÁS ARIAS FERNÁNDEZ

Sanxillao - Proendos
27460 Sober (Lugo)
☎: 982 460 055

PROENCIA AMANDI 2003 RED

82 Brilliant bigarreau cherry. Slightly intense aroma of well-characterised ripe fruit (strawberries, blackberries, bilberries). Round, flavourful palate with a fleshy edge, a good expression of ripe fruit and a degree of persistence.

TOMÁS RODRÍGUEZ GONZÁLEZ

Proendos, 104
27460 Sober (Lugo)
☎: 982 460 489 - Fax: 982 460 252

BODEGA BARBADO

VAL DE QUIROGA

Carretera N-120, km. 489
27320 Quiroga (Lugo)
☎: 982 428 580 - Fax: 982 428 580

Established: 1947

📦 500,000 litres 🍇 20 has.

🍷 98% 🍇2%: -FR

VIÑA DE NEIRA GODELLO 2003 WHITE
100% godello

DO RIBEIRA SACRA

78 Golden yellow. Powerful aroma of ripe fruit, with fine reduction (nuts, withered petals) and balsamic notes. Flavourful palate with hints of mountain herbs, lacking fruit expression.

VIÑA DE NEIRA RED
100% mencía

74 Garnet red cherry. Not very intense aroma with hints of fermentation and red fruit. Better on the palate; fruity, quite flavourful, well-mannered overall.

VAL DE QUIROGA WHITE
VAL DE QUIROGA RED

Adegas VERAO

Outeiro 20 - Bolmente
27423 Sober (Lugo)
☎: 982 152 981

CIVIDADE 2003 RED
100% mencía

76 Cherry with a lively violet edge. Medium-intensity aroma of ripe red fruit with a mild evolution. Somewhat flavourful, light palate with blackberries, pleasant.

Adegas e Viñedos VÍA ROMANA

A Ermida - Belesar
27514 Chantada (Lugo)
☎: 982 454 005 - Fax: 982 454 094
viaromana@viaromana.es
www.viaromana.es
Established: 1998
250,000 litres ❦ 12 has. 85% 15%

VÍA ROMANA SELECCIÓN DE AÑADA
MAGNUM 1999 RED
100% mencía

83 Garnet red cherry with a brick red hue. Intense aroma of ripe red fruit with fine notes of spices and reduction. Flavourful palate with a good varietal and crianza expression, notes of toasted nuts, liquorice and good acidity.

VÍA ROMANA MENCÍA 2002 RED
100% mencía

80 Intense cherry with a dark red edge. Powerful, ripe aroma of red fruit with fine hints of reduction and a hint of the freshness of grapeskins. Flavourful, fleshy palate with quite marked tannins (a mild hint of greeness), spicy with hints of earth.

VÍA ROMANA MENCÍA 2003 RED
100% mencía

83 Garnet red cherry with a violet hue. Intense aroma of foresty red fruit and fine herbaceous hints. Fleshy, fruity palate with spicy hints of skins, slightly marked but flavourful tannins and good acidity.

VICENTA VAQUEZ RIVERA

Vilachá de Salvadur
27413 Puebla de Brollón (Lugo)
☎: 982 430 329

XILA JOVEN RED

VICENTE GALLEGO GONZÁLEZ

General Franco, 100
27320 Quiroga (Lugo)
☎: 982 428 393 - Fax: 982 421 205
Established: 1989
❦ 5 has. 100%

VIÑA HERMIDA JOVEN WHITE
SEÑORÍO DE QUIROGA JOVEN RED

VICTORIANO PÉREZ VÁZQUEZ

Seara, 69 -Anllo San Estevo
27466 Sober (Lugo)
☎: 982 460 457 - Fax: 982 402 363

VIÑA SEARA

VIÑA CAZOGA

Amandi- Pacio, 5
27423 Sober (Lugo)
☎: 982 152 780 - Fax: 982 472 293
Established: 1700
2 25,100 litres ❦ 7 has. 100%

VIÑA CAZOGA 2003 JOVEN RED
100% mencía

75 Lively garnet red cherry. Fresh, fine, expressive aroma of ripe red fruit and violet hints. Fleshy, fruity palate with very marked and drying tannins.

VIÑA CAZOGA 2003 JOVEN WHITE
DON DIEGO 2002 OAK AGED RED

Adega VIÑA GAROÑA

Nogueira de Abaixo
27515 Chantada (Lugo)
☎: 982 171 636 - Fax: 982 171 636
Established: 1988
23 120,000 litres ❦ 4 has 100%

MARQUÉS DE GAROÑA MENCÍA 2003
JOVEN RED
100% mencía

60 Garnet red cherry. With very strong off-odours, lacking cleanliness.

VIRXEN DOS REMEDIOS

Diomondi
27548 O Saviñao (Lugo)
☎: 982 171 720

VIÑA VELLA GODELLO 2003 WHITE
100% godello

76 Brilliant pale with golden nuances. Slightly intense, fruity aroma with hints of fine herbs. Fresh palate with fine spicy notes and citrus fruit, lacking fruit expression.

VIÑA VELLA MENCÍA 2003 RED
100% mencía

73 Brilliant cherry with a violet edge. Medium-intensity aroma of blackberries and a suggestion of mild off-odours. Light and slightly fruity on the palate, pleasant.

XOSÉ VÁSQUEZ RODRÍGUEZ

Ana Blanca, s/n
32765 A Teixeira (Ourense)
☎: 629 818 701

Established: 2000

🛢 15,000 litres 🍇 1 has. 🇪🇸 100%

SÉCULO 2003 RED

79 Cherry with a lively violet edge. Expressive aroma of good intensity with jammy red fruit and very sweet notes. Flavourful, fruity and varietal on the palate, very pleasant.

DO RIBEIRO

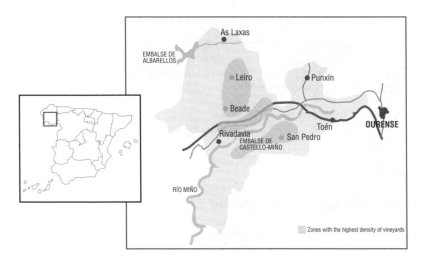

As Laxas

EMBALSE DE ALBARELLOS

Leiro

Punxín

Beade

OURENSE

Toén

Rivadavia

EMBALSE DE CASTELLO-MIÑO

San Pedro

RÍO MIÑO

Zones with the highest density of vineyards

NEWS. Of the 2003 harvest, the aromatic quality of the white wines stands out, thanks to the good health of the grapes and the excellent varietal expression of the *Treixadura*, which has ripened exceptionally well this year. In total, two million more grapes were harvested than in 2002.

Among the most outstanding wines is the Viña Magnavía, with a high percentage (40%) of *Torrontés* (a very promising variety, but which is used very little in significant percentages) and which costs less than € 5. It achieved 90 points, above Viña Meín (88), and was only surpassed by an excellent Emilio Rojo which reached 91 points.

Hectares of Vineyard	No. of Viticulturists	No. of Bodegas	2003 Harvest	2003 Production	Marketing
3,000	5,930	102 (28 bottlers)	Excellent	10,500,00 litres	97% Spain 2% export

Mention should also be made of the attempts by the Ribeiro cooperative to recover the 'Tostadillo', a traditional variety of the region, which was very successful in Europe in the 15th and 16th centuries. An as yet experimental wine, which was officially presented at the Vinoble fair of sweet wines.

LOCATION. In the west of the province of Orense. The region comprises 13 municipal districts marked by the Miño and its tributaries.

CLIMATE. Atlantic, with low temperatures in winter, a certain risk of spring frosts, and high temperatures in the summer months. The average annual rainfall varies between 800 mm and 1,000 mm.

SOIL. Predominantly granite, deep and rich in organic matter, although in some areas clayey soils predominate. The vineyards are on the slopes of the mountains (where higher quality wines are produced) and on the plains.

VARIETIES:
White: Preferred: *Treixadura, Torrontés, Palomino, Godello, Macabeo, Loureira* and *Albariño*. Authorized: *Albilla, Macabeo, Jerez*. Experimental: *Lado*.
Red: Preferred: *Caíño, Alicante, Sousón, Ferrón, Mencía, Tempranillo, Brancellao*. Authorized: *Tempranillo, Garnacha*.

REGULATORY COUNCIL.
Salgado Moscoso, 9. 32400 Ribadavia (Orense).
Tel: 988 47 72 00. Fax: 988 47 72 01.
E-mail: conselloregulador@do-ribeiro.com
Website: www.do-ribeiro.com

GENERAL CHARACTERISTICS OF THE WINES:

Whites	These are the most characteristic of the DO. The wines, produced from the autochthonous varieties (mainly *Treixadura* and *Torrontés*, although *Lairo*, *Loureira* and *Godello* are also used), are characterised by their fresh and fruity aroma with notes of green apple, fennel and hints of flowers; on the palate they have good acidity, which makes them very fresh. Those produced from *Palomino*, however, are much more neutral, aromatically limited and less expressive on the palate.
Reds	The production is limited compared to the white wines. The most common are based on a non-local grape variety, the *Alicante*, exported after the phylloxera outbreak, which gives wines of medium quality and which are somewhat aggressive and acidic. Those of Mencía, on the other hand, have greater aromatic potency; they are fresh, light and pleasant to drink. Another line, still quite new, are the reds that experiment with other autochthonous grapes (*Brancellao, Caíño, Sousón* and *Ferrón*), which are more characteristic, but which, on some occasions, provide slight vegetative and herb sensations.

Sociedad Agraria de Transformación
A PORTELA

Piñeiros, s/n
32431 Beade (Orense)
☎: 988 480 050 - Fax: 988 480 201
beadeprimicia@airtel.net
www.aler-sl.es/aportela

Established: 1987

250,000 litres 🍇 9 has.
🍷 98% 🌐2%: -UK -CH

BEADE PRIMACÍA 2003 JOVEN WHITE
treixadura

84 Pale with golden nuances. Intense, very fine aroma with notes of ripe white fruit, hints of flowers and fine herbs. Flavourful, fruity palate with excellent fruit-acidity balance, bitter quality citrus hints.

SEÑORÍO DE BEADE 2003 JOVEN WHITE
treixadura, torrontes, otras

83 Brilliant pale with greenish nuances. Intense aroma of white fruit (apples), with hints of fennel and fine herbs. Fresh, flavourful palate with fine bitter notes and excellent acidity.

SEÑORÍO DE BEADE 2003 JOVEN RED
caíno, brancellao, ferrón

78 Dark cherry with a violet hue. Intense aroma of slightly reduced ripe fruit and mild off-odours from the tank. Fresh, flavourful palate with a light carbonic hint, bitter notes (slightly green tannins) and good acidity.

ALANÍS

Carretera de Vigo 22-24
32450 Barbantes (Orense)
☎: 988 280 405 - Fax: 988 280 346
alanis@byb.es
www.byb.es

Established: 1910

518,600 litres

GRAN ALANÍS 2003 WHITE

82 Brilliant pale. Quite intense aroma with a certain finesse and notes of fennel. Flavourful palate with white fruit (pears) and fine spicy hints of skins, hints of aniseed.

SAN TROCADO 2003 WHITE
treixadura, torrontés

83 Pale yellow with greenish nuances. Quite intense aroma of fruit and white flowers with the freshness of citrus fruit. Flavourful palate with fine bitter and herby notes, good acidity.

ALEMPARTE

Gomariz
32496 Leiro (Ourense)
☎: 988 488 295 - Fax: 988 271 256

Established: 1979

80,000 litres 🍇 7 has. 🍷 100%

AIRÓN 2003 WHITE
torrontés, treixadura, godello, loureira

78 Pale with greenish nuances. Quite intense and fruity aroma with floral hints. Very fresh, flavourful palate with spicy notes and slightly marked acidity.

ALEMPARTE WHITE

ANTONIO GARCÍA VÁZQUEZ

Ventosela, 43-45
32417 Ribadavia (Ourense)
☎: 988 470 248

CANGALLO WHITE

ANTONIO MONTERO SOBRINO

Santa María
32430 Castrelo do Miño (Ourense)
☎: 988 471 132

ANTONIO MONTERO WHITE

ANTONIO SOUSA PAZ

Souto
32232 Castrelo de Miño (Ourense)
☎: 988 489 080

GRAN CRUCEIRO WHITE
VIÑA CRUCEIRO WHITE

Adegas ÁUREA LUX (MANUEL GARCÍA CARRASCO)

Esposende
32400 Ribadavia (Ourense)
☎: 986 470 368

AUREA LUX WHITE
treixadura, otras

76 Pale gold. Intense aroma without great fruit expression and mild suggestion of reduction (nuts, cumin). Quite flavourful, bitter palate with hints of fine herbs.

LEIVE 2003 WHITE
treixadura

DO RIBEIRO

79 Brilliant gold. Powerful aroma of very ripe white stone fruit with hints of flowers (acacia) and herbs, a nuance of wax. Flavourful, fruity palate with creamy overtones.

BARBANTIÑO

Barbantes
32457 Puxin (Ourense)
☎: 988 280 352 - Fax: 988 280 352
Established: 1968
210,000 litres 100%

AMANECER WHITE
REAL BANTIÑO WHITE

Bodegas CAMPANTE

Finca Reboreda
32941 Puga (Ourense)
☎: 988 261 212 - Fax: 988 261 213
info@campante.com
www.campante.com
Established: 1940
2,000,000 litres 20 has.
80% 20%: -US -UK -DE -CH -BE -NL V-E

CAMPANTE 2003 WHITE
palomino, torrontés

75 Brilliant pale. Quite intense and fruity aroma without great fruit expression. Fresh palate with fine bitter notes and a slightly acidic edge.

GRAN REBOREDA 2003 WHITE
80% treixadura, 12% godello, 8% loureira

85 Brilliant pale. Intense, very fine aroma of flowers and white fruit with hints of fennel and quite jammy fruit. Flavourful, fresh palate with fine bitter notes and a nuance of herbs and citrus fruit, expressive, long.

VIÑA REBOREDA 2003 WHITE
70% treixadura, torrontés, godello, 30% palomino

80 Pale. Quite intense aroma with a certain finesse, fruit and white flowers and hints of herbs. Fresh, flavourful palate with fine notes of spices and citrus fruit.

VIÑA REBOREDA 2003 RED
mencía, caíno, brancellao

79 Intense cherry. Fresh, fruity aroma with somewhat varietal herbaceous hints, spices and underbrush. Flavourful, bitter palate with slightly marked, fresh tannins and good acidity.

VIÑA DO RECANTO 2003 WHITE

Bodega CASTRO REI

Sampaio
32400 Ribadavia (Ourense)
☎: 615 323 221 - Fax: 988 472 069
castrorei@hotmail.com
www.castrorei.com
Established: 1998
80,000 litres 2 has. 90% 10%

CASTRO REI 2003 WHITE
treixadura, lado, loureira, palomino, torrontés

78 Pale gold. Intense aroma of ripe white fruit with hints of flowers and herbs (bay, fennel) and a suggestion of grapes. Flavourful palate with a certain spicy freshness.

CASTRO REI 2003 RED
garnacha, brencellao, caíno, sousón

78 Cherry with a violet hue. Intense aroma of forest fruit with spicy hints of skins and a very varietal herbaceous hint. Flavourful, bitter palate with an acidic edge.

CUNQUEIRO

Prado do Miño, s/n
32230 Castrelo de Miño (Orense)
☎: 988 489 023 - Fax: 988 489 082
info@bodegascunqueiro.es
www.bodegascunqueiro.es
Established: 1960
600,000 litres 8 has. 88% 12%: -CH -DE

CUNQUEIRO III MILENIUM 2003 WHITE
MAIS DE CUNQUEIRO 2003 WHITE
CUNQUEIRA 2003 WHITE
ANCIÑO RED

EMILIO ROJO

Puente
32233 Arnoia (Orense)
☎: 988 488 050
Established: 1987
5 300 litres 7,5 has.
90% 10%

EMILIO ROJO 2003 JOVEN WHITE
lado, torrontés

91 Straw-coloured, with a greenish glint. Intense aroma, with predominant white fruit notes and fine notes of balsamic herbs. Fresh palate with fruity notes, generous, slightly oily texture, a powerful hint of green grass in the retronasal passage.

FRANCISCO FERNÁNDEZ SOUSA

Prado, 14
32430 Castrelo do Miño (Ourense)
☎: 988 489 077 - Fax: 986 272 148
casalbrais@telefonica.net

Established: 1960

🗄 30,000 litres 🍇 2 has. 🍷 100%

CASAL BRAIS 2003 WHITE
100% palomino

78 Pale with a greenish hue. Quite intense aroma of green grass, without great fruit expression. Fresh, flavourful, bitter palate with good acidity.

TERRA MINEI 2003 WHITE
80% treixadura, 20% torrontés

75 Pale with a greenish hue. Intense aroma with notes of herbs and aniseed but poor fruit expression. Flavourful, bitter palate with a marked citrus character.

LAGAR DE BRAIS 2003 WHITE

FREIJIDO

Avenida Ribeiro, 32
32400 Ribadavia (Ourense)
☎: 988 470 066 - Fax: 988 472 242
info@bodegasfreijido.com
www.bodegasfreijido.com

Established: 1892

🗄 150,000 litres 🍇 9 has.

🍷 90% 🌐10%: -NL -FR -UK

DO AVOENGO 2001 WHITE
70% treixadura, 10% albariño, 10% torrontés, 10% loureira

84 Pale yellow with a lemony nuance. Intense aroma of ripe white fruit with exotic hints and fine notes of petals. Flavourful, fruity palate with a slightly oily texture, notes of fine herbs and good acidity.

FREIJIDO WHITE
VIÑA DOS CONDES 2002 WHITE

GALLAECIA PREMIUM

Fray Pedro Payo Piñeiro, 17 bajo
15009 A Coruña (A Coruña)
☎: 670 522 577 - Fax: 881 924 492
delispain@delispain.com
www.gallaeciapremium.com

Established: 2003

VIÑA MAGNAVIA 2003 WHITE
40% torrontés, 20% treixadura, 20% loureira, 20% godello

90 Golden straw. Complex aroma with a rich fruit expression and fine herbs (lavender, fennel, mint). Full, oily palate rich in nuances of fruit and fragrant herbs, very persistent.

VIÑA MAGNAVIA PREMIUM 2003 WHITE

HEREDEROS DE JESÚS FREIJIDO

Jose Antonio, 30-5º 1
32400 Ribadavia (Ourense)
☎: 988 471 969 - Fax: 988 471 969

AGAS DO TEMPO WHITE

JAIME LÓPEZ VÁZQUEZ

Esposende
32400 Ribadavia (Ourense)
☎: 988 471 161

VIÑA GUIMERÁNS WHITE

JOSÉ ARMANDO BANGUESES LÓPEZ

Barral
32430 Castrelo do Miño (Ourense)
☎: 988 493 065

GRAN BARUXO WHITE

JOSÉ CAMILO LÓPEZ RODRÍGUEZ

Carballeda de Avia
32420 Carballeda de Avia (Ourense)
☎: 988 487 024

VIÑA TEIXEIRA WHITE

JOSÉ ESTÉVEZ FERNÁNDEZ

Ponte
32224 Arnoia (Ourense)
☎: 988 492 833

MAURO E. ALVAREZ 2003 WHITE
treixadura, torrontés, lado

84 Pale yellow with a greenish hue. Powerful aroma of white fruit, with fine notes of herbs and fennel fresh mineral and citrus fruit overtones.

Flavourful palate with white fruit, fine bitter notes and good acidity.

JOSÉ GONZÁLEZ ALVAREZ

32496 Gomariz - Leiro (Ourense)

PAZO LALÓN WHITE

JOSÉ MANUEL BLANCO PÉREZ

Souto, 34
32430 Castrelo do Miño (Ourense)
☎: 988 303 878
Established: 2000
⊞ 8 📖 21,500 litres 🌱 1,5 has. 🍷 100%

GRAN SOUTO WHITE
VIÑA SOUTO WHITE

JOSÉ MERENS MARTÍNEZ

Chaos
32224 Arnoia (Ourense)
☎: 988 493 045
Established: 2001
⊞ 4 📖 10,900 litres 🌱 2,6 has.

LAGAR DO MERENS 2003 BARREL AGED WHITE
treixadura, lado, godello

84 Brilliant pale with greenish nuances. Intense, very fine aroma of white fruit, with the spicy freshness of skins and hints of limestone. Fresh, flavourful palate with excellent fruit-acidity balance.

LOEDA

Sampaio
32414 Ribadavia (Ourense)
☎: 988 471 043 - Fax: 988 470 734
info@bodegasloeda.com
www.bodegasloeda.com
🍷 100%

VIÑA LEDA 2003 WHITE

LUIS A. RODRÍGUEZ VÁZQUEZ

Laxa, 7
32234 Arnoia (Ourense)
☎: 988 492 977
Established: 1987
📖 20,000 litres 🌱 1,8 has. 🍷 100%

VIÑA DE MARTÍN WHITE

A TORNA DOS PASAS RED
EIDOS ERMOS RED

LUIS CARNERO PÉREZ

Puga
32941 Toén (Ourense)
☎: 988 268 913

VIÑA CABADIÑA WHITE
VIÑA CABADIÑA RED

MARÍA ALVAREZ SERRANO

Barro de Gomariz
32429 Leiro (Ourense)
☎: 988 488 249 - Fax: 988 488 249
Established: 1987
📖 30,000 litres 🌱 6 has. 🍷 100%

COTO DE GOMARIZ WHITE

Bodega MERLOT IBÉRICA

Rodríguez Valcárcel, 15
32400 Ribadavia (Ourense)
☎: 988 471 508 - Fax: 988 471 508
merlotiberica@yahoo.es
Established: 1989
📖 120,000 litres 🌱 6 has.
🍷 88% 🌐12%: -UK - VE

VEIGA D'OURO 2003 WHITE
treixadura, torrontés, albariño, godello

82 Pale with greenish nuances. Intense aroma of green fruit and fine herbs with floral hints. Flavourful palate with fine bitter notes, a spicy hint (anise) and excellent acidity.

COTO D'AGUIA MENCÍA RED
mencía

77 Garnet red cherry with a violet hue. Fresh, quite varietal aroma of red fruit, with a herbaceous (balsamic) hint. Flavourful palate with slightly marked tannins (a mild hint of greeness) and marked acidity.

Bodegas NAIROA

A Ponte
32224 Arnoia (Ourense)
☎: 988 492 867 - Fax: 988 492 422

GRAN NAIROA 2003 WHITE
treixadura, otras

80 Pale with greenish nuances. Intense aroma with a certain finesse and varietal expression (green fruit, fennel). Flavourful palate with the freshness of spices and citrus fruit.

NEXUS PROMOCIONES

Fechos - Arrabaldo
32593 Santa Cruz de Arrabaldo (Ourense)
☎: 988 384 196 - Fax: 988 341 196

Established: 2000

🗄 40,000 litres 🍇 14 has. 🍷 85% 🍊15%

PAZO CASANOVA WHITE

Bodegas O'VENTOSELA

Carretera N-120, s/n
32574 Grova-Rivadabia (Ourense)
☎: 988 471 947 - Fax: 988 471 205
bodegas@oventosela.es

Established: 1987

🗄 1,000,000 litres 🍇 20 has.
🍷 90% 🍊10%: -US -CH -PR

GRAN LEIRIÑA 2002 WHITE
GRAN LEIRIÑA SELECCIÓN 1958 2002
WHITE
JUAN MIGUEZ ALITIA 2002 WHITE
O'VENTOSELA 2002 WHITE
VIÑA LEIRIÑA 2002 WHITE
JUAN MIGUEZ ALITIA 2002 RED
O'VENTOSELA TINTO 2002 RED

PAZO CASANOVA

Fechos - Arrabaldo
32593 Santa Cruz de Arrabaldo (Ourense)
☎: 988 384 196 - Fax: 988 341 196
casanova@pazocasanova.com
www.pazocasanova.com

Established: 2000

🗄 100,000 litres 🍇 14 has.
🍷 85% 🍊15%: -CH -NL -DK -UK

PAZO CASANOVA 2003 WHITE
85% treixadura, 5% loureira, 5% albariño, 5% godello

82 Pale with greenish nuances. Intense aroma of white fruit with exotic hints, fine floral notes and hints of pollen and fine herbs. Flavourful palate with a certain spicy freshness and rich hints of citrus fruit.

Adega PAZO DO MAR

Carretera Ourense-Castrelo, km. 12, 5
32940 Feá (Ourense)
☎: 988 261 256 - Fax: 988 261 264
info@pazodomar.com
www.pazodomar.com

Established: 2002

🗄 1,800,000 litres 🍇 2 has.
🍷 90% 🍊10%: -BE -CH

PAZO DO MAR 2003 WHITE
NEREIDA 2003 WHITE
TORRE DO OLIVAR 2003 WHITE

PEÑA

Vide
32430 Castrelo do Miño (Ourense)
☎: 988 489 094

SEÑORÍO DO LANCERO WHITE

PRADOMINIO

Boa Vista, 49
32430 Castrelo do Miño (Ourense)
☎: 988 489 052
info@pradominio.com
www.pradominio.com

Established: 1989

🗄 7,000 litres 🍇 2.2 has. 🛢 4000 litres.
🍷 90% 🍊10%

PRADOMINIO 2003 WHITE

77 Pale with golden nuances. Quite intense aroma of white fruit with slightly tropical and fine herbaceous hints. Quite flavourful and fruity palate with fresh overtones.

REY LAFUENTE

Prado Do Miño
32230 Castrelo do Miño (Ourense)
☎: 988 489 025 - Fax: 988 489 125

Established: 1985

🗄 500,000 litres 🍇 4 has.
🍷 85% 🍊15%: -DE -IE -CH

REY LAFUENTE 2003 WHITE
REY LAFUENTE DORADO 2003 WHITE
REY LAFUENTE SUMUM 2003 WHITE
REY LAFUENTE 2003 RED

Adegas RIVERA

Carretera de Vigo, s/n
32450 A Barca de Barbantes (Ourense)
☎: 988 280 028 - Fax: 988 280 028
valeiras@adegasrivera.com
www.adegasrivera.com

Established: 1886

🗄 500,000 litres 🍇 5 has.

98% 2%: -BE

GRAN RIVERA 2003 WHITE
80% treixadura, 15% torrontés, 5% albariño, godello, loureira, lado

76 Pale with greenish nuances. Intense aroma of white fruit with hints of flowers and citrus fruit. Flavourful palate with fresh overtones and a slightly acidic edge.

RIVERA 2003 WHITE
palomino, torrontés

77 Brilliant pale. Quite intense aroma of fruit and white flowers with a nuance of fine herbs. Fresh, flavourful palate without great fruit expression, with rich hints of citrus fruit.

MOUCHIÑO 2003 WHITE
80% treixadura, 15% torrontés, 5% albariño, godello, loureira, lado

80 Pale yellow with lemony nuances. Quite intense aroma of ripe white fruit (slightly reduced) with hints of petals and fine lees. Flavourful palate with fine bitter and fruity notes and spicy hints.

VIÑA XINADAS 2003 WHITE
VIÑAL DO REL 2003 RED
RIVERA 2003 RED

RODRÍGUEZ MÉNDEZ

Barral
32430 Castrelo do Miño (Ourense)
☎: 988 493 006 - Fax: 988 493 211
Established: 1964
800,000 litres 2 has.
80% 20%: -DE -IT -AD

SOLBEIRA 2003 WHITE
VIÑA BARRAL 2003 WHITE
GRAN SOLBEIRA 2003 WHITE
VIÑA BARRAL 2003 RED

SERVANDO MARTÍNEZ GÓMEZ

Casardeita
32430 Castrelo do Miño (Ourense)
☎: 988 475 096

VIÑA CULMIÑAS WHITE

VALDEPUGA

Carretera de Ourense a Cortegada, km 10
32940 Alongos -Toén (Ourense)
☎: 988 222 772 - Fax: 988 222 561
valdepuga@infonegocio.com
Established: 1999

50,000 litres 7 has. 100%

VALDEPUGA 2003 WHITE
treixadura, torrontés, godello, loureira

83 Brilliant pale. Quite intense aroma of ripe white fruit (slightly reduced) with hints of petals. Flavourful, quite fruity palate with hints of herbs and spicy skins, good acidity.

VICENTE GIRALDEZ FERNÁNDEZ

Cenlle
32454 Cenlle (Ourense)
☎: 988 404 030

ALECRIN WHITE
ALECRIN RED

VILERMA

Villerma - Gomariz
32429 Leiro (Ourense)
☎: 988 228 702 - Fax: 988 248 580

VILERMA 2003 WHITE

79 Brilliant pale yellow. Intense, quite fresh aroma with green apples and hints of herbs. Flavourful, quite fruity palate with a slightly oily texture and a spicy hint of skins.

VILERMA 2002 RED

77 Dark garnet red cherry. Powerful aroma with toasty notes of skins, a balsamic hint (eucalyptus) and damp earth. Flavourful palate with slightly marked tannins (a mild suggestion of greeness).

VIÑA MEIN

Mein, s/n San Clodio
32420 Leiro (Ourense)
☎: 617 326 248 - Fax: 915 761 019
vinamein@wol.es
www.vinamein.com
Established: 1988
7 150,000 litres 16 has.
80% 20%: -US -UK -FR -CH -BE -NL -DK -DE

VIÑA MEIN 2002 WHITE
80% treixadura, 15% godello, 5% loureira

88 Brilliant pale gold. Intense, very fine aroma of fruit and white flowers with hints of smokiness and hay. Flavourful palate with fine bitter notes, very fine oak tannins and the freshness of minerals and citrus fruit in the finish.

VIÑA MEIN 2003 WHITE
80% treixadura, 10% godello, 5% loureira, 2% albariño, 2% torrontés, 1% lado, albilla

85 Pale with greenish nuances. Intense aroma of fruit and white flowers with hints of fine herbs and a spicy hint. Flavourful, elegant palate, rich in herby nuances (mint, fennel) with excellent acidity.

VIÑA MEIN 2002 RED
50% caíño, 25% mencía, 25% ferrón

75 Medium-hue cherry. Fresh, sharp aroma of green peppers. Drying palate with hints of greeness and hints of underripe fruit in the retronasal passage.

Cooperativa
VITIVINÍCOLA DEL RIBEIRO

Valdepereira
32417 Ribadavia (Ourense)
☎: 988 477 210 - Fax: 988 470 330
mcastro@pazoribeiro.com

Established: 1967
🍇 670 has.

PAZO 2003 WHITE

72 Very pale. Intense aroma of grapes without great nuances. Fresh, quite flavourful palate, lacking acidity.

VIÑA COSTEIRA 2003 WHITE

77 Pale. Fine aroma of fruit and white flowers with hints of herbs. Fresh, flavourful palate without great nuances.

ALÉN DA ISTORIA 2003 RED

81 Dark cherry with a purplish edge. Powerful, fruity aroma with spicy hints of skins and very varietal herbaceous hints. Flavourful palate with fine bitter notes slightly marked tannins and good acidity.

XOSE A. CARRASCO GONZÁLEZ

Cenlle
32454 Cenlle (Ourense)
☎: 988 404 027
🍷 32,000 litres 🍇 2.2 has.

CENLLE SELECCIÓN WHITE
SEÑORÍO DE CENLLE WHITE
CENLLE SELECCIÓN RED

XOSE VILLAR FERNÁNDEZ

Laxa
32224 Arnoia (Ourense)
☎: 988 492 955

LOURAL WHITE

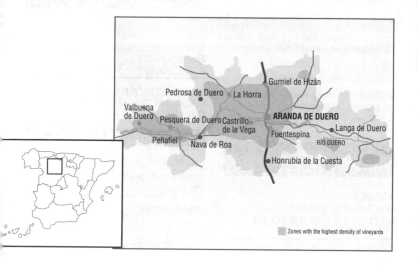

Zones with the highest density of vineyards

NEWS. There were concerns in the Ribera del Duero (fourth denomination in Spain in terms of production and second in terms of business volume) and fear of a second consecutive bad harvest, after the disaster that the rains brought to the region in 2002. Under these conditions, only the choice of grapes and great care in the production process saved the quality. The enemy in 2003 was very different: the heat, although the water reserves of the subsoil (there were abundant rains during the winter and spring) seem to have been sufficient to be able to complete the growth cycle and the ripening process successfully. Moreover, in 2003, there was a record harvest: 76 million kilograms of grapes.

Hectares of Vineyard	No. of Viticulturists	No. of Bodegas	2003 Harvest	2003 Production	Marketing
18,600	8,200	178	Very Good	76,265,000 Kg	70% Spain 30% export

As always happens in denominations where young wines (some of which spend little time in barrels) make up merely 18% of the total of the samples tasted, the conclusions regarding quality have to go beyond the mere reference to the year in question, because good ageing (together with a rigorous selection and sensible oenology) can save the worst harvests. This is the case of the condemned 2002 harvest, as opposed to the highly-praised 2001 harvest. With almost the same number of wines tasted (73 in 2002 compared to 80 in 2001), 35 surpassed 85 points in 2002 compared to 48 in 2001, and 6 reached or surpassed 90 points in 2002 compared to 10 in 2001.

We have also noticed that most of the wines of the DO are marketed without the traditional labels Crianza, Reserva and Gran Reserva, which shows that the freedom of the oenologist is becoming the best guarantor of quality and is forcing the Regulatory Council to seriously reflect on the matter.

LOCATION. Between the provinces of Burgos, Valladolid, Segovia and Soria. This region comprises 19 municipal districts in the east of Valladolid, 5 in the north west of Segovia, 59 in the south of Burgos (most of the vineyards are concentrated in this province with 10,000 Ha) and 6 in the west of Soria.

CLIMATE. Continental in nature, with slight Atlantic influences. The winters are rather cold and the summers hot, although mention must be made of the significant difference in day-night temperatures contributing to the slow ripening of the grapes, enabling excellent acidity indexes to be achieved. The greatest risk factor in the region is the spring frosts, which are on many occasions responsible for sharp drops in production. The average annual rainfall is between 450 mm and 500 mm.

SOIL. In general, the soils are loose, not very fertile and with a rather high limestone content. Most of the sediment is composed of layers of sandy limestone or clay. The vineyards are located on the interfluvial hills and in the valleys at an altitude of between 700 and 850 m.

VARIETIES:
White: *Albillo.*
Red: *Tinto del País* (*Tempranillo* – majority with 81% of all vineyards), *Garnacha Tinta, Cabernet Sauvignon, Malbec* and *Merlot.*

REGULATORY COUNCIL.
c/ Hospital, 6. 09300 Roa (Burgos).
Tel: 947 54 12 21. Fax: 947 54 11 16.
E-mail: info@doriberadelduero.es
Website: www.riberadelduero.es

GENERAL CHARACTERISTICS OF THE WINES:

Rosés	They are onion skin coloured, fruity and flavourful, although on occasions they may be a little alcoholic and heavy.
Reds	These are the top wines of the DO. Produced mainly from a red grape variety of the country (*Tempranillo*), they are an intense cherry colour. On the nose, they are characterised by their aromas of very ripe fruit, with the great character of the skins which is normally reminiscent of the smell of ink, although there are also young wines with rustic notes. Ageing in barrels allows these powerful wines to mellow and to acquire greater elegance. Their solid tannins and fine structure make them exceptional products for ageing in wood and in the bottle. On the palate, the red wines from Ribera are powerful, with body and a good balance between alcohol and acidity.

DO RIBERA DEL DUERO

AALTO, BODEGAS Y VIÑEDOS

Ctra. de Peñafiel, s/n
09300 Roa (Burgos)
☎: 947 540 781 - Fax: 947 540 790
aalto@aalto.es
www.aalto.es
Established: 1999
🌐 1,000 📦 225 litres 🍇 42 has. 🍷 60%
🌐40%: -US -DE -CH -JP -FI -AT -CA

AALTO 2001 OAK AGED RED
100% tinto fino

90 Intense cherry. Aroma with notes of very ripe fruit (jammy blackberries) and fine toasty oak. Round, elegant palate with fine toasty notes in the retronasal passage (cocoa, coffee) and very well-crafted silky tannins.

AALTO PS 2001 OAK AGED RED
100% tinto fino

94 Intense cherry. Aroma of very fine toasty (cocoa, tobacco) and creamy notes with ripe fruit (jammy black plums). Oily palate with silky tannins and dates and jammy fruit in the retronasal passage, warm, slightly spirituous, full and elegant with great persistence.

ADRADA ECOLÓGICA

La Ermita, 3
09462 Adrada de Aza (Burgos)
☎: 947 531 096 - Fax: 947 531 096
adradaecologica@yahoo.es
www.adradaecologica.com
Established: 2001
🌐 18 📦 60,000 litres 🍇 7 has.
🍾 26,000 litres.

🍷 70% 🌐30%

KIRIOS DE ADRADA 2003 JOVEN RED
KIRIOS DE ADRADA 2001 OAK AGED RED
KIRIOS DE ADRADA 2002 OAK AGED RED

ALEJANDRO FERNÁNDEZ TINTO PESQUERA

Real nº 2
47315 Pesquera de Duero (Valladolid)
☎: 983 870 039 - Fax: 983 870 088
pesquera@pesquera.com
www.grupopesquera.com
Established: 1972
🌐 6,000 📦 40 litres 🍇 200 has.
🍷 60% 🌐40%

TINTO PESQUERA 2001 CRIANZA RED
100% tempranillo

89 Intense cherry. Powerful aroma with rich notes of ripe skin maceration and toasty oak, ripe fruit and the hallmark of this vineyard's red wines. Fleshy and powerful palate with a rich expression of ripe fruit and oak with very well-assembled and marked tannins; flavourful and long.

TINTO PESQUERA JANUS 1995 GRAN RESERVA RED

87 Dark cherry with a brick red rim. Spicy aroma with animal notes (leather, tobacco, cigar box) and slightly jammy fruit. Powerful, fleshy, flavourful and spicy on the palate (pepper, leather) with ripe, round tannins in the retronasal passage.

Bodegas y Viñedos ALIÓN

Ctra. N-122, km. 312, 4
47300 Padilla de Duero (Valladolid)
☎: 983 881 236 - Fax: 983 881 246
alion@bodegasalion.com
www.vega.sicilia.com
Established: 1991
🌐 1,200 📦 400,000 litres 🍷 50% 🌐50%

ALIÓN 2001 OAK AGED RED
100% tinto fino   🌐 13

92 Intense cherry with a brilliant garnet red edge. Medium-intensity aroma of fine toasty flavours, cocoa, coffee and ripe fruit. Round, flavourful palate with powerful tannins well cloaked by the alcohol, fine toasty notes in the retronasal passage and an elegant finish.

Hijos de ANTONIO POLO

La Olma, 5 Pl. Los Comuneros
47300 Peñafiel (Valladolid)
☎: 983 881 083 - Fax: 983 873 183
pago.penafiel@terra.es
www.pagopenafiel.com
Established: 1999
🌐 300 📦 85,000 litres 🍇 10 has. 🍷 30%
🌐70%: -US -PR -JP -CH -DE -FR -DK -BE -UK -AT -MX -PL

PAGOS DE PEÑAFIEL 2003 ROBLE RED
100% tinto fino

87 Intense cherry with a lively violet edge. Intense aroma of very ripe fruit (viscous notes) and well-assembled wood, fine. Powerful palate with concentrated and jammy fruit and ripe tannins, very sweet with chocolate in the finish, long.

PAGOS DE PEÑAFIEL 2003 JOVEN RED
100% tinto fino

80 Cherry with a lively violet edge. Medium intensity aroma with unusual notes of cereal and a suggestion of black fruit. Better on the palate: flavourful and prominent with sweet fruit and polished tannins, very pleasant.

PAGOS DE PEÑAFIEL 2001 CRIANZA RED
100% tinto fino

87 Intense cherry with a garnet red-orangey edge. Intense aroma with ripe black fruit and fine wood (cocoa), harmonious. Powerful, flavourful, generous palate with black fruit, well-integrated wood and oily and ripe tannins.

PAGOS DE PEÑAFIEL 2000 RESERVA RED
100% tinto fino

87 Quite intense cherry with a garnet red edge. Fine harmonious aroma of creamy oak notes and ripe black fruit. Flavourful, powerful palate of ripe black fruit and a long toasty finish (white chocolate).

ARCO DE CURIEL

Calvario, s/n
47316 Curiel del Duero (Valladolid)
☎: 983 880 481 - Fax: 983 881 766
info@arcocuriel.com
www.arcocuriel.com

Established: 1998

🌐 500 🛢 315,000 litres 🍇 40 has.

🍷 70% 🍇30%: -US -PR -BE -LU

ARCO DE CURIEL 2002 ROBLE RED
ARCO DE CURIEL 2000 CRIANZA RED

Bodegas ARROCAL

Eras de Santa María, s/n
09443 Gumiel de Mercado (Burgos)
☎: 669 403 169 - Fax: 947 511 861
info@bodegasconde.com

Established: 2002

🌐 120 🛢 130,000 litres 🍇 15 has.

🍷 30% 🍇70%: -US -DE -PR -DK -CH -UK

ARROCAL 2003 OAK AGED RED
100% tempranillo   🌐 4

87 Very dark cherry with a violet edge. Powerful aroma of jammy black fruit, slightly varietal with hints of damp earth. Flavourful, fleshy palate with a good fruit/oak integration, predominant fruit notes (macerated skins) and liquorice.

ARZUAGA NAVARRO

Ctra. N-122, km. 325
47350 Quintanilla de Onésimo (Valladolid)

☎: 983 681 146 - Fax: 983 681 147
bodeg@arzuaganavarro.com
www.arzuaganavarro.com

Established: 1993

🌐 3,000 🛢 1,000,000 litres 🍇 150 has.

🍷 45% 🍇55%

VIÑEDOS Y BODEGAS LA PLANTA 2003 JOVEN RED
100% tinto fino

84 Red with an orangey rim. Aroma with overtones of reduction and very ripe red fruit. Flavourful palate with wood and well-integrated fruit.

GRAN ARZUAGA 2002 OAK AGED RED
100% tinto fino

90 Intense cherry. Intense aroma with very ripe and slightly jammy fruit notes (jam), spirituous notes and fine toasty oak. Powerful and fleshy palate rich in ripe fruit, fine toasty and creamy sensations, sweet and flavourful tannins.

TINTO ARZUAGA 2001 CRIANZA RED
90% tinto fino, 8% cabernet sauvignon, 2% merlot

87 Cherry with an orangey rim. Aroma of ripe red fruit, jammy tomatoes and spices. Well polished tannins on the palate, well-balanced fruit-wood, a smoky nuance, evoking fruit.

ARZUAGA 2001 RESERVA ESPECIAL RED
100% tinto fino

89 Cherry. Aroma of jammy red fruit with a smoky character, nuts and mild balsamic hints. Good tannic symmetry, intense, well-balanced, round.

Viñedos y Bodegas ÁSTER

Ctra. Aranda - Palencia, km. 55, 1.
09312 Término El Caño (Anguix)
☎: 947 561 028 - Fax: 947 561 018
aster@riojalta.com
www.riojalta.com

Established: 1990

🌐 2,777 🍇 95 has.

ÁSTER 2000 RESERVA RED

87 Dark garnet red cherry with a coppery edge. Intense, very fine aroma with predominant smoky notes, spicy wood and the freshness of macerated skins. Flavourful, fleshy palate with a good fruit/oak integration, spicy and bitter (dark-roasted flavours, dry earth) with quite ripe, polished tannins long.

áster
RESERVA 2000

RIBERA DEL DUERO
DENOMINACIÓN DE ORIGEN

BALBÁS

La Majada s/n
09331 La Horra (Burgos)
☎: 947 542 111 - Fax: 947 542 112
bodegas@balbas.es
www.balbas.es

Established: 1988
🍷 2,000 🛢 990,000 litres 🌿 72 has.
🍇 60% 🌐40%

BALBÁS 2001 CRIANZA RED

87 Deep cherry. Expressive aroma of ripe, jammy black fruit, mineral notes and very fine wood reduction. Fleshy, powerful palate with fruity tannins dominating the wood, fresh and long.

ARDAL 1999 CRIANZA RED

85 Deep cherry. Aroma of expressive black fruit, mineral notes and very fine toasty flavours. Fleshy palate, with character, excellent flavour, fresh and fruity tannins (blackberries), a pleasant bitterness in the finish.

ARDAL 1999 RESERVA RED

78 Dark garnet red with a brick red hue. Aroma of menthol and pine with good wood and some sweet notes. Drying palate with wood tannins over marked, fresh and slightly short.

BALBÁS 1999 RESERVA RED

86 Deep cherry. Elegant aroma with notes of varnish, terroir a suggestion of fine reduction. Fleshy palate with ripe, flavourful tannins, freshness, a good crianza-fruit balance and a pleasant bitterness in the finish.

ALITUS 1996 RESERVA RED

89 Intense cherry. Powerful aroma rich in mineral notes and fine toasty flavours in an excellent bottle evolution (cocoa, tobacco, old leather. cedar wood). Full, round, oily and warm palate with lively but flavourful tannins and leather and spices in the retronasal passage.

ARDAL 2001 CRIANZA RED

BRIEGO

Del Rosario, 32
47311 Fompedraza (Valladolid)
☎: 983 892 156 - Fax: 983 892 156
comercial@bodegasbriego.com
www.bodegasbriego.com

Established: 1992
🍷 450 🛢 180,000 litres 🌿 32 has.
🍇 50% 🌐50%

BRIEGO TIEMPO 2002 ROBLE RED

88 Quite intense cherry. Fine and creamy toasty aroma (cocoa) of ripe fruit with a slight varietal expression. Full palate with oily, very elegant tannins, flavourful and persistent.

GONDOMAR 2002 ROBLE RED

🍷4

85 Dark cherry with a dark red edge. Powerful aroma of black fruit with hints of macerated skins and a suggestion of toasty oak. Powerful palate with an excellent expression of varietal fruit well sustained by the wood and hints of liquorice.

GONDOMAR 2000 CRIANZA RED

84 Dark cherry. Powerful aroma, of slightly varietal and reduced ripe fruit with a suggestion of spicy oak and notions of terroir. Flavourful, fleshy palate with a good fruit/oak integration, notes of slightly overripe fruit and liquorice, long.

GONDOMAR 1999 RESERVA RED

85 Dark cherry with a dark red-saffron edge. Intense, ripe aroma with reduction notes typical of Ribera Tempranillo (a suggestion of animals, mild lack of racking) and a spicy and creamy hint of oak. Powerful, fleshy palate with a good Reserva expression, spicy, slightly fruity and long.

BRIEGO CRIANZA RED
BRIEGO FIEL RESERVA RED
BRIEGO RESERVA RED
BRIEGO GRAN RESERVA RED
GONDOMAR GRAN RESERVA RED

CACHOPA

Ctra. N-122, km. 259
09491 Vadocondes (Burgos)
☎: 947 528 133 - Fax: 947 528 151
bodegascachopa@wanadoo.es

Established: 1997

⊞ 635 ▤ 200,000 litres ▧ 20 has.
▼ 70% 💧30%

CACHOPA CRIANZA RED
CACHOPA RESERVA RED
AVAN CEPAS CENTENARIAS RED
VALDOLÉ RED

Bodegas del CAMPO

Camino Fuentenavares, s/n
09370 Quintana del Pidío (Burgos)
☎: 947 561 034 - Fax: 947 561 034
bodegas@pagosdequintana.com
www.pagosdequintana.com

Established: 1992

▤ 280,000 litres ▧ 30 has.▼ 80% 💧20%: -
FR -DE -CH -AT -US -MX -PR -DO -BR -JP

PAGOS DE QUINTANA 2003 ROBLE RED
PAGOS DE QUINTANA "PAGO
CARRAMONZÓN" 2001 OAK AGED RED
PAGOS DE QUINTANA 2002 CRIANZA RED
PAGOS DE QUINTANA 1999 RESERVA RED

CARRALBA

Ctra. N-122 , km. 306
47300 Peñafiel (Valladolid)
☎: 983 881 910 - Fax: 983 881 659
info@carralba.com
www.carralba.com

Established: 2001

⊞ 140 ▤ 140,000 litres ▧ 40 has.
▼ 90% 💧10%

CARRALBA 2003 JOVEN RED
CARRALBA 2001 CRIANZA RED
CARRALBA 2000 CRIANZA RED
CARRALBA 2000 RESERVA RED

CASTILLALTA

Ctra. Aranda - Salas, s/n
09490 San Juan del Monte (Burgos)
☎: 947 552 233 - Fax: 947 552 233
castillalta@eresmas.com

Established: 1995

⊞ 210 ▤ 1,000,000 litres ▮ 100%

CASTILLALTA JOVEN RED
CASTILLALTA CRIANZA RED

CASTILLO DE PEÑAFIEL

Ctra. Pesquera, 12
47300 Peñafiel (Valladolid)
☎: 983 873 029 - Fax: 983 873 029
viejocoso@wanadoo.es

Established: 1993

⊞ 180 ▤ 40,000 litres ▼ 90% 💧10%

VIEJO COSO CRIANZA RED
VIEJO COSO RESERVA RED

CEPAS Y BODEGAS

La Horra
La Horra (Burgos)
☎: 983 376 979 - Fax: 983 340 824
b.burlon@terra.es

Established: 1998

⊞ 200 ▤ 50,000 litres ▼ 1% 💧99%: -DE -
CH -US -FR -PR -NL -BE -DK -MX -UK -CA

VILLACAMPA 2003 ROBLE RED
VILLACAMPA 2001 CRIANZA RED
VILLACAMPA 2000 RESERVA RED

CILLAR DE SILOS

Paraje El Soto s/n
09443 Quintana del Pidio (Burgos)
☎: 947 545 126 - Fax: 947 545 605
bodega@cillardesilos.es
www.cillardesilos.es

Established: 1994

⊞ 600 ▤ 275,000 litres ▧ 50 has.
▼ 75% 💧25%

CILLAR DE SILOS 2001 CRIANZA RED
100% tempranillo

80 Deep cherry. Not very intense aroma of red fruit and vanilla. Very dry palate due to the wood yet structured and well-balanced.

TORRESILO 2001 CRIANZA RED
100% tempranillo

88 Very deep cherry with a coppery edge. Powerful, very fine aroma of jammy black fruit with fine toasty oak notes and hints of terroir. Powerful, concentrated palate with a good oak/fruit integration, ripe and oily tannins, fine bitter notes (chocolate, liquorice) and refreshing acidity.

CILLAR DE SILOS 2003 RED

COMARCAL LA MILAGROSA

Ctra. Madrid/Irun, km. 147
09460 Milagros (Burgos)
☎: 947 548 026 - Fax: 947 548 026

Established: 1962
⬚ 100 ▊ 1,250,000 litres
🍇 240 has. 🍷 100%

MILCAMPOS 2003 ROSÉ

68 Raspberry. Aroma with marked off-odours (racking flaw). Better in the mouth, fresh and fruity.

MILCAMPOS 2002 JOVEN RED
90% tinto fino, 10% otras

79 Garnet red cherry. Medium-intensity aroma with pleasant red berries. Ripe red fruit character on the palate, easy drinking and pleasant.

MILCAMPOS 2002 OAK AGED RED
90% tinto fino, 10% otras   ⬚ 3

75 Garnet red cherry. Not very intense aroma with notes of greeness and a nuance of red fruit. Fairly fruity palate, mildly vegetative yet well-mannered as a whole.

SOLAR DE VALDEFERREROS 2002 OAK AGED RED
90% tinto fino, 10% otras

78 Ruby red cherry. Perfumed aroma of red stone fruit. Some herbaceous notes on the palate with drying tannins in the finish.

MILCAMPOS 2000 CRIANZA RED
90% tinto fino, 10% otras

78 Cherry with an orangey edge. Aroma with a rustic touch (skins, ink) and lacking in fruit. The same character but flavourful on the palate, well-mannered.

SOLAR DE VALDEFERREROS JOVEN ROSÉ
SOLAR DE VALDEFERREROS 2002 JOVEN RED

Bodegas y Viñedos COMENGE

Camino del Castillo, s/n
47316 Curiel de Duero (Valladolid)
☎: 983 880 363 - Fax: 983 880 717

www.comenge.com
Established: 2000
⬚ 302 ▊ 132,000 litres
🍇 36 has. 🝆 90,000 litres.

COMENGE 2001 RED
100% tempranillo

86 Ruby red cherry. Aroma of creamy and toasty wood and spices. Flavourful palate with slightly marked though well-balanced wood tannins with coffee and tobacco in the finish.

COMENGE 2002 CRIANZA RED
100% tempranillo

86 Deep cherry with a violet edge. Intense, very fine aroma of jammy red fruit and toasty oak notes with a mild balsamic note. Flavourful palate with promising yet quite marked tannins and a slightly oily texture; balanced.

CON CLASS

Ctra. Madrid-Coruña km. 170, 6
47490 Rueda (Valladolid)
☎: 983 868 336 - Fax: 983 868 432
bodegasbccv@interbook.net
www.bodegasdecastilla.com

Established: 1988
⬚ 300 ▊ 150,000 litres 🝆 20%
🌐80%: -DE -CH -NL -BE

VALLEBUENO 2000 CRIANZA RED
100% tinto fino

83 Garnet red cherry with a saffron hue. Intense, ripe aroma with a mild nuance of woody freshness. Flavourful palate with quite marked oak tannins, a nuance of black fruit and hints of terroir.

CRIANZA 2000
VALLEBUENO
RIBERA DEL DUERO
DENOMINACIÓN DE ORIGEN
75 cl.e   14% Vol.
EMBOTELLADO POR CON CLASS, S.L. - PESQUERA DE DUERO (VALLADOLID) ESPAÑA
RE 8.155 VA 00

CONDADO DE HAZA

Ctra. La Horra, s/n
09300 Roa (Burgos)
☎: 947 525 254 - Fax: 947 561 098
www.condadodehaza.com

Established: 1988

⊞ 4,000 ▤ 800,000 litres 🍇 200 has.
🍷 65% ◉35%

CONDADO DE HAZA SELECCIÓN 1999 RESERVA RED

84 Intense cherry. Toasty aroma of black fruit (hints of maceration) and creamy oak. Fruity pala-te, with notes of crianza dominant over the fruit and wood tannins, lacks harmony.

Bodegas CONDE

Pizarro, s/n
09400 Aranda de Duero (Burgos)
☎: 947 511 61/ - Fax: 947 511 861
info@bodegasconde.com
www.bodegasconde.com

Established: 2000

⊞ 63 ▤ 21,000 litres 🍇 7 has.
🍷 30% ◉70%

NEO COUPAGE 2002 OAK AGED RED
100% tinta del país   ⊞ 15

88 Intense cherry. Powerful aroma of toasty cask (dark-roasted flavour, chocolate) with ripe black fruit. Fleshy, full palate with well-displayed tan-nins, warm, well-structured with fruity persistence.

NEO PUNTA ESENCIA 2001 OAK AGED RED
100% tinta del país   ⊞ 20

91 Intense cherry. Aroma with considerably mar-ked oak with a mild suggestion of minerals (earthy, damp underbrush). Powerful palate with sweet ripe fruit tannins and dry perfumed oak tannins (cre-amy), flavourful.

NEO 2000 OAK AGED RED
100% tinta del país   ⊞ 14

89 Dark cherry with a very lively garnet red edge. Fine aroma of good toasty wood and ripe fruit with good varietal character. Generous, flavourful and round palate; very fine tannins with considerable fruity complexity and a suggestion of minerals; excellent acidity-alcohol symmetry.

NEO 2001 RED
100% tinta del país

87 Intense cherry. Powerful aroma with a rich, ripe fruit expression (jammy prunes) and toasty hints of oak (peat, pitch). Fleshy, full and flavour-ful palate with slightly drying tannins.

CONVENTO DE OREJA

Lago Salado, 8
28017 Madrid ()
☎: 659 920 752
convento@conventooreja.com

Established: 2002

⊞ 100 ▤ 60,000 litres 🇪🇸 100%

CONVENTO OREJA 2002 ROBLE RED
100% tinta del país   ⊞ 4

80 Quite dark cherry with a violet edge. Intense aroma with notes of macerated black fruit, smoky hints of oak and terroir. Flavourful palate with slightly drying tannins (quite fresh oak) and hints of wax and spices in the retronasal passage.

CONVENTO SAN FRANCISCO

Calvario, 22
47300 Peñafiel (Valladolid)
☎: 983 878 052 - Fax: 983 873 052
bodega@bodegaconvento.com
www.bodegaconvento.com

Established: 1998

⊞ 335 ▤ 100,000 litres 🍷 60% ◉40%: -US -PR -DE -IT -FR -CH -AT -NL -PT -AD

CONVENTO SAN FRANCISCO 2001 RED
CONVENTO SAN FRANCISCO 2002 RED

Hermanos CUADRADO GARCÍA

Ctra. de Soria, km. 322
47350 Quintanilla de Onésimo (Valladolid)
☎: 983 238 400 - Fax: 983 239 000

Established: 1994

⊞ 100 ▤ 50,000 litres 🍇 40 has.
🍷 20% ◉80%

ORBEN 2000 RED

88 Intense cherry with a lively garnet red edge. Powerful aroma of toasty flavours, (coffee, dark-roasted flavours) ripe black fruit with a mineral nuance. Powerful, full and fleshy palate. Dry but ripe tannins, toasty oak in the retronasal passage. Good acidity.

DEHESA DE LOS CANÓNIGOS

Ctra. Renedo-Pesquera, km. 39
47315 Pesquera de Duero (Valladolid)
☎: 983 484 001 - Fax: 983 870 359
bodegadehesadeloscanonigos@bodegadehesadeloscanonigos.com
www.bodegadehesadeloscanonigos.com

Established: 1988

🌐 1,600 🍇 62 has.

🍷 90% 🌐10%: -US -PR -MX

SOLIDEO 2000 RESERVA RED
85% tempranillo, 12% cabernet sauvignon, 3% albillo

85 Fairly dark cherry. Fruity, very even oak flavour and fresh on the palate with mild earthy hints. Round, oak/fruit well-blended on the palate, toasty in the retronasal passage with reduction notes (tobacco, cedar), supple tannins.

SOLIDEO 2002 CRIANZA RED
SOLIDEO 2001 RESERVA RED

Bodegas DIEZ LLORENTE

Ctra. Circunvalación R-30 s/n
09300 Roa (Burgos)
☎: 615 293 031 - Fax: 947 540 341
bodegas@diezllorente.com
www.diezllorente.com

Established: 2001

🌐 300 📊 200,000 litres 🍇 50 has.

🍷 60% 🌐40%

SEÑORÍO DE BRENDA 2001 OAK AGED RED
100% tinto fino   🌐3

83 Garnet red cherry with a coppery edge. Fairly intense aroma with spicy oak notes and quite ripe red stone fruit. Flavourful on the palate with slightly marked tannins, herbaceous hints and bitter notes (liquorice), good acidity.

DÍEZ LLORENTE 2002 OAK AGED RED
100% tinta del país   🌐4

82 Garnet red cherry with a brick red glint. Intense, ripe aroma with spicy hints of oak and a reduction nuance. Flavourful on the palate with slightly marked tannins (hints of greeness), fresh overtones and well-integrated fruit/oak.

SEÑORÍO DE BRENDA 2002 CRIANZA RED
100% tinto fino

83 Garnet red cherry with a coppery edge. Not very intense aroma with a certain finesse, macerated fruit and well-integrated toasty notes of oak. Flavourful and well-balanced on the palate with fine bitter notes and mineral overtones.

DÍEZ LLORENTE 2002 CRIANZA RED
100% tinto fino

85 Garnet red cherry with a brick red edge. Powerful aroma with predominant spicy oak notes, hints of fruit and sun-drenched skins and evoking terroir freshness. Flavourful on the palate with good crianza expression, well-balanced and long.

SEÑORÍO DE BRENDA 2001 CRIANZA RED
100% tinta del país

83 Garnet red cherry with a coppery edge. Intense aroma, toasty notes, jammy fruit with hints of sour cherries in liqueur. Flavourful and fleshy on the palate, with a certain spicy freshness and well-integrated fruit/oak, slightly warm.

SEÑORÍO DE BRENDA 2003 JOVEN RED
DÍEZ LLORENTE 2003 JOVEN RED
SEÑORÍO DE BRENDA 2001 RESERVA RED
DÍEZ LLORENTE 2001 RESERVA RED

Bodega DOMINIO BASCONCILLO

Condado de Treviño, 55
09001 Burgos (Burgos)
☎: 947 473 300 - Fax: 947 473 360
info@dominiobasconcillos.com
www.dominiobasconcillos.com

Established: 2000

🌐 360 📊 151,000 litres 🍇 50 has.

🍷 90% 🌐10%: -PR

VIÑA MAGNA 2001 CRIANZA RED
VIÑA MAGNA 2000 CRIANZA RED

DOMINIO DE ATAUTA

Ctra. de Morcuera s/n
42345 Atauta (Soria)
☎: 913 020 247 - Fax: 917 661 941
dominiodeatauta.ribera@arrakis.es

Established: 2000

🌐 330 🍇 15 has. 🍷 30% 🌐70%

DOMINIO DE ATAUTA 2002 OAK AGED RED
100% tinto fino   🌐15

89 Intense cherry. Powerful, spicy aroma with mineral and fruit expression with fine toasty notes (chocolate, coffee). Oily, elegant and mineral on the palate with flavourful and fine tannins, ripe fruit and notions of minerals.

DOMINIO DE ATAUTA LLANOS DEL ALMENDRO 2002 OAK AGED RED
100% tinto fino   🌐18

95 Intense cherry. Powerful, complex aroma, with abundant mineral notes, dried mountain herbs (thyme and broom) with toasty oak (cocoa, chocolate). Generous, oily and very original palate with ripe fruit expression and a ripe nuance with fine toasty notes and oily tannins, very long and elegant.

DOMINIO DE ATAUTA LA MALA 2002 OAK AGED RED
100% tinto fino   🌐20

92 Very intense cherry. Deep, toasty aroma (pitch, dark chocolate, carpentry) of black fruit and flowers (violets, bilberries) with nuances of incense and minerals. Full, fleshy palate with fresh fruit in the retronasal passage, an expression of dried mountain herbs and ripe tannins.

DO RIBERA DEL DUERO

DOMINIO DE PINGUS

Hospital s/n (Apdo. 93, Peñafiel)
47350 Quintanilla de Onésimo (Valladolid)
☎: 639 833 854

Established: 1995

⊞ 150 ⚘ 5 has.

FLOR DE PINGUS 2002 RED
100% tinto fino

89 Garnet red cherry. Powerful aroma with a rich expression of fresh fruit (redcurrants, blackberries) and very fine and delicate toasty, creamy oak. Round, elegant, fine, delicate palate with fresh red fruit and fine toasty oak in the retronasal passage, light and silky tannins, great persistence.

DURÓN

Ctra. Roa-La Horra km. 3, 800
09300 Roa (Burgos)
☎: 902 227 700 - Fax: 902 227 701
bodega@cofradiasamaniego.com
www.cofradiasamaniego.com

Established: 1982

⊞ 1,105 🗓 542,500 litres ⚘ 120 has.

🍷 75% 🍇25%: -UK -DE -FR -NL -CH -DK -BE -US -JP

DURÓN 2002 ROBLE JOVEN RED

82 Medium-hue cherry. Toasty aroma of wood, slightly lactic with a balsamic suggestion. Well-balanced on the palate with slightly marked tannins though a little short in fruit weight.

DURÓN 2000 CRIANZA RED
90% tinta del pais, 10% cabernet sauvignon

83 Not very deep cherry. Spicy aroma of new wood, menthol and light reduction. Slightly drying palate with marked ripe tannins and liquorice and cedar in the retronasal passage.

DURÓN 1996 RESERVA RED

78 Garnet red with an orangey hue. Aroma with reduction character (leather, wet dog, cloves). Light and well-balanced on the palate with slightly characterless tannins and balsamic hints in the retronasal passage.

DURÓN 2003 ROBLE JOVEN RED
DURÓN 1999 RESERVA RED
DURÓN 1989 GRAN RESERVA RED

ÉBANO VIÑEDOS Y BODEGAS

Ctra. Palencia, km. 15.5
09440 Gumiel de Mercado (Burgos))
☎: 986 609 060 - Fax: 986 609 313

ebano@ebanovinedosybodegas.com

⊞ 200 ⚘ 43 has.

ÉBANO CRIANZA 2001 RED
100% tempranillo

EL MOLAR

Avenida Rotura s/n
47315 Pesquera de Duero (Valladolid)
☎: 983 210 750 - Fax: 983 210 929
info@bodegaselomar.com
www.bodegaselmolar.com

Established: 1998

⊞ 1,000 🗓 300,000 litres ⚘ 30 has.

🍷 60% 🍇40%: -CH -BE -US -CA -MX -IT -JP -TW

ARAVIÑAS 2003 ROSÉ
NELEO 2001 RED
LAGAR VIEJO 2000 RED
VIÑA TREBLA 2000 RED
ARAVIÑAS SEMICRIANZA 2002 OAK AGED RED
ARAVIÑAS 2000 CRIANZA RED
ARAVIÑAS 1999 RESERVA RED

Bodegas EMILIO MORO

Ctra. Peñafiel - Valoria, s/n
47315 Pesquera de Duero (Valladolid)
☎: 983 878 400 - Fax: 983 870 195
bodega@emiliomoro.com
www.emiliomoro.com

Established: 1988

⊞ 1,500 🗓 850,000 litres ⚘ 105 has.

🍷 65% 🍇35%: -US -PR -MX -PE -DO - PA -BR -SE -FI -CH -DE -FR -IE -IT -RU -IL -BE -AT -JP -AD -NL -CU -AU

FINCA RESALSO 2003 OAK AGED RED
100% tempranillo

83 Deep garnet red with a purplish rim. Aroma of brambles, not very intense red fruit and vanilla. Fleshy palate with flavourful tannins, earthy, persistent with medium-high body.

MALLEOLUS DE VALDERRAMIRO 2002 OAK AGED RED
100% tempranillo

94 Very intense cherry. Very complex, toasty aroma (dark-roasted coffee, cocoa, chocolate) with creamy hints of fine wood, very ripe fruit and a slightly mineral hint (dry stones). Powerful, fleshy palate with ripe fruit, slightly spirituous with sweet tannins and a dry and powerful finish, flavourful and very persistent.

EMILIO MORO 2001 OAK AGED RED
100% tempranillo

86 Deep cherry. Fine spicy aroma (cloves, black pepper) with an elegant crianza and a black fruit suggestion. Fleshy, powerful palate with good oak/fruit balance and very supple but fleshy tannins.

MALLEOLUS 2001 OAK AGED RED
100% tempranillo

85 Intense cherry. Aroma with fine toasty notes and ripe fruit. Fleshy, ripe palate with harmony between wood and fruit and marked oak tannins in the finish.

EMILIO MORO 2002 OAK AGED RED
MALLEOLUS 2002 OAK AGED RED
MALLEOLUS DE SANCHO MARTÍN 2002 OAK AGED RED
FINCA RESALSO 2003 OAK AGED RED

EMINA

Ctra. Quintanilla
47359 Olivares de Duero (Valladolid)
☎: 983 107 100 - Fax: 983 107 104
jvalenzuela@bodegamatarromera.es
www.matarromera.es

Established: 1995

🌐 400 ▦ 90,000 litres 🍇 42 has.

🍷 70% 🌐30%: -DE -AD -AT -BE -BR -CA -CU -CL -DK -EC -FR -UK -NL -IT -JP -MX - DK -PA -PE -PR -SE -CH -US -CZ -DM

EMINA 2003 ROBLE RED
100% tinto fino   🌐 4

83 Deep intense cherry. Aroma of well-ripened black fruit with notes of complex skins (flowers, minerals). Fleshy palate with fresh and fruity but weighty tannins; generously earthy finish.

RIBERA DE DUERO
DENOMINACIÓN DE ORIGEN

EMINA 2001 CRIANZA RED
100% tinto fino

85 Deep cherry with a garnet red edge. Earthy aroma of a fine wood reduction with hints of minerals and ripe skins. Fleshy palate with round and oily yet fresh tannins and well-integrated wood; a pleasant finish.

Bodegas y Viñedos ESCUDERO

Camino El Ramo, s/n
09311 Olmedillo de Roa (Burgos)
☎: 947 551 070 - Fax: 947 551 070

Established: 1999

🌐 100 ▦ 167,000 litres 🍇 20 has.

🍷 95% 🌐5%

COSTAVAL 2003 JOVEN RED
100% tempranillo

80 Cherry with a violet hue. Fresh, fruity, expressive aroma (blackberries, raspberries) and a nuance of flowers (violets). Flavourful, fresh and lively palate with slightly astringent tannins

COSTAVAL 2001 CRIANZA RED
100% tempranillo

81 Intense cherry with an orangey edge. Not very intense aroma with oak notes and a ripe fruit hint. Flavourful palate of concentrated fruit with a viscous touch and very marked tannins.

COSTAVAL 2000 RESERVA RED
100% tempranillo

82 Deep garnet red. Smoky aroma with toasty oak and a hint of reduction. Fleshy, powerful palate with wood-fruit harmony and an expressive finish, persistente. persistent.

COSTAVAL 2003 OAK AGED RED

Hermanos ESPINOSA RIVERA

Plazuela del Postigo, 10
47315 Pesquera de Duero (Valladolid)
☎: 983 870 137 - Fax: 983 870 201

Established: 1998

🌐 57 ▦ 45,000 litres 🍇 7,22 has. 🍷 100%

HESVERA 2002 OAK AGED RED
100% tempranillo   🌐 18

87 Dark cherry with a purple edge. Powerful aroma, with fine toasty and lactic crianza notes, a suggestion of superripened fruit and balsamic hints. Flavourful, fleshy palate with slightly drying yet promising tannins, bitter (cocoa, coffee, liquorice).

HESVERA 2001 ROBLE RED
100% tempranillo

80 Very deep garnet red. Aroma with a mild viscous suggestion and ripe red fruit, balsamic. Drying tannins on the palate, fresh and slightly bitter.

HESVERA 2002 CRIANZA RED
100% tempranillo

86 Dark cherry with a purplish edge. Powerful aroma of jammy black fruit and fine toasty oak with a slightly balsamic suggestion and hints of fallen leaves. Flavourful, fleshy palate with an excellent crianza expression, bitter (liquorice, dark-roasted flavours) and very long.

HESVERA 2003 ROBLE JOVEN RED

FEDERICO

Real, 154
47315 Pesquera de Duero (Valladolid)
☎: 983 870 105 - Fax: 983 870 105
info@bodegasfederico.com
www.bodegasfederico.com

Established: 1986

🌐 700 📊 175,000 litres 🌿 35 has.

🍷 75% 🍇25%: -CA -PR -CH

TINTO FEDERICO 2002 ROBLE RED
TINTO FEDERICO 2001 CRIANZA RED
TINTO FEDERICO 1999 RESERVA RED
TINTO FEDERICO 1996 GRAN RESERVA RED

FÉLIX CALLEJO

Avenida Aranda, 4
09441 Sotillo de la Ribera (Burgos)
☎: 947 532 312 - Fax: 947 532 304
bfc@ctv.es
www.bodegasfelixcallejo.com

Established: 1989

🌐 2,000 📊 600,000 litres 🌿 60 has.

🍷 40% 🍇60%: -UE -US -CA

VIÑA PILAR 2003 ROSÉ
100% tinto fino

80 Brilliant strawberry. Clear aroma of well-ripened, clean strawberries, with fine notes of flower petals, slightly artificial. Flavourful palate with a slight bead, with good freshness, reminiscent of strawberry yoghurt.

FÉLIX CALLEJO SELECCIÓN VIÑEDOS DE LA FAMILIA 2002 OAK AGED RED
100% tinta fina   🌐 16

91 Almost opaque cherry with a raspberry edge. Fine smoky aroma with toasty flavours (pitch), jammy black fruit and earthy and balsamic hints. Fleshy palate with character, round and oily fruit tannins, very elegant unharmonised crianza with a nuance of old vine (Pedernal) and forest fruit.

CALLEJO CUATRO MESES EN BARRICA 2003 OAK AGED RED
100% tinta fina

85 Very deep cherry with a violet edge. Aroma of black bramble fruit, very concentrated (liquorice, flowers). Fleshy, flavourful palate, very fruity (blackberries, bilberries), yet to be assembled; a toasty finish.

CALLEJO 2002 CRIANZA RED
100% tinta fina

87 Almost opaque cherry. Complex aroma of black fruit with integrated toasty notes, pitch and flowers. Powerful and fleshy palate, with excellent ripe fruit tannins; fresh with dry stones in the retronasal passage.

CALLEJO 2001 RESERVA RED
100% tinta fina

84 Very dark intense cherry. Aroma of jammy red fruit, toasty flavours and a nuance of violets. Flavourful palate with very elegant but slightly limp tannins, fruity, well-balanced but without character.

GRAN CALLEJO 1998 GRAN RESERVA RED
100% tinta fina

83 Cherry with a strawberry edge. Smoky aroma of fine crianza reduction, minerals. Fleshy palate with marked oak tannins, "very Ribera" with a slightly dry but complex finish.

DO RIBERA DEL DUERO

CALLEJO MAGNUM 1999 RESERVA RED

Bodegas FÉLIX SANZ

Ronda Aradillas, s/n
47490 Rueda (Valladolid)
☎: 983 868 044 - Fax: 983 868 133

info@bodegasfelixsanz.es
www.bodegasfelixsanz.es

Established: 1934

🌐 260 📊 400,000 litres 🍇 30 has.

🏴 95% 🌐5%: -US -NL -CH -UK -DE -FI

MONTENEGRO 2003 ROSÉ
MONTENEGRO 2002 ROBLE JOVEN RED
MONTENEGRO 2003 JOVEN RED
MONTENEGRO 2001 CRIANZA RED

FINCA VILLACRECES

Ctra. Soria, km. 322
47350 Quintanilla de Onésimo (Valladolid)
☎: 945 609 086 - Fax: 945 609 261

Established: 1994

🌐 800 📊 150,000 litres 🍇 43 has.

🏴 60% 🌐40%

NEBRO 2001 RED
tempranillo

90 Intense cherry. Powerful aroma, rich in ripe fruit expression with creamy oak and a mineral hint (aromatic coffee, peat and cocoa) . Full, flavourful palate with ripe black fruit and very powerful and persistent fruit and oak tannins, fleshy and long.

FINCA VILLACRECES 2000 RESERVA RED
75% tinto fino, merlot, cabernet sauvignon

88 Dark garnet red cherry. Intense aroma with predominant toasty creamy (toffee) wood notes, jammy black fruit and balsamic hints. Flavourful palate with supple sweetish tannins, fine bitter notes and refreshing acidity.

FINCA VILLACRECES 2001 OAK AGED RED

FUENTENARRO

Cruce
09311 La Horra (Burgos)
☎: 947 542 092 - Fax: 947 542 083
fuentenarro@eresmas.com

Established: 2002

🌐 150 📊 170,000 litres 🍇 16 has.

🏴 75% 🌐25%: -UK -DE -US -RU -CA -
MX -AU -DK

VIÑA FUENTENARRO 2003 JOVEN RED
VIÑA FUENTENARRO 2002 JOVEN RED
VIÑA FUENTENARRO 2003 ROBLE RED
VIÑA FUENTENARRO 2002 ROBLE RED
VIÑA FUENTENARRO 2003 CRIANZA RED
VIÑA FUENTENARRO 2002 CRIANZA RED

FUENTESPINA

Camino Cascajo, s/n
09470 Fuentespina (Burgos)
☎: 921 596 002 - Fax: 921 596 035
ana@avelinovegas.com
www.avelinovegas.com

Established: 1960

🌐 2,000 📊 2,000,000 litres 🍇 385 has.

🏴 80% 🌐20%: -US -CA -MX -PR -DO -
BR -PE -UK -SE -FI -NL -BE -DE -CZ -AT

FUENTESPINA 2003 RED
100% tempranillo

80 Cherry. Lactic aroma with fine lees and fruit. Flavourful, not very structured yet balanced palate.

CORONA DE CASTILLA ESTILO 2002 RED
100% tempranillo

78 Very dark cherry with a violet edge. Powerful, fruity palate with good varietal expression, a fine toasty oak nuance and hints of red fruit syrup. Flavourful, fleshy and sweet palate with well-integrated fruit/oak.

FUENTESPINA 2002 ROBLE RED
100% tempranillo   🌐4

87 Cherry with a brick red hue. Aroma of very new wood, ripe red fruit and vanilla. Fleshy, warm and flavourful palate with evident tannins.

CORONA DE CASTILLA PRESTIGIO 2001 RED
100% tempranillo

78 Very deep garnet red cherry. Intense aroma with predominant toasty oak notes. Flavourful palate with slightly marked and sweet tannins, a jammy black fruit nuance and bitter notes, lacks balance.

CORONA DE CASTILLA ÉLITE 1999 RED
100% tempranillo

82 Very deep garnet red cherry. Intense aroma of jammy red fruit with fine reduction notes. Flavourful palate with ripe and sweet tannins and fine bitter notes, pleasant.

FUENTESPINA 2001 CRIANZA RED
100% tempranillo

84 Cherry with an orangey edge. Aroma of toasty wood and balsamic flavours, Ribera typification. Good balance on the palate between the wood tannins and the fruit.

FUENTESPINA 1998 RESERVA RED
100% tempranillo

83 Cherry with an orangey edge. Good crianza aroma (toasty flavours, spices) and light reduction (tobacco). Round, well-balanced palate with polished tannins.

FUENTESPINA 1998 RESERVA ESPECIAL RED

85 Quite dark cherry with an orangey edge. Aroma evoking a good reduction (tobacco, spices) with a ripe fruit nuance. Powerful, flavourful palate with ripe tannins and toasty notes, well-balanced.

CORONA DE CASTILLA ELITE 1998 RESERVA RED
100% tempranillo

86 Garnet red cherry. Fine aroma of toasty skins and elegant crianza (vanilla, pitch), with notions of terroir. Flavourful palate with wood tannins well-integrated with the fruit and crianza expression (Bordeaux-style); a generous and round finish.

Bodegas GARCÍA DE ARANDA

Ctra. de Soria, s/n
09400 Aranda de Duero (Burgos)
☎: 947 501 817 - Fax: 947 506 355
bodega@bodegasgarcia.com
www.bodegasgarcia.com

Established: 1966

800 ▯ 2,000,000 litres 30 has.

80% 20%: -CA -US -MX -CH -PA -NL

SEÑORÍO DE LOS BALDÍOS 2003 JOVEN RED
tinta del país

79 Garnet red. Aroma of red fruit with light hints of reduction. High acidity on the palate, light, without great expressivity.

VEGARANDA 2003 JOVEN RED

73 Garnet red. Aroma with notes of tank and not very ripe fruit. Warm and light on the palate, without great nuances.

SEÑORÍO DE LOS BALDÍOS 2000 CRIANZA RED
100% tempranillo

84 Garnet red with a ruby red hue. Toasty aroma of jammy red fruit and sweet notes. Medium-bodied palate, with robust tannins fleshy with coffee and liquorice in the retronasal passage.

VEGARANDA 1999 CRIANZA RED
tinta del país

77 Strawberry with an orangey hue. Aroma of new wood and balsamic flavours (pine, resins). Well-balanced palate without rich nuances.

SEÑORÍO DE LOS BALDÍOS 1998 RESERVA RED

78 Red with orangey hue. Spicy aroma with quite sweet woody notes and a notion of red fruit. Light palate, without great expression of the long crianza.

VEGARANDA 1998 RESERVA RED

75 Brick red. Not very expressive aroma with hints of reduction. Unbalanced acidity on the palate, light, fairly ripe.

Viñedos y Bodegas GARCÍA FIGUERO

Ctra. La Horra-Roa, km. 2
09311 La Horra (Burgos)
☎: 947 542 066

TINTO FIGUERO CRIANZA RED

GORMAZ

Avenida de Soria, s/n
42330 San Esteban de Gormaz (Soria)
☎: 975 350 404 - Fax: 975 351 313
bodegasgormaz@bodegasgormaz.com
www.bodegasgormaz.com

Established: 1974

3,500 ▯ 2,000,000 litres 530 has.

80% 20%

DOCE LINAJES JOVEN RED
VIÑA GORMAZ JOVEN RED
DOCE LINAJES ROBLE RED
DOCE LINAJES CRIANZA RED

Bodegas HERMANOS SASTRE

San Pedro, s/n
09311 La Norra (Burgos)
☎: 947 542 108 - Fax: 947 542 108
sastre@vinasastre.com
www.vinasastre.com

Established: 1992

800 ▯ 300,000 litres 42 has.

60% 40%: -DE -UK -CH -SE -BE -NL -US -PR -DO -PA -BR -MX -JP -RU -PL

REGINA VIDES 2001 ROBLE RED
100% tinta del país

92 Intense cherry. Aroma with notes of concentrated ripe fruit but rich in fruit expression and toasty nuances of high quality oak. Round, flavourful, warm palate with fleshy overtones that almost match the '99 vintage, well-displayed but very ripe tannins.

PESUS 2001 OAK AGED RED
tinta del país, merlot, cabernet sauvignon

95 Intense cherry. Very toasty and creamy aroma of oak with hints of jammy fruit (plums and cherries) and a spirituous and mineral suggestion. Powerful, fleshy palate with obvious wood just as in last year's tasting, a toasty retronasal effect (dark-roasted flavours) and a hint of carpentry with bitter hints of oak combined with a good alcoholic graduation.

VIÑA SASTRE 2001 CRIANZA RED
100% tinta del país

86 Intense cherry. Aroma with notions of ripe fruit (black plums) and toasty creamy oak (coffee and cocoa). Fleshy, warm palate with ripe fruit, fine toasty oak and flavourful and ripe yet very noticeable tannins.

VIÑA SASTRE PAGO DE SANTA CRUZ 1999 GRAN RESERVA RED
100% tinta del país

93 Intense cherry. Powerful aroma rich in very ripe fruit sensations and well-assembled spicy toasty oak. Powerful, fleshy, very ripe, warm, slightly spirituous and flavourful palate with powerful tannins.

VIÑA SASTRE 2003 ROBLE RED
VIÑA SASTRE 2000 GRAN RESERVA RED

HORNILLOS BALLESTEROS

Camino Tenerías, 9
09300 Roa de Duero (Burgos)
☎: 947 541 071 - Fax: 947 541 071
hornillosballesteros@hotmail.com

Established: 2002
⊕ 150 🍇 40 has. 🍶 67,000 litres.

MIBAL 2003 JOVEN RED

82 Garnet red with a purplish hue. Intense aroma of ripe red fruit and lactics. Fleshy, powerful palate with good structure.

MIBAL 2002 OAK AGED RED
tinta del país   ⊕ 8

88 Very dark deep cherry. Powerful aroma of black fruit with nuances of sun-drenched skins and a fine toasty hint. Flavourful, fleshy palate with excellent fruit (minerals, skins, jammy black fruit); well-balanced fine toasty flavours.

MIBAL SELECCIÓN 2002 CRIANZA RED

88 Very deep garnet red. Toasty aroma of wood (coffee, toffee), balsamic flavour and slightly muted fruit. Fruity, flavourful and powerful on the palate with well-integrated wood and hints of fine toasty wood notes.

Bodega y Viñedos HOZ SUALDEA

Ctra., 7
09315 Fuentemolinos (Burgos)

☎: 947 531 289 - Fax: 947 531 289
www.lariberadelduero.com

Established: 2000
⊕ 400 🍶 420,000 litres 🍇 25 has.
🍷 70% 🌐30%

TARIENZO 2000 RED
TARIENZO 2001 RED
TARIENZO 2003 RED

Bodegas IMPERIALES

Ctra. Madrid - Irun, km. 171
09370 Gumiel de Izán (Burgos)
☎: 609 506 358 - Fax: 629 558 749
direccion@bodegasimperiales.com
www.bodegasimperiales.com

Established: 1998
⊕ 1,035 🍶 700,000 litres 🍇 25 has.
🍷 65% 🌐35%

ABADÍA DE SAN QUIRCE 2000 CRIANZA RED
tinta del país

83 Dark cherry with a dark red edge. Intense aroma with predominant toasty oak notes and a ripe red fruit hint. Flavourful palate with a good oak/fruit integration and oak with a fresh, spicy touch.

ABADÍA DE SAN QUIRCE 1999 RESERVA RED
tempranillo

80 Garnet red cherry. Intense aroma of very ripe, slightly reduced fruit with spicy oak notes and hints of aged wood. Flavourful palate with slightly drying tannins, slightly warm and lacking crianza expression.

ISMAEL ARROYO

Los Lagares, 71
09441 Sotillo de la Ribera (Burgos)
☎: 947 532 309 - Fax: 947 532 487
bodega@valsotillo.com
www. valsotillo.com

Established: 1979
⊕ 1,200 🍶 500,000 litres 🍇 20 has.
🍷 70% 🌐30%

MESONEROS DE CASTILLA 2003 ROSÉ

83 Very deep raspberry with a coppery hue. Quite intense and fruity aroma with spicy hints of skins. Flavourful, fresh palate with red stone fruit, very spicy and long with excellent acidity.

MESONEROS DE CASTILLA 2003 JOVEN RED

82 Intense cherry. Pleasant aroma of jammy black forest fruits and a spicy hint. Fleshy, very fruity, powerful palate with ripe tannins.

MESONEROS DE CASTILLA 2002 ROBLE RED

82 Intense cherry with a violet edge. Aroma of well-ripened black fruit with flor and complex liquorice. Fleshy, fruity palate, with consistent wood tannins well-balanced with the fruit and a fresh finish.

VALSOTILLO 2001 CRIANZA RED

82 Intense cherry with a garnet red edge. Not very intense aroma with spicy oak, sun-drenched skins and ink. Flavourful palate with a toasty skins character with dry and marked oak tannins.

VALSOTILLO 1999 RESERVA RED

84 Intense cherry with a garnet red-orange edge. Powerful aroma with a strong character of skins, sun-drenched notes and ink. Flavourful, powerful palate with concentrated fruit and rough tannins.

VALSOTILLO 1996 GRAN RESERVA RED

85 Intense cherry with an orangey edge. Aroma with reduction notes (tobacco, leathers) and bitter chocolate. Intense palate with abundant toasty wood, ripe black fruit and incisive tannins.

J.A. CALVO CASAJÚS

Cercados s/n
09443 Quintana del Pidío (Burgos)
☎: 947 545 699 - Fax: 947 545 626
info@bodegascasajus.com
www.bodegascasajus.com

Established: 1993

⊞ 225 ▤ 150,000 litres ▦ 20 has.
▮ 90% ◉10%

CASAJÚS 2003 JOVEN RED

83 Deep cherry with a violet edge. Powerful aroma of jammy black fruit, notes of cocoa from the skins and a suggestion of liquorice. Fleshy palate with character, marked black fruit and a slightly astringent finish.

CASAJÚS 2002 OAK AGED RED

⊜6

79 Very deep garnet red. Aroma of red fruit with lees, slightly spicy and toasty. Drying wood tannins on the palate with medium acidity and toasty suggestions in the retronasal passage.

CASAJÚS 2001 CRIANZA RED

82 Dark garnet red. Aroma of toasty wood, chocolate and toffee with elegant reduction notes. Drying, flavourful palate, with good persistence.

Bodegas y Viñedos del JARO

Ctra. Pesquera-Valbuena, s/n.
Finca El Quiñón
47315 Peñafiel (Valladolid)

☎: 900 505 855 - Fax: 956 852 339
info@bodegajaro.com
www.bodegajaro.com

Established: 2000

⊞ 615 ▤ 225,000 litres ▦ 105 has.
▮ 70% ◉30%: -US -UK -DE -CH -BE -KR

SEMBRO 2003 ROSÉ
100% tinta del país

84 Raspberry. Powerful, very fruity aroma of red fruit (strawberries, raspberries, jelly). Powerful, warm, fruity palate, slightly foresty and very ripe.

JAROS 2001 RED
100% tinta del país

88 Intense cherry. Aroma with toasty notes of black fruit, a mineral hint (dry earth, clay) and toasty oak. Fleshy, powerful palate, rich in ripe fruit and toasty oak, persistent.

CHAFANDÍN 2001 RED
100% tinta del país

89 Intense cherry. Deep, complex aroma with fine mineral notes and black fruit, smoky (chocolate, peat). Generous, full, fleshy and toasty palate (dark-roasted flavours), spirituous and warm with powerful and ripe tannins, persistent.

SED DE CANÁ 2001 RED
100% tinta del país

91 Very intense cherry. Aroma with fruit and mineral expression, fine toasty scents (coffee, cocoa), very toasty almonds and creamy oak. Fleshy, full, flavourful, complex and well-balanced palate, persistent and very long with pronounced but ripe tannins.

JAROS LEÓN DE NEMEA 2002 RED
100% tinta del país

85 Intense cherry. Aroma with light reduction notes of the oak(toast, pitch), lacks airing. Fleshy, warm and quite concentrated on the palate with stewed black fruit.

JESÚS RIVERA

Las Eras, s/n
47315 Pesquera de Duero (Valladolid)
☎: 983 870 010 - Fax: 983 870 010
valdemoral@eresmas.com

Established: 1994

⊞ 66 ▤ 40,000 litres ▦ 15 has.
▮ 90% ◉10%: -CH

VALDEMORAL 2001 OAK AGEDRED

JOSÉ CABESTRERO

Dionisio Camarero, 29
09462 Moradillo de Roa (Burgos)

☎: 947 324 551 - Fax: 947 324 551
Established: 1994
📥 100.000 litres 🌱 10 has. 🍷 100%

JOSÉ CABESTRERO 2002 ROSÉ
JOSÉ CABESTRERO 2002 JOVEN RED

Cooperativa Nuestra Señora de LA ASUNCIÓN

Eras de Arriba, s/n
09454 Quemada (Burgos)
☎: 947 553 133 - Fax: 947 553 133
roquesanq@terra.es
Established: 1964
🍷 124 📥 1,100,000 litres 🍷 100%

ROQUESÁN ROSÉ
LAGAR DEL ROLLO JOVEN RED
ROQUESÁN JOVEN RED
ROQUESÁN CRIANZA RED
ROQUESÁN RESERVA RED

Cooperativa LA ASUNCIÓN DE NUESTRA SEÑORA

Ctra. Madrid-Irún, s/n
09370 Gumiel de Izán (Burgos)
☎: 947 544 021 - Fax: 947 525 827
morozan@eresmas.com
www.asunciongumiel.com
Established: 1963
🍷 200 📥 1,800,000 litres 🍷 100%

MOROZÁN 2003 ROSÉ
MOROZÁN 2003 OAK AGED RED
MOROZÁN 2003 RED
ARCO MOROZÁN 2001 RED

Bodega y Viñedos LA CEPA ALTA

Ctra. Quintanilla, 28
47359 Olivares de Duero (Valladolid)
☎: 983 681 010 - Fax: 983 681 010
Established: 1992
🍷 724 📥 320,000 litres 🌱 64 has.
🍷 90% 🌍10%: -DE -BE -CH

LAVEGUILLA 2002 ROBLE RED
LAVEGUILLA 1999 CRIANZA RED
LAVEGUILLA 1998 RESERVA RED
LAVEGUILLA 1995 GRAN RESERVA RED

Señorío de LA SERNA

Ctra. Nacional 122, km. 291

09318 Valdezate (Burgos)
☎: 947 550 327 - Fax: 947 550 327
bodegadelaserna@hotmail.com
www.bodegadelaserna.com
Established: 1996
🍷 1,000 📥 850,000 litres 🍷 70%
🌍30%: -UE -MX

GRAN JERARQUÍA 1999 ROBLE RED
100% tempranillo 🍷 36

81 Garnet red cherry. Intense aroma of ripe black fruit with hints of reduction notes (animals, dried flowers). Flavourful palate with a good fruit/oak integration, dark-roasted and bitter notes, good acidity.

GRAN JERARQUÍA 2000 ROBLE RED
100% tinto fino 🍷 6

77 Dark garnet red cherry. Intense aroma with light off-odours (late racking), very ripe reduced fruit and notes of stables. Better on the palate and flavourful with predominant ripe fruit and a spicy nuance.

GRAN JERARQUÍA 2000 CRIANZA RED
100% tinto fino

82 Dark garnet red cherry. Powerful aroma of slightly reduced black fruit with a suggestion of animals and terroir. Flavourful palate with fine bitter notes and a good fruit/oak structure, slightly warm.

GRAN JERARQUÍA 1999 CRIANZA RED
100% tinto fino

80 Dark cherry. Intense aroma with reduction notes (overripe fruit, animals) and a spicy oak nuance. Flavourful palate with slightly marked and oily tannins and fine bitter notes.

GRAN JERARQUÍA 1999 RESERVA RED
100% tempranillo

83 Deep cherry with a coppery edge. Intense aroma of jammy black fruit with fine toasty oak. Flavourful palate with a good fruit/oak integration and predominant bitter notes (liquorice, dark-roasted flavours).

GRAN JERARQUÍA 1996 GRAN RESERVA RED
100% tinto fino

82 Garnet red cherry with a coppery glint. Powerful aroma of jammy black fruit with toasty oak notes. Flavourful, fleshy palate with slightly reduced ripe fruit and ripe and oily tannins, bitter notes (dark-roasted flavours) in the finish.

LAGAR DE ISILLA

Isilla, 18
09400 Aranda de Duero (Burgos)
☎: 947 504 316 - Fax: 947 504 316
bodegas@lagarisilla.es - lagarisilla.es
Established: 1997
🍷 320 📥 200,000 litres 🌱 35 has.

🐂 80% 🍇20%: -DE -UK -US -MX -CH

ZALAGAR 2003 ROSÉ
tempranillo

75 Pale blush. Quite intense, fruity aroma with spicy and waxy hints. Flavourful, bitter palate with an acidic edge.

VALDEUSILLO 2002 JOVEN RED
100% tempranillo

83 Dark cherry with a garnet red edge. Powerful, ripe aroma with slightly reduced fruit, hints of skins and terroir. Fleshy, flavourful palate with spicy hints (cocoa, pepper) and an excellent ripe fruit expression.

EL LAGAR DE ISILLA 2000 CRIANZA RED
100% tempranillo

85 Dark cherry with a garnet red glint. Powerful aroma with predominant toasty notes of oak and skins and bitter chocolate. Fleshy palate with quite rough yet promising tannins, dark-roasted flavours and notions of wax, flavourful with excellent acidity.

84 Deep garnet red. Slightly warm aroma of ripe black fruit, and reduction notes (earth, tobacco). Fleshy, powerful palate of round, ripe black fruit with dry wood tannins in the finish.

EL LAGAR DE ISILLA 2000 RESERVA RED

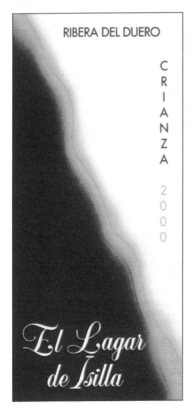

EL LAGAR DE ISILLA 1999 RESERVA RED
100% tempranillo

ZALAGAR 2002 ROBLE RED
100% tempranillo

82 Deep cherry with a violet edge. Aroma of jammy black fruit, a nuance of minerals and slightly spicy. Fleshy, powerful palate with abundant fruit, marked toasty oak and a slightly drying finish.

LAMBUENA

Ctra. Fuentecén, s/n
09300 Roa (Burgos)
☎: 947 540 034 - Fax: 947 540 614
lambuena@bodegaslambuena.com
www.bodegaslambuena.com
Established: 1989

⊞ 400 ▤ 300,000 litres ⚘ 40 has.
🍷 80% ⊕20%: -DE -US -CH

LAMBUENA 2002 JOVEN RED
LAMBUENA 2001 CRIANZA RED
LAMBUENA 1998 RESERVA RED
LAMBUENA 1995 GRAN RESERVA RED

Bodegas y Viñas LAS PINZAS

Ctra. Peñafiel-Pesquera, km. 6
47316 Curiel de Duero (Valladolid)
☎: 983 880 489 - Fax: 983 880 489
valdecuriel@yahoo.com
Established: 2000

⊞ 200 ▤ 80,000 litres ⚘ 15 has.
🍷 90% ⊕10%: -DE -UK

VALDECURIEL 2003 OAK AGED RED
100% tempranillo

84 Cherry with a purplish edge. Aroma of strawberry pulp with black pepper, balsamic hints and flowers. Fleshy palate with bitter fruit tannins, fine notes of oak and a fruity finish (liquorice).

VALDECURIEL 2001 CRIANZA RED
100% tempranillo

87 Almost opaque cherry. Powerful aroma of black fruit with elegant wood notes (spices, liquorice, cocoa) . Fleshy palate with a good acidity-alcohol balance, marked fruit and wood tannins; powerful and with a long and fruity aftertaste.

VALDECURIEL 2002 OAK AGED RED

LEGARIS

Ctra. Peñafiel Encinas de Esgueva km. 2, 5
47316 Curiel de Duero (Valladolid)
☎: 983 878 088 - Fax: 983 881 034
info@legaris.es/smartin@codorniu.es
www.legaris.com
Established: 2000

⊞ 1,058 ⚘ 93.5 has. 🍷 76% ⊕24%

LEGARIS 1999 RESERVA RED
100% tinto fino

84 Garnet red cherry. Concentrated aroma with notes of truffles and earth (fine reduction), a hint of minerals and jammy black fruit. Fleshy, powerful palate with oily and round fruit tannins well-assembled with the wood and a dry yet fresh finish.

LOS ASTRALES

Ctra. Olmedillo, s/n
09313 Anguix (Burgos)
☎: 979 744 626 - Fax: 979 703 095
astrales2001@hotmail.com

ASTRALES 2002 RED

87 Intense cherry. Fine toasty aroma of oak and ripe fruit with light vegetative notes. Fleshy palate, ripe fruit, toasty oak and grapes, long.

LÓPEZ CRISTÓBAL

Barrio Estación s/n
09300 Roa de Duero (Burgos)
☎: 947 540 106 - Fax: 947 540 606
lopezcristobal@wanadoo.es
Established: 1994

⊞ 484 ▤ 250,000 litres ⚘ 50 has.
🍷 70% ⊕30%

BAGÚS VENDIMIA SELECIONADA 2001 ROBLE RED
tinta del pais, cabernet sauvignon, merlot   ⊞14

85 Cherry with a blueish edge. Slightly alcoholic aroma of toast with balsamic hints and ripe red fruit. Good acidity on the palate, lacking integration of the still marked wood tannins, a suggestion of ripe fruit.

LÓPEZ CRISTOBAL 2003 ROBLE RED
tempranillo, cabernet sauvignon, merlot   ⊞3

82 Cherry with a purplish hue. Aroma of vanilla, menthol and red fruit with good intensity. Slightly light on the palate, well-balanced with a good fruit weight.

LÓPEZ CRISTOBAL 2001 CRIANZA RED
tempranillo, cabernet sauvignon, merlot

84 Garnet red with shades of brick red. Toasty aroma of wood with jammy black fruit and smokiness. Vinous, fleshy palate with slightly marked wood tannins and a suggestion of black fruit.

LÓPEZ CRISTOBAL 2000 RESERVA RED

84 Garnet red with a reddish hue. Aroma of toasty wood, balsamic with reduction notes and ripe red fruit. Drying, fleshy palate with good acidity and weighty fruit, slightly bitter.

BAGÚS 2003 ROBLE RED
BAGÚS 2001 CRIANZA RED
BAGÚS 2000 RESERVA RED

MARQUÉS DE VALPARAISO

Paraje los Llanillos s/n
09443 Quintana del Pidío (Burgos)
☎: 947 545 286 - Fax: 947 545 163
m.valparaiso@fer.es
www.paternina.com

Established: 2000

🌐 1,500 📦 800,000 litres 🍇 41 has.

🍷 80% 🌐20%

MARQUÉS DE VALPARAÍSO 2002 ROBLE RED
100% tinta del pais

74 Not very deep cherry. Slight aroma of tank off-odours, damp wood and jammy fruit. Light reduction tones on the palate and bitter notes, without persistence.

MARQUÉS DE VALPARAÍSO 1998 CRIANZA RED
tinto fino

81 Brick red. Animal aroma of leather with notes of reduction. Supple palate with integrated tannins and good acidity, slightly short with hints of elegant reduction in the retronasal passage.

MARQUÉS DE VALPARAÍSO 2002 CRIANZA RED
MARQUÉS DE VALPARAÍSO 1999 RESERVA RED

MARQUÉS DE VELILLA

Ctra. de Sotillo, s/n
09311 La Horra (Burgos)
☎: 947 542 166 - Fax: 947 542 165
central@marquesdevelilla.es
www.marquesdevelilla.es

Established: 1985

🌐 4,500 📦 1,250,000 litres 🍇 200 has.

🍷 60% 🌐40%: -DE -CH -UK -SE -BE -FR -RU -BR -EC -US -PR -DK -JP -AT -AU -CU

MARQUÉS DE VELILLA 2003 JOVEN RED
100% tinta del pais

82 Medium-hue garnet red. Perfumed aroma, with flowers, ripe strawberries, raspberries and light notes of the tank. Flavourful and well-balanced with a good varietal expression.

MONTE VILLALOBÓN 2000 OAK AGED RED
90% tinta del país, 10% cabernet sauvignon   🌐6

83 Deep garnet red. Aroma of ripe red fruit with toasty wood and slightly balsamic notes. Well-balanced, flavourful, slightly drying palate and a suggestion of wood in the retronasal passage.

MARQUÉS DE VELILLA 2000 CRIANZA RED
100% tinta del pais

82 Not very deep cherry. Not very clean aroma with lees and light notes of toasty wood. Drying palate with marked wood tannins, short with hints of salted meat in the retronasal passage.

MARQUÉS DE VELILLA 1999 RESERVA RED
90% tinta del país, 10% cabernet sauvignon

84 Medium-high hue garnet red. Toasty aroma of wood, vanilla, cedar and sweet notes. Slightly drying palate with marked ripe tannins, flavourful.

Bodegas y Viñedos
MARTÍN BERDUGO

Camino de la Colonia, s/n
09400 Aranda de Duero (Burgos)
☎: 947 506 331 - Fax: 947 506 602
bodega@martinberdugo.com
www.martinberdugo.com

Established: 2000

🌐 484 📦 300,000 litres 🍇 104 has.

🍷 60% 🌐40%: -US -CH -DE -BE -TR -IE -MX -CO -NL -DK

MARTÍN BERDUGO 2003 JOVEN RED
100% tinto fino

83 Dark cherry with a violet edge. Intense, varietal aroma (red fruit, hints of vine shoots), and a nuance of damp earth. Flavourful palate with ripe fruit and fleshy overtones, slightly warm.

MARTÍN BERDUGO 2002 OAK AGED RED
100% tinto fino

86 Dark garnet red cherry. Powerful aroma with a good varietal fruit expression (red fruit, underbrush), a hint of spicy oak and balsamic nuance. Flavourful palate with notes of fresh skins fine bitterness (liquorice, dark-roasted flavours) and excellent acidity.

MARTÍN BERDUGO 2001 CRIANZA RED
100% tinto fino

84 Intense cherry. Intense balsamic aroma, with notes of toasty skins and a suggestion of minerals. Fleshy, fruity palate with fine toasty notes and flavourful fruit tannins well-blended with those of the oak.

MARTÍN MEDINA

Valbuena, 3
47359 San Bernardo-Valbuena de Duero (Valladolid)
☎: 983 683 103 - Fax: 983 683 103
jayala2@etb.net.co

Established: 1992

🌐 200 📦 60,000 litres 🍇 40 has.

SAN BERNARDO 2003 ROBLE RED
100% tempranillo

78 Dark cherry with a purplish hue. Aroma of strawberry jelly with lactic notes and notions of liquorice (maceration). Powerful palate with black fruit (foresty) and abundant slightly drying wood tannins and sweetish fruit in the finish.

SAN BERNARDO 2001 CRIANZA RED
100% tempranillo

81 Deep cherry. Concentrated aroma of jammy fruit with notes of cocoa and earth (slightly mineral). Fleshy, with full-throttle fruit on the palate (bitter cocoa) with liquorice notes, well-assembled wood and a suggestion of reduction notes (oak).

SAN BERNARDO 2000 RESERVA RED
100% tempranillo

78 Deep garnet red. Spicy aroma (pepper, cloves) with hints of crianza (animals). Fleshy palate with oily fruit tannins, smoky wood and a slightly drying but flavourful finish.

MATARROMERA

Ctra. Renedo-Pesquera, km. 30
47359 Valbuena de Duero (Valladolid)
☎: 983 107 100 - Fax: 983 107 104
gperez@bodegamatarromera.es
www.matarromera.es

Established: 1988

🍷 2,000 🛢 600,000 litres 🌱 81 has.

🏴 70% 🌐30%: -DE -AD -AT -BE -BR -CA -CU -CL -DK -EC -FR -UK -NL -IT -JP -MX -DK -PA -PE -PR -SE -CH -US -CZ -DM

MELIOR 2003 OAK AGED RED
95% tinto fino, 5% cabernet sauvignon   🛢 5

83 Cherry with a violet edge. Medium intensity aroma of bramble fruit with a suggestion of smoky oak. Flavourful, slightly warm palate with notes of liquorice and creamy oak.

PAGO DE LAS SOLANAS 2000 ROBLE RED
100% tinto fino

90 Intense cherry. Toasty and spicy aroma with nuances of a fine reduction in the bottle(cedar wood and leather). Round, spicy, elegant palate with body and good oak/fruit integration, flavourful.

MATARROMERA 2001 CRIANZA RED
100% tinto fino

85 Quite intense cherry with a garnet red edge. Medium intensity aroma with spicy oak (sandalwood) and jammy fruit. Flavourful, powerful palate with well-assembled ripe fruit and wood, elegant and long.

MATARROMERA PRESTIGIO 1998 RED
100% tinto fino

93 Intense cherry. Toasty aroma (dark-roasted flavours, peat), with a hint of spicy notes (leather and pipe tobacco), and ripe fruit (jammy plums). Round, fleshy, full, warm palate with well-displayed but ripe tannins, persistent with ripe fruit in the retronasal passage.

MATARROMERA 1999 RESERVA RED
100% tinto fino

87 Intense cherry with a garnet red edge. Powerful aroma with a suggestion of ink, chimneys and smoky oak. Powerful, flavourful palate, with character, ripe and polished fruit tannins and dry oak tannins, a cherry liqueur finish.

MATARROMERA 1996 GRAN RESERVA RED
100% tinto fino

83 Cherry with an orangey edge. Aroma with reduction notes (tobacco, dried peaches, leathers) but a suggestion of finesse. Flavourful palate with jammy fruit and dry wood tannins in the finish.

MATARROMERA MAGNUM 1995 CRIANZA RED
MATARROMERA MAGNUM 1996 CRIANZA RED
MATARROMERA MAGNUM 2001 CRIANZA RED
MATARROMERA MAGNUM 1994 RESERVA RED
MATARROMERA NUEVO MILENIO MAGNUM 1995 RESERVA RED
MATARROMERA NUEVO MILENIO MAGNUM 1996 RESERVA RED

MONASTERIO

Ctra. Pesquera - Valbuena, s/n
47315 Pesquera de Duero (Valladolid)
☎: 983 484 002 - Fax: 983 484 020
bmonasterio@vodafone.es

Established: 1991

🛢 500,000 litres 🌱 70 has. 🏴 40%

🌐60%: -US -MX -CA -PA -PE -DO -PR -FR -PT -UK -DE -CH -SE -BE -NL -AT -DK -JP

DO RIBERA DEL DUERO

HACIENDA MONASTERIO 2001 OAK AGED RED
80% tinto fino, 10% merlot, 10% cabernet sauvignon

88 Intense cherry. Slightly fruity aroma, mildly reduced notes (leather, tobacco). Fleshy palate with highly polished tannins, oily palate with toasty hints (pitch, coffee, peat), flavourful, pleasant finish.

HACIENDA MONASTERIO ESPECIAL 1998 RESERVA RED
75% tinto fino, 15% merlot, 10% cabernet sauvignon

91 Intense cherry with a slightly brick red edge. Quite closed and spicy aroma of coffee, peat, chocolate, with notes of tobacco and old leather. Oily and round palate, caressing, flavourful, fine toasty fruit and oak with leather and tobacco in the retronasal passage, oily and sweet tannins.

HACIENDA MONASTERIO 2000 RESERVA ESPECIAL RED
75% tinto fino, 10% merlot, 10% malbec, 5% cabernet sauvignon

90 Intense cherry. Fine, toasty aroma (coffee, cocoa), with notes of creamy vanilla and ripe black fruit. Oily and round palate, with well-integrated fresh tannins, ripe fruit.

Bodegas y Viñedos MONTE AIXA

Ctra. Aranda de Duero - Palencia
09442 La Horra (Burgos)
☎: 610 227 123 - Fax: 947 542 067

Established: 1997

150 ▤ 122,500 litres 🍇 32 has.

🍷 80% 🌐20%

ZUMEL JOVEN RED
MONTE AIXA CRIANZA RED
ZUMEL CRIANZA RED
MONTE AIXA RESERVA RED

Bodegas y Viñedos MONTEABELLÓN

Calvario s/n
09318 Nava de Roa (Burgos)
☎: 947 550 000 - Fax: 947 550 219
info@monteabellon.com
www.monteabellon.com

Established: 2000

400 ▤ 290,000 litres 🍇 45 has.

🍷 80% 🌐20%: -UE -US

MONTEABELLÓN 2003 OAK AGED RED
100% tinta del pais   ▤ 4

80 Garnet red with a purplish hue. Aroma of ripe red fruit (blackberries, raspberries), a suggestion of lees and spices. Fruity and flavourful on the palate, with somewhat green fruit tannins, persistent.

MONTEABELLÓN 2001 CRIANZA RED

85 Very deep cherry. Concentrated aroma of jammy plums with predominant toasty flavours, hints of slate and a suggestion of fine reduction. Fleshy, powerful palate with abundant black fruit, round and marked fruit tannins over the smoky wood and a slightly dry and long finish.

MONTEABELLÓN 2002 CRIANZA RED
100% tinta del pais

86 Dark garnet red with a purplish rim. Aroma with very sweet notes, balsamic hints (menthol) and well-integrated wood. Fleshy palate with well-assembled tannins, fresh with good fruit weight.

MONTEABELLÓN 2002 OAK AGED RED
MONTEABELLÓN 2001 RESERVA RED

MONTEBACO

Finca Monte Alto, s/n
47359 Valbuena de Duero (Valladolid)
☎: 983 485 128 - Fax: 983 485 128
montebaco@cerocinco.es
montebaco@bodegasmontebaco.com
www.bodegasmontebaco.com

Established: 1989

560 ▤ 220,000 litres 🍇 50 has.

🍷 60% 🌐40%: -US -DO -PR -PE -BR -FR -CH -DE -BE -AT -IT -JP -SG

SEMELE 2002 ROBLE RED
90% tinto fino, 10% merlot

85 Intense cherry. Powerful, fruity aroma with light notes of creamy and toasty wood. Flavourful, fruity palate, rich in varietal expression.

MONTEBACO 2002 CRIANZA RED
100% tinto fino

88 Intense cherry. Fine, mineral aroma with toasty, creamy hints (cocoa, vanilla, coffee) and ripe skins. Fleshy, round palate with sweet, flavourful tannins and a fine, toasty and flavourful effect in the retronasal passage; long.

MONTEBACO SELECCIÓN ESPECIAL 2001 RED
100% tinto fino

92 Intense cherry. Elegant, complex aroma, rich in creamy expression of lees and toasty oak (coffee, cocoa, toasty vanilla). Round, oily and elegant on the palate with balance between the fresh fruit and well-integrated oak and a persistent flavour.

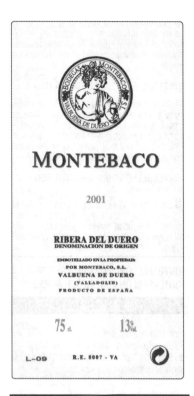

MONTEBACO

2001

RIBERA DEL DUERO
DENOMINACION DE ORIGEN

EMBOTELLADO EN LA PROPIEDAD:
POR MONTEBACO, S.L.
VALBUENA DE DUERO
(VALLADOLID)
PRODUCTO DE ESPAÑA

75 d.   13%Vol.

L-09   R.E. 8007 - VA

MONTEGAREDO

Ctra. Boada - Pedrosa, km. 1
09314 Boada de Roa (Burgos)
☎: 947 530 003 - Fax: 947 530 017
montegaredo@terra.com

Established: 1999

🍷 395 📊 480,000 litres 🍇 60 has.

🍷 80% 🌐20%: -UK -DE -CH -JP

MONTEGAREDO 2003 JOVEN RED
100% tinto fino

82 Dark cherry with a violet edge. Powerful, fruity aroma with light reduction notes (withered petals, and hints of sulphur). Powerful, and concentrated on the palate with slightly drying tannins, bitter and slightly warm.

MONTEGAREDO 2003 ROBLE RED
100% tinto fino

83 Dark cherry with a garnet red glint. Powerful, fruity aroma of fine toasty oak and skins. Flavourful, fleshy palate with slightly drying tannins, a spicy, bitter hint (cocoa, liquorice) and slightly sweet fruit.

PIRÁMIDE 2003 OAK AGED RED
100% tinto fino

77 Not very deep cherry. Aroma of not very ripe skins, grape seeds and under-ripe fruit. Drying palate with green notes, slightly bitter

PIRÁMIDE 2001 CRIANZA RED
100% tinto fino

86 Dark cherry with a dark red edge. Powerful aroma of jammy black fruit and fine oak (spices, smoky notes). Powerful palate with rough, oily tannins, and fine bitter notes (liquorice, dark-roasted flavours, hints of graphite).

MONTEGAREDO 2001 CRIANZA RED
100% tinto fino

85 Dark cherry with a saffron edge. Quite quite closed aroma with a certain finesse, toasty oak, a nuance of jammy black fruit and notions of terroir. Flavourful, fleshy and concentrated on the palate with a good oak/fruit integration, bitter and long.

PIRÁMIDE 1999 RESERVA RED
100% tinto fino

81 Deep cherry. Aroma of ripe black fruit, toasty skins, hints of pepper and terroir. Flavourful palate with fresh tannins, a good crianza; a fruity finish.

MONTEGAREDO 2001 ROBLE RED

MONTEVANNOS

Santiago, s/n
09450 Baños de Valdearados (Burgos)
☎: 947 534 277 - Fax: 947 534 016
bodega@montevannos.es
www.montevannos.es

Established: 1987

🍷 750 📊 400,000 litres 🍇 50 has.

🍷 30% 🌐70%: -US -DE -CH -UK

MONTEVANNOS 2001 CRIANZA RED
95% tinto fino, 5% merlot

84 Very deep cherry. Deep toasty aroma of spices, dry earth and very ripe black fruit. Fleshy, powerful palate with well-integrated oak tannins and an expressive fruit hint.

MONTEVANNOS 2000 RESERVA RED
95% tinto fino, 5% merlot

86 Deep cherry. Aroma with notes of black pepper, cedar and a fine crianza expression. Round palate with very flavourful, polished tannins; an elegant expression of skins and wood, persistent.

OPIMIUS 2002 RED
100% tinto fino

83 Intense cherry. Aroma of toasty skins, red fruit and vanilla notes of wood. Fleshy, fruity palate with integrated oak and a fresh finish.

MONTEVANNOS 2003 RED
100% tinto fino

83 Intense cherry with a violet edge. Concentrated aroma of jammy blackberries (brambles), fine spices and toasty skins. Fleshy, powerful palate with fruity tannins (blackberries, redcurrants) and a fresh finish.

MARQUÉS DE VANNOS 2003 ROBLE RED

NUESTRA SEÑORA DEL ROSARIO

Ctra. Boada, s/n
09314 Quintanamanvirgo (Burgos)
☎: 947 554 075 - Fax: 947 554 036
torremoron@wanadoo.es
www. torremoron.com

Established: 1957

🌐 650 🍷 2,000,000 litres 🌿 240 has.

🍇 90% 🌐10%: -US -MX -DE -DO

TORREMORÓN 2003 RED
100% tinta del país

82 Cherry with a violet edge. Complex aroma of jammy black fruit and liquorice notes. Flavourful, very sweet palate with marked red fruit tannins and a pleasant finish (blackberries).

TORREMORÓN 2000 CRIANZA RED
100% tinta del país

77 Garnet red with a reddish hue. Aroma of ripe red fruit and jammy tomatoes with some smoky notes. Fleshy palate with marked tannins and a smoky suggestion in the retronasal passage.

TORREMORÓN 1998 RESERVA RED
100% tinta del país

82 Deep cherry. Balsamic aroma of wood, notes of pepper and flowers; a suggestion of dried fruit. Fruity (blackberries plums), very fresh and quite spicy on the palate with a fresh finish.

TORREMORÓN 2003 ROSÉ
SENDERILLO 2003 JOVEN RED
TORREMORÓN 2002 OAK AGED RED
TIBERIO 2000 CRIANZA RED
TORREMORÓN 1999 GRAN RESERVA RED

NUESTRAS CEPAS

Ctra. Circunvalación, R-30, s/n
09300 Roa (Burgos)
☎: 947 541 191 - Fax: 947 541 192
comercial@paramodeguzman.com
www.paramodeguzman.com

Established: 1998

🌐 750 🍷 450,000 litres 🌿 25 has.

🍇 60% 🌐40%: -US -PR -DE -MX -NL -

CH -FR -JP -UK

PÁRAMO DE GUZMÁN 2000 CRIANZA RED
100% tempranillo

83 Garnet red cherry. Medium intensity aroma with a good reduction (tobacco, acetaldehydes) and vanilla. Flavourful palate with ink, quite intensewith fruit-wood harmony and polished tannins.

RAÍZ DE GUZMÁN 2000 CRIANZA RED
100% tempranillo

87 Garnet red cherry. Not very intense but fine aroma with lactic hints and creamy oak. Flavourful palate with toasty wood, ripe fruit and oily tannins, very pleasant and long.

PÁRAMO DE GUZMÁN 2001 CRIANZA RED
100% tempranillo

85 Garnet red cherry. Aroma with spicy oak notes and ripe fruit, not very intense yet harmonious. Flavourful, powerful, warm palate with well-assembled superripe fruit and wood, very sweet.

PÁRAMO DE GUZMÁN 1999 RESERVA RED
100% tempranillo

85 Garnet red cherry. Medium intensity aroma with spicy oak (cinnamon, sandalwood) and ripe fruit. Flavourful palate with polished tannins and good fruit/wood symmetry, slightly persistent.

PÁRAMO DE GUZMÁN 2003 JOVEN RED

Bodegas y Viñedos O. FOURNIER

Finca El Pinar, s/n
09316 Berlangas de Roa (Burgos)
☎: 947 533 006 - Fax: 947 533 010
roobmartin@terra.es

Established: 1979

🌐 300 🍷 400,000 litres 🌿 60 has.

🍇 80% 🌐20%: -US -DK -DE -SE

ASPICA 2002 RED

88 Very deep cherry. Aroma of black fruit with fine smoky and toasty hints, pitch and terroir and a suggestion of fresh skins. Fresh, flavourful palate, with fruit tannins, very fresh with harmonious wood and a finish that evokes bramble fruit.

OSBORNE RIBERA DEL DUERO

San Roque, s/n
09300 Roa (Burgos)
☎: 925 860 903 - Fax: 925 860 905
comunicacion@osborne.es
www.osborne.es

🌐 500 🍇 50% 🌐50%: -US

SEÑORIO DEL CID 2000 OAK AGED RED

PAGO DE CARRAOVEJAS

Camino de Carraovejas, s/n
47300 Peñafiel (Valladolid)
☎: 983 878 020 - Fax: 983 878 022
bodega@pagodecarraovejas.com

Established: 1988

🌐 1,600 📊 600,000 litres 🍇 80 has.
🍷 85% 🌐15%

PAGO DE CARRAOVEJAS 2002 CRIANZA RED

89 Dark cherry. Intense, very fine aroma with black fruit notes well-integrated with the wood (pepper, coffee, dried flowers, terroir). Powerful, concentrated and very spicy palate (paprika) with jammy fruit, hints of graphite and liquorice.

PAGO DE CARRAOVEJAS 2001 RESERVA RED

88 Deep cherry. Aroma of jammy black fruit, with notes of graphite, fine smoky hints and a complex crianza suggestion. Fleshy, powerful palate with noticeable yet oily wood tannins, traces of earthiness, a good expression of red fruit and a dry finish (cocoa).

PAGO DE LOS CAPELLANES

Camino de la Ampudia s/n
09314 Pedrosa de Duero (Burgos)
☎: 947 530 068 - Fax: 947 530 111
bodega@pagodeloscapellanes.com
www.pagodeloscapellanes.com

Established: 1996

🌐 1,400 📊 375,000 litres 🍇 100 has.
🍷 50% 🌐50%: UE -RU -US -MX -PR -SAM

PAGO DE LOS CAPELLANES 2003 ROBLE RED
80% tinto fino, 10% cabernet sauvignon, 10% merlot

88 Cherry with a garnet red-violet edge. Medium-intensity, fine aroma with smoky oak, ripe red fruit with fresh overtones and a suggestion of skins. Flavourful, with toasty oak on the palate, well-balanced with an uncommon fruity expression and depth.

PAGO DE LOS CAPELLANES 2000 OAK AGED RED
90% tinto fino, 10% cabernet sauvignon   🌐 16

86 Quite intense cherry. Fruity, ripe aroma with fine toasty oak well-integrated with the wine. Fleshy, full, warm, fruity palate with powerful tannins, flavourful.

PAGO DE LOS CAPELLANES 2001 OAK AGED RED
90% tinto fino, 10% cabernet sauvignon   🌐 12

86 Intense cherry. Very fine, toasty aroma of oak (dark-roasted flavour carpentry) with ripe fruit. Fleshy, flavourful palate with quite well-displayed but fine and creamy oak tannins.

PAGO DE LOS CAPELLANES PARCELA EL PICÓN 1999 CRIANZA RED
100% tinto fino

93 Intense cherry. Medium-intensity aroma but with fine toasty oak (cocoa, toffee), ripe fruit and a suggestion of minerals. Round, fleshy, full, vourful palate with fine reduction notes (tobacco and cedar), silky, polished tannins and a complex retronasal effect.

PAGO DE LOS CAPELLANES "MAGNUM" 1999 CRIANZA RED
PAGO DE LOS CAPELLANES "MAGNUM" 2001 CRIANZA RED

PAGOS DE REY

Ctra. Aranda-Palencia, km. 23
09311 Olmedillo de Roa (Burgos)
☎: 947 551 111 - Fax: 947 551 311
administracion@pagosdelrey.com

Established: 2002

🌐 4,500 📊 7,420,000 litres 🍷 90%
🌐10%: -DE -CH -JP -UK -RU -CZ -PL -LT -
EE -LV -FR -SE -PH -FI.

ALTOS DE TAMARÓN 2002 RED

80 Garnet red cherry with a violet edge. Intense aroma of ripe fruit with spicy hints. Flavourful and fruity on the palate with fine bitter notes (liquorice) and a slight varietal expression.

CONDADO DE ORIZA 2002 RED

82 Intense cherry with a violet edge. Aroma of red fruit with fine notes of skins and a smoky hint. Flavourful palate with fresh fruit tannins and toasty sensations of the skins, harmonious.

ALTOS DE TAMARÓN 2002 ROBLE RED
tinta del país   🌐 3

81 Very deep red cherry. Intense aroma of jammy black fruit with fine toasty oak hints and a nuance of terroir. Flavourful palate with slighty marked yet promising oak tannins and a ripe fruit nuance with spicy, bitter hints (chocolate, liquorice) of quality.

CONDADO DE ORIZA 2002 ROBLE RED
tinta del país

82 Cherry with a violet edge. Aroma with very creamy oak notes (white chocolate) which conceal the fruit. Flavourful on the palate with both ripe fruit and very heavy wood (lead pencil finish).

CONDADO DE ORIZA 2003 JOVEN RED
ALTOS DE TAMARÓN 2003 JOVEN RED

Hermanos PÁRAMO ARROYO

Ctra. de Roa s/n
09314 Pedrosa de Duero (Burgos)
☎: 947 530 041 - Fax: 947 530 036
paramo.arroyo@navegalia.com
www.riberaduero.net/vinaeremos

Established: 2000

🛢 225 🛢 180,000 litres ⚘ 35 has.
🍷 90% ⦿10%: -CZ -DE -JP

VIÑA EREMOS 2001 JOVEN RED
VIÑA EREMOS 2003 JOVEN RED
EREMUS 2001 CRIANZA RED

PÁRAMO DE CORCOS

Ctra. Aranda s/n
09462 Moradillo de Roa (Burgos)
☎: 947 530 735 - Fax: 947 530 735
paramodecorcos@terra.es

PÁRAMO DE CORCOS RED

PARÍS TRIMIÑO MORENO

Barrio San Roque, s/n
09300 Roa de Duero (Burgos)
☎: 947 540 033 - Fax: 947 540 033
bodegaparis@bodegaparis.com
www.bodegaparis.com

Established: 2001

🛢 86 🛢 215,000 litres ⚘ 19 has. 🍷 100%

TRIMIÑO 2003 JOVEN RED
100% tempranillo

81 Cherry with a violet hue. Not very intense yet clean aroma of red fruit and brambles. Fruity, light palate with a certain expression, pleasant.

TRIMIÑO GONZÁLEZ 2003 JOVEN RED
100% tempranillo

82 Cherry with a lively violet edge. Not very intense, clean aroma of ripe bramble fruit and a floral hint. Flavourful, expressive palate of ripe fruit; a good young wine.

TRIMIÑO GONZALEZ 2001 OAK AGED RED
95% tempranillo, 5% cabernet sauvignon   🍷 4

83 Garnet red cherry with a violet edge. Intense, ripe aroma with light reduction notes (wax, prunes) and a balsamic hint. Flavourful palate with slightly marked tannins, spicy oak notes and good fruit weight.

TRIMIÑO GONZÁLEZ 2002 OAK AGED RED
95% tempranillo, 5% cabernet sauvignon   🍷 4

82 Cherry with a violet hue. Not very intense yet clean aroma of brambles and balsamic hints.

Flavourful, fruity palate with light notes of well-integrated oak.

PARÍS TRIMIÑO 2002 CRIANZA RED
95% tempranillo, 5% cabernet sauvignon

86 Cherry with a garnet red edge. Fine aroma with toasty, creamy oak notes and spices. Full, flavourful palate with powerful fruit, well-integrated wood and liquorice in the finish.

TRIMIÑO GONZÁLEZ 2003 JOVEN RED
PARÍS TRIMIÑO 2001 CRIANZA RED

PARXET

Ctra. de Valoria , km. 7
47315 Pesquera de Duero (Valladolid)

☎: 983 870 185 - Fax: 983 870 185
parxet@parxet.es
www.parxet.es

Established: 1995

🛢 300 🛢 150,000 litres ⚘ 30 has.
🍷 85% ⦿15%: -US -UK -JP -DE -BE -DK

AUSTUM 2002 OAK AGED RED
100% tinto fino

82 Garnet red cherry. Fresh aroma of red berries and blackberries, with a certain elegance and moderate oak presence. Flavourful and fresh palate, with good expression of red fruit, well-balanced with an agreeable toasty finish.

AUSTUM
Ribera del Duero
DENOMINACIÓN DE ORIGEN
2002

TIONIO 2000 CRIANZA RED

PASCUAL

Comarcal 114, km. 145, 5
09471 Fuentelcesped (Burgos)
☎: 947 557 351 - Fax: 947 557 312
tinto@bodegaspascual.com

www.bodegaspascual.com

Established: 1986

⊞ 800 🍶 500,000 litres 🍇 25 has.

🍷 70% 🌐30%

HEREDAD DE PEÑALOSA 2003 ROSÉ

69 Onion skins. Aroma with fermentation off-odours and a nuance of red fruit. Light palate with notes of red fruit, not very expressive.

CASTILDIEGO 2003 JOVEN RED
100% tempranillo

83 Cherry with a lively violet hue. Not very intense yet clean aroma with a good expression of ripe fruit (blackberries, bilberries). Fruity, fresh flavourful palate, a good young wine.

BURÓ 2002 OAK AGED RED
100% tempranillo   ⊞ 10

84 Intense cherry with a lively garnet edge. Intense aroma of macerated skins with a notion of terroir and well-integrated wood. Flavourful, well-balanced palate with well-integrated fruit and wood tannins.

HEREDAD DE PEÑALOSA 2003 OAK AGED RED
90% tempranillo, 10% cabernet sauvignon   ⊞ 4

82 Dark cherry with a violet edge. Medium intensity aroma with sun-drenched skins, ink and a hint of earthiness. Flavourful palate with a good fruit expression and barely perceptible wood, long.

HEREDAD DE PEÑALOSA 2000 CRIANZA RED

84 Cherry with a garnet red edge. Medium intensity aroma with crianza character (vanilla) and black fruit, harmonious. Flavourful palate with red fruit, well-integrated wood and a degree of persistence.

CASTILDIEGO 2000 CRIANZA RED

85 Garnet red cherry. Good intensity aroma with creamy and spicy oak notes (vanilla, white pepper). Flavourful palate with ripe and polished tannins well-assembled with the wood tannins, slightly oily, very pleasant and with good persistence.

HEREDAD DE PEÑALOSA 1999 RESERVA RED

83 Cherry with a garnet red edge. Medium intensity aroma with ink, black fruit and well-integrated wood. Flavourful, medium bodied palate with fresh and ripe fruit, toasty oak, and polished tannins.

GRAN BURÓ 1999 RESERVA RED
100% tempranillo

84 Garnet red cherry. Aroma with crianza character (vanilla, toasty flavours) and ripe fruit, not very intense yet harmonious. Flavourful, intense, medium bodied palate with polished tannins and a toasty finish.

Bodegas PEÑAFIEL

Ctra. N-122, km. 311
47300 Peñafiel (Valladolid)
☎: 983 881 622 - Fax: 983 881 622
bodegaspenafiel@bodegaspenafiel.com
www.bodegaspenafiel.com

Established: 2002

⊞ 625 🍶 155,000 litres 🍇 28 has.

BARÓN DE FILAR 2001 CRIANZA RED
BARÓN DE FILAR 1999 RESERVA RED

PEÑALBA LÓPEZ-FINCA TORREMILANOS

Finca Torremilanos
09400 Aranda de Duero (Burgos)
☎: 947 501 /77 - Fax: 947 508 044
torremilanos@torremilanos.com
www.torremilanos.com

Established: 1903

⊞ 6,500 🍶 6,000,000 litres 🍇 200 has.

🍷 60% 🌐40%: -US -MX -JP -PE -CO -IN -UK -DE -SE -DK -CH -FR -IT -NL -BE

MONTE CASTRILLO 2003 ROBLE RED
tinto fino   ⊞ 46

85 Very dark cherry. Powerful aroma with predominant burnt notes (toasty oak and skins) and a suggestion of jammy fruit. Flavourful palate with a good fruit/oak integration, liquorice, dark-roasted flavours and a hint of graphite in the finish.

TORREMILANOS 2000 CRIANZA RED

86 Deep cherry. Elegant aroma of jammy black fruit and fine wood notes (cocoa, spices). Fleshy, powerful palate with very spicy wood and a good fruit hint; for keeping.

TORREMILANOS 2001 CRIANZA RED
tempranillo

82 Not very deep garnet red with a brick red hue. Earthy aroma of toffee with a balsamic hint and black fruit (blackberries). Flavourful, fresh palate with slightly aggressive tannins and medium persistence.

TORRE - ALBENIZ 1999 RESERVA RED
75% tempranillo, 15% cabernet sauvignon, 10% merlot

82 Deep cherry. Aroma with crianza reduction notes (varnish, cigar box), slightly warm with a ripe black fruit suggestion. Fleshy, slightly rustic palate with oak tannins and a toasty finish.

TORREMILANOS 1999 RESERVA RED
100% tempranillo

87 Dark cherry with a dark red edge. Powerful aroma of toasty oak, skins, terroir and jammy fruit. Flavourful palate with rough, slightly oily tannins, fine bitter notes, hints of wax and excellent acidity.

TORREMILANOS 1996 GRAN RESERVA RED
100% tempranillo

86 Intense cherry with a slightly brick red edge. Aroma with predominant bottle reduction nuances (wet leather, cigar box). Round, velvety palate with jammy fruit, flavourful with spicy notes in the retronasal passage and supple tannins.

Hermanos PÉREZ PASCUAS

Ctra. Roa, s/n
09314 Pedrosa de Duero (Burgos)
☎: 947 530 100 - Fax: 947 530 002
vinapedrosa@perezpascuas.com
www.perezpascuas.com
Established: 1980
🍾 2,500 🛢 600,000 litres 🍇 110 has.
🍷 60% 🌐40%: -CH -MX -DK -SE -DK -FI -US -CA -PR -BR -PE -PA -DO -UK -DE -FR -BE -NL -LU -IE -SG -RU -PL

PÉREZ PASCUAS GRAN SELECCIÓN 1999 OAK AGED RED
100% tinta del país   🍾 26

87 Garnet red cherry with a ruby red edge. Aroma with animal notes (wet leather) and spices (tobacco, cedar wood). Round, elegant, flavourful palate with medium expression and hints of very premature reduction for a Ribera.

CEPA GAVILÁN 2002 OAK AGED RED
100% tinta del país   🍾 12

85 Garnet red cherry with a coppery edge. Powerful aroma of ripe black fruit with a spicy, toasty (cocoa, coffee) oak suggestion. Flavourful, fleshy palate with rough, slightly oily tannins, fine notes of dark-roasted flavours, liquorice and excellent acidity.

VIÑA PEDROSA 2001 CRIANZA RED
100% tinta del país

85 Cherry with a brick red edge. Aroma of toasty wood, vanilla, blackberries and light lactic notes. Flavourful, well-balanced and creamy on the palate with good wood tannins and good persistence.

VIÑA PEDROSA 2002 CRIANZA RED
100% tinta del país

85 Intense cherry. Toasty, fruity, ripe aroma of fine oak. Fruity palate with good acidity, fine toasty flavours and slightly ripe tannins.

VIÑA PEDROSA 2000 RESERVA RED
90% tinta del país, 10% cabernet sauvignon

84 Medium-high hue garnet red. Aroma with light hints of reduction (leather, tobacco) and jammy tomatoes. Fleshy, well-balanced palate with some bitter notes.

VIÑA PEDROSA 1998 GRAN RESERVA RED
90% tinta del país, 10% cabernet sauvignon

88 Intense cherry with a brick red edge. Aroma with spicy notes of long crianza (wax, carpentry) and nuances of a good bottle evolution (leather, tobacco). Fleshy, full, flavourful palate with spices in the retronasal passage, a pleasantly bitter oaky aftertaste and polished tannins.

PINGÓN

Ctra. N-122, km. 311
47300 Peñafiel (Valladolid)
☎: 983 880 623 - Fax: 983 880 623
carramimbre@bodegaspingon.com
www.bodegaspingon.com
Established: 1997
🍾 800 🛢 225,000 litres 🍇 25 has.
🍷 85% 🌐15%: -US -PR -CH -SE -NL -BE -DK -UK

CARRAMIMBRE 2003 ROBLE RED

84 Intense cherry. Aroma with an intense suggestion of ripe bunches, maceration and ripe fruit with a mild hint of oak. Fleshy, fruity, powerful, warm palate with very ripe and flavourful tannins.

ALTAMIMBRE SELECCIÓN ESPECIAL 2001 OAK AGED RED

88 Garnet red cherry. Powerful aroma with toasty oak notes over a nuance of very varietal fruit (jammy black fruit, spices), well-balanced. Flavourful palate with slightly drying oak tannins although promising with age and with suggestion of slightly sweet fruit and terroir in the retronasal passage,spicy, long.

CARRAMIMBRE 2001 CRIANZA RED

81 Intense cherry. Slightly fruity aroma without great nuances and with toasty oak. Slightly fleshy palate with ripe fruit and a nuance of mature Tempranillo, sun-drenched with slightly dry tannins.

CARRAMIMBRE 2002 CRIANZA RED

86 Intense cherry. Intense aroma of very ripe black fruit with hints of minerals (dry clay) and toasty oak notes. Fleshy, powerful palate with something of a fruity-varietal character and a notion of terroir, flavourful with toasty hints of oak.

Bodegas PINNA FIDELIS

Camino Llanillos, s/n
47300 Peñafiel (Valladolid)
☎: 983 878 034 - Fax: 983 878 035
info@pinnafidelis.com
www.pinnafidelis.com

Established: 2001

🍷 1,500 🗄 1,000,000 litres 🌿 225 has.

🍷 70% 💧30%: -UK -DE -BE -US

PINNA FIDELIS 2002 ROBLE RED
100% tempranillo

85 Deep cherry with a violet edge. Intense aroma and toasty oak notes over a nuance of ripe fruit, warm hints. Flavourful, slightly fleshy palate with marked oak, good fruit-wood symmetry and good acidity.

PINNA FIDELIS 2003 ROBLE RED
100% tempranillo

86 Cherry with a violet hue. Intense aroma of black fruit with hints of sun-drenched skins and fine toasty oak notes. Very dry, fleshy, flavourful palate with well-integrated wood and oak, fine spicy notes of ripe fruit and liquorice in the retronasal passage.

PINNA FIDELIS VENDIMIA SELECCIONADA MAGNUM 2002 OAK AGED RED
100% tempranillo 🍷 10

86 Garnet red cherry. Powerful, ripe aroma with notes of macerated black fruit and a toasty oak nuance. Flavourful, concentrated palate slightly marked yet promising tannins, a slightly oily texture, a good fruit weight and a powerful effect in the retronasal passage.

PINNA FIDELIS 2002 CRIANZA RED

POMAR VIÑEDOS

Camino Carralaceña, s/n
09318 Valdezate (Burgos)
☎: 947 550 064 - Fax: 947 550 064
pomardeburgos@wanadoo.es

Established: 1999

🍷 150 🗄 105,000 litres 🌿 24 has.

🍷 90% 💧10%

POMAR DE BURGOS JOVEN RED
POMAR DE BURGOS ROBLE RED
QUINTA DE BACO CRIANZA RED
POMAR DE BURGOS CRIANZA RED
POMAR DE BURGOS RESERVA RED

PRADO DE OLMEDO

Paraje El Salegar, s/n
09443 Quintana del Pidío (Burgos)
☎: 947 546 902 - Fax: 947 546 902
pradodeolmedo@terra.es
www.pradodeolmedo.com

Established: 1999

🍷 290 🌿 20 has. 🍷 90%

💧10%: -PR -DE -UK

MONASTERIO DE SAN MIGUEL 2003 RED
100% tempranillo

80 Very deep garnet red. Aroma of strawberry syrup, sweet notes of very ripe fruit, perfumed. Fleshy, intense and slightly warm on the palate with hints of violets in the retronasal passage.

MONASTERIO DE SAN MIGUEL 2000 RESERVA RED
100% tempranillo

77 Cherry with an orange edge. Ripe aroma of black berries in liqueur and spices. Flavourful palate with woody tannins and spicy oak over the fruit with an earthy finish.

MONASTERIO DE SAN MIGUEL 2000 CRIANZA RED

PROTOS BODEGAS RIBERA DUERO DE PEÑAFIEL

Bodegas Protos, 24-28
47300 Peñafiel (Valladolid)
☎: 983 878 011 - Fax: 983 878 012
bodega@bodegaprotos.com
www.bodegasprotos.com

Established: 1927

🍷 8,500 🗄 3,000,000 litres 🌿 100 has.

🍷 80% 💧20%: -US -CH -PA -MX -DE

PROTOS RIBERA DUERO 2002 ROBLE RED
100% tinto fino

84 Dark garnet red cherry. Powerful aroma of black fruit with a suggestion of the spicy freshness of skins and a hint of fine oak. Fleshy palate with quite rough but flavourful tannins, fresh fruit and a spicy and balsamic hint, excellent acidity.

PROTOS SELECCIÓN 2001 RED

89 Intense cherry. Aroma with excellent, fine toasty oak nuances well-integrated with the fruit. Round palate, oily, elegant, flavourful, well-harmonised oak tannins with the alcohol and the fruit tannins.

PROTOS ESPECIAL 2001 RED

89 Very deep garnet red. Dark-roasted, toasty, balsamic aroma with menthol and ripe red fruit. Marked and slightly drying wood tannins on the palate with a good fruit weight and a suggestion of coffee and toffee.

PROTOS 2001 CRIANZA RED
100% tinto fino

86 Dark garnet red cherry. Quite intense, very fine aroma with good expression of crianza and

DO RIBERA DEL DUERO

varietal fruit. Flavourful palate with a good fruit/oak integration and a suggestion of the freshness of skins and minerals.

PROTOS 2000 RESERVA RED
100% tinto fino

87 Dark cherry with a garnet red edge. Intense, very fine aroma with notes of red fruit, hints of fresh skins and smoky oak notes. Flavourful palate with a good oak/fruit integration, slightly warm with a good crianza expression, quite potential.

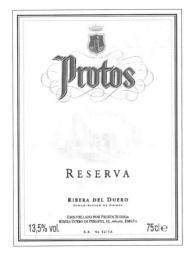

PROTOS 1996 GRAN RESERVA RED
PROTOS 1999 RESERVA ESPECIAL RED

REAL SITIO DE VENTOSILLA

Ctra. Aranda-Palencia, km. 10
09443 Gumiel de Mercado (Burgos)
☎: 947 546 900 - Fax: 947 546 999
bodega@pradorey.com - pradorey.com

Established: 1996
6,200 ▦ 2,000,000 litres 520 has.
75% 25%

PRADO REY 2003 ROBLE RED

84 Intense cherry. Powerful aroma, reminiscent of ripe black fruit (grape bunches). Very fruity palate, flavourful, ripe skins, slightly oaky hint well-integrated in the wine.

PRADO REY 2001 CRIANZA RED

83 Dark garnet red cherry. Fruity aroma, slightly rustic Tempranillo notes of La Ribera, oak notes. Slightly fleshy palate, well-balanced, retronasal effect of ripe fruit, jammy blackberries, quite sweet tannins.

PRADO REY 1999 RESERVA RED

86 Quite dark cherry. Fine aroma, jammy fruit and toasty oak well-integrated (cocoa and coffee). Round palate, oily tannins, flavourful, tobacco and creamy vanillas in the retronasal passage.

PRADO REY ÉLITE 2001 RESERVA

87 Intense cherry with an orangey edge. Powerful aroma, rich in ripe fruit, mild mineral notes, toasty oak, unassembled with the toasty hints of grapes. Fleshy palate, very marked fruit tannins, good varietal expression and complex overtones.

DO RIBERA DEL DUERO

RENACIMIENTO

Ctra. Renedo-Pesquera, km. 30
Santa María, 36
47359 Olivares de Duero (Valladolid)
☎: 983 107 100 - Fax: 983 107 104
gperez@bodegamatarromera.es
www.matarromera.es

⊞ 100 ⚜ 85 has.

☞ 70% ⚐30%: -DE -AD -AT -BE -BR -CA
-CU -CL -DK -EC -FR -UK -NL -IT -JP -MX -
DK -PA -PE -PR -SE -CH -US -CZ -DM

RENTO 2001 OAK AGED RED
100% tinto fino

87 Very deep garnet red. Aroma of red fruit with dark-roasted and very subtle toasty flavours. Fleshy, flavourful palate, with wood/fruit symmetry, long.

Bodegas RESALTE DE PEÑAFIEL

Ctra. N-122, km. 312
17300 Peñafiel (Valladolid)
☎: 983 878 160 - Fax: 983 880 601
info@resalte.com
www.resalte.com

Established: 2000

⊞ 1,500 🗄 480,000 litres

☞ 60% ⚐40%: -US -JP -SE -CA -NL -BE

RESALTE 2003 ROBLE JOVEN RED
100% tempranillo   ⊞ 2

84 Very deep cherry with a violet edge. Intense aroma of black fruit, fine smoky notes of oak, spicy hints of skins, notions of graphite and underbrush. Flavourful palate, ripe, rough tannins, slightly drying yet promising, an excellent fruit expression with liquorice and balsamic notes.

RESALTE 2000 CRIANZA RED
100% tempranillo

87 Lively garnet red cherry. Powerful, ripe aroma with predominant spicy oak notes, a suggestion of black fruit and hints of smoky earth. Powerful, concentrated palate with well-integrated oak/fruit, and fine bitter notes (dark-roasted flavours, liquorice) in the retronasal passage.

RESALTE 2001 CRIANZA RED
100% tempranillo

89 Very deep cherry. Powerful aroma of ripe red fruit, spicy oak notes balsamic hints, sour cherries in liqueur and fresh mineral overtones. Powerful palate with promising but slightly marked tannins, an excellent fruit/oak association, good acidity and quality bitter notes.

RESALTE 2000 RESERVA RED
100% tempranillo

88 Intense garnet red cherry. Intense aroma though somewhat quite closed with predominant toasty, creamy (vanilla) oak notes, fine balsamic and salted meat hints. Flavourful palate, with slightly marked but ripe and promising tannins, an excellent fruit expression, fine bitter notes and good acidity.

Bodegas REYES

Ctra. Va-So, km. 54, 300 Apdo. 41
47300 Peñafiel (Valladolid)
☎: 983 873 015 - Fax: 983 873 017
info@teofiloreyes.com

Established: 1994

⊞ 900 🗄 350,000 litres ⚜ 60 has.

☞ 80% ⚐20%: -DE -DK -AT -MX -PR

TAMIZ 2003 OAK AGED RED

81 Very dark cherry. Powerful aroma, warm, fruity and slightly spicy suggestion, hints of skins. Flavourful palate, marked herbaceous tones, bitter, high in acidity, lacking balance.

TAMIZ 2001 OAK AGED RED
tempranillo

83 Very deep cherry. Concentrated aroma of black fruit with fine hints of fresh skins, a nuance of earth and fine wood. Flavourful, elegant palate, with fine, flavourful, earthy tannins and a toasty oak finish.

DO RIBERA DEL DUERO

TEÓFILO REYES 2001 CRIANZA RED
97% tempranillo, 3% albillo

86 Cherry with an orangey edge. Not very intense aroma but with a certain finesse, toasty oak and jammy fruit. Flavourful, warm, fleshy palate with powerful fruit and well-integrated wood.

RIBERALTA

Ctra. Madrid-Irún, km. 168
09370 Gumiel de Izán (Burgos)
☎: 947 544 101 - Fax: 947 525 722
riberalta@bodegasriberalta.com
www.bodegasriberalta.com
Established: 1988
🌐 1,800 📖 1,000,000 litres 🍇 10 has.
🍷 80% 🌐20%: -PR -CH -DE -MX -NL

VEGA IZÁN 2003 ROSÉ

77 Dark raspberry with a coppery hue. Quite intense aroma of slightly reduced ripe fruit with hints of withered petals. Flavourful palate with bittersweet notes and a slightly acidic edge.

VEGA IZÁN 2003 JOVEN RED
100% tempranillo

81 Garnet red cherry with a violet hue. Powerful aroma of black fruit, with notes of sun-drenched skins and an earthy suggestion. Fleshy palate with slightly drying tannins, fine bitter notes and liquorice.

VEGA IZÁN 2002 ROBLE RED
100% tempranillo

80 Garnet red cherry. Intense aroma with spicy oak notes and hints of reduction. Flavourful, fleshy palate with slightly drying tannins, warm hints and a ripe fruit suggestion.

VEGA IZÁN 2000 CRIANZA RED
100% tempranillo

77 Deep cherry. Smoky, spicy aroma with a suggestin of reduction. Flavourful, sweetish palate with ripe fruit and spicy oak.

VEGA IZÁN 1999 RESERVA RED
100% tempranillo

81 Garnet red cherry. Toasty aroma with smoky hints and an earthy hint (reduction). Fleshy palate of ripe black fruit with obvious oak tannins and a dry finish.

VEGA IZÁN 1994 GRAN RESERVA RED
100% tempranillo

77 Garnet red with a brick red edge. Ripe aroma with noticeable crianza reduction notes (dry earth, tobacco, animal fur). Flavourful palate with fresh, supple tannins; rancid sensations, toffee finish.

GOMEL 2003 JOVEN RED
GOMEL 2000 CRIANZA RED

DO RIBERA DEL DUERO

Viñedos y Bodegas RIBÓN

Basilón, 15
47350 Quintanilla de Onésimo (Valladolid)
☎: 983 680 015 - Fax: 983 680 015
bodegasribon@telefonica.net

Established: 1995

🌐 250 ▦ 90,000 litres ⚘ 25 has.

🍷 50% 🌐50%: -PR -DE -CH -PT -LU -BE

RIBÓN 2002 ROBLE RED
85% tempranillo, 15% merlot

82 Deep cherry. Aroma of very ripe black fruit with sweet and balsamic toasty hints. Fleshy palate with black fruit, consistent fruit tannins and bitter overtones (oak, cocoa).

RIBÓN 2001 CRIANZA RED
90% tempranillo, 10% merlot

85 Dark cherry with a dark red-saffron edge. Powerful aroma with an excellent expression of varietal fruit well-integrated with the oak (toasty flavours, spices). Fleshy, flavourful palate with predominant bitter notes (dark-roasted flavours, liquorice), slightly warm.

RIBÓN 1999 RESERVA RED
TINTO RIBÓN 2001 RESERVA RED

Bodegas RÍOS PRIETO

Ctra. Valbuena, s/n
47315 Pesquera de Duero (Valladolid)
☎: 983 880 383@filete
fax:cdelosrios@wanadoo.es

Established: 2002

🌐 450 ▦ 249,000 litres ⚘ 27 has.

🍷 72% 🌐28%: -MX -DE

PRIOS MAXIMUS 2003 ROBLE RED
tempranillo   🌐6

84 Dark cherry with a violet edge. Powerful aroma of black fruit with an excellent varietal profile (damp earth), spices and fine toasty oak. Flavourful palate with slightly marked yet fine and promising tannins with bitter notes and hints of overextraction.

PRIOS MAXIMUS 2002 CRIANZA RED
tempranillo

86 Dark cherry. Powerful aroma with a good fruit/oak integration and predominant toasty and balsamic notes. Flavourful palate with rough tannins, a suggestion of sweet fruit and fine bitter notes (liquorice, dark-roasted flavours), promising.

PRIOS MAXIMUS 2002 ROBLE RED
PRIOS MAXIMUS 2003 ROBLE RED
PRIOS MAXIMUS 2002 OAK AGED RED

RODERO

Ctra. Boada, s/n
09314 Pedrosa de Duero (Burgos)
☎: 947 530 046 - Fax: 947 530 097
rodero@bodegasrodero.com
www.bodegasrodero.com

Established: 1991

🌐 1,000 ▦ 500,000 litres ⚘ 81 has.

🍷 65% 🌐35%

CARMELO RODERO 2003 JOVEN RED

84 Bigarreau cherry with a violet rim. Intense aroma of blackberries, ripe plums, liquorice and a floral nuance (violets). Full, flavourful palate with a good expression of ripe fruit and well-integrated alcohol; an excellent young wine.

CARMELO RODERO 2001 CRIANZA RED

82 Intense cherry. Lactic aroma and an elegant reduction (leather) with vanilla and red stone fruit. Good acidity, persistent and fleshy on the palate with balsamic notes.

CARMELO RODERO 2000 RESERVA RED

88 Cherry with an orangey edge. Intense aroma of fine, spicy wood (cocoa, vanilla), yet to be assembled and a suggestion of ripe fruit. Full, very flavourful and spicy on the palate; creamy, well-balanced and with toasty notes in the retronasal passage.

CARMELO RODERO 1996 GRAN RESERVA RED

88 Cherry with a brick red edge. Medium-intensity, fine aroma; viscous with vanilla and cocoa. Powerful, flavourful palate with spicy toasty notes, jammy fruit, good evolution with crianza complexity, ripe.

CARMELO RODERO VENDIMIA SELECCIONADA 2000 GRAN RESERVA RED
100% tinto fino

88 Cherry with an orangey edge. Aroma of toasty wood with sweetish notes, liquorice and spices. Fleshy, well-balanced palate with very well-integrated tannins.

CARMELO RODERO 2002 OAK AGED RED
CARMELO RODERO 1999 RESERVA RED

S. ARROYO

Avenida del Cid, 99
09441 Sotillo de la Ribera (Burgos)
☎: 947 532 444 - Fax: 947 532 444
info@tintoarroyo.com
www.tintoarroyo.com

Established: 1960

🌐 1,500 📊 1,000,000 litres 🍷 90 has.
🚩 60% 🌐40%: -DE -UK -IE -RU -US -CA
-BE -DK -FR -NL -CH -AD -MX -PA -PR -SG

VIÑARROYO 2003 JOVEN ROSÉ
TINTO ARROYO 2003 JOVEN RED
TINTO ARROYO 2003 ROBLE RED
TINTO ARROYO 1999 CRIANZA RED
TINTO ARROYO 2000 CRIANZA RED
TINTO ARROYO 1998 RESERVA RED
TINTO ARROYO 1998 RESERVA RED
TINTO ARROYO 1995 GRAN RESERVA RED

Hermanos SAN JUAN LÓPEZ

Finca El Plnar, s/n
09316 Berlangas de Roa (Burgos)
☎: 947 533 006 - Fax: 947 533 010
marian_santa@hotmail.com

Established: 1979
🌐 250 📊 180,000 litres 🍷 60 has.
🚩 80% 🌐20%

BLASÓN DE SAN JUAN 2000 ROBLE RED
100% tinto fino

81 Garnet red with a very deep orangey edge. Aroma of black olives, jammy tomatoes and ripe black fruit. Slightly warm palate with tannins still marked, fruity.

BLASÓN DE SAN JUAN 2000 CRIANZA RED
100% tinto fino

82 Dark garnet red. Aroma of mild reduction (leathers) with paprika, and ripe red fruit.Fresh, flavourful palate, with good wood/fruit tannin integration.

BLASÓN DE SAN JUAN 1999 RESERVA RED
100% tinto fino

83 Medium-hue dark garnet red. Aroma with sweet notes, red fruit and toasty wood. Green notes on the palate, slightly bitter with a balsamic suggestion.

Bodega SAN MAMÉS

Ctra. Valladolid, s/n
09315 Fuentecén (Burgos)
☎: 947 532 693 - Fax: 947 532 653
bodegasanmames@wanadoo.es
www.lariberadelduero.com/sanmames

Established: 1964
🌐 100 📊 3,500,000 litres 🍷 380 has.
🚩 95% 🌐5%: -DK -NL -DE -UK

VIÑA EL GUIJARRAL ROSÉ
CARRALAVEGA ROSÉ
VIÑA EL GUIJARRAL JOVEN RED
CARRALAVEGA RED

Sociedad Agraria de Transformación SAN PABLO

Camino de Cantaburros, s/n
09400 Aranda de Duero (Burgos)
☎: 947 500 484 - Fax: 947 501 302
irenusa@teleline.es

Established: 1998
🌐 400 📊 320,000 litres 🍷 35 has.
🚩 80% 🌐20%

CANTABURROS 2001 ROBLE RED

83 Cherry with an orangey edge. Medium intensity and very spicy aroma (cumin, vanilla, pepper). Flavourful, medium bodied palate with a toasty and pleasant finish.

CANTABURROS 2001 CRIANZA RED

82 Dark cherry with an orangey edge. Not very intense aroma with ink and a rustic and balsamic suggestion. Flavourful palate, fruitier than in the nose with well-integrated oak.

CANTABURROS 1999 RESERVA RED

83 Cherry with a garnet red-orange edge. Medium intensity aroma of fruit in liquor and toasty oak. Not very well-structured but flavourful on the palate with jammy fruit.

Cooperativa SAN PEDRO REGALADO

Ctra. de Aranda, s/n
09370 La Aguilera (Burgos)
☎: 947 545 017 - Fax: 947 545 017
bspregalado@terra.es

Established: 1958
📊 1,500,000 litres 🍷 297 has. 🚩 100%

EMBOCADERO 2003 JOVEN ROSÉ
50% tempranillo, 50% otras

55 Pale pink. Off-odours and notes of dirt very noticeable in the nose and on the palate.

EMBOCADERO 2001 JOVEN RED
100% tempranillo

79 Garnet red cherry with a saffron edge. Intense, spicy aroma of skins and hints of reduction. Flavourful, bitter and warm on the palate with fine toasty notes in the retronasal passage.

EMBOCADERO 2002 JOVEN RED
100% tempranillo

76 Not very deep cherry with an orangey hue. Salted meat aroma with skins and ripe fruit. Light palate with fruit concealed by the alcohol.

EMBOCADERO 2002 JOVEN ROSÉ
EMBOCADERO 2003 JOVEN RED
CANTAPERDICES JOVEN RED

Cooperativa SAN ROQUE DE LA ENCINA

San Roque, 73
09391 Castrillo de la Vega (Burgos)
☎: 947 536 001 - Fax: 947 536 001

Established: 1957

🍷 180 📊 1,700,000 litres 🍇 230 has.

🍷 95% 🌐5%

CERRO PIÑEL ROSÉ
MONTE PINADILLO ROSÉ
CERRO PIÑEL CRIANZA RED
CERRO PIÑEL RED
MONTE PINADILLO RED

Bodega Cooperativa SANTA ANA

Ctra. De Salas s/n
09410 Peñaranda de Duero (Burgos)
☎: 947 552 011
www.bodegasantaana.com

Established: 1964

🍷 150 📊 2,000,000 litres 🍇 350 has.

🍷 95% 🌐5%: -UK -FR

CASTILLO DE PEÑARANDA 2003 ROSÉ
CASTILLO DE PEÑARANDA 2002 RED
CASTILLO DE PEÑARANDA 2003 RED
CASTILLO DE PEÑARANDA 2002 ROBLE RED
CASTILLO DE PEÑARANDA 1999 CRIANZA RED

Bodegas SANTA EULALIA

Malpica, s/n
09442 La Horra (Burgos)
☎: 947 542 051 - Fax: 947 580 180
comercial.tvillar@cic.es

Established: 1950

🍷 1,500 📊 1,200,000 litres 🍇 210 has.

🍷 60% 🌐40%

CONDE DE SIRUELA 2003 JOVEN RED
100% tempranillo

80 Very deep garnet red with a ruby red hue. Medium-intensity aroma of fresh fruit. Flavourful tannins on the palate, fruity and slightly bitter.

CONDE DE SIRUELA 2002 OAK AGED (4) RED

84 Dark cherry with a garnet red edge. Intense aroma of ripe red fruit, smoky notes. Flavourful on

the palate with fresh red fruit well-integrated with hints of creamy oak, well-balanced.

CONDE DE SIRUELA 1999 CRIANZA RED
100% tempranillo

83 Cherry with an orangey rim. Lactic aromas, very ripe fruit, mildly spicy. Slight toastiness on the palate with medium acidity and smokiness in the retronasal passage.

RIBERAL 1999 CRIANZA RED

83 Deep garnet red cherry with a coppery edge. Intense aroma of jammy black fruit with toasty and creamy oak notes and a balsamic nuance. Flavourful and fleshy on the palate with slightly marked tannins, quite potential with fine toasty flavours and liquorice in the retronasal passage.

CONDE DE SIRUELA ÉLITE 2001 CRIANZA RED

85 Deep cherry. Spicy aroma of new wood and ripe fruit. Wood tannins yet to be assembled on the palate, good acidity, very flavourful.

CONDE DE SIRUELA 1998 RESERVA RED
100% tempranillo

80 Garnet red with a brick red hue. Aroma with fine reduction notes, vinous, toasty. Drying palate with predominat wood, slightly warm and light.

CONDE DE SIRUELA ELITE 2000 RESERVA RED

86 Intense cherry. Toasty, creamy aroma of fine wood and ripe black fruit; overtones of a very clean and clear Ribera varietal character. Fleshy palate with traces of fruit and wood tannins despite a good integration, flavourful, persistent.

RIBERAL 2003 ROBLE RED
LA HORRA COSECHA 2003 RED
RIBERAL 1996 RESERVA RED
CONDE DE SIRUELA 1994 GRAN RESERVA RED

Bodegas y Viñedos SANTO DOMINGO

Camino de Sarmentero, s/n
47360 Quintanilla de Arriba (Valladolid)
☎: 609 085 201 - Fax: 983 484 052
info@bodegasantodomingo.com

Established: 1993

🍷 120 📊 100,000 litres 🍇 20 has.

SANDO ROBLE RED
SANDO RED

Vinos SANTOS ARRANZ

Ctra. de Valbuena s/n
47315 Pesquera de Duero (Valladolid)
☎: 983 870 008 - Fax: 983 870 008

lagrimanegra82@hotmail.com

Established: 1982

🌐 375 📊 95.000 litres 🍇 21 has.

🍷 80% 🌐20%: -DE -DK -CH

LAGRIMA NEGRA 2001 OAK AGED RED
95% tempranillo, 5% cabernet sauvignon 🌐 6

83 Cherry with a violet edge. Aroma of jammy black forest fruits with a complex liquorice hint. Fleshy, flavourful palate with rough yet oily wood tannins and fruit expression.

LAGRIMA NEGRA 2000 RESERVA RED

86 Deep cherry. Aroma with fine crianza notes (terroir, smoky hints, spices), a suggestion of very ripe black fruit and character. Fleshy, very flavourful palate with fresh but marked fruit tannins and an elegant crianza expression.

LÁGRIMA NEGRA 1999 GRAN RESERVA RED
95% tempranillo, 5% cabernet sauvignon

87 Intense cherry. Fine aroma with toasty hints, spices (cinnamon, pepper, tobacco) and jammy fruit. Fleshy, powerful and flavourful palate with spicy, seasoned oak in the retronasal passage, persistent.

LÁGRIMA NEGRA 2000 CRIANZA RED
LÁGRIMA NEGRA 2001 CRIANZA RED
POLO SANTOS 2000 RED

Bodegas SEÑORÍO DE NAVA

Ctra. Valladolid - Soria, s/n
09813 Nava de Roa (Burgos)
☎: 987 209 790 - Fax: 987 209 800
snava@senoriodenava.es
www.senoriodenava.es

Established: 1986

🌐 3,046 📊 2,454,000 litres 🍇 120 has.

🍷 87% 🌐13%: -CA -US -SE -CH -DK -DE -RU -LU -LT -BE -PE -VE -HK

SEÑORÍO DE NAVA 2002 ROBLE RED
85% tinto fino, 15% cabernet sauvignon

74 Slightly intense cherry with a garnet red edge. Intense aroma of creamy wood, greeness (vine shoots) and red fruit. Medium-bodied, fruity palate but also with pronounced greeness.

SEÑORÍO DE NAVA 2000 CRIANZA RED
100% tinto fino

82 Cherry with a garnet red edge. Medium-intensity aroma of ripe fruit well-blended with the oak. Flavourful palate with abundant fruit; medium bodied with ripe toasty wood.

SEÑORÍO DE NAVA FINCA SAN COBATE 1999 RESERVA RED
100% tinto fino

88 Intense cherry. Aroma with predominant toasty notes, jammy black fruit and hints of terracotta. Flavourful, slightly fleshy palate with a good oak/fruit integration, and fine bitter notes (dark-roasted flavours, liquorice) in the finish.

SEÑORÍO DE NAVA 1999 RESERVA RED
100% tinto fino

80 Cherry with a brick red edge. Not very intense aroma of liquorice, lactics and ripe red fruit. Fleshy with slightly marked wood tannins on the palate.

Bodegas SURCO

Picote s/n
09400 Aranda de Duero (Burgos)
☎: 947 512 069 - Fax: 947 512 069
mcalvo@valdrinal.com - valdrinal.com

Established: 2000

🌐 450 📊 135,000 litres 🍇 30 has.

🍷 40% 🌐60%: -CH -MX -DE -UK

VALDRINAL 2002 ROBLE RED
100% tempranillo

84 Intense cherry. Toasty aroma of ripe fruit with a suggestion of half-ripe skins, toasty. Fruity, warm, flavourful palate, with a suggestion of classic Ribera, earthy notes and brambles.

VALDRINAL 2000 CRIANZA RED
100% tempranillo

84 Deep garnet red cherry. Intense aroma with predominant toasty oak notes and a ripe fruit suggestion (hints of prunes). Flavourful, fleshy palate with well-integrated oak/fruit, a slightly oily texture, fresh spicy overtones and good acidity.

VALDRINAL RESERVA 2000 RED

DO RIBERA DEL DUERO

Bodegas y Viñedos TAMARAL

Ctra. N-122 Valladolid-Soria, km. 310, 6
47314 Peñafiel (Valladolid)
☎: 983 878 017 - Fax: 983 878 089
Info@tamaral.com
www.tamaral.com

Established: 1997

🌐 650 📦 350,000 litres 🍇 50 has.

🍷 80% 🌐20%: -US -DE -CH -DO U.K -FR
-BE -NL -VE -DK -MX

TAMARAL 2000 CRIANZA RED
100% tempranillo

80 Intense cherry. Aroma of ripe red fruit, notes
of fresh skins and a spicy hint. Flavourful, fresh
palate with ripe skins, spicy and well-mannered.

TAMARAL 1999 RESERVA RED
100% tempranillo

80 Deep cherry. Aroma of toasty skins, spicy oak
and a smoky hint. Flavourful, very fresh palate with
supple wood tannins and a spicy finish.

TAMARAL 2000 ROBLE RED
TAMARAL 2002 ROBLE RED
TAMARAL 1999 CRIANZA RED

TARSUS

Ctra. De Roa-Anguix, km. 3
09312 Anguix (Burgos)
☎: 947 554 218 - Fax: 947 541 804
tarsus@byb.es
www.byb.es

Established: 1998

🌐 1,300 📦 35,400 litres 🍇 86 has.

QUINTA DE TARSUS 2000 ROBLE RED
100% tinta del pais

87 Cherry with a garnet red edge. Medium-intensity yet fine aroma with balsamic tones (bay,
eucalyptus) and well-assembled fruit and wood.
Flavourful, fairly powerful and very balsamic on
the palate with light toasty oak, well-integrated
fruit and wood tannins, elegant and original.

TARSUS 2000 RED
90% tinta del pais, 10% cabernet sauvignon

85 Intense cherry. Aroma of red berries and aromatic herbs with very pleasant toasty notes of
cocoa and flowers. Fleshy on the palate with
powerful yet flavourful wood tannins and an aftertaste of Mediterranean herbs with good acidity.

**TARSUS VENDIMIA SELECCIONADA 1999
ROBLE RED**

Compañía de Vinos de TELMO RODRÍGUEZ

Siete Infantes de Lara, 5 Oficina 1
26006 Logroño (La Rioja)
☎: 941 511 128 - Fax: 941 511 131
cia@fer.es

GAZUR 2003 JOVEN RED
100% tinto fino

86 Intense cherry. Aroma with notes of fresh fruit
and creamy oak. Fruity, flavourful palate with good
varietal expression and typification.

MATALLANA 2001 OAK AGED RED
100% tinto fino

93 Intense cherry. Powerful aroma rich in fruity
nuances, creamy toasty oak (cocoa, toffee) and a
mild hint of minerals. Oily palate with excellent
oily tannins, slightly spirituous with fine toasty
notes in the retronasal passage, complex.

M2 DE MATALLANA 2002 OAK AGED RED
100% tinto fino

85 Quite dark cherry. Aroma with notes of ripe
fruit and very delicate toasty oak with mild spicy
and animal hints. Round, medium-bodied, flavourful palate with ripe tannins and ripe fruit.

Bodegas TIERRAS DE PEÑAFIEL

Las Damas 10 2°A
47300 Peñafiel (Valladolid)
☎: 983 881 350 - Fax: 983 881 350
jorge@temera.com

Established: 2001

🌐 60 📦 40,000 litres 🍇 9 has. 🇪🇸 100%

RUBÉN RAMOS 2002 ROBLE JOVEN RED
100% tempranillo

80 Very deep cherry. Intense aroma of very ripe
fruit with hints of petals and a toasty oak nuance.
Flavourful palate with somewhat rough tannins,
lacks balance.

RUBÉN RAMOS 2001 CRIANZA RED
100% tempranillo

83 Garnet red cherry. Powerful aroma of very ripe
black fruit with reduction hints (slightly aged
wood). Flavourful palate with ripe grape tannins,
bitter hints of oak, pleasant with somewhat high
acidity.

TORRECORCOS

Ctra. Valladolid, km. 289, 300
09318 Fuentelisendo (Burgos)
☎: 947 532 627 - Fax: 947 532 731

administrador@torrecorcos.com
www.torrederos.com

Established: 2000

🌐 400 📊 450,000 litres 🍇 90 has.

🍷 80% 🍇20%: -US -DE -CH -MX -DK -BO -FR

TORREDEROS 2001 CRIANZA RED
100% tempranillo

85 Deep cherry. Slightly viscous aroma of ripe black, fruit notes of cocoa and spices. Fleshy palate with powerful tannins, hints of jammy black fruit and a flavourful, well-balanced finish.

TORREDEROS 2000 RESERVA RED
100% tempranillo

84 Dark garnet red cherry. Intense aroma with predominant black fruit notes and a hint of spicy oak. Fresh, flavourful palate with good oak/fruit integration, very pleasant although without strong Reserva expression.

TORREDEROS 2003 RED
TORREDEROS 2001 ROBLE RED

TORRES DE ANGUIX

Camino La Tejera s/n
09312 Angüix (Burgos)
☎: 947 554 008 - Fax: 947 554 129
bodega@torresdeanguix.com
www.torresdeanguix.com

Established: 2000

🌐 1,798 📊 1,400,000 litres 🍇 105 has.

🍷 80% 🍇20%: -CH -DE -US -UK

TORRES DE ANGUIX 2003 ROSÉ
100% tinto fino

71 Blush. Aroma with a mild off-odour and a fruity, herby nuance. Quite fruity, bitter palate with weak fruit.

TORRES DE ANGUIX 2003 JOVEN RED
100% tinto fino

83 Garnet red with a violet rim. Aroma with aniseed notes, very sweet skins and red bramble fruit. Flavourful, earthy palate with supple tannins and medium persistence.

D´ANGUIX 2001 ROBLE RED
100% tinto fino   🌐 12

82 Dark garnet red. Spicy aroma with very sweet notes of toasty wood and jammy black fruit. Drying palate with obvious yet round wood tannins and a good suggestion of red fruit in the finish.

TORRES DE ANGUIX 2002 OAK AGED RED
100% tinto fino   🌐 4

80 Garnet red with a violet rim. Aroma of incense and wood with a suggestion of skins. Well-balanced palate with well-integrated tannins and a suggestion of wood.

TORRES DE ANGUIX 2000 CRIANZA RED
100% tinto fino

86 Deep cherry. Jammy aroma of plums and dates with fine wood (cocoa, cedar), well-integrated. Fleshy, powerful palate with good fruit expression and wood tannins well-integrated with the fruit, an elegant and round finish.

TORRES DE ANGUIX 2000 RESERVA RED
100% tinto fino

87 Dark cherry. Powerful aroma with excellent varietal expression (black fruit, spices, fallen leaves) and well-cloaked by the spicy finesse of the oak. Flavourful, fleshy palate with a good oak/fruit integration, bitter (pitch, graphite, liquorice), long and promising.

URBAN WINES

Finca El PInar, s/n
09316 Berlangas de Roa (Burgos)
☎: 947 533 006 - Fax: 947 533 010
msantamaria@ofournier.com

Established: 1979

🌐 250 📊 180,000 litres 🍇 60 has.

🍷 80% 🍇20%

URBAN OAK 2003 RED
100% tinto fino

82 Cherry with a purplish hue. Clear aroma of intense red fruit with hints of liquorice and mountain herbs. Fleshy, very flavourful palate with fruity tannins; cocoa and flowers in the finish.

URBAN OAK 2002 ROBLE RED
100% tinto fino

82 Cherry with a garnet red edge. Aroma of ripe red fruit with balsamic notes (fallen leaves) and an earthy hint. Fleshy, very flavourful palate with earthy sensations; fruity and fresh with a slightly sweet finish.

UVAGUILERA

Ctra. La Aguilera, km. 5
09400 Aranda de Duero (Burgos)
☎: 947 545 419 - Fax: 947 546 904
uvaguilera@lycos.es

Established: 1998

🌐 250 📊 100,000 litres 🍇 10 has.

🍷 50% 🍇50%

PALOMERO VENDIMIA SELECCIONADA 1999 OAK AGED RED
tinto fino   🌐 25

88 Intense cherry. Powerful aroma, rich in ripe fruit nuances with a suggestion of minerals and fine toasty oak well-blended with the wine. Powerful, full, fleshy, flavourful palate with lively and persistent tannins.

PALOMERO VENDIMIA SELECCIONADA 2000 OAK AGED RED
tinto fino   🍷 36

84 Intense cherry. Toasty aroma of unassembled oak with foresty hints of ripe fruit. Fleshy palate with oak, flavourful with ripe fruit, less complex than the previous year.

Bodegas y Viñedos VALDERIZ

Ctra. Pedrosa, km 1
09300 Roa (Burgos)
☎: 947 540 460 - Fax: 947 541 032
bodvalderiz@hotmail.com

Established: 1997

🍷 400 🛢 350,000 litres 🍇 60 has.
🍷 60% 🌐40%

SEÑORÍO DE VALDEHERMOSO JOVEN RED
VALDERIZ TOMÁS ESTEBAN RED
VALDERIZ TOMÁS ESTEBAN OAK AGED RED
VALDERIZ OAK AGED RED
SEÑORÍO DE VALDEHERMOSO CRIANZA RED

Bodegas VALDEVIÑAS

Ctra. Nacional 122, km. 245
42320 Langa de Duero (Soria)
☎: 609 113 675 - Fax: 923 181 522

Established: 2003

🍷 200 🛢 200,000 litres 🍇 16 has.
🍷 80% 🌐20%: -BE -FR -CH

MIRAT 2001 CRIANZA RED
100% tempranillo

89 Very deep garnet red cherry. Intense aroma with great finesse, black fruit and well-integrated oak with hints of terroir. Concentrated, flavourful palate, ripe fruit, well-balanced and with a powerful retronasal effect with notes of liquorice and spices; excellent acidity.

TINAR 2000 CRIANZA RED

VALDUBÓN

Antigua N-I, km. 151
09003 Milagros (Burgos)
☎: 947 546 251 - Fax: 947 546 250
valdubon@valdubon.es
www.valdubon.com

Established: 1997

🍷 1,300 🛢 800,000 litres 🍇 50 has.
🍷 70% 🌐30%: -MX -DE -FR -UK -US

VALDUBÓN 2003 ROBLE RED
VALDUBÓN 2002 CRIANZA RED
VALDUBÓN 2000 RESERVA RED

VALDUERO

Ctra. de Aranda, s/n
09440 Gumiel de Mercadol (Burgos)
☎: 947 545 459 - Fax: 947 545 609
valduerocom@bodegasvalduero.com
www.bodegasvalduero.com

Established: 1982

🍷 2,600 🛢 1,200,000 litres 🍇 250 has.
🍷 680,000 litres. 🍷 50% 🌐50%: -CH -DE -UK -US -PR -DO -JP -AT -BE -NL -CA

VALDUERO 1999 CRIANZA RED
100% tempranillo

85 Cherry with an orangey edge. Aroma of toasty skins, with notes of petals, slightly balsamic and a fine toasty hint. Flavourful palate of considerable freshness and complexity (terroir, flowers, a certain reduction).

VALDUERO 2000 CRIANZA RED
100% tempranillo

81 Deep cherry. Slightly warm aroma of very ripe black fruit and very toasty hints of wood. Fleshy, powerful palate with slightly drying wood tannins and sweetish black fruit.

VALDUERO 6 AÑOS PREMIUM 1996 RESERVA RED
100% tempranillo

88 Garnet red with an orange edge. Intense aroma with elegant notes of a long crianza (terroir, animal skins, tobacco), ripe skins and balsamic flavours. Flavourful palate with consistent black fruit tannins well-integrated with the wood, good freshness, complex notes of skins and a flavourful finish (minerals, long).

VALDUERO 1998 RESERVA RED
100% tempranillo

87 Cherry with an orangey edge. Intense aroma of terroir, pitch and fine reduction (animal skins). Flavourful palate with supple integrated tannins, good acidity and a long finish with suggestions of tobacco and spices.

VALDUERO 12 AÑOS 1990 GRAN RESERVA RED
100% tempranillo

82 Brick red. Aroma of long crianza (toasty flavours, pepper, orange peel) with a nuance of sun-drenched fruit. Flavourful palate with very fine, almost flabby tannins, toasty hints and a bitter finish, quite evolved.

VALDUERO 1995 GRAN RESERVA RED
100% tempranillo

88 Cherry with a garnet red edge. Complex toasty aroma of a long crianza (reduction, earth, tobacco) and a suggestion of balsamic black fruit. Long, flavourful palate with a good fruit weight under the crianza notes and round tannins.

VALPINCIA

Ctra. de Melida, km. 3, 5
47318 Peñafiel (Valladolid)
☎: 983 878 007 - Fax: 983 880 620
penafiel@bodegasvalpincia.com
www.valpincia.lesein.es

Established: 1991

⊞ 600 🗄 600,000 litres 🍇 110 has.

🍷 90% 🌐10%: -BE -NL -MX -DE

VALPINCIA 2003 RED
PAGOS DE VALCERRACIN 2003 RED
PAGOS DE VALCERRACIN 2002 OAK AGED RED
PAGOS DE VALCERRACIN 2001 OAK AGED RED
VALPINCIA 2001 RED
VALPINCIA 2000 RESERVA RED
GLORIA MAYOR 1998 RESERVA RED

VALSARDO DE PEÑAFIEL

Pago de Fuentecilla, s/n
47300 Peñafiel (Valladolid)
☎: 983 878 080 - Fax: 983 880 618
valsardo@valsardo.com
www.valsardo.com

Established: 1998

⊞ 428 🗄 170,000 litres 🍇 8.57 has.

🍷 80% 🌐20%

VALSARDO 2001 OAK AGED RED
100% tempranillo   🍷 24

84 Dark garnet red cherry. Intense, very fine aroma of toasty oak, well-integrated skins, minerals and spices. Flavourful palate with slightly drying yet promising tannins, fine bitter notes and good acidity.

VALDEYUSO 2001 CRIANZA RED
100% tempranillo

83 Garnet red cherry with a coppery edge. Powerful aroma with predominant smoky wood notes and varietal, slightly reduced, fruit. Flavourful, fleshy palate with a good fruit/oak integration, and bitter notes (liquorice, dark-roasted flavours), slightly warm.

VALSARDO 1998 RESERVA RED
90% tempranillo, cabernet sauvignon, merlot

82 Garnet red cherry with a brick red edge. Intense aroma with predominant reduction notes

(animals, cigar box) and a spicy hint. Flavourful, and supple on the palate with a good Reserva expression, black pepper and good acidity.

VALSARDO 1999 RESERVA RED
90% tempranillo, cabernet sauvignon, merlot

83 Dark cherry with a garnet red edge. Powerful aroma with a fine expression of the crianza (tanned hide, spices, old furniture). Flavourful palate with slightly drying tannins, quite potential, spicy, supple and slightly oily with good acidity.

VALDEYUSO 2000 OAK AGED RED

Bodegas y Viñedos VALTRAVIESO

Finca La Revilla, s/n
47316 Pinel de Arriba (Valladolid)
☎: 983 484 030 - Fax: 983 484 030

Established: 1994

⊞ 1,000 🗄 300,000 litres 🍇 85 has.

🍷 80% 🌐20%: -US -PR -MX -FR -UK -DE

VT DE VALTRAVIESO 2002 JOVEN RED
75% tinto fino, 18% cabernet sauvignon, 7% merlot

88 Intense cherry. Aroma with fruity fresh and unblended woody notes, with fine toasty hints of oak, elegant. Powerful and flavourful palate of ripe fruit but with expression, dry tannins well-blended in the alcohol.

DOMINIO DE NOGARA 2003 JOVEN RED
90% tinto fino, 5% cabernet sauvignon, 5% merlot

79 Intense cherry with a vilet edge. Powerful, fruity aroma of macerated black fruit and an underbrush nuance. Flavourful palate with fine tannins well-integrated with the ripe fruit notes and fresh acidity.

VALTRAVIESO 2001 CRIANZA RED
90% tinto fino, 5% cabernet sauvignon, 5% merlot

85 Very deep cherry. Powerful aroma of jammy plums, integrated toasty wood notes and a complex nuance (pitch). Some dryness of the wood on the palate, oily fruit tannins, with good expression (notes of liquorice, pitch) and a long finish.

VALTRAVIESO 1999 RESERVA RED
90% tinto fino, 5% cabernet sauvignon, 5% merlot

81 Very deep garnet red cherry. Intense aroma with predominant spicy oak notes and a nuance of fruit and fine reduction. Flavourful on the palate with slightly fresh tannins, fine bitter hints (dark-roasted flavours, spices) and with an acidic edge.

VALLE DE MONZÓN

Paraje El Salegar, s/n
09443 Quintana del Pidío (Burgos)
☎: 947 545 694 - Fax: 947 545 694
vallemonzon@retemail.es

www.vallemonzon.com
Established: 1993
⊞ 350 ▤ 530,000 litres ☙ 90 has.
🍷 75% 🌐25%: -CH -PR -DE

HOYO DE LA VEGA 2002 OAK AGED RED
100% tinto fino

80 Garnet red. Smoky aroma with notes of oak over the fruit and rustic hints. Fleshy, flavourful palate with oak tannins well-associated with the fruit and a well-balanced finish.

HOYO DE LA VEGA 2000 CRIANZA RED
100% tinto fino

80 Cherry with an orangey rim. Toasty aroma of wood, resins and liquorice. Very marked drying wood tannins on the palate, good acidity.

HOYO DE LA VEGA 1999 RESERVA RED
100% tinto fino

78 Not very deep cherry. Toasty, spiced, balsamic aroma. Fleshy, and well-balanced on the palate with medium persistence and a balsamic suggestion in the retronasal passage.

GROMEJÓN 2003 ROSÉ
GROMEJÓN 2003 JOVEN RED
GROMEJÓN 2002 ROSÉ
GROMEJÓN 2002 JOVEN RED
GROMEJÓN 2001 ROBLE RED
GROMEJÓN 1999 CRIANZA RED
HOYO DE LA VEGA 1999 CRIANZA RED
GROMEJÓN 1998 RESERVA RED

Bodegas y Viñedos VEGA DE YUSO

Basilón, 9
47350 Quintanilla de Onésimo (Valladolid)
☎: 983 680 054 - Fax: 983 335 001
bodega@vegadeyuso.com
www.vegadeyuso.com
Established: 2002
⊞ 120 ▤ 60,000 litres ☙ 8 has.
🍷 80% 🌐20%: -DE -BE -US

VEGA DE YUSO 2003 OAK AGED RED
100% tempranillo   ⊚3

80 Deep cherry with a violet edge. Intense aroma of jammy plums and blackberries with notes of flowers and of slightly sun-drenched maceration. Fleshy and powerful on the palate, concentrated black fruit, astringent bitterness (cocoa).

Bodegas y Viñedos VEGA REAL

Ctra. N-122, km. 298, 6
47318 Castrillo de Duero (Valladolid)
☎: 983 881 580 - Fax: 983 873 188
bodegas@vegareal.com

www.vegareal.com
Established: 1997
⊞ 700 ▤ 275,000 litres ☙ 5 has.
🍷 70% 🌐30%: -DE -CH -BE -NL -UK -JP -MX -US -BR

VEGA REAL 2003 OAK AGED UNDEFINED
VEGA REAL 2002 CRIANZA RED
VEGA REAL 2001 RESERVA RED

VEGA SICILIA

Ctra. N-122, km. 323
47359 Valbuena de Duero (Valladolid)
☎: 983 680 147 - Fax: 983 680 263
vegasicilia@vega-sicilia.com
www.vega-sicilia.com
Established: 1864
⊞ 2200 ▤ 350,000 litres ☙ 140 has.
🍷 65% 🌐35%

VEGA SICILIA RESERVA ESPECIAL AÑADAS 81-85-96 RED

98 Quite intense cherry with an orange-very lively brick red hue. Powerful aroma, rich in crianza expression (toasty pastries, jammy fruit and floral notes -violets-), with notions of classic crianza. Powerful, fleshy, full, warm palate with spicy sensations, a spicy and slightly floral retronasal effect, oak tannins well-integrated with the wine and a warm alcoholic and bitter cloaked wood finish.

VEGA SICILIA ÚNICO 1994 OAK AGED RED
85% tinto fino, 15% cabernet sauvignon, 5% merlot

97 Quite intense cherry with a brick red edge. Fine, slightly closed aroma with a rich expression of ripe black fruit and spicy notes (old leather, carpentry, hints of incense, liquorice). Generous, fleshy palate with very obvious fruit and oak tannins, well-cloaked by the alcohol, spices and creamy toast in the retronasal passage (chocolate, coffee) and a pleasantly bitter oak tannin finish.

VALBUENA 5º 2000 OAK AGED RED
85% tinto fino, 15% merlot, malbec

95 Intense cherry with an orangey-brick red edge. Medium-intensity aroma with a mild fruit and mineral expression (coffee, notes of peat, a hint of carpentry) and very ripe fruit, well-assembled. Powerful, fleshy palate with quite closed expression and powerful tannins, flavourful and spicy with jammy fruit in the retronasal passage.

VINÍCOLA DE CASTILLEJO DE ROBLEDO

Camino de las Bodegas, s/n
42328 Castillejo de Robledo (Soria)
☎: 975 355 062 - Fax: 975 355 060

DO RIBERA DEL DUERO

bodrobledo.3017@cajarural.com
www.castillejoderobledo.com

SILENTIUM 2000 CRIANZA RED

87 Fairly dark cherry with a garnet red-orange rim. Fine elegant aroma with good assemblage of wood in the wine (red cherries and creamy vanilla). Round and elegant palate with flavourful and harmonious tannins.

VIÑA ARNAIZ

Ctra. N-122 Km. 281
09316 Haza (Burgos)
☎: 947 561 066 - Fax: 947 561 066
rarevalo@jgc.es
www.vinosdefamilia.com

Established: 1998
🌐 2,200 🪣 1,500,000 litres 🍇 50 has.
🍷 80% 🌍20%: -UK -DE -US -DK

MAYOR DE CASTILLA 2002 ROBLE RED

84 Garnet red cherry. Good intensity aroma of ripe, macerated fruit. Flavourful, powerful and expressive on the palate with great fruit character and a toasty wood finish.

VIÑA ARNÁIZ 1999 CRIANZA RED
85% tinta del pais, 15% cabernet sauvignon

85 Intense garnet red cherry. Powerful aroma with a good varietal expression of the Cabernet, toasty oak notes and hints of underbrush. Flavourful on the palate with quite fresh although promising tannins and fine bitter notes (chocolate, liquorice), spicy and long.

MAYOR DE CASTILLA 2001 CRIANZA RED

84 Garnet red cherry with a saffron edge. Intense aroma with predominant toasty oak notes and a reduction nuance (varnish, leathers). Flavourful on the palate with well-integrated fruit/oak, fine bitter notes, notions of liquorice and slightly mineral hints.

VIÑA ARNÁIZ 1998 RESERVA RED
85% tinto fino, 15% cabernet sauvignon

84 Garnet red cherry with a coppery edge. Intense aroma with predominant spicy oak notes and a reduction nuance (new leather, varnish). Flavourful and slightly fleshy on the palate with well-integrated oak/fruit and good acidity.

VIÑA BUENA

Avenida Portugal, parcela 96
09400 Aranda de Duero (Burgos)
☎: 947 506 694 - Fax: 947 506 694

Established: 1986
🌐 300 🪣 500,000 litres 🍇 20 has.

FUERO REAL 2003 RED

82 Cherry with a violet edge. Intense, ripe aroma of black fruit with hints of sun-drenched skins and fresh balsamic overtones. Ripe, flavourful palate with predominant fruity notes, hints of spices and liquorice in the retronasal passage.

FUERO REAL 2002 RED

80 Cherry with a coppery glint. Intense, ripe aroma with predominant ripe fruit notes and a spicy nuance. Fresh palate with slightly green tannins, good acidity.

SEÑORÍO DE VALDERRAMA 2002 OAK AGED RED
tempranillo

80 Dark garnet red cherry. Powerful aroma of jammy black fruit with a suggestion of toasty oak. Flavourful palate with a good oak/fruit integration, bitter and pleasant.

FUERO REAL 1999 CRIANZA RED

80 Garnet red cherry. Intense aroma of well-associated fruit and oak with a balsamic suggestion of overripe fruit and fine reduction notes. Flavourful palate with fine bitter notes and hints of reduction, lacks balance.

SEÑORÍO DE VALDERRAMA 1999 CRIANZA RED
tempranillo

79 Dark cherry with a coppery edge. Intense aroma with toasty oak notes and a suggestion of ripe fruit. Flavourful palate with good crianza expression and hints of aged wood.

SEÑORÍO DE VALDERRAMA 1996 RESERVA RED
100% tempranillo

79 Dark cherry with a saffron rim. Powerful, ripe aroma with hints of reduction (animals, withered petals) and toasty wood. Flavourful, fleshy palate with a slightly oily texture, a liquorice hint and hints of damp earth.

VIÑA BUENA 2003 RED

VIÑA MAMBRILLA

Ctra. Pedrosa s/n
09318 Mambrilla de Castrejón (Burgos)
☎: 947 540 234 - Fax: 947 540 234
bodega@mambrilla.com
www.mambrilla.com

Established: 2000
🌐 222 🪣 220,000 litres 🍇 40 has.
🍷 90% 🌍10%

ALIDIS 2003 JOVEN RED

80 Cherry with a purple hue. Aroma of fresh red fruit, maceration notes and slightly spicy. Fruity, very fresh palate with liquorice and balsamic flavours in the finish.

ALIDIS 2002 OAK AGED RED
tempranillo 🏺 4

82 Lively garnet red cherry. Quite intense aroma with predominant spicy oak notes. Flavourful palate with a good oak/fruit integration and fresh overtones of the skins, warm, liquorice and dark-roasted flavours in the finish.

ALIDIS 2001 CRIANZA RED

80 Very deep garnet red. Aroma of toasty wood, balsamic flavour and slightly alcoholic. Drying palate with quite aggressive wood tannins but with good fruit weight and nuances of smoke.

Bodegas y Viñedos VIÑA MAYOR

Ctra. Valladolid - Soria, km. 325, 6
47350 Quintanilla de Onésimo (Valladolid)
☎: 915 006 000 - Fax: 914 763 713
barcelo@habarcelo.es
www.habarcelo.es

Established: 1986

🛢 8,000 📊 4,500,000 litres 🍇 10 has.

🏷 75% 🌐25%: -UE -UK -CA -US -SAM -SDV

VIÑA MAYOR 2003 ROBLE RED
100% tinto fino

78 Cherry. Aroma of ripe red fruit and earth with light toasty notes and vanilla. Good acidity, light bitter notes and well-integrated tannins on the palate.

VIÑA MAYOR 2001 CRIANZA RED
100% tinto fino

82 Cherry with a brick red edge. Aroma of toasty wood, smoky, tobacco. Slightly marked wood tannins on the palate with toasty notes, well-balanced.

SECRETO VIÑA MAYOR 2000 RESERVA RED
100% tinto fino

86 Ruby red cherry. Medium-intensity, balsamic aroma of very ripe red fruit. Fleshy, well-balanced palate with well-integrated wood and fruit tannins, medium persistence.

VIÑA MAYOR 2000 RESERVA RED
100% tinto fino

82 Cherry with an orangey rim. Aroma of toasty wood, balsamic and sweet red fruit notes. Well-balanced on the palate with medium persistence and oak in the retronasal passage.

SECRETO VIÑA MAYOR 1999 RESERVA RED
100% tinto fino

80 Cherry with a garnet red edge. Medium-intensity aroma, not very expressive, with notes of wood and fruit. Round, flavourful palate, better than in the nose.

VIÑA MAYOR 1996 GRAN RESERVA RED
100% tinto fino

80 Cherry with a brick red nuance. Aroma with reduction notes (tobacco), toasty wood and red fruit in liqueur. Round, pleasant palate with polished tannins.

VIÑA SOLORCA

Ctra. Circunvalación, s/n
09300 Roa de Duero (Burgos)
☎: 947 561 109 - Fax: 947 540 035
info@vina-solorca.com
www.viña-solorca.com

Established: 1998

⊕ 1,300 ▦ 500,000 litres ⚘ 70 has.

🚩 70% 🌐30%: -US -UK -NL -DK -BE -DK -CH -AT -JP

GRAN SOLORCA 1999 RESERVA RED
100% tempranillo

84 Dark cherry with a garnet red rim. Powerful aroma with predominant toasty oak notes and hints of terracotta. Flavourful palate with promising but somewhat fresh tannins, bitter and quite concentrated.

VIÑA SOLORCA 2003 RED
100% tempranillo

80 Dark cherry with a purplish hue. Powerful aroma of black fruit with notes of macerated skins, sweet with damp earth. Flavourful palate with slightly drying tannins that conceal the fruit, a spicy nuance.

VIÑA SOLORCA 2002 OAK AGED RED
VIÑA SOLORCA 2000 CRIANZA RED
BARÓN DEL VALLE 2000 CRIANZA RED
VIÑA SOLORCA VENDIMIA SELECCIONADA
2001 CRIANZA RED
BARÓN DEL VALLE 1999 RESERVA RED

VIÑA TUELDA

Camino de las Bodegas, 23
09310 Villatuelda (Burgos)
☎: 947 551 145 - Fax: 947 551 145
mauroh@terra.es

Established: 1998

⊕ 300 ▦ 120,000 litres ⚘ 15 has.

🚩 80% 🌐20%: -AT -US -DE

VIÑA TUELDA 2003 JOVEN RED
VIÑA TUELDA 2001 OAK AGED RED
VIÑA TUELDA 2001 CRIANZA RED
VIÑA TUELDA 2000 RESERVA RED

VIÑA VILANO

Ctra. de Anguix, 10
09314 Pedrosa de Duero (Burgos)
☎: 947 530 029 - Fax: 947 530 037
info@vinavilano.com
www.vinavilano.com

Established: 1957

⊕ 800 ▦ 2,200,000 litres ⚘ 350 has.

🚩 70% 🌐30%: -DE -SE -BE -CH -CA -US -MX -AT

VIÑA VILANO 2000 RESERVA RED

88 Deep cherry with a ruby red edge. Intense aroma, subtle, fruity, reminiscent of stewed red fruit, fresh skins, smoky. Flavourful, very fresh palate, fruity tannins, well-balanced toasty notes, unlike a Reserva.

VIÑA VILANO 2003 ROSÉ
VIÑA VILANO 2003 RED
VIÑA VILANO 2002 RED
VIÑA VILANO 2001 CRIANZA RED
VIÑA VILANO 1999 RESERVA RED

VIÑALCASTA

Pago de los Quiñones
49810 Morales de Toro (Zamora)
☎: 983 376 979 - Fax: 983 340 824
b.burlon@terra.es

Established: 1998

⊕ 600 ▦ 150,000 litres ⚘ 40 has.

🚩 50% 🌐50%

VILLACAMPA DEL MARQUÉS 2002 ROBLE
RED
VILLACAMPA DEL MARQUÉS 2000 CRIANZA
RED

Cooperativa Virgen de las VIÑAS

Ctra. Madrid-Burgos, s/n
09400 Aranda de Duero (Burgos)
☎: 947 501 311 - Fax: 947 501 219

Established: 1963

⊕ 300 ▦ 2,000,000 litres ⚘ 350 has.

🚩 90% 🌐10%

TIERRA ARANDA ROSÉ
VEGA PRIVANZA ROSÉ
TIERRA ARANDA RED
VEGA PRIVANZA RED
TIERRA ARANDA CRIANZA RED

DO RIBERA DEL DUERO

VIRGEN DE LA ASUNCIÓN

Las Afueras, s/n
09311 La Horra (Burgos)
☎: 947 542 057 - Fax: 947 542 057
info@virgendelaasuncion.com
www.virgendelaasuncion.com

Established: 1957

🏭 700 🍶 1,200,000 litres 🍇 450 has.
🇪🇸 55% 🌐45%

VIÑA VALERA JOVEN ROSÉ
VIÑA VALERA JOVEN RED
VIÑA VALERA ROBLE RED
VIÑA VALERA CRIANZA RED
VIÑA VALERA RESERVA RED

VIRGEN DE LA VEGA

Ctra. de Pedrosa s/n
09300 Roa (Burgos)
☎: 947 540 224 - Fax: 947 541 811
informacion@vinos-roa-rauda.com
www.vinos-roa-rauda.com

Established: 1956

🏭 550 🍶 3,000,000 litres 🍇 440 has.
🇪🇸 92% 🌐8%: -DE -CH

RAUDA 2003 JOVEN RED
100% tinto fino

78 Cherry with a violet rim. Vinous aroma with regional character. Light palate, a little flat and without great expressivity.

RAUDA 2001 CRIANZA RED
100% tinto fino

83 Garnet red with shades of Bigarreau cherry. Aroma of lactics and red fruit with jammy hints. Round tannins on the palate, good body and acidity, slightly drying, well-assembled with the wood, coffee in the finish.

RAUDA 2003 JOVEN ROSÉ
RAUDA 2002 JOVEN RED
RAUDA VIEJO 1998 RESERVA RED

Bodegas VIYUELA

Ctra. de Quintanamanvirgo, s/n
09314 Boada de Roa (Burgos)
☎: 947 530 072 - Fax: 947 530 075
andres.gonzalez@novodelta.com

Established: 2003

🏭 240 🍶 141,000 litres 🍇 3,5 has.
🍶 93,000 litres. 🇪🇸 100%

VIYUELA 2003 ROBLE RED
100% tinta del país   🏭 4

82 Dark cherry. Fruity aroma with hints of skin maceration and ripe fruit. Fresh, fruity, flavourful palate with body.

VIYUELA 2003 ROBLE RED
100% tinta del país

86 Intense cherry. Quite ripe and expressive fruity aroma with fine toasty notes. Powerful, flavourful palate with ripe but fresh and fine fruit and toasty notes in the retronasal passage.

VIZCARRA-RAMOS

Ctra. Roa Peñafiel, 17
09317 Membrilla de Castrejón (Burgos)
☎: 947 540 340 - Fax: 947 540 340
bodegas-vizcarra@wanadoo.es
www.masbytes.es/vizcarra

Established: 1991

🏭 350 🍶 250,000 litres 🍇 22 has. 🇪🇸 70%
🌐30%: -US -DE -FR -PR -NL -CH -MX

VIZCARRA SENDA DEL ORO 2003 ROBLE RED
100% tinto fino

87 Intense cherry. Aroma with notes of ripe fruit with toasty, very elegant nuances (coffee and dark chocolate). Powerful palate with character, flavourful with good fruit/toasty oak integration and a persistent finish. Much better than the 2000 vintage.

VIZCARRA TORRALVO 2001 OAK AGED RED
100% tinto fino

88 Intense cherry. Spicy aroma of jammy fruit with animal nuances (new leather, pipe tobacco). Oily, round flavourful palate with spices in the retronasal passage and supple and polished tannins.

VIZCARRA 2001 CRIANZA RED
100% tinto fino

88 Intense cherry. Powerful, complex, original aroma with fine toasty flavours of creamy oak and jammy fruit but quite expressive. Oily, powerful palate rich in toasty fine nuances, and solid but ripe tannins, very flavourful. A great change in this vineyard's wines.

VIZCARRA 2003 MACERACIÓN CARBÓNICA RED
CELIA VIZCARRA 2003 RED

WILLIAMS & HUMBERT

Ctra. N-IV, km. 641, 75
11408 Jerez de la Frontera (Cádiz)
☎: 956 353 400 - Fax: 956 353 411
williams@williams-humbert.com

www.williams-humbert.com

Established: 1877

🌐 70,000 📊 35,000,000 litres 🍇 500 has.

🍷 35% 🌐65%

MARQUÉS DE POLAVIEJA 2002 RED

77 Garnet red with a brick red edge. Spicy aroma with dry earth and a long crianza. Ripe palate with fresh, light tannins and notes of very sweet wood (vanilla).

MARQUÉS DE POLAVIEJA CRIANZA RED

84 Deep cherry. Aroma of long crianza (leather, mild varnish) with jammy black fruit and a notion of terroir. Fleshy palate with noticeable but supple oak tannins, flavourful with a spicy and toasty finish.

MARQUÉS DE POLAVIEJA 1998 RESERVA RED

78 Garnet red with a brick red edge. Toasty aroma of crianza with reduction notes (animals, leather). Fleshy palate with silky oak tannins yet predominating the fruit, a suggestion of reduction and oak in the finish.

WINNER WINES

Adelfas, 18 3ºB
28007 Madrid
☎: 915 019 042 - Fax: 915 017 794
rsaseta@winnerwines.es
www.winnerwines.es

Established: 1986

🌐 550 📊 1,200,000 litres 🍇 400 has.

🍷 8% 🌐92%: -US -CA -MX -DO -PR -SG -JP -CH -IT -FR -DE -SE -FI -DK -BE -AT -DK

IBERNOBLE 2001 ROBLE RED
90% tempranillo, 10% cabernet sauvignon

80 Deep cherry with a garnet red edge. Slightly closed aroma with notes of toastiness and soil and a suggestion of jammy prunes. Fleshy, powerful palate with oily and woody tannins and a vanilla and slightly bitter finish.

IBERNOBLE 2000 CRIANZA RED
90% tempranillo, 10% cabernet sauvignon

78 Garnet red with a brick red edge. Aroma with notes of animal skins and tobacco (reduction), with a toasty suggestion. Fleshy palate with slightly rough wood tannins and rustic traces; fresh.

IBERNOBLE 1999 RESERVA RED
90% tempranillo, 10% cabernet sauvignon

81 Garnet red with an orange edge. Toasty aroma with predominant hints of oak and reduction and a suggestion of earth. Fleshy palate with astringent wood and dry tannins, graphite in the finish, fresh.

IBERNOBLE COSECHA 2003 RED
90% tempranillo, 10% cabernet sauvignon

80 Cherry with a purplish hue. Fruity aroma with warm and slightly ripe strawberries and a hint of liquorice. Fleshy, flavourful palate with fruity tannins (strawberry pulp).

Grupo YLLERA

Ctra. Madrid - Coruña, km. 173, 5
47490 Rueda (Valladolid)
☎: 983 868 097 - Fax: 983 868 177
grupoyllera@grupoyllera.com
www.grupoyllera.com

Established: 1972

🌐 13,500 📊 6,000,000 litres 🍇 70 has.

🍷 85% 🌐15%: -UE -CH -US -MX -GT -DO -BR -JP

VIÑA DEL VAL 2003 JOVEN RED
100% tempranillo

84 Lively garnet red cherry. Powerful aroma with excellent varietal expression (black fruit, underbrush) and toasty skins. Fleshy palate with slightly marked but flavourful tannins, fine spicy notes and terroir.

BRACAMONTE 2002 ROBLE RED
100% tempranillo

81 Dark garnet red cherry. Intense aroma with not very fine reduction notes (petals,stewed meat) and a spicy suggestion of oak. Better on the palate, fleshy with good fruit/oak integration and bitter (hints of overextraction), long.

BRACAMONTE 2000 CRIANZA RED
100% tempranillo

82 Black cherry. Powerful aroma with predominant burnt notes and a suggestion of jammy black fruit. Fleshy palate with slightly marked yet promising tannins and bitter hints (liquorice, dark-roasted flavours).

BRACAMONTE 1999 RESERVA RED
100% tempranillo

80 Cherry with an orangey hue. Aroma with balsamic notes, toasty wood and dark-roasted flavours. Flavourful, warm palate with hints of red fruit.

DO RIBERA DEL GUADIANA

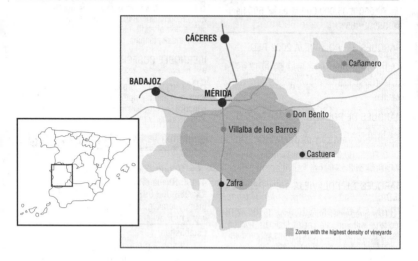

NEWS. In 2003, a winter that was colder than usual and a summer of infernal heat caused a decrease in the harvest, besides affecting the quality of the earlier varieties (*Merlot* and *Macabeo*) harvested at the beginning of August, forcing many batches to be rejected. The *Tempranillo* had better luck. This grape variety, which makes up 50% of the wines rated in 2003, showed better quality, except for those harvested on plots with poorer soil that really suffered the consequences of the heatwave.

Hectares of Vineyard	No. of Viticulturists	No. of Bodegas	2003 Harvest	2003 Production	Marketing
22,000	2,603	111(46 bottlers)	Good	-	60% foreign 40% Spain

Ribera del Guadiana is still pushing its export policy, given the reasonable prices of its wines. In fact, in 2003, it exported almost a million litres. However, of the 83 wines tasted, only 20 surpassed 80 points and none reached 85, the most outstanding being the Leyendas of Vega Esteban, from Ventura de Vega, with 84 points. This same cellar also achieved the highest score for a 2003 Harvest wine, within a rather poor year, as its Cadencias de Vega Esteban hardly surpassed 80 points.

LOCATION. Covering the 6 wine-growing regions of Extremadura, with a total surface of more than 87,000 Ha as described below.

SUB-REGIONS:

Cañamero. To the south east of the province of Cáceres, in the heart of the Sierra de Guadalupe. It comprises the municipal districts of Alia, Berzocana, Cañamero, Guadalupe and Valdecaballeros. The vineyards are located on the mountainside, at altitudes of between 600 m to 800 m. The terrain is rugged and the soil is slaty and loose. The climate is mild without great temperature contrasts, and the average annual rainfall is 750 mm to 800 mm. The main grape variety is the white *Alarije*.

Montánchez. Comprising 27 municipal districts. It is characterised by its complex terrain, with numerous hills and small valleys. The vineyards are located on brown acidic soil. The climate is Continental in nature and the average annual rainfall is between 500 mm and 600 mm. The white grape variety *Borba* occupies two thirds of the vineyards in the region.

Ribera Alta. This covers the Vegas del Guadiana and the plains of La Serena and Campo de Castuera and comprises 38 municipal districts. The soil is very sandy. The most common varieties are *Alarije, Borba* (white), *Tempranillo* and *Garnacha* (red).

Ribera Baja. Comprising 11 municipal districts. The vineyards are located on clayey-limy soil. The climate is Continental, with a moderate Atlantic influence and slight contrasts in temperature. The most common varieties are: *Cayetana Blanca* and *Pardina* among the whites, and *Tempranillo* among the reds.

Matanegra. Rather similar to Tierra de Barros, but with a milder climate. It comprises 8 municipal districts, and the most common grape varieties are *Beba, Montua* (whites), *Tempranillo, Garnacha* and *Cabernet Sauvignon* (reds).

Tierra de Barros. Situated in the centre of the province of Badajoz and the largest (4475 Ha and 37 municipal districts). It has flat plains with fertile soils which are rich in nutrients and have great water retention capacity (Rainfall is low: 350 mm to 450 mm per year). The most common varieties are the white *Cayetana Blanca* and *Pardina*, and the red *Tempranillo, Garnacha* and *Cabernet Sauvignon*.

VARIETIES:

White: *Alarije, Borba, Cayetana Blanca, Pardina, Macabeo, Chardonnay, Chelva or Montua, Malvar, Parellada, Pedro Ximénez, Verdejo, Eva, Cigüente, Perruno, Moscatel de Alejandría, Moscatel de Grano Menudo* and *Sauvignon Blanc.*

Red: *Garnacha Tinta, Tempranillo, Bobal, Cabernet Sauvignon, Garnacha Tintorera, Graciano, Mazuela, Merlot, Monastrell, Syrah, Pinot Noir* and *Jaén Tinto.*

REGULATORY COUNCIL.

Ctra. Sevilla-Gijón, Km 114. 06200 Almendralejo (Badajoz). Apdo. Correos 299.
Tel: 924 671 302. Fax: 924 664 703.
E-mail: informacion@riberadelguadiana.org

GENERAL CHARACTERISTICS OF THE WINES:

Whites	With the differences that may appear between the different sub-regions, the white wines are substantial, with a Mediterranean character (mountain herbs, undergrowth, supple on the palate, but at the same time, persistent and very flavourful).
Rosés	Except for some modern wine production with the usual raspberry flavour, they are, in general, warm, very fruity and with a point of sweetness produced by the high alcohol content.
Reds	The red wines are powerful, warm, supple, with sweet tannins and smoothness, even those based on the *Tempranillo*. Flavours of sunny vineyards with *Garnacha* that provide the ripe and fruity nuance characteristic of this grape variety.

Bodegas AGAPITA RUBIO BRAVO

José Manuel Durán, 17
10136 Cañamero (Cáceres)
☎: 927 369 192 - Fax: 927 369 437
Established: 1948
⬚ 180 ▪ 1,100,000 litres ⬚ 30 has.
⬚ 100%

CAMPO ROYERO 2001 CRIANZA RED

ANTONIO MEDINA E HIJOS

Cestería, 4
06300 Zafra (Badajoz)
☎: 924 575 060 - Fax: 924 575 076
amedina@coeba.es
www.bodegasmedina.net
Established: 1931
⬚ 4,000 ▪ 3,000,000 litres ⬚ 250 has.
⬚ 65% ⬚35%: -JP -CH -DE -HU -AT -
BE -DK -FR -UK -IE -IT -NL -SE -RU -CA -
MX -TW

DIFERENTE 2002 JOVEN RED
tempranillo

78 Garnet red cherry with a brick red edge.
Intense aroma of somewhat varietal, reduced ripe
fruit. Flavourful, fleshy palate with fine bitter notes
(liquorice, chocolate).

DIFERENTE 2000 CRIANZA RED
tempranillo, cabernet sauvignon

70 Not very deep cherry. Aroma with reduction notes, balsamic flavours, strawberries and
sweet blackberries. Very marked, dry wood tannins on the palate although with suggestions of
light reduction and red fruit in the retronasal
passage.

BERNARDA GONZÁLEZ PACHECO

Alberca, 34
06200 Almendralejo (Badajoz)
☎: 924 671 268 - Fax: 924 671 268
bodegasbernarda@bodegasbernarda.com
www.bodegasbernarda.com

NOBLEZA DE BARROS JOVEN RED

CASIMIRO TORIBIO BORAITA

Luis Chamizo, 12 y 21
06310 Puebla de Sancho Pérez (Badajoz)

☎: 924 551 449 - Fax: 924 551 449
info@bodegastoribio.com
www.bodegastoribio.com
Established: 1953
⬚ 250 ▪ 800,000 litres ⬚ 50 has.
⬚ 95% ⬚5%: -DE -NL -SE

VIÑA PUEBLA 2003 FERMENTADO EN
BARRICA WHITE
100% macabeo

81 Brilliant pale yellow. Intense aroma of fine
smoky oak, a white fruit hint and hints of fennel.
Flavourful and bitter on the palate, slightly warm,
and oily with good acidity.

VIÑA PUEBLA MACABEO 2003 WHITE
100% macabeo

74 Pale yellow with a golden hue. Quite intense,
fruity aroma without great nuances. Quite flavourful palate with a slightly acidic edge.

VIÑA PUEBLA 2003 JOVEN RED
tempranillo

78 Not very deep Bigarreau cherry. Intense, clean
aroma of strawberries, lactics and flowers. Sweet
palate, quite low in acidity with well-integrated
fruit tannins and medium persistence.

VIÑA PUEBLA 2001 CRIANZA RED
100% tempranillo

79 Garnet red cherry with a brick red glint.
Powerful aroma with predominant toasty wood
notes. Flavourful, bitter palate (dark-roasted flavours); without great nuances.

LAGAR DE PUEBLA WHITE
LAGAR DE PUEBLA RED
CHAPARRAL CRIANZA RED
SEÑORIO DE PUEBLA CRIANZA RED
VIÑA TORIBIO CRIANZA RED
VIÑA PUEBLA 2001 RESERVA RED

CASTELAR

Avenida de Extremadura, 1
06228 Hornachos (Badajoz)
☎: 924 533 073 - Fax: 924 533 493
bodega@bodegascastelar.com
www.bodegascastelar.com
Established: 1963
⬚ 800 ▪ 2,000,000 litres ⬚ 120 has.
⬚ 90% ⬚10%: -UE -US

CASTELAR 2003 WHITE
CASTELAR 2003 RED
PAGO DE LAS MONJAS 2002 RED
CASTELAR 2001 CRIANZA RED
CASTELAR 1997 RESERVA RED

DOLORES MORENAS

Polígono Industrial La Nava
06230 Los Santos de Maimona (Badajoz)
☎: 924 544 158 - Fax: 924 572 342
dmorenas@doloresmorenas.com
www.doloresmorenas.com

Established: 1930

🛢 300 📊 500,000 litres 🌿 63 has.

🚩 60% 🌐40%: -DE -AT -BE -DK -FR -NL -CH -UK

ZAGALÓN 2003 JOVEN WHITE
100% macabeo

78 Pale steel. Short, quite fruity aroma with a nuance of hay. Flavourful palate, slightly oily, hay; very pleasant with good acidity.

ZAGALÓN 2003 JOVEN RED
tempranillo, garancha

77 Garnet red cherry. Not very intense yet fresh aroma of red fruit. Flavourful, fresh, light and expressive on the palate.

MELITHON 2001 CRIANZA RED
80% tempranillo, 20% garnacha

82 Garnet red with an orange edge. Aroma of black pepper, fine toasty notes and jammy ripe fruit. Fleshy, powerful palate with marked wood tannins, abundant ripe fruit and a long, sweet finish.

REAL PROVISIÓN 2002 CRIANZA RED
100% tempranillo

80 Cherry with a raspberry edge. Aroma of very ripe strawberries, spicy notes and with a suggestion of viscosity. Fleshy, fresh palate with fruity tannins and a slightly green finish.

REAL PROVISIÓN 2001 RESERVA RED
100% tempranillo

80 Deep garnet red. Spicy aroma with fine notes of oak (cedar, pepper) over the fruit. Fleshy palate with ripe, flavourful tannins, marked toasty wood and a fresh finish.

KARAVEL 2002 WHITE SWEET
REAL PROVISIÓN 2002 OAK AGED RED

EXAGRAVÍN

Carretera Olivenza, km. 8, 5
06005 Badajoz (Badajoz)
☎: 924 248 135 - Fax: 924 261 820
exagravin@hotmail.com

Established: 1961

🛢 700 📊 4,700,000 litres 🌿 480 has.

🚩 70% 🌐30%

TELENA MACABEO 2003 JOVEN WHITE
TELENA JOVEN ROSÉ
TELENA 2002 RED
TELENA 2000 CRIANZA RED

Hijos de FRANCISCO ESCASO

Carretera Villafranca, 15
06360 Fuente del Maestre (Badajoz)
☎: 924 530 012 - Fax: 924 531 703
bodegasescaso@infonegocio.com

Established: 1942

⊕ 300 📖 2,000,000 litres 🌱 120 has.
🍷 100%

VALLARCAL 2003 JOVEN WHITE
100% cayetana blanca

79 Pale straw. Clean, fresh aroma of hay and a ripe white fruit hint. Fresh, flavourful palate, slightly oily with good bitter-acidic balance.

VALLARCAL 2002

72 Yellow straw. Aroma of slightly reduced fruit yet well-mannered. Somewhat fruity with an edge of acidity on the palate.

VALLARCAL 2002 ROBLE RED
100% tempranillo

80 Very deep intense cherry. Aroma of ripe black fruit, toasted hints of skins, pepper and dust. Fleshy, powerful palate (jammy fruit) with ripe, earthy tannins and a ripe finish.

VALLARCAL 2002 CRIANZA RED
80% tempranillo, 20% garnacha

77 Dark garnet red. Perfumed, earthy, and slightly sweet, spicy aroma. Drying palate with bitter notes, good acidity and a suggestion of toasted wood in the retronasal passage.

FLOR DE LÍBANO 2003 WHITE
VIÑA MAGNA 2003 WHITE
DOÑANA 2003 WHITE
SIERRAPINO 2003 WHITE
VALLARCAL 2003 JOVEN RED
FLOR DE LÍBANO 2003 RED
VIÑA MAGNA 2003 RED
DOÑANA 2003 RED
SIERRAPINO 2003 RED

FRANCO-SÁNCHEZ

Pilones, 24
10100 Miajadas (Cáceres)
☎: 927 347 274 - Fax: 927 348 751
francosanchez@francosanchez.com
www.francosanchez.com

Established: 1955
⊕ 45 📖 280,000 litres 🍷 100%

BÚRDALO 2001 RED
100% tempranillo

75 Cherry with an orangey hue. Not very intense yet clean aroma with a nuance of jammy fruit. Quite fruity and ripe on the palate, without great nuances but well-mannered.

CASA ALBADRI 2000 CRIANZA RED
100% tempranillo

75 Dark cherry with a coppery edge. Powerful, toasty aroma with reduction notes (aged wood).

Flavourful, bitter palate without great nuances and not very clean.

Compañía Vinícola del GUADIANA

Labrador, 5
06200 Almendralejo (Badajoz)
☎: 924 661 080 - Fax: 924 671 413
vigua@vinicolaguadiana.com
www.vinicolaguadiana.com

Established: 2000
⊕ 100 📖 1,000,000 litres 🌱 200 has.
🍷 70% 🌐30%: -DK -UK -DE -DK -SE -FI -PT

BASANGUS 2000 RED

80 Deep garnet red cherry. Aroma of jammy fruit and toasty dark-roasted flavours; hints of reduction. Fleshy palate with marked oak tannins over the slightly ripe fruit; a slightly drying finish and warm overtones assembling the ensemble.

VIGUA 2001 RED
100% tempranillo

78 Garnet red cherry. Intense aroma, good varietal expression (black fruit, spices), fine smoky oak. Fleshy palate, flavourful, slightly astringent wood tannins that conceal the fruit; notes of terroir in the finish.

BASANGUS 2001 CRIANZA RED
100% tempranillo

78 Medium-high hue garnet red. Aroma of toasted wood, vanilla and light reduction. Drying tannins on the palate, long with green notes.

J. SILVA

Avenida de Mérida, 10
06810 Calamonte (Badajoz)
☎: 924 324 005 - Fax: 924 324 005

Established: 1949
📖 500,000 litres

SEÑORÍO DE SILVA JOVEN WHITE
SEÑORÍO DE SILVA JOVEN RED

JUAN ROMERO FUENTES

Avenida Magaz, s/n
06392 El Raposo (Badajoz)
☎: 924 570 448 - Fax: 924 570 448
romero@bodegasromero.com
www.bodegasromero.com

Established: 1954
⊕ 80 📖 400,000 litres 🌱 20 has.
🍷 90% 🌐10%: -CH -DE

DOMINIO DE CAELES 2001 JOVEN RED
100% tempranillo

75 Brilliant deep cherry. Aroma of very ripe, jammy black fruit and sun-drenched skins. Fleshy, warm palate with ripe tannins, sun-drenched fruit and a round finish.

PRADOMAYO ECOLOGICO 2002 OAK AGED RED
DOMINIO DE CAELES 2000 CRIANZA RED

LAR DE BARROS-INVIOSA

La Fuente, 8
06200 Almendralejo (Badajoz)
☎: 924 671 235 - Fax: 924 665 932
info@lardebarros.com
www.lardebarros.com

Established: 1931

🌐 2,500 📊 2,000,000 litres 🍷 400 has.

🍷 60% 🌐40%: -US -MX -CA -JP -PR -TW -PL -CH -SE -DK -DE -DK -UK -NL -BE -FR

LAR DE BARROS MACABEO 2003 WHITE
LAR DE BARROS 2003 ROSÉ
LAR DE BARROS TEMPRANILLO 2003 JOVEN RED
LAR DE BARROS 2003 ROBLE RED
LAR DE BARROS 2001 CRIANZA RED

LAR DE LARES 1998 RESERVA RED

LAS GRANADAS

Avenida de Madrid, s/n
10200 Trujillo (Cáceres)
☎: 927 312 048 - Fax: 927 321 300
jmgarcia@hotelasciguenas.com

Established: 1975

🌐 1,600 📊 1,000,000 litres 🍷 110 has.

🍷 90% 🌐10%: -DK -NL

TARYALA 2001 CRIANZA RED
tempranillo

79 Dark garnet red cherry. Intense aroma of fine smoky oak and jammy black fruit notes. Flavourful palate with slightly marked, sweet tannins, bitter hints and a slightly acidic edge.

TORRE JULIA 2000 RESERVA RED
90% cabernet sauvignon, 10% tempranillo

78 Cherry with an orangey edge. Ripe, slightly varietal aroma of liquorice, and ink. Palate with very toasty oak (almost burnt) and ripe fruit; well-mannered.

ALTAMIRANO 2003 WHITE
PITARRA 2003 RED
LAGARES 2002 CRIANZA RED

MARCELINO DÍAZ

López de Ayala, 13
06200 Almendralejo (Badajoz)
☎: 924 677 548 - Fax: 924 660 977
bodega@madiaz.com
www.madiaz.com

Established: 1931

🌐 500 📊 150,000 litres 🍷 100 has.

🍷 60% 🌐40%: -DE -BE -DK -NL -AT -PT -FR IS -UK -MT -CH -NO.-US -CA -MX -NI -JP -TH

PUERTA PALMA 2002 ROBLE RED
80% tempranillo, 15% cabernet sauvignon, 5% graciano
🌐 6

78 Medium-hue garnet red. Spicy, lactic aroma with an element of ripe fruit. Drying, bitter palate with medium persistence.

PUERTA PALMA FINCA LAS TENDERAS 2001 CRIANZA RED
90% tempranillo, 10% cabernet sauvignon

75 Cherry with a brick red hue. Spicy, toasty aroma of ripe red fruit. Drying palate with very marked wood tannins.

PUERTA PALMA FINCA EL CAMPILLO 2001 RESERVA RED
80% tempranillo, 15% graciano

82 Dark cherry with a dark red edge. Powerful, spicy aroma with ripe fruit and notes of damp wood. Flavourful, fleshy palate with slightly marked tannins, bitter hints and a light touch of greenness.

PUERTA PALMA 2003 WHITE

MARTÍNEZ PAYVA

Carretera Gijón - Sevilla, N-630, km. 646
06200 Almendralejo (Badajoz)
☎: 924 671 130 - Fax: 924 663 056
bodega@depayva.net

DO RIBERA DEL GUADIANA

www.depayva.net
Established: 1979
🏭 900 🛢 1,800,000 litres 🍇 350 has.
🍷 70% 🌐30%: -US -CA -NL -DE

PAYVA CAYETANA BLANCA 2003 WHITE
100% cayetana blanca

59 Straw-coloured with a golden glimmer. Obvious off-odours in the nose and on the palate.

RÍO PAYVA 2003 WHITE DE AGUJA
100% moscatel

70 Pale with a greenish nuance. Ripe, fresh, grapey aroma with a slightly vegetative hint. Sweet palate with bitter notes and lemon sorbet.

DOÑA FRANCISQUITA 2003 JOVEN RED
90% tempranillo, 10% garnacha

75 Deep cherry. Herbaceous aroma of black fruit and earth. Flavourful palate with ripe tannins, a suggestion of red berries and a flavourful finish.

PAYVA 2001 CRIANZA RED
80% tempranillo, 20% graciano

78 Garnet red with an orange edge. Spicy aroma with notes of oak reduction, ripe fruit and hints of earth. Fleshy, warm palate with noticeable wood tannins over the ripe fruit; quite sweet.

JM ORTEA TEMPRANILLO 2000 CRIANZA RED
tempranillo

74 Intense cherry with an orangey edge. Aroma with strong toasted notes (coffee, popcorn). Rough, incisive tannins on the palate; lacking both fruity and fleshy overtones.

PAYVA 2000 CRIANZA RED
100% cabernet sauvignon

79 Intense cherry. Aroma with notes of toasty oak and ripe fruit (jammy cherries and blackberries). Round, flavourful, fruity palate, an aftertaste of toasty oak.

SEÑORÍO DE PAYVA 1998 RESERVA RED
80% tempranillo, 20% graciano

78 Garnet red with a brick red edge. Warm aroma with reduction notes (leather, cigar box) and ripe fruit. Fleshy palate with ripe fruit tannins, pungent wood overtones and an element of greeness.

PAYVA CHARDONNAY 2003 WHITE
PAYVA 2003 WHITE
RÍO PAYVA 2003 JOVEN RED

MIGUEL A. MATAMOROS

San Isidro, 23
06310 Puebla de Sancho (Badajoz)
☎: 924 551 431 - Fax: 924 551 431

VEGA DE LA MOTA 2003 JOVEN RED

80 Intense cherry. Smoky aroma with a viscous edge, earthy notes and very ripe red fruit. Fleshy palate with bramble fruit, astringent tannins (liquorice) and a fruity finish.

Sociedad Cooperativa MONTEVIRGEN

Hermano Rocha, 18
06208 Villalba de los Barros (Badajoz)
☎: 924 685 025 - Fax: 924 685 050
cooperativa@montevigen.com
www.montevirgen.com
Established: 1962
🏭 100 🛢 22,000,000 litres 🍇 3.700 has.
🍷 75% 🌐25%: -PT -IT -BE -US

MARQUÉS M. DE VILLALBA 2003 WHITE
pardina

74 Straw-coloured with a greenish hue. Not very intense aroma with notes of scrubland and a nuance of white fruit. Light palate with good acid-bitter balance although without great expression of the vine variety.

SEÑORÍO DE VILLALBA 2003 ROSÉ
tempranillo, pardina

74 Pale pink. Not very intense yet clear, fruity aroma. Light, fresh palate with red fruit and lively acidity.

MARQUÉS M. DE VILLALBA 2003 RED
tempranillo

79 Garnet red cherry. Not very intense yet clean aroma of red berries. Slightly warm palate of ripe red fruit with earthy notes and character.

MARQUÉS M. DE VILLALBA 2001 CRIANZA RED
tempranillo

75 Garnet red cherry. Medium intensity aroma of jammy fruit with notes of oak. Light palate with drying wood tannins; well-mannered overall.

NUESTRA SEÑORA DE LA CABEZA

Carretera de Zafra, s/n
06360 Fuente del Maestre (Badajoz)
☎: 924 530 120 - Fax: 924 531 408

VIÑA RONIEL 2003 JOVEN WHITE

73 Brilliant pale. Quite intense, fruity aroma without great nuances. Flavourful palate with spicy citrus fruit notes.

VIÑA RONIEL 2003 JOVEN RED

80 Bigarreau cherry. Spicy aroma of light reduction and ripe red fruit. Well-balanced palate with earthy notes and medium persistence.

Sociedad Cooperativa NUESTRA SEÑORA DE LA SOLEDAD

Santa Marta, s/n
06207 Aceuchal (Badajoz)
☎: 924 680 228 - Fax: 924 680 228
nssoledad@terra.es

Established: 1976

▦ 40,000,000 litres ⚘ 7,500 has.
⚑ 25% ◔75%: -PT

ORGULLO DE BARROS 2003 JOVEN WHITE
ORGULLO DE BARROS MACABEO 2003 JOVEN WHITE
ORGULLO DE BARROS 2003 JOVEN ROSÉ
ORGULLO DE BARROS 2003 JOVEN RED

Sociedad Cooperativa de OLIVAREROS

Avenida de Extremadura, 62
06225 Ribera del Fresno (Badajoz)
☎: 924 537 001 - Fax: 924 536 286
administración@olivareros.com
www.olivareros.com

Established: 1953
▦ 22 ▦ 4,950 litres ⚑ 70% ◔30%: -DE -AT -TW -US -FR -PT -UK -SE

BATILO TEMPRANILLO 2003 JOVEN RED
100% tempranillo

74 Garnet red cherry. Warm aroma with notes of lightly evolved fruit. Better on the palate: fruity and pleasant with slightly incisive tannins.

REGIANA 2000 CRIANZA RED
100% tempranillo

68 Cherry with an orangey edge. Unusual, medicinal aroma (cough medicine). Without fruit on the palate, medicinal.

CASTILLO DE REGIANA 1998 RESERVA RED
100% tempranillo

74 Cherry with a brick red hue. Ripe aroma with reduction notes (leathers) and aged wood. Supple, round palate with crianza character and dry oak tannins.

VALLEGARZÓN JOVEN WHITE
VALLEJUELO 2003 JOVEN WHITE
BATILO CAYETANA PARDINA 2003 JOVEN WHITE
VALLEGARZÓN JOVEN ROSÉ
VALLEJUELO 2003 JOVEN ROSÉ
VALLEGARZÓN JOVEN RED
CASTILLO DE VILLAFRESNO 2000 OAK AGED RED

VALLEJUELO 2003 JOVEN RED

Bodegas ORTIZ

Sevilla, 34
06200 Almendralejo (Badajoz)
☎: 924 662 811 - Fax: 924 665 406
info@bodegasortiz.com
www.bodegasortiz.com

Established: 1940

▦ 600 ▦ 2,350,000 litres ⚘ 20 has.
⚑ 90% ◔10%: -DE -NL -DO -CA

VIÑA ROJA TEMPRANILLO 2003 JOVEN RED
100% tempranillo

77 Cherry with a violet edge. Not very intense yet fruity aroma (red berries). Somewhat bitter palate with pleasant notes of red fruit; well-mannered overall.

CASTILLO DE FERIA 1999 CRIANZA RED
100% tempranillo

76 Garnet red cherry with a brick red glint. Intense, spicy aroma with a certain oaky freshness and notes of slightly reduced fruit. Flavourful, slightly fleshy palate, lacking balance.

Castillo de Feria
Crianza 1999
Ribera del Guadiana
Denominación de Origen
Bodegas Ortiz, S.L.

PEDRO CUPIDO

Barranco, 1
06810 Calamonte (Badajoz)
☎: 924 323 516
▦ 100,000 litres ⚑ 50% ◔50%

PEDRO CUPIDO WHITE
PEDRO CUPIDO RED

Bodegas PUENTE AJUDA

Carretera Olivenza-Elvas, km 105
06100 Olivenza (Badajoz)
☎: 924 126 280 - Fax: 924 126 280
bodegaspuenteajuda@mesasdelrio.com
www.bodegaspuenteajuda.com

Established: 1999

🍶 800 📊 1,500,000 litres 🍷 100 has.

🐗 90% 🌐10%: -DE -NL -FI

DUQUE DE CADAVAL 2000 RESERVA RED

Bodegas ROMALE

Gonzalo Hernandez, 8
06200 Almendralejo (Badajoz)
☎: 924 667 255 - Fax: 924 665 877
romale@romale.com
www.romale.com

Established: 1989

🍶 600 📊 12,500,000 litres 🐗 60%

🌐40%: -PT -DE -NL -AT -US

VIÑA ROMALE 2003 JOVEN WHITE
macabeo

76 Pale with a greenish nuance. Not very intense, slightly rustic aroma with light vegetative hints. Better in the mouth; fresh with ripe fruit and good acidity.

VIÑA ROMALE 2003 ROSÉ
tempranillo

79 Salmon blush. Clean aroma with red fruit and a floral edge. Flavourful and fresh on the palate with red fruit, easy drinking.

VIÑA ROMALE TEMPRANILLO 2003 JOVEN RED
tempranillo

77 Dark garnet red cherry. Powerful aroma of black fruit, toasty hints of skins and quite varietal touches (underbrush). Flavourful palate with slightly marked tannins (a certain greeness).

VIÑA ROMALE MERLOT 2003 RED
merlot

70 Cherry with a garnet red edge. Aroma with quite a viscous edge, very ripe red fruit and notes of damp earth. Fleshy, ripe palate with oily and slightly warm tannins.

PRIVILEGIO DE ROMALE 2000 CRIANZA RED
100% tempranillo

77 Dark cherry with a saffron edge. Powerful aroma with predominant toasty oak notes and a suggestion of jammy fruit. Fleshy, flavourful palate with slightly marked tannins and bitter notes, slightly lacking in balance.

PRIVILEGIO DE ROMALE 1999 RESERVA RED
tempranillo

77 Cherry red. Aroma of menthol, spices and toasty wood notes. Very marked acidity on the palate with unintegrated wood tannins, without great nuances.

PRIVILEGIO DE ROMALE 2001 CRIANZA RED
tempranillo

76 Intense garnet red. Aroma of ripe black fruit and crianza reduction notes (hints of varnish). Fleshy, ripe palate with flavourful but sweet tannins; spicy wood.

PRIVILEGIO DE ROMALE
RIBERA DEL GUADIANA
Denominación de Origen
75 cl. e   12,5% Vol.
CRIANZA
EMBOTELLADO POR: R.E. EX-06-046/0 - 06200
PARA: ANTONIA ORTIZ CIPRIAN - C/. GONZALO HERNANDEZ, 8
ALMENDRALEJO · BADAJOZ
Ribera del Guadiana

VIÑA ROMALE 2003 WHITE
VIÑA ROMALE 2003 JOVEN RED
VIÑA ROMALE 2003 RED

RUIZ TORRES

Cañadahonda, 61
10136 Cañamero (Cáceres)
☎: 927 369 024 - Fax: 927 369 302
info@ruiztorres.com
www.ruiztorres.com

Established: 1870

🍶 1,200 📊 4,000,000 litres 🍷 250 has.

🐗 70% 🌐30%: -DE -CH -LT -LV -CZ -UK

-EE -TW -JP -TW BY -BE -MX -AR -CA

ATTELEA TEMPRANILLO 2003 ROBLE RED
tempranillo

81 Bigarreau cherry with a lively violet hue. Good intensity aroma of red fruit, with good expression and light vegetative hints. Flavourful, fresh palate of concentrated fruit (blackberries, bilberries) with good acidity with evident but unaggressive tannins.

ATTELEA 2001 CRIANZA RED

86 Dark cherry. Aroma with toasty notes between stewed black fruit and new wood, notions of terroir. Fruity palate and very well-assembled oak, toasty, a suggestion of liquorice and ripe tannins.

Sociedad Cooperativa Agr Vinícola Extremeña "SAN JOSÉ"

Carretera de Palomas, s/n km. 1, 8
06220 Villafranca de los Barros (Badajoz)
☎: 924 524 417 - Fax: 924 526 045
cavesanjose@ceme.es
www.bodegascave.com

Established: 1963

⬜ 350 🗄 33,000,000 litres 🍇 5,500 has.
🍷 80% 🌐20%: -PT -FR -JP -SE -UK -DE -IE -DK -NO

VIÑA CANCHAL 2003 WHITE
VIÑA CANCHAL 2003 WHITE SEMIDULCE
VIÑA CANCHAL 2003 ROSÉ
VIÑA CANCHAL 2000 RED
VIÑA CANCHAL 2002 RED
VIÑA CANCHAL 2003 RED
VIÑA CANCHAL ECOLÓGICO 2003 RED
VIÑA CANCHAL CABERNET SAUVIGNON 2003 RED
VIÑA CANCHAL 1998 RESERVA RED

Cooperativa del Campo SAN ISIDRO

La Paz , 2
06197 Entrín Bajo (Badajoz)
☎: 924 481 031 - Fax: 924 481 017
coopentrin@hotmail.com

Established: 1966

⬜ 20 🗄 7,500,000 litres 🍇 1,800 has.
🍷 70% 🌐30%: -PT -IT

VEGA HERRERA 2003 JOVEN RED
tempranillo

80 Garnet red cherry. Medium intensity, fresh aroma with pleasant notes of red berries. Light, flavourful and expressive on the palate with red fruit and an earthy hint, very pleasant.

Sociedad Cooperativa SAN ISIDRO DE VILLAFRANCA

Carretera Fuente del Mestre, 12
06220 Villafranca de los Barros (Badajoz)
☎: 924 524 020 - Fax: 924 524 136
cssanisidro22@navegalia.com
www.cooperativasanisidro.com

Established: 1960

⬜ 50 🗄 13,000,000 litres 🍇 2,500 has.
🍷 100%

VALDEQUEMAO 2003 JOVEN WHITE
100% macabeo

75 Pale yellow. Intense, fruity aroma with fresh overtones of citrus fruit. Flavourful, fresh and fruity on the palate.

VALDEQUEMAO 2003 JOVEN RED
100% tempranillo

78 Cherry with a purplish hue. Aroma of under-ripe red fruit and skins. Watery, light palate with bitter notes.

VALDEQUEMAO 2001 CRIANZA RED
100% tempranillo

77 Deep cherry. Aroma of jammy black fruit notas de cacao amargo y with notes of bitter cocoa

DO RIBERA DEL GUADIANA

and earth and toasty skins. Fleshy palate with powerful black fruit, oily tannins and a slightly astringent finish (green seeds).

Sociedad Cooperativa Comarcal-Vitivinícola
SAN JUAN

Pozo Nuevo, s/n
06420 Castuera (Badajoz)
☎: 924 760 802 - Fax: 924 760 802
coop.sanjuan@eresmas.com

PALIQUE JOVEN WHITE

Cooperativa SAN MARCOS DE ALMEDRALEJO

Carretera Aceuchal, s/n
06200 Almendralejo (Badajoz)
☎: 924 670 410 - Fax: 924 665 505
angel@campobarro.com
www.campobarro.com

Established: 1980
🌐 1,445 🛢 1,800,000 litres 🍇 3,000 has.
🍷 50% 🍇50%

CAMPOBARRO MACABEO 2003 WHITE
macabeo

74 Pale yellow. Powerful, ripe aroma with white fruit and a nuance of perfumed soap. Flavourful, bitter and not very fine on the palate.

CAMPOBARRO PARDINA 2003 WHITE
100% pardina

79 Straw-coloured. Expressive aroma with a certain finesse, white fruit and fragrant herbs. Fruity, light, freshand pleasant on the palate.

CAMPOBARRO ROSÉ
100% cencibel

70 Blush. A slightly unusual aroma with medicinal notes and a red fruit hint. Light palate with green notes, fresh but without great nuances.

CAMPOBARRO TEMPRANILLO 2003 RED
100% tempranillo

70 Garnet red cherry. Not very intense aroma with vegetative notes and red berries. Red fruit on the palate with caramelised, sweet notes, lacking liveliness.

CAMPOBARRO CENCIBEL 2002 RED
100% cencibel

80 Cherry with a brick red hue. Aroma of toasted wood, vanilla, smoky notes and ripe red fruit. Flavourful palate with a good fruit /wood tannin integration and a suggestion of strawberries in the retronasal passage.

HEREDAD DE BARROS 2000 CRIANZA RED
100% cencibel

74 Garnet red cherry. Intense, fruity and fresh aroma with smoky hints of oak though without great crianza expression. Flavourful, bitter palate with a good fruit/oak integration, without great nuances.

CASTILLO DE BELMIRO 2001 CRIANZA RED
100% cencibel

74 Intense cherry. Aroma of ripe plums, sun-drenched notes and toasty skins. Fleshy palate with ripe, fruity tannins, good weight but lacking freshness.

VALDEGRACIA JOVEN WHITE
QUINTA DEL SANTO 2003 WHITE
VALDEGRACIA JOVEN RED
QUINTA DEL SANTO 2003 RED
JUMERO CRIANZA RED
VIÑA MORÁN CRIANZA RED
VALDEGRACIA CRIANZA RED
HEREDAD DE BARROS 1999 RESERVA RED
CASTILLO DE BELMIRO 2001 RESERVA RED

Sociedad Cooperativa
SANTA MARÍA EGIPCIACA

Carretera Entrín Bajo, s/n
06196 Corte de Peleas (Badajoz)
☎: 924 693 014 - Fax: 924 693 270
staegipciaca@terra.es

CONDE DE LA CORTE JOVEN RED

SANTA MARTA VIRGEN

Cordelillo, s/n
06150 Santa Marta de los Barros (Badajoz)
☎: 924 690 218 - Fax: 924 690 083
info@bodegasantamarta.com
www.bodegasantamarta.com

Established: 1963
🌐 300 🛢 21,000,000 litres 🍇 2,800 has.
🍷 90% 🍇10%: -US -DE Sudamérica -UK

BLASÓN DEL TURRA 2003 JOVEN WHITE
100% macabeo

74 Pale yellow with a greenish hue. Powerful aroma with a hint of precocious reduction. Flavourful, bitter and not very fine on the palate.

BLASÓN DEL TURRA 2003 JOVEN WHITE
cayetana blanca, pardina

72 Pale with a golden hue. Slightly intense, fruity aroma without great nuances. Quite flavourful and bitter on the palate, without fruit expression.

BLASÓN DEL TURRA 2003 ROSÉ
100% tempranillo

75 Deep raspberry. Powerful, fruity aroma with notes of sun-drenched skins. Flavourful and bitter on the palate with a slightly acidic edge.

BLASÓN DEL TURRA 2003 RED
100% tempranillo

74 Garnet red cherry. Not very intense yet fresh aroma with a vegetative hint and red fruit. Light palate with red fruit and liquorice, well-mannered.

VALDEBLASÓN 2000 RED
100% tempranillo

74 Cherry with an orange hue. Ripe aroma (orange peel) of toasty oak. Light palate with drying oak tannins; lacking fruit.

VALDEAURUM 2000 CRIANZA RED
100% tempranillo

74 Cherry with an orange hue. Ripe aroma with toasty oak and spices (cinnamon). Light palate with ripe fruit, liquorice, earthy notes and dry oak tannins.

VALDEBLASÓN 2002 RED

VALDEANÁS

Prolongación c/Sol s/n
06196 Aldea de Cortegana (Badajoz)
☎: 924 687 927 - Fax: 924 687 951
bodegas@valdeanas.com
www.valdeanas.com

PEÑA DE HITA TEMPRANILLO 1999 CRIANZA RED
tempranillo

70 Cherry with a brick red nuance. Aroma with crianza character (aged wood, acetaldehydes). Light palate with drying oak tannins, without great nuances.

PEÑA DE HITA JOVEN RED

Bodegas VENTURA DE VEGA

Badajoz, 70
06200 Almendralejo (Badajoz)
☎: 924 671 105 - Fax: 924 677 205
bodegas@vegaesteban.com
www.vegaesteban.com
Established: 1927
🍇 400 📊 5,000,000 litres 🍇 300 has.
🍷 5% 🍇95%: -UK -DE -SE -CH -BE -NL -DK -JP

VEGA ESTEBAN 2003 JOVEN WHITE
100% viura

76 Pale. Medium intensity aroma of ripe white fruit with a nuance of herbs. Light palate with lively acidity; without great nuances but well-mannered.

CADENCIAS DE VEGA ESTEBAN 2003 JOVEN RED
100% tempranillo

81 Garnet red cherry with a coppery edge. Powerful aroma of jammy black fruit with smoky notes of skins and hints of sweetness and terroir. Fleshy palate with slightly marked and flavourful tannins and bitter notes (liquorice).

VEGA ESTEBAN 2003 JOVEN RED
100% tempranillo

76 Cherry with a purplish hue. Aroma of red fruit, with sweet lactic notes and slightly alcoholic. Flavourful slightly warm palate with supple tannins and medium persistence.

LEYENDAS DE VEGA ESTEBAN 2002 RED
tempranillo

84 Cherry with an orangey hue. Spicy aroma with liquorice, ripe black fruit and mild lactic notes. Slightly marked wood tannins on the palate but with good fruit weight and medium persistence.

VEGA ESTEBAN 2001 CRIANZA RED
100% tempranillo

83 Very dark cherry. Powerful aroma with predominant toasty oak notes, a suggestion of jammy black fruit and hints of spices and terroir. Flavourful palate with elements of drying (somewhat fresh oak) but promising tannins, bitter notes and refreshing acidity.

LEYENDAS DE VEGA ESTEBAN 2000 CRIANZA RED
100% tempranillo

83 Dark garnet red cherry. Intense aroma with predominant spicy oak notes and hints of quite fresh oak. Flavourful palate with slightly marked tannins, a suggestion of sweet fruit, and bitterness, quite potential.

VÍA DE LA PLATA

Zugasti, 9
06200 Almendralejo (Badajoz)
☎: 924 660 235 - Fax: 924 661 155
hermanosmesias@teleline.net
www.bodegasviadeplata.com
Established: 1985
🍇 88 📊 175,000 litres 🍇 15 has. 🍷 100%

VÍA DE LA PLATA WHITE
VIÑA PROMETIDA 2002 JOVEN RED
VÍA DE LA PLATA 2001 RED
VIÑA TIZA 2001 CRIANZA RED

VINIFICACIONES EXTREMEÑAS

Camino de las Huertas, 9
06498 Lobón (Badajoz)
☎: 924 447 492 - Fax: 924 447 492
viniexsa@wanadoo.es
www.viniexsa.com

Established: 1979

🌐 50 🛢 2,000,000 litres 🍇 120 has.

🍷 90% 🍇10%: -NL

LYKAÓN 2003 JOVEN WHITE
100% cayetana blanca

79 Pale straw. Aroma with notes of ripe fruit (tropical) and hay. Oily palate with ripe fruit, more expressive than in the nose, very pleasant.

LYKAÓN 2001 ROBLE RED
100% tempranillo

70 Cherry with an orange edge. Slightly short aroma with toasty oak and mild off-odours. Light palate with considerable oak weight.

LYKAÓN 2002 JOVEN WHITE
LYKAÓN 2001 CRIANZA RED

VIÑA EXTREMEÑA

Carretera de Alange, s/n
06200 Almendralejo (Badajoz)
☎: 924 670 158 - Fax: 924 670 159
info@vinexsa.com - borja@vinexsa.com
www.vinexsa.com

Established: 1971

🌐 10,000 🛢 4,700,000 litres 🍇 1,100 has.

🍷 30% 🍇70%: -UE Asia -US

TORRE DE SANDE

VIÑA SANTA MARINA

Carretera N-630, km. 634 - Apdo. 714
06800 Mérida (Badajoz)
☎: 924 027 670 - Fax: 924 027 675
bodega@vsantamarina.com
www.vsantamarina.com

Established: 1999

🌐 400 🍇 59 has. 🍷 79% 🍇21%: -DE -BE -NL -UK -AT -CH -IT -US -JP -PT -KY

TORREMAYOR TEMPRANILLO 2001 CRIANZA RED
100% tempranillo

83 Lively garnet red cherry. Fine aroma with a good expression of ripe red berries well-integrated with the wood. Flavourful, fresh palate of red fruit with slightly marked tannins, yet pleasant.

TORREMAYOR TEMPRANILLO 2000 RESERVA RED
100% tempranillo

82 Cherry with an orange edge. Fine, spicy aroma (pepper, vanilla) with jammy red fruit. Powerful palate with a good fruit/oak integration and dry oak tannins in the finish.

Sociedad Cooperativa VIÑAOLIVA

Polígono Industrial, Parcela 4-17
06200 Almendralejo (Badajoz)
☎: 924 677 321 - Fax: 924 660 989
acoex@bme.es

Established: 1998

🛢 170,000,000 litres 🍇 55,000 has.

🍷 50% 🍇50%

ZALEO PARDINA WHITE
ZALEO MACABEO WHITE
ZALEO TEMPRANILLO RED

VIÑAS DE ALANGE

Carretera Almendralejo - Palomas, km 6
06840 Alange (Badajoz)
☎: 924 670 175 - Fax: 957 650 135
alvearsa@alvear.es

Established: 2000

PALACIO QUEMADO 2001 OAK AGED RED
100% tempranillo 🛢4

81 Dark cherry. Powerful, ripe aroma with jammy black fruit and hints of fine reduction (varnish). Flavourful, fleshy palate with rough and slightly oily tannins, hints of liquorice and notions of terroir.

VIÑAS DE ALANGE

PALACIO QUEMADO

Ribera del Guadiana
DENOMINACIÓN DE ORIGEN

COSECHA 2001

Ribera
del Guadiana
Denominación de Origen

ALVEAR
Elaborado por: Viñas de Alange, S.A. - 06840 Alange (España)

75 cl
13% vol

PALACIO QUEMADO 2000 RESERVA RED
100% tempranillo

84 Deep cherry. Toasty aroma with balsamic notes and cedar over black fruit. Flavourful, well-balanced palate with fruity tannins and Mediterranean expression; slightly dry and bitter finish.

Sociedad Cooperativa
VIRGEN DE LA ESTRELLA

Calle Mérida, 1
06230 Los Santos de Maimona (Badajoz)
☎: 924 544 094 - Fax: 924 572 490
export@maimona.com
www.maimona.com

Established: 1963
🛢 45 🛢 9,000,000 litres 🍇 2.500 has.
🍷 95% 🌐 5%: -DE -AT -PT

VIÑA MAIMONA 2003 RED
VIÑA MAIMONA 2001 CRIANZA RED
VIÑA MAIMONA 2001 CRIANZA RED

DO RIBERA DEL JÚCAR

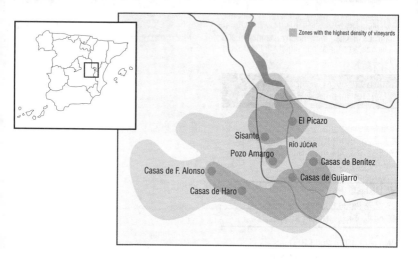

Zones with the highest density of vineyards

El Picazo
Sisante
RÍO JÚCAR
Pozo Amargo
Casas de F. Alonso
Casas de Benítez
Casas de Guijarro
Casas de Haro

NEWS. 2003 was the first year in which wines were marketed with the label Ribera del Júcar, once the creation of this DO was ratified by the Agricultural Council of Castilla-La Mancha. 300,000 bottles were sold in the first three months of 2004, compared to the half a million bottles of the previous year, which indicates that last year's figures will more than likely be doubled.

One of the peculiarities of the new DO, the spearhead in the application of the Wine Law in all of Spain, is that the wines will be rated by a consultancy with no links to the Regulatory Council, which will then send its certification to the IVICAM (Instituto de la Vid y el Vino de Castilla-La Mancha). From a qualitative point of view, however, within a very correct mid level, the wines seem to lack variety and, although they reach scores of 80 points, they struggle to achieve higher scores. Perhaps the cellars of the DO should abandon their single-variety policy (along with the local *Cencibel*, one is starting to see fine examples of *Syrah*, *Cabernet Sauvignon* and *Merlot*) and start making blends in search of greater complexity.

Hectares of Vineyard	No. of Viticulturists	No. of Bodegas	2003 Harvest	2003 Production	Marketing
9,141	1,425	8	Very Good	750,000 litres	60% Spain 40% foreign

LOCATION. The 7 wine producing municipal districts that make up the DO are located on the banks of the Júcar, in the south of the province of Cuenca. They are: Casas de Benítez, Casas de Guijarro, Casas de Haro, Casas de Fernando Alonso, Pozoamargo, Sisante and El Picazo. The region is at an altitude of between 650 and 750 m above sea level.

CLIMATE. Continental in nature, dry, and with very cold winters and very hot summers. The main factor contributing to the quality of the wine is the day-night temperature contrasts during the ripening season of the grapes, which causes the process to be carried out slowly.

SOIL. The most common type of soil consists of pebbles on the surface and a clayey subsoil, which provides good water retention capacity in the deeper levels.

VARIETIES:
Red: *Cencibel* or *Tempranillo, Cabernet Sauvignon, Merlot, Syrah* and *Bobal.*

REGULATORY COUNCIL.
Avda. de España, 21 1º. 16611 Casas de Haro (Cuenca).
Tel: 969 380 840. Fax: 969 380 518.
E-mail: riberadeljucar@navegalia.com

GENERAL CHARACTERISTICS OF THE WINES:

Reds	With an intense cherry colour and violet edge when they are young, they resemble the wines of the peripheral regions of La Mancha, characterised by less rusticity. On the nose, the notes of blackberries, red berries and earthy nuances stand out. On the palate, they are expressive, with tannins which are flavourful and liverly; freshly acidic with varietal reminders of the principal grape variety, the *Cencibel*.

COOPERJUCAR

Matas Altas s/n
16700 Sisante (Cuenca)
☎: 969 380 511 - Fax: 969 380 511

RAMBLILLA 2003 RED
tempranillo

80 Dark cherry with a violet edge. Powerful aroma of ripe red fruit (sweet notes). Flavourful palate with ripe tannins and hints of slight overripeness.

RAMBLILLA 2000 CRIANZA RED
tempranillo

80 Not very deep cherry. Slightly alcoholic aroma with sweet notes of toasty wood and light notes of reduction. Warm, drying palate with metallic notes, short with a suggestion of wood in the retronasal passage.

Cooperativa del Campo DULCE NOMBRE DE JESÚS

Calvario, 7
Casas de Guijarro (Cuenca)
☎: 969 382 227

MONTE MANUEL JOVEN RED

Sociedad Cooperativa LA MAGDALENA

Carretera de la Roda, s/n
16611 Casas de Haro (Cuenca)
☎: 967 380 722 - Fax: 967 380 722
vmoragona@ucaman.es

Established: 1958

⊞ 250 ▤ 6,400,000 litres ☙ 1,400 has.
🍷 85% 🍇15%

VEGA MORAGONA 1999 CRIANZA RED
100% cencibel

74 Cherry with a brick red rim. Toasty wood aroma with light reduction notes. Without expression on the palate, with toasty notes, well-mannered.

VEGA MORAGONA VIÑAS VIEJAS ALTA SELECCIÓN 2000 CRIANZA RED
100% cencibel

75 Cherry with an orange edge. Toasty, smoky aroma of ripe red fruit. Bitter notes on the palate; quite light.

VEGA MORAGONA 2003 JOVEN RED

NUESTRA SRA DE LA CABEZA

Tapias, 8
16708 Pozoamargo (Cuenca)

☎: 969 387 173 - Fax: 969 387 202
info@casagualda.com
www.casagualda.com

Established: 1958

⊞ 535 ▤ 5,000,000 litres ☙ 900 has.
🍷 80% 🍇20%: -US -NL -DE -CH -UK

CASARRIBA 2001 ROBLE RED
cencibel   ⊞ 4

82 Cherry with an orange edge. Perfumed aroma of ripe red fruit and jammy forest fruits. Warm, bitter, medium-bodied palate.

Cooperativa NUESTRO PADRE JESÚS DE NAZARENO

Deportes, 4
16700 Sisante (Cuenca)
☎: 969 387 094 - Fax: 969 387 094
sisante_nazareno@yahoo.es

Established: 1943

⊞ 20 ▤ 5,782,000 litres 🍷 100%

CASA DON JUAN 2003 RED

Sociedad Cooperativa PURÍSIMA CONCEPCIÓN

Carretera Minaya-San Clemente, s/n
16610 Casas de Fernando Alonso (Cuenca)
☎: 969 383 043 - Fax: 969 383 153
purisima@ucaman.es

Established: 1958

⊞ 300 ▤ 15,000,000 litres ☙ 2,300 has.
🍷 70% 🍇30%: -UK -US -PT -NL

TEATINOS TEMPRANILLO 2003 JOVEN RED
tempranillo

80 Dark cherry. Powerful, fruity aroma with sweet hints and toasty skins. Flavourful, fleshy palate with slightly marked tannins and good acidity.

TEATINOS SELECCIÓN 40 BARRICAS 2000 CRIANZA RED
tempranillo

83 Deep ruby red. Aroma of vanilla with sweet notes and new wood, balsamic and slightly short on fruit. Fleshy palate with polished tannins although the wood subdues the fruit, flavourful.

TEATINOS CABERNET SAUVIGNON 2002 RED
cabernet sauvignon

81 Deep cherry. Fruity aroma (forest black fruit) with balsamic notes and a suggestion of the vine variety (pepper). Powerful palate with very expressive vine variety; fleshy and oily tannins with fallen leaves in the finish.

Sociedad Cooperativa SAN GINÉS

Virgen del Carmen, 6
16707 Casas de Benitez (Cuenca)
☎: 969 382 037 - Fax: 969 382 449
cincoalmudes@cincoalmudes.es
www.cincoalmudes.es
Established: 1956
🍷 500 🛢 12,000,000 litres 🍇 40%
🌐60%: -DE -DK -FI -US -AT -SV -FR

CINCO ALMUDES CABERNET SAUVIGNON 2003 JOVEN RED
100% cabernet sauvignon

80 Very deep cherry with a violet edge. Intense, fruity aroma with a good varietal expression (paprika) and hints of damp earth. Flavourful palate with slightly marked tannins (hints of greeness), a spicy nuance, rich in nuances of a young vine and slightly mineral.

CINCO ALMUDES 2003 JOVEN RED
100% tempranillo

80 Cherry with a violet rim. Aroma of red fruit. Creamy palate, tannins present but flavourful, good acidity and medium persistence.

CINCO ALMUDES MERLOT 2003 JOVEN RED
100% merlot

81 Very intense cherry with a violet edge. Clear, fruity aroma of sweet strawberries and maceration notes (flowers). Flavourful, fruity palate (red fruit pulp), very fresh.

CINCO ALMUDES SYRAH 2003 JOVEN RED
100% syrah

81 Cherry with a violet hue. Powerful aroma of jammy black fruit with toasty notes of skins and hints of petals and underbrush. Fleshy, flavourful palate with slightly marked tannins and an acidic edge.

CINCO ALMUDES 2003 RED
100% tempranillo

80 Cherry with a violet hue. Powerful, fruity, very varietal aroma of ripe red fruit and underbrush with hints of sun-drenched skins. Flavourful palate with slightly marked yet elegant tannins and a ripe fruit nuance, pleasant.

ALMUDES 5 DÉCADAS 1999 CRIANZA RED
100% tempranillo

82 Cherry with an orangey rim. Toasty, smoky, spicy and lactic aroma. Well-integrated tannins on the palate although the wood tends to conceal the fruit somewhat.

CINCO ALMUDES 1999 CRIANZA RED
100% tempranillo

82 Dark cherry with a saffron edge. Intense aroma with a certain finesse, jammy fruit, toasty oak, lactic hints and fine reduction (tobacco). Fleshy palate with rough, somewhat sweet tannins and notes of cocoa and terroir in the retronasal passage.

CINCO ALMUDES 2000 CRIANZA RED
100% tempranillo

81 Cherry with a garnet red edge. Aroma with fine notes of reduction (toasty skins, tobacco). Flavourful palate with predominant notes of crianza over the fruit, well-integrated alcohol-acidity and chocolate in the finish.

CINCO ALMUDES BOBAL 2003 JOVEN RED

DOCa. RIOJA

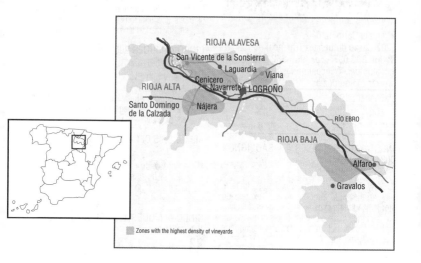

Zones with the highest density of vineyards

NEWS. Despite the criticism and the crisis with which Rioja saw out the 20th century, the flagship of our wine industry is in great shape, at least in qualitative terms, and seems to have more than sufficient arguments and resources to weather any storm. Rioja is reinventing itself, and together with the more 'traditional' styles (the classic Rioja thinned by ageing and the young wine of carbonic maceration) and the 'designer' or 'high range' red wines produced with varying success, the essential attribute of modern wines is coming to the fore: freshness, as opposed to the traditional reds that have bored so many palates of late.

1,452 wines referenced, 805 wines tasted, 47 with scores above 90 points, 278 surpassing 85 points, 490 between 85 and 75 points, and only 52 below this mark are scores that undeniably have to be taken into account.

Hectares of Vineyard	No. of Viticulturists	No. of Bodegas	2003 Harvest	2003 Production	Marketing
62,146	19,399	517	Good	291,000,000 litres	59% Spain 41% foreign

The quality of the 2003 harvest equally appears certain, with the Erre Punto of Remírez de Ganuza (86 points) as the best example of traditional carbonic maceration. Also worthy of mention, as in the Ribera del Duero, is the progressive abandonment of the regulatory labels of Crianza, Reserva and Gran Reserva, in favour of greater liberty for the oenologist.

LOCATION. Occupying the Ebro valley. To the north it borders with the Sierra de Cantabria and to the south with the Sierra de la Demanda, and is made up of different municipal districts of La Rioja, the Basque Country and Navarra. The most western region is Haro and the easternmost, Alfaro, with a distance of 100 km between the two. The region is 40 km wide.

CLIMATE. Quite variable depending on the different sub-regions. In general, there is a combination of Atlantic and Mediterranean influences, the latter becoming more dominant as the terrain descends from west to east, becoming drier and hotter. The average annual rainfall is slightly over 400 mm.

SOIL. Various types: the clayey calcareous soil arranged in terraces and small plots which are located especially in Rioja Alavesa, la Sonsierra and some regions of Rioja Alta; the clayey ferrous soil, scattered throughout the region, with vineyards located on reddish, strong soil with hard, deep rock; and the alluvial soil in the area close to the rivers; these are the most level vineyards with larger plots; here the soil is deeper and has pebbles.

VARIETIES:
White: *Viura* (7,045 Ha), *Malvasía* and *Garnacha Blanca*.
Red: *Tempranillo* (majority with 38,476 Ha), *Garnacha, Graciano* and *Mazuelo*.

SUB-REGIONS:
Rioja Alta. This has Atlantic influences; it is the most extensive with some 20,500 Ha and produces wines well suited for ageing.
Rioja Alavesa. A mixture of Atlantic and Mediterranean influences, with an area under cultivation of some 11,500 Ha; both young wines and wines suited for ageing are produced.
Rioja Baja. With approximately 18,000 Ha, the climate is purely Mediterranean; white wines and rosés with a higher alcohol content and extract are produced.

REGULATORY COUNCIL. Estambrera, 52. 26006 Logroño (La Rioja).
Tel: 941 500 400. Fax: 941 500 672.
E-mail: info@riojawine.com - Website: www.riojawine.com

GENERAL CHARACTERISTICS OF THE WINES:

Whites	These are produced from *Viura*. One can find young wines (straw yellow, fruity aromas and herbaceous notes, characteristic of the variety), wines fermented in barrels (slightly golden yellow, with aromas that combine fruit with the creamy notes of wood, and which are flavourful and well-balanced on the palate), and traditional aged wines (golden yellow colour in which the notes of the oak predominate on the palate and on the nose).
Rosés	These are basically produced from *Garnacha*, almost always cultivated in Rioja Baja. The have a raspberry pink colour and reflect the character of the variety they are produced from: they are fruity, fresh and pleasant on the palate.
Reds	As far as young wines are concerned, there are the wines from Rioja Alavesa, harvested traditionally and produced by carbonic maceration, which gives them great aromatic strength: intense cherry coloured, with notes of ripe, sunny fruit (they are to be drunk within the year). Other young wines, produced with prior destemming, have slightly less colour and fruit intensity: they are light, fresh and easy drinking. As for the wines aged in wood, their characteristics are determined by the length of time they remain in contact with the oak, which determines the intensity of their colour. So, in the Crianza wines, the fruity notes of the grapes are slightly toned down by the action of the wood, while in the Reserva wines, and especially in the Gran Reserva wines (aged for at least two years in barrels and three years in the bottle), the roundness and harmony of the wines increases. On the nose, aromas of vanilla, toast and tobacco appear, together with the complexity typical of the reduction in the bottle. In the younger wines, it is common to find notes reminiscent of leather and animal aromas.

Bodegas 501 DEL PUERTO

Valdés, 9
11500 El Puerto de Sta. María (Cádiz)
☎: 956 855 511 - Fax: 956 873 053
brandy501@infonegocio.com
www.bodegas501.com
Established: 1783
⊕ 3,800 ▤ 4,000,000 litres ☛ 58% ⦿42%:
-NG -SK -MT -GQ -AD -DE -BE -UK -ZA

501 ABADIA 1999 CRIANZA RED

ABADÍA

Santiago, 2
01307 Villabuena (Álava)
☎: 607 817 202

ROZANKO RED

ABEICA

Paraje El Calvario, s/n
26339 Ábalos (La Rioja)
☎: 941 308 009 - Fax: 941 334 392
abeica@sp-editores.es
⊕ 350 ▤ 800,000 litres ⦿ 35 has.

CHULATO JOVEN RED
LONGRANDE CRIANZA RED
LONGRANDE RESERVA RED
LONGRANDE GRAN RESERVA RED

ABEL MENDOZA MONGE

Carretera Peñacerrada, 7
26338 San Vicente de la Sonsierra (La Rioja)
☎: 941 308 010 - Fax: 941 308 010
jarrarte@datalogic.es
Established: 1987
⊕ 94 ▤ 117,000 litres ⦿ 18 has.
☛ 75% ⦿25%: -UE -US

ABEL MENDOZA GARNACHA BLANCA 2003 OAK AGED WHITE
100% garnacha blanca

89 Yellow. Aroma with light smoky and oxidative notes (nuts), scrubland herbs and sweet fruit. Full, fresh, herby palate, very Mediterranean, warm, dry scrubland, flavourful.

ABEL MENDOZA MALVASÍA 2003 FERMENTADO EN BARRICA WHITE
100% malvasía

88 Pale with golden nuances. Slightly intense aroma with predominant floral, smoky and hone-

yed notes over a suggestion of ripe stone fruit. Flavourful palate with slightly fresh oak tannins and fine notes of caramel well-integrated with the ripe fruit.

ABEL MENDOZA TORRONTÉS 2003 FERMENTADO EN BARRICA WHITE
100% torrontés

86 Straw-coloured with a brilliant coppery hue. Aroma with musky notes, herbs and flowers and fruity hints. Fresh, light palate with a fine retronasal effect of fragrant herbs, flavourful.

ABEL MENDOZA VIURA 2003 FERMENTADO EN BARRICA WHITE
100% viura

86 Straw-coloured with a yellow glimmer. Aroma with light notes of evolution, toasty hints and scrubland herbs. Sweet notes and hints of sweet fruit on the palate with a fine toasty retronasal effect, flavourful and long.

ABEL MENDOZA SELECCIÓN PERSONAL 2001 RED
100% tempranillo

91 Intense cherry. Powerful aroma with toasty notes and a mild animal hint (cocoa, leather). Fleshy, full, flavourful palate with fruit and crianza expression and fine toasty notes in the retronasal passage.

ABEL MENDOZA SELECCIÓN PERSONAL 2002 CRIANZA RED
100% tempranillo

90 Deep cherry with a purplish edge. Powerful aroma of jammy red fruit with hints of skins and fine toasty oak. Flavourful and fruity palate with ripe and fine oak tannins, powerful balsamic and liquorice in the retronasal passage, fine bitter notes.

JARRARTE 2001 OAK AGED RED
100% tempranillo

87 Dark cherry with a purplish edge. Powerful aroma of macerated red fruit with spicy hints of oak and the freshness of damp earth. Flavourful palate with round and oily tannins well-integrated with the fruit (jammy hints) and a balsamic and liquorice suggestion.

JARRARTE 2003 MACERACIÓN CARBÓNICA RED
100% tempranillo

81 Dark cherry with a violet edge. Powerful aroma of red fruit with the typical freshness of car-bonic maceration. Flavourful palate with firm and fine tannins, ripe fruit, spicy notes of skins and excellent acidity.

AFERSA

Carretera Logroño, s/n
26340 San Asensio (La Rioja)

☎: 941 457 394 - Fax: 941 457 394

Established: 1988

🍷 400 ▨ 300,000 litres 🍇 8 has. 🍾 100%

EL AGOZAL JOVEN WHITE
EL AGOZAL ROSÉ
CERRILLO VERBALLE JOVEN RED
CERRILLO VERBALLE CRIANZA RED
CERRILLO VERBALLE RESERVA RED

Bodegas AGE

Barrio de la Estación, s/n
26360 Fuenmayor (La Rioja)
☎: 941 293 500 - Fax: 941 293 501
bodegasage@byb.es
www.byb.es

Established: 1881

🍷 35,000 ▨ 8,622,500 litres 🍇 500 has.
🇪🇸 60% 🌐40%: -CA -US -MX -GT -HN -
PA -CU -PR -CO -PE -BR -IS -DK -SE -FI -
DK -UK -IE -PT -BE -NL -DE -CH -IT -CY -
MT -EL -AT -PL -CZ -SK -SY -LV -LT -RU -
KZ -MA -AE -AU -JP -PH -TW -SG -MY

SIGLO 1881 2002 RED
tempranillo, garnacha

80 Glacé cherry. Aroma of vanilla, toasty wood and light notes of red fruit. Round, and supple on the palate with good acidity, very well-mannered.

SIGLO 1881 2001 CRIANZA RED
30% garnacha, 70% tempranillo

78 Cherry with a brick red edge. Aroma with mild toasty wood notes and spices. Light, somewhat spicy and flavourful palate.

SIGLO SACO 2001 CRIANZA RED
75% tempranillo, 15% garnacha, 10% mazuelo

79 Brilliant cherry with an orangey glint. Fairly intense aroma of red stone fruit with spicy hints of wood and a light suggestion of sackcloth. Flavourful and supple on the palate with fine bitter notes, easy drinking.

SIGLO 1998 RESERVA RED
80% tempranillo, 10% mazuelo, 10% graciano

83 Ruby red with a brick red hue. Aroma with good reduction notes (tobacco, cloves) and a suggestion of aged wood. Round, supple and flavourful palate, a classic with well-integrated wood and a spicy finish.

AZPILICUETA 2000 RESERVA RED
85% tempranillo, 5% mazuelo, 10% graciano

87 Dark cherry. Intense aroma with ripe black fruit, fine toasty wood and a viscous, balsamic hint. Flavourful palate with a good fruit/oak integration, and fine bitter notes, slightly warm and promising.

MARQUÉS DEL ROMERAL 1993 GRAN RESERVA RED
75% tempranillo, 15% mazuelo, 10% graciano

83 Glacé cherry. Medium-intensity aroma of sour cherries in liqueur and vanilla. Round, supple and flavourful on the palate with good crianza; very polished.

SIGLO 1881 2001 ROBLE RED
AZPILICUETA 1999 RESERVA RED
AZPILICUETA 2000 CRIANZA RED

AGUIRRE

Camino del Soto, s/n
01306 La Puebla de Labarca (Álava)
☎: 945 607 148

Established: 1980

DO Ca. RIOJA

🍇 15 📊 240,000 litres 🍷 12 has. 🍴 100%

AGUIRRE-VITERI 2003 RED

74 Fairly deep cherry. Somewhat intense aroma without obvious fruit expression and with spicy hints of skins. Flavourful palate with quite bitter tannins and poor fruit expression (an element of greeness).

AGUIRRE-VITERI 2001 CRIANZA RED

82 Fairly deep cherry with a purplish edge. Powerful aroma of very ripe fruit (hints of prunes) with toasty and creamy notes of oak. Flavourful palate with a good fruit/oak integration and bitter and toasty notes in the retronasal passage.

AGUIRRE-VITERI SELECCIÓN 2002 RED

80 Dark cherry with a purplish edge. Powerful aroma with predominant toasty oak notes and ripe fruit (jammy hints). Flavourful palate with ripe fruit, fine bitter notes (dark-roasted flavours) and slightly drying oak tannins.

AIDA NARRO MARÍN

Escuelas, 14
26224 Alesanco (La Rioja)
☎: 941 379 151
comercial@ignaciomarin.com
www.ignaciomarin.com

Established: 1996
📊 50,000 litres 🍷 6 has. 🇪🇸 100%

M. ENSENADA WHITE
M. ENSENADA ROSÉ
SAÚL REINARES NARRO RED

Bodegas ALAVESAS

Carretera De Elciego s/n
01300 Laguardia (Álava)
☎: 902 227 700 - Fax: 902 227 701
bodega@cofradiasamaniego.com
www.cofradiasamaniego.com

Established: 1970
🍇 4,841 📊 1,287,700 litres 🍷 95 has.
🍴 75% 🌐25%: -UK -DE -FR -NL -CH -BE -US -JP

BODEGAS ALAVESAS 2003 JOVEN RED
100% tempranillo

77 Cherry with a violet hue. Aroma of ripe red fruit, short. Bitter, light palate, of vinous character.

SOLAR DE SAMANIEGO GRACIANO 2001 RED
100% graciano

85 Deep cherry with a raspberry edge. Aroma of fresh red fruit with a character of skins, fine smoky flavours and a nuance of spices. Fresh, flavourful palate with well-balanced wood and fruit; firm, fresh tannins.

SOLAR DE SAMANIEGO 2001 CRIANZA RED
100% graciano

81 Cherry with a copper edge. Light toasty crianza notes, fine reduction (without great fruitiness). Flavourful, pleasant palate with good fruit-wood balance.

SOLAR DE SAMANIEGO VENDIMIA SELECCIONADA 1998 RED
75% tempranillo, 25% graciano

85 Cherry with an orangey edge. Fine, spicy aroma (vanilla) with well-integrated fruit/wood. Flavourful and round on the palate with ripe and polished tannins and a complex crianza, very pleasant drinking with a spicy finish.

SOLAR DE SAMANIEGO 1999 RESERVA RED
92% tempranillo, 8% graciano

85 Garnet red. Aroma of ripe black fruit with well-integrated mild smoky flavours, concentrated (elegant reduction). Fleshy, flavourful palate with fine toasty oak notes harmonised with the fruit; oily, powerful tannins

SOLAR DE SAMANIEGO 1998 RESERVA RED

82 Brick red garnet. Reduction aroma (leathers, orange peel) with hints of acetaldehyde. Fresh, flavourful palate, toasty, good acidity, pleasant.

SOLAR DE SAMANIEGO 2003 JOVEN RED

ALEJOS

Polígono Industrial El Sequero - Parcela 27
26509 Agoncillo (La Rioja)
☎: 941 437 051 - Fax: 941 437 077
b.a.alabanza@teleline.es
www.bodegasalejos.com

Established: 1988
🍇 1,250 📊 1,453,000 litres 🍷 25 has.
🍴 80% 🌐20%: -DE -AD -AT -UK -NL -MX

ALABANZA 2003 JOVEN RED
85% tempranillo, 15% otras

76 Cherry with an orangey edge. Balsamic aroma with notes of broom over foresty red berries. Flavourful, fruity palate with carbonic traces and good freshness but slightly sweet.

ALABANZA SELECCIÓN 2001 OAK AGED RED
90% tempranillo, 7% mazuelo, 3% graciano

89 Garnet red cherry with a violet edge. Intense aroma, rich in nuances (toasty flavours, red flowers, bilberries). Flavourful, fleshy palate with ripe tannins well-complemented by equally ripe fruit, generous and oily.

ALABANZA SELECCIÓN 2002 OAK AGED RED
90% tempranillo, 7% mazuelo, 3% graciano

89 Dark cherry. Powerful aroma of jammy black fruit with macerated skins, smoky oak notes and a balsamic hint. Flavourful, fleshy palate with a good fruit/oak integration, bitter with excellent acidity.

ALABANZA 2001 CRIANZA RED
95% tempranillo, 5% mazuelo

84 Garnet red cherry with a saffron edge. Powerful aroma with predominant spicy wood notes and a suggestion of slightly reduced fruit (prunes). Flavourful, bitter palate with excellent crianza expression, spicy and long.

ALABANZA 1999 RESERVA RED
90% tempranillo, 7% mazuelo, 3% garnacha

83 Garnet red cherry with a brick red glint. Not very intense aroma of slightly reduced ripe fruit with fine hints of tobacco and leather. Flavourful palate with ripe and oily tannins, spicy and long.

TORNASOL ECOLÓGICO 2002 RED
90% tempranillo, 5% mazuelo, 5% garnacha

80 Garnet red cherry with a violet hue. Powerful, fruity aroma with fine smoky skins and crianza. Flavourful palate with red stone fruit, slightly warm with a liquorice hint and good acidity.

ALICIA ROJAS

Carretera Nacional 232, km. 376 - 377
26513 Ausejo (La Rioja)
☎: 941 430 010 - Fax: 941 430 286
info@bodegasaliciarojas.com
www.bodegasaliciarojas.com

Established: 1962

700 📦 1,100.000 litres 🍇 125 has.

📦 80% 🌐 20%: -US -DE -UK -CH -BR -BE -AT -DK

SOLARCE 2003 JOVEN RED

78 Intense cherry with a violet edge. Intense aroma, very varietal red fruit over a suggestion of skins and brambles. Flavourful palate, fruity, with bitter nuances and marked acidity.

FINCA ALICIA ROJAS 2001 CRIANZA RED

80 Intense garnet red cherry. Intense aroma, toasty oak, with a suggestion of red fruit and nuances of new oak and stewed fruit. Flavourful, very bitter palate, with a suggestion of sweet fruit but predominant drying oak notes.

FINCA ALICIA ROJAS SELECCIÓN 2000 RESERVA RED

77 Dark garnet red cherry. Powerful aroma, with predominant notes of oak, a hint of precocious reduction. Flavourful, bitter (dark-roasted flavours) on the palate, lacking balance.

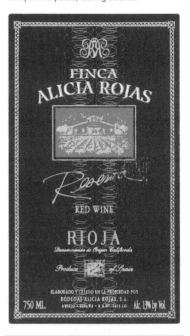

SOLARCE 2003 JOVEN WHITE
SOLARCE 2003 JOVEN ROSÉ
SOLARCE ECOLÓGICO 2003 JOVEN WHITE
SOLARCE ECOLÓGICO 2003 JOVEN ROSÉ
SOLARCE ECOLÓGICO 2003 JOVEN RED
FINCA ALICIA ROJAS 2003 WHITE
COLLADO DE LA ESTRELLA 2003
JOVEN RED
COLLADO DE LA ESTRELLA 2001
CRIANZA RED
SOLARCE 2001 CRIANZA RED
SOLARCE ECOLÓGICO 2001 CRIANZA RED
SOLARCE 1999 RESERVA RED
SOLARCE ECOLÓGICO 1999 RESERVA RED
FINCA ALICIA ROJAS 1999 RESERVA RED

Bodegas ALONSO GONZÁLEZ

Hospital, 9
26339 Ábalos (La Rioja)
☎: 941 334 164 - Fax: 941 334 164

Established: 1985

150 📦 180,000 litres 🍇 15 has. 📦 100%

CARLOS ALONSO 2003 WHITE
90% viura, 10% otras

76 Pale yellow with golden nuances. Intense, fruity aroma with hints of flowers and lees. Flavoured palate with fine bitter notes and an acidic edge.

CARLOS ALONSO 2002 ROSÉ
90% viura, 10% tempranillo

78 Pale salmon (classic Claret) Not very intense, slightly fruity aroma, with fine spicy hints of skins. Fresh, quite flavourful palate with hints of spicy fruit and good acidity.

CANTAURI 2003 JOVEN RED
90% tempranillo, 10% viura

84 Intense cherry with a violet edge. Powerful aroma of black fruit with a slight varietal and maceration expression. Flavourful palate with fine toasty and spicy notes of skins, ripe and firm grape tannins, excellent acidity and a hint of terroir.

VIÑA GORTU 2000 CRIANZA RED
100% tempranillo, 10% otras

84 Garnet red cherry with a brick red edge. Slightly intense aroma of fine toasty oak with a jammy fruit nuance and light reduction notes (leather). Flavourful palate with fine bitter notes, round tannins, spices and liquorice in the retronasal passage.

ALTANZA

Carretera Nacional 232, km. 419, 5
26360 Fuenmayor (Rioja)
☎: 941 450 860 - Fax: 941 450 804
altanza@bodegasaltanza.com
www.bodegasaltanza.com

Established: 1998

7,600 ▯ 3,900,000 litres ▯ 40 has.

▯ 70% ▯30%: -MX -CH -US -UK -IT -IE -DE -JP -PA -DO -CA -AT -TR

ALTANZA 1999 RESERVA ESPECIAL RED
100% tempranillo

85 Intense cherry. Aroma with notes of reduction in the bottle (leather, cedar wood, black tobacco) and slightly jammy fruit. Round, oily, spicy palate with hints of animals, flavourful with good acidity.

LEALTANZA 1999 RESERVA RED
100% tempranillo

85 Cherry with an garnet red-orangey edge. Medium-intensity aroma with a good reduction (leather, vanilla, cigar box) and a certain finesse. Round and flavourful on the palate with good fruit and wood symmetry and very pleasant.

CLUB LEALTANZA 1998 RESERVA RED
100% tempranillo

86 Cherry with a garnet red-orangey edge. Not very intense yet fine and harmonious aroma (vanilla, tobacco, jammy fruit). Flavourful and round on

the palate with polished tannins, intense with excellent harmony between fruit and wood.

LEALTANZA 1998 GRAN RESERVA RED
100% tempranillo

86 Quite intense cherry. Toasty, creamy aroma (cocoa and coffee) with notes of a fine reduction in the bottle (leather and cedar). Round, oily palate with polished tannins, spices in the retronasal passage and jammy fruit, flavourful.

EDULIS 2000 CRIANZA RED

AMADOR GARCÍA CHÁVARRI

Avenida Río Ebro, 70
01307 Baños de Ebro (Álava)
☎: 945 290 385 - Fax: 945 290 373

Established: 1980

▯ 250,000 litres ▯ 6 has. ▯ 100%

PEÑAGUDO WHITE
PEÑAGUDO ROSÉ
PEÑAGUDO RED
BALCORRE RED
HERENCIA BERSATXOA RED
IBARREDI RED

AMÉZOLA DE LA MORA

Paraje Viña Vieja, s/n
26359 Torremontalbo (La Rioja)
☎: 941 454 532 - Fax: 941 454 537

Established: 1986

▯ 2,700 ▯ 500,000 litres ▯ 65 has.

▯ 60% ▯40%: -UK -CH -US

IÑIGO AMÉZOLA 2002 OAK AGED RED
85% tempranillo, 10% mazuelo, 5% graciano

87 Fairly deep, brilliant cherry. Intense aroma of redcurrants, red stone fruit, a spicy suggestion and slightly sweet oak with fresh overtones. Flavourful, concentrated palate with ripe, slightly oily tannins, and spicy and liquorice notes in the retronasal passage.

VIÑA AMÉZOLA 2002 CRIANZA RED
85% tempranillo, 10% mazuelo, 5% graciano

87 A more intense cherry than the previous vintage. Aroma with very subtle notes of seasoned oak that allow the jammy fruit to come through. Slightly fleshy, flavourful palate with spices and seasoned oak in the retronasal passage.

VIÑA AMÉZOLA 2001 CRIANZA RED
85% tempranillo, 10% mazuelo, 5% graciano

85 Dark lively garnet red cherry. Fine, spicy and elegant aroma. Flavourful palate with jammy fruit and spices in the retronasal passage (tobacco, vanilla, cedar).

VIÑA AMÉZOLA 2000 CRIANZA RED
85% tempranillo, 10% mazuelo, 5% graciano

81 Brilliant cherry with a brick red glint. Intense aroma with a certain fruity and oaky freshness and a light spicy suggestion and reduction, very fine. Flavourful on the palate with bitter hints of oak and a slightly overripe suggestion.

SEÑORÍO AMÉZOLA 1999 RESERVA RED
85% tempranillo, 10% mazuelo, 5% graciano

83 Intense cherry with a brick red glint. Intense aroma with predominant spicy oak notes, fresh fruity and terroir overtones. Flavourful, supple palate with a good fruit/oak integration and good acidity.

SOLAR AMÉZOLA 1996 GRAN RESERVA RED

ÁNGEL Y VICENTE MARTÍNEZ ÁLVAREZ

San Cristóbal, 46
26360 Fuenmayor (La Rioja)
☎: 941 450 320
Established: 1990
240,000 litres ☙ 25 has.

HERENCIA MARTÍNEZ ALVAREZ ROSÉ
HERENCIA MARTÍNEZ ALVAREZ RED

ANTIGUA USANZA

Camino Garraguelle, s/n
26338 San Vicente de la Sonsierra (La Rioja)
☎: 941 334 156 - Fax: 941 334 156
usanza@prorioja.es
www.prorioja.es
Established: 1989
2,200 3,000,000 litres ☙ 7 has.
80% 20%: -DE -FR -US -MX

ANTIGUA USANZA 1998 RESERVA RED
90% tempranillo, 5% graciano, 5% mazuelo

81 Fairly deep cherry with a very lively copper edge. Not very intense aroma with well-integrate fruit/oak and a ripe and slightly warm suggestion. Flavourful on the palate with quite marked and drying tannins, warm with jammy fruit and liquorice in the finish.

VIÑA AZAI 2003 JOVEN RED
ANTIGUA USANZA 2000 CRIANZA RED
ANTIGUA USANZA PREMIUM 2001 CRIANZA RED
VIÑA AZAI 2000 CRIANZA RED
ANTIGUA USANZA PREMIUM 1996 RESERVA RED
VIÑA AZAI 1998 RESERVA RED

ANTONIO RAMÍREZ-PECIÑA

La Lleca, s/n
01307 Villabuena (Álava)
☎: 945 609 088

BIKAIN RED
VIÑA SOCARRE RED

ARABARTE

Carretera Samaniego, s/n
01307 Villabuena (Álava)
☎: 945 609 408 - Fax: 945 609 409
arabarte@arabarte.es
www.arabarte.es
Established: 1990
600 750,000 litres ☙ 42 has.
88% 12%

ARABARTE 2003 JOVEN WHITE
100% viura

79 Pale with golden nuances. Intense aroma of slightly reduced white fruit and hints of lees. Flavourful, somewhat fruity palate with quality bittersweet notes and good acidity.

ARABARTE 2003 JOVEN ROSÉ
85% tempranillo, 15% viura

77 Brilliant salmon pink. Not very intense aroma of red fruit and floral hints. Flavourful palate with bitter notes and pronounced citrus acidity.

ARABARTE 2003 MACERACIÓN CARBÓNICA RED
85% tempranillo, 15% viura

77 Cherry with a violet hue. Intense, fruity aroma, light fermentative off-odours. Better on the palate, flavourful with noticeable tannins (elements of greeness) and hints of liquorice.

ARABARTE TEMPRANILLO 2002 MACERACIÓN CARBÓNICA RED
100% tempranillo

80 Garnet red cherry with a violet edge. Fruity aroma with a fermentative and not altogether clear hint and hints of skins. Better palate, fleshy with slightly sweet hints and notions of terroir, flavourful tannicity.

ARABARTE 2000 CRIANZA RED
90% tempranillo, 10% viura

80 Dark cherry with a saffron edge. Slightly intense aroma with predominant toasty, quite sweet wood notes. Flavourful palate with slightly reduced fruit and ripe, sweet tannins, without great nuances.

ARABARTE 1999 RESERVA RED
90% tempranillo, 10% viura

82 Red cherry with a coppery edge. Intense aroma of very ripe, slightly reduced fruit and toasty oak notes. Flavourful palate with ripe, oily tannins, and fine bitter notes, fresh and supple overtones.

ARABARTE 2002 MACERACIÓN CARBÓNICA WHITE
ARABARTE 2002 MACERACIÓN CARBÓNICA ROSÉ
ARABARTE 2002 MACERACIÓN CARBÓNICA RED

ARACO

Carretera Lapuebla, s/n
01300 Laguardia (Álava)
☎: 945 600 209 - Fax: 945 600 067
araco@bodegasaraco.com
www.bodegasaraco.com

Established: 1986

⊕ 600 🗄 1,200,000 litres 🍇 200 has.
🍷 90% 🌐10%: -US -AT -LV

SEÑORÍO ARACO 2003 JOVEN RED
100% tempranillo

82 Garnet red with a violet edge. Medium-intensity, fruity aroma (blackberries, plums). Flavourful palate with a good fruit expression, well-integrated alcohol and spices (pepper), well-balanced, long.

ARACO SELECCIÓN 2000 CRIANZA RED
tempranillo

85 Garnet red cherry. Powerful palate with spicy oak notes, a suggestion of reduction with a certain animal character (leather, stables). Flavourful, and fleshy palate, with supple overtones, well-integrated fruit/oak and good crianza expression.

SEÑORÍO ARACO 2001 CRIANZA RED
100% tempranillo

86 Garnet red cherry with a coppery edge. Powerful aroma of jammy black fruit, spicy oak notes and balsamic hints. Flavourful palate with fleshy overtones, a good oak/fruit integration, hints of liquorice, pepper and refreshing acidity.

SEÑORÍO ARACO 2002 ROSÉ
SEÑORÍO ARACO 2002 WHITE

ARNÁEZ

Acosta, 15
26223 Hormilla (La Rioja)
☎: 941 417 734

Established: 1980

🗄 35,000 litres 🍇 4 has. 🍷 100%

S.B. ARNÁEZ ROSÉ
S.B. ARNÁEZ JOVEN RED

ARTADI-COSECHEROS ALAVESES

Carretera de Logroño, s/n
01300 Laguardia (Álava)
☎: 945 600 119 - Fax: 945 600 850
info@artadi.com

Established: 1985

⊕ 1,300 🗄 900,000 litres 🍇 70 has.
🍷 40% 🌐60%:

ARTADI 2003 JOVEN RED
85% tempranillo, 15% viura

85 Intense cherry. Powerful aroma rich in ripe fruit nuances (skin maceration). Very fruity, ripe, sweet palate with skins and maceration.

ARTADI PAGOS VIEJOS 2002 OAK AGED RED
tempranillo

94 Intense cherry. Quite closed but very fine aroma (cocoa, After Eights) of creamy toast and black, very fresh fruit (bilberries, redcurrants). Oily, round and elegant palate with a creamy toasty retronasal effect, sweet and very flavourful tannins, and notions of ripe bunches in the retronasal palate, persistent, long.

ARTADI VIÑAS DE GAIN 2002 OAK AGED RED
tempranillo

89 Intense cherry. Fine, toasty aroma (coffee, cocoa) with fresh fruit and creamy vanilla oak notes. Powerful, fruity, flavourful palate with excellent fruit/oak assemblage.

VIÑA EL PISÓN 2002 OAK AGED RED
99% tempranillo, 1% otras

98 Very intense cherry. Powerful aroma rich in fine toasty sensations (cocoa, aromatic coffee, fine carpentry), and ripe black fruit but rich in nuances that has maintained its freshness during grape ripening. Round, oily, elegant palate that fills the mouth, a toasty retronasal effect (aromatic coffee), ripe but perceptible tannins and ripe grapes in the retronasal passage.

ARTADI GRANDES AÑADAS OAK AGED RED

AYESA

Páganos, 92
01300 Laguardia (Álava)
☎: 945 600 008
vinaayesa@terra.es

Established: 1975

⊕ 200 🗄 300,000 litres 🍇 60 has.
🍷 80% 🌐20%

REAL ONEAN RED
VIÑA AYESA RED

AZPILLAGA-URARTE

Camino Elvillar, s/n
01308 Lanciego (Álava)
☎: 945 608 045

Established: 1989

145,000 litres 🍇 15 has. 🍷 100%

SEÑORÍO DE ARTULE RED
VIÑA EL PAGO RED

Bodegas BAGORDI

Carretera de Estella, km. 32
31261 Andosilla (Navarra)
☎: 948 674 860 - Fax: 948 674 238
info@bagordi.com
www.bagordi.com

Established: 1996

1,200 1,000,000 litres 🍇 60 has.
🍷 40% 🌐60%

NAVARDIA 2003 JOVEN RED
90% tempranillo, 10% garnacha

83 Intense cherry. Powerful, fruity aroma with toasty hints of skins and the freshness of damp earth. Flavourful, fleshy palate with fine, spicy hints of skins, firm tannins and excellent acidity.

USOA DE BAGORDI 2003 JOVEN RED
75% tempranillo, 15% merlot, 10% graciano

82 Brilliant cherry. Powerful aroma of red fruit with fresh overtones of herbs and fallen leaves and spicy hints of skins. Flavourful, fresh palate, slightly warm yet with a good fruit weight, fine spicy notes and refreshing acidity.

BAGORDI 2003 OAK AGED RED
100% tempranillo

79 Dark cherry. Powerful aroma with an excellent varietal expression (black fruit, underbrush), hints of skins and fine smoky oak. Flavourful palate with slightly marked tannins (a touch of greeness) and fresh acidity.

USOA DE BAGORDI SELECCIÓN 2002 OAK AGED RED
80% tempranillo, 20% merlot

76 Cherry. Balsamic aroma with pine, resins and leather. Very marked wood tannins on the palate; a little lacking in fruit.

BAGORDI 2001 CRIANZA RED
100% tempranillo

84 Dark garnet red cherry. Intense aroma with predominant toasty oak notes and a suggestion of ripe stone fruit. Flavourful palate with a good

oak/fruit integration, bitter notes (liquorice, dark-roasted flavours) and excellent acidity.

NAVARDIA 2000 CRIANZA RED
90% tempranillo, 10% garnacha

82 Fairly deep cherry with a saffron edge. Powerful aroma of toasty oak notes, with hints of sun-drenched skins, a balsamic bouquet and damp fallen leaves. Flavourful palate of red fruit with slightly marked but fine tannins, fresh and supple overtones.

BAGORDI GARNACHA 2000 RESERVA RED
100% garnacha

86 Cherry with a brick red hue. Good intensity aroma of ripe but fine wine, spices (pepper, vanilla) and a balsamic varietal notion (red fruit). Round on the palate, spicy, warm with toasty notes and a good barrel aged Garnacha.

USOA DE BAGORDI RESERVA ESPECIAL 2000 RED
60% graciano, 40% merlot

88 Garnet red cherry with a coppery edge. Intense aroma with fine spicy notes, cedar, a suggestion of balsamic hints and red fruit and mineral fresh overtones. Flavourful, supple palate with a good fruit/oak integration, spicy notes of skins, balsamic hints and minerals.

BAIGORRI

Carretera Vitoria-Logroño, km. 53
01307 Samaniego (Álava)
☎: 945 609 420 - Fax: 945 609 407
mail@bodegasbaigorri.com
www.bodegasbaigorri.com

Established: 1997

1,500 720,000 litres 🍇 2 has. 🍷 100%

BAIGORRI 2002 FERMENTADO EN BARRICA WHITE
100% viura

80 Yellow straw. Not very intense aroma with toasty wood notes and a herby suggestion. Flavourful, well-balanced palate with well-assembled wood; pleasant.

BAIGORRI SOLAR DE BAI 2002 FERMENTADO EN BARRICA WHITE
100% viura

84 Golden. Herbaceous aroma, spices (ginger, anise), well-assembled smoky hints of the wood. Flavourful palate, slightly warm, toasty and spicy notes and fruit; slightly woody finish.

BAIGORRI 2002 MACERACIÓN CARBÓNICA RED
100% tempranillo

83 Garnet red cherry with a ruby red edge. Medium-intensity aroma, fruity with a slight varietal expression. Fresh, fruity palate with a mild vegetative hint that does not alter its character.

BAIGORRI 2003 MACERACIÓN CARBÓNICA RED
100% tempranillo

84 Somewhat open garnet red cherry. Varietal aroma with good fruit expression. Flavourful, medium-bodied palate with varietal hints in the retronasal passage, pleasant.

BAIGORRI DE GARAGE 2000 CRIANZA RED

84 Garnet red cherry. Aroma with toasty notes of oak over the fruit. Quite fruity in the mouth with oak tannin notes, fruit concealed by the wood; flavourful.

BAIGORRI VENDIMIA SELECCIONADA 2002 CRIANZA RED

86 Dark cherry. Fruity aroma with undertones of varietal character and woody notes. Round, medium-bodied, flavourful palate, oak in the retronasal passage.

BAIGORRI 2003 FERMENTADO EN BARRICA WHITE
BAIGORRI 2003 FERMENTADO EN BARRICA WHITE
BAIGORRI 2003 MACERACIÓN CARBÓNICA RED
BAIGORRI DE GARAGE 2002 CRIANZA RED
BAIGORRI VIÑAS VIEJAS 2002 RESERVA RED

BARÓN DE LEY

Carretera Mendavia - Lodosa, km. 5, 5
31587 Mendavia (Navarra)
☎: 948 694 303 - Fax: 948 694 304
info@barondeley.com
www.barondeley.com

Established: 1985
🍷 11,000 📊 3,000,000 litres 🍇 140 has.
🏆 50% 🌐50%

BARÓN DE LEY 2003 WHITE
viura

82 Brilliant pale yellow. Powerful, ripe aroma with white fruit notes, floral hints (acacia), fine lees and mountain herbs. Fresh, bitter, spicy palate with good acidity.

BARÓN DE LEY 2003 ROSÉ
tempranillo

83 Brilliant raspberry. Slightly intense aroma with predominant spicy and herby notes. Fresh, flavourful palate with bitter and spicy notes, noticeable acidity.

BARÓN DE LEY FINCA MONASTERIO 2001 OAK AGED RED
tempranillo, otras

87 Dark cherry. Powerful aroma, dark-roasted flavours, smoky oak, jammy black fruit and balsamic notes. Flavourful palate with a certain concentration, predominant dark-roasted notes of pitch and bitter hints; somewhat oily and warm.

BARÓN DE LEY 1999 RESERVA RED

84 Garnet red cherry with a brick red rim. Powerful aroma with mild reduction notes (tobacco, leather), and a suggestion of spices and ripe fruit. Flavourful palate with fine bitter notes and hints of spices and terracotta in the finish.

BENIGNO BASOCO

Herrería, 31
01307 Villabuena (Álava)
☎: 945 609 142

Established: 1997
📊 410,000 litres 🍇 25 has. 🏆 100%

BASOCO RED
BENIGNO BASOCO RED

Vinos de BENJAMÍN ROMEO

Amorebieta 6, bajo
26338 San Vicente de la Sonsierra (La Rioja)
☎: 941 334 228 - Fax: 955 601 672

Established: 1996
🍷 75 🍇 7 has.

CONTADOR 2001 OAK AGED RED
tempranillo

93 Intense cherry. Slightly quite closed aroma with mineral and fruit expression (blackplums) and fine toasty oak. Powerful palate with vigourous tannins enveloped by the alcohol, warm and slightly mineral.

LA CUEVA DEL CONTADOR 2002 OAK AGED RED
100% tempranillo

91 Intense cherry. Slightly closed yet fine and mineral aroma with hints of very ripe fruit, floral nuances (violets) and excellent and fine crianza. Round, complex palate with excellent wood, ripe fruit and a mineral hint.

LA VIÑA DE ANDRÉS ROMEO 2001 OAK AGED RED
tempranillo

87 Intense, almost opaque cherry. Powerful, concentrated aroma of jammy black fruit with spicy oak notes and a hint of reduction (stables). Flavourful, fleshy palate with ripe tannins, warm notes, a good fruit weight and hints of pitch and chocolate in the finish.

LA VIÑA DE ANDRÉS ROMEO 2002 OAK AGED RED
tempranillo

89 Dark cherry. Powerful aroma with an excellent ripe fruit expression (redcurrants, cherries), fine toasty wood and a balsamic hint. Flavourful palate with fleshy overtones, jammy fruit, and spicy hints. Warm, with a new Riojan dimension and fresh notes of skins and cocoa in the retronasal passage.

CONTADOR 2002 OAK AGED RED

BERBERANA

Carretera de Vitoria, km. 182-183
26360 Cenicero (La Rioja)
☎: 941 453 100 - Fax: 941 450 101
info@berberana.com
www.berberana.com

Established: 1877

🍶 10,000 📦 26,000,000 litres 🍇 3,000 has.

🍷 56% 🌐44%: -UK -NL -DE PAÍSES DEL ESTE -JP -US -OTROS

BERBERANA VIÑA ALARDE 2000 CRIANZA RED
100% tempranillo

80 Brilliant cherry with a coppery edge. Intense aroma with predominant smoky and spicy notes of wood. Flavourful on the palate with fine bitter notes, well-integrated fruit and oak although without great nuances.

BERBERANA VIÑA ALARDE 1999 RESERVA RED
80% tempranillo, 20% garnacha

84 Garnet red cherry with a brick red rim. Intense aroma of smoky oak and fine reduction notes (leathers, varnish). Flavourful and supple palate with a good oak/fruit integration, freshness of spices and fruit (dates), balsamic hints.

BERBERANA SELECCIÓN ESPECIAL WHITE
VIÑA CANDA VINO DE VENDIMIA WHITE
VIÑA CANDA VINO DE VENDIMIA ROSÉ
BERBERANA VIÑA MARA TEMPRANILLO RED
BERBERANA MARINO JOVEN RED
CARTA DE ORO ROBLE RED
BERBERANA CARTA DE ORO RED
BERBERANA CARTA DE PLATA RED
BERBERANA TIERRA DEL SOL RED
BERBERANA VIÑA ALARDE 2º AÑO RED
VIÑA CANDA VINO DE VENDIMIA RED
BERBERANA RED
BERBERANA CARTA DE ORO ETIQUETA NEGRA RED
BERBERANA SELECCIÓN ESPECIAL OAK AGED RED

BERBERANA CARTA DE ORO 2000 CRIANZA RED
BERBERANA SELECCIÓN ORO CRIANZA RED
BERBERANA VIÑA MARA 2000 CRIANZA RED
BERBERANA VIÑA ALARDE 1997 GRAN RESERVA RED

Bodegas BERCEO

Cuevas, 32-34-36
26200 Haro (La Rioja)
☎: 941 310 744 - Fax: 941 310 744
bodegas@gurpegui.es
www.gurpegui.es

Established: 1872

🍶 4,000 📦 1,200,000 litres 🍇 50 has.

🍷 80% 🌐20%

VIÑA BERCEO 2003 FERMENTADO EN BARRICA WHITE
100% viura

81 Straw-coloured. Aroma with creamy wood notes (nuts) over a nuance of fresh tropical fruit and herbs. Bitter palate (green fruit pulp), fresh with vine variety character and well-integrated wood.

LOS DOMINIOS DE BERCEO PREFILOXÉRICO 2001 CRIANZA RED
100% tempranillo

88 Deep, intense cherry. Fine aroma with grape expression and well-integrated and elegant toasty notes (smoke, earth), very elegant. Flavourful, very harmonious palate with wood well-integrated with the grape notes; fine fruit tannins with character.

VIÑA BERCEO 2001 CRIANZA RED
graciano, tempranillo, mazuelo

85 Deep garnet red. Aroma of terroir, fine crianza (liquorice, smoky flavours) with a nuance of ripe black fruit. Fleshy palate with good black fruit in harmony with the toasty flavours, oily tannins, improves with age.

GONZALO DE BERCEO 1999 RESERVA RED
graciano, tempranillo, mazuelo

82 Pale garnet red. Fruity aroma of fine herbs, spices, pleasant. Flavourful with fresh acidity on the palate, marked wood but fine and well-integrated; fresh redcurrants in the finish.

LOS DOMINIOS DE BERCEO 2000 RESERVA RED
100% tempranillo

89 Fine smoky and earthy flavours (slightly mineral) well-integrated with the very ripe red fruit and without loss of freshness. Fleshy palate with round, polished and very flavourful tannins; good acidity for ageing with wood-fruit symmetry, cocoa and oak spices.

VIÑADRIÁN 2003 WHITE
VIÑADRIÁN 2003 JOVEN ROSÉ
VIÑADRIÁN 2003 JOVEN RED
VIÑA BERCEO 2003 JOVEN ROSÉ
GONZALO DE BERCEO 1996 GRAN RESERVA RED

BERONIA

Carretera Ollauri - Nájera, km. 1, 800
26220 Ollauri (La Rioja)
☎: 941 338 000 - Fax: 941 338 266
beronia@beronia.es
www.beronia.es

Established: 1973

⊕ 20,000 ▤ 8,000,000 litres ❧ 10 has.

▰ 65% ◐35%: -DE -UK -CH -JP -MX -EC -CA -US

BERONIA VIURA 2003 JOVEN WHITE
viura

76 Straw-coloured. Fine aroma of white fruit with nuances of flowers. Flavourful palate with fresh acidity and hardly any fruit; short, a hint of beads.

BERONIA VIURA 2001 FERMENTADO EN BARRICA WHITE
100% viura

78 Golden. Honeyed aroma of toasty casks with a hint of ripe fruit. Oily, fresh palate with predominant wood and alcohol-acidity balance; a toasty finish.

BERONIA TEMPRANILLO 2001 OAK AGED RED
100% tempranillo

80 Brilliant cherry with a coppery glint. Intense aroma with fine reduction notes (leathers) and fresh overtones of red fruit. Flavourful palate, with slightly drying tannins, warm notes, without obvious nuances; round with a certain structure; pleasant.

BERONIA 2001 CRIANZA RED
tempranillo, garnacha, mazuelo

85 Brilliant garnet red cherry. Slightly intense aroma with a certain finesse, toasty oak notes and a suggestion of ripe black fruit. Flavourful palate with fleshy overtones and slightly rough tannins, an oily texture and fine bitter notes (liquorice, chocolate) in the retronasal passage.

BERONIA 1999 RESERVA RED
tempranillo, graciano, mazuelo

84 Garnet red. Fine aroma of long crianza (toasty flavours, orange peel) with a nuance of terroir notes. Flavourful, very well-balanced palate with creamy wood notes; fresh and pleasant.

BERONIA MAZUELO 1998 RESERVA RED
100% mazuelo

87 Garnet red. Aroma of red fruit with well-assembled fine spices and smoky flavours and an expression of toasty skins. Flavourful palate with varietal character, elegant well-balanced toasty flavours and fine tannins, pleasant.

BERONIA 1995 GRAN RESERVA RED
tempranillo, mazuelo, graciano

80 Garnet red with a brick red hue. Animal aroma (reduction) with very long crianza notes and overtones of oxidation and earth. Flavourful palate with elegant tannins, notes of animals and leathers, short but with good freshness.

BERRUECO

Herrería, travesía-2, nf 2
01307 Villabuena (Álava)
☎: 945 609 034
gontzalb@hotmail.com
www.jazzfree.com/jazz1/gamberru

Established: 1970

⊕ 150 ▤ 500,000 litres ❧ 28 has. ▰ 100%

BERRUECO RED
BERRUECO CRIANZA RED
BERRUECO RESERVA RED

Hermanos BERZAL TRONCOSO

Avenida del Puente, 24
01307 Baños de Ebro (Álava)
☎: 945 623 368 - Fax: 945 623 368
dominioberzal@euskalnet.net

Established: 1958

🏭 300 📦 67,500 litres 🍇 50 has.

🍷 75% 🍾25%: -DE -BE -NL -LU -US

DOMINIO DE BERZAL 2003 JOVEN RED
90% tempranillo, 10% viura

85 Cherry with a violet edge. Aroma of skins, flowers and red fruit (blackberries, raspberries). Fresh, somewhat bitter and persistent on the palate with red fruit in the retronasal passage.

DOMINIO DE BERZAL 2001 CRIANZA RED
100% tempranillo

78 Cherry. Perfumed aroma of vanilla, not very intense. Light, round palate, well-mannered.

DOMINIO DE BERZAL SELECCIÓN PRIVADA 2001 RED
100% tempranillo

80 Cherry with a blueish rim. Quite alcoholic with light woody notes and ripe red fruit. Warm, somewhat bitter, medium bodied palate.

Bodegas BILBAÍNAS

Estación, 3
26200 Haro (La Rioja)
☎: 941 310 147 - Fax: 941 310 706
smartin@codorniu.es
www.grupocodorniu.com

Established: 1859

🏭 18,000 📦 7,000,000 litres 🍇 256 has.

🍷 97% 🍾3%:

VIÑA PACETA 2000 CRIANZA RED
100% tempranillo

82 Garnet red cherry with a brick red edge. Slightly intense, elegant aroma with toasty hints of oak and skins and a fine vanilla nuance. Flavourful palate with a good fruit/oak integration, hints of sweetish fruit and an oily texture.

LA VICALANDA 1999 RESERVA RED
100% tempranillo

89 Dark cherry with an orange rim. Fine, spicy, complex aroma (cigar box, blond tobacco) with less nuances of tanned oak (classic). Round, oily, elegant palate with polished but perceptible tannins, flavourful, long, with spicy, very delicate notes in the retronasal passage.

VIÑA POMAL 1998 RESERVA RED
85% tempranillo, 15% mazuelo, graciano

86 Ruby red with a brick red hue. Aroma with notes of tanned wood, spices (pepper, cedar, tobacco) and light jammy fruit. Round, oily palate with a classic hint yet elegant flavourful, with perfect integration of tannins and alcohol.

VIÑA POMAL SELECCIÓN CENTENARIO 1998 RESERVA RED
100% tempranillo

86 Ruby red with a brick red hue. Aroma rich in Crianza-in-cask expression (tobacco, vanilla, cedar) and a jammy fruit nuance; elegant. Very supple palate with somewhat muted tannins; much better in the nose than on the palate.

LA VICALANDA 1997 GRAN RESERVA RED
100% tempranillo

87 Brilliant cherry with a saffron glint. Intense aroma with fresh overtones of red stone fruit, spicy with traditional crianza expression. Flavourful on the palate with promising although slightly marked tannins; fine bitter crianza notes and good acidity.

LA VICALANDA 1996 GRAN RESERVA RED

BIURKO GORRI

Ponibal, s/n
31229 Bargota (Navarra)
☎: 948 648 370 - Fax: 948 648 399
ocijo@biurkogorri.com
www.biurkogorri.com

Established: 1993

🏭 1,000 📦 700,000 litres 🍇 30 has.

🍷 60% 🍾40%:

ARBANTA JOVEN RED
BIURKO MACERACIÓN CARBÓNICA RED
BIURKO SELECCIÓN GARNACHA RED
BIURKO TEMPRANILLO OAK AGED RED
JOANES DE BARGOTA CRIANZA RED

BODEGAS Y VIÑAS DEL CONDE

Bodegas, 98
01306 La Puebla de Labarca (Álava)
☎: 656 780 938 - Fax: 945 607 017
b.casado@euskalnet.net
casadomorales.com

Established: 2001

🏭 50 📦 40,000 litres 🍇 3 has.

🍷 60% 🍾40%: -DE -UK -IE -FR

CONDE DE ÁLAVA 2002 JOVEN RED
CONDE DE ÁLAVA 1999 CRIANZA RED

DO Ca. RIOJA

BONIFACIO MARTÍNEZ BOBADILLA

La Iglesia, s/n
26311 Cárdenas (La Rioja)
☎: 941 367 219

CASTILLANTICO WHITE
CASTILLANTICO ROSÉ
CASTILLANTICO RED

Bodegas BRETÓN CRIADORES

Carretera de Fuenmayor, km. 1, 5
26370 Navarrete (La Rioja)
☎: 941 440 840 - Fax: 941 440 812
info@bodegasbreton.com
www.bodegasbreton.com

Established: 1985

🏭 6,000 🛢 2,000,000 litres 🍇 106 has.

🍷 55% 🌍45%: -US -DE -UK -SE -FI -DK
-RU -PL -CA -PR -AT -VE -NL -BE -MX

LORIÑON 2003 FERMENTADO EN BARRICA WHITE
100% viura

79 Straw-coloured. Medium-intensity aroma and burnt, smoky oak notes with a suggestion of citrus fruit. Marked oak character on the palate and a suggestion of fresh fruit; needs time for the cuvée.

LORIÑON 2001 CRIANZA RED
85% tempranillo, 5% garnacha, 5% mazuelo, 5% graciano

84 Dark cherry. Toasty creamy aroma of ripe fruit. Fleshy, warm palate with flavourful wood tannins.

ALBA DE BRETÓN 2001 RESERVA RED
100% tempranillo

91 Intense cherry. Aroma of ink and creamy toast (dark-roasted flavours, dark chocolate). Powerful, fleshy and very sweet on the palate, riper, with a hint of flavourful tannins.

PAGOS DEL CAMINO 2001 RED
100% garnacha

91 Intense cherry. Complex aroma, rich in expression, with floral notes (violets). Full, flavourful palate, with copious fruit expression, warm.

DOMINIO DE CONTE 2001 RESERVA RED
90% tempranillo, 10% graciano

89 Intense cherry. Toasty aroma (coffee, cereals) of the cask with quite closed fruit and a fruit expression. Powerful, toasty palate with long flavour.

LORIÑÓN 1999 RESERVA RED
85% tempranillo, 5% garnacha, 5% mazuelo, 5% graciano

85 Intense cherry. Aroma with notes of oak, unassembled fruit, and toasty hints (coffee, cocoa). Fleshy palate with ripe, lively oak tannins.

ALBA DE BRETÓN 1998 RESERVA RED
100% tempranillo

85 Intense cherry with a coppery edge. Intense aroma with fine smoky oak and a suggestion of jammy red fruit, balsamic and quite varietal (underbrush) notes. Flavourful, fleshy palate with slightly rough tannins, lacking balance (marked acidity).

DOMINIO DE CONTE 1998 RESERVA RED
90% tempranillo, 10% graciano

83 Quite dark cherry with an orangey edge. Medium-intensity aroma of vanilla, varnish and ink. Flavourful palate with toasty notes, pitch and bitter polished tannins.

LORIÑÓN 1997 GRAN RESERVA RED
85% tempranillo, 5% garnacha, 5% mazuelo, 5% graciano

86 Ruby red with a brick red hue. Fine reduction aroma (tobacco leather) with pepper spices. Oily, round and spicy on the palate. A ìmodern classicî.

BURGO VIEJO

Concordia, 8
26540 Alfaro (La Rioja)
☎: 941 183 405 - Fax: 941 181 603
bodegas@burgoviejo.com
www.burgoviejo.com

Established: 1960

🏭 1,150 🛢 3,800,000 litres 🍇 210 has.

🍷 70% 🌍30%

BURGO VIEJO 2003 JOVEN WHITE
100% viura

74 Pale yellow. Intense aroma with fresh overtones, of ripe white fruit with hints of herbs. Flavourful on the palate without great fruit expression, pleasant.

BURGO VIEJO 2003 JOVEN ROSÉ
100% garnacha

73 Intense salmon pink with an orangey glint. Intense aroma without great fruit expression, toasty hints of skins (varietal character) and a suggestion of fallen leaves. Quite fresh on the palate with bitter and citrus fruit notes, slightly oily.

BURGO VIEJO 2003 JOVEN RED
70% tempranillo, 20% garnacha, 10% mazuelo

78 Garnet red cherry. Intense aroma of macerated red fruit and violet petals. Fresh on the palate with flavourful grape tannicity, hints of damp earth and good acidity.

BURGO VIEJO 2001 CRIANZA RED
80% tempranillo, 20% graciano

77 Garnet red cherry with a coppery edge. Intense aroma of black fruit with spicy oak notes and hints of a fine reduction (tobacco). Flavourful on the palate with well-integrated creamy oak and fruit notes and a spicy nuance; pleasant.

BURGO VIEJO 1998 RESERVA RED
85% tempranillo, 10% mazuelo, 5% graciano

77 Cherry with a brick red edge. Not very intense aroma of spicy oak notes and hints of a fine reduction (leathers). Flavourful on the palate with a fruity nuance, fine bitter notes and a good expression of traditional crianza.

Bodega CAMPANILE

Barrihuelo, 73
01340 Elciego (Álava)
☎: 944 807 295 - Fax: 944 630 938
www.diez-caballero@terra.es

Established: 1975

⊞ 650 ▤ 246,000 litres ▧ 26 has.
▼ 90% ✪10%

DIEZ-CABALLERO 2001 CRIANZA RED
95% tempranillo, 5% graciano

87 Dark cherry. Intense aroma of black fruit, fresh overtones of macerated skins and toasty hints of oak. Flavourful palate with a good oak/fruit integration, fine notes of fruit, liquorice, damp earth and spicy oak, long.

DÍEZ-CABALLERO 2000 RESERVA RED
90% tempranillo, 5% mazuelo, 5% graciano

86 Dark cherry with a coppery edge. Intense aroma of jammy black fruit with spicy hints of oak and a balsamic suggestion. Flavourful palate with a good fruit/oak integration, quality bitter notes (liquorice dark-roasted flavours) and good acidity, very original.

DÍEZ-CABALLERO VENDIMIA SELECCIONADA 2000 RESERVA RED
100% tempranillo

84 Garnet red cherry. Slightly intense aroma of ripe red fruit, with fine toasty and balsamic notes. Flavourful palate with fleshy overtones, a good oak/fruit integration and fine bitter notes of liquorice.

DÍEZ-CABALLERO VENDIMIA SELECCIONADA 2001 RESERVA RED
100% tempranillo

85 Dark, garnet red cherry. Intense aroma with a certain finesse, macerated black fruit and spicy notes of oak. Flavourful, fleshy palate, round,

slightly oily tannins, with fine spicy notes, liquorice and fresh fruit in the finish.

DÍEZ-CABALLERO 1998 RESERVA RED
DÍEZ-CABALLERO 2000 CRIANZA RED

CAMPILLO

Carretera de Logroño, s/n
01300 Laguardia (Álava)
☎: 945 600 826 - Fax: 945 600 837
info@bodegascampillo.es

Established: 1990

⊞ 12,000 ▤ 1,500,000 litres ▧ 50 has.
▼ 80% ✪20%

CAMPILLO 1998 RESERVA RED

86 Garnet red with a brick red edge. Aroma of ripe black fruit with hints of sour cherries in liqueur and good crianza notes (animals, pitch). Dry and very flavourful on the palate with supple wood tannins, fresh acidity and well-balanced toasty and creamy notes.

CAMPILLO CRIANZA 2000 RED

85 Cherry with a garnet red edge. Aroma with crianza notes (coffee-flavoured toffee, animals) and balsamic hints. Flavourful on the palate with polished wood tannins and oily fruit tannins, fresh acidity, cocoa and animal skins in the finish.

CAMPILLO RESERVA ESPECIAL 1996 RED

87 Deep garnet red. Medium-intensity aroma, elegant smoky scents, peat and vanilla with a nuance of black fruit. Dry palate, wood tannins well-integrated with the fruit, slightly oily, for keeping; with features of a good crianza.

CAMPILLO 1994 GRAN RESERVA RED
tempranillo

84 Cherry with an orangey hue. Balsamic aroma (mint, eucalyptus) with spicy notes, chocolate, vanilla and a fine reduction. Good acidity on the palate with well-assembled tannins and medium persistence.

CÁNDIDO BESA

Errementari, 27
01307 Villabuena - Eskuernaga (Álava)
☎: 945 609 089

Established: 1970

▤ 128,000 litres ▧ 8,5 has. ▼ 100%

CÁNDIDO BESA RED

CARDEMA

Las Huertas, 7
26360 Fuenmayor (La Rioja)

DO Ca. RIOJA

☎: 941 451 083 - Fax: 941 451 083
Established: 1993
⊕ 40 🍇 20 has. 🍷 100%

SEÑORÍO DE CARCEDO RED

CARLOS OLASOLO

Frontón, 4 bis
26360 Fuenmayor (La Rioja)
☎: 941 450 334
olasolofuenmayor@yahoo.es
Established: 1985
⊕ 50 ▤ 100,000 litres 🍇 15 has.
🍶 12,500 litres.

OLASOLO 2002 RED
95% tempranillo, 5% graciano

79 Dark garnet red cherry. Slightly intense, fruity aroma with fine toasty notes and spicy skins. Flavourful, bitter palate with a slight hint of greeness and good acidity.

CARLOS SAMPEDRO

Páganos, 44
01300 Laguardia (Álava)
☎: 945 600 146 - Fax: 945 600 146
bodegascarlossampedro@telefonica.net -
www.bodegascarlossampedro.com
⊕ 100 ▤ 120,000 litres 🍇 10 has.
🍷 85% 🌐15%: -UK

BRILLADOR 2003 JOVEN RED
tempranillo

80 Cherry with a violet hue. Powerful aroma with predominant varietal and maceration notes (skins, nettles, underbrush). Fresh, flavourful palate with fine tannins and excellent acidity.

VIÑASPERI 2003 JOVEN RED

79 Dark cherry with a violet edge. Intense aroma with good varietal and maceration expression, hints of damp earth. Flavourful, sweet and warm on the palate with hints of liquorice.

VIÑASPERI 2001 RESERVA RED

80 Dark cherry with a coppery edge. Slightly intense aroma with predominant toasty oak and skins. Flavourful, supple palate with ripe oily tannins and bitter notes.

CASTILLO DE PEÑALTA 2003 RED
GOBELET ROJO 2001 RED
VIÑA CONSTANTINA 2000 CRIANZA RED

CARLOS SERRES

Avenida Santo Domingo, 40

26200 Haro (La Rioja)
☎: 941 310 294 - Fax: 941 310 418
info@carlosserres.com - serres@fer.es
www.carlosserres.com
Established: 1896
⊕ 4,500 ▤ 2,000,000 litres 🍇 50 has.
🍷 65% 🌐35%: -FR -UK -DE -NL -SE -BE -PL -RU -US -MX -HN -PR -FI -JP -TW -DK -AT -AU

SERRES VIURA LÁGRIMA 2003 WHITE
viura

81 Pale yellow with golden nuances. Intense, fruity aroma with fine floral and sweet notes. Flavourful, bitter palate with pronounced citrus acidity, very pleasant.

SERRES 2003 ROSÉ
garnacha

80 Pale raspberry with an orangey hue. Not very intense aroma, somewhat fruity and spicy. Fresh, flavourful palate with hints of spices, quality citrus fruit and good acidity.

SERRES 2003 RED
tempranillo

82 Dark cherry with a violet edge. Slightly intense aroma of black fruit and the freshness of grapeskins. Flavourful palate with ripe, somewhat sweet tannins, hints of liquorice and good acidity.

CARLOS SERRES 2001 CRIANZA RED
90% tempranillo, 10% graciano

82 Garnet red cherry. Slightly intense aroma of black fruit and toasty oak notes. Flavourful palate with quite rough, promising tannins; spicy with liquorice in the retronasal passage.

CARLOS SERRES 1998 RESERVA RED
90% tempranillo, 10% graciano

85 Garnet red cherry with a saffron edge. Intense aroma with predominant notes of toasty oak and fine reduction (tobacco, old furniture). Flavourful palate with fleshy overtones, ripe, slightly oily tannins, fine bitter notes and good acidity.

ONOMÁSTICA 1995 RESERVA RED
90% tempranillo, 10% graciano

89 Brilliant cherry with a coppery glint. Powerful aroma, rich in nuances with well-combined wood and fruit, a red fruit stone nuance, spices, blond tobacco and a rich oily (wax) texture. Flavourful on the palate with promising although quite marked tannins; well-structured and balanced with fine bitter crianza notes.

CARLOS SERRES 1994 GRAN RESERVA RED
90% tempranillo, 10% graciano

81 Ruby red cherry with an orangey glint. Slightly intense aroma with quality reduction notes (wax, old furniture, cigar box) and a suggestion of prune. Flavourful, supple palate with fine spicy notes, a degree of fruit weight and good acidity.

CARLOS SERRES 1995 GRAN RESERVA RED

CASA JUAN

Paseo Sancho Abarca, 22
01300 Laguardia (Álava)
☎: 945 621 241 - Fax: 945 621 241
angel@bodegas-casajuan.com
www.bodegas-casajuan.com

Established: 1995
500 ▯ 800,000 litres 10 has.

CUARTETO 2003 MACERACIÓN CARBÓNICA RED
SONETO 2000 OAK AGED RED
SEÑOR DE LESMOS 1999 CRIANZA RED
SEÑOR DE LESMOS 1998 CRIANZA RED
SEÑOR DE LESMOS 2001 RESERVA ESPECIAL RED
SEÑOR DE LESMOS 1997 GRAN RESERVA RED
SEÑOR DE LESMOS 1995 GRAN RESERVA RED

Bodegas y Viñedos
CASADO MORALES

Avenida de la Pobeda, 12-14
01306 La Puebla de Labarca (Álava)
☎: 945 607 017 - Fax: 945 607 017
b.casado@euskalnet.net
www.casadomorales.com

Established: 1925
1,000 ▯ 530,.000 litres 32 has.
80% 20%: -DE -UK -IE -FR -AD

CASADO MORALES 2001 FERMENTADO EN BARRICA WHITE
viura, malvasía

74 Golden yellow. Intense aroma with predominant spicy oak notes, hints of citrus fruit peel. and mild reduction (varnish). Flavourful palate of slightly fresh oak; lacking balance.

NOBLEZA 2003 MACERACIÓN CARBÓNICA RED
tempranillo, graciano

84 Cherry. Fruity aroma (fresh red fruit) with a slightly complex (earth, maceration) suggestion. Fleshy, fruity, quite warm yet flavourful palate with good freshness; strawberry pulp in the finish.

NOBLEZA DIMIDIUM 1999 RED

83 Garnet red cherry. Fresh, fruity aroma of liquorice and a certain finesse. Flavourful palate

with red fruit well-assembled with the wood; feels much younger than a ë99.

CASADO MORALES 1999 CRIANZA RED
tempranillo, graciano

79 Not very deep cherry with orangey glints. Intense aroma with predominant reduction notes (leather, dates) and a spicy oak suggestion. Flavourful, supple palate with hints of aged wood; pleasant.

CASADO MORALES 1998 RESERVA RED
tempranillo, graciano

76 Garnet red cherry with a brick red edge. Slightly intense aroma of slightly reduced fruit with hints of spices and varnish. Flavourful, supple palate with fine bitter notes and quite a sweet oak suggestion.

LADERAS SUR CASADO MORALES CARÁCTER 1998 RESERVA RED
60% tempranillo, 40% graciano

88 Dark cherry with a saffron edge. Powerful aroma of jammy black fruit with fine toasty oak and balsamic hints. Flavourful, supple, fleshy palate with a good oak/fruit integration and predominant bitter notes (chocolate liquorice, pitch, dark-roasted flavours), good acidity.

CASADO MORALES 2003 ROSÉ
NOBLEZA ALTA EXPRESIÓN 2003 JOVEN RED
CASADO MORALES 1988 GRAN RESERVA RED
NOBLEZA VENDIMIA SELECCIONADA 2001 RED

CASTILLO DE CUZCURRITA

San Sebastián, 1
26214 Cuzcurrita del Río Tirón (La Rioja)
☎: 941 328 022 - Fax: 941 301 620
castillodecuzcurrita@cuzcurrita.com

140 ▯ 60.000 litres 12 has.
90% 10%: -US

SEÑORÍO DE CUZCURRITA 2001 OAK AGED RED
100% tempranillo

86 Deep cherry. Intense aroma of ripe black fruit, fine toasty notes and spicy oak. Flavourful palate with a good oak/fruit integration, promising but quite marked tannins, a slightly oily texture, with fine bitter and terroir notes, long.

CASTILLO DE MAETIERRA

Vara de Rey, 5
26003 Logroño (La Rioja)
☎: 619 111 918 - Fax: 941 248 211
ventas@castillodemaetierra.com
www.castillodemaetierra.com

Established: 2002

🍷 350 🛢 300,000 litres 🌿 80 has.

GAVANZA 2002 OAK AGED RED
80% tempranillo, 5% garnacha, 15% graciano

86 Dark garnet red cherry. Intense aroma of black fruit jammy with fine toasty oak, notes of sun-drenched skins and smoky earth. Flavourful, fleshy palate with slightly marked but promising tannins and hints of spices and wax, excellent acidity.

GAVANZA SELECCIÓN 2002 OAK AGED RED
80% tempranillo, 5% garnacha, 15% graciano

87 Dark cherry. Powerful aroma with predominant toasty oak notes, a suggestion of jammy black fruit and balsamic hints. Flavourful palate with fleshy overtones, quite noticeable tannins, a ripe fruit nuance and a certain spicy freshness (pepper), liquorice and terroir in the retronasal passage.

CASTILLO DE MENDOZA

Juan XXIII, 20
26338 San Vicente de la Sonsierra (La Rioja)
☎: 941 334 496 - Fax: 941 334 496

Established: 1994

🍷 590 🛢 450,000 litres 🌿 40 has.

🍇 50% 🍇50%

VIÑA VITARÁN 2001 CRIANZA RED
tempranillo

85 Quite intense cherry with a brick red edge. Intense aroma with a certain finesse, predominant reduction notes (leather, tobacco) and a suggestion of red fruit. Flavourful palate with a good oak/fruit integration, ripe, oily tannins and spices in the retronasal passage.

CASTILLO DE MENDOZA 1999 RESERVA RED

85 Garnet red cherry. Intense aroma with predominant spicy oak notes, a suggestion of black fruit and hints of terroir. Flavourful supple palate with a good fruit/oak integration, round, oily tannins, fine spicy notes in the finish and excellent acidity.

CÉSAR DEL RÍO

San Martín, 57
26311 Cordovín (La Rioja)
☎: 941 367 061 - Fax: 941 367 061

Established: 1988

🛢 260,000 litres 🍇 100%

CÉSAR DEL RÍO WHITE
CÉSAR DEL RÍO ROSÉ
CÉSAR DEL RÍO RED

Sociedad Cooperativa Limitada
COMARCAL DE NAVARRETE

Carretera de Entrena, s/n
26370 Navarrete (La Rioja)
☎: 941 440 626 - Fax: 941 440 835
comarcal@fer.com

Established: 1989

🍷 750 🛢 6,500,000 litres 🌿 550 has.

🍇 25% 🍇75%: -DE

CAMPO BABIERO 2001 CRIANZA RED
90% tempranillo, 10% mazuelo

80 Brilliant cherry. Fairly intense aroma with notes of ripe red fruit and spicy and slightly creamy hints (vanilla) of wood. Without great nuances on the palate, pleasant, with a certain fruity freshness.

CAMPO BABIERO 2003 JOVEN WHITE
CAMPO BABIERO 2003 JOVEN ROSÉ
CAMPO BABIERO 2003 JOVEN RED

CONSEJO DE LA ALTA

Avenida de Fuenmayor, s/n
26350 Cenicero (La Rioja)
☎: 941 455 005 - Fax: 941 455 010
comercial@consejodelaalta.com
www.consejodelaalta.com

Established: 1989

🍷 3,000 🛢 1,500,000 litres 🌿 140 has.

🍇 55% 🍇45%

ALTA RÍO 1998 RESERVA RED
tempranillo

78 Cherry with a brick red glint. Intense, ripe aroma with predominant reduction notes (leathers, wet dog), light sulphuric and damp off-odours. Better in the mouth, flavourful with fine bitter notes.

CATA DEL CONSEJERO RESERVA RED

82 Garnet red cherry with a brick red edge. Not very intense aroma with spicy oak notes, light hints of reduction (leather) and a suggestion of redcurrants. Flavourful on the palate with slightly marked tannins and a note of greeness, spicy and balsamic hints (pepper, liquorice).

CONSEJO DE LA ALTA 2001 RESERVA RED

83 Garnet red cherry with a coppery edge. Intense aroma with predominant toasty oak notes and a reduction nuance (hints of animals). Flavourful on the palate with rough tannins (a note of oaky greeness) and a ripe fruit nuance.

Bodegas CORRAL

Carretera de Logroño, km. 10
26370 Navarrete (La Rioja)
☎: 941 440 193 - Fax: 941 440 195
info@donjacobo.es
www.donjacobo.es

Established: 1898

5,000 6,000,000 litres 40 has.
40% 60%

DON JACOBO 2003 JOVEN WHITE
100% viura

74 Very pale. Intense aroma with fresh overtones and green fruit, fine floral and jammy notes and hints of fennel. Fresh and slightly flavourful on the palate, with an acidic edge.

DON JACOBO 2003 ROSÉ
70% garnacha, 30% tempranillo

72 Brilliant blush. Slightly short aroma with barely any fruit expression. Flavourful and bitter on the palate with a slightly acidic edge.

DON JACOBO 2002 OAK AGED RED
85% tempranillo, 10% garnacha, 5% mazuelo, graciano

84 Garnet red cherry. Intense, ripe aroma of jammy black fruit with hints of chocolate, fine hints of spices and sweet oak. Flavourful on the palate, well-integrated oak/fruit, with toasty hints and a slightly subdued fruit expression, very pleasant.

DON JACOBO 2000 CRIANZA RED
80% tempranillo, 15% garnacha, 5% mazuelo

73 Cherry with a brick red edge. Perfumed aroma with light viscous notes and toasty wood. Round on the palate, well-mannered, with a woody finish.

ALTOS DE CORRAL 1998 RESERVA RED
100% tempranillo

84 Intense cherry with a coppery edge. Intense aroma, quite typical of a Riojan Reserva, although not very prominent. Flavourful palate of red stone fruit, with quite ripe, sweet tannins, spicy, creamy (vanilla) oak notes and high acidity.

DON JACOBO 1998 RESERVA RED
85% tempranillo, 10% garnacha, 5% mazuelo

80 Deep cherry with a saffron edge. Intense aroma with toasty oak notes and a jammy red fruit sugges-

tion. Flavourful palate with fine bitter crianza notes and the freshness of spices and fruit in the finish.

DON JACOBO 1996 GRAN RESERVA RED
90% tempranillo, 10% mazuelo

80 Fairly deep cherry with a coppery glint. Fairly intense aroma with a certain finesse, with well-integrated oak/fruit and creamy hints of oak. Flavourful on the palate without obvious crianza nuances, with fine hints of reduction and good acidity.

DON JACOBO 1994 GRAN RESERVA RED
85% tempranillo, 10% garnacha, 5% mazuelo

84 Garnet red cherry with a brick red edge. Intense aroma with predominant fine reduction notes (leathers, old furniture, prunes). Flavourful palate with sweet hints of oak and crianza (dates, vanilla) and tobacco in the retronasal passage, a classic with excellent acidity.

ALTOS DE CORRAL 1995 RESERVA RED

COVIAL

San Andrés, 7
01300 Laguardia (Álava)
☎: 945 600 776 - Fax: 945 600 776

Established: 1984

150,000 litres 80 has. 100%

BASTARRICA 2003 JOVEN RED
BASTARRICA 2002 JOVEN RED
VIÑA LOSILLA 2003 JOVEN RED
VIÑA LOSILLA 2002 JOVEN RED

COVILA

Camino del Soto, 26
01306 La Puebla de Labarca (Álava)
☎: 945 627 232 - Fax: 945 627 295
bodegas@covila.es
www.covila.es

Established: 1989

1,900 3,500,000 litres 315 has.
75% 25%: -DE -NL -DK -UK -US

PAGOS DE LABARCA 2003 WHITE
100% viura

80 Brilliant pale yellow. Intense aroma with fine smoky oak, a suggestion of ripe white stone fruit and hints of herbs. Flavourful palate, slightly bitter and warm, lacking balance with notes of vanilla in the finish.

COVILA 2003 RED
100% tempranillo

80 Brilliant garnet red cherry. Intense aroma of red fruit with good varietal and young wine expression. Flavourful, fruity palate with fresh maceration overtones, slightly oily and warm, with good acidity.

VIÑA GURÍA 2001 CRIANZA RED
90% tempranillo, 5% graciano, 5% mazuelo

79 Garnet red cherry with a brick red edge. Intense aroma with predominant reduction notes (leather, dates). Flavourful, supple palate with a good fruit/oak integration and a suggestion of spices and leather.

COVILA 1998 RESERVA RED
90% tempranillo, 5% graciano, 5% mazuelo

82 Not very deep cherry with an orange hue. Slightly intense, spicy aroma with a mild reduction nuance (leather, varnish). Flavourful palate with a good fruit/oak integration, a dried fruit suggestion, liquorice, slightly warm and oily.

PAGOS DE LABARCA 2001 RESERVA RED
90% tempranillo, 5% graciano, 5% macabeo

84 Dark garnet red cherry. Powerful, fruity aroma with good varietal expression, with spicy creamy oak notes and balsamic hints. Flavourful, fleshy palate with a good fruit/oak integration and liquorice and dark-roasted flavours in the retronasal passage.

COVILA 2003 WHITE
COVILA 2003 ROSÉ
COVILA 2002 CRIANZA RED
VIÑA GURÍA 2003 WHITE
VIÑA GURÍA 2003 ROSÉ
VIÑA GURÍA 2003 RED
MESA MAYOR 2003 RED
PAGOS DE LABARCA 2002 CRIANZA RED
PAGOS DE LABARCA 2001 RESERVA RED
VIÑA GURÍA 2001 RESERVA RED

CRIADORES DE RIOJA

Carretera de Clavijo, s/n
26141 Alberite (La Rioja)
☎: 941 436 702 - Fax: 941 436 072
info@criadoresderioja.es
www.criadoresderioja.es

Established: 2000
⊞ 18,000 ▤ 8,690,000 litres ❦ 40 has.
🇪🇸 95% 🌐5%:

MONTE CLAVIJO VIURA 2003 JOVEN WHITE
100% viura

77 Pale lemony yellow. Slightly intense aroma of white fruit, exotic hints, citrus fruit and fine herbs. Flavourful, slightly oily and fruity on the palate with fine bitter notes and an acidic edge.

MONTE CLAVIJO GARNACHA 2003 JOVEN ROSÉ
100% garnacha

76 Pale raspberry. Slightly intense and fruity aroma with spicy hints of skins. Flavourful, very fresh palate and a slightly acidic edge.

MONTE CLAVIJO TEMPRANILLO 2003 JOVEN RED
100% tempranillo

78 Brilliant cherry with a coppery glint. Intense, ripe aroma with good varietal expression (berries, underbrush) and hints of maceration. Flavourful palate with quite marked grape tannins, pleasant.

CASTILLO DE CLAVIJO 1999 CRIANZA RED
90% tempranillo, 10% garnacha

79 Dark red cherry with a brick red edge. Not very intense aroma with a suggestion of ripe fruit and spicy oak. Flavourful palate with fine bitter notes and hints of aged wood, a hint of spicy freshness in the retronasal passage.

CASTILLO DE CLAVIJO 1995 RESERVA RED
90% tempranillo, 10% mazuelo

84 Garnet red cherry with a brick red edge. Intense aroma of fine spicy and reduction notes (tobacco, old furniture) with hints of dates. Flavourful, supple palate with fine bitter notes, good acidity and a suggestion of dark-roasted flavours and jammy fruit.

CASTILLO DE CLAVIJO 1994 GRAN RESERVA RED
80% tempranillo, 10% graciano, 10% mazuelo

77 Quite intense cherry with an orangey edge. Powerful aroma with fine reduction notes (cedar, varnish). Flavourful, supple palate with reduced fruit, bitter notions (aged wood) and a slightly acidic edge.

CUNA DE REYES

Carretera Najera - Uruñuela, s/n
26300 Najera (La Rioja)
☎: 941 228 608 - Fax: 941 206 287
gruasgarte@fer.es

Established: 2001
⊞ 707 ▤ 1,100,000 litres
❦ 25 has 🍷 100%

CUNA DE REYES 2003 JOVEN RED
tempranillo, garnacha

78 Medium-hue garnet red cherry. Clean aroma of red berries and brambles. A carbonic element on the palate, light, pleasant and easy drinking.

CUNA DE REYES 2001 CRIANZA RED
85% tempranillo, 15% garnacha, mazuelo

78 Quite dark cherry with a garnet red edge. Intense, toasty (coffee, vanilla), woody aroma with partially concealed fruit. Round, light palate with considerable wood weight but well-mannered overall.

CVNE

Barrio de la Estacion s/n
26200 Haro (La Rioja)
☎: 941 304 800 - Fax: 941 304 815
haro@cvne.com
www.cvne.com

Established: 1879

🏭 42,000 🛢 80% 🍇20%: -CH -MX -UK -US -DE -DK -JP -VE-PR -DO -IE

CUNE 2003 JOVEN WHITE
100% viura

83 Pale with greenish nuances. Not very intense aroma with notes of ripe white fruit and fresh herby and citrus fruit overtones. Flavourful, slightly fruity palate (hints of citrus fruit), fine bitter notes and excellent acidity.

MONOPOLE 2003 JOVEN WHITE
malvasía, garnacha blanca

81 Yellow straw with a greenish hue. Aromas of hay and green grass, fresh. Warm palate, high in acidity, light.

CORONA 2001 WHITE SEMIDULCE
100% viura

85 Pale yellow. Intense aroma of ripe white fruit with exotic hints and dried grass. Sweetish, slightly unctuous on the palate with hints of fresh fruit and fine bitter and citrus notes in the finish, well-balanced.

CUNE 2003 JOVEN ROSÉ
100% garnacha

78 Salmon. Medium-intensity aroma with anise-ed notes and a nuance of red fruit. Flavourful, pleasant and fresh on the palate, well-mannered.

CUNE 2001 CRIANZA RED
tempranillo, garnacha, mazuelo

85 Cherry with a garnet red edge. Concentrated aroma of smoky wood with overtones of reduction and a nuance of black fruit. Fleshy, very flavourful palate with balanced wood and fruit; polished and supple tannins.

CUNE 2000 RESERVA RED
90% tempranillo, 5% garnacha, 5% graciano

85 Ruby red cherry. Fruity aroma with a certain expression and a good assemblage of very light toasty wood notes and fruit. Round and elegant on the palate with supple and oily tannins and good acidity, a typical Rioja Alta.

IMPERIAL 1998 RESERVA RED
85% tempranillo, 10% graciano, 5% mazuelo

88 Cherry with an orangey glint and a saffron edge. Intense aroma with fresh overtones (red stone fruit), fine reduction notes and hints of terroir. Flavourful on the palate with polished and fairly sweet tannins; excellent crianza expression.

IMPERIAL 1999 RESERVA RED

86 Cherry with a subtle ruby red hue. Spicy aroma, seasoned wood (wax, cedar). Round, oily, flavourful and fine on the palate with spicy and ripe flavours in the retronasal passage.

IMPERIAL 1996 GRAN RESERVA RED
85% tempranillo, 10% graciano, 5% mazuelo

88 Ruby red with a slightly brick red hue. Spicy aroma with notes of a fine reduction in the bottle (leather, tobacco, cinnamon) and notions of seasoned oak (wax, old furniture). Round, oily and spicy on the palate (cloves, pepper) with well-polished flavourful oak and stewed fruit tannins.

REAL DE ASÚA 2000 RED
95% tempranillo, 5% graciano

88 Quite intense cherry. Fine, complex aroma of toasty oak (cocoa, creamy vanilla and coffee) and jammy fruit. Round, supple and elegant on the palate with seasoned oak in the retronasal passage, stewed fruit, cocoa and vanilla, flavourful and persistent.

CUNE 2002 CRIANZA RED

Bodegas DANIEL PURAS

Calle Cuesta Dulce, 1
26330 Briones (La Rioja)
☎: 941 322 263 - Fax: 941 322 294
info@miguelmerino.com

Established: 2004

🏭 55 🛢 100,000 litres 🍇 11 has.

CANTIGA 2003 CRIANZA RED
100% tempranillo

77 Intense cherry. Smoky aroma with a suggestion of reduction over ripe fruit. Flavourful palate with dominant crianza notes and fresh overtones.

Bodegas DARIEN

Avenida Mendavia, 29
26006 Logroño (La Rioja)
☎: 941 258 130 - Fax: 941 270 352
info@darien.es
www.darien.es

Established: 1999

🏭 1,727 🛢 2,130,000 litres 🍇 66 has.

🛢 60% 🍇40%: -US -UK -CH -BE -NL -DK -FR -PR

DARIEN TEMPRANILLO 2003 RED
100% tempranillo

82 Garnet red cherry with a violet hue. Intense aroma of red fruit, with hints of skins, and fine herbaceous notes of maceration. Flavourful palate with slightly marked tannins, fine notes of spices and terroir and good acidity.

DARIEN SELECCIÓN 2001 OAK AGED RED
75% tempranillo, 10% graciano, 8% mazuelo, 7% garnacha

86 Garnet red cherry with a coppery glint. Intense aroma with well-integrated oak/fruit, fresh overtones of red fruit and oak and a spicy suggestion. Flavourful, and supple on the palate, slightly warm (ripe fruit partially concealed by the alcohol).

DARIEN 2001 CRIANZA RED
60% tempranillo, 17% garnacha, 17% mazuelo, 6% graciano

87 Garnet red cherry with a saffron edge. Intense, ripe aroma with fine smoky, creamy (vanilla, cocoa) oak notes. Powerful, fleshy palate with good fruit/oak integration, generous, oily, and spicy with notions of terroir and cocoa in the retronasal passage.

DARIEN 2000 RESERVA RED
66% tempranillo, 20% garnacha, 11% mazuelo, 3% graciano

85 Garnet red cherry with a saffron edge. Intense aroma of ripe fruit (redcurrants, cherries) and spicy oak notes. Flavourful palate with good fruit/oak integration, slightly warm with waxy hints, quite promising.

DAVID MORENO

Carretera de Villar de Torre s/n
26310 Badarán (La Rioja)
☎: 941 367 338 - Fax: 941 418 685
davidmoreno@davidmoreno.com
www.davidmoreno.com

Established: 1981

🍷 2,000 📦 1,500,000 litres 🌿 15 has.

🇪🇸 80% 🌐20%: -UK -CH -DE -BE -NL -AT -JP -LU -NI

DAVID MORENO 2003 JOVEN RED
80% tempranillo, 20% garnacha

78 Garnet red cherry. Intense, fruity aroma with spicy hints of skins (maceration) and fresh overtones. Fresh, flavourful palate with ripe and sweet tannins and hints of liquorice.

DAVID MORENO 2002 OAK AGED RED
80% tempranillo, 20% garnacha

77 Not very deep cherry with brick red glints. Slightly intense, ripe aroma with spicy hints. Flavourful, bitter palate with a suggestion of sweet fruit and warm notes.

DAVID MORENO 2001 CRIANZA RED
90% tempranillo, 10% garnacha

84 Brilliant cherry with a coppery-saffron edge. Intense aroma with a certain concentration, predominant notes of ripe black fruit, light reduction notes of classic Rioja. Flavourful on the palate with a good oak/fruit integration, ripe.

DAVID MORENO COLECCIÓN PRIVADA 1999 CRIANZA RED
85% tempranillo, 15% garnacha

82 Medium-hue cherry with an orangey edge. Intense, spicy aroma (pepper, vanilla, cedar) and tobacco. Round, flavourful and light on the palate, very polished, a good crianza.

DAVID MORENO SELECCIÓN DE LA FAMILIA 2001 CRIANZA RED
100% tempranillo

81 Garnet red cherry with a brick red edge. Intense aroma of jammy black fruit, spicy hints and fine reduction notes (tobacco). Flavourful, and bitter on the palate (with a good fruit/oak integration); slightly warm, spicy and with good acidity.

DAVID MORENO 1998 RESERVA RED
100% tempranillo

80 Brilliant cherry with an orangey glint. Intense aroma with predominant spicy and sweet oak notes and a light suggestion of reduction. Flavourful on the palate with well-integrated fruit/oak and pleasant bitter hints in the retronasal passage.

DAVID MORENO JOVEN WHITE
DAVID MORENO JOVEN ROSÉ
DAVID MORENO 1995 GRAN RESERVA RED
MONASTERIO DE YUSO 1998 RESERVA RED
MONASTERIO DE YUSO 2001 CRIANZA RED

Bodegas DINASTÍA VIVANCO

Carretera Nacional 232
Briones (La Rioja)
☎: 941 322 332 - Fax: 941 322 316
infobodega@dinastiavivanco.es

Established: 1915

🍇 300 has.

DINASTÍA VIVANCO SELECCIÓN DE FAMILIA 1998 RESERVA RED
90% tempranillo, 10% graciano

83 Brilliant cherry with a coppery glint. Intense aroma with predominant reduction notes (varnish) and toasty oak. Flavourful palate with a suggestion of fruit partially concealed by the alcohol and an oily texture, pleasant.

DINASTÍA VIVANCO 2001 CRIANZA RED
DINASTÍA VIVANCO SELECCIÓN DE FAMILIA 2001 CRIANZA RED
DINASTÍA VIVANCO 1998 RESERVA RED

DOMECQ

Carretera de Villanueva n¥9
01340 Elciego (Álava)
☎: 945 606 001 - Fax: 945 606 235
rioja@domecq.es
www.domecq.es

Established: 1973

🍷 21,000 🛢 19,500,000 litres 🍇 300 has.

🇪🇸 60% 🌐40%: -UK -SE -DK -FI -IS -DK - BE -NL -EE -LV -US Sudamérica

MARQUÉS DE ARIENZO 2000 CRIANZA RED
95% tempranillo, 5% graciano, mazuelo

79 Garnet red cherry with a coppery edge. Intense aroma of ripe black fruit, fine spicy oak notes and mineral fresh overtones. Flavourful palate with slightly fresh oak tannins, hints of greeness.

VIÑA EGUÍA 2001 CRIANZA RED
95% tempranillo, 5% graciano, mazuelo

81 Brilliant cherry with a brick red hue. Not very intense aroma with predominant spicy oak notes. Flavourful, supple palate with a good oak/fruit integration, fine toasty notes in the retronasal passage and a hint of black pepper.

100% tempranillo

MARQUÉS DE ARIENZO 1999 RESERVA RED
95% tempranillo, 5% graciano, mazuelo

82 Intense cherry with a brick red rim. Somewhat intense aroma of jammy red fruit and hints of reduction (wax, tanned hide). Flavourful palate with slightly drying oak tannins, warm notes and spices.

MARQUÉS DE ARIENZO RESERVA ESPECIAL 1998 RESERVA ESPECIAL RED
75% tempranillo, 25% graciano

85 Dark cherry with a saffron edge. Powerful aroma of jammy black fruit and fine toasty and spicy oak notes. Flavourful palate with a certain fleshy overtones, fine bitter notes (good oak/fruit integration), dark-roasted hints and good acidity.

MARQUÉS DE ARIENZO 1995 GRAN RESERVA RED

85 Brilliant cherry with a brick red rim. Intense aroma with predominant toasty notes, fine hints of jam and reduction (dates, old furniture). Flavourful, supple and well-balanced on the palate with tobacco and spices in the retronasal passage.

MARQUÉS DE ARIENZO 2003 JOVEN WHITE

Bodegas DON BALBINO

Avenida La Poveda, 26
01306 Lapuebla de Labarca (Álava)
☎: 945 607 018 - Fax: 945 607 018
donbalbino@navegalia.com

Established: 1924

🍷 500 🛢 1,000,000 litres 🍇 40 has.

🇪🇸 50% 🌐50%: -DE -UK -CH -DK

DON BALBINO 2001 CRIANZA RED
100% tempranillo

77 Not very deep cherry. Aroma of dark-roasted flavours, coffee with reduction notes (leather). Slightly marked tannins on the palate with a dark-roasted finish.

MERITISIMUS VENDIMIA SELECIONADA 2001 RED
100% tempranillo

77 Cherry with a brick red edge. Smoky aroma of incense with sweet notes. Slightly drying on the palate with marked wood tannins.

DON BALBINO 1998 CRIANZA RED
100% tempranillo

76 Not very deep brick red. Aroma of leather and wet dog, somewhat rancid with cloves. Warm palate with elements of acidity, lacking great nuances.

DON BALBINO 1997 RESERVA RED

78 Cherry with an orangey hue. Aroma with notes of liquorice and almost overripe red fruit. Very marked wood tannins on the palate, warm with medium acidity, somewhat short.

DON BALBINO 1987 GRAN RESERVA RED
100% tempranillo

76 Not very deep amber. Chocolate, rancid aroma with notes of reduction. Light palate with slight bitter notes.

DON BALBINO 1994 GRAN RESERVA RED
100% tempranillo

76 Amber. Very toasty aroma of spices and leather with sweet notes. Integrated wood tannins on the palate, light and a little fleshy.

PUENTEGRIJOS 2000 JOVEN RED
DON BALBINO 1997 RESERVA RED

DUNVIRO

Carretera Logroño, km. 362, 800
26500 Calahorra (La Rioja)
☎: 941 148 161 - Fax: 941 130 626
bodegasdunviro@hotmail.com
www.bodegasdunviro.com

Established: 1958

🌐 500 🛢 2,500,000 litres 🍇 215 has.

🍷 80% 🍇20%: -DE -UK

DUNVIRO 2003 JOVEN WHITE
100% viura

72 Yellow straw with a coppery glint. Fairly intense, fruity aroma with herbaceous hints. Flavourful, bitter palate; lacking balance.

DUNVIRO 2003 JOVEN ROSÉ
100% garnacha

78 Lively raspberry. Intense, fruity aroma with warm hints. Fresh, flavourful, slightly warm and oily palate with notes of red fruit, pleasant.

DUNVIRO 2003 JOVEN RED
60% tempranillo, 40% garnacha

79 Brilliant cherry. Not very intense aroma of red stone fruit, fresh overtones. Flavourful palate with very expressive grape tannins; refreshing acidity, pleasant.

NASICA 2003 JOVEN RED
60% tempranillo, 40% garnacha

74 Fairly deep cherry with a violet glint. Fresh aroma of black fruit with not very clean maceration notes. Flavourful, fresh palate with overtones of greeness to the grape tannins.

DUNVIRO 2001 CRIANZA RED
90% tempranillo, 5% graciano, 5% mazuelo

75 Garnet red cherry. Intense aroma of black fruit with toasty wood notes and vegetative fresh overtones. Flavourful palate with a note of greeness to the tannins.

DUNVIRO 1998 RESERVA RED
90% tempranillo, 5% graciano, 5% mazuelo

73 Ruby red with an orange glint. Not very intense aroma with hints of reduction over a nuance of black fruit. Flavourful palate with a nuance of sweet fruit and bitter hints.

MONTEPADILLARES 2003 JOVEN RED
DUNVIRO 1998 RESERVA RED

EDUARDO GARRIDO

Plaza de la Constitución, 2
26339 Abalos (La Rioja)
☎: 941 334 187 - Fax: 941 334 010

Established: 1950

🌐 150 🛢 100,000 litres 🍇 2 has.

🍷 60% 🍇40%: -UK -CH -DE

EDUARDO GARRIDO GARCIA 1995 GRAN RESERVA RED
90% tempranillo, 10% mazuelo

76 Brilliant cherry with a coppery glint. Fairly intense, ripe aroma with reduction notes, without remarkable nuances. Flavourful on the palate, with fine bitter notes, and hints of aged wood; with a certain expression of traditional crianza.

EDUARDO GARRIDO GARCÍA RED
EDUARDO GARRIDO GARCÍA 2000 CRIANZA RED
EDUARDO GARRIDO GARCÍA 1998 RESERVA RED

EL COTO DE RIOJA

Camino Viejo de Logroño, 26
01320 Oyón (Álava)
☎: 945 622 216 - Fax: 945 622 315
cotorioja@elcoto.com

DO Ca. RIOJA

www.elcoto.com
Established: 1970
🍷 70,000 📊 15,000,000 litres 🍇 325 has.
🇪🇸 70% 🌐30%: Centro -UE Sudamérica - US Asia

EL COTO 2001 CRIANZA RED
100% tempranillo

79 Cherry with an orangey edge. Toasty aroma of ripe fruit. Warm palate with good acidity, slightly marked tannins and a toasty finish.

COTO REAL 2000 RESERVA RED
70% tempranillo, 20% garnacha, 10% graciano

89 Deep cherry with a saffron hue. Powerful aroma of fine toasty notes of oak and skins with a spicy and balsamic nuance. Flavourful, fleshy, vigorous palate with a good oak/fruit integration and balsamic flavours and terracotta in the retronasal passage, excellent acidity.

COTO DE IMAZ 2000 RESERVA RED
100% tempranillo

84 Medium-hue cherry. Balsamic aroma of vanilla with some sweet notes. Warm, expressive palate with polished tannins.

COTO DE IMAZ SELECCIÓN 25 ANIVERSARIO 1998 RESERVA RED
100% tempranillo

88 Garnet red cherry. Intense aroma with a good Reserva expression (a good fruit/oak integration), balsamic hints and fine reduction notes (new leather). Flavourful palate with quite rough, sweet tannins, a degree of fruit weight, spices, toasty flavours and fine wax in the retronasal passage.

COTO DE IMAZ 1995 GRAN RESERVA RED
100% tempranillo

86 Ruby red cherry with orangey glints. Intense aroma with predominant toasty oak and reduction notes (animals, varnish). Flavourful and supple palate with a good oak/fruit integration, jammy hints and rich spicy notes of tobacco and leather in the retronasal passage.

EL FABULISTA

Plaza San Juan, s/n
01300 Laguardia (Álava)
☎: 945 621 192 - Fax: 945 600 110
bfabulista@dieznet.com
🍷 38 📊 64,000 litres 🍇 4 has.

DECIDIDO 2003 JOVEN RED
DECIDIDO XXXX 2003 OAK AGED RED
BODEGA EL FABULISTA 2001 CRIANZA RED
FÁBULA 2001 CRIANZA RED

Bodega Cooperativa EL PATROCINIO

Carretera Cenicero
26313 Uruñuela (La Rioja)
☎: 941 371 319
Established: 1986
🍷 1,102 📊 8,000,000 litres 🍇 500 has.
🇪🇸 99% 🌐1%: -AT -DK

SEÑORÍO DE UÑUELA 2001 FERMENTADO EN BARRICA WHITE
100% viura

74 Pale straw. A slightly unusual aroma (oak, balsamic flavours, burnt smells). Heavy oak weight on the palate that conceals the fruit.

SEÑORÍO DE UÑUELA 2003 RED
100% tempranillo

79 Brilliant cherry. Intense, not very fine, quite fruity aroma. Better palate, flavourful and fleshy with fresh overtones, notions of liquorice and a slightly oily texture.

SANCHO GARCÉS 2000 CRIANZA RED
100% tempranillo

79 Garnet red cherry. Fairly intense aroma with notes of red fruit and spicy hints of oak. Flavourful palate with well-integrated oak and fruit, well-mannered without great nuances.

SEÑORÍO DE UÑUELA 2001 CRIANZA RED
100% tempranillo

80 Garnet red cherry with a coppery glint. Intense, fruity aroma with toasty oak and a fine reduction nuance. Flavourful, and fleshy palate of well-integrated ripe fruit and oak, with fine spicy notes, very pleasant.

ZINIO (VENDIMIA SELECCIONADA) 2000 CRIANZA RED
100% tempranillo

77 Garnet red cherry with a brick red edge. Intense aroma with predominant toasty wood notes and a jammy red fruit nuance. Flavourful palate with dark-roasted notes, without character.

SANCHO GARCÉS 2003 RED
100% tempranillo

79 Red with a violet glimmer. Slightly vinous aroma of underripe fruit. Slightly vegetative, medium-bodied palate, but well-mannered overall.

EL SANTUARIO VINÍCOLA RIOJANO

Carretera Arnedo, km. 14
26589 Arnedillo (La Rioja)
☎: 941 394 063 - Fax: 941 394 200

ritual@pegarrido.com
www.pegarrido.com

Established: 1980

120 📦 150,000 litres 🍇 10 has.

🍷 80% 🌐20%: -JP -UK -DE

RITUAL ECOLÓGICO 2003 RED
RITUAL ECOLÓGICO 2001 RED
RITUAL 2002 RED
RITUAL ECOLÓGICO 2000 RED
VIÑA RITUAL 2000 CRIANZA RED
VIÑA RITUAL 1997 RESERVA RED
VIÑA RITUAL 1996 RESERVA RED
VIÑA RITUAL 1994 RESERVA RED
VIÑA RITUAL 1989 GRAN RESERVA RED

Bodegas ESCUDERO

Carretera de Arnedo, s/n
26587 Gravalos (La Rioja)
☎: 941 398 008 - Fax: 941 398 070
www.bodegasescudero.com

Established: 1952

1,300 📦 800,000 litres 🍇 120 has.

🍷 80% 🌐20%: -CH -DE -UK -DK -FR

SOLAR DE BECQUER 1999 FERMENTADO
EN BARRICA WHITE
60% chardonnay, 40% viura

84 Brilliant pale yellow. Intense aroma with predominant spicy wood notes, a slightly fruity suggestion and mountain herbs. Generous palate, rich in crianza nuances with fine bitter notes, well-balanced.

SOLAR DE BECQUER 2003 JOVEN RED
60% garnacha, 40% tempranillo

80 Cherry with a violet hue. Powerful, very fruity aroma (strawberry jelly) with toasty notes of skins and an element of sweetness. Flavourful and fruity on the palate with firm tannins, sweetish and oily with a spicy nuance.

SOLAR DE BECQUER 2000 CRIANZA RED
70% tempranillo, 20% mazuelo, 10% garnacha

80 Garnet red cherry with a brick red edge. Slightly intense aroma with fine reduction notes (tobacco) and a ripe red fruit nuance. Flavourful on the palate with fleshy overtones, a good fruit/oak integration and subtle bitter, spicy and balsamic notes.

BECQUER 2001 OAK AGED RED
70% tempranillo, 30% garnacha

84 Deep cherry. Powerful aroma of ripe black fruit with toasty oak notes and spicy hints of skins. Flavourful and fleshy on the palate with a good fruit/oak integration and a certain fruity and mineral freshness.

SOLAR DE BÉCQUER 1998 RESERVA RED
70% tempranillo, 20% mazuelo, 10% garnacha

82 Cherry with an orangey hue. Aroma of jammy tomatoes, slightly alcoholic, with ripe red fruit. Fleshy, well-balanced and flavourful on the palate.

SOLAR DE BECQUER 1996 GRAN RESERVA
RED
70% tempranillo, 15% mazuelo, 15% garnacha

80 Not very deep cherry with an orangey glint. Not very intense aroma with reduction notes (leather, dates). Flavourful and supple palate with ripe fruit, toasty hints and supple and integrated tannins.

ESPADA OJEDA

Avenida La Poveda, 8
01306 Lapuebla de Labarca (Álava)
☎: 945 627 349 - Fax: 945 627 349
espadaojeda@navegalia.com

Established: 1989

📦 350,000 litres 🍇 25 has.

🍷 100%

DA LAUSAN 2003 RED

ESTRAUNZA

Avenida La Poveda, s/n
01306 Lapuebla de Labarca (Álava)
☎: 945 627 245 - Fax: 945 627 293
www.bodegasestraunza.com

Established: 1990

1,500 📦 1,000,000 litres 🍷 85%

🌐15%: -UK -DE -LV -FR -US

BLAS DE LEZO 2001 CRIANZA RED
95% tempranillo, 5% otras

79 Dark red cherry with a coppery edge. Slightly intense aroma with predominant fruit notes and hints of spices and reduction. Flavourful palate with juicy, slightly sweet tannins, spicy notes and fresh fruit and damp earth in the retronasal passage.

SOLAR DE ESTRAUNZA VENDIMIA
SELECCIONADA 2002 RED
100% tempranillo

87 Deep cherry with a garnet red edge. Intense aroma of very spicy oak (vanilla, sandalwood, cedar) and a ripe fruit suggestion. Flavourful, intense palate of concentrated fruit and very toasty fine creamy wood; well-elaborated and long.

SOLAR DE ESTRAUNZA 2001 CRIANZA RED
95% tempranillo, 5% otras

73 Garnet red cherry. Not very intense aroma of red fruit and a light suggestion of off-odours. Light and fruity on the palate with drying oak tannins.

SOLAR DE ESTRAUNZA 1997 RESERVA
RED
95% tempranillo, 5% otras

83 Garnet red cherry with brick red hue. Intense aroma with predominant dark-roasted reduction notes (tobacco, wax). Flavourful palate, a good oak/fruit integration, and a spicy suggestion; slightly rough and spicy in the retronasal passage.

SOLAR DE ESTRAUNZA WHITE
SOLAR DE ESTRAUNZA ROSÉ
BLAS DE LEZO RED
SOLAR DE MUSKIZ RED
SUPERBE RED
SOLAR DE ESTRAUNZA 1995 GRAN
RESERVA RED

Bodegas FAUSTINO

Carretera de Logroño, s/n
01320 Oyón (Álava)
☎: 945 622 500 - Fax: 945 622 106

⊕ 25,000 ⚑ 650 has.

FAUSTINO DE AUTOR RESERVA ESPECIAL
1998 RESERVA RED
86% tempranillo, 14% graciano

88 Dark cherry with a saffron edge. Intense aroma with fine toasty oak, macerated black fruit and a balsamic suggestion. Flavourful palate with supple overtones, a good oak/fruit integration, hints of liquorice, glacé cherries in liqueur and spices; excellent acidity.

FAUSTINO V 2000 RESERVA RED
90% tempranillo, 10% mazuelo

83 Cherry with a brick red edge. Medium-intensity aroma with spicy notes, tobacco, ink and crianza. Flavourful, round palate with ripe black fruit well-assembled with the wood and polished tannins, well-balanced.

FAUSTINO I 1995 GRAN RESERVA RED
85% tempranillo, 10% graciano, 5% mazuelo

85 Deep cherry with a brick-red edge. Intense aroma with excellent crianza notes well-integrated with the ripe fruit notes and a hint of spicy oak. Flavourful, fleshy palate with ripe tannins, slightly oily with a suggestion of sweet fruit.

FAUSTINO I 1996 RED

87 Cherry with a brick red edge. Medium-intensity aroma with mild reduction notes (tobacco, leather), spices, good crianza. Intense, flavourful palate; spicy, very well-balanced and with quite persistent.

FAUSTINO V 2003 FERMENTADO EN
BARRICA WHITE
FAUSTINO V 2003 WHITE
FAUSTINO V 2003 ROSÉ
FAUSTINO 2001 CRIANZA RED
FAUSTINO DE AUTOR 1995 RESERVA RED

FAUSTINO RIVERO ULECIA

Carretera de Garray, km. 73- Apdo. 75
26580 Arnedo (La Rioja)
☎: 941 380 057 - Fax: 941 385 072
faustino@faustinorivero.com
www.faustinorivero.com

⊕ 3,000 ▤ 3,000,000 litres ⬛ 60%
🍷40%

FAUSTINO RIVERO ULECIA WHITE
FAUSTINO RIVERO ULECIA ROSÉ
FAUSTINO RIVERO ULECIA RED

FEDERICO PATERNINA

Avenida Santo Domingo, 11
26200 Haro (La Rioja)
☎: 941 310 550 - Fax: 941 312 778
marketing@paternina.com
www.paternina.com

Established: 1896

⊕ 40,000 ▤ 20,000,000 litres ⬛ 50%

🌐50%: -GK-UE -SE -UK -CH -DK -NL -DK -IE -FR -BE -FI -DE -PL -LU -US -MX -PR - CR -CA -CU -DM -CO -CA -PE -RU -JP -MU -EE -CY

GRACIELA 1997 CRIANZA WHITE
90% viura, 10% malvasía

79 Brilliant gold. Aroma with crianza character (toasty oak) and a nuance of crystallised fruit. Flavourful, sweet palate with notes of herbs and marked oak tannins.

PATERNINA BANDA ORO 1998 CRIANZA RED
80% tempranillo, 15% garnacha, 5% mazuelo

83 Garnet red cherry with an orangey glint. Slightly intense aroma of toasty oak with hints of spices and ripe fruit (dates). Flavourful, quite fleshy, spicy palate with a good expression of traditional crianza and sweet and bitter hints in the finish.

PATERNINA 1995 RESERVA RED

86 Ruby red cherry with an orangey glint. Powerful aroma with predominant fine reduction notes (tobacco, wax, old furniture) and a suggestion of cedar and jammy fruit. Flavourful, supple palate with a good oak/fruit integration (good weight of the latter), slightly warm and oily.

CONDES DE LOS ANDES 1995 RESERVA RED
80% tempranillo, 15% garnacha, 5% mazuelo

84 Ruby red cherry with an orangey hue. Somewhat intense aroma with a certain finesse and reduction notes (tobacco, leather) over a suggestion of jammy fruit. Flavourful, supple palate with a good fruit/oak integration and a sweet and bitter hint of the crianza in oak, good fruit and acidity weight.

CONDES DE LOS ANDES 1991 GRAN RESERVA RED
90% tempranillo, 10% mazuelo

79 Orangey ruby red. Intense aroma with predominant notes of oak and reduction (spices, tanned hide, animal hints). Quite flavourful on the palate but lacking balance and expressivity with fairly obvious acidity.

PATERNINA 1994 GRAN RESERVA RED
80% tempranillo, 15% garnacha, 5% mazuelo

86 Ruby red cherry with an orangey rim. Slightly intense aroma with predominant reduction notes (leather, cigar box) and a nuance of ripe fruit (jammy redcurrants, dates). Flavourful, fleshy, supple with a slightly oily and spicy texture (white pepper) and good acidity.

BANDA DORADA 2003 JOVEN WHITE
BANDA ROSA 2003 JOVEN WHITE
PATERNINA BANDA AZUL 1999 CRIANZA RED

PATERNINA ESPECIAL CRIANZA RED
CLOS PATERNINA 1997 RESERVA RED
PATERNINA BANDA ROJA 1998 RESERVA RED
CONDES DE LOS ANDES 1989 GRAN RESERVA RED
PATERNINA 1995 GRAN RESERVA RED

FÉLIX IBÁÑEZ BUJANDA

Avenida Gasteiz, 2
01306 Lapuebla de Labarca (Álava)
☎: 945 627 342 - Fax: 945 627 342
📖 80.000 litres 🍇 19 has.
📇 95% 🌐5%

IBÁÑEZ BUJANDA JOVEN RED
IBÁÑEZ BUJANDA VIÑAS VIEJAS RED

FÉLIX SOLÍS

Autovía de Andalucía, km. 199
13300 Valdepeñas (Ciudad Real)
☎: 926 322 400 - Fax: 926 322 417
bfs@felixsolix.com
www.felixsolis.com

Established: 1952

🌐 40,000 📖 192,000,000 litres 🍇 500 has.
📇 62% 🌐38%: -UK -DE -NL -DK -FI -SE - BE -GQ -CH TG -MX -BE -AT -JP -PH -NC - DO -US -AO TAHITI -CA -CO -SE -DK -CZ - DZ -PE -VE -IT -LU -CF -PA -KE CM -VN - TW -LB -GT -MY CD -SG -EC -BR -JO -GA TZ -CR -EL -AU -SV -SB -GM -IE -NI -PT

ABADÍA DE ALTILLO 2003 WHITE

71 Straw-coloured. Slightly short, clear aroma with quite weak fruit. Slightly unctuous first impression but without great fruit expression.

ABADÍA DE ALTILLO 2003 ROSÉ

76 Brilliant raspberry. Fairly intense, fresh aroma with hints of red fruit. Flavourful, somewhat fruity palate with an oily texture and spicy skins.

ABADÍA DE ALTILLO 2003 RED

76 Garnet red cherry. Not very intense aroma with a fruity nuance and spicy hints of skins. Flavourful on the palate with a good expression of young wine, ripe tannins and a slightly oily texture.

MARQUÉS DE ALTILLO 2003 JOVEN RED

78 Garnet red cherry with a violet edge. Fairly intense aroma of ripe red fruit with fresh tannic notions of young wine (brambles). Fresh, flavourful and fruity on the palate with a slightly oily texture, pleasant.

Bodegas y Viñedos
FERNÁNDEZ DE MANZANOS

Çarretera San Adrian-Azaga (Na-134 Km.47
31560 Azagra (Navarra)
☎: 948 692 500 - Fax: 948 692 500
info@bodegasfernandezdemanzanos.com -
bodegasfernandezdemanzanos.com

Established: 1890
🏺 1.000 📦 1.500.000 litres 🍇 150 has.
🍷 90% 🌐10%: -DE -AT -FR

VIÑA MARICHALAR 2003 JOVEN RED
80% tempranillo, 10% mazuelo, 10% garnacha

81 Garnet red cherry with a violet hue. Quite intense aroma of blackberries and macerated skins with sweet hints, spices and damp earth. Flavourful palate with somewhat noticeable tannins, liquorice and spices.

VIÑA BERRI 2003 RED
80% tempranillo, 15% garnacha, 5% mazuelo

77 Garnet red cherry with a violet hue. Quite intense, fruity aroma with the freshness of macerated skins and hints of nettles. Flavourful palate with somewhat noticeable tannins and a slightly acidic edge.

V. FERNÁNDEZ DE MANZANOS 2000 CRIANZA RED
90% tempranillo, 5% garnacha, 5% mazuelo

80 Not very deep cherry with a coppery glint. Fairly intense aroma with predominant spicy and sweetish oak notes. Flavourful on the palate with quite marked and fresh oak tannins and a suggestion of ripe red fruit.

VIÑA MARICHALAR 2000 CRIANZA RED
90% tempranillo, 5% garnacha, 5% mazuelo

82 Cherry with a coppery glint. Slightly intense aroma with a certain finesse of jammy fruit, hints of spices and reduction (tobacco, leather). Flavourful palate with good oak/fruit integration, sweetish hints, spicy notes and liquorice.

VIÑA MARICHALAR 1998 RESERVA RED
95% tempranillo, 5% garnacha

81 Ruby red cherry with an orange glint. Quite intense, spicy aroma with predominant reduction notes (tobacco, old furniture). Flavourful, supple palate with a good Reserva expression, spicy and rich in acidity.

VIÑA BERRI WHITE
VIÑA BERRI ROSÉ
VIÑA MARICHALAR WHITE
VIÑA MARICHALAR JOVEN ROSÉ
VIÑA BERRI CRIANZA RED
VIÑA MARICHALAR MAGNUM RESERVA RED
V. FERNÁNDEZ DE MANZANOS CRIANZA RED

FERNÁNDEZ DE PIEROLA

Carretera Logroño s/n Finca El Somo
01322 Moreda (Álava)
☎: 945 622 480 - Fax: 945 622 489
bodegas@pierola.com
www.pierola.com

Established: 1996
🏺 1,500 📦 555,000 litres 🍇 25 has.
🍷 90% 🌐10%: -CH -UK

FERNÁNDEZ DE PIÉROLA 2003 FERMENTADO EN BARRICA WHITE
viura

80 Pale golden yellow. Powerful aroma with predominant smoky and creamy wood notes and hints of herbs. Flavourful palate with fine spicy notes of oak, slightly warm.

FERNÁNDEZ DE PIÉROLA 2000 CRIANZA RED
tempranillo

84 Garnet red cherry with a brick red edge. Intense aroma with predominant burnt notes and good crianza expression. Flavourful palate with well-integrated oak/fruit and ripe, oily tannins.

FERNÁNDEZ DE PIÉROLA 1998 RESERVA RED
tempranillo

79 Garnet red cherry with a brick red rim. Not very intense aroma with fine reduction notes (tobacco, varnish) and a suggestion of prunes. Flavourful, slightly warm palate; spicy and without remarkable nuances.

VITIUM 1999 RESERVA RED

86 Deep cherry. Intense aroma with predominant animal reduction notes and jammy black fruit. Flavourful, fleshy palate with a good fruit/oak integration, a powerful aroma of liquorice and dark-roasted flavours in the retronasal passage; slightly oily and warm.

Bodegas FERNÁNDEZ EGUILUZ

Los Morales, 7

26339 Abalos (La Rioja)
☎: 941 334 166 - Fax: 941 308 055
p.larosa@terra.es
www.bodegasfdezeguiluz.es

Established: 1989

⊞ 25 ▥ 156,000 litres ※ 10 has.

PEÑA LA ROSA 2003 MACERACIÓN CARBÓNICA RED

82 Cherry with a violet hue. Intense, fruity and slightly sweet aroma with a certain spicy freshness of skins. Fresh and fleshy on the palate with flavourful grape tannins and ripe black fruit, excellent acidity.

PEÑA LA ROSA VENDIMIA SELECCIONADA 2001 OAK AGED RED

79 Garnet red cherry with a coppery edge. Intense, fruity aroma of spicy oak notes (slightly fresh). Flavourful palate with a note of greeness to the tannins, a ripe fruit nuance and a spicy finish.

FERNANDO REMÍREZ DE GANUZA

Constitución, 1
01307 Samaniego (Álava)
☎: 945 609 022 - Fax: 945 623 335
remirez@eniac.es - rdeganuza@eniac.es
www.remirezdeganuza.com

Established: 1989

⊞ 900 ▥ 350,000 litres ※ 53 has.
▮ 150,000 litres.
▼ 50% ◐50%: -US -DE -UK

ERRE PUNTO 2003 MACERACIÓN CARBÓNICA RED
90% tempranillo, 5% graciano, 5% otros

86 Dark garnet red cherry. Powerful aroma, rich in expression of ripe fruit (grape bunches, blackberries, liquorice) with hints of dry earth. Slightly carbonic on the palate and very fruity, flavourful and very ripe.

TRASNOCHO 2001 RESERVA RED
90% tempranillo, 10% graciano

93 Intense cherry. Toasty aroma (dark-roasted flavours, chocolate, peat), with jammy black fruit and hints of carpentry (new oak). Fleshy, powerful palate with oak tannins that stand out from the fruit, flavourful and persistent.

REMÍREZ DE GANUZA 2000 RESERVA RED
90% tempranillo, 10% graciano

92 Intense cherry. Toasty, fine aroma with notes of fresher yet less complex fruit than previous years (aromatic coffee, cocoa). Flavourful, powerful palate rich in fruit expression, creamy toasty hints and fresh and ripe tannins.

FINCAS DE GANUZA 1999 RESERVA RED
83% tempranillo, 17% graciano

89 Cherry with a saffron edge. Fine aroma with a suggestion of reduction (tobacco, leather, petals). Round, oily, complex palate with a fine even floral, retronasal effect and supple and polished tannins, flavourful and persistent.

FERVIÑO

Carretera de Ollauri, s/n
26323 Hormilla (La Rioja)
☎: 941 417 722 - Fax: 941 417 884
fervino@fervino.com
www.fervino.com

Established: 1995

⊞ 150 ▥ 100,000 litres ※ 30 has.
▼ 80% ◐20%

PAZALUCIA ROSÉ
PAZALUCIA RED
EL REBECO RED

FINCA ALLENDE

Plaza Ibarra, 1
26330 Briones (La Rioja)
☎: 941 322 301 - Fax: 941 322 302
allende@finca-allende.com
www.finca-allende.com

Established: 1995

⊞ 2,240 ▥ 1,000,000 litres ※ 42 has.
▼ 25% ◐75%

ALLENDE 2001 OAK AGED RED
100% tempranillo

92 Very deep cherry. Intense, ripe aroma with well-integrated oak/fruit, a jammy fruit hint and fine toasty oak. Flavourful palate with promising but quite marked tannins, a slightly oily texture and fine toasty notes in the retronasal passage.

AVRVS 2001 OAK AGED RED
85% tempranillo, 15% graciano   ⊞ 24

95 Very deep cherry. Slightly quite closed, very concentrated aroma with an excellent fruit/oak blend (toasty flavours, jammy fruit, pitch, new leathers, oriental spices). Powerful palate, rich in nuances, with rough tannins that boost the black fruit notes, with creamy, toasty oak notes, balsamic hints and excellent acidity, very long.

AVRVS 2000 OAK AGED RED
85% tempranillo, 15% graciano

96 Intense cherry with a garnet red-orange edge. Fine and elegant palate with creamy toasty flavours (cocoa, aromatic coffee, blond tobacco) and ripe fruit but with expression. Powerful, round, oily, warm and full palate with an elegantly toasty retronasal effect, caressing tannins.

ALLENDE 2000 CRIANZA RED
100% tempranillo

89 Quite intense cherry. Fine toasty aroma, fruity, light reduction notes (tobacco, cedar). Flavourful palate, medium bodied, good fruit expression with fine toasty notes well-integrated with the wine, supple but precise tannins.

CALVARIO 2001 CRIANZA RED
90% tempranillo, 8% garnacha, 2% graciano

94 Almost opaque cherry. Intense, concentrated aroma rich in nuances (ripe fruit, balsamic notes, cedar, pitch, mountain herbs, sun-drenched skins and spicy hints of wood). Generous, fleshy palate with ripe, oily tannins.

CALVARIO 2002 CRIANZA RED
90% tempranillo, 8% garnacha, 2% graciano

94 Intense cherry with a lively garnet red edge and an orange hue. Toasty aroma, of fresh fruit, well-balanced grape ripeness, fine toasty, creamy flavours. Powerful, fleshy and flavourful palate, good acidity with fresh fruit in the retronasal passage, complex overtones.

FINCA LA GRAJERA

Carretera Burgos km. 6
26006 Logroño (La Rioja)
☎: 941 291 364 - Fax: 941 291 723
gestion.medios@larioja.org

VIÑA GRAJERA 1999 RESERVA RED
tempranillo

84 Deep cherry with a coppery hue. Intense, fruity aroma with toasty oak notes and a spicy hint of light sweetness. Flavourful, fleshy palate with well-integrated oak/fruit, well-balanced, mild hints of overripening.

FINCA VALPIEDRA

El Montecillo, s/n
26360 Fuenmayor (La Rioja)
☎: 945 622 188 - Fax: 941 122 111
info@fincavalpiedra.com
www.martinezbujanda.com
Established: 1999
🌐 4,200 🍇 80 has.
🍷 50% 🌐50%: -US -DE -UK

FINCA VALPIEDRA 1999 RESERVA RED
90% tempranillo, 5% cabernet sauvignon, 3% graciano, 2% mazuelo

88 Deep cherry with a coppery-saffron edge. Intense aroma with a Riojan Reserva (leather, balsamic flavours, hints of animals) and varietal (Tempranillo) good expression, hints of dry flowers. Flavourful palate with well-integrated oak/fruit, expressive, well-balanced and very long.

FINCA VALPIEDRA 1998 RESERVA RED
90% tempranillo, 5% cabernet sauvignon, 3% graciano, 2% mazuelo

86 Garnet red. Expressive aroma with notes of a crianza reduction, notions of terroir and a suggestion of jammy black fruit. Fleshy palate with fresh yet ripe fruit tannins, powerful and persistent.

FINCA VALPIEDRA 1997 RESERVA RED
90% tempranillo, 5% cabernet sauvignon, 3% graciano, 2% mazuelo

87 Garnet red with an orangey edge. Aroma with reduction notes (leather, animals, chocolate) and a suggestion of ripe plums and dates. Fleshy palate with dominant oak tannins (slightly earthy) but oily and powerful with a bitter finish (stones).

FLORENTINO DE LECANDA

Cuevas, 36
26200 Haro (La Rioja)
☎: 941 303 477 - Fax: 941 312 707
florentinodelecanda@fer.es
Established: 1965
🌐 800 🍇 300,000 litres 🍷 70% 🌐30%: -
CH -DE UK

FLORENTINO DE LECANDA 2001 CRIANZA RED
FLORENTINO DE LECANDA 1996 RESERVA RED
FLORENTINO DE LECANDA 1995 GRAN RESERVA RED

FLORENTINO MARTÍNEZ

Ermita, 33
26311 Cordovín (La Rioja)
☎: 941 418 614 - Fax: 941 418 614
Established: 1992
🌐 162 🍇 16 has.
🍷 95% 🌐5%: -UK

FLORENTINO MARTÍNEZ 2001 FERMENTADO EN BARRICA WHITE
FLORENTINO MARTÍNEZ 2003 JOVEN WHITE
FLORENTINO MARTÍNEZ 2003 JOVEN ROSÉ
FLORENTINO MARTÍNEZ 2003 JOVEN RED
FLORENTINO MARTÍNEZ 2000 CRIANZA RED
FLORENTINO MARTÍNEZ 1998 RESERVA RED

FRANCO ESPAÑOLAS

Cabo Noval, 2
26006 Logroño (La Rioja)
☎: 941 251 300 - Fax: 941 262 948
marketing@francoespanolas.com
www.francoespanolas.com
Established: 1890

🏭 15,000 📦 30,000,000 litres 🍇 50 has.
🍷 60% 🍾40%: -UE: -SE -UK -CH -DK -
NL -DK -IE -FR -BE -FI -DE -PL -US -MX -
PR -CR -CU -DO -CO.-RU -JP

VIÑA SOLEDAD 2003 JOVEN WHITE
100% viura

78 Pale gold. Intense aroma of ripe and somewhat reduced white stone fruit with hints of petals (acacia). Flavourful palate with fresh overtones, without great fruit expression.

VIÑA SOLEDAD TÍTE DE CUVÉE 1995 JOVEN WHITE
60% viura, 30% malvasía, 10% garnacha

82 Golden. Powerful, ripe aroma with predominant creamy (vanilla) oak notes and a suggestion of nuts and fragrant herbs. Flavourful palate with good crianza expression, slightly oily with good acidity.

RIOJA BORDÓN 1998 RESERVA RED
75% tempranillo, 25% garnacha, mazuelo

83 Cherry with a brick red glint. Intense aroma with predominant reduction notes (tobacco, leather old furniture). Flavourful, supple and bitter on the palate with a good traditional Reserva expression.

BARON DÍANGLADE 1995 RESERVA RED
tempranillo, mazuelo, graciano

88 Cherry with an orangey hue. Intense, fine aroma with spicy wood notes, hints of reduction and a ripe fruit nuance. Flavourful on the palate with round and oily tannins; hints of tobacco and slightly spicy and sweet oak in the retronasal passage, slightly marked acidity.

RIOJA BORDÓN 1999 CRIANZA RED
75% tempranillo, 25% garnacha

83 Garnet red cherry with a brick red glint. Somewhat intense, clean aroma with a good expression of traditional crianza (hints of fine reduction).

Flavourful palate with fine bitter notes, a sweet oaky hint, dark-roasted flavours and liquorice.

DIAMANTE CVC JOVEN WHITE

RINSOL 2003 JOVEN WHITE
RIOJA BORDÓN 2003 JOVEN ROSÉ
ROYAL 1995 RESERVA RED
EXCELSO 1982 GRAN RESERVA RED
RIOJA BORDÓN 1994 GRAN RESERVA RED

Hermanos FRÍAS DEL VAL

Herrerías, s/n
01307 Villabuena (Álava)
☎: 945 609 172 - Fax: 945 609 172
friasdelval@wanadoo.es

Established: 1980
🏭 8 📦 272,000 litres 🍇 20 has. 🇪🇸 100%

HERMANOS FRÍAS DEL VAL 2002 OAK FERMENTED WHITE
DON PEDUZ SELECCIÓN 2002 JOVEN RED
HERMANOS FRÍAS DEL VAL 2002 JOVEN RED
HERMANOS FRÍAS DEL VAL SELECCIÓN 2001 OAK AGED RED

Bodegas FUENMAYOR

P. Buicio, Parcelas 5 - 6
26360 Fuenmayor (La Rioja)
☎: 941 450 935 - Fax: 941 450 936
bodegasfuenmayor@bodegasfuenmayor.com
www.bodegasfuenmayor.com

Established: 1998
🏭 650 📦 350,000 litres
🍇 12,5 has. 🇪🇸 100%

NOCEDAL 1999 RESERVA RED
100% tempranillo

86 Dark cherry with a coppery edge. Somewhat intense aroma of jammy black fruit with fine toasty oak. Flavourful, supple palate with round and oily tannins and an excellent expression of Reserva.

GAILUR

Puente del Ebro, 76
01307 Baños del Ebro (Álava)
☎: 945 609 158 - Fax: 943 835 952
bodegasgailur@euskalnet.net

Established: 1985
⊕ 350 🗄 300,000 litres 🍷 100%

ARDANDEGI RED
GAILUR RED
SEÑORÍO DE LAURGAIN RED
SOLAR GAILUR RED

GARCÍA DE OLANO

Carretera de Laguardia-Vitoria s/n
01309 Paganos - La Guardia (Álava)
☎: 945 121 146 - Fax: 945 621 146
garciadeolano@terra.es
www.bodegasgarciadeolano.com

Established: 1991
⊕ 270 🗄 662,100 litres 🍇 25 has. 🍷 100%

HEREDAD GARCÍA DE OLANO 2003 RED
95% tempranillo, 5% graciano

78 Cherry with a violet hue. Quite alcoholic, clear aroma of strawberries and Bigarreau cherries. Light palate with not very marked tannins and bitter notes.

HEREDAD GARCÍA DE OLANO 1999
CRIANZA RED
95% tempranillo, 5% graciano

76 Garnet red cherry. Not very intense aroma of spicy notes and the freshness of red fruit. Flavourful palate without great crianza expression and with a toasty nuance of sweetish fruit.

HEREDAD GARCÍA DE OLANO 1998
CRIANZA RED
95% tempranillo, 5% graciano

79 Brilliant cherry with a brick red glint. Slightly intense aroma with predominant spicy and reduction notes (stewed meat) Flavourful and supple palate and a good fruit/oak integration and mild hints of aged wood.

HEREDAD GARCÍA DE OLANO SELECCIÓN
1998 CRIANZA RED

Bodegas y Viñedos GÓMEZ CRUZADO

Avenida Vizcaya, 6
26200 Haro (La Rioja)
☎: 941 312 502 - Fax: 941 303 567
gcruzado@infonegocio.com
www.gomezcruzado.com

Established: 1886
⊕ 2,500 🗄 2,500,000 litres 🍇 15 has.
🍷 85% 🍷15%: -MX -DE -CH -DK

VIÑA DORANA 1999 CRIANZA RED
VIÑA DORANA 1997 RESERVA RED
VIÑA ANDREA 1995 GRAN RESERVA RED

GÓMEZ DE SEGURA IBÁÑEZ

Barrio El Campillar, 7
01300 Laguardia (Álava)
☎: 945 600 227 - Fax: 945 600 227
gomez_segura@hotmail.com
www.gomezdesegura.com

Established: 1942
⊕ 200 🗄 350,000 litres 🍇 50 has.
🍷 90% 🍷10%: -UK -LV -MX -NL -CH

GÓMEZ DE SEGURA 2003 JOVEN WHITE
100% viura

79 Pale with greenish nuances. Slightly intense, fruity aroma with hints of flowers and spicy skins. Flavourful palate with fresh overtones of white fruit, citrus fruit and good acidity.

GÓMEZ DE SEGURA 2003 MACERACIÓN
CARBÓNICA RED
95% tempranillo, 5% viura

81 Cherry with shades of violet. Intense, fruity aroma with varietal and macerated skins, freshness. Fleshy palate with sweetish fruit, firm and fine grape tannins and excellent acidity.

GÓMEZ DE SEGURA 2001 CRIANZA RED
100% tempranillo

82 Intense cherry. Powerful aroma of jammy black fruit with spicy oak notes and balsamic and terracota notions. Flavourful palate with rough and sweet tannins, spicy and bitter.

GÓMEZ DE SEGURA 2003 JOVEN ROSÉ
GÓMEZ DE SEGURA IBÁÑEZ
SELECCIONADA CRIANZA RED

GRANJA NUESTRA SEÑORA DE REMELLURI

Carretera Rivas, s/n
01330 Labastida (Álava)
☎: 945 331 801 - Fax: 945 331 802
info@remelluri.com
www.remelluri.com

Established: 1967

🛢 5,000 📊 1,044,567 litres 🍇 105 has.

🍷 75% 🌐25%: -US -CH -DE -FI -JP -MX

REMELLURI 2002 WHITE

91 Yellow straw. Intense, fine, perfumed and complex aroma (hay, fine herbs, ripe white fruit, smoky flavours). Powerful, oily and flavourful on the palate with an important fruity presence (grapey) and pleasant herby hints; long.

REMELLURI COLECCIÓN JAIME RODRÍGUEZ 2001 RED

88 Intense cherry with a garnet red edge. Intense, spicy (cloves, tobacco), fine aroma with well-integrated red fruit and wood. Flavourful and powerful on the palate with a good expression of jammy ripe fruit and a mineral hint.

REMELLURI 2000 RESERVA RED
tempranillo, garnacha, graciano

85 Cherry with an orangey edge. Medium-intensity aroma with spicy notes and red fruit. Flavourful on the palate with well-assembled, fresh red fruit and toasty wood, very well-balanced, quite persistent.

LA GRANJA REMELLURI 1997 GRAN RESERVA RED

GREGORIO MARTÍNEZ

Polígono 1. Parcela 12
26190 Nalda (La Rioja)
☎: 941 220 266 - Fax: 941 203 849
cc112682@cconline.es
www.gregoriomartinez.com

Established: 2001

🛢 600 📊 370,000 litres 🍇 35 has.

GREGORIO MARTÍNEZ 2003 WHITE

82 Brilliant pale yellow. Fresh aroma with green apples, fine notes of petals and spicy hints of skins. Flavourful palate with fresh and fleshy overtones, white fruit with warm notes, hints of crystallised fruit, good acidity.

GREGORIO MARTÍNEZ VENDIMIA SELECCIONADA 2001 CRIANZA RED
100% tempranillo

82 Dark garnet red cherry. Powerful, very ripe aroma with fine toasty oak notes and a certain balsamic freshness. Flavourful, fleshy palate with a good oak/fruit integration and excellent acidity.

GREGORIO MARTÍNEZ 2000 CRIANZA RED
90% tempranillo, 10% mazuelo

82 Dark garnet red cherry. Slightly intense aroma with a certain finesse, jammy black fruit and toasty hints of oak. Flavourful, fleshy palate with fine bitter notes, hints of slightly reduced fruit in the finish, good acidity.

GREGORIO MARTÍNEZ 1999 RESERVA RED
90% tempranillo, 10% mazuelo

87 Dark garnet red cherry. Intense aroma of jammy black fruit with fine toasty oak and balsamic notions of terroir. Flavourful palate with round and oily tannins and a powerful finish with predominant notes of dark-roasted flavours and liquorice.

CAVES 2001 CRIANZA RED

HACIENDA MARQUÉS DE LA CONCORDIA

Avenida del Ebro, s/n
26540 Alfaro (La Rioja)
☎: 914 365 900 - Fax: 914 365 932
adelgado@haciendas-espana.com
www.haciendas-espana.com

Established: 1998

🛢 1,000 🍇 15 has.

MARQUÉS DE LA CONCORDIA 2000 CRIANZA RED
tempranillo

84 Garnet red cherry. Intense aroma, slightly fruity, good expression of the Tempranillo (spices) over a hint of fine reduction. Flavourful palate, sweet and smoky oak tannins integrated with the fruit; fresh finish.

MARQUÉS DE LA CONCORDIA 2001 CRIANZA RED
tempranillo

84 Garnet red cherry with a coppery-saffron edge. Intense aroma of black fruit, spicy hints of oak and fine reduction notes (cigar box). Flavourful palate with a good oak/fruit integration, fine bitter notes (liquorice), slightly warm with creamy and jammy notes in the retronasal passage.

MARQUÉS DE LA CONCORDIA HACIENDA SUSAR 2001 RESERVA RED
tempranillo

89 Very deep cherry. Powerful aroma, rich in nuances with macerated black fruit, a toasty oak nuance and a balsamic hint, notions of terroir. Powerful, fleshy palate with ripe tannins and a fairly oily and warm texture, a fruity nuance, spicy, liquorice, very long.

MARQUÉS DE LA CONCORDIA 1999 RESERVA RED
100% tempranillo

84 Garnet red cherry. Intense, ripe aroma with fine reduction notes and a spicy oak nuance. Flavourful palate with slightly marked yet promising oak tannins and a powerful retronasal effect with predominant ripe fruit and liquorice notes.

Bodegas y Viñedos HERAS CORDÓN

Carretera Lapuebla, km.2
26360 Fuenmayor (La Rioja)
☎: 941 451 413 - Fax: 941 450 265
bodegas@herascordon.com
www.herascordon.com
Established: 1997
🌐 2,000 🍾 500,000 litres 🍇 50 has.
🍷 75% 🌐25%: -CH -AT -PR -UK -US

HERAS CORDÓN 2001 RESERVA RED
HERAS CORDÓN VENDIMIA SELECCIONADA 2002 RED
HERAS CORDÓN VENDIMIA SELECCIONADA 2001 CRIANZA RED

HEREDAD DE ADUNA

Matarredo, 39
01307 Samaniego (Álava)
☎: 945 623 343 - Fax: 945 609 290
baduna@arrakis.es
www.heredadaduna.com
Established: 1961
🌐 350 🍾 480,000 litres 🍇 43 has.
🍷 70% 🌐30%: -US -CA -MX -BR -FR -DE -UK -IE -CH -BE -NL -AL LV -DK -JP

HEREDAD DE ADUNA 2003 MACERACIÓN CARBÓNICA RED
90% tempranillo, 10% viura

83 Dark cherry with a violet edge. Powerful, fruity aroma with notes of skins and underbrush. Flavourful, fleshy palate with ripe tannins, a slightly warm texture spicy notes and liquoric

RETVM 2003 MACERACIÓN CARBÓNICA RED
90% tempranillo, 10% viura

84 Garnet red cherry with a violet hue. Intense, fruity aroma with a good varietal expression and maceration (skins, damp earth). Flavourful, fleshy palate with fine, ripe tannins, rich bitter notes and excellent acidity.

ADUNA 2000 CRIANZA RED
95% tempranillo, 5% mazuelo, graciano

81 Garnet red cherry. Not very intense aroma with a good oak/fruit integration. Flavourful, fleshy palate with good crianza expression (sweet fruit and spices).

RETVM 2000 CRIANZA RED
95% tempranillo, 5% mazuelo, graciano

80 Garnet red cherry. Slightly intense aroma of red fruit and a spicy oak freshness. Flavourful palate with slightly rough tannins and warm touches that subdue the best of the fruit expression.

ADUNA 1999 RESERVA RED
95% tempranillo, 5% mazuelo, graciano

76 Brick red. Aroma of toast, liquorice with some reduction notes. Not very polished wood tannins on the palate, slightly warm and light without much persistence.

RETVM 1999 RESERVA RED
95% tempranillo, 5% mazuelo, graciano

85 Garnet red cherry with a brick red rim. Intense aroma with predominant notes of fine reduction (leather, tobacco, old furniture) and a nuance of dates. Flavourful, supple palate with hints of aged wood and a certain fruit-alcohol-crianza balance.

ADUNA 2001 CRIANZA RED
ADUNA 2002 CRIANZA RED
RETVM 2001 CRIANZA RED
ADUNA 2000 RESERVA RED

HEREDAD DE BAROJA

Cercas Altas, 6
01309 Elvillar (Álava)
☎: 945 604 068 - Fax: 945 604 105
info@heredadbaroja.com
www.heredadbaroja.com
Established: 1984
🌐 1,800 🍾 1,200,000 litres 🍷 65%
🌐35%: -FR -DE -BE -DK -NL -JP -UK -US -SE -MX -FI -DK -CY -IE

CAUTIVO 2003 JOVEN RED
100% tempranillo

83 Dark cherry with a purplish edge. Powerful, fruity aroma of sun-drenched skins with hints of sweetness and very varietal notions of terroir. Flavourful, fleshy palate with ripe fruit, spicy, vigorous and very rich.

LAR DE PAULA 2001 OAK AGED RED
100% tempranillo   🌐 14

87 Dark cherry with a coppery edge. Somewhat intense aroma of jammy black fruit with the freshness of skins and a nuance of toasty oak. Flavourful, fruity palate with round and oily oak tannins, fine bitter notes (liquorice, dark-roasted flavours) and excellent acidity.

CAUTIVO 2001 CRIANZA RED
100% tempranillo

79 Garnet red cherry. Somewhat intense aroma with predominant toasty oak notes. Flavourful palate with well-integrated ripe fruit and wood, spicy with bitter hints in the finish.

CAUTIVO 1998 RESERVA RED
100% tempranillo

80 Garnet red cherry with a brick red edge. Not very intense aroma with fine toasty and reduction notes (prunes, tobacco). Flavourful palate with a good fruit/oak integration and fleshy overtones, without great nuances.

CAUTUM 1995 GRAN RESERVA RED
100% tempranillo

87 Garnet red cherry with a brick red edge. Powerful aroma with fine reduction notes (leather, varnish) and a nuance of jammy red fruit. Flavourful palate with a good fruit/oak integration, rich bitter notes and a good fruit and acidity weight, promising.

RINCÓN DE BAROJA 2001 CRIANZA RED
HEREDAD BAROJA 1998 RESERVA RED
CAUTIVO 1996 GRAN RESERVA RED
GRAN BAROJA 1995 GRAN RESERVA RED

HEREDAD GUZMÁN ALDAZÁBAL

Madrid, 10
01309 Navaridas (Álava)
☎: 945 605 172 - Fax: 945 605 172
guzmanaldazabal@terra.es

Established: 1935

150 📦 250,000 litres 🍇 21 has.

🍷 70% 🌐30%: -US

GUZMÁN ALDAZÁBAL 2000 RED
GUZMÁN ALDAZÁBAL "EXALTACIÓN" 2001 RED
PAGO GUZMÁN ALDAZÁBAL RED

HEREDAD UGARTE

Carretera Vitoria-Logroño, km. 61
01309 Laguardia (Álava)
☎: 945 282 844 - Fax: 945 271 319
info@herredadugarte.com
www.herredadugarte.com

Established: 1989

3,100 📦 850,000 litres 🍇 125 has.

🍷 70% 🌐30%: -DE -US -JP

TÉRMINO DE UGARTE 2003 RED
85% tempranillo, 15% garnacha

80 Garnet red cherry with a violet hue. Intense aroma with a good varietal expression (red fruit, underbrush) and spicy hints of skins. Flavourful palate with ripe firm tannins, fine bitter notes and good acidity.

UGARTE 2002 RED
80% tempranillo, 20% garnacha

77 Cherry with a brick red glint. Not very intense aroma of jammy black fruit and hints of damp earth. Flavourful palate, with a slightly warm, oily texture, a light touch of greeness to the tannins and fresh overtones.

HEREDAD UGARTE 2001 CRIANZA RED
92% tempranillo, 8% garnacha

77 Garnet red cherry with a saffron edge. Somewhat intense aroma with predominant toasty oak notes. Flavourful, bitter and slightly oily on the palate with hints of wax; not very expressive overall.

DOMINIO DE UGARTE 1999 RESERVA RED
95% tempranillo, 5% graciano

80 Red cherry with a coppery rim. Not very intense aroma with spicy oak notes. Flavourful palate with quite promising though slightly marked tannins, a suggestion of spices, jammy red fruit and wax.

MARTÍN CENDOYA 1998 RESERVA RED
80% tempranillo, 15% graciano, 5% mazuelo

86 Dark cherry with a deep red edge. Intense, very fine aroma with good fruit/oak integration and predominant jammy red fruit notes. Flavourful palate with round, somewhat oily tannins. Warm, spicy and long.

Vinos de los HEREDEROS DEL MARQUÉS DE RISCAL

Torrea, 1
01340 Elciego (Álava)
☎: 945 606 000 - Fax: 945 606 023
marquesderiscal@marquesdrriscal.com
www.marquesderiscal.com

Established: 1860

37,000 📦 9,000,000 litres 🍇 220 has.

🍷 45% 🌐55%: -UE América -Asia -Africa -Oceanía

MARQUÉS DE RISCAL 2000 RESERVA RED
90% tempranillo, 10% graciano, mazuelo

87 Cherry with a brick red edge. Balsamic aroma with vanilla, wood and light notes of red stone fruit. Fleshy palate with good acidity, persistence and varietal typification; hints of tobacco and bitter chocolate in the retronasal passage.

BARÓN DE CHIREL 1999 RESERVA RED
54% tempranillo, 46% otras

92 Cherry with an orangey rim. Spicy aroma with a suggestion of jammy prunes, toasty oak with leather and pepper. Generous, oily and flavourful on the palate with polished tannins and classic tones (the complexity comes more from the Crianza than the fruit).

MARQUÉS DE RISCAL 1996 GRAN RESERVA RED
65% tempranillo, 25% otras, 10% graciano

87 Intense cherry with a brick red rim. Intense, concentrated aroma of fine toasty notes with a jammy fruit nuance and balsamic hints. Flavourful, and fleshy on the palate with a good tannin/fruit integration, a slightly oily texture and a vigour uncommon in the Gran Reservas.

Bodegas HERMOSILLA

Avd. Rio Ebro, 36 y Las Piscinas, s/n
01307 Baños de Ebro (Álava)
☎: 945 609 161 - Fax: 945 609 161
bodegashermosilla@euskal.net

🏛 112 📖 500,000 litres 🍇 16 has. 🚩 100%

BODEGAS J.I. HERMOSILLA 2003 JOVEN RED
BODEGAS J.I. HERMOSILLA 2000 CRIANZA RED
BODEGAS J.I. HERMOSILLA 2001 CRIANZA RED
BODEGAS J.I. HERMOSILLA 1998 RESERVA RED

HONORIO RUBIO VILLAR

Carretera Baderán 36
26311 Cordovín (La Rioja)
☎: 941 367 343 - Fax: 941 367 343
bodegashonoriorubio@hotmail.com

TREMENDUS 2003 RED
100% tempranillo

76 Intense cherry with a violet edge. Intense aroma with red fruit notes (strawberry jelly) and light hints of liquorice and nettle. Fresh and bitter on the palate with poor fruit expression, slightly woody hints and high in acidity.

HONORIO RUBIO 2000 OAK AGED RED
85% tempranillo, 10% garnacha, 5% mazuelo   🛢 5

87 Garnet red cherry with a saffron edge. Intense aroma, rich in red fruit nuances with hints of macerated skins, fine toasty oak and a terroir nuance. Flavourful, concentrated palate rich in sweet notes, toasty oak and skins.

PASUS 2001 CRIANZA RED
90% tempranillo, 10% mazuelo

84 Intense cherry with a coppery hue. Intense aroma with predominant spicy oak notes (vanilla, pepper). Flavourful palate with a good crianza expression yet without great nuances; slightly warm, with a fruity, liquorice suggestion.

IDIÁQUEZ

San Vicente, 33
01307 Baños de Ebro (Álava)
☎: 945 623 395 - Fax: 945 623 395
bodegasidiaquez@msn.com

Established: 1972
🏛 10 📖 200,000 litres 🍇 12 has. 🚩 100%

IDIÁQUEZ JOVEN WHITE
IDIÁQUEZ JOVEN RED
MAYORAZGO DE IDIÁQUEZ 2002 CRIANZA RED

Bodegas y Viñedos ILURCE

Avenida de Logroño, 7
26540 Alfaro (La Rioja)
☎: 941 180 829 - Fax: 941 183 897
ilurce@fer.es

Established: 1940
🏛 110 📖 1,350,000 litres 🍇 55 has.
🚩 100%

ILURCE 2003 JOVEN ROSÉ
100% garnacha

77 Pale blush. Somewhat intense, fruity aroma with fresh overtones. Fresh and flavourful palate with spicy notes of skins, hints of citrus fruit and good acidity, lacking great fruit expression.

ILURCE 2000 CRIANZA RED
100% graciano

85 Dark cherry with a coppery edge. Powerful aroma of fine toasty oak with very varietal fruit (fresh skins, vine shoots) and a suggestion of dried leaves. Flavourful, fruity palate with slightly fresh yet very elegant tannins, warm and spicy hints, very varietal.

ILURCE VENDIMIA SELECCIONADA 2001 CRIANZA RED
60% tempranillo, 40% garnacha

84 Deep cherry. Intense, very elegant aroma of ripe black fruit with toasty oak and balsamic notes. Flavourful palate with jammy fruit, ripe and firm tannins, dark-roasted wood notes and good acidity.

ILURCE 2003 JOVEN RED

Vinos IRADIER

Avenida La Rioja, 17
26339 Abalos (La Rioja)
☎: 941 334 251 - Fax: 945 290 081
vinosiradier@vinosiradier.euskalnet.net
Established: 1983
▤ 500,000 litres ▼ 100%

IRADIER 2003 WHITE
viura

79 Pale with greenish nuances. Intense aroma with fresh overtones, white fruit and floral hints. Fresh and flavourful palate with green fruit and good acidity.

IRADIER 2003 ROSÉ
50% viura, 50% tempranillo

71 Brilliant blush. Slightly short aroma with spicy hints of skins. Fresh palate with citrus and carbonic hints, warm with an acidic edge.

IRADIER 2003 WHITE
IRADIER 2003 ROSÉ
IRADIER 2003 RED
IRAIL 2003 RED

IRONDA

Carretera Burgos, 53
26370 Navarrete (La Rioja)
☎: 941 446 180 - Fax: 941 440 548
bodegas-ironda@terra.es
Established: 1973
⊕ 2,000 ▤ 3,500,000 litres ▼ 60 has.
▼ 80% ◔20%

BOYAL JOVEN RED
HURTADO JOVEN RED
VIÑA IRONDA JOVEN RED
VIÑA IRONDA CRIANZA RED
HURTADO I GRAN RESERVA RED

JOSÉ BASOCO BASOCO

Carretera de Samaniego, s/n
01307 Villabuena (Álava)
☎: 945 331 619 - Fax: 945 331 619
j.basoco@euskalnet.net
Established: 1997
⊕ 50 ▤ 200,000 litres ▼ 8 has.▼ 100%

BETIKOA 2003 JOVEN WHITE
BETIKOA 2003 JOVEN RED
FINCA BARRONTE 2001 CRIANZA RED

JOSÉ CÓRDOBA

Plaza El Plano, 5 1ſ
01306 Lapuebla de Labarca (Álava)
☎: 945 627 212 - Fax: 945 627 212
josecordobabode@mixmail.com
Established: 1986
▤ 50,000 litres ▼ 18 has.▼ 100%

JOSÉ CÓRDOBA 2003 RED

JOSE MARÍA SÁENZ COSECHEROS Y CRIADORES

Carretera LR-123, km.61
26511 El Villar de Arnedo (La Rioja)
☎: 941 159 034 - Fax: 941 159 034
Established: 1990
⊕ 230 ▤ 200,000 litres ▼ 24 has.▼ 100%

PRESAGIO 2002 CRIANZA RED
80% tempranillo, 20% graciano

83 Garnet red cherry with with a purplish edge. Powerful aroma of smoky oak, jammy black fruit and a balsamic hint. Flavourful palate with slightly marked although promising oak tannins, fine bitter notes (liquorice, dark-roasted flavours), a certain length.

PRESAGIO 2001 RESERVA RED
80% tempranillo, 20% graciano

84 Garnet red cherry. Intense, very fine aroma with predominant spicy oak notes and a nuance of jammy black fruit. Flavourful palate with a good fruit/oak integration, spicy and balsamic notes and liquorice.

PRESAGIO 2003 RED

DO Ca. RIOJA

JUAN ALCORTA

Camino de la Puebla, 50
26006 Logroño (La Rioja)
☎: 941 279 900 - Fax: 941 279 901
info@byb.es
www.byb.es

Established: 2001

🌐 70,000 📦 30,000,000 litres 🍇 413 has.

🍷 60% 🍾40%

CAMPO VIEJO 2001 CRIANZA RED
85% tempranillo, 10% garnacha, 5% mazuelo

82 Intense cherry. Spicy aroma with vanilla notes over red fruit, toasty. Flavourful palate with fresh tannins, very pleasant with a slightly bitter finish.

VIÑA ALCORTA 2001 CRIANZA RED
100% tempranillo

82 Cherry. Fine smoky aroma of spices and jammy fruit with an elegant earthy hint. Flavourful palate with fresh and fruity tannins, character of the vine variety and a pleasantly bitter finish.

CAMPO VIEJO LA FINCA 2001 CRIANZA RED
85% tempranillo, 10% garnacha, 5% mazuelo

84 Cherry with a garnet red edge. Aroma of red fruit with toasty notes and a balsamic suggestion. Flavourful palate with good freshness, fresh fruit and a slightly bitter finish (minerals).

MARQUÉS DE VILLAMAGNA 2001 CRIANZA RED
100% tempranillo

82 Intense cherry. Spicy aroma with crianza vanilla over red fruit. Flavourful palate with a fruit expression and a very elegant and well-assembled crianza; fresh fruit tannins.

AZPILICUETA 2001 CRIANZA RED
75% tempranillo, 10% graciano, 15% mazuelo

87 Deep cherry. Elegant aroma of black fruit (plums), spices and fine crianza (complex). Flavourful, fleshy palate with round and oily wood tannins; good freshness and a toasty finish.

CAMPO VIEJO 1998 RESERVA RED
tempranillo, graciano, mazuelo

84 Garnet red cherry with a coppery edge. Powerful aroma of red berries with the spicy freshness of oak and a balsamic hint of damp earth. Flavourful, supple palate with round and oily tannins, balanced with a spicy finish and good acidity.

CAMPO VIEJO LA FINCA 1998 RESERVA RED
85% tempranillo, 10% garnacha, 5% mazuelo

86 Brilliant cherry with a coppery edge. Intense aroma of fine toasty oak, a ripe fruit suggestion and hints of flowers (pot purri). Flavourful, supple palate with well-integrated oak and fruit and hints of liquorice and terroir in the retronasal passage.

MARQUÉS DE VILLAMAGNA 1998 RESERVA RED
100% tempranillo

82 Cherry with an orangey edge. Spicy aroma with fine crianza notes (orange peel). Flavourful palate with fresh and fruity tannins, spicy with an aftertaste of reduction notes.

VIÑA ALCORTA 1998 RESERVA RED
100% tempranillo

84 Brilliant garnet red cask. Aroma with a fine crianza reduction (vanilla, smoky hints), a slightly earthy nuance and ripe fruit (dates). Flavourful palate with fruity tannins and wood assembled perfectly and with complex overtones.

CAMPO VIEJO 1997 GRAN RESERVA RED
tempranillo, garnacha, mazuelo

84 Deep cherry. Aroma of well-ripened red fruit, toasty with a suggestion of earth and reduction. Flavourful palate with well-harmonised ripe fruit; round tannins.

MARQUÉS DE VILLAMAGNA 1997 GRAN RESERVA RED
75% tempranillo, 15% mazuelo, 10% graciano

85 Intense cherry with a saffron edge. Not very intense aroma of fine notes of well-integrated oak and fruit. Flavourful on the palate with red stone fruit and spicy wood notes; quite complex.

AZPILICUETA 2000 RESERVA RED

JUAN JOSÉ MENDIETA GARCÍA

Curillos, 16
01308 Lanciego (Álava)
☎: 945 608 134 - Fax: 945 608 140
bodegamendieta@hotmail.com

Established: 1982

📦 160,000 litres 🍇 14 has.

ZABALMENDI 2003 MACERACIÓN
CARBÓNICA RED
80% tempranillo, 15% mazuelo, 5% viura

81 Cherry with a purplish edge. Intense aroma of black fruit with spicy hints of skins and fresh overtones. Flavourful, fruity palate with notions of liquorice, slightly warm.

JUAN JOSÉ URARTE ESPINOSA

Finca El Redondo de Assa, s/n
01300 Laguardia (Álava)
☎: 945 600 102 - Fax: 945 625 063
www.vinaemiliano.com

▦ 485 ▤ 350,000 litres ☙ 30 has.
▼ 100%

VIÑA EMILIANO 2002 JOVEN RED
VIÑA EMILIANO 1999 CRIANZA RED
VIÑA EMILIANO 1998 RESERVA RED

JULIÁN FERNÁNDEZ GARRIDO

Avenida de La Rioja, 12
26339 Abalos (La Rioja)
☎: 941 334 166

PEÑA LA ROSA 2003 RED
PEÑA LA ROSA 2001 RED

Bodegas KEFRÉN

Blas de Otero 5-5/C
01010 Vitoria (Álava)
☎: 945 175 466
info@bodegaskefren.com
www.bodegaskefren.com

Established: 2000
▦ 64 ▤ 80,000 litres ☙ 10 has.
▼ 90% ☙10%

KEFRÉN 2001 OAK AGED RED
KEFRÉN VENDIMIA SELECCIONADA 2000 OAK AGED RED

Bodegas L. CASADO

Avenida de la Poveda, 46
01306 Lapuebla de Labarca (Álava)
☎: 945 607 096 - Fax: 945 607 412
bodegaslcasado@airtel.net
www.vintiumexport.es

Established: 1968
▦ 380 ▤ 342,000 litres ☙ 25 has.
▼ 85% ☙15%

COVARA 2003 JOVEN RED
85% tempranillo, 10% viura, 5% mazuelo, graciano

76 Cherry with a garnet red edge. Slightly warm aroma with notes of oak, very sweet raspberries and sun-drenched skins. Warm palate with light bitter notes.

JAUN DE ALZATE 2001 CRIANZA RED
90% tempranillo, 5% graciano, 5% mazuelo

84 Garnet red cherry with a brick red edge. Intense aroma with predominant reduction notes (varnish, leather). Supple palate with fine bitter crianza notes and a traditional Rioja expression, very flavourful.

JAUN DE ALZATE SELECCIÓN 2002 RED

84 Fairly deep cherry. Powerful, fruity aroma with an excellent varietal expression (redcurrants, damp earth) and fine toasty notes. Fleshy, fruity palate with flavourful, firm tannins and toasty and spicy hints in the retronasal passage.

COVARA 2003 JOVEN WHITE
COVARA 2003 JOVEN ROSÉ
JAUN DE ALZATE 1995 RESERVA RED
JAUN DE ALZATE 1994 GRAN RESERVA RED

Agrícola LA BASTIDA

El Olmo s/n
01330 Labastida (Álava)
☎: 945 331 230 - Fax: 945 331 257

Established: 1992
▦ 100 ▤ 150,000 litres ☙ 25 has.
▼ 90% ☙10%

TIERRA FERNÁNDEZ GÓMEZ 2003
FERMENTADO EN BARRICA WHITE
TIERRA FERNÁNDEZ GÓMEZ 2003 RED
BELISARIO 2002 RED
TIERRA FIDEL 2001 RED
TIERRA FERNÁNDEZ GÓMEZ 2001 CRIANZA RED

Bodegas LA EMPERATRIZ

Carretera Sto. Domingo - Haro, km. 31, 500
26241 Baños de Rioja (La Rioja)
☎: 941 300 105 - Fax: 941 300 231
correo@bodegaslaemperatriz.com
www.bodegaslaemperatriz.com

Established: 1999
▦ 1,500 ▤ 1,800,000 litres ☙ 125 has.
▼ 90% ☙10%: -DE -US -UK

VIÑA ACEDO 2001 CRIANZA RED
95% tempranillo, 2,5% garnacha, 2,5% mazuelo

80 Cherry with an orangey edge. Medium-intensity, clean aroma with a good fruit/oak integration.

DO Ca. RIOJA

Flavourful, medium bodied and spicy palate (black pepper).

VIÑA ACEDO 2000 RESERVA RED
96% tempranillo, 4% mazuelo

84 Intense cherry with a coppery hue. Intense aroma of fresh fruit and flowers with spicy oak notes and light hints of reduction. Flavourful, supple palate with a certain freshness and fine bitter notes; very pleasant without an obvious fruit expression.

VIÑA ACEDO 2003 JOVEN WHITE
VIÑA ACEDO 2003 JOVEN ROSÉ

LA ENCINA BODEGAS Y VIÑEDOS

Carretera N 124 Logroño-Vitoria, km. 45
26290 Briñas (La Rioja)
☎: 941 305 630 - Fax: 941 313 028
reinoso@laencina.es
www.laencinabodegas.com
Established: 1999

🌐 950 📊 250,000 litres 🍇 10 has.
🍷 90% 🌐10%: -CH -UK -NL -BE

TAHÓN DE TOBELOS 2001 RED

85 Cherry with an orangey edge. Medium-intensity, spicy aroma (cinnamon, vanilla), fine. Flavourful, intense palate, creamy wood well-assembled with the fruit, well-balanced, long, ripe tannins.

TOBELOS 2001 CRIANZA RED
90% tempranillo, 10% garnacha

83 Medium-hue cherry with brick red edge. Medium-intensity aroma of ink and spicy crianza notes. Supple, and flavourful on the palate with notes of red berries well-assembled with the wood, well-balanced.

TAHON DE TOBELOS 1999 RESERVA RED
100% tempranillo

85 Cherry with an orangey edge. Medium-intensity, fine, spicy aroma (cinnamon, vanilla). Flavourful, intense palate with creamy wood well-assembled with the fruit; well-balanced and long with ripe tannins.

LA RIOJA ALTA

Avenida Vizcaya, s/n
26200 Haro (La Rioja)
☎: 941 310 346 - Fax: 941 312 854
riojalta@riojalta.com
www.riojalta.com
Established: 1890

🌐 52,000 🍇 425 has.
🍷 75% 🌐25%: -UK -DE -US -MX

VIÑA ALBERDI 2000 CRIANZA RED
tempranillo, mazuelo

88 Ruby red with quite a dark brick red hue. Slightly closed, spicy and fine aroma (tobacco, cedar, used leather) with mild waxy hints and a very light suggestion of jammy fruit. Good symmetry between slightly jammy crianza fruit and seasoned wood, well-integrated and flavourful on the palate with a mildly floral effect in the retronasal passage (violets).

VIÑA ARANA 1997 RESERVA RED
tempranillo, graciano

88 Ruby red with a brick red hue. Medium-intensity aroma with creamy notes of vanilla and wax, a hint of jammy fruit and mild floral nuances. Round palate with spices in the retronasal passage, polished tannins and a bitter oak finish.

VIÑA ARDANZA 1998 RESERVA RED
tempranillo, graciano

89 Ruby red with quite a dark brick red hue. Creamy and slightly spicy aroma (cocoa, tobacco, old leather). Round, generous palate with polished tannins and spices in the retronasal passage, mildly floral rather than fruity, has barely changed in a year, a modernised classic.

LA RIOJA ALTA GRAN RESERVA 890 1989 GRAN RESERVA RED
90% tempranillo, 10% mazuelo, graciano

88 Dark cherry with a brick red edge. Aroma with notes of jammy fruit and spices and nuances of evolution in the bottle (leather, tobacco, cedar wood, pepper, old furniture, a waxy hint). Round, slightly velvety palate with supple tannins, a suggestion of acidity and spices and animals in the retronasal passage, a bitter oak finish. A classic Rioja.

LA RIOJA ALTA GRAN RESERVA 904 1994 GRAN RESERVA RED
90% tempranillo, 10% graciano

83 Orangey ruby red. Fairly intense aroma with fine crianza expression, hints of aged wood and red meat with spicy hints of wax and pepper. Better on the palate, flavourful and rich in long crianza nuances with a spicy aroma in the retronasal passage; somewhat lacking in crianza expression, slightly quite closed.

LAGUNILLA

Carretera de Elciego, s/n
26350 Cenicero (La Rioja)
☎: 941 453 100 - Fax: 941 453 114
info@lagunilla.com
www.lagunilla.com

Established: 1885

🏭 50,000 🍇 5000 has.

🍷 50% 🌐50%: -UK -DE -NL -CH -Asia -JP -US

LAGUNILLA CASA DEL COMENDADOR 2001 CRIANZA RED
80% tempranillo, 20% garnacha

83 Garnet red cherry with a brick red edge. Not very intense aroma of fine spicy and reduction notes with hints of ripe fruit (redcurrants, dates). Flavourful and supple on the palate with a good oak/fruit integration, good acidity.

LAGUNILLA CASA DEL COMENDADOR 1999 RESERVA RED
80% tempranillo, 20% garnacha

84 Fairly deep cherry with a coppery glint. Intense aroma with fine spicy and reduction notes and a suggestion of ripe red fruit. Flavourful on the palate with good turns between sweet fruit and bitter oak notes, well-balanced and very pleasant.

LAGUNILLA VIÑA ARTAL 2000 CRIANZA RED
LAGUNILLA RESERVA RED
LAGUNILLA VIÑA ARTAL 1999 RESERVA RED
LAGUNILLA GRAN RESERVA RED
LAGUNILLA CASA DEL COMENDADOR 1997
 GRAN RESERVA RED
LAGUNILLA VIÑA ARTAL 1997 GRAN
 RESERVA RED

Bodegas LAN

Paraje del Buicio, s/n
26360 Fuenmayor (La Rioja)
☎: 941 450 950 - Fax: 941 450 567
info@bodegaslan.com
www.bodegaslan.com

Established: 1974

🏭 25,000 📦 13,000,000 litres 🍇 8 has.

🍷 60% 🌐40%: -DE -AT -BE -NL -SE -EE -FI -IE -UK -CH -RU -US -CA -MX -CO -CR -PA -DO -VN -JP

LAN 2002 OAK AGED RED
85% tempranillo, 10% mazuelo, 5% graciano

93 Very deep cherry with a violet edge. Powerful, concentrated aroma of jammy black fruit with spicy and toasty hints (pitch) of the oak. Concentrated, flavourful palate with well-integrated oak/fruit, promising but quite marked tannins and notes of chocolate and spices in the retronasal passage.

CULMEN 2001 OAK AGED RED
75% tempranillo, 20% mazuelo, 5% graciano

87 Intense cherry. Slightly overripe aroma of yet to be assembled toasty wood. Powerful, fleshy, spirituous palate with jammy black berries, oak and ripe fruit tannins.

LAN 1999 CRIANZA RED
85% tempranillo, 10% garnacha, 5% mazuelo

82 Intense cherry. Intense aroma of very ripe fruit notes (prunes, dates) with a spicy oak nuance. Flavourful palate with a good oak/fruit integration, slightly warm with toasty hints of fruit and oak in the retronasal passage.

LAN 1998 RESERVA RED
80% tempranillo, 10% garnacha, 10% mazuelo

84 Dark cherry with a coppery edge. Aroma with a certain finesse and predominant toasty notes of oak and very ripe fruit. Flavourful and slightly fleshy on the palate with a good fruit/oak integration and dark-roasted and balsamic notes.

MENCIÓN 1998 RESERVA RED
80% tempranillo, 20% mazuelo

87 Intense cherry with a saffron edge. Powerful aroma with predominant dark-roasted and fine reduction notes and a spicy, jammy suggestion. Flavourful, fleshy and supple palate with good fruit/oak integration and hints of graphite in the retronasal passage.

VIÑA LANCIANO 1999 RESERVA RED

86 Dark cherry. Intense, fruity aroma of jammy black fruit with fine toasty and balsamic notes. Flavourful and bitter palate with promising but somewhat fresh tannins, toasty hints of oak and skins and good acidity.

VIÑA LANCIANO EDICIÓN LIMITADA 1996 RESERVA RED
80% tempranillo, 15% mazuelo, 5% graciano

89 Deep cherry with a saffron edge. Intense aroma, excellent long crianza character (spices, leathers, cigar box) over a suggestion of jammy red fruit. Flavourful palate with fleshy overtones and well-integrated oak/fruit, refreshing acidity.

VIÑA LANCIANO EDICIÓN LIMITADA 1998 RESERVA RED
80% tempranillo, 15% mazuelo, 5% graciano

88 Deep cherry. Powerful aroma of great finesse with predominant toasty notes (oak, skins). Flavourful, fleshy palate with promising but slightly marked tannins, excellent expression of jammy black fruit, slightly warm.

LAN 1997 GRAN RESERVA RED
85% tempranillo, 5% garnacha, 10% mazuelo

84 Dark cherry with a brick red edge. Intense aroma with predominant burnt notes and a balsamic nuance. Flavourful and slightly fleshy on the palate with promising but slightly marked tannins, a bitter nuance (chocolate, dark-roasted flavours) and balsamic fresh overtones of terroir.

LARCHAGO

La Poveda, 41
01306 Lapuebla de Labarca (Álava)
☎: 945 231 974 - Fax: 945 135 512
bodegaslarchago@terra.es
www.bodegaslarchago.es
Established: 1898
⊕ 3,000 ▤ 1,500,000 litres ⬚ 60 has.
▼ 30% ⬥70%:

LARCHAGO 2003 JOVEN WHITE
LARCHAGO 2003 JOVEN RED
VIÑEDOS DE TAHOLA 2000 CRIANZA RED
IZARBE RESERVA SELECCIÓN 1996 RESERVA RED
LARCHAGO 2001 CRIANZA RED
LARCHAGO 1998 RESERVA RED
VIÑEDOS DE TAHOLA 1997 RESERVA RED
IZARBE 1995 GRAN RESERVA RED

Hermanos LAREDO VILLANUEVA

Mayor, 18
01309 Leza (Álava)
☎: 945 605 018 - Fax: 945 605 178
abra@riojalavesa.com
Established: 1963
⊕ 450 ▤ 452,000 litres ⬚ 32 has.
▼ 85% ⬥15%: -FR -DE

LAREDO ANAIAK 2003 RED
90% tempranillo, 10% viura

70 Cherry with a purplish edge. Aroma of phosphorus (mild off-odours). Bitter on the palate with a mild greeness.

SEÑORÍO DE LAREDO 1999 CRIANZA RED
80% tempranillo, 10% graciano, 10% mazuelo

82 Cherry with an orangey edge. Toasty aroma of jammy red fruit with light reduction notes. Fleshy palate with well-polished tannins and a toasty finish.

SEÑORÍO DE LAREDO 1998 RESERVA RED
80% tempranillo, 10% graciano, 10% mazuelo

73 Cherry with a brick red hue. Reduction notes and ripe aroma. Supple palate, well-mannered but without great nuances.

SEÑORÍO DE LAREDO 1994 GRAN RESERVA RED
80% tempranillo, 10% graciano, 10% mazuelo

80 Brick red. Slightly viscous aroma with light reduction notes (leather, tobacco). Warm and supple on the palate with bitter notes.

LAS ORCAS

Camino de la Hoya, 1
01300 Laguardia (Álava)
☎: 945 621 148 - Fax: 945 621 124
lasorcas@jet.es
www.riojalavesa.com
Established: 1994
⊕ 1,200 ▤ 1,500,000 litres ⬚ 90 has.
▼ 60% ⬥40%: -US -NL -DK -PL -BE

DECENIO 2003 JOVEN RED
LAGUSAN 2003 JOVEN RED
SOLAR DE RANDEZ 2003 JOVEN RED
VIÑA TORSAL 2003 JOVEN RED
DECENIO 2001 CRIANZA RED
LAGUSAN 2001 CRIANZA RED
SOLAR DE RANDEZ 2001 CRIANZA RED
VIÑA TORSAL 2001 CRIANZA RED
DECENIO 1997 RESERVA RED
LAGUSAN 1997 RESERVA RED
SOLAR DE RANDEZ 1997 RESERVA RED

VIÑA TORSAL 1997 RESERVA RED
PAGOS DE VALDEORCA 2001 RED

Señorío de LAS VIÑAS

Mayor, s/n
01309 Laserna (Álava)
☎: 945 621 110 - Fax: 945 621 110

Established: 1991

🍶 500 🍷 36 has.

🍇 90% 🍷10%: -UK -MX

SEÑORÍO DE LAS VIÑAS 2003 RED
SEÑORÍO DE LAS VIÑAS 1999 CRIANZA RED
SEÑORÍO DE LAS VIÑAS 1995 RESERVA RED
SELLADO 1994 RESERVA RED

LAVALLE

Mayor 51
01307 Navaridas (Álava)
☎: 945 605 032 - Fax: 945 605 032

Established: 1994

🍶 100,000 litres 🍷 16 has.🍇 100%

LAVALLE 2003 JOVEN RED
85% tempranillo, 10% otras, 5% graciano

82 Dark cherry with a violet hue. Powerful aroma of black fruit with hints of nettles and fresh maceration notes. Fresh on the palate with spicy notes of skins and flavourful, firm tannins.

LECEA

Cſ Santo Domingo, 6
26340 San Asensio (La Rioja)
☎: 941 457 444 - Fax: 941 457 444

🍶 180 🍶 250,000 litres 🍷 20 has.🍇 100%

LECEA 2003 RED
LECEA 1999 CRIANZA RED
LECEA 1998 RESERVA RED
LECEA 1994 GRAN RESERVA RED

LEZA GARCÍA

San Ignacio, 26
26313 Uruñuela (La Rioja)
☎: 941 371 142 - Fax: 941 371 035
bodegalezagarcia@bodegasleza.com
wwww.bodegasleza.com

Established: 1982

🍶 285 🍶 1,000,000 litres 🍷 45 has.

🍇 85% 🍷15%: -DE -UK -MX -CH

VALDEPALACIOS 2003 JOVEN WHITE
100% viura

71 Brilliant pale. Intense, not very fine aroma (mild reduction and tank off-odours). Flavourful and slightly oily palate with very ripe white stone fruit.

LEZA GARCÍA 2003 FERMENTADO EN BARRICA WHITE
100% viura

74 Brilliant gold. Slightly intense aroma with a mild hydrogen sulphide off-odour and slightly fresh oak. Slightly better on the palate with ripe fruit, smoky oak hints, slightly drying tannins and a herby suggestion.

VALDEPALACIOS 2003 ROSÉ
90% garnacha, 10% viura

69 Onion-skins. Slightly vinous, not very clear aroma. Light and bitter palate. with weak fruit.

VALDEPALACIOS 2001 CRIANZA RED
90% tempranillo, 5% garnacha, 5% mazuelo

82 Dark garnet red cherry. Not very intense aroma with predominant fruity notes and a leather nuance. Flavourful palate with a good oak/fruit integration, spicy and waxy hints, pleasant.

LEZA GARCÍA 2001 OAK AGED RED
100% tempranillo   🍶 7

75 Brilliant cherry. Aroma with ripe fruit and fine reduction notes (tobacco, animals), hints of petals and a light sulphurous suggestion. Flavourful palate with slightly drying oak tannins, bitter notes and light hints of dilution.

VALDEPALACIOS VENDIMIA SELECCIONADA 2002 OAK AGED RED
95% tempranillo, 5% garnacha

81 Dark garnet red cherry with a brick red edge. Intense aroma, with spicy oak notes and a suggestion of ripe fruit (hints of macerated skins) and damp earth. Flavourful palate with slightly drying tannins and a suggestion of spices, bitter (liquorice, dark-roasted flavours).

VALDEPALACIOS 2003 JOVEN RED
90% tempranillo, 5% garnacha, 5% mazuelo

82 Garnet red cherry. Intense, fruity aroma with good varietal expression of the Tempranillo (terroir). Flavourful palate of ripe black fruit with fine spicy notes of skins and excellent acidity.

LEZA GARCÍA 1998 RESERVA RED
90% tempranillo, 10% garnacha

83 Ruby red cherry with a brick red glint. Intense aroma with mild reduction notes (prunes, tobacco, leather) and spicy hints of oak. Flavourful, supple palate with a good oak/fruit integration, very pleasant.

LEZA GARCÍA 1996 GRAN RESERVA RED
90% tempranillo, 10% garnacha

80 Garnet red cherry with a brick red edge. Intense aroma with predominant toasty oak and mild reduction notes (cigar box, old furniture). Flavourful palate with slightly drying tannins, jammy fruit notes and an element of bitterness.

LÓPEZ HEREDIA-VIÑA TONDONIA

Avenida Vizcaya, 3
26200 Haro (La Rioja)
☎: 941 310 244 - Fax: 941 310 788
bodega@lopezheredia.com
www.lopezheredia.com

Established: 1877

🌐 15,000 📊 9,000,000 litres 🍇 170 has.

🇪🇸 90% 🌐10%: -DE -AD -AT -BE -CA -DO -
US -FR -NL -UK -IL -JP -MX -DK -SE -PR -CH

VIÑA GRAVONIA 1994 CRIANZA WHITE
100% viura

78 Brilliant golden yellow. Somewhat intense aroma with predominant smoky, creamy and spicy crianza notes. Flavourful palate of nuts, with hints of wax and perfumed soap, hardly any fruit nuances.

VIÑA TONDONIA 1987 RESERVA WHITE
90% viura, 10% malvasía

83 Golden. Somewhat intense aroma with fine oxidised crianza notes, hints of wax and aged wood. Somewhat flavourful, warm and oily on the palate with fine spicy hints in the finish

VIÑA TONDONIA 1981 GRAN RESERVA WHITE
90% viura, 10% malvasía

84 Golden yellow. Powerful aroma with a certain finesse, very reduced white stone fruit, creamy wood notes, vanilla, oriental spices and crystallised citrus fruit peel. Flavourful, fleshy, slightly warm and oily on the palate with a nuance of nuts, slightly aged and damp wood, good acidity

VIÑA CUBILLO 1999 CRIANZA RED
65% tempranillo, 25% garnacha, 5% graciano, mazuelo

83 Garnet red cherry with a brick red rim. Intense aroma of fine toasty and reduction notes (horsehair, old furniture), and ripe fruit with notions of raisins. Flavourful palate with bitter crianza notes and a good expression of traditional crianza.

VIÑA TONDONIA 1996 RESERVA RED
75% tempranillo, 15% garnacha, 5% graciano, 5% mazuelo

85 Ruby red cherry with an orangey hue. Intense aroma with good crianza expression (leather, spices, hints of wax), and fresh overtones of red fruit. Flavourful on the palate with well polished oak and fruit tannins and hints of sweet spices; a little lacking in balance (high in acidity).

VIÑA TONDONIA 1985 GRAN RESERVA RED
75% tempranillo, 15% garnacha, 10% graciano, mazuelo

84 Ruby red cherry with an orangey hue. Intense aroma of fine reduction notes (old furniture, nuts, cumin). Flavourful, supple on the palate with predominant spicy notes and hints of tobacco and aged wood.

VIÑA TONDONIA 1993 CRIANZA ROSÉ
VIÑA BOSCONIA 1996 RESERVA RED
VIÑA BOSCONIA 1981 GRAN RESERVA RED

LOS ARLOS

Avenida La Póveda, 16
01306 La Puebla de Labarca (Álava)
☎: 945 607 003 - Fax: 945 607 003

Established: 1999

🌐 100 📊 120,000 litres 🍇 25 has.🇪🇸 100%

VIÑA ISAFE 2002 RED
VIÑA ISAFE 2000 RED

Bodegas LUBERRI

Las Piscinas, s/n
01307 Baños de Ebro (Álava)
☎: 945 609 317 - Fax: 945 609 317
bodegasluberri@euskalnet.net
www.bodegasluberri.com

Established: 1989

🌐 330 📊 400,000 litres 🍇 35 has.

🐗 95% 🌐5%: -US -NL -UK -CH -DE

ALBIKER 2003 RED
90% tempranillo, 10% viura

80 Deep cherry with a violet rim. Aroma of ripe red fruit, sweet notes and grape harvest bunches. Fruity on the palate with quite incisive, bitter tannins.

EVEREST DE ALTÚN 2001 OAK AGED RED
100% tempranillo

84 Brilliant garnet red cherry. Intense aroma of fine toasty oak notes, well-integrated with ripe black fruits and a spicy nuance. Flavourful palate, ripe, slightly sweet tannins, fine spicy notes of liquorice and fresh overtones.

ALTÚN 2001 CRIANZA RED
100% tempranillo

84 Garnet red cherry with a coppery edge. Not very intense aroma with a certain finesse, jammy red fruit and spicy hints of oak. Flavourful palate with slightly marked tannins (slightly fresh oak), with fleshy overtones and structure.

ALTÚN 1999 RESERVA RED
100% tempranillo

85 Garnet red cherry. Elegant but moderate fruit and wood aroma with a fine expression of the skins. Dry, fresh palate, very round tannins, wellbalanced fruit/oak and a spicy finish.

ALTÚN SELECCIÓN 1999 RESERVA RED
100% tempranillo

88 Intense cherry with a brick red edge. Intense aroma with predominant toasty oak notes and a fine reduction nuance (prunes, old furniture). Flavourful palate, with excellent crianza expression and a slightly oily and warm texture.

ALBIKER 2003 RED

Bodegas LUIS ALEGRE

Carretera Navaridas, s/n
01307 Laguardia (Álava)
☎: 945 600 089 - Fax: 945 600 089
luisalegre@bodegasluisalegre.com
www.larioja.com/bodegas/luisalegre/

Established: 1968

750 ▯ 300,000 litres 🍇 20 has.

80% 🍷20%: -DK -CH -VE -US

LUIS ALEGRE 2003 FERMENTADO EN BARRICA WHITE
90% viura, 10% malvasía

86 Pale yellow. Intense, very fine aroma of fennel and white fruit with floral hints and a good varietal presence (syrup, orange blossom) of the Malvasía grape. Flavourful palate with fine smoky oak, ripe fruit, aniseed and excellent acidity.

LUIS ALEGRE 2003 MACERACIÓN CARBÓNICA RED
85% tempranillo, 10% viura, 5% garnacha

83 Dark cherry with a purplish rim. Powerful, fruity aroma with varietal notes and maceration freshness. Fruity palate with flavourful and firm grape tannins, spicy hints and good fruit-alcohol-acidity balance.

LUIS ALEGRE 2001 CRIANZA RED
85% tempranillo, 15% mazuelo, garnacha

85 Garnet red cherry. Intense aroma of fine smoky oak over a suggestion of ripe red fruit with hints of damp earth. Flavourful palate with a certain oaky freshness, a good fruit association, rich spicy notes and a certain balsamic and acidic freshness.

LUIS ALEGRE SELECCIÓN PRIVADA 2001 RESERVA RED
90% tempranillo, 10% graciano

86 Dark cherry with a purplish edge. Powerful aroma of black fruit, with a certain finesse and an oaky freshness (very spicy). Flavourful palate with promising, fine, toasty but quite noticeable tannins, ripe fruit, liquorice, balsamic notes and notes of damp earth in the retronasal passage.

LUIS ALEGRE VENDIMIA SELECCIONADA 2000 RESERVA RED
95% tempranillo, 5% graciano

87 Deep garnet red cherry. Intense, very fine aroma of well-associated ripe red fruit and oak with a certain spicy freshness of terroir. Flavourful palate with promising but slightly marked tannins and slightly fresh fruit, good acidity.

LUIS CAÑAS

Carretera Samaniego, 10
01307 Villanueva (Álava)
☎: 945 623 373 - Fax: 945 609 289
bodegas@luiscanas. com
www.luiscanas.com

Established: 1970

4,300 ▯ 2,000,000 litres 🍇 90 has.

75% 🍷25%: -DE -UK -NL -CH -SE -DK -AT -FR -DK -US -CA -JP -PR -MX -BR -CY -BE -DK -TH

LUIS CAÑAS 2003 JOVEN RED
90% tempranillo, 10% viura

85 Intense cherry. Aroma of expressive black fruit with complex overtones, mineral notes and a suggestion of fresh fruit pulp. Fleshy palate with fruity tannins, varietal and fresh.

HIRU 3 RACIMOS 2002 RED
100% tempranillo

88 Dark cherry. Intense aroma with an excellent expression of very ripe fruit (redcurrants, cherries), toasty oak notes and a balsamic hint. Flavourful, fleshy and warm on the palate with rough, oily tannins and waxy hint.

AMAREN GRACIANO 2002 CRIANZA RED
100% graciano

88 Deep cherry. Powerful aroma of jammy black fruit, with fine toasty oak (pitch, coffee), a balsamic hint and notions of terroir. Flavourful, fleshy palate with fine bitter crianza notes and a good fruit weight despite the alcohol.

LUIS CAÑAS 2001 CRIANZA RED
95% tempranillo, 5% garnacha

84 Cherry. Aroma of wood with lactics and red fruit. Drying palate with light bitter notes, little fruit weight, medium persistence and a suggestion of wood in the retronasal passage.

LUIS CAÑAS 1998 RESERVA RED
95% tempranillo, 5% graciano, mazuelo, garnacha

86 Garnet red cherry. Slightly intense aroma with a certain finesse, black fruit, spicy oak and wax. Flavourful, somewhat fleshy palate with good oak/fruit integration, fine bitter notes (cocoa dark-roasted flavours, liquorice) and elements of a mild reduction in the retronasal passage.

LUIS CAÑAS SELECCIÓN DE LA FAMILIA 1999 RESERVA RED
85% tempranillo, 15% otras

84 Dark cherry with a garnet red edge. Intense, very fine aroma of black fruit, toasty with a good varietal and terroir expression. Flavourful palate with marked though promising tannins and fine bitter notes, slightly warm.

AMAREN TEMPRANILLO 1999 RESERVA RED
100% tempranillo

88 Very deep cherry. Intense aroma with jammy black fruit and toasty oak notes very well-integrated and a spicy and waxy nuance. Powerful and concentrated on the palate, rich in bitter nuances (jammy fruit, toasty oak, liquorice, chocolate) with excellent acidity.

LUIS CAÑAS 2002 FERMENTADO EN BARRICA WHITE
LUIS CAÑAS 1996 GRAN RESERVA RED

LUIS GURPEGUI MUGA

Avenida Celso Muerza, 8
31570 San Adrián (Navarra)
☎: 948 670 050 - Fax: 948 670 259
bodegas@gurpegui.es
www.gurpegui.es

Established: 1921
🌐 14,000 📊 10,250,000 litres
🇪🇸 80% 🌍20%

PRIMI 2003 RED
tempranillo, graciano, garnacha

85 Cherry red. Aroma of ripe red fruit, redcurrants, blackberries, slightly viscous. Warm palate with round tannins.

DOMINIO DE LA PLANA 2003 JOVEN RED
DOMINIO DE LA PLANA 2000 CRIANZA RED
DOMINIO DE LA PLANA 1998 RESERVA RED
DOMINIO DE LA PLANA 1996 GRAN RESERVA RED

LUIS MARÍA PALACIOS SÁEZ

Termino Vialva s/n
01340 Elciego (Álava)
☎: 659 871 287 - Fax: 945 606 348

Established: 1969
🌐 400 📊 300,000 litres 🍇 12 has.
🇪🇸 100%

PALACIOS SAEZ 2003 RED

75 Garnet red cherry. Not very intense yet clear aroma of red berries. Bitter palate with weak yet well-mannered fruit.

HACIENDA PALACIANA 2001 CRIANZA RED

80 Garnet red cherry with a coppery edge. Intense aroma of jammy black fruit with a toasty oak nuance. Flavourful and fruity palate without great crianza expression and with ripe and slightly sweet tannins, pleasant.

ALBA PAL & BER 2000 RESERVA RED
graciano

84 Garnet red cherry with a saffron edge. Intense aroma with predominant toasty oak notes. Flavourful and fleshy palate with supple overtones, well-integrated tannins and fruit and rich toasty notes (coffee).

PALACIOS SAEZ 2000 RESERVA RED

79 Garnet red cherry. Jammy aroma with well-assembled smoky and toasty notes and a slight hint of vanilla. Supple, fresh palate with well-balanced crianza and fruit; integrated tannins.

LUIS MARÍN DIEZ

Paraje La Asomante
26270 Navarrete (La Rioja)
☎: 944 630 024 - Fax: 944 644 105

Established: 1970
🌐 495 📊 470,000 litres 🍇 4 has.
🇪🇸 99,5% 🌍,5%

BASAPE RED
BASAPE CRIANZA RED
BASAPE RESERVA RED
VIÑA ASOMANTE RESERVA RED

M. A. PASCUAL LARRIETA

Camino Santa Lucía, s/n
01307 Samaniego (Álava)
☎: 609 415 872 - Fax: 945 609 306
pascualLarrieta@hotmail.com
www.riojalavesa.com

Established: 1994
🌐 102 📊 114,000 litres 🇪🇸 90% 🌍10%:

PASCUAL LARRIETA 2003 JOVEN RED
PASCUAL GÓMEZ DE SEGURA 2001 CRIANZA RED
PASCUAL GÓMEZ DE SEGURA COSECHA ESPECIAL 2001 RED

DO Ca. RIOJA

MARIANO ANTÓN SAENZ

Carretera de Vitoria, s/n
01300 Laguardia (Álava)
☎: 945 600 189

Established: 1982

🛢 23 🗄 152,700 litres 🍇 9 has. 🍷 100%

MARIANO ANTÓN SÁENZ 2003 JOVEN RED
CASTILLARES 2001 RED
CASTILLARES 2000 RED

MARÍN PALACIOS

Santorcuato, 5
01307 Villabuena (Álava)
☎: 945 609 045 - Fax: 945 609 045
bodegasmarin@hotmail.com
www.marinpalacios.net

Established: 1985

🗄 400,000 litres 🍷 90% 🌐10%: -FR

MARÍN PALACIOS ANAIAK 2003 WHITE
MARÍN PALACIOS ANAIAK 2003 ROSÉ
MARÍN PALACIOS ANAIAK 2003 RED

MARQUÉS DE CÁCERES

Carretera Logroño, s/n
26350 Cenicero (La Rioja)
☎: 941 454 000 - Fax: 941 454 400
dc.marquesdecaceres@fer.es

Established: 1970

🍷 40,000 🍷 50% 🌐50%

MARQUÉS DE CÁCERES 2003 JOVEN WHITE
100% viura

82 Straw-coloured. Powerful, fresh aroma (green apples) of herbs and grapefruit. Fresh, fruity and very harmonious on the palate.

ANTEA 2003 FERMENTADO EN BARRICA WHITE
viura, malvasía

85 Straw-coloured. Fresh, fruity aroma with a suggestion of dry stone and forest herbs. Body on the palate, flavourful with light toasty notes.

SATINELA 2003 WHITE SEMIDULCE
viura, malvasía

84 Straw-coloured. Very powerful aroma, full of white fruit expression and fragrant herbs (lavender and fennel). Fresh, supple and fruity palate, less spectacular than in the nose.

MARQUÉS DE CÁCERES 2003 ROSÉ
80% tempranillo, 20% garnacha tinta

87 Salmon pink. Powerful, fresh, and fruity aroma (strawberries and raspberries). Powerful, very expressive and fresh on the palate with intense fruit. The best Rosé of all time.

MC MARQUÉS DE CÁCERES 2002 RED
tempranillo

93 Intense cherry. Powerful aroma of fresh fruit with varietal expression, fine and creamy toasty notes and a mineral hint. Powerful, fleshy palate with a complex fruit expression and elegant tannins.

MARQUÉS DE CÁCERES 2001 CRIANZA RED
85% tempranillo, 15% garnacha tinta, graciano

84 Garnet red cherry. Fresh, fruity aroma with fine toasty hints (pepper, cloves, cocoa). Fleshy, flavourful palate with fresh yet ripe fruit and good oak/fruit integration.

GAUDIUM GRAN VINO 1998 RED
85% tempranillo, 15% garnacha tinta, graciano

91 Quite intense cherry. Fresh aroma of Fino (coffee, creamy vanilla), fruity with light floral hints. Round and elegant on the palate, with flavourful, fine tannins and a flor and spicy retronasal effect, very harmonious.

GAUDIUM GRAN VINO 1996 RESERVA RED
85% tempranillo, 15% garnacha y graciano

90 Brilliant cherry with a saffron edge. Intense, very fine aroma with a well- characterised crianza (spicy and ripe fruit notes) and balsamic hints. Flavourful palate with ripe, slightly rough tannins, a suggestion of fallen leaves and spiced fruit, powerful in the retronasal passage.

MARQUÉS DE CÁCERES 1996 RESERVA RED
85% tempranillo, 15% garnacha tinta, graciano

88 Quite intense cherry with a brick red edge. Fine aroma (cocoa, tobacco), spices (pepper) and excellent evolution in the bottle. Round, velvety palate with perfect tannins and acidity, a spicy retronasal effect.

MARQUÉS DE CÁCERES 1995 GRAN RESERVA RED
85% tempranillo, 15% garnacha tinta, graciano

90 Intense cherry. Slightly closed yet fine aroma (spices, pepper, cinnamon, vanilla) with stewed fruit and slightly more modern ìGran Reservaî typification. Powerful, oily and elegant on the palate, a typical Rioja without being a classic, with ripe, flavourful tannins.

MARQUÉS DE CÁCERES 1994 GRAN RESERVA RED
85% tempranillo, garnacha, graciano

89 Ruby red cherry with a brick-red rim. Fairly intense aroma with spicy oak notes, hints of reduction (leather, cigar box) and ripe fruit. Flavourful on the palate with excellent crianza expression, well-integrated fruit and oak; powerful aroma in the retronasal passage with spicy and slightly sweet notes, long.

MARQUÉS DE CAMPO NUBLE

Avenida del Ebro, s/n
26540 Alfaro (La Rioja)
☎: 941 183 502 - Fax: 941 183 157
camponuble@camponuble.com

🍷 3,000 🛢 4,500,000 litres 🍇 1 has.
🍇 70% 🍇30%: -US -MX -DE -UK

CAMPO BURGO 2003 WHITE
100% viura

75 Pale gold. Intense, slightly fruity aroma with spicy hints. Flavourful, bitter palate without great fruit expression.

CAMPO BURGO 2003 ROSÉ
tempranillo, garnacha

72 Raspberry with a coppery glint. Intense, slightly fruity and floral aroma with a suggestion of not very fine reduction. Flavourful palate with bitter notes and hints of evolution.

CAMPO BURGO 2003 RED
90% tempranillo, 10% garnacha

74 Garnet red cherry with a coppery edge. Quite intense, ripe aroma with spicy hints. Flavourful palate with quite bitter tannins and without much young wine expression.

CAMPO BURGO 1999 CRIANZA RED
90% tempranillo, 5% graciano, 5% mazuelo

80 Cherry with a brick red glint. Quite intense aroma of jammy fruit with a spicy suggestion of oak. Flavourful palate with a good fruit/oak integration, creamy hints of crianza and a suggestion of toastiness and slightly sweet fruit.

MARQUÉS DE CAMPO NUBLE 1999 CRIANZA RED
85% tempranillo, 10% garnacha, 5% mazuelo

77 Garnet red cherry with a coppery rim. Intense aroma with predominant toasty oak notes and a suggestion of jammy fruit. Flavourful palate, slightly lacking in symmetry (hints of aged wood, an acidic edge).

CAMPO BURGO 1998 RESERVA RED
tempranillo, graciano, mazuelo

82 Fairly deep cherry with a brick red edge. Intense aroma with predominant toasty wood notes. Flavourful palate with a good fruit/oak integration and quality bitter notes (dark-roasted flavours, liquorice).

MARQUÉS DE CAMPO NUBLE 1996 GRAN RESERVA RED
90% tempranillo, 10% garnacha

80 Dark garnet red cherry with a coppery hue. Quite intense aroma of toasty oak with a sugges-

tion of jammy fruit. Flavourful palate with a good fruit/oak integration and hints of sweet fruit, lacking Gran Reserva expression.

MARQUÉS DE CAMPO NUBLE 1998 RESERVA RED

MARQUÉS DE CARRIÓN

c/Camino de la Estación, s/n
26330 Briones (La Rioja)
☎: 941 322 246 - Fax: 941 301 010
eromero@jgc.es
www.vinosdefamilia.com
Established: 1942

🍷 3,426 🛢 3,500,000 litres
🍇 70% 🍇30%

ANTAÑO 2003 JOVEN RED
70% tempranillo, 25% garnacha, 5% graciano

82 Garnet red cherry with a saffron edge. Fairly intense aroma of jammy black fruit with spicy and slightly toasty hints of skins. Flavourful and fleshy on the palate with toasty hints (short period in oak barrel) and good acidity.

ANTAÑO 2001 CRIANZA RED
70% tempranillo, 25% garnacha, 5% mazuelo

83 Cherry with an orangey rim. Fruity aroma with predominant sweet, toasty wood notes. Medium-bodied, flavourful palate with quite evident tannins.

MARQUÉS DE CARRIÓN 2001 CRIANZA RED
70% tempranillo, 20% garnacha, 10% mazuelo

77 Garnet red cherry. Toasty aroma with notes of cedar, hints of varnish and a suggestion of ripe fruit. Fleshy, bitter palate with slightly green fruit and drying wood notes.

MARQUÉS DE CARRIÓN 1998 RESERVA RED
80% tempranillo, 15% mazuelo, 5% graciano

83 Cherry with an orangey hue. Balsamic aroma of toasty wood, red fruit jam and spices. Well-balanced, flavourful palate with toasty wood in the retronasal passage.

MARQUÉS DE GRIÑÓN

Avenida del Ebro, s/n
26540 Alfaro (La Rioja)
☎: 941 453 100 - Fax: 941 453 114
adelgado@haciendas-espana.com
www.marquesdegrinon.com
Established: 1994

🍷 2,000 🛢 2,954,000 litres 🍇 15 has.
🍇 50% 🍇50%

MARQUÉS DE GRIÑÓN ALEA 2000 CRIANZA RED
tempranillo

81 Garnet red with a ruby red edge. Aroma of macerated red fruit, fine oak flavours and spices. Flavourful, very fresh palate of ripe red fruit, harmonised wood.

MARQUÉS DE GRIÑÓN TEMPRANILLO 2002 RED
tempranillo

83 Deep cherry. Spicy aroma, with smoky notes integrated with the fruit (redcurrants), a varietal hint. Flavourful palate with a fine crianza reduction, round fruity tannins and flavourful.

MARQUÉS DE GRIÑÓN COLECCIÓN PERSONAL 2000 RESERVA RED

85 Deep cherry. Elegant aroma with notes of terroir and underbrush, fine crianza, with well-harmonised red fruit. Supple, flavourful palate, with ripe fruit and persistent tannins, perfectly assembled wood, a fruity finish.

MARQUÉS DE MATAFLORIDA

Cº de los Vinateros, s/n
26141 Alberite (La Rioja)
☎: 941 436 729 - Fax: 941 436 729

Established: 1996
🛢 350 🗓 400,000 litres 🍇 8 has.
🍷 75% 🍇25%

MARQUÉS DE MATAFLORIDA WHITE
MATAFLORIDA WHITE
MATAFLORIDA RED
MOZO ROSALES RED
MARQUÉS DE MATAFLORIDA CRIANZA RED
MARQUÉS DE MATAFLORIDA COLECCIÓN
 PRIVADA ALTA EXPRESIÓN CRIANZA RED
MARQUÉS DE MATAFLORIDA COLECCIÓN
 PRIVADA ALTA EXPRESIÓN RESERVA RED
MARQUÉS DE MATAFLORIDA COLECCIÓN
 PRIVADA ALTA EXPRESIÓN GRAN RESERVA
 RED

MARQUÉS DE MURRIETA

Finca Ygay. Ctra Logroño-Zaragoza, km. 5
26006 Logroño (La Rioja)
☎: 941 271 370 - Fax: 941 251 606
rrpp@marquesdemurrieta.com
www.marquesdemurrieta.com

Established: 1852
🛢 16,000 🗓 1,500,000 litres 🍇 300 has.
🍷 45% 🍇55%

MARQUÉS DE MURRIETA 2000 RESERVA WHITE
100% viura

89 Golden yellow. Powerful aroma rich in crianza nuances (wax, nuts). Full, oily, complex and warm on the palate with dried mountain herbs and bitter tannins well compensated by the alcohol.

DALMAU 2000 RESERVA RED
85% tempranillo, 10% cabernet sauvignon, 5% graciano

96 Very intense cherry. Deep aroma rich in black fruit (more pronounced than the previous vintage), with hints of minerals, fine toasty oak and dark-roasted flavours. Powerful, warm, full and wide on the palate with ripe yet virile tannins, spirituous and long.

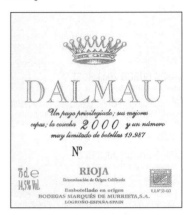

MARQUÉS DE MURRIETA 2000 RESERVA RED
88% tempranillo, 4% mazuelo, 8% garnacha

92 Intense cherry. Slightly closed aroma of very ripe fruit with fine toasty hints of oak. Fleshy, well-structured palate with well-balanced fruit and wood and powerful, fruity tannins in the retronasal passage.

DALMAU 1999 RESERVA RED
85% tempranillo, 10% cabernet sauvignon, 5% graciano

95 Intense cherry with a coppery edge. Powerful aroma of jammy red fruit, fine toasty oak, with hints of sun-drenched skins balsamic notes and a flint hint. Flavourful, fleshy palate with ripe, oily tannins, an excellent constitution and a jammy fruit and bitter chocolate finish.

MARQUÉS DE MURRIETA 1999 RESERVA RED
88% tempranillo, 4% mazuelo, 8% garnacha

91 Intense cherry with a slightly orangey edge. Spicy aroma with toasty hints, classic spices (dark-roasted flavours, cedar wood, cigar box). Fleshy, spicy palate with dry oak and fruity grape tannins, warm and very Mediterranean.

CASTILLO YGAY ESPECIAL 1978 GRAN RESERVA RED
78% tempranillo, 15% mazuelo, 6% garnacha, 1% graciano

89 Intense cherry with a brick red edge. Slightly closed aroma with a hint of Fino (leather, incense, cedar). Fresh palate of high acidity yet with alcohol, supple and flavourful tannins with a complex, spicy retronasal passage.

MARQUÉS DE REINOSA

Carretera Rincón de Soto, s/n
26560 Autol (La Rioja)
☎: 941 742 015 - Fax: 941 742 015
bodegas@marquesdereinosa.com
www.marquesdereinosa.com

Established: 1956

900 ▯ 7,553,800 litres ▯ 1.075 has.
▯ 90% ▯10%: -DE -NL -MX

MARQUÉS DE REINOSA VITICULTURA ECOLÓGICA 2002 JOVEN RED
60% tempranillo, 40% garnacha

78 Brilliant garnet red cherry. Intense aroma with predominant toasty oak notes, ripe skins and a certain spicy freshness. Flavourful palate with the red fruit partially concealed by the alcohol and high acidity.

MARQUÉS DE REINOSA TEMPRANILLO 2003 OAK AGED RED
100% tempranillo

77 Intense cherry with a violet rim. Intense, fruity aroma with toasty hints of oak and not very ripe red fruit. Flavourful on the palate, with light carbonic hints, somewhat fresh oak and equally as marked grape tannins.

MARQUÉS DE REINOSA 2000 CRIANZA RED
100% tempranillo

84 Intense cherry with a violet rim. Not very intense aroma with a certain finesse, jammy black fruit, a spicy oak nuance and balsamic hints. Flavourful and fleshy on the palate with a good fruit/oak integration, fine bitter notes and good acidity.

MARQUÉS DE REINOSA 2000 RESERVA RED
100% tempranillo

80 Garnet red cherry. Toasty aroma of nuts with light sweet notes (honey). Dry wood tannins on the palate, well-balanced although slightly lacking in fruit.

VIÑESTRAL 2003 JOVEN ROSÉ
VIÑESTRAL 2003 JOVEN RED
VIÑESTRAL 2000 CRIANZA RED

Bodegas MARQUÉS DE VARGAS

Carretera Zaragoza, km. 6
26006 Logroño (La Rioja)
☎: 941 261 401 - Fax: 941 238 696
bvargas@jet.es

Established: 1990

2,900 ▯ 700,000 litres ▯ 65 has.
▯ 65% ▯35%: -US -SE -UK -IE -CA -JP -MX -AT -DE -CH -DK

MARQUÉS DE VARGAS 2001 RESERVA RED
75% tempranillo, 10% mazuelo, 10% otras, 5% garnacha

88 Quite intense cherry. Fruity, toasty and creamy aroma with a suggestion of spices (cedar wood, coffee, pepper), well-assembled. Slightly fleshy, warm palate with excellent acidity, a good ripe fruit/oak integration and a mineral hint.

MARQUÉS DE VARGAS HACIENDA PRADOLAGAR 2001 RESERVA RED
40% tempranillo, 40% otras, 10% garnacha, 10% mazuelo

91 Intense cherry. Powerful aroma, with a rich toasty expression of ripe fruit and oak (dark-roasted flavour, toasty hazelnuts), a slight floral hint (violets). Generous, full, flavourful and powerful palate with ripe oak and fruit tannins.

MARQUÉS DE VARGAS RESERVA PRIVADA 2001 RESERVA RED
60% tempranillo, 20% otras, 10% garnacha, 10% mazuelo

90 Intense cherry. Complex aroma rich in toasty and mineral nuances and ripe fruit with a lively and fresh expression. Fleshy, full and warm palate with a toasty and creamy retronasal effect, fine oak and fruit tannins, flavourful and persistent.

MARQUÉS DE VITORIA

Camino de Santa Lucía, s/n
01320 Oyón (Álava)
☎: 945 622 134 - Fax: 945 601 496
info@bodegasmarquesdevitoria.es
www.marquesdevitoria.com

Established: 1988

16,500

MARQUÉS DE VITORIA 2000 CRIANZA RED
100% tempranillo

83 Garnet red cherry with coppery glints. Slightly intense aroma of ripe black fruit, fresh overtones of macerated skins and spicy oak notes. Flavourful palate with a good fruit/oak integration, ripe, oily tannins and excellent acidity.

MARQUÉS DE VITORIA 1998 RESERVA RED
100% tempranillo

82 Quite dark cherry with an orangey edge. Medium-intensity aroma with crianza notes, spices and jammy fruit. Flavourful, round palate, well-balanced and very pleasant.

MARQUÉS DE VITORIA 1995 GRAN RESERVA RED
100% tempranillo

78 Brilliant cherry with coppery glints. Not very intense aroma with hints of fine reduction (leather, tobacco). Flavourful, supple and slightly warm on the palate, lacking in fruit and crianza expression.

ORIGINAL 2001 OAK AGED RED
tempranillo

86 Intense cherry. Aroma with notes of macerated skins (bunches, jam), fruity and slightly toasty hints. Fleshy palate of ripe fruit (brambles), hints of maceration, skins and fruit and oak tannins in the retronasal passage.

ORIGINAL 2003 OAK AGED RED
tempranillo

85 Dark cherry with a dark red edge. Intense, ripe aroma of black fruit with notes of macerated skins and fine creamy hints of oak. Powerful, fleshy palate with ripe fruit (jammy hints of skins), slightly marked tannins and bitter hints of oak, pleasant.

MARQUÉS DE VITORIA 2003 WHITE
MARQUÉS DE VITORIA 2003 ROSÉ
MARQUÉS DE VITORIA 1999 CRIANZA RED

MARQUÉS DEL PUERTO

Carretera de Logroño, s/n
26360 Fuenmayor (La Rioja)
☎: 941 450 001 - Fax: 941 450 051
bmp@mbrizard.com

Established: 1972

🌐 6,500 🗄 2,370,000 litres 🍷 72% 🍇28%

MARQUÉS DEL PUERTO 2003 FERMENTADO EN BARRICA WHITE

80 Straw-coloured with a greenish hue. Intense aroma of fine and smoky woods that conceal the fruit a little. Flavourful on the palate with abundant creamy wood notes, pleasant.

MARQUÉS DEL PUERTO 2003 WHITE
viura

79 Straw-coloured with a coppery hue. Medium-intensity, fruity (apples) and harmonious aroma. Fruity on the palate, easy drinking and well-mannered.

MARQUÉS DEL PUERTO 2003 ROSÉ
tempranillo, garnacha

82 Blush. Intense, fine aroma of ripe red fruit with a floral edge. Fresh, flavourful and fruity on the palate with a bitter counterpoint, well-crafted.

MARQUÉS DEL PUERTO 2001 CRIANZA RED
90% tempranillo, 10% mazuelo

82 Garnet red cherry with a coppery edge. Not very intense aroma with overtones of finesse, jammy black fruit and creamy oak notes. Flavourful palate with a good oak/fruit integration, fleshy overtones and a slightly acidic edge.

MARQUÉS DEL PUERTO 1998 RESERVA RED
90% tempranillo, 10% mazuelo

85 Cherry-ruby red with an orangey edge. Elegant aroma with abundant creamy oak notes (cocoa, toffee) and a suggestion of jammy fruit. Flavourful and round on the palate with polished tannins and quite persistent.

MARTÍNEZ LACUESTA

La Ventilla, 71
26200 Haro (La Rioja)
☎: 941 310 050 - Fax: 941 303 748
bodega@martinezlacuesta.com
www.martinezlacuesta.com

Established: 1895

🌐 7,500 🗄 4,000,000 litres 🌿 8 has.

🍷 92% 🍇8%: -US -UK -DE -MX -CH -JP -SE -NL -BE -DK

MARTÍNEZ LACUESTA 2002 OAK AGED RED
85% tempranillo, 10% graciano, 5% mazuelo   🌐 6

88 Garnet red cherry with a coppery-violet edge. Powerful aroma with well-integrated wood/fruit, hints of macerated skins and a creamy oak suggestion. Flavourful palate with fleshy overtones, oily tannins and a well-crafted crianza rich in nuances (chocolate, jammy fruit, toasty flavours, liquorice).

MARTÍNEZ LACUESTA SELECCIÓN AÑADA 2001 CRIANZA RED
tempranillo, garnacha

83 Brilliant cherry with a saffron hue. Intense aroma with fresh oak overtones and a ripe red fruit suggestion. Flavourful, slightly warm palate with a predominant bitter notes (chocolate) and spices.

FÉLIX MARTÍNEZ LACUESTA AÑADA 100 1995 GRAN RESERVA RED
garnacha, tempranillo, mazuelo

82 Cherry with an orangey edge. Intense aroma of ripe stone fruit with reduction notes (fine leathers, tobacco) with hints of sackcloth and spring onions. Flavourful and supple on the palate with notes of evolution, lacking balance (high in acidity).

MARTÍNEZ LACUESTA 2000 CRIANZA RED
SELECCIÓN AÑADA 2001 CRIANZA RED
CAMPEADOR 1999 RESERVA RED
FÉLIX MARTÍNEZ LACUESTA 2000
RESERVA RED

MARTÍNEZ LAORDEN

Huércanos, s/n
26350 Cenicero (La Rioja)
☎: 941 454 446 - Fax: 941 454 446
bmlrioja@eniac.es

Established: 1994

🍷 202 📖 300,000 litres 🍇 40 has.
🍷 285,000 litres. 🌿 80% 🌐20%: -DE -NL -US -MX -BE

LANZADO 2003 JOVEN RED

83 Cherry with shades of violet. Powerful aroma with an excellent varietal expression of maceration (red fruit, nettle, damp earth). Flavourful, fleshy and very fruity on the palate with fine spicy notes and excellent acidity.

LA ORBE 2001 CRIANZA RED
100% tempranillo

83 Intense cherry with a violet edge. Aroma with predominant toasty notes of quite sweet, ripe fruit. Flavourful, bitter palate with hints of possible ove-rextraction, spicy and pleasant.

LANZADO 1999 CRIANZA RED
tempranillo

83 Garnet red cherry with a brick red hue. Slightly intense aroma with predominant toasty oak and of slightly reduced ripe fruit. Flavourful palate with round, oily tannins, fine bitter crianza notes and good acidity.

POR TÍ 2002 CRIANZA RED
100% graciano

88 Brilliant garnet red cherry. Intense aroma with good varietal expression (black fruit, hints of herbs and underbrush), spicy oak notes and bal-samic hints. Flavourful, concentrated palate with well-integrated oak/fruit and fine toasty bitter notes (liquorice, chocolate), very long.

EL TALUD 2003 RED
100% tempranillo

79 Intense cherry with a violet glint. Intense, fresh aroma with a light note of greeness over the well-crafted fruit hint, a slight varietal expression and notions of terroir. Flavourful on the palate, high in acidity and predominant characteristic woody overtones and green fruit.

Bodegas MARTÍNEZ PALACIOS

Real, 22
26220 Ollauri (Rioja)

☎: 941 338 023 - Fax: 941 338 023
bodegasmtzpalacios@yahoo.es

Established: 1999

🍷 180 📖 100,000 litres 🍇 8 has. 🌿 100%

MARTÍNEZ PALACIOS PAGO CANDELA
2002 OAK AGED RED
90% tempranillo, 10% graciano

89 Very deep cherry. Intense, concentrated aroma with predominant toasty oak notes, black fruit (an overripe touch) and balsamic hints. Powerful, flavourful palate of jammy black fruit with ripe, somewhat oily tannins.

ORMAEGUI 2003 FERMENTADO EN
BARRICA WHITE
MARTÍNEZ PALACIOS 2003 RED
MARTÍNEZ PALACIOS 2001 CRIANZA RED

MAYOR DE MIGUELOA

Mayor, 20
01300 Laguardia (Álava)
☎: 945 621 175 - Fax: 945 621 022

MAYOR DE MIGUELOA CRIANZA RED
MAYOR DE MIGUELOA RESERVA RED

MEDRANO IRAZU

San Pedro, 14
01309 Elvillar (Álava)
☎: 945 604 064 - Fax: 945 604 064
Amamviana@teleline.es
www.bodegasmedranoirazu.com

Established: 1985

🍷 450 📖 900,000 litres 🍇 21 has.
🌿 85% 🌐15%

AEDENS RED
MEDRANO IRAZU CRIANZA RED
MEDRANO IRAZU RESERVA RED

MENTOSTE

Niño Jesús, 15
26280 Briñas (La Rioja)
☎: 941 312 226 - Fax: 941 312 226
mentoste@hotmail.com

Established: 1946

🍷 317 🍇 15 has.

MENTOSTE CRIANZA RED
MENTOSTE RESERVA RED
VENDIGORNA RED

Vinos MERINO

Camino de la Lucera, 11

26512 Tudelilla (La Rioja)
☎: 945 384 098 - Fax: 945 384 098

Established: 1981

▦ 125.000 litres ▼ 100%

IBASTRAL 2º AÑO 2002 RED
VIÑA PEDRIZA 2003 RED

MIGUEL ÁNGEL MURO

Avenida Diputación, 4
01306 Lapuebla de Labarca (Álava)
☎: 945 607 081
www.juloem.com

Established: 1972

⊕ 180 ▦ 300,000 litres ❦ 25 has.▼ 100%

MIGUEL ÁNGEL MURO 2003 MACERACIÓN
CARBÓNICA RED
80% tempranillo, 15% viura, 5% graciano

81 Dark cherry with a violet edge. Powerful, fruity aroma with fine varietal and maceration notes and herbaceous hints (vine shoots). Flavourful, bitter palate with slightly marked tannins and good acidity.

MURO BUJANDA 2001 CRIANZA RED
100% tempranillo

80 Cherry with a garnet red hue. Powerful, ripe aroma with toasty oak notes over a suggestion of black fruit (hints of macerated skins). Powerful, concentrated palate with a good fruit/oak integration and a mild hint of overextraction, bitter (liquorice, dark-roasted flavours).

MURO VENDIMIA SELECCIONADA 2001
RED
100% tempranillo

84 Dark cherry with a deep red edge. Powerful aroma with fine smoky and spicy notes and predominant notes of black fruit and macerated skins. Powerful, concentrated palate with good crianza expression and a good fruit weight.

MIGUEL MERINO

Carretera de Logroño, 16
26330 Briones (La Rioja)
☎: 941 322 263 - Fax: 941 322 294
info@miguelmerino.com
www.miguelmerino.com

Established: 1993

⊕ 364 ▦ 70,000 litres ❦ 2 has.

▼ 20% ◑80%:

VITOLA DE MIGUEL MERINO 1999
RESERVA RED

85 Garnet red cherry with a saffron edge. Intense aroma with predominant notes of a very fine reduction (leather, old furniture), a nuance of spi-

ces and fruit in liqueur. Flavourful, supple palate with slightly marked tannins, expressive, with a certain vigour, freshness and promising.

MIGUEL MERINO 1995 GRAN RESERVA RED
tempranillo, graciano

88 Cherry with a brick red glint. Powerful aroma, rich in balsamic and ripe fruit nuances with a nuance of spices and fine reduction. Very flavourful, supple palate with a good fruit/oak integration, slightly warm, spicy, long.

UNUM 2001 CRIANZA RED

Bodegas MITARTE

Avenida Rioja, 5
01330 Labastida (Álava)
☎: 945 331 292
bodegas@mitarte.com

Established: 1992

⊕ 30 ▦ 300,000 litres ❦ 30 has.

▼ 95% ◑5%

S Y C (SANTIAGO Y CARMEN) DE MITARTE
2002 OAK AGED RED

85 Dark cherry with a coppery edge. Powerful aroma of red fruit with hints of balsamic notes and petals and fine toasty wood notes. Flavourful palate with a good fruit/oak integration and predominant dark-roasted notes in the finish.

MITARTE 2000 CRIANZA RED
85% tempranillo, 15% graciano

81 Dark cherry. Powerful aroma with predominant toasty oak notes, jammy red fruit and balsamic notes. Flavourful palate with slightly drying oak tannins and a good fruit weight, spicy hints, liquorice and damp earth.

MITARTE 2001 CRIANZA RED
85% tempranillo, 15% graciano

85 Dark cherry with a purplish edge. Powerful aroma rich in fruit nuances (jammy red fruit, macerated skins), spicy oak notes and a suggestion of balsamic freshness. Flavourful palate slightly drying tannins yet promising, fresh fruit and a spicy suggestion of damp earth.

MONJE AMESTOY

Camino de Rehoyos, s/n
01340 Elciego (Álava)
☎: 945 606 010 - Fax: 945 606 482
luberri@luberri.com

Established: 1995

⊕ 350 ▦ 400,000 litres ❦ 32 has. ▼ 85%

◑15%: -DE -DK -NL -US -UK -CH -IT -LV

LUBERRI 2003 MACERACIÓN CARBÓNICA RED
95% tempranillo, 5% viura

83 Dark cherry with a violet edge. Intense aroma of ripe fruit with hints of fresh macerated skins. Flavourful palate with carbonic hints and spicy notes of skins, ripe and fine tannins, bitter (liquorice) and long.

BIGA 2001 CRIANZA RED
100% tempranillo

85 Dark garnet red cherry. Intense aroma with fine toasty oak notes over a nuance of jammy red fruit. Flavourful palate with a good oak/fruit integration, fine bitter notes and a somewhat warm and spicy finish.

LUBERRI CEPAS VIEJAS 2000 CRIANZA RED
95% tempranillo, 5% cabernet sauvignon

88 Dark garnet red cherry. Powerful aroma of jammy black fruit, toasty notes of oak, skins, balsamic hints and terroir. Flavourful, fleshy and concentrated palate with a good fruit/oak integration, fine bitter notes (liquorice, dark-roasted flavours), warm, oily and long.

MONJE AMESTOY 2000 RESERVA RED
95% tempranillo, 5% otras

85 Dark cherry with a purplish edge. Intense aroma of jammy black fruit, fine toasty oak and hints of damp earth. Flavourful palate with slightly marked oily tannins and fine bitter notes (liquorice, dark-roasted flavours, balsamic flavours), warm and long.

SEIS DE LUBERRI 2002 CRIANZA RED

MONTECILLO

San Cristobal, 34
26360 Fuenmayor (La Rioja)
☎: 941 440 125 - Fax: 941 440 663
comunicacion@osborne.es
www.osborne.es

Established: 1874
29,700 🛢 4,000,000 litres 🍷 50%
🍇50%: -NL -DE -UK -US -NO -DK -IS -FI

MONTECILLO 2000 CRIANZA RED
100% tempranillo

85 Garnet red cherry with a brick red edge. Intense, ripe aroma of fine spicy oak notes with a mild reduction note. Fleshy palate with ripe fruit, slightly marked but flavourful tannins and a spicy finish of oak/fruit integration, somewhat oily.

MONTECILLO SELECCIÓN ESPECIAL 1982 GRAN RESERVA RED
100% tempranillo

90 Ruby red with an orangey rim. Intense aroma with fine reduction notes (coffee, spices, leather) and a ripe fruit and rich oak nuance. Flavourful and fleshy on the palate with excellent crianza expression, oily tannins and a glycerin texture, powerful aroma of spices and jammy fruit in the retronasal passage.

MONTECILLO SELECCIÓN ESPECIAL 1991 GRAN RESERVA RED
100% tempranillo

89 Intense cherry with a brick red edge. Powerful, ripe aroma with predominant reduction notes (leather, stables, cigar box). Flavourful and fleshy on the palate with ripe and oily tannins, fine spicy notes, liquorice, balsamic notes, and an excellent expression of traditional Gran Reserva.

MONTECILLO 1998 RESERVA RED
100% tempranillo

85 Garnet red cherry with a coppery glint. Not very intense aroma with fine hints of toasty oak and jammy black fruit. Powerful and vigorous on the palate with a good oak/fruit integration, excellent symmetry and hints of balsamic notes and leather in the retronasal passage.

MONTECILLO 1995 GRAN RESERVA RED
100% tempranillo

87 Garnet red cherry with a brick red rim. Powerful aroma of spicy oak notes with a fine reduction nuance (animals). Flavourful and fleshy on the palate with quite marked tannins although well-integrated with the abundant fruit, spicy and vigorous with liquorice and chocolate, very long.

MORAZA

Carretera Peñacerrada, s/n
26338 San Vicente de la Sonsierra (La Rioja)
☎: 941 334 473 - Fax: 941 334 473
moraza2001@jazzfree.com

Established: 1983
170 🛢 340,000 litres 🍷 16 has.
🍷 95% 🍇5%: -DE -FR

MORAZA 2003 RED
MORAZA 2000 CRIANZA RED
SEÑORÍO DE MORAZA 1998 RESERVA RED
SEÑORÍO DE MORAZA 1994 GRAN RESERVA RED

Bodegas MUGA

Barrio de la Estación, s/n
26200 Haro (La Rioja)
☎: 941 311 825 - Fax: 941 312 867
info@bodegasmuga.com
www.bodegasmuga.com

Established: 1932

🌐 17,000 🍇 150 has.

🚩 70% 🌐30%: -US -MX -CA -UE Caribe Asia

MUGA 2003 FERMENTADO EN BARRICA WHITE
90% viura, 10% malvasía

88 Pale with golden nuances. Intense aroma with smoky oak notes over ripe white fruit and hints of lees. Flavourful palate with good fruit/oak integration, sweet hints with spices (vanilla, cumin) and herbs in the finish, excellent acidity.

ARO 2001 RED
75% tempranillo, 30% graciano

93 Dark cherry. Powerful aroma with predominant toasty oak notes, jammy black fruit, a balsamic hint and a suggestion of bark. Fleshy, concentrated palate with promising yet slightly rough tannins and fine bitter notes (pitch, liquorice), slightly warm notes.

TORRE MUGA 2001 RED
75% tempranillo, 15% mazuelo, 10% graciano

90 Intense cherry. Elegant aroma with an exotic hint (cedar wood, incense), fine toasty oak and slightly fresh but ripe fruit. Round palate with dry oak tannins blended with the sweetness of alcohol, toasty in the retronasal passage and a suggestion of spices with mild reduction hints (tanned leather), flavourful.

MUGA 2001 CRIANZA RED
70% tempranillo, 20% mazuelo, 10% graciano

87 Dark cherry with a coppery edge. Powerful aroma with well-integrated toasty and fruity notes and balsamic hints. Flavourful, fleshy palate with quite rough and oily tannins and excellent fruit weight and crianza expression, long.

MUGA SELECCIÓN ESPECIAL 2000 RESERVA RED
70% tempranillo, 20% mazuelo, 10% graciano

86 Dark cherry. Powerful aroma of jammy black fruit with toasty hints of oak (coffee, pitch). Flavourful, fleshy palate with a good fruit/oak integration, fine bitter notes (liquorice, dark-roasted flavours) and excellent acidity and fruit weight.

TORRE MUGA 2001 RED

MURIEL

Carretera de Laguardia, s/n
01340 Elciego (Álava)
☎: 945 606 268 - Fax: 945 606 371
bodegasmuriel@eniac.es

🌐 10,000 🛢 6,000,000 litres 🚩 80%
🌐20%: -UK -DK -DE -SE -DE -CH -AT -US -JP

BARON DE BARBÓN 2003 OAK AGED RED
BARON DE BARBÓN 2001 OAK AGED RED
MURIEL 1999 CRIANZA RED
BARON DE BARBÓN 1999 RESERVA RED
MURIEL 1997 RESERVA RED
MURIEL 1994 GRAN RESERVA RED

MURILLO VITERI

Avenida Azcárraga, 27-29
26350 Cenicero (La Rioja)
☎: 944 495 839 - Fax: 944 263 725
www.imurilloeuskainet.net

Established: 1900

🌐 1,000 🛢 700,000 litres 🍇 10 has.
🚩 95% 🌐5%: -NL -FR

MURILLO VITERI JOVEN RED
ARANZUBIA CRIANZA RED
MURILLO VITERI CRIANZA RED
MURILLO VITERI RESERVA RED

Bodegas MURUA

Ctra. Laguardia s/n
01340 Elciego (Álava)
☎: 945606260 - Fax: 945606326
info@bodegasmurua.com
www.bodegasmurua.com

Established: 1974

🌐 2,300 🍇 110 has. 🚩 85%
🌐15%: -DE -UK -US -JP -CH -BE

MURUA 2001 FERMENTADO EN BARRICA WHITE
60% viura, 40% garnacha blanca

81 Brilliant pale yellow. Powerful aroma with fine smoky oak, a spicy nuance (aniseed, cumin) and fine herbs. Flavourful palate with slightly marked tannins and a spicy nuance, slightly warm with good acidity.

MURUA M 2001 RED

90 Intense cherry. Concentrated aroma of ripe black fruit and to5asty flavours (chocolate, coffee, creamy wood). Powerful, fleshy, full, warm palate, ripe tannins very well-harmonised with the oak tannins, flavourful and long.

MURUA 1998 RESERVA RED
75% tempranillo, 15% graciano, 10% mazuelo

82 Garnet red cherry with a brick red edge. Slightly intense aroma of jammy red fruit, a balsamic hint, toasty oak and hints of fine reduction. Flavourful, supple and quite light on the palate with bitter notes of the crianza.

VEGUIN DE MURUA 1995 RESERVA RED
75% tempranillo, 15% graciano, 10% mazuelo

85 Garnet red cherry with a brick red edge. Somewhat intense aroma of spices, fine reduction notes (tobacco) and a dried stone fruit hint. Flavourful palate with a good Reserva expression, a bitter hint of jammy fruit and good acidity.

MURUA 1994 GRAN RESERVA RED
75% tempranillo, 15% graciano, 10% mazuelo

85 Dark cherry with a brick red edge. Intense aroma with a certain finesse, predominant reduction notes (varnish, cigar box) and a dried stone fruit hint. Flavourful and supple on the palate, slightly warm and oily with fine bitter notes.

Bodegas NAVA-RIOJA

Carretera Eje del Ebro, s/n
31261 Andosilla (Navarra)
☎: 948 690 454 - Fax: 948 674 491
nava-rioja@telefonica.net

Established: 1999

🌐 200 📦 800,000 litres 🍇 50 has.

PARDOÑO 2003 JOVEN RED
80% tempranillo, 20% garnacha

79 Garnet red cherry. Fresh, fruity, slightly vegetative aroma. Quite flavourful with notes of skins and slightly warm on the palate.

PARDOÑO 2001 CRIANZA RED
85% tempranillo, 10% mazuelo, 5% graciano

82 Slightly intense cherry with a garnet red edge. Aroma of ripe red fruit, toasty oak and a balsamic hint. Flavourful, quite concentrated and very toasty on the palate.

PARDOÑO 2003 JOVEN RED
PARDOÑO 2000 CRIANZA RED

NAVAJAS

Valgarauz, 2
26370 Navarrete (La Rioja)
☎: 941 440 140 - Fax: 941 440 657
bodegas.navajas@terra.es

Established: 1918

🌐 3,500 📦 3,500,000 litres 🍇 10 has.

🍷 30% 🌐70%: -DE -NL -FR -BE -LU -CH -UK -CZ

NAVAJAS 2001 CRIANZA WHITE
100% viura

73 Pale golden yellow. Powerful, not very fine aroma of ripe fruit with light reduction off-odours (lees) and creamy hints of oak. Flavourful palate with predominant drying wood notes.

NAVAJAS 2003 WHITE
viura

77 Pale with greenish nuances. Intense aroma of white stone fruit with floral hints and fresh overtones. Green fruit and bitter notes on the palate, without remarkable nuances.

NAVAJAS 2003 RED
tempranillo

80 Intense cherry. Powerful, fruity aroma with hints of ripe skins and fresh notes of carbonic maceration. Fresh, flavourful and fruity palate with firm and fine tannins (a touch of greeness) and spicy notes of skins.

NAVAJAS 2001 CRIANZA RED
tempranillo

77 Cherry with an orangey hue. Aroma of wood with red fruit jam. Slighlty glyceric marked acidity on the palate, without great nuances.

NAVAJAS 2000 CRIANZA RED
100% graciano

74 Cherry with an orangey hue. Very noticeable crianza aroma (wood; tobacco) with vanilla. Light palate without great expression with a toasty finish.

NAVAJAS 1998 RESERVA RED
tempranillo

75 Glacé cherry. Balsamic aroma (eucalyptus, menthol) with wood and vanilla. Warm palate with light bitter notes.

NAVAJAS 2003 ROSÉ
ARJONA 2003 RED
VEGA DEL RÍO 2003 RED
GENTES DE FORASTIA 2000 RED
ARJONA 2001 CRIANZA RED
VEGA DEL RÍO 2001 CRIANZA RED
GUSTALES 1998 RESERVA RED
VEGA DEL RÍO 1998 RESERVA RED

NAVARRSOTILLO

Carretera N-232, km. 354
26500 Calahorra (La Rioja)
☎: 941 146 523 - Fax: 941 146 523
info@navarrsotillo.com
www.navarrsotillo.com

Established: 1998

🌐 500 📦 350,000 litres 🍇 60 has.

🍷 40% 🌐60%: -DE -CA -AT -UK -NL -SE -DK -PL -US -FR -CZ

COMIȘATIO 2003 MACERACIÓN CARBÓNICA RED
100% tempranillo

80 Cherry with a violet hue. Expressive aroma of ripe red fruit. Flavourful on the palate with carbonic hints, fine bitter notes, a certain concentration and lacking fruit expression, with a slight note of greeness.

MAGISTER BIBENDI GARNACHA 2001 OAK AGED RED
100% garnacha

80 Garnet red with a coppery edge. Intense, quite fruity aroma with floral hints, a toasty oak suggestion, varietal expression and warm notes that tone the varietals down. Flavourful palate with fine tannins and warm overtones.

NOEMUS 2003 JOVEN WHITE
NOEMUS 2003 JOVEN ROSÉ
NOEMUS 2003 JOVEN RED
COMISATIO 2003 ORGANIC RED
MAGISTER BIBENDI 2001 CRIANZA RED
MAGISTER BIBENDI 1998 RESERVA RED
MAGISTER BIBENDI GARNACHA 2002 RED
MAGISTER BIBENDI SELECCIÓN ESPECIAL GRACIANO 2003 RED
MAGISTER BIBENDI SELECCIÓN ESPECIAL MAZUELO 2002 RED

NUESTRA SEÑORA DEL VICO

Polígono El Raposal, parc. 77
26580 Arnedo (La Rioja)
☎: 941 380 257 - Fax: 941 380 257

Established: 1957

⊕ 150 🗄 2,500,000 litres 🍇 450 has.

🍷 98% 🍇2%

CIENCUEVAS 2002 WHITE
CANTOBLANCO ROSÉ
CANTOBLANCO RED
CIENCUEVAS 1998 CRIANZA RED
CIENCUEVAS TEMPRANILLO 2001 RED

Bodegas OLARRA

Poligono de Cantabria 1, s/n
26006 Logroño (La Rioja)
☎: 941 235 299 - Fax: 941 253 703
bodegasolarra@bodegasolarra.es
www.bodegasolarra.es

Established: 1973

⊕ 25,000 🍷 50% 🍇50%

SUMMA AÑARES 1998 RESERVA RED
60% tempranillo, 25% mazuelo, 15% graciano

86 Deep cherry with a coppery hue. Intense aroma with predominant jammy fruit notes and reduction (leather, spices and nuts). Flavourful palate with fine bitter notes, ripe fruit, a slightly acidic edge and a certain length.

AÑARES 1999 RESERVA RED
75% tempranillo, 15% mazuelo, 10% garnacha, graciano

89 Garnet red cherry. Powerful aroma with predominant smoky oak notes over the red stone fruit; hints of minerals. Flavourful palate with promising yet slightly drying tannins, a suggestion of the freshness of red fruit, liquorice in the finish, good acidity.

CERRO AÑÓN 2001 CRIANZA RED
80% tempranillo, 10% mazuelo, 5% garnacha, 5% graciano

86 Garnet red cherry with an orange edge. Fairly complex, smoky aroma of leather and tobacco over a nuance of spicy fruit. Flavourful palate with well-balanced fruit and toasty wood; round and long.

SUMMA AÑARES 1999 RESERVA RED
60% tempranillo, 25% mazuelo, 15% graciano

88 Garnet red cherry. Powerful aroma of red stone fruit with smoky oak notes and mineral hints. Flavourful palate with promising but slightly drying tannins, hints of liquorice in the retronasal passage and fresh overtones.

RECIENTE 2003 JOVEN WHITE
AÑARES 2003 WHITE
AÑARES 2003 ROSÉ
OTOÑAL 2003 ROSÉ
OTOÑAL 2003 JOVEN RED
AÑARES 2001 CRIANZA RED
CERRO AÑÓN 1999 RESERVA RED

Bodegas ONDALÁN

Carretera de Logroño nʃ 22
01320 Oyón (La Rioja)
☎: 945 622 537 - Fax: 945 622 538
ondalan@ondalan.es - ondalan.es

Established: 1976

ONDALÁN 2000 RESERVA RED
50% tempranillo , 50% graciano

82 Garnet red cherry. Not very intense aroma with spicy oak notes and a ripe fruit nuance. Flavourful, fleshy palate with creamy crianza notes, ripe tannins and a slightly oily texture.

Bodegas ONDARRE

Carretera de Aras, s/n
31230 Viana (Navarra)
☎: 948 645 300 - Fax: 948 646 002
bodegasondarre@bodegasondarre.es
www.bodegasondarre.es

Established: 1984

⊕ 12,000 🍷 55% 🍇45%

MAYOR DE ONDARRE 1999 RESERVA RED
tempranillo, mazuelo

87 Intense cherry with a brick red edge. Intense, ripe aroma with fine reduction nuances and a balsamic suggestion. Flavourful palate with a good fruit/oak integration, good expression of reduction crianza (leather, tobacco) and fine bitter notes.

DO Ca. RIOJA

ONDARRE 1998 RESERVA RED
75% tempranillo, 15% mazuelo, 10% garnacha

85 Garnet red cherry with a coppery edge. Intense aroma of ripe fruit with a woody suggestion well-integrated with the fruit, hints of spices and of damp earth. Flavourful palate with slightly marked tannins, a red fruit stone nuance and fresh overtones.

ONDARRE FERMENTADO EN BARRICA WHITE

ONTAÑÓN

Avenida de Aragón, 3
26006 Logroño (La Rioja)
☎: 941 234 200 - Fax: 941 234 200
ontanon@ontanon.es
www.bodegasontanon.com
Established: 1984
🍷 4,000 📊 1,400,000 litres 🍇 180 has.
🍷 80% 🌐20%: -FR -CH -AT -SE -DE -NL -BE -CA -MX -DK -BR -US -UK

ARTESO 2002 RED
tempranillo, garnacha, mazuelo

87 Brilliant cherry with a violet hue. Intense aroma of red stone fruit, with hints of sun-drenched skins, fresh overtones of wet foliage and fine toasty notes. Fleshy palate with ripe and oily tannins, fruity, concentrated and rich in terroir expression.

ONTAÑÓN 2001 CRIANZA RED
90% tempranillo, 10% garnacha

82 Cherry. Fruity aroma (ripe strawberries) of smoky meats and spices, pleasant. Round on the palate with flavourful and ripe fruit tannins, fine oak spices.

ONTAÑÓN 1998 RESERVA RED
95% tempranillo, 5% graciano

78 Clear garnet red. Aroma of ripe black fruit with a crianza reduction smell (animals). Flavourful, spicy palate with supple tannins and good acidity but short in crianza expression.

ONTAÑÓN MITOLOGÍA EN LA BODEGA 1994 GRAN RESERVA RED
95% tempranillo, 5% graciano

81 Garnet red with a brick red edge. Aroma with reduction crianza notes (animal fur, leathers), ripe black fruit and absorbing spices. Supple, spicy palate (cloves, pepper); acidity-alcohol in harmony, smokiness predominating the fruit.

LINAJE DE VETIVER 2001 CRIANZA WHITE

OSOTI VIÑEDOS ECOLÓGICOS

Julián Gayarre, 1
31261 Andosilla (Navarra)

☎: 948 674 010 - Fax: 948 674 832
info@anpiwines.com
Established: 1998
🍷 130 📊 300,000 litres 🍇 22 has.
🍷 30% 🌐70%: -DE -CH -UK -IE -US -NL -MX -SDV

OSOTI 2003 CRIANZA RED
70% tempranillo, 20% garnacha, 10% mazuelo

79 Cherry with a garnet red edge. Fresh, balsamic aroma of red fruit. Fruity on the palate, slightly astringent and fiery in the finish.

OSOTI 2001 CRIANZA RED
80% tempranillo, 20% mazuelo

81 Cherry with an orange edge. Medium-intensity aroma of jammy fruit and spicy crianza notes. Flavourful, medium-bodied palate with well-assembled ripe red fruit and wood, pleasant.

OSOTI LA ERA 2001 CRIANZA RED
100% tempranillo

80 Dark garnet red cherry. Intense aroma of black fruit with toasty oak. Flavourful, slightly spicy palate with fruit partially concealed by the alcohol.

OSTATU

Carretera Vitoria, 1
01307 Samaniego (Álava)
☎: 945 609 133 - Fax: 945 623 338
bodostatu@euskalnet.net
www.ostatu.com
Established: 1970
🍷 375 📊 350,000 litres 🍇 32 has.
🍷 85% 🌐15%: -CH -US -DE -PR -CA -AT -DK

OSTATU 2003 WHITE

79 Yellow with a greenish hue. Perfumed aroma of white fruit (pears), and light hints of herbs. Slightly warm on the palate with bitter tannins.

OSTATU 2003 MACERACIÓN CARBÓNICA RED
85% tempranillo, 10% garnacha, 5% viura

80 Cherry with a purple edge. Powerful aroma of black fruit, with good varietal expression (skins, underbrush) and faint off-odours of maceration. Flavourful palate with slightly marked tannins; fruity with good acidity.

GLORIA DE OSTATU 2002 ROBLE RED
100% tempranillo

91 Almost opaque cherry. Powerful aroma rich in toasty nuances of wood and skins and balsamic notes. Flavourful, concentrated palate with a good oak/fruit integration, expressive and vigorous with fine dark-roasted (pitch) and balsamic notes and hints of graphite and liquorice in the retronasal passage.

OSTATU 2001 CRIANZA RED
85% tempranillo, 15% graciano

85 Dark cherry. Intense aroma with a good fruit/oak integration, with predominant toasty and somewhat sweet notes. Flavourful and fleshy on the palate with slightly marked tannins, a jammy fruit nuance, fine bitter hints (liquorice) and excellent acidity

MAZARREDO 2001 CRIANZA RED
100% tempranillo

81 Garnet red cherry. Powerful aroma of black fruit, fine toasty oak, hints of leather and terroir. Flavourful, fleshy palate with slightly ripe, oily tannins, fine spicy notes (pepper), a good fruit weight and hints of liquorice and terroir in the retronasal passage.

OSTATU 2000 RESERVA RED
85% tempranillo, 15% graciano

84 Garnet red cherry. Intense aroma with predominant toasty oak notes, a ripe fruit nuance and balsamic and waxy notes. Flavourful palate with promising but quite marked tannins and fine bitter notes.

Hermanos OTERO MUÑOZ

Plaza de la Constitución, 16
01307 Baños de Ebro (Álava)
☎: 945 609 134 - Fax: 945 609 134

Established: 1990
🌐 50 📊 120,000 litres 🍇 8 has. 🇪🇸 100%

HERMANOS OTERO RED

PAGO DE LARREA

Cantón de la Concepción, 6
01340 Elciego (Álava)
☎: 945 606 063 - Fax: 945 606 063
bodega@pagodelarrea.com

Established: 2003
🌐 80 📊 124,000 litres 🍇 12 has. 🇪🇸 100%

CAECUS 2003 OAK AGED JOVEN RED
95% tempranillo, 5% garnacha

83 Garnet red cherry. Aroma with good fruit expression with nuances of very clean maceration. Fresh, fruity palate, modern with bitter tannins from the wine and the barrel.

PAISAJES Y VIÑEDOS

Plaza Ibarra, 1
26330 Briones (La Rioja)
☎: 941 322 301 - Fax: 941 322 302

PAISAJES I 2001 RED
100% garnacha

86 Garnet red cherry. Slightly closed, fresh and varietal aroma (pepper, grape bunches, violets). Fresh fruit on the palate, varietal with nice tannins, medium-bodied and flavourful.

PAISAJES IX 2001 RED
50% garnacha, 50% tempranillo

87 Intense cherry. Aroma with notes of maceration and fine toasty flavours. Dry, fruity palate with fine toasty flavours. Fresh, fruity palate with good acidity and a fine, toasty retronasal effect.

PAISAJES V VALSALADO 2001 RED
40% garnacha, 40% tempranillo, 10% mazuelo, 10% graciano

88 Fairly intense cherry. Fruity aroma (brambles) with mild bottle reduction notes (leather, tobacco), and fine toasty flavours. Slightly fleshy, fresh, spicy palate (pepper, cloves) with fresh fruit, oak and slightly fruity tannins.

PAISAJES VII 2001 RED
100% garnacha

90 Intense cherry with a very lively garnet red edge. Powerful aroma rich in toasty nuances (cocoa, aromatic coffee), ripe fruit and spices. Retronasal effect on the palate of brambles and pepper, elegant, fresh and fruity, with hints of minerals (dry stone) and flavourful tannins.

PAISAJES VIII 2001 RED
100% tempranillo

89 Fairly intense cherry. Powerful aroma of ripe fruit and fine toasty flavours (cocoa). Fruity and varietal expression on the palate (brambles), fresh fruit and oak tannins.

Bodegas PALACIO

San Lázaro, 1
01300 Laguardia (Álava)
☎: 945 600 151 - Fax: 945 600 297
barcelo@habarcelo.es
www.habarcelo.es

Established: 1894
🌐 12,000 📊 6,500,000 litres 🇪🇸 75%

🌐25%: -UE -CA -US -SAM -UK -SDV

MILFLORES 2003 JOVEN RED

77 Brilliant pale cherry. Intense, fruity aroma with the freshness of red fruit and warm hints. Fresh, flavourful palate with hints of maceration and fruit partially concealed by the alcohol.

BODEGAS PALACIO 2000 RESERVA ESPECIAL RED
100% tempranillo

86 Dark garnet red cherry. Fairly intense aroma of jammy red fruit, nuances of sun-drenched skins and spicy hints of oak. Flavourful, fleshy palate with supple overtones, well-integrated oak/fruit (slightly sweet), liquorice, some red stone fruit freshness and minerals.

GLORIOSO 2000 RESERVA ESPECIAL RED

83 Dark garnet red cherry. Intense, ripe aroma with fine toasty hints of oak. Powerful, rather supple palate with jammy fruit, predominant toasty notes (coffee, dark-roasted notes) and good acidity.

COSME PALACIO Y HERMANOS 2002 CRIANZA RED
tempranillo

87 Dark cherry with a purplish edge. Intense aroma with predominant notes of red fruit and macerated skins. Flavourful palate with a good fruit/oak integration, slightly oily with excellent acidity.

GLORIOSO 2001 CRIANZA RED

84 Dark garnet red cherry. Intense, fruity aroma with fine toasty oak and a balsamic suggestion. Flavourful, fleshy palate with excellent Crianza expression, a liquorice suggestion and slightly sweet fruit.

Bodegas PALACIOS REMONDO

Avenida Zaragoza, 8
26540 Alfaro (La Rioja)
☎: 941 180 207 - Fax: 941 181 628
hremondo@vinosherenciaremondo.com
www.vinosherenciaremondo.com

Established: 1945

⊕ 2,000 🛢 1,000,000 litres 🍇 95 has.

🍷 75% 🌐25%: -US -CH -DE -UK -FR -NL -BE -RU -FI

PLÁCET 2003 WHITE
100% viura

89 Straw-coloured with a yellow glimmer. Complex aroma rich in nuances of herbs and fresh fruit (apples, lavender). Fresh, fruity palate, complex overtones, flavourful and persistent.

LA VENDIMIA 2003 JOVEN RED
100% tempranillo

79 Dark cherry with a violet edge. Powerful aroma of red fruit with fine toasty skins and subtle herbaceous (vine shoots) and slightly warm hints. Flavourful palate with slightly marked and drying tannins and fruit partially concealed by the alcohol.

PROPIEDAD HERENCIA REMONDO 2001 OAK AGED RED
40% garnacha, 35% tempranillo, 15% mazuelo, 10% graciano   ⊕ 13

90 Very deep garnet red cherry. Powerful aroma of very ripe red stone fruit, toasty oak notes, hints of underbrush and acid fresh overtones. Powerful, concentrated palate with tannins of excellent ripeness, a slightly oily texture, toasty notes and liquorice and jammy fruit in the retronasal passage.

HERENCIA REMONDO LA MONTESA 2001 CRIANZA RED
40% tempranillo, 35% garnacha, 15% mazuelo, 10% graciano

83 Intense cherry. Aroma of black fruit with a suggestion of fine smoky meats and earthy notes. Fleshy palate with ripe fruit tannins, spices and crianza smokiness, round.

HERENCIA REMONDO LA MONTESA 2000 RESERVA RED
40% tempranillo, 35% garnacha, 15% mazuelo, 10% graciano

86 Intense cherry with a purplish edge. Intense aroma of fine reduction notes (leather, wax), hints of ripe fruit and spicy oak notes. Flavourful, fleshy palate with noticeable tannins of promise and good fruit weight; well-balanced.

HERENCIA REMONDO 1994 GRAN RESERVA RED
50% garnacha, 45% tempranillo, 5% mazuelo

87 Intense cherry with a brick red glint. Powerful aroma of fine toasty oak with an excellent expression of the Reserva and a suggestion of dried fruit (plums, dates). Flavourful palate with a good oak/fruit integration and rich in nuances (leather, tobacco, spices).

HERENCIA REMONDO 2000 RESERVA RED

PASTOR DOMECO

Camino del Cristo, 8
26559 Aldeanueva de Ebro (La Rioja)
☎: 941 142 390 - Fax: 941 142 391
pastordomeco@infonegocio.com
wwwpastordomeco.com

Established: 1995
🍷 1,500 🛢 1,800,000 litres 🍇 150 has.
🍷 80% 🌐20%

CASTROVIEJO 2003 JOVEN RED

76 Dark cherry with a violet edge. Intense aroma of ripe black fruit with mild reduction off-odours in the tank. Flavourful and fruity palate with fleshy overtones, slightly fresh and lively tannins and good acidity.

CASTROVIEJO TEMPRANILLO 2001 RED
tempranillo

79 Garnet red cherry. Slighyly short aroma, quite fruity and clean. Round on the palate, flavourful and easy drinking; uncomplicated.

CASTROVIEJO 2000 CRIANZA RED
tempranillo, garnacha

77 Cherry with a brick red edge. Fairly intense aroma with predominant spicy oak notes and a ripe fruit hint. Flavourful on the palate with firm tannins and without crianza expression.

CASTROVIEJO 1998 RESERVA RED
tempranillo, garnacha

77 Ruby red with a brick red hue. Short aroma with mild spicy notes. Light, round palate with dry wood tannins; well-mannered but without great expression.

CASTROVIEJO 1995 GRAN RESERVA RED

79 Garnet red cherry with a brick red edge. Not very intense aroma with toasty oak notes, ripe fruit, spicy, fresh overtones and a suggestion of fallen leaves. Flavourful and supple palate with slightly rough tannins and a good fruit/oak integration, spicy.

Hermanos PECIÑA

Carretera de Vitoria, km. 47
26338 San Vicente de la Sonsierra (La Rioja)
☎: 941 334 366 - Fax: 941 334 180
esdrope@teleline.es

Established: 1992
🍷 2,500 🛢 1,000,000 litres 🍇 50 has.
🍷 85% 🌐15%

SEÑORÍO DE P. PECIÑA 2003 RED

72 Garnet red cherry with a coppery hue. Not very intense aroma with toasty notes. Flavourful palate with bitter crianza notes; slightly warm without much character.

SEÑORÍO DE P. PECIÑA 1999 CRIANZA RED

80 Garnet red cherry with a brick red edge. Intense aroma with predominant animal reduction notes. Flavourful palate with slightly marked tannins, fine toasty notes of oak and fruit and hints of prunes and bitter chocolate in the retronasal passage.

PECIÑA VENDIMIA SELECCIONADA 1997 RESERVA RED
95% tempranillo, 3% graciano, 2% garnacha

84 Fairly deep cherry with a coppery-saffron edge. Intense aroma with predominant reduction notes and a ripe red fruit hint. Flavourful on the palate with fleshy overtones, well-integrated fruit/oak and fine bitter notes, very pleasant.

SEÑORÍO DE P. PECIÑA 1998 RESERVA RED

82 Garnet red cherry with a brick red edge. Powerful, ripe aroma of fine toasty reduction notes (tobacco) and a suggestion of black fruit. Flavourful, fleshy palate with fine, bitter, balsamic notes, a good fruit weight; rich and very spicy in the retronasal passage.

SEÑORÍO DE P. PECIÑA 1998 GRAN RESERVA RED

82 Garnet red cherry with a saffron edge. Intense aroma with predominant spicy oak notes, hints of ripe fruit and slightly aged wood. Flavourful palate of reduced fruit with ripe, slightly oily tannins and tobacco and spices in the retronasal passage.

PEDRO BENITO URBINA

Campillo, 33-35
26214 Cuzcurrita de Río Tirón (La Rioja)
☎: 941 224 272 - Fax: 941 224 272
urbina@fer.es
www.urvinavinos.com

🔲 1,600 📖 1,600,000 litres 🍷 75 has.
🍷 40% 🌐60%: -UK -DE -DK -CH -NL -HK -JP -PH

URBINA 2003 WHITE
viura

76 Yellow straw. Aroma of white flowers and delicate notes of lees. Light palate with medium acidity.

URBINA 2003 RED
100% tempranillo

72 Ruby red cherry with a brick red glint. Somewhat intense aroma of toasty notes of skins and oak with an unusual element of evolution for such a young wine. Flavourful and somewhat oily on the palate with hints´of sweet fruit.

URBINA SELECCIÓN ESPECIAL 2001 OAK AGED RED
90% tempranillo, 5% graciano, 5% mazuelo

80 Garnet red cherry with a coppery edge. Not very intense aroma of ripe black fruit and spicy notes of oak. Flavourful, fleshy palate of jammy fruit with ripe tannins but without fruit integration; lacking balance.

URBINA 2000 CRIANZA RED
95% tempranillo, 2,5% graciano, 2,5% mazuelo

72 Glacé cherry. Aroma with reduction notes, leather, wet hide, toasty flavours and fruit in liquor. Slightly supple, light palate with no outstanding nuances.

URBINA SELECCIÓN ESPECIAL 1997 CRIANZA RED
95% tempranillo, 2,5% graciano, 2,5% mazuelo

84 Ruby red cherry with an orangey hue. Powerful aroma with predominant fine reduction notes (tobacco, old furniture) and spicy hints of oak. Flavourful palate with a good oak/fruit integration, and fine, bitter, spicy notes in the retronasal passage; a classic Riojan expression.

URBINA ESPECIAL 1994 GRAN RESERVA RED
90% tempranillo, 5% graciano, 5% mazuelo

84 Ruby red cherry with an orange glint. Intense aroma with predominant reduction notes (old furniture, raisins). Flavourful and supple on the palate with fine bitter notes and a good expression of traditional crianza.

URBINA 1996 RESERVA ESPECIAL RED
URBINA 1991 GRAN RESERVA RED

PEDRO MARTÍNEZ ALESANCO

José García, 20
26310 Badarán (La Rioja)
☎: 941 367 075 - Fax: 941 367 075
bodegasmartinezalesanco@telefonica.net
Established: 1985

🔲 1,000 📖 1,800,000 litres 🍷 70 has.
🍷 100%

PEDRO MARTÍNEZ ALESANCO 2003 FERMENTADO EN BARRICA WHITE
100% viura

75 Brilliant pale yellow. Intense aroma of fine smoky and vanilla-flavoured oak over a suggestion of white stone fruit with hints of herbs. Flavourful palate with slightly drying tannins, lacks balance.

PEDRO MARTÍNEZ ALESANCO CLARETE 2003
90% garnacha, 10% viura

70 Onion-skin with a salmon-pink glint. Not very fine aroma (stewed meat) with a hint of red fruit. Flat on the palate with a slightly oily texture and light, spicy hints of skins.

PEDRO MARTÍNEZ ALESANCO 2003 RED
70% tempranillo, 30% garnacha

82 Brilliant cherry. Fresh, fruity aroma with good varietal expression. Fresh palate with ripe and somewhat sweet grape tannins, the freshness of vine shoots and good acidity.

PEDRO MARTÍNEZ ALESANCO 2001 CRIANZA RED
90% tempranillo, 10% garnacha

84 Garnet red cherry with a coppery edge. Intense, fruity aroma with fine creamy and spicy oak notes. Fresh and flavourful overtones, a good oak/fruit integration with predominant fruit.

PEDRO MARTÍNEZ ALESANCO SELECCIÓN 2001 CRIANZA RED
50% tempranillo, 50% garnacha

83 Garnet red with a violet edge. Balsamic aroma of ripe red stone fruit and good wood. Well-balanced palate with polished wood tannins which do not conceal the fruit tannins.

PEDRO MARTÍNEZ ALESANCO 1999 RESERVA RED
100% tempranillo

80 Garnet red cherry with a saffron edge. Powerful aroma of jammy fruit with toasty oak notes and balsamic hints. Flavourful palate with a good oak/fruit integration and the freshness of spices and fruit, pleasant although without Reserva character.

PEDRO MARTÍNEZ ALESANCO 2003 WHITE

PÉREZ BASOCO

Carretera de Samaniego, 1ſ Travesía, 5
01307 Villabuena (Álava)
☎: 945 609 028 - Fax: 945 609 028

Established: 1983

241,000 litres 🍇 22 has. 100%

ECHAZARRETA BANDA NEGRA RED
HERMANOS PÉREZ BASOCO RED

PERICA

Avenida de la Rioja, 59
26340 San Asensio (La Rioja)
☎: 941 457 152 - Fax: 941 457 240
correo@bodegasperica.net
www.bodegasperica.net

Established: 1949

3,500 🍾 2,200,000 litres 🍇 90 has.
80% 🌐20%

VIÑA OLAGOSA 2001 CRIANZA RED

PERICA ORO 1998 RESERVA ESPECIAL RED

MI VILLA 2003 JOVEN WHITE
MI VILLA 2003 JOVEN ROSÉ
MI VILLA 2003 JOVEN RED
VIÑA OLAGOSA 1995 OAK FERMENTED RED
VIÑA OLAGOSA 1996 RESERVA RED

PRIMICIA

Camino de la Hoya, 1
01300 Laguardia (Álava)
☎: 945 600 296 - Fax: 945 621 252
albertoherrero@bodegasprimicia.com
www.araex.com

Established: 1985

5,500 🍾 2,000,000 litres 🍇 45 has.
40% 🌐60%: -SE -UK -DE -JP -AT -CH
-NL -DK -IE -RU -US

FLOR DE PRIMICIA 2003 FERMENTADO EN BARRICA WHITE
100% viura

83 Pale yellow. Intense aroma of fruit and white flowers with a good varietal expression and smoky hints of oak. Flavourful palate rich in fruit nuances, well-cloaked by subtle oak notes, fine bitter notes; slightly warm.

FLOR DE PRIMICIA 2003 MACERACIÓN CARBÓNICA RED
100% tempranillo

83 Cherry with a violet rim. Fresh aroma of skins and red fruit. Palate with polished tannins, a good fruit weight and red fruit in the retronasal passage.

CURIUM 2001 RED

88 Very deep garnet red cherry. Spicy aroma (pepper, paprika), leather and ripe red fruit (blackberries, raspberries). Fleshy palate with well-balanced tannins; persistent with good fruit/wood integration.

VIÑA DIEZMO 2001 CRIANZA RED
100% tempranillo

83 Deep cherry. Aroma of new wood with vanilla, resins and light notes of ripe fruit. Light bitter notes on the palate, fleshy, with medium persistence.

DIEZMO MAZUELO 2000 CRIANZA RED
100% mazuelo

82 Garnet red cherry. Not very intense yet fine aroma with balsamic notes and spicy. Round, flavourful palate with well-assembled fruit and wood, but less varietal character than in the nose.

CARRAVALSECA 1999 RESERVA RED
50% tempranillo, 50% otras

81 Dark, garnet red cherry. Powerful aroma of somewhat reduced ripe fruit, withered flowers and creamy Crianza notes. Flavourful palate with slightly ripe, oily tannins, lactic hints and spices.

JULIÁN MADRID 1999 RESERVA RED
80% tempranillo, 20% otras

83 Cherry with a brick red hue. Strong aroma of jammy tomatoes and balsamic notes. Palate with well-integrated tannins and medium persistence.

VIÑA DIEZMO 1999 RESERVA RED
100% tempranillo

82 Cherry with an orangey hue. Aroma with fleshy notes, spices and ripe red fruit. Palate with polished tannins, well-balanced.

PROPIEDAD GRIAL

Carretera Logroño - Vitoria, s/n
26360 Fuenmayor (La Rioja)
☎: 941 450 194

Established: 1982

700 🗄 500,000 litres 🌿 30 has.

GRIBEÑA 1999 CRIANZA RED
GRIBEÑA 1996 RESERVA RED
GRIBEÑA 1995 GRAN RESERVA RED

Bodegas PUELLES

Camino de los Molinos, s/n
26339 Abalos (La Rioja)
☎: 941 334 415 - Fax: 941 334 132
informacion@bodegaspuelles.com
www.bodegaspuelles.com

800 🗄 500,000 litres 🌿 17,5 has.
🍷 80% 🌐20%: -US -UK -DE -CH -NL -BE -SE -DK -AT

PUELLES 2003 JOVEN RED
95% tempranillo, 5% garnacha, graciano, mazuelo

80 Cherry with an intense raspberry edge. Fruity aroma (strawberries, blackberries) with hints of liquorice. Fleshy, flavourful, fresh palate with strawberries, clear.

EL MOLINO DE PUELLES ECOLÓGICO 2002 OAK AGED RED
100% tempranillo

80 Deep cherry with a violet edge. Intense, concentrated aroma with toasty oak and a very ripe fruit suggestion (hints of raisins). Flavourful, warm palate slightly drying tannins, with fruit concealed by the alcohol and good acidity.

PUELLES 2001 CRIANZA RED
95% tempranillo, 5% garnacha, graciano, mazuelo

82 Deep cherry. Aroma of fine red smoky fruit with notes of fresh skins. Fleshy palate, slightly dominated by the wood; spicy with good crianza in the retronasal passage.

PUELLES 1996 GRAN RESERVA RED
95% tempranillo, 5% garnacha, graciano, mazuelo

85 Garnet red with an ochre edge. Peppery aroma of cumin with complex toasty oak and a nuance of jammy black fruit. Fleshy palate with promising fruit; well-balanced fruit-wood; a generous Reserva finish.

PUELLES ZENUS 1998 RED
98% tempranillo, 2% garnacha, graciano, mazuelo

85 Deep garnet red. Toasty oak aroma over jammy plums with a smoky and cocoa nuance. Fleshy palate with harmonised acidity-alcohol and a good fruit weight, round with chocolate and black fruit finish.

PUELLES 2003 JOVEN WHITE
PUELLES ZENUS 1998 OAK AGED RED
PUELLES 1998 RESERVA RED

Bodegas PUENTE DEL EA

Camino Aguachal s/n
26212 Sajazarra (La Rioja)
☎: 941 320 210 - Fax: 941 320 406
puentedea@terra.es

Established: 2002

100 🗄 350,000 litres 🌿 25 has. 🍷 100%

ERIDANO 2003 ROSÉ
ERIDANO 2002 MACERACIÓN CARBÓNICA RED
ERIDANO 2003 MACERACIÓN CARBÓNICA RED

Bodegas y Viñedos PUJANZA

Carretera del Villar s/n
01300 Laguardia (Álava)
☎: 945 600 548 - Fax: 945 600 522
bvpujanza@jet.es

Established: 1998

305 🗄 450,000 litres 🌿 30 has.
🍷 50% 🌐50%

PUJANZA 2002 CRIANZA RED
tempranillo

85 Intense cherry. Aroma with notes of ripe fresh fruit (blackberries, small bunches, maceration) and with mild nuances of toasty oak. Fruity palate with ripe fruit and oak tannins, quite fleshy with fine toasty notes in the retronasal passage, flavourful.

PUJANZA NORTE 2002 CRIANZA RED
tempranillo

88 Very intense cherry. Quite intense aroma with toasty nuances of ripe fruit and oak (chocolate, spices). Fleshy, warm spicy palate with fine toasty flavours, ripe and very flavourful tannins with long flavour.

RAMIREZ DE LA PISCINA

Carretera Vitoria-Laguardia s/n
26338 San Vicente de la Sonsierra (La Rioja)
☎: 941 334 506 - Fax: 941 334 506
rampiscina@knet.es
www.welcome.to/bodegas-ramirez

Established: 1980

⊕ 1,000 📖 500,000 litres 🍇 8 has.

🍷 85% 🍇15%: -US -UK -CH -DK -NL -IS
-DE -AT

RAMÍREZ DE LA PISCINA 2003 JOVEN
WHITE

71 Pale yellow. Not very intense, slightly fruity
aroma, without great expression. Flavourful palate
with a slightly oily texture, without character.

ENTARI 2003 JOVEN RED
100% tempranillo

77 Garnet red cherry with a purplish edge.
Slightly intense aroma of jammy red fruit with
toasty hints of skins. Flavourful palate with slightly
marked tannins (woody hints) and the freshness of
spice and fruit.

RAMÍREZ DE LA PISCINA 2003 JOVEN RED
100% tempranillo

79 Garnet red cherry with a purplish edge.
Intense, fruity aroma with fine herbaceous (nettle)
and fresh maceration notes. Flavourful palate with
slightly marked grape tannins and good acidity.

RAMÍREZ DE LA PISCINA 2001 CRIANZA
RED
100% tempranillo

81 Dark garnet red cherry. Intense aroma with
spicy oak notes (slightly fresh) and a hint of red
fruit. Flavourful palate with fleshy overtones,
slightly marked tannins, quite promising, with fine
bitter notes.

RAMÍREZ DE LA PISCINA 2000 CRIANZA
RED
100% tempranillo

84 Brilliant cherry with a brick red rim. Intense
aroma with predominant mild reduction notes
(leather, dates, old furniture). Flavourful palate
with slightly ripe and oily tannins, fine bitter notes
(cocoa, liquorice) and good acidity.

RAMÍREZ DE LA PISCINA SELECCIÓN 2001
CRIANZA RED
100% tempranillo

84 Garnet red cherry with a saffron edge.
Powerful palate of toasty oak notes, a balsamic
and macerated black fruit hint. Flavourful, fleshy
palate, well-integrated oak/fruit, light salted meat
hints and minerals in the retronasal passage.

RAMÍREZ DE LA PISCINA 1998 RESERVA RED
100% tempranillo

76 Ruby red cherry with orangey glints. Not very
intense aroma with a spicy suggestion and a fine
reduction. Flavourful palate with fine bitter notes,
slightly warm and without great expression.

SANTA MARÍA DE LA PISCINA 1996 GRAN
RESERVA RED
100% tempranillo

82 Ruby red cherry with orangey glints. Intense
aroma with predominant classic reduction notes
(tobacco, leather, old furniture). Flavourful, spicy
palate with a hint of slightly reduced fruit (dates),
pleasant.

RAMÍREZ DE LA PISCINA 2003 JOVEN
ROSÉ
ENTARI 1999 CRIANZA RED

RAMÓN BILBAO

Avenida Santo Domingo, 34
26200 Haro (La Rioja)
☎: 941 310 295 - Fax: 941 310 832
info@bodegasramonbilbao.es
www.bodegasramonbilbao.es

Established: 1924

⊕ 7,100 📖 2,100,000 litres 🍇 50 has.

🍶 2,000,000 litres. 🍷 70% 🍇30%

RAMÓN BILBAO 2003 FERMENTADO EN
BARRICA WHITE
viura

83 Brilliant pale. Powerful aroma of ripe white
fruit, smoky oak, hints of fine lees and withered
petals. Flavourful palate with fleshy overtones,
freshness (herbs, bitter almonds) and a slightly
mineral nuance.

MIRTO DE RAMÓN BILBAO 2001 CRIANZA
RED
100% tempranillo

91 Very deep cherry. Slightly quite closed aroma
of toasty oak with a balsamic nuance and light
reduction. Slightly more expressive on the palate
with rough, oily, ripe tannins; concentrated,
somewhat lacking in nuances yet promising.

RAMÓN BILBAO TEMPRANILLO EDICIÓN
LIMITADA 2001 CRIANZA RED
tempranillo

88 Garnet red cherry. Good intensity aroma of
ripe fruit, well-integrated with fine woods (vanilla,
biscuits). Varietal, fresh, generous, flavourful palate with fruit-wood harmony, persistent.

RAMÓN BILBAO 2001 CRIANZA
100% tempranillo

82 Garnet red. Not very intense, balsamic and slightly floral aroma. Round palate with quite noticeable tannins; warm and pleasant.

RAMÓN BILBAO 1996 GRAN RESERVA RED
90% tempranillo, 5% graciano, 5% garnacha

82 Cherry with an orangey hue. Aromas of toasty wood, cocoa, dark-roasted flavours, jammy red fruit and good varietal character. Warm palate with polished tannins and toasty notes in the retronasal passage.

RAMÓN BILBAO 1999 RESERVA RED
90% tempranillo, mazuelo, garnacha, graciano

83 Cherry. Aromas of toasty wood, smoky meat, spices, coffee and black fruit. Balanced, fleshy palate with polished tannins.

VIÑA TURZABALLA 1996 GRAN RESERVA RED
100% tempranillo

84 Cherry with an orangey edge. Aroma of dark-roasted flavours, light reduction notes (leather), of ripe red fruit and sweet. Balanced palate with polished tannins.

RAMÓN DE AYALA E HIJOS

Fuentecilla, s/n
26290 Briñas (La Rioja)
☎: 941 312 212 - Fax: 941 312 544
rayala@ conlared.com

🏭 500 📊 270,000 litres 🍇 30 has.
🍷 90% 🌍10%: -DE -UK -US -CZ

VIÑA SANTURNIA 2003 JOVEN RED
100% tempranillo

78 Garnet red with a violet rim. Lactic aromas, strawberry jelly, red fruit and skins. Warm palate with good acidity and varietal character.

DEÓBRIGA SELECCIÓN FAMILIAR 2001 OAK AGED RED
100% tempranillo

84 Dark cherry. Intense aroma with predominant toasty notes of oak, skins, balsamic notes and underbrush. Flavourful palate with quite robust but fine tannins and ripe fruit; somewhat warm with a certain concentration and potential.

VIÑA SANTURNIA 2001 CRIANZA RED
100% tempranillo

75 Cherry with a brick red edge. Slightly warm aroma with a suggestion of mild off-odours. Light, round palate, well-mannered but without great nuances.

VIÑA SANTURNIA 1999 RESERVA RED
90% tempranillo, 5% graciano, 5% mazuelo

80 Garnet red cherry with a coppery hue. Somewhat intense aroma with toasty oak and a suggestion of jammy fruit. Flavourful palate with good oak/fruit integration and a spicy hint of quite sweet fruit.

VIÑA SANTURNIA 1998 GRAN RESERVA RED

Bodegas REAL DIVISA

Divisa Real, s/n
26339 Abalos (La Rioja)
☎: 941 258 133 - Fax: 941 258 155
realdivisa@fer.es
Established: 1971
🏭 1,200 📊 670,000 litres 🍇 40 has.
🍷 85% 🌍15%: -DE -UK -CH -US -PH

MARQUÉS DE LEGARDA 2001 CRIANZA RED
95% tempranillo, 5% graciano

79 Not very deep cherry with saffron glints. Not very intense aroma, jammy fruit, with a mild reduction hint (spices, varnish). Flavourful palate, supple overtones, pleasant but without potential.

MARQUÉS DE LEGARDA 1998 RESERVA RED
90% tempranillo, 10% graciano

80 Ruby red cherry with orangey glints. Not very intense aroma, tobacco, leather, and spicy oak. Flavourful palate with reduced fruit (dates), slightly oily and warm with a spicy hint.

MARQUÉS DE LEGARDA 1995 GRAN RESERVA RED
MARQUÉS DE LEGARDA RESERVA DE LA FAMILIA 1994 RED

REAL JUNTA

San Cristóbal, 20-21
26360 Fuenmayor (La Rioja)
☎: 941 450 141 - Fax: 941 450 441
bodegas@realjunta.com
Established: 1787
🏭 1,000 📊 100,000 litres 🍷 90% 🌍10%

REAL JUNTA 1999 CRIANZA RED
MARQUÉS DE LA REAL JUNTA 1996 RESERVA RED

Bodegas REY DE VIÑAS

Camino Viejo Fuenmayor s/n
26006 Logroño (La Rioja)
☎: 941 203 944 - Fax: 941 214 802
reydevinas@hisa.com
Established: 1990
🏭 750 📊 100,000 litres 🍷 80%
🌍20%: -DE -CH -IT

DO Ca. RIOJA

REY DE VIÑAS 2003 OAK AGED RED
REY DE VIÑAS 1999 CRIANZA RED
REY DE VIÑAS 1995 RESERVA RED
REY DE VIÑAS 1988 GRAN RESERVA RED

RIOFRANCOS RUIZ DE VERGARA

Avenida Marqués del Riscal, 21
01340 Elciego (Álava)
☎: 616 228 251 - Fax: 645 606 282
riofrancosruizdevergara@latinmail.com
Established: 1981
⊕ 25 ▤ 142,344 litres ☙ 17 has. ⛴ 100%

RIOFRANCOS RUIZ DE VERGARA 2003 RED
98% tempranillo, 2% viura

83 Dark cherry with a violet edge. Intense aroma of ripe red fruit with hints of sun-drenched skins and an excellent varietal expression (damp earth). Flavourful, fleshy palate with slightly marked but fine tannins and excellent acidity.

RIOJA SANTIAGO

Barrio Estación, s/n
26200 Haro (La Rioja)
☎: 941 310 200 - Fax: 941 312 679
riojasantiago@fer.es
www.bodegasriojasantiago.com
Established: 1870
⊕ 2,600 ▤ 1,811,000 litres ⛴ 17% ☙83%:
-DE -UK -NL -DK -FR -RU -PL -US -MX

RIOJA SANTIAGO VENDIMIA
SELECCIONADA 2003 RED
100% tempranillo

80 Deep cherry. Lactic aromas, strawberry jelly with good varietal character. Warm palate with light vegetative notes and evident but flavourful tannins.

RIOJA SANTIAGO 1999 CRIANZA RED
100% tempranillo

83 Garnet red cherry. Intense, ripe aroma with predominant creamy oak notes. Flavourful, with fleshy overtones on the palate, quite marked but promising tannins, spicy notes and good acidity.

VIZCONDE DE AYALA 1999 CRIANZA RED

80 Deep cherry with a coppery edge. Not very intense aroma of jammy black fruit with creamy oak (vanilla) notes. Flavourful and fleshy on the palate with a good oak/fruit integration and ripe, slightly oily tannins.

RIOJA SANTIAGO 1997 RESERVA RED
100% tempranillo

81 Deep cherry with a coppery edge. Intense aroma with toasty notes and a light reduction nuance (animal fur). Better in the mouth; flavourful with fleshy overtones on the palate and quite ripe, oily tannins, good acidity.

VIZCONDE DE AYALA 1997 RESERVA RED

79 Garnet red cherry with a brick red edge. Fairly intense aroma with fine reduction notes and a toasty suggestion of oak and fruit. Flavourful, bitter palate with a slightly acidic edge.

RIOJA SANTIAGO 1994 GRAN RESERVA RED
100% tempranillo

83 Garnet red cherry with a brick red edge. Fairly intense aroma with a suggestion of macerated red fruit, spicy hints of oak and fine reduction notes (varnish). Flavourful, supple and slightly warm and oily on the palate with fine bitter notes (good oak/fruit integration).

VIZCONDE DE AYALA 1994 GRAN RESERVA RED

85 Deep garnet red cherry. Intense aroma with predominant toasty oak and fine jammy notes, spicy with a mineral hint. Flavourful palate with fresh and fleshy overtones and a ripe fruit suggestion, spicy and long.

RIOJA VEGA

Carretera Logroño-Mendavia, km. 92
31230 Viana (Navarra)
☎: 948 646 263 - Fax: 948 645 612
info@riojavega.com
www.riojavega.com
Established: 1882
⊕ 6,000 ▤ 3,700,000 litres ☙ 70 has.
⛴ 70% ☙30%: -FR -US -CA -MX -JP -MY-
SG -PH -SE -DK -DE -AT -CH -UK -IE -NL

RIOJA VEGA 2003 FERMENTADO EN
BARRICA WHITE
viura, malvasía

81 Pale gold. Intense aroma with predominant smoky and creamy (vanilla) oak notes and an aromatic white fruit nuance (herbs). Flavourful palate with fine tannins and a slightly sweet wood nuance, good acidity.

MUERZA VENDIMIA SELECCIONADA 2002
OAK AGED RED
tempranillo, graciano, mazuelo, garnacha

83 Dark cherry with a purplish edge. Powerful aroma of black fruit with hints of macerated skins, the freshness of damp earth and spicy hints of oak. Flavourful, fruity palate with slightly drying tannins and warm hints, quite promising.

RIOJA VEGA 2001 CRIANZA RED
tempranillo, mazuelo, garnacha

82 Garnet red cherry with a brick red rim. Intense aroma of ripe fruit with fine spicy notes of oak and elements of a mild reduction. Flavourful palate with somewhat noticeable tannins and a ripe fruit hint, spicy and long.

RIOJA VEGA 1999 RESERVA RED
tempranillo, graciano, mazuelo

79 Dark cherry with a purplish edge. Somewhat intense aroma with a certain finesse, jammy black fruit and toasty notes of oak. Flavourful palate with promising but slightly marked tannins, a somewhat sweet fruity hint, liquorice and balsamic notes.

RIOJA VEGA 2003 JOVEN WHITE
RIOJA VEGA 2003 JOVEN ROSÉ
RIOJA VEGA 2003 JOVEN RED
RIOJA VEGA 2003 OAK FERMENTED WHITE
RIOJA VEGA VENDIMIA SELECIONADA 2002 OAK AGED RED
RIOJA VEGAVENDIMIA SELECIONADA 2003 OAK AGED RED

Bodegas RIOJANAS

Estación, 1
26350 Cenicero (La Rioja)
☎: 941 454 050 - Fax: 941 454 529
bodegas@bodegasriojanas.com
www.bodegasriojanas.com
Established: 1890
24,000 ▦ 10,000,000 litres 200 has.
60% 40%: -UK -DE -DK -BE -DK -AT -FI -FR -NL -IE -CH -SE -CA -CR -US -MX -JP

PUERTA VIEJA 2003 JOVEN WHITE
100% viura

75 Brilliant pale yellow. Intense aroma of ripe white fruit with spicy hints of herbs. Slightly fresh and flavourful palate with a warm and oily texture, without remarkable nuances.

VIÑA ALBINA 2003 FERMENTADO EN BARRICA WHITE DRY
100% viura

81 Brilliant pale yellow. Slightly intense aroma with a certain finesse, green fruit notes and hints of herbs and smoky oak. Flavourful, fresh palate with fine bitter notes and citrus fruit.

VIÑA ALBINA VENDIMIA TARDÍA 1998 RESERVA WHITE
viura, malvasía

80 Brilliant gold. Intense, smoky aroma with predominant oak notes (vanilla, wax) and hints of fine herbs. Flavourful with rich bittersweet notes and somewhat unctuous on the palate with hints of jammy fruit, good acidity.

PUERTA VIEJA 2003 ROSÉ
80% tempranillo, 20% viura

72 Pale raspberry. Not very intense, slightly fruity aroma. Flavourful palate with herbaceous hints and an acidic edge.

CANCHALES 2003 JOVEN RED
80% tempranillo, 15% mazuelo, 5% graciano

75 Not very deep cherry. Not very intense aroma of lactic notes and strawberries. Marked tannins on the palate and reminiscent of red stone fruit in the retronasal passage.

GRAN ALBINA 2001 OAK AGED RED
34% tempranillo, 33% mazuelo, 33% graciano

86 Very intense cherry with a saffron edge. Somewhat intense aroma of black fruit with spicy oak notes and an underbrush nuance. Flavourful and fleshy on the palate with slightly marked oak tannins and a good fruit weight, spicy and vigorous with liquorice and balsamic notes in the retronasal passage.

MONTE REAL 2001 CRIANZA RED
tempranillo

82 Medium-hue cherry with an orangey edge. Aroma of new wood, spicy, balsamic, light reduction notes (leather). Warm palate with polished wood tannins but lacking fruit.

PUERTA VIEJA 1999 CRIANZA RED
80% tempranillo, 15% mazuelo, 5% graciano

82 Intense cherry with a brick red edge. Slightly intense aroma of fine reduction notes (leather, tobacco) and a spicy oak hint. Flavourful palate with fine bitter notes (a good oak/fruit integration) and spices in the retronasal passage (pepper, nutmeg).

GRAN ALBINA 1998 RESERVA RED
80% tempranillo, 15% mazuelo, 5% graciano

85 Cherry with a brick red hue. Aroma of wood with a balsamic bouquet (mint, liquorice) and elegant reduction notes. Well-balanced on the palate with good acidity and good assemblage of wood and fruit tannins.

MONTE REAL 1998 RESERVA RED
80% tempranillo, 15% mazuelo, 5% graciano

83 Garnet red with a brown rim. Balsamic and reduction aromas (leathers, ink). Light palate with good acidity and fine reduction notes, a classic wine.

VIÑA ALBINA 1998 RESERVA RED
80% tempranillo, 15% mazuelo, 5% graciano

85 Intense cherry with an orangey rim. Slightly intense, ripe aroma with predominant reduction notes (leather, cigar box). Flavourful, supple palate with fleshy overtones and predominant toasty and sweet notes.

MONTE REAL 1994 GRAN RESERVA RED
80% tempranillo, 15% mazuelo, 5% graciano

84 Garnet red cherry with a brick red edge. Intense aroma with predominant reduction notes (aged wood). Flavourful, supple palate with a slightly oily texture and a good expression of traditional Rioja Gran Reserva.

VIÑA ALBINA 1994 GRAN RESERVA RED
80% tempranillo, 15% mazuelo, 5% graciano

85 Intense cherry with a brick red rim. Powerful aroma with predominant reduction notes (animals). Flavourful palate with a good expression of Gran Reserva, and an oily texture, spicy, with certain vigour and powerful in the retronasal passage (toasty flavours, tobacco, white pepper).

CANCHALES 2003 JOVEN WHITE
CANCHALES 2003 ROSÉ
VIÑA ALBINA 2003 JOVEN WHITE SEMIDULCE
MONTE REAL 1996 RESERVA RED
VIÑA ALBINA 1996 RESERVA RED
MONTE REAL 1964 GRAN RESERVA RED
MONTE REAL 1981 GRAN RESERVA RED

ROBERTO DE MIGUEL

Mayor, 2
01307 Baños de Ebro (Álava)
☎: 945 623 323 - Fax: 945 623 323
www.artuke.com

Established: 1985

🌐 10 ▪ 120,000 litres ❦ 14 has. 🐗 100%

VIÑA ARTUKE 2003 JOVEN RED
VIÑA ARTUKE JOVEN RED
VIÑA ARTUKE MEDALLA DE PLATA 2001 RED
VIÑA ARTUKE SELECCIÓN 2000 CRIANZA RED

RODA

Avenida de Vizcaya, 5
26200 Haro (Haro)
☎: 941 303 001 - Fax: 941 312 703
rodarioja@roda.es
www.roda.es

Established: 1987

🌐 2,000 ▪ 300,000 litres ❦ 60 has.

🐗 50% 🌐50%: -US -PR -FR -SE -DK -BR -DE -MX -AU -FR -JP -FI -DK -CH -CA -UK -DO -AU

RODA I 2001 RESERVA RED
100% tempranillo

93 Cherry with a garnet red and orange edge. Very complex toasty aroma (cocoa, aromatic coffee, creamy). Round, oily, full, elegant and complex palate, velvety tannins with fresh fruit in the retronasal passage, very îfeminineî.

RODA II 2001 RESERVA RED
92% tempranillo, 5% garnacha, 3% graciano

88 Quite intense cherry. Powerful aroma with toasty notes of creamy oak (cocoa, dark-roasted flavours) and ripe fruit. Round, oily, full and generous on the palate with hints of oak tannins.

CIRSION 2001 RED
100% tempranillo

95 Very deep cherry. Powerful, concentrated aroma of fine toasty notes, spices (pepper, cumin), jammy black fruit, pitch, and balsamic hints. Powerful palate with a perfect fruit-oak association, liquorice and balsamic notes in the retronasal passage; well-balanced and very long.

RODA I 2000 RESERVA RED
100% tempranillo

92 Intense cherry with an orangey edge. Fine, toasty aroma with hints of underbrush, cocoa and vanilla, with great expression. Powerful, flavourful palate with polished tannins and fine toasty notes in the retronasal passage, ripe, fresh and flavourful tannins, a certain complexity.

RODA II 2000 RESERVA RED
92% tempranillo, 5% garnacha, 3% graciano

88 Garnet red cherry. Fine toasty creamy aroma of fresh fruit. Round, oily, elegant palate with silky tannins, full, persistent, with cocoa and aromatic coffee.

CIRSION 2003 RED

RODOLFO GARCÍA MARTELO

Vitoria, 3
01309 Navaridas (Álava)
☎: 670 448 057 - Fax: 945 605 141
interalimentaria@maitaren.net

Established: 1990

⊕ 60 📖 80,000 litres 🍇 11 has. 🍷 100%

MAITAREN 2001 JOVEN RED
80% tempranillo, 10% graciano, 10% mazuelo

79 Deep cherry. Intense aroma with predominant spicy oak notes over a nuance of macerated black fruit. Flavourful palate with ripe tannins and a fine herbaceous nuance with spicy hints.

RODOLFO GARCÍA MARTELO 2003 JOVEN RED
tempranillo, viura

78 Brilliant cherry with a violet edge. Intense, fresh aroma of red stone fruit with vine shoot expression. Fresh palate with very flavourful grape tannins and good acidity, pleasant.

RODOLFO GARCÍA MARTELO 2001 CRIANZA RED

Bodegas RUCONIA

Ctra de San Asensio, s/n. (off N-120)
26300 Nájera (La Rioja)
☎: 941 362 059 - Fax: 941 362 467
bodegasruconia@telefonica.net
www.bodegasruconia.com

Established: 2000

⊕ 330 📖 1,000,000 litres 🍇 20 has.
🍷 90% 🌐10%: -UK -BE

MOSANROSO 2003 WHITE
100% viura

65 Pale. Not very clear aroma with notes of menthol. No fruit on the palate, rustic and not very clean.

MOSANROSO 2003 ROSÉ
100% garnacha

72 Onion skins. Short, slightly vinous aroma, without great expression. Light, well-mannered palate, without obvious nuances and with a certain sweetness.

MOSANROSO 2003 RED
100% tempranillo

78 Intense cherry. Clear aroma of strawberries, fresh. Flavourful palate with a fruity character and spicy notes, pleasant.

REY DON GARCÍA 2000 CRIANZA RED
100% tempranillo

78 Cherry with a garnet red edge. Aroma of long crianza (toasty and smoky) with notes of ripe skins. Flavourful palate with notes of wood over the fruit, fresh tannins and reduction overtones.

TUBAL 2001 CRIANZA RED
100% tempranillo

84 Deep cherry. Aroma of jammy black fruit with a fine smoky and toasty hint and overall harmony. Flavourful palate with well-balanced toasty tannins, fruity, uncomplicated, round in structure; smoky finish.

Bodegas y Viñedos RUYAVÍ

Avenida La Poveda s/n
01306 Lapuebla de Labarca (Álava)
☎: 945 607 156

Established: 1996

📖 140,000 litres 🍇 14 has. 🍷 100%

RUYAVÍ RED

SÁENZ DE SANTAMARÍA

Carretera N-232, km. 431
26350 Cenicero (La Rioja)
☎: 941 454 008 - Fax: 941 454 688
bsantamaria@jet.es

Established: 1993

⊕ 1,800 📖 1,200,000 litres 🍇 60 has.
🍷 80% 🌐20%

RONDAN 2001 FERMENTADO EN BARRICA WHITE
RONDAN 1999 CRIANZA RED
RONDAN 1998 RESERVA RED
SEÑORÍO DE RONDAN 1994 GRAN RESERVA RED

SAN ASENSIO

Pʃ de Urumea, 21
20014 San Sebastián (Guipúzcoa)
☎: 943 468 455

CASTILLO DE SAN ASENSIO JOVEN RED

Cooperativa SAN JUSTO Y SAN ISIDRO

Estación, s/n
26570 Quel (La Rioja)
☎: 941 392 030 - Fax: 941 392 030

Established: 1947

📖 2,000,000 litres 🍇 200 has. 🍷 100%

FUENTEYEDRA RED
MANCUERA RED

Sociedad Cooperativa SAN MIGUEL

Carretera de Zaragoza, 7
26513 Ausejo (La Rioja)
☎: 941 430 005 - Fax: 941 430 209
Established: 1956
⊕ 363 🗄 5,230,000 litres ⚜ 700 has.
🐏 95% 🍇5%

CAMPOLOSA ROSÉ
CAMPOLOSA JOVEN RED
CAMPOLOSA CRIANZA RED

SAN PEDRO

Camino de la Hoya, s/n
01300 Laguardia (Álava)
☎: 945 121 204
sanpedro@fer.es
Established: 1987
⊕ 1,100 🗄 400,000 litres ⚜ 70 has.
🐏 90% 🍇10%

VALLOBERA CRIANZA RED
VALLOBERA RESERVA RED
VALLOBERA CAZADOR RESERVA RED
VALLOBERA TEMPRANILLO RED

Cooperativa SAN ROQUE

Carretera de Logroño, s/n
01309 Elvillar (Álava)
☎: 945 604 005 - Fax: 945 604 005
san.roke@euskalnet.net
Established: 1951
🗄 2,500,000 litres ⚜ 300 has. 🐏 100%

PAULEJAS VINO DEL AÑO RED

Cooperativa SAN SIXTO

San Sixto, 12
01322 Yecora (Álava)
☎: 945 601 448 - Fax: 945 622 925
sansixto@fcae.org
Established: 1954
🗄 2,000,000 litres 🐏 100%

CAMPO LENGO RED
VALSIERRA RED

SANTAMARÍA LÓPEZ

Camino de la Hoya, 3

01300 Laguardia (Álava)
☎: 945 621 212 - Fax: 945 621 222
santamaria@santamarialopez.com
www.santamarialopez.com
Established: 1937
⊕ 4,800 🗄 2,500,000 litres ⚜ 60 has.
🐏 80% 🍇20%

ANGEL SANTAMARÍA 2000 CRIANZA RED
100% tempranillo

76 Deep cherry. Perfumed aroma with sweet notes of ripe black fruit, an element of reduction and black olives. Fleshy and slightly drying palate.

SOLAR VIEJO 2001 CRIANZA RED
tempranillo

79 Garnet red cherry. Intense, fruity aroma of toasty oak notes. Flavourful on the palate with a certain crianza expression, hints of somewhat aged wood and a spicy and fruity nuance.

SEÑORÍO DE ARANA

La Cadena, 20
01330 Labastida (Álava)
☎: 945 331 150 - Fax: 944 212 738
senoriodearana@infonegocio.com
www.señoriodearana.com
Established: 1905
⊕ 2,500 🗄 2,000,000 litres ⚜ 8 has.
🐏 85% 🍇15%: -DE -AT

VIÑA DEL OJA 2003 RED
80% tempranillo, 10% garnacha, 10% viura

75 Garnet red. Fresh, fruity aroma. Light, quite flavourful palate, easy drinking, uncomplicated.

VIÑA DEL OJA 2000 CRIANZA RED
80% tempranillo, 10% garnacha, 10% mazuelo

82 Garnet red cherry with a brick red edge. Intense aroma of red fruit, with spicy hints of oak and aged wood. Flavourful, spicy palate with a good expression of a traditional crianza and with spices (pepper) and leather in the retronasal passage.

VIÑA DEL OJA 1998 RESERVA RED
90% tempranillo, 5% garnacha, 5% mazuelo

80 Not very deep cherry with a brick red edge. Intense aroma with predominant spicy and reduction notes. Flavourful, supple palate with sweet oak notes and hints of reduced fruit, slightly oily and warm.

VIÑA DEL OJA 2003 WHITE
VIÑA DEL OJA 2003 ROSÉ

SEÑORÍO DE LÍBANO

Del Río, s/n
26212 Sajazarra (La Rioja)

☎: 941 320 066 - Fax: 941 320 251
bodega@castillo-de-sajazarra.com
www.castillo-de-sajazarra.com

Established: 1978

🏭 3,200 📊 500,000 litres 🍇 52 has.
🍷 70% 🌐30%

LÍBANO LA ROMA 1998 RESERVA RED
tempranillo

87 Ruby red cherry with a saffron-coppery hue. Intense aroma of ripe fruit, a spicy oak suggestion and fine reduction. Flavourful palate with well-integrated oak and fruit, hints of leather, ripe, slightly oily tannins and refreshing acidity.

SOLAR DE LÍBANO 1999 RESERVA RED

85 Garnet red cherry with a brick red rim. Powerful aroma with predominant spicy oak notes and a suggestion of fine reduction (leathers, old furniture, prunes). Flavourful palate with well-integrated oak/fruit and an excellent expression of traditional crianza.

CASTILLO DE SAJAZARRA 1998 RESERVA RED

Señorío de SAN VICENTE

Los Remedios, 27
26338 San Vicente de la Sonsierra (La Rioja)
☎: 941 308 040 - Fax: 941 334 371
info@eguren.com
www.eguren.com

Established: 1991

🏭 500 📊 425,000 litres 🍇 18 has.
🍶 50,000 litres. 🍷 50% 🌐50%: -US -UE -CH -JP -MX

SAN VICENTE 2001 OAK AGED RED
tempranillo

93 Intense cherry with a very lively purple edge. Aroma with great fruit expression with fine toasty notes (cocoa, tobacco) and something of a varietal character. Generous, full, flavourful palate with excellent vine variety and crianza expression, with fine toasty flavours, elegant.

SAN VICENTE 2000 OAK AGED RED
tempranillo

90 Garnet red cherry. Intense aroma with predominant toasty oak notes, a suggestion of reduction (wet horsehair) and spices. Flavourful palate with well-integrated oak/fruit, bitter notes, ripe tannins, an excellent fruit weight and liquorice in the retronasal passage.

SEÑORÍO DE SOMALO

Carretera de Baños, 62
26321 Bobadilla (La Rioja)
☎: 941 202 351 - Fax: 941 202 351
exclusivassomalo@telefonica.net
www.riojasomalo.com

Established: 1998

🏭 300 📊 300,000 litres 🍇 10 has.
🍷 95% 🌐5%

SEÑORÍO DE J.A. SOMALO 2003 WHITE
100% viura

80 Pale yellow with golden nuances. Slightly intense aroma of white stone fruit with a suggestion of fennel and fine herbs. Flavourful palate with fine bitter notes, slightly fruity, good acidity.

SEÑORÍO DE J.A. SOMALO CLARO 2003 ROSÉ
75% garnacha, 25% viura

75 Onion-skin with a coppery glint. Not very intense aroma with fine notes of skins. Flavourful palate with bitter notes and notes of red stone fruit, fresh with good acidity.

SEÑORÍO DE J.A. SOMALO 2003 ROSÉ
80% garnacha, 20% viura

81 Brilliant blush. Not very intense aroma of forest strawberries with spicy hints of skins. Fresh, flavourful palate with hints of citrus fruit and excellent acidity.

SEÑORÍO DE J.A. SOMALO 2003 JOVEN RED
75% tempranillo, 25% garnacha

78 Brilliant cherry with a violet edge. Intense aroma of black fruit with toasty hints of skins and the freshness of vine leaves. Flavourful, fruity palate with slightly marked tannins, high in acidity.

SEÑORÍO DE J.A. SOMALO 2000 CRIANZA RED
80% tempranillo, 20% garnacha

78 Garnet red cherry with a brick red rim. Slightly intense aroma with spicy oak notes and a suggestion of fine reduction smells (leather). Flavourful palate with a good oak/fruit integration, a slightly oily texture, hints of aged wood and a spicy aroma in the retronasal passage.

SEÑORÍO DE J.A. SOMALO 1998 RESERVA RED
85% tempranillo, 15% garnacha

82 Garnet red cherry with a brick red edge. Not very intense aroma with fine spicy notes of reduction and Garnacha (pepper, petals). Flavourful palate with fleshy overtones, marked yet fine tannins and fine bitter notes.

SEÑORÍO DE ULÍA

Carretera Logroño, s/n
01330 Labastida (Álava)
☎: 941 450 950 - Fax: 941 450 567

⊕ 4.000 🝔 80% 🍷20%: -DE -CH -US -FI

MARQUÉS DE ULÍA 2000 CRIANZA RED
100% tempranillo

80 Dark garnet red cherry with a brick red edge. Intense aroma with predominant toasty oak notes and hints of jammy red fruit. Flavourful palate with slightly drying tannins, a good fruit weight (overripe) and dark-roasted flavours in the retronasal passage.

MARQUÉS DE ULÍA 1998 RESERVA RED
90% tempranillo, 10% mazuelo

84 Fairly deep cherry. Powerful aroma of fine toasty oak, a jammy red fruit hint, spices, flowers and damp earth. Flavourful, quite supple palate with a good oak/fruit integration and a very spicy, tobacco finish (black pepper),

Bodegas SER

Planig.ela 426 Polígono 10
26314 Huereanos (La Rioja)
☎: 617 328 629 - Fax: 941 231 515

Established: 2000
⊕ 510 🝧 200,000 litres 🝔 100%

426 2003 ROSÉ
426 2003 JOVEN RED
EGOISTE 2003 ROSÉ
EGOISTE 2003 JOVEN RED
PLANIGUELA 2003 JOVEN RED
SEÑORÍO DE AZOFRA 2003 JOVEN RED
426 2001 OAK AGED RED
LARGO PLAZO 2001 OAK AGED RED
SEÑORÍO DE AZOFRA 1999 OAK AGED RED

SIERRA CANTABRIA

Amorebieta, 3
26338 San Vicente de la Sonsierra (La Rioja)
☎: 941 334 080 - Fax: 941 334 371
info@eguren.com
www.eguren.com

Established: 1957
⊕ 2,500 🝧 1,500,000 litres 🝓 90 has.

🝧 1,000,000 litres. 🝔 50% 🍷50%: -US -UE -CH -JP -MX

MURMURÓN 2003 MACERACIÓN CARBÓNICA RED
100% tempranillo

79 Cherry with a violet hue. Intense aroma with a suggestion of red fruit less pronounced than in previous years, slightly unripe stone fruit and a light sulphurous element. Flavourful and concentrated on the palate with fleshy overtones, quite marked tannins, slightly warm and lacking balance.

AMANCIO 2001 OAK AGED RED
100% tempranillo

96 Intense cherry. Toasty, complex aroma of minerals with a rich expression of ripe fruit and creamy and fine notes of oak. Oily, powerful palate, rich in fine toasty nuances (aromatic coffee, peat, pipe tobacco) with abundant and sweet tannins, full-bodied.

SIERRA CANTABRIA COLECCIÓN PRIVADA 2002 OAK AGED RED
tempranillo

87 Deep garnet red cherry. Intense aroma with a good varietal profile, a spicy hint, creamy oak and hints of nettles. Flavourful, fleshy palate with ripe, slightly oily tannins, good fruit weight, rich in crianza expression and fine toasty notes in the retronasal passage.

EL BOSQUE 2002 RED

92 Intense cherry. Powerful aroma, rich in toasty nuances (cocoa, chocolate, coffee) with ripe fruit and ripe fruit expression. Generous, oily, flavourful palate with wood and ripe fruit tannins, full, persistent.

FINCA EL BOSQUE 2001 OAK AGED RED
100% tempranillo   ⊕ 16

92 Very deep cherry with a coppery edge. Slightly quite closed aroma with a tightly-knit suggestion of black fruit, toasty oak, balsamic hints and flint. Powerful, concentrated palate with promising but quite noticeable tannins and a slightly oily texture, fine bitter notes in the retronasal passage, excellent acidity (good ageing potential).

Bodega y Viñedos SOLABAL

Camino San Bartolomé, 6
26339 Abalos (La Rioja)
☎: 941 334 492 - Fax: 941 334 492
solabal@terra.es

Established: 1988
⊕ 1,400 🝧 1,200,000 litres 🝓 120 has.
🝔 70% 🍷30%: -DE -NL -CH -US -UK

SOLABAL 1999 RESERVA RED
100% tempranillo

85 Brilliant cherry with an orangey hue. Intense, quite fruity aroma with spicy hints of oak and fine reduction. Flavourful palate with fine bitter and lactic notes, ripe tannins, good acidity and a suggestion of light sweetness.

SOLABAL 2003 JOVEN WHITE
SOLABAL 2003 JOVEN ROSÉ
MUÑARRATE 2003 JOVEN RED
ESCULLE DE SOLABAL 2001 CRIANZA RED
SOLABAL 2001 CRIANZA RED

SOLANA DE RAMÍREZ RUIZ

Arana 24
26339 Abalos (La Rioja)
☎: 941 308 049 - Fax: 941 308 049
solramirez@infonegocio.com
www.valsarte.com
Established: 1986
⊕ 600 🗄 1,200,000 litres ✦ 50 has.
🍷 80% ✦20%

SOLANA DE RAMÍREZ 2002 JOVEN RED
SOLANA DE RAMÍREZ 2003 JOVEN RED
VALSARTE 1999 CRIANZA RED
VALSARTE 2000 CRIANZA RED
VALSARTE 2001 CRIANZA RED
VALSARTE 1996 RESERVA RED
VALSARTE 1997 RESERVA RED
VALSARTE 1998 RESERVA RED
VALSARTE 1997 GRAN RESERVA RED

SONSIERRA

El Remedio, s/n
26338 San Vicente de la Sonsierra (La Rioja)
☎: 941 334 031 - Fax: 941 334 245
sonsierra@sonsierra.com
www.sonsierra.com
Established: 1962
⊕ 3,200 🗄 8,000,000 litres ✦ 640 has.
🍷 60% ✦40%: -UK -AT -DE -US -NL -BE -FR -CH

SONSIERRA VIURA 2003 JOVEN WHITE
100% viura

81 Pale yellow with a coppery glint. Not very intense aroma of white fruit with floral hints. Fresh, slightly fruity palate with fine bitter notes and excellent acidity.

SONSIERRA TEMPRANILLO 2003 JOVEN ROSÉ
100% tempranillo

82 Brilliant raspberry. Slightly intense aroma of foresty strawberries with spicy hints of skins. Fresh palate with fine bitter notes and excellent acidity.

SONSIERRA 2001 CRIANZA RED
100% tempranillo

79 Intense cherry with a coppery edge. Intense aroma of fine toasty notes with spicy hints (oak, skins) and wax. Flavourful palate with rough and slightly drying tannins, warm notes, and very spicy in the retronasal passage.

SONSIERRA VENDIMIA SELECCIONADA 2000 CRIANZA RED
100% tempranillo

83 Dark cherry with a garnet red edge. Intense aroma of roasted coffee and vanilla that conceals something of the fruit. Flavourful, very toasty palate; powerful and concentrated with unpolished wood.

PAGOS DE LA SONSIERRA 1999 RESERVA RED
100% tempranillo

85 Intense cherry with coppery glints. Intense aroma of ripe fruit with hints of reduction (stable) and toasty oak. Flavourful palate with fine bitter notes, slightly herbaceous hints, quite typical of a long Rioja crianza, well-balanced, with citrus hints (orange peel) in the retronasal passage.

PAGOS DE LA SONSIERRA 2000 RESERVA RED
100% tempranillo

85 Intense garnet red cherry. Powerful aroma with predominant ripe red fruit notes and fine toasty oak. Flavourful and fleshy palate with promising but slightly marked tannins and a sweetish suggestion of fruit, liquorice and hints of balsamic notes and terroir.

SONSIERRA 2000 RESERVA RED
100% tempranillo

80 Garnet red. Aroma with lactic hints, toasty notes and earth. Unpolished tannins but flavourful on the palate and with quite persistent.

SONSIERRA 1997 GRAN RESERVA RED
100% tempranillo

84 Intense cherry with a brick red edge. Intense aroma of jammy black fruit, toasty hints of oak and fine reduction (varnish, leather, prunes). Flavourful fleshy palate with ripe, oily tannins, fruity fresh overtones; excellent in the retronasal passage (liquorice, damp earth).

SONSIERRA 2001 FERMENTADO EN BARRICA WHITE
SONSIERRA TEMPRANILLO 2003 JOVEN RED
SONSIERRA VENDIMIA SELECCIONADA 2001 CRIANZA RED
SONSIERRA 1999 RESERVA RED

Compañía de Vinos de
TELMO RODRÍGUEZ

Siete Infantes de Lara, 5 Oficina 1
26006 Logroño (La Rioja)
☎: 941 511 128 - Fax: 941 511 131
cia@fer.es

LZ 2003 JOVEN RED
100% tempranillo

80 Garnet red cherry. Fruity, fresh aroma with a mild suggestion of reduction. Fresh palate with a hint of sweetness, flavourful and fruity.

ALTOS DE LANZAGA 2002 OAK AGED RED
100% tempranillo

94 Intense cherry. Fine aroma, rich in mineral and fruit expression, toasty (cocoa, coffee). Oily, elegant palate, with fresh and ripe fruit, fine and persistent tannins and creamy toast in the retronasal passage (vanilla and chocolates).

LANZAGA 2002 OAK AGED RED
100% tempranillo

88 Quite intense cherry. Very fine toasty aroma (cocoa, coffee), creamy with ripe fruit (blackberries). Slightly fleshy, powerful palate, rich in fine toasty notes of oak and ripe fruit with very perceptible and persistent tannins.

TOBÍA

Carretera Nac. 232, km. 438 , s/n
26340 San Asensio (La Rioja)
☎: 941 457 425 - Fax: 941 457 401
tobia@bodegastobia.com
www.bodegastobia.com

Established: 1994

950 ▦ 500,000 litres 🍇 17 has.

🇪🇸 70% 🌐30%: -UK -DE -CH -AT -BE -DK -SE -FR -PR -US

VIÑA TOBÍA BLANCO DE LÁGRIMA 2003 WHITE
100% viura

83 Brilliant pale with greenish nuances. Fresh aroma of green fruit with hints of petals and a suggestion of fine lees. Fresh, flavourful palate with fine notes of citrus fruit and green apples.

ALMA DE TOBÍA 2002 FERMENTADO EN BARRICA WHITE
70% malvasía, 30% viura

83 Pale yellow with golden nuances. Intense aroma with predominant smoky and creamy oak notes and a suggestion of herbs and fennel. Flavourful palate with a certain oaky freshness and fine bitter notes, well-balanced.

TOBÍA 2000 CRIANZA WHITE
50% malvasía, 50% viura

82 Pale yellow with golden nuances. Intense aroma with predominant smoky oak notes, toasty and fine lees hints. Flavourful palate with bitter notes and fine herbs, good acidity.

VIÑA TOBÍA ROSADO DE LÁGRIMA 2003 JOVEN ROSÉ
100% garnacha

80 Brilliant raspberry. Slightly intense and fruity aroma with fine spicy notes of skins and hints of high quality citrus fruit. Fresh, flavourful palate with fine bitter notes, slightly oily and warm.

ALMA DE TOBÍA 2002 FERMENTADO EN BARRICA ROSÉ
tempranillo

81 Pale cherry with a coppery hue. Not very intense aroma of red stone fruit and spicy hints of skins. Flavourful palate with slightly fresh oak tannins and a slightly acidic edge.

VIÑA TOBÍA 2003 JOVEN RED
85% tempranillo, 15% mazuelo

78 Intense cherry with a violet edge. Slightly intense aroma with black fruit, spicy hints of skins and warm notes of damp earth. Flavourful palate with slightly drying tannins (a mild note of greeness), an oily texture and a spicy nuance.

ALMA DE TOBÍA TINTO DE AUTOR 2001 OAK AGED RED
80% tempranillo, 10% garnacha, 10% mazuelo

86 Intense cherry with a saffron edge. Intense, ripe aroma with predominant reduction notes (leather, wet horsehair) and a toasty oak hint. Flavourful palate, with slightly biting tannins, a ripe fruit hint; slightly oily with spicy hints of oak.

ALMA DE TOBÍA TINTO DE AUTOR 2002 OAK AGED RED
80% tempranillo, 10% garnacha, 10% mazuelo

88 Very deep cherry. Powerful aroma of jammy red fruit, a spicy oak suggestion and balsamic hints. Flavourful palate with a certain concentration, promising although slightly marked tannins, ripe stone fruit, quality bitter hints (chocolate, liquorice) and excellent acidity.

TOBÍA 2001 CRIANZA RED
100% tempranillo

84 Garnet red cherry with a brick red edge. Intense aroma with toasty oak notes, a jammy fruit suggestion, balsamic hints and fine reduction notes (new leather). Flavourful and fleshy on the palate with a good fruit/oak integration, somewhat drying tannins and notes of dark-roasted flavours and liquorice.

TOBÍA 2000 RESERVA RED
100% tempranillo

86 Dark cherry. Powerful, vigorous aroma with fine toasty oak notes, a suggestion of jammy red fruit and fresh damp earth overtones. Flavourful, fleshy palate with slightly marked but promising tannins, ripe fruit, dark-roasted flavours, balsamic notes and mineral.

TOBÍA 1999 RESERVA RED

TORRE DE OÑA

Finca San Martín s/n
01307 Paganos - Laguardia (Álava)
☎: 945 621 154 - Fax: 945 621 171
BARON@riojalta.com
www.riojalta.com

Established: 1985
🍾 4,000 🌿 50 has.
🍷 65% 🌐35%: -UK -DE -US -HN -MX

BARÓN DE OÑA 1998 RESERVA RED
96% tempranillo, 4% mazuelo

85 Cherry with a brick red hue. Intense aroma with mild reduction notes (cedar, leather, tobacco,

dates, dried peaches). Flavourful, supple and well-balanced on the palate with a good traditional Reserva expression and hints of aged wood.

TORRES LIBRADA

Carretera de Corella - Finca Estarijo
26540 Alfaro (La Rioja)
☎: 941 741 003 - Fax: 941 741 005
dang@fer.es

Established: 1987
🍾 300 🗄 300,000 litres 🌿 28 has.
🍷 60% 🌐40%: -SE -CA -BE -CO -US -NL -DE

ESTARIJO 1998 CRIANZA RED
TORRESCUDO 2000 CRIANZA RED
TORRESCUDO 1997 RESERVA RED

TREVIÑO RUIZ DE LAS HERAS

Avenida La Escobosa, s/n
26380 El Cortijo (La Rioja)
☎: 941 227 991 - Fax: 941 214 625

Established: 1993
🍾 400 🗄 300,000 litres 🌿 25 has.
🍷 90% 🌐10%

MARQUÉS DE TREVIÑO WHITE
MARQUÉS DE TREVIÑO RED
TREVIÑO RUIZ DE LAS HERAS RED
MARQUÉS DE TREVIÑO CRIANZA RED
MARQUÉS DE TREVIÑO RESERVA RED
MARQUÉS DE TREVIÑO (MAGNUM) RESERVA RED

UNIÓN DE COSECHEROS DE LABASTIDA

Avenida Diputación, 53
01330 Labastida (Álava)
☎: 945 331 161 - Fax: 945 331 118
bodegas@solaguen.com
www.solaguen.com

Established: 1965
🍾 6,000 🗄 6,000,000 litres 🌿 500 has.
🍷 50% 🌐50%

MONTEBUENA 2003 RED
100% tempranillo

73 Cherry with a purplish rim. Aroma of sundren ched skins, yeast and light notes of red fruit. Bitter tannins on the palate.

SOLAGÜEN 2001 CRIANZA RED
100% tempranillo

81 Cherry with brick red nuances at the edge. Not very intense aroma of ripe fruit and spicy oak. Flavourful palate with intense fruit and wood tannins in the finish.

MANUEL QUINTANO 1998 RESERVA RED

85 Garnet red cherry with a brick red glint. Intense aroma with predominant spicy oak notes, and fine reduction (tobacco, new leather). Flavourful palate with ripe and oily tannins and good oak/fruit integration; slightly warm with good acidity.

SOLAGÜEN 1998 RESERVA RED

83 Cherry with a brick red edge. Medium-intensity aroma with crianza notes (vanilla). Flavourful and round on the palate, more expressive than in the nose, with good assemblage of fruit and wood.

UNIÓN DE VITICULTORES RIOJANOS

Carretera de Cenicero, s/n. Apdo. Correo, 3
26360 Fuenmayor (La Rioja)
☎: 941 451 129 - Fax: 941 450 297
uvrioja@apdo.com
www.marquesdetomares.es

Established: 1997

⊞ 2,100 ▤ 850,000 litres ⚘ 25 has.

▰ 60% ◔40%

DON ROMÁN 2002 OAK AGED RED
MARQUÉS DE TOMARES EXCELLENCE 2002 OAK AGED RED
MARQUÉS DE TOMARES 2001 CRIANZA RED
MARQUÉS DE TOMARES 1998 RESERVA RED
MARQUÉS DE TOMARES 1996 GRAN RESERVA RED

VALDELACIERVA

Carretera Burgos, km. 13
26370 Navarrete (La Rioja)
☎: 941 440 620 - Fax: 941 440 787
manuel.zaldivar@teleline.es

Established: 1988

⊞ 1,000 ▤ 1,670,000 litres ⚘ 5 has.

▰ 90% ◔10%: USA -MX -DO -DE -UK

VALDELACIERVA 2003 JOVEN WHITE

77 Pale golden yellow. Slightly intense aroma of ripe white stone fruit with a suggestion of fine herbs. Flavourful palate with fresh overtones, fine bitter notes and a slightly oily texture.

VALDELACIERVA 2003 ROSÉ

75 Blush with an orangey glint. Not very intense, slightly flat aroma with spicy hints of skins. Flavourful palate of red stone fruit, slightly oily and warm.

VALDELACIERVA 2003 JOVEN RED
98% tempranillo, 2% mazuelo

75 Garnet red cherry with a coppery glint. Intense aroma of red fruit with a slight note of greenness. Flavourful, somewhat fruity palate, with slightly marked tannins and unripe fruit, high in acidity.

ALCALLER 2000 CRIANZA RED
95% tempranillo, 4% graciano, 1% mazuelo

73 Garnet red cherry. Intense aroma of smoky oak notes with the freshness of red fruit and a vegetative element. Flavourful palate with slightly marked tannins, lacks balance.

VALDELACIERVA 2001 CRIANZA RED
95% tempranillo, 4% graciano, 1% mazuelo

77 Garnet red cherry with a coppery glint. Not very intense aroma of fine toasty oak (slightly fresh). Flavourful, slightly fruity and spicy palate with slight notes of greenness.

VALDELACIERVA 1999 RESERVA RED
95% tempranillo, 5% mazuelo

77 Garnet red cherry with a coppery edge. Somewhat intense aroma with predominant spicy oak notes, a suggestion of red fruit and herbaceous hints. Flavourful palate with slightly marked tannins, toasty notes of fruit and oak and an element of greeness.

VALDELACIERVA 2000 CRIANZA RED

VALDELANA

Puente Barricuelo, 67
01340 Elciego (Álava)
☎: 945 606 055 - Fax: 945 606 055
bodegasvaldelana@wanadoo.es

Established: 1877

⊞ 1,800 ▤ 800,000 litres ⚘ 75 has.

▰ 50% ◔50%: -DE -UK -US -IL -CH -AT -MX -FR -BE -LU -NL -DK -JP

VALDELANA 2000 RESERVA RED
90% tempranillo, 5% graciano, 5% mazuelo

84 Dark cherry with a saffron edge. Powerful aroma of toasty oak with lactic hints of fine reduction (tobacco) over a suggestion of jammy fruit. Flavourful, fleshy palate with good crianza expression and a suggestion of slightly sweet fruit and oak, bitter and long.

JUAN DE VALDELANA 2003 RED
90% tempranillo, 5% graciano, 5% viura

82 Dark cherry with a dark red-violet edge. Powerful, fruity aroma with fine maceration notes and sweet and herbaceous hints (nettles). Flavourful, fleshy palate with slightly marked tannins, good acidity and young wine expression.

JUDIT DE VALDELANA 2001 CRIANZA RED
90% tempranillo, 5% graciano, 5% mazuelo

85 Dark garnet red cherry. Powerful aroma with fine smoky and spicy oak notes and a suggestion of ripe fruit. Fleshy, flavourful palate with slightly rough and promising tannins and good crianza expression (well-integrated notes of fruit, oak and reduction).

Bodegas VALDEMAR

Camino Viejo, s/n
01320 Oyón (Álava)
☎: 945 622 188 - Fax: 945 622 111
bujanda@bujanda.com
www.martinezbujanda.com
Established: 1889
🌐 15,000 🍷 450 has.
🍷 50% 🌐50%: -US -DE -CA -UK

VALDEMAR 2003 JOVEN WHITE
90% viura, 10% malvasía

81 Yellow with a golden glimmer. Aromas of white flowers, perfumed, citrus fruit. Fresh palate with light bitter hints, medium persistence.

CONDE DE VALDEMAR 2002 FERMENTADO EN BARRICA WHITE
100% viura

80 Yellow. Aroma of ripe quince and butters, mildly toasty. Toasty palate, evoking ripeness with good acidity and light bitter notes.

VALDEMAR 2003 JOVEN ROSÉ
100% garnacha

81 Fresh pink. Aroma of strawberries, lactic with red fruit and light notes of sweetness. Warm palate, high in acidity, light.

CONDE DE VALDEMAR 2001 CRIANZA RED
85% tempranillo, 15% mazuelo

84 Dark garnet red cherry. Slightly intense, fruity aroma with fine creamy notes (vanilla, lactic flavours) and spicy oak. Flavourful, fleshy, supple palate with ripe and slightly oily tannins, fine bitter notes, good crianza expression and a suggestion of slightly sweet fruit.

CONDE DE VALDEMAR 1999 RESERVA RED
85% tempranillo, 15% mazuelo

82 Cherry with an orangey hue. Aroma of new wood, balsamic (menthol, liquorice), with hints of light red fruit. Astringent, light palate with good acidity.

VALDEMAR 2003 JOVEN RED
CONDE DE VALDEMAR VENDIMIA SELECCIONADA 1999 RESERVA RED

CONDE DE VALDEMAR 1996 GRAN RESERVA RED
CONDE DE VALDEMAR VENDIMIA SELECCIONADA 1995 GRAN RESERVA RED

Compañía Bodeguera de VALENCISO

Apartado 227
Plaza Pintores Tubia y Santamaría, 7
26200 Haro (La Rioja)
☎: 941 304 724 - Fax: 941 304 728
valenciso@valenciso.com
www.valenciso.com
Established: 1998
🌐 367 🍷 80%
🌐20%: -UK -CH -DE -BE -FR -RU

VALENCISO 2000 RESERVA RED
100% tempranillo

87 Very deep cherry. Intense aroma of ripe black fruit, toasty and spicy (ginger) oak hints with fine reduction hints. Flavourful, fleshy and supple on the palate with a powerful effect of flowers and fresh fruit in the retronasal passage (skins) and refreshing acidity.

VALENTIN PASCUAL WEIGAND

Dr. Azcárraga, 23 y Plaza España, 2
26350 Cenicero (La Rioja)
☎: 941 454 053
🛢 64,000 litres 🍷 14 has. 🍷 100%

VALENTIN PASCUAL RED

VALGRANDE

Carretera de Briones, s/n
26338 San Vicente de Sonsierra (La Rioja)
☎: 947 545 459 - Fax: 947 545 609

VALGRANDE 1998 CRIANZA RED
100% tempranillo

88 Garnet red cherry with a brick red edge. Powerful aroma of toasty oak, skins and a jammy fruit hint. Flavourful palate with a good oak/fruit integration, fine bitter notes (pitch, coffee, liquorice) and leather and spices in the retronasal passage.

VALGRANDE 1997 RESERVA RED

78 Deep garnet red. Toasty aroma with smoky hints and reduction notes. Flavourful palate with supple wood tannins but pungent oak; a ripe finish (plums).

VALGRANDE 1995 RESERVA RED

VALORIA

Carretera de Burgos, km. 5
26006 Logroño (La Rioja)

☎: 941 204 059 - Fax: 941 204 155
bodegas@vina-valoria.es
www.vina-valoria.es

Established: 1860

🍶 1,000 📊 1,500,000 litres 🍇 25 has.
🇪🇸 60% 🌐40%: -DE -AT -DK -US -FI -NL -
IT -DK -UK -SE -CH

VIÑA VALORIA 1998 CRIANZA WHITE
100% viura

80 Golden yellow. Slightly intense aroma of toasty and creamy oak notes with hints of wax and fine herbs. Flavourful palate with slightly drying oak tannins, toffee, vanilla overtones.

VIÑA VALORIA 2002 RED
80% tempranillo, 10% graciano, 10% mazuelo

83 Garnet red cherry with a coppery edge. Not very intense aroma of ripe black fruit and hints of smoky earth. Flavourful, slightly fleshy and supple on the palate with ripe fruit, a slightly oily texture and fine spicy hints in the retronasal passage.

VIÑA VALORIA SELECCIÓN ESPECIAL 2000 OAK AGED RED
100% tempranillo

84 Brilliant cherry with a brick red edge. Slightly intense aroma with spicy oak notes and hints of jammy red fruit. Flavourful supple palate with a good oak/fruit integration, fine bitter crianza notes, dark-roasted hints and refreshing acidity.

VIÑA VALORIA 2000 CRIANZA RED
70% tempranillo, 20% graciano, 10% mazuelo

77 Ruby red cherry with a brick red rim. Slightly intense aroma with fine reduction notes (tobacco, old furniture) and a suggestion of red fruit. Flavourful palate of spicy notes and a slightly warm texture.

VIÑA VALORIA 1998 RESERVA RED
80% tempranillo, 10% graciano, 10% mazuelo

83 Ruby red cherry with an orangey rim. Slightly intense aroma of fine reduction notes (tobacco, old furniture) and hints of dates. Flavourful, supple, slightly warm on the palate with refreshing acidity.

VIÑA VALORIA 1992 GRAN RESERVA RED
70% tempranillo, 20% graciano, 10% mazuelo

82 Ruby red cherry with an orangey hue. Not very intense aroma with a certain finesse, and predominant reduction notes (old furniture, dates, cigar box). Supple, light palate with fine spicy notes in the retronasal passage.

VALSACRO

Carretera N-232, km. 364
26510 La Rioja (Pradejón)
☎: 941 398 008 - Fax: 941 398 070
www.valsacro.com

Established: 1998

🍶 1,300 📊 1,200,000 litres 🍇 120 has.
🇪🇸 50% 🌐50%: -US -CH -DK -DE -UK

VALSACRO 1998 CRIANZA WHITE
60% chardonnay, 40% viura

86 Brilliant golden yellow. Powerful aroma with predominant spicy and creamy (vanilla) oak notes and a suggestion of fine lees. Flavourful palate, rich in nuances with excellent crianza expression and elements of minerals and fine herbs in the retronasal passage.

VALSACRO DIORO 2001 OAK AGED RED
100% vidau

92 Very deep cherry. Intense, concentrated aroma with notes of black fruit well-integrated with the oak and fine hints of reduction (leather, prunes). Flavourful palate slightly warm but with a good fruit combination, powerful in the retronasal passage (bitter cocoa, toasty flavours) with mineral hints.

VALSACRO 1999 RED
50% tempranillo, 40% vidau, 10% mazuelo

88 Fairly deep cherry with a brick red glint. Intense aroma of fine toasty oak with a jammy fruit nuance and balsamic hints. Flavourful palate with fleshy overtones, a good oak/fruit integration, fine bitter notes (liquorice, cocoa) and excellent acidity.

VALSANZO SELECCIÓN

Manuel Azaña, 9. Edif. Ambassador, L-15
47014 (Valladolid)
☎: 677 448 608 - Fax: 983 784 096
valsanzo@telefonica.net

🍶 250 📊 150,000 litres 🍇 80 has.
🇪🇸 30% 🌐70%

SAURÓN 2001 CRIANZA RED
60% tempranillo, 40% graciano

87 Dark garnet red cherry. Slightly quite closed aroma of jammy black fruit with toasty hints of oak and a nuance of terroir. Flavourful palate with a good oak/fruit integration and fine bitter notes (liquorice, pitch), spicy (pepper), promising.

LACRIMUS 2001 CRIANZA RED
85% tempranillo, 15% graciano

86 Garnet red cherry. Not very intense yet fine aroma with balsamic notes and well-integrated spices and fruit. Very flavourful on the palate with pleasant toasty wood, ripe fruit and polished tannins, persistent.

VALLEMAYOR

Carretera Logroño-Vitoria 38
26360 Fuenmayor (La Rioja)
☎: 941 450 142 - Fax: 941 450 376
vallemayor@fer.es
www.vallemayor.com

Established: 1985

⊕ 2,500 📊 2,500,000 litres ⚜ 40 has.
🍇 65% 🌐35%: -UE -US -MX -CH -SG

VALLEMAYOR 2003 FERMENTED EN BARRICA WHITE

72 Brilliant pale yellow with golden nuances. Intense, not very fine aroma of white stone fruit (exotic hints) and a nuance of slightly fresh oak. Fresh on the palate without obvious fruit expression, with slightly green tannins and an acidic edge.

VALLEMAYOR 2000 CRIANZA RED
80% tempranillo, 12% mazuelo, 8% graciano

78 Cherry with an orangey hue. Aromas of toasty wood and jammy tomatoes. Polished tannins on the palate, noticeable wood and sweet notes in the retronasal passage.

VALLE MAYOR VIÑA ENCINEDA 2002 RED
100% tempranillo

78 Cherry. Lactic aromas of red fruit. Warm palate with good wood tannins, sweet notes of alcohol and a slight greeness.

VALLEMAYOR VIÑA CERRADILLA 2001 CRIANZA RED
85% tempranillo, 15% mazuelo

80 Garnet red with an orangey edge. Spicy, smoky and balsamic aroma. Warm palate with dry wood tannins.

VALLE MAYOR VIÑA CERRADILLA 2000 RESERVA RED
85% tempranillo, 15% mazuelo

83 Brick red cherry. Lactic aromas of red stone fruit with light hints of wood. Fleshy overtones on the palate and a smoky toasty finish.

VALLEMAYOR 1998 RESERVA RED
80% tempranillo, 12% mazuelo, 8% graciano

77 Cherry with a brick red edge. Slightly short, balsamic aroma of jammy red fruit. Warm, light palate without notes of any importance.

VALLEMAYOR 1995 GRAN RESERVA RED
80% tempranillo, 12% mazuelo, 8% graciano

85 Garnet red cherry with an orangey edge. Intense aroma with predominant fine reduction notes and a jammy fruit hint. Flavourful, with fleshy overtones on the palate and ripe, oily tannins, slightly complex and long.

SEÑORIO DE LA LUZ 2003 WHITE
SEÑORIO DE LA LUZ 2003 ROSÉ
SEÑORIO DE LA LUZ 2003 JOVEN RED
TONDELUNA 2003 WHITE
TONDELUNA 2002 OAK AGED RED
TONDELUNA 2000 CRIANZA RED

Bodegas VARAL

San Vicente, 40
01307 Baños de Ebro (Álava)
☎: 945 623 321 - Fax: 945 623 321
bodegasvaral@euskalnet.net

Established: 1987

⊕ 110 📊 500,000 litres ⚜ 50 has. 🍇 100%

TRUJALERO 2003 WHITE
100% viura

83 Pale yellow with golden glints. Powerful aroma of ripe white fruit with hints of flowers and dried grass. Flavourful, fruity, slightly warm and oily on the palate with the freshness of citrus fruits and excellent acidity.

TRUJALERO 2003 MACERACIÓN CARBÓNICA RED
95% tempranillo, 5% viura

82 Intense garnet red cherry. Powerful, fruity aroma of foresty strawberries with the freshness of carbonic maceration and hints of nettle. Fresh, flavourful palate with firmish tannins, spicy hints of skins and liquorice, refreshing acidity.

MAYOR TRUJALERO 2001 CRIANZA RED
100% tempranillo

78 Garnet red cherry with a purplish edge. Powerful aroma of red fruit with a suggestion of oaky freshness and warm hints. Flavourful palate with slightly drying oak tannins and a suggestion of fruit slightly concealed by the alcohol.

MAYOR TRUJALERO 2000 OAK AGED RED

VILLARNEDO

Prolongación El Cortijo, 25
26511 El Villar de Arnedo (La Rioja)
☎: 941 159 036 - Fax: 941 159 210

Established: 1991

⊕ 200 📊 100,000 litres 🍇 90%
🌐10%: -DE -NL

D'ORDUÑO 2001 WHITE
D'ORDUÑO 2001 ROSÉ
D'ORDUÑO VINO 2001 RED
EL YAQUE 2000 CRIANZA RED
D'ORDUÑO 1997 RESERVA RED
D'ORDUÑO 1996 RESERVA RED
D´ORDUÑO 1998 RESERVA RED
D'ORDUÑO 1999 RESERVA RED
D'ORDUÑO 1995 GRAN RESERVA RED

VINÍCOLA DE RODEZNO

Plaza Asunción, 8
26222 Rodezno (La Rioja)
☎: 941 338 296 - Fax: 941 340 387
avillaluenga@teleline.es
Established: 1997
🍷 800 📊 250,000 litres 🍇 2 has.
🍷 90% 🌐10%: -DE -UK

VIÑA OLARTIA 1999 CRIANZA RED
100% tempranillo

76 Garnet red cherry with a coppery rim. Slightly intense aroma with predominant toasty oak notes. Flavourful palate with slightly drying tannins and glyceric hints that spoil the fruit expression.

CONDE DE MAYALDE 1997 RESERVA RED
100% tempranillo

83 Garnet red cherry with a brick red rim. Slightly intense aroma with fine reduction notes (leather, tobacco, prunes) and a spicy hint. Flavourful, supple palate with slightly drying but elegant tannins, a very spicy finish with hints of wax.

SEÑORÍO DE OLARTIA 1997 RESERVA RED
100% tempranillo

77 Garnet red cherry with an orangey glint. Somewhat intense aroma with predominant reduction notes (tobacco, leather). Flavourful palate with slightly marked oak tannins and hardly any fruit balance, bitter.

SEÑORIO DE OLARTIA 1996 GRAN RESERVA RED
100% tempranillo

74 Ruby red cherry with orangey glints. Intense aroma with spicy, reduction notes (leather, tobacco), slightly warm. Flavourful on the palate with predominant alcohol notes that conceal other nuances.

VIÑA OLARTIA 1999 RED
ZUMALACARREGUI 1999 CRIANZA RED
CONDE DE MAYALDE 1996 GRAN RESERVA RED

VINÍCOLA REAL

Santiago Aldaz, s/n
26120 Albelda de Iregua (La Rioja)

☎: 941 444 233 - Fax: 941 444 233
info@vinicolareal.com
www.vinicolareal.com
Established: 1997
🍷 900 🍇 10 has. 🍷 70% 🌐30%

VIÑA LOS VALLES 2000 OAK AGED RED
70% tempranillo, 15% graciano, 15% graciano

79 Brilliant cherry with a coppery hue. Fairly intense aroma with toasty oak notes, a ripe fruit suggestion and acid fresh overtones. Flavourful palate with well-integrated wood/fruit, warm notes that conceal the fruit, fine toasty and liquorice notes in the retronasal passage.

200 MONGES 1999 RESERVA RED
85% tempranillo, 10% graciano, 5% mazuelo

85 Deep cherry with a saffron edge. Intense, spicy aroma with a balsamic, slightly reduced suggestion. Flavourful, supple palate with well-integrated oak/fruit, warm and fine bitter notes; pleasant.

CUEVA DEL MONGE 2003 OAK AGED WHITE
200 MONGES 1995 GRAN RESERVA RED
LITURGIA 2001 RED

VINÍCOLA RIOJANA DE ALCANADRE

San Isidro, 46
26509 Alcanadre (La Rioja)
☎: 941 165 036 - Fax: 941 165 289
vinicola@riojanadealcanadre.com
www.vinicolariojanadealcanadre.com
Established: 1957
🍷 322 📊 6,000,000 litres 🍇 600 has.
🍷 60% 🌐40%: -UK -DE -NL -US -SE -CH -FR -AT

ARADÓN 2003 WHITE
100% viura

80 Pale. Aroma of very ripe white stone fruit. Fresh, flavourful palate with hints of citrus fruit and herbs, refreshing acidity.

BARZAGOSO 2003 WHITE
100% viura

80 Pale. Intense aroma of very ripe white stone fruit. Flavourful palate with fresh spicy overtones and fine hints of citrus fruit and herbs, pleasant.

VIÑA ROMITA 2003 WHITE
100% viura

80 Pale yellow. Intense, fruity aroma (hints of exotic fruit) with fresh overtones. Fresh, flavourful palate with good fruit expression, slightly oily.

ARADÓN 2003 ROSÉ
100% garnacha

80 Quite pale raspberry. Intense aroma of red stone fruit with fine spicy notes of skins. Fresh, flavourful palate with hints of high quality citrus fruit and a slightly acidic edge.

VIÑA ROMITA 2003 ROSÉ
100% garnacha

81 Brilliant pale raspberry. Not very intense aroma with spicy, citrus fresh overtones. Fresh, flavourful palate with red fruit and excellent acidity.

ARADÓN 2003 JOVEN RED
50% tempranillo, 50% garnacha

83 Brilliant cherry. Intense aroma of red fruit notes with good Garnacha expression and faint vegetative hints. Flavourful, fruity, well-crafted palate with carbonic hints; good turns between sweet fruit notes and grape tannins, fairly warm.

SILVAL 2003 JOVEN RED
50% tempranillo, 50% garnacha

82 Brilliant cherry. Slightly intense aroma of black fruit with fine toasty notes of skins and hints of underbrush. Flavourful and fleshy on the palate with quite firm grape tannins and ripe fruit, spicy and very rich.

VIÑA ROMITA 2003 JOVEN RED
50% tempranillo, 50% garnacha

81 Brilliant cherry with a violet glint. Intense aroma of ripe red fruit with hints of violets and a notion of terroir. Flavourful and fleshy on the palate with ripe and sweet grape tannins, fresh nettle overtones, good acidity.

BARZAGOSO 2001 CRIANZA RED
70% tempranillo, 15% garnacha, 15% mazuelo

80 Garnet red cherry with a brick red edge. Intense, ripe aroma with predominant reduction notes (wet horsehair, attics). Flavourful palate with a ripe fruit nuance, bitter and spicy notes, somewhat fresh oak, pleasant.

SILVAL 2000 CRIANZA RED
70% tempranillo, 15% garnacha, 15% mazuelo

81 Intense cherry with a brick red glint. Somewhat intense aroma of fine spicy and reduction notes (tobacco, dates, nuts) and balsamic and underbrush notes. Flavourful palate with slightly marked tannins, bitter notes and a slightly acidic edge.

BARZAGOSO 1999 RESERVA RED
70% tempranillo, 20% mazuelo, 10% garnacha

79 Fairly deep cherry with a brick red edge. Intense aroma with typical fine reduction notes (tobacco, notes of leather and stables), without remarkable nuances. Flavourful on the palate with certain balance and a Rioja crianza expression.

ARADÓN 2º AÑO 2002 RED
BARZAGOSO 1999 RESERVA RED

VIÑA ALMUDENA

Carretera Cenicero s/n
01340 Elciego (Álava)
☎: 945 606 525 - Fax: 945 606 526
www.melquior.com

MELQUIOR COLECCIÓN FAMILIAR MMI 2001 OAK AGED RED

84 Ruby red with an orange hue. Somewhat short, clear aroma, without expression, with toasty nuances and quite fresh fruit. Round, supple palate with a suggestion of elegance, flavourful and light tannins.

MELQUIOR COLECCIÓN FAMILIAR MMI ECOLÓGICO 2001 OAK AGED RED

84 Fairly dark cherry with a garnet red edge. Aroma with fruity notes and hints of foresty berries (brambles). Fruity palate with fresh fruit and flavourful tannins, pleasant.

MELQUIOR COLECCIÓN FAMILIAR MMI 1994 RESERVA RED

85 Cherry with an orangey edge. Aroma with fine notes of reduction in the bottle (leather, tobacco, vanilla), fruity. Round, oily palate, a good texture with a slight complexity and supple tannins.

MELQUIOR COLECCIÓN FAMILIAR MMI 1995 RESERVA RED

VIÑA BERNEDA

Carretera Somalo, 59
26131 Uruñuela (La Rioja)
☎: 941 371 304 - Fax: 941 371 304
Established: 1989
🌐 110 🗄 250,000 litres 🍇 120 has.
🍷 100%

VIÑA BERNEDA OAK AGED RED

VIÑA EL FUSTAL

Camino del Cristo, 2
01308 Samaniego (Álava)
☎: 945 140 450 - Fax: 945 143 810
Established: 1987
🌐 160 🗄 740,000 litres 🍇 7 has.
🍷 85% 🌐15%: -US -LV

VIÑA ALELXAL WHITE
VIÑAS LAS NAVAS JOVEN RED
ENARA CRIANZA RED
VIÑAS LAS NAVAS CRIANZA RED
ENARA RESERVA RED
VIÑAS VIEJAS RESERVA RED

DO Ca. RIOJA

VIÑA HERMINIA

Camino de los Agudos, 1
26559 Aldeanueva de Ebro (La Rioja)
☎: 941 142 305 - Fax: 941 142 303
vherminia@vherminia.es
www.vherminia.es

Established: 1998

🍷 5,000 🌿 3 has.

🍷 50% 🌐50%: -DE -SE -FI -DK -UK -DK -US -RU -NL -CH -AT

VIÑA HERMINIA 2002 FERMENTADO EN BARRICA WHITE
84% viura, 10% malvasía, 6% garnacha blanca

79 Pale yellow. Slightly intense aroma of smoky oak notes (somewhat fresh) with a light fruity suggestion. Flavourful palate with the freshness of citrus fruits and rich bitter notes.

PREFERIDO TEMPRANILLO 2003 RED
100% tempranillo

82 Brilliant cherry. Fruity aroma of ripe red fruit with toasty hints of skins and fresh brambles overtones. Flavourful palate with firm tannins, a ripe fruit nuance, a slightly oily texture and good acidity.

DUQUE DE HUÉSCAR 1996 OAK AGED RED
86% tempranillo, 10% graciano, 4% garnacha

85 Intense cherry with a brick red glint. Intense on the palate with fine toasty oak, jammy red stone fruit (raisiny hints), and a light reduction note. Flavourful, supple palate with fine bitter notes, an element of spices (pepper) and good acidity.

PREFERIDO DE LAS VIÑAS VIEJAS 2002 OAK AGED RED
86% tempranillo, 14% graciano

79 Garnet red cherry with a brick red glint. Intense, fruity aroma with a spicy oak nuance. Flavourful and fruity on the palate with a good oak/fruit integration, fresh overtones of red fruit and skins, good acidity.

VIÑA HERMINIA EXCELSUS 2001 OAK AGED RED
60% tempranillo, 40% garnacha

85 Intense cherry. Powerful aroma with predominant spicy (pepper) oak notes, ripe fruit (jammy hints) and a terroir nuance. Flavourful palate with fleshy overtones, a good fruit/oak integration and excellent symmetry.

VIÑA HERMINIA 2000 CRIANZA RED
85% tempranillo, 15% garnacha

77 Ruby red cherry with an orangey glint. Not very intense aroma with spicy oak notes and hints of reduction (varnish). Better in the mouth, flavourful and supple, thinned out by the crianza and lacking expression.

VIÑA HERMINIA 1996 RESERVA RED
85% tempranillo, 15% garnacha

84 Ruby red cherry with a brick red rim. Somewhat intense aroma of fine spicy and reduction notes (animals). Flavourful palate with fleshy overtones, with rough, sweet tannins and a spicy finish with notes of ripe fruit and a raisiny flavour (dates).

VIÑA HERMINIA 1996 RESERVA RED
100% graciano

85 Garnet red cherry. Slightly intense aroma of black fruit with fine toasty oak, creamy hints and notes of damp earth. Flavourful and supple palate with fleshy overtones, a good fruit weight, spicy hints (pepper) and excellent acidity.

VIÑA HERMOSA

Avenida de la Rioja, s/n
26221 Gimileo (La Rioja)
☎: 941 304 231 - Fax: 941 304 326
santiagoijalba@fer.es
www.santiagoijalba.es

Established: 1998

🍷 1,500 📖 650,000 litres 🌿 10 has.

🍷 73% 🌐27%: -UK -AT -MX -FR -DE -BE

ABANDO 2003 FERMENTADO EN BARRICA WHITE
viura

79 Greenish straw. Medium-intensity aroma with fairly evident lactic notes that somewhat smother the fruit. Quite flavourful palate with citrus fruit and good acidity but with excessive wood weight.

VIÑA HERMOSA 2002 RED
tempranillo

75 Cherry. Aroma of jammy fruit, vinous. Well-balanced palate, somewhat short, well-mannered.

JARRERO 2000 CRIANZA RED
tempranillo

80 Brilliant cherry with a coppery glint. Fairly intense aroma with spicy hints of oak. Flavourful on the palate with slightly marked tannins though with notes of ripeness, fine bitter notes, fresh overtones, pleasant.

JARRERO 2001 CRIANZA RED
tempranillo

82 Cherry with a ruby red hue. Aroma of red fruit, vanilla (wood) and viscous. High acidity yet warmth on the palate with toasty aromas and ripe tannins in the retronasal passage.

VIÑA HERMOSA 2001 CRIANZA RED
tempranillo

74 Cherry with an orangey rim. Aroma of jammy fruit with light toasty and balsamic flavours. Well-integrated wood on the palate with good acidity and medium persistence.

OGGA 2000 RESERVA RED
tempranillo

85 Deep cherry. Intense, ripe aroma of slightly overripe stone fruit (dates) with fine balsamic hints and reduction notes. Flavourful palate with fresh overtones of red fruit, supple with spicy hints of oak and fresh fruit in the retronasal passsage.

VIÑA HERMOSA 1996 GRAN RESERVA RED
tempranillo

78 Cherry with brick-red edge. Slightly intense aroma, with notes of fine reduction over a hint of ripe fruit suggestion, hints of fruit stones and prunes. Predominant drying wood notes on the palate; with a hint of bitterness, well-mannered.

VIÑA HERMOSA 1998 RESERVA RED
ABANDO 2001 CRIANZA RED

VIÑA IJALBA

Carretera Pamplona, km. 1
26006 Logroño (La Rioja)
☎: 941 261 100 - Fax: 941 261 128
vinaijalba@ijalba.com
www.ijalba.com

Established: 1991

🍾 2,500 🛢 1,100,000 litres 🍇 80 has.

🇪🇸 50% 🌍 50%

IJALBA VITICULTURA ECOLÓGICA 2003 FERMENTADO EN BARRICA WHITE
100% maturana blanca

80 Pale gold. Quite intense aroma with fine smoky oak notes and a nuance of white fruit. Flavourful palate with fine bitter and smoky wood notes and a nuance of lees, lacking fruit expression.

SOLFERINO 2003 MACERACIÓN CARBÓNICA RED
100% tempranillo

81 Garnet red cherry with a violet hue. Intense aroma with red fruit, fresh grapeskins overtones and a nuance of damp earth. Fresh, fruity palate with flavourful, fine tannins and liquorice hints.

DIONISIO RUIZ IJALBA 2002 OAK AGED RED
100% maturana tinta

87 Intense cherry red. Intense aroma of ripe red fruit, a spicy and creamy oak suggestion. Flavourful on the palate with fleshy overtones, well-integrated oak/fruit, notes of chocolate, liquorice, a balsamic hint and fallen leaves well-balanced.

IJALBA GRACIANO 1998 OAK AGED RED
100% graciano

88 Deep cherry with a garnet red hue. Powerful, concentrated aroma with toasty oak notes, a suggestion of ripe black fruit, hints of terroir, chocolate and spices. Fleshy palate with rough, oily tannins, jammy red fruit and fine reduction notes; well-balanced.

MÚRICE 2000 CRIANZA RED
90% tempranillo, 5% graciano, 5% mazuelo

81 Garnet red cherry with a coppery edge. Intense aroma with predominant smoky oak notes and fine reduction hints (tobacco). Flavourful, supple and spicy on the palate with a hint of fresh oak and good acidity.

IJALBA 1998 RESERVA RED
80% tempranillo, 20% graciano

82 Dark garnet red cherry with a saffron edge. Intense aroma of smoky oak notes, jammy black fruit and mild reduction hints (new leather). Flavourful, supple palate with hints of quite fresh oak and liquorice, spicy and warm.

IJALBA SELECCIÓN ESPECIAL 1994 RESERVA RED
50% tempranillo, 50% graciano

88 Cherry with a brick red edge. Intense aroma with fine reduction notes (leathers, cigar box) over a suggestion of ripe fruit and of toasty oak. Flavourful palate rich in long crianza nuances, with supple overtones and refreshing acidity.

GENOLI VITICULTURA ECOLÓGICA 2003 JOVEN WHITE
ALOQUE VITICULTURA ECOLÓGICA 2003 JOVEN ROSÉ
LIVOR VITICULTURA ECOLÓGICA 2003 JOVEN RED
IJALBA VITICULTURA ECOLÓGICA 2000 CRIANZA RED

VIÑA IZADI

Herrería Travesia, 2-5
01307 Villabuena (Álava)
☎: 945 609 086 - Fax: 945 609 261
izadi@izadi.com
www.izadi.com

Established: 1987

⊕ 9,000 ▭ 2,500,000 litres ▼ 80%
♠20%

VIÑA IZADI 2003 FERMENTADO EN BARRICA WHITE
80% viura, 20% malvasía

81 Brilliant pale yellow. Intense aroma with predominant notes of ripe white fruit and a creamy nuance of smoky oak. Flavourful palate with fine bitter notes, herbs, fresh overtones and a slightly acidic edge.

VIÑA IZADI EXPRESIÓN 2000 ROBLE RED
100% tempranillo

91 Very deep cherry. Powerful aroma with predominant burnt notes and balsamic hints. Flavourful, fleshy palate with promising but slightly marked tannins, fine toasty notes, black fruit and hints of graphite.

VIÑA IZADI SELECCIÓN 2000 RED
80% tempranillo, 20% graciano

86 Very deep cherry. Powerful aroma of ripe fruit, with fine toasty oak notes and fresh spicy overtones of the skins. Flavourful, fleshy palate with fine, quite ripe tannins, an oily texture and liquorice, balsamic and terracotta notes in the retronasal passage.

VIÑA IZADI 2001 CRIANZA RED
100% tempranillo

87 Intense cherry with a violet edge. Powerful aroma with good varietal and crianza expression (fine toasty oak). Fleshy palate with well-integrated oak/fruit, rich in nuances (jammy fruit, liquorice, balsamic notes, terroir).

VIÑA IZADI 2001 RESERVA RED
73% tempranillo, 15% graciano, 12% otras

86 Deep cherry. Intense aroma with predominant spicy oak notes, a ripe red fruit and underbrush suggestion. Flavourful, fleshy palate with promising but quite marked tannins, a slightly oily texture and fine bitter notes in the retronasal passage.

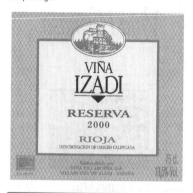

VIÑA OLABARRI

Carretera Haro-Anguciana, s/n
26200 Haro (La Rioja)
☎: 941 310 937 - Fax: 941 311 602
info@bodegasolabarri.com
www.bodegasrubi.es

Established: 1989

⊕ 3,500 ▭ 1,000,000 litres ❦ 12 has.
▼ 90% ♠10%

VIÑA OLABARRI 2001 CRIANZA RED
100% tempranillo

81 Dark cherry. Powerful aroma of jammy black fruit and macerated skins with fine spicy and toasty oak notes and balsamic hints. Flavourful palate with slightly drying oak tannins and a good fruit expression, quite promising.

BIKANDI VENDIMIA SELECCIONADA 1996 RESERVA RED
100% tempranillo

85 Very deep cherry with a purplish edge. Powerful aroma of very ripe black fruit (hints of prune) with fine toasty oak and notes of damp earth. Flavourful palate with fleshy overtones, slightly marked tannins but promising with good acidity.

VIÑA OLABARRI 1998 RESERVA RED
80% tempranillo, 20% mazuelo, garnacha

80 Garnet red cherry with a brick red glint. Slightly intense aroma, rich in traditional Reserva expression (reduced fruit, tobacco, spices). Flavourful palate with slightly fresh oak tannins and a spicy hint.

VIÑA OLABARRI 1996 GRAN RESERVA RED
80% tempranillo, 20% mazuelo, garnacha

81 Dark cherry with a coppery edge. Intense aroma of jammy red fruit, fine toasty oak and reduction notes. Flavourful palate with slightly drying tannins, hints of wax and a spicy suggestion of fresh fruit.

VIÑA REAL

Carretera Logroño - Laguardia, km. 4, 8
01300 Laguardia (Álava)
☎: 945 625 210 - Fax: 945 625 209
laguardia@cvne.com
www.cvne.com

Established: 2004
🛢 14,000 🌱 150 has.

🍷 20% 🌐80%: -CH -MX -UK -US -DE -
DK -JP -VE -PR -DO -IE

PAGOS DE VIÑA REAL 2001 ROBLE RED
100% tempranillo

90 Intense cherry. Toasty aroma of ripe fruit and oak, varietal expression, hints of minerals (hot stone) and creamy oak. Fleshy, full and warm on the palate with ripe fruit and fine toasty new oak enveloped by the fruit.

VIÑA REAL 2001 CRIANZA RED
85% tempranillo, 15% garnacha, mazuelo

84 Quite dark cherry. Aroma with notes of fresh, ripe fruit and toasty oak. Round on the palate with fruity and toasty flavours in the retronasal passage, flavourful and with very well-combined oak and wine.

VIÑA REAL 2000 RESERVA RED
90% tempranillo, 5% garnacha, 5% graciano

84 Cherry with a garnet red-orangey edge. Fine, classic aroma with spicy notes and orange peel. Flavourful on the palate with a good crianza, round and polished tannins.

VIÑA REAL 1996 GRAN RESERVA RED
95% tempranillo, 5% graciano

89 Garnet red cherry with a brick red edge. Aroma with seasoned oak notes (wax, old furniture) and spicy hints (cloves and pepper) and a fine reduction in bottle (leather and cedar wood). Round and with jammy fruit on the palate with a spicy aroma in the retronasal passage, silky and polished tannins, an excellent wood association, fruit and reduction.

VIÑA REAL 2003 FERMENTADO EN BARRICA WHITE

VIÑA SALCEDA

Carretera de Cenicero, km. 3
01340 Elciego (Álava)

☎: 945 606 125 - Fax: 945 606 069
info@vinasalceda.com
Established: 1969
🛢 8,000 🛢 2,367,000 litres 🌱 40 has.
🍷 85% 🌐15%

VIÑA SALCEDA 2001 CRIANZA RED
85% tempranillo, 15% mazuelo, graciano

82 Quite intense cherry. Aroma with fruity and spicy oak notes with medium expression. Fruity palate with a suggestion of animal notes (leather, cedar), slightly spicy and flavourful.

CONDE DE LA SALCEDA 2000 RESERVA RED
95% tempranillo, 5% graciano

91 Intense cherry. Complex aroma with a rich expression of well-integrated fruit and creamy oak, complex, fine and jammy. Fleshy, full palate with toasty fruit and fine and creamy oak, flavourful with harmonious tannins.

VIÑA SALCEDA 1999 RESERVA RED
90% tempranillo, 5% mazuelo, 5% graciano

89 Intense cherry. Fine toasty aroma (cocoa and coffee) with well-integrated and quite fresh fruity nuances (bunches). Fleshy palate with a good fruity and toasty oak note integration, well-balanced with round overtones and dry but ripe and well-assembled tannins.

VIÑA SALCEDA 1998 GRAN RESERVA RED
90% tempranillo, 5% mazuelo, 5% graciano

88 Quite dark ruby red with a brick red edge. Slightly closed, spicy aroma with subtle notes of leather and cigar boxes, fruit and a suggestion of varietal notes. Round, oily, elegant, spicy palate with silky tannins, a very lively and promising Gran Reserva.

CONDE DE LA SALCEDA 1998 RESERVA RED

VIÑEDOS DE ALDEANUEVA

Avenida Juan Carlos I, 100
26559 Aldeanueva de Ebro (La Rioja)
☎: 941 163 039 - Fax: 941 163 585
va@aldeanueva.com
www.aldeanueva.com

Established: 1956

🍾 12,000 🗄 28,700,000 litres 🍇 2.450 has.
🏴 65% 🌐35%: -UK -DE -SE -FI -CH -AT -

JP -US -MX

AZABACHE 2003 FERMENTADO EN BARRICA WHITE
100% viura

83 Brilliant straw. Powerful aroma with predominant smoky oak notes and a suggestion of white fruit (slightly exotic). Flavourful palate with fine tannins and rich bitter notes, good acidity.

AZABACHE ECOLÓGICO 2003 JOVEN RED
60% tempranillo, 30% garnacha, 10% graciano

81 Garnet red cherry. Powerful, fruity aroma with notes of macerated skins. Flavourful, quite fleshy palate with rough and slightly sweet tannins and fruit expression slightly muted by the alcohol.

AZABACHE TEMPRANILLO 2003 JOVEN RED
100% tempranillo

81 Brilliant cherry. Fresh aroma with fresh notes of macerated skins and hints of the underside of leaves. Flavourful and quite fruity on the palate with firm tannins, good acidity and warm hints (13,5) which subdue the fruit expression.

AZABACHE ECOLÓGICO 2002 CRIANZA RED
60% tempranillo, 30% garnacha, 10% graciano

75 Brilliant cherry. Fairly intense aroma with hardly any suggestion of the fruit (excessive alcohol). Equally warm palate with smoky hints of oak and an acidic edge.

AZABACHE 1999 RESERVA RED
70% tempranillo, 20% garnacha, 10% graciano

84 Dark cherry with a deep red edge. Not very intense aroma with a certain finesse, toasty oak, a nuance of jammy fruit and a waxy suggestion. Flavourful palate with slightly marked but promising tannins, slightly warm.

AZABACHE 2000 CRIANZA RED
70% tempranillo, 20% garnacha, 10% mazuelo

85 Dark cherry with a coppery hue. Intense, ripe aroma of red stone fruit, and light reduction notes (varnish). Flavourful palate with a good oak/fruit integration, with rough, slightly sweet tannins and a toasty oak hint; very pleasant.

AZABACHE TRADICIÓN 2000 CRIANZA RED
100% tempranillo

85 Dark garnet red cherry. Intense aroma of black fruit with hints of macerated skins and fine spicy hints of oak. Flavourful palate with a good fruit/oak integration and bitter notes (dark-roasted flavours, liquorice), promising.

AZABACHE MAZUELO 2000 CRIANZA RED
100% mazuelo

84 Garnet red cherry with a coppery edge. Intense aroma of macerated red berries and spicy oak notes with fresh damp earth overtones. Flavourful palate with rough and slightly sweet tannins and a good varietal and crianza expression.

AZABACHE GRACIANO 1999 RESERVA RED
100% graciano

82 Dark garnet red cherry. Powerful aroma with predominant toasty notes (oak, skins) and a jammy fruit and damp earth hint. Flavourful, concentrated palate with slightly drying tannins and a slight varietal expression, warm.

AZABACHE TRADICIÓN 1998 RESERVA RED
70% tempranillo, 20% garnacha, 10% graciano

78 Deep cherry with a saffron edge. Intense, fruity aroma with a fine reduction hint. Flavourful on the palate with predominant bitter and spicy oak notes without Reserva character.

AZABACHE TRADICIÓN 1996 GRAN RESERVA RED
70% tempranillo, 20% garnacha, 10% graciano

86 Dark cherry with a saffron edge. Powerful aroma of jammy fruit (redcurrants, cherries) and toasty oak (pitch). Fleshy, concentrated palate with ripe and vigorous tannins, will age well.

VIÑA AZABACHE 2003 FERMENTADO EN BARRICA WHITE
AZABACHE 2003 JOVEN ROSÉ
AZABACHE ECOLÓGICO 2001 CRIANZA RED

VIÑEDOS DEL CONTINO

Finca San Rafael, s/n
01321 Laserna (Álava)
☎: 945 600 201 - Fax: 945 621 114
laserna@contino-sa.com
www.cvne.com
Established: 1973
🌐 2,000 🍇 62 has. 🛢 350,000 litres.
🍷 85% 🌍15%: -US -DE -SE -CH -MX

VIÑEDOS DEL CONTINO GRACIANO 2003 OAK AGED RED
100% graciano

88 Very deep Bigarreau cherry. Aroma of ripe red fruit (redcurrants, blackberries), lactics and balsamic flavours. Round on the palate with good fruit tannins, toasty flavours and vanilla.

CONTINO 2001 RED
90% tempranillo, 10% mazuelo, garnacha

88 Dark red cherry. Spicy aroma with hints of fine wood, nuances of cedar and black tobacco. Round palate with polished tannins and spices in the retronasal passage, oily and very flavourful.

CONTINO ÎVIÑA DEL OLIVOÎ 2001 CRIANZA RED
90% tempranillo, 10% graciano

90 Intense cherry. Somewhat closed-in aroma but with spicy and toasty notes (tobacco, coffee, cedar wood). Full, generous, fleshy and powerful on the palate with spices in the retronasal passage, rich in crianza and ripe fruit expression with flavourful and ripe tannins.

CONTINO 1999 RESERVA RED
85% tempranillo, 10% graciano, 5% mazuelo

88 Cherry with an orangey edge. Aroma with nuances of flowers and delicate fruit with toasty notes of cocoa and chocolate liqueurs. Round, oily palate with highly polished tannins, jammy fruit and spicy cask notes in the retronasal passage.

VIÑEDOS DE PÁGANOS

Carretera Navaridas, s/n
01307 Páganos - Laguardia (Álava)
☎: 941 334 080 - Fax: 941 334 371
info@eguren.com
www.eguren.com
Established: 1998
🛢 400,000 litres 🍇 45 has. 🛢 12,000 litres.
🍷 50% 🌍50%: -US -UE -CH -JP -MX

EL PUNTIDO 2001 OAK AGED RED
100% tempranillo

90 Very intense cherry. Deep aroma of very ripe stewed black fruit with toasty hints (chocolate, pitch, peat). Powerful, fleshy, concentrated and warm on the palate, very Mediterranean with toasty hints and sweet, very flavourful tannins.

LA NIETA

VIÑEDOS RUIZ JIMÉNEZ

Carretera Comarcal LR-115 Km. 43, 5
26559 Aldeanueva de Ebro (La Rioja)
☎: 941 163 577 - Fax: 941 163 577
vrjimenez@masbytes.com
Established: 1998
🌐 110 🛢 525,000 litres 🍇 55 has.
🍷 95% 🌍5%: -DE -UK -US -BE -NL

PERSEUS GARNACHA (ECOLÓGICO) 2002 OAK AGED RED
100% garnacha

83 Deep cherry with a violet edge. Powerful aroma with toasty oak, toasty skins, spicy and very varietal notes, warm hints. Flavourful, slightly fleshy palate with slightly marked tannins; very warm.

PERSEUS VENDIMIA SELECCIONADA 2002 OAK AGED RED
tempranillo, garnacha

76 Brilliant cherry. Intense aroma with floral notes (rose petals and violets) and sweet alcoholic overtones that conceal the fruit. Quite warm, flavourful palate of fine toasty oak.

VALCALIENTE 2002 OAK AGED RED
tempranillo, graciano

88 Fairly deep cherry with a violet edge. Intense aroma of ripe red fruit, hints of toasty oak and skins. Flavourful palate, with promising but quite marked tannins, fleshy, with powerful chocolate, spices, jammy fruit and fine hints of terroir in the retronasal passage.

PERSEUS 2002 RED

82 Cherry. Aroma of very ripe red fruit and balsamic notes. Drying on the palate with good acidity, light bitter notes and medium persistence, pleasant.

VIÑEDOS Y BODEGAS DE LA MARQUESA

Herrería, 76
01307 Villabuena (Álava)
☎: 945 609 085 - Fax: 945 623 304
lamarquesa@worldonline.es

Established: 1880

🌐 3,000 📊 1,000,000 litres 🍇 60 has.

🍷 50% 🌍50%: -US -RU -DE -CH -BE -NL -SE -FI -HU -DO -MX

VALSERRANO 2003 FERMENTADO EN BARRICA WHITE
100% viura

83 Pale yellow with a golden hue. Fresh aroma of white stone fruit with fine smoky oak and fragrant herbs. Flavourful, bitter palate with a slightly acidic edge, quite fresh and unintegrated oak tannins, promising.

VALSERRANO GRACIANO 2001 RED
100% graciano

84 Dark cherry. Powerful, fruity aroma with a slight varietal expression (black fruit, spices, petals) and toasty oak notes. Flavourful, fleshy palate with fine bitter notes and good crianza expression.

VALSERRANO MAZUELO 2001 RED
100% mazuelo

88 Dark cherry with a dark red edge. Intense aroma with a certain finesse, forest fruit, hints of macerated skins and fine toasty, creamy crianza notes. Fleshy, flavourful palate with good fruit/oak integration, slightly warm and oily.

VALSERRANO 2001 CRIANZA RED
90% tempranillo, 10% mazuelo

83 Dark deep red cherry. Intense aroma with predominant notes of toasty, creamy oak. Flavourful, fleshy palate with good fruit/oak integration, a sweet and spicy hint, good acidity.

VALSERRANO 1999 RESERVA RED
90% tempranillo, 10% graciano

83 Garnet red cherry with a coppery hue. Intense aroma with predominant spicy wood notes and a suggestion of reduction (animals). Flavourful palate with hints of slightly aged wood, bitterness and marked acidity.

VALSERRANO SELECCIÓN LIMITADA 1996 RESERVA RED
90% tempranillo, 10% graciano

84 Dark cherry with a brick red rim. Powerful aroma with predominant reduction notes (animals, old furniture). Flavourful palate with good fruit/oak integration, bitter hints (liquorice, dark-roasted flavours, jam) and hints of cocoa in the finish.

VALSERRANO FINCA MONTEVIEJO 2002 RED
95% tempranillo, 5% graciano, garnacha

87 Dark garnet red cherry. Intense aroma with predominent jammy fruit notes over a suggestion of spicy oak. Fleshy, concentrated palate with good fruit/oak integration, excellent bitter notes (liquorice, dark-roasted flavours), good acidity and potential.

VIÑEGRA DON TEÓFILO 1º

Vitoria, 7 3º A
01309 Elvillar (Álava)
☎: 947 201 645 - Fax: 947 201 645
rcascos@wanadoo.es

Established: 1916

🌐 270 📊 90,000 litres 🍇 8 has.
🍷 70% 🌍30%

DON TEÓFILO 1º CRIANZA RED
DON TEÓFILO 1º RESERVA RED
DON TEÓFILO 1º GRAN RESERVA RED

VIRGEN DEL VALLE

Carretera a Villabuena, 3
01307 Samaniego (Álava)
☎: 945 609 033 - Fax: 945 609 106
bodegavirvalle@sea.es

Established: 1987

DO Ca. RIOJA

🌐 1.421 🛢 1.000.000 litres 🍷 77,5%
🌍22,5%: -UK -DE -DK -NL -CH

CINCEL 2001 CRIANZA RED

CINCEL 1989 GRAN RESERVA RED
CINCEL 1990 GRAN RESERVA RED
CINCEL 1994 GRAN RESERVA RED
CINCEL COSECHA FAMILIAR 1987 GRAN
 RESERVA RED
CINCEL MAGNUM 1995 GRAN RESERVA
 RED
CINCEL 1999 RESERVA ESPECIAL RED

CINCEL 1998 RESERVA RED

WILLIAMS & HUMBERT

Carretera N-IV, km. 641, 75
11408 Jerez de la Frontera (Cádiz)
☎: 956 353 400 - Fax: 956 353 411
williams@williams-humbert.com
www.williams-humbert.com

Established: 1877
🌐 70,000 🛢 35,000,000 litres 🍇 500 has.
🍷 35% 🌍65%

VIÑA PAUL RED

WINNER WINES

Adelfas, 18 3ℑB
28007 Madrid (Madrid)
☎: 915 019 042 - Fax: 915 017 794
rsaseta@winnerwines.es
www.winnerwines.es

Established: 1986
🌐 550 🛢 1,200,000 litres 🍇 400 has.
🍷 8% 🌍92%: -US -CA -MX -DO -PR -SG -
JP -CH -IT -FR -DE -SE -FI -DK -BE -AT -DK

VIÑA SASETA 2001 CRIANZA RED
90% tempranillo, 5% graciano, 5% mazuelo

83 Dark cherry with a garnet red edge. Intense aroma with predominant toasty and fine reduction notes (prunes, tobacco). Flavourful, fleshy palate with a good oak/fruit integration, a sweet fruit hint and liquorice, slightly warm and oily.

VIÑA SASETA 1999 RESERVA RED
90% tempranillo, 5% graciano, 5% mazuelo

81 Ruby red cherry with brick red glints. Intense aroma of slightly reduced ripe fruit with spicy hints of oak, tobacco and aged wood. Flavourful, supple palate with good crianza expression and a suggestion of sweet fruit.

VIÑA SASETA JOVEN RED

YSIOS

Camino de la Hoya s/n
01300 Laguardia (Álava)
☎: 945 600 640 - Fax: 945 600 520
isios@byb.es
www.byb.es
Established: 1998
🍷 1,500 🌿 50 has. 🇪🇸 85% 🌐15%

YSIOS 2000 RESERVA RED
100% tempranillo

84 Garnet red cherry with a saffron edge. Intense aroma with a certain finesse, with ripe fruit (bilberries, cherries) and spicy oak notes. Flavourful palate with ripe, slightly oily tannins and fine bitter notes.

YSIOS VENDIMIA SELECCIONADA 2000 RESERVA RED
100% tempranillo

84 Garnet red cherry with a brick red edge. Intense aroma with an excellent expression of the Reserva (leather, prunes, spices, toast, lactics). Flavourful, fleshy palate with a good fruit/oak integration, rich in nuances with a slightly oily texture.

Bodegas y Viñedos ZUAZO GASTÓN

Las Norias, 12
01320 Oyón (Álava)
☎: 945 601 526 - Fax: 945 622 917
zuazogaston@zuazogaston.com
www.zuazogaston.com
Established: 1998
🍷 520 🍶 950,000 litres 🌿 52 has.
🇪🇸 70% 🌐30%: -NL -CH -DE -UK -US

ZUAZO GASTÓN TEMPRANILLO 2003 RED
100% tempranillo

74 Garnet red cherry. Slightly evolved aroma of windfall fruit. Quite flavourful and slightly flabby on the palate with sweet fruit.

ZUAZO GASTÓN VENDIMIA SELECCIONADA 2003 RED
95% tempranillo, 5% graciano

80 Brilliant cherry. Intense aroma with good varietal and young wine expression, fresh maceration overtones, nettles and damp earth. Fruity palate with quite firm but flavourful tannins and good acidity.

ZUAZO GASTÓN 2001 CRIANZA RED

Bodegas ZUGOBER

Tejerías, 13-15
01306 Lapuebla de Labarca (Álava)
☎: 945 627 228 - Fax: 945 627 281
zugober@zugober.com
www.zugober.com
Established: 1987
🍷 400 🍶 245,000 litres 🌿 22 has.
🇪🇸 40% 🌐60%: -UK -DE -AT -MX -LV

BELEZOS 2003 FERMENTADO EN BARRICA WHITE
95% viura, 5% malvasía

78 Pale with golden nuances. Intense aroma with well-integrated fruit notes and smoky oak. Flavourful palate with rich bitter notes and hints of woody sweetness (luke-warm butter, caramel).

BELEZOS 2003 RED
95% tempranillo, 5% viura

81 Dark cherry with a violet edge. Intense, fruity aroma (redcurrants, cherries) with hints of sun-drenched skins and underbrush. Flavourful palate with ripe, firm tannins, notes of liquorice, spices and hints of terroir in the retronasal passage, slightly warm.

BELEZOS VENDIMIA SELECCIONADA 2001 RED
100% tempranillo

79 Garnet red cherry. Intense aroma of black fruit, balsamic notes and spicy hints of wood. Flavourful, somewhat fruity palate with hints of quite fresh oak.

BELEZOS 1998 RESERVA RED
95% tempranillo, garnacha, graciano

78 Cherry. Aroma of ripe red fruit, earth and sweet, toasty wood notes. Warm palate with well-integrated, polished tannins and toasty hints and coffee in the retronasal passage.

BELEZOS 2003 WHITE
BELEZOS 2003 ROSÉ
BELEZOS 2003 RED
BELEZOS 2000 CRIANZA RED
BELEZOS 2001 CRIANZA RED
BELEZOS 1999 RESERVA RED
BELEZOS 1996 GRAN RESERVA RED
BELEZOS 1998 GRAN RESERVA RED

DO RUEDA

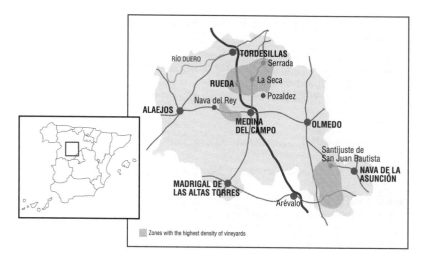

Zones with the highest density of vineyards

NEWS. On the eve of the 25th anniversary of the DO, the Regulatory Council is working harder than ever on the control of the new plantations and on improving the vine-growing register, they have even promised to divide the DO into sub-regions. As far as the climate is concerned, 2003 was characterised by a wet winter and a very hot summer that brought with it a harvest that was early by about nine days with respect to 2002. The mechanization statistics of the harvest are interesting: 52% was harvested by machines, 56% in the case of *Verdego*. This autochthonous variety, the flagship of the DO, of which 19 million kg was harvested in 2003 (almost 60% of the white grapes), has increased its presence in the vineyards of Rueda to 45.7%.

In the end, 2003 was a good year as far as quality was concerned, and a record harvest too (15% increase on the previous year); in addition, sales increased by 6% in the midst of a full-blown recession in all the markets.

Hectares of Vineyard	No. of Viticulturists	No. of Bodegas	2003 Harvest	2003 Production	Marketing
7,491	1,280	36	Very Good	27,027,984 litres	83,4% Spain 16,6% foreign

It is interesting how some of its red wines, particularly those from Bodegas Antaño (Cobranza and Viña Cobranza) started to rise above 80 points and approach the 90 mark (as was the case with Cobranza Vendimia Seleccionada). As for the white wines, the best were Naia (90) and Náiades (92), Basa and José Pariente (91) and Finca La Colina (91), most of which cost less than € 7. What more could one ask for?

LOCATION. In the provinces of Valladolid (53 municipal districts), Segovia (17 municipal districts) and Avila (2 municipal districts). The vineyards are situated on the undulating terrain of a plateau and are conditioned by the influence of the river Duero that runs through the northern part of the region.

CLIMATE. Continental in nature, with cold winters and short hot summers. Rainfall is concentrated in spring and autumn. The average altitude of the region is between 600 m and 700 m, and only in the province of Segovia does it exceed 800 m.

SOIL. Many pebbles on the surface. The terrain is stony, poor in organic matter, with good aeration and drainage. The texture of the soil is variable although, in general, sandy limestone and limestone predominate.

VARIETIES:
White: *Verdejo* (52%), *Viura* (22%), *Sauvignon Blanc* (7%) and *Palomino Fino* (19%).
Red: *Tempranillo, Cabernet Sauvignon, Merlot* and *Garnacha.*

REGULATORY COUNCIL.
Real, 8. 47490 Rueda (Valladolid).
Tel: 983 868 248. Fax: 983 868 135.
E-mail: crdo.rueda@dorueda.com
Website: www.dorueda.com.

GENERAL CHARACTERISTICS OF THE WINES:

Whites	These are produced mainly from *Verdejo*. As the percentage of this grape variety increases (from Rueda to Rueda Verdejo), a more characteristic style is obtained. Greenish straw coloured, they offer fine and elegant aromas, fruity, with hints of fennel, mint and apple. On the palate they are fresh, fruity and with a characteristic bitter aftertaste, which contrasts with the sensation of ripe grapes, sweetness and freshness. Those produced from *Sauvignon Blanc* offer good aromatic potency, with floral notes and, in most cases, notes of tropical fruit. They are flavourful with a certain oily character.
Espumosos	These are produced according to the traditional method of a second fermentation in the bottle. They are fresh with hints of yeast, although, in general, they are slightly heavier than the Cavas.
Reds	These are based mainly on the *Tempranillo*, with the participation of especially *Cabernet Sauvignon*. They have a quite intense cherry colour and are fruity, meaty and flavourful; they may be reminiscent of the red wines of Cigales.
Classic Whites	The so-called 'Dorado' fits the pattern of the traditional Generoso wines. Produced from a minimum of 40% *verdejo* and an alcohol content not less than 15°, they have a golden colour and a slightly toasted taste due to the long oxidation process they are subjected to in the wooden barrels. There is also a 'Palido' labelling for wines of this style with shorter ageing in wood.

AGRÍCOLA CASTELLANA

Sociedad Cooperativa Limitada

Carretera Rodilana, s/n
47491 La Seca (Valladolid)
☎: 983 816 320 - Fax: 983 816 562
agricast1@terra.es
www.agricolacastellana.com

Established: 1935

📦 500 🛢 10,000,000 litres 🍇 2,000 has.

🍷 90% (🍇10%: -DE -UK -SE -DK -IT -US -JP -MX -AT

CUATRO RAYAS 2004 WHITE

85 Brilliant yellow with a greenish hue. Intense aroma, fruit and white flowers, exotic and slightly mineral hints. Flavourful palate, varietal expression (green fruit, a bitter nuance), slightly oily, marked acidity.

AZUMBRE SAUVIGNON 2003 WHITE
100% sauvignon blanc

84 Pale gold. Powerful, fruity aroma with hints of ripe melon and a hint of citrus freshness. Fresh, flavourful palate with fine notes of fruit, bitter hints and marked citrus acidity.

AZUMBRE VERDEJO VENDIMIA SELECCIONADA 2003 WHITE
100% verdejo

86 Brilliant pale yellow. Intense, very fine and varietal aroma (fruit and white flowers, tropical hints, herbs). Fresh, flavourful palate with very varietal bitter notes, slightly warm with good acidity.

CUATRO RAYAS VERDEJO 2003 WHITE SECO
VELITERRA 2003 WHITE SECO
PAMPANO 2003 WHITE SEMISECO
PALACIO DE VIVERO 2003 WHITE SECO
VACCEOS TEMPRANILLO 2003 JOVEN RED
VACCEOS 2003 CRIANZA RED

AGRONANCLARES

San Judas, 2
47491 La Seca (Valladolid)
☎: 983 816 669 - Fax: 983 816 639

Established: 1990

🛢 1,000,000 litres 🍇 104 has.

🍷 60% (🍇40%: -DE

HEREDEROS DE DON AGUSTÍN NANCLARES RUEDA VERDEJO 2003 JOVEN WHITE
85% verdejo, 15% viura

84 Pale with greenish nuances. Slightly intense aroma of white fruit (exotic hint) with hints of wit-

hered petals. Fresh, flavourful palate with very varietal fine bitter notes and fine toasty skins.

ORDEN TERCERA RUEDA 2003 WHITE
HEREDEROS DE DON AGUSTÍN NANCLARES RUEDA 2003 WHITE
HEREDEROS DE DON AGUSTÍN NANCLARES SAUVIGNON BLANC 2003 WHITE

ALDOR

Carretera Renedo-Pesquera, km. 30
47359 Valbuena de Duero (Valladolid)
☎: 983 107 100 - Fax: 983 107 104
aclavero@matarromera.com
www.matarromera.com

ALDOR 2003 WHITE
100% verdejo

86 Pale yellow with a golden hue. Powerful aroma of very varietal fruit with fine hints of herbs. Fresh, flavourful palate with rich bitter notes and excellent acidity.

ÁLVAREZ Y DÍEZ

Juan Antonio Carmona, 12
28020 Nava del Rey (Valladolid)
☎: 983 850 136 - Fax: 983 850 761
bodegas@alvarezydiez.com
www.alvarezydiez.com

Established: 1941

🛢 1,500,000 litres 🍇 75 has.

🍷 70% (🍇30%

MANTEL BLANCO 2003 JOVEN WHITE
85% verdejo, 15% viura

86 Pale gold with a greenish hue. Powerful, ripe aroma of fruit and white flowers with fine exotic notes of lees. Powerful, flavourful palate with very varietal bitter notes and marked citrus acidity.

MANTEL BLANCO SAUVIGNON BLANC 2003 JOVEN WHITE
100% sauvignon blanc

88 Pale yellow with a greenish glint. Intense aroma with a fine varietal expression, white fruit (exotic hints) and notes of flowers and fine herbs. Very fresh and fruity palate with citrus notes (limes) and excellent acidity.

MANTEL BLANCO 2001 FERMENTADO EN BARRICA WHITE
100% verdejo

89 Straw-coloured with a golden glimmer. Aroma of ripe fruit and fine smoky wood. Fresh, fruity palate with a smoky, creamy retronasal effect, flavourful and persistent.

DO RUEDA

ÁNGEL LORENZO CACHAZO

Estación, 53
47220 Pozaldes (Valladolid)
☎: 983 822 481 - Fax: 983 822 012
bodegamartivilli@jet.es
www.martivilli.com

Established: 1988

▦ 500,000 litres ❦ 25 has ⚘ 85% ◔15%

MARTIVILLÍ SAUVIGNON BLANC 2003 FERMENTADO EN BARRICA WHITE
100% sauvignon blanc

79 Pale with golden nuances. Slightly intense aroma with a certain varietal fruit expression (partially concealed by the alcohol). Flavourful palate with fine bitter notes, slightly warm and oily.

MARTIVILLÍ 2002 FERMENTADO EN BARRICA WHITE
100% verdejo

86 Pale gold. Slightly intense aroma of white stone fruit, with well-integrated smoky oak and fine lees. Flavourful, slightly fleshy and warm on the palate, with fine herbs, hints of citrus fruit and ripe fruit, good acidity.

LORENZO CACHAZO 2003 WHITE
50% viura, 50% verdejo

78 Pale. Slightly intense aroma of white fruit. Fresh, flavourful palate with bitter notes and quality citrus fruit.

MARTIVILLÍ VERDEJO 2003 WHITE
100% verdejo

88 Pale with greenish nuances. Powerful, very fine aroma of white fruit (exotic hints), and fine notes of flowers and herbs. Flavourful palate with very varietal fruity and bitter notes, excellent acidity, and spicy hints of skins.

MARTIVILLÍ RESERVA BRUT

80 Pale gold with fine beads. Intense aroma with ripe white fruit (exotic hints), hints of withered petals

and honey. Fresh and dry on the palate with bitter notes (herbs, nuts); lacking crianza expression.

LORENZO CACHAZO 2002 JOVEN ROSÉ
LORENZO CACHAZO 2002 JOVEN RED
CACHAZO 2000 CRIANZA RED

ÁNGEL RODRÍGUEZ VIDAL

Torcido, 1
47491 La Seca (Valladolid)
☎: 983 816 302 - Fax: 983 816 302

Established: 1780
▦ 300,000 litres ❦ 60 has.

MARTINSANCHO RUEDA SUPERIOR WHITE

ANTAÑO

Arribas, 7-9
47490 Rueda (Valladolid)
☎: 983 868 533 - Fax: 983 868 514
info@bodegas-antano.com
www.bodegas-antano.com

Established: 1989

⊕ 3,000 ▦ 3,000,000 litres ❦ 250 has.

⚘ 80% ◔20%: -DE -BE -CH -SE -IE -JP -US -CY -NL -DK

VIÑA MOCÉN VERDEJO 2000 FERMENTADO EN BARRICA WHITE
100% verdejo

86 Pale with a coppery hue. Powerful aroma of white stone fruit with hints of peach skins and fragrant herbs. Flavourful, fresh palate with fine notes of fruit, bitter hints and good acidity.

VIÑA MOCÉN SAUVIGNON BLANC 2003 WHITE
100% sauvignon blanc

87 Brilliant golden yellow. Powerful, ripe aroma with predominant exotic fruit notes (bananas, pineapples, guava) and fine herbs. Flavourful palate with fine notes of fruit and bitterness and marked citrus acidity.

VEGA BRAVÍA 2002 RED
85% tempranillo, 15% cabernet sauvignon

80 Dark cherry with a purplish edge. Powerful aroma of toasty oak with hints of earth and a suggestion of jammy fruit. Flavourful palate with quite marked tannins (notes of greeness), bitter.

COBRANZA VENDIMIA SELECCIONADA 2001 OAK AGED RED
100% tempranillo   ⊕ 16

89 Very dark cherry. Powerful aroma with predominant toasty oak notes and a suggestion of underbrush. Powerful, concentrated palate, with slightly marked but very promising tannins, fine bitter notes and excellent acidity.

VIÑA COBRANZA 2000 CRIANZA RED
85% tempranillo, 15% cabernet sauvignon

84 Dark cherry with a coppery-brick red edge. Powerful aroma with predominant smoky (cedar), and fine reduction notes with a notion of terroir. Flavourful palate with slightly marked but promising tannins, bitter.

VIÑA COBRANZA 1998 RESERVA RED
85% tempranillo, 15% cabernet sauvignon

85 Dark garnet red cherry with a coppery edge. Powerful aroma with predominant spicy and reduction notes (leather, cigar box) and a suggestion of jammy fruit. Flavourful, smoky palate with fine spicy notes and a good Reserva expression.

ALTA PLATA RUEDA 2003 JOVEN WHITE
VIÑA MOCÉN RUEDA 2003 JOVEN WHITE
VIÑA MOCÉN VERDEJO 2003 JOVEN WHITE
ANTAÑO CHARDONNAY 2000 WHITE
ALTA PLATA VERDEJO 2003 WHITE
VEGA BRAVÍA 2003 JOVEN ROSÉ
VEGA BRAVÍA 2003 JOVEN ROSÉ
MONTESTRELLA 1999 RED
VIÑA COBRANZA 1996 GRAN RESERVA RED

AURA

Autovía del Noroeste, km. 175
47490 Rueda (Valladolid)
☎: 983 868 286 - Fax: 983 868 168
mgonzalo@byb.es
www.byb.es
Established: 1990
⊞ 102 ▤ 578,000 litres ▒ 32 has.

AURA VENDIMIA SELECCIONADA 2002 FERMENTADO EN BARRICA WHITE
100% sauvignon blanc

87 Pale with golden nuances. Powerful aroma with predominant spicy and creamy oak notes, a suggestion of ripe white fruit and hints of flowers and herbs. Flavourful palate with ripe fruit and hints of exotic fruit, fine bitter notes and hints of smokiness and herbs in the retronasal passage, spicy notes.

AURA VERDEJO 2003 WHITE
98% verdejo, 2% sauvignon blanc

85 Pale yellow with golden nuances. Powerful aroma of ripe white stone fruit with the freshness of citrus fruit and fresh herbs and fine toasty skins. Flavourful palate with fine spicy notes of ripe fruit, excellent acidity.

BELONDRADE

Quinta San Diego. Camino del Puerto
47491 La Seca (Valladolid)
☎: 983 481 001 - Fax: 600 590 024
belondrade@vodafone.es
Established: 1994
⊞ 223 ▤ 70,000 litres ▒ 13 has.
▨ 70% ⏺30%: -JP -US -UK -CH -DK -FR -PR -IT -BE

BELONDRADE Y LURTON 2002 FERMENTADO EN BARRICA WHITE
100% verdejo

89 Lively golden. Elegant aroma with ripe fruit and somewhat excessive smoky oak that hides the fruit expression. Fresh and fruity on the palate; better than in the nose, full, creamy, flavourful and spirituous in the retronasal passage.

BUIL & GINÉ

Apdo. de Correo 63
43730 Falset (Tarragona)
☎: 977 830 483 - Fax: 977 830 373
esther@builgine.com
www.builgine.com
Established: 1996

NOSIS 2003 JOVEN WHITE
100% verdejo

86 Pale yellow with a golden hue. Powerful aroma of white fruit with light tropical notes (pineapples, limes) and fine herbs. Flavourful palate with fine bitter notes and excellent citrus acidity.

Bodegas CASTELO DE MEDINA

Villaverde de Medina
47465 (Valladolid)
☎: 983 831 932 - Fax: 983 831 857
castelodemedina@yahoo.es
Established: 1995
⊞ 500 ▤ 1,100,000 litres ▒ 160 has.
▨ 70% ⏺30%: -UK -DE -NL -CH -FR -DK -BE -CA -US -MX -PR

CASTELO DE MEDINA SAUVIGNON 2003 JOVEN WHITE
100% sauvignon blanc

86 Pale gold. Intense aroma of ripe white stone fruit with fine exotic notes and fine herbs. Flavourful, fresh palate with excellent fruit-alcohol-acidity symmetry, a slight varietal expression and hints of aniseed, long.

CASTELO DE MEDINA VERDEJO 2003 JOVEN WHITE
100% verdejo

86 Brilliant pale with lemony nuances. Powerful aroma of ripe white fruit with exotic notes (pineapple, passion fruit) and fine notes of herbs. Powerful, flavourful, slightly oily palate with jammy hints and somewhat scarce acidity.

REAL CASTELO 2003 JOVEN WHITE
85% verdejo, 10% sauvignon blanc, 5% viura

88 Pale with brilliant nuances. Intense aroma of great finesse with excellent varietal expression (green fruit, exotic hints, fine herbs). Flavourful, well-balanced palate with fine bitter notes, spicy hints of skins, herbs and excellent acidity.

CASTELO NOBLE 2001 FERMENTADO EN BARRICA WHITE
85% verdejo, 15% sauvignon blanc

83 Brilliant golden yellow. Powerful aroma with predominant smoky and creamy oak notes with a suggestion of somewhat exotic ripe fruit (pineapple). Flavourful, creamy palate with drying and vanilla notes of oak.

CASTELO ÁMBAR 2003 WHITE SEMIDULCE
100% sauvignon blanc

84 Greenish straw. Intense aroma with a fresh Sauvignon character (grapefruit, green fruit). Flavourful, fresh, very lively palate with well-balanced sweetness and acidity and green grass in the finish.

CASTELO DE MEDINA 2000 CRIANZA RED
tempranillo, cabernet sauvignon

79 Cherry with an orangey hue. Aroma of vanilla, toasty and spicy with jammy tomatoes. Dry wood tannins on the palate, fruity and balsamic (resins).

VEGA BUSIEL 2000 CRIANZA RED
tempranillo, cabernet sauvignon

82 Garnet red cherry with a saffron edge. Intense aroma with predominant spicy oak notes and a balsamic nuance. Flavourful palate with fleshy overtones, slightly drying tannins and and rich bitter notes.

CASTELO BURGO 2002 BRUT NATURE
100% verdejo

79 Brilliant yellow with a fine persistent bead. Intense aroma with a certain finesse, ripe white fruit hints of herbs and fine lees. Flavourful palate with bitter notes, citrus fruits, fresh fruit and hints of not very fine yeast in the retronasal passage.

CASTELO DE LA DEHESA 2003 WHITE
VEGA BUSIEL 2002 RED
VEGA BUSIEL 2000 RESERVA RED
CASTELO DE MEDINA 2000 RESERVA RED

Bodegas CERROSOL

Camino Villagonzalo, s/n
40460 Santituste de San Juan Bautista (Segovia)
☎: 921 596 002 - Fax: 921 596 035
fernandovegas@avelinovegas.com
www.avelinovegas.com

Established: 1985

🍷 200 ⬛ 3,500,000 litres 🍇 80%

🌐20%: -US -CA -MX -PR -DO -BR -PE -UK -SE -FI -NL -BE -DE -CZ -AT

DOÑA BEATRIZ VERDEJO 2002 FERMENTADO EN BARRICA WHITE
100% verdejo

87 Golden yellow. Powerful aroma of smoky oak notes, lees and fine ripe fruit (apples). Flavourful, slightly warm palate with notes of nuts, mountain herbs and a smoky retronasal effect.

DOÑA BEATRIZ SAUVIGNON 2003 WHITE
100% sauvignon blanc

87 Brilliant gold. Powerful aroma of ripe and very varietal fruit (apricots, flowers, exotic hints). Flavourful, fruity palate with fine bitter notes, spicy, slightly warm and oily with excellent acidity.

DOÑA BEATRIZ VERDEJO 2003 WHITE
100% verdejo

84 Yellow straw. Intense, fine aroma of tropical fruit with a nuance of green grass evoking freshness. Flavourful palate with hay and ripe fresh fruit, expressive.

DOÑA BEATRIZ VERDEJO VIURA 2003 WHITE
50% verdejo, 50% viura

82 Straw-coloured with a greenish hue. Medium-intensity aroma of ripe fruit (tropical fruits). Oily, ripe palate with good expression.

VALLE DE LA VEGA 2003 WHITE
50% verdejo, 50% viura

83 Brilliant golden yellow. Quite intense aroma with a good expression of slightly varietal and exotic white fruit and hints of herbs. Flavourful, fresh, fruity palate with notes of crystallised fruit and fine bitter notes.

VALLE DE LA VEGA SAUVIGNON 2003 WHITE
100% sauvignon blanc

85 Straw-coloured with a greenish hue. Intense, fresh aroma of grapefruit and green grass, powerful. Oily, flavourful, very fresh palate with an excellent fruit expression, very varietal and long.

VALLE DE LA VEGA 2003 WHITE
100% verdejo

85 Brilliant gold. Intense aroma of fruit and white flowers with exotic hints and fragrant herbs. Flavourful, fruity palate with very varietal, spicy and bitter hints, excellent acidity.

Bodegas de CRIANZA DE CASTILLA LA VIEJA

Carretera Madrid-Coruña km. 170, 6
47490 Rueda (Valladolid)
☎: 983 868 116 - Fax: 983 868 432
bodegasbccv@interbook.net
www.bodegasdecastilla.com

Established: 1976

🏛 883 📖 3,000,000 litres 🍷 200 has.

🍷 63% 🍇37%: -UK -NL -BE -DE -DK -AT -CH -US -IE -HU -JP -IT -PL

BORNOS SAUVIGNON BLANC 2003 JOVEN WHITE
100% sauvignon blanc

86 Straw-coloured. Intense aroma of grapefruit, ripe fruit and hay. Flavourful, powerful, fresh palate with notes of herbs and expressive fruit, varietal and quite persistent.

PALACIOS DE BORNOS VERDEJO 2003 WHITE
100% verdejo

89 Straw-coloured with a greenish nuance. Powerful, varietal aroma of fennel, lavender and ripe fruit, expressive. Oily, generous, flavourful and very Verdejo palate with pleasant bitter notes, long.

BORNOS SAUVIGNON BLANC 2003 WHITE
sauvignon blanc

88 Pale with greenish nuances. Powerful aroma of aniseed and white fruit with notes of hay and jammy tropical fruit (pineaple). Flavourful palate with fine bitter and bittersweet notes, refreshing acidity.

EXXENCIA 1999 WHITE DULCE
100% verdejo

89 Ambery gold. Powerful, complex aroma of crystallised fruit with an aniseed nuance and new wood. Flavourful and unctuous on the palate with notes of botrytis, reminiscent fresh fruit and pleasant bitter hints in the finish.

PALACIO DE BORNOS SAUVIGNON BLANC VENDIMIA SELECCIONADA 2002 WHITE
sauvignon blanc

86 Greenish straw. Intense aroma of fine wood (smokiness) with a ripe fruit hint (tropical fruits). Flavourful, oily palate with powerful toasty wood yet to be assembled, fresh acidity.

PALACIO DE BORNOS VERDEJO VENDIMIA SELECCIONADA 2000 WHITE
100% verdejo

88 Golden with a greenish nuance. Intense aroma of quince with honeyed and smoky notes, a citrus fruit and herby hint and a good reduction. Unctuous, flavourful palate with smoky notes, lively, with good acidity.

SEÑORÍO DE ILLESCAS 1999 CRIANZA RED
100% tempranillo

79 Garnet red cherry with a purplish edge. Intense, fruity aroma with toasty notes of oak, skins and a varietal character (damp earth). Flavourful palate with predominant fruit notes, slightly sweet, oily and liquorice hints.

PALACIO DE BORNOS BRUT NATURE
50% verdejo, 50% viura

76 Brilliant pale yellow. Intense, fresh and fruity aroma (green apples, exotic hints) and hints of fine herbs. Fresh palate with rich bittersweet notes, without great Crianza expression.

BORNOS SEMIDULCE 2003 JOVEN WHITE
COLAGON RUEDA 2003 JOVEN WHITE
PALACIO DE BORNOS VERDEJO 2003 FERMENTADO EN BARRICA WHITE
PALACIO DE BORNOS BRUT

CUEVAS DE CASTILLA

Carretera Madrid-Coruña, km. 171
47490 Rueda (Valladolid)
☎: 983 868 336 - Fax: 983 868 432
bodegasbccv@interbook.net
www.bodegasdecastilla.com

Established: 1986

📖 1,500,000 litres 🍷 200 has.

🍷 70% 🍇30%: -UK -NL -BE -DE -DK -AT -CH -US -SE

CON CLASS 2003 JOVEN WHITE
60% verdejo, 40% viura

79 Brilliant pale. Intense aroma of ripe white fruit, exotic hints, hints of flowers and fine herbs. Flavourful, fruity palate with a slightly oily, warm texture.

PALACIO DE MENADE SAUVIGNON BLANC 2003 JOVEN WHITE
100% sauvignon blanc

87 Pale with a greenish nuance. Intense aroma of grapefruit, passion fruit, fresh fruit and green grass. Flavourful, varietal and fresh palate with pleasantly bitter notes.

RUEDA
DENOMINACIÓN DE ORIGEN

PALACIO DE MENADE

COSECHA 2003

EMBOTELLADO PARA CUEVAS DE CASTILLA, S.A.
POR R.E. 5695-VA - RUEDA (VALLADOLID)
75 cl
12,5% vol
Producto de España

PALACIO DE MENADE VERDEJO 2003 WHITE
90% verdejo, 8% viura, 2% sauvignon blanc

85 Greenish straw. Intense, fresh, varietal aroma of fresh fruit and fennel. Flavourful, fresh palate of ripe fruit and hay with pleasantly bitter notes in the finish.

DELISPAIN

Fray Pedro Payo Piñeño, 17 bajo
15009 A Coruña (A Coruña)
☎: 670 522 577 - Fax: 881 924 492
delispain@delispain.com
www.delispain.com

VEGA SUPERATU VERDEJO 2003 WHITE
100% verdejo

79 Straw-coloured with brilliant golden nuances. Powerful, ripe aroma with a good varietal fruit expression (exotic hints). Flavourful, slightly warm and oily on the palate with ripe fruit and notes of herbs.

VEGA SUPERATU TINTA FINA 2002 CRIANZA RED
100% tinto fino

80 Intense cherry with a purplish edge. Powerful aroma of black fruit with hints of macerated skins, slightly warm. Flavourful, fleshy palate with fine fruity notes partially concealed by the alcohol and a spicy hint.

Bodegas y Viñas DOS VICTORIAS

Juan Mora, s/n
47530 San Román de Hornija (Valladolid)
☎: 983 784 029 - Fax: 983 784 029
info@dosvictorias.com

www.dos victorias.com

Established: 1998

🍷 450 📊 200,000 litres 🍇 16 has.

🇪🇸 60% 🌐40%: -DE -UK -IE -SE -BE -DK -IT -FI -AT - US

JOSÉ PARIENTE 2003 JOVEN WHITE
100% verdejo

91 Straw-coloured. Powerful aroma with maceration notes, sweet fruit (passion fruit) and fragrant herbs. Fresh, flavourful palate, rich in nuances with excellent green fruit, freshness and persistence.

VIÑAS ELÍAS MORA 2002 OAK AGED RED
100% tinta de toro   🛢5

85 Very dark cherry. Powerful aroma of black fruit, prunes (a light reduction note) with a slight varietal expression (damp earth) and toasty oak. Flavourful palate with slightly rough tannins; spicy and bitter (pitch, liquorice), long with cocoa and jammy fruit.

FÉLIX LORENZO CACHAZO

Carretera Medina del campo, km. 9
47220 Pozáldez (Valladolid)
☎: 983 822 008 - Fax: 983 822 008
bodegas@cachazo.com
www.cachazo.com

Established: 1945

🍷 120 📊 800,000 litres 🇪🇸 85% 🌐15%: -DE -NL -BE -DK -FR

CARRASVIÑAS VERDEJO 2003 WHITE
100% verdejo

84 Greenish straw. Intense, varietal aroma of white fruit and fennel, fresh. Flavourful, fresh palate with good fruit expression, lemony notes and lively acidity.

GRAN CARDIEL RUEDA VERDEJO 2003 WHITE
100% verdejo

86 Brilliant pale. Powerful, fruity aroma (exotic touches) and fine herbs. Fresh palate with a light carbonic touch, bitter notes of citrus fruits and good acidity.

CARRASVIÑAS 2002 FERMENTADO EN BARRICA WHITE
GRAN CARDIEL 2003 JOVEN WHITE
LARRUA RUEDA 2003 JOVEN WHITE
LARRUA RUEDA 2003 JOVEN WHITE

Bodegas FÉLIX SANZ

Ronda Aradillas, s/n
47490 Rueda (Valladolid)
☎: 983 868 044 - Fax: 983 868 133

info@bodegasfelixsanz.es
www.bodegasfelixsanz.es

Established: 1934

🏭 260 🛢 400,000 litres 🍇 30 has.

🍷 95% 🌐5%: -US -NL -CH -UK -DE -FI

VIÑA CIMBRÓN RUEDA 2003 JOVEN WHITE
50% verdejo, 50% viura

78 Pale with greenish nuances. Intense, ripe, fruity aroma (hints of melon) with a certain citrus freshness. Flavourful palate with fresh fruit, fine bitter notes and citrus fruit.

VIÑA CIMBRÓN RUEDA SAUVIGNON 2003 JOVEN WHITE
100% sauvignon blanc

80 Pale golden yellow. Intense aroma of quite varietal fresh fruit (green fruit, exotic and floral hints). Flavourful palate with ripe fruit, a slightly oily texture and a toasty suggestion of skins.

VIÑA CIMBRÓN RUEDA VERDEJO 2003 JOVEN WHITE
85% verdejo, 15% viura

78 Brilliant pale. Slightly intense aroma of white stone fruit with hints of flowers and citrus fruit. Flavourful palate with bitter notes; lacking fruit expression, but with good acidity.

VIÑA CIMBRÓN VERDEJO 2001 FERMENTADO EN BARRICA WHITE
100% verdejo

71 Golden. Intense aroma with predominant smoky wood notes. Quite flavourful palate, fruit expression subdued by the oak and warm notes.

FÉLIX SOLÍS

Autovía de Andalucía, km. 199
13300 Valdepeñas (Ciudad Real)
☎: 926 322 400 - Fax: 926 322 417
bfs@felixsolis.com
www.felixsolis.com

Established: 1952

🏭 40,000 🛢 192,000,000 litres 🍇 500 has.

🍷 62% 🌐38%: -UK -DE -NL -DK -FI -SE -BE -GQ -CH TG -MX -BE -AT -JP -PH -NC -DO -US -AO Tahiti -CA -CO -SE -DK -CZ -DZ -PE -VE -IT -LU -CF -PA -KE CM -VN -TW -LB -GT -MY CD -SG -EC -BR -JO -GA TZ -CR -EL -AU -SV -SB -GM -IE -NI -PT

ANALIVIA 2003 JOVEN WHITE

80 Pale yellow with a golden glint. Intense, ripe aroma of white stone fruit, oily hints and a spicy nuance of skins. Fresh and flavourful on the palate with fine bitter notes and good acidity.

ANALIVIA VERDEJO 2003 JOVEN WHITE
verdejo

82 Straw-coloured. Medium-intensity aroma with tropical fruit and hay. Flavourful, intense palate with ripe fruit and hay and good acidity, quite persistent.

GARCI GRANDE

Aradillas, s/n
47490 Rueda (Valladolid)
☎: 983 868 561 - Fax: 983 868 449

Established: 1989

🏭 515 🛢 1,000,000 litres 🍇 40 has.

🍷 95% 🌐5%

ANIER VERDEJO VENDIMIA SELECCIONADA 2003 WHITE
100% verdejo

85 Pale yellow with greenish nuances. Powerful aroma with fine spicy notes of skins, green fruit, minerals and citrus fruit. Fresh, flavourful palate with very varietal bitter notes, hints of herbs and good acidity.

SEÑORÍO DE GARCI GRANDE RUEDA 2003 WHITE
verdejo, viura

76 Pale. Slightly intense aroma of ripe white fruit with exotic hints. Flavourful palate with a citrus and bitter freshness, slightly warm.

SEÑORÍO DE GARCI GRANDE SAUVIGNON BLANC 2003 WHITE
100% sauvignon blanc

75 Pale with brilliant golden nuances. Intense aroma of ripe white fruit, exotic hints and slightly warm notes. Fresh, flavourful palate of fruity notes, bitter hints (herbs) and an acidic edge.

SEÑORÍO DE GARCI GRANDE VERDEJO 2003 WHITE
100% verdejo

80 Pale yellow. Slightly intense aroma with light varietal freshness. Flavourful palate with bitter notes, quality herbs, a suggestion of citrus fruit and good acidity.

SEÑORÍO DE GARCI GRANDE 2003 ROSÉ

78 Brilliant deep raspberry. Intense aroma of red fruit with sweet and spicy hints of skins. Fresh palate with forest fruit, bitter notes of citrus fruit and an acidic edge.

VIÑA TORÍO 1999 CRIANZA RED

80 Dark cherry with a brick red edge. Powerful aroma with predominant toasty oak notes and reduction hints (tobacco). Flavourful, fleshy palate with a good fruit/oak integration, slightly warm.

GARCÍAREVALO

Pza. San Juan, 4
47230 Matapozuelos (Valladolid)

DO RUEDA

☎: 983 832 914 - Fax: 983 832 986
garciarevalo@garciarevalo.com

Established: 1991

🌐 100 📊 500,000 litres 🍇 80 has.

🍷 80% 🌐20%: -UK -NL -BE -DE

CASAMARO 2003 WHITE
50% verdejo, 50% viura

75 Brilliant pale. Slightly intense, fruity aroma with floral hints. Fresh, flavourful palate with bitter, citrus notes and a slightly acidic edge.

TRES OLMOS 2003 WHITE
100% verdejo

79 Pale green. Slightly intense aroma with green fruit notes and hints of quite varietal spices and fennel. Flavourful, fresh and bitter on the palate with a slightly acidic edge.

VIÑA ADAJA 2003 WHITE
100% verdejo

87 Pale with greenish nuances. Intense aroma of ripe fruit with a good varietal character (pineapple, herbs). Flavourful palate with a certain spicy freshness, bitter notes and excellent acidity.

TRES CANTOS 2003 WHITE
TRES OLMOS 2003 JOVEN RED
LA TORREVIEJA 1998 CRIANZA RED

HERMANOS DEL VILLAR

Zarcillo, s/n
47490 Rueda (Valladolid)
☎: 983 868 904 - Fax: 983 868 905
hvillar@infonegocio.com
www.orodecastilla.com

Established: 1995

🌐 150 📊 350,000 litres 🍇 102 has.

🍷 76% 🌐24%

ORO DE CASTILLA 2003 FERMENTADO EN BARRICA WHITE
verdejo

83 Brilliant pale. Intense, fresh aroma of green fruit and fine lees with hints of citrus fruit (sweet limes) and smoky oak. Flavourful palate with slightly noticeable oak tannins, creamy notes integrated with the fruit and fine herbs in the retronasal passage.

ORO DE CASTILLA SAUVIGNON BLANC 2003 WHITE
100% sauvignon blanc

80 Pale. Slightly short aroma with a certain varietal freshness (pineapple, grapefruit). Fresh palate with rich bitter notes and an acidic edge.

ORO DE CASTILLA VERDEJO 2003 WHITE
100% verdejo

83 Pale yellow. Intense aroma with predominant smoky notes of skins, herbs and a slightly mineral hint. Flavourful, fresh, bitter and slightly warm on the palate, lacking fruit expression.

Bodegas HIJOS DE ALBERTO GUTIÉRREZ

Carretera de Valdestillas, 2
47239 Serrada (Valladolid)
☎: 983 559 107 - Fax: 983 559 084
aguti@losalbertos.com
www.losalbertos.com

Established: 1949

🌐 1,600 📊 15,000,000 litres 🍇 250 has.

🍷 50% 🌐50%: -DE Escandinavia -NL KR -BE -LT -US -UK

MONASTERIO DE PALAZUELOS 2003 WHITE
100% verdejo

83 Pale straw. Medium intensity, clean, varietal, fresh aroma of grapefruit and herbs. Flavourful palate with hay with a herby complexity, well-balanced and pleasant.

MONASTERIO DE PALAZUELOS 2003 ROSÉ
100% tempranillo

82 Brilliant raspberry. Intense, fresh aroma of red fruit with sweet hints and quality citrus fruits. Fresh, fruity palate with fine notes of spices and citrus fruit.

MONASTERIO DE PALAZUELOS 2001 CRIANZA RED
80% tempranillo, 20% cabernet sauvignon

81 Deep cherry. Spicy aroma (pepper) of ripe black fruit and a suggestion of sun-drenched skins. Fleshy palate with flavourful yet bitter tannins; a dry woody finish.

MONASTERIO DE PALAZUELOS 2003 WHITE
MONASTERIO DE PALAZUELOS 2003 RED
MONASTERIO DE PALAZUELOS 1999
RESERVA RED

J. & F. LURTON

Mostenses, 4
47400 Medina del Campo (Valladolid)
☎: 983 850 025 - Fax: 983 850 025
jflurton@jflurton.com
www.jflurton.com

HERMANOS LURTON WHITE

J. GARCÍA CARRIÓN

Joint-Venture con Agrícola Castellana
47491 La Seca (Valladolid)
☎: 914 355 556 - Fax: 915 766 607
tonig@jgc.es
www.vinosdefamilia.com

SOLAR DE LA VEGA VENDIMIA
SELECCIONADA 2003 WHITE
60% verdejo, 40% viura

74 Straw-coloured with a greenish hue. Slightly short but clean and fruity aroma. Slightly flabby palate, well-mannered but without great fruit expression.

SOLAR DE LA VEGA VERDEJO 2003 WHITE
100% verdejo

80 Straw-coloured with a greenish hue. Not very intense yet clean, fresh, citrus fruit aroma (grape-

fruit). Fresh, fruity palate, good acidity and well-mannered.

JAVIER SANZ VITICULTOR

Santiago Sanz, 24
47491 La Seca (Valladolid)
☎: 983 816 669 - Fax: 983 816 639
bodega@jsviticultor.com
www.jsviticultor.com

Established: 1990

🛢 200 📊 1,000,000 litres 🍇 104 has.

🍷 50% 🍇50%: -US -MX -PR -JP -RU - DE -BE -NL -UK -CH -DK

VILLA NARCISA VERDEJO 2003 WHITE
100% verdejo

80 Brilliant pale. Slightly intense aroma with predominant notes of oak, spicy skins and a suggestion of fresh fruit. Fresh, flavourful and fruity on the palate with bitter notes, slightly warm and oily.

VILLA NARCISA FERMENTADO EN BARRICA
 WHITE
VILLA NARCISA SAUVIGNON BLANC 2003
 JOVEN WHITE
REY SANTO 2003 JOVEN WHITE
VILLA NARCISA 1997 RESERVA RED
JAVIER SANZ VITICULTOR 1998 RESERVA
 RED

MARQUÉS DE IRÚN

Nueva, 7-9
47491 La Seca (Valladolid)
☎: 956 851 711 - Fax: 956 853 462
mirun@marquesdeirun.es

Established: 1990

🛢 100 🍇 60 has. 🍷 90% 🍇10%

MARQUÉS DE IRÚN VERDEJO 2003 WHITE
100% verdejo

81 Pale yellow with a greenish hue. Intense aroma of ripe white fruit with hints of flowers and fragrant herbs. Flavourful, bitter palate with marked acidity, lacking fruit expression (hint of slightly green bananas).

MARQUÉS DE VELILLA

Carretera de Sotillo, s/n
09311 La Horra (Burgos)
☎: 947 542 166 - Fax: 947 542 165
central@marquesdevelilla.es
www.marquesdevelilla.es

Established: 1985

🛢 4,500 📊 1,250,000 litres 🍇 200 has.

🍷 60% 🍇40%: -DE -CH -UK -SE -BE -FR -RU -BR -EC -US -PR -DK -JP -AT -AU -CU

CATALINA DE MERCADO 2003 FERMENTADO EN BARRICA WHITE

MONTE PEDROSO RICARDO RODRÍGUEZ

Hospital s/n
47491 La Seca (Valladolid)
☎: 983 816 572 - Fax: 983 816 572
wedlirondo@mixmail.com

Established: 2000
🛢 30 🛢 5,000 litres 🇪🇸 100%

LIRONDO 2001 FERMENTADO EN BARRICA WHITE

Bodegas PEDRO ESCUDERO

Carretera Pozaldez, s/n
47491 La Seca (Valladolid)
☎: 983 816 616 - Fax: 983 816 616
bodegasescudero@wanadoo.es

Established: 2002
🛢 30 🛢 281,900 litres 🍇 32 has.
🍷 70% 🍇30%: -CA -US -DE -BE -CH -UK

FUENTE ELVIRA VERDEJO 2003 FERMENTADO EN BARRICA WHITE
100% verdejo

87 Pale with greenish nuances. Intense, very fine aroma of very varietal fruit notes (green fruit, fragrant herbs) with a nuance of citrus fruit. Fresh, flavourful palate with excellent fruit-acidity balance, fine bitter notes and good acidity.

VALDECHIMOZA VERDEJO 2003 WHITE
85% verdejo, 15% viura

75 Pale yellow with greenish nuances. Intense, fruity aroma, with smoky skins and notes of dried herbs. Flavourful, fruity aroma; slightly warm and oily.

VALDELAINOS VERDEJO 2003 WHITE
85% verdejo, 15% viura

78 Pale with brilliant golden nuances. Intense, fruity aroma with exotic hints (bananas) and hints of hay. Fresh, flavourful palate with quality bittersweet notes and good acidity.

PREDIO DE VASCARLÓN

Carretera Rueda s/n
47491 La Seca (Valladolid)
☎: 983 816 325 - Fax: 983 816 326

Established: 2003

🛢 500,000 litres 🍇 100 has.

ATELIER 2003 JOVEN WHITE
100% verdejo

83 Straw-coloured with a greenish hue. Intense aroma of grapefruits, hay and citrus fruit, very fresh with a hint of fennel. Notes of bitter fruit on the palate (grapefruit), quite structured but fresh, long.

ATELIER 2003 JOVEN WHITE

Vinos SANZ

Carretera Madrid-La Coruña, km. 170, 5
47490 Rueda (Valladolid)
☎: 983 868 100 - Fax: 983 868 117
vinossanz@vinossanz.com
www.vinossanz.es

Established: 1870
🛢 1,000,000 litres 🍇 100 has.
🍷 80% 🍇20%: -DE -FI -BE -NL USA -UK -MX -CH -CV -IE

SANZ SAUVIGNON 2003 WHITE
100% sauvignon blanc

89 Straw-coloured. Fresh, fruity and mineral aroma (grind stone). Generous, flavourful, fresh and very varietal palate, excellent Rueda Sauvignon without tropical sensations.

SANZ CLÁSICO 2003 FERMENTADO EN BARRICA WHITE
85% verdejo, 15% viura

87 Straw-coloured. Fresh, fruity aroma with complex overtones. Light, flavourful palate with a mild expression of green herbs and fresh fruit.

SANZ RUEDA VERDEJO 2003 WHITE
85% verdejo, 15% viura

88 Straw-coloured. Powerful, fruity, fresh and varietal aroma. Fruity palate with carbonic traces, flavourful with a bitter finish and considerable typification.

FINCA LA COLINA 2003 WHITE
100% sauvignon blanc

90 Straw-coloured. Aroma with notes of ripe fruit with a suggestion of minerals, fresh and complex. Generous, full, original palate with hints of mineral Sauvignon (pebbles), fine, flavourful and persistent.

SANZ RUEDA 2003 WHITE

Bodegas SEÑORÍO DE NAVA

Carretera Valladolid - Soria, s/n
09813 Nava de Roa (Burgos)
☎: 987 209 790 - Fax: 987 209 800
snava@senoriodenava.es
www.senoriodenava.es

Established: 1986

📦 3,046 🛢 2,454,000 litres 🍇 120 has.

🍷 87% 🌍13%: -CA -US -SE -CH -DK -DE -RU -LU -LT -BE -PE -VE -HK

VAL DE LAMAS RUEDA 2003 WHITE
50% verdejo, 50% viura

80 Pale with golden nuances. Not very intense aroma of ripe white fruit. Flavourful palate rich in ripe fruit nuances with hints of bitterness, herbs and good acidity.

VAL DE LAMAS RUEDA VERDEJO 2003 WHITE
85% verdejo, 15% viura

79 Brilliant pale. Not very intense aroma with fruit notes partially concealed by the alcohol and hints of herbs. Flavourful palate with fine bitter notes; slightly oily and warm.

VAL DE LAMAS VERDEJO-SAUVIGNON 2003 WHITE
50% verdejo, 50% sauvignon blanc

77 Brilliant straw. Not very intense aroma with ripe fruit, exotic hints and withered petals. Fresh, flavourful palate with the freshness of white fruit, warm, bitter notes and an acidic edge.

SOLAR DE MUÑOSANCHO

Plaza de la Olma, s/n
47491 La Seca (Valladolid)
☎: 983 291 540 - Fax: 983 291 540

Established: 1996

📦 300 🛢 67,500 litres 🍇 60 has.

🍷 90% 🌍10%

PRIUS DE MORAÑA VERDEJO WHITE
PRIUS VERDEJO FERMENTADO EN BARRICA WHITE
PRIUS DE MORAÑA CRIANZA RED
SEÑOR DE MORAÑA RESERVA RED

Compañía de Vinos de TELMO RODRÍGUEZ

Siete Infantes de Lara, 5 Oficina 1
26006 Logroño (La Rioja)
☎: 941 511 128 - Fax: 941 511 131
cia@fer.es

BASA 2003 JOVEN WHITE
85% verdejo, 5% sauvignon blanc, 15% viura

91 Brilliant straw. Fine, fresh aroma of fragrant herbs (lavender) and sweet fruit (mangoes, a hint of passion fruit). Powerful, very fruity palate with freshness without the cloying sensations from the macerating wheels, good acidity, excellent price.

TONELERÍA BURGOS

Seco, 20
47500 Nava del Rey (Valladolid)
☎: 983 850 114 - Fax: 983 850 900

Established: 1990

🛢 80,000 litres 🍷 100%

EL TONELERO WHITE

VAL DE VID

Finca La Revilla
47316 Piñel de Arriba (Valladolid)
☎: 983 484 030 - Fax: 983 484 012

Established: 1996

🍇 20 has. 🍷 80% 🌍20%

CONDESA EYLO WHITE

VALSANZO SELECCIÓN

Manuel Azaña, 9
Edificio Ambassador, Local 15
47014 (Valladolid)
☎: 677 448 608 - Fax: 983 784 096
valsanzo@telefonica.net

⊞ 250 🗄 150000 litres ❦ 80 has.

🍷 30% 🍇70%

VIÑA SANZO 2003 JOVEN WHITE
verdejo

85 Straw-coloured with a greenish nuance. Good intensity, very fresh aroma with notes of grapefruit, green grass and hay. Flavourful palate of sweet fruit, an oily texture, good acidity and a characteristic, bitter finish.

VEGA DE LA REINA

Los Moros, 10
47490 Rueda (Valladolid)
☎: 983 868 089 - Fax: 983 868 594
fjmerino@grupo22.com

Established: 1966

⊞ 1,100 🗄 1,200,000 litres ❦ 100 has.

🍷 95% 🍇5%: -MX -NI -NL -US

VEGA DE LA REINA RUEDA VERDEJO 2003
WHITE
100% verdejo

84 Pale gold with a lemony hue. Powerful, ripe aroma of white stone fruit, exotic hints (pineapple, passion fruit), a certain spicy freshness of skins. Flavourful palate with ripe fruit, and very varietal, fine bitter notes, slightly warm and oily, excellent overall.

VEGA DE LA REINA EXPRESIÓN 2001 OAK
AGED RED
tempranillo, merlot, cabernet sauvignon

78 Brick red cherry of medium-intensity. Perfumed, spicy aroma with flowers and menthol. Light on the palate with greeness, medium acidity and hints of green peppers.

VEGA DE LA REINA RUEDA 2003 WHITE
verdejo, viura

78 Brilliant pale yellow. Intense aroma of ripe white stone fruit and fine herbaceous notes. Flavourful, fruity palate with fine bitter notes, ripe citrus fruit peel and good acidity.

VEGA DE LA REINA SAUVIGNON BLANC 2003 WHITE
100% sauvignon blanc

80 Pale gold. Intense aroma with a fine, very varietal fruit expression (white fruit, tropical hints), a suggestion of flowers and fine herbs. Flavourful, fruity aroma with a slightly warm, oily texture, quality bitter and citrus fruit notes, good acidity.

Bodegas VERACRUZ

Juan A. Carmona, 1
47500 Nava del Rey (Valladolid)
☎: 630 107 300 - Fax: 983 850 761
b.veracruz@terra.es
Established: 2003
100,000 litres 🍷 50% 🌐50%

ERMITA VERACRUZ VERDEJO 2003 WHITE
100% verdejo

89 Pale yellow with a golden hue. Intense aroma of very varietal ripe fruit (exotic) with hints of fennel and spicy skins. Fresh, flavourful palate, slightly warm and oily but with good fruit weight and a suggestion of bitterness.

VICENTE SANZ

Las Flores, 5
47240 Valdestillas (Valladolid)
☎: 983 551 197 - Fax: 983 551 197
bodegavicentesanz@telefonica.net
Established: 1992
100 🍷 200,000 litres 🌿 30 has.
🍷 85% 🌐15%

VICARAL RUEDA VERDEJO 2003 WHITE
VICARAL RUEDA 2003 WHITE
CAÑADA REAL 2003 ROBLE RED
CAÑADA REAL 2001 CRIANZA RED

VIDAL SOBLECHERO

Plaza España, 13
47491 La Seca (Valladolid)
☎: 983 816 363 - Fax: 983 816 526
bodegas.soblechero@wanadoo.es

www.bodegasvidalsoblechero.com
Established: 1999
150 🍷 70,000 litres 🌿 42 has.
🇪🇸 70% 🌐30%: -US -DE -MX

VIÑA CLAVIDOR VERDEJO 2003 WHITE
100% verdejo

83 Greenish straw. Medium-intensity aroma of ripe fruit (tropical fruit) with notes of hay. Flavourful palate with ripe fruit and notes of sweetness, pleasant.

VIÑA CLAVIDOR TINTA FINA 2002 OAK AGED RED
100% tinta de pais

78 Dark cherry with a violet rim. Powerful aroma of jammy black fruit (light raisiny nuance), petals and toasty oak. Flavourful, fleshy palate with dark-roasted and liquorice notes, slightly warm and oily.

VIÑA CLAVIDOR 2001 FERMENTADO EN BARRICA WHITE
PAGOS DE VILLA VENDIMIA 2001 CRIANZA RED

VINOS BLANCOS DE CASTILLA

Carretera N-IV, km. 172, 600
47490 Rueda (Valladolid)
☎: 983 868 029 - Fax: 983 868 563
vinosblancosdecastilla@arrakis.es
Established: 1972
1,500 🍷 5,134,920 litres 🌿 354 has.
🍷 53,08% 🌐46,92%: -DE -AT -BE -BB -BR -CA -CY -CO -CR -CU -DK -US -SV -AE -PH -FR -GT -NL -HN -IE -IT -KY -JP LB -LU -MT -MY -MX -NI -DK -PR -PA -PE -PL -PT -DO -UK -RU -SE -CH -UA -UY

MARQUÉS DE RISCAL SAUVIGNON BLANC 2003 WHITE
100% sauvignon blanc

84 Straw-coloured with a greenish nuance. Good intensity, fresh aroma of hay, green fruit and herbs. Flavourful palate with pleasant bitter notes well-balanced with the acidity.

MARQUÉS DE RISCAL LIMOUSIN 2000 WHITE
100% verdejo

85 Lively golden. Aroma with crianza complexity (smoky notes, vanilla) and a pleasant suggestion of white fruit. Very oily, flavourful palate with abundant toasty notes, persistent.

MARQUÉS DE RISCAL 2003 WHITE
85% verdejo, 15% viura

88 Pale straw. Intense, fresh, varietal aroma, hay, ripe fruit and a herb suggestion (fennel). Fresh, grapey, oily and expressive palate with herby notes that give a complexity, very characteristic.

Bodega VIÑA BAJOZ

Avenida de los Comuneros, 90
49810 Morales de Toro (Zamora)
☎: 980 698 023 - Fax: 980 698 020
info@vinabajoz.com
www.vinabajoz.com

Established: 1962
⊕ 3,000 📊 6,500,000 litres 🍇 1.100 has.
🍷 65% 🌐35%

OVACIÓN VERDEJO 2003 JOVEN WHITE
100% verdejo

79 Pale yellow. Not very intense, fresh aroma with hints of flowers and white fruit. Fresh, flavourful palate with bitter notes, slightly warm and oily with a slightly acidic edge.

OVACIÓN 2003 JOVEN WHITE
60% verdejo, 40% viura

81 Very pale with greenish nuances. Slightly intense fresh aroma of white fruit (green apples) and hints of herbs. Fresh, flavourful palate with a good fruit (in spite of 13.5% alcohol) and varietal (bitter notes) expression.

VIÑA DEL SOPIÉ

Pol. Industrial La Alberquería, s/n
31230 Viana (Navarra)
☎: 948 645 008 - Fax: 948 645 166
info@lanavarra.com
www.lanavarra.com

Established:
⊕ 📊 litres 🍇 has. 🍷 90% 🌐10%: -UE

ASIA -US -CA -CAM

VIÑA DEL SOPIÉ 2003 WHITE
50% viura, 50% verdejo

78 Straw-coloured. Medium-intensity aroma of tropical fruit (passion fruit), but with a hint of freshness. Quite flavourful on the palate, pleasant and fruity.

VIÑA DEL SOPIÉ VERDEJO 2003 WHITE
100% verdejo

82 Straw-coloured with a greenish nuance. Intense aroma of fennel and green grass, expressive. Flavourful palate with Verdejo character, easy drinking.

VIÑA SILA

Juan Antonio Carmona, s/n
28020 Nava del Rey (Valladolid)
☎: 609 119 248 - Fax: 916 160 246
victorre@telefonica.net

Established: 2002
⊕ 50 📊 400,000 litres 🍇 34 has.
🍷 30% 🌐70%: -US -JP -DE -NL

NAIA 2003 JOVEN WHITE

90 Brilliant straw. Fine aroma of fragrant herbs with a nuance of minerals, elegant. Flavourful, fresh palate with a mineral retronasal effect (dry stones), complex and with volume, persistent.

LAS BRISAS 2003 JOVEN WHITE
verdejo, viura, sauvignon blanc

85 Brilliant straw. Fresh aroma with mild tropical nuances. Fresh, flavourful palate, rich in fruity nuances.

NAIADES 2003 FERMENTADO EN BARRICA WHITE
100% verdejo
92 Golden straw. Fine, smoky aroma with well-blended fine lees and fruit. Oily, powerful, smoky, fresh and flavourful palate, long with elegant, creamy hints in the retronasal passage.

VIÑEDOS DE NIEVA

Camino Real s/n
40447 Nieva (Segovia)
☎: 921 594 628 - Fax: 921 420 929
vinedosdenieva@infonegocio.com
www.infonegocio.com/vinedosdenieva

Established: 1989
📊 425,000 litres 🍇 50 has. 🍷 90% 🌐10%

BLANCO NIEVA 2003 FERMENTADO EN BARRICA WHITE
85% verdejo, 15% sauvignon blanc

86 Brilliant pale yellow. Powerful aroma with varietal expression (white fruit, herbs) and fine smoky oak notes. Flavourful palate with a good oak/fruit integration (bitter notes) and excellent acidity.

BLANCO NIEVA PIE FRANCO WHITE
100% verdejo

87 Greenish straw. Fine intense aroma of ripe fruit (apricots, peaches) with a suggestion of fennel and lavender, very expressive. Flavourful, fresh, varietal palate with herbs in the retronasal passage and a mineral finish.

BLANCO NIEVA SAUVIGNON 2003 WHITE
100% sauvignon blanc

86 Brilliant pale. Intense aroma of ripe white fruit with notes of flowers and fragrant herbs. Flavourful palate with ripe fruit (hints of exotic fruit), fine bitter notes and a good fruit weight, slightly oily with smoky notes of skins in the finish.

LOS NAVALES 2003 WHITE
100% verdejo

78 Pale straw. Not very intense, slightly fruity aroma, but poor in expression. Better in the mouth, fresh, fruity and bitter.

VIÑEDOS SECA

Carretera Rodilana, s/n
47491 La Seca (Valladolid)
☎: 620 212 111 - Fax: 913 294 950
vlaseca@rueda.net
Established: 1998
⊟ 36,000 litres 🌱 22 has. 🇪🇸 100%

VIÑA PRETEL WHITE

WILLIAMS & HUMBERT

Carretera N-IV, km. 641, 75
11408 Jerez de la Frontera (Cádiz)
☎: 956 353 400 - Fax: 956 353 411
williams@williams-humbert.com
www.williams-humbert.com
Established: 1877
⊞ 70,000 ⊟ 35,000,000 litres 🌱 500 has.
🍷 35% 🌐65%

VIÑA SALTES WHITE

Grupo YLLERA

Carretera Madrid - Coruña, km. 173, 5
47490 Rueda (Valladolid)
☎: 983 868 097 - Fax: 983 868 177
grupoyllera@grupoyllera.com
www.grupoyllera.com
Established: 1972
⊞ 13,500 ⊟ 6,000,000 litres 🌱 70 has.
🍷 85% 🌐15%: -UE -CH -US -MX -GT -DO -BR -JP

TIERRA BUENA 2003 JOVEN WHITE
60% verdejo, 40% viura

69 Pale. Short aroma, weak in fruit. Rustic, and light on the palate, without fruit expression.

VIÑA CANTOSÁN 2003 JOVEN WHITE
100% verdejo

80 Pale with a greenish nuance. Not very intense yet clean aroma with notes of tropical fruit. Oily, flavourful palate with hay, pleasant.

VIÑA CANTOSÁN 2002 FERMENTADO EN BARRICA WHITE
100% verdejo

81 Greenish straw. Medium intensity aroma with toasty wood that subdues the fruit. Oily, flavourful palate with varietal Verdejo carácter, well-balanced, unintegrated oak.

CANTOSÁN ESPUMOSO BRUT
verdejo

81 Pale yellow with greenish nuances. Powerful palate with ripe fruit, and fine Crianza notes (lees, withered petals). Flavourful, creamy palate with a bitter, spicy nuance and hints of fresh herbs.

CANTOSÁN ESPUMOSO BRUT NATURE
verdejo

80 Pale yellow. Powerful, ripe aroma with predominant floral notes and yeast. Dry palate with well-integrated beads, white stone fruit notes, spicy and slightly mineral hints.

CANTOSÁN ESPUMOSO DEMI-SEC
verdejo

81 Pale with greenish nuances and a fine bead. Powerful, fruity aroma with a floral nuance, hints of aniseed and yeast. Flavourful palate with fine bittersweet notes (slightly jammy), a bitter nuance (almonds) and fine herbs.

DO SOMONTANO

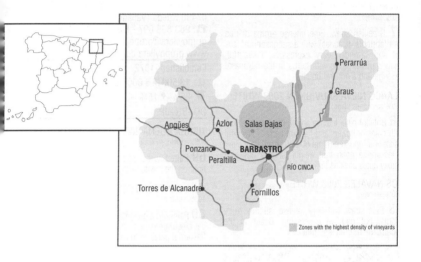

NEWS. 2003 was a record year for sales of the DO Somontano, with more than 10 million bottles sold, an increase of almost a million bottles on the previous year. As for production, 19.5 million kg were harvested, almost 5 million kg more (30% more) than in 2002. The most harvested grape variety was the *Cabernet Sauvignon*, with almost 6.5 million kg, followed at a distance by the *Merlot* and the *Tempranillo*. As for quality, the first places were shared almost equally by Viñas del Vero (93 points for its Blecua) and Enate (also 93 for the new vintage of its Reserva Especial). The white wine category was won by the Chardonnay Colección of Viñas del Vero with 90 points, the only one of its kind to achieve this score. Regarding the controversy about native or foreign varieties, mention should be made of the formidable defence of the *Garnacha* in the Secastilla of Viñas del Vero (90) or the Mascún of Bodegas Osca (85). Also interesting is the Marboré of Bodegas Pirineos, a blend of three local varieties (*Parraleta, Moristel* and *Tempranillo*) together with *Merlot* and *Cabernet Sauvignon*, the third bodega in the firmament of the Somontanos.

Hectares of Vineyard	No. of Viticulturists	No. of Bodegas	2003 Harvest	2003 Production	Marketing
4,317	530	15	Very Good	13,530,700 litres	75% Spain 25% foreign

LOCATION. In the province of Huesca, around the town of Barbastro. The region comprises 43 municipal districts, mainly centred round the region of Somontano and the rest of the neighbouring regions of Ribagorza and Monegros.

CLIMATE. Characterised by cold winters and hot summers, with sharp contrasts in temperature at the end of spring and autumn. The average annual rainfall is 500 mm, although the rains are scarcer in the south and east.

SOIL. The soil is mainly brownish limestone, not very fertile, with a good level of limestone and good permeability.

VARIETIES:
White: *Macabeo, Garnacha Blanca, Alcañón, Chardonnay* and *Gewürztraminer.*
Red: *Tempranillo, Garnacha Tinta, Cabernet Sauvignon, Merlot, Moristel, Parraleta, Pinot Noir* and *Syrah.*

REGULATORY COUNCIL.
Avda. de la Merced, 64. 22300 Barbastro (Huesca).
Tel: 974 313 031. Fax: 974 315 132.
E-mail: somontano@dosomontano.com
Website: www.dosomontano.com

GENERAL CHARACTERISTICS OF THE WINES:

Whites	The traditional wines of the region, they are based on the *Macabeo* variety, giving young wines with a straw yellow colour, which are fresh and easy drinking (worthy of mention is the only existing example of late harvest *Macabeo*, which has revealed a complexity uncommon to this variety). Although of higher quality, they are generally produced from *Chardonnay*, whether for young wines or wines fermented in barrels, which gives white wines with powerful aromas, with good varietal definition, oily and flavourful on the palate.
Rosés	Produced from autochthonous or foreign grapes, they follow the line of the modern rosés: raspberry pink in colour, good fruit intensity, light, fresh and easy drinking.
Reds	The traditional red wine of the region, produced from *Moristel* and *Tempranillo*, is notably fruity and intense. There have also been very interesting experiences with single variety wines produced from local grapes, specifically *Moristel* and *Parraleta*, of notable quality; both produced as young wines and characterised by an excellent fruity character and a certain complexity of notes. In the rest of the red wines the foreign varieties impose themselves, blended with the local grapes or presented separately. The aged *Cabernet* and *Merlot* wines stand out for their Atlantic influence, varietal character, aromatic potency and fine blend with the wood due to not excessive ageing periods; they have a good structure on the palate.

BLECUA

Carretera Barbastro - Naval, km. 3
22300 Barbastro (Huesca)
☎: 974 302 216 - Fax: 974 302 098
info@bodegablecua.com

Established: 2000

🌐 1,650 📊 50,000 litres 🍇 14 has.

🍷 75% 🌐25%

BLECUA 2001 RED

93 Intense cherry. Aroma with great expression of ripe fruit and toasty, creamy oak (peat, chocolate, vanilla, pastries) with a somewhat mineral hint. Full, fleshy and ripe palate with fine creamy toasty flavours (chocolate, peat), lively and ripe tannins, promising with time.

DALCAMP

Constitución, 4
22415 Monesma de San Juan (Huesca)
☎: 973 760 018 - Fax: 973 760 523
rdalfo@mixmail.com

Established: 1994

🌐 300 📊 534,000 litres 🍇 26,5 has.

🍷 30% 🌐70%: -DE -AT -BE -UK -NL -DK

CASTILLO DE MONESMA 2000 CRIANZA RED
95% cabernet sauvignon, 5% merlot

89 Intense cherry. Toasty aroma of ripe fruit with mild notes of overripening and a suggestion of minerals. Fleshy, powerful, spirituous palate with jammy fruit (jam) and with tannins between sweet and sour.

CASTILLO DE MONESMA CABERNET SAUVIGNON - MERLOT 2002 OAK AGED RED
70% cabernet sauvignon, 30% merlot

85 Dark cherry with a coppery hue. Powerful aroma of overripe black fruit with spicy oak notes and hints of fine reduction. Flavourful palate with quite rough and oily tannins, quite promising with varietal character.

CASTILLO DE MONESMA 1999 RESERVA RED
100% cabernet sauvignon

89 Intense cherry with an orange edge. Toasty aroma with animal notes (leather), complex (peat) and blackcurrants. Round, oily, complex, slightly mineral palate with ripe fruit and a slightly viscous retronasal effect.

CASTILLO DE MONESMA CABERNET SAUVIGNON-MERLOT 2002 JOVEN RED

84 Dark cherry with a slightly orangey rim. Toasty aroma of very ripe fruit (jammy blackberries and plums). Spirituous, mineral hints (dry earth) and mild hints of jammy fruit. Fleshy, warm, flavourful palate with ripe fruit and slightly vegetative Cabernet. Very Mediterranean with a spicy expression.

ENATE (VIÑEDOS Y CRIANZAS DEL ALTO ARAGÓN)

Avenida de las Artes, 1
22314 Salas Bajas (Huesca)

☎: 974 302 580 - Fax: 974 300 046
bodega@enate.es
www.enate.es

Established: 1991

🍾 4,200 🛢 4,500,000 litres 🍇 500 has.

🇪🇸 70% 🌐30%: -DE -NL -DK -FI -EE -BE -AT -DK -SE -CH -UK -US -CA -MX -BR -PR -IN -RU -SG -VN -PH -TW -HK

ENATE CHARDONNAY 2002 FERMENTADO EN BARRICA WHITE
100% chardonnay

87 Brilliant golden yellow. Powerful aroma with a good varietal expression (ripe apples) predominant oak notes (smoky, vanilla) and a suggestion of exotic fruit and lees. Powerful, flavourful palate with slightly marked oak tannins, slightly fruity with mountain herbs, warm with smoky notes in the finish, lacking acidity.

ENATE CHARDONNAY-234 2003 WHITE
100% chardonnay

85 Straw-coloured with a yellow hue. Aroma rich in expression of ripe fruit, herbs (lavender), and light nuances of spirits. Dense and oily on the palate, rich in varietal nuances, warm with excellent acidity that stays in the mouth; very flavourful.

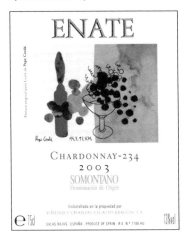

ENATE GEWÜRZTRAMINER 2003 JOVEN WHITE
100% gewürztraminer

84 Brilliant straw. Fresh, fruity aroma with musky notes (fresh laundry) and lightly grapey. Fresh on the palate; fruity but with less expression than the previous vintage.

ENATE CABERNET SAUVIGNON 2003 ROSÉ
100% cabernet sauvignon

82 Strawberry pink. Not very intense yet fine aroma of red fruit and flowers. Slightly carbonic on the palate with good acidity, slightly warm.

ENATE TEMPRANILLO CABERNET SAUVIGNON 2001 CRIANZA RED
cabernet sauvignon, tempranillo

84 Cherry with an orangey edge. Peppery aroma with varietal typification and pleasant toasty notes. Flavourful palate with good acidity, well-balanced.

ENATE CABERNET SAUVIGNON 2000 RESERVA RED
100% cabernet sauvignon

90 Quite intense cherry. Powerful, toasty aroma (coffee oak, chocolate) of ripe fruit with a fresh and elegant expression. Round, oily palate with excellent varietal fruit character of ripe, fresh Cabernet.

ENATE RESERVA ESPECIAL 2000 RED
50% cabernet sauvignon, 50% merlot

93 Intense cherry. Concentrated, mineral aroma of very ripe, almost jammy black fruit and a poweful toasty oak expression. Palate rich in southern Cabernet varietal expression, with superb, oily tannins, full and generous.

ENATE VARIETALES DEL DOS MIL UNO 2001 RESERVA RED
cabernet sauvignon, merlot, tempranillo

85 Intense cherry. Aroma with superripe notes (jammy plums) and quite vegetative skins with toasty hints (cocoa, pepper). Warm, round and oily on the palate, quite spirituous with slightly muted fruit. Inferior to the previous vintage.

ENATE MERLOT-MERLOT 2002 RED
100% merlot

84 Garnet red cherry with a coppery-saffron glint. Powerful aroma, with an excellent varietal fruit expression (redcurrants, underbrush), and herbaceous hints (nettles, fresh bunches) and dry stones, fine smoky oak. Flavourful palate, slightly woody character which mutes the good fruit expression, slightly warm and oily, bitter, not the best year for Merlot.

FÁBREGAS

Cerler, s/n "Barrio San Juan"
22300 Barbastro (Huesca)
☎: 974 310 498 - Fax: 974 310 898

info@bodegasfabregas.com
www.bodegasfabregas.com

Established: 1884
🌐 100 📊 300,000 litres 🍇 38 has.
🍷 70% 🌍30%

FÁBREGAS CHARDONNAY 2003 FERMENTADO EN BARRICA WHITE
100% chardonnay

85 Brilliant gold. Powerful aroma with toasty wood notes, vanilla, ripe white fruit and a suggestion of fine lees. Flavourful palate with good fruit/oak integration and a smoky nuance.

FÁBREGAS 2003 ROSÉ
100% cabernet sauvignon

84 Very deep raspberry with coppery nuances. Powerful aroma of red stone fruit, sweet, hints of toasty skins and damp earth. Flavourful palate with an excellent fruit expression and a ripe citrus fruit nuance, slightly warm with good acidity.

FÁBREGAS CABERNET-MERLOT 2002 OAK AGED RED
50% cabernet sauvignon, 50% merlot

80 Cherry with an orange edge. Aroma of green peppers, not very ripe red fruit and black olives. Good acidity on the palate with quite noticeable wood tannins.

VEGA FERRERA 2000 CRIANZA RED
70% cabernet sauvignon, 30% merlot

77 Not very deep cherry. Aroma with sweet notes of wood and a hint of reduction notes. Light, well-mannered palate, but without great nuances.

FÁBREGAS 2003 WHITE
FÁBREGAS 2003 RED

LALANNE

Torre de San Marcos, s/n
22300 Barbastro (Huesca)
☎: 974 310 689 - Fax: 974 310 689
blalanne@jazzfree.com

Established: 1842
🌐 1,017 📊 420,000 litres 🍇 35 has.
🍷 40% 🌍60%: -AT -NL -DE -CH -FR -US

VIÑA SAN MARCOS WHITE
80% macabeo, 20% chardonnay

75 Yellow straw. Aroma of ripe white stone fruit. Fresh, light palate with noticeable acidity.

LAURA LALANNE WHITE DE AGUJA
60% macabeo, 40% chardonnay

75 Straw-coloured. Pungent aroma of hay and herbs. Carbonic and light on the palate with good acidity.

DO SOMONTANO

LAURA LALANNE ROSÉ DE AGUJA
60% tempranillo, 40% moristel

73 Strawberry red. Aroma of strawberries and red fruit. Carbonic on the palate, good acidity.

VIÑA SAN MARCOS 2003 ROSÉ
60% moristel, 40% tempranillo

73 Strawberry pink. Not very intense, somewhat lactic, fresh aroma. Noticeable acidity on the palate with quite perceptible tannins.

VIÑA SAN MARCOS 2003 RED
60% tempranillo, 40% moristel

79 Garnet red cherry. Somewhat intense aroma of toasty skins with ripe and somewhat reduced fruit. Flavourful palate with spicy notes and notions of terroir and somewhat reduced fruit (dried peaches).

LEONOR LALANNE MERLOT 1999 CRIANZA RED
100% merlot

86 Garnet red cherry with a brick red edge. Powerful aroma with an excellent Bordeaux crianza expression (cedar, tobacco, dates). Flavourful, supple palate, a slightly oily texture, fine spicy notes and reduced fruit (plums) in the retronasal passage.

LALANNE CABERNET SAUVIGNON - MERLOT 1996 RESERVA RED
70% cabernet sauvignon, 30% merlot

83 Cherry with brick red nuances. Intense, very fine aroma with predominant reduction notes of quality (cedar, cigar box, old furniture, raisins). Flavourful, spicy palate with acidic and tannic vigour, well-balanced.

LALANNE CABERNET SAUVIGNON-MERLOT 2001 RED
60% cabernet sauvignon, 40% merlot

83 Garnet red cherry with a brick red edge. Powerful aroma with predominant spicy and reduction notes and a red stone fruit nuance. Flavourful palate with slightly marked tannins, a very varietal herbaceous nuance with the freshness of minerals and skins in the finish.

Bodegas MONCLÚS

Carretera Radiquero - Alquezar s/n
22145 Radiquero (Huesca)
☎: 974 318 120 - Fax: 974 318 120

INÉS DE MONCLÚS RED
VIÑAS DE RADIQUERO

Bodegas y Viñedos OLVENA

Carretera Nacional , 123
22300 Barbastro (Huesca)
☎: 974 308 481 - Fax: 974 308 842
info@bodegasolvena.com

OLVENA CHARDONNAY 2003 FERMENTADO EN BARRICA WHITE
chardonnay

84 Brilliant gold. Powerful aroma of ripe white fruit, with fine smoky, creamy oak notes and an excellent varietal expression. Flavourful palate with well-integrated smoky fruit notes and vanilla, slightly warm.

OLVENA 2002 RED
tempranillo, merlot, cabernet sauvignon

86 Dark cherry. Intense aroma of jammy black fruit, with fine spicy notes of skins, balsamic notes and damp earth. Flavourful palate with slightly drying oak tannins, quality bitter notes and fine toasty flavours in the retronasal passage.

OLVENA MERLOT 2002 RED

OSCA

La Iglesia, 1
22124 Ponzano (Huesca)
☎: 974 319 017 - Fax: 974 319 175
satborruel@micromat.es
www.bodegasosca.com

Established: 1903
🍷 350 📦 190,000 litres 🌿 25 has.

🚩 70% 🌐30%

OSCA CHARDONNAY 2001 FERMENTADO EN BARRICA WHITE
100% chardonnay

84 Pale with golden nuances. Intense aroma of ripe white fruit and mild reduction notes (withered petals). Flavourful palate with bitter notes (almonds, fine herbs) and creamy overtones; some freshness lost since last year.

OSCA 2003 ROSÉ
tempranillo , moristel

84 Deep raspberry with a coppery hue. Intense aroma of red stone fruit, petals and spicy hints of skins. Flavourful, fresh palate with a mineral freshness and overtones of the skins.

MASCÚN MERLOT 2002 OAK AGED RED
100% merlot   3

84 Dark cherry. Powerful aroma of jammy black fruit, with a certain varietal character (spices, paprika, fallen leaves). Flavourful, fleshy palate with fine toasty oak, chocolate and balsamic notes and good acidity.

MASCÚN GARNACHA 2001 OAK AGED RED
100% garnacha   12

85 Garnet red cherry with a coppery edge. Intense, fruity aroma with notes of spicy oak, skins (varietal) and hints of petals. Flavourful palate with a good oak/fruit integration, good fruit weight and quality bitter and balsamic notes.

OSCA MERLOT 2000 CRIANZA RED
100% merlot

83 Dark cherry with a purplish edge. Powerful aroma with fine toasty oak, jammy black fruit, hints of fallen leaves and reduction. Flavourful, fleshy palate, good fruit/oak integration and toasty and sweet fruit notes in the finish.

CASTILLO DE L'AINSA 2001 CRIANZA RED
tempranillo, cabernet sauvignon

87 Dark cherry. Powerful aroma of ripe black fruit with fine spicy notes and quality varietal hints (paprika, fallen leaves, balsamic flavours). Flavourful palate, good fruit/oak integration and an excellent expression of the Crianza.

OSCA MORISTEL 2001 CRIANZA RED
moristel

81 Dark cherry. Powerful aroma of slightly reduced red stone fruit (overripe), toasty hints of oak, fallen leaves and damp earth. Flavourful palate with good fruit/oak integration, and an original and reduction varietal expression.

OSCA 2001 CRIANZA RED
tempranillo, cabernet sauvignon

84 Dark garnet red cherry. Powerful aroma with toasty oak, a suggestion of ripe black fruit, balsamic notes and liquorice. Flavourful palate with ripe, oily tannins and bitter notes.

OTTO BESTUE

Carretera A-138, km. 05
22312 Enate (Huesca)
☎: 974 305 157 - Fax: 974 314 842
bodegasottobestue@grupo7.com
www.bodega-ottobestue.com

Established: 1999

🌐 186 📦 243,000 litres 🍇 30 has.

🚩 70% 🌐30%: -CH -BE -UK -IE -US -DE -FR

BESTUÉ DE OTTO BESTUÉ 2003 ROSÉ
50% cabernet sauvignon, 50% tempranillo

83 Very lively deep raspberry. Powerful aroma with predominant notes of herbs and spicy skins, a nuance of stone fruit. Fresh, flavourful palate with fine bitter notes, rich in acidity.

BESTUÉ DE OTTO BESTUÉ FINCA RABLEROS 2002 OAK AGED RED
50% cabernet sauvignon, 50% tempranillo

85 Dark garnet red cherry. Powerful aroma of very ripe fruit (hints of mild reduction, prunes), fine toasty oak and leather notes. Flavourful palate with slightly marked but fine tannins and excellent Crianza expression, bitter and long.

Bodega PIRINEOS

Carretera Barbastro-Naval, km. 3, 5
22300 Barbastro (Huesca)
☎: 974 311 289 - Fax: 974 306 688
info@bodegapirineos.com
www.bodegapirineos.com

Established: 1993

🍾 5,000 📊 6,000,000 litres 🍇 140 has.

BODEGA PIRINEOS CHARDONNAY 2002 FERMENTADO EN BARRICA WHITE
100% chardonnay

84 Brilliant yellow. Powerful aroma of smoky oak with a very varietal ripe fruit nuance, rich hints of vanilla and toffee. Flavourful palate with slightly drying oak tannins, spicy and quite persistent.

BODEGA PIRINEOS MACABEO VENDIMIA TARDÍA 2002 FERMENTADO EN BARRICA WHITE
100% macabeo

85 Pale yellow with lemony nuances. Intense aroma of fine smoky oak, slightly fruity (exotic hints), with hints of aniseed and fine lees. Flavourful, ripe palate with spicy notes, slightly warm and oily.

BODEGA PIRINEOS MERLOT-CABERNET 2003 JOVEN ROSÉ
50% merlot, 50% cabernet sauvignon

85 Pale pink. Intense aroma with notes of skins and sweet, floral hints. Fresh, unctuous palate with ripe red fruit.

BODEGA PIRINEOS MORISTEL 2002 OAK AGED RED
moristel

83 Dark cherry with a garnet red edge. Powerful aroma with spicy notes of skins, black fruit and fine toasty oak. Flavourful, supple palate with quality lactic notes and a good fresh fruit expression with a correct oak contribution.

BODEGA PIRINEOS MERLOT-CABERNET 2001 CRIANZA RED
50% merlot, 50% cabernet sauvignon

85 Dark cherry with a garnet red edge. Powerful aroma with very ripe red stone fruit, spicy hints of skins, fine toasty notes and balsamic notes. Flavourful palate with fresh and fleshy overtones of the fruit, spicy oak; vigorous and long.

MARBORÉ 2001 CRIANZA RED
tempranillo, cabernet sauvignon, moristel, merlot, parraleta

90 Dark garnet red cherry. Powerful aroma of foresty black fruit with fine toasty oak notes, a balsamic hint and a suggestion of graphite. Flavourful, slightly fleshy palate with quite ripe and oily tannins, fine bitter notes (liquorice), and a suggestion of minerals.

SEÑORÍO DE LAZÁN 2000 RESERVA RED
50% tempranillo, 45% cabernet sauvignon, 5% moristel

82 Garnet red cherry with a saffron edge. Intense, spicy aroma with ripe fruit and mild balsamic notes. Flavourful, fleshy palate with quite rough, rich tannins, promising though still lacks Reserva expression.

MONTESIERRA 2001 CRIANZA RED
50% tempranillo, 25% cabernet sauvignon, 25% moristel

84 Dark garnet red cherry. Intense aroma of ripe black fruit and smoky oak with a suggestion of wax and damp earth. Flavourful, fleshy palate with somewhat obvious tannins but with a promising spicy nuance, hints of leather, balsamic notes and terroir.

BODEGA PIRINEOS GEWÜRZTRAMINER 2003 JOVEN WHITE

Bodegas SIERRA DE GUARA

Carretera de Abiego, km. 0, 2
22124 Lascellas (Huesca)
☎: 974 319 363 - Fax: 974 319 363
idrias@bodegassierradeguara.es
www.bodegassierradeguara.es

Established: 1997

🍷 300 🛢 700,000 litres 🍇 70 has.
🍷 75% 🌐25%: -US -CH -DE -UK

IDRIAS CHARDONNAY 2003 CRIANZA WHITE
100% chardonnay

88 Yellow straw. Powerful, varietal, expressive aroma with very ripe fruit yet crafted with finesse. Flavourful, fresh, oily palate with sensations of fresh, ripe fruit over a suggestion of citrus fruit, very well-balanced.

IDRIAS MERLOT 2003 ROSÉ
100% merlot

79 Lively raspberry blush. Not very intense aroma although fresh and fruity (strawberry jelly). Light fresh palate, a well-mannered ensemble.

IDRIAS ABIEGO 2003 ROBLE RED
50% tempranillo, 25% cabernet sauvignon, 25% merlot

89 Garnet red cherry with a violet hue. Powerful aroma of black fruit with notes of macerated skins and fine toasty oak notes. Powerful, flavourful, very concentrated on the palate with ripe and oily tannins, fine spicy and bitter notes, liquorice, balsamic notes and a mineral suggestion.

IDRIAS SEVIL 2002 CRIANZA RED

VALDOVINOS

Camino de la Almunia, s/n
22133 Antillón (Huesca)
☎: 974 260 330 - Fax: 974 260 147
jvaldovinos@terra.es
bodegasvaldovinos.com

Established: 1995

🍷 500 🛢 250,000 litres 🍇 10 has.
🍷 80% 🌐20%: -CH -AT -DE -FR

VIÑAS DE ANTILLÓN 2003 WHITE
100% macabeo

82 Pale steel. Intense, fresh aroma of apples with a herbal complexity, harmonious. Flavourful palate with hay, well-balanced and very pleasant.

VIÑAS DE ANTILLÓN 2003 ROSÉ
100% cabernet sauvignon

82 Intense raspberry. Powerful, fruity aroma with toasty hints of skins. Flavourful palate with red stone fruit, fine bitter notes and excellent citrus acidity.

VIÑAS DE ANTILLÓN 2003 RED
40% cabernet sauvignon, 40% merlot, 20% tempranillo

77 Cherry with a raspberry rim. Intense aroma of fresh skins with notes of petals (maceration). Flavourful, light, fruity palate with strawberries in the finish.

VIÑAS DE ANTILLÓN CABERNET SAUVIGNON 2000 CRIANZA RED
100% cabernet sauvignon

76 Garnet red cherry. Spicy, toasty aroma with a nuance of sun-drenched fruit. Flavourful palate with fresh acidity and notes of sweetness.

VIÑAS DE ANTILLÓN CABERNET - MERLOT 2001 CRIANZA RED
70% cabernet sauvignon, 30% merlot

77 Ruby red with an orange edge. Toasty aroma with dark-roasted notes over ripe fruit. Fleshy palate with marked oak tannins; fresh with a slightly viscous finish.

VALDOVINOS 2003 RED
VALDOVINOS 2002 CRIANZA RED

VIÑAS DEL VERO

Finca de San Marcos
Carretera Barbastro - Naval, km. 3, 7
22300 Barbastro (Huesca)
☎: 974 302 216 - Fax: 974 302 098

DO SOMONTANO

info@vinasdelvero.com
www.vinasdelvero.com

Established: 1986

6,000 🛢 4,500,000 litres 🍇 950 has.

🍷 75% 🍇 25%

COLECCIÓN VIÑAS DEL VERO CHARDONNAY 2002 FERMENTADO EN BARRICA WHITE
chardonnay

90 Lively and brilliant golden yellow. Powerful aroma, rich in smoky notes and scented herbs with a nuance of hay. Oily, powerful, flavourful, elegant palate with varietal expression, warm with perfect oak and fine lees.

VIÑAS DEL VERO CHARDONNAY 2003 WHITE
100% chardonnay

88 Straw-coloured with a golden glimmer. Fresh aroma of fine green herbs with hints of ripe yet very elegant fruit. Fresh, varietal, flavourful palate with good acidity, long with abundant Chardonnay fruit.

VIÑAS DEL VERO CLARIÓN SELECCIÓN 2002 WHITE

89 Straw-coloured. Powerful aroma, rich in nuances of minerals, flowers and fresh scented herbs. Sweet, slightly musky notes on the palate, flavourful, fruity and original.

VIÑAS DEL VERO 2003 ROSÉ
tempranillo, cabernet sauvignon, moristel

81 Deep raspberry with a coppery glint. Fresh, quite intense aroma of red stone fruit with hints of fennel and spicy skins. Flavourful, creamy palate with fine toasty notes of grapes, sweet hints and excellent acidity.

VIÑAS DEL VERO GEWÜRZTRAMINER COLECCIÓN 2003 WHITE
100% gewürztraminer

85 Pale yellow. Intense aroma of somewhat varietal ripe fruit (tropical) with floral and somewhat spicy notes. Flavourful palate with bittersweet notes, oily, with jammy hints, somewhat bitter with pollen notes in the retronasal passage.

VIÑAS DEL VERO 2001 CRIANZA RED
tempranillo, cabernet sauvignon

86 Dark garnet red cherry. Aroma of excellent crianza in oak with ripe fruit and a slight varietal expression. Somewhat fleshy, fruity, ripe palate with robust but flavourful and persistent tannins, quite full-bodied.

VIÑAS DEL VERO 2003 RED
tempranillo, cabernet sauvignon, moristel

81 Dark cherry with a lively garnet red edge. Powerful aroma of ripe fruit with smoky hints of skins and a suggestion of damp earth. Flavourful palate with quite lively and fine tannins and a hint of the freshness of under-ripe skins, good acidity.

VIÑAS DEL VERO GRAN VOS 2001 RESERVA RED
garnacha

88 Intense cherry. Aroma with toasty notes and slightly jammy ripe fruit. Fleshy, full, flavourful palate with powerful but ripe tannins and a fine toasty oak retronasal effect.

COLECCIÓN VIÑAS DEL VERO LOS SASOS 2002 RED
cabernet sauvignon

90 Intense cherry. Powerful aroma, rich in ripe varietal expression (paprika) with fine toasty notes (cocoa, coffee). Full, generous, fleshy palate, rich in balsamic and varietal nuances with lively but ripe tannins, a complex retronasal effect, highly flavourful and complex.

SECASTILLA 2002 RED
garnacha

90 Intense cherry. Aroma with balsamic notes (fallen leaves) and very ripe black fruit with spicy hints of Garnacha (pepper and cloves). Warm, fleshy and ripe palate with flavourful and sweet tannins and spices and forest flowers in the retronasal passage, riper than the previous vintage.

COLECCIÓN VIÑAS DEL VERO MERLOT 2002 RED
merlot

85 Garnet red cherry. Aroma with varietal notes and well-integrated toasty scents, fruity. Fruity, flavourful palate with very harmonious oak, fresh with lively but moderate tannins.

DO TACORONTE - ACENTEJO

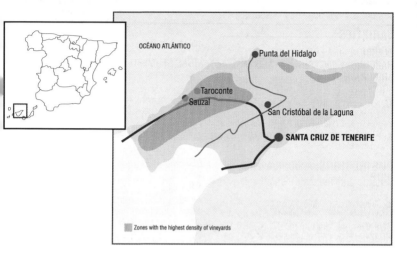

OCÉANO ATLÁNTICO

Punta del Hidalgo

Taroconte
Sauzal

San Cristóbal de la Laguna

SANTA CRUZ DE TENERIFE

Zones with the highest density of vineyards

NEWS. Climatically, 2003 was characterized by a wet winter, a spring with sharp jumps in temperature and good contrasts in day-night temperatures. The hot summer prevented the appearance of diseases in the grapes, all of which lead the Regulatory Council to rate the year as 'very good', although it is evident that the red wines are better than the whites. In the lower-lying regions, generally warmer, the ripening of the grapes was better, although the wines are slightly less expressive, whilst at an altitude of 200 m to 500 m the trade wind cooled the vines and the grapes took longer to ripen, resulting in the wines from these altitudes having a greater richness in nuances.

Hectares of Vineyard	No. of Viticulturists	No. of Bodegas	2003 Harvest	2003 Production	Marketing
1,723	2,340	48	Very Good	1,650,000 litres	99% Islands and Peninsula 1% foreign

There were 40 wines with scores in excess of 80 points, compared with only 17 for the 2004 harvest. This is the result of not only of a better harvest, but also of better production techniques.

LOCATION. Situated in the north of Tenerife, stretching for 23 km and is composed of 9 municipal districts: Tegueste, Tacoronte, El Sauzal, La Matanza de Acentejo, La Victoria de Acentejo, Santa Úrsula, La Laguna, Santa Cruz de Tenerife and El Rosario.

CLIMATE. Typically Atlantic, affected by the orientation of the island and the relief which give rise to a great variety of microclimates. The temperatures are in general mild, thanks to the influence of the trade winds, which provide high levels of humidity, around 60%, although the rains are scarce.

SOIL. The soil is volcanic, reddish, and is made up of organic matter and trace elements. The vines are cultivated both in the valleys next to the sea and higher up at altitudes of up to 1,000 m.

VARIETIES:
White:
Preferred: *Güal, Malvasía, Listán Blanco* and *Marmajuelo*.
Authorized: *Pedro Ximénez, Moscatel, Verdello, Vijariego, Forastera Blanca* and *Torrontés*.
Red:
Preferred: *Listán Negra* and *Negramoll*.
Authorized: *Tintilla, Moscatel Negro* and *Malvasía Rosada*.

SUB-REGIONS: Anaga (covering the municipal areas of La Laguna, Santa Cruz de Tenerife and Tegueste) which falls within the limits of the Anaga Rural Park.

REGULATORY COUNCIL.
Ctra. General del Norte, 97. 38350 Tacoronte.
Tel: 922 560 107. Fax: 922 561 155.
E-mail: consejo@tacovin.com
Website: www.tacovin.com

GENERAL CHARACTERISTICS OF THE WINES:

Whites	These are light and fruity; they are produced in small quantities.
Rosés	Produced mainly from *Listán Negro*, they maintain the varietal character of this stock and are fresh and pleasant to drink.
Reds	These are the most characteristic wines of the DO. The young red wines have a deep cherry-red or deep red ruby colour; on the nose they develop aromas with a good intensity; they are fresh and fruity and transmit a somewhat wild character, but are original from the *Listán* grape. Recently, Crianza wines aged in barrels have also been produced.

BUTEN

San Nicolás, 122
38360 El Sauzal (Santa Cruz de Tenerife)
☎: 922 573 272 - Fax: 922 561 225
crater@bodegasbuten.com

Established: 1998

🍷 64 📊 31,500 litres 🍷 75%

🌍 25%: -US -CH

CRÁTER 2003 OAK AGED RED
70% listán negro, 30% negramoll   🛢 5

89 Quite dark cherry. Fine aroma of creamy toast (coffee and chocolates), fresh, fruity. Flavourful, fruity palate with a varietal character and considerable typification, elegant with fresh and creamy tannins.

CALDOS DE ANAGA

Cruz de Candelaria, 20
38203 La Laguna (Santa Cruz de Tenerife)
☎: 922 255 478 - Fax: 922 255 478
caldo@caldosdeanaga.com
www.caldosdeanagas.com

Established: 1999

🍷 6 📊 6,000 litres 🍇 1 has. 🍷 100%

CUEVAS DE LINO 2003 RED

CÁNDIDO HERNÁNDEZ PÍO

Limeras con Avenida Tinguaro
38370 La Matanza de Acenjo (Tenerife)
☎: 922 577 270 - Fax: 922 577 390
candher2@teleline.es

Established: 1975

📊 210,000 litres 🍇 30 has. 🍷 100%

BALCÓN CANARIO 2002 JOVEN RED
VIÑA RIQUELAS 2002 JOVEN RED

DOMÍNGUEZ IV GENERACIÓN

Calvario, 79
38350 Tacoronte (Tenerife)
☎: 922 572 435 - Fax: 922 274 924

DOMÍNGUEZ RED

EDUADO HERNÁNDEZ TORRES

Real Orotava, 298
38360 El Sauzal (Tenerife)
☎: 922 584 221 - Fax: 922 584 221

EL MORAL RED

EL LOMO

Ctra. El Lomo, 52
38280 Tegueste (Tenerife)
☎: 922 545 254 - Fax: 922 241 587
afecan@bodegaellomo.com
www.bodegaellomo.com

Established: 1990

🍷 12 📊 80,000 litres 🍇 9 has. 🍷 100%

EL LOMO MALVASÍA DULCE 2003 WHITE
100% malvasía

80 Slightly pale gold. Slightly short aroma without varietal expression with a crystallised fruit essence. Sweet, flavourful palate with good varietal character and better than in the nose, bitter finish of the vine variety.

EL LOMO 2003 JOVEN RED

82 Garnet red cherry. Fresh, fruity aroma with ripe skins and varietal character. Fresh, fruity, flavourful palate with notes of the vine variety.

EL LOMO 2003 OAK AGED RED

85 Intense cherry. Powerful aroma of fresh and ripe skins, fruity with a mature and typical varietal suggestion. Flavourful, fruity palate, rich in varietal expression, typical.

EL MOCANERO

Carretera General, 347
38350 Tacoronte (Santa Cruz de Tenerife)
☎: 922 560 762 - Fax: 922 560 762
elmocanero@teleline.es

Established: 1993

🍷 10 📊 105,000 litres 🍇 8,5 has. 🍷 100%

EL MOCANERO 2003 JOVEN RED
listán negro, negramoll

81 Garnet red cherry. Fruity, fresh aroma with a hint of varietal expression. Fruity palate with varietal character and a suggestion of tannins, flavourful.

EL MOCANERO 2003 FERMENTADO EN BARRICA RED
listan, negramoll, tintillo

83 Dark cherry. Fruity aroma with smoky nuances of the oak well-integrated with the fruit (foresty), fresh. Flavourful palate, rich in fruit expression with creamy smokiness well-integrated with the wine, supple tannins.

ZERAFINA 2003 VINO DE LICOR

DO TACORONTE-ACENTEJO

ESCUELA DE CAPACITACIÓN AGRÍCOLA DE TACORONTE

Guayonje, 68
38350 Tacoronte (Tenerife)
☎: 922 573 360 - Fax: 922 573 361

VIÑA MAIMONA ROBLE RED

GRAN TINERFE

San Antonio, 61
38370 La Matanza (Tenerife)
☎: 922 578 042 - Fax: 922 578 581
divican@terra.es

GRAN TINERFE TRADICIONAL RED

GUAYONJE

Candelaria, 4 El Cantillo
38350 Tacoronte (Tenerife)
☎: 922 561 780
bodegasguayonge@teleline.net

GUAYONJE 2003 JOVEN RED

77 Dark cherry with a carbonic edge. Aroma somewhere between red fruit and balsamic flavours. Fresh, fruity palate, pleasant and well-mannered.

Comunidad de Bienes
HERMANOS PÍO HERNÁNDEZ

Real, 197
38370 La Matanza de Acenjo (Tenerife)
☎: 922 577 828 - Fax: 922 578 761
ferreteriapio@telefonica.net
Established: 1987
🗄 12,000 litres 🍇 2 has. 🚩 100%

FUENTECILLA 2003 JOVEN RED

81 Dark cherry. Fresh, toasty, fruity aroma (raspberries). Fresh, fruity palate with balsamic hints (fallen leaves and eucalyptus), flavourful.

HIMACOPASA

Avenida Reyes Católicos, 23
38005 Santa Cruz de Tenerife (Tenerife)
☎: 922 218 155 - Fax: 922 215 666
sofusa@gruposocas.com
Established: 1996
🌐 150 🗄 300,000 litres 🍇 76 has. 🚩 100%

SANSOFÉ 2003 OAK AGED WHITE

88 Straw-coloured. Complex aroma of mountain herbs with a suggestion of typification, elegant and fruity. Powerful, flavourful palate, rich in varietal expression, with a slightly smoky retronasal effect, elegant and complex.

SANSOFÉ 2003 OAK AGED JOVEN RED 🌐3

79 Dark cherry. Aroma with sweet and toasty notes and fresh fruit. Fruity, balsamic palate with fallen leaves and barely perceptible oak.

SANSOFÉ 2003 RED

79 Garnet red cherry. Fresh, fruity aroma with notes of forest herbs, balsamic. Fresh, fruity palate, typical and balsamic.

SANSOFÉ 2003 ROSÉ
PUERTO DE LA MADERA 2003 RED
TINTO TRADICIONAL 2003

IGNACIO DÍAZ GONZÁLEZ

Capitan Brotons, 1 ATICO
38200 La Laguna (Santa Cruz de Tenerife)
☎: 922 252 610 - Fax: 922 252 088
Established: 1983
🗄 35,000 litres 🍇 17 has. 🚩 100%

VIÑA ORLARA 2003 JOVEN RED

80 Garnet red cherry. Fruity aroma with mild post-fermentative nuances, fresh and varietal. Fresh, fruity, flavourful palate with varietal character.

VIÑA ORLARA 2003 MACERACIÓN CARBÓNICA RED

81 Garnet red cherry. Fresh, fruity aroma with a hint of varietal nuances. Fresh, fruity, well-balanced palate with a slight varietal expression, flavourful.

INSERCASA

Finca El Fresal/Camino Juan Fernandez, s/n
38270 Valle de Guerra-La Laguna (Santa Cruz de Tenerife)
☎: 922 285 316 - Fax: 922 270 626
info@vinobronce.com
www.tacovin.com
Established: 2001
🌐 9 🗄 18,000 litres 🍇 2 has 🚩 100%

BRONCE 2003 OAK AGED RED
70% listán negro, 30% negramoll

85 Garnet red cherry. Powerful, very fruity and slightly floral aroma (petals), quite complex, elegant and fresh. Fresh palate with creamy oak in the retronasal passage, flavourful, varietal and interesting.

Bodegas INSULARES TENERIFE

Vereda del Medio, 8B
38350 Tacoronte (Tenerife)
☎: 922 570 617 - Fax: 922 570 043
bitsa@cistia.es
www.bodegasinsulares.es

Established: 1992

🌐 300 🗎 1,700,000 litres 🇪🇸 95% 🌍5%

VIÑA NORTE 2003 JOVEN SECO WHITE
100% listán blanca

83 Straw-coloured. Fruity, delicado (delicate aroma (fragrant herbs, lavender), clear and fresh. Slightly carbonic on the palate, dry and fruity with a bitter finish, well-crafted with balsamic notes in the retronasal passage.

VIÑA NORTE 2003 JOVEN WHITE
100% güal

70 Straw-coloured. Aroma with light rustic notes of early evolution and muted fruit. Fresh, unexpressive palate with light oxidative notes. Is this a characteristic of the vine variety?

VIÑA NORTE 2003 JOVEN ROSÉ
100% listán negro

80 Lively raspberry. Powerful aroma with copious fruity nuances (blackberries, brambles), fresh. Fresh, fruity, slightly balsamic palate (fallen leaves, vegetative) but flavourful.

VIÑA NORTE 2003 OAK AGED MACERACIÓN CARBÓNICA RED
90% listán negro, 10% negramoll

84 Intense cherry. Powerful aroma of fresh fruit and ripe skins (brambles). Slightly fleshy, very fruity (strawberries and brambles), flavourful and fresh palate with good varietal character.

VIÑA NORTE 2003 OAK AGED MACERACIÓN CARBÓNICA RED
90% listán negro, 10% negramoll   🌐4

87 Garnet red cherry. Aroma with good fruity and varietal expression and notes of ripe but fresh fruit. Flavourful, full palate with excellent fruit expression, elegant balsamic hints and supple tannins from the casks.

BREZAL 2003 JOVEN RED
90% listán negro, 10% negramol

81 Garnet red cherry. Slightly short but clear aroma with a slight varietal and fruit expression. Light, fresh, flavourful and well-balanced palate, well-crafted and with fresh fruit.

VIÑA NORTE 2003 JOVEN RED
90% listán negro, 10% negramoll

83 Dark cherry. Aroma with a hint of varietal strength, fruity (brambles and fallen leaves) and fresh. Fresh, flavourful, good acidity with good varietal expression.

HUMBOLDT 2001 OAK AGED RED SWEET
100% listán negro

91 Intense cherry. Powerful, sweet and toasty aroma (dark-roasted flavours, minerals), spirituous with hints of ripeness and overripening. Sweet, powerful, flavourful palate, similar to a young vintage Oporto wine, flavourful, complex and long.

VIÑA NORTE 2003 OAK AGED RED
90% listán negro, 10% negramoll   🌐6

89 Dark cherry. Powerful aroma with copious toasty and fresh fruit nuances and balsamic and very elegant notes. Round, generous, flavourful palate, rich in fruit expression with fine toasty oak (cocoa), elegant balsamic flavours.

VIÑA NORTE 2001 CRIANZA RED
90% listán negro, 10% negramoll

88 Quite intense cherry. Toasty aroma of ripe skins with a slight varietal expression and creamy oak notes. Slightly fleshy, powerful, flavourful palate with a rich expression of fresh but ripe fruit and a smoky retronasal effect of fine oak.

BREZAL 2003 WHITE
VIÑA NORTE 1997 ROBLE WHITE DULCE
VIÑA NORTE VENDIMIA SELECCIONADA
 2001 OAK AGED RED
BREZAL 1999 CRIANZA RED

J.A. FLORES

Cuchareras Bajas, 2
38370 La Matanza de Acentejo (Tenerife)
☎: 922 577 194 - Fax: 922 577 194

Established: 1972

🗎 26,000 litres 🍇 6,5 has. 🇪🇸 100%

VIÑA FLORES 2003 JOVEN RED

80 Garnet red cherry. Fruity and balsamic aroma (eucalyptus and bay). Fresh, fruity, balsamic palate, flavourful.

VIÑA FLORES 2001 CRIANZA RED

81 Garnet red cherry. Aroma with crianza in bottle reduction notes (leather, tobacco, cedar). Supple palate with classic crianza notes, hints of animals (leather) and supple tannins.

VIÑA FLORES WHITE

JUAN FUENTES TABARES

Camino El Boquerón, s/n
38200 La Laguna (Tenerife)
☎: 922 543 375 - Fax: 922 541 004

VIÑA EL DRAGO 2003 JOVEN RED
100% merlot

80 Intense cherry with a luminous edge. Aroma with slightly shrunken fruit, closed-in with predominant toasty note. Fresh, fruity, quite balsamic palate with noticeable oak tannins and a slightly muted varietal character (new vineyard?).

VIÑA EL DRAGO 2002 JOVEN RED

81 Dark cherry. Aroma with mild and well-balanced toasty and fruity notes, fresh with varietal expression. Slightly fleshy, flavourful palate with fruit and oak and balsamic hints in the retronasal passage.

VIÑA EL DRAGO 2003 JOVEN RED
100% cabernet sauvignon

81 Intense cherry. Aroma with mild fruity and slightly vegetative notes, balsamic nuances and hints of paprika. Fleshy, flavourful palate with a slightly muted varietal character and still supple tannins, the wood is too well-balanced for the Merlot.

EL DRAGO WHITE

JUAN GUTIERREZ LEÓN

Pérez Díaz, 44
38380 La Victoria (Tenerife)
☎: 922 581 003 - Fax: 922 581 831

HACIENDA ACENTEJO 2003 JOVEN RED

80 Garnet red cherry. Balsamic, fresh, slightly fruity aroma. Fruity and typical with fallen leaves on the palate, flavourful and light.

JUAN JOSÉ TORRES GARCÍA

Real Orotava, 300
38360 El Sauzal (Tenerife)
☎: 922 560 752 - Fax: 922 560 752

EL TIMPLILLO JOVEN RED

JUAN ZACARÍAS REYES GARCÍA

Pérez Cáceres, 47
38370 La Matanza (Santa Cruz de Tenerife)
☎: 922 577 088

BREÑA REYES RED

JULIO SUÁREZ NEGRIN

Taganana, 1
38130 Santa Cruz de Tenerife (Tenerife)
☎: 922 590 082 - Fax: 922 294 058
taganana@msn.es
Established: 1955

🍃 10 🛢 9,225 litres 🍇 36 has. 🍷 100%

LAS FAJANETAS 2003 JOVEN WHITE

78 Straw-coloured. Very ripe fruity aroma, warm with mild viscous notes. Warm, vinous palate with scrubland herbs, somewhat flavourful.

LAS FAJANETAS 2001 OAK AGED WHITE

70 Golden. Aroma with notes of oak with rancid nuances (generous) and a nuance of toasty pâtisserie. Warm palate with slightly woody oak and generous and spirituous hints.

LAS FAJANETAS JOVEN RED

LA ISLETA

José Rodríguez Amador, 21
38260 Tejina-La Laguna (Santa Cruz de Tenerife)
☎: 922 541 805 - Fax: 922 540 082
bodegaisleta@tiscali.es

LA ISLETA 2003 JOVEN WHITE

80 Straw-coloured. Fresh, somewhat fruity aroma of wet forest herbs. Fruity, fresh palate with a balsamic hint in the retronasal passage, wild fallen leaves, interesting.

LA ISLETA 2003 JOVEN DULCE WHITE

89 Straw-coloured with a golden glimmer. Fresh, varietal aroma with hints of minerals (stones) and sweet fruit. Fresh palate with abundant fruit expression and fine fragrant herbs, sweet yet bitter, typical of the vine variety.

LA ISLETA MOSCATEL 2003 DULCE WHITE

85 Golden yellow. Powerful, varietal aroma with notes of exotic fruit and crystallised, floral hints. Flavourful palate with bitter sweet notes, unctuous with ripe fruit, minerals, herby hints and a slightly acidic edge.

LA ISLETA 2003 JOVEN SECO RED

70 Dark cherry. Slightly fruity aroma with a varietal nuance (brambles, dry earth). Fresh, slightly fruity palate, discreet.

LA PALMERA

La Herrera nº85
38360 El Sauzal (Tenerife)
☎: 922 661 282 - Fax: 922 652 566
robertotorresdelcastillo@terra.es
Established: 1969
🛢 45,000 litres 🍇 5 has. 🍷 100%

LA PALMERA 2003 JOVEN RED

80 Quite dark cherry. Toasty aroma of jammy fruit (a hint of overripening from some bunches). Flavourful palate with ripe fruit and fresh overtones.

LA PALMERA WHITE

LA ROSA

Las Mesetas, 3 - Agua García
38350 Tacoronte (Tenerife)
☎: 922 584 242

Established: 1960
🛢 8 ⬚ 10,000 litres 🍇 1 has. 🏆 100%

ATLANTES RED
ATLANTES LISTÁN RED
ATLANTES OAK AGED RED
ATLANTES CRIANZA RED

MARBA

Carretera del Socorro, 253
38280 Tegueste (Tenerife)
☎: 922 638 305 - Fax: 922 638 305
bodegas_marba@telefonica.net

Established: 1993
🛢 14 ⬚ 35,000 litres 🍇 4 has.
🏆 99% 🌼1%

MARBA 2003 JOVEN RED
listán negro

76 Intense cherry. Aroma with mild nuances of overripening (jam), fruity. Slightly fleshy, flavourful palate with a slightly weak fruit expression.

MARBA 2003 MACERACIÓN CARBÓNICA RED
listán negro

81 Quite intense cherry. Aroma with a fruity essence and mild vegetative notes evoking minimal ripening, clear. Fruity, fresh, flavourful, moderately expressive palate.

MARBA 2003 JOVEN WHITE
MARBA 2003 OAK AGED WHITE

MIGUEL PACHECO MESA

El Calvario, 67
El Sauzal ()
☎: 922 330 557 - Fax: 922 331 223
miguel@pacheco.es
www.baldesa.com

LA BALDESA 2003 JOVEN WHITE

80 Straw-coloured. Fruity, fresh aroma with a good varietal expression (fragrant herbs, sweet fruit) Fresh, dry, flavourful and fruity with a bitter finish.

LA BALDESA 2003 JOVEN RED
listán negro

70 Garnet red. Very short, imprecise, clear aroma. Unexpressive sweet notes on the palate, discreet.

MONJE

Camino Cruz de Leandro, 36
38359 El Sauzal (Santa Cruz de Tenerife)
☎: 922 585 027 - Fax: 922 585 027
monje@bodegasmonje.com
www.bodegasmonje.com

Established: 1956
🛢 95 ⬚ 160,000 litres 🍇 14 has.
🏆 90% 🌼10%: -DE

EVENTO 2001 FERMENTADO EN BARRICA WHITE
100% listán blanca

83 Straw-coloured. Powerful aroma, rich in notes of fine herbs and sweet fruit (custard apples and melons). Fresh, fruity, flavourful palate with good varietal character, fine.

DRAGOBLANCO 2002 WHITE
100% listán blanca

82 Straw-coloured. Fresh, quite fruity aroma with a mild essence of wet forest herbs and sweet fruit. Notes of sweetness on the palate with fine herbs (lavender, mint), flavourful, fresh and fruity.

BIBIANA MONJE 2003 ROSÉ
100% listán negro

82 Strawberry. Fresh, fruity, pleasant aroma, clear and clean. Powerful, fruity palate, good acidity, flavourful and varietal.

MONJE LISTAN NEGRO 2001 FERMENTADO EN BARRICA JOVEN RED
100% listán negro

84 Garnet red cherry. Aroma with balsamic notes, fresh fruit and smoky hints, slightly woody. Flavourful, fresh, fruity and balsamic palate.

HOLLERA MONJE 2003 MACERACIÓN CARBÓNICA RED
100% listán negro

80 Quite dark garnet red cherry. Aroma with mild post fermentative notes (toasty flavours, lees), and a fruity and slightly balsamic essence (fallen leaves, vine shoots). Fresh, fruity, flavourful and clear palate with balsamic notes in the retronasal passage.

VINO PADRE DULCE 1999 OAK AGED RED DULCE
100% listán negro

87 Intense cherry. Aroma of pâtisserie, and jammy fruit, fine with hints of caramelised sugar. Round, flavourful, sweet palate with toasty pâtisserie in the retronasal passage.

DO TACORONTE-ACENTEJO

MONJE 2003 OAK AGED RED
80% listan negro, 15% listán blanco, 5% negramoll

79 Garnet red cherry. Fresh, fruity aroma with light toasty notes well-integrated with the wine. Fresh, slightly balsamic palate with half-ripe fruit.

MONJE DE AUTOR ALFREDO KRAUS 1998 RESERVA RED
70% listán negro, 20% negramoll, 10% listán blanca

81 Garnet red cherry with an orange edge. Slightly closed aroma with a suggestion of spices and hints of reduction (tobacco and leather). Supple, round palate with jammy fruit, a smoky retronasal effect and reduction hints.

MONJE MOSCATEL 2000 GENEROSO DULCE
100% moscatel

88 Golden. Aroma of ripe grapes with toasty and honeyed notes. Powerful palate, rich in expression of ripe and sun-drenched Muscatel, flavourful, complex and full.

PRESAS OCAMPO

Los Alamos de San Juan, 5
38350 Tacoronte (Tenerife)
☎: 922 571 689 - Fax: 922 561 700
presasocampo@terra.es

Established: 1991
12 📊 150,000 litres 🍇 15 has.
🍷 95% 🌿5%

PRESAS OCAMPO FERMENTADO EN BARRICA WHITE
PRESAS OCAMPO WHITE
PRESAS OCAMPO ROSÉ
PRESAS OCAMPO OAK AGED RED
PRESAS OCAMPO RED

REJANERO

Rejanero, 3 - El Socorro
38280 Tegueste (Tenerife)
☎: 922 540 120 - Fax: 922 544 773

REJANERO 2003 MACERACIÓN CARBÓNICA RED
100% listán negro

72 Quite dark cherry. Fresh, fruity aroma, without great nuances. Fresh, slightly fruity palate, only well-mannered.

RUIZ

Simón Bolivar, 4
Urb. Lomo Román
38390 Santa Ursula (Santa Cruz de Tenerife)
☎: 922 300 802 - Fax: 922 153 227

bodega@bodegaruiz.com
www.bodega-ruiz.com

MILLENIUM ROSÉ
LA BASTONA RED

SAN DIEGO

Camino Botello, 2
38370 La Matanza de Acentejo (Tenerife)
☎: 922 577 636 - Fax: 922 578 804
sandiego@ideanet.com
www.tacovin.com

Established: 1980
📊 400,000 litres 🍇 4,5 has 🍷 100%

SAN DIEGO WHITE
SAN DIEGO AFRUTADO RED
SAN DIEGO RED

TAGOROR

Salto del Gato, 61
38360 El Sauzal (Santa Cruz Tenerife)
☎: 922 572 097 - Fax: 922 204 284
cogosa@infonegocio.com

Established: 1995
📊 500,000 litres 🍇 15 has. 🍷 100%

TAGOROR 2003 JOVEN WHITE
TAGOROR 2002 JOVEN RED
EL ENGAZO 2002 JOVEN RED
TAGOROR 2003 JOVEN RED
IDENTIDAD 2003 JOVEN RED
EL ENGAZO 2003 JOVEN RED
EL SACHO RED

TEXIMAR

Carretera General El Socorro, 53 San Luis
38292 Tegueste (Tenerife)
☎: 922 542 605 - Fax: 922 542 790
teximar@stl.logiccontrol.es
www.teximar.com

Established: 1967
40 📊 100,000 litres 🍇 12 has.
🍷 95% 🌿5%: -DE

VALLE MOLINA 2003 JOVEN WHITE SEMI DULCE
malvasía

79 Pale gold. Aroma with mild varietal character with a nuance of herbs and sweet fruit. Supple, fresh and bitter palate.

VALLE MOLINA 2003 OAK AGED RED
cabernet sauvignon, listán negro   6

78 Garnet red cherry. Slightly muted fruity aroma with smoky oak notes, without great nuances. Fresh, fruity palate with a vegetative hint, pleasant.

VIÑA SANTO DOMINGO 2003 WHITE
VIÑA SANTO DOMINGO 2003 RED

TRINIDAD LAURA DIAZ HERNÁNDEZ

Tostada, 14
Tejina (La Laguna)
☎: 922 543 754

TRINIDAD 2003 JOVEN WHITE
listán blanca

67 Straw-coloured. Aroma with mild reduction notes and a hint of evolution, quite weak fruit. Dry, unexpressive palate with a suggestion of reduction in the retronasal passage.

TRINIDAD 2003 JOVEN RED
100% listán negro

67 Lively garnet red cherry. Short aroma, without fruit expression, discreet. Slightly sweet and vegetative notes on the palate, muted fruit.

VIÑA EL MATO

Calvario, 270
38350 Tacoronte (Tenerife)
☎: 922 561 752 - Fax: 922 561 752
Established: 1984
▤ 50,000 litres ♚ 0.8 has. ☛ 100%

VIÑA EL MATÓ 2003 JOVEN RED

60 Garnet red. Aroma with an off-odour (poor racking) and concealed fruit. Flat palate, discreet.

VIÑA EL MATÓ 2003 MACERACIÓN CARBÓNICA RED

82 Garnet red. Aroma with a hint of fruit expression, fresh with varietal notes. Fresh, fruity palate with balsamic notes in the retronasal passage, flavourful.

VIÑA TOGALEZ

San Cristóbal, 63
38370 La Matanza (La Matanza)
☎: 922 577 968

VIÑA TOGALEZ JOVEN RED

ZAHIRA NASSER EDDIN

18 de Julio, 50-4° Izda.
38004 Sta Cruz de Tenerife (Tenerife)
☎: 922 286 898 - Fax: 922 240 095
zahiranasser@hotmail.com

VIÑA JANA RED

DO TARRAGONA

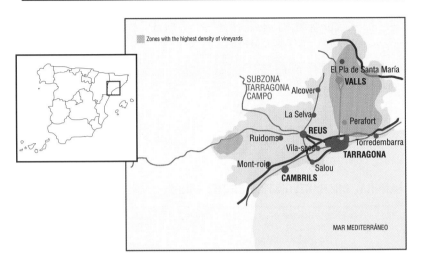

Zones with the highest density of vineyards

SUBZONA TARRAGONA CAMPO · Alcover · La Selva · Ruidoms · Vila-seca · Mont-roig · Salou · El Pla de Santa María · VALLS · Perafort · REUS · Torredembarra · TARRAGONA · CAMBRILS · MAR MEDITERRÁNEO

NEWS. The new regulations of the DO Tarragona, approved on 30th October 2001, did not make provision for sub-regions and prepared a series of changes which, amongst other things, were to include the *Sumoll* variety. These are some of the signs that show the desire for change in this historic Spanish wine region, from which regions have broken off during the last few years to become the DO Montsant. Tarragona seems to be in search of a balance between its traditional sweet wines (the famous Mistelas from Tarraco) and the Crianza red wines, amongst which the Clos Barenys, from the bodega of Josep M. Bach Voltas e Hijos stands out, with excellent blends of the two main grape varieties from Bordeaux (*Merlot* and *Cabernet Sauvignon*) which have adapted so well in Catalonia, even in the far south of the province.

Hectares of Vineyard	No. of Viticulturists	No. of Bodegas	2003 Harvest	2003 Production	Marketing
7,280	2,500	44 producers 22 bottlers	Very Good	45,000,000 litres	80% Spain 20% foreign

LOCATION. The region is situated in the province of Tarragona. It comprises two different wine-growing regions: El Camp and Ribera d'Ebre, with a total of 72 municipal areas.

CLIMATE. Mediterranean in the region of El Camp, with an average annual rainfall of 500 mm. The region of the Ribera has a rather harsh climate with cold winters and hot summers; it also has the lowest rainfall in the region (385 mm per year).

SOIL. El Camp is characterized by its calcareous, light terrain, and the Ribera has calcareous terrain and also some alluvial terrain.

VARIETIES:

White: *Chardonnay, Macabeo, Xarel·lo, Garnacha Blanca, Parellada, Moscatel de Alejandría, Moscatel de Frontignan, Sauvignon Blanc, Malvasía.*
Red: *Samsó (Cariñena), Garnacha, Ull de Llebre (Tempranillo), Cabernet Sauvignon, Merlot, Monastrell, Pinot Noir, Syrah.*

SUB-REGIONS: El Camp and Ribera d'Ebre (See specific characteristics in previous sections).

REGULATORY COUNCIL.

Avda. Catalunya, 50. 43002 Tarragona.
Tel: 977 217 931. Fax: 977 229 102.
E-mail: dotarragona@ctmail.net

GENERAL CHARACTERISTICS OF THE WINES:

Whites	These have a markedly Mediterranean character, with notes reminiscent of mountain herbs. Yellow straw in colour, they are fresh, fruity and flavourful on the palate.
Rosés	Most of these have a colour that ranges from salmon to raspberry. They are fresh, fruity, light and pleasant to drink.
Reds	The young wines are the most characteristic. They have a cherry colour and are fruity, flavourful, with a slightly warm hint due to the Mediterranean influence, although much less meaty and powerful than those of Montsant.
Traditional Wines	These are the Licorosos (sweet) and the so-called Rancios Secos, with an alcohol content of between 13.5° and 23°, and the Generosos (dry), with an alcohol content of between 14° and 23°. Some also undergo the traditional processes.

ADOLF TOUS I ANDREU

Carretera Salmella, km. 1
43817 El Pont D'Armentera (Tarragona)
☎: 977 638 381 - Fax: 977 238 631
ata@tinet.fut.es
www.tousandreu.com

Established: 1994
🌐 35 📊 50,000 litres 🍇 10 has. 🍷 100%

TOUS ANDREU WHITE
TOUS ANDREU CABERNET SAUVIGNON RED
TOUS ANDREU PINOT NOIR RED
TOUS ANDREU CRIANZA RED
TOUS ANDREU RESERVA RED

ALBESA FIGUEROLA

D'Avall, 34
43886 Vilabella (Tarragona)
☎: 977 620 190 - Fax: 977 620 130
alfiscp@hotmail.com

📊 180,000 litres 🍇 30 has. 🍷 100%

DORSER 2003 WHITE

Cooperativa Agrícola de BRAFIM

Major, 50
43894 Brafim (Tarragona)
☎: 977 620 061 - Fax: 977 620 061
brafimcoop@retemail.es

Established: 1930
📊 8,000,000 litres 🍇 700 has. 🍷 100%

PUIG RODÓ 2003 WHITE
100% macabeo

78 Very pale yellow. Intense aroma of white fruit (hints of light reduction), a floral and herby suggestion. Flavourful, slightly bitter and mineral on the palate with a minor fruit expression and an acidic edge, pleasant.

PUIG RODÓ 2003 ROSÉ
100% tempranillo

79 Very deep raspberry. Powerful, fruity aroma with fine notes of toasty skins. Flavourful palate with bitter notes and hints of slightly sweet fruit, pleasant.

PUIG RODÓ 2003 JOVEN RED
70% tempranillo, 30% merlot

82 Dark cherry with a dark red-violet edge. Powerful, fruity aroma with a good varietal expression of young wine (redcurrants, underbrush). Fleshy palate with slightly sweet fruit, marked yet flavourful tannins and good acidity.

Unió Agraria Cooperativa CELLERS UNIÓ

Joan Oliver, 16-24 Mas de les Animes
43206 Reus (Tarragona)
☎: 977 330 055 - Fax: 977 330 070
f.gimenez@cellersunio.com
www.cellersunio.com

Established: 1942
🌐 6,500 📊 6,000,000 litres 🍇 2,110 has.
🍷 25% 🌍75%: -DE -DK -US -NL -JP

ROUREDA BLANC DE BLANCS 2003 WHITE SECO
70% garnacha blanca, 30% macabeo

75 Pale gold. Quite intense aroma with predominant spicy notes of skins and a nuance of fruit and perfumed soap. Fresh, dry palate with fine bitter notes (herbs, nuts).

ROUREDA RUBÍ 2003 ROSÉ
85% garnacha tinta, 15% merlot

79 Fairly deep raspberry. Somewhat intense aroma with predominant spicy notes of skins. Flavourful palate with red stone fruit and fine bitter notes.

ROUREDA 2003 JOVEN RED
33% garnacha tinta, 33% tempranillo, 33% cabernet sauvignon

82 Red cherry with a violet rim. Intense aroma with red stone fruit, a spicy hint (black pepper) and balsamic hints. Flavourful, fruity palate with ripe, firm tannins, peppery hints of Cabernet and good acidity.

ROUREDA 1999 CRIANZA RED
40% garnacha tinta, 20% tempranillo, 20% cabernet sauvignon, 20% cariñena

81 Garnet red cherry with a coppery edge. Somewhat intense, fruity aroma (hints of black olives) with spicy oak notes. Flavourful palate with a good fruit/oak integration, ripe and slightly oily tannins and a waxy nuance.

ROUREDA 2000 CRIANZA RED

DE MULLER

Camí Pedra Estela, 34
43205 Reus (Tarragona)
☎: 977 757 473 - Fax: 977 771 129
demuller1@infonegocio.com

Established: 1851
🌐 1,200 📊 3,850,000 litres 🍇 132 has.
🍷 35% 🌍65%: -US; -CA -MX -CO -PE -
SE -UK -FR -FI -DK -DE -RU -LT -JP -BJ -
ET -CH -DE -SE

DE MULLER SOLIMAR 2003 JOVEN WHITE
70% macabeo, 10% sauvignon blanc, 20% muscat de Alejandria

78 Pale yellow. Intense, very fresh, slightly fruity palate with herby hints. Very fresh, bitter palate with marked citrus acidity.

DE MULLER CHARDONNAY 2003 FERMENTADO EN BARRICA WHITE
100% chardonnay

82 Intense gold. Powerful aroma with quite varietal, very ripe fruit (apples) and a suggestion of caramelised oak. Flavourful, generous palate with an oily, warm texture, fine smoky and spicy notes.

DE MULLER MUSCAT 2003 WHITE
100% moscatel

79 Pale yellow with a golden hue. Powerful, ripe aroma with a good varietal expression (musk, acacia, honey). Fleshy palate of white stone fruit, exotic hints and a slightly acidic edge.

DE MULLER PINOT NOIR 2003 JOVEN ROSÉ
100% pinot noir

75 Fairly deep raspberry with an orangey hue. Powerful aroma of very ripe fruit, sweet hints, toasted skins and a slightly viscous suggestion. Flavourful, bitter palate with a toasty suggestion lacking freshness and varietal expression.

DE MULLER SOLIMAR 2003 JOVEN ROSÉ
60% tempranillo, 40% cabernet sauvignon

79 Fairly deep raspberry with a coppery hue. Intense aroma of superripe red fruit, slight reduction, a balsamic and viscous hint. Flavourful, smoky and spicy on the palate (varietal paprika) with fresh overtones.

DE MULLER CABERNET SAUVIGNON 2001 OAK AGED RED
100% cabernet sauvignon

84 Dark garnet red cherry. Intense aroma with toasty oak notes, a nuance of jammy fruit and fine reduction (cedar, tobacco). Flavourful, supple palate with fine reduction hints, slightly warm.

DE MULLER PINOT NOIR 2001 CRIANZA RED
100% pinot noir

76 Not very deep cherry with an orangey glint. Intense aroma with predominant reduction notes (damp horsehair, old furniture, tobacco). Flavourful, supple palate with a slight reduction and varietal expression.

DE MULLER SOLIMAR 2001 CRIANZA RED
60% cabernet sauvignon, 40% merlot

83 Garnet red cherry with brick red nuances. Intense aroma of toasty oak, spicy, jammy fruit with hints of cedar. Flavourful palate with a good fruit/oak integration, bitter with a suggestion of sweet fruit, liquorice and spices.

DE MULLER MERLOT 2001 RED
100% merlot

79 Deep cherry with a saffron edge. Quite intense aroma with spicy crianza notes and a suggestion of jammy fruit. Flavourful, warm palate without great varietal expression, pleasant.

AUREO SECO MUY VIEJO VINO DE LICOR
60% garnacha, 40% garnacha blanca

82 Very old gold. Aroma with pâtisserie notes, aldehydes, varnish and toasted nuts. Flavourful palate with quite pungent alcohol, marked wood notes and quite a discreet finish.

AUREO SEMI-DULCE MUY VIEJO VINO DE LICOR

82 Old gold. Slightly short aroma with fine notes of Solera (pastries), hints of varnish and fruit in liqueur. Flavourful palate with sweet notes well-integrated with the freshness, Solera sensation but lacking complexity.

DE MULLER GARNACHA MOSCATEL SOLERA 1926 VINO DE LICOR

85 Copper with a yellow edge. Toasty aroma with spices, rancid and nutty hints and a viscous hint. Flavourful palate with notes of toasted nuts, Solera complexity, rancid hints and orange peel, long.

DE MULLER MOSCATEL AÑEJO DULCE

84 Amber. Clean aroma of sun-drenched grapes with notes of peaches, oranges and a suggestion of honey and vanilla. Sweet palate with a pleasant sensation of bitter orange, a good fresh finish, crystallised fruit.

DE MULLER RANCIO SECO VINO DE LICOR

80 Coppery. Rancid aroma (salted meat) with notes of oak and pâtisserie. Flavourful palate with bitter hints and good freshness, slightly flat finish.

PAJARETE SOLERA 1851 VINO DE LICOR
garnacha tinta, garnacha blanca

86 Dark mahogany with a yellow rim. Dark-roasted aroma (coffee) with toasty crianza notes, a suggestion of jammy dates, raisins and rancid hints. Powerful, fleshy palate, slightly cloying, lacking some freshness, a bitter cocoa finish.

AUREO MUY VIEJO VINO DE LICOR

EDETÀRIA

Finca El Mas, Ctra. Gandesa - Vilalba s/n
43780 Gandesa (Tarragona)
☎: 630 966 957 - Fax: 938 605 147
www.edetaria.es

Established: 2003
🍇 38 has.

EDETÀRIA 2003 OAK AGED WHITE
garnacha blanca, macabeo

81 Pale yellow with a golden hue. Powerful aroma with fine smoky oak, fragrant herbs, a slightly fruity hint. Flavourful, bitter palate (slightly marked tannins unintegrated with the fruit), a smoky suggestion, spices (vanilla) and a nuance of Catalonian cream custard.

EMILIO MIRÓ SALVAT

Adria Gual, 10
43206 Reus (Tarragona)
☎: 977 312 958 - Fax: 977 320 321
miro.salvat@trr.servicom.es
www.mirosalvat.com

🌿 3,5 has 🍷 75% 🍇25%

MIRÓ RANCIO CRIANZA GENEROSO
FARLATÍ MOSCATEL DULCE
MIRALVA MISTELA
MIRÓ VINO DE MISA DULCE

Bodegas JOSEP M. BACH VOLTAS I FILLS

Apartado de Correos, 155
43480 Vila Seca (Tarragona)
☎: 977 388 593 - Fax: 977 382 226
clos_barenys@hotmail.com
www.closbarenys.com

Established: 1995

🍾 80 🛢 48,000 litres 🌿 7 has.
🍷 70% 🍇30%: -NL -DE

CLOS BARENYS 2003 RED
50% merlot, 50% syrah

84 Nearly opaque cherry. Slatey aroma with smoky hints, spices and concentrated black fruit. Powerful, slightly pungent palate with abundant fruit well-integrated with the toasted oak (cocoa); for keeping.

CLOS BARENYS 2001 CRIANZA RED
50% cabernet sauvignon, 50% merlot

83 Dark garnet red cherry with a saffron edge. Intense aroma with predominant toasty oak notes and balsamic hints. Flavourful palate with round, oily tannins, well-balanced with good crianza expression (dark-roasted flavours, liquorice, jammy fruit, terroir).

CLOS BARENYS 2000 CRIANZA RED
50% cabernet sauvignon, 50% merlot

82 Garnet red cherry. Ripe aroma with reduction notes (animal skins, old leather) and earthy hints. Earthy, very toasty palate with ripe but slightly pungent wood tannins, a warm finish.

CLOS BARENYS 1998 CRIANZA RED
50% cabernet sauvignon, 50% merlot

85 Very dark cherry with a brick red rim. Powerful aroma with predominant toasty notes of crianza oak and a suggestion of jammy fruit. Fleshy, bitter palate (cocoa) with an excellent crianza expression, hints of liquorice and terroir.

CLOS BARENYS 2000 CRIANZA RED
50% cabernet sauvignon, 50% merlot

82 Garnet red cherry. Ripe aroma with reduction notes (animal skins, old leather) and earthy hints. Earthy, very toasty palate with ripe but slightly pungent wood tannins, a warm finish.

CLOS BARENYS 2000 RESERVA RED
50% cabernet sauvignon, 50% merlot

87 Deep garnet red. Aroma of jammy black fruit with notes of cocoa, cloves and pepper (crianza well-integrated with the fruit). Powerful, fleshy palate with ripe, earthy tannins and a complex aftertaste (liquorice, black fruit).

CLOS BARENYS 1998 RESERVA RED
50% cabernet sauvignon, 50% merlot

86 Dark garnet red with a brownish edge. Earthy aroma with some good crianza reduction (cocoa, pepper, animals) and jammy plums. Fleshy, powerful palate with an earthy, crianza character, oily tannins and a fresh finish.

CLOS BARENYS 1997 RESERVA RED
50% cabernet sauvignon, 50% merlot

84 Dark cherry with a brick red rim. Powerful aroma with predominant burnt notes (pitch, dark-roasted flavours) and a suggestion of jammy fruit. Flavourful, fleshy palate with fine bitter notes, slightly warm and oily, quite promising.

MONESTIR DEL TALLAT

Carretera Reus-El Morell, Km. 738
43760 El Morrell (Tarragona)
☎: 977 840 655 - Fax: 977 842 146
vermut@vermutzyaguirre.com
www.vermutzaguirre.com

Established: 1995

🍾 130 🛢 88,000 litres 🌿 45 has.
🍷 75% 🍇25%: -BE -NL -IT -AD -CH -DE -LV -RU -IE

MOSCATEL J. SALLA DULCE

Cooperativa Agrícola MONTBRIÓ DEL CAMP

Avenida Sant Jordi, 19
43340 Montbrió del Camp (Tarragona)
☎: 977 826 039 - Fax: 977 826 576
montebrione@retmail.es
www.montebrione.com

Established: 1964

🛢 120,000 litres 🍷 100%

VINO DE MISA MONTEBRIONE 2003 OAK
 AGED WHITE
MONTEBRIONE 2003 MOSCATEL

DO TARRAGONA

Vinos PADRÓ

Avenida Catalunya, 56-58
43812 Brafim (Tarragona)
☎: 977 620 012 - Fax: 977 620 486
padro@tinet.org

Established: 1916

🌐 440 📦 4,400,000 litres 🍇 50 has.
🍷 70% 🌍30%: -CR -US -JP -NL -DE -CH
-AT -FR

CRINEL 2003 WHITE
CRINEL 2003 ROSÉ
CRINEL 2003 RED
BACANAL 1999 CRIANZA RED
CRINEL 2000 CRIANZA RED

Cooperativa Agrícola SANT JAUME DE BENISSANET

Carmenes, 4
43747 Benissanet (Tarragona)
☎: 977 407 105

ENNIS WHITE
LLIMS WHITE
ENNIS RED

VINÍCOLA DE NULLES

Raval Sant Joan, 7
43887 Nulles (Tarragona)
☎: 977 602 622 - Fax: 977 602 622
casinulles@casinulles.com
www.casinulles.com

Established: 1917

🌐 26 📦 3,500,000 litres 🍇 440 has.
🍷 80% 🌍20%: -JP -DE -CH

ADERNATS CHARDONNAY WHITE
ADERNATS BLANC DE BLANCS 2003 WHITE
CAMPASSOS 2003 WHITE
ADERNATS TEMPRANILLO 2003 ROSÉ
CAMPASSOS 2003 ROSÉ
ADERNATS CABERNET SAUVIGNON 2000
RED
ADERNATS MERLOT 2002 RED
ADERNATS TEMPRANILLO 2003 RED
CAMPASOS 2003 RED
1917 1999 CRIANZA RED
ADERNATS TEMPRANILLO 1999 CRIANZA
RED

VINS FONT

Disseminat El Canyet - St. Marçal
Apdo. Correos nº 298
08732 Castellet i la Gornal (Barcelona)
☎: 938 980 301 - Fax: 938 186 020
vinsfont@logiccontrol.es

Established: 1981

📦 30,000,000 litres 🍇 20 has.
🍷 95% 🌍5%

COSTERS MILENARIS WHITE
COSTERS MILENARIS RED

VINYA JANINE

Anselm Clavé, 1
43812 Rodonyá (Tarragona)
☎: 977 628 305 - Fax: 977 628 305
vjanine@tinet.org
www.vinyajanine.com

Established: 1994

🌐 60 📦 35,000 litres 🍇 15 has.
🍷 70% 🌍30%

VINYA JANINE XAREL.LO VARIETAL WHITE
VINYA JANINE ULL DE LLEBRE JOVEN RED
VINYA JANINE CABERNET SAUVIGNON
 1998 RESERVA RED

DO TERRA ALTA

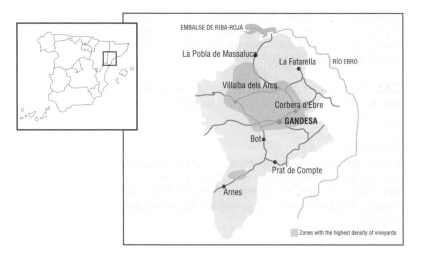

EMBALSE DE RIBA-ROJA

La Pobla de Massaluca

La Fatarella   RÍO EBRO

Villalba dels Arcs

Corbera d'Ebre

GANDESA

Bot

Prat de Compte

Arnes

Zones with the highest density of vineyards

NEWS. In the centre of one of the historic Catalonian wine regions (besides being the furthest south), the DO has in the last few years shown a real commitment to quality. Besides filling the map with different varieties, with the inclusion of experimental varieties of some interest, they are trying to set rather moderate yields per hectare: 8,000 kg for red varieties and 10,000 for whites. This quest for quality seems to have paid off last year, with a 10% increase in the sales of bottled wine. The hot summer in 2003, however, seems to have affected the expression of the exquisite *Garnacha Blanca* of the region – without a doubt its best point – which perhaps has not achieved the scores of previous years, as it displays less expression of fruit, masked as much by the oak as by the alcohol. The best examples hardly surpassed 85 points (Dardell, Ilercavonia, Llàgrimes de Tardor and a blend, the Vila-Closa of La Botera).

Hectares of Vineyard	No. of Viticulturists	No. of Bodegas	2003 Harvest	2003 Production	Marketing
9,224	1,880	33	Very Good	11,123,550 litres	48% Spain 52% foreign

The work of Piñol bodega was excellent, with a magnificent L'Avi Arrufí, which returns to the podium even after the difficult 2002 harvest, or the Mil·lennium of Clúa, which shows off the goodness of the local *Garnacha* outside sweet wine production. The 2001 harvest was impeccable in various Crianza red wines, amongst which, besides the two examples mentioned, a large group stands out, including the Torremadrina of Tarroné, the L'Aube of Batea, the Clos Pinell of Cellers Unió, the Varvall of the Gandesa Cooperativa, the Fill del Temps and the Vall de Verrús of Covilalba, or the Bàrbara Forés.

LOCATION. In the southeast of Catalonia, in the province of Tarragona. It covers the municipal districts of Arnes, Batea, Bot, Caseres, Corbera d´Ebre, La Fatarella,

Gandesa, Horta de Sant Joan, Pinell de Brai, La Pobla de Massaluca, Prat de Comte and Vilalba dels Arcs.

CLIMATE. Mediterranean, with continental influences. It is characterized by its hot, dry summers and very cold winters, especially in the higher regions in the east. The average annual rainfall is 400 mm. Another vital aspect is the wind: the 'Cierzo' and the 'Garbi' (Ábrego) winds.

SOIL. The vineyards are located on an extensive plateau at an altitude of slightly over 400 m. The soil is calcareous and the texture mainly clayey, poor in organic matter and with many pebbles.

VARIETIES:

White: *Chardonnay, Garnacha Blanca, Parellada, Macabeo, Moscatel, Sauvignon Blanc, Chenin, Pedro Ximénez.* Experimental: *Viognier.*
Red: *Cabernet Sauvigon, Cariñena, Garnacha Tinta, Garnacha Peluda, Syrah, Tempranillo, Merlot, Samsó, Cabernet Franc.* Experimental: *Petit Verdot, Marselane, Caladoc.*

REGULATORY COUNCIL.

Avinguda Catalunya, 31. 43780 Gandesa (Tarragona).
Tel: 977 421 278. Fax: 977 421 623.
E-mail: info@doterraalta.com
Website: www.doterraalta.com

GENERAL CHARACTERISTICS OF THE WINES:

Whites	These are the most interesting products of the region. They are produced from the *Garnacha Blanca* variety, and have a purely Mediterranean character. With yellowish nuances, they have aromas of ripe fruit and mountain herbs; they are supple, warm, complex and very expressive on the palate.
Rosés	Mainly produced from *Garnacha*, they offer all the fruitiness and tastiness on the palate that one expects from this variety.
Reds	Cherry-coloured, they are characterised by their ripe fruit aromas; they are quite flavourful on the palate.
Generosos	This is another of the traditional wines of the region, whether in its Rancio or Mistela version.

AGRÍCOLA FUSTER

Méndez Núñez, 15
43780 Gandesa (Tarragona)
☎: 977 232 671 - Fax: 977 234 665
dardell@dardell.es
www.dardell.es

Established: 1996

🏭 35 📊 200,000 litres 🍇 20 has.

🍷 50% 🌐50%: -JP -NL -DE

DARDELL 2003 JOVEN WHITE
90% garnacha, 10% macabeo

83 Pale gold with a coppery hue. Intense, quite fruity aroma with smoky hints of skins. Flavourful with fine bitter notes, hints of fine herbs and excellent acidity.

DARDELL 2003 FERMENTADO EN BARRICA WHITE
100% garnacha blanca

86 Reddish golden hue. Deep aroma of fine lees (toasty flavours) and forest herbs, warm Dried mountain herbs notes on the palate (lavender, rosemary), warm with a hint of sweetness combined with oak notes.

DARDELL GARNACHA Y SYRAH 2003 RED
50% garnacha, 50% syrah

79 Dark cherry with a purplish edge. Powerful aroma of toasty oak and skins well-integrated with the fruit. Flavourful palate with slightly drying tannins and a mild note of greeness, slightly varietal, fleshy and bitter.

DARDELL ENVEJECIDO EN BARRICA 2002 OAK AGED RED
40% garnacha, 40% syrah, 20% cabernet sauvignon 🛢 6

85 Dark cherry. Powerful aroma with predominant burnt notes (pitch dark-roasted flavours), a balsamic hint and viscous hints. Flavourful, fleshy palate with a good oak/fruit integration and bitter hints (liquorice coffee, graphite).

DARDELL 2003 ROSÉ

ALTAVINS VITICULTORS

Tarragona, 42
43786 Batea (Tarragona)
☎: 977 430 596 - Fax: 977 430 371
altavins@hotmail.com
www.altavins.com

Established: 2001

🏭 140 📊 56,000 litres 🍷 25% 🌐75%: -CH -DE -NL -AT -BE -UK -US

ILERCAVONIA 2003 JOVEN WHITE
garnacha

85 Coppery gold. Powerful aroma of ripe stone fruit (peaches) with exotic hints (papaya) and balasamic herbs, hints of lees and flowers. Powerful palate with smoky hints of wood, spicy, slightly warm and oily.

ALMODÍ 2003 JOVEN RED
garnacha, syrah, cabernet sauvignon, cariñena

83 Intense cherry. Clear aroma of foresty strawberries, fresh with maceration notes. Fresh, flavourful palate, with traces of ripe strawberry pulp, expressive.

TEMPUS 2003 OAK AGED RED
garnacha, syrah, merlot, cabernet sauvignon, cariñena
🛢 6

87 Dark cherry with a dark red-violet edge. Intense, fruity aroma with fine smoky, creamy oak notes. Fleshy palate with good fruit/oak integration, and a nuance of jammy fruit, fine bitter notes (liquorice) and good acidity, warm with good fruit weight.

DOMUS PENSI 2002 CRIANZA RED
garnacha, syrah, merlot, cabernet sauvignon, cariñena

85 Deep cherry. Aroma of jammy red fruit, slightly warm with earthy and light smoky notes and jammy hint. Fleshy, powerful palate with flavourful and fruity tannins, notions of raspberries and an earthy and liquorice finish.

ANDREU ROCA VAQUE

Sant Vicent, 31, 1º, 2º
43870 Amposta (Tarragona)
☎: 977 430 060 - Fax: 977 705 773

VALL DE VINYES BATEA WHITE
VALL DE VINYES ROSÉ
VALL DE VINYES RED

ANNA MARÍA VILLAGRASA SANJUAN

Carretera de Maella
43786 Batea (Tarragona)
☎: 977 430 137

Established: 1963

🏭 40 📊 200,000 litres 🍇 17 has.

VI DEL TANCAT CRIANZA WHITE
VI DEL TANCAT CRIANZA RED

Celler BÁRBARA FORÉS

Santa Anna, 28
43780 Gandesa (Tarragona)
☎: 977 420 160 - Fax: 977 421 399
bfores@nil.fut.es

DO TERRA ALTA

Established: 1889
🛢 200 📦 58,000 litres 🍇 21 has.
🍷 60% 🌐40%: -FR -BE -UK -DE -NL -DK -CH -US

EL QUINTA BÁRBARA FORES 2002 FERMENTADO EN BARRICA WHITE
100% garnacha blanca

83 Golden. Powerful aroma with a rich suggestion of dried mountain herbs, smoky and lactic hints and traces of oak. Dry palate with fruit slightly muted by the wood (bitter).

BÀRBARA FORÉS 2003 WHITE
85% garnacha blanca, 15% viognier

84 Pale. Slightly intense aroma with a fine varietal expression (herbs, cumin) hints of flowers and lees, lacking fruit expression. Flavourful palate with rich bitter notes, warm hints and a spicy suggestion.

BÀRBARA FORÉS 2003 ROSÉ
50% garnacha tinta, 50% syrah

85 Intense cherry. Grapey aroma with powerful and ripe red fruit, hints of maceration (flowers, liquorice). Flavourful palate with good alcohol-acidity balance, long, unctuous and very fruity, with complex overtones of the vine varieties.

BÀRBARA FORÉS 2002 OAK AGED RED
51% garnacha tinta, 42% syrah, 7% otras

85 Intense garnet red. Earthy, spicy aroma with notes of sun-drenched skins and aromatic herbs (petals, lavender). Flavourful, fresh palate with macerated black fruit and a spicy finish.

BÁRBARA FORÉS 2001 CRIANZA RED
60% garnacha tinta, 25% syrah, 15% cariñena

86 Garnet red cherry. Intense aroma with fruity and toasty notes and a hint of minerals, warm. Powerful, flavourful palate with not very incisive sweet tannins, spirituous

COMA D'EN POU BÀRBARA FORÉS 2001 CRIANZA RED
30% garnacha tinta, 30% cabernet sauvignon, 27% syrah, 13% merlot

88 Garnet red cherry with an orange edge. Powerful aroma of very ripe fruit, light mineral notes and dry earth, and fine toasty oak flavours, spirituous. Warm, round and ripe palate, slightly sweet supple tannins; an earthy-mineral and flavourful retronasal effect.

BÀRBARA FORÉS 2002 FERMENTADO EN BARRICA WHITE DULCE

Celler BATEA

Moli, 30
43786 Batea (Tarragona)
☎: 977 430 056 - Fax: 977 430 589

cellerbatea@cellerbatea.com
www.cellerbatea.com
Established: 1961
🛢 500 📦 8,000,000 litres 🍇 1,200 has.
🍷 90% 🌐10%

VALLMAJOR 2003 JOVEN WHITE

81 Reddish gold hue. Aroma with smoky and toasty notes, nuts (bitter almonds) and dried mountain herbs. Fresh, quite fruity palate with bitter oak notes and a hint of early evolution.

PRIMICIA 2003 FERMENTADO EN BARRICA WHITE

80 Golden with a coppery hue. Aroma with notes of oxidative evolution (nuts, wax) and mountain herbs. Warm, dry palate with oak tannins and medium fruit expression, bitter.

VALLMAJOR 2002 ROSÉ
100% garnacha

79 Deep raspberry. Powerful, fruity aroma (raspberries, cherries) with sweet hints and toasty skins. Flavourful palate with fine bitter notes and marked acidity.

VALLMAJOR 2002 RED
70% garnacha, 10% merlot, 5% tempranillo, 5% cariñena, 10% syrah

81 Lively garnet red cherry. Intense, fruity aroma with spicy hints, toasty skins, a suggestion of lavender and terroir. Flavourful palate with quite rough, fresh tannins and fine notes of bitterness and minerals.

L'AUBE "SELECCIÓ VINYES VELLES" 2001 CRIANZA RED
60% merlot, 20% garnacha, 10% syrah, 5% tempranillo, 5% cabernet sauvignon

88 Intense cherry. Aroma with notes of ripe black fruit (jammy plums) and toasty notes (coffee, chocolate). Powerful, fleshy palate with powerful ripe tannins and a suggestion of toasty oak well-blended with the wine.

VIVERTELL 1999 RESERVA RED
tempranillo, garnacha, syrah

81 Dark cherry with a coppery glint. Quite intense aroma with fine reduction and spicy notes, suggestion of ripe fruit, hints of skins and underbrush. Flavourful, bitter palate (liquorice, dark-roasted flavours, balsamic flavours), with round tannins and good acidity.

VALLMAJOR 2002 JOVEN WHITE
PRIMICIA 2002 FERMENTADO EN BARRICA WHITE

CASTELL BEL ART

Carretera Vilalba, s/n
43780 Gandesa (Tarragona)

DO TERRA ALTA

☎: 977 420 014 - Fax: 977 420 014

Established: 1997

🏳 50 📊 4,595,800 litres 🍇 24 has.

🍷 40% 🌐60%

BLANC DE BEL ART WHITE
MISTELA DE BEL ART WHITE
RANCI DE BEL ART WHITE
BEL ART CABERNET GARNATXA RED
BEL ART MERLOT RED
BEL ART JOVEN RED
SEÑORÍO DEL MAR CRIANZA RED
VIÑA MATER RESERVA RED

Unió Agraria Cooperativa CELLERS UNIÓ

Joan Oliver, 16-24 Mas de les Animes
43206 Reus (Tarragona)
☎: 977 330 055 - Fax: 977 330 070
f.gimenez@cellersunio.com
www.cellersunio.com

Established: 1942

🏳 6,500 📊 600,0000 litres 🍇 2,110 has.

🍷 25% 🌐75%: -DE -DK -US -NL -JP

CLOS DEL PINELL 2003 WHITE SECO
80% garnacha blanca, 15% macabeo, 5% moscatel

84 Pale gold. Powerful aroma with spicy, very varietal notes, fine, musky hints of overripening, flowers, wax and zest. Flavourful quite warm, a plate with bitter notes.

CLOS DEL PINELL 2º ANY 2001 CRIANZA RED
45% garnacha tinta, 35% garnacha peluda, 20% cariñena

88 Dark cherry with a purplish edge. Powerful aroma with ripe black fruit, toasty oak, mild reduction notes (animals) and a balsamic hint. Flavourful, fleshy palate with excellent concentration and fruit-oak fusion, spicy with waxy hints.

Vinyes i Cellers CLÚA

Vall de Sant Isidre, 41
43782 Vilalba dels Arcs (Tarragona)
☎: 977 439 003 - Fax: 977 439 003
info@cellerclua.com
www.cellerclua.com

Established: 1995

🏳 69 📊 25,800 litres 🍇 12 has.

🍷 20% 🌐80%

MAS D'EN POL 2003 JOVEN WHITE

84 Straw-coloured. Fine, creamy, fruity and warm aroma. Flavourful palate with a fruit expression evoking fine herbs, with mineral notes.

VINDEMIA 2002 FERMENTADO EN BARRICA WHITE

83 Intense golden. Quite intense aroma with smoky notes, creamy wood and a ripe fruit hint. Flavourful, spicy and fresh on the palate with a slightly acidic edge, lacking balance.

MAS D'EN POL 2003 JOVEN RED

84 Dark cherry with a lively garnet red edge. Powerful, fruity aroma with notes of macerated skins, a spicy hint and fresh mineral overtones. Powerful, fleshy palate with a slightly oily, warm texture, a good fruit weight and toasty, spicy notes in the finish.

MIL.LENNIUM 2001 RED
60% garnacha tinta, 20% cabernet sauvignon, 15% syrah, 5% tempranillo , pinot noir

91 Intense cherry. Powerful aroma with good assemblage of ripe fruit notes with fine oak and a mild hint of minerals (burnt stone). Toasty hints on the palate (coffee and chocolate) with ripe fruit, integrated yet obvious oak and quite complex. Better in the mouth than the previous vintage.

MIL.LENNIUM 2002 DULCE RED
garnacha tinta

88 Intense cherry. Ripe, toasty aroma of skins with fine smoky and earthy notes and a suggestion of fresh black fruit, complex. Fleshy palate with ripe but very flavourful tannins, perfect acidity-sweetness symmetry, jammy raspberries in the finish, slightly less subtle than in the nose.

Cooperativa Agrícola de
CORBERA D'EBRE

Ponent, 21
43784 Corbera D'Ebre (Tarragona)
☎: 977 420 432 - Fax: 977 420 432
coop@corbera.tinet.org

Established: 1960

🏳 31 📊 3,500,000 litres 🍇 625 has.

🍷 95% 🌐5%: -NL -IE

MIRMIL-LÓ PARELLADA 2003 WHITE
100% parellada

80 Pale yellow with a golden hue. Quite intense aroma of green fruit and fragrant herbs. Fresh, flavourful palate with fine spicy notes and marked citrus acidity.

MIRMIL-LÓ 2003 ROSÉ
100% garnacha

60 Rose with a salmon hue. Aroma of weak fruit, without expression. Evolved on the palate.

MIRMIL-LÓ 2003 RED
45% garnacha, 30% syrah, 15% cariñena, 5% tempranillo, 5% merlot

79 Garnet red cherry. Intense aroma of slightly reduced ripe fruit. Flavourful, fleshy and very bitter on the palate, with a slightly oily, warm texture and notions of terroir.

DO TERRA ALTA

VALL EXCELS 2001 CRIANZA RED
garnacha tinta, tempranillo

74 Lively garnet red cherry. Intense aroma with predominant spicy and reduction notes (not very fine hint of animals). Quite flavourful, bitter palate with notes of overripe fruit, lacking balance.

POBLE VELL 2003 VINO DE LICOR WHITE
garnacha blanca, pedro ximénez, esquitxagos

82 Old gold with a coppery hue. Fresh aroma of orange peel and peaches in syrup with a nuance of raisins. Generous, flavourful palate with crystallised fresh fruit, slightly pasty, long.

MIRMIL-LÓ 2003 JOVEN WHITE
VALL EXCELS 2002 CRIANZA WHITE
POBLE VELL 2003 VINO DE LICOR RED

Bodegas CORTIELLA

Plaça de Catalunya, 1
43784 Corbera D´Ebre (Tarragona)
☎: 977 420 434 - Fax: 977 420 434
bodegasc@tinet.org
Established: 1920
🍮 250 📗 1,800,000 litres 🍇 25 has.
🍷 90% 🌐10%

CORTIELLA 2001 WHITE
70% garnacha blanca, 30% otras

71 Intense golden. Powerful, ripe aroma with expression of oxidative crianza (mountain herbs,withered petals, nuts, toasty flavours). Flavourful, spicy palate, slightly warm and oily with a hint of perfumed soap.

SOVATERRES 2000 RESERVA RED
40% tempranillo, 30% syrah, 30% cabernet sauvignon

65 Garnet red. with a coppery hue. Slightly short aroma without great nuances. Flavourful palate with bitter notes and hints of aged oak.

CORTIELLA 2000 RESERVA RED
tempranillo, syrah, cabernet sauvignon

74 Fairly deep cherry with an orangey glint. Slightly intense aroma with predominant reduction notes (tobacco, old furniture). Flavourful, supple palate with a certain crianza expression and spicy hints of slightly aged wood in the retronasal passage.

SOVATERRES 2003 WHITE
SOVATERRES 2003 ROSÉ
CORTIELLA 2003 ROSÉ

COVILALBA

Cervantes, 1
43782 Vilalba dels Arcs (Tarragona)
☎: 977 438 010 - Fax: 977 438 294
covilalba@covilalba.com
www.covilalba.com
Established: 1965
🍮 300 📗 3,000,000 litres 🍇 700 has.
🍷 40% 🌐60%: -US -UK -CH -DE -CR

FARISTOL 2003 RED
100% garnacha tinta

79 Lively garnet red cherry. Intense aroma with notes of lightly reduced fruit, balsamic hints and terroir. Flavourful palate with slightly lively tannins and fine spicy notes of liquorice with marked acidity.

SUPREM SELECCIÓ 2003 RED
garnacha tinta, tempranillo, syrah

77 Brilliant cherry with a coppery hue. Intense, fruity aroma with a suggestion of vegetative character (nettles, vine shoots) and smoky hints of skins. Flavourful palate with fruit expression slightly muted by the alcohol.

VALL DE BERRÚS 2001 ROBLE RED
garnacha tinta, cariñena, cabernet sauvignon

86 Dark cherry. Powerful aroma of jammy black fruit with fine smoky and balsamic notes. Flavourful palate with a good oak/fruit integration, a warm and and oily texture and a suggestion of ripe fruit and dark-roasted flavours, with a hint of minerals.

FILL DEL TEMPS GRAN SELECCIÓ 2001 OAK AGED RED
garnacha tinta, cariñena

87 Dark cherry with a dark red edge. Powerful, ripe aroma with fine smoky oak notes a suggestion of slightly varietal fruit and notions of terroir. Flavourful, bitter palate (liquorice graphite, dark-roasted flavours), slightly warm with a good fruit/oak integration.

FILL DEL TEMPS 2000 CRIANZA RED
garnacha tinta, cariñena, cabernet sauvignon, tempranillo

83 Dark garnet red cherry. Intense aroma with predominant crianza notes (spices, tobacco, suggestions of wax). Flavourful palate with quite rough, oily tannins, bitter notes (dark-roasted flavours, dry earth) and good acidity.

RANCI 1928 RANCIO
100% garnacha blanca

85 Old gold with a reddish glint. Aroma with rancid notes of hazelnuts and almonds and hints of varnish and carpentry. Dry, pungent palate with varnish and aldehyde, very bitter.

MISTELA ARCS MISTELA
VI DE L'ALBA 2002 FERMENTADO EN BARRICA WHITE
SUPREM 2003 WHITE

DE MULLER

Camí Pedra Estela, 34

43205 Reus (Tarragona)
☎: 977 757 473 - Fax: 977 771 129
demuller1@infonegocio.com

Established: 1851

🍷 1,200 🛢 3,850,000 litres 🍇 132 has.

🇪🇸 35% 🌐65%: -US; -CA -MX -CO -PE -
SE -UK -FR -FI -DK -DE -RU -LT -JP -BJ -
ET -CH -DE -SE

VINO DE MISA SUPERIOR DE MULLER
VINO DE LICOR

ECOVITRES

La Verge, 6
43782 Vilalba dels Arcs (Tarragona)
☎: 977 438 196@filete
fax:ecotres69@yahoo.es

Established: 2003

🍷 10 🛢 25,000 litres 🍇 50 has.

🇪🇸 90% 🌐10%: -UK

CATXAP 2003 OAK AGED JOVEN RED
ASPIRALL 2003 JOVEN RED

Cooperativa Agraria de
EL PINELL DE BRAI

Carretera de Mora, s/n Calle Pilonet, 8
43594 El Pinell de Brai (Tarragona)
☎: 977 426 234 - Fax: 977 426 290
cellerpinell@retemail.es

Established: 1919

🍷 32 🛢 30,000 litres 🇪🇸 100%

FONT DE LA TEULA VI BRISAT 2003
FERMENTADO EN BARRICA WHITE
FONT DE LA TEULA FERMENTACIÓN
CONTROLADA 2003 OAK AGED WHITE

Celler Cooperatiu GANDESA

Avenida Catalunya, 28
43780 Gandesa (Tarragona)
☎: 977 420 017 - Fax: 977 420 403
gandesa@ccae.es

Established: 1919

🍷 225 🛢 5,000,000 litres 🍇 900 has.

🇪🇸 90% 🌐10%: -BE -DE -NL

ANTIC CASTELL 2003 JOVEN WHITE
10% macabeo, 90% garnacha blanca

74 Pale gold. Quite intense aroma with fruity and
varietal hints (fragrant herbs). Warm, somewhat
oily and spicy palate with good acidity.

ANTIC CASTELL 2003 ROSÉ
50% garnacha, 50% cariñena

76 Deep raspberry. Powerful aroma of ripe red
fruit with a sweet and spicy hint of skins.
Flavourful, slightly fruity, warm palate with fine
bitter notes.

ANTIC CASTELL GANDESA 2003 OAK AGED
RED
100% cariñena

81 Dark cherry with a purplish edge. Intense, ripe
aroma with fine toasty oak, hints of macerated
skins and terroir. Flavourful, fleshy palate with a
good oak/fruit integration and balsamic hints.

VARVALL CABERNET 2001 RED
100% cabernet sauvignon

87 Dark cherry with a dark red edge. Powerful
aroma of ripe fruit, fine reduction notes (leather)
and a suggestion of peat. Flavourful, fleshy and
spicy on the palate with predominant lactic notes,
balsamic hints and slightly viscous in the finish.

MISTELA GANDESA VINO DE LICOR
100 % garnacha blanca

81 Golden. Grapey aroma with spicy notes, vanilla (crianza) with a nuance of Mistelle. Sweet palate with notes of peaches, slightly pasty, without
great freshness.

MESSEROLS 2001 CRIANZA RED
90% tempranillo, 10% merlot

81 Dark cherry with a dark red edge. Intense aroma
with predominant crianza notes (toasty flavours, old
furniture, suggestions of wax). Fleshy, flavourful palate with ripe, oily tannins and fine bitter notes.

VARVALL 2001 RESERVA RED
85% garnacha, 15% tempranillo

80 Dark cherry with a brick red edge. Powerful,
ripe aroma with predominant crianza notes and
fine reduction (leather, wax, aged wood). Fleshy
palate with a good fruit/oak integration, flavourful,
with a slightly viscous hint.

VI DE LICOR 1919 VINO DE LICOR
100% garnacha blanca

83 Dark amber. Expressive aroma with crianza
notes (toasted hints orange peel, pâtisserie) and
varnish. Dry, expressive palate with notes of nuts
and a suggestion of orange (fresh); long
(almonds, rancid flavours).

GARIDELLS 2003 OAK AGED WHITE
GARIDELLS 2003 JOVEN ROSÉ
GARIDELLS 2003 JOVEN RED
CESAR MANINELL 2001 CRIANZA WHITE
VARVALL 1994 GRAN RESERVA RED
GANDESA RANCIO

HERETAT DE VIDAL

San Isidro, 48

43782 Villalba dels Arcs (Tarragona)
☎: 977 439 011 - Fax: 977 439 011
vvidal@tinet.org
www.heretatdevidal.org

Established: 1940

🍶 80 📦 100,000 litres 🍇 35 has.

🍷 25% 🌐75%

LES LLOSSANES CRIANZA WHITE
TOSSAL DE VIDAL WHITE
VITORI WHITE DULCE
TOSSAL DE VIDAL RED
TADEUS CRIANZA RED

JOSÉ VALLS

Pol. Ind. La Plana, Parc. 25
43780 Gandesa (Tarragona)
☎: 977 420 835 - Fax: 977 420 835

Established: 1967

🍶 10 📦 300,000 litres 🍇 10 has. 🍷 100%

VIÑAVI 2003 JOVEN WHITE
VIÑAVI 2003 JOVEN RED
GRAN VIÑAVI TEMPRANILLO CRIANZA RED

JOSEP SANTIAGO
VICENS VALLESPÍ

Av. Aragó, 20
43780 Gandesa (Tarragona)
☎: 977 421 080
josepvicensv@wanadoo.es

Established: 1874

🍶 7 📦 33,000 litres 🍇 10 has. 🍷 100%

VINYES DEL GRAU 2002 JOVEN WHITE
macabeo, garnacha blanca

78 Pale gold. Powerful aroma with smoky hints, a nuance of fruit, white flowers and mountain herbs. Flavourful, warm palate without great nuances.

VINYES DEL GRAU SYRAH 2003 RED
100% syrah

82 Dark cherry with a purplish edge. Powerful, ripe aroma with a nuance of slightly reduced fruit, a viscous and terroir nuance. Powerful, flavourful palate with macerated skins, fine bitter notes and an oily texture.

VINYES DEL GRAU 2002 OAK AGED RED
cariñena, garnacha, syrah   🍶 3

84 Dark cherry. Powerful aroma with smoky oak, jammy fruit, balsamic hints and terroir. Fleshy palate with slightly fresh tannins and flavourful overtones, a mineral character with notes of liquorice and dark-roasted flavours, bitterness and good acidity.

VINYES DEL GRAU 2003 JOVEN WHITE
VINYES DEL GRAU 2002 JOVEN RED

LA BOTERA

Sant Roc, 26
43786 Batea (Tarragona)
☎: 977 430 009 - Fax: 977 430 009

L'ARNOT 2003 WHITE
60% macabeo, 40% garnacha blanca

76 Pale gold. Quite intense aroma with smoky notes and a hint of varietal character (fragrant herbs). Dry, bitter palate with good acidity, without great nuances.

VILA-CLOSA 2003 WHITE
macabeo, garnacha blanca, chardonnay

86 Golden straw. Aroma with smoky notes and mountain herbs, slightly fruity. Fresh, fruity aroma with herbs and a smoky-toasty retronasal effect, with oak tannins.

VILA-CLOSA 2003 JOVEN RED
syrah, garnacha, cariñena

80 Dark garnet red cherry. Intense aroma of ripe fruit with hints of macerated skins. Flavourful, slightly fleshy palate with ripe tannins and a suggestion of jammy fruit, spicy and balsamic hints in the finish.

L'ARNOT 2003 RED

65 Dark cherry with a dark red edge. Powerful aroma with not very fine notes of the tank. Bitter on the palate and not very pleasant.

Celler LAUREANO
SERRES MONTAGUT

Gaudí, 1
43594 El Pinell de Brai (Tarragona)
☎: 977 426 356 - Fax: 977 426 192
laureano@lasm.com
www.serres.net

Established: 2001

🍶 10 📦 7,500 litres 🍇 2 has.

🍷 90% 🌐10%

LAUREANO SERRES 2003 WHITE

79 Golden. Powerful, balsamic aroma with spicy notes, flowers and citrus fruit peel. Flavourful, bitter palate with a slight varietal expression and slight oxidation, original.

LAUREANO SERRES 2003 RED

81 Dark cherry with a dark red edge. Powerful, ripe aroma of jammy fruit with a toasty hint, balsamic and slightly viscous. Flavourful palate with ripe fruit, spicy hints (paprika) and notions of terroir.

LAUREANO SERRES 2002 OAK AGED RED
🍇6

84 Dark cherry with a saffron edge. Powerful aroma with toasty oak notes, a slightly balsamic suggestion, a viscous edge and hints of jammy fruit. Flavourful palate with a good oak/fruit integration, slightly oily, bitter and original with good acidity.

Celler MARIOL

Les Forques, s/n
43786 Batea (Tarragona)
☎: 934 367 628 - Fax: 934 500 281
celler@cellermariol.es
www.cellermariol.es

Established: 1945

600 🍷 3,100,000 litres 🍇 50 has.

🍷 50% 🍇50%

VINYA PUBILLA 2003 JOVEN WHITE
macabeo, garnacha blanca

73 Brilliant pale. Quite intense and fruity aroma with fresh overtones. Somewhat flavourful, fresh palate, lacking expression.

VINYA SEDOSA BLANC DE BLANCS WHITE
macabeo, moscatel, garnacha

80 Pale with golden nuances. Quite intense aroma of fruit and white flowers with fine herbs. Flavourful, fruity palate with fine bitter and herby notes, excellent acidity.

VINYA PUBILLA OAK AGED RED
tempranillo, garnacha

81 Lively garnet red cherry. Intense, fruity aroma with the freshness of minerals, skins and smoky hints of oak. Flavourful palate with somewhat lively tannins, a good fruit/oak integration and a nuance of bitterness and jammy fruit.

CELLER MARIOL RESERVA SELECCIÓ 1996 CRIANZA RED
30% merlot, 30% syrah, 40% cabernet sauvignon

85 Dark cherry with a brick red edge. Powerful aroma with predominant crianza notes (toasted hints, spices, old furniture), an earthy hint and slightly viscous. Fleshy palate with a good fruit/oak integration, warm and rich in bitter nuances (liquorice, pitch, dark-roasted flavours).

LA CLAU 2001 CRIANZA RED
tempranillo, garnacha

78 Fairly deep cherry with a saffron-copper glint. Quite intense aroma with smoky oak notes and the freshness of minerals and skins. Flavourful, bitter palate (well-integrated wood, slightly aged).

MAS MONTASELL CABERNET SAUVIGNON 1998 RESERVA RED
100% cabernet sauvignon

82 Fairly deep cherry with a brick red rim. Powerful, ripe aroma with toasty oak notes, a fine reduction hint. and hints of black olives. Flavourful, fleshy palate with bitter crianza notes (dark-roasted flavours, pitch).

MAS MONTASELL SYRAH 1999 RESERVA RED
100% syrah

80 Garnet red cherry with a coppery rim. Not very intense aroma with spicy oak notes and a jammy fruit hint, lacking varietal expression. Flavourful, bitter palate with a hint of burnt caramel and good acidity.

VI DE PAGÉS 2003 WHITE
VINYA SEDOSA 2003 ROSÉ
VINYA PUBILLA 2003 ROSÉ
VI DE PAGÉS SEMICRIANZA RED
CELLER MARIOL CABERNET SAUVIGNON
 CRIANZA RED
CELLER MARIOL MERLOT RESERVA RED
VI DE PAGÉS 2003 ROSÉ

Celler MAS BLANCH

Pista Batea - La Pobla s/n
43782 Vilalba dels Arcs (Tarragona)
☎: 977 438 018 - Fax: 977 438 043

Established: 2000

🍷 60,000 litres 🍇 40 has. 🍷 100%

CELLER MAS BLANCH JOVEN WHITE
CELLER MAS BLANCH JOVEN RED

Celler MENESCAL

Joan Amades, 2
43785 Bot (Tarragona)
☎: 977 428 095 - Fax: 977 428 261
info@cellermenescal.com
www.cellermenescal.com

Established: 1907

200 🍷 200,000 litres 🍇 20 has.

🍷 85% 🍇15%: -DE -BE -FR -UK -NL

VALL DE RACÓ 2003 WHITE
VALL DEL POU 2003 WHITE
AVUS 2002 FERMENTADO EN BARRICA
 WHITE
VALL DE RACÓ 2003 RED
VALL DEL POU 2003 RED
AVUS 2002 ROBLE RED

Celler Vinos PIÑOL

Avenida de Aragón, 9
43786 Batea (Tarragona)
☎: 977 430 505 - Fax: 977 430 498
info@vinospinol.com
www.vinospinol.com

Established: 1945

🍷 200 🍶 125,000 litres 🍇 42 has.

🍷 30% 🍷70%

L'AVI ARRUFI 2002 OAK AGED RED

30% cabernet sauvignon, 20% merlot, 20% garnacha, 15% syrah, 15% tempranillo 🍷 15

92 Very deep garnet red cherry. Powerful aroma with predominant creamy oak notes (vanilla) and macerated black fruit. Powerful, concentrated palate with ripe and oily tannins, an excellent crianza expression, bitter notes (liquorice, balsamic flavours) and excellent acidity.

SACRA NATURA 2003 OAK AGED RED

50% cariñena, 30% merlot, 10% syrah, 10% tempranillo

88 Garnet red cherry with a violet edge. Powerful aroma of macerated black fruit and fine toasty oak. Powerful, concentrated palate with quite rough though ripe tannins; an oily texture with fine bitter notes (chocolate, liquorice).

NUESTRA SEÑORA DEL PORTAL 2003 OAK AGED RED

30% merlot, 30% cabernet sauvignon, 20% garnacha, 10% tempranillo, 10% syrah

90 Opaque cherry with a violet edge. Intense aroma of macerated black fruit and creamy oak notes. Powerful, concentrated palate with quite rough but ripe and sweet tannins and well-integrated oak and fruit; a slightly oily texture and a powerful aroma in the retronasal passage.

MISTELA JOSEFINA PIÑOL 2003 VINO DE LICOR

100% garnacha blanca

90 Amber. Good intensity aroma with toasty notes, nuts, mountain herbs and crystallised fruit, fine. Sweet palate with dried peaches and toasty flavours, powerful, very flavourful and oily with an excellent sweet-acidity combination.

MATHER TERESINA SELECCIÓN 2001 RED

30% cabernet sauvignon, 20% garnacha, 15% merlot, 15% syrah, 5% morenillo

89 Garnet red cherry with a coppery edge. Powerful aroma of macerated black fruit with fine toasty wood notes and a balsamic nuance slightly mineral. Flavourful, very concentrated palate with predominant long bitter crianza notes and ripe fruit (hints of prunes), well-integrated with the oak, chocolate, spices and liquorice.

MISTELA JOSEFINA PIÑOL 2003 VINO DE LICOR

90% garnacha tinta, 10% syrah

90 Deep cherry. Powerful aroma of jammy plums and cherry liqueur, fine with a perfumed nuance. Velvety texture, very flavourful and powerful on the palate with a strong fruit expression, well-integrated fine toasty flavours, sweet and persistent.

L'AVI ARRUFI 2002 JOVEN WHITE
NUESTRA SEÑORA DEL PORTAL 2003 WHITE
RAIG DE RAIM 2003 JOVEN WHITE
RAIG DE RAIM 2003 JOVEN RED

Cooperativa Agrícola
SANT JOSEP DE BOT

Estació, 2
43785 Bot (Tarragona)

DO TERRA ALTA

☎: 977 428 035 - Fax: 977 428 192
coopbot@retemail.es
Established: 1944
🍷 140 🍾 3,500,000 litres 🍇 563 has.
🍷 95% 🍇5%: -CH -DK -DE -NL -BE -PA -TR

CLOT D'ENCÍS 2003 JOVEN WHITE
90% garnacha, 10% sauvignon blanc

82 Straw-coloured. Powerful aroma with a varietal expression, peach skins and fragrant herbs. Dry, flavourful, bitter and slightly oily palate with a suggestion of spices and herbs.

LLÀGRIMES DE TARDOR 2002 FERMENTADO EN BARRICA WHITE
100% garnacha blanca

85 Gold with a reddish glimmer. Complex aroma with fine notes of smoky oak and fine lees, elegant. Fresh, fruity palate, oak in the retronasal passage with a slightly tannic edge.

CLOT D'ENCÍS 2003 JOVEN ROSÉ
100% garnacha

74 Lively blush. Intense aroma with a hint of freshness, without great fruit expression. Flavourful palate with fine bitter notes, hints of greeness and a slightly acidic edge.

CLOT D'ENCÍS 2003 JOVEN RED
45% garnacha, 30% syrah, 15% cabernet sauvignon, 10% merlot

79 Cherry. Clean, fresh red fruit aroma with hints of greeness. Fresh, fruity palate with good acidity, pleasant.

LA PLANA DE'N FONOLL 2003 OAK AGED RED
32,5% garnacha, 19% syrah, 5% ull de llebre, 8% merlot, 13,5% cabernet sauvignon, 22% cariñena 🍷4

75 Cherry with a violet edge. Aroma with lactic notes, metals and jammy tomatoes. Drying and warm on the palate with quite agressive tannins.

LLÀGRIMES DE TARDOR 2002 CRIANZA RED
60% garnacha, 14% syrah, 12% cariñena, 14% ull de llebre

86 Garnet red cherry. Powerful aroma of black fruit, fine smoky oak, with a hint of ash and dry earth. Flavourful, supple palate with a good fruit/oak integration, with excellent balance and a mineral suggestion.

LA PLANA D'EN FONOLL 2002 OAK AGED RED

SERRA DE CAVALLS

Bonaire, 1
43594 El Pinell de Brai (Tarragona)
☎: 977 426 049 - Fax: 977 426 196

serradecavall@terralta.com
www.terralta.com
Established: 2001
🍷 20 🍾 20,000 litres 🍇 8 has. 🍷 100%

SERRA DE CAVALLS 2003 WHITE
50% garnacha, 50% chardonnay

84 Brilliant pale gold. Intense aroma with notes of slightly varietal fruit, fragrant herbs and hints of hydrocarbon. Flavourful, quite fruity palate with fine bitter notes, an oily texture fondo especiado. and a spicy hint.

SERRA DE CAVALLS 2003 RED
cariñena, garnacha, ull de llebre, cabernet sauvignon

80 Lively garnet red cherry. Quite intense, fruity aroma with notes of fresh skins and warm hints. Flavourful, vigorous palate with a light touch of greeness to the tannins.

SERRA DE CAVALLS 2001 CRIANZA RED
40% cariñena, 30% garnacha, 20% ull de llebre, 10% cabernet sauvignon

84 Dark cherry with a coppery edge. Powerful aroma with predominant toasty oak notes (vanilla, cocoa) and spices. Powerful, fleshy and concentrated on the palate with notes of chocolate, terroir and fine bitter notes.

Cellers TARRONÉ

Calvario, 22
43786 Batea (Tarragona)
☎: 977 430 109 - Fax: 977 430 183
ctarrone@jazzfree.com
Established: 1942
🍷 30 🍇 35 has. 🍷 90% 🍇10%

MERIAN 2003 WHITE
100% garnacha

78 Brilliant pale with a coppery hue. Quite intense aroma of smoky skins and the varietal (fragrant herbs). Flavourful, bitter and warm palate with fruit expression muted by the alcohol.

MERIAN RED
garnacha, cariñena

73 Lively garnet red cherry. Quite intense aroma of black fruit with hints of skins. Flavourful palate with notes of bitterness, spices and a suggestion of damp earth.

TORREMADRINA 2001 CRIANZA RED
cabernet sauvignon, tempranillo, merlot, syrah

88 Very dark cherry. Powerful, concentrated palate with an excellent crianza expression, jammy fruit notes, toasted hints and well-integrated fine oak and terroir. Powerful, fleshy palate with round, oily tannins and fine bitter notes.

MAS TARRONÉ RED

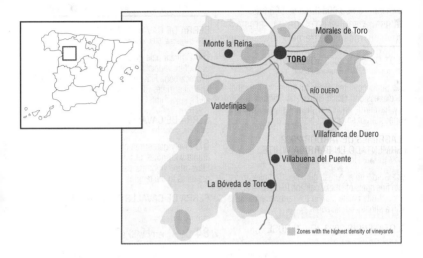

Morales de Toro
Monte la Reina
TORO
RÍO DUERO
Valdefinjas
Villafranca de Duero
Villabuena del Puente
La Bóveda de Toro

Zones with the highest density of vineyards

NEWS. The 2003 harvest was rated as excellent in Toro and confirmed by our tasting. Possibly, the key to this excellence lies in the soil of the region which is capable of storing the abundant rainwater of the winter in its water table to face the especially hot summers. Equally, the relative absence of frosts favoured an abundant harvest, with a 30% increase on the previous year and a record harvest with more than 16 million kg harvested. The main red grape variety, *Tinta de Toro*, made up more than 13 million kg, with the white grape varieties lagging behind.

Hectares of Vineyard	No. of Viticulturists	No. of Bodegas	2003 Harvest	2003 Production	Marketing
5.329	1.171	34	Excellent	7.500.000 litres	70% Spain 30% Foreign

Of the 109 wines tasted, 50 achieved or surpassed 85 points, although of these, only two (Dehesa Gago of Telmo Rodríguez and Primero of Fariña) were young wines, from which it is plain to see that the best expression of the notable local grape is to age them in oak. Equally worthy of mention of this year's tasting was the good quality of the *Garnacha* produced by the Estancia Piedra firm with a percentage of 25% in its new La Garona (91 points); apart from this exceptional example, the stock only participated, always in minimum percentages, in barely 8 wines of the total of the brands tasted.

LOCATION. Comprising 12 municipal districts of the province of Zamora (Argujillo, Boveda de Toro, Morales de Toro, El Pego, Peleagonzalo, El Piñero, San Miguel de la Ribera, Sanzoles, Toro, Valdefinjas, Venialbo and Villanueva del Puente) and three in the province of Valladolid (San Román de la Hornija, Villafranca de Duero and the vineyards of Villaester de Arriba and Villaester de Abajo in the municipal district of Pedrosa del Rey), which practically corresponds to the agricultural region of Bajo

Duero. The production area is to the south of the course of the Duero, which crosses the region from east to west.

CLIMATE. Extreme continental, with Atlantic influences and quite arid, with an average annual rainfall of between 350 mm and 400 mm. The winters are harsh (which means extremely low temperatures and long periods of frosts) and the summers short, although not excessively hot, with significant contrasts in day-night temperatures.

SOIL. The geography of the DO is characterised by a gently-undulating terrain. The vineyards are situated at an altitude of 620 m to 750 m and the soil is mainly brownish-grey limestone. However, the stony alluvial soil is better.

VARIETIES:
White: *Malvasía* and *Verdejo*.
Red: *Tinta de Toro* (majority) and *Garnacha*.

REGULATORY COUNCIL.
c/ de la Concepción, 3. Palacio de los condes de Requena 49800 Toro (Zamora).
Tel: 980 690 335. Fax: 980 693 201.
E-mail: consejo@dotoro.es
Website: www.dotoro.es

GENERAL CHARACTERISTICS OF THE WINES:

Whites	Produced mainly from the *Malvasía* variety, they have a colour ranging from pale yellow to greenish yellow; on the nose, rustic notes may appear, and on the palate, they have a slightly bitter aftertaste.
Rosés	The *Tinta de Toro* and *Garnacha* varieties are used, and are blended or used alone to produce single variety wines. Rosy coloured, they have notes of ripe red berries; they are meaty and fruity on the palate.
Reds	These are the most characteristic of the region. They have an astringency typical of the *Tinta de Toro* variety, and a high alcohol content (13° or more) and good acidity levels. When the wines are young, they have a dark cherry colour with violet nuances; on the nose they have good intensity with notes reminiscent of blackberries and black berry fruit in general; on the palate, they are powerful, flavourful, meaty, slightly overripe and have a good persistency. Those aged in wood maintain the notes of ripe fruit together with the contribution of the oak and the meatiness on the palate.

A. VELASCO E HIJOS

Polígono Industrial Norte. Parc. 17-18
49800 Toro (Zamora)
☎: 980 692 455 - Fax: 980 692 455

Established: 1999

🛢 120 🗄 130,000 litres 🍇 12 has. ⚑ 100%

PEÑA REJAS 2002 JOVEN RED
100% tinta de Toro

80 Cherry. Spicy slightly sweet aroma of ripe red fruit. Flavourful palate with fruity tannins and an element of evolution, fresh.

PEÑA REJAS 2003 ROSÉ
100% tinta de Toro

69 Deep raspberry. Slightly intense and fruity aroma without great nuances. Bittersweet palate; hints of sweetness and an acidic edge.

PEÑA REJAS 2001 CRIANZA RED
100% tinta de Toro

78 Brilliant cherry. Aroma of ripe red fruit and toasty hints. Fleshy, flavourful and spicy on the palate with a slightly acidic edge; long.

PEÑA REJAS 2002 ROBLE RED

ÁLVAREZ Y DÍEZ

Juan Antonio Carmona, 12
28020 Nava del Rey (Valladolid)
☎: 983 850 136 - Fax: 983 850 761
bodegas@alvarezydiez.com
www.alvarezydiez.com

Established: 1941

🗄 1,500,000 litres 🍇 75 has.

⚑ 70% 🌐30%

VALMORO 2002 OAK AGED RED
🛢 12

82 Garnet red cherry. Medium-intensity aroma of sun-drenched skins with an earthy hint. Flavourful and warm on the palate with black fruit well-assembled with the wood.

BIENVENIDA DE VINOS

Las Bodegas s/n
49810 Morales de Toro (Zamora)
☎: 607 323 636 - Fax: 983 403 146
p-originales@airtel.net

Established: 2001

🛢 100 🍇 1.5 has.

SITIO DE EL PALO BIENVENIDA 2001 RED
tinta de toro

89 Intense cherry. Typical Toro wine aroma (jammy black fruit, earthy hints) with a suggestion of fine toasty oak (cocoa). Powerful, fleshy palate with bitter oak tannins, warm and persistent.

SITIO DE EL PALO BIENVENIDA 2002 RED
tinta de toro

93 Intense cherry. Concentrated aroma with mineral hints, toasty with ripe black fruit but with great expression. Powerful, warm, spirituous palate with highly flavoured intense and sweet tannins, rich in retronasal expression, very persistent.

CEPAS Y BODEGAS

Pago de los Quiñones
47320 Morales de Toro (Zamora)
☎: 983 376 979 - Fax: 983 340 824
b.burlon@terra.es

Established: 1998

🛢 200 🗄 140,000 litres 🍇 40 has.

⚑ 1% 🌐99%: -DE -CH -US -FR -PR -NL -BE -DK -MX -UK -CA

ARCO DE GUÍA 2000 RESERVA RED
ARCO DE GUÍA 2003 RED
ARCO DE GUÍA 2002 CRIANZA RED
CEPAS DE VIÑALCASTA 2002 CRIANZA RED

COVITORO

Carretera de Tordesillas, 13
49800 Toro (Zamora)
☎: 980 690 347 - Fax: 980 690 143
covitoro@covitoro.com
www.covitoro.com

Established: 1974

🛢 900 🍇 1,100 has.

⚑ 65% 🌐35%: -UK -DE -US -CH -NL -BE -DK -FR -IT -PL -MX -JP -AT -CZ -SE -BR

CERMEÑO 2003 WHITE
100% malvasía

77 Brilliant yellow with a lemony hue. Quite intense, not very fine aroma of white fruit with exotic notes (pineapples), hints of petals and a light varietal hint. Quite flavourful and fresh palate, bitter with an acidic edge.

CERMEÑO 2003 ROSÉ
tinta de toro, garnacha

78 Brilliant very deep raspberry. Powerful, ripe aroma of reduced fruit with a slight suggestion of off-odours. Slightly better on the palate, flavourful, fruity and with good citrus acidity.

DO TORO

CAÑUS VERUS 2002 ROBLE RED

82 Intense cherry. Spicy aroma of black bramble fruits with notes of dried herbs. Fleshy palate with fresh but powerful fruit tannins, well-assembled fine wood and a smoky finish of the vine variety.

GRAN CERMEÑO 2000 CRIANZA RED
100% tinta de Toro

82 Cherry with a garnet red edge. Slightly rustic, spicy aroma of jammy black fruit. Fleshy, flavourful palate with expressive fruit and a toasty finish.

CERMEÑO 2003 CRIANZA RED
100% tinta de Toro

80 Deep purplish cherry. Clean aroma of red bramble fruit and herbaceous notes. Fleshy palate with firm, fruity tannins and notions of terroir, slightly warm.

MARQUÉS DE LA VILLA 1997 RESERVA RED
100% tinta de Toro

82 Deep garnet red. Aroma with crianza notes (varnish, a certain reduction), jammy fruit and a suggestion of minerals. Fleshy palate with good ripe fruit, terroir, and firm, quite dry but oily tannins, for keeping.

MARQUÉS DE LA VILLA 1998 RESERVA RED
100% tinta de Toro

80 Cherry with an orangey edge. Spicy aroma (tobacco, cinnamon) with crianza character and stewed fruit hint. Round, warm palate with slightly marked wood tannins and polished fruit tannins and a toasty finish.

GRAN CERMEÑO 2001 OAK AGED RED

DELISPAIN

Fray Pedro Payo Piñeño, 17 bajo
15009 A Coruña (A Coruña)
☎: 670 522 577 - Fax: 881 924 492
delispain@delispain.com
www.delispain.com

VIÑA PRÓDIGUS 2001 ROBLE RED
90% tinta de Toro, 10% garnacha 🍇4

86 Dark red cherry. Intense aroma with predominant toasty oak notes, a nuance of spices and sun-drenched skins. Fleshy palate with good fruit/oak integration and hints of fresh fruit, spicy, flavourful and long.

VIÑA PRÓDIGUS 1998 RESERVA RED
95% tinta de Toro, 5% garnacha

88 Garnet red cherry. Powerful aroma with toasty oak and fine reduction notes (leather, prunes). Flavourful palate with good fruit/oak integration, predominant dark-roasted notes, hints of wax and minerals.

VIÑA PRÓDIGUS 2000 CRIANZA RED

Bodegas y Viñas DOS VICTORIAS

Juan Mora, s/n
47530 San Román de Hornija (Valladolid)
☎: 983 784 029 - Fax: 983 784 029
info@dosvictorias.com
www.dosvictorias.com
Established: 1998
🍾 450 📦 200,000 litres 🍇 16 has.
🍷 60% 🍇40%: -DE -UK -IE -SE -BE -DK -IT -FI -AT -US

GRAN ELÍAS MORA 2001 OAK AGED RED
100% tinta de Toro 🍇17

89 Dark cherry with a violet edge. Powerful aroma with predominant toasty oak notes (pitch), skins, spices, balsamic and mineral nuance. Flavourful, fleshy palate with good fruit/oak integration, bitter with excellent balance.

ELÍAS MORA 2001 CRIANZA RED
100% tinta de Toro

87 Dark cherry with a garnet red edge. Powerful, fruity aroma (redcurrants, ripe cherries) with toasty oak, skins, balsamic and damp earth nuance. Powerful, concentrated palate with rough, ripe, oily tannins and excellent varietal fruit expression of the crianza.

ESTANCIA PIEDRA

Carretera Toro-Salamanca, km 8
49800 Toro (Zamora)
☎: 980 693 900 - Fax: 980 693 901
info@estanciapiedra.com
www.estanciapiedra.com
Established: 1999
🍾 400 📦 225,000 litres 🍇 60 has.
🍷 45% 🍇55%

ESTANCIA PIEDRA 2001 CRIANZA RED
93% tinta de Toro, 7% garnacha 🍇8

87 Garnet red with a violet rim. Aroma with light mineral notes and red fruit. Well-balanced with a good fruit weight, with supple, integrated wood tannins, fleshy with long persistence.

LA GARONA 2001 CRIANZA RED
75% tinta de Toro, 25% garnacha

with fleshy, oily, not very rough tannins; with excellent freshness and a generous aftertaste (minerals, earth, cherries).

ESTANCIA PIEDRA PAREDINAS 2000 CRIANZA RED
100% tinta de Toro

90 Dark cherry. Powerful aroma with predominant burnt notes, balsamic suggestion, jammy black fruit and hints of graphite. Fleshy, concentrated palate with rough tannins well-blended with the fruit; hints of liquorice and pitch; well-balanced and long.

ESTANCIA PIEDRA SELECCIÓN 2000 CRIANZA RED
100% tinta de Toro

88 Dark red cherry. Intense aroma with predominant toasty wood notes, spices, balsamic and sun-drenched skin suggestion. Flavourful, fleshy palate with marked yet promising tannins and the freshness of spices and minerals, long.

ESTANCIA PIEDRA 1999 RED
ESTANCIA PIEDRA 2000 ROBLE RED
ESTANCIA PIEDRA PAREDINAS 1999 CRIANZA RED
ESTANCIA PIEDRA SELECCIÓN 1999 CRIANZA RED
CANTADAL RED

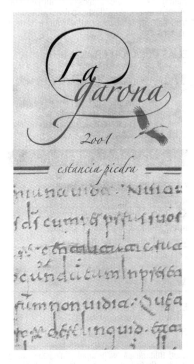

91 Deep cherry. Complex, smoky aroma with notes of terroir and fresh red fruit. Powerful palate

FARIÑA

Camino del Palo, s/n
49800 Toro (Zamora)
☎: 980 577 673 - Fax: 980 577 720
comercial@bodegasfarina.com
www.bodegasfarina.com

Established: 1942
⊞ 2,500 ▨ 3,000,000 litres ❦ 250 has.
▮ 50% ◉50%

COLEGIATA 2003 JOVEN WHITE
malvasia

81 Pale. Intense, fresh aroma of orange peel and apricots with a suggestion of aniseed and herbs. Unctuous and flavourful on the palate with aniseed, well-balanced and pleasant.

COLEGIATA 2003 JOVEN ROSÉ
tinta de toro

79 Pale raspberry. Intense aroma of red stone fruit and hints of petals (roses). Slightly fruity palate with a spicy suggestion of skins and good acidity.

PRIMERO 2003 MACERACIÓN CARBÓNICA RED
tinta de toro

87 Very intense deep cherry. Powerful aroma of concentrated bramble fruit, expressive with hints of liquorice andflowers. Flavourful palate with fruity, fresh tannins, complex hints of skins and a finish with good character.

GRAN COLEGIATA ROBLE FRANCES 1999 OAK AGED RED
tinta de toro

86 Intense cherry. Aroma of black fruit, subtle smoky, toasty notes and a suggestion of mountain herbs. Fleshy, powerful palate with obvious yet elegant wood tannins and a round oily finish.

GRAN COLEGIATA CAMPUS 2000 OAK AGED RED
tinta de toro   ⊞ 15

87 Deep cherry. Concentrated and slightly warm aroma of black fruit, graphite and fine earthy hints (mountain herbs). Powerful palate with oily, jammy fruit tannins, very elegant wood and expression of old vineyard in the finish.

GRAN COLEGIATA 1996 RESERVA RED
tinta de toro

83 Deep garnet red. Concentrated aroma of jammy black fruit with smoky notes of fine varnish. Fleshy, slightly rustic palate with firm fruit and wood tannins; flavourful.

COLEGIATA 2003 JOVEN RED
GRAN COLEGIATA 1999 ROBLE RED
GRAN COLEGIATA 2000 OAK AGED RED

Bodegas FRANCISCO CASAS

San Cosme, 6
28600 Navalcarnero (Madrid)
☎: 918 110 207 - Fax: 918 110 798
f.casas@bodegascasas.com
www.bodegascasas.com

Established: 1965
⊞ 400 ▨ 2,000,000 litres ▮ 50% ◉50%

CAMPARRÓN 2003 JOVEN RED
100% tinta de Toro

77 Cherry with an intense purple hue. Aroma of red fruit, slightly rustic and liquorice hints. Fleshy, fruity palate with fresh tannins and a blackberry finish.

CAMPARRÓN SELECCIÓN 2000 ROBLE RED
100% tinta de Toro

85 Garnet red cherry with a brick red rim. Quite intense aroma of toasty oak and jammy fruit with fresh overtones (spices, damp earth). Flavourful, vigorous palate with a good oak/fruit integration, liquorice and dark-roasted flavours, very long.

CAMPARRÓN 1999 CRIANZA RED
100% tinta de Toro

81 Deep garnet red. Aroma with reduction notes (animals, tobacco) over jammy black fruit, slightly rustic. Fleshy, earthy palate with noticeable oak tannins; slightly warm.

CAMPARRÓN 2001 CRIANZA RED
100% tinta de Toro

85 Dark cherry with a coppery rim. Powerful aroma with toasty notes of oak, skins and creamy spices. Flavourful, bitter palate (rough tannins, jammy fruit, dark-roasted flavours) with good acidity, promising.

CAMPARRÓN 1999 RESERVA RED
100% tinta de Toro

83 Dark cherry with a brick red edge. Intense aroma with predominant reduction notes (leather, prunes). Flavourful palate with a good oak/fruit integration, excellent balance and a spicy hint.

GAMAZO RED
GAMAZO ROBLE RED
GAMAZO CRIANZA RED

FRUTOS VILLAR

Carretera Burgos, km. 113, 7
47270 Cigales (Valladolid)
☎: 983 586 868 - Fax: 983 580 180
frutosvillar@cic.es
www.frutosvillar.com

Established: 1960
⊞ 2,100 ▨ 3,000,000 litres ❦ 110 has.

🐂 80% 🌐20%: -DE -FR -UK -US -RU - MX - PT

MIRALMONTE 2002 JOVEN RED

77 Garnet red cherry. Not very intense, but clear aroma of ripe fruit with an earthy nuance. Round palate with a flavourful edge and dry tannins in the finish.

MURUVE ELITE 2001 RED

84 Cherry. Aroma with light reduction notes, fine red fruit and jammy tomatoes. Warm, medium-bodied palate with good acidity and toasty notes in the retronasal passage.

MURUVE 2001 ROBLE RED

80 Cherry. Aroma of new wood with light hints of varnish, ripe red fruit and slightly viscous notes. Fleshy, flavourful palate with dry oak tannins.

MIRALMONTE 1999 CRIANZA RED

76 Cherry with an orangey hue. Slightly alcoholic aroma with mild spicy notes. Medium-bodied, without great nuances but very well-mannered.

MURUVE 2000 CRIANZA RED

81 Very deep cherry with an orangey hue. Fresh aroma with mild lactic notes and red fruit (strawberries, cherries). Flavourful palate with the wood dominating the fruit.

GRAN MURUVE 1999 RESERVA RED

84 Cherry with an orangey hue. Vinous aroma of toasty wood and red fruit. Flavourful, fruity palate with well-assembled wood and somewhat obvious tannins.

MIRALMONTE 2000 RED

Bodegas y Viñedos GARANZA

Finca La Calera s/n
49800 Toro (Zamora)
☎: 666 548 751 - Fax: 914 152 288
garanza@garanza.es
www.garanza.es

Established: 1999

🍷 550 🛢 190,000 litres 🍇 96 has.
🐂 40% 🌐60%: -US -DE -CH -SE -NO

CYAN 2002 CRIANZA RED
100% tinta de Toro

87 Dark cherry with a purplish edge. Powerful aroma with notes of skins, black fruit well-integrated with the toasty oak and fine hints of reduced fruit. Fleshy palate with ripe, oily tannins, excellent varietal and crianza expression, balsamic hints and good acidity.

CYAN 2001 CRIANZA RED
100% tinta de Toro

88 Very deep cherry. Powerful, ripe aroma of black fruit with toasty hints of skins, fine, spicy and creamy oak notes and a notion of terroir. Fleshy and very flavourful on the palate with quite marked but promising tannins, fine notes of sour cherries in liqueur, chocolate, spices, very long.

CYAN VENDIMIA SELECCIONADA 2001 RESERVA RED
100% tinta de Toro

89 Garnet red cherry with a violet edge. Powerful aroma of jammy black fruit (reduction hints) and spicy oak notes with a balsamic hint. Powerful and very concentrated on the palate with quite marked but promising tannins and an excellent varietal expression (terroir), very long.

Bodegas GIL LUNA

Carretera Toro - Salamanca, km. 4, 7
49800 Toro (Zamora)
☎: 686 481 196 - Fax: 980 698 294
pbgiluna@giluna.com

Established: 2004

🍷 50 🛢 30,000 litres 🍇 7 has.
🍷 16,000 litres. 🐂 100%

GIL LUNA 2000 OAK AGED RED
95% tinta de Toro, 5% garnacha   🍷 24

88 Quite intense cherry. Aroma of ripe fruit with moderate varietal expression and fine wood. Powerful, fresh palate, more expressive than in the nose; flavourful and warm with good oak and fruit tannins.

STRABON 2000 CRIANZA RED
95% tinta de Toro, 5% garnacha

86 Dark cherry. Aroma of ripe fruit with slightly marked toasty notes of fine and new oak. Warm palate with unassembled tannins of ripe fruit and dry oak, flavourful ensemble.

J. & F. LURTON

Mostenses, 4
47400 Medina del Campo (Valladolid)
☎: 983 850 025 - Fax: 983 850 025
jflurton@jflurton.com
www.jflurton.com

EL ALBAR OAK AGED RED
EL ALBAR EXCELENCIA CRIANZA RED

LIBERALIA ENOLÓGICA

Camino del Palo, s/n
49800 Toro (Zamora)
☎: 980 692 571 - Fax: 980 692 571
byvliberalia@hotmail.com
www.liberalia.es

Established: 2000

🍇 350 ▦ 150,000 litres 🍃 30 has.

🐂 60% 🍇40%: -DE -BE -UK -IE -JP -MX -PR -US -AT

LIBERALIA CABEZA DE CUBA 2001 OAK AGED RED
tinta de toro 🍇 12

87 Deep purplish cherry. Aroma with concentrated bramble fruit and fine elegant toasty and smoky notes. Powerful, fleshy palate with rough and pungent yet fine tannins with a bitter finish (cocoa, liquorice), for keeping.

LIBERALIA TRES 2003 OAK AGED RED
tinta de toro 🍇 4

85 Dark garnet red cherry. Powerful aroma of very varietal red fruit with fresh overtones of macerated skins and spicy hints of oak. Flavourful, fruity and supple on the palate with good fruit weight despite the alcohol (14,2%).

LIBERALIA CUATRO 2001 CRIANZA RED
tinta de toro

84 Deep cherry. Toasty aroma of red fruit with hints of liquorice and spices. Fleshy palate, oily tannins with pleasantly bitter overtones; flavour and body in the finish.

LIBERALIA CINCO 2001 RESERVA RED
tinta de toro

88 Dark cherry. Powerful aroma of black fruit, sun-drenched skins and toasty oak (pitch, dark-roasted flavours). Flavourful, bitter palate with tannins well-blended with the fruit, hints of graphite and minerals.

LIBERALIA CERO 2003 FERMENTADO EN BARRICA RED

MARQUÉS DE IRÚN

Nueva, 7-9
47491 La Seca (Valladolid)
☎: 956 851 711 - Fax: 956 853 462
mirun@marquesdeirun.es
Established: 1990
🍇 100 🍃 60 has. 🐂 90% 🍇10%

SANTUARIO 1999 CRIANZA RED
tinta de toro

86 Garnet red cherry. Toasty aroma of jammy black fruit, enveloping spices and balsamic flavours. Fleshy, powerful palate with oily, fleshy tannins and good acidity, long (smoky hints, terroir).

Bodegas MARQUÉS DE OLIVARA

Eras de Santa Catalina, s/n
49800 Toro (Zamora)
☎: 980 693 425 - Fax: 980 693 409

bmarquesolivares@hotmail.com

VALDEVÍ 2002 RED

80 Dark cherry with a coppery edge. Intense aroma of slightly reduced ripe fruit (prunes) with hints of toasty flavours and terroir. Flavourful, fleshy palate with fine bitter notes and warm hints.

VALDEVÍ MADURADO EN ROBLE 2000 OAK AGED RED

79 Dark cherry with a coppery glint. Intense aroma of ripe fruit with a spicy hint of oak. Flavourful palate, with a good fruit/oak integration and a spicy finish with slightly varietal fruit.

CASTILLO DEL RÍO 2000 CRIANZA RED

80 Dark garnet red cherry with a brick red edge. Powerful, ripe aroma with toasty oak and a suggestion of tobacco. Flavourful, fleshy, slightly warm and varietal palate with a suggestion of sweet fruit.

MARQUÉS DE OLIVARA 1998 RESERVA RED
100% tinta de Toro

82 Dark cherry with a dark red edge. Powerful aroma with predominant reduction notes (animals, old furniture). Flavourful palate with round, oily tannins, fine notes of bitterness and quite sweet fruit.

MATARREDONDA

Carretera Toro-Valdefinjas, s/n
47006 Valladolid ()
☎: 983 226 047 - Fax: 983 222 352
libranzatoro@hotmail.com
Established: 2001
🍇 300 ▦ 105,000 litres 🍃 25 has.
🐂 100%

LIBRANZA 2001 ROBLE RED
tinta de toro 🍇 14

88 Deep cherry with a violet edge. Deep smoky aroma of earth and minerals with well-ripened black fruit and expression of the vine variety. Fleshy palate with marked but fine and fresh wood tannins and a nuance of terroir and minerals.

LIBRANZA 2002 ROBLE RED
tinta de toro

90 Deep cherry with a violet edge. Aroma of fine crianza (cedar, tobacco) with subtle traces of minerals and dry earth and grape character. Fleshy, expressive, spicy palate with smoky oak tannins over the fruit, long with a mineral and flavourful finish.

Bodegas y Viñedos MAURODOS

Carretera N-122, km. 412 Villaester
47112 Pedrosa del Rey (Valladolid)

☎: 983 784 118 - Fax: 983 784 018
info@bodegasmauro.com

Established: 1998

🌐 800 📊 175,000 litres 🍇 35 has.

🇪🇸 60% 🌐40%: -US -PR -DE Asia -DK

SAN ROMÁN 2001 CRIANZA RED
100% tinta de Toro

93 Almost opaque cherry. Elegant aroma of fresh fruit skins, smoky notes, blended dark-roasted flavours, hints of pitch and terroir. Powerful finish with oily yet firm oak tannins, an expression of a fine red wine, a persistent finish of dry earth, liquorice and bitter cocoa.

Bodega NUMANTHIA TERMES

Real s/n
49882 Valdefinjas (Zamora)
☎: 980 699 147 - Fax: 980 699 147
info@eguren.com
www.eguren.com

Established: 1998

🌐 480 📊 120,000 litres 🍇 40 has.

🍷 44,000 litres.

NUMANTHIA 2002 RED

89 Intense cherry. Powerful aroma with an excellent expression of fresh but ripe fruit and fine toasty oak notes. Fruity palate with body and good acidity, flavourful with fresh overtones and an elegant note.

TERMANTHIA 2002 RED

93 Very intense cherry. Powerful aroma, rich in varietal and mineral expression with fine toasty flavours (chocolate, coffee). Powerful, fleshy, full and flavourful palate with wood tannins lacking an impenetrable fruit expression. Will improve over the next few months.

NUMANTHIA RED
TERMANTHIA RED

PALACIO DE VILLACHICA

Carretera Nacional 122, km. 433
49800 Toro (Zamora)
☎: 983 372 289 - Fax: 983 381 356
correo@palaciovillachica.com
www.palaciosdevillachica.com

Established: 2000

🌐 430 📊 230,000 litres 🍇 40 has.

🇪🇸 95% 🌐5%: -CA

PALACIO DE VILLACHICA 3T 2003 RED
100% tinta de Toro

81 Dark cherry. Intense aroma of slightly reduced ripe red fruit with a suggestion of macerated skins

and notes of damp earth. Flavourful palate with slightly marked tannins (a mild hint of greeness) and liquorice, slightly balsamic with marked acidity.

PALACIO DE VILLACHICA 2001 ROBLE RED
🌐6

81 Cherry with an orangey edge. Medium-intensity aroma of ripe black fruit and smoky oak. Round, powerful palate with very ripe fruit (quite viscous) and a toasty wood finish.

PALACIO DE VILLACHICA 4T 2001 OAK AGED RED
100% tinta de Toro
🌐5

83 Garnet red cherry with a coppery-saffron glint. Intense aroma of toasty oak notes, macerated black fruit, spicy hints and a fine reduction. Flavourful, fleshy palate with the fruit well-enveloped by the oak tannins and fine bitter notes.

PALACIO DE VILLACHICA 5T 2001 OAK AGED RED
100% tinta de Toro
🌐10

84 Garnet red cherry with a saffron edge. Intense aroma with predominant toasty oak notes and a fine reduction nuance. Fleshy, flavourful palate, well-integrated fruit/oak, hints of liquorice, sour cherries in liqueur and mineral notes in the retronasal passage.

VILLACHICA 2000 CRIANZA RED
100% tinta de Toro

80 Cherry with an orangey edge. Medium-intensity aroma with considerable weight oak and a nuance of ripe fruit. Round, flavourful palate with marked very toasty oak tannins.

Bodegas y Viñedos PINTIA

Carretera de Morales s/n
47530 San Román de Hornija (Valladolid)
☎: 983 784 178
vegasicilia@vega-sicilia.com
www.vega-sicilia.com

Established: 2001

🌐 650 📊 400,000 litres 🍇 80 has.

🇪🇸 50% 🌐50%

PINTIA 2002 OAK AGED RED
100% tinta de Toro
🌐13

95 Very intense cherry with a purplish edge. Powerful aroma, rich in toasty and mineral notes, with dry stone, clay, hints of ripe but fresh fruit with good varietal expression and spirituous notes. Powerful, full, fleshy, generous palate, rich in ripe but firm tannins, with jammy but quite fresh and elegant fruit in the retronasal passage, good varietal expression.

QUINTA DE LA QUIETUD

Camino de Bardales, s/n
Apartado de Correos 34

49800 Toro (Zamora)
☎: 980 568 019 - Fax: 980 568 019
info@quintaquietud.com

Established: 1999

⊕ 350 ▯ 80,000 litres ⚘ 22 has.

QUINTA DE LA QUIETUD 2002 OAK AGED RED
100% tinta de Toro

89 Very dark cherry. Powerful aroma with fine toasty (coffee, pitch) wood notes, jammy black fruit and hints of graphite. Concentrated palate with good fruit/oak integration, dark-roasted flavours, minerals and toasty skins.

QUINTA DE LA QUIETUD 2001 CRIANZA RED
100% tinta de Toro

88 High hue garnet red. Aroma with light hints of reduction (leather, cedar), toasty wood and mineral notes. Spiritous, warm palate with drying tannins and a reduced retronasal.

QUINTA DE LA QUIETUD 2000 CRIANZA RED

RAMÓN RAMOS

Pozo, 35
49153 Venialbo (Zamora)
☎: 980 573 080 - Fax: 980 573 241
ramonramoscarrilo@eresmas.com
www.ramonramos.com

Established: 1963

⊕ 250 ▯ 950,000 litres ⚘ 25 has.

🍷 30% 🌐70%: -US -JP -DE -UK -CH -RU -IT -FR -MX -TW

MONTE TORO WHITE
MONTE TORO 2003 JOVEN RED
MONTE TORO 2003 RED
TARDENCUBA 2001 ROBLE RED
RAMÓN RAMOS 2003 OAK AGED MOSCATEL
TARDENCUBA 2001 CRIANZA RED
MONTE TORO 1996 RESERVA RED
MONTE TORO 1995 GRAN RESERVA RED
MONTE TORO 1999 CRIANZA RED

REJADORADA

Reja Dorada, 11
49800 Toro (Zamora)
☎: 980 693 089 - Fax: 980 693 089
rejadorada@rejadorada.com
www.rejadorada.com

Established: 1999

⊕ 400 ▯ 75,000 litres 🍷 40% 🌐60%: -
US -DE -UK -BE -CH -NL -AT -MX -PR

REJADORADA 2002 ROBLE RED
100% tinta de Toro ⊕ 6

82 Garnet red-violet. Aroma with notes of cheese, wood and a hint of ripe red fruit. Drying, fleshy palate with very marked tannins, slightly warm and long.

REJADORADA 2001 CRIANZA RED
100% tinta de Toro

85 Medium-hue garnet red. Toasty aroma of wood, chocolate, dark-roasted flavours and foresty red fruits. Fleshy and round on the palate with quite aggressive tannins, long with toasty wood in the retronasal passage.

SANGO DE REJADORADA 2000 RESERVA RED
100% tinta de Toro

81 Very deep garnet red. Aroma of elegant wood, balsamic spices and ripe sweet red fruit. Flavourful palate with very marked wood tannins that mask the fruit.

SIETECERROS

Carretera N-122, Km. 410 (Villaester de Arriba)
47540 Pedrosa del Rey (Valladolid)
☎: 983 784 142 - Fax: 983 784 142
sietecerros@eresmas.net
www.bodegasietecerros.com

Established: 2001

⊕ 150 🗟 100,000 litres ⅋ 50 has.
🐄 80% 🌐20%: -CH -NL -DE -LI -US

QUEBRANTARREJAS 2002 JOVEN RED
tinta de toro

86 Dark cherry with a violet edge. Intense, varietal aroma of black fruit, smoky hints of skins, hints of nettles and damp earth. Flavourful palate with marked tannins and good fruit weight; slightly warm, spicy and long.

VALDELAZARZA 2002 ROBLE RED
tinta de toro

82 Intense cherry. Aroma of powerful, well-ripened red fruit with well-integrated fine smoky wood. Fleshy, fresh palate with pungent yet flavourful wood tannins and a spicy finish.

VALDELAZARZA 2001 CRIANZA RED
tinta de Toro

81 Cherry. Slightly warm vanilla aroma with noticeable oak notes over the red fruit. Fleshy, powerful palate with well-balanced fruit and wood and a certain fruit expresión, flavourful.

SOBREÑO

Carretera N-122, km. 423
49800 Toro (Zamora)
☎: 980 693 417 - Fax: 980 693 416
bodegassobreno@terra.es

Established: 1998

⊕ 1,300 🗟 990,000 litres ⅋ 80 has.
🐄 25% 🌐75%

FINCA SOBREÑO 2001 CRIANZA RED
tinta de toro

86 Dark cherry with a garnet red edge. Powerful aroma of jammy black fruit with fresh overtones of macerated skins and fine toasty oak. Flavourful, fleshy palate with ripe, oily tannins and bitter notes in the finish.

FINCA SOBREÑO SELECCIÓN ESPECIAL 1999 OAK AGED RED
100% tinta de Toro

90 Dark garnet red cherry. Intense aroma with predominant burnt notes, a nuance of graphite and macerated skins. Powerful, fleshy palate with ripe, oily tannins, slightly warm and long.

FINCA SOBREÑO 2003 ROBLE RED
tinta de toro

85 Dark cherry with a violet edge. Powerful, fruity aroma of macerated skins, smoky oak notes and terracotta. Fleshy palate with promising but slightly marked tannins, a sweet fruit hint and bitter notes (liquorice, dark-roasted flavours), warm, quite long.

Compañía de Vinos de
TELMO RODRÍGUEZ

Siete Infantes de Lara, 5 Oficina 1
26006 Logroño (La Rioja)
☎: 941 511 128 - Fax: 941 511 131
cia@fer.es

DEHESA GAGO 2003 JOVEN RED
100% tinta de Toro

88 Intense cherry. Powerful aroma rich in black fruit notes but with fresh overtones and toasty nuances. Fleshy palate with sweet tannins, slightly jammy, spirituous yet flavourful and persistent.

PAGO LA JARA 2002 ROBLE RED
100% tinta de Toro

93 Very intense cherry. Powerful aroma of sun-drenched skins and toasty oak with a hint of stewed fruit aromas, warm and spirituous with foresty herbs. Powerful, fleshy palate with sweet and very flavourful tannins and a spirituous and mineral retronasal passage.

GAGO 2002 OAK AGED RED
100% tinta de Toro

87 Intense cherry. Powerful aroma of ripe fruit with hints of dry earth (minerals), and fine toasty flavours. Jammy black fruit on the palate, warm with sweet and spirituous tannins, persistent.

TORESANAS

Carretera N-122 s/n
Polígono Carabizal
49800 Toro (Zamora)
☎: 983 868 336 - Fax: 983 868 432
bodegasbccv@interbook.net
www.bodegasdecastilla.com

Established: 1997

⊕ 500 🗟 500,000 litres ⅋ 25 has.
🐄 90% 🌐10%: -UK -NL -DE -BE -DK -JP -HU -US -AT

AMANT 2002 ROBLE RED
100% tinta de Toro

84 Garnet red cherry with a violet hue. Intense aroma with a good varietal fruit expression (reduction notes, underbrush) and smoky oak. Flavourful palate with fleshy overtones and a sweet fruit hint, spicy with hints of dark-roasted flavours and terracotta.

OROT 2001 CRIANZA RED
100% tinta de Toro

85 Medium-hue cherry. Aroma of sun-drenched skins, light toasty notes and red fruit. Notes of greeness on the palate, warm with toasty wood in the retronasal passage and medium persistence.

OROT 1998 RESERVA RED
100% tinta de Toro

87 Dark cherry. Powerful aroma with toasty oak, macerated skins and hints of graphite. Fleshy palate with a good oak/fruit integration, alternate sweet and bitter notes of quality and good acidity.

TORREDUERO

Polígono Industrial Norte, Parcela 5, Apartado de Correo 81
49800 Toro (Zamora)
☎: 980 693 421 - Fax: 980 693 422
torreduero.3085@cajarural.com
www.bodegastorreduero.com

Established: 2000
600 🛢 1,800,000 litres 🍇 94 has.
🍷 70% 🌍 30%

PEÑAMONTE 2003 JOVEN ROSÉ
85% tinta de Toro, 15% garnacha

74 Brilliant raspberry. Intense aroma of red stone fruit with spicy hints of skins. Flavourful palate with bittersweet hints and a suggestion of overripe fruit.

PEÑAMONTE 2003 JOVEN RED
100% tinta de Toro

78 Cherry with a violet edge. Balsamic, smoky aroma of quite unripe black fruit. Fleshy palate with slightly vegetative tannins, slightly warm with a predominantly oaky finish.

PEÑAMONTE 2002 OAK AGED RED
100% tinta de Toro 🛢 3

82 Intense cherry. Spicy aroma with smoky notes that envelop the black fruit. Fleshy, powerful palate with firm fruit tannins and well-integrated toasty oak; long.

MARQUÉS DE PEÑAMONTE 2001 CRIANZA RED
100% tinta de Toro

84 Cherry with a garnet red-orange edge. Medium-intensity, viscous aroma of spicy wood (sandalwood), fine. Flavourful, fleshy palate with a good fruit/wood integration and round tannins.

PEÑAMONTE 2001 CRIANZA RED
100% tinta de Toro

82 Intense cherry. Aroma of expressive black fruit and well-assembled toasty and smoky notes. Flavourful palate with noticeable toasty tannins over the fruit, good acidity and a spicy finish.

PEÑAMONTE 2003 OAK AGED RED

VALDUERO

Carretera de Aranda, s/n
09440 Gumiel de Mercadol (Burgos)
☎: 947 545 459 - Fax: 947 545 609
valduerocom@bodegasvalduero.com
www.bodegasvalduero.com

Established: 1982
2,600 🛢 1,200,000 litres 🍇 250 has.

📏 680,000 litres.

🍷 50% 🌐50%: -CH -DE -UK -US -PR - DO -JP -AT -BE -NL -CA

VAL VIADERO 2002 JOVEN RED
100% tempranillo

86 Cherry with a garnet red edge. Intense aroma of ripe black fruit, jammy red fruit and hints of sun-drenched skins. Fleshy palate with good wood/fruit integration and a suggestion of red fruit in the retronasal passage.

VAL VIADERO 2001 OAK AGED RED
100% tempranillo

85 Medium-hue cherry. Fresh aroma of toasty wood, vanilla, red fruit (blackberries) and varietal typification. Flavourful, flesh palate with slightly drying tannins, long with fruity hints.

VALSANZO SELECCIÓN

Manuel Azaña, 9
Edificio Ambassador, Local 15
47014 (Valladolid)
☎: 677 448 608 - Fax: 983 784 096
valsanzo@telefonica.net

🏛 250 📊 150,000 litres 🍇 80 has.
🍷 30% 🌐70%

DAMALISCO 1999 RESERVA RED
tinta de toro

87 Deep cherry with a garnet red edge. Intense aroma of fine toasty woods and concentrated black fruit. Powerful, flavourful and fleshy on the palate with a good assemblage of fruit and wood, a balsamic nuance and sweet, ripe tannins.

DAMALISCO 2000 CRIANZA RED
tinta de toro

85 Cherry with a garnet red edge. Intense, expressive and very fruity aroma (blackberries and macerated cherries), expressive. Flavourful and fleshy on the palate with a character of ripe red fruit, well-integrated wood and a pleasantly toasty finish.

Bodegas VEGA SAUCO

Avenida Comuneros, 108
49810 Morales de Toro (Zamora)
☎: 980 698 294 - Fax: 980 698 294
vegasauco@vegasauco.com
www.vegasauco.com

Established: 1991
🏛 750 📊 700,000 litres 🍇 22 has.
🍷 40% 🌐60%

VEGA SAUCO 2002 ROBLE RED
100% tinta de Toro

84 Garnet red. Slightly warm aroma of jammy black fruit with toasty oak notes. Round, powerful palate with oily but dry wood tannins and a good fruit hint, long.

PAGO SANTA OLALLA 1999 CRIANZA RED
100% tinta de Toro

82 Cherry with an orangey edge. Aroma of jammy fruit with toasty oak and sensations of ripeness. Warm palate with marked oak tannins, well-mannered and pleasant but lacking fruit.

VEGA SAUCO 2000 CRIANZA RED
100% tinta de Toro

84 Intense cherry. Harmonious aroma of well-ripened black fruit, smoky notes and earth. Fleshy palate with powerful, flavourful fruit tannins and well-integrated wood, warm, with a mineral finish.

ADOREMUS 1999 RESERVA RED
100% tinta de Toro

83 Cherry with a brick red edge. Intense aroma of spicy wood (sandalwood) and ripe fruit. Flavourful, warm, fleshy palate with toasty wood well-assembled with the ripe fruit.

ADOREMUS 1998 RESERVA RED
100% tinta de Toro

83 Cherry with an orangey edge. Slightly short aroma with mild reduction notes (tobacco), spicy wood and jammy hint. Quite dry wood tannins on the palate, round and flavourful with a toasty finish.

VEGA SAUCO 1997 RESERVA RED
100% tinta de Toro

82 Cherry with an orangey edge. Aroma of long crianza (tobacco, spices) over jammy black fruit. Fleshy palate with flavourful tannins, good crianza expression (toasty notes) and a mineral finish.

WENCES 1999 RESERVA RED
80% tinta de Toro, 20% cascajera

86 Dark cherry with an evolved edge. Aroma with sweet notes of wood, spices and balsamic flavour. Fleshy palate with good acidity, long with medium persistence.

WENCES 2001 RESERVA RED
80% tinta de Toro, 20% cascajera

86 Intense cherry with a garnet red-orange edge. Medium-intensity aroma with powerful and spicy wood and jammy black fruit. Generous, fleshy, round palate with ripe and oily tannins and a good fruit/oak integration.

Bodega VIÑA BAJOZ

Avenida de los Comuneros, 90
49810 Morales de Toro (Zamora)
☎: 980 698 023 - Fax: 980 698 020
info@vinabajoz.com
www.vinabajoz.com

Established: 1962

🍷 3,000 🛢 6,500,000 litres 🌿 1.100 has.
🍷 65% 🍷 35%

BAJOZ MALVASÍA 2003 JOVEN WHITE
100% malvasía

75 Pale with golden nuances. Intense, ripe aroma of slightly reduced white fruit with a nuance of withered petals and yeast. Dry, flavourful palate with bitter notes and not very fine varietal hints (herbal soap).

BAJOZ 2003 JOVEN ROSÉ
100% garnacha

75 Brilliant raspberry. Intense aroma of ripe and slightly sweet fruit with petals and spicy varietal hints. Flavourful, quite fresh palate with bittersweet notes and pronounced citrus acidity.

BAJOZ COSECHA 2003 JOVEN RED
tinta de toro

82 Dark cherry with a purplish edge. Powerful, ripe aroma with excellent varietal expression (black fruit, underbrush) and toasty skins. Flavourful, fleshy palate with quite bitter tannins (overripening) and liquorice, long.

GRAN BAJOZ 2000 ROBLE RED
tinta de toro

87 Medium-hue not very deep cherry. Fresh aroma of toasty wood, dark-roasted hints, coffee, ripe red fruit, notes of elegant evolution. Fleshy, unctous and round on the palate with good wood/fruit integration, good fruit weight and hints of cinnamon in the retronasal passage.

BAJOZ 2002 ROBLE RED
tinta de toro

83 Dark red cherry. Intense aroma with predominant notes of ripe fruit and spicy oak. Flavourful, fleshy palate with well-balanced lactic hints.

BAJOZ 2000 CRIANZA RED
100% tinta de Toro

85 Brilliant cherry with a brick red glint. Intense aroma with predominant notes of fine reduction (tobacco, leather, dates) and smoky oak notes. Flavourful, and supple on the palate with good crianza expression, cigar box and spices in the finish.

BAJOZ 1999 RESERVA RED
tinta de toro

87 Garnet red cherry with a violet hue. Powerful, very varietal aroma (black fruit, balsamic flavours, underbrush) with fine toasty oak. Flavourful palate with rough, slightly oily tannins, bitter hints (liquorice, graphite, dark-roasted flavours) and a sweet fruit hint.

VIÑAGUAREÑA

Carretera Toro-Salamanca, km. 12, 5
49800 Toro (Zamora)
☎: 980 568 013 - Fax: 980 568 013
info@vinotoro.com
www.vinotoro.com

Established: 1999

🍷 367 🛢 180,000 litres 🌿 30 has.

VIÑAGUAREÑA 2001 OAK AGED RED
100% tinta de Toro

79 Garnet red with a ruby red hue. Aroma of overripe red fruit, toasty, smoky, slightly alcoholic. Somewhat warm palate with toasty flavours that conceal the ripe fruit, with body.

VIÑAGUAREÑA 2003 RED
100% tinta de Toro

80 Deep cherry. Fruity aroma, floral with marked hints of maceration. Fleshy palate with abundant fruit, sweet ripe tannins; flowers and liquorice in the finish.

VIÑAGUAREÑA 2001 CRIANZA RED
100% tinta de Toro

81 Deep cherry. Not very intense aroma, toasty notes and of jammy black fruit. Flavourful palate with skins, red fruit and well-integrated alcohol, a fleshy touch.

VIÑAGUAREÑA 2001 RESERVA RED
100% tinta de Toro

84 Very deep cherry. Fine aroma of ripe fruit, toasty skins and light smoky notes integrated with the fruit, complex (pepper, cocoa). Powerful palate with good fruit, fleshy fruit and oak tannins; toasty finish, for keeping.

VIÑAGUAREÑA ESPECIAL 2002 RED
100% tinta de Toro

83 Brilliant deep cherry. Fruity aroma with fine smoky notes, a nuance of mineral hints. Fleshy, flavourful palate with powerful yet lively tannins, somewhat dry oak in the finish.

VIÑALCASTA

Pago de los Quiñones
49810 Morales de Toro (Zamora)
☎: 983 376 979 - Fax: 983 340 824
b.burlon@terra.es

Established: 1998

⊕ 600 🗍 150,000 litres 🌿 40 has.

🍷 50%🌐50%

VIÑALCASTA 2000 RESERVA RED

VIÑEDOS DE VILLAESTER

Villaester de Arriba
47540 Pedrosa del Rey (Valladolid)
☎: 948 712 193 - Fax: 948 712 343
info@lanavarra.com

Established: 2001

⊕ 300 🗍 180,000 litres 🌿 100 has.

🍷 75%🌐25%: -UE Asia Oriental -US -CA
Centroamérica

TAURUS 2002 ROBLE RED
100% tinta de Toro

77 Ruby red cherry. Aroma of skins, alcohol and underripe red fruit. Notes of greenness on the palate; warm and very well-mannered.

VILLAESTER 2001 CRIANZA RED
100% tinta de Toro

85 Deep cherry with an orangey edge. Elegant reduction notes (leather, animals), spicy and with jammy ripe red fruit. Well-balanced with well-integrated tannins on the palate, fleshy and long.

Grupo YLLERA

Carretera Madrid - Coruña, km. 173, 5
47490 Rueda (Valladolid)
☎: 983 868 097 - Fax: 983 868 177
grupoyllera@grupoyllera.com
www.grupoyllera.com

Established: 1972

⊕ 13,500 🗍 6,000,000 litres 🌿 70 has.

🍷 85% 🌐15%: -UE -CH -US -MX -GT -
DO -BR -JP

GARCILASO 2000 CRIANZA RED

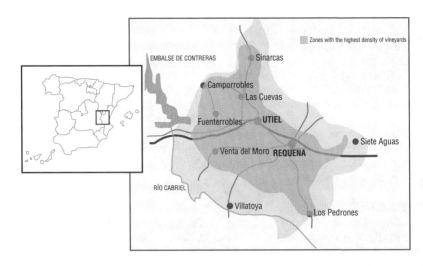

NEWS. The 2003 harvest, one of the most abundant in recent years in the region, was up 18% on the previous year, thanks to (as with other regions in the Peninsula) the abundant rains during spring that provided the plants with sufficient water to face the exceptionally hot summer. Of the 296 million kg harvested, more than 238 were *Bobal*, true queen of the DO, which blended with *Tempranillo* has to date not yet produced wines of exceptional quality. The highest scores were achieved either by the single-variety wines or by blends of *Tempranillo* and *Cabernet Sauvignon*.

Hectares of Vineyard	No. of Viticulturists	No. of Bodegas	2003 Harvest	2003 Production	Marketing
40,000	7,000	110	Good	155,000,000 litres	-

As for *Bobal*, which makes up 80% of the surface of the vineyards, the plenary of the Regulatory Council has just approved the designation 'Bobal Clásico' for wine from vineyards grwoing this variety that are more than 50 years old, which may not be irrigated and must yield less than 3,000 kg/Ha.

In general, in terms of quality, it is also true that the hot 2003 harvest left its mark with uneven ripening between the must and the skin. The most notable, surprisingly, is the Vega Infante, a white wine of the Vinícola Cooperative of Utiel, whose 89 points makes it the best single-variety *Macabeo* wine in the whole of Spain. Good expectations for the red wines, which occupy the top of the table of the DO, although, of the more than 40 wines that surpassed 80 points, only 18 include some percentage of the autochthonous variety *Bobal*. Other novelties worthy of mention: the Labor de Almadeque range of Finca San Blas, which is excellent value for money, and the Coronillas range of Murviedro, a firm which has been leading the way for various years with impeccable oenology, by experimenting with all types of grape varieties and with a clarity of objectives in the foreign market that is considered quite remarkable.

LOCATION. In the west of the province of Valencia. It comprises the municipal districts of Camporrobles, Caudete de las Fuentes, Fuenterrobles, Requena, Siete Aguas, Sinarcas, Utiel, Venta del Moro and Villagordo de Cabriel.

CLIMATE. Continental, with Mediterranean influences, cold winters and slightly milder summers than in other regions of the province. Rainfall is quite scarce with an annual average of 400 mm.

SOIL. Mainly brownish-grey, almost red limestone, poor in organic matter and with good permeability. The horizon of the vineyards are broken by the silhouette of the odd tree planted in the middle of the vineyards, which, bordered by woods, offer a very attractive landscape.

VARIETIES:
White: *Macabeo, Merseguera, Planta Nova, Chardonnay* and *Sauvignon Blanc.*
Red: *Bobal (*majority), *Tempranillo, Garnacha, Cabernet Sauvignon, Merlot, Syrah.*

REGULATORY COUNCIL.
Sevilla, 12. Apdo. Correos 61. 46300 Utiel (Valencia).
Tel: 962 171 062. Fax: 962 172 185.
E-mail: comunicacion@utielrequena.org
Website: www.utielrequena.org

GENERAL CHARACTERISTICS OF THE WINES:

Whites	Firstly, there are the most traditional from *Merseguera*, fresh with wild notes; secondly, the more modern variety from *Macabeo*, with greater aromatic potency, fresh and light; and finally, single variety wines from *Chardonnay*, some fermented in barrels.
Rosés	Produced from *Bobal*, they have a pink to salmon colour; their aromas are fresh and fruity, with somewhat wild and vegetative aromas; on the palate they are fresh and pleasant.
Reds	As opposed to the traditional wines from *Bobal*, with a lot of colour but with somewhat rustic notes, the *Garnacha* variety gives rise to young, fresh, fruity and very correct red wines. For the Crianza wines some *Bobal* is included. Those of this type are flavourful, rounded and, on occasion, somewhat warm.
Espumosos	Cavas and Espumosos are produced according to the traditional methods not included in the DO Cava.

ASTURIANA DE VINOS

Carretera As-18, km. 20, 8
33392 Porceyo-Gijón (Asturias)
☎: 985 307 132 - Fax: 985 307 553
comercial@asturvisa.com
www.asturvisa.com

Established: 1984
▤ 1,000,000 litres

ALOYÓN WHITE
macabeo

79 Brilliant yellow. Aroma of ripe white fruit, yeasts. Warm palate, good acidity, oily, medium persistence.

ALOYÓN ROSÉ
bobal

77 Coppery. Slightly warm aroma of petals and ripe red fruit. Flavourful palate with balanced bittersweetness; quite alcoholic.

ALOYÓN RED
tempranillo, garnacha

73 Not very deep cherry. Aroma of red fruit with mild liquorice notes. Drying on the palate with slightly green tannins, not very expressive.

C. AUGUST EGLI, A.G. CASA LO ALTO

Carretera Venta del Moro-Los Isidros, s/n
46310 Venta del Moro (Valencia)
☎: 962 139 101 - Fax: 962 139 097
ca-egli@cae.ch - cae.ch

FINCA CASA LO ALTO CRIANZA RED

Bodegas CASA DEL PINAR

Carretera Isidros-Venta del Moro, Km
46310 Venta del Moro (Valencia)
☎: 962 139 21 - Fax: 962 139 121
dinent@wanadoo.es

Established: 2000
⊕ 30 ❧ 2 has. ◆ 50% ◉50%: -UK -US

SANFIR 2001 CRIANZA RED
34% bobal, 33% tempranillo, 23% cabernet sauvignon , 5% merlot, 5% syrah

79 Intense cherry. Aroma with reduced notes and overripe bunches, slightly fruity and mildly evolved. Fruity palate with a mild varietal expression, flavourful, cask well infused with the wine.

CASA DEL PINAR 2000 RESERVA RED
50% cabernet sauvignon, 18% merlot, 17% bobal, 13% tempranillo, 5% syrah

84 Intense cherry. Aroma with fine notes of new oak and ripe fruit with hints of minerals. Fleshy, flavourful, warm, toasty palate (dark-roasted) with sweet, very ripe tannins, persistent.

Bodegas CASA PASTOR

Travesía Industria, 5
46352 Campo Arcís - Requena (Valencia)
☎: 687 953 512 - Fax: 962 138 009

Established: 2001
⊕ 80 ▤ 150,000 litres

CASA PASTOR LAMBIES 2003 ROBLE RED
100% tempranillo

76 Cherry. Spicy, slightly earthy aroma with a hint of black fruit. Fleshy, slightly warm palate with marked wood tannins, a floral and slightly alcoholic finish.

CASA PASTOR LAMBIES 2002 CRIANZA RED
90% tempranillo, 10% cabernet sauvignon

84 Dark cherry with a violet hue. Powerful aroma, jammy black fruit, slightly floral, fine spicy and terroir notes. Powerful palate, flavourful, varietal, well-assembled fruit/oak, fine bitter notes (chocolate, liquorice) in the finish, good acidity

CASA PASTOR SELECCIÓN 2002 ROBLE RED

Cooperativa Vinícola COVIÑAS

Rafael Duyos s/n
46340 Requena (Valencia)
☎: 962 300 680 - Fax: 962 302 127
covinas@covinas.com
www.covinas.com

Established: 1965
⊕ 5,140 ▤ 4,566,000 litres ❧ 11,000 has.
◆ 35% ◉65%: -BR -CA -CZ -TW -DE -DK -
FI -FR -IT -JP -MX -NL -DK -PL -RU -SE -US

VIÑA ENTERIZO 2003 WHITE
VIÑA ENTERIZO 2003 ROSÉ
AULA TEMPRANILLO/CABERNET 2002 OAK
 AGED RED
VIÑA ENTERIZO 1999 CRIANZA RED
AULA MERLOT 2002 CRIANZA RED
VIÑA ENTERIZO TEMPRANILLO 2003
 CRIANZA RED
ENTERIZO 1997 RESERVA RED
ENTERIZO 1993 GRAN RESERVA RED

CRIADORES ARTESANOS

Avenida Virgen de Tejeda, 28
46320 Sinarcas (Valencia)

☎: 962 170 028 - Fax: 962 305 032
xriadoresartesanos@hotmail.com

Established: 1997

🍶 45 ▯ 8,000 litres 🍇 15 has. 🍷 100%

PASIEGO 2001 CRIANZA RED
80% tempranillo, 20% cabernet sauvignon

83 Garnet red cherry. Fresh, fruity, pleasant aroma with varietal character. Fresh, fruity palate with a hint of black berries in the retronasal passage, flavourful.

PASIEGO 2000 RESERVA RED
40% tempranillo, 40% cabernet sauvignon, 20% bobal

80 Dark cherry with an orangey edge. Slightly short, imprecise aroma with a mild spicy nuance. Round palate with jammy fruit, spicy notes of oak and flavourful and persistent tannins.

CRIANZO

San Agustín, 13
46340 Requena (Valencia)
☎: 962 300 016 - Fax: 962 304 256
crianzo@hotmail.com

Established: 1994

🍶 34 ▯ 6,000 litres 🍷 100%

ALTIPLANO FERMENTADO EN BARRICA
WHITE
VIÑA IRANZO RESERVA RED
ALTIPLANO RESERVA RED

CULTIVO UVAS ECOLÓGICAS, VINOS Y AFINES

Mayor, 2
46357 La Portera (Valencia)
☎: 962 345 025@filete
fax:cuevasl@ono.com

CUEVA CRIANZA RED

CHERUBINO VALSANGIACOMO

Carretera Cheste-Godelleta, km. 1
46370 Chiva (Valencia)
☎: 962 510 451 - Fax: 962 511 361
cherubino@cherubino.es
www.cherubino.es

Established: 1831

🍶 9,000 ▯ 80,000,000 litres 🍷 20%
🌐80%

MARQUÉS DE CARO ROSÉ
SELECCION DE OTOÑO CRIANZA RED

CHOZAS CARRASCAL

Finca Carrascal, vereda San Antonio
46390 San Antonio de Requena (Valencia)
☎: 963 410 395 - Fax: 963 168 067
chozas@xpress.es

🍇 30 has.

LAS TRES 2003 FERMENTADO EN BARRICA WHITE
chardonnay, macabeo, sauvignon blanc

89 Brilliant straw. Fine aroma with mild smoky hints and foresty mountain herbs, fruity and quite expressive. Fruity palate, rich in fruit expression with a very fine smoky retronasal passage; very fresh with excellent acidity.

LAS CUATRO 2003 JOVEN ROSÉ
tempranillo, garnacha, merlot, syrah

83 Strawberry. Very fruity aroma with expression and ripe hints, fresh. Powerful, very fruity, sweet palate with ripe fruit, flavourful.

DISCOSTA NORTE BODEGAS CASTILLO SAN DAMIÁN

Dompiñor, s/n
27715 Ribadeo (Lugo)
☎: 982 128 900 - Fax: 982 128 641
discosta@hotmail.com

Established: 1978

▯ 1,000,000 litres 🍷 99% 🌐1%

CANDEAL WHITE
CANDEAL ROSÉ
CANDEAL RED

DOMINIO DE ARANLEÓN

Carretera Caudete, s/n
46310 Los Marcos (Valencia)
☎: 963 631 640 - Fax: 963 900 481
maria@aranleon.com
www.aranleon.com

Established: 1927

🍶 300 ▯ 3,000 litres 🍷 80%
🌐20%: -US -DE -IE -FR -AT -IT

ARANLEÓN 2001 CRIANZA RED
50% tempranillo, 50% cabernet sauvignon

75 Cherry with an orangey hue. Quite short aroma of ripe fruit with notes of oak. A touch of flavour on the palate, warm and ripe with slightly aggresive wood.

ARANLEÓN 2000 RESERVA RED
50% tempranillo, 50% cabernet sauvignon

79 Cherry with an orangey edge. Not very intense yet clean aroma of woody vanilla with a balsamic hint. Flavourful palate with a good wood/fruit integration, pleasant.

DOMINIO DE LA VEGA

Carretera Madrid - Valencia, km. 270, 650
46390 San Antonio. Requena (Valencia)
☎: 962 320 570 - Fax: 962 320 330
info@dominiodelavega.com
www.dominiodelavega.com

Established: 2001

AÑACAL DOMINIO DE LA VEGA 2003 WHITE
100% macabeo

75 Straw-coloured. Tropical aroma (passion fruit), with a suggestion of ripeness. Fresh, light palate, flavourful with white fruit.

AÑACAL DOMINIO DE LA VEGA 2003 ROSÉ
100% bobal

79 Intense pink. Clear, fresh aroma of red berries. Dry, fresh palate with pleasant fruit.

DOMINIO DE LA VEGA 2002 FERMENTADO EN BARRICA RED
bobal, cabernet sauvignon, tempranillo

73 Deep cherry with a purple hue. Spicy aroma of slightly ripe black fruit and oily notes. Fleshy, powerful palate with toasty nuances and ripe fruit; a dry finish.

DOMINIO DE LA VEGA 2001 CRIANZA RED
bobal, tempranillo , cabernet sauvignon

78 Intense cherry. Aroma with notes of ripe black fruit, a hint of oak well-assembled with the fruit and a mild nuance of overripening. Fleshy, flavourful palate with overripe bunches and a hint of oak.

DOMINIO DEL ARENAL

Pedanía de San Juan, s/n
46390 San Juan (Valencia)
☎: 962 320 001 - Fax: 962 320 624
educan@dominiodelarenal.com
www.dominiodelarenal.com

Established: 1908
🍇 200 🍇 80 has.
🍷 30% 🌐70%: -DE -US -UK -CA -TW -DK

DOMINIO DEL ARENAL CERRADO DEL ESPINO 2003 RED
100% tempranillo

78 Garnet red cherry. Powerful aroma with black fruit notes, hints of Mediterranean herbs and petals and a nuance of lees. Flavourful on the palate with an edge of greeness to the grape tannins and an acidic edge.

DOMINIO DEL ARENAL SHIRAZ 2002 RED
100% shiraz

82 Very deep cherry. Powerful, fruity aroma with a toasty oak nuance, viscous and without great varietal expression. Flavourful, fleshy and fairly concentrated on the palate with promising although slightly marked tannins; notions of fruit and terroir.

DOMINIO DEL ARENAL 1998 CRIANZA RED
50% tempranillo, 50% shiraz

82 Garnet red cherry with a violet edge. Intense aroma with spicy notes of the oak well-integrated with the ripe fruit notes. Flavourful on the palate with slightly marked oak tannins, a fresh fruity overtone and an acidic edge.

DOMINIO DEL ARENAL 1998 RESERVA RED
50% tempranillo, 50% shiraz

85 Very deep cherry. Aroma of jammy black fruit with fine smoky flavours, hints of spices and flowers. Flavourful palate with full-throttle fruit (notes of red fruit pulp), hints of cocoa in the finish, tannins yet to be assembled.

VIÑA CALDERÓN 2000 CRIANZA RED
DOMINIO DEL ARENAL DULCE DE BOBAL RED

ECOVITIS

Polígono Industrial El Romeral, 13-D
46340 Requena (Valencia)
☎: 962 323 099 - Fax: 962 323 048
info@ecovitis.com
www.ecovitis.com

Established: 1999
🍇 25 🍇 650,000 litres 🍇 90 has.
🍷 75% 🌐25%: -DK -BE -US -IT

ANANTO 2003 WHITE
ANANTO 2003 ROSÉ
ANANTO 2003 RED
ANANTO 2000 CRIANZA RED

EJARQUE

Barcelona, 5-7
46391 El Rebollar (Valencia)
☎: 916 508 344 - Fax: 916 502 219
lalcacer@infonegocio.com

Established: 1998
🍇 200 🍇 40,000 litres 🍇 50 has.
🍷 75% 🌐25%

LAUREL DORADO JOVEN WHITE
VIÑA EJARQUE CRIANZA RED
EIXARCH RESERVA RED

DO UTIEL-REQUENA

EMILIO CLEMENTE

Camino de San Blas, s/n
46340 Requena (Valencia)
☎: 963 466 402 - Fax: 963 465 359
e.clemente@infonegocio.com

Established: 1999

⊕ 126 🍇 98 has.

🍷 50% 🌍50%: -BE -CH -US -PL

PEÑAS NEGRAS 2003 JOVEN RED
EMILIO CLEMENTE 2001 CRIANZA RED

Hijos de ERNESTO CÁRCEL

Bodegas, 5
46391 Rebollar - Requena (Valencia)
☎: 962 303 608 - Fax: 962 303 608

Established: 1948

⊕ 128 📊 230,000 litres 🍇 20 has.

🍷 70% 🌍30%

VALLE DEL TEJO JOVEN WHITE
VALLE DEL TEJO FERMENTADO EN BARRICA
 WHITE
VALLE DEL TEJO JOVEN ROSÉ
VALLE DEL TEJO MACERACIÓN CARBÓNICA
 RED
VALLE DEL TEJO FERMENTADO EN BARRICA
 RED
VALLE DEL TEJO CRIANZA RED

FINCA SAN BLAS

Partida San Blas s/n
46340 Requena (Valencia)
☎: 962 300 888 - Fax: 963 370 707
info@fincasanblas.com
www.fincasanblas.com

Established: 1992

⊕ 150 📊 60,000 litres 🍇 76 has. 🍷 100%

LABOR DEL ALMADEQUE 2000 CRIANZA RED
60% tempranillo, 40% cabernet sauvignon

87 Cherry with a garnet red edge. Elegant aroma of integrated wood (vanilla, peat, toffee) and a nuance of ripe skins. Flavourful palate with good alcohol-acidity balance and nutty notes in the finish, very harmonious.

LABOR DE ALMADEQUE 2001 CRIANZA RED
60% tempranillo, 40% cabernet sauvignon

88 Intense cherry. Slightly short aroma with a notion of carob and liquorice, fine hints of toasty oak and ripe black fruit. Fleshy, powerful, warm palate, with excellent balance between fruit and wood; elegant, for keeping.

LABOR DEL ALMADEQUE 2002 CRIANZA
RED
100% merlot

87 Intense cherry. Aroma with notes of ripe black fruit (plums and blackberries) evoking pressed bunches with fine notes of toasty oak. Fleshy palate with ripe black fruit and flavourful and sweet tannins and toasty and dark-roasted notes.

LABOR DE ALMADEQUE RESERVA DE LA
FAMILIA 2001 RED
100% cabernet sauvignon

83 Intense garnet red cherry. Intense aroma of smoky oak notes, a slightly varietal fruit suggestion with warm notes and earth. Flavourful, fleshy palate with slightly fresh oak tannins, warm notes and a spicy suggestion.

FUSO

Carretera Utiel, 10
46357 El Pontón-Requena (Valencia)
☎: 962 304 212 - Fax: 962 304 212
bodegasfuso@teleline.es
www.bodegasfuso.com

Established: 1999

⊕ 100 📊 500,000 litres 🍇 50 has.

🍷 98% 🌍2%

ALUVIÓN 2003 JOVEN WHITE
ALUVIÓN 2003 JOVEN ROSÉ
ALUVIÓN SUPERIOR 2002 OAK AGED RED
ALUVIÓN 2001 CRIANZA RED

ALUVIÓN 100 AÑOS (CEPAS VIEJAS) 2003
CRIANZA RED

IBERVINO

Avenida Arrabal, 52
46340 Requena (Valencia)
☎: 962 304 803 - Fax: 962 305 246
ibervino@terra.es

Established: 1977

🌐 500 🛢 200,000 litres 🍇 50 has.

🍷 50% 🍇50%

VEGANO RED

Bodegas del INTERIOR

Valencia, 9
46391 Rebollar (Valencia)
☎: 962 300 584 - Fax: 962 323 079
epm@e2000.es

VIDUEÑO 2001 OAK AGED RED
VITA LONGA 1999 CRIANZA RED
VITA LONGA 2001 CRIANZA RED

Bodegas IRANZO

Carretera de Madrid, 60
46315 Caudete de las Fuentes (Valencia)
☎: 962 319 282 - Fax: 962 319 282
iranzoperezduque@@yahoo.es
www.bodegasiranzo.com

Established: 1896

🌐 100 🛢 750,000 litres 🍇 50 has.

🍷 10% 🍇90%: -US -DE -BE -NL -DK

CAÑADA HONDA TEMPRANILLO-
CABERNET SAUVIGNON 2003 JOVEN RED
50% tempranillo, 50% cabernet sauvignon

75 Cherry. Aroma of black fruit with hints of sun-drenched skins (liquorice). Fleshy, slightly tannic palate; fruity with overtones of dryness in the finish.

FINCA CAÑADA HONDA 2002 OAK AGED
RED
50% tempranillo, 50% cabernet sauvignon

79 Garnet red cherry. Fresh, fruity aroma with a mild nuance of overripening. Fruity palate with flavourful tannic notes and a long finish.

FINCA CAÑADA HONDA 2001 CRIANZA RED
50% tempranillo, 50% cabernet sauvignon

80 Quite dark cherry. Slightly fruity aroma with a fairly short expression and fine oak notes. Flavourful palate with oak/fruit balance, light with good persistence.

VERTUS 2001 CRIANZA RED
100% tempranillo

83 Strawberry with hints of Bigarreau cherry. Balsamic aroma (mint, liquorice) with violets, roses and very light toasty flavours. Round palate, good acidity, a little short.

BODEGAS IRANZO TEMPRANILLO
SELECCIÓN 2002 RED
100% tempranillo

82 Garnet red cherry. Fresh, fruity aroma of red berries. Flavourful, expressive palate, varietal with terroir notes, quite persistent.

LA BARONÍA DE TURIS

Carretera de Godelleta, 22
46389 Turis (Valencia)
☎: 962 526 011 - Fax: 962 527 282
baronia@sistelcom.com
www.baroniadeturis.bypermat.net

Established: 1920

🌐 1,660 🛢 11,100,000 litres 🍇 1,460 has.

🍷 55% 🍇45%: -DE -BE -CA -DK -UK -IE
-DK -US -EE -PL -RU -FI -GT -NL -LV

CASTILLO DE BAYREN 2001 RED

Cooperativa Vinícola LA PROTECTORA

Román Ochando, 1
46320 Sinarcas (Valencia)
☎: 962 315 434 - Fax: 962 315 436
coop-sinarcas@resone.es
www.bodegasinarcas.com

CERRO CARPIO ROSÉ

70 Coppery blush. Ripe aroma with a hint of red fruit, without great fruit expression. Fresh, dry palate; without fruit nuances, well-mannered.

CERRO CARPIO ROSÉ DE AGUJA

72 Clear blush. Discreet aroma of slightly ripe red fruit. Flavourful palate, slightly sweet with heavy beads, persistent.

CERRO CARPIO 1999 CRIANZA RED
100% tempranillo

74 Quite intense cherry. Aroma with mild evolution notes (overripe bunches), and a hint of oak. Supple palate, fruity but without great expression with slightly faded oak tannins.

CERRO CARPIO 1999 RED
100% tempranillo

74 Cherry with a garnet red edge. Fairly short aroma of red fruit with a vegetative nuance. Slightly vegetative, fruity palate, well-mannered yet without great nuances.

DO UTIEL-REQUENA

ARCAZ 1999 RESERVA RED

81 Cherry with an orange edge. Aroma with woody notes of oak well-assembled with the ripe fruit, quite complex with mild suggestions of minerals. Round, flavourful palate with bitter hints of oak and jammy fruit.

Cooperativa Nuestra Señora de LAS VIÑAS

Cl. Almendro, 1
46315 Caudete de las Fuentes (Valencia)
☎: 962 319 023 - Fax: 962 319 023
coopcau@ccae.es

Established: 1943
▤ 8,000,000 litres ※ 1,300 has.
🍷 70% 🌐30%: -IT

CELIN 2003 RED

LATORRE AGROVINÍCOLA

Carretera Requena, 2
46310 Venta del Moro (Valencia)
☎: 962 185 028 - Fax: 962 185 422
vinos@latorreagrovinicola.com
www.latorreagrovinicola.com

Established: 1968
⊕ 140 ▤ 8,500,000 litres ※ 190 has.
🍷 95% 🌐5%: -DE -CZ

EL PARREÑO MACABEO 2003 WHITE
100% macabeo

75 Pale yellow. Slightly intense, fruity aroma, without great nuances. Fresh, fruity palate with bitter hints and pronounced citrus acidity.

EL PARREÑO BOBAL 2003 JOVEN ROSÉ
100% bobal

78 Brilliant raspberry. Slightly intense aroma of red fruit with hints of sweetness. Flavourful palate with fine bitter notes, a slightly acidic edge and a toasty hint of skins.

EL PARREÑO 1999 CRIANZA RED
75% bobal, 25% tempranillo

80 Garnet red cherry. Fine aroma of crianza and fruit (cocoa, vanilla). Round, oily palate with a good evolution in the bottle, harmony between oak and fruit and silky tannins, has improved since the 2004 Wine Guide.

EL PARREÑO TEMPRANILLO 1999 CRIANZA RED
tempranillo

69 Cherry with a brick red edge. Not very clean aroma (stables). Better on the palate despite slightly aged wood.

EL PARREÑO BOBAL 1999 RESERVA RED
100% bobal

82 Cherry with a garnet red-orange-edge. Medium-intensity aroma of chimneys, toasty notes and slightly aged wood. Flavourful, balanced, very round palate with a good fruit/wood assemblage; good crianza.

EL PARREÑO 2003 JOVEN RED
EL PARREÑO BOBAL 1999 CRIANZA RED
EL PARREÑO 1996 GRAN RESERVA RED

Bodegas y Viñedos LUIS TORRES

Cardona, 1
46352 Campo Arcis - Requena (Valencia)
☎: 699 917 543@filete
luistorres@terra.com

Established: 2000
⊕ 12 ▤ 10,000 litres ※ 40 has. 🍷 100%

GRAN FIDEL FERMENTADO EN BARRICA RED
GRAN FIDEL CABERNET SAUVIGNON OAK AGED RED
GRAN FIDEL CABERNET SAUVIGNON RED
GRAN FIDEL CRIANZA RED

MAS DE BAZÁN

Carretera Villar de Olmos, km. 2
46340 Requena (Valencia)
☎: 962 303 586 - Fax: 962 138 160
agrodebazan@agrodebazansa.es

Established: 1998
⊕ 600 ▤ 1,000,000 litres 🍷 96% 🌐4%:
-CH -US -DE

MAS DE BAZÁN 2003 ROSÉ
ROBURT 2002 RED
MAS DE BAZÁN 2001 CRIANZA RED
MAS DE BAZÁN SELECCIÓN DE AÑADAS 2000 RESERVA RED

Bodegas MURVIEDRO

Ampliación Polígono El Romeral, s/n
46340 Requena (Valencia)
☎: 962 329 003 - Fax: 962 329 002
murviedro@murviedro.es
www.murviedro.es

Established: 1927
⊕ 1,500 ▤ 7,100,000 litres 🍷 5% 🌐95%

SANTERRA BOBAL ROSÉ 2003 ROSÉ
100% bobal

79 Blush with a coppery edge. Aroma of red fruit with toasty hints of skins, fresh. Dry, flavourful palate, slightly alcoholic with good acidity.

SANTERRA TEMPRANILLO 2003 RED
tempranillo, bobal

82 Garnet red with a raspberry edge. Intense aroma of red fruit (redcurrants, raspberries), clean. Flavourful, very fresh and fruity palate with varietal hints.

CORONILLA 2003 ROBLE JOVEN RED
100% bobal

78 Intense cherry with a garnet red glint. Aroma with notes of ripe grape bunches with a hint of fruity freshness. Flavourful, fresh palate with good acidity and hints of forest fruit.

SANTERRA TEMPRANILLO 2002 RED
100% tempranillo

84 Cherry. Very perfumed aroma of sweet fruit and a mild reduction, intense. Drying palate with very pleasant acidity and good tannicity, reminiscent of sweetness.

CORONILLA 2000 RESERVA RED
100% bobal

86 Intense cherry. Slightly closed aroma of ripe black berries with fine notes of smoky oak, a suggestion of minerals (stones and dry earth) and jammy fruit. Full, fleshy, flavourful palate with jammy black fruit and firm and very ripe tannins; mild overripening in the retronasal passage.

CORONILLA 2001 CRIANZA RED
100% bobal

89 Aroma with great varietal expression (hints of brambles and flowers), hints of ripe fruit and well-integrated fine nuances of oak. Fresh, very fruity palate, with character, good varietal expression with flavourful fruit tannins and toasty fine wood in the retronasal passage, persistent.

PALMERA

Bodegas, 11
46391 El Rebollar (Valencia)
☎: 962 320 720 - Fax: 962 320 720
Established: 1998
⊕ 47 ▤ 120,000 litres ⚘ 14,3 has.
🍷 5% 🌐95%: -BE -NL -FI -UK -CH -AT -DE

BOBAL Y TEMPRANILLO 2002 RED
50% tempranillo, 40% bobal, 10% merlot

83 Garnet red cherry with a violet edge. Intense, fruity aroma with hints of sun-drenched skins and good varietal expression (underbrush). Flavourful, fleshy, and spicy on the palate with slightly marked tannins and symmetry between fruit and acidity.

VIÑA CABRIEL SUPERIOR 2002 OAK AGED RED
80% tempranillo, 10% cabernet sauvignon, 10% merlot

79 Deep garnet red cherry with a violet edge. Intense, slightly fruity aroma with toasty hints of oak. Flavourful on the palate with quite marked oak tannins and a fruity nuance, a suggestion of freshness.

L'ANGELET 2001 CRIANZA RED
70% tempranillo, 20% cabernet sauvignon, 10% merlot

91 Intense cherry. Concentrated aroma of black fruit (jammy bilberries) with fine toasty oak notes (coffee, chocolate), Powerful, fleshy, full, flavourful palate with ripe and slightly sweet tannins; creamy toasty oak in the retronasal passage, very persistent.

PEDRO MORENO 1940

Bodegas, s/n
46311 Jaraguás.Venta del Moro (Valencia)
☎: 962 185 208 - Fax: 962 185 208
comercial@bodegaspedromoreno1940.es
Established: 1940
⊕ 67 ▤ 2,000,000 litres ⚘ 180 has.
🍷 40% 🌐60%

DULCE TERTULIA ROSÉ
VIÑA TURQUESA ROSÉ
VIÑA TURQUESA CRIANZA RED

PROEXA

Carretera Caudete, s/n
46310 Los Marcos-Venta del Moro (Valencia)

DO UTIEL-REQUENA

☎: 963 890 877 - Fax: 963 890 877
bproexa@wanadoo.es

Established: 1995

🌐 57 📊 250,000 litres 🍇 40 has.

🍷 10% 🌐90%: -DE -UK

VEGA VALTERRA DE AÑADA 2003 RED
VEGA VALTERRA 2000 CRIANZA RED
VEGA VALTERRA 1997 RESERVA RED

RESERVAS Y CRIANZAS REQUENENSES

Santa Ana, 18
46390 San Antonio (Valencia)
☎: 962 304 353 - Fax: 962 323 020
recrire@hotmail.com

MARMITÓN CRIANZA RED
MARMITÓN RESERVA RED

ROMERAL VINÍCOLA

Pol. Industrial "El Romeral" Parcela 1-2
46340 Requena (Valencia)
☎: 962 303 665 - Fax: 962 304 991
romeral@eurociber.es

Established: 1991

🌐 860 📊 7,000,000 litres 🍇 400 has.

🍷 60% 🌐40%: -CH -SE -IT -PL -DE
-US -UK -FR -NL -BE

CASTILLO DE REQUENA 2003 WHITE
100% macabeo

84 Yellow straw. Aroma with good varietal expression, ripe white stone fruit (pears, apricots). Well-balanced palate, good acidity, persistent.

CASTILLO DE REQUENA 2003 ROSÉ
100% bobal

78 Garnet red cherry. Fresh, fruity aroma, slightly foresty but well-balanced. Fresh, fruity palate with hints of foresty yet clean and clear Bobal, good acidity.

CASTILLO DE REQUENA 2002 OAK AGED RED
100% tempranillo

83 Garnet with a violet rim. Aroma of ripe red stone fruit, very new wood and vanilla, somewhat alcoholic. Slightly drying palate with light bitter notes and moderate acidity.

CASTILLO DE REQUENA 2000 CRIANZA RED
80% tempranillo, 20% bobal

80 Garnet red cherry. Aroma with spicy notes and forest fruit with a slight varietal expression.

Flavourful, well-balanced palate, with toasty notes of well-integrated oak/fruit.

CASTILLO DE REQUENA 1999 RESERVA RED
90% bobal, 10% tempranillo

80 Garnet red cherry with a brick red edge. Short, mildly spicy aroma with a hint of reduction (leather, cigar box). Round palate with ripe fruit and well-balanced hints of oak, flavourful.

LOMAS DEL CASTILLO 2001 OAK AGED RED
CAÑADA ALTA 2001 OAK AGED RED
CASTILLO DE REQUENA 2003 RED
LOMAS DEL CASTILLO 2000 CRIANZA RED
LOMAS DEL CASTILLO 1998 RESERVA RED

Cooperativa Vinícola Vitivinicultores
SANTA RITA

Patrocinio, s/n
46314 Fuenterrobles (Valencia)
☎: 962 183 008 - Fax: 962 183 008
entidad@copsantarita.jazztel.es

Established: 1959

📊 8,000,000 litres 🍇 1,164.59 has. 🍷 100%

REGAJO ROSÉ
REGAJO RED

SEBIRAN

Pérez Galdos, 1
46352 Campo Arcis-Requena (Valencia)
☎: 962 303 321 - Fax: 962 303 966
bodegassebiran@bodegassebiran.com
www.bodegassebiran.com

Established: 1914

🌐 500 🍇 133 has.

🍷 60% 🌐40%: -DE -CH

SEÑORIO DE ARCIS 2003 ROSÉ
100% bobal

80 Strawberry blush. Aroma of sweetish strawberries, evoking jelly. Dry palate with good freshness that sustains the sweetness; fleshy and bitter notes (foresty strawberries).

COTO D´ARCIS 2001 FERMENTADO EN BARRICA WHITE
SEÑORÍO DE ARCIS 2003 WHITE
TERRÁNEO BOBAL RED
COTO D´ARCIS BOBAL 2001 FERMENTADO EN BARRICA RED
COTO D´ARCIS TEMPRANILLO 2000 RED
SEÑORÍO DE ARCIS 2001 RED
SEÑORÍO DE ARCIS 1999 CRIANZA RED
COTO D´ARCIS 1998 RESERVA RED
COTO D´ARCIS 1997 GRAN RESERVA RED

Cavas y Vinos TORRE ORIA

Carretera Pontón - Utiel, km. 3
46390 Derramador - Requena (Valencia)
☎: 962 320 289 - Fax: 962 320 311
info.torreoria@natra.es
www.torreoria.com

Established: 1897

🍷 4,500 📊 4,500,000 litres 🍇 20 has.

🍷 35% 🌍65%: -DK -DK -SE -FI -DE -UK -NL -BE -CH -RU -LT -JP -PH MK -US -MX

MARQUÉS DE REQUENA 2003 WHITE
100% macabeo

78 Straw-coloured. Medium-intensity, tropical aroma with a slightly ripe nuance. Flavourful palate with good acidity and exotic fruity notes (pineapple); long.

MARQUES DE REQUENA 2003 ROSÉ
100% bobal

75 Pale blush. Quite ripe aroma with a nuance of red fruit, slightly herbaceous. Flavourful palate, slightly alcoholic, without freshness, well-mannered.

TORRE ORIA 2002 RED
100% tempranillo

76 Cherry with an orangey edge. Aroma of sun-drenched skins, ink and overripe fruit. Fruity palate with a ripe character, slightly flavourful.

LOS CLAUSTROS DE TORRE ORIA 2001 CRIANZA RED
70% cabernet sauvignon, 20% tempranillo, 5% merlot, 5% bobal

82 Cherry with an orangey edge. Toasty aroma with crianza reduction notes over ripe black fruit. Fresh, flavourful palate with sweetish and pleasant tannins; fruit-wood symmetry.

MARQUES DE REQUENA 2001 CRIANZA RED
100% tempranillo

71 Cherry with an orangey edge. Aroma with ver green notes (small vine shoots, asparagus) that are repeated on the palate, together with overtones of fruit and wood.

TORRE ORIA CABERNET 2001 CRIANZA RED
80% cabernet sauvignon, 20% merlot

74 Dark cherry. Aroma with mild notes of ripe fruit and slightly brittle wood. Light, flavourful palate with a hint of animal notes, well-mannered.

LOS CLAUSTROS DE TORRE ORIA 1999 RESERVA RED
70% cabernet sauvignon, 20% tempranillo, 5% merlot, 5% bobal

80 Cherry with an orangey edge. Aroma with reduction notes (tobacco, pepper) and jammy fruit. Vegetative but flavourful overtones on the palate with well-integrated wood.

MARQUÉS DE REQUENA 1999 RESERVA RED
100% tempranillo

71 Cherry with an orangey edge. Aroma with notes of greeness (small vine shoots) that are repeated on the palate. A nuance of fruit on the palate and an astringent finish.

TORRE ORIA CABERNET 1999 RESERVA RED
80% cabernet sauvignon, 20% merlot

79 Quite intense cherry with an orangey rim. Aroma with predominant oak over fruit. Fleshy palate with slightly brittle oak tannins.

MARQUÉS DE REQUENA 1997 GRAN RESERVA RED
100% tempranillo

76 Garnet red cherry. Toasty aroma (old wood) with notes of ripe black fruit and overtones of crianza reduction. Fleshy palate with dry wood tannins and sweet vanillas in the finish.

TORRE ORIA 1997 GRAN RESERVA RED
80% cabernet sauvignon, 20% merlot

82 Garnet red with a brick red hue. Aroma with notes of elegant reduction and oak with a fairly viscous nuance. Round and supple on the palate with a toasty aroma in the retronasal passage, long.

Bodegas TORROJA

Nueva, 1 Azagador
46357 Requena (Valencia)
☎: 962 304 232 - Fax: 962 303 833
bodegas@bodegastorroja.com
www.bodegastorroja.com

Established: 1994

🍷 1,000 📊 1,000,000 litres 🍇 43 has.

🍷 20% 🌍80%: -DK -DE -US -LT -LV -TR -TW -MY

SYBARUS TARDANA 2003 WHITE
100% tardana

80 Very pale yellow. Intense, ripe aroma of white fruit with fine, spicy hints of skins. Dry and flavourful on the palate with fine bitter notes and a slightly oily texture, excellent acidity.

CAÑADA MAZÁN BOBAL 2003 ROSÉ
100% bobal

80 Brilliant raspberry. Powerful aroma with fresh overtones, notes of red fruit (foresty strawberries), citrus hints (grapefruit pulp) and slightly spicy. Fresh, fruity palate, somewhat oily and warm.

SYBARUS CABERNET SAUVIGNON 2002 RED
100% cabernet sauvignon

74 Quite intense cherry. Aroma with mild sweetish notes (very ripe) and toasty oak. Fresh, flavourful palate with hints of fermentation in the retronasal passage and slightly overripe fruit.

CAÑADA MAZÁN 2001 FERMENTADO EN BARRICA RED
tempranillo, bobal

78 Garnet red cherry. Sweet, dark-roasted aroma of caramel and a jammy fruit nuance. Flavourful palate of quite ripe fruit yet integrated with the acidity and with a spicy wood finish.

SYBARUS BOBAL 2002 FERMENTADO EN BARRICA RED
100% bobal

84 Garnet red cherry with a saffron edge. Fairly intense aroma of well-integrated fruit and oak with hints of fine lees. Flavourful and fleshy on the palate with hints of ripe fruit (blackberries) and excellent acidity, notes of liquorice and terroir in the retronasal passage.

SYBARUS MERLOT 2002 FERMENTADO EN BARRICA RED
100% merlot

76 Garnet red cherry with a coppery edge. Intense, not very fine aroma (late racking) with a ripe fruit and toasty oak nuance. Flavourful and fruity on the palate with toasty wood and a slightly acidic edge.

SYBARUS SYRAH 2002 FERMENTADO EN BARRICA RED
100% syrah

80 Quite intense cherry. Quite impenetrable aroma with fine notes of toasty oak well-integrated with the wine. Fresh, fruity and flavourful palate, pleasant and slightly lighter than the previous vintage.

CAÑADA MAZÁN CABERNET SAUVIGNON TEMPRANILLO 1998 CRIANZA RED
75% tempranillo, 25% cabernet sauvignon

81 Cherry with a garnet red edge. Spicy aroma with tobacco notes and well-integrated ripe black fruit. Fleshy palate with oily tannins, crianza character and a round finish.

SYBARUS 1996 RESERVA RED
tempranillo, cabernet sauvignon, merlot

80 Garnet red cherry with an orange edge. Spicy and slightly reduced aroma (tobacco, leather). Round, flavourful palate with ripe tannins well-assembled with the fruit.

CAÑADA MAZÁN TARDANA 2003 WHITE
VIÑA REQUENA ESPECIAL 2003 RED
VIÑA REQUENA 1995 RESERVA RED
SYBARUS 1998 RESERVA RED

Bodegas y Viñedos de UTIEL

Finca el Renegado, s/n
46315 Caudete de las Fuentes (Valencia)
☎: 962 174 029 - Fax: 962 171 432
entrevinas@ainia.es
www.bodegasdeutiel.com

Established: 1999
🌐 135 🛢 3,500,000 litres 🍇 250 has.
🇪🇸 80% 🌐20%

VIÑA CAPELLANA TEMPRANILLO 2002 RED
VALLEJO DEL CAMPILLO 1999 CRIANZA RED
VIÑA CAPELLANA 2000 CRIANZA RED

Cooperativa Agrícola
UTIEL VINÍCOLA

San Fernando, 18
46300 Utiel (Valencia)
☎: 962 171 157 - Fax: 962 170 801
vino.utiel@coop.credit.es

Established: 1927
🌐 500 🛢 30,000,000 litres 🍇 4,000 has.
🇪🇸 100%

CASTILLO DE UTIEL 2003 WHITE
100% macabeo

78 Brilliant pale. Intense, quite fruity aroma with fresh citrus overtones. Flavourful palate with fine bitter notes, pleasant.

VEGA INFANTE 2003 FERMENTADO EN BARRICA WHITE
100% macabeo

89 Straw-coloured. Fresh, fruity aroma (green apples) with great varietal expression and fine smoky nuances. Full palate, rich in nuances of fine herbs with a smoky retronasal passage, very sweet; fine, fruity and ripe.

SEÑORÍO DE UTIEL 2003 WHITE
macabeo

72 Pale. Medium-intensity, grapey aroma of crystallised fruit. Green notes on the palate, slightly rustic.

CASTILLO DE UTIEL 2003 ROSÉ
100% bobal

70 Raspberry blush. Medium-intensity aroma with almost overripe fruit and a nutty hint. Light palate, well-mannered but lacking fruit and freshness.

SEÑORIO DE UTIEL 2003 ROSÉ
100% bobal

78 Brilliant raspberry. Intense, fruity aroma with fine smoky notes of the skins and fresh overtones. Flavourful, fresh palate with good acidity but lacking fruit expression.

CASTILLO DE UTIEL 2003 JOVEN RED
80% bobal, 20% tempranillo

74 Garnet red cherry. Medium-intensity aroma of bramble berries, fresh. Light, fruity, slightly astringent palate.

SEÑORÍO DE UTIEL 2003 JOVEN RED
60% bobal, 40% tempranillo

75 Garnet red cherry. Fresh, fruity aroma (foresty brambles). Fresh, fruity palate with mild vegetative nuances without diminishing the ensemble.

VEGA INFANTE 2003 OAK AGED RED
70% tempranillo, 30% bobal

87 Dark cherry with a purplish edge. Powerful, very fine aroma with predominant smoky oak notes and a suggestion of jammy black fruit. Powerful, fleshy palate with slightly marked and flavourful tannins, slightly warm with fine bitter notes and a suggestion of fresh fruit, quite promising.

CASTILLO DE UTIEL 2001 CRIANZA RED
100% tempranillo

75 Dark garnet red cherry. Slightly vinous aroma of overripe bunches with unharmonised oak and a hint of evolution. Fresh, fruity palate with oak tannins, discreet.

CASTILLO DE UTIEL 2000 RESERVA RED
100% tempranillo

79 Cherry with an orange-brick red rim. Aroma with light nuances of evolution (jammy fruit). Ripe fruit and oak on the palate, without great varietal expression.

Cooperativa Agrícola VCIANA. VIRGEN DE LORETO - (COVILOR)

Antonio Bartual, 21
46313 Cuevas de Utiel (Valencia)
☎: 962 182 053 - Fax: 962 182 053
coop-cuevas@resone.es
www.resone.es/coop-cuevas

Established: 1955
🍶 166 📊 15,400,000 litres 🍇 1,740 has.
🇪🇸 90% 🌍10%

ALTO CUEVAS 2003 FERMENTADO EN BARRICA WHITE

66 Straw-coloured. Ripe aroma of reduced fruit with nutty notes. Dry, fresh palate, without fruit nuances and with bitter overtones.

ALTO CUEVAS 2002 ROSÉ

60 Raspberry. Highly evolved aroma and palate (a 2002).

ALTO CUEVAS 2003 RED
tempranillo

77 Cherry. Clear aroma of strawberries with hints of fermentation and liquorice notes. Fleshy, somewhat oily, fruity palate with quite bitter tannins.

Viñedos y Bodegas VEGALFARO

Carretera Pontón - Utiel, km. 3
46340 Requena (Valencia)

☎: 616 982 817 - Fax: 639 118 301
rodolfo@vegalfaro.com
www.vegalfaro.com

Established: 1999
🍶 180 📊 450,000 litres 🍇 65 has.

🇪🇸 40% 🌍60%: -DE -BE -SE -CH -IE -UK -US -NL

VEGALFARO 2003 ROSÉ
VEGALFARO 2003 OAK AGED WHITE
VEGALFARO 2002 CRIANZA RED
PAGO DE LOS BALAGUESES 2002 CRIANZA RED

VERA DE ESTENAS

Junto Carretera N-III , km. 266 Finca La Cabezuela
46300 Utiel (Valencia)
☎: 962 171 141 - Fax: 962 174 352
info@veradeestenas.es
www.veradeestenas.es

Established: 1919
🍶 500 📊 400,000 litres 🍇 42 has.
🇪🇸 50% 🌍50%: -US -IE -CH

VIÑA LIDON CHARDONNAY FERMENTADO EN BARRICA 2004 WHITE

74 Golden with a coppery hue. Quite intense aroma with fruity hints, without great nuances. Flavourful palate, with sweet oak notes, lacking expression.

MARTÍNEZ BERMELL MERLOT 2003 FERMENTADO EN BARRICA RED

83 Cherry with a violet hue. Quite intense aroma, fruity, with quality varietal notes (redcurrants, spices). Fresh, flavourful palate, red fruit, slightly marked oak tannins and excellent acidity.

VERA DE ESTENAS 2001 CRIANZA RED

82 Garnet red cherry with a coppery edge. Intense aroma, toasty and creamy crianza notes. Flavourful, fleshy palate, jammy black fruit, with slightly marked but promising oak tannins, oily, long.

VERA DE ESTENAS 1999 RESERVA RED

80 Garnet red cherry, with a coppery edge. Intense, spicy aroma, a fruity nuance, hints of reduction. Flavourful palate, with predominant bitter crianza notes (liquorice, dark-roasted flavours), ripe and oily.

CVCRE BLANCO FLOR 2003 JOVEN WHITE
VIÑA CARMINA BOBAL 2003 ROSÉ
CASA DON ANGEL 2000 OAK AGED RED
VIÑA MARIOLA TEMPRANILLO 2001 CRIANZA RED

DO UTIEL-REQUENA

CVCRE 1995 GRAN RESERVA RED
JUAN DE ARGÉS BRUT

VEREDA REAL

Vereda Real, 2-A
46340 Requena (Valencia)
☎: 962 303 656 - Fax: 962 302 543
veredareal@wanadoo.es
www.bodegaveredareal.com

Established: 2000

⊞ 140 🖩 65,000 litres 🍇 10 has 🍷 100%

VEREDA REAL 2003 JOVEN WHITE
100% macabeo

79 Pale gold. Intense aroma of white fruit with exotic (ripe pineapples) and floral hints. Flavourful, bitter palate with hints of herbs and a slightly acidic edge.

VEREDA REAL 2003 FERMENTADO EN BARRICA WHITE
100% macabeo

79 Straw-coloured. Aroma with mild nuances of evolution, notes of unharmonised oak, fresh, fruity. Ripe palate with toasty oak in the retronasal passage, overripe fruit.

VEREDA REAL 2003 FERMENTADO EN BARRICA RED

80 Dark cherry. Toasty aroma with remnents of fermentation, wood and unintegrated fruit, slightly reduced notes. Fleshy palate, full, flavourful; hints of oak without harmony and without finish.

VEREDA REAL 2001 OAK AGED RED
VEREDA REAL 1999 CRIANZA RED
MAGNUM 1999 RESERVA RED
VEREDA REAL 1999 RESERVA RED
VEREDA REAL 2000 RESERVA RED
VEREDA REAL MAGNUM 2000 RESERVA RED
CAMPOS DE OLEANA 2000 GRAN RESERVA RED
CAMPOS DE OLEANA MAGNUM 2000 GRAN RESERVA RED

VICENTE GANDÍA PLA

Carretera Cheste-Godelleta, s/n
46370 Chiva (Valencia)
☎: 962 524 242 - Fax: 962 524 243
gandia@gandiawines.com
www.gandiawines.com

Established: 1885

⊞ 14,000 🖩 28,000,000 litres 🍇 200 has.
🍷 10% 🍇90%

GANDÍA SELECCIÓN CHARDONNAY 2003 JOVEN WHITE
100% chardonnay

79 Straw-coloured with golden nuances. Intense aroma of very ripe white fruit and hints of withered petals. Fresh on the palate, without great varietal expression; with a slightly oily texture and an acidic edge.

HOYA DE CADENAS 2003 WHITE
chardonnay, sauvignon blanc, macabeo

80 Brilliant yellow straw. Aroma of ripe white stone fruit and fine notes of yeast. Flavourful, fresh palate of medium persistence.

HOYA DE CADENAS 2003 ROSÉ
100% bobal

77 Brilliant blush. Slightly intense aroma of foresty strawberries with warm hints. Flavourful, slightly fruity palate with the spicy freshness of skins and good acidity.

MIL AROMAS (DEL MEDITERRÁNEO) 2003 ROSÉ
100% bobal

80 Pale raspberry. Not very intense aroma of red fruit and fresh overtones. Flavourful, fresh palate with fine spicy, citrus hints, a slightly oily texture and good acidity.

GANDÍA SELECCIÓN TEMPRANILLO 2002 RED
100% tempranillo

79 Fairly brilliant deep cherry. Intense, ripe aroma, with light hints of skins and reduced fruit. Flavourful, fleshy palate of jammy black fruit and fine spicy oak notes in the retronasal passage.

GANDÍA SELECCIÓN CABERNET SAUVIGNON 2001 RED
100% cabernet sauvignon

75 Deep cherry. Fruity aroma of fine spicy varietal notes (paprika, vine leaves) and spicy hints of skins. Flavourful palate with slightly drying tannins (hints of greeness), slightly fruity.

GANDÍA SELECCIÓN MERLOT 2001 RED
100% merlot

78 Garnet red cherry with a saffron edge. Intense, ripe aroma, with spicy hints (paprika); varietal notes and a damp earthy hint. Flavourful palate with slightly drying oak tannins, ripe fruit and spicy hints in the retronasal passage.

VICENTE GANDÍA GENERACION 1 2001 OAK AGED RED
50% bobal, 20% garnacha, 15% merlot, 15% cabernet sauvignon ⊞ 12

90 Black cherry. Powerful, very concentrated aroma, rich in nuances (black fruit, violets, toasty, creamy oak notes, damp earth). Flavourful, concentrated palate with ripe, oily tannins, jammy fruit, a balsamic nuance and notes of liquorice and pitch.

CASTILLO DE LIRIA 2001 CRIANZA RED
100% tempranillo

868

78 Garnet red cherry with a coppery edge. Intense, fruity aroma of spicy oak notes and fresh overtones of slightly green skins. Flavourful palate with vegetative overtones, spicy and slightly warm.

CEREMONIA 2000 OAK AGED RED
tempranillo, cabernet sauvignon, bobal

83 Dark cherry with a coppery edge. Intense aroma with predominant spicy wood notes, a ripe red fruit suggestion with balsamic fresh overtones. Flavourful palate with quite fresh tannins and fine bitter notes.

HOYA DE CADENAS RESERVA PRIVADA 1999 RED
85% tempranillo, 15% cabernet sauvignon

80 Intense cherry with a saffron edge. Intense aroma of ripe fruit, with hints of sun-drenched skins and a toasty creamy oak suggestion. Flavourful palate with slightly drying tannins, somewhat herbaceous, varietal hints, lacking balance.

HOYA DE CADENAS 1999 RESERVA RED
90% tempranillo, 10% garnacha

84 Garnet red cherry with a purplish edge. Intense, fruity, very varietal aroma of fine toasty wood. Flavourful palate with slightly marked tannins yet fine and promising; spicy notes of creamy oak with hints of liquorice and terroir.

VIRASA VINÍCOLA

Bodega Casa de don Pedro
Carretera Chera, km. 5, 2
46340 Requena (Valencia)
☎: 962 170 301 - Fax: 962 174 135
info@virasa.com

Established: 1997

🍇 152 ▤ 112,000 litres ⚘ 102 has.

🍷 60% 🍾40%: -NL -BE -UK -CH -MX -DE -US

CERRO BERCIAL BOBAL 2003 ROSÉ
100% bobal

78 Very intense blush. Slightly short aroma of strawberries with slightly sweet overtones. Fresh palate with bitter overtones (hints of grape pips), warm.

CERRO BERCIAL 2002 OAK AGED RED
75% bobal, 25% tempranillo

83 Quite intense cherry. Fine aroma with creamy notes of the oak and ripe fruit. Powerful, fresh palate with well-assembled hints of oak and fruit, flavourful with hints of foresty berries.

CERRO BERCIAL TEMPRANILLO 2001 CRIANZA RED
100% tempranillo

71 Strawberry with shades of violet. Aroma with a nuance of acetaldehyde concealing the fruit. Light palate, a little unbalanced.

CERRO BERCIAL "EL PERDÍO" 2001 RED
100% tempranillo

89 Quite dark garnet red cherry. Fruity, fresh, elegant aroma with a well-balanced mineral hint of expressive oak. Flavourful palate with fresh fruit, foresty notes and well-integrated nuances of oak.

CERRO BERCIAL 1999 RESERVA RED
50% tempranillo, 50% bobal

80 Intense cherry. Slightly short aroma with quite overripe fruit, slightly reduced. Round, flavourful palate with very obvious oak tannins, differing slightly from last year.

CERRO BERCIAL 2003 RED

Vinos VIURE

Luis Santangel, 22 Bajo
46005 Valencia (Valencia)
☎: 963 950 013 - Fax: 963 740 363
puntok@xpress.es

VIURE 2003 WHITE
VIURE 2003 ROSÉ
VIURE 2002 RED
VIURE 1998 RESERVA RED
VIURE 1994 GRAN RESERVA RED

DO VALDEORRAS

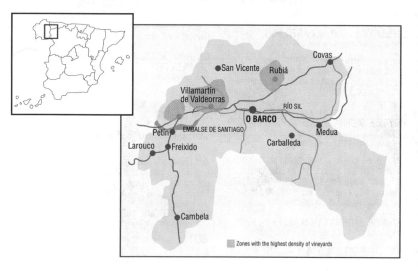

NEWS. An interesting and revealing point: the volume of disqualified wine in the DO Valdeorras in 2003 was almost equal to that considered worthy of carrying the official label, which gives one an idea, amongst other things, of how difficult the harvest was and the poor wine producing practices still in force in part of the region.

Hectares of Vineyard	No. of Viticulturists	No. of Bodegas	2003 Harvest	2003 Production	Marketing
1,329	2,022	35	Excellent	2,792,525 litres	100% Spain

The novelty that most stands out is the inclusion of red grape varieties from previous years in the vineyards of the region: *Brancellao (Albarello), Tempranillo* and *Negreda (Mouratón)*. However, Godello for whites and Mencía for reds are still the best bets of the DO.

As for the 2003 harvest, the good, abundant *Godello* harvest was reflected in our tasting, where this variety took most of the scores above 80 points, with the *Mencía* not living up to its full potential at those latitudes.

LOCATION. The DO Valdeorras is situated in the northeast of the province of Orense. It comprises the municipal areas of Larouco, Petín, O Bolo, A Rua, Vilamartín, O Barco, Rubiá and Carballeda de Valdeorras.

CLIMATE. Continental, with Atlantic influences. The average annual temperature is 11°C and the average annual rainfall ranges between 850 mm and 1,000 mm.

SOIL. Quite varied. There are three types: the first type which is settled on shallow slate with many stones and a medium texture; the second type on deeper granite with a lot of sand and finally the type that lies on sediments and terraces, where there are usually a lot of pebbles.

VARIETIES:

White: *Godello, Doña Blanca, Palomino (Jerez).*
Red: *Mencía, Merenzao, Grao Negro* and *Garnacha.*

REGULATORY COUNCIL.

Ctra. Nacional 120, Km 463. 32340 Vilamartín de Valdeorras (Orense).
Tel: 988 300 295. Fax: 988 336 887.
E-mail: conselloreg@teleline.es

GENERAL CHARACTERISTICS OF THE WINES:

Whites	Produced from the *Godello* variety, they offer high quality. They are straw yellow or pale yellow in colour. Aromatically, they are not excessively intense, although fine and delicate, with pleasant floral notes. On the palate, they are characterised by their tastiness, excellent acidity and, often, by their oily essence.
Reds	The *Mencía* variety is used, with which mainly young red wines are produced with a markedly Atlantic character, defined aromas of blackberries; they are dry and fruity on the palate.

DO VALDEORRAS

Adegas A COROA

Valencia do Sil
32314 Vilamartin de Valdeorras (Ourense)
☎: 636 964 680

COROA 2003 WHITE
100% godello

79 Pale with a greenish hue. Quite intense, fruity aroma of fragrant herbs. Fresh, fruity palate with good fruit-alcohol-acidity balance.

A TAPADA

Finca A Tapada
32310 Rubiá (Ourense)
☎: 988 324 195 - Fax: 988 324 197

Established: 1993

🍾 80 📊 220,000 litres 🌿 10 has.
🇪🇸 60% 🌐 40%

GUITIÁN GODELLO SOBRE LÍAS WHITE
godello

86 Very pale with greenish nuances. Intense aroma of great finesse with fruit, white flowers, hints of citrus fruit and fine lees. Fresh, flavourful palate with fine bitter notes (mint, anise) and excellent acidity.

GUITIÁN GODELLO 2002 FERMENTADO EN BARRICA WHITE
godello

86 Pale with golden nuances. Slightly intense aroma with a certain finesse, white fruit, exotic hints (pineapple), fine smoky oak and aniseed. Flavourful, bitter palate with slightly drying tannins and good acidity.

GUITIÁN GODELLO 2003 WHITE
godello

83 Pale with greenish nuances. Somewhat intense, very fresh aroma with fine notes of fruit, white flowers, exotic touches and herbs. Fresh, flavourful palate with fine bitter notes, spicy hints of skins, perfumed soap and excellent acidity.

Adega ALAN

San Roque, 36
32350 A Rúa (Orense)
☎: 988 311 457 - Fax: 988 311 457

Established: 1993

📊 30,000 litres 🌿 8 has.
🍷 95% 🌐 5%: -UK

ALAN DE VAL MENCÍA 2003 JOVEN RED
90% mencía, 10% brancellao, garnacha

80 Intense cherry. Aroma of sweet strawberries with earthy notes and a varietal edge. Flavourful, fresh and fruity on the palate (red fruit pulp) with a well-integrated slight bitterness.

ALAN DE VAL GODELLO 2003 JOVEN WHITE

AVELINA VÁZQUEZ FERRER

Córgomo
32316 Vilamartín de Valdeorras (Ourense)
☎: 988 324 533

CASAL DE FURCOS GODELLO 2003 WHITE
godello

79 Brilliant pale yellow. Quite intense, fruity aroma with mild exotic hints (bananas) and fragrant herbs. Flavourful, fruity palate with marked citrus acidity.

Bodegas BENÉITEZ

Santa Cruz del Bollo
32375 O Bolo (Ourense)
☎: 988 323 033

📊 12,000 litres 🌿 2 has. 🍷 100%

VIÑA FALCUEIRA WHITE
godello

72 Brilliant gold. Intense aroma of ripe white fruit and a hint of reduction in the tank. Better on the palate, flavourful with spicy and herby notes without great nuances.

VIÑA FALCUEIRA RED
mencía

80 Dark cherry with a purplish edge. Powerful aroma of black fruit, a rich herbaceous hint, fresh overtones of skins and underbrush. Flavourful, bitter palate with ripe fruit, a balsamic hint and marked acidity.

CARBALLAL

Carretera de Carballal, km 2, 2
32356 Petin de Valdeorras (Ourense)
☎: 988 311 281 - Fax: 988 311 281

Established: 1998

📊 180,000 litres 🌿 12 has.
🍷 80% 🌐 20%

EREBO 2003 WHITE
100% godello

80 Pale greenish. Intense, very fine aroma with a good varietal expression (exotic hints, fennel, green grass). Flavourful, fruity palate, slightly warm and oily with good acidity.

EREBO 2003 RED
100% mencia

78 Intense cherry with a violet edge. Aroma of red fruit, earthy hints and a suggestion of ripeness. Fruity palate with sweet notes of jam and strawberry jelly.

SILENO 2003 JOVEN WHITE
SILENO 2003 JOVEN RED

Adegas DÍA-NOITE

Carretera Carballal, s/n
32356 Petin de Valdeorras (Ourense)
☎: 988 311 462 - Fax: 988 311 462
cmurgaliciano@yahoo.es
www.galiciano.com
Established: 1986
🛢 10 🛢 125,000 litres 🌿 9 has.
🍷 80% 🌐20%: -US -DE -PR -FI -UK

GALICIANO GODELLO DÍA 2003 WHITE
100% godello

83 Pale yellow with a greenish hue. Quite intense, very fine, and varietal aroma (white fruit, exotic and fennel hints). Intense, flavourful palate with fine bitter notes and citrus fruit, slightly warm.

GALICIANO MENCÍA NOITE 2003 RED
100% mencia

83 Dark cherry with a dark red-violet edge. Intense aroma with very varietal ripe fruit (spices, skins, underbrush), herbaceous and smoky hints. Fleshy palate with rough, slightly oily tannins and flavourful notes of cocoa and liquorice, slightly warm and long.

GALICIANO ARBORE 2002 FERMENTADO EN BARRICA WHITE
VIÑA LADEIRA 2003 JOVEN WHITE

Adegas DON MARIO

Portela, s/n
32371 Larouco (Ourense)
☎: 696 967 516
Established: 1997
🛢 500,000 litres 🌿 20 has.
🍷 80% 🌐20%

DON MARIO GODELLO 2003 WHITE
godello

84 Straw-coloured with a golden hue. Powerful, fruity aroma with fine spicy notes of skins. Flavourful, bitter and very varietal on the palate with fragrant herbs and excellent acidity.

GERMÁN RODRÍGUEZ PRADA

Progreso, 24
32350 A Rua (Ourense)
☎: 619 350 638
Established: 1998
🛢 50,000 litres 🌿 6 has. 🍷 100%

GALGUEIRA 2003 RED

82 Cherry. Aroma of black fruit, spices, with a good Mencía expression. Fruity, quite earthy palate, fresh, concentrated red fruit.

GERMÁN RODRÍGUEZ SALGADO

Fernández Latorre, 20 bajo
15006 La Coruña (La Coruña)
☎: 981 249 373 - Fax: 981 151 968
Established: 1988
🛢 40,000 litres 🌿 2 has 🍷 100%

VIÑA DE FORNOS GODELLO WHITE
VIÑA ARADAS RED

Bodegas GODEVAL

Avenida de Galicia, 20
32300 El Barco de Valdeorras (Ourense)
☎: 988 325 309 - Fax: 988 325 309
godeval@godeval.com
www.godeval.com
Established: 1986
🌿 20 has. 🍷 70% 🌐30%: -US -UK -FI -
NL -BE -CH

VIÑA GODEVAL 2003 JOVEN WHITE
100% godello

83 Pale yellow with a coppery hue. Intense, very fine aroma with a good varietal expression (white fruit, exotic and aniseed hints). Fresh, flavourful and slightly fruity on the palate with spicy notes of skins and excellent acidity.

Cooperativa JESÚS NAZARENO

Avenida Florencio Delgado Gurriarán, 62
32300 O Barco de Valdeorras (Ourense)
☎: 988 320 262 - Fax: 988 320 242
coopbarco@infonegocio.com
Established: 1957
🛢 150 🛢 2,300,000 litres 🌿 4 has.
🍷 95% 🌐5%: -CH -NL

DO VALDEORRAS

ALBAR 2003 JOVEN WHITE
100% palomino

72 Pale yellow. Intense, quite fruity aroma and an unrefined hint of the tank. Sweet on the palate without great nuances.

MOZAFRESCA 2003 JOVEN WHITE
80% palomino, 20% godello

74 Pale yellow with a greenish hue. Slightly intense aroma of slightly reduced ripe white fruit (petals). Fresh, flavourful and slightly fruity on the palate; pleasant.

VIÑA ABAD GODELLO 2003 JOVEN WHITE
100% godello

73 Pale with a greenish hue. Quite intense aroma of slightly reduced white fruit (withered petals, lees). Flavourful palate with not very fine bittersweet notes, bitter.

AURENSIS GODELLO 2001 FERMENTADO EN BARRICA WHITE
100% godello

81 Pale gold with a greenish hue. Intense aroma with predominant smoky oak notes and a ripe white fruit hint. Fresh, flavourful palate with tannins well-integrated with the fruit, spicy, good acidity.

MENCIÑO 2003 JOVEN RED
100% mencía

78 Cherry with a violet edge. Ripe aroma with spices and hints of maceration. Flavourful, fruity on the palate (redcurrants, blackberries) with a certain character of the vine variety.

VALDOURO MENCIA 2002 ROBLE RED
85% mencía, 15% alicante

77 Cherry. Toasty oak aroma and a ripe red fruit hint. Fresh palate of intense red fruit, good wood balance in the mouth and a slightly toasty finish.

ALBAR 2003 JOVEN RED

JESÚS RAFAEL NÚÑEZ RODRÍGUEZ

Rua Da Baixo, 23
32310 O Val Rubiá de Valdeorras (Ourense)
☎: 988 307 789 - Fax: 988 327 146
Established: 1993
▯ 15,000 litres ❦ 2 has. ▼ 100%

VIÑA TREVAL 2003 WHITE
godello

81 Pale greenish. Intense aroma with a certain finesse, fruit and white flowers, fresh citrus notes and herbs. Flavourful, fruity palate with bitter notes, marked citrus acidity and a suggestion of minerals.

JOAQUÍN REBOLLEDO

San Roque, s/n
32350 A Rúa (Ourense)
☎: 988 336 023 - Fax: 988 336 089
jrebolledo@teleline.es
www.infonegocio.com/jrebolledo

JOAQUÍN REBOLLEDO 2003 WHITE
godello

78 Pale with a golden hue. Intense, quite fruity aroma with smoky hints and fragrant herbs. Flavourful, bitter and slightly warm on the palate, fruit expression partially concealed by the alcohol.

JOAQUÍN REBOLLEDO OAK AGED RED
mencía

82 Dark cherry with a purplish edge. Powerful, ripe aroma of quite varietal black fruit and a nuance of toasty oak. Flavourful, fleshy palate with slightly marked, oily tannins, spices and hints of cocoa in the finish.

JOAQUÍN REBOLLEDO MENCÍA 2003 RED
mencía

76 Dark cherry. Powerful aroma of ripe black fruit, with hints of skins and slight reduction. Flavourful palate with slightly marked tannins, hints of overextraction and a terroir nuance.

JOSÉ M. RODRÍGUEZ GONZÁLEZ

Vilachá - Doade
27424 Sober (Lugo)
☎: 982 460 613

A SILVEIRA 2003 WHITE
godello

80 Brilliant gold. Intense aroma of quite varietal ripe white fruit, exotic and slightly reduced hints with fragrant herbs. Flavourful, fruity palate with fine spicy notes, well-balanced.

JUAN ARES VICENTE

Plaza José Luis Núñez, s/n
32340 Vilamartín de Valdeorras (Orense)
☎: 988 300 018

VIÑA FORAL WHITE
godello

81 Pale lemon yellow yellow. Intense aroma with fruit, white flowers, exotic fruit notes (pineapples), and fragrant herbs. Flavourful, slightly fruity on the palate, with fine bitter notes and good acidity.

M. REMEDIOS BARANGA REAL

Plaza José Luis Núñez, s/n
32340 Vilamartin de Valdeorras (Orense)
☎: 988 300 097

RONCAL GODELLO WHITE
RONCAL MENCÍA RED

MAJLU

Carretera de Cernego, s/n
32340 Vilamartin de Valdeorras (Ourense)
☎: 986 419 367 - Fax: 986 419 367
ruchel@terra.es

Established: 1989
🌐 20 ▦ 250,000 litres 🍷 99% 🔺1%

RUCHEL GODELLO 2003 WHITE
godello

80 Straw-coloured. Fruity aroma with a hint of pineapple and a slightly honeyed hint. Fresh, oily palate with hints of sweet fruit, stewed fruit in the finish.

RUCHEL GODELLO OAK AGED WHITE
100% godello

80 Brilliant gold. Intense aroma with creamy, spicy (vanilla) oak notes and a nuance of slightly reduced ripe fruit (acacia petals). Flavourful, slightly warm and oily on the palate with toffee in the retronasal passage.

RUCHEL MENCÍA 2003 RED
100% mencía

75 Cherry. Aroma of ripe red berries, slightly spicy. Light, fresh palate, flavourless.

MANUEL CORZO MACÍAS

Chandoiro
32370 O Bolo (Ourense)
☎: 629 893 649
▦ 25,000 litres 🍷 100%

VIÑA CORZO 2003 RED
mencía

78 Dark cherry with a dark red edge. Powerful varietal aroma of slightly reduced ripe fruit (mild off-odours from the tank). Flavourful, fleshy palate with slightly marked tannins, warm.

Adega O CASAL

Pumarega, 22
32310 Rubiá (Ourense)
☎: 988 342 067

CASAL NOVO GODELLO 2003 WHITE

86 Straw-coloured. Aroma with notes of ripe fruit with tropical nuances. Notes of sweetness on the palate, flavourful with quite complex overtones and very ripe, better than the previous vintage.

CASAL NOVO MENCÍA 2003 RED
mencía

85 Intense cherry. Powerful aroma of macerated ripe fruit, fresh with toasty ripe skins. Powerful palate with ripe sweet fruit (blackberries), fruity tannins and slightly low acidity, very fruity.

Adegas O RIBOUZO

Valencia do Sil
32349 Vilamartin de Valdeorras (Ourense)
☎: 670 519 752 - Fax: 981 935 913
ribouzo@yahoo.es

Established: 1996
🌐 10 ▦ 100,000 litres 🌿 3.5 has.

GODELLO RIBOUZO WHITE
MENCÍA RIBOUZO RED
MISTURA RIBOUZO RED

OS CINCO IRMANS

Seoane, s/n
32358 Larouco (Ourense)
☎: 988 348 026

Established: 1991
▦ 25,000 litres 🌿 6.5 has 🍷 100%

VARIETAL GODELLO ANUAL WHITE

Señorío de ROBLIDO

Curros Enríquez, 10 Bajo
32350 A Rua (Ourense)
☎: 988 312 343 - Fax: 988 312 343
bdga.sr.roblido@teleline1

Established: 1998
▦ 150,000 litres 🌿 2 has. 🍷 100%

SEÑORÍO DE ROBLIDO GODELLO WHITE

Bodegas SAMPAYOLO

Felgar, 1 - 1º
32350 A Rua (Orense)
☎: 679 157 977

SAMPAYOLO GODELLO 2003 WHITE
godello

80 Pale gold with a greenish hue. Quite intense aroma of green fruit, fine herby and citrus fruit

DO VALDEORRAS

notes. Flavourful, slightly fruity palate with spicy notes, a hint of minerals and marked citrus acidity.

SAMPAYOLO MENCÍA 2003 RED
mencía

82 Dark cherry with a garnet red edge. Intense, ripe aroma with a good varietal expression (black fruit, fresh skins, underbrush). Fresh, fleshy palate with slightly marked but flavourful tannins and good fruit-acidity balance.

Cooperativa SANTA MARÍA DE LOS REMEDIOS

Langullo, 11
32358 Larouco (Orense)
☎: 988 348 043 - Fax: 988 348 043

Established: 1957

2,400,000 litres 95% 5%: -DE -FR -CH -BE -NL

ARUME 2003 JOVEN WHITE
godello

76 Pale gold. Intense aroma with ripe fruit, smoky hints, spices and a suggestion of fragrant herbs. Flavourful, slightly fruity palate with fresh citrus and mineral overtones.

SILVIÑO 2003 WHITE
MEDULIO 2003 JOVEN RED
SILVIÑO 2003 RED

SANTA MARTA

Córgomo
32340 Villamartin de Valdeorras (Ourense)
☎: 988 324 559 - Fax: 988 324 559
santamarta@teleline.es

Established: 1998

210,000 litres 14 has.
90% 10%

VIÑAREDO GODELLO 2003 WHITE
100% godello

76 Straw-coloured. Ripe aroma with notes of bakery and a suggestion of tropical fruit. Fruity, fresh palate without great Godello nuances.

VIÑAREDO MENCÍA 2003 JOVEN RED
100% godello

80 Dark cherry with a violet edge. Intense aroma with fresh varietal overtones (skins, brambles, sweet and herbaceous hints). Flavourful, fleshy palate with slightly marked tannins, bitter, good fruit weight.

Bodegas TESTEIRO

Somoza, 3
32350 A Rua de Valdeorras (Ourense)
☎: 988 311 659 - Fax: 988 311 659

Established: 1991

100,000 litres 6 has. 100%

LAVANDEIRA WHITE
100% godello

75 Pale with a greenish glint. Ripe aroma with very sweet, white fruit notes and no grape expression. Simple palate, flat in fruit, without nuances.

ENTRE NÓS RED
mencía, otras

77 Dark cherry with a dark red edge. Powerful aroma of very ripe fruit with mild reduction off-odours from the tank. Flavourful, fleshy palate with spicy hints and toasty crianza.

LAVANDEIRA RED
100% mencía

80 Brilliant cherry. Aroma of red fruit pulp with hints of flowers and maceration. Fleshy, fresh palate with varietal notes, round but without great flavour.

VAL DE TORRES

Iglesia Alvariño, 13
32004 Ourense (Ourense)
☎: 659 965 828

TERRA LOMBARDA WHITE
godello

82 Brilliant gold. Intense aroma of ripe white fruit, exotic and spicy hints and fragrant herbs. Flavourful palate with fine bitter notes varietal hints, excellent acidity and good fruit-alcohol balance.

Bodegas VALDERROA

Córgomo, s/n
32348 Vilamartin de Valdeorras (Ourense)
☎: 988 337 900 - Fax: 988 337 901
valderroa@valderroa.com
www.valderroa.com

Established: 1990

25 650,000 litres 15 has.
70% 30%: -US -DE -UK -BE -DK -SE -MX -AD

PEZAS DA PORTELA 2002 JOVEN WHITE
100% godello

78 Golden with a greenish glint. Herbaceous aroma (fennel) with a green fruit pulp and a hint of ripeness. Oily palate with fresh overtones and slightly ripe fruit without nuances.

VALDESIL GODELLO 2003 WHITE
100% godello

78 Straw-coloured. Aroma with mild notes of tropical fruit and ripeness. Fruity palate with very sweet, ripe notes, fresh, very persistent and slightly oily.

MONTENOVO GODELLO 2003 WHITE
100% godello

77 Straw-coloured. Aroma of muted fruit with signs of reduction. Fresh, fruity palate though without great Godello expression.

VALDESIL GODELLO 2002 WHITE
100% godello

85 Straw-coloured with a golden glint. Aroma of ripe, exotic fruit (papaya, pineapples) and a nuance of stewed fruit. Expressive, mildly smoky, enveloping and glyceric on the palate with good fruit weight and good acidity, very long.

VALDERROA MENCÍA 2002 RED
100% mencía

79 Dark garnet red cherry. Powerful, ripe aroma with a slight varietal expression (red fruit, nettles) and a suggestion of terroir. Flavourful palate with marked tannins (green overtones), good acidity and a fresh mineral hint.

VELAIÑO

Portela
32316 Villamartín de Valdeorras (Ourense)
☎: 988 324 526
cambavelaino@virtuooras.com
Established: 1986
⊞ 100 ▤ 700,000 litres 🍇 4 has.
🍷 100%

VELAIÑO GODELLO WHITE
VELAIÑO MENCÍA RED

VIÑA SOMOZA BODEGAS Y VIÑEDOS

Rua do Pombar, s/n
32350 A Rua (Ourense)
☎: 656 407 857 - Fax: 916 757 538
vinosomoza@telefonica.net
Established: 1981
▤ 200,000 litres 🍇 25 has.
🍷 60% 🌐40%: -US -BE -FR

VIÑA SOMOZA 2003 WHITE
100% godello

82 Pale yellow with a golden hue. Intense, fresh aroma with white fruit, hints of flowers and citrus fruits. Flavourful, bitter palate with fruit partially concealed by the alcohol and marked citrus acidity.

VIRGEN DE LAS VIÑAS

Campo Grande, 97
32350 A Rúa de Valdeorras (Ourense)
☎: 988 310 607 - Fax: 988 312 016
market-rua@telefonica.net
Established: 1964
▤ 9,000,000 litres 🍇 300 has.
🍷 90% 🌐10%

BRISEL WHITE
MARQUESIÑO WHITE
PINGADELO RED

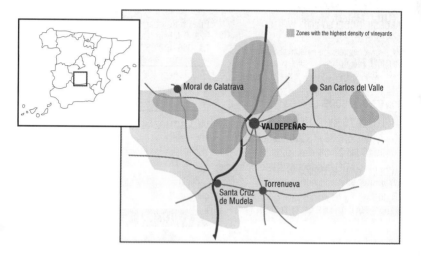

NEWS. Valdepeñas is still operating between the traditional custom of refreshing old harvests and producing new brands that are appearing on the marketplace. The latter, although they more closely define the *Tempranillo* variety, have not managed to do away with that rough edge, making it difficult to compare them with top quality wines. Valdepeñas has not yet managed to produce fresh, modern wines to match the fame that its 'Manchados' white wines once had in the taverns of Madrid.

Still behind the more modern wines of La Mancha, only 3 of the 112 wines rated for this Guide reached or surpassed 85 points. What is happening is that the best brands are joining the ever larger designation of 'Vinos de la Tierra' (Wines of the Land). In spite of this, Valdepeñas still represents 35% of the exports of national DO wines.

Hectares of Vineyard	No. of Viticulturists	No. of Bodegas	2003 Harvest	2003 Production	Marketing
29,616	4,018	35	Very Good	55,236,701 litres	62% Spain 38% foreign

Despite the conversion from white to red wine over the last few years, due to the poor expectations and results of the *Airén* grape variety, the volume of the red grapes still does not cover all the production needs. Among the three wines rated as outstanding in the DO, the Dionisos Tempranillo 2003 stands out for its young wine character, the defence of the best expression (single-variety) of the local *Tempranillo*, and its condition as an organic wine.

LOCATION. On the southern border of the southern plateau, in the province of Ciudad Real. It comprises the municipal districts of Alcubillas, Moral de Calatrava, San Carlos del Valle, Santa Cruz de Mudela, Torrenueva and Valdepeñas and part of

Alhambra, Granátula de Calatrava, Montiel and Torre de Juan Abad.

CLIMATE. Continental in nature, with cold winters, very hot summers and little rainfall, which is usually around 250 and 400 mm per year.

SOIL. Mainly brownish-red and brownish-grey limestone soil with a high lime content and quite poor in organic matter.

VARIETIES:
White: *Airén* (majority) and *Macabeo*.
Red: *Cencibel (Tempranillo), Garnacha* and *Cabernet Sauvignon*.

REGULATORY COUNCIL.
Constitución, 23. 13300 Valdepeñas (Ciudad Real).
Tel: 926 32 27 88. Fax: 926 32 10 54.
E-mail: c.r.DOvaldepenas@telefonica.net
Website: www.dovaldepenas.es

GENERAL CHARACTERISTICS OF THE WINES:

Whites	These are produced from *Airén*. They have a pale or straw yellow colour; on the nose they are fresh and fruity and may develop aromas reminiscent of banana or pineapple; on the palate, they are fresh and pleasant, although they have slightly low acidity.
Rosés	Raspberry pink or salmon pink in colour, they are fresh, fruity, pleasant and easy drinking.
Reds	The young wines from *Cencibel* have a deep cherry-red colour with violet nuances; the aroma is fresh and fruity, almost always with good intensity; on the palate, the freshness and the fruity nuances that make them so pleasant to drink are very noticeable. Those aged in wood start to benefit from the cleaner aromas of oak due to the use of newer barrels. They are supple and quite flavourful on the palate.

ANTONIO CAÑAVERAS

Gloria, 42
13730 Santa Cruz de Mudela (Ciudad Real)
☎: 926 342 128
vinosjuanele@telefonica.net

Established: 1901

🍷 100 📊 1,200,000 litres 🍇 50 has.

🍷 95% 🌐 5%

VIÑA JUANELE 2003 JOVEN WHITE
VIÑA JUANELE 2003 JOVEN RED
VIÑA JUANELE 1997 CRIANZA RED
VIÑA JUANELE 1997 RESERVA RED

ARÚSPIDE

Francisco Morales, 102
13300 Valdepeñas (Ciudad Real)
☎: 926 347 075 - Fax: 926 347 875
baruspide@jazzfree.com
www.aruspide.com

Established: 1999

🍷 450 📊 180,000 litres 🍇 70 has.

🍷 80% 🌐 20%: -DE -AT -BE -US -UK -IE -NL -DK -CA

ÁGORA 2003 MACERACIÓN CARBÓNICA WHITE
100% airén

82 Pale. Powerful aroma with typical Airén notes (bananas, pineapples) and a pleasant nuance of fine herbs. Fresh, light, pleasant palate with the sweetness of the vine variety, flavourful with well-balanced acidity.

ÁGORA LÁGRIMA 2003 SEMISECO WHITE
100% airén

76 Straw-coloured. Short aroma with mild notes of must. A carbonic element on the palate, fresh and fruity, better on the palate than in the nose.

ÁGORA 2003 MACERACIÓN CARBÓNICA RED
100% tempranillo

80 Garnet red cherry with a purplish edge. Fresh, fruity aroma with mild vegetative notes. Fleshy palate, quite powerful with obvious oak and fruit, flavourful. Less complex than the previous vintage.

ÁGORA NOBLE VENDIMIA SELECCIONADA 2000 OAK AGED RED
100% tempranillo

73 Garnet red. Aroma with notes of evolution (orange peel) and slightly overripe fruit. Better on the palate, flavourful and with toasty oak notes but slightly drying in the finish.

ODRE VIEJO TEMPRANILLO 2001 SEMICRIANZA RED
100% tempranillo

73 Garnet red cherry. Medium-intensity aroma of caramelised, slightly flawed fruit. Slightly fruity on the palate with drying wood tannins, lacks harmony.

ÁGORA GENUINO TEMPRANILLO 2000 CRIANZA RED
100% tempranillo

72 Garnet red cherry. Not very intense aroma with a fruity nuance, rubber and notes of oak. Slightly drying on the palate with toasty hints and burnt smells, a well-mannered ensemble.

ÁGORA 1999 RESERVA RED
100% tempranillo

81 Garnet red cherry. Spicy aroma with hints of underbrush and cigar box and a suggestion of ripe fruit. Flavourful palate with a fine tuned crianza expression and toasty oak in the retronasal passage.

ÁGORA 2003 FERMENTADO EN BARRICA RED

DO VALDEPEÑAS

CADEVI

Carretera de la Solana a Infantes, km. 15
13248 Alhambra (Ciudad Real)
☎: 926 696 044 - Fax: 926 696 068
www.byb.es

Established: 1857

6,500,000 litres 🍇 250 has.

CASA DE LA VIÑA 2002 OAK AGED RED
100% cencibel   7

84 Garnet red cherry with a violet hue. Intense, fruity aroma with fine toasty oak notes and hints of macerated skins. Flavourful palate with quite rough and oily tannins, fine notes of spices and liquorice.

CASA DE LA VIÑA VENDIMIA
SELECCIONADA 2000 OAK AGED RED
100% cencibel   10

83 Dark cherry with a garnet red edge. Quite intense aroma with notes of spices and red stone fruit and warm hints. Flavourful palate with promising but slightly marked tannins, red fruit, spices, and balsamic notions.

CASA DE LA VIÑA 2003 RED
100% cencibel

83 Dark cherry with a purplish rim. Powerful aroma of black fruit, somewhat sweet with notes of macerated skins and hint of damp earth. Flavourful, fleshy palate with quite noticeable and oily tannins, liquorice and a balsamic essence.

CASA DE LA VIÑA 2003 RED

CANCHOLLAS

Solanilla, 2
13300 Valdepeñas (Ciudad Real)
☎: 926 322 357 - Fax: 926 322 357

Established: 1889

2,000,000 litres 🍇 55 has.🍷 100%

CANCHOLLAS JOVEN BOTIJA 2003 JOVEN
WHITE
100% airén

71 Very pale. Not very intense, fresh aroma with hints of citrus fruit. Fresh and flavourful on the palate with a slightly acidic edge.

CANCHOLLAS GRAN BOTIJA 1999 RED
15% airén, 85% cencibel

74 Ruby red with shades of brick red. Short aroma with notes of attics and aged wood. Better on the palate, light with pleasant notes of well-integrated fruit and wood.

VIEJO BOTIJA 1997 CRIANZA RED
15% airén, 85% cencibel

67 Brick red. Aroma with mild off-odours, aged wood. Light on the palate with dry oak tannins.

CANCHOLLAS VIEJO BOTIJA 1993 WHITE
VIÑA BOTIJA WHITE
VIÑA BOTIJA RED

CANUTO BODEGAS DE VALDEPEÑAS

Caldereros, 33
13300 Valdepeñas (Ciudad Real)
☎: 926 322 009 - Fax: 926 322 009
jcanuto@grupobbva.net

Established: 1964

🍷 125 1,800,000 litres 🍇 50 has.
🍷 80% 🌐20%: -DE -NL

MONTECLARO 2003 JOVEN WHITE
100% airén

73 Pale yellow. Not very intense aroma of white stone fruit with fresh overtones. Fresh on the palate with bitter notes and a slightly acidic edge.

MONTECLARO 2003 JOVEN RED
100% tempranillo

82 Garnet red with a violet edge. Medium-intensity aroma of berries and ripe foresty berries, clean. Expressive on the palate with ripe fruit and sweet tannins, very pleasant with an earthy and toasty finish.

MONTECLARO 2000 CRIANZA RED
100% tempranillo

69 Cherry with an orangey hue. Short aroma without prominent fruit or wood and hints of overripe bunches. Slightly fruity on the palate, slightly woody, discreet.

MONTECLARO 1999 RESERVA RED
100% tempranillo

82 Garnet red with an orangey edge. Not very intense yet clean aroma with spicy hints. Round and flavourful on the palate with well-assembled red fruit and wood; pleasant and easy drinking.

MONTECLARO 1998 GRAN RESERVA RED
100% tempranillo

70 Quite dark cherry. Aroma with reduced notes and a hint of overripe fruit and slightly woody oak. Flabby palate, without expression, discreet.

MONTECLARO VALDEPEÑAS RED
CALDOPEÑAS 2000 CRIANZA RED
ALVIJES 1996 RESERVA RED

DIONISOS

Unión, 82

13300 Valdepeñas (Ciudad Real)
☎: 926 313 248 - Fax: 926 322 813
ta@agrobio-dionisos.com
www.agrobio-dionisos.com

Established: 1970

🌐 200 ▦ 475,000 litres 🍇 42 has.🍷 20%
🍷80%: -DE -NL -DK -BE -CH -AT -JP

DIONISOS TEMPRANILLO 2003 JOVEN RED
100% tempranillo

86 Very deep cherry with a violet hue. Intense aroma of ripe black fruit with hints of sun-drenched skins and a nuance of terroir. Fleshy on the palate with ripe grape tannins well-integrated with the notes of ripe fruit, a bitter nuance (chocolate, damp earth) and good acidity.

DIONISOS PAGO DEL CONUCO 2002 FERMENTADO EN BARRICA RED
100% tempranillo

78 Dark cherry. Aroma with postfermentative notes and reduced hints, toasty. Fleshy palate with body and ripe but obvious fruit tannins, flavourful, persistent.

DIONISOS VINUM VITAE 2001 OAK AGED RED
90% tempranillo, 10% cabernet sauvignon   🌐 12

78 Dark cherry with a garnet red edge. Aroma with mild notes of oxidative evolution (jammy foresty blackberries) and smoky hints of oak. Fleshy palate with a suggestion of evolutive nuances, flavourful with ripe fruit.

DIONISOS MACABEO 2003 WHITE
DIONISOS TEMPRANILLO 2003 JOVEN RED
DIONISOS 2000 CRIANZA RED
DIONISOS 2001 CRIANZA RED

ESPINOSA

Carretera Madrid-Cádiz, km. 198
13300 Valdepeñas (Ciudad Real)
☎: 926 321 854 - Fax: 926 322 493
bodegasespinosa@hotmail.com

Established: 1966

🌐 1,200 ▦ 8,000,000 litres 🍇 110 has.
🍷 85% 🍷15%

CONCEJAL 2003 WHITE

78 Pale. Fresh, fruity aroma (apples and ripe pears). Flavourful and fruity on the palate with an oily note, without great acidity but well-mannered.

VIÑA DEL LUGAR ROSÉ

63 Salmon blush. Not very clear aroma (lacks racking). Light on the palate with weak fruit.

CONCEJAL 2003 ROSÉ

73 Brilliant raspberry. Fairly intense, fruity aroma with fresh overtones. Fresh on the palate, lacks balance, poor fruit expression.

CENCIPEÑAS 1998 CRIANZA RED

75 Ruby red with a brick red hue. Fairly short aroma of aged wood with overtones of reduction. Light and supple on the palate with dry wood tannins.

CONCEJAL 2000 CRIANZA RED
100% tempranillo

72 Cherry with an orange edge. Aroma with poor strength and fruit expression. Slightly concealed oak and fruit tannins on the palate, discreet.

SEÑORÍO DE VALDEÑAS 1995 RESERVA RED

70 Ruby red with a brick red hue. Aroma with reduction notes (leather), acetaldehydes and hints of attics. Light with drying tannins and bitter oak on the palate, in decline.

VIÑA DEL LUGAR 1999 RESERVA RED

78 Ruby red with a brick red hue. Not very intense aroma with earthy and woody notes. Well-assembled red fruit and wood on the palate, round and pleasant.

VIÑA DEL LUGAR JOVEN WHITE
VIÑA DEL LUGAR JOVEN RED

FÉLIX SOLÍS

Autovía de Andalucía, km. 199
13300 Valdepeñas (Ciudad Real)
☎: 926 322 400 - Fax: 926 322 417
bsf@felixsolix.com
www.felixsolis.com

Established: 1952

🌐 40,000 ▦ 192,000,000 litres 🍇 500 has.
🍷 62% 🍷38%: -UK -DE -NL -DK -FI -SE -BE -GQ -CH TG -MX -BE -AT -JP -PH -NC -DO -US -AO Tahiti -CA -CO -SE -DK -CZ -DZ -PE -VE -IT -LU -CF -PA -KE CM -VN -TW -LB -GT -MY CD -SG -EC -BR -JO -GA TZ -CR -EL -AU -SV -SB -GM -IE -NI -PT

LOS MOLINOS TRADICIÓN 2003 WHITE
100% airén

73 Pale yellow. Fairly intense aroma of ripe fruit with fresh overtones. Fresh and flavourful on the palate with hints of high quality citrus fruit and an acidic edge.

VIÑA ALBALI AIRÉN 2003 WHITE
100% airén

80 Pale yellow with a golden hue. Intense aroma of ripe white fruit with hints of petals and honey. Fresh on the palate with fine bittersweet notes, bitter notes of skins and good acidity.

DO VALDEPEÑAS

VIÑA ALBALI AIRÉN 2003 SEMIDULCE WHITE
100% airén

77 Pale yellow. Intense, perfumed aroma (acacia, passion fruit, crystallised hints of citrus fruits). Sweet and slightly oily on the palate with fine citrus notes and good acidity.

VIÑA ALBALI MACABEO 2003 WHITE
100% macabeo

79 Pale yellow with golden nuances. Not very intense aroma of ripe fruit with a nuance of hay, petals and toasty hints of grapeskins. Generous, fruity, and slightly oily on the palate.

LOS MOLINOS TRADICIÓN 2003 ROSÉ
100% tempranillo

72 Quite pale raspberry with coppery hues. Slightly short, fruity aroma. Flavourful and slightly oily on the palate with hardly any fruit expression, hints of citrus fruit.

LOS MOLINOS TRADICIÓN 2003 RED
100% tempranillo

78 Garnet red cherry with an orange edge. Short aroma, without fruity nuances, discreet. Pleasant, fruity palate, balsamic, fresh and very light.

VIÑA ALBALI TEMPRANILLO 2003 RED
100% tempranillo

80 Garnet red cherry. Fresh aroma of forest fruit with light notes of oak, slightly less obvious than previous vintages. Great fruity potential, fresh and flavourful with very light notes of oak.

VIÑA ALBALI 2000 RED
100% tempranillo

79 Garnet red cherry. Fresh fruity aroma with unassembled notes of oak, flavourful with balsamic notes.

DIEGO DE ALMAGRO 2000 CRIANZA RED
90% tempranillo, 5% cabernet sauvignon, 5% garnacha

78 Garnet red cherry. Intense aroma of red fruit with a mild nuance of off-odours that disapear with airing. Fruity on the palate with a flavourful edge and a toasty oak finish.

LOS MOLINOS 2000 CRIANZA RED
100% tempranillo

75 Garnet red cherry. Fresh, fruity, slightly short aroma without great nuances. Light, fruity and flavourful palate, well-mannered.

VIÑA ALBALI 2001 CRIANZA RED
100% tempranillo

79 Dark cherry with a garnet red edge. Aroma of unassembled fruit and wood with notes of brambles and red fruit. Fresh, flavourful palate with slightly short fruit expression, different to the 2004 Wine Guide.

VIÑA ALBALI 1999 RED RESERVA

80 Garnet red with an orangey edge. Medium-intensity aroma with a good reduction, spicy and oak notes. Round and flavourful on the palate with well-assembled wood; well-balanced.

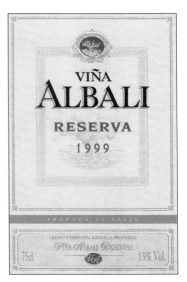

DIEGO DE ALMAGRO 1999 RESERVA RED
100% tempranillo

77 Ruby red with an orangey edge. Aroma with a good reduction and without great nuances. Round and light on the palate with ink, more expressive than in the nose, well-integrated wood.

LOS MOLINOS 1999 RESERVA RED
100% tempranillo

73 Not very deep cherry with an orangey edge. Aroma with predominant wood and burnt notes. Red fruit on the palate and slightly drying wood.

DIEGO DE ALMAGRO 1997 GRAN RESERVA RED

79 Garnet red cherry. Short aroma without nuances of crianza or reduction and with a hint of fruity notes. Fresh, fruity palate with oak in the retronasal passage, very fresh for a Gran Reserva.

VIÑA ALBALI 1998 RED

82 Ruby red with a brick red edge. Intense, balsamic aroma with a jammy fruit nuance and well-integrated wood. Round and supple, good crianza, harmonious.

LOS MOLINOS 1997 GRAN RESERVA RED
100% tempranillo

77 Garnet red cherry. Fresh, not very intense, fruity aroma with barely noticeable wood. Light palate with the thickness of this vineyard's wines.

VIÑA ALBALI 1997 GRAN RESERVA RED
100% tempranillo

79 Garnet red cherry. Aroma with fine reduction notes (leather, tobacco), ripe fruit and oak. Fruity palate with oak, without great nuances although with mild spicy notes.

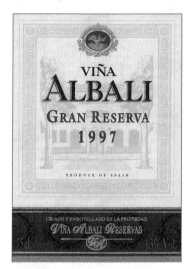

VIÑA ALBALI 1996 GRAN RESERVA RED

80 Garnet red cherry. Fresh, fruity aroma with oak notes. Flavourful palate with mild fine reduction notes (tobacco, pepper, leather).

VIÑA ALBALI GRAN RESERVA DE LA FAMILIA 1996 GRAN RESERVA RED
tempranillo, cabernet sauvignon

85 Garnet red cherry. Aroma with fine bottle reduction notes (leather, cedar, tobacco, cocoa) and hints of fruit. Light, round, fine, flavourful palate with silky tannins, quite persistent and elegance.

CASTILLO DE SOLDEPEÑAS 2003 WHITE
CASTILLO DE SOLDEPEÑAS 2003 ROSÉ
CASTILLO DE SOLDEPEÑAS 2003 RED
VIÑA ALBALI BATANEROS RED
VIÑA ALBALI CABERNET TEMPRANILLO
2000 RESERVA RED

Bodegas FERNANDO CASTRO

Paseo Castelar, 70
13730 Santa Cruz de Mudela (Ciudad Real)
☎: 926 342 168 - Fax: 926 349 029
fcastro@infor4.es
www.bodegasfernandocastro.com

Established: 1850

🍾 900 📊 3,000,000 litres 🌿 120 has.

🇪🇸 30% 🌐70%: -DE -NL -UK -SE -FI -DK -PL -MX -CA -RU -AT

CASTILLO DE BAÑOS 1998 RESERVA RED
RAÍCES 1997 GRAN RESERVA RED

GALÁN

Salida de los Llanos, 15
13300 Valdepeñas (Ciudad Real)
☎: 926 321 752 - Fax: 926 324 766
bodegasgalan@bodegasgalan.com
www.bodegasgalan.com

Established: 1876

🍾 200 📊 200,000 litres 🍾 95%
🌐5%: -DE

VIÑA LUPARIA 2003 JOVEN WHITE
VIÑA LUPARIA 2000 RED
VIÑA LUPARIA 2001 CRIANZA RED

Bodegas J.A. MEGÍA E HIJOS

Magdalena, 33
13300 Valdepeñas (Ciudad Real)
☎: 926 347 828 - Fax: 926 347 829
jamegia@corcovo.com
www. corcovo.com

Established: 1994

🍾 500 📊 1,000,000 litres 🌿 100 has.

🍾 65% 🌐35%: -UK -FR -DE -DK -BE - US -CA

CORCOVO 2003 JOVEN WHITE
100% airén

80 Pale yellow. Intense and very fragrant aroma (flowers, ripe white fruit), with a nuance of hay and spicy skins typical of maceration at a low temperature. Flavourful, slightly oily and rich in nuances on the palate; fine bitter and citrus notes.

CORCOVO 2003 JOVEN ROSÉ
100% tempranillo

78 Salmon. Fairly short, quite closed, fruity aroma. Fruity, fresh, pleasant palate, better than in the nose.

CORCOVO 2003 ROBLE JOVEN RED
100% tempranillo

79 Quite dark cherry. Fruity aroma with barely noticeable oak notes, slightly closed. Slightly fleshy, fruity palate with oak tannins well-assembled with the wine, flavourful, good persistence.

CORCOVO 2003 JOVEN RED
100% cencibel

79 Lively garnet red cherry. Fresh, slightly foresty, fruity aroma (brambles, dry earth). Fruity, fresh, flavourful, clean palate with varietal overtones.

DO VALDEPEÑAS

CORCOVO 2000 CRIANZA RED
100% tempranillo

80 Dark cherry. Fresh, fruity, not very intense, clean aroma. Fruity palate with mild wood hints ensembled in the wine, flavourful, better on the palate.

CORCOVO 1998 RESERVA RED
100% tempranillo

80 Dark cherry with a garnet red edge. Aroma with toasty notes of well-balanced oak and fruit. Fresh, flavourful palate, well-balanced with a good assemblage of oak and fruit nuances.

CORCOVO MAGNUM 1999 CRIANZA RED

J4 BODEGAS

Chalanes, 50
13300 Valdepeñas (Ciudad Real)
☎: 926 324 269 - Fax: 926 324 269
j4bodegas@eresmas.com
Established: 2003
🌐 30 📊 100,000 litres 🍇 50 has. 🏴 100%

FORJADO 2003 WHITE
FORJADO TEMPRANILLO 2003 JOVEN RED
FORJADO TEMPRANILLO 2001 CRIANZA RED

Bodegas JUAN RAMÍREZ

Torrecillas, 138
13300 Valdepeñas (Ciudad Real)
☎: 926 322 021 - Fax: 926 320 495
info@bodegasjuanramirez.com
www.bodegasjuanramirez.com
Established: 1914
🌐 150 📊 800,000 litres 🍇 14 has.
🏴 70% 🌍30%: -DE -BE -NL -PL -LT -LV

ALBA 2002 FERMENTADO EN BARRICA WHITE
100% airén

77 Straw-coloured. Fresh aroma with wood notes but without the complexity of fine lees, slightly fruity. Fruity palate with dry notes of oak which persist on the palate; well-mannered.

ALBA DE LOS INFANTES TEMPRANILLO 2003 MACERACIÓN CARBÓNICA RED
100% tempranillo

69 Intense cherry. Aroma with mild notes of over-ripening (raisins), fruity and fresh. Fleshy, flavourful, fresh palate with ripe fruit.

ALBA DE LOS INFANTES 1999 CRIANZA RED
100% tempranillo

80 Dark cherry. Toasty aroma of unintegrated crianza and ripe fruit with foresty hues. Fleshy, powerful palate, with wood tannins and a fruity suggestion, pleasant and flavourful.

ALBA DE LOS INFANTES 1998 RESERVA RED

80 Slightly intense cherry. Fruity, fresh, woody aroma without great varietal expression. Unintegrated fruit and wood on the palate, a flavourful ensemble.

ALBA DE LOS INFANTES TEMPRANILLO 1999 RED
100% tempranillo

78 Garnet red cherry. Medium-intensity aroma with mild reduction notes (tobacco), spices and a suggestion of caramelised fruit. Flavourful on the palate with a good fruit expression but drying oak in the finish.

TANIS 2000 CRIANZA RED

Sociedad Cooperativa LA INVENCIBLE

Torrecillas, 130
13300 Valdepeñas (Ciudad Real)
☎: 926 321 700 - Fax: 926 311 080
invencible@ucaman.es
www.ucaman.es/invencible
Established: 1943
🌐 600 📊 20,000,000 litres 🍇 1,000 has.
🏴 75% 🌍25%: -NL -DK -DE

VALDEAZOR MÁXIMA 2000 OAK AGED RED
100% tempranillo   🌐 15

80 Dark garnet red cherry. Powerful aroma of jammy black fruit and dark-roasted flavours with a slightly viscous essence. Flavourful, bitter palate (coffee, pitch), without varietal expression.

NOCTURNO 2001 CRIANZA RED
100% tempranillo

79 Dark cherry. Quite intense, fruity aroma with toasty oak notes. Fleshy palate with quite flavourful tannins and bitter notes, without great nuances and pleasant.

VALDEAZOR 2000 CRIANZA RED
100% cencibel

84 Dark cherry. Medium-intensity aroma of ripe black fruit with a viscous edge. Flavourful and fleshy on the palate with a good fruit-wood balance, quite persistent.

NOCTURNO 2000 RESERVA RED
100% tempranillo

80 Dark red cherry. Intense, ripe aroma of black fruit with a light hint of reduction (withered petals, prunes) and hints of slightly aged wood. Flavourful, fleshy palate, pleasant.

VALDEAZOR TEMPRANILLO 1998 RESERVA RED
100% tempranillo

82 Cherry with a garnet red edge. Clean, medium-intensity aroma of perfectly ripe fruit;

DO VALDEPEÑAS

expressive. Flavourful on the palate with earthy notes, ripe red fruit and toasty oak, well-balanced.

NOCTURNO 1998 GRAN RESERVA RED
100% tempranillo

81 Dark cherry. Powerful, ripe aroma with hints of petals and creamy oak notes. Flavourful palate with a good oak/fruit integration, bitter with good acidity.

VIÑA LASTRA 2003 JOVEN WHITE
VIÑA LASTRA AIRÉN SEMISECO 2003 WHITE
VALDEMONTE 2003 JOVEN WHITE
VIÑA LASTRA ROSADO 2003 ROSÉ
VALDEMONTE 2003 JOVEN ROSÉ
VIÑA LASTRA TEMPRANILLO 2003 RED
VALDEMONTE 2003 JOVEN RED
VALDEAZOR TRADICIONAL 2000 RED
VALDEMONTE 2001 CRIANZA RED

LOS LLANOS (COSECHEROS ABASTECEDORES)

Carretera N-IV, km. 200, 5
13300 Valdepeñas (Ciudad Real)
☎: 926 347 860 - Fax: 926 322 742
losllanos@coabsa.com
www.coabsa.com

Established: 1875
⊞ 23,000 🛢 85,000,000 litres 🍇 350 has.
🍷 55% 🌐45%: -SE -FI -DE -UK -GK -CH -BE -NL -BE -GA -VE -PR

ARMONIOSO 2003 WHITE
100% airén

76 Pale with a golden glint. Intense aroma of ripe apples and exotic hints with faint off-odours from the tank. Fresh and dry on the palate with fine bitter, slightly varietal notes.

LOMA DE LA GLORIA CABERNET SAUVIGNON 2000 CRIANZA RED
100% cabernet sauvignon

72 Garnet red cherry. Medium-intensity, very vegetative aroma (vine shoots, asparagus). Slightly fruitier on the palate yet also vegetative.

SEÑORÍO DE LOS LLANOS 2001 CRIANZA RED
100% tempranillo

78 Garnet red cherry. Short but clean aroma with mild nuances of oak and fruit. Slightly light on the palate with notes of skins and ink and well-integrated oak.

PATA NEGRA 1997 GRAN RESERVA RED
100% cencibel

75 Garnet red with a brick red edge. Aroma with reduction notes (leather) and spices (vanilla).

Light and round on the palate with an obvious presence of oak and an element of acidity.

SEÑORÍO DE LOS LLANOS 1998 GRAN RESERVA RED
100% cencibel

77 Garnet red cherry. Short aroma without great nuances of fruit and wood. Slightly flavourful, well-balanced, light-bodied palate, well-mannered.

DON OPAS WHITE
ARMONIOSO 2003 ROSÉ
TORNEO CRIANZA RED
SEÑORÍO DE LOS LLANOS CRIANZA RED
DON OPAS RED
SEÑORÍO DE LOS LLANOS 2000 RESERVA RED
SEÑORÍO DE LOS LLANOS 125 ANIVERSARIO 1993 GRAN RESERVA RED

LOS MARCOS

Cristo, 2
13730 Santa Cruz de Mudela (Ciudad Real)
☎: 926 349 028 - Fax: 926 349 030
bodegaslosmarcos@ctv.es
www.bodegaslosmarcos.com

Established: 1875
⊞ 100 🛢 1,500,000 litres 🍷 70%
🌐30%: -DE -UK -DK -NL -NO

MONTECRUZ 2003 JOVEN WHITE
airén

75 Pale. Fairly intense aroma of ripe white fruit. Fresh and fruity on the palate with a slightly oily texture, high quality bitter notes.

MONTECRUZ 2003 ROSÉ
tempranillo

72 Brilliant raspberry. Fairly intense aroma of red fruit with hints of lees. Flavourful on the palate with fresh overtones, hints of citrus fruit and an acidic edge.

MONTECRUZ TEMPRANILLO 2002 RED
tempranillo

73 Cherry with a garnet red edge. Medium-intensity aroma with the weight of the wood concealing the fruit. Slightly drying and astringent on the palate with red fruit and without great nuances.

MONTECRUZ TEMPRANILLO SELECCIÓN 2001 ROBLE RED
tempranillo, cabernet sauvignon   ⊞8

81 Garnet red cherry. Medium-intensity aroma of skins with notes of oak. Red fruit on the palate with character and a slightly drying woody finish although flavourful and quite persistent.

MONTECRUZ 2000 CRIANZA RED
100% tempranillo

77 Garnet red cherry with a coppery edge. Intense aroma with predominant toasty notes of oak, jammy black fruit and faint off-odours (late racking). Flavourful and fleshy on the palate with slightly marked tannins, a creamy oak nuance and hints of liquorice.

MONTECRUZ 1998 RESERVA RED
tempranillo

79 Garnet red cherry. Spicy oak aroma (vanilla, white pepper). Light and round on the palate with a flavourful edge and dry wood tannins in the finish.

MONTECRUZ TRADICIONAL 2003 RED

Bodegas LUIS MEGIA

C/Cruces, 27
13300 Valdepeñas (Ciudad Real)
☎: 926 347 908 - Fax: 926 347 908

DON LUIS MEGIA CRIANZA RED

75 Garnet red with an orangey edge. Not very intense yet clean aroma with notes of nuts. Light on the palate with hints of red fruit and dry oak tannins.

DON LUIS MEGIA 1998 RESERVA RED

55 Garnet with brick red edge. Aroma with off-odours, lacks racking. Greeness on the palate.

MARQUÉS GASTAÑAGA RED

Bodegas MARÍN PERONA

Castellanos, 99
13300 Valdepeñas (Ciudad Real)
☎: 926 313 296 - Fax: 926 313 347
bodegas@merxi.com
www.merxi.com
Established: 1986

TEJERUELAS AIRÉN 2003 JOVEN WHITE
100% airén

79 Pale. Slightly short aroma without fruit expression, fresh. Light, fruity, fresh palate, easy drinking.

VIÑA ALDANTE WHITE

70 Very pale. Not very intense aroma of white fruit with a herby nuance. Fresh on the palate without great fruit expression.

CALAR VIEJO 2000 CRIANZA RED
tempranillo

80 Garnet red cherry with a brick red edge. Intense aroma with predominant toasty notes of oak and hints of jammy fruit. Flavourful on the palate with well-integrated oak and fruit and a bitter nuance (liquorice, terroir).

CALAR VIEJO 1999 CRIANZA RED
100% tempranillo

81 Intense cherry with an orangey edge. Intense on the palate with predominant spicy oak notes and a fine reduction nuance (leather). Flavourful and supple on the palate with well-integrated oak and fruit.

MARÍN PERONA 2000 RESERVA RED
tempranillo

78 Garnet red cherry with an orange edge. Fresh, fruity aroma with fine notes of oak well-integrated with the wine. Flavourful, fresh palate with a suggestion of fruit expression and very precise hints of oak.

MARÍN PERONA 1999 RESERVA RED
tempranillo

81 Garnet red with a brick red edge. Spicy aroma with oak and a suggestion of ripe red fruit. Flavourful, fresh palate, very balanced fruit-crianza, fine reduction in the finish.

TEJERUELAS CENCIBEL 2003 RED
tempranillo

82 Cherry with a violet hue. Intense aroma of fresh and ripe black fruit and liquorice. Flavourful, powerful, very fruity and expressive on the palate; a good example of a young Tempranillo.

VIÑA ALDANTE RED

68 Garnet red. Fairly short aroma without great fruit expression and with mild off-odours. Sweet red fruit and very astringent on the palate, lacking harmony.

MÁRQUEZ

Travesía de la Unión, 14
13300 Valdepeñas (Ciudad Real)
☎: 926 322 545 - Fax: 926 322 545
Established: 1889
🌐 100 ▯ 400,000 litres 🍇 55 has.
🍷 60% 🌿40%: -FR -DE

LINDEROS 2001 CRIANZA RED
85% cencibel, 15% otras

78 Garnet red cherry with an orange glint. Intense aroma of ripe red fruit with hints of creamy and spicy (vanilla, luke-warm butter) oak. Flavourful and supple palate with a marked lactic and strawberry jelly character, without great crianza expression.

LAS CABEZAS 1998 RED
100% cencibel

79 Not very deep garnet red. Aroma with creamy wood notes (vanilla, white chocolate, cocoa). Light notes of fruit and very toasty wood on the palate; well-mannered.

MÁRQUEZ JOVEN WHITE
VIÑAPERAL 2002 WHITE

VIÑAPERAL 2002 ROSÉ
MÁRQUEZ RED
VIÑAPERAL 2002 RED

MIGUEL CALATAYUD

Postas, 20
13300 Valdepeñas (Ciudad Real)
☎: 926 348 070 - Fax: 926 322 150
vegaval@vegaval.com
www.vegaval.com

Established: 1960

🍾 3,000 🛢 4,000,000 litres 🍇 50 has.

🍷 55% 🍇45%: -US -UK -DE -NL -DK -CH
-JP -FR -AT -VE -PR -CA -HK -LU -BE -DK -
FI -HU -BR -IE -PL -SG -MY

VEGAVAL PLATA MACABEO 2003 WHITE
100% macabeo

78 Pale yellow with a golden glint. Fairly intense
aroma of fairly ripe white stone fruit with fresh
overtones. Fresh and flavourful on the palate with
fine bitter and citrus notes and an acidic edge.

VEGAVAL PLATA TEMPRANILLO 2002 RED
100% tempranillo

74 Garnet red cherry. Aroma with mild reduction
notes in the tank and a fruity hint. Fresh, fruity
palate, discreet.

VEGAVAL PLATA 2001 CRIANZA RED
100% tempranillo

81 Garnet red with an orangey edge. Aroma with
spicy notes (vanilla, pepper) and mild toasty oak.
Flavourful on the palate with well-assembled red
fruit and wood; pleasant with dry oak tannins in
the finish.

VEGAVAL PLATA 1999 RESERVA RED
100% tempranillo

80 Cherry with an orangey edge. Not very intense aroma with light reduction notes and a fruity
nuance. Round and flavourful on the palate with
well-integrated fruit and wood, pleasant.

VEGAVAL PLATA 1996 GRAN RESERVA RED
100% tempranillo

74 Garnet red cherry with a brick red edge. Short,
slightly reduced aroma, without nuances. Round
palate with a fruity nuance, discreet.

VEGAVAL PLATA 1993 RESERVA RED
VEGAVAL PLATA MAGNUM 1991 GRAN
 RESERVA RED

MIGUEL MARTÍN

Torrecilla, 118
13300 Valdepeñas (Ciudad Real)
☎: 926 322 174 - Fax: 926 322 174

Established: 1942

🍾 45 🛢 1,600,000 litres 🍇 36 has.

🍷 99% 🍇1%: -DE

DESTELLOS 2003 JOVEN WHITE
100% airén

74 Pale yellow. Not very intense aroma of very
ripe white fruit with a light and not very fine nuance (withered petals). Fresh on the palate with bitter
notes and lacking balance.

DESTELLOS 1998 CRIANZA RED
100% tempranillo

76 Not very deep garnet red. Not very intense
aroma of red berries with an aniseed nuance.
Slightly vegetative on the palate with enough fruit
presence to be a 98, drying tannins.

VIÑA M.MARTIN 1999 CRIANZA RED
70% tempranillo, 30% airén

79 Garnet red cherry with coppery hues. Intense,
fruity aroma with creamy hints of wood. Flavourful
on the palate with slightly drying tannins and supple overtones; pleasant.

VALDEMESO 1996 RESERVA RED
100% tempranillo

75 Ruby red with a brick red hue. Aroma with
notes of reduction and toasty oak. Round and light
on the palate with bitter wood tannins, without
great nuances.

VALDEMESO 2003 JOVEN WHITE
DESTELLOS 2002 JOVEN ROSÉ
VALDEMESO 2003 JOVEN RED

Bodegas NAVARRO LÓPEZ

Autovía Madrid-Cádiz, km. 193
13300 Valdepeñas (Ciudad Real)
☎: 902 193 431 - Fax: 902 193 432
laboratorio@navarrolopez

Established: 1988

🍾 6,000 🛢 6,000,000 litres 🍇 150 has.

🍷 25% 🍇75%

DON AURELIO MACABEO 2003 WHITE
100% macabeo

80 Pale with a golden glint. Powerful aroma of
very ripe white stone fruit with hints of hay and
citrus fruit. Flavourful on the palate, rich in fruit
nuances, a bitter suggestion, a slightly oily texture and excellent acidity.

DON AURELIO AIRÉN 2003 WHITE

76 Straw-coloured with a greenish hue. Slightly
short but fruity aroma (lemony notes) with herbs.
Fruity on the palate, herbs, somewhat lacking in
acidity yet well-mannered.

DO VALDEPEÑAS

DON AURELIO TEMPRANILLO 2003 RED
tempranillo

83 Cherry with a violet hue. Intense, ripe, fruity aroma with a good varietal expression (underbrush) and fresh overtones. Fleshy on the palate with very flavourful grape tannins and excellent fruit-alcohol-acidity symmetry.

DON AURELIO 2000 CRIANZA RED
100% tempranillo

79 Dark garnet red cherry. Aroma of ripe black fruit, hints of blackberries, barely evident oak. Fruity, quite intense palate, fresh, flavourful.

DON AURELIO 1998 RESERVA RED
100% cencibel

75 Dark cherry. Slightly closed aroma, different to the 2004 Wine Guide, slightly lacking in fruit expression with unobvious wood. Slightly flavourful fruity palate with oak tannins and foresty hints.

DON AURELIO 1996 GRAN RESERVA RED
100% tempranillo

78 Garnet red cherry. Fresh, fruity, refreshing aroma. Fresh, fruity, flavourful palate, unlike a Gran Reserva.

PEDRO SÁNCHEZ MOLERO LARA

Postas, 62
13300 Valdepeñas (Ciudad Real)
☎: 926 321 710 - Fax: 926 320 304
Established: 1945
34 ▪ 380,000 litres 90 has.
99% 1%

CALAHOYA JOVEN WHITE
CALAHOYA CENCIBEL RED
CALAHOYA CRIANZA RED
CALAHOYA RESERVA RED

RAFAEL LÓPEZ-TELLO

Avenida Estudiantes nº 5
13300 Valdepeñas (Ciudad Real)
☎: 926 322 165 - Fax: 926 312 457
pedidos@lopeztello.com
www.lopeztello.com
Established: 1893
300 ▪ 300,000 litres 30 has.
75% 25%: -DE -BE -IE -AT

LÓPEZ-TELLO 2003 JOVEN WHITE
airén

78 Pale with a golden hue. Fairly short aroma with a ripe fruit nuance. Better, flavourful palate with fine bitter notes, hints of citrus fruit and good acidity.

MOHINO RED

68 Cherry with a violet edge. Aroma with fermentation off-odours and a nuance of ripe fruit. Copious fruit on the palate unbalanced by the acidity; an astringent finish.

LÓPEZ-TELLO 2000 CRIANZA RED
100% cencibel

79 Garnet red cherry. Medium-intensity aroma with obvious oak (lard) and a suggestion of fruit. Fruitier on the palate, pleasant with dry wood tannins in the finish.

GRAN MOHINO 1988 RED
cencibel

76 Cherry with a brick red edge. Aroma with reduction notes, old furniture and attics. Round and flavourful on the palate evoking black fruit and toasty wood notes

LOPEZ-TELLO TEMPRANILLO 1998 RESERVA RED
100% tempranillo

77 Cherry with a brick-red hue. Aroma with notes of slightly rough, brittle oak with a hint of fruit. Slightly flavourful palate with hints of oak and fruit, medium-bodied and well-mannered.

LÓPEZ-TELLO TEMPRANILLO MOHINO 2003 JOVEN RED
LÓPEZ-TELLO AFRUTADO 2003 ROSÉ
SEÑORÍO LÓPEZ-TELLO 1997 RESERVA RED

Hijos de RAMÓN HIDALGO

Balbuena, 108
13300 Valdepeñas (Ciudad Real)
☎: 926 347 953 - Fax: 926 347 954
ramidal@antonia.com
Established: 1865
200 ▪ 1,000,000 litres 10 has.
70% 30%: -DE -SE -JP

VIÑA DEL CALAR 2003 WHITE
VIÑA DEL CALAR "TEMPRANILLO" 2003 RED
CORTIJO LOS CLÉRIGOS 1999 CRIANZA RED
CORTIJO LOS CLÉRIGOS 1997 RESERVA RED

Bodegas REAL

Finca Marisanchez. Ctra. a Cózar, km. 12'800
13300 Valdepeñas (Ciudad Real)
☎: 926 338 001 - Fax: 926 338 079
comunicacion@bodegas-real.com
www.bodegas-real.com
Established: 1989
500 ▪ 3,000,000 litres 280 has.
35% 65%: -DE -UK -US -IE -BE -FR

DO VALDEPEÑAS

-CA -SE -DK -NL -CH -JP

BONAL TEMPRANILLO 2003 JOVEN RED
100% tempranillo

78 Garnet red cherry with a violet edge. Medium-intensity, perfumed aroma (violet eau de toilette) and with a suggestion of sweet fruit. Flavourful and with copious fruit on the palate, an earthy finish.

PALACIO DE IBOR 1998 RESERVA RED
85% tempranillo, 15% cabernet sauvignon

87 Quite intense cherry. Toasty aroma with a nuance of paprika, black fruit and a suggestion of minerals. Fleshy, flavourful, toasty palate with a peppery essence and oak infused in the wine.

VICENTE NAVARRO Y HERMANOS

Sebastián Bermejo, 50
13300 Valdepeñas (Ciudad Real)
☎: 926 323 354

Established: 1959
🍶 1,200,000 litres 🍇 70 has. 🍷 100%

RACIMO DE ORO RED
RACIMO DE ORO CRIANZA RED
RACIMO DE ORO GRAN RESERVA RED

VIDEVA

Travesía Horno, 16
13300 Valdepeñas (Ciudad Real)
☎: 926 322 351 - Fax: 926 320 092
bodegasvideva@terra.es

Established: 1967
🍾 500 🍶 2,000,000 litres 🍇 515 has.
🍷 80% 🌐20%

GRAN VIDEVA JOVEN WHITE
OSTRERO OAK AGED WHITE
ANIVERSARIO RED
VIDEVA CRIANZA RED
VIDEVA RESERVA RED

VINOS DE SANCTI PAULI

Paseo de la estación, 43
13300 Valdepeñas (Ciudad Real)
☎: 926 316 938 - Fax: 926 316 007
sanctipauli@wanadoo.es

SANCTI PAULI 2002 RED

87 Intense cherry. Powerful, ripe aroma, toasty grapes, jammy and earthy hints. Fleshy, warm, flavourful palate, with a good ripe fruit/wood balance.

Viñedos y Bodegas VISÁN

Paseo Castelar, 92
13730 Santa Cruz de Mudela (Ciudad Real)
☎: 926 342 075 - Fax: 926 342 050
vinvisan@teleline.es

Established: 1996
🍾 300 🍶 1,050,000 litres 🍷 70%
🌐30%: -CA -FR -NL-DK

CASTILLO DE MUDELA 2002 JOVEN RED
100% cencibel

80 Dark cherry. Aroma with good fruit expression (cherries and petals), fresh, good intensity. Fleshy, fresh, fruity palate, with a youthful expression, flavourful.

CASTILLO DE CALATRAVA 2000 RESERVA RED
100% tempranillo

78 Ruby red cherry. Aroma of casks with woody notes, a fruity suggestion and mild hints of evolution. Slightly flavourful palate, well-balanced, with oak tannins that predominate over the fruit.

CASTILLO DE CALATRAVA SELECCIÓN ESPECIAL RED
CASTILLO DE LOS INFANTES CRIANZA RED
VILLA DEL DUQUE RESERVA RED

DO VALENCIA

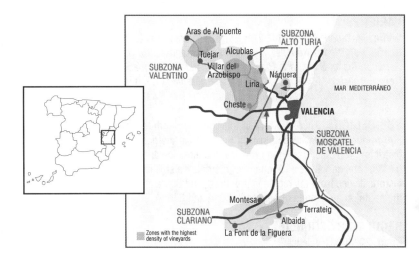

NEWS. The level of quality in the region is basically the same as last year. The cooperatives have still not jumped onto the quality bandwagon of the private bodegas, which is all too evident from the scores and is an impediment to the DO as a whole.

Significant differences are also coming to light between the different sub-regions. For example, whilst Valentino appears half asleep, in Clariano (the highest region in Valencia) the greatest hope for new wine from Valencia is starting to appear, to the point that it may acquire its own designation, and the name 'Vinos de la Tierra' of Albaida is already used for its wines that are warm but with very fresh tannins. Here is where we find the enthusiasm for the creation of single-variety wines of J. Belda and, of course, the extraordinary Maduresa of Celler del Roure.

Hectares of Vineyard	No. of Viticulturists	No. of Bodegas	2003 Harvest	2003 Production	Marketing
19,490	12,411	46	Very Good	70,433,400 litres	30% Spain 70% Foreign*

Also noteworthy is the 30% increase in the amount of wine exported, accompanied by an equal increase in national sales. And all in spite of the climate of uncertainty after the restructuring of the vineyards, with the substitution of the *Bobal* for the *Tempranillo* which is being paid at a miserable € 0.19 per kilo, which translates into wines with poor varietal expression.

LOCATION. In the province of Valencia. It comprises 66 municipal districts in 4 different sub-regions: Alto Turia, Moscatel de Valencia, Valentino and Clariano.

CLIMATE. Mediterranean, marked by strong storms and downpours in summer and autumn. The average annual temperature is 15°C and the average annual rainfall is 500 mm.

SOIL. Mostly brownish-grey with limestone content; there are no drainage problems.

VARIETIES:
White: *Macabeo, Malvasía* (1,700 Ha), *Merseguera* (majority 4,440 Ha), *Moscatel* (3,100 Ha), *Pedro Ximénez, Plantafina, Plantanova, Tortosí, Verdil, Chardonnay, Semillon Blanc, Sauvignon Blanc* and *Moscatel de Hungria*.
Red: *Garnacha, Monastrell* (1,180 Ha), *Tempranillo* (1,680 Ha), *Tintorera, Forcayat, Bobal, Cabernet Sauvignon, Merlot, Pinot Noir* and *Syrah*.

SUB-REGIONS: There are four in total: Alto Turia, the highest sub-region (700 to 800 m above sea level) comprising 6 municipal districts; Valentino (23 municipal districts), in the centre of the province; the altitude varies between 250 m and 650 m; Moscatel de Valencia (9 municipal districts), also in the central region where the historical wine from the region is produced; and Clariano (33 municipal districts), to the south, at an altitude of between 400 m and 650 m.

REGULATORY COUNCIL.
Quart, 22. 46001 Valencia.
Tel: 963 910 096. Fax: 963 910 029.
E-mail: info@vinovalencia.org
Website: www.vinovalencia.org

GENERAL CHARACTERISTICS OF THE WINES:

Whites	The most classic, young and fresh with pleasant wild nuances, are produced from *Merseguera*. Also typical are those made from *Moscatel* (the historic variety of the region), and are used both for dry white wines, very aromatic and light, and for the characteristic Mistelas of the region, which have a pale colour when they are from the latest harvest and golden yellow if they are older. They are all characterised by their musky and grapy aromas.
Rosés	The current trend is towards raspberry pink coloured rosés, which are fresh and light, with a good fruity and aromatic potency.
Reds	The most characteristic wines are produced from *Monastrell* and *Garnacha*; the wines are slightly warm with notes of ripe fruit, although with less vigour than those from Utiel-Requena and lighter than those from Alicante. Wines from other varieties have begun to be produced recently, mainly *Tempranillo* and *Cabernet Sauvignon*, which give supple, flavourful red wines with a Mediterranean character.

Sociedad Cooperativa AGROVINÍCOLA DE MONTSERRAT

Doctor Marañón, s/n
46192 Montserrat (Valencia)
☎: 962 999 042 - Fax: 962 999 042
montserrat@fecoav.es

Established: 1972

🗄 1,700,000 litres 🍷 100%

MISTELA NOVA DULCE

ANTONIO ARRAEZ

Arcediano Ros, 35
46630 Fuente La Higuera (Valencia)
☎: 962 290 031 - Fax: 962 290 339
bodegasarraez@ono.com

🛢 400 🗄 2,000,000 litres 🍇 50 has.
🍷 80% 🍾20%

ARRÁEZ JOVEN RED
CABEZUELAS RED
LAGARES CRIANZA RED

BATALLER

Camí Real, 94-96
46841 Castelló de Rugat (Valencia)
☎: 962 813 017 - Fax: 962 813 017
vinosbenicadell@telepolis.com

Established: 1945

🛢 100 🗄 1,300,000 litres 🍇 4 has 🍷 100%

BENICADELL WHITE
BENICADELL ROSÉ
BENICADELL RED
BENICADELL CRIANZA RED

BENAVENT

Maestro Giner, 9
46837 Quatretonda (Valencia)
☎: 962 264 692

Established: 2001

🛢 20 🗄 300,000 litres 🍇 2 has. 🍷 100%

REAL CASA TORRELLA WHITE
REAL CASA TORRELLA ROSÉ
REAL CASA TORRELLA RED

CARMELITANO

Avenida de Castellón s/n
12560 Benicasim (Castellón)
☎: 964 300 849 - Fax: 964 304 489
mblasco@telefonica.net
www.telefonica.net/carmelitano

Established: 1913

🛢 50 🗄 250,000 litres 🍷 90% 🍾10%

MOSCATEL CARMELITANO 2003
VINO DE MISA CARMELITANO 2003
VINO AÑEJO CARMELITANO 2003

COMECHE

Ingeniero Tamarit, 10
46170 Villar del Arzobispo (Valencia)
☎: 962 720 078 - Fax: 961 645 126
bodegascomeche@bodegascomeche.com
www.bodegascomeche.com

Established: 1947

🛢 100 🗄 500,000 litres 🍇 15 has. 🍷 100%

PARTANA RED
COMECHE CRIANZA RED
VEGA SERRANA CRIANZA RED
COMECHE CABERNET SAUVIGNON
RESERVA RED

COVIBEX

Carretera Nacional III, km. 314
46370 Chiva (Valencia)
☎: 962 522 200 - Fax: 962 521 678
covibex@covibex.com
www.covibex.com

Established: 1991

🛢 500 🗄 225 litres 🍇 2,000 has.
🍷 95% 🍾5%: -CH -FI

BÁRBARA GRIAL ALTO TURIA 2003 WHITE
100% merseguera

79 Straw-coloured with a greenish glint. Fairly intense aroma of ripe white fruit and hints of flowers (acacia) with quite an oily character. Flavourful on the palate, with a slightly oily texture and a ripe fruit nuance; pleasant.

BÁRBARA GRIAL SEMILLON 2003 WHITE
100% semillon

80 Golden yellow. Fairly intense aroma of green fruit with a spicy nuance of skins, hints of citrus fruit and dried grass. Flavourful on the palate with light carbonic notions and fine bitter notes, very pleasant.

VIÑA BÁRBARA ALTO TURIA 2003 WHITE
100% merseguera

79 Pale yellow. Not very intense, fruity aroma with a nuance of fine herbs. Flavourful on the palate with fruit concealed by the alcohol, fine bitter hints and good acidity.

BÁRBARA GRIAL 2003 ROSÉ
tempranillo

79 Pale raspberry. Fairly intense aroma with a good expression of ripe red fruit and fresh overtones. Fresh, dry on the palate with fine bittersweet notes and bitter hints.

VIÑA BÁRBARA TEMPRANILLO 2003 ROSÉ
100% tempranillo

75 Lively raspberry. Not very intense aroma, slightly fruity with fresh overtones and a nuance of citrus fruit (grapefruit pulp). Fresh flavourful palate with an acidic edge.

BÁRBARA GRIAL 2003 RED
50% tempranillo, 50% bobal

82 Cherry with a violet edge. Intense aroma of jammy black fruit with a toasty and creamy oak nuance. Flavourful and fleshy on the palate with oak tannins well-integrated with the grape tannins, a slight varietal expression and hints of liquorice and terroir.

VIÑA BÁRBARA 2003 OAK AGED RED
50% bobal, 50% tempranillo

79 Brilliant garnet red cherry. Fairly intense aroma of ripe red fruit with fine creamy and toasty hints. Flavourful on the palate with slightly marked tannins, fresh overtones and a bitter nuance.

VIÑA BÁRBARA 1999 CRIANZA RED
monastrell, tempranillo

83 Garnet red cherry with a coppery edge. Powerful aroma with spicy oak notes and a fine reduction nuance. Flavourful on the palate with fresh red stone fruit overtones and well-integrated oak and fruit, well-balanced.

VIÑA BÁRBARA 1997 RESERVA RED
75% tempranillo, 25% cabernet sauvignon

79 Cherry with a brick red edge. Aroma with toasty and oak notes (vanilla, cocoa). Round and light on the palate with toasty notes, pleasant.

VIÑA BÁRBARA SEMILLÓN 2003 WHITE

CHERUBINO VALSANGIACOMO

Carretera Cheste-Godelleta, km. 1
46370 Chiva (Valencia)
☎: 962 510 451 - Fax: 962 511 361
cherubino@cherubino.es
www.cherubino.es

Established: 1831

🌐 9,000 📖 80,000,000 litres

🍷 20% 🌐 80%

GRAN NATURAL WHITE DE AGUJA
merseguera, macabeo

75 Pale yellow with a greenish hue. Not very intense, fresh aroma with notes of green apples and citrus fruit and hints of crystallised fruit. Very fresh in the mouth with fine carbonic hints, good acidity and without great fruit expression.

MARQUÉS DE CARO 2003 WHITE
merseguera, moscatel

82 Straw-coloured with a greenish edge. Intense aroma of herbs with green fruit pulp and perfumed soap. Fresh on the palate, bitter with green fruit, long.

VALL DE SANT JAUME 2003 WHITE
100% merseguera

79 Pale yellow. Intense aroma of ripe apples with hints of white stone fruit and fresh overtones. Ripe and flavourful on the palate with a slightly oily texture and a bitter nuance, very pleasant.

VALL DE SANT JAUME 2003 ROSÉ
100% bobal

78 Brilliant raspberry with a coppery glint. Intense, fruity aroma with spicy hints of skins. Flavourful palate of red stone fruit and bitter hints; with overtones of fruit-alcohol-acidity symmetry.

MARQUÉS DE CARO TEMPRANILLO 2003 RED
100% tempranillo

75 Garnet red cherry with a violet edge. Medium-intensity aroma of red fruit with a vegetative and metallic nuance. Flavourful on the palate with ripe red fruit and pleasant.

VALL DE SANT JAUME 2003 RED
bobal, tempranillo

76 Brilliant cherry. Powerful aroma of ripe red fruit with hints of sun-drenched skins and a good expression of young wine. Flavourful on the palate with quite marked tannins (vegetative hints) and oily.

MARQUÉS DE CARO 2000 CRIANZA RED
tempranillo, cabernet sauvignon

79 Garnet red cherry. Not very intense aroma of fruity and woody notes. Flavourful, more expressive and fruity on the palate although wood is very present at the back of the mouth.

MARQUÉS DE CARO 1999 RESERVA RED
50% tempranillo, 50% cabernet sauvignon

80 Garnet red cherry. Fruity, ripe, fresh aroma with very well-balanced oak notes. Varietal notes on the palate, flavourful, fresh and light with well-balanced wood.

VITTORE MOSCATEL DE VALENCIA

77 Golden straw. Aroma of Muscatel grapes with fine tropical fruit and orange peel. Sweet, quite heavy and warm on the palate with notes of crystallised fruit.

Cooperativa CHESTE AGRARIA

María Carbonell, 2
46380 Cheste (Valencia)

hint. Flavourful palate with mineral expression, well-balanced oak tannins and a very fresh finish.

HERETAT DE TAVERNERS 2000 RESERVA RED
55% cabernet sauvignon, 15% monastrell, 15% merlot, 15% tempranillo

86 Deep garnet red. Elegant aroma of very ripe black fruit, fine toasty wood, earth and minerals. Fleshy palate, slightly warm but with good freshness and complex toasty skins; long and flavourful.

HERETAT DE TAVERNERS GRACIANO 2000 RESERVA RED
100% graciano

89 Intense cherry. Powerful aroma, rich in fruit expression (bilberries) with hints of foresty berries and earth, original. Powerful, fleshy and warm on the palate with wild but flavourful and slightly sweet tannins.

J. BELDA

Salvaterra, 54
46635 Fontanars dels Alforins (Valencia)
☎: 608 962 365 - Fax: 962 222 245
daniel.belda@vinsbjb.com
www.vinsbjb.com

Established: 1931

🛢 450 ⬛ 500,000 litres 🍇 120 has. 🍷 100%

VERDIL DANIEL BELDA 2003 JOVEN WHITE
100% verdil

77 Straw-coloured. Fruity aroma (grapefruit, citrus fruit) with a suggestion of sun-drenched skins. Flavourful, very fresh palate without great varietal expression and sweetish finish.

CHARDONNAY DANIEL BELDA 2003 FERMENTADO EN BARRICA WHITE
100% chardonnay

85 Golden. Fresh aroma of ripe apples, with well-balanced toasty and nutty notes, a suggestion of fine herbs. Flavourful, slightly oily palate with supple oak tannins, well-structured apples and wood, good persistence.

DANIEL BELDA CABERNET SAUVIGNON 2003 JOVEN ROSÉ
100% cabernet sauvignon

77 Cherry with a coppey edge. Aroma of ripe red fruit (bilberries) with warm overtones. Flavourful with good fruit on the palate, slightly alcoholic but fresh, long (red berries).

DANIEL BELDA PONSALET 2003 JOVEN RED
100% monastrell

80 Garnet red cherry. Aroma of lightly smoky, quite spicy red berries and warm notes. Flavourful, very fresh palate; balsamic notes of skins.

PINOT NOIR DANIEL BELDA 1999 FERMENTADO EN BARRICA RED
100% pinot noir

78 Mahogany cherry. Aroma with hints of animals, toasty oak and a slightly warm fruity hint. Fleshy, slightly rustic palate (reduction), with flavourful yet fine tannins and a spicy finish.

EUSEBIO LA CASTA CABERNET SAUVIGNON 2000 CRIANZA RED
100% cabernet sauvignon

82 Deep garnet red. Strong mineral aroma of ripe black fruit and hints of earth. Fleshy, highly flavourful and very fresh palate, mineral sensations; ripe in the finish.

EUSEBIO LA CASTA TEMPRANILLO 2000 CRIANZA RED
100% tempranillo

85 Deep cherry with a garnet red edge. Spicy aroma of dried, aromatic herbs and a suggestion of foresty black berries. Fleshy palate of toasty skins, mineral expression and quite bitter (cocoa), well-integrated, fresh tannins.

SHIRAZ DANIEL BELDA 2001 RESERVA RED
100% shiraz

84 Very deep cherry. Concentrated aroma with notes of toasty and sun-drenched skins, minerals, dry stone and slightly varietal. Fleshy palate, spicy, with very pleasant fresh tannins and a dry stone (mineral) finish.

DANIEL BELDA 2000 RESERVA RED
100% merlot

84 Garnet red cherry. Aroma of slightly ripe red fruit, spices, hints of juniper and heather, fine integrated smoky notes. Flavourful palate with good freshness, fruity tannins with mineral notes and a spicy finish.

DANIEL BELDA CABERNET SAUVIGNON 1995 RESERVA RED
100% cabernet sauvignon

83 Garnet red cherry. Intense, slightly mineral aroma, of ripe black fruit, toasty oak and hints of animals. Fleshy palate with marked wood tannins (smoky notes, spices) over warm, ripe fruit with a balsamic finish.

DANIEL BELDA SELECCIÓN RESERVA RED
35% tempranillo, 15% monastrell, 10% pinot noir, 10% cabernet sauvignon

81 Intense cherry. Fresh, fruity, pleasant aroma with a mild nuance of well-assembled oak. Fresh, fruity, flavourful palate, well-balanced.

DANIEL BELDA TEMPRANILLO 1995 RESERVA RED
100% tempranillo

80 Deep garnet red. Aroma of ripe black fruit, Mediterranean expression (eucalyptus, mountain herbs) and toasty skins. Fleshy palate with slightly drying wood tannins, ripe fruit (chocolate), fresh.

DANIEL BELDA 1994 GRAN RESERVA RED

LA BARONÍA DE TURIS

Carretera de Godelleta, 22
46389 Turis (Valencia)
☎: 962 526 011 - Fax: 962 527 282
baronia@sistelcom.com
baroniadeturis.bypermat.net

Established: 1920

🍾 1,660 📖 11,100,000 litres 🍇 1,460 has.

🍷 55% 🍇45%: -DE -BE -CA -DK -UK -IE -DK -US -EE -PL -RU -FI -GT -NL -LV

BARÓN DE TURIS MALVASÍA 2003 WHITE
100% malvasía

71 Pale yellow. Not very intense aroma with fresh overtones, lacking varietal and fruit expression. Fresh palate with bitter hints, without great nuances.

VIÑAMALATA 2003 JOVEN WHITE
100% moscatel

78 Pale gold. Intense, perfumed aroma with fine musky, very varietal notes of white flowers. Flavourful, fresh, supple palate with fine bitter notes and toasty skins.

CASTELL DE VEZA MERLOT 2002 RED
100% merlot

77 Dark garnet red cherry. Powerful aroma of ripe fruit with notes of reduction in the tank, balsamic and terroir notes. Flavourful, fleshy palate with slightly sweet fruit, warm with spicy hints.

CASTELL DE VEZA CABERNET SAUVIGNON 2002 RED
100% cabernet sauvignon

80 Dark garnet red cherry. Powerful, quite varietal aroma (paprika, redcurrants), a suggestion of Mediterranean herbs and damp fallen leaves. Fleshy, flavourful palate with ripe, oily tannins, slightly warm.

BARÓN DE TURÍS 2000 RESERVA RED
90% tempranillo, 10% garnacha

75 Garnet red cherry. Fruity aroma with mild spicy oak notes and nuances of carpentry without altering the ensemble. Fresh, light, flavourful palate, well-mannered.

MISTELA MOSCATEL TURÍS 2003 VINO DE LICOR
100% moscatel

85 Brilliant pale gold. Intense aroma with crystallised white fruit, fine hints of grapes and musk, notes of flowers and pollen. Flavourful palate with fine bittersweet notes, fresh overtones, hints of crystallised citrus fruit peel and good acidity.

VIÑAMALATA 2003 ROSÉ
BARÓN DE TURIS 2002 ROSÉ
BARÓN DE TURIS 2002 RED
GRAN BARÓN DE TURIS 2001 CRIANZA
RED
CASTILLO DE TURIS 1999 GRAN RESERVA
RED

Vitivinícola de LA POBLA DEL DUC

Marxillent, 58
46840 Pobla del Duc (Valencia)
☎: 962 250 017 - Fax: 962 927 210
roscardi@inicia.es
Established: 1930
🛢 5,.000,000 litres 🍇 663 has. 🡆 100%

ROSCARDÍ WHITE
ROSCARDÍ ROSÉ
ROSCARDÍ RED

Cooperativa Vinícola LA VIÑA

Portal de Valencia, 52
46630 Fuente La Higuera (Valencia)
☎: 962 290 052 - Fax: 962 290 442
Established: 1945
🌐 1,800 🛢 10,000,000 litres 🍇 3200 has.
🡆 10% 🌐90%: -FI -DK -DE -US -IE -UK -
CZ -NL Centro América -PL -AT -BE -RU

PALACIO DEL CONDE 2003 WHITE
macabeo, merseguera, malvasía

79 Straw-coloured with a greenish edge. Fruity, clear and fresh aroma. Pleasant with considerable freshness on the palate, notes of pears, well-crafted and simple.

ICONO SYRAH 2002 RED
syrah

79 Slightly intense cherry. Slightly fruity aroma without subtle varietal nuances. Fresh, fruity palate with flavourful tannins.

SEQUIOT TEMPRANILLO 2002 RED
tempranillo

81 Quite dark garnet red cherry. Fresh, slightly fruity, well-balanced aroma with perfect ripeness. Fresh, fruity, slightly flavourful palate, well-mannered.

RINCÓN DE ESCRIBANOS 2000 CRIANZA
RED

LEOPOLDO

San Jaime, 3
03760 Ondara (Alicante)
☎: 965 766 314 - Fax: 965 766 241
correo@bodegasleopoldo.com
www.bodegasleopoldo.com

ALFATARA VARIETAL MUSCAT 2003 WHITE
ALFATARA 2003 RED
ALFATARA VARIETAL TEMPRANILLO 2003
RED
ALFATARA 2000 CRIANZA RED

LOS FRAILES

Casa Los Frailes
46635 Fontanares (Valencia)
☎: 963 339 845

CASAMONFRARE MONASTRELL 2003 RED
monastrell

82 Cherry. Clear aroma of ripe red berries (bilberries), balsamic notes and intense dried herbs. Flavourful, very fresh palate, with fine and very pleasant tannins.

CASAMONFRARE MONASTRELL CABERNET
SAUVIGNON 2003 OAK AGED RED
monastrell, cabernet sauvignon   🛢 3

84 Intense cherry. Intense aroma of clear red fruit, spices, very well-integrated oak and a suggestion of mountain herbs. Flavourful palate with fresh fruit tannins; notes of foresty red berries.

LOS PINOS

Casa Los Pinos
46635 Fontanars dels Alforins (Valencia)
☎: 962 222 090 - Fax: 962 222 086
domlospinos@wanadoo.es
Established: 1863
🌐 140 🛢 300,000 litres 🍇 60 has.
🡆 2% 🌐98%: -DE -UK -CH -US -FI

DOMINIO LOS PINOS CUM LAUDE 2002
FERMENTADO EN BARRICA WHITE
40% sauvignon blanc, 30% moscatel, 30% viognier

70 Pale yellow. Intense aroma with smoky and mildly creamy notions of oak and a not very fine nuance of varnish. Dry and very warm on the palate, without fruit expression.

DOMINIO LOS PINOS CUM LAUDE 2000
CRIANZA RED
30% monastrell, 30% merlot, 20% cabernet sauvignon

83 Almost opaque cherry. Aroma of jammy black fruit, slightly warm, with sweet smoky notes. Fleshy palate with earthy but fresh tannins, black fruit and spices and cocoa in the finish; pleasantly fresh.

L. OLAECHEA 2002 CRIANZA RED
monastrell, merlot, cabernet sauvignon, syrah

85 Deep cherry. Concentrated aroma with fine spices, toasty oak, a suggestion of ripe black berries and hints of broom. Fleshy palate of excellent flavour with flabby fruit tannins and Mediterranean character.

DOMINIO LOS PINOS 2000 RESERVA RED

79 Garnet red cherry. Fresh, fruity aroma with mild toasty notes of oak. Fresh, fruity, pleasant, simple palate.

DOMINIO LOS PINOS 2002 OAK AGED RED
DOMINIO LOS PINOS SELECCIÓN 2001 RED

MANUEL POLO MONLEON

Carretera Alpuente, 12
46178 Titaguas (Valencia)
☎: 961 634 148 - Fax: 961 634 148

Established: 1953

🍶 20 📊 640,000 litres 🍇 9 has.

🍷 90% 🍾10%

HOYA DEL CASTILLO ALTO TURIA 2003 JOVEN WHITE
merseguera, macabeo

77 Brilliant pale with greenish nuances. Not very intense aroma of ripe white fruit with a nuance of not very fine lees. Better on the palate, flavourful, bitter and with good acidity.

HOYA DEL CASTILLO CRIANZA RED
tempranillo

73 Cherry. Aroma of skins and red fruit (blackberries). Acidic and light on the palate, not very well-balanced.

HOYA DEL CASTILLO ALTO TURIA 1999 CRIANZA RED
tempranillo

77 Garnet red. Slightly discreet aroma of ripe fruit with a suggestion of oak notes. Fleshy, fresh and fruity on the palate with round tannins.

Bodegas MURVIEDRO

Ampliación Polígono El Romeral, s/n
46340 Requena (Valencia)
☎: 962 329 003 - Fax: 962 329 002
murviedro@murviedro.es
www.murviedro.es

Established: 1927

🍶 1,500 📊 7,100,000 litres 🍷 5% 🍾95%

LOS MONTEROS 2003 WHITE

76 Pale. Intense aroma of ripe white fruit with hints of freshness. Fresh and flavourful on the palate with good expression of white fruit and notions of herbs.

MURVIEDRO 2003 WHITE
merseguera, macabeo, moscatel

81 Pale with coppery nuances. Intense, fragrant aroma of fruit and white flowers with hints of fine herbs. Flavourful palate with fine bitter notes and spicy hints of skins, very rich.

MURVIEDRO 2003 ROSÉ
bobal, monastrell, tempranillo

80 Cherry with coppery nuances. Powerful, fruity aroma with toasty hints of skins and a suggestion of sweetness. Flavourful palate with fine bitter notes, somewhat warm and spicy.

LOS MONTEROS 2002 RED
50% tempranillo, 50% monastrell

80 Garnet red cherry with a violet edge. Powerful, fruity aroma with a good Monastrell varietal expression (spices, sun-drenched skins). Flavourful on the palate with slightly fresh tannins, black fruit, balsamic hints and good acidity.

LOS MONTEROS 2001 CRIANZA RED
monastrell, merlot

83 Intense cherry. Fresh, slightly fruity aroma although not very intense or precise with unobvious oak yet well-integrated with the fruit. Fresh, fruity palate, with mild hints of wood, flavourful and harmonious.

MURVIEDRO 2001 CRIANZA RED
monastrell, bobal

78 Garnet red cherry. Fresh, fruity aroma with subtle nuances. Fresh, flavourful, warm palate, better in the mouth.

MURVIEDRO 1998 RESERVA RED
tempranillo, cabernet sauvignon, otras

83 Garnet red cherry. Fresh, fruity aroma with spicy nuances of oak. Fresh, fruity palate, well-balanced and flavourful with toasty hints of oak well-integrated with the wine.

SANTERRA DRY MUSCAT 2003 MOSCATEL SECO
moscatel

79 Pale. Not very intense aroma, fragrant with musky notes, flowers, and hints of aniseed. Dry, flavourful palate with quality bitter notes.

MURVIEDRO 2002 RED

Hermanos NOGUEROLES

Carretera Tabernes a Liria, km. 61
46389 Turis (Valencia)
☎: 962 526 768 - Fax: 962 526 768
Established: 1991
⊞ 50 🗟 1,000,000 litres 🍇 25 has.
🇪🇸 100%

VINYA MERAVELLA FERMENTADO EN BARRICA WHITE
LLANOS DE TURIS WHITE
LLANOS DE TURIS RED
LLANOS DE TURIS CRIANZA RED

Cooperativa Vinícola ONTENIENSE

Avenida Almansa, 17
46870 Ontinyent (Valencia)
☎: 962 380 849 - Fax: 962 381 149
info@coopontinyent.com
roberto@coopontinyent.com
Established: 1968
⊞ 30 🗟 2,650,000 litres 🇪🇸 100%

CODOLLA 2003 JOVEN WHITE
50% macabeo, 25% merseguera, 25% malvasía

67 Golden yellow. Intense aroma with a mild reduction off-odour (herbs, nuts) and without fruit expression. Quite flavourful, bitter, vinous palate with notions of sweetened must.

DON CARLOS 2003 JOVEN RED
100% tempranillo

74 Cherry. Aroma of foresty red fruit with aromatic notes, clear. Flavourful, fruity palate with slightly drying fruit tannins, uncomplicated.

DON CARLOS 2002 FERMENTADO EN BARRICA RED
50% tempranillo, 50% monastrell

72 Cherry with a garnet red edge. Predominant, smoky aroma of ash over black fruit. Fleshy palate with astringent wood tannins, good freshness but structured with the dryness of oak.

VIÑA UMBRIA RED
100% monastrell

60 Garnet red cherry with an orange edge. Aroma with reduction off-odours, geraniums and varnish. Slightly better on the palate, spicy and warm.

Cooperativa Vinícola de QUATRETONDA

Avenida Pais Valencia, 1
46837 Quatretonda (Valencia)
☎: 962 264 575 - Fax: 962 264 016
Established: 1953
⊞ 250 🗟 400,000 litres 🍇 175 has.
🇪🇸 100%

ROSETONDA RED

RAFAEL CAMBRA

Plaza Concepción, 13 - 19
46870 Onteniente (Valencia)
☎: 616 463 245
ibervin@fer.es
Established: 2001
⊞ 30 🍇 25 has.
🇪🇸 5% 🌐95%: -DE -NL -BE

RAFAEL CAMBRA DOS 2002 RED
cabernet sauvignon, cabernet franc

83 Intense cherry. Aroma with mildly vegetative but fresh and fruity varietal Cabernet notes. Fresh, fruity, flavourful, very varietal palate with dry but sufficiently ripe tannins.

RAFAEL CAMBRA UNO RED
monastrell

84 Intense cherry. Fruity aroma with foresty and slightly vegetative notes. Fruity, ripe, flavourful palate, better than in the nose, long and persistent.

Celler del ROURE

Carretera de Les Alcusses, km. 2, 5
46640 Moixent (Valencia)
☎: 962 295 020 - Fax: 962 295 142
cellerdelroure@hotmail.com
Established: 1995
⊞ 200 🗟 150,000 litres 🍇 22 has.
🇪🇸 40% 🌐60%

LES ALCUSSES 2002 RED

88 Slightly intense cherry with a slightly orangey edge. Warm aroma of ripe fruit with hints of dry earth. Fleshy, warm and Mediterranean on the palate with supple and sweet ripening tannins.

DO VALENCIA

MADURESA 2001 RED

90 Intense cherry. Aroma with toasty notes of oak and ripe fruit with earthy and mineral nuances, sun-drenched. Powerful, warm and flavourful on the palate with dry and sweet oak and ripe fruit tannins, long.

LES ALCUSSES 2000 RED

84 Slightly intense cherry. Lightly jammy aroma (jammy plums). Round, oily, warm, full, flavourful and slightly spirituous on the palate.

MADURESA 2000 RED

92 Intense cherry. Fine, elegant aroma of fine toasty oak (cocoa, vanilla, coffee). Slightly fleshy, fruity palate with very fine toasty notes and a mineral suggestion, warm with oak tannins diminished by the alcohol, very Mediterranean and complex.

MADURESA 2002 RED

90 Intense cherry. Aroma rich in expression of ripe black fruit with hints of minerals (dry earth) and fine toasty oak (cocoa, coffee). Powerful, fleshy, full, warm, minerals and flavourful palate, rich in expression of black fruit and minerals.

Cooperativa Vinícola
SAN PEDRO APÓSTOL

Mayor, 79
46388 Godelleta (Valencia)
☎: 961 800 017 - Fax: 961 800 017
godelleta.fruitsecs@serich.com
Established: 1950
100%

CASTILLO DE GODELLETA WHITE
GODELLETA MISTELA MOSCATEL

Cooperativa SANTA BÁRBARA

Carretera de Alpuente, 27
46178 Titaguas (Valencia)
☎: 961 634 030 - Fax: 961 634 030
Established: 1955
3,000,000 litres 300 has. 100%

LLANOS DE TITAGUAS WHITE

Cooperativa Agrícola
STA BÁRBARA DE CASINOS

Pelayo, 8
46171 Casinos (Valencia)
☎: 962 700 056 - Fax: 962 700 663
Established: 1952
250 3,000,000 litres 250 has.

100%

EL TOLLET WHITE
SERVERET WHITE
VI DOLÇ CRIANZA WHITE
VI RANCI CRIANZA WHITE
SERVERET ROSÉ
SERVERET RED

Bodegas TORREVELLISCA

Carretera L'Ombria, km. 1
46635 Fontanars dels Alforins (Valencia)
☎: 962 222 261 - Fax: 962 222 257
botorrevellisca@teleline.es
www.bodegas-torrevellisca.com
Established: 1990
900 2,000,000 litres 350 has.
25% 75%: -DE -NL -DK -SE -BE

TORREVELLISCA MACABEO 2003 WHITE
100% macabeo

78 Straw-coloured. Not very intense aroma with fresh white fruit overtones. Fresh and fruity on the palate with bitter hints and notions of herbs.

VERDIL TORREVELLISCA 2003 WHITE
100% verdil

74 Very pale. Not very intense aroma of green fruit with a herbaceous nuance with fresh overtones. Dry, quite flavourful and warm on the palate with hints of herbs and without fruit expression.

TORREVELLISCA 2003 WHITE SEMISECO
100% pedro ximénez

73 Pale. Not very intense aroma with hardly any fruit expression and hints of herbs. Flavourful on the palate with a slightly oily texture, hints of hay and a mild nuance of crystallised fruit.

TORREVELLISCA 2001 CRIANZA WHITE
50% macabeo, 50% verdil

71 Pale yellow with a golden glint. Fairly intense aroma with predominant, slightly toasty wood notes. Dry on the palate with an oily and warm texture, oak, without fruit expression.

TORREVELLISCA 2003 ROSÉ
100% tempranillo

80 Brilliant cherry. Intense aroma of ripe red stone fruit with floral hints. Fresh, flavourful palate with red fruit, fine spicy notes of skins and good acidity.

TORREVELLISCA 2003 RED
70% tempranillo, 20% monastrell, 10% cabernet sauvignon

78 Garnet red cherry. Not very intense, fruity aroma with toasty notes of skins. Fresh, flavourful palate with ripe grape tannins, slightly oily (hints of wax) and lacking fruit expression.

TORREVELLISCA 2000 CRIANZA RED
100% cabernet sauvignon

79 Garnet red cherry with a saffron edge. Not very intense aroma of toasty oak and jammy black fruit, without great varietal expression. Flavourful and fleshy on the palate with well-integrated fruit and oak; without great nuances.

TORREVELLISCA 2000 CRIANZA RED
80% tempranillo, 20% cabernet sauvignon

77 Cherry. Not very intense aroma of not very new woods, strawberries and raspberries. Light palate with somewhat oily, bitter notes.

TORREVELLISCA MERLOT 2002 CRIANZA RED
merlot

79 Garnet red cherry. Fruity, somewhat toasty aroma (sun-drenched skins) and sweet notes of the vine variety. Flavourful palate with slightly drying wood tannins and fruit spices in the aftertaste.

TORREVELLISCA 1998 RESERVA RED
80% tempranillo, 20% cabernet sauvignon

80 Not very deep cherry. Aroma of toasty wood, smoky hints and cedar. Unctuous palate with supple, fleshy tannins and a good though slightly short persistence in the retronasal passage.

TORREVELLISCA 1999 RESERVA RED
100% cabernet sauvignon

80 Garnet red cherry with a violet edge. Fairly intense aroma with a ripe fruit nuance, toasty hints of oak and reduction notes. Flavourful and fleshy on the palate with ripe and somewhat oily tannins.

TORREVELLISCA MOSCATEL 2003 VINO DE LICOR DULCE
100% moscatel

85 Intense gold. Classic aroma of Muscatel (jammy grapes, musky notes) with a herby nuance. Flavourful and sweet palate with light toasty oak, musky and sweet.

TORREVELLISCA 2000 CRIANZA RED

Bodegas TORROJA

Nueva, 1 Azagador
46357 Requena (Valencia)
☎: 962 304 232 - Fax: 962 303 833
bodegas@bodegastorroja.com
www.bodegastorroja.com

Established: 1994

🌐 1,000 📦 1,000,000 litres 🍇 43 has.

🍷 20% 🌍80%: -DK -DE -US -LT -LV -TR -TW -MY

AZALEA CHARDONNAY FERMENTADO EN BARRICA WHITE

Compañía VALENCIANA DE VINS I ESPIRITUOSOS

Plaza Maestro Serrano, 3
46380 Cheste (Valencia)
☎: 963 375 874 - Fax: 933 371 861

Established: 1996

🌐 50 🍷 70% 🌍30%

VIÑA CORDIAL ROSÉ
VIÑA CORDIAL RED
VIÑA CORDIAL CRIANZA RED
VIÑA CORDIAL RESERVA RED
CORDIAL GRAN RESERVA RED
CORDIAL MOSCATEL

Vinos VALTUILLE

La Fragua, s/n
24530 Valtuille de Abajo (León)
☎: 987 562 112 - Fax: 987 549 425

Established: 2000

📦 90,000 litres 🍇 12 has.

VIÑA SOLER 2001 CRIANZA RED

68 Garnet red cherry. Aroma with mild notes of oxidative evolution. Warm, slightly fleshy palate with a hint of evolution.

Viñedos y Bodegas VEGALFARO

Carretera Pontón - Utiel, km. 3
46340 Requena (Valencia)
☎: 616 982 817 - Fax: 639 118 301
rodolfo@vegalfaro.com
www.vegalfaro.com

Established: 1999

🌐 180 📦 450,000 litres 🍇 65 has.

🍷 40% 🌍60%: -DE -BE -SE -CH -IE -UK - US -NL

ARTIUS 2002 JOVEN RED
bobal, merlot

77 Quite dark cherry. Fruity aroma although with mild vegetative notes, fresh. Fruity, slightly flavourful and fresh palate, only well-mannered.

ARTIUS VIURA 2003 WHITE

VICENTE GANDÍA PLA

Carretera Cheste-Godelleta, s/n
46370 Chiva (Valencia)
☎: 962 524 242 - Fax: 962 524 243
gandia@gandiawines.com

DO VALENCIA

www.gandiawines.com
Established: 1885
🍷 14,000 🛢 28,000,000 litres 🍇 200 has.
🍷 10% 🌐90%: 75 paises de los 5 continentes

CASTILLO DE LIRIA 2003 JOVEN WHITE SEMIDULCE
viura, merseguera

73 Straw-coloured. Aroma of white flowers with aniseed notes. Light palate with good acidity but without expression.

CASTILLO DE LIRIA 2003 ROSÉ
100% bobal

76 Brilliant blush. Not very intense aroma with fresh overtones. Fresh, flavourful palate with fine spicy and bitter notes and good acidity.

CASTILLO DE LÍRIA 2002 JOVEN RED
tempranillo, bobal

79 Brilliant garnet red cherry. Not very intense aroma of ripe red stone fruit and spicy hints of skins. Flavourful palate of ripe fruit; fine bitter notes and hints of liquorice.

CASTILLO DE LIRIA 2000 RESERVA RED
tempranillo, garnacha

76 Garnet red cherry. Intense aroma of red fruit and quite fresh oak notes. Flavourful palate with bitter notes and a slight hint of greeness; lacking balance.

CASTILLO DE LIRIA MOSCATEL
100% moscatel

74 Yellow with a golden edge. Mild aroma of white flowers and citrus fruit. Sweet palate, with good acidity, slightly warm.

FUSTA NOVA 2003 MOSCATEL
100% moscatel

83 Pale yellow with shades of green. Aroma of orange peel and white flowers (jasmine). Sweet palate with good acidity; unctuous.

HOYA DE CADENAS CRIANZA RED
CASTILLO DE LIRIA RESERVA RED

Bodegas VIDAL

Valencia, 16
12550 Almanzora (Castellón)
☎: 964 503 300 - Fax: 964 560 604
info@bodegasvidal.com
www.bodegasvidal.com
Established: 1899
🍷 120 🛢 650,000 litres 🍷 85% 🌐15%: -
FR -DE -BE -AD -UE Centroamérica

UVA D'OR MOSCATEL VINO DE LICOR
100% moscatel

80 Straw-coloured with golden nuances. Intense aroma of grapes and crystallised fruit. Sweet, flavourful palate with herbs, slightly warm and very well-mannered.

CASTILLO DE PEÑISCOLA 2003 WHITE
CASTILLO DE PEÑISCOLA 2003 ROSÉ
CASTILLO DE PEÑISCOLA 2003 RED
ARTESANO MOSCATEL VINO DE LICOR
UVA D'OR SELECCIÓN ALLIER 2003 VINO DE LICOR

Cooperativa Vinícola VINICA CHIVANA

Plaza Aniceto Blasco, s/n
46370 Chiva (Valencia)
☎: 962 520 039 - Fax: 962 520 039
bodega@vinicachivana.com
www.vinicachivana.com
🍷 100 🛢 2,200,000 litres 🍇 350 has.
🍷 60% 🌐40%

CASTILLO DE CHIVA 2003 SECO WHITE
100% moscatel

79 Greenish straw-coloured. Not very intense aroma although fresh and musky with a nuance of white flowers. A hint of flavour on the palate with notes of herbs, very pleasant.

CASTILLO DE CHIVA 2003 WHITE
merseguera

73 Straw-coloured with a greenish nuance. Not very intense yet fresh and fruity aroma. Quite fruity palate with vegetative notes, easy drinking.

CASTILLO DE CHIVA 2001 WHITE
100% merseguera

68 Brilliant gold. Intense aroma with notes of evolution (cumin, mountain herbs) without fruit expression. Dry, quite flavourful palate without nuances.

CASTILLO DE CHIVA 2003 ROSÉ
bobal

65 Onion skins. Quite short aroma with weak fruit. Rustic palate, without fruit and with unbalanced acidity.

CASTILLO DE CHIVA 2003 RED
monastrell, tempranillo

78 Garnet red cherry with a brick red glint. Intense aroma of very ripe and slightly reduced fruit (prunes). Flavourful, fleshy palate with ripe tannins, a toasty hint and a suggestion of sweetness.

ABADÍA DE CHIVA 2000 RED
100% tempranillo

77 Dark cherry with a garnet red edge. Powerful aroma of slightly reduced ripe fruit with toasty oak. Flavourful palate with slightly marked tannins and a mild note of overextraction.

CASTILLO DE CHIVA 1998 CRIANZA RED
100% tempranillo

76 Cherry with an orangey hue. Aroma with viscous notes, slightly sweet, quince and very ripe red fruit. Warm palate with suggestions of almost overripe fruit and imperceptible tannins.

MOSCATEL CASTILLO DE CHIVA VINO DE LICOR
100% moscatel

82 Golden. Grapey aroma of sun-drenched skins with notes of honey and orange peel. Sweet palate evoking pâtisserie, slightly pasty, without freshness; slightly warm.

VIÑAS DEL PORTILLO

P.I. El Llano F2 P4
46360 Buñol (Valencia)
☎: 962 504 827 - Fax: 962 500 937
vinasportillo@teleline.es

Established: 1997
⊕ 80 █ 1,000,000 litres ⵌ 200 has.
▟ 20% ⵌ 80%

CASTILLO DE BUÑOL WHITE
CASTILLO DE BUÑOL ROSÉ
AROMA DEL LLANO RED
CASTILLO DE BUÑOL RED
CASTILLO DE BUÑOL CRIANZA RED
CASTILLO DE BUÑOL RESERVA RED

DO VALLE DE GÜÍMAR

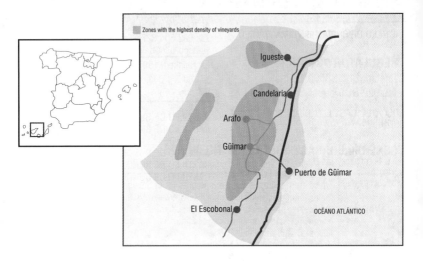

Zones with the highest density of vineyards

Igueste
Candelaria
Arafo
Güimar
Puerto de Güimar
El Escobonal
OCÉANO ATLÁNTICO

NEWS. Half of the barely 20 wines rated reached or surpassed 80 points, which is indicative of the quality. The almost two-week delay in the ripening of the grapes in 2003 with respect to previous years pointed to better quality, which was later confirmed in our tasting. And all this in a bumper harvest: 450,000 kilos controlled by the Regulatory Council, which is an increase of 67% on 2002.

Hectares of Vineyard	No. of Viticulturists	No. of Bodegas	2003 Harvest	2003 Production	Marketing
711.46	899	20	Good	385,000 litres	100% Spain

LOCATION. On the island of Tenerife. It practically constitutes a prolongation of the Valle de la Orotava region to the southeast, forming a valley open to the sea, with the Las Dehesas region situated in the mountains and surrounded by pine forests where the vines grow in an almost Alpine environment. It covers the municipal districts of Arafo, Candelaria and Güímar.

CLIMATE. Although the influence of the trade winds is more marked than in Abona, the significant difference in altitude in a much reduced space must be pointed out, which gives rise to different microclimates, and pronounced contrasts in day-night temperatures, which delays the harvest until 1st November.

SOIL. Volcanic at high altitudes, there is a black tongue of lava crossing the area where the vines are cultivated on a hostile terrain with wooden frames to raise the long vine shoots.

VARIETIES:

White: *Gual, Listán Blanco, Malvasía, Moscatel, Verdello* and *Vijariego.*
Red: *Bastardo Negro, Listán Negro* (15% of total), *Malvasía Rosada, Moscatel Negro, Negramoll, Vijariego Negro, Cabernet Sauvignon, Merlot, Pinot Noir, Ruby Cabernet, Syrah* and *Tempranillo.*

REGULATORY COUNCIL.

Tafetana, 14. 38500 Güímar.
Tel: 922 51 47 09. Fax: 922 51 44 85.
E-mail: consejo@vinosvalleguimar.com
Website: www.vinosvalleguimar.com

GENERAL CHARACTERISTICS OF THE WINES:

Whites	These are the most characteristic product of the area, with more than 80% of the production. They are produced from *Listán Blanco*, and the best stand out for their expressivity, refinement and complexity. They have a pale yellow colour; delicate aromas of flowers and fruit; on the palate they are complex, flavourful and persistent.
Reds	These play a minor role in the overall production. Deep cherry-red coloured, they tend to be fruity with wild nuances; on the palate they are dry, fruity and light.

DO VALLE DEL GÜIMAR

A. RAUL FUENTES BRITO

Príncipe Ruyman, 39-1º Barrio de la Salud
38008 Santa Cruz de Tenerife (Tenerife)
☎: 922 217 788 - Fax: 922 217 788

Established: 1998

🛢 6 ▯ 13,800 litres 🍇 3 has. 🍷 100%

TIZÓN DEL SUR 2003 JOVEN RED

80 Quite dark cherry. Slightly short but clear aroma with adequate skins ripeness (red fruit, blackberries). Dry, flavourful, clear palate with something of a varietal character and better ripeness than other reds from the region.

AGUSTÍN J. HERNÁNDEZ

Carretera General del Sur, 15 - Pájara
38500 Güimar (Tenerife)
☎: 610 707 487

GUIMASOL ROSÉ
GUIMASOL RED

ARCA DE VITIS

Chinguaro, 26 (Barrio San Francisco Javier)
38500 Güimar (Tenerife)
☎: 922 512 552 - Fax: 922 512 552
agrovolcan@telefonica.net
www.arcadevitis.com

Established: 2003

🛢 10 ▯ 35,500 litres 🍇 13 has. 🍷 100%

CONTIEMPO MALVASÍA SECO 2003 ROBLE
JOVEN SECO WHITE
100% malvasía

80 Slightly golden yellow. Aroma with ripe and smoky notes, somewhat fruity. A suggestion of oak on the palate with ripe fruit notes, flavourful and persistent.

CONTIEMPO 2003 OAK AGED SECO WHITE
30% moscatel, 20% güal, 20% marmajuelo, 20% verdello,
10% vijariego

85 Straw-coloured. Fresh, fruity, somewhat musky and grapey aroma. Character on the palate, fresh with fine bitter notes, flavourful and persistent.

CONTIEMPO 2003 SEMISECO WHITE
100% moscatel

82 Straw-coloured. Aroma with grapey, fruity, somewhat musky notes. Retronasal effect on the palate of fragrant herbs and tropical fruit, flavourful, sweet but good acidity.

CONTIEMPO 2003 OAK AGED RED
100% castellana

80 Quite intense cherry. Fruity aroma of ripe skins with a suggestion of notes of scrubland herbs. Somewhat fleshy, flavourful palate with medium fruit expression and a slightly foresty retronasal effect.

CONTIEMPO 2003 RED

COMARCA DE GÜIMAR

Carretera Subida Los Loros, km. 4
38550 Arafo (Tenerife)
☎: 922 510 437 - Fax: 922 510 437
info@bodegacomarcalguimar.com
www.bodegacomarcalguimar.es

Established: 1990

🛢 20 ▯ 600,000 litres 🍷 95%

🌐5%: -DE -US

BRUMAS DE AYOSA 2003 AFRUTADO
WHITE
50% listán blanca, 50% moscatel

83 Straw-coloured. Fresh, fruity aroma with varietal character, notions of terroir and notes of Muscatel well-integrated with the Listán forest herbs. Sweet, supple, fruity and fresh palate, pleasant.

BRUMAS DE AYOSA MALVASÍA 2003
DULCE WHITE
100% malvasía

81 Straw-coloured. Aroma with toasty and ripe notes with a nuance of minerals and tropical fruit. Sweet, unctuous palate with a dry aftertaste of the vine variety, flavourful with a foresty hint.

BRUMAS DE AYOSA 2000 RESERVA BRUT
NATURE
100% listán blanca

80 Straw-coloured. Aroma with notes of yeast, a classic sparkling wine with lees and withered flowers. Generous, dry, flavourful, quite fat palate with yeast, slightly vinous.

BRUMAS DE AYOSA 2001 BRUT NATURE
100% listán blanca

80 Straw-coloured. Fresh, slightly fruity aroma with notes of forest herbs and lees in reduction (toasty). Fresh, dry palate with good lees evolution and foresty hints.

PICO CHO MARCIAL 2001 BRUT NATURE
100% listán blanca

79 Straw-coloured. Aroma with notes of forest herbs, with yeast and nuts. Fresh palate with forest herbs, very dry and quite fat.

BRUMAS DE AYOSA 2003 WHITE
PICO CHO MARCIAL 2003 WHITE
BRUMAS DE AYOSA 2003 ROSÉ
PICO CHO MARCIAL 2003 ROSÉ

BRUMAS DE AYOSA 2003 RED
PICO CHO MARCIAL 2003 RED

EL BORUJO

Carretera de la Cumbre, km. 4, 2
38550 Arafo (Santa Cruz de Tenerife)
☎: 922 511 676 - Fax: 925 513 643
juanfra_f@hotmail.com

Established: 1995

🛢 8,000 litres 🌿 0.5 has. 🍷 100%

EL BORUJO 2003 JOVEN WHITE
95% listán blanca, 5% moscatel

75 Straw-coloured. Fresh aroma of sweet fruit with notes of dried mountain herbs. Dry, somewhat flavourful and fruity palate, only well-mannered.

EL BORUJO 2003 JOVEN RED
100% listán negro

67 Garnet red. Slightly fruity aroma, without nuances. Flat, vegetative palate, discreet.

JOSÉ M. GARCÍA DELGADO

Barranco Las Abejeras
38509 Güimar (Tenerife)
☎: 922 501 797 - Fax: 922 501 797
josemanuelgarciad@yahoo.com

Established: 1991

🛢 12,000.litres 🌿 1.5 has. 🍷 100%

LAS ABEJERAS

JUAN TACORONTE CEJAS

Las Dehesas
38500 Güimar (Tenerife)
☎: 922 513 092 - Fax: 922 513 092

DIVINO WHITE

LA ROCIERA (EL TRINQUE)

Camino Real, 11
38500 Güimar (Santa Cruz de Tenerife)
☎: 922 513 170 - Fax: 922 513 170

Established: 2000

🛢 5,000 litres 🌿 2 has. 🍷 90% 🍇10%

EL TRINQUE 2003 WHITE
EL TRINQUE 2003 ROSÉ

LOS CERCADOS

Ecuador, s/n P M 3º izq. 78
38500 Güimar (Tenerife)

☎: 922 513 092

EL MOLLERO

LUIS OLIVA RODRÍGUEZ

La Hoya, 7 Finca La Mocana
38500 Güimar (Tenerife)
☎: 922 512 039

🌿 3 has.

VIÑA OLIVA WHITE
VIÑA OLIVA ROSÉ
VIÑA OLIVA RED

M. DEL CARMEN HERNÁNDEZ GARCÍA

Obispo Pérez Cáceres, 12
38600 San Isidro (Granadilla)
☎: 922 243 850

🌿 1.5 has.

VIÑA CENLLADA WHITE

MIGUEL ANGEL HERNÁNDEZ

Morras del Tanque
38550 Arafo (Santa Cruz de Tenerife)
☎: 922 511 405 - Fax: 922 290 064
mangel3@comtl.es

Established: 1995

🌐 7 🛢 9,000 litres 🌿 7,000 has.

VIÑAS HERZAS 2002 WHITE
VIÑAS HERZAS 2002 OAK AGED RED

RUPERTO GÓMEZ GÓMEZ

Hoya Cartaya, 32 - Chacona
38500 Güimar (Tenerife)
☎: 922 512 788

LOS PELADOS WHITE

TOMÁS GUZMÁN MESA RODRÍGUEZ

Sosa, 2
38550 Arafo (Tenerife)
☎: 922 510 450

VIÑAS MESA 2003 WHITE

64 Straw-coloured. Aroma with mild reduction off-odours, somewhat fruity. Not very clear palate, reduced and discreet.

VIÑAS MESA 2003 JOVEN RED

69 Quite clear garnet red cherry. Short, imprecise aroma. Flat palate, without fruity nuances, discreet.

VIÑA CHAGUA

Barranco Badajoz-La Ladera
38500 Güimar (Santa Cruz de Tenerife)
☎: 922 511 168 - Fax: 922 511 168
vinachagua@terra.es

Established: 1990

🍷 4 ▮ 80,000 litres 🍇 2 has. 🍷 100%

VIÑA CHAGUA 2003 WHITE
VIÑA CHAGUA 2003 WHITE
VIEJACEPA 2003 OAK AGED RED
VIÑA CHAGUA 2003 RED

VIÑA DEL MACHADO

Camino Hoya Martín - Chogo
38500 Güimar (Santa Cruz de Tenerife)
☎: 922 512 544 - Fax: 922 512 544

Established: 1989

🍷 12 ▮ 50,000 litres 🍇 3 has 🍷 100%

HEREDAMIENTO 2003 JOVEN WHITE
75% listán blanca, 25% malvasía

75 Straw-coloured. Fresh, varietal aroma with notes of forest herbs and a hint of reduction. Dry, fresh palate with acidic overtones, flavourful.

VIÑA MELOSAR 2003 SECO WHITE
100% listán blanca

80 Pale. Fresh, fruity aroma with a certain varietal character, somewhat complex. Fresh, varietal, flavourful palate with good acidity.

VIÑA MELOSAR 2003 SEMISECO WHITE
50% moscatel, 50% malvasía

75 Straw-coloured. Aroma with notes of forest herbs, fruity. Sweet, flavourful, fresh palate with a nuance of aromatic herbs.

VIÑA MELOSAR 2003 JOVEN RED
80% listán negro, 20% tintilla

72 Garnet red cherry. Fresh, slightly fruity aroma, lacking fruit expression with a slightly weak harvest. Light palate without prominent nuances.

HEREDAMIENTO 2003 RED
80% listán negro, 10% syrah, 10% malvasía

70 Quite dark cherry. Aroma with light notes of overripening as well as vegetative notes. Light, slightly flavourful and fresh palate.

DO VALLE DE LA OROTAVA

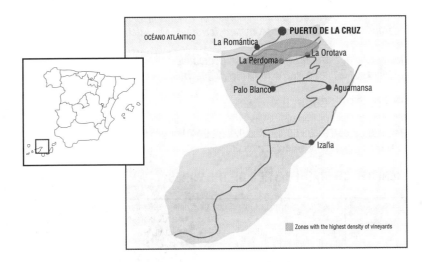

OCÉANO ATLÁNTICO

PUERTO DE LA CRUZ

La Romántica

La Orotava

La Perdoma

Palo Blanco

Aguamansa

Izaña

Zones with the highest density of vineyards

NEWS. In this region, with a similar climate to Tacoronte, the harvest has been significantly better than last year. Of the 29 wines tasted, 18 brands achieved scores above 80 points, whilst in the 2004 edition (which reviewed the 2002 harvest) only 5 wines surpassed this mark. La Orotava leads the DOs of the island in production, with a harvest of almost 3 million kilograms. Noteworthy is the excellent work of the Cecilia Farrais Lorenzo wine cellar (with its Tajinaste brand), especially red wines, two of which surpassed 85 points and have excellent varietal expression.

Hectares of Vineyard	No. of Viticulturists	No. of Bodegas	2003 Harvest	2003 Production	Marketing
679	854	24	Good	887,241 kilos	100% Canary Islands

LOCATION. In the north of the island of Tenerife. It borders to the west with the DO Ycoden-Daute-Isora and to the east with the DO Tacoronte-Acentejo. It extends from the sea to the foot of the Teide, and comprises the municipal districts of La Orotava, Los Realejos and El Puerto de la Cruz.

CLIMATE. As with the other regions on the islands, the weather is conditioned by the trade winds, which in this region result in wines with a moderate alcohol content and a truly Atlantic character. The influence of the Atlantic is also very important, in that it moderates the temperature of the costal areas and provides a lot of humidity. Lastly, the rainfall is rather low, but is generally more abundant on the north face and at higher altitudes.

SOIL. Light, permeable, rich in mineral nutrients and with a slightly acidic pH due to the volcanic nature of the island. The vineyards are at an altitude of between 250 mm and 700 m.

VARIETIES:
White:

Main: *Güal, Malvasía, Verdello, Vijariego.*

Authorized: *Bastardo Blanco, Forastera Blanca (Gomera), Listán Blanco, Marmajuelo, Moscatel, Pedro Ximénez, Torrontés, Moscatel.*

Red:

Main: *Listán Negro, Malvasía Rosada, Negramoll.*

Authorized: *Bastardo Negro, Moscatel Negra, Tintilla, Vijariego Negra.*

REGULATORY COUNCIL.
Casa de la Cultura Rómulo Betancourt. c/ San Juan, 34. 38300 La Orotava.
Tel: 922 32 09 79 / 33 68 42. Fax: 922 32 09 79.
E-mail: orotava@vinos-de-canarias.org

GENERAL CHARACTERISTICS OF THE WINES:

Whites	These are similar to those from Tacoronte in that they share the same Atlantic character. They have a straw yellow colour and are fresh and fruity with somewhat herbaceous notes, and in the best of the examples can reproduce the refinement of fennel or mint.
Rosés	Although the production is much lower, there are some fine examples of modern rosés with a raspberry colour, very fruity aromas, which are fresh and pleasant on the palate.
Reds	These are young wines, with a deep cherry-red colour, good aromatic intensity and notes of red berries in line with their Atlantic character; on the palate they are light, flavourful and pleasant.

DO VALLE DE LA OROTAVA

CECILIA FARRAIS LORENZO

La Habanera, 5 El Ratiño
38300 La Orotava (Tenerife)
☎: 922 308 720 - Fax: 922 308 720
www.vtajinaste.net

Established: 1980
⊞ 12 ▯ 60,000 litres ▽ 1.3 has. ▼ 100%

TAJINASTE 2003 JOVEN WHITE

79 Straw-coloured. Fresh, slightly fruity aroma of wet forest herbs. Fresh, dry, fruity palate, pleasant.

TAJINASTE 2003 JOVEN SEMISECO WHITE

79 Straw-coloured. Fruity aroma with notes of fresh herbs. Sweet notes on the palate but not as sweet as a demi-sec, flavourful.

TAJINASTE 2003 JOVEN RED

84 Intense cherry. Fruity, slightly ripe aroma with something of a fruity and varietal expression (blackberries). A hint of fruit expression on the palate, with typification, flavour and notes of a good maturity, flavourful and well-crafted.

TAJINASTE MACERACIÓN 2003 MACERACIÓN CARBÓNICA RED

85 Quite intense cherry. Medium-intensity aroma with a hint of varietal expression (cherries and red-currants), fresh and fruity. Powerful, fruity, fresh palate with fruit and varietal expression, flavourful.

TAJINASTE 2003 OAK AGED RED

86 Intense cherry. Medium-intensity aroma with a fruity hint and light toasty oak nuances. A hint of fruit on the palate although with less expression than the maceration, slightly more tannic than the other reds (oak), flavourful and more elegant.

EL CALVARIO

Calvario, 39 La Perdoma
38315 La Orotava (Santa Cruz de Tenerife)
☎: 922 308 725 - Fax: 922 308 144
bodegacalvario@telefonica.net

Established: 1926
⊞ 30 ▯ 100,000 litres ▽ 700,002 has. ▼ 100%

VINOS DE HIGA 2003 JOVEN WHITE
VINOS DE HIGA 2002 JOVEN RED
VINOS DE HIGA 2003 OAK AGED RED

EL PENITENTE

La Habanera, 288
38300 La Orotava (Tenerife)
☎: 922 309 024 - Fax: 922 309 710
ventas@bodegasdemiranda.com
www.bodegasdemiranda.com

Established: 1998
⊞ 30 ▯ 245,000 litres ▽ 12 has. ▼ 100%

ARAUTAVA 2003 JOVEN WHITE
100% listán blanca

83 Straw-coloured. Fresh, fruity aroma evoking fresh herbs, very well-crafted. Fresh, oily, elegant and flavourful palate with a varietal retronasal effect, excellent Listán.

BODEGAS DE MIRANDA 2003 WHITE
100% listán blanca

80 Straw-coloured. Slightly short but clear aroma with a suggestion of herbs and fresh fruit. Fresh, flavourful, slightly oily palate, elegant.

BODEGAS DE MIRANDA 2003 SEMISECO WHITE
100% listán blanca

82 Straw-coloured. Fresh aroma of sweet fruit with wet forest herbs. Supple palate with a hint of sweetness that emphasises its qualities, flavourful.

BODEGAS DE MIRANDA 2003 ROSÉ
100% listán negro

82 Raspberry blush. Powerful aroma with copious notes of brambles and strawberries, very fruity. Fresh, aromatic, flavourful palate, dry and harmonious.

ARAUTAVA 2003 FERMENTADO EN BARRICA JOVEN RED
100% listán negro

80 Quite intense cherry. Aroma with balsamic notes (eucalyptus, bay), hints of slightly woody oak and a fruity hint. Dry, flavourful, well-balanced palate, lacking a little varietal expression and grape ripeness.

ARAUTAVA 2003 JOVEN RED
100% listán negro

80 Intense cherry. Slightly toasty aroma with good maturation, black fruit and a slight varietal expression. Fresh, slightly fruity palate, low in nuances.

ARAUTAVA 2003 JOVEN RED
100% tintilla

82 Quite intense cherry. Aroma with a hint of toasty black fruit expression and a mineral and foresty hint. Flavourful, quite fleshy palate with ripe fruit and a slight hint of supple tannins.

BODEGAS DE MIRANDA 2003 JOVEN RED

80 Garnet red cherry. Fruity, fresh aroma with a slight varietal expression. Fresh, light, flavourful palate with varietal character and a balsamic suggestion in the retronasal passage.

DO VALLE DE LA OROTAVA

BODEGAS DE MIRANDA 2003 MACERACIÓN CARBÓNICA RE

82 Quite dark cherry. Aroma with a good expression of the vine variety and hints of slightly ripe skins, fruity. Flavourful, fresh, fruity palate, quite full-bodied.

BODEGAS DE MIRANDA 2003 FERMENTADO EN BARRICA RED

79 Very deep cherry with a violet edge. Powerful, fruity, ripe aroma of toasty oak with quality herbaceous hints. Flavourful palate with ripe fruit and slightly marked tannins, slightly bitter and mineral.

ARAUTAVA 2001 CRIANZA RED
100% listán negro

84 Quite intense cherry. Aroma with good varietal expression and fine notes of oak well-integrated with the wine (damp earth, redcurrants), elegant. Round palate quite expressive, flavourful with predominant oak tannins.

EL VALLE

Carretera de Medianía, 156
38400 La Orotava (Tenerife)
☎: 922 213 813 - Fax: 922 213 477
Established: 1993
⊕ 40 ▯ 150,000 litres ☙ 1 has. ▜ 100%

VIÑA EL VALLE WHITE
VIÑA EL VALLE ROSÉ
VIÑA EL VALLE RED
SEÑORÍO DEL VALLE RED

ERAS DEL MARQUÉS

Higa San Jerónimo, 3. La Perdoma
38315 La Orotava (Tenerife)
☎: 922 308 760 - Fax: 922 343 785
Established: 1993
▯ 60,000 litres ☙ 2 has.

BODEGA ERAS DEL MARQUÉS 2003 RED

FINCA LA SIERRA

Carretera General La Torrita, 64
38310 La Orotava (Tenerife)
☎: 922 330 677 - Fax: 922 330 677

FINCA LA SIERRA RED

HORACIO LLANOS DÉVORA

Carretera El Mocan, 57
38411 Los Realejos (Santa Cruz Tenerife)
☎: 922 343 148

Established:

VINOS LOS LLANOS WHITE
VINOS LOS LLANOS RED

JUAN E. LUIS BRAVO

Cancela, 14
38300 La Orotava (Tenerife)
☎: 922 335 548 - Fax: 922 335 548

TREVIÑA RED

LOS GÜINES

Pista Los Guines, s/n
38410 Los Realejos (Tenerife)
☎: 922 353 865 - Fax: 922 353 855
Established: 1986
⊕ 18 ▯ 45,000 litres ▜ 100%

LOS GÜINES 2003 JOVEN SEMISECO WHITE

70 Straw-coloured. Aroma with slight off-odours from reduction in the tank (late racking), somewhat fruity. Dry palate without great nuances, underripe grapes.

LOS GÜINES 2003 JOVEN RED

67 Quite clear garnet red. Aroma with a slight off-odour (high airing) and weak fruit. Flat, without nuances and slightly fruity on the palate.

LOS GÜINES 2003 ROSÉ

MIGUEL LUIS GONZÁLEZ GONZÁLEZ

Taoro s/n
38300 La Orotava (Tenerife)
☎: 922 322 032 - Fax: 922 320 129

VIÑA ESPALDERA RED

MONTESCLAROS

Carretera El Mocán, 12
38411 Los Realejos (Tenerife)
☎: 922 340 629

MONTESCLAROS WHITE

MONTIJO

Camino Montijo, 24
38300 La Orotava (Tenerife)
☎: 922 301 250 - Fax: 922 302 536
karincanarias@jazzfree.com

25 🍷 185,000 litres 🍷 100%

MONTIJO WHITE
MONTIJO RED

RAIMUNDO J. HERNÁNDEZ JORGE

Hacienda Perdida, 20
38300 La Orotava (Tenerife)
☎: 922 219 171 - Fax: 922 332 043

HACIENDA PERDIDA RED

ROTER OROTAVA

Avenida Fernando Alonso de Lugo, 2
38300 La Orotava (Tenerife)
☎: 922 326 481 - Fax: 922 324 454

BALCÓN DEL VALLE WHITE
BALCÓN DEL VALLE RED

Vinos TAFURIASTE

Las Candias Altas, 11
38312 La Orotava (Tenerife)
☎: 922 335 978 - Fax: 922 336 027

VINOS TAFURIASTE WHITE
VINOS TAFURIASTE ROSÉ
VINOS TAFURIASTE RED

VALLEORO

Ctra. Gral La Oratova - Los Realejos, km. 4.5
38315 La Pedoma (Santa Cruz de Tenerife)
☎: 922 308 600 - Fax: 922 308 233
info@bodegavalleoro.com
www.bodegavalleoro.com
Established: 1988
150 🍷 1,000,000 litres 🍇 120 has.
🍷 100%

GRAN TEHYDA 2003 AFRUTADO WHITE
100% listán blanca

83 Straw-coloured. Aroma with an abundance of varietal expression and with a suggestion of aromatic herbs (mint, fennel, lavender). Fresh, light, flavourful palate with an excellent sweet hint in harmony with the acidity.

VALLEORO 2003 AFRUTADO WHITE
100% listán blanca

82 Straw-coloured. Fresh, fruity aroma with a suggestion of fragrant herbs, clear. Generous, flavourful palate with a suggestion of herbs and tropical fruit, persistent.

GRAN TEHYDA 2003 JOVEN WHITE
100% listán blanca

81 Straw-coloured. Fresh, fruity aroma with a suggestion of fragrant herbs. Light, fresh, flavourful palate with sweet fruit (custard apples) and fragrant herbs, flavourful.

VALLEORO TRADICIÓN 2003 FERMENTADO EN BARRICA WHITE
100% listán blanco

78 Pale. Fresh, fruity aroma with slightly pronounced toasty notes of lees. Dry, fresh, fruity palate.

GRAN TEHYDA 2003 ROSÉ
100% listán negro

80 Raspberry. Fresh, fruity aroma with varietal notes. Fruity palate with varietal and balsamic notes.

GRAN TEHYDA 2003 RED
100% listán negro

75 Lively garnet red. Slightly short, clear aroma, concealed fruit (difficult harvest). Supple, fresh, slightly fruity palate, flavourful and with slightly low acidity.

VALLEORO 2003 JOVEN RED
100% listán negro

70 Garnet red. Imprecise aroma with scarcely any fruit. Flat palate, weak harvest, without nuances.

GRAN TEHYDA 2003 MACERACIÓN CARBÓNICA RED
100% listán negro

79 Quite dark cherry. Not very intense aroma for a c. maceration with a clean fruity hint and something of a varietal character. Fruity, fresh, flavourful palate.

VALLEORO TRADICCIÓN 2003 ROBLE RED

74 Garnet red. Fresh, fruity aroma with a good wood assemblage. Fresh, fruity, slightly flavourful palate.

VALLEORO ESPUMOSO 2000 BRUT
100% listán blanca

79 Straw-coloured. Fresh aroma of aged lees with foresty notes and yeast. Fresh palate with a strong carbonic hint and a slightly vinous suggestion.

GRAN TEHYDA 2001 CRIANZA RED
VALLEORO ESPUMOSO BRUT NATURE

VIÑA MARZAGANA

Calvario, 2 Icod el Alto
38411 Los Realejos (Tenerife)
☎: 922 359 195 - Fax: 922 340 342

VIÑA MARZAGANA 2003 ROSÉ

75 Brilliant raspberry with a coppery hue. Quite intense, fruity aroma with hints of petals and light

DO VALLE DE LA OROTAVA

reduction. Slightly better on the palate, flavourful with spicy hints of skins, a slightly oily texture and a slightly sweet suggestion of fruit.

VIÑA MARZAGANA WHITE
VIÑA MARZAGANA RED

VIÑA MOCAN

Carretera General de Palo Blanco, s/n
38411 Los Realejos (Tenerife)
☎: 922 330 684 - Fax: 922 330 684

Established: 1973
🛢 5 📦 160,000 litres 🍇 12 has.

VIÑA EL MOCÁN AFRUTADO WHITE
VIÑA EL MOCÁN AFRUTADO SEMIDULCE WHITE
VIÑA EL MOCÁN AFRUTADO ROSÉ
VIÑA EL MOCÁN AFRUTADO RED

VIÑA PIÑERA

Carretera Palo Blanco, 93
38411 Los Realejos (Tenerife)
☎: 922 342 803 - Fax: 922 249 939

VIÑA PIÑERA 2003 JOVEN WHITE

80 Straw-coloured. Fresh, fruity aroma with nuances of green herbs and tropical fruit. Light, fresh, fruity palate, pleasant and with varietal character.

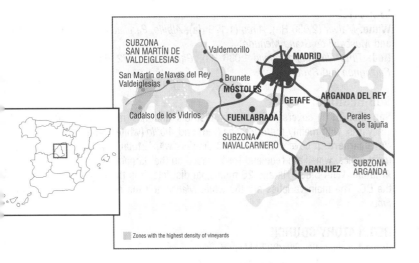

SUBZONA SAN MARTÍN DE VALDEIGLESIAS

Valdemorillo

MADRID

San Martín de Valdeiglesias — Navas del Rey

Brunete

MÓSTOLES

GETAFE

ARGANDA DEL REY

Cadalso de los Vidrios

FUENLABRADA

Perales de Tajuña

SUBZONA NAVALCARNERO

ARANJUEZ

SUBZONA ARGANDA

Zones with the highest density of vineyards

NEWS. Although the frosts did not affect the vineyards in Madrid during the spring, and a good harvest was expected for 2003, the hot summer finally caused the harvest to be brought forward which resulted in a reduction of 30% with respect to the 2002 harvest, accompanied by a certain loss in acidity. The only good effect of the heat was that the grapes did not contract any diseases and entered the cellars in excellent health. The Regulatory Council has already confirmed the definite incorporation of the *Moscatel de Grano Menudo* and the *Syrah*, the latter already present as a fundamental grape variety in two wines of Bodegas Jeromín, and which are amongst the best rated in the region: Grego and Manu.

Hectares of Vineyard	No. of Viticulturists	No. of Bodegas	2003 Harvest	2003 Production	Marketing
11,591	3,084	37	Very Good	-	80% Spain 20% export

With the *Garnacha* giving ground (only two wines based on this variety surpassed 80 points), the *Tempranillo* from Madrid was the most outstanding as regards quality, whether in single-variety wines or blended with the main foreign varieties (*Cabernet Sauvignon, Merlot* and *Syrah*) which are finally reaching a certain age and quality in the vineyards of the capital.

LOCATION. In the south of the province of Madrid, it covers three distinct sub-regions: Arganda, Navalcarnero and San Martín de Valdeiglesias.

CLIMATE. Extreme continental, with cold winters and hot summers. The average annual rainfall ranges from 461 mm in Arganda to 658 mm in San Martín.

SOIL. Rather unfertile soil and granite subsoil in the sub-region of San Martín de Valdeiglesias; in Navalcarnero the soil is brownish-grey, poor, with a subsoil of coarse sand and clay; in the sub-region of Arganda the soil is brownish-grey, with an acidic pH and granite subsoil.

VARIETIES:

White: *Malvar* (2,056 Ha), *Airén* (1,179 Ha), *Albillo, Parellada, Macabeo, Torrontés* and *Moscatel de Grano Menudo.*
Red: *Tinto Fino* (*Tempranillo* 1,036 Ha), *Garnacha* (2,772 Ha), *Merlot, Cabernet Sauvignon* and *Syrah.*

SUB-REGIONS:

San Martín. It covers 9 municipal districts and has more than 3,821 Ha of vineyards, with mainly the *Garnacha* (red) and *Albillo* (white) varieties.
Navalcarnero. It covers 19 municipal districts with a total of about 2,107 Ha. The most typical wines are reds and rosés based on the Garnacha variety.
Arganda. With 5,830 Ha and 26 municipal districts, it is the largest sub-region of the DO. The main varieties are the white *Malvar* and the red *Tempranillo* or *Tinto Fino.*

REGULATORY COUNCIL.

Bravo Murillo, 101, 3º. 28020 Madrid.
Tel: 915 348 511 / 7 240. Fax: 915 538 574.
E-mail: consejo@vinosdemadrid.es
Website: www.vinosdemadrid.es

GENERAL CHARACTERISTICS OF THE WINES:

Whites	The most characteristic are those produced from *Malvar* in the sub-region of Arganda. Fruity and pleasant, on occasion they have wild notes; on the palate they are fresh, flavourful and supple. They are also produced from traditional 'sobremadre' wines (they follow a barrelling process with the skins lasting about three months) and, in line with more modern trends, white wines fermented in barrels.
Rosés	Mainly produced from *Garnacha*, they have a pink colour; on the nose they are fresh, powerful and fruity; on the palate, they have the tastiness typical of this variety.
Reds	Firstly, there are those produced from *Tinto Fino*, mainly from Arganda. They are mostly young wines, light and fruity, in line with the wines from La Mancha. In Navalcarnero and San Martín, the *Garnacha* variety is used. In the latter area, the aromas and flavours of the red wines are concentrated, with a character of ripe fruit, earthy notes, meaty and flavourful on the palate.

Bodega Ecológica ANDRÉS MORATE

Camino del Horcajuelo, s/n
28390 Belmonte de Tajo (Madrid)
☎: 918 747 165 - Fax: 918 747 165
bodegas@andresmorate.com
andresmorate.com

Established: 1999

🛢 12 🛢 90,000 litres 🍇 18 has.

🍷 40% 🌐 60%: -DE

VIÑA BOSQUERA 2003 WHITE
100% airén

75 Straw-coloured. Short, clear, fresh, slightly fruity aroma. Supple palate with a hint of sweetness, flavourful.

VIÑA BOSQUERA 2002 OAK AGED RED
100% tempranillo 🛢 6

86 Garnet red cherry. Intense, concentrated aroma, with predominant fruit notes over fine toasty oak. Powerful, flavourful palate with a nuance of sweet fruit and ripe and oily tannins, spicy, long.

VIÑA BOSQUERA 2003 RED
100% tempranillo

85 Intense cherry with a violet rim. Powerful, fruity aroma with excellent varietal expression (black fruit, underbrush). Powerful, concentrated palate with grape tannins of an excellent quality, spicy notes of skins and a hint of jammy fruit, excellent acidity.

Cooperativa de ARGANDA

Los Silos, 21
28500 Arganda del Rey (Madrid)
☎: 918 710 201 - Fax: 918 710 201

Established: 1952

🛢 200 🛢 3,000,000 litres 🍇 700 has.

VIÑA RENDERO 2002 OAK AGED RED
100% tempranillo

75 Cherry with a coppery glint. Intense, spicy and ripe aroma with a suggestion of mild reduction. Dry, flavourful palate with bitter notes (nutty overtones), good acidity.

VIÑA RENDERO SELECCIÓN ESPECIAL 2002 OAK AGED RED
100% tempranillo

73 Intense cherry with a brick red edge. Intense aroma with notes of oak over a hint of red stone fruit and a suggestion of reduction, slightly warm. Slightly flavourful palate with drying tannins, a hint of sweet fruit and dark-roasted flavours, lacking balance.

CASTEJÓN

Ronda de Watres, 29
28500 Arganda del Rey (Madrid)
☎: 918 710 264 - Fax: 918 713 343
castejon@bodegascastejon.com
www.bodegascastejon.com

Established: 1959

🛢 1,200 🛢 4,000,000 litres 🍇 62 has.

🍷 90% 🌐 10%

VIÑA REY "70 BARRICAS" 2003 OAK AGED RED
100% tempranillo

85 Garnet red cherry. Powerful, ripe aroma of well-integrated fruit and oak with a spicy nuance of oak and prune stones. Flavourful palate with very complementary fruit and oak; notes of coffee and liquorice in the retronasal passage.

VIÑA REY TEMPRANILLO 2003 RED
100% tempranillo

83 Intense cherry with a violet edge. Powerful, fruity, ripe aroma with overtones of tannin and acidity freshness and varietal expression (underbrush). Flavourful palate with slightly marked grape tannins and a spicy nuance of skins.

DON ÁLVARO DE LUNA

Carretera de Avila s/n
28680 San Martín de Valdeiglesias (Madrid)
☎: 918 676 007 - Fax: 918 610 272
alva2@donalvarodeluna.com
www.bodegadonalvarodeluna.com

Established: 1960

🛢 250 🛢 6,000,000 litres 🍇 1,800 has.

🍷 95% 🌐 5%

QVOD 1 GARNACHA JOVEN ROSÉ
100% garnacha

84 Fairly deep brilliant raspberry. Not very intense aroma, with good varietal expression (red stone fruit, spicy notes). Fresh, flavourful palate with spicy notes of skins, good acidity.

1434 TEMPRANILLO 2003 CRIANZA RED
100% tempranillo

84 Lively garnet red cherry. Aroma with foresty notes, ripe fruit and a slight varietal expression. Fresh, fruity palate with foresty notes, slightly varietal.

QVOD 1 ALBILLO 2003 WHITE
NOVUSS ALBILLO 2003 WHITE
1434 ALBILLO VARIETAL 2003 ROBLE
 WHITE
NOVUSS 2003 JOVEN ROSÉ

QVOD 1 GARNACHA TEMPRANILLO 2003 RED
ANDREVO GARNACHA 2003 RED
NOVUSS GARNACHA 2003 RED
QVOD 1 GARNACHA TEMPRANILLO 2003 RED
1434 GARNACHA 2001 CRIANZA RED

EL ARCO

Camino de San Juan, 7
28380 Colmenar de Oreja (Madrid)
☎: 918 943 150 - Fax: 918 938 691

Established: 1974
⊕ 80 🍾 2,000,000 litres
🍇 600 has. 🍷 100%

CANTERAS WHITE
CANTERAS RED
EL ARCO CRIANZA RED

FIGUEROA

Convento, 19
28380 Colmenar de Oreja (Madrid)
☎: 918 944 859

Established: 1962
🍾 150,000 litres 🍇 15 has.

FIGUEROA WHITE
FIGUEROA OAK AGED RED

Bodegas FRANCISCO CASAS

San Cosme, 6
28600 Navalcarnero (Madrid)
☎: 918 110 207 - Fax: 918 110 798
f.casas@bodegascasas.com
www.bodegascasas.com

Established: 1965
⊕ 400 🍾 2,000,000 litres 🍷 50% 🌐50%

TOCHUELO 2003 WHITE
100% malvar

80 Straw-coloured. Intense aroma with fine notes of ripe white fruit and overtones of freshness. Flavourful palate with rich bitter notes over a nuance of fruit, good acidity.

TOCHUELO 2003 ROSÉ
100% garnacha

79 Salmon with a coppery glint. Somewhat intense, ripe aroma with red stone fruit and good varietal expression (spices). Dry, fresh palate with fine bitter notes and a suggestion of spices and red fruit.

LOS CAMINILLOS 2003 ROSÉ
100% garnacha

75 Brilliant salmon. Not very intense aroma with a suggestion of fresh fruit. Fresh palate with bitter notes, without subtle nuances, good acidity, pleasant.

LOS CAMINILLOS 2003 RED
50% garnacha, 50% tempranillo

80 Intense cherry. Fresh, fruity aroma with good varietal expression (black fruit, a nuance of underbrush). Flavourful, fresh palate with slightly marked grape tannins and hints of sun-drenched skins, good acidity.

TOCHUELO TEMPRANILLO-GARNACHA 2003 RED
75% garnacha, 25% tempranillo

77 Fairly deep cherry. Intense, ripe aroman with spicy hints of Garnacha. Flavourful palate with slightly marked grape tannins, elevated acidity and overtones of warmth.

Bodegas del FRESNO

Finca Navayuncosa
28620 Aldea del fresno (Madrid)
☎: 915 421 504

DEHESA NAVAYUNCOSA 2003 JOVEN ROSÉ
100% garnacha

77 Raspberry with a coppery glint. Intense, ripe aroma of red stone fruit with a nuance of sweetness and hints of glue. Flavourful, fleshy, slightly unctuous, very warm palate with bitter notes, lacking balance.

DO VINOS DE MADRID

DEHESA NAVAYUNCOSA 2002 OAK AGED RED

88 Dark garnet red cherry. Complex aroma with a suggestion of minerals and fine lees with toasty oak nuances. Round palate with supple and warm tannins, flavourful and mineral.

Bodegas y Viñedos GOSÁLBEZ ORTI

Real, 14
28813 Pozuelo del Rey (Madrid)
☎: 918 725 399 - Fax: 918 725 202
bodega@bodegagosalbezorti.com
www.bodegagosalbezorti.com

Established: 2000

🌐 33 📦 21,300 litres 🍇 10 has.

🍷 95% 🍷5%: -US -DE -BE

QUBÉL 2001 CRIANZA RED
tempranillo

91 Intense cherry. Powerful aroma, rich in toasty creamy notes of oak (coffee and cocoa) with fresh ripe fruit. Generous, fleshy, powerful, flavourful palate, rich in fruit expression and wood, flavourful and ripe tannins.

QUBÉL 2002 OAK AGED RED
80% tempranillo, 10% syrah, 10% cabernet sauvignon
🌐 10

84 Very deep garnet red cherry. Powerful, ripe aroma of black fruit over a hint of well-integrated oak. Powerful, flavourful palate with slightly drying yet promising oak tannins, a nuance of ripe fruit and hints of spices and chocolate.

JESÚS DÍAZ

Convento, 38
28380 Colmenar de Oreja (Madrid)
☎: 918 943 378 - Fax: 918 944 585
bodegasjdiaz@interbook.net

Established: 1898

🌐 60 📦 450,000 litres 🍇 8 has.

🍷 90% 🍷10%

JESÚS DÍAZ WHITE

79 Straw-coloured with coppery hues. Not very intense aroma with a fine suggestion of white fruit and overtones of freshness. Dry, flavourful palate with notes of sun-drenched skins and dried herbs, good acidity, pleasant.

JESÚS DÍAZ 2003 ROSÉ

82 Fairly deep raspberry. Intense, ripe aroma with a nuance of sweet red fruit and spicy hints of skins. Dry, flavourful, slightly warm palate with hints of red stone fruit, very pleasant.

JESÚS DÍAZ 2003 RED

80 Garnet red cherry. Not very intense aroma with notes of ripe stone fruit and a spicy nuance of skins. Fresh, flavourful palate with slightly marked grape tannins but with a hint of sweetness, spicy, very rich.

HEREDAD TORRESANO 2001 CRIANZA RED

80 Garnet red cherry with a brick red edge. Intense, ripe aroma with reduction notes (varnishes, leathers) and a hint of ripe fruit, slightly sweet. Flavourful, fleshy palate with ripe oak tannins well-integrated with the fruit, warm hints, spicy, pleasant.

JULIO HERRERA SOLERA

Arco, 14
28380 Colmenar de Oreja (Madrid)
☎: 918 943 407 - Fax: 915 720 372

Established: Mitad s. XIX

🌐 7 📦 90,000 litres 🍇 18 has. 🍷 100%

JULIO HERRERO JOVEN WHITE
JULIO HERRERO RED
MOURIZ VIÑAS VIEJAS RED
MOURIZ CRIANZA RED

Cooperativa Nuestra Señora de
LA SOLEDAD

Paseo Avilés nº 2
28607 El Álamo (Madrid)
☎: 915 120 462 - Fax: 918 120 462
Established: 1964
▤ 2,000,000 litres

VALFRÍO WHITE
VALFRÍO ROSÉ
VALFRÍO RED

Bodega Ecológica LUIS SAAVEDRA

Plaza de los Caños, 70
28650 Cenicientos (Madrid)
☎: 918 642 896 - Fax: 916 893 400
alonso1986@wanadooadsl.net
www.bodegasaavedra.com
Established: 1996
⬡ 50 ▤ 38,500 litres 🍇 16 has.
🍷 60% 🌐40%

CORUCHO ALBILLO-MOSCATEL 2002
FERMENTADO EN BARRICA WHITE
85% albillo, 15% moscatel de grano menudo

84 Golden with a reddish glint. Slightly musky aroma of ripe fruit with nutty notes (toasty almonds). Powerful, sweet, very flavourful and warm palate with Muscatel in the retronasal passage. Better than the previous vintage.

LUIS SAAVEDRA 2002 RED
garnacha, tinto fino

88 Quite lively garnet red cherry. Aroma with fresh fruit notes, nuances of minerals and good grape ripeness. Medium-bodied palate with presence of fruit and wood, flavourful with a suggestion of finesse in the finish.

CORUCHO ECOLÓGICO 2001 OAK AGED RED
CORUCHO ECOLÓGICO 2002 OAK AGED RED
CORUCHO ECOLÓGICO 2002 OAK AGED RED

ORUSCO

Alcalá, 54
28511 Valdilecha (Madrid)
☎: 918 738 006 - Fax: 918 738 336
bodegasorusco@servicom.com
Established: 1896
⬡ 130 ▤ 2,300,000 litres 🍇 9 has.
🍷 85% 🌐15%

VIÑA MAÍN 2003 WHITE

80 Straw-coloured. Fresh, fruity aroma with herbaceous notes. Fresh, fruity, light, flavourful palate, with character.

VIÑA MAÍN 2003 ROSÉ
100% tempranillo

80 Brilliant raspberry. Intense, very fruity aroma with fine spicy notes of skins and excellent varietal expression (berries, juniper, underbrush), ripe. Dry, flavourful palate with ripe grape tannins, a nuance of sweetness and spices in the retronasal passage.

MAÍN 2001 JOVEN RED

78 Intense cherry. Aroma with mild vegetative with overtones of phenolic immaturity. Palate with a suggestion of sweetness, jammy, very ripe, slightly viscous.

VIÑA MAÍN 2003 JOVEN RED
100% tempranillo

83 Fairly deep cherry with a violet edge and carbonic hints. Intense, fruity aroma with excellent varietal expression. Fresh palate with very flavourful grape tannins and a suggestion of ripe fruit, good acidity.

MAÍN 2002 ROBLE RED
tempranillo

79 Deep cherry with a coppery glint. Intense aroma with spicy notes of oak, a ripe fruit nuance and a hint of mild reduction. Flavourful, fleshy, slightly warm palate with drying hints of oak, pleasant.

MAÍN 2001 CRIANZA RED
100% tempranillo

84 Very deep garnet red cherry. Intense aroma with well-integrated oak and fruit, overtones of finnesse and varietal expression. Powerful palate with slightly drying oak tannins, a hint of ripe red fruit (prunes) and a spicy and creamy effect in the retronasal passage, good acidity.

PABLO MORATE-MUSEO
DEL VINO

Avenida Generalísimo, 30 - 31
28391 Valdelaguna (Madrid)
☎: 918 937 172 - Fax: 918 937 172
Established: 1873
⬡ 60 ▤ 550,000 litres 🍇 16 has.
🍷 95% 🌐5%

VIÑA CHOZO 2003 WHITE

75 Straw-coloured. Fresh, fruity aroma. Light, fruity palate, well-mannered.

VIÑA CHOZO 2003 ROSÉ
100% tempranillo

79 Blush with a coppery glint. Intense, ripe aroma with spicy notes of skins and hints of fine reduction. Flavourful, slightly fleshy, warm and spicy palate; a suggestion of sweetness, good acidity.

SEÑORÍO DE MORATE GRAN SELECCIÓN 2001 CRIANZA RED
tempranillo

79 Garnet red cherry with a brick red edge. Intense, ripe aroma with predominant toasty notes of oak and a suggestion of reduction. Flavourful palate with slightly drying tannins, warm.

SEÑORÍO DE MORATE GRAN SELECCIÓN 2000 CRIANZA RED
tempranillo

80 Garnet red cherry with a saffron edge. Intense, ripe aroma with toasty oak notes over a suggestion of fruit and varietal hints. Flavourful palate with good crianza expression (leathers); well-integrated wood/fruit, good acidity.

SEÑORÍO DE MORATE GRAN SELECCIÓN 1999 RESERVA RED
tempranillo

82 Garnet red cherry with a brick red edge. Intense aroma with spicy notes of oak, a hint of jammy prunes and fine reduction notes. Flavourful palate with good crianza expression, ripe and slightly oily tannins, good acidity.

Bodegas y Viñedos
PEDRO GARCÍA CARRERO

Soledad, 10
28380 Colmenar de Oreja (Madrid)
☎: 918 943 278 - Fax: 918 942 589

Established: 1931
⊞ 25 ▤ 500,000 litres ☙ 35 has.
⬗ 80% ◔20%

VIÑA EL CARRASCAL 2002 WHITE
ISLA DE SAN PEDRO 2002 RED
ISLA DE SAN PEDRO ECOLÓGICO 2003 RED
ISLA DE SAN PEDRO 1999 CRIANZA RED
ISLA DE SAN PEDRO 2000 RESERVA RED

Bodegas **PERAL (LUIS ANTONIO PERAL HEREZA)**

Bajada de las Monjas, 4
28380 Colmenar de Oreja (Madrid)
☎: 918 943 237 - Fax: 918 943 237
Established: 1866
⊞ 15 ▤ 500,000 litres ☙ 10 has. ⬗ 100%

PERAL 2003 WHITE
malvar

76 Straw-coloured with a golden hue. Intense, quite fruity aroma with reduction overtones, hints of lees and characteristic spices of over-ripening. Fresh, dry and flavourful palate with carbonic, spicy and herby hints, good acidity.

PERAL 2003 ROSÉ

77 Pale blush. Intense, spicy aroma with hints of withered petals, without fruit expression. Flavourful, fresh palate with fine bitter notes, slightly warm with good acidity.

LA MENINA RED
tinto fino

78 Garnet red cherry with a violet edge. Powerful aroma of slightly reduced ripe fruit, spices and terroir. Flavourful palate with fresh overtones, hints of cocoa, terracotta and fine bitter notes.

PERAL 2003 RED
tinto fino

76 Medium-hue cherry. with a coppery nuance. Quite intense aroma of red stone fruit with hints of flowers and lees. Fresh, light palate with a hint of terracotta and bitterness, slightly warm.

RICARDO BENITO

Las Eras, 5
28600 Navalcarnero (Madrid)
☎: 918 110 097 - Fax: 918 112 663
bodega@ricardobenito.com
www.ricardobenito.com

Established: 1940
⊞ 800 ▤ 2,500,000 litres ☙ 50 has.
⬗ 80% ◔20%

DUAN 2003 RED

84 Brilliant garnet red cherry. Fine aroma, creamy toasty flavours (cocoa), quite fresh fruit and hints of ripe skins. Fruity, clean aroma, medium-bodied, very well-balanced, flavourful palate, good acidity and freshness, a good wine for everyday consumption.

DIVO GRAN VINO DE GUARDA 2002 RED

90 Intense cherry. Aroma with fine notes of toasty oak (coffee, chocolate), hints of ripe fruit and slightly fresh red fruit nuances, mineral notes, terroir. Fleshy, full palate, drier but ripe and persistent tannins, elegant although with a close nuance in the retronasal passage. Will improve in bottle.

ASIDO VINO DE GUARDA RED

86 Dark garnet red cherry. Aroma with toasty and mineral notes and forest fruity hints. Fruity, flavourful palate, good clean oak tannins, a complex retronasal effect, fresh fruit.

DIVO GRAN VINO DE GUARDA 2000 RED

92 Intense cherry. Mineral aroma, black fruit, complex, fine toasty oak (coffee, chocolate). Warm palate, sweet tannins, powerful, slightly spirituous, good acidity, generous palate.

SAN ANDRÉS DE VILLAREJO DE SALVANÉS

Valdelaguna, s/n
28590 Villarejo de Salvanés (Madrid)
☎: 918 744 597 - Fax: 918 744 597

Established: 1961

🛢 4,051,800 litres 🍇 900 has. 🌰 100%

SAN ANDRÉS WHITE
SAN ANDRÉS RED

Sociedad Agraria de Transformación
SAN ESTEBAN PROTOMÁRTIR

Plaza de los Caños, 30
28650 Cenicientos (Madrid)
☎: 918 642 487 - Fax: 918 642 487

Established: 1959

🛢 200 🛢 3,100,000 litres

PIEDRA ESCRITA 2002 ROSÉ

68 Raspberry with a coppery glint. Not very intense aroma with reduction off-odours (varnishes). Dry, slightly flavourful, warm palate with poor fruit expression.

PIEDRA ESCRITA 2003 RED

74 Cherry with a saffron edge. Not very intense aroma of ripe fruit with a mild hint of reduction and spicy hints of skins. Dry palate with slightly marked tannins, bitter notes, without great fruit expression.

SAN ISIDRO DE BELMONTE

Avenida Felipe Serrano, 9
28390 Belmonte de Tajo (Madrid)
☎: 918 747 234 - Fax: 918 747 234
vinoscerravin@eresmas.com

Established: 1956

🛢 2,200,000 litres 🍇 400 has. 🌰 100%

VINOS CERRAVIN WHITE
VINOS CERRAVIN ROSÉ
VINOS CERRAVIN RED

Bodegas TAGONIUS

Carretera Ambite, km. 44
28550 Tielmes (Madrid)
☎: 918 737 505 - Fax: 918 746 161

Established: 2000

🛢 320 🛢 850,000 litres 🍇 5 has.
🌰 90% 🌍 10%: -BE

TAGONIUS 2002 ROBLE RED
tempranillo, cabernet sauvignon, merlot, syrah

86 Very deep garnet red cherry. Powerful aroma with toasty and creamy notes of oak over a suggestion of ripe fruit. Flavourful palate with slightly marked yet promising oak tannins, a hint of jammy fruit and notions of liquorice.

TAGONIUS GRAN VINO SELECCIÓN 2000 ROBLE RED
cabernet sauvignon, tempranillo, syrah

92 Intense cherry. Aroma with good fruit and mineral expression, fine and creamy toasty wood (chocolate, dark-roasted flavors) and very ripe fruit. Full, generous palate rich in powerful and ripe tannins, slightly warm and spirituous with a mineral retronasal effect, excellent Madrid red wine.

TAGONIUS 2000 CRIANZA RED
tempranillo, cabernet sauvignon, syrah

89 Intense cherry. Complex aroma with mineral notes, very ripe fruit and fine toasty wood (dark-roasted flavour) Fleshy, flavourful palate, rich in ripe fruit and fine toasty oak tannins.

TIKUAH 2003 RED
TIKUAH 2000 CRIANZA RED

VALLE DEL SOL

Ctra. de Cadalso de los Vidrios, km. 0.3
28600 Navalcarnero (Madrid)
☎: 918 110 926 - Fax: 918 110 926

🍷 120 📗 4,000,000 litres
🍇 1,200 has. 🍷 100%

ANTÏNOS 2003 WHITE
100% malvar

80 Pale yellow with a golden glint. Aroma with notes of white fruit, overtones of freshness (acidity, fruit stone) and spicy hints of skins. Flavourful palate with fine bitter notes, good acidity.

ANTÏNOS 2003 ROSÉ
100% garnacha

78 Brilliant cherry. Intense, ripe aroma with spicy hints of skins and slight overtones of reduction. Flavourful, fruity palate with overtones of varietal freshness, good acidity.

ANTÏNOS 2003 ROBLE RED
100% cabernet sauvignon   🛢 6

74 Very deep garnet red cherry. Intense, ripe aroma with a suggestion of spicy oak. Flavourful palate with marked tannins, scarce varietal expression and a sweetish suggestion of oak and overripe grapes (pitch).

VALDECEPA 2003 RED
100% garnacha

77 Garnet red cherry. Quite intense, ripe aroma with warm hints and scarce varietal expression. Flavourful palate with ripe black fruit, and slightly marked grape tannins well-integrated with the fruit, lacking acidity.

VALLE DEL SOL "PREMIUM" 2001 RED
100% tempranillo

85 Dark cherry. Powerful aroma rich in fine oak notes (coffee, chocolate) and ripe but quite expressive fruit. Warm, flavourful, round palate with ripe fruit and ripe tannins.

VINOS JEROMÍN

San José, 8
28590 Villarejo de Salvanés (Madrid)
☎: 918 742 030 - Fax: 918 744 139
vinosjeromin@telefonica.net
www.vinosjeromin.com

Established: 1956

🍷 700 📗 4,000,000 litres 🍇 50 has.
🍷 75% 🌐25%: -DE -FR -UK -US -CH -DK -BE -SE

VEGA MADROÑO 2003 WHITE
50% airén, 50% malvar

75 Straw-coloured. Fresh, not very intense aroma, without great character. Fruity, light, flavourful palate, well-mannered.

PUERTA DE ALCALÁ 2003 ROSÉ
85% tempranillo, 15% garnacha

77 Blush. Fresh, fruity aroma (strawberries, blackberries) of medium-intensity. Slightly flavourful, vinous, fruity.

VEGA MADROÑO 2003 ROSÉ
50% tempranillo, 30% garnacha, 20% malvar

75 Raspberry. Not very intense aroma with overtones of freshness and a nuance of ripe red fruit. Fresh, flavourful palate, without great fruit expression, pleasant.

PUERTA DE ALCALÁ 2003 RED
100% tempranillo

81 Deep cherry with a violet edge. Powerful, fruity, ripe aroma with hints of sun-drenched skins. Flavourful palate with overtones of tannic freshness, a nuance of sweet fruit, slightly oily and warm, very pleasant.

VEGA MADROÑO 2003 RED
60% tempranillo, 40% garnacha

78 Brilliant cherry with a violet edge. Not very intense aroma with fine notes of ripe fruit, spicy hints of skins and a suggestion of vine shoots. Flavourful, fresh palate with bitter notes, a hint of ripe fruit and elevated acidity.

GREGO 2003 ROBLE RED
tempranillo, syrah

85 Intense cherry. Aroma with notes of very ripe forest fruits. Fleshy palate with slightly foresty hints of rapid ripening, flavourful.

PUERTA DEL SOL VARIETALES 2002 ROBLE WHITE
100% malvar

81 Yellow with a golden glint. Intense aroma with fine spicy notes of oak (vanilla), and a nuance of ripe white fruit. Flavourful palate with well-integrated fruit/oak, overtones of freshness and good acidity with spicy hints and a suggestion of herbs in the retronasal passage.

GREGO 2001 CRIANZA RED
50% syrah, 40% tempranillo, 10% otras

89 Dark cherry. Fruity aroma with jammy notes and a hint of brambles and oak. Fleshy palate with good expression of fruit and fine toasty flavours; hints of ripe fruit, highly flavourful.

MANU VINO DE AUTOR 2001 CRIANZA RED
45% syrah, 40% tempranillo, 10% cabernet sauvignon, 5% garnacha, merlot

90 Intense cherry. Powerful aroma with nuances of skins and bunches, notes of fine oak. Fleshy palate with ripe fruit, notes of pitch and a viscous suggestion; flavourful with sweet and flavourful tannins.

PUERTA DE ALCALÁ 2000 CRIANZA RED
100% tempranillo

82 Garnet red cherry with a coppery edge. Intense aroma with fine notes of reduction, a nuance of ripe fruit and spicy hints. Flavourful palate with slightly marked tannins but a good suggestion of ripe fruit (prunes); spicy, pleasant, long.

PUERTA DEL SOL TEMPRANILLO 2000 CRIANZA RED
100% tempranillo

80 Garnet red cherry with a saffron rim. Powerful aroma with spicy notes of oak over a hint of ripe fruit. Flavourful palate with a good crianza expression (leathers, spices) and a suggestion of sweet fruit.

PUERTA DEL SOL VARIETALES 2000 CRIANZA RED
tempranillo, cabernet sauvignon, syrah, merlot

78 Deep cherry with a coppery glint. Intense aroma with toasty notes of oak and a hint of ripe fruit. Flavourful palate with slightly drying tannins, slightly warm with poor fruit expression and a spicy suggestion of wood.

FÉLIX MARTÍNEZ CEPAS VIEJAS 1999 RESERVA RED
90% tempranillo, 5% merlot, 5% cabernet sauvignon

88 Intense cherry. Spicy aroma of crianza (cedar, leather and Havana cigars) with ripe fruit. Round, oily, spicy, flavourful and full palate.

PUERTA DE ALCALÁ 2000 RESERVA RED
100% tempranillo

87 Intense cherry. Powerful aroma, rich in fruit expression, ripe with fine creamy notes of oak. Fleshy palate with a mineral suggestion, flavourful with ripe fruit.

PUERTA CERRADA 2003 JOVEN WHITE
PUERTA DE ALCALÁ 2003 JOVEN WHITE
PUERTA DEL SOL 2002 FERMENTADO EN BARRICA WHITE
PUERTA CERRADA 2003 JOVEN ROSÉ
PUERTA CERRADA 2003 JOVEN RED

VINOS Y ACEITES LAGUNA

Illescas, 3
28360 Villaconejos (Madrid)
☎: 918 938 196 - Fax: 918 938 344
vyalaguna@eresmas.com

Established: 1890

🍞 200 🍷 3,000,000 litres 🍇 130 has.
🍷 95% 🌍 5%

ALMA DE VALDEGUERRA 2003 WHITE
100% malvar

77 Straw-coloured. Fresh, very fruity aroma (sweet fruit, pineapples). Fresh, light, clear palate, well prepared and dry.

ALMA DE VALDEGUERRA 2003 JOVEN RED
100% tempranillo

84 Cherry with a violet edge. Intense, fruity aroma with excellent varietal expression. Fresh, flavourful, fleshy palate with slightly marked tannins but with a hint of sweetness, spicy hints of skins and good acidity.

LACUNA 2001 CRIANZA RED
100% tempranillo

84 Cherry with a saffron edge. Intense aroma of well-integrated ripe fruit and toasty notes of oak with good varietal expression. Flavourful palate with ripe and oily tannins and hints of chocolate and liquorice in the finish.

VIÑA BAYONA

Grande, 28
28359 Titulcia (Madrid)
☎: 918 010 445 - Fax: 918 010 445

Established: 1945

⊞ 25 ▊ 200,000 litres ☙ 7 has. ⚑ 100%

VIÑA BAYONA SOBREMADRE JOVEN WHITE
100% malvar

79 Straw-coloured. Fresh aroma of ripe fruit (apples, pineapples). Fresh, fruity palate with good acidity and some character.

VIÑA BAYONA SOBREMADRE 2002 JOVEN RED
75% tempranillo, 25% malvar

74 Intense cherry with a coppery glint. Intense aroma of ripe fruit with hints of lees and mild reduction off-odours. Fresh palate with slightly marked grape tannins, overtones of freshness, spicy hints of skins and good acidity.

VIÑA BAYONA 2000 CRIANZA RED
50% merlot, 50% cabernet sauvignon

70 Ruby red cherry with a brick red edge. Intense aroma with fine reduction notes (varnishes, leather, tobacco) and a spicy oak nuance. Flavourful, warm palate with predominant acetaldehydes that conceal the flavours.

VIÑA BAYONA MERLOT 2000 RED

VIÑAS DE EL REGAJAL

Diplomaticos, 8
28023 Madrid (Madrid)
☎: 651 522 198 - Fax: 913 079 636
agarip@terra.es

Established: 1998

⊞ 40 ▊ 25,000 litres ☙ 10 has.

⚑ 67% ◷33%: -US -CH -DE -NL -BE

EL REGAJAL SELECCIÓN ESPECIAL 2002 OAK AGED RED
tempranillo, cabernet sauvignon, syrah, merlot, petit verdot

92 Intense cherry. Powerful aroma, rich in expression of ripe fruit but with fresh nuances (blackcurrants, brambles) and fine notes of creamy oak. Fleshy, powerful, flavourful palate, rich in ripe fruit expression with mineral notes.

VIRGEN DE LA POVEDA

Camino de Méntrida, 20
28630 Villa del Pardo (Madrid)
☎: 918 620 068 - Fax: 918 604 520

Established: 1963

⊞ 250 ▊ 6,000,000 litres ☙ 1,500 has.

ACEÑA AFRUTADO WHITE
ACEÑA ROSÉ
ACEÑA RED
ALFAMÍN CRIANZA RED

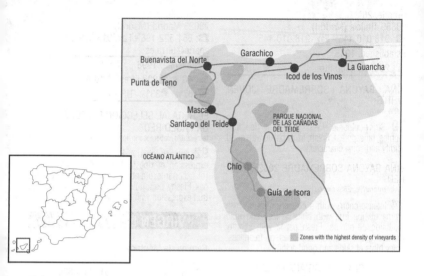

Zones with the highest density of vineyards

NEWS. As with several of the denominations of the island vineyards, of the 35 wines tasted, 15 obtained 80 points or more, whilst in the previous edition only 6 achieved or surpassed this mark. This proves that in the regions where the trade winds blow, the quality of the grapes was better in 2003 than in the previous year, although it must also be mentioned that 2002 was a particularly bad year regarding quantity and quality, and therefore not a valid reference point. Also worthy of mention is how the white wines (especially the sweet wines) and even the rosés outdid the red wines, which moreover occupy the tail end of the DO as far as the ratings are concerned, with a significant number of defects.

Hectares of Vineyard	No. of Viticulturists	No. of Bodegas	2003 Harvest	2003 Production	Marketing
435	964	27	Good	900,000 litres	95% The Canary Islands 5% export

LOCATION. Occupying the northeast of the island of Tenerife and comprising the municipal districts of San Juan de La Rambla, La Guancha, Icod de los Vinos, Los Silos, El Tanque, Garachico, Buenavista del Norte, Santiago del Teide and Guía de Isora.

CLIMATE. Mediterranean, characterised by the multitude of microclimates depending on the altitude and other geographical conditions. The trade winds provide the humidity necessary for the development of the vines. The average annual temperature is 19°C and the average annual rainfall is around 540 mm.

SOIL. Volcanic ash and rock on the higher grounds, and clayey lower down. The vines are cultivated at very different heights, ranging from 50 to 1,400 m.

VARIETIES:

White:

Preferred: *Bermejuela (or Marmajuelo), Güal, Malvasía, Moscatel, Pedro Ximénez, Verdello, Vijariego and Albillo.*

Authorized: *Bastardo Blanco, Forastera Blanca, Listán Blanco* (majority), *Sabro, Torrontés.*

Red:

Preferred: *Tintilla, Listán Negro* (majority), *Malvasía Rosada, Negramoll and Castellana.*

Authorized: *Bastardo Negra, Moscatel Negra, Vijariego Negra.*

REGULATORY COUNCIL.

La Palmita, 10. 38440 La Guancha - Tenerife.
Tel: 922 130 246. Fax: 922 828 159.
E-mail: ycoden@ycoden.com
Website: www.ycoden.com

GENERAL CHARACTERISTICS OF THE WINES:

Whites	The most characteristic wines of the DO are the white wines produced from *Listán*, which are fresh, flavourful and quite expressive. They are produced as dry, semi sec and sweet wines and there are also examples of wines fermented in barrels.
Rosés	These have a strawberry colour, good fruit expression and are pleasantly herbaceous.
Reds	These have a deep cherry-red colour; they are fruity and fresh; on occasion they develop soothing aromas: eucalyptus and autumn leaves.

DO YCODEN-DAUTE-ISORA

BILMA

Carretera Chio Boca Tauce
38680 Guía de Isora (Tenerife)
☎: 922 863 538

TAGARA 2003 FERMENTADO EN BARRICA JOVEN WHITE

80 Straw-coloured. Aroma with light toasty notes of lees and wood with slightly concealed fruit, fresh. Dry palate with a smoky retronasal effect, fresh and slightly fruity.

TÁGARA 2003 AFRUTADO WHITE
100% listán blanca

81 Straw-coloured. Clear, fresh aroma with a suggestion of wet forest herbs and sweet fruit. Supple, fresh, sweet and flavourful palate, persistent.

TAGARA 2003 JOVEN WHITE

78 Straw-coloured. Quite short, fruity aroma. Dry, slightly bitter, fruity palate.

TÁGARA 2003 JOVEN ROSÉ
100% listán negro

81 Garnet red raspberry. Fresh, fruity aroma with varietal notes of ripe fruit (blackberries and plums). Fresh, fruity palate with a good alcohol-acidity, flavourful.

TÁGARA 2003 OAK AGED JOVEN RED
95% listán negro, 5% tintilla   🍷4

70 Garnet red. Unexpressive aroma without fruit. Fresh, slightly better palate, discreet.

TÁGARA 2003 GENEROSO LICOR NOBLE
100% listán blanca

86 Slightly golden. Sweet aroma of very ripe or crystallised fruit with honeyed notes. Sweet, warm, powerful and spirituous palate with toasty honey, flavourful and persistent.

CUEVA DE SAN MARCOS

Carretera El Amparo, 97
38430 Icod de los Vinos (Tenerife)
☎: 922 812 442

Established: 1983
🛢 20 📒 30,000 litres 🍇 0.7 has.🍷 100%

CUEVA DE SAN MARCOS WHITE
CUEVA DE SAN MARCOS RED

CUEVA DEL REY

Camino Cuevas del Rey, 8
38430 Icod de los Vinos (Tenerife)
☎: 922 121 414 - Fax: 922 121 414

CUEVA DEL REY WHITE
CUEVA DEL REY ROSÉ
CUEVA DEL REY RED

CUEVAS DEL VIENTO

Camino La Manca, 4
38430 Icod de los Vinos (Tenerife)
☎: 922 811 796 - Fax: 922 811 796
web@cuevadelviento.com
www.cuevadelviento.com

Established: 1988
🛢 32 📒 120,000 litres 🍇 3.5 has.
🍷 98% 🍇2%

CUEVAS DEL VIENTO 2003 AFRUTADO WHITE
80% listán blanca, 20% otras

82 Pale. Fresh, fruity aroma with certain varietal nuances (wet forest herbs) An expression of sweet fruit on the palate (custard apples, melons), fresh, with a slightly bitter finish typical of the region.

CUEVAS DEL VIENTO 2003 SEMISECO WHITE
80% listán blanca, 20% otras

70 Straw-coloured. Slightly fruity aroma with a hint of reduction, fresh. Not very clear palate, late racking.

CUEVAS DEL VIENTO 2003 SECO WHITE
80% listán blanca, 20% otras

78 Straw-coloured. Fresh, fruity, pleasant and clear aroma. Light, flavourful, fruity palate with a nuance of forest herbs, quite bitter.

CUEVAS DEL VIENTO 2003 JOVEN ROSÉ
80% listán negro, 20% listán blanco

78 Dark raspberry. Short, fruity, clear aroma. Fruity palate with varietal notes and a foresty hint.

CUEVAS DEL VIENTO 2003 JOVEN RED
90% listán negro, 10% otras

59 Clear garnet red. Aroma with an off-odour, without fruit, harvest and preparation problems.

CUEVAS DEL VIENTO 1998 CRIANZA RED
CUEVAS DEL VIENTO 2002 CRIANZA RED

CUMBRES DE BOLICO

Era del Llano, 3 Tamaimo
38436 Santiago del Teide (Tenerife)
☎: 922 863 154

CUMBRES DE BOLICO RED

Cooperativa Agraria CHINYERO

Avenida General Franco, s/n

38436 Santiago del Teide (Tenerife)
☎: 922 864 089 - Fax: 922 864 089

MARQUÉS DE SANTIAGO
2003 SEMISECO WHITE

70 Straw-coloured. Slightly fruity aroma with a nuance of the tank, fresh. Sweet, quite flavourful, discreet palate.

FAYCAN

El Norte, 20
38680forest herbs Guía de Isora (Tenerife)
☎: 922 850 120

FAYCAN 2003 JOVEN WHITE

78 Straw-coloured. Short aroma with hardly any fruit expression, clear and fresh. Dry, flavourful, light, slightly fruity palate.

FAYCAN 2003 JOVEN RED

63 Glacé cherry. Short aroma, without fruit or nuances. Light, unexpressive, slightly flat palate.

FRANCISCO JAVIER GÓMEZ PIMENTEL

La Palita, 63
38430 Icod de los Vinos (Tenerife)
☎: 922 810 237 - Fax: 922 810 237

ACEVIÑO 2003 JOVEN WHITE

80 Straw-coloured. Fresh, fruity, clean aroma with a suggestion of herbs and sweet fruit. Fresh, flavourful, fruity palate with sweet overtones and slightly bitter.

ACEVIÑO 2003 JOVEN SEMISECO WHITE

78 Straw-coloured. Short, imprecise aroma with a clear and slightly fruity hint. Sweetness on the palate, slightly drier than usual, flavourful.

ACEVIÑO 2003 ROSÉ
100% listán negro

82 Strawberry. Fresh, fruity, very varietal aroma (brambles, blackberries). Fresh, clear flavourful palate, very fruity and varietal.

ACEVIÑO 2003 JOVEN RED
100% listán negro

70 Garnet red. Clear aroma with quite scarce but clean and slightly varietal fruit. Scarcely any fruit on the palate, discreet.

ACEVIÑO 2003 MACERACIÓN CARBÓNICA RED
100% listán negro

73 Quite dark cherry with a carbonic edge. Aroma with barely any fruity nuances, slightly vegetative and fresh. Fresh, slightly fruity palate, discreet.

ACEVIÑO OAK AGED RED

HIMACOPASA

Avenida Reyes Católicos, 23
38005 Santa Cruz de Tenerife (Tenerife)
☎: 922 218 155 - Fax: 922 215 666
sofusa@gruposocas.com

Established: 1996

⊞ 150 🗟 300,000 litres 🍇 76 has.

🚩 100%

MALVASÍA TASANA CLÁSICO 2001 JOVEN DULCE WHITE
100% malvasía

87 Golden. Aroma with notes of nuts and honey, crystallised and jammy fruit. Sweet, fresh, supple, elegant and complex palate with mild notes of aldehyde, flavourful and long with persistence.

LA PALMITA

Carretera General Santa Bárbara 131
38430 Icod de los vinos (Tenerife)
☎: 922 121 424

Established: 1993

⊞ 40 🗟 40,000 litres 🍇 0.5 has. 🚩 100%

EL JABLE SECO WHITE
LA PALMITA WHITE
EL JABLE ROSÉ
LA PALMITA ROSÉ
EL JABLE RED
LA PALMITA RED

MARDIAZ

José Rodríguez Ramírez, s/n San José
38420 San Juan de la Rambla (Tenerife)
☎: 922 360 363

LOS QUEVEDOS WHITE
TASANA CLÁSICO MALVASÍA DULCE WHITE
LOS QUEVEDOS RED

PATIO REAL

Camino Real, 8 Valle de Arriba
38436 Santiago del Telde (Tenerife)
☎: 922 861 306 - Fax: 922 861 669

PATIO REAL 2003 JOVEN RED

60 Garnet red with a carbonic hue. Flat aroma without fruit or nuances. Sweet notes on the palate, barely perceptible fruit and low acidity.

DO YCODEN-DAUTE-ISORA

Sociedad Agraria de Transformación
TAJINASTE

Cecilio Montes, 17
38430 Icod de los Vinos (Tenerife)
☎: 922 122 395 - Fax: 922 122 395

Established: 1994
🍷 12 📊 240,600 litres 🍇 75 has. 🍷 100%

MIRADERO 2001 CRIANZA RED

81 Quite dark cherry. Aroma with toasty notes of oak and ripe fruit with balsamic nuances. Flavourful, fruity palate with persistent toasty oak tannins in the retronasal passage.

TEÓFILO SOCAS HERNÁNDEZ
BODEGAS SOCAS

Avenida de los Chincanayros, 31
38430 Icod de los Vinos (Tenerife)
☎: 922 810 513 - Fax: 922 810 513
socas@nexo.es

Established: 1860
🍷 30 📊 500,000 litres 🍇 5.3 has. 🍷 100%

7 ISLAS WHITE
BODEGAS SOCAS WHITE
VIÑAS TEIDE WHITE
7 ISLAS ROSÉ
BODEGAS SOCAS ROSÉ
VIÑAS TEIDE ROSÉ
7 ISLAS RED
BODEGAS SOCAS RED
VIÑAS TEIDE RED

VIÑA ACOSTA
(VALERIANO ACOSTA PEREZ)

El Teléfono, 4 (Tierra del Trigo)
38470 Los Silos (Tenerife)
☎: 922 840 995 - Fax: 922 840 995

VIÑA ACOSTA 2003 JOVEN RED

70 Garnet red. Slightly fresh and quite fruity aroma, clear. Light, balsamic palate with barely any fruit, well-mannered.

VIÑA EL PALMAR

Albóndiga, 8
38480 Buenavista del Norte (Tenerife)
☎: 922 127 064 - Fax: 922 127 675

VIÑA EL PALMAR 2003 WHITE
VIÑA EL PALMAR 2003 RED

VIÑA LA GUANCHA

El Sol, 3
38440 La Guancha (Santa Cruz de Tenerife)
☎: 922 828 166 - Fax: 922 828 166
zanata@zanata.net
www.zanata.net

Established: 1893
🍷 45 📊 140,000 litres 🍇 5 has. 🍷 100%

VIÑA ZANATA 2001 FERMENTADO EN BARRICA WHITE
VIÑA ZANATA 2003 WHITE
ZANATA 2003 MACERACIÓN CARBÓNICA RED
VIÑA ZANATA 2002 OAK AGED RED

VIÑA SPINOLA

Camino Esparragal, s/n
38470 Los Silos (Tenerife)
☎: 922 860 418 - Fax: 922 840 977

VIÑA SPINOLA MALVASÍA JOVEN WHITE

VIÑAMONTE

Avenida Villanueva, 34
35440 La Guancha (Tenerife)
☎: 922 828 085 - Fax: 922 130 037
🍷 20 📊 42,000 litres 🍷 80% 🍇20%

VIÑAMONTE 2003 JOVEN WHITE

77 Straw-coloured. Aroma with sweet herbaceous notes, fresh and slightly fruity. Fresh, light, slightly dry palate, very well-mannered.

VIÑAMONTE 2003 JOVEN SEMISECO WHITE

81 Straw-coloured. Fresh, quite fruity aroma with certain foresty varietal nuances. Supple, sweet and flavourful palate with a bitter hint, pleasant and stylish.

VIÑAMONTE 2003 JOVEN ROSÉ
100% listán negro

74 Subdued strawberry. Aroma with notes of slightly overripe fruit with hints of sweetness. Slightly foresty and vegetative palate with a nuance of fruitiness.

VIÑAMONTE 2003 OAK AGED JOVEN RED
100% listán negro

58 Quite dark cherry. Aroma with reduction off-odours, flawed harvest. Flat palate, without nuances, slightly vinegarish.

VIÑAMONTE 2003 JOVEN RED
100% listán negro

66 Glacé cherry. Aroma with a slight off-odour, without fruit. Light palate with hardly fleshy overtones or fruit, discreet.

VIÑAMONTE 2002 BARREL AGED WHITE

80 Straw-coloured. Slightly toasty aroma of oak with a suggestion of forest herbs and sweet fruit. Toasty retronasal effect on the palate with dominant oak tannins; slightly fruity.

VIÑAMONTE DULCE WHITE

VIÑÁTIGO

Cabo Verde, s/n
38440 La Guancha (Tenerife)
☎: 922 828 768 - Fax: 922 829 936
vinatigo@vinatigo.com
www.vinatigo.com

Established: 1990

🛢 120 🛢 300,000 litres 🍇 20 has.

🍷 70% 🌐30%: -DE -US

VIÑÁTIGO MALVASÍA 2003 OAK AGED DULCE WHITE
malvasía   🛢 2

89 Brilliant golden yellow. Powerful aroma, with fine toasty notes of grapes, smoky and creamy oak notes and a fine suggestion of overripening. Powerful palate with fresh overtones, caramel, quality bittersweet notes and excellent acidity.

VIÑÁTIGO 2003 SECO WHITE
100% listán blanca

79 Pale with a coppery hue. Intense aroma with notes of fruit and white flowers and fine spicy notes of skins. Flavourful, slightly fruity palate with bitter notes and marked citrus acidity.

AÑATERVE 2003 WHITE

82 Pale yellow with a golden hue. Intense, floral, spicy aroma (cumin, anise) with fine notes of herbs. Fresh, flavourful, spicy palate, rich in nuances with excellent acidity.

VIÑÁTIGO GUALFOREST HERBS 2003 WHITE
güal

77 Golden. Powerful aroma of ripe fruit with fine smoky oak and a suggestion of spices and herbs. Flavourful palate with slightly fresh and drying tannins, warm with good acidity and poor fruit expression.

VIÑÁTIGO MARMAJUELOFOREST HERBS 2003 WHITE
marmajuelo

80 Pale yellow with a golden hue. Intense, slightly fruity aroma with hints of citrus fruit (limes) and fragrant herbs. Fresh, flavourful, bitter palate with excellent acidity, lacking fruit expression.

VIÑÁTIGO NEGRAMOLL 2003 CRIANZA RED
100% listán negro

85 Garnet red cherry with a coppery hue. Powerful, highly perfumed and varietal aroma (red stone fruit, petals, hints of vine shoots) with spicy hints. Fleshy palate, with quite marked and flavourful tannins, fine herbaceous and soil notes and good acidity.

VIÑÁTIGO ALLIER 2003 FERMENTADO EN BARRICA WHITE
VIÑÁTIGO 2003 SEMISECO WHITE
VIÑÁTIGOFOREST HERBS 2003 ROSÉ
VIÑÁTIGOFOREST HERBS 2003 JOVEN RED
VIÑÁTIGO TINTILLA 2003 CRIANZA RED

DO YECLA

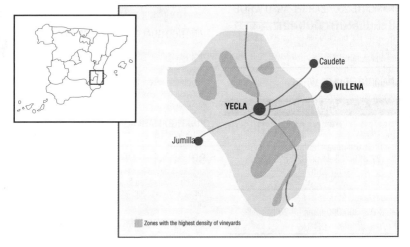

Zones with the highest density of vineyards

NEWS. In a denomination whose vineyards are 92.5% red (and 85% *Monastrell*), it is not surprising that the wines have achieved a certain level of quality in a year such as 2003, with a good deal of hot weather and little rainfall, prefect conditions for its flagship variety. As for quantity, the predicted fall in production eventually did not transpire, thanks to the rains in September. As we have become accustomed to of late, Bodegas Castaño leads the way in quality and is still leading the region, with only two wines from other cellars (Bellum El Remate, a sweet red wine of Antonio Candela e Hijos, and the Mira Salinas of Bodegas Laus) making inroads of quality beyond 85 points.

Hectares of Vineyard	No. of Viticulturists	No. of Bodegas	2003 Harvest	2003 Production	Marketing
4,600	-	7	Very Good	5,000,000 litres	-

LOCATION. In the northeast of the province of Murcia, within the plateau region, and comprising a single municipal district, Yecla.

CLIMATE. Continental, with a slight Mediterranean influence, with hot summers and cold winters, and little rainfall, which is usually around 300 mm per annum.

SOIL. Fundamentally deep limestone, with good permeability. The vineyards are on undulating terrain at a height of between 400 m and 800 m above sea level.

VARIETIES:
White: *Merseguera, Airén, Macabeo, Malvasía, Chardonnay.*
Red: *Monastrell* (majority 85% of total), *Garnacha Tinta, Cabernet Sauvignon, Cencibel (Tempranillo), Merlot, Tintorera, Syrah.*

SUB-REGIONS: Yecla Campo Arriba, with *Monastrell* as the most common variety and alcohol contents of up to 14°, and Yecla Campo Abajo, whose grapes produce a lower alcohol content (around 12° for reds and 11.5° for whites).

REGULATORY COUNCIL.

Centro de Desarrollo Local.
Poeta Francisco A. Jiménez, s/n. Polígono Industrial Urbayecla II.
Tel / Fax: 968 792 352.
E-mail: info@yeclavino.com
Website: www.yeclavino.com

GENERAL CHARACTERISTICS OF THE WINES:

Whites	These have a straw yellow colour; they are fruity and have quite a good aromatic intensity, although on the palate their acidity is somewhat low.
Rosés	Although they are not the most representative wines of the region, the best wines are produced according to modern techniques for this type of wine and they are therefore quite fruity, fresh and pleasant.
Reds	Thes are the most characteristic wines of the region and also the most abundant. Produced mainly from *Monastrell*, they have either a violet cherry or deep cherry-red colour. Their aroma is of ripe fruit and there may sometimes be hints of raisining, due to the strong sunshine of the region. They are meaty, warm and supple on the palate.

ANTONIO CANDELA E HIJOS

Avenida de la Paz, 58
30510 Yecla (Murcia)
☎: 968 790 281 - Fax: 968 792 351
info@bodegasantoniocandela.com
www.barahonda.com

Established: 1925

🌐 190 🍇 110 has.

🍷 80% 🌐20%: -US -CA -UK -DE -IE -NL

BARAHONDA 2003 JOVEN WHITE
90% airén, 10% macabeo

79 Pale with a golden hue. Powerful aroma of ripe white fruit with exotic notions (melons, papaya) and flowers. Flavourful, slightly fruity palate with bitter and rich citrus fruit notes.

BARAHONDA 2003 JOVEN ROSÉ
100% monastrell

75 Pale cherry with an orange glint. Powerful aroma of ripe red fruit with an element of sweetness and spicy, herby notes. Flavourful, slightly fruity and warm on the palate.

BARAHONDA 2003 JOVEN RED
100% monastrell

82 Dark cherry with a purplish edge. Powerful, ripe aroma, with good varietal expression and hints of sun-drenched skins. Flavourful palate with somewhat firm though ripe tannins, a good fruit weight and fine bitter notes, pleasant.

BARAHONDA CABERNET SAUVIGNON 2003 RED
100% cabernet sauvignon

79 Very deep cherry with a violet edge. Powerful aroma of ripe black fruit (hints of prunes) with a suggestion of withered petals and without great varietal expression. Flavourful palate with slightly rough tannins, ripe fruit and spicy hints.

BARAHONDA SELECCIÓN 2003 OAK AGED RED
70% monastrell, 30% cabernet sauvignon

79 Dark cherry with a violet edge. Powerful aroma of very ripe black fruit (raisiny hints), petals and lees (mild reduction off-odours in the tank). Better in the mouth, flavourful and fleshy on the palate with notes of ripe fruit, sweet.

BELLUM EL REMATE 2003 OAK AGED DULCE RED
100% monastrell   🌐 5

86 Black cherry. Powerful aroma with predominant notes of macerated red fruit, hints of petals and toasty oak. Fleshy, flavourful and very concentrated on the palate with rough, fine tannins, quality bittersweet notes, slightly warm with a sweet hint.

BARAHONDA 2001 OAK AGED RED
70% monastrell, 30% cabernet sauvignon

81 Deep cherry. Powerful aroma of jammy black fruit, fine reduction notes (withered petals, leathers, slightly dried fruit) and toasty oak. Flavourful palate with fleshy overtones, slightly marked tannins and bitter notes.

BARAHONDA 2002 JOVEN RED
100% monastrell

81 Deep cherry. A deep aroma of black fruit, smoky notes and wet earth (ripe skins). Fleshy palate with noticeable ripe fruit tannins, quite warm notes and correct acidity.

BARAHONDA 1999 OAK AGED RED
70% monastrell, 30% cabernet sauvignon

79 Garnet red cherry with a coppery edge. Intense aroma with predominant reduction notes (wet horsehair, aged wood). Flavourful and warm on the palate with fine bitter notes (a good fruit/oak integration).

BARAHONDA 2000 OAK AGED RED
70% monastrell, 30% cabernet sauvignon

82 Garnet red cherry with a coppery edge. Not very intense aroma of red stone fruit (raisiny hints), toasty and reduction (tobacco) notes. Flavourful supple palate with a good oak/fruit integration; very pleasant.

BARAHONDA CRIANZA DULCE RED

Bodegas CASTAÑO

Carretera Fuentealamo, 3
30510 Yecla (Murcia)
☎: 968 791 115 - Fax: 968 791 900
info@bodegascastano.com
www.bodegascastano.com

Established: 1950
2,000 ▤ 4,000,000 litres ⚘ 400 has.
🍷 30% ▼70%: -DE -NL -CH -UK -DK -JP -MX -SE -CA -US -PL -AT -DK

CASTAÑO MACABEO-CHARDONNAY 2003 WHITE
60% macabeo, 40% chardonnay

82 Pale with a golden hue. Fairly intense aroma of white fruit with fine hints of herbs. Flavourful, fresh palate with fine bitter notes, smoky hints of oak, a slightly oily texture and complex overtones.

CASTAÑO MONASTRELL 2003 JOVEN RED
100% monastrell

79 Garnet red cherry. Intense aroma of red plums and skins. Slightly warm on the palate with a nuance of red fruit and skins and very bitter tannins.

CASTAÑO CABERNET SAUVIGNON 2003 RED
100% cabernet sauvignon

86 Deep cherry with a garnet red edge. Powerful, balsamic aroma of ripe black fruit with notes of paprika. Powerful, concentrated palate with ripe redcurrants, sweet fruit and obvious yet ripe tannins, a spicy finish.

CASTAÑO MERLOT 2003 RED
100% merlot

87 Garnet red cherry. Intense aroma of ripe black fruit and toasty skins. Powerful, flavourful palate with very ripe fruit, expressive, with an earthy finish, strong character.

CASTAÑO SYRAH 2003 RED
100% syrah

87 Intense cherry with a garnet red edge. Powerful, varietal aroma of very ripe red fruit with a spicy hint. Powerful, flavourful palate with sun-drenched skins and notes of terroir, persistent.

CASTAÑO COLECCIÓN 2002 OAK AGED RED
80% monastrell, 20% cabernet sauvignon   🌐 14

90 Intense cherry. Powerful aroma of ripe fruit and creamy toast (cocoa, dark-roasted flavour). Fleshy, powerful, warm, flavourful palate with a nuance of minerals, long with sweet but persistent tannins, spirituous.

DOMINIO ESPINAL 2002 OAK AGED RED
85% monastrell, 15% tempranillo   🌐 1

80 Garnet red cherry with a coppery edge. Fairly intense aroma of black fruit with spicy hints of oak. Flavourful palate with slightly marked tannins and a sweet fruit nuance, lacks expression.

HÉCULA 2002 OAK AGED RED
100% monastrell

86 Very deep cherry with a violet rim. Intense aroma of jammy black fruit with spicy notes of oak. Powerful and creamy on the palate with well-integrated tannins and fruit and fine bitter notes (chocolate, liquorice), with hints of terroir.

DETRÁS DE LA CASA TINTORERA 2002 RED
100% tintorera

90 Very intense cherry. Slightly closed aroma of ripe fruit (grape bunches) with hints of skins and fine toasty wood and a suggestion of minerals. Fleshy palate with acid fresh overtones and sweet alcoholic notes with dry but very persistent tannins.

VIÑA AL LADO DE LA CASA 2002 RED
80% monastrell, 15% cabernet sauvignon, 5% syrah

91 Intense cherry. Powerful aroma with a rich toasty expression (cocoa, coffee, creamy vanilla), ripe fruit and mineral notes. Fleshy, warm and mineral palate with excellent toasty oak nuances and flavourful tannins.

DETRÁS DE LA CASA SYRAH 2002 RED
100% syrah

88 Intense cherry. Aroma of fresh ripe fruit with spicy and toasty hints and a hint of moderately ripe varietal Syrah contrasting with slightly ove-rripe notes. Fresh fruit and mineral notes on the palate with a toasty hint of oak and wood and fruit tannins.

CASTAÑO MONASTRELL 2001 DULCE RED
100% monastrell

86 Intense cherry. Viscous aroma of stewed black fruit with very mild raisiny hints. Sweet palate with very ripe foresty black fruit, viscous, flavourful with sweet tannins.

DETRÁS DE LA CASA MONASTRELL 2001 RED
100% monastrell

87 Intense cherry. Aroma of black fruit with foresty notes and a hint of fine toasty oak. Warm, flavourful palate with nice tannins and ripe black bramble fruit.

VIÑA AL LADO DE LA CASA 2001 RED
85% monastrell, 15% cabernet sauvignon

90 Dark cherry. Toasty chocolate aroma with ripe fruit and foresty hints (brambles). Fleshy, warm, flavourful palate with a slight mineral expression, persistent.

DETRÁS DE LA CASA CABERNET SAUVIG-NON-TINTORERA 2001 CRIANZA RED
60% cabernet sauvignon, 40% garnacha tintorera

88 Very intense cherry. Medium-intensity aroma with fine toasty notes (cocoa, coffee, cigar box) and stewed fruit. Fleshy, full, tannic and mineral palate (dry earth) with foresty hints, slightly acidic, flavourful.

POZUELO 2001 CRIANZA RED
85% monastrell, 10% cabernet sauvignon

83 Very deep cherry with a violet edge. Fairly intense aroma of jammy black fruit with toasty hints of wood. Flavourful palate with well-integra-ted oak/fruit, fine bitter notes, a slightly mineral nuance and good acidity.

POZUELO 2000 RESERVA RED
80% monastrell, 10% tempranillo, 10% cabernet sauvignon

80 Deep cherry with a saffron edge. Intense aroma with predominant spicy oak notes. Flavourful palate oak tannins with an element of greeness, lacking crianza expression.

CASTAÑO MONASTRELL 2003 ROSÉ
DOMINIO ESPINAL SELECCIÓN 2001 OAK AGED RED
CASTAÑO MONASTRELL DULCE RED

Bodegas LAUS

Carretera N-240, km 154, 8
22300 Barbastro (Huesca)
☎: 974 308 565 - Fax: 974 308 566
info@bodegaslaus.com

MIRA SALINAS 2001 RED
monastrell, cabernet, garnacha tintorera

88 Very intense cherry. Toasty oak aroma with notes of jammy fruit, warm, dry earth. Fleshy, spirituous jammy palate with dates and raisins in the retronasal passage and oak tannins; powerful and persistent.

Cooperativa del Vino de Yecla
LA PURÍSIMA

Carretera de Pinoso, 3 Apdo. Correos 27
30510 Yecla (Murcia)
☎: 968 751 257 - Fax: 968 795 116
info@calpyecla.com
www.calpyecla.com

Established: 1954

🏭 1,000 📦 12,000,000 litres 🍇 3,200 has.
🍷 70% 🌐30%: -UK -NL -DE -BE -FR -DK -NO

ESTÍO 2003 JOVEN WHITE
100% macabeo

77 Brilliant pale gold. Intense, quite fruity aroma with hints of flowers and spicy skins. Flavourful, bitter palate without great nuances.

VALCORSO 2003 FERMENTADO EN BARRICA WHITE
100% macabeo

78 Pale. Intense aroma of slightly reduced white fruit with not very fine oak notes and hints of fen-nel. Flavourful, quite fresh palate without great nuances.

ESTÍO 2003 JOVEN ROSÉ
60% monastrell, 40% tempranillo

79 Lively raspberry. Powerful, quite fruity aroma with hints of aniseed and grapefruit. Flavourful, bitter palate with a fruity hint and an acidic edge.

ESTÍO 2003 JOVEN RED
70% monastrell, 30% tempranillo

80 Dark cherry with a purplish edge. Powerful, concentrated aroma of black fruit, notes of mace-rated skins, a suggestion of toastiness and terroir. Fleshy palate with ripe, oily tannins.

VALCORSO CABERNET SAUVIGNON 2003 JOVEN RED
100% cabernet sauvignon

82 Dark cherry with a dark red glint. Powerful, ripe aroma with quite varietal fruit (jammy redcurrants) and the freshness of grapeskins. Fleshy, flavourful palate with fine bitter notes, terroir and spices long.

VALCORSO SYRAH 2003 JOVEN RED
100% syrah

78 Dark cherry with a coppery edge. Powerful, fruity aroma (black fruit, plums), quite warm without a substancial varietal profile. Flavourful, spicy palate with the fruit expression slightly muted by the alcohol.

VALCORSO MONASTRELL ECOLÓGICO 2003 RED
100% monastrell

83 Dark cherry with a purplish edge. Powerful, slightly varietal aroma with hints of sun-drenched skins, terroir and a spicy hint. Flavourful, fleshy palate with slightly marked tannins, a suggestion of toastiness, jammy fruit and liquorice, long.

VALCORSO MONASTRELL 2002 OAK AGED RED
100% monastrell

82 Dark garnet red cherry. Intense aroma of black fruit with a spicy, slightly varietal hint and smoky hints of oak. Flavourful, slightly fleshy and ripe palate with a powerful effect in the retronasal passage (spices, terroir).

VALCORSO TEMPRANILLO 2002 OAK AGED RED
100% tempranillo   3

79 Dark cherry with a purplish edge. Powerful aroma with slightly varietal ripe fruit, a suggestion of flowers and toasty oak. Flavourful palate with slightly marked tannins and predominant bitter notes in the finish.

IGLESIA VIEJA 2001 CRIANZA RED
70% monastrell, 15% tempranillo, 15% cabernet sauvignon

80 Dark cherry with a dark red edge. Powerful aroma with predominant crianza notes (toast, spices) and a suggestion of jammy fruit. Flavourful, somewhat spicy and and warm on the palate with fine bitter notes.

IGLESIA VIEJA 1999 RESERVA RED
70% monastrell, 15% tempranillo, 15% cabernet sauvignon

82 Garnet red cherry with a coppery edge. Intense aroma of fine reduction (tobacco, leather, old furniture) and a nuance of jammy fruit. Flavourful palate with fleshy overtones and slightly rough tannins, warm with waxy hints.

ESTÍO ECOLÓGICO 2002 CRIANZA RED

ESPUMOSO WINES – TRADITIONAL METHOD

All the wines reviewed in this section are produced according to the traditional method known as second fermentation in the bottle, the same method used for the production of Cava, and come from regions which do not fall under the DO Cava or any other DOs.

In fact, they represent a very small portion of the sparkling wines produced in Spain and their production figures do not come close to those of Cava. As far as the quality of these wines is concerned, they are generally somewhat inferior to the Catalonian Cavas.

IBAÑEZ ARDO APARTSUAK

General, s/n
31396 Oloriz (Navarra)
☎: 948 720 293 - Fax: 948 720 293
basondoa@coaatnavarra.org

Established: 1995
🗄 10,000 litros 🍷 97% 🌐3%: -DE

BASONDOA GARNACHA 2001 CRIANZA
 BRUT
BASONDOA 2001 BRUT

BODEGAS AND WINE TASTING
OF VINOS DE LA TIERRA

The different *Vinos de la Tierra* designations have been listed in alphabetical order. The list is not exhaustive and not all the associations in Spain are referenced on the following pages, but rather those that produce the most outstanding wines or that have submitted their wines to be tasted.

Theoretically, the *Vinos de la Tierra* are one step below the DO wines, and are equivalent to the French *Vins de Pays*, pioneers in the promotion of this status. Spain, however, has some unique circumstances. For example, the fact that the designation *Vinos de la Tierra* is not always the goal in itself, but is used as a springboard to achieving the highly desired DO category. In addition, as has happened in other countries, many producers have opted for this type of association with less stringent codes to produce their wines with greater freedom. Therefore, in this section there is a bit of everything: from great wines to other simpler and more ordinary wines. But the broad spectrum of these wines also offers a chance to experiment with new tastes that are different, and with all types of local or regional varieties.

The new *Ley del Vino* (Wine Law) maintains the classification of Vinos de la Tierra, but establishes an intermediate step between these and DO wines. They are the so-called '*Vinos de Calidad con Indicación Geográfica*' (Quality Wines with Geographic Indication), a stepping-stone to the DO, in which the region in question must remain for a minimum of five years.

In the light of the ratings carried out for this section, a steady improvement in the quality of these wines was noted and also fewer misgivings by the bodegas about joining these associations.

VT ARRIBES DEL DUERO

Given the status of *Vino de la Tierra* in 1998, the wines of the 2004 harvest may well go on sale with the official DO label. The region is in the southwest of Zamora and the northeast of Salamanca, on the border with Portugal and near the Duero, a region with a long wine-growing tradition. The region enjoys a Mediterranean climate with Atlantic influences, shallow, sandy soils, with a presence of quartz and granite, poor in organic material and abundant slate in the subsoil, which acts as a temperature regulator. It has 1,260 Ha of vineyards, with very old vines (an average of 65 years old), mainly arranged without supporting wires. The main variety is *Juan García*, an autochthonous variety that performs quite well in ageing, with the *Rufete*, the *Tempranillo* and the *Garnacha* as complementary varieties. The main white variety is the *Malvasía*, with the *Verdejo* and the *Albillo* as complementary varieties. The autochthonous *Bruñal* variety, which only exists in Arribes del Duero, will soon be admitted.

VT BAJO ARAGÓN

The most Mediterranean region in Aragón, bordering Tarragona, Castellón and Teruel, and consisting of four different regions: Campo de Belchite, Bajo Martín, Bajo Aragón and Matarraña, which all share clay and limestone soil, very rich in minerals with a high potash content. The altitude never rises above 600 m in this semi-desert region (the average annual rainfall is a mere 350 mm), where the cooling effect of the 'Cierzo' (north wind), together with the day-night temperature contrasts, are fundamental for the correct ripening of the grapes. The main varieties are the *Garnacha* (both red and white, with the former occupying 80% of the vineyards), although *Syrah, Cabernet Sauvignon, Merlot* and *Chardonnay*, as well as *Tempranillo* and *Cariñena*, and the little known *Royal, Romero de Híjar* and *Muniesa* are also present.

VT CÁDIZ

This includes the municipal districts of Arcos, Prado del Rey, Setenil de las Bodegas, Olvera and Villamartín, as well as those of the Jerez March (Sanlúcar de Barrameda, El Puerto,

Trebujana, Chiclana, Chipiona, Rota, Puerto Real and Jerez), whose DO, strangely, controls the raw material (the grapes) but not the wines produced. The authorised white varieties are: *Garrido, Palomino, Chardonnay, Moscatel de Chipiona, Macabeo* and *Colombard* (which means the definite exclusion of two historic varieties from the vineyards of the region: *Perruno* and *Mantúa*, practically extinct and of very low yield); and the red varieties: *Tempranillo, Syrah, Cabernet Sauvignon, Garnacha, Monastrell, Merlot, Tintilla de Rota* and *Pinot Noir*.

VT CAMPO DE CARTAGENA

The only two VTs of Murcia, Abanilla and Campo de Cartagena share a common code that stipulates the authorised varieties (Red: *Bonicaire, Cabernet Sauvignon, Forcallat Tinta, Garnacha Tintorera, Merlot, Moravia Dulce (Crujidera), Syrah* and *Petit Verdot*; White: *Chardonnay, Malvasía, Moscatel de Grano Menudo* and *Sauvignon Blanc*) and the recommended varieties (Red: *Garnacha, Monastrell, Tempranillo*; White: *Airén, Merseguera, Moscatel de Alejandría, Pedro Ximénez, Verdil* and *Viura (Macabeo)*). The only production comes from Bodegas Serrano, which has 25 Ha of vineyards.

VT CANGAS

The vineyards around the municipality of Cangas del Narcea in Asturias, on the provincial border with León, are located on siliceous, slatey soil, with very loose sand, somewhat similar to the Priorat in Cataluña in the structure of the terrain, in the form of terraces. The high annual rainfall (1,000 mm) is the most distinctive climatic condition. Autochthonous varieties predominate: *Verdejo Negro, Carrasquín (María Ordoña), Mencía* and *Albarín Negro* for red wines, and *Albarín Blanco* for white wines.

VT CASTILLA

Castilla-La Mancha, which accommodates the largest vineyard on the planet (600,000 Ha, equivalent to 6% of the total surface of vineyards in the world, and to half of Spain's) used this geographic indication of *Vinos de la Tierra* in 1999 to take in all the wines produced outside the DO in the region: Valdepeñas, La Mancha, Manchuela, Méntrida, Mondéjar, Ribera del Júcar, Almansa and part of Jumilla. There has been some conflict of interest with the VT Castilla y León regarding the use of the word 'Castilla' on its labels, which, given the size of the vineyards and the volume bottled in Castilla-La Mancha, has increased the exports of Castilla-La Mancha to the detriment of those of Castilla y León.

VT CASTILLA Y LEÓN

Another of the regional 'macro-denominations' for wines from vineyards of a total of 317 regions of the provinces of Ávila, Burgos, León, Palencia, Salamanca, Segovia, Soria, Valladolid and Zamora. A continental climate with little rainfall, together with the diverse soils, are the most distinctive characteristics of the region, which, on the whole, can be divided into the Duero basin and part of the central plateau, alongside the mountainous perimeter that surrounds them.

VT CONTRAVIESA-ALPUJARRA

The high altitude of the vineyards (up to 1,300 m, the highest of all European vineyards) of this region of Granada poses difficulties for the cultivation of grapes, seeing as, in spite of the many hours of sunlight, the cool climate and the absence of irrigation makes it difficult to complete the growth cycle. In the production of white wines, red wines and rosés from *Contraviesa-Alpujarra*, the *Tempranillo, Garnacha, Vijiriego Negra, Cabernet Sauvignon* and *Merlot* are used for red wines, and *Chardonnay* and *Sauvignon Blanc* for white wines.

VT CÓRDOBA

Constituted in 2002 as a geographic indication to take in red and rosé wines from the province of Córdoba, as well as quality table wines not covered by the DO Montilla-Moriles. In total, around 300 Ha of vineyards with the following varieties: *Merlot, Syrah, Tempranillo, Pinot Noir* and *Tintilla de Rota*.

VT DESIERTO DE ALMERÍA

Approved in the summer of 2003, the production region consists of the municipal districts of Alcudia de Monteagud, Benitagla, Benizalón, Castro de Filabres, Lubrín, Lucainena de las Torres, Olula de Castro, Senés, Sorbas, Tabernas, Tahal, Turrillas, Uleila del Campo and Velefique. It produces white wines from the *Chardonnay, Moscatel, Macabeo* and *Sauvignon Blanc* varieties, and red and rosé wines from the *Tempranillo, Cabernet Sauvignon, Monastrell, Merlot, Syrah* and *Garnacha* varieties.

VT EIVISSA

The production area includes the entire island of Ibiza (Eivissa), with the vineyards located in small valleys amongst the mountains of the island – which never surpass 500 m in height – on brownish-reddish soil covered by a thin limestone crust. The low rainfall and the hot, humid summers are the most interesting climatic characteristics. The autochthonous varieties are the red *Monastrell, Tempranillo, Cabernet Sauvignon, Merlot* and *Syrah*, and the white *Macabeo, Parellada, Malvasía, Chardonnay* and *Moscatel*.

VT EL TERRERAZO

The production area is limited exclusively to the region known as El Terrerazo, within the municipal area of Utiel, in Valencia, an estate that belongs to the Sarrión family, the owners of the only bodega registered with the Mustiguillo DO, with the ubiquitous Sara Pérez in charge of oenology.

VT EXTREMADURA

One of the great unknowns of the Spanish wine-growing landscape, the total production of this VT in the 2002-2003 season was 350,000 hectolitres, which makes it the second largest *Vinos de la Tierra* producer after Castilla-La Mancha in terms of production volume in Spain. It includes the vineyards of the two provinces of Extremadura.

VT GRANADA SUROESTE

The VT covers the wines produced in a production area which includes around 53 municipal districts of the province of Granada, from the *Vijariego, Macabeo, Pedro Ximénez, Palomino, Moscatel de Alejandría, Chardonnay* and *Sauvignon Blanc* white grape varieties and the *Garnacha, Perruna, Tempranillo, Cabernet Sauvignon, Merlot, Syrah* and *Pinot Noir* red grape varieties.

VT ILLA DE MENORCA

In Minorca, recently declared a biosphere reserve, the production of wine has long been of singular importance, especially during the English occupation of the island, which began in 1708 and ended in the 19th century. The gentle slopes, the brownish limy soil with a complex lithological substratum of limestone, sandstone and slate, the Mediterranean climate, and the winter winds from the north are the most significant characteristics from a wine-growing view point. Of all the different varieties (the red *Cabernet Sauvignon, Merlot, Monastrell, Tempranillo* and *Syrah*; and the white *Chardonnay, Macabeo, Moscatel, Parellada, Moll* and *Malvasía*), the latter produces the best Mediterranean examples.

VT ILLES BALEARS

The production area covers the islands which make up the archipelago, with the vineyards established on brownish-red soil (rich in siliceous sandstone sediments) and a Mediterranean climate with moderate temperatures (especially the minimum temperatures). The red varieties are *Cabernet Sauvignon, Merlot, Syrah, Monastrell, Tempranillo, Fogoneu, Callet* and *Manto Negro,* and the white varieties *Chardonnay, Moscatel, Moll, Parellada, Macabeo* and *Malvasía.*

VT LA GOMERA

See DO La Gomera.

VT LAUJAR-ALPUJARRA

This includes some 700 Ha of vineyard in the region of Laujar in Almeria, situated in the munic-ipal areas of Alcolea, Bayárcal, Paterna del Río, Laujar del Andarax, Fondón, Fuente Victoria, Benecid, Baires, Almócita, Padules, Ohanes and Canjáyar.

VT NORTE DE GRANADA

This includes the vineyards of a total of 43 municipal areas in the region of Guadix, with the white *Chardonnay, Baladí Verdejo, Airén* and *Torrontés* and the red *Tempranillo, Monastrell* and *Garnacha* as the main varieties, besides the *Palomino, Pedro Ximénez* and *Macabeo* (white), and *Cabernet Sauvignon* and *Merlot* (red) as complementary varieties, suitable for the pro-duction of white, red and rosé wines.

VT RIBERA DEL ANDARAX

This covers the municipal areas of Alboloduy, Alhabia, Alhama de Almería, Alicún, Almócita, Alsodux, Beires, Bentarique, Canjáyar, Enix, Félix, Jergal, Huécija, Illar, Instinción, Nacimiento, Ohanes, Padules, Rágol, Santa Cruz de Marchena and Terque in Almeria.

VT RIBERA DEL ARLANZA

With a spectacular growth of about 40% in sales in 2003 over the previous year, the VT Ribera del Arlanza, whose mention was authorized in 1998, has long been awaiting its forthcoming conversion to a DO. This region in Burgos, with 350 Ha of vineyards in the vicinity of the municipal district of Lerma (besides another 44 municipal areas – among which the excep-tional enclave of Covarrubias stands out – 5 of which are found in the neighbouring province of Palencia), shares similar climatic characteristics with the neighbouring Ribera del Duero, although another flagship, Rioja, is also not more than a stone's throw away. Therefore, it comes as no surprise that the star variety is the *Tempranillo,* as the high average altitude (the majority of the vineyards are found between 700 m and 1000 m) confers very particular char-acteristics on this variety, given the slower ripening of the grapes in these conditions.

VT RIBERA DEL QUEILES

A new geographic indication for wines produced exclusively from the varieties *Cabernet Sauvignon, Graciano, Garnacha, Tempranillo, Merlot* and *Syrah,* and which covers nine municipal districts in Aragón (Grisel, Lituénigo, Los Fayos, Malón, Novallas, Santa Cruz de Moncayo, Tarazona, Torrellas and Vierlas) and seven in Navarra (Ablitas, Barillas, Cascante,

Monteagudo, Murchante, Tulebras and the area of the town of Tudela situated to the south of the Ebro) in the vicinity of the Queiles valley. The initiative of the project sprung from the Bodegas Guelbenzu, in Cascante, which was initially hoping to gain exclusive rights over the denomination.

VT SERRA DE TRAMUNTANA-COSTA NORD

This VT covers 18 Majorcan municipal areas, situated between the cape of Formentor and the southwest coast of Andratx, with mainly brownish-grey and limy soil. Both the single-variety wines produced with white grapes (especially *Malvasía* and *Chardonnay*) and the red *Cabernet Sauvignon* and *Merlot* from Bordeaux stand out.

VT TIERRA DE LEÓN

Another of the 'important' VTs within Castilla-León (jointly applying for conversion to DO with Ribera del Arlanza), which has more than 20 registered bodegas with a total of 2,000 Ha of vineyards currently registered, and an average production of three million kilograms, although reduced by half in the last few years due to the inclemency of the weather. Its main asset is the indigenous variety, the Prieto Picudo. The vineyards are situated at an altitude of between 750 m and 860 m, and the average rainfall is 500 mm per year. The traditional production in the region is the fresh, slightly acidic claret with an average alcohol content of 12° and a very distinct trend to conserving its carbonic nature which is achieved during the ancient operation of 'madreo' (the adding of whole grapes to the must to produce a second partial fermentation which enhances the fruity notes), although the young and aged red wines are currently better winning the quality argument. The regulations specify the Prieto Picudo and the Mencía as main varieties, and the *Tempranillo (Tinto Fino), Garnacha Tinta, Verdejo* and *Palomino* as complementary varieties.

VT TIERRA DEL VINO DE ZAMORA

This covers the vineyards situated on both sides of the Duero as it flows through the province of Zamora, in the well-known vicinity of Toro, Rueda and Arribes del Duero. It consists of 61 towns, 51 of which belong to province of Zamora and 10 to the province of Salamanca. The multiple river courses in the region determine the alluvial character of the soil, which is clayey, poor in organic matter and, on occasions, with abundant pebbles. With respect to the varieties, the main ones are the red *Tempranillo (Tinto del País)* and the white *Malvasía* and *Moscatel*, with the *Garnacha, Cabernet Sauvignon, Albillo, Palomino* and *Verdejo* as complementary. As with the other VTs, the transposition of the *Ley del Vino* (Wine Law) to the autonomous area places *Tierra del Vino* de Zamora one step away from its conversion to DO.

VT VAL DO MIÑO

Annex I of the Order of the Ministry of Agriculture, Fisheries and Food, of 7th January 1998, defines the geographic area of this VT as being the municipal districts in Orense of Pereiro de Aguiar, Coles, Barbadás, San Cibrao das Viñas, Toén and the city of Orense itself, as well as the various parishes associated with them, with the vineyards always close to the course of the Miño.

VT VALDEJALÓN

Established in 1998, this covers 36 municipal districts in the mid- and lower-Jalón valley and its tributaries, the Aranda, Isuela and Grío. The vineyards are situated on brownish-grey, limy and alluvial soil, with a low rainfall of around 350 mm per year. The drought and the mass uprooting campaigns significantly reduced the size of the vineyards, dropping from 14,600 Ha in 1975 to hardly 1,000 at present. They are planted with the white varieties *Macabeo,*

Garnacha Blanca, Moscatel and *Airén*, and the red *Garnacha, Tempranillo, Cabernet Sauvignon, Syrah, Monastrell* and *Merlot.*

VT VALLE DEL CINCA

Situated in the southeast of the province of Huesca, the Valle del Cinca offers a very favourable climate and soil conditions for the cultivation of vines, similar to a certain extent to those of the Somontano and the Costers del Segre. The soil is limy and clayey, with the average annual rainfall barely reaching 300 mm, and so irrigation is usually required.

VT VALLE DEL JILOCA

The Jiloca is, together with the Jalón, one of the main tributaries of the Ebro. Close to the Moncayo, the wine-growing region is centred in the valley in three distinct areas: the Sierra de Santa Cruz (with the town of Abanto, in the northeast), the Jiloca valley and the Sierras de Peco-Herrera (northeast). The cooperative bodegas represent 95% of the production and marketing of wine in the region. Other villages with bodegas of interest are Daroca, San Martín del Río and Báguena. As with the nearby DO Calatayud, the vineyards are established on the former stony and limy river terraces, with the *Garnacha* as the main variety, followed by the white *Macabeo.* The dry climate, the abundant annual sunshine and the cold winters are determining factors for the excellent quality of the local grapes.

VT VALLES DE BENAVENTE

Recognized by the Autonomous Government of Castilla y León since September 2000, the VT currently covers over 50 towns and 3 bodegas located in the towns of Benavente, Santibáñez de Vidriales and San Pedro de Ceque. The region has 5 wine-growing regions: Valle Vidriales, Valle del Tera, Valle Valverde, La Vega and Tierra de Campos, which surround Benavente as a natural centre, and 4 rivers (Tera, Esla, Órbigo and Valderadey, all tributaries of the Duero) which mark the outline of the geographical area of the region.

VT VALLES DE SADACIA

A designation created to cover the wines produced from the *Rioja Moscatel*, a variety which was practically lost due to grape phylloxera but today recovered for the production of two types of wine: the liqueur wine (a blend of wine and must, to which Aguardiente or distilled spirit may be added), and the white *Moscatel* wine which, depending on its production, may either be dry, semi-dry or sweet.

VINOS DE LA TIERRA

V.T. ARRIBES DE DUERO

ARRIBES DE DUERO

Carretera Masueco, s/n
37250 Corporario-Aldeavila de la Ribera
(Salamanca)
☎: 923 169 195 - Fax: 923 169 195
secretaria@bodegasarribesdelduero.com
www.bodegasarribesdelduero.com

Established: 1992
🍷 600 🛢 1,000,000 litres 🍇 203 has.
🍷 80% 🍇20%: -US -PR -DK

ARRIBES DE VETTONIA 2000 FERMENTADO EN BARRICA WHITE
100% malvasía

76 Brilliant gold. Powerful aroma with predominant oak notes (spices, toast, resins). Flavourful, slightly warm, oily and spicy on the palate, pleasant though with barely any fruit expression.

ARRIBES DE VETTONIA 2003 WHITE
malvasía

73 Pale with a greenish nuance. Medium intensity, slightly rustic aroma with a nuance of green herbs. Better on the palate: fresh, with very sweet notes, pleasant.

ARRIBES DE VETTONIA 2003 ROSÉ
100% juan garcía

78 Deep raspberry. Powerful aroma with red stone fruit and hints of petals. Flavourful palate with fine bitter notes, a ripe fruit hint and hints of liquorice.

ARRIBES DE VETTONIA 2003 RED
100% juan garcía

78 Intense cherry. Aroma of jammy plums and marked balsamic notes. Fleshy palate with fruity tannins and slightly high acidity; red berries in the finish.

ARRIBES DE VETTONIA 1999 OAK AGED RED
100% juan garcía 🍷 24

74 Garnet red with a brick red edge. Toasty aroma with notes of oak over slightly ripe fruit, warm. Flavourful, ripe palate with supple tannins and without great expression.

ARRIBES DE VETTONIA VENDIMIA SELECCIONADA 2000 CRIANZA RED
75% brunal, 12,5% juan garcía, 12,5% tempranillo

82 Garnet red cherry. Aroma with notes of oak and fine smoky wood with a hint of earthiness and a nuance of fruity ripeness. Fleshy palate with drying wood tannins and jammy fruit, fresh.

ARRIBES DE VETTONIA 2000 SEMICRIANZA RED

ARRIBES DE VETTONIA 1999 CRIANZA RED
ARRIBES TINTO JUAN GARCÍA 1999 RESERVA RED

Cooperativa Virgen de LA BANDERA

Avenida General Franco, 24
49220 Fermoselle (Zamora)
☎: 980 613 023 - Fax: 980 613 023

VIÑA BORBÓN OAK AGED RED
100% juan garcía 🍷 12

69 Not very deep cherry with a brick red glint. Intense aroma with not very fine reduction notes (animals, varnish, aged wood). Quite flavourful palate, without great nuances.

VIÑA BORBÓN RED
100% juan garcía

78 Dark cherry. Powerful aroma of very ripe fruit with hints of toasty skins and damp earth and a balsamic suggestion. Flavourful, bitter palate with rough tannins and hints of liquorice, pleasant.

VIÑA BORBÓN WHITE
VIÑA BORBÓN ROSÉ
VIÑA CARACOSTA ROSÉ
VIÑA CARACOSTA RED

Sociedad Cooperativa NUESTRA SEÑORA DEL CASTILLO

Avenida Constitución, 2
37175 Pereña de la Ribera (Salamanca)
☎: 923 573 069 - Fax: 923 573 209

VIÑA CIBRERA 2001 ROSÉ
juan garcía, malvasía

63 Deep raspberry with an orangey hue. Aroma with notes of evolution (nail varnish). Warm, bitter palate without nuances.

ALDANA 2001 RED
juan garcía

75 Garnet red cherry with a coppery glint. Quite intense, fruity aroma with spicy hints and a balsamic suggestion. Flavourful, bitter palate with mild overextraction and hints of liquorice.

VIÑA SABALDÍN RED

Bodegas y Viñedos OCELLVM DURII

San Juan 56 - 58
49220 Fermoselle (Zamora)
☎: 983 390 606 - Fax: 983 394 224
ocellumdurii@hotmail.com

CONDADO DE FERMOSEL 2000 ROBLE RED
80% juan garcía, 10% tempranillo, 5% rufete, 5% otras

78 Garnet red with an orangey edge. Ripe aroma with a suggestion of reduction (earthiness, animals). Fresh palate with expressive fruit with dominant crianza notes and flavourful tannins.

CONDADO DE FERMOSEL 2001 ROBLE RED
80% juan garcía, 15% tempranillo, 5% rufete, otras 🍷 3

80 Garnet red cherry with a saffron hue. Powerful aroma with predominant toasty notes (oak, skins) and notions of terroir. Flavourful, fleshy palate with slightly sweet fruit yet well-integrated with the oak, dark-roasted flavours.

Bodegas RIBERA DE PELAZAS

Carretera de la Ermita, s/n
37175 Pereña de la Ribera (Salamanca)
☎: 923 166 001 - Fax: 923 573 153
administracion@grupolancia.com

Established: 1997
🍷 210 ▤ 95,000 litres 🌱 5 has. 🍇 100%

ABADENGO 2001 OAK AGED RED
100% juan garcía 🍷 12

84 Dark garnet red cherry. Intense aroma of fine toasty oak and skins with jammy fruit and notions of terroir. Flavourful palate with slightly marked tannins, very bitter (dark-roasted flavours and liquorice).

Cooperativa SAN BARTOLOMÉ

Eras 26, bajo
37250 Aldeadávila de la Ribera
(Salamanca)
☎: 923 505 008 - Fax: 923 505 008

LAGAR DE PAZOS JOVEN RED

Cooperativa del Campo SAN ROQUE

Revuelta s/n
37160 Villarino de los Aires (Salamanca)
☎: 923 573 053

LAXON JOVEN WHITE

V.T. BAJO ARAGÓN

DOMINIO MAESTRAZGO

Royal, 13
44550 Alcorisa (Teruel)
☎: 978 840 642 - Fax: 978 840 642
bodega@dominiomaestrazgo.com
www.dominiomaestrazgo.com

Established: 2001
🍷 36 ▤ 50,000 litres 🌱 4 has.
🍇 90% 🌍10%: -UK

DOMINIO MAESTRAZGO 2002 OAK AGED RED
85% garnacha, 10% cabernet sauvignon, 5% tempranillo
🍷 12

76 Cherry with a garnet red edge. Aroma with creamy oak notes that mask the fruit somewhat. Quite flavourful palate although also with heavy oak and dry tannins.

SANTOLEA 2003 OAK AGED RED
60% garnacha, 20% tempranillo, 20% cariñena 🍷 3

80 Ruby red-garnet red. Warm aroma of not very ripe red fruit. Unassembled wood tannins on the palate, fruity and flavourful.

FANBAR

Camino del Descanso, s/n
44520 Samper de Calanda (Teruel)
☎: 978 822 778 - Fax: 978 822 778
fanbar@fanbar.es
www.fanbar.es

Established: 2000
🍷 75 ▤ 200,000 litres 🌱 80 has.
🍇 98% 🌍2%: -DE

FANDOS Y BARRIUSO 2003 RED
FANDOS Y BARRIUSO 2001 ROBLE RED
FANDOS Y BARRIUSO 2002 ROBLE RED

Vinos MONTANER

Avenida Aragón 85
50710 Maella (Zaragoza)
☎: 976 638 384 - Fax: 976 638 384
vinosmontaner@teleline.es

Established: 1994
🍷 15 ▤ 500,000 litres 🌱 12 has. 🍇 100%

BARONO 2001 OAK AGED RED

Cooperativa SANTA MARÍA LA MAYOR

San Cristóbal, 63
44580 Valderrobres (Teruel)
☎: 978 850 082 - Fax: 978 890 181

Established: 1958
🍷 4 ▤ 2,452,000 litres 🌱 67.36 has.
🍇 100%

PEÑA LAGAYA ESPECIAL 2002 CRIANZA WHITE

VINOS DE LA TIERRA

PEÑA LAGAYA 2002 WHITE
PEÑA LAGAYA 2002 ROSÉ
PEÑA LAGAYA 2002 RED
PEÑA LAGAYA 2002 RED

Bodegas TEMPORE

Carretera Zaragoza-Montalbán, s/n
50131 Lécera (Zaragoza)
☎: 976 835 040 - Fax: 976 835 040
info@bodegastempore.com
www.bodegastempore.com

Established: 2002

🍾 70 📦 250,000 litres 🍇 20 has.

🇪🇸 95% 🌐5%: -UE

TEMPORE 2003 JOVEN RED
tempranillo, garnacha

75 Cherry with an orangey hue. Ripe aroma of sour cherry liqueur, quite evolved. Flavourful, spicy, slightly viscous palate with a toasty finish (skins).

TEMPORE TEMPRANILLO 2002 ROBLE RED
100% tempranillo

80 Deep garnet red. Dark-roasted aroma with a nuance of ripe black fruit. Fleshy palate with powerful black fruit in symmetry with the oak; a slight hint of vanilla.

TEMPORE VIÑA CENTURIA 2002 OAK AGED RED
100% garnacha   🍾10

77 Cherry with a brick red hue. Not very intense yet clean aroma of ripe fruit and toasty notes. Some vegetative notes on the palate with a flavourful edge, well-mannered.

TEMPORE TEMPRANILLO 2002 OAK AGED RED

VENTA D'AUBERT

Apdo. Correos, 20
44580 Valderrobres (Teruel)
☎: 978 769 021 - Fax: 978 769 031

Established: 1988

🍾 450 📦 100,000 litres 🍇 18 has.

🇪🇸 30% 🌐70%: -US -CH -DE -BE -NL -DK -JP -MX -AT -UK

VENTA D'AUBERT VIOGNIER 2003 JOVEN WHITE
100% viognier

93 Straw-coloured. Fine aroma with a suggestion of sweet fruit, fragrant herbs and notes of flowers. Full, perfumed palate (lavender, fennel) rich in fruit expression.

VENTA D'AUBERT 2003 FERMENTADO EN BARRICA WHITE
chardonnay, viognier, garnacha blanca

91 Pale yellow. Intense, very fine aroma with excellent expression of white stone fruit well-integrated with the smoky oak and floral notes. Powerful, flavourful palate with fruit well cloaked by the oak tannins and with good citrus acidity.

DIONUS 2000 OAK AGED RED
cabernet sauvignon, merlot, garnacha , syrah

88 Intense cherry. Mineral aroma with creamy toast (cocoa, coffee, pipe tobacco) and very ripe black fruit. Fleshy, powerful palate rich in oak and fruit tannins, less expressive and complex than previous harvests.

VENTA D'AUBERT 2000 OAK AGED RED
cabernet sauvignon, merlot, garnacha , syrah

85 Intense cherry. Toasty aroma of oak, dark-roasted flavours and ripe fruit (stewed fruit). Fleshy, powerful, warm, slightly spirituous palate with oak and fruit tannins flavourful.

VENTUS 2000 RED
cabernet sauvignon, garnacha, merlot

83 Intense cherry with a purple edge. Fresh, fruity, clear aroma without great nuances but fruity and with a suggestion of ripeness. Fleshy, fruity, flavourful palate rich in fruit tannins.

V.T. CÁDIZ

BARBADILLO

Luis de Eguilaz, 11
11540 Sanlúcar de Barrameda (Cádiz)
☎: 956 385 500 - Fax: 956 385 501
barbadillo@barbadillo.com
www.barbadillo.com

Established: 1821

🍾 50,000 📦 5,000,000 litres 🍇 500 has.

🇪🇸 60% 🌐40%: -UK -DE -US -NL -BE

CASTILLO DE SAN DIEGO 2003 WHITE
MAESTRANTE 2003 WHITE SEMIDULCE

Complejo Bodeguero BELLAVISTA

Carretera Circunvalaión s/n Complejo Bellavista
11407 Jerez de la Frontera (Cádiz)
☎: 956 319 650 - Fax: 956 319 824
atencionalcliente@grupogarvey.com
www.grupogarvey.com

VIÑA MONTEGIL 2002 OAK AGED WHITE
100% palomino

74 Pale yellow with a golden hue. Powerful aroma with smoky oak and a suggestion of sherry (lees, oxidative hints). Dry, quite flavourful palate with notes of green olives.

HEREDEROS DE ARGÜESO

Mar, 8
11540 Sanlúcar de Barrameda (Cádiz)
☎: 956 385 116 - Fax: 956 368 169
argueso@argueso.es
www.argueso.es

Established: 1822

⊕ 12,000 🗐 6,000,000 litres 🍇 50 has.

🍷 85% 🍏15%: -DE -UK -NL -BE -US -CA

QUINTA DEL CARMEN WHITE

J. FERRIS M.

Carretera CA-602, km. 16
11500 Sanlucar de Barrameda (Cádiz)
☎: 956 235 100 - Fax: 956 235 011
bodega@bodegasferris.com

Established: 1975

⊕ 10,000 🗐 2,000,000 litres 🍇 35 has.

🍷 5% 🍏95%

SEÑORIO DE J. FERRIS 2001 RED
syrah, merlot, cabernet sauvignon, tempranillo

77 Dark cherry. Fruity aroma (muted fruit) with slight notes of overripening and oak. A hint of overripe fruit and slightly sweet on the palate, with good oak notes.

SEÑORIO DE J. FERRIS 2000 RED
syrah, merlot, tempranillo, cabernet sauvignon

58 Fairly subdued cherry. Negative, sweetish, flawed aroma. Greeness on the palate, sweetish and mediocre.

MANUEL ARAGÓN BAIZÁN

Calle Olivo, 1
11130 Chiclana de la Frontera (Cádiz)
☎: 956 400 756 - Fax: 956 532 907
granero@teleline.es

Established: 1795

⊕ 800 🗐 250,000 litres 🍇 60 has.

🍷 85% 🍏15%: -FR -IT -UK

M. ARAGÓN 2003 JOVEN WHITE
SAUVIGNON BLANC M. ARAGÓN 2003 SECO

OSBORNE Y CÍA

Fernán Caballero, 3

11500 El Puerto de Sta. María (Cádiz)
☎: 956 869 000 - Fax: 956 869 078
comunicacion@osborne.es
www.osborne.es

Established: 1772

⊕ 17,500 🗐 10,000,000 litres 🍇 210 has.

🍷 50% 🍏50%: -NL -DE -UK -US

GADIR WHITE
chardonnay, palomino

78 Pale straw. Medium-intensity, fruity, fresh aroma. Light, flavourful palate, uncomplicated.

Hijos de RAINERA PÉREZ MARÍN

Misericordia, 1
11540 Sanlúcar de Barrameda (Cádiz)
☎: 956 319 564 - Fax: 956 319 869
laguita@laguita.com
www.laguita.com

Established: 1852

⊕ 50 🗐 5,204,000 litres 🍇 275 has.

🍷 90% 🍏10%: -PH -PL -NZ -LV -RU

PAGO DE MIRAFLORES 2003 FERMENTADO EN BARRICA RED
cabernet sauvignon, tempranillo, syrah

82 Garnet red cherry. Short aroma without varietal nuances, clear and warm with well-integrated fine toasty oak notes. Medium structured, warm palate with ripe fruit and a mild sensation of slightly vegetative skins.

PAGO DE MIRAFLORES 2002 FERMENTADO EN BARRICA WHITE
CASTILLO DE MIRAFLORES 2003 WHITE

SÁNCHEZ ROMATE HERMANOS

Lealas 26-28
11403 Jerez de la Frontera (Cádiz)
☎: 956 182 212 - Fax: 956 185 276
comercial@romate.com
www.romate.com

Established: 1781

⊕ 6,500 🗐 500,000 litres 🍇 110 has.

🍷 40% 🍏60%

MO & MO 2003 WHITE

VIÑA LA CALLEJUELA

Camino Reventón Chico, s/n
11540 Sanlucar de Barrameda (Cádiz)
☎: 956 361 553
callejuela@vodafone.es

Established: 1998

🌐 400 📊 500,000 litres 🍇 35 has. 🍷 100%

VIÑA LA CALLEJUELA 2003 WHITE

V.T. CAMPO DE CARTAGENA

SERRANO

Finca La Cabaña, 30
30594 Pozo Estrecho (Cartagena) (Murcia)
☎: 968 556 298 - Fax: 968 556 298
bodegaserrano@teleline.es
www.bodegaserrano.com

Established: 1941

🌐 10 📊 98,000 litres 🍇 15 has.
🍷 95% 🌍5%: -DE

DARIMUS 2003 WHITE SEMIDULCE
VIÑA GALTEA 2003 WHITE SEMIDULCE
DARIMUS 2003 FERMENTADO EN BARRICA
 RED
VIÑA GALTEA 2003 RED SEMIDULCE
DARIMUS 2003 RED DULCE

V.T. CANGAS

CHACÓN-BUELTA

Carretera General, s/n
33812 Cerredo (Asturias)
☎: 985 818 190 - Fax: 985 818 190
alejandrobuelta@hotmail.com

Established: 2000

📊 50,000 litres 🍇 1.5 has. 🍷 100%

CHACÓN-BUELTA 2003 RED
mencía, verdejo

80 Garnet red cherry. Intense, fruity aroma with toasty notes of skins. Flavourful palate with the freshness of skins, spicy with good acidity.

MONASTERIO DE CORIAS

Monasterio de Corias Apdo. de correos 100
33800 Cangas del Narcea (Asturias)
☎: 985 810 493
vinoscangas@narceadigital.com

Established: 2000

🌐 60 📊 40,800 litres 🍇 3.5 has.
🍷 90% 🌍10%: América Sur

MONASTERIO DE CORIAS VIÑA GRANDIELLA 2003 FERMENTADO EN BARRICA WHITE
albarín, moscatel

82 Pale yellow with a golden hue. Intense aroma of fruit and white flowers with fine smoky and creamy oak notes. Flavourful, fruity aroma with spicy wood notes, citrus and bitter hints and a slightly acidic edge.

MONASTERIO DE CORIAS 2002 OAK AGED RED
verdejo, mencía, carrasquín, albarín

81 Not very deep brilliant cherry. Powerful aroma of foresty red fruit with macerated skins and a spicy, slightly creamy hint (lactic flavours) of damp earth. Fresh flavourful palate with ripe sweet fruit and a slightly oily texture, original.

OBANCA

Obanca 12
33800 Cangas del Narcea (Asturias)
☎: 985 811 539

VIÑEDOS OBANCA RED

Bodegas VICENTE

La Muriella-Vega de Rengos
33812 Cangas del Narcea (Asturias)
☎: 985 911 097 - Fax: 985 911 097

MURIELLA 2003 WHITE
MURIELLA 2002 RED

V.T. CASTILLA

ALBAVINSA

Lepanto, 23 Bajo
02003 Albacete (Albacete)
☎: 967 217 711 - Fax: 967 242 066
info@albavinsa.com
www.albavinsa.com

Established: 1999

🌐 300 📊 500,000 litres 🍇 70 has.
🍷 90% 🌍10%: -DE -CZ -SB UK -NL -BE

ALDONZA 1999 CRIANZA RED
70% tempranillo, 30% cabernet sauvignon

78 Cherry with an orangey hue. Aroma of new wood with ripe fruit, not very intense. Light, watery palate, without great expression.

ALDONZA 1999 RESERVA RED

ARÚSPIDE

Francisco Morales, 102
13300 Valdepeñas (Ciudad Real)
☎: 926 347 075 - Fax: 926 347 875
baruspide@jazzfree.com
www.aruspide.com

Established: 1999

🌐 450 📊 180,000 litres 🍇 70 has.

🍷 80% 🌐20%: -DE -AT -BE -US -UK -IE -NL -DK -CA

ARDALES DE ARÚSPIDE 2003 WHITE
airén

80 Pale. Intense, fruity aroma of green grass and lavender. Flavourful, oily palate with ripe white fruit and good expression.

ARDALES DE ARÚSPIDE SELECCIÓN DE BARRICA 2001 OAK AGED RED
🌐 8

83 Garnet red cherry. Aroma of ripe black fruit with toasty skins and fine wood (spices, vanilla). Original and flavourful palate with fruity and fresh tannins and integrated but evident oak in the finish; well-rounded structure.

ARDALES DE ARÚSPIDE 2002 RED
tempranillo

81 Dark cherry with a violet rim. Powerful aroma of black fruit and macerated skins, quite sweet with a nuance of damp earth. Flavourful, fleshy palate with a hint of overripening, sweet, earthy and long.

ARVA-VITIS

Ctro. Empresas-Vía Principal
13200 Manzanares (Ciudad Real)
☎: 926 611 065 - Fax: 926 613 961
arvavitis@terra.es
www.arvavitis.com

Established: 1998

🌐 250 📊 1,000,000 litres 🍷 10% 🌐90%

ARVA VITIS SELECCIÓN 2003 SECO WHITE
macabeo, sauvignon blanc

82 Yellow straw. Intense aroma of ripe but fresh fruit, prominent. Oily, flavourful palate with hay, very pleasant with fine bitter notes.

ARVA VITIS 2003 RED
cabernet sauvignon, syrah

82 Intense cherry with a violet edge. Clean, intense aroma of ripe red fruit. Flavourful palate with pleasant tannins, medium persistence and a suggestion of red fruit in the retronasal passage.

ARVA VITIS 2001 ROBLE RED
tempranillo
🌐 6

82 Medium-hue cherry red. Aroma with sweet notes of ripe fruit, balsamic flavours and lactics. Good fruit weight on the palate and sweet with good acidity, well-integrated wood tannins and suggestions of ripe fruit.

ARVA VITIS SELECCIÓN TEMPRANILLO 2000 ROBLE RED
tempranillo
🌐 12

81 Not very deep cherry. Aroma of jammy black fruit, balsamic notes and violets. Good varietal expresión on the palate, slightly short and not very persistent.

AVALÓN DE ARVA VITIS 2001 RED
100% tempranillo

80 Garnet red cherry. Aroma of very ripe fruit (plums, raisins), and ripeness (dried peaches). Flavourful, with toasted oak well-integrated with the ripe fruit; livelier than in the nose.

ARVA VITIS NATURALIS 2003 WHITE

Bodegas ASOCIADAS

Plaza Santa Quiteria, 24, 1 Pt
13600 Alcázar de San Juan (Ciudad Real)
☎: 926 547 404 - Fax: 926 547 702
baco@dominiodebaco.com
www.ofimanchega.com/b.a.co

AMALIA RED
cencibel

80 Cherry red. Not very intense aroma of slightly reduced red fruit. Warm, bitter palate with smoky notes in the retronasal passage.

Bodegas y Viñedos BARREDA

Ramalazo, 2
45880 Corral de Almaguer (Toledo)
☎: 925 207 223 - Fax: 925 207 223
bodegas-barreda@bodegas-barreda.com
www.bodegas-barreda.com

Established: 1945

🌐 200 📊 300,000 litres 🍇 170 has.

🍷 50% 🌐50%

TORRE DE BARREDA 2002 ROBLE RED
100% tempranillo

85 Garnet red cherry with a violet edge. Intense aroma of black fruit, with toasty notes of skins and the freshness of spicy oak. Flavourful palate with ripe and oily tannins, excellent symmetry and a hint of mineral freshness.

TORRE DE BARREDA SELECCIÓN 2001 OAK AGED RED
100% tempranillo

86 Very deep garnet red cherry. Powerful aroma with predominant red fruit notes, smoky hints of oak and a slightly mineral nuance. Flavourful, supple palate with well-integrated oak/fruit, excellent symmetry and crianza expression, a suggestion of balsamics and terroir and refreshing acidity.

TORRE DE BARREDA AMIGOS 2000 RED
100% tempranillo

86 Intense garnet red cherry. Intense aroma with predominant toasty oak notes over the ripe fruit notes, a balsamic hint and a fine reduction. Flavourful, supple palate, fleshy overtones, with a good oak/fruit integration and spices and minerals in the retronasal passage.

BERBERANA

Carretera de Vitoria, km. 182-183
26360 Cenicero (La Rioja)
☎: 941 453 100 - Fax: 941 450 101
info@berberana.com
www.berberana.com

Established: 1877

🌐 10,000 🛢 26,000,000 litres 🍇 3,000 has.

🍷 56% 🌐44%: -UK -NL -DE -JP -US

BERBERANA DRAGÓN OAK AGED RED
50% tempranillo, 50% cabernet sauvignon ⊕ 6

80 Garnet red cherry with a saffron edge. Fruity aroma with creamy and spicy notes of wood. Flavourful palate with fresh varietal overtones (herbs, paprika) and slightly marked tannins, pleasant.

Bodegas CANTÓ

Carretera Jaen, km. 3'400
02400 Hellín (Albacete)
☎: 967 300 121 - Fax: 967 300 975

Established: 1956

🌐 325 🛢 500,000 litres 🍇 39 has.

🍷 100%

CANTOFINO INTENSO 2003 JOVEN RED
100% garnacha titorera

85 Bigarreau cherry with a violet edge. Intense aroma with ripe and fresh fruit (blackberries, raspberries) and a nuance of flowers (violets), fine. Flavourful, powerful, expressive and varietal palate, a good young wine.

FINCA MINATEDA ROBLE 2001 ROBLE RED
100% garnacha

85 Dark cherry with a violet edge. Not very intense yet fine harmonious aroma of ripe black fruit and balsamic notes. Flavourful, balsamic palate of concentrated fruit, with well-integrated wood and noticeable tannins, long.

FINCA MINATEDA SYRAH 2002 ROBLE RED
100% syrah

80 Lively garnet red cherry. Intense, unusual aroma (aniseed, incense) with ripe fruit. Fruitier on the palate, flavourful with toasty oak yet to be integrated.

FINCA MINATEDA TEMPRANILLO 2002 ROBLE RED
100% tempranillo

74 Cherry with a garnet red edge. Aroma with notes of greeness (vine shoots) and a hint of red fruit. Quite flavourful palate but also with notes of greeness; astringent.

FINCA MINATEDA SELECCIÓN PEDRO SARRIÓN 2000 ROBLE RED
90% tempranillo, 10% syrah

87 Deep cherry. Smoky aroma of jammy red fruit, a spicy hint and a suggestion of earth. Fleshy, deep palate (slightly mineral) with polished, oily tannins, a good oak-fruit balance and liquorice and bitter cocoa in the finish.

FINCA MINATEDA SELECCIÓN PEDRO SARRIÓN 1999 ROBLE RED
90% tempranillo, 10% syrah

84 Intense cherry with a garnet red edge. Quite intense aroma of spicy oak and black fruit. Flavourful, powerful, fleshy palate with good expression of ripe fruit and oak yet to be integrated; promising.

CASA DE LA VIÑA

Carretera de la Solana a Infantes, km. 15
13248 Alhambra (Ciudad Real)
☎: 943 445 700 - Fax: 943 445 292
iadrianl@byb.es
www.byb.es

Established: 1857
⊕ 1,000 🗄 6,500,000 litres 🍇 250 has.

ALBOR 2003 JOVEN RED

Pago CASA DEL BLANCO

Carretera Manzanares a Moral de Calatrava, km. 24-26
13200 Manzanares (Ciudad Real)
☎: 917 480 606 - Fax: 913 290 266
fincaelblanco@terra.es

Established: 2003
⊕ 800 🗄 300,000 litres 🍇 120 has.
🍷 20% 🌐80%: -JP -DE -UK -US

QVIXOTE 2001 CRIANZA RED
cabernet sauvignon, syrah

83 Dark cherry with a saffron edge. Powerful aroma of jammy black fruit with balsamic notes, toasty oak and a nuance of damp earth. Flavourful, concentrated palate with hints of overripening that subdue the varietal expression, spicy, warm and oily.

QVIXOTE 02 2002 CRIANZA RED
QVIXOTE 03 2003 CRIANZA RED

Bodegas y Viñedos CASA DEL VALLE

Carretera de Yepes - Añover, km. 47, 700
(Finca Valdelagua)
45313 Yepes (Toledo)
☎: 925 147 019 - Fax: 925 155 533
casadelvalle@bodegasolarra.es

www.bodegacasadelvalle.es

Established: 2000
⊕ 2,000 🍇 100 has. 🍷 70% 🌐30%

HACIENDA CASA DEL VALLE CABERNET SAUVIGNON 2002 RED
100% cabernet sauvignon

84 Garnet red cherry. Intense, ripe aroma with predominant creamy oak notes and a slight varietal expression (black fruit, hints of brambles). Flavourful and bitter on the palate with ripe tannins and herbaceous hints, high in acidity.

ACANTUS 2003 WHITE
ACANTUS 2003 ROSÉ
ACANTUS 2002 RED

CASAGRANDE

Matadero, 1
45749 Villamuelas (Toledo)
☎: 925 346 524 - Fax: 925 346 524
gmdiego@mixmail.com

Established: 1975
⊕ 420 🗄 3,500,000 litres 🍷 70%
🌐30%: -SE -JP -AD -UK

DIERA 2000 OAK AGED RED
DIERA 2001 OAK AGED RED

Bodegas y Viñedos CASTIBLANQUE

Isaac Peral 19
13610 Campo de Criptana (Ciudad Real)
☎: 926 589 147 - Fax: 926 589 148
info@bodegascastiblanque.com
www.bodegascastiblanque.com

Established: 2001
⊕ 192 🗄 2,120,000 litres 🍇 175 has.
🍷 90% 🌐10%: -PA -FR -CAM-CA -DE -UK

ILEX AIRÉN 2003 JOVEN WHITE
100% airén

80 Pale gold. Intense aroma of white fruit (hints of apricot skins) with a spicy hint of skins. Flavourful palate with fine bitter notes (hay, cumin) and good acidity.

ILEX MACABEO 2003 JOVEN WHITE
100% macabeo

82 Pale gold. Intense aroma of very varietal perfume with fruit and white flowers and hints of fragrant herbs. Flavourful palate with fine bitter notes and excellent acidity.

ILEX CHARDONNAY 2003 OAK AGED WHITE
100% chardonnay

82 Golden yellow. Intense aroma of slightly varietal white fruit, spicy notes and creamy oak

VINOS DE LA TIERRA

with citrus fruit peel and fragrant herbs. Flavourful palate with slightly drying tannins, warm hints and fine bitter notes.

BALDOR TRADICIÓN SYRAH 2002 OAK AGED RED
100% syrah   🍷 6

82 Garnet red with a strawberry edge. Very balsamic, earthy aroma of black fruit. Good varietal expression on the palate, good fruit weight and fruity, round tannins.

BALDOR TRADICIÓN TEMPRANILLO 2002 OAK AGED RED
100% tempranillo   🍷 6

83 Cherry with a violet edge. Aroma of ripe red fruit, fine spices of the vine variety and a complex smoky hint. Fresh, round and very fruity on the palate with well-integrated wood, original with a varietal finish.

ILEX COUPAGE 2002 OAK AGED RED
40% tempranillo, 40% syrah, 20% cabernet sauvignon

83 Garnet red cherry. Quite intense aroma of red fruit, hints of fresh skins and spicy oak. Flavourful, supple, slightly warm on the palate evoking the freshness of fruit and terroir.

Bodegas CELAYA

Poligono Industrial El Salvador Avenida 1, Parcelas 56-57
02630 La Roda (Albacete)
☎: 967 440 101 - Fax: 967 548 496
correo@bodegascelaya.com

Established: 1927
🍷 100 🛢 2,500,000 litres 🇪🇸 100%

MIZANTAR CENCIBEL RED
100% cencibel

78 Garnet red cherry with a coppery glint. Intense, ripe aroma with spicy hints of skins. Flavourful palate with fleshy overtones and slightly bitter tannins.

MIZANTAR 2001 ROBLE RED
cencibel   🍷 6

78 Cherry with an orangey edge. Aroma with tobacco notes, spices and sloes in liqueur. Fresh, flavourful palate with light and spicy tannins; a pleasant, slightly bitter finish.

CERVANTINO

Grande, 66
13670 Villarubia de los Ojos (Ciudad Real)
☎: 926 898 018 - Fax: 926 266 514
cervantino@b-lozano.com

Established: 2000
🛢 150,000 litres 🇪🇸 75% 🌐25%

CONDELIER WHITE
CONDELIER RED

Sociedad Agraria de Transformación COLOMAN

Goya, 17
13620 Pedro Muñoz (Ciudad Real)
☎: 926 586 410 - Fax: 926 586 656
coloman@satcoloman.com
www.satcoloman.com

Established: 1965
🍷 50 🛢 27,800,000 litres 🍇 4,210 has.
🍷 99% 🌐1%: -FR

PEDROTEÑO AIRÉN WHITE
airén

78 Pale yellow. Intense aroma of fruit and white flowers, with fresh citrus overtones and fragrant herbs. Flavourful, and fruity on the palate, a slightly oily texture, bitter.

PEDROTEÑO CENCIBEL RED
cencibel

82 Cherry with a garnet red edge. Aroma of red fruit, spices, slightly earthy and varietal. Fleshy, very fresh and flavourful palate, reminiscent of the vine variety.

CORONADO VINOS Y BODEGAS

Carretera San Isidro, s/n
16620 La Alberca de Zancara (Cuenca)
☎: 620 287 825 - Fax: 967 150 107

Established: 2002
🍷 20 🛢 250,000 litres 🍇 20 has.🍷 100%

VIÑA CHARCÓN CABERNET SAUVIGNON 2003 RED
VIÑA CHARCÓN 2002 ROBLE RED
VIÑA CHARCÓN SYRAH 2003 RED

COSECHEROS Y CRIADORES

Diputación, s/n
01320 Oyón (Alava)
☎: 945 601 944 - Fax: 945 622 488
nacional@cosecherosycriadores.com
www.martinezbujanda.com

Established: 1951
🍷 5,000 🍷 40% 🌐60%: -US -CA -DE -UK

INFINITUS 2003 WHITE
viura, chardonnay

82 Pale with coppery nuances. Intense aroma of white stone fruit, notes of flowers, syrup and fine lees. Flavourful, quite fruity palate with fine bitter notes, citrus fruits and excellent acidity.

INFINITUS 2000 OAK AGED RED
tempranillo, cabernet sauvignon

78 Cherry with a garnet red edge. Intense, warm and viscous aroma. Round and ripe on the palate with toasty wood and slightly drying tannins.

DEHESA DEL CARRIZAL

13140 Retuerta del Bullaque (Ciudad Real)
☎: 914 841 385 - Fax: 916 624 209
jalcubilla@investblue.es
www.dehesadelcarrizal.com

Established: 1987

🍷 800 📊 242,000 litres 🍇 22 has.

🍷 70% 🌐30%: -US -CH -UK -DE -MX -EC

DEHESA DEL CARRIZAL MV 2002 OAK AGED RED
55% cabernet sauvignon, 25% syrah, 20% merlot   🍷 12

90 Dark garnet red cherry. Powerful aroma rich in mineral nuances (earth and dry stones), fine and creamy toasty oak and slightly jammy, well-balanced fruit. Round, spicy, toasty, complex palate, very Mediterranean with jammy fruit and sweet tannins, spirituous and warm

DEHESA DEL CARRIZAL CABERNET SAUVIGNON 2002 OAK AGED RED
100% cabernet sauvignon

88 Quite dark cherry with a garnet red hue. Aroma with fruity notes and with a mild vegetative hint, fine toasty flavours. Fruity, flavourful and pleasant on the palate but with less varietal complexity than the previous vintage.

DEHESA DEL CARRIZAL CHARDONNAY 2003 OAK AGED WHITE
100% chardonnay

88 Intense gold. Powerful, creamy aroma with predominant toasty oak notes (slightly sweet) over a nuance of ripe apples. Flavourful palate with fine bitter notes, well-integrated fruit and oak, smoky hints and jammy citrus fruit in the retronasal passage.

DEHESA DEL CARRIZAL COLECCIÓN PRIVADA 2000 OAK AGED RED
40% cabernet sauvignon, 30% syrah, 30% merlot

89 Quite intense cherry. Spicy aroma with fine reduction nuances (tobacco, leather) and toasty flavours (coffee, cocoa). Round, oily, spicy palate with powerful and ripe tannins, toasty oak and jammy fruit, spirituous and warm.

DEHESA DEL CARRIZAL CABERNET SAUVIGNON 2001 OAK AGED RED
100% cabernet sauvignon

91 Dark cherry. Fine toasty aroma (cocoa, coffee and peat) with stewed fruit and a suggestion of minerals, warm. Powerful, very varietal palate (overripe redcurrants, paprika) with fine and very ripe Cabernet tannins, very long.

DEHESA DEL CARRIZAL SYRAH 2002 OAK AGED RED

VINOS DE LA TIERRA

DEL SAZ (VIDAL DEL SAZ RODRÍGUEZ)

Maestro Manzanares, 57
13610 Campo de Criptana (Ciudad Real)
☎: 926 562 424 - Fax: 926 562 659
bodegasdelsaz@infonegocio.com
Established: 1974
⊞ 60 ▤ 6,000,000 litres ⚘ 70 has.
🍇 100%

RIBERA DEL SAZ TEMPRANILLO 2003 RED
RIBERA DEL SAZ 2003 SEMIDULCE

DUELA MAESTRA

Avenida de Nazaret, 4
28009 Madrid (Madrid)
☎: 915 745 534 - Fax: 915 745 534
duelamaestra@terra.es
Established: 2000
⊞ 5 ▤ 500 litres 🍇 100%

ZUMAQUE DE BROTEAS 2001 RED
syrah, cabernet sauvignon

92 Intense cherry. Powerful aroma of ripe, toasty skins with fine notes of creamy oak and ripe fruit. Fleshy, powerful palate rich in warm sensations of ripe fruit (jam) and hints of minerals and earth.

EGUREN

Avenida del Cantábrico, s/n
01013 Vitoria (Alava)
☎: 945 282 844 - Fax: 945 271 319
info@heredadugarte.com
www.heredadugarte.com
Established: 1957
⊞ 120 ▤ 1,200,000 litres 🍇 75% ⚬25%

REINARES 2003 WHITE
100% viura

80 Pale straw. Fresh, fruity, clean, delicate aroma with fine green herbs. Light, flavourful, fresh, pleasant, fruity and very clean on the palate.

REINARES 2003 ROSÉ
tempranillo, garnacha

79 Lively raspberry. Slightly intense, fruity aroma with hints of herbs and spicy skins. Fresh flavourful palate with bitter notes and marked citrus acidity.

PAGOS DE EGUREN 2003 RED
100% tempranillo

82 Intense cherry. Powerful aroma with very ripe fruity notes and hints of dry earth. Fleshy palate with ripe black fruit and foresty hints, flavourful.

REINARES 2003 RED
100% tempranillo

75 Garnet red cherry. Slightly short aroma with barely any fruit and notions of a slight reduction in the tank. Fresh, flavourful palate, better than in the nose, warm and mildly sweet.

CONDADO DE EGUREN 2001 RED
100% tempranillo

78 Quite dark cherry. Slightly fruity aroma with mild notes of early reduction. Flavourful, fruity palate, better than in the nose.

EGUREN FRESCO WHITE
EGUREN FRESCO RED

Cooperativa Agrícola EL PROGRESO

Avenida de la Virgen, 89
13670 Villarubia de los Ojos (Ciudad Real)
☎: 926 896 088 - Fax: 926 896 135
cooprogres@isid.es
Established: 1917
⊞ 200 ▤ 45,000 litres ⚘ 9,700 has.

MI CHUPITO WHITE
airén

79 Pale. Somewhat intense aroma of white fruit with hints of herbs. Fresh, flavourful palate with fine spices, herby notes, hints of aniseed and good acidity.

Bodegas ERCAVIO

Plazuela de la Iglesia, 1
45311 Dosbarrios (Toledo)
☎: 626 481 146 - Fax: 941 302 606
masquevinos@fer.es
Established: 1999
⊞ 200 ▤ 200,000 litres ⚘ 15 has.
🍇 15% ⚬85%: -DE -BE -CH -AT -FI -DK - IE -UK -US -MX -JP

ERCAVIO 2003 WHITE
airén

84 Straw-coloured with a greenish nuance. Intense, fine, fresh aroma of apples and complex mountain herbs. Fresh and light on the palate with an excellent Airén expression, easy drinking.

ERCAVIO TEMPRANILLO 2003 ROBLE RED
100% tempranillo

87 Biggareau cherry with a lively violet edge. Intense aroma of very ripe black fruit (quite viscous) with spicy oak (sandalwood), harmonious. Generous, flavourful palate with very ripe fruit well-integrated with the spicy oak, ripe tannins and a degree of persistence.

ERCAVIO TEMPRANILLO CABERNET SAUVIGNON 2003 JOVEN RED
70% tempranillo, 30% cabernet sauvignon

85 Cherry with a violet hue. Intense aroma with a good fruit expression (blackberries, plums, cherries), clean with a balsamic hint. Generous, flavourful palate with lively fruit and a touch of liquorice, well-balanced with black fruit in the retronasal passage.

ERCAVIO LIMITED RESERVE 2001 OAK AGED RED
75% tempranillo, 25% merlot   🛢 12

86 Cherry with an orangey edge. Intense aroma with crianza character (fine wood), very spicy (tobacco, pepper, cloves, cinnamon) with jammy fruit. Flavourful, round, spicy palate with an excellent crianza.

LA PLAZUELA 2002 RED

FÉLIX SOLÍS

Autovía de Andalucía, km. 199
13300 Valdepeñas (Ciudad Real)
☎: 926 322 400 - Fax: 926 322 417
bsf@felixsolix.com

www.felixsolis.com

Established: 1952

🍶 40,000 🛢 192,000,000 litres 🍇 500 has.

🍷 62% ⌖38%: -UK -DE -NL -DK -FI -SE -BE -GQ -CH TG -MX -BE -AT -JP -PH -NC -DO -US -AO Tahiti -CA -CO -SE -DK -CZ -DZ -PE -VE -IT -LU -CF -PA -KE CM -VN -TW -LB -GT -MY CD -SG -EC -BR -JO -GA TZ -CR -EL -AU -SV -SB -GM -IE -NI -PT

SENDAS DEL REY 2003 WHITE
viura, airén

72 Pale steel. Not very intense yet clear aroma with aniseed notes, fruity. Light, slightly flabby palate, quite sweet yet well-mannered.

CALIZA TEMPRANILLO 2003 OAK AGED RED
90% tempranillo, 10% cabernet sauvignon

81 Intense cherry with a purplish edge. Intense, fruity aroma with good varietal expression (underbrush), toasty hints of oak. Flavourful, concentrated and fruity on the palate with promising although quite marked tannins and good acidity.

SENDAS DEL REY 2000 OAK AGED RED
tempranillo, garnacha

78 Dark cherry with a coppery edge. Fairly intense, fruity aroma with a spicy and mildly creamy oak nuance. Flavourful palate with slightly marked tannins, a nuance of sweet fruit and notions of liquorice, pleasant.

FINCA LA ESTACADA

Carretera N-400, km. 103
16400 Tarancón (Cuenca)
☎: 969 327 099 - Fax: 969 327 199
fincalaestacada@fincalaestacada.com
www.fincalaestacada.com

Established: 2001

🍶 2,000 🛢 1,000,000 litres 🍇 400 has.

🍷 75% ⌖25%: -US -NL -AT -DE -UK -CH -DK-PT -PR

FINCA LA ESTACADA 2003 OAK AGED RED
100% tempranillo   🍶 6

83 Deep garnet red. Slightly alcoholic aroma of honey, new wood and cedar. Quite polished wood tannins on the palate with bitter notes, slightly short with hints of new wood in the retronasal passage.

FINCA LA ESTACADA 2002 OAK AGED RED
100% tempranillo   🍶 12

87 Lively garnet red cherry. Intense aroma with fine toasty oak, a suggestion of superripened fruit and notions of wax and dry earth. Powerful palate with slightly rough yet promising tannins, flavourful and bitter with an excellent mineral character in the finish.

FINCA LA ESTACADA SELECCIÓN VARIETALES 2001 OAK AGED RED
tempranillo, cabernet sauvignon, merlot, syrah, mazuelo
🌐 18

88 Dark cherry with a dark red-violet edge. Powerful, ripe aroma with fine smoky oak notes, a suggestion of slightly reduced fruit (cedar, jammy prunes) and notions of terroir. Flavourful, very bitter palate (liquorice, graphite, dark-roasted flavours) with excellent acidity.

FINCA LORANQUE

45593 Bargas (Toledo)
☎: 669 476 849 - Fax: 925 512 450
fincaloranque@miportal.es
Established: 1996
🛢 200 📦 250,000 litres 🍇 42 has.
🍷 80% 🌐20%: -US -CH

FINCA LORANQUE 2002 OAK AGED RED
55% syrah, 35% tempranillo, 10% cabernet sauvignon

86 Dark cherry. Powerful, ripe aroma (cherries, black fruit) with hints of petals, toasty oak and a nuance of damp earth. Flavourful, fleshy palate with a good oak/fruit integration and fine bitter notes, slightly warm with toasty hints in the retronasal passage.

FINCA LORANQUE 2002 RED
100% cabernet sauvignon

84 Very dark garnet red. Aroma of toasty wood, spicy (pepper, cloves) with varietal expression. Somewhat green fruit tannins and slightly marked wood tannins on the palate with a suggestion of tobacco and cedar in the retronasal passage.

FINCA LORANQUE TEMPRANILLO 2002 RED
tempranillo

83 Quite dark cherry. Fruity and ripe aroma with fine notes of oak well-integrated with the wine. Flavourful, ripe, fruity and warm palate, minerals in the retronasal passage.

FONTANA

Extramuros, s/n
16411 Fuente de Pedro Naharro (Cuenca)
☎: 969 125 433 - Fax: 969 125 387
bf@bodegasfontana.com
www.bodegasfontana.com
Established: 1997
🛢 2,150 📦 5,000,000 litres 🍇 500 has.
🍷 60% 🌐40%: -US -CH -DK -DE -NL -UK -PR -JP

MESTA 2003 WHITE

74 Pale with coppery nuances. Slightly intense aroma of ripe fruit with hints of lees and withered petals. Flavourful, bitter palate with a slightly acidic edge.

MESTA 2003 ROSÉ

79 Pale cherry. Slightly intense aroma of foresty red fruit with hints of macerated skins. Flavourful, bitter palate with a spicy hint and excellent acidity.

MESTA TEMPRANILLO 2003 RED
100% tempranillo

83 Dark cherry with a coppery edge. Intense, fruity aroma with a certain varietal character (black fruit, underbrush). Flavourful, fruity palate with spicy hints of skins, rough and fine tannins, slightly oily.

DUETO 2002 CRIANZA RED
50% cabernet sauvignon, 50% merlot

93 Very intense cherry. Powerful aroma, rich in ripe varietal expression (sun-drenched grapes) without losing its character (redcurrants and mineral notes). Powerful, ripe and very flavourful palate with a certain mineral complexity; excellent grape harvest and perfect wood.

QUERCUS 2001 CRIANZA RED
100% tempranillo

86 Dark cherry with a garnet red edge. Quite impenetrable aroma with fine notes of jammy fruit well-integrated with the wood, balsamic notes. Flavourful, fleshy, ripe palate with excellent crianza expression and a spicy hint, slightly viscous and oily.

PAGO EL PÚLPITO 1999 VINO DE LICOR
100% tempranillo

84 Cherry with an orangey edge. Aroma of nearly overripe fruit (stewed pear, plums), with sun-drenched skins and cinnamon. Flavourful, generous palate, not too sweet with jammy black fruit and viscous notes, very polished and silky.

GALÁN

Salida de los Llanos, 15
13300 Valdepeñas (Ciudad Real)
☎: 926 321 752 - Fax: 926 324 766
bodegasgalan@bodegasgalan.com
www.bodegasgalan.com
Established: 1876
🛢 200 📦 200,000 litres 🍷 95% 🌐5%: -DE

VEGA FRÍA 2003 JOVEN RED

GARVA

Topete, 72
45930 Méntrida (Toledo)
☎: 918 177 304 - Fax: 918 177 304

ELISA MACABEO 2003 WHITE

83 Excellent bright yellow colour. Aroma with good varietal expression, well-integrated with the creamy nuances of the cask. Dry, flavourful palate, evident wood due to the lesser glycerin content of the Macabeo variety. Flavourful palate, with oak nuances but slightly shorter on the palate than on the nose, ripe vine variety in the retronasal passage.

SEÑORÍO DE TOLEDO MAIUS 2003

84 Garnet red. Slightly short aroma of black berries, redcurrants, with spicy hints, quite warm. Fleshy palate, slightly spirituous, supple, with sweet and polished tannins.

Cooperativa JESÚS DEL PERDÓN

Polígono Industrial, s/n
13200 Manzanares (Ciudad Real)
☎: 926 610 309 - Fax: 926 610 516
yuntero@yuntero.com
www.yuntero.com

Established: 1954

⊞ 2,000 🗃 25,000,000 litres 🍇 3,605 has.

🍷 60% 🍇40%: -UE -CH -JP -AU -US -CO -PH

LAZARILLO 2003 WHITE SEMIDULCE
airén

76 Pale straw. Short but clear aroma, fresh and fruity. Sweet palate with a suggestion of bitterness and notes of herbs; very well-mannered.

LAZARILLO AIRÉN 2003 WHITE
airén

80 Straw-coloured. Medium-intensity, fresh aroma of ripe apples with a nuance of herbs. Light, quite flavourful, fruity palate, easy drinking.

LAZARILLO 2003 RED
tempranillo

77 Intense cherry. Fruity aroma (brambles) with green and balsamic notes. Flavourful palate with fresh and fruity tannins; red fruit in the finish.

Bodegas y Viñedos JESÚS RECUERO

La Puebla, 14
45810 Villanueva de Alcardete (Toledo)
☎: 925 166 396 - Fax: 925 166 396
jesusrecuero@teleline.es

Established: 1954

⊞ 30 🗃 150,000 litres 🍇 30 has.

🍷 90% 🍇10%: -BE -DE

TERRA SIGILLATA 2001 FERMENTADO EN
  BARRICA WHITE
TERRA SIGILLATA 2003 WHITE
TERRA SIGILLATA 2003 RED
TERRA SIGILLATA 1998 ROBLE RED

Bodegas JUAN RAMÍREZ

Torrecillas, 138
13300 Valdepeñas (Ciudad Real)
☎: 926 322 021 - Fax: 926 320 495
info@bodegasjuanramirez.com
www.bodegasjuanramirez.com

Established: 1914

⊞ 150 🗃 800,000 litres 🍇 14 has.

🍷 70% 🍇30%: -DE -BE -NL -PL -LT -LV

AMPELO 2003 OAK AGED RED
tempranillo   ⊞ 3

75 Ruby red cherry. Aroma of vanilla, lactics and ripe red fruit. Drying on the palate with slightly pungent wood tannins and light bitter notes.

Sociedad Cooperativa LA INVENCIBLE

Torrecillas, 130
13300 Valdepeñas (Ciudad Real)
☎: 926 321 700 - Fax: 926 311 080
invencible@ucaman.es
www.ucaman.es/invencible

Established: 1943

⊞ 600 🗃 20,000,000 litres 🍇 1,000 has.

🍷 75% 🍇25%: -NL -DK -DE

MAJANO MERLOT RED

Cooperativa Agrícola LA REMEDIADORA

Alfredo Atienza, 149
02630 La Roda (Albacete)
☎: 967 440 600 - Fax: 967 441 465
remediador@ucaman.es
www.laremediadora.com

Established: 1946

⊞ 150 🗃 33,750 litres 🍇 1,500 has.

🍷 95% 🍇5%: -BE -DE

CASTILLO DE RODA 2003 JOVEN WHITE
100% airén

80 Brilliant pale yellow. Intense aroma with good expression of white stone fruit and spicy hints of skins. Flavourful palate with bitter notes, herbs and a slightly acidic edge.

CASTILLO DE RODA 2003 JOVEN RED
100% tempranillo

77 Cherry with a dark violet hue. Somewhat intense aroma of black fruit, notes of sun-drenched skins and damp earth. Flavourful palate with bitter notes and hints of overextraction.

Bodegas y Viñedos LA SOLANA

Ctra Porzuna-Cno. Cristo del Humilladero km. 7
13420 Malagón (Ciudad Real)
☎: 983 681 446 - Fax: 983 681 147
bodega@pagoflorentino.com
www.pagoflorentino.com

Established: 1999
🍷 200 🛢 300,000 litres 🍇 70 has.

PAGO FLORENTINO 2002 RED
100% cencibel

87 Intense cherry. Powerful, very ripe aroma (jammy blackberries) with notes of skins maceration and hints of dry earth. Powerful, fleshy palate with sweet tannins, spirituous, full and flavourful; mild wood well-integrated in the wine.

Cooperativa del Campo LA UNIÓN

Barrio San José, s/n
02100 Tarazona de la Mancha (Albacete)
☎: 967 480 074 - Fax: 967 480 294
cclaunion@terra.es
www.cop-launion.com

Established: 1956
🍷 400 🛢 30,000,000 litres
🍷 60% 🍇40%

VALDEMEMBRA 2002 RED

70 Cherry with a brick red hue. Viscous aroma with notes of rancid wine, oxidised. Acidic, dry palate without noteworthy notes.

Bodegas LÓPEZ PANACH

Torpedero Tucumán, 33
28016 Madrid
☎: 913 500 422
lopezpanach@ono.com

LÓPEZ PANACH 2002 RED
merlot, syrah, tempranillo, cabernet

85 Intense cherry. Aroma with notes of ripe fruit (sun-drenched bunches), a rustic hint and toasty oak nuances. Fruity, ripe, flavourful and warm palate; pleasant tannins but with a rustic finish.

LÓPEZ PANACH CABERNET SAUVIGNON 2002 RED
cabernet sauvignon

86 Intense cherry. Aroma of red fruit with very varietal nuances (spices, fallen leaves). Flavourful and very fresh palate with red berries and maceration notes; long.

Cooperativa Nuestra Señora de LOS REMEDIOS

Cooperativa, 2
45100 Sonseca (Toledo)
☎: 925 380 322 - Fax: 925 381 617

Established: 1967
🍷 60 🛢 7,000,000 litres 🍇 3,000 has.
🍷 100%

FRAY GABRIEL 2003 ROSÉ

76 Lively raspberry. Medium-intensity aroma of strawberry jelly. Flavourful, fruity palate, slightly weak acidity.

Bodegas MARTÚE

Campo de la Guardia s/n
45760 Laguardia (Toledo)
☎: 925 123 333 - Fax: 925 123 1/2
bodegasenlaguardia@martue.com
www.martue.com

Established: 2000
🍷 1,000 🛢 20,000 litres 🍇 85 has.
🍷 80% 🌐20%: -DE -US -JP -NL -CH -CA -BE -AL

MARTÚE CHARDONNAY 2003 FERMENTADO EN BARRICA WHITE
100% chardonnay

85 Golden yellow. Medium-intensity aroma of hay with fresh and ripe fruit and a nuance of herbs. Oily, flavourful, intense palate with considerable fruit expression (hay, ripeness), perfectly integrated with the smoky oak and slightly warm in the finish.

MARTÚE 2002 OAK AGED RED
38% tempranillo, 28% merlot, 26% cabernet sauvignon, 8% syrah

83 Deep garnet red. Spicy aroma of wood with lactic notes and slightly balsamic. Flavourful palate with good fruit weight, well-integrated wood and toasty wood in the retronasal passage.

MARTÚE 2003 OAK AGED RED
ESPECIAL DE MARTÚE 2003 OAK AGED RED
MARTÚE SYRAH 2003 OAK AGED RED

Bodegas MÁXIMO

Camino Viejo de Logroño, 26
01320 Oyón (Alava)
☎: 945 622 216 - Fax: 945 622 315

Established: 2003

🌐 2,400 ⬛ 3,000,000 litres 🍷 10%

📍90%: CENTRO -UE SUDAMÉRICA -US ASIA

MÁXIMO SAUVIGNON BLANC 2002 WHITE
100% sauvignon blanc

80 Brilliant pale yellow. Intense aroma with a slight varietal expression (green fruit, hints of exotic fruit, a suggestion of fine herbs). Fresh and flavourful palate with fine bitter notes, hints of citrus fruit and good acidity.

MÁXIMO CABERNET SAUVIGNON 2002 OAK AGED RED
100% cabernet sauvignon

80 Garnet red cherry. Powerful aroma of jammy black fruit with a spicy and creamy oak hint. Fleshy, flavourful palate with ripe tannins and fine bitter notes (toasty flavours, liquorice) without great varietal character.

MÁXIMO MERLOT 2002 OAK AGED RED
100% merlot

78 Garnet red cherry with a coppery edge. Fairly intense aroma of red fruit with spicy hints of oak. Flavourful palate with slightly marked tannins (a slight greeness) and hardly any varietal expression.

MÁXIMO TEMPRANILLO CABERNET SAUVIGNON 2001 BARREL AGED RED
75% tempranillo, 25% cabernet sauvignon

74 Intense cherry with a violet-coppery edge. Not very intense aroma of black fruit with a creamy oak nuance. Flavourful palate with astringent overtones and an acidic edge.

MÁXIMO SYRAH CABERNET 2002 RED

MIGUEL CALATAYUD

Postas, 20
13300 Valdepeñas (Ciudad Real)
☎: 926 348 070 - Fax: 926 322 150
vegaval@vegaval.com
www.vegaval.com

Established: 1960

🌐 3,000 ⬛ 4,000,000 litres 🍷 50 has.

🍷 55% 📍45%: -US -UK -DE -NL -DK -CH
-JP -FR -AT -VE -PR -CA -HK -LU -BE -DK -

FI -HU -BR -IE -PL -SG -MY

MIGUEL CALATAYUD SELECCIÓN MACABEO ALLIER 2002 ROBLE WHITE
100% macabeo

79 Straw-coloured. Fresh aroma with very marked oak notes but with a certain finesse and a perfumed hint. Oak tannin structure on the palate with herbal tea, lacks fruit.

MIGUEL CALATAYUD SELECCIÓN 1999 OAK AGED RED
tempranillo, cabernet sauvignon, merlot

80 Garnet red with an orangey edge. Aroma with reduction crianza notes (cigar box, leather) and a nuance of jammy fruit. Fleshy palate with noticeable wood tannins, spicy.

MONTALVO WILMOT

Finca Los Cerrillos
Carretera Ruidera km. 10, 200
13170 Argamasilla de Alba (Ciudad Real)
☎: 926 699 069 - Fax: 926 699 069
alejandromontalvo@ya.com

Established: 2001

🌐 218 ⬛ 694,000 litres 🍷 34 has.

🍷 70% 📍30%: -IE -CH -DE -UK

MONTALVO WILMOT 2002 ROBLE RED
100% tempranillo

83 Very deep garnet red cherry. Intense, ripe fruit aroma (jammy fruit), with fine toasty oak notes and hints of terroir. Fleshy on the palate with rough, flavourful and firm tannins, well-integrated oak/fruit, well-balanced.

Bodegas del MUNI

Carretera de Lillo, 48
45310 Villatobas (Toledo)
☎: 925 152 511 - Fax: 925 152 511
info@bodegasdelmuni.com
www.bodegasdelmuni.com

Established: 2001

🌐 132 ⬛ 260,000 litres 🍷 115 has.

🍷 65% 📍35%: -DE-US-UK -CH -AT -DK -JP

CORPUS DEL MUNI 2003 OAK AGED RED
79% tempranillo, 7% syrah, 4% garnacha

84 Quite intense cherry. Fine toasty aroma (cocoa, coffee) with hints of jammy black fruit and earthy notes. Powerful, fleshy, very ripe and fruity on the palate with foresty hints.

CORPUS DEL MUNI "VIÑA LUCÍA" 2002 OAK AGED RED
100% tempranillo

88 Intense cherry. Powerful aroma, rich in toasty nuances (dark-roasted flavours, chocolate) and black bramble fruit. Powerful, fleshy, and warm on the palate, with jammy hints, earth, black fruit (grape bunches) and sweet tannins.

Viñedos y Bodegas MUÑOZ

Carretera Villarrubia, 11
45350 Noblejas (Toledo)
☎: 925 140 070 - Fax: 925 141 334
vibomu@teleline.es

Established: 1940

⊞ 600 ▦ 7,500,000 litres ⚜ 70 has.

▰ 25% ✇75%

FINCA MUÑOZ 2002 OAK AGED RED
100% tempranillo

84 Dark red cherry with a purplish rim. Intense aroma of ripe black fruit with a slight varietal expression (damp earth) and fine toasty oak. Flavourful palate with fleshy overtones, a good oak/fruit integration and fine bitter notes (liquorice, dark-roasted flavours).

LEGADO MUÑOZ MERLOT 2003 RED
100% merlot

82 Almost opaque cherry. Intense aroma of ripe black fruit with fine toasty skins, hints of very varietal spices and petals. Flavourful palate with fleshy overtones, slightly marked tannins but promising, balsamic notes.

LEGADO MUÑOZ CABERNET SAUVIGNON 2003 RED
100% cabernet sauvignon

84 Dark cherry with a purplish rim. Powerful, and fruity aroma with a good varietal expression (redcurrants, paprika, damp earth). Flavourful, fleshy palate with fine toasty skins, firm tannins, a slightly oily texture, spicy, with good acidity.

Sociedad Cooperativa NUESTRA SEÑORA DEL ESPINO

San Miguel, 34
13230 Membrilla (Ciudad Real)
☎: 926 637 475 - Fax: 926 636 616
coopvirgenespino@eresmas.com

Established: 1957

⊞ 60 ▦ 21,000,000 litres
⚜ 2,300 has. ▰ 100%

JARIQUE WHITE
JARIQUE RED

Sociedad Cooperativa NUESTRA SEÑORA DEL PILAR

Extramuros, s/n

45810 Villanueva de Alcardete (Toledo)
☎: 925 166 375 - Fax: 925 166 611
coopnspilar.3081@cajarural.com

Established: 1973

⊞ 35 ▦ 24,500,000 litres ⚜ 3,800 has.

FINCA ALMEDO 2003 JOVEN RED
FINCA ALMEDO 2002 ROBLE RED
FINCA ALMEDO 2003 RED

OSBORNE MALPICA

Finca El Jaral
Carretera Malpica-Pueblanueva, Km 6
45692 Malpica de Tajo (Toledo)
☎: 925 860 903 - Fax: 925 860 905
comunicacion@osborne.es
www.osborne.es

Established: 2002

⊞ 5,300 ▦ 5,500,000 litres ⚜ 1,040 has.

▰ 50% ✇50%: -NL -DE -UK -US - SDV

SOLAZ 2002 OAK AGED RED
tempranillo, cabernet sauvignon

84 Garnet red cherry. Quite intense aroma with a certain finesse, with predominant toasty oak and fruit (sun-drenched skins). Flavourful, fleshy, spicy palate with quite vigorous tannins, fresh fruit and liquorice and balsamic notes in the retronasal passage.

SOLAZ SHIRAZ-TEMPRANILLO 2003 RED
shiraz, tempranillo

85 Dark cherry with a purplish edge. Intense aroma of blackberries, notes of petals and macerated skins with a suggestion of damp earth. Flavourful on the palate with slightly sweet ripe fruit, ripe and fine tannins, fine notes of liquorice and balsamic flavours.

DOMINIO DE MALPICA 2001 OAK AGED RED
cabernet sauvignon

87 Garnet red cherry with a saffron edge. Powerful aroma with spicy and very varietal notes of oak (paprika) and notions of terroir. Flavourful palate with a good fruit/oak integration, fine bitter notes (spices, liquorice, dark-roasted flavours) and excellent acidity.

PAGO DEL VICARIO

Juan II 7, 3ª planta
13001 Ciudad Real
☎: 926 211 401 - Fax: 926 273 515
susana@pagodelvicario.com
www.pagodelvicario.com

TALVA 2003 WHITE
chardonnay, sauvignon blanc, macabeo, airén

82 Yellow straw. Medium-intensity aroma of hay and ripe white fruit. Oily, flavourful palate with a certain complexity of lees, very pleasant.

AGIOS 2002 OAK AGED RED

86 Almost opaque cherry. Quite impenetrable, very fine aroma with predominant fruit notes (jammy black fruit) and fine toasty oak. Powerful, concentrated palate, rich in nuances, with promising yet quite marked tannins and excellent symmetry.

Bodegas PECES-BARBA

Finca El Retamar
45100 Sonseca (Toledo)
☎: 925 380 375 - Fax: 925 380 950
bodega@peces-barba.com
www.peces-barba.com

Established: 1995
🍷 160 📟 250,000 litres 🌱 60 has.
🍾 70% 🌐30%: -DE -BE -MX

BARBASOL WHITE DE AGUJA
85% macabeo, 15% sauvignon blanc

68 Straw-coloured. Aroma with very prominent green notes (vine shoots). An edge of acidity on the palate, carbonic and light.

CONDE DE ORGAZ 2003 WHITE
100% sauvignon blanc

63 Straw-coloured with a golden hue. Short, rustic aroma with herby notes but without character of the vine variety. Without fruit on the palate, coarse.

BARBAROS RED DE AGUJA
75% garnacha, 25% cencibel

70 Dusky pink. Somewhat ripe aroma of strawberry jelly. Very sweet on the palate, lacking freshness.

CONDE DE ORGAZ MERLOT 2003 RED
100% merlot

83 Very deep cherry with a violet edge. Aroma of very ripe black fruit, toasty skins, earthy notes (minerals), hints of pitch and ink. Fleshy palate with powerful fruit, sweet overtones and a toasty oak finish.

CONDE DE ORGAZ CABERNET-MERLOT 2001 OAK AGED RED
50% cabernet sauvignon, 50% merlot

84 Garnet red cherry. Intense aroma with fine reduction notes (cedar leathers) and an excellent varietal (redcurrants, fallen leaves) and crianza expression. Flavourful palate with fairly solid tannins, supple, spicy and quite potential.

CONDE DE ORGAZ 2000 RED
50% cabernet sauvignon, 50% merlot

80 Cherry with a brick red hue. Powerful aroma with vanilla and ripe red fruit. Flavourful palate with slightly drying wood tannins balsamic notes

in the retronasal passage.

PINTO POLO

Finca El Colmenar
45310 Villatobas (Toledo)
☎: 915 425 143 - Fax: 912 110 128
pintopolo@pintopolo.com
www.pintopolo.com

Established: 2000
📟 25,000 litres 🌱 25 has. 🍾 100%

CAÑADA DE "EL VALLE" RIESLING 2002 WHITE
100% riesling

77 Straw-coloured with a golden glint. Not very varietal aroma of very ripe fruit (bananas) with a nuance of herbs. Light, bitter palate with ripe fruit, well-mannered overall.

Bodegas REAL

Finca Marisanchez. Cta a Cózar, km. 12.800
13300 Valdepeñas (Ciudad Real)
☎: 926 338 001 - Fax: 926 338 079
comunicacion@bodegas-real.com
www.bodegas-real.com

Established: 1989
🍷 500 📟 3,000,000 litres 🌱 280 has.
🍾 35% 🌐65%: -DE -UK -US -IE -BE -FR
-CA -SE -DK -NL -CH -JP

FINCA MARISÁNCHEZ CHARDONNAY 2003 WHITE
100% chardonnay

85 Golden yellow. Intense, fruity aroma with good varietal expression (ripe apples), hints of exotic fruit and hay. Flavourful and fruity on the palate with fine hints of skins, slightly warm with mineral notes in the retronasal passage.

VEGA IBOR 2001 OAK AGED RED
100% tempranillo

82 Garnet red cherry with a violet edge. Intense aroma with predominant creamy oak notes, and a ripe red fruit nuance. Flavourful on the palate with slightly drying oak tannins and a fruity and spicy nuance.

FINCA MARISÁNCHEZ 2001 ROBLE RED
80% tempranillo, 15% cabernet sauvignon, 5% merlot

82 Intense cherry with a saffron edge. Fairly intense aroma with predominant spicy oak notes and a ripe red fruit nuance. Flavourful and fleshy on the palate with slightly marked oak tannins and oily and warm hints.

Sociedad Cooperativa AgroVitivinícola
SAN ISIDRO

Dos de Mayo, 21
13620 Pedro Muñoz (Ciudad Real)
☎: 926 586 057 - Fax: 926 568 380
mail@viacotos.com
www.viacotos.com

Established: 1954

⊕ 50 ⚘ 4,500 has. 🍷 80% 🌐20%

CARRIL DE COTOS 2003 WHITE
CARRIL DE COTOS 2003 RED
CARRIL DE COTOS 2002 OAK AGED

Bodegas y Viñedos
SÁNCHEZ MULITERNO

Tesifonte Gallego, 5 1º
02002 Albacete (Albacete)
☎: 967 193 222 - Fax: 967 193 292
bodega@muliterno.com
www.muliterno.com

Established: 1993

⊕ 500 ⚘ 70 has. 🍷 100%

DIVINUS 2003 WHITE
100% chardonnay

86 Golden yellow. Intense aroma with predominant creamy and smoky oak notes and a nuance of ripe apples, fairly warm. Flavourful palate with fine oak tannins, smoky hints and herbs in the retronasal passage.

MAGNIFICUS 2002 CRIANZA RED
90% syrah, 10% cabernet sauvignon

88 Opaque cherry. Powerful, concentrated aroma with fine toasty and spicy oak notes over a nuance of ripe fruit and hints of minerals. Concentrated, flavourful palate with well-integrated grape and oak tannins, a nuance of ripe fruit and spicy hints of liquorice in the retronasal passage.

VEGA GUIJOSO 2001 CRIANZA RED
60% merlot, 40% cabernet sauvignon

83 Garnet red cherry. Intense aroma of spicy oak notes with a nuance of ripe black fruit, hints of cedar and paprika. Predominant bitter oak notes on the palate, lacks balance, quite promising.

VIÑA CONSOLACIÓN 1999 RESERVA RED
85% cabernet sauvignon, 10% tempranillo, 5% syrah

82 Cherry with a coppery edge. Powerful, ripe aroma with a nuance of reduction (new leather).

Flavourful palate with fleshy overtones, well-assembled oak and grape tannins and slightly acidic edges.

Sociedad Cooperativa Limitada
SANTA CATALINA

Cooperativa, 2
13240 La Solana (Ciudad Real)
☎: 926 632 194 - Fax: 926 631 085
losgalanes@ucaman.es

Established: 1959

⊕ 102 🗄 18,000,000 litres ⚘ 14,000 has.

🍷 70% 🌐30%: -DK -DE -FR

CAMPECHANO 2003 WHITE
100% airén

76 Pale with golden nuances. Somewhat intense, fruity aroma without great nuances. Fresh, quite flavourful palate with hints of herbs and good citrus acidity.

CAMPECHANO 2003 ROSÉ
100% tempranillo

72 Intense raspberry. Not very intense aroma with a spicy suggestion of skins. Fresh palate with scarcely any fruit expression.

CAMPECHANO 2003 RED
100% tempranillo

68 Cherry with a purple rim. Vinous aroma of ripe red fruit and delicate notes of lees. Drying on the palate with noticeable tannins.

TORRE DE LA SOLANA RED

70 Not very deep cherry. Aroma of sun-drenched skins, lees, alcohol. Light palate without great nuances.

SEÑORÍO DEL JÚCAR

Avenida Albacete, 23
02230 Madrigueras (Albacete)
☎: 967 484 334 - Fax: 967 485 065
bodegas@bsjucar.e.telefonica.net

Established: 1982

⊕ 300 🗄 2,000,000 litres ⚘ 60 has.

🍷 90% 🌐10%: -DE -UK -US -CI

SEÑORÍO DEL JÚCAR 2003 JOVEN WHITE
100% macabeo

75 Straw-coloured. Medium intensity aroma of tropical fruit (bananas). Light palate, with very ripe fruit, well-mannered but lacking freshness.

SEÑORÍO DEL JÚCAR 2003 JOVEN ROSÉ

73 Pale pink. Fresh, fruity aroma with subtle yet pleasant vegetative hints. More noticeable vegetative notes on the palate and red fruit.

SEÑORÍO DEL JÚCAR 2003 JOVEN RED
100% tempranillo

78 Intense cherry. Fresh aroma with red bramble fruit and maceration notes. Fresh, flavourful and fruity on the palate (strawberries, blackberries), simple.

SEÑORÍO DEL JUCAR 2001 OAK AGED RED
80% tempranillo, 20% cabernet sauvignon

80 Deep cherry. Toasty aroma with a black fruit hint and warm hints. Flavourful with high acidity on the palate and black fruit in the aftertaste.

Grupo SOLIS VINTNERS

Carretera Santa Cruz km. 4, 5
16400 Tarancón (Cuenca)
☎: 969 320 200 - Fax: 969 321 274
gruposolis@gruposolis.net
www.gruposolis.net

Established: 2000

🌐 900 ▯ 25,000,000 litres 🍷 80% 🍇20%

ATENEA 2003 JOVEN RED
tempranillo

83 Cherry with a violet rim. Intense aroma of caramelised strawberry jelly with lactic notes. A little acidic and fleshy on the palate with a good fruit weight, sweet hints and red fruit notions.

MONTE DEL MARQUÉS 2002 RED
tempranillo

76 Not very deep cherry. Slightly short, fruity aroma with very sweet notes. Short palate with notes of greeness.

Cooperativa UNIÓN CAMPESINA INIESTENSE

c/San Idefonso, 1
16235 Iniesta (Cuenca)
☎: 967 490 120 - Fax: 967 490 777
comercial@cooperativauci.com

Established: 1944

🌐 800 ▯ 54,000,000 litres 🍇 7,000 has.

🍷 70% 🍇30%: -FR -IT -PT -DE -BE -US -NL -AT

SEÑORÍO DE INIESTA 2003 JOVEN WHITE
100% viura

70 Yellow straw. Quite short aroma with mild off-odours and a nuance of hay and dried grass. Slightly rustic palate with weak fruit.

SEÑORÍO DE INIESTA 2003 JOVEN ROSÉ
100% bobal

78 Brilliant raspberry. Slightly intense, fruity palate with the freshness of grapeskins. Flavourful palate with fruit expression slightly muted by the alcohol.

SEÑORÍO DE INIESTA 2003 JOVEN RED
100% tempranillo

80 Cherry with a violet edge. Aroma of ripe strawberries and strawberry yoghurt, very varietal. Quite robust tannins but with good presence on the palate, varietal.

URBEA S.A.

Finca Aguileros, s/n
☎: 952 789 070 - Fax: 915 783 901

LOS AGUILEROS SYRAH 2003 RED

75 Intense cherry. Vegetative aroma with notes of skins and overripening. Warm palate, sweetness, with dried fruit in the retronasal passage, very flabby.

URIBES MADERO

Carretera Huete a Cuenca, km. 3.2
16500 Huete (Cuenca)
☎: 969 143 020 - Fax: 969 147 047
www.pagodecalzadilla.net

Established: 1995

🌐 200 ▯ 100,000 litres 🍇 15 has.

🍷 65% 🍇35%: -CH -US -BE -MX -PR -UK

CALZADILLA SYRAH 2001 RED
syrah

84 Intense cherry. Toasty aroma with balsamic notes and a mild vegetative hint, ripe fruit. Fruity, ripe, toasty palate with supple tannins, slightly fleshy.

CALZADILLA 2001 RESERVA RED
60% tempranillo, 30% cabernet sauvignon, 10% garnacha

85 Intense cherry. Aroma with light reduction notes (cedar wood, tobacco, leather), toasty (coffee). Fleshy, powerful, warm palate with reduction notes in the retronasal passage (leather) and ripe tannins.

GRAN CALZADILLA 2000 RESERVA RED
60% tempranillo, 40% cabernet sauvignon

88 Intense cherry. Toasty aroma of oak (dark-roasted flavours, chocolate) with ripe black fruit with a hint of reduction notes. Powerful, warm palate with ripe tannins, flavourful with jammy ripe black fruit and persistent tannins with sweet overtones.

Pago de VALLEGARCÍA

Finca Vallegarcía, s/n
13194 Retuerta de Bullaque (Ciudad Real)
☎: 915 745 534 - Fax: 915 745 534
fvallegarcia@terra.es

Established: 1999

190 20,000 litres 25 has.

70% 30%: -US -CH

VALLEGARCÍA VIOGNIER 2002 FERMENTADO EN BARRICA WHITE
100% viognier

91 Brilliant gold. Aroma with notes of sweet ripe fruit, scrubland herbs and a smoky hint. Oily, powerful, warm palate with a retronasal passage of herbs and sweet fruit, warm, flavourful and very Mediterranean.

VALLEGARCÍA CABERNET Y MERLOT 2001 RED
cabernet sauvignon, merlot

91 Intense cherry with a luminous edge. Powerful aroma with toasty minerals and slightly jammy fruit whilst maintaining its varietal character. Warm, fruity, mineral palate with a suggestion of good varietal expression, flavourful with toasty hints of oak.

VIDEVA

Travesía Horno, 16
13300 Valdepeñas (Ciudad Real)
☎: 926 322 351 - Fax: 926 320 092
bodegasvideva@terra.es

Established: 1967

500 2,000,000 litres 515 has.

80% 20%

PAGO LUCONES CRIANZA RED
PAGO LUCONES VIÑAS VIEJAS RED

VINOS Y BODEGAS

Carretera de las Mesas, km. 1
13630 Socuéllanos (Ciudad Real)
☎: 926 531 067 - Fax: 926 532 249
export@vinosybodegas.com
www.vinosybodegas.com

Established: 1996

300 4,500,000 litres 10%

90%: -UE - AFRICA ASIA AMÉRICA

MIRADOR DE CASTILLA WHITE
100% airén

80 Golden with a coppery hue. Powerful, slightly fruity aroma with hints of flowers and exotic fruit. Flavourful, fruity palate with bitter notes and good acidity.

MIRADOR DE CASTILLA CABERNET SAUVIGNON RED
100% cabernet sauvignon

78 Fairly deep cherry with a violet edge. Powerful, fruity aroma with hints of vine shoots

and a suggestion of terracotta and smoky skins. Flavourful palate with slightly marked tannins and a suggestion of spicy and varietal greenness.

LA NUNCIATURA 2002 RED

78 Intense cherry. Aroma with notes of foresty black berries and earthy traces. Fleshy, warm palate with ripe fruit and typically regional foresty hints, slightly short in fruit expression.

MIRADOR DE CASTILLA TEMPRANILLO RED

VIÑEDOS CIGARRAL SANTA MARÍA

Cerro del Emperador, s/n
45001 Toledo (Toledo)
☎: 925 252 991 - Fax: 925 253 198
vinedos@adolfo-toledo.com
www.adolfo-toledo.com

Established: 1999

21 15,000 litres 5 has.

66% 34%: -US

PAGO DEL AMA SYRAH 2001 OAK AGED RED
syrah

93 Very intense cherry. Concentrated aroma, very ripe (bilberry jam) with a mineral nuance (burnt stone) and fine notes of toasty wood. Generous, fleshy, warm, very sweet palate with very flavourful tannins and minerals and forest fruit in the retronasal passage.

PAGO DEL AMA SYRAH 2002 OAK AGED RED
syrah

93 Very intense cherry. Powerful aroma, dark-roasted flavours, chocolate, dates, mineral notes, clay. Powerful, fleshy and spirituous palate, viscous, stewed black fruit.

PAGO DEL AMA COLECCIÓN 2002 RED
merlot, syrah, tempranillo

92 Intense cherry. Toasty aroma of jammy black fruit, spirituous notes, toasty creamy oak, very ripe. Powerful, fleshy and spirituous palate, very ripe fruit, sweet tannins; slightly fiery retronasal effect, mild notes of dry stone and clay, and slightly viscous.

PAGO DEL AMA COLECCIÓN 2001 RED
merlot, syrah, tempranillo

90 Intense cherry. Aroma with character and hints of salted meat, stone and toasty fruit and wood. Powerful, warm palate, with hints of sweetness from the optimum ripening level. Fine notes of wood and very ripe forest fruit, flavourful and persistent.

VIÑEDOS Y CRIANZAS

Avenida Juan Carlos I, 28
16400 Tarancón (Cuenca)

☎: 969 327 099 - Fax: 969 327 199
viñedosycrianzas@telefonica.net

Established: 2000

🌐 1,000 🛢 800,000 litres 🍇 300 has.

🍷 95% 🌐5%

VIÑANSAR MACERACIÓN CARBÓNICA RED
VIÑANSAR CABERNET - TEMPRANILLO RED

VIÑEDOS Y RESERVAS

Carretera Quintanar, km. 2
45810 Villanueva de Alcardete (Toledo)
☎: 925 167 536 - Fax: 925 167 558
vr@fedeto.es
www.cuevassantoyo.com

Established: 1987

🍇 100 has. 🍷 90% 🌐10%: -DE -US

CELLA VINARIA 2000 OAK AGED RED

V.T. CASTILLA Y LEÓN

ABADÍA RETUERTA

Abadía Santa María de Retuerta s/n
47540 Sardón de Duero (Valladolid)
☎: 983 680 314 - Fax: 983 680 286
abadia.retuerta@abadia-retuerta.com
www.abadia-retuerta.com

Established: 1996

🌐 3,200 🛢 1,700,000 litres 🍇 206 has.

🍷 30% 🌐70%: -US -CH -JP

ABADÍA RETUERTA PRIMICIA 2003 RED
80% tempranillo, 20% cabernet sauvignon, 20% merlot

83 Garnet red with a violet edge. Aroma of sun-drenched skins and ripe red fruit. Fleshy, well-balanced palate with good persistence.

ABADÍA RETUERTA RIVOLA 2002 ROBLE RED
60% tempranillo, 40% cabernet sauvignon

81 Garnet red with a violet rim. Aroma of jammy red fruit and sun-drenched skins. Drying palate with slightly aggressive tannins and medium persistence.

PAGO NEGRALADA 2000 OAK AGED RED
100% tempranillo 🌐 24

88 High hue garnet red. Intense, spicy, balsamic and toasty aroma with a hint of red fruit. Fleshy palate with balanced wood tannins and a good fruit weight.

ABADÍA RETUERTA SELECCIÓN ESPECIAL
2000 ROBLE RED
75% tempranillo, 20% cabernet sauvignon, 5% merlot

85 Garnet red with a violet rim. Not very intense aroma of red fruit, quite spicy. Drying palate with slightly marked tannins and a suggestion of green pepper in the retronasal passage.

PAGO VALDEBELLÓN 2000 OAK AGED RED
100% cabernet sauvignon

91 Garnet red with a very deep ruby red rim. Spicy, balsamic aroma of ripe red fruit and bell pepper. Fleshy, unctuous and well-balanced palate with a suggestion of minerals and a spicy retronasal effect.

CUVÉE EL CAMPANARIO 2000 CRIANZA RED
100% tempranillo

86 Very deep garnet red. Aroma of pepper and cedar with a lactic hint and notions of stewed fruit. Unctuous, well-balanced palate with well-integrated wood tannins.

CUVÉE EL PALOMAR 2000 CRIANZA RED
50% tempranillo, 50% cabernet sauvignon

87 Very deep garnet red. Jammy aroma of red fruit, quite spicy. Fleshy, well-structured palate with a suggestion of toasty wood and balsamic flavours in the retronasal passage.

Sociedad Cooperativa Limitada
AGRÍCOLA CASTELLANA

Carretera Rodilana, s/n
47491 La Seca (Valladolid)
☎: 983 816 320 - Fax: 983 816 562
agricast1@terra.es
www.agricolacastellana.com

Established: 1935

🌐 500 🛢 10,000,000 litres 🍇 2,000 has.

🦃 90% 🌐10%: -DE -UK -SE -DK -IT -US -JP -MX -AT

CASA MARÍA 2003 WHITE

80 Brilliant pale yellow. Quite intense and fruity aroma with floral hints. Flavourful, fruity palate with fine spicy notes of skins and good acidity.

CASA MARÍA 2003 ROSÉ SEMISECO

79 Brilliant blush. Quite intense, fruity aroma with spicy and sweet hints. Flavourful, quite fruity palate with fine jammy and citrus notes, good acidity.

CASA MARÍA 2002 RED

75 Ruby red with a purple rim. Aroma with light reduction notes and green fruit. Warm palate with underripe fruit.

CASA MARÍA TEMPRANILLO 2001 OAK AGED RED
tempranillo

72 Cherry with an orange rim. Viscous aroma of very ripe red fruit with a mild hint of acetone. Light palate without great nuances.

AVELINO VEGAS

Real del Pino, 36
40460 Santituste (Segovia)
☎: 921 596 002 - Fax: 921 596 035
general@avelinovegas.com
www.avelinovegas.com

Established: 1950
🍷 300 🛢 225 litres 🦃 80% 🌐20%

ABADÍA REAL 2003 WHITE

84 Yellow straw. Aroma with notes of white stone fruit, fresh herbs. Light palate with overtones of bitter notes (almonds).

CASA LA LUNA VERDEJO-VIURA 2003 WHITE
verdejo, viura

81 Yellow straw. Aroma of fresh herbs, floral and perfumed. Good acidity on the palate, persistent, slightly warm.

CONDADO REAL VERDEJO-VIURA 2003 WHITE
verdejo, viura

76 Straw-coloured. Slighlty short aroma of ripe fruit with toasty notes. Dry, fresh, quite flavourful palate without great fruit nuances.

CASA LA LUNA TEMPRANILLO 2003 JOVEN RED
100% tempranillo

77 Cherry with and orangey rim. Aroma of jammy strawberries, somewhat short. Drying palate with wood tannins, warm and unexpressive.

ABADÍA REAL 2003 RED
tempranillo

83 Cherry. Aroma of ripe red fruit, jam, balsamic flavours. Powerful, generous palate, evokes balsamic flavours, good acidity, medium persistence.

CONDADO REAL TEMPRANILLO 2003 RED
tempranillo

85 Cherry with a red garnet red edge. Clear, varietal aroma with spicy notes of skins, flowers and well-balanced fine oak. Fleshy, fresh palate; fruity and very pleasant, elegant oak tannins.

CONDADO REAL 2002 RED
tempranillo

78 Bigarreau cherry. Aroma of red fruit and lactics, quite sweet. Some wood dryness on the palate, warm with light persistence and vanilla in the retronasal passage.

BEGOÑA CARRILLO ROMERO

San Pedro Cardeña, 32 bajo
09002 Burgos (Burgos)
☎: 947 205 289 - Fax: 947 205 289
info@asovintcal.com

BESARDILLA
DEHESA VERDE
SEÑORÍO DE ALBILLOS

BELONDRADE

Quinta San Diego. Camino del Puerto
47491 La Seca (Valladolid)
☎: 983 481 001 - Fax: 600 590 024
belondrade@vodafone.es

Established: 1994
🍷 223 🛢 70,000 litres 🍇 13 has.

🦃 70% 🌐30%: -JP -US -UK -CH -DK -FR -PR -IT -BE

QUINTA APOLONIA 2003 JOVEN WHITE
100% verdejo

84 Pale with brilliant greenish nuances. Powerful aroma with excellent varietal expression (fruit, white flowers, fennel, ripe citrus fruit, hints of pineapple). Flavourful palate with bitter notes; slightly warm and oily.

QUINTA CLARISA 2003 ROSÉ

84 Salmon pink. Powerful aroma with notes of sweet fruit and maceration. Fresh, fruity, light and pleasant palate with excellent acidity.

BENITO BLÁZQUEZ E HIJOS

Carretera Venta del Obispo, s/n
05260 Cebreros (Ávila)

☎: 918 630 025 - Fax: 918 630 635
info@vinosperlado.com
www.vinosperlado.com

Established: 1947

🏭 500 🍾 15,000,000 litres 🍷 75% 🌐25%

MONTEPERLADO RED
PERLA PLATA 2001 JOVEN RED
PERLA PLATA 1998 ROBLE RED

Bodega Ecológica BRUNO RUIZ

La Luna, 9
45790 Quero (Toledo)
☎: 914 675 38/ - Fax: 926 552 283
ecobruno@terra.es

Established: 1995

🏭 220 🍾 160,000 litres 🌱 71 has.

🍷 35% 🌐65%: -DE -CH -DK -NL

RUIZ VILLANUEVA CENCIBEL 2003
MACERACIÓN CARBÓNICA RED
100% cencibel

83 Dark cherry with a purplish edge. Powerful aroma of black fruit with hints of macerated skins and sweet notes. Flavourful, fleshy palate with ripe and fine grape tannins, varietal expression (liquorice, underbrush) and excellent acidity.

RUIZ VILLANUEVA 2001 ROBLE RED
80% cencibel, 10% syrah, 10% cabernet sauvignon 🛢6

85 Dark garnet red cherry. Powerful aroma with a fine varietal and (crianza expression (spices, jammy fruit, hints of leather and petals). Flavourful, fleshy palate with a good oak/fruit integration and a suggestion of cocoa and slightly sweet fruit.

RUIZ VILLANUEVA AIRÉN 2003
 MACERACIÓN CARBÓNICA WHITE
RUIZ VILLANUEVA CHARDONNAY 2003
 FERMENTADO EN BARRICA WHITE
RUIZ VILLANUEVA SYRAH 2003
 FERMENTADO EN BARRICA RED

Bodegas CASTELO DE MEDINA

Villaverde de Medina
47465 (Valladolid)
☎: 983 831 932 - Fax: 983 831 857
castelodemedina@yahoo.es

Established: 1995

🏭 500 🍾 1,100,000 litres 🌱 160 has.

🍷 70% 🌐30%: -UK -DE -NL -CH -FR -DK
-BE -CA -US -MX -PR

VIÑA CASTELO 2003 ROSÉ
CASTELO ROJO 2000 OAK AGED RED
CASTELO ROJO 2001 RED

Bodegas de CRIANZA DE CASTILLA LA VIEJA

Carretera Madrid-Coruña km. 170, 6
47490 Rueda (Valladolid)
☎: 983 868 116 - Fax: 983 868 432
bodegasbccv@interbook.net
www.bodegasdecastilla.com

Established: 1976

🏭 883 🍾 3,000,000 litres 🌱 200 has.

🍷 63% 🌐37%: -UK -NL -BE -DE -DK -AT
-CH -US -IE -HU -JP -IT -PL

PALACIO DEL ALMIRANTE 2003 WHITE
100% chardonnay

84 Pale yellow with a golden hue. Intense, fruity aroma with excellent varietal expression (apples, flowers) and hints of exotic fruit and aromatic herbs. Fresh, flavourful palate with fine bitter and spicy notes (fennel) and good acidity.

HUERTA DEL REY TEMPRANILLO-
GARNACHA 2003 JOVEN ROSÉ
90% tempranillo, 10% garnacha

80 Brilliant blush. Aroma of red stone fruit with jammy strawberry notes. Flavourful and fruity on the palate, slightly warm but with balanced acidity, persistent.

ALMIRANTAZGO 2000 RED
100% tempranillo

78 Garnet red. Aroma of ripe black fruit, smoky flavours and slightly rustic notes. Flavourful on the palate with well-balanced fruit and wood, pleasant acidity.

DEHESA DE RUBIALES

Real, s/n
24234 Villamartin - Villacalbiel (León)
☎: 980 667 095 - Fax: 986 657 371
infernandez@galiciano.com

Established: 1999

🏭 150 🍾 800,000 litres 🌱 200 has.

🍷 90% 🌐10%

DEHESA DE RUBIALES 2001 OAK AGED RED
ALAIA 2001 OAK AGED RED

FARIÑA

Carretera Moraleja s/n
49151 Casaseca de las Chanas (Zamora)
☎: 980 577 673 - Fax: 980 577 720
comercial@bodegasfarina.com
www.bodegasfarina.com

VAL DE REYES 2001 SEMIDULCE WHITE
50% moscatel, 50% albillo

82 Golden straw. Intense, fresh aroma, grapey, musky and very varietal. Sweet palate with a lot of fresh fruit and herbs, very well-balanced and pleasant.

FÉLIX LORENZO CACHAZO

Carretera Medina del campo, km. 9
47220 Pozáldez (Valladolid)
☎: 983 822 008 - Fax: 983 822 008
bodegas@cachazo.com
www.cachazo.com

Established: 1945

🛢 120 🛢 800,000 litres 🍷 85% 🌐15%: -DE -NL -BE -DK -FR

CARRILES 2003 JOVEN ROSÉ
100% tempranillo

78 Lively blush. Powerful aroma of foresty red fruit with fresh citrus overtones. Fresh, flavourful palate with good acidity.

CARRILES 2003 JOVEN RED
100% tempranillo

76 Cherry with a violet edge. Fruity aroma with light off-odours that disappear with airing. Light palate, fruity and very pleasant.

CARRILES 2000 RED
100% tempranillo

78 Dark cherry with an orangey edge. Not very intense aroma with toasty oak and black fruit. Light, quite flavourful and very toasty on the palate (coffee), easy drinking.

Hija de FRANCISO PÉREZ ADRIÁ

Antigua Ctra. Madrid - La Coruña, km. 408
24500 Villafranca del Bierzo (León)
☎: 987 540 048 - Fax: 987 540 279

Established: 1948

🛢 100 🛢 1,500,000 litres 🍷 10 has.
🍷 95% 🌐5%

VALTORAL GODELLO 2003 WHITE
VALTORAL 2003 RED
VALTORAL 1996 RED

FRUTOS VILLAR

Carretera Burgos, km. 113, 7
47270 Cigales (Valladolid)
☎: 983 586 868 - Fax: 983 580 180
frutosvillar@cic.es
www.frutosvillar.com

Established: 1960

🛢 2,100 🛢 3,000,000 litres 🍷 110 has.
🍷 80% 🌐20%: -DE -FR -UK -US -RU -MX - PT

SEÑORÍO DE BALBOA 2003 ROBLE RED

80 Not very deep cherry. Not very intense aroma with salted meat notes, smoky hints and spices. Drying palate with slightly marked wood tannins, warm and not very varietal.

Bodegas y Viñedos GARMENDIA

Finca Santa Rosalia
09260 Vizmalo (Burgos)
☎: 947 166 246 - Fax: 947 166 246
info@bodegasgarmendia.com
www.bodegasgarmendia.com

Established: 1995

🛢 545 🛢 155,000 litres 🍷 48 has.
🍷 80% 🌐20%: -DE

GARMENDIA 2003 WHITE
GARMENDIA 2003 ROSÉ
GARMENDIA 2001 OAK AGED RED

Bodegas GORDONZELLO

Alta de Santa Marina, s/n
24294 Gordoncillo (León)
☎: 987 758 030 - Fax: 987 757 201
gordonzello@terra.es

Established: 1994

🛢 100 🛢 1,000,000 litres 🍷 205 has.
🍷 75% 🌐25%: -DE -NL -UK -CH -SE -AT

CANDIDUS 2003 WHITE SEMIDULCE
100% verdejo

75 Pale gold. Powerful aroma of ripe fruit, with smoky notes and light off-odours from the tank. Flavourful, sweet palate with toasty, bitter hints, lacking acidity.

CANDIDUS VERDEJO 2003 WHITE
100% verdejo

81 Pale gold. Intense aroma of ripe fruit with hints of apricot skin and a toasty suggestion of skins. Flavourful, slightly warm and oily on the palate with fine bitter notes.

INICIO VERDEJO WHITE
100% verdejo

79 Brilliant gold. Intense aroma of ripe fruit with exotic hints, flowers and a mild sweetness (skins). Powerful, creamy palate lacking varietal presence.

INICIO PRIETO PICUDO ROSÉ
100% prieto picudo

81 Deep raspberry with a coppery glint. Quite intense aroma of red stone fruit and hints of herbs. Flavourful, somewhat fruity, varietal and spicy on the palate with smoky hints of skins.

INICIO PRIETO PICUDO RED
100% prieto picudo

78 Cherry. Aroma of ripe black fruit with a nuance of sweetness. Fresh, spicy palate with light fruity tannins and a suggestion of ripeness.

PEREGRINO MACERACIÓN PECULIAR 2003 RED
prieto picudo

88 Intense cherry. Powerful aroma, rich in expression of fruit and maceration with nuances of fresh black fruit (bilberries). Powerful, fleshy, full, ripe and very flavourful palate with varietal character, great fruitiness creating persistence.

PEREGRINO 2002 JOVEN ROSÉ
PEREGRINO 2002 JOVEN RED
PEREGRINO 2000 OAK AGED RED

HACIENDAS DURIUS

Carretera Zamora - Fermoselle, km. 56
49220 Fermoselle (Zamora)
☎: 980 613 163 - Fax: 914 365 920
adelgado@haciendas-espana.com
www.haciendas-espana.com

Established: 1999
🛢 1,000 📊 800,000 litres 🍇 70 has.
🍷 50% 🌐50%

HACIENDA ZORITA 2001 CRIANZA RED

83 Very deep garnet red cherry. Powerful aroma of ripe black fruit notes with balsamic hints and a suggestion of sun-drenched skins and fresh (spices, smoky flavours) woody overtones. Flavourful, fleshy palate with slightly marked yet promising oak tannins, liquorice, long.

Bodegas HIJOS DE ALBERTO GUTIÉRREZ

Carretera de Valdestillas, 2
47239 Serrada (Valladolid)
☎: 983 559 107 - Fax: 983 559 084
aguti@losalbertos.com
www.losalbertos.com

Established: 1949
🛢 1,600 📊 15,000,000 litres 🍇 250 has.
🍷 50% 🌐50%: -DE SDV -NL KR -BE -LT -US -UK

VIRTANA 2003 JOVEN WHITE
viura, sauvignon blanc

78 Straw-coloured. Medium-intensity, clean aroma of ripe fruit. Slightly oily, quite flavourful palate with hay, pleasant and easy drinking.

PUCELA 2001 ROBLE RED

Bodegas y Viñedos LA MEJORADA

Finca La mejorada
Olmedo (Valladolid)
☎: 913 110 500 - Fax: 914 595 700

Established: 1997
🛢 200 📊 20,000 litres.
🍷 55% 🌐45%: -US -MX

LA MEJORADA 2001 ROBLE RED
50% tempranillo, 45% syrah, 5% malbec

92 Dark garnet red cherry. Elegant aroma of creamy fresh fruit (cocoa, chocolates). Fine, elegant palate with feminine subtlety, lighter than the previous vintage.

Bodegas LEDA VIÑAS VIEJAS

Mayor, 48
47320 Tudela de Duero (Valladolid)
☎: 983 521 976 - Fax: 983 403 146

Established: 1998
🛢 155

LEDA VIÑAS VIEJAS 2002 RED
tempranillo

94 Intense cherry. Aroma with fine toasty notes (cocoa, aromatic coffee, creamy vanilla), ripe fruit and light mineral notes. Fleshy, flavourful, powerful palate with ripe fruit and tannic hints of oak, less complex than the previous vintage.

LIBERALIA ENOLÓGICA

Camino del Palo, s/n
49800 Toro (Zamora)
☎: 980 692 571 - Fax: 980 692 571
byvliberalia@hotmail.com
www.liberalia.es

Established: 2000
🛢 350 📊 150,000 litres 🍇 30 has.
🍷 60% 🌐40%: -DE -BE -UK -IE -JP -MX -PR -US -AT

LIBERALIA UNO 2003 JOVEN DULCE NATURAL

Bodega y Viñedos LUNA BEBERIDE

Carretera Madrid-Coruña, km. 402
24540 Cacabelos (León)
☎: 987 549 002 - Fax: 987 549 214

VINOS DE LA TIERRA

info@lunabeberide.com
www.lunabeberide.com

Established: 1987

🍷 400 🗄 400,000 litres 🌿 80 has.

TIERRAS DE LUNA 2000 OAK AGED RED
50% cabernet sauvignon, 20% tempranillo, 15% merlot, 15% mencía

91 Intense cherry. Powerful, very toasty aroma (dark-roasted flavours, chocolate) with ripe yet not jammy fruit and a suggestion of mineral notes. Fleshy, fruity, fresh and flavourful palate with toasty and creamy oak tannins integrated with the wine fruit, persistent.

TIERRAS DE LUNA 2001 OAK AGED RED
merlot, cabernet sauvignon, tempranillo, mencía

84 Intense cherry. Aroma with notes of jammy fruit and creamy toast (chocolate, dates). Fleshy, powerful palate with mildly Porty flavours in the retronasal passage (overripening), flavourful.

LUNA BEBERIDE 2000 CRIANZA RED
merlot, cabernet sauvignon, tempranillo

92 Intense cherry. Deep, toasty aroma (chocolate, coffee) with ripe fruit and mineral notes (stone and sand). Powerful palate with fresh fruit and peat in the retronasal passage and solid but ripe tannins, flavourful and very long.

MAURO

Cervantes, 12
47320 Tudela de Duero (Valladolid)
☎: 983 521 972 - Fax: 983 521 973
info@bodegasmauro.com
www.bodegasmauro.com

Established: 1980

🍷 1,200 🗄 215,000 litres 🌿 45 has.

🏴 65% 🌐35%: -UE -US Asia -PR

MAURO VENDIMIA SELECCIONADA 2000 OAK AGED RED
100% tinto fino

90 Intense cherry. Aroma of very ripe fruit (jammy plums) and fine toasty oak (dark-roasted flavour, chocolate). Generous, full, fleshy, warm palate with oak and ripe fruit tannins and a toasty retronasal effect (peat, pitch), flavourful.

MAURO 2002 CRIANZA RED
90% tinto fino, 10% syrah

84 Intense cherry. Fruity aroma with notes of stewed fruit and fine toasty oak. Fleshy palate with flavourful and consistent tannins, ripe fruit and a fine, toasty retronasal effect.

PALACIO DE ARGANZA

Bernardo Diez Obelar, 17
24500 Villafranca del Bierzo (León)

☎: 987 540 322 - Fax: 987 540 516
vinos@palaciodearganza.com

Established: 1805

🍷 5,000 🗄 4,500,000 litres 🌿 75 has.

🏴 75% 🌐25%: -DE -BE -NL -DK -FI -SE -DK -CH -CU -DO -MX -US -RU

PALACIO DE ARGANZA 2003 WHITE
PALACIO DE ARGANZA 1997 ROBLE RED
PALACIO DE ARGANZA 2000 ROBLE RED

PEÑASCAL

Carretera Valladolid - Segovia (N-601) km. 7, 3. Polígono 2. Parc. 273
47140 Laguna de Duero (Valladolid)
☎: 983 546 080 - Fax: 983 546 091
habarcelo@habarcelo.es
www.habarcelo.com

Established: 1970

🍷 4,000 🗄 11,000,000 litres 🌿 400 has.

🏴 70% 🌐30%: -UE -UK -CA -US - SAM -SDV

PEÑASCAL SAUVIGNON BLANC 2003 WHITE
100% sauvignon blanc

81 Pale yellow. Not very intense aroma with a certain finesse (green fruit, white flowers) and a mild exotic note (pineapples, bananas). Flavourful, bitter palate with good acidity.

REALEZA 2002 RED
100% tempranillo

80 Intense cherry. Aroma of foresty red fruit with balsamic notes and liquorice, clear. Flavourful, fruity palate (blackberries) with earthy notes, very pleasant.

PEÑASCAL TEMPRANILLO 2001 RED
tempranillo

83 Cherry with a raspberry hue. Spicy aroma with notes of sun-drenched skins and ripe red fruit. Flavourful palate with a rustic nuance, fine oak, polished tannins and a fresh finish.

REAL SITIO DE VENTOSILLA

Carretera Aranda-Palencia, km. 10
09443 Gumiel de Mercado (Burgos)
☎: 947 546 900 - Fax: 947 546 999
bodega@pradorey.com
www.pradorey.com

Established: 1996

▦ 6,200 ▤ 2,000,000 litres ❦ 520 has.
🍷 75% 🍇25%

SALGÜERO 2003 ROSÉ
50% tempranillo, 50% merlot

80 Raspberry blush. Medium-intensity, fresh aroma of red fruit and herbs. Flavourful, fresh, very pleasant on the palate.

SALGÜERO FERMENTADO EN BARRICA 2003 ROSÉ
50% Tempranillo, 50% Merlot

80 Raspberry blush. Medium-intensity aroma, fresh, red fruit, herbs. Flavourful, fresh palate, very pleasant.

SALGÜERO TEMPRANILLO 2001 RED
100% tempranillo

80 Deep-red. Aroma of flowers and red stone fruit, vanilla and balsamic flavours. Flavourful tannins on the palate, round, with body and medium persistence.

SALGÜERO TEMPRANILLO 2001 RED

80 Garnet red. Aroma of flowers, red stone fruit, vanilla, balsamic hints. Flavourful tannins on the palate, round, with body, medium persistence.

SALGÜERO CABERNET 2000 RED

85 Intense cherry. Toasty aroma, peppery, nuances of oak and ripe fruit, good skins and berry ripening. Fleshy, warm, flavourful palate, sweet tannins, mature Cabernet.

SALGÜERO MERLOT 2000 RED
100% merlot

82 Intense cherry. Aroma with hints of jammy fruit (jammy blackberries), an earthy suggestion, brambles. Fleshy palate, flavourful, toasty, a warm suggestion with a mild vegetative hint at the same time.

SALGÜERO TEMPRANILLO 1999 RED
100% tempranillo

80 Deep cherry. Aroma with spicy oak notes and a nuance of not overly ripe black fruit. Flavourful palate with slightly marked tannins, slightly bitter with good fruity freshness.

Bodegas y Viñedos
RIBERA DEL DURATÓN

Carretera Valtiendas - Aranda, s/n
40314 Valtiendas (Segovia)
☎: 921 527 285 - Fax: 921 527 049
sofia@riberadelduraton.com

▦ 450 ▤ 500,000 litres ❦ 22 has.

🍷 60% 🍇40%: -CH -DE -FR -JP -AT -US -DK -NL -BE -IT -FI

DURATÓN 2001 ROBLE RED
50% tempranillo, 35% syrah, 15% cabernet sauvignon

88 Intense cherry. Powerful, toasty aroma offine oak, ripe fruit and mineral overtones. Toasty, slightly fleshy palate with fresh overtones.

PAGO DE LA MORAVIA 2002 2000 ROBLE RED
100% tempranillo

89 Very intense cherry. Fresh, ripe aroma with fine notes of oak well-integrated with the wine. Fleshy palate with flavourful, lively tannins and excellent acidity, flavourful and elegant.

DURATÓN SYRAH 2002 ROBLE RED
100% syrah

93 Very intense cherry with a brilliant lively edge. Aroma rich in fruit and varietal expression, earthy and mineral hints. Powerful palate with solid, very flavourful tannins, fine toasty oak and elegant fruit. A very "French" Syrah.

DURATÓN 2000 ROBLE RED

Vinos SANZ

Carretera Madrid-La Coruña, km. 170, 5
47490 Rueda (Valladolid)
☎: 983 868 100 - Fax: 983 868 117
vinossanz@vinossanz.com
www.vinossanz.es

Established: 1870

▤ 1,000,000 litres ❦ 100 has.

🍷 80% 🍇20%: -DE -FI -BE -NL USA -UK -MX -CH -CV -IE

CAMPO SANZ 2003 ROSÉ
CAMPO SANZ 2001 RED

VAGAL

La Fuente, 19
40314 Valtiendas (Segovia)
☎: 921 527 331 - Fax: 921 527 332
vagal@vagal.es

VINOS DE LA TIERRA

www.vagal.es

Established: 1998

🛢 300 📦 200,000 litres 🌿 30 has.

🍷 65% 🌐35%: -CH -DE -US

VAGAL CUVÉE JOANA 2003 OAK AGED RED
100% tempranillo 🛢7

85 Intense cherry. Aroma of jammy black fruit with earthy hints (dry clay) and toasty oak notes. Fleshy, warm palate with ripe black fruit, sweet tannins and toasty flavours (sunny vineyards).

VAGAL FELI 2001 RED
tempranillo

81 Intense cherry. Powerful aroma of very ripe fruit and toasty grapes and oak with notes of an early reduction. Ripe fruit on the palate, warm and flavourful with somewhat short varietal expression.

VAGAL JOSÉ Mª GALINDO 2001 RED
tempranillo

83 Intense cherry. Powerful aroma with suggestions of overripening (jam) and toasty hints. Fleshy, warm palate with ripe fruit tannins and an overripe retronasal effect.

VAGAL PAGO ARDALEJOS 2001 RED
tempranillo

89 Quite intense cherry. Aroma with fruit and mineral expression and fine toasty scents, slightly better than last year's vintage. Fleshy, full, flavourful, complex palate with excellent fruit/oak balance and ripe tannins.

VEGA DE LA REINA

Los Moros, 10
47490 Rueda (Valladolid)
☎: 983 868 089 - Fax: 983 868 594
fjmerino@grupo22.com

Established: 1966

🛢 1,100 📦 1,200,000 litres 🌿 100 has.

🍷 95% 🌐5%: -MX -NI -NL -US

VEGA DE LA REINA 2003 JOVEN RED
tempranillo, merlot

83 Brilliant raspberry. Expressive aroma of foresty red fruit, maceration notes and flowers. Light, very fresh and flavourful on the palate with red fruit and suggestions of petals.

VEGA DE LA REINA TRADICIÓN 1999 OAK AGED RED
tempranillo, cabernet sauvignon 🛢12

80 Fairly deep cherry with a brick red glint. Intense aroma, with predominant reduction notes (cocoa, tobacco, old furniture). Flavourful, bitter palate, fresh overtones, with a suggestion of red fruit, marked acidity.

VINOS BLANCOS DE CASTILLA

Carretera N-IV, km. 172, 600
47490 Rueda (Valladolid)
☎: 983 868 029 - Fax: 983 868 563
vinosblancosdecastilla@arrakis.es

Established: 1972

🛢 1,500 📦 5,134,920 litres 🌿 354 has.

🍷 53.08% 🌐46.92%: -DE -AT -BE -BB -BR -CA -CY -CO -CR -CU -DK -US -SV -AE -PH -FR -GT -NL -HN -IE -IT -KY -JP LB -LU -MT -MY -MX -NI -DK -PR -PA -PE -PL -PT -DO -UK -RU -SE -CH -UA -UY

RISCAL 1860 2002 ROBLE RED
100% tinta de Toro

84 Deep cherry. Fresh aroma with notes of fresh skins, hints of petals and a very fine smoky hint. Fleshy, powerful palate with fruity and very fresh tannins and sensations of well-ripened fruit; a suggestion of bitterness in a very pleasant finish (red fruit pulp) with character of the vine variety.

VIÑAS VIEJAS DE CEBREROS

Finca La Piñonera
05260 Cebreros (Avila)
☎: 916 409 797 - Fax: 916 409 797

PEGASO 2001 ROBLE RED
100% garnacha

89 Intense cherry. Complex aroma of minerals with hints of foresty herbs and brambles and creamy notes. Warm, flavourful, mineral palate (hotstone) with herbs and sweet, supple tannins and a viscous retronasal effect.

VIÑAS ZAMORANAS

Pago de la Vega, s/n
49530 Coreses (Zamora)
☎: 980 590 995 - Fax: 980 500 611
zamoranas@terra.es

Established: 2000

🛢 350 📦 500,000 litres 🍷 50% 🌐50%: -US -LU -DE -AT -NL -JP

VERBO DIVINO FERMENTADO EN BARRICA JOVEN WHITE SEMI-SWEET
60% moscatel, 40% albillo

82 Brilliant gold. Intense, grapey aroma of crystallised white fruit (exotic hints), with spicy hints and skins, musky. Flavourful palate with bittersweet notes, slightly marked oak tannins and a slightly acidic edge.

VIÑA MALVA VERDEJO 2003 WHITE
100% verdejo

73 Straw-coloured with a coppery glimmer. Not very intense aroma of weak fruit. Palate with an element of acidity and a bitter finish; poor fruit content.

TRESANTOS VENDIMIA SELECCIONADA 2001 ROBLE RED
60% tinta de Toro, 40% tempranillo

89 Garnet red cherry with a purple rim. Aroma with toasty notes of fine oak, very ripe fruit, slightly spirituous. Warm palate, spirituous with very flavourful sweet tannins and a creamy toasty retronasal effect, good persistence.

TRESANTOS 2002 ROBLE RED
OINOS TRESANTOS VIÑAS VIEJAS 2000 RED
NOVO 2002 MACERACIÓN CARBÓNICA RED
TRESANTOS 2001 OAK AGED RED
TRESANTOS VENDIMIA SELECCIONADA
 2001 RED
NOVO 2001 RED
OINOS TRESANTOS VIÑAS VIEJAS 2001 RED

Grupo YLLERA

Carretera Madrid - Coruña, km. 173, 5
47490 Rueda (Valladolid)
☎: 983 868 097 - Fax: 983 868 177
grupoyllera@grupoyllera.com
www.grupoyllera.com

Established: 1972

⊕ 13,500 📇 6,000,000 litres 🍇 70 has.

🍷 85% 🌐15%: -UE -CH -US -MX -GT -
DO -BR -JP

CUVI 2003 ROSÉ
100% tempranillo

80 Lively blush. Intense, fresh aroma with a good varietal expression, hints of citrus fruit and notions of terroir. Fleshy, slightly warm and fruity palate with slightly marked and flavourful grape tannins.

ALMENADA 2003 ROSÉ
100% tempranillo

77 Lively blush. Slightly intense and fruity aroma without great nuances. Fresh, flavourful palate with spicy hints of skins.

ALMENADA 2002 ROBLE RED
100% tempranillo

80 Intense cherry with a coppery nuance. Slightly intense aroma with toasty oak notes, hints of skins and ripe fruit. Flavourful palate with somewhat ripe, oily tannins, bitter, with waxy hints and flint in the retronasal passage.

CUVI 2002 ROBLE RED
100% tempranillo

78 Dark garnet red cherry with a brick red edge. Intense aroma of toasty oak with balsamic hints. Flavourful, bitter palate with a suggestion of earthiness and without great nuances.

YLLERA 1998 ENVEJECIDO EN ROBLE RED
100% tempranillo

79 Dark cherry with a saffron rim. Intense aroma with predominant toasty oak notes. Flavourful, bitter palate with dark-roasted crianza notes and good acidity.

YLLERA 2000 CRIANZA RED
100% tempranillo

84 Garnet red. Aroma of jammy plums, fine toasty notes and a suggestion of minerals. Fleshy palate with oily, round tannins well-integrated with the crianza and a generous finish (earth, toasty flavours).

YLLERA DOMINUS 2000 RESERVA RED
100% tempranillo

84 Deep cherry. Quite complex aroma of jammy black fruit (plums), and fine toasty, smoky notes. Fleshy palate with marked but ripe (cocoa, cloves) wood tannins, traces of bitterness and a good fresh finish.

YLLERA 1991 GRAN RESERVA RED
100% tempranillo

78 Garnet red cherry with a brick red glint. Intense aroma with toasty wood notes and hints of reduction (varnish). Flavourful, very bitter palate (dark roasted flavours, pitch), lacking complexity.

ZARRAGUILLA

Iglesia, 14
40237 Sacramenia (Segovia)
☎: 921 527 126 - Fax: 913 240 140
zarraguilla.bog@mibbva.com
www.bodegaszarraguilla.es

Established: 1997

⊕ 120 📇 65,000 litres 🍇 15 has.

🍷 90% 🌐10%: -CH

ZARRAGUILLA 2002 ROBLE RED
VENNUR 2002 ROBLE RED

V.T. CONTRAVIESA-ALPUJARRA

BARRANCO OSCURO

Cortijo Barranco Oscuro
18440 Cádiar (Granada)
☎: 958 343 066 - Fax: 958 343 066
info@barrancooscuro.com

VINOS DE LA TIERRA

www.barrancooscuro.com

Established: 1872

🛢 85 📊 30,000 litres 🍇 15 has.

🍷 70% 🌐30%: -DE -DK

BARRANCO OSCURO BLANCO DE BLANCAS NOBLES 2003 WHITE
vigiriega, riesling, vermentino, viognier, morisco

85 Golden yellow. Powerful, ripe aroma of fine lees and creamy oak notes. Flavourful palate of ripe white fruit with spicy hints of skins, an oily and warm texture and fine bitter notes, spicy notes and fine herbs in the retronasal passage.

1368 BARRANCO OSCURO 2001 CRIANZA RED
45% garnacha, 25% cabernet sauvignon, 10% merlot, 5% tempranillo, 10% syrah, 5% cabernet franc

87 Deep cherry. Very concentrated aroma of black fruit, fine hints of reduction (tobacco, smoky woods) and balsamic flavours. Dry, fresh palate, polished fruit and wood tannins, slightly oily and spicy with a generous finish.

1368 BARRANCO OSCURO 2000 CRIANZA RED
45% garnacha, 30% cabernet sauvignon, 10% merlot, 5% tempranillo, 7% syrah, 3% cabernet franc

84 Deep garnet red cherry. Powerful aroma of ripe red fruit and spicy oak notes with a suggestion of aromatic herbs. Flavourful palate with quite fresh tannins, fine bitter notes and excellent acidity.

1368 BARRANCO OSCURO 2002 CRIANZA RED
45% garnacha, 25% cabernet sauvignon, 10% merlot, 5% tempranillo, 10% syrah, 5% cabernet franc

86 Dark cherry. Powerful aroma of ripe black fruit with fine crianza notes (smokiness, spices, balsamic notes) and a nuance of graphite. Fleshy, concentrated palate with rough and oily tannins, spicy (cocoa, pitch) with good acidity.

BORGOÑÓN GRANATE 2002 CRIANZA RED
100% pinot noir

84 Very deep cherry with a violet hue. Intense aroma of red fruit with fine reduction notes (animals) and slightly varietal with a spicy oak nuance. Flavourful palate with slightly marked although promising tannins, ripe fruit and fine bitter notes (liquorice, damp earth).

BARRANCO OSCURO 2002 BRUT NATURE
90% vigiriega, 10% pinot noir

73 Pale yellow. Fresh, quite intense aroma with notes of green fruit, a spicy nuance (cumin), hints of lees and slightly foresty. Very dry, flavourful palate with very bitter, citrus fruit notes and an acidic edge.

1368 BARRANCO OSCURO 1999 CRIANZA RED
TEMPRANILLO Y MÁS 2002 CRIANZA RED

CUATRO VIENTOS

Finca Cuatro Vientos
Carretera de Murtas, PK-4
18490 Murtas (Granada)
☎: 958 343 325
fmcvinos@terra.es
www.grupofernando.es

Established: 2001

🛢 120 📊 300,000 litres 🍇 110 has.

🍷 100%

MARQUÉS DE LA ABUXARRA WHITE
MARQUÉS DE LA ABUXARRA ROSÉ
MARQUÉS DE LA ABUXARRA RED

DOMINIO BUENAVISTA

Carretera de Almería, s/n
18480 Ugíjar (Granada)
☎: 958 767 254 - Fax: 958 767 254
dominiobuenavista@terra.es
www.dominiobuenavista.com

Established: 1996

🛢 100 📊 40,000 litres 🍇 24 has.

🍷 60% 🌐40%: -US

DOMINIO DE BUENAVISTA 2003 WHITE
chardonnay

84 Yellow with a golden glimmer. Aroma with oak notes that stand out from the wine and a nuance of ripe nuances (apples). Powerful, warm and flavourful on the palate with a spirituous suggestion, good acidity and somewhat notorious oak tannins.

DOMINIO DE BUENAVISTA 2002 RED
tempranillo, syrah

85 Intense cherry. Toasty aroma of ripe black fruit with a nuance of fermentative notes, warm, with a spirituous suggestion. Fleshy, flavourful and ripe palate with unharmonised notes of oak and fruit and light fermentative off-odours.

VELETA 2002 RED
cabernet sauvignon

85 Very intense cherry. Powerful aroma, with a rich expression of very ripe black fruit, a nuance of minerals and integrated oak. Powerful, fleshy palate with good acidity and warmth at the same time and flavourful and ripe tannins.

DOMINIO BUENAVISTA 2002 ROBLE RED

EL SOTILLO

Los Carros, s/n
18760 La Rábita (Granada)
☎: 958 829 019 - Fax: 958 829 402

al.garcia@bodegaelsotillo.com
www.odegaelsotillo.com

Established: 1868

🛢 50 ⑧ 52,600 litres 🍇 10 has. 🍷 100%

RAÑOL 2001 CRIANZA RED
85% tempranillo, 15% cabernet sauvignon

57 Fairly dark cherry with a muted orange edge. Evolved, slightly foresty aroma with muted fruit. Vegetative notes and unbalanced acidity on the palate, mediocre.

RAÑOL 2001 FERMENTADO EN BARRICA WHITE
VINICOLA ALPUJARREÑA 1930 GRAN RESERVA WHITE
RAÑOL LICOROSO 1991 DULCE
ADRAVIÑA COSTA 2001 CRIANZA RED
RAÑOL 2001 CRIANZA RED
RAÑOL 2002 CRIANZA RED

GARCÍA DE VERDEVIQUE

Cortijo Los García de Verdevique
18439 Castaras (Granada)
☎: 958 859 030

Established: 1990

🛢 18 ⑧ 9,000 litres 🍇 4 has. 🍷 100%

LOS GARCÍA DE VERDEVIQUE FERMENTADO EN BARRICA WHITE
100% tempranillo

80 Brilliant yellow. Aroma with ligh duction notes (late ranking) and ripe fruit. Notes of sweetness on the palate, powerful and flavour full, better than in the nose.

LOS GARCÍA DE VERDEVIQUE 2001 ROBLE RED
100% tempranillo

86 Deep cherry. Intense aroma of jammy black fruit with notes of thyme and broom and a hint of soil. Fleshy, slightly warm palate with oily fruit tannins and bitterness (earth), a complex finish.

LOS GARCÍA DE VERDEVIQUE 2003 RED
100% tempranillo

83 Deep cherry. Earthy, very Mediterranean aroma (thyme and dried herbs) with a nuance of black fruit. Flavourful with high acidity on the palate and bitter notes that make up for the ripe fruit; a spicy finish, pleasant.

LOS GARCÍA DE VERDEVIQUE WHITE

JOSÉ CARA E HIJOS

Molino, s/n
Albodón(Granada)
☎: 958 826 382

SEÑORIO DE ÇEHEL
100% tempranillo

59 Dull cherry. Mineral aroma of slightly overripe fruit, a littlel volatile. Sweet palate, without nuances, flawed.

Bodegas LORENTE

Cortijo Los Amates
18700 Albuñol (Granada)
☎: 958 826 172 - Fax: 958 826 291
bodegaml@terra.es

🛢 50 ⑧ 35,000 litres 🍇 10 has. 🍷 100%

GRAN CEMEL 2003 WHITE
MACABEO CERRO DEL GATO 2003 WHITE
TINTO CERRO DEL GATO 2003 RED
ALDAMAYAR 2002 CRIANZA RED

LOS BARRANCOS

Carretera Cádiar-Albuñol, km. 9, 4
18449 Lobras (Granada)
☎: 958 343 218 - Fax: 969 425 309
info@lavineria.de

Established: 2000

🛢 60 ⑧ 50,000 litres 🍇 6.8 has.
🍷 5% ⑤95%

CERRO DE LA RETAMA 2002 OAK AGED RED
95% tempranillo, 5% cabernet sauvignon

84 Dark cherry with a purplish edge. Powerful, fruity aroma with balsamic hints (Mediterranean herbs, liquorice) and toasty oak. Powerful, flavourful and concentrated palate with rough tannins, less expressive than in the nose, promising.

CERRO DE LA RETAMA 2001 OAK AGED RED
95% tempranillo, 5% cabernet sauvignon

81 More or less intense cherry. Slightly short but well-balanced aroma (light notes of toasty vanilla, cocoa and fresh fruit). Medium bodied, fresh, flavourful palate, slightly less expressive than the 2002 vintage.

CORRAL DE CASTRO 2002 OAK AGED RED
80% tempranillo, 20% cabernet sauvignon

87 Very deep garnet red cherry. Powerful aroma of black fruit (redcurrants, blackberries) with smoky oak notes, fine lavender notes and Mediterranean herbs. Flavourful and fleshy on the palate with perfectly ripe fruit, well-integrated fruit and oak tannins, fresh overtones, fine spicy notes and excellent acidity.

CORRAL DE CASTRO 2001 OAK AGED RED
80% tempranillo, 20% garnacha

84 Quite intense brilliant cherry. Slightly short, clear, fruity aroma with fine toasty notes (vanilla, tobacco). Round, supple palate with fresh fruit, notes of forest herbs and tannins and fresh fruit, good acidity.

PIEDRAS BLANCAS

Cortijo Piedras Blancas
18430 Torvizcón (Granada)
☎: 958 343 135

Established: 1988
⊕ 18 ▤ 32,000 litres ❦ 9 has. 🍷 100%

PIEDRAS BLANCAS WHITE

73 Golden. Aroma with notes of slightly woody oak and nuts (almonds, walnuts). Warm palate with oak, slightly rough tannins that stand out from the wine and hints of evolution in the cask.

PIEDRAS BLANCAS WHITE
PIEDRAS BLANCAS ROSÉ
PIEDRAS BLANCAS RED

V.T. CÓRDOBA

Cooperativa Agrícola LA UNIÓN

Avenida de Italia, 1
14550 Montilla (Córdoba)
☎: 957 651 855 - Fax: 957 651 855
coop_launion@terra.es

Established: 1979
⊕ 2,700 ▤ 15,000,000 litres ❦ 1,500 has.
🛢 14,500,000 litres.
🍷 80% ⦿20%: -IT -FR -PT

LOS OMEYA JOVEN RED
syrah, cabernet sauvignon, merlot, tempranillo

80 Dark cherry. Powerful, fruity aroma with toasty notes (macerated skins), an earthy hint and overripe fruit. Fleshy palate with slightly marked tannins and a slightly oily, warm texture and bitter hints (liquorice, cocoa, toast).

LOS OMEYA 2001 ROBLE RED
syrah, tempranillo, cabernet sauvignon, merlot

81 Dark cherry with a saffron edge. Powerful aroma with predominant spicy, toasted notes (cocoa) of oak and a suggestion of jammy fruit. Flavourful, fleshy palate with quite rough, oily tannins, cocoa, chocolate, hints of earthiness and liquorice, quite warm.

LAMA

Ronda Povedano, 9
14860 Doña Mencía (Córdoba)
☎: 957 676 016 - Fax: 957 676 023
bodegaslama@terra.es

www.geocities.com/bodegaslama
Established: 1885
⊕ 25 ▤ 300,000 litres 🍷 100%

SEÑORÍO VALERA 2001 ROBLE RED

V.T. DESIERTO DE ALMERÍA

AGROSOL

Finca Los Rubiales
Carretera N-340, km. 488
04210 Lucainena de las Torres (Almería)
☎: 950 364 247 - Fax: 933 620 661
info@agrosol.es
www.agrosol.es

Año de fundación: 1970
⊕ 300 ▤ 400,000 litres ❦ 99 has.
🍷 60% ⦿40%: -BE -NL -DE -DK -IT -IE -US

PERS 2003 WHITE

73 Pale yellow. Slightly intense, and fruity aroma, hints of herbs without great nuances. Quite fresh on the palate, bitter, and a suggestion of perfumed soap.

PERS 2003 ROSÉ

77 Brilliant raspberry, with a coppery hue. Slightly intense aroma of foresty red fruit. Flavourful, bitter palate with toasty hints and spicy skins, good acidity.

VIÑA SALVANA 2003 JOVEN RED
monastrell, tempranillo, cabernet sauvignon

78 Deep cherry. Fresh palate with foresty red fruit, maceration nuances, liquorice notes. Meaty, slightly warm palate, reminiscent of strawberry pulp, a certain bitterness in the finish.

PERS LOS RUBIALES 2003 RED
monastrell, merlot

81 Intense cherry. Earthy aroma with red bramble fruit and a smoky essence. Fruity, meaty, flavourful palate, well-balanced wood-fruit.

PERS LA DIONISIA 2003 RED
cabernet sauvignon, tempranillo, monastrell

84 Deep cherry. Concentrated aroma of well-ripened black fruit and notes of liquorice and earth; a balsamic suggestion. Meaty, concentrated palate with black fruit, good freshness; integrated oak.

PERS LAS MAGAÑAS 2003 CRIANZA RED
syrah, tempranillo, monastrell

80 Deep cherry. Aroma of foresty red fruit, clean and clear. Meaty, very fresh palate with a sensation of strawberries and slightly balsamic; an earthy finish.

PERS LAS MAGAÑAS 2002 CRIANZA RED
syrah, tempranillo, monastrell

79 Garnet red. Toasty aroma with notes of crianza reduction and an essence of macerated red fruit. Flavourful, earthy on the palate, polished wood tannins; slightly warm.

PERS CABERNET SAUVIGNON 2002 RED
cabernet sauvignon

83 Brilliant deep garnet red. Aroma of ripe black fruit, peppery hints and a well-assembled smoky wood essence. Meaty palate with flavourful and consistent tannins, good alcohol-acidity balance; a spicy finish, varietal.

PERS CRIANZA ESCOGIDA 2002 RED

74 Dark garnet red with a brick red edge. Aroma with reduction notes (smoky, animal skins). Evolved, flavourful, toasty warm palate.

PERS LA DIONISIA 2002 RED
cabernet sauvignon, tempranillo, monastrell

78 Garnet red with a ruby red edge. Aroma of black fruit, quite viscous palate, an earthy and sun-drenched essence. Flavourful palate with supple but dominant oak tannins, fresh.

PERS MONASTRELL 2002 RED
monastrell

82 Cherry with a light garnet red edge. Fruity aroma (ripe strawberries) of sour cherries in liqueur, earth. Spicy palate with quite rough but ripe tannins, quite warm, reminiscent of strawberries, flavourful.

PERS TEMPRANILLO 2002 RED
tempranillo

78 Deep cherry. Spicy aroma of foresty red berries and slightly vegetative. Flavourful warm palate with flabby tannins and slightly earthy.

VIÑA SALVANA 1996 RED

77 Ruby red with a brick red hue. Aroma of red fruit in liqueur, warm hints, sun-drenched. Meaty palate with flabby and flavourful tannins, spices and bitter cocoa well-blended with the rest.

PERS SELECCIÓN ESPECIAL 2003 RED

V.T. EIVISSA

Vinos CAN MAYMÓ

Casa Can Maymó
07816 Sant Mateu d'Albarca (Balears)
☎: 971 805 100 - Fax: 971 805 100
Established: 1995
🍇 10 🗄 25,000 litres 🍇 4 has. 🇪🇸 100%

CAN MAYMÓ 2003 JOVEN WHITE
100% malvasia

80 Pale with a golden hue. Intense aroma of ripe fruit with hints of petals and fine lees. Fresh, quite fruity, flavourful palate with good acidity.

CAN MAYMÓ 2003 JOVEN ROSÉ
100% monastrell

81 Pale raspberry. Slightly intense aroma with fruity and floral notes, hints of sweetness and notions of terroir. Flavourful palate with fine bitter and toasty notes, a slightly mineral suggestion and good acidity.

CAN MAYMÓ TRADICIÓN 2003 JOVEN RED
100% monastrell

80 Fairly deep cherry with a dark red edge. Intense, very fine aroma with fresh forest fruit overtones and a suggestion of skins and Mediterranean herbs. Flavourful, supple palate, slightly warm and oily with a bitter finish.

CAN MAYMÓ 2003 OAK AGED RED
merlot, tempranillo, monastrell

83 Garnet red cherry with a coppery glint. Intense aroma with jammy fruit notes and fine toasty oak. Flavourful, fleshy palate with rough and oily tannins, a good fruit/oak integration and hints of liquorice and balsamic flavours in the finish.

CAN MAYMÓ 2002 JOVEN RED

CAN RICH DE BUSCATELL

Cami de Sa Vorera, s/n
07820 San Antonio (Baleares)
☎: 971 803 377 - Fax: 971 803 377
info@bodegascanrich.com
www.bodegascanrich.com
Established: 2000
🍇 68 🗄 120,000 litres 🍇 17 has.
🍷 80% 🍇20%

CAN RICH 2003 JOVEN WHITE
80% malvasía, 20% chardonnay

80 Pale yellow with a golden hue. Quite intense, fruity aroma with hints of exotic fruit and fine herbs. Flavourful palate with rich bitter notes and a mineral hint.

CAN RICH 2003 JOVEN ROSÉ
70% tempranillo, 30% cabernet sauvignon

83 Very deep raspberry. Intense aroma with very ripe red stone fruit and a toasty suggestion of skins. Flavourful palate with sweet notes, spicy hints of skins and a slightly mineral suggestion, excellent acidity.

CAN RICH COSECHA 2002 JOVEN RED
60% monastrell, 10% tempranillo, 30% merlot

67 Dark cherry. Aroma with reduction off-odours (late racking) and a fruity and toasty hint. Somewhat flat palate, without nuances, discreet.

CAN RICH SELECCIÓN 2002 RED
60% cabernet sauvignon, 40% merlot

85 Intense cherry. Aroma with peppery notes, jammy fruit, toasty oak, a nuance of minerals and scrubland herbs. Powerful, fleshy palate with paprika and very ripe sweet tannins, flavourful and long.

CAN RICH SELECCIÓN 2001 RED

SA COVA

07816 Sant Mateu D'Albarca (Baleares)
☎: 971 187 046 - Fax: 971 187 046
Established: 1993
🌐 70 🗄 45,000 litres 🍇 9 has.
🎗 85% 🌐15%: -DE

SA COVA BLANC DE BLANCS 2003 WHITE
100% malvasía

83 Pale yellow with a golden hue. Intense aroma with predominant notes of herbs and anise and a suggestion of fruit and white flowers. Fresh, very flavourful palate with fine spicy and mineral notes.

SA COVA 2003 OAK AGED ROSÉ
100% monastrell

70 Deep blush with an orangey hue. Intense, ripe, slightly evolved aroma (nuts, mountain herbs) with smoky hints. Flavourful, slightly warm, oily and bitter on the palate, without great nuances.

SA COVA 9 2003 JOVEN RED
100% monastrell

81 Dark garnet red cherry. Quite intense, very fine aroma with notes of fruit and toasty skins and hints of Mediterranean herbs. Flavourful palate with fleshy overtones and slightly marked grape tannins, warm and slightly oily.

SA COVA RED ROBLE 2000

84 Cherry with a brick red hue. Aroma with toasty notes of oak, a nuance of forest berries (scrubland) and light reduction notes (tobacco). Light, round palate with slightly weak tannins, flavourful and spicy with reduction and spicy notes in the retronasal passage.

SA COVA PRIVAT 2002 OAK AGED RED
90% tempranillo, 10% syrah   🌐 12

83 Quite intense cherry with an orange edge. Aroma with toasty notes, hillside herbs, balsamic notes and ripe fruit. Somewhat fleshy, warm, flavourful palate with ripe fruit, a medium-expression and toasty oak.

SA COVA PRIVAT 1998 OAK AGED RED
70% monastrell, 30% tempranillo

79 Dark cherry with a brick red glint. Powerful aroma with predominant burnt notes (dark-roasted flavours, tyres, varnish). Flavourful palate, warm and oily with a bitter and dark-roasted suggestion.

SA COVA 1998 CRIANZA RED

Vins de TANYS MEDITERRANIS

D'es Tudó, 13-15
07830 Sant Josep de Sa Talaia (Baleares))
☎: 971 399 167 - Fax: 971 305 440
enotecum@telefonica.net
Established: 2001
🌐 15 🗄 10,000 litres 🎗 60% 🌐40%

COS D'UC 2002 OAK AGED RED
100% monastrell

84 Dark cherry with a purplish edge. Powerful aroma of black fruit, petals, balsamic hints and a hint of spicy oak. Flavourful, concentrated palate with quite rough, oily tannins and a slightly acidic edge.

ES DIVI 2002 OAK AGED RED
100% monastrell

84 Dark, garnet red cherry. Powerful aroma of very varietal, slightly reduced fruit, balsamic hint, damp earth and spicy hints of oak. Flavourful palate with rough, oily tannins, spicy and long.

ES DIVI SA SELECCIÓ 2002 CRIANZA RED
95% monastrell, 5% garnacha

83 Very deep cherry with a dark red edge. Powerful aroma of very ripe fruit with hints of reduction (withered petals) and creamy hints of oak. Fleshy palate with ripe, oily tannins, bitter, balsamic and slightly warm with a notion of terroir.

SOMNI 2002 RED DULCE

V.T. EL TERRERAZO

MUSTIGUILLO

Carretera N-330, km 195
46300 Las Cuevas de Utiel (Valencia)
☎: 620 216 227 - Fax: 618 308 288
info@bodegamustiguillo.com
Established: 1999
🌐 370 🗄 90,000 litres 🍇 90 has.
🎗 40% 🌐60%

FINCA TERRERAZO 2001 OAK AGED RED
60% bobal, 20% tempranillo, 20% cabernet sauvignon

94 Intense cherry. Toasty aroma (dark-roasted flavours, minerals, peat) of stewed black fruit. Generous, fleshy, full, flavourful and original palate with abundant but oily and polymerised tannins, persistent.

QUINCHA CORRAL 2001 OAK AGED RED
90% bobal, 6% tempranillo, 4% cabernet sauvignon

93 Intense cherry. Slightly closed aroma of minerals rich in fruit expression, ripe with fine toasty oak and ripe fruit. Powerful and fleshy palate, good acidity and dry tannins, slightly foresty and mineral suggestion in the retronasal passage and fine toasty flavours.

MESTIZAJE 2002 OAK AGED RED
50% bobal, tempranillo, cabernet sauvignon, syrah, merlot, garnacha

91 Intense cherry with a very lively violet edge. Aroma with good fruit expression and well-integrated fine, toasty and creamy oak notes with a light mineral nuance. Fresh but ripe fruit on the palate with flavourful and well-balanced tannins; warm and very expressive in the retronasal passage (mineral and fruity, very good finish).

V.T. EXTREMADURA

Bodegas AGAPITA RUBIO BRAVO

José Manuel Durán, 17
10136 Cañamero (Cáceres)
☎: 927 369 192 - Fax: 927 369 437

Established: 1948

🍷 180 📊 1,100,000 litres 🌿 30 has.

🍇 100%

GARRUCHO 2002 ROBLE RED
SEÑORÍO DE LA RAÑA 2002 CRIANZA RED

ALVEAR

Carretera Almendralejo - Paloma, km. 8
06840 Alange (Badajoz)
☎: 957 650 100 - Fax: 957 650 135
info@alvear.es - www.alvear.es

VIÑALANGE TEMPRANILLO 2002 RED
100% tempranillo

75 Dark garnet red. Aroma of ripe plums and slightly sunny, earthy notes (varnish). Fleshy palate with quite rough tannins but without a strong fruit presence.

VIÑALANGE TEMPRANILLO 2003 RED
100% tempranillo

87 Intense cherry with a raspberry edge. Blackberry aroma (maceration) with earthy notes and a hint of aromatic herbs, expressive and concentrated. Flavourful, fleshy palate with good fruit tannins and traces of very typical Tempranillo (flowers liquorice, black fruit), persistent.

VIÑALANGE TEMPRANILLO 2001 ROBLE RED

Bodegas y Viñedos ANGEL SÁNCHEZ REDONDO

Finca El Palomar - Sierra Santa Bárbara
10600 Plasencia (Cáceres)
☎: 927 418 159 - Fax: 927 418 102
jesus@fincaelpalomar.com
www.fincaelpalomar.com

Established: 1990

🍷 125 📊 55,000 litres 🌿 4 has.

🍇 40% 🍷60%: -FI -SE -DK -DK -DE

VIÑA PLACENTINA 2002 ROBLE RED
100% cabernet sauvignon

81 Garnet red with an orange edge. Aroma of very ripe plums with notes of toasty skins and a nuance of minerals. Flavourful palate with well-assembled wood tannins, very fresh.

ANTONIO MEDINA E HIJOS

Cestería, 4
06300 Zafra (Badajoz)
☎: 924 575 060 - Fax: 924 575 076
amedina@coeba.es
www.bodegasmedina.net

Established: 1931

🍷 4,000 📊 3,000,000 litres 🌿 250 has.

🍇 65% 🍷35%: -JP -CH -DE -HU -AT -BE
-DK -FR -UK -IE -IT -NL -SE -RU -CA -MX -TW

MARQUES DE BADAJOZ FERMENTADO EN
 BARRICA WHITE
JALOCO ZAFRA WHITE
CASTA BRAVA WHITE

JALOCO ZAFRA ROSÉ
MARQUES DE BADAJOZ OAK AGED RED
JALOCO ZAFRA OAK AGED RED
JALOCO RED
PITARRA DEL ABUELO RED
CASTA BRAVA RED
MARQUÉS DE BADAJOZ OAK AGED
 VINO DE LICOR

COLOMA

Finca Torre Bermeja del Colmenar
Carretera EX-363, km. 5, 6
06170 Alvarado (Badajoz)
☎: 924 440 028 - Fax: 924 440 409
coloma@bodegascoloma.com
www.bodegascoloma.com

Established: 1966
⊕ 750 ⚘ 200 has.

COLOMA VIURA 2003 WHITE
COLOMA-VIÑA AMELIA 2003 WHITE
COLOMA CABERNET/MERLOT 2003 RED
COLOMA GARNACHA ROJA 2003 RED
COLOMA-VIÑA AMELIA 2003 JOVEN RED
COLOMA CUVÉE 2003 JOVEN RED
COLOMA SELECCIÓN GRAN MERLOT NOIR
 2003 OAK AGED RED
COLOMA SELECCIÓN CABERNET SAUVIG-
NON 2003 OAK AGED RED
COLOMA-CASTILLO "TORRE BERMEJA"
2001 CRIANZA RED

EXPLOTACIONES AGROINDUS
TRIALES DE BADAJOZ

Plaza de los Alféreces, 11
06005 Badajoz (Badajoz)
☎: 924 235 705 - Fax: 924 235 705
vinajara@cempresarial.com

VIÑA JARA RED

JUAN ROMERO FUENTES

Avenida Magaz, s/n
06392 El Raposo (Badajoz)
☎: 924 570 448 - Fax: 924 570 448
romero@bodegasromero.com
www.bodegasromero.com

Established: 1954
⊕ 80 ⚗ 400,000 litres ⚘ 20 has.
🍷 90% 🍇10%: -CH -DE

AMONAZAR WHITE
AMONAZAR RED

LAR DE BARROS-INVIOSA

La Fuente, 8
06200 Almendralejo (Badajoz)
☎: 924 671 235 - Fax: 924 665 932
info@lardebarros.com
www.lardebarros.com

Established: 1931
⊕ 2,500 ⚗ 2,000,000 litres ⚘ 400 has.
🍷 60% 🍇40%: -US -MX -CA -JP -PR -TW
-PL -CH -SE -DK -DE -DK -UK -NL -BE -FR

LAR DE ORO 2003 RED

LUIS GURPEGUI MUGA

Avenida Celso Muerza, 8
31570 San Adrián (Navarra)
☎: 948 670 050 - Fax: 948 670 259
bodegas@gurpegui.es
www.gurpegui.es

⊕ 1,500 🍷 80% 🍇20%

GURPEGUI TEMPRANILLO CABERNET
SAUVIGNON 2003 RED
tempranillo, cabernet sauvignon

74 Cherry with a violet rim. Aroma of red fruit,
fresh. Slightly drying, supple, tannic and light on
the palate.

CINCO VIÑAS 2003 WHITE
RANCHO VIEJO 2003 WHITE
RANCHO VIEJO 2003 ROSÉ
GURPEGUI 2003 ROSÉ
CINCO VIÑAS 2003 ROSÉ
CINCO VIÑAS 2002 ROBLE RED
RANCHO VIEJO 2003 ROBLE RED

Bodegas ORTIZ

Sevilla, 34
06200 Almendralejo (Badajoz)
☎: 924 662 811 - Fax: 924 665 406
info@bodegasortiz.com
www.bodegasortiz.com

Established: 1940
⊕ 600 ⚗ 2,350,000 litres ⚘ 20 has.
🍷 90% 🍇10%: -DE -NL -DO -CA

SEÑORÍO DE ORÁN 2001 OAK AGED RED
100% tempranillo

79 Cherry with a garnet red edge. Aroma of black
fruit, spicy with viscous hints. Fleshy, warm palate with slightly rough yet round tannins, a well-
balanced plummy and wood finish.

VIÑA ROJA SELECCIÓN 1998 OAK AGED RED

79 Intense cherry with a saffron edge. Intense, spicy aroma, jammy red fruit, hints of reduction. Flavourful palate, fresh overtones, slightly warm and oily, high in acidity.

VIÑA ROJA COUPAGE 2001 OAK AGED RED

79 Dark cherry with a coppery edge. Intense aroma, red stone fruit, nuances of dried fruit, a terracotta suggestion. Better on the palate, flavourful, fresh fruit, with spicy hints, high in acidity.

SEÑORÍO DE ORÁN 2003 WHITE
CHARNECAL 2003 ROSÉ
CHARNECAL 2003 RED

Bodegas PUENTE AJUDA

Carretera Olivenza-Elvas, km 105
06100 Olivenza (Badajoz)
☎: 924 126 280 - Fax: 924 126 280
bodegaspuenteajuda@mesasdelrio.com
www.bodegaspuenteajuda.com

Established: 1999

🍇 800 📊 1,500,000 litres 🍇 100 has.

🍷 90% 🌐10%: -DE -NL -FI

VIÑA ALOR 2000 CRIANZA RED
80% tempranillo, 20% cabernet sauvignon

72 Cherry with a brick red hue. Aroma of toasty wood, an element of reduction and a mild hint of paprika. Not very well-balanced palate with slightly marked wood; not very expressive.

MARBEAN 2001 CRIANZA RED

RUIZ TORRES

Cañadahonda, 61
10136 Cañamero (Cáceres)

☎: 927 369 024 - Fax: 927 369 302
info@ruiztorres.com
www.ruiztorres.com

Established: 1870

🍇 1,200 📊 4,000,000 litres 🍇 250 has.

🍷 70% 🌐30%: -DE -CH -LT -LV -CZ -UK -EE -TW -JP -TW BY -BE -MX -AR -CA

TRAMPAL 2000 CRIANZA RED
RUIZ TORRES CABERNET SAUVIGNON 1998 CRIANZA RED
FELIPE RUIZ 1998 RESERVA RED

VINIFICACIONES EXTREMEÑAS

Camino de las Huertas, 9
06498 Lobón (Badajoz)
☎: 924 447 492 - Fax: 924 447 492
viniexsa@wanadoo.es
www.viniexsa.com

Established: 1979

🍇 50 📊 2,000,000 litres 🍇 120 has.

🍷 90% 🌐10%: -NL

VIÑA MONJÍAS 2002 JOVEN RED
VIÑA MONJÍAS ENVEJECIDO 2001 RED

VIÑA EXTREMEÑA

Carretera de Alange, s/n
06200 Almendralejo (Badajoz)
☎: 924 670 158 - Fax: 924 670 159
info@vinexsa.com   borja@vinexsa.com
www.vinexsa.com

Established: 1971

🍇 10,000 📊 4,700,000 litres 🍇 1,100 has.

🍷 30% 🌐70%: -UE ASIA -US

VEGA ADRIANA RED
CASTILLO DE VALDESTRADA RED
PALACIO DE VADEINFANTE RED
MONASTERIO DE TENTUDIA 2000 RED
CORTE REAL 2000 RED
MONASTERIO DE TENTUDIA TRADICIÓN 2000 RED
ADVENTUS 2000 RED
CORTE REAL PLATINUM 2000 RED
PALACIO DE MONSALUD 2001 RED

VIÑA SANTA MARINA

Carretera N-630, km. 634 - Apdo. 714
06800 Mérida (Badajoz)
☎: 924 027 670 - Fax: 924 027 675
bodega@vsantamarina.com
www.vsantamarina.com

VINOS DE LA TIERRA

Established: 1999

🍇 400 🍷 59 has.

🐷 79% (🍇)21%: -DE -BE -NL -UK -AT -CH -IT -US -JP -PT -KY

ALTARA 2003 JOVEN SECO WHITE
60% montúa, 30% pardina, 10% cayetana blanca

78 Pale with a greenish hue. Medium-intensity aroma with notes of hay, green grass and white fruit. Pleasant, fruity and slightly oily on the palate, somewhat lacking in freshness.

CELTUS TEMPRANILLO 2002 SECO RED
100% tempranillo

82 Garnet red cherry. Fresh, fruity aroma, a suggestion of violet flowers. Flavourful, expressive palate with good fresh fruit expression,. well-balanced.

VIÑA SANTA MARINA CABERNET SAUVIGNON - SYRAH 2001 OAK AGED RED
75% cabernet sauvignon, 25% syrah

81 Dark garnet red cherry. Powerful aroma with smoky oak, hints of ripe fruit and slightly varietal (redcurrants, paprika, damp earth). Flavourful palate with a good oak/fruit integration and quite fresh oak notes.

VIÑA SANTA MARINA TEMPRANILLO 2001 OAK AGED RED
85% tempranillo, 11% cabernet sauvignon, 4% syrah

84 Cherry with an orangey edge. Not very intense aroma with ripe fruit, spicy skins and a balsamic hint. Flavourful palate with very lively red fruit

and excellent acidity, medium bodied though very pleasant drinking.

EQUUS 2001 OAK AGED RED
85% tempranillo, 10% cabernet sauvignon, 5% syrah

83 Intense cherry with a violet edge. Aroma of quite ripe red stone fruit with a nuance of smoky oak. Flavourful, spicy palate (black pepper), fruit without great nuances, easy drinking.

MIRACULUS 1999 RESERVA RED
50% tempranillo, 30% cabernet sauvignon, 20% syrah

83 Cherry with an orangey hue. Aroma with crianza character (spices, leather). Round palate with hints of red fruit and good acidity, less woody presence, fresh.

V.T. GRANADA SUROESTE

Bodegas H. CALVENTE

Viñilla, 6
18699 Jete (Granada)
☎: 958 644 179 - Fax: 958 644 179
bodegasmar@arrakis.es

Established: 1996

🍷 8.5 has. 🍶 50,000 litres.

CALVENTE 2003 WHITE
100% moscatel

86 Brilliant straw. Fresh, very fruity aroma with hints of Muscatel and notes of herbs and flowers. Sweet overtones on the palate, flavourful, full with excellent dried Muscatel experience without the bitterness of its skin.

CALVENTE 2002 WHITE
100% moscatel

86 Brilliant golden yellow with a lemony hue. Powerful aroma with an excellent varietal fruit expression (musk, exotic hints and flowers) and a slightly smoky and mineral suggestion. Fresh, dry, flavourful palate with slightly fresh tannins, crystallised hints and fine minerals.

CALVENTE 2001 OAK AGED RED
Cabernet sauvignon, syrah, merlot, tempranillo

83 Intense cherry. Aroma with toasty notes of oak and jammy fruit (plums) with mineral hints, warm. Fleshy palate with balsamic flavours in the retronasal passage, slightly well-displayed oak tannins and jammy ripe fruit.

BODEGA LOS MORENOS

Silencio, 2
18230 Atarfe (Granada)
☎: 958 43 45 33

VINOS DE LA TIERRA

RIBERA DEL GENIL 2003 FERMENTADO EN
BARRICA WHITE
100% chardonnay

85 Straw-coloured with a yellow hue. Smoky
aroma with ripe fruit, lees, very varietal of
Chardonnay.Oily, smoky and warm palate with cut
grass in the retronasal passage (hay), expressive
and with a suggestion of very ripe fruit.

RIBERA DEL GENIL 2002 OAK AGED RED
% Cabernet Sauvignon, tempranillo

78 Deep garnet red cherry with an orange edge.
Aroma with fruity and early reduction notes (wet
leather). Quite fresh on the palate and fruity, without great nuances, flavourful, ripe.

EL VIÑEDO 2003 RED

80 Garnet red cherry. Fruity, fresh aroma with
expression. Fruity, flavourful palate with a slightly
foresty hint.

BODEGA **LOS NEVEROS**

Camino de Zote 21
Huetor Vega (Granada)
☎: 958 50 17 32

LOMAS ALTAS ROSÉ

75 Salmon pink. Aroma with ripe fruit and foresty
notes (earth, broom). Supple palate, slightly
foresty and warm with very ripe fruit.

CERRO DE LOS GUARDAS 2003 OAK AGED
RED
tempranillo, garnacha   🍷 12

77 Intense cherry. Aroma with hardly any fruit,
hints of overripe fruit and nuances of evolution.
Warm, quite flavourful, rustic palate with hardly
any fruitiness.

CERRO DE LOS GUARDAS 2001 OAK AGED
RED
tempranillo, garnacha   🍷 12

78 Garnet red cherry. Aroma with traces of old
wood (Solera) but with overtones of fresh
Garnacha expression. Fresh, flavourful palate with
hints of oak that cloak the freshness of the wine.

SEÑORÍO DE NEVADA

Autovía Granada - Motril (salida 153)
Carretera de Cónchar, s/n
18659 Villamena (Granada)
☎: 902 300 028 - Fax: 958 777 062
bodegass_nevada@teleline.es
Established: 1996

🌐 250 📊 200.000 litres 🍇 10,8 has.
🍷 80% 🌐20%: -DE -CH -SE

SEÑORÍO DE NEVADA CABERNET
SAUVIGNON/MERLOT 2002 RED

83 Garnet red cherry. Intense aroma, fine oak
notes well-integrated with those of the ripe fruit, a
terracotta and mountain herbs suggestion and
slightly vegetative notes (heatstroke). Powerful,
flavourful palate, an oily texture, excellent crianza
expression (chocolate, spices), long.

SEÑORÍO DE NEVADA CABERNET
SAUVIGNON/MERLOT 2003 RED

86 Garnet red cherry. Quite intense aroma, with
predominant spicy oak notes, a suggestion of ripe
stone fruit and a mineral suggestion. Flavourful
palate, marked but promising tannins, mineral and
perfectly ripened fruit nuances.

SEÑORÍO DE NEVADA SYRAH-MERLOT
2003 RED

85 Garnet red cherry. Quite intense aroma with
mild varietal notes (brambles, petals, underbrush)
and fine oak notes. Flavourful palate, nuances of
sun-drenched skins, unpolished tannins, excellent
acidity, long, hints of Mediterranean forest.

SEÑORÍO DE NEVADA VENDIMIA
SELECCIONADA 2002 RED

87 Garnet red cherry. Powerful aroma with predominant toasty oak notes, mineral nuances.
Powerful, flavourful palate, excellent crianza
expression, bitter hints (liquorice, chocolate,
terracotta), well-structured and long with slightly
sweet tannins.

V.T. ILLA DE MENORCA

CRISPÍN MARIANO VADELL

Camí de Tramuntana, km. 1
07740 Es Mercadal (Menorca)
☎: 971 375 391 - Fax: 971 375 467

VINOS DE LA TIERRA

www.bodegasmenorquinas@mns.net

FERRER DE MUNT PALAU RED

Compañía Vitivinícola de MENORCA

Finca Sa Cúdia Nova. Parque Natural de
S'Albufera
07702 Mahón (Menorca)
☎: 629 330 162 - Fax: 971 353 607
vinyasacudia.com
www.vinyasacudia.com

Established: 1999
▯ 7,500 litres ☘ 6 has. ▼ 100%

VINYA SA CUDÍA 2003 WHITE
100% malvasía

87 Golden yellow. Warm, mineral, spirituous
aroma with ripe fruit and exotic hints of Malvasía.
Warm palate with volume, flavourful yet fruity, very
Mediterranean.

V.T. ILLES BALEARS

ÁN NEGRA VITICULTORS

3ª Volta 18
07200 Falanitx (Balears)
☎: 971 584 481 - Fax: 971 584 482
annegra@hotmail.com

Established: 1994
▦ 450 ▯ 180,000 litres ☘ 25 has.
▼ 40% ◉60%: -UE -MX -BR

AN/2 2002 OAK AGED RED
50% callet, 50% syrah, cabernet sauvignon, manto negro,
otras   ▯ 10

84 Quite dark garnet red cherry. Aroma with fruity
notes, slightly balsamic with fine toasty notes.
Fresh, fruity palate with a balsamic and vegetative
retronasal effect, a foresty hint and supple tannins.

À.N. SON NEGRE 2001 CRIANZA RED
100% callet

93 Garnet red cherry with an orange edge.
Elegant, not very intense aroma (slightly closed in)
with notes of fine evolution (tobacco, delicate spices). Round, oily, fine palate with integrated flavourful tannins and a subtle fruit expression.
Somewhat impenetrable as a whole.

ÀN 2001 CRIANZA RED
90% callet, 10% fogoneu, mantonegro

91 Quite dark garnet red cherry. Fresh, fruity
aroma with subtle notes of fallen leaves (balsamic)
and fine toasty (cocoa) and reduction notes. Fine,
elegant palate with a balsamic retronasal effect,
fresh, light and well-integrated tannins, good per-

sistence. Has more expression and elegance than
last year's vintage.

CAN MAJORAL

Carrer Campanar, s/n
07210 Algaida (Balears)
☎: 971 665 867 - Fax: 971 665 867
bodega@canmajoral.com
www.canmajoral.com

Established: 1994
▦ 96 ▯ 50,000 litres ☘ 12 has.
▼ 90% ◉10%: -DE

CAN MAJORAL GALDENT 2003 WHITE

ES VERGER

S'Hort d'es Verger s/n
07190 Esporles ()
☎: 971 716 267 - Fax: 971 665 867

Established: 1999
▦ 15 ▯ 10,000 litres ☘ 4 has.

SES MARJADES 2002 CRIANZA RED

87 Dark cherry. Aroma with good fruit expression, fine toasty nuances and a balsamic hint (dry
leaves). Round palate with a good expression of
fruit and crianza, a fine retronasal effect and oily,
elegant tannins.

ES ROJALS 2003 CRIANZA RED

FLORIANÓPOLIS

Carretera Andratx - Capdella, km. 40
07150 Andratx (Baleares)
☎: 971 235 413 - Fax: 971 235 519
florianopolis@eresmas.com
www.santa-catarina.com

Established: 1985
▦ 750 ▯ 500,000 litres ☘ 80 has.
▼ 90% ◉10%: -DE -CH

SANTA CATARINA 2003 JOVEN WHITE
100% chardonnay

80 Pale gold. Intense aroma of white fruit with
floral notes and toasty and spicy hints of skins.
Flavourful palate with fine bitter notes and fragrant
herbs, slightly warm and oily.

SANTA CATARINA 2003 JOVEN ROSÉ
cabernet sauvignon

76 Intense raspberry with a coppery hue.
Powerful aroma of slightly reduced ripe fruit with a
spicy and warm suggestion. Flavourful, bitter
palate with nuts and fruit expression slightly
muted by the alcohol.

SANTA CATARINA SON ALOY 2003 JOVEN RED
50% cabernet sauvignon, 50% merlot

80 Dark garnet red cherry. Intense aroma of ripe red stone fruit with toasty notes of skins, smoky flavours and a notion of terroir. Flavourful, fleshy palate with slightly marked tannins, pleasant.

SANTA CATARINA 2001 CRIANZA RED
SANTA CATARINA SON BOSCH 2001 CRIANZA RED
SANTA CATARINA 1998 RESERVA RED

Bodegas RIBAS

Montanya, 2
07330 Consell (Balears)
☎: 971 622 673 - Fax: 971 622 746
hhribas@hotmail.com

Established: 1986

🛢 220 📦 170,000 litres 🍇 40 has.

🍷 70% 🍇30%

HEREUS DE RIBAS 2002 ROBLE RED
57% manto negro, 27% cabernet sauvignon, 11% Syrah, 5% merlot

85 Dark cherry. Aroma with a mineral expression, balsamic notes (iodine, eucalyptus) and well-integrated fine toasty wood. Round palate with oily tannins, flavourful with a varietal retronasal effect.

SIÓ DE RIBAS 2001 CRIANZA RED
55% manto negro, 25% cabernet sauvignon, 20% syrah

88 Glacé cherry. Fruity aroma with well-integrated light toasty oak notes. Round, spicy palate with a fine toasty retronasal effect, silky and flavourful tannins and an elegant finish.

RIBAS DE CABRERA 2001 RED
50% manto negro, 15% syrah, 35% cabernet sauvignon

86 Dark cherry. Aroma with a fruit expression and elegant toasty scents (cocoa, coffee). Oily palate with good fruit expression and with silky tannins well-integrated in the wine, flavourful and elegant.

HEREUS DE RIBAS 2003 JOVEN WHITE
HEREUS DE RIBAS 2003 JOVEN ROSÉ

Finca SON BORDILS

Carretera Inca-Sineu, km. 4
07300 Inca (Illes Balears)
☎: 971 182 200 - Fax: 971 612 583
info@sonbordils.es
www.sonbordils.es

Established: 1998

🛢 750 📦 400,000 litres 🍇 40 has.

🍷 60% 🍇40%: -US -CH -DE

SON BORDILS 2003 WHITE
100% chardonnay

84 Pale gold. Intense, ripe aroma with excellent varietal expression (apples, hay), floral and spicy hints. Flavourful, generous palate with ripe fruit, warm and oily.

SON BORDILS BLANC DE RAÏM BLANC 2003 WHITE
100% prensal blanc

83 Brilliant pale yellow. Intense, fresh, quite varietal aroma (ripe white fruit, fragrant herbs) and spicy. Flavourful, generous palate rich in ripe fruit expression, with fine bitter notes, good acidity and a suggestion of minerals.

SON BORDILS MUSCAT 2003 WHITE
100% moscatel de grano menudo

84 Pale with a golden hue. Intense aroma with a fine varietal expression (musk, white flowers, exotic and, fennel hints). Fresh palate with fine bitter notes and excellent acidity.

SON BORDILS 2001 RED

88 Intense cherry. Varietal aroma (damp earth, blackcurrants), with fine toasty scents (coffee, chocolate). Fleshy, full, flavourful warm palate with ripe tannins and fine toasty creamy oak.

VINORICA (CASTELL MIQUEL)

Polígono 3, Parcela 259/261
07340 Alaró (Mallorca)
☎: 971 510 698
www.castellmiquel.de

CASTELL MIQUEL SYRAH 2002 RED
syrah

80 Quite intense cherry. Aroma with light notes of overripening (jammy raisins), toasty. Round, warm palate with ripe fruit, flavourful.

VINOS DE LA TIERRA

CASTELL MIQUEL CABERNET SAUVIGNON 2002 RED

V.T. LA GOMERA

EFRAIN GÁMEZ CORDERO

El Palmar Viejo
38840 Vallehermoso (Tenerife)
☎: 922 800 024

EFRAIN GÁMEZ CORDERO WHITE
EFRAIN GÁMEZ CORDERO JOVEN RED

HUMBERTO ASCANIO MONTESINOS

38840 Hermigua (Tenerife)
☎: 922 146 218

MONTESINOS AFRUTADO WHITE
MONTESINOS JOVEN RED

JORGE SUÁREZ COELLO

El Tanque
38840 Vallehermoso (Tenerife)
☎: 922 800 025

LA ZOQUILLA AFRUTADO WHITE
LA ZOQUILLA JOVEN RED

RAMÓN MARICHAL FELIPE

Macayo
38840 Vallehermoso (Tenerife)
☎: 922 800 095

ROQUE CANO AFRUTADO WHITE
ROQUE CANO JOVEN RED

V.T. LAUJAR-ALPUJARRA

CORTIJO EL CURA

Paraje de Jáncor, s/n
04470 Laujar de Andarax (Almería)
☎: 950 228 436 - Fax: 950 228 436
milan@almerilim.com
www.almerilim.com

Established: 1997
🛢 100 🗄 120,000 litres 🍇 25 has.
🍷 90% 🌿10%: -DE -CH

ORO DEL LLANO 2003 JOVEN WHITE
INFANTE FRANCISCO DOMINGO 2003 ROSÉ
JANCOR 2001 CRIANZA RED
SÁNCHEZ VIZCAINO 1999 RESERVA RED

VALLE DE LAUJAR

Carretera de Laujar a Berja, km. 2, 2
04470 Laujar de Andarax (Almería)
☎: 950 524 026 - Fax: 950 524 026

VIÑA LAUJAR FERMENTADO EN BARRICA RED

V.T. NORTE DE GRANADA

ANTONIO VILCHEZ VALENZUELA

18516 Marchal (Granada)

NARANJUEZ 2003 WHITE

83 Yellow with a golden glimmer. Aroma with notes of slightly ripe sweet fruit with hints of scrubland herbs. Warm, oily, flavourful palate with a nuance of dried mountain herbs and mineral notes.

NARANJUEZ 2003 RED

86 Intense cherry with a garnet red edge. Fine aroma of ripe but quite fresh fruit and toasty oak notes. Round, powerful palate, rich in toasty oak nuances with a mild suggestion of minerals and fresh fruit.

NARANJUEZ 2002 RED

81 Intense cherry. Powerful aroma of toasty oak, black fruit with mild post-fermentative notes and macerated skins. Meaty palate with dry red fruit tannins, good acidity and toasty oak in the retro-nasal passage.

PAGO DE ALMARAES

Calle Generalife, 10
18360 Huertor Tajar (Granada)
☎: 629 588 742

RIBERA DEL FARDES RED

80 Intense cherry. Aroma with notes of mace-rated skins (ink) with mild notes of overripe-ness, fruit and an earthy essence (damp clay). Meaty, full, flavourful palate with earth in the retronasal passage.

RAMÓN SAAVEDRA SAAVEDRA

Graena-Guadix

18517 (Granada)

CAUZON 2003 WHITE

82 Slighty dull straw. Aroma with mild notes of mountain herbs, foresty with a suggestion of sweet fruit. Oily, warm palate with good acidity, flavourful, slightly foresty but original.

CAUZON 2003 RED

84 Intense cherry. Powerful aroma, rich in ripe fruit expression but with fresh nuances, fine toasty notes. Powerful palate with high acidity relatively well compensated by the alcohol, dry tannins and fine toasty oak.

TORCUATO GARCIA

18516 Policar (Granada)

VERTIJANA 2003 RED

87 Intense brilliant cherry. Aroma with toasty notes of fine oak and fresh fruit in the retronasal passage (brambles, plums). Powerful, fresh palate with very incisive dry oak and fruit tannins, well-balanced acidity and a good fruit expression.

VERTIJANA 2002 RED

89 Intense cherry. Fine aroma with a good fruit expression, fresh (redcurrants, damp earth) and toasty hints of fine oak (cocoa, coffee). Full, flavourful, fresh palate with excellent northern wine acidity and fresh fruit despite its 14 degrees, ripe, varietal.

Bodegas VILLAGRAN

C/ Sol, 2
18815 Campocámara-Cortes de Baza (Granada)
☎:954 457 757 - Fax: 954 457 757
boegavillagran@terra.es

CORTIJO DE ANAGIL 1998 RED
tempranillo, cabernet sauvignon , merlot

78 Fairly intense cherry. Reduced aroma (lacks airing, tank wine) without fruit expression. Slightly better, flavourful palate, ripe fruit with mild jammy notes, warm.

CORTIJO DE ANAGIL 2002 RED
tempranillo, cabernet sauvignon , merlot

80 Intense cherry. Short, fruity aroma, clearer than the 98 vintage, reminiscent of brambles. Flavourful, fruity palate, with fresh overtones and ripe fruit tannins, very well-mannered.

CORTIJO DE BALSILLAS 2000 RED
tempranillo

69 Cherry with an orange edge. Slightly overripe aroma, reduced, even evolved. Slightly flat palate, without nuances, discreet.

V.T. RIBERA DEL ANDARAX

FINCA LA MORALEA (PACO FERRE)

La Rueda, s/n
04458 Padules (Almería)
☎: 950 608 308 - Fax: 950 608 430
bodegapacoferre@hotmail.com

Established: 1998

🍷 50 225,000 litres 🍇 10 has.
🍷 80% 🌿20%

ERMITA DE TICES 2002 OAK AGED RED
60% tempranillo, 30% cabernet sauvignon, 10% syrah

70 Cherry with an ochre glint. Not very clear with notes of esparto grass and overripe fruit. Unintegrated wood and fruit in the retronasal passage (a little overripe), sweetish.

BARJALÍ 2000 RED
60% tempranillo, 30% cabernet sauvignon, 10% merlot

79 Cherry with an orangey hue. Warm, ripe and slightly alcoholic aroma with earthy notes of very ripe fruit. Warm, spirituous palate with sweet, light tannins.

V.T. RIBERA DEL ARLANZA

ARLANZA

Carretera Madrid-Irún km 203, 800
09390 Villamanzo (Burgos)
☎: 947 171 066 - Fax: 947 170 400
info@bodegasarlanza.com
www.bodegasarlanza.com

Established: 2001

🍷 239 600,000 litres 🍷 100%

DOMINIO DE MANCILES 2003 ROSÉ

82 Raspberry with a violet hue. Fresh, powerful and clean aroma with abundant fresh fruit. Flavourful palate with well-balanced sweetness-acidity-bitterness.

DOMINIO DE MANCILES 2003 JOVEN RED

80 Garnet red cherry with a violet edge. Good intensity aroma of well defined red fruit and quite a floral hint. Flavourful, fruity and pleasant on the palate.

DOMINIO DE MANCILES 2001 OAK AGED RED

78 Garnet red cherry. Medium-intensity aroma with predominant wood over the fruit. Pleasant, light palate, well-mannered overall.

DOMINIO DE MANCILES 2002 OAK AGED RED

78 Garnet red cherry. Aroma of mildly overripe fruit (orange peel) and oak notes. Well-mannered and pleasant on the palate with wood tannins in the finish.

DOMINIO DE MANCILES 2001 CRIANZA RED

82 Garnet red cherry. Not very intense yet clean aroma with well-assembled fruit and wood. Flavourful palate with some concentration of the fruit, toasty wood.

ARLESE NEGOCIOS

Pol. Industrial de Villamanzo
Parcela 109
09390 Villamanzo (Burgos)
☎: 661 612 426

Established: 2002
🍇 30 🌿 2 has.

ALMANAQUE ROBLE RED

COVARRUBIAS SALUD

Finca La Nebreda, s/n
09346 Covarrubias (Burgos)
☎: 607 863 537

VEGA RUBIAS ROSÉ
VEGA RUBIAS JOVEN RED
VEGA RUBIAS CRIANZA RED
VEGA RUBIAS RESERVA RED

LA COLEGIADA

Carretera N-I, km. 202
Femal S.A. Apdo 40
09340 Lerma (Burgos)
☎: 947 177 030 - Fax: 947 177 004
andres@marialuisanavarro.com
www.bodegalacolegiada.com

Established: 1998
🍇 300 🛢 225,000 litres 🌿 20 has.
🍷 30% 🌐70%: -BE -NL -DE -FI -DK -CH

TINTO LERMA 2000 OAK AGED RED
100% tempranillo 🍇 12

84 Dark cherry. Intense aroma of ripe fruit, spicy with a good oaky hint. Flavourful, spicy palate with well-integrated alcohol and ripe tannins.

TINTO LERMA 2001 OAK AGED RED
🍇 12

85 Garnet red cherry. Good intensity aroma with spices (vanilla), ripe fruit, well-integrated wood

and Fino. Flavourful, fairly powerful, full and expressive on the palate with well structured wood and a toasty finish (peanuts).

RISCO VENDIMIA SELECIONADA 2000

Hijos de
MÁXIMO ORTÍZ GONZÁLEZ

Gómes Salazar, 18
09346 Covarrubias (Burgos)
☎: 947 406 533 - Fax: 947 406 533
bodega@hotelarlanza.com
www.circulopyme.com/bodega

Established: 1995
🍇 80 🛢 100,000 litres 🌿 18 has. 🍷 100%

VIÑA VALDABLE 2001 OAK AGED RED
100% tempranillo

85 Cherry with a violet hue. Intense and powerful aroma with a good fruit expression and a floral hint. Very flavourful, powerful aroma with a toasty finish and bitter but pleasant tannins.

VIÑA VALDABLE 2000 CRIANZA RED
100% tempranillo

84 Quite intense cherry. Good intensity, fruity aroma with toasty oak notes. Flavourful palate with red fruit and evident tannins.

VIÑA LETICIA 1999 RESERVA RED
100% tempranillo

79 Garnet red cherry. Aroma with predominat wood. Flavourful palate with a suggestion of fruit and fresh acidity, oak tannins in the finish.

VIÑA VALDABLE 2003 JOVEN RED

Bodegas MONTE AMÁN

Carretera Santo Domingo de Silos, s/n
09348 Castrillo de Solarana (Burgos)
☎: 947 173 304 - Fax: 947 173 308
monteaman@wanadoo.es

Established: 1989
🍇 280 🛢 222,500 litres 🌿 30 has.
🍷 60% 🌐40%

MONTE AMÁN 2001 OAK AGED RED
100% tinta del país 🍇 5

80 Garnet red cherry. Fresh aroma with a varietal suggestion (red fruit) and well-integrated oak. Flavourful palate with lively acidity and good fruit.

MONTE AMÁN 2001 CRIANZA RED
95% tinta del país, 5% cabernet sauvignon

84 Garnet red cherry. Aroma of fresh red fruit with a touch of liquorice and light toasty notes of oak. Flavourful, full, fleshy palate with considerable depth.

MONTE AMÁN 1999 CRIANZA RED
95% tinta del país, 5% cabernet sauvignon

82 Garnet red cherry. Aroma with a suggestion of red berries and woody notes. Flavourful, lively palate with well-integrated wood, fairly persistent.

MONTE AMÁN 2003 JOVEN RED
MONTE AMÁN 1998 RESERVA RED

PALACIO DE LERMA

Carretera Madrid-Irún, km. 203
09340 Lerma (Burgos)
☎: 947 170 089 - Fax: 947 170 089
info@palaciodelerma.com
www.palaciodelerma.com

Established: 2000

173 ▤ 150,000 litres ❦ 2 has.

🍾 90% 🍷10%

PALACIO DE LERMA 2003 JOVEN RED

75 Garnet red cherry with a violet edge. Slightly short, fruity aroma. Fruity, light palate, well-mannered overall.

VALDEDIOS 2001 OAK AGED RED
▤ 12

85 Fairly deep cherry. Aroma with spicy wood notes (vanilla, pepper) and a nuance of ripe fruit (plums). Concentrated palate with fruit well covered by the wood, full-bodied with a spicy finish.

PALACIO DE LERMA 2000 RESERVA RED

82 Garnet red cherry. Medium-intensity, spicy aroma with wood that slightly dominates on the fruit. Flavourful, round palate, pleasant.

Bodegas SIERRA

Carretera Madrid-Irún km 203, 700
09390 Villalmanzo (Burgos)
☎: 947 170 083 - Fax: 947 170 083
bodegassierra@terra.es

Established: 1997

100 ▤ 185,000 litres ❦ 20 has.
🍾 90% 🍷10%: -US -GQ -DE

CASCAJUELO 2003 ROSÉ
100% tempranillo

80 Salmon blush. Fresh, fruity aroma. A touch of sharpness on the palate, flavourful, expressive and fresh.

CASTILLO DE URA 2000 OAK AGED RED
100% tempranillo

79 Cherry with a brick red edge. Aroma with crianza character and noticeable wood. Round, flavourful and pleasant on the palate.

CASTILLO DE URA 2001 OAK AGED RED
100% tempranillo

76 Garnet red cherry with a slightly orangey edge. Aroma with slightly overripe fruit and notes of oak. Slightly drying wood tannins on the palate but well-mannered overall.

CASTILLO DE URA 1998 RESERVA RED
100% tempranillo

79 Cherry with a brick red hue. Slightly short aroma with a suggestion of vanilla. Round, light and quite flavourful on the palate with a toasty finish.

CASCAJUELO 2001 ROBLE RED

V.T. RIBERA DEL QUEILES

GUELBENZU

San Juan, 14
31520 Cascante (Navarra)
☎: 948 850 055 - Fax: 948 850 097
guelbenzu@masbytes.es
www.guelbenzu.com

Established: 1851

1,000 ▤ 325,000 litres ❦ 92 has.

🍾 30% 🍷70%: -US -CA -UK -FR -BE -DE
-DK -NL -LU -DK -SE -IS -AT -MT -BR -AU
-MX -PE -SG -IE

GUELBENZU VIERLAS 2003 OAK AGED JOVEN RED
syrah, tempranillo, merlot, garnacha, cabernet sauvignon
▤ 2

84 Dark cherry with a purplish edge. Powerful aroma of black fruit, macerated skins and toasty hints of oak. Flavourful, spicy palate with meaty overtones, rough tannins, fine bitter notes and excellent acidity.

GUELBELZU JARDÍN 2003 JOVEN RED

84 Garnet red cherry. Fresh, fruity aroma with some varietal nuances. Fresh, fruity and pleasant on the palate with Bordeaux notes in the retronasal passage, flavourful.

GUELBENZU AZUL 2002 OAK AGED RED
46% tempranillo, 30% cabernet sauvignon, 24% merlot
9 ▤

84 Garnet red cherry. Intense aroma with fine spicy oak notes over an essence of fresh fruit skins (redcurrants). Flavourful, spicy palate with slightly marked but fine tannins (black pepper), herbace.

GUELBENZU EVO 2002 OAK AGED RED
55% cabernet sauvignon, 33% merlot, 12% tempranillo
🌐 12

87 Quite intense cherry. Aroma of fresh fruit notes with a mild vegetative nuance, damp earth notes and toasty oak. Flavourful on the palate with good crianza in fine, toasty oak, of "Bordeaux-style" in the retronasal effect, fruity. Slightly inferior to the previous vintage.

GUELBENZU LAUTUS 1999 OAK AGED RED
50% tempranillo, 20% merlot, 20% cabernet sauvignon, 10% garnacha

86 Intense cherry. Aroma with notes of ripe black fruit, fine hints of reduction (vanilla, tobacco, coffee). Round and supple on the palate with fine toasty oak in the retronasal passage; oak tannins, flavourful overtones and with ripe fruit. ous, varietal hints and fine mineral notes.

V.T. SIERRA DE TRAMUNTA-NA COSTA NORD

CAN VIDALET

Carretera Alcudia-Pollença km. 4, 8
Apartado 10
07460 Pollença (Mallorca)
☎: 971 531 719 - Fax: 971 531 719
vidalet@wanadoo.es
www.canvidalet.com

Established: 2001

🍷 150 ▯ 77,000 litros 🍇 8 has.

🍾 20% 🌐80%: -DE -UK

CA'N VIDALET 2002 WHITE
100% chardonnay

80 Very pale. Fresh, very fine aroma with fruit and white flowers and a suggestion of varietal character (apples). Fresh, flavourful palate with fine bitter and herby notes, marked citrus acidity.

CA'N VIDALET CABERNET SAUVIGNON & MERLOT 2002 CRIANZA RED
cabernet sauvignon, merlot

84 Garnet red cherry with a brick red edge. Intense aroma with a good varietal (redcurrants, paprika) and crianza expression. Flavourful palate with a good oak/fruit integration, a suggestion of jammy fruit and liquorice and terroir in the retronasal passage.

CA'N VIDALET BARQUEE 2003 FERMENTADO EN BARRICA WHITE
CA'N VIDALET CHARDONNAY 2003 WHITE

SA VINYA DE CAN SERVERA

Carrer Noblesa, 41
07313 Selva (Balears)
☎: 651 555 945

DIVINS CABERNET 2003 RED

82 Very deep cherry with a purplish edge. Aroma of red bramble berries with hints of maceration, earthy, with a balsamic nuance. Fleshy, powerful palate, abundant jammy fruit, hints of cocoa and bay; not evident wood.

VINORICA (CASTELL MIQUEL)

Polígono 3, Parcela 259/261
07340 Alaró (Mallorca)
☎: 971 510 698
www.castellmiquel.de

STAIRWAY TO HEAVEN CABERNET SAUVIGNON 2002 RED
cabernet sauvignon

84 Intense cherry. Toasty aroma of the vine variety (paprika), with ripe fruit and a suggestion of minerals. Powerful, warm palate with Cabernet tannins (between pepper and paprika), flavourful.

VINOS DE LA TIERRA

V.T. TIERRA DE LEÓN

Cooperativa COMARCAL DEL CEA

Carretera Castrobol s/n
47680 Mayorga (Valladolid)
☎: 983 751 182 - Fax: 983 751 363

CAÑASECAS 2003 ROSÉ
mencía

76 Deep raspberry with a coppery hue. Intense aroma of red fruit and spicy notes of skins. Flavourful palate with fruit expression slightly muted by the alcohol.

CAÑASECAS 2003 ROBLE RED
prieto picudo   ⬤ 4

85 Deep cherry with a violet edge. Jammy aroma of plums, blackberries, spicy notes and toasty skins, complex. Fleshy, powerful palate with abundant black fruit, notes of pitch and terroir, fresh.

CAÑASECAS RED
mencía

80 Intense cherry with a purplish hue. Intense aroma of red bramble fruit with hints of maceration (liquorice, lactics). Fruity palate (blackberries) with ripe tannins, flavourful with fresh overtones.

FERNÁNDEZ LLAMAZARES

Camino Valdeperales, s/n
24209 Pajares de los Oteros (León)
☎: 987 752 025 - Fax: 987 750 612
pajares@bornet.es

PAJARES

Bodegas GONZALEZ NAVA

La Barrera, 7
24209 Pajares de los Oteros (León)
☎: 987 750 814 - Fax: 987 750 814

VEGA SILVERA 2003 ROSÉ
prieto picudo

83 Brilliant blush. Powerful, quite fruity aroma with fine smoky notes of the skins. Flavourful palate with fine bitter notes and hints of red stone fruit, slightly warm with excellent acidity.

VEGA SILVERA 2003 RED
Prieto Picudo

83 Opaque cherry. Powerful, ripe aroma of sun-drenched skins, jammy black fruit, spicy (cocoa) and terroir hints. Flavourful, fleshy palate with liquorice and a bitter nuance (toasty flavours, liquorice).

Señorío de LOS ARCOS

La Iglesia, s/n
24392 Ardoncino (León)
☎: 987 226 594 - Fax: 987 226 594
Established: 1999
⬛ 43 ▐ 700,000 litres ▐ 100%

VEGA CARRIEGOS 2003 ROSÉ
100% prieto picudo

73 Brilliant raspberry with a coppery hue. Reduced aroma of sour cherries in liqueur. Quite flavourful, fruity palate with freshness and an acidic edge.

VEGA CARRIEGOS 2003 OAK AGED RED

78 Dark cherry with a purplish edge. Powerful, ripe aroma of jammy black fruit (hints of reduction), with a nuance of toasty oak. Flavourful, concentrated palate of jammy and very sweet fruit with hints of ripe skins in the finish.

VEGA CARRIEGOS 2003 RED
80% prieto picudo, 15% tempranillo, 5% mencia

75 Cherry with a violet hue. Powerful, ripe aroma of black fruit with hints of macerated skins and a nuance of damp earth. Fruity, quite sweet palate with hints of overripening.

EL CARRIEGO ROSÉ
EL CARRIEGO OAK AGED RED

Cooperativa LOS OTEROS

La Bodega, 7
24209 Pajares de los Oteros (León)
☎: 987 753 047 - Fax: 987 753 047
www.prietopicudo.com
Established: 1968
⬛ 40 ▐ 166,000 litres ▐ 100%

VIÑA BRICAR ROSÉ
100% prieto picudo

76 Brilliant cherry. Intense, fruity aroma with slightly toasty and sweet hints of skins. Fleshy palate with fine spicy notes, slightly ripe and oily tannins.

AUTEROLO 2003 ROSÉ
100% prieto picudo

80 Deep raspberry. Powerful aroma of very ripe red stone fruit with toasty hints of skins, slightly warm. Flavourful palate with fruit expression slightly muted by the alcohol.

AUGUSTA ROBLE 2001 OAK AGED RED
prieto picudo   ⬤ 12

82 Very deep cherry. Concentrated aroma with toasty notes (ink, pitch, liquorice) and fine integrated smoky flavours. Fleshy, powerful palate with fine, slightly astringent tannins, flavourful; slightly impenetrable nuances.

PRIETO REAL 2003 ROSÉ
PRIETO REAL 2003 RED

LLAMAZARES MARINELLI

Avenida de Valderas, 26
24200 Valencia de Don Juan (León)
☎: 987 752 407 - Fax: 987 750 597
llamazaresmarinelli@telefonica.net

🌐 14 ▤ 12,000 litres 🍇 8 has. 🍷 100%

VIÑA COLUMBIANO 2003 ROSÉ
100% prieto picudo

84 Brilliant cherry. Powerful, fruity aroma (redcurrants, blackberries, cherries) with petals, slightly sweet hints and toasty skins. Flavourful, fruity palate with excellent fruit-acid-alcohol balance and fine bitter notes.

VIÑA COLUMBIANO 2000 OAK AGED RED
100% prieto picudo

65 Cherry with a violet rim. Aroma of toasty casks, cough medicine, smokiness and cedar. Very aggressive wood tannins on the palate and a suggestion of new wood in the retronasal passage.

MARI CRUZ MARINELLI 2003 WHITE
VIÑA COLUMBIANO 2002 OAK AGED RED

Bodegas MELWA

Calvo Sotelo 4
24230 Valdevimbre (León)
☎: 987 304 149 - Fax: 987 304 149

Established: 1965

🌐 25 ▤ 50,000 litres 🍇 10 has 🍷 100%

VALLE GUDIN 2002 ROSÉ
VALLE GUDIN 2002 CRIANZA RED

NICOLÁS REY E HIJOS

Palomares 6
24230 Valdevimbre (León)
☎: 987 304 218 - Fax: 987 304 236

VIÑA EL PICO DE LOS CERROS

Bodegas y Viñedos PARDEVALLES

Carretera de León, km. 2, 5
24230 Valdevimbre (León)
☎: 987 304 222 - Fax: 987 304 077

pardevalles@canal21.com

Established: 1949

🌐 60 ▤ 150,000 litres 🍇 27 has. 🍷 100 %

PARDEVALLES 2003 WHITE
PARDEVALLES 2003 ROSÉ
PARDEVALLES 2003 RED
PARDEVALLES OAK AGED RED
PARDEVALLES 2001 CRIANZA RED

Bodegas y Viñedos PEDRO CASIS

Las Bodegas, s/n
24325 Gordaliza del Pino (León)
☎: 987 699 618 - Fax: 987 699 618
casis@jet.es
www.bodegascasis.com

Established: 1960

🌐 60 ▤ 200,000 litres 🍇 15 has. 🍷 100%

CASIS 2003 ROSÉ
prieto picudo, mencía

77 Very deep raspberry. Powerful aroma of ripe fruit with a hint of sweetness and toasty hints of skins. Flavourful palate, without great varietal character with a nuance of sweetness and good acidity.

CASIS 2002 RED
tempranillo, mencía, prieto picudo

79 Garnet red cherry. Intense aroma of black fruit with toasty oak notes and a nuance of mild reduction (prunes). Flavourful palate with ripe tannins, bitter hints with overripe fruit.

CONDELIZE 2003 WHITE
CASIS 2003 RED

PELÁEZ

Grajal de la Ribera
24796 La Antigua (León)
☎: 987 202 350 - Fax: 987 202 350
bodegaspelaez@terra.es

Established: 1950

🌐 10 ▤ 300,000 litres 🍷 100%

SENOEL JOVEN ROSÉ
SENOEL JOVEN RED
SENOEL CRIANZA RED

Cooperativa Vinícola RIBERA DEL CEA

Avenida Panduro y Villafañe, s/n
24220 Valderas (León)
☎: 987 762 191 - Fax: 987 762 191

Established: 1970

🌐 14 ▤ 2,200,000 litres 🍇 400 has.

☙ 100%

VIÑA TRASDERREY 2003 ROSÉ
100% prieto picudo

74 Pale cherry with a coppery hue. Intense aroma of ripe and slightly reduced red fruit with hints of withered petals. Intense palate with sweet fruit, without great nuances.

VIÑA CUESTASBUENAS 2003 RED
tempranillo, garnacha, mencía, prieto picudo

65 Cherry with a not very deep violet edge. Aroma of stables. Light, short palate without persistence.

VIÑA TRASDERREY 2003 RED
prieto picudo

73 Garnet red with a violet rim. Not very clean, vinous aroma of skins with a hint of red fruit. Light palate, without persistence.

VIÑA CUESTASBUENAS 2003 WHITE
VIÑA TRASDERREY 2003 OAK AGED RED

Cooperativa Vinícola
UNIÓN DEL PÁRAMO

Carretera Sahagún, s/n
24325 Gordaliza del Pino (León)
☎: 987 784 057 - Fax: 987 784 057
cooperativalaunion@wanadoo.es

Established: 1962
🗄 3,766,000 litres 🍇 300 has. ☙ 100%

EL TESORO DEL PÁRAMO ROSÉ
EL TESORO DEL PÁRAMO RED

Cooperativa Vinícola
UNIÓN DEL VALLE

Camino Real s/n
24234 Villacalbiel (León)
☎: 987 767 032 - Fax: 987 767 032

Established: 1965
🗄 204,000 litres

VIVAZ 2003 ROSÉ
VIVAZ 2003 RED

Cooperativa Vinícola de VALDEVIMBRE

Carretera de León, s/n
24230 Valdevimbre (León)
☎: 987 304 195 - Fax: 987 304 195
valdevim@ccac.es

Established: 1970
🌐 100 🗄 6,150,000 litres

🍇 575 has. ☙ 100%

ABADÍA DE BALDEREDO 2003 ROSÉ
SEÑORÍO DE VALDÉS 2003 ROSÉ
ABADÍA DE BALDEREDO 2003 RED
SEÑORÍO DE VALDÉS 2003 RED

VILLACEZÁN

San Juan, 10
24274 Gordoncillo (León)
☎: 987 758 031 - Fax: 987 758 031
villacezan@villacezan.com
www.villacezan.com

Established: 1920
🌐 110 🗄 275,000 litres 🍇 60 has.
☙ 70% 🌐30%: -US -DK

MOLENDORES 2003 JOVEN ROSÉ
100% prieto picudo

80 Lively blush. Fresh, fruity aroma of red berries with a perfumed hint. Flavourful, fresh palate, evoking skins and with a hint of raspberries, varietal.

DEHESA DE VILLACEZÁN 2003 JOVEN RED
40% tempranillo, 30% prieto picudo, 30% mencia

76 Cherry with a lively violet edge. Aroma with slight fermentation off-odours and quite expressive lively red fruit. Flavourful, fresh palate with red fruit, easy drinking.

VILLACEZÁN DOCE MESES 2001 OAK AGED RED
40% tempranillo, 40% prieto picudo, 20% mencia   🌐 2

82 Quite intense cherry with a garnet red edge. Intense, spicy aroma (vanilla, cinnamon) with ripe fruit. Flavourful, intense palate with well-assembled black fruit and toasty oak.

VILLACEZÁN SEIS MESES 2002 OAK AGED RED
40% tempranillo, 40% prieto picudo, 20% mencía   🌐 6

76 Quite intense cherry with a garnet red edge. Aroma with slightly overripe fruit and spicy oak notes. Better on the palate, flavourful with well-assembled ripe fruit and wood.

VILLACEZÁN COLECCIÓN 2000 CRIANZA RED
40% tempranillo, 40% prieto picudo, 20% mencia

81 Deep cherry. Aroma of black berries, spicy with smoky wood notes and an earthy hint. Fleshy, flavourful palate with earthy tannins and a slightly drying woody finish.

ELVERITE 2003 JOVEN WHITE

VINÍCOLA VALMADRIGAL

Constitución, 16
24323 Castrotierra de Valmadrigal (León)

☎: 987 784 047 - Fax: 987 784 047
Established: 1969
🛢 50 🛢 200,000 litres 🍷 100%

CASTILLO VALMADRIGAL 2003 ROSÉ
CASTILLO VALMADRIGAL 2003 JOVEN RED
CASTILLO VALMADRIGAL 2001 ROBLE RED

Bodegas VINOS DE LEÓN

La Vega, s/n
24011 Armunia (León)
☎: 987 209 712 - Fax: 987 209 800
info@bodegasvinosdeleon.es
www.bodegasvinosdeleon.es
Established: 1967
🛢 2,000 🛢 4,000,000 litres 🍇 20 has.
🍷 90% 🍷10%: -UK -CH -SE -DK -DE -
MX -US -JP -LV -LT

VALJUNCO 2003 ROSÉ
100% prieto picudo

81 Raspberry blush. Medium-intensity, fresh aroma of ripe raspberries, varietal. Slightly carbonic palate with fresh and ripe red fruit, very expressive with the originality of the Prieto Picudo.

DON SUERO 1999 OAK AGED RED
100% prieto picudo

79 Dark garnet red cherry. Intense aroma of jammy black fruit with fine toasty oak notes, spicy. Flavourful palate with slighlty marked tannins and notions of wax, without great nuances.

VALJUNCO 2000 OAK AGED RED
100% prieto picudo

83 Medium-hue cherry with a garnet red hue. Not very intense aroma but with a certain finesse (toasty oak, red fruit, balsamic flavour). Round, flavourful and well-balanced on the palate with good wood/oak integration.

PALACIO DE LOS GUZMANES 1999 OAK AGED RED
50% prieto picudo, 50% tempranillo

80 Cherry with an orangey hue. Aroma of ripe red fruit and balsamic notes, fresh. Flavourful tannins on the palate, slightly warm with good balance and a hint of toasty wood.

V.T. TIERRA DEL VINO DE ZAMORA

Bodegas y Viñedos ALIZÁN

Industrias nº 6
49150 Moraleja del Vino (Zamora)

☎: 980 571 517 - Fax: 980 571 982
bodega@alizan.net
www.alizan.net
Established: 1999
🛢 500 🛢 320,000 litres 🍇 35 has.
🍷 80% 🍷20%: -DE -DK -US -BE -AU

ALIZÁN 2002 OAK AGED RED
90% tempranillo, 10% cabernet sauvignon   🛢 6

85 Deep cherry. Concentrated aroma of jammy black fruit with a fine spicy hint and dry earth. Fleshy, flavourful palate with round wood tannins well-integrated with the fruit; pleasant.

ALIZÁN ÉLITE 2001 CRIANZA RED
100% tempranillo

88 Dark cherry with a garnet red edge. Aroma with notes of ripe fruit and fine nuances of toasty, lightly spiced, creamy oak. Round, ripe, warm and flavourful palate, an earthy finish.

ALIZÁN 2000 OAK AGED RED
100% tempranillo   🛢 12

84 Cherry with an orangey hue. Aroma of new casks with balsamic notes and black fruit. Pronounced wood tannins and a good fruit weight on the palate, fleshy with medium persistence.

ALIZÁN SELECCIÓN 2001 OAK AGED RED
100% tempranillo   ⊕ 12

86 Deep cherry. Aroma of black fruit with notes of fallen leaves, a suggestion of minerals and fine smoky notes. Fleshy, fresh palate with well-integrated wood and a notion of terroir, expressive.

ALIZÁN PRESTIGIO 2001 RESERVA RED
ALIZÁN AÑADA 2003 RESERVA RED

Bodegas Seleccionadas ARMANDO

"Viña Concita y Adilen"
Carretera N-630, km. 270
49192 Zamora (Zamora)
☎: 980 538 683 - Fax: 980 538 683
armando@bodegas-armando.com
www.bodegas-armando.com

Established: 1992

🐂 80% 🍇20%

AÑORADO 2003 JOVEN WHITE
malvasía, moscatel

72 Golden. Powerful, ripe, very sweet aroma with not very fine hints of reduction in the tank. Fleshy, slightly unctuous palate with bittersweet notes, lacking acidity.

Bodegas EL SOTO

Carretera de Circunvalación, s/n
49708 Villanueva de Campeán (Zamora)
☎: 980 560 330 - Fax: 980 560 330
info@bodegaselsoto.com
www.bodegaselsoto.com

Established: 2001

⊕ 65 🍶 600,000 litres 🌿 250 has.

PAGO DE CAMPEÁN MOSCATEL 2003
JOVEN SEMIDULCE WHITE
100% moscatel

74 Very pale yellow. Intense aroma with white fruit, floral and musky notes, a suggestion of aniseed and citrus fruits. Intense bitter palate with not very fine bittersweet notes.

PAGO DE CAMPEÁN MALVASÍA 2003
WHITE
100% malvasía

69 Yellow straw. Quite short aroma with aniseed notes and weak fruit. Rustic palate, without fruit.

PAGO DE CAMPEÁN 2003 JOVEN RED
tempranillo

81 Dark cherry. Powerful, fruity aroma with toasty notes of skins, earthy hints and cocoa. Flavourful, bitter palate with spicy hints of skins and damp earth.

PAGO DE CAMPEÁN CLARETE
TRADICIONAL 2003 JOVEN RED
malvasía, tempranillo

80 Brilliant cherry. Powerful, fruity aroma (redcurrants, cherries) with hints of skins and a suggestion of sweetness. Flavourful, fruity palate with fine bitter notes (liquorice, herbs), slightly warm.

PAGO DE CAMPEÁN 2002 JOVEN RED
tempranillo

82 Dark cherry with a dark red edge. Powerful, fruity aroma with spicy hints and petals. Flavourful palate with fine bitter notes (liquorice, cocoa); well-structured with complex overtones.

CUÉVANO 2001 JOVEN RED
tempranillo

74 Cherry with an orangey hue. Aroma of paprika, jammy tomatoes and overripe fruit. Unbalanced palate without noteworthy notes.

PAGO DE CAMPEÁN 2001 OAK AGED RED
tempranillo   ⊕ 6

80 Opaque cherry. Powerful aroma of jammy fruit, hints of fine reduction (prunes), toasty oak and cocoa. Flavourful, fleshy and concentrated palate with liquorice, cocoa and quite promising though without great nuances.

JUAN MIGUEL FUENTES SARDÓN

Larga, 12
49709 Cabañas de Sayago (Zamora)
☎: 620 748 253 - Fax: 980 560 055
bodetgesoblanco@wanadoo.es

🍶 50000 litres

BROCHERO 2003 RED
tempranillo

82 Cherry with an intense raspberry hue. Fresh aroma of forest red berries (blackberries, redcurrants) with a nuance of liquorice. Fleshy, fruity palate (jammy black fruit) with fresh tannins and a pleasant finish.

BROCHERO 2003 ROSÉ

Sociedad Cooperativa NUESTRA SEÑORA DEL CASTILLO

Avenida Constitución, 2
37175 Pereña de la Ribera (Salamanca)
☎: 923 573 069 - Fax: 923 573 209

VINOS DE LA TIERRA

CARROVALLE 2003 JOVEN RED
100% tinta del país

82 Clear cherry. Spicy aroma with floral and balsamic notes and a nuance of red berries. Flavourful palate with pleasant, bitter traces of ripe fruit with spices and cocoa in the finish.

VIÑA ESCUDEROS

Carretera Cubo del Vino, s/n
49719 Villamor de los Escuderos (Zamora)
☎: 980 609 204 - Fax: 980 609 154
bodega@vinaescudero.com
www.vinaescudero.com

Established: 2002

🍇 100 📖 350,000 litres 🌿 200 has.

🍷 95% 🍇5%: -AT -DE -BE -NL

GAVIÓN 2003 WHITE
90% verdejo, 10% moscatel

72 Yellow straw. Quite short aroma with mild off-odours and a nuance of fresh fruit. Mildly fruity palate; well-mannered overall.

GAVIÓN 2003 JOVEN RED
100% tempranillo

81 Cherry with a violet edge. Clear, clean aroma of red bramble fruit with notes of liquorice and dry earth. Fleshy palate with oily and bitter tannins and good freshness; very pleasant red fruit finish.

GAVIÓN 2002 ROBLE RED
100% tempranillo   🍇 12

78 Garnet red with an orange edge. Peppery aroma of spices (toasty oak) over sun-drenched black fruit. Flavourful palate with fresh tannins, a vanilla sensations and a pleasant finish.

GAVIÓN 2001 ROBLE RED
100% tinta del país

77 Deep cherry. Aroma of slightly overripe black fruit with a suggestion of Port. Ripe, fleshy palate with round fruit tannins; sweet sensations.

GAVIÓN 2003 ROBLE JOVEN RED
GAVIÓN ROSÉ

WINELAND

Carretera de Circunvalación, s/n
49708 Villanueva de Campeán (Zamora)
☎: 609 119 248 - Fax: 916 160 246
victorre@telefonica.net

Established: 2002

🍇 600 📖 200,000 litres 🌿 15 has.

🍷 30% 🍇70%: -US -CA -JP -DE -NL -CH

VENTA MAZARRÓN 2003 JOVEN RED
tempranillo

88 Intense cherry. Aroma of ripe, slightly jammy fruit with foresty hints. Powerful palate rich in varietal expression and sweet tannins, warm, fleshy and vigorous.

V.T. VAL DO MIÑO

LAGARIÑOS

Ferreiros, 15
32950 Coles (Ourense)
☎: 988 205 067 - Fax: 988 205 067
bodega@bodegaslagariños.com
www.bodegaslagariños.com

Established: 1979

🍇 10 📖 200,000 litres 🌿 4,5 has.

🍷 95% 🍇5%

CONDE DE LAGARIÑOS WHITE
MARQUÉS DO MIÑO WHITE
MENCÍA LAGARIÑOS RED

V.T. VALDEJALÓN

Cooperativa del Campo
SAN PEDRO ARBUÉS

Carretera de Muel, 50
50290 Épila (Zaragoza)
☎: 976 603 211 - Fax: 976 603 437
epila@sanpedroarbues.com
www.sanpedroarbues.com

Established: 1959

🍇 30 📖 5,100,000 litres 🍷 100%

VIÑA ARBUES 2003 RED
80% garnacha, 20% monastrell

75 Deep cherry with a violet edge. Aroma with notes of maceration, ripe fruit. Fleshy, quite viscous palate, with ripe fruit notes.

VIÑA ARBUÉS 2002 OAK AGED RED
70% tempranillo, 30% merlot

72 Garnet red with a brick red edge. Aroma with a slightly viscous edge, spices over evolved fruit. Ripe palate without expression of the vine varieties, flavourful.

VIÑA ARBUÉS 2002 OAK AGED RED
20% monastrell, 20% tempranillo, 60% garnacha

72 Garnet red with an orange edge. Ripe aroma with sun-drenched notes without grape notes. Spicy, quite warm palate, without fruit yet flavourful.

VIÑA ARBUES 2003 WHITE
VIÑA ARBUES 2003 ROSÉ

VINOS LÓPEZ

San Agustín 7
50290 Épila (Zaragoza)
valdecella@terra.es

Established: 1974

🏭 7 📊 175,000 litres 🍇 30 has 🛢 100%

VALDECELLA 2003 JOVEN WHITE
VALDECELLA 2003 JOVEN ROSÉ
VALDECELLA 2003 JOVEN RED
VALDECELLA 2003 JOVEN RED
VALDECELLA 2001 OAK AGED RED
VALDECELLA 2003 VINO DE LICOR

V.T. VALLE DEL CINCA

MONTE JULIA

Finca Monte Julia
22536 Monte Julia (Huesca)
☎: 974 469 319 - Fax: 974 468 439
mdg@bodegasmontejulia.com
www.bodegasmontejulia.com

Established: 1998

🏭 280 📊 725,000 litres 🍇 130 has.
🛢 90% 🌐10%: -FR

VALCINCA MOSCATEL 2002 OAK AGED
SEMIDULCE WHITE
100% moscatel

72 Pale gold. Intense aroma of ripe white fruit (exotic hints) with flowers and a hint of grapey and varietal character. Flavourful palate with bitter hints of oak, a slightly sweet character and an acidic edge.

VALCINCA 2002 OAK AGED RED
60% cabernet sauvignon, 20% cabernet franc, 20% merlot
🛢 4

74 Dark cherry. Intense aroma of black fruit, toasty oak, a balsamic nuance with a not very clea nuance. Flavourful palate with slightly marked tannins, a certain herbaceous, balsamic and very varietal carácter, lacking balance.

VALCINCA PRESTIGIO 2002 OAK AGED
RED
85% merlot, 15% graciano   🛢 6

79 Garnet red cherry. Somewhat intense aroma of ripe red fruit and a sweet, balsamic hint. Flavourful, bitter palate with a degree of fruit expression (hints of overextraction), lacking balance.

GRAN VALCINCA 2001 CRIANZA RED
70% cabernet sauvignon, 30% graciano

80 Dark garnet red cherry with a saffron edge. Powerful aroma of black fruit and not very fine reduction notes. Flavourful palate with quite promising though slightly marked tannins and a good fruit weight. Spicy, bitter and long.

VALCINCA 2001 CRIANZA RED

NUVIANA

Carretera A-1241 Zaidín-Tamarite, km 11
22549 San Miguel-Belver de Cinca
(Huesca)
☎: 974 478 800 - Fax: 974 478 802
smartin@codorniu.es
www.nuviana.com

Established: 2002

🏭 1,500 🛢 68% 🌐32%: -DK -SE -CH -DE -LU

NUVIANA CABERNET SAUVIGNON MERLOT
2003 JOVEN RED
60% cabernet sauvignon, 40% merlot

81 Medium-hue cherry with an orangey edge. Medium-intensity, balsamic aroma of ripe red fruit. Flavourful, pleasant and fruity on the palate, easy drinking.

VALONGA

Monte Valonga, s/n
22500 Belver de Cinca (Huesca)
☎: 974 435 127 - Fax: 974 339 101
josemaria@valonga.com
www.valonga.com

Established: 1931

🏭 400 📊 900,000 litres 🍇 85 has.
🛢 90% 🌐10%

VALONGA CHARDONNAY 2003 WHITE
100% chardonnay

80 Golden yellow. Intense aroma with a good varietal expression (ripe apples, hay) and spicy creamy notes. Flavourful, ripe palate, a slightly oily texture with spicy hints (vanilla) of wood.

VALONGA CABERNET SAUVIGNON 2000
CRIANZA RED
90% cabernet sauvignon, 10% tempranillo

78 Garnet red cherry with a brick red edge. Slightly intense aroma of toasty oak and a slightly varietal ripe fruit nuance (paprika). Flavourful palate with ripe, oily tannins, bitter notes and good acidity.

VALONGA CABERNET SAUVIGNON 2003 RED
100% cabernet sauvignon

VINOS DE LA TIERRA

78 Intense cherry with a garnet red edge. Intense aroma of black fruit with the spicy freshness of skins and slightly varietal. Flavourful, fruity palate with slightly marked tannins; slightly warm and oily.

VALONGA 1999 RESERVA RED
70% cabernet sauvignon, 15% tempranillo, 15% merlot

77 Garnet red cherry with brick red glints. Intense aroma of toasty oak, reduction notes (tobacco) and dried fruit. Flavourful, slightly oily and warm on the palate with bitter notes and hints of aged wood.

VALONGA ROSÉ

V.T. VALLE DEL JILOCA

Bodega SANTO TOMÁS DE AQUINO

Avenida Madrid, 39
50360 Daroca (Zaragoza)
☎: 976 800 277 - Fax: 976 800 277
coopdaroca.3092@cajarural.com
Established: 1960
3,000,000 litres 100%

PUERTA BAJA 2002 WHITE
PUERTA BAJA 2002 ROSÉ
PUERTA BAJA 2002 RED
PUERTA BAJA 2002 RED

V.T. VALLES DE BENAVENTE

Bodegas OTERO

Avenida General Primo de Rivera, 22
49600 Benavente (Zamora)
☎: 980 631 600 - Fax: 980 631 722
info@bodegasotero.com
www.bodegasotero.com
Established: 1965
200 3,400,000 litres 20 has.
95% 5%

PAGO DE VALLEOSCURO 2003 WHITE
malvasía, verdejo

79 Pale with a greenish glint. Fairly intense, fresh aroma with notes of green fruit and spicy hints of skins. Fresh on the palate with fine bitter notes of fresh fruit, bittersweet hints and excellent acidity.

PAGO DE VALLEOSCURO 2003 ROSÉ
tempranillo, prieto picudo

84 Brilliant raspberry. Intense aroma of ripe red fruit with spicy hints of skins. Flavourful and fruity on the palate with fresh overtones and a slightly oily texture, good acidity.

PAGO DE VALLEOSCURO 2003 RED
tempranillo, prieto picudo

83 Intense cherry with a violet edge. Aroma of very well-ripened red fruit with an elegant hint of liquorice. Fleshy palate with a jammy sensation, supple tannins; a very fresh and long finish.

Bodegas VERDES

Carretera Benavente, s/n
49610 Santibáñez de Vidriales (Zamora)
☎: 980 648 308 - Fax: 980 648 005
Established: 1998
30 400,000 litres 22 has. 100%

SEÑORÍO DE VIDRIALES 2003 ROSÉ

80 Brilliant raspberry. Intense, slightly fruity aroma with fine smoky skins. Flavourful, slightly warm palate, lacking fruit expression, with good acidity.

VIÑA VERÓNICA 2002 ROBLE RED
tempranillo, prieto picudo

78 Cherry with a strawberry hue. Aroma of red bramble fruit with balsamic hints (fallen leaves) and well-assembled smoky wood. Flavourful, fruity palate with good freshness; without oak presence.

SEÑORÍO DE VIDRIALES 2002 RED

80 Cherry with an intense strawberry hue. Balsamic aroma with spicy notes and skins. Flavourful palate with good freshness, red bramble fruit and a long slightly bitter finish.

V.T. VALLES DE SADACIA

CASTILLO DE MAETIERRA

Vara de Rey, 5
26003 Logroño (La Rioja)
☎: 619 111 918 - Fax: 941 248 211
ventas@castillodemaetierra.com
www.castillodemaetierra.com
Established: 2002
350 300,000 litres 80 has.

ALISÉ 2002 WHITE
MELANTE VENDIMIA TARDÍA 2002 WHITE DULCE

LIBALIS 2002 WHITE

Avenida de Aragón, 3
26006 Logroño (La Rioja)
☎: 941 234 200 - Fax: 941 234 200
ontanon@ontanon.es
www.bodegasontanon.com

Established: 1984

4,000 ▤ 1,400,000 litres 🌿 180 has.

🍷 80% 🍇20%: -FR -CH -AT -SE -DE -NL -BE -CA -MX -DK -BR -US -UK

RIBERAS DE MARCO FABIO DULCE WHITE
100% moscatel

84 Pale yellow. Not very intense aroma of very varietal fine musky notes, with floral hints. Fresh, fruity palate with crystallised white fruit and good acidity.

COLECCIÓN MITOLÓGICA 1994 GRAN RESERVA RED

BODEGAS AND WINE TASTING
OF OTHER REGIONS

OTHER REGIONS – OTHER WINES

The different wines reviewed below are produced in geographical regions which are not included in any DO or integrated into any association of *Vinos de la Tierra*, although many of them are produced in regions with a certain wine-making tradition.

What follows is not an exhaustive summary of the usually mundane *Vinos de Mesa*, but rather an attempt to rescue the most qualitatively outstanding wines of the remaining 'unlabelled' wines within the Spanish wine-making arena.

All the bodegas are sorted by Autonomous Communities. Amongst the brands tasted, the reader will discover wines with singular characteristics and, on many occasions, of excellent quality which may be of great interest for all those in search of interesting novelties and alternatives to serve at the table.

OTHER REGIONS - OTHER WINES

ANDALUCIA

A. MUÑOZ CABRERA

San Bartolomé, 5
29738 Moclinejo (Málaga)
☎: 952 400 594 - Fax: 952 400 743
dimobe@terra.es
Established: 1927
⊕ 70 📊 146,000 litres 🍇 2 has. 🍷 100%

VIÑA AXARKIA MISTELA

COLONIAS DE GALEÓN

Plazuela, 39
41370 Cazalla de la Sierra (Sevilla)
☎: 607 530 495 - Fax: 955 710 093
info@coloniasdegaleon.com
www.coloniasdegaleon.com
Established: 1999
⊕ 50 📊 40,000 litres 🍇 9 has. 🍷 100%

COLONIAS DE GALEÓN 2002 OAK AGED
WHITE
100% chardonnay

71 Slightly cloudy intense yellow. Intense aroma with predominant creamy and spicy oak notes (vanilla). Flavourful palate, with slightly drying and bitter tannins, warm, lacking fruit expression.

COLONIAS DE GALEÓN 2003 MACERACIÓN
CARBÓNICA RED

84 Garnet red cherry. Powerful aroma, ripe fruit, with maceration notes, fresh bunches. Unctuous, flavourful, and warm palate; blackberry and raspberry in the retronasal passage.

COLONIAS DE GALEÓN 2002 OAK AGED RED
merlot, syrah, cabernet franc, tempranillo   ⊕ 4

82 Cherry with a saffron edge. Aroma of jammy fruit with hints of oak, notions of carpentry and a suggestion of earthiness. Supple, fleshy and warm palate with a hint of drying tannins, quite flavourful.

COLONIAS DE GALEÓN 2003 MACERACIÓN
CARBÓNICA RED
COLONIAS DE GALEÓN 2002 OAK AGED RED

Bodega y Viñedos EL CHANTRE

Pueblo Verde, 17
Urbanización Simón Verde
41120 Gelves (Sevilla)
☎: 670 851 480 - Fax: 954 181 818
elchantre@telefonica.net
Established: 2001

⊕ 600 📊 210,000 litres 🍇 25 has.

RAMOS PAUL 2002 RED

F. SCHATZ

Finca Sanguijuela s/n.
Apdo. Correos 131
29400 Ronda (Málaga)
☎: 952 871 313 - Fax: 952 161 825
bodega@f-schatz.com
www.f-schatz.com
Established: 1982
⊕ 50 📊 20,000 litres 🍇 3 has.
🍷 70% 🍇30%

ACINIPO 2002 CRIANZA RED
lemberger, otras

82 Cherry with a garnet red edge. Not very intense yet harmonious aroma with balsamics and ripe fruit. Flavourful, concentrated palate with well-assembled red fruit and wood, well-balanced.

FINCA SANGUIJUELA 2001 WHITE
100% riesling

83 Brilliant pale yellow. Intense aroma with a good varietal profile (hydrocarbons, white stone fruit, citrus fruit) and fine smoky oak. Flavourful on the palate with a slightly oily texture, an element of fruity freshness and good acidity.

SCHATZ 2002 ROSÉ
100% muskattrollinger

85 Very deep brilliant raspberry. Powerful aroma of red fruit with fine spicy notes of skins and a balsamic nuance. Flavourful on the palate with fine smoky notes, hints of earth and citrus fruit (orange peel) and excellent acidity.

Bodegas GONZÁLEZ PALACIOS

Consolación, 60
41005 Lebrija (Sevilla)
☎: 655 972 785 - Fax: 955 974 084
gonzalezpalacios@arrakis.es
Established: 1960
⊕ 800 📊 500,000 litres 🍇 30 has.
🍷 85% 🍇15%: -BE -FR -UK

CASTILLO DE GONZÁLEZ PALACIOS 2003
WHITE
100% palomino

80 Pale. Fruity aroma with tropical fruit notes (papaya, green fruit pulp) and a suggestion of ripeness. Flavourful on the palate with good alcohol-acidity and notes of tropical fruit; pleasant.

GONZÁLEZ PALACIOS CREAM ROBLE VINO
DE LICOR SEMIDULCE
100% palomino

83 Light mahogany. Aroma with notes of Solera, toasty flavours and reduction (orange peel). Very sweet, slightly pungent palate with notes of pastries and marzipan, fresh and flavourful.

GONZÁLEZ PALACIOS OLOROSO ROBLE VINO DE LICOR
100% palomino

85 Light mahogany. Toasty aroma with fine notes of Solera (pâtisserie, nuts). Dry palate with hints of casks and bitter almonds, round.

M. FINA GONZÁLEZ PALACIOS EL POETA ROBLE VINO DE LICOR
100% palomino

82 Straw-coloured. Clean flor aroma (saline flavours, flowers) with hints of iodine. Fresh, bitter palate with character and generous notes of Fino; slightly vinous with a warm finish.

GONZÁLEZ PALACIOS MANZANILLA DE LEBRIJA
100% palomino

75 Straw-coloured with a golden edge. Aroma of ripe fruit with notes of cask reduction (nuts). Flavourful, fresh palate with rancid hints and a slightly oily finish.

VINO DE PASAS EL POETA DULCE
100% moscatel

87 Dark mahogany. Dark-roasted aroma of sultanas with a pleasant suggestion of Solera. Round, very flavourful palate with good acidity, a syrupy texture and hints of vanilla and fine cask.

HACIENDAS ÁNDALUS

Estación de Parchite, 104
29400 Ronda (Málaga)
☎: 952 114 124 - Fax: 952 114 124
adelgado@haciendas-espana.com
www.haciendas-espana.com

Established: 1992

🌐 500 🛢 100,000 litres 🍇 15 has.

🍷 65% 🌐35%

ÁNDALUS PETIT VERDOT 2001 RED
100% petit verdot

91 Very intense cherry. Powerful aroma of almost jammy black fruit, toasty with fine woods and a mild varietal nuance. Strong, fresh fruity sensation on the palate with flavourful tannins and a very pleasant oaky finish, very long.

PRÍNCIPE ALFONSO RESERVA PRIVADA 2001 RED

JOSÉ GALLEGO GÓNGORA

Cristo de la Vera Cruz, 59
41808 Villanueva del Ariscal (Sevilla)

☎: 954 113 700 - Fax: 954 113 239
gongora@bodegasgongora.com
www.bodegasgongora.com

Established: 1682

🌐 1,500 🛢 2,000,000 litres 🍇 60 has.

🍷 75% 🌐25%: -DE -BE -AT -UK -US -DO -CU -JP -PH

ALJARAFE FINO
60% garrido, 30% palomino, 10% listán

75 Straw-coloured. Quite warm, grapey aroma with expressive notes of white fruit and flor masked by the wood. Flavourful, fresh and slightly bitter palate without notes of flor; vinous.

EXTRA FINÍSIMA ANDANITA FINO
75% garrido, 25% listán

78 Straw-coloured. Original aroma of very ripe white fruit with notes of flowers and a hint of reduced flor. Flavourful and enveloping on the palate with discreet notes of Fino; a short finish.

PATA DE HIERRO FINO
100% garrido

80 Yellow straw. Aroma with mild notes of varnish, saline hints, slightly ripe (suggestion of reduction). Flavourful, warm palate with good freshness; notes of sweet almonds.

AMONTILLADO MUY VIEJO
100% garrido

83 Dark amber. Aroma with toasty reduction notes (varnish, toasted nuts) and saline hints. Dry, almondy and flavourful on the palate with flor-crianza balance, long.

AMONTILLADO MUY VIEJO SELECCIÓN IMPERIAL
100% garrido,

82 Dark amber. Aroma of hazelnuts, nutty with marked notes of Solera and aged flor. Flavourful, expressive palate with light toasty notes distinguishable under a notion of Fino, an almondy nuance.

DUQUE DE CARMONA ORANGE WINE OLOROSO DULCE
75% garrido, 25% moscatel

82 Old gold. Expressive and clear aroma of orange peel with a creamy and coffee hint. Very fresh, flavourful palate with sweetness compensated by the freshness, orange liqueur-style.

GÓNGORA SOLERA 1840 OLOROSO DULCE
75% garrido, 25% pedro ximénez

80 Old gold. Aroma of mild varnish with hints of nuts and Solera. Sweet, fresh and flavourful palate with slightly flat nuances and traces of creamy vanilla.

OLOROSO GÓNGORA DULCE
100% garrido

81 Mahogany with a yellowish edge. Aroma of vanilla (toasted raisins), fine crianza notes (toffee, vanilla) and a suggestion of varnish. Flavourful palate with fresh notes and toasty crianza, a round finish with saline touches.

GÓNGORA P.X. DULCE
60% pedro ximénez, 20% moscatel, 20% garrido

81 Mahogany. Aroma of Mistelle with notes of cedar and spices and a suggestion of old Solera. Flavourful, fresh palate evoking carpentry, spicy with a toasty finish.

GÓNGORA PX DULCE AÑEJO SELECCIÓN IMPERIAL
100% pedro ximénez,

86 Almost opaque mahogany. Aroma of chocolate and jammy figs with very subtle Solera and marked dark-roasted flavours, very complex. Long, syrupy palate with notes of coffee, nuts and dried fruit, freshness.

GRAN VINO MOSCATEL GÓNGORA DULCE
60% moscatel, 20% pedro ximénez, 20% garrido

83 Mahogany with an orange edge. Toasty aroma with notes of raisins, orange peel and a Muscatel edge. Fruity, very flavourful palate, fresh and a generous aftertaste of toffee and sun-drenched skins.

SEÑORÍO DE HELICHE WHITE SEMISECO
MARQUÉS DE HELICHE JOVEN WHITE SECO
OLOROSO VIEJÍSIMO SELECCIÓN
IMPERIAL OLOROSO SECO

Cooperativa Agrícola LA AURORA

Carretera Córboba - Málaga, km. 44
14550 Montilla (Córdoba)
☎: 957 650 362 - Fax: 957 654 642

LA AURORA TEMPRANILLO JOVEN RED

Bodegas PÁEZ MORILLA

Avenida Medina Sidonia, 20
11406 Jerez de la Frontera (Cádiz)
☎: 956 181 717 - Fax: 956 181 534
bodegas@paezmorilla.com
www.paezmorilla.com
Established: 1945
450 261,000 litres 38 has.
90% 10%: -DE -FR

TIERRA BLANCA WHITE
TIERRA BLANCA WHITE SEMIDULCE
VIÑA LUCÍA RED
LA VICARÍA OLOROSO
SANTA LUCÍA MOSCATEL

Bodegas PRIVILEGIO DEL CONDADO

San José, 2
21710 Bollullos del Condado (Huelva)
☎: 959 410 261 - Fax: 959 410 171
comercial@vinicoladelcondado.com
www.vinicoladelcondado.com
Established: 1955
1,000 40,000,000 litres 2,000 has.
95% 5%

LANTERO TEMPRANILLO 2003 RED
50% tempranillo, 50% syrah

75 Dark cherry with a violet edge. Intense, slightly fruity aroma with spicy notes of skins and fine herbaceous hints. Fleshy on the palate with slightly astringent grape tannins and quite flavourful.

RAPOSO (J.A. RAPOSO)

Miguel Hernández, 37
21710 Bollullos Par del Condado (Huelva)
☎: 959 410 565 - Fax: 959 413 821
Established: 1929
1,000 1,000,000 litres 3 has.
100%

VIÑA LA NUEZ CRIANZA WHITE
ROSA MORENA CRIANZA WHITE
MORENA CLARA CRIANZA WHITE
AVELLANERO CRIANZA DULCE WHITE
AVELLANERO CRIANZA DULCE WHITE
VIÑA NUEZ WHITE
LA CACHIFA CRIANZA FINO
M.F. LA NUEZ CRIANZA FINO
SELECTO M.C. CRIANZA FINO

SOCIEDAD ANDALUZA DE LA VID SANTA GERTRUDIS

Prolongacion Baeza, s/n ó Ctra. N IV Km. 296
23710 Bailen (Jaen)
☎: 953 671 256 - Fax: 953 671 256
sta_gertrudis@bailen.org
Established: 1964
72 2,500,000 litres 190 has.
95% 5%: -UK -DE -FR

ATARDECER ANDALUZ WHITE
DUQUE DE BAILEN RED
BATALLA 1808 TEMPRANILLO RED

ARAGÓN

DALCAMP

Constitución, 4
22415 Monesma de San Juan (Huesca)
☎: 973 760 018 - Fax: 973 760 523
rdalfo@mixmail.com

Established: 1994
⊞ 300 ▤ 534,000 litres ⛭ 26,5 has.
🍷 30% 🌐70%: -DE -AT -BE -UK -NL -DK

MONTE NERI CABERNET SAUVIGNON 2001 OAK AGED RED
33% cabernet sauvignon, 33% merlot, 34% garnacha

81 Cherry with an orangey hue. Medium-intensity, balsamic aroma with ripe fruit. Flavourful, medium bodied, balsamic and expressive on the palate, very pleasant.

MONTE NERY 1999 CRIANZA RED
85% cabernet sauvignon, 45% merlot

82 Garnet red with an orangey edge. Aroma of a long crianza with a suggestion of reduction (animals, dark-roasted flavours) and a jammy plum hint. Fleshy palate with oily, quite ripe, fruit tannins, noticeable oak and an earthy, woody finish.

MONTE NERY 1998 CRIANZA RED
85% cabernet sauvignon, 15% merlot

80 Garnet red with a brick red edge. Aroma of dark-roasted flavours, toasty oak and reduction overtones. Fleshy palate with marked wood tannins, slightly warm with a ripe, earthy finish.

Cooperativa SANTA MARÍA LA MAYOR

San Cristóbal, 63
44580 Valderrobres (Teruel)
☎: 978 850 082 - Fax: 978 890 181

Established: 1958
⊞ 4 ▤ 2,452,000 litres ⛭ 67,36 has.
🍷 100%

VALDERROBRES WHITE
VALDERROBRES ROSÉ
VALDERROBRES RED

BALEARES

CAN VIDALET

Carretera Alcudia-Pollença km. 4, 8

Apartado 10
07460 Pollença (Mallorca)
☎: 971 531 719 - Fax: 971 531 719
vidalet@wanadoo.es
www.canvidalet.com

Established: 2001
⊞ 150 ▤ 77,000 litres ⛭ 8 has.
🍷 20% 🌐80%: -DE -UK

CA'N VIDALET CABERNET SAUVIGNON 2001 OAK AGED RED
100% cabernet sauvignon

83 Dark cherry. Powerful aroma with predominant burnt notes, balsamic hints and a notion of terroir. Powerful, concentrated palate with good fruit/oak integration, bitter (liquorice dark roasted flavours, terracotta) with notions of wax, lacking varietal expression.

CA'N VIDALET SYRAH & CABERNET SAUVIGNON 2001 CRIANZA RED
syrah, cabernet sauvignon

79 Dark cherry with a purplish edge. Intense, ripe aroma with spicy crianza notes. Fleshy palate with slightly marked tannins and unintegrated with the fruit, marked acidity.

CA'N VIDALET MERLOT 2001 CRIANZA RED
100% merlot

79 Dark cherry with a dark red edge. Powerful aroma with a hint of varietal fruit expression (redcurrants, fallen leaves), warm. Flavourful, fleshy palate with fine bitter notes and excessively warm.

Vins MIQUEL GELABERT

Salas, 50
07500 Manacor (Balears)
☎: 971 821 444 - Fax: 971 821 444
vinsmq@vinsmiquelgelabert.com
www.vinsmiquelgelabert.com

Established: 1985
⊞ 104 ▤ 40,000 litres ⛭ 8 has.
🍷 70% 🌐30%: -DE

BLANC SA VALL SELECCIÓ PRIVADA 2003 FERMENTADO EN BARRICA WHITE

87 Pale yellow with a golden hue. Intense, ripe aroma with predominant creamy, smoky wood notes and exotic hints (banana skins). Flavourful palate with fine bitter notes, aniseed and herbs in the retronasal passage, warm hints and minerals.

BLANC SA VALL 2002 OAK AGED WHITE
90% riesling, 10% gewürztraminer

83 Pale yellow with a golden hue. Intense aroma with notes of ripe white fruit, hints of peach skins, spices and smoky oak. Flavourful, bitter, and warm on the palate lacking varietal expression.

VINYA DES MORÈ 2001 OAK AGED RED
100% pinot noir

88 Intense cherry. Aroma with a certain complexity, hints of earthiness and bramble patches and very delicate toasty, creamy oak. Round, oily, original palate, an unusual Pinot Noir with a balsamic retronasal effect and notes of scrubland herbs (broom).

Vins de TANYS MEDITERRANIS

D'es Tudó, 13-15
07830 Sant Josep de Sa Talaia (Ibiza (Baleares))
☎: 971 399 167 - Fax: 971 305 440
enotecum@telefonica.net
Established: 2001
🛢 15 🛢 10,000 litres 🚩 60% 🌐40%

COS DE SAL DMIII RED

Vins TONI GELABERT

Camí dels Horts de Llodrá km. 1, 3 Son Fangos
07500 Manacor (Balears)
☎: 971 552 409 - Fax: 971 552 409
info@vinstonigelabert.com
www.vinstonigelabert.com
Established: 1980
🛢 65 🛢 24,000 litres 🍇 5 has.
🚩 90% 🌐10%: -DE

TORRES DES CANONGE 2003 WHITE
100% giró

88 Golden yellow. Powerful aroma, with fine smoky oak, a spicy hint (cumin, anise, vanilla) and fragrant herbs. Flavourful, and creamy on the palate with a good oak/fruit integration, bitter and warm with good acidity.

TORRES DES CANONGE 2001 OAK AGED RED
60% pinot noir, 20% syrah, 20% merlot   🛢 15

82 Quite dark cherry with an orange edge. Fruity aroma with hints of bramble patches and old leather. Round, somewhat light palate with supple tannins and a suggestion of foresty berries in the retronasal passage, curious.

VINORICA (CASTELL MIQUEL)

Polígono 3, Parcela 259/261
07340 Alaró (Mallorca)
☎: 971 510 698
www.castellmiquel.de

CASTELL MIQUEL GARNATXA 2002 RED
garnacha

83 Dark garnet red cherry. Intense aroma with predominant toasty oak notes. Flavourful, fleshy palate with a good fruit/oak integration, slightly warm and oily with spicy hints, liquorice and Mediterranean herbs.

CASTELL MIQUEL TEMPRANILLO 2002 RED
tempranillo

79 Very dark cherry with a coppery-saffron edge. Powerful aroma with toasty and spicy notes of oak, jammy fruit and scarce varietal expression. Flavourful, fleshy palate with slightly drying tannins and fine bitter notes, slightly warm.

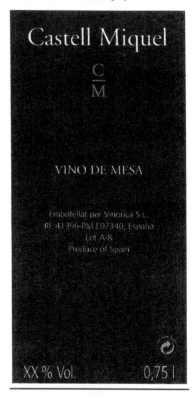

CASTELL MIQUEL CABERNET 2002 RED
CASTELL MIQUEL RED

CANARIAS

JUAN MATÍAS TORRES PÉREZ

Ciudad Real 10 Canarios
38740 Fuentecaliente de la Palma (Tenerife)
☎: 922 444 219 - Fax: 922 444 219

Established: 1895
🌐 42 🛢 32,000 litres 🍇 2 has. 🚩 100%

VINO DE MESA DE CANARIAS 2003 OAK
AGED ROSÉ

VEGA GRANDE DE GUADALUPE

Doctor Verneau, 1 Oficina 306
35001 Las Palmas de Gran Canaria (Las
Palmas de Gran Canaria)
☎: 928 336 279 - Fax: 928 310 876
Established: 2002
🌐 25 🛢 40,000 litres 🍇 4.3 has.

VEGA GRANDE 2003 CRIANZA RED

CASTILLA- LA MANCHA

Bodegas CELAYA

Poligono Industrial El Salvador Avenida 1,
Parcelas 56-57
02630 La Roda (Albacete)
☎: 967 440 101 - Fax: 967 548 496
correo@bodegascelaya.com
Established: 1927
🌐 100 🛢 2,500,000 litres 🚩 100%

CASTILLO RODAFUERTE WHITE
AVE DE PRESA WHITE
CASTILLO RODAFUERTE RED
AVE DE PRESA RED

CORONADO VINOS Y BODEGAS

Carretera San Isidro, s/n
16620 La Alberca de Zancara (Cuenca)
☎: 620 287 825 - Fax: 967 150 107
Established: 2002
🌐 20 🛢 250,000 litres 🍇 20 has. 🚩 100%

CHARCÓN 2003 RED

FÉLIX SOLÍS

Autovía de Andalucía, km. 199
13300 Valdepeñas (Ciudad Real)
☎: 926 322 400 - Fax: 926 322 417
bsf@felixsolis.com
www.felixsolis.com
Established: 1952

🌐 40,000 🛢 192,000,000 litres 🍇 500 has.
🚩 62% 🌐38%: -UK -DE -NL -DK -FI -SE -
BE -GQ -CH TG -MX -BE -AT -JP -PH -NC -
DO -US -AO -PF -CA -CO -SE -DK -CZ -DZ -
PE -VE -IT -LU -CF -PA -KE CM -VN -TW -
LB -GT -MY CD -SG -EC -BR -JO -GA TZ -
CR -EL -AU -SV -SB -GM -IE -NI -PT

SENDAS DEL REY 2003 RED

Sociedad Coop. Agraria INMACULADA CONCEPCIÓN

Carretera de Campillo, s/n
16200 Motilla del Palancar (Cuenca)
☎: 969 331 071 - Fax: 969 331 680
coopmotilla.3064@cajarural.com
Established: 1952
🛢 6,000,000 litres 🍇 1,100 has.
🚩 70% 🌐30%

INMACULADA CONCEPCIÓN WHITE
INMACULADA CONCEPCIÓN ROSÉ
INMACULADA CONCEPCIÓN RED

MONTE LA VILLA

Haza del Santo, s/n
45850 Villa de Don Fadrique (Toledo)
☎: 925 195 672 - Fax: 925 195 990
montelavilla@terra.es
www.agrocaja.es
Established: 1987
🛢 7,200,000 litres 🍇 1,274 has. 🚩 100%

MONTE LA VILLA WHITE
MONTE LA VILLA RED

Sociedad Cooperativa Agraria NUESTRA SEÑORA DE RUS

Carretera Almarcha, 50
16600 San Clemente (Cuenca)
☎: 969 300 155 - Fax: 969 300 281
cooprus@puentederus.com
www.puentederus.com
Established: 1945
🌐 200 🛢 30,000,000 litres 🍇 3,500 has.
🚩 80% 🌐20%: -PT -FR -DE

NUESTRA SEÑORA DE RUS 2003 WHITE
NUESTRA SEÑORA DE RUS 2003 ROSÉ
NUESTRA SEÑORA DE RUS 2003 RED

Cooperativa del Campo SAN ISIDRO

Extramuros, s/n
02215 Alborea (Albacete)
☎: 967 477 067 - Fax: 967 477 096

Established: 1959

🍷 120 📊 4,500,000 litres 🌿 920 has.

🍇 99% 🌐1%: -UK -BE

CERAJONES RED

Bodegas UGENA

Reina Sofía, 29
13620 Pedro Muñoz (Ciudad Real)
☎: 926 568 416 - Fax: 926 568 416
vinos@bodegasugena.com
www.bodegasugena.com

Established: 1830

🍷 63 📊 216,000 litres 🍇 100%

VIÑA OBDULIA CÁPSULA BURDEOS 2002
OAK AGED RED
VIÑA OBDULIA CÁPSULA NEGRA 2002
CRIANZA RED

Cooperativa UNIÓN CAMPESINA INIESTENSE

C/San Idefonso, 1
16235 Iniesta (Cuenca)
☎: 967 490 120 - Fax: 967 490 777
comercial@cooperativauci.com

Established: 1944

🍷 800 📊 54,000,000 litres 🌿 7,000 has.

🍇 70% 🌐30%: -FR -IT -PT -DE -BE -US -
NL -AT

MIRABUENO

CASTILLA Y LEÓN

Bodegas y Viñedos ALONSO TORIBIO

Santibáñez de Valcorba
47331 Santibáñez de Valcorba (Valladolid)
☎: 983 682 108 - Fax: 983 682 484

Established: 1997

🍷 300 📊 100,000 litres 🍇 80% 🌐20%: -
CH

FACUS GRAN VINO DE GUARDA 2000 RED

MATIZALES 2001 RED
PICALCÓN 2001 RED

ALTA PAVINA

Camino de Santibáñez, s/n
47328 La Parrilla (Valladolid)
☎: 983 681 521 - Fax: 983 339 890

Established: 1988

🍷 300 📊 153,000 litres 🌿 10.5 has.

🍇 70% 🌐30%

ALTA PAVINA PINOT NOIR 1999 CRIANZA RED
ALTA PAVINA TINTO FINO 2000 CRIANZA RED
ALTA PAVINA CABERNET SAUVIGNON 1999
 CRIANZA RED

Bodegas Seleccionadas ARMANDO

"Viña Concita y Adilen"
Carretera N-630, km. 270
49192 Zamora (Zamora)
☎: 980 538 683 - Fax: 980 538 683
armando@bodegas-armando.com
www.bodegas-armando.com

Established: 1992

🍇 80% 🌐20%

CATHEDRAL DE ZAMORA 2000 RESERVA
RED
tinta de toro, juan garcía, merlot

83 Dark cherry with a saffron edge. Powerful,
ripe aroma with predominant toasty wood notes.
Flavourful, concentrated palate with a good
oak/fruit integration and bitter notes (dark-roasted
flavours, liquorice).

NOVISSIMO QUINTA DURI 2003 RED
QUINTA DURI 2002 RED

ARZUAGA NAVARRO

Carretera N-122, km. 325
47350 Quintanilla de Onésimo (Valladolid)
☎: 983 681 146 - Fax: 983 681 147
bodeg@arzuaganavarro.com
www.arzuaganavarro.com

Established: 1993

🍷 3,000 📊 1,000,000 litres 🌿 150 has.

🍇 45% 🌐55%

FAN D'ORO 2003 FERMENTADO EN
BARRICA WHITE
100% chardonnay

79 Brilliant yellow. Aroma of very new woods
(resins), toasty, smoky with light hints of tropical

fruit. Drying wood tannins on the palate, good acidity, slightly warm.

CASTRO VENTOSA

Finca El Barredo, s/n
24530 Valtuille de Abajo (León)
☎: 987 562 148 - Fax: 987 562 191
bodegascastrov@terra.es

Established: 1987

🛢 250 litres 🍇 60 has.

👕 90% 🌐10%: -PR -DE -UK

AIROLA CHARDONNAY 2003 WHITE
100% chardonnay

82 Yellow straw. Aroma of peaches, ripe pears and tropical fruit. Warm on the palate with good acidity, medium persistence and reminiscent of ripe white fruit in the retronasal passage.

COVITORO

Carretera de Tordesillas, 13
49800 Toro (Zamora)
☎: 980 690 347 - Fax: 980 690 143
covitoro@covitoro.com
www.covitoro.com

Established: 1974

🛢 900 🍇 1,100 has.

👕 65% 🌐35%: -UK -DE -US -CH -NL -BE -DK -FR -IT -PL -MX -JP -AT -CZ -SE -BR

VIÑA VIRGEN WHITE DULCE
verdejo, moscatel

73 Pale golden yellow. Intense aroma of fruit and white flowers with the spicy freshness of skins. Flavourful, sweet palate with crystallised fruit, slightly warm.

Bodegas y Viñedos
FERNÁNDEZ RIVERA

Finca La Granja
49420 Vadillo de la Guareña (Zamora)
☎: 980 566 009 - Fax: 980 566 009
www.dehesalagranja.com

Established: 1998

🛢 3,000 🛢 400,000 litres 🍇 150 has.

👕 70% 🌐30%: -CA -US -MX

DEHESA LA GRANJA 2000 RED
100% tempranillo

88 Intense cherry. Powerful warm aroma, with toasty hints of oak and jammy fruit (plums, blackberries). Fleshy, spicy palate with well-integrated fruit/oak tannins, flavourful with a foresty hint.

Bodega y Viñedos LUNA BEBERIDE

Carretera Madrid-Coruña, km. 402
24540 Cacabelos (León)
☎: 987 549 002 - Fax: 987 549 214
info@lunabeberide.com
www.lunabeberide.com

Established: 1987

🛢 400 🛢 400,000 litres 🍇 80 has.

LB 2003 WHITE

PÉREZ CARAMÉS

Peña Picón, s/n
24500 Villafranca del Bierzo (León)
☎: 987 540 197 - Fax: 987 540 314
1018fp@teleline.es

Established: 1986

🛢 156 🍇 32 has.

👕 30% 🌐70%: -CH -FI -DE -BE -JP -MX

CASAR DE SANTA INÉS CHARDONNAY 2001 WHITE
100% chardonnay

83 Straw-coloured with a golden hue. Aroma with fine reduction notes (lees, quince, honey). Oily, unctuous palate with ripe fruit (dried peaches) and hay, well-balanced.

CASAR DE SANTA INÉS CHARDONNAY 2002 WHITE
100% chardonnay

83 Golden yellow. Ripe aroma (quince, honey, very sweet notes). Oily palate with notes of herbs and nuts with hints of sweetness and good acidity.

CASAR DE SANTA INÉS 1994 OAK AGED RED
50% cabernet sauvignon, 33% mencía, 17% tempranillo
🛢 24

84 Garnet red cherry with a coppery hue. Intense aroma with predominant reduction notes (old furniture, tobacco, prunes). Flavourful palate with good crianza expresión, spicy and quite vigorous.

CASAR DE SANTA INÉS 1998 OAK AGED RED
50% cabernet sauvignon, 25% mencía, 15% merlot, 10% tempranillo
🛢 27

84 Cherry with an orangey hue. Aroma with crianza character and reduction notes (tobacco, pepper) yet firm. Flavourful and round on the palate with hints of red fruit, balsamic flavour and toasty oak.

CASAR DE SANTA INÉS 1997 CRIANZA RED
37% merlot, 29% cabernet sauvignon, 25% mencía, 9% tempranillo

87 Dark cherry with a coppery edge. Powerful aroma rich in crianza nuances (cedar, cigar box, old furniture). Flavourful palate with a good oak/fruit integration, fine bitter notes and excellent acidity, still promising.

CASAR DE SANTA INÉS MENCÍA-CABERNET SAUVIGNON 2001 RED
60% mencía, 40% cabernet sauvignon

87 Intense cherry. Aroma of jammy plums with a suggestion of minerals and fine smoky oak, intense. Fleshy, powerful palate with oily but consistent tannins and well-integrated wood, for keeping.

CASAR DE SANTA INÉS PINOT NOIR 1999 RED
100% pinot noir

73 Cherry with a brick red hue. Spicy aroma (flowers), slightly viscous with ripe black fruit. Fresh, very flavourful palate with oily and spicy tannins; sloes in the finish.

CASAR DE SANTA INÉS CABERNET SAUVIGNON 1999 RED

80 Cherry with an orangey edge. Intense aroma evoking a good crianza (pepper, balsamic notes), varietal. Flavourful palate with vegetative notes, slightly aggressive dry wood tannins in the finish. palate with slightly weak tannins, flavourful and spicy with reduction and spicy notes in the retronasal passage.

CASAR DE SANTA INÉS MERLOT 1998 RED

83 Garnet red cherry with a coppery edge. Powerful aroma of smoky oak with a slight varietal expression (redcurrants, paprika). Flavourful, very bitter palate (dark-roasted flavours, liquorice) with good acidity.

QUINTA SARDONIA

Granja Sardón, s/n
47340 Sardon de Duero (Valladolid)
☎: 650 398 353
@telefonica.net

Established: 2002
🍶 90 🖥 60,000 litres 🌿 17 has. 🇪🇸 100%

QUINTA SARDONIA 2002 ROBLE RED
48% tinto fino, 22% cabernet sauvignon, 16% merlot, 5% syrah

95 Intense cherry. Powerful, fine, delicate aroma (cocoa, chocolates) with creamy toast and ripe fruit (plums, blackberries). Full, toasty and creamy on the palate with sweet, very flavourful tannins, elegant.

Cooperativa Vinícola RIBERA DEL CEA

Avenida Panduro y Villafañe, s/n
24220 Valderas (León)
☎: 987 762 191 - Fax: 987 762 191

Established: 1970

🍶 14 🖥 2,200,000 litres
🌿 400 has. 🍷 100%

VIÑA CUESTASBUENAS 2003 ROSÉ
tempranillo, garnacha, mencía, prieto picudo

68 Dark raspberry with an orangey hue. Flat aroma with hardly any nuances, toasty oak. Sweet and warm palate.

Bodegas ROMÁNTICAS DEL MONASTERIO DE SP DE CARDEÑA

Lg/Monasterio de San Pedro de Cardeña
09193 Castillo de Val (Burgos)
☎: 947 290 033

CARDEÑA RED
VALDEVEGÓN RED
VALDEVEGÓN SELECCIÓN MÍO CID CRIANZA RED

Cooperativa SAN ESTEBAN

Chorrito, s/n
37671 San Esteban de la Sierra (Salamanca)
☎: 923 435 028 - Fax: 923 435 028

Established: 1959
🍶 50 🖥 1,200,000 litres 🌿 250 has.
🇪🇸 90% 🌐10%

CORRETAJERO JOVEN RED
TIRIÑUELO OAK AGED RED
TIRIÑUELO 2003 ROSÉ
GRAN TIRIÑUELO 2000 CRIANZA RED
TIRIÑUELO CUMBRE 1999 RESERVA RED
TIRIÑUELO 2003 RED

Bodega Cooperativa SANTA ANA

Carretera De Salas s/n
09410 Peñaranda de Duero (Burgos)
☎: 947 552 011 -
www.bodegasantaana.com

Established: 1964
🍶 150 🖥 2,000,000 litres 🌿 350 has.
🍷 95% 🌐5%: -UK -FR

MATARREDONDA 2003 WHITE

VALDUERO

Carretera de Aranda, s/n
09440 Gumiel de Mercadol (Burgos)
☎: 947 545 459 - Fax: 947 545 609
valduerocom@bodegasvalduero.com
www.bodegasvalduero.com

Established: 1982

⊕ 2,600 ▤ 1,200,000 litres ⛆ 250 has. ⫯ 680,000 litres.

🍷 50% ☕50%: -CH -DE -UK -US -PR -DO -JP -AT -BE -NL -CA

GARCÍA VIADERO ALBILLO 2003 WHITE
100% albillo

81 Pale yellow. Intense, very fine aroma of fruit and white flowers with hints of hay. Fresh, flavourful palate with white fruit, rich bitter notes and excellent citrus acidity.

VERMILIÓN DE VALBUENA DE DUERO

Carretera Renedo-Pesquera, km. 30
47395 Valbuena de Duero (Valladolid)
☎: 983 107 100 - Fax: 983 107 104
gperez@bodegamatarromera.es
www.matarromera.es

Established: 1995

⊕ 90 ⛆ 4 has.

🍷 70% ☕30%: -DE -AD -AT -BE -BR -CA -CU -CL -DK -EC -FR -UK-NL -IT -JP -MX -DK -PA -PE -PR -SE -CH -US -CZ -DM

VERMILIÓN 1999 OAK AGED RED
100% tinto fino

90 Intense cherry. Aroma of finely toasted oak (milk chocolate, dark-roasted flavour), with stewed ripe fruit (blackberries and plums). Fleshy, full, flavourful, warm palate with powerful, ripe tannins.

VINÍCOLA VALMADRIGAL

Constitución, 16
24323 Castrotierra de Valmadrigal (León)
☎: 987 784 047 - Fax: 987 784 047

Established: 1969

⊕ 50 ▤ 200,000 litres 🍷 100%

CASTRO IUVARA 2003 WHITE

VIÑEDOS DE ARGANZA Y CANEDO (CASTILLO D'ULVER)

Castillo D'Ulver
24540 Cacabelos (León)
☎: 987 546 367 - Fax: 987 546 367
castillodeulver@castillodeulver.com
www.castillodeulver.com

Established: 1998

▤ 20,000 litres ⛆ 8 has.

🍷 85% ☕15%: -DE

CASTILLO DE ULVER 2002 RED

82 Intense cherry. Peppery aroma with intense, toasty crianza over concentrated black fruit. Powerful, fresh palate with dry oak tannins and pleasant fruit (flowers, ripe black fruit), a bitter finish.

CASTILLO DE ULVER TEMPRANILLO RED

CATALUÑA

Celler CAN SAIS

Raval de Dalt, 10
17253 Vall-llobrega (Girona)
☎: 972 318 033 - Fax: 972 918 033
correu@cellercansais.com
www.cellercansais.com

Established: 1999

⊕ 30 ▤ 40,000 litres ⛆ 12 has.

🍷 90% ☕10%

CAN SAIS 2003 JOVEN WHITE
CAN SAIS MALVASÍA 2003 WHITE DULCE NATURAL
CAN SAIS 2003 JOVEN RED
CAN SAIS SELECCIÓ 2001 OAK AGED RED

CASTILLO DE CAPMANY

Plaza del Fort, 5
17750 Capmany (Girona)
☎: 972 549 043 - Fax: 972 549 043
castillodecapmany@terra.es

Established: 1994

⊕ 55 ▤ 60,000 litres ⛆ 11 has. 🍷 60% ☕40%: -DE -FR

CASTILLO OLIVARES MISTELA MISTELA

77 Golden. Intense aroma with musky notes, fine herbs and hints of honey and young quince. Fleshy, unctuous palate, slightly warm and spicy in the retronasal passage.

CAVAS DEL AMPURDÁN

Plaza del Carme, 1
17491 Perelada (Girona)
☎: 972 538 011 - Fax: 972 538 277
perelada@castilloperelada.com
www.perelada.com

Established: 1923

▤ 1,800,000 litres 🍷 99% ☕1%

BLANC PESCADOR WHITE DE AGUJA
50% macabeo, 25% parellada, 25% xarel.lo

78 Pale with greenish nuances. Not very intense, fresh aroma with a certain finesse, with fruit, white flowers and a nuance of lees. Fresh palate with carbonic hints, bitter notes and good acidity.

CRESTA AZUL WHITE DE AGUJA
macabeo, parellada, xarel.lo, moscatel

80 Pale yellow with greenish nuances. Intense, fruity aroma with hints of honey and flowers. Fresh, dry and creamy palate (fine carbonic hints) with quality bittersweet notes, bitter and very rich.

CRESTA ROSA ROSÉ DE AGUJA
60% garnacha, 40% tempranillo

78 Pale raspberry with an orangey hue. Fresh, fruity palate with citrus hints. Flavourful, slightly creamy palate (fine carbonics) with fine bitter notes.

ENBLAVE

Penedés, 24
08420 Canovelles (Barcelona)
☎: 938 496 863 - Fax: 938 400 889
enblaje@teleline.es
www.vinyesdelbruguer.com

VINYES DEL BRUGUER CHARDONNAY 2002 FERMENTADO EN BARRICA WHITE
chardonnay

79 Brilliant pale gold. Powerful aroma with predominant smoky and creamy oak notes and a slightly varietal suggestion (ripe apples). Powerful, flavourful palate with unintegrated oak tannins and good acidity.

VINYES DEL BRUGUER GARNATXA 2002 JOVEN ROSÉ
100% garnacha

80 Dark raspberry with a coppery hue. Intense aroma with slightly sweet ripe fruit, toasty skins and a balsamic hint. Flavourful, fresh, bitter palate with toasty hints in the finish.

VINYES DEL BRUGUER CABERNET SAUVIGNON - GARNATXA 2002 RED
65% cabernet sauvignon, 35% garnacha

83 Dark garnet red cherry. Powerful, ripe aroma with notes of cedar, spicy wood, balsamic hints and notions of terroir. Flavourful palate with a good oak/fruit integration, bitter, with notions of wax and flint and liquorice in the finish.

VINYES DEL BRUGUER MERLOT 2002 RED
90% merlot, 10% cabernet sauvignon

80 Dark garnet red cherry. Powerful, ripe aroma of black fruit with a hint of reduction, cocoa and toasty oak. Fleshy palate with a good fruit/oak integration, slightly warm and oily.

HERETAT MONT-RUBÍ

Abellà, 1
08736 Font Rubí (Barcelona)
☎: 938 979 066 - Fax: 934 732 292
mont.rubi@salvat-lab.es

Established: 1985
🍶 30 🍶 30,000 litres 🌿 340 has.
🍷 75% 🍇25%: -US -CH

DOLÇ DE PALLER 2001 OAK AGED SWEET
100% xarel.lo

87 Coppery gold. Aroma of acetone and varnish, with toasty notes, orange peel and mountain herbs, complex overtones. Unctuous palate with pleasant toasty, creamy oak, crystallised fresh fruit and good acidity, well-balanced.

GAINTUS 2001 OAK AGED RED
85% sumoll, 15% merlot, cabernet sauvignon   🛢 12

81 Garnet red cherry. Fine toasty aroma of oak (cocoa, coffee, vanilla) with fresh fruit. Flavourful, fresh, fruity palate with fine toasty wood in the retronasal passage and fresh tannins.

DURONA 2002 OAK AGED RED
17,25% garnacha, 17,25% sumoll, 30% cariñena, 17,25% merlot, 17,25% cabernet sauvignon   🛢 8

90 Intense cherry. Complex aroma with an expression of macerated skins, slightly mineral with fine toasty oak. Fleshy, full, flavourful palate with sweet yet full and persistent tannins.

MASIA GIRONELLA

Carretera Encias, km. 32
17172 Planes Hostoles (Girona)
☎: 972 449 021 - Fax: 934 532 974
Established: 1990
🍶 100 🍶 110,000 litres 🌿 22 has.
🍷 100%

MASIA GIRONELLA CHARDONNAY WHITE
MASIA GIRONELLA SAUVIGNON BLANC
 WHITE
MASIA GIRONELLA SEMILLÓN WHITE
MASIA GIRONELLA VIOGNIER WHITE
MASIA GIRONELLA CABERNET RED
MASIA GIRONELLA MERLOT RED
MASIA GIRONELLA PINOT NOIR RED

MASIA VILA-RASA

Masia Vila-Rasa
08552 Taradell (Barcelona)
☎: 932 892 700 - Fax: 934 243 830
riera@riera.es

Established: 1989

⊞ 40 ▤ 18,000 litres ⚲ 2 has.

🍷 6,000 litres.

🇪🇸 95% 🌐5%: -NL

MASIA VILA-RASA 1999 OAK AGED RED
66% pinot noir, 34% merlot   ⊞ 12

86 Garnet red cherry with a coppery edge. Powerful aroma, excellent Pinot varietal expression, fine notes of Burgundy style reduction (animals, sour cherries in liqueur), exotic spices. Flavourful and slightly fruity palate with supple overtones, fine viscous and earthy notions, rich in crianza nuances, bitter, very original.

MONESTIR DEL TALLAT

Adminstracion. Carretera Reus-El Morell, Km. 738
43760 El Morrell (Tarragona)
☎: 977 840 655 - Fax: 977 842 146
vermut@vermutzyaguirre.com
www.vermutyzaguirre.com

Established: 1995

⊞ 130 ▤ 88,000 litres ⚲ 45 has.

🍷 75% 🌐25%: -BE -NL -IT -AD -CH -DE -LV -RU -IE

VINO DE MISA J. SALLA DULCE

SERRAT DE MONTSORIU

Can Serrat
17451 Sant Feliu de Buixalleu (Girona)
☎: 972 870 552 - Fax: 972 870 552
info@serratdemontsoriu.com
www.serratdemontsoriu.com

Established: 1995

⊞ 30 ⚲ 10 has. 🍷 100%

VINYA ILARIA 2001 FERMENTADO EN BARRICA WHITE
ESCLAT D´ODINA 2003 JOVEN ROSÉ
BRI DE MONROIG 2003 JOVEN RED
FLOR D ´ALVA 2003 JOVEN RED
CLOT DE L´ESPINA 2000 OAK AGED RED
VINYA DELS TONS 2001 CRIANZA RED

Celler SORT DEL CASTELL

Carretera Reus-El morell Km. 738
43760 El Morell (Tarragona)
☎: 977 840 655 - Fax: 977 842 146
vermut@vermutzyaguirre.com
www.vermutyzaguirre.com

Established: 1982

⊞ 80 ▤ 700,000 litres 🍷 85%

🌐15%: -BE -NL -IT -AD -CH -DE -IE -LV - RU -US -MX -JP -FR -PR

MOSCATEL J. SALLA MOSCATEL DULCE
VINO DE MISA J. SALLA DULCE

EXTREMADURA

Bodegas AGAPITA RUBIO BRAVO

José Manuel Durán, 17
10136 Cañamero (Cáceres)
☎: 927 369 192 - Fax: 927 369 437

Established: 1948

⊞ 180 ▤ 1,100,000 litres ⚲ 30 has.

🍷 100%

CERRO CABRERO 2003 ROBLE RED

CATALINA ARROYO

Carretera Don Benito-Miajadas, km. 19
06400 Don Benito (Badajoz)
☎: 924 841 852 - Fax: 924 841 852
catalina.arroyo@terra.es

Established: 1940

⊞ 500 ▤ 450,000 litres ⚲ 32 has.

🍷 100%

CATALINA ARROYO ANAS WHITE
CATALINA ARROYO ROSÉ
CATALINA ARROYO CABERNET SAUVIGNON RED
CATALINA ARROYO CLÁSICO RED
CATALINA ARROYO MERLOT RED

FRANCO-SÁNCHEZ

Pilones, 24
10100 Miajadas (Cáceres)
☎: 927 347 274 - Fax: 927 348 751
francosanchez@francosanchez.com
www.francosanchez.com

Established: 1955

⊞ 45 ▤ 280,000 litres 🍷 100%

VIÑA ZANJO RED

LÓPEZ MORENAS

Melilla, 13
06360 Fuente del Maestre (Badajoz)
☎: 924 530 016 - Fax: 924 530 305

Established: 1943

🌐 200 🛢 20,000,000 litres 🍇 250 has. 🇪🇸 90% 🌐10%

PONDERADO RED
VEGAS DEL BADIÓN RED

Sociedad Cooperativa VIRGEN DE LA ESTRELLA

Calle Mérida, 1
06230 Los Santos de Maimona (Badajoz)
☎: 924 544 094 - Fax: 924 572 490
export@maimona.com
www.maimona.com

Established: 1963
🌐 45 🛢 9,000,000 litres 🍇 2,500 has.
🇪🇸 95% 🌐5%: -DE -AT -PT

VALDECACHO 2002 WHITE

GALICIA

DICOSTA NORTE BODEGAS CASTILLO SAN DAMIÁN

Dompiñor, s/n
27715 Ribadeo (Lugo)
☎: 982 128 900 - Fax: 982 128 641
discosta@hotmail.com

Established: 1978
🛢 1,000,000 litres 🇪🇸 99% 🌐1%

CASTILLO DE SAN DAMIAN WHITE
HOJA DORADA WHITE
CASABELLA WHITE
FONTEMIÑA WHITE
CASTILLO DE SAN DAMIÁN ROSÉ
HOJA DORADA ROSÉ
CASABELLA ROSÉ
CASTILLO DE SAN DAMIAN RED
HOJA DORADA RED
CASABELLA RED
FONTEMIÑA RED

Bodegas MARQUÉS DE VIZHOJA

Finca La Moreira
36430 Arbo (Pontevedra)
☎: 986 665 825 - Fax: 986 665 960
marquesdevizhoja.@marquesdevizhoja.com
www.marquesdevizhoja.com

Established: 1966
🛢 1,125,000 litres 🍇 35 has.

🇪🇸 80% 🌐20%: -DE -IT -CH -UK -BE -JP -PR -US -AD

MARQUÉS DE VIZHOJA 2004 WHITE

83 Straw-coloured. Intense aroma, fruit and white flowers, exotic nuances, ripe, varietal. Fresh palate, white stone fruit, excellent citrus acidity, quite long.

LA RIOJA

FAUSTINO GARCÍA MARTÍNEZ

Aguadilla 5,
26511 El Villar de Arnedo (La Rioja)
☎: 941 159 036 - Fax: 941 159 210

Established: 1960
🛢 2,000,000 litres 🇪🇸 95%
🌐5%: -DE -NL -ID

FAUSTINO GARCÍA MARTÍNEZ WHITE
DON ORTUÑO WHITE
FAUSTINO GARCÍA MARTÍNEZ ROSÉ
DON ORTUÑO ROSÉ
FAUSTINO GARCÍA MARTÍNEZ RED
DON ORTUÑO AROMATIZADO DULCE

Hermanos GÓMEZ AMELIVIA

Carretera Pancorbo-Camino de los Lirios
26214 Cuzcurrita del Rio Tirón (La Rioja)
☎: 941 328 018 - Fax: 941 328 019
amelivia@fer.es
www.fer.es/amelivia

Established: 1998
🌐 1,200 🛢 2,000,000 litres 🍇 26 has.
🇪🇸 50% 🌐50%: -CH -DE -PT -MX

BUENAVENTURA MACABEO 2003 WHITE
BUENAVENTURA CHARDONNAY 2003 WHITE
LOS LIRIOS MACABEO 2003 WHITE
BUENAVENTURA GARNACHA 2003 ROSÉ
LOS LIRIOS TEMPRANILLO 2002 RED
LOS LIRIOS GARNACHA 2003 RED
BUENAVENTURA TEMPRANILLO 1999
CRIANZA RED
BUENAVENTURA CABERNET SAUVIGNON
1999 CRIANZA RED
BUENAVENTURA MERLOT 1999 CRIANZA
RED
BUENAVENTURA SYRAH 1999 CRIANZA RED
BUENAVENTURA MERLOT MAGNUM 1999
CRIANZA RED
BUENAVENTURA MERLOT MAGNUM 2000
CRIANZA RED
BUENAVENTURA SYRAH 2000 CRIANZA RED
BUENAVENTURA MERLOT 2000 CRIANZA
RED
BUENAVENTURA CABERNET SAUVIGNON
2000 CRIANZA RED
BUENAVENTURA TEMPRANILLO 2000
CRIANZA RED
BUENAVENTURA TEMPRANILLO 1999
RESERVA RED
BUENAVENTURA CABERNET SAUVIGNON
1999 RESERVA RED
BUENAVENTURA MERLOT 1999 RESERVA
RED
BUENAVENTURA SYRAH 1999 RESERVA RED
BUENAVENTURA MERLOT MAGNUM 1999
RESERVA RED
BUENAVENTURA MERLOT MAGNUM 2000
RESERVA RED
BUENAVENTURA SYRAH 2000 RESERVA RED
BUENAVENTURA MERLOT 2000 RESERVA
RED
BUENAVENTURA CABERNET SAUVIGNON
2000 RESERVA RED
BUENAVENTURA TEMPRANILLO 2000
RESERVA RED

MADRID

FORO DE FORMACIÓN Y CULTURA DEL VINO

Alcalá, 177 - 6ºA
28009 Madrid
☎: 918 598 737

AMISTAD AMICUM COUPAGE 2002

83 Garnet red cherry. Powerful aroma, rich in very ripe fruit (jammy plums, foresty hints and terroir). Slightly fleshy palate, flavourful although slightly rustic tannins, warm and persistent.

VIÑEDOS DE SAN MARTÍN

Castelló, 20, 4º D
28001 Madrid
☎: 915 770 005 - Fax: 915 776 527

MONTAZO 2002 RED
garnacha, cariñena, otras

91 Quite dark cherry. Powerful aroma, rich in mineral and fruit expression with a toasty hint of oak, fine and elegant. Round, mineral, flavourful palate, complex and flavourful with oily but persistent tannins and a spirituous retronasal effect.

MURCIA

Bodegas CASTAÑO

Carretera Fuentealamo, 3
30510 Yecla (Murcia)
☎: 968 791 115 - Fax: 968 791 900
info@bodegascastano.com
www.bodegascastano.com
Established: 1950
🛢 2,000 🛢 4,000,000 litres 🍇 400 has.
🍷 30% 🍇70%: -DE -NL -CH -UK -DK -JP -MX -SE -CA -US -PL -AT -DK

CASA CISCA 2002 RED
100% monastrell

93 Intense cherry with a purplish edge. Aroma of not overly ripe fresh black fruit with fine notes of oak and subtle hints of minerals (dry earth). Boca lleno, Full, original, original, flavourful and spirituous palate with sweet yet abundant tannins and toasty fine oak in the retronasal passage.

VALENCIA

Vins del COMTAT

Alcudia, 104
03820 Concentaina (Alicante)
☎: 651 487 694 - Fax: 965 592 307
vinsdelcomtat@wanadoo.es
www.perso.wanadoo.es/vinsdelcomtat
Established: 1996
🛢 300 🛢 150,000 litres 🍇 13 has.
🍷 80% 🍇20%: -UE

VERDEVAL ESPECIAL 2003 ROBLE WHITE SECO
VERDEVAL 2003 WHITE SECO
CRISTAL - L 2003 WHITE

PENYA CADIELLA 2001 OAK AGED RED
MONTCABRER CABERNET SAUVIGNON
 2001 OAK AGED RED
PENYA CADIELLA SELECCIÓ 2002 OAK
 AGED RED
MOSCATEL ESPECIAL 2002 DULCE

PAGO DE THARSYS

Carretera Nacional III, Km 278, 5
46340 Requena (Valencia)
☎: 962 303 354 - Fax: 962 329 000
pagodetharsys@pagodetharsys.com
www.pagodetharsys.com

Established: 2002
⊕ 100 ▤ 130,000 litres ❦ 12 has.
⬤ 70% ⊕30%: -CH -US -DE -UK

PAGO DE THARSYS VENDIMIA NOCTURNA
2003 WHITE
albariño, godello

87 Straw-coloured with a golden hue.
Expressive aroma with fresh fruit, sun-drenched
skins and fine, very clean herbaceous hints.
Fruity, fresh palate with pleasant bitter notes,
slightly oily with excellent acidity and a generous finish (slightly mineral).

THE PODIUM

THE BEST WINES FROM EACH REGION

THE BEST BUYS

WINEMAKING GROUPS

WINE-PRODUCING REGIONS BY
AUTONOMOUS COMMUNITY

THE PODIUM

There are 64 more wines than last year in the Olympus of wines in the frenetic race by the large number of bodegas in the search for 90 points. They make up a large pyramid of 292 wines, many of which have joined for the first time, while others have changed positions.

Rioja, the Rioja which sometimes surprises us and at times disappoints us, reigns supreme with 45 wines, while Ribera del Duero is far behind with only 25 wines. It is also significant that Castilla and Castilla-Leon between them have no fewer than 18 wines on the podium. The most notable absentee is Pingus, who did not want to take the risk with the 2002 vintage, and being aware that they could lose positions used their stock for their second brand of wine, Flor de Pingus, which on this occasion is knocking at the door of the best.

As far as Generoso wines go, Jerez was even more reluctant and sluggish in sending in samples than usual, even after being encouraged to do so by their Regulatory Council. The fact that they are the wines which proportionally have the best scores in the Guide does not seem to interest them at all. There are even absentees among wines which were on the podium in previous years. There seems to be a general disillusionment about the future of Generoso wines. A sector in which the sales of the most commercial brands are dropping, whilst the relics are growing: the most carefully looked after old wines typical of their history. The classic wines of Andalusia need new blood in their laboratories and vineyards.

FINE TABLE WINE

98 VEGA SICILIA RESERVA ESPECIAL RED (81, 85 AND 96 VINTAGES)
RIBERA DEL DUERO

The best kept 'secret' of the house. They still retain the old Spanish tradition of blending vintages and the long maturations of the old Reservas. And moreover, Vega Sicilia can afford the luxury of stating the different vintages used in the blends. Just when we thought that the new style of more concentrated reds, with new wood and ripe fruit was unbeatable, this exceptional classic wine appeared exhibiting floral nuances that are only reserved for the great vintages. At any event, this wine combines the selection and the blending of the best wines of Vega Sicilia. Therefore, it should be the best.

98 VIÑA EL PISÓN 2002 RED
RIOJA

This elegant red has always been a wine with a future. It struggles to come alive in the bottle and therefore its score rises after four months in bottle. Quite recently bottled, the bodega was on the verge

of not sending in the new vintages as they were afraid they would get the low score of the previous year's vintage (90 points) which we acknowledged a few months later when we reviewed the wine for GP magazine. However, surprisingly this vintage is in its prime. Is the vintage not showing its full expression as a premonition of its short life? What impressed me most was the complexity and fineness of certain floral hints the wine retained for the seven hours the tasting session lasted.

97 L'ERMITA 2002 RED
PRIORAT

Nothing, not even the bad weather has been able to oust this wine from the top positions. Only the hints of minerals remind us it is a Priorat, the rest is entirely another case. The almost impossible objective of combining elegance and strength which the great oenologists yearn for these days is palpable in this wine. Alvaro Palacios is an expert in this field. His ancestors from Rioja were known for their 'fine wines' a reputation which they treasured. And this seems evident in this earthy wine where the mountainside Garnacha reign supreme.

97 VEGA SICILIA ÚNICO 1994 RED
RIBERA DEL DUERO

The vintages of Vega Sicilia are in another league when we compare them to those of the DO. Even though 1994 was a good year, the exquisite work of this company achieves miracles in a continuous battle with the climate. It has two points more than the 1991 vintage, the last one on the market, but the result is the same: this legendary wine is always on the podium.

96 AMANCIO 2001 RED ✪
RIOJA

The Eguren brothers have a hatful of surprises and never fail to surprise one. It is an oenological workshop where Termanthia, Numanthia, San Vicente, El Bosque and now Amancio alternate, the result of their untiring search for perfection. Their wines are profound, full of complex fruit and fine wood thanks to their dedication and tenacity.

96 AURUS 2000 RED
RIOJA

It is clear that this wine is a 'long distance' wine. It has always had a lower score than Calvario due to its slow evolution and arriving at the Guide without having had time to reveal its charms. An example of this is the 2000 vintage which got 90 points in the 2004 edition. A year later (when the bodega had sold out their stock) it got no less than 96 points, with the hope that the few bottles that remain on the market 'benefit' from this score; the best score ever for this wine from Rioja.

New wines on the market are marked with a ✪

1023

96 DALMAU 2000 RED
RIOJA

This heterodox wine from the Bodegas Marqués de Murrieta is climbing up the list point by point. The breath of fresh air and the courage of the oenologist María Vargas has converted this red wine into a true depiction of the Ygay terroir. It is the sum of the values of the grape, the soil and meticulous winemaking. They have retained many of the old Rioja ageing techniques but without any of the defects which in the past were considered typical of Riojan wines.

95 AURUS 2001 RED
RIOJA

Another wine the winemaker was hesitant to send us due to the wine's slow evolution and it not being ready for sampling. Will the 2001 vintage be the one to show off its charms sooner? An Aurus has never had such a high score on just being released.

95 CALCHETAS 2001 RED ✪
NAVARRA

This is the first time that a red wine from Navarra has had such a high score. The only other bodega I can think of would be Magaña, whose owner was more attached to the art of ageing than aging on the lees and without racking. The best of its kind, so much so that people not associated with it such as Quim Vila or Xavier Coppel (Primo Palatum) from France chose this way of making wines which in no way resembles theirs.

95 CIRSION 2001 RED
RIOJA

This is another wine which is on the podium again, but with a better score than the 92 points it received in the 2004 edition. This is a perfect example of grape selection and work in the bodega. The 'artistic' culmination of the old Riojan tradition of making a wine from the sum of various model vineyards.

95 CLOS D'AGON 2003 WHITE
CATALUNYA

This is the first white to achieve this score. A wine filled to the brim with aromatic sensations as well as taste sensations. A typical Rhone wine made from Rousanne, Marsanne and Viognier varieties. Never has a multi-varietal wine expressed so many nuances linked to the different varieties. An extraordinary wine which could only be the creation of Peter Sisseck. It is his white 'Pingus'

95 CLOS MARTINET 2001 RED
PRIORAT

This is another red that has 'grown' in the bottle. From 91 points in the 2004 edition to 95 points in this edition. The 2002 vintage has not developed yet. It is a symphony of Garnacha, Syrah, Cariñena and Cabernet Sauvignon that needs more time to break in than the majority of the Priorat wines in which Garnacha usually makes up more than 70%.

95 DOMINIO DE ATAUTA LLANOS ✪
DEL ALMENDRO 2002 RED
RIBERA DEL DUERO

The most 'hidden' vineyards in Ribera del Duero. In the province of Soria, over 900m above sea level, but with a valley micro-climate, this miracle comes from the soil and the climate. Betrand Sourdais chose this small plot because of the connection with nature, herbs and brush. A prodigy of minerals which does not identify it with any other in use.

95 FINCA GARBET DEL CASTILLO DE ✪
PERELADA 2001 RED
EMPORDÁ - COSTA BRAVA

At last, and with the permission of the north wind, this slatey vineyard which lies on the Mediterranean Sea and a stone's throw away from the border has borne fruit. An explosion of the mineral Syrah with the tannins of the Cabernet, with a liqueurish touch due to its high alcohol content and assembled with hints of herbs and black fruit. A superb wine.

95 PESUS 2001 RED
RIBERA DEL DUERO

As we stated in the previous guide (94 points), it needed more time in bottle to reach the Olympic 95 points and more. This wine will still go a long way. The Sastre Brothers have culminated their work by breaking in a wine made from Tempranillo accompanied by Merlot and Cabernet Sauvignon. Few people will argue about the superb level of this wine venerated by the great connoisseurs of the Ribera.

95 PINTIA 2002 RED
TORO

From the 2001 Alquiriz to the 2002 Pintia. A cooler year in Toro is a blessing when they are able to maintain the expression of fruit within the heavy ripening of the region. After many years of experimenting which culminated in the previous vintage, Vega Sicilia has become famous with this Pintia full of mineral expression and black fruit. Xavier Ausàs has worked with some liberty but within the limits of an exceptionally fast ripening which irremissibly leads to the robust Toro which must be avoided.

95 QUINTA SARDONIA 2002 RED ✪
RIBERA DEL DUERO

Daniel Pita, the owner of El Regajal de Aranjuez, came and conquered. With 18 hectares of vineyards and 90 barrels he has obtained 95 points at the hands of Peter Sisseck who has given his blessing to this wine from Sardón de Duero. A curious conglomeration for a fine red, Cabernet Sauvignon, Merlot, Syrah, Petit Verdot and Malbec. An extraordinary display of originality and character.

95 SOT LEFRIEC 2001 RED
PENEDÈS

Three consecutive vintages with the same score. The tastings were almost identical, tasted on the same dates. This is possibly as a result of making a small amount – barely 5,000 bottles - which enables the selection of the best, even though the vintages are different. It is not that difficult as the best is almost always identical. Only if the owners change the varietal composition - Cabernet Sauvignon, Merlot and Cariñena – could it mean a change of style, but they would run the risk of making an inferior quality wine.

95 VALBUENA 5º 2000 RED
RIBERA DEL DUERO

Only one point less shows the slight difference between this vintage and the previous one which was better. The selection and the care taken in the vineyards that Vega Sicilia pride themselves on dampens the differences in vintages and this wine seems to have a little more secretive fruit expression if we compare it to Valbuena 99. Except for very unusual cases, this wine always gets similar points which proves it is great wine.

94 POINTS

Finca Sandoval 2002 has moved up from the 90 points it received for the previous vintage. Even though the 2002 vintage has been sold out by the bodega, a few bottles may still be found at restaurants or in shops which may benefit from this excellent rating. Another development is the ascent of **Reserva Real** de Torres, from the 91 points of the 2000 vintage. **Pagos Viejos** paid for the wine's harshness when we tasted the wine in July 2003 with 88 points, to the 2002 vintage which is complete and rich. **Finca Dofi** is reaching the Olympus point by point and catching up with its famous brother L'Ermita. It is more reasonably priced and there are more bottles available. **Finca Terrerazo**, Mustiguillo's second wine, has surpassed its elder brother Quincha Corral by one point, thanks to the greater fruit expression which could be due to less Bobal and more Tempranillo marrying exceptionally well with the oak and the complexity from a larger percentage of Cabernet. **Aalto PS** gains points as a result of a better vintage. **Dominio de Tares Cepas Viejas 2002** continues its ascent, at least in our guide, which makes it the leading wine in Bierzo. **Valtosca 2003** has the same score as the 2001 vintage. **Malleolus de Valderramiro 2002** gains a point with a vintage which in theory is inferior to the previous one. The excellent **Olivares 2000** is completely different to the 2001 vintage which appeared in the 2004 Guide. This sweet wine expresses like no other wine the qualities of Monastrell when the harvest is delayed.

AALTO PS 2001 OAK AGED R
RIBERA DEL DUERO
ALTOS DE LANZAGA 2002 OAK AGED RED
RIOJA
ARTADI PAGOS VIEJOS 2002 OAK AGED RED
RIOJA
CALVARIO 2001 CRIANZA RED
RIOJA
CALVARIO 2002 CRIANZA RED
RIOJA

DOMINIO DE TARES CEPAS VIEJAS 2002 OAK AGED RED
BIERZO.
EL BUGADER 2001 CRIANZA RED
MONTSANT
FINCA DOFÍ 2002 CRIANZA RED
PRIORAT
FINCA SANDOVAL 2002 RED
MANCHUELA
FINCA TERRERAZO 2001 OAK AGED RED
VT EL TERRERAZO
LEDA VIÑAS VIEJAS 2002 RED
VT CASTILLA Y LEÓN
MALLEOLUS DE VALDERRAMIRO 2002 OAK AGED RED
RIBERA DEL DUERO
RESERVA REAL 2000 RED
PENEDÈS
VALTOSCA 2003 OAK AGED RED
JUMILLA

93 POINTS

Sitio del Palo de Bienvenida 2002 is a new wine from Toro made by the enterprising Cesar Muñoz (Leda). Thermantia is in this group but with two points less. The 2002 vintage could not beat its predecessor. **MC 2002** de Marqués de Cáceres is a welcome surprise as the bodega put all its efforts into Gaudium. There is a better fruit expression and breadth in this red. **Duratón Syrah 2002** has risen spectacularly, as well as **Dueto 2002** of the Quintana Bodegas in Cuenca. Roda I 2001 has achieved the maximum score in its history due to a good harvest. **Viognier 2003** of Venta D'Aubert is excellent. A resounding success by the Julia Roch bodega from Jumilla which has four wines with a score in the nineties. **Las Gravas 2001** and **Valtosca 2002** are placed in this section with 93 points. Finally, the surprise of a Petit Verdot from **Arrayán 2003**, the best wine ever produced by this bodega from Toledo and a first for the restaurant-owner Adolfo with his **Pago del Ama Syrah 2002**, a micro-wine which is practically all exported to the United States.

À.N. SON NEGRE 2001 CRIANZA RED
VT ILLES BALEARS
ABADAL SELECCIÓ 2001 OAK AGED RED
PLA DEL BAGES
ARO 2001 RED
RIOJA
ARRAYÁN PETIT VERDOT 2003 OAK AGED RED
MÉNTRIDA
ARRAYÁN SYRAH 2002 RED
MÉNTRIDA
BLECUA 2001 RED
SOMONTANO
CASA CASTILLO PIE FRANCO 2000 OAK AGED RED
JUMILLA
CASA CISCA 2002 RED
OTHER REGIONS
CASTILLO DE PERELADA EX EX 4 2001 RED ✪
EMPORDÀ - COSTA BRAVA
CLOS D'AGON 2001 OAK AGED RED
CATALUNYA
CONTADOR 2001 OAK AGED RED
RIOJA

New wines on the market are marked with a ✪

CHIVITE COLECCIÓN 125 2002 FERMENTADO EN
BARRICA WHITE
NAVARRA

CHIVITE COLLECTION 125 VENDIMIA TARDIA
2002 WHITE DULCE
NAVARRA

DUETO 2002 CRIANZA RED✪
VT CASTILLA

DURATÓN SYRAH 2002 ROBLE RED
VT CASTILLA Y LEÓN

ENATE RESERVA ESPECIAL 2000 RESERVA RED
SOMONTANO

JANÉ VENTURA 'MAS VILELLA' 2001 CRIANZA RED
PENEDÈS

LAN 2002 OAK AGED RED
RIOJA

LAS GRAVAS 2001 CRIANZA RED
JUMILLA

MATALLANA 2001 OAK AGED RED
RIBERA DEL DUERO

MATARROMERA PRESTIGIO 1998 RED
RIBERA DEL DUERO

MC MARQUÉS DE CÁCERES 2002 RED
RIOJA

PAGO DE LOS CAPELLANES PARCELA
EL PICÓN 1999 CRIANZA RED
RIBERA DEL DUERO

PAGO DEL AMA SYRAH 2001 OAK AGED RED
VT CASTILLA

PAGO DEL AMA SYRAH 2002 OAK AGED RED
VT CASTILLA

PAGO LA JARA 2002 ROBLE RED
TORO

QUINCHA CORRAL 2001 OAK AGED RED
VT EL TERRERAZO

RODA I 2001 RESERVA RED
RIOJA

SAN ROMÁN 2001 CRIANZA RED
TORO

SAN VICENTE 2001 OAK AGED RED
RIOJA

SITIO DE EL PALO BIENVENIDA 2002 RED✪
TORO

TERMANTHIA 2002 RED
TORO

TORRENT NEGRE 2001 OAK AGED RED
PLA I LLEVANT

TRASNOCHO 2001 RESERVA RED
RIOJA

VALTOSCA 2002 RED
JUMILLA

VENUS 2001 RED
MONTSANT

VIÑA SASTRE PAGO DE SANTA CRUZ 1999
GRAN RESERVA RED
RIBERA DEL DUERO

VENTA D'AUBERT VIOGNIER 2003 WHITE
BAJO ARAGÓN

92 POINTS

The most relevant new developments are Otazu with **Palacio de Otazu Reserva Especial 1999**, the improvement of **Valsacro Dioro 2001** in bottle and the ascent and incorporation of certain wines from Madrid such as **El Regajal 2002** and **Tagonius 2000** with other wines from Toledo such as **Zumaque de Broteas** from the untiring Ignacio de Miguel and the surprising **Pago del Ama Colección 2002**. **Emeritvs 2000** has improved in bottle over the last year. The 2001 vintage was being bottled at the moment of going to press. With 92 points, **Allende 2001** is no longer Miguel Ángel de Gregorio's second wine. It has gone up in points without going up in price; being able to produce 200,000 bottles at this fantastic level is a tribute to the oenologist. And finally, at this rate, Alejandro Fernández is going to surpass his legendary Pesqueras de Ribera with his **El Vínculo 2002** from La Mancha.

ALBARIÑO FILLABOA SELECCIÓN FINCA
MONTE ALTO 2002 WHITE
RÍAS BAIXAS

ALIÓN 2001 OAK AGED RED
RIBERA DEL DUERO

ALLENDE 2001 OAK AGED RED
RIOJA

ARRAYÁN SYRAH 2003 RED
MÉNTRIDA

BALTASAR GRACIÁN GARNACHA VIÑAS
VIEJAS 2002 OAK AGED RED
CALATAYUD

BARÓN DE CHIREL 1999 RESERVA RED
RIOJA

CASTA DIVA FONDILLÓN 15 AÑOS
OAK AGED DULCE
ALICANTE

DOMINIO DE ATAUTA LA MALA
2002 OAK AGED RED
RIBERA DEL DUERO

EL BOSQUE 2002 RED
RIOJA

EL REGAJAL SELECCIÓN ESPECIAL
2002 OAK AGED RED
VINOS DE MADRID

EL VÍNCULO 2002 ROBLE RED
LA MANCHA

ENRIQUE MENDOZA SANTA ROSA 1999
RESERVA RED
ALICANTE

FAGUS DE COTO DE HAYAS 2002 OAK AGED RED
CAMPO DE BORJA

FINCA L'ARGATA 2002 CRIANZA RED
MONTSANT

L'AVI ARRUFI 2002 OAK AGED RED
TERRA ALTA

LA MEJORADA 2001 ROBLE RED
CASTILLA Y LEÓN

LES ONES 2002 CRIANZA RED
PRIORAT

LUNA BEBERIDE 2000 CRIANZA RED
CASTILLA Y LEÓN

MADURESA 2000 RED
VALENCIA

MARQUÉS DE GRIÑÓN EMERITVS 2000
RESERVA RED
DOMINIO DE VALDEPUSA

MARQUÉS DE MURRIETA 2000 RESERVA RED
RIOJA

MONTEBACO SELECCIÓN ESPECIAL 2001 RED
RIBERA DEL DUERO

NAIADES 2003 FERMENTADO EN BARRICA WHITE
RUEDA

NONA 2002 FERMENTADO EN BARRICA WHITE
PRIORAT

NORA 2003 WHITE
RÍAS BAIXAS

PAGO DEL AMA COLECCIÓN 2002 RED
CASTILLA

PALACIO DE OTAZU RESERVA ESPECIAL 1999 RED
NAVARRA

REGINA VIDES 2001 ROBLE RED
RIBERA DEL DUERO

REMÍREZ DE GANUZA 2000 RESERVA RED
RIOJA

RODA I 2000 RESERVA RED
RIOJA

TAGONIUS GRAN VINO SELECCIÓN 2000 ROBLE RED
VINOS DE MADRID

TORCAS 2002 RED
NAVARRA

VALSACRO DIORO 2001 OAK AGED RED
RIOJA

ZUMAQUE DE BROTEAS 2001 RED
CASTILLA

91 POINTS

New wines such as **Qubél** from Madrid, **L'Angelet** from Utiel Requena, **Absis** from Parés Baltà or **Mestizaje** from Mustiguillo amongst others, liven up the podium. Bretón has gone from having a few hiccups in quality over the past few years to having a great vintage such as the 2001 in which **Alba de Bretón** and the Garnacha of **Pagos del Camino** have gone up with the previously praised Dominio de Conté. The matchless Emilio Rojo has placed its variety on the podium: their tenacity has paid off after masterfully managing the assembly of Torrontés.

1780 2000 RESERVA RED
COSTERS DEL SEGRE

ABADÍA RETUERTA PAGO VALDEBELLÓN 2000 OAK AGED RED
VT CASTILLA Y LEÓN

ABEL MENDOZA SELECCIÓN PERSONAL 2001 RED
RIOJA

ABSIS 2000 RESERVA RED ✪
PENEDÈS

AGUSTÍ TORELLÓ MATA MAGNUM 1998 GRAN RESERVA BRUT NATURE
CAVA

ALBA DE BRETÓN 2001 RESERVA RED
RIOJA

ALTAR 1999 RESERVA ESPECIAL RED ✪
NAVARRA

ÀN 2001 CRIANZA RED
VT ILLES BALEARS

ÁNDALUS PETIT VERDOT 2001 RED
OTHER REGIONS

BASA 2003 WHITE
RUEDA

BORIÀ SUMARROCA 2001 RED✪
PENEDÈS

BROJAL 2000 RESERVA RED✪
NAVARRA

CAPRICHO DE GOYA VINO DE LICOR SWEET
NAVARRA

CARE 2001 BAREL AGED RED
CARIÑENA

CASTILLO DE PERELADA FINCA MALAVEÏNA 2001 RED
EMPORDÀ - COSTA BRAVA

CÉRVOLES SELECCIÓ EN VINYA 2001 RESERVA RED
COSTERS DEL SEGRE

CLOS MASET SELECCIÓN ESPECIAL 2000 CRIANZA RED
PENEDÈS

CLOS MOGADOR 2002 CRIANZA RED
PRIORAT

CLOS VALMAÑA 2001 CRIANZA RED
CATALUNYA

CONDE DE LA SALCEDA 2000 RESERVA RED
RIOJA

DÁVILA 2003 WHITE
RÍAS BAIXAS

DEHESA DEL CARRIZAL CABERNET SAUVIGNON 2001 OAK AGED RED
VT CASTILLA

DOLÇ DE MENDOZA 2001 RED DULCE
ALICANTE

EMILIO ROJO 2003 WHITE
RIBEIRO

ÈTIM SELECTION SYRAH 2001 OAK AGED RED
MONTSANT

FÉLIX CALLEJO SELECCIÓN VIÑEDOS DE LA FAMILIA 2002 OAK AGED RED
RIBERA DEL DUERO

FLOR DE PRIMAVERA 2001 ROBLE RED
MONTSANT

GAUDIUM GRAN VINO 1998 RED
RIOJA

GEOL 2003 OAK AGED RED ✪
COSTERS DEL SEGRE

GLORIA DE OSTATU 2002 ROBLE RED
RIOJA

HACIENDA MONASTERIO ESPECIAL 1998 RESERVA RED
RIBERA DEL DUERO

HUMBOLDT 2001 OAK AGED RED DULCE
TACORONTE-ACENTEJO

JANE VENTURA 'MAS VILELLA' 2000 CRIANZA RED
PENEDÈS

JAUME CODORNÍU MAGNUM 450 ANIVERSARIO BRUT
CAVA

JAVIER ASENSIO 2000 RESERVA RED
NAVARRA

JOSÉ PARIENTE 2003 WHITE
RUEDA

L'ANGELET 2001 CRIANZA RED
UTIEL-REQUENA

LA CUEVA DEL CONTADOR 2002 OAK AGED RED
RIOJA

LA GARONA 2001 CRIANZA RED✪
TORO

LUSCO 2003 WHITE
RÍAS BAIXAS

New wines on the market are marked with a ✪

MARQUÉS DE MURRIETA 1999 RESERVA RED
RIOJA

MARQUÉS DE VARGAS HACIENDA PRADOLAGAR 2001 RESERVA RED
RIOJA

MAS LA PLANA 2000 OAK AGED RED
PENEDÈS

MAS ROIG 2001 CRIANZA RED
MONTSANT

MESTIZAJE 2002 OAK AGED RED
VT EL TERRERAZO

MIL.LENNIUM 2001 RED
TERRA ALTA

MONTAZO 2002 RED
OTHER REGIONS

MONTSALVAT 2001 RED
PRIORAT

NEO PUNTA ESENCIA 2001 OAK AGED RED ✪
RIBERA DEL DUERO

OLIVARES 2000 RED DULCE
JUMILLA

PAGOS DEL CAMINO 2001 RED
RIOJA

QUBÉL 2001 CRIANZA RED
VINOS DE MADRID

REMELLURI 2002 WHITE
RIOJA

SED DE CANÁ 2001 RED✪
RIBERA DEL DUERO

SIGNAT RESERVA IMPERIAL BRUT
CAVA

TIERRAS DE LUNA 2000 OAK AGED RED
VT CASTILLA Y LEÓN

VALLEGARCÍA CABERNET AND MERLOT 2001 RED✪
VT CASTILLA

VALLEGARCÍA VIOGNIER 2002 FERMENTADO EN BARRICA WHITE
VT CASTILLA

VENTA D'AUBERT 2003 FERMENTADO EN BARRICA WHITE
VT BAJO ARAGÓN

VIÑA AL LADO DE LA CASA 2002 RED
YECLA

VIÑA IZADI EXPRESIÓN 2000 ROBLE RED
RIOJA

90 POINTS

Torre Muga is on the podium due to the 2001 harvest after a few years absence. Valencia with **Maduresa 2001 and the 2002** of Pablo Calatayud is a pleasant surprise. A newcomer is the white wine Montsant **Étim Vereda Tardana 2002**, a 100% white *Garnacha*. On the top are **Al lado and Arriba dela Casa** from the wine cellar of the ineffable Quim Vila who makes the selections at Bodegas Castaño. The flamboyant **Pagos de Viña Real 2001** from the new and much spoken about Cyne bodega from Alavés just made it.

AALTO 2001 OAK AGED RED
RIBERA DEL DUERO

ABEL MENDOZA SELECCIÓN PERSONAL 2002 CRIANZA RED
RIOJA

ABELLARS 2002 CRIANZA RED✪
PRIORAT

ALBARIÑO FILLABOA 2002 FERMENTADO EN BARRICA WHITE
RÍAS BAIXAS

ALBARIÑO FILLABOA 2003 FERMENTADO EN BARRICA WHITE
RÍAS BAIXAS

ALBET I NOYA RESERVA MARTÍ 1998 RED
PENEDÈS

ALTOS DE LUZÓN 2002 CRIANZA RED
JUMILLA

ARRAYÁN CABERNET SAUVIGNON 2002 RED
MÉNTRIDA

CABRIDA 2001 OAK AGED RED
MONTSANT

CASTA DIVA COSECHA MIEL 2002 WHITE DULCE
ALICANTE

CASTA DIVA RESERVA REAL 2002 WHITE DULCE
ALICANTE

CASTAÑO COLECCIÓN 2002 OAK AGED RED
YECLA

CÉSAR PRÍNCIPE 2001 ROBLE RED
CIGALES

COLECCIÓN VIÑAS DEL VERO CHARDONNAY 2002 FERMENTADO EN BARRICA WHITE
SOMONTANO

COLECCIÓN VIÑAS DEL VERO ✪

LOS SASOS 2002 RED
SOMONTANO

CONTINO 'VIÑA DEL OLIVO' 2001 CRIANZA RED
RIOJA

CORULLÓN 2002 RED
BIERZO.

CHIVITE COLECCIÓN 125 2000 RESERVA RED
NAVARRA

DEHESA DEL CARRIZAL MV 2002 OAK AGED RED
VT CASTILLA

DETRÁS DE LA CASA TINTORERA 2002 RED✪
YECLA

DOIX 2001 CRIANZA RED
PRIORAT

DOMINIO DE VALDEPUSA CABERNET SAUVIGNON 2001 RED
DOMINIO DE VALDEPUSA

EL PUNTIDO 2001 OAK AGED RED ✪
RIOJA

EMBRUIX DE VALL-LLACH 2002 OAK AGED RED
PRIORAT

ENATE CABERNET SAUVIGNON 2000 RESERVA RED
SOMONTANO

ESTANCIA PIEDRA PAREDINAS 2000 CRIANZA RED
TORO

ÈTIM VEREMA TARDANA 2002 WHITE DULCE
MONTSANT

FINCA LA COLINA 2003 WHITE
RUEDA

FINCA SOBREÑO SELECCIÓN ESPECIAL 1999 OAK AGED RED
TORO

GAUDIUM GRAN VINO 1996 RESERVA RED
RIOJA

GRAMONA COLECCIÓN DE ARTE MILENIO GRAN RESERVA BRUT NATURE
CAVA

GRAMONA GRA A GRA 2001 WHITE DULCE NATURAL
PENEDÈS

GRAN ARZUAGA 2002 OAK AGED RED
RIBERA DEL DUERO

GRAN CLAUSTRO 2000 OAK AGED RED
EMPORDÁ - COSTA BRAVA

GRAN CLAUSTRO DE CASTILLO DE PERELADA 2001 RESERVA RED
EMPORDÁ - COSTA BRAVA

GRAN FEUDO 2003 WHITE DULCE
NAVARRA

HACIENDA MONASTERIO 2000 RESERVA ESPECIAL RED
RIBERA DEL DUERO

IDOIA NEGRE 2003 FERMENTADO EN BARRICA RED
CATALUNYA

JAVIER ASENSIO 2000 CRIANZA RED
NAVARRA

L'O DE L'ORIGAN BRUT NATURE ✪
CAVA

LIBRANZA 2002 ROBLE RED
TORO

MADURESA 2001 RED
VALENCIA

MADURESA 2002 RED
VALENCIA

MANO A MANO 2003 ROBLE RED✪
LA MANCHA

MANU VINO DE AUTOR 2001 CRIANZA RED
VINOS DE MADRID

MARBORÉ 2001 CRIANZA RED
SOMONTANO

MARQUÉS DE CÁCERES 1995 GRAN RESERVA RED
RIOJA

MARQUÉS DE VARGAS 2001 RESERVA PRIVADA RED
RIOJA

MAURO VENDIMIA SELECCIONADA 2000 OAK AGED RED
CASTILLA Y LEÓN

MISTELA JOSEFINA PIÑOL 2003 VINO DE LICOR WHITE
TERRA ALTA

MISTELA JOSEFINA PIÑOL 2003 VINO DE LICOR RED
TERRA ALTA

MOLINO REAL 2002 WHITE DULCE
MÁLAGA Y SIERRAS DE MÁLAGA

MONTECILLO SELECCIÓN ESPECIAL 1982 GRAN RESERVA RED
RIOJA

NAIA 2003 WHITE
RUEDA

NEBRO 2001 RED✪
RIBERA DEL DUERO

NUESTRA SEÑORA DEL PORTAL 2003 OAK AGED RED
TERRA ALTA

ODYSSEUS 2001 OAK AGED RED
PRIORAT

ODYSSEUS R 2003 ROSÉ
PRIORAT

OLIVER CONTI 2000 RED
EMPORDÁ - COSTA BRAVA

PAGO DE LAS SOLANAS 2000 ROBLE RED
RIBERA DEL DUERO

PAGO DEL AMA COLECCIÓN 2001 RED✪
VT CASTILLA

PAGOS DE VIÑA REAL 2001 ROBLE RED✪
RIOJA

PAISAJES VII 2001 RED
RIOJA

PAIXAR MENCÍA 2001 RED✪
BIERZO.

PASANAU FINCA LA PLANETA 2001 RED
PRIORAT

PAZO DE BARRANTES ALBARIÑO 2003 WHITE
RÍAS BAIXAS

PROPIEDAD HERENCIA REMONDO 2001 OAK AGED RED
RIOJA

SECASTILLA 2002 RED
SOMONTANO

SES FERRITGES 2001 RESERVA RED
PLA I LLEVANT

TORRE MUGA 2001 RED
RIOJA

TORRENT NEGRE SELECCIÓ PRIVADA 2001 OAK AGED RED
PLA I LLEVANT

TRASLANZAS 2001 OAK AGED RED
CIGALES

VALL-LLACH 2002 OAK AGED RED
PRIORATO

VEIGADARES 2003 FERMENTADO EN BARRICA WHITE
RÍAS BAIXAS

VERMILIÓN 1999 OAK AGED RED
OTHER REGIONS

VICENTE GANDÍA GENERACIÓN 1 2001 OAK AGED RED
UTIEL-REQUENA

VIÑA AL LADO DE LA CASA 2001 RED
YECLA

VIÑA MAGNAVIA 2003 WHITE✪
RIBEIRO

GENEROSO WINES

There are no surprises here except for the resurrection of 1830 of Alvear and the new PXs which have joined the podium, particularly Emilio Hidalgo's Santa Ana.

98 ALVEAR PX SOLERA 1830 ✪
MONTILLA-MORILES

This has returned to re-establish its position. It is not the very old and concentrated 1830 of a few years ago but a light and exceptionally refreshing wine from this solera which has gained in registers and the character of the Pedro Ximénez raisin- a trait that characterises the wines from this genre - complex from the ageing, cleaner and more emphatic. On the brink of perfection.

New wines on the market are marked with a ✪

97 SAN LEÓN MANZANILLA
JEREZ

What I look for in a Manzanilla is the saline and iodine taste one found before somebody in the marketing department invented the less aged and very light wine - watered down for my taste - which is now available. This wine is sold at fairs and when it has acquired a little more body, it is marketed. Argüeso has found the exact point where one minute more with the fleur would result in a 'dated Manzanilla'. With this in mind, he has created his San León, which in my opinion is not only the best Manzanilla in the world but as a wine with fleur; in other words, this also includes all Finos.

97 SANTA ANA SOLERA 1861 PEDRO XIMÉNEZ
JEREZ

With due respect to Osborne and its 30 year old rare sherry, this is the second best Pedro Ximénez from Jerez. Emilio Hilgado has made a dense, concentrated wine that is rich in registers from the raisins and the ageing without discarding the fact that it has been touched up as seems to be the custom within the Jerez framework, with an old oloroso to remove that overly sweet, and sometimes cloying, flavour.

95 OSBORNE RARE SHERRY SOLERA INDIA OLOROSO
JEREZ

The Rare range is becoming the most magnificent exhibition of the great 'holy of holies' or premium Jerez wines. This wine represents the tolerable limit of the most exquisite old Olorosos without acquiring the bitterness from long ageing in casks.

95 OSBORNE RARE SHERRY PX VORS 30 AÑOS
JEREZ

This is not as sublime or as concentrated as the PX that received the Critic's Prize two years ago. It is the best sample of a typical PX from the Jerez temple in which wise blending of old Oloroso hides the sticky sweetness of the Pedro Ximénez.

95 ROYAL AMBROSANTE PEDRO XIMÉNEZ
JEREZ

Sandeman had not produced treasures of this type in their quest to commercialise insignificant and easy wines. This new path chosen by the company should pay off and this PX is proof of this.

95 VENERABLE 30 AÑOS PEDRO XIMÉNEZ
JEREZ

This Pedro Ximénez de Domecq has always been on the podium with its score varying by just a point each time. Over the years the wine caramelises and goes darker until it reaches the culmination of all the relevant processes of the raisin and the toasted and the spiced notes from the solera.

BETWEEN 90 AND 94 POINTS.

Don **Guido**, a Pedro Ximénez from Williams & Humbert is new to the podium. The unwavering **Tio Pepe** remains faithful to its tradition. **La Ina** has gone down two points due to a slight move to more commercial tastes, although it has not lost the essence which for years has made it the best Fino in Spain. The Manzanilla Pasada **Pastrana** has climbed onto the podium going up two points due to a better definition of the fleur in its enveloping sensations. Alvear has improved its level overall. In the 2004 edition it only had one wine on the podium and this year there are four and the scores of some of the others have risen too. Another **Rare Sherry** from Osborne stands out, the Solera BC, an elegant and expressive Oloroso as well as the magnificent **Rare Sherry Palo Cortado**, an exceptional portrait of a complex and complicated wine.

94 POINTS

FINO QUINTA
JEREZ
OSBORNE RARE SHERRY SOLERA BC 200 OLOROSO
JEREZ

93 POINTS

CAPUCHINO VORS AMONTILLADO
JEREZ
DON GUIDO PEDRO XIMÉNEZ
JEREZ
FERNANDO DE CASTILLA PEDRO XIMÉNEZ
JEREZ
LA INA FINO
JEREZ
TÍO PEPE FINO
JEREZ

92 POINTS

DEL DUQUE AMONTILLADO
JEREZ
DON P.X. 1975 PEDRO XIMÉNEZ
MONTILLA-MORILES
NOÉ PEDRO XIMÉNEZ SOLERA
OSBORNE RARE SHERRY PALO CORTADO SEMIDULCE
JEREZ
TÍO MATEO FINO
JEREZ

91 POINTS

ALVEAR RESERVA 1998 PEDRO XIMÉNEZ
MONTILLA-MORILES
AMONTILLADO 51-1ª VORS
JEREZ
BOTAINA AMONTILLADO SOLERA
JEREZ
COQUINERO FINO AMONTILLADO
JEREZ

GRAN ORDEN PEDRO XIMÉNEZ
JEREZ

OÑANA AMONTILLADO
JEREZ

90 POINTS

ALVEAR FINO EN RAMA 2000
MONTILLA-MORILES

CAPATAZ FINO
MONTILLA-MORILES

COVADONGA OLOROSO
JEREZ

DELGADO 1874 AMONTILLADO NATURAL MUY VIEJO
MONTILLA-MORILES

DELGADO 1874 OLOROSO VIEJO
MONTILLA-MORILES

DON JUAN PEDRO XIMÉNEZ DULCE DE LICOR
MÁLAGA Y SIERRAS DE MÁLAGA

DON SALVADOR MOSCATEL DULCE DE LICOR
MÁLAGA Y SIERRAS DE MÁLAGA

DUQUESA PEDRO XIMÉNEZ
JEREZ

EL MAESTRO SIERRA VIEJÍSIMO PEDRO XIMÉNEZ
JEREZ

FERNANDO DE CASTILLA AMONTILLADO
JEREZ

GONZÁLEZ BYASS DE AÑADA 1978 OLOROSO
JEREZ

INOCENTE FINO
JEREZ

JARANA FINO
JEREZ

LA SACRISTÍA DE ROMATE OLOROSO
JEREZ

NPU AMONTILLADO
JEREZ

OSBORNE RARE SHERRY AMONTILLADO SECO
JEREZ

OXFORD 1970 PEDRO XIMÉNEZ
JEREZ

PALO CORTADO VIEJO HIDALGO V.O.R.S. 30 YEARS
JEREZ

PASTRANA MANZANILLA
JEREZ

PASTRANA AMONTILLADO
JEREZ

PEDRO ROMERO MANZANILLA
JEREZ

SIBARITA VORS OLOROSO VIEJO
JEREZ

New wines on the market are marked with a ✪

THE BEST WINES FROM EACH REGION

JUMILLA

LA GOMERA

LA MANCHA

83 FILL DEL TEMPS 2000 CRIANZA RED 834
83 VI DE LICOR 1919 VINO DE LICOR 835
83 VINDEMIA 2002 FERMENTADO EN
BARRICA WHITE 833
82 CLOT D'ENCÍS 2003 WHITE 839
82 MAS MONTASELL CABERNET SAUVIGNON 1998
RESERVA RED 837
82 POBLE VELL 2003 VINO DE LICOR WHITE 834
82 VINYES DEL GRAU SYRAH 2003 RED 836
81 ANTIC CASTELL GANDESA 2003 OAK AGED RED ..835
81 LAUREANO SERRES 2003 RED 836
81 MESSEROLS 2001 CRIANZA RED 835
81 MISTELA GANDESA VINO DE LICOR 835
81 VALLMAJOR 2002 RED 832
81 VALLMAJOR 2003 WHITE 832
81 VINYA PUBILLA 2003 OAK AGED RED 837
81 VIVERTELL 1999 RESERVA RED 832
80 MAS MONTASELL SYRAH 1999 RESERVA RED 837
80 MIRMIL-LÓ PARELLADA 2003 WHITE 833
80 PRIMICIA 2003 FERMENTADO EN BARRICA
WHITE 832
80 SERRA DE CAVALLS 2003 RED 839
80 VARVALL 2001 RESERVA RED 835
80 VILA-CLOSA 2003 RED 836
80 VINYA SEDOSA BLANC DE BLANCS WHITE 837

TORO

95 PINTIA 2002 OAK AGED RED 848
93 PAGO LA JARA 2002 ROBLE RED 850
93 SAN ROMÁN 2001 CRIANZA RED 848
93 SITIO DE EL PALO BIENVENIDA 2002 RED 842
93 TERMANTHIA 2002 RED 848
91 LA GARONA 2001 CRIANZA RED ....
90 ESTANCIA PIEDRA PAREDINAS 2000
CRIANZA RED 844
90 FINCA SOBREÑO SELECCIÓN ESPECIAL
1999 OAK AGED RED 850
90 LIBRANZA 2002 ROBLE RED 847
89 CYAN VENDIMIA SELECCIONADA 2001
RESERVA RED 846
89 GRAN ELÍAS MORA 2001 OAK AGED RED 843
89 NUMANTHIA 2002 RED 848
89 QUINTA DE LA QUIETUD 2002 OAK AGED RED ...849
89 SITIO DE EL PALO BIENVENIDA 2001 RED 842
88 CYAN 2001 CRIANZA RED 846
88 DEHESA GAGO 2003 RED 850
88 ESTANCIA PIEDRA SELECCIÓN 2000
CRIANZA RED 844
88 GIL LUNA 2000 OAK AGED RED 846
88 LIBERALIA CINCO 2001 RESERVA RED 847
88 LIBRANZA 2001 ROBLE RED 847
88 QUINTA DE LA QUIETUD 2001 CRIANZA RED 849
88 VIÑA PRÓDIGUS 1998 RESERVA RED 843
87 BAJOZ 1999 RESERVA RED 853
87 CYAN 2002 CRIANZA RED 846
87 DAMALISCO 1999 RESERVA RED 852
87 ELÍAS MORA 2001 CRIANZA RED 843
87 ESTANCIA PIEDRA 2001 CRIANZA RED 843
87 GAGO 2002 OAK AGED RED 850
87 GRAN BAJOZ 2000 ROBLE RED 853
87 GRAN COLEGIATA CAMPUS 2000 OAK
AGED RED 845
87 LIBERALIA CABEZA DE CUBA 2001 OAK
AGED RED 847
87 OROT 1998 RESERVA RED 851
87 PRIMERO 2003 RED 845
86 FINCA SOBREÑO 2001 CRIANZA RED 850
86 GRAN COLEGIATA ROBLE FRANCES 1999
OAK AGED RED 845
86 QUEBRANTARREJAS 2002 RED 850
86 SANTUARIO 1999 CRIANZA RED 847
86 STRABON 2000 CRIANZA RED 846
86 VAL VIADERO 2002 RED 852
86 VIÑA PRÓDIGUS 2001 ROBLE RED 843
86 WENCES 1999 RESERVA RED 852
86 WENCES 2001 RESERVA RED 853
85 BAJOZ 2000 CRIANZA RED 853
85 CAMPARRÓN 2001 CRIANZA RED 845
85 CAMPARRÓN SELECCIÓN 2000 ROBLE RED 845
85 DAMALISCO 2000 CRIANZA RED 852
85 FINCA SOBREÑO 2003 ROBLE RED 850
85 LIBERALIA TRES 2003 OAK AGED RED 847
85 OROT 2001 CRIANZA RED 851
85 REJADORADA 2001 CRIANZA RED 849

85 VAL VIADERO 2001 OAK AGED RED 852
85 VILLAESTER 2001 CRIANZA RED 854

UTIEL-REQUENA

91 L'ANGELET 2001 CRIANZA RED 863
90 VICENTE GANDÍA GENERACION 1 2001
OAK AGED RED 868
89 CERRO BERCIAL "EL PERDÍO" 2001 RED 869
89 CORONILLA 2001 CRIANZA RED 863
89 LAS TRES 2003 FERMENTADO EN
BARRICA WHITE 858
89 VEGA INFANTE 2003 FERMENTADO EN BARRICA
WHITE 866
88 LABOR DE ALMADEQUE 2001 CRIANZA RED 860
88 LABOR DE ALMADEQUE 2000 CRIANZA RED 860
87 LABOR DE ALMADEQUE 2002 CRIANZA RED 860
87 VEGA INFANTE 2003 OAK AGED RED 867
86 CORONILLA 2000 RESERVA RED 863
85 DOMINIO DEL ARENAL 1998 RESERVA RED 859
84 CASA DEL PINAR 2000 RESERVA RED 857
84 CASA PASTOR LAMBIES 2002 CRIANZA RED 857
84 CASTILLO DE REQUENA 2003 WHITE 864
84 HOYA DE CADENAS 1999 RESERVA RED 869
84 SANTERRA TEMPRANILLO 2002 RED 863
84 SYBARUS BOBAL 2002 FERMENTADO EN
BARRICA RED 866
83 BOBAL Y TEMPRANILLO 2002 RED 863
83 CASTILLO DE REQUENA 2002 OAK AGED RED 864
83 CEREMONIA 2000 OAK AGED RED 869
83 CERRO BERCIAL 2002 OAK AGED RED 869
83 LABOR DE ALMADEQUE RESERVA DE LA
FAMILIA 2001 RED..860
83 LAS CUATRO 2003 ROSÉ 858
83 MARTÍNEZ BERMELL MERLOT 2003 FERMENTADO
EN BARRICA RED 867
83 PASIEGO 2001 CRIANZA RED 858
83 VERTUS 2001 CRIANZA RED 861
82 BODEGAS IRANZO TEMPRANILLO SELECCIÓN
2002 RED 861
82 DOMINIO DEL ARENAL 1998 CRIANZA RED 859
82 DOMINIO DEL ARENAL SHIRAZ 2002 RED 859
82 EL PARREÑO BOBAL 1999 RESERVA RED 862
82 LOS CLAUSTROS DE TORRE ORIA 2001
CRIANZA RED 865
82 SANTERRA TEMPRANILLO 2003 RED 863
82 TORRE ORIA 1997 GRAN RESERVA RED 865
82 VERE DE ESTENAS 2001 CRIANZA RED 867
81 ARCAZ 1999 RESERVA RED 862
81 CAÑADA MAZÁN CABERNET SAUVIGNON
TEMPRANILLO 2002 CRIANZA RED...........................866
80 CAÑADA MAZÁN BOBAL 2003 ROSÉ 865
80 CASTILLO DE REQUENA 1999 RESERVA RED 864
80 CASTILLO DE REQUENA 2000 CRIANZA RED 864
80 CERRO BERCIAL 1999 RESERVA RED 869
80 EL PARREÑO 1999 CRIANZA RED 862
80 FINCA CAÑADA HONDA 2001 CRIANZA RED 861
80 HOYA DE CADENAS 2003 WHITE 868
80 HOYA DE CADENAS RESERVA PRIVADA 1999
RESERVA PRIVADA RED 869
80 LOS CLAUSTROS DE TORRE ORIA 1999
RESERVA RED 865
80 MIL AROMAS (DEL MEDITERRÁNEO) 2003
ROSÉ 868
80 PASIEGO 2000 RESERVA RED 858
80 SEÑORÍO DE ARCIS 2003 ROSÉ 864
80 SYBARUS 1996 RESERVA RED 866
80 SYBARUS SYRAH 2002 FERMENTADO EN
BARRICA RED 866
80 SYBARUS TARDANA 2003 WHITE 865
80 VERA DE ESTENAS 1999 RESERVA RED 867
80 VEREDA REAL 2003 FERMENTADO EN
BARRICA RED 868

VALDEORRAS

86 CASAL NOVO GODELLO 2003 WHITE 875
86 GUITIÁN GODELLO 2002 FERMENTADO
EN BARRICA WHITE 872
86 GUITIÁN GODELLO SOBRE LÍAS WHITE 872
85 CASAL NOVO MENCÍA 2003 RED 875
85 VALDESIL GODELLO 2002 WHITE 877
84 DON MARIO GODELLO 2003 WHITE 873
83 GALICIANO GODELLO DÍA 2003 WHITE 873
83 GALICIANO MENCÍA NOITE 2003 RED 873

83 GUITIÁN GODELLO 2003 WHITE 872
83 VIÑA GODEVAL 2003 WHITE................................873
82 GALGUEIRA 2003 RED.......................................873
82 JOAQUÍN REBOLLEDO OAK AGED RED...............874
82 SAMPAYOLO MENCÍA 2003 RED...........................876
82 TERRA LOMBARDA WHITE 876
82 VIÑA SOMOZA 2003 WHITE 877
81 AURENSIS GODELLO 2001 FERMENTADO
   EN BARRICA WHITE..874
81 VIÑA FORAL WHITE 874
81 VIÑA TREVAL 2003 WHITE 874
80 A SILVEIRA 2003 WHITE.....................................874
80 ALAN DE VAL MENCÍA 2003 RED.........................872
80 EREBO 2003 WHITE..872
80 LAVANDEIRA RED 876
80 RUCHEL GODELLO 2003 WHITE 875
80 RUCHEL GODELLO OAK AGED WHITE..................875
80 SAMPAYOLO GODELLO 2003 WHITE....................875
80 VIÑA FALCUEIRA RED 872
80 VIÑAREDO MENCÍA 2003 RED.............................876

VALDEPEÑAS

87 PALACIO DE IBOR 1998 RESERVA RED.................890
86 DIONISOS TEMPRANILLO 2003 RED 882
85 VIÑA ALBALI GRAN RESERVA DE LA FAMILIA
   1996 GRAN RESERVA RED..................................884
84 CASA DE LA VIÑA 2002 OAK AGED RED 881
84 VALDEAZOR 2000 CRIANZA RED 885
83 CASA DE LA VIÑA 2003 RED................................881
83 CASA DE LA VIÑA VENDIMIA SELECCIONADA
   2000 OAK AGED RED 881
83 DON AURELIO TEMPRANILLO 2003 RED 889
82 ÁGORA 2003 WHITE 880
82 MONTECLARO 1999 RESERVA RED......................881
82 MONTECLARO 2003 RED 881
82 TEJERUELAS CENCIBEL 2003 RED 887
82 VALDEAZOR TEMPRANILLO 1998 RESERVA RED ..885
82 VIÑA ALBALI 1998 RED..883
81 ÁGORA 1999 RESERVA RED.................................880
81 CALAR VIEJO 1999 CRIANZA RED 887
81 MARÍN PERONA 1999 RESERVA RED 887
81 MONTECRUZ TEMPRANILLO SELECCIÓN 2001
   ROBLE RED..886
81 NOCTURNO 1998 GRAN RESERVA RED................886
81 VEGAVAL PLATA 2001 CRIANZA RED 888
80 ÁGORA 2003 RED..880
80 ALBA DE LOS INFANTES 1998 RESERVA RED 885
80 ALBA DE LOS INFANTES 1999 CRIANZA RED........885
80 CALAR VIEJO 2000 CRIANZA RED 887
80 CASTILLO DE MUDELA 2002 RED.........................890
80 CORCOVO 1998 RESERVA RED............................885
80 CORCOVO 2000 CRIANZA RED..............................885
80 CORCOVO 2003 WHITE 884
80 DON AURELIO MACABEO 2003 WHITE 888
80 NOCTURNO 2000 RESERVA RED..........................885
80 VALDEAZOR MÁXIMA 2000 OAK AGED RED...........885
80 VEGAVAL PLATA 1999 RESERVA RED 888
80 VIÑA ALBALI 1996 GRAN RESERVA RED................884
80 VIÑA ALBALI 1999 RED RESERVA 883
80 VIÑA ALBALI AIRÉN 2003 WHITE..........................882
80 VIÑA ALBALI TEMPRANILLO 2003 RED 883

VALENCIA

92 MADURESA 2000 RED..902
90 MADURESA 2001 RED..902
90 MADURESA 2002 RED..902
89 HERETAT DE TAVERNERS GRACIANO 2000
   RESERVA RED..897
88 FOSC 2002 RED..896
88 LES ALCUSSES 2002 RED....................................901
86 HERETAT DE TAVERNERS 2000 RESERVA RED 897
85 CASTILLO DE ENGUERA 2003 CRIANZA RED 896
85 CHARDONNAY DANIEL BELDA 2003
   FERMENTADO EN BARRICA WHITE 897
85 EUSEBIO LA CASTA TEMPRANILLO 2000
   CRIANZA RED...897
85 L. OLAECHEA 2002 CRIANZA RED.......................900
85 MISTELA MOSCATEL TURÍS 2003 VINO DE LICOR 898
85 TORREVELLISCA MOSCATEL 2003 VINO DE
   LICOR DULCE...903
84 CASAMONFRARE MONASTRELL CABERNET
   SAUVIGNON 2003 OAK AGED RED 899
84 DANIEL BELDA 2000 CRIANZA RED.......................898

84 HERETAT DE TAVERNERS 2000 CRIANZA RED 896
84 LA CARTUJA VIACOELI MISTELA DULCE 895
84 LES ALCUSSES 2000 RED...................................902
84 NATURANE VINO DE LICOR DE MOSCATEL
   DULCE...895
84 RAFAEL CAMBRA UNO RED.................................901
84 SHIRAZ DANIEL BELDA 2001 RESERVA RED.........897
83 CASTILLO DE ENGUERA 2002 CRIANZA RED 896
83 DANIEL BELDA CABERNET SAUVIGNON 1995
RESERVA RED...898
83 DOMINIO LOS PINOS CUM LAUDE 2000
   CRIANZA RED...899
83 FUSTA NOVA 2003 MOSCATEL 904
83 LOS MONTEROS 2001 CRIANZA RED 900
83 MURVIEDRO 1998 RESERVA RED.........................900
83 RAFAEL CAMBRA DOS 2002 RED 901
83 VIÑA BÁRBARA 1999 CRIANZA RED 894
82 BÁRBARA GRIAL 2003 RED 894
82 BODEGAS FERNANDO FRANCÉS CHARDONNAY
   2002 FERMENTADO EN BARRICA WHITE 896
82 CASAMONFRARE MONASTRELL 2003 RED 899
82 EUSEBIO LA CASTA CABERNET SAUVIGNON
   2000 CRIANZA RED 897
82 LADERAS TEMPRANILLO RED 895
82 MARQUÉS DE CARO 2003 WHITE 894
82 MOSCATEL CASTILLO DE CHIVA VINO DE LICOR .904
82 TEMPRANILLO SELECCIÓN VARIETAL 2003 RED....896
82 VIÑA NORA 2001 CRIANZA RED............................895
81 DANIEL BELDA SELECCIÓN RESERVA RED...........898
81 MURVIEDRO 2003 WHITE 900
81 SEQUIOT TEMPRANILLO 2002 RED......................899
80 BÁRBARA GRIAL SÉMILLON 2003 WHITE 893
80 BODEGAS FERNANDO FRANCÉS TEMPRANILLO
   2002 RED...896
80 BONICAIRE SELECCIÓN VARIETAL 2003 RED 896
80 CASTELL DE VEZA CABERNET SAUVIGNON 2002 RED
898
80 DANIEL BELDA PONSALET 2003 RED 897
80 DANIEL BELDA TEMPRANILLO 1995
   RESERVA RED..898
80 LOS MONTEROS 2002 RED 900
80 MARQUÉS DE CARO 1999 RESERVA RED...............894
80 MURVIEDRO 2003 ROSÉ.....................................900
80 TORREVELLISCA 1998 RESERVA RED...................903
80 TORREVELLISCA 1999 RESERVA RED...................903
80 TORREVELLISCA 2003 ROSÉ 902
80 UVA D'OR MOSCATEL VINO DE LICOR 904

VALLE DE GÜIMAR

85 CONTIEMPO 2003 OAK AGED WHITE SECO 908
83 BRUMAS DE AYOSA 2003 WHITE 908
82 CONTIEMPO 2003 WHITE SEMI-SECO 908
81 BRUMAS DE AYOSA MALVASÍA 2003
   WHITE DULCE..908
80 BRUMAS DE AYOSA 2000 RESERVA
   BRUT NATURE...908
80 BRUMAS DE AYOSA 2001 BRUT NATURE 908
80 CONTIEMPO 2003 OAK AGED RED 908
80 CONTIEMPO MALVASÍA 2003 ROBLE
   WHITE SECO 908
80 TIZÓN DEL SUR 2003 RED 908
80 VIÑA MELOSAR 2003 WHITE SECO 910

VINOS DE MADRID

92 DIVO GRAN VINO DE GUARDA 2000
   OAK AGED RED...924
92 EL REGAJAL SELECCIÓN ESPECIAL 2002
   OAK AGED RED...927
92 TAGONIUS GRAN VINO SELECCIÓN 2000
   ROBLE RED..925
91 QUBÉL 2001 CRIANZA RED 921
90 DIVO GRAN VINO DE GUARDA 2002
   OAK AGED RED...923
89 MANU VINO DE AUTOR 2001 CRIANZA RED 926
89 GREGO 2001 CRIANZA RED.................................926
89 TAGONIUS 2000 CRIANZA RED.............................925
88 DEHESA NAVAYUNCOSA 2002 OAK AGED RED 921
88 FÉLIX MARTÍNEZ CEPAS VIEJAS 1999
   RESERVA RED..926
88 LUIS SAAVEDRA 2002 RED..................................922
87 PUERTA DE ALCALÁ 2000 RESERVA RED..............926
86 ASIDO VINO DE GUARDA 2002 RED 924
86 TAGONIUS 2002 ROBLE RED 924

86 VIÑA BOSQUERA 2002 OAK AGED RED.............919
85 GREGO 2003 ROBLE RED 926
85 VALLE DEL SOL "PREMIUM" 2001 RED 925
85 VIÑA BOSQUERA 2003 RED 919
85 VIÑA REY "70 BARRICAS" 2003 OAK AGED RED ...919
84 1434 TEMPRANILLO 2003 CRIANZA RED 919
84 ALMA DE VALDEGUERRA 2003 RED 926
84 CORUCHO ALBILLO-MOSCATEL 2002
FERMENTADO EN BARRICA WHITE 922
84 DUÁN 2003 RED 923
84 LACUNA 2001 CRIANZA RED 926
84 MAÍN 2001 CRIANZA RED 922
84 QUBÉL 2002 OAK AGED RED 921
84 QVOD 1 GARNACHA ROSÉ 919
83 VIÑA MAÍN 2003 RED 922
83 VIÑA REY TEMPRANILLO 2003 RED 919
82 JESÚS DÍAZ 2003 ROSÉ 921
82 PUERTA DE ALCALÁ 2000 CRIANZA RED 926
82 SEÑORÍO DE MORATE GRAN SELECCIÓN 1999
RESERVA RED 923
81 PUERTA DE ALCALÁ 2000 RED 925
81 PUERTA DEL SOL VARIETALES 2002
ROBLE WHITE 926
81 ANTINOS 2003 WHITE 925
80 HEREDAD TORRESANO 2001 CRIANZA RED 921
80 JESÚS DÍAZ 2003 RED 921
80 LOS CAMINILLOS 2003 RED 920
80 PUERTA DEL SOL TEMPRANILLO 2000
CRIANZA RED 926
80 SEÑORÍO DE MORATE GRAN SELECCIÓN 2000
CRIANZA RED 923
80 TOCHUELO 2003 WHITE 920
80 VIÑA MAÍN 2003 ROSÉ 922
80 VIÑA MAÍN 2003 WHITE 922

YCODEN-DAUTE-ISORA

89 VIÑÁTIGO MALVASÍA 2003 OAK AGED
WHITE DULCE 933
87 MALVASÍA TASANA CLÁSICO 2001 WHITE DULCE 931
86 TÁGARA 2003 GENEROSO LICOR NOBLE 930
85 VIÑÁTIGO NEGRAMOLL 2003 CRIANZA RED 933
82 ACEVIÑO 2003 ROSÉ 931
82 AÑATERVE 2003 WHITE 933
82 CUEVAS DEL VIENTO 2003 WHITE................930
81 MIRADERO 2001 CRIANZA RED 932
81 TÁGARA 2003 ROSÉ 930
81 TÁGARA 2003 WHITE 930
81 VIÑAMONTE 2003 WHITE SEMI-SECO...............932
80 ACEVIÑO 2003 WHITE 931
80 TÁGARA 2003 FERMENTADO EN BARRICA WHITE..930
80 VIÑAMONTE 2002 OAK AGED WHITE 933
80 VIÑÁTIGO MARMAJUELO 2003 WHITE 933

YECLA

91 VIÑA AL LADO DE LA CASA 2002 RED 937
90 CASTAÑO COLECCIÓN 2002 OAK AGED RED 937
90 DETRÁS DE LA CASA TINTORERA 2002 RED 937
90 VIÑA AL LADO DE LA CASA 2001 RED 938
88 DETRÁS DE LA CASA CABERNET SAUVIGNON-
TINTORERA 2001 CRIANZA RED 938
88 DETRÁS DE LA CASA SYRAH 2002 RED 938
88 MIRA SALINAS 2001 RED 938
87 CASTAÑO MERLOT 2003 RED 937
87 CASTAÑO SYRAH 2003 RED 937
87 DETRÁS DE LA CASA MONASTRELL 2001 RED 938
86 BELLUM EL REMATE 2003 OAK AGED
RED DULCE 936
86 CASTAÑO CABERNET SAUVIGNON 2003 RED 937
86 CASTAÑO MONASTRELL 2001 RED DULCE 938
86 HÉCULA 2002 OAK AGED RED 937
83 POZUELO 2001 CRIANZA RED 938
83 VALCORSO MONASTRELL ECOLÓGICO 2003 RED..939
82 BARAHONDA 2000 OAK AGED RED 937
82 BARAHONDA 2003 RED 937
82 CASTAÑO MACABEO-CHARDONNAY 2003 WHITE ..937
82 IGLESIA VIEJA 1999 RESERVA RED...............939
82 VALCORSO CABERNET SAUVIGNON 2003 RED 939
82 VALCORSO MONASTRELL 2002 OAK AGED RED ...939
81 BARAHONDA 2001 OAK AGED RED 936
81 BARAHONDA 2002 RED 936
80 DOMINIO ESPINAL 2002 OAK AGED RED 937
80 ESTÍO 2003 RED 938
80 IGLESIA VIEJA 2001 CRIANZA RED 939

80 POZUELO 2000 RESERVA RED 938

V.T. ARRIBES DEL DUERO

84 ABADENGO 2001 OAK AGED RED 950
82 ARRIBES DE VETTONIA VENDIMIA SELECCIONADA
2000 CRIANZA RED 949
80 CONDADO DE FERMOSEL 2001 ROBLE RED 950

V.T. BAJO ARAGÓN

93 VENTA D'AUBERT VIOGNIER 2003 WHITE 951
91 VENTA D'AUBERT 2003 FERMENTADO EN
BARRICA WHITE 951
88 DIONUS 2000 OAK AGED RED 951
85 VENTA D'AUBERT 2000 OAK AGED RED 951
83 VENTUS 2000 RED 951
80 SANTOLEA 2003 OAK AGED RED 950
80 TEMPORE TEMPRANILLO 2002 ROBLE RED 951

V.T. CANGAS

82 MONASTERIO DE CORIAS VIÑA GRANDIELLA
2003 FERMENTADO EN BARRICA WHITE 953
81 MONASTERIO DE CORIAS 2002 OAK AGED RED ..953
80 CHACÓN-BUELTA 2003 RED 953

V.T. CASTILLA

93 DUETO 2002 CRIANZA RED 961
93 PAGO DEL AMA SYRAH 2001 OAK AGED RED 969
93 PAGO DEL AMA SYRAH 2002 OAK AGED RED 969
92 PAGO DEL AMA COLECCIÓN 2002 RED.............969
92 ZUMAQUE DE BROTEAS 2001 RED 959
91 DEHESA DEL CARRIZAL CABERNET SAUVIGNON
2001 OAK AGED RED 958
91 VALLEGARCÍA CABERNET Y MERLOT 2001 RED ...969
91 VALLEGARCÍA VIOGNIER 2002 FERMENTADO
EN BARRICA WHITE 969
90 DEHESA DEL CARRIZAL MV 2002 OAK AGED RED 958
90 PAGO DEL AMA COLECCIÓN 2001 RED.............969
89 DEHESA DEL CARRIZAL COLECCIÓN PRIVADA
2000 OAK AGED RED.............................958
88 CORPUS DEL MUNI "VIÑA LUCÍA" 2002 OAK
AGED RED 964
88 DEHESA DEL CARRIZAL CABERNET SAUVIGNON
2002 OAK AGED RED.............................958
88 DEHESA DEL CARRIZAL CHARDONNAY 2003 OAK
AGED WHITE 958
88 FINCA LA ESTACADA SELECCIÓN VARIETALES
2001 OAK AGED RED 961
88 GRAN CALZADILLA 2000 RESERVA RED............968
88 MAGNIFICUS 2002 CRIANZA RED 967
87 DOMINIO DE MALPICA 2001 OAK AGED RED.......965
87 ERCAVIO TEMPRANILLO 2003 ROBLE RED..........959
87 FINCA LA ESTACADA 2002 OAK AGED RED 960
87 FINCA MINATEDA SELECCIÓN PEDRO SARRIÓN
2000 ROBLE RED 956
87 PAGO FLORENTINO 2002 RED 963
86 AGIOS 2002 OAK AGED RED......................966
86 DIVINUS 2003 WHITE 967
86 ERCAVIO LIMITED RESERVE 2001 OAK
AGED RED 960
86 FINCA LORANQUE 2002 OAK AGED RED 961
86 LÓPEZ PANACH CABERNET SAUVIGNON
2002 RED 963
86 QUERCUS 2001 CRIANZA RED 961
86 TORRE DE BARREDA AMIGOS 2000 RED 955
86 TORRE DE BARREDA SELECCIÓN 2001 OAK
AGED RED 955
85 CALZADILLA 2001 RESERVA RED 968
85 CANTOFINO INTENSO 2003 RED 955
85 ERCAVIO TEMPRANILLO CABERNET SAUVIGNON
2003 RED 960
85 FINCA MARISÁNCHEZ CHARDONNAY
2003 WHITE 966
85 FINCA MINATEDA ROBLE 2001 ROBLE RED 955
85 LÓPEZ PANACH 2002 RED 963
85 MARTÚE CHARDONNAY 2003 FERMENTADO EN
BARRICA WHITE 963
85 SOLAZ SHIRAZ-TEMPRANILLO 2003 RED 960
85 TORRE DE BARREDA 2002 ROBLE RED 954
84 CALZADILLA SYRAH 2001 RED 968
84 CONDE DE ORGAZ CABERNET-MERLOT 2001
OAK AGED RED 966

V.T. CASTILLA Y LEÓN

V.T. CONTRAVIESA-ALPUJARRA

V.T. CÓRDOBA

V.T. DESIERTO DE ALMERÍA

V.T. EIVISSA

85 CAN RICH SELECCIÓN 2002 RED 983
84 COS D'UC 2002 OAK AGED RED 983
84 ES DIVI 2002 OAK AGED RED 983
84 SA COVA 2000 ROBLE RED 983
83 CAN MAYMÓ 2003 OAK AGED RED 982
83 CAN RICH 2003 ROSÉ 982
83 ES DIVI SA SELECCIÓ 2002 CRIANZA RED 983
83 SA COVA BLANC DE BLANCS 2003 WHITE 983
83 SA COVA PRIVAT 2002 OAK AGED RED....................983
81 CAN MAYMÓ 2003 ROSÉ 982
81 SA COVA 9 2003 RED 983
80 CAN MAYMÓ 2003 WHITE 982
80 CAN MAYMÓ TRADICIÓN 2003 RED 982
80 CAN RICH 2003 WHITE 982

V.T. EL TERRERAZO

94 FINCA TERRERAZO 2001 OAK AGED RED 983
93 QUINCHA CORRAL 2001 OAK AGED RED 984
91 MESTIZAJE 2002 OAK AGED RED 984

V.T. EXTREMADURA

87 VIÑALANGE TEMPRANILLO 2003 RED 984
84 VIÑA SANTA MARINA TEMPRANILLO 2001
OAK AGED RED 987
83 EQUUS 2001 OAK AGED RED 987
83 MIRACULUS 1999 RESERVA RED 987
82 CELTUS TEMPRANILLO 2002 RED SECO 987
81 VIÑA PLACENTINA 2002 ROBLE RED 984
81 VIÑA SANTA MARINA CABERNET SAUVIGNON -
SYRAH 2001 OAK AGED RED 987

V.T. GRANADA SUROESTE

87 SEÑORÍO DE NEVADA VENDIMIA SELECCIONADA
2002 RED 988
86 CALVENTE 2002 WHITE..987
86 CALVENTE 2003 WHITE..987
86 SEÑORÍO DE NEVADA CABERNET S./MERLOT
2003 RED 988
85 RIBERA DEL GENIL 2003 FERMENTADO EN
BARRICA WHITE 988
85 SEÑORÍO DE NEVADA SYRAH-MERLOT
2003 RED 988
83 CALVENTE 2001 OAK AGED RED 987
83 SEÑORÍO DE NEVADA CABERNET S./MERLOT
2002 RED 988
80 EL VIÑEDO 2003 RED 988

V.T. ILLA DE MENORCA

87 VINYA SA CUDÍA 2003 WHITE 989

V.T. ILLES BALEARS

93 À.N. SON NEGRE 2001 CRIANZA RED 989
91 AN 2001 CRIANZA RED 989
88 SIÓ DE RIBAS 2001 CRIANZA RED 990
86 RIBAS DE CABRERA 2001 RED 990
85 HEREUS DE RIBAS 2002 ROBLE RED 990
84 AN/2 2002 OAK AGED RED 989
84 SON BORDILS 2003 WHITE..990
84 SON BORDILS MUSCAT 2003 WHITE.......................990
83 SON BORDILS BLANC DE RAÏM BLANC
2003 WHITE 990
80 CASTELL MIQUEL SYRAH 2002 RED 990
80 SANTA CATARINA 2003 WHITE 989
80 SANTA CATARINA SON ALOY 2003 RED 990
88 SON BORDILS 2001 RED 990
87 SES MARJADES 2002 CRIANZA RED 989

V.T. NORTE DE GRANADA

89 VERTIJANA 2002 RED...992
87 VERTIJANA 2003 RED 992
86 NARANJUEZ 2003 RED 991
84 CAUZON 2003 RED 992
83 NARANJUEZ 2003 WHITE 991
82 CAUZON 2003 WHITE 992
81 NARANJUEZ 2002 RED 991

---

80 CORTIJO DE ANAGIL 2002 RED 992
80 RIBERA DEL FARDES RED 991

V.T. RIBERA DEL ARLANZA

85 TINTO LERMA 2001 OAK AGED RED 993
85 VALDEDIOS 2001 OAK AGED RED 994
85 VIÑA VALDABLE 2001 OAK AGED RED 993
84 MONTE AMÁN 2001 CRIANZA RED 993
84 TINTO LERMA 2000 OAK AGED RED 993
84 VIÑA VALDABLE 2000 CRIANZA RED 993
82 DOMINIO DE MANCILES 2001 CRIANZA RED..........993
82 DOMINIO DE MANCILES 2003 ROSÉ 992
82 MONTE AMÁN 1999 CRIANZA RED 994
82 PALACIO DE LERMA 2000 RESERVA RED 994
80 CASCAJUELO 2003 ROSÉ 994
80 DOMINIO DE MANCILES 2003 RED 992
80 MONTE AMÁN 2001 OAK AGED RED 993

V.T. RIBERA DEL QUEILES

87 GUELBENZU EVO 2002 OAK AGED RED 995
86 GUELBENZU LAUTUS 1999 OAK AGED RED 995
84 GUELBELZU JARDÍN 2003 RED 994
84 GUELBENZU AZUL 2002 OAK AGED RED 994
84 GUELBENZU VIERLAS 2003 OAK AGED RED 994

V.T. SERRA DE TRAMUNTANA-COSTA NORD

84 CA'N VIDALET CABERNET SAUVIGNON & MERLOT
2002 CRIANZA RED 995
82 DIVINS CABERNET 2003 TINTO 995
80 CA'N VIDALET 2002 WHITE...995

V.T. TIERRA DE LEÓN

85 CAÑASECAS 2003 ROBLE RED 996
84 VIÑA COLUMBIANO 2003 ROSÉ................................997
83 VALJUNCO 2000 OAK AGED RED 999
83 VEGA SILVERA 2003 RED 996
83 VEGA SILVERA 2003 ROSÉ 996
82 AUGUSTA ROBLE 2001 OAK AGED RED 996
82 VILLACEZÁN DOCE MESES 2001 OAK AGED RED ..998
81 VALJUNCO 2003 ROSÉ 999
81 VILLACEZÁN COLECCIÓN 2000 CRIANZA RED 998
80 AUTEROLO 2003 ROSÉ 996
80 CAÑASECAS RED 996
80 MOLENDORES 2003 ROSÉ 998
80 PALACIO DE LOS GUZMANES 1999 OAK
AGED RED...999

V.T. TIERRA DEL VINO DE ZAMORA

88 ALIZÁN ÉLITE 2001 CRIANZA RED............................999
86 ALIZÁN SELECCIÓN 2001 OAK AGED RED 1000
85 ALIZÁN 2002 OAK AGED RED 999
84 ALIZÁN 2000 OAK AGED RED 999
82 BROCHERO 2003 RED 1000
82 CARROVALLE 2003 RED 1001
82 PAGO DE CAMPEÁN 2002 RED 1000
81 GAVIÓN 2003 RED 1001
81 PAGO DE CAMPEÁN 2003 RED 1000
80 PAGO DE CAMPEÁN 2001 OAK AGED RED 1000
80 PAGO DE CAMPEÁN CLARETE TRADICIONAL
2003 RED 1000
88 VENTA MAZARRÓN 2003 RED 1001

V.T. VALLE DEL CINCA

81 NUVIANA CABERNET SAUVIGNON MERLOT
2003 RED 1002
80 GRAN VALCINCA 2001 CRIANZA RED 1002
80 VALONGA CHARDONNAY 2003 WHITE 1002

V.T. VALLES DE BENAVENTE

84 PAGO DE VALLEOSCURO 2003 ROSÉ 1003
83 PAGO DE VALLEOSCURO 2003 RED 1003
80 SEÑORÍO DE VIDRIALES 2002 RED 1003
80 SEÑORÍO DE VIDRIALES 2003 ROSÉ.....................1003

V.T. VALLES DE SADACIA

84 RIBERAS DE MARCO FABIO DULCE WHITE 1004

OTRAS ZONAS - OTROS VINOS

95 QUINTA SARDONIA 2002 ROBLE RED 1015
93 CASA CISCA 2002 RED 1020
91 ANDALUS PETIT VERDOT 2001 RED 1008
91 MONTAZO 2002 RED 1020
90 DURONA 2002 OAK AGED RED 1017
90 VERMILIÓN 1999 OAK AGED RED 1016
88 DEHESA LA GRANJA 2000 RED 1014
88 TORRES DES CANONGE 2003 WHITE 1011
88 VINYA DES MORE 2001 OAK AGED RED 1011
87 BLANC SA VALL SELECCIÓ PRIVADA 2003
  FERMENTADO EN BARRICA WHITE 1010
87 CASAR DE SANTA INÉS 1997 CRIANZA RED 1014
87 CASAR DE SANTA INÉS MENCÍA-CABERNET
  SAUVIGNON 2001 RED 1015
87 DOLÇ DE PALLER 2001 OAK AGED DULCE 1017
87 PAGO DE THARSYS VENDIMIA NOCTURNA 2003
  WHITE 1021
87 VINO DE PASAS EL POETA DULCE.........................1008
86 GÓNGORA PX DULCE AÑEJO SELECCIÓN
  IMPERIAL PEDRO XIMÉNEZ DULCE 1009
86 MASIA VILA-RASA 1999 OAK AGED RED 1018
85 GONZÁLEZ PALACIOS OLOROSO ROBLE VINO
  DE LICOR 1008
85 SCHATZ 2002 ROSÉ..1007
84 CASAR DE SANTA INÉS 1994 OAK AGED RED.....1014
84 CASAR DE SANTA INÉS 1998 OAK AGED RED 1014
84 COLONIAS DE GALEÓN 2003 RED 1007
83 AMISTAD AMICUM COUPAGE 2001 TINTO 1020
83 AMONTILLADO MUY VIEJO AMONTILLADO 1008
83 BLANC SA VALL 2002 OAK AGED WHITE 1010
83 CA'N VIDALET CABERNET SAUVIGNON 2001
  OAK AGED RED 1010
83 CASAR DE SANTA INÉS CHARDONNAY
  2001 WHITE 1014
83 CASAR DE SANTA INÉS CHARDONNAY
  2002 WHITE 1014

83 CASAR DE SANTA INÉS MERLOT 1998 RED..........1015
83 CASTELL MIQUEL GARNATXA 2002 RED 1011
83 CATHEDRAL DE ZAMORA 2000 RESERVA RED 1013
83 FINCA SANGUIJUELA 2001 WHITE 1007
83 GONZÁLEZ PALACIOS CREAM ROBLE VINO
  DE LICOR SEMI-DULCE...1007
83 GRAN VINO MOSCATEL GÓNGORA DULCE...........1009
83 MARQUÉS DE VIZHOJA WHITE 1019
83 VINYES DEL BRUGUER CABERNET SAUVIGNON -
  GARNATXA 2002 RED 1017
82 ACINIPO 2002 CRIANZA RED 1007
82 AIROLA CHARDONNAY 2003 WHITE 1014
82 AMONTILLADO MUY VIEJO SELECCIÓN
  IMPERIAL 1008
82 CASTILLO DE ULVER 2002 RED 1016
82 COLONIAS DE GALEÓN 2002 OAK AGED RED 1007
82 DUQUE DE CARMONA ORANGE WINE
  OLOROSO DULCE 1008
82 M. FINA GONZÁLEZ PALACIOS EL POETA
  ROBLE VINO DE LICOR 1008
82 MONTE NERY 1999 CRIANZA RED.........................1010
82 TORRES DES CANONGE 2001 OAK AGED RED.....1011
81 GAINTUS 2001 OAK AGED RED 1017
81 GARCÍA VIADERO ALBILLO 2003 WHITE 1016
81 GÓNGORA P.X. DULCE DULCE 1009
81 OLOROSO GÓNGORA OLOROSO DULCE...............1008
80 CASAR DE SANTA INÉS CABERNET SAUVIGNON
  1999 RED 1015
80 CASTILLO DE GONZÁLEZ PALACIOS
  2003 WHITE 1007
80 CRESTA AZUL WHITE DE AGUJA 1017
80 GÓNGORA SOLERA 1840 OLOROSO DULCE 1008
80 MONTE NERY 1998 CRIANZA RED.........................1010
80 PATA DE HIERRO FINO 1008
80 VINYES DEL BRUGUER GARNATXA 2002 ROSÉ....1017
80 VINYES DEL BRUGUER MERLOT 2002 RED 1017

WINEMAKING GROUPS

WINEMAKING GROUPS
BODEGAS   DO

ALLIED DOMECQ
Pedro Domecq
Pedro Domecq ....DO Jerez
Domecq (Marqués de Arienzo) ....DO Ca. Rioja
Bodegas y Bebidas
AGE...DO Ca. Rioja
Aura ....DO Rueda
Bodegas Alanís ....DO Ribeiro
Cadevi ....DO Valdepeñas
Casa de la Viña...VT Castilla
Juan Alcorta ....DO Ca. Rioja
Pazo de Villarei ....DO Rías Baixas
Señorío del Condestable ....DO Jumilla
Tarsus...DO Ribera del Duero
Vinícola Navarra ....DO Navarra
Ysios ....DO Ca. Rioja

ALTA ALELLA - CARMENET

Alta Alella ....DO Alella
Alta Alella ....DO Catalunya
Alta Alella ....DO Cava

ALVEAR
Alvear ....DO Montilla-Moriles
Alvear ....DO Ribera del Guadiana
Alvear..VT Extremadura

ANECOOP
Cooperativa Agrícola Virgen de Loreto ....DO Utiel-Requena
Covibex ....DO Valencia
La Baronía de Turis ....DO Valencia

ARCO BODEGAS UNIDAS
Berberana ....DO Ca. Rioja
Lagunilla ....DO Ca. Rioja
Haciendas de España
Haciendas Andalus...Otras Zonas
Haciendas Durius ....VT Castilla y León
Hacienda Marqués de la Concordia ....DO Ca. Rioja
Marqués de Griñón ....DO Ca. Rioja
Marqués de Monistrol ....DO Cava
Marqués de Monistrol ....DO Penedès
Masía L'Hereu ....DO Penedès

ARTADI – COSECHEROS ALAVESES
Artadi ....DO Ca. Rioja
Bodegas y Viñedos Artazu ....DO Navarra
Ladera de Pinoso ....DO Alicante

ARZUAGA-NAVARRO
Arzuaga-Navarro ....DO Ribera del Duero
La Colegiada ....VT Ribera del Arlanza

AVELINO VEGAS
Avelino Vegas ....VT Castilla y León
Cerrosol ....DO Rueda
Fuentespina ....DO Ribera del Duero

BARÓN DE LEY
Barón de Ley...DO Ca. Rioja
El Coto de Rioja ....DO Ca. Rioja
Finca Museum ....DO Cigales
Bodegas Máximo ....VT Castilla

BODEGAS DE CRIANZA DE CASTILLA LA VIEJA
Bodegas de Crianza de Castilla la Vieja.......................................DO Rueda
Bodegas Toresanas ....DO Toro

Con Class ....DO Ribera del Duero
Cuevas de Castilla ....DO Rueda

BODEGAS RIOJANAS
Bodegas Riojanas ....DO Ca. Rioja
Torreduero ....DO Toro

BODEGAS LAN
LAN ....DO Ca. Rioja
Santiago Ruiz ....DO Rías Baixas
Señorío de Ulía ....DO Ca. Rioja

BUIL & GINÉ
Buil & Giné...DO Montsant
Buil & Giné...DO Priorat
Buil & Giné..DO Rueda

CASA MASAVEU
Murúa ....DO Ca. Rioja
Fillaboa ....DO Rías Baixas

CASTELL DEL REMEI
Castell del Remei ....DO Costers del Segre
Celler de Cantonella ....DO Costers del Segre

CELLERS UNIÓ
Cellers Unió ....DO Ca. Priorat
Cellers Unió ....DO Terra Alta
Cellers Unió ....DO Montsant
Cellers Unió ....DO Cava
Cellers Unió ....DO Tarragona

CHIVITE
Chivite...DO Navarra
Señorío de Arínzano ....DO Navarra
Viña Salceda ....DO Ca. Rioja

CODORNÍU
Abadia de Poblet..DO Conca de Barberá
Bodegas Bilbaínas...DO Ca. Rioja
Cellers Scala Dei..DO Priorat
Codorníu ....DO Cava
Legaris ....DO Ribera del Duero
Masia Bach ....DO Cava
Masia Bach ....DO Penedès
Nuviana...VT Valle del Cinca
Raimat..DO Costers del Segre
Rondel...DO Cava

COMPAÑÍA DE VINOS DE TELMO RODRÍGUEZ
Compañía de Vinos de Telmo Rodríguez ....DO Alicante
Compañía de Vinos de Telmo Rodríguez ....DO Cigales
Compañía de Vinos de Telmo Rodríguez ....DO Málaga y Sierras de Málaga
Compañía de Vinos de Telmo Rodríguez ....DO Ribera del Duero
Compañía de Vinos de Telmo Rodríguez ....DO Ca. Rioja
Compañía de Vinos de Telmo Rodríguez ....DO Rueda
Compañía de Vinos de Telmo Rodríguez ....DO Toro
Viñas Viejas de Cebreros ....VT Castilla y León
Viñedos de San Martín...Otras Zonas

CVNE
CVNE..DO Ca. Rioja
Viña Real ....DO Ca. Rioja
Viñedos del Contino ....DO Ca. Rioja

DELISPAIN
Delispain ....DO Méntrida
Delispain ....DO Rueda
Delispain ....DO Toro

Gallaecia Premium ....DO Ribeiro
Gallaecia Premium ....DO Rías Baixas

FRUTOS VILLAR
Bodegas Santa Eulalia ....DO Ribera del Duero
Frutos Villar ....DO Cigales
Frutos Villar ....DO Toro

GARCÍA CARRIÓN
Bodegas 1890 ....DO Jumilla
García Carrión ....DO Rueda
García Carrión ....DO La Mancha
Jaume Serra ....DO Cava
Jaume Serra ....DO Penedès
Jaume Serra ....DO Catalunya
Marqués de Carrión ....DO Ca. Rioja
Viña Arnáiz ....DO Ribera del Duero

GRUPO BODEGAS OLARRA
Bodegas Olarra ....DO Ca. Rioja
Bodegas Ondarre ....DO Navarra
Bodegas y Viñedos Casa del Valle ....VT Castilla

GRUPO ZAMORA
Ramón Bilbao ....DO Ca. Rioja
Mar de Frades...DO Rías Baixas

GRUPO ESTÉVEZ
Marqués del Real Tesoro ....DO Jerez
Valdespino ....DO Jerez

GRUPO FAUSTINO
Faustino ....DO Ca. Rioja
Campillo ....DO Ca. Rioja
Leganza ....DO La Mancha
Marqués de Vitoria ....DO Ca. Rioja
Valcarlos ....DO Navarra

GRUPO FÉLIX SOLÍS
Félix Solís (Altos de Tamarón) ....DO Ribera del Duero
Félix Solís (Viña Albali) ....DO Valdepeñas
Félix Solís (Analivia) ....DO Rueda
Félix Solís (Abadía de Altillo) ....DO Ca. Rioja
Félix Solís (Sendas del Rey)..VT Castilla
Pagos del Rey ....DO Ribera del Duero

GRUPO FREIXENET
Freixenet ....DO Cava
Castellblanch ....DO Cava
Segura Viudas ....DO Cava
Conde de Caralt..DO Cava
Conde de Caralt ....DO Catalunya
René Barbier ....DO Penedès
René Barbier ....DO Cava

GRUPO GALICIANO
Adegas Día-Noite ....DO Valdeorras
Adegas Galegas ....DO Rías Baixas
Viticultores Bercianos ....DO Bierzo
Terres de Codols i Llicorella..DO Montsant

GRUPO GARVEY
Bodegas Marqués de Olivara ....DO Toro
Complejo Bodeguero Bellavista...VT Cádiz
Garvey-José de Soto ....DO Jerez
Marqués de Campo Nuble ....DO Ca. Rioja
Viña Buena ....DO Ribera del Duero

GRUPO LA NAVARRA
Marco Real ....DO Navarra
Señorío de Andión ....DO Navarra

Viña del Sopié ....DO Rueda
Viñedos de Villaester ....DO Toro

GRUPO SCHENK
Bodegas Murviedro ....DO Alicante
Bodegas Murviedro ....DO Valencia
Bodegas Murviedro ....DO Utiel-Requena

GRUPO SIERRA CANTABRIA
Numanthia Termes ....DO Toro
Señorío de San Vicente...DO Ca. Rioja
Sierra Cantabria ....DO Ca. Rioja
Viñedos de Páganos ....DO Ca. Rioja

GONZÁLEZ BYASS
González Byass ....DO Jerez
Beronia ....DO Ca. Rioja
Castell de Vilarnau...DO Cava
Castell de Vilarnau...DO Penedès

GURPEGUI
Bodegas Berceo ....DO Ca. Rioja
Luis Gurpegui Muga ....DO Ca. Rioja
Luis Gurpegui Muga ....DO Navarra
Luis Gurpegui Muga ....VT Extremadura

HIJOS DE ANTONIO BARCELÓ
Bodegas Palacio ....DO Ca. Rioja
Peñascal ....VT Castilla y León
Viña Mayor ....DO Ribera del Duero

HIJOS DE RAINERA PÉREZ-MARÍN Y BODEGAS M. GIL LUQUE
Hijos de Rainera Pérez-Marín ....DO Jerez
Hijos de Rainera Pérez-Marín ....VT Cádiz
Bodegas M. Gil Luque ....DO Jerez

LA RIOJA ALTA
Bodegas y Viñedos Áster ....DO Ribera del Duero
La Rioja Alta ....DO Ca. Rioja
Lagar de Fornelos...DO Rías Baixas
Torre de Oña ....DO Ca. Rioja

LUIS CABALLERO
Marqués de Irún ....DO Rueda
Marqués de Irún ....DO Toro
Viña Herminia ....DO Ca. Rioja

MARQUÉS DE MURRIETA
Marqués de Murrieta ....DO Ca. Rioja
Pazo de Barrantes...DO Rías Baixas

MARQUÉS DE RISCAL
Herederos del Marqués de Riscal ....DO Ca. Rioja
Vinos Blancos de Castilla ....DO Rueda
Vinos Blancos de Castilla ....VT Castilla y León

MATARROMERA
Émina ....DO Ribera del Duero
Matarromera..DO Ribera del Duero
Renacimiento ....DO Ribera del Duero
Valdelosfrailes ....DO Cigales
Vermilión ....Otras Zonas

MARTÍNEZ BUJANDA
Bodegas Valdemar ....DO Ca. Rioja
Cosecheros y Criadores ....VT Castilla
Finca Antigua ....DO La Mancha
Finca Valpiedra ....DO Ca. Rioja

MAURO
Bodegas y Viñedos Paixar ....DO Bierzo
Mauro ....VT Castilla y León
Maurodos ....DO Toro

MONT-FERRANT
Mont-Ferrant ....DO Cava
Mont-Ferrant ....DO Penedès
Rogert Goulart ....DO Cava

OLIVEDA
Freixa Rigau ....DO Cava
Oliveda ....DO Catalunya
Oliveda ....DO Empordà-Costa Brava

OSBORNE
Montecillo ....DO Ca. Rioja
Osborne y Cía. ....DO Jerez
Osborne Malpica ....VT Castilla
Osborne Ribera del Duero ....DO Ribera del Duero

PATERNINA
Federico Paternina ....DO Ca. Rioja
Federico Paternina ....DO Jerez
Franco-Españolas ....DO Ca. Rioja
Marqués de Valparaíso ....DO Ribera del Duero

PERELADA
Castillo de Perelada ....DO Cava
Castillo de Perelada ....DO Empordà-Costa Brava
Cims de Porrera ....DO Ca. Priorat

PESQUERA
Alejandro Fernández-Tinto Pesquera ....DO Ribera del Duero
Condado de Haza ....DO Ribera del Duero
El Vínculo ....DO La Mancha
Bodegas y Viñedos Fernández Rivera ....Otras Zonas

PINORD
Pinord ....DO Penedès
Marrugat ....DO Cava
Monasterio de Corias ....VT Cangas

PRÍNCIPE DE VIANA
Príncipe de Viana ....DO Navarra
Rioja Vega ....DO Ca. Rioja

TERRAS GAUDA
Pittacum ....DO Bierzo
Terras Gauda ....DO Rías Baixas

TORRES
Jean León ....DO Catalunya
Jean León ....DO Penedès
Miguel Torres ....DO Catalunya
Miguel Torres ....DO Conca de Barberá
Miguel Torres ....DO Penedès

VALDUERO
Valduero ....Otras Zonas
Valduero ....DO Ribera del Duero
Valduero ....DO Toro
Valgrande ....DO Ca. Rioja

VALSANZO SELECCIÓN
Valsanzo Selección (Terras Cúa) ....DO Bierzo
Valsanzo Selección (Lacrimus, Saurón) ....DO Ca. Rioja
Valsanzo Selección (Viña Sanzo) ....DO Rueda
Valsanzo Selección (Damalisco) ....DO Toro

VEGA SICILIA
    Bodegas y Viñedos Alión ....DO Ribera del Duero
    Bodegas y Viñedos Pintia ....DO Toro
    Vega Sicilia...DO Ribera del Duero

VIÑA IZADI
    Finca Villacreces..DO Ribera del Duero
    Viña Izadi ....DO Ca. Rioja

WINNER WINES
    Winner Wines ....DO Cariñena
    Winner Wines (Juvenals) ....DO Cava
    Winner Wines (Juvenals)...DO Penedès
    Winner Wines (Ibernoble) ....DO Ribera del Duero
    Winner Wines (Viña Saseta) ....DO Ca. Rioja

YLLERA
    Yllera ....DO Ribera del Duero
    Yllera...DO Rueda
    Yllera ....DO Toro
    Yllera ....VT Castilla y León

WINE PRODUCING REGIONS BY AUTONOMOUS COMMUNITY

NAVARRA

PAIS VASCO

VALENCIA

NAVARRA - ARAGON

WINE-TASTING DICTIONARY
INDEX

VOCABULARY

TERMINOLOGY RELATED TO COLOUR.

AMBER. The first oxidation phase in Generoso wines, brandies, whiskies and rum (between yellow and reddish tones).

BEADS. The slow rising chain of bubbles in a sparkling wine.

BRICK RED. A nuance of reds that have been matured in bottle for longer than 10 years or in barrel for longer than 6 years. A tone similar to brick.

BRILLIANT. Related to the youth and cleanness of the wine.

CLEAN. Absolutely clean, without defects.

CLOUDY. The first sign of cloudiness in the wine.

COPPERY Similar to copper, a reddish nuance that can be seen in whites that have been aged for a long time in barrel, usually Amontillados and some Palos Cortados.

CHERRY. A term commonly used to express the colour. When the term bigarreau is used or very intense it means it is a very dark or almost black cherry.

DARK. This often refers to a tone slightly lighter than "intense", something similar to "medium-intensity".

DEEP. A red with a very dark colour which hardly lets one see the bottom of the glass.

DULL. A wine lacking liveliness, tending to have ochre borders.

GARNET RED. This is a common nuance in medium to light reds. If the wine is an intense cherry red it could have a garnet border or rim only if it comes from less sunny regions. It is more luminous and open than the violet border of a very dark wine, generally from the latest vintage.

GLACE CHERRY. This is used to define a colour lighter than a red but darker than a rosé.

GOLDEN. Golden with yellowy to reddish tones, but with a predominance of yellow tones.

GLIMMER. Not well defined hues, a certain nuance.

IODINE. A tone similar to the stains from iodine (old gold and brown) which Rancio and Generosos have after long oxidative maturation.

LIVELY. This reflects the youth of the wine with very bright and brilliant colours.

MAHOGANY. The second phase of ageing in brandies, rum and Generoso wines. A tone between brown and yellow which wines generally have when they are older.

OCHRE. The last colour phase of a table wine which is usually found in wines with a long oxidative maturation and is indicative of its decline.

OILY. A wine that appears dense to the eye, usually high alcohol content and sweet.

OLD GOLD. Golden with the brownish tones found in many Amontillados which do not have the mahogany nuances that predominate in Olorosos.

ONION SKIN. This is a tone lighter than salmon.

OPAQUE. A wine with a very intense colour and one cannot see the bottom of the glass. Generally found in very old Pedro Ximénez and therefore has a very caramelised colour.

OPEN. Very pale, not very intense.

ORANGEY EDGE. Intermediate phase between a deep red and brick red which is found towards the rim or edge of red wines and indicates an intermediate age. It is a feature that appears sooner in wines with higher alcohol content. It is also a typical tone found in wines made from Pinot Noir.

RASPBERRY. This is the best shade of a rosé that denotes youth, good acidity and freshness. Pinkish with a bluish rim.

RIM. This is also known as the border or edge. It is the colour of the wine at the far top edge when we incline the glass. It is not as dark as at the centre of the glass. If it is a red from the latest vintage, it will normally be a violet or raspberry colour; if it is slightly older, it will be a deeper red and if has been in bottle for more than five years it will be similar in colour to a brick red or an Arab tile.

RUBY. Slightly orangey tone with a yellow hue found in old wines that have lost part of their cherry red colour.

SALMON. A tone slightly redder than pink found in rosés with less acidity and more alcohol.

STEELY. Pale colour with metallic reflections (steel) which identifies some whites.

STRAW-COLOURED. This term should be understood as straw yellow. This is the colour found in the majority of young whites, halfway between yellow and green. It can also be described as "lemony".

TERMINOLOGY RELATED TO AROMA.

ACETONE. The same tones as varnish. It is a smell very close to nail varnish, typical of very old eau-de-vie.

ALCOHOL. This is not a perjorative term for an excess of alcohol – in which case we would say fiery - but a dominant aroma that is not aggressive.

ALDEHYDE. A sensation of alcohol but at the same time rancid, of old wines with a high alcohol content that have undergone oxidative maturation.

ANIMAL. Not a very positive aroma, which is caused by long storage in bottle (hints of wet dog or wet hide) and is normally associated with a lack of hygiene. If the smell is found in more recent vintages then it is a symptom of "brett" (see brett).

ATTIC. A smell of old dry wood and the sensation of the dust that is very typical of attics. Typical of some fortified wines aged in wood or old casks. It is also a typical trait found in very old wines that have been in bottle for more than ten years and which have been aged for a long period in well-used barrels.

BALSAMIC This aroma is produced by ageing in wood accelerated by the high temperatures in warm regions. It also refers to the aroma of dry leaves (eucalyptus, bay), incense and pitch.

BLACK FRUIT. This is the toasty aroma of ripe fruit that is found in reds that have undergone a long skin maceration.

"BRETT". This is the abbreviation for a new term (brettanomyces) to describe an old problem: the aroma of stables, chicken coops, and wet, un-tanned leather...normally found in reductive state wines that have been in bottle for over ten years. These aromas, in small doses, were integrated into the cluster of complex aromas in old wines and they were tolerated. Nowadays, due to more precision in the aromas and more hygienic working conditions in the wine cellars, they are detected better by the senses. In addition, brett is more often found in wines that are not very old as this yeast develops in wines with a higher ph level. The increase in the ph of wines is quite common these days due to the climate, riper grapes and the soils being constantly bombarded with fertilizers over the past 35 years.

BROOM. This is an aroma reminiscent of Mediterranean scrubland.

CARPENTRY. Sharp aroma of varnished wood, typical of wines aged for long periods in oak barrels, during which process the alcohol oxidises and gives off an aroma of acetone, nail varnish or varnish.

CAROB. Anybody who has chewed or smelt one of these beans cannot fail to notice the sweetness and the toasted notes at the same time, as well as the slightly rustic notes. It is usually found in old brandy aged in Pedro Ximénez Soleras and in concentrated wines made from very ripe grapes.

CEDAR. The somewhat perfumed aroma of cedar, a soft wood commonly found in Morocco.

CITRUS. An aroma somewhat similar to lemon, orange and grapefruit.

CLASSIC RIOJA. This is the best known Rioja, with a large presence of wood (normally very old). The spicy characters dominate and notes of candle wax appear with fruity nuances from the increased action of oxygen during the maturation in oak.

CLEAR. A wine that has no defects, in neither the taste nor the aroma.

CLOSED. A term used to refer to an aroma that is very faint, not developed or has not opened. Almost always found in very concentrated wines, from an excellent vintage, which evolve very slowly in the bottle. It can also be found in recently bottled wines.

COCOA. Slightly toasted and fine aroma found in moderately wood aged wines and which have evolved very well in bottle.

COMPLEX. A wealth of aromas and tastes from the variety, soil and ageing, but without clearly defining any of them.

CREAMY. Aroma of finely toasted oak (usually French oak) with hints of caramelised vanilla.

CRYSTALLISED FRUIT. This is a sweet nuance, something between toasted and jammy, which is found in some whites with a long oxidative evolution and in some sweet white wines.

DARK-ROASTED FLAVOUR. Seen in terms of taste.

DATES. A sweet aroma with hints of dates and the inclusion of toasted and raisiny notes.

EARTHY. An aroma somewhere between clay and dust which is typical of red wines made from ripe grapes and which have a high alcohol content. It is also a mineral note in some wines.

ELEGANT. This is the combination of a series of noble nuances (perfumed wood, light and pleasantly complex (see complex), without being excessively intensely aromatic, but fully harmonised).

ETHEREAL. This is used to define fortified wines and wines with a certain intensity of alcohol in their oxidative evolution; the strength of the alcohol reveals the rancid-type aromas. It has a lot to do with the age.

FADED FLOR (FLEUR). This is the toasted nuance typical of good champagnes with a high percentage of

Pinot Noir and champagnes which have evolved perfectly on their lees for a long time in the bottle.

FINE. Synonym of elegant.

FINE LEES. This is an aroma between herbaceous and lightly toasted, produced by the yeasts that die (autolysis) after the fermentation, and which are used during a certain period to make the wine more complex and give it a richer aroma.

FLOR (FLEUR). This is a pungent, saline, salty meat aroma, that is typically found in Finos, Manzanillas and to a lesser degree in Amontillados. It is caused by the taste-smell transfer of the yeast cap (fleur) that covers the surface of these wines.

FLORAL. Reminiscent of the petals of certain flowers such as roses and jasmine which is produced in certain white wines from the north or in excellent red wines after they have developed in bottle and in which spicy aromas also come out.

FRAGRANT HERBS. An aroma similar to soaps and perfumes made from lavender, rosemary, lemon, orange blossom or jasmine. It is found in white wines subjected to pre-fermentation skin maceration.

FRESH. Lively aroma of a wine without a hint of alcohol.

FRESH FRUIT. These are fruity notes which are produced at the height of a slow ripening of the grape, typical of moderate climates.

FRUIT EXPRESSION. This is the character produced by various tastes and aromas reminiscent of fine herbs and fruit trees.

FRUITY. This is a trace of vegetative notes close to the fruit, but also enveloped in hints of green grass

INTENSE. The strength of the aroma that can be immediately noticed when taking the glass to the nose.

IODINE. This refers to the tincture of iodine (a combination of a sweet smell of alcohol, toast, liniment and varnish or lacquer).

JAM. This is a trace of very ripe black fruit, caramelised by the oxidation caused by the oak. Very similar to forest fruit jam (prunes, blackberries, blueberries, redcurrants, cherries). Found in red wines with a high concentration of fruitiness which have been skin macerated for long periods. The skins come from very ripe grapes from vineyards in the south.

MACERATION. These are aromas which persist in the wine and are similar to those given off by the container in which the red wine was fermented.

MEDITERRANEAN TYPE. This is an aroma where the alcohol, burnt, sweet, raisiny, caramelised notes concur and are transmitted to the wine by the grapes from vineyards found in warm regions.

MINERAL NOTES. This is used for wines that have a slight nose, reminiscent of flint, slate, hot stones or sand.

MUSK. A relative term for the sweet and grapey aromas of aromatic varieties such as the Moscatel, Riesling and Gewürztraminer.

MUTED FRUIT. These are generally the aromas produced by a rapid ripening of the grape, and are very typical of warmer climates.

NOTES OF EVOLUTION. This is generally used for wines prematurely aged by the action of the air or heat; e.g. wine that has been left in a glass for several hours.

NUTS. Notes which are normally found in white wines with oxidative ageing; the movement of air generates aromas and tastes reminiscent of nuts (bitter almonds, hazelnuts, walnuts…). When the ageing is longer and above all in old barrels, it includes aromas and flavours that are closer to figs, dates, raisins, etc.

ORANGE PEEL. Spicy and, at the same time, the fruit tree aroma found in certain white wines.

ORGANIC NOTES. A way of defining the aroma of the fermentation yeasts in young wines (usually found in white wines) and maturation yeasts (fleur).

OVERRIPE FRUIT. This is typical of wines that are slightly oxidised and have not been aged in wood. An aroma of bunches of grapes with the first signs of going rotten or an aroma of bruised and pressed bunches.

OXIDATIVE EVOLUTION. The tendency of a wine to age by the action of the oxygen through the pores of the cask or barrel (micro-oxidation), or by airing through the racking.

PATISSERIE. This is an aroma between sweet and toasted with hints of caramelised sugar and vanilla, typical of freshly-baked cakes. It is found in wines that have been aged for a long time in oak, normally sweet wines, and is caused by the oxidative evolution and from the odoriferous compounds (vanilla) of the oak containers.

PEAT. A lightly burnt aroma which occurs when associating the ripe grape with the toasted aromas of new oak in wines with a high alcohol content.

PHENOLIC. This is a derivative of the polyphenols (a combination of the tannins and anthocyanins, or vegetal part of the grape), and it defines an aroma from extensively macerated grapeskins which evoke a nuance of something between black grapes and a pressed bunch of grapes.

PITCH. The slightly tarrish aromas of very toasted wood, associated with concentrated red wines with lots of colour, structure and alcohol.

PORTY. This is the sweet aroma of a wine made from somewhat raisiny or overripe grapes which is reminiscent of the vintage Ports made with a short oxidative ageing phase

PUNGENT. A prominent aromatic note developed from the alcohol, the wood and the flor of Fino wines.

RANCID. This is not a defect but a note better known as "sherrified", caused by the oxidative ageing.

RED FRUIT. This refers to foresty red fruit (blackberries, redcurrants, mulberries) and not very ripe cherries and plums.

REDUCTION. This is the aroma of a wine caused by the lack of air during its long stay in bottle (tobacco, old leather, vanilla, cinnamon, cocoa, attic, dust, etc).

REDUCTION OFF-ODOURS. This is a negative aroma produced by the decay of the lees in a wine that has not been oxygenated or because of late racking. Halfway between boiled cabbage and boiled eggs.

REDUCTION OFF-ODOURS IN THE TANK. A smell between metal and boiled, typical of wines stored in large tanks and at high temperatures, which means that excessive amounts of sulphur have to be added and this combines with the wine, reducing its fruity freshness. This phenomenon is found in the large storage tanks of common wines.

RIPE SKIN. This is similar to the writing ink aroma that a very ripe grape gives off when we squeeze it between our fingers, or that is given off from the accumulation of ripe pressed bunches.

SALINE. This is the note acquired by a Fino that has aged in soleras with a lot of flor.

SCRUBLAND. An aroma typical of the herbs found in Mediterranean scrubland (a mixture of rosemary, thyme and other semi-arid herbs). This is the dry herbaceous note which is found especially in white and red wines from warm regions.

SEASONED WOOD. Notes which appear in wine aged in barrel for more than four or five years and that have lost the fine toasted aromas and flavours of new oak.

SOLERA-FLAVOURED. This expresses an aroma close to the wet smell of an Oloroso bodega

SPICY. This refers to household spices (pepper, cloves, cinnamon) which appear in wines aged by the action of the oxygen in the barrels.

SPIRITUOUS. Taste and olfactory feature of a wine with a high alcohol content but without it having a burning sensation. An intellectual word to define alcohol that is nothing else but the "spirit of wine".

STEWED FRUIT. Notes of stewed or cooked fruit, which comes from grapes well-ripened on the vine, without being overripe. Hints of the fruit in jam.

TERROIR. An aroma which is determined by the soil and climate, a nuance between mountain herbs, minerals, stones, etc.

TOASTED SUGAR. Sweet caramelised aromas.

TOFFEE. This is typical of the white coffee sweets (lactic and toasty notes) of some Crianza red wines.

TROPICAL NOTES. These are the sweet aromas of white wines whose grapes have ripened very quickly, and are similar to sweet ripe fruit that are very low in acidity.

TRUFFLE. Similar to a mixture of wet earth and mushroom.

UNDERBRUSH. This is the aromatic nuance between damp earth, grass and fallen leaves which is found in well-assembled, medium-aged reds that have a certain fruity and phenolic concentration, and which have been aged in wood.

VANILLA. A typical trait of wines and fortified wines aged in oak. The vanilla contained in the wood is a component which is transmitted to the wine.

VARIETAL EXPRESSION. This is the taste and aroma of the variety or varieties that make up the wine.

VARNISH. A typical smell found in very old or fortified wines due to alcohol oxidation after long ageing in wood. The traces of varnished wood are similar to the aromas of eau-de-vie aged in wood.

VEGETABLE. This is a vague aroma of vine shoots, thickets and geranium leaves which is produced by the incomplete ripening of the grape skin.

VISCOUS. The sweet aromas and flavours of wines with high alcohol content.

VOLATILE This is a characteristic of wines with high "volatile acidity"; that is, with the first signs of turning into vinegar. It is typical of wines that have been badly stabilised when they are young or else in old wines with a high alcohol content which, by means of its oxidative phase in barrel and therefore increased contact with the air, have taken on this nuance. However, this nuance is not negative in the case of Generoso wines.

WINE PRESS. The aroma of the vegetal parts of the grape after fermentation, faintly reminiscent of eau de vie, grapeskins and ink.

WITH CHARACTER. Used to express the singularity of wine above the rest. It could refer to the making, terroir or a particular or different crianza.

WOODY. An excessive taste and aroma of wood due to excessive ageing in oak or due to a weak structure of the wine.

YEAST. A dry aroma of bread yeast that can be perceived in young cavas or wines that have just been bottled.

TERMINOLOGY RELATED TO THE PALATE

ALCOHOL. The sensation of spirits but without being aggressive; it is not a defect.

ALCOHOLIC EDGES. A slight excess of alcohol which is appreciated on the tongue, but which does not harm the whole.

BITTER. A nuance of bitterness, but not aggressive, and it is often found in Finos, Amontillados and the white wines from Rueda. A touch of bitterness is not necessarily negative; on the contrary, it can moderate the soft or slightly sweet sensations that prolong the perceptions; it is a counterpoint.

CARAMELISED. A very sweet and toasted taste which is typical of some dense wines that have been aged in Oloroso or Pedro Ximénez casks

DARK-ROASTED FLAVOUR. This is the sensation between sweet and toasted caramelised sugar; a typical taste found in wines aged in barrels whose staves have been burnt, or else the taste of very ripe grapes or almost raisiny grapes.

DENSE. This is related to the body of the wine, a dense sensation on the palate.

FATNESS. A term used in Jerez vocabulary to define a wine with body; it is the antonym of fine.

FLABBY. This is a wine low in acidity and with a lack of freshness.

FLAVOURFUL. A pronounced and pleasant sensation on the palate with the combination of numerous slightly sweet nuances.

FULL. A sensation of volume, rich in nuances of sweetness and "round" tannins; that is, a gentle meatiness and an oily feel.

GENEROUS. A term used to describe a wealth of tastes, as though it were filling the mouth. It is a sensation that is experienced as the wine enters the mouth.

LIGHT. This is the opposite of meaty, dense, concentrated; that is, a wine with little body.

LONG. This is the persistence of the taste after swallowing the wine.

MEATY. A wine that has body, structure and which one "chews" is said to be meaty.

NOTES OF WOOD. Very defined notes of wood (a touch between wood and resin) which is normally found in wines aged in younger casks.

OILY. This is the supple, pleasantly fatty sensation of a wine produced by the glycerin which comes out more in old wines due to the reduction of the acidity or in certain varieties such as *Riesling*, *Gewürztraminer*, *Chardonnay*, *Albariño* and *Godello*.

OXIDATIVE AGEING. This expression comes from the influence of the air on the evolution of the wine. Depending on the quantity of oxygen the air oxidises the wine to a greater or lesser extent. Oxidative ageing is produced by the air which enters through the pores of the wood and comes into contact with the wine, or else during the rackings. This procedure ages the wine faster, and at the same time the wine acquires the aromas and tastes of the oak

PASTY. This is not a disparaging term. It is a very sweet and dense taste.

ROUGH TANNINS, Tannins normally from the oak or skins that have not ripened.

ROUND. This is an expression commonly used in wines to define a drink without rough edges, supple, but at the same time with volume, with body.

SWEETENED. Related to sweetness.

SWEETNESS. A slightly sweet taste which stands out between a mainly dry taste and the tannins of the wine.

SWEET TANNINS. These are the tannins whose bitterness is neutralised by the alcohol and the ripeness of the grape. They are also called oily tannins.

TANNIC. This is a derivative of tannin, a substance with a sensation of harshness which is normally found in the skins and in the wood. In wines, it is the slightly harsh feel which comes from the wood of the barrel.

UNCTUOUS. This refers to the oily and warm feel, and the slight sickly sweetness found in some sweet wines.

VELVETY. This is a smooth, caressing and pleasant sensation on the palate, and is typical of great wines in which the edges of the tannins and the alcohol have been rounded off during its ageing in bottle.

VIGOROUS. This is a wine with a high alcohol content.

WARM. This explains the good side of alcohol. It is a sensation that is less spirituous than alcoholic.

WELL-BALANCED. This is a term which is used to define a good wine: the balance of all its components (alcohol, acidity, extract and the taste of oak if it is a Crianza wine) without any one of the taste nuances standing out.

WINE INDEX

WINE INDEX

F

M

S

1123

WINE INDEX

WINE INDEX

WINE INDEX

X

Y

Z

INDEX OF BODEGAS

INDEX OF BODEGAS